PUBLIC LIBRARY CATALOG

TENTH EDITION

STANDARD CATALOG SERIES

JULIETTE YAAKOV, GENERAL EDITOR

CHILDREN'S CATALOG
JUNIOR HIGH SCHOOL LIBRARY CATALOG
SENIOR HIGH SCHOOL LIBRARY CATALOG
FICTION CATALOG
PUBLIC LIBRARY CATALOG

PUBLIC LIBRARY CATALOG

Guide to Reference Books
and
Adult Nonfiction

TENTH EDITION

EDITED BY
JULIETTE YAAKOV

THE H. W. WILSON COMPANY
NEW YORK
1994

Printed in the United States of America

Library of Congress Cataloging-in-Publication Data

Public library catalog : guide to reference books and adult nonfiction / edited by Juliette Yaakov. — 10th ed.

    p.   cm. — (Standard catalog series)

Includes index.
ISBN 0-8242-0859-5 (lib. bdg. : alk. paper)
1. Public libraries—United States—Book lists.   I. Yaakov, Juliette.   II. Series.

Z1035.P934   1994
025.2′187473—dc20

94-15986
CIP

PREFACE

PUBLIC LIBRARY CATALOG is a list of recommended reference and nonfiction books for adults, classified by subject. The Public Library Catalog service consists of this basic volume and four annual supplements for the years 1994, 1995, 1996, and 1997. They will be distributed on publication to purchasers of the tenth edition without further charge.

History

PUBLIC LIBRARY CATALOG had its inception in the first decade of this century when The H. W. Wilson Company considered ways to meet the needs of the general library patron. The initial response was the publication in 1908 of a modest version of FICTION CATALOG. The first of several installments of the "Standard Catalog" for the general library was published in 1918. It was called Standard Catalog: Sociology Section and was to be considered a "test section," issued with the expectation that helpful criticism would be forthcoming from librarians before the full catalog was published. Additional installments of the test sections, covering Biography; Fiction; Fine Arts; History and Travel; Science and Useful Arts; Literature and Philology; and Philosophy, Religion and General Works were issued over the next fourteen years. Finally, it was determined that the test sections had proven themselves, and a fully integrated first edition of the STANDARD CATALOG FOR PUBLIC LIBRARIES * was assembled and published in 1934. The contents were displayed under the rubrics of the latest version of the Dewey Decimal Classification—a practice that has continued with each succeeding edition of the Catalog.

Although a Fiction Section was issued in 1923, followed by supplements in 1928 and 1931, fiction was omitted from the first edition of the Catalog in 1934. The omission seems to have been for two reasons: the need to keep the Catalog to a manageable size and the desire to develop an improved subject approach to works of fiction. A new expanded edition of FICTION CATALOG was published in 1942. In its preface the Catalog referred to itself as "a companion volume to the Standard Catalog for Public Libraries." This complementary relationship has continued to the present. Users of the latest edition of FICTION CATALOG and its four supplements will find criticism, books about the writing of fiction, essays, and literary history in generous measure in the PUBLIC LIBRARY CATALOG.

Scope and Purpose

The Catalog lists nonfiction books published in the United States, or published in Canada or the United Kingdom and distributed in the United States. It excludes nonprint materials; periodicals; non-English items, with the exception of dictionaries, aids to language learning, and similar materials; and works that quickly become outdated, such as versions of computer software. All books were in print at the time of listing. A work that was elected to the Catalog but has since gone out of print will be considered for one of the annual supplements if it is reprinted. Paperbacks are included when they are the only available format for a work and when a work published in hardcover is also available in paper. This edition consists of 7,735 titles and 3,999 analytical entries. Over 4,000 additional titles will appear in the four supplements.

Satisfying the needs of a broad readership requires a catalog of extraordinary range. Each new edition of PUBLIC LIBRARY CATALOG is a mixture of the old and the new. Older titles, some in updated versions, are included if they continue to meet the needs of the contemporary adult. Newer books in this latest edition of the Catalog reflect the pressures and interests of contemporary life: child rearing, crime, substance abuse, health issues, and environmental concerns. In response to the demand for information in all areas, the emphasis on reference materials has been increased. Biography, poetry and literary criticism have been given comprehensive coverage.

---

* The name was changed to PUBLIC LIBRARY CATALOG with the publication of the fifth edition in 1969.

The Catalog is intended to serve the needs of public and undergraduate libraries. Its admixture of old and current titles should enable the librarian to make informed decisions on weeding a collection. The newer titles should help in identifying areas that need to be updated or strengthened. With its classified arrangement, complete bibliographical data, and descriptive and critical annotations, the Catalog provides useful information for the acquisitions librarian, the reference librarian, and the cataloger. Analytical entries in the Index augment the local catalog by affording access to composite works and to topics for which whole books may not be available. This feature, which increases the usefulness of the library's resources by making the contents of the collection more accessible, should prove especially helpful to readers' advisers and reference librarians.

Preparation

The voting list for this edition was prepared with the assistance of subject specialists. The titles were elected by experienced librarians representing public library systems across the United States. The names of participating libraries are listed in the Acknowledgments.

Organization

The Catalog is organized into three parts: Classified Catalog; Author, Title, Subject, and Analytical Index; Directory of Publishers and Distributors.

Part 1. Classified Catalog. This is arranged according to the Dewey Decimal Classification. Within classes, arrangement is by main entry, with complete bibliographical and cataloging information given for each book. The classified arrangement, along with the descriptive and critical annotations, provides a useful guide to book selection. Entries include such information as price and ISBN to facilitate acquisitions.

Part 2. Author, Title, Subject, and Analytical Index. This is a comprehensive key to Part 1. As mentioned earlier in this Preface, an important feature of this section is the detailed indexing given to composite works. Analytic entries are provided in order to exploit fully the contents of compilations.

Part 3. Directory of Publishers and Distributors. This provides the full name and address of the publisher or distributor for each title listed in Part 1.

For further information consult the Directions for Use of the Catalog.

Acknowledgments

The H. W. Wilson Company is grateful to those publishers who supplied copies of their titles and information on prices and editions. James E. Bobick, Head, Science & Technology Division, Carnegie Library of Pittsburgh, and Charles Willard, Librarian, Andover-Harvard Theological Library, Harvard University, assisted in compiling the voting list. The Company wishes to express its appreciation to the members of the following library systems who participated in the selection of titles for this Catalog:

Boston Public Library
Boston, Massachusetts

Norfolk Public Library System
Norfolk, Virginia

Broward County Library
Fort Lauderdale, Florida

Providence Public Library
Providence, Rhode Island

Cuyahoga County Public Library
Cleveland, Ohio

Public Library of Des Moines
Des Moines, Iowa

East Orange Public Library
East Orange, New Jersey

Sacramento Public Library
Sacramento, California

Martin Memorial Library
York, Pennsylvania

Salt Lake City Public Library
Salt Lake City, Utah

Wake County Department of the Public Library
Raleigh, North Carolina

DIRECTIONS FOR USE OF THE CATALOG

Part 1. Classified Catalog

The Classified Catalog is arranged by the Dewey Decimal Classification in numerical order from 000 to 999. Biographies of individual artists and musicians will be found in class 709.2 and 780.92 respectively. Other individual biographies are classed at 92 and follow the 920's (collective biography). An Outline of Classification, which is reproduced on page 2, serves as a table of contents for the Classified Catalog. It should be noted that many books can be classified in more than one discipline. If a particular title is not found where it might be expected, the Index in Part 2 should be consulted to determine if the title is classified elsewhere.

Within classes, each book is listed under its main entry, usually the author. The name of the author is given in conformity with *Anglo-American Cataloguing Rules,* 2nd edition, 1988 revision. References are made in Part 2 from variant forms of the name.

Each listing consists of a full bibliographical description. Prices, which are always subject to change, have been obtained from the publisher and are as current as possible. Entries include recommended subject headings derived from the *Sears List of Subject Headings,* a suggested classification number from the *Abridged Dewey Decimal Classification and Relative Index,* a brief description of the contents, and, whenever possible, an evaluation from a quoted source.

Part 2. Author, Title, Subject, and Analytical Index

This is a complete index to Part 1. Each book listed in the Catalog is entered under author, title, and subject in a single, alphabetical arrangement. Also included are author and title analytics for works contained in anthologies and collections, and subject analytics for parts of books not covered under the subject heading for the whole. The classification number, displayed in boldface type, is the key to the location of the main entry of the book in Part 1.

Access is provided from names of joint authors and editors. Cross references are made from variant forms of name, from terms not used as subject headings to the preferred term, and from terms used as subject headings to related or more specific headings.

Examples of analytical entries for author, title, and subject are given below.

> **Du Bois, Shirley Graham, 1906-1977**
> I gotta home
> *In* Black female playwights p225-79   **812.08**
>
> I gotta home. Du Bois, S. G.
> *In* Black female playwights p225-79   **812.08**
>
> **Eating disorders**
> *See/See also pages in the following book(s):*
> Dowling, C. You mean I don't have to feel this way?
> p106-26   **616.85**

Part 3. Directory of Publishers and Distributors

This Directory provides the full name, address, and other pertinent information for the publisher or distributor of the books listed in Part 1.

CONTENTS

Outline of Classification

Reproduced below is the Second Summary of the Dewey Decimal Classification.* As Part 1 of this Catalog is arranged according to this classification, the outline will serve as a table of contents for it. Please note, however, that the inclusion of this outline is not to be considered a substitute for consulting the Dewey Decimal Classification itself.

000 Generalities
010   Bibliography
020   Library & information sciences
030   General encyclopedic works
040
050   General serials & their indexes
060   General organizations & museology
070   News media, journalism, publishing
080   General collections
090   Manuscripts & rare books

100 Philosophy & psychology
110   Metaphysics
120   Epistemology, causation, humankind
130   Paranormal phenomena
140   Specific philosophical schools
150   Psychology
160   Logic
170   Ethics (Moral philosophy)
180   Ancient, medieval, Oriental philosophy
190   Modern Western philosophy

200 Religion
210   Natural theology
220   Bible
230   Christian theology
240   Christian moral & devotional theology
250   Christian orders & local church
260   Christian social theology
270   Christian church history
280   Christian denominations & sects
290   Other & comparative religions

300 Social sciences
310   General statistics
320   Political science
330   Economics
340   Law
350   Public administration
360   Social services; association
370   Education
380   Commerce, communications, transport
390   Customs, etiquette, folklore

400 Language
410   Linguistics
420   English & Old English
430   Germanic languages   German
440   Romance languages   French
450   Italian, Romanian, Rhaeto-Romanic
460   Spanish & Portuguese languages
470   Italic languages   Latin
480   Hellenic languages   Classical Greek
490   Other languages

500 Natural sciences & mathematics
510   Mathematics
520   Astronomy & allied sciences
530   Physics
540   Chemistry & allied sciences
550   Earth sciences
560   Paleontology   Paleozoology
570   Life sciences
580   Botanical sciences
590   Zoological sciences

600 Technology (Applied sciences)
610   Medical sciences   Medicine
620   Engineering & allied operations
630   Agriculture
640   Home economics & family living
650   Management & auxiliary services
660   Chemical engineering
670   Manufacturing
680   Manufacture for specific uses
690   Buildings

700 The arts
710   Civic & landscape art
720   Architecture
730   Plastic arts   Sculpture
740   Drawing & decorative arts
750   Painting & paintings
760   Graphic arts   Printmaking & prints
770   Photography & photographs
780   Music
790   Recreational & performing arts

800 Literature & rhetoric
810   American literature in English
820   English & Old English literatures
830   Literatures of Germanic languages
840   Literatures of Romance languages
850   Italian, Romanian, Rhaeto-Romanic
860   Spanish & Portuguese literatures
870   Italic literatures   Latin
880   Hellenic literatures   Classical Greek
890   Literatures of other languages

900 Geography & history
910   Geography & travel
920   Biography, genealogy, insignia
930   History of ancient world
940   General history of Europe
950   General history of Asia   Far East
960   General history of Africa
970   General history of North America
980   General history of South America
990   General history of other areas

* Reproduced from Edition 12 of the Dewey Decimal Classification, published in 1990, by permission of OCLC Forest Press, a division of OCLC Online Computer Library Center, owner of copyright.

PUBLIC LIBRARY CATALOG
TENTH EDITION
CLASSIFIED CATALOG

000 GENERALITIES

001.4 Research. Grants, prizes, scholarships

Awards, honors, & prizes. Gale Res. 2v v1 $180, v2 $210   **001.4**

1. Rewards (Prizes, etc.)
ISSN 0196-6316

First published 1969. (10th edition 1993-1994) Periodically revised

Contents: v1 United States and Canada; v2 International and foreign

Volume one is an alphabetical directory of organizations in the United States and Canada sponsoring awards, honors and prizes in a wide range of endeavors from academic awards to prizes in sports. Volume two provides coverage of awards originating in other countries

Government research directory. Gale Res. $405   **001.4**

1. Research—Directories
ISSN 0882-3766

First published 1980-1981 in three volumes with title: Government research centers directory. (7th edition 1993-1994) Periodically revised

"A descriptive guide to approximately 3,900 U.S. and Canadian government research and development centers, institutes, laboratories, bureaus, test facilities, experiment stations, data collection and analysis centers, and grants management and research coordinating offices in agriculture, commerce, education, energy, engineering, environment, the humanities, medicine, military science, and basic and applied sciences." Title page

"For all reference collections." N Y Public Libr. New Tech Books

001.9 Controversial knowledge

Bauer, Henry H.
The enigma of Loch Ness; making sense of a mystery. University of Ill. Press 1986 243p il $27.50; pa $11.95   **001.9**

1. Loch Ness monster
ISBN 0-252-01284-4; 0-252-06031-8 (pa)

LC 85-24554

An account of the sightings of the legendary monster and of efforts to determine its existence

Includes bibliography

Dinsdale, Tim, 1924-1987
Loch Ness monster. 4th ed. Routledge & Kegan Paul 1982 218p il hardcover o.p. paperback available $14.95   **001.9**

1. Loch Ness monster
ISBN 0-415-04550-9 (pa)

LC 81-17899

First published 1961

This book describes the ongoing search for explanations to account for the mysterious creatures which seem to inhabit Scotland's Loch Ness

Earth energies; by the editors of Time-Life Books. Time-Life Bks. 1991 144p il (Mysteries of the unknown) $19.93 **001.9**

1. Parapsychology 2. Earth 3. Nature   LC 90-20666

An illustrated look at spirituality based on the natural world. Among the topics discussed are grain circles, the power of trees and the art of Feng Shui

Includes bibliography

Good, Timothy
Above top secret; the worldwide U.F.O. cover-up; with a foreword by Lord Hill-Norton. Morrow 1988 592p il $19.95; pa $14   **001.9**

1. Unidentified flying objects
ISBN 0-688-07860-5; 0-688-09202-0 (pa)

LC 87-34869

First published 1987 in the United Kingdom

"This volume chronicles the continuing involvement of world military forces and intelligence agencies with the UFO phenomenon. The author concentrates on military cases from Great Britain and the U.S., although there are substantial chapters on France, Australia, Canada, China, the USSR, and other countries. . . . One of the best-documented UFO books ever written." Booklist

Mysterious creatures; by the editors of Time-Life Books. Time-Life Bks. 1988 144p il (Mysteries of the unknown) $19.93 **001.9**

1. Monsters   LC 88-2124

An illustrated look at legendary monsters and their reported sightings

Includes bibliography

Rovin, Jeff
The encyclopedia of monsters. Facts on File 1989 390p il $35; pa $19.95   **001.9**

1. Monsters
ISBN 0-8160-1824-3; 0-8160-2303-4 (pa)

LC 89-30417

Rovin, Jeff—*Continued*

This work "covers a variety of fiends, specters, were-wolves, mummies, and other creatures and demons. . . . Information includes: the common name or nickname; where and when the monster first appeared; its size, gender and species; its distinguishing features and powers; a biographical sketch, from origin to demise; and a bibliography or filmography." SLJ

Vallée, Jacques

Confrontations: a scientist's search for alien contact. Ballantine Bks. 1990 263p hardcover o.p. paperback available $4.95
001.9

1. Unidentified flying objects
ISBN 0-345-36501-1 (pa)   LC 89-91790

The author "considers some of the more puzzling cases concerning alleged sightings and examines the physical characteristics of UFOs in an intriguing investigation that promises to be popular for research and personal reading." Booklist

Includes bibliographic references

Walters, Ed (Edward)

The Gulf Breeze sightings; the most astounding multiple sightings of UFO's in U.S. history; [by] Ed Walters [and] Frances Walters; introduction by Budd Hopkins; photo analysis by Bruce S. Maccabee. Morrow 1990 248p il $21.95   **001.9**

1. Unidentified flying objects
ISBN 0-688-09087-7   LC 89-13255

Also available in paperback from Avon Bks.

"The Walters' book is a frightening account of 20 UFO encounters occurring near their Florida home. Their position in the community, the collaboration of over 100 other area witnesses, and the authenticated photographs and videotape they took make this account more trustworthy than most." Libr J

002 The book

Olmert, Michael

The Smithsonian book of books. Smithsonian Bks. 1992 319p il $45   **002**

1. Books—History
ISBN 0-89599-030-X   LC 91-39590

"The nearly 350 illustrations in this well-designed volume are mostly in color, and range from reproductions of art depicting people of all cultures throughout history reading, writing, and making books, to photographs of the latest in computerized print technology. Olmert's anecdotal commentary offers a fluid overview of the evolution of writing from ancient cuneiform tablets to elegant medieval manuscripts and the earliest printed books." Booklist

002.075 Book collecting

Ahearn, Allen

Collected books; the guide to values; [by] Allen and Patricia Ahearn. Putnam 1991 636p $50   **002.075**

1. Book collecting
ISBN 0-399-13663-0   LC 90-14559

This is a "source for prices of many collectible books, mainly first editions published since 1800, and includes brief notes to identify first printings." Libr J

Includes bibliographic references

Carter, John, 1905-1975

ABC for book collectors. 6th ed, with corrections & additions by Nicolas Barker. Oak Knoll Bks. 1992 219p il $25 **002.075**

1. Book collecting—Dictionaries 2. Book industries—Dictionaries
ISBN 0-938768-30-1   LC 91-30020

First published 1951(?) by Knopf; present edition first published 1980 in the United Kingdom

"An alphabetical dictionary of bibliographic and booksellers' terms with definitions as used in Great Britain and the United States." Sheehy. Guide to Ref Books. 10th edition

Includes bibliographic references

003 Systems

Gleick, James

Chaos: making a new science. Viking 1987 352p il $22.95   **003**

1. Chaos (Science)
ISBN 0-670-81178-5   LC 87-40025

Also available in paperback from Penguin Bks.

The author chronicles the development of chaos theory, which attempts to find order in seemingly random phenomena

"The average reader may have difficulty grasping the technical points, but in general the author has done a remarkable job of translating new research into accessible language. As valuable for its thumbnail biographies of unorthodox thinkers as for its clear exposition of new ideas, this book should command wide attention." Booklist

Includes bibliography

Lewin, Roger

Complexity: life at the edge of chaos. Macmillan 1992 208p il $22   **003**

1. Science—Philosophy 2. Chaos (Science)
ISBN 0-02-570485-0   LC 92-30314

"The basic idea of the complexity movement is that all things in nature are driven to organize themselves into patterns. . . . [This book sets] out to explore this ambitious attempt to unify the sciences." N Y Times Book Rev

A "vivid and engaging discussion of complexity for general readers." Libr J

Includes bibliographic references

Rheingold, Howard
Virtual reality. Summit Bks. 1991 415p
$22.95; pa $12 **003**
1. Cybernetics
ISBN 0-671-69363-8; 0-671-77897-8 (pa)
LC 91-10955

"The term 'virtual reality' describes the computer-generated simulation of reality with physical, tactile, and visual dimensions. This interactive technology is used by science and engineering researchers as well as by the entertainment industry, especially in the form of video games. In this book, Rheingold . . . reports on his visits to virtual reality labs in industry and universities around the world." Libr J
"The book offers an interesting insight into the problems of bringing information from diverse fields into a single focus because virtual reality is fundamentally a convergence of existing technologies. . . . Rheingold's book is thorough and thoughtful. He writes with clarity and from a wide-ranging perspective." New Sci

Includes bibliographic references

004 Data processing. Computer science

Barry, John A.
Technobabble. MIT Press 1991 268p
$22.50 **004**
1. Computers and civilization 2. Technology—Philosophy
ISBN 0-262-02333-4 LC 91-12488

"Such words as 'access,' 'network,' 'crash,' and 'dump' have taken on new shades of meaning since their adoption by the computer industry, while new words from the jargon of the field, such as 'interface,' 'download,' 'realtime,' and 'end user' have infiltrated the common vernacular. Some characteristics of technobabble are the use of nouns for verbs, the proliferation of acronyms, and excessive use of the passive voice. Barry's book explores this new phenomenon in a style that is entertaining and 'user-friendly.'" Libr J

Includes bibliography

Bear, John, 1938-
Computer wimp no more; the intelligent beginner's guide to computers; by John Bear and David M Pozerycki with the help of Justine Roberts [et al.] Ten Speed Press 1992 285p il pa $14.95 **004**
1. Computers
ISBN 0-89815-432-4 LC 91-17554

This introduction to computers discusses what to look for when purchasing computers and software. Computer troubleshooting is also examined

Includes bibliographic references

Communications; by the editors of Time-Life Books. [rev ed]. Time-Life Bks. 1990 128p il (Understanding computers) $21.27 **004**
1. Data transmission systems 2. Computer networks
LC 89-20548

First published 1986

An illustrated look at the applications of data transmission systems and computer networking in the communications industry

Includes bibliography

Computer basics; by the editors of Time-Life Books. [rev ed]. Time-Life Bks. 1989 128p il (Understanding computers) $21.27 **004**
1. Computers
First published 1985

Among the topics discussed in this volume are the binary code, the evolution of the microchip, and microcomputer-related entrepreneurship

Includes bibliography

Computers. Time-Life Bks. 1990 144p il (How things work) $19.93 **004**
1. Computers LC 90-47450

Illustrated with numerous photographs, charts, diagrams, and cutaway drawings, this volume explains how computers work

Covington, Michael A., 1957-
Dictionary of computer terms; [by] Michael Covington, Douglas Downing. 3rd ed. Barron's Educ. Ser. 1992 xx, 364p il pa $8.95 **004**
1. Computers—Dictionaries
ISBN 0-8120-4824-5 LC 91-21529

First published 1986 with authors' names in reverse order

This guide to computer terminology contains some 1,000 entries

The entries "are far from comprehensive yet provide an excellent starting point for beginners, while also serving more experienced users who seek brief and only moderately technical definitions." Am Ref Books Annu, 1993

Dictionary of computing. 3rd ed. Oxford Univ. Press 1990 510p il (Oxford science publications) $39.95; pa $11.95 **004**
1. Electronic data processing—Dictionaries 2. Computers—Dictionaries
ISBN 0-19-853825-1; 0-19-286131-X (pa)
LC 89-26662

First published 1983

General editor: Valerie Illingworth

This computer dictionary includes terms from the related fields of electronics, mathematics, and logic

This work "has become a standard among computer science dictionaries. . . . The book is strongly recommended for purchase by most libraries." Sci Books Films

Freedman, Alan
The computer glossary; the complete illustrated desk reference. AMACOM il $36.95; pa $24.95 **004**
1. Computers—Dictionaries 2. Electronic data processing—Dictionaries

First published by Computer Language Co. (6th edition, 1993) Periodically revised

Includes more than 5,300 computer terms, abbreviations, and acronyms. "Covers systems design, programming, communications, LANs, computer graphics, desktop publishing, multimedia, PCs, Macintoshes, workstations, and more." Publisher's note

Glossbrenner, Alfred
The complete handbook of personal computer communications. all new 3rd ed. St. Martin's Press 1990 405p $24.95; pa $18.95 **004**
1. Computers 2. Online data processing 3. Computer networks
ISBN 0-312-03311-7; 0-312-03312-5 (pa)
LC 89-34838
First published 1983
This guide covers modems and software needed to link various database lines to personal computers. Among areas covered are: online utilities; business, financial and investment services; and electronic mail

Henle, Richard A.
Desktop computers; in perspective; [by] Richard A. Henle, Boris W. Kuvshinoff; editor, C. M. Kuvshinoff; illustrator, A. L. Kundratic; programmer, R. D. Bucy. Oxford Univ. Press 1992 xxiv, 650p il (Johns Hopkins applied physics laboratory ser. in science and engineering) pa $24.95 **004**
1. Microcomputers
ISBN 0-19-507031-3
LC 91-45410
This book explains personal computer equipment, programs, networking strategies, and applications such as text processing, spreadsheets and graphics
"This remarkable new book provides the global overview needed to truly understand and benefit from the huge capabilities offered by today's desktop technology. It is a treasury of issues, technical considerations, perspectives, and other must-know information." Univ Press Books for Public and Second Sch Libr

Macmillan encyclopedia of computers; edited by Gary G. Bitter. Macmillan 1992 2v il $175 **004**
1. Computers—Dictionaries
ISBN 0-02-897045-4
LC 91-45339
"This two-volume encyclopedia describes the role computers have come to play in many areas of our world: farming, insurance, government, and astronomy to name a few. The 200 articles deal with technical considerations, theoretical questions, and current developments, but historical and biographical information is provided as well. Hardware and software concerns are dealt with generically to avoid becoming immediately outdated." Am Libr
For a fuller review see: Booklist, Sept. 1, 1992

The New hacker's dictionary; compiled by Eric S. Raymond; foreword and cartoons by Guy L. Steele, Jr. 2nd ed. MIT Press 1993 xxi, 505p il $30; pa $14.95 **004**
1. Computers—Dictionaries 2. Electronic data processing—Dictionaries
ISBN 0-262-18154-1; 0-262-68079-3 (pa) LC 93-2464
First published 1991
This volume collects and defines the jargon used by computer hackers and programmers. It also includes hacker history and folklore

Owen, Barry, 1952-
Personal computers for the computer illiterate. HarperPerennial 1990 181p il pa $12 **004**
1. Computers
ISBN 0-06-096839-7
LC 90-55005
This "introduction to purchasing and using a computer . . . covers standard software—i.e., word processors and spread sheets—and standard hardware, from the monitor to the keyboard to the central processing unit." Sci Books Films

Parker, R. Wayne
The computer buyer's handbook; how to select & buy personal computers for your home or business. 2nd ed rev. Fast Forward Pub. 1992 284p il pa $17.95 **004**
1. Computers 2. Consumer education
ISBN 0-9627370-7-0
LC 91-77813
First published 1991
This guide to buying personal computers covers hardware and software basics, buying strategies, upgrading an existing system, CD-ROM technology, and related topics

Pearson, Olen R.
Personal computer buying guide; [by] Olen R. Pearson and the editors of Consumer Reports Books. rev ed. Consumer Repts. Bks. 1993 216p pa $14.95 **004**
1. Computers 2. Consumer education
ISBN 0-89043-622-3
LC 92-28806
First published 1990
The author outlines seven basic steps to follow in planning, purchasing, and using a personal computer system. The book includes checklists for assessing needs and evaluating hardware, software, and dealers

The **Personal** computer; by the editors of Time-Life Books. rev ed. Time-Life Bks. 1993 128p il (Understanding computers) $19.93 **004**
1. Microcomputers 2. Computer software
LC 92-40576
First published 1989
An illustrated introduction to microcomputer systems, software and applications
Includes bibliography

Revolution in science; by the editors of Time-Life Books. [rev ed]. Time-Life Bks. 1990 128p il (Understanding computers) $21.27 **004**
1. Computers 2. Electronic data processing
LC 90-10884
First published 1987
An account of the development of data processing technology in response to the needs of science, this book begins with a description of the punched card calculator, ca. 1890, and ends with a discussion of computer systems used today
Includes bibliography

Sinclair, Ian Robertson
The HarperCollins dictionary of computer terms; [by] Ian R. Sinclair. HarperCollins Pubs. 1991 261p il $25; pa $10.95 **004**
1. Computers—Dictionaries 2. Electronic data processing—Dictionaries
ISBN 0-06-271505-4; 0-06-461016-0 (pa)
LC 90-55516
First published 1986 in the United Kingdom with title: Collins dictionary of computing
This work contains 1,700 entries on computer subjects. It has "see references and uses boldface print to designate words within a definition that appear elsewhere as entries. Computer Terms provides information on selected tradenames (e.g., Apple and Epson)." Booklist

Space; by the editors of Time-Life Books. [rev ed]. Time-Life Bks. 1991 128p il (Understanding computers) $21.27 **004**
1. Astronautics—Data processing LC 90-24705
First published 1987
The applications of high-speed data processing in the fields of astronautics and space flight are discussed
Includes bibliography

Speed and power; by the editors of Time-Life Books. [rev ed]. Time-Life Bks. 1990 128p il (Understanding computers) $21.27 **004**
1. Computers 2. Electronic data processing
LC 90-11079
First published 1987
Examines the ways in which technology has increased the speed and power of computers and computer-processing, and current applications
Includes bibliography

005 Computer programming, programs, data

Computer languages; by the editors of Time-Life Books. [rev ed]. Time-Life Bks. 1990 128p il (Understanding computers) $21.27 **005**
1. Programming languages (Computers) LC 89-20429
First published 1986
An illustrated introduction to basic components and applications of BASIC, FORTRAN, COBOL and other computer programming languages
Includes bibliography

Software; by the editors of Time-Life Books. [rev ed]. Time-Life Bks. 1990 128p il (Understanding computers) $21.27 **005**
1. Computer software LC 89-39522
First published 1985
An illustrated introduction to computer software, programs, and their applications
Includes bibliography

The **Software** encyclopedia. Bowker 2v pa set $222 **005**
1. Computer software
Annual. First published 1985

Contents: v1 Titles, publishers; v2 System compatibility/applications
A guide to currently available microcomputer software packages including publishing-related programs, word processing programs, database programs and spreadsheet programs
"This annually updated work is considered the most comprehensive and current list available." Nichols. Guide to Ref Books for Sch Media Cent. 4th edition

Software Reviews on File. Facts on File $210 per year **005**
1. Computer software—Bibliography
ISSN 8755-7169
Monthly. First published 1985
Looseleaf file. "Reviews over 600 software programs per year—educational, word processing, computer graphics, recreational, business, personal, and more—designed for all major microcomputer systems and languages. Each 64-page issue condenses reviews of 50 new software programs published in 125 journals. Each monthly issue contains cumulative indexing by subject and computer (e.g., IBM, Apple, Macintosh). The entries for each program include publisher, address, and price; a lengthy publisher's description; and a 100-word condensation of reviews, citing journal, date, page, and name of reviewer." Nichols. Guide to Ref Books for Sch Media Cent. 4th edition

006.3 Artificial intelligence

Johnson, George, 1952-
Machinery of the mind. Times Bks. 1986 336p o.p.; Microsoft Press paperback available $9.95 **006.3**
1. Artificial intelligence
ISBN 1-55615-010-5 (pa) LC 86-1313
The author "describes research in a variety of areas within artificial intelligence, including natural language processing, vision, learning, the fine arts, theorem-proving, and robotics. Johnson's presentation is sufficiently nontechnical so as to be understood by the general reader." Choice
Includes bibliography

Jubak, Jim
In the image of the brain; breaking the barrier between the human mind and intelligent machines. Little, Brown 1992 348p il $24.95 **006.3**
1. Artificial intelligence
ISBN 0-316-47555-6 LC 91-41771
"Neural networks are computing devices capable of learning and evolving. Modeled after the neurobiology of the human brain, with immense numbers of processors, they are either simulated in computer programs or actually built out of silicon. . . . Jubak takes readers to the cutting edge of this field by interviewing neural network researchers at their drawing-boards." Publ Wkly
Includes bibliographic references

Kurzweil, Raymond
The age of intelligent machines. MIT
Press 1990 565p il $39.95; pa $24.95
006.3

1. Artificial intelligence
ISBN 0-262-11121-7; 0-262-61079-5 (pa)
LC 89-13606

In this overview of artificial intelligence the author
"disscusses its philosophical, mathematical, psychological
and technical roots; the outstanding problems in contemporary research on artificial intelligence; the history and
current state of the industry; the impact of artificial intelligence on the arts, and the future of the discipline."
N Y Times Book Rev

"A fascinating, yet understandable, book. . . . Easily
accessible to nonspecialists." Choice

Includes bibliographic references

Levy, Steven
Artificial life; quest for a new creation.
Pantheon Bks. 1992 390p il $25; pa $13
006.3

1. Artificial intelligence
ISBN 0-679-40774-X; 0-679-74389-8 (pa)
LC 91-50749

"Can an engineered creation be alive? This centuries-
old question is the starting point for Steven Levy's . .
. new book. . . . The title refers neither to the products
of genetic engineering nor to artificial intelligence's goal
of creating a thinking machine. The subject matter of
artificial life (or 'a-life' as its adherents call it) is the
making of computer programs that reproduce themselves,
exhibit unexpected behavior and evolve. . . . [This] is
not only exhilarating reading but an all-too-rare case of
a scientific popularization that breaks new ground." NY
Times Book Rev

Includes bibliographic references

Moravec, Hans P.
Mind children; the future of robot and
human intelligence. Harvard Univ. Press
1988 214p il $22.95; pa $8.95
006.3

1. Artificial intelligence 2. Robotics
ISBN 0-674-57616-0; 0-674-57618-7 (pa)
LC 88-21343

The author "explores the role of the human mind in
a world where superior computer power seemingly makes
our contributions superfluous. . . . Computer viruses and
cellular automation programs also receive attention. Appendixes provide technical details. This volume has a
special appeal for science fiction fans and the computer
literate, and it serves up provocative ideas to adventurous general readers." Booklist

Includes bibliography

Penrose, Roger
The emperor's new mind; concerning
computers, minds and the laws of physics;
foreword by Martin Gardner. Oxford Univ.
Press 1989 466p il $30
006.3

1. Artificial intelligence 2. Thought and thinking
3. Science—Philosophy 4. Computers
ISBN 0-19-851973-7
LC 89-8548

Also available in paperback from Penguin Bks.

The author "attempts to sketch the outlines of a future theory that would link relativity, quantum physics
and the phenomenon of intelligence. . . . [The book]

is just about as rigorous as it could be, so much so
that readers lacking at least a graduate student's
comprehension of physics will find parts of it rough
going. Yet it is also as clear as it could be; Mr. Penrose
has obviously taken pains to make his book accessible
without compromising his subject matter." N Y Times
Book Rev

Includes bibliography

Thro, Ellen
The artificial intelligence dictionary.
Microtrend Bks. 1991 407p (Lance A.
Leventhal microtrend ser) pa $24.95 **006.3**

1. Artificial intelligence—Dictionaries
ISBN 0-915391-36-8
LC 89-43542

"This dictionary contains over 1,300 terms from AI
and related subjects like expert systems, data structures,
computer languages, robotics, probability, and software.
The writing style is everyday English, and there are examples throughout the text. Each entry provides
syllabication and contains a brief, two- to four-sentence
description." Booklist

Waldrop, M. Mitchell
Man-made minds; the promise of artificial
intelligence. Walker & Co. 1987 280p il
$22.95; pa $14.95
006.3

1. Artificial intelligence
ISBN 0-8027-0899-4; 0-8027-7297-8 (pa)
LC 86-22370

The author "traces the history of artificial-intelligence
research, exploring the nature of its problems and
crediting its scientists. . . . He also analyzes controversial
modern issues: parallel processing, the 'fifth generation'
and military funding, and future AI possibilities, both
practical and esoteric. Waldrop's painstaking presentation
of multiple sides of the issues, along with provocative
reflections on emotions, teamwork, and process, promotes
thoughtful reading." Booklist

Includes bibliography

011 General bibliographies

American reference books annual. Libraries
Unlimited $85
011

1. Reference books—Bibliography 2. Reference
books—Reviews
ISSN 0065-9959

Cumulative index available for 1985-1989

Annual. First published 1970

Editor: 1970- Bohdan S. Wynar

"Each issue covers the reference book output
(including reprints) of the previous year (i.e., the 1970
volume covers 1969 publications). Offers descriptive and
evaluative notes (many of them signed by contributors),
with references to selected reviews. Classed arrangement;
author-subject-title index." Sheehy. Guide to Ref Books.
10th edition

Best reference books; titles of lasting value
selected from American reference books
annual; edited by Bohdan S. Wynar.
Libraries Unlimited
011

1. Reference books—Bibliography 2. Reference
books—Reviews

Best reference books—*Continued*
Volume covering 1970-1980 o.p.; volumes available cover 1981-1985 $45 (ISBN 0-87287-544-7); 1986-1990 $67.50 (ISBN 0-87287-936-4)

A selection of reference titles with annotations and references to reviews selected from volumes of American reference books annual

Bibliographic index; a cumulative bibliography of bibliographies. Wilson, H.W. service basis **011**
1. Bibliography—Bibliography 2. Bibliography—Indexes
ISSN 0006-1255
Also available on CD-ROM
Published April and August with bound cumulation in December

This is a subject list of bibliographies, in both English and foreign languages, which contain 50 or more bibliographic citations. Bibliographies published separately as books and pamphlets or appearing as parts of books and pamphlets are included. In addition, approximately 2,800 periodicals are regularly examined for bibliographic material

Enoch Pratt Free Library
Reference sources: a brief guide. Enoch Pratt Free Lib. Publs. pa $7.95 **011**
1. Reference books—Bibliography

First published 1938 with title: A guide to reference books. (9th edition, 1988) Periodically revised. Variant title: Reference books: a brief guide

This guide now includes computerized databases and resources in microform. It "is meant to be suggestive rather than complete. It covers general reference books, the humanities, sciences, and social sciences. Materials in genealogy, medicine, and law are excluded. This guide continues to help librarians identify significant reference sources." Nichols. Guide to Ref Books for Sch Media Cent. 4th edition

Guide to reference books; edited by Eugene P. Sheehy; with the assistance of Rita G. Keckeissen [et al.]; science, technology, and medicine compiled by Richard J. Dionne, Elizabeth E. Ferguson, Robert C. Michaelson. 10th ed. American Lib. Assn. 1986 1560p $80 **011**
1. Reference books—Bibliography
ISBN 0-8389-0390-8   LC 85-11208
First published 1902 as: Guide to the study and use of reference books, by Alice B. Kroeger

"The most complete compilation of reference books currently available. More than 16,000 entries provide details on general reference works and on reference books on specialized subjects in the humanities, social and behavorial sciences, history and area studies, and science, technology, and medicine." N Y Public Libr Book of How & Where to Look It Up

Guide to reference books; covering materials from 1985-1990; edited by Robert Balay; special editorial advisor, Eugene P. Sheehy. supplement to the tenth edition. American Lib. Assn. 1992 613p $85
011
1. Reference books—Bibliography
ISBN 0-8389-0588-9   LC 92-6463
This supplement contains 4,668 entries

International directory of little magazines and small presses. Dustbooks $42.95; pa $26.95 **011**
1. Periodicals—Bibliography 2. Periodicals—Directories 3. Publishers and publishing—Directories
ISSN 0092-3974

Annual. First published 1965 with title: Directory of little magazines

"Entries for little magazines and for small presses appear in a single alphabetical listing. In addition to the expected directory information, listings usually include comments by the editors regarding policies and types of material published, and lists of recent contributors." Sheehy. Guide to Ref Books. 10th edition

Magazines for libraries; for the general reader and school, junior college, college, university, and public libraries; [edited by] Bill Katz and Linda Sternberg Katz. Bowker $139.95 **011**
1. Periodicals—Bibliography
ISSN 0000-0914

First published 1969. (7th edition, 1992) Frequently revised

"Annotated classified guide to recommended periodicals for the general reader and school, college, and public libraries. Provides comparative evaluations and grade- and age-level recommendations for all periodicals included." N Y Public Libr Book of How & Where to Look It Up

The **Reader's** adviser; a layman's guide to literature. Bowker 6v ea $110; set $500
011
1. Books and reading—Best books 2. Literature—Bio-bibliography 3. Reference books—Bibliography
ISSN 0094-5943

First published 1921 with title: The Bookman's manual. Title varies. (14th edition, 1993) Frequently revised

Contents: v1 The best in reference books, British literature, and American literature; v2 The best in world literature; v3 The best in social sciences, history, and the arts; v4 The best in philosophy and religion; v5 The best in science, technology, and medicine; v6 Indexes

"Designed primarily for the bookseller and librarian, this is an up-to-date, standard work useful in any library." Sheehy. Guide to Ref Books. 10th edition

Recommended reference books for small and medium-sized libraries and media centers. Libraries Unlimited $39.50 **011**
1. Reference books—Bibliography 2. Reference books—Reviews
ISSN 0277-5948

Annual. First published 1981

Editor: 1981- Bohdan S. Wynar

Each annual volume includes reviews of about 550 titles chosen by the editor as the most valuable reference titles published during the previous year

"Where budget restrictions are a consideration, this is an invaluable asset; for small libraries, a superior selection/acquisitions tool. Highly recommended." Voice Youth Advocates

Recommended reference books in paperback; Andrew L. March, editor. 2nd ed. Libraries Unlimited 1992 263p $37.50

011

1. Reference books—Bibliography 2. Paperback books—Bibliography
ISBN 1-56308-067-2   LC 92-15875

First published 1981 under the editorship of Mary Alice Deveny

"The editor annotates nearly 1,000 works in 37 broad categories from general reference to subjects ranging from agriculture to zoology. Sixty-two percent of the titles cost less than $15, and 98 percent cost less than $40. Some government documents and free publications are also listed. Each entry includes author, title, imprint, collation, series, price, LC card number, ISBN, and an annotation. . . . Annotations are evaluative and especially useful." Booklist

The Standard periodical directory. Oxbridge Communications; [distributed by] Gale Res. $495

011

1. Periodicals—Bibliography 2. Periodicals—Directories
ISSN 0085-6630

Annual. First published 1964/1965

A guide to more than 75,000 periodicals published in the United States and Canada

"Alphabetical subject arrangement with index of titles and subjects. Information given includes name and address of publisher, editorial content and scope, year founded, frequency, subscription rate, total circulation, advertising rate, etc." Sheehy. Guide to Ref Books. 10th edition

Ulrich's international periodicals directory; including Irregular serials & annuals. Bowker 5v $395

011

1. Periodicals—Bibliography 2. Periodicals—Directories
ISSN 0000-0175

Also available on CD-ROM

Annual since 1980. First published 1932 with title: Periodicals directory. Variant title: Ulrich's Periodicals directory

"A classified list of current domestic and foreign periodicals, including irregular serials and annuals, arranged under some 550 subject headings. Provides complete publishing and subscription information. Indications of where each is indexed or abstracted. Also includes a list of serials that have ceased or suspended publication since last edition." Ref Sources for Small & Medium-sized Libr. 5th edition

Words on cassette. Bowker $134.95   **011**

1. Sound recordings—Bibliography

Annual. First published 1992. Formed by the merger of On cassette and Words on tape

This work "lists spoken-word audiocassettes in many and varied subject areas. . . . Information on each includes reader's name, author, title, playing time, number of cassettes, purchase/rental price, order number, and publisher. Many titles have an annotation." Nichols. Guide to Ref Books for Sch Media Cent. 4th edition

011.6 General bibliographies of works for specific kinds of users

Best books for senior high readers; John T. Gillespie, editor. Bowker 1991 931p $46

011.6

1. Young adults' literature—Bibliography 2. Books and reading—Best books
ISBN 0-8352-3021-X   LC 91-26666

"This volume annotates material appropriate for grades 10-12 (ages 15-18). . . . 10,805 titles are mentioned in 9,979 annotated entries. . . . Entries include author, title, grade level, publication date, publisher, price, and ISBN. Annotations of a sentence or two describe the book. Each entry concludes with the Dewey classification number; some cite reviews." Booklist

Books for college libraries; a core collection of 50,000 titles. 3rd ed. American Lib. Assn. 1988 6v set $550   **011.6**

1. Books and reading—Best books 2. Academic libraries
ISBN 0-8389-3353-X   LC 88-16714

First published 1967

"A project of the Association of College and Research Libraries." Title page

Contents: v1 Humanities; v2 Language and literature; v3 History; v4 Social sciences; v5 Psychology, science, technology, Bibliography; v6 Index

"The titles chosen represent a core collection of books for four-year college libraries. Individual entries contain full cataloging and classification information and are arranged in Library of Congress call number sequence. Entries carried over from the previous edition are flagged." Coll Res Libr

Children's catalog. 16th ed, edited by Juliette Yaakov, with the assistance of Anne Price. Wilson, H.W. 1991 1346p $90

011.6

1. Catalogs, Classified 2. Children's literature—Bibliography 3. School libraries—Catalogs
ISBN 0-8242-0805-6   LC 91-27841

"Standard catalog series"

First published 1909

Kept up to date by annual supplements which are included in price of main volume

This collection of recommended materials includes 6,061 titles and 7,189 analytical entries of books for children from preschool to grade six. Entries contain full bibliographic information, Dewey Decimal classification number, subject headings, reading level, descriptive, and when possible, critical annotations

"A reliable and important guide for collection development." Wynar. Guide to Ref Books for Sch Media Cent. 3d edition

Dreyer, Sharon Spredemann
The best of Bookfinder; a guide to children's literature about interests and concerns of youth aged 2-18. American Guidance Service 1992 xxi, 451p $75; pa $40   **011.6**

1. Children's literature—Bibliography
ISBN 0-88671-440-0; 0-88671-439-7 (pa)
    LC 91-76898

Dreyer, Sharon Spredemann—*Continued*

"This volume describes 676 children's books selected from volumes 1-3 [of the Bookfinder, published 1977-1989] that are still useful. They are categorized in more than 450 psychological, developmental, and behavioral topics of high interest to children and young people ages 2-18. . . . The 100-page subject index is easy to read and easy to use. Its usefulness is increased by cross-references. . . . Libraries and media centers having the original volumes will want to have *The Best of Bookfinder*, since outdated material has been dropped. Those who do not have the original volumes will certainly want this selected volume." Booklist

Junior high school library catalog. 6th ed, edited by Juliette Yaakov. Wilson, H.W. 1990 802p $105   **011.6**

1. Catalogs, Classified 2. High school libraries—Catalogs
ISBN 0-8242-0799-8   LC 90-44498

"Standard catalog series"

First published 1965

Kept up to date by annual supplements which are included in price of main volume

This collection of recommended materials includes 3,219 titles and some 3,600 analytical entries of books for grades seven through nine. Entries contain full bibliographic information, Dewey Decimal classification number, subject headings, descriptive, and when possible, critical annotations

"This series belongs on every school and public library shelf as a valuable reference tool." Booklist

Lipson, Eden Ross

The New York Times parent's guide to the best books for children. rev & updated. Times Bks. 1991 508p il pa $15   **011.6**

1. Children's literature—Bibliography 2. Books and reading—Best books
ISBN 0-8129-1889-4   LC 91-2675

First published 1988

This work "contains over 1700 listings of children's books for every age group. Fifty-five indexes enable readers to browse through pocket reviews organized according to minorities; religion; picture books; funny books to read aloud to toddlers; dinosaur books for babies; and more." Libr J

Includes bibliographic references

Nichols, Margaret Irby

Guide to reference books for school media centers. 4th ed. Libraries Unlimited 1992 463p $38.50   **011.6**

1. Reference books—Bibliography 2. School libraries—Catalogs
ISBN 0-87287-833-3   LC 91-45242

First edition by Christine Gehrt Wynar published 1973

This guide to reference sources for elementary, middle, and high schools contains 2,280 annotated entries for titles published between 1985 and early 1991 as well as some significant older titles

Rasinski, Timothy V.

Sensitive issues; an annotated guide to children's literature, K-6; by Timothy V. Rasinski and Cindy S. Gillespie. Oryx Press 1992 277p pa $29.95   **011.6**

1. Children's literature—Bibliography 2. Children—Books and reading
ISBN 0-89774-777-1   LC 92-18682

The main part of this "book consists of eight chapters, each devoted to a sensitive issue: divorce, substance abuse, death and dying, nontraditional home environments, child abuse, prejudice and cultural differences, moving, and illness and disability. Each chapter includes an alphabetical listing of 25 to 30 titles, with some chapters divided into fiction and nonfiction. Each entry includes grade-level information . . . bibliographic information, a summary of the book, a critique, and activities that can be used to heighten students' understanding and appreciation of the text. . . . A directory of publishers and an index of subjects, authors, and titles complete the book." Booklist

Reference books for young readers; authoritative evaluations of encyclopedias, atlases, and dictionaries; Marion Sader, editor; Brent Allison, Shirley A. Fitzgibbons, Rebecca L. Thomas, consultants. Bowker 1988 615p il (Bowker buying guide ser) $49.95   **011.6**

1. Reference books—Bibliography
ISBN 0-8352-2366-3   LC 87-38234

This "is a compilation of indepth reviews of 400 general reference books, including encyclopedias, atlases, and dictionaries." Libr J

Rosenberg, Judith K.

Young people's books in series: fiction and non-fiction, 1975-1991; [by] Judith K. Rosenberg with the assistance of C. Allen Nichols. Libraries Unlimited 1992 424p $27.50   **011.6**

1. Children's literature—Bibliography 2. Young adults' literature—Bibliography
ISBN 0-87287-882-1   LC 91-36646

Originally published 1972 and 1973 with titles: Young people's literature in series: fiction and Young people's literature in series: publishers' and non-fiction series; supplementary volume combining fiction and non-fiction published 1977

This reference work lists and describes "series published for young people from early elementary grades through high school. . . . Fiction series from 1976 through 1990 (and new titles in existing series through 1991) are included as well as nonfiction series, which are limited to in-print items only. Each entry includes the publisher, a brief description of the series, a list of books and their publication dates, and recommended grade level." Publisher's note

Senior high school library catalog. 14th ed, edited by Brenda Smith and Juliette Yaakov. Wilson, H.W. 1992 1467p $115   **011.6**

1. Catalogs, Classified 2. High school libraries—Catalogs
ISBN 0-8242-0831-5   LC 92-26946

"Standard catalog series"

Senior high school library catalog — *Continued*

First published 1926-28 with title: Standard catalog for high school libraries

Kept up to date by annual supplements included in price of main volume

This collection of recommended materials includes 5,762 titles and some 10,578 analytical entries of books for grades nine through twelve. Entries contain full bibliographic information, Dewey Decimal classification number, subject headings, descriptive, and when possible, critical annotations

This "has been a standard work for more than 60 years in collection development and maintenance, selection and purchasing, cataloging and classification, general reference, and readers' advisory work." Nichols. Guide to Ref Books for Sch Media Cent. 4th edition

Wilson, George, 1920-

Books for children to read alone; a guide for parents and librarians; [by] George Wilson, Joyce Moss. Bowker 1988 184p $41

011.6

1. Children's literature—Bibliography 2. Books and reading—Best books
ISBN 0-8352-2346-9   LC 88-10430

This is an annotated bibliography of over 350 fiction and non-fiction titles recommended for readers ages 5-8. The book is divided into seven chapters according to half-year readability levels, starting with books for beginning readers through books for the second half of grade three. There are separate subject, readability, author, and title indexes

The **Young** adult reader's adviser; general editor, Myra Immell; consulting editor, Marion Sader. Bowker 1992 2v il set $79.95   **011.6**

1. Young adults' literature—Bibliography 2. Books and reading—Best books
ISBN 0-8352-3068-6   LC 92-3232

Companion to The reader's adviser, entered in class 011

Contents: v1 The best in literature and language arts, mathematics and computer science; v2 The best in social sciences and history, science and health

"Selected by a wide geographical range of authorities, it parallels the courses of study in American schools and closely follows the needs of curricula. It's a bibliographic tool, a critical compendium, and a biographical encyclopedia covering literature, language arts, math, computer science, social studies, history, science and health. Full bibliographic information is included." SLJ

For a fuller review see: Booklist, June, 1992

015.73 Bibliographies and catalogs of works issued or printed in the United States

Bailey, William G., 1947-

Guide to popular U.S. government publications; compiled by William G. Bailey. 3rd ed. Libraries Unlimited 1993 xxiv, 289p $39.50   **015.73**

1. United States—Government publications—Bibliography
ISBN 1-56308-031-1   LC 93-17573

First edition compiled by LeRoy C. Schwarzkopf published 1986

"The book identifies and describes more than 1,400 federal publications of current or long-term popular interest. . . . Arrangement is by subject. Each entry includes bibliographic description, issuing agency, SuDocs number, GPO stock number and price, and a brief descriptive annotation. . . . This volume covers the period from June of 1989 to January of 1993." Publisher's note

Books in print. Bowker 10v set $425   **015.73**

1. Bibliography
ISSN 0068-0214

Also available on CD-ROM

Annual. First published 1948

Updated by Books in print Supplement (3v) published annually in Spring, available at $229.95 (ISSN 0000-0310)

Contents: v1-4 Authors; v5-8 Titles; v9 Out of print, out of stock indefinitely; v10 Publishers

Lists titles available during the current year from American publishers, supplying such information as authors, co-authors, title, price, publisher, year of publication, and International Standard Book Numbers of cooperating publishers

The **Complete** directory of large print books and serials. Bowker pa $141   **015.73**

1. Large print books—Bibliography
ISSN 0000-1120

Also available on CD-ROM

Annual. First published 1970 with title: Large type books in print

This directory covers books, periodicals, and newspapers printed in 14 point type or larger. Books are indexed by subject, author and title, with complete bibliographic and ordering information

Cumulative book index; world list of books in the English language. Wilson, H.W. service basis   **015.73**

1. Bibliography 2. Books—Indexes
ISSN 0011-300X

Also available on CD-ROM

Monthly except August, cumulating at intervals with permanent bound annual cumulations

This is a single-alphabet author, title, and subject index to books published in the English language. 50,000 to 60,000 books are indexed each year. Author entries include complete bibliographic information: full title, paging, price, ISBN if available, publication date, publisher, edition, and LC card number

Forthcoming books. Bowker $227 per year   **015.73**

1. Bibliography
ISSN 0015-8119

Also available on CD-ROM

Bimonthly. First published 1966

This supplement to Books in print, entered above, and Subject guide to Books in print, entered below, provides a cumulative author-title-subject index to books that are to appear in the next five-month period. Information includes price, publisher, ISBN and LC card numbers and expected publication date

Government reference books; a biennial guide to U.S. government publications. Libraries Unlimited $55 **015.73**
1. United States—Government publications—Bibliography
ISSN 0072-5188
Biennial. First published 1970
An annotated listing of "atlases, bibliographies, catalogs, compendiums, dictionaries, directories, guides, handbooks, indexes, and other reference tools. Serials, except those of a monographic nature . . . are now listed in a separate work, *Government Reference Serials* (Libraries Unlimited, 1988). Annotated entries include detailed bibliographic citations, LC card numbers, ISBNs and ISSNs, OCLC numbers, *Monthly Catalog* numbers, GPO stock numbers, current price as of date of publication, and SuDocs classification numbers." Nichols. Guide to Ref Books for Sch Media Cent. 4th edition

Monthly catalog of United States Government publications; issued by the Superintendent of Documents. U.S. Govt. Ptg. Office $199 per year **015.73**
1. United States—Government publications—Bibliography
ISSN 0362-6830
Monthly. Subscription includes Periodicals supplement, semiannual and annual cumulative indexes, which are also available separately. Also available on CD-ROM
First published 1895. Title varies
"Each issue includes between 1500 and 3000 new documents, arranged by Superintendent of Documents classification number. Includes sales information and complete cataloging data. Utilizes Anglo-American cataloging rules and Library of Congress subject headings. Author, title, subject, and series/report index in each issue." Ref Sources for Small & Medium-sized Libr. 5th edition

Paperbound books in print. Bowker 6v set $202 **015.73**
1. Paperback books—Bibliography
ISSN 0031-1235
Also available on CD-ROM
Semi-annual. First published 1955
Published in Spring and Fall, each six-volume set gives title, author, subject and publisher information for paperback books currently available

Robinson, Judith Schiek, 1947-
Tapping the government grapevine; the user friendly guide to U.S. government information sources. 2nd ed. Oryx Press 1993 227p il pa $34.50 **015.73**
1. United States—Government publications—Bibliography
ISBN 0-89774-712-7 LC 92-40201
First published 1988
"Various types of federal government information searches are discussed, such as legislation and regulations, statistics, patents, scientific reports, Freedom of Information Act requests, and National Archives material. . . . [A] concise, well-designed guide to many mystifying realms of government information." Booklist

Subject guide to Books in print. Bowker 5v set $281 **015.73**
1. Catalogs, Subject 2. Bibliography
ISSN 0000-0159

Also available on CD-ROM
Annual. First published 1957
This companion publication to Books in print, entered above, lists titles currently available from United States publishers indexing them under LC subject headings

United States. Superintendent of Documents
Subject bibliographies. U.S. Govt. Ptg. Office gratis **015.73**
1. United States—Government publications—Bibliography
"Over 270 subject bibliographies listing publications available for sale by the Superintendent of Documents. Many deal with topics of current interest." Ref Sources for Small & Medium-sized Libr. 5th edition

U.S. Government books; publications for sale by the Government Printing Office. U.S. Govt. Ptg. Office gratis **015.73**
1. United States—Government publications—Bibliography
First published 1982. Issued irregularly
This catalog contains annotations of hundreds of currently available government publications, organized into subject categories. Each entry includes date, pages, GPO stock number, and price

Vertical file index; guide to pamphlets and references to current topics. Wilson, H.W. pa $50 per year **015.73**
1. Pamphlets—Bibliography 2. Pamphlets—Indexes
ISSN 0042-4439
First published 1932 with title: Vertical file service catalog. Issued monthly except August
"A list of free and inexpensive pamphlets, booklets, leaflets, and similar material considered to be of interest to general libraries. Subjects range from those suitable for school libraries to specialized technical reports. Arranged alphabetically by subject headings (deemed suitable for vertical file use) with title index." Sheehy. Guide to Ref Books. 10th edition

016 Bibliographies and catalogs of works on specific subjects or in specific disciplines

The **Schocken** guide to Jewish books; where to start reading about Jewish history, literature, culture, and religion; edited by Barry W. Holtz. Schocken Bks. 1992 357p il $25; pa $16 **016**
1. Jews—Bibliography 2. Judaism—Bibliography 3. Jewish literature—Bibliography
ISBN 0-8052-4108-6; 0-8052-1005-9 (pa)
LC 91-17760
Analyzed in Essay and general literature index
"The purpose of this book is to help the general reader find his or her way through the maze of Jewish books in the marketplace. . . . A variety of experts guide us through topics such as Bible, Talmud, Jewish history, the Holocaust, contemporary Israel, religious life and customs, mysticism, Hebrew and Yiddish literature, and Jewish feminism. There is also a chapter recommending books for the young adult of Bar or Bat Mitzvah age." Publisher's note

016.3713   Bibliographies of instructional materials

El-hi textbooks and serials in print. Bowker $133   **016.3713**

1. Textbooks—Bibliography   2. Periodicals—Bibliography
ISSN 0000-0825

Annual. Title varies

"Index to textbooks, dictionaries, encyclopedias, maps, atlases, professional books, teaching aids and auxiliary AV materials for grades K-12, plus adult and special education. Subject index contains grade and reading level; also author and title indexes and series index. Lists information not in 'Books in Print.'" N Y Public Libr. Ref Books for Child Collect. 2d edition

016.78   Bibliographies of music

Duckles, Vincent, 1913-1985
Music reference and research materials; an annotated bibliography; [by] Vincent H. Duckles, Michael A. Keller. 4th ed. Schirmer Bks. 1988 714p $39.95   **016.78**

1. Music—Bibliography
ISBN 0-02-870390-1   LC 88-18530

New edition in preparation

First published 1964

"Long regarded as one of the most significant works of its type. . . . The strength of this work is the complete citations and analytical annotations." Ref Sources for Small & Medium-sized Libr. 5th edition

016.79143   Bibliographies of motion pictures

Cella, Catherine
Great videos for kids; a parent's guide to choosing the best. Citadel Press 1992 144p pa $7.95   **016.79143**

1. Videotapes—Catalogs
ISBN 0-8065-1377-2   LC 92-31006

This guide focuses on the home video market and excludes feature films. "Chapters include animation, book-based videos, family topics, folk and fairy tales, holidays, and instruction films. . . . The appendices, which are particularly valuable, list 12 different best lists, including 'best videos with positive female roles' and 'positive black roles.' Highly recommended." Libr J

016.8   Bibliographies of literature

Anatomy of wonder; a critical guide to science fiction; edited by Neil Barron. 3rd ed. Bowker 1987 874p $48   **016.8**

1. Science fiction—Bibliography 2. Science fiction—History and criticism
ISBN 0-8352-2312-4   LC 87-9305

First published 1976

"Gives concise summaries and evaluations of more than 2000 adult and juvenile science fiction titles published through 1986. Includes sections on English-language science fiction, foreign-language science fiction, and research aids, covering history and criticism, science

fiction magazines, science fiction on film and television, and a core collection checklist." Ref Sources for Small & Medium-sized Libr. 5th edition

Anderson, Vicki, 1928-
Fiction sequels for readers 10 to 16; an annotated bibliography of books in succession. McFarland & Co. 1990 150p pa $19.95   **016.8**

1. Children's literature—Bibliography 2. Young adults' literature—Bibliography
ISBN 0-89950-519-8   LC 89-43686

The author has compiled a list of 1500 titles by about 350 authors. . . . Information is arranged alphabetically by author and provides the title, placement in the sequence, publisher, publication date, and a brief annotation of the content." Voice Youth Advocates

For a fuller review see: Booklist, Aug. 1990

Barzun, Jacques, 1907-
A catalogue of crime; [by] Jacques Barzun & Wendell Hertig Taylor. rev & enl ed. Harper & Row 1989 xxxvi, 952p $50   **016.8**

1. Mystery and detective stories—Bibliography
ISBN 0-06-010263-2   LC 88-45884

First published 1971

This work "provides bibliographic information and brief plot summaries for novels, short stories, criticism, and true crime. Arrangement is alphabetical by author and then by title, with indexes to authors, titles, and names." Ref Sources for Small & Medium-sized Libr. 5th edition

Burgess, Michael, 1948-
Reference guide to science fiction, fantasy, and horror. Libraries Unlimited 1992 403p $45   **016.8**

1. Science fiction—Bibliography 2. Fantastic fiction—Bibliography 3. Horror—Fiction—Bibliography
ISBN 0-87287-611-X   LC 91-44853

"This title provides a crisp and clear introduction to the entire domain of reference works that deal with perhaps the most exciting of modern literature genres. Every type of reference source known . . . is succinctly described and intelligently evaluated. Included is a very practical 'Core Collections' listing that recommends individual works appropriate for libraries. . . . This reference book is now the standard guide to the field." Am Libr

Fantasy literature; a reader's guide; edited by Neil Barron. Garland 1989 xxvii, 586p (Garland reference lib. of the humanities) $55   **016.8**

1. Fantastic fiction—Bibliography
ISBN 0-8240-3148-2   LC 89-23693

The editor covers "over 1700 works of fiction and nonfiction. History and criticism, reference works, film and television, art, magazines, core collections, awards, and organizations are surveyed. Modern titles for children and young adults receive attention. Numerous works combining science fiction and fantasy are carefully delineated." Libr J

Fiction catalog. 12th ed, edited by Juliette Yaakov and John Greenfieldt. Wilson, H.W. 1991 943p $98 **016.8**

1. Fiction—Bibliography 2. Fiction—Indexes
ISBN 0-8242-0804-8 LC 91-2355

"Standard catalog series"

First begun in 1908 as a paperback

Kept up to date by annual supplements which are included in price of main catalog

"A standard annotated bibliography of 5159 works of classical and popular fiction. Serves both as a selection aid and as a source for identifying outstanding works of fiction. Entries, arranged alphabetically by author, contain full bibliographic information and brief descriptive summaries, along with excerpts from critical reviews. Includes out-of-print titles and a special section for large-print books. Title and subject indexes." Ref Sources for Small & Medium-sized Libr. 5th edition

Horror literature; a reader's guide; edited by Neil Barron. Garland 1989 xxvii, 596p (Garland reference lib. of the humanities) $55 **016.8**

1. Horror—Fiction—Bibliography
ISBN 0-8240-4347-2 LC 89-27454

"Signed chapters cover historical periods, research sources, and special topics such as film and television, art, and magazines. . . . Concludes with a section listing a recommended core collection, award-winning works, organizations, and works published in series. Author, title, and theme indexes." Sheehy. Guide to Ref Books. 10th edition. suppl

Husband, Janet, 1942-
Sequels; an annotated guide to novels in series; [by] Janet Husband and Jonathan F. Husband. 2nd ed. American Lib. Assn. 1990 576p $45 **016.8**

1. Fiction—Bibliography
ISBN 0-8389-0533-1 LC 90-180

First published 1982

"A selective, annotated list of the best, most enduring, and most popular novels in series. Short stories and children's books are excluded; classics, mysteries, and science fiction are included. Each work is listed in the best current edition, in the preferred order for reading. Arranged by author, with a title and subject index." Ref Sources for Small & Medium-sized Libr. 5th edition

Reginald, R., 1948-
Science fiction and fantasy literature, 1975-1991; a bibliography of science fiction, fantasy, and horror fiction books and nonfiction monographs; associate editors, Mary A. Burgess, Daryl F. Mallett; editorial assistants and advisors, Scott Alan Burgess [et al.] Gale Res. 1992 1512p $199 **016.8**

1. Science fiction—Bibliography 2. Fantastic fiction—Bibliography 3. Horror—Fiction—Bibliography
ISBN 0-8103-1825-3 LC 92-28219

Companion volume to the author's Science fiction and fantasy literature: a checklist, 1700-1974 (1979)

This is "an alphabetical listing of authors and their works. Excluded are stage plays, poetry, songs, and graphic novels and comic books, but nonfiction works about the field and compilations of sf art are included. Each author entry notes titles, place of publication, publisher, date, pagination, binding, type (novel, collection, anthology, television/movie adaptation, nonfiction), and series." Libr J

Rosenberg, Betty
Genreflecting; a guide to reading interests in genre fiction; [by] Betty Rosenberg, Diana Tixier Herald. 3rd ed. Libraries Unlimited 1991 xxv, 345p $33.50 **016.8**

1. Fiction—Bibliography 2. Fiction—History and criticism 3. Books and reading
ISBN 0-87287-930-5 LC 91-28074

First published 1982

"Annotated guide to genre fiction, including westerns, thrillers, romance, science fiction, fantasy, and horror. Written to familiarize librarians with popular-reading interests of the public as well as to aid libraries and bookstores in identifying and selecting genre fiction. Arranged by genre and then by themes and types. Indexes to genre authors and to secondary materials." Ref Sources for Small & Medium-sized Libr. 5th edition

016.80881 Bibliographies of poetry collections

Katz, William A., 1924-
The Columbia Granger's guide to poetry anthologies; [by] William Katz, Linda Sternberg Katz. Columbia Univ. Press 1990 231p $45 **016.80881**

1. Poetry—Collections—Bibliography
ISBN 0-231-07244-9 LC 90-2469

Also available as part of Columbia Granger's world of poetry on CD-ROM, which also includes Granger's index to poetry, 8th edition, and The Columbia Granger's index to poetry, 9th edition

This volume provides "critical annotations for all the anthologies indexed in the ninth edition of Granger's [entered in class 808.81]. Almost 400 anthologies are arranged in 60 categories. . . . Useful for library collection development and readers' advisory work." Booklist

016.8093 Bibliographies of fiction history and criticism

Walker, Warren S.
Twentieth century short story explication: new series; with checklists of books and journals used. v1: 1989-1990. Shoe String Press 1993 366p $49.50 **016.8093**

1. Short stories—History and criticism—Bibliography
ISBN 0-208-02340-2 LC 92-22790

The third edition (1977) of the original series, its five supplements and index are still available

Contains nearly 6000 entries that provide a bibliography of interpretations for short stories published between 1989 and 1990

016.812   Bibliographies of American drama

Eddleman, Floyd Eugene
American drama criticism; interpretations, 1890-1977; compiled by Floyd Eugene Eddleman. 2d ed. Shoe String Press 1979 488p $45   **016.812**
1. American drama—History and criticism—Bibliography 2. Theater—United States—Bibliography
ISBN 0-208-01713-5   LC 78-31346

Updated by Supplement I, covering the years 1978-1982 $39.50 (ISBN 0-208-01978-2); Supplement II, covering the years 1983-1987 $47.50 (ISBN 0-208-02138-8); Supplement III, covering the years 1988-1990 $55 (ISBN 0-208-02270-8)

First published 1967 with title: American drama criticism; interpretations, 1890-1965; compiled by Helen H. Palmer and Jane Anne Dyson

This work lists criticism and interpretations of American plays published in books and periodicals. Entries are arranged by playwright and then by title of play

018   Catalogs arranged by author and date

American book prices current. Bancroft-Parkman, Box 1236, Washington, CT 06793 price varies   **018**
1. Books—Prices   2. Autographs—Prices   3. Rare books
ISSN 0091-9357

Annual. First published 1894/95. Quadrennial indexes

"Arrangement and information given vary somewhat but usually include author, title, edition, place and date of publication, size, binding, condition, where sold, date of sale, catalog number of lot, and price. . . . Generally considered the most accurate of the auction record compilations." Sheehy. Guide to Ref Books. 10th edition

Bookman's price index; a guide to the values of rare and other out-of-print books. Gale Res. $218   **018**
1. Books—Prices 2. Rare books
ISSN 0068-0141

Semi-annual. First published 1964 as an annual

"Two volumes per year provide . . . current price information from the year's catalogs of nearly 200 book-dealers located in the United States, England, and elsewhere. The entries are arranged alphabetically by author." Publisher's note

020   Library and information sciences

ALA handbook of organization and membership directory. American Lib. Assn. $30   **020**
1. American Library Association—Directories 2. Librarians—Directories
ISSN 0273-4602

Annual. First published for 1980/1981

Combined edition of ALA handbook of organization (available separately, pa $20) and ALA membership directory, first published 1972 and 1940 respectively

The Handbook provides names of current officials, committee members, Council members, and representatives. It also provides information regarding the units of ALA, and lists the periodicals of the association. The Membership Directory includes the name and brief address of personal and organizational members

Information U.S.A. [compiled by] Matthew Lesko; research director, Sharon Zarozny. rev ed. Viking 1986 1253p o.p.; Penguin Bks. paperback available $24.95   **020**
1. Information services 2. United States—Government publications 3. United States—Officials and employees
ISBN 0-14-046745-9 (pa)   LC 85-40628

First published 1983

"Addresses, telephone numbers, advice and comments (some pleasantly irreverent), and a user-friendly slant with a sound sense of the needs and wishes of readers . . . make this guide to obtaining information from federal sources an attractive reference." Recomm Ref Books in Paperback. 2d edition

Library literature. Wilson, H.W. service basis   **020**
1. Library science—Bibliography 2. Library science—Periodicals—Indexes
ISSN 0024-2373

Also available on CD-ROM

Published bimonthly with bound annual cumulations

This is a single-alphabet author and subject index to materials in library and information science published in the United States and abroad. About 220 journals and more than 600 monographs are indexed each year. Other materials indexed include selected state journals, conference proceedings, pamphlets, and library school theses

020.5   Library and information sciences—Serial publications

The **Bowker** annual library and book trade almanac. Bowker $142   **020.5**
1. Libraries 2. Book industries
ISSN 0068-0540

Also available on CD-ROM as part of Library reference plus

Annual. First published 1956. Title varies

"A compendium of statistical and directory information relating to most aspects of librarianship and the book trade. Professional reports from the field; international library news; library legislation; grants; survey articles of developments during the preceding year." Ref Sources for Small & Medium-sized Libr. 5th edition

Library Journal. Bowker $79   **020.5**
1. Library science—Periodicals 2. Libraries—Periodicals
ISSN 0363-0277

Semimonthly February through June and September through November. Monthly January, July, August and December. First published 1876

Each issue contains "news, feature articles, columns on magazines, people, a calendar of events, and reviews. . . . No other library science journal can compare to this one for timeliness, coverage of the library world, and reviewing services, all in one neat package. An

Library Journal—*Continued*
essential purchase for all library collections." Katz. Mag for Libr. 6th edition

Wilson Library Bulletin. Wilson, H.W. $52
020.5
1. Library science—Periodicals 2. Libraries—Periodicals 3. Books and reading—Periodicals
ISSN 0043-5651

Monthly except July and August. First published 1914 with title: The Wilson Bulletin

Articles, special reports and reviews assess children's literature, reference books, audio-visual materials, special collections, online services and other topics of interest to librarians
"A basic purchase for most professional collections." Katz. Mag for Libr. 6th edition

021.7 Promotion of libraries, information centers

Friends of libraries sourcebook; edited by Sandy Dolnick. 2nd ed. American Lib. Assn. 1990 247p il pa $25 **021.7**
1. Public relations—Libraries
ISBN 0-8389-0525-0 LC 89-17889
First published 1981

This work "covers just about every issue involved in organizing and operating Friends, including such diverse items as tax-exempt status, management by objectives, programming, and group dynamics. . . . This will be of help to directors seeking outside support for any type of library." Libr J
Includes bibliographic references

Schaeffer, Mark
Library displays handbook. Wilson, H.W. 1991 250p il $39 **021.7**
1. Libraries—Exhibitions 2. Public relations—Libraries
ISBN 0-8242-0801-3 LC 90-49442
"Schaeffer presents techniques for the design and lettering of signs, posters, wall displays, bulletin boards, and exhibits, discussing such up-to-date means to those end products as computer-generated graphics, including clip art. Many sample projects are carefully presented step-by-step, and appendixes provide materials sources, computer software suggestions, further reading suggestions." Booklist

025.04 Automated information storage and retrieval systems

Gale directory of databases. Gale Res. 2v + update volumes pa v1 $199, v2 $119, set $280 **025.04**
1. Information systems—Directories
ISSN 1066-8934
Each price includes update service
Also available on CD-ROM
Annual. First published 1993. Formed by the merger of Directory of online databases, Directory of portable databases, and Computer-readable databases
Contents: v1 Online databases; v2 CD-ROM, diskette, magnetic tape, handheld, and batch access database products

"Descriptive entries include such details as producer name and contact information, summary of content, database language, geographic coverage, year first available, time span, updating, availability, rates, and more." Publisher's note

025.1 Library administration

Give 'em what they want! managing the public's library; [by] the Baltimore County Public Library's Blue Ribbon Committee. American Lib. Assn. 1992 169p il (Public lib. administration ser) pa $30 **025.1**
1. Libraries—Administration 2. Public libraries 3. Public relations—Libraries
ISBN 0-8389-0592-7 LC 92-13756
"From a how-to perspective, the text treats building (i.e., how to establish service where people want it), materials (i.e., how to monitor the need for types and quantities of books wanted), and service delivery (i.e., how to put user and stuff together quickly). It's easy to read and full of useful advice. . . . An excellent overview of a controversial and exciting concept in library service." Booklist
Includes bibliographic references

Swan, James
Fundraising for the small public library; a how-to-do-it manual for librarians. Neal-Schuman 1990 238p (How-to-do-it manuals for libraries) pa $37.50 **025.1**
1. Library finance
ISBN 1-55570-077-2 LC 90-6457
"Swan outlines very practical ways (donations, memorials, grants, direct mail, auctions, annual events, etc.) for small libraries to raise the extra dollars they need." Booklist
Includes bibliographic references

Weingand, Darlene E.
Administration of the small public library. 3rd ed. American Lib. Assn. 1992 213p pa $25 **025.1**
1. Libraries—Administration 2. Public libraries
ISBN 0-8389-0583-8 LC 91-42064
First published 1965 under the authorship of Dorothy Sinclair
"Weingand integrates principles of public library namagement with a marketing approach to library service. . . . The marketing emphasis is found throughout the text, influencing programs, staffing, finances, and all aspects of library administration." Publisher's note
"A helpful overview for administrators in small libraries, even for those who don't insist that they are 'marketing' 'products' to 'clients.'" Libr J
Includes bibliographic references

025.17 Administration of collections of special materials

Appel, Marsha C., 1953-
Illustration index. Scarecrow Press **025.17**
1. Pictures—Indexes

Appel, Marsha C., 1953-—*Continued*

First and second editions by Lucile E. Vance and Esther M. Tracy, published 1957 and 1966 respectively; third edition by Roger C. Greer published 1973; fourth edition by Marsha C. Appel published 1980; o.p.

Volumes available are: fifth edition covering the years 1977-1981, published 1984 $34 (ISBN 0-8108-1656-3); sixth edition covering the years 1982-1986, published 1988 $42.50 (ISBN 0-8108-2146-X)

"Comprehensive guide to many thousand of photographs, paintings, drawings, and diagrams appearing in popular periodicals. Publications were chosen for the richness of illustration and availability of back issues in libraries." Ref Sources for Small & Medium-sized Libr. 5th edition

Morehead, Joe, 1931-

Introduction to United States government information sources; [by] Joe Morehead and Mary Fetzer. 4th ed. Libraries Unlimited 1992 xxxii, 474p $38.50; pa $32.50 **025.17**

1. United States—Government publications
ISBN 0-87287-909-7; 1-56308-066-4 (pa)
LC 92-13251

First published 1975 with title: Introduction to United States public documents

This guide covers government publications in both print and nonprint formats. Included are chapters on the Government Printing Office, the Superintendent of Documents, the depository library system, publications of the Presidency and of the judiciary, technical report literature, geographic sources, government periodicals and serials, and statistical sources

"Highly recommended . . . as a reference source for public and academic librarians who deal with government information." Libr J

025.3 Bibliographic analysis and control

ALA filing rules; [prepared by the] Filing Committee, Resources and Technical Services Division, American Library Association. American Lib. Assn. 1980 50p pa $13 **025.3**

1. Files and filing 2. Library catalogs
ISBN 0-8389-3255-X
LC 80-22186

Successor to: ALA Rules for filing catalog cards, second edition

"This edition of ALA's library catalog 'Filing Rules' was issued to correspond with requirements of the 'Anglo-American Cataloguing Rules' 2d ed. [entered below] and machine filing applications." Wynar. Guide to Ref Books for Sch Media Cent. 3d edition

According to a 1981 announcement of the American Library Association, this may be considered as an alternative to, rather than a definite replacement for, the 1968 edition of ALA Rules for filing catalog cards. Libraries may choose to continue using the earlier publication

Anglo-American cataloguing rules, 2d ed., 1988 revision; prepared under the direction of the Joint Steering Committee for Revision of AACR, a committee of the American Library Association [et al.]; the Australian Committee on Cataloguing, the British Library; edited by Michael Gorman and Paul W. Winkler. American Lib. Assn. 1988 xxv, 677p $40; pa $30 **025.3**

1. Cataloging
ISBN 0-8389-3346-7; 0-8389-3360-2 (pa)
LC 88-19349

Also available in loose-leaf format $60 (ISBN 0-8389-3361-0)

First published 1967

"These rules are designed for use in the construction of catalogues and other lists in general libraries of all sizes. . . . The rules cover the description of, and the provision of access points for, all library materials commonly collected at the present time. . . . Part I deals with the provision of information describing the item being catalogued and part II deals with the determination and establishment of headings (access points) under which the descriptive information is to be presented to catalogue users, and with the making of references to those headings." General Introduction

Gorman, Michael, 1941-

The concise AACR2, 1988 revision. American Lib. Assn. 1989 161p pa $24 **025.3**

1. Anglo-American cataloguing rules 2. Cataloging
ISBN 0-8389-3362-9
LC 89-15110

Based on Anglo-American cataloguing rules, 2nd edition, 1988 revision entered above

"Many smaller libraries will find this volume more helpful than the complete *AACR2*, although some may eventually progress to the full set of rules. . . . Capitalization rules, glossary and comparative table of *AACR2* and *Concise AACR2* rules appended." Booklist

Maxwell, Margaret F., 1927-

Handbook for AACR2; explaining and illustrating the Anglo-American cataloguing rules; with a new chapter by Judith A. Carter. 1988 rev ed. American Lib. Assn. 1989 436p pa $37 **025.3**

1. Anglo-American cataloguing rules—Handbooks, manuals, etc. 2. Cataloging—Handbooks, manuals, etc.
ISBN 0-8389-0505-6
LC 88-36703

First published 1980

This "manual furnishes hundreds of examples of the application of specific rules to data typically found on materials being cataloged. . . . Maxwell should be part of every student-cataloger's bookshelf and all professional collections." Libr J

Miller, Rosalind E.

Commonsense cataloging; a cataloger's manual; [by] Rosalind E. Miller & Jane C. Terwillegar. 4th ed rev. Wilson, H.W. 1990 180p pa $26 **025.3**

1. Cataloging
ISBN 0-8242-0789-0
LC 89-70716

Miller, Rosalind E.—*Continued*
First edition by Esther J. Piercy published 1965; this is a revision of the fourth edition published 1989

This practical manual for the beginning cataloger discusses such topics as: applications of AACR2; subject organization; Dewey classification; subject access; cataloging with copy; mechanical preparation and maintenance; special problems posed by serials, maps, kits and electronic software; computers and cataloging

Includes bibliography

025.4 Subject analysis and control

Dewey, Melvil, 1851-1931
Abridged Dewey decimal classification and relative index; devised by Melvil Dewey. ed 12, edited by John P. Comaromi. Forest Press (Albany) 1990 857p $80   **025.4**
1. Dewey Decimal Classification
ISBN 0-910608-42-3   LC 90-31428
First abridged edition published 1894

This edition is an abridgement of the 20th edition, entered below. Adapted to the needs of small and growing libraries, the 12th Abridged Edition is designed primarily for school and public libraries with collections of up to 20,000 titles

Dewey decimal classification and relative index; devised by Melvil Dewey. ed 20, edited by John P. Comaromi. Forest Press (Albany) 1989 4v set $250   **025.4**
1. Dewey Decimal Classification
ISBN 0-910608-37-7   LC 88-24629
First published anonymously in 1876

Contents: v1 Introduction, tables; v2 Schedules 000-599; v3 Schedules 600-999; v4 Relative index, manual

Library of Congress. Office for Subject Cataloging Policy
Library of Congress subject headings; prepared by the Office for Subject Cataloging Policy, Collections Services. Library of Congress 4v $170   **025.4**
1. Subject headings
Also available on CD-ROM
Editions 1-7 published with title: Subject headings used in the dictionary catalogs of the Library of Congress. Published annually since 1988

This work contains the headings and cross-references established and applied by the Library of Congress

Sears list of subject headings. 14th ed, edited by Martha T. Mooney. Wilson, H.W. 1991 731p $42   **025.4**
1. Subject headings
ISBN 0-8242-0803-X   LC 91-10290
Also available: Canadian companion to 14th edition $18 (ISBN 0-8242-0832-3); Spanish version of 12th edition with title: Sears Lista de encabezamientos de materia $45 (ISBN 0-8242-0704-1)
First published 1923 with title: List of subject headings for small libraries, by Minnie Earl Sears

This list of headings follows the Library of Congress form of headings with appropriate adaptations to meet the needs of smaller libraries. This edition features suggested classification numbers for the subject headings. The numbers are based upon the Twelfth Edition of the Abridged Dewey decimal classification and relative index

025.5 Services to users

Berliner, Barbara
The book of answers; the New York Public Library Telephone Reference Service's most unusual and entertaining questions; [by] Barbara Berliner with Melinda Corey and George Ochoa. Prentice Hall Press 1990 311p $21.45; pa $9.95   **025.5**
1. Questions and answers
ISBN 0-13-957432-8; 0-13-406554-9 (pa)
LC 90-34337

A Stonesong Press book developed with the Telephone Reference Service, Mid-Manhattan Library, the Branch Libraries, the New York Public Library

"More than 1,000 queries and their answers are arranged [in 27 subject areas]. . . . Besides supplying a quick ready reference source, the book gives patrons insight into the work performed by a reference librarian and the possibilities for information service available at the local library." Booklist

Katz, William A., 1924-
Introduction to reference work. McGraw-Hill 2v v1 $30.61, v2 $30.24   **025.5**
1. Reference services (Libraries) 2. Reference books—Bibliography
First published 1969. (6th edition 1992) Periodically revised

Contents: v1 Basic information sources; v2 Reference services and reference processes

Volume one opens with a general introduction to the reference process and online reference services. Types of services include: bibliographies; indexing and abstracting services; encyclopedias; ready-reference; biographies; government documents. Volume two covers community reference services; interviewing; online searching; and library and bibliographic instruction, as well as evaluation of reference services

The **New** York Public Library book of how and where to look it up; Sherwood Harris, editor-in-chief. Prentice-Hall 1991 382p $30   **025.5**
1. Reference books—Bibliography   2. Research
3. Libraries—Handbooks, manuals, etc.
ISBN 0-13-614728-3   LC 91-25660
"A Stonesong Press book"
This work "is a mixture of bibliographic and directory information. . . . The book consists of six sections, covering Reference Books, Telephone, Government, and Picture sources, Special Collections, and Electronic Databases. . . . Within each category, entries are alphabetical by subject. . . . Virtually all entries are annotated. . . . It will prove an outstanding purchase for small libraries, and larger ones will welcome it as a ready reference tool at the public service desk." Libr J
For a fuller review see: Booklist, Dec. 15, 1991

Saricks, Joyce G.
Readers' advisory service in the public library; [by] Joyce G. Saricks and Nancy Brown. American Lib. Assn. 1989 84p pa $18   **025.5**
1. Reader services (Libraries) 2. Reference services (Libraries) 3. Fiction—Bibliography
ISBN 0-8389-0511-0   LC 89-30717
The authors "describe the key reference sources used by readers' advisors, describe how an advisory interview is conducted, review the need for such advisors in offering popular fiction, indicate how the work of such advisors can best be promoted, and conclude with a two-page epilogue that focuses on the administrative and personal commitment that an effective program demands. It is an essential tool for any librarian whose job involves helping users select reading material." Wilson Libr Bull

025.7 Physical preparation for storage of library materials

Greenfield, Jane
Books: their care and repair. Wilson, H.W. 1984 204p il $38   **025.7**
1. Books—Conservation and restoration
ISBN 0-8242-0695-9   LC 83-25926
"Geared to librarians, this useful handbook explains in clear, precise language how major and minor book repairs can be performed in-house without costly materials. . . . [The author] also furnishes basic background material on the structure of books and how proper care prevents deterioration. Simple line drawings supplement the text." Booklist
Includes bibliography

Lavender, Kenneth
Book repair; a how-to-do-it manual for librarians; [by] Kenneth Lavender, Scott Stockton. Neal-Schuman 1992 119p il (How-to-do-it manuals for school and public librarians) $37.50   **025.7**
1. Books—Conservation and restoration
ISBN 1-55570-103-5   LC 92-8109
Step-by-step instructions and illustrations detail recasing, rebacking, tightening hinges and mending tears
Includes bibliography

025.8 Maintenance and preservation of library collections

Morris, John, 1912-
The library disaster preparedness handbook. American Lib. Assn. 1986 129p il pa $25   **025.8**
1. Libraries—Security measures 2. Library resources—Conservation and restoration
ISBN 0-8389-0438-6   LC 86-1155
"Although water and fire are still serious threats in libraries, mutilation, theft, and problem patrons also have become major concerns in the area of preservation of materials. Morris covers all these topics in this useful study of how library collections can be protected from

all forms of disaster. . . . A bibliography on disaster preparedness is appended." Booklist

Swartzburg, Susan G., 1938-
Preserving library materials; a manual. Scarecrow Press 1980 282p il $17.50
                                               025.8
1. Library resources—Conservation and restoration
ISBN 0-8108-1302-5   LC 80-11742
This discussion of collection maintenance covers the various media found in library collections: books, photographs, prints, slides, microforms, records, tapes, and film and the problems each present
Includes bibliography

026 Libraries, information centers devoted to specific disciplines and subjects

Directory of special libraries and information centers. Gale Res. v1 (pt.1-2) $415, v2 $355, v3 inter-edition subscription pa $360
                                               026
1. Special libraries—Directories
ISSN 0731-633X
First published 1963. (16th edition 1993) Frequently revised. Volume one is kept up to date between editions by New special libraries (designated volume three)
Contents: v1 pt.1 A-M; v1 pt.2 N-Z; v2 Geographic and personnel indexes; v3 New special libraries (ISSN 0193-4287)
This is a guide to nearly 21,000 special libraries and information centers maintained by government agencies and business, education, non-profit, and professional organizations

Subject collections; a guide to special book collections and subject emphasis in libraries. Bowker 2v $275   **026**
1. Special libraries
ISSN 0000-0140
First published 1958. (7th edition 1993) Periodically revised
Compiled by Lee Ash and others
Arranged alphabetically by subject, then geographically. This volume covers over 18,000 collections in some 11,000 academic, public, and special libraries as well as in museums, located in the United States and Canada. Information given for each entry includes name and address of library, number of volumes within collection and holdings other than books

Subject directory of special libraries and information centers. Gale Res. 3v ea $265, set $695   **026**
1. Special libraries—Directories
ISSN 0732-927X
First published 1975. (16th edition 1992) Frequently revised
A rearrangement of entries from the Directory of special libraries and information centers, entered above
Contents: v1 Business, government, and law libraries; v2 Computers, engineering, and science libraries; v3 Health science libraries

027 General libraries, information centers

American library directory. Bowker 2v $225

027

1. Libraries—Directories
ISSN 0065-910X

Also available on CD-ROM as part of Library reference plus

Annual. First published 1923

"Includes U.S. and Canadian public, academic, and special libraries arranged by state or province, city, and institution. Gives personnel and statistical data, subject interests, and special collections." Ref Sources for Small & Medium-sized Libr. 5th edition

Dickson, Paul
The library in America; a celebration in words and pictures. Facts on File 1986 242p il $40; pa $19.95

027

1. Libraries—United States 2. Public libraries
ISBN 0-8160-1365-9; 0-8160-1887-1 (pa) LC 86-8981

A "history of the public library movement in the United States. Dickson has collocated a wealth of charming black-and-white photographs that vividly illustrate the fundamental social and intellectual appeal of the public library, as well as capture the undeniably romantic aura of this singularly American institution." Booklist

Eberhart, George M.
The whole library handbook; current data, professional advice, and curiosa about libraries and library services; compiled by George M. Eberhart. American Lib. Assn. 1991 490p il pa $25

027

1. Library science 2. Libraries—United States 3. Library services
ISBN 0-8389-0573-0 LC 91-17311

"This compact quick-reference manual is well organized, attractive, and packed with useful library-related information for all levels of librarianship. The book will be a valuable resource tool as well as an excellent browsing item." Voice Youth Advocates

For a fuller review see: Booklist, Nov. 15, 1991

Includes bibliographic references

Harris, Michael H.
History of libraries in the western world. compact textbook ed. Scarecrow Press 1984 289p $22.50

027

1. Libraries—History
ISBN 0-8108-1666-0 LC 83-20133

First published 1965 under the authorship of Elmer D. Johnson and Michael H. Harris

"Traces the history of libraries in the Western world and shows how they developed, influenced, and were influenced by their coeval cultures." Publisher's note

Includes bibliographic references

027.5 Government libraries

Goodrum, Charles A.
Treasures of the Library of Congress; photography by Michael Freeman and Jonathan Wallen. rev and expanded ed. Abrams 1991 344p il $75

027.5

1. Library of Congress
ISBN 0-8109-3852-9 LC 90-1147

First published 1980

"The author selects 500 . . . 'treasures' to highlight, among them: the Gutenberg Bible; Ptolemy's 1482 atlas; Dorothea Lange's photographs; and ancient Chinese, Japanese and Arabic texts. . . . Anecdotes about the Library's administrators and patrons enliven the history of the institution." Publ Wkly

Includes bibliographic references

027.62 Libraries for children and young adults

Bauer, Caroline Feller, 1935-
Read for the fun of it; active programming with books for children; drawings by Lynn Gates Bredeson. Wilson, H.W. 1992 xx, 372p il $45

027.62

1. Children—Books and reading 2. Children's literature 3. Children's libraries
ISBN 0-8242-0824-2 LC 91-31450

This volume "demonstrates how to promote children's recreational reading. . . . Among the topics covered are reading aloud, reaching parents, author visits, storytelling with visual aids, teaching children to present stories and poetry, and using puppetry and magic tricks in storytelling." Booklist

Includes bibliographic references

Cullum, Carolyn N.
The storytime sourcebook; a compendium of ideas and resources for storytellers. Neal-Schuman 1990 177p pa $24.95

027.62

1. Storytelling 2. Children's libraries
ISBN 1-55570-067-5 LC 90-49657

"Neatly arranged by subject, each page contains all you will need for one story hour session, including five titles, four or five filmstrips or a film, songs, fingerplays, crafts, and activities." Booklist

Includes bibliographies

Greene, Ellin, 1927-
Books, babies, and libraries; serving infants, toddlers, their parents & caregivers. American Lib. Assn. 1991 187p il pa $25

027.62

1. Children's libraries 2. Children—Books and reading
ISBN 0-8389-0572-2 LC 91-17050

The author "begins with a look at some model early childhood centers in libraries, an overview of major theories of early child development, and a discussion of the roles of parents and librarians in fostering literacy. Subsequent chapters cover the development of collections (both for toddlers themselves and for their parents), program planning, networking and outreach, and the overall

Greene, Ellin, 1927-—*Continued*
planning, implementation, and evaluation of library service to early childhood." SLJ

Includes bibliographies

027.8 School libraries

American Association of School Librarians
Information power; guidelines for school library media programs; prepared by the American Association of School Librarians and Association for Educational Communications and Technology. American Lib. Assn.; Association for Educ. Communications & Technology 1988 171p il pa $15   **027.8**

1. School libraries 2. Instructional materials centers
ISBN 0-8389-3352-1   LC 88-3480

Replaces Media programs: district and school, published 1975

"The book begins with the mission statement—to ensure that students and staff are effective users of ideas and information—and lists five challenges that library media specialists face. Following are individual chapters, complete with helpful bibliographies, that discuss programs; roles and responsibilities; leadership, planning, and management; personnel; resources and equipment; facilities; and district, regional and state leadership." Booklist

028 Reading and use of other information media

Adler, Mortimer Jerome, 1902-
How to read a book; revised and updated by Mortimer J. Adler and Charles Van Doren. Simon & Schuster 1972 hardcover o.p. paperback available $12   **028**

1. Books and reading 2. Reading
ISBN 0-671-21209-5 (pa)

First published 1940

This guide "is dedicated to the virtues of a disciplined and structured approach to reading. . . . The authors distinguish four levels: elementary reading; inspectional reading (e.g., skimming); analytical reading; and 'syntopical' reading, where complex ideas are pursued through more than one book. . . . Appendix A is a recommended reading list. . . . Appendix B consists of exercises and tests. Recommended as stimulating and (nowadays) provocative." Recomm Ref Books in Paperback. 2d edition

Alter, Robert
The pleasures of reading; in an ideological age. Simon & Schuster 1989 250p hardcover o.p. paperback available $8.95   **028**

1. Books and reading 2. Literature—History and criticism
ISBN 0-671-70627-6 (pa)   LC 88-36590

"In his defense of reading, the author examines basic components of literature—character, perspective, style, allusion, structure—and draws on the Bible, poetry and, above all, novels to illustrate how these varied elements . . . provide readers with pleasure in part because they resist inclusion within the grand schemes of now-popular theoretical models." Publ Wkly

"A readable book that opponents of recent critical theory will readily embrace." Booklist

Booktalk! 2-5. Wilson, H.W. 1985-1993 4v pa ea $32   **028**

1. Books and reading
ISBN 0-8242-0716-5 (v2); 0-8242-0764-5 (v3); 0-8242-0835-8 (v4); 0-8242-0836-6 (v5)

Original Booktalk! published 1980 o.p.

Edited by Joni Bodart-Talbot

Volume 2 explains what booktalks are and contains 250 examples; volume 3 offers 500 booktalks and has a combined index to booktalks in volumes 2-3; volume 4 is a collection of 350 booktalks and 5 articles which appeared in the Booktalker section of Wilson Library Bulletin between September 1989 and May 1992; volume 5 adds 320 more talks and 4 articles on booktalking

Fadiman, Clifton, 1904-
The lifetime reading plan. 3rd ed. Harper & Row 1988 291p hardcover o.p. paperback available $10   **028**

1. Books and reading—Best books
ISBN 0-06-096174-0 (pa)   LC 87-46135

First published 1960 by Crowell

The author has selected and provided commentaries on some one hundred significant works, from Homer to contemporary authors, including both fiction and nonfiction titles

Includes bibliography

Rubin, Joan Shelley, 1947-
The making of middlebrow culture. University of N.C. Press 1992 xx, 416p il $34.95; pa $14.95   **028**

1. Books and reading 2. United States—Intellectual life 3. United States—Popular culture
ISBN 0-8078-2010-5; 0-8078-4354-7 (pa)

     LC 91-22241

Analyzed in Essay and general literature index

"Exploring the democratization of culture in a consumer society, Rubin concentrates on . . . the establishment of book clubs, including the founding of the Book-of-the-Month Club; the beginnings of 'great books' programs; the creation of the New York Herald Tribune's book-review section; the popularity of such works as Will Durant's The Story of Philosophy; and the emergence of literary radio programs. Rubin also . . . [examines individuals involved in] these middlebrow enterprises." Publisher's note

"Supported by its extensive bibliography, this study is a treasure trove for all students of American studies and popular culture." Choice

Van Doren, Charles Lincoln, 1926-
The joy of reading; 210 favorite books, plays, poems, essays, etc.: what's in them, why read them. Harmony Bks. 1985 479p $19.95   **028**

1. Books and reading—Best books
ISBN 0-517-55580-8   LC 85-5424

The author's "210 selections for discussion are unabashedly personal, ranging across centuries, subjects, and genres. . . . His enthusiastic, unpedantic entries provide fine capsule introductions useful to anyone

Van Doren, Charles Lincoln, 1926- — *Continued*
seeking a '*good* book.' For readers and readers' advisors alike." Libr J

Includes bibliography

028.1 Reviews of books and other media

The **Best** in children's books; the University of Chicago guide to children's literature, 1966-1972—1985-1990; written and edited by Zena Sutherland. University of Chicago Press 1973-1991 4v 028.1
1. Children's literature—Bibliography 2. Books and reading—Best books 3. Books—Reviews
LC 85-31820

1985-1990 volume written and edited by Zena Sutherland, Betsy Hearne, and Roger Sutton

Volumes available are: 1966-1972 $25 (ISBN 0-226-78057-0); 1973-1978 $25 (ISBN 0-226-78059-7); 1979-1984 $35 (ISBN 0-226-78060-0); 1985-1990 $37.50 (ISBN 0-226-78064-3)

These volumes bring together reviews originally published in The Bulletin of the Center for Children's Books. Some 1400 recommended titles from each period are covered in each volume. The listings are arranged alphabetically by author, with title, developmental values, curricular use, reading level, subject, and type of literature indexes

Book review digest. Wilson, H.W. service basis 028.1
1. Books—Reviews
ISSN 0006-7326

Also available on CD-ROM
All annual cumulations 1905-to date available
Published monthly, except February and July. Quarterly cumulations. Permanent bound annual cumulations

This work "provides excerpts from, and citations to, reviews of adult and juvenile fiction and nonfiction, trade books, and reference books. It currently covers reviews of almost 7,000 English-language publications each year that appear in 95 (26 recent additions) American, British, and Canadian periodicals in the humanities, social sciences, and general sciences, plus library review media. Entries, arranged alphabetically by author or title (as appropriate), give author, title, paging, price, publisher and year, ISBN, a descriptive introduction to the book, age or grade level (for juvenile works), suggested Sears subject headings, and LC card number. Reviewing information includes citations of reviews, name of reviewers, approximate length of each review, and up to four review excerpts chosen to provide a balance of opinion." Nichols. Guide to Ref Books for Sch Media Cent. 4th edition

An author/title index covering 1975-1984 is available for $65 (ISBN 0-8242-0729-7); index covering 1905-1974 is o.p.

Book review index. Gale Res. 028.1
1. Books—Reviews—Indexes
ISSN 0524-0581

Bimonthly. Began publication in 1965 as a monthly. Annual cumulations available for $210 each. Master cumulation covering the years 1965-1984 available 10v $1275 (ISBN 0-8103-0577-1)

"This comprehensive index cites all reviews appearing in more than 500 popular and professional periodicals. Included are adult and juvenile fiction, nonfiction, and reference books—some 132,000 review citations for about 74,000 new books each year. Arranged alphabetically by author, *BRI* gives only author, title, and the review. There is a title index. No descriptive summaries or excerpts from reviews, such as those found in *Book Review Digest*, are offered; nor is any subject access provided." Nichols. Guide to Ref Books for Sch Media Cent. 4th edition

Booklist. American Lib. Assn. $60 per year 028.1
1. Books—Reviews 2. Books and reading—Best books
ISSN 0006-7385

Semimonthly September through June; monthly July and August. First published 1905 with title: A.L.A. Booklist. Merged with Subscription Books Bulletin in 1956

"*Booklist's* clear organizational format facilitates selective scanning. Only recommended titles are reviewed, allowing the reader a quick, high-quality overview of the best in new books. . . . Regular sections review new books for young adults and children and survey the latest films, videos, classroom filmstrips, and selected, educational microcomputer software. . . . An inserted section, 'Reference Books Bulletin,' appearing in each issue [and available in an annual cumulation for $25] constitutes a separate publication with longer profiles of major reference works and more abbreviated entries on continuations, supplements, and serials. *Booklist* is an essential and increasingly valuable selection tool for public and school libraries." Katz. Mag for Libr. 6th edition

Choice. Association of College & Res. Libs. $155 per year 028.1
1. Books—Reviews 2. Academic libraries—Periodicals
ISSN 0009-4978

Monthly with a combined July-August issue. First published 1964

"This publication has become one of the most indispensable book review tools for academic and large public library acquisitions. . . . Issues feature a regular section with a changing bibliographic essay topic and follow with the precisely stated 100-to 150-word reviews themselves, grouped by academically oriented subject categories." Katz. Mag for Libr. 6th edition

Yardley, Jonathan
Out of step; notes from a purple decade. Villard Bks. 1991 263p $20 028.1
1. Books—Reviews
ISBN 0-394-58910-6
LC 90-36283

This selection of the author's Washington Post columns is "divided into three sections (literary, social, and personal commentaries). . . . The book serves well as a commentary on life in the Eighties as well as an excellent introduction to Yardley's readable style and curmudgeonly views." Libr J

028.5 Reading and use of other information media by children and young adults

Atlas, James
Battle of the books; the curriculum debate in America. Norton 1992 157p $17.95 028.5
1. Books and reading 2. Colleges and universities—Curricula 3. Higher education
ISBN 0-393-03413-5
LC 92-20032

Atlas, James—*Continued*

The author outlines the "curriculum debate that embroils American college campuses today. He explains why the multiculturalists believe that the nation's educational heritage is racist, paternalistic, and elitist. But he also presents the view of the traditionalists, who see themselves as guardians of an approved canon of literature." Publisher's note

Carpenter, Humphrey

The Oxford companion to children's literature; [by] Humphrey Carpenter and Mari Prichard. Oxford Univ. Press 1984 586p il $49.95   **028.5**

1. Children's literature—Dictionaries
ISBN 0-19-211582-0   LC 83-15130

"One volume work with brief critiques of authors, illustrators, books, characters, and radio and television programs. Largely British in coverage of materials but does include most Newbery winners as well as well-known American, Australian and Canadian authors. Contemporary and historical subjects related to children's literature are examined." N Y Public Libr. Ref books for Child Collect

Secret gardens; a study of the golden age of children's literature. Houghton Mifflin 1985 235p hardcover o.p. paperback available $9.70   **028.5**

1. Children's literature—History and criticism
ISBN 0-395-57374-2 (pa)   LC 85-5213

"Carpenter's examination of the works of Charles Kingsley, Lewis Carroll, George MacDonald, Louisa Alcott, Kenneth Grahame, E. Nesbit, Beatrix Potter, J. M. Barrie, and A. A. Milne avoids the pretensions frequent in literary criticism of children's books and appeals to more than specialists only. . . . There is a balance here between cultural comment and personal detail that's informative without becoming bogged down." Booklist

Children's books: awards & prizes; includes prizes and awards for young adult books; compiled & edited by the Children's Book Council. Children's Bk. Council $85; pa $57.50   **028.5**

1. Literary prizes 2. Children's literature—Bibliography 3. Young adults' literature—Bibliography
ISSN 0069-3472

First published 1969. (1992 edition published 1993) Periodically revised

This publication lists 190 awards divided as follows: Part I: United States awards selected by adults; Part II: United States awards selected by young readers; Part III: Australian, Canadian, New Zealand, and United Kingdom (UK) awards; Part IV: Selected international and multinational awards; Part V: Awards classified; Part VI: Publications and lists for selecting U. S. children's and young adult books. A brief history of each award precedes the list of winners

Copperman, Paul

Taking books to heart; how to develop a love of reading in your child. Addison-Wesley 1986 273p il hardcover o.p. paperback available $10.53   **028.5**

1. Children—Books and reading
ISBN 0-201-05717-4 (pa)   LC 86-7923

The author discusses ways in which parents can promote reading and its enjoyment in their young children

"Copperman's recurring emphasis on the value of children's literature—and the value of helping youngsters become avid readers—is the overriding strength of this book." Christ Sci Monit

Includes bibliographies

Field, Carolyn W., 1916-

Values in selected children's books of fiction and fantasy; [by] Carolyn W. Field, Jaqueline Shachter Weiss. Library Professional Publs. 1987 298p $32.50   **028.5**

1. Children's literature—History and criticism
ISBN 0-208-02100-0; 0-208-02101-9 (pa) LC 87-3874

This "selection tool identifies more than 700 books of fiction and fantasy that have positive values inherent to their story lines. . . . Each section categorizes books into age ranges . . . and concludes with ashort summary and bibliographic reference. . . . Librarians as well as parents and other adults looking for reading materials that support positive values but are not didactic will want to add this excellent title to their collections." Booklist

Fox, Barbara J.

Rx for reading; how the schools teach your child to read and how you can help. Penguin Bks. 1989 226p il pa $10.95   **028.5**

1. Children—Books and reading 2. Reading
ISBN 0-14-010703-7   LC 88-37323

The author "explains the basal reading and whole-language approaches to teaching reading and describes reading problems such as dyslexia. Methods of stimulating interest in reading, sharing books with children, parent cooperation with teachers and librarians, and learning activities for teaching phonics, vocabulary, and comprehension are stressed. A chapter on matching children with books cites a number of recommended books and series." Libr J

Includes bibliography

Griswold, Jerome

Audacious kids; coming of age in America's classic children's books; [by] Jerry Griswold. Oxford Univ. Press 1992 285p il $24.95   **028.5**

1. Children's literature—History and criticism 2. Children—Books and reading
ISBN 0-19-505888-7   LC 91-31115

Analyzed in Essay and general literature index

This "survey of 12 classic children's stories (including *Rebecca of Sunnybrook Farm, Little Lord Fauntleroy, The Wizard of Oz, Tarzan of the Apes,* and *Hans Brinker*) is . . . [a] blend of literary and social history. . . . Griswold asserts that these stories are quintessentially American, that is, they are symbolic of our nation's fight for independence and struggle toward maturity." Booklist

"Griswold writes clearly, convincingly, and even entertainingly. This thoughtful union of the scholarly and the readable deserves a very wide audience." Libr J

Includes bibliographic references

Innocence & experience; essays & conversations on children's literature; compiled and edited by Barbara Harrison and Gregory Maguire from programs presented at Simmons College Center for the Study of Children's Literature. Lothrop, Lee & Shepard Bks. 1987 xxi, 569p il $20   **028.5**

1. Children's literature—History and criticism
ISBN 0-688-06123-0   LC 86-10344

"The contributors to this volume share a fundamental and unswerving interest in the good story, how it comes about, what it means to them and to children. . . . This seven part work deals with various authors and the genres of interest to them, as well as illustrators, editors, critics and such nationally known librarians as Frances Sedney, Caroline Ward Romans and Therese Bigelow. 'Innocence and Experience' is for every student and lover of children's literature." Voice Youth Advocates

Includes bibliography

Kimmel, Margaret Mary

For reading out loud! a guide to sharing books with children; [by] Margaret Mary Kimmel & Elizabeth Segel; drawings by Michael Hays; foreword by Fred M. Rogers. rev & expanded ed. Delacorte Press 1988 266p il $16.95   **028.5**

1. Children—Books and reading 2. Children's literature—Bibliography 3. Books—Reviews
ISBN 0-385-29660-6   LC 87-30515

Also available in paperback from Dell

First published 1983

"Practical tips couple with descriptions of more than 300 child-tested titles to help librarians, teachers, parents, and other adults wanting to find quality read-aloud titles to bring children and books together. . . . An invaluable offering from two top-notch professionals." Booklist

Kobrin, Beverly

Eyeopeners! how to choose and use children's books about real people, places, and things; photographs by Richard Steinheimer, and Shirley Burman. Viking 1988 317p il o.p.; Penguin Bks. paperback available $10.95   **028.5**

1. Children's literature—History and criticism 2. Children—Books and reading
ISBN 0-14-046830-7 (pa)   LC 88-40115

"Following an introduction by Jim Trelease and several short chapters on promoting, using and choosing good books, a bibliography of more than 500 titles appears. Arranged by subject, the selections include complete imprint information and meaningful annotations, as well as tips for linking the books to other offerings. Kobrin's enthusiasm is contagious, and her knowledge of nonfiction is stimulating and far reaching. Her book provides a quick reference source for librarians, teachers, parents, and other adults working with children." Booklist

Larrick, Nancy

A parent's guide to children's reading; illustrated with drawings from favorite children's books. 5th ed, completely rev. Westminster Press 1982 271p il $13 **028.5**

1. Children—Books and reading 2. Children's literature—History and criticism 3. Children's literature—Bibliography
ISBN 0-664-32705-2   LC 82-24702

First published 1958 by Doubleday

In addition to providing bibliographies, the author covers such topics as reading aloud to babies, helping beginning readers, wordless picture books, developing children's interests, movie and TV tie-ins, discovering poetry, using reference books, buying books, using the library, and the teaching of reading

Masterplots II, juvenile and young adult fiction series; edited by Frank N. Magill. Salem Press 1991 4v set $365   **028.5**

1. Children's literature—Stories, plots, etc. 2. Young adults' literature—Stories, plots, etc.
ISBN 0-89356-579-2   LC 91-4509

Focusing "on fiction that is of interest to readers aged 10 to 18 . . . [this set] covers more than 500 titles. . . . The selection criteria are exceptionally broad, allowing for the inclusion of children's classics, works written for a general audience but of particular interest to children and young adults, those from past eras, and those of contemporary writers." Am Ref Books Annu, 1992

For a fuller review see: Booklist, Aug. 1991

Includes bibliography

Newbery and Caldecott Medal books, 1966-1975; with acceptance papers, biographies and related material chiefly from The Horn Book magazine; edited by Lee Kingman. Horn Bk. 1975 xx, 321p il $22.95   **028.5**

1. Newbery Medal books 2. Caldecott Medal books 3. Children's literature—History and criticism 4. Authors 5. Illustrators
ISBN 0-87675-003-X

"Brings up to date the volumes, 'Newbery Medal books: 1922-1955 [entered below], Caldecott Medal books: 1938-1957.' and 'Newbery and Caldecott Medal books: 1956-1965' [both o.p.] Gives for each Newbery or Caldecott award winner his acceptance speech, a biographical note, and a book note. An excerpt from each Newbery book gives an example of the writer's style; a sample illustration from each Caldecott book is supplemented by notes on size, medium, printing process, number of illustrations and type used." Choice

Newbery and Caldecott Medal books, 1976-1985; with acceptance papers, biographies, and related material chiefly from The Horn Book magazine; edited by Lee Kingman. Horn Bk. 1986 358p il $24.95   **028.5**

1. Newbery Medal books 2. Caldecott Medal books 3. Children's literature—History and criticism 4. Authors 5. Illustrators
ISBN 0-87675-004-8   LC 86-15223

This volume "compiles the winning speeches, biographies and book notes for the 1976 through 1985 awards. It includes essays by Barbara Bader, Ethel Heins and Zena Sutherland." Bookbird

Newbery Medal books, 1922-1955; with their authors' acceptance papers & related material chiefly from The Horn Book magazine; edited by Bertha Mahony Miller and Elinor Whitney Field. Horn Bk. 1955 458p il $22.95   **028.5**

1. Newbery Medal books 2. Children's literature—History and criticism 3. Authors
ISBN 0-87675-396-9

Companion volume to Caldecott Medal books, 1938-1957 (o.p.)

"Largely biographical notes about award recipients and the acceptance papers." Ref Sources for Small & Medium-sized Libr. 5th edition

Oppenheim, Joanne
Choosing books for kids; how to choose the right book for the right child at the right time; authors, Joanne F. Oppenheim, Barbara Brenner, Betty D. Boegehold; consultant, Claudia Lewis; editor, William H. Hooks. Ballantine Bks. 1986 345p il pa $9.95   **028.5**

1. Children—Books and reading 2. Children's literature—Bibliography
ISBN 0-345-32683-0   LC 86-90730

"A Bank Street book"

The text is "structured around age-arranged book lists, allowing parents easy access to the multitude of suggested titles, all of which are briefly annotated. . . . The introduction explains the importance of combining books and children and offers techniques designed to create a lifelong interest in reading. Tips on buying and borrowing books are appended along with lists of sources for software, records, tapes, and magazines." Booklist

Sendak, Maurice
Caldecott & Co.: notes on books and pictures. Farrar, Straus & Giroux 1988 216p il $18.95; pa $8.95   **028.5**

1. Children's literature—History and criticism 2. Illustrators
ISBN 0-374-22598-2; 0-374-52218-9 (pa)
LC 87-19772

"Michael di Capua books"

A collection of 32 essays, speeches and reviews culled from the author/illustrator's critical work of the past 33 years

The author offers a "remarkably clear and consistent vision of excellence in both children's picture books and popular culture." N Y Times Book Rev

Smith, Laura J.
Children's book awards international; a directory of awards and winners, from inception through 1990. McFarland & Co. 1992 xxii, 649p $75   **028.5**

1. Literary prizes 2. Children's literature—Bibliography 3. Young adults' literature—Bibliography 4. Books and reading—Best books
ISBN 0-89950-686-0   LC 91-50940

Organized alphabetically by country this guide lists "the winners of more than four hundred awards from forty-six nations. Within each country's section, awards

are listed alphabetically by their official names. . . . The authors or books honored are then listed chronologically by year of award. Illustrator, author, and title indexes pinpoint award winners." Wilson Libr Bull

For a fuller review see: Booklist, Jan. 1, 1993

Sutherland, Zena, 1915-
Children and books; [by] Zena Sutherland, May Hill Arbuthnot; chapters contributed by Dianne L. Monson. HarperCollins Pubs. il $47.50   **028.5**

1. Children's literature—History and criticism

First edition by May Hill Arbuthnot published 1947 by Scott, Foresman. (8th edition, 1991) Periodically revised

This "work, this standard textbook for courses in children's literature also serves as a handbook and selection aid for the field. Arranged in five major sections, it provides extensive information on all aspects of children's literature. The introductory section surveys developmental needs and interests, trends, and evaluation criteria. The second section treats picture books and their authors and illustrators, and the third section focuses on books and authors for older children. The last two sections discuss the use of books with children and current issues in children's literature." Nichols. Guide to Ref Books for Sch Media Cent. 4th edition

Trelease, Jim
The new read-aloud handbook. 2nd rev ed. Penguin Bks. 1989 xxvi, 290p il pa $10.95   **028.5**

1. Children—Books and reading 2. Children's literature—Bibliography
ISBN 0-14-046881-1   LC 89-31925

First published 1982 with title: The read-aloud handbook

"Trelease shares his firm belief in books. A pep talk, with new research on the value of reading aloud and new methods for its encouragement, is followed by the 'Treasury of Read-Alouds,' featuring 300 children's books . . . all nicely annotated and with notes leading to even more titles. An essential library book, of value to parents and professionals." Booklist

Includes bibliography

028.7   Use of books and other media as sources of information

Gates, Jean Key
Guide to the use of libraries and information sources. McGraw-Hill pa $17.70   **028.7**

1. Reference books 2. Libraries—Handbooks, manuals, etc.

First published 1962 with title: Guide to the use of books and libraries. (6th edition, 1989) Periodically revised

"After introductory sections on the history of books and libraries, and the arrangement of materials in libraries, the bulk of the work emphasizes how to use information sources through a sampling of the better basic reference materials as reviewed in evaluative bibliographies. It covers not only general reference sources but those in subject fields." Ref Sources for Small & Medium-sized Libr. 5th edition

031 American general encyclopedic works

Academic American encyclopedia. Grolier 21v il maps apply to publisher for price **031**

1. Encyclopedias and dictionaries

Also available CD-ROM version, The New Grolier electronic encyclopedia

First published 1980 by Aretê Publishing Company. Frequently revised

This "general encyclopedia, geared to the informational needs of students at the high school and college levels and for the inquiring adult, fills the gap between the young people's encyclopedia and the scholarly encyclopedia. . . . This work allows its audience to have an intelligible overview of a subject without an intricate analysis and serves as an excellent starting place for more research." Ref Sources for Small & Medium-sized Libr. 5th edition

Collier's encyclopedia; with bibliography and index. Macmillan Educ. Co. 24v il maps apply to publisher for price **031**

1. Encyclopedias and dictionaries

First published 1949-1951 by Crowell-Collier Educational Corporation. Frequently revised

Supplemented by: Collier's yearbook

"An adult encyclopedia suitable for junior and senior high school students as well as the adult reader. Almost all articles are signed by scholars of international renown. . . . The arts, humanities, social sciences, and biography are particularly well represented in articles that include integrated subtopics. . . . Objectivity is consistent in the set's handling of controversial topics." Ref Sources for Small & Medium-sized Libr. 5th edition

The **Columbia** encyclopedia; edited by Barbara A. Chernow and George A. Vallasi; consultants: Peter J. Awn [et al.] 5th ed. Columbia Univ. Press 1993 3048p il maps $125 **031**

1. Encyclopedias and dictionaries

ISBN 0-395-62438-X   LC 92-26989

First published 1935. Fourth edition published with title: The New Columbia encyclopedia

"Sold and distributed by Houghton Mifflin Company." Title page

This "is the oldest, largest, most prestigious, and most expensive single-volume general encyclopedia in the English language. . . . It provides international coverage of basic knowledge, yet it remains, in the words of the editors, an 'American encyclopedia written for American readers.'" Libr J

For a fuller review see: Booklist, Sept. 15, 1993

The **Concise** Columbia encyclopedia. 2nd ed. Columbia Univ. Press 1989 920p $39.95 **031**

1. Encyclopedias and dictionaries

ISBN 0-231-06938-3   LC 89-15877

First published 1983

This work contains approximately 15,000 entries. "Articles are written for those of average reading ability, and technical terms are defined. Lack of redundancy contributes to the book's conciseness, but over 50,000 cross-references help assure thorough coverage." Am Ref Books Annu, 1990

For a fuller review see: Booklist, Jan. 1, 1990

The **Encyclopedia** Americana. Grolier 30v il maps apply to publisher for price **031**

1. Encyclopedias and dictionaries

First published 1829. Frequently revised

Supplemented by: The Americana annual

"An encyclopedia suitable for junior and senior high school students as well as adults and college-level students. A broad base of scholarship supports the authority of *Americana*. . . . The sciences, mathematics, American history, and the social sciences are particularly well developed. Practical as well as historical and theoretical aspects of subjects are covered. Continuous revision ensures that content is reasonably current. The text is clear, concise, and understandable." Ref Sources for Small & Medium-sized Libr. 5th edition

A **First** dictionary of cultural literacy: what our children need to know; edited by E.D. Hirsch, Jr.; associate editors, William G. Rowland, Jr. & Michael Stanford. Houghton Mifflin 1989 271p il maps $14.95; pa $9.70 **031**

1. Culture—Dictionaries 2. Encyclopedias and dictionaries

ISBN 0-395-51040-6; 0-395-59901-6 (pa)

LC 89-33776

Presents an outline of the knowledge that, according to the Cultural Literacy Foundation, should be acquired by the end of sixth grade, in such categories as literature, religion and philosophy, history, geography, mathematics, science, and technology

For a review see: Booklist, Jan. 15, 1990

Hirsch, E. D. (Eric Donald), 1928-

The dictionary of cultural literacy; [by] E. D. Hirsch, Jr., Joseph F. Kett, James Trefil. 2nd ed, rev and updated. Houghton Mifflin 1993 619p il maps $24.95 **031**

1. Civilization—Dictionaries 2. English language—Dictionaries 3. United States—Civilization—Dictionaries

ISBN 0-395-65597-8   LC 93-19568

First published 1988

This dictionary of general cultural information is divided into twenty-three sections, each dealing with a major field of knowledge. Within each section entries identify ideas, events, and individuals. More than 250 maps, charts and illustrations accompany the text

Kohl, Herbert

From archetype to Zeitgeist; powerful ideas for powerful thinking; by Herbert Kohl with the assistance of Erica Kohl and Dee Garner [et al.]; illustrated by Deborah Hohenber [et al.] Little, Brown 1992 246p il $19.95 **031**

1. Encyclopedias and dictionaries

ISBN 0-316-50138-7   LC 91-37658

"Organized according to subject area (literature, philosophy, critical thinking, and political science, etc.), each section presents an informative introduction to the vocabulary used by a particular discipline. . . . Definitions surpass those found in a traditional dictionary; thorough discussions include word derivation, historical development, famous figures in the field, and related and contrasting concepts." SLJ

For a fuller review see: Booklist, Oct. 15, 1992

The **New** Encyclopaedia Britannica. 15th ed. Encyclopaedia Britannica 32v il maps apply to publisher for price **031**

1. Encyclopedias and dictionaries

First published 1768 in England; in the United States 1902. Now published with the editorial advice of the University of Chicago. First published with current title 1974. Frequently revised

"In three sections: Propaedia, or outline of knowledge; Macropaedia, with longer in-depth articles covering major topics; and Micropaedia, with shorter A-to-Z ready reference entries. *Britannica's* reputation as the basic encyclopedia for all libraries and reference collections is based on the writing and knowledge of thousands of expert contributors and consultants. Updated between major editions by the Britannica *Book of the Year.*" NY Public Libr Book of How & Where to Look It Up

The **Random** House encyclopedia; James Mitchell, editor in chief; Jess Stein, editorial director. new rev 3rd ed. Random House 1990 2781, 130p il maps $129.95 **031**

1. Encyclopedias and dictionaries
ISBN 0-394-58450-3 LC 90-38567

First published 1977

Divided into four sections: "Colorpedia," "Time Chart," "Alphapedia," and "Atlas," this "one-volume encyclopedia contains some three million words augmented by 13,500 illustrations, most in color." Libr J

For a fuller review see: Booklist, Jan. 1, 1991

The **Treasury** of the Encyclopaedia Britannica; more than two centuries of facts, curiosities, and discoveries from the most distinguished reference work of all time; general editor, Clifton Fadiman; contributing editors, Bruce L. Felknor, Robert McHenry. Viking 1992 xxix, 704p il $40 **031**

1. Encyclopedias and dictionaries
ISBN 0-670-83568-4 LC 92-54069

This "book is a heavily edited compilation of the more interesting and memorable articles from the distinguished life of the *Britannica*, in which are recorded both the musings of great minds and the propounding of total misconceptions as verified fact. . . . Part 1 contains extracts from articles on various topics arranged under broad subject categories, such as Living Things and Technology. . . . Part 2 reprints articles, either whole or in excerpts, by some of the most renowned contributors from *Britannica's* past: e.g., Shaw on socialism, Trotsky on Lenin, Freud on psychoanalysis." Libr J

"Public and academic libraries will want to consider this interesting volume for their circulating collections. Browsing in it provides a glimpse of the history of this esteemed reference source." Booklist

The **World** Book encyclopedia. World Bk. 22v il maps apply to publisher for price **031**

1. Encyclopedias and dictionaries

Also available CD-ROM version, Information finder

First published 1917-1918 by Field Enterprises. Frequently revised

Supplemented by: The World Book year book; another available annual supplement is Science year

"Curriculum-oriented, this superior encyclopedia is well-edited and produced to meet the reference and informational needs of students from grade four through high

school. Long standing tradition of excellence for readability, accuracy, authoritativeness, objectivity, judicious and extensive use of outstanding graphics and timeliness." N Y Public Libr. Ref Books for Child Collect

031.02 American books of miscellaneous facts

Facts & fallacies. Reader's Digest Assn. 1988 448p il maps $25.95 **031.02**

1. Curiosities and wonders
ISBN 0-89577-273-6 LC 87-20627

At head of title: Reader's Digest

Among the topics discussed are wonders of the natural world, feats of building and engineering, oddities and eccentricities, unsolved mysteries, and the world tomorrow

Feldman, David, 1950-
Do penguins have knees? an Imponderables book; illustrated by Kassie Schwan. HarperCollins Pubs. 1991 265p il $19; pa $10 **031.02**

1. Questions and answers
ISBN 0-06-016294-5; 0-06-092327-X (pa)
LC 91-55100

This book offers "questions and answers explaining the unusual and heretofore unanswered questions of life. Researchers can use the index to locate specific information and browsers can just enjoy." SLJ

Imponderables; the solution to the mysteries of everyday life; illustrations by Kas Schwan. Morrow 1986 262p il $15.95; pa $9 **031.02**

1. Questions and answers
ISBN 0-688-05913-9; 0-688-05914-7 (pa)
LC 85-21428

A question-and-answer format is used to explain commonplace but rarely pondered phenomena

"While not an everyday sort of reference work, there are some days this may come in handy, especially in public and high school libraries." Wilson Libr Bull

When do fish sleep? and other imponderables of everyday life; illustrated by Kassie Schwan. Harper & Row 1989 260p il hardcover o.p. paperback available $10 **031.02**

1. Questions and answers
ISBN 0-06-092011-4 (pa) LC 89-45038

"Feldman offers answers to such 'imponderables' as Why are rented bowling shoes so ugly? and Why do doctors tap on our backs during physical exams? Delightful and informative browsing fare." Booklist

Why do clocks run clockwise? and other imponderables; mysteries of everyday life; explained by David Feldman; illustrated by Kas Schwan. Harper & Row 1987 251p il hardcover o.p. paperback available $10 **031.02**

1. Questions and answers
ISBN 0-06-091515-3 (pa) LC 87-45045

Feldman, David, 1950-—*Continued*

The author "answers such recurring questions as 'What causes the ringing sound in your ears?' 'Why do nurses wear white?' and 'Why doesn't a "two-by-four" measure two inches by four inches?' Feldman answers them as authoritatively and truthfully as he can, relying on as trustworthy sources as he can find and sometimes, when the query submits to no single answer, fielding several different probable responses." Booklist

Why do dogs have wet noses? and other imponderables of everyday life; illustrated by Kassie Schwan. HarperPerennial 1990 249p il hardcover o.p. paperback available $10
031.02

1. Questions and answers
ISBN 0-06-092111-0 (pa)   LC 89-46529

"Feldman poses such questions as, 'Why Are Racquetballs Blue?' 'How Did the Football Get Its Strange Shape?' . . . The answers are supplied with the consultation of experts." Booklist

The **Guinness** book of records 1492; the world five hundred years ago; editor, Deborah Manley; editorial consultant, Geoffrey Scammell. Facts on File 1992 192p il maps $24.95   **031.02**

1. Curiosities and wonders   2. World records
3. Fifteenth century
ISBN 0-8160-2772-2   LC 91-58588

"Grouped by eleven broad subjects, the thousands of factual tidbits presented here bring the world of Columbus to life for researchers and browsers. Topics range from the academic, such as science, architecture, and religion to such informal activities as sports, the arts, and entertainment." SLJ

Includes bibliographic references

Information please almanac, atlas & yearbook. Houghton Mifflin il maps $21.95; pa $8.95   **031.02**

1. Almanacs   2. Statistics   3. United States—Statistics
ISSN 0073-7860

Annual. First published 1947 by Doubleday. Publisher varies

"Statistical and factual material organized by subject area; contains special articles by experts. Illustrated, with a color map section and detailed index." N Y Public Libr Book of How & Where to Look It Up

Kane, Joseph Nathan, 1899-

Famous first facts; a record of first happenings, discoveries, and inventions in American history. 4th ed expanded & rev. Wilson, H.W. 1981 1350p $80   **031.02**

1. Encyclopedias and dictionaries   2. United States—History—Dictionaries
ISBN 0-8242-0661-4   LC 81-3395

First published 1933

"This unusual work focuses on 'firsts' on the North American continent (1,007 to date) that concern a wide range of subjects (e.g., events, inventions, discoveries)—9,000 in all. Arrangement is by subject with appropriate cross-references and concise explanations for each entry. Indexing is by year and month/date of occurrence, names of persons directly and indirectly involved, and location of the event." Nichols. Guide to Ref Books for Sch Media Cent. 4th edition

The **New** York Public Library desk reference. 2nd ed. Prentice Hall General Ref. 1993 930p il maps $40   **031.02**

1. Encyclopedias and dictionaries
ISBN 0-671-85014-8   LC 93-18299

"A Stonesong Press book"

First published 1989 by Webster's New World

Divided into twenty-six chapters, this reference features charts, tables, lists, and illustrations providing information in such categories as signs and symbols, mathematics and science basics, the arts, grammar and punctuation, etiquette, personal finance, first aid, and household tips

The **People's** almanac presents The book of lists; [by] David Wallechinsky and Amy Wallace. 90's ed. Little, Brown 1993 xxxii, 491p il $17.95   **031.02**

1. Encyclopedias and dictionaries
ISBN 0-316-92079-7   LC 93-17197

First published 1977

A compendium of curious information in list form. Among the categories featured in this volume are: illfated foreign products, names of things you didn't know had names, FDA-accepted filth levels for foods, celebrities who were cheerleaders, and odd jobs held by famous people

Wilson, Colin, 1931-

Unsolved mysteries past and present; [by] Colin Wilson with Damon Wilson. Contemporary Bks. 1992 xxii, 426p il pa $13.95   **031.02**

1. Curiosities and wonders
ISBN 0-8092-4091-2   LC 92-4008

"The Wilsons provide some 34 chapters on historical and contemporary mysteries, including ancient astronauts, fairies, sea-monsters, telepathies, and vampires. . . . Readers seeking titillation rather than knowledge will enjoy this book." Libr J

The **World** almanac and book of facts. Pharos Bks. il maps $19.95; pa $8.95
031.02

1. Almanacs   2. Statistics   3. United States—Statistics
ISSN 0084-1382

Annual. First published 1868. Publisher varies

"This is the most comprehensive and well-known of almanacs. . . . Contains a chronology of the year's events, consumer information, historical anniversaries, annual climatological data, and forecasts. Color section has flags and maps. Includes detailed index." N Y Public Libr Book of How & Where to Look It Up

032 English general encyclopedic works

The **Cambridge** encyclopedia; edited by David Crystal. Cambridge Univ. Press il maps $49.95   **032**

1. Encyclopedias and dictionaries

First published 1990. Updated and corrected with each printing

The Cambridge encyclopedia—*Continued*
This international one-volume encyclopedia consists of a main body of alphabetically arranged biographical, geographical and topical entries, and a separate Ready Reference section which presents information in tabular form

032.02 English books of miscellaneous facts

Guinness book of records. Facts on File il $22.95 **032.02**
1. Curiosities and wonders
ISSN 0300-1679

Also available on CD-ROM; paperback edition available from Bantam Bks.

Annual. First published 1955 in the United Kingdom; in the United States 1962. Variant title: Guinness book of world records

Editors vary

"Ready reference for current record holders in all fields, some esoteric. Index provides access to information arranged in broad subject categories. Must be replaced annually." N Y Public Libr. Ref Books for Child Collect

050 General serials and their indexes

Humanities index. Wilson, H.W. service basis **050**
1. Humanities—Periodicals—Indexes
ISSN 0095-5981

Also available on CD-ROM

Quarterly with bound annual cumulations
Started publication in June 1974 as a result of the division of the Social sciences & humanities index, entered below, to form the Humanities Index and the Social science index, the latter entered in class 300.5

A subject index to nearly 350 periodicals in a broad range of subject fields in the humanities. Author and subject entries are arranged in a single alphabet. Complete bibliographic information is given with each entry. Book reviews are indexed by author in a separate section

Nineteenth century Reader's guide to periodical literature, 1890-1899; with supplementary indexing, 1900-1922; edited by Helen Grant Cushing and Adah V. Morris. Wilson, H.W. 1944 2v $180
050
1. Periodicals—Indexes
ISBN 0-824200584-7

"An author, subject, and illustrator index to the material in 51 periodicals (1,003 volumes) mainly in the period from 1890 to 1899. . . . Periodicals indexed are mainly general and literary, but some are included from special fields." Sheehy. Guide to Ref Books. 10th edition

Social sciences & humanities index v19-27. Wilson, H.W. 1965-1974 9v ea $115
050
1. Social sciences—Periodicals—Indexes
2. Humanities—Periodicals—Indexes

This index, which was superseded by the two indexes, Humanities index, entered above and Social sciences index, entered in class 300.5, covered 202 periodicals in the fields of social sciences and humanities. The first 18 volumes were published under the title: International Index (volumes available ea $115)

051 American general serial publications and their indexes

Abridged readers' guide to periodical literature. Wilson, H.W. $90 per year
051
1. Periodicals—Indexes
ISSN 0001-334X

Also available on CD-ROM

First published July 1935. Monthly except June, July, and August (The indexing for these months is included in the September issue). Permanent bound annual cumulations

An index to over 80 periodicals of general interest which have been chosen by the subscribers to the index from the approximately 200 periodicals covered by the unabridged Readers' guide to periodical literature. The form of indexing is the same as that used in the unabridged Readers' guide

"Designed especially for school and small public libraries unable to afford the regular Readers' guide." Sheehy. Guide to Ref Books. 10th edition

Draper, Robert
Rolling Stone magazine; the uncensored history. Doubleday 1990 389p il o.p.; HarperPerennial paperback available $10.95
051
1. Wenner, Jann S. 2. Rolling stone (Periodical)
ISBN 0-06-097393-5 (pa) LC 89-25627

A history of the "magazine and its wunderkind founder, Jann Wenner." Booklist

"This highly entertaining behind-the-scenes study of the fortunes of the 'little music paper from San Francisco,' founded in 1967, benefits from extensive interviews with the writers—including reclusive 'wild man' Hunter S. Thompson—who made *Rolling Stone* one of the most noted American newspapers of the late '60s and early '70s." Publ Wkly

Readers' guide to periodical literature. Wilson, H.W. $180 per year **051**
1. Periodicals—Indexes
ISSN 0034-0464

Also available on CD-ROM

First published 1900. Semi-monthly in September, October, December, March, April and June; monthly in January, February, May, July, August and November. Permanent bound annual cumulations

A free pamphlet: How to use the Reader's guide to periodical literature, is available upon request

A cumulative author and subject index to over 200 periodicals. Coverage includes computers, business, health, fashion, politics, education, science, sports, arts and literature with criticism of individual dramatic works, videodiscs and videotapes, operas, ballets, musicals, movies, phonograph records, dance, and television and radio programs

"This is a modern index of the best type." Sheehy. Guide to Ref Books. 10th edition

Tebbel, John William, 1912-
The magazine in America, 1741-1990; [by] John Tebbel, Mary Ellen Zuckerman. Oxford Univ. Press 1991 432p $35   **051**

1. American periodicals—History
ISBN 0-19-505127-0   LC 90-7874

This work "traces the development of significant American magazines including special interest periodicals for women, blacks, and children, and magazines with unusual formats, such as the news weekly and the photo journal." Booklist

Includes bibliographic references

060.25 General organizations— Directories

Directories in print. Gale Res. 2v $270, suppl pa $165   **060.25**

1. Directories
ISSN 0275-5580

Annual. First published 1980 by Information Enterprises with title: The Directory of directories. Beginning 1991 incorporates International directories in print

"An annotated guide to over 14,000 directories published worldwide, including business and industrial directories; professional and scientific rosters; entertainment, recreation, and cultural directories; directory databases and other non-print products; and other lists and guides of all kinds." Title page of 1993 edition

The **World** of learning. Europa Publs. [distributed by] Gale Res. $370   **060.25**

1. Societies—Directories 2. Colleges and universities—Directories
ISSN 0084-2117

Annual. First published 1947

"The standard international directory for the nations of the world, covering learned societies, research institutes, libraries, museums and art galleries, and universities and colleges. Includes for each institution address, officers, purpose, foundation date, publications, etc." Ref Sources for Small & Medium-sized Libr. 5th edition

060.4 General rules of order (Parliamentary procedure)

Robert, Henry Martyn, 1837-1923
The Scott, Foresman Robert's Rules of order newly revised. a new and enl ed, by Sarah Corbin Robert, with the assistance of Henry M. Robert III, William J. Evans. Scott, Foresman $25; pa $12.50   **060.4**

1. Parliamentary practice
A simplified paperback version The new Robert's Rules of order, by Mary A. De Vries, is available from New Am. Lib.

First published 1876 known as Robert's Rules of order

"Long the standard compendium of parliamentary law, explaining methods of organizing and conducting the business of societies, conventions, and other assemblies. Includes convenient charts and tables. Subject index." Ref Sources for Small & Medium-sized Libr. 5th edition

Sturgis, Alice
Standard code of parliamentary procedure. 3rd ed new and rev. McGraw-Hill 1988 xxiv, 275p $18.95; pa $9.95   **060.4**

1. Parliamentary practice
ISBN 0-07-062399-6; 0-07-062522-0 (pa)
                    LC 88-460194

First published 1950

"A somewhat simpler and clearer presentation of the rules of parliamentary procedure, supported by explanations of the underlying purpose of the rules and examples of their use. Revised with the assistance of the Revision Committee, American Institute of Parliamentarians." Ref Sources for Small & Medium-sized Libr. 5th edition

Includes bibliography

061.025 American organizations—Directories

Encyclopedia of associations. Gale Res. 3v in 5 v1 $340, v2 $275, v3 pa $275   **061.025**

1. Societies 2. Trade and professional associations
ISSN 0071-0202

Also available on CD-ROM

Also available: International organizations 2v + suppl set $455 (ISSN 1041-0023); Regional, state, and local organizations 5v ea $99

Annual with supplement. First published 1956 with title: Encyclopedia of American associations

Contents: v1 pt 1-3 National organizations of the U.S.; v2 Geographic and executive indexes; v3 Supplement

This is a guide to more than 23,000 national and international organizations, including trade, professional, cultural, and recreational associations

The **Foundation** directory; compiled by The Foundation Center. Foundation Center $175, pa $150   **061.025**

1. Endowments—Directories 2. Charities—Directories
ISSN 0071-8092

Annual with supplement. First published 1960 by Russell Sage. Replaces American foundations and their fields

"Lists nongovernmental, nonprofit organizations having assets of $1 million or more or making annual grants totaling at least $100,000. Data elements covered for each include donor, purpose, assets, expenditures, officers, and grant application information. Arranged by states. Four indexes: by state and city; donors, trustees, and administrators; foundation name; and fields of interest." Ref Sources for Small & Medium-sized Libr. 5th edition

The **Foundation** grants index; a cumulative listing of foundation grants; compiled by The Foundation Center. Foundation Center pa $125   **061.025**

1. Endowments—Directories 2. Subsidies—Indexes
Annual. First published for 1970/71 in 1972

This work lists grants of $5,000 or more. "Entries include the recipient's name and the amount, length, and intended use of the grant. The work is indexed by subject and subject category, by recipient's name, and geographically." Recomm Ref Books in Paperback. 2d edition

The **National** directory of addresses and telephone numbers. Omnigraphics $89.95, pa $79.95   **061.025**

1. Telephone—Directories 2. Business—Directories
ISSN 0740-7203

Annual. First published 1981

Divided into an alphabetical "white pages" section and a classified "yellow pages" section, this directory provides addresses, phone numbers, fax numbers, and toll-free numbers for businesses and organizations throughout the United States. A smaller preliminary section profiles sixty of the largest U.S. cities, giving travel-related information for each

National trade and professional associations of the United States. Columbia Bks. pa $75   **061.025**

1. Trade and professional associations

Annual. First published 1966 with title: Directory of national trade and professional associations of the United States

"Includes nearly 6500 organizations arranged by subject. Indexed by title, key word, geographical location, size of budget, and executive officers. Particularly valuable for its data on the annual budget as well as such general information as date of establishment, address, headquarters staff, size of membership, publications, and telephone number." Ref Sources for Small & Medium-sized Libr. 5th edition

069 Museum science

Park, Edwards
Treasures of the Smithsonian. Smithsonian Bks. 1983 xxv, 470p il $42.96   **069**

1. Smithsonian Institution
ISBN 0-89599-012-1   LC 83-40203

This is a tour of the Smithsonian collections including the Air and Space Museum, the Museum of American History, the Freer Gallery and the Museum of African Art

"The text, accompanied by over 400 superb color plates, not only deals with the individual masterworks illustrated but weaves them into an enthralling fabric of history, fact, invention, and art in a most enlightening and exciting style, presenting an intimate overview of that diverse institution." Choice

Preston, Douglas
Dinosaurs in the attic. St. Martin's Press 1986 244p pl $18.95   **069**

1. American Museum of Natural History
ISBN 0-312-21098-1   LC 86-13478

"This behind-the-scenes look at the American Museum of Natural History is divided into two parts. The first half of the book deals with the scientists, explorers, and expeditions that amassed the museum's collections; the second half takes the reader on a tour of the museum. . . . Truly enjoyable reading." Sci Books Films

069.025 Museums—Directories

The **Directory** of museums & living displays; [compiled by] Kenneth Hudson and Ann Nicholls. 3rd ed. Stockton Press 1986 c1985 1047p $195   **069.025**

1. Museums—Directories
ISBN 0-943818-17-6   LC 85-9967

First published 1975 by Columbia University Press with title: The Directory of world museums; British edition had title: The Directory of museums. Present edition first published 1985 in the United Kingdom

"Over 35,000 entries are listed for museums in places ranging from Afghanistan to Zimbabwe. Each entry includes an address and a brief description of the collections. Arranged by country, the listings for each are preceded by an essay on the state of museums in that country today." Ref Sources for Small & Medium-sized Libr. 5th edition

Hudson, Kenneth
The Cambridge guide to the museums of Europe; [by] Kenneth Hudson and Ann Nicholls. Cambridge Univ. Press 1991 509p il $29.95   **069.025**

1. Museums—Directories
ISBN 0-521-37175-9   LC 90-27183

"Organized by country and city, the book provides concise information on locations, telephone numbers, hours, restrictions, and special collections of 1500 Western European museums, regardless of size and orientation. Symbols indicate available parking, handicapped facilities, restaurants, libraries, and other amenities." Libr J

For a fuller review see: Booklist, June 15, 1991

Museums of the world. 4th rev & enl ed. Saur 1992 642p il $325   **069.025**

1. Museums—Directories
ISBN 3-598-20533-3   LC 93-187321

First published 1973

"Arranged alphabetically by country, and by city within the country, the museums are listed by name, address, type, founding date, and subject description of collections and facilities. Appendix lists museum associations of the world." Ref Sources for Small & Medium-sized Libr. 5th edition

The **Official** museum directory. American Assn. of Mus.; Bowker $179   **069.025**

1. Museums—Directories
ISSN 0090-6700

Annual. Supersedes the Museums directory of the United States and Canada, first published 1961 by The American Association of Museums and the Smithsonian Institution

This is "the standard directory for North America and includes such information as address, officers, hours, major holdings, and activities. Arranged by state or province and then by city, coverage is of all types of museums: art, history, natural history, science, etc. Several helpful indexes." Ref Sources for Small & Medium-sized Libr. 5th edition

070 News media, journalism, publishing

Mills, Kay

A place in the news; from the women's pages to the front page; with a new preface by the author. Columbia Univ. Press 1990 378p il $39.50; pa $16.50 **070**

1. Women journalists
ISBN 0-231-07416-6; 0-231-07417-4 (pa)

LC 90-37380

A reissue of the title first published 1988 by Dodd, Mead

The author "provides an excellent history of women working in the newspaper field. She lets the women—publishers, writers, editors, and photographers—share their own accounts of their lives in journalism. These stories, together with the author's astute analysis, reveal a picture of great change from the 1930's." Libr J

Includes bibliographic references

Stephens, Mitchell

A history of news; from the drum to the satellite. Viking 1988 401p il $24.95 **070**

1. Journalism 2. Reporters and reporting
ISBN 0-670-81378-8

LC 87-40455

Also available in paperback from Penguin Bks.

The author attempts "to define those aspects of the news that are eternal, universal, common to the village square and the fully wired condominium. . . . As a critical historian, [Mr. Stephens'] analysis is not only astute, but often eloquent." N Y Times Book Rev

Includes bibliography

070.025 Newspapers and journalism—Directories

Gale directory of publications and broadcast media. Gale Res. 3v $290 **070.025**

1. Newspapers—Directories 2. Periodicals—Directories
ISSN 1048-7972

Annual. First published 1880. Variant titles: Gale directory of publications and Ayer directory of publications

"An annual guide to publications and broadcasting stations including newspapers, magazines, journals, radio stations, television stations, and cable systems." Title page

Contents: v1 Alabama-New Mexico; v2 New York-Wyoming, Canada; v3 Indexes, tables and maps

"Covers U.S. and Canada. Arranged alphabetically by state (for Canada, by province), then by city. For print media, information includes publisher, address and telephone, beginning date, description, advertising rates, circulation, etc.; for broadcast media, call letters and frequency, address, format, advertising rates, etc." Sheehy. Guide to Ref Books. 10th edition. suppl

070.1 News media

Bliss, Edward, 1912-

Now the news; the story of broadcast journalism; [by] Edward Bliss, Jr. Columbia Univ. Press 1991 575p $34.95; pa $19.95 **070.1**

1. Broadcast journalism
ISBN 0-231-04402-X; 0-231-04403-8 (pa)

LC 90-22546

"The pioneers of radio news like Lowell Thomas and Elmer Davis are chronicled. And then there are the journalists who made the transition from radio to television, most notably Edward R. Murrow. And today's young news 'stars.' Bliss also recalls the news stories that were landmarks in the development of broadcast reporting." Libr J

Includes bibliographic references

Broder, David S.

Behind the front page; a candid look at how the news is made. Simon & Schuster 1987 393p hardcover o.p. paperback available $9.95 **070.1**

1. Journalism 2. Reporters and reporting 3. Press—Government policy
ISBN 0-671-65721-6 (pa)

LC 86-31630

This is a "discussion of the way presidential campaigns are covered, the relationship between journalists and public officials in general and, in particular, the relationship between the White House press corps and what [the author] calls 'the White House propaganda machine.'" Publ Wkly

"This book should assist readers in seeing how reporters shape what they write, and why." Libr J

Includes bibliography

Donovan, Robert J.

Unsilent revolution; television news and American public life, 1948-1991; [by] Robert J. Donovan and Ray Scherer. Woodrow Wilson Int. Center for Scholars; Cambridge Univ. Press 1992 357p $49.95; pa $17.95 **070.1**

1. Broadcast journalism 2. United States—Politics and government
ISBN 0-521-41829-1; 0-521-42862-9 (pa)

LC 91-41189

The authors discuss "how television news over the last four decades 'has affected American moods, American society and institutions, American politics and politicians.'" N Y Times Book Rev

Includes bibliographic references

Goldberg, Robert

Anchors: Brokaw, Jennings, and Rather and the evening news; by Robert and Gerald Jay Goldberg. Carol Pub. Group 1990 399p il $19.95 **070.1**

1. Brokaw, Tom 2. Jennings, Peter, 1938- 3. Rather, Dan 4. Broadcast journalism
ISBN 1-55972-019-0

LC 90-40480

"A Birch Lane Press book"

Goldberg, Robert—*Continued*

This book is a "look at the networks' top three newscasters—Tom Brokaw, Peter Jennings and Dan Rather—and, beyond them, at the overall field of TV news." Publ Wkly

Joyce, Ed, 1932-

Prime times, bad times. Doubleday 1988 561p $19.95; pa $9.95   **070.1**

1. CBS Inc. 2. Broadcast journalism
ISBN 0-385-23923-8; 0-385-26102-0 (pa)

                  LC 87-36587

In this book the author presents an account of his experiences as head of CBS News

"Joyce has written a defensive, descriptive, dialogue-filled account of the dirty deeds done to him by the network. He depicts himself as a talented and misunderstood manager who did the best he could with budget and personnel in troubled times." Libr J

Paisner, Daniel

The imperfect mirror; inside stories of television newswomen. Morrow 1989 270p il $18.95   **070.1**

1. Women journalists 2. Broadcast journalism
ISBN 0-688-07499-5   LC 88-29063

This work discusses the careers of various women working in television journalism, including Chere Avery, Denise Franklin, Renee Poussaint, Bree Walker, Deborah Norville and Connie Chung

Parenti, Michael, 1933-

Inventing reality; the politics of news media. 2nd ed. St. Martin's Press 1993 274p $19.95; pa $18.70   **070.1**

1. Mass media 2. Public opinion
ISBN 0-312-08629-6; 0-312-02013-9 (pa)

                  LC 92-50023

First published 1986 with subtitle: The politics of the mass media

The author discusses the role of the news media in formulating public opinion, charging that selective coverage of news events distorts perceptions

Whittemore, Hank

CNN; the inside story. Little, Brown 1990 319p il $22.95   **070.1**

1. Turner, Ted, 1938- 2. Cable News Network 3. Broadcast journalism
ISBN 0-316-93761-4   LC 89-14001

"The story of CNN and the man behind the network, Ted Turner. Whittemore describes how Turner took a small Atlanta, Georgia, television station and turned it into a media giant—the foundation of Cable Network News and other cable channels. Using an anecdotal format, the author covers in an informal style Turner's colorful career as an entrepreneur. Present and former employees of CNN add their own stories of triumphs and debacles." Booklist

070.4 Journalism

Brady, John Joseph, 1942-

The craft of interviewing; [by] John Brady. Writer's Digest Bks. 1976 244p o.p.; Vintage Bks. paperback available $12   **070.4**

1. Journalism 2. Reporters and reporting
ISBN 0-394-72469-0 (pa)

A "guide to arranging, researching, and conducting journalistic interviews, whether over the phone, by mail, or face-to-face. Brady discusses means of recording the interview (by notes, tape, or memory), suggests how to handle balky subjects, and by and large considers every occupational hazard imaginable. He generously suggests other sources for further study." Libr J

Friedlander, E. J.

Feature writing for newspapers and magazines; the pursuit of excellence; [by] Edward Jay Friedlander, John Lee. 2nd ed. HarperCollins College Pubs. 1993 351p $34   **070.4**

1. Journalism
ISBN 0-06-500661-5   LC 92-18918

First published 1988

Through suggestions and examples this guide for the novice writer provides tips from Pulitzer Prize winning journalists and other magazine and newspaper feature writers

Gelman, Mitch

Crime scene; on the streets with a rookie police reporter. Times Bks. 1992 277p $21   **070.4**

1. Crime 2. Reporters and reporting 3. New York (N.Y.)—Social conditions
ISBN 0-8129-2084-8   LC 92-5139

"Gelman recounts his days on the [New York City] police beat and his zeal to get the story and the newsworthy quote, ending with his sense of burnout and move to other areas of reporting. While he relates plenty of crime stories, this is also the tale of a young man's growth in his profession." Libr J

"A riveting exposé of the often tawdry nature of the free press and a superior contribution to the true crimes genre." Booklist

Klatell, David A.

Sports for sale; television, money, and the fans; [by] David A. Klatell and Norman Marcus. Oxford Univ. Press 1988 253p $22.95   **070.4**

1. Sports 2. Television broadcasting
ISBN 0-19-503836-3   LC 88-18789

The authors "explore the history, economics, and sociology of TV sports. . . . [They argue] that such programs 'are nothing more than diversions manufactured for the purpose of filling time, selling commercials, and making profits.'" Libr J

"Seldom has the interrelationship between money and television sports been as closely and as carefully examined as it is in this book." Publ Wkly

Includes bibliography

Knightley, Phillip

The first casualty; from the Crimea to Vietnam; the war correspondent as hero, propagandist, and myth maker. Harcourt Brace & Co. 1975 465p il hardcover o.p. paperback available $16.95 **070.4**

1. Journalism 2. War
ISBN 0-15-631130-5 (pa)

"Surveying major armed hostilities the world over since the middle of the last century, Knightley assesses correspondents' influence on the dissemination of truth, and as a consequence, their impact on public opinion. . . . Vastly instructive, and prepared with reason." Booklist

Includes bibliography

Malcolm, Janet

The journalist and the murderer. Knopf 1990 161p o.p.; Vintage Bks. paperback available $10.95 **070.4**

1. MacDonald, Jeffrey R. 2. Journalistic ethics 3. Homicide
ISBN 0-679-73183-0 (pa)　　　　LC 89-45866

"An engrossing analysis of the tricky issues of libel and journalistic fair play, specifically focusing on infamous convicted murderer Jeffrey MacDonald's lawsuit against true-crime author Joe McGinniss." Booklist

070.5　Publishing

Appelbaum, Judith

How to get happily published. 4th ed. HarperCollins Pubs. 1992 317p hardcover o.p. paperback available $11 **070.5**

1. Authors and publishers 2. Publishers and publishing
ISBN 0-06-273133-5 (pa)　　　　LC 91-58282
First published 1978 with co-author Nancy Evans

Covers the mechanics of writing and manuscript preparation, selling the book to a publisher, stages of publication and the self-publishing option, promotional ideas, and posible markets such as poetry and children's books

Includes bibliographic references

Blake, Barbara Radke

Creating newsletters, brochures, and pamphlets; a how-to-do-it manual; [by] Barbara Radke Blake, Barbara L. Stein. Neal-Schuman 1992 129p il (How-to-do-it manuals for school and public librarians) $29.95 **070.5**

1. Newsletters 2. Pamphlets 3. Public relations— Libraries
ISBN 1-55570-107-8　　　　LC 92-1370

This work "addresses such practical concerns as mailing rates, when to use a pamphlet and when to use a flyer, different kinds of folds . . . the difference between desktop publishing and word processing, and many others. As in other How-to-Do-It series titles, information is presented in a well-designed, easily accessible format. . . . [This] effort is recommended to all libraries interested or involved in producing newsletters and such." Booklist

Includes bibliographic references

Clurman, Richard M.

To the end of Time; the seduction and conquest of a media empire. Simon & Schuster 1992 368p $23; pa $13 **070.5**

1. Time Warner Inc.
ISBN 0-671-69227-5; 0-671-86739-3 (pa)
　　　　LC 91-41293

This is the "story of how Time Inc., the straitlaced journalistic company, was courted by and married to Warner Communications, the racy movie venture, to form the biggest American media conglomerate ever; written by a former chief of correspondents for Time magazine." N Y Times Book Rev

"An informative, entertaining, and often compelling story." Libr J

Curtis, Richard

Beyond the bestseller; a literary agent takes you inside the book business. New Am. Lib. 1989 xx, 380p hardcover o.p. paperback available $9.95 **070.5**

1. Book industries 2. Publishers and publishing 3. Authors and publishers
ISBN 0-452-26432-4 (pa)　　　　LC 88-35322

"In these 53 short chapters, previously published in 'Locus,' the science fiction trade paper, a New York literary agent describes the publishing scene in general and explains many aspects of his profession." Publ Wkly

"Most writers will gather insight from these pages, learning why checks from publishers are so slow, how movie rights work, or what agents can and cannot do." Libr J

Holt, Robert Lawrence

How to publish, promote, and sell your own book. St. Martin's Press 1985 366p il $16.95; pa $8.95 **070.5**

1. Publishers and publishing
ISBN 0-312-39618-X; 0-312-39619-8 (pa)
　　　　LC 85-11748

"A new version, revised by the author, of Publishing for schools, small presses, and entrepreneurs, which was first published in 1982 by California Financial Publications." Verso of title page

The author offers a "grounding in editorial, production and marketing basics, and provides tips to aid neophytes avoid common pitfalls. . . . The sections on marketing and on selling reprint rights are particularly valuable. Holt's lucid writing and business-like approach will appeal to many." Publ Wkly

Hudson, Howard Penn

Publishing newsletters. rev ed. Scribner 1988 240p il pa $13.95 **070.5**

1. Newsletters 2. Publishers and publishing
ISBN 0-684-18954-2　　　　LC 87-32925
First published 1982

After covering the history and basic format of newsletters, the author discusses markets, editorial content, design, subscriptions, management, and desktop publishing

Includes bibliography

The **Publish-it-yourself** handbook; edited by
Bill Henderson. 3rd rev ed. Pushcart Press
1987 352p il pa $11.95   **070.5**

1. Publishers and publishing
ISBN 0-916366-44-8

First published 1973

An anthology of articles about how to publish without
the assistance of commercial or vanity publishers.
Includes contributions by Anaïs Nin, Stewart Brand,
Leonard Woolf, and Alan Swallow

070.5025   Publishing—Directories

American book trade directory. Bowker $205
     070.5025

1. Book industries—Directories 2. Publishers and publishing—Directories 3. Book collecting
ISSN 0065-759X

Also available on CD-ROM as part of Library
reference plus

Annual. First published 1915 with title: American
book trade manual

"Includes lists of booksellers, wholesalers, and publishers in the United States, with related information on the
book trade in Canada, the United Kingdom, and Ireland.
Bookstores are arranged under state and city with
speciality of each noted. Separate lists include exporters,
importers, and dealers in foreign books. Index of retailers
and wholesalers in the United States and Canada." Ref
Sources for Small & Medium-sized LIbr. 5th edition

International literary market place: ILMP.
Bowker pa $164   **070.5025**

1. Publishers and publishing—Directories
ISSN 0074-6827

Also available on CD-ROM as part of Library
reference plus

Annual. First published 1965

This "directory to publishing worldwide covers 160
countries. . . . Profiles of more than 14,000 book related
concerns include book trade organizations; trade reference
books and journals; publishers; literary agents; book
manufacturers; book clubs; major booksellers and
libraries; literary associations; suppliers; periodicals and
prizes; and translation agencies." Publisher's note [1993
edition]

Literary market place: LMP; the directory
of the American book publishing industry
with industry yellow pages. Bowker pa
$148   **070.5025**

1. Publishers and publishing—Directories
ISSN 0075-9899

Also available on CD-ROM as part of Library
reference plus

Annual. First published 1940. In 1972 absorbed
Names & numbers

"Directory of U.S. and Canadian book publishers and
related businesses such as book clubs, literary agents,
translators, and manufacturers. Gives names of executives
and addresses, telephone numbers, and fields of
specialization for each publishing company." N Y Public
Libr Book of How & Where to Look It Up

Publishers, distributors, and wholesalers of
the United States. Bowker 2v $165
     070.5025

1. Publishers and publishing—Directories
ISSN 0000-0671

Also available on CD-ROM as part of Library
reference plus

Annual. First published 1979 with title: Publishers and
distributors of the United States

"A directory of publishers, distributors, associations,
wholesalers, software producers and manufacturers listing
editorial and ordering addresses, and an ISBN publisher
prefix index; now including publisher FAX information."
Title page of 1993-94 edition

070.503   Publishing— Encyclopedias and dictionaries

The **Bookman's** glossary; edited by Jean
Peters. 6th ed rev and enl. Bowker 1983
223p $39.95   **070.503**

1. Book industries—Dictionaries 2. Printing—Dictionaries 3. Bibliography—Dictionaries
ISBN 0-8352-1686-1   LC 83-2775

First published 1924 in pages of Publishers Weekly;
in book form 1925

Provides definitions of terms used in book publishing,
book manufacturing, bookselling, the antiquarian trade,
and librarianship

Includes bibliography

071   Journalism and newspapers—North America

Bates, Douglas
The Pulitzer Prize; the inside story of
America's most prestigious award; by J.
Douglas Bates. Carol Pub. Group 1991 291p
$19.95   **071**

1. Pulitzer, Joseph, 1847-1911 2. Pulitzer prizes
ISBN 1-55972-070-0   LC 91-13659

"A Birch Lane Press book"

A "look at the history, mechanics, and politics of
American journalism's best-known award. . . . The
author also investigates the story behind the story as he
tells why certain sure winners were passed over, and he
describes the constant controversies within certain
categories." Booklist

Includes bibliography

Kluger, Richard
The paper: the life and death of the New
York herald tribune; [by] Richard Kluger
with the assistance of Phyllis Kluger. Knopf
1986 801p il o.p.; Vintage Bks. paperback
available $16.95   **071**

1. New York herald tribune
ISBN 0-394-75565-0 (pa)   LC 86-45276

The author, literary editor for the New York Herald
Tribune during its final four years, chronicles the paper's
history from its 1835 origins to its closing in 1966

"It is Richard Kluger's contention that 'the Tribune
was not inferior to the Times—only less successful.' He
argues very convincingly on behalf of that premise. His

Kluger, Richard—*Continued*
is a thorough and sensitive study' . . . it is also brilliantly written." Christ Sci Monit

The New York Times Index. New York Times $760 per year; includes 3 quarterly cumulations and annual cumulation **071**
ISSN 0147-538X

This index "has provided coverage since 1851. It is currently in a dictionary arrangement with cross-references to names and related topics. Entries, chronologically arranged with topics, include brief abstracts of the news stories, which often can be used instead of the actual newspaper accounts. Book and theater reviews are grouped in a separate section." Nichols. Guide to Ref Books for Sch Media Cent. 4th edition

Talese, Gay
The kingdom and the power. World Pub. 1969 555p il o.p.; Dell paperback available $6.95 **071**

1. New York times
ISBN 0-440-34525-1 (pa)

"A former New York Times reporter who began writing a magazine profile of The Times managing editor, Clifton Daniel, in 1966, has ended with [a] book about the personal struggles within . . . [that] newspaper. . . . The story concentrates on The Times from the midfifties to [1969]." N Y Times Book Rev

"I know of no book about a great institution which is so detailed, so intensely personalized, or so dramatized as this volume." Christ Sci Monit

080 General collections

Essay and general literature index. Wilson, H.W. $115 per year **080**

1. Essays—Indexes 2. Literature—Indexes
ISSN 0014-083X

Also available on CD-ROM

Also available: Works indexed, 1900-1969 $43 (ISBN 0-8242-0503-0) which cites the 9,917 titles analyzed in the first seven permanent cumulations

Basic volume and permanent retrospective volumes available at $230 each

Continues the "A.L.A. index to general literature." The basic volume published 1934 covered the period 1900-1933. Kept up to date by semi-annual supplements, cumulating annually, with five year permanent cumulations

"This subject-author index provides access to essays and articles in collections and anthologies published in English. It emphasizes the humanities and social sciences but analyzes some collections in science and other areas. Literature receives special attention, making this an excellent source for criticism of authors around the world." Nichols. Guide to Ref Books for Sch Media Cent. 4th edition

Great treasury of Western thought; a compendium of important statements on man and his institutions by the great thinkers in Western history; edited by Mortimer J. Adler & Charles Van Doren. Bowker 1977 xxv, 1771p $49.50 **080**

1. Quotations
ISBN 0-8352-0833-8
LC 77-154

"Quotations are often long ones, the average lengths being about 100 words. . . . Arranged in twenty chapters (Man, Family, Love, Emotion, Mind, Knowledge, etc.) with introductory notes for each chapter and subsection. Overall subject and proper name index." Sheehy. Guide to Ref Books. 10th edition

098 Prohibited works, forgeries, hoaxes

Burress, Lee
Battle of the books; literary censorship in the public schools, 1950-1985. Scarecrow Press 1989 385p il $42.50 **098**

1. Books—Censorship 2. School libraries 3. Academic freedom
ISBN 0-8108-2151-6
LC 88-30775

"The topics range from reasons for censorship, places where censorship issues have surfaced, publishers as censors (omissions, deletions, and/or changes in texts and anthologies), and a discussion of secular humanism. . . . Half of the book is comprised of footnotes, appendixes containing listings of specific titles that have been banned or have been the focus of controversy, and an extensive, selected bibliography." SLJ

A "comprehensive, readable report." J Youth Serv Libr

Censorship; 500 years of conflict; [published in association with] The New York Public Library. Oxford Univ. Press 1984 144p il $34.50 **098**

1. Books—Censorship
ISBN 0-19-503529-1
LC 84-8320

Published in association with an exhibition held at the New York Public Library, June 1-Oct. 15, 1984

Nine essays provide an historical overview of censorship of written and visual material from the Renaissance to the 20th century

Green, Jonathon
The encyclopedia of censorship. Facts on File 1990 388p $45 **098**

1. Censorship—Dictionaries
ISBN 0-8160-1594-5
LC 89-1210

"This A-to-Z encyclopedia summarizes major censorship cases, tells the tales of books and films that have incited censors' wrath, describes censorship and freedom of information laws and practices in various countries, explains relevant legal concepts, and profiles both perpetrators and victims of censorship." Wilson Libr Bull

For a fuller review see: Booklist, March 15, 1990

100 PHILOSOPHY AND PSYCHOLOGY

Adler, Mortimer Jerome, 1902-
Ten philosophical mistakes. Macmillan 1985 xx, 200p hardcover o.p. paperback available $7.95 **100**

1. Philosophy
ISBN 0-02-064120-6 (pa)
LC 84-26144

Adler, Mortimer Jerome, 1902-—*Continued*
"Among the fallacies Adler dissects are selfish hedonism, taking ideas as objects, solipsism and modern linguists' presumption that language controls thought, when actually it is the other way around." Publ Wkly
"A most satisfying essay that should entertain and enlighten even those who think philosophy is too recondite for them." Booklist

Includes bibliographic references

Buber, Martin, 1878-1965
Pointing the way; collected essays; edited and translated with an introduction by Maurice S. Friedman. Harper & Row 1957 239p o.p.; Humanities Press Int. paperback available $15 **100**
1. Philosophy
ISBN 0-391-03655-6 (pa)
Also available in hardcover from Ayer
Analyzed in Essay and general literature index
These essays "range from education and politics to literature and religion but all reflect the central concept of the author's thought: the necessity for revitalizing man's relationship with his fellow man. Scholarly but lucidly written pieces." Booklist

Danto, Arthur Coleman, 1924-
Connections to the world; the basic concepts of philosophy. Harper & Row 1989 281p $22.95; pa $9 **100**
1. Philosophy
ISBN 0-06-015960-X; 0-06-091641-9 (pa)
LC 88-45571
This is a "discussion of some of the basic issues in philosophy of one of America's leading philosophers. . . . This is not only an excellent introduction to philosophy for the general reader but also a superb example of a philosopher engaged in the activity of thinking about the world." Libr J

Masterpieces of world philosophy; edited by Frank N. Magill; selection by John K. Roth; with an introduction by John K. Roth. HarperCollins Pubs. 1990 684p $40 **100**
1. Philosophy
ISBN 0-06-016430-1 LC 89-46545
This book "examines and summarizes nearly one hundred influential works through critical essays that focus on their themes and major points. Based on the . . . five-volume reference, *World Philosophy* [1982] each essay explains the historical background of the work, the life of its author, and its influence on modern thought. Alternate views of the philosopher's ideas are provided through reviews of important critical works." Publisher's note
For a review see: Booklist, Jan. 15, 1991

Nagel, Thomas
What does it all mean? a very short introduction to philosophy. Oxford Univ. Press 1987 101p $16.95; pa $8.95 **100**
1. Philosophy
ISBN 0-19-505292-7; 0-19-505216-1 (pa)
LC 87-14316

The author's intent "is to equip the average, intelligent person to think philosophically. This exercise . . . scratches the surface of some questions concerning death, justice, right and wrong, how we know, the meaning of words and the mind-body problem." Publ Wkly
"Nagel makes no apologies for his own positions on these questions but still presents the uncertainty surrounding them in a fair and balanced manner. His style is clear and free of technical terms, and the book should appeal to those who know little or nothing of the discipline." Libr J

Russell, Bertrand, 1872-1970
The problems of philosophy **100**
1. Philosophy
Hardcover and paperback editions available from various publishers
First published 1912 by Holt
The author discusses: appearance and reality, matter, idealism, theories of knowledge, universals, intuition, and truth
"The work is concise, free from technical terms and perfectly clear to the general reader with no prior knowledge of the subject." Booklist

103 Philosophy—Encyclopedias and dictionaries

A **Dictionary** of philosophy; editorial consultant, Anthony Flew. rev 2nd ed. St. Martin's Press 1984 380p $24.95; pa $12.95 **103**
1. Philosophy—Dictionaries
ISBN 0-312-20924-X; 0-312-20923-1 (pa)
LC 78-68699
First published 1979
"A dictionary of key words, phrases, and people in philosophy. Length varies from very brief to several pages as the subject warrants. Emphasis is on the philosophy of the Western world." Ref Sources for Small & Medium-sized Libr. 5th edition

The **Encyclopedia** of philosophy; Paul Edwards, editor in chief. Free Press 1973 c1967 8v in 4 set $425 **103**
1. Philosophy—Dictionaries
ISBN 0-02-909200-0
A reissue of the title first published 1967 in eight volumes
This is a "clear, readable compendium of articles by authorities in many areas; includes Eastern and Western thought." N Y Public Libr Book of How & Where to Look It Up

109 Philosophy—History

Adler, Mortimer Jerome, 1902-
The great ideas; a lexicon of Western thought. Macmillan 1992 xxxviii, 957p $35 **109**
1. Great books of the Western world 2. Philosophy—History
ISBN 0-02-500573-1 LC 92-127
Originally published as v2-3 (1952) of Great books of the Western World

Adler, Mortimer Jerome, 1902-—_Continued_
This is a collection of 102 philosophical essays in which Adler attempts to synthesize the ideas of philosophers from ancient to modern times. A new essay discussing the intellectual climate of the twentieth century introduces the volume

Includes bibliographic references

Durant, William James, 1885-1981
The story of philosophy; the lives and opinions of the great philosophers; by Will Durant. [2nd ed]. Simon & Schuster 1933 412p hardcover o.p. paperback available $14.95   **109**
1. Philosophy—History 2. Philosophers
ISBN 0-671-20159-X (pa)

First published 1926

A selective account of western thinkers from Socrates and Kant to Schopenhauer and Dewey

Includes bibliography

Hamlyn, D. W., 1924-
A history of Western philosophy. Viking 1987 345p o.p.; Penguin Bks. paperback available $10   **109**
1. Philosophy—History 2. Philosophers
ISBN 0-14-013752-1 (pa)   LC 86-51116

The author chronicles "the lives of the greater philosophers from Thales to Merleau-Ponty . . . [and shows] the influence of their ideas within a wider social and historical context." Libr J
"For its compactness, philosophical acumen, fairness, and clarity of prose this book will be a welcome, even necessary, resource in all libraries." Choice

Includes bibliographic references

Jaspers, Karl, 1883-1969
The great philosophers; edited by Hannah Arendt; translated by Ralph Manheim. Harcourt Brace & Co. 1962-1993 3v v1-2 o.p.; v3 $29.95   **109**
1. Philosophy—History 2. Philosophers
ISBN 0-15-136942-9 (v3)

Volume four in preparation

Analyzed in Essay and general literature index

Originally published in Germany

Volume three edited by Michael Ermarth and Leonard H. Ehrlich; translated by Edith Ehrlich and Leonard H. Ehrlich

Contents: v1 The foundations: The paradigmatic individuals; Socrates; Buddha; Confucius; Jesus. The seminal founders of philosophical thought: Plato; Augustine; Kant; v2 The original thinkers: Anaximander; Heraclitus; Parmenides; Plotinus; Anselm; Nicholas of Cusa; Spinoza; Lao-Tzu; and Nagarjuna; v3 Xenophanes; Democritus; Empedocles; Bruno; Epicurus; Boehme; Schelling; Leibniz; Aristotle; Hegel

Includes bibliographies

Russell, Bertrand, 1872-1970
A history of Western philosophy; and its connection with political and social circumstances from the earliest times to the present day. Simon & Schuster 1945 xxiii, 895p hardcover o.p. paperback available $17.95   **109**
1. Philosophy—History 2. Philosophers
ISBN 0-671-20158-1 (pa)

Analyzed in Essay and general literature index

Originally designed and partly delivered as lectures at the Barnes Foundation in Pennsylvania

Contents: Ancient philosophy; Catholic philosophy; Modern philosophy. A summary is given of the main contributions of each period

"My purpose is to exhibit philosophy as an integral part of social and political life; not as the isolated speculations of remarkable individuals." Preface

111 Ontology

Adler, Mortimer Jerome, 1902-
Six great ideas; truth, goodness, beauty, liberty, equality, justice: ideas we judge by, ideas we act on; [by] Mortimer J. Adler. Macmillan 1981 243p hardcover o.p. paperback available $7.95   **111**
1. Truth 2. Good and evil 3. Aesthetics 4. Justice 5. Equality 6. Freedom
ISBN 0-02-072020-3 (pa)   LC 80-28945

"In the first half of this book, Adler discusses the question whether truth, goodness, and beauty are objective features of the world. . . . The second half of the book . . . distinguishes different ideals of equality, analyzes several senses of liberty, and argues for the priority of justice over equality and liberty." Libr J

Heidegger, Martin, 1889-1976
Being and time; translated by John Macquarrie & Edward Robinson. Harper & Row 1962 589p $26   **111**
1. Ontology 2. Phenomenology
ISBN 0-06-063850-8

Original German edition, 1927

"All of Heidegger's work revolves around the essential inquiry: what is the nature of being? In his most important book, . . . he distinguishes between two types of being: human existence (_Dasein_) and nonhuman presence (_Vorhandensein_)." Reader's Ency. 3d edition

Includes bibliographic references

On time and being; translated by Joan Stambough. Harper & Row 1972 84p hardcover o.p. paperback available $10
                                                              111
1. Ontology 2. Phenomenology
ISBN 0-06-131941-4 (pa)

Original German edition, 1969

This volume by the 20th Century philosopher "contains four items: a 1962 lecture, 'Time and Being,' and a seminar report on it by Alfred Guzzoni; a 1964 lecture, 'The End of Philosophy and the Task of Thinking'; and a 1963 Festschrift essay, 'My Way to Phenomenology.'" Libr J

113   Cosmology (Philosophy of nature)

Barrow, John D., 1952-
Theories of everything; the quest for ultimate explanation. Clarendon Press 1991 223p il $22.95   **113**
1. Universe 2. Physics 3. Science—Philosophy
ISBN 0-19-853928-2   LC 90-47394
Also available in paperback from Fawcett Columbine
The author "evaluates the claims widely made during the past few years that recent progress in theoretical physics will shortly bring the subject to an end, with the final discovery of a Theory of Everything, or TOE as it is now commonly referred to." Times Lit Suppl
Barrow "explores a large number of interesting and exciting topics, but he does so at a level that may not be accessible to everyone, as some familiarity with the basic concepts of physics is required for a full understanding." Choice
Includes bibliographic references

Staguhn, Gerhard, 1952-
God's laughter; man and his cosmos; translated from the German by Steve Lake and Caroline Mahl. HarperCollins Pubs. 1992 255p il $23   **113**
1. Universe 2. Religion and science
ISBN 0-06-019004-3   LC 91-58351
Original German edition, 1990
"Addressing the perceived conflict between science and religion, Staguhn asserts advances in scientific understanding have not negated theology, but have led to the abandonment of simplistic views of divinity. In fact, his central thesis is that science and religion are allied." SLJ
"The philosophical discussions do offer the nonspecialist an understanding of many central issues, without the bafflement of mathematical derivation. Still, some readers may balk at the author's curious wedding of European science and Asian mysticism." Booklist
Includes bibliographic references

Teilhard de Chardin, Pierre
The heart of matter; translated by René Hague. Harcourt Brace Jovanovich 1979 276p hardcover o.p. paperback available $7.95   **113**
1. Universe 2. Christianity—Philosophy
ISBN 0-15-640004-9 (pa)   LC 78-21707
"A Helen and Kurt Wolff book"
Original French edition, 1976; this translation first published 1978 in the United Kingdom
This "volume of Père Teilhard's essays includes 'The Heart of Matter,' a spiritual autobiography written in 1950, and 'The Christic,' a brief summation of religious vision, which was written just a month before his death, as well as a number of short pieces." Booklist
Includes bibliography

The phenomenon of man; with an introduction by Julian Huxley. Harper & Row 1959 318p hardcover o.p. paperback available $12   **113**
1. Universe 2. Evolution 3. Man
ISBN 0-06-090495-X (pa)

Original French edition, 1955; this translation by Bernard Wall
The author integrates scientific findings with the tenets of Christian faith in this study of human evolution and destiny

Whitehead, Alfred North, 1861-1947
Process and reality; an essay in cosmology. corrected ed, edited by David Ray Griffin, Donald W. Sherburne. Free Press 1978 xxxi, 413p $19.95; pa $16.95   **113**
1. Universe 2. Science—Philosophy
ISBN 0-02-934580-4; 0-02-934570-7 (pa)
                                        LC 77-90011
First published 1929
Gifford lectures delivered in the University of Edinburgh during the session, 1927-28
This book presents a condensed scheme of cosmological ideas developed by confrontation with various topics of experience. The aesthetic, moral and religious interests are thus brought into relation with those elements of knowledge which have their origin in natural science
Includes bibliographic references

121   Epistemology (Theory of knowledge)

Locke, John, 1632-1704
An essay concerning human understanding   **121**
1. Knowledge, Theory of 2. Thought and thinking
Hardcover and paperback editions available from various publishers
This essay first published 1690, deals "with the origin and scope of human knowledge. Its basic premise is the empirical origin of ideas, which can be described as the raw material with which the mind works. The mind of man at birth, Locke claimed, is like a blank sheet of paper and possesses no 'innate ideas.' Man acquires knowledge through experience, which is made up of sensation, impressions of the external world derived through the senses, and reflection, the internal operation of the mind. Knowledge stems from the perception of relationships among ideas. Locke's essay contributed greatly to the growth of 18th-century rationalism." Reader's Ency. 3d edition

Sartre, Jean Paul, 1905-1980
Truth and existence; original text established and annotated by Arlette Elkaïm-Sartre; translated by Adrian van den Hoven; edited and with an introduction by Ronald Aronson. University of Chicago Press 1992 xlix, 94p $18.95   **121**
1. Knowledge, Theory of
ISBN 0-226-73522-2   LC 92-5889
Written in 1948; original French edition, 1989
This book "presents Sartre's ontology of truth in terms of his characteristic key moral questions of freedom, action, and bad faith. Here is Sartre the existentialist at his most original and most provocative." Univ Press Books for Public and Second Sch Libr
Includes bibliographic references

126 The self

Dennett, Daniel Clement
Consciousness explained; [by] Daniel C. Dennett; illustrated by Paul Weiner. Little, Brown 1991 511p il $27.95; pa $14.95
126

1. Consciousness 2. Mind and body
ISBN 0-316-18065-3; 0-316-18066-1 (pa)
LC 91-15614

The author seeks to "revise our traditional view of consciousness. . . . He claims we must abandon not just the dualism of mind and body that is our legacy from Descartes, but also what he dubs the Cartesian Theatre, the mythical place in the brain 'where it all comes together' for 'presentation' in consciousness. . . . [Dennett's] model of consciousness is based on new facts and theories from the realms of neuroscience, psychology, and Artificial Intelligence." Publisher's note

"A triumph of perspicuous organisation, as well as a fine piece of philosophical writing." London Rev Books

Includes bibliography

128 Humankind

Adler, Mortimer Jerome, 1902-
Intellect: mind over matter; [by] Mortimer J. Adler. Macmillan 1990 205p $16.95
128

1. Mind and body 2. Intellect
ISBN 0-02-500350-X
LC 89-15924

The author attempts "to resolve the old philosophical question of mind/body dualism; in other words, is mind (Adler's 'intellect') a purely physical phenomenon, or is it something else? Adler argues that intellect is a non-material component of humans, though having a physiological base. It is this quality of intellect that distinguishes humanity from other species and that endows us with certain duties and characteristics. In the course of his examination of the question, Adler looks at both artificial and extraterrestrial intelligence, as well as the uses and abuses of intellect." Libr J

Humphrey, Nicholas
A history of the mind. Simon & Schuster 1992 238p il $22
128

1. Consciousness 2. Mind and body 3. Senses and sensation
ISBN 0-671-68644-5
LC 92-18734

The author attempts "to develop a theory of consciousness. . . . Humphrey's theory has two main parts: 1. a distinction between sensation and perception, with consciousness attaching directly only to the former; and 2. the suggestion that to have a sensation is for the brain to initiate a feedback loop from its core to its periphery." London Rev Books

Includes bibliographic references

Mumford, Lewis, 1895-1990
The conduct of life. Harcourt Brace & Co. 1951 342p hardcover o.p. paperback available $7.95
128

1. Life 2. Human behavior
ISBN 0-15-621600-0 (pa)

The final volume of a series that includes Technics and civilization (entered in class 609); The culture of cities (entered in class 307.7) and The condition of man (entered in class 909)

"This is a consideration of the individual's role in the new civilization; it explores the need for a philosophy and religion that will teach man individual human worth and also equip him to act as a member of a group." Booklist

Includes bibliography

When the worst that can happen already has; conquering life's most difficult times; [interviewed by] Dennis Wholey. Hyperion 1992 362p $19.95
128

1. Suffering 2. Adjustment (Psychology) 3. Loss (Psychology)
ISBN 1-56282-985-8
LC 92-8338

Also available in paperback from Berkley Pub. Group

"This collection of interviews focuses on the personal stories of 50 individuals who have experienced great adversity and have courageously overcome it. The interviews, presented as short essays and prefaced by the author's succinct comments, focus on such hardships as physical handicap, divorce, addiction, disease, and the death of loved ones. . . . An inspirational and beneficial resource for those in pain, and a thought-provoking book for those whose minor problems loom large." Libr J

133 Parapsychology and occultism

Encyclopedia of occultism & parapsychology; edited by Leslie Shepard. 3rd ed. Gale Res. 1991 2v set $295
133

1. Occultism—Dictionaries 2. Parapsychology—Dictionaries
ISBN 0-8103-4907-8

First published 1978

"A compendium of information on the occult sciences, magic, demonology, superstitions, spiritism, mysticism, metaphysics, psychical science, and parapsychology, with biographical and bibliographical notes and comprehensive indexes." Title page

"If this encyclopedia is used carefully, and supplemented by the use of critical studies, it will be a valuable resource. In any case, it is the most comprehensive and useful encyclopedia on the occult and paranormal by far." Choice

Goodman, Linda, 1925-
Linda Goodman's star signs; the secret codes of the universe: forgotten rainbows and forgotten melodies of ancient wisdom. St. Martin's Press 1987 xli, 477p il hardcover o.p. paperback available $6.99
133

1. Occultism 2. Parapsychology 3. Astrology 4. New Age movement
ISBN 0-312-95191-4 (pa)
LC 87-28375

"Goodman explains numerology, lexigrams (secret codes of words, names, and titles), the power of sound, and the power of color. . . . Along with explanations of karma and other modes of spiritual growth, she interweaves her own experiences with avatars and gurus, as well as common folk who are on their own spiritual path." Booklist

Guiley, Rosemary Ellen

Harper's encyclopedia of mystical &
paranormal experience; foreword by Marion
Zimmer Bradley. HarperSanFrancisco 1991
666p il $35.95; pa $19.95   **133**

1. Occultism—Dictionaries   2. Parapsychology—Dictionaries 3. Supernatural—Dictionaries
ISBN 0-06-250365-0; 0-06-250366-9 (pa)

LC 90-21718

This work "provides 500 cross-referenced entries which
emphasize major personalities, mystical techniques and
traditions, locations of interest, and mystic and paranormal phenomena. While the coverage is not completely
inclusive, Guiley manages to detail most areas and personalities particularly well—albeit with a slight New Age
bias. . . . This reference should prove useful to both
serious researchers and curious browsers." Libr J

Includes bibliographic references

MacLaine, Shirley

Going within; a guide for inner
transformation. Bantam Bks. 1989 263p
$18.95; pa $5.99   **133**

1. Parapsychology
ISBN 0-553-05367-1; 0-553-28331-6 (pa)

LC 88-47942

The author "focuses on mediational techniques that
will help readers locate their chakras and put them to
good use. When she's not instructing, MacLaine is discoursing on the nature of the universe." Booklist

New Age encyclopedia; by J. Gordon Melton
[et al.] Gale Res. 1990 586p $59.50

133

1. New Age movement
ISBN 0-8103-7159-6

"The book's more than 300 entries provide information on terms, individuals, and organizations from the
nineteenth century (Madame Blavatsky, mesmerism)
through the present day (Shirley MacLaine, crystals, channeling.) Not limited to the spiritual, it also covers
holistic health." Booklist

"Aimed at both believers and nonbelievers, this work
provides a comprehensive and clear overview of the
many concepts, leaders, and works that have helped to
develop the still-evolving movement." Am Libr

Randi, James

Flim-flam! psychics, ESP, unicorns and
other delusions. Prometheus Bks. 1982 342p
il pa $15.95   **133**

1. Parapsychology 2. Occultism
ISBN 0-87975-198-3   LC 82-60953

First published 1980 by Lippincott & Crowell

The author, a critic of supernaturalism, seeks to show
that the evidence for paranormal powers does not hold
up under examination

Includes bibliography

133.1   Apparitions

Guiley, Rosemary Ellen

The encyclopedia of ghosts and spirits.
Facts on File 1992 374p il $40; pa $20

133.1

1. Ghosts—Dictionaries   2. Parapsychology—Dictionaries
ISBN 0-8160-2140-6; 0-8160-2846-X (pa)

LC 91-37427

This "compendium of the supernatural documents the
fascinating world of ghosts, goblins, and spirits. In over
400 alphabetical entries, the author provides descriptions
of and explanations for strange spiritual phenomena,
apparitions, and other ghostly events, including both
those based in folk traditions and those investigated by
scientific method. . . . In addition, the work also
provides numerous biographical sketches of persons involved in the reporting or debunking of ghosts and psychical research. Some entries are illustrated and each
entry ends with a short bibliography for further study."
Am Libr

Roberts, Nancy, 1924-

Haunted houses; tales from 30 American
homes. Globe Pequot Press 1988 181p il
$19.95; pa $11.95   **133.1**

1. Ghosts
ISBN 0-87106-775-7; 0-87106-768-4 (pa)

LC 87-20598

These "essays tell of eerie events in 30 American
haunted houses, many of which are easily accessible to
the tourist and are open to public view. . . . Roberts'
carefully written guidebook mixes just enough terror with
commonplace descriptions. Each essay features touring
information (when available) and exact locations." Booklist

133.3   Divinatory arts

Nostradamus, 1503-1566

The complete prophecies of Nostradamus;
translated, edited and interpreted by Henry
C. Roberts. new rev ed, re-edited by Lee
Roberts Amsterdam and Harvey Amsterdam.
Nostradamus; [distributed by] Crown 1982
360p il $15   **133.3**

1. Prophecies (Occult sciences)
ISBN 0-517-54956-5   LC 83-153468

First published 1947

Bilingual edition of the prophecies of Nostradamus,
the sixteenth century Frenchman who is said to have
predicted the deeds of Hitler and Mussolini and World
War II. French and English texts are in parallel columns

Visions and prophecies; by the editors of
Time-Life Books. Time-Life Bks. 1988
160p il (Mysteries of the unknown) $19.93

133.3

1. Prophecies (Occult sciences)   LC 87-33638

This work examines the practice of divination
throughout history and includes sections on numerology,
astrology, dreams, palmistry, the I Ching, and the Tarot

Includes bibliography

133.4 Demonology and witchcraft

Adler, Margot

Drawing down the moon; witches, Druids, goddess-worshippers, and other pagans in America today. rev and expanded ed. Beacon Press 1986 595p il pa $16.95

133.4

1. Witchcraft
ISBN 0-8070-3253-0   LC 86-70551

First published 1979 by Viking

A survey of goddess worship and witchcraft movements discussing their basic philosophies and practices

"Despite its clear anti-Judaic and anti-Christian bias, this book is recommended for general and college audiences interested in religion, the occult, and modern social phenomena." Choice [review of 1979 edition]

Includes bibliography

Cavendish, Richard

A history of magic. Taplinger 1977 180p il o.p.; Penguin Bks. paperback available $9.95

133.4

1. Occultism
ISBN 0-14-019279-4 (pa)   LC 76-56613

The author "covers, in depth, ancient times, the Middle Ages, and the Renaissance, with a shorter coverage of the occult in modern times. Brief biographies of major figures in the history of magic and the occult are included." Libr J

A "reader can learn a great deal from this book regarding the varieties, complexities, and social manifestations of magic and witchcraft in Western culture." Choice

Includes bibliography

Guiley, Rosemary Ellen

The encyclopedia of witches and witchcraft. Facts on File 1989 488p il $45; pa $19.95

133.4

1. Witchcraft—Dictionaries
ISBN 0-8160-1793-X; 0-8160-2268-2 (pa)
          LC 89-11776

This volume contains over 500 essay "entries on modern Wiccan philosophy, practices, and beliefs plus a wealth of historical information on the various witch trials in Europe and America during the persecution of folk magic practitioners, midwives, and healers. . . . It also offers an impressive collection of current biographies of contemporary 20th-century witches." Libr J

Includes bibliography

Hansen, Chadwick, 1926-

Witchcraft at Salem. Braziller 1969 252p il $17.95; pa $8.95

133.4

1. Witchcraft 2. Salem (Mass.)—History
ISBN 0-8076-0492-5; 0-8076-1137-9 (pa)

The author examines the practice of witchcraft and its effect upon the people of colonial New England

Includes bibliography

Huxley, Aldous, 1894-1963

The devils of Loudun. Harper 1952 340p il o.p.; Carroll & Graf Pubs. paperback available $5.95

133.4

1. Grandier, Urbain, 1590-1634 2. Loudun (France). Ursuline Convent 3. Demoniac possession
ISBN 0-88184-228-1 (pa)

"A reconstruction of sensational occurrences in the early 1600's at the Ursuline Convent in Loudun, where a group of nuns . . . were so affected by reports of the debauches of Loudun's notorious parson, Urbain Grandier, as to be swept into a prolonged state of frenzy and sexual excitement." Libr J

Includes bibliography

Karlsen, Carol F., 1940-

The devil in the shape of a woman; witchcraft in colonial New England. Norton 1987 360p o.p.; Vintage Bks. paperback available $12.95

133.4

1. Witchcraft 2. New England—History—1600-1775, Colonial period
ISBN 0-679-72184-3 (pa)   LC 87-16615

The author presents a "social history of witchcraft in Puritan New England (1620-1725). She unearths detailed evidence which demonstrates that prosecuted and accused witches generally were older, married women who had violated the religious and/or economic Puritan social hierarchy. . . . A well-written, provocative addition to the recent scholarship on New England witchcraft." Libr J

Includes bibliographic references

Witches and witchcraft; by the editors of Time-Life Books. Time-Life Bks. 1990 144p il (Mysteries of the unknown) $19.93

133.4

1. Witchcraft   LC 89-28091

An illustrated look at witchcraft throughout history. This volume describes witchcraft trials and the portrayal of witches in literature and the mass media

Includes bibliographic references

133.5 Astrology

Goodman, Linda, 1925-

Linda Goodman's sun signs. Taplinger 1968 xxiii, 549p $24.95

133.5

1. Astrology 2. Zodiac
ISBN 0-8008-4900-0

Also available in paperback from Bantam Bks.

The author tells how to identify and deal with people according to their astrological signs

"This book is part astrology, part psychology, and always entertaining." Libr J

133.9   Spiritualism

Moody, Raymond A.
The light beyond; [by] Raymond A.
Moody, Jr. with Paul Perry; foreword by
Andrew Greeley. Bantam Bks. 1988 161p
$15.95; pa $4.95   **133.9**
1. Future life
ISBN 0-553-05285-3; 0-553-27813-4 (pa)   LC 88-6388
Companion volume to Life after life (1975)
The author presents descriptions of near-death experiences. "The accounts of supposedly dying and being revived related by adults and children are strikingly similar as are cases here reported by other researchers." Publ Wkly
Includes bibliography

Psychic voyages; by the editors of Time-Life
Books. Time-Life Bks. 1987 144p il
(Mysteries of the unknown) $19.93 **133.9**
1. Spiritualism 2. Reincarnation   LC 87-18126
This book explores near-death experiences, out-of-the-body experiences and reincarnation. Providing historical perspectives as well as discussions of present-day research, this book also includes testimonials by Charles Lindbergh, George Patton, and Ernest Hemingway
Includes bibliography

Zaleski, Carol Goldsmith
Otherworld journeys; accounts of
near-death experience in medieval and
modern times; [by] Carol Zaleski. Oxford
Univ. Press 1987 275p $30; pa $9.95
      133.9
1. Death 2. Spiritualism
ISBN 0-19-503915-7; 0-19-505665-5 (pa)
      LC 86-17983
This book "considers accounts from medieval Christiendom and then the works of current near-death researchers and their critics. . . . [Zaleski also] touches on such issues as literary tradition, truth claims, scientific methodology and evidence, and the effect of visionary experience on the visionary and on those who accept his or her testimony." Libr J
"Well written and readable, the book is thoroughly researched and documented. . . . The scholarly approach and measured conclusions on the concept of life after death make it a valuable volume in every library to put the more popular books on the subject in proper perspective." Choice
Includes bibliography

142   Critical philosophy

Barrett, William, 1913-1992
Irrational man; a study in existential
philosophy. Doubleday 1958 278p o.p.;
Anchor Bks. paperback available $9.95
      142
1. Existentialism
ISBN 0-385-03138-6 (pa)
This discussion of existentialism traces its origins and analyzes the contributions of chief exponents of existentialist thought—Nietzsche, Kierkegaard, Heidegger and Sartre

Existentialism from Dostoevsky to Sartre.
rev and expanded, edited, with an
introduction, prefaces, and new
translations by Walter Kaufmann. New
Am. Lib. 1975 384p pa $10.95   **142**
1. Existentialism
ISBN 0-452-00930-8
Also available in hardcover from P. Smith
"A Meridian book"
First published 1956 by World Pub.
This book contains selections from the basic writings of Dostoevsky, Kierkegaard, Nietzsche, Rilke, Ortega y Gasset, Jaspers, Heidegger, Sartre and Camus

Sartre, Jean Paul, 1905-1980
Being and nothingness; an essay on
phenomenological ontology; translated and
with an introduction by Hazel E. Barnes.
Philosophical Lib. 1956 638p o.p.;
Washington Sq. Press paperback available
$6.99   **142**
1. Existentialism
ISBN 0-671-49606-9 (pa)
Original French edition, 1943
This is "Sartre's major attempt to systematize his theoretical analysis of the human condition and human consciousness which underlies 'Existentialism." Reader's Ency. 3d edition

Existentialism and human emotions.
Philosophical Lib. 1957 96p o.p.; Citadel
Press paperback available $4.95   **142**
1. Existentialism
ISBN 0-8065-0902-3 (pa)
"The section on 'Existentialism' is taken from the book of that name; translated by Bernard Frechtman; all other selections are from 'Being and nothingness' [listed above] translated by Hazel E. Barnes"
Contents: Existentialism; Freedom and responsibility; The desire to be God; Existentialist psychoanalysis; The hole; Ethical implications

150   Psychology

The **Oxford** companion to the mind; edited
by Richard L. Gregory, with the assistance
of O. L. Zangwill. Oxford Univ. Press
1987 856p il $49.95   **150**
1. Psychology—Dictionaries   2. Philosophy—Dictionaries 3. Mind and body—Dictionaries
ISBN 0-19-866124-X   LC 87-1671
This book "discusses human behavior both normal and abnormal, and features major articles on key concepts as well as brief definitions of specialist terms. Entries are arranged alphabetically and are linked by a network of helpful cross-references." Univ Press Books for Public Libr

150.19 Psychological systems, schools, viewpoints

Bettelheim, Bruno
Freud and man's soul. Knopf 1983 111p
hardcover o.p. paperback available $7.95
150.19
1. Freud, Sigmund, 1856-1939 2. Psychoanalysis
ISBN 0-394-71036-3 (pa)   LC 82-47809
The author argues that Freud was a great humanist
and that mistranslation of his work has lead American
psychoanalysis astray

Freud's Vienna, and other essays. Knopf
1990 281p $22.95; pa $12.95   **150.19**
1. Psychoanalysis
ISBN 0-394-57209-2; 0-679-73188-1 (pa)
LC 89-45286
Analyzed in Essay and general literature index
"In 18 essays collected under three headings—Freud,
children, and the Holocaust—the author recalls how he
got involved in psychoanalysis, influential books and
movies, how Annie Sullivan's work with the severely
handicapped Helen Keller foreshadowed his 'milieu
therapy' with autistic children, and how the psychological
scars of children of Holocaust survivors rarely heal due
to an inability to mourn adequately." Libr J
The author "succeeds in communicating complex ideas
in the eloquent yet unpretentious prose. . . . Filled with
unimpeachably sound thinking." Booklist

Carpenter, Finley
The Skinner primer: behind freedom and
dignity. Free Press 1974 224p $14.95; pa
$12.95   **150.19**
1. Skinner, B. F. (Burrhus Frederic), 1904-1990
2. Behaviorism 3. Free will and determinism
ISBN 0-02-905290-4; 0-02-905900-3 (pa)
"Carpenter examines Skinnerian psychology in an unbiased way, then examines the meaning, value and
paradoxical nature of the concept of freedom. Cognitive
freedom, especially in its relation to art, government and
education, is discussed at some length." Sci Books
Includes bibliographies

Freud, Sigmund, 1856-1939
The basic writings of Sigmund Freud;
translated, and edited with an introduction
by A. A. Brill. Modern Lib. 1938 1001p
$19.95   **150.19**
1. Psychoanalysis
ISBN 0-394-60400-8
Contents: Psychopathology of everyday life; Interpretation of dreams; Three contributions to the theory of sex;
Wit and its relation to the unconscious; Totem and
taboo; History of the psychoanalytic movement

The Freud reader; edited by Peter Gay.
Norton 1989 832p hardcover o.p. paperback
available $15.95   **150.19**
1. Psychoanalysis
ISBN 0-393-95806-X (pa)   LC 89-2949
This "work includes some 50 of Freud's texts, organized chronologically with headnotes. The selections
range from case studies and theoretical discussions about
dreams, anxiety and anal eroticism to essays on lay

analysis and religion as humankind's obsessional
neurosis." Libr J
Includes bibliographic references

Fromm, Erich, 1900-1980
Greatness and limitations of Freud's
thought. Harper & Row 1980 147p $11.95
150.19
1. Freud, Sigmund, 1856-1939 2. Psychoanalysis
ISBN 0-06-011389-8   LC 79-2730
Original German edition, 1979
The author seeks to "differentiate the lasting insights
within Freud's thought from those aspects which are
more delimited and socially relative. En route, he integrates his own . . . work on scientific methodology,
character, dreams, the Oedipus complex, narcissism, and
the seductions of contemporary consumer culture." Libr
J
Includes bibliography

Psychoanalysis and religion. Yale Univ.
Press 1950 119p hardcover o.p. paperback
available $8   **150.19**
1. Psychoanalysis 2. Religion—Psychology
ISBN 0-300-00089-8 (pa)
Based on the series given as the Terry lectures at Yale
University
Contents: The problem; Freud and Jung; Analysis of
some types of religious experience; Psychoanalyst as
"physician of the soul"; Is psychoanalysis a threat to
religion

Gay, Peter, 1923-
A Godless Jew; Freud, atheism, and the
making of psychoanalysis; [published] in
association with Hebrew Union College
Press. Yale Univ. Press 1987 182p $20; pa
$9.95   **150.19**
1. Freud, Sigmund, 1856-1939 2. Psychoanalysis
3. Atheism
ISBN 0-300-04008-3; 0-300-04608-1 (pa) LC 87-8267
Based on lectures presented at Hebrew Union College,
Cincinnati, in 1986
The author "reviews the various claims for the Jewish-
ness of psychoanalysis and finds them to be wholly
without merit. Paradoxically, he argues that Freud's position as an outsider—an atheist and Jew—enabled him
to pierce the taboo topics of sexuality and the unconscious which led to his momentous discoveries." Publ
Wkly
Includes bibliography

Horney, Karen, 1885-1952
New ways in psychoanalysis. Norton 1939
313p hardcover o.p. paperback available
$4.95   **150.19**
1. Psychoanalysis
ISBN 0-393-00132-6 (pa)
"A critical re-evaluation of psychoanalysis, accepting
Freud's theories as a basis but showing how modern
practice is in some ways departing from the limitations
set by Freud's viewpoint, particularly in giving more
importance to cultural factors." Booklist

Jung, C. G. (Carl Gustav), 1875-1961
The basic writings of C. G. Jung; edited with an introduction by Violet Staub de Laszlo. Modern Lib. 1993 xxxiii, 691p $17
150.19
1. Psychoanalysis
ISBN 0-679-60071-X   LC 93-17801
Also available in paperback from Princeton Univ. Press
This is a reissue of the 1959 edition
This volume contains excerpts from Symbols of transformation, On the nature of the psyche, Relations between the ego and the unconscious, Psychological types, Psychology of the transference, and Psychology and religion. It also includes Archetypes of the collective unconscious, Psychological aspects of the mother archetype, On the nature of dreams, On the psychogenesis of schizophrenia, Introduction to the religious and psychological problems of alchemy, and Marriage as a psychological relationship
Includes bibliographic references

The essential Jung; selected and introduced by Anthony Storr. Princeton Univ. Press 1983 447p hardcover o.p. paperback available $12.95   150.19
1. Psychoanalysis
ISBN 0-691-02455-3 (pa)   LC 82-61441
"This book is an attempt to distill the essential features of Jung's psychology as it developed during the course of his life by means of extracts from his own writings." Preface
Storr's "selections from Jung's writings are lucid and accessible; linked by skillful explanatory passages, they provide both interested laypersons and students with a perspective on Jung." Libr J
Includes bibliography

Man and his symbols; [by] Carl G. Jung [et al.] Doubleday 1964 320p il $22.95
150.19
1. Symbolism 2. Psychology 3. Dreams
ISBN 0-385-05221-9
Also available in paperback from Dell
Analyzed in Essay and general literature index
"The basic ideas of Jungian psychology are presented in popular language in six essays by Dr. Jung and [four] of his pupils; these are correlated to dreams and symbols and are shown in their archetypal relationships to ancient myths, present-day thought and art." Libr J
Includes bibliography

The portable Jung; edited with an introduction by Joseph Campbell; translated by R. F. C. Hull. Viking 1971 xli, 659p o.p.; Penguin Bks. paperback available $11
150.19
1. Psychoanalysis
ISBN 0-14-015070-6 (pa)
"The Viking portable library"
A collection of writings spanning the career of the pioneering psychoanalyst. Includes a chronology and bibliography

May, Rollo
The discovery of being; writings in existential psychology. Norton 1983 192p hardcover o.p. paperback available $7.95
150.19
1. Existentialism 2. Psychotherapy
ISBN 0-393-30315-2 (pa)   LC 83-4282
The author "provides the reader with principles of his existential psychotherapy; delineates his view of the cultural-historical context that gave rise to both psychoanalysis and existentialism; and sets forth what he considers to be the contributions to therapy of an existential approach." Choice
Includes bibliographic references

Menninger, Karl A. (Karl Augustus), 1893-1990
Love against hate; [by] Karl Menninger with the collaboration of Jeanetta Lyle Menninger. Harcourt Brace & Co. 1942 311p hardcover o.p. paperback available $10.95   150.19
1. Psychoanalysis 2. Sexual behavior 3. Love 4. Instinct
ISBN 0-15-653892-X (pa)
Analyzed in Essay and general literature index
The author "rehearses first the various frustrations which inhibit and misguide human energies, and then, in a series of chapters on Work, Play, Faith, Hope and Love considers how the destructive tendencies may be guided into creative channels." Wis Libr Bull
Includes bibliography

Rogers, Carl R. (Carl Ransom), 1902-1987
A way of being. Houghton Mifflin 1980 395p hardcover o.p. paperback available $9.70   150.19
1. Psychology 2. Humanism
ISBN 0-395-30067-3 (pa)   LC 80-20275
The author offers a "collection of papers, talks, autobiographical sketches and vignettes of patients' experiences in workshops and therapy." Publ Wkly
"This is a book rich in theoretical insights and experiential sharing, and full of invigorating optimism." Libr J
Includes bibliography

Skinner, B. F. (Burrhus Frederic), 1904-1990
About behaviorism. Knopf 1974 256p hardcover o.p. paperback available $9
150.19
1. Behaviorism
ISBN 0-394-71618-3 (pa)
The author defines, analyzes and defends the science of behaviorism with chapters exploring the causes of behavior, operant behavior, verbal behavior, thinking, causes and reasons, knowledge, emotion and self
Includes bibliography

Beyond freedom and dignity. Knopf 1971 225p $25   150.19
1. Behaviorism 2. Free will and determinism
ISBN 0-394-42555-3
Also available in paperback from Bantam Bks.

Skinner, B. F. (Burrhus Frederic), 1904-1990—*Continued*

The author "challenges two of man's cherished attributes—his individual freedom and his self-dignity. Skinner takes an extreme, environmentalistic approach in asserting that man's nature and attributes are shaped by his society. . . . His second main thesis deals with the futility of punishment as a reinforcement and emphasizes reward as the only logical way to proceed." Choice

Includes bibliographic references

Reflections on behaviorism and society. Prentice-Hall 1978 209p (Century psychology ser) $40   **150.19**
1. Behaviorism
ISBN 0-13-770057-1   LC 77-28636

In this collection of essays Skinner comments on such topics as: the ethics of helping people, cognitive psychology, designing higher education, freedom and dignity, and human behavior and democracy

Includes bibliographic references

Watson, John Broadus, 1878-1958

Behaviorism. rev ed. Norton 1930 308p il hardcover o.p. paperback available $9.95   **150.19**
1. Behaviorism
ISBN 0-393-00524-0 (pa)

First published 1925 by Peoples Institute, N.Y.

The author applies the concept of physiological stimuli to the study of human behavior. He rejects conscious and unconscious mental activity as bases of human behavior and believes that man differs from other animals in terms of the types of behavior he displays

150.3 Psychology—Encyclopedias and dictionaries

Encyclopedia of psychology; Raymond J. Corsini, editor. 2nd ed. Wiley 1994 4v set $399   **150.3**
1. Psychology—Dictionaries
ISBN 0-471-55819-2   LC 93-22638
"A Wiley-Interscience publication"
First published 1984

"A major tool that provides access to all important aspects of the field of psychology. Two-thirds of the material is subject entries and the remaining third covers people of influence. . . . It is written for the average intelligent person with an interest in psychological theory and practice." Ref Sources for Small & Medium-sized Libr. 5th edition

152 Sensory perception, movement, emotions, physiological drives

Garrett, Henry Edward, 1894-

Great experiments in psychology; [by] Henry E. Garrett. Irvington Pubs. 1980 c1951 358p il $39.50   **152**
1. Psychophysiology 2. Psychology—History
ISBN 0-89197-190-4   LC 79-24362

First published 1930; this is a reprint of the 3rd edition published 1951 by Appleton-Century-Crofts

This book stresses the personal element in the study of psychology by presenting the discoveries and experimental methods of those who have contributed most to its development. There are chapters on Binet's scale for measuring intelligence, Ebbinghaus's studies in memory and forgetting, Pavlov and the conditioned reflex, Galton and the measurement of individual differences, Weber's and Fechner's laws, etc.

152.1 Sensory perception

Ackerman, Diane

A natural history of the senses. Random House 1990 331p $19.95; pa $11   **152.1**
1. Senses and sensation
ISBN 0-394-57335-8; 0-679-73566-6 (pa)
                                              LC 89-43416

"Ackerman celebrates the senses by examining their biological bases and the various and bizarre ways we have come to indulge them. Her catalog of the senses is itself a sensuous journey, with prose rich in imagery and rhythm. Ackerman's book is a provocative and entertaining treat whose details will bestir the reader's imagination." Libr J

Includes bibliographic references

152.3 Movements and motor functions

Coren, Stanley

The left-hander syndrome; the causes and consequences of left-handedness. Free Press 1992 308p $24.95   **152.3**
1. Left- and right-handedness
ISBN 0-02-906682-4   LC 91-26505
Also available in paperback from Vintage Bks.

The author argues that left-handed people have a shorter life expectancy than right-handers. He maintains that "left-handedness is associated with birth and pregnancy complications—the likely cause of much left-handedness; greater risk for a variety of behavioural and medical problems; and an 89% higher rate of accidental injury, the result primarily of the world's functioning for the convenience of right-handers." Quill Quire

"The book is readable without oversimplifying the topic." Libr J

Includes bibliographic references

152.4 Emotions and feelings

Allport, Gordon, 1897-1967

The nature of prejudice; [by] Gordon W. Allport; introduction by Kenneth Clark, foreword by Thomas Pettigrew. unabridged, 25th anniversary ed. Addison-Wesley 1979 xxxii, 537p il hardcover o.p. paperback available $11.49   **152.4**
1. Prejudices 2. Social psychology
ISBN 0-201-00179-9 (pa)   LC 79-112200
Also available in paperback from Anti-Defamation League of B'nai B'rith
First published 1954

Allport, Gordon, 1897-1967—*Continued*
The author examines the roots of prejudice as well as its manifestations. The effects of prejudice on the "in-group" and the "out-group" are discussed, as are the ways in which children form their perceptions of groups

Includes bibliographic references

Borysenko, Joan
Guilt is the teacher, love is the lesson. Warner Bks. 1990 239p $18.95; pa $10.95
152.4

1. Spiritual life 2. Mind and body
ISBN 0-446-51465-9; 0-446-39224-3 (pa)
LC 89-27834

"Postulating that guilt is the root cause of many physical and emotional ailments, the author presents a mind/body system intended to eradicate guilt and promote well-being. Rejecting both formal religions and science, she develops a psycho-spiritual program that focuses inward on the human psyche. . . . Borysenko affirms the reality of visions and relates instances of her patients' seeing the light—literally—and recovering from physical pain." Libr J

Includes bibliography

Bradshaw, John E., 1933-
Creating love; the next great stage of growth; [by] John Bradshaw. Bantam Bks. 1992 374p il $23
152.4

1. Love
ISBN 0-553-07510-1
LC 92-23230

Also available G.K. Hall large print edition

The author "explains the concept of 'mystification'—a type of identity confusion rooted in the 'defective love' encouraged by our culture and passed along by even the best intentioned parents. Then he suggests how to replace it with 'soulful' love, which remains grounded in reality but also calls the creative spirit into play. Borrowing from 12-step programs, transactional analysis and conventional psychology as well as theology, Bradshaw outlines a four-step program to overcome the 'trance' that perpetuates mystification." Publ Wkly

Buscaglia, Leo F.
Born for love; reflections on loving; edited by Daniel Kimber. Slack 1992 298p $19
152.4

1. Love 2. Self-realization 3. Human relations
ISBN 0-679-41393-6
LC 91-51071

Also available large print edition $21 (ISBN 0-679-41381-2)

This is a collection of the author's thoughts on love accompanied by quotes from a variety of sources

Darwin, Charles, 1809-1882
The expression of the emotions in man and animals
152.4

1. Emotions 2. Psychology, Comparative 3. Instinct
Hardcover and paperback editions available from various publishers

First published 1872

In this classic work the author discusses the general principles of expression in both man and animals, dealing specifically with weeping; low and high spirits, reflection, ill-temper, and determination; hatred and anger, disgust, guilt, pride, and patience; surprise and fear; self-attention and shyness

Forward, Susan
Obsessive love; when passion holds you prisoner; [by] Susan Forward and Craig Buck. Bantam Bks. 1991 305p $21.50; pa $5.99
152.4

1. Human relations
ISBN 0-553-07385-0; 0-553-29674-4 (pa)
LC 90-23099

The author "describes the effects and consequences of out-of-control passions. . . . She portrays situations where one partner seeks to completely dominate the supposed object of his or her affection, and highlights unrealistic expectations that can turn unrequited love into violent anger. Forward devotes her third and most important section to 'Freeing Yourself from Obsession.'" Libr J

Includes bibliographic references

Freeman, Lucy, 1916-
Guilt; letting go; Lucy Freeman, Herbert S. Strean. Wiley 1986 270p $14.95; pa $9.95
152.4

1. Guilt
ISBN 0-471-83636-2; 0-471-61679-6 (pa)
LC 86-15873

This is a "Freudian-oriented guide to coping with a nagging conscience. The first part of the text explores the roots of guilt—in anxiety about a forbidden wish for sexual satisfaction or aggression. . . . The book's second part contains the authors' advice to end the guilt trip by accepting the sexual and aggressive desires within oneself." Publ Wkly

Fromm, Erich, 1900-1980
The anatomy of human destructiveness. Holt, Rinehart & Winston 1973 521p o.p.; Holt & Co. paperback available $16.95
152.4

1. Aggressiveness (Psychology) 2. Violence
ISBN 0-8050-1604-X (pa)
"An Owl book"

The author examines the origins and causes of human agression from biological, psychological and philosophical points of view

Includes bibliographic references

The art of loving. Harper & Row 1956 hardcover o.p. paperback available $9
152.4

1. Love
ISBN 0-06-091594-3 (pa)

Also available in hardcover from Borgo Press

"World perspectives"

"Dr. Fromm discusses love in all its aspects, not only romantic love, so surrounded by false conceptions, but also the love of parents for children, brotherly love, erotic love, self-love and love of God." Publisher's note

Includes bibliographic references

Gaylin, Willard
The rage within; anger in modern life. Simon & Schuster 1984 224p o.p.; Penguin Bks. paperback available $9.95   **152.4**
1. Anger
ISBN 0-14-012003-3 (pa)   LC 84-13968
An examination of the psychological and physiological causes of anger
"Jargon-free, written in an appealing style, interspersed with personal anecdotes and observations, 'The Rage Within' reveals Gaylin's own share in the rages and petty humiliations so common in everyday life today." Libr J

Includes bibliography

Jampolsky, Gerald G., 1925-
Love is the answer: creating positive relationships; [by] Gerald G. Jampolsky and Diane V. Cirincione. Bantam Bks. 1990 242p il $16.95; pa $11   **152.4**
1. Human relations 2. Love
ISBN 0-553-05725-1; 0-553-35268-7 (pa)
                                        LC 89-18520
The authors suggest "moving past our illusions and perceptions; transforming fear, blame, and guilt into love; communicating with love in all our relationships; transforming relationships of control into relationships of freedom; finding peace, love, and happiness within ourselves; forgiving ourselves; forgiving ourselves and others; and achieving holy relationships. This is a 'New Age' book from which all readers can benefit." Libr J

Jeffers, Susan J.
Feel the fear and do it anyway; [by] Susan Jeffers. Harcourt Brace Jovanovich 1987 227p il $14.95   **152.4**
1. Fear
ISBN 0-15-130559-5   LC 86-18414
Also available in paperback from Fawcett Columbine
"By mixing positive thinking with situational exercises that examine basic fear responses, psychologist Jeffers shows that fear is what you make it and that in most cases it is unfounded." Libr J
Includes bibliography

Lorenz, Konrad
On aggression; translated by Marjorie Kerr Wilson. Harcourt Brace & World 1966 306p hardcover o.p. paperback available $9.95   **152.4**
1. Aggressiveness (Psychology)   2. Psychology, Comparative
ISBN 0-15-668741-0 (pa)
Also available in hardcover from P. Smith
"A Helen and Kurt Wolff book"
Original German edition published 1963 in Austria
The author examines aggression in animals and humans, noting both the positive and destructive manifestations of such behavior
Includes bibliography

Man and aggression. 2nd ed. Oxford Univ. Press 1973 278p map hardcover o.p. paperback available $7.95   **152.4**
1. Ardrey, Robert 2. Lorenz, Konrad 3. Aggressiveness (Psychology) 4. Human behavior
ISBN 0-19-501680-7 (pa)
Analyzed in Essay and general literature index
First published 1968
This is a collection of articles that "refute the views on human nature expressed by Robert Ardrey in The territorial imperative and African genesis and by Konrad Lorenz in his On aggression." N Y Times Book Rev

May, Rollo
Love and will. Norton 1969 352p $19.95   **152.4**
1. Love 2. Free will and determinism 3. Sexual behavior
ISBN 0-393-01080-5
Also available in paperback from Doubleday
The author "centers on three interconnected themes: eros, or the capacity to be responsive; the daimonic, a potentially creative force present in every personality; and intentionality, the imaginative attention which should rightfully connect intention and action. . . . May says important things with great lucidity." Booklist
Includes bibliographic references

Montagu, Ashley, 1905-
The nature of human aggression. Oxford Univ. Press 1976 381p il $16.95; pa $8.95   **152.4**
1. Aggressiveness (Psychology)
ISBN 0-19-501822-2; 0-19-502373-0 (pa)
Montagu "attempts to rebut the thesis advanced by Lorenz, Morris and Ardrey that innate human aggressivity is the major factor behind war and other forms of social violence." Sci Books Films
Includes bibliographic references

Nichols, Michael P.
No place to hide; facing shame so we can find self-respect. Simon & Schuster 1991 366p hardcover o.p. paperback available $12   **152.4**
1. Shame 2. Self-respect
ISBN 0-671-68181-8 (pa)   LC 90-47416
According to the author "'shame plays a poorly understood but central role in our lives'. Its manifestations are explored here and interpolated with vignettes illustrating approaches to understanding and coping with this alienating emotion, which is believed to spring from a sense of one's unworthiness." Publ Wkly
Includes bibliographic references

Rubin, Theodore Isaac
Real love; what it is, and where to find it. Continuum 1990 219p $17.95   **152.4**
1. Love 2. Human relations
ISBN 0-8264-0453-7   LC 89-22109
The author "offers observations on the nature of love. Short meditations (most one page, some a sentence) on the attributes of love ('Loving is even more important than being loved') and its enemies, which he calls 'cor-

Rubin, Theodore Isaac—*Continued*
rosives' and which include jealousy, pride, secretiveness
and mastery, support Rubin's indisputable view that
loving—God, parents, children, mates, friends—is our
most redeeming activity. Optimistic and encouraging."
Publ Wkly

Russianoff, Penelope
When am I going to be happy? how to
break the emotional bad habits that make
you miserable. Bantam Bks. 1988 287p
$17.95; pa $5.99   **152.4**

1. Emotions 2. Habit
ISBN 0-553-05054-0; 0-553-28215-8 (pa)
                                    LC 88-10473
"Drawing primarily from the cognitive and behavioral
schools of psychology, [the author] shows how mild yet
persistent forms of depression, self-defeating behavior,
guilt, inferiority, anger, anxiety, phobias, obsessions, and
the like are amenable to change by correcting the er-
roneous thinking that leads to these problems in the first
place." Booklist
Includes bibliography

Tavris, Carol
Anger; the misunderstood emotion. rev ed.
Simon & Schuster 1989 383p pa $11
                                             152.4
1. Anger
ISBN 0-671-67523-0   LC 89-33129
"A Touchstone book"
First published 1983
The author argues that anger is a complex, socially
learned response that is not necessarily cathartic
Includes bibliography

153   Conscious mental processes and intelligence

Arendt, Hannah
The life of the mind. Harcourt Brace
Jovanovich 1981 2v in 1 pa $12.95   **153**
1. Intellect 2. Philosophy 3. Free will and deter-
minism
ISBN 0-15-651992-5
First published 1978 as two separate volumes with
titles: v1 Thinking and v2 Willing
An exploration of the nature of mind and thought.
Among the concepts discussed are: appearance versus
reality, free will, determinism, and necessity
Includes bibliographic references

Jastrow, Robert, 1925-
The enchanted loom: mind in the
universe. Simon & Schuster 1981 183p
$13.95   **153**
1. Brain 2. Intellect 3. Evolution
ISBN 0-671-43308-3   LC 81-13532
Companion volume to: Until the sun dies, entered in
class 577, and Red giants and white dwarfs (1990)
The author presents an account of the evolution of
the human brain and the nature of the thinking process
Includes bibliography

Sagan, Carl, 1934-
The dragons of Eden; speculations on the
evolution of human intelligence. Random
House 1977 263p il $10.95   **153**
1. Intellect 2. Brain 3. Genetics
ISBN 0-394-41045-9   LC 76-53472
Also available in paperback from Ballantine Bks.
In this study of human intellect "Sagan is principally
preoccupied with the neocortex, with its left hemisphere,
responsible for language and logic, a right hemisphere
in charge of intuition and spatial dimension, and a cor-
pus callosum that mediates and synthesizes the two."
Atlantic
Includes bibliography

153.1   Memory and learning

Johnson, George, 1952-
In the palaces of memory; how we build
the worlds inside our heads. Knopf 1991
255p $22.95; pa $11   **153.1**
1. Memory 2. Nervous system
ISBN 0-394-58348-5; 0-679-73759-6 (pa)
                                    LC 90-53170
This book looks at "the current state of understanding
of the brain as the source of memory. Johnson identifies
three major approaches, following the work over the last
20 years of three investigators: Gary Lynch, a biologist
. . . [studying brain synapses]; Leon Cooper, a theoretical
physicist working towards a mathematical theory of brain
interactions; [and] Patricia Churchland, a philosopher."
Antioch Rev
"This elegantly written report is science on the cutting
edge—messy, intuitive and exciting." Publ Wkly
Includes bibliographic references

Moss, Robert A.
Why Johnny can't concentrate; coping
with attention deficit problems; [by] Robert
A. Moss with Helen Huff Dunlap. Bantam
Bks. 1990 225p pa $9.95   **153.1**
1. Attention
ISBN 0-553-34968-6   LC 90-404
"After discussing the characteristics of ADD [Attention
Deficit Disorder] and how it is diagnosed, the book is
broadly organized by age group, including a chapter on
ADD in adults. Moss utilizes case studies to illustrate
the role of the physician, the parents, the schools, and
the teacher in treating this problem." Libr J
Includes bibliography

153.3   Imagination and imagery. Creativity

May, Rollo
The courage to create. Norton 1975 143p
o.p.; Bantam Bks. paperback available $4.95
                                             153.3
1. Creative ability
ISBN 0-553-26361-7 (pa)
The author argues that creativity is an act of encounter and draws on examples from literature, art, and psychoanalysis
Includes bibliographic references

Storr, Anthony
Churchill's black dog, Kafka's mice, and other phenomena of the human mind. Grove Press 1988 310p o.p.; Ballantine Bks. paperback available $9.95   **153.3**
1. Creative ability 2. Psychoanalysis
ISBN 0-345-36547-X (pa)   LC 88-21307
The author "examines, among other topics, people whose remarkable accomplishments in art (Kafka) or science (Newton) or politics (Churchill) have co-existed with periods of extreme depression. . . . Mr. Storr writes clearly and unpretentiously, and if his conclusions are less than earthshaking, the route by which he reaches them is always interesting." Atlantic

Includes bibliographies

153.4 Knowledge (Cognition)

Dewey, John, 1859-1952
How we think; a restatement of the relation of reflective thinking to the educative process. Heath 1933 301p $19.50
    153.4
1. Thought and thinking 2. Educational psychology
ISBN 0-669-20024-7
Also available in paperback from Prometheus Bks.
First published 1910
"A study of the nature and logical process of reflective thinking as applied to the problem of training children to scientific habits of thought." A L A Cat, 1926

Lorenz, Konrad
Behind the mirror; a search for a natural history of human knowledge; translated by Ronald Taylor. Harcourt Brace Jovanovich 1977 261p il hardcover o.p. paperback available $7.95   **153.4**
1. Knowledge, Theory of 2. Psychology, Comparative
ISBN 0-15-611776-2 (pa)   LC 76-55029
Also available in hardcover from P. Smith
"A Helen and Kurt Wolff book"
Original German edition, 1973
This work examines the roots of higher mental processes and human culture

Includes bibliography

Piaget, Jean, 1896-1980
Six psychological studies; translated from the French by Anita Tenzer and David Elkind; edited with an introduction and notes, by David Elkind. Random House 1967 xx, 169p hardcover o.p. paperback available $6.95   **153.4**
1. Knowledge, Theory of 2. Child psychology
ISBN 0-394-70462-2 (pa)
Original French edition, 1964
These studies examine the behavioral and mental development of children

Includes bibliographic references

Wegner, Daniel M., 1948-
White bears and other unwanted thoughts; suppression, obsession, and the psychology of mental control. Viking 1989 207p o.p.; Penguin Bks. paperback available $9.95
    153.4
1. Thought and thinking 2. Self-control
ISBN 0-14-011599-4 (pa)   LC 88-40410
"The author explores how suppression can lead to obsession, how mood and mind control can be useful, and what affinity exists between mind and body." Libr J
"Wegner presents his subject intriguingly, with a sense of humor that may frequently have the reader laughing out loud. A 'must read' for anyone who has tried to no avail to avoid a recurring worry, fear, or thought of any kind." Booklist

Includes bibliographic references

153.6 Communication

Elgin, Suzette Haden
The last word on the gentle art of verbal self-defense. Prentice Hall Press 1987 245p pa $9.95   **153.6**
1. Invective 2. Communication 3. Language and languages
ISBN 0-13-524083-2   LC 86-12195
The author "explains ways of reducing verbal abuse and promoting verbal harmony in one's environment. Her system for achieving control of language around us . . . is based on perceiving the sensory (visual, aural, etc.) and behavioral (blaming, placating, etc.) modes of normal human discourse." Booklist

Includes bibliography

Fast, Julius, 1918-
Body language. Evans & Co. 1970 192p $12.95   **153.6**
1. Body language
ISBN 0-87131-039-2
This book discusses the "science of kinesics, the use of non-verbal communication through the means of body movements which may support or contradict our verbal expressions." Best Sellers

Includes bibliography

Glass, Lillian
Say it—right; how to talk in any social or business situation. Putnam 1991 240p $18.95; pa $9.95   **153.6**
1. Communication 2. Conversation
ISBN 0-399-13588-X; 0-399-51699-9 (pa) LC 90-8746
"This is not a how-to book on speaking before groups; it is about communication one-to-one with others. Talking to the boss or to strangers at a party can be nerve wracking, and Glass gives advice on breathing exercises, facial expression, and physical movements." Libr J

153.8   Will (Volition)

Rubin, Theodore Isaac
Overcoming indecisiveness; the eight stages of effective decisionmaking. Harper & Row 1985 208p o.p.; Avon Bks. paperback available $4.99   **153.8**

1. Success 2. Decision making
ISBN 0-380-69977-X (pa)   LC 84-48189

"The causes and remedies of indecision are presented in short, example-filled and headlined paragraphs for easy reference. Rubin lists a series of decision blockers, suggests ways to order priorities and divides the decision-making process into eight stages." Publ Wkly

153.9   Intelligence and aptitudes

Gould, Stephen Jay, 1941-
The mismeasure of man. Norton 1983 352p il hardcover o.p. paperback available $9.95   **153.9**

1. Mental tests 2. Ability—Testing
ISBN 0-393-30056-0 (pa)   LC 81-38430

This book "examines the history of the various scientific methods used to measure intelligence as a single quantity. Gould demonstrates how such research was used, both consciously and unconsciously, to perpetuate the myth of the intellectual superiority of the white male." SLJ

Includes bibliography

Jensen, Arthur Robert
Bias in mental testing; Arthur R. Jensen. Free Press 1980 786p $32.95   **153.9**

1. Mental tests 2. Educational tests and measurements
ISBN 0-02-916430-3   LC 79-7583

This book presents an "analysis, based on psychometrics and statistical techniques, of the merits and validity of standardized tests. Jensen . . . examines the various allegations against standardized tests, including cultural bias, the inadequacy of any general definition of intelligence, and the criticism that IQ tests fail to measure innate ability." Publisher's note

Includes bibliography

Tests; a comprehensive reference for assessments in psychology, education, and business; Richard C. Sweetland, Daniel J. Keyser, general editors. 3rd ed. PRO-ED 1990 1250p $69; pa $44   **153.9**

1. Mental tests 2. Educational tests and measurements 3. Ability—Testing
ISBN 0-89079-255-0; 0-89079-256-9 (pa)
    LC 89-78495

First published 1983 by Test Corp. of America

This is a "quick reference catalog that classifies thousands of tests now available. Each entry provides very brief information about the test's purpose, cost, scoring, and publisher as well as a description of the test. Material is classified and cross-referenced for easy access. The use of plain English makes this a tool that nonprofessionals can easily master." Ref Sources for Small & Medium-sized Libr. 5th edition

154.6   Sleep phenomena

Freud, Sigmund, 1856-1939
Interpretation of dreams   **154.6**

1. Dreams 2. Psychoanalysis

Hardcover and paperback editions available from various publishers

Original German edition, 1900; first English translation published 1913

Groundbreaking analysis of dreams as manifestations of suppressed unconscious desires

Fromm, Erich, 1900-1980
The forgotten language; an introduction to the understanding of dreams, fairy tales and myths. Rinehart 1951 263p o.p.; Grove Press paperback available $10.95   **154.6**

1. Dreams 2. Psychoanalysis 3. Symbolism
ISBN 0-8021-3050-X (pa)

Against the background of a history of dream interpretation, Dr. Fromm offers his own concepts with the aid of a great many case histories on modern psychoanalytic work. He also studies the Oedipus myth, as well as other myths and fairy tales. The book outlines the different approaches of Freud and Jung and relates the author's own views to modern life

155   Differential and developmental psychology

Kotre, John N.
Seasons of life; our dramatic journey from birth to death; [by] John Kotre and Elizabeth Hall. Little, Brown 1990 421p $24.95   **155**

1. Psychology 2. Socialization 3. Aging—Psychological aspects
ISBN 0-316-50252-9   LC 90-40376

The authors "illustrate human development from infancy to late adulthood through a series of biographical sketches of real people representing all of life's stages, or 'seasons.' The narratives are bound together with . . . details of our biological, social, and psychological 'clocks.'" Libr J

Includes bibliographic references

155.2   Individual psychology

Allport, Gordon, 1897-1967
Becoming; basic considerations for a psychology of personality. Yale Univ. Press 1955 106p hardcover o.p. paperback available $8   **155.2**

1. Personality 2. Psychology
ISBN 0-300-00002-2 (pa)

"The Terry lectures"

In this work Allport attempts "to correlate and interpret psychology's views on human welfare and religion." Booklist

Brim, Gilbert, 1923-
Ambition; how we manage success and failure throughout our lives. Basic Bks. 1992 205p $23; pa $12   **155.2**
1. Success 2. Failure (Psychology)
ISBN 0-465-09190-3; 0-465-00118-1 (pa)
LC 91-55453

The author "here delivers an antidote to the rat race and a meditation on ambition, rather than a how-to-succeed primer to placate those who haven't yet realized their dreams." Publ Wkly

This "volume is a sane, sentient exposition of how people can strike a happy balance between their ambitions and their abilities." Libr J

Includes bibliographic references

Cheek, Jonathan
Conquering shyness; the battle anyone can win; [by] Jonathan M. Cheek and Bronwen Cheek with Larry Rothstein. Putnam 1989 224p o.p.; Dell paperback available $8.95
155.2
1. Bashfulness
ISBN 0-440-50319-1 (pa)   LC 89-3475

After elucidating the sources and symptoms of three types of shyness the author offers suggestions for combating them

Includes bibliography

Csikszentmihalyi, Mihaly
Flow: the psychology of optimal experience. Harper & Row 1990 303p hardcover o.p. paperback available $11
155.2
1. Happiness 2. Attention 3. Psychology, Applied
ISBN 0-06-092043-2 (pa)   LC 89-45645

This book offers a discussion of "'flow,' a field of behavioral science examining connections between satisfaction and daily activities. [According to the author], a flow state ensues when one is engaged in self-controlled, goal-related, meaningful actions." Libr J

"As an analysis of individual psychology, flow is important, for it illuminates the accuracy of what philosophers have been saying for centuries: that the way to happiness lies not in mindless hedonism but in mindful challenge." N Y Times Book Rev

Includes bibliographic references

Hunt, Morton M., 1920-
The compassionate beast; what science is discovering about the humane side of humankind; [by] Morton Hunt. Morrow 1990 287p $18.95   **155.2**
1. Altruism 2. Helping behavior
ISBN 0-688-07577-0   LC 89-38546

Also available in paperback from Anchor Bks.

"Hunt begins by exploring studies that have proven that animals are instinctively altruistic. . . . [He] describes the natural history of altruistic behavior by charting the different stages of its development in children . . . [and] provides a general outline of the 'altruistic personality.'" Publisher's note

This book "is well-illustrated with examples of heroism, including an impressive study on altruism during the Holocaust." Libr J

Includes bibliography

Jung, C. G. (Carl Gustav), 1875-1961
Undiscovered self; translated from the German by R.F.C. Hull. Little, Brown 1958 113p hardcover o.p. paperback available $9.95   **155.2**
1. Self
ISBN 0-316-47694-3 (pa)
"An Atlantic Monthly Press book"
Original German edition, 1957

"This deals with the plight of the individual in today's highly organized world. Points out man's surrender of more & more of his freedom—political freedom, religious freedom, moral & intellectual freedom—to the subjugating forces of modern mass society." Libr J

Lasch, Christopher
The minimal self; psychic survival in troubled times. Norton 1984 317p $16.95; pa $10.95   **155.2**
1. Self 2. Human ecology
ISBN 0-393-01922-5; 0-393-30263-6 (pa) LC 84-4103

The author "maintains that our society's reaction to nuclear and environmental threats and the current mood of retrenchment inadvertently breed emotional disengagement and self-depletion." Libr J

"One of Lasch's more interesting undertakings is a comparative analysis of three political tendencies: neoconservative, liberal, and countercultural. He captures well their mode of argument and contrasts in an illuminating way their views of the state as a source of values." New Repub

Includes bibliography

Maslow, Abraham Harold
The farthest reaches of human nature. Viking 1971 xxi, 423p o.p.; Penguin Bks. paperback available $9.95   **155.2**
1. Personality
ISBN 0-14-004265-2 (pa)

Also available in hardcover from P. Smith
"An Esalen book"

The author's discussion "arranges itself around biology, creativeness, values, education, society, cognition and transcendence. This is heady reading for the serious reader who is willing and able to follow Maslow's logic, which pursues some penetrating insights by a series of leaps and bounds." Publ Wkly

Includes bibliography

Toward a psychology of being. 2nd ed. Van Nostrand Reinhold 1982 240p hardcover o.p. paperback available $15.95
155.2
1. Personality 2. Motivation (Psychology)
ISBN 0-442-03805-4 (pa)   LC 82-2071
"Van Nostrand insight books"
First published 1962

The author presents his theory of psychological health and motivation and explains his belief that human beings can be loving and creative, and capable of pursuing the

Maslow, Abraham Harold—*Continued*
highest values and aspirations

Includes bibliography

Seligman, Martin E. P.
Learned optimism. Knopf 1990 319p
$19.95   **155.2**
1. Self-perception 2. Adjustment (Psychology)
ISBN 0-394-57915-1   LC 90-53075

Also available in paperback from Pocket Bks.

The author "documents the effects of optimism on
the quality of life, provides tests to determine the degree
of . . . negative and positive orientation, and offers a
program of specific exercises to help . . . break the habit
of pessimism and learn the habit of optimism."
Publisher's note

The author "has written a lively, very accessible book.
. . . Presented for lay readers, this book can be highly
recommended to professionals as well for its lucid and
informative introduction to cognitive therapy and its approach to issues of mood and depression." Libr J

Includes bibliographic references

Steinem, Gloria
Revolution from within; a book of
self-esteem. Little, Brown 1992 377p $22.95
     155.2
1. Self-respect 2. Feminism
ISBN 0-316-81240-4   LC 91-11356

The author discusses the importance of self-esteem and
offers practical advice on ways of acquiring it

Steinem's "book unfolds like a flower: it offers literature, art, nature, meditation, and connectedness as ways
of finding and exploring the self. . . . Her focus is
women, but she is clear that what she has to say is
for men, too, and she is neither strident nor dismissive."
Libr J

Includes bibliography

155.3   Sex psychology and psychology of the sexes

Barbach, Lonnie Garfield, 1946-
For each other; sharing sexual intimacy.
Anchor Press/Doubleday 1982 305p il
hardcover o.p. paperback available $10.95
     155.3
1. Women—Sexual behavior
ISBN 0-385-17297-4 (pa)   LC 81-43538

Also available in paperback from New Am. Lib.

Clinical psychologist Barbach "addresses the couple
from the standpoint of the woman who is either nonor-
gasmic, uninterested, or uncomfortable with sex. She
prescribes some 50 exercises in detail—some solo, some
with partner—involving physical and psychological effort
and, usually, reward." Libr J

Brothers, Joyce
What every woman should know about
men. Simon & Schuster 1982 268p o.p.;
Ballantine Bks. paperback available $5.95
     155.3
1. Men—Psychology 2. Sex role
ISBN 0-345-35372-2 (pa)   LC 81-14435

The author "first explains that maleness is determined
in the embryo, then goes on to describe the roots of
men's insecurity, frail ego, physical weaknesses—causes
of the male's need to dominate the female." Publ Wkly

Friday, Nancy
Jealousy. Morrow 1985 539p o.p.; Bantam
Bks. paperback available $5.99   **155.3**
1. Jealousy 2. Human relations
ISBN 0-553-26165-7 (pa)   LC 85-4911

"A Perigord Press book"

An exploration of jealousy and the effect it has on
interpersonal relationships

This book's "analysis strips away some of the subterfuges that cloak our jealous behavior, revealing the more
dreadful demon, slit-eyed envy, and then explores . . .
the healing balms of gratitude, reparation and love." NY
Times Book Rev

Includes bibliographic references

Hite, Shere
The Hite report; a nationwide study on
female sexuality. Macmillan 1976 438p il
o.p.; Dell paperback available $6.95   **155.3**
1. Women—Sexual behavior 2. Women—Psychology
ISBN 0-440-13690-3 (pa)

This report is based on responses of 3,000 women
to a series of questionnaires on their sexual behavior

Includes bibliography

The Hite report on male sexuality. Knopf
1981 xxxiii, 1129p il o.p.; Ballantine Bks.
paperback available $6.95   **155.3**
1. Men—Sexual behavior 2. Men—Psychology
ISBN 0-345-35248-3 (pa)   LC 80-2709

"Using the responses of more than 7000 men to a
sexuality questionnaire, Hite presents a comprehensive
report on topics pertaining to men's perception and experience of sexuality." Libr J

Hudson, Liam
The way men think; intellect, intimacy
and the erotic imagination; [by] Liam
Hudson & Bernadine Jacot. Yale Univ.
Press 1991 219p il $28; pa $13   **155.3**
1. Men—Psychology 2. Intellect 3. Sex differences
(Psychology)
ISBN 0-300-04997-8; 0-300-05753-9 (pa)
     LC 91-21918

This is a psychoanalytic study of masculinity and male
behavior. The authors argue "that the male of the human
species is a wounded creature. . . . To become a male
like other males, the boy child has to reject womanliness
and the primitive comfort it has given him, and launch
out on his own. This painful process creates the wound.
It accounts for misogyny, . . . for aggressivity and a
need to be in control." Times Lit Suppl

Includes bibliographic references

Jack, Dana Crowley
Silencing the self; women and depression.
Harvard Univ. Press 1991 256p $19.95
155.3

1. Women—Psychology 2. Depression, Mental
ISBN 0-674-80815-0   LC 91-15472
Also available in paperback from HarperPerennial

"Based on data from a longitudinal study of 12 depressed white women of varying ages and social classes, this excellent book explains how cultural expectations about gender contribute to depression in women." Sci Books Films

Includes bibliographic references

Masters, William H.
Human sexual inadequacy; by William H. Masters, Virginia E. Johnson. Little, Brown 1970 467p il $39   **155.3**

1. Sex (Biology) 2. Sexual disorders
ISBN 0-316-54985-1
Also available in paperback from Bantam Bks.

The authors report on "treatment of 790 individual cases of sexual dysfunction. [The book] describes the methods of treatment and their results." Book World

Includes bibliography

Human sexuality; [by] William H. Masters, Virginia E. Johnson, Robert C. Kolodny. 4th ed. HarperCollins Pubs. 1992 748p il $50.50; pa $19.50   **155.3**

1. Sexual behavior 2. Sex (Biology)
ISBN 0-673-46362-1; 0-673-46481-4 (pa)
LC 90-24006

First published 1982 by Little, Brown

The authors discuss the dimensions of sexuality, the historical perspectives, and look at the methods and limitations of sex research. Other subjects covered are intimacy and communication; childhood/adolescent and adult development; sexually transmitted diseases, and the principles of sex research

Includes bibliographic references

Masters and Johnson on sex and human loving; [by] William H. Masters, Virginia E. Johnson, Robert C. Kolodny. Little, Brown 1986 598p il hardcover o.p. paperback available $19.95   **155.3**

1. Sexual behavior 2. Sex (Biology)
ISBN 0-316-50160-3 (pa)   LC 85-23950

"Provides complete coverage of the biological, psychological, and social aspects of human sexuality. Examines both cultural and historical trends and practices." N Y Public Libr Book of How & Where to Look It Up

Includes bibliography

Moir, Anne
Brain sex; the real difference between men and women; [by] Anne Moir and David Jessel. Carol Pub. Group 1991 242p il $17.95   **155.3**

1. Sex differences (Psychology) 2. Brain
ISBN 0-8184-0543-0   LC 91-7569
Also available in paperback from Dell
"A Lyle Stuart book"

The authors contend that "'the sexes are different because their brains are different.' After anticipating and countering the myriad objections to such a stance, they proceed to explain the mechanics of sex differentiation in the womb and the role male hormones play in the sexing of the brain. . . . Two dozen pages of notes support their lucid, entertaining, provocative, and potentially controversial claims." Booklist

Moore, Robert L., 1942-
The warrior within; accessing the knight in the male psyche; [by] Robert Moore and Douglas Gillette. Morrow 1992 301p il $22
155.3

1. Men—Psychology
ISBN 0-688-09592-5   LC 92-9494
Also available in paperback from Avon Bks.

Companion volume to King, warrior, magician, lover (1990) and The king within (1992)

The authors explain the Jungian concepts of "archetypes, the Ego, the Transpersonal Other (God for many individuals), the Self and the Shadow. Their thesis is simple: the Warrior is an integral part of the male psyche, but it must be socialized so that it does not lead the man to either sadism or masochism, and it must be incorporated with the King, the Magician and the Lover to achieve its fullest expression." Publ Wkly

Ross, John Munder
The male paradox. Simon & Schuster 1992 350p $23   **155.3**

1. Men—Psychology 2. Sex role
ISBN 0-671-70517-2   LC 92-21639
"Men, Ross surmises, wish for what they fear the most: love, oneness and emotionality, all of which they stereotypically associate with women. . . . His party-line psychoanalytic view that homosexual men subconsciously fear effeminization and pulverization by women is highly debatable, but in almost all other areas Ross unmasks the essential vulnerability behind male posturing with rare insight and sensitivity." Publ Wkly

Includes bibliographic references

155.4 Child psychology

Bettelheim, Bruno
Love is not enough; the treatment of emotionally disturbed children. Free Press 1950 386p il $27.95   **155.4**

1. Sonia Shankman Orthogenic School 2. Emotionally disturbed children 3. Child psychiatry
ISBN 0-02-903280-6

A report with case studies of a University of Chicago experimental school and its program to help socially and emotionally disturbed children

Brazelton, T. Berry, 1918-
The earliest relationship; parents, infants, and the drama of early attachment; [by] T. Berry Brazelton, Bertrand G. Cramer. Addison-Wesley 1990 252p $19.95; pa $10.95   **155.4**

1. Child psychology 2. Parent and child
ISBN 0-201-10639-6; 0-201-56764-4 (pa)
LC 89-39839

Brazelton, T. Berry, 1918——_Continued_
"A Merloyd Lawrence book"

An examination of "the first bewildering stages of parent-infant interaction and development. Parents are warned about the natural roller coaster of responses they will undergo, from anxiety over the newborn through the resentment often felt when a child displays those first physical signs of independence." Booklist

Includes bibliographic references

On becoming a family; the growth of attachment. rev ed. Delacorte Press; Lawrence, S. 1992 217p il $27.50; pa $16   **155.4**

1. Child psychology 2. Parent and child
ISBN 0-385-30768-3; 0-385-30770-5 (pa)
       LC 91-47567

"A Merloyd Lawrence book"

First published 1981

The author discusses the process of parent-child bonding from pregnancy on. Scientific commentary alternates with first-person remarks by couples raising young children

Includes bibliographic references

To listen to a child; understanding the normal problems of growing up; photographs by B.A. King. Addison-Wesley 1984 184p il hardcover o.p. paperback available $10.95   **155.4**

1. Child development 2. Child psychology 3. Emotionally disturbed children 4. Parent and child
ISBN 0-201-63270-5 (pa)   LC 84-6174

"A Merloyd Lawrence book"

The author "advises parents on children's transient developmental problems such as fears, thumbsucking, eating and sleeping deviations, enuresis, and stomachaches." Libr J

"Brazelton's sensible, authoritative, clear approach provides parents with the kinds of information they need to relax over the long pull, and to understand and cope with day-to-day difficulties." Publ Wkly

Carlsson-Paige, Nancy

Who's calling the shots? how to respond effectively to children's fascination with war play and war toys; [by] Nancy Carlsson-Paige and Diane E. Levin. New Soc. Pubs. 1990 188p il $39.95; pa $12.95   **155.4**

1. Child psychology 2. Toys
ISBN 0-86571-164-X; 0-86571-165-8 (pa)

The authors "explore the often developmentally necessary role of agressive play in childhood, demonstrate how most of the current Rambo-type toys actually undermine the potential value of such play, offer a number of creative alternatives to these toys, and suggest ways in which individuals can help to affect public policy to discourage this trend." Libr J

Includes bibliography

Coles, Robert

The moral life of children. Atlantic Monthly Press 1986 302p il o.p.; Houghton Mifflin paperback available $10.70   **155.4**

1. Moral education 2. Child psychology 3. Child development
ISBN 0-395-59921-0 (pa)   LC 85-18590

A study of the moral status of children in a diversity of cultures

The author "is at his best when he is listening to children talk, recording their talk and then transforming their talk into a kind of narrative poetry. . . . [His book is] a major contribution to our understanding of how children become socialized." N Y Times Book Rev

Includes bibliography

Their eyes meeting the world; the drawings and paintings of children; edited by Margaret Sartor. Houghton Mifflin 1992 133p il $30   **155.4**

1. Child artists
ISBN 0-395-61129-6   LC 92-18677

This book "is a collection of 50 full-color drawings by preteen children from around the world. It brings together the insights Coles gained working with children in the South during the 1960s, in New Mexico during the '70s, and throughout the US and other countries more recently. The drawings come from the hands of black and white children experiencing early integration efforts in the South, suburban children of privilege, children living in ghettos, and children with what are considered terminal illnesses." Christ Sci Monit

Gesell, Arnold Lucius, 1880-1961

The child from five to ten; Arnold Gesell, Frances L. Ilg, and Louise Bates Ames, in collaboration with Glenna E. Bullis. rev ed. Harper & Row 1977 461p il $29.95 **155.4**

1. Child psychology 2. Child development
ISBN 0-06-011501-7   LC 76-5123

Also available companion volumes Infant and child in the culture of today and The Gesell Institute's child from one to six

First published 1946

"Part One is intended to give the reader preliminary orientation to the central theme of development. . . . Part Two describes the progressive stages in the growth of the child's mind, by means of a series of cross-sectional characterizations. . . . Part Three deals with the total growth complex." Introduction

Includes bibliography

Greenspan, Stanley I.

First feelings; milestones in the emotional development of your baby and child; [by] Stanley I. Greenspan, Nancy Thorndike Greenspan. Viking 1985 247p il o.p.; Penguin Bks. paperback available $9.95   **155.4**

1. Child psychology 2. Emotions
ISBN 0-14-011988-4 (pa)   LC 84-40471

The authors outline discernable steps in the emotional development from infancy

Includes bibliography

Healy, Jane M.

Endangered minds; why our children don't think. Simon & Schuster 1990 382p il hardcover o.p. paperback available $11

155.4

1. Learning, Psychology of
ISBN 0-671-74920-X (pa)   LC 90-39897

"According to the author, the present generation is not receiving the educational foundation needed to foster analytical thought processes. The current trend toward preschool preparedness and the use of such programs as Sesame Street to enhance the child's learning may teach the child to read but fails to develop critical reasoning processes." Libr J

"This is an essential book for those looking for widened perspectives, a broad range of mental skills, and open-ended imagination." Readings

Includes bibliography

Your child's growing mind; a parent's guide to learning from birth to adolescence. Doubleday 1987 324p il $17.95; pa $10.95

155.4

1. Learning, Psychology of 2. Brain 3. Child psychology 4. Parent and child
ISBN 0-385-23149-0; 0-385-23150-4 (pa) LC 86-2058

The author "discusses learning, problem-solving, creativity, perception, memory and other standard aspects of cognitive development as these develop in children in general and in children individually." Sci Books Films

"Excellent reading for parents and pre-school teachers." Libr J

Includes bibliography

Klaus, Marshall H.

The amazing newborn; [by] Marshall H. Klaus and Phyllis Klaus. Addison-Wesley 1985 145p il pa $12.95

155.4

1. Infants 2. Child psychology
ISBN 0-201-11672-3   LC 85-9048

Also available in hardcover from P. Smith

"A Merloyd Lawrence book"

"The Klauses describe six different states of consciousness experienced by newborns—from quiet sleep to crying. They then outline the development of sight, hearing, touch, taste and smell, as well as patterns of movement, automatic reflexes and facial expressions." Publ Wkly

"This lucid explication of the fascinating process of sensory development will appeal to parents eager to fathom the mysterious world of the newborn." Booklist

Includes bibliographic references

McGrath, Ellie

My one and only: the special experience of the only child. Morrow 1989 250p $16.95

155.4

1. Only child 2. Parent and child
ISBN 0-688-06488-4   LC 88-37064

"Herself an only child, McGrath . . . grew up hearing the popular clichés about only children: They are selfish, spoiled, lonely, and socially maladjusted. This book, the result of interviews with over 100 only children . . . of all ages shows how the myths may come true, but are not inescapable." Libr J

Includes bibliographic references

Montessori, Maria, 1870-1952

The absorbent mind; translated from the Italian by Claude A. Claremont. Holt, Rinehart & Winston 1967 304p il o.p.; Dell paperback available $9.95

155.4

1. Child development 2. Child psychology 3. Educational psychology
ISBN 0-440-55056-4 (pa)

"In these lectures Dr. Montessori dwells, not so much on the techniques used in her schools, but on her insight into the development of children, physically and psychologically, from birth to adulthood." Publ Wkly

Piaget, Jean, 1896-1980

The essential Piaget; edited by Howard E. Gruber and J. Jacques Vonèche. Basic Bks. 1977 xlii, 881p il hardcover o.p. paperback available $23.95

155.4

1. Child psychology 2. Knowledge, Theory of
ISBN 0-465-02064-X (pa)   LC 76-9337

"An anthology of 47 selections from the Swiss psychologist's writings, including translations of pieces previously unavailable in English. The editors emphasize a coherent presentation of the development of Piaget's ideas rather than a summarization of Piaget's final position on a topic." Booklist

Includes bibliography

The moral judgment of the child; [translated by Marjorie Gabain] Free Press 1948 418p $19.95; pa $15.95

155.4

1. Child psychology 2. Human behavior 3. Ethics
ISBN 0-02-925230-X; 0-02-925240-7 (pa)

Original French edition, 1932

Piaget studies, not the moral behavior of children, but their ideas about right and wrong, the rules of a game, adult authority, and cooperation and justice

Play, dreams, and imitation in childhood; translated by C. Gattegno and F. M. Hodgson. Norton 1951 296p hardcover o.p. paperback available $9.95

155.4

1. Child psychology 2. Play 3. Dreams
ISBN 0-393-00171-7 (pa)

Also available in hardcover from P. Smith

Original French edition, 1945; this translation first published 1951 in the United Kingdom

The author tries to show that "the acquisition of language is itself subordinated to the working of a symbolic function which can be seen in the development of imitation and play as well as in that of verbal mechanisms." Introduction

Restak, Richard M., 1942-

The infant mind. Doubleday 1986 274p il $18.95

155.4

1. Infants—Development 2. Brain 3. Child psychology
ISBN 0-385-19531-1   LC 86-2033

In this study Restak clarifies current "theory regarding brain development, tracing the fetal brain through various stages in utero, explaining the changes it undergoes after birth, and viewing how it controls infant behavior." Booklist

Includes bibliographic references

Roiphe, Herman, 1924-

Your child's mind; the complete book of infant and child mental health care; [by] Herman Roiphe, Anne Roiphe. St. Martin's/Marek 1985 429p o.p. paperback available $10.95   **155.4**

1. Child psychology
ISBN 0-312-89784-7 (pa)
     LC 85-1742

The Roiphes "explore the child's emotional development from infancy to age ten. Taking a Freudian perspective, the authors emphasize sexuality and toilet training, but discuss more than 150 different subjects such as bonding, colic, infantile depression, stuttering, TV, cruelty to animals." Libr J

Segal, Marilyn M.

Your child at play; three to five years; [by] Marilyn Segal and Don Adcock. Newmarket Press 1986 218p il $16.95; pa $10.95   **155.4**

1. Play 2. Child development
ISBN 0-937858-72-2; 0-937858-73-0 (pa)
     LC 86-60294

Other available titles in authors' Your child at play series are: Your child at play: birth to one year; Your child at play: one to two years; Your child at play: two to three years

This volume offers "ideas for encouraging children's creativity. . . . It is divided into five sections: conversational play, discovery play, creative play, letters and numbers, and playing with friends. The text, highlighted by photographs and entertaining anecdotes, is both stimulating and thorough." Libr J

Includes bibligraphy

Sifford, Darrell, 1931-1992

The only child; being one, loving one, understanding one, raising one. Putnam 1989 221p $17.95   **155.4**

1. Only child 2. Parent and child
ISBN 0-399-13394-1
     LC 88-11498

Also available in paperback from HarperPerennial

The author explores the following questions: "What drives the only child to achieve at levels above and beyond other children; Why is it so hard for the only child to forgive and forget; How can parents keep from spoiling and overvaluing their only child; How can only children break the chains of parental dependency." Publisher's note

"Readers are likely to conclude that there's not much difference between an only child and one with a sibling when it comes to capabilities, faults, virtues and other human characteristics." Publ Wkly

White, Burton L., 1929-

The first three years of life. new & rev ed. Prentice Hall Press 1991 380p il pa $10.95   **155.4**

1. Infants—Development 2. Child psychology
ISBN 0-13-317678-9
     LC 89-23107

First published 1975

This volume provides "a week-by-week guide to the mental, physical, and emotional development of the young child [and] covers all the topics parents ask about most, including: how to discipline effectively, how to defuse sibling rivalry, when and how to toilet train, how

to avoid the spoiled-child syndrome, what toys you should (and should not) buy, which early tests are crucial, [and] substitute care." Publisher's note

Includes bibliographic references

155.45   Exceptional children

Greenfeld, Josh

A client called Noah; a family journey continued. Holt & Co. 1987 371p o.p.; Harcourt Brace & Co. paperback available $7.95   **155.45**

1. Greenfeld, Noah Jiro, 1966- 2. Mentally handicapped children 3. Parent and child
ISBN 0-15-618168-1 (pa)
     LC 86-14210

Sequel to A place for Noah, entered below

The author "presents his 'graphic' diary notes, which record his suffering family's attempts to live with the severely brain-damaged Noah." Publ Wkly

A place for Noah. Holt, Rinehart and Winston 1978 310p o.p.; Harcourt Brace & Co. paperback available $7.95   **155.45**

1. Greenfeld, Noah Jiro, 1966- 2. Mentally handicapped children 3. Parent and child
ISBN 0-15-672000-0 (pa)
     LC 77-13354

"A journal kept from 1971 to 1977 records events in the life of Greenfeld's severely brain-damaged son from age 5-11. First writing about the boy in 'A Child Called Noah' the noted playwright and screenwriter continues to reveal facets of the burden placed on each member of the family, the indecision about institutionalizing him, and the quest for a place that could provide special education." Booklist

Stehli, Annabel

The sound of a miracle; a child's triumph over autism. Doubleday 1991 226p $19.95   **155.45**

1. Stehli, Georgiana 2. Autism
ISBN 0-385-41140-5
     LC 90-37456

Also available in paperback from Avon Bks.

The author "relates the details of living and coping with her unresponsive, autistic child. . . . When Georgie began auditory training in Switzerland, she became a different person as her hearing changed." SLJ

"Stehli's is a powerful story of courage, hope, and determination." Libr J

155.5   Psychology of young adults

Ames, Louise Bates

Your ten- to fourteen-year-old; by Louise Bates Ames, Frances L. Ilg, Sidney M. Baker. Delacorte Press 1988 346p $16.95; pa $9.95   **155.5**

1. Adolescent psychology 2. Child development 3. Child psychology
ISBN 0-385-29631-2; 0-385-29699-1 (pa)
     LC 87-20214

Replaces Youth: the years from ten to sixteen, under the authorship of Arnold Gesell, Frances L. Ilg and Louise Bates Ames

Ames, Louise Bates—*Continued*
"After replicating their 1956 study of adolescents in the late 1970s and early 1980s, the authors concluded that the tasks of adolescence remained constant: to get free of parents, establish a sense of one's own personality, and gradually become interested and involved in a relationship with a member of the opposite sex." Libr J
"This straightforward, informative survey of the whys and whats of pre- and early teens should help parents cope with the ups and downs of these tumultuous years." Booklist

Includes bibliography

Brown, Lyn Mikel, 1956-
Meeting at the crossroads; women's psychology and girls' development; [by] Lyn Mikel Brown, Carol Gilligan. Harvard Univ. Press 1992 258p $19.95   **155.5**
1. Adolescent psychology 2. Women—Psychology
ISBN 0-674-56464-2   LC 92-14312
Also available in paperback from Ballantine Bks.

The authors, "interested in the effects of adolescence on the development of girls and the psychological health of women, conducted interviews of 100 girls over a five-year period. Excerpts from these interviews tell, in the compelling voices of preadolescent and adolescent girls, of 'lost voices and lost strengths.'" SLJ

Includes bibliographic references

155.6 Psychology of adults

Braiker, Harriet B., 1948-
The type E* woman; how to overcome the stress of being *everything to everybody. Dodd, Mead 1986 274p o.p.; New Am. Lib. paperback available $5.99   **155.6**
1. Stress (Psychology) 2. Women—Psychology 3. Success
ISBN 0-451-14999-8 (pa)   LC 86-8934
The author "identifies the Everything to Everybody syndrome, a syndrome experienced by today's high-achieving woman who suffers stress while trying to excel in both personal life and career. Braiker compares this syndrome to Type A behavior in men. After presenting a self-test that helps readers determine whether they suffer from this syndrome, she goes on to describe some of the false premises that contribute to its development." Libr J

Estés, Clarissa Pinkola
Women who run with the wolves; myths and stories of the wild woman archetype. Ballantine Bks. 1992 520p $23; pa $14   **155.6**
1. Women—Folklore 2. Women—Psychology
ISBN 0-345-37744-3; 0-345-38321-4 (pa)   LC 91-58630
In this "introduction to feminine psychology, a Jungian analyst . . . endeavors to define and describe the wild woman archetype. Arguing that it can be best elucidated through stories and myths, Estés examines traditional tales from various world cultures and explains their symbolism. By studying the meaning of these stories, she claims, a woman gains insight into her inner nature and can tap the wild woman within herself to bring forth new measures of self-determination and fresh expressions of creativity, thus achieving a state of greater empowerment and freedom. Written in a clear, richly evocative style." Libr J

Includes bibliographic references

Forward, Susan
Men who hate women & the women who love them; [by] Susan Forward and Joan Torres. Bantam Bks. 1986 294p $16.95; pa $5.99   **155.6**
1. Women—Psychology 2. Men—Psychology
ISBN 0-553-05135-0; 0-553-28037-6 (pa)   LC 85-48235

"Many men need to control their relationships completely and consequently are mentally (if not physically) abusive. . . . Women with low self-esteem are drawn to these men because they can also be charming and devoted. Forward devotes the first half of the book to an analysis of the problem, the second half to breaking the pattern and getting outside help." Libr J
"Plentifully sprinkled with handy checklists and real-life examples of emotionally abusive relationships, this guide will help both the victims of abuse and those who care about them." Booklist

Includes bibliography

Friday, Nancy
My mother/my self; the daughter's search for identity. Delacorte Press 1977 425p o.p.; Dell paperback available $5.99   **155.6**
1. Women—Psychology 2. Mothers 3. Parent and child
ISBN 0-440-15664-5 (pa)   LC 77-23571
The author explores the psychological aspects of the mother-daughter relationship

Includes bibliography

Gerzon, Mark
Coming into our own; understanding the adult metamorphosis. Delacorte Press 1992 315p $19; pa $12.95   **155.6**
1. Middle age 2. Self-realization
ISBN 0-385-30492-7; 0-385-30831-0 (pa)   LC 91-35686

"The author claims that although adult changes are less dramatic than childhood changes, adults are still undergoing a constant re-examination of who they are and what they want from their lives. This is a good, thought-provoking choice for psychology and self-help collections." Libr J

Includes bibliographic references

Johnson, Karen
Trusting ourselves; the sourcebook on psychology for women; [by] Karen Johnson and Tom Ferguson. Atlantic Monthly Press 1990 477p hardcover o.p. paperback available $12.95   **155.6**
1. Women—Psychology
ISBN 0-87113-447-0 (pa)   LC 89-38637
A "compilation of information on the various psychologies and the way women are affected by their practice; it also considers emotional illness to which women are particularly prone. Johnson and Ferguson are espe-

Johnson, Karen—*Continued*
cially good in these areas, including body image, abuse, and depression. As a woman consumer's guide to the therapies, this is an excellent addition to self-help collections." Booklist

Includes bibliographic references

Kiley, Dan
Living together, feeling alone; healing your hidden loneliness. Prentice Hall Press 1989 205p o.p.; Fawcett Bks. paperback available $4.95   **155.6**
1. Women—Psychology
ISBN 0-449-21919-4 (pa)   LC 89-33433
The author "applies his counseling techniques, which he calls 'Spiritual Behaviorism,' to the problem of loneliness of married or otherwise coupled women. He presents case studies from his clinical work with women whose undefined feelings of loneliness produce destructive symptoms such as eating disorders and workaholism, even though outwardly their marriages exemplify togetherness." Publ Wkly

Includes bibliography

The Peter Pan syndrome; men who have never grown up; Dan Kiley. Dodd, Mead 1983 281p o.p.; Avon Bks. paperback available $4.95   **155.6**
1. Men—Psychology 2. Boys
ISBN 0-380-68890-5 (pa)   LC 83-8907
Companion volume to The Wendy dilemma (1984)
The author "coined the term Peter Pan Syndrome to describe men who refuse to grow up and to accept adult responsibilities. 'Usually the oldest male child of a traditional family,' A Peter Pan passes through the stages of irresponsibility, anxiety, loneliness, sex role conflicts, narcissism, and chauvinism to arrive at social impotence and despondency in adulthood. The final section instructs parents, wives, and friends on how to help the PPS victim." Libr J

Includes bibliography

What to do when he won't change; getting what you need from the man you love. Putnam 1987 218p o.p.; Fawcett Bks. paperback available $4.95   **155.6**
1. Men—Psychology 2. Human relations
ISBN 0-449-21616-0 (pa)   LC 87-6053
"Understanding oneself, the psychologist-author counsels, is the first step to getting what you need from the man you love. Questionnaires included in the text are meant to establish this groundwork, then the reader moves on to Kiley's program for improving relationships." Publ Wkly
The advice "is generally sound, focusing on the need for inner-directedness and for changing one's behavior in order to be a catalyst for change in one's partner." Booklist

Lerner, Harriet Goldhor
The dance of intimacy; a woman's guide to courageous acts of change in key relationships. Harper & Row 1989 255p $17.95; pa $12   **155.6**
1. Women—Psychology 2. Human relations
ISBN 0-06-016067-5; 0-06-091646-X (pa)
      LC 88-45519

The author explains "how to operate more effectively in key relationships—whether it be with a distant or unfaithful spouse, a depressed sister, a difficult mother, an alcoholic father, an uncommitted lover, a dying parent, or a family member that we have written off." Publisher's note

Includes bibliographic references

Levinson, Daniel J.
The seasons of a man's life; by Daniel J. Levinson [et al.] Knopf 1978 363p $24.95   **155.6**
1. Men—Psychology 2. Middle age
ISBN 0-394-40694-X   LC 77-20978
Also available in paperback from Ballantine Bks.

The Levinson theory divides a man's "life cycle into five overlapping eras. . . . Each era is marked by periods of stability during which life structures are built. These stable periods alternate with transition periods during which life structures change." Saturday Rev

Includes bibliographic references

Miller, Jean Baker
Toward a new psychology of women. 2nd ed. Beacon Press 1986 xxv, 154p $20; pa $10.95   **155.6**
1. Women—Psychology
ISBN 0-8070-2910-6; 0-8070-2909-2 (pa)
      LC 86-47553

First published 1976
This study of women's psychological and emotional states also examines feminist scholarship on the subject

Includes bibliography

Scarf, Maggie, 1932-
Unfinished business; pressure points in the lives of women. Doubleday 1980 581p $14.95   **155.6**
1. Women—Psychology 2. Depression, Mental
ISBN 0-385-12248-9   LC 78-22352
Also available in paperback from Ballantine Bks.

"In examining the issues that women typically face at different periods of life, the thesis is that failure to resolve the problems of one period increases vulnerability to difficulties later. A major topic discussed throughout is female depression." Choice

Includes bibliography

155.8 Ethnopsychology and national psychology

Lévi-Strauss, Claude
The savage mind. University of Chicago Press 1966 290p il (Nature of human society ser) hardcover o.p. paperback available $13.95   **155.8**
1. Ethnopsychology 2. Anthropology
ISBN 0-226-47484-4 (pa)
Original French edition, 1962

Lévi-Strauss, Claude—*Continued*
"An anthropological study of the nature of thought, concepts and systems as they occur in various cultures." Chicago Public Libr

Includes bibliography

155.9 Environmental psychology

Bettelheim, Bruno
Surviving, and other essays. Knopf 1979 432p hardcover o.p. paperback available $14.95 **155.9**
1. Adjustment (Psychology) 2. Social psychology
ISBN 0-394-74264-8 (pa)   LC 78-20388
Analyzed in Essay and general literature index
These essays cover topics such as the Holocaust, education, sexual mores, violence, and contemporary youth
Includes bibliographic references

Borg, Susan, 1947-
When pregnancy fails; families coping with miscarriage, ectopic pregnancy, stillbirth, and infant death; Susan Borg and Judith Lasker. rev and updated ed. Bantam Bks. 1989 298p pa $8.95 **155.9**
1. Miscarriage 2. Abortion 3. Bereavement 4. Death
ISBN 0-553-34594-X   LC 88-21671
First published 1981 by Beacon Press
The authors discuss topics ranging from "how loss affects the single woman and grandparents . . . and the disappointment among grieving parents with the lack of emotional support coming from the medical community, to when and how to consider a malpractice suit." Publisher's note
Includes bibliography

Cramer, Kathryn D.
Staying on top when your world turns upside down. Viking 1990 332p il o.p.; Penguin Bks. paperback available $8.95 **155.9**
1. Adjustment (Psychology) 2. Stress (Psychology)
ISBN 0-14-012772-0 (pa)   LC 89-40649
The author presents a "four-stage system to help people cope with traumatic life events—death, divorce, financial setbacks, job loss, major illness—by developing inner strength and resilience. Based on the adage that 'Rough weather makes good timber,' the system involves confronting the challenge, exploring the ramifications, identifying new possibilities, and finally achieving personal transformation." Libr J
Includes bibliographic references

Explaining death to children; edited by Earl A. Grollman; with an introduction by Louise Bates Ames. Beacon Press 1967 296p hardcover o.p. paperback available $12.95 **155.9**
1. Child psychology 2. Death
ISBN 0-8070-2385-X (pa)
The contributors "include an anthropologist, a biologist, a librarian, a psychiatrist, a psychologist, a sociologist, and Protestant, Jewish and Catholic clergy.

The title is the theme of each of the essays." Libr J
Includes bibliographic references

Fitzgerald, Helen
The grieving child; a parent's guide. Simon & Schuster 1992 207p pa $9 **155.9**
1. Death 2. Bereavement 3. Child rearing
ISBN 0-671-76762-3   LC 91-48211
"A Fireside book"
This book "is intended as a guide for parents seeking to explain the death of a parent, relative, friend, or even a pet to a child. . . . Fitzgerald believes in using a clear, direct approach when explaining death to a child, yet her tone is gentle and loving." Libr J
Includes bibliographic references

Friedman, Rochelle
Surviving pregnancy loss; [by] Rochelle Friedman, Bonnie Gradstein; with a foreword by Robert H. Glass, M.D. rev and updated ed. Little, Brown 1992 302p pa $12.95 **155.9**
1. Miscarriage 2. Pregnancy 3. Death
ISBN 0-316-29396-2
First published 1982
This book provides "information on how to deal with the trauma associated with miscarriage, stillbirth, ectopic pregnancy, and loss after amniocentesis. Also covered: the husband's experience, explaining the loss to children, and in-depth information about future options—trying again or adoption." Publisher's note
Includes bibliography

Jewett, Claudia L., 1939-
Helping children cope with separation and loss. Harvard Common Press 1982 146p $14.95; pa $8.95 **155.9**
1. Child psychology 2. Joy and sorrow
ISBN 0-916782-27-1; 0-916782-53-0 (pa)
                                LC 82-11823
This book "focuses on the effects of a major loss (through death, divorce, hospitalization, etc.) on children. Directed toward parents and/or other helping adults . . . who may be assisting a child through the grieving process, the text stresses the importance of the resolution of one's grief. Specific methods to be used in dealing with a mourning child are outlined in a clear, concise fashion." Libr J
Includes bibliography

Kübler-Ross, Elisabeth
Living with death and dying. Macmillan 1981 181p il hardcover o.p. paperback available $9 **155.9**
1. Death 2. Terminal care
ISBN 0-02-086490-6 (pa)   LC 80-26984
The author argues that caring for, and living with the terminally ill need not be a solely negative experience

Kübler-Ross, Elisabeth—*Continued*

On children and death. Macmillan 1983
279p hardcover o.p. paperback available $10
155.9

1. Death 2. Child psychology
ISBN 0-02-089144-X (pa)   LC 83-11252

A look at how one copes with a child's death by
disease, accident or murder

Includes bibliography

On death and dying. Macmillan 1991
c1969 260p $50; pa $10   **155.9**

1. Death
ISBN 0-02-567111-1; 0-02-089141-5 (pa)
    LC 90-22561

A reissue of the title first published 1969

A look at the psychological, sociological and theological issues faced by the terminally ill and their caregivers

Includes bibliographic references

Lifton, Robert Jay, 1926-

The broken connection; on death and the
continuity of life. Simon & Schuster 1979
495p o.p.; Basic Bks. paperback available
$15.95   **155.9**

1. Death
ISBN 0-465-00776-7 (pa)   LC 79-12886

"Lifton explores the individual life cycle and discusses
anxiety and tension, conscience and guilt, anger, violence
and depression as central not only to all mental suffering
but to the life process." Publisher's note

Includes bibliography

Death in life; survivors of Hiroshima.
University of N.C. Press 1991 594p pa
$18.95   **155.9**

1. Atomic bomb victims 2. Hiroshima (Japan)—Bombardment, 1945
ISBN 0-8078-4344-X   LC 91-50248

Also available Basic Bks. 1982 edition

A reprint with new preface of the title first published
1967 by Random House

Based on interviews, this is an "analysis and description in psychological and social terms of the immediate
and long-term effects on the survivors of the Hiroshima
atom bomb." Libr J

Includes bibliographic references

Lukas, Christopher

Silent grief; living in the wake of suicide;
[by] Christopher Lukas & Henry M. Seiden.
Scribner 1988 c1987 240p o.p.; Bantam Bks.
paperback available $9.95   **155.9**

1. Suicide 2. Bereavement
ISBN 0-553-34832-9 (pa)   LC 87-23328

The author addresses the physical and psychological
problems that arise in the aftermath of a suicide

"A sensible popular manual on 'postvention' of suicide
and the dangers of unspoken sorrow and anger." Libr
J

Includes bibliography

Matheny, Kenneth B.

Stress and strategies for lifestyle
management; [by] Kenneth B. Matheny,
Richard J. Riordan. Georgia State Univ.
Business Press 1992 258p pa $29.95 **155.9**

1. Stress (Psychology)
ISBN 0-88406-250-3   LC 92-7078

The authors discuss ways "to bring about change by
suggesting techniques to control stressful thoughts, alter
stress-inducing habits, increase coping resources, prevent
runaway emotions, and lower stressful arousal. Although
much of the book's emphasis is on self-treatment, readers
are also directed to helpful literature, self-help groups,
and professional resources." Publisher's note

Includes bibliographic references

Schiff, Harriet Sarnoff

Living through mourning; finding comfort
and hope when a loved one has died.
Viking 1986 300p o.p.; Penguin Bks.
paperback available $10   **155.9**

1. Death 2. Bereavement
ISBN 0-14-010309-0 (pa)   LC 85-40801

The author addresses sorrow, denial, anger, guilt,
depression, and acceptance. The uses of faith are also
considered

Storr, Anthony

Solitude; a return to the self. Free Press
1988 216p $24.95   **155.9**

1. Self 2. Adjustment (Psychology)
ISBN 0-02-931620-0   LC 88-7187

Also available in paperback from Ballantine Bks.

In this book Storr "considers the impact of voluntary
as well as enforced solitude, particularly on creative persons such as composers, writers, and philosophers. Their
efforts take place chiefly in solitude, and Storr argues
that solitude has restorative value for the ordinary individual as well." Libr J

Includes bibliography

158   Applied psychology

Bradshaw, John E., 1933-

Homecoming; reclaiming and championing
your inner child; [by] John Bradshaw.
Bantam Bks. 1990 288p il $20; pa $12.50
    158

1. Self-realization
ISBN 0-553-05793-6; 0-553-35389-6 (pa)
    LC 90-33688

The author "offers a series of progressive meditations
and exercises for resolving the trauma that results from
a dysfunctional family." Libr J

Includes bibliographic references

Branden, Nathaniel

How to raise your self-esteem. Bantam
Bks. 1987 164p $14.95; pa $4.99   **158**

1. Self-respect 2. Psychology, Applied
ISBN 0-553-05185-7; 0-553-26646-2 (pa)
    LC 86-14644

Branden, Nathaniel—*Continued*
"Intended for use without the aid of a psychotherapist, Branden's book shows that there are many paths to self-esteem, as exemplified by accounts culled from his own private-practice files." Libr J

Includes bibliography

Burns, David D.
Feeling good; the new mood therapy; preface by Aaron T. Beck. Morrow 1980 393p il $25   158
1. Depression, Mental 2. Psychotherapy
ISBN 0-688-03633-3   LC 80-12694
Also available in paperback from Avon Bks. and New. Am. Lib.

"The author reports on results of treating depression (from mild blues to serious cases) with 'cognitive thinking.' . . . The therapy involves fighting automatic responses to disappointments by intelligent thinking that can put one's shortcomings into perspective." Publ Wkly
"The author . . . writes simply, clearly, and without any jargon; better yet, he has a sense of compassion and a sense of humor, and is aware of his own limitations." Libr J

Includes bibliography

The feeling good handbook; using the new mood therapy in everyday life. Morrow 1989 587p il $19.95   158
1. Psychotherapy
ISBN 0-688-01745-2   LC 89-30573
Also available in paperback from New Am. Lib.

"Burns argues that while medication is necessary in treating serious cases of destructive mood problems, the therapy he uses in his own practice—cognitive therapy, or new mood therapy, as he calls it—should prove an effective means of dealing with everyday problems. . . . Recommended as a real help." Libr J

Buscaglia, Leo F.
Loving each other; the challenge of human relationships. Slack 1984 208p $13.95   158
1. Love 2. Human relations
ISBN 0-943432-27-8   LC 84-50590
Also available in paperback from Fawcett Columbine
The author offers practical suggestions for improving human relationships

Includes bibliography

Carnegie, Dale, 1888-1955
How to win friends and influence people; editorial consultant, Dorothy Carnegie, editorial assistance, Arthur R. Pell. rev ed. Simon & Schuster 1981 299p $17.45   158
1. Success 2. Psychology, Applied
ISBN 0-671-42517-X   LC 80-28759
First published 1936
An examination of the psychology of business and social success

Includes bibliographic references

Charlesworth, Edward A., 1949-
Stress management; a comprehensive guide to wellness; [by] Edward A. Charlesworth and Ronald G. Nathan. rev & updated ed. Atheneum Pubs. 1984 xxiv, 327p o.p.; Ballantine Bks. paperback available $5.99
                                          158
1. Stress (Psychology)
ISBN 0-345-32734-9 (pa)   LC 84-45060
First published 1982
The authors have written a "manual for stress management which moves from the basics to practical applications in an easily usable format." Libr J

Includes bibliographies and discographies

Dyer, Wayne W.
Real magic; creating miracles in everyday life. HarperCollins Pubs. 1992 260p $20
                                          158
1. Success 2. Psychology, Applied
ISBN 0-06-016678-9   LC 92-52588
In this work the author "prods readers into recognizing a spiritual essence and then using that awareness to transform themselves. . . . The miracles of reformation for the individual, family, community, and world discussed here range from enhancing mental prowess or breaking addictions to eliminating apartheid." Booklist

Fensterheim, Herbert
Don't say yes when you want to say no; how assertiveness training can change your life; by Herbert Fensterheim and Jean Baer. McKay, D. 1975 275p o.p.; Dell paperback available $5.99   158
1. Assertiveness (Psychology) 2. Behavior modification
ISBN 0-440-15413-8 (pa)
This book "deals with methods of altering the life style of an individual. It presents a cookbook set of procedures which, if followed, should result in an individual becoming more assertive. Sufficient historical and empirical background is presented so that the interested reader may delve further. Although the overview is brief, it is accurate and relevant to the points under discussion." Libr J

Fisher, Roger, 1922-
Getting to yes; negotiating agreement without giving in; by Roger Fisher and William Ury, with Bruce Patton, editor. 2nd ed, by Fisher, Ury, and Patton. Houghton Mifflin 1991 200p $22.45   158
1. Negotiation
ISBN 0-395-63124-6   LC 91-32444
Also available in paperback from Penguin Bks.
First published 1981
"The authors treat negotiating as an integral part of everyday life and illustrate this with a . . . selection of examples (ranging from labor-management to counseling for marital problems). This work is an offshoot of the Harvard Negotiating Project. . . . The volume is written for a very broad audience and is well suited for public, professional, and academic libraries." Choice

Flanigan, Beverly

Forgiving the unforgivable. Macmillan 1992 270p $20 **158**

1. Psychology, Applied
ISBN 0-02-538681-6   LC 91-30875

The author "offers readers a six-step program on how to cope with the 'unforgivable'—betrayals and wounds inflicted by loved ones that go beyond everyday slights and insults—and eventually forgive the offender. . . . Case histories illustrate the points made. This inspiring and thought-provoking guide should give comfort to those who thought they could never trust a loved one again." Publ Wkly

Includes bibliographic references

Freeman, Arthur M.

The 10 dumbest mistakes smart people make and how to avoid them; simple and sure techniques for gaining greater control of your life; [by] Arthur Freeman, Rose DeWolf. HarperCollins Pubs. 1992 xxxii, 284p il $20; pa $10   **158**

1. Psychology, Applied   2. Human behavior   3. Decision making 4. Errors
ISBN 0-06-016685-1; 0-06-092199-4 (pa)

LC 91-50440

The authors present "cognitive therapy techniques which focus on common habits of thinking that 'cause us to misinterpret experience, misjudge others and misjudge ourselves.'. . . Also discussed is the role stress plays in faulty thinking. Final chapters summarize techniques and give suggestions for putting changes into action, using such practices as time scheduling, problem solving, and role-playing." Libr J

Harris, Thomas Anthony, 1913-

I'm OK, you're OK; a practical guide to transactional analysis. Harper & Row 1969 278p il o.p.; Avon Bks. paperback available $4.95   **158**

1. Transactional analysis
ISBN 0-380-00772-X (pa)

This book describes the method of psychiatric group treatment, and applies the system to problems in marriage and child rearing, violence and revolution, racial prejudice, creativity, and international problems

Includes bibliographic references

Hyatt, Carole

When smart people fail; by Carole Hyatt and Linda Gottlieb. Simon & Schuster 1987 240p o.p.; Penguin Bks. paperback available $9.95   **158**

1. Failure (Psychology) 2. Success 3. Psychology, Applied
ISBN 0-14-010727-4 (pa)   LC 86-26205

The authors "explore the effects of failure on people in success-oriented America. Interviewing men and women in various fields, they glean interesting information from those who accepted defeat only temporarily." Publ Wkly

Includes bibliography

James, Muriel

Born to win; transactional analysis with gestalt experiments; by Muriel James and Dorothy Jongeward. Addison-Wesley 1971 286p il hardcover o.p. paperback available $6.68   **158**

1. Transactional analysis 2. Gestalt psychology
ISBN 0-201-55016-4 (pa)

Also available in paperback from New Am. Lib.

An introduction to Transactional analysis, a method which attempts to increase human self-awareness in relating to others

Includes bibliographic references

Kaminer, Wendy

I'm dysfunctional, you're dysfunctional; the recovery movement and other self-help fashions. Addison-Wesley 1992 180p $18.22   **158**

1. Psychology, Applied
ISBN 0-201-57062-9   LC 91-42471

Also available in paperback from Vintage Bks.

The author critiques the "self-help and recovery movements sweeping middle-class America. Taking a skeptical look at the books, groups, gurus, and philosophy the recovery movement vends, she says that if we listen to the jargon of recovery, we'd think that Americans are a passive, dependent, abused, and victimized people. . . . Biting and sharp, Kaminer doesn't go easy on her subject as she raises some very cogent questions about its greater implications." Booklist

Includes bibliographic references

Katz, Stan J.

The codependency conspiracy; how to break the recovery habit and take charge of your life; [by] Stan J. Katz and Aimee E. Liu. Warner Bks. 1991 233p $18.95; pa $10.99   **158**

1. Psychology, Applied
ISBN 0-446-51595-7; 0-446-39377-0 (pa)

LC 90-50532

The authors "argue that many self-help books and programs promote an almost addictive dependence on groups and meetings. They reject labeling an individual as 'codependent,' 'victim,' or continually 'recovering.' The authors offer an eight-point program designed to foster healthy independence and further self-development." Libr J

Includes bibliographic references

Luks, Allan

The healing power of doing good; the health and spiritual benefits of helping others; [by] Allan Luks with Peggy Payne. Fawcett Columbine 1992 330p $18   **158**

1. Altruism 2. Voluntarism
ISBN 0-449-90451-2   LC 91-37771

The author's "purpose is to show exactly how one's physical health, not just emotional well-being, is improved through helping others." Libr J

Includes bibliographic references

May, Rollo

Freedom and destiny. Norton 1981 275p $14.95 **158**

1. Psychology, Applied 2. Free will and determinism 3. Fate and fatalism

ISBN 0-393-01477-0   LC 81-4009

Also available in paperback from Delacorte Press

This book examines "the continuing tension in our lives between the possibilities freedom offers and the various limitations imposed upon us by our particular fate or destiny." America

Includes bibliographic references

McGrath, Ellen

When feeling bad is good. Holt & Co. 1992 350p il $22.50 **158**

1. Depression, Mental 2. Women—Psychology

ISBN 0-8050-1474-8   LC 92-14573

The author "distinguishes culturally based, healthy depression from biologically rooted, unhealthy depression (which requires professional treatment). Both conditions are effected by a core of traditional values and expectations which influence women's behavior. . . . McGrath identifies six types of healthy depression and examines the social and cultural sources for each. She offers such strategies as exercise and activities which promote a positive self-image." Libr J

Includes bibliographic references

Peck, M. Scott (Morgan Scott)

The road less traveled; a new psychology of love, traditional values, and spiritual growth. Simon & Schuster 1978 312p hardcover o.p. paperback available $10.95 **158**

1. Psychology, Applied 2. Love

ISBN 0-671-25067-1 (pa)   LC 78-15776

Also available Walker & Co. large print edition

This book attempts to bring together "psychology and religion. It is divided into four areas—discipline, love, religion and growth, and grace—and within each Peck tackles the . . . struggle between stagnation and progress which goes on in all of us throughout our lives." Libr J

Includes bibliographic references

Robbins, Anthony

Awaken the giant within; how to take immediate control of your mental, emotional, physical & financial destiny! Summit Bks. 1991 539p il $22; pa $12 **158**

1. Success 2. Psychology, Applied

ISBN 0-671-72734-6; 0-671-79154-0 (pa)

LC 91-27218

The author offers advice and techniques for achieving personal success

"Robbins' system is somewhat elaborate, but his advice is based on common sense and on psychological and sociocultural reality." Booklist

Shaffer, Martin

Life after stress. Plenum Press 1982 273p il $15.95 **158**

1. Stress (Psychology)

ISBN 0-306-40869-4   LC 81-17785

Also available in paperback from Contemporary Bks.

This "offering on stress control presents clear, concise, practical information in a pleasing, easy-to-read format, offering readers the opportunity to grasp the full scope of stress and its management with permanent results." Libr J

Includes bibliography

Simon, Sidney B.

Getting unstuck; breaking through your barriers to change; produced by The Philip Lief Group, Inc. Warner Bks. 1988 296p hardcover o.p. paperback available $9.95 **158**

1. Psychology, Applied 2. Motivation (Psychology) 3. Self-realization

ISBN 0-446-39024-0 (pa)   LC 88-40092

"Stressing that the key to change is the recognition of one's problems, [Simon] provides readers with exercises that help determine their goals and shows them how to effectively meet those goals." Publisher's note

Skinner, B. F. (Burrhus Frederic), 1904-1990

Enjoy old age; a program of self-management; [by] B. F. Skinner & M. E. Vaughan. Norton 1983 157p $11.95 **158**

1. Psychology, Applied 2. Old age

ISBN 0-393-01805-9   LC 83-8326

"This book is an account of the author's recommendations, including those based on behavior management, for remaining productive and intellectually active in old age. Published in large print, this small volume is sprinkled with literary references that relate mainly to the positive nature of aging. Free of jargon, the book gives practical advice for those who have lived active lives and wish to continue doing so." Sci Books Films

Smith, Manuel J., 1934-

When I say no, I feel guilty; how to cope—using the skills of systematic assertive therapy. Dial Press 1975 302p o.p.; Bantam Bks. paperback available $5.99 **158**

1. Assertiveness (Psychology)

ISBN 0-553-26390-0 (pa)

"A practical book for those people who feel they are always being talked into doing what others want them to do." Libr J

Includes bibliography

Spezzano, Charles

What to do between birth and death; the art of growing up. Morrow 1992 189p $15 **158**

1. Self-realization

ISBN 0-688-10399-5   LC 91-27037

Also available in paperback from Avon Bks.

Spezzano, Charles—*Continued*

In these short essays the author offers "insights and advice on various aspects of self-actualization. Some of his more unusual topics include discussions of how attachments work, and the need to be alone in the presence of others. . . . His straightforward style is enhanced with humor and memorable passages." Libr J

Ury, William

Getting past no; negotiating with difficult people; [by] William L. Ury. Bantam Bks. 1991 161p $20; pa $9.95   **158**

1. Negotiation
ISBN 0-553-07274-9; 0-553-37131-2 (pa)
                                    LC 91-10101

"Ury presents a five-step agenda to deal successfully with opponents, be they unruly teenagers, labor leaders, terrorists or international politicians. Strategies focus on self-discipline, or tactics for defusing the adversary's attacks, and suggestions for developing options designed to lead to a mutually satisfactory agreement." Publ Wkly

Includes bibliographic references

160 Logic

Copi, Irving M.

Introduction to logic; Irving M. Copi, Carl Cohen. Macmillan il $43   **160**

1. Logic   LC 89-37742
First published 1953 (9th edition 1993) Periodically revised

This introduction to logic covers language, fallacies, definitions, categories, arguments, deduction, probability and other areas of logical inquiry such as thought and reasoning

Includes bibliographic references

Dewey, John, 1859-1952

Logic, the theory of inquiry. Holt & Co. 1938 546p o.p.; Irvington Pubs. reprint available $49.50   **160**

1. Logic
ISBN 0-89197-831-3

This study on the nature of logical theory "ranges over a wide field from formal logic and mathematics to the methodology of the social sciences." Nation

170 Ethics (Moral philosophy)

Aristotle, 384-322 B.C.

Ethics   **170**

1. Ethics
Hardcover and paperback editions available from various publishers

Variant titles: Ethica Nichomachea and Nichomachean ethics

According to Aristotle's ethical treatises, "happiness is the goal of life. Pleasure, fame, and wealth, however, will not bring one the highest happiness, which is achieved only through the contemplation of philosophic truth, because it exercises man's peculiar virtue, the rational principle." Reader's Ency. 3d edition

Dewey, John, 1859-1952

Theory of the moral life; with an introduction by Arnold Isenberg. Irvington Pubs. 1980 c1960 179p pa $12.95   **170**

1. Ethics
ISBN 0-8290-3150-2   LC 80-18200

A reprint of the edition first published 1960 by Holt, Rinehart & Winston

"A redaction . . . of part II of Dewey and Tufts' Ethics, from the revised edition of 1932"

This introduction to the study of moral philosophy is a compact examination of basic moral theories and major theorists, including Aristotle, Kant, Mill, Bentham, Spencer, and others. In addition, one of the aims of the book is to provide the individual with a set of principles which will help him follow a moral path

Includes bibliographies

Edelman, Marian Wright

The measure of our success; a letter to my children and yours. Beacon Press 1992 97p $15   **170**

1. Ethics 2. Human behavior 3. Child rearing 4. United States—Moral conditions
ISBN 0-8070-3102-X   LC 91-42743

Also available in paperback from HarperPerennial

The author presents her "beliefs on child rearing and moral values. . . . She includes a personal letter to her three sons, who were born into a family with a shared African American and Jewish heritage, and offers 25 lessons, or 'road maps', for life." Libr J

The **Encyclopedia** of ethics; Lawrence C. Becker, editor, Charlotte B. Becker, co-editor. Garland 1992 2v (Garland reference lib. of the humanities) set $150   **170**

1. Ethics—Dictionaries
ISBN 0-8153-0403-X   LC 91-4978

This first general encyclopedia on ethics [contains] . . . surveys on trends and eras; summaries of leading concepts, principles, and theoretical problems; and biographical entries for philosophers key to ethical theory. The majority of the articles are topical, covering metaethics, ethical theory, moral problems, and political, social, and legal theory. Each has a bibliography with see also and cross-references." Choice

For a fuller review see: Booklist, Oct. 1, 1992

Smedes, Lewis B.

Choices; making right decisions in a complex world. Harper & Row 1986 121p hardcover o.p. paperback available $7.95   **170**

1. Ethics 2. Christian ethics 3. Decision making
ISBN 0-06-067411-3 (pa)   LC 86-45025

In this book, the author seeks to present guidelines for ethical conduct. "Smedes believes that love and justice are the two moral absolutes; beyond this, he sifts through various categories for evaluating behavior (is it forgivable? permissible?) and discriminates among other conditional guidelines (rules of strategy, propriety, etc.)." Libr J

171 Ethical systems and doctrines

Fromm, Erich, 1900-1980
Man for himself; an inquiry into the psychology of ethics. Rinehart 1947 254p o.p.; Holt & Co. paperback available $10.95 **171**

1. Ethics 2. Psychology
ISBN 0-8050-1403-9 (pa)

The author "believes that mental therapy can be effective only if it recognizes that psychology cannot be divorced from ethics; that human personality depends on moral values as well as unconscious, irrational desires." Booklist

174 Economic, professional, occupational ethics

Lappé, Marc
Broken code; the exploitation of DNA. Sierra Club Bks. 1985 354p il $17.95 **174**

1. Genetic engineering 2. Recombinant DNA
ISBN 0-87156-835-7   LC 84-22190

The author "reviews recombinant-DNA research, the economic/corporate motives behind its direction, and the moral questions raised for society. He covers both the medical uses of this biotechnology and the agricultural." Libr J

"A well-written, thought-provoking book that is generally quite successful in demystifying the scientific and technological jargon of genetic engineering and in examining ethical and environmental concerns generated by its growing presence." Choice

Macklin, Ruth
Mortal choices; bioethics in today's world; Ruth Macklin. Pantheon Bks. 1987 245p o.p.; Houghton Mifflin paperback available $12.70 **174**

1. Medical ethics 2. Bioethics
ISBN 0-395-46847-7 (pa)   LC 86-42970

An examination of ethical questions brought about by developments in medical technology

This book "provides a lively and useful primer for the rapidly expanding field of bioethics." N Y Times Book Rev

Includes bibliographic references

Suzuki, David T., 1936-
Genethics; the clash between the new genetics and human values; [by] David Suzuki & Peter Knudtson. Harvard Univ. Press 1989 384p il $27.50; pa $14 **174**

1. Genetic engineering
ISBN 0-674-34565-7; 0-674-34566-5 (pa)
          LC 88-26013

"The first third of this text is a . . . primer on the scientific basis of genetics and its relationship to evolution. . . . The remainder of the book explores a number of issues related to research on molecular genetics, the implications of the research, and the practical applications for humans, other animals, society, and the ecosystem." Sci Books Films

Includes bibliography

Zussman, Robert
Intensive care; medical ethics and the medical profession. University of Chicago Press 1992 252p il $29.95 **174**

1. Medical ethics
ISBN 0-226-99634-4   LC 91-36919

The author uses case studies to reveal "deep conflicts of opinion among patients and their families, physicians, hospital administrators, and medical ethicists on how best to allocate treatment and resources in intensive care units." Univ Press Books for Public and Second Sch Libr

Includes bibliographic references

177 Ethics of social relations

Bok, Sissela
Secrets; on the ethics of concealment and revelation. Pantheon Bks. 1983 332p o.p.; Vintage Bks. paperback available $11 **177**

1. Right of privacy 2. Social ethics 3. Professional ethics
ISBN 0-679-72473-7 (pa)   LC 82-47891

Bok "examines both private or individual occasions for secrecy (secret societies, self-deception, confessions, and gossip) as well as more 'large-scale collective practices of secrecy, revelation, and probing' in areas such as medicine, industry, government, and the law." Libr J

179 Other ethical norms

Alvarez, A. (Alfred), 1929-
The savage god; a study of suicide. Random House 1972 299p o.p.; Norton paperback available $8.95 **179**

1. Suicide
ISBN 0-393-30657-7 (pa)

First published 1971 in the United Kingdom

"The author traces changing attitudes toward suicide, from primitive societies, Greek, Roman and Christian interpretations, to Durkheim, Freud, and the alienation in the twentieth century. He also examines the relationship between suicide and creative imaginations from Dante to the present. Included is a personal memoir of Sylvia Plath." Publisher's note

Includes bibliographic references

Durkheim, Émile, 1858-1917
Suicide, a study in sociology; translated by John A. Spaulding and George Simpson; edited with an introduction by George Simpson. Free Press 1951 405p maps $27.95; pa $14.95 **179**

1. Suicide
ISBN 0-02-908650-7; 0-02-908660-4 (pa)

Durkheim's "Suicide is a major sociological classic, one that is still read today, not so much for its data, which are limited and out-of-date, but for the brilliance of his analysis of suicide rates and other data that had been initially obtained for administrative rather than

Durkheim, Émile, 1858-1917—*Continued*
scientific purposes." Reader's Adviser
Includes bibliographic references

Fox, Michael Allen
The case for animal experimentation; an evolutionary and ethical perspective. University of Calif. Press 1986 262p $35; pa $11 **179**
1. Vivisection 2. Animal experimentation
ISBN 0-520-05501-2; 0-520-06023-7 (pa) LC 85-1036
The author contends that animal experimentation "is essential for further scientific advances that benefit mankind and that humans have a moral right to use animals for this purpose." N Y Times Book Rev
"The level of erudition is high, and the step-by-step construction of the author's thesis is extraordinarily tight. . . . A great many different types of people should read this book. It is important." Sci Books Films
Includes bibliography

Fox, Michael W., 1937-
Inhumane society; the American way of exploiting animals; introduction by Cleveland Amory. St. Martin's Press 1990 268p $18.95; pa $9.95 **179**
1. Animal welfare
ISBN 0-312-04274-4; 0-312-07808-0 (pa)
LC 89-70299
The author "looks at the exploitative and inhumane treatment of domestic, agriculture, and laboratory animals." Booklist
This book "is very readable and takes a strong stance while presenting a creditably balanced treatment of the issues." Libr J
Includes bibliographic references

Hendin, Herbert
Suicide in America. Norton 1982 252p hardcover o.p. paperback available $19.95 **179**
1. Suicide
ISBN 0-393-30163-X (pa) LC 81-16988
The author examines the personal and social factors contributing to suicide and presents theories about prevention

Humphry, Derek, 1930-
Dying with dignity; understanding euthanasia. Carol Pub. Group 1992 215p $16.95 **179**
1. Euthanasia
ISBN 1-55972-105-7 LC 91-46786
"A Birch Lane Press book"
In this work the author discusses the ethics of euthanasia and assisted suicide and describes the effects of related court decisions
Includes bibliographic references

Final exit; the practicalities of self-deliverance and assisted suicide for the dying. Hemlock Soc. 1991 192p $16.95 **179**
1. Suicide 2. Right to die
ISBN 0-9606030-3-4 LC 90-83673
Also available in paperback from Dell
This volume offers information on how to commit suicide
"Mr Humphry stresses that his book is only for those terminally ill people who have made a 'rational' decision to end their lives. . . . For Mr Humphry, to commit suicide or to request euthanasia is part of 'the most important of civil liberties, to govern one's own life'." Economist
Includes bibliographic references

Regan, Tom
The case for animal rights. University of Calif. Press 1983 425p $35; pa $14 **179**
1. Animal welfare
ISBN 0-520-04904-7; 0-520-05460-1 (pa) LC 83-1087
This book is "divided into three parts. First Regan develops an argument for the view that many animals are not only conscious, but also enjoy a mental life of some complexity. . . . In the second part, he sets down and defends a general ethical theory, which he calls 'the rights view.' . . . Third, Regan deduces specific conclusions from the premises of Part 1 and 2 concerning the obligations of humans vis-à-vis animals." Choice
"Mr. Regan is to be commended for coming forth with a careful, sophisticated and reasoned statement about the moral status of animals." N Y Times Book Rev

Tada, Joni Eareckson
When is it right to die? suicide, euthanasia, suffering, mercy; foreword by C. Everett Koop. Zondervan; HarperSanFrancisco 1992 189p $15.99 **179**
1. Suicide 2. Euthanasia 3. Right to die 4. Handicapped
ISBN 0-310-58570-8 LC 92-60215
The author "frames her view of the 'right to die' issue in the context of personal growth through tragedy. . . . In a compassionate response to proponents of 'suicide machines' and assisted death, the author advocates such alternatives as hospice care and refers frequently to the advice and consolation provided by Scripture." Publ Wkly

Tillich, Paul, 1886-1965
The courage to be. Yale Univ. Press 1952 197p hardcover o.p. paperback available $10 **179**
1. Courage
ISBN 0-300-00241-6 (pa)
The author offers advice on how to conquer the anxiety caused by the loss of meaning in one's life

Wennberg, Robert N.
Terminal choices; euthanasia, suicide, and the right to die. Eerdmans 1989 246p pa $14.95   **179**
1. Euthanasia 2. Suicide 3. Right to die
ISBN 0-8028-0454-3   LC 89-39127
The author "outlines the dissenting moral stances on active and passive euthanasia. He reaches back to the Greek and Roman philosophers in tracing his study of social approbation and disapproval and applies such historical thinking to the quandaries created by modern medicine." Booklist
Wennberg's "simple and elegant prose makes this book a delight to read despite its sombre themes. Worthwhile for any library." Libr J
Includes bibliographic references

181   Oriental philosophy

Buber, Martin, 1878-1965
I and Thou; a new translation with a prologue "I and You" and notes by Walter Kaufmann. Scribner 1970 185p $35; pa $10   **181**
1. Philosophy, Jewish 2. God 3. Ontology
ISBN 0-684-15575-3; 0-684-71725-5 (pa)
Original German edition, 1923
In this book, the author "conceived the individual as in permanent relationship with all forms of life, finding his fulfillment in the reciprocity of the relationship—the 'Thou' being God." Reader's Adviser

Confucius
The analects of Confucius   **181**
1. Philosophy, Chinese 2. Ethics, Chinese
Hardcover and paperback editions available from various publishers
"One of the Chinese 'Four Books.' A brief, unsystematic collection of fragmentary writings attributed to Confucius and his school. . . . It is one of the most influential works in the history of Chinese thought." Reader's Ency

The wisdom of Confucius; edited and translated with notes by Lin Yutang. Modern Lib. 1938 290p $13.50   **181**
1. Philosophy, Chinese 2. Ethics, Chinese
ISBN 0-394-60426-1
Also available in hardcover from Amereon
A selection of writings by the Chinese political and ethical philosopher who advocated a form of rationalism based on humanity, reverence for ancient sages, and government by personal virtue

183   Sophistic, Socratic and related Greek philosophies

Stone, I. F. (Isidor Feinstein), 1907-1989
The trial of Socrates. Little, Brown 1988 282p o.p.; Anchor Bks. paperback available $10.95   **183**
1. Socrates
ISBN 0-385-26032-6 (pa)   LC 87-22855
The author attempts "to show that Athens was totally committed to free speech and did not normally place any check on it, and, therefore, that the trial of Socrates was a singular aberration which might be explicable, if finally not justifiable." Commentary

184   Platonic philosophy

Hare, R. M. (Richard Mervyn)
Plato. Oxford Univ. Press 1982 82p (Past masters ser) $14.95; pa $7.95   **184**
1. Plato
ISBN 0-19-287586-8; 0-19-287585-X (pa)
LC 83-159441
The author examines the chief Platonic concepts in their political and intellectual contexts
Includes bibliography

185   Aristotelian philosophy

Adler, Mortimer Jerome, 1902-
Aristotle for everybody; difficult thought made easy; by Mortimer J. Adler. Macmillan 1978 206p hardcover o.p. paperback available $12.95   **185**
1. Aristotle, 384-322 B.C.
ISBN 0-02-064111-7 (pa)   LC 78-853
Adler traces "in the simplest language and with occasional modern analogues, the logic and growth of Aristotle's basic doctrines." Publ Wkly
Includes bibliographic references

188   Stoic philosophy

Marcus Aurelius, Emperor of Rome, 121-180
Meditations   **188**
Hardcover and paperback editions available from various publishers
"An emperor and Stoic philosopher records his thoughts as he struggles for composure and order in the face of national disaster." Good Read

189   Medieval Western philosophy

The **Renaissance** philosophy of man; [by] Petrarca [and others]; selections in translation, edited by Ernst Cassirer, Paul Oskar Kristeller, John Herman Randall, Jr. University of Chicago Press 1948 405p hardcover o.p. paperback available $12.95   **189**
1. Philosophy, Medieval
ISBN 0-226-09604-1 (pa)
Analyzed in Essay and general literature index
This book provides English translations from selected writings of six early Italian Renaissance philosophers from about the middle of the fourteenth century to the end of the sixteenth. Francesco Petrarca, Lorenzo Valla, Marsilio Ficino, Giovanni Pico della Mirandola, Pietro Pomponazzi, and Juan Luis Vives are represented. An

The Renaissance philosophy of man—*Continued*

introduction accompanies each of the translations

Includes bibliography

Thomas, Aquinas, Saint, 1225?-1274

Introduction to Saint Thomas Aquinas; edited with an introduction by Anton C. Pegis. Modern Lib. 1948 xxx, 690p pa $7.43   **189**

ISBN 0-394-30974-X

"Modern Library college editions"

This volume contains selections from the Basic writings of St. Thomas Aquinas (1945)

Selected writings; translated, with introductions and notes, by Robert P. Goodwin. Bobbs-Merrill 1965 xxi, 162p o.p.; Macmillan paperback available $7.95   **189**

ISBN 0-02-345050-9 (pa)

"The principles of nature, On being and essence, On the virtues in general, On free choice." Title page

Includes bibliography

190   Modern Western philosophy

Ayer, A. J. (Alfred Jules), 1910-1989

Philosophy in the twentieth century. Random House 1982 283p $22.50; pa $11   **190**

1. Philosophy, Modern
ISBN 0-394-50454-2; 0-394-71655-8 (pa)

LC 82-40131

The author discusses main issues in "critical and speculative Western philosophy, primarily of the Anglo-American varieties." Libr J

"Ayer is unabashed in emphasizing the philosophical currents to which he is most sympathetic, e.g., pragmatism and language theory. . . . Still, Ayer's short course will hold much interest for those who have read his previous work and for readers who are fairly well acquainted with philosophical history." Booklist

Includes bibliographic references

Barzun, Jacques, 1907-

Darwin, Marx, Wagner; critique of a heritage. 2nd ed. Doubleday 1958 xx, 373p o.p.; University of Chicago Press paperback available $13.95   **190**

1. Darwin, Charles, 1809-1882 2. Marx, Karl, 1818-1883 3. Wagner, Richard, 1813-1883
ISBN 0-226-03859-9 (pa)

First published 1941 by Little, Brown

The thesis is that these three "intellectual imperialists," who were all collators rather than originators of ideas, really established the mechanistic, pseudo-scientific "system" which is the root of all communism and fascism

Bronowski, Jacob, 1908-1974

The Western intellectual tradition; from Leonardo to Hegel; [by] Jacob Bronowski, Bruce Mazlish. Harper & Row 1960 522p hardcover o.p. paperback available $12   **190**

1. Philosophy, Modern—History 2. Civilization, Occidental
ISBN 0-06-133001-9 (pa)

Also available in hardcover from Ayer

Analyzed in Essay and general literature index

The ideas of Machiavelli, Copernicus, Luther, Descartes, Rousseau, Jefferson, and many other thinkers are analyzed

Includes bibliographic references

Gay, Peter, 1923-

The Enlightenment: an interpretation. Knopf 1966-1969 2v o.p.; Norton paperbacks available v1 $14.95, v2 $16.95   **190**

1. Philosophy, Modern 2. Europe—Intellectual life 3. Eighteenth century

Contents: v1 The rise of modern paganism (ISBN 0-393-00870-3); v2 The science of freedom (ISBN 0-393-00875-4)

Gay examines the ideas, experiences and impact of leading Enlightenment figures in 18th century Europe and America

Includes bibliography

Great thinkers of the Western world; edited by Ian P. McGreal. HarperCollins Pubs. 1992 572p $40; pa $15   **190**

1. Philosophy 2. Theology 3. Science
ISBN 0-06-270026-X; 0-06-272017-1 (pa)

LC 91-38362

"The major ideas and classic works of more than 100 outstanding Western philosophers, physical and social scientists, psychologists, religious writers, and theologians." Title page

"This guide to 116 selected authors . . . spans the ancient Greeks to the first half of the twentieth century. . . . The guide is arranged chronologically by the birthdate of the writer. Each entry contains birth and death dates, a list of the author's major ideas, an essay of three to five pages, and a short annotated list of secondary sources. . . . Its readable essays . . . are accessible to the layperson." Booklist

191   North American philosophy

Baker, James Thomas

Ayn Rand; [by] James T. Baker. Twayne Pubs. 1987 168p (Twayne's United States authors ser) $21.95   **191**

1. Rand, Ayn, 1905-1982
ISBN 0-8057-7497-1   LC 86-29569

The author "gives a good sketch of Rand's life, routine summaries of her books, and very useful outlines of her themes and theories and of the published attacks on and defenses of her work." Booklist

Includes bibliography

Dewey, John, 1859-1952
The philosophy of John Dewey; edited with an introduction and commentary by John J. McDermott. University of Chicago Press 1981 2v in 1 pa $22.95   **191**

ISBN 0-226-14401-1   LC 80-39766

"Phoenix edition"

First published 1973 in two volumes by Putnam and analyzed in Essay and general literature index

Contents: v1 The structure of experience; v2 The lived experience

A digest of extracts from the American philosopher's most important works

Includes bibliography

Fuller, R. Buckminster, 1895-1983
Synergetics; explorations in the geometry of thinking; in collaboration with E. J. Applewhite; preface and contribution by Arthur L. Loeb. Macmillan 1975 xxxii, 876p il hardcover o.p. paperback available $21.95   **191**

1. Mathematics—Philosophy 2. Thought and thinking 3. Science—Philosophy
ISBN 0-02-065320-4 (pa)

Companion volume to Synergetics 2 (1979)

"Fuller approaches nature and human society holistically, as inseparably inter-related coordinates in the Whole System of the Universe. 'Synergetics' is the term Fuller ascribes to his integrated study of the universe." Best Sellers

Includes bibliography

Hook, Sidney, 1902-1989
Convictions; introduction by Paul Kurtz. Prometheus Bks. 1990 310p $25.95   **191**

1. Philosophy   2. Education   3. Political science   4. Social ethics
ISBN 0-87975-473-7   LC 89-3676

Analyzed in Essay and general literature index

In this collection of essays "Hook argues that American freedoms are threatened by the increasing politicization of education. The topics of his polemics range from Stanford University's decision to scrap its course on Western civilization to an exchange with the historian Howard Zinn on 'How Democratic is America?' Other essays reflect on euthanasia, suicide, anti-Semitism, Whittaker Chambers and Joseph McCarthy." N Y Times Book Rev

This volume "captures as well as anything Hook's remarkable ability to examine principles in their concrete contexts." Libr J

Rand, Ayn, 1905-1982
The voice of reason; essays in objectivist thought; edited and with an introduction by Leonard Peikoff; and with additional essays by Leonard Peikoff and Peter Schwartz. New Am. Lib. 1989 c1988 353p hardcover o.p. paperback available $12   **191**

1. Philosophy, American
ISBN 0-452-01046-2 (pa)   LC 88-18192

The late author opposed liberalism and championed "capitalism, self-interest, and objective reality against collectivism, altruism, and mysticism. . . . These lectures, newspaper columns, and magazine articles are entirely characteristic of her—surprisingly emotional and dogmatic for a professed rationalist. Additional essays by editor Peikoff and disciple Peter Schwartz are of a piece." Booklist

Includes bibliographic references

192 British philosophy

Russell, Bertrand, 1872-1970
Basic writings, 1903-1959; edited by Robert R. Egner snd Lester E. Denonn. Simon & Schuster 1961 736p hardcover o.p. paperback available $17.95   **192**

ISBN 0-671-20154-9 (pa)

"An authorized selection of 81 essays, short stories and excerpts from Lord Russell's many writings between 1903 and 1959, presenting . . . his views as philosopher, historian, psychologist, mathematician, biographer, etc." N Y Her Trib Books

Includes bibliography

193 German and Austrian philosophy

Hegel, Georg Wilhelm Friedrich, 1770-1831
The philosophy of Hegel; edited with an introduction by Carl J. Friedrich. Modern Lib. 1954 lxiv, 552p o.p.; McGraw-Hill paperback available $7.43   **193**

ISBN 0-07-553655-2 (pa)

"Modern Library college editions"

Selections from Hegel's writings on aesthetics, history of philosophy, phenomenology of spirit, philosophy of history, philosophy of right and law, political essays, and science of logic

Heidegger, Martin, 1889-1976
Basic writings; from Being and time (1927) to The task of thinking (1964); edited, with general introduction and introductions to each selection by David Farrell Krell. rev and expanded ed. HarperSanFrancisco 1993 452p $15   **193**

ISBN 0-06-063763-3   LC 91-58187

This anthology first published 1977 by Harper & Row

Contents: Being and time: introduction; What is metaphysics?; On the essence of truth; The origin of the work of art; Letter on humanism; Modern science, metaphysics, and mathematics; The question concerning technology; Building dwelling thinking; What calls for thinking?; The way to language; The end of philosophy and the task of thinking

Includes bibliographic references

Kant, Immanuel, 1724-1804
Critique of pure reason   **193**

1. Knowledge, Theory of 2. Reason

Kant, Immanuel, 1724-1804—*Continued*

Hardcover and paperback editions available from various publishers

Original German edition, 1781

In this philosophical work Kant "maintained that all sense experience must be inherently rational and therefore that rational knowledge about experience is possible. However, although reason can understand a thing considered as an object of experience, reason cannot understand the 'thing in itself.'" Reader's Ency. 3d edition

The philosophy of Kant; Immanuel Kant's moral and political writings; edited with an introduction by Carl J. Friedrich. Modern Lib. 1993 lxii, 525p $17.50   **193**

ISBN 0-679-60068-X   LC 93-44979

A reissue of the 1949 edition

A selection of Kant's writings on the metaphysics of morality and politics

Nietzsche, Friedrich Wilhelm, 1844-1900

The portable Nietzsche; selected and translated, with an introduction, prefaces, and notes, by Walter Kaufmann. Viking 1954 687p o.p.; Penguin Bks. paperback available $12   **193**

ISBN 0-14-015062-5 (pa)

"The Viking portable library"

Includes the complete texts of Thus spoke Zarathustra, Twilight of the idols, The antichrist, and Nietzsche contra Wagner. Selections from other works, notes and letters complete the volume

Thus spake Zarathustra   **193**

Hardcover and paperback editions available from various publishers

Written between 1883-1892

A philosophical narrative "in which the ancient Persian philosopher Zarathustra. . . is used as a mouthpiece for the author's views. In it, Nietzsche develops his doctrine of the 'Übermensch,' and the quasi-biblical style he uses underlines the prophetic character of his ideas." Reader's Ency. 3d edition

The will to power; a new translation by Walter Kaufmann and R. J. Hollingdale; edited with commentary by Walter Kaufmann; with facsimiles of the original manuscript. Random House 1967 xxxii, 576p hardcover o.p. paperback available $15   **193**

ISBN 0-394-70437-1 (pa)

Partial contents: European nihilism: Critique of morality; The will to power as knowledge; The will to power as art; Discipline and breeding

194   French philosophy

Descartes, René, 1596-1650

The philosophical writings of Descartes; translated by John Cottingham, Robert Stoothoff, Dugald Murdoch. Cambridge Univ. Press 1984-1991 3v il ea $69.95   **194**

1. Philosophy, French   LC 84-9399

Also available in paperback editions

Descartes: selected philosophical writings (1988) also available for $44.95 (ISBN 0-521-35264-9)

Contents: v1: Early writings; Rules for the direction of the mind; The world; Treatise on man; Discourse on the method; Optics; Principles of philosophy; Comments on a certain broadsheet; Description of the human body; Passions of the soul (ISBN 0-521-24594-X); v2 Meditations; Objections and replies; Letter to Father Dinet; Search for truth (ISBN 0-521-24595-8); v3 Correspondence (ISBN 0-521-40323-5)

Includes bibliographic references

Sartre, Jean Paul, 1905-1980

Life/Situations; essays written and spoken; translated by Paul Auster and Lydia Davis. Pantheon Bks. 1977 216p hardcover o.p. paperback available $10   **194**

ISBN 0-394-73460-2 (pa)   LC 76-54561

Original French edition, 1975

This book "comprises three interviews, a preface, an introduction, a public lecture, and an article. . . . For those who find Sartre an interesting person and thinker, and particularly for those who are interested in his political thought, this book will prove to be both enjoyable and enlightening. Although these pieces are not at all technical, a familiarity with Sartre's philosophy will enrich a reader's appreciation of the book." Choice

Teilhard de Chardin, Pierre

Toward the future; translated by René Hague. Harcourt Brace Jovanovich 1975 224p hardcover o.p. paperback available $4.95   **194**

ISBN 0-15-690780-1 (pa)

"A Helen and Kurt Wolff book"

Original French edition, 1973

A collection of essays written between 1929 and 1954 concerning the spiritual future of mankind. The function of art, Eastern mysticism and the concept of chastity are among the topics discussed

Includes bibliographic references

196   Spanish and Portuguese philosophy

Ortega y Gasset, José, 1883-1955

What is philosophy? translated from the Spanish by Mildred Adams. Norton 1961 c1960 252p hardcover o.p. paperback available $8.95   **196**

1. Philosophy

ISBN 0-393-00126-1 (pa)

"The Norton library"

Ortega y Gasset, José, 1883-1955 — *Continued*

This volume by the influential Spanish philosopher, essayist and critic "consists of a series of lectures begun in 1929 at the University of Madrid. Interrupted when the University was closed as a result of political troubles, they were resumed in a Madrid theatre. Part of the lectures had been given earlier in Buenos Aires." N Y Times Book Rev

199 Philosophy in other geographic areas

Spinoza, Benedictus de, 1632-1677

Chief works of Benedict de Spinoza; translated from the Latin with an introduction by R. H. M. Elwes; with a bibliographical note by Francesco Cordasco. Dover Publs. 1955 c1951 2v o.p.   **199**

Available in hardcover from P. Smith

An unabridged replication of the Bohn Library edition translated by R. H. M. Elwes and published by Bell in 1883. This edition first published 1951 by Dover in one volume

Contents: v1 Theologico-political treatise; Political treatise; v2 On the improvement of the understanding; The ethics; Spinoza's correspondence (abridged)

200 RELIGION

Parrinder, Edward Geoffrey

A dictionary of religious and spiritual quotations; compiled by Geoffrey Parrinder. Simon & Schuster 1990 218p $40   **200**

1. Religion—Quotations 2. Spiritual life—Quotations
ISBN 0-13-210121-1   LC 90-33251

This book "presents over 3,000 brief quotations under 177 topical headings. Typically, a section includes one quotation each from the Old and New Testaments and the *Koran*, then a broad selection by philosophers, theologians, poets, sociologists, psychologists, and even skeptics throughout the ages. The work provides worldwide coverage, with Islamic, Eastern, and aboriginal religions receiving almost as much representation as Judeo-Christianity. The universality of religious thought provides the collection's underlying theme." Libr J

Treasury of religious quotations; compiled and edited by Gerald Tomlinson. Prentice-Hall 1991 341p $39.95; pa $14.95   **200**

1. Religion—Quotations 2. Spiritual life—Quotations
ISBN 0-13-276429-6; 0-13-276411-3 (pa)
                                            LC 91-18940

This compendium contains over 2,000 quotes from 30 different religions that draw on religious history, literature, myth and humor. Arranged topically, the subjects range from ambition and atheism to values and zeal

Includes bibliographic references

The **World** treasury of modern religious thought; edited by Jaroslav Pelikan; with a foreword by Clifton Fadiman, general editor. Little, Brown 1990 635p $29.95   **200**

1. Religion
ISBN 0-316-69770-2   LC 89-37290

"Pelikan collects some 66 articles or excerpts from 19th- and 20th-century literature, anthropology, religion, psychology, theology, and philosophy that touch upon religion and religious experience. The writers are as diverse as Kierkegaard and Black Elk, Teilhard de Chardin and Martin Luther King, with representatives of all the major world religions, East and West. While many of the pieces are well known, Pelikan includes a number of less familiar but welcome articles." Libr J

200.1 Religion—Philosophy and theory

James, William, 1842-1910

The varieties of religious experience; study in human nature   **200.1**

1. Religion—Philosophy 2. Psychology 3. Conversion
Hardcover and paperback editions available from various publishers

First published 1902 by Longman

"Based on material James had collected on the psychology and philosophy of religion for lectures at the University of Edinburgh in 1901 and 1902. The varieties of religious experience contains numerous descriptions of religious states of consciousness, which James presented from a pragmatic point of view." Benet's Reader's Ency of Am Lit

Jung, C. G. (Carl Gustav), 1875-1961

Psychology and religion. Yale Univ. Press 1938 131p hardcover o.p.   paperback available $7.95   **200.1**

1. Religion—Philosophy 2. Psychology 3. Symbolism
ISBN 0-300-00137-1 (pa)

Three lectures delivered at Yale University in 1937 present the eminent Swiss psychoanalyst's understanding of the relationship between psychology and religion

Includes bibliographic references

200.3 Religion—Encyclopedias and dictionaries

The **Encyclopedia** of religion; Mircea Eliade, editor in chief. Macmillan 1987 16v il set $1400   **200.3**

1. Religion—Dictionaries
ISBN 0-02-909480-1   LC 86-5432

"Treats theoretical (e.g., doctrines, myths, theologies, ethics), practical (e.g., cults, sacraments, meditations), and sociological (e.g., religious groups, ecclesiastical forms) aspects of religion; includes extensive coverage of non-Western religions. . . . Has quickly become the standard work." Sheehy. Guide to Ref Books. 10th edition. suppl

Includes bibliographies

The **Encyclopedia** of world faiths; an illustrated survey of the world's living religions; general editors, Peter Bishop & Michael Darton; the contributors, Duane Wade-Hampton Arnold [et al.] Facts on File 1988 c1987 352p il $40   **200.3**

1. Religions—Dictionaries
ISBN 0-8160-1860-X   LC 88-118151

First published 1987 in the United Kingdom

Contains "articles on twelve major religions: Judaism, Zoroastrianism, Christianity, Islam, Babism and the Baha'i Faith, Hinduism, Jainism, Buddhism, Sikhism, Confucianism, Taoism, and Shinto. . . . Chapters are also included on the general nature of religion, the relevance of religion in the modern world, and on new religious movements in modern Western society and among primal peoples." Am Ref Books Annu, 1989

200.9   Religion—Historical and geographic treatment

Encyclopedia of the American religious experience; studies of traditions and movements; Charles H. Lippy and Peter W. Williams, editors. Scribner 1988 3v set $259   **200.9**

1. United States—Religion
ISBN 0-684-18062-6   LC 87-4781

Analyzed in Essay and general literature index

This "source presents 105 essays written by religious scholars for the general reader. Topics include all major denominations as well as indigenous movements, and religion's interaction with society and politics." Ref Sources for Small & Medium-sized Libr. 5th edition

Macquarrie, John
Twentieth-century religious thought. 4th ed. SCM Press; Trinity Press Int. 1989 468p pa $19.95   **200.9**

1. Philosophy, Modern 2. Theology
ISBN 0-334-01709-2   LC 89-5026

First published 1963 by Harper & Row

The author discusses major twentieth century theologians and philosophers. Contemporary developments such as hope and liberation theologies, neo-Marxism, and problems in hermeneutics are examined

Includes bibliographic references

Melton, J. Gordon
The encyclopedia of American religions. 4th ed. Gale Res. 1993 1217p $175 **200.9**

1. United States—Religion—Dictionaries 2. Sects—Dictionaries
ISBN 0-8103-6904-4   LC 93-123526

Companion volume to The Encyclopedia of American religions: religious creeds, entered in class 291

First published 1978 by McGrath Publishing Company

This study of religious and spiritual bodies in the United States provides information on approximately 1,600 groups, ranging from Adventists to Zen Buddhists

Religious bodies in the United States; a directory. Garland 1992 313p (Religious information systems ser) $55   **200.9**

1. United States—Religion—Directories
ISBN 0-8153-0806-X   LC 91-41564

First published 1977 with title: A directory of religious bodies in the United States

This volume contains addresses, telephone, fax and cable numbers for American religious groups of all faiths plus a list of periodicals which serve each group

This directory is "a gold mine of information and is indispensable for any general reference collection." Am Ref Books Annu, 1993

Includes bibliographic references

201   Christianity—Philosophy and theory

Lewis, C. S. (Clive Staples), 1898-1963
Mere Christianity; an anniversary edition of the three books, The case for Christianity, Christian behaviour, and Beyond personality; edited and with an introduction by Walter Hooper. Macmillan 1981 c1952 xliv, 211p il $12.95   **201**

1. Christianity—Philosophy
ISBN 0-02-570590-3   LC 81-12339

Analyzed in Essay and general literature index

This combined edition first published 1952

This omnibus edition includes most of C. S. Lewis' writings on Christian theology and moral philosophy

The world's last night, and other essays. Harcourt Brace & Co. 1960 113p hardcover o.p. paperback available $6.95   **201**

1. Christianity—Philosophy
ISBN 0-15-698360-5 (pa)

Analyzed in Essay and general literature index

These seven essays cover topics such as culture, democracy, education, good works, prayers, the second coming of Christ, and space exploration

Niebuhr, Reinhold, 1892-1971
Beyond tragedy; essays on the Christian interpretation of history. Scribner 1937 306p o.p.   **201**

1. Christianity—Philosophy 2. History—Philosophy

Available in hardcover from Ayer

Analyzed in Essay and general literature index

"Sermonic essays elaborating one theme in various aspects. The theme is Christianity's dialectical conception of the relation of time and eternity, of God and the world, of nature and grace." Preface

Teilhard de Chardin, Pierre
Christianity and evolution; translated by René Hague. Harcourt Brace Jovanovich 1971 255p hardcover o.p. paperback available $6.95   **201**

1. Theology
ISBN 0-15-617740-4 (pa)

"A Helen and Kurt Wolff book"

Teilhard de Chardin, Pierre—*Continued*
Original French edition, 1969

These essays "covering a wide expanse of Teilhard's thought . . . stimulate the reader to reflect seriously on the Christian dogma of creation, the role of Christ in evolution as a cosmic phenomenon, and on the relationship of the church to the modern world." Choice

Includes bibliographic references

The divine milieu; an essay on the interior life. Harper & Row 1960 144p hardcover o.p. paperback available $10

201

1. Christianity—Philosophy
ISBN 0-06-090487-9 (pa)

Original French edition, 1957

In this book Father de Chardin describes his spiritual philosophy

Tillich, Paul, 1886-1965
Theology of culture; edited by Robert C. Kimball. Oxford Univ. Press 1959 213p hardcover o.p. paperback available $8.95

201

1. Christianity—Philosophy 2. Culture
ISBN 0-19-500711-5 (pa)

Selected essays by the influential theologian focus on ethics, education, science, aesthetics, psychology, and existential philosophy

Trueblood, Elton, 1900-
Philosophy of religion. Harper & Row 1957 324p o.p.; Greenwood Press paperback available $35

201

1. Christianity—Philosophy 2. Religion—Philosophy
ISBN 0-8371-8514-9 (pa)

The author discusses the logic of religion, realism, challenges to faith, the problem of evil and such concepts as God and freedom

Includes bibliography

203   Christianity—Encyclopedias and dictionaries

The **Oxford** Dictionary of the Christian Church; edited by F. L. Cross and E. A. Livingstone. 2nd ed. Oxford Univ. Press 1974 xxxi, 1518p $65

203

1. Theology—Dictionaries 2. Christianity—Dictionaries
ISBN 0-19-211545-6

First published 1957

This work contains "more than 6,000 articles, some of considerable length. Although about half the entries were written by contributing scholars, in the interests of uniformity none is signed. Bibliographies are appended to most articles. Coverage is broad, including historical and doctrinal development, many biographies, definitions of ecclesiastical terms and customs, etc." Sheehy. Guide to Ref Books. 10th edition

World Christian encyclopedia; a comparative study of churches and religions in the modern world, AD 1900-2000; edited by David B. Barrett. Oxford Univ. Press 1982 1010p il $195

203

1. Religions—Dictionaries 2. Christianity—Dictionaries
3. Sects—Dictionaries
ISBN 0-19-572435-6   LC 82-199409

"A survey of the state of Christianity in the world today. Each country is covered by a chapter describing its religious history and present-day status along with detailed statistical information. This volume also has a dictionary of terms, an atlas, a chronology, a who's who, a bibliography, a directory, and encyclopedic articles on various aspects of evangelization and culture." Ref Sources for Small & Medium-sized Libr. 5th edition

210   Natural theology

Huxley, Aldous, 1894-1963
The perennial philosophy. Harper & Row 1945 312p hardcover o.p. paperback available $11

210

1. Philosophy and religion 2. Religion—Philosophy
ISBN 0-06-090191-8 (pa)

Also available in hardcover from Ayer and Borgo Press

Analyzed in Essay and general literature index

An anthology of and commentary on Chinese, Latin, Greek, Catholic and Protestant mysticism

Includes bibliography

Schweitzer, Albert, 1875-1965
The words of Albert Schweitzer; selected by Norman Cousins. Newmarket Press 1984 110p il $12.95

210

1. Quotations
ISBN 0-937858-41-2   LC 84-18890

Quotations from Schweitzer's speeches and writings on reverence for life, faith, music, civilization, peace, and other topics

Teilhard de Chardin, Pierre
Hymn of the universe. Harper & Row 1965 157p hardcover o.p. paperback available $12

210

1. Natural theology 2. Mysticism 3. Universe
ISBN 0-06-131910-4 (pa)

Original French edition, 1961

"The poetic mysticism of the Jesuit philosopher-scientist and author is revealed in a selection which includes three meditations and a group of 81 'pensées.'" Booklist

211 Concepts of God

Russell, Bertrand, 1872-1970
Why I am not a Christian, and other essays on religion and related subjects; edited, with an appendix on the "Bertrand Russell Case", by Paul Edwards. Simon & Schuster 1957 266p hardcover o.p. paperback available $9.95 **211**
1. Free thought
ISBN 0-671-20323-1 (pa)
The essays in this collection present Bertrand Russell's views on religious, moral, and ethical questions

Turner, James, 1946-
Without God, without creed; the origins of unbelief in America. Johns Hopkins Univ. Press 1985 316p (New studies in American intellectual and cultural history) $42.50; pa $14.95 **211**
1. Religion 2. Faith
ISBN 0-8018-2494-X; 0-8018-3407-4 (pa)
LC 84-15397
The author traces the development of agnosticism and atheism in the United States
"Mr. Turner allows us to see clearly the decline of transcendental Christianity and its replacement by ever softer religions and ever harder systems of social metaphysics." N Y Times Book Rev
Includes bibliography

212 Existence, knowability, attributes of God

Adler, Mortimer Jerome, 1902-
How to think about God; a guide for the 20th-century pagan; Mortimer J. Adler. Macmillan 1980 175p hardcover o.p. paperback available $9 **212**
1. God
ISBN 0-02-016022-4 (pa) LC 79-25098
"The central question to which the book addresses itself is whether or not God exists—whether or not there is anything in reality that corresponds to the notion we have of God. Dr. Adler examines and refutes several traditional arguments, proposing instead his own theory." Publisher's note
Includes bibliography

213 Creation

Scientists confront creationism; edited by Laurie R. Godfrey. Norton 1983 xxvi, 324p il hardcover o.p. paperback available $10.95 **213**
1. Creation—Study and teaching 2. Evolution
ISBN 0-393-30154-0 (pa) LC 82-12500
Analyzed in Essay and general literature index
"These articles refute point by point the claims of the Institute of Creation Research that schools must give 'equal' time to 'scientific' Creationist positions. The book demonstrates that scientific methods and practices demand constant testing and questioning and that

Creationists seek verification of their positions in the Bible as God's word, rather than through open experimentation." Sci Books Films
Includes bibliographic references

220.1 Bible—Origins and authenticity

The **Cambridge** History of the Bible. Cambridge Univ. Press 1963-1970 3v il hardcover o.p. paperback available set $100 **220.1**
1. Bible—History 2. Bible—Versions
ISBN 0-521-29018-X (pa)
Contents: v1 From the beginnings to Jerome, edited by P. R. Ackroyd and C. F. Evans, published 1970; v2 The West, from the Fathers to the Reformation, edited by G. W. H. Lampe, published 1969; v3 The West, from the Reformation to the present day, edited by S. L. Greenslade, published 1963
Volume 1 shows how the Bible came into being in the original tongues, and how its various component books came to be organized into a canon. Volumes 2 and 3 give accounts of the use, study and influence, the translations, and the physical form of the Bible in the Western world from the time of Jerome to the New English Bible

220.3 Bible—Encyclopedias and topical dictionaries

The **Anchor** Bible dictionary; David Noel Freedman, editor-in-chief; associate editors, Gary A. Herion, David F. Graf, John David Pleins; managing editor, Astrid B. Beck. Doubleday 1992 6v il maps set $360 **220.3**
1. Bible—Dictionaries
ISBN 0-385-42583-X LC 91-8385
Contents: v1 A-C; v2 D-G; v3 H-J; v4 K-N; v5 O-Sh; v6 Si-Z
"The 6,000 separate subject entries reflect many of the changes that have taken place in biblical research over the last 30 years. . . . There are individual entries for all the different books of the Bible, major figures, places, names, and biblical terms. Substantial bibliographies and numerous cross references enhance the usefulness of this as a reference source." Am Libr
"With its sound scholarship, good organization, and readable prose, the ABD deserves a place in all academic and public libraries." Libr J

The **Dictionary** of Bible and religion; William H. Gentz, editor. Abingdon Press 1986 1147p il maps $26.95 **220.3**
1. Bible—Dictionaries 2. Theology—Dictionaries
ISBN 0-687-10757-1 LC 85-15011
"The authoritative, comprehensive result of the work of twenty-eight scholars. All aspects of the Bible and its times are covered. The Jewish and Christian religious traditions receive better coverage than Hinduism, Buddhism, or Islam. Careful scholarship makes this a fine dictionary that libraries will really use." Ref Sources for Small & Medium-sized Libr. 5th edition

The **Eerdmans** Bible dictionary; revision editor, Allen C. Myers; associate editors, John W. Simpson, Jr. [et al.] Eerdmans 1987 1094p il $32.50 **220.3**

1. Bible—Dictionaries
ISBN 0-8028-2402-1   LC 87-13239

Revised augmented translation of Dutch work published 1975

"The nearly 5,000 entries identify all persons, places, plants, animals, and objects mentioned in the Bible, apocryphal and canonical books, literary genres, geographical regions, theological and interpretative concepts, ancient Near Eastern civilizations, and some aspects of the early and medieval church. Each entry includes an indication of pronunciation, and—where appropriate—the transliterated Greek, Hebrew, or other ancient language." Booklist

Harper's Bible dictionary; general editor, Paul J. Achtemeier; associate editors, Roger S. Boraas [et al.] with the Society of Biblical Literature. Harper & Row 1985 xxii, 1178p il maps $39; thumb-indexed $42   **220.3**

1. Bible—Dictionaries
ISBN 0-06-069862-4; 0-06-069863-2 (thumb-indexed)
LC 85-42767

"Explains terms of current biblical scholarship. Extended entries define terms in relation to their biblical usage, then explain where problems, if any, arise from that usage. Entries also give the general or specific background of names and places, as well as their location in the Bible. The books of both Old and New Testaments are outlined and key texts given. Designed to be compatible with any translation; entries written by Protestant, Catholic, and Jewish authorities." N Y Public Libr Book of How & Where to Look It Up

The **International** standard Bible encyclopedia; general editor, Geoffrey W. Bromiley [et al.] fully rev. Eerdmans 1979-1988 4v il maps set $220   **220.3**

1. Bible—Dictionaries
ISBN 0-8028-8160-2   LC 79-12280

First published 1915 in five volumes by the Howard-Severance Company

"A substantial revision, actually a rewriting, of a standard Bible encyclopedia. Its purpose is to define, identify, and explain terms and topics of interest for both the more advanced student and the average pastor or Bible student." Ref Sources for Small & Medium-sized Libr. 5th edition

The **Interpreter's** dictionary of the Bible. Abingdon Press 1962-1976 5v il maps set $179.95   **220.3**

1. Bible—Dictionaries
ISBN 0-687-19268-4

Volumes 1-4 edited by George Arthur Buttrick. Supplementary volume (v5) published 1976 and edited by Keith Crim, available separately for $39.95 (ISBN 0-687-19269-2)

"An illustrated encyclopedia identifying and explaining all proper names and significant terms and subjects in the Holy Scriptures, including the Apocrypha, with attention to archaeological discoveries and researches into the life and faith of ancient times." Subtitle

"A scholarly encyclopedic dictionary designed for the preacher, scholar, student, teacher, and general reader, based on recent discoveries and referring to both the King James Version and the Revised Standard Version, to the Aprocrypha, the Pseudepigrapha, the Dead Sea Scrolls, and other ancient manuscripts. . . . Indispensable for modern Biblical study." Sheehy. Guide to Ref Books. 10th edition

Unger, Merrill Frederick, 1909-1980
The new Unger's Bible dictionary; R.K. Harrison, editor; Howard F. Vos, Cyril J. Barber, contributing editors. rev & updated ed. Moody Press 1988 1400p il maps $32.99   **220.3**

1. Bible—Dictionaries
ISBN 0-8024-9037-9   LC 88-9189

First published 1957 with title: Bible dictionary

This dictionary "claims four special emphases: (1) archaeological information based on the latest contributions to scientific biblical archaeology, (2) historical-geographical characteristics of Near Eastern lands as they affected the Bible, (3) biographical entries about figures connected to biblical places and events, and (4) doctrinal beliefs widely held throughout Christendom. *The New Unger's* is based on the *New American Standard Bible,* with additional quotations from the King James Version and the *New International Version.* . . . Students, pastors, and researchers will be pleased with this solid and reliable source, with its fine physical appearance and accurate definitions." Best Ref Books, 1986-1990

Includes bibliographies

220.5 Bible—Modern versions

Bible
The Anchor Bible. Doubleday 1964-1993 54v apply to publisher for price   **220.5**

Contents: v1 Genesis; v3 Leviticus 1-16; v4 Numbers 1-20; v5 Deuteronomy 1-11; v6 Joshua; v6A Judges; v7 Ruth; v7A Lamentations; v7B Esther; v7C Song of songs; v8 I Samuel; v9 II Samuel; v11 II Kings; v12 I Chronicles; v13 II Chronicles; v14 Ezra & Nehemiah; v15 Job. Rev. ed; v16 Psalms I: 1-50; v17 Psalms II: 51-100; v17A Psalms III: 101-150; v18 Proverbs & Ecclesiastes; v20 II Isaiah; v21 Jeremiah; v22 Ezekiel I-XX; v23 The book of Daniel; v24 Hosea; v24A Amos; v25B Haggai, Zechariah 1-8; v25C Zechariah 9-14; v26 Matthew; v27 Mark; v28 Gospel according to Luke I-IX; v28A Gospel according to Luke X-XXIV; v29 Gospel according to John I-XII; v29A Gospel according to John XIII-XXI; v30 Epistles of JOhn; v31 Acts of the Apostles; v32 I Corinthians; v32A II Corinthians; v33 Romans; v34 Ephesians 1-3; v34A Ephesians 4-6; v35 The letter to Titus; v36 To the Hebrews; v37 Epistles of James, Peter and Jude; v37C 2 Peter, Jude; v38 Revelation; v39 The wisdom of Ben Sira; v40 Judith; v41 I Maccabees; v41A II Maccabees; v42 I and II Esdras; v43 Wisdom of Solomon; v44 Daniel, Esther and Jeremiah: the additions

Good news Bible; today's English version. American Bible Soc. prices vary   **220.5**

Available in various bindings and editions including a large print edition

"Begun in 1964 with the Gospel of Mark, The New Testament was completed in 1966, with rev. eds. in 1971 and 1976. The whole Bible was published in 1976. An extremely popular, inexpensive translation using contemporary American English. . . . Especially useful for youth or lay Bible study as well as for private reading." Bollier. Lit of Theology

Bible—*Continued*

The Holy Bible; containing the Old and New Testaments; translated out of the original tongues; and with the former translations diligently compared and revised by King James's special command, 1611. Oxford Univ. Press prices vary **220.5**

Available in various bindings and editions

The authorized or King James Version originally published 1611

The Holy Bible: new revised standard version; containing the Old and New Testaments with the Apocryphal/Deuterocanonical books. Nelson, T. maps prices vary **220.5**

Available in various bindings and editions including a large print edition

This version first published 1989

"Intended for public reading, congregational worship, private study, instruction, and meditation, it attempts to be as literal as possible while following standard American English usage, avoids colloquialism, and prefers simple, direct terms and phrases." Sheehy. Guide to Ref Books. 10th edition. suppl

Holy Bible: the new King James Version; containing the Old and New Testaments. Nelson, T. prices vary **220.5**

Available in various bindings and editions

This version first published 1982

"Protestant. This edition replaces 17th Century verb forms and second person pronouns. Updates archaic terms. Psalms and Job appear as poetry." N Y Public Libr. Ref Books for Child Collect. 2d edition

The new American Bible; with revised New Testament; translated from the original languages, with critical use of all the ancient sources by members of the Catholic Biblical Association of America; sponsored by the Bishops' Committee of the Confraternity of Christian Doctrine. Benziger 1987 1347, 513, 16p maps $10.92 **220.5**

ISBN 0-02-641640-9

First published 1970 by Kenedy

"Roman Catholic version based on modern English translations; replaces the Douay edition." N Y Public Libr Book of How & Where to Look It Up

New American standard Bible **220.5**

Available in various bindings and editions from various publishers

This translation, completed 1971, is a modernization of the American Standard Version of 1901

The new Jerusalem Bible. Doubleday maps prices vary **220.5**

Available in various bindings and editions

First published in this format 1966 with title: The Jerusalem Bible

General editor: Henry Wansbrough

"Derives from the French version edited at the Dominican Ecole Biblique de Jerusalem and known as 'La Bible de Jerusalem.' The introductions and notes are 'a direct translation from the French, though revised and brought up to date in some places' but translation of the Biblical text goes back to the original languages." Sheehy. Guide to Ref Books. 10th edition

The new Oxford annotated Bible; new revised standard version. Oxford Univ. Press maps prices vary **220.5**

Available in various bindings with and without the Apocrypha

This study Bible incorporates the full text of the New revised standard version translation, with cross-referenced annotations, a collection of essays and introductions, and a section of maps

The revised English Bible. Oxford Univ. Press; Cambridge Univ. Press 1989 prices vary **220.5**

Available in various bindings with and without the Apocrypha

A revised edition of The new English Bible, published 1970

This version is based upon a re-examination of the original Greek, Hebrew, and Aramaic texts, and is written in contemporary English

Cruden, Alexander

Cruden's Complete concordance to the Old and New Testaments **220.5**

1. Bible—Concordances

Hardcover and paperback editions available from various publishers

First edition 1737. Frequently revised

"The special value of this title is that Cruden provides an index to the Apocrypha. Note that some reprints of the work omit the Apocrypha in the concordance." Ref Sources for Small & Medium-sized Libr. 5th edition

Day, A. Colin (Arthur Colin), 1935-

Roget's thesaurus of the Bible. HarperSanFrancisco 1992 927p $28; indexed ed $30 **220.5**

1. Bible—Concordances

ISBN 0-06-061773-X; 0-06-061772-1 (indexed ed)

LC 92-53896

"This book replaces neither concordance nor dictionary, but uses the classified format of the various Roget's thesauruses of English words and phrases to provide for the English Bible a topical approach to its language. It provides access, for instance, to such topics of contemporary interests as 'incest,' 'gay,' and 'litigation.' There are indexes of subjects and Bible verses and a category list. This work will prove useful alongside the standard Bible translations, concordances, and dictionaries." Choice

The **Eerdmans** analytical concordance to the Revised Standard Version of the Bible; compiled by Richard E. Whitaker; with James E. Goehring and research personnel of the Institute for Antiquity and Christianity. Eerdmans 1988 1548p $59.99 **220.5**

1. Bible—Concordances

ISBN 0-8028-2403-X

LC 88-19217

The Eerdmans analytical concordance to the Revised Standard Version of the Bible —*Continued*

"The basis of this computer-generated concordance is an alphabetical listing in English of almost every word found in the RSV. Each English word (or sometimes phrase) is followed by the Hebrew, Greek, Aramaic, or Latin expressions that correspond to it." Am Ref Books Annu, 1989

"Because of the extensive analytical treatment that this work provides, it will be particularly valuable in collections that support the scholarly study of the Bible." Booklist

Strong, James, 1822-1894

The new Strong's concordance of the Bible; a popular edition of the exhaustive concordance. Nelson, T. 1985 749p $14.99 **220.5**

1. Bible—Concordances
ISBN 0-8407-4951-1 LC 85-344

First published 1980 with title: Strong's concordance of the Bible

An abridgment of The new Strong's exhaustive concordance of the Bible (1984), also available for $26.95 (ISBN 0-8407-6750-1)

220.6 Bible—Interpretation and criticism

Every, George

Christian legends. Bedrick Bks. 1987 144p il (Lib. of the world's myths and legends) $24.95 **220.6**

1. Legends, Christian
ISBN 0-87226-046-1 LC 86-22242

This book "illustrates the central biblical stories (Creation, the Flood, the Fall and Redemption, etc.) as well as the apocryphal legends of the apostles and other saints, the life of the Virgin Mary, and the visions of the afterlife prevalent in Christian art and practice." Booklist

Includes bibliography

Greeley, Andrew M., 1928-

The Bible and us; a priest and a rabbi read scripture together; [by] Andrew M. Greeley and Jacob Neusner. Warner Bks. 1990 288p $24.95; pa $14.95 **220.6**

1. Bible—Criticism, interpretation, etc.
ISBN 0-446-51522-1; 0-446-39247-2 (pa)

LC 89-40472

"The authors alternate chapters, sometimes agreeing with, sometimes arguing against, sometimes criticizing or confronting the other. They cover both the Hebrew Scriptures and the Christian New Testament. In the course of the conversation, each tries to understand the things most cherished by the other. Finally, they talk about the possibility of dialogue between Judaism and Christianity, with Neusner denying it and Greeley confirming it. Recommended for all religion collections." Booklist

The Literary guide to the Bible; edited by Robert Alter and Frank Kermode. Belknap Press 1987 678p $35; pa $14.95 **220.6**

1. Bible—Criticism, interpretation, etc. 2. Bible as literature
ISBN 0-674-87530-3; 0-674-87531-1 (pa)

LC 86-32172

This volume aims "to provide a survey of the literary dimensions of the Bible. General essays precede separate articles on the books of the Old and New Testaments, and there are also . . . essays on larger topics pertaining to the literary study of the Bible." America

This collection "reflects a significant shift in scholarly approaches and, what is more important, it communicates the impact of that shift to all readers of the Bible." N Y Times Book Rev

Includes bibliography

220.7 Bible—Commentaries

Asimov, Isaac, 1920-1992

Asimov's guide to the Bible; maps by Rafael Palacios. Doubleday 1968-1969 2v maps o.p.; Avon Bks. paperbacks available v1 $10.95, v2 $9.95 **220.7**

1. Bible—Commentaries

Contents: v1 The Old Testament (ISBN 0-380-01032-1); v2 The New Testament (ISBN 0-380-01031-3)

The author discusses the Bible book by book, verse by verse, letting us in on the actual historical, geographical, and biographical aspects of Biblical history

"Asimov is relaxed, down-to-earth, calmly analytical, not irreverent but also not 'pious' in his approach." Publ Wkly

Harper's Bible commentary; general editor, James L. Mays; associate editors, Joseph Blenkinsopp [et al.] with the Society of Biblical Literature. Harper & Row 1988 1326p il maps $37.95; thumb-indexed $39.95 **220.7**

1. Bible—Commentaries
ISBN 0-06-065541-0; 0-06-065542-9 (thumb-indexed)
LC 88-45148

This volume "contains numerous introductory essays on the whole Bible and on the seven parts into which the *Commentary* divides it, and provides an introductory essay, concise commentary, and current bibliography for each book, including the Apocrypha. Cross-references to *Harper's Bible dictionary* [entered in class 220.3]" Sheehy. Guide to Ref Books. 10th edition. suppl

The Interpreter's Bible; the Holy Scriptures in the King James and Revised Standard versions. Abingdon Press 1951-1957 12v set $414.95 **220.7**

1. Bible—Commentaries
ISBN 0-687-19206-4

Commentary editor: George Arthur Buttrick
"With general articles and introduction, exegesis, exposition for each book of the Bible." Title page

"A guide and commentary to the Bible by some 125 scholars, prepared for the general reader, the teacher, and the preacher. Includes long introductions with bibliographies to the whole Bible, to each Testament, and to each book. Each is written and signed by an individual scholar. Includes the text of both versions, exegesis and exposition." Sheehy. Guide to Ref Books. 10th edition

The **Interpreter's** one-volume commentary on the Bible; introduction and commentary for each book of the Bible; including the Apocrypha; with general articles; edited by Charles M. Laymon. Abingdon Press 1971 1386p il mpas $34.95; thumb-indexed $39.95   **220.7**

1. Bible—Commentaries
ISBN 0-687-19299-4; 0-687-19300-1 (thumb-indexed)

"The results of the past hundred years of Anglo-American liberal biblical scholarship. Useful for its well-organized introductory chapters as well as commentaries on each book. Subject index." Ref Sources for Small & Medium-sized Libr. 5th edition

220.9   Bible—Geography, history, biography, stories

Aharoni, Yohanan, 1919-1976
The Macmillan Bible atlas; [by] Yohanan Aharoni and Michael Avi-Yonah; designed and prepared by Carta. completely rev 3rd ed, [by] Anson F. Rainey, Ze'ev Safrai. Macmillan 1993 unp il maps $35   **220.9**

1. Bible—Geography 2. Bible—History of biblical events 3. Palestine—Maps
ISBN 0-02-500605-3   LC 92-27895
First published 1968

This atlas contains over 200 maps and depicts events from 3,000 B.C. to A.D. 200 including migrations, conquests, economic developments, archeological excavations, and church growth. It incorporates Egyptian, Assyrian, Greek, and Roman sources in addition to recent biblical studies

For a review see: Booklist, Oct. 1, 1993

Calvocoressi, Peter
Who's who in the Bible. Viking 1987 xxxi, 269p maps $19.95   **220.9**

1. Bible—Biography
ISBN 0-670-81188-2   LC 87-50540
Also available in paperback from Penguin Bks.

"This work provides profiles, ranging in length from a sentence to several pages, of some 450 biblical characters. It is unusual in discussing the literature, visual arts, and music associated with many of these characters." Libr J

Deen, Edith
All of the women of the Bible. Harper & Row 1955 xxii, 410p hardcover o.p. paperback available $14   **220.9**

1. Bible—Biography 2. Women in the Bible
ISBN 0-06-061852-3 (pa)

"Good or bad, they are all here: three hundred and sixteen of them. They are not vague historical personages but living women whom we get to know well. Most of the portraits are preceded by the Bible chapters and verses which are the sources and by an outline sketch that establishes the background." Cincinnati Public Libr

The **Harper** atlas of the Bible; edited by James B. Pritchard. Harper & Row 1987 254p il maps $49.95   **220.9**

1. Bible—Geography 2. Bible—History of biblical events
ISBN 0-06-181883-6   LC 86-675550

"This work presents biblical geography and social and cultural history in topical entries, all illustrated by full-color maps, charts, diagrams, photographs, and drawings. The chronological arrangement, extending from prehistoric times to A.D. 135, relates the Bible to ancient history, including major events, customs, beliefs, and everyday life." Nichols. Guide to Ref Books for Sch Media Cent. 4th edition

The **Harper** concise atlas of the Bible; edited by James B. Pritchard. HarperCollins Pubs. 1991 151p il maps $30   **220.9**

1. Bible—Geography 2. Bible—History of biblical events
ISBN 0-06-270029-4
Published in the United Kingdom with title: The Times concise atlas of the Bible

"This concise version of *The Harper Atlas of the Bible* [entered above] is reduced both in number of pages and in page size. . . . This new edition contains most of the attractive, colorful photographs and art found in the original. New features include a bibliography, an index of personal names, and an index of biblical references. The index of place-names from the parent set is retained, but the concordance of personal names has been dropped." Booklist

"The first *Atlas* commends itself without reservation; having that, the smaller version probably is not necessary. Lacking the full edition, however, consider the concise edition for those collections serving the general public." Libr J

New Bible atlas; contributing editors, J. J. Bimson, J. P. Kane, consulting editors, J. H. Paterson, D. J. Wiseman, organizing editor, D. R. W. Wood. Tyndale House 1985 128p il maps $16.99   **220.9**

1. Bible—Geography 2. Bible—History of biblical events
ISBN 0-8423-4675-9   LC 84-52722

"The maps, more than two-thirds of which are in color, illustrate numerous events and phases of biblical history and also many aspects of its geographical and cultural setting: topography, geological features, vegetation, climate, economy, trade routes, archaeological sites, etc. . . . The text, which consists mostly of brief summaries of biblical history, also includes judicious references to textual sources and archaeological evidence, and some discussion of difficulties and controversies." Best Ref Books, 1986-1990

Oxford Bible atlas; edited by Herbert G. May; with the assistance of G.N.S. Hunt; in consultation with R.W. Hamilton. 3rd ed, rev for the 3rd ed by John Day. Oxford Univ. Press 1984 144p il maps $30; pa $14.95   **220.9**

1. Bible—Geography
ISBN 0-19-143452-3; 0-19-143451-5 (pa)
    LC 84-10052
First published 1962

"An introductory essay supported by 50 photos and two chronological tables surveys the geography and climate of the area, and traces the history of the Is-

Oxford Bible atlas—*Continued*
raelites from 1025 B.C. to the fall of Jerusalem in A.D. 70. The map section contains 26 revised colored maps showing topography, climate, historical periods, and archaeological sites." Wynar. Guide to Ref Books for Sch Media Cent. 3d edition

Reader's Digest atlas of the Bible; an illustrated guide to the Holy Land. Reader's Digest Assn. 1982 c1981 256p il maps $30   **220.9**
1. Bible—Geography 2. Bible—History of biblical events 3. Middle East—Antiquities
ISBN 0-89577-097-0   LC 80-53426
Editor: Joseph L. Gardner
In this atlas the text "places the Bible's stories in their proper geographical and historical context. The many accompanying maps are clearly keyed to the text. Numerous full color illustrations (drawings, photographs, and representative works of art) convey vivid impressions of the biblical times and places. Special aids include an index, chronology, and gazetteer." Libr J
"Superb topographic maps are the most distinctive and valuable asset of this popular-level biblical handbook." Booklist

Rogerson, J. W. (John William), 1935-
Atlas of the Bible; [by] John Rogerson. Facts on File 1985 237p il maps $45   **220.9**
1. Bible—Geography 2. Bible—History of biblical events
ISBN 0-8160-1207-5   LC 84-25980
This volume "treats the subject geographically rather than historically. . . . Part one of the book is devoted to a discussion of the composition and transmission of biblical literature, while part two presents an outline of biblical history and a pictographic account of the Bible in art. But the discussion of the geography of the Bible in part three constitutes by far the largest portion of his study." Booklist
This atlas is "an admirably brisk and comprehensive presentation of an enormous amount of information." Atlantic

221.5 Bible. Old Testament— Modern versions

Bible. O.T.
Tanakh; a new translation of the Holy Scriptures according to the traditional Hebrew text. Jewish Publ. Soc. 1985 xxvi, 1624p prices vary   **221.5**
     LC 85-10006
Available in various bindings and editions
This volume represents a "collaboration between rabbis from the Orthodox, Conservative, and Reform branches of Judaism, and scholars in Semitic languages and biblical studies. The translators relied on the Hebrew tenth-century Masoretic text that is Judaism's standard. The Torah, Prophets, and Writings are here in a single volume." Publisher's note

221.6 Bible. Old Testament— Interpretation and criticism

Alter, Robert
The world of biblical literature. Basic Bks. 1992 225p $23; pa $12   **221.6**
1. Bible. O.T.—Criticism, interpretation, etc. 2. Bible as literature
ISBN 0-465-09255-1; 0-465-09256-X (pa)
     LC 91-55462
This is a collection of "essays analyzing the Hebrew Bible as a literary work." N Y Times Book Rev
"Examples of Alter's detailed literary analyses of several typically laconic texts reveal the hidden richness of syntax, motifs, and allusion. While it is not the purpose of literary analysis to confirm faith, Alter maintains that neither is it detrimental to faith or the spiritual authority of the texts." Libr J
Includes bibliographic references

221.9 Bible. Old Testament— Geography, history, biography, stories

Rogerson, J. W. (John William), 1935-
The Old Testament world; [by] John Rogerson, Philip Davies. Prentice-Hall 1989 384p il maps $39   **221.9**
1. Bible. O.T.—History of Biblical events 2. Palestine—Antiquities
ISBN 0-13-634049-0
"This book is divided into four parts. Part 1 places the Old Testament and its people in geographical, social, and political context. Part 2 reconstructs the history of Israel using sound historical method. And while Part 3 breaks down the Old Testament into genres, subjecting each to literary analysis, Part 4 tells how the Old Testament was formed. There is nothing new here, but that isn't the point; the authors' purpose is to teach the essentials of modern biblical scholarship. Clearly written." Libr J
Includes bibliography

222 Historical books of Old Testament

Bible. O.T. Pentateuch
The book of J; translated from the Hebrew by David Rosenberg; interpreted by Harold Bloom. Grove Weidenfeld 1990 340p $21.95   **222**
1. Bible. O.T.—Criticism, interpretation, etc.
ISBN 0-8021-1050-9   LC 90-37391
Also available in paperback from Vintage Bks.
This volume "contains three works: David Rosenberg's translation of those parts of the Pentateuch that have been attributed to the J Writer (most of Genesis and Exodus, parts of Numbers and Deuteronomy), Bloom's introduction, and, following the translation, his [commentary]." Voice Lit Suppl

Bible. O.T. Pentateuch—*Continued*
The Torah: the five books of Moses; a new translation of the Holy Scriptures according to the Masoretic text; first section. Jewish Publ. Soc. 1963 1962 393p $14.95
222

ISBN 0-8276-0015-1

This "translation of Genesis, Exodus, Leviticus, Numbers, and Deuteronomy was prepared . . . to present a version of the Bible that takes into account modern insights and knowledge of ancient times. . . . Of chief value to persons of the Jewish religion but of interest to Bible scholars of any religion." Booklist

Blenkinsopp, Joseph, 1927-
The Pentateuch; an introduction to the first five books of the Bible. Doubleday 1992 273p (Anchor Bible reference lib) $28
222

1. Bible. O.T. Pentateuch—Criticism, interpretation, etc.
ISBN 0-385-41207-X   LC 91-22988

The author focuses on "unraveling the radical scholarly opinions on who has written the Pentateuch, how it was written, and what significance it has today." Publisher's note

"This is an interesting and self-consistent analysis of the Pentateuchal narratives, the Deuteronomistic history, and much of the prophetic corpus. . . . Fairly technical but very readable." Choice

Includes bibliographic references

Friedman, Richard Elliott
Who wrote the Bible? Prentice-Hall 1987 299p maps $20
222

1. Bible. O.T. Pentateuch—Criticism, interpretation, etc.
ISBN 0-13-958513-3   LC 87-1978

Also available in paperback from HarperPerennial

The author describes the documentary hypothesis in Bible exegesis which ascribes the Torah to four sources: "J" (the Yahwist), "E" (the Elohist), "P" (the priestly writer), and "D" (the Deuteronomist). He then attempts to discover the authors of the four documents

Friedman "turns a potentially dry scholarly inquiry into a lively detective story. . . . This book is neither comprehensive nor unduly complex, making it a good introductory text for beginners and nonspecialists." Libr J

Kolatch, Alfred J., 1916-
This is the Torah. David, J. 1988 418p $16.95
222

1. Bible. O.T. Pentateuch—Criticism, interpretation, etc. 2. Judaism—Customs and practices
ISBN 0-8246-0330-3   LC 87-33624

"Popular in its orientation, this book uses a question-and-answer format to address over 500 questions frequently asked about the Torah. Included are queries regarding its origin (divine or human?), its handling in the synagogue, and its use in the liturgy and service. Kolatch's authoritative answers encompass all branches of Judaism but lean heavily to a traditional approach." Libr J

Includes bibliography

223   Poetic books of Old Testament

Safire, William
The first dissident; the book of Job and today's politics. Random House 1992 xxix, 304p il $23; pa $12
223

1. Bible. O.T. Job—Criticism, interpretation, etc.
2. Dissent 3. Politics, Practical
ISBN 0-679-41755-9; 0-679-74858-X (pa)

                   LC 92-50167

The author "uses the Bible's Book of Job to illustrate the relationship between authority and dissent. He finds in Job a justification for 'defiance of unjust authority.' . . . Even readers who do not agree with Safire's interpretation can appreciate the insights he offers into fundamental questions of political philosophy and practical politics. Because of Safire's considerable writing skills, the book can be profitably read by both general readers and scholars." Libr J

224   Prophetic books of Old Testament

Heschel, Abraham Joshua, 1907-1972
The prophets. Harper & Row 1962 2v hardcover o.p. paperbacks available v1 $12, v2 $13
224

1. Bible. O.T. Prophets—Criticism, interpretation, etc.
2. Prophets
ISBN 0-06-131421-8; 0-06-131557-5

"Essays on the individual prophets—most of the pre-exilic, and of the post-exilic only the Second Isaiah—take up about a third of the book. The main effort . . . is to analyze the significance of prophecy in the history of religion, and the nature and meaning of prophetic inspiration." America

Includes bibliographic references

225.5   Bible. New Testament— Modern versions

Bible. N.T.
The New Testament in modern English; [translated by] J.B. Phillips. rev ed. Macmillan 1973 c1972 558p il hardcover o.p. paperback available $9.95
225.5

Also available in other bindings and editions

Originally published 1958; this edition first published 1972 in the United Kingdom

This version of the New Testament is a translation from the Greek text published by the United Bible Societies in 1966

Morrison, Clinton, 1924-
An analytical concordance to the "Revised Standard Version" of the New Testament. Westminster Press 1979 773p maps $20
225.5

1. Bible. N.T.—Concordances
ISBN 0-664-20773-1   LC 77-26210

Morrison, Clinton, 1924—— *Continued*
"This is the first concordance for the Revised Standard Version (RSV) of the New Testament that relates the RSV English directly to the original Greek. It is an invaluable tool for any serious student of the Bible who lacks a knowledge of the original Greek and who is therefore dependent upon translations of the New Testament." Ref Sources for Small & Medium-sized Libr. 5th edition

225.7 Bible. New Testament— Commentaries

Harvey, A. E. (Anthony Ernest)
The new English Bible companion to the New Testament. Oxford Univ. Press 1970 850p maps hardcover o.p. paperback available $13.95 **225.7**
1. Bible. N.T.—Commentaries
ISBN 0-19-826168-3 (pa)

Also available in paperback from Cambridge Univ. Press

The author "presents a brief, popular commentary on the New Testament of 'The New English Bible.' He provides short introductions to each of the New Testament books and a short index of main words and themes. Though non-technical in style, the book is based on the results of (generally conservative British) scholarship and is quite reliable. It is well written and clear, though not so colloquial as 'The New English Bible' itself." Libr J

225.9 Bible. New Testament— Geography, history, biography, stories

Bouquet, Alan Coates
Everyday life in New Testament times; [by] A. C. Bouquet; illustrated from drawings by Marjorie Quennell. Scribner 1954 c1953 235p il maps lib bdg $55 **225.9**
1. Bible. N.T.—Antiquities 2. Palestine—Social life and customs
ISBN 0-684-14833-1

"Hudson River editions"

A look at how people lived in Palestine under Roman rule

226 Gospels and Acts

Ayo, Nicholas
The Lord's prayer; a survey theological and literary. University of Notre Dame Press 1992 258p $29.95; pa $14.95 **226**
1. Lord's prayer
ISBN 0-268-01291-1; 0-268-01292-X (pa)
LC 90-50929

"Ayo combines a word by word biblical and exegetical study with a modern commentary on the Lord's Prayer, quoting writers such as Origen, Thomas Aquinas, Teresa of Avila, and Simone Weil. Finally, Ayo includes a personal meditation on the overall significance of this unique prayer in spiritual life." Univ Press Books for Public and Second Sch Libr

Includes bibliographic references

Bonhoeffer, Dietrich, 1906-1945
The cost of discipleship; containing material not previously translated. rev and unabridged ed. Macmillan 1959 hardcover o.p. paperback available $6.95 **226**
1. Bible. N.T. Gospels—Criticism, interpretation, etc.
2. Sermon on the mount
ISBN 0-02-083850-6 (pa)

Also available in hardcover from P. Smith

Original German edition, 1937. This edition translated by R. H. Fuller with some revision by Irmgard Booth

The first part of the book "is an exposition of the conception of discipleship that is to be found in the Synoptic Gospels, together with an interpretation of the Sermon on the Mount. The second part consists of Bonhoeffer's attempt to show how the terminology used by the evangelists has been translated into the language of the Church of the Apostle Paul." Magill. Masterpieces of Christ Lit in Summary Form

Mitchell, Stephen
The gospel according to Jesus; a new translation and guide to his essential teachings for believers and unbelievers. HarperCollins Pubs. 1991 310p $23; pa $12 **226**
1. Jesus Christ—Teachings 2. Bible. N.T. Gospels—Criticism, interpretation, etc.
ISBN 0-06-016641-X; 0-06-092321-0 (pa)
LC 90-56390

Chiefly commentary on biblical excerpts

"Consisting of three parts (an introduction, a translation of the teachings and deeds of Jesus that Mitchell considers authentic, and a series of comments on each reading) this book is modeled after Thomas Jefferson's The Life and Morals of Jesus Christ, presenting a human Jesus whose teachings harmonized with Eastern (i.e., Zen, Hindu, Chinese) sages." Choice

Includes bibliographic references

229 Apocrypha, pseudepigrapha, intertestamental works

Bible. O.T. Apocrypha
The Apocrypha **229**

Available in various versions, including the New revised standard version, in hardcover and paperback from various publishers

"These books form part of the sacred literature of the Alexandrian Jews. . . . Some of them form an historical link between the Old and New Testament, others have a linguistic value in connexion with the Hellenistic phraseology of the latter. The narratives of Apocrypha are partly historical records, and partly allegorical." Oxford Univ. Press

Dead Sea scrolls

The Dead Sea scriptures; in English translation with introduction and notes by Theodor H. Gaster. 3rd ed rev and enl. Anchor Press/Doubleday 1976 580p pa $12
229

ISBN 0-385-08859-0

Also available in hardcover from P. Smith

First published 1956 by Doubleday

A translation, with commentary and notes, of the scrolls relating the life and faith of the Dead Sea sect

Includes bibliographic references

The Dead Sea scrolls uncovered; the first complete translation and interpretation of 50 key documents withheld for over 35 years; [edited by] Robert H. Eisenman and Michael Wise. Element Bks. 1992 286p il $24.95
229

ISBN 1-85230-368-9   LC 93-108131

Also available in paperback from Penguin Bks.

Text of scrolls in Aramaic and Hebrew with translation into English; introductions in English

"Eisenman and Wise have reconstructed fifty texts from the scrolls found in Cave 4 near the Dead Sea. They divide the documents into eight categories: messianic and visionary recitals; prophets and pseudo-prophets; biblical interpretation; calendrical texts and priestly courses; testaments and admonitions; works reckoned as righteousness-legal texts; hymns and mysteries; and divination, magic and miscellaneous." Libr J

Includes bibliographic references

The **Secret** teachings of Jesus; four Gnostic gospels; translated, with an introduction and notes, by Marvin W. Meyer. Random House 1984 129p hardcover o.p. paperback available $9   **229**

1. Jesus Christ—Teachings 2. Gnosticism
ISBN 0-394-74433-0 (pa)   LC 84-42528

"Four texts from the Coptic Gnostic library discovered in Egypt in 1945 are translated here—the Secret Book of James, the Gospel of Thomas, the Book of Thomas and the Secret Book of John—all ostensibly containing secret teachings of Jesus transmitted to his disciples. . . Meyer also provides helpful explanatory comments on the texts. For the general reader this is the most accessible version of these texts presently available." Libr J

Includes bibliographic references

230 Christian theology

Bonhoeffer, Dietrich, 1906-1945

Letters and papers from prison; edited by Eberhard Bethge. enl ed. Macmillan 1972 c1971 437p il maps $17.95; pa $8.95 **230**

ISBN 0-02-513110-9; 0-02-083920-0 (pa)

Original German edition 1951; this translation first published 1953 in the United Kingdom and 1954 in the United States with title: Prisoner for God

These letters cover the years of Bonhoeffer's imprisonment to his execution in 1945. Emphasis is also placed on the private sphere of Bonhoeffer's life. References to his fiancée and to their plans for marriage are included, as is her article containing excerpts from his personal letters

A testament to freedom; the essential writings of Dietrich Bonhoeffer; edited by Geffrey B. Kelly and F. Burton Nelson. HarperSanFrancisco 1990 xxii, 579p il $32.95   **230**

1. Theology
ISBN 0-06-060813-7   LC 89-45514

This collection "follows Bonhoeffer through the various stages of his life and career, including his final years in the underground resistance against the Nazi government and his subsequent martyrdom. This book features previously untranslated writings, sermons, and selections from letters spanning his entire pastoral-theological career, including his prison letters." Publisher's note

This book will not "subsitute for the individual volumes of Bonhoeffer's best-known works. But as a single volume collection of Bonhoeffer's writings, however, there is none better." Christ Today

Includes bibliography

Kierkegaard, Søren, 1813-1855

The present age, and Of the difference between a genius and an apostle; translated by Alexander Dru; introduction by Walter Kaufman. Harper & Row 1962 108p pa $10
230

1. Theology
ISBN 0-06-130094-2

"Harper torchbooks. The Cloister library"

First published 1846. This translation "originally published, together with a third essay, by Oxford University Press under the title 'The Present Age and Two Minor Ethico-Religious Treatises in 1940'." Verso of title page

"Those who would know Kierkegaard, the intensely religious humorist, the irrepressibly witty critic of his age and ours, can do no better than to begin with this book." Introduction

Thomas, Aquinas, Saint, 1225?-1274

St. Thomas Aquinas on politics and ethics; a new translation, backgrounds, interpretations; translated and edited by Paul E. Sigmund. Norton 1988 xxix, 248p hardcover o.p. paperback available $7.95
230

1. Theology 2. Christian ethics
ISBN 0-393-95243-6 (pa)   LC 87-12196

"A Norton Critical edition"

This volume contains selections from The summa against the Gentiles; On kingship, or, The governance of rulers; and The summa of theology. It also includes selections from the writings of Aristotle, St. Augustine, and Dionysius the Areopagite; and critical writings on the influence of Aquinas' thought on subsequent political, social and religious thought, as well as on modern issues such as war, contraception, and abortion

Includes bibliography

Tillich, Paul, 1886-1965

The essential Tillich; an anthology of the writings of Paul Tillich; edited with a preface by F. Forrester Church. Macmillan 1987 281p hardcover o.p. paperback available $9.95 **230**

1. Theology
ISBN 0-02-018920-6 (pa)   LC 87-17177

"This volume, compiled by a noted minister and scholar, offers to the theological student, church worker, or, indeed, any serious reader struggling with the existential question, a tantalizing and illuminating introduction to perhaps the greatest mind of twentieth-century Protestant theology. An essential complement to religion collections." Booklist

Systematic theology. University of Chicago Press 1967 c1951-1963 3v in 1 $55 **230**

1. Theology
ISBN 0-226-80336-8

Also available separately in paperback

Contents: v1 Reason and revelation; Being and God (1951); v2 Existence and The Christ (1957); v3 Life and the spirit; History and the Kingdom of God (1963)

My purpose "has been to present the method and the structure of a theological system written from an apologetic point of view and carried through in a continuous correlation with philosophy." Preface

The **Westminster** dictionary of Christian theology; edited by Alan Richardson and John S. Bowden. [rev ed]. Westminster Press 1983 614p $30 **230**

1. Theology—Dictionaries
ISBN 0-664-21398-7   LC 83-14521

First published 1969 with title: A dictionary of Christian theology; this edition published in the United Kingdom with title: A new dictionary of Christian theology

"Wide-ranging signed articles that explain Christian belief, practice, and experience, primarily in the mainstream of Protestant thought, cover the interlocking areas of theology and philosophy. Biographical entries, bibliographic sources, and a name index are included." Ref Sources for Small & Medium-sized Libr. 5th edition

231.7 God's relation to the world

Boyer, Paul S., 1935-

When time shall be no more; prophecy belief in modern American culture; [by] Paul Boyer. Belknap Press 1992 468p il (Studies in cultural history) $29.95 **231.7**

1. Millennium 2. United States—Religion
ISBN 0-674-95128-X   LC 91-45302

A survey of the persistence of prophetic belief in American culture. Among the proponents of apocalyptic thinking discussed are: Hal Lindsey, Billy Graham, Tim LaHaye and Jerry Falwell

Boyer's "portrayal of other people's views is straightforward and accurate. Though some readers may find much in this book to laugh at, Boyer himself never sneers at his subject and treats prophecy believers with respect. In short, his analysis is judicious and well-nuanced." Christ Today

Includes bibliographic references

Lewis, C. S. (Clive Staples), 1898-1963

Miracles; a preliminary study. Macmillan 1947 220 hardcover o.p. paperback available $3.95 **231.7**

1. Miracles
ISBN 0-02-086760-3 (pa)

"Mr. Lewis casts his net fairly wide and, under the guise of a book on miracles, offers a rational justification both of theism and of doctrinal Christianity." Times Lit Suppl

Niebuhr, H. Richard (Helmut Richard), 1894-1962

The meaning of revelation. Macmillan 1941 196p hardcover o.p. paperback available $5.95 **231.7**

1. Revelation
ISBN 0-02-087750-1 (pa)

"An eloquent plea for the vital realization of God—a personal God who denies that man is a cog in an impersonal, universal machine." Cincinnati Public Libr

232 Jesus Christ and his family. Christology

Charlesworth, James H.

Jesus and the Dead Sea Scrolls; [by] James H. Charlesworth, with internationally renowned experts. Doubleday 1992 xxxvii, 370p il maps (Anchor Bible reference lib) $28 **232**

1. Jesus Christ 2. Dead Sea scrolls
ISBN 0-385-24863-6   LC 92-2617

These essays "explore the question of Jesus' relationship to those who wrote the scrolls, and whether or not the scrolls' original scholars were hiding something profound or damaging to the Christian faith." Booklist

This book is "a solid contribution to the current debate that will inform and challenge both scholars and lay readers." Libr J

Includes bibliographic references

232.9 Family and life of Jesus

Bishop, Jim, 1907-1987

The day Christ died; [introduction by Paul L. Maier] HarperSanFrancisco 1991 c1957 272p pa $9 **232.9**

1. Jesus Christ—Crucifixion
ISBN 0-06-060816-1   LC 90-42233

First published 1957

An hour-by-hour account of the Last Supper, and Jesus' trial and crucifixion

Includes bibliography

The day Christ was born; [with a new introduction by Paul L. Maier] Harper & Row 1977 107p il map pa $8 **232.9**

1. Jesus Christ—Nativity
ISBN 0-06-060794-7   LC 77-10021

Also available Walker & Co. large print edition

First published 1960

Bishop, Jim, 1907-1987—*Continued*

A "Catholic retelling of the story of Jesus' birth and his first days, up to the return to Nazareth from Egypt. [The author] amplifies the story from what is known of the marriage customs, the taxes, the clothing and food and other aspects of the history and life of the time." Publ Wkly

Dimont, Max I.

Appointment in Jerusalem; the search for the historical Jesus. St. Martin's Press 1991 194p $17.95   **232.9**

1. Jesus Christ—Historicity 2. Bible. N.T. Gospels—Criticism, interpretation, etc.

ISBN 0-312-06291-5   LC 91-21449

The author "explores seven portraits of Jesus as they emerge in the gospel and the letters of Paul. Covering the images of Jesus as Christian Messiah, Jewish Messiah, zealot, mastermind of his own Crucifixion, Essene, theological Christ, and Gnostic Christian, Dimont shows the politics and sociology that surround the making of the Gospels and the creation of Jesus images. . . . This book is recommended for those who want to explore the various facets of the myth surrounding Jesus." Booklist

Includes bibliographic references

Meier, John P.

A marginal Jew; rethinking the historical Jesus. v1: The roots of the problem and the person. Doubleday 1991 484p (Anchor Bible reference lib) $25   **232.9**

1. Jesus Christ—Historicity

ISBN 0-385-26425-9   LC 91-10538

The first of a projected two-volume work on the historical Jesus

The author "adopts a two-tier approach: he delineates up-to-date research on the Jesus of history with discussions geared toward well-read general readers, while his extensive notes discuss technical matters of interest to doctoral students and scholars. Meier explains issues of method, definitions and sources, and then turns to the birth, years of development, and cultural background of Jesus." Libr J

"Meier is meticulous and prudent, and openly impatient with tendentious conclusions based more on imagination than on hard evidence or rigorous thought. There is an added bonus: he can write." Commonweal

Includes bibliographic references

Muggeridge, Malcolm, 1903-1990

Jesus; the man who lives. Harper & Row 1975 191p il hardcover o.p. paperback available $12.95   **232.9**

1. Jesus Christ—Biography

ISBN 0-06-066042-2 (pa)

His comments on the life of Jesus seek to prove Muggeridge's belief that the New Testament account is the source of the greatest art, literature, architecture and music in Western civilization

Oursler, Fulton, 1893-1952

The greatest story ever told; a tale of the greatest life ever lived. Doubleday 1949 299p o.p.; Image Bks. paperback available $9.95   **232.9**

1. Jesus Christ—Biography

ISBN 0-385-08028-X (pa)

"This is the story of Jesus. It is a chronology of events from the betrothal of Mary and Joseph to the days after the Resurrection, and the episodes are taken from the four Gospels. What is imaginative in the narrative is largely detail to fill in chinks left open in the Bible accounts; nothing has been included that did not seem a reasonable assumption from the records." Preface

Pelikan, Jaroslav Jan, 1923-

Jesus through the centuries; his place in the history of culture. Yale Univ. Press 1985 270p il $30   **232.9**

1. Jesus Christ—Historicity

ISBN 0-300-03496-2   LC 85-2428

Also available in paperback from HarperCollins

In these essays the author "proposes that, while the figure of Jesus provides the chief continuity in the history of Christianity, each age has depicted him in accordance with its own character." Libr J

This work "bridges scholarly and popular discourse on the prophet from Nazareth over the past 2,000 years. Believers and skeptics alike will find it a sweeping visual and conceptual panorama." N Y Times Book Rev

Schweitzer, Albert, 1875-1965

The quest of the historical Jesus; a critical study of its progress from Reimarus to Wrede; introduction by James M. Robinson. Macmillan 1968 xxiii, 413p pa $18   **232.9**

1. Jesus Christ—Biography

ISBN 0-02-089240-3

"Macmillan paperbacks"

A reprint of the title first published in English, 1910. Translated by W. Montgomery from the first German edition, 1906

This book surveys various critical, imaginative and sentimental theological attempts which were made between 1778 and 1901 to explain the Gospel narratives of Jesus' life and mission

Includes bibliography

Wilson, A. N. (Andrew Norman), 1950-

Jesus. Norton 1992 269p $22.95   **232.9**

1. Jesus Christ—Biography 2. Jesus Christ—Historicity

ISBN 0-393-03087-3   LC 92-37046

The author attempts to understand Jesus as a historical figure and ethical teacher within the context of first-century Judaism

Includes bibliography

Wilson, Ian, 1941-
The mysterious shroud; photographs by Vernon Miller. Doubleday 1986 158p il maps hardcover o.p. paperback available $9.95   **232.9**

1. Holy Shroud
ISBN 0-385-24748-6 (pa)   LC 83-45570

The author "details the results of the 1978 investigation of the garment by a team of U.S. scientists expert in electronic, microscope, and computer technology." Natl Rev

Includes bibliography

232.91   Mary, mother of Jesus

Zimdars-Swartz, Sandra, 1949-
Encountering Mary; from La Salette to Medjugorje. Princeton Univ. Press 1991 342p il $24.95   **232.91**

1. Mary, Blessed Virgin, Saint 2. Apparitions
ISBN 0-691-07371-6   LC 90-46215

Also available in paperback from Avon Bks.

The author examines apparitions of the Virgin Mary reported between 1846 and the present—at Fatima, La Salette, Lourdes, Melleray (Ireland), San Damiano (Italy), San Sebastián de Garabandal (Spain) and Medjugorje (Yugoslavia)

"Zimdars-Swartz provides a guide to the literature, as well as a balanced, comprehensive examination of the anatomy of a Marian apparition." Choice

234   Salvation and grace

Tillich, Paul, 1886-1965
Dynamics of faith. Harper & Row 1957 127p hardcover o.p. paperback available $11
234

1. Faith
ISBN 0-06-130042-X (pa)

"World perspectives"

"The author considers what faith is and is not, the symbols and types of faith and the truth and the life of faith. The discussion treats of history, science, the Bible, the individual and the community and the claims of Judaism, Mohammedanism, Protestantism and Catholicism." N Y Times Book Rev

235   Spiritual beings

Adler, Mortimer Jerome, 1902-
The angels and us. Macmillan 1982 205p $11.95; pa $7.95   **235**

1. Angels
ISBN 0-02-500550-2; 0-02-016021-6 (pa)
LC 81-20810

The author "examines here the concept of angels from philosophical and theological standpoints. Philosophically, he builds an Aquinas-derived argument for their existence as soul entities. Theologically, he is most interested in their persistence as objects of religious belief." Booklist

Includes bibliography

Godwin, Malcolm
Angels; an endangered species. Simon & Schuster 1990 255p il $22.50   **235**

1. Angels
ISBN 0-671-70650-0   LC 90-33122

"Complete with a 'Who's Who of the Underworld,' the book is the only reference guide to angels you'll ever need. It traces the complicated angelic family tree and maps out, in detail, the hierarchy of angelic political life." Voice Lit Suppl

Graham, Billy, 1918-
Angels; God's secret agents. rev & expanded ed. Word Bks. 1986 131p o.p. Random House edition available $11   **235**

1. Angels
ISBN 0-394-29860-8   LC 85-31578

First published 1975 by Doubleday

The author draws upon scriptural citations and his interpretations of contemporary events to support his assertion that angels have a direct influence on the living

236   Eschatology

Küng, Hans, 1928-
Eternal life? life after death as a medical, philosophical, and theological problem; translated by Edward Quinn. Doubleday 1984 271p o.p.; Crossroad paperback available $16.95   **236**

1. Future life 2. Death 3. Heaven 4. Eschatology
ISBN 0-8245-1120-4 (pa)   LC 82-45112

Original German edition, 1982

"This collection of nine expanded lectures deals with such topics as reincarnation, belief in heaven and hell, the Resurrection and dying with dignity." Publ Wkly

McDannell, Colleen
Heaven; a history; [by] Colleen McDannell and Bernhard Lang. Yale Univ. Press 1988 410p il $38   **236**

1. Heaven 2. Future life
ISBN 0-300-04346-5   LC 88-10765

Also available in paperback from Vintage Bks.

The authors "describe and interpret the ways in which believers—from biblical authors to medieval mystics, from Jesus to present-day religious thinkers—have pictured Heaven, not just in doctrine but also in poetry, art, literature, and popular culture. In so doing, they shed new light into both the private and public dimensions of western culture." Univ Press Books for Public Libr

Includes bibliography

241   Christian moral theology

Encyclopedia of Biblical and Christian ethics; R.K. Harrison, general editor. rev ed. Nelson, T. 1992 472p pa $14.99   **241**

1. Christian ethics—Dictionaries 2. Ethics—Dictionaries
ISBN 0-8407-3391-7   LC 92-3120

First published 1987

Encyclopedia of Biblical and Christian ethics—*Continued*

This volume explains biblical and Christian teachings about issues such as abortion, bioethics, capital punishment, euthanasia, racism, and war, in over 540 alphabetical entries

Niebuhr, H. Richard (Helmut Richard), 1894-1962

The responsible self; an essay in Christian moral philosophy; with an introduction by James M. Gustafson. Harper & Row 1963 183p hardcover o.p. paperback available $10
241

1. Christian ethics
ISBN 0-06-066211-5 (pa)

"This work, based on lectures given by Dr. Niebuhr at Glasgow University, is concerned with the concept of responsibility as the central characteristic of man's moral life." Cincinnati Public Libr

Includes bibliographic references

Pagels, Elaine H., 1943-

Adam, Eve, and the serpent. Random House 1988 xxviii, 189p $17.95; pa $9
241

1. Bible. O.T.—Criticism, interpretation, etc. 2. Sexual behavior
ISBN 0-394-52140-4; 0-679-72232-7 (pa)
LC 87-43227

The author "focuses on six schools of early Christian opinion concerning sexuality, marriage, family, procreation, celibacy, moral freedom, and human nature, as reflected in various interpretations on Genesis 1-3." Choice
"Pagels writes with a rare combination of formidable knowledge and easy fluency. The old controversies she discusses become, in her hands, matters of immediate interest." Economist

Includes bibliographic references

The Westminster dictionary of Christian ethics; edited by James F. Childress and John Macquarrie. Westminster Press 1986 678p $35
241

1. Christian ethics—Dictionaries 2. Ethics—Dictionaries
ISBN 0-664-20940-8
LC 85-22539

First published 1967 with title: Dictionary of Christian ethics

With 620 signed entries, this work "includes among its subjects key ethical concepts as well as entries on biblical ethics, theological ethics, philosophical traditions in ethics, non-Christian ethical traditions, various nonethical concepts relevant to Christian ethics, and a host of ethical problems. Obviously not every topic important to Christian ethical reflection can be included in a single volume. However, this book is a must buy for any library with an interest in Christian ethics. Appropriate for general readers, college and university collections." Choice

Includes bibliographies

242 Devotional literature

Augustine, Saint, Bishop of Hippo

The confessions of St. Augustine
242

Hardcover and paperback editions available from various publishers

"These confessions were written at the end of the fourth century by the most distinguished of the Latin fathers as a revelation of his spiritual experience. They have been a source of religious inspiration through the centuries." Pratt Alcove

Dillard, Annie

Holy the firm. Harper & Row 1977 76p hardcover o.p. paperback available $9
242

1. Meditations
ISBN 0-06-091543-9 (pa)
LC 77-6883

A lyrical meditation on God and nature
"Few pilgrims of the spirit can avoid sounding cheaply pious or painfully oversincere. Dillard's literary salvation is her sense of wonder and intensity. . . . At their best, Dillard's sentences have a clean, penetrating edge." Time

Francis, of Assisi, Saint, 1182-1226

The little flowers of St. Francis. Image Bks. 1958 357p il pa $7
242

ISBN 0-385-07544-8

Also available Walker & Co. large print edition

"A Doubleday Image book"

These "simple anecdotes exemplify [St. Francis'] love of nature, man and of God." Bookman's Manual

Imitation of Christ

The imitation of Christ; [by] Thomas à Kempis
242

Hardcover and paperback editions available from various publishers

This devotional classic originally written in Latin in the 15th century "traces in four books the gradual progress of the soul to Christian perfection, its detachment from the world, and its union with God." Oxford Companion to Engl Lit. Concise edition

The Macmillan book of earliest Christian prayers; edited by F. Forrester Church and Terrence Mulry. Macmillan 1988 242p hardcover o.p. paperback available $9.95
242

1. Prayers
ISBN 0-02-031080-3 (pa)
LC 87-28233

This book includes "liturgicals and private prayers from the New Testament, the early Gnostic writings, and prayers composed by women and the earliest Fathers. The editors provide . . . introductions to each section. This collection covers Armenian, Coptic, Syriac, and Ethiopic prayers, as well as Latin and Greek sources." Publisher's note

Pascal, Blaise, 1623-1662

The thoughts of Blaise Pascal. Greenwood Press 1978 320p $55
242

1. Apologetics 2. Christianity
ISBN 0-313-20530-2
LC 78-12814

Also available in paperback from Penguin Bks. with title: Pensées

A reprint of the 1961 edition published by Dolphin Bks. with title: Pensées

Pascal, Blaise, 1623-1662—*Continued*
"A collection of reflections on religion by Blaise Pascal, found in fragmentary form after his death. The first edition (1670) abridged the *Pensées* in order to soften their strongly Jansenist tone, but the edition of 1844 is faithful to the original manuscript." Reader's Ency. 3d edition

248 Christian experience, practice, life

Lewis, C. S. (Clive Staples), 1898-1963
Letters to Malcolm: chiefly on prayer. Harcourt Brace & World 1964 124p hardcover o.p. paperback available $6.95   **248**

1. Christian life 2. Prayer
ISBN 0-15-650880-X (pa)

The author's "reflections on prayer are here set down in the form of thoughtful and engaging letters to his friend Malcolm." Cincinnati Public Libr

The Screwtape letters. Macmillan 1943 o.p.   **248**

1. Christian life 2. Satire

Available in hardcover from Amereon

"A popular work on Christian moral and theological problems. . . . It is in the form of a series of letters in which a devil, Screwtape, advises his nephew, Wormwood, on how to deal with his human 'patients.'" Reader's Ency. 3d edition

Marshall, Catherine, 1914-1983
Beyond our selves. McGraw-Hill 1961 266p o.p.; Avon Bks. paperback available $8   **248**

1. Christian life 2. Faith
ISBN 0-380-72202-X (pa)

Also available in paperback from Baker Bk. House

The author "re-examines her personal experiences and relationships in childhood, college, and adulthood to illuminate the quest for abiding faith in God and the concern of one's fellow man that have helped her and others to sustain the trials of life." Booklist

Merton, Thomas, 1915-1968
The Asian journal of Thomas Merton; edited from his original notebooks by Naomi Burton, Patrick Hart & James Laughlin; consulting editor: Amiya Chakravarty. New Directions 1973 xxviii, 445p il hardcover o.p. paperback available $12.95   **248**

1. Spiritual life
ISBN 0-8112-0570-3 (pa)

This volume is based on "notes written during [Merton's] last journey which took him to the monasteries of the Orient and ended with his accidental death in Bangkok." Libr J

Includes bibliography

Love and living; edited by Naomi Burton Stone & Patrick Hart. Farrar, Straus & Giroux 1979 232p o.p.; Harcourt Brace & Co. paperback available $7.95   **248**

1. Spiritual life
ISBN 0-15-653895-4 (pa)   LC 79-14717

These essays include "aspects of the perennial themes of love, death, life and the divine and also demonstrate the ease with which Merton assimilated the spiritual heritages of East and West." Publ Wkly

New seeds of contemplation. New Directions 1962 c1961 297p hardcover o.p. paperback available $8.95   **248**

1. Spiritual life
ISBN 0-8112-0099-X (pa)

First published 1949 with title: Seeds of contemplation and analyzed in Essay and general literature index

Meditations on integrity, fear, faith, liberty, love and renunciation

No man is an island. Harcourt Brace & Co. 1955 264p hardcover o.p. paperback available $7.95   **248**

1. Spiritual life 2. God
ISBN 0-15-665962-X (pa)

Also available Walker & Co. large print edition

Analyzed in Essay and general literature index

This book contains "innumerable answers for those who have attempted a spiritual way of life in day-to-day living and are confronted with doubts about real love, the will of God, wisdom of charity, asceticism, conscience, and sincerity." Cincinnati Public Libr

Peale, Norman Vincent
The power of positive living. Doubleday 1990 398p $18.95   **248**

1. Psychology, Pastoral 2. Psychology, Applied 3. Success
ISBN 0-385-41635-0   LC 90-36544

Also available Doubleday large print edition and in paperback from Fawcett Bks.

In this volume "Peale strings together dozens of personal success stories ('success' is always materialistic) that make readers feel good. Believing (in yourself, others, values, God) is all-important, and the stories of wealthy business executives who made it on their own grab center stage." Libr J

Teresa, Mother, 1910-
The love of Christ; spiritual counsels; edited by Georges Gorrée and Jean Barbier. Harper & Row 1982 115p $10.95   **248**

1. Christian life
ISBN 0-06-068229-9   LC 81-23746

A selection of Mother Teresa's writings, speeches, letters and commentaries. A chronology of her life is included

252 Texts of sermons

King, Martin Luther, 1929-1968
Strength to love; [by] Martin Luther King, Jr. Harper & Row 1963 146p o.p.; Fortress Press paperback available $7.95   252
1. Sermons
ISBN 0-8006-1441-0 (pa)
Also available Walker & Co. large print edition
A collection of sermons addressing social injustice and racism
Includes bibliography

Marshall, Peter, 1902-1949
Mr. Jones, meet the Master; sermons and prayers. Revell 1949 192p o.p.; Baker Bk. House paperback available $8   252
1. Sermons 2. Prayers
ISBN 0-8007-5095-0 (pa)
A collection of sermons and prayers of the late chaplain of the Senate. The sermons were preached in the New York Avenue Presbyterian Church in Washington, D.C., and the prayers were offered in the United States Senate

Schweitzer, Albert, 1875-1965
Reverence for life; translated by Reginald Fuller. Harper & Row 1969 153p o.p.
            252
1. Sermons
Available in hardcover from Irvington Pubs.
Original German edition, 1966
This collection contains "seventeen meditations originally given at the Church of St. Nicolai in Strasbourg, 1900-19. . . . The messages included here are all based on New Testament scriptures and concern primarily the themes of gratitude, hope, suffering, death, missions, and ethics." Choice

Tillich, Paul, 1886-1965
The eternal now. Scribner 1963 185p hardcover o.p. paperback available $9.95
            252
1. Sermons
ISBN 0-684-71907-X (pa)
Also available in hardcover from P. Smith
"A collection of sixteen sermons on man's isolation, loneliness, and perplexity and on God's eternal Presence." Chicago Public Libr
"This is a very good place to begin an acquaintance with Tillich's thought." Libr J

The new being. Scribner 1955 179p hardcover o.p. paperback available $9.95
            252
1. Sermons
ISBN 0-684-71908-8 (pa)
Also available in hardcover from P. Smith
"This book contains sermons which I gave mostly in colleges and universities, especially in Union Theological Seminary, New York, and in Connecticut College, New London, Connecticut." Preface

"Tillich's insights into the philosophical, psychological and sociological implications of Christianity are embodied in these sermons." N Y Her Trib Books

253.5 Pastoral counseling and spiritual direction

Peale, Norman Vincent
The positive principle today; how to renew and sustain the power of positive thinking. Prentice-Hall 1976 239p o.p.; Fawcett Bks. paperback available $5.95
            253.5
1. Psychology, Pastoral 2. Psychology, Applied 3. Success
ISBN 0-449-20029-9 (pa)
The author "expands on his theme [of positive thinking] by exploring ways of vitalizing our lives in a stressful environment." Publ Wkly

The power of positive thinking   253.5
1. Psychology, Pastoral 2. Psychology, Applied 3. Success
Hardcover and paperback editions available from various publishers. Also available Walker & Co. large print edition
First published 1952 by Prentice-Hall
The author argues that a positive attitude can change lives, win success and overcome obstacles

255 Religious congregations and orders

Bianco, Frank, 1931-
Voices of silence: lives of the Trappists today. Paragon House 1991 xx, 220p il $18.95   255
1. Trappists
ISBN 1-55778-305-5   LC 90-46762
Also available in paperback from Anchor Bks.
The author describes the lives of Trappist monks whom he observed in monasteries in the United States and France
"Seekers of all faiths will be intrigued by and gain respect for the contemplative life as portrayed in these pages." Publ Wkly
Includes bibliographic references

261 Christian social theology and interreligious relations and attitudes

Niebuhr, H. Richard (Helmut Richard), 1894-1962
Christ and culture. Harper & Row 1951 259p hardcover o.p. paperback available $12
            261
1. Sociology, Christian 2. Civilization, Christian 3. Culture
ISBN 0-06-130003-9 (pa)
Also available in hardcover from P. Smith

Niebuhr, H. Richard (Helmut Richard), 1894-1962—*Continued*

"Important, scholarly study presents five viewpoints of Christ and culture held over the centuries: (1) Christ against culture—a separation from 'the world;' (2) the Christ of culture—the identification of Christianity and civilization; (3) Christ above culture—the Thomist position; (4) Christ and culture in paradox—Luther's position; (5) Christ transforming culture—exemplified by Augustine and Calvin." Cincinnati Public Libr

261.2 Christianity and other systems of belief

Cox, Harvey Gallagher

Many mansions; a Christian's encounter with other faiths; [by] Harvey Cox. Beacon Press 1988 216p hardcover o.p. paperback available $12   **261.2**

1. Christianity and other religions
ISBN 0-8070-1213-0 (pa)   LC 88-47656

The author "here delineates his travels and explorations of how Jesus is perceived by adherents to Muslim, Buddhist, Hindu and Jewish faiths, as well as to the Catholic Church and Protestant denominations." Publ Wkly

"A warm and informative book that introduces some of the central issues confronting opponents of interfaith dialogue." N Y Times Book Rev

Includes bibliography

DiNoia, J. A., 1943-

The diversity of religions; a Christian perspective. Catholic Univ. of Am. Press 1992 199p $29.95; pa $17.95   **261.2**

1. Christianity and other religions 2. Theology
ISBN 0-8132-0763-0; 0-8132-0769-X (pa)
LC 91-33001

This volume on the theology of religions "explores new territories and recasts old debates in a fresh and intelligent manner. It will appeal to philosophers, theologians, indologists and those concerned with the meeting of Christianity and the world religions." Univ Press Books for Public and Second Sch Libr

Includes bibliographic references

261.5 Christianity and secular disciplines

Davies, P. C. W., 1946-

God and the new physics. Simon & Schuster 1983 255p il hardcover o.p. paperback available $11   **261.5**

1. Physics 2. Religion and science
ISBN 0-671-52806-8 (pa)   LC 83-14866

The author "outlines the physicist's view of the nature of time, space, and causality. He describes the way that natural processes can bring about things that were once thought to require the intervention of the Deity." Libr J

"The uninitiated reader will find in this volume brief presentations on quarks and black holes and a stimulating introduction to science as a helpful path in the search for God. Highly recommended for public and undergraduate libraries." Choice

Redondi, Pietro

Galileo heretic (Galileo eretico); translated by Raymond Rosenthal. Princeton Univ. Press 1987 356p il $49.50; pa $12.95
261.5

1. Galilei, Galileo, 1564-1642 2. Religion and science 3. Catholic Church—History
ISBN 0-691-08451-3; 0-691-02426-X (pa)
LC 86-30581

Original Italian edition, 1983

The author argues that an anonymous denunciation of the scientist for atomism, a physical theory thought to challenge Catholic orthodoxy concerning the Eucharist, was the real motive behind Galileo's trial. The accusation of Copernicanism was used by Pope Urban VIII, Redondi maintains, to shield Galileo from a more serious charge of heresy brought by the Jesuits

261.7 Christianity and political affairs

Weigel, George

The final revolution; the resistance church and the collapse of communism. Oxford Univ. Press 1992 255p $25   **261.7**

1. Communism and religion 2. Eastern Europe—Politics and government
ISBN 0-19-507160-3   LC 92-9607

In this study of the collapse of Soviet Communism, the author argues that, in addition to Mikhail Gorbachev and Ronald Reagan, "credit for the anti-Communist revolution should be given to another world figure, Pope John Paul II. It is Weigel's contention that the Pope's role, and the role of religious belief generally, have been much undervalued in the various assessments of the overthrow of Communism in Eastern Europe." Commentary

261.8 Christianity and socioeconomic problems

Berryman, Phillip

Liberation theology; essential facts about the revolutionary movement in Latin America—and beyond. Temple Univ. Press 1987 231p $34.95   **261.8**

1. Liberation theology 2. Catholic Church—Latin America
ISBN 0-87722-479-X   LC 87-162179

Also available in paperback from Pantheon Bks.

The author "recounts the changes in Catholic thinking in the 1960's that gave birth to liberation theology and how this in turn provided a religious justification for social action." N Y Times Book Rev

Includes bibliography

Cone, James H.

A black theology of liberation. 20th anniversary ed. Orbis Bks. 1990 xx, 214p pa $14.95   **261.8**

1. Church and race relations 2. Blacks—Religion
ISBN 0-88344-685-5   LC 90-43041

First published 1970 by Lippincott

Cone, James H.—*Continued*

The author "takes as his theme the belief that 'Christian theology is a theology of liberation.' He then proceeds to relate the struggle for black liberation to the development of black theology in reaction to the indifference of white Christians to the plight of their fellow church members." Libr J

Includes bibliographic references

Merton, Thomas, 1915-1968

The hidden ground of love; the letters of Thomas Merton on religious experience and social concerns; selected and edited by William H. Shannon. Farrar, Straus & Giroux 1985 669p hardcover o.p. paperback available $17.95   **261.8**

1. Church and social problems
ISBN 0-374-51963-3 (pa)   LC 84-26045

Also available in paperback from Harcourt Brace & Co.

A collection of Merton's letters addressing spiritual and social issues of the 1940s through the 1960s. Among his correspondents are: the Berrigans, Dorothy Day, Erich Fromm, Aldous Huxley, Pope John XXIII, Coretta Scott King and Paul Tillich

Seeds of destruction. Farrar, Straus & Giroux 1965 c1964 328p hardcover o.p. paperback available $8.95   **261.8**

1. Church and race relations 2. Christianity
ISBN 0-374-51586-7 (pa)

This volume is divided into three parts. Part one, Black revolution, contains two essays concerning the race question. Part two, The Diaspora, contains three essays on the role of the Catholic Church in a non-Catholic world. Part three, entitled Letters in a Time of Crisis, contains Fr. Merton's correspondence with such people as Jacques Maritain, the mayor of Hiroshima, James Baldwin, a Quaker, a Moslem, a rabbi, Dorothy Day, Mark Van Doren, and others

264 Public worship

Episcopal Church

The book of common prayer prices vary
264

Available in various bindings and editions
The official liturgy of the Episcopal Church

The **Macmillan** book of earliest Christian hymns; edited by F. Forrester Church and Terrence J. Mulry. Macmillan 1988 233p $19.95   **264**

1. Hymns
ISBN 0-02-525581-9   LC 88-15339

In this selection of "worship from Christianity's first 600 years . . . chapters draw on both early orthodox and gnostic traditions, the Johannine 'Odes of Solomon,' the New Testament Apocrypha, St. Ephrem's theological and pastoral 'Harp of the Spirit,' and the hagiographic and ascetic hymnody of the eastern church. . . . An excellent devotional anthology that is also a distinguished literary collection." Booklist

The **New** Westminster dictionary of liturgy and worship; edited by J. G. Davies. Westminster Press 1986 544p il $30
264

1. Liturgies—Dictionaries 2. Worship—Dictionaries
ISBN 0-664-21270-0   LC 86-9219

First published 1972 with title: The Westminster dictionary of worship

This dictionary offers an "ecumenical approach concerned with the structures and rationale of liturgical functions. Sects, rites, sacraments, and some subjects, e.g., architecture and vestments, are treated at length, with illustrations and bibliographies. . . . It relates historical background to contemporary subjects of interest, with fresh ideas on the role of women, liturgical dance and movement-prayer, cremation, childen and family worship, the disabled, drama, laity, law and worship, and media worship." Ref Sources for Small & Medium-sized Libr. 5th edition

266 Missions

Pettifer, Julian

Missionaries; [by] Julian Pettifer and Richard Bradley. BBC/Parkwest Publs. 1991 272p il $33.95   **266**

1. Missions 2. Missionaries, Christian
ISBN 0-563-20702-7   LC 91-72331

This companion volume to the PBS television series focuses on "Christian missions, and both the famous (e.g., Mother Theresa, Billy Graham) and the unusual (e.g., Pastor Bonnke) are depicted. . . . This highly readable and fascinating account is enhanced by a vivid array of photos, many in full color. Highly recommended." Libr J

Includes bibliographic references

269 Spiritual renewal

Balmer, Randall Herbert

Mine eyes have seen the glory; a journey into the evangelical subculture in America; [by] Randall Balmer. Oxford Univ. Press 1989 246p $24.95; pa $10.95   **269**

1. Evangelicalism   2. Fundamentalism   3. Pentecostalism
ISBN 0-19-505117-3; 0-19-507985-X (pa)

LC 88-34315

The author "presents a cross section of modern evangelical Christianity in America in 11 chapters each sketching some aspect of this world from church camps and seminaries to missions and tent meetings. Every chapter is a narrative account of the author's experiences and conversations plus his own interpretations." Libr J

Includes bibliographies

Sims, Patsy

Can somebody shout amen! St. Martin's Press 1988 234p $15.95   **269**

1. Revivals   2. United   States—Church   history
3. Evangelistic work
ISBN 0-312-01397-3   LC 87-27955

"A Thomas Dunne book"

This study of Southern revivalism contains chapters on such evangelists as H. Wayne Simmons, Tommy Walker, R.W. Schambach, Ernest Angley, H. Richard

Sims, Patsy—*Continued*

Hall, and Mike Shreve, and considers their beliefs and activities

"There is much to be thankful for here. Ms. Sims has ventured out onto the geographical margins and into the institutional gaps, and she has taken us with her. . . . She has conveyed, without preaching, her conviction that it is important to understand them." N Y Times Book Rev

Includes bibliography

270 Christian church history

Atlas of the Christian church; edited by Henry Chadwick and G.R. Evans. Facts on File 1987 240p il maps $45   **270**

1. Church history
ISBN 0-8160-1643-7   LC 86-32894

"An Equinox book"

"This is a beautifully illustrated handbook on the development of Christianity, not a true atlas. The text is elegant, concise, and highlighted with lavish color in photographs, maps, charts, and diagrams. A vast amount of information is packed into this slim volume, which should be useful to all libraries in need of readable introductory material on the history of Christianity." Ref Sources for Small & Medium-sized Libr. 5th edition

Includes bibliography

Dictionary of Pentecostal and charismatic movements; Stanley M. Burgess and Gary B. McGee, editors; Patrick H. Alexander, associate editor. Regency Ref. Lib. 1988 914p il $34.99   **270**

1. Pentecostalism—Dictionaries
ISBN 0-310-44100-5   LC 88-28341

"A biographical, biblical, theological, and topical dictionary of Pentecostal and charismatic movements in North America and Europe. Signed articles with bibliographies provide coverage of pentecostal denominations with more than 2000 members. Historical and contemporary photographs." Ref Sources for Small & Medium-sized Libr. 5th edition

Dictionary of the ecumenical movement; edited by Nicholas Lossky [et al.] Eerdmans 1991 1196p il $79.99   **270**

1. Christian unity—Dictionaries
ISBN 0-8028-2428-5   LC 91-180933

In this dictionary "doctrinal themes, ecumenical activity in every region of the world, historical overviews of interdenominational dialogue, and Christian perspectives on sociopolitical and ethical issues are all given thorough coverage, as are the many people instrumental in the movement. Representative entries include birth control, Buddhist-Christian dialogue, human rights, ordination, John Paul II, and Theology—African. Each entry ends with a short bibliography for further study." Am Libr

Encyclopedia of the early church; produced by the Institutum Patristicum Augustinianum and edited by Angelo Di Berardino; translated from the Italian by Adrian Walford; with a foreword and bibliographic amendments by W.H.C. Frend. Oxford Univ. Press 1992 2v il maps set $195   **270**

1. Early Christian literature—Dictionaries 2. Church history—30(ca.)-600, Early church—Dictionaries
ISBN 0-19-520892-7   LC 91-23934

Original Italian edition, 1983-1988

This reference work provides "concise and precise information on all topics concerning the first eight centuries of Chistianity. Valuable to classicists, historians, archaeologists, philosophers, and philologists as well as theologians, the work extends the knowledge of how Christianity evolved. Approximately 2,300 articles by a range of scholars from many disciplines focus on all the major and most of the minor people, works, ideas, and issues of the formative period of Christianity." Univ Press Books for Public and Second Sch Libr

Lane Fox, Robin

Pagans and Christians. Knopf 1987 799p maps o.p.; HarperSanFrancisco paperback available $20   **270**

1. Christianity and other religions 2. Rome—Religion 3. Church history—30(ca.)-600, Early church
ISBN 0-06-062852-9 (pa)   LC 86-2752

An "historical study of pagans and Christians together, as they lived and worked in the same cities, with the same language, and within the same empire. The author uses not only textual sources but also inscriptions and other archaeological data to depict life in the years before and after the conversion of Constantine in A.D. 313." Booklist

Includes bibliography

Latourette, Kenneth Scott, 1884-1968

A history of Christianity. rev ed. Harper & Row 1975 2v maps hardcover o.p. paperbacks available ea $20   **270**

1. Church history
First published 1953

Contents: v1 To A.D. 1500 (ISBN 0-06-064952-6) cover title: Beginnings to 1500; v2 A.D. 1500-A.D. 1975 (ISBN 0-06-064953-4) cover title: Reformation to the present

This book endeavors "to be a well-rounded summary of the entire history of Christianity in all its phases and in its setting in the human scene." Preface

The **Oxford** illustrated history of Christianity; edited by John McManners. Oxford Univ. Press 1990 724p il maps $45; pa $25   **270**

1. Church history
ISBN 0-19-822928-3; 0-19-285259-0 (pa)
          LC 90-30280

"This volume provides a relatively concise overview of the major Occidental religion in three parts: 'From the Origins to 1800,' 'Christianity since 1800,' and 'Christianity Today and Tomorrow.' The chapters, each by a prominent scholar, trace the development of Christian belief, Christianity's relationship to other world religions,

The Oxford illustrated history of Christianity—*Continued*
and the practice of Christianity in different parts of the
world." Booklist
This is a work "full of wise insights, balance of information, reliable scholarship and precision of writing."
Times Lit Suppl

Includes bibliographic references

270.6   Christian church— Reformation

The **Reformation**; edited by Pierre Chaunu.
St. Martin's Press 1990 c1986 296p il
$49.95   **270.6**
1. Reformation 2. Calvinism
ISBN 0-312-03750-3   LC 89-37008

Original French edition, 1986
"Composed in the spirit of 'true ecumenism,' 'The
reformation' combines the efforts of 17 scholars of
various religious and academic persuasions. . . . Framed
by editor Chaunu's pointed and debatable reflections on
the signs of the times, the essays, diverse and expert,
cover all aspects of the subject, from theology to daily
life, and they are abundantly reinforced by a splendid
menu of pictures." Christ Sci Monit

Includes bibliographic references

Spitz, Lewis William, 1922-
The Protestant reformation, 1517-1559.
Harper & Row 1985 444p il (Rise of
modern Europe) hardcover o.p. paperback
available $12   **270.6**
1. Reformation
ISBN 0-06-132069-2 (pa)   LC 83-48805

The author analyzes the events of the Protestant
Reformation and discusses its significance and influence
on the course of European history
This book "is history at its best—broadly researched,
skillfully written, judiciously argued, and also spiritually
insightful." Christ Today

Includes bibliography

271   Religious orders in church history

Barthel, Manfred, 1924-
The Jesuits; history & legend of the
Society of Jesus; translated & adapted by
Mark Howson. Morrow 1984 324p
hardcover o.p. paperback available $8.70
      271
1. Jesuits
ISBN 0-688-06970-3 (pa)   LC 84-60446

The author tells "the story of Ignatius Loyola and of
the generations of priests who have followed his call.
Barthel focuses upon the multiple roles Jesuits have
adopted throughout history and their contributions to
society as scholars, missionaries, playwrights, scientists,
etc." Booklist
Although this book "breaks no significant new ground,
it does offer a fascinating compendium of observations."
N Y Times Book Rev

Includes bibliography

272   Persecutions in church history

Foxe, John, 1516-1587
Foxe's Book of martyrs   **272**
1. Martyrs 2. Persecution 3. Church history
Hardcover and paperback editions available from
various publishers
First complete version published 1563 in England
under title: Actes and monuments of these latter and
perilous days
"The *Actes and Monuments* was tremendously influential, being used practically as a companion volume to
the Bible in English churches and households for many
years. The work is of interest historically for its many
accounts of the deaths of contemporary Protestant martyrs." Reader's Ency. 3d edition

277   Christian Church—North America

Dictionary of Christianity in America;
coordinating editor, Daniel G. Reid;
consulting editors, Robert D. Linder,
Bruce L. Shelley, Harry S. Stout.
InterVarsity Press 1990 xxix, 1305p $44.99
      277
1. Christianity—Dictionaries 2. United States—Church
history—Dictionaries
ISBN 0-8308-1776-X   LC 89-29953

"This convenient source for authoritative information
on Christianity in English-speaking North America gives
a broad coverage in a historical perspective. Information
on movements, denominations, and individuals who left
their mark on Christianity are among the 4,000 topics
included in this source. Signed articles, many
bibliographies, and cross-references are useful features."
Ref Sources for Small & Medium-sized Libr. 5th edition

Yearbook of American and Canadian
churches. Abingdon Press pa $29.95 **277**
1. Churches—United States—Directories 2. Churches—Canada—Directories
ISSN 0195-9043
Annual. First published 1916. Title and publisher vary
"Directory, statistical, and historical information on
many religious and ecumenical organizations and service
agencies, accredited seminaries, colleges and universities,
and depositories of church history materials. Also a list
of religious periodicals." Ref Sources for Small &
Medium-sized Libr. 5th edition

277.3   Christian Church—United States

Backman, Milton Vaughn
Christian churches of America; origins and
beliefs; [by] Milton V. Backman, Jr. rev ed.
Scribner 1983 278p il o.p.; Macmillan
paperback available $34   **277.3**
1. United States—Church history 2. United States—
Religion
ISBN 0-02-305090-X (pa)   LC 83-8695
First published 1976 by Brigham Young University
Press

Backman, Milton Vaughn—*Continued*
This is a "guidebook to the history and beliefs of the major Christian denominations in the United States, updated to include the charismatic and fundamentalist movements that have gained much influence and membership in recent years. This invaluable reference book, presented in a scholarly, objective manner, makes for interesting reading for both clergy and laypersons." Booklist

Includes bibliography

Hudson, Winthrop Still
Religion in America; an historical account of the development of American religious life; [by] Winthrop S. Hudson, John Corrigan. 5th ed. Macmillan 1992 450p pa $32   **277.3**
1. United States—Religion
ISBN 0-02-357830-0   LC 91-3853
First published 1965
A survey of American religious life from 1607 to the present
Includes bibliography

Lincoln, C. Eric (Charles Eric), 1924-
The black church in the African American experience; [by] C. Eric Lincoln and Lawrence H. Mamiya. Duke Univ. Press 1990   519p   hardcover   o.p.   paperback available $19.95   **277.3**
1. Blacks—Religion 2. United States—Church history
ISBN 0-8223-1073-2 (pa)   LC 90-34050
This book was "developed from a ten-year field study that investigated the black church as it relates to the history of African Americans and to contemporary black culture. . . . [It considers] the church's relationships to politics, economics, women (attitudes of clergy as pastors), youth, music, civil rights, and trends for the next century." Libr J
Includes bibliography

Marty, Martin E., 1928-
Modern American religion. University of Chicago Press 1986-1991 2v il v1 $24.95; v2 $27.50   **277.3**
1. United States—Religion 2. United States—Church history   LC 85-16524
Contents: v1 The irony of it all, 1893-1919 (ISBN 0-226-50893-5); v2 The noise of conflict, 1919-1941 (ISBN 0-226-50895-1)
The first two titles of a projected four volume cultural history of religion in America
This "is a cultural history, with the emphasis on the American aspect of religion during the decades under discussion." Booklist
Includes bibliographic references

Pilgrims in their own land; 500 years of American religion. Little, Brown 1984 500p il $25   **277.3**
1. United States—Church history 2. United States—Religion
ISBN 0-316-54867-7   LC 84-821
Also available in paperback from Penguin Bks.

This book examines "the force of religion in the United States since colonial times. Marty considers not only the religious beliefs and rituals brought to America by the various European settlers, but also those of native Americans. The clashes between Protestant, Catholic, Judaic, and other religious groups are perceived in light of their influence upon the development of this nation up to the present." Booklist

280 Christian denominations and sects

Mead, Frank Spencer, 1898-1982
Handbook of denominations in the United States; [by] Frank S. Mead. Abingdon Press $13.95   **280**
1. Sects 2. United States—Religion
First published 1951. (9th edition 1990) Periodically revised
9th edition edited by Samuel S. Hill
"History and present structure of Christian religious bodies in the United States. Reports on doctrines of different churches. Includes bibliography and index." NY Public Libr Book of How & Where to Look It Up

282 Roman Catholic Church

Catholic almanac. Our Sunday Visitor pa $15.95   **282**
1. Catholic Church—Directories 2. Almanacs
ISSN 0069-1208
Annual. First published 1904. Title varies
This almanac "includes information on the whole panoply of matters touching on the Catholic Church. Sections are devoted to such things as Protestant churches, ecumenism, events of the year, papal journeys, the hierarchy of the Catholic Church, brief biographies of cardinals and American bishops, the books of the Bible, national Catholic conferences, the Catholic population of the United States, missions, and houses of retreat and renewal." Recomm Ref Books in Paperback. 2d edition

The Catholic encyclopedia; Robert C. Broderick, editor; Virginia Broderick, illustrator. rev and updated ed. Nelson, T. 1987 613p pa $19.99   **282**
1. Catholic Church—Dictionaries
ISBN 0-8407-3175-2   LC 86-18245
First published 1976
"This work is best used to look up a broad range of traditional Catholic terms, such as the papacy, indulgences, and canonization, and its views on such things as Marxism, evolution, an euthanasia. New articles are added on such topics as liberation theology and the ordination of women, but the main thrust is historical." Recomm Ref Books in Paperback. 2d edition

Deedy, John G.
The Catholic fact book. Thomas More Press 1986 412p hardcover o.p. paperback available $15.95   **282**
1. Catholic Church—Dictionaries
ISBN 0-88347-252-X (pa)   LC 86-215323

Deedy, John G.—*Continued*
"This one-volume fact book in dictionary style includes almanac data, intended to explain Roman Catholicism to the Catholic and non-Catholic alike. A historical section includes the saints and famous Catholics. The beliefs, teachings, dogmas, traditions, rituals, sacraments, and sacramentals are explained. Descriptions are given of various institutions, orders, organizations, movements, and the communication media. A miscellany section covers other items." Ref Sources for Small & Medium-sized Libr. 5th edition

Dolan, Jay P., 1936-
The American Catholic experience; a social history from colonial times to the present. Doubleday 1985 504p o.p.; University of Notre Dame Press paperback available $15.95   **282**
1. Catholic Church—United States—History 2. United States—Church history
ISBN 0-268-00639-3 (pa)   LC 84-26026
The author presents a "history of American Catholicism from colonial times to the present. Coverage includes the inception of the Spanish and French mission in North America, the era of the beginning of the American republic, the nineteenth-century influx of immigrant Catholics, and the 'Catholic Reformation' in the years leading up to and following the Second Vatican Council." Booklist
"Elucidating a vast subject with engaging economy, this popular history of the people who comprise the country's single largest religious denomination sets a standard for future researchers." Publ Wkly

Greeley, Andrew M., 1928-
The Catholic myth; the behavior and beliefs of American Catholics. Scribner 1990 322p $21.95   **282**
1. Catholic Church—United States 2. Catholics—United States
ISBN 0-684-19184-9   LC 89-39259
Also available in paperback from Macmillan
"Greeley debunks the popular myth that American Catholicism is virtually moribund. Employing . . . concrete sociological data to support his thesis, he asserts that Catholicism is thriving in the U.S. Though many American Catholics have lost faith in the institutionalized hierarchy of the Church, they remain assiduously devoted to the essential poetry of their religion." Booklist
"This lively, readable assessment of contemporary Catholicism may affront some readers, but will likely stimulate and challenge others." Publ Wkly

Hardon, John A.
Modern Catholic dictionary. Doubleday 1980 635p pa $22.50   **282**
1. Catholic Church—Dictionaries 2. Theology—Dictionaries
ISBN 0-385-12162-8   LC 77-82945
Also available in abridged paperback edition with title: Pocket Catholic dictionary for $7.95 (ISBN 0-385-23238-1)
This work defines "terms in many fields from a Catholic viewpoint, while also covering the significant concepts of the Roman Catholic faith, morals, rituals, canon law, liturgy, mysticism, spirituality, history, and organization. . . . Included are biographies of biblical persons, descriptions of selected organizations and

institutes, abbreviations, and basic terms from scholastic philosophy and theology." Libr J

Hennesey, James J.
American Catholics; a history of the Roman Catholic community in the United States; with a foreword by John Tracy Ellis. Oxford Univ. Press 1981 397p $35; pa $13.95   **282**
1. Catholics—United States 2. Catholic Church—United States—History
ISBN 0-19-502946-1; 0-19-503268-3 (pa) LC 81-1074
A general survey of American Catholic history. Emphasis is placed on social, political and moral issues confronting the church
"This fascinating book will be permanently useful for browsing, for looking things up, for checking a date here, a name there." N Y Times Book Rev

Lernoux, Penny, 1940-1989
People of God; the struggle for world Catholicism. Viking 1989 466p o.p.; Penguin Bks. paperback available $9.95   **282**
1. Christianity and politics 2. Catholic Church
ISBN 0-14-009816-X (pa)   LC 88-40282
"Lernoux examines the rift between the Catholic church of Rome and its followers throughout the world, especially in the U.S. and Latin America." Booklist
The author "offers a fresh perspective on the challenges of Vatican II in the modern-day church, presenting her views cogently, evenhandedly, and with insight." Libr J
Includes bibliography

New Catholic encyclopedia; prepared by an editorial staff at the Catholic University of America. Heraty & Assocs. 1981 c1967-1979 17v + supplement il set $875   **282**
1. Catholic Church—Dictionaries 2. Theology—Dictionaries
ISBN 0-07-010235-X   LC 80-84921
A reprint of the 15 volume set published 1967 and the two supplementary volumes designated 16 and 17, published 1974 and 1979. Also included in price of set is supplementary volume 18 published 1989
"Highly objective, modern, and ecumenical in tone, with many non-Catholic contributors, its high level of scholarship is generally more readable than its predecessor. Partially replaces and supersedes the *Catholic encyclopedia*, which should be retained for older, more historical points of view. Recent supplementary volumes reflect the accelerating tempo of change in the world and in the church." Ref Sources for Small & Medium-sized Libr. 5th edition
Includes bibliographies

Occhiogrosso, Peter
Once a Catholic; prominent Catholics and ex-Catholics discuss the influence of the Church on their lives and work. Houghton Mifflin 1987 371p o.p.; Ballantine Bks. paperback available $4.95   **282**
1. Catholics 2. Catholic Church—United States
ISBN 0-345-35670-5 (pa)   LC 87-2772

Occhiogrosso, Peter—*Continued*

The twenty-six current and former Catholics interviewed "share their attitudes toward the Church as authority, culture, mystery, and purveyor of an often-skewed sexuality." Libr J

"There is much to ponder in these pages about the past, present, and possible future of America's largest cultural-denominational group. A thoughtful collection likely to provoke discussion." Choice

Includes bibliography

The **Official** Catholic directory. Bowker $169

282

1. Catholic Church—Directories
ISSN 0078-3854

Also available with midyear supplement for $199

Annual. First published 1886 with title: Hoffman's Catholic directory, almanac and clergy list. Title varies

"Useful annual, containing a large amount of detailed directory, institutional, and statistical information about the organization, clergy, churches, missions, schools, religious orders, etc., of the Catholic church in the United States and its possessions. Coverage varies." Sheehy. Guide to Ref Books. 10th edition

Ranke-Heinemann, Uta, 1927-

Eunuchs for the kingdom of heaven; women, sexuality and the Catholic Church; translated by Peter Heinegg. Doubleday 1990 360p $21.95

282

1. Christian ethics 2. Women in Christianity 3. Sexual ethics
ISBN 0-385-26527-1   LC 89-48951

Also available in paperback from Penguin Bks.

Original German edition, 1988

"A historical critique of the Roman Catholic Church's attitude toward women and sexuality by a German Catholic and professor of the history of religion; few theologians have targeted church sexual teaching from so many angles or as trenchantly." N Y Times Book Rev

Includes bibliographic references

Rice, David, 1945-

Shattered vows; priests who leave. Morrow 1990 215p $18.95

282

1. Ex-priests 2. Catholic Church—Clergy
ISBN 0-688-07805-2   LC 90-39287

Also available in paperback from Liguori Publs.

The author's "subject is the exodus of 100,000 Catholic priests from the church in the past 20 years, and he has criss-crossed the globe in collecting personal stories on this theme." New Statesman Soc

The author "cannot be commended enough for his brilliant study." Libr J

Includes bibliographic references

Woodward, Kenneth L.

Making saints; how the Catholic Church determines who becomes a saint, who doesn't, and why. Simon & Schuster 1990 461p il hardcover o.p. paperback available $12

282

1. Christian saints 2. Catholic Church
ISBN 0-671-74743-6 (pa)   LC 90-10117

A study of the politics and procedures of the modern process of canonization in the Roman Catholic church

This is "the most comprehensive, critical and up-to-date look at saint making so far written." N Y Times Book Rev

Includes bibliography

285 Presbyterian churches, Reformed churches centered in America, Congregational churches

Lesser, M. X.

Jonathan Edwards. Twayne Pubs. 1988 153p (Twayne's United States authors ser) $22.95

285

1. Edwards, Jonathan, 1703-1758
ISBN 0-8057-7519-6   LC 87-34994

The author "draws on Edward's letters, diaries, journals and other personal writings to provide a . . . sketch of his life. Presenting his writings as a series of arguments for the Calvinist doctrine of divine sovereignty, he reviews Edwards's complete career." Publisher's note

Includes bibliography

289 Other denominations and sects

Sprigg, June

Shaker—life, work, and art; [by] June Sprigg and David Larkin; photographs by Michael Freeman. Stewart, Tabori & Chang 1987 272p il $50

289

1. Shakers
ISBN 1-55670-011-3   LC 87-9957

Also available in paperback from Houghton Mifflin

"A David Larkin book"

An illustrated look at Shaker's history, lifestyle, religious practices, and crafts

Includes bibliography

Stein, Stephen J., 1940-

The Shaker experience in America; a history of the United Society of Believers. Yale Univ. Press 1992 xx, 554p il $40

289

1. Shakers
ISBN 0-300-05139-5   LC 91-30836

A historical look at the evolution of Shakerism focusing on the movement's cultural values, religion and artifacts

Includes bibliographic references

289.3 Latter-Day Saints (Mormons)

Book of Mormon

The Book of Mormon. Herald House prices vary

289.3

1. Mormons

Available in various bindings and editions

Book of Mormon—_Continued_
First published 1830

"Based on golden plates which Joseph Smith claimed were revealed to him, and which he unearthed from Cumorah Hill, New York, this book is roughly similar in structure to the _Bible_. . . . Emphasized are the doctrines of pre-existence, perfection, the after-life, and Christ's second coming." Haydn. Thesaurus of Book Dig

Bushman, Richard L., 1931-
Joseph Smith and the beginnings of Mormonism. University of Ill. Press 1984 262p maps $24.95; pa $10.95   **289.3**

1. Smith, Joseph, 1805-1844 2. Church of Jesus Christ of Latter-day Saints
ISBN 0-252-01143-0; 0-252-06012-1 (pa)   LC 84-2451

The author surveys the historical background of the Mormon church with particular emphasis on the spiritual growth of its founder, Joseph Smith

"Resulting from many years of careful research and reflections, this book will stand for decades as a major contribution in the field." Choice

Includes bibliography

Coates, James, 1943-
In Mormon circles; gentiles, jack Mormons, and Latter-Day Saints. Addison-Wesley 1990 235p il $22.95; pa $12.45   **289.3**

1. Mormons 2. Church of Jesus Christ of Latter-day Saints
ISBN 0-201-51758-2; 0-201-60811-1 (pa)
     LC 90-42231

"Writing as an outsider, though with a deep appreciation of the Latter-day Saints, Coates traces the history of the sect and the various controversies surrounding it, including the issues of polygamy, blood atonement, and fundamentalism. . . . A fascinating look at the interface between religion and culture." Booklist

Includes bibliographic references

Shipps, Jan, 1929-
Mormonism; the story of a new religious tradition. University of Ill. Press 1985 211p il hardcover o.p. paperback available $12.95   **289.3**

1. Church of Jesus Christ of Latter-day Saints 2. Mormons
ISBN 0-252-01417-0 (pa)   LC 84-2672

An introduction to the origin, development, social structure, and dogma of the Church of Jesus Christ of Latter-day Saints

"Superbly researched and well written, this is a landmark study that will profoundly shape the thinking of future students of Mormonism." Libr J

Includes bibliography

Tobler, Douglas F.
The history of the Mormons; in photographs and text: 1830 to the present; [by] Douglas F. Tobler and Nelson B. Wadsworth. St. Martin's Press 1989 294p il $17.95   **289.3**

1. Church of Jesus Christ of Latter-day Saints
ISBN 0-312-03359-1   LC 89-32762

"Intended for the general reader, this book has three goals: to give a survey of Mormon history, to provide background on the history of photographing the Mormons, and finally to provide a visual record with abundant, interesting, and often beautiful historical photographs." Libr J

Includes bibliographic references

289.5   Church of Christ, Scientist (Christian Science)

Eddy, Mary Baker, 1821-1910
Science and health, with key to the Scriptures; Trustees under the will of Mary Baker G. Eddy. Christian Science Pub. Soc. prices vary   **289.5**

1. Christian Science
Available in various bindings
First published 1875

This work is the foundation of the Christian Science religion, setting forth Mrs. Baker's interpretations of the Holy Scriptures and the method of healing. It has not been revised since her death in 1910

289.6   Society of Friends (Quakers)

Barbour, Hugh
The Quakers; [by] Hugh Barbour and J. William Frost. Greenwood Press 1988 407p maps (Denominations in America) $65
     289.6

1. Society of Friends
ISBN 0-313-22816-7   LC 88-10240

"In the first part of this work, [the authors] sketch the English origins of the [Quaker] movement, devoting primary attention to the events and personalities that shaped the various branches of the American denomination. The second part of their book consists of biographical sketches of persons important in the development of Quakerism in America." Choice

This book is "a very important addition to Quaker history." J Am Hist

Includes bibliography

Trueblood, Elton, 1900-
The people called Quakers. Harper & Row 1966 298p o.p.; Friends United Press paperback available $10.95   **289.6**

1. Society of Friends
ISBN 0-913408-02-6 (pa)

"The author traces the development of Quakerism, its beliefs, practices and original contributions to religious thought, using the approach of a religious philosopher rather than that of a historian." Chicago Public Libr

289.7   Mennonite churches

Amish roots; a treasury of history, wisdom, and lore; [edited by] John A. Hostetler. Johns Hopkins Univ. Press 1989 319p il $35; pa $16.95   **289.7**
1. Amish
ISBN 0-8018-3769-3; 0-8018-4402-9 (pa)
                                                   LC 88-31688
This is a compilation of "writing by and about the Amish from journals and letters, family and farm records, newspaper stories, poems, songs and stories. Ranging from the observations of the first Anabaptist immigrants in the 1700s to the present, the over 150 entries—commenting on church, family life, work, school and the rich Amish agricultural heritage—form a remarkably complete portrait." Publ Wkly
Includes bibliography

Hostetler, John A., 1918-
Amish society. 4th ed. Johns Hopkins Univ. Press 1993 435p il maps $45; pa $14.95   **289.7**
1. Amish
ISBN 0-8018-4441-X; 0-8018-4442-8 (pa)
                                                   LC 92-19304
First published 1963
This book discusses the sectarian origins of the Amish, immigration history, family and community life, population trends, farming practices, technological innovations, education, medicine and the effects of government regulation
Includes bibliographic references

Hutterite society. Johns Hopkins Univ. Press 1974 403p il maps $49.50   **289.7**
1. Hutterian Society of Brothers
ISBN 0-8018-1584-3   LC 74-6827
An introduction to the history, culture and social structure of the Hutterites, a Mennonite sect of North America
"Hostetler succeeds, not only with his analysis but with his well-written prose, his haunting illustrations and his carefully worked-out and charted data." Libr J

Kraybill, Donald B.
The riddle of Amish culture. Johns Hopkins Univ. Press 1989 304p il maps $40; pa $9.95   **289.7**
1. Amish
ISBN 0-8018-3681-6; 0-8018-3682-4 (pa)
                                                   LC 88-19868
This study "examines the history of Amish adherence to tradition and adaptation to innovation within Lancaster County, Pennsylvania." Booklist
Includes bibliography

The **Mennonite** encyclopedia; a comprehensive reference work on the Anabaptist-Mennonite movement. Herald Press 1955-1959 4v set $160   **289.7**
1. Mennonites—Dictionaries
ISBN 0-8361-1018-8
Supplementary volume, designated volume 5, published 1990 available $80 (ISBN 0-8361-3105-3)

"Treats historical and contemporary topics relating to the Anabaptist-Mennonite movement from its beginning in the 16th century to the present time. Covers theology, ethics, history, and biography with special emphasis on existing and extinct congregations and institutions. Articles vary in length from a few lines to several columns, are signed, and include bibliographies." Sheehy. Guide to Ref Books. 10th edition

Seitz, Ruth Hoover
Amish ways; photography by Blair Seitz. RB Bks. 1991 117p il $24.95   **289.7**
1. Amish
ISBN 1-879441-77-2   LC 90-063838
"Focusing mainly on Lancaster County, Pa., the major locus of the 'plain people' settlement, which was established there in the 1720s, the photos pause briefly at other Amish and Mennonite communities in Ohio and Canada. The text provides a historical context as well as intimate glimpses of the daily life that promotes continuity of values and skills from generation to generation." Publ Wkly

291   Comparative religion and religious mythology

Anderson, Sherry Ruth
The feminine face of God; the unfolding of the sacred in women; [by] Sherry Ruth Anderson and Patricia Hopkins. Bantam Bks. 1991 253p $20; pa $12   **291**
1. Women—Religious life 2. Femininity of God
ISBN 0-553-07561-6; 0-553-35266-0 (pa) LC 91-6657
This book is "an attempt to see the divine face as mirrored on the faces of more than 100 women from all walks of life who were willing to describe their inner lives in open and intimate detail. . . . What these women have in common, the authors tell us, is that they were willing to trust their own essential natures and become their own teachers." N Y Times Book Rev
Includes bibliographic references

Appel, Willa
Cults in America; programmed for paradise. Holt & Co. 1983 204p hardcover o.p. paperback available $8.95   **291**
1. Cults 2. United States—Religion
ISBN 0-8050-0524-2 (pa)   LC 82-15538
The author examines various cults (Unification Church, Hare Krishnas, etc.) and analyzes how they succeed in American society
This book is "a readable and useful introduction to a fascinating and complex subject." Sci Books Films
Includes bibliography

Bloom, Harold, 1930-
The American religion; the emergence of the post-Christian nation. Simon & Schuster 1992 288p $22; pa $12   **291**
1. United States—Religion 2. Sects 3. Gnosticism
ISBN 0-671-67997-X; 0-671-86737-7 (pa)
                                                   LC 91-47559
"Bloom claims that American religion is more gnostic than Christian. He sees this American Gnosis expressed most powerfully in early Mormonism and in the modern

Bloom, Harold, 1930——*Continued*
Southern Baptist tradition, though it thrives in virtually every denomimation and cult. By turns brilliant and wrong-headed, provocative and repetitious, this work belongs in most libraries less for what it achieves than what it attempts." Libr J

Bulfinch, Thomas, 1796-1867
Bulfinch's mythology   **291**
1. Mythology 2. Folklore—Europe 3. Chivalry
Hardcover and paperback editions available from various publishers
First combined edition published 1913 by Crowell. Originally published in three separate volumes 1855, 1858 and 1862 respectively
Contents: The age of fable; The age of chivalry; Legends of Charlemagne
"The classic work on mythology, Bulfinch's gives brief summations of Greek, Roman, Norse, Arthurian, and other miscellaneous myths and includes notes on the *Iliad*, the *Odyssey*, and the *Aeneid*." N Y Public Libr Book of How & Where to Look It Up

Campbell, Joseph, 1904-1987
Historical atlas of world mythology. HarperCollins Pubs. 1988-1989 2v in 5 parts il maps ea $50   **291**
1. Mythology
Each part also available in paperback for $24.95
Volume one first published 1983 by Alfred van der Marck Eds.
Contents: v1 The way of the animal powers: pt 1 Mythologies of the primitive hunters and gatherers (ISBN 0-06-055148-8); pt2 Mythologies of the great hunt (ISBN 0-06-055149-6); v2 The way of the seeded earth: pt 1 The sacrifice (ISBN 0-06-055150-X); pt2 Mythologies of the primitive planters: the northern Americas (ISBN 0-06-055158-5); pt3 Mythologies of the primitive planters: the middle and southern Americas (ISBN 0-06-055159-3)
"No one but Joseph Campbell could conceive of such a scheme or carry it out as boldly as he does." N Y Times Book Rev

The masks of God. Viking 1959-1968 4v o.p.; Penguin Bks. paperbacks available ea $9.95   **291**
1. Mythology 2. Mythology in literature
Contents: v1 Primitive mythology (ISBN0-14-004304-7); v2 Oriental mythology (ISBN 0-14-004305-5); v3 Occidental mythology (ISBN 0-14-004306-3); v4 Creative mythology (ISBN 0-14-004307-1)
In the first three volumes the author deals "with the anonymous mythological past; in . . . [the final volume he shifts] the emphasis to individual creators of modern myths—from Dante to James Joyce, Thomas Mann, and T.S. Eliot." Libr J
Includes bibliographies

The mythic image; assisted by M. J. Abadie. Princeton Univ. Press 1975 c1974 552p il maps hardcover o.p. paperback available $24.95   **291**
1. Mythology 2. Symbolism
ISBN 0-691-01839-1 (pa)
"Bollingen series C"

Starting with the relation of dreams to myth, Campbell interweaves nonliterate folk traditions with those of the "literate civilizations that culminated in the triad of the great world religions, Buddhism, Christianity, and Islam." Publisher's note
Campbell "manages to be selective and brief while avoiding superficiality. It's heady stuff. . . . Yet it is convincing, and elegantly supported by hundreds of excellent reproductions of art." Newsweek
Includes bibliographic references

The power of myth; [by] Joseph Campbell, with Bill Moyers; Betty Sue Flowers, editor. Doubleday 1988 231p il $35; pa $22.95   **291**
1. Mythology 2. Religious art and symbolism 3. Spiritual life
ISBN 0-385-24773-7; 0-385-24774-5 (pa)   LC 88-4218
This companion to a public television series records conversations between Campbell and Bill Moyers. Campbell reflects on themes and symbols from world religions and mythologies and explores their relevance for his own spiritual journey
"Campbell is the hero on his own voyage of discovery. This well-bound book on lovely paper with helpful illustrations from art is highly recommended for all libraries." Choice

Transformations of myth through time. Perennial Lib. 1990 263p il hardcover o.p. paperback available $17.95   **291**
1. Mythology
ISBN 0-06-096463-4 (pa)   LC 89-45788
"This book consists of 13 chapters, each of which is a slightly edited version of one of the lectures in the PBS series of the same title. Drawing on his vast knowledge, Campbell explains in simple language, with copious examples from all times and cultures, how the same myths occur everywhere in slightly different forms." Libr J

Earhart, H. Byron
Religions of Japan; many traditions within one sacred way. Harper & Row 1984 142p il (Religious traditions of the world) pa $10   **291**
1. Japan—Religion
ISBN 0-06-062112-5   LC 84-47722
Following a brief historical background on Japanese culture and society the author then discusses the country's religious traditions
Includes bibliography

Eastern mysteries; by the editors of Time-Life Books. Time-Life Bks. 1991 160p il (Mysteries of the unknown) $19.93   291
1. Asia—Religion   LC 90-11281
An illustrated look at Asiatic religion, spirituality and mysticism. The book also explores the growing appeal of Eastern faiths in the Western world
Includes bibliography

Eerdmans' handbook to the world's religions. Eerdmans 1982 448p il $29.95   291
1. Religions 2. Religion
ISBN 0-8028-3563-5   LC 82-137503

Eerdmans' handbook to the world's religions—*Continued*

This "work compresses essential, factual information on beliefs and practices of the world's religions, past and living. . . . The book is designed for rapid fact-finding, with charts, boxed information, bold headings and subheadings, and summaries. The whole is brightly, intelligently illustrated. A cross-referenced glossary of hundreds of terms and concepts concludes the work." Booklist

Eliade, Mircea, 1907-1986

The Eliade guide to world religions; [by] Mircea Eliade, Ioan P. Couliano, with Hillary S. Wiesner. HarperSanFrancisco 1991 301p $22.95   **291**

1. Religions
ISBN 0-06-062145-1   LC 90-56452

Intended as an abridgement of Eliade's 3 volume History of religious ideas (entered below), this work is largely based on the Encyclopedia of religion (entered in class 200.3)

This is a "guide to the world's major religious traditions, present and past. . . . The macro-dictionary contains . . . accounts of the thirty-three major religious traditions, from African religions to Zoroastrianism. The micro-dictionary offers both an index and brief identifications of key religious figures, sacred books, and spiritual themes." Publisher's note

This "work is unbiased and scholarly, yet accessible to the informed lay reader." Libr J

Includes bibliographic references

A history of religious ideas; translated from the French by Willard R. Trask. University of Chicago Press 1978-1985 3v pa ea $18.95   **291**

1. Religion 2. Religions   LC 77-16784

Volume one also available in hardcover for $27.50 (ISBN 0-226-20400-6)

Contents: v1 From the Stone Age to the Eleusinian mysteries, original French edition 1976 (ISBN 0-226-20401-4); v2 From Gautama Buddha to the triumph of Christianity, original French edition 1978 (ISBN 0-226-20403-0); v3 From Muhammad to the Age of Reform, original French edition 1983 (ISBN 0-226-20405-7)

Eliade has chosen "to focus on moments and movements in which religious creativity has found expression. He gives attention not only to the major religions but also to less familiar religious creations. . . . [The author has] contributed immeasurably to our understanding of the nature and varieties of religious experience." Christ Century

Includes bibliographies

The **Encyclopedia** of American religions: religious creeds; J. Gordon Melton, editor. Gale Res. 1988 xxiii, 838p $125   **291**

1. Creeds 2. Doctrinal theology
ISBN 0-8103-2132-7   LC 87-30384

New edition in preparation

"A compilation of more than 450 creeds, confessions, statements of faith, and summaries of doctrine of religious and spiritual groups in the United States and Canada." Title page

"Not intended to replace other sources, this volume emphasizes contemporaneity by including only creeds currently acknowledged. Texts are arranged by the 'religious family' groupings used in Melton's *Encyclopedia of American Religions* [entered in class 200.9]. A superb reference

that also makes fascinating reading; highly recommended." Libr J

Frazer, Sir James George, 1854-1941

The new golden bough; a new abridgment of the classic work; edited and with notes and foreword by Theodor H. Gaster. Phillips 1959 xxx, 738p $37.95   **291**

1. Mythology 2. Religions 3. Superstition
ISBN 0-87599-036-3

Also available in paperback from New Am. Lib.

First published with imprint Criterion Books

This edition is based on the 12 volumes of The golden bough and its supplements with revisions, commentary and annotations

"A comparative study of world religions, magic, vegetation and fertility beliefs and rites, kingship, taboos, totemism and the like." New Century Handb of Engl Lit

Includes bibliographic references

Hopfe, Lewis M., d. 1992

Religions of the world. 5th ed. Macmillan 1991 474p il pa $37   **291**

1. Religions
ISBN 0-02-357205-1   LC 90-43368

First published 1976 by Glencoe

New edition in preparation

In exploring the major religions of the world, the author traces the historical development of each, its founders, teachings, and present status

Includes bibliographic references

Leach, Marjorie, 1911-

Guide to the gods; edited by Michael Owen Jones, Frances Cattermole-Tally. ABC-CLIO 1992 995p $150   **291**

1. Gods and goddesses
ISBN 0-87436-591-0   LC 91-35820

This book "acts as a 'finding list' that identifies and classifies over 20,000 gods and goddesses. . . . In a unique anthropological approach, these many thousand beings are arranged, on the basis of their religious function and personal attributes, under eight major headings—Celestial, Atmospheric, Terrestrial, and so forth—and within these broad headings into 53 subgroupings such as love, war, fertility, and justice." Am Libr

For a fuller review see: Booklist, March 15, 1992

Includes bibliographic references

Leeming, David Adams, 1937-

The world of myth. Oxford Univ. Press 1990 362p il $24.95; pa $13.95   **291**

1. Mythology
ISBN 0-19-505601-9; 0-19-507475-0 (pa)
                                           LC 89-48070

This volume "is organized thematically, with sections on cosmic myths, myths of the gods, hero myths, and place and object myths. Modern myths, such as the idea of Earth as Gaia, intermingle . . . with their ancient counterparts." Booklist

Includes bibliographic references

Marty, Martin E., 1928-
The glory and the power; the fundamentalist challenge to the modern world; [by] Martin E. Marty and R. Scott Appleby. Beacon Press 1992 225p il $30; pa $15   **291**
1. Fundamentalism
ISBN 0-8070-1216-5; 0-8070-1217-3 (pa)
         LC 92-32840
"This work serves as a companion to a series of PBS and NPR documentaries which aired in June 1992. . . . The coverage includes interviews not only with Christian fundamentalists (from such groups as the Moral Majority and Operation Rescue), but also with members of the Israeli group Gush Emunin . . . and members of the Egyptian Muslim Brotherhood. The authors discuss the movements in an nonjudgmental manner, and provide keen insights into fundamentalism as a sociological phenomenon." Libr J
Includes bibliographic references

Melton, J. Gordon
Encyclopedic handbook of cults in America. rev & updated ed. Garland 1992 407p (Religious information systems ser) $65; pa $18.95   **291**
1. Cults
ISBN 0-8153-0502-8; 0-8153-1140-0 (pa)
         LC 92-11540
First published 1986
"A fascinating survey of cults that should provide answers to many questions on cult origins and founders, beliefs and practices, current status and controversies. The opening chapter surveys the topic of cults as alternative religion and is followed by sections reviewing thirty-seven movements active today. Counter-cult groups are discussed and an excellent section on violence and cults ends the book. Well written, thoroughly documented and indexed." Ref Sources for Small & Medium-sized Libr. 5th edition [review of 1986 edition]

Mythologies; compiled by Yves Bonnefoy; a restructured translation of Dictionnaire des mythologies et des religions des sociétés traditionnelles et du monde antique prepared under the direction of Wendy Doniger; translated by Gerald Honigsblum [et al.] University of Chicago Press 1991 2v il set $250   **291**
1. Mythology
ISBN 0-226-06453-0   LC 90-46982
Also available in four paperback editions: American, African and Old European mythologies (1993); Asian mythologies (1993); Greek and Egyptian mythologies (1992); Roman and European mythologies (1992)
Original French edition, 1981
This is a collection of 395 essays by French scholars on various aspects of mythology. "Volume 1 has chapters on Africa; the ancient Near East; the Celts, Norse, Slavs, Caucasians, and their neighbors; Greece; and Rome. Sections in volume 2 cover Western civilization in the Christian era; south Asia, Iran, and Buddhism; southeast Asia; east Asia and inner Asia; and the Americas and the South Pacific." Christ Sci Monit
This work is "fascinatingly original if somewhat quirky and idiosyncratic." Libr J
Includes bibliographic references

Walsh, Roger N.
The spirit of shamanism. Tarcher, J.P. 1990 285p $18.95   **291**
1. Shamanism
ISBN 0-87477-562-0   LC 89-48642
In this "guide to shamans' practices and beliefs, Walsh ranges from Iglulike Eskimos to South American Jivaro Indians to Tibetan yogis, tracing parallels between the shaman's work and the archetypal 'hero's journey' identified by Joseph Campbell. A shaman's effectiveness as a therapist or doctor, in Walsh's view, is due to a combination of placebo effects, spiritual insight into the patient's condition and, possibly, to paranormal abilities." Publ Wkly
Includes bibliography

World religions; from ancient history to the present; editor, Geoffrey Parrinder. Facts on File 1983 c1971 528p il $35; pa $15.95   **291**
1. Religions
ISBN 0-87196-129-6; 0-8160-1289-X (pa) LC 83-1510
First published 1971 with title: Religions of the world
This volume examines each religion in terms of its historical, geographical, social, international, and doctrinal contexts
Includes bibliography

291.03   Comparative religion— Encyclopedias and dictionaries

Cotterell, Arthur
A dictionary of world mythology. Putnam 1980 c1979 256p il hardcover o.p. paperback available $9.95   **291.03**
1. Mythology—Dictionaries
ISBN 0-399-50619-5 (pa)   LC 79-65889
First published 1979 in the United Kingdom
"Contains some five hundred brief entries for mythic figures and themes, arranged according to the seven 'great traditions of world mythology' (West Asia, South and Central Asia, East Asia, Europe, America, Africa, and Oceania). For each tradition there is an overview article of several pages that discusses the historical background of the area's mythology." Wilson Libr Bull
Includes bibliography

The Macmillan illustrated encyclopedia of myths & legends. Macmillan 1989 260p il maps $29.95   **291.03**
1. Mythology—Dictionaries 2. Legends—Dictionaries
ISBN 0-02-580181-3   LC 89-8282
Published in the United Kingdom with title: The illustrated encyclopedia of myths & legends
"A section of brief introductory surveys of the mythology of specific countries or regions is followed by 'Characters and concepts: an A-Z of myths' (the major portion of the book). A 'Micropedia' consisting of 'more than one thousand short entries alphabetically arranged' (p.180) treats names not dealt with in the previous section." Sheehy. Guide to Ref Books. 10th edition. suppl
Includes bibliography

A **Dictionary** of comparative religion; general editor: S. G. F. Brandon. Scribner 1970 704p $60   **291.03**
ISBN 0-684-15561-3   LC 76-11390

A Dictionary of comparative religion—*Continued*

"Descriptions of the history and current practices of world religions and denominations, together with related subjects. Provides detailed coverage of eastern and ancient religions. Many terms are defined under one heading and these are cross-referenced and indexed (alphabetically and synoptically). Bibliographies are appended to entries." N Y Public Libr Book of How & Where to Look It Up

The Facts on File dictionary of religions; edited by John R. Hinnells. Facts on File 1984 550p il maps $40   **291.03**

1. Religions—Dictionaries
ISBN 0-87196-862-2   LC 83-20834

"Definitions of terms used in various world religions. Entries run from several descriptive sentences to many paragraphs. Terms are defined within one heading, and these are cross-referenced and indexed (alphabetically and synoptically). Includes extensive bibliography." N Y Public Libr Book of How & Where to Look It Up

Mercatante, Anthony S.

The Facts on File encyclopedia of world mythology and legend. Facts on File 1988 807p il $95   **291.03**

1. Mythology—Dictionaries   2. Folklore—Dictionaries
3. Legends—Dictionaries
ISBN 0-8160-1049-8   LC 84-21218

"A comprehensive reference on world mythologies covered in thematic, biographical, and narrative essays." N Y Public Libr Book of How & Where to Look It Up

Includes bibliography

Parrinder, Edward Geoffrey

Dictionary of non-Christian religions; [by] Geoffrey Parrinder. 2nd ed. Hulton 1981 320p il   **291.03**

1. Religions—Dictionaries   LC 82-143597

Available in hardcover from State Mutual Bk. & Periodical Service

First published 1971 in the United Kingdom; 1973 in the United States by Westminster Press

"Short, clear, well-formulated, and easy to understand definitions reflect recent scholarship on contemporary and historical religions. The book features the terms and concepts of non-Christian religions, with an emphasis on Hinduism, Buddhism, and Islam. Dynasty tables, short bibliography, drawings, photographs, and cross-references prove helpful." Ref Sources for Small & Medium-sized Libr. 5th edition [review of 1971 edition]

Senior, Michael, 1940-

Illustrated who's who in mythology; consultant editor, Geoffrey Parrinder. Macmillan 1985 223p il $50   **291.03**

1. Mythology—Dictionaries
ISBN 0-02-923770-X   LC 85-18814

This encyclopedia of "world mythology includes myths from many cultures—Greek, Egyptian, Hindu, Hebrew, Indian, Mayan, Japanese, Russian, and Scandinavian, among others. More than twelve hundred alphabetically arranged entries . . . briefly describe their subject and, in numerous instances, refer the user to the source of the myth." Am Ref Books Annu, 1987

291.3 Public worship and other religious practices

The Mystical year; by the editors of Time-Life Books. Time-Life Bks. 1992 144p il (Mysteries of the unknown) $19.93   **291.3**

1. Fasts and feasts 2. Religion   LC 91-42780

An illustrated look at various religious customs around the world. Fasts, feasts, and religious calendars are discussed

Includes bibliography

291.4 Religious experience, life, practice

Coles, Robert

The spiritual life of children. Houghton Mifflin 1990 358p il $22.95; pa $10.70   **291.4**

1. Children—Religious life
ISBN 0-395-55999-5; 0-395-59923-7 (pa)
    LC 90-40097

"A Peter Davison book"

In this book the author presents "his research regarding children's understanding of and reflections on spiritual matters." Libr J

"One of the delights of his presentation is the combination of the children's searching comments and the struggle the author makes to hear beyond his own conceptions." J Youth Serv Libr

Includes bibliographic references

Fitzpatrick, Jean Grasso

Something more: nurturing your child's spiritual growth. Viking 1991 237p $18.95   **291.4**

1. Children—Religious life
ISBN 0-670-83706-7   LC 90-50516

Also available in paperback from Penguin Bks.

"This book points out the need for parents to teach their children spirituality as well as the basic skills for surviving in an achievement-oriented world. With the word *spiritual*, Fitzpatrick refers to an 'awareness of our sacred connection with all life.' She quickly puts readers at ease by stating that becoming spiritual is not necessarily the product of formal religious education. Instead, using discussions with real parents to make her points, she emphasizes the spirituality inherent in children and their enjoyment of life." Booklist

Heller, David

Talking to your child about God. Bantam Bks. 1988 167p $12.95   **291.4**

1. Children—Religious life
ISBN 0-553-05325-6   LC 88-47644

This book provides suggestions on how parents can guide their children's growing spiritual development. Brief descriptions of the major beliefs of Jewish, Catholic, and Protestant religions are included

The **Oxford** book of prayer; general editor, George Appleton. Oxford Univ. Press 1985 397p $29.95; pa $10.95   **291.4**
1. Prayers
ISBN 0-19-213222-9; 0-19-282108-3 (pa)
LC 85-176243
This collection contains "prayers from the Bible and other sacred texts and personal prayers of people as diverse as St. Thomas Aquinas, Dr. Johnson, and Solzhenitsyn. . . . While some are given in modern (often 'newspeak') translations, many are in their beautiful traditional forms. A welcome addition to general and academic collections." Libr J
Includes bibliographic references

292 Classical religion and religious mythology

Bell, Robert E., 1926-
Dictionary of classical mythology, symbols, attributes, & associations; illustrations by John Schlesinger. ABC-CLIO 1982 390p $52
292
1. Mythology, Classical—Dictionaries
ISBN 0-87436-305-5   LC 81-19141
"A topical dictionary of Greek and Roman mythology. Under subjects (bear, indigestion, sculpture) various mortal and immortal personae are listed with a brief identification and a description of their relationship to the subject." Ref Sources for Small & Medium-sized Libr. 5th edition

Women of classical mythology; a biographical dictionary. ABC-CLIO 1991 462p $52   **292**
1. Mythology, Classical—Dictionaries 2. Gods and goddesses—Dictionaries
ISBN 0-87436-581-3   LC 91-26649
Also available in paperback from Oxford Univ. Press
This "dictionary contains the names of both notable and not so notable women of classical myth who are not easily found in other convenient sources on myth. . . . The biographical entries, ranging from a single sentence to three pages in length, are easily understood and provide sufficient information for further study." Choice
For a fuller review see: Booklist, Nov. 15, 1991

Graves, Robert, 1895-1985
Greek myths   **292**
1. Mythology, Classical
Hardcover and paperback editions available from various publishers
First published 1955 by Penguin Bks.
A collection of the author's interpretations of Greek myths based on anthropological and archaeological findings

Grimal, Pierre, 1912-
A concise dictionary of classical mythology; edited by Stephen Kershaw from the translation by A.R. Maxwell-Hyslop. Blackwell 1990 456p $35   **292**
1. Mythology, Classical—Dictionaries
ISBN 0-631-16696-3   LC 90-32787

Based on The dictionary of classical mythology, entered below
"The entries range overall from one sentence to seven pages in length, the exception being the Heracles entry, which is 12 pages long. . . . The format follows the same pattern [as the unabridged dictionary], starting with the English name, the name in Greek, the evidence, and genealogy. Many times the story is also retold." Choice

The dictionary of classical mythology; translated by A.R. Maxwell-Hyslop. Blackwell 1986 603p il $50   **292**
1. Mythology, Classical—Dictionaries
ISBN 0-631-13209-0   LC 85-7387
Original French edition, 1951; this translation first published 1985 in the United Kingdom
"The dictionary is a comprehensive source dealing with every mythological creature and character, from Abas to Zeuxippe, and all the versions of the associated myths and legends. Articles are clear and readable, explain historical and literary allusions, and are attractively illustrated. . . . An essential purchase for both school and public libraries." Am Libr
Includes bibliography

Hamilton, Edith, 1867-1963
Mythology; illustrated by Steele Savage. Little, Brown 1942 497p il $19.95   **292**
1. Mythology, Classical 2. Mythology, Norse
ISBN 0-316-34114-2
Also available in paperback from New Am. Lib.
A retelling of Greek, Roman and Norse myths

Perowne, Stewart, 1901-1989
Roman mythology. new rev ed. Bedrick Bks. 1984 144p il (Lib. of the world's myths and legends) $24.95   **292**
1. Mythology, Classical
ISBN 0-911745-56-4   LC 84-6446
First published 1969 in the United Kingdom; this edition first published 1983
This volume discusses mythology and religion within the culture of ancient Rome
Includes bibliography

Pinsent, John, 1922-
Greek mythology. new rev ed. Bedrick Bks. 1983 144p il (Lib. of the world's myths and legends) $24.95; pa $14.95   **292**
1. Mythology, Classical
ISBN 0-911745-08-4; 0-87226-250-2 (pa)
LC 83-71479
First published 1969 in the United Kingdom; this edition first published 1982
This volume combines a survey of mythology with Greek history
Includes bibliography

294 Religions of Indic origin

Ions, Veronica
Indian mythology. new rev ed. Bedrick
Bks. 1984 144p il (Lib. of the world's myths
and legends) $24.95 **294**

1. Mythology, Indic 2. Mythology, Hindu
ISBN 0-911745-55-6 LC 84-6483

First published 1967 in the United Kingdom

The author "interweaves the legends and tales with
the pageant of India's history. She tells why Indra, storm
god and bringer of rain, became a more dignified and
less active deity after the Aryans consolidated their
power. She lucidly explains the Brahman cycle of creation and destruction, the Hindu concept of rebirth, Buddha's search for enlightenment, Tantric spiritual union
through sexual rapture." Publ Wkly

Includes bibliography

294.3 Buddhism

The **Dalai** Lama; a policy of kindness: an
anthology of writings by and about the
Dalai Lama; foreword by Claiborne Pell;
compiled and edited by Sidney Piburn.
Snow Lion Publs. 1990 150p pa $6.95
294.3

1. Dalai Lama XIV, 1935-
ISBN 0-937938-91-2 LC 90-31752

This collection of writings includes "both biographical
essays and the Dalai Lama's discussions of science and
religion, human rights, the environment, and spiritual
subjects." Antioch Rev
This book is "accessible to those who know nothing
of Buddhism or of Tibet." Libr J

Includes bibliographic references

Matthiessen, Peter
Nine-headed dragon river; Zen journals,
1969-1985. Shambhala Publs. 1986 288p
hardcover o.p. paperback available $19
294.3

1. Zen Buddhism 2. Japan—Description
ISBN 0-87773-401-1 (pa) LC 85-27918

Companion volume: The snow leopard, entered in
class 915.4

This book includes "thoughts on Japanese culture and
history from a Zen perspective along with the author's
spiritual experiences. [It] is well written and full of
memorable incidents and impressions of various important Zen teachers. This authentic account by a Western
seeker is recommended for public libraries." Libr J

Ross, Nancy Wilson, 1905?-1986
Buddhism, a way of life and thought.
Knopf 1980 208p il hardcover o.p.
paperback available $12 **294.3**

1. Buddhism
ISBN 0-394-74754-2 (pa) LC 80-7652

The author "presents the basic data of Buddha's life,
his teachings, and Buddhist practice. . . . [She] describes
Theravada Buddhism (of Southeast Asia), Tantra Buddhism (of Tibet), and Zen Buddhism (of Japan). . . .
The book is a clear introduction to Buddhism, enthusiastically written and designed for the general public

or beginning student." Choice
Includes bibliography

Sogyal, Rinpoche
The Tibetan book of living and dying;
edited by Patrick Gaffney and Andrew
Harvey. HarperSanFrancisco 1992 425p il
$22 **294.3**

1. Buddhism 2. Death
ISBN 0-06-250793-1 LC 90-56214

This "modern reinterpretation of the classic *Tibetan
Book of the Dead* is a manual on learning to accept
death, on caring for the dying, and on spiritual growth.
Rinpoche, . . . draws parallels between contemporary
Western near-death experiences and the afterlife journey
through *bardos*, or intermediate planes between death and
rebirth, described in sacred Tibetan texts." Publ Wkly
The author "is well qualified to pass on his tradition.
He does this beautifully, in limpid prose free of the
scholastic list making that deadens many Tibetan Buddhist primers." N Y Times Book Rev

Suzuki, Daisetz Teitaro, 1870-1966
Manual of Zen Buddhism. Grove Press
1960 192p il pa $10.95 **294.3**

1. Zen Buddhism
ISBN 0-8021-3065-8

"An Evergreen original"

Fisrt published 1950 in the United Kingdom

In this volume, D. T. Suzuki has brought together
some of Zen Buddhism's original sources. Included are
the sutras or sermons of the Buddha: the gathas or
hymns; the philosophical puzzles known as koan; and
the dharanis or invocations to expel evil spirits. In addition to the written selections there are reproductions of
Buddhist drawings and paintings, including religious
statues found in Zen temples

Tibetan book of the dead
The Tibetan book of the dead; or, The
afterdeath experiences on the Bardo plane,
according to Láma Kazi Dawa-Samdup's
English rendering; by W. Y. Evans-Wentz;
with a psychological commentary by C. G.
Jung, introducing foreward by Láma
Anagarika Govinda, and foreword by John
Woodroffe. 3rd ed. Oxford Univ. Press 1957
xxxiv, 249p il hardcover o.p. paperback
available $8.95 **294.3**

This translation first published 1927

A translation of the Bardo thödol, a Tibetan Buddhist
scriptural work describing the mind's projections immediately after death. The accompanying commentary
explains the symbolism and outlines applications of the
teachings of the Bardo for living

Watts, Alan, 1915-1973
The way of Zen; by Alan W. Watts.
Pantheon Bks. 1957 236p il o.p.; Vintage
Bks. paperback available $9 **294.3**

1. Zen Buddhism
ISBN 0-679-72301-3 (pa)

Watts, Alan, 1915-1973—*Continued*
This is an historical and cultural survey of Zen, tracing its origins in Indian and Chinese thought. The author describes the Zen way of living and its techniques for overcoming the mind's conflict between symbolic thought and actual experience

Includes bibliography

294.5 Hinduism

Basham, Arthur Llewellyn
The origins and development of classical Hinduism; [by] A. L. Basham; edited and annotated by Kenneth G. Zysk. Beacon Press 1989 159p il o.p.; Oxford Univ. Press paperback available $8.95 **294.5**
1. Hinduism
ISBN 0-19-507349-5 (pa) LC 88-43314
This illustrated history "traces the spiritual life of India from the time of the Indus Culture (around 2700 B.C.E) through the crystallization of classical Hinduism in the first centuries of the common era. It chronicles as well the rise of other mystical and ascetic traditions, such as Buddhism and Jainism, and follows Hinduism's later incarnations in the West." Publisher's note

Includes bibliographic references

Herman, A. L.
A brief introduction to Hinduism; religion, philosophy, and ways of liberation. Westview Press 1991 xxi, 181p il $42.50; pa $14.95 **294.5**
1. Hinduism 2. Philosophy, Hindu
ISBN 0-8133-8109-6; 0-8133-8110-X (pa)
LC 90-25262
The author "identifies three major strands of Hinduism: (1) the way of devotion exemplified by A. C. Bhaktivedanta, (2) the way of selfless action exemplified by Gandhi, and (3) the way of mystical knowledge exemplified by Ramana Maharshi. He then traces these strands to their roots in the Vedas, Upanisads, and the Indus civilization." Choice

Includes bibliographic references

Isherwood, Christopher, 1904-1986
The wishing tree; Christopher Isherwood on mystical religion; edited by Robert Adjemian; introduction by Gavin Lambert. Harper & Row 1987 xx, 208p pa $9.95 **294.5**
1. Vedanta
ISBN 0-06-250402-9 LC 87-45178
A collection of the author's writings on the Vedantic (Hindu) philosophy and Eastern thought, including a piece on the guru Ramakrishna

296 Judaism

American Jewish year book. Jewish Publ. Soc. $30 **296**
1. Jews—Periodicals 2. Jews—United States
ISSN 0065-8987
Annual. First published 1989

"International in scope. Embraces all aspects of Jewish activities and includes population statistics, directories of organizations, and Jewish periodicals, necrology, American Jewish bibliography, and Jewish calendar." Ref Sources for Small & Medium-sized Libr. 5th edition

The **Cambridge** history of Judaism; edited by W. D. Davies, Louis Finkelstein. Cambridge Univ. Press 1984-1988 2v il maps **296**
1. Judaism—History LC 77-85704
First two volumes of a projected four volume set
Contents: v1 Introduction; The Persian period $84.95 (ISBN 0-521-21880-2); v2 The Hellenistic age $94.95 (ISBN 0-521-21929-9)
The scope of this work is intended "to cover from the Babylonian exile to the codification of the Mishnah, and to include extensive background on the context in which Judaism developed." Sheehy. Guide to Ref Books. 10th edition

Includes bibliography

The **Encyclopedia** of Judaism; editor-in-chief Geoffrey Wigoder. Macmillan 1989 768p il $75 **296**
1. Judaism—Dictionaries
ISBN 0-02-628410-3 LC 89-8184
"Articles range from a few lines to about a page and a half, with most in the half-column category. The articles are unsigned but the contributors are listed. Most are well-known scholars in different fields and of differing ideological backgrounds, including Reform, Orthodox, and Conservative Judaism." Choice

Fackenheim, Emil L.
What is Judaism? Summit Bks. 1987 320p o.p.; Collier Bks. paperback available $10.95 **296**
1. Judaism
ISBN 0-02-032191-0 (pa) LC 87-10880
The author presents an interpretation of Judaism "in light of the Holocaust and the creation of the state of Israel. Beginning with the religious situation of the Jew today, he examines such concepts as Jewish peoplehood, Zionism, God, and the Bible; such issues as anti-Semitism, assimilation, and the relationship between Judaism and other religions; and the meaning of prayer, repentance, and the Messiah for today's Jew." Libr J
This book offers "a refreshingly honest and insightful glimpse into modern Judaism." Christ Today

Includes bibliographic references

Glazer, Nathan
American Judaism. 2nd ed rev, with a new introd. University of Chicago Press 1989 xxix, 214p (Chicago history of American civilization) pa $11.95 **296**
1. Judaism 2. Jews—United States
ISBN 0-226-29843-4 LC 89-161422
First published 1957
Focusing upon Jews as a people and as a religious group, the author surveys the history of Jews in the United States beginning with the first Jewish settlement in New Amsterdam in 1654. Among the topics considered are the German and East European immigrants, the Sephardic communities, and the Orthodox,

Glazer, Nathan—*Continued*
Reform and Conservative movements
Includes bibliographic references

Liebman, Charles S.
Two worlds of Judaism; the Israeli and American experiences; [by] Charles S. Liebman and Steven M. Cohen. Yale Univ. Press 1990 202p $27.95; pa $11   **296**

1. Judaism 2. Jews—United States
ISBN 0-300-04726-6; 0-300-05231-6 (pa)

LC 89-28457

This is an exploration of the ways in which Jews in Israel and the United States conceive of Judaism
"Liebman and Cohen's comparison of Jewish life in the United States and Israel offers new insights into the strengths and weaknesses of both cultures and a deeper understanding of the current situation in Israel. Highly recommended for all collections." Libr J

Includes bibliographic references

Wiesel, Elie, 1928-
Sages and dreamers; biblical, Talmudic and Hasidic portraits and legends. Summit Bks. 1991 443p $25; pa $13   **296**

1. Bible. O.T.—Biography 2. Talmud—Biography 3. Hasidism
ISBN 0-671-74679-0; 0-671-79778-6 (pa)

LC 91-26454

"Based on a series of lectures, this collection's focus is 25 Jewish figures. . . . The subjects are mostly men—Noah, Rabbi Akiba, The Ostrowitzer Rabbi—though Ruth and Esther get a nod. These figures each represent a specific era, but Wiesel shows, in surprisingly accessible, even colloquial, prose, that their problems and dreams are not so very different from our own. . . . This is a rich, provocative volume." Booklist

Wouk, Herman, 1915-
This is my God: the Jewish way of life. Little, Brown 1987 345p $14.95   **296**

1. Judaism
ISBN 0-316-95514-0   LC 87-3245

Also available Walker & Co. large print edition and in paperback from Simon & Schuster

Reprint of the title first published 1959 by Doubleday

The author, an orthodox Jew, writes a personal declaration of faith. He also explains the holy days and the fasts and presents the historical background of Judaism, taking his readers back some five thousand years

Includes bibliography

296.1 Judaism—Sources

Baigent, Michael
The Dead Sea scrolls deception; [by] Michael Baigent and Richard Leigh. Summit Bks. 1991 268p il $20; pa $12   **296.1**

1. Dead Sea scrolls
ISBN 0-671-73454-7; 0-671-79797-2 (pa)

LC 91-41879

This "account of the events surrounding the discovery and translation of the scrolls attempts to . . . [establish] theological and political efforts by individuals, governments, and religious institutions to keep controversial documents unpublished, ostensibly to preserve orthodox interpretations." Libr J
This is a "crystalline, well-documented work. . . . The authors advance startling theories that should change the way we view ancient Judaism and nascent Christianity." Publ Wkly

Includes bibliography

Cohen, A. (Abraham), b. 1887
Everyman's Talmud; with an introduction to the new American edition by Boaz Cohen. Dutton 1949 xli, 403p o.p.; Schocken Bks. paperback available $17   **296.1**

1. Talmud 2. Judaism
ISBN 0-8052-0497-0 (pa)

First published 1932 in the United Kingdom

"Its aim is to provide a summary of the teachings of the Talmud on Religion, Ethics, Folk-lore, and Jurisprudence. . . . All that is offered is a sufficient number of extracts to give [the] reader a general idea of the Talmudic doctrine." Preface
"A comprehensive and satisfactory summary of Talmudic doctrine . . . prefaced by an excellent introduction." Commonweal

Includes bibliography

Frankel, Ellen
The classic tales; 4,000 years of Jewish lore. Aronson, J. 1989 659p $40; pa $29.95   **296.1**

1. Legends, Jewish 2. Legends, Hasidic
ISBN 0-87668-904-7; 1-56821-038-8 (pa)

LC 88-35119

"Frankel selects and retells a wide selection of tales arranged in broadly thematic sections. Biblical, hasidic, and midrashic sources predominate, but the oral tradition is also represented. Likewise, the balance between Ashkenazi and Sephardic stories aims for a broader geographical representation. Frankel also takes the opportunity to personalize the woman's role in many of these tales and makes the references to God genderless." Booklist

Includes bibliography

Neusner, Jacob, 1932-
Invitation to the Talmud; a teaching book. rev & expanded ed. Harper & Row 1984 xxxi, 359p hardcover o.p. paperback available $13.95   **296.1**

1. Talmud 2. Judaism
ISBN 0-06-066112-7 (pa)   LC 83-48422

First published 1973

Text in Aramaic, English, and Hebrew

The author discusses the Mishnah (law), Tosefta (supplementary statements), and Gemara (commentary) and illustrates each with a classic Talmudic debate

Includes bibliographic references

Understanding the Dead Sea scrolls; a reader from the Biblical archaeology review; edited by Hershel Shanks. Random House 1992 xxxviii, 336p il maps $22.50; pa $13
296.1

1. Dead Sea scrolls
ISBN 0-679-41448-7; 0-679-74445-2 (pa)

LC 91-45727

This is a compilation of "22 articles from the pages of BAR and *Bible Review* dealing with the discovery of the Scrolls, the ancient community that stored them away, and their impact upon the study of the Bible, Rabbinic Judaism, and early Christianity. Three chapters on the controversy surrounding the publication (and in many cases non-publication) of the materials round out the volume. . . . The articles included are written by scholars but are easily accessible to laypersons. Coverage is balanced, including opposing viewpoints." Libr J

Includes bibliographic references

296.3 Judaism—Doctrinal, moral, social theology

Kushner, Harold S., 1935-
When bad things happen to good people; with a new preface by the author. 2nd ed. Schocken Bks. 1989 148p pa $19   **296.3**

1. Providence and government of God 2. Suffering
ISBN 0-8052-4089-6   LC 89-38662

Also available G.K. Hall large print edition and in paperback from Avon Bks.

First published 1981

"A bright and happy infant, Rabbi Kushner's first-born son gradually succumbed to progeria, 'rapid aging': he never grew beyond three feet tall, looked like a hairless, wizened old man, and died in his teens. This book is his father's attempt to make sense out of his son's fate, his own pain, and the pain of others enduring undeserved misfortunes." Libr J

296.4 Judaism—Traditions, rites, public services

Greenberg, Irving, 1933-
The Jewish way; living the holidays. Summit Bks. 1988 463p $24.95   **296.4**

1. Fasts and feasts—Judaism 2. Judaism—Customs and practices
ISBN 0-671-49399-X   LC 88-20085

The author "explains and interprets each holiday's origin and background, ceremonial rituals, and religious significance. He shows how the holidays relate to one another and to Judaism's central themes and how they offer the individual the capacity to experience the full range of Judaism's and humankind's values." Publisher's note

Includes bibliography

Lewit, Jane
The bar/bat mitzvah planbook; [by] Jane Lewit and Ellen Epstein; foreword by Joshua O. Haberman. Scarborough House 1991 178p il pa $14.95   **296.4**

1. Bar mitzvah 2. Bat mitzvah
ISBN 0-8128-8529-5   LC 91-13691
First published 1982 by Stein & Day
New edition in preparation

"Emphasizing the bar/bat mitzvah ceremony itself, and the preparation leading up to it, the *Planbook* also offers succinct discussions of many associated customs and rituals. Informative and accessible, this guide answers many questions. A section on study aids as well as helpful charts and timetables are included." Libr J

Includes bibliographic references

Raphael, Chaim
Festival days; a history of Jewish celebrations. Grove Weidenfeld 1991 144p $19.95   **296.4**

1. Fasts and feasts—Judaism
ISBN 0-8021-1147-5   LC 90-25371

This "volume covers the cycle of Jewish holidays, beginning with their historical underpinnings and wrapping up with personal accounts and poetry from a variety of contemporary and historical persons." Booklist

Includes bibliographic references

Strassfeld, Michael
The Jewish holidays; a guide and commentary; illustrated by Betsy Platkin Teutsch; commentaries by Arnold Eisen [et al.] Harper & Row 1985 248p il hardcover o.p. paperback available $18   **296.4**

1. Fasts and feasts—Judaism 2. Judaism—Customs and practices
ISBN 0-06-091225-1 (pa)   LC 84-48196

This book examines the history and customs surrounding the major Jewish holidays

296.7 Judaism—Religious experience, life, practice

Diamant, Anita
Living a Jewish life; a guide for starting, learning, celebrating, and parenting; [by] Anita Diamant, Howard Cooper. HarperCollins Pubs. 1991 xx, 330p $24.95; pa $11   **296.7**

1. Jews—Social life and customs
ISBN 0-06-271508-9; 0-06-273025-8 (pa)

LC 90-56092

This book "is written as a kind of handbook to help those who are perhaps new to the faith or rebuilding for themselves as adults the traditions with which they were (or were not) brought up. It would also make an excellent introduction for anyone unacquainted with Jewish customs." Booklist

Includes bibliographic references

Kaplan, Aryeh

Jewish meditation; a practical guide. Schocken Bks. 1985 165p hardcover o.p. paperback available $12　　　**296.7**

1. Meditation 2. Judaism—Customs and practices
ISBN 0-8052-0781-3 (pa)　　　LC 84-23589

The author "outlines various forms of meditation based on Jewish writings and practices. He discusses mantra meditation, visualization, and ways to contemplate God. With an eye toward traditional Judaism, Kaplan also explains how following the many commandments of the Bible is also a form of meditation. A profound book that is complex in subject matter yet simple in methodology." Booklist

Kushner, Harold S., 1935-

Who needs God. Summit Bks. 1989 208p o.p.; Pocket Bks. paperback available $5.99
296.7

1. God—Judaism
ISBN 0-671-68027-7 (pa)　　　LC 89-35140

Also available Walker & Co. large print edition

The author "believes that 'human life has meaning . . . but only in religious terms.' According to this crucial realization, it is religion that connects us to God and community." Libr J

296.8 Judaism—Sects and movements

Wiesel, Elie, 1928-

Somewhere a master; further Hasidic portraits and legends; translated from the French by Marion Wiesel. Summit Bks. 1982 221p hardcover o.p. paperback available $7.95　　　**296.8**

1. Hasidism 2. Legends, Hasidic
ISBN 0-671-50823-7 (pa)　　　LC 82-10370

"Told with eloquence and drama, these moving tales resound with the age-old wisdom of a people imbued with faith and fervor." Publ Wkly

Souls on fire; portraits and legends of Hasidic masters; translated from the French by Marion Wiesel. Summit Bks. 1982 c1972 268p hardcover o.p. paperback available $9.95　　　**296.8**

1. Hasidism 2. Legends, Hasidic
ISBN 0-671-44171-X (pa)　　　LC 82-5984

Also available in hardcover from J. Aronson

A reissue of the title first published 1972 by Random House

"A collection of legends and portraits of the founder of the Hasidic movement and his disciples. . . . Wiesel assumes the role of a storyteller, who simply transmits tales he heard as faithfully as his personal experience will allow." Publ Wkly

297 Islam and religions originating in it

Armstrong, Karen

Muhammad; a biography of the prophet. HarperSanFrancisco 1992 290p maps $23
297

1. Muhammad, d. 632
ISBN 0-06-250014-7　　　LC 91-55407

First published 1991 in the United Kingdom with subtitle: A Western attempt to understand Islam

In this "quest for the historical Muhammad, Armstrong first traces the West's long history of hostility toward Islam. . . . [This] biography portrays Muhammad (ca. 570-632) as a passionate, complex, fallible human being—a charismatic leader possessed of political as well as spiritual gifts, and a prophet whose monotheistic vision intuitively answered the deepest longings of his people." Publ Wkly

Includes bibliography

Esposito, John L.

Islam; the straight path. expanded ed. Oxford Univ. Press 1991 251p il $21.95; pa $15.95　　　**297**

1. Islam
ISBN 0-19-506225-6; 0-19-507472-6 (pa)
LC 90-30148

First published 1988

A study of Islamic history, law, ritual and contemporary Islamic society

Includes bibliographic references

Glassé, Cyril

The concise encyclopedia of Islam; introduction by Huston Smith. Harper & Row 1989 472p il maps $59.95; pa $24.95
297

1. Islam—Dictionaries
ISBN 0-06-063123-6; 0-06-063126-0 (pa)
LC 88-45658

The author "explains the philosophy, metaphysical beliefs, rituals, laws, and observances that permeate Islamic life. . . . There are a large number of biographical entries for prophets, religious and military leaders, and rulers." Best Ref Books, 1986-1990

Includes bibliography

Hiro, Dilip

Holy wars; the rise of Islamic fundamentalism. Routledge 1989 334p il $42; pa $14.95　　　**297**

1. Islam 2. Islam and politics 3. Middle East—Politics and government
ISBN 0-415-90207-X; 0-415-90208-8 (pa)
LC 89-10190

Published in the United Kingdom with title: Islamic fundamentalism

This book examines "tensions within the Muslim world (Chapters 1-3) and considers the emergence of 'fundamentalist' ideologies in five modern nation-states: Egypt and Syria, Saudi Arabia, Iran, and Afghanistan (Chapters 4-7)." Choice

Hiro, Dilip—*Continued*
"This clearly written work is an excellent introduction to Islamic political assertiveness." Libr J
Includes bibliography

Jomier, Jacques
How to understand Islam. Crossroad 1989 168p il pa $12.95   **297**
1. Islam
ISBN 0-8245-0981-1   LC 89-7854
Translated from the French by John Bowden
This study begins with an historical overview of the origins and development of Islam, then discusses the fundamental precepts of the religion. Islamic philosophy, social life, political life and civilization are examined
Includes bibliography

Koran
The Koran   **297**
Some editions are:
Penguin Bks. (Penguin classics) pa $5.95 Translated by N. J. Dawood (ISBN 0-14-044558-7)
Tuttle (Everyman's lib) $4.95 Translated by J. M. Rodwell (ISBN 0-460-87134-X)
"The sacred scripture of Islam, regarded by Muslims as the Word of God, and except in sūra I.—which is a prayer to God—and some few passages in which Muhammad or the angels speak in the first person, the speaker throughout is God." Ency Britannica

Lippman, Thomas W.
Understanding Islam; an introduction to the Moslem world. New Am. Lib. 1982 196p pa $4.99   **297**
1. Islam
ISBN 0-451-62760-1   LC 81-85142
"A Mentor book"
The author explains fundamental Islamic beliefs and practices. The life and work of Muhammad is examined in depth
Includes bibliography

Naipaul, V. S. (Vidiadhar Surajprasad), 1932-
Among the believers; an Islamic journey. Knopf 1981 430p hardcover o.p. paperback available $14   **297**
1. Islam
ISBN 0-394-71195-5 (pa)   LC 81-47503
"Based on his seven-month journey across the Asian continent, Naipaul explores the life, the culture, the ferment inside the nations of Islam." Publisher's note

Rahman, Fazlur, 1919-1988
Islam. 2nd ed. University of Chicago Press 1979 285p hardcover o.p. paperback available $10.95   **297**
1. Islam
ISBN 0-226-70281-2 (pa)   LC 78-68547
First published 1966 by Holt, Rinehart & Winston

The author discusses the origin and development of the Islamic faith, stressing its moral, legal, social, and philosophical bases
Includes bibliography

Renard, John, 1944-
In the footsteps of Muhammad; understanding the Islamic experience. Paulist Press 1992 173p il pa $9.95   **297**
1. Islam
ISBN 0-8091-3316-4   LC 92-11396
The author "approaches the world of Islam spiritually and experientially, using the image of 'journey' or 'pilgrim path' as his metaphor. He explores the three paradigmatic journeys of Muhammad—leaving home/emigrating (Hijra), pilgrimage to Makka (Hajj) and a mystical experience or trip to the beyond (Isra' and Mi'raj)—for understanding the Islamic tradition as a whole." Publisher's note
Includes bibliographic references

Ruthven, Malise
Islam in the world. Oxford Univ. Press 1984 400p maps $27.95; pa $12.95   **297**
1. Islam
ISBN 0-19-520453-0; 0-19-520454-9 (pa)
                    LC 84-18944
This book combines "a historical overview of the rise of Islam, the prophethood of Muhammad, and the development of Islamic community, with careful examination of Islam law, religious factionalism, and mysticism in Islamic society." Libr J
"Ruthven has combined scholarship with lucidity, a rare achievement. His self-confessed agnosticism gives strength and objectivity to his admirable work." New Statesman

299 Other religions

Blofeld, John Eaton Calthorpe, 1913-1987
Taoism; the road to immortality; [by] John Blofeld. Shambhala Publs. 1978 195p il pa $16   **299**
1. Taoism
ISBN 0-394-73582-X   LC 77-90882
The author seeks to explain the fundamental concepts of Taoism, tells stories of its masters and offers reflections on Taoist verse. In addition, he describes his visits to Taoist monasteries in China and discussions he had with contemporary masters

Burland, C. A. (Cottie Arthur), 1905-
North American Indian mythology; [by] Cottie Burland. new rev ed, revised by Marion Wood. Bedrick Bks. 1985 144p il (Lib. of the world's myths and legends) $24.95; pa $16.95   **299**
1. Indians of North America—Religion
ISBN 0-87226-016-X; 0-87226-248-0 (pa)
                    LC 85-70555
First published 1965 in the United Kingdom

Burland, C. A. (Cottie Arthur), 1905- —
Continued

Arranged geographically, this survey looks at North American Indian beliefs, festivals, crafts and ceremonial life

Includes bibliography

Castaneda, Carlos

The teachings of Don Juan; a Yaqui way of knowledge. University of Calif. Press 1968 196p $32.50; pa $13   **299**

1. Juan, Don 2. Yaqui Indians—Religion
ISBN 0-520-00217-2; 0-520-02258-0 (pa)

Also available in paperback from Pocket Bks.

"This book is the record of a young anthropologist's experiences as the apprentice of a [Yaqui] Indian sorcerer. Over a period of four years, Mr. Castaneda paid intermittant visits to Don Juan, first in Arizona, then in Sonora, Mexico." N Y Times Book Rev

Other available titles about Don Juan are:
The art of dreaming (1993)
The eagle's gift (1981)
The fire from within (1984)
Journey to Ixtlan (1972)
The power of silence (1987)
The second ring of power (1977)
A separate reality (1971)
Tales of power (1974)

Ellis, Peter Berresford

Dictionary of Celtic mythology. ABC-CLIO 1992 232p $52   **299**

1. Mythology, Celtic—Dictionaries
ISBN 0-87436-609-7   LC 92-872

This alphabetically-arranged guide to Celtic mythology and culture draws primarily on Irish and Welsh sources, but also includes coverage of Scottish, Cornish, Manx, and Breton traditions

"The entries are thorough and well written. An excellent selected bibliography rounds out this interesting reference." Libr J

The **Fireside** treasury of light; edited by Mary Olsen Kelly. Simon & Schuster 1990 pa $12   **299**

1. New Age movement
ISBN 0-671-68505-8   LC 90-40629

"A Fireside book"

"The editor describes the 'foundations' of the New Age movement and introduces each of the 11 sections with background information. Chapters cover topics such as healing and alternative medicine, new psychology, channels and psychics, and global change and social transformation, featuring excerpts from books by a diverse set of authors including M. Scott Peck, Baba Ram Dass, Carl Jung, Robert M. Pirsig, Sondra Ray, Lynn Andrews, and Starhawk." Booklist

"Whether or not one agrees with its thinking, this book is important to understanding many aspects of contemporary culture: it serves as a useful introduction, a ready reference, and a challenge. Highly recommended." Libr J

Gill, Sam D., 1943-

Dictionary of Native American mythology; [by] Sam D. Gill, Irene F. Sullivan. ABC-CLIO 1992 xxx, 425p il maps $65   **299**

1. Indians of North America—Religion—Dictionaries
ISBN 0-87436-621-6   LC 92-27053

"The authors have included entries representing more than 150 Native American language groups. . . . For each of the alphabetically arranged entries, tribal source and culture area are included. A collection of vivid black-and-white illustrations is reprinted. A comprehensive bibliography and index by tribe complete this excellent reference work." Libr J

Hart, George, 1945-

A dictionary of Egyptian gods and goddesses. Routledge & Kegan Paul 1986 229p il hardcover o.p. paperback available $13.95   **299**

1. Mythology, Egyptian 2. Egypt—Religion
ISBN 0-7102-0167-2 (pa)   LC 85-11862

The author has "tried to include all the important deities that figure in magical medicine and daily life of ancient Egypt." Preface

"The entries are arranged alphabetically and often include line illustrations. . . . Hart's entries are . . . detailed and informative. Hart also includes a map of ancient Egypt and a selected bibliography. This dictionary will be extremely useful to anyone needing concise and informative material in this area." Coll Res Libr

Hirschfelder, Arlene B.

The encyclopedia of Native American religions; [by] Arlene Hirschfelder, Paulette Molin. Facts on File 1991 367p il maps $40   **299**

1. Indians of North America—Religion—Dictionaries
ISBN 0-8160-2017-5   LC 91-21145

"The entries in this encyclopedia provide descriptions of religious ceremonies and terminology; biographies of native American religious leaders, missionaries, and others who have influenced the practice of these religions; summaries of major court cases affecting native religious practices; healing and other ceremonial practices that are spiritual rather than religious in nature; and some . . . mythology. . . . Most academic and public libraries should consider it for their collections." Booklist

Includes bibliography

Hultkrantz, Åke

The religions of the American Indians; translated by Monica Setterwall. University of Calif. Press 1979 335p il $32.50; pa $15.95   **299**

1. Indians—Religion
ISBN 0-520-02653-5; 0-520-04239-5 (pa)

LC 73-90661

Both sections of this book on North and South American Indians "provide fundamental knowledge and point to genetic connections between cultural areas. A well-researched work with a comprehensive bibliography, sure to be of interest to historians of religion and those interested in American culture." Libr J

I ching
The I ching; or, Book of changes   **299**
1. Divination
Hardcover and paperback editions available from various publishers
A "book of divinations to which, according to legend, 'Confucius', as editor, appended some commentaries. It consists of sixty-four hexagrams made of broken and unbroken lines, with accompanying text. By throwing coins or manipulating yarrow stalks the petitioner chooses any one or, usually, two of these hexagrams by lot. The corresponding text reveals the questioner's prospects or provides guidance in what to do." Reader's Ency. 3d edition

Ions, Veronica
Egyptian mythology. [rev ed]. Bedrick Bks. 1983 c1982 144p il map (Lib. of the world's myths and legends) $24.95; pa $16.95   **299**
1. Mythology, Egyptian 2. Egypt—Religion
ISBN 0-911745-07-6; 0-87226-249-9 (pa)
LC 83-71478
First published 1965 in the United Kingdom; this edition first published 1982
Containing 150 illustrations, 50 of them in color, this book presents the gods of ancient Egypt, the more human deities, and the pharoahs Rameses, Tutankhamen, and Akhenaten
Includes bibliography

Lao-tzu, 6th cent. B.C.
Tao te ching   **299**
Hardcover and paperback editions available from various publishers
"Chinese Taoist text attributed to Lao Tzu. A brief work in eighty-one paragraphs in both verse and prose, it probably dates from the 4th or 3rd century BC, although some believe it may be as early as the 6th century BC. The meaning is obscure and subject to many interpretations, the two principal ones being that it is a mystical book about union with the absolute, and that it is a political handbook on how to rule and survive in chaotic times." Reader's Ency. 3d edition

MacCana, Proinsias
Celtic mythology. new rev ed. Bedrick Bks. 1985 c1983 143p il (Lib. of the world's myths and legends) $24.95; pa $14.95   **299**
1. Mythology, Celtic 2. Celts
ISBN 0-87226-002-X; 0-87226-242-1 (pa)
LC 84-45597
First published 1970 in the United Kingdom; this edition first published 1983
Describes the gods, myths, and epic legends of the Celts, discussing their sources, their relationship with Celtic history, and the influence of the Romans
Includes bibliography

Native American religions: North America; edited by Lawrence E. Sullivan. Macmillan 1989 220p (Religion, history, and culture) pa $12.95   **299**
1. Indians of North America—Religion
ISBN 0-02-897402-6
LC 89-12086

This volume contains selections from The encyclopedia of religion, entered in class 200.3
Includes bibliography

Pagels, Elaine H., 1943-
The gnostic Gospels; by Elaine Pagels. Random House 1979 xxxvi, 182p hardcover o.p. paperback available $9   **299**
1. Gnosticism
ISBN 0-679-72453-2 (pa)
LC 79-4764
An examination of the origins of early Christianity based on Gnostic texts rediscovered in the 20th century
Pagels "writes for the layman, which is refreshing, and she does so lucidly, which is a challenge, especially when 'gnosticism' was regarded by its own adherents to be for the initiated only." Christ Sci Monit
Includes bibliographic references

Parrinder, Edward Geoffrey
African mythology; [by] Geoffrey Parrinder. new rev ed. Bedrick Bks. 1986 c1982 144p il map (Lib. of the world's myths and legends) $24.95; pa $16.95   **299**
1. Mythology, African
ISBN 0-87226-042-9; 0-87226-243-X (pa)
LC 85-22967
First published 1967 in the United Kingdom; this edition first published 1982
Text and numerous illustrations explore the diversity of the myths, fables and traditional tales of the African continent
Includes bibliography

Piggott, Juliet
Japanese mythology. new rev ed. Bedrick Bks. 1983 c1982 144p il map (Lib. of the world's myths and legends) $24.95; pa $16.95   **299**
1. Mythology, Japanese
ISBN 0-911745-09-2; 0-87226-251-0 (pa)
LC 83-71480
First published 1969 in the United Kingdom; this edition first published 1982
This presentation of Japanese mythology is illustrated with about 50 color photographs of temples and artifacts and over 100 black-and-white photographs
Includes bibliography

Popol vuh
Popol Vuh; the definitive edition of the Mayan book of the dawn of life and the glories of gods and kings; translated by Dennis Tedlock, with commentary based on the ancient knowledge of the modern Quiché Maya. Simon & Schuster 1985 380p il maps hardcover o.p. paperback available $10.95   **299**
1. Mayas—Legends 2. Indians of Central America—Religion
LC 84-23644
A modern translation of the 16th century Mayan holy book

Popol vuh—*Continued*
"Tedlock's translation splendidly combines scholarship, imagination, and literary sensitivity. His photographs (derived from field work in Guatemala) vividly illustrate the text, and the notes (based on his collaboration with a contemporary Quiché shaman) fascinate and inform." Libr J

Includes bibliography

The **Spirit** world; by the editors of Time-Life Books. Time-Life Bks. 1992 176p il (American Indians) $19.93   **299**
1. Indians of North America—Religion 2. Indians of North America—Rites and ceremonies   LC 92-7592
This work explores creation myths, magical rituals, medical practices and other aspects of the spiritual life of various Native American peoples. There are many color photographs depicting artifacts and modern ceremonies, as well as historic black-and-white photographs
Includes bibliography

300   SOCIAL SCIENCES

300.3   Social sciences— Encyclopedias and dictionaries

International encyclopedia of the social sciences; David L. Sills, editor. Macmillan 1968 17v il o.p.   **300.3**
1. Social sciences—Dictionaries
Supplements available are: Biographical, published 1979, $95 (ISBN 0-02-895690-7); Social science quotations, published 1991, $95 (ISBN 0-02-928751-0)

300.5   Social sciences—Serial publications

Social sciences index. Wilson, H.W. service basis   **300.5**
1. Social sciences—Periodicals—Indexes
ISSN 0094-4920
Also available CD-ROM version
Quarterly with bound annual cumulations
"Author-subject index to over 300 periodicals in the social sciences. Specific subject headings and many cross-references aid research. Book reviews indexed by author in a separate section." Ref Sources for Small & Medium-sized Libr. 5th edition

301   Sociology and anthropology

Encyclopedia of sociology; Edgar F. Borgatta, editor-in-chief, Marie L. Borgatta, managing editor. Macmillan 1992 4v il set $340   **301**
1. Sociology—Dictionaries
ISBN 0-02-897051-9   LC 91-37827
"This set contains 370 lengthy, signed articles written by more than 300 national and international sociologists. The encyclopedia covers not just the traditional issues, concepts, and theories of sociology, but also the newer aspects of social research." Am Libr
For a fuller review see: Booklist, May 1, 1992

302   Social interaction

Fromm, Erich, 1900-1980
For the love of life; translated from the German by Robert and Rita Kimber; edited by Hans Jürgen Schultz. Free Press 1986 152p $24.95   **302**
1. Human behavior 2. Civilization, Modern—1950-
ISBN 0-02-910930-2   LC 85-20518
The author "analyzes the psychopathology he sees everywhere—in consumerism, in the power mania of dictators on the right and left, in our success ethic whose emphasis on ruthlessness and greed is at odds with Judeo-Christian morals. These radio interviews and talks from the last decade of Fromm's life form a succinct, clear summary of his ideas and a provocative statement by a major thinker." Publ Wkly

To have or to be? Harper & Row 1976 xxiv, 215p $13.95   **302**
1. Human behavior 2. Ontology 3. Civilization
ISBN 0-06-011379-0
Also available in paperback from Bantam Bks.
"World perspectives"
The author maintains "that two modes of existence are struggling for the spirit of humankind: the *having* mode, which concentrates on material possession, acquisitiveness, power, and aggression . . . and the *being* mode, which is based in love." Publisher's note
Includes bibliography

302.2   Communication

Adler, Mortimer Jerome, 1902-
How to speak, how to listen. Macmillan 1983 280p hardcover o.p. paperback available $9   **302.2**
1. Communication
ISBN 0-02-079590-4 (pa)   LC 82-25907
The author seeks to "describe various kinds of speeches—sales talks, lectures, courtroom arguments—with advice and examples from his own experiences and the classics. The second part of the book stresses active listening—taking notes during and after a speech, later reflection on what has been said, etc." Libr J

Boettinger, H. M.
Moving mountains; or, The art and craft of letting others see things your way. Macmillan 1969 340p il hardcover o.p. paperback available $8.95   **302.2**
1. Communication
ISBN 0-02-030660-1 (pa)
This book "deals not only with the nuts and bolts of persuasive speaking but [also] with the philosophy of communicating. . . . Boettinger is not for the patron who has limited time. Still, this book has real literary merit and will appeal to anyone who enjoys stimulating ideas." Libr J

Dreyfuss, Henry, 1904-1979
Symbol sourcebook; an authoritative guide to international graphic symbols. McGraw-Hill 1972 292p il o.p.; Van Nostrand Reinhold paperback available $29.95　　　　**302.2**

1. Signs and symbols
ISBN 0-442-21806-0 (pa)

"Approximately one-half of this . . . reference book is given over to graphic symbols, arranged by subject, from accommodations and travel, to engineering, to vehicle control. . . . The second half is a listing of basic graphic forms and how they are employed for a variety of duties. The first part is a ready reference aid, the second an inspiration to designers and artists." Libr J

Liungman, Carl G., 1938-
Dictionary of symbols. ABC-CLIO 1991 596p $65　　　　**302.2**

1. Signs and symbols 2. Picture writing
ISBN 0-87436-610-0　　　　LC 91-36657

Original Swedish edition, 1974

This dictionary groups "icons according to their graphical style rather than their meaning. For example, all symbols based upon the cross are included in one chapter, those based upon the triangle in another, and those based upon the circle in yet another. Each symbol is succinctly defined and a source of origin (if known) is given. To enhance access, both name and form indexes are provided. This work will certainly become one of the key sources for tracing symbols and their meanings." Am Libr

For a fuller review see: Booklist, Jan. 1, 1992

Includes bibliography

Tannen, Deborah
You just don't understand; women and men in conversation. Morrow 1990 330p $18.95　　　　**302.2**

1. Conversation 2. Sex differences (Psychology)
ISBN 0-688-07822-2　　　　LC 89-49000

Also available in paperback from Ballantine Bks.

The author "ponders gender-based differences that, she claims, define and distinguish male and female communication. . . . She asserts that for most women conversation is a way of connecting and negotiating. . . . Men, on the other hand, use conversation to achieve or maintain social status." Publ Wkly

"Aside from the vivid examples and lively prose, what makes this book particularly engaging is that the author makes linguistics . . . interesting and usable." N Y Times Book Rev

Includes bibliography

302.23 Media (Means of communication)

Alterman, Eric
Sound and fury; the Washington punditocracy and the collapse of American politics. HarperCollins Pubs. 1992 352p $23　　　　**302.23**

1. Journalism 2. United States—Politics and government
ISBN 0-06-016874-9　　　　LC 91-59934

The author presents an analysis of non-objective political columnists and television commentators and their influence upon politicians and the public

"Successful both as political history and as media criticism." Publ Wkly

Includes bibliographic references

Bacon-Smith, Camille
Enterprising women; television fandom and the creation of popular myth; photographs by Stephanie A. Hall. University of Pa. Press 1992 338p il $39.95; pa $17.95　　　　**302.23**

1. Television programs 2. United States—Popular culture
ISBN 0-8122-3098-1; 0-8122-1379-3 (pa)
　　　　　　　　　　　　　　LC 91-29875

"A study of the worldwide community of fans of *Star Trek* and other genre television series who create and distribute fiction and art based on their favorite series." Univ Press Books for Public and Second Sch Libr

Includes bibliographic references

McLuhan, Marshall, 1911-1980
The global village; transformations in world life and media in the 21st century; [by] Marshall McLuhan and Bruce R. Powers. Oxford Univ. Press 1989 220p il (Communication and society) $29.95; pa $9.95　　　　**302.23**

1. Mass media 2. Technology and civilization
ISBN 0-19-505444-X; 0-19-507910-8 (pa)
　　　　　　　　　　　　　　LC 88-22718

This book "was written, according to Powers, between 1974 and 1980 . . . and 'put together' between 1976 and 1984. McLuhan's thesis has always been that electronic technologies have been altering and reconstituting people in ways they don't understand and causing them to lose their private identities. This book probes the same theme from different angles, but with the same McLuhanesque all-over-the-place reasoning." Libr J

Includes bibliography

Understanding media. McGraw-Hill 1964 359p o.p.; New Am. Lib. paperback available $4.95　　　　**302.23**

1. Communication 2. Mass media 3. Technology and civilization
ISBN 0-451-62496-3 (pa)

The premise of the book is that the form of any medium, rather than its content, determines what is being communicated. The author examines the various media to show how their forms affect "the patterning of human associations"

Medved, Michael
Hollywood vs. America; popular culture and the war on traditional values. HarperCollins Pubs. 1992 386p $20; pa $12　　　　**302.23**

1. Religions 2. Motion picture industry 3. Television broadcasting 4. United States—Popular culture
ISBN 0-06-016882-X; 0-06-092435-7 (pa)
　　　　　　　　　　　　　　LC 92-52604

Medved, Michael—*Continued*

Medved presents a critique of the entertainment industry in general and Hollywood in particular. Arguing "that 'the dream factory has become the poison factory,' he criticizes Hollywood movies for portraying religion unfavorably, glamorizing violence, and celebrating immorality." Libr J

This "is a passionate and immensely readable polemic about the entertainment industry's self-destructive assault on the ideas and mores of its American audience." Commentary

Meyrowitz, Joshua

No sense of place; the impact of electronic media on social behavior. Oxford Univ. Press 1985 416p $30; pa $10.95
302.23

1. Mass media 2. Communication 3. Social change
ISBN 0-19-503474-0; 0-19-504231-X (pa) LC 84-3950

"Television, the author argues, has so shifted the contexts of communication that modern Americans are losing the sense of place that helps us choose contextually appropriate social behaviors." Libr J

"Meyrowitz has produced a masterful study, a fine combination of perceptive analysis and creative synthesis." Choice

Includes bibliography

Postman, Neil

Amusing ourselves to death; public discourse in the age of show business. Viking 1985 184p o.p.; Penguin Bks. paperback available $10
302.23

1. Mass media 2. Television broadcasting 3. United States—Civilization
ISBN 0-14-009438-5 (pa) LC 85-5335

"Elisabeth Sifton books"

The author argues that the constant exposure to television has contributed to a decline in America's intellectual life

"A sustained, withering and thought-provoking attack on television and what it is doing to us." Publ Wkly

Includes bibliography

Spigel, Lynn

Make room for TV; television and the family ideal in postwar America. University of Chicago Press 1992 236p il $42; pa $15.95
302.23

1. Television
ISBN 0-226-76966-6; 0-226-76967-4 (pa)
LC 91-32770

"Spigel concentrates on the changing role TV has played in our society. Interesting to note is that TV has been a center of attention from its inception. . . . Although academic in tone, her book is still accessible—even fun—to read. She draws on a variety of sources, from ads in women's magazines to controlled university studies, so there's a wide range in levels of information." Booklist

Includes bibliographic references

Twitchell, James B., 1943-

Carnival culture; the trashing of taste in America. Columbia Univ. Press 1992 306p il $24.95
302.23

1. Mass media 2. United States—Popular culture
ISBN 0-231-07830-7 LC 91-32227

This study looks at "how changes in publishing, movie making, and television since the 1960s have affected taste." Univ Press Books for Public and Second Sch Libr

Includes bibliographic references

Wurman, Richard Saul, 1935-

Information anxiety. Doubleday 1989 356p il $19.95
302.23

1. Mass media
ISBN 0-385-24394-4 LC 88-25787

Also available in paperback from Bantam Bks.

The author "argues that 'learning is remembering what you are interested in,' and proposes to help the anxious individual to select personally relevant information from the body of raw data or 'non-information.'" Publ Wkly

"Beyond the very useful advice, this book is built on a profound appreciation for something often overlooked, the wonder of conversation." Christ Sci Monit

Includes bibliography

302.3 Social interaction within groups

Sher, Barbara

Teamworks! building support groups that guarantee success; [by] Barbara Sher and Annie Gottlieb. Warner Bks. 1989 230p hardcover o.p. paperback available $12.95
302.3

1. Social groups
ISBN 0-446-39244-8 (pa) LC 88-40097

"Along with details on establishing the support unit, the authors provide success stories, tips on overcoming problems within the group, and detailed instructions on such trivia as serving food at meetings and sharing the work of record keeping. An excellent book for anyone who succeeds best in a group or who needs the encouragement of others in order to tackle life's difficulties." Booklist

303.3 Social coordination and control

Cousins, Norman

The pathology of power; foreword by George F. Kennan. Norton 1987 228p hardcover o.p. paperback available $8.95
303.3

1. Power (Social sciences) 2. United States—Military policy
ISBN 0-393-30541-4 (pa) LC 86-21658

The author seeks to "trace the way national power becomes enlarged and institutionalized. . . . This book is based largely on reports issued by the U.S. General Accounting Office and congressional committees—reports documenting waste, fraud, and incompetence in excess of ten billion dollars." Publisher's note

Cousins, Norman—*Continued*
"A rigorously reasoned, carefully articulated position paper on a public-affairs issue of vital concern." Booklist
Includes bibliography

Galbraith, John Kenneth, 1908-
The anatomy of power. Houghton Mifflin 1983 206p hardcover o.p. paperback available $10.70   303.3
1. Power (Social sciences)
ISBN 0-395-38170-3 (pa)   LC 83-12622
The author analyses the nature and use of both institutional and private power
This book "focuses on a wide range of organizations and their power. He argues persuasively that property and personality, once independent sources of power, can effectively be used today only with the help of organizational structures." N Y Times Book Rev

Huxley, Aldous, 1894-1963
Brave new world revisited. Harper & Row 1958 147p hardcover o.p. paperback available $6   303.3
1. Propaganda 2. Totalitarianism 3. Brainwashing 4. Culture
ISBN 0-06-080984-1 (pa)
Also available in hardcover from Borgo Press
In response to his 1932 novel Brave new world "Huxley reconsiders his prophecies and fears that some of these may be coming true much sooner than he thought." Oxford Companion to Engl Lit. 5th edition

Koppes, Clayton R., 1945-
Hollywood goes to war; how politics, profits, and propaganda shaped World War II movies; [by] Clayton R. Koppes, Gregory D. Black. Free Press 1987 374p il $22.50
303.3
1. World War, 1939-1945—Motion pictures and the war 2. Propaganda, American 3. Motion pictures—Censorship
ISBN 0-02-903550-3   LC 87-10698
Also available in paperback from University of Calif. Press
This book considers the "influence of the US Office of War Information over the content and presentation of Hollywood movies, and the industry's own concern with the censorship of film content to coincide with an assumed need for [supporting] the war effort." Choice
"Thoroughly thought out and well written, this is an important, ground-breaking work." Libr J
Includes bibliography

303.4 Social change

Hardison, O. B.
Disappearing through the skylight; culture and technology in the twentieth century. Viking 1989 389p il o.p.; Penguin Bks. paperback available $14   303.4
1. Technology and civilization 2. Social change 3. Culture
ISBN 0-14-011582-X (pa)   LC 88-40477

This book "reviews changes in cultural concepts of nature, history, language, art, and human evolution since the beginning of the 20th century. Historical events that reflect evolutionary and sudden changes of concepts are presented. . . . The increased accessibility of science and technology is leading the styles of architecture, dress, and even eating toward universality." Sci Books Films
"Challenging but highly readable, the book should spark discussion." Libr J
Includes bibliography

Hoffman, Abbie
The best of Abbie Hoffman; foreword by Norman Mailer; edited by Dan Simon with the author. Four Walls Eight Windows 1989 421p il $21.95; pa $14.95   303.4
1. Radicals and radicalism 2. United States—Civilization
ISBN 0-941423-27-1; 0-941423-42-5 (pa)
LC 89-23585
This volume contains selections from Revolution for the hell of it, Woodstock Nation, Steal this book, and New writings

Naisbitt, John
Megatrends; ten new directions transforming our lives. Warner Bks. 1982 290p hardcover o.p. paperback available $5.95   303.4
1. Social change 2. United States—Social conditions
ISBN 0-446-35681-6 (pa)   LC 82-6959
"Among the ten 'Megatrends' Naisbitt describes are: a global economy edging out national economies; a north-to-south population shift; a move from an industrial to an information-based society. Naisbitt advocates that such trends should influence planning. . . . Fascinating reading." Libr J
Includes bibliographic references

Megatrends 2000; ten new directions for the 1990's; [by] John Naisbitt and Patricia Aburdene. Morrow 1990 384p $21.95
303.4
1. Social change 2. United States—Social conditions
ISBN 0-688-07224-0   LC 89-13301
Also available in paperback from Avon Bks.
The authors "examine what they see as ten 'millennial megatrends: gateways to the 21st Century.' They are: the global economy; a renaissance in arts; the emergence of free-market socialism; global lifestyles and cultural nationalism; the privatization of the welfare state; rise of the Pacific Rim; the decade of women in leadership; the age of biology; the religious revival especially in what . . . [they call] 'new age' religion; [and] the triumph of the individual." Christ Sci Monit
Includes bibliographic references

Postman, Neil
Technopoly; the surrender of culture to technology. Knopf 1992 222p $21; pa $11
303.4
1. Technology and civilization
ISBN 0-394-58272-1; 0-679-74540-8 (pa)
LC 91-53121

Postman, Neil—*Continued*
According to Postman, "the history of the world can be retold from the perspective of technological advances. In 'technopoly,' the present stage in Western culture, our tools, especially the computer, have committed a palace revolt, 'redefining what we mean by religion, by art, by family, by politics, by history, by privacy, by intelligence, so that our definitions fit its new requirements.'" Natl Rev

Postman's "style is comfortable, his exposition incisive, and his reasoning hard to ignore." Christ Sci Monit

Includes bibliographic references

Toffler, Alvin
Future shock. Random House 1970 505p $18.95   **303.4**
1. Social change 2. Technology and civilization 3. Civilization, Modern—1950-
ISBN 0-394-42586-3
Also available in paperback from Bantam Bks.

According to the author, "future shock is 'the dizzying disorientation brought on by the premature arrival of the future.' . . . Toffler outlines some interesting strategies for survival, writing in a clear popular style." Publ Wkly

Includes bibliography

Powershift; knowledge, wealth, and violence at the edge of the 21st century. Bantam Bks. 1990 xxii, 585p hardcover o.p. paperback available $6.99   **303.4**
1. Social change 2. Power (Social sciences) 3. Civilization, Modern—1950-
ISBN 0-553-29215-3 (pa)   LC 90-1068

The author "argues that the control of knowledge has become the principal means to create wealth and power. Aided by the widespread use of computers and other communications technologies, this 'powershift,' Toffler predicts, will dramatically alter the world's political balance." Libr J

Includes bibliography

The third wave. Morrow 1980 544p o.p.; Bantam Bks. paperback available $5.95
                                               303.4
1. Social change 2. Technology and civilization 3. Civilization, Modern—1950-
ISBN 0-553-24698-4 (pa)   LC 79-26690

Toffler argues that mankind, having already experienced the agricultural age and the industrial age, is on the verge of a new age characterized by "new technical systems, especially those in electronics, genetics and biology." N Y Times Book Rev

Includes bibliography

303.49 Social forecasts

Halberstam, David, 1934-
The next century. Morrow 1991 126p $16.95   **303.49**
1. Forecasting 2. World politics—1965- 3. Twenty-first century
ISBN 0-688-10391-X   LC 90-46188
Also available in paperback from Avon Bks.

"Essentially this book is an analysis of America's declining world position and how her economic dominance has been eroded by more industrious and dynamic rivals." Libr J

303.6 Social conflict

Arendt, Hannah
On revolution   **303.6**
1. Revolutions
Hardcover and paperback editions available from various publishers
First published 1963 by Viking

The author "believes that war and revolution are the central facts of our time. But while war may become obsolete through nuclear terror, revolution seems likely to persist as the order of the day, and those who understand revolution may well be the masters of the future." Atlantic

Camus, Albert, 1913-1960
The rebel; an essay on man in revolt; with a foreword by Sir Herbert Read; a revised and complete translation of L'homme révolté by Anthony Bower. Vintage Bks. 1991 c1956 306p pa $11
                                                   303.6
1. Revolutions 2. Nihilism
ISBN 0-679-73384-1   LC 91-50022
Original French edition, 1951; this translation first published 1956 by Knopf

The author describes how the theories of philosophers have been used with disastrous effect by political leaders from the French Revolution through the nihilist revolutions of Russia and the governments of Lenin, Hitler and Stalin. The conclusion calls for a return to a political philosophy having as its aim the happiness and development of living human beings

MacDonald, Eileen
Shoot the women first. Random House 1992 xxi, 241p $20   **303.6**
1. Terrorism 2. Women—Political activity
ISBN 0-679-41596-3   LC 92-3867

This book is based on interviews with "members of the Basque separatist movement, the Italian Red Brigades, the Palestine Liberation Organization, the Irish Republican Army and the German Red Army Faction." Publ Wkly

This is "a thoughtful analysis of the oppressions and ideologies that have convinced some women to engage in political violence." Booklist

304.2 Human ecology

Commoner, Barry, 1917-
Making peace with the planet. Pantheon Bks. 1990 292p $19.95   **304.2**
1. Pollution 2. Man—Influence on nature 3. Environmental protection 4. Nature conservation
ISBN 0-394-56598-3   LC 89-43241
Also available in paperback from New Press (NY)

The author offers an "analysis of our contemporary environmental crisis, using the metaphor of a war between the natural ecosphere and the human-made technosphere." Libr J

"Visionary yet specific, his urgent essay is a blueprint of our possible future and a beacon for the environmental struggles of the '90s." Publ Wkly

Includes bibliographic references

Gore, Albert, Jr.
Earth in the balance; ecology and the human spirit; [by] Al Gore. Houghton Mifflin 1992 407p il maps $22.95   **304.2**

1. Human ecology 2. Environmental protection
ISBN 0-395-57821-3   LC 91-42676

Also available in paperback from New Am. Lib.

In this discussion of the global environment and civilization the author "argues that only a radical rethinking of our relationship with nature can save the earth's ecology for future generations." Publisher's note

"The author exhibits little of the clichéd myopia of his profession and is aware of the political obstacles posed by such an integrated approach. He identifies the root of our current problems as spiritual. If civilization is to persist, he maintains, it must make the rescue of the environment its organizing principle." N Y Times Book Rev

Includes bibliography

McPhee, John A.
The control of nature. Farrar, Straus & Giroux 1989 272p $17.95; pa $10   **304.2**

1. Environmental protection 2. Man—Influence on nature
ISBN 0-374-12890-1; 0-374-52259-6 (pa) LC 89-1052

The three essays which make up this book first appeared in the New Yorker. They describe "efforts to pit human ingenuity against the might of Mother Nature . . . in the lower Mississippi Valley, on the volcanic islands of Iceland, and in the canyons of Los Angeles's San Gabriel mountains. In each case, [McPhee argues], people risk their lives and incur colossal expense to live in places where geology and weather say they have no business to be." Libr J

"The book is a fascinating, if sometimes disjointed, report. . . . Once caught up in the drama, it is difficult to put these stories aside." N Y Times Book Rev

Ornstein, Robert E. (Robert Evan), 1942-
New world new mind; moving toward conscious evolution; [by] Robert Ornstein, Paul Ehrlich. Doubleday 1989 302p il o.p.; Simon & Schuster paperback available $9.95   **304.2**

1. Human ecology 2. Environmental protection
ISBN 0-671-69606-8 (pa)   LC 87-36605

According to the authors "the 'new world' of short-term technological and environmental change requires a 'new mind' capable of perceiving long-term, slow-motion calamity. . . . The authors therefore recommend a formal effort to train minds to filter in, not filter out, imperceptible changes in global ecology and the large-scale consequences of economic growthmanship." Libr J

Includes bibliography

Sagan, Carl, 1934-
A path where no man thought; nuclear winter and the end of the arms race; [by] Carl Sagan and Richard P. Turco. Random House 1990 xx, 499p il $27.45   **304.2**

1. Nuclear warfare 2. Arms control
ISBN 0-394-58307-8   LC 89-43155

This book attempts to "describe what determines the global climate of the Earth, and how nuclear war could change that climate; what the long-term consequences of

nuclear war would be like, for individuals and societies." Prologue

The authors' "detailed proposals for reducing arsenals to achieve a 'minimum sufficient deterrance' make this a book that neither concerned citizens nor policymakers can ignore." Publ Wkly

304.6   Population

Ehrlich, Paul R.
The population explosion; [by] Paul R. Ehrlich & Anne H. Ehrlich. Simon & Schuster 1990 320p hardcover o.p. paperback available $11   **304.6**

1. Population 2. Human ecology
ISBN 0-671-73294-3 (pa)   LC 89-48263

This book examines "the detonation of and fall out from the overpopulation of the Earth. The dimensions of the problem—depletion of natural resources and the reduction in the Earth's biodiversity—are up-dated to include global warming, rain forest destruction, ozone depletion, and AIDS. The authors clearly portray the magnitude of the problem and offer viable solutions. This is an important book." Libr J

Includes bibliographic references

Hartmann, Betsy
Reproductive rights and wrongs; the global politics of population control and contraceptive choice. Harper & Row 1987 368p $24.95; pa $13   **304.6**

1. Birth control 2. Population
ISBN 0-06-055065-1; 0-06-096171-6 (pa)

           LC 86-46070

A "sociopolitical treatise that debunks the myth of global overpopulation and warns of gross worldwide abuses of human (but especially female) rights in the name of birth control." Booklist

"An important book both for its arguments and for its scrutiny of specific programs in India, Kenya, Indonesia, Bangladesh, and of China's new one-child policy." Christ Sci Monit

Includes bibliography

Malthus, T. R. (Thomas Robert), 1766-1834
An essay on the principle of population   **304.6**

1. Population

Hardcover and paperback editions available from various publishers

First published 1798

This is "the Malthusian doctrine that population increases in a geometric ratio, while the means of subsistence increases in an arithmetic ratio, and that crime, disease, war, and vice are necessary checks on population." Reader's Ency. 3d edition

Mattson, Mark T.
Atlas of the 1990 census. Macmillan 1992 168p il maps $90   **304.6**

1. United States—Census—Maps 2. United States—Population—Maps
ISBN 0-02-897302-X   LC 92-24006

Mattson, Mark T.—*Continued*

"This work is organized into six sections containing maps that graphically depict the statistical results of the 1990 census of population and housing. Population includes density, age, sex, death and birth rates, etc. Information about households depicts families, marital status, female-headed, nonfamily, etc." Booklist

United Nations. Statistical Office

Demographic yearbook. U.N. Publs. $125

304.6

1. Population—Statistics

Annual. First issue for 1948 published 1949. Text in English and French

"Official compilation of international demographic data in such fields as area and population, natality, mortality, marriage, divorce, and international migration. Each year some aspect of demographic statistics is treated intensively." Ref Sources for Small & Medium-sized Libr. 5th edition

Wattenberg, Ben J.

The first universal nation; leading indicators and ideas about the surge of America in the 1990s. Free Press 1991 418p il hardcover o.p. paperback available $12.95

304.6

1. Forecasting 2. United States—Population
ISBN 0-02-934002-0 (pa)   LC 90-3803

A study of American demographic and geopolitical trends

"The topics range over the environment, presidential elections, definitions of poverty, and much more. Most show Wattenberg at his debunking best." Commentary

304.8   Movement of people

Gregory, James Noble

American exodus; the Dust Bowl migration and Okie culture in California. Oxford Univ. Press 1989 338p il $30; pa $11.95

304.8

1. Migration, Internal   2. Agricultural laborers
3. Oklahoma—History 4. California—Social life and customs
ISBN 0-19-504423-1; 0-19-507136-0 (pa)

LC 88-36230

This is a "study of the migration of Oklahomans, Arkansans, Texans, and Missourians to California in the years of . . . the Great Depression." Libr J

"By examining oral history collections, the records of investigators from the 1940s, and mimeographed newspapers emanating from migrant farm labor camps, Gregory has unearthed grassroots attitudes and observations, thereby transforming the Okies from anonymous victims of the system into real people." Rev Am Hist

Includes bibliographic references

305.23   Young people

Blume, Judy

Letters to Judy: what your kids wish they could tell you. Putnam 1986 284p o.p.; Pocket Bks. paperback available $4.50

305.23

1. Children 2. Parent and child
ISBN 0-671-62696-5 (pa)   LC 85-30119

The author presents letters from children to her confiding their concerns with friendships, families, illness, sexuality, and other problems; and in return, Ms. Blume shares similar moments from her own life, both as a child and as a parent

"Blume wrote 'Letters to Judy' to share kids' letters with other kids to let them know they are not alone, and to let their parents know what kids cannot seem to tell them directly. As she addresses the whole family, Blume is remarkably successful in her dual purpose." Voice Youth Advocates

Includes bibliography

Cosby, Bill, 1937-

Childhood; introduction by Alvin F. Poussaint. Putnam 1991 188p o.p.; Berkley Pub. Group paperback available $7.95

305.23

1. Children 2. Parent and child
ISBN 0-425-13476-8 (pa)   LC 91-16722

Also available Thorndike Press large print edition

The author "features the eternal conflict between parents and kids while comparing the dull, structured, affluent lives of today's children with his own richly adventurous, independent years growing up in the 1940s." Publ Wkly

Elkind, David, 1931-

The hurried child; growing up too fast too soon. rev ed. Addison-Wesley 1989 xx, 217p pa $10.53   **305.23**

1. Stress (Psychology) 2. Child psychology 3. Child rearing
ISBN 0-201-07397-8   LC 88-7523

First published 1981

The author "suggests that the general fast pace of life and the demands of the current generation of upwardly mobile parents have conspired to—albeit inadvertently—increase stress on children, who too often must mimic adult schedules and life-styles. Written clearly and cohesively, Elkind's text is backed up with much of the current research on children and adolescents." Booklist

Includes bibliography

Hawes, Joseph M.

The children's rights movement of the United States; a history of advocacy and protection. Twayne Pubs. 1991 169p (Social movements past and present) $26.95; pa $13.95   **305.23**

1. Children—Civil rights
ISBN 0-8057-9747-5; 0-8057-9748-3 (pa)

LC 91-10922

The author presents an "overview of the 'many disparate social actions' that might pass as a children's rights 'movement.' Hawes begins his narrative with the

Hawes, Joseph M.—*Continued*
'stubborn child' law (1641); he continues through (among other significant happenings) the founding of the Society for the Prevention of Cruelty to Children (1875), the creation of the U.S. Children's Bureau (1912), the establishment of the Children's Defense League (1973), and the ACLU's stance on behalf of child welfare victims in 1990." Libr J

Includes bibliographic references

Hopson, Darlene Powell
Different and wonderful; raising black children in a race-conscious society; [by] Darlene Powell Hopson and Derek S. Hopson; foreword by Alvin F. Poussaint. Prentice Hall Press 1990 xxiii, 241p $19.95
305.23
1. Black children 2. Child rearing
ISBN 0-13-211509-3   LC 89-70909
Also available in paperback from Fireside Bks.

This is a "guide to child development, which concentrates on engendering positive self-images for black children of all ages." Booklist
"The approaches of this work make it imperative reading for concerned parents everywhere. Highly recommended." Libr J

Ianni, Francis A. J.
The search for structure; a report on American youth today. Free Press 1989 336p $24.95
305.23
1. Youth—United States 2. United States—Social conditions
ISBN 0-02-915360-3   LC 88-30945
This is a report of "Ianni's research into the influences shaping the behaviors and identities of American teens, from 1973 to 1985. . . . The author has a good feel for the inner journey that characterizes adolescence and a genuine empathy with the youngsters he and his associates interviewed." America

Includes bibliography

Kotlowitz, Alex
There are no children here; the story of two boys growing up in the other America. Doubleday 1991 324p $21.95; pa $12.95
305.23
1. Children 2. Family 3. Public housing 4. Chicago (Ill.)—Social conditions
ISBN 0-385-26526-3; 0-385-26556-5 (pa)
LC 90-45225
"A sensitive and unremitting survey of the life and times of Lafeyette and Pharoah Rivers, their family and the Chicago housing project they live in." N Y Times Book Rev

Includes bibliographic references

Morris, Desmond
Babywatching. Crown 1992 214p il $15
305.23
1. Infants
ISBN 0-517-58845-5   LC 91-43202

Through observation the author sets out to explain infant behavior and development. He also offers his insights into popular baby myths and misconceptions

Steinberg, Laurence D., 1952-
You and your adolescent; a parent's guide for ages 10 to 20; [by] Laurence Steinberg and Ann Levine. HarperCollins Pubs. 1990 417p $19.95; pa $12
305.23
1. Adolescence 2. Parent and child
ISBN 0-06-016241-4; 0-06-272002-3 (pa)
LC 89-45720
"After debunking popular myths—e.g., adolescents are inherently difficult, peer pressure is evil, the nuclear family is in a decline—the authors offer practical information and suggestions. . . . Age-appropriate chapters discuss physical health, psychological development, and socialization skills, and an introductory section cites the components of a 'good parent.'" Libr J
"Wide ranging, well documented, and generally middle-of-the-road, this book's counsel is well worth considering, and its encouraging attitude is like a breath of fresh air." Booklist

Includes bibliographic references

Winn, Marie
Children without childhood. Pantheon Bks. 1983 224p o.p.; Penguin Bks. paperback available $9.95
305.23
1. Children—United States 2. Family 3. United States—Social conditions
ISBN 0-14-007105-9 (pa)   LC 82-48951
This is an "account of the many facets that have contributed to the establishment and alteration of the phenomenon of childhood. The author interviewed numerous individuals to gather impressions of the contemporary demeanor of American children and how parents' attitudes have moved from an 'age of protection' to an 'age of preparation.' Current and past children's behavioral patterns are described, explained, and compared with the theories and research of many well-established authorities on childhood." Choice

Includes bibliographic references

305.24   Adults

Sheehy, Gail
Pathfinders. Morrow 1981 494p o.p.; Bantam Bks. paperback available $6.99
305.24
1. Adulthood 2. Quality of life 3. Self-realization
ISBN 0-553-27084-2 (pa)   LC 81-11306
The author examines the lives and careers of people who are able to confront crises and turn them into opportunities
The author "reports cogently on the theories and research, both old and new, of psychologists, sociologists, anthropologists, historians, and philosophers on almost every imaginable aspect of personality, development, and social change." Psychol Today

Includes bibliography

305.26 Late adulthood

Biracree, Tom, 1947-
Over 50; the resource book for the better half of your life; [by] Tom and Nancy Biracree. HarperPerennial 1991 495p hardcover o.p. paperback available $15.95
305.26

1. Middle age 2. Elderly 3. Retirement
ISBN 0-06-273000-2 (pa)   LC 90-55490

"This is a guide to resources useful to those approaching retirement, and it includes discussions of personal finance, health, housing, employment, and leisure activities. Chapters begin with overviews of the topic followed by lists of resource organizations and related publications, most of which are inexpensive or free." Libr J

Cheney, Walter J.
The second 50 years; a reference manual for senior citizens; [by] Walter J. Cheney, William J. Diehm, Frank E. Seeley. Paragon House 1992 445p il pa $21.95   **305.26**

1. Elderly 2. Retirement
ISBN 1-55778-531-7   LC 91-42339

"This compendium provides facts, advice, and sources of additional information on everything from healthcare to travel tips, dealing with con artists, and proper use of crutches. The large-type format and positive tone make this a popular reference for patrons and librarians alike." Libr J

A **Consumer's** guide to aging; [by] David H. Solomon [et al.] Johns Hopkins Univ. Press 1992 526p il $45; pa $22.95
305.26

1. Elderly 2. Retirement
ISBN 0-8018-4301-4; 0-8018-4302-2 (pa)
LC 91-41587

"A comprehensive guide to the questions and concerns of the later years with sound advice on issues ranging from health and housing to fitness and finances." Univ Press Books for Public and Second Sch Libr

Includes bibliographic references

Cort-Van Arsdale, Diana
Transitions: a woman's guide to successful retirement; [by] Diana Cort-Van Arsdale and Phyllis Newman. HarperCollins Pubs. 1991 334p $21.95; pa $11   **305.26**

1. Retirement 2. Women
ISBN 0-06-016278-3; 0-06-092147-1 (pa)
LC 90-55929

"The authors outline the number of choices and options retirees have, how to gain access to them, and where to get necessary information. Besides social, financial, and career implications, they emphasize the emotional adjustment to retirement and, accordingly, proffer self-assessment quizzes to help the reader identify feelings and coping styles." Booklist

Includes bibliographic references

The **Encyclopedia** of aging; George L. Maddox, editor-in-chief; Robert C. Atchley [et al.], associate editors; Raymond J. Corsini, managing editor. Springer 1987 xxv, 890p il $96   **305.26**

1. Gerontology—Dictionaries 2. Elderly—Dictionaries
ISBN 0-8261-4840-9   LC 86-27965

"Signed articles, alphabetically arranged, treat key topics in aging, legislation, government agencies, foundations, and membership organizations. Entries (typically two to three columns, some as long as 16—e.g., Social security) include Asian-American aged, Cell morphology, Demography, Congressional committees, Gray Panthers, Health care policy, Sexuality, and World Assembly on Aging. Separate list of headwords; tables, diagrams, and figures; list of 224 contributors. 128 pages of references; detailed general index." Sheehy. Guide to Ref Books. 10th edition. suppl

Includes bibliography

Falk, Ursula A.
On our own; independent living for older persons. Prometheus Bks. 1989 159p il (Golden age bks) $19.95; pa $15.95
305.26

1. Elderly
ISBN 0-87975-502-4; 0-87975-449-4 (pa)
LC 88-32141

The author explores "ways in which older people can continue to live successfully on their own. The book outlines services available, such as meal programs, alternative living arrangements, and medical plans, and touches on subjects crucial to meaningful independent living, including leisure activities and advocacy." Libr J

Kaplan, Lawrence J. (Lawrence Jay), 1915-
Retiring right; planning for your successful retirement. Avery Pub. Group 1990 352p pa $12.95   **305.26**

1. Retirement
ISBN 0-89529-461-3   LC 90-280
First published 1986

The author focuses mainly on the financial aspects of retirement planning and "deals largely with practical matters such as budgeting, taxes, investments, health insurance, Social Security and pension benefits, and housing (including nursing homes)." Libr J

Includes bibliographic references

LeShan, Eda J.
It's better to be over the hill than under it; thoughts on life over sixty; [by] Eda LeShan. Newmarket Press 1990 227p $18.95; pa $11.95   **305.26**

1. Elderly
ISBN 1-55704-071-0; 1-55704-102-4 (pa)
LC 90-41274

"In these collected essays, LeShan discusses the terrors of failing health, dwindling social security payments, and abusive relations. Still, most of her pieces are laced with humor and portray the positive side of growing older." Booklist

Palder, Edward L.

The retirement sourcebook; your complete guide to health, leisure, and consumer information. Woodbine House 1989 521p $14.95   **305.26**

1. Retirement 2. Consumer education
ISBN 0-933149-24-7   LC 88-40219

"Readers can find lists of brochures available on buying apartment insurance and catalogs of mail-order pet supplies, as well as information on the National Senior Olympics and how to request presidential birthday or anniversary greetings. Also included is information on health care and crime prevention volunteer programs. Entries are short and include brief introductions to topics and annotated lists of additional resources, including telephone hotlines, publications, and clearing-houses." Libr J

Petras, Kathryn

The only retirement guide you'll ever need; [by] Kathryn & Ross Petras. Poseidon Press 1991 544p il hardcover o.p. paperback available $14.95   **305.26**

1. Retirement
ISBN 0-671-70060-X (pa)   LC 91-25536

The authors "discuss relocation after retirement, keeping healthy, and post-retirement employment. Chapters on the pros and cons of early retirement and last-minute retirement planning are a plus." Libr J

Includes bibliographic references

Roy, Frederick Hampton

The encyclopedia of aging and the elderly; [by] F. Hampton Roy and Charles Russell. Facts on File 1992 308p il $45   **305.26**

1. Gerontology—Dictionaries 2. Elderly—Dictionaries
ISBN 0-8160-1869-3   LC 91-23435

This "work covers such topics as estate planning, living with adult children, guardianships, living wills, and the like, as well as social activities, volunteering, TV watching, and coping with taxes. Practical advice is offered on selecting a nursing home and on visiting the homebound elderly. . . . This work will prove useful in any public or academic library." Booklist

Includes bibliographic references

Sinclair, Carole

When women retire; the problems they face & how to solve them. Crown 1992 178p $20   **305.26**

1. Women 2. Retirement
ISBN 0-517-58499-9   LC 91-25769

In this work the author "outlines steps for researching and structuring a retirement plan, including such elements as insurance. . . . Sinclair presents scenarios of pre-retirement preparation that cover the differing situations of women who are married, divorced or single, business owners or employees. Various kinds of pension plans are described, as are individual retirement accounts, Keough plans, annuities and Social Security payments." Publ Wkly

Smith, Wesley J.

The senior citizens' handbook; a nuts and bolts approach to more comfortable living. Price/Stern/Sloan 1989 214p pa $9.95
                                          305.26

1. Elderly 2. Retirement
ISBN 0-89586-795-8   LC 88-39744

Medicare, housing, crime prevention, estate planning and budgeting are among the topics examined in this volume

"This handbook, which offers basic information supplemented with names and addresses of resource organizations, provides a useful point for coping with the many challenges of growing old." Libr J

305.3   Men and women. Sex role

Banner, Lois W.

In full flower; aging women, power, and sexuality: a history. Knopf 1992 422p il $25; pa $13   **305.3**

1. Women—History 2. Sex role
ISBN 0-394-57943-7; 0-679-74474-6 (pa) LC 91-4266

The author "shows how, from antiquity on, stereotypes have restricted the power that knowledge and experience should naturally confer on older women. . . . Other themes covered are menopause, older women and young men duos." Publ Wkly

"The disparate influences of Ovid, Chaucer, Shakespeare, Freud, Margaret Fuller, and Colette all come under Banner's clear-eyed scrutiny, resulting in a vibrant synthesis of scholarship and thought that challenges the cult of youth and reductive views of women." Booklist

Includes bibliographic references

Berkowitz, Bob

What men won't tell you but women need to know; [by] Bob Berkowitz with Roger Gittines. Morrow 1990 203p $16.95 **305.3**

1. Men—Psychology
ISBN 0-688-08779-5   LC 89-12953

Also available in paperback from Avon Bks.

This book "offers advice to women on getting men to open up, dating divorced men, extramarital affairs, gauging a man's true intentions regarding commitment, dealing with his fears of impotence, and so forth." Publ Wkly

Written "in a chattily informal tone. . . . Optimistic, frequently humorous." Booklist

French, Marilyn, 1929-

Beyond power; on women, men, and morals. Summit Bks. 1985 640p o.p.; Ballantine Bks. paperback available $14
                                          305.3

1. Sex role 2. Women—Social conditions
ISBN 0-345-33405-1 (pa)   LC 85-2718

The author examines the evolution of sex roles and the relationship between the sexes

"That there is so much to argue with in Beyond Power is of course one of the book's most attractive virtues. If it fails to achieve dialectical thinking, it certainly elicits dialectical thinking." Psychol Today

Includes bibliography

305.31 Men

Bly, Robert
Iron John; a book about men. Addison-Wesley 1990 268p $19.18 **305.31**
1. Men—Psychology
ISBN 0-201-51720-5   LC 90-37877
Also available in paperback from Vintage Bks.
"Drawing vitally upon such diverse sources as ancient mythology, classic literature (including his own poetry), anthropology, psychology, and even the responses of the real-life men who have participated in his seminars ('gatherings'), Bly staunchly redefines male identity, emphasizing the importance of what he calls 'warrior energy' and all its positive implications." Booklist

Duneier, Mitchell
Slim's table; race, respectability, and masculinity in America. University of Chicago Press 1992 192p il $19.95 **305.31**
1. Blacks—Chicago (Ill.) 2. Men—Psychology 3. Chicago (Ill.)—Race relations
ISBN 0-226-17030-6   LC 91-45637
"This book deals with the lives of older working-class African American men of the South Side ghettos of Chicago." Libr J
"Duneier's contribution in this small book—and there is one—is to point out that neither scholars nor journalists attend to the majority of the black American population, the solid working class." Nation
Includes bibliographic references

Keen, Sam
Fire in the belly; on being a man. Bantam Bks. 1991 272p $19.95; pa $12.50 **305.31**
1. Men—Psychology
ISBN 0-553-07188-2; 0-553-35137-0 (pa)
     LC 90-19474
"Keen argues that if the old gender/sex differentiations are wrong, so are modern unisex approaches. The difference between men and women is more than biological. Keen does not articulate the difference, however, calling it a mystery. Describing what being a man has historically meant, he argues forcefully that we need a new understanding." Libr J
Includes bibliographic references

305.4 Women

Aburdene, Patricia
Megatrends for women; [by] Patricia Aburdene and John Naisbitt. Villard Bks. 1992 xxiv, 388p $22.50 **305.4**
1. Women—Social conditions 2. Social change
ISBN 0-679-40337-X   LC 92-431
"Aburdene and Naisbitt scan what women have accomplished so far and what comes next in politics, sports, work, religion, medicine, fashion, the family, social activism, and the 'New World Order.' . . . Most readers will pick up useful factoids and solid food for thought here." Booklist
Includes bibliographic references

Anderson, Bonnie S.
A history of their own; women in Europe from prehistory to the present; [by] Bonnie S. Anderson, Judith P. Zinsser. Harper & Row 1988 2v il hardcover o.p. paperbacks available ea $16 **305.4**
1. Women—Europe 2. Europe—History
ISBN 0-06-091452-1 (v1); 0-06-091563-3 (v2)
     LC 87-11933
This two-volume social history discusses early traditions about women; the lives of peasant women; women in the church; feudal women; town women from the twelfth to the seventeenth centuries; women of the courts from the fifteenth to the eighteenth centuries; and women of the cities through the twentieth century
"Combining superb scholarship and sheer readability, this is a revelatory, much-needed survey of women in European history." Publ Wkly
Includes bibliography

Beauvoir, Simone de, 1908-1986
The second sex; translated and edited by H.M. Parshley. Knopf 1993 lv, 786p (Everyman's lib) $20 **305.4**
1. Women
ISBN 0-679-42016-9   LC 92-54303
Original French edition, 1949; this translation first published 1953
This "thorough analysis of women's secondary status in society, became a classic of feminist literature." Reader's Ency. 3d edition

Berg, Barbara J.
The crisis of the working mother; resolving the conflict between family and work. Summit Bks. 1986 249p $16.95 **305.4**
1. Women—Employment 2. Mothers
ISBN 0-671-49956-4   LC 85-31717
An analysis of the challenges and conflicts facing working mothers
"Berg's crisp treatment distinguishes itself with a good mix of real-life examples and constructive suggestions." Booklist
Includes bibliography

Bergmann, Barbara R.
The economic emergence of women. Basic Bks. 1986 372p il $19.95; pa $14 **305.4**
1. Women—Employment 2. Sex discrimination 3. Homemakers
ISBN 0-465-01796-7; 0-465-01797-5 (pa)
     LC 85-73876
A historical survey of the economic impact of women in modern society
"Bergmann has constructed a lucid synthesis of the economic and sociological literatures on gender inequality. Her most important accomplishment is to make complex scholarly and policy issues accessible to a lay audience. The book would be profitably read by policymakers interested in employment issues and could be used to good advantage in courses on the sociology or economics of work." Am J Sociol
Includes bibliography

Brownmiller, Susan

Femininity. Linden Press/Simon & Schuster 1984 270p o.p.; Fawcett Bks. paperback available $10   **305.4**

1. Women—Psychology 2. Feminism
ISBN 0-449-90142-4 (pa)   LC 83-20004

"Much of 'Femininity' is an exploration of feminine conventions—body, hair, clothes, voice—through the centuries and across cultures. Some of it is well-plowed turf. . . . But much of it is fresh and revealing." Newsweek

Davis, Angela Yvonne, 1944-

Women, culture, & politics; [by] Angela Y. Davis. Random House 1989 238p $17.95; pa $11   **305.4**

1. Black women 2. Blacks—Social conditions 3. Sexism 4. Racism
ISBN 0-394-56976-8; 0-679-72487-7 (pa)
     LC 88-42674

In this "collection of essays based on speeches delivered between 1983 and 1987, Ms. Davis . . . discusses the interconnectedness of sexism, racism and classism. . . . Ms. Davis's arguments for justice are formidable. While some may be put off by her persistent propagandizing for 'the eventual advent of communism,' the power of her historical insights and the sweetness of her dreams cannot be denied." N Y Times Book Rev

Davis, Flora

Moving the mountain; the women's movement in America since 1960. Simon & Schuster 1991 604p $27.50; pa $14   **305.4**

1. Women's movement 2. Feminism 3. Women—United States
ISBN 0-671-60207-1; 0-671-79292-X (pa)
     LC 91-25144

"In a book about women's activism since 1960, Davis discusses political realities as well as issues such as abortion, lesbian feminism, radical equality, and the ERA." Booklist

"This balanced, gripping, inspirational chronicle of the contemporary women's movement in the U.S. should be a standard resource for years to come." Publ Wkly

Includes bibliography

Doress, Paula Brown

Ourselves, growing older; women aging with knowledge and power; [by] Paula Brown Doress and Diana Laskin Siegal and the Midlife and Older Women Book Project; in cooperation with the Boston Women's Health Book Collective; illustrations by Roselaine Perkis. Simon & Schuster 1987 xxvi, 511p il hardcover o.p. paperback available $18   **305.4**

1. Women—Psychology 2. Aging
ISBN 0-671-64424-6 (pa)   LC 87-12898

This work focuses "on the health, social, and psychological concerns of women in midlife and beyond. . . . Discussions of diet, health, and family relationships are interspersed with quotes from over 300 women who share their thoughts on growing older. Highly recommended for most collections." Libr J

Includes bibliography

Evans, Sara M. (Sara Margaret), 1943-

Born for liberty: a history of women in America. Free Press 1989 386p il $24.95; pa $16.95   **305.4**

1. Women—United States—History 2. Women—Social conditions
ISBN 0-02-902990-2; 0-02-903090-0 (pa)
     LC 88-33544

"This history of women in America is a concise, comprehensive review of what women were doing from the 16th century to the present. . . . Ms. Evans traces the long and honorable history of women's reform efforts and restores to women the credit they deserve for many of the major social movements in this country." N Y Times Book Rev

Includes bibliographic references

Faludi, Susan

Backlash; the undeclared war against American women. Crown 1991 xxiii, 552p $24   **305.4**

1. Feminism 2. Women—United States 3. Women—Psychology
ISBN 0-517-57698-8   LC 90-29172

Also available in paperback from Doubleday

This volume examines the current status of women in American life and culture. The author argues that a growing backlash against women is systematically preventing them from realizing the goals of the feminist movement

The author "argues that women's anger and resentment are not due to their feminism, but occur because women have not yet been the beneficiaries of the justice, fairness, and equity they deserve. . . . This is [a] most important book." Libr J

Fox-Genovese, Elizabeth, 1941-

Within the plantation household; black and white women of the Old South. University of N.C. Press 1988 544p il (Gender & American culture) $37.50; pa $13.95   **305.4**

1. Women—Southern States 2. Plantation life 3. Slavery—United States
ISBN 0-8078-1808-9; 0-8078-4232-X (pa)
     LC 88-40139

"In this study, Fox-Genovese examines class, race, and gender in the antebellum South. . . . In her narrative, Fox-Genovese draws upon the letters, diaries, and journals of white women, and . . . the WPA slave narratives." Choice

"An illuminating and solid book of social history, with appeal to those who take a serious interest in historical research." Booklist

Includes bibliography

Fraser, Antonia, 1932-

The weaker vessel. Knopf 1984 544p il o.p.; Vintage Bks. paperback available $16   **305.4**

1. Women—England
ISBN 0-394-73251-0 (pa)   LC 84-47751

The author's "survey of women's lives and roles in seventeenth-century England represents an attempt to reconstruct through documentary evidence a remarkable and often shocking world. The parts played by sex, love,

Fraser, Antonia, 1932-—*Continued*
marriage, politics, children, and religion in women's existence are . . . threaded together and elaborated on." Booklist

"A substantial contribution to women's history that is free of specious argument and ideological cant." Newsweek

Includes bibliography

French, Marilyn, 1929-
The war against women. Summit Bks. 1992 223p $20   **305.4**
1. Women—Social conditions 2. Sex discrimination 3. Sexism
ISBN 0-671-77829-3   LC 92-705
Also available in paperback from Ballantine Bks.

The author writes "of how the world's major religions and the military complex institutionalize violence against women as well as the violation of their basic human rights. Her graphic accounts of the grueling nature of women's lives in Africa, India, and the Mideast are genuinely shocking while her reports on the political and cultural oppression of women in Western societies are simply infuriating." Am Libr

Includes bibliographic references

Friedan, Betty
The feminine mystique. 20th anniversary ed. Norton 1983 xxviii, 452p $17.50
305.4
1. Women—United States 2. Feminism
ISBN 0-393-01775-3   LC 83-11375
Also available in paperback from Dell
First published 1963
An "analysis of the dilemma facing the educated American woman; the post-war emphasis on the feminine image of the role as wife and mother has caused the American woman to lose her identity, says the author." Cincinnati Public Libr

Includes bibliographic references

The second stage; with a new introduction and afterword by the author. rev ed. Summit Bks. 1986 366p o.p.; Dell paperback available $5.95   **305.4**
1. Women—United States 2. Feminism 3. Women's movement
ISBN 0-440-20843-2 (pa)   LC 86-12388
First published 1981
The author examines the successes and failures of the first stage of the women's movement, and suggests that the second stage requires cooperative planning between men and women in order to restructure traditional roles

Giddings, Paula
When and where I enter; the impact of black women on race and sex in America. Morrow 1984 408p $22.95   **305.4**
1. Black women 2. United States—Race relations
ISBN 0-688-01943-9   LC 84-164770
Also available in paperback from Bantam Bks.

The author has "compiled a narrative history of black women from the 17th century to the present, with particular emphasis on the black women's club movement of the early 1890's to the 1940's. It was a labor of commitment and love—and it shows. What emerges is

a jarringly fresh and challenging interpretation." N Y Times Book Rev

Includes bibliography

Greer, Germaine, 1939-
The madwoman's underclothes; essays and occasional writings. Atlantic Monthly Press 1987 xxvii, 305p hardcover o.p. paperback available $8.95   **305.4**
1. Feminism 2. Women—Social conditions
ISBN 0-87113-308-3 (pa)   LC 87-11475
First published 1986 in the United Kingdom
A collection of the British feminist's nonfiction writings spanning her career from the 1960s to the 1980s

Hite, Shere
The Hite report: Women and love; a cultural revolution in progress. Knopf 1987 xxi, 922p o.p.; St. Martin's Press paperback available $5.95   **305.4**
1. Women—Psychology 2. Love 3. Human relations 4. Sex role
ISBN 0-312-91378-8 (pa)   LC 87-45129
"Following The Hite Report: a Nationwide Study of Female Sexuality and The Hite Report on Male Sexuality [both entered in class 155.3] the final volume of the Hite trilogy reports on the responses of 4500 women to open-ended questionnaires about their emotional relations with men and with each other." Libr J

Includes bibliography

Jones, Jacqueline, 1948-
Labor of love, labor of sorrow; black women, work, and the family from slavery to the present. Basic Bks. 1985 432p il $25.95   **305.4**
1. Black women
ISBN 0-465-03756-9   LC 84-24310
Also available in paperback from Vintage Bks.

"Jones examines the nature of employment and home life for the black woman through such socioeconomic eras as the period of bondage in the South, the so-called freedom that came with Reconstruction, the years between emancipation and the great migration to the North, the northern flight itself, the Depression, and the civil rights and feminist movements." Booklist
"Ambitious in scope, bold in interpretation, and comprehensive in its scholarship, Jones's book is a rare blend of seminal study and synthesis." Libr J

Includes bibliography

Lanker, Brian
I dream a world: portraits of black women who changed America; photographs and interviews by Brian Lanker; edited by Barbara Summers; foreword by Maya Angelou. Stewart, Tabori & Chang 1989 167p il $40; pa $24.95   **305.4**
1. Black women
ISBN 1-55670-063-6; 1-55670-092-X (pa)
                    LC 88-32697

Lanker, Brian—*Continued*
"A doubled-paged format of photographs, brief biographical information, and first-person accounts of women from all walks of life. . . . The book can function as art, history, literature, or social commentary. Though Barbara Jordan, Alice Walker, and Priscilla Williams inspired this white man's project, many other women provide the names he needed to produce the final 75. Amazingly beautiful and moving." Libr J

Montagu, Ashley, 1905-
The natural superiority of women. new & rev ed. Collier Bks. 1992 280p pa $9.95
     305.4
1. Women
ISBN 0-02-035128-3   LC 90-32712
First published 1953 in hardcover by Macmillan
"This book is designed to bring the sexes closer together, not to set them apart by placing one above the other. . . . Natural superiority does not imply social inequality; on the other hand, the plea of this book is for more mutual love and understanding and complete social equality of the sexes." Foreword
Includes bibliographic references

Scott, Kesho
The habit of surviving; black women's strategies for life; [by] Kesho Yvonne Scott. Rutgers Univ. Press 1991 208p $19.95
     305.4
1. Black women
ISBN 0-8135-1646-3   LC 90-48068
Also available in paperback from Ballantine Bks.
"In this combination of oral history, biography, and autobiography, Scott chronicles the lives of five black women, including her own, as they struggle to achieve success and survive as women of color in America. Not only would this book be a good addition to black studies and women's studies collections, its human interest stories would appeal to the general reader." Libr J
Includes bibliography

Sisterhood is powerful; an anthology of writings from the Women's Liberation Movement; [edited by] Robin Morgan. Random House 1970 xli, 602p il hardcover o.p. paperback available $15
     305.4
1. Women's movement 2. Feminism
ISBN 0-394-70539-4 (pa)
This collection includes articles, poems, photographs and manifestos from groups as well as individuals covering the range of problems considered by the movement
Includes bibliography

Statistical handbook on women in America; compiled and edited by Cynthia Taeuber. Oryx Press 1991 385p il $54.50   **305.4**
1. Women—United States
ISBN 0-89774-609-0   LC 90-41624
Taeuber "has selected and in some cases edited 437 tables from a variety of federal government publications to illustrate trends in the life patterns of women." Libr J
Includes bibliographic references

Steinem, Gloria
Outrageous acts and everyday rebellions. Holt, Rinehart & Winston 1983 370p o.p.; New Am. Lib. paperback available $7.95
     305.4
1. Feminism
ISBN 0-452-25579-1 (pa)   LC 83-222
The topics in this collection range from "personal accounts of political leaders and individual women (including Marilyn Monroe and Jackie Onassis) to general theoretical material regarding the feminist movement to articles addressing specific feminist issues." Libr J
Includes bibliographic references

Wolf, Naomi
The beauty myth; how images of beauty are used against women. Morrow 1991 348p $21.95   **305.4**
1. Women 2. Sex role
ISBN 0-688-08510-5   LC 90-49983
Also available in paperback from Anchor Bks.
A "book about the ways women enslave themselves—and their bank accounts—to an industry that promises physical perfection." N Y Times Book Rev
The author "presents a provocative and persuasive account of the pervasiveness of the beauty ideal in all facets of Western culture." Libr J

Woolf, Virginia, 1882-1941
A room of one's own. Harcourt Brace Jovanovich 1991 c1929 125p $15.95; pa $5.95   **305.4**
1. Women—Social conditions 2. Women authors
ISBN 0-15-178733-6; 0-15-678733-4 (pa)
     LC 91-17953
"An HBJ modern classic"
A reissue of the title first published 1929
"Woolf begins by announcing her basic thesis: that 'a woman must have money and a room of her own if she is to write fiction.' . . . She then examines the educational, social, and financial disadvantages and prejudices which have thwarted women writers throughout (English) history." Camb Guide to Lit in Engl

305.5   Social classes

Birmingham, Stephen
America's secret aristocracy. Little, Brown 1987 334p il o.p.; Berkley Pub. Group paperback available $4.95   **305.5**
1. Upper classes 2. United States—Social life and customs
ISBN 0-425-11912-2 (pa)   LC 87-4229
A sociological history of America's wealthiest families from the 18th to 20th century
"Birmingham's work is lively and based on research into family documents and interviews with current family members. . . . A popular, entertaining history." Libr J
Includes bibliography

Ehrenreich, Barbara

Fear of falling; the inner life of the middle class. Pantheon Bks. 1989 292p o.p.; HarperCollins Pubs. paperback available $11
305.5

1. Middle classes
ISBN 0-06-097333-1 (pa)   LC 88-43202

This book examines the changing political complexion of the American middle class since the 1950s

Harrington, Michael, 1928-1989

The new American poverty. Holt, Rinehart & Winston 1984 271p o.p.; Penguin Bks. paperback available $8.95
305.5

1. Poor—United States 2. Economic assistance, Domestic 3. Social problems
ISBN 0-14-008112-7 (pa)   LC 84-3746

The author traces the causes and manifestations of poverty—among them: "the Vietnam War, the emergence of a fiercely competitive global economy, and a growing negative attitude of Americans toward the impoverished. After this . . . analysis of the problem, Harrington attempts to offer some solutions." Booklist

"A balanced combination of objective analysis and principled advocacy." Libr J

Mayle, Peter

Acquired tastes. Bantam Bks. 1992 229p $20; pa $9.95   **305.5**

1. Wealth
ISBN 0-553-09027-5; 0-553-37183-5 (pa) LC 92-3354

Also available Thorndike Press large print edition

This is a collection of "articles on 'the spending habits of the rich,' which . . . half poke fun at those habits but at the same time assert the qualities of quality." Booklist

"This delightful celebration of the little (and not-so-little) extravagances that make life worth living scintillates with wit, brio and trenchant observations on the best and the second-rate." Publ Wkly

Newman, Katherine S., 1953-

Falling from grace; the experience of downward mobility in the American middle class; [by] Katherine S. Newman. Free Press 1988 320p il $29.95   **305.5**

1. Middle classes 2. United States—Social conditions
ISBN 0-02-923121-3   LC 88-1201

Also available in paperback from Vintage Bks.

The author "begins with an overview of the nature and extent of downward mobility. She then focuses on four different groups of downwardly mobile Americans: former managers and executives; air traffic controllers; plant workers caught in a shutdown; and divorced mothers. . . . The book is thoughtfully organized and masterly written; the bibliography is thorough and interdisciplinary." Choice

Packard, Vance Oakley, 1914-

The ultra rich; how much is too much? [by] Vance Packard. Little, Brown 1989 358p $22.95   **305.5**

1. Wealth 2. Millionaires
ISBN 0-316-68752-9   LC 88-23071

The author reports on his interviews with thirty of the richest people in America

The author "proposes a wealth tax, (as a supplement to the income tax) and a limitation on individual fortunes. Readers may not agree with Packard's conclusions and proposals, but they likely will enjoy the opportunity to learn how the super-rich view, use, and protect their money." Libr J

Riis, Jacob A. (Jacob August), 1849-1914

How the other half lives; studies among the tenements of New York; with illustrations chiefly from photographs taken by the author. Scribner 1890 304p il o.p.; Dover Publs. paperback available $9.95
305.5

1. Poor—New York (N.Y.) 2. Tenement houses 3. New York (N.Y.)—Social conditions
ISBN 0-486-22012-5 (pa)

The classic exposé of slum conditions in the tenements of New York City's Lower East Side in the late 19th century by a journalist, social reformer, and photographer. It touched the conscience of the nation and led to major social reforms

Veblen, Thorstein, 1857-1929

The theory of the leisure class   **305.5**

1. Social classes

Hardcover and paperback editions available from various publishers

First published 1899 by Macmillan

In this economic treatise, "Veblen held that the feudal subdivision of classes had continued into modern times, the lords employing themselves uselessly . . . while the lower classes labored at industrial pursuits to support the whole of society. The leisure class, Veblen said, justifies itself solely by practicing 'conspicuous leisure and conspicuous consumption'; he defined waste as any activity not contributing to material productivity." Reader's Ency

305.8 Racial, ethnic, national groups

Allen, James Paul, 1936-

We the people; an atlas of America's ethnic diversity; [by] James Paul Allen, Eugene James Turner. Macmillan 1988 315p maps $160   **305.8**

1. United States—Population
ISBN 0-02-901420-4   LC 87-28194

"A comprehensive guide to the immigrant, ethnic, and racial groups in the US. Its 13 chapters treat European, Asian, South American, and African immigrants, and native North Americans. Each chapter contains copious historical information, statistics, and vivid color maps depicting settlement patterns. The appendix lists the ancestries of state populations and ethnic populations for

Allen, James Paul, 1936—— *Continued*
states and counties." Choice

Includes bibliography

Bell, Derrick A.
Faces at the bottom of the well; the permanence of racism. Basic Bks. 1992 222p $20 **305.8**

1. Racism   2. United   States—Race   relations
3. Blacks—Civil rights
ISBN 0-465-06817-0   LC 91-59020

The author argues "that racism is not a passing phase but a permanent feature of American life. . . . [Mr. Bell] approaches his theme indirectly, through allegory, fables and dialogues with a fictional 'lawyer-prophet.'" N Y Times Book Rev

Bell "has written a provocative and creative book. . . . His 'interweaving of fact and fiction' and an 'unorthodox form' make for stimulating reading. . . . An especially important and relevant publication for public and academic libraries." Libr J

Includes bibliographic references

Bettelheim, Bruno
Social change and prejudice, including Dynamics of prejudice; [by] Bruno Bettelheim and Morris Janowitz. Free Press 1964 337p $27.95 **305.8**

1. Prejudices 2. Social change 3. Minorities
ISBN 0-02-903480-9

A reprinting of the author's: Dynamics of prejudice (1950), with a reexamination of its findings

An assessment of prejudice based on sociological and psychological research

Includes bibliographic references

Birmingham, Stephen
"The rest of us"; the rise of America's eastern European Jews. Little, Brown 1984 392p il $19.95 **305.8**

1. Jews—United States
ISBN 0-316-09647-4   LC 84-9658

The author combines "facts, gossip, and insight to chronicle the rise of such famous and not-so-famous Eastern Europeans as Rose Pastor Stokes, Samuel Goldwyn, Meyer Lansky, and Samuel Bronfman. . . . The narrative is engaging and the vignettes are well chosen." Libr J

Includes bibliography

Blauner, Bob
Black lives, white lives; three decades of race relations in America. University of Calif. Press 1989 347p $32.50; pa $12.95 **305.8**

1. United States—Race relations
ISBN 0-520-06261-2; 0-520-06950-1 (pa)
                                       LC 88-27769

This study "combines individual narrative with . . . Blauner's historical commentary and analysis. Seventeen men, eleven women (black and white), mostly residents of northern California, speak eloquently in their own words. Cross sections of three periods (1968, 1979, 1986) when interviews were conducted are presented. . . . A

substantial, absorbing work." Libr J

Includes bibliography

Buckley, William F. (William Frank), 1925-
In search of anti-Semitism; [by] William F. Buckley, Jr. Continuum 1992 207p $19.95 **305.8**

1. Antisemitism
ISBN 0-8264-0619-X   LC 92-16268

This volume "consists of a long editorial essay Buckley wrote examining instances of alleged anti-Semitic writing, primarily from the right; responses from journalists and lay people; and comments on Buckley's comments. He addresses columns by Joe Sobran, formerly of the *National Review*, and Pat Buchanan; allegations of anti-Semitism in the pages of the *Dartmouth Review*, a conservative magazine published at Dartmouth College; and a column by Gore Vidal in *The Nation*." Libr J

Cleaver, Eldridge, 1935-
Soul on ice; with an introduction by Maxwell Geismar. McGraw-Hill 1968 210p o.p.; Dell paperback available $5.99 **305.8**

1. Blacks
ISBN 0-440-21128-X (pa)

"A Ramparts book"

In a collection of essays and open letters written from California's Folsom State Prison, the author writes about the forces which shaped his life

There are sections "on the Watts riots, on Cleaver's religious conversion, on the black man's stake in the Vietnam War, on fellow-writers and white women." Saturday Rev

Du Bois, W. E. B. (William Edward Burghardt), 1868-1963
The souls of black folk; essays and sketches; by W.E. Burghardt Du Bois **305.8**

1. Blacks

Hardcover and paperback editions available from various publishers

First published 1903 by McClurg

"A collection of fifteen essays and sketches by W.E.B. Du Bois. In it he describes the lives of African American farmers, sketches the role of music in their churches, details the history of the Freedman's Bureau, discusses the career of Booker T. Washington, and advocates a commitment to higher education for the most talented African American youth." Benet's Reader's Ency of Am Lit

Encyclopedia of African-American civil rights; from emancipation to the present; edited by Charles D. Lowery and John F. Marszalek; foreword by David J. Garrow. Greenwood Press 1992 xxv, 658p il $59.95 **305.8**

1. Blacks—Civil rights—Dictionaries
ISBN 0-313-25011-1   LC 91-27814

This "compilation of information covering the general area of civil rights since the Emancipation Proclamation contains over 800 entries written by 157 experts in African American history. . . . In addition to people, also included are important laws, books, newspapers,

Encyclopedia of African-American civil rights—*Continued*

journals, events, and landmark court cases. All entries provide bibliographies and are cross-referenced. . . . This is a fine work, unique in its focus and comprehensive in its coverage." Libr J

For a fuller review see: Booklist, Aug. 1992

Encyclopedia of black America; W. Augustus Low, editor, Virgil A. Clift, associate editor. McGraw-Hill 1981 xx, 921p il $124   **305.8**

1. Blacks—Dictionaries 2. Blacks—Biography
ISBN 0-07-038834-2   LC 80-13247

Also available in paperback from Da Capo Press

"A comprehensive one-volume general encyclopedia on Afro-American life and culture. About 1700 A-Z articles, of which 1400 are biographical and 125 others are major topical articles (artists, civil disobedience, newspapers, etc.) Bibliographical references append many entries. Black-and-white illustrations; tables and graphs." Ref Sources for Small & Medium-sized Libr. 5th edition

Franklin, John Hope, 1915-

From slavery to freedom; a history of Negro Americans; [by] John Hope Franklin, Alfred A. Moss, Jr. Knopf il maps $37; pa $19.95   **305.8**

1. Blacks—History 2. Slavery—United States
ISBN 0-394-56362-X; 0-394-37013-9 (pa)

First published 1947. (6th edition 1987) Periodically revised

"A history of African-Americans from Africa to the present. It also explores the history of Blacks in Canada, Latin America, and the Caribbean. Covers the African homelands and their sociology, the slave trade, the Caribbean, and slavery as an American institution. In the 20th century, the author documents the Harlem Renaissance, the New Deal, and developments up to the death of Martin Luther King, Jr." N Y Public Libr Book of How & Where to Look It Up

Includes bibliography

Glazer, Nathan

Beyond the melting pot; the Negroes, Puerto Ricans, Jews, Italians, and Irish of New York City; by Nathan Glazer and Daniel Patrick Moynihan. 2nd ed. MIT Press 1970 xcviii, 363p hardcover o.p. paperback available $14.95   **305.8**

1. Minorities 2. New York (N.Y.)—Foreign population
ISBN 0-262-57022-X (pa)

First published 1963

A study of the different levels of achievement of the five major ethnic groups of New York City in education, business, and politics

Includes bibliographic references

Griffin, John Howard, 1920-1980

Black like me. 2nd ed, with a new epilogue by the author. Houghton Mifflin 1977 208p o.p.; New Am. Lib. paperback available $4.95   **305.8**

1. Blacks—Southern States 2. Prejudices
ISBN 0-451-16317-6 (pa)   LC 76-47690

First published 1961

The author, "who is white, a Catholic, and a Texan, conceived and carried out the unusual notion of blackening his skin with a newly developed pigment drug and traveling through the Deep South as a Negro. This book, part of which appeared in the Negro magazine Sepia, is a journal account of that experience." New Yorker

Hacker, Andrew

Two nations; black and white, separate, hostile, unequal. Scribner 1992 257p $24.95   **305.8**

1. Blacks—Social conditions 2. United States—Race relations
ISBN 0-684-19148-2   LC 91-34003

Also available in paperback from Ballantine Bks.

In this discussion of race in America the author analyzes "such problems as crime, unemployment, family instability, and the role of race in politics." Publisher's note

"The real value of this book, despite its wealth of data, is in Mr. Hacker's calm, analytical eye, his unblinking view of American history and his unwillingness to accept cant and 'common sense' as facts." N Y Times Book Rev

Includes bibliography

Harvard encyclopedia of American ethnic groups; Stephan Thernstrom, editor; Ann Orlov, managing editor, Oscar Handlin, consulting editor. Belknap Press 1980 xxv, 1076p maps $95   **305.8**

1. Ethnic groups—Dictionaries 2. Minorities—Dictionaries
ISBN 0-674-37512-2   LC 80-17756

"Defining *ethnic* in the widest possible way, this book contains substantial articles on American ethnic groups. Origins, migration and settlement, history in America, socioeconomic structure, religion and politics, and many other topics are addressed. Includes demographic information, individual bibliographies, and appendices." N Y Public Libr Book of How & Where to Look It up

Hosokawa, Bill

Nisei; the quiet Americans: the story of a people. University Press of Colo. 1992 550p il $19.95   **305.8**

1. Japanese Americans
ISBN 0-87081-273-4   LC 92-38737

First published 1969 by Morrow

This book "traces the story of Japanese Americans from the first immigrants to the tragedy of the World War II detention camps." Univ Press Books for Public and Second Sch Libr

The author "cuts through the haze and, without any special pleading, in stark dispassionate reporting limns a classic laboratory case of governmental and human fallibilities suddenly converging in monstrous injustice." N Y Times Book Rev

Howe, Irving
World of our fathers; with the assistance of Kenneth Libo. Harcourt Brace Jovanovich 1976 xx, 714p il $34.95   **305.8**
1. Jews—New York (N.Y.) 2. New York (N.Y.)—Social conditions
ISBN 0-15-146353-0

Also available in paperback from Schocken Bks.

"A comprehensive study of the East European, Yiddish-speaking Jewish migration to the U.S. in the late 19th and early 20th centuries, the community and subculture that developed from it on New York's East Side, and the influence of this culture of 'Yiddishkeit' on American life in general and its meaning for the more recent American Jewish experience in particular." Choice

Includes bibliography

Hughes, Langston, 1902-1967
A pictorial history of Blackamericans; [by] Langston Hughes, Milton Meltzer, and C. Eric Lincoln. 5th ed. Crown 1983 379p il $29.95   **305.8**
1. Blacks—History—Pictorial works 2. Slavery—United States 3. United States—Race relations
ISBN 0-517-55072-5   LC 83-7742

First published 1956 with title: A pictorial history of the Negro in America

"The 1,200 black-and-white illustrations depict the history of blacks in America from the earliest times to 1983. The illustrations are accompanied by brief text. The purpose is to provide a simple but authentic story of black American life and history. All names, events, and organizations mentioned in the text are indexed." Wynar. Guide to Ref Books for Sch Media Cent. 3d edition

Jewish-American history and culture; an encyclopedia; edited by Jack Fischel and Sanford Pinsker. Garland 1991 xxvi, 710p $95   **305.8**
1. Jews—United States—Dictionaries 2. United States—Civilization
ISBN 0-8240-6622-7   LC 91-14188

"This encyclopedia takes a comprehensive look at U.S. history and culture from the context of Jewish experience. Long and short signed essays cover a wide variety of topics: individuals, movements, literature, religion, and history from the colonial period to modern-day America. . . . A brief bibliography follows each entry." Am Libr

For a fuller review see: Booklist, May 1, 1992

The **Jewish** people in America. Johns Hopkins Univ. Press 1992 5v set $145   **305.8**
1. Jews—United States
ISBN 0-8018-4486-X

Edited by Henry L. Feingold

Contents: v1 A time for planting, by E. Faber; v2 A time for gathering, by H. Diner; v3 A time for building, by G. Sorin; v4 A time for searching, by H. Feingold; v5 A time for healing, by E. Shapiro

"The authors explore the roots of Jewish immigration, the experience of settling in America, economic and social adjustment, religious developments and educational aspirations, political involvements and, above all, the experience from generation to generation of what it means to be at once Jewish and American." Univ Press Books for Public and Second Sch Libr

Katz, William Loren
The black West. 3rd ed rev & expanded. Open Hand 1988 c1987 348p il $29.95; pa $15.95   **305.8**
1. Blacks—History 2. Frontier and pioneer life—West (U.S.)
ISBN 0-940880-17-2; 0-940880-18-0 (pa)
        LC 87-28067

First published 1971 by Doubleday

Using pictures, documents and text, this book relates the story of the part blacks played in U.S. westward expansion as fur trappers, missionaries, cowboys, poets, soldiers, rodeo stars, etc.

Includes bibliography

Kaufman, Jonathan
Broken alliance; the turbulent times between blacks and Jews in America. Scribner 1988 311p $19.95   **305.8**
1. Blacks 2. Jews and Gentiles 3. United States—Race relations
ISBN 0-684-18699-3   LC 88-1948

Also available in paperback from New Am. Lib.

An "account of the growth and collapse of the 'civil rights' alliance between American Jews and blacks. By focusing on the lives and attitudes of seven persons, Kaufman creates a deeply personal analysis of the connections and tensions between the two communities." Libr J

Includes bibliography

Kimbro, Dennis
Think and grow rich: a black choice; [by] Dennis Kimbro & Napoleon Hill. Fawcett Columbine 1991 306p $20; pa $5.99   **305.8**
1. Blacks 2. Success
ISBN 0-449-90612-4; 0-449-21998-4 (pa)
        LC 91-70654

Companion volume to Napoleon Hill's Think and grow rich (1937)

"Some time after his death in 1970, it was reported that [motivationalist Napoleon] Hill had left an unfinished manuscript targeting black America with his message of self-confidence and affirmative outlook. Now Kimbro, a black writer and lecturer for the Napoleon Hill Foundation, has adapted and updated Hill's manuscript. Acknowledging such barriers as lack of opportunity, racism, and discrimination, Kimbro argues that these should not be self-defeating obstacles." Booklist

Lukas, J. Anthony, 1933-
Common ground; a turbulent decade in the lives of three American families. Knopf 1985 659p il maps $19.95; pa $15   **305.8**
1. Boston (Mass.)—Race relations 2. Busing (School integration) 3. School integration
ISBN 0-394-41150-1; 0-394-74616-3 (pa)   LC 85-127

"By focusing on three families—one of them welfare black, one upper-middle-class white and one working-class Irish—a veteran journalist recreates the school-busing struggles of Boston in the 1970s, and delineates . . .

Lukas, J. Anthony, 1933—*Continued*
the moral complexities of caste and class in America."
Newsday

Mills, Nicolaus
Like a holy crusade; Mississippi, 1964—
the turning of the civil rights movement in
America. Dee, I.R. 1992 222p $22.50
305.8

1. Blacks—Civil rights 2. Blacks—Mississippi 3. Mississippi—Race relations
ISBN 0-929587-96-0   LC 92-13846

Mills presents an account of the Mississippi Freedom
Project in which some one thousand volunteers, many
of them white college students from the North, came
to Mississippi in 1964 to assist in efforts aimed at
securing voting rights for black Mississippians

"An extremely readable and fair-minded short history
of one of the central events of the civil rights movement." N Y Times Book Rev

Includes bibliographic references

Morris, Aldon D.
The origins of the civil rights movement;
black communities organizing for change.
Free Press 1984 354p $24.95; pa $14.95
305.8

1. Blacks—Civil rights 2. Southern States—Race relations
ISBN 0-02-922120-X; 0-02-922130-7 (pa)
                                      LC 84-10272

An "analysis of the civil rights movement, 1953-63.
Rejecting collective behavior, charismatic, and resource
mobilization models, Morris asserts that an 'indigenous'
perspective best explains the movement's success. Thus
carefully organized and planned local and regional institutions and networks, like the black church, were largely
responsible for the movement's power." Libr J

Includes bibliography

The **Negro** almanac; a reference work on the
Afro-American; compiled and edited by
Harry A. Ploski and James Williams. Gale
Res. $110   **305.8**

1. Blacks 2. Almanacs
First edition under the editorship of Harry A. Ploski
published 1967 by Bellwether. Periodically revised. (5th
edition 1989) Publisher varies

"Reference covering the cultural and political history
of Black Americans. Includes generous amount of
statistical information and biographies of Black Americans, both historical and contemporary." N Y Public
Libr Book of How & Where to Look It Up

Robeson, Paul, 1898-1976
Here I stand; with a preface by Lloyd L.
Brown and a new introduction by Sterling
Stuckey. Beacon Press 1988 c1958 xxxvi,
121p hardcover o.p. paperback available
$9.95   **305.8**

1. Blacks—Civil rights
ISBN 0-8070-6445-9 (pa)   LC 87-47882
First published 1958 by Othello Associates

"Combining a narrative of his life and travels with
commentary on history and the events of his time, [the
author] relates the fight against segregation to social
progress for all Americans, white and black, claiming that
'white supremacy' disenfranchises and impoverishes white
workers and white farmers as well as black." Libr J

Robinson, Jo Ann Gibson, 1912-
The Montgomery bus boycott and the
women who started it; the memoir of Jo
Ann Gibson Robinson; edited, with a
foreword, by David J. Garrow. University
of Tenn. Press 1987 190p il $32.50; pa
$14.95   **305.8**

1. Blacks—Segregation 2. Black women 3. Montgomery (Ala.)—Race relations
ISBN 0-87049-524-0; 0-87049-527-5 (pa)
                                      LC 86-14684

Examines the role of black women during the organization of the boycott; the events leading up to it; and
the involvement of various civic groups, including the
Women's Political Council

Sachar, Howard Morley, 1928-
A history of the Jews in America; by
Howard M. Sachar. Knopf 1992 1051p $40
305.8

1. Jews—United States
ISBN 0-394-57353-6   LC 91-4261

The author examines "two different subjects. One is
the rich, sometimes dark, ultimately triumphant story of
Jews in the United States. The other is the relation
between American Jews and Israel, a matter of the
widest interest, for probably no other group in this country is so deeply committed to the success of a foreign
state. That poses problems that Mr. Sachar confronts
unflinchingly and in detail, making his narrative not only
good history but a contribution to the current debate
over American-Israeli relations." N Y Times Book Rev

Includes bibliographic references

Shorris, Earl, 1936-
Latinos; a biography of the people. Norton
1992 520p $25   **305.8**

1. Hispanic Americans
ISBN 0-393-03360-0   LC 91-39720

Shorris presents a "portrait of the Spanish-speaking
peoples—Cubans, Puerto Ricans, Mexicans and others—
who now live in the United States as Latinos or
Hispanics." Newsweek

"Considering the wide range of topics covered—history, religion, politics, education, business, the arts, music,
literature, employment and world view—Mr. Shorris does
a laudable job of maintaining the boundary between the
actual and the stereotypical. . . . 'Latinos' is a powerful,
beautifully written and thoughtful book." N Y Times
Book Rev

Includes bibliography

Sowell, Thomas, 1930-
The economics and politics of race; an international perspective. Morrow 1983 324p hardcover o.p. paperback available $9.95
305.8

1. Race relations
ISBN 0-688-04832-3 (pa)   LC 83-715

"Through a comparative examination of migrants (Chinese, Germans, Italians, blacks, and others), each studied in a variety of overseas settings, the author seeks to discount the factor of race or racism as a lasting, or seriously disruptive, determinant in socioeconomic and political development." Choice

This book is "thoroughly, almost dauntingly, researched, yet it is as readable as a novel." Commentary

Includes bibliographic references

Ethnic America; a history. Basic Bks. 1981 353p hardcover o.p. paperback available $14
305.8

1. Minorities 2. Ethnic groups
ISBN 0-465-02075-5 (pa)   LC 80-68957

"Offering concise accounts of the Old World experiences of European groups (Irish, German, Jews, Italians) and Asians (Chinese, Japanese) as well as blacks, Puerto Ricans and Mexicans, the author examines the complexities and nuances of their American stories." Publ Wkly

"While bringing together the best of primary and secondary source materials from several vast fields, the book's extraordinary merit is its application of demographic and economic analysis to historical and social materials." New Repub

Statistical record of black America; compiled and edited by Carrell Peterson Horton and Jessie Carney Smith. 2nd ed. Gale Res. 1993 xli, 955p $95   **305.8**

1. Blacks—Statistics
ISBN 0-8103-8351-9   LC 84-643570
First published 1990

Statistical graphs and tables are divided into nineteen broad subject areas, including the arts; business and economics; crime, law enforcement and legal justice; education; the family; health and medical care; housing; labor and employment; the professions; and sports and leisure

Steele, Shelby
Content of our character; a new vision of race in America. St. Martin's Press 1990 175p $15.95   **305.8**

1. Blacks—Social conditions 2. United States—Race relations
ISBN 0-312-05064-X   LC 90-36889
Also available in paperback from HarperPerennial

The author offers his perspective on the current state of race relations in the United States. He "argues that it is time for blacks to look beyond racism and stop thinking of themselves as victims." N Y Times Book Rev

Takaki, Ronald T., 1939-
Strangers from a different shore; a history of Asian Americans; [by] Ronald Takaki. Little, Brown 1989 570p il $24.95   **305.8**

1. Asian Americans
ISBN 0-316-83109-3   LC 89-2816

Also available in paperback from Penguin Bks.

In this history, based on primary sources, the author covers a "diverse group that includes Chinese, Japanese, Filipinos, Koreans, Vietnamese, Laotians, Cambodians, and Asian Indians. An excellent popular history with a far-ranging epic sweep." Booklist

Includes bibliographic references

Terkel, Studs, 1912-
Race; how blacks and whites think and feel about the American obsession. New Press (NY) 1992 403p $24.95   **305.8**

1. United States—Race relations
ISBN 1-56584-000-3   LC 91-66864

Also available in paperback from Anchor Bks.

"In this new oral history, Terkel explores Americans' inner feelings and values pertaining to the subject of race. . . . His study is primarily centered in Chicago, but the people chosen to be interviewed represent a broad spectrum of society. . . . Terkel demonstrates how very skilled he is at drawing out interviewees' intrinsic feelings pertaining to race." Libr J

Wiesel, Elie, 1928-
The Jews of silence; a personal report on Soviet Jewry; translated from the Hebrew by Neal Kozodoy; with a new preface by Elie Wiesel and a new afterword by Martin Gilbert. Schocken Bks. 1987 116p pa $8.95
305.8

1. Jews—Russia
ISBN 0-8052-0826-7   LC 86-26134
First published 1966 by Holt

Based on a series of articles written for an Israeli newspaper, this account of the author's trip to the Soviet Union during the 1965 High Holy Days describes the celebration of Simhat Torah and the service at the Great Synagogue of Moscow

"Wiesel does not portray a self-pitying Soviet Jewry. Rather, he stresses the indomitable strength of their belief." Christ Sci Monit

Wiley, Ralph
Why black people tend to shout; cold facts and wry views from a black man's world. Carol Pub. Group 1991 200p $15.95
305.8

1. Blacks—Social conditions
ISBN 1-55972-073-5   LC 90-28665

Also available in paperback from Penguin Bks.

"A Birch Lane Press book"

The author "offers his opinions and observations on a variety of current concerns affecting Black Americans. He discusses such topics as racism, AIDS, politicians, television, the South, IQ tests, culture, food, and athletics. He also profiles Michael Jackson, Meadowlark Lemon, Marion Barry, Jesse Jackson, and other noted black people." Libr J

Woodward, C. Vann (Comer Vann), 1908-
The strange career of Jim Crow. 3rd rev ed. Oxford Univ. Press 1974 233p hardcover o.p. paperback available $8.95 **305.8**
1. Blacks—Segregation
ISBN 0-19-501805-2 (pa)
First published 1955
An account of segregation in the South which analyzes events from 1877 to the Nixon administration
Includes bibliography

306 Culture and institutions

Chenevière, Alain
Vanishing tribes: primitive man on Earth. Doubleday 1987 267p il maps $35 **306**
1. Nonliterate folk society 2. Ethnology
ISBN 0-385-23897-5 LC 86-29047
"A Dolphin book"
Original French edition, 1986
"This book focuses on 20 tribes, ranging from the Cuna of Panama to the Washkuk of Papua, New Guinea. Each tribe is represented by a brief narrative, a splendid photographic essay with captions describing aspects of the culture, and a myth taken directly from their oral tradition." Libr J

Freeman, Derek
Margaret Mead and Samoa; the making and unmaking of an anthropological myth. Harvard Univ. Press 1983 379p il $29.95 **306**
1. Mead, Margaret, 1901-1978 2. Ethnology—Samoan Islands
ISBN 0-674-54830-2 LC 82-15620
The author examines "Mead's depiction of Samoan culture. . . . He concludes that 'many of the assertions appearing in Mead's depiction of Samoa are fundamentally in error, and some of them preposterously false.'" Science
"Freeman's brilliant study reaches far beyond Samoa to illuminate how cultural myths are made and the ways that biases can endanger the social sciences." Publ Wkly
Includes bibliographic references

Freud, Sigmund, 1856-1939
Totem and taboo; some points of agreement between the mental lives of savages and neurotics **306**
1. Totems and totemism 2. Psychoanalysis 3. Taboo
Hardcover and paperback editions available from various publishers
Original German edition published 1912-1913 in Vienna
In the four essays in this volume Freud seeks to bridge the gap between psychoanalysis and such disciplines as social anthropology, philology and folklore
Includes bibliography

Gay, Peter, 1923-
The bourgeois experience: Victoria to Freud. Oxford Univ. Press 1984-1993 3v v1-2 ea $35, v3 $30 **306**
1. Middle classes 2. Nineteenth century 3. Social conditions LC 83-8187
Also available in paperback
Volume three published by Norton
Contents: v1 Education of the senses (ISBN 0-19-503352-3); v2 The tender passion (ISBN 0-19-503741-3; v3 The cultivation of hatred (ISBN 0-393-03398-8)
The first three volumes of a projected five volume study of 19th century middle-class life. In these volumes the author explores sexual behavior, romantic love, and aggression

Leinberger, Paul, 1947-
The new individualists; the generation after The organization man; [by] Paul Leinberger, Bruce Tucker. HarperCollins Pubs. 1991 454p $22.95; pa $13 **306**
1. Whyte, William Hollingsworth. Organization man 2. Individualism 3. Social ethics 4. United States—Social conditions
ISBN 0-06-016591-X; 0-06-092154-4 (pa)
LC 90-55932
The authors present an "analysis based upon seven years of interview research with some of the original 'organization men' described in William Whyte Jr.'s classic *The Organization Man* and their adult children. They describe the shift in commitment from a generation whose careers meant devotion to one company to a generation that rejects such blind loyalty and seeks to find their own place. . . . A valuable, well-written work that is highly recommended for all types of collections." Libr J

Mead, Margaret, 1901-1978
Coming of age in Samoa; a psychological study of primitive youth for Western civilisation; foreword by Franz Boas. Morrow 1928 297p il hardcover o.p. paperback available $12.50 **306**
1. Adolescence 2. Samoan Islands—Social life and customs 3. Sex differences (Psychology)
ISBN 0-688-30974-7 (pa)
Also available in hardcover from P. Smith
An anthropological study of adolescent Samoan girls

Growing up in New Guinea; a comparative study of primitive education. Morrow 1930 372p il hardcover o.p. paperback available $13.45 **306**
1. Children—New Guinea 2. Adolescence 3. New Guinea—Social life and customs 4. Manus (Papua New Guinea people)
ISBN 0-688-07989-X (pa)
Also available in hardcover from P. Smith
The author studies the children of a primitive community on the island of Manus from infancy to adolescence
Includes bibliography

Nance, John, 1935-

The gentle Tasaday; a stone age people in the Philippine rain forest; foreword by Charles A. Lindbergh. Harcourt Brace Jovanovich 1975 465p il o.p.; Godine paperback available $14.95   **306**

1. Tasaday (Philippine people)
ISBN 0-87923-604-3 (pa)

This book chronicles the author's visits with the Tasaday (believed at the time to be a Stone Age tribe), shortly after their 'discovery' in 1971

Primitive worlds; people lost in time; prepared by the Special Publications Division. National Geographic Soc. 1973 211p il maps $8.95   **306**

1. Nonliterate folk society 2. Ethnology
ISBN 0-87044-127-2

Chapters by six authors portray the societies of the Mbotgate in the New Hebrides, the Tifalmin in New Guinea, the Turkana in Kenya, the Somba in Dahomey, the Yanomamo in Venezuela and the Tarahumara in Mexico. They "report on such topics as the tribes' patterns of behavior, etiquette and rituals, religious beliefs and superstitions, and morality." Booklist

Includes bibliographic references

Turnbull, Colin M., 1924-

The mountain people. Simon & Schuster 1972 309p il maps hardcover o.p. paperback available $12   **306**

1. Ik (African people)
ISBN 0-671-64098-4 (pa)

Also available in hardcover from P. Smith

A study of an African tribe, the Ik, a small group of hunters in northern Uganda, who have lost their ancestral hunting grounds by the creation of a National Game Reserve

306.4 Specific aspects of culture

Language loyalties; a source book on the official English controversy; edited by James Crawford; with an afterword by Geoffrey Nunberg. University of Chicago Press 1992 522p $45.95; pa $14.95   **306.4**

1. English language—Social aspects
ISBN 0-226-12015-5; 0-226-12016-3 (pa)
                LC 91-29445

This guide to the Official English debate presents more than eighty-five key documents and articles

Includes bibliographic references

Schor, Juliet

The overworked American; the unexpected decline of leisure; [by] Juliet B. Schor. Basic Bks. 1991 247p $21; pa $12   **306.4**

1. Leisure 2. Hours of labor 3. United States—Social conditions
ISBN 0-465-05433-1; 0-465-05434-X (pa)
                LC 91-70057

The author argues that "between 1969 and 1987, time on the job for the average employed American increased by 163 hours a year, or an extra month. . . . Schor offers two explanations for today's long hours. First, it lowers costs for management to impose longer hours. . . . Second, the 'consumerist treadmill and long-hour jobs' have combined to form a cycle of work and spend." Christ Sci Monit

"Ms. Schor has crammed a great deal of data and insight into a short, powerful book. One can take issue with some of her conclusions or points of emphasis, yet still admire the overall product." N Y Times Book Rev

Includes bibliography

306.7 Institutions pertaining to relations of the sexes

D'Emilio, John

Intimate matters; a history of sexuality in America; [by] John D'Emilio and Estelle B. Freedman. Harper & Row 1988 xx, 428p il hardcover o.p. paperback available $12   **306.7**

1. Sexual behavior 2. United States—Social conditions
ISBN 0-06-091550-1 (pa)   LC 87-45608

A survey of sex and sexuality in America from colonial times to the present

This book "summarizes the state of our knowledge about sexual behavior in the United States in clear prose and with discriminating insight. This fine book will be definitive for some time to come." Nation

Includes bibliography

Kirk, Marshall

After the ball; how America will conquer its hatred and fear of gays in the '90s; [by] Marshall Kirk and Hunter Madsen. Doubleday 1989 398p il o.p.; New Am. Lib. paperback available $12   **306.7**

1. Gay liberation movement 2. Homosexuality
ISBN 0-452-26498-7 (pa)   LC 88-36860

Kirk and Madsen offer their views on how gay men can gain acceptance in American society

"The authors proceed to debunk myths that have been used to justify anti-gay abuse and to show how gays cope with homophobia. Data from public opinion polls, law, psychology, and sociology are presented." Choice

Includes bibliography

Margulis, Lynn, 1938-

Mystery dance; on the evolution of human sexuality; [by] Lynn Margulis and Dorion Sagan. Summit Bks. 1991 224p $19.95; pa $12   **306.7**

1. Sexual behavior 2. Sex (Biology)
ISBN 0-671-63341-4; 0-671-79226-1 (pa)
                LC 91-18450

This is an "account of the evolution of human sexuality. The 'mystery dance' is depicted as an 'evolutionary striptease,' in which our sexuality is denuded to reveal its primate, reptilian, and, ultimately, even protist origins. Through the dance, the authors suggest the possible significance of anatomical and behavioral aspects of our sexual selves. Some of the possibilities are intriguing, some disturbing, but all are

Margulis, Lynn, 1938-—*Continued*
thought-provoking." Libr J

Includes bibliographic references

Pittman, Frank S. (Frank Smith), 1935-

Private lies; infidelity and the betrayal of intimacy; [by] Frank Pittman. Norton 1989 309p hardcover o.p. paperback available $10.95   **306.7**

1. Adultery
ISBN 0-393-30707-7 (pa)   LC 88-15170

"Using over a hundred case histories, psychiatrist/ therapist Frank Pittman details personalities and marriage situations that lead to infidelity and provides guidelines for avoiding the betrayal of marital vows." West Coast Rev Books

"For people who suspect their spouses are having a secret romantic affair, or are coping with the aftermath of one, this primer offers sensible counsel, albeit in pedestrian, chatty prose." Publ Wkly

Includes bibliography

Reinisch, June

The Kinsey Institute new report on sex; what you must know to be sexually literate; [by] June M. Reinisch with Ruth Beasley; edited and compiled by Debra Kent. St. Martin's Press 1990 xx, 540p il $22.95; pa $14.95   **306.7**

1. Sexual behavior
ISBN 0-312-05268-5; 0-312-06386-5 (pa)
                                            LC 90-41444

This volume offers information about sexual matters, divided into general areas, including "body image and self esteem, problems with sexual functioning, sex and aging, contraception, [and] sexually transmitted diseases." Libr J

Talese, Gay

Thy neighbor's wife. Doubleday 1980 568p o.p.; Dell paperback available $6.99   **306.7**

1. Sexual behavior 2. United States—Social life and customs
ISBN 0-440-38497-4 (pa)   LC 76-51988

In this report on sex in America "the focus is on two major topics: the struggle to publish sexually explicit material in a censorship-oriented society, and the attempts of certain individuals to live lives of greater sexual freedom." Libr J

"Taken as a record of one man's social observations, the book can be regarded as a success. Mr. Talese is always a readable writer, and his finely etched profiles of well known and unknown Americans make for absorbing and often titillating reading." Economist

306.8 Marriage and family

Anderson, Joan, 1947-

The single mother's book; a practical guide to managing your children, career, home, finances, and everything else. Peachtree Pubs. 1990 304p pa $12.95
                                                306.8

1. Mothers 2. Single parent family
ISBN 0-934601-84-4   LC 89-28640

"Topics as diverse as plumbing, raising psychologically as well as physically healthy children, and nutrition, are covered in brief narratives. Valuable more for inspiration and encouragement than for in-depth instruction, this is an affordable addition to life skills sections of public libraries." Libr J

Includes bibliographic references

Ashner, Laurie

When parents love too much; what happens when parents won't let go; [by] Laurie Ashner and Mitch Meyerson. Morrow 1990 312p $18.95   **306.8**

1. Child rearing 2. Parent and child
ISBN 0-688-08766-3   LC 89-48252

Also available in paperback from Avon Bks.

"In the view of the therapist-authors of this study, emotional overinvolvement by parents, often an effort to control their children's lives, is a powerful, painful capacity that cuts across all economic strata. . . . To examine this type of co-dependency or enabling behavior in its variety, the authors supply case histories that trace patterns of personal and familial dysfunction." Publ Wkly

"This highly readable guide is packed with insights gleaned from real-life cases, many of them vividly detailed here." Booklist

Includes bibliographic references

Barker, Robert L.

The green-eyed marriage; surviving jealous relationships. Free Press 1987 256p $27.95
                                                306.8

1. Jealousy 2. Human relations
ISBN 0-02-901791-2   LC 87-19860

This book discusses the nature of jealousy "as it arises in marriages, families, and work. The more and less destructive forms of jealousy are distinguished, and strategies and resources for helping both the jealous person and his/her spouse are discussed." Choice

Includes bibliography

Bernstein, Anne C., 1944-

Yours, mine, and ours; how families change when remarried parents have a child together. Scribner 1989 337p il o.p.; Norton paperback available $10.95   **306.8**

1. Stepfamily 2. Remarriage 3. Brothers and sisters
ISBN 0-393-30668-2 (pa)   LC 88-26538

Based on "interviews with parents and children, the book [aims to] take the perspective of all family members as it traces the changes in stepfamilies from the decision to have a mutual child through to the maturity of all the children." Publisher's note

Includes bibliography

Bloomfield, Harold H., 1944-
Making peace with your parents; [by]
Harold H. Bloomfield with Leonard Felder.
Random House 1983 220p o.p.; Ballantine
Bks. paperback available $5.95   **306.8**
1. Parent and child 2. Family life
ISBN 0-345-30904-9 (pa)   LC 83-42771

"Based on the premise that many of our problems
can be traced to unresolved conflicts with parents, [this
book] suggests a means of resolution. Personal anecdotes
provide psychological insights in an entertaining and nontechnical way. . . . An appealing and very practical
book." Libr J

Includes bibliographic references

Brothers, Joyce
What every woman ought to know about
love and marriage. Simon & Schuster 1984
335p o.p.; Ballantine Bks. paperback
available $5.95   **306.8**
1. Marriage 2. Dating (Social customs) 3. Women—
Psychology
ISBN 0-345-32113-8 (pa)   LC 84-10584

The author "looks at marriage chronologically—from
the early years, parenthood, the seven-year itch, the dol-
drums to the 20-year ditch—and explains the perils of
each. She also offers suggestions on what to do about
difficult times involving money, sex, kids, in-laws." Publ
Wkly

Widowed. Simon & Schuster 1990 256p
o.p.; Ballantine Bks. paperback available
$5.99   **306.8**
1. Widows 2. Loss (Psychology)
ISBN 0-345-37400-2 (pa)   LC 90-10174

Also available Thorndike Press large print edition

"Having for years advised women on how to face
widowhood or other grievously damaging emotional experiences, popular psychologist Brothers . . . here
recounts how she rebuilt her own life after briefly
considering suicide upon the 1989 death by cancer of
her husband of 39 years." Publ Wkly

Burns, Cherie
Stepmotherhood; how to survive without
feeling frustrated, left out, or wicked. Times
Bks. 1985 222p o.p.; HarperCollins Pubs.
paperback available $10   **306.8**
1. Stepfamily
ISBN 0-06-097064-2 (pa)   LC 85-40271

The author "offers a multitude of ways to negotiate
this difficult role with comfort. . . . Burns shows how
crippling stereotypes and the realities of mothering
someone else's children can handicap even the most
promising marriage. But part of the book's charm is its
avoidance of glib reassurance and false cheer. Instead,
there is healthy common sense." Publ Wkly

Caine, Lynn
Being a widow. Arbor House 1988 261p
$18.95   **306.8**
1. Widows
ISBN 0-87795-966-8   LC 88-15280

Also available in paperback from Penguin Bks.

"An Eleanor Friede book"

The author discusses the emotional, practical, and
physical problems that arise when coping with terminal
illness and sudden death

"Caine's direct, articulate writing, full of compassion
and understanding, assure a large readership for this special book." Libr J

Includes bibliography

Caron, Ann F.
"Don't stop loving me"; a reassuring guide
for mothers of adolescent daughters. Holt &
Co. 1990 228p il $19.95   **306.8**
1. Mothers and daughters 2. Teenagers
ISBN 0-8050-1136-6   LC 90-4273

Also available in paperback from HarperCollins Pubs.

This book "provides mothers with insights into the
volatile behavior of teenage daughters, practical information on risks, and thoughtful advice on a range of
problems. . . . She covers the big problems of anorexia,
bulimia, drugs and alcohol, and the touchy subjects of
underage drinking, sexuality, peer friendships, and
mother-daughter relations." Booklist

Includes bibliographic references

Cocola, Nancy Wasserman
How to manage your mother; skills and
strategies to improve mother-daughter
relationships; [by] Nancy Wasserman Cocola,
Arlene Modica Matthews. Simon & Schuster
1992 286p $20; pa $11   **306.8**
1. Mothers and daughters
ISBN 0-671-74216-7; 0-671-86678-8 (pa)
          LC 91-48204

"This course on improving diplomatic maternal relations is directed at adult daughters of various ages who
feel their mothers may be chronically worried, hyper-
critical, controlling, competitive, pseudo-perfect, or living
through a daughter. After an overview of the ways mothers behave that drive their female offspring to distraction, Cocola and Matthews supply skills and strategies
for coping, conversing, and maintaining healthy ties."
Booklist

Includes bibliographic references

Coontz, Stephanie
The way we never were; American
families and the nostalgia trap. Basic Bks.
1992 391p $27   **306.8**
1. Family 2. United States—Social conditions
ISBN 0-465-00135-1   LC 91-59009

"Arguing that 'Americans have tended to discover a
crisis in family structure and standards whenever they
are in the midst of major changes in socioeconomic
structure and standards,' Coontz [attempts to put] contemporary challenges facing the family into . . . historical
perspective." Libr J

"The historical vignettes are interesting and, though
geared to prove Coontz's points, are still informative."
Choice

Includes bibliographic references

Cosby, Bill, 1937-

Fatherhood; introduction and afterword by Alvin F. Poussaint. Doubleday 1986 178p $14.95 **306.8**

1. Fathers
ISBN 0-385-23410-4 LC 86-2100

Also available in paperback from Berkley Pub. Group "A Dolphin book"

Cosby's "advice on surviving the vagaries of one's offspring consists of a succession of . . . [anecdotes and] observations, all designed to encourage the application of love and patience." Atlantic

This volume "is like a prose version of a Cosby comedy performance—informal, commiserative anecdotes delivered in a sardonic style that's as likely to prompt a smile of recognition as a belly laugh." Newsweek

Love and marriage; introduction by Alvin F. Poussaint. Doubleday 1989 xxvi, 188p o.p.; Bantam Bks. paperback available $5.99 **306.8**

1. Marriage
ISBN 0-553-28467-3 (pa) LC 88-35242

The author "has produced a scrapbook of the happier side of romance. . . . Though some of the dialogue sounds as if it were part of a stand-up comedy routine—meant to be said, not read—Mr. Cosby captures the give and take of happy marriages." N Y Times Book Rev

Cowan, Connell

Smart women, foolish choices; finding the right men and avoiding the wrong ones; by Connell Cowan & Melvyn Kinder. Potter 1985 204p o.p.; New Am. Lib. paperback available $5.99 **306.8**

1. Marriage 2. Dating (Social customs) 3. Women—Psychology
ISBN 0-451-15885-7 (pa) LC 84-22656

The authors "speak about the changing nature of the male/female relationship. The women they counsel are careerists, therefore 'smart,' but as the case studies indicate, inclined to indulge in frustrating relationships with men and to do so with disturbing frequency. Various causes such as low self-esteem, unrealistic expectations and game playing are cited." Publ Wkly

Cowan, Paul

Mixed blessings; marriage between Jews and Christians; [by] Paul Cowan with Rachel Cowan. Doubleday 1987 275p $19.95 **306.8**

1. Interfaith marriage 2. Jews and Gentiles
ISBN 0-385-19502-8 LC 87-480

Also available in paperback from Penguin Bks.

The authors examine the problems that arise within interfaith marriages

"Contemporary interfaith couples, not traditionally religious, often do not realize the time bomb—as the authors call it—that their different backgrounds can constitute. Reading this book should help such couples defuse that time bomb by making them aware of the problems and offering concrete advice on dealing with them." Libr J

Field, Martha A.

Surrogate motherhood. Harvard Univ. Press 1988 215p $24.95; pa $10.95 **306.8**

1. Surrogate mothers
ISBN 0-674-85748-8; 0-674-85749-6 (pa) LC 88-17459

In this book the author discusses "federal regulation of surrogacy, the rights of biological fathers, and custody and adoption law." Libr J

"If you want a clear, comprehensive overview of the legal status of surrogate motherhood in the United States (and the world) today, together with a calm discussion of all the moral and practical pros and cons, this book is the one to read." Women's Rev Books

Fishel, Elizabeth

Family mirrors; what our children's lives reveal about ourselves. Houghton Mifflin 1991 xxii, 295p $21 **306.8**

1. Family 2. Parenting
ISBN 0-395-44261-3 LC 91-2005

In this "examination of parent-child relationships, Fishel adheres to family systems theory, searching multigenerational diagrams (genograms) of family characteristics and difficulties for clues to current family problems. The wisdom of such eminent psychologists as D. W. Winnicott, Margaret Mahler, Selma Fraiberg and Bruno Bettelheim is interwoven with observations by current family therapy practitioners and anecdotes culled from parental support groups." Publ Wkly

Includes bibliography

Gates, Philomene A., 1918-

Suddenly alone; a woman's guide to widowhood; [by] Philomene Gates. Harper & Row 1990 xxii, 248p hardcover o.p. paperback available $9.95 **306.8**

1. Widows
ISBN 0-06-092089-0 (pa) LC 89-46092

The author "discusses how to adjust initially to a profound loss, how to find a job, make new friends, obtain a lawyer, attend to one's physical and mental health over a sustained period and even look again for male companionship." Publ Wkly

"Practical, commonsense approach to the myriad problems created by the loss of a spouse. . . . Empathetic and down-to-earth, Gates offers a plethora of systematically organized information." Libr J

Gies, Frances

Marriage and the family in the Middle Ages; [by] Frances and Joseph Gies. Harper & Row 1987 372p il hardcover o.p. paperback available $11 **306.8**

1. Marriage—History 2. Family—History
ISBN 0-06-091468-8 (pa) LC 87-45048

"Among other topics the authors treat family definition and size, marriage rules and customs, and sexual relations. Especially because it offers the general reader a critical sense of the scholarship that resulted in this material, this is recommended for public and college libraries." Libr J

Includes bibliography

Graham, Virginia, 1912-
Life after Harry; my adventures in widowhood. Simon & Schuster 1988 191p o.p.; Dell paperback available $7.95   **306.8**
1. Widows
ISBN 0-440-50183-0 (pa)   LC 87-28766
This "is a manual on how to cope after the first grief has passed; how to get on with your life. . . . Graham adopts a chatty, upbeat style. She covers such topics as dating (including how to meet men); going back to work; and handling well-meaning relatives." Libr J
Includes bibliography

Hochschild, Arlie Russell, 1940-
The second shift; working parents and the revolution at home; [by] Arlie Hochschild with Anne Machung. Viking 1989 309p o.p.; Avon Bks. paperback available $9.95   **306.8**
1. Children of working parents 2. Sex role
ISBN 0-380-71157-5 (pa)   LC 88-40280
A sociological study of the two-career family. Hochschild conducted detailed interviews and home observations of 50 working couples raising children under six years of age to see how they balanced careers, household, and child rearing tasks." Libr J
The author's "insights into family dynamics are astute and her standard of fairness is beyond challenge." N Y Times Book Rev
Includes bibliography

Katz, Donald, 1952-
Home fires; an intimate portrait of one middle-class family in postwar America. HarperCollins Pubs. 1992 619p $25; pa $14   **306.8**
1. Family 2. United States—Social conditions
ISBN 0-06-019009-4; 0-06-099502-5 (pa)
     LC 91-58347
"An Aaron Asher book"
"The middle-class parents are, in this instance, New Yorkers, Eve and Sam Gordon, and [this book] . . . is the true story—the names unchanged, the traumas apparently unretouched—of their family. . . . 'Home Fires' novelistically chronicles—year by year, from 1945 to 1990—the Gordons' turbulent lives and trying times." NY Times Book Rev
"Perhaps the fractured Gordon family cannot serve as metaphor for all of America, but most readers will find at least a few points of correspondence in their chaotic saga. This book will stir shocks of recognition—and conjecture about the future." Booklist

Lang, Susan S.
Women without children; the reasons, the rewards, the regrets. Pharos Bks. 1991 278p $18.95   **306.8**
1. Childlessness 2. Women—Psychology
ISBN 0-88687-532-3   LC 91-7437
"While Lang does explore the sorrow and grief infertile women experience, her interviews and research uncovered a high degree of satisfaction and happiness in women who, for one reason or another, have not had children. Lang moves smoothly from the societal context, such as a discussion of women and careers, to the articulate and eye-opening attitudes and goals of in-

dividuals." Booklist
Includes bibliographic references

Leman, Kevin
Growing up firstborn; the pressure and privilege of being number one. Delacorte Press 1989 280p il o.p.; Dell paperback available $4.95   **306.8**
1. Psychology, Applied 2. Parent and child
ISBN 0-440-20743-6 (pa)   LC 89-7743
The author discusses "how one's position in the family directly shapes a personality for life, the special focus here being on those who are first-born (either first-born overall, first-born male or female, or 'only' children). . . . Using case studies, a welcome sense of humor, and his all-too-perceptive sense of family dynamics, Leman offers coping strategies for first-borns." Booklist
Includes bibliographic references

Levin, Laurie
You can't hurry love; an intimate look at first marriages after 40; [by] Laurie Levin and Laura Golden Bellotti. Dutton 1992 268p $20   **306.8**
1. Marriage 2. Middle age 3. Single people
ISBN 0-525-93402-2   LC 91-24576
Also available in paperback from Signet Bks.
"Section one discusses the reasons why legal cohabitation is avoided, such as career demands, the 'I don't wanna grow up' view of marriage, and psychic baggage (controlling parents, previous failed relationships), among others. (Each chapter includes quotes and longer, interesting case histories from the 40 men and women who served as willing guinea pigs). Section two is a miniprimer on making these (or any) marriages work." Booklist
Includes bibliographic references

Maynard, Joyce, 1953-
Domestic affairs; enduring the pleasures of motherhood and family life. Times Bks. 1987 313p il $17.95   **306.8**
1. Mothers 2. Family life 3. Parent and child
ISBN 0-8129-1244-6   LC 86-30033
Also available in paperback from McGraw-Hill
"Here is a testimony to the joys and sadness to be found in the most routine events of family life. The author is a keen observer and skilled at making the important connections between those routine events and the larger picture. This will have great appeal to young parents." Libr J

Page, Susan
If I'm so wonderful, why am I still single? ten strategies that will change your love life forever. Viking 1988 255p il o.p.; Bantam Bks. paperback available $5.99   **306.8**
1. Dating (Social customs) 2. Women—Psychology
ISBN 0-553-28299-9 (pa)   LC 87-40320
The author presents a 10-step regimen for single men and women who desire a committed intimate relationship

Pearsall, Paul

The power of the family; strength, comfort, and healing. Doubleday 1990 372p $19.95 **306.8**

1. Family

ISBN 0-385-26005-9   LC 90-2982

Also available in paperback from Bantam Bks.

The author "explores the thesis that there is power in family relationships to promote healthy human development. . . . In practical steps that he calls the '10 Rxs' of healthy family living, Pearsall lays out prescriptions with which family members, alone or in the group, may experiment." Publ Wkly

This is "an instructive and occasionally inspirational primer on the fine art of having and belonging to a family." Booklist

Includes bibliography

Pogrebin, Letty Cottin

Family politics; love and power on an intimate frontier. McGraw-Hill 1983 278p $14.95; pa $6.95   **306.8**

1. Family 2. Power (Social sciences)

ISBN 0-07-050386-9; 0-07-050399-0 (pa)   LC 83-9818

"Pogrebin defines and discusses the positive bonds, support systems, and beliefs that operate within the family and [attempts] to expose the misuse and manipulation of the family in the political arena." Libr J

"Throughout this multilayered examination, Pogrebin retains her very pragmatic outlook. The result is a book that not only evaluates and explains contemporary family life, but that also offers no-nonsense solutions for sustaining and improving it." Booklist

Poston, Carol H.

Reclaiming our lives; hope for adult survivors of incest; by Carol Poston and Karen Lison. Little, Brown 1989 279p il $17.45   **306.8**

1. Incest 2. Child molesting

ISBN 0-316-71472-0   LC 88-28375

Also available in paperback from Bantam Bks.

"Writing to help adult women whose childhood was marred by incest, each co-author approaches this once-taboo topic from a different perspective. Poston writes . . . of her shatteringly abusive childhood, while therapist Lison adds painful case studies and analyzes the shared characteristics of each victim's experiences." Libr J

Robertson, John, 1927-

Suddenly single; learning to start over through the experience of others; [by] John Robertson, Betty Utterback; foreword by Sally Jessy Raphael. Simon & Schuster 1986 223p $15.95   **306.8**

1. Divorce 2. Widows 3. Widowers

ISBN 0-671-54442-X   LC 85-27889

The authors discuss how to cope with the loss of a spouse through death or divorce

"This sensitive and easy-to-read book is a good introduction to its subject." Libr J

Includes bibliography

Russell, Diana E. H.

The secret trauma; incest in the lives of girls and women. Basic Bks. 1986 426p $24.95; pa $16   **306.8**

1. Incest 2. Child molesting

ISBN 0-465-07595-9; 0-465-07596-7 (pa)

LC 85-43107

Based on interviews with over 900 women, this book examines the incidence and psychological ramifications of incest

This "will be invaluable in helping to combat the denial of incestuous abuse and remediate its effects." NY Times Book Rev

Includes bibliography

Sachs, Brad, 1956-

Things just haven't been the same; making the transition from marriage to parenthood. Morrow 1992 272p $20 **306.8**

1. Parenting 2. Marriage

ISBN 0-688-10183-6   LC 92-13322

The author examines how parenthood places stress on marriages

"Case studies abound as Sachs underscores the immense tensions of parenthood. All in all, this is a most thoughtful, realistic, and readable book." Libr J

Salk, Lee, 1926-1992

Familyhood; nurturing the values that matter. Simon & Schuster 1992 206p $21   **306.8**

1. Family 2. Child rearing

ISBN 0-671-72936-5   LC 92-8195

"Salk uses anecdotes and stories to show how children can be taught values which will remain with them throughout their lives. Although his treatment is value oriented, it is ultimately a guide to raising a good child. Salk covers a wide range of subjects: marriage, homework, discipline, teenagers, drugs and alcohol, divorce, single parents, etc." Libr J

Sander, Joelle

Before their time; four generations of teenage mothers; with a foreword by Robert Coles. Harcourt Brace Jovanovich 1991 192p $19.95   **306.8**

1. Teenage mothers 2. Black women

ISBN 0-15-111638-5   LC 91-19965

An oral history "of the lives of four related black women from succeeding generations who all became teenage mothers. . . . Here we meet firsthand a great-grandmother, a grandmother, a mother, and a daughter from the New York City area whose family dynamic becomes painfully clear in a repetitive cycle of violence, poverty, neglect, and teenage motherhood that typifies the lives of many other young, unwed mothers nationwide." Booklist

Includes bibliographic references

Sanders, Darcie, 1953-
Staying home; from full-professional to full-time parent; [by] Darcie Sanders and Martha M. Bullen. Little, Brown 1992 239p il $19.95　　**306.8**

1. Mothers 2. Parenting
ISBN 0-316-77061-2　　　　　LC 92-2839

The authors "surveyed 600 women who have taken sabbaticals from their careers to devote themselves to full-time mothering. Drawing on the information gathered, the authors offer suggestions for coping with reduced income, changing relationships, and altered self-image. They also explore home-based employment." Libr J

"In all, an indisputably worthwhile effort to help with issues many women have felt they faced alone." Booklist

Includes bibliographic references

Scarf, Maggie, 1932-
Intimate partners; patterns in love and marriage. Random House 1987 428p $18.95　　**306.8**

1. Marriage
ISBN 0-394-55485-X　　　　　LC 86-10111
Also available in paperback from Ballantine Bks.

This book is intended to "provide insight on the way marriages are made, the basic materials used in their construction and how these affect the structure of the relationship as it changes and develops over time. . . . The book chronicles . . . the marriages of five couples selected by the author to represent the problems and tasks associated with different phases of life and particular stages of an intimate relationship." Psychol Today
"Profoundly arresting, this excellent work is of practical use to marriage counselors and general readers alike." Booklist

Includes bibliography

Secunda, Victoria
When you and your mother can't be friends; resolving the most complicated relationship of your life. Delacorte Press 1990 xxii, 406p $19.95; pa $10　　**306.8**

1. Mothers and daughters
ISBN 0-385-29883-8; 0-385-30423-4 (pa)
　　　　　　　　　　　　　　LC 89-27800

A "study of troubled mother-daughter relationships and how these relationships can be improved, usually through the efforts of the daughter. Dysfunctional parents usually raise dysfunctional children who pass the same behavior on to their children unless a conscientious effort, often with the help of therapy, is made to break the chain. Practical advice on how to come to terms with, and often improve, unhealthy mother-daughter bonds is offered through excerpts from many interviews and quotes from experts." Libr J

Includes bibliographic references

Whitehead, Mary Beth
A mother's story; the truth about the Baby M case; [by] Mary Beth Whitehead with Loretta Schwartz-Nobel. St. Martin's Press 1989 xx, 220p il $17.95　　**306.8**

1. Stern, Melissa, 1986- 2. Surrogate mothers 3. Child custody—Personal narratives
ISBN 0-312-02614-5　　　　　LC 88-29892

"By presenting her surrogate mother story . . . from the birth of Sara/Melissa [in 1986] to the final court decision two years later, Whitehead allows many readers to sympathize with her for the first time, and to revise unwarranted assumptions about this famous case." Libr J

Yarrow, Andrew L.
Latecomers; children of parents over 35. Free Press 1991 244p $19.95　　**306.8**

1. Parent and child
ISBN 0-02-935685-7　　　　　LC 90-45944

The author "evaluates the impact of delayed childbearing on the children born to not-so-youthful parents—some of whom here cite the advantages of having more mature, emotionally and financially secure progenitors, while others emphasize the drawbacks." Publ Wkly

306.89　Separation and divorce

Adler, Robert E., 1946-
Sharing the children; how to resolve custody problems and get on with your life. Adler & Adler 1988 254p $17.95; pa $9.95　　**306.89**

1. Children of divorced parents 2. Child custody 3. Divorce
ISBN 0-917561-50-3; 0-917561-56-2 (pa)
　　　　　　　　　　　　　　LC 87-19532

The authors provide guidelines for divorcing parents on how to best meet the needs of their children
"Summary outlines and appendixes—which include a self-help checklist, a comparison of children's needs at different ages, and a sketch of the custody laws of the different states—are extremely helpful." Libr J

Arendell, Terry
Mothers and divorce; legal, economic, and social dilemmas; foreword by Arlie Russell Hochschild. University of Calif. Press 1986 221p $32.50; pa $9.95　　**306.89**

1. Women—Social conditions 2. Divorce 3. Mothers
ISBN 0-520-05708-2; 0-520-06215-9 (pa) LC 86-6959

Based on a series of interviews with sixty women, this book addresses the economic and social aspects of divorce
The author "has clearly and movingly illuminated the effects of divorce on the lives of women and children." Am J Sociol

Beal, Edward W.
Adult children of divorce. Delacorte Press 1991 421p $18.95; pa $10　　**306.89**

1. Children of divorced parents
ISBN 0-385-29924-9; 0-385-30593-1 (pa)
　　　　　　　　　　　　　　LC 90-23184

A "volume devoted to helping adults resolve relationship problems connected with the failure of their parents' marriage. (The authors consider the divorce itself only one factor in the adult child's trauma)." Booklist

Belli, Melvin M., 1907-
Divorcing; [by] Melvin M. Belli, Sr. and Mel Krantzler with Christopher S. Taylor. St. Martin's Press 1988 434p hardcover o.p. paperback available $14.95   **306.89**
1. Divorce
ISBN 0-312-03816-X (pa)   LC 87-38264
The authors discuss the legal and psychological aspects of divorce
"Readers needing sound, well-written, and practical advice will find it here." Libr J
Includes bibliography

Francke, Linda Bird
Growing up divorced. Linden Press/Simon & Schuster 1983 303p o.p.; Fawcett Bks. paperback available $4.95   **306.89**
1. Divorce 2. Children of divorced parents
ISBN 0-449-20570-3 (pa)   LC 83-9336
This is a survey of the effects of divorce on children
"Francke combines numerous case histories and extensive interviews with experts in the field, as well as with parents and children, to provide a cogent discussion of the psychology of these children." N Y Times Book Rev

Gardner, Richard A., 1931-
The parents book about divorce. rev ed. Creative Therapeutics 1991 xxi, 393p $22
                306.89
1. Divorce 2. Parent and child 3. Child psychology
ISBN 0-933812-27-2   LC 91-21283
First published 1977 by Doubleday
Among the topics covered in this guide are when and how to tell the children, dealing with guilt feelings, visitation problems, and meeting children's emotional needs

Krantzler, Mel
Creative divorce; a new opportunity for personal growth. Evans & Co. 1974 268p $8.95   **306.89**
1. Divorce
ISBN 0-87131-131-3
Also available in paperback from New Am. Lib.
The author "considers divorce the 'death' of a relationship, necessitating a mourning period followed by serious reevaluation and planning. That process is explored through anecdotal case histories from Krantzler's divorce workshop." Libr J

Lansky, Vicki
Vicki Lansky's divorce book for parents; helping your children cope with divorce and its aftermath. New Am. Lib. 1989 255p hardcover o.p. paperback available $4.50
                306.89
1. Divorce 2. Children of divorced parents
ISBN 0-451-16977-8 (pa)   LC 88-27227
Among the areas covered, "all from the perspective of doing what is best for the child, are breaking the news, the danger of continuing conflict, deciding when professional help is needed, organizing—and surviving—departure, dealing with the ex-spouse, and long-term

adjustment. . . . Highly recommended for all public library collections." Libr J
Includes bibliography

Vaughan, Diane
Uncoupling: turning points in intimate relationship. Oxford Univ. Press 1986 250p o.p.; Vintage Bks. paperback available $10
                306.89
1. Divorce
ISBN 0-679-73002-8 (pa)   LC 86-5401
This "examination of the breakup of relationships from a sociological and psychological perspective identifies the key steps in uncoupling from both partner's points of view. This schema is supported by 103 indepth interviews and solid documentation from the professional literature." Libr J
Includes bibliography

Wallerstein, Judith S.
Second chances; men, women, and children a decade after divorce; [by] Judith S. Wallerstein and Sandra Blakeslee. Ticknor & Fields 1989 xxi, 329p hardcover o.p. paperback available $9.70   **306.89**
1. Divorce 2. Children of divorced parents
ISBN 0-89919-949-6 (pa)   LC 88-23320
In 1971 the author "began a study of 131 children and adolescents from 60 families and their divorcing parents, in Marin County, California. . . . The researchers reinterviewed all family members 18 months later, again 5 years after divorce, and again 10 years after divorce. . . . 'Second Chances' is Ms. Wallerstein's account of the course and consequences of divorce for these parents and children." N Y Times Book Rev
Includes bibliography

307 Communities

Human settlement; general editor, John Rennie Short. Oxford Univ. Press 1992 256p i¹ maps $45   **307**
1. Cities and towns 2. Population
ISBN 0-19-520944-3   LC 92-25044
"An Equinox book"
The focus of this "volume is the human urban experience, especially as expressed in the late 20th century. . . . The inhabited world is divided into 22 regions . . . each of which is briefly discussed in turn, with an emphasis on the interplay between physical geography, climate, human settlement patterns, culture, and history. . . . Reading this book is pure enjoyment and, at the same time, quite a learning experience." Sci Books Films

Peck, M. Scott (Morgan Scott)
The different drum; community-making and peace. Simon & Schuster 1987 334p $14.95; pa $12   **307**
1. Community life 2. Peace 3. Spiritual life
ISBN 0-671-64633-8; 0-671-66833-1 (pa) LC 87-4825
The author argues that successful community-making is a way to achieve international peace

Peck, M. Scott (Morgan Scott)—*Continued*
The author "draws exciting analogies between the ways communities emerge and the dynamics of individual spiritual development." Libr J

307.7 Specific kinds of communities

Boyer, Rick
Places rated almanac; your guide to finding the best places to live in America; [by] Richard Boyer & David Savageau. Prentice-Hall il maps pa $19   **307.7**
1. Cities and towns—United States 2. Quality of life
First published 1981 by Rand McNally. (revised edition 1993) Frequently revised
Ranking "metropolitan areas as to factors that affect the quality of life—namely, the arts, economics, education, crime, transportation, environment, housing, climate, and health care—this compendium provides statistical information on American cities and towns. People planning to move will find it useful." Ref Sources for Small & Medium-sized Libr. 5th edition

Ford, Norman D., 1921-
The 50 healthiest places to live and retire in the United States. Mills & Sanderson Pubs. 1991 255p map pa $12.95   **307.7**
1. Retirement communities 2. Quality of life
ISBN 0-938179-25-X   LC 90-49964
Also available in paperback from Ballantine Bks.
This is a "report on 50 cities' ability to provide a high 'quality of life.' Environmental factors include elevation and water and soil condition as well as 'terrain therapy.' Some life-style considerations are stress level (evaluated using a survey taken by Zero Population Growth); opportunities for volunteer work, spiritual growth, and social contacts; and health awareness of the population." Booklist
Includes bibliographic references

Mumford, Lewis, 1895-1990
The city in history; its origins, its transformation, and its prospects. Harcourt Brace & World 1961 657p il hardcover o.p. paperback available $21.95   **307.7**
1. Cities and towns—History 2. City life 3. Civilization—History
ISBN 0-15-618035-9 (pa)
More than a history of the forms and functions of the city throughout the ages, this is a portrait of the development of man as a religious, a political, an economic, a cultural, and a sexual being
Includes bibliography

The culture of cities. Harcourt Brace & Co. 1938 586p il hardcover o.p. paperback available $19.95   **307.7**
1. Cities and towns 2. City planning 3. Regional planning
ISBN 0-15-623301-0 (pa)
Also available in hardcover from Greenwood Press

The second in a series which begins with Technics and civilization (entered in class 609) and continues with The condition of man (entered in class 909) and The conduct of life (entered in class 128)
Traces the growth of cities from medieval times to the twentieth century
Includes bibliography

Savageau, David
Retirement places rated; all you need to plan your retirement or select your second home. 3d ed. Prentice Hall Press 1990 237p il maps pa $16.95   **307.7**
1. Retirement communities
ISBN 0-13-778929-7   LC 90-7714
First published 1983 with title: Places rated retirement guide
"Evaluates and ranks more than 100 places in the United States for characteristics of importance to retirees. Compares in considerable detail each location for climate, housing, money matters, personal safety, services (including health and transportation), and leisure activities." Ref Sources for Small & Medium-sized Libr. 5th edition

Whyte, William Hollingsworth
City; rediscovering its center; by William H. Whyte; photos by the author. Doubleday 1988 386p il o.p.; Anchor Bks. paperback available $14.95   **307.7**
1. Cities and towns 2. City life 3. City planning
ISBN 0-385-26209-4 (pa)   LC 88-3977
"Whyte's Street Life Project studied the use of urban spaces for 16 years. This follow-up to *The Social Life of Small Urban Spaces* [1980] is an engaging look at the variety of human interactions which make 'downtown' vibrant. Whyte looks at such diverse topics as pedestrian movement, concourses and skyways, sunlight and its effects—all from the perspective of a confirmed city-lover." Libr J
Includes bibliographies

310.5 General statistics—Serial publications

The **Europa** world year book. Europa Publs. [distributed by] Gale Res. 2v $530
    310.5
1. Statistics 2. Political science
ISSN 0956-2273
Annual. First published 1959 with title: The Europa year book
Contents: v1 International organizations; Afghanistan-Jordan; v2 Kazakhstan-Zimbabwe
"The best annual directory of the nations of the world. For each country it includes demographic and economic statistics, and facts about constitution and government, political parties, press, trade and industry, publishers, etc. Also incorporates a substantive section with listings and information about international organizations." Ref Sources for Small & Medium-sized Libr. 5th edition

The **Statesman's** year-book; statistical and historical annual of the states of the world. St. Martin's Press $79.95 **310.5**

1. Statistics 2. Political science
ISSN 0081-4601

Annual. First published 1864

"Descriptive and statistical information about international organizations and countries of the world—brief history, area, political status, economy, etc." N Y Public Libr. Ref Books for Child Collect. 2d edition

United Nations. Statistical Office
Statistical yearbook. U.N. Publs. $150 **310.5**

1. Statistics

First published 1948. Text in English and French

An annual giving statistics under the following headings: Population; Manpower; Production summary; Agriculture; Forestry; Fishing; Mining, quarrying; Manufacturing; Construction; Electricity, gas, consumption; Transport; Communications; Internal trade; External trade; Balance of payments; International economic aid; Wages and prices; National income; Public finance; Housing statistics; Education, culture

314.1 General statistics of Great Britain

Whitaker's almanack. Whitaker; [distributed by] Gale Res. $72 **314.1**

1. Great Britain—Statistics 2. Almanacs 3. Statistics

Annual. First published 1869, founded by Joseph Whitaker. Subtitle varies

"This annual contains an enormous amount of statistical and descriptive information concerning Great Britain, plus brief information for other parts of the world. Detailed index." Ref Sources for Small & Medium-sized Libr. 5th edition

317.1 General statistics of Canada

Canada, a portrait. Statistics Canada; [distributed by] International Specialized Bk. Services pa $25 **317.1**

1. Canada—Statistics
ISSN 0840-6014

Biennial. First published 1980

"Provides historical and current information on all aspects of Canadian society. Concise textual surveys, photographs, and statistical tables." Ref Sources for Small & Medium-sized Libr. 5th edition

Canadian almanac & directory. Canadian Almanac & Directory; [distributed by] Gale Res. $145 **317.1**

1. Canada—Directories 2. Almanacs
ISSN 0068-8193

Annual. First published 1990

"The standard directory source for Canada, including addresses and officers of associations, institutions, professional and trade organizations, government departments, etc. Statistical and factual data. Arranged alphabetically

by topic. Detailed subject index." Ref Sources for Small & Medium-sized Libr. 5th edition

317.3 General statistics of the United States

County and city data book. U.S. Govt. Ptg. Office $36 **317.3**

1. Cities and towns—United States 2. United States—Statistics

First published 1949. (1988 edition available) Periodically revised

"Presents the latest available census figures for each county, and for the larger cities in the United States. Also has summary figures for states, geographical regions, urbanized areas, standard metropolitan areas, and unincorporated places." Sheehy. Guide to Ref Books. 10th edition

United States. Bureau of the Census
Statistical abstract of the United States. U.S. Govt. Ptg. Office $19.95 **317.3**

1. United States—Statistics 2. Statistics

Annual. First published for the year 1878

"Compendium of statistics on the social, political and economic organization of the U.S. presented in tables. Lists other sources of such information." N Y Public Libr. Ref Books for Child Collect. 2d edition

320 Political science

Aristotle, 384-322 B.C.
Politics **320**

1. Political science

Hardcover and paperback editions available from various publishers

"Discussion of public affairs by the most eminent of the Greek philosophers in terms applicable to many of the problems of modern political science." Pratt Alcove

Coles, Robert
The political life of children. Atlantic Monthly Press 1986 341p il o.p.; Houghton Mifflin paperback available $10.70 **320**

1. Children and politics 2. Child psychology 3. Child development
ISBN 0-395-59922-9 (pa) LC 85-22821

This volume in the author's series of behavior studies on childhood explores children's concepts of politics

Coles has "an expert psychological knowledge about children's attitudes and choices. Moreover, he has a keen appreciation for the complex social forces that shape those views about the world." Psychol Today

Includes bibliography

Machiavelli, Niccolò, 1469-1527
The prince **320**

1. Political science 2. Political ethics

Hardcover and paperback editions available from various publishers

Written in 1513

Machiavelli, Niccolò, 1469-1527—_Continued_
"A handbook of advice on the acquisition, use, and
maintenance of political power, dedicated to Lorenzo de
Medici." Haydn. Thesaurus of Book Dig

Paine, Thomas, 1737-1809
Common sense   **320**
1. United States—Politics and government—1775-
1783, Revolution
Hardcover and paperback editions available from
various publishers
"Published anonymously at Philadelphia (Jan. 10,
1776). At a time of rising passion against the British
government, the work was the first unqualified argument
for complete political independence, and helped turn
colonial thought in the direction that, six months later,
culminated in the Declaration of Independence. Over
100,000 copies were sold by the end of March, and it
is generally considered the most important literary influence on the movement for independence." Oxford
Companion to Am Lit. 5th edition

The rights of man   **320**
1. Political science 2. France—History—1789-1799,
Revolution
Hardcover and paperback editions available from
various publishers
First published 1791-1792
A political work "defending the French Revolution
against attacks made on it by Edmund Burke. In it Paine
argues that civil government exists only through a contract with a majority of the people for the safeguarding
of the individual, and that if man's 'natural rights' are
interfered with by the government, revolution is permissible." Reader's Ency

320.025 Political science—
Directories

Washington   information   directory.
Congressional Quarterly $89.95   **320.025**
1. Washington (D.C.)—Directories 2. United States—
Executive departments—Directories
ISSN 0887-8064
Annual. First published 1975/76
"Lists names, telephone numbers, addresses, and
responsibilities of 5,000 key personnel and agencies, both
private and governmental, in the Washington, DC area;
includes detailed indexes." N Y Public Libr Book of
How & Where to Look It Up

320.03 Political science—
Encyclopedias and dictionaries

Plano, Jack C.
The American political dictionary; [by]
Jack C. Plano, Milton Greenberg. Harcourt
Brace & Co. pa $21.75   **320.03**
1. Political science—Dictionaries 2. United States—
Politics and government—Dictionaries
First published 1962. (9th edition 1993) Frequently
revised
"Combination dictionary and subject-arranged overview
of important terms, concepts, and court cases." N Y
Public Libr Book of How & Where to Look It Up

Safire, William
Safire's New political dictionary; the
definitive guide to the new language of
politics. Random House 1993 930p $35
    320.03
1. Political science—Dictionaries 2. United States—
Politics and government—Dictionaries
ISBN 0-679-42068-1   LC 93-14554
First published 1968 with title: The new language of
politics
In over 1100 essaylike entries "Safire defines and explores the terms and expressions, the catchwords and
slogans, that have burst into the American language
through politics." Publisher's note
"Mr. Safire's admirers will relish his forensic way with
the clichés of the inside-the-Beltway crowd." N Y Times
Book Rev

Shafritz, Jay M.
The HarperCollins dictionary of American
government and politics. HarperCollins Pubs.
1992 656p il $50; pa $10   **320.03**
1. Political science—Dictionaries 2. United States—
Politics and government—Dictionaries
ISBN 0-06-270031-6; 0-06-461021-7 (pa)
    LC 91-55389
"This is a comprehensive dictionary of 5000 terms,
phrases, and processes central to an understanding of
American government and politics at all levels. Concepts,
persons, laws, court cases, political slang, and organiza-
tions make up entries of up to 400 words." Libr J
For a fuller review see: Booklist, May 1, 1992
Includes bibliographic references

320.1 The state

Hobbes, Thomas, 1588-1679
Leviathan   **320.1**
1. Political science 2. State, The
Hardcover and paperback editions available from
various publishers
First published 1651
"A treatise on the origin and ends of government. .
. . This work, a defense of secular monarchy, written
while the Puritan Commonwealth ruled England, contains
Hobbes's famous theory of the sovereign state." Reader's
Ency

Locke, John, 1632-1704
Two treatises of government   **320.1**
1. Political science 2. State, The
Hardcover and paperback editions available from
various publishers
First published 1690
Locke's Two treatises written in "defense of the
Glorious Revolution, revealed his belief in the natural
goodness and cooperative spirit of man and his theory
that the state should operate according to natural laws
of reason and tolerance. He advocated religious tolerance
and rights to personal property." Reader's Ency. 3d edition

Rousseau, Jean-Jacques, 1712-1778
The social contract   **320.1**
1. Political science
Hardcover and paperback editions available from various publishers
First published 1762
"A treatise on the origins and organization of government and the rights of citizens. Rousseau's thesis states that, since no man has any natural authority over another, the social contract, freely entered into, creates natural reciprocal obligations between citizens." Reader's Ency. 3d edition

320.4 Structure and functions of government

Government by the people; national, state and local edition; [by] James McGregor Burns [et al.] Prentice-Hall $53.33   **320.4**
1. United States—Politics and government—Handbooks, manuals, etc. 2. State governments 3. Local government
Also available in other versions
Originally published 1952 as two separate works, one covering national government and the other covering state and local government. (15th edition 1993) Frequently revised
This book "tries to get away from dry exposition of structures and powers in order to 'picture American government as an alive and dynamic thing.'" Ann Am Acad Polit Soc Sci

320.5 Political ideologies

Dionne, E. J., Jr.
Why Americans hate politics; [by] E.J. Dionne, Jr. Simon & Schuster 1991 430p hardcover o.p. paperback available $12
320.5
1. Right and left (Political science) 2. United States—Politics and government
ISBN 0-671-77877-3 (pa)   LC 91-10030
The author "argues that American liberal and conservative ideologies since the 1960s have presented the public with false choices, preventing the framing of issues in ways that are conducive to their resolution. He calls for a 'new political center' that incorporates some ideas of both the political left and right." Libr J
Includes bibliographic references

Lappé, Frances Moore
Rediscovering America's values. Ballantine Bks. 1989 325p hardcover o.p. paperback available $12.95   **320.5**
1. Political ethics 2. Values 3. Right and left (Political science)
ISBN 0-345-36953-X (pa)   LC 88-47875
The author "here envisions a more democratic economy, one in which big corporations would be responsive to community needs, while workers would win decision-making power in their companies. . . . Her brave, challenging essay is valuable for its power to encourage people to assess the kind of society we now have—and to envision alternative scenarios for the fu-

ture." Publ Wkly
Includes bibliographic references

Malcolm X, 1925-1965
Malcolm X talks to young people; speeches in the U.S., Britain, and Africa. Pathfinder Press 1991 110p il $40; pa $9.95
320.5
1. Blacks—Civil rights 2. Black Muslims 3. United States—Race relations
ISBN 0-87348-631-5; 0-87348-628-5 (pa)
LC 90-64197
"Providing, a sense of Malcolm X's voice as well as his beliefs, this book presents transcripts and excerpts of speeches given to teenagers in the U.S., Africa, and England during the last year of his life. Most of the material is unavailable elsewhere." Booklist

Malcolm X: the last speeches; edited by Bruce Perry. Pathfinder Press 1989 189p il $40; pa $15.95   **320.5**
1. Black Muslims 2. Blacks—Civil rights 3. United States—Race relations
ISBN 0-87348-544-0; 0-87348-543-2 (pa)
LC 89-61591
"Perry provides four previously unpublished speeches and two interviews given by Malcolm X immediately prior to his 1965 assassination. . . . The speeches and interviews are introduced by brief editorial comments. An important addition to the literature of Malcolm X and the Black Power movement." Booklist
Includes bibliographic references

Malcolm X; in our own image; Joe Wood, editor. St. Martin's Press 1992 246p $18.95   **320.5**
1. Malcolm X, 1925-1965
ISBN 0-312-06609-0   LC 92-4015
This book "presents various African American intellectuals' consideration of Malcolm X's significance and legacy. Each writer—from Amiri Baraka to Angela Davis to John Edgar Wideman—has a separate chapter to evaluate the political message of Malcolm X from black, gay, and feminist perspectives. Some of the essays are beautifully composed and soothing, while others are angry; all are thoughtful and lend valuable depth and solidity to the contemporary debate." Booklist
Includes bibliographic references

321 Systems of governments and states

More, Sir Thomas, Saint, 1478-1535
Utopia   **321**
1. Utopias
Hardcover and paperback editions available from various publishers
Originally published 1516 in Latin; 1551 in English
In his study of the ideal state, "More assigns the narrative to a Raphael Hythloday ('Hythloday' is Greek for 'talker of nonsense'). . . . Book I treats of the evils of the world and asserts the need for an ideal commonwealth, which Book II describes." Haydn. Thesaurus of Book Dig

Mumford, Lewis, 1895-1990

The story of utopias; with an introduction by Hendrik Willem Van Loon. Boni and Liveright 1922 315p o.p.   **321**

1. Utopias

Available in hardcover from P. Smith

The book "connects up the classic Utopias from Plato onward with modern social myths and schemes for reform showing the contrasts as well as the points common to all." Am J Sociol

Includes bibliography

321.9   Authoritarian systems

Arendt, Hannah

Origins of totalitarianism. new ed with added prefaces. Harcourt Brace Jovanovich 1973 xliii, 527p pa $14.95   **321.9**

1. Totalitarianism 2. Imperialism 3. Antisemitism
ISBN 0-15-670153-7

Also available as three separate paperbacks with titles: Antisemitism; Imperialism; Totalitarianism

"A Harvest book"

First published 1951 in the United Kingdom with title: The burden of our time

In this book, the author documents her "belief that Nazism and Communism had their roots in the anti-Semitism and imperialism of the 19th century." Reader's Ency

Includes bibliography

Rubin, Barry M.

Modern dictators; Third World coup makers, strongmen, and populist tyrants; [by] Barry Rubin. McGraw-Hill 1987 385p il o.p.; New Am. Lib. paperback available $10.95   **321.9**

1. Dictators
ISBN 0-452-01036-5 (pa)   LC 86-18543

This "book details the rise of one-party rule after 1945 and examines various dictatorial styles in the Third World. Rubin's cool analysis of these despots, their effect on the U.N., and the ambivalence [of] the United States toward them is completed by a useful bibliography." Libr J

322   Relation of the state to organized groups and their members

Wills, Garry, 1934-

Under God; religion and American politics. Simon & Schuster 1990 445p $22.95; pa $12   **322**

1. Presidents—United States—Election—1988 2. Christianity and politics 3. Church—Government policy—United States 4. United States—Politics and government—1974-1989 5. United States—Church history
ISBN 0-671-65701-1; 0-671-74746-0 (pa)

LC 90-44624

"Anchoring his arguments that understanding Protestantism—especially evangelical Protestantism—is crucial to understanding American politics, Wills recovers

much fascinating lost, suppressed, and misunderstood history while accounting for the varying fortunes and foibles of five candidates: the official evangelicals Robertson, Jackson, and Bush; the apostate evangelical Hart; and the rigid secularist Dukakis." Booklist

Includes bibliographic references

322.4   Political action groups

Alinsky, Saul

Rules for radicals; a practical primer for realistic radicals; by Saul D. Alinsky. Random House 1971 196p hardcover o.p. paperback available $5.95   **322.4**

1. Community organization 2. Radicals and radicalism
ISBN 0-394-71736-8 (pa)

The author discusses how radicals should organize and work within the system to effect social change

Includes bibliographic references

Chalmers, David Mark

Hooded Americanism: the history of the Ku Klux Klan. 3rd ed. Duke Univ. Press 1987 c1981 477p il $39.95; pa $16.95

    322.4

1. Ku Klux Klan
ISBN 0-8223-0730-8; 0-8223-0772-3 (pa)

    LC 86-29133

First published 1965 by Doubleday; this is a reissue of the 1981 edition published by Watts

This book recounts the history of the Klan. It describes the sociological and psychological forces behind the Klan, and sets forth its dogmas

"The book is written in a breezy, journalistic style. . . . Especially instructive and sobering is Chalmers' account of the role of the Klan in politics." J Am Hist

Includes bibliography

Gandhi, Mahatma, 1869-1948

Gandhi on non-violence; selected texts from Mohandas K. Gandhi's Non-violence in peace and war; edited with an introduction by Thomas Merton. New Directions 1965 82p pa $4.95   **322.4**

1. Passive resistance 2. India—Politics and government
ISBN 0-8112-0097-3

"A New Directions paperbook"

In an introductory essay Merton "considers Gandhi's ideas, not in relation to their Indian context, but in terms of their applicability to all men's lives. Brief quotations from Gandhi's writings make up most of the book." Asia: a Guide to Paperbacks

Livingstone, Neil C.
Inside the PLO; covert units, secret funds, and the war against Israel and the United States; [by] Neil C. Livingstone and David Halevy in cooperation with the Ethics and Public Policy Center, Washington, D.C. Morrow 1990 336p il $21.95; pa $13
322.4
1. Palestine Liberation Organization 2. Jewish-Arab relations
ISBN 0-688-09335-3; 0-688-10742-7 (pa)
LC 89-38232
The authors discuss the structure and activities of the Palestine Liberation Organization
"This is essential reading for an appreciation of Middle East developments, the PLO, and terrorism." Libr J
Includes bibliography

Mailer, Norman
The armies of the night; history as a novel, the novel as history. New Am. Lib. 1968 288p hardcover o.p. paperback available $5.99
322.4
1. Vietnam War, 1961-1975—Protests, demonstrations, etc.
ISBN 0-451-14070-2 (pa)
The author chronicles his experiences during the four days of events surrounding the peace march on the Pentagon in October, 1967. In a final section, he presents an evaluation of the march and its implications for American life and politics

Ture, Kwame, 1941-
Black power; the politics of liberation in America; [by] Stokely Carmichael & Charles V. Hamilton. Random House 1967 198p hardcover o.p. paperback available $6.95
322.4
1. Black power
ISBN 0-394-70033-3 (pa)
The authors "explain the origins, development, and goals of the Black Power movement." Saturday Rev
Includes bibliography

323   Civil and political rights

The **Amnesty** International handbook; compiled and edited by Marie Staunton, Sally Fenn, and Amnesty International U.S.A. Hunter House 1991 145p il pa $9.95
323
1. Human rights
ISBN 0-89793-081-9
LC 91-12255
"This handbook educates readers on AI's three major goals: the release of 'prisoners of conscience,' fair and prompt trials for all political prisoners, and the abolishment of torture and the death penalty. It also discusses other major AI issues: the 'disappearances' of prisoners, the rights of children and women, refugees, and human rights education. The book's second half covers AI's structure and what volunteers can do." Libr J

Drinan, Robert F.
Cry of the oppressed; the history and hope of the human rights revolution. Harper & Row 1987 210p $17.95
323
1. Civil rights
ISBN 0-06-250261-1
LC 87-45173
Ex-congressman Drinan argues that "ratification of economic and political [human rights] covenants has come slowly or not at all, due in part to socialist insistence on the right to work and a decent standard of living, and in part to U.S. reluctance to seek compliance from aid recipients." Libr J
Includes bibliography

Walker, Samuel, 1942-
In defense of American liberties: a history of the ACLU. Oxford Univ. Press 1990 479p il $27.95; pa $12.95
323
1. American Civil Liberties Union
ISBN 0-19-504539-4; 0-19-507141-7 (pa)
LC 89-32843
This history of the ACLU covers its involvement in famous causes such as the Scopes "Monkey Trial," the internment of Japanese-Americans during World War II, the Cold War anti-Communist witch hunts, and the civil rights movement
Includes bibliography

323.1   Civil and political rights of nondominant aggregates

Cagin, Seth
We are not afraid; the story of Goodman, Schwerner, and Chaney and the civil rights campaign for Mississippi; [by] Seth Cagin and Philip Dray. Macmillan 1988 500p il o.p.; Bantam Bks. paperback available $14.95
323.1
1. Chaney, James Earl, 1943-1964 2. Schwerner, Michael Henry, 1939-1964 3. Goodman, Andrew, 1943-1964 4. Blacks—Civil rights 5. Mississippi—Race relations
ISBN 0-553-35252-0 (pa)
LC 87-24069
This is an account of the murder of three civil rights workers who went to Mississippi in the summer of 1964 to help blacks register to vote
"The book resembles a good documentary film, and in explaining how the three men happened to be where they were when they were killed it clarifies both the public and the private aspects of the tragedy." New Yorker

Durham, Michael
Powerful days; the civil rights photography of Charles Moore; [by] Michael S. Durham; introduction by Andrew Young. Stewart, Tabori & Chang; Eastman Kodak. Professional Photography Div. 1990 207p il $35; pa $24.95
323.1
1. Moore, Charles 2. Blacks—Civil rights—Pictorial works 3. Southern States—Race relations—Pictorial works
ISBN 1-55670-171-3; 1-55670-202-7 (pa)
LC 90-10327

Durham, Michael—*Continued*

This is a photographic record of leaders and events in the civil rights campaign of the 1950s and 1960s

"Disturbing yet inspiring, the 180 duotones presented here are a needed and welcome document of a struggle that still continues." Libr J

The **Eyes** on the prize civil rights reader; documents, speeches, and firsthand accounts from the black freedom struggle, 1954-1990; general editors, Clayborne Carson [et al.] Penguin Bks. 1991 764p pa $16   323.1

1. Blacks—Civil rights 2. United States—Race relations

ISBN 0-14-015403-5   LC 91-9507

First published 1987 with title: Eyes on the prize: America's civil rights years, a reader and guide

"An anthology of primary material important in the historiography of this country's civil rights movement. . . . Not simply for reference use, this compilation makes provocative cover-to-cover reading and is extremely worthy of consideration by every library." Booklist

Includes bibliographic references

Hampton, Henry

Voices of freedom; an oral history of the civil rights movement from the 1950s through the 1980s; [by] Henry Hampton and Steve Fayer with Sarah Flynn. Bantam Bks. 1990 xxviii, 692p hardcover o.p. paperback available $15.95   323.1

1. Blacks—Civil rights 2. United States—Race relations

ISBN 0-553-35232-6 (pa)   LC 89-18297

This companion to the public television series "Eyes on the Prize" contains chronologically arranged excerpts from interviews recorded in the process of producing the series. The thirty-one chapters cover events in the history of the civil rights struggle from the 1955 lynching of Emmett Till to the controversy over affirmative action (Atlanta, 1973-1980)

Includes bibliography

Jackson, Helen Hunt, 1830-1885

A century of dishonor; a sketch of the United States Government's dealings with some of the Indian tribes. new ed, enlarged by the addition of the report of the needs of the mission Indians of California. Scholarly Press 1972 c1885 514p $79

323.1

1. Indians of North America—Government policy

ISBN 0-403-00382-2

Also available from Reprint Services Corp.

First published 1881 by Harper

A major thesis of this title "was that the United States had followed an outrageous Indian policy in defiance of the basic principles of justice and of the laws of all nations. The book described maltreatment of the Indians from the period of the American Revolution." Introduction

King, Martin Luther, 1929-1968

The papers of Martin Luther King, Jr; senior editor, Clayborne Carson; volume editors, Ralph E. Luker, Penny A. Russell; advisory editor, Louis R. Harlan. v1: Called to serve, January 1929-June 1951. University of Calif. Press 1992 484p il $35   323.1

1. Blacks—Civil rights 2. United States—Race relations

ISBN 0-520-07950-7   LC 91-42336

"The first of a projected multivolume series of the famed civil rights leader's papers. This volume consists largely of essays and papers King wrote while a student at Crozer Theological Seminary. . . . An excellent introduction and document inventory . . . help make this an indispensable resource for college, university, and major public libraries." Libr J

Includes bibliographic references

Stride toward freedom; the Montgomery story; by Martin Luther King, Jr. Harper & Row 1958 230p il hardcover o.p. paperback available $10   323.1

1. Blacks—Civil rights 2. Blacks—Segregation 3. Montgomery (Ala.)—Race relations

ISBN 0-06-250490-8 (pa)

An account of the bus boycott organized by Montgomery blacks in December, 1955, to protest discriminatory practices

A testament of hope; the essential writings of Martin Luther King, Jr. edited by James Melvin Washington. Harper & Row 1986 xxvi, 676p $24.95; pa $18   323.1

1. Blacks—Civil rights 2. United States—Race relations

ISBN 0-06-250931-4; 0-06-064691-8 (pa)

LC 85-45370

"King's most important writings are gathered together in one source. The arrangement is topical: philosophy, sermons and public addresses, essays, interviews and excerpts of his books. The material within each of these categories is arranged chronologically. Included are Dr. King's writings on nonviolence, integration and politics." SLJ

Includes bibliography

Where do we go from here: chaos or community? [by] Martin Luther King, Jr. Harper & Row 1967 209p o.p.; Beacon Press paperback available $12.95   323.1

1. Blacks—Civil rights 2. United States—Race relations

ISBN 0-8070-0571-1 (pa)

The author reaffirms his belief in the power of nonviolence to achieve full citizenship for black people in America and defines his attitude toward the Black Power movement and the white backlash

Includes bibliographic references

Why we can't wait; [by] Martin Luther King, Jr. Harper & Row 1964 178p il o.p.; New Am. Lib. paperback available $4.50

323.1

1. Blacks—Civil rights 2. Birmingham (Ala.)—Race relations

ISBN 0-451-62754-7 (pa)

King, Martin Luther, 1929-1968 — Continued
The author first reviews the background of the 1963 civil rights demands. He then describes the strategy of the Birmingham campaign and outlines future action

The words of Martin Luther King, Jr. selected by Coretta Scott King. Newmarket Press 1983 112p il $12.95; pa $7.95
323.1

1. Blacks—Civil rights 2. United States—Race relations
ISBN 0-937858-28-5; 0-937858-79-X (pa)
LC 83-17306

This "volume of selections from Dr. King's speeches and writings . . . focuses on seven areas of his concerns: 'The Community of Man, Racism, Civil Rights, Justice and Freedom, Faith and Religion, Nonviolence, and Peace.'" Publisher's note
Includes bibliography

Lyon, Danny, 1942-
Memories of the Southern civil rights movement; with a foreword by Julian Bond. University of N.C. Press 1992 192p il (Lyndhurst ser. on the South) $39.95; pa $19.95
323.1

1. Student Nonviolent Coordinating Committee 2. Blacks—Civil rights—Pictorial works 3. Southern States—Race relations—Pictorial works
ISBN 0-8078-2054-7; 0-8078-4386-5 (pa) LC 92-5961
Published for the Center for Documentary Studies, Duke University
"Lyon, a young Jewish New Yorker, joined the Student Nonviolent Coordinating Committee (SNCC) in 1962 as a photographer. The 212 black-and-white photographs shown here, taken from 1962 to 1965, document that short-lived influential civil rights organization. . . . The book is an honest, rich statement, transmitting the tumult, cross-purposes and devotion of the era." Publ Wkly
Includes bibliography

Powledge, Fred
Free at last? the civil rights movement and the people who made it. Little, Brown 1990 xxiii, 711p il $29.95
323.1

1. Blacks—Civil rights 2. United States—Race relations
ISBN 0-316-71632-4
LC 90-41332
Also available in paperback from HarperCollins
"An ample history, frankly partisan but generously comprehensive of the nonviolent activists of the 1960's and their opponents." N Y Times Book Rev
Includes bibliographic references

Seeger, Pete
Everybody says freedom; [by] Pete Seeger, Bob Reiser; including many songs collected by Guy and Candie Carawan. Norton 1989 266p il music hardcover o.p. paperback available $18.95
323.1

1. Blacks—Civil rights 2. Black songs
ISBN 0-393-30604-6 (pa)
LC 88-23341

This narrative of the American civil rights movement of the 1960s "is illustrated with music and words to three dozen songs. . . . Profiles of 15 people active in the movement, anecdotes about . . . others, and a chronological outline/commentary on events from 1955 to 1968 are linked by the songs." Libr J
Includes discography and bibliography

Sowell, Thomas, 1930-
Civil rights; rhetoric or reality? Morrow 1984 164p hardcover o.p. paperback available $6.95
323.1

1. Civil rights 2. Affirmative action programs 3. United States—Race relations
ISBN 0-688-06269-5 (pa)

The author's "thesis is that the civil rights vision is based on three premises: that statistical disparities in incomes, occupations, and education between whites and blacks represent moral inequities and are caused by society; that a belief in the innate inferiority of blacks has further exacerbated the inequitable conditions of the races; and that political activity is the key to improving the lot of the disadvantaged. Through probing statistical comparisons, Sowell casts considerable doubt on the validity of this 'civil rights vision.'" Choice
Includes bibliographic references

Williams, Juan
Eyes on the prize: America's civil rights years, 1954-1965; [by] Juan Williams with the Eyes on the prize production team; introduction by Julian Bond. Viking 1987 300p il o.p.; Penguin Bks. paperback available $11.95
323.1

1. Blacks—Civil rights 2. United States—Race relations
ISBN 0-14-009653-1 (pa)
LC 86-40271

"A Robert Lavelle book"
"This companion volume to the PBS TV series of the same name is an . . . account of black America's struggle for social and political equality, covering the civil rights battle from the landmark Brown v. Board of Education decision in 1954 to the Selma protest marches, and Voting Rights Act of 1965." Libr J
"Highly recommended both as a socio-historical document and as a heartfelt, poignant remembrance of a movement and its activists." Booklist
Includes bibliographic references

323.44 Freedom of action (Liberty)

Blanchard, Margaret A.
Revolutionary sparks; freedom of expression in modern America. Oxford Univ. Press 1992 572p $49.95
323.44

1. Free speech 2. Freedom of the press
ISBN 0-19-505436-9
LC 91-16147

A "discussion of freedom of expression in America, this book begins by studying the period after the Civil War and Reconstruction when new and unsettling ideas appeared with great regularity on the American scene. Blanchard traces this contest for control through the Watergate scandal of the 1970s and the Reagan and early Bush administrations." Univ Press Books for Public and

Blanchard, Margaret A.—*Continued*
Second Sch Libr

Includes bibliographic references

Commager, Henry Steele, 1902-
Freedom, loyalty, dissent. Oxford Univ.
Press 1954 155p $19.95   **323.44**

1. Freedom
ISBN 0-19-500510-4

Five essays dealing with various aspects of the function and character of loyalty in democratic society

The **First** freedom today; critical issues relating to censorship and intellectual freedom; edited by Robert B. Downs and Ralph E. McCoy. American Lib. Assn. 1984 341p $20   **323.44**

1. Censorship 2. Freedom of information 3. Free speech
ISBN 0-8389-0412-2   LC 84-461

First published 1960 with title: First freedom

"The editors have assembled an anthology of . . . writings on censorship. . . . The virtue of the volume is its thoroughness. It will be useful for a long time as a reference history of censorship in the United States." Libr J

Includes bibliographic references

Intellectual freedom manual; compiled by the Office for Intellectual Freedom of the American Library Association. 4th ed. American Lib. Assn. 1992 283p pa $25   **323.44**

1. Intellectual freedom 2. Libraries—Censorship
ISBN 0-8389-3412-9   LC 92-10699

This "manual remains an essential document for all libraries and librarians because it sets the standard for preserving intellectual freedom while providing practical direction for librarians under fire from censors. . . . An index provides quick reference to key concepts, issues, names, places, and legal cases." Libr J

Includes bibliographic references

Mill, John Stuart, 1806-1873
Three essays. Oxford Univ. Press 1975 xxv, 550p pa $12.95   **323.44**

1. Freedom 2. Representative government and representation 3. Women—Civil rights
ISBN 0-19-283013-9

On liberty was published 1859, Representative government in 1861 and The subjection of women in 1869

Mill's "works were of vital importance in enhancing the value placed on individual action and judgement, a value affirmed by the century's poets and novelists. Mill was sharp in analysis and lucid in exposition. He had a prophetic power in nosing out the issues that have become important." Penguin Companion to Engl Lit

Patterson, Orlando, 1940-
Freedom. v1: Freedom in the making of Western culture. Basic Bks. 1991 487p $29.95; pa $15   **323.44**

1. Freedom
ISBN 0-465-02535-8; 0-465-02532-3 (pa)
     LC 90-55593

Patterson "argues that the idea of freedom is the supreme value in the Western world and increasingly so in the rest of the world. This book, the first of a projected two-volume inquiry, seeks to answer the question of how it became such a powerful and popular value." Libr J

Includes bibliographic references

Rothfeder, Jeffrey
Privacy for sale; how computerization has made everyone's private life an open secret. Simon & Schuster 1992 224p $22   **323.44**

1. Right of privacy 2. Computers—Access control
ISBN 0-671-73492-X   LC 92-364

The author examines the collection of personal information about individuals by "institutions like medical bureaus and credit reporting companies. . . . [He] suggests that the misuse of personal information in the United States is on the increase because of the growing computerization of records and a largely ineffective hodgepodge of Federal and state laws." N Y Times Book Rev

Includes bibliographic references

324   The political process

Germond, Jack
Whose broad stripes and bright stars? the trivial pursuit of the presidency, 1988; [by] Jack W. Germond & Jules Witcover. Warner Bks. 1989 478p hardcover o.p. paperback available $12.95   **324**

1. Presidents—United States—Election—1988 2. United States—Politics and government—1981-
ISBN 0-446-39187-5 (pa)   LC 88-40566

The authors offer a report on what went on in the 1988 presidential "campaign, an analysis of how the process has changed over their three decades of personal observing, and what [in their view] this means for future elections." Publisher's note

This is "a well-researched and beautifully crafted account." Libr J

Greider, William
Who will tell the people; the betrayal of American democracy; [by] William B. Greider. Simon & Schuster 1992 464p $25; pa $13   **324**

1. Democracy 2. Lobbying and lobbyists 3. Corruption in politics 4. United States—Politics and government—1981-
ISBN 0-671-68891-X; 0-671-86740-7 (pa) LC 92-3514

"Greider charges that America's two major political parties, unions, the press and mass media no longer mediate between citizens and the powerful moneyed elites that control the political process. The result of this collective failure, he asserts, is a near-total breakdown of democracy." Publ Wkly

Greider, William—*Continued*

The author "has written an indispensable and comprehensive guide to the continuing meltdown of the American political system." N Y Times Book Rev

Includes bibliographic references

Morris, Celia

Storming the statehouse; running for governor with Ann Richards and Dianne Feinstein. Scribner 1992 325p il $25   **324**

1. Richards, Ann 2. Feinstein, Dianne 3. Elections—United States 4. Texas—Politics and government 5. California—Politics and government

ISBN 0-684-19328-0   LC 91-25644

"Morris takes readers on the campaign trails of two seemingly contrasting yet similar women . . . who met with quite different results in their respective 1990 runs for governor of two of the nation's largest and most politically influential states. . . . She offers a well-balanced view of both Richards and Feinstein, tracing their personal and political development over the years. But what makes this book a real winner is its skill at analyzing the specifics of the election process." Booklist

Includes bibliographic references

324.025 The political process—Directories

Political handbook of the world. CSA Publs. $94.95   **324.025**

1. Political science—Handbooks, manuals, etc. 2. Political parties

ISSN 0913-175X

Annual. First published 1927 with title: A political handbook of Europe

Editor 1975- Arthur S. Banks

"Provides data for each country on chief officials, government and politics, political parties, and news media. Sections devoted to intergovernmental organizations and to issues concerned with particular regions; e.g., Middle East, Latin America. Index to geographical, organizational, and personal names." Ref Sources for Small & Medium-sized Libr. 5th edition

324.2 Political parties

Frank, Barney

Speaking frankly; what's wrong with the Democrats and how to fix it. Times Bks. 1992 164p $18.50   **324.2**

1. Democratic Party (U.S.)

ISBN 0-394-57642-X   LC 91-50134

The author "outlines a pragmatic approach for liberating the Democratic Party from the imprisoning grasp of its ideological purists—without sacrificing the liberal principles on which the party rests. Focusing on defense, crime, and national security (and to a lesser extent, taxation), Frank supplies cogent arguments, strategies, and tactics to overcome self-inflicted negative public images and to win over the many 'swing voters' who elect Democrats for offices other than the presidency." Libr J

McCarthy, Eugene J., 1916-

Up 'til now; a memoir; [by] Eugene McCarthy. Harcourt Brace Jovanovich 1987 273p $16.95   **324.2**

1. Democratic Party (U.S.) 2. United States—Politics and government—1900-1999 (20th century)

ISBN 0-15-193170-4   LC 86-14313

A collection of personal reflections and political opinions from the former senator and presidential candidate

"'Up 'Til Now' certainly proves that Mr. McCarthy is still the poetic Isaiah whose plain literacy puts many other politicians to shame." N Y Times Book Rev

324.6 Election systems and procedures; suffrage

America votes; a handbook of contemporary American election statistics; compiled and edited [for] Governmental Affairs Institute. Congressional Quarterly maps $125   **324.6**

1. Elections—United States—Statistics

ISSN 0065-678X

Biennial. First volume published for the year 1954/55

"Arranged alphabetically by state. Statistics, by state, of vote since 1945 for president, governor, senator, congressman; statistics, by county and ward, of vote in most recent election for president, governor, senator; with maps of each state and of large cities and congressional districts, and brief statements of basic political information and special situations in each state." Sheehy. Guide to Ref Books. 10th edition

Congressional Quarterly's guide to U.S. elections. 2nd ed. Congressional Quarterly 1985 1308p il $155   **324.6**

1. Elections—United States—Statistics

ISBN 0-87187-339-7   LC 85-6912

First published 1975

"This first purchase for election statistics contains state-level data on elections for president, governor, senator, and representative through 1984. . . . Valuable overviews of political parties, political conventions, and southern primaries as well as of presidential, gubernatorial, Senate, and House elections supplement the most complete one-stop source of U.S. election data available in print." Ref Sources for Small & Medium-sized Libr. 5th edition

Presidential elections since 1789. Congressional Quarterly il $19.95   **324.6**

1. Presidents—United States—Election

First published 1975. (5th edition 1991) Periodically revised

Tables, charts and maps provide statistical data on primaries, nominating conventions, and candidates for every election

Sheehy, Gail

Character; America's search for leadership. Morrow 1988 303p o.p.; Bantam Bks. paperback available $5.95   **324.6**

1. Presidents—United States—Election

ISBN 0-553-27924-6 (pa)   LC 88-9221

Sheehy, Gail—*Continued*

This book contains chapters on such political figures as Gary Hart, Jesse Jackson, Robert Dole, George Bush, Albert Gore, Jr., Michael Dukakis, and Ronald Reagan

"The book assumes that an informed electorate should know more about those who would be president than is conveyed by a slick PR image. . . . Artistic and compelling." Libr J

White, Theodore H., 1915-1986

The making of the president, 1960. Atheneum Pubs. 1988 c1961 400p pa $14.95

324.6

1. Nixon, Richard M. (Richard Milhous), 1913-1994
2. Kennedy, John F. (John Fitzgerald), 1917-1963
3. Presidents—United States—Election 4. United States—Politics and government—1953-1961

ISBN 0-689-70803-3   LC 88-27604

Also available in paperback from New Am. Lib.

A reissue of the title first published 1961

A chronological account of the 1960 Presidential campaign "beginning with the first primaries in New Hampshire and Wisconsin and continuing through Inauguration Day, and into the White House." New Repub

324.7   Conduct of election campaigns

Beaudry, Ann E.

Winning local and state elections; the guide to organizing your campaign; [by] Ann Beaudry, Bob Schaeffer. Free Press 1986 217p $27.95

324.7

1. Politics, Practical 2. Elections—United States

ISBN 0-02-902490-0   LC 85-28066

The authors discuss the essential techniques of managing a professional local campaign: scheduling the candidate, building a field organization, working with media, fundraising, budgeting, and voter contact. They also provide record-keeping forms, checklists, sample letters and press releases

Includes bibliography

Cramer, Richard Ben

What it takes: the way to the White House. Random House 1992 1047p $27.50; pa $15

324.7

1. Presidents—United States—Election

ISBN 0-394-56260-7; 0-679-74649-8 (pa)

LC 91-52676

In this chronicle of the 1988 presidential campaign, the author examines the lives and motivations of six of the candidates

Cramer "set out to write neither campaign history nor political biography—though his book contains both. Instead, his main goal is to examine what leads a person to enter the cement mixer of Presidential politics and what happens to him once he does. Recurring phenomena, relevant now and in elections to come, fascinate Mr. Cramer." N Y Times Book Rev

325   International migration and colonization

Szulc, Tad

The secret alliance; the extraordinary story of the rescue of the Jews since World War II. Farrar, Straus & Giroux 1991 327p il maps $24.95

325

1. Berihah (Organization) 2. Refugees, Jewish 3. Palestine—Immigration and emigration 4. Israel—Immigration and emigration

ISBN 0-374-24946-6   LC 91-25542

"Szulc examines the covert movement of European, Middle Eastern, and North African Jews to an independent Palestine homeland following World War II." Booklist

"The story is updated with the saga of 'rescuing' the Jewish communities of Morocco, Yemen, Iraq, and most recently Ethiopa. Highlighted are the efforts of the American Jewish Joint Distribution Committee and the Hebrew Immigrant Aid Society, whose organizational talents essentially make it all happen. An excellent historical drama." Libr J

Includes bibliographic references

325.73   Immigration to the United States

Daniels, Roger

Coming to America; a history of immigration and ethnicity in American life. HarperCollins Pubs. 1990 450p il maps $29.95; pa $14

325.73

1. United States—Immigration and emigration 2. Minorities

ISBN 0-06-016098-5; 0-06-092100-5 (pa)

LC 89-46524

The author provides a "worldwide study of immigration to the US from 1500 to the present. He treats Colonial European immigrants from England, France, and Spain; African slaves; later arrivals from Ireland and Germany; Eastern European immigrants during the rise of industrialization; and the Latin American and Asian immigrants of the present era." Choice

Includes bibliographic references

Handlin, Oscar, 1915-

The uprooted. 2nd ed. Little, Brown 1973 333p hardcover o.p. paperback available $10.95

325.73

1. United States—Foreign population 2. Acculturation

ISBN 0-316-34313-7 (pa)

"An Atlantic Monthly Press book"

First published 1951

This account of the American immigrant experience and the acculturation process describes employment, religion, ghetto life, benevolent societies, boss politics, family life, and social alienation

Kennedy, John F. (John Fitzgerald), 1917-1963

A nation of immigrants; introduction by Robert F. Kennedy. rev and enl ed. Harper & Row 1964 111p il map hardcover o.p. paperback available $10   **325.73**

1. United States—Immigration and emigration 2. United States—Foreign population
ISBN 0-06-091367-3 (pa)

A reissue of a booklet written 1958 for the "One Nation Library" series of the Anti-Defamation League of B'nai B'rith

"An account of the struggles of successive waves of immigrants, their contributions to America, and their repeated triumphs over prejudice and discrimination. Expounds the need for an enlargement of our immigration laws." Guide to Read in Am Hist

Includes bibliography

Portes, Alejandro, 1944-

Immigrant America; a portrait; [by] Alejandro Portes and Rubén G. Rumbaut. University of Calif. Press 1990 xxiii, 300p il maps $39.95; pa $11.95   **325.73**

1. United States—Immigration and emigration
ISBN 0-520-06894-7; 0-520-07038-0 (pa)
LC 89-20444

"A Centennial book"

Using "charts and statistics, the authors discuss the nature of foreign influx over the years, relating diverse patterns to U.S. official and unofficial policy as well as politics and living conditions in the immigrants' countries of origin. They characterize immigrant America in its variety, from common laborer to educated elite, identifying those who 'make it' and those who don't." Libr J

The authors "have written a wonderful book, a richly textured map of the new immigration that is as diverse and pluralistic as the new America they rightly celebrate." New Repub

Includes bibliographic references

Santoli, Al, 1949-

New Americans: an oral history; immigrants and refugees in the U.S. today. Viking 1988 392p il o.p.; Ballantine Bks. paperback available $10.95   **325.73**

1. United States—Immigration and emigration 2. Refugees
ISBN 0-345-36455-4 (pa)
LC 87-40633

The author "selects 18 individual immigrants and families who relate their stories in a feeling, sympathetic, instructive oral history." Publ Wkly

Tifft, Wilton S.

Ellis Island; foreword by Lee Iacocca. Contemporary Bks. 1990 239p il $35
325.73

1. Ellis Island Immigration Station 2. United States—Immigration and emigration
ISBN 0-8092-4418-7
LC 89-22352

This photodocumentary "traces the history of the island from its Indian days, to private ownership, use as a fort and arsenal, and finally as an immense immigrant-receiving station. Photographs from archives and by Lewis Hine capture the strength, patience, and faith of the immigrants, while Tifft's text recounts the various phases of immigration laws, procedures, confusion, fraud, and their consequences." Booklist

Includes bibliographic references

326 Slavery and emancipation

Blockson, Charles L.

The Underground Railroad. Prentice Hall Press 1987 308p il o.p.; Berkley Bks. paperback available $4.99   **326**

1. Slavery—United States 2. Underground railroad
ISBN 0-425-11588-7 (pa)
LC 86-43173

"Blockson compiled more than 50 accounts by slaves and their rescuers, gleaned primarily from histories published in the 1800s. The selections are arranged geographically, with Blockson providing introductions to each section. The effect is to produce an overall perspective on the Underground Railroad phenomenon." Booklist

Includes bibliography

Free at last; a documentary history of slavery, freedom, and the Civil War; [edited by] Ira Berlin [et al.] New Press (NY) 1992 xxxiii, 571p il $27.50   **326**

1. Slavery—United States 2. United States—History—1861-1865, Civil War—Sources
ISBN 1-56584-015-1
LC 92-53726

"Drawn from letters, affidavits, records, and other documents collected by The Freedmen and Southern Society Project, *Free at Last* gives voice to compelling observations about slavery written by both blacks and whites, in the North and South, during the Civil War." Libr J

"This superb anthology makes available to general readers selected materials originally published in, or projected for, the multivolume reference work *Freedom: A Documentary History of Emancipation* (Cambridge University Press)." Publ Wkly

Includes bibliographic references

Genovese, Eugene D., 1930-

Roll, Jordan, roll; the world the slaves made. Pantheon Bks. 1974 xxii, 823p o.p.; Vintage Bks. paperback available $17   **326**

1. Slavery—United States
ISBN 0-394-71652-3 (pa)

"As a historical narrative, as a sensitive functional analysis of a major region and a period of American society in general, and the Afro-American community in particular, Roll, Jordan, Roll is without modern peer." New Repub

Includes bibliography

327.1 General topics of international relations

Bundy, McGeorge

Danger and survival; choices about the bomb in the first fifty years. Random House 1988 735p $24.95; pa $12.95   **327.1**

1. Nuclear warfare 2. United States—Military policy
ISBN 0-394-52278-8; 0-679-72568-7 (pa)
LC 88-42824

Bundy, McGeorge—*Continued*

"This political history of the nuclear age . . . [concerns] the choices made by scientists and statesmen of the major powers." Libr J

This "is both vivid and illuminating, narrative and analysis in one." Economist

Gorbachev, Mikhail

Perestroika; new thinking for our country and the world. Harper & Row 1987 254p $19.95; pa $12   327.1

1. World politics—1965- 2. Soviet Union—Foreign relations 3. Soviet Union—Politics and government
ISBN 0-06-039085-9; 0-06-091528-5 (pa)

LC 87-46197

Also available from Borgo Press

"A Cornelia & Michael Bessie book"

"Gorbachev's approach to East-West relations is sketched out clearly and passionately as he takes his case directly to the people by presenting his views and concerns on the international scene and the world's future." Booklist

Waller, Douglas C.

Congress and the nuclear freeze; an inside look at the politics of a mass movement; foreword by Edward M. Kennedy. University of Mass. Press 1987 346p $35; pa $16.95   327.1

1. United States. Congress 2. Arms control
ISBN 0-87023-559-1; 0-87023-560-5 (pa)

LC 86-19336

The author aims to "trace the origins of the freeze movement and show how . . . it became a major foreign policy issue. . . . He describes the organizing, lobbying, and maneuvering that eventually brought the Nuclear Freeze Resolution before Congress for a vote." Publisher's note

Includes bibliography

327.12 Espionage and subversion

Agee, Philip, 1935-

Inside the Company: CIA diary. Stonehill 1975 639p o.p.; Bantam Bks. paperback available $6.95   327.12

1. United States. Central Intelligence Agency 2. Intelligence service—United States
ISBN 0-553-26012-X (pa)

An exposé of the U.S. Central Intelligence Agency by a former secret agent. "Written in diary form . . . Agee traces his development from a Midwestern Catholic university through tours with Air Force intelligence at the beginning of his CIA career to specialized covert training, assignments in Ecuador, Uruguay, Washington, D.C. and Mexico, and ultimately, to his estrangement from the agency." Nation

Andrew, Christopher M.

Her Majesty's Secret Service; the making of the British intelligence community; [by] Christopher Andrew. Viking 1986 c1985 619p il $25   327.12

1. Great Britain. MI6 2. Intelligence service—Great Britain
ISBN 0-670-80941-1   LC 85-40574

Also available in paperback from Penguin Bks.

"Elisabeth Sifton books"

First published 1985 in the United Kingdom with title: Secret Service: the making of the British intelligence community

This is "a narrative history of the British intelligence and security services from their origins in the first decade of this century to [the 1980s]." N Y Times Book Rev

This "is an extraordinary and authoritative portrait of men and institutions." Times Lit Suppl

Includes bibliography

KGB; the inside story of its foreign operations from Lenin to Gorbachev; [by] Christopher Andrew and Oleg Gordievsky. HarperCollins Pubs. 1990 776p il $29.95; pa $16   327.12

1. KGB 2. Intelligence service—Soviet Union
ISBN 0-06-016605-3; 0-06-092109-9 (pa)

LC 90-55525

This is a "chronological history of the K.G.B., beginning more than 400 years ago, in 1565, with the secret police of Ivan the Terrible. It ends . . . with a description of the organization under Mikhail Gorbachev." NY Times Book Rev

"Treasures from the KGB's secret 'memory room'—photographs, drawings, and documents—and other scenes of spies in action illustrate this fascinating, cogent, lengthy history." Booklist

Black, Ian

Israel's secret wars; the untold history of Israeli intelligence; [by] Ian Black and Benny Morris. Grove Weidenfeld 1991 603p $24.95; pa $14.95   327.12

1. Intelligence service—Israel
ISBN 0-8021-1159-9; 0-8021-3286-3 (pa)

LC 90-49373

This book traces the history of Israel's intelligence services from the pre-state 1930s to the present. The authors cover "all three branches of the Israeli intelligence community; the Shin Bet, in charge of internal security and counter-espionage; Aman, the corps within the IDF (Israeli Defense Force) charged with the assessment of enemy capabilities and intentions; and Mossad whose brief is espionage and special operations abroad." London Rev Books

Includes bibliographic references

Earley, Pete

Family of spies; inside the John Walker spy ring. Bantam Bks. 1988 385p $19.95; pa $5.99   327.12

1. Walker, John Anthony 2. Walker family 3. Whitworth, Jerry A. 4. Espionage, Russian
ISBN 0-553-05283-7; 0-553-28222-0 (pa)

LC 88-19432

Earley, Pete—*Continued*
"Based on family papers, wiretapped conversations, trial transcripts and interviews with the principals, this is the most comprehensive look we are likely to get at the inception and operation of what has been called the most damaging spy ring in America's history." Publ Wkly

Kessler, Ronald
Inside the CIA; revealing the secrets of the world's most powerful spy agency. Pocket Bks. 1992 xxiii, 283p il $23; pa $5.99 **327.12**
1. United States. Central Intelligence Agency 2. Intelligence service—United States
ISBN 0-671-73457-1; 0-671-73458-X (pa)
LC 92-11084
"Writing with the cooperation of active and retired personnel, Kessler offers a working portrait of the contemporary CIA. His background in journalistic study of intelligence, augmented by an unusual array of other resources, enables him to provide an account unique for balance, perspective, clarity of writing, and the large amount of factual material." Booklist

Knightley, Phillip
The second oldest profession; spies and spying in the twentieth century. Norton 1987 c1986 436p il $19.95 **327.12**
1. Espionage 2. Intelligence service 3. Spies
ISBN 0-393-02386-9
LC 86-28548
Also available in paperback from Penguin Bks.
First published 1986 in the United Kingdom
A history of British, French, German, Russian and American intelligence operations in the twentieth century
Includes bibliography

Marchetti, Victor
The CIA and the cult of intelligence; [by] Victor Marchetti and John D. Marks; introduction by Melvin L. Wulf. Knopf 1974 xxvi, 398p o.p.; Dell paperback available $5.95 **327.12**
1. United States. Central Intelligence Agency 2. Intelligence service—United States
ISBN 0-440-20336-8 (pa)
This book examines the organization and operation of the Central Intelligence Agency and seeks to show how its original purpose—the gathering and processing of intelligence information—has been subverted by its obsession with clandestine operations

Ostrovsky, Victor
By way of deception; [by] Victor Ostrovsky and Claire Hoy. St. Martin's Press 1990 371p maps $22.95; pa $5.99 **327.12**
1. Israel. Mossad 2. Intelligence service—Israel
ISBN 0-312-05613-3; 0-312-92614-6 (pa)
An expose of Mossad, Israel's intelligence organization by a former member of the department
Includes glossary

Prados, John
Presidents' secret wars; C.I.A. and Pentagon covert operations since World War II. Morrow 1986 480p hardcover o.p. paperback available $14 **327.12**
1. United States. Central Intelligence Agency 2. Intelligence service—United States
ISBN 0-688-07759-5 (pa)
LC 86-12854
"Prados argues that presidents have too much freedom of action in covert operations and that at the same time congressional oversight committees have very limited impact." Publ Wkly
Includes bibliography

Raviv, Daniel
Every spy a prince; the complete history of Israel's intelligence community; [by] Dan Raviv and Yossi Melman. Houghton Mifflin 1990 466p il hardcover o.p. paperback available $12.70 **327.12**
1. Intelligence service—Israel
ISBN 0-395-58120-6 (pa)
LC 90-4353
"A Marc Jaffe book"
This is an account of the three "branches of the Israeli intelligence community: the Mossad, responsible for foreign operations; Aman, the intelligence-gathering arm of the military; and Shin Bet, the agency in charge of internal security. . . . The book also discusses the threat of future use of chemical, biological, and nuclear weapons in the Middle East." Publisher's note
Includes bibliography

Wise, David, 1930-
Molehunt; the secret search for traitors that shattered the CIA. Random House 1992 325p il $21.50 **327.12**
1. United States. Central Intelligence Agency 2. Intelligence service—United States 3. Espionage, Russian
ISBN 0-394-58514-3
LC 91-53114
An account of the Central Intelligence Agency's search for Soviet spies within its own ranks
This "well-researched volume will serve as a vital source for both intelligence buffs and scholars seeking to weigh the danger of Soviet subversion of American society against the cost that the internal security investigations of the cold war exacted upon American lives and institutions." N Y Times Book Rev
Includes bibliographic references

Woodward, Bob, 1943-
VEIL; the secret wars of the CIA, 1981-1987. Simon & Schuster 1987 543p il o.p.; Pocket Bks. paperback available $5.99 **327.12**
1. United States. Central Intelligence Agency 2. Intelligence service—United States
ISBN 0-671-66159-0 (pa)
LC 87-20520
This is an "account of six years of the CIA under William Casey. Woodward details U.S. involvement in covert action in Lebanon, Libya, and especially in Nicaragua." Libr J
"Despite one's qualms about the book's accuracy, it makes for fascinating reading as Woodward exposes the CIA's modus operandi." Booklist

327.51   China—Foreign relations

Fairbank, John King, 1907-1991
The United States and China. 4th ed enl.
Harvard Univ. Press 1983 xxvi, 632p il
(American foreign policy lib) hardcover o.p.
paperback available $12.50   **327.51**

1. China—Foreign relations—United States 2. United
States—Foreign relations—China 3. China—History
ISBN 0-674-92438-X (pa)   LC 83-8492
First published 1948

The author presents a survey of Chinese history dating
from prehistoric times, an analysis of Chinese society,
and an account of Sino-American relations through the
events of 1982

Includes bibliography

327.73   United States—Foreign relations

Bailey, Thomas Andrew, 1902-1983
A diplomatic history of the American
people; [by] Thomas A. Bailey. 10th ed.
Prentice-Hall 1980 1093, xxxix p il $58
    327.73

1. United States—Foreign relations
ISBN 0-13-214726-2   LC 79-17620
First published 1940 by Crofts

"An introductory textbook which gives a clear
interpretation of the United States diplomatic history
from colonial times. It shows how diplomatic policies
evolved, and stresses the roles that public opinion played
in the development." Booklist

Includes bibliography

Ball, George W.
The passionate attachment; America's
involvement with Israel, 1947 to the present;
[by] George W. Ball with Douglas B. Ball.
Norton 1992 382p maps $24.95   **327.73**

1. United States—Foreign relations—Israel 2. Israel—
Foreign relations—United States
ISBN 0-393-02933-6   LC 90-37033

This volume offers a discussion "of U.S. policy toward
the Middle East and Israel especially, beginning with its
creation in 1948 up through the Bush administration."
Libr J

"George Ball has made many contributions to American public life. It is sad that the most 'passionate attachment' in this book is to unrelenting and one-sided
denunciation of Israel. This work does not help the cause
of peace." N Y Times Book Rev

Includes bibliographic references

Barnet, Richard J.
The rockets' red glare; when America goes
to war: the presidents and the people.
Simon & Schuster 1990 476p $24.95; pa
$10.95   **327.73**

1. War—Public opinion 2. United States—History,
Military 3. United States—Foreign relations—Public
opinion
ISBN 0-671-63376-7; 0-671-73287-0 (pa)
    LC 89-22044

This work offers an "account of the role public opin-
ion has played in the foreign policy process from George
Washington's administration through the Reagan years."
Libr J

"'Public opinion' is indeed a complex matter and
Richard Barnet has not fully plumbed its mysteries, or
taken into account such variables as region, class, gender,
and ethnicity. He is most penetrating when analyzing his
most familiar subject—the upper reaches of the American
government." Commonweal

Includes bibliographic references

Brzezinski, Zbigniew
Power and principle; memoirs of the
national security advisor, 1977-1981. Farrar,
Straus & Giroux 1983 587p il hardcover
o.p. paperback available $11.95   **327.73**

1. Carter, Jimmy, 1924- 2. United States—Foreign
relations 3. United States—National security
ISBN 0-374-51877-7 (pa)   LC 83-1598

Among the topics covered in this memoir by Carter's
national security advisor are: relations with China and
the Soviet Union, the Camp David peace process, the
fall of the Shah and the Panama Canal treaty

Fulbright, J. William
The price of empire; [by] J. William
Fulbright with Seth P. Tillman. Pantheon
Bks. 1989 243p $17.95   **327.73**

1. United States—Foreign relations 2. United States—
Economic conditions—1900-1999 (20th century)
3. World politics
ISBN 0-394-57224-6   LC 88-42717

"Here Fulbright decries the costs of 40 years of the
cold war, the U.S. policy of interventionism, and the
near bankruptcy of our economy. . . . [He] calls for a
new kind of leadership committed to a new manner of
thinking—a leadership of intellect, judgment, tolerance,
and rationality 'committed to human values, to world
peace, and to the improvement of the human condition.'
Fulbright, a distinguished and influential former politician, offers an important work on the state of the
world." Booklist

Higgins, Trumbull
The perfect failure; Kennedy, Eisenhower,
and the CIA at the Bay of Pigs. Norton
1987 224p hardcover o.p. paperback
available $7.95   **327.73**

1. Kennedy, John F. (John Fitzgerald), 1917-1963
2. Eisenhower, Dwight D. (Dwight David), 1890-1969
3. United States. Central Intelligence Agency 4. United States—Foreign relations 5. Cuba—History—1961,
Invasion
ISBN 0-393-30563-5 (pa)   LC 87-5720

An exploration of United States foreign policy that
led to the Bay of Pigs debacle, with a description of
the military operations and an analysis of its aftermath

The author's "solid research—in memoirs, declassified
documents and interviews—leads to stark and damning
conclusions." N Y Times Book Rev

Includes bibliography

Ishihara, Shintaro
The Japan that can say no; translated by Frank Baldwin; foreword by Ezra F. Vogel. Simon & Schuster 1991 158p $18.95; pa $10
327.73

1. United States—Foreign relations—Japan 2. Japan—Foreign relations—United States
ISBN 0-671-72686-2; 0-671-75853-5 (pa)
LC 90-22466

This book discusses "Japan's new role as a major world power and its potential repercussions for the United States. . . . [The author argues that] if there is to be bilateral cooperation between the two nations, America must overcome its self-defeating superior attitudes and Japan must speak out in defense of its needs and concerns." Publisher's note

Kennan, George Frost, 1904-
American diplomacy; [by] George F. Kennan. expanded ed. University of Chicago Press 1984 179p hardcover o.p. paperback available $7.95
327.73

1. United States—Foreign relations 2. United States—Foreign relations—Soviet Union 3. Soviet Union—Foreign relations—United States
ISBN 0-226-43147-9 (pa)
LC 84-24085

First published 1951 with title: American diplomacy, 1900-1950

A group of essays by a former counselor of the State Department, on the various types of diplomacy used by the United States. Topics discussed include the escalation of the nuclear arms race, and the American involvement in Vietnam

Includes bibliographic references

Moynihan, Daniel P. (Daniel Patrick), 1927-
On the law of nations. Harvard Univ. Press 1990 211p $22.50; pa $10.95 **327.73**

1. International law 2. United States—Foreign relations
ISBN 0-674-63575-2; 0-674-63576-0 (pa)
LC 90-33227

"In the seven essays in this volume, Moynihan traces U.S. attitudes toward international law from the American Revolution to the current administration, and he makes a powerful argument for a return to the conventions of international behavior set out by Woodrow Wilson and the United Nations." Libr J

Nixon, Richard M. (Richard Milhous), 1913-1994
1999; victory without war. Simon & Schuster 1988 336p $19.95; pa $10.95
327.73

1. United States—Foreign relations 2. World politics
ISBN 0-671-62712-0; 0-671-70626-8 (pa) LC 88-4547
Also available in paperback from Pocket Bks.

The former President presents prescriptions for foreign diplomatic relations
"Nixon makes two particularly significant contributions. He attempts to draw the moderate conservative sector of the American political spectrum toward cautious support for negotiations with the Soviet Union on arms control and a low-keyed management of the competitive relationship. And he seeks to arouse Americans of both the right and the left to reject the temptations of isolationism." N Y Times Book Rev

Seize the moment; America's challenge in a one-superpower world; [by] Richard Nixon. Simon & Schuster 1992 322p $25 **327.73**

1. United States—Foreign relations
ISBN 0-671-74343-0
LC 91-37743

The author's "thesis is that the collapse of the Soviet Union presents the U.S. both with an unparalleled chance to help shape a more stable and peaceful world and with a great danger of a lapse into chaos and turmoil if the nation misguidedly turns its attention totally inward. He offers . . . advice on what to do about specific areas of potential trouble . . . [and] insists on the continued importance of military power." Time
"A forceful argument for a classical, geopolitical American internationalism." N Y Times Book Rev

Tuchman, Barbara Wertheim
Stilwell and the American experience in China, 1911-45; [by] Barbara W. Tuchman. Macmillan 1971 621p il maps $60 **327.73**

1. Stilwell, Joseph Warren, 1883-1946 2. United States—Foreign relations—China 3. China—Foreign relations—United States 4. World War, 1939-1945—China
ISBN 0-02-620290-5
Also available in paperback from Bantam Bks.

Using the career of General "Vinegar Joe" Stilwell as a vehicle, this is a history of America's relations with China from the end of the Manchu Empire to the rise of Mao Tse-tung

Includes bibliography

328.73 The legislative process in the United States

Barone, Michael
The almanac of American politics; [by] Michael Barone and Grant Ujifusa. National Journal il maps $56.95; pa $44.95 **328.73**

1. United States. Congress 2. United States—Politics and government 3. Almanacs

First published 1972 by Gambit. (1990 edition) Frequently revised

Subtitle and publisher vary
"The senators, the representatives and the governors; their records and elections results, their states and districts." Subtitle
"A political overview for each individual state is followed by a district-by-district summary of political background and information on the legislators. A very useful compilation." Sheehy. Guide to Ref Books. 10th edition

Congress A to Z; a ready reference encyclopedia. 2nd ed. Congressional Quarterly 1993 547p il maps $110
328.73

1. United States. Congress
ISBN 0-87187-826-7
LC 93-25926
First published 1988

This overview contains entries that examine the procedures, traditions and structure of Congress. Significant personalities and historical highlights are included

Includes bibliographic references

Congress and the Nation; a review of government and politics. Congressional Quarterly 1965-1988 7v il maps v1 o.p.; v2-7 ea $189.95   **328.73**

1. United States. Congress 2. Legislation 3. United States—Politics and government—1900-1999 (20th century)

Contents: v1 1945-1964 o.p.; v2 1965-1968 (ISBN 0-87187-004-5); v3 1969-1972 (ISBN 0-87187-055-X); v4 1973-1976 (ISBN 0-87187-112-2); v5 1977-1980 (ISBN 0-87187-216-1); v6 1981-1984 (ISBN 0-87187-334-6); v7 1985-1988 (ISBN 0-87187-532-2)

"Overview and detailed coverage of presidential, legislative, and political events in every major subject area." N Y Public Libr Book of How & Where to look It Up

Congressional Quarterly almanac. Congressional Quarterly $205   **328.73**

1. United States. Congress 2. United States—Politics and government 3. Almanacs

Annual. First published 1945

"Each volume now offers a survey of legislation for one session of Congress. . . . Major congressional action is summarized in sections dealing with categories of legislation . . . subdivided according to specific topics. Includes voting information on individual measures. Several useful appendixes. Fully indexed." Sheehy. Guide to Ref Books. 10th edition

Congressional Quarterly's guide to Congress. Congressional Quarterly il $179.95
328.73

1. United States. Congress

First published 1971 with title: Congressional Quarterly's guide to the Congress of the United States. (4th edition 1991) Periodically revised

"Covers history and workings of Congress, with biographical data on all members." N Y Public Libr Book of How & Where to look It Up

Congressional Quarterly's politics in America. CQ Press il maps $74.95, pa $49.95   **328.73**

1. United States. Congress 2. Elections—United States

Biennial. First published 1981

Current editor: Phil Duncan

Profiles each current member of Congress, providing political background, statistical information, committee assignments, etc.

United States. Congress
Biographical directory of the United States Congress, 1774-1989; the Continental Congress, September 5, 1774, to October 21, 1788, and the Congress of the United States, from the First through the One Hundredth Congresses, March 4, 1789, to January 3, 1989, inclusive. Bicentennial ed. U.S. Govt. Ptg. Office 1989 2104p $82   **328.73**

1. United States. Congress 2. United States—Biography—Dictionaries   LC 88-600335

First published 1869 with title: Dictionary of the United States Congress

"Brief biographies of members of Congress from the Continental Congress and from the first through the one-hundredth Congress of the United States. Lists executive

officers by administration and senators and representatives by Congress. Updated by the *Official congressional directory* [entered below]." Ref Sources for Small & Medium-sized Libr. 5th edition

Includes bibliographies

Official Congressional directory. U.S. Govt. Ptg. Office $20, pa $15   **328.73**

1. United States. Congress
ISSN 0160-9890

Biennial

"Covers biographical information, committee assignments of members of Congress, and officers of Congress." N Y Public Libr Book of How & Where to Look It Up

Will, George F.
Restoration; Congress, term limits, and the recovery of deliberative democracy. Free Press 1992 260p maps $19.95   **328.73**

1. United States. Congress 2. Politics, Practical 3. United States—Politics and government
ISBN 0-02-934437-9   LC 92-26005

In this book Will argues that "the tireless quest to hang on to office has left individual members of both parties dependent on pleasing special interests, which has all but robbed Congress of any larger notion of the public good. . . . Term limits, Will says, can help restore public faith, deliberative democracy, and congressional supremacy." New Repub

Includes bibliographic references

330   Economics

Galbraith, John Kenneth, 1908-
The affluent society. 4th ed. Houghton Mifflin 1984 xxxvii, 291p $18.45   **330**

1. Economics 2. United States—Economic conditions—1900-1999 (20th century)
ISBN 0-395-36613-5   LC 84-12880

Also available in paperback from New Am. Lib.

First published 1958

The author surveys the economic upheavals that have changed the economic climate of the world. He also discusses the proper goals and management of a modern society and the question of how the production and distribution of wealth should be organized

Includes bibliographic references

Economics in perspective; a critical history. Houghton Mifflin 1987 324p $19.95; pa $9.70   **330**

1. Economics
ISBN 0-395-35572-9; 0-395-48346-8 (pa)   LC 87-3644

The author examines the development of economics from ancient Greece to the modern welfare state, arguing that its "history cannot be understood apart from the circumstances that shaped the economic beliefs of the time." Publisher's note

Samuelson, Paul Anthony, 1915-
Economics. McGraw-Hill il $41.03   **330**

1. Economics

First published 1948. (13th edition 1989) Frequently revised

Samuelson, Paul Anthony, 1915- — *Continued*

Covers important policy and analytical questions and promotes greater understanding of our institutions and of macro- and micro-economic analysis. The book presents the operations of individual business and how it affects—and is affected by—the operations of the economic system

Includes bibliographic references

Silk, Leonard Solomon, 1918-

Economics in plain English. Updated & expanded ed. Simon & Schuster 1986 237p pa $10 **330**

1. Economics
ISBN 0-671-60613-1 LC 85-22226
First published 1978

The author "discusses economic theory and its history and assesses the state of the art of economics in business, government, and society." Libr J

Includes bibliography

330.03 Economics—Encyclopedias and dictionaries

The **McGraw-Hill** encyclopedia of economics; Douglas Greenwald, editor in chief. 2nd ed. McGraw-Hill 1993 1093p $99.50 **330.03**

1. Economics—Dictionaries
ISBN 0-07-024410-3 LC 93-9805
First published 1982

Over 200 economists have contributed signed articles on economics, econometrics and statistics. Concepts, institutions and historical periods are covered
For a review see: Booklist, Jan. 15, 1994

330.1 Economic systems and theories

Friedman, Milton, 1912-

Free to choose; a personal statement; [by] Milton & Rose Friedman. Harcourt Brace Jovanovich 1980 338p $16.95; pa $7.95 **330.1**

1. Capitalism 2. United States—Economic conditions 3. Public welfare
ISBN 0-15-133481-1; 0-15-633460-7 (pa) LC 79-1821
Also available in paperback from Avon Bks.

The authors "paint a picture in which a marketplace sensitive to the people's wants and needs is frustrated by governmental interference, extreme government costs, and governmentally induced inflation. . . . Citing sociological and economic laws, the Friedmans set out to prove that the harder a nation tries to control capitalism, the worse things get." Libr J

Includes bibliographic references

Galbraith, John Kenneth, 1908-

American capitalism; the concept of countervailing power; with a new introduction by the author. Transaction Pubs. 1993 208p (Classics in economics) $17.95 **330.1**

1. Capitalism 2. United States—Economic conditions—1900-1999 (20th century)
ISBN 1-560-00674-9 LC 92-43232
First published 1952 by Houghton Mifflin; this is a reissue of the revised 1956 edition

The author "presents an interesting theory about American economic development primarily since World War II. He believes American Capitalism has survived its test and though changed in places has come up with 'countervailing power.' (Labor unions against great corporations, strong buyers against weak sellers)." Cincinnati Public Libr

Includes bibliographic references

Heilbroner, Robert L.

The worldly philosophers; the lives, times, and ideas of the great economic thinkers. Simon & Schuster $10.95 **330.1**

1. Economists 2. Economics
First published 1953. (6th edition 1987) Periodically revised

The author traces the story of economics and the great economists from Adam Smith, Malthus, Ricardo, the Utopians, Marx, Veblen and Keynes to those working with the problems of our contemporary world

Includes bibliography

Keynes, John Maynard, 1883-1946

The general theory of employment, interest and money. Harcourt Brace & Co. 1936 403p hardcover o.p. paperback available $9.95 **330.1**

1. Economics 2. Money 3. Interest (Economics)
ISBN 0-15-634711-3 (pa)

This work "revolutionized economic theory by showing how unemployment could occur 'involuntarily'. For 30 years after the Second World War governments of western nations pursued 'Keynesian' full-employment policies." Oxford Companion to Engl Lit. 5th edition

Marx, Karl, 1818-1883

Capital; a critique of political economy 3v **330.1**

1. Capital 2. Economics
Hardcover and paperback editions available from various publishers
Edited by Friedrich Engels
Contents: v1 The process of capitalist production; v2 The process of circulation of capital; v3 The process of capitalist production as a whole

"A systematic critical study of capitalist economy by Karl Marx, based on the ideas which he formulated, with Friedrich Engels, in 'The Communist Manifesto,' [entered in class 335.4]. Volume one appeared in 1867; volumes two and three were completed by Engels from Marx's notes (1885-1894)." Reader's Ency

Smith, Adam, 1723-1790
The wealth of nations   **330.1**
1. Economics

Hardcover and paperback editions available from various publishers

First published 1776

Variant title: An inquiry into the nature and causes of the wealth of nations

This treatise "is the first comprehensive treatment of the whole subject of political economy, and is remarkable for its breadth of view. . . . [In it, the author presents an] attack on the mercantile system, and an advocacy of freedom of commerce and industry." Oxford Companion to Engl Lit. 5th edition

330.9 Economic situation and conditions

Reich, Robert B.
The work of nations; preparing ourselves for 21st-century capitalism. Knopf 1991 331p $25; pa $12   **330.9**
1. Capitalism 2. United States—Economic policy 3. Twenty-first century
ISBN 0-394-58352-3; 0-679-73615-8 (pa) LC 90-5123

The author "argues that in a world without economic borders all people will rise or fall to their market values; the skilled and talented will prosper, while the uneducated and unskilled will not. In his view, then, the 'work' of a nation is to improve the skills of its people so that they will flourish in this new world order." NY Times Book Rev

Includes bibliography

330.973 United States—Economic conditions

Galbraith, John Kenneth, 1908-
The culture of contentment. Houghton Mifflin 1992 195p $22.95; pa $9.70
     330.973
1. United States—Economic conditions—1974- 2. United States—Economic policy 3. Social values
ISBN 0-395-57228-2; 0-395-66919-7 (pa)
     LC 91-47038

"This is Galbraith's analysis of the bind we Americans have put ourselves in since Reagan-Bush. His thesis is that we have become a 'culture of contentment' wherein the majority of those who vote are socially and economically advantaged and will fight like tigers to maintain that advantage by voting against increased taxation that would reduce the federal deficit and respond to aching social problems." Libr J

"A compelling analysis of contemporary society and one that may make readers conclude that the U.S. is turning into a third-world society." Booklist

The Great Crash, 1929; with a new introduction by the author. Houghton Mifflin 1988 xx, 206p il hardcover o.p. paperback available $8.70   **330.973**
1. United States—Economic conditions—1919-1933 2. Depressions, Economic 3. Business cycles
ISBN 0-395-47805-7 (pa)   LC 88-134280
First published 1955

Beginning with the bull market of Coolidge and Hoover and continuing through the stock market crash, the author analyzes its causes and speculates about the chances of another crash

Includes bibliographic references

Lehmann, Michael B.
The Dow Jones-Irwin guide to using the Wall Street journal. 3rd ed. Dow Jones-Irwin 1990 382p il $24.95   **330.973**
1. Wall Street journal 2. United States—Economic conditions 3. Business cycles
ISBN 1-55623-242-X   LC 89-17232
First published 1984

"Intends to 'show the reader how to use *The Wall Street journal* to be your own economist' (Pref.), focusing on key economic indicators and describing what they measure, how they are computed, and when they appear in the *Journal*. Also explains how each indicator is used to track the economy and includes excerpts from *Journal* articles that illustrate the contexts in which specific statistics are used." Sheehy. Guide to Ref Books. 10th edition. suppl

Includes bibliographic references

Malabre, Alfred L.
Beyond our means; how America's long years of debt, deficits and reckless borrowing now threaten to overwhelm us. Random House 1987 174p hardcover o.p. paperback available $6.95   **330.973**
1. United States—Economic conditions—1900-1999 (20th century)
ISBN 0-394-75816-1 (pa)   LC 86-22002

The author considers such subjects as the American national debt, federal spending, and taxation. Other topics include banking, the business cycle, wages, and economic theories

Includes bibliography

Thurow, Lester C.
The zero-sum society; distribution and the possibilities for economic change. Basic Bks. 1980 230p $14.50   **330.973**
1. United States—Economic conditions—1974- 2. United States—Economic policy 3. Income
ISBN 0-465-09384-1   LC 79-2758
Also available in paperback from Penguin Bks.

The author advocates "a redistribution of income that would markedly reduce the economic gap between the top and bottom fifths of the population. He proposes to achieve this . . . by means of a massive Federal 'guaranteed job program,' offering employment at a wide range of salary levels." N Y Times Book Rev

Includes bibliographic references

The zero-sum solution; building a world-class American economy. Simon & Schuster 1985 414p hardcover o.p. paperback available $9.95   **330.973**
1. United States—Economic conditions—1974- 2. United States—Economic policy
ISBN 0-671-62814-3 (pa)   LC 85-14480

Thurow, Lester C.—*Continued*
Building on his arguments in The zero-sum society, entered above, Thurow examines the decline of United States dominance in the world economy

Includes bibliography

331.1 Labor force and market

Sowell, Thomas, 1930-
Preferential policies; an international perspective. Morrow 1990 221p hardcover o.p. paperback available $9   **331.1**
1. Affirmative action programs 2. Race discrimination
ISBN 0-688-10969-1 (pa)   LC 89-49712

This book discusses the effects of "laws favoring specific racial, religious or ethnic groups and government policies stating that individuals are not to be judged by the same criteria or subjected to the same procedures. . . . [Sowell concentrates] on India, Nigeria, Malaysia, South Africa, Eastern Europe, Sri Lanka and the United States." Publisher's note

331.2 Compensation and other conditions of employment

Levering, Robert, 1944-
The 100 best companies to work for in America; [by] Robert Levering, Milton Moskowitz. Doubleday 1993 503p il $27.50
          331.2
1. Corporations 2. Job satisfaction 3. Personnel management
ISBN 0-385-26548-4   LC 92-20442

First published 1984 by Addison-Wesley under the authorship of Robert Levering, Milton Moskowitz and Michael Katz

The one hundred companies profiled here have been selected acording to such criteria as pay, benefits, job security, opportunity for advancement, and work environment

A great place to work; what makes some employers so good (and most so bad). Random House 1988 xxii, 312p $18.95
          331.2
1. Job satisfaction 2. Work
ISBN 0-394-55725-5   LC 87-43226

Also available in paperback from Avon Bks.

This book "focuses on 23 firms, describing their philosophies and offering direct comment from their employees. . . . In addition, the text charts the lives and ideologies of corporate thinkers such as Peter Drucker and Elton Mayo." Booklist

Includes bibliography

Terkel, Studs, 1912-
Working; people talk about what they do all day and how they feel about what they do. Pantheon Bks. 1974 xlix, 589p o.p.; Ballantine Bks. paperback available $6.95
          331.2
1. Labor—United States 2. Work 3. United States—Social conditions
ISBN 0-345-32569-9 (pa)

Based on interviews, this study describes the working lives and feelings of people engaged in occupations ranging from interstate truck driver to stockbroker to bookbinder to corporation president

This "is not a dry, academic treatise but a sensitive portrayal of the experience of working, with all its pain, tension, frustrations, and occasional satisfactions." Best Sellers

331.4 Women workers

Bravo, Ellen
The 9 to 5 guide to combating sexual harassment; candid advice from 9 to 5, the National Association of Working Women; [by] Ellen Bravo, Ellen Cassedy. Wiley 1992 151p pa $9.95   **331.4**
1. Sexual harassment
ISBN 0-471-57576-3   LC 92-9793

This book "takes an anecdotal approach, recounting numerous examples of questionable behavior to define what is harassment and what is not. Authors Bravo and Cassedy . . . cover the role managers, unions, and employers should play in preventing harassment and they devote a chapter to what to do if you are a victim of harassment. The advice in this book is basic, sometimes simplistic, but it is generally a good overview." Libr J

Canape, Charlene
The part-time solution; the new strategy for managing your career while managing motherhood. Harper & Row 1990 278p $18.95; pa $8.95   **331.4**
1. Part-time employment 2. Women—Employment
ISBN 0-06-016237-6; 0-06-092040-8 (pa)
          LC 89-45638

"Canape advocates the option of part-time employment for women desiring to track the ideal career path. . . . Utilizing examples from questionnaire results and interviews, she shows how to find part-time positions, negotiate benefits, garner emotional support, and return ultimately to full-time work." Booklist

Includes bibliographic references

331.6 Categories of workers by racial, ethnic, national origin

Conover, Ted
Coyotes; a journey through the secret world of America's illegal aliens. Vintage Bks. 1987 264p pa $11   **331.6**
1. Illegal aliens 2. Mexicans—United States 3. Migrant labor
ISBN 0-394-75518-9   LC 87-6101

"Vintage departures"

"The title refers to the name given to those people who smuggle illegal aliens into the United States. Conover lived among the people who pay 'coyotes' enormous sums of money to be secretly brought into this country under conditions that are full of physical threat." SLJ

331.7 Labor by industry and occupation

Bird, Caroline
Second careers; new ways to work after 50. Little, Brown 1992 357p hardcover o.p. paperback available $14.95   **331.7**

1. Career changes 2. Elderly—Employment
ISBN 0-316-09599-0 (pa)   LC 91-20604

The author "provides a fresh perspective to those people 50 years old and older who desire to continue in the workplace for financial, social, physical, and emotional reasons. Using actual reader responses to an AARP *Modern Maturity* questionnaire, she offers the older worker a framework in which to examine basic life/work planning issues such as kind of work enjoyed, type of careers to consider, new skills, networking, résumé writing, and age discrimination." Libr J

Bolles, Richard Nelson
What color is your parachute? a practical manual for job-hunters & career changers. Ten Speed Press il $18.95; pa $14.95
                                        331.7

1. Applications for positions 2. Vocational guidance
First published 1973. (1993 edition) Frequently revised

This job-hunter's manual explains how to organize and conduct a self-initiated career search that makes optimum use of one's chief skills. The author also addresses the psychological aspects of an extended job search

Encyclopedia of career change and work issues; edited by Lawrence K. Jones; consulting editors, Consuelo Arbona [et al.] Oryx Press 1992 xxvii, 379p il $67.50
                                        331.7

1. Vocational guidance 2. Career changes 3. Labor—United States
ISBN 0-89774-610-4   LC 91-33913

"This compilation treats varied issues and problems of the workplace from the point of view of the employee. Its purpose is to enable readers to deal effectively with these issues and problems. Among the more than 160 topics covered are the expected (such entries as *Résumé, Career Planning, Discrimination: People with Disabilities,* and *Law in the Workplace)* and the unexpected *(Low Back Pain, Fear of Flying, Nonstandard English,* and *Self-Esteem)."* Booklist

The **Encyclopedia** of careers and vocational guidance; William E. Hopke, editor-in-chief. Ferguson, J.G. 4v il set $129.95   **331.7**

1. Occupations 2. Vocational guidance
First published 1967. (9th edition 1993) Periodically revised

Contents: v1 Industry profiles; v2 Professional careers; v3 General and specific careers; v4 Technicians' careers

A "basic reference source to careers and jobs. . . . Material is well written, direct, and clear. It is drawn from government, industry, and professional sources. . . . Frequent examples and photographs lend a human tone that is useful to those searching for career possibilities. Each volume contains a complete, well-laid out index of job titles leading to material in all four books. Appendixes provide resources for disabled individuals

and internship and training programs." Am Ref Books Annu, 1991

Job hunter's sourcebook; where to find employment leads and other job search resources; Michelle LeCompte, editor; Charity Anne Dorgan and Edward F. Nakfoor, project coordinators. Gale Res. 1991 1106p $44.95   **331.7**

1. Job hunting 2. Vocational guidance
ISBN 0-8103-7717-9

This volume "identifies information sources on job opportunities for 155 professions and occupations. Alphabetically arranged, each entry provides sources of help-wanted ads, placement services, employment directories and networking lists, handbooks and manuals, and employment agencies. Another section addresses 20 general employment topics." Libr J
For a fuller review see: Booklist, April 15, 1991

Krantz, Les
The jobs rated almanac. rev ed. World Almanac 1992 345p $24.95; pa $15.95
                                        331.7

1. Occupations 2. Vocational guidance
ISBN 0-88687-717-2; 0-88687-679-6 (pa)
                                        LC 92-32168
First published 1988

This book ranks the best and worst jobs by more than a dozen criteria including salary, stress, benefits and travel

Petras, Kathryn
Jobs; [by] Kathryn and Ross Petras. Prentice Hall Press pa $16   **331.7**

1. Vocational guidance 2. Applications for positions 3. Occupations
Annual. First published 1990

This survey of the job market and career opportunities lists and rates companies, discusses trends, and contains a section on minorities, women and the handicapped

United States. Bureau of Labor Statistics
Occupational outlook handbook. U.S. Govt. Ptg. Office il $22.95; pa $18.95
                                        331.7

1. Occupations 2. Vocational guidance
Biennial. First published 1949. Supplemented by Occupational Outlook Quarterly, subscription $8

"Gives information on employment trends and outlook in more than 800 occupations. Indicates nature of work, qualifications, earnings and working conditions, how to enter, where to go for more information, etc." Sheehy. Guide to Ref Books. 10th edition

VGM's Careers encyclopedia; [by] the editors of VGM Career Horizons. 3rd ed. VGM Career Horizons 1991 502p $39.95 **331.7**

1. Occupations 2. Vocational guidance
ISBN 0-8442-8692-3   LC 90-50726
First published 1980

This volume reports "on 200 careers, alphabetically arranged, with a description of the job, places of employment and working conditions, qualifications, education and training, potential advancement, and income as well

VGM's Careers encyclopedia—*Continued*
as additional sources of information. An excellent starting point for anyone in the process of exploring careers."
Booklist

331.8 Labor unions and labor-management relations

Dulles, Foster Rhea, 1900-1970
Labor in America; a history; [by] Foster Rhea Dulles, Melvyn Dubofsky. 5th ed. Davidson, H. 1993 434p il pa $24.95
331.8
1. Labor unions—United States 2. Labor—United States
ISBN 0-88295-900-X   LC 92-16104
First published 1949 by Crowell
A study of the social and political impact of the American labor movement since colonial times
Includes bibliography

Foner, Philip Sheldon, 1910-
Women and the American labor movement; [by] Philip S. Foner. Free Press 1979-1980 2v il   **331.8**
1. Labor unions—United States 2. Women—Employment   LC 79-63035
Contents: v1 From colonial times to the eve of World War I pa $17.95 (0-685-01684-6); v2 From World War I to the present $37.95, pa $19.95 (ISBN 0-02-910380-0, 0-02-910470-X)
Includes bibliographies

Freeman, Richard B. (Richard Barry), 1943-
What do unions do? [by] Richard B. Freeman & James L. Medoff. Basic Bks. 1984 293p $22.95; pa $17   **331.8**
1. Labor unions—United States
ISBN 0-465-09133-4; 0-465-09132-6 (pa)
LC 81-68407
An appraisal and summation of union activities in the United States. Among the points covered are wages, productivity, political involvement and corruption
Includes bibliographic references

Geoghegan, Thomas
Which side are you on? trying to be for labor when it's flat on its back. Farrar, Straus & Giroux 1991 287p $19.95   **331.8**
1. Labor unions—United States 2. Labor—United States 3. United States—Social conditions
ISBN 0-374-28919-0   LC 90-21759
Also available in paperback from New Am. Lib.
The author contends that "post-industrial Reaganomics have caused a widening rift between the working and professional middle classes. In related episodes, he demonstrates how the combined effects of steel mill closings, leveraged buyouts and Third World competitive labor have contributed to the decline of American organized labor." Publ Wkly

332 Financial economics

Volcker, Paul A.
Changing fortunes; the world's money and the threat to American leadership; [by] Paul A. Volcker, Toyoo Gyohten. Times Bks. 1992 359p il $24.50; pa $14   **332**
1. International finance
ISBN 0-8129-2018-X; 0-8129-2218-2 (pa)
LC 91-51035
The authors "returned to their alma mater, Princeton University, in the spring of 1991 to conduct a joint seminar on international monetary affairs. This volume is a record of their seminar lectures. . . . The book surveys the evolution of international monetary affairs since the late 1950's when both authors began their careers in public service—Mr. Volcker at the Federal Reserve Bank of New York, Mr. Gyohten at Japan's Finance Ministry." N Y Times Book Rev
Includes bibliography

332.024 Personal finance

Belin, David W.
Leaving money wisely; creative estate planning for middle- and upper-income Americans for the 1990s. Scribner 1990 325p $19.95   **332.024**
1. Estate planning
ISBN 0-684-19227-6   LC 90-8502
Also available in paperback from Collier Bks.
"After outlining estate problems caused by such situations as blended families, prenuptial agreements, and the need for equitable distribution among siblings [the author] proceeds to a more technical discussion of the subject." Libr J
"An authoritative, comprehensive guide." Booklist

Bove, Alexander A., 1938-
The Medicaid planning handbook; a guide to protecting your family's assets from catastrophic nursing home costs; [by] Alexander A. Bove, Jr. Little, Brown 1992 163p pa $10.95   **332.024**
1. Personal finance 2. Medicaid 3. Estate planning 4. Elderly—Medical care
ISBN 0-316-10365-9   LC 91-23271
"To Bove, protecting one's savings, investments, and retirement funds from bankruptcies through Medicaid planning is a moral obligation. How Medicaid works, various states' eligibility rules, and how marriage affects benefits occupy Bove's opening chapters, while understanding such planning issues as asset transfer, exempt assets, jointly held assets, and the role children can play in sheltering assets are all critically reviewed later." Booklist

Cheeks, James E.
The Dow Jones-Irwin guide to Keoghs. Dow Jones-Irwin 1989 230p $32.50
332.024
1. Personal finance 2. Investments
ISBN 1-55623-167-9   LC 88-33617

Cheeks, James E.—*Continued*

"A Keogh is a tax-deferred pension plan for the self-employed. . . . This guide systematically outlines the complexities of Keogh plans. . . . Cheeks's description and explanation of Keoghs is easily understood and not overly technical. His mathematical examples are fully explained and illustrated." Libr J

Clifford, Denis

Plan your estate with a living trust. 2nd ed. Nolo Press (Berkeley) 1992 various paging il pa $19.95   332.024

1. Estate planning
ISBN 0-87337-142-9

First published 1989 with title: Plan your estate

"Clifford outlines what estate planning is, what options exist, and the pros and cons of each. He targets readers with a net worth of under $600,000 and provides them with the forms needed to create what he feels are the key components of a viable estate plan—a living trust and a will." Libr J

Esperti, Robert A.

The handbook of estate planning; [by] Robert A. Esperti, Renno L. Peterson. 3rd ed. McGraw-Hill 1991 294p il $39.95
332.024

1. Estate planning
ISBN 0-07-019684-2   LC 90-24714

First published 1983

This volume covers such topics as property, wills, taxes, trusts, and working with estate advisers

Gaudio, Peter E., 1950-

Your retirement benefits; [by] Peter E. Gaudio, Virginia S. Nicols. Wiley 1992 254p il (ICFP personal wealth-building guides) $29.95; pa $10.95   332.024

1. Retirement income 2. Pensions
ISBN 0-471-53965-1; 0-471-53966-X (pa)
                                      LC 91-37446

"While Gaudio and Nicols provides sound, easy-to-follow direction on how to determine one's future financial needs and calculate postretirement costs and benefits, their main achievement is the careful, detailed, and understandable explanations of each of the various financial retirement plans available today. . . . Highly recommended for both reference and circulating collections in all public libraries." Booklist

Givens, Charles J.

Financial self-defense; how to win the fight for financial freedom. Simon & Schuster 1990 488p $22.95   332.024

1. Personal finance
ISBN 0-671-70099-5   LC 90-10212

The author presents strategies applicable to numerous financial situations, and offers advice about banks, insurance companies, brokers, car dealers, and the Federal government

More wealth without risk; how to develop a personal fortune without going out on a limb: updated and expanded for 1991 and beyond. Simon & Schuster 1991 xxi, 599p il $24   332.024

1. Personal finance 2. Investments
ISBN 0-671-70101-0   LC 91-36227

First published 1988 with title: Wealth without risk

The author outlines strategies for successful investment and accumulation of capital

Gordon, Harley

How to protect your life savings from catastrophic illness and nursing homes; a handbook for financial survival; [by] Harley Gordon with Jane Daniel. 2nd ed. Financial Planning Inst. 1991 281p pa $19.95
332.024

1. Personal finance 2. Medicaid 3. Estate planning 4. Elderly—Medical care
ISBN 0-9625667-1-3   LC 92-129157

First published 1990

The author "explains the basic principles of Medicare financing, including countable and noncountable assets, trusts, and the Spousal Impoverishment Act. He presents family scenarios requiring either immediate or long-term planning and provides options to protect ' . . . a lifetime of accumulated assets' from the enormous costs of nursing home care. Advice for choosing a lawyer experienced in Medicare law is included, along with state-by-state charts of income allowances." Libr J [review of 1990 edition]

Includes bibliographic references

Hallman, G. Victor

Personal financial planning; [by] G. Victor Hallman, Jerry S. Rosenbloom. 5th ed. McGraw-Hill 1993 xxi, 565p il $39.95
332.024

1. Personal finance
ISBN 0-07-025680-2   LC 92-40274

First published 1975

This guide "is solid on difficult legal issues. It would be especially useful to well-educated, prosperous business-people." Libr J

Klott, Gary L., 1949-

The complete financial guide to the 1990s. Times Bks. 1990 430p il maps $22.50
332.024

1. Personal finance 2. Investments
ISBN 0-8129-1814-2   LC 89-40189

The author provides an overview of what the 1990s "may be like with respect to jobs, energy, the environment, taxation, education, the family structure, consumer purchasing, real estate, retirement, and health care. . . . Many charts are used to show the trends and to explain more clearly the essence of this well-written, to-the-point text." Libr J

Loeb, Marshall

Marshall Loeb's money guide. Little, Brown pa $15.95 **332.024**

1. Personal finance 2. Investments
Annual. First published 1983

The author discusses such "subjects as investments, financing a home, taxes, retirement, estates, and many other subjects relating to personal and family finances. Organized by topic, with an index." N Y Public Libr Book of How & Where to Look It Up

Porter, Sylvia Field, 1913-1991

Sylvia Porter's your finances in the 1990s. Prentice Hall Press 1990 346p il $22.95 **332.024**

1. Personal finance
ISBN 0-13-879776-5 LC 90-42572

"Porter divides her advice into three sections: acquiring money (jobs, savings, investments), preserving holdings (tax considerations, insurance, retirement security), and trends for the 1990s (financial planning)." Booklist

Quinn, Jane Bryant

Making the most of your money; smart ways to create wealth and plan your finances in the '90s. Simon & Schuster 1991 934p il $27.50 **332.024**

1. Personal finance 2. Investments
ISBN 0-671-65952-9 LC 90-25050

This guide includes information about investing, savings options, college aid, retirement planning, and more

The author "provides comprehensive, knowledgeable, easy-to-understand coverage of virtually every aspect of personal and family finance. . . . An indispensable reference." Booklist

Siegel, Joel G.

Dictionary of personal finance; [by] Joel G. Siegel, Jae K. Shim, Stephen Hartman. Macmillan 1992 391p il $70; pa $20 **332.024**

1. Personal finance—Dictionaries
ISBN 0-02-897393-3; 0-02-897394-1 (pa)
LC 91-14276

This work provides "jargon-free definitions for 3,500 entries covering the topics of consumer economics; career planning; consumer credit; education financing; personal banking, budgeting, savings, and debts; retirement income; and tax planning. Appropriate even for high-schoolers, it also has appendixes that include annuity and monthly mortgage tables and lists of federal information centers and state government consumer protection offices." Booklist

Sloane, Leonard

The New York Times book of personal finance; updated to reflect the latest tax law changes. rev ed. Times Bks. 1992 323p pa $13 **332.024**

1. Personal finance
ISBN 0-8129-1995-5 LC 91-58078
First published 1985

This guide covers insurance, real estate, investments, as well as estate and retirement planning

Tobias, Andrew P.

The only other investment guide you'll ever need; [by] Andrew Tobias. Simon & Schuster 1987 271p o.p.; Bantam Bks. paperback available $9.95 **332.024**

1. Investments 2. Personal finance
ISBN 0-553-34665-2 (pa) LC 87-20494

"Among the many topics discussed are household budgets, insurance, the ins and outs of investing, and alternatives to traditional financing. Popular investment targets . . . are also briefly profiled." Booklist

VanCaspel, Venita, 1922-

Money dynamics for the 1990s. Simon & Schuster 1988 544p il $25 **332.024**

1. Personal finance
ISBN 0-671-66158-2 LC 87-38119

"The author identifies what she feels are important business and social trends that will affect economic conditions in the years to come, then evaluates the role of various investment strategies in a personal money management plan. VanCaspel covers not only the conventional investment instruments—stocks, bonds, mutual funds, and Treasury securities—but also more esoteric items such as jewelry, fine art and oil exploration." Booklist

Vicker, Ray

The Dow Jones-Irwin guide to retirement planning. 2nd ed. Dow Jones-Irwin 1987 332p $30 **332.024**

1. Retirement income 2. Personal finance
ISBN 1-55623-005-2 LC 86-72973
First published 1985

The author "shows how to start a lifetime money management program with only a handful of dollars and to build nest eggs exceeding six figures. Step-by-step the book explains how to develop savings habits, organize records, estimate one's net worth and make personal financial statements." Publisher's note

Warfield, Gerald

How to read and understand the financial news. Harper & Row 1986 214p $21.95; pa $11 **332.024**

1. Personal finance 2. Investments
ISBN 0-06-015647-3; 0-06-091474-2 (pa)
LC 86-45161

This "introduction to a wide range of business information presented daily in the financial press will be helpful to the uninitiated. Warfield includes lucid explanations for such . . . products as stock index and financial futures as well as for more traditional investment instruments." Libr J

332.03 Financial economics— Encyclopedias and dictionaries

Encyclopedia of banking & finance; [edited by] Glenn G. Munn [et al.] Salem Press 3v set $235   **332.03**
1. Banks and banking—Dictionaries 2. Finance—Dictionaries

First published 1924 by Bankers (9th edition 1993). Publisher varies

"Definition of terms and articles on money, credit, banking, investments, insurance, and other financial matters." N Y Public Libr Book of How & Where to Look It Up

The New Palgrave dictionary of money & finance; edited by Peter Newman, Murray Milgate, John Eatwell. Stockton Press 1992 3v set $595   **332.03**
1. Finance—Dictionaries
ISBN 1-56159-041-X   LC 92-28016
Companion set The New Palgrave: a dictionary of economics (1987)

This dictionary covers "both domestic and international aspects of money, banking, and finance. . . . It provides essays on public accounting, investment, consumption spending, and balanced budgets, as well as the money systems of most major countries." Libr J
For a fuller review see: Booklist, Feb. 15, 1993

332.1 Banks and banking

Greider, William
Secrets of the temple; how the Federal Reserve runs the country. Simon & Schuster 1987 798p hardcover o.p. paperback available $16   **332.1**
1. Federal Reserve System (U.S.). Board of Governors 2. Banks and banking—United States 3. Monetary policy—United States
ISBN 0-671-67556-7 (pa)   LC 87-16712
An investigation of the structure and influence of the Federal Reserve System during the Reagan era
"This well-researched study, with its lively style, will certainly provide fuel for the conspiracy theorists but also sheds much-needed light on an often-baffling institution." Booklist
Includes bibliography

332.3 Credit and loan institutions

Mayer, Martin, 1928-
The greatest-ever bank robbery; the collapse of the savings and loan industry. Scribner 1990 354p o.p.; Collier Bks. paperback available $12.95   **332.3**
1. Savings and loan associations
ISBN 0-02-012620-4 (pa)   LC 90-34790
"Mayer traces what happened and documents the activities of key personalities; however, what distinguishes this book are Mayer's pertinent questions regarding the impact of the debt both in general and on the future of the industry itself." Libr J
Includes bibliographic references

Pizzo, Stephen
Inside job; the looting of America's savings and loans; [by] Stephen Pizzo, Mary Fricker, and Paul Muolo. [updated ed]. HarperPerennial 1991 578p pa $10.95   **332.3**
1. Savings and loan associations
ISBN 0-06-098600-X   LC 90-56097
First published 1989 by McGraw-Hill
The author examines how, since deregulation in 1982, the savings and loans were plundered by organized crime
Includes bibliographic references

332.6 Investment and investments

Auletta, Ken
Greed and glory on Wall Street; the fall of the house of Lehman. Random House 1986 253p il $19.95   **332.6**
1. Lehman Brothers Kuhn Loeb Incorporated 2. Wall Street (New York, N.Y.)
ISBN 0-394-54410-2   LC 85-10700
Also available in paperback from Warner Bks.

In this work, the author seeks to "chronicle the activity at Lehman Brothers during the months between July 1983 and April 1984, immediately preceding the firm's takeover by Shearson/American Express." Libr J
"To Auletta's credit, one comes away with a better understanding of how deals are made . . . on Wall Street." Christ Sci Monit

Brill, Jack A.
Investing from the heart; a guide to socially responsible money management and investments; [by] Jack A. Brill and Alan Reder. Crown 1992 414p $20   **332.6**
1. Investments
ISBN 0-517-58495-6   LC 91-22420
Updated paperback edition also available $12 (ISBN 0-517-88069-5)

The authors "discuss the concept of socially responsible investing, which involves the 'channeling of personal, community, or workplace capital toward just, peaceful, healthy, environmentally sound purposes and away from destructive uses.' Investments that can be considered for these purposes are discussed in detail; what is available, sources for information, and performance data for certain investments are provided." Libr J
Includes bibliography

Business One Irwin business and investment almanac; edited by Sumner N. Levine. Business One Irwin $75   **332.6**
1. Business 2. Almanacs
ISSN 1057-5014
Annual. First published 1977 with title: The Dow Jones-Irwin business almanac. Title and publisher's name vary
"Covering stock market averages, price/earnings ratios, futures markets, mutual fund performance, foreign stock markets, and many other topics relating to investments." N Y Public Libr Book of How & Where to Look It Up

Carlson, Charles B.

Buying stocks without a broker. McGraw-Hill 1992 367p $29.95; pa $16.95

332.6

1. Investments 2. Stocks
ISBN 0-07-009951-0; 0-07-009952-9 (pa)

LC 91-32447

This book show how investors may buy stock directly from the company issuing it thus avoiding broker's fees. Dividend reinvestment plans (DRIPs) are examined in detail

Includes bibliographic references

Downes, John

Barron's finance & investment handbook; [by] John Downes, Jordan Elliot Goodman. 3rd ed. Barron's Educ. Ser. 1990 1234p il $29.95

332.6

1. Personal finance 2. Investments
ISBN 0-8120-6188-8

LC 89-18307

First published 1986

"This handbook defines 3,000 investment terms, explains in great detail how to read annual reports and financial pages, describes 30 major personal investment vehicles (e.g., annuities, option contracts), and provides information on various market indexes." Booklist

Includes bibliographic references

The Handbook for no-load fund investors.

Business One Irwin $49

332.6

1. Investments
ISSN 0736-6264

Annual. First published 1981

Current editor: Sheldon Jacobs

Published by No-Load Fund Investor

"This annual presents principles of purchasing various types of funds. Tables track fund performance over the past ten years. About one-third of the book is a directory of 1700 funds, giving their investment policy and other information. Libraries will want to buy every year for the statistics." Libr J

Lewis, Michael

Liar's poker: rising through the wreckage on Wall Street. Norton 1989 249p $18.95

332.6

1. Salomon Brothers Inc. 2. Wall Street (New York, N.Y.)
ISBN 0-393-02750-3

LC 89-30819

Also available in paperback from Penguin Bks.

"Lewis describes his four years with the Wall Street firm Salomon Brothers, from his bizarre hiring through the training program to his years as a successful bond trader." Libr J

"This is a story with much irony. Here is one of America's top investment banking and securities trading firms, an adviser to the largest corporations and money managers, unable to run itself. Its management style is one of warring individuals and factions." N Y Times Book Rev

Lynch, Peter

One up on Wall Street; how to use what you already know to make money in the market; by Peter Lynch with John Rothchild. Simon & Schuster 1989 318p $19.95

332.6

1. Investments 2. Stocks 3. Speculation
ISBN 0-671-66103-5

LC 88-32741

Also available in paperback from Penguin Bks.

The authors argue that "average investors can beat Wall Street professionals by using the information that they encounter in their everyday lives. . . . The book is also a primer on how the stock market works and is written in a light, entertaining style." Publ Wkly

Miller, Theodore J.

Kiplinger's invest your way to wealth. rev & updated. Kiplinger Bks. 1993 386p $23.95

332.6

1. Investments
ISBN 0-938721-30-5

LC 93-44560

First published 1991

The author "analyzes investment vehicles, explaining which to avoid and how to select investments for a portfolio." Libr J

Tolchin, Martin

Selling our security; the erosion of America's assets; [by] Martin and Susan J. Tolchin. Knopf 1992 427p $25

332.6

1. Foreign investments 2. United States—National security 3. United States—Economic policy
ISBN 0-394-58309-4

LC 92-4499

Also available in paperback from Penguin Bks.

The authors "maintain that the United States, accustomed to defining national security within the narrow confines of military preparedness, has permitted critical companies and even entire industries crucial to its future to slip under the control of other countries. . . . They call upon the U.S. government to enhance regional trade agreements, allow consortia and the positive characteristics of cartels, and subsidize critical industries." Libr J

"The Tolchins marshal impressive research to bolster their claims." Booklist

Includes bibliography

Wurman, Richard Saul, 1935-

The Wall Street journal guide to understanding money & markets; [by] Richard Saul Wurman, Alan Siegel, Kenneth M. Morris. Access Press (NY); Simon & Schuster [1992] c1990 119p il pa $13.95

332.6

1. Investments 2. Finance—United States
ISBN 0-671-76691-0

"A Fireside book"

First published 1989 by Prentice Hall Press

Cover title

This guide explains how to purchase stocks, bonds, mutual funds, and futures, and how to read the financial pages. It also discusses concepts related to money

332.7   Credit

Dorfman, John
The mortgage book; [by] John R. Dorfman and the editors of Consumer Reports Books. Consumer Repts. Bks. 1992 246p pa $15.95   **332.7**

1. Mortgages
ISBN 0-89043-457-3   LC 92-11957

The author "discusses in detail refinancing, home equity mortgages, prepayments, and reverse mortgages, and he covers . . . consumer protection legislation. Although Dorfman represents a very conservative financial viewpoint, he presents the pros and cons on each issue. Worksheets are included." Libr J

333.3   Real estate

Allen, Robert G.
Nothing down for the 90's; how to buy real estate with little or no money down. new rev ed. Simon & Schuster 1990 362p il $22.95   **333.3**

1. Real estate investment
ISBN 0-671-72558-0   LC 90-10221

First published 1980 with title: Nothing down

The author provides strategies for locating good buys, negotiating, dealing with realtors and managing properties. Suggestions on how to solve immediate cash-flow problems and build equity are included

Janik, Carolyn
How to sell your home in the '90s; with less stress and more profit. Penguin Bks. 1991 246p pa $9.95   **333.3**

1. Houses—Buying and selling 2. Real estate
ISBN 0-14-013269-4   LC 90-7891

Such "factors as arriving at a fair market price, packaging the home (cleaning, repairing, and beautifying), marketing the property with signs, brochures, and advertising, showing the home . . . and finalizing the sale are covered in a clear, comprehensive fashion." Booklist

333.7   Natural resources and energy

Shoumatoff, Alex
The world is burning. Little, Brown 1990 377p il maps $19.95   **333.7**

1. Mendes, Chico 2. Rain forests 3. Conservation of natural resources
ISBN 0-316-78739-6   LC 90-37151

Also available in paperback from Avon Bks.

This is an analysis of the issues involved in the 1988 murder of the Brazilian union leader Chico Mendes

"Supportive of Mendes and his position, though not uncritical, Shoumatoff interviews friend and foe alike, including Mendes' alleged killers, the reputedly murderous Alves da Silva family." Booklist

Includes bibliographic references

333.75   Forest lands

The **Conservation** atlas of tropical forests: Africa; edited by Jeffrey A. Sayer, Caroline S. Harcourt, N. Mark Collins; editorial assistant: Clare Billington; map editor: Mike Adam. Simon & Schuster 1992 288p il maps $95   **333.75**

1. Rain forests 2. Africa—Maps 3. Man—Influence on nature 4. Conservation of natural resources
ISBN 0-13-175332-0   LC 91-39120

Published for the World Conservation Union

This atlas provides an analysis of Africa's "ecological history, superb maps based on satellite imagery of country-by-country forest resources, and a discussion of biodiversity, conservation areas, and initiatives for conservationists. . . . An excellent single-volume source, this is highly recommended." Libr J

333.95   Biological resources

Ehrlich, Paul R.
Extinction; the causes and consequences of the disappearance of species; [by] Paul and Anne Ehrlich. Random House 1981 305p $16.95   **333.95**

1. Nature conservation 2. Ecology 3. Endangered species
ISBN 0-394-51312-6   LC 80-6036

Also available in paperback from Ballantine Bks.

The authors maintain that mankind endangers its own species by extinguishing others. They discuss the economic benefits of preserving species as well as the indirect benefits. Three final chapters focus on the politics of extinction, the tactics and the strategy of conservation

"A definitive manual of hard-headed arguments for environmental debates to come." Saturday Rev

Includes bibliographic references

335   Socialism and related systems

Harrington, Michael, 1928-1989
Socialism: past and future. Arcade Pub. 1989 320p o.p.; New Am. Lib. paperback available $9.95   **335**

1. Socialism 2. Forecasting
ISBN 0-452-26504-5 (pa)   LC 89-6555

The author "describes the various world socialisms—utopian, scientific, authoritarian, Keynesian, Third World, and so on—which, despite their ultimate failure, have in his view done more for humanity over the past 100 years than other social movements. . . . This book is a valuable summary of the ideas of one of America's leading social democrats." Choice

335.4 Marxian systems

Brzezinski, Zbigniew
The grand failure; the birth and death of communism in the twentieth century. Scribner 1989 278p o.p.; Collier Bks. paperback available $11   **335.4**
1. Communism
ISBN 0-02-030730-6 (pa)   LC 88-38050

The author presents a history of Marxism, Leninism, and Stalinism; describes the attempts at political and socioeconomic reforms in the Soviet Union; and predicts the collapse of Communism

Marx, Karl, 1818-1883
The Communist manifesto of Karl Marx and Friedrich Engels   **335.4**
1. Communism

Hardcover and paperback editions available from various publishers

First published 1848

This document "analyzes history in terms of class conflict, predicts the imminent overthrow of the ruling bourgeoisie by the oppressed proletariat, and envisions a resulting classless society in which personal property would be abolished. The 'Manifesto' calls upon the proletariat of the world to unite and strengthen itself for this final revolution." Reader's Ency. 3d edition

336.2 Taxes and taxation

H & R Block income tax guide. Collier Bks. pa $12.95   **336.2**
1. Income tax

Annual. First published 1967 by Macmillan with title: H & R Block income tax workbook

This is a line-by-line tax-preparation workbook and guide to specific situations. Tax tables and sample forms are appended

J.K. Lasser's your income tax; prepared by the J.K. Lasser Tax Institute. Prentice Hall General Ref. pa $14   **336.2**
1. Income tax
ISSN 0084-4314

Annual. First published by Simon & Schuster. Began publication with 1936 issue. Title varies. Early issues prepared by J.K. Lasser

A standard aid for filing income tax returns

336.3 Public borrowing, debt, expenditure

Friedman, Benjamin M.
Day of reckoning; the consequences of American economic policy under Reagan and after; [by] Benjamin Friedman. Random House 1988 323p $19.45; pa $11   **336.3**
1. Fiscal policy—United States 2. Public debts
3. United States—Economic conditions—1974-
ISBN 0-394-56553-3; 0-679-72569-5 (pa)
LC 88-11693

"Friedman's economic projections encompass a belief that the U.S. must stop funding the government deficit. . . . [He] summarizes the policies of each presidential administration since World War II, leveling special criticism at the Reagan White House." Booklist

This book "is cool, solid, well reasoned and clearly written." N Y Times Book Rev

Includes bibliography

337 International economics

Thurow, Lester C.
Head to head; the coming economic battle among Japan, Europe, and America; [by] Lester Thurow. Morrow 1992 336p $25
337
1. International economic relations 2. Economic forecasting 3. Japan—Economic policy 4. Europe—Economic policy 5. United States—Economic policy
ISBN 0-688-11150-5   LC 91-33300

Also available in paperback from Warner Bks.

The author argues that "the United States is facing head-to-head, winner-take-all economic competition with the newly integrated Europe and with Japan. Those trading partners now take the remaining superpower for granted. . . . The United States stands a good chance of coming in third in this race." N Y Times Book Rev

"As always, Thurow has a knack for the telling phrase and the discovery of a significant trend." Libr J

Includes bibliographic references

338.1 Agriculture. Food supply

Rodale, Robert
Save three lives; a plan for famine prevention; [by] Robert Rodale with Mike McGrath. Sierra Club Bks. 1991 253p $20
338.1
1. Food supply 2. Agriculture
ISBN 0-87156-621-4   LC 91-15224

In this book the author presents "a plan to save the Third World from starvation through natural, simple foods. Expressed in a down-to-earth and down-home style, Rodale's ideas seem eminently sensible." Booklist

Includes bibliography

338.2 Mineral industries

Yergin, Daniel
The prize; the epic quest for oil, money, and power. Simon & Schuster 1991 877, xxxii p il maps $27.50; pa $16   **338.2**
1. Petroleum industry 2. World politics
ISBN 0-671-50248-4; 0-671-75705-9 (pa)
LC 90-47575

This is a "history of the oil industry, from the first oil well ever drilled (near Titusville, Pennsylvania, in 1859) to the Iraqi invasion of Kuwait. It recalls advances in technology, innovations in salesmanship, and wars and truces among corporations and nations." New Yorker

"A comprehensive careful book that pulls together reams of information." N Y Times Book Rev

Includes bibliographic references

338.4   Secondary industries and services

Halberstam, David, 1934-
The reckoning. Morrow 1986 752p o.p.;
Avon Bks. paperback available $6.50 **338.4**
1. Nissan Motor Co. Ltd. 2. Ford Motor Co. 3. Automobile industry
ISBN 0-380-70447-1 (pa)   LC 86-16427
An examination of the automobile industry in the United States and Japan. "Halberstam takes two companies—Ford and Nissan—and compares their growth, their reaction to labor problems, their philosophy, and their leadership in developing the various potentials of these organizations." Choice

Includes bibliography

338.7   Business enterprises and their structure

Directory of corporate affiliations; who owns whom. National Register 5v set $875
     338.7
1. Corporations—Directories
Available on CD-ROM
Volumes also available separately. Apply to publisher for prices
Annual with quarterly updates. First published as separate publications. Title varies
Contents: v1-2 U.S. public companies; v3 U.S. private companies; v4 International public and private companies; [v5] Master index
Provides statistical, financial, personnel and other data on parent companies and their subsidiaries

Enrico, Roger
The other guy blinked; how Pepsi won the cola wars; [by] Roger Enrico and Jesse Kornbluth. Bantam Bks. 1986 280p $17.95; pa $4.95   **338.7**
1. PepsiCo, Inc. 2. Coca-Cola Company 3. Soft drink industry
ISBN 0-553-05177-6; 0-553-26632-2 (pa)
     LC 86-17485
After "relating a bit of personal history and the story of his rise up the corporate ladder, Enrico, with the assistance of veteran journalist Kornbluth, offers the Pepsi side of the 'cola wars'." Booklist
"Since Enrico is the president and CEO of Pepsi-Cola USA, his account of the battles between his company and Coca-Cola is something less than objective. Yet he has both a sense of perspective and a sense of humor, so . . . his book is lively business history." Publ Wkly

Everybody's business; a field guide to the 400 leading companies in America; edited by Milton Moskowitz, Robert Levering, and Michael Katz. Doubleday 1990 732p il $49.95; pa $22.50   **338.7**
1. Corporations
ISBN 0-385-26547-6; 0-385-41629-6 (pa)
     LC 90-38923
"This almanac of curious facts is a popular and often irreverent look at 400 U.S. companies. The facts presented here range from market rankings, sales/profits, and

address information to reviews of a company's ethics and the inclusion of interesting pictures from various pivotal events in a company's history." Booklist

Love, John F.
McDonald's: behind the arches. Bantam Bks. 1986 470p il $24.50   **338.7**
1. Kroc, Ray 2. McDonald's Corp. 3. Food industry
ISBN 0-553-05127-X   LC 85-48111
This history of McDonald's "is not the story of Ray Kroc, McDonald's . . . founder, but that of all of the individuals including the McDonald brothers, suppliers, financiers, franchises, as well as the early employees, who [were connected with McDonald's]." Libr J

Standard and Poor's register of corporations, directors, and executives. Standard & Poor's Corp. 3v $525   **338.7**
1. Corporations—Directories   2. Executives—Directories
ISSN 0079-3825
Also available CD-ROM version
Annual. First published 1928
This "reference provides essential information on virtually all of the nation's corporations and their key people. Updated with supplements in April, July, and October. Volume 1: Profiles of more than 55,000 corporations in alphabetical order. Volume 2: Brief biographies of directors and executives. Volume 3: Indexes according to geography, industry, and other parameters." N Y Public Libr Book of How & Where to Look It Up

Von Hoffman, Nicholas
Capitalist fools; tales of American business, from Carnegie to Forbes to the Milken gang. Doubleday 1992 313p $22.50   **338.7**
1. Forbes, Malcolm Stevenson 2. Forbes, Bertie Charles 3. Capitalists and financiers 4. Businessmen
ISBN 0-385-41674-1   LC 92-11597
"By interweaving anecdotes and biographical sketches of Malcolm Forbes and his father B.C. Forbes with those of business titans who were their contemporaries, von Hoffman blends solid historical research with social criticism." Libr J

Includes bibliographic references

Zemke, Ron
The service edge; 101 companies that profit from customer care; by Ron Zemke with Dick Schaaf; foreword by Tom Peters. New Am. Lib. 1989 584p hardcover o.p. paperback available $14   **338.7**
1. Corporations 2. Customer relations
ISBN 0-452-26493-6 (pa)   LC 88-28869
The author have produced a "list of the best service organizations in the country. Before describing their choices, they elaborate upon the fundamental principles underlying distinctive service. They then present their selections . . . in categories by industry, ranging from travel, hotels, and health care to manufacturing, entertainment, and public service." Libr J

Includes bibliographic references

338.8 Business combinations

Burrough, Bryan, 1961-
Barbarians at the gate: the fall of RJR Nabisco; [by] Bryan Burrough and John Helyar. Harper & Row 1990 528p il $22.95; pa $12   **338.8**

1. RJR Nabisco Inc. 2. Conglomerate corporations
ISBN 0-06-016172-8; 0-06-092038-6 (pa)

LC 89-45635

The authors "describe the battle to control RJR Nabisco, providing a behind-the-scenes account of the deal through interviews with Wall Street power brokers and comments on the restructuring of corporations today." Publ Wkly

This book "contains enough individual examples of greed, egoism, conniving and sheer incompetence to stun even more jaundiced observers of the Wall Street madhouse. . . . [The authors] have done a solid job of American reportage; in other words, they tell a good story without getting bogged down in analysis." Economist

338.9 Economic development and growth

Glouchevitch, Philip
Juggernaut; the German way of business: why it is transforming Europe—and the world. Simon & Schuster 1992 239p $21   **338.9**

1. Industrial management 2. Germany—Economic policy
ISBN 0-671-74410-0   LC 92-19015

"In this examination of German business practices, Glouchevitch warns that we ignore Germany, both as a trading partner and as a competitor, at our own risk. . . . He profiles Germany's banking system, tax structure, and labor practices—all of which have an impact on German business. He also discusses reunification's effects and prospects, and looks at Germany's role in the future world economy." Booklist

Includes bibliographic references

Lesko, Matthew
Getting yours; the complete guide to government money. 3rd ed. Penguin Bks. 1987 368p pa $11.95   **338.9**

1. Economic assistance, Domestic
ISBN 0-14-046760-2   LC 86-22688

First published 1982

A directory of funds available from federal and state governments. Entries include type of assistance, eligibility requirements, program objectives, and address and phone numbers of contacts

338.973 United States—Economic policy

Galbraith, John Kenneth, 1908-
The new industrial state. 4th ed. Houghton Mifflin 1985 xxxv, 438p $19.95   **338.973**

1. Corporations 2. Industry—Government policy—United States 3. United States—Economic conditions—1900-1999 (20th century)
ISBN 0-395-38991-7   LC 85-11956

Also available in paperback from New Am. Lib.

First published 1967

The author's thesis is that our economy is dominated by some 500 powerful corporations which not only plan new products but also, through advertising, create demand, thus destroying the free market and consumer choice

Includes bibliographic references

Janeway, Eliot
The economics of chaos; on revitalizing the American economy. Dutton 1989 402p hardcover o.p. paperback available $12.95   **338.973**

1. United States—Economic policy 2. United States—Economic conditions—1974-
ISBN 0-525-48545-7 (pa)   LC 88-16063

"A Truman Talley book"

The author "believes that this country is mired in traditional free-market philosophies that may be appropriate for smaller nations as England or France, but fail to take into account our unique and unsurpassed economic and military power. Drawing on a parade of great thinkers . . . [the author] tries to develop a new philosophy that can rejuvenate America's economy by better exploiting its resources, its vast market, its entrepreneurial spirit and the leverage it has throughout the world." N Y Times Book Rev

Includes bibliography

Phillips, Kevin P.
The politics of rich and poor; wealth and the American electorate in the Reagan aftermath; [by] Kevin Phillips. Random House 1990 xxiii, 262p maps $19.95   **338.973**

1. Wealth 2. United States—Economic policy 3. United States—Politics and government—1981-
ISBN 0-394-55954-1   LC 89-43419

Also available in paperback from HarperPerennial

The author presents an analysis of the economic policies of the Reagan administration and their consequences. He argues that these policies have led to an increasing gap between rich and poor

"No one else has assembled a more scathing assault on the 1980s as a time of economic exploitation." NY Rev Books

Includes bibliographic references

339.4 Factors affecting national product, wealth, income

Galbraith, John Kenneth, 1908-
The nature of mass poverty. Harvard Univ. Press 1979 150p $12.95; pa $5.95
339.4

1. Poverty 2. Developing countries—Economic conditions
ISBN 0-674-60533-0; 0-674-60535-7 (pa)
LC 78-11839

Originally given as lectures at the Graduate Institute of International Studies at the University of Geneva, and later at Radcliffe Institute

The author discusses "mass poverty—its nature, causes, and why present methods of aid haven't erased it—and proposes a radical cure to fit his diagnosis." Booklist

Includes bibliographic references

340 Law

Belli, Melvin M., 1907-
Everybody's guide to the law; [by] Melvin M. Belli, Sr. & Allen P. Wilkinson. Harcourt Brace Jovanovich 1986 xxi, 649p $19.95
340

1. Law—United States
ISBN 0-15-142166-8
LC 86-14305

Also available in paperback from HarperCollins

"The first 14 chapters cover subjects ranging from marriage, automobiles, and estate planning to products liability, contracts and consumer credit, debt collection, and bankruptcy." Booklist

"This well-written and clearly organized book is packed with valuable information that will enable people to deal more expeditiously and intelligently with their legal affairs." Libr J

Coughlin, George Gordon, 1900-1986
Your handbook of everyday law; [by] George Gordon Coughlin, Jr. 5th ed. HarperPerennial 1993 452p $25; pa $13
340

1. Law—United States
ISBN 0-06-271572-0; 0-06-273240-4 (pa)
LC 93-25283

First published 1963 by Barnes & Noble with title: Your introduction to law

The author uses "cases and examples to illustrate the essential points of the laws that govern business and personal affairs. Some of the more common areas of law that he covers include: marriage and divorce, accidents and injuries, employment . . . environmental law, consumer protection and civil rights." Publisher's note

Elias, Stephen
Legal research; how to find and understand the law; by Stephen Elias and Susan Levinkind. 3rd natl ed. Nolo Press (Berkeley) 1992 various paging il $16.95
340

1. Law—Research
ISBN 0-87337-144-5
LC 92-1378

First published 1982

"A popular title and a true step-by-step guide to locating legal material, this book covers standard procedures for getting at the important sources and provides sample research problems and their solutions." Libr J

Includes bibliographic references

You and the law. [3rd rev ed]. Reader's Digest Assn. 1984 861p $21.95   **340**

1. Law—United States
ISBN 0-89577-164-0

First published 1971

At head of title: Reader's Digest

"A practical guide to everyday law and how it affects you and your family. Has 651 sections that cover, in clear, understandable terms, all the legal problems that confront the average person. Includes charts and tables that show differences from state to state. Has a glossary of more than 1,000 legal terms and an index." N Y Public Libr Book of How & Where to Look It Up

340.03 Law—Dictionaries

Black, Henry Campbell, 1860-1927
Black's law dictionary. West $27.95
340.03

1. Law—Dictionaries

Also available in an abridged paperback edition

First published 1891 with title: A dictionary of law. (6th edition 1991) Periodically revised to bring terms up to date

"Definitions of the terms and phrases of American and English jurisprudence, ancient and modern." Subtitle

"This comprehensive work is the standard law dictionary for ready reference." Sheehy. Guide to Ref Books. 10th edition

Bruno, Carole A.
Legal secretary's standard desk book. Prentice-Hall 1987 559p il $39.95   **340.03**

1. Office practice—Handbooks, manuals, etc.
2. Law—Dictionaries
ISBN 0-13-529397-9
LC 86-9492

Provides explanation of various legal terms in layman's language, and sample legal forms

Garner, Bryan A.
A dictionary of modern legal usage. Oxford Univ. Press 1987 587p $45; pa $15.95
340.03

1. Law—Dictionaries 2. English language—Usage
ISBN 0-19-504377-4; 0-91-506578-6 (pa)
LC 87-13276

"The ideal companion to standard law dictionaries, this definitive guide to style and usage for the legal writer offers accessible, authoritative, and up-to-date information enabling lawyers, judges, students, journalists, and others to write with clarity and precision." Univ Press Books for Public Libr

The **Guide** to American law; everyone's legal encyclopedia. West 1983-1985 12v il set $1624.75 **340.03**

1. Law—United States—Dictionaries
ISBN 0-314-73224-1 LC 83-1134

"The single most valuable legal reference source and a first purchase for all collections. Alphabetically arranged entries lucidly explain legal principles and concepts, landmark documents, law, famous trials, and historical movements. Lengthy, signed articles by legal scholars provide in-depth analysis of selected topics." Ref Sources for Small & Medium-sized Libr. 5th edition

Supplemented annually since 1990 by The guide to American law supplement (ISSN 0895-0989)

341.23 United Nations

United Nations. Dept. of Public Information
Everyone's United Nations. U.N. Publs. $14.95; pa $9.95 **341.23**

1. United Nations

First published 1948 with title: Everyman's United Nations. Periodically revised

"This tenth edition is a self-contained volume, covering all 40 years of the Organization's existence. It focuses on the period 1978 to 1985." Title page of 1986 edition

Yearbook of the United Nations. U.N. Publs. il $115 **341.23**

1. United Nations—Periodicals
ISSN 0082-8521

First published 1947

"Describes the proceedings and activities of the United Nations and its related inter-governmental agencies during [the year]. . . . Political, security, economic, social, legal, administrative, and budgetary questions are covered." Publ Wkly

Your United Nations: the official guidebook. U.N. Publs. $11.95; pa $6.95 **341.23**

1. United Nations

First published 1952. (1987 edition) Periodically revised

The official guidebook to the United Nations contains photographs and text highlighting the architecture and art of the complex itself and an introduction to the organization's day to day operations

341.6 Law of war

Brackman, Arnold C., 1923-1983
The other Nuremberg; the untold story of the Tokyo war crimes trials. Morrow 1987 432p il hardcover o.p. paperback available $9.95 **341.6**

1. War crime trials 2. World War, 1939-1945—Atrocities 3. Japan—Politics and government
ISBN 0-688-07957-1 (pa) LC 86-21834

This is an account of the 1946-1948 International Military Tribunal for the Far East, the Japanese counterpart to the Nuremberg Trials. Representatives of the eleven Allied nations served as judges in these war crimes trials of twenty-eight Japanese leaders. The author of this book was a correspondent for United Press at the time, report-

ing on the Tokyo court proceedings
Includes bibliography

342 Constitutional and administrative law

Adler, Mortimer Jerome, 1902-
We hold these truths; understanding the ideas and ideals of the Constitution. Macmillan 1987 278p hardcover o.p. paperback available $6.95 **342**

1. United States—Constitutional law
ISBN 0-02-064130-3 (pa) LC 86-23458

This "interpretation of the wellspring of our democratic system also includes the complete texts of the so-termed 'American Testament': the Declaration of Independence, the Constitution, and the Gettysburg Address." Booklist

Alderman, Ellen
In our defense: the Bill of Rights in action; [by] Ellen Alderman, Caroline Kennedy. Morrow 1990 430p il $22.95 **342**

1. United States. Supreme Court 2. United States. Constitution. 1st-10th amendments 3. Civil rights 4. United States—Constitutional law
ISBN 0-688-07801-X LC 90-48844

Also available in paperback from Avon Bks.

The authors use "accounts of real-life controversies to introduce the general reader to the Bill of Rights. Nineteen vignettes illuminate virtually all rights guarantees and demonstrate their contemporary relevance. Of particular interest are the stories about the development of public land held sacred by Native Americans (First Amendment) and the attempt to protect minors testifying in molestation cases (Sixth Amendment)." Libr J

Includes bibliographic references

Berns, Walter, 1919-
Taking the Constitution seriously. Simon & Schuster 1987 287p o.p.; University Press of Am. paperback available $17.95 **342**

1. United States—Constitutional law 2. United States—Constitutional history
ISBN 0-8191-7970-1 (pa) LC 87-4309

An exploration of the Constitution and its central place in the political, social, and moral development of the nation

Includes bibliography

Bowen, Catherine Drinker, 1897-1973
Miracle at Philadelphia; the story of the Constitutional Convention, May to September, 1787; foreword by Warren E. Burger. Little, Brown 1986 c1966 346p $18.95; pa $10.95 **342**

1. United States. Constitutional Convention (1787) 2. United States—Constitutional history
ISBN 0-316-10378-0; 0-316-10398-5 (pa)
LC 86-205421

"An Atlantic Monthly Press book"
A reissue of the title first published 1966

Bowen, Catherine Drinker, 1897-1973 —
Continued

"Writing from sources—delegates' letters and diaries; contemporary reports; James Madison's faithful minutes— Catherine Drinker Bowen draws [a] . . . picture of the men, issues and background of the Constitutional Convention held at Philadelphia in the hot summer of 1787." Publ Wkly

Includes bibliographic references

Carter, Stephen L.
Reflections of an affirmative action baby. Basic Bks. 1991 286p $23; pa $12   **342**

1. Affirmative action programs 2. Race discrimination—Law and legislation
ISBN 0-465-06871-5; 0-465-06869-3 (pa)
                                              LC 91-70054

The author begins by "discussing the positive and negative effects of affirmative action on his life. He then expands his study to include other topics such as the increase of racial incidents in America, dealing with political correctness and the conflicts between the mainstream liberal black community and the increasingly vocal so-called black conservatives." Libr J

Cox, Archibald, 1912-
The court and the Constitution. Houghton Mifflin 1987 434p hardcover o.p. paperback available $9.70   **342**

1. United States. Supreme Court 2. United States—Constitutional law
ISBN 0-395-48071-X (pa)
                                              LC 87-3772

Cox's "discussion of the making of the Constitution and the major controversies surrounding the role of the Supreme Court in American history provides a valuable perspective on the . . . debate over the Judiciary's proper bounds. The book is not a polemic for either judicial activism or institutional restraint." Choice

Includes bibliography

Cushman, Robert Fairchild, 1918-
Leading constitutional decisions; [by] Robert F. Cushman. Prentice-Hall pa $37.33
                                              342

1. United States—Constitutional law 2. United States—Constitutional history
First published 1925 by Appleton. (18th edition 1991) Periodically revised

This collection of landmark Supreme Court cases that have left an enduring mark on the political and social history of the United States is intended primarily to serve the needs of students of American government and American history

Encyclopedia of the American Constitution; Leonard W. Levy, editor-in-chief; Kenneth L. Karst, associate editor; Dennis J. Mahoney, assistant editor. Macmillan 1986 4v o.p.   **342**

1. United States—Constitutional law   LC 86-3038
Two volume reissue (published 1990) and supplement (published 1990) available set $275 (ISBN 0-02-897256-2)

"A collection of essays by historians, lawyers, and political scientists on doctrinal concepts, legislation, people, historical periods, and decisions of the Supreme Court involving the American Constitution. Most essays

should be accessible to the general reader." N Y Public Libr Book of How & Where to Look It Up

The **Federalist**; edited, with introduction and notes, by Jacob E. Cooke. Wesleyan Univ. Press 1982 c1961 xxx, 672p pa $19.95
                                              342

1. United States. Constitution
ISBN 0-8195-6077-4   LC 82-2815
A reissue of the 1961 edition

"From 27 Oct. 1787 to 2 April 1788, 77 essays were published in the semi-weekly 'Independent Journal' of New York, entitled 'The Federalist,' and signed first 'A Citizen of New York' then 'Publius.' Eight more were added when they were collected in book form [in 1789]. . . . They were so acute and massively learned in their exposition of the true intent of the Constitution, that even the courts have accepted them as authoritative comments in doubtful cases; and they are held by all the civilized world as among the noblest storehouses of political philosophy in existence. A classic textbook of political science." Ency Americana

Findlay, Bruce Allyn
Your rugged Constitution; how America's house of freedom is planned and built; [by] Bruce Allyn Findlay, Esther Blair Findlay; illustrated by Richard Dawson. 2nd rev ed. Stanford Univ. Press 1969 290p il $24.50; pa $10.95   **342**

1. United States. Constitution
ISBN 0-8047-0405-8; 0-8047-0407-4 (pa)
First published 1950

The authors describe the Constitution of the United States, from its Preamble through its Amendments. Their purpose is to show how each part of this document is as functional today as it was when it was originally written

Friendly, Fred W.
The Constitution—that delicate balance; [by] Fred W. Friendly, Martha J.H. Elliott. Random House 1984 339p il o.p.; McGraw-Hill paperback available $15.77
                                              342

1. United States. Supreme Court 2. United States—Constitutional law
ISBN 0-07-554612-4 (pa)   LC 84-42656

"The focus is on the conflicts behind 16 major Supreme Court cases, and each chapter is a lucid, informative account of such controversial issues as abortion, school prayer, the insanity plea and the treatment of illegal aliens. By tracing each conflict back in time . . . the authors allow us to follow its evolution and court efforts to balance individual and societal rights." Publ Wkly

Includes bibliography

Hentoff, Nat
Free speech for me—but not for thee; how the American left and right relentlessly censor each other. HarperCollins Pubs. 1992 405p $25   **342**

1. Free speech 2. Censorship
ISBN 0-06-019006-X   LC 92-52550

Hentoff, Nat—*Continued*

"An Aaron Asher book"

This is a collection of pieces from the author's weekly columns in The Village Voice and The Washington Post

"Anyone sitting down to read [this book] should be prepared for a hard but rewarding experience. . . . Its importance lies in its accounting, in rich detail, of the major assaults upon our freedom to think, read, write and speak that have taken place since the days of Joseph McCarthy. It is exceptional, too, in that it contains mostly eyewitness material." N Y Times Book Rev

Irons, Peter H., 1940-

The courage of their convictions; [by] Peter Irons. Free Press 1988 420p il $24.95
342

1. United States. Supreme Court 2. Civil rights
ISBN 0-02-915670-X   LC 88-21406

Also available in paperback from Penguin Bks.

This book contains accounts of sixteen plaintiffs in civil rights cases that were examined by the United States Supreme Court

A "work that not only shows the judicial process at work but also the real-life people whose cases make constitutional law. More than that, however, this is an excellent primer on civil liberties in the U.S. in the 20th century." Choice

Lieberman, Jethro K. (Jethro Koller)

The evolving Constitution; how the Supreme Court has ruled on issues from abortion to zoning. Random House 1992 751p $26   **342**

1. United States. Supreme Court 2. United States—Constitutional law
ISBN 0-679-40530-5   LC 92-16590

This "reference work details the manner in which the U.S. Supreme Court has interpreted the Constitution for almost 200 years. . . . [It] is well organized, digesting about 2370 Supreme Court cases into roughly 1200 concise, pertinent, and easily understood essays on constitutional issues." Libr J

For a fuller review see: Booklist, April 15, 1993

Marwick, Christine M.

Your right to government information. Bantam Bks. 1985 xxxii, 252p (American Civil Liberties Union handbook)   **342**

1. Government information—Law and legislation
2. Freedom of information   LC 85-179643

Available from Southern Ill. Univ. Press pa $4.95 (ISBN 0-8093-9960-1)

This "volume sets forth data regarding the rights of an individual to have access to government files. Our rights to expression, privacy, equal protection, and due process are all discussed thoroughly." Booklist

Includes bibliographic references

McDonald, Laughlin

The rights of racial minorities; the basic ACLU guide to racial minority rights; [by] Laughlin McDonald, John A. Powell. 2nd ed completely rev & updated. Southern Ill. Univ. Press 1993 288p (American Civil Liberties Union handbook) $34.95; pa $7.95
342

1. Race discrimination 2. Blacks—Civil rights
ISBN 0-8093-1899-7; 0-8093-1888-1 (pa)
LC 93-15756

First published 1980 under the authorship of E. Richard Larson and Laughlin McDonald

"Individual chapters explain the federal civil laws and procedures protecting the rights of racial minorities in voting, employment, education, housing, public accommodations, federally assisted programs, and jury selection and trials. Relevant criminal statutes and the use of race-conscious remedies are covered as well." Publisher's note

The **Origins** of the American Constitution;

a documentary history; edited with an introduction by Michael Kammen. Penguin Bks. 1986 xxxv, 407p pa $8.95
342

1. United States—Constitutional history
ISBN 0-14-008744-3   LC 86-8173

The editor "presents supporting documents dealing with the earliest period of constitutional history. Excerpts from 'The Federalist' papers, correspondence between various founders of the nation, as well as voices in opposition are also included, as is an earlier version of and amendments to the Constitution." Booklist

Includes bibliography

The **Right** to protest; the basic ACLU guide

to free expression; [by] Joel M. Gora [et al.] Southern Ill. Univ. Press 1991 344p pa $7.95   **342**

1. Protests, demonstrations, etc. 2. United States—Constitutional law 3. Free speech 4. Freedom of assembly
ISBN 0-8093-1699-4   LC 90-19977

This volume provides description of the Constitution's provisions, legal doctrines, and laws which govern protest activities

Includes bibliographic references

United States. Constitution

The Constitution of the United States of America; analysis and interpretation; prepared by the Congressional Research Service, Library of Congress. U.S. Govt. Ptg. Office $70   **342**

1. United States—Constitutional law

First published 1953. Periodically revised and kept up to date by supplements

Under PL 589, 91st Congress this work "will become a decennial publication with biennial cumulative supplements. The Constitution is presented with citations to important cases concerning it, given clause-by-clause. It also contains a section on acts of Congress which were declared unconstitutional. Often referred to as the 'Annotated Constitution.'" Wynkoop. Subject Guide to Gov Ref Books

344 Social, labor, welfare, & related law

The **Americans** with Disabilities Act handbook; Maureen Harrison, Steve Gilbert, editors. Excellent Bks. 1992 246p pa $15.95   **344**

1. Handicapped—Law and legislation 2. Handicapped—Civil rights

ISBN 1-880780-00-3   LC 92-72951

Title on spine: The ADA handbook

"A series of questions about the act are answered before it is spelled out, with helpful definitions and analysis. While all the questions one could raise are not answered here, the guide is useful because it carries both explanation of the act's passage and its actual wording." Booklist

Includes bibliographic references

De Grazia, Edward

Girls lean back everywhere; the law of obscenity and the assault on genius. Random House 1992 814p $29.50   **344**

1. Censorship 2. Obscenity (Law)

ISBN 0-394-57611-X   LC 90-53153

The author presents a "history of literary censorship and [discusses] the continuing legal and constitutional struggle to define 'obscenity.'" Libr J

"Had law professor de Grazia stayed within his professional purview, he would have written a book for every nonprofessional concerned with censorship in the arts. But because he places censorship trials in their social contexts (and because he is not above gossip), he has written a book that also should be read by everyone interested in the worlds of American literature and publishing." Booklist

Dziech, Billie Wright

On trial; America's courts and their treatment of sexually abused children; [by] Billie Wright Dziech and Charles B. Schudson. Beacon Press 1989 227p pa $16   **344**

1. Child abuse—Law and legislation

ISBN 0-8070-0408-1   LC 87-42843

"Balancing the need to protect sexually abused children against the rights of defendants who may have been unfairly accused is a dilemma confronting the legal system. The authors of this clear, cogent brief propose reforms to foster better communication with child witnesses, thus allowing their voices to be heard without intimidation or embarrassment, while permitting more informed judgments about their veracity." Publ Wkly

Includes bibliography

Epstein, Lee, 1958-

The Supreme Court and legal change; abortion and the death penalty; [by] Lee Epstein, Joseph F. Kobylka. University of N.C. Press 1992 417p $45; pa $16.95 **344**

1. United States. Supreme Court 2. Abortion—Law and legislation 3. Capital punishment

ISBN 0-8078-2051-2; 0-8078-4384-9 (pa)

LC 92-53618

This study examines how the Court is influenced in politically volatile cases by amicus curiae briefs filed before them

Includes bibliographic references

Faux, Marian

Roe v. Wade; the untold story of the landmark Supreme Court decision that made abortion legal. Macmillan 1988 370p il $22.50   **344**

1. McCorvey, Norma 2. Wade, Henry, 1914- 3. Roe v. Wade 4. Abortion—Law and legislation

ISBN 0-02-537151-7   LC 87-34827

Also available in paperback from New Am. Lib.

This is an account of the events leading up to the Supreme Court's 1973 decision to overturn state laws banning abortion during the first six months of pregnancy

"A solid work of cultural and legal history, useful even for those familiar with the story." N Y Times Book Rev

Includes bibliography

Lieberson, Alan D.

The living will handbook. Hastings House 1992 170p il pa $12.95   **344**

1. Right to die

ISBN 0-8038-9334-5   LC 91-73925

"A living will is a document that provides a series of written instructions to doctors as to what care the patient wishes to accept or reject. The Patient-Self Determination Act has become law as of December 1, 1991, which means that hospitals receiving Medicaid or Medicare funds must advise patients of the right to sign a living will or select a proxy." Booklist

Outten, Wayne N.

The rights of employees and union members; the basic ACLU guide to the rights of employees and union members; [by] Wayne N. Outten, Robert J. Rabin, Lisa R. Lipman. 2nd ed completely rev & updated. Southern Ill. Univ. Press 1994 604p (American Civil Liberties Union handbook) $39.95; pa $14.95   **344**

1. Employees—Civil rights 2. Labor unions—United States

ISBN 0-8093-1913-6; 0-8093-1914-4 (pa)

LC 93-16895

A revised, combined edition of The rights of employees, by Wayne N. Outten, first published 1984 by Bantam Bks., and The rights of union members, by Clyde Summers and Robert J. Rabin, published 1979 by Avon Bks.

The authors use a "question-and-answer format to examine . . . such topics as the employment relationship, compensation and benefits, the union workplace, and workplace protections. They also answer questions about discrimination, including discrimination based on race, ethnicity, sex, religion, age, disability, AIDS, sexual orientation, and veteran and reserve status." Publisher's note

The **Rights** of prisoners; the basic ACLU guide to prisoners' rights; [by] David Rudovsky [et al.] 4th ed. Southern Ill. Univ. Press 1988 127p (American Civil Liberties Union handbook) pa $7.95 **344**

1. Prisoners—Law and legislation 2. Prisoners—Civil rights
ISBN 0-8093-1452-5   LC 87-23577
First published 1973 by Richard W. Baron

"Topics covered include freedom from cruel and unusual punishment, due process, prison censorship, religious and racial discrimination, special concerns of women prisoners, medical care, rehabilitation, parole, and remedies and procedures for challenging conditions of confinement." Publisher's note

Rubin, David, 1932-
The rights of teachers; the basic ACLU guide to a teacher's constitutional rights; [by] David Rubin with Steven Greenhouse. rev ed. Bantam Bks. 1984 351p (American Civil Liberties Union handbook)   **344**

1. Teachers—Law and legislation 2. Teachers—Civil rights   LC 84-149150
Available from Southern Ill. Univ. Press pa $4.95 (ISBN 0-8093-9957-1)
First published 1968

Guide to teachers' rights, covering information on unfair dismissals, denied promotions, student discipline, right to strike and privacy

Zimring, Franklin E.
The citizen's guide to gun control; Franklin E. Zimring and Gordon Hawkins. Macmillan 1987 201p il maps $19.95; pa $14.95   **344**

1. Firearms—Law and legislation
ISBN 0-02-934830-7; 0-02-897505-7 (pa) LC 87-5503

"Topics examined include the relationship between firearms and interpersonal violence, general patterns of gun ownership, gun control legislation, and the forces that will shape the future of gun control." Booklist

Includes bibliographic references

345 Criminal law

Couric, Emily
The trial lawyers; the nation's top litigators tell how they win. St. Martin's Press 1988 380p $19.95; pa $13.95   **345**

1. Trials 2. Lawyers
ISBN 0-312-02305-7; 0-312-05172-7 (pa)
                                  LC 88-16893

The author has "compiled a study of ten of the most prominent attorneys in the States, concentrating on one case in particular. Five of the cases are criminal, of which one is distinguished mainly by the fact that the judge, the prosecutor, and the alleged victim are all women." West Coast Rev Books

Davies, Nick
White lies; rape, murder, and justice, Texas style. Pantheon Bks. 1991 402p $23   **345**

1. Brandley, Clarence, 1952- 2. Trials (Homicide) 3. Racism 4. Corruption in politics
ISBN 0-679-40167-9   LC 90-53407
Also available in paperback from Avon Bks.

This is an account of the case of Clarence Brandley, a black janitor convicted on circumstantial evidence in Conroe Texas in 1980 of the rape and murder of a white high school student. He was freed from Death Row on appeal
"Extremely well written, dramatic, and thought-provoking, this is highly recommended." Libr J

Dershowitz, Alan M.
The best defense. Random House 1982 xxii, 425p il hardcover o.p. paperback available $7.95   **345**

1. Trials
ISBN 0-394-71380-X (pa)   LC 81-40208
The author offers his reflections upon the practice of law and the American criminal justice system. He describes a number of controversial cases in which he served as defense attorney

Reversal of fortune; inside the von Bülow case. Random House 1986 xxvi, 276p il $19.95   **345**

1. Von Bulow, Claus 2. Trials (Homicide)
ISBN 0-394-53903-6   LC 85-25722
Also available in paperback from Pocket Bks.

An inside account of Claus Von Bulow's second trial by his defense attorney

Fletcher, George P.
A crime of self-defense; Bernhard Goetz and the law on trial. Free Press 1988 253p $29.95   **345**

1. Goetz, Bernhard 2. Trials
ISBN 0-02-910311-8   LC 88-7170
Also available in paperback from University of Chicago Press

"Goetz, the so-called 'subway vigilante,' shot four black teenagers on the subway in New York City. His main alibi was self-defense. Fletcher . . . discusses the judicial history and interpretation of self-defense. He then leads us through the trial, which resulted in Goetz's acquittal on all charges except gun possession." Libr J

Includes bibliographic references

Heilbroner, David
Rough justice; days and nights of a young D.A. Pantheon Bks. 1990 286p $19.95   **345**

1. Criminal justice, Administration of
ISBN 0-394-58191-1   LC 89-43239
Also available in paperback from Dell

The author discusses his experiences as an assistant district attorney in Manhattan
This is "a comprehensive portrayal of court life, a fine primer on the way individual prosecutors make decisions. . . . It is accurate, engaging and unsettling." NY Times Book Rev

Lewis, Anthony, 1927-
Make no law; the Sullivan case and the First Amendment. Random House 1991 354p $25; pa $13   **345**

1. Sullivan, L. B. 2. New York Times Company v. Sullivan 3. Libel and slander 4. Press—Law and legislation
ISBN 0-394-58774-X; 0-679-73939-4 (pa)   LC 91-6618

The author chronicles the historic First Amendment case of Sullivan v. The New York Times. Lewis discusses the effect the case has had on both libel laws and press freedoms

Markman, Ronald, 1936-
Alone with the devil; famous cases of a courtroom psychiatrist; [by] Ronald Markman and Dominick Bosco. Doubleday 1989 368p il $18.95   **345**

1. Trials 2. Mental illness—Jurisprudence
ISBN 0-385-24427-4   LC 88-13869

Also available in paperback from Bantam Bks.

The author "has written a riveting account of some of his more famous cases, including the Hillside Strangler and the Manson family murders. Markman's job is to evaluate the criminal's state of mind at the time of the crime, a decision that can determine whether the criminal serves prison time or is rehabilitated in a psychiatric setting." Libr J

Nizer, Louis
Catspaw; the famous trial attorney's heroic defense of a man unjustly accused. Fine, D.I. 1992 299p il $21.95   **345**

1. Gold, Murray 2. Trials (Homicide)
ISBN 1-55611-276-9   LC 91-57891

Also available in paperback from Carroll & Graf Pubs.

This is an account of the legal efforts made in order to overturn an unjust murder accusation. In "1974, Louis Pasternak, a 71-year-old lawyer, and his wife were murdered in cold blood in their Waterbury, Connecticut home. Because of loose circumstantial evidence, the Pasternak's former son-in-law, Murray Gold, became the prime suspect and was indicted by the grand jury. At trial, evidence was introduced—but excluded as hearsay—that a Satanist, Bruce Sanford, had the motive and opportunity to commit the murders. Although he later committed suicide, Sanford had also confessed to friends that he killed the Pasternaks. After 17 years and four trials, Nizer filed a writ of *habeus corpus* in a last-ditch effort to clear Gold's name. The writ was granted in 1991." Libr J

Vise, David A.
Eagle on the Street; based on the Pulitzer prize-winning account of the SEC's battle with Wall Street; [by] David A. Vise, Steve Coll. Scribner 1991 395p il $24.95; pa $14   **345**

1. United States. Securities and Exchange Commission 2. Insider trading 3. Stock exchange
ISBN 0-684-19314-0; 0-02-008162-6 (pa)   LC 91-9529

This work offers an "account of a decade of mergers, junk bonds and insider trading scandals as seen through two struggles: one between the Securities and Exchange Commission in Washington and the powerful financial institutions in New York, the other within the commis-

sion itself." N Y Times Book Rev

Includes bibliographic references

346   Private law

Bove, Alexander A., 1938-
The complete book of wills & estates; [by] Alexander A. Bove, Jr. Holt & Co. 1989 268p hardcover o.p. paperback available $10.95   **346**

1. Wills
ISBN 0-8050-1464-0 (pa)   LC 88-31380

Among the topics covered in this look at probate law and the tax system are how to set up a living trust, how to minimize inheritance taxes, and how to choose and deal with a lawyer

Includes glossary

Elias, Stephen
How to file for bankruptcy; by Stephen Elias, Albin Renauer, Robin Leonard. Nolo Press (Berkeley) 1989 various paging $24.95   **346**

1. Bankruptcy
ISBN 0-87337-079-1   LC 89-37115

"This book focuses almost exclusively on personal or so-called 'straight' bankruptcy under Chapter 7 of the Bankruptcy Code, and excludes detailed consideration of Chapter 13 repayment plans. The authors . . . provide step-by-step information necessary to determine whether or not, and how, to file." Libr J

Includes bibliographic references

Simple contracts for personal use; by Stephen Elias & Marcia Stewart; edited by Mary Randolph & Barbara Kate Repa; illustrated by Linda Allison. natl 2nd ed. Nolo Press (Berkeley) 1991 various paging il pa $16.95   **346**

1. Contracts
ISBN 0-87337-155-0   LC 91-17629

First published 1986

"All kinds of everyday forms for commonplace circumstances are represented in this book. Each form is clearly marked as to the kind of situation for which it is designed, with good explanations on the fine points. Forms range from a contract for housekeeping services to an animal-boarding agreement." Libr J

Includes bibliographic references

Fehrenbacher, Don Edward, 1920-
The Dred Scott case; its significance in American law and politics; [by] Don E. Fehrenbacher. Oxford Univ. Press 1978 741p $45   **346**

1. Scott, Dred 2. Slavery—United States
ISBN 0-19-502403-6   LC 78-4665

This study discusses the "case of 1857 in which the Supreme Court ruled on . . . questions of Negro citizenship, congressional power over the territories, and the constitutionality of the Missouri Compromise." Choice

Includes bibliographic references

Jordan, Cora, 1941-
Neighbor law; fences, trees, boundaries and noise; edited by Mary Randolph; illustrations by Linda Allison; with a foreword by Ernest Callenbach. Nolo Press (Berkeley) 1991 various paging il pa $14.95
346
1. Law—United States
ISBN 0-87337-158-5   LC 91-21036
"The potential trouble areas between neighbors are represented here: noise, trees, fences, boundary lines, obstruction of view, trespassing, and fallen fruit. This book offers guidance in resolving disputes; included are citations to nuisance laws, fence statutes, and damages penalties for injury to trees. Sample complaint letters to neighbors are an added benefit." Libr J
Includes bibliographic references

Nicholas, Ted, 1934-
How to form your own corporation without a lawyer for under $75.00. Enterprise pa $19.95   **346**
1. Corporations
First published 1972 with title: How to form your own corporation without a lawyer for under $50.00. (1992 edition) Periodically revised
A step-by-step guide to forming a corporation, with sample forms, minutes, and by-laws
Includes bibliography

346.01 Law of persons and domestic relations

Brown, Robert N., 1944-
The rights of older persons; [by] Robert N. Brown with Legal Counsel for the Elderly. 2nd ed completely rev & up-to-date. Southern Ill. Univ. Press 1989 413p (American Civil Liberties Union handbook) pa $7.95   **346.01**
1. Elderly—Law and legislation 2. Elderly—Medical care
ISBN 0-8093-1432-0   LC 88-2030
First published 1979 by Avon Bks.
This guide focuses on legal rights in the areas of income (Social Security, pensions, jobs), health care, property transfers, guardianship and tax status

Chesler, Phyllis
Mothers on trial; the battle for children and custody. McGraw-Hill 1986 651p o.p.; Harcourt Brace & Co. paperback available $12.95   **346.01**
1. Child custody 2. Mothers
ISBN 0-15-662167-3 (pa)   LC 85-11318
The author argues that child custody and protection laws often treat mothers unfairly
Includes bibliography

Forer, Lois G., 1914-
Unequal protection; women, children, and the elderly in court. Norton 1991 256p $22.95; pa $10.95   **346.01**
1. Law—United States 2. Age discrimination 3. Sex discrimination
ISBN 0-393-02949-2; 0-393-30954-1 (pa)
LC 90-34876
"Forer explores the origins and manifestations of ingrained legal prejudices, concluding with a call for 'a new concept of equality that acknowledges and protects differences.'" Libr J
Includes bibliographic references

Hunter, Nan
The rights of lesbians and gay men; the basic ACLU guide to a gay person's rights; [by] Nan D. Hunter, Sherryl E. Michaelson, Thomas B. Stoddard. 3rd ed. Southern Ill. Univ. Press 1992 220p (American Civil Liberties Union handbook) pa $7.95
346.01
1. Gay men—Civil rights 2. Gay women—Civil rights
ISBN 0-8093-1634-X   LC 91-40607
First published 1975
This is a "survey of the rights of lesbians and gay men under present law, specifically in regard to freedom of speech and association, employment, housing, the military, family relationships, criminal matters, security clearances, and HIV disease." Publisher's note
Includes bibliography

Kaminer, Wendy
A fearful freedom; women's flight from equality. Addison-Wesley 1990 250p $18.22; pa $9.57   **346.01**
1. Sex discrimination 2. Women—Employment
ISBN 0-201-09234-4; 0-201-57701-1 (pa)
LC 89-28509
The author argues that "protective laws governing work place and home hurt women by advancing debilitating sterotypes of passivity, dependence, and weakness." Libr J

The **Rights** of women; the basic ACLU guide to women's rights; [by] Susan Deller Ross [et al.] 3rd ed, completely rev and up-to-date. Southern Ill. Univ. Press 1993 317p (American Civil Liberties Union handbook) $24.95; pa $7.95   **346.01**
1. Women—Law and legislation 2. Women—Civil rights
ISBN 0-8093-1898-9; 0-8093-1633-1 (pa)
LC 92-34244
First published 1973 by Sunrise Books/Dutton
Topics covered "include employment, education, parenting, family law, and reproductive freedom. This handbook also examines criminal proceedings, insurance, the military, credit, and the rights of homeless women." Publisher's note
Includes bibliographic references

Sitarz, Daniel, 1948-
Divorce yourself; the national no-fault divorce kit. 2nd ed rev & updated. Nova Pub. Co. 1991 331p (Legal self-help ser) $24.95   **346.01**

1. Divorce—Law and legislation
ISBN 0-935755-06-3   LC 91-23431

First published 1990

This volume contains "guidelines on division of property, custody and visitation issues, support questions, and tax information. The bibliography of divorce books for individual states is a wise addition. Forms, sample clauses, questionnaires, and summaries of all 50 states' laws make this book indispensable." Libr J

The **State-by-state** guide to women's legal rights; [by the] NOW Legal Defense and Education Fund and Renée Cherow-O'Leary. McGraw-Hill 1987 523p $19.95; pa $12.95   **346.01**

1. Women—Law and legislation 2. Women—Civil rights
ISBN 0-07-047779-5; 0-07-047778-7 (pa)   LC 86-2972

"A historic overview of women's changing legal status and a state-by-state guide to women's rights in education, family, employment, and the community. Appendices list factors considered by the courts in divorce and custody, and list civil rights offices around the country." N Y Public Libr Book of How & Where to Look It Up

Includes bibliography

346.03   Law of torts (delicts)

Dill, Barbara
The journalist's handbook on libel and privacy. Free Press 1986 262p il $27.95   **346.03**

1. Libel and slander 2. Right of privacy 3. Mass media—Law and legislation
ISBN 0-02-908070-3   LC 86-551

"As a manual for journalists, editors, and others in the media, Dill's guide is without peer, but it is also an intriguing resource for anyone with an interest in how the legal system perceives slander, libel, and rights of privacy." Booklist

Matthews, Joseph L.
How to win your personal injury claim; edited by Barbara Kate Repa. Nolo Press (Berkeley) 1992 various paging il $24.95   **346.03**

1. Liability (Law) 2. Accident insurance
ISBN 0-87337-189-5   LC 92-10996

The author "discusses the principles of liability and offers instruction on the valuation of a claim and negotiating and finalizing a settlement." Libr J

346.04   Property law

Everyone's guide to copyrights, trademarks, and patents; the comprehensive handbook for protecting your writing, inventions, and other creative work. Running Press 1990 176p pa $14.95   **346.04**

1. Copyright 2. Trademarks 3. Patents
ISBN 0-89471-725-9

A "how-to for the intimidating undertakings of copyrighting, trademarking, and patenting creative works. The text is taken from the most recent U.S. Copyright Office and U.S. Patent and Trademark Office materials, including a section on international copyright and the 1989 U.S. Supreme Court definition of 'work made for hire,' which gave free-lancers more protection. An essential tool for writers, graphic designers, musicians, video artists, and inventors, this guide cuts through the legalese that often obscures the basics." Booklist

Fishman, Stephen
The copyright handbook; how to protect and use written works. Nolo Press (Berkeley) 1991 various paging il $24.95   **346.04**

1. Copyright
ISBN 0-87337-130-5   LC 91-29495

The author "concentrates on copyright protection for printed matter (books, articles, scripts, songs, etc.) and offers one of the better 'how to' sections on copyright registration. His handbook reflects current changes in copyright law, fees, and Copyright Office phone numbers." Libr J

Johnston, Donald F.
Copyright handbook. 2nd ed. Bowker 1982 381p $39.95   **346.04**

1. Copyright
ISBN 0-8352-1488-5   LC 82-4218

First published 1978

"Copyright law explained simply. Treated along with other topics are remedies for infringement, how to register, restrictions, and duration. Includes lengthy appendices and index." N Y Public Libr Book of How & Where to Look It Up

Includes bibliography

McGrath, Kate, 1952-
Trademark; how to name a business & product; by Kate McGrath, Stephen Elias, with Sarah Shena. Nolo Press (Berkeley) 1992 various paging il pa $29.95   **346.04**

1. Trademarks
ISBN 0-87337-157-7   LC 92-14968

"Includes all official forms & instructions necessary to register with U.S. Patent & Trademark Office." On cover

"Designed for small businesses, this book shows how to: choose a name competitors can't copy, conduct a trademark search, know your rights if there's a dispute over use of a trademark." Publisher's note

Woodhouse, Violet, 1948-
Divorce and money; everything you need to know about dividing property; by Violet Woodhouse and Victoria Felton-Collins, with M.C. Blakeman; edited by Robin Leonard and Stephen Elias. Nolo Press (Berkeley) 1992 various paging $19.95   **346.04**
1. Divorce—Law and legislation 2. Property—Law and legislation
ISBN 0-87337-143-7   LC 91-31761
A guide to financial problems that arise as a result of divorce proceedings

346.05 Law regarding inheritance, succession, trusts

Clifford, Denis
Nolo's simple will book; how to prepare a legally valid will. 2nd ed. Nolo Press (Berkeley) 1989 various paging il $17.95
346.05
1. Wills
ISBN 0-87337-108-9   LC 92-223999
First published 1986
"The author thoroughly covers the reasons to make a will, the basic legal requirements for validating such a document, and differing state laws. Finally, he walks the reader through the specifics of preparing a will, with necessary discussion of requisite statements and provisions." Booklist

Plotnick, Charles
How to settle an estate; a manual for executors and trustees; [by] Charles K. Plotnick, Stephan R. Leimberg, and the editors of Consumer Reports Books. Consumer Repts. Bks. 1991 324p $18.95
346.05
1. Executors and administrators
ISBN 0-89043-443-3   LC 91-16585
Revised edition of: The executor's manual, published 1986 by Doubleday
"Intended for the nonlawyer, this book covers every facet of handling an estate, including organ donation, probate, insurance, government benefits, and taxes. Detailed checklists provide a step-by-step guide for the executor to follow in settling an estate. The guide also explains when and how to obtain expert legal and financial advice—and how to negotiate fees for these services." Libr J

Sitarz, Daniel, 1948-
Prepare your own will; the national will kit. 3rd ed. Nova Pub. Co. 1991 240p (Legal self-help ser) pa $15.95   **346.05**
1. Wills
ISBN 0-935755-07-1   LC 91-23432
New edition in preparation
First published 1988 with title: Prepare your own last will and testament—without a lawyer
"This is an exceedingly simple treatment that allows the user to work through the questionnaires, clauses, and checklists toward the creation of a valid will. Complex

issues involving trusts and guardianships are successfully presented." Libr J

347 Civil procedure and courts

Bork, Robert H., 1927-
The tempting of America; the political seduction of the law. Free Press 1990 432p $24.95   **347**
1. United States. Supreme Court 2. United States—Constitutional law
ISBN 0-02-903761-1   LC 89-39128
In this book the American jurist discusses Constitutional law and examines the circumstances that led to Senate rejection of his Supreme Court nomination
This "is a lucid, elegant, provocative work of legal scholarship." N Y Times Book Rev
Includes bibliographic references

Bronner, Ethan
Battle for justice; how the Bork nomination shook America. Norton 1989 399p il $22.50   **347**
1. Bork, Robert H., 1927- 2. United States. Supreme Court
ISBN 0-393-02690-6   LC 89-3248
Also available in paperback from Doubleday
"An excellent account of Robert Bork's unsuccessful nomination to the U.S. Supreme Court. . . . Bronner uncovers conflicts in Bork's legal positions and how these disparities led to major controversies in the Senate hearings." Libr J
"Offers a well-crafted and insightful overview of the nomination struggle." Nation
Includes bibliography

Cox, Archibald, 1912-
The Warren Court; Constitutional decision as an instrument of reform. Harvard Univ. Press 1968 144p hardcover o.p. paperback available $5.95   **347**
1. United States. Supreme Court
ISBN 0-674-94742-8 (pa)
Lectures on constitutional developments under the Warren Court originally given in shorter form at a summer school conducted in Honolulu in 1967 by the Harvard Law School in conjunction with the University of Hawaii

Lewis, Anthony, 1927-
Gideon's trumpet. Random House 1964 262p hardcover o.p. paperback available $10
347
1. Gideon, Clarence Earl 2. United States. Supreme Court 3. Law—United States
ISBN 0-679-72312-9 (pa)
An account of the case of a Florida man convicted of burglary which brought about a historic decision of the Supreme Court decreeing that in all states a defendant is entitled to counsel
Includes bibliographic references

O'Brien, David M.
Storm center; the Supreme Court in American politics. 3rd ed. Norton 1993 479p il $24.95; pa $13.95   347

1. United States. Supreme Court
ISBN 0-393-03521-2; 0-393-96356-X (pa)
LC 92-17079

First published 1986

The author discusses "the day-to-day workings of the Court justices and their law clerks, how cases are accepted for hearing, what negotiations and compromises go on, how case opinions get written—and what happens to American society when two conservative presidents, Reagan and Bush, appoint the majority of justices." Publisher's note

Includes bibliographic references

Olson, Walter
The litigation explosion; what happened when America unleashed the lawsuit; [by] Walter K. Olson. Dutton 1991 388p $24.95   347

1. Litigation 2. Legal ethics
ISBN 0-525-24911-7
LC 90-49985

Also available in paperback from New Am. Lib.

"A Truman Talley book"

Olson "examines the 20-year evolution of America's sue-and-be-damned society. . . . [He explains] why the litigation explosion developed, what it means, and who profits and who loses." Libr J

Includes bibliographic references

The **Oxford** companion to the Supreme Court of the United States; editor in chief, Kermit L. Hall; editors, James W. Ely, Jr., Joel B. Grossman, William M. Wiecek. Oxford Univ. Press 1992 xx, 1032p il $49.95   347

1. United States. Supreme Court
ISBN 0-19-505835-6
LC 92-3863

"Entries, arranged alphabetically, cover the internal operations and history of the Court; biographical information on all of the justices plus other relevant historical figures; definitions of basic legal and constitutional terminology; and the process of selecting, nominating, and confirming justices. More than 400 entries examine the Court's most significant decisions. . . . This is a landmark publication." SLJ

For a fuller review see: Booklist, Dec. 1, 1992

Phelps, Timothy M.
Capitol games; Clarence Thomas, Anita Hill, and the story of a Supreme Court nomination; [by] Timothy M. Phelps, Helen Winternitz. Hyperion 1992 458p $24.95   347

1. Thomas, Clarence 2. Hill, Anita 3. United States. Supreme Court 4. Sexual harassment
ISBN 1-56282-916-5
LC 92-9168

Also available in paperback from HarperCollins

The authors present an "overview of the whole Clarence Thomas story, from his rise from poverty in Pinpoint, Ga., through his first year of service on the Supreme Court. Much of the account is based on the authors' own research, some of which is published for

the first time." N Y Times Book Rev

Includes bibliographic references

Race-ing justice, en-gendering power; essays on Anita Hill, Clarence Thomas, and the construction of social reality; edited and with an introduction by Toni Morrison. Pantheon Bks. 1992 xxx, 475p il pa $15   347

1. Thomas, Clarence 2. Hill, Anita 3. United States. Supreme Court 4. Blacks—Social conditions 5. Racism 6. Sexism
ISBN 0-679-74145-3
LC 92-54119

Analyzed in Essay and general literature index

This is a collection of essays by eighteen contributors on issues related to the Senate hearings on Clarence Thomas's nomination to the United States Supreme Court and the testimony of Anita Hill accusing him of sexual harrassment

Includes bibliographic references

Rehnquist, William H.
The Supreme Court: how it was, how it is. Morrow 1987 338p il hardcover o.p. paperback available $13   347

1. United States. Supreme Court 2. Judges
ISBN 0-688-08668-3 (pa)
LC 87-12271

"Rehnquist outlines the particulars of a number of seminal cases and describes the characters and personalities of several of the court's most distinguished and notable members. In addition, he also discusses the influential role the Court plays in the American political process. However, the most interesting discourse involves his insider's view of the everyday minutiae of the institution." Booklist

Includes bibliography

Simon, Paul, 1928-
Advice & consent; Clarence Thomas, Robert Bork, and the intriguing history of the Supreme Court's nomination battles. National Press Bks. 1992 328p $23.95 347

1. United States. Congress. Senate 2. United States. Supreme Court 3. Judges
ISBN 0-915765-98-5
LC 92-16107

"Senator Simon (D.-Ill.), a member of the Senate Judiciary Committee, gives an . . . account of the confirmation process for Supreme Court nominees. He examines recent . . . confirmation hearings, especially for Clarence Thomas and Robert Bork, and earlier confirmation battles beginning with George Washington's administration." Libr J

The author "offers a thoughtful, modest and shrewd appraisal of his and the Senate's performance." N Y Times Book Rev

Includes bibliographic references

Spence, Gerry
With justice for none; destroying an American myth. Times Bks. 1989 370p $19.95   347

1. Justice, Administration of
ISBN 0-8129-1696-4
LC 88-40165

Also available in paperback from Penguin Bks.

Spence, Gerry—*Continued*
The author "takes on the whole legal system—the law schools, the attorneys, the judiciary, and so on—and tells where he believes it is going wrong." Libr J
This "should be read by anyone who cares about justice for all." N Y Times Book Rev

Tribe, Laurence H.
God save this honorable court; how the choice of Supreme Court Justices shapes our history. Random House 1985 171p $17.95
347
1. United States. Supreme Court 2. Judges
ISBN 0-394-54842-6   LC 85-2324
Also available in paperback from New Am. Lib.
The author attempts to "show how the choice of Supreme Court Justices shape our lives and the destiny of the nation. . . . [Tribe argues] for fuller involvement by the Senate, and by the American public, in the process of selection." Publisher's note
Includes bibliographic references

Warner, Ralph E.
Everybody's guide to small claims court; [by] Ralph Warner; edited by Annie Tillery and Cora Jordan; illustrated by Linda Allison. natl 5th ed. Nolo Press (Berkeley) 1991 various paging il $15.95   **347**
1. Small claims court
ISBN 0-87337-161-5   LC 91-31345
First published 1980 by Addison-Wesley
The author "discusses filing court papers, paying fees, and using witnesses and examines typical kinds of small claims. The appendixes detail procedures, list monetary thresholds, and reference statutory citations." Libr J

Wilber, Wanda K.
Small claims court without a lawyer; [by] W. Kelsea Wilber. Sourcebooks Trade 1992 218p pa $18.95   **347**
1. Small claims court 2. Debtor and creditor
ISBN 0-942061-32-2   LC 91-28539
"Small businesses and landlords seeking to enforce contract or lease payments or performance as well as consumers seeking contract performance or compensation for nonperformance from service firms will appreciate Wilbur's clear, step-by-step explanation of small-claims court procedures and requirements, as well as her outline of small-claims court specifics by state, samples of collection and contract enforcement letters and legal forms, address list of state bar associations, and glossary of relevant terms." Booklist

Wishman, Seymour
Anatomy of a jury; the system on trial. Times Bks. 1986 322p o.p.; Penguin Bks. paperback available $9.95   **347**
1. Jury
ISBN 0-14-009851-8 (pa)   LC 85-40845
The "author dramatizes a composite murder trial, based primarily on one actual case, and uses it to illustrate his fundamental concerns about the American jury system." Booklist

"Deftly lacing information and statistics about the history, psychology and sociology of the jury into an often compelling narrative . . . the author manages to keep an interesting subject interesting." N Y Times Book Rev
Includes bibliographic references

Woodward, Bob, 1943-
The brethren: inside the Supreme Court; [by] Bob Woodward & Scott Armstrong. Simon & Schuster 1979 467p il o.p.; Avon Bks. paperback available $5.95   **347**
1. United States. Supreme Court
ISBN 0-380-52183-0 (pa)   LC 79-19955
This book examines the workings of the Supreme Court and the personalities of its members in the period 1969-1976. The information, the authors "claim, is based on interviews with more than 200 people, including several justices, more than 170 former law clerks, and several dozen former employees of the Court." N Y Times Book Rev

Yant, Martin, 1949-
Presumed guilty; when innocent people are wrongly convicted. Prometheus Bks. 1991 231p il $23.95   **347**
1. Justice, Administration of 2. Trials
ISBN 0-87975-643-8   LC 90-26301
The author discusses the wrongful convictions of innocent people by American courts, citing case histories
Includes bibliographic references

349 Law of specific jurisdictions

Johnson, John W., 1946-
Historic U.S. court cases, 1690-1990; an encyclopedia. Garland 1992 xxix, 754p (Garland reference lib. of social science) $125   **349**
1. Law—United States
ISBN 0-8240-4430-4   LC 91-40175
The cases in this compendium "run the gamut of legal categories, including criminal law, governmental power, civil liberties, trade and commerce, labor, due process, and discrimination. The editor wisely selects multiple cases on the same topic, often with differing viewpoints on legal issues and social implications. . . . Each case review is concise, well-written, easily understood, and straightforward." Libr J
For a fuller review see: Booklist, June 1, 1992

351.3 Civil service examinations

Bobrow, Jerry
How to prepare for the civil service examinations for stenographer, typist, clerk, and office machine operator; by Jerry Bobrow, in collaboration with Peter Z. Orton, William Covino. Barron's Educ. Ser. pa $11.95   **351.3**
1. Civil service—Examinations

Bobrow, Jerry—*Continued*

First published 1967 under the authorship of Edwin Riemer and Louis Liebling with title: Barron's how to prepare for civil service examinations. (3rd edition 1994) Periodically revised

Provides both instruction and practice tests for a variety of civil service jobs

Civil service arithmetic and vocabulary. Prentice Hall General Ref. pa $12 **351.3**

1. Civil service—Examinations

First published 1951 by Arco. (11th edition 1993) Periodically revised

Contains basic instructions for working every type of math problem found on the exams. The vocabulary section includes a review of vocabulary words, verbal analogies, and sentence completion problems

351.6   Civil service system

Civil service handbook. Prentice Hall General Ref. pa $10   **351.6**

1. Civil service—United States 2. Civil service—Examinations

First published 1948 by Arco. (10th edition 1992) Periodically revised

Information on the Civil Service employment set-up tells how to apply for a job and how to get the best job available. Includes sample examination questions given on typical federal tests

Complete guide to U.S. civil service jobs. Prentice Hall General Ref. pa $10 **351.6**

1. Civil service—United States

First published 1957 by Arco. (10th edition 1991) Periodically revised

Information for those who have, and those who want to obtain a government job in the Federal Civil Service System. Includes material on the types of positions available, applications, requirements, working conditions, unions, retirement, and veteran's preference

351.9   Malfunctioning of administration

Garment, Suzanne

Scandal; the culture of mistrust in American politics. Times Bks. 1991 335p $23   **351.9**

1. Corruption in politics 2. Political ethics 3. United States—Politics and government

ISBN 0-8129-1942-4   LC 91-50185

Also available in paperback from Anchor Bks.

"The past 15 years, according to Garment, have seen unprecedented numbers of scandals erupt in national politics. . . . [In her view] the mistrust of politics and government that began during the Vietnam era and reached full bloom in Watergate has become pervasive." Christ Sci Monit

The author "clearly makes the case for a fresh look at the way the United States upholds standards of conduct in the federal government." Commentary

Includes bibliographic references

Glazer, Myron

The whistleblowers; exposing corruption in government and industry; [by] Myron Peretz Glazer & Penina Migdal Glazer. Basic Bks. 1989 286p $19.95; pa $9.95   **351.9**

1. Whistle blowing 2. Corruption in politics 3. Corporations

ISBN 0-465-09173-3; 0-465-09174-1 (pa)

LC 88-47896

The authors "document remarkable examples of persons who have risked careers, reputations, marriages, and even lives to expose corruption in industry and government. Some 15 detailed cases vividly illustrate the battle to make ethical resistance legitimate, the campaign of retaliation sometimes waged by management, and the unfortunate price whistle-blowers can be forced to pay." Booklist

352   Administration of local governments

The **Municipal** year book. International City Mgt. Assn. $77.50   **352**

1. Municipal government—United States—Periodicals

ISSN 0077-2186

Annual. First published 1934

"Very complete statistical data on individual cities and counties, combined with articles on contemporary urban management trends and issues. Includes directory of city officials and bibliography for major areas of local government administration." Ref Sources for Small & Medium-sized Libr. 5th edition

353   Administration of United States federal and state governments

Burnham, David, 1933-

A law unto itself; power, politics, and the IRS. Random House 1990 419p $22.50; pa $12.95   **353**

1. United States. Internal Revenue Service 2. Taxation—United States

ISBN 0-394-56097-3; 0-679-73283-7 (pa)

LC 89-42778

The author "describes the history of taxes, the rise of the Internal Revenue Service (IRS), and the process by which taxes are assessed and collected within the United States' voluntary compliance system. . . . He outlines the IRS's alarmingly expansive institutional powers, most notably its vast computer files, which threaten the privacy of every individual." Libr J

Includes bibliography

Chelekis, George C.

The official government auction guide; foreword by Sonny Bloch. Crown 1992 494p il pa $25   **353**

1. Surplus government property 2. Auctions

ISBN 0-517-58938-9   LC 91-42573

This guide to buying property at bargain prices at government auctions describes types of auctions, bidding strategies, specific government agencies and their auction procedures and includes a directory of certified auctioneers

Osborne, David

Reinventing government; how the entrepreneurial spirit is transforming the public sector; [by] David Osborne and Ted Gaebler. Addison-Wesley 1992 xxii, 405p $22.95 **353**

1. Public administration 2. Bureaucracy 3. United States—Politics and government
ISBN 0-201-52394-9 LC 91-31307
Also available in paperback from New Am. Lib.
"A William Patrick book"

This book "examines state and local governments, plus a few federal bureaucracies, to find out what constitutes governmental success and to see how the lessons of success could be applied where governments now fail." Atlantic

This book "offers both a vision and a road map, and it will intrigue and enlighten anyone interested in government." N Y Times Book Rev

Includes bibliographic references

Rehnquist, William H.

Grand inquests; the historic impeachments of Justice Samuel Chase and President Andrew Johnson. Morrow 1992 303p il $23 **353**

1. Chase, Samuel 2. Johnson, Andrew, 1808-1875 3. Impeachments
ISBN 0-688-05142-1 LC 91-31681

An "account of two of the most significant trials and 'cases' in American legal and political history: the 1804 impeachment of Justice Samuel Chase and the 1868 impeachment of President Andrew Johnson." Libr J

This is an "informative and readable account of two pivotal trials that imparted safety and responsibility to that most draconian and potentially destructive feature of the Constitution's system of checks and balances, the impeachment process." N Y Times Book Rev

Includes bibliographic references

Smith, James Allen, 1948-

The idea brokers; think tanks and the rise of the new policy elite. Free Press 1991 xxi, 313p $27.95 **353**

1. Group problem solving 2. Political science
ISBN 0-02-929551-3 LC 90-39735

The author "argues cogently that think tanks such as the Brookings Institution, the Urban Institute, and the Heritage Foundation are becoming a new political elite. Through extensive interviewing and primary source research, he provides information on the emergence and impact of these private, nonprofit research organizations." Libr J

Includes bibliography

United States government manual; Office of the Federal Register, National Archives and Records Service, General Services Administration. Superintendent of Docs. pa $23 **353**

1. United States—Politics and government—Handbooks, manuals, etc.
Annual. First published 1935. Variant title: United States government organization manual

"Official handbook of the Federal government describing the purposes and programs of most Government agencies and listing the top personnel." N Y Public Libr. Ref Books for Child Collect. 2d edition

Wilson, James Q.

Bureaucracy; what government agencies do and why they do it. Basic Bks. 1989 433p $26.95; pa $14 **353**

1. United States—Executive departments 2. Bureaucracy
ISBN 0-465-00784-8; 0-465-00785-6 (pa)
LC 89-42527

The author "attempts to explain bureaucratic behavior, beginning with a contrast of similar institutions (armies, prisons, and schools) that have succeeded and failed. He finds that neither the liberal view (more money, new programs) or the conservative ideology (smaller government) provide the single answer." Libr J

Includes bibliographic references

353.03 President and vice-president

Congressional Quarterly's guide to the presidency; Michael Nelson, editor. Congressional Quarterly 1989 xx, 1521p $179.95 **353.03**

1. Presidents—United States
ISBN 0-87187-500-4 LC 89-7184

"This tome provides an in-depth survey of the history, politics, and people who have held and assisted the office of president of the United States. In well-organized, readable sections, the origins and development, selection and removal, the powers and structure of the executive branch are presented as well as biographies of presidents and vice-presidents. . . . Where possible, George Bush is included; otherwise the book is current through Ronald Reagan." SLJ

The **Presidency** A to Z; a ready reference encyclopedia; Michael Nelson, advisory editor. Congressional Quarterly 1992 574p il (CQ's encyclopedia of American government) $85 **353.03**

1. Presidents—United States—Dictionaries
ISBN 0-87187-667-1 LC 92-20360

"Approximately 300 entries describe the background of the presidents, their public experiences, daily and family life, powers and life in the White House, and deaths. Extensive essays explore concepts relating to the presidency such as Constitutional powers, the budget process, diplomatic activity, the cabinet, and the relationship of the presidency to Congress and the courts." Libr J

For a fuller review see: Booklist, March 15, 1993

Schlesinger, Arthur M., 1917-

The imperial presidency; Arthur M. Schlesinger, Jr.; with a new epilogue by the author. Houghton Mifflin 1989 588p pa $12.70 **353.03**

1. Executive power 2. Presidents—United States
ISBN 0-395-51561-0 LC 89-35462
This is a reissue of the title first published 1973

Schlesinger, Arthur M., 1917——*Continued*

Covering all the presidents from Washington through Nixon, the author "traces the growth of power in the United States presidency and shows how this power has expanded with each involvement in war." Chicago Public Libr

Includes bibliographic references

Speeches of the American presidents; edited by Janet Podell, Steven Anzovin. Wilson, H.W. 1988 xxv, 820p il $63   **353.03**

1. Presidents—United States—Messages 2. Speeches, addresses, etc. 3. United States—History—Sources

ISBN 0-8242-0761-0   LC 87-29833

This volume "contains 180 speeches of the 40 Presidents, from Washington through Reagan. . . . Most speeches are included in their entirety, while some of the longer ones are excerpted. Each speech is prefaced by date, place, and historical context." SLJ

Witcover, Jules

Crapshoot: rolling the dice on the vice-presidency; from Adams to Jefferson to Truman and Quayle. Crown 1992 450p $25   **353.03**

1. Vice-presidents—United States

ISBN 0-517-58480-8   LC 91-38980

The author discusses the history of the Vice-Presidency of the United States. "Eight Presidents have died in office, and another resigned. That fact, along with the current widespread assumption that the Vice President is the natural heir to the top job, should, Mr. Witcover argues, dissuade us from accepting a person picked primarily to help win the general election or to satisfy the whim of a party's standard-bearer." N Y Times Book Rev

"Most of the book is an astute, scathingly ironic history of vice-presidential politics—generally colorful, if at times inevitably tinged with the dullness that clings to that office." Publ Wkly

Includes bibliographic references

353.09   Special agencies and commissions

From the secret files of J. Edgar Hoover; edited with commentary by Athan Theoharis. Dee, I.R. 1991 370p $24.95; pa $12.95   **353.09**

1. Hoover, J. Edgar (John Edgar), 1895-1972 2. United States. Federal Bureau of Investigation 3. Internal security—United States 4. Anticommunist movements 5. Subversive activities

ISBN 0-929587-67-7; 1-56663-017-7 (pa) LC 91-3478

After a history of the Federal Bureau of Investigation, the first section of the book "presents selected files examining the alleged and real sexual indiscretions of JFK, Robert Kennedy, Eleanor Roosevelt, and Martin Luther King Jr. . . . Subsequent chapters examine the FBI's 'investigative' techniques, its relationship with Presidents and the McCarthy committee, and the uses of public relations and the role of the director." Libr J

353.9   State governments

The **Book** of the states. Council of State Govts. $79   **353.9**

1. State governments

Biennial. Began publication 1935

"In addition to general articles on various aspects of state government, this source provides many statistical and directory data, the principal state officials, and such information as the nickname, motto, flower, bird, song, and tree of each state." Ref Sources for Small & Medium-sized Libr. 5th edition

355   Military science

Atkinson, Rick

The long gray line. Houghton Mifflin 1989 592p il $24.45   **355**

1. United States Military Academy. Class of 1966 2. United States. Army 3. Soldiers—United States

ISBN 0-395-48008-6   LC 89-34223

Also available in paperback from Pocket Bks.

This book "chronicles the fortunes of West Point's class of 1966, who entered the academy in 1962 during the golden age of the Kennedy administration. . . . Most of them served in Vietnam; a great many of them died there; and, upon their return home, many more eventually resigned their commissions, disillusioned by the war, the army, a nation rended by social upheaval, and a growing hatred for all things military." Booklist

"The book is a poignant, thought-provoking account of the struggles of young men who pledged themselves to 'Honor, Duty, Country.'" Publ Wkly

Includes bibliography

Clausewitz, Carl von, 1780-1831

On war; [by] Carl von Clausewitz; edited and translated by Michael Howard and Peter Paret; introductory essays by Peter Paret, Michael Howard and Bernard Brodie; with commentary by Bernard Brodie. Princeton Univ. Press 1976 717p $49.50   **355**

1. Military art and science 2. War

ISBN 0-691-05657-9

Original German edition, 1833

"Drawing on the experiences of Frederick the Great and Napoleon, Clausewitz tried to analyze the workings of military genius by isolating the factors that decide success in war. His conclusions have remained generally applicable, and since his work contains a minimum of technical discussion, it has retained a wide appeal." Ency Britannica

Dupuy, R. Ernest (Richard Ernest), 1887-1975

The Harper encyclopedia of military history; from 3500 BC to the present; [by] R. Ernest Dupuy and Trevor N. Dupuy. 4th ed. HarperCollins Pubs. 1993 xxi, 1654p il maps $65   **355**

1. Military history—Dictionaries

ISBN 0-06-270056-1   LC 92-17853

Dupuy, R. Ernest (Richard Ernest), 1887-1975—*Continued*

First published 1970 with title: The encyclopedia of military history

This volume covers battles, leaders, tactics, and weapons from ancient times through the Persian Gulf War. It is arranged chronologically and has over 170 maps and illustrations

For a review see: Booklist, Nov. 1, 1993

Hersh, Seymour M.

The Samson option; Israel's nuclear arsenal and American foreign policy. Random House 1991 354p $23; pa $12

355

1. Israel—Military policy 2. Israel—Foreign relations—United States 3. United States—Foreign relations—Israel 4. Nuclear weapons

ISBN 0-394-57006-5; 0-679-74331-6 (pa)

LC 91-52678

This is an account of Israel's nuclear weapons program and its influence on diplomatic relations between Israel and the United States

Hersh "manages in a readable and fascinating account to convey a keen sense of the dynamic propelling Israel's nuclear program. . . . He provides compelling portraits of key figures in the drama." N Y Times Book Rev

Nalty, Bernard C.

Strength for the fight; a history of black Americans in the military. Free Press 1986 424p il $29.95; pa $14.95

355

1. Black soldiers 2. United States—Armed forces

ISBN 0-02-922410-1; 0-02-922411-X (pa)   LC 86-536

This work examines the history of black soldiers in the United States from colonial times through the 1980s

The author's "readable narrative is humanized by frequent individual vignettes and highlights of salient events. . . . Nalty's is a superb contribution to military history—and much more. This is, properly, social and political history as well." J Am Hist

Includes bibliography

Schell, Jonathan, 1943-

The fate of the earth. Knopf 1982 244p $19.95

355

1. Nuclear warfare

ISBN 0-394-52559-0   LC 81-48610

Also available in paperback from Avon Bks.

This book considers "the perils of a possible nuclear holocaust and global annihilation. First, [Schell] analyzes the technical and strategic aspects of nuclear arms and speculates on several scenarios. . . . Then he explores the human, philosophical, and behavioral consequences for all generations—past, present, and future. He concludes with . . . [a discussion] of deterrence doctrine and its grim companion, retaliatory strike. A brillant and chilling book." Libr J

Timmerman, Kenneth R.

The death lobby; how the West armed Iraq. Houghton Mifflin 1991 443p $21.95

355

1. Hussein, Ṣaddām 2. Iraq—Military policy 3. Iraq—Foreign relations 4. Munitions

ISBN 0-395-59305-0   LC 91-28557

The author examines "Iraq's strategies to procure conventional, chemical, and nuclear weapons from the West over the past two decades. . . . [He argues that] the West chose to ignore Iraq's military ambitions." Choice

"The power of 'The Death Lobby' lies not in the detail—of which there is a surfeit, some of it dubious—but in the overall portrayal of Western greed, cupidity and stupidity in arming Saddam Hussein's Iraq." N Y Times Book Rev

355.2   Military resources

Practice for Army placement tests. Prentice Hall General Ref. $8.95   355.2

1. United States. Army—Examinations

First published 1975 by Arco with title: Practice for Army classification battery. (4th edition 1989) Periodically revised

Exam questions and answers focus on material concerning the U.S. Army placement test

Practice for the Armed Forces tests. Prentice Hall General Ref. il pa $10.95   355.2

1. United States—Armed forces—Examinations

First published 1942 by Arco with title: Practice for the Army tests. (13th edition 1988) Periodically revised

Covers material on the general test given to candidates of all military branches; study guidelines; and discussion of career opportunities for military and civilian occupations

355.3   Organization and personnel of military forces

Holm, Jeanne, 1921-

Women in the military; an unfinished revolution. rev ed. Presidio Press 1992 544p il $27.50   355.3

1. Women in the armed forces 2. United States—Armed forces

ISBN 0-89141-450-9   LC 92-17981

First published 1982

This history of American military women covers the role of women in World War II, the Korean, Vietnam, and Persian Gulf wars, the changing role of military women in the 1980s, the draft, and combat exclusion policies

Includes bibliography

355.6   Military administration

Weiner, Tim
Blank check; the Pentagon's black budget.
Warner Bks. 1990 273p $21.95; pa $11.99
355.6

1. United States. Dept. of Defense 2. United States—Military policy 3. United States—Appropriations and expenditures
ISBN 0-446-51452-7; 0-446-39275-8 (pa)
LC 90-50291

The author "argues that the portion of the defense budget that is exempt from the normal public hearings is a secret cache of funds free from control and accountability. According to Mr. Weiner, this hidden defense treasury . . . is used to finance secret wars, to back international espionage activities and to support the development of specialized nuclear weapons." N Y Times Book Rev

Includes bibliographic references

355.8   Military equipment and supplies

Bull, Stephen
An historical guide to arms and armor; edited by Tony North. Facts on File 1991 224p il $35
355.8

1. Arms and armor
ISBN 0-8160-2620-3
LC 91-36681

The author "has compiled an evolutionary history of small arms (swords, knives, pistols, and rifles) and armor (helmets and body armor) beginning with the Graeco-Roman world and ending with the advent of World War I. The history is supported with over 300 photographs, mostly from works of art and individual pieces in European art museums." Libr J

For a fuller review see: Booklist, Dec. 1, 1991

358   Air and other specialized forces and warfare

Burrows, William E.
Deep black; space espionage and national security. Random House 1986 xxi, 401p il $22.50
358

1. Space warfare 2. United States—National security
ISBN 0-394-54124-3
LC 86-10220

Also available in paperback from Berkley Pub. Group

The author offers an "account of 'black' (satellite-derived) intelligence from the 1960s to the present. He covers the technical aspects of both electronic and photographic intelligence as well as the political infighting for control of satellites and the data they gather." Booklist

"In addition to being fascinating to read, Burrows's book asks some hard questions about how much leaders, policymakers, and citizens can trust each other and other nations." Christ Sci Monit

Includes bibliography

358.4   Air forces and warfare

Gann, Ernest Kellogg, 1910-1991
The black watch: the men who fly America's secret spy planes; by Ernest K. Gann. Random House 1989 210p $18.95
358.4

1. United States. Air Force 2. Aerial reconnaissance 3. Airplanes, Military 4. Aeronautics, Military
ISBN 0-394-57507-5
LC 89-3919

The author "looks at the 99th Squadron of the U.S. Air Force, responsible for flying the U-2 and SR-71 high-altitude reconnaissance planes. After describing the surprisingly fragile crafts, he concentrates on the men who fly them, dedicated, highly skilled and supremely confident; he sketches several . . . portraits, especially of the higher-ranking officers." Publ Wkly

"The result is informative and entertaining—nonfiction that reads like a novel." Libr J

359   Sea (Naval) forces and warfare

Beach, Edward Latimer, 1918-
The United States Navy; 200 years; [by] Edward L. Beach. Holt & Co. 1986 264p il o.p.; Houghton Mifflin paperback available $12.70
359

1. United States. Navy 2. United States—History, Naval
ISBN 0-395-55996-0 (pa)
LC 85-8617

The author "covers the story of the U.S. Navy in its formative years, including the War of 1812, the Civil War, and the Spanish-American War, and also relates many peacetime episodes and post-World War II events. . . . Full of insight, wit, and compassion, Beach makes his highly readable book less of a straightforward chronology and more of a sailor's tribute." Booklist

Includes bibliography

Howarth, Stephen, 1953-
To shining sea; a history of the United States Navy, 1775-1991. Random House 1991 620p il maps $25
359

1. United States. Navy 2. United States—History, Naval
ISBN 0-394-57662-4
LC 90-52889

"This history covers the military, political and technological evolution of the U.S. Navy from the days of sail to the nuclear era." Publ Wkly

Includes bibliographic references

Love, Robert William, 1944-
History of the U.S. Navy; [by] Robert W. Love, Jr. Stackpole Bks. 1992 2v ea $39.95
359

1. United States. Navy 2. United States—History, Naval
ISBN 0-8117-1862-X (v1); 0-8117-1863-8 (v2)
LC 91-27510

Contents: v1 1775-1941; v2 1942-1991

"This pragmatic chronicle pays as much attention to the government context out of which naval policy proceeded as to campaigns at sea. The Navy's main

Love, Robert William, 1944-—*Continued*
business, in Love's view, has always been to serve as a handmaid to diplomacy and at the same time as the clenched fist of foreign policy. . . . A comprehensive, thoroughly researched review." Publ Wkly

Includes bibliographic references

359.4 Naval operations

Hoyt, Edwin Palmer
Submarines at war; the history of the American silent service; [by] Edwin P. Hoyt. Madison Bks. 1983 329p il $18.95   **359.4**
1. Submarines 2. United States—History, Naval
ISBN 0-8128-2833-X   LC 81-40808
Also available in paperback from Jove Publs.

First published by Stein & Day

An "account of American undersea warfare from the Revolution to the nuclear-powered navy. Much of the work naturally focuses on World War II, but there is an excellent and hard-to-find account of American submarine activities during World War I. This is a useful introduction to the subject for the lay reader." Libr J

Includes bibliography

359.9 Specialized combat forces

Cohen, Barney
The proud; inside the Marine Corps; [by] Bernard Halsband Cohen. Morrow 1992 282p il $22   **359.9**
1. United States. Marine Corps
ISBN 0-688-11737-6   LC 92-1299
This portrait of the U.S. Marine Corps "covers both basic and advanced training, amphibious operations, sea duty, both fixed-wing and helicopter aviation, and the viewpoint of marines' families. . . . [This] is an admirably clear presentation of how marines see themselves and why they see being a marine as something unique and wonderful." Booklist

361 General social problems and welfare

Encyclopedia of social work. National Assn. of Social Workers 3v $90   **361**
1. Social work—Dictionaries
ISSN 0071-0237
First published 1929. (18th edition 1987) Updated between editions by supplementary volume

"Theoretical and practical approach to societal problems, including family and housing, for social workers and social-science students and practitioners." N Y Public Libr Book of How & Where to Look It Up

361.2 Social action

Hollender, Jeffrey
How to make the world a better place; a guide to doing good. Morrow 1990 303p il $22.95; pa $9.95   **361.2**
1. Social action 2. Social problems 3. Human ecology 4. Consumer education
ISBN 0-688-09577-1; 0-688-08479-6 (pa)
    LC 89-13132
"Protecting the environment; food, hunger, and agriculture; responsible banking and investing; responsible consumerism; and peace, nonviolence and human rights are the topics contained in this activists' manual. From the hows and whys of recycling, to whom to boycott and whom to support, Hollender offers specific responses to 120 problems in the aforementioned areas. . . . Informative, current, biased, easily read through or just consulted, occasionally outrageous, this work's greatest value lies in the breadth of issues treated." Libr J

361.6 Governmental welfare action

Buckley, William F. (William Frank), 1925-
Gratitude; reflections on what we owe to our country. Random House 1990 xxi, 169p $16.95   **361.6**
1. United States—Social policy 2. Voluntarism
ISBN 0-394-57674-8   LC 90-53126
The author discusses "whether the young should be encouraged or even compelled to give a year of 'national service' to help the nation cope with its social problems." Libr J

Ellwood, David T.
Poor support; poverty in the American family. Basic Bks. 1988 271p il $19.95; pa $12   **361.6**
1. United States—Social policy 2. Economic assistance, Domestic 3. Public welfare 4. Poor—United States
ISBN 0-465-05996-1; 0-465-05995-3 (pa)
    LC 87-47779
The author "analyzes the causes of poverty for three different kinds of families: the working poor, the single-parent family and the ghetto poor. . . . Mr. Ellwood's signal achievement is that by addressing the causes of their poverty, he is able to design solutions that may hold some promise of helping each group work itself out of poverty, and, in the process, solve the whole welfare mess." N Y Times Book Rev

Includes bibliography

Glazer, Nathan
The limits of social policy. Harvard Univ. Press 1988 215p $25; pa $10.95   **361.6**
1. Public welfare 2. United States—Social policy
ISBN 0-674-53443-3; 0-674-53444-1 (pa) LC 88-4029
This is a "collection of Glazer's articles and speeches from the 1970s and 1980s. . . . He argues that social scientists' efforts to design governmental programs that deal effectively with social problems have failed because the deleterious effect of such programs on traditional structures, such as the family, were ignored." Choice

Includes bibliography

Making a difference; the Peace Corps at twenty-five; edited by Milton Viorst; with a foreword by Ronald Reagan. Weidenfeld & Nicolson 1986 218p $16.95   **361.6**

1. Peace Corps (U.S.)
ISBN 1-55584-010-8   LC 86-9055

This "book is a compilation of essays and excerpts by individuals who were involved in the formative years of the Peace Corps." Libr J

"A thoughtful, idealistic anthology." Booklist

361.7 Private welfare action. Fund raising

Charitable organizations of the U.S. a descriptive and financial information guide; Doris Morris Maxfield, editor; Joseph M. Palmisano, associate editor; Karen Hill, contributing editor. 2nd ed. Gale Res. 1992 xxiv, 565p $139.50   **361.7**

1. Charities—Directories
ISBN 0-8103-8081-1
First published 1990

This "book is designed to help individuals become informed donors. . . . After an introduction on how to evaluate a charity, nearly 800 national charities . . . are listed alphabetically. . . . Areas represented include health, religion, education, the environment, veterans' affairs, children's welfare, and other social issues. The profiles . . . include contact information, history, activities, board members and administrators, fund-raising events, and recent financial figures." Booklist

Flanagan, Joan

The grass roots fundraising book; how to raise money in your community; by Joan Flanagan for The Youth Project. Swallow Press 1977 219p o.p.; Contemporary Bks. paperback available $14.95   **361.7**

1. Fund raising
ISBN 0-8092-5746-7 (pa)   LC 77-79610

"Emphasis is on financial solvency, and the roles of salesmanship, publicity, and record keeping are seen as vital elements in success. Flanagan introduces a wealth of techniques, from simple book and bake sales through complex TV marathons and tennis tournaments. Explicit how-tos, a list of training schools, and a bibliography are appended." Booklist

Gershen, Howard

A guide for giving; 250 charities and how they use your money. Pantheon Bks. 1990 341p il pa $14.95   **361.7**

1. Charities
ISBN 0-679-73275-6   LC 90-52562

"250 charities are briefly decribed from the Account for POW/MIAs to Zero Population Growth. Among the data provided for each group are: purpose, income, overhead, fund-raising expenses, program costs, ratings, registrations, and little-known facts." Booklist

Includes bibliographic references

The **Nonprofit** organization handbook; Tracy Daniel Connors, editor in chief. 2nd ed. McGraw-Hill 1988 various paging $84.95   **361.7**

1. Charities—Handbooks, manuals, etc. 2. Corporations—Handbooks, manuals, etc.
ISBN 0-07-012432-9   LC 87-26276
First published 1980

This handbook provides practical guidelines on several aspects of the successful management and operation of nonprofit public service organizations. Topics covered include organization and corporate principles, leadership, sources of revenue, public relations, and financial management

362.1 Physical illness. Medical care

The **AIDS** caregiver's handbook; edited by Ted Eidson. rev ed. St. Martin's Press 1993 xx, 364p $25.95; pa $14.95   **362.1**

1. AIDS (Disease)
ISBN 0-312-08497-8; 0-312-08129-4 (pa)
    LC 92-49770
First published 1988

This guide offers information and advice to those who care for AIDS patients including nutritional and psychological aspects of treatment, home care, dealing with caregiver's stress, and financial and practical problems

Includes bibliographic references

The **AIDS** reader; social, political, ethical issues; edited by Nancy F. McKenzie. New Am. Lib. 1991 597p $15   **362.1**

1. AIDS (Disease)
ISBN 0-452-01072-1   LC 90-20125

"Starting with a discussion of the medical facts, the 32 previously published articles by leading researchers, scientists, and social commentators focus on the problems of risk populations, the issues of prevention and testing, and the role of the community in responding to the crisis." Libr J

Includes bibliographic references

AIDS: the women; edited by Ines Rieder and Patricia Ruppelt. Cleis Press 1988 251p $24.95; pa $9.95   **362.1**

1. AIDS (Disease)
ISBN 0-939416-20-4; 0-939416-21-2 (pa)
    LC 88-28561

"This book includes essays by spouses, parents, siblings, and lovers of AIDS victims; women with AIDS, ARC, or HIV-positive blood; doctors, nurses, and counselors; lesbians; prostitutes; and AIDS educators, attorneys, and activists." Libr J

These essays "unfailingly relate the personal to the political and social efforts necessary to effectively stanch the epidemic." Booklist

Includes bibliography

Arno, Peter S., 1954-
Against the odds; the story of AIDS drug development, politics, and profits; [by] Peter S. Arno and Karyn L. Feiden. HarperCollins Pubs. 1992 314p $23; pa $12   **362.1**
1. AIDS (Disease)
ISBN 0-06-018309-8; 0-06-092359-8 (pa)
LC 90-55947
"The book details how the travails of AIDS therapies have caused the emergence of parallel-track testing and community-based clinical trials, redefined placebo standards and private-use pharmaceutical importation, and recast the Orphan Drug Act and medical journal publication embargos." Publ Wkly
Includes bibliographic references

Arnot, Robert Burns
The best medicine; how to choose the top doctors, the top hospitals, and the top treatments; [by] Robert Arnot. Addison-Wesley 1992 468p $22.07; pa $14.38   **362.1**
1. Medicine 2. Consumer education
ISBN 0-201-57792-5; 0-201-62478-8 (pa)
LC 92-17849
The author "proffers two consumers' guides, one to operations and procedures, the other to chronic diseases. In each chaper of these guides, he outlines steps to follow to obtain the best possible care for the particular procedure or complaint. Procedures covered include those for the heart, obstetrics and gynecology, the abdomen, orthopedics, the brain, the eyes, and burns. Chronic diseases discussed are AIDS, arthritis, asthma, cancer, coronary artery disease, depression, diabetes, epilepsy, high blood pressure, osteoporosis, and peptic ulcer disease." Booklist
Includes bibliographic references

Bartlett, John G.
The guide to living with HIV infection; developed at the Johns Hopkins AIDS Clinic; [by] John G. Bartlett and Ann K. Finkbeiner. Johns Hopkins Univ. Press 1991 337p $38.95; pa $15.95   **362.1**
1. AIDS (Disease)
ISBN 0-8018-4193-3; 0-8018-4194-1 (pa)
LC 90-15643
This guide offers advice "on such topics as what to do when diagnosed, how to prevent transmission, and how to maintain positive attitudes. The glossary is especially helpful in understanding HIV/ARC/AIDS terminology." Libr J

Bayer, Ronald
Private acts, social consequences; AIDS and the politics of public health. Free Press 1989 282p $29.95   **362.1**
1. AIDS (Disease)
ISBN 0-02-901961-3
LC 88-21221
Also available in paperback from Rutgers Univ. Press
The author "reviews the record of public agencies in dealing with AIDS-created biological, social and political problems, including resolution of conflicts between privacy and the public good. . . . A valuable fact-finding study that should interest a lay as well as professional

audience." Publ Wkly
Includes bibliography

Beasley, Joseph D.
The betrayal of health; the impact of nutrition, environment, and lifestyle on illness in America. Times Bks. 1991 274p $22.50   **362.1**
1. Social medicine 2. Medical care 3. United States—Social conditions
ISBN 0-8129-1897-5
LC 90-71448
The author contends "that poor diet, substance abuse, and pollution are major contributors to chronic disease; hence, break-throughs in medical technology or pharmacology are less important for the future of public health than major lifestyle changes on the part of individuals and society. Beasley thinks that public policy needs to be altered to reflect this perspective." Libr J

Berger, Stuart
What your doctor didn't learn in medical school—and what you can do about it. Morrow 1988 336p il o.p.; Avon Bks. paperback available $4.95   **362.1**
1. Medicine, Popular 2. Nutrition 3. Diseases
ISBN 0-380-70319-X (pa)
LC 87-36562
The author "explains what is wrong with certain aspects of the modern medical system. . . . Practical tips are offered on how to go about obtaining quality health care." Booklist

Bogdanich, Walt
The great white lie; how America's hospitals betray our trust and endanger our lives. Simon & Schuster 1991 320p $23; pa $11   **362.1**
1. Hospitals
ISBN 0-671-68452-3; 0-671-79290-3 (pa)
LC 91-28389
The author "names names, cites hospitals and makes it shockingly clear that the staggering cost of health care, the growing number of uninsured and indigent patients, the scourge of AIDS and crack abuse, and Government determination to reduce hospital costs have coalesced into a disastrous economic crunch—one that has turned hospitals from compassionate social service institutions into a careless, profit-motivated industry." N Y Times Book Rev
"This is a searing indictment of our most important health-care institution." Libr J
Includes bibliographic references

Brown, Marie Annette
Caring for a loved one with AIDS; the experiences of families, lovers, and friends; [by] Marie Annette Brown, Gail M. Powell-Cope. University of Wash. Press 1992 64p il pa $4.95   **362.1**
1. AIDS (Disease)
ISBN 0-295-97183-5
LC 92-2695
"Published for the University of Washington School of Nursing." Title page

Brown, Marie Annette—*Continued*

The authors address the feelings and emotions involved in living with the challenges that the AIDS sufferer presents

Includes bibliographic references

Califano, Joseph A., 1931-

America's health care revolution; who lives? who dies? who pays? [by] Joseph A. Califano, Jr. Random House 1986 241p $17.95   **362.1**

1. Medical economics
ISBN 0-394-54291-6   LC 84-45771

This is a survey of the health-care crisis in America, and proposed solutions for the current system's ills

Includes bibliographies

Callahan, Daniel, 1930-

What kind of life; the limits of medical progress. Simon & Schuster 1990 318p $19.95   **362.1**

1. Medical care 2. Medical economics 3. Medical ethics
ISBN 0-671-67096-4   LC 89-21894

The author "argues that centralized planning and control are indispensable to reform. . . . Our top priorities, he says, should be preventive medicine and the needs of groups at particular risk—for instance, prenatal care for the poor—while our lowest priority should be high-cost interventions in marginal cases." N Y Times Book Rev

"Essential for collections in health, medicine, and the social sciences, but heavy going for most lay readers." Libr J

Includes bibliographic references

Callen, Michael, 1955-1993

Surviving AIDS. Harper & Row 1990 243p il $18.95; pa $10   **362.1**

1. AIDS (Disease)
ISBN 0-06-016148-5; 0-06-092125-0 (pa)
                  LC 89-45636

This study of long-time survivors of AIDS was written eight years after the author's own AIDS diagnosis

Includes bibliographic references

Charting the journey; an almanac of resources for cancer survivors; [by] The National Coalition for Cancer Survivorship; edited by Fitzhugh Mullan, Barbara Hoffman and the editors of Consumer Reports Books. Consumers Union of U.S. 1990 225p il map pa $14.95   **362.1**

1. Cancer
ISBN 0-89043-304-6   LC 90-2013

This book "addresses cancer survivors' special medical, psychological, and legal needs." Publisher's note

Includes bibliography

Corea, Gena

The invisible epidemic; the story of women and AIDS. HarperCollins Pubs. 1992 356p il $23   **362.1**

1. AIDS (Disease) 2. Women—Diseases
ISBN 0-06-016648-7   LC 91-58369

The author "charges that the medical establishment in this country has vastly underreported and misdiagnosed cases of AIDS in women, thereby shortening the lives of infected women and falsely suggesting to the rest of the female population—especially middle-class women—that their chance of contracting the disease is relatively small." N Y Times Book Rev

"Corea's sermon is for the converted. Her anger is heartbreaking but doesn't effectively counter impressions that AIDS is a disease of minorities and drug users, and no real threat to white suburbia; unwittingly, it underscores them. Still, this book breaks some ground." Booklist

Includes bibliographic references

Diamond, Timothy

Making gray gold; narratives of nursing home care. University of Chicago Press 1992 280p (Women in culture and society) $24.95
               362.1

1. Nursing homes
ISBN 0-226-14473-9   LC 91-45755

In this account of nursing home residents and their caregivers, the author argues that "residents and workers share common experiences of poverty, powerlessness, and regimentation." Libr J

"This is a riveting book, an important book: thoroughly informed, it is also thoroughly readable, relegating its scholarly apparatus unostentatiously to the footnotes." Women's Rev Books

Includes bibliographic references

Doelp, Alan

In the blink of an eye; inside a children's trauma center. Prentice Hall Press 1989 220p o.p.; Fawcett Bks. paperback available $4.95   **362.1**

1. Children's Hospital National Medical Center 2. Children—Health and hygiene
ISBN 0-449-21830-9 (pa)   LC 88-25556

This "description of a Washington, D.C., hospital trauma center fuses engrossing accounts of young patients with observations on the caring role of physicians, social workers, and other professionals." Booklist

Forrest, Mary Brumby

Nursing homes; the complete guide; [by] Mary Brumby Forrest, Christopher B. Forrest, Richard Forrest. Facts on File 1990 287p il $24.95   **362.1**

1. Nursing homes
ISBN 0-8160-2170-8   LC 90-40851

"The goal of this book is to provide criteria for making an informed choice for an elder needing care. It covers . . . evaluating prospective facilities, roles of staff members, visiting residents, preparing a relative for nursing home life." Libr J

Includes bibliographic references

Frohock, Fred M.

Healing powers; alternative medicine, spiritual communities, and the state. University of Chicago Press 1992 340p (Morality and society) $29.95   **362.1**

1. Alternative medicine   2. Spiritual healing   3. Medicine, State

ISBN 0-226-26584-6   LC 91-36941

This "is a book about a single issue: whether unorthodox beliefs on health and healing ought to be shielded from state regulation when (a) life is at stake and (b) the competence of individuals to select therapies cannot be demonstrated successfully. . . . [The book] explores a variety of claims for extraordinary healings . . . and also examines the lives of those who engage in healing practices." Preface

Includes bibliography

Fumento, Michael

The myth of heterosexual AIDS. Basic Bks. 1989 411p il $22.95; pa $14.95   **362.1**

1. AIDS (Disease)

ISBN 0-465-09803-7; 0-89526-729-2 (pa)   LC 89-42518

"A New Republic book"

The author contends that AIDS does not pose a threat to heterosexuals. In his conception the "magnitude of the [AIDS] epidemic has been amplified by a variety of interest groups, all trying to promote their own particular political, economic, or moral agenda." Society

Includes bibliographic references

Glaser, Elizabeth

In the absence of angels; a Hollywood family's courageous story; [by] Elizabeth Glaser and Laura Palmer. Putnam 1991 318p il o.p.; Berkley Pub. Group paperback available $5.99   **362.1**

1. AIDS (Disease)

ISBN 0-425-13023-1 (pa)   LC 90-21290

"This is the autobiographical story of a mother's (Glaser's) inadvertent infection with the AIDS virus through blood transfusion, her passing of the virus to her two children, the elder child's sickening and death, and her founding of an organization dedicated to financing research into pediatric AIDS." Booklist

"This is a valuable addition to the growing body of AIDS literature." Libr J

Goldsmith, Seth B.

Choosing a nursing home. Prentice Hall Press 1990 267p pa $10.95   **362.1**

1. Nursing homes

ISBN 0-13-298779-1   LC 89-48844

The author "provides a detailed checklist for individuals and families to use in evaluating nursing homes, along with sample admissions forms, agreements, and fee schedules. Perhaps most useful are the profiles of nursing home staff members . . . and how they contribute to the quality of care and life provided by the facility." Libr J

Includes bibliography

Harpham, Wendy Schlessel

Diagnosis: cancer; your guide through the first few months; illustrations by Ann Bliss Pilcher. Norton 1992 xxiv, 136p il $22.95; pa $9.95   **362.1**

1. Cancer

ISBN 0-393-03187-X; 0-393-30892-8 (pa)   LC 91-37302

"The author, a physician and cancer survivor, answers the questions that any newly diagnosed cancer patient is likely to have. Her information is practical; her calm logic and straightforward data . . . encourage confidence." Publ Wkly

Includes bibliography

Horowitz, Lawrence C.

Taking charge of your medical fate. Random House 1988 319p $18.95   **362.1**

1. Medical care   2. Consumer education

ISBN 0-394-56336-0   LC 88-2001

Horowitz encourages those in need of medical assistance to participate in the decisions regarding the nature and quality of their care

This book "provides an informative, if unsettling, indictment of modern medicine and detailed instructions about how to navigate around some of its perils." NY Times Book Rev

Includes bibliographies

How to resolve the health care crisis; affordable protection for all Americans; [by] the editors of Consumer Reports. Consumer Repts. Bks. 1992 270p il pa $8.95   **362.1**

1. Medical care—Costs   2. Medical economics

ISBN 0-89043-626-6   LC 92-82813

"The editors critically examine each aspect of the current health-care crisis, exposing wasted health-care dollars, profit made on illness by insurance companies and physicians . . . and the abuses of the Medicare system and long-term care insurance. The second half of the book, in search of a better way, reviews the Canadian, Hawaiian, and Minnesota health plans and compares coverage with US plans. . . . Well done, timely, easy to read. A must for every citizen!" Choice

Inlander, Charles B.

Take this book to the hospital with you; a consumer guide to surviving your hospital stay; [by] Charles B. Inlander, Ed Weiner. rev & updated ed. Pantheon Bks. 1991 253p il pa $14.95   **362.1**

1. Hospitals   2. Consumer education

ISBN 0-679-72841-4   LC 90-42188

"A People's Medical Society book"

Originally published 1985 in different form, in paperback, by Rodale Press

Medical and financial consumer information for hospital patients

Includes bibliography

Kirp, David L.
Learning by heart; AIDS and schoolchildren in America's communities; [by] David L. Kirp, with Steven Epstein [et al.] Rutgers Univ. Press 1989 304p $30; pa $14.95   **362.1**

1. AIDS (Disease)
ISBN 0-8135-1396-0; 0-8135-1609-9 (pa)
LC 88-29789

This book provides "descriptions of how nine communities responded to the challenge of whether to admit children with HIV infection—whether symptomatic or not—to school." Nation

"These charged stories should encourage parents, neighborhoods, and school officials to promote open forums and make informed decisions about risk assessment and individual rights." Libr J

Includes bibliographic references

Kübler-Ross, Elisabeth
AIDS: the ultimate challenge. Macmillan 1987 329p hardcover o.p. paperback available $10   **362.1**

1. AIDS (Disease)
ISBN 0-02-089143-1 (pa)   LC 87-24016

This book examines "the suffering of individuals with AIDS, presents case histories, provides dialogue from public meetings where citizens debate the issues of providing care to AIDS patients within their community, and looks at AIDS from the perspectives of mothers, babies, prisoners, drug addicts, and homosexuals." Choice

Kwitny, Jonathan
Acceptable risks. Poseidon Press 1992 466p $24   **362.1**

1. Delaney, Martin 2. Corti, Jim 3. AIDS (Disease) 4. Drugs
ISBN 0-671-73244-7   LC 92-17548

This book on the "efforts of AIDS activists to both circumvent and revolutionize the drug approval process in the United States . . . [focuses on] Martin Delaney and Jim Corti. Both activists have successfully fought to bring treatments for HIV to the infected and ailing." Columbia J Rev

"Absorbing and informative, his book is highly recommended." Libr J

Lapierre, Dominique
Beyond love; translated from the French by Kathryn Spink. Warner Bks. 1991 400p $22.95; pa $12.95   **362.1**

1. AIDS (Disease)
ISBN 0-446-51438-1; 0-446-39346-0 (pa)
LC 90-39515

Original French edition, 1990

This is an account of the AIDS epidemic and the search for a cure

"Lapierre is a master storyteller who has found a subject worthy of his skills and creates a compelling work." Libr J

McCormack, Thomas P., 1944-
The AIDS benefits handbook; everything you need to know to get social security, welfare, medicaid, medicare, food stamps, housing, drugs, and other benefits. Yale Univ. Press 1990 257p $30; pa $10   **362.1**

1. AIDS (Disease) 2. Social security
ISBN 0-300-04736-3; 0-300-04721-5 (pa)
LC 89-70591

The author gives "advice on how to get Social Security and disability benefits, Medicaid, AIDS drug AZT, food stamps, housing and foreclosure prevention, burial assistance, and other benefits. In the course of providing this concise, accessible, yet exhaustive information, he also manages to take some of the confusion out of that bureaucratic nightmare, the public benefit eligibility process. Hence, his handbook is invaluable not only for PWAs (persons with AIDS) but also for the poor, aged, and disabled and their advocates." Libr J

Includes bibliographic references

Monette, Paul
Borrowed time; an AIDS memoir. Harcourt Brace Jovanovich 1988 342p $18.95   **362.1**

1. AIDS (Disease)
ISBN 0-15-113598-3   LC 88-7215

Also available in paperback from Avon Bks.

"In March 1985, after a period of intermittent ill-health, Roger Horwitz was diagnosed as having AIDS, he died in October 1986. [This volume] is his lover's memoir." New Statesman Soc

"The memoir transcends the particulars of the AIDS epidemic to stand as an eloquent testimonial to the power of love and the devastation of loss." Publ Wkly

Munley, Anne
The hospice alternative; a new context for death and dying. Basic Bks. 1983 349p hardcover o.p. paperback available $8.95   **362.1**

1. Hospices
ISBN 0-465-03061-0 (pa)   LC 82-72402

The author "provides readers with a sympathetic but measured evaluation of the work and meaning of hospice as viewed by patients, staff, and families. . . . Chapters on the larger issues of death and the place of hospice in American society round out the contents of a sensitively written book on an important subject." Best Sellers

Includes bibliography

Pogash, Carol
As real as it gets; the life of a hospital at the center of the AIDS epidemic; foreword by Randy Shilts. Carol Pub. Group 1992 255p $18.95   **362.1**

1. San Francisco General Hospital (Calif.) 2. AIDS (Disease)
ISBN 1-55972-127-8   LC 92-28516

"A Birch Lane Press book"

"Encapsulating the AIDS crisis in a profile of San Francisco's General Hospital . . . [the author] tells an engrossing story through the voices of the hospital's physicians and other health care workers." Publ Wkly

Rhea, Joseph C.
The Facts on File dictionary of health care management; [by] Joseph C. Rhea, J. Steven Ott, Jay M. Shafritz. Facts on File 1988 692p $50   **362.1**

1. Medical care—Dictionaries
ISBN 0-8160-1637-2   LC 87-6831

This is a "compilation of definitions of the words and acronyms used to describe various aspects of the health-care delivery system. Court decisions that have had a major impact on the system are also cited, government bodies and private organizations related to health care are defined and described, and jargon used by health-care planners, administrators, and health professionals is defined." Sci Books Films

Includes bibliography

Rolde, Neil, 1931-
Your money or your health; America's cruel, bureaucratic, and horrendously expensive health care system: how it got that way and what we can do about it. Paragon House 1992 285p $23.95   **362.1**

1. Medical care—Costs 2. Medical economics
ISBN 1-55778-520-1   LC 92-11904

The author "tells how the country got in its present inefficient and costly health care situation and examines the major players in this story. He then looks at the health care programs in other countries; devotes 50 pages to a levelheaded description . . . of Canada's single-payer system; and surveys programs in 12 states." Booklist

Includes bibliography

Shilts, Randy
And the band played on; politics, people, and the AIDS epidemic. St. Martin's Press 1987 xxiii, 630p $24.95   **362.1**

1. AIDS (Disease)
ISBN 0-312-00994-1   LC 87-16528

Also available in paperback from Penguin Bks.

A "chronicle of the five-year political, scientific, and social battle to force government, the medical and blood-bank establishments, the news media, and gay men to take AIDS seriously." Booklist

"Shilts successfully weaves comprehensive investigative reporting and commercial page-turner pacing, political intrigue and personal tragedy into a landmark work." Publ Wkly

Includes bibliographic references

Smith, John M., 1942-
Women and doctors; a physician's explosive account of women's medical treatment, and mistreatment, in America today and what you can do about it. Atlantic Monthly Press 1992 241p $20.95
362.1

1. Women—Health and hygiene
ISBN 0-87113-523-X   LC 91-44367

Also available in paperback from Dell

The author "questions the appropriateness of males as gynecologists, claiming that a male cannot emphathize with, or even fully understand, a female patient's problems. He says a male gynecologist is too quick to operate, suggesting a female physician would make different, and perhaps, better decisions. He also questions a male doctor's reasons for choosing the field of gynecology." Libr J

Smith "gives excellent examples for a variety of situations, then offers practical advice for selecting a personal physician. An important book for all women." Booklist

Includes bibliographic references

Sontag, Susan, 1933-
AIDS and its metaphors. Farrar, Straus & Giroux 1988 95p $14.95   **362.1**

1. AIDS (Disease)
ISBN 0-374-10257-0   LC 88-21173

"Sontag examines the ways AIDS is conceptualized for public discourse. She finds that the historical habit of visualizing incidence of disease and attempts to control it as a military process—as a war—harms persons with AIDS." Booklist

Stevens, Rosemary
In sickness and in wealth; American hospitals in the twentieth century. Basic Bks. 1989 432p $25.95; pa $12.95   **362.1**

1. Hospitals 2. Medical care
ISBN 0-465-03223-0; 0-465-03224-9 (pa)

LC 88-47903

This book aims to "document the rise, development, and present state of hospitals in America." Choice

"Its complexity and profundity of analysis make this a book that will be a valuable source for students of American medicine and health economics for many years to come." Sci Books Films

Includes bibliography

Strong, Maggie
Mainstay; for the well spouse of the chronically ill. Little, Brown 1988 323p $17.95   **362.1**

1. Sick 2. Adjustment (Psychology)
ISBN 0-316-81923-9   LC 87-16873

Also available in paperback from Penguin Bks.

The author "addresses the issues she has confronted as the spouse of a chronically ill husband." Booklist

"This is at once an affecting personal yet practical and specific guide." Publ Wkly

Includes bibliography

Szasz, Suzy
Living with it; why you don't have to be healthy to be happy. Prometheus Bks. 1991 243p $22.95   **362.1**

1. Lupus erythematosus, Systemic
ISBN 0-87975-659-4   LC 90-27045

The author gives an account of her life as a sufferer of Systemic lupus erythematosus, with advice to others with chronic illnesses

Watstein, Sarah B.

AIDS and women; a sourcebook; [by] Sarah Barbara Watstein & Robert Anthony Laurich. Oryx Press 1990 159p il $36.50
362.1

1. AIDS (Disease) 2. Women—Diseases
ISBN 0-89774-577-9   LC 90-7732

"The 14 chapters cover transmission, risk factors, prevention, demographics, occupational issues, and resources for support and education. . . . There are four appendixes that list audiovisual resources, hotlines and other organizations providing information and support services, a glossary of AIDS-related terms, and materials and methods for continuing research." Booklist

362.2 Mental and emotional illnesses and disturbances

Evans, Glen

The encyclopedia of suicide; [by] Glen Evans and Norman L. Farberow. Facts on File 1988 xxvii, 434p $45   **362.2**

1. Suicide—Dictionaries
ISBN 0-8160-1397-7   LC 88-11173

"Arranged in A-Z format, over 500 entries explore everything from 'psychological concerns to political and legal factors, from socioeconomic aspects to educational and religious considerations' in nontechnical language. . . . Because of its scope, authority, and coherent presentation of the myriad aspects of the subject, *The Encyclopedia of Suicide* will be essential for guidance counselors, public health workers, and for high school, public, and academic libraries." Booklist

Grollman, Earl A.

Suicide; prevention, intervention, postvention. 2nd ed updated & expanded. Beacon Press 1988 151p $17.50; pa $12
362.2

1. Suicide 2. Euthanasia
ISBN 0-8070-2708-1; 0-8070-2707-3 (pa)
LC 87-47880

First published 1971

This book provides an "overview of the statistics about suicide and of the religious, philosophical, and psychological views of it. . . . Includes a list of crisis intervention centers." Publisher's note

Includes bibliography

Isaac, Rael Jean

Madness in the streets; how psychiatry and the law abandoned the mentally ill; [by] Rael Jean Isaac, Virginia C. Armat. Free Press 1991 436p $27.95; pa $12.95 **362.2**

1. Mentally ill
ISBN 0-02-915380-8; 0-02-915381-6 (pa)
LC 90-37735

The authors argue that the "mentally ill have become pawns in the hands of advocates for the homeless, civil libertarians, and even the media in order to distort the size and nature of the homelessness problem and to divert attention from finding appropriate care for the homeless, 30 to 50 percent of whom are mentally ill." Booklist

Includes bibliographic references

Johnson, Ann Braden, 1945-

Out of bedlam; the truth about deinstitutionalization. Basic Bks. 1990 xxvi, 306p $22.95; pa $13   **362.2**

1. Mentally ill
ISBN 0-465-05427-7; 0-465-05428-5 (pa)
LC 90-80253

The author provides an analysis of the rationale behind deinstitutionalization of mental patients. "She illustrates how bureaucratic complexity and confusion make it inevitable that many of the severely mentally ill will fall through the cracks. . . . Money, she argues, drives the system; the chase to garner funds distorts priorities and fragments services." N Y Times Book Rev

Includes bibliographic references

The **Self-help** sourcebook; finding & forming mutual aid self-help groups. Self-Help Clearinghouse pa $10   **362.2**

1. Associations—Directories 2. Community services—Directories
ISSN 8756-1425

First published 1986. (4th edition 1992) Frequently revised

Lists self-help groups under subject headings and gives address, telephone number, date founded, and purpose for each group

"This handy paperback is an essential reference source for public libraries, providing easy access to valuable information." Booklist

Torrey, E. Fuller (Edwin Fuller)

Nowhere to go; the tragic odyssey of the homeless mentally ill. Harper & Row 1988 256p $18.95; pa $11   **362.2**

1. Mentally ill 2. Homeless people
ISBN 0-06-015993-6; 0-06-091597-8 (pa)
LC 88-45065

In his discussion of the situation of the homeless mentally ill, Torrey "argues that the closing of mental hospitals, the exodus of mental health workers into private practice, and the failure of the community mental health centers have forced many severely ill mental patients out on the streets." Libr J

This book "is clearly written and will appeal to general readers, students, and specialists." Choice

Includes bibliography

362.29 Substance abuse

Adult children of alcoholics remember; true stories of abuse and recovery by ACOAs; edited by E. Nelson Hayes. Harmony Bks. 1989 220p $17.95   **362.29**

1. Adult children of alcoholics 2. Codependency (Psychology)
ISBN 0-517-57207-9   LC 89-1751

Also available in paperback from Ivy Bks.

"Seventeen stories by adult children of alcoholics (ACOAs) attest to the painful legacies such parents bestow. The storytellers describe their depression, low self-esteem, and other manifestations of unhealthy behavior and sometimes how they became alcoholics themselves. . . . Lists of suggested readings, organizations, and the 12 steps of Alcoholics Anonymous appended." Booklist

Becoming your own parent; the solution for adult children of alcoholic or other dysfunctional families; [edited by] Dennis Wholey. Doubleday 1988 285p $17.95

362.29

1. Adult children of alcoholics
ISBN 0-385-24591-2   LC 88-9710

"Written as if it were a series of support-group meetings (patterned after AA), the book presents the histories of 14 individuals who describe their progress from abysmal dysfunctioning to recovery. References to Wholey's own family strife and alcoholism are intermingled with the case histories. . . . Comforting, constructive advice well grounded in concrete examples." Booklist

Cahalan, Don
Understanding America's drinking problem; how to combat the hazards of alcohol. Jossey-Bass 1987 xx, 234p $30.95

362.29

1. Alcoholism
ISBN 1-55542-057-5   LC 87-45418

The author "examines the background of America's drinking problem, reviews the successes and failure of various treatment programs, and suggests methods to minimize the problem. . . . This well-researched and scholarly work is recommended for both academic and general audiences." Choice

Includes bibliography

Cermak, Timmen L.
A time to heal; the road to recovery for adult children of alcoholics. Tarcher, J.P. 1988 227p o.p.; Avon Bks. paperback available $8.95   **362.29**

1. Adult children of alcoholics
ISBN 0-380-70722-5 (pa)   LC 87-29127

Dr. Cermak "portrays the manner in which homes controlled by the chaos of substance abuse inflict traumatic damage on young children and adolescents. Then . . . the author shows how varied self-healing techniques operate, including such Twelve-Step, self-help groups as Al-Anon and Alcoholics Anonymous." Publisher's note

Includes bibliography

Cocores, James
The 800-COCAINE book of drug and alcohol recovery. Villard Bks. 1990 255p $18.95   **362.29**

1. Alcoholism 2. Drug addiction
ISBN 0-394-57404-4   LC 89-43462

Also available in paperback from Fireside Bks.

The author outlines the effects of alcoholism and drug addiction on health, family, and work, and describes stages of recovery and treatment programs

Includes bibliography

Conrad, Barnaby, 1922-
Time is all we have; four weeks at the Betty Ford Center. Arbor House 1986 272p o.p.; Cameron paperback available $9.95

362.29

1. Betty Ford Center 2. Alcoholism
ISBN 0-918684-37-4 (pa)   LC 86-14163

"A Belvedere book"

"This is an account of a noted author's lifelong struggle with alcoholism and his decision, at age 63, to enter a four-week alcoholism treatment program at the prestigious Betty Ford Center. . . . The book describes Conrad's day-to-day experiences as an inpatient at the center." Libr J

Dorris, Michael
The broken cord; with a foreword by Louise Erdrich. Harper & Row 1989 300p il $18.95; pa $11   **362.29**

1. Alcoholism 2. Fathers and sons 3. Indians of North America
ISBN 0-06-016071-3; 0-06-092287-7 (pa)
                                      LC 88-45893

Also available G.K. Hall large print edition

This is a memoir about Dorris' "adopted son, Adam, a victim of fetal alcohol syndrome (FAS). Although the book began as an anthropological investigation of FAS and its effect on native American communities, Dorris soon realized that he couldn't separate the theoretical from the personal." Booklist

"The alarming statistics and consequences of fetal alcohol syndrome are skillfully interwoven with the human story of one of its victims in 'The Broken Cord.' Mr. Dorris's prose is clear and affecting." N Y Times Book Rev

Includes bibliography

Falco, Mathea
The making of a drug-free America; programs that work. Times Bks. 1992 254p $22   **362.29**

1. Drug abuse 2. Drug addicts—Rehabilitation
ISBN 0-8129-1957-2   LC 92-53667

The author "emphasizes that reducing demand for drugs is a more viable goal than trying to cut the supply. Believing that both legalization of drugs and a draconian crackdown are unwise, she surveys a broad range of programs, including those that teach prevention in the schools; that test for drugs in the workplace and offer confidential assistance to users; and that operate therapeutic communities to treat addicts." Publ Wkly

"An enlightening, encouraging study." Booklist

Flynn, John C.
Cocaine; an in-depth look at the facts, science, history, and future of the world's most addictive drug. Carol Pub. Group 1991 167p il $18.95; pa $10.95   **362.29**

1. Cocaine
ISBN 1-55972-060-3; 0-8065-1432-9 (pa)   LC 91-201

"A Birch Lane Press book"

The author maintains "that viewing cocaine as just another part of the nation's drug problem is outrageous and does a major disservice. It is the most highly addictive drug, he argues, quickly and insidiously stimulating the body's pleasure receptors and capable, in some cases,

Flynn, John C.—*Continued*
of causing almost instant addiction. In his book, he delves into the science of cocaine, along the way imparting the drug's infamous history." Booklist

Francis, Charlie
Speed trap; inside the biggest scandal in Olympic history; [by] Charlie Francis with Jeff Coplon. St. Martin's Press 1991 306p il $18.95   362.29
1. Johnson, Ben 2. Athletes—Drug use 3. Drug abuse
ISBN 0-312-04877-7   LC 90-49392
Francis was the track coach of Canadian sprinter Ben Johnson, who had to forfeit his gold medal at the 1988 Seoul Olympics after failing a drug test. Francis discusses the use of "performance enhancing" drugs by athletes on the international track circuit

Hoffman, Abbie
Steal this urine test; fighting drug hysteria in America; [by] Abbie Hoffman with Jonathan Silvers. Penguin Bks. 1987 262p pa $11   362.29
1. Drug testing—Government policy
ISBN 0-14-010400-3   LC 87-12093
An examination of the legal and social issues that surround drug testing
Includes bibliography

Marlin, Emily
Hope; new choices and recovery strategies for adult children of alcoholics; produced by the Philip Lief Group. Harper & Row 1987 287p $15.95; pa $8.95   362.29
1. Adult children of alcoholics 2. Alcoholism
ISBN 0-06-015769-0; 0-06-091511-0 (pa)
                    LC 86-46158
"The work is divided into three major areas of study: anger and grief over lost childhood, the tasks needed for recovery . . . and rebuilding relationships with parents and siblings." Booklist
"Interesting and readable; an excellent self-help or source book." Libr J
Includes bibliography

O'Brien, Robert, 1932-
The encyclopedia of alcoholism; [by] Robert O'Brien and Morris Chafetz; edited by Glen Evans. 2nd ed. Facts on File 1991 xx, 346p il $45   362.29
1. Alcoholism—Dictionaries
ISBN 0-8160-1955-X   LC 89-23333
First published 1983
"A concise compilation of more than 500 alphabetically arranged entries on the substance alcohol, the socioeconomic interrelations that have an impact on alcoholism, and the physical and psychological effects of the disease. The definitions, ranging from one sentence to several pages, are nontechnical, informative, and cross-referenced." Ref Sources for Small & Medium-sized Libr. 5th edition

Robertson, Nan
Getting better; inside Alcoholics Anonymous. Morrow 1988 298p $17.95
                    362.29
1. Alcoholics Anonymous
ISBN 0-688-06869-3   LC 87-31153
Also available in paperback from Fawcett Bks.
"A Thomas Congdon book"
This is an account of the history of the self-help movement, Alcoholics Anonymous, and the author's experiences as a recovering alcoholic with the program
Includes bibliography

Schwebel, Robert
Saying no is not enough: raising children who make wise decisions about drugs and alcohol. Newmarket Press 1989 239p $18.95; pa $10.95   362.29
1. Youth—Alcohol use 2. Youth—Drug use 3. Parenting
ISBN 1-557-04041-9; 1-55704-078-8 (pa)
                    LC 89-33775
"This book offers basic information about types of drugs and their effects. The author explains what life skills and attitudes are vital to prevent drug abuse by children and how to teach them to youth of varying ages. Prevention is stressed, but intervention is given appropriate coverage." Voice Youth Advocates
Includes bibliographic references

Seymour, Richard, 1937-
Drugfree; a unique, positive approach to staying off alcohol and other drugs; [by] Richard B. Seymour & David E. Smith. Facts on File 1987 261p $18.95; pa $10.95
                    362.29
1. Drug abuse 2. Alcoholism
ISBN 0-8160-1363-2; 0-8160-2143-0 (pa)   LC 87-455
"Sarah Lazin books"
"Geared to the recovering abuser, the heart of the book deals with how to stay off alcohol and drugs and conquer 'white knuckle sobriety.' Also deals with physical and psychological effects of alcohol and drug use and addiction and ways of getting help." N Y Public Libr Book of How & Where to Look It Up
Includes bibliography

Szasz, Thomas Stephen, 1920-
Our right to drugs; the case for a free market; [by] Thomas Szasz. Praeger Pubs. 1992 199p $19.95   362.29
1. Drugs—Law and legislation
ISBN 0-275-94216-3   LC 91-30378
The author "advocates a free market in drugs, both for pharmaceutical medicines (including opiates) and for substances like heroin and marijuana. Szasz believes that state-sanctioned coercions to protect people from their own vices are futile and violate our fundamental rights." Publ Wkly
Includes bibliographic references

Taylor, C. Barr (Craig Barr), 1945-
The facts about smoking; [by] C. Barr Taylor, Joel D. Killen, and the editors of Consumer Reports Books. Consumer Repts. Bks. 1991 198p il $18.95   **362.29**
1. Smoking
ISBN 0-89043-475-1   LC 91-20626
This is a report on the effects of smoking on mind and body with suggested methods for quitting
Includes bibliographic references

Tessina, Tina B.
The real thirteenth step; discovering confidence, self-reliance and autonomy beyond the 12-step programs; [by] Tina Tessina. Tarcher, J.P. 1991 293p hardcover o.p. paperback available $12.95   **362.29**
1. Compulsive behavior 2. Alcoholism 3. Self-reliance
ISBN 0-87477-713-5 (pa)   LC 91-22183
"This work addresses a question that many 12-step program (Alcoholics Anonymous, etc.) participants have undoubtedly asked: 'Where do I go from here?' While never denying the benefits of these programs in helping to maintain abstinence from addictive behavior, Tessina . . . suggests that program involvement may not have to be lifelong, and that many participants may be able to 'graduate' to autonomous living. . . . The premise of this intelligently written title is bound to cause some controversy." Libr J
Includes bibliography

Yoder, Barbara
The recovery resource book. Simon & Schuster 1990 314p il pa $13.95   **362.29**
1. Substance abuse 2. Medical care
ISBN 0-671-66873-0   LC 89-26278
"A Fireside book"
This volume "gives a broad overview of the major programs, lists and reviews the popular books, and provides names, addresses, and phone numbers for many organizations." Libr J

362.4 Problems of and services to people with physical disabilities

AFB directory of services for blind and visually impaired persons in the United States and Canada. American Foundation for the Blind $75   **362.4**
1. Blind—Directories
ISSN 1067-5833
First published 1926 with title: Agencies for the blind in America. (24th edition 1993) Periodically revised. Title varies
"Information on federal agencies, national voluntary agencies, and state, local, and regional services, including low vision clinics. . . . Entry information: agency name, address, phone, name of key official, services offered, accreditation, memberships." Ref Sources for Small & Medium-sized Libr. 5th edition

The **Complete** directory for people with disabilities. Grey House $125; pa $69.95   **362.4**
1. Handicapped—Directories
Annual. First published 1991
"Products, resources, books, services; a one-stop sourcebook for individuals and professionals." Title page
This directory "is in four sections: institutions, media, products, and programs. The first section includes associations, camps, housing, and libraries. The second lists books, newsletters, videos, and conferences. The third covers assistive devices, clothing, and computer products. The fourth and largest section lists educational programs, funding, recreation, rehabilitation, and travel. Each of the more than 5,600 entries includes contact name, address, telephone number, and a one- or two-sentence annotation." Booklist
This "is a tool that should be available somewhere in every community." Voice Youth Advocates

Gallaudet encyclopedia of deaf people and deafness; John V. Van Cleve, editor in chief. McGraw-Hill 1987 3v il set $345   **362.4**
1. Deaf—Dictionaries 2. Deafness—Dictionaries
ISBN 0-07-079229-1   LC 86-15396
"Contains 273 alphabetically arranged signed articles treating characteristics of the deaf, educational practices, specific individuals, organizations, periodicals, etc. Many entries are divided into sections and subsections, . . . and most include cross-references and bibliographies." Sheehy. Guide to Ref Books. 10th edition. suppl

Hoffa, Helynn
Yes you can; a helpbook for the physically disabled; [by] Helynn Hoffa and Gary Morgan. Pharos Bks. 1990 309p pa $12.95   **362.4**
1. Physically handicapped
ISBN 0-88687-480-7   LC 90-43239
This is a book of "practical advice for handicapped persons. Tips for selecting living quarters, choosing a personal care attendant, finding a job, traveling, and doing appropriate exercise are among the topics covered. . . . A comprehensive appendix contains listings of distributors of specialized equipment and products, addresses of organizations, and even computer bulletin boards for the disabled." Libr J
Includes bibliographic references

Lane, Harlan L.
The mask of benevolence; disabling the deaf community; [by] Harlan Lane. Knopf 1992 310p $23; pa $13   **362.4**
1. Deaf 2. United States—Social policy
ISBN 0-679-40462-7; 0-679-73614-X (pa)
LC 91-31478
"Lane asserts that the audist (hearing) community is, with benevolent intent, disabling the structure and power of the deaf community through such devices and practices as the cochlear ear implant and the continuing insistence on having deaf children speak, lip-read, and undergo painful surgery, which may only leave them in a limbo between the two communitites." Booklist
The author "is thorough, detailed, and intensive in relating the deaf world to the hearing, and he backs up his opinions with facts, research, and vivid detail." Libr J
Includes bibliographic references

Lane, Harlan L.—*Continued*

When the mind hears; a history of the deaf. Random House 1984 537p il $29.95; pa $15.95   **362.4**

1. Deaf—Education

ISBN 0-394-50878-5; 0-679-72023-5 (pa)

LC 83-43201

In this history of education for the deaf, the author traces "the controversy between the sign and oral schools. The book focuses first on France, then on the introduction of the French tradition of sign to the United States in the early 19th century . . . and on subsequent developments both in this country and in Europe to 1900." N Y Times Book Rev

"A monumental example of scholarship. . . . This volume appears to be a fair and objective presentation of the facts concerning the development of educational theory associated with deaf education." Choice

Includes bibliography

Rezen, Susan V.

Coping with hearing loss; a guide for adults and their families; [by] Susan V. Rezen and Carl Hausman; foreword by Richard Dysart. rev and updated ed. Barricade Bks. 1993 217p il $17.95   **362.4**

1. Deafness

ISBN 0-942637-83-6   LC 92-36728

First published 1985

The authors discuss "the social, psychological, vocational, and emotional aspects, offering as a realistic description of what to expect with a hearing loss and outlining attitude and behavior adjustments. Chapters dispensing practical advice summarize salient points and end with question-and-answer sections." Libr J

Sacks, Oliver W.

Seeing voices; a journey into the world of the deaf; [by] Oliver Sacks. University of Calif. Press 1989 180p il $22   **362.4**

1. Deaf 2. Sign language

ISBN 0-520-06083-0   LC 89-4817

Also available in paperback from HarperPerennial

The author "scrutinizes the history of treatment of the deaf, investigates the expressive capabilities of sign language and gauges the linguistic and social pressures faced by deaf people. The closing section documents a 1988 student revolt at Gallaudet that led to the appointment of the school's first deaf president." Publ Wkly

"With his philosopher's penchant for profound discovery and his neurologist's knowledge of biology and the brain, Sacks offers provocative connections and acute observations about the nature of language and culture." Booklist

Includes bibliography

Sardegna, Jill

The encyclopedia of blindness and vision impairment; [by] Jill Sardegna and T. Otis Paul. Facts on File 1991 329p $45   **362.4**

1. Blind—Dictionaries   2. Vision disorders—Dictionaries

ISBN 0-8160-2153-8   LC 90-3374

"The basic guide aimed at both professionals and general readers; treats all aspects of blindness, including health issues, education, adaptive aids, and organizations. Over 500 entries include both brief definitions and main articles (one to two pages in length), some of which include short lists of references. Provides an extensive bibliography and a subject and name index." Sheehy. Guide to Ref Books. 10th edition. suppl

Walker, Lou Ann

A loss for words; the story of deafness in a family. Harper & Row 1986 208p $16.95; pa $11   **362.4**

1. Deaf

ISBN 0-06-015644-9; 0-06-091425-4 (pa)

LC 85-42597

"Walker is one of three hearing daughters of Gale and Doris Jean Walker, both deafened as babies by illnesses. As the oldest child, the author served as her parents' 'interpreter,' dealing with outsiders. There is humor in her recollections but nothing lighthearted in accounts of crude or condescending reactions to her father and mother from indifferent people. Walker is candid in detailing her own frustrations and the burdens of life with the deaf." Publ Wkly

Winefield, Richard, 1949-

Never the twain shall meet; Bell, Gallaudet, and the communications debate. Gallaudet Univ. Press 1987 129p il $19.95   **362.4**

1. Bell, Alexander Graham, 1847-1922 2. Gallaudet, Edward Miner, 1837-1917 3. Deaf—Means of communication 4. Deaf—Education

ISBN 0-913580-99-6   LC 87-11885

The author describes "the long-standing dissension between 'oralists' (those who favor the education of deaf students via speech reading and oral communication) and 'combinists' (who favor sign language as well as speech and speech reading, when possible). In tracing the history of this debate, Winefield focuses on the adversarial relationship between . . . Alexander Graham Bell (the oralist) and Edward Miner Gallaudet (the combinist)." Booklist

Includes bibliography

362.5   Problems of and services to the poor

Blau, Joel

The visible poor; homelessness in the United States. Oxford Univ. Press 1992 235p $25; pa $10.95   **362.5**

1. Homeless people

ISBN 0-19-505743-0; 0-19-508353-9 (pa)

LC 91-29828

The author "argues that because our economic system produced the homeless, it is poorly equipped to solve their problems, the amelioration of which would require policies that conflict with the profit motive, the American ethos of self-sufficiency and the contemporary tendency to 'commodify' basic needs. New York City's response to the homeless comes in for close scrutiny here." Publ Wkly

"The last part of this highly readable and eye-opening book recommends solutions to the problem, some of them controversially innovative." Booklist

Includes bibliographic references

Coates, Robert C.
A street is not a home; solving America's homeless dilemma. Prometheus Bks. 1990 356p il pa $15.95   **362.5**
1. Homeless people
ISBN 0-87975-621-7   LC 90-43193
The author discusses various subpopulations of the homeless, the concept of empowerment, and possible solutions to the problem
Includes bibliographies

Hombs, Mary Ellen
American homelessness; a reference handbook. ABC-CLIO 1990 193p (Contemporary world issues) $39.50 **362.5**
1. Homeless people
ISBN 0-87436-547-3   LC 90-30936
This study of homelessness in the United States includes a chronology, a bibliography, biographies of individuals and a documents section focusing on legislation and court cases
For a review see: Booklist, Nov. 15, 1990

The **Homeless** problem; edited by Matthew A. Kraljic. Wilson, H.W. 1992 162p (Reference shelf, v64 no2) pa $15 **362.5**
1. Homeless people
ISBN 0-8242-0826-9   LC 92-5909
A collection of articles looking at the problem of homelessness from a variety of perspectives. Causes of homelessness and various suggestions for social and political responses are suggested
Includes bibliographic references

Katz, Michael B.
In the shadow of the poorhouse; a social history of welfare in America. Basic Bks. 1986 338p $22.95; pa $15   **362.5**
1. Public welfare 2. United States—Social policy
ISBN 0-465-03225-7; 0-465-03226-5 (pa)
          LC 85-73875
A historical look at the American government's attempts to eliminate or reduce the plight of the impoverished
Includes bibliography

The undeserving poor; from the war on poverty to the war on welfare. Pantheon Bks. 1990 293p $22.95; pa $15.95 **362.5**
1. Poor—United States 2. Discrimination 3. Economic assistance, Domestic
ISBN 0-394-53457-3; 0-679-72561-X (pa)
          LC 89-42676
Katz aims to "trace the U.S. government's political and financial policies vis-à-vis the least affluent U.S. citizens from the 1960s through the Reagan administration. He argues that the overwhelming tendency historically has been to identify 'the poor' as a culturally defined sub-unit of society, lacking ambition and moral standards, undeserving recipients of public assistance." Libr J
This is a "careful and convincing social history." Commonweal
Includes bibliographic references

Koplow, Lesley
The way home; a child therapist looks at the inner lives of city children. Dutton 1992 196p $20   **362.5**
1. Homeless people
ISBN 0-525-93517-7   LC 92-52886
The author, a psychotherapist, "describes the lives of some of her young clients who live in New York City. Her stories reflect a wide spectrum of problems emanating from either actual homelessness, or from an experiential dread of displacement." Libr J

Kozol, Jonathan
Rachel and her children; homeless families in America. Crown 1988 261p o.p.; Fawcett Columbine paperback available $10 **362.5**
1. Homeless people
ISBN 0-449-90339-7 (pa)   LC 87-22273
The author introduces us to "the residents of a hotel for the homeless in New York. . . . Kozol faults everyone involved: governments, social agencies, landlords, the courts, and indifferent Americans in general." Libr J
"While the individual stories that Kozol tells so affectingly point out the vivid realities of urban poverty, the book also supplies statistics that detail the more abstract—and inhuman—attitudes that contemporary society assumes when attempting to deal with its victims." Booklist

Rossi, Peter Henry, 1921-
Down and out in America; the origins of homelessness; [by] Peter H. Rossi. University of Chicago Press 1989 247p hardcover o.p. paperback available $9.95
          362.5
1. Homeless people
ISBN 0-226-72829-3 (pa)   LC 89-31598
This is a report and "an academic analysis of the homeless and the extremely poor [that provides] . . . comparative research data on homelessness: age, gender, marital status, income, appearance, health, alcoholism, drug use, and criminal record." Libr J
Includes bibliography

Schorr, Lisbeth B.
Within our reach; breaking the cycle of disadvantage; by Lisbeth B. Schorr with Daniel Schorr. Anchor Press/Doubleday 1988 xxix, 398p $19.95; pa $10.95   **362.5**
1. Poor—United States 2. United States—Social policy 3. United States—Social conditions
ISBN 0-385-24243-3; 0-385-24244-1 (pa)
          LC 87-27886
"Schorr describes programs that have worked to weaken the cycle of disadvantage—some short-term, limited demonstration models; others (community health centers, Headstart) of longer duration and broader scale." Libr J
Includes bibliography

Wilson, William Julius
The truly disadvantaged; the inner city, the underclass, and public policy. University of Chicago Press 1987 254p maps $19.95; pa $12.95   **362.5**

1. Poor—United States 2. United States—Social policy 3. Blacks—Economic conditions 4. United States—Race relations
ISBN 0-226-90130-0; 0-226-90131-4 (pa)
               LC 87-10822

An analysis of the causes of black urban poverty in the United States
"Mr. Wilson takes on conservatives, liberals and civil rights leaders alike as he develops persuasive alternative explanations of what has gone wrong in the inner city and supports them with extensive data and research." N Y Times Book Rev

Includes bibliography

362.6 Problems of and services to persons in late adulthood

Carlin, Vivian F., 1919-
Where can mom live? a family guide to living arrangements for elderly parents; by Vivian F. Carlin, Ruth Mansberg. Lexington Bks. 1987 206p il hardcover o.p. paperback available $13.95   **362.6**

1. Elderly—Housing
ISBN 0-669-13666-2 (pa)
               LC 86-45526

"The authors explore housing arrangements for senior citizens, including shared homes, 'congregate communities' and live-in help and provide examples of them. Special heed is given to the older person's need for independence, physical safety and social comfort. Checklists, addresses and various governmental agencies are provided." Publ Wkly

Includes bibliography

Heath, Angela
Long distance caregiving; a survival guide for far away caregivers; advisory panel: Evelyn Aker [et al.] American Source Bks. 1993 122p il (Working caregiver ser) pa $9.95   **362.6**

1. Elderly—Care
ISBN 0-9621333-9-6
               LC 92-42895

The author "helps families identify health, community, and social services in unfamiliar cities and develop care plans to coordinate these services. Checklists organize everything from travel plans to family meetings. Especially valuable is information on international caregiving." Libr J

Koch, Thomas, 1949-
Mirrored lives; aging children and elderly parents; [by] Tom Koch. Praeger Pubs. 1990 xxii, 217p $19.95   **362.6**

1. Elderly—Home care 2. Parent and child
ISBN 0-275-93671-6
               LC 90-7457

This book "chronicles the daily stresses of living with an aged, ill parent whose physical disabilities are heightened by loss of independence and self-esteem. The final chapter outlines a family plan for dealing with prolonged illness in an elderly relative." Libr J

Includes bibliographic references

Levy, Michael T.
Parenting mom & dad; a guide for the grown-up children of aging parents. Prentice Hall Press 1991 267p pa $10.95   **362.6**

1. Elderly—Care 2. Parent and child
ISBN 0-13-603101-3
               LC 90-35807

Areas covered "range from financial planning to mental and physical disabilities, from how to adapt the home environment when an elderly person moves in to when to look into skilled care facilities. The intricacies of Medicare and Medicaid are discussed as well." Booklist

Includes bibliography

Matthews, Joseph L.
Elder care; choosing & financing long-term care; by Joseph Matthews; edited by Barbara Kate Repa. Nolo Press (Berkeley) 1990 various paging pa $16.95   **362.6**

1. Elderly—Care
ISBN 0-87337-113-5
               LC 90-7129

The author "focuses on the economics of long-term health care and housing for older citizens. He advises on how to assess the type of care that is needed and where to find the services, agencies, caregivers, and residences. . . . Social Security, Medicare, and other benefit programs and reports on taxes and estate planning are described." Booklist

Rob, Caroline
The caregiver's guide; helping elderly relatives cope with health and safety problems; [by] Caroline Rob, with Janet Reynolds. Houghton Mifflin 1991 458p $22.95; pa $12.70   **362.6**

1. Elderly—Home care
ISBN 0-395-50086-9; 0-395-58780-8 (pa) LC 91-4221

The authors "provide home caregivers practical advice on the management of health problems commonly associated with aging. Indicators of illness change with age, they note, as they counsel how to recognize problems related to vision and hearing; memory loss and depression; skin, digestive, heart, lung, and kidney problems; as well as how to manage diabetes and cancer therapy." Booklist
"Recommended for popular medical collections because of its comprehensive coverage, practical tips, and sound advice." Libr J

Smith, Kerri S., 1960-
Caring for your aging parents; a sourcebook of timesaving techniques and tips; advisory panel Susan C. Aldridge [et al.] American Source Bks. 1992 117p (Working caregiver ser) pa $8.95   **362.6**

1. Elderly—Home care
ISBN 0-9621333-8-8
               LC 91-33909

The author "includes information on where to find free or low-cost health services, how to modify the home environment of elderly parents and how to organize their financial and legal affairs. Smith also describes how to cope with long-distance care-giving, balance care-giving

Smith, Kerri S., 1960-—*Continued*
with professional responsibilities and hands-on care-giving techniques. Particularly helpful are listings of national organizations that provide information on elder-care topics and a home shopping guide for difficult-to-find products often needed by the elderly." Publ Wkly

362.7 Problems of and services to young people

The **Adoption** directory; Ellen Paul, editor. Gale Res. 1989 xx, 515p $55 **362.7**
1. Adoption
ISBN 0-8103-2240-4 LC 90-103919

"The most comprehensive guide to family-building options including state statutes on adoption, public and private adoption agencies, adoption exchanges, foreign requirements and adoption agencies, independent adoption services, foster parenting, biological alternatives, and support groups." Title page

"Describes organizations that match children with families, foster care agencies and groups, support groups, and facilities providing biological alternatives such as in vitro fertilization and artificial insemination. Describes agencies and adoption criteria for Colombia, Guatemala, India, Korea, Philippines, and Taiwan." Sheehy. Guide to Ref Books. 10th edition. suppl

Alexander, Sherry
The home day-care handbook; a complete guide for establishing your own day-care home. Human Sciences Press 1987 197p $31.95; pa $16.95 **362.7**
1. Child care centers
ISBN 0-89885-344-3; 0-89885-365-6 (pa)
LC 86-27184

Contents: Responsibilities of a day-care provider; How to establish your business; Records to keep for taxes; Meal planning; Toys that teach fun; Activities, games, crafts, books; Child-safe; Sample forms

"An invaluable resource for the novice interested in establishing and maintaining a healthy, safe, and nurturing environment for the children of working parents." Booklist

The **Battered** child; edited by Ray E. Helfer and Ruth S. Kempe. 4th ed rev & expanded. University of Chicago Press 1987 470p il $37.50; pa $17.95 **362.7**
1. Child abuse
ISBN 0-226-32631-4; 0-226-32632-2 (pa)
LC 86-19342

First published 1968

Specialists from various disciplines analyze the causes, handling, and prevention of child abuse in terms of medical, psychiatric, social and legal aspects. Also considered is the possibility of reeducating the injuring parents

Includes bibliographies

Berezin, Judith
The complete guide to choosing child care. Random House 1990 258p il pa $12.95 **362.7**
1. Child care
ISBN 0-679-73100-8 LC 90-45487

At head of title: The National Association of Child Care Resource and Referral Agencies in cooperation with Child Care, Inc.

"Checklists of pertinent questions; diverse personal observations; suggested considerations and sampler forms related to in-home family daycare; infant/toddler/early childhood centers; *in loco parentis* for school age children; and summer camps are all included, plus a section on child abuse issues." Libr J

Besharov, Douglas J.
Recognizing child abuse; a guide for the concerned. Free Press 1990 270p il $27.95; pa $12.95 **362.7**
1. Child abuse
ISBN 0-02-903081-1; 0-02-903082-X (pa)
LC 89-25638

"The aim of this book is to increase awareness of the evidence of probable child abuse, the reporting requirements, and the investigative procedures. With its illustrations of abuse injuries, this book is no mere summary of a shocking social problem but an in-depth, serious examination that will be especially useful for those who are uncertain about whether or not to report their suspicions." Booklist

Includes bibliographic references

Dash, Leon, 1944-
When children want children; the urban crisis of teenage childbearing. Morrow 1989 270p il $18.95 **362.7**
1. Teenage mothers 2. Teenage pregnancy 3. Black women
ISBN 0-688-06957-6 LC 88-8280
Also available in paperback from Penguin Bks.

This report focuses on teenage pregnancy among black adolescents in a ghetto neighborhood of Washington, D.C.

"In exploring why so many black teenagers are caught up in the syndrome and its devastating consequences, Dash became more than a working reporter. At times confidant and friend, he has written a sociological report that reaches to the roots of early childbearing patterns." Publ Wkly

Includes bibliographic references

Finkelhor, David
Child sexual abuse; new theory and research. Free Press 1984 260p $29.95 **362.7**
1. Child molesting
ISBN 0-02-910020-8 LC 84-47889

The author addresses "critical problems posed by child sexual abuse as both a social and psychological phenomenon, reevaluates its moral implications, and profiles . . . both offenders and high-risk victims." Publisher's note

Includes bibliography

Flating, Sonja
Child care; a parent's guide. Facts on File 1990 173p $24.95 **362.7**
1. Child care
ISBN 0-8160-2232-1 LC 90-40850

Flating, Sonja—*Continued*

The author "discusses the advantages and disadvantages of in-home care, licensed family day care, child care centers, and babysitting co-ops. There is a wealth of information about how to put one's plans into action, such as a sample classified ad, an employment agreement, and a list of questions to ask when researching prospective day care arrangements." Libr J

Includes bibliographic references

Gilman, Lois

The adoption resource book. 3rd ed. HarperPerennial 1992 421p il hardcover o.p. paperback available $12   **362.7**

1. Adoption
ISBN 0-06-273043-6 (pa)   LC 91-36432
First published 1984

The author "shows how to pursue various paths with or without an agency, within or outside the U.S. Additionally, she discusses preparations that need to be made while the parents wait for their child and how to handle the necessary adjustments once the child has arrived." Booklist [review of 1984 edition]

Includes bibliographic references

Hayden, Torey L.

Ghost girl; the true story of a child in peril and the teacher who saved her. Little, Brown 1991 307p $19.95   **362.7**

1. Child abuse 2. Satanism
ISBN 0-316-35167-9   LC 90-19944
Also available in paperback from Avon Bks.

This is the "story of a young special education teacher who suspects that one of her students, a young girl who is habitually hunched over and mute, may be the victim of sexual abuse and a black magic cult." Booklist

Hewlett, Sylvia Ann, 1946-

When the bough breaks; the cost of neglecting our children. Basic Bks. 1991 346p il $22.95; pa $12   **362.7**

1. Child welfare
ISBN 0-465-09165-2; 0-465-09165-2 (pa)
                   LC 90-55663

The author outlines the societal problems which have led to the neglect of children, and suggests ways to rectify the situation, including changes in education, in the workplace, and in government policies

This book is "almost encyclopedic in its recitation of studies and intriguing cost-benefit analyses of some very urgent human dilemmas. Very accessible and utterly convincing—a 'must' for all libraries." Booklist

Includes bibliographic references

Jewett, Claudia L., 1939-

Adopting the older child. Harvard Common Press 1978 308p hardcover o.p. paperback available $9.95   **362.7**

1. Adoption
ISBN 0-916782-09-3 (pa)   LC 77-26973

The author explains "the process of adoption, from the first tentative decision through the home study, waiting period, placement, and follow-up. She discusses a wide variety of problems encountered in adopting and rearing older children and offers possible solutions,

drawing frequently on the theories of Transactional Analysis and Parent Effectiveness Training." Libr J

Includes bibliography

Kempe, Ruth S.

Child abuse; [by] Ruth S. Kempe and C. Henry Kempe. Harvard Univ. Press 1978 136p il (Developing child ser) $20; pa $6.95   **362.7**

1. Child abuse 2. Parent and child
ISBN 0-674-11425-6; 0-674-11426-4 (pa) LC 78-5104

"Viewing child abuse as a cyclical pattern: abused children become abusive parents, and, similarly, children of inadequate parenting become inadequate parents, the authors discuss the nature of child abuse, its forms and origins, and then present ways to help the victims." Booklist

Includes bibliography

The common secret; sexual abuse of children and adolescents; [by] Ruth S. and C. Henry Kempe. Freeman, W.H. 1984 284p il hardcover o.p. paperback available $14.95   **362.7**

1. Child molesting 2. Incest
ISBN 0-7167-1625-9 (pa)   LC 84-4093

"This volume explains the nature of incest and other sexual child abuse, destroys myths about who the victims and perpetrators usually are, describes what is likely to happen to victims of sexual child abuse, and discusses the positive effects of skillful treatment." Booklist

Includes bibliography

Lindsay, Jeanne Warren

Parents, pregnant teens and the adoption option; help for families. Morning Glory Press 1989 204p hardcover o.p. paperback available $8.95   **362.7**

1. Adoption 2. Teenage pregnancy
ISBN 0-930934-28-8 (pa)   LC 88-8359

This book relates the problems faced by teenage mothers who give up babies for adoption

"The author clearly indicates that the final choice—keeping the baby or adoption—should be the birthmothers and birthfathers rather than their parents'. Sympathetically treated is the position of the birthfather and his legal rights." Sci Books Films

Includes bibliography

Rappaport, Bruce M.

The open adoption book; a guide to adoption without tears. Macmillan 1992 195p $20   **362.7**

1. Adoption
ISBN 0-02-601105-0   LC 91-42800

A "guide that explains the basic procedures of open adoption and sensitively addresses the concerns and fears of prospective adoptive parents. . . . Highly practical, informative, and compassionately written." Booklist

Register, Cheri, 1945-
"Are those kids yours?"; American families with children adopted from other countries. Free Press 1991 240p $24.95   **362.7**

1. Interracial adoption
ISBN 0-02-925750-6   LC 90-37734

The author "interviewed 31 adoptive families and 15 adoptees ranging in age from 6 to 30 to learn how they cope, day to day, with the somewhat controversial situation of cross-cultural adoption. . . . Register's main focus is on how the emotional bonds between these parents and children are 'sealed, maintained, and tested.'" Booklist

Includes bibliographic references

Sennott, Charles M.
Broken covenant. Simon & Schuster 1992 373p il $23   **362.7**

1. Ritter, Bruce, 1927- 2. Covenant House (New York, N.Y.)
ISBN 0-671-76715-1   LC 92-26312

This is an account of alleged misuse of funds and sexual misconduct by Father Bruce Ritter, the founder of Covenant House, a private Catholic charity for street kids under 21

Includes bibliographic references

Somers, Suzanne
Wednesday's children; adult survivors of abuse speak out. Putnam 1992 319p $22.95
362.7

1. Child abuse
ISBN 0-399-13743-2   LC 92-8688

Also available in paperback from Jove Publs.

"Such famous people as Angie Dickinson, Patti Davis, Cindy Williams, and Suzanne Somers share their stories. Through their accounts, readers see the effects of emotional, physical, and/or sexual abuse and the ways each individual dealt with the trauma." SLJ

Stavsky, Lois
The place I call home; voices and faces of homeless teens; [by] Lois Stavsky and I.E. Mozeson; photographs by Bob Hirschfield. Shapolsky Pubs. 1990 172p il $14.95; $9.95
362.7

1. Youth 2. Homeless people
ISBN 0-944007-81-3; 1-56171-071-7 (pa) LC 90-8668

This book presents "narratives from teens who live or have lived in city shelters, welfare hotels, juvenile and adult correctional facilities, psychiatric wards and drug rehab centers, . . . [as well as] city streets and mass-transit stations." Publisher's note

Tower, Cynthia Crosson
Secret scars; a guide for the adult survivor of child sexual abuse. Viking 1988 207p o.p.; Penguin Bks. paperback available $7.95
362.7

1. Child molesting
ISBN 0-14-012229-X (pa)   LC 87-40430

In this study of child sexual abuse the author "covers such topics as emotional baggage, self-defeating cycles, the psyche of the perpetrator, and consequences for victims' own children." Libr J

Includes bibliography

362.82 Problems of and services to families

Finkelhor, David
License to rape; sexual abuse of wives; by David Finkelhor and Kersti Yllo. Holt, Rinehart & Winston 1985 258p o.p.; Free Press paperback available $14.95   **362.82**

1. Rape 2. Wife abuse
ISBN 0-02-910401-7 (pa)   LC 84-19808

This book "was written in order to raise 'awareness about the seriousness of the problem of marital rape. . . ' and to detail 'the ways in which the problem is ignored or minimized.' . . . This excellent study will be a valuable addition to women's studies, sociology, psychology, and criminal justice collections." Libr J

Forward, Susan
Toxic parents: overcoming their hurtful legacy and reclaiming your life; [by] Susan Forward with Craig Buck. Bantam Bks. 1989 326p hardcover o.p. paperback available $5.95   **362.82**

1. Child abuse
ISBN 0-553-28434-7 (pa)   LC 89-6812

The authors identify types of hurtful parents, including alcoholics, verbal and physical abusers, and those who emotionally neglect their children. They also offer advice to adult child abuse victims on how to overcome the harm done

Includes bibliographic references

Gelles, Richard J.
Intimate violence; [by] Richard J. Gelles, Murray A. Straus. Simon & Schuster 1988 297p il hardcover o.p. paperback available $12   **362.82**

1. Family violence
ISBN 0-671-68296-2 (pa)   LC 88-3271

In this study of family violence "the authors use case histories and surveys to explore in depth the kinds of physical and sexual abuse of children, elderly adults, and spouses taking place in American families. They also analyze methods used by victims to cope with and combat violence, and they suggest appropriate social deterrents." Booklist

Includes bibliography

Greif, Geoffrey L.
When parents kidnap; the families behind the headlines. Free Press 1992 [i.e. 1993] 321p $22.95   **362.82**

1. Parental kidnapping
ISBN 0-02-912975-3   LC 92-23855

This is an "analysis of the burgeoning problem of parental abduction. . . . The authors address the traumas to the abducting parent, the searching parent, the chil-

Greif, Geoffrey L.—*Continued*
dren, their siblings and the extended family, which is
often involved, and suggest ways the incidence of parental kidnapping can be reduced." Publ Wkly

Includes bibliographic references

Gunderson, Ted L.
How to locate anyone anywhere without
leaving home; [by] Ted Gunderson with
Roger McGovern. Dutton 1989 238p il o.p.;
New Am. Lib. paperback available $10

362.82

1. Missing persons
ISBN 0-452-26715-3 (pa)   LC 88-27093

The authors "provide a logical step-by-step guide to
locating missing persons by mail or telephone. . . . Discussed are a few basic reference works, local, state and
federal records, and miscellaneous sources such as ads
and insurance and religious records. There are sections
on missing children and adoptee searches, some useful
addresses, and suggested content for letters." Libr J

Kritsberg, Wayne, 1942-
The invisible wound; the new approach
to healing childhood sexual trauma. Bantam
Bks. 1992 xxi, 261p il $22.50; pa $11.95

362.82

1. Child molesting
ISBN 0-553-08984-6; 0-553-37265-3 (pa)
    LC 92-20158

This is a self-help manual written for those who have
experienced sexual abuse in childhood. The first section
discusses types of childhood sexual abuse. . . . The next
section analyzes the process of healing and recovery,
using case histories derived from the author's clinical
practice. The third section details how to keep a 'healing
journal,' in which the reader can perform exercises in
self-exploration and self-affirmation." Libr J

"This is a supportive and coherent guide." Publ Wkly

Includes bibliographic references

Maltz, Wendy
The sexual healing journey; a guide for
survivors of sexual abuse; illustrations by
Carol Arian. HarperCollins Pubs. 1991 347p
il $19.95; pa $12

362.82

1. Child molesting
ISBN 0-06-016661-4; 0-06-092155-2 (pa)
    LC 90-55934

The author offers a self-help guide to victims of sexual abuse. Opening with information on how to use the
book, Maltz covers such topics as "achieving awareness,
acknowledging the abuse, identifying the sexual impact,
and gaining control over one's sexuality. . . . This book
is highly recommended for survivors of sexual abuse and
as a valuable addition to the libraries of those who work
with them." Readings

NiCarthy, Ginny
The ones who got away; women who left
abusive partners. Seal Press 1987 329p pa
$11.95

362.82

1. Abused women 2. Wife abuse
ISBN 0-931188-49-0   LC 87-20470

This book relates "the stories of 33 women who
successfully escaped their abusive partners. . . . NiCarthy
describes why these women stayed in abusive relationships as long as they did and what finally compelled
them to leave. The women surveyed come from a wide
variety of socioeconomic and ethnic backgrounds, making
the book especially valuable for readers trapped in
similar situations and looking for examples of how others
with the same sort of resources were able to find help."
Booklist

Includes bibliography

Sanford, Linda Tschirhart
Strong at the broken places; overcoming
the trauma of childhood abuse; [by] Linda
T. Sanford. Random House 1990 191p
$18.95

362.82

1. Child abuse
ISBN 0-394-56563-0   LC 89-43429

Also available in paperback from Avon Bks.

"Various traumas and coping mechanisms are discussed here, and case histories provide examples not only
of how the abused child feels and reacts but also of
how the adult survivor still carries the memories and
works through them. Sanford gives alternative healing
approaches that present options for overcoming common
problems. The whole tone of the book is optimistic
about survivors' prospects for rising above their pasts
and leading satisfying lives." Booklist

Wexler, Richard, 1953-
Wounded innocents; the real victims of
the war against child abuse. Prometheus
Bks. 1990 369p $22.95

362.82

1. Child abuse 2. Child molesting 3. Foster home
care
ISBN 0-87975-602-0   LC 90-40334

This "book takes the stance that child protection services in America do more harm than good. Citing broad-
based interpretations of laws that allow agencies to coer-
cively intervene in family situations, Wexler cites case
after case where a family has been devastated by the
accusation of child abuse where none actually exists."
Booklist

"This extensively researched volume deserves to be
read by anyone concerned with child abuse." Libr J

Includes bibliographic references

362.83   Problems of and services to women

Bass, Ellen
The courage to heal; a guide for women
survivors of child sexual abuse; by Ellen
Bass and Laura Davis. Harper & Row 1988
493p hardcover o.p. paperback available $20

362.83

1. Child molesting
ISBN 0-06-096931-8 (pa)   LC 87-45598

The authors "set forth a three-part recovery program:
taking stock, healing, and changing patterns. Along with
counsel on how to move through the three stages, the
text includes testimonials from actual survivors. . . . An
excellent choice for all public library collections." Booklist

Includes bibliography

Sidel, Ruth

Women and children last; the plight of poor women in affluent America. Viking 1986 236p o.p.; Penguin Bks. paperback available $10 **362.83**

1. Poor 2. Public welfare 3. Women—United States
ISBN 0-14-016766-8 (pa) LC 85-40629

The author "uses interviews, federal data, and other current materials [in an attempt] to synthesize the history of women's economic status in the United States and calls for the adoption of a radical national family policy predicated upon allowances for child-care leave, comprehensive health care, day care, and welfare reform." Libr J

Includes bibliographic references

362.88 Problems of and services to victims of crimes

McEvoy, Alan W.

If she is raped; a guidebook for husbands, fathers, and male friends; [by] Alan W. McEvoy and Jeff B. Brookings. 2nd ed. Learning Publs. 1991 132p pa $12.95 **362.88**

1. Rape
ISBN 1-55691-062-2
First published 1984

"This book states that a rape victim's ultimate recovery from the emotional effects of the attack is seriously affected by the male behavior she experiences right after the attack and beyond. . . . A unique but very valuable handbook for public libraries of any size. Appended: case studies of national rape-crisis centers; suggested readings." Booklist [review of 1984 edition]

Noël, Barbara

You must be dreaming; [by] Barbara Noël, with Kathryn Watterson. Poseidon Press 1992 333p $21 **362.88**

1. Rape
ISBN 0-671-74153-5 LC 92-16265

The author "charges she was repeatedly drugged and raped during an 18-year course of therapy by an eminent Chicago psychiatrist." Publ Wkly

Includes bibliographic references

Sykes, Charles J.

A nation of victims; the decay of the American character. St. Martin's Press 1992 289p hardcover o.p. paperback available $12.95 **362.88**

1. United States—Social conditions 2. United States—Moral conditions
ISBN 0-312-09882-0 (pa) LC 92-21704

The author argues that Americans "have allowed psychotherapy to run amok and now routinely accept the illness excuse in cases of public misconduct or personal sloth. . . . This perception of ourselves as a nation of victims represents nothing less than the decay of the American character. Sykes calls for a 'moratorium on blame' and a return to the acceptance of personal responsibility for one's actions along with stiff penalties for criminal behavior." Libr J

Includes bibliographic references

Warshaw, Robin

I never called it rape; the Ms. report on recognizing, fighting, and surviving date and acquaintance rape; afterword by Mary P. Koss. Harper & Row 1988 229p $17.95; pa $10 **362.88**

1. Rape
ISBN 0-06-055126-7; 0-06-096276-3 (pa) LC 87-46180

"Ms. magazine/Sarah Lazin books"

A study of date and acquaintance rape and the myths and cultural attitudes that surround it

The author "handles an inherently sensational subject with compassion and restraint." Publ Wkly

Includes bibliography

363.1 Public safety programs

Adato, Michelle

Safety second; the NRC and America's nuclear power plants; [by] the Union of Concerned Scientists; contributors, Michelle Adato, principal author, James MacKenzie, Robert Pollard, Ellyn Weiss. Indiana Univ. Press 1987 194p $25 **363.1**

1. U.S. Nuclear Regulatory Commission 2. Nuclear power plants—Security measures
ISBN 0-253-35034-4 LC 86-45408

The Union of Concerned Scientists seeks to evaluate the performance of the U.S. Nuclear Regulatory Commission (NRC) since its creation in 1975. The book argues that the commission has not fulfilled its responsibilities to be "a 'tough, independent protector of the public health and safety.' . . . The material is free of jargon and technical detail, and is thus accessible to the general reader." Libr J

Cox, Matthew

Their darkest day; the tragedy of Pan Am 103 and its legacy of hope; by Matthew Cox and Tom Foster. Grove Weidenfeld 1992 233p il map $19.95 **363.1**

1. Pan Am Flight 103 Bombing Incident, 1988 2. Terrorism
ISBN 0-8021-1382-6 LC 91-33079

"In an account that personalizes the victims and their families, the authors recall the unforgettable Pan American flight 103 tragedy in which all 259 passengers and crew were killed after an exploding bomb sent the aircraft plunging into Lockerbie, Scotland." Booklist

Includes bibliographic references

Dadd, Debra Lynn

Nontoxic, natural, & earthwise; how to protect yourself and your family from harmful products and live in harmony with the earth; [by] Debra Lynn Dadd in collaboration with Steve Lett and Judy Collins. Tarcher, J.P. 1990 360p pa $12.95 **363.1**

1. Environmental health 2. Consumer education 3. Environmental protection
ISBN 0-87477-584-1 LC 90-38920

First published 1984 with title: Nontoxic & natural

Dadd, Debra Lynn—*Continued*

This volume contains a "listing of healthful products available through retail and mail order sources, and a rating system that indicates both their safety and their environmental impact." Publisher's note

Exposure; victims of radiation speak out; the Chugoku newspaper; translated by Kirsten McIvor; foreword by Robert J. Lifton. Kodansha Int./U.S.A. 1992 327p il $25

363.1

1. Radiation
ISBN 4-7700-1623-9   LC 92-15044

First published 1989-1990 as a series of newspaper articles in Japan

This "report details nuclear contamination's appalling toll: the still-lethal effects of the 1986 Chernobyl disaster; the destruction British, French and Japanese nuclear tests and refineries have caused in the South Pacific; the danger the ongoing development of nuclear power for 'peaceful' uses poses to the planet and its inhabitants." Publ Wkly

Feshbach, Murray, 1929-

Ecocide in the USSR; health and nature under seige; [by] Murray Feshbach and Alfred Friendly, Jr.; foreword by Lester Brown. Basic Bks. 1992 376p maps $24; pa $15

363.1

1. Public health—Soviet Union 2. Environment—Government policy—Soviet Union 3. Pollution
ISBN 0-465-01664-2; 0-465-01781-9 (pa)

LC 91-55456

The authors argue that "70 years of unregulated industrial pollution have both devastated the Soviet environment and created a host of medical problems that Russia's . . . health service is inadequate to handle." Libr J

"Not since the harrowing accounts of the famines and purges of the Stalin years has so much new and damning information been brought together to expose the monumental brutality behind the Soviet cause." Economist

Includes bibliographic references

Fradkin, Philip L.

Fallout; an American nuclear tragedy. University of Ariz. Press 1989 300p maps $29.95; pa $16.95

363.1

1. Radioactive fallout 2. Nuclear weapons
ISBN 0-8165-1086-5; 0-8165-1143-8 (pa)

LC 88-27813

"This book discusses nuclear testing in Nevada in the 1950's and its effect on off-site civilians in the surrounding region. The framework is a trial . . . [in which] the plaintiffs were cancer victims and surviving relatives." Libr J

"Fradkin's carefully researched book is a welcome addition to the growing body of work describing an atmospheric testing program so aggressive that it amounted to nothing less than an undeclared domestic nuclear war." N Y Times Book Rev

Includes bibliography

Gale, Robert Peter

Final warning; the legacy of Chernobyl; [by] Robert Peter Gale and Thomas Hauser. Warner Bks. 1988 230p $18.95; pa $12.95

363.1

1. Chernobyl Nuclear Accident, Chernobyl, Ukraine, 1986 2. Nuclear power plants
ISBN 0-446-51409-8; 0-446-39008-9 (pa)

LC 87-40606

This is an account of "a medical doctor specializing in bone marrow transplants, who went to the USSR to help care for the victims of Chernobyl. What happened inside the installation, Dr. Gale's participation there, and the lessons the incident should teach the world are addressed here. . . . This is a moving, touching, sobering, but, more importantly, an edifying book." Booklist

Goldman, Benjamin A.

The truth about where you live; an atlas for action on toxins and mortality. Times Bks. 1991 416p maps pa $17

363.1

1. Environmental health 2. Diseases
ISBN 0-8129-1898-3   LC 90-50676

"Interpreting statistics gleaned largely from the Census Bureau and other government sources, Goldman has created over 100 maps, ranked by county, of mortality rates, toxin emissions and concentrations, and demographics. The text raises disturbing questions about the relationship between pollution and disease, and the tremendous geographic disparities in mortality rates." Libr J

For a fuller review see: Booklist, Feb. 1, 1992

Includes bibliographic references

Gough, Michael, 1939-

Dioxin, Agent Orange; the facts. Plenum Press 1986 289p il $19.95

363.1

1. Agent Orange 2. Dioxins
ISBN 0-306-42247-6   LC 86-467

This study of the effects of human exposure to dioxin examines the scientific data and the controversy over the seriousness of the health risks involved

Includes bibliography

Jacobs, James B.

Drunk driving; an American dilemma; foreword by Franklin E. Zimring. University of Chicago Press 1989 c1988 xxii, 259p (Studies in crime and justice) hardcover o.p. paperback available $13.95

363.1

1. Drunk driving
ISBN 0-226-38979-0 (pa)   LC 88-17383

The author presents a synthesis of the academic research and an evaluation of public policy concerning drunk driving

"The book is essential to students and professionals." Contemp Sociol

Includes bibliography

Le Riche, W. Harding (William Harding), 1916-
A chemical feast. Facts on File 1982 204p
$22.95 **363.1**
1. Food contamination 2. Diet in disease
ISBN 0-87196-643-3 LC 82-2442
The author seeks to "demonstrate that the three greatest food hazards are microbiological infection, poor nutrition, and accidental environmental contamination. Among other topics covered are common food additives, naturally occurring poisons, pesticides, water purity, and the relationship of diet to cancer and heart disease." Libr J

Includes bibliography

Medvedev, Grigorii
The truth about Chernobyl; translated from the Russian by Evelyn Rossiter; with a foreword by Andrei Sakharov and author's preface to the American edition. Basic Bks. 1991 274p $22.95; pa $12 **363.1**
1. Chernobyl Nuclear Accident, Chernobyl, Ukraine, 1986 2. Nuclear power plants
ISBN 0-465-08775-2; 0-465-08776-0 (pa)
LC 90-55599
This is an account of the 1986 nuclear accident at Chernobyl
"Mr. Medvedev describes forthrightly how incompetence in the Soviet nuclear industry led to the disaster, and how a lack of foresight and a desire to evade responsibility needlessly exacerbated its consequences." Economist

Medvedev, Zhores Aleksandrovich
The legacy of Chernobyl; [by] Zhores A. Medvedev. Norton 1990 352p il maps $24.95; pa $10.95 **363.1**
1. Radioactive pollution 2. Chernobyl Nuclear Accident, Chernobyl, Ukraine, 1986 3. Nuclear power plants
ISBN 0-393-02802-X; 0-393-30814-6 (pa)
LC 89-39757
This study of the Chernobyl accident "addresses environmental, agricultural, technological, public health, and political repercussions." Libr J
The author "offers everything from a detailed scientific account of the disaster to the Moscow office politics which led to the fatal accident. . . . Medvedev is best on the sheer horror of the disaster itself." New Statesman

Includes bibliographic references

Miller, Richard L. (Richard Lee), 1947-
Under the cloud; the decades of nuclear testing. Free Press 1986 547p il maps $24.95 **363.1**
1. Nuclear weapons 2. Radioactive fallout
ISBN 0-02-921620-6 LC 86-4651
This is an "account of United States and Soviet efforts to develop the bomb and the history of nuclear testing in the US from the first bomb up to the abolishing of the Atomic Energy Commission in 1974." Christ Sci Monit
Includes bibliography

Mott, Lawrie
Pesticide alert; a guide to pesticides in fruits and vegetables; by Lawrie Mott and Karen Snyder. Sierra Club Bks. 1988 179p $15.95; pa $6.95 **363.1**
1. Pesticides
ISBN 0-87156-728-8; 0-87156-726-1 (pa)
LC 87-42965
"This guide identifies the pesticide residues found in 26 fresh fruits and vegetables, charting the pesticides' effects on general health and describing how washing, peeling, or cooking the produce will reduce toxic matter. Mott and Snyder also discuss the government's regulation of pesticides." Booklist
"A good reference for concerned consumers." Libr J
Includes bibliography

Moyers, Bill
Global dumping ground; the international traffic in hazardous waste; [by the] Center for Investigative Reporting and Bill Moyers. Seven Locks Press 1990 152p il pa $11.95 **363.1**
1. Hazardous wastes
ISBN 0-932020-95-X LC 90-43079
"A 'companion book' to the . . . PBS documentary hosted by Bill Moyers, 'Global Dumping Ground' makes a strong case against the export of hazardous waste." N Y Times Book Rev
This is "one of the most accessible introductions to the problem of waste available today." Small Press
Includes bibliographic references

363.2 Police services

Bouza, Anthony
The police mystique; an insider's look at cops, crime, and the criminal justice system. Plenum Press 1990 299p $23.50 **363.2**
1. Police—United States 2. Crime
ISBN 0-306-43464-4 LC 89-29450
The author "discusses police culture, agencies, and organization; the nature of criminals and how to control them; and the future of criminal justice. . . . Bouza is an interesting, sympathetic, and independent thinker who expresses some surprising views." Libr J

Includes bibliographic references

Daley, Robert
Prince of the city; the true story of a cop who knew too much. Houghton Mifflin 1978 311p o.p.; Berkley Pub. Group paperback available $5.50 **363.2**
1. Leuci, Bob, 1940- 2. Police—New York (N.Y.)
ISBN 0-425-09789-7 (pa) LC 78-15137
Daley recounts the story of Detective Robert Leuci, who in February 1971, "became an undercover agent assisting federal prosecutors to ferret out corruption within the [New York Police Department]. . . . Leuci, according to this account, had become enmeshed in [the corruption]. Yet his efforts as an undercover agent led to the indictment of dishonest cops, crooked lawyers, and organized crime figures." Libr J

Davis, James Kirkpatrick
Spying on America; the FBI's domestic counterintelligence program. Praeger Pubs. 1992 192p $21.95   **363.2**
1. United States. Federal Bureau of Investigation 2. Eavesdropping 3. Political crimes and offenses 4. Intelligence service
ISBN 0-275-93407-1   LC 91-23131
In this account of the FBI's COINTELPRO operations, the author summarizes surveillance techniques used against such groups as the American Communist Party, the Socialist Workers' Party, the Ku Klux Klan, the Black Panthers, and antiwar activists
Includes bibliographic references

Fallis, Greg
Be your own detective; [by] Greg Fallis and Ruth Greenberg. Evans & Co. 1989 xxi, 248p pa $9.95   **363.2**
1. Detectives
ISBN 0-87131-579-3   LC 89-23676
The authors "discuss how to do surveillance; how to follow the paper trail of public and private records (even sifting through trash); how to trace missing persons; do interviews; and examine evidence. This instruction, plus numerous anecdotes, provides an entertaining, informative, and interesting look at a little-known occupation." Libr J
Includes bibliographic references

Goddard, Donald
The insider; the FBI's undercover "wiseguy" goes public. Pocket Bks. 1992 344p $21; pa $5.99   **363.2**
1. Breen, Billy 2. United States. Federal Bureau of Investigation
ISBN 0-671-70335-8; 0-671-70336-6 (pa)
     LC 91-29370
The author "documents the real life, times, and escapades of ex-cop Billy Breen, a former FBI informant responsible for the downfall of well over 1,000 professional criminals. . . . His book chronicles how Breen skillfully maneuvered into the heart of drug rings, loan-shark operations, money-laundering schemes, and the like. But this is more an indictment of FBI bureaucracy . . . than a glorification of an undercover agent's lifestyle." Booklist

Greene, Marilyn
Finder; [by] Marilyn Greene and Gary Provost. Crown 1988 225p o.p.; Pocket Bks. paperback available $4.50   **363.2**
1. Missing persons 2. Detectives
ISBN 0-671-68326-8 (pa)   LC 87-15449
The author tells how she "started a voluntary service involving search and rescue in the Adirondack region. The success of that venture led to her current occupation as a private investigator specializing in missing persons." Booklist

Jeffers, H. Paul (Harry Paul), 1934-
Bloody business; an anecdotal history of Scotland Yard. Pharos Bks. 1992 278p il $19.95   **363.2**
1. Great Britain. Metropolitan Police Office 2. Criminal investigation
ISBN 0-88687-678-8   LC 92-5136
The author discusses the history of London's Metropolitan Police Office at Scotland Yard and examines the investigation of such criminals as Jack the Ripper and Dr. Crippen
"Readers will derive pleasure from this lively and entertaining history of the world's most famous police force. . . . The most interesting sections of the book deal with the evolution of forensic science and are backed up with case studies showing how criminals were caught by then state-of-the-art technology." Libr J

Mitgang, Herbert
Dangerous dossiers; exposing the secret war against America's greatest authors. Fine, D.I. 1988 331p il $18.95   **363.2**
1. United States. Central Intelligence Agency 2. United States. Federal Bureau of Investigation 3. Censorship 4. Authors, American
ISBN 1-55611-077-4   LC 87-46257
Also available in paperback from Ballantine Bks.
"Gaining access to FBI files through the Freedom of Information Act, Mitgang learned how America's writers and artists—including Pearl S. Buck, Thomas Mann, Georgia O'Keefe, and E. B. White—have been subject to investigation and their ideas subject to distortion through misinformation. . . . Mitgang's argument that artistic creations and freedom of speech in America have, at times, met government-sponsored innuendo makes for bone-chilling reading for both expert and casual readers." Libr J

Robins, Natalie S.
Alien ink; the FBI's war on freedom of expression; [by] Natalie Robins. Morrow 1992 495p il $27.50   **363.2**
1. Hoover, J. Edgar (John Edgar), 1895-1972 2. United States. Federal Bureau of Investigation 3. Censorship 4. Authors, American
ISBN 0-688-06885-5   LC 91-25559
Also available in paperback from Rutgers Univ. Press
The author "shows how the FBI—before, during and after J. Edgar Hoover's reign—far exceeded its proper investigative role to intimidate, harass and wage war against American writers." Publ Wkly
"Ms. Robins has accomplished more than just an assembly of dusty files. . . . She has made an admirable effort to be fair-minded, though sometimes her editorial remarks seem overstated. Still, she has written a book that should be required reading for anyone interested in modern American intellectual history." N Y Times Book Rev
Includes bibliographic references

Simon, David, 1960-
Homicide: a year on the killing streets. Houghton Mifflin 1991 599p $24.95   **363.2**
1. Homicide 2. Police—Baltimore (Md.)
ISBN 0-395-48829-X   LC 91-11526

Simon, David, 1960-—*Continued*

After spending 1988 with a squad of Baltimore detectives the author "gives detailed reports on investigations of the 234 homicides that occurred in Baltimore that year, and follows the lives of 19 homicide detectives who investigated many of them. The murders and the painstaking, often heartbreaking investigations that ensued—especially the yearlong search for a child killer—are engrossing. But perhaps best of all are the profiles of the individual detectives." N Y Times Book Rev

Wambaugh, Joseph

Lines and shadows. Morrow 1984 383p o.p.; Bantam Bks. paperback available $4.50

363.2

1. Police—San Diego (Calif.)
ISBN 0-553-24607-0 (pa)   LC 83-13313

The author chronicles the activities of the Border Alien Robbery Force between 1976 and 1978 when they were charged with cracking down on crime against illegals entering San Diego from Mexico

363.3 Other aspects of public safety

The **Gun** control debate; you decide; edited by Lee Nisbet. Prometheus Bks. 1990 341p (Contemporary issues) pa $16.95

363.3

1. Firearms—Law and legislation
ISBN 0-87975-618-7   LC 90-9138

This volume contains "more than 20 studies and essays that examine both sides of the controversial gun control issue." Booklist

Includes bibliographies

National Fire Protection Association

Fire protection handbook. National Fire Protection Assn. il $125   **363.3**

1. Fire prevention

First published 1896. (16th edition 1986) Periodically revised. Title varies

"A handbook of approved practice in the fields of fire prevention and fire protection. Will be useful to owners and superintendents of buildings, and to architects and engineers interested in designing safe buildings and planning for their protection against fire." Carnegie Libr of Pittsburgh

Pyne, Stephen J., 1949-

Fire on the rim; a firefighter's season at the Grand Canyon. Weidenfeld & Nicolson 1989 323p o.p.; Ballantine Bks. paperback available $4.95   **363.3**

1. Forest fires 2. Fire fighters 3. Grand Canyon (Ariz.)
ISBN 0-345-36219-5 (pa)   LC 88-33763

The author "recalls his fifteen summers working on a fire crew at the Grand Canyon." Libr J

Smith, Dennis, 1940-

Firefighters; their lives in their own words. Doubleday 1988 xxiii, 320p il $18.95

363.3

1. Fire fighters
ISBN 0-385-24121-6   LC 88-11815

Also available in paperback from Dell

"Smith is a fire fighter turned journalist. . . . His own experiences open each of these chapters packed with the highly personal remarks of various fire-fighting citizens, professional and volunteer, in cities, towns, and forests. The lengthy, anonymous quotes describe exactly what it's like to be a fire fighter in training, in action, around the station, and away from work." Booklist

363.4 Controversies related to public morals and customs

Baulieu, Etienne-Emile

The abortion pill; RU-486, a woman's choice; [by] Etienne-Emile Baulieu with Mort Rosenblum. Simon & Schuster 1991 238p il $22   **363.4**

1. Mifepristone 2. Abortion
ISBN 0-671-73816-X   LC 91-5054

Original French edition, 1990

"The discoverer of the antihormone RU-486 lucidly explains the discovery and its workings, his views on social responsibility and the political barriers, here and elsewhere, the drug has run into." N Y Times Book Rev

The **Choices** we made; 25 women and men speak out about abortion; edited and with an introduction by Angela Bonavoglia. Random House 1991 xxxiii, 201p $19.95; pa $10   **363.4**

1. Abortion
ISBN 0-394-58463-5; 0-679-74247-6 (pa)

LC 90-53138

"Twenty-three women and two men recount their experiences with abortion. . . . [The contributors include] Rita Moreno, Polly Bergen, Linda Ellerbee and Whoopi Goldberg." N Y Times Book Rev

Hertz, Sue

Caught in the crossfire; a year on abortion's front line. Prentice Hall Press 1991 242p $20   **363.4**

1. Abortion 2. Pro-choice movement
ISBN 0-13-381914-0   LC 91-2676

This is an account of "the experiences of a group of providers and patients at a Brookline, Mass., abortion clinic in 1989, the year that the United States Supreme Court upheld a Missouri law that restricted access to abortion." N Y Times Book Rev

"Hertz captures the violence, tragedy, and courage of human beings caught up in the complex set of legal, ethical, and moral dilemmas surrounding the abortion issue." Booklist

Includes bibliographic references

Kleiman, Mark

Against excess; drug policy for results; [by] Mark A.R. Kleiman. Basic Bks. 1992 474p $26; pa $16   **363.4**

1. Drugs—Law and legislation 2. Drug abuse
ISBN 0-465-01103-9; 0-465-00086-X (pa)

LC 91-55459

The author "discusses the principles of a drug policy, the characteristics of various illicit drugs, users and other victims, plus the laws and problems with enforcing them." Booklist

"Kleiman makes a case for a middle road between prohibition and permissiveness, i.e., for taxes, regulations and personal-use licenses that might avoid the pitfalls of criminalization." Publ Wkly

Includes bibliographic references

Lader, Lawrence

RU 486; the pill that could end the abortion wars and why American women don't have it. Addison-Wesley 1991 172p $16.95; pa $9.50   **363.4**

1. Mifepristone 2. Abortion
ISBN 0-201-57069-6; 0-201-60819-7 (pa)

LC 90-24451

This is a discussion of the "pill developed by a French pharmaceutical company that produces a safe and effective abortion through body chemistry. . . . Lader covers the current state of abortion politics, showing how RU 486 was created, how it works, and what women think about its use. In advocating RU 486's early release in the American market, Lader describes the drug's other medical uses in treating brain tumors and Cushing's disease." Booklist

Includes bibliographic references

Luker, Kristin

Abortion and the politics of motherhood. University of Calif. Press 1984 324p (California ser. on social choice and political economy) $29.95; pa $12.95   **363.4**

1. Abortion
ISBN 0-520-04314-6; 0-520-05597-7 (pa)

LC 83-47849

In this "study of the abortion controversy in the United States, Luker . . . examines the social and environmental factors that led to the pro-choice and pro-life movements." Libr J

"Anyone concerned with this issue should welcome the publication of this excellent sociological study. . . . The book can be read with profit by partisans of either side." New Repub

Includes bibliography

Miller, Richard Lawrence

The case for legalizing drugs. Praeger Pubs. 1991 247p $21.95   **363.4**

1. Drugs—Law and legislation
ISBN 0-275-93459-4

LC 90-7379

The author advocates legalizing the manufacture, distribution, sale, purchase, possession and use of drugs such as heroin, cocaine, marijuana and LSD

Includes bibliographic references

Rosenblatt, Roger

Life itself; abortion in the American mind. Random House 1992 194p $20; pa $10   **363.4**

1. Abortion
ISBN 0-394-58244-6; 0-679-74373-1 (pa)

LC 91-52686

The author "views individual Americans as truly ambivalent about abortion. Just as the nation has found ways to live with such other 'normal, unresolvable problems' as capital punishment and free speech, he argues, a reasonable policy can be built on that ambivalence. After tracing the history of public policy toward abortion, Rosenblatt explains the special problems Americans have with this issue. . . . Life Itself is a well-reasoned contribution to the 'real discussion about abortion' the author advocates." Booklist

Includes bibliographic references

Shannon, Elaine

Desperados; Latin drug lords, U.S. lawmen, and the war America can't win. Viking 1988 xx, 499p il o.p.; Penguin Bks. paperback available $5.95   **363.4**

1. Drugs and crime
ISBN 0-451-82207-2 (pa)

LC 87-40448

This "book concentrates on the case of Enrique Camarena, the DEA [Drug Enforcement Agency] agent who was kidnapped, tortured, and murdered . . . in Mexico in 1985." N Y Rev Books

"An incisive and gripping account." Libr J

Includes bibliography

Tribe, Laurence H.

Abortion: the clash of absolutes. new ed. Norton 1992 318p pa $10.95   **363.4**

1. Abortion
ISBN 0-393-30956-8

LC 93-111762

First published 1990

The author examines both pro-life and pro-choice arguments and analyzes major court and legislative decisions

Includes bibliographic references

Weddington, Sarah Ragle, 1945-

A question of choice. Putnam 1992 306p il $21.95   **363.4**

1. Roe v. Wade 2. Abortion
ISBN 0-399-13790-4

LC 92-14311

"Starting with her years at the University of Texas Law School at Austin, Weddington, the attorney who won Roe v. Wade, traces the history of her involvement with this . . . Supreme Court case and its aftermath." Libr J

"This description of the background and legal significance of the 1973 Supreme Court decision . . . provides a sense of how Roe happened that is at once more personal and more knowledgeable than most popular summaries. . . . A sound addition to legal history and current affairs collections." Booklist

Includes bibliographic references

Whitney, Catherine
Whose life? a balanced, comprehensive view of abortion from its historical context to the current debate. Morrow 1991 272p $21   **363.4**

1. Abortion 2. Pro-choice movement
ISBN 0-688-09622-0   LC 90-19899

A survey of the abortion debate in the United States focusing on legal cases, political manifestations, and women's personal stories

Includes bibliographic references

363.7 Environmental problems and services

Asimov, Isaac, 1920-1992
Our angry earth; [by] Isaac Asimov, Frederik Pohl. TOR Bks. 1991 323p il $19.95; pa $5.99   **363.7**

1. Environmental protection 2. Pollution 3. Nature conservation
ISBN 0-312-85252-5; 0-8125-2096-3 (pa)
LC 91-19919

"A Tom Doherty Associates book"

The authors "take a comprehensive look at the major threats to our planet's ecosystem and present a prescription by which humanity might rescue itself from self-destruction." Publ Wkly

"The various aspects of the crisis, the urgency, and both individual and organizational plans of action are set out in prose of generally admirable clarity and reasonable balance. As an introduction to the subject, this volume is highly recommended." Booklist

Branson, Gary D.
The complete guide to recycling at home; how to take responsibility, save money, and protect the environment. Betterway Publs. 1991 176p il pa $14.95   **363.7**

1. Recycling (Waste, etc.)
ISBN 1-55870-189-3   LC 90-21380

"The author's suggestions for personal action include making purchase selections based upon the waste that will be left over; using grass clippings and leaves for mulch; recycling used paper, glass, and plastics; making our homes as energy efficient as we can; and keeping our automobiles tuned to hold air pollution down." Booklist

Brown, Lester Russell, 1934-
Saving the planet; how to shape an environmentally sustainable global economy; [by] Lester R. Brown, Christopher Flavin, Sandra Postel. Norton 1991 224p hardcover o.p. paperback available $8.95   **363.7**

1. Environmental protection 2. Economic conditions
ISBN 0-393-30823-5 (pa)   LC 91-24623

According to the authors, "the world economy suffers from a failure to consider the costs of environmental disruption. They argue that, in the absence of coordinated international efforts, environmental problems . . . will continue to worsen. . . . They discuss the potential gains to human quality of life from increasing energy efficiency, creating a solar economy, using more recycled materials, and protecting the planet's fragile bio-

logical base." Choice

Includes bibliographic references

Brown, Michael H.
The toxic cloud. Harper & Row 1987 307p o.p. paperback available $9.95   **363.7**

1. Air pollution 2. Hazardous wastes
ISBN 0-06-091509-9 (pa)   LC 87-45027

This book looks at the causes and effects of atmospheric pollution in the United States

Caldicott, Helen
If you love this planet; a plan to heal the earth. Norton 1992 231p $19.95; pa $10.95   **363.7**

1. Environmental protection
ISBN 0-393-03045-8; 0-393-30835-9 (pa)
LC 91-30322

The author describes the earth's environmental problems and suggests solutions

Caldicott's "diagnosis of our planetary ills is comprehensive, her etiology fascinating, and her prescription bracing." Libr J

Includes bibliographic references

Carless, Jennifer
Taking out the trash; a no-nonsense guide to recycling. Island Press (Covelo) 1992 249p $35; pa $16   **363.7**

1. Recycling (Waste, etc.)
ISBN 1-55963-171-6; 1-55963-170-8 (pa)
LC 91-43855

This guide to recycling in the United States "presents an overview of recycling efforts around the country, an analysis of the various materials that can be reused, and a discussion of issues that need to be resolved in the future. . . . This well-written and practical book will be useful to concerned citizens." Libr J

Includes bibliographic references

Carson, Rachel, 1907-1964
Silent spring; drawings by Lois and Louis Darling; foreword by Paul Brooks. 25th anniversary edition. Houghton Mifflin 1987 c1962 368p il $19.45; pa $8.70   **363.7**

1. Pesticides—Environmental aspects 2. Pesticides and wildlife
ISBN 0-395-45389-5; 0-395-45390-9 (pa)
LC 87-406420

Companion volume Silent spring revisited available from American Chemical Soc.

First published 1962

"An important, controversial account . . . of the way in which man's use of poisons to control insect pests and unwanted vegetation is changing the balance of nature." Booklist

Includes bibliography

Coffel, Steve
But not a drop to drink! the lifesaving guide to good water. Rawson Assocs. 1989 323p $19.95 **363.7**
1. Water supply 2. Water pollution
ISBN 0-89256-328-1 LC 87-43084
Also available in paperback from Ivy Bks.

This book describes "how pollutants have gotten into our water supply, how natural and constructed water purification systems work, how toxic materials in water influence human health, and what individuals can do both in their communities and in their own homes to clean up and conserve this . . . resource." Libr J
"A sound treatment of a complex subject." Booklist

Davidson, Art, 1943-
In the wake of the Exxon Valdez; the devastating impact of the Alaska oil spill. Sierra Club Bks. 1990 333p maps $19.95 **363.7**
1. Exxon Valdez (Ship) 2. Oil spills 3. Petroleum industry
ISBN 0-87156-614-1 LC 89-29294
In this examination of the oil spill "Davidson recounts the critical event, the response of Exxon and governmental authorities, and the long-range effects of the disaster on parks, wildlife, and coastal communities." Booklist
Includes bibliographic references

Ehrlich, Paul R.
Healing the planet; strategies for resolving the environmental crisis; [by] Paul R. Ehrlich and Anne H. Ehrlich. Addison-Wesley 1991 366p $22.95; pa $12.95 **363.7**
1. Man—Influence on nature 2. Environmental protection 3. Population
ISBN 0-201-55046-6; 0-201-63224-1 (pa) LC 91-2734
"A Robert Ornstein book"
A Publication of the Center for Conservation Biology, Stanford University
The authors discuss "such issues as energy, global warming, acid rain, ozone depletion, water and land use problems . . . [population], economic growth, environmental economics, and environmental vs. military security." Sci Books Films
Includes bibliographic references

Elkington, John
The green consumer; [by] John Elkington, Julia Hailes, and Joel Makower. Penguin Bks. 1990 342p il pa $9.95 **363.7**
1. Consumption (Economics) 2. Environmental protection
ISBN 0-14-012708-9 LC 89-48639
"A Tilden Press book"
"This book raises a 'green' consciousness by listing products and services that work toward environmental preservation. The consumption of products—from cars, groceries, personal care items, and home energy and furnishings to gardening, gifts, and traveling—and the purchase of environmentally sound substitutes are persuasively presented." Booklist
Includes bibliographic references

Epstein, Samuel S.
Hazardous waste in America; [by] Samuel S. Epstein, Lester O. Brown, Carl Pope. Sierra Club Bks. 1982 593p hardcover o.p. paperback available $12.95 **363.7**
1. Hazardous wastes
ISBN 0-87156-807-1 (pa) LC 82-3304
The authors present a "review of the important aspects of the problems of hazardous waste: the nature, composition, toxic properties, and sources of these wastes; major case studies; legislation belatedly enacted by Congress; and some predictions about our ability to handle hazardous wastes, to cleanse them from our environment, and to prevent further contamination." Sci Books Films
Includes bibliography

Fisher, David E., 1932-
Fire & ice; the greenhouse effect, ozone depletion, and nuclear winter. Harper & Row 1990 232p $19.95 **363.7**
1. Air pollution 2. Greenhouse effect
ISBN 0-06-016214-7 LC 89-45652
This volume "addresses such subjects as: the atmospheric phenomenon known as 'the greenhouse effect'; the history of the ice ages and their possible recurrence; the effects of chemical and biological warfare on the planet; and the planet's ever changing climate and temperature." Publisher's note
"The reader who fears formulas and detailed technical explanations will find the book readable and relatively free of jargon." Sci Books Films

Foreman, Dave
Confessions of an eco-warrior; [by] David Foreman. Harmony Bks. 1991 228p $19.95 **363.7**
1. Environment—Government policy—United States 2. Ecology
ISBN 0-517-58123-X LC 90-48729
Memoirs of the founder of the radical environmental organization Earth First! Foreman examines the movement in practical, ethical and philosophical terms
Includes bibliographic references

Franck, Irene M.
The green encyclopedia; [by] Irene Franck and David Brownstone. Prentice Hall General Ref. 1992 486p il maps $35; pa $20 **363.7**
1. Environmental protection—Dictionaries 2. Nature conservation—Dictionaries
ISBN 0-13-365685-3; 0-13-365677-2 (pa) LC 92-12240
This sourcebook includes biographies of environmentalists and entries on animals, pesticides, wildlife preserves, organizations and government agencies
For a review see: Booklist, Dec. 15, 1992

The **Global** ecology handbook; what you can do about the environmental crisis; the Global Tomorrow Coalition; edited by Walter J. Corson. Beacon Press 1990 414p il $35; pa $16.95 **363.7**

1. Environmental protection 2. Social action
ISBN 0-8070-8500-6; 0-8070-8501-4 (pa)

LC 88-43318

This book is "broken down into 14 issue-oriented chapters that cover, among other topics, population growth, food and agriculture, biological diversity, tropical forest, fresh water, energy, air, hazardous substances, and global security. As a reference tool, this handbook will be indispensable; it is well documented, well organized, quite comprehensive and comprehensible, instructive, and easy to use." Booklist

The **Green** lifestyle handbook; Jeremy Rifkin, editor. Holt & Co. 1990 xxii, 198p hardcover o.p. paperback available $10.95 **363.7**

1. Pollution 2. Man—Influence on nature 3. Environmental protection
ISBN 0-8050-1369-5 (pa)

LC 89-26944

"This book examines the consumption and convenience-oriented American life-style and suggests actions and products that can create a more environmentally sound or 'green' lifestyle and sustainable future. This book takes the 'green' philosophy beyond products, . . . to an entire way of life, covering the broad topics of home, work, play, shopping, diet, investment, and religion." Libr J

Includes bibliographic references

The **Green** pages; your everyday shopping guide to environmentally safe products; [by] the Bennett Information Group. Random House 1990 237p il pa $8.95 **363.7**

1. Environmental protection 2. Consumer education
ISBN 0-679-73130-X

LC 90-37831

"This guide lists products designed with the environment in mind that can be purchased in retail stores or through the mail. Thousands of recommended products that are phosphate-free, biodegradable, recyclable, etc., are arranged by point of use (kitchen, bath, yard, garage)." Booklist

The **Greenhouse** effect; edited by Matthew A. Kraljic. Wilson, H.W. 1992 155p (Reference shelf, v64 no3) pa $15 **363.7**

1. Greenhouse effect
ISBN 0-8242-0827-7

LC 92-5990

A collection of reprinted articles from various sources concerning the greenhouse effect, its measurement and causes, consequences and possible solutions

Includes bibliography

Gribbin, John R.
The hole in the sky; man's threat to the ozone layer; [by] John Gribbin. Bantam Bks. 1988 192p pa $4.95 **363.7**

1. Ozone 2. Air pollution
ISBN 0-553-27537-2

LC 88-3302

"Though he describes many possibilities for the dissolution of the ozone layer, Gribbin makes a compelling case for chlorine as the culprit. . . . The text concludes with vital discussion on what can and should be done about this potentially grave hazard to human health. An accessible paperback." Booklist

Includes bibliographic references

The **HarperCollins** dictionary of environmental science; [by] Gareth Jones [et al.] HarperCollins Pubs. 1992 453p il maps $25; pa $12.95 **363.7**

1. Human ecology—Dictionaries 2. Environmental protection—Dictionaries
ISBN 0-06-271533-X; 0-06-461040-3 (pa)

LC 91-55392

This dictionary of over 2,000 entries focuses on four areas of study: the physical world, the biological world, the man-made environment and the agro-economic structures. Emphasis is on international interpretation

The **Information** please environmental almanac; compiled by World Resources Institute. Houghton Mifflin $21.45; pa $10.70 **363.7**

1. Environmental protection 2. Conservation of natural resources 3. Almanacs
ISSN 1057-8293

Annual. First published 1992

"In charts and graphs covering energy use and production, waste, pollutant releases, and environmental policies, the almanac supplies environmental portraits of . . . individual countries, each of the U.S. states and Canadian provinces, and . . . major U.S. cities. Here is a welcome compilation of data on industrial pollution, land deregulation, deforestation, wildlife preservation, and endangered species—all in a single handy source." Am Libr

Ingram, Colin, 1936-
The drinking water book; a complete guide to safe drinking water. Ten Speed Press 1991 195p il maps pa $11.95 **363.7**

1. Water supply 2. Water pollution 3. Water—Purification
ISBN 0-89815-436-7

LC 91-14714

The author examines potential drinking water "pollutants and their sources. . . . He offers ideas for reducing pollutants in the home water supply . . . [and discusses] possible alternatives, from purchasing bottled water to using a home treatment system." Libr J

"A good introduction to the myriad of water-quality problems facing the general public." Choice

Includes bibliographic references

Kimball, Debi
Recycling in America; a reference handbook. ABC-CLIO 1992 254p il map (Contemporary world issues) $39.50 **363.7**

1. Recycling (Waste, etc.)
ISBN 0-87436-663-1

LC 92-29984

This handbook "includes an overview of the topic; biographies of important people in the field; facts on recyclable products; state-by-state laws and regulations; a directory of organizations; and a bibliography that includes books, articles, journals, educational materials, databases, and video tapes." SLJ

For a fuller review see: Booklist, Feb. 1, 1993

Lewis, Martin W.

Green delusions; an environmentalist critique of radical environmentalism. Duke Univ. Press 1992 288p $24.95   **363.7**

1. Environmental protection 2. Radicals and radicalism

ISBN 0-8223-1257-3   LC 92-5671

This study of the radical environmental movement argues that the policies advocated by its adherents would, if enacted, result in ecological disaster. The author defines "'five main variants of eco-extremism,' namely 'antihumanist anarchism,' 'primitivism,' 'humanist eco-anarchism,' 'green Marxism' and 'radical eco-feminism.'" N Y Times Book Rev

Lewis "hits his target cleanly and forcefully, making the book essential for environmental collections. Its clarity, detail, and solid documentation could also make it a suprise success in general circulation." Libr J

Includes bibliographic references

Lyman, Francesca

The greenhouse trap; what we're doing to the atmosphere and how we can slow global warming; [by] Francesca Lyman, with Irving Mintzer, Kathleen Courrier, and James Mackenzie. Beacon Press 1990 190p il $21.95; pa $9.95   **363.7**

1. Greenhouse effect

ISBN 0-8070-8502-2; 0-8070-8503-0 (pa)

LC 89-43080

"A WRI guide to the environment"

This book provides a "survey of past, present, and probable future atmospheric degradation that touches upon nearly every aspect and facet of the topic. Sources are quoted, and prognostications are tentative and carefully qualified. . . . A number of commonsense measures to counteract atmospheric problems are outlined." Sci Books Films

Includes bibliography

Manes, Christopher, 1957-

Green rage; radical environmentalism and the unmaking of civilization. Little, Brown 1990 291p hardcover o.p. paperback available $9.95   **363.7**

1. Environmental protection 2. Radicals and radicalism 3. Human ecology

ISBN 0-316-54532-5 (pa)   LC 90-5697

The author, "a member of the ecology group Earth First!, here offers a spirited defense of radical environmentalism. He charges that mainstream enviromental groups see our relationship with nature only in utilitarian terms, that they have become too conservative. . . . Readers interested in preserving our environment will find the book very much worth their time." Publ Wkly

Includes bibliographic references

Mason, Robert J., 1955-

Atlas of United States environmental issues; [by] Robert J. Mason, Mark T. Mattson. Macmillan 1990 252p il maps $95   **363.7**

1. Conservation of natural resources 2. Pollution 3. Man—Influence on nature

ISBN 0-02-897261-9   LC 90-43707

"Using numerous full-color maps, tables, charts, and photographs, the atlas illustrates demographic, scientific, economic, political, and governmental aspects of the current and prospective environmental situation in the U.S." Am Libr

For a fuller review see: Booklist, Feb. 15, 1991

McKibben, Bill

The end of nature. Random House 1989 226p $19.95   **363.7**

1. Man—Influence on nature 2. Greenhouse effect

ISBN 0-394-57601-2   LC 89-42791

Also available in paperback from Anchor Bks.

"McKibben warns that due to culprits such as the greenhouse effect and genetic engineering, nature as we know it is nearing an end. He describes recent work on possible climatic change and suggests measures to allay the greenhouse effect. He also warns against the effects of biotechnology." Libr J

"Essential reading for anyone concerned with life on this planet." Booklist

Mitchell, George J.

World on fire; saving an endangered earth. Scribner 1991 247p $22.50   **363.7**

1. Environmental protection

ISBN 0-684-19231-4   LC 90-8578

This book discusses "the greenhouse effect, ozone depletion, deforestation, and acid rain. Mitchell has done his homework, reeling off page after page of data about the consequences of these scourges. He has also investigated the solutions and concludes that while they are difficult, they are do-able." Booklist

Includes bibliography

Null, Gary

Clearer, cleaner, safer, greener; a blueprint for detoxifying your environment. Villard Bks. 1990 xxvi, 293p $18.95; pa $12   **363.7**

1. Environmental health 2. Pollution

ISBN 0-394-58316-7; 0-679-74248-4 (pa)

LC 89-43467

"An Omni book"

An "analysis of the myriad sources of pollution and how they affect us through food, water, and the 'sick-building' syndrome. Null offers suggestions for detoxifying home and office, as well as assessing the broader arenas." Booklist

Includes bibliography

Oppenheimer, Michael

Dead heat; the race against the greenhouse effect; [by] Michael Oppenheimer, Robert H. Boyle. Basic Bks. 1990 268p $19.95; pa $10.95   **363.7**

1. Greenhouse effect 2. Environmental protection

ISBN 0-465-09804-5; 0-465-09808-8 (pa)

LC 89-18532

"A New Republic book"

The authors' thesis is that "industry and government can become vehicles for solving, instead of causing, the global environmental crisis." Publisher's note

Oppenheimer, Michael—*Continued*

Oppenheimer and Boyle "present the usual fictive scenarios about the greenhouse effect, based in this case on computer projections that they acknowledge may be wrong. They do, however, make a real contribution to the literature by their inventiveness in proposing political and economic solutions to the problems." Libr J

Includes bibliographic references

The **Poisoned** well; new strategies for groundwater protection; [by] Sierra Club Legal Defense Fund; Eric P. Jorgensen, editor. Island Press (Covelo) 1989 xxi, 422p il $35; pa $19.95 **363.7**

1. Water pollution 2. Water supply 3. Environment—Government policy—United States
ISBN 0-933280-56-4; 0-933280-55-6 (pa) LC 89-1940

The first part of this volume discusses "groundwater systems, health effects of groundwater contamination, sources of contamination, methods of testing, and analyzing the extent of groundwater contamination. . . . The next three parts consider citizen action plans, federal groundwater programs, and state and local programs." Choice

Includes bibliographic references

Rathje, William L.

Rubbish! the archaeology of garbage; [by] William L. Rathje and Cullen Murphy. HarperCollins Pubs. 1992 250p il $23; pa $12 **363.7**

1. Garbage Project 2. Refuse and refuse disposal 3. Excavations (Archeology)—United States
ISBN 0-06-016603-7; 0-06-092228-1 (pa)
LC 91-50452

"Since 1973, a group of anthropologists at the University of Arizona has been conducting a series of systematic archeological digs, . . . sifting, classifying and recording the contents of [urban landfills]. . . . The garbage project is based on [the] . . . premise: 'That what people have owned—and thrown away—can speak more eloquently, informatively, and truthfully about the lives they lead than they themselves ever may." N Y Times Book Rev

"A very accessible and entertaining book that never descends into academic gobbledygook or self-righteous environmentalism." Libr J

Ray, Dixy Lee

Trashing the planet; how science can help us deal with acid rain, depletion of the ozone, and nuclear waste (among other things); [by] Dixy Lee Ray and Lou Guzzo. Regnery Gateway 1990 206p $19.95 **363.7**

1. Pollution 2. Environmental protection 3. Science and civilization
ISBN 0-89526-544-3 LC 90-8344

Also available in paperback from HarperPerennial

The authors argue "that nuclear power is a safe and cheap source of energy; that acid rain is a vastly exaggerated problem; that chemical pesticides are not as dangerous as they have been made out to be; and that worry over the ozone hole is just an environmental scare tactic." Libr J

Ray "offers what may be the definitive statement of the pro-science, pro-technology approach to environmentalism."

Includes bibliographic references

Roan, Sharon

Ozone crisis; the 15-year evolution of a sudden global emergency. Wiley 1989 270p il $18.95; pa $9.95 **363.7**

1. Ozone 2. Air pollution
ISBN 0-471-61985-X; 0-471-52823-4 (pa)
LC 88-33952

"Wiley science editions"

The author discusses research into the effects of chloroflurocarbons (CFC's) on stratospheric ozone. She also examines government policy on this issue

"A sober, well-researched, and well-written book. . . . This is clearly one of the best case studies of the evolution of science-intensive public policy." Choice

Includes bibliography

Schneider, Stephen Henry

Global warming; are we entering the greenhouse century? [by] Stephen H. Schneider. Sierra Club Bks. 1989 317p maps $20 **363.7**

1. Greenhouse effect 2. Climate 3. Environment—Government policy—United States
ISBN 0-87156-693-1 LC 89-6048

Also available in paperback from Vintage Bks.

The author "explains the greenhouse effect, recounts . . . scientific work on atmospheric warming, including uncertainties and controversies, and gives advice on what could be done to ameliorate potential rapid climate change." Libr J

"Global Warming is lucid enough to clarify many matters for laypeople and, one would think, evenhanded enough to satisfy most scientists." N Y Rev Books

Includes bibliography

Steger, Will

Saving the earth; a citizen's guide to environmental action; by Will Steger and Jon Bowermaster; illustrations by Mike Mikos. Knopf 1990 xxiii, 306p il maps pa $19.95 **363.7**

1. Environmental protection 2. Social action
ISBN 0-679-73026-5 LC 89-43366

"A Byron Preiss book"

"Grouped into four general sections (atmosphere, land, water, and people), this environmental guide is further subdivided by specific problems—offering, for each one, description of cause, effect, and solutions." Booklist

This volume "is carefully written, with reasoned suggestions for action and informative diagrams. The authors prefer to build a case for their views rather than bludgeon the reader into submission." N Y Times Book Rev

Stevenson, L. Harold, 1940-

The Facts on File dictionary of environmental science; [by] L. Harold Stevenson, Bruce C. Wyman. Facts on File 1990 294p $24.95 **363.7**

1. Environmental protection—Dictionaries
ISBN 0-8160-2317-4 LC 90-28139

"Words, phrases, acronyms, and jargon from the new interdisciplinary field of environmental science are covered in this handy dictionary. Containing more than

Stevenson, L. Harold, 1940- —*Continued*
3,000 entries, this book presents concise, easy-to-understand explanations of organizations, processes, legislation, and other terminology." Am Libr
For a fuller review see: Booklist, Feb. 1, 1992

363.8 Food supply

Kutzner, Patricia L.
World hunger; a reference handbook. ABC-CLIO 1991 359p il (Contemporary world issues) $39.50   **363.8**
1. Hunger 2. Food supply
ISBN 0-87436-558-9   LC 90-25185
This book provides a broad overview of the many dimensions of world hunger, focusing specifically on the context of economic, social, political, and scientific constraints that affect global food security
"The chronology, biographies, directory and data sections are thorough and provide evaluative discussions." Choice

364 Criminology

Buchanan, Edna
The corpse had a familiar face; covering Miami, America's hottest beat. Random House 1987 364p $17.95   **364**
1. Crime 2. Police—Miami (Fla.)
ISBN 0-394-55794-8   LC 86-26185
Also available in paperback from Berkley Pub. Group
"Buchanan recollects her more than 15 years as a Florida crime reporter in a frank but not emotionalized autobiography that graphically captures the gritty, violent world she has come to know and the cops, victims, and villains with whom she has shared it." Booklist

364.03 Criminology— Encyclopedias and dictionaries

Encyclopedia of crime and justice; Sanford H. Kadish, editor in chief. Free Press 1983 4v set $375   **364.03**
1. Crime—Dictionaries   2. Criminals—Dictionaries
3. Criminal justice, Administration of
ISBN 0-02-918110-0   LC 83-7156
"In-depth, signed, authoritative articles ranging from 1000 to 10,000 words draw from all disciplines to explore the nature and causes of criminal behavior, the prevention of crime, punishment and treatment of offenders, the institutions of criminal justice, and the body of law that defines criminal behavior. Extensive cross references, a clear style, and selective bibliographies for further research make this a valued resource for a wide variety of general users and students." Ref Sources for Small & Medium-sized Libr. 5th edition

Encyclopedia of world crime; criminal justice, criminology, and law enforcement; [editor-in-chief] Jay Robert Nash. CrimeBooks 1990 6v il set $600   **364.03**
1. Crime—Dictionaries 2. Criminals—Dictionaries
ISBN 0-923582-00-2   LC 88-92729
Also available on CD-ROM

"Volumes 1-4 contain biographical, historical, and literary entries from early history to the present. Personal entries give full name, aliases, date and place of birth and death, profession, and type of crime. Bibliographic references follow each entry, including any film or fictionalized elaborations. These references are fully indexed and documented in Volume 6. Volume 5 is a dictionary of crime terms." SLJ
For a fuller review see: Booklist, Oct. 1, 1990

Nash, Jay Robert
World encyclopedia of 20th century murder. Paragon House 1992 693p il $49.95
364.03
1. Homicide—Dictionaries
ISBN 1-55778-506-6   LC 91-40492
This volume presents information condensed from the Encyclopedia of world crime (entered above). It contains some 1,000 alphabetically arranged entries for murderers and murders
For a review see: Booklist, April 15, 1992

World encyclopedia of organized crime. Paragon House 1992 624p il $49.95
364.03
1. Organized crime—Dictionaries
ISBN 1-55778-508-2   LC 91-40697
Condensed from Encyclopedia of world crime, entered above
"This is primarily a biographical collection concerning American mobsters, the Mafia predominantly. . . . A separate section—20 percent of the book—has very brief listings arranged geographically. . . . The coverage is extensive but uneven. . . . Despite weaknesses, this book is unique and is recommended for libraries with strong organized crime collections." Libr J

364.1 Criminal offenses

Abrahamsen, David, 1903-
Murder & madness; the secret life of Jack the Ripper. Fine, D.I. 1992 219p il map $21
364.1
1. Jack the Ripper
ISBN 1-55611-279-3   LC 91-58655
The author "pieces together a 'documentary theory' based on evidence 'overlooked by previous investigators,' including previously unreleased files from Scotland Yard. Abrahamsen asserts that Jack the Ripper was actually two men, Prince Albert Victor Edward (Prince Eddy) and James Kenneth Stephen, Prince Eddy's tutor; his theory centers on misogyny, which he claims motivated their killings of five East End prostitutes." Publ Wkly
Includes bibliographic references

Adams, James Ring
The big fix; inside the S & L scandal: how an unholy alliance of politics and money destroyed America's banking system. Wiley 1990 308p il $19.95; pa $12.95
364.1
1. Savings and loan associations
ISBN 0-471-51535-3; 0-471-53844-2 (pa)
LC 89-27378

Adams, James Ring—*Continued*

In this "exposé of the savings-and-loan crisis, Adams shows how accidents of history and a series of understandable but ill-conceived policies helped turn federal deposit insurance into a virtually unlimited government subsidy for fraud." Booklist

Includes bibliographic references

A full service bank; how BCCI stole billions around the world; [by] James Ring Adams and Douglas Frantz. Pocket Bks. 1992 381p $22; pa $10   **364.1**

1. Bank of Credit and Commerce International SA 2. Banks and banking
ISBN 0-671-72911-X; 0-671-72912-8 (pa)
                                         LC 91-44520

"A penetrating treatment of the underlying forces in the Bank of Commerce and Credit International scandal and of the detective work by several nations that ran the thieves to earth." N Y Times Book Rev

Includes bibliographic references

Alexander, Shana

Nutcracker; money, madness, murder: a family album. Doubleday 1985 444p o.p.; Dell paperback available $5.99   **364.1**

1. Schreuder, Frances 2. Schreuder, Marc 3. Homicide
ISBN 0-440-16512-1 (pa)   LC 85-7042

This is an account of the 1978 murder of Franklin Bradshaw, a Salt Lake City millionaire, plotted by his daughter and carried out by his grandson

Alexander "spins this yarn with brio, keeping the narrative rolling along, holding the reader's interest with deft infusions of telling detail." N Y Times Book Rev

Baldwin, James, 1924-1987

The evidence of things not seen. Holt & Co. 1985 125p hardcover o.p. paperback available $7.95   **364.1**

1. Williams, Wayne B., 1958- 2. Homicide 3. Atlanta (Ga.)—Race relations
ISBN 0-8050-0138-7 (pa)   LC 85-924

This book is "about the Atlanta child murders. . . . Baldwin believes that [the alleged murderer] Wayne Williams was a scapegoat—a necessary sacrifice—in order to solve the 28 murders of Black children and leave Atlanta an untarnished Southern city." Voice Youth Advocates

This "is a book of brilliant parts which fails to work as a whole. . . . 'Evidence of Things Not Seen' is nonetheless provocative and reiterates the themes that have made James Baldwin a significant writer." Christ Sci Monit

Barker, Rodney, 1946-

The broken circle; a true story of murder and magic in Indian country. Simon & Schuster 1992 367p $23   **364.1**

1. Homicide 2. Navajo Indians 3. Hate crimes
ISBN 0-671-74146-2   LC 91-39402

Also available in paperback from Ivy Bks.

"In the spring of 1975, three Navajo men were brutally murdered near Farmington, New Mexico. Three local high school students committed the murders but only served two years in a juvenile reformatory. Barker, who that same year had encountered a group of Navajos in Farmington protesting the killings, returned in 1988 to chronicle the saga and its aftermath." Libr J

This "is the story of a search for harmony, and that is the true mystery it explores. Read this book and you will know why there is friction between the Indian and non-Indian communities in this nation, why there will be no quick and easy solutions and why our differences are things worth cherishing and well worth knowing." N Y Times Book Rev

Barthel, Joan

Love or honor; the true story of an undercover cop who fell in love with a Mafia boss's daughter. Morrow 1989 263p o.p.; Avon Bks. paperback available $4.95   **364.1**

1. Police—New York (N.Y.) 2. Mafia
ISBN 0-380-71105-2 (pa)   LC 89-2872

"New York City policeman Chris Anastos infiltrated organized crime as an undercover agent in 1975. In the process, he began dating the daughter of a Mafioso." Libr J

"Expertly written, the book tells Anastos' story with the force and flair of a high-caliber TV miniseries." Publ Wkly

Baumann, Edward

Step into my parlor; the chilling story of serial killer Jeffrey Dahmer; [by] Ed Baumann. Bonus Bks. 1991 305p il $19.95   **364.1**

1. Dahmer, Jeffrey 2. Homicide
ISBN 0-929387-64-3   LC 91-76192

The author discourses "straightforwardly on the pathetic path of Dahmer's life, leading up to his two-year spree (1989-91) of killing a minimum of 17 young men before his apprehension." Booklist

Benedict, Helen

Virgin or vamp; how the press covers sex crimes. Oxford Univ. Press 1992 309p $25   **364.1**

1. Sex crimes 2. Press 3. Public opinion
ISBN 0-19-506680-4   LC 92-3821

The author discusses "the Greta and John Rideout case, the first case of marital rape in this country; the New Bedford gang rape, which became the source of the Jodie Foster movie The Accused; the Jennifer Levin-Robert Chambers case, known in the press as the 'Preppy Murder' case; and the case of the Central Park jogger." Columbia J Rev

"This is an essential purchase for communications and women's studies collections." Libr J

Includes bibliographic references

Berry, Jason

Lead us not into temptation; Catholic priests and the sexual abuse of children. Doubleday 1992 xxi, 407p $22.50   **364.1**

1. Child molesting 2. Catholic Church—Clergy
ISBN 0-385-42436-1   LC 92-8503

In this exposé "Berry documents scores of cases of sexual abuse of boys by Roman Catholic priests across the U.S. Tracking this tragic story from Louisiana to Washington, D.C., and then to New York, Berry reports

Berry, Jason—*Continued*
that most child-molesting priests are simply reassigned
to a different parish. He accuses the Catholic bishops
of evasion and cover-up." Publ Wkly

Includes bibliographic references

Bledsoe, Jerry
Blood games; a true account of family
murder. Dutton 1991 451p il $22.95
364.1

1. Pritchard, Chris 2. Homicide
ISBN 0-525-93369-7   LC 91-28485
Also available in paperback from New Am. Lib.

"On July 25, 1988, in the early morning hours, the
Von Stein house in Washington, North Carolina was
invaded and the Von Steins brutally attacked. Lieth was
murdered, and Bonnie, severely injured, barely survived.
Their son Chris was away at college, but suspicion quickly focused on him and his friends. Chris, a very bright
but totally unmotivated student, had become immersed
in a world of drugs, alcohol, and the game Dungeons
and Dragons." Libr J

"The book is far more than a true-crime study: it
is a devastating and profoundly disturbing portrait of a
certain kind of family life." Publ Wkly

Blumenthal, Ralph
Last days of the Sicilians; at war with the
Mafia: the FBI assault on the pizza
connection. Times Bks. 1988 354p $18.95
364.1

1. United States. Federal Bureau of Investigation
2. Mafia 3. Organized crime 4. Drug traffic
ISBN 0-8129-1594-1   LC 87-40597
Also available in paperback from Pocket Bks.

This book tells of the FBI investigation of a "heroin
and money-laundering network. Known as 'The Pizza
Connection,' this drug distribution pipeline operated here
through anonymous pizzerias and involved some of
America's largest financial institutions." Libr J

Bommersbach, Jana
The trunk murderess, Winnie Ruth Judd;
the truth about an American crime legend
revealed at last. Simon & Schuster 1992
270p il $20   364.1

1. Judd, Winnie Ruth, 1905- 2. Homicide
ISBN 0-671-74007-5   LC 92-27493

In 1931 Winnie Ruth Judd "was found guilty of killing her two friends in Phoenix and dismembering the
body of one. She spent almost forty years in prisons
and insane asylums. In setting out to research the crime,
Bommersbach uncovers a welter of lies and unanswered
questions." Libr J

Brown, Arnold R.
Lizzie Borden; the legend, the truth, the
final chapter. Rutledge Hill Press 1991 382p
il $18.95   364.1

1. Borden, Lizzie, 1860-1927 2. Homicide
ISBN 1-55853-099-1   LC 91-19250
Also available in paperback from Dell

"The infamous 1892 hatchet murders of Andrew and
Abby Borden are examined . . . by Brown, who offers
convincing evidence that the couple was killed by Liz-

zie's illegitimate half-brother, William." Booklist

Includes bibliographic references

Browne, Angela
When battered women kill. Free Press
1987 228p $22.95; $11.95   364.1

1. Wife abuse 2. Homicide
ISBN 0-02-903880-4; 0-02-903881-2 (pa)
LC 86-25789

This is a "study of 42 abused women charged with
the murder or attempted murder of their partners." NY
Times Book Rev

"Browne's book, like most of the literature on battering, focuses on the victims because, as Browne points
out, there is little information about the perpetrators of
the crime: the husbands. But Browne never loses sight
of them. . . . Browne also examines the shocking inversion that allows society, through sex-role stereotyping and
legal precedent to condone husbands' brutality while
blaming wives." Psychol Today

Includes bibliography

Bugliosi, Vincent
And the sea will tell; [by] Vincent Bugliosi
with Bruce B. Henderson. Norton 1991 574p
il $22.95   364.1

1. Jenkins, Jennifer 2. Walker, Buck 3. Homicide
4. Trials (Homicide)
ISBN 0-393-02919-0   LC 90-37457
Also available in paperback from Ivy Bks.

The author recounts how he successfully defended Jennifer Jenkins of murder charges relating to the 1974
slaying of a couple on a remote Pacific island

"Skillfully guiding the reader through the labyrinthine
legal process, Bugliosi provides true-crime fans with both
a juicy case and a bonanza of back-room detail." Booklist

Helter skelter; the true story of the
Manson murders; [by] Vincent Bugliosi with
Curt Gentry. Norton 1974 502p il maps
o.p.; Bantam Bks. paperback available $6.99
364.1

1. Manson, Charles, 1934- 2. Homicide
ISBN 0-553-25529-0 (pa)

This book "by the prosecutor at the Tate-LaBianca
murder trial tells the inside story of the Manson Family
murders, the investigations, and the trial." Libr J

Capote, Truman, 1924-1984
In cold blood; a true account of a
multiple murder and its consequences.
Random House 1966 c1965 343p $24.95
364.1

1. Hickock, Richard, 1931-1965 2. Smith, Perry,
1928-1965 3. Homicide
ISBN 0-394-43023-9
Also available G.K. Hall large print edition and in
paperback from New Am. Lib.

"A breathtaking account of a grotesque series of
murders by two men in Kansas, which Capote called
a 'nonfiction novel.'" Reader's Ency

Demaris, Ovid

The last Mafioso; the treacherous world of Jimmy Fratianno. Times Bks. 1981 463p il o.p.; Bantam Bks. paperback available $4.95 **364.1**

1. Fratianno, Jimmy, 1913-1993 2. Organized crime
ISBN 0-553-25474-X (pa)   LC 80-50926

"Recounting Fratianno's varied career as enforcer, hit man, schemer, and womanizer, Demaris tells how the Weasel entered his life of crime, rose through the ranks to become the Cosa Nostra's Los Angeles boss, and was 'persuaded' to turn state's evidence via a witness protection plan." Booklist

DeSantis, John

For the color of his skin; the murder of Yusuf Hawkins and the trial of Bensonhurst; introduction by Alan M. Dershowitz. Pharos Bks. 1991 240p il $18.95 **364.1**

1. Hawkins, Yusuf 2. Homicide 3. Hate crimes 4. Bensonhurst (New York, N.Y.)
ISBN 0-88687-621-4   LC 91-16557

The author recounts the murder of sixteen-year-old Yusuf Hawkins by a group of white youths in the Bensonhurst section of Brooklyn in 1989 and the racial tension and trial that ensued

DeSantis "provides a thorough and unbiased investigative account of all facets of the case. The roles of the media, the political system, law enforcement, community and civic leaders, and personal prejudice are all examined in turn and their impact assessed. . . . Highly recommended for public and academic libraries." Libr J

Duncan, Lois, 1934-

Who killed my daughter? Delacorte Press 1992 289p il $20 **364.1**

1. Arquette, Kaitlyn Clare, 1970-1989 2. Homicide
ISBN 0-385-30781-0   LC 92-89

"Duncan, a highly acclaimed author of young adult literature, here tells the story of her agonizing search for her daughter's murderers. The police wrote off the crime as a 'random shooting,' but Duncan could not accept that verdict and set about her own investigation of what really happened." Libr J

"Readers critical of either Duncan's contacts with paranormals or her talking to God and to her dead daughter may be put off by the book, but many will be sympathetic to this mother's plight." Publ Wkly

Earley, Pete

Prophet of death; the Mormon blood-atonement killings. Morrow 1991 448p il $21 **364.1**

1. Lundgren, Jeffrey 2. Homicide 3. Cults 4. Mormons
ISBN 0-688-10584-X   LC 91-25557

Also available in paperback from Avon Bks.

This book recounts the 1989 Mormon cult murders of the Avery family by a group led by Jeff Lundgren. The author emphasizes the dynamics within the cult and Lundgren's growing psychosis

"Perhaps as interesting as how the group came together is the disintegration that followed when the individuals realized they were facing murder charges. Their faith in Lundgren only seemed as strong as his ability to protect them." Libr J

Includes bibliographic references

Eddy, Paul, 1944-

The cocaine wars; [by] Paul Eddy, Hugo Sabogal, Sara Walden. Norton 1988 399p il o.p.; Bantam Bks. paperback available $4.95 **364.1**

1. Cocaine 2. Drugs and crime
ISBN 0-553-28171-2 (pa)   LC 87-33946

This "look at the cocaine trade concentrates on one source country, Bolivia; one American city, Miami, reputed to be the gateway to the U.S. for 80 percent of all cocaine; and one cartel of wealthy Colombian dealers." Booklist

"The authors avoid sensationalism and marshall their massive documentation impressively." Publ Wkly

Includes bibliography

Egginton, Joyce

From cradle to grave; the short lives and strange deaths of Marybeth Tinning's nine children. Morrow 1989 363p il $18.95 **364.1**

1. Tinning, Marybeth 2. Homicide 3. Trials (Homicide)
ISBN 0-688-07566-5   LC 88-64106

Also available in paperback from Jove Publs.

"Schenectady housewife Marybeth Tinning gave birth to eight children and adopted one. Over a 14-year period, all of those children died, most from unexplained causes. After confessing to killing three of the kids, Marybeth was convicted of second-degree murder in 1987 and sentenced to 20 years in prison." Booklist

"Egginton has written a moving, sympathetic account of human tragedy, including insights into what triggers infanticide." Libr J

Elkind, Peter

The death shift; the true story of nurse Genene Jones and the Texas baby murders. Viking 1989 351p il o.p.; New Am. Lib. paperback available $4.95 **364.1**

1. Jones, Genene 2. Homicide
ISBN 0-451-40196-4 (pa)   LC 89-5513

"In 1981 Genene Jones was a nurse in pediatric intensive care at Medical Center Hospital in San Antonio. Although her bizarre behavior made Jones a suspect when babies began dying inexpicably on her shift, she was allowed to leave the hospital with a glowing reference. Jones then moved to a smaller clinic in a nearby town and killed again. . . . This is true-crime reporting at its most compelling." Booklist

Fisher, Jim, 1939-

The Lindbergh case. Rutgers Univ. Press 1987 480p il $22.95 **364.1**

1. Lindbergh, Charles, Jr. 2. Hauptmann, Bruno Richard 3. Kidnapping 4. Trials (Kidnapping)
ISBN 0-8135-1233-6   LC 86-28023

"Refuting those who claim that Bruno Richard Hauptmann was framed, the author presents a convincing case that he was guilty of the kidnap-murder of 20-month-old Charles A. Lindbergh Jr." Publ Wkly

Fisher, Jim, 1939-—_Continued_

"The author simply lets the facts stand alone—and, ultimately, they are more than sufficient to drive the reader through the book." N Y Times Book Rev

Includes bibliography

Fox, Stephen R. (Stephen Russell)

Blood and power; organized crime in twentieth-century America; [by] Stephen Fox. Morrow 1989 512p il o.p.; Penguin Bks. paperback available $10.95   **364.1**

1. Organized crime 2. Mafia 3. Criminal justice, Administration of
ISBN 0-14-013438-7 (pa)   LC 89-3128

The author "explores the ethnic and class dimension of organized crime, from Irish, Jewish and Italian bootleggers of the Prohibition era to the latest influx of newer immigrant groups, especially Latin and Asian gangsters." Publ Wkly

"In chronicling the lives and activities of various gangland chieftains, Fox writes with a kind of grim verve that illuminates his subject without romanticizing it. . . . An appalling but fascinating book." Booklist

Includes bibliography

Ganey, Terry

St. Joseph's children; a true story of terror and justice. Carol Pub. Group 1989 237p il $17.95   **364.1**

1. Hatcher, Charles R., 1929-1984 2. Homicide
ISBN 0-8184-0509-0   LC 89-22291

"A Lyle Stuart book"

"This is the story of Charles Hatcher who, in his lifetime, [allegedly] murdered at least 16 people, including three children. Throughout his 37-year career of crime . . . [psychiatrists] repeatedly failed to identify him as a multiple murderer." Publisher's note

The author "has written a gripping tale of murder, pursuit, and justice." Libr J

Gugliotta, Guy F.

Kings of cocaine; inside the Medellín Cartel, an astonishing true story of murder, money, and international corruption; [by] Guy Gugliotta and Jeff Leen. Simon & Schuster 1989 391p il o.p.; HarperCollins Pubs. paperback available $4.95   **364.1**

1. Medellin Cartel 2. Cocaine 3. Drugs and crime
ISBN 0-06-100027-2 (pa)   LC 88-36756

"The authors trace the cocaine routes of supply and demand back to their source in Colombia, covering each step in the production and distribution chain. They also show how the narcotics ring gained a foothold in the U.S. market and how organized crime involved itself." Booklist

Includes bibliographic references

Hafner, Katie

Cyberpunk; outlaws and hackers on the computer frontier; [by] Katie Hafner and John Markoff. Simon & Schuster 1991 368p hardcover o.p. paperback available $12   **364.1**

1. Computer crimes
ISBN 0-671-77879-X (pa)   LC 91-11598

The authors "detail stories of three recent cases of major computer misdeeds. They portray Kevin Mitnick's penetration of Digital Equipment Corporation's top-secret computer system, West Berliner Pengo's international espionage scheme, and Robert Morris' 'worm' that disabled many of the nation's computer networks. The authors present objective, well-researched reporting while telling spellbinding tales that raise issues but leave conclusions to the reader." Booklist

Includes bibliographic references

Hinckle, Warren

Deadly secrets; the CIA-Mafia war against Castro and the assassination of J.F.K. [by] Warren Hinckle, William W. Turner. Thunder's Mouth Press 1992 lxiii, 464p $21.95; pa $14.95   **364.1**

1. Castro, Fidel, 1927- 2. United States. Central Intelligence Agency 3. United States—Foreign relations—Cuba 4. Cuba—Foreign relations—United States 5. Mafia
ISBN 1-56025-046-1; 1-56025-053-4 (pa)
                                                 LC 92-22925

A revised edition of The fish is red, published 1981 by Harper & Row

The authors contend "that RFK cut private deals with the Mafia which solidified the mob's ties with the Central Intelligence Agency. Furthermore, the authors charge, the CIA was involved in at least a dozen attempts on Castro's life through 1987. . . . [This book] supports current speculation that the murderers of JFK were part of a CIA-Mafia hit team." Publ Wkly

Includes bibliographic references

Horton, Sue

The Billionaire Boys Club. St. Martin's Press 1989 354p il hardcover o.p. paperback available $4.95   **364.1**

1. Hunt, Joe 2. Homicide
ISBN 0-312-92232-9 (pa)   LC 89-4249

"Like an unfolding mystery, this true-crime account describes how a mesmerizing young man from Los Angeles named Joe Hunt gathered together a group of his privileged peers in an investment corporation. When the business went sour, he convinced several of the boys to become involved in murder." Booklist

Humes, Edward

Buried secrets; a true story of serial murder, black magic, and drug-running on the U.S. border. Dutton 1991 412p il o.p.; New Am. Lib. paperback available $5.99
                                                  364.1

1. Kilroy, Mark 2. Homicide 3. Drug traffic 4. Cults
ISBN 0-451-17164-0 (pa)   LC 90-46461

Humes, Edward—*Continued*
"The 1989 disappearance of a Texas college student led authorities to a dangerous group of satanic worshipers who kidnapped, mutilated, and killed him. Humes' frank, riveting account of the Mexican cult and their bizarre activities is suggested for . . . readers who can handle some of the more gruesome descriptions of devil worship." Booklist

Hurt, Henry
Reasonable doubt; an investigation into the assassination of John F. Kennedy. Holt & Co. 1986 c1985 555p il hardcover o.p. paperback available $15.95 **364.1**
1. Kennedy, John F. (John Fitzgerald), 1917-1963—Assassination
ISBN 0-8050-0360-6 (pa)   LC 85-7571

The author "assembles an overview of evidence, circumstances and theory about the assassination of John F. Kennedy in 1963. In addition to reviewing the eight official inquiries and the various conspiracy theories, he minutely examines seemingly outlandish notions." Publ Wkly

Includes bibliography

Johnson, Joyce, 1935-
What Lisa knew: the truths and lies of the Steinberg case. Putnam 1990 302p o.p.; Zebra Bks. paperback available $4.95
                                            364.1
1. Steinberg, Joel 2. Nussbaum, Hedda, 1942- 3. Steinberg, Lisa, d. 1987 4. Homicide 5. Child abuse
ISBN 0-8217-3387-7 (pa)   LC 89-48171

This book is a psychological examination of the circumstances and persons involved in the 1987 death of six-year-old Lisa Steinberg
"In an eloquent re-creation of the emotional and psychological history behind the crime, novelist Joyce Johnson suggests . . . [that Nussbaum] was equally guilty. . . . Through extensive interviews with people who knew the couple, Johnson paints a horrifying picture of a sadomasochistic relationship." Newsweek

Jones, Ann, 1937-
Women who kill. Holt, Rinehart & Winston 1980 408p o.p.; Fawcett Bks. paperback available $4.95 **364.1**
1. Homicide 2. Criminals
ISBN 0-449-21609-8 (pa)   LC 80-12329

"Jones contends that the restricted sphere of women and their subordinate status pushed them into areas of activity viewed as criminal. For colonial women a particular kind of murder was common—infanticide. . . . Beyond the American colonial period, Jones examines murderers from Lizzie Borden to Alice Crimmins." Best Sellers

Includes bibliographic references

Jones, Jack
Let me take you down; inside the mind of Mark David Chapman, the man who killed John Lennon. Villard Bks. 1992 281p il $21 **364.1**
1. Chapman, Mark David 2. Homicide
ISBN 0-679-41144-5   LC 92-53655

"This account of [Chapman's] life and the obsessive forces that culminated in the death of his former idol is based largely on Chapman's recollections. Jones's book would have been strengthened by a critical analysis of Chapman's pathology . . . but nonetheless it is engrossing reading." Libr J

Kaplan, Joel
Murder of innocence; the tragic life and final rampage of Laurie Dann; [by] Joel Kaplan, George Papajohn, and Eric Zorn. Warner Bks. 1990 335p $19.95; pa $4.99
                                            364.1
1. Dann, Laurie Wasserman, d. 1988 2. Homicide
ISBN 0-446-51572-8; 0-446-36002-3 (pa)
                                        LC 90-50293

The authors tell the story of Laurie Dann, who on May 20, 1988, "went on a rampage on Chicago's North shore. . . . In little more than two hours, Dann tried to burn down a house with three people inside, started a fire in an elementary school, attempted to poison about 50 people, shot and killed an 8-year-old in front of his classmates, wounded five more young children and fired a bullet into a young man she was holding hostage." N Y Times Book Rev
"This is a fascinating, fast-paced, and well-written story that almost immediately engages the reader." Libr J

Kent, David, 1923-
Forty whacks; new evidence in the life and legend of Lizzie Borden; with foreword by Robert A. Flynn. Yankee Bks. 1992 231p il $19.95 **364.1**
1. Borden, Lizzie, 1860-1927 2. Homicide
ISBN 0-89909-351-5   LC 92-9799

"It is known with certainty that Andrew and Abby Borden were killed in 1892. All else is conjecture. . . . Kent reveals new evidence about the case, although he does not advocate a suspect. . . . Still, *Forty Whacks* gives a good presentation of the social history of the time. It also shows Lizzie as she probably was instead of the way the late Victorian tabloids portrayed her." Libr J

Includes bibliographic references

Levine, Dennis B.
Inside out; an insider's account of Wall Street; [by] Dennis B. Levine, with William Hoffer. Putnam 1991 431p il $22.95 **364.1**
1. Insider trading 2. Wall Street (New York, N.Y.)
ISBN 0-399-13655-X   LC 91-3149

Also available in paperback from Berkley Pub. Group

Levine describes and reflects upon his use of inside knowledge concerning mergers and acquisitions. He was convicted in 1986 for illegal stock trading and served seventeen months in prison

Levine, Dennis B.—*Continued*
"Levine's chronicle is free of business-world jargon and obtuse concepts, the pace is intense, and the events are fascinating." Libr J

Levine, Michael
Deep cover; the inside story of how DEA infighting, incompetence, and subterfuge lost us the biggest battle of the drug war. Delacorte Press 1990 319p il $19.95 **364.1**
1. United States. Drug Enforcement Administration 2. Drug traffic
ISBN 0-385-30128-6   LC 90-144091
Also available in paperback from Dell
"For 25 years Michael Levine was . . . an undercover agent . . . for the Federal Drug Enforcement Administration. As he sees it, drug dealers were not his only enemy, merely the ones who carried weapons and threatened bodily harm. At times far more vexing to him were, as he terms them, 'the suits,' those bureaucrats entrusted with guiding this country's battle against controlled substances. . . . Mr. Levine has woven a fascinating, exciting and sometimes horrifyingly comic tale." N Y Times Book Rev

Lindsey, Robert
A gathering of saints; a true story of money, murder, and deceit. Simon & Schuster 1988 397p il o.p.; Dell paperback available $4.95   **364.1**
1. Hofmann, Mark 2. Homicide 3. Forgery 4. Mormons
ISBN 0-440-20558-1 (pa)   LC 88-18318
This is an "account of the notorious document forgeries and 1985 bomb-killings by disaffected Latter-day Saint Mark Hofmann. . . . [The author] offers a straightforward if hardly simple . . . chronological tracing of the case." Booklist

Maas, Peter, 1929-
In a child's name; the legacy of a mother's murder. Simon & Schuster 1990 378p il $15.95; pa $5.99   **364.1**
1. Taylor, Kenneth Z. 2. Taylor, Teresa, d. 1984 3. Homicide 4. Child custody
ISBN 0-671-72627-7; 0-671-74619-7 (pa)
       LC 90-47526
True crime drama about a sociopathic dentist, his wife's murder, and the prolonged courtroom battles over the custody of his son
The author "lets the inherent drama in this case speak for itself, without sensationalized embellishments." Booklist

Manhunt. Random House 1986 301p $17.95   **364.1**
1. Wilson, Edwin P. 2. Criminals 3. Munitions—Libya
ISBN 0-394-55293-8   LC 85-25762
This is the "story of Edwin P. Wilson, a CIA operative turned international arms dealer, who grew rich providing restricted explosives and aid to Libya's Qaddafi." Publ Wkly
"It's an old story, and Mr. Maas tells it well, with a fine eye for character and setting and a good reporter's tenacity in finding out things a whole lot of people don't want him to know." N Y Times Book Rev

Malkin, Peter Z.
Eichmann in my hands; [by] Peter Z. Malkin & Harry Stein. Warner Bks. 1990 272p il hardcover o.p. paperback available $5.95   **364.1**
1. Eichmann, Adolf, 1906-1962 2. Intelligence service—Israel
ISBN 0-446-36095-3 (pa)   LC 89-40464
Also available Thorndike Press large print edition
"An Israeli secret agent relates his role in the capture and extradition of Nazi war criminal Adolf Eichmann." Booklist
Includes bibliographic references

McGinniss, Joe
Blind faith. Putnam 1988 381p il o.p.; New Am. Lib. paperback available $5.95
       364.1
1. Homicide
ISBN 0-451-16806-2 (pa)   LC 88-6754
"In 1984, Rob Marshall, a well-to-do New Jersey businessman, was knocked unconscious at a picnic area, and Maria, his wife, was killed. Police investigation led to Marshall's trial and, for two of his sons, to the anguishing discovery that their father was behind Maria's murder." Libr J
"This is an excellent example of the true-detective 'genre.'" West Coast Rev Books

Cruel doubt. Simon & Schuster 1991 460p il hardcover o.p. paperback available $5.99
       364.1
1. Von Stein, Bonnie 2. Pritchard, Chris 3. Homicide
ISBN 0-671-77539-1 (pa)   LC 91-27633
In July 1988 in Washington, North Carolina, Lieth Von Stein was fatally stabbed and his wife Bonnie was injured. In January 1990, Bonnie Von Stein's son Chris Pritchard was sentenced to life imprisonment plus twenty years for engineering the crime. This is an account of those events

Fatal vision. Putnam 1983 663p o.p.; New Am. Lib. paperback available $6.99 **364.1**
1. MacDonald, Jeffrey R. 2. Homicide
ISBN 0-451-16566-7 (pa)   LC 82-24127
"The complex story of Jeffrey MacDonald, a Princeton-educated doctor and Green Beret captain who was accused of brutally murdering his wife and their two young daughters on a dreary February night in 1970." Best Sellers
"This is a wisely observant, well-written, and understated book." Harpers
Includes bibliography

Mokhiber, Russell
Corporate crime and violence; big business power and the abuse of the public trust. Sierra Club Bks. 1988 450p hardcover o.p. paperback available $16   **364.1**
1. Business—Corrupt practices 2. Crime 3. Corporations
ISBN 0-87156-608-7 (pa)   LC 87-4730
Mokhiber offers us thirty-six cases of corporate misconduct that killed people or destroyed the environment. . . . [The author] is not dealing in 'exposés.' He is reviewing history for the purpose of suggesting reform.

Mokhiber, Russell—*Continued*
And he does it beautifully, masterfully." Nation

Includes bibliographies

Mones, Paul A.
When a child kills; abused children who kill their parents. Pocket Bks. 1991 331p $21; pa $5.99   **364.1**
1. Homicide 2. Child abuse 3. Incest
ISBN 0-671-67420-X; 0-671-67421-8 (pa) LC 91-4212

"Mones, a children's rights advocate, presents a disturbing look at the crime of parricide. . . . In eight separate case studies, he deals with boys and girls who kill their fathers or mothers and children who kill both parents or who hire others to commit the parricide." Booklist

Naifeh, Steven W., 1952-
The Mormon murders; a true story of greed, forgery, deceit, and death; [by] Steven Naifeh and Gregory White Smith. Weidenfeld & Nicolson 1988 458p il o.p.; New Am. Lib. paperback available $5.95
                                             364.1
1. Hofmann, Mark 2. Homicide 3. Forgery 4. Mormons
ISBN 0-451-40152-2 (pa)   LC 88-5712

An account of the investigation and trial of Mark Hofmann, the forger of the so-called Salamander Letter who resorted to killing his associates

Olsen, Jack
Predator; rape, madness, and injustice in Seattle. Delacorte Press 1991 366p $19.95
                                             364.1
1. Smith, McDonald J., 1952- 2. Titus, Steve G. (Steve Gary), 1949-1985 3. Rape
ISBN 0-385-29935-4   LC 90-19228

Also available in paperback from Dell

This is "a biographical exploration of a sociopath who raped more than 50 Seattle-area women at knifepoint. . . . Olsen details the life of pseudonymous Mac Smith—his dysfunctional family, early sexual experimentation, and bent toward crime. . . . A young Seattle man, Steve Titus, was arrested, tried, and convicted for one of Smith's rapes and saved from prison only by the Pulitzer Prize-winning efforts of journalist Paul Henderson." Booklist

Outrage: the story behind the Tawana Brawley hoax; by Robert D. McFadden [et al.] Bantam Bks. 1990 408p $21.95
                                             364.1
1. Brawley, Tawana 2. Rape 3. United States—Race relations
ISBN 0-553-05756-1   LC 90-32338

"The Tawana Brawley case attracted national attention in 1987 when the black teenager from Wappingers Falls, N.Y., claimed that she had been kidnapped, gang-raped and defiled by white racists, among them law officers. . . . In an impressive exposé that distills much . . . information from scores of interviews, McFadden and a team of fellow *New York Times* journalists present evidence that Brawley concocted her story, with her mother's complicity." Publ Wkly

Includes bibliographic references

Posner, Gerald L.
Warlords of crime; Chinese secret societies—the new Mafia. McGraw-Hill 1988 289p il o.p.; Penguin Bks. paperback available $9.95   **364.1**
1. Organized crime 2. Drug traffic
ISBN 0-14-012340-7 (pa)   LC 88-9667

"The Chinese virtually invented organized crime, asserts Posner, and their secret societies, called Triads, not only control the heroin trade in the U.S., but the 'Chinese crime dragon has systematically spread its tentacles around the world.' Posner researched the Chinese warlords in 19 countries on five continents." Booklist

"Posner's research is prodigious and often extremely courageous. . . . 'Warlords of Crime' is powerful, frightening and, unfortunately, nonfiction." N Y Times Book Rev

Includes bibliography

Prouty, L. Fletcher (Leroy Fletcher), 1917-
JFK; the CIA, Vietnam, and the plot to assassinate John F. Kennedy; with an introduction by Oliver Stone. Carol Pub. Group 1992 xxxv, 366p il $22   **364.1**
1. Kennedy, John F. (John Fitzgerald), 1917-1963—Assassination 2. United States. Central Intelligence Agency
ISBN 1-55972-130-8   LC 92-1655

"A Birch Lane Press book"

The author proposes "that a super-powerful, avaricious power elite engineered the Cold War and all its pivotal events—Korea, Vietnam, the U-2 incident, the Bay of Pigs, and the Kennedy assassination. Although they are never identified, these shadowy technocrats, working through the CIA, allegedly had Kennedy murdered because he was on the brink of ending America's commitment to Vietnam, along with its billions of dollars of military contracts." Libr J

Includes bibliographic references

Provost, Gary, 1944-
Perfect husband; the true story of the trusting bride who discovered her husband was a coldblooded killer. Pocket Bks. 1991 248p il $20; pa $5.50   **364.1**
1. Fotopoulos, Konstantin 2. Fotopoulos, Lisa 3. Hunt, Deidre Michelle, 1969- 4. Homicide
ISBN 0-671-72493-2; 0-671-72494-0 (pa)
                                       LC 91-25331

This "is the true story of a man who tried to murder his wife—not once, but seven times. Provost recounts Floridian Lisa Fotopoulos' courtship and marriage to a man her relatives picked out for her. . . . Only during the investigation of the last bungled attempt on her life . . . was it found that Konstantin was also a counterfeiter, a thief, a pimp, and a drug dealer." Booklist

The author "tells the tale well, creating an ominous picture of how attractive a sociopath can be." Publ Wkly

Radish, Kris
Run, Bambi, run; the beautiful ex-cop and convicted murderer who escaped to freedom and won America's heart. Carol Pub. Group 1992 291p il $18.95   **364.1**
1. Bembenek, Laurie 2. Homicide 3. Escapes
ISBN 1-55972-103-0   LC 91-43175

Radish, Kris—*Continued*

Also available in paperback from New Am. Lib.

"A Birch Lane Press book"

"Former Milwaukee police officer Lawrencia 'Bambi' Bembenek made headlines in 1990 when she escaped from the Wisconsin prison in which she had been held since a 1982 murder conviction. The former model, convicted of killing her police detective husband's ex-wife, was eventually located in Canada. . . . Bembenek vehemently denies any involvement in the murder and cites Milwaukee police department corruption and shoddy investigative work as reasons for her arrest and conviction." Booklist

Ressler, Robert K.

"Whoever fights monsters—"; [by] Robert K. Ressler & Tom Shachtman. St. Martin's Press 1992 256p il $22.95; pa $4.99

364.1

1. Homicide
ISBN 0-312-07883-8; 0-312-95044-6 (pa) LC 92-4013

"A Thomas Dunne book"

An "account of Ressler's 30-year FBI career and the development of the Violent Criminal Apprehension Program. Ressler's numerous interviews with convicted killers (David Berkowitz, Ted Bundy, etc.), use of behavioral sciences principles, and many years of detective experience have given him an uncanny ability to 'read' a crime scene and develop a criminal profile of the offender. Detailing multiple serial killing investigations in which his profiling was instrumental in the apprehension of criminals gives the reader an insider's view into police work." Libr J

Rubin, Lillian B.

Quiet rage; Bernie Goetz in a time of madness. Farrar, Straus & Giroux 1986 246p $16.95 **364.1**

1. Goetz, Bernhard 2. Trials
ISBN 0-374-24063-9 LC 86-18433

Also available in paperback from University of Calif. Press

The author, a clinical psychologist, "tackles the case of Bernhard Goetz, New York's 'subway vigilante' who, in 1984, gunned down four black youths he assumed meant him harm." Booklist

"'Quiet Rage' is a book that takes a look at much more than just an event. It is a critical analysis of the criminal justice system, the media, and the malady in American society." Best Sellers

Rule, Ann

Everything she ever wanted; a true story of obsessive love, murder, and betrayal. Simon & Schuster 1992 527p il $23

364.1

1. Allanson, Patricia Radcliffe Taylor 2. Homicide
ISBN 0-671-69070-1 LC 92-21541

"Spoiled rotten by her family, Patricia Vann Radcliffe Taylor Allanson, a Georgia beauty whose goal in life was to emulate Scarlett O'Hara, led a life of deadly horror. . . . Her presence was a constant danger to people who stood in her way: her brother a suicide, her new in-laws shot dead, her grandparents-in-law nearly poisoned by arsenic, her employer severely overdosed, her daughter, who finally saw the awful truth about her mother, possibly poisoned. Rule's tautly written study of this

diabolical woman constantly fascinates the reader." Libr J

Scott, Peter Dale

Cocaine politics; drugs, armies, and the CIA in Central America; [by] Peter Dale Scott and Jonathan Marshall. University of Calif. Press 1991 279p $24.95; pa $13

364.1

1. Drug traffic 2. Central America—Politics and government
ISBN 0-520-07312-6; 0-520-07781-4 (pa)

LC 90-48813

This book explores the "connection between the Nicaraguan Contras, U.S. support for them, and drugs. Marshall and Scott argue that the United States might actually have furthered the flow of cocaine from Central America to the States by colluding with anti-Sandinista forces. . . . An authoritative account." Libr J

Includes bibliographic references

Sessions, Shelley

Dark obsession; a true story of incest and justice; [by] Shelley Sessions with Peter Meyer. Putnam 1990 316p o.p.; Berkley Pub. Group paperback available $4.95

364.1

1. Incest 2. Child molesting
ISBN 0-425-12296-4 (pa) LC 89-36591

"Sessions suffered years of sexual abuse by her stepfather, a Texas rancher-millionaire, portrayed as a manipulator obsessed with total control of her life. Shelly's mother, 'fragile and malleable,' failed to intervene. Using his connections, Mr. Sessions served just six months in a private hospital for the crime of incest—it was not until Shelly successfully sued him for $10 million that justice was done." Libr J

Siegel, Barry

A death in White Bear Lake; the true chronicle of an all-American town. Bantam Bks. 1990 448p il $19.95; pa $5.99 **364.1**

1. Jurgens, Lois 2. Homicide 3. Child abuse
ISBN 0-553-05790-1; 0-553-29048-7 (pa)

LC 90-32487

"Siegel tells the story of Harold and Lois Jurgens, a Minnesota couple who adopted two children and beat the younger one, Dennis, to death in 1963. The Jurgens later adopted four more children, all of whom were also abused. Lois Jurgens was successfully prosecuted for third-degree murder after Dennis's natural mother came looking for her son and expressed suspicions about his death, 22 years after it happened." Libr J

The author "interviewed hundreds of people and examined endless documents dating back more than 30 years. This is a work of genuine journalism." N Y Times Book Rev

Sifakis, Carl

The Mafia encyclopedia. Facts on File 1987 367p il $40; pa $17.95 **364.1**

1. Mafia—Dictionaries 2. Organized crime—Dictionaries
ISBN 0-8160-1172-9; 0-8160-1856-1 (pa)

LC 84-21220

Sifakis, Carl—*Continued*
Entries "cover U.S. crime figures and related places, incidents, and figures of speech during the twentieth century. The term 'Mafia' covers the crime network that exists in the U.S. and is not limited to Italian criminal activity." Booklist

Sillitoe, Linda, 1948-
Salamander; the story of the Mormon forgery murders; [by] Linda Sillitoe and Allen Roberts; technical appendix by George Throckmorton. Signature Bks. (Salt Lake City) 1988 556p hardcover o.p. paperback available $5.95   **364.1**
1. Hofmann, Mark 2. Homicide 3. Forgery 4. Mormons
ISBN 0-941214-87-7 (pa)   LC 87-32466
An account of the investigation and trial of Mark Hofmann, the forger of the so-called Salamander Letter who resorted to killing his associates

Stein, Benjamin, 1944-
A license to steal; the untold story of Michael Milken and the conspiracy to bilk the nation; [by] Benjamin J. Stein. Simon & Schuster 1992 219p il $23   **364.1**
1. Milken, Michael R. 2. Drexel Burnham Lambert Incorporated 3. Junk bonds 4. Stock exchange
ISBN 0-671-74272-8   LC 92-31121
The author argues that Michael "Milken was very much in charge of the Drexel Burnham Lambert junk bond operation in its heyday in the 1980s and knew that he was selling a product that was based on deeply flawed financial analysis." Libr J
"This concise, punchy exposé is the best and clearest guide yet to the workings of Milken's money machine." Publ Wkly

Stevens, Mark, 1947-
Sudden death; the rise and fall of E.F. Hutton. NAL Bks. 1989 298p hardcover o.p. paperback available $9.95   **364.1**
1. E. F. Hutton Group Inc.
ISBN 0-452-26438-3 (pa)   LC 89-9454
An account "of the legendary brokerage firm's downfall and subsequent buyout by Shearson Lehman. . . . [The author] crafts the events and personalities involved in a manner that will hold the interest of even readers who normally would be bored with or nonplused by business news and corporate hi-jinks." Libr J

Stewart, James B.
Den of thieves. Simon & Schuster 1991 493p il hardcover o.p. paperback available $12   **364.1**
1. Insider trading 2. Wall Street (New York, N.Y.)
ISBN 0-671-79227-X (pa)   LC 91-28819
The author "tracks the fateful convergence of four figures (Martin Siegel, Ivan Boesky, Dennis Levine, and Michael Milken) whose actions resulted in the collapse of the mighty investment firm Drexel Burnham Lambert and nearly brought down Wall Street. . . . A masterful, revealing portrait." Booklist
Includes bibliographic references

Stoll, Clifford
The cuckoo's egg: tracking a spy through the maze of computer espionage. Doubleday 1989 326p $19.95   **364.1**
1. Hess, Markus 2. Computer crimes 3. Espionage, Russian
ISBN 0-385-24946-2   LC 89-7808
Also available in paperback from Pocket Bks.
"Stoll, an astrophysicist at the Lawrence Berkeley Laboratory, became a computer security expert when his persistence in chasing a computer hacker in West Germany led to the crackdown of an international spy ring. His documentation of a year-long tailing of the intruder reveals the vulnerability of computer networks, the bureaucratic politics of government agencies, and the irresponsible, damaging actions of hackers. . . . Succinct explanations of computer jargon make this an intelligible text for general readers." Libr J
Includes bibliography

Taibbi, Mike
Unholy alliances; working the Tawana Brawley story; by Mike Taibbi & Anna Sims-Phillips. Harcourt Brace Jovanovich 1989 375p il $18.95   **364.1**
1. Brawley, Tawana
ISBN 0-15-188050-6   LC 89-31093
"New York television reporters Mike Taibbi and Anna Sims-Phillips . . . tell how they covered [the 1988] Tawana Brawley case. Ms. Brawley, a 15-year-old black high school student alledged that she had been beaten and raped by a gang of white men." Christ Sci Monit

Talese, Gay
Honor thy father. World Pub. 1971 526p il o.p.; Ivy Bks. paperback available $5.99   **364.1**
1. Bonanno family 2. Mafia
ISBN 0-8041-1058-1 (pa)
This study of the Mafia focuses on three generations of the Bonanno family

Taylor, Lawrence, 1942-
To honor and obey. Morrow 1992 381p il $22   **364.1**
1. Fratt, Louann 2. Homicide
ISBN 0-688-09854-1   LC 91-22454
"One fall dawn in 1988, wealthy Upper East Side Manhattanite Louann Fratt, mother of three, went to the apartment of her estranged husband, Charles, to whom she had been married for 30 years, and fatally stabbed him. After reporting her crime to the police, she retained as counsel scruffy-looking Michael Dowd, a downtown lawyer in every sense, famed for his pro bono defenses of battered women." Publ Wkly
"A real page-turner, this is true-crime writing at its best." Booklist

Terry, Maury

The ultimate evil; an investigation into America's most dangerous satanic cult. Doubleday 1987 512p il $17.95   **364.1**

1. Berkowitz, David Richard, 1953- 2. Homicide 3. Satanism
ISBN 0-385-23452-X   LC 86-29203

Also available in paperback from Bantam Bks.

"A Dolphin book"

"On the basis of a ten-year investigation, journalist Terry argues that convicted 'Son of Sam' killer David Berkowitz did not act alone, but rather was part of a satanic cult conspiracy. He identifies Charles Manson as a member of a cult and reviews other murders allegedly committed by devil-worshipping groups." Libr J
"A fascinating docudrama not for the faint-hearted." Booklist

Thompson, Thomas, 1933-1982

Blood and money. Doubleday 1976 450p o.p.; Dell paperback available $5.95   **364.1**

1. Hill, Joan Olive Robinson, 1931-1969 2. Hill, John Robert, 1931-1972 3. Homicide
ISBN 0-440-10679-6 (pa)

"The high society of Houston's ultra rich is the setting of a spellbinding account of mysterious death and the bizarre consequences set in motion by the murderous grudge it produced. . . . A variegated, brilliantly woven documentary." Libr J

Traub, James

Too good to be true: the outlandish story of Wedtech. Doubleday 1990 379p il $21.95   **364.1**

1. Wedtech Corporation 2. Corruption in politics 3. Government purchasing
ISBN 0-385-26182-9   LC 90-30172

The author examines Wedtech "from its start in the late 1970s with a fraudulent application in the minority set-aside program, to its heyday of lucrative defense contracts, followed by the fall, trials, and prison sentences." Libr J
"Traub's is by far the best of the Wedtech chronicles. It is elegant, funny and, for the most part, exciting." N Y Times Book Rev

Wambaugh, Joseph

The blooding. Morrow 1989 288p $18.95   **364.1**

1. Homicide 2. Rape
ISBN 0-688-08617-9   LC 88-13679

Also available in paperback from Bantam Bks.

"A Perigord Press book"

This is an account of "two British sex murders and the police hunt for the killer. The title stems from a procedure of genetic fingerprinting detected by examining blood samples, and used by the police to catch the murderer." Libr J
"Wambaugh's tale is captivating. A terrific crime story." West Coast Rev Books

Echoes in the darkness. Morrow 1987 415p $18.95   **364.1**

1. Homicide
ISBN 0-688-06889-8   LC 86-23708

Also available in paperback from Bantam Bks.

"A Perigord Press book"

The setting for the crime recounted in this book is "an upper middle-class suburban Philadelphia high school. English teacher Susan Reinert and her two children were the victims of a . . . [conspiracy devised] by her colleague William Bradfield and her former principal Jay Smith. Both men were convicted after a seven-year investigation." Libr J
"Wambaugh chooses the cop's-eye view, telling much of the story as developed by the state police investigation and dispensing considerable amounts of macabre station-house humor." Time

Williams, Terry M., 1948-

The cocaine kids; the inside story of a teenage drug ring; [by] Terry Williams. Addison-Wesley 1989 140p il $16.95; pa $9.57   **364.1**

1. Drug traffic 2. Juvenile delinquency
ISBN 0-201-09360-X; 0-201-57003-3 (pa) LC 89-6505

"From 1982 to 1986, sociologist Williams followed the activities of a teenage cocaine ring in New York's Spanish Harlem. He tells their story in their own street language." Libr J
"Mr. Williams's detailed observations yield a fascinating picture of an underground economy that is remarkably similar to the world of respectable commerce. . . . Most important, Mr. Williams makes clear that the drug trade flourishes in direct response to the absence of legitimate opportunity." N Y Times Book Rev

Wilson, Kirk, 1946-

Unsolved: great mysteries of the 20th century. Carroll & Graf Pubs. 1990 264p hardcover o.p. paperback available $10.95   **364.1**

1. Homicide
ISBN 0-88184-703-8 (pa)   LC 89-30220

"Wilson documents 10 unsolved crimes. . . . Investigations into the mysterious disappearance of candy heiress Helen Brach and Teamster boss Jimmy Hoffa mix provocatively with probes on Marilyn Monroe's alleged suicide and John F. Kennedy's assassination." Booklist

Wolfe, Linda

The professor and the prostitute, and other true tales of murder and madness. Houghton Mifflin 1986 228p il $16.95   **364.1**

1. Homicide
ISBN 0-395-40049-X   LC 86-397

Also available in paperback from Ballantine Bks.

This is a collection of nine true crime stories
"More clinical expertise or literary skill would have made this collection much better, but its subject matter alone makes compelling reading for true-crime buffs." Booklist

Wasted; the preppie murder. Simon & Schuster 1989 303p il hardcover o.p. paperback available $4.95   **364.1**

1. Levin, Jennifer Dawn, d. 1986 2. Chambers, Robert 3. Homicide
ISBN 0-671-70900-3 (pa)   LC 89-35480

Wolfe, Linda—*Continued*
An "account of the much-publicized Central Park murder of Jennifer Levin by Robert Chambers. Wolfe's research has produced a fascinating, in-depth look at the head-line grabbing case." Booklist

364.3 Offenders

Bing, Léon, 1950-
Do or die. HarperCollins Pubs. 1991 277p $19.95; pa $11   **364.3**
1. Juvenile delinquency
ISBN 0-06-016326-7; 0-06-092291-5 (pa)
                                                    LC 90-55922
"L.A. gang members tell it like it is in a disturbing yet compelling portrait of gangbangers that goes beyond stereotype to give face to individuals who exist in a world of incredible violence." Booklist

Campbell, Anne
The girls in the gang. 2nd ed. Blackwell 1991 295p il pa $15.95   **364.3**
1. Juvenile delinquency
ISBN 1-55786-120-X   LC 90-1216
First published 1984
A sociological examination of the structure and trappings of girl street gangs in New York City. Psychological profiles of members are included

The **Gunfighters**; by the editors of Time-Life Books; with text by Paul Trachtman. Time-Life Bks. 1974 238p il map (Old West) $19.93   **364.3**
1. Robbers and outlaws 2. Frontier and pioneer life—West (U.S.)
This book describes the exploits of such western gunfighters as Jesse and Frank James, Butch Cassidy, and Billy the Kid. The apprehension of outlaws by sheriffs and marshalls, and the exercise of frontier justice by courts and by vigilance committees are also discussed
Includes bibliography

Sander, Daryl
Focus on teens in trouble; a reference handbook. ABC-CLIO 1991 182p (Teenage perspectives) $39   **364.3**
1. Juvenile delinquency
ISBN 0-87436-207-5   LC 90-24777
Discusses such aspects of juvenile delinquency as gangs, drug abuse, running away, and crime. Provides resources for additional information
"Because the volume is intended for youth, treatment is somewhat simplistic, and the general tone is moralistic. This source would interest adults serving youth as well, especially for the core information and lists of sources." Booklist

364.6 Penology

Congregation of the condemned; voices against the death penalty; edited by Shirley Dicks; with essays by Edward Kennedy [et al.] Prometheus Bks. 1991 290p il $24.95   **364.6**
1. Capital punishment
ISBN 0-87975-679-9   LC 91-26108
This "collection of forty-nine essays . . . calls for an end to the death penalty. . . . [It] features writings by death-row inmates, members of victims' families, legal and medical experts, religious and political figures, journalists, entertainers, and spokespersons from such . . . organizations as Amnesty International, the NAACP, and the National Coalition to Abolish the Death Penalty." Publisher's note
"This is gripping reading. . . . Among their persuasive conclusions: it is the poor who are executed, and some of them are innocent." Publ Wkly

Trombley, Stephen
The execution protocol; inside America's capital punishment industry. Crown 1992 342p il $20   **364.6**
1. Capital punishment
ISBN 0-517-59113-8   LC 92-22805
Also available in paperback from Anchor Bks.
This is a study of execution procedures at Missouri's Potosi Correctional Center. The author presents interviews with "Fred Leuchter, who invented the lethal injection machine; the chaplain; the psychologist; correctional officers; and men on death row." Libr J
This book "is all the more thought-provoking and chilling for being written in a straightforward, nonjudgmental manner." Publ Wkly

White, Welsh S., 1940-
The death penalty in the nineties; an examination of the modern system of capital punishment. University of Mich. Press 1991 223p hardcover o.p. paperback available $19.95   **364.6**
1. United States. Supreme Court 2. Capital punishment
ISBN 0-472-06461-4 (pa)   LC 90-49339
An updated version of The death penalty in the eighties, published 1987
The author surveys the Supreme Court's major capital punishment decisions, and examines their effects. Cases include racial discrimination, plea bargaining, and defendants who elect execution
Includes bibliographic references

365 Penal and related institutions

Abbott, Jack Henry, 1944-
In the belly of the beast; letters from prison; with an introduction by Norman Mailer. Random House 1981 166p hardcover o.p. paperback available $10
                                                         365
1. Prisoners 2. Prisons—United States
ISBN 0-679-73237-3 (pa)   LC 80-6038

Abbott, Jack Henry, 1944-—*Continued*

The writer of these letters began them while "chained to the crossbar of his bed in the Butner, North Carolina Federal Correctional Institution. He addressed his letter to Norman Mailer. . . . [In these letters he] wished to convey something about the effect of [prison life on the individual]." Nation

Abbott's "letters belong with the best prison literature, not because of their accounts of atrocity, but for their disturbing picture of daily life behind bars." Time

Earley, Pete

The hot house: life inside Leavenworth Prison. Bantam Bks. 1992 383p $22.50; pa $5.99   365

1. United States Penitentiary (Leavenworth, Kan.) 2. Prisons—United States

ISBN 0-553-07573-X; 0-553-56023-9 (pa)

LC 91-25400

The author "spent two years interviewing the inmates and employees of Leavenworth Prison. Here, he provides portraits of five convicts, two guards, and the warden." Libr J

"The convicts themselves provide a deep and enduring picture, not just of the criminal mind, but also of the rules of conduct that govern every act in prison. . . . An exposé that is nearly as hard to think about as it is to forget." Booklist

Mitford, Jessica, 1917-

Kind and usual punishment; the prison business. Knopf 1973 340p o.p.; Vintage Bks. paperback available $8.76   365

1. Prisons—United States

ISBN 0-394-71093-2 (pa)

From her analyses the author finds American prisons ineffective, inhuman and costly. In the last of 15 chapters devoted to these, and other defects, she suggests as remedies shorter sentences, abolition of parole and the elimination of the indeterminate sentence

Includes bibliographic references

Solzhenitsyn, Aleksandr, 1918-

The Gulag Archipelago, 1918-1956; an experiment in literary investigation; [Pts] I-VII. Harper & Row 1974-1978 3v il maps   365

1. Political prisoners 2. Soviet Union—Politics and government

Also available in an abridged edition for $25, pa $14.95 (ISBN 0-06-015474-8; 0-06-091280-4)

v1 pa $16 (ISBN 0-06-092102-1); v2 $20.95, pa $4.95 (ISBN 0-06-013911-0; 0-06-080345-2); v3 $20.95, pa $16 (ISBN 0-06-013912-9; 0-06-092104-8)

"The unspeakable terror of Stalin's reign, long a forbidden topic, finds impassioned expression in much of Solzhenitsyn's work, particularly in 'The Gulag Archipelago', which in its relentless march of grisly detail leaves no reader unmoved nor fails to evoke in the reader its author's own moral indignation." Reader's Ency

368   Insurance

Nader, Ralph

Winning the insurance game; the complete consumer's guide to saving money; [by] Ralph Nader and Wesley J. Smith; foreword by J. Robert Hunter. rev ed. Doubleday 1993 538p il pa $14.95   368

1. Insurance

ISBN 0-385-46838-5   LC 92-32964

"A Main Street book"

First published 1990 by Knightsbridge

"Nader's guide reveals how to save money on automobile, health, life, homeowners', and other types of insurance. He explains the legal aspects, always with a strong pro-consumer attitude." Libr J

Includes bibliographic references

Taylor, Barbara J., 1933-

How to get your money's worth in home and auto insurance; [by] Barbara Taylor; edited by Lynn Brenner. McGraw-Hill 1991 184p il $19.95; pa $12.95   368

1. Insurance

ISBN 0-07-063178-6; 0-07-063179-4 (pa)

LC 90-40327

This book "surveys property, automobile, and other related policies. . . . Factors affecting insurance premiums are discussed, along with helpful hints for reducing costs." Booklist

368.3   Insurance against death, old age, illness, injury

Berman, Henry

Choosing the right health care plan; [by] Henry S. Berman and Louisa Rose. Consumers Union of U.S. 1990 261p pa $14.95   368.3

1. Health insurance

ISBN 0-89043-218-X   LC 88-71029

This overview of health insurance practices offers advice and information about indemnity insurance, HMOs, Medicare, getting good medical care, and how to compare various types of health insurance plans

Includes bibliographic references

Dacey, Norman F., 1908-1994

What's wrong with your life insurance. Macmillan 1989 452p $24.95   368.3

1. Life insurance

ISBN 0-02-529350-8   LC 89-2504

First published 1963

The author argues that the insurance industry is guilty of numerous abuses and deceptions that leave customers inadequately insured

Enteen, Robert

Health insurance; how to get it, keep it, or improve what you've got. Paragon House 1992 196p pa $12.95 **368.3**

1. Health insurance
ISBN 1-55778-511-2   LC 91-47065

The author compares costs, assesses private health insurance, group and individual plans, and tells how to get the most out of one's policy. He also covers government health insurance, including programs for federal employees, as well as veterans' benefits, Medicaid, Medicare and Medigap. Most chapters are presented in a checklist format, making the book extremely user-friendly." Publ Wkly

Korn, Donald Jay

Your money or your life; how to save thousands on your health-care insurance. Collier Bks. 1992 308p pa $10   **368.3**

1. Health insurance
ISBN 0-02-080441-5   LC 91-35827

The author explains "basic health insurance, disability income insurance, and long-term care insurance. . . . Illustrations provide true-to-life examples that will help readers protect their assets, shop for coverage, and intelligently evaluate their options. . . . This is a coherent view of a complicated subject and it is therefore highly recommended for public library collections." Libr J

Life insurance; how to buy the right policy from the right company at the right price; [by] the editors of Consumer Reports Books with Trudy Lieberman. Consumers Union of U.S. 1988 289p il pa $12   **368.3**

1. Life insurance
ISBN 0-89043-095-0   LC 87-71006

"The book first tackles general information, such as how to determine if you need life insurance; the four major types of life insurance policies; and dealing with salespersons and company hype. Part 2 consists of tables and charts that rate the life insurance policies of major firms and explain how to calculate the real cost of policies. An eminently practical compendium." Booklist

Life insurance fact book. American Council of Life Insurance pa gratis   **368.3**

1. Life insurance
ISSN 0075-9406

Biennial. First published 1946

"A useful source, with tables, charts, and interpretive text, to all U.S. legal reserve life insurance companies. Data are taken from annual statements and give statistics, yearly statements, ownership, payments, assets, officials, etc." Ref Sources for Small & Medium-sized Libr. 5th edition

368.4 Government-sponsored insurance

Hardy, Dorcas

Social insecurity; the crisis in America's social security system and how to plan now for your own financial survival; [by] Dorcas R. Hardy, C. Colburn Hardy. Villard Bks. 1991 xxv, 178p $16   **368.4**

1. Social security
ISBN 0-679-40290-X   LC 91-50062

"Former Social Security commissioner Hardy and her father, financial adviser Colburn, here allege that unless a national retirement policy that retains Social Security as a base is adopted soon, the resources of a weakened and wounded Social Security will be exhausted by 2010. Having sounded the alarm, the authors offer suggestions on how to calculate and provide for post-retirement income needs, advising on tax strategies, IRAs, pensions, annuities and other profitable, safe investments." Publ Wkly

Inlander, Charles B.

Medicare made easy; [by] Charles B. Inlander, Charles K. MacKay. Addison-Wesley pa $13.95   **368.4**

1. Medicare

First published 1989. (3rd edition 1992) Frequently revised

"Guide for Medicare recipients and advocates. A tour through the system strips away the confusion and helps recipients get the benefits to which they are entitled." N Y Public Libr Book of How & Where to Look It Up

Jehle, Faustin F.

The complete & easy guide to Social Security & Medicare. Fraser-Vance Pub. pa $10.95   **368.4**

1. Social security 2. Medicare

Annual. First published 1983

"This guide helps reader understand the complex interrelationships between Social Security, Medicare, Medicaid, SSI, and government disability insurance coverage." Libr J

Medicare explained. Commerce Clearing House pa $15   **368.4**

1. Medicare

Annual

"Concise, thorough explanation for the average reader of all aspects of federal health insurance for the aged and disabled. Includes recent legal changes. Also includes inpatient/outpatient benefits, nursing home services, services excluded from coverage, and miscellaneous provisions." N Y Public Libr Book of How & Where to Look It Up

Robertson, A. Haeworth

Social security; what every taxpayer should know. Retirement Policy Inst. 1992 xxiv, 321p $40; pa $14.95   **368.4**

1. Social security 2. Medicare
ISBN 0-9632345-4-4; 0-9632345-5-2 (pa)

LC 92-80166

The author "explains what Social Security is, how it works, and what it costs and then comments on specific issues that could possibly affect the future of Social Security." Booklist

"Robertson clarifies with graphs, charts, tables and a remarkably lucid text the immensely complex functions of our federal retirement, health-care, disability and survivors-benefit insurance programs." Publ Wkly

Includes bibliographic references

Snyder, Harry

Medicare/Medigap; the essential guide for older Americans and their families; [by] Harry Snyder, Carl Oshiro, and the editors of Consumer Reports Books. Consumers Union of U.S. 1990 212p hardcover o.p. paperback available $12.95   **368.4**

1. Medicare 2. Elderly—Medical care 3. Consumer education
ISBN 0-89043-329-1 (pa)   LC 90-2020

Areas covered include supplemental insurance, abusive insurance practices, medical claim forms, and long term care. Appended are sample letters, forms, names of insurance companies, and sources of further information

Social Security handbook; United States Department of Health and Human Services, Social Security Administration. U.S. Govt. Ptg. Office pa $13   **368.4**

1. Social security

First published 1960 by United States. Bureau of Old Age and Survivors Insurance. Subtitle varies. (10th edition 1988) Periodically revised

"Detailed explanation without commentary of the federal retirement, survivors, disability, black lung benefits, supplementary security income, and health insurance programs, who is entitled to benefits, and how such benefits may be obtained." Ref Sources for Small & Medium-sized Libr. 5th edition

370   Education

Cetron, Marvin J.

Educational renaissance; our schools at the turn of the century; [by] Marvin Cetron and Margaret Gayle; introduction by Bill Honig. St. Martin's Press 1991 352p $21.95; pa $14.95   **370**

1. Education—United States 2. Forecasting
ISBN 0-312-05422-X; 0-312-07739-4 (pa)

LC 90-48936

This book "provides forecasts and ideas for reshaping U.S. education in the 1990s and beyond by employing a multitude of reforms already in place. . . . The authors present a roster of 75 trends in education, short biographies of 12 educators they feel are making a difference, and an appendix of vital educational statistics for comparing state initiatives." Libr J

Includes bibliographic references

Leinwand, Gerald

Public education. Facts on File 1992 140p (American issues) $16.95   **370**

1. Public schools 2. Education—United States
ISBN 0-8160-2100-7   LC 91-39721

"The author sketches the increasing importance of education in the coming century, the mission and achievements of U.S. schools over the past two centuries, and critical issues Americans must soon resolve: who should be taught, what should be taught, and who should teach?" Booklist

Includes bibliographic references

Ravitch, Diane

The schools we deserve; reflections on the educational crises of our times. Basic Bks. 1985 337p $19.95; pa $16   **370**

1. Education—United States 2. Education—Aims and objectives
ISBN 0-465-07236-4; 0-465-07234-8 (pa)

LC 84-45303

These critical essays "treat such issues as racial integration, tuition tax credits, bilingual education, standardized tests, scapegoating teachers for school failures, and the role of the federal government in education." Booklist

Includes bibliographic references

The troubled crusade; American education, 1945-1980. Basic Bks. 1985 384p $19.95; pa $17   **370**

1. Education—United States
ISBN 0-465-08756-6; 0-465-08757-4 (pa)

LC 83-70750

A "survey of developments in American education at all levels over a period marked by political, racial, and cultural upheaval. Ravitch shows how changing philosophies, shifting alliances, and the influence of applied social science radically altered the nature of 'education' from its traditional, intellectual emphasis to a concern for personal adjustment and social utility." Libr J

Includes bibliographic references

370.1   Education—Philosophy

Adler, Mortimer Jerome, 1902-

Reforming education; the opening of the American mind; [by] Mortimer J. Adler; edited by Geraldine Van Doren. Macmillan 1988 xxxiii, 362p hardcover o.p. paperback available $8.95   **370.1**

1. Education—Philosophy
ISBN 0-02-030175-8 (pa)   LC 88-8339

"This collection of programmatic essays and occasional pieces argues for the restoration of form and substance to . . . education in America. Adler . . . writes eloquently and passionately in defense of a truly 'democratic' vision of education." Libr J

Includes bibliography

Dewey, John, 1859-1952
Democracy and education; an introduction to the philosophy of education. Macmillan 1916 434p o.p.; Free Press paperback available $13.95   **370.1**
1. Education—Philosophy
ISBN 0-02-907370-7 (pa)
"The author's aim here is to detect and state the ideas implied in a democratic society and to apply those ideas to the problems of education." Boston Transcr

John Dewey on education; selected writings; edited and with an introduction by Reginald D. Archambault. Modern Lib. 1964 xxx, 439p o.p.; University of Chicago Press paperback available $14.95   **370.1**
1. Education—Philosophy
ISBN 0-226-14390-2 (pa)
"This book represents an attempt to collect, in systematic form, Dewey's major writings on education, together with certain basic statements of his philosophic position that are relevant to understanding his educational views." Preface

Illich, Ivan, 1926-
Deschooling society. Harper & Row 1971 xx, 116p hardcover o.p. paperback available $9   **370.1**
1. Education—Aims and objectives 2. Education—United States 3. Educational sociology
ISBN 0-06-132086-2 (pa)
In this critique of compulsory education, the author suggests that the school system be disestablished and replaced by opportunities for self-motivated learning
Includes bibliographic references

Kilpatrick, William, 1940-
Why Johnny can't tell right from wrong; [by] William K. Kilpatrick. Simon & Schuster 1992 366p $23   **370.1**
1. Moral education 2. Education—United States
ISBN 0-671-75801-2   LC 92-25864
"Attacking the moral relativism of such current approaches to the teaching of ethics as 'Values Clarification,' Kilpatrick . . . calls for a return to a traditional model of teaching morality based on content rather than decision-making. . . . His jeremiad hits the mark when aimed at ambiguous approaches to drug and sex education." Publ Wkly
Includes bibliographic references

Lickona, Thomas
Educating for character; how our schools can teach respect and responsibility. Bantam Bks. 1991 478p $22.50; pa $12.50   **370.1**
1. Moral education 2. Students 3. Values
ISBN 0-553-07570-5; 0-553-37052-9 (pa)
    LC 91-16853
The author "views the school as a major force in responding to America's moral crisis. He defines values, discusses how they may be taught, and outlines the role of school and family. He emphasizes values as an important factor in the well being of a nation, family, and individual." Libr J

"This important study will be a resource for those concerned with the 'ethical illiteracy' of children." Publ Wkly
Includes bibliographic references

370.15   Educational psychology

Gardner, Howard
The unschooled mind; how children think and how schools should teach. Basic Bks. 1991 303p $23; pa $13   **370.15**
1. Educational psychology 2. Education—Aims and objectives 3. Thought and thinking
ISBN 0-465-08895-3; 0-465-08896-1 (pa)
    LC 91-70058
In this work the author "reviews child development theories (about the growth of the 'natural' learner), provides a description of schooling, and ends with a plea for education based on apprenticeship and museum learning models. . . . Gardner's summary of recent research on naive conceptions in science, math, social sciences, humanities, and the arts brings together a wide range of material in a readable format." Sci Books Films
Includes bibliographic references

Ginott, Haim G.
Teacher and child; a book for parents and teachers. Macmillan 1972 323p $14.95; pa $9   **370.15**
1. Educational psychology 2. Child psychology
ISBN 0-02-543340-7; 0-02-013974-8 (pa)
Also available in paperback from Avon Bks.
"Short scenarios show how a considerate teacher can make his students happier, his job easier and his teaching more effective." Chicago Public Libr
Includes bibliography

Holt, John Caldwell, 1923-1985
How children learn; [by] John Holt. rev ed. Delacorte Press; Lawrence, S. 1983 303p hardcover o.p. paperback available $9.95
    370.15
1. Educational psychology 2. Elementary education 3. Knowledge, Theory of
ISBN 0-440-55051-3 (pa)   LC 82-17311
"A Merloyd Lawrence book"
First published 1967 by Pitman
The author "describes the ways in which bright or normal children tackle learning by themselves, experimentally and as a game." Publ Wkly
This is "a poetic, humane, perceptive account of some of the author's own teaching experiences with the very young. . . . Like all other first-rate books [it] is really about a great deal more than its stated subject." Nation

370.19   Education—Social aspects

Council on International Educational Exchange

Work, study, travel abroad; the whole world handbook. St. Martin's Press pa $12.95   **370.19**

1. Education—Directories   2. Foreign study—Directories

First published 1972 by Council on International Educational Exchange with title: Whole world handbook. (11th edition 1991-1993) Frequently revised

"An unparelleled handbook for anyone wishing to undertake work, study, or travel in foreign countries. Facilities, organizations, and programs are listed with addresses. The book's coverage stretches from Canada and Europe to Australia, Asia, Latin America, Africa, and the Middle East. National profiles are included." Recomm Ref Books in Paperback. 2d edition

D'Souza, Dinesh, 1961-

Illiberal education; the politics of race and sex on campus. Free Press 1991 319p $19.95   **370.19**

1. Colleges and universities—United States   2. Discrimination in education   3. Minorities—Education
ISBN 0-02-908100-9   LC 90-47055

Also available in paperback from Vintage Bks.

"D'Souza believes that preferential-treatment admissions policies weaken educational standards and foster separatism and racial tension on campus. . . . [He] calls for 'nonracial affirmative action policies' based strictly on socioeconomic disadvantage." Publ Wkly

This book "recounts, in a manner both responsible and chilling, the atrocities that ravage our campuses. Whatever your politics, read it." New Repub

Includes bibliographic references

Formisano, Ronald P., 1939-

Boston against busing; race, class, and ethnicity in the 1960s and 1970s. University of N.C. Press 1991 323p $34.95; pa $12.95   **370.19**

1. Busing (School integration)   2. Boston (Mass.)—Race relations
ISBN 0-8078-1929-8; 0-8078-4292-3 (pa)
     LC 90-12587

This is a study of opposition in Boston to court-ordered busing to achieve school desegregation

The author "argues persuasively that although simple racism was a key factor, the real reasons for the opposition were much more complex. . . . The writing style is a nice blend of journalism and serious scholarly prose." Choice

Includes bibliographic references

Graff, Gerald, 1937-

Beyond the culture wars; how teaching the conflicts can revitalize American education. Norton 1992 214p $19.95   **370.19**

1. Colleges and universities—Curricula   2. Colleges and universities—United States
ISBN 0-393-03424-0   LC 92-12855

In this assessment of the current state of American higher education the author argues "for a curriculum that includes political debates and multicultural texts. . . . He suggests that the ideological conflicts that accompany the curricular problem are getting students to grapple with ideas." Publ Wkly

"This provocative and controversial book is an essential acquisition for balanced subject collections." Libr J

Includes bibliographic references

Hirsch, E. D. (Eric Donald), 1928-

Cultural literacy; what every American needs to know; with an appendix: What literate Americans know [by] E.D. Hirsch, Jr., Joseph Kett, and James Trefil. Houghton Mifflin 1987 251p $19.45   **370.19**

1. Literacy   2. Education—United States   3. Culture
ISBN 0-395-43095-X   LC 86-21352

Also available in paperback from Vintage Bks.

Hirsch advocates the incorporation of a strong base of factual information and traditional lore in the curriculum. Appended is a list of names and terms that he and his colleagues think should be common knowledge to all Americans

"This is a delightful book. E. D. Hirsch says something new. He is probably wrong. He certainly is iconoclastic; but he should be read." N Y Times Book Rev

Includes bibliographic references

Kozol, Jonathan

Death at an early age; the destruction of the hearts and minds of Negro children in the Boston public schools. Houghton Mifflin 1967 240p o.p.; New Am. Lib. paperback available $10   **370.19**

1. Discrimination in education   2. Public schools—Boston (Mass.)   3. Blacks—Education
ISBN 0-452-26292-5 (pa)

The author relates his experience as a fourth-grade teacher in 1964 at a predominantly black Boston school, emphasizing poorly trained teachers, biased text books, overcrowded conditions, prejudiced school administrators, and their effects upon the students

Includes bibliographic references

Illiterate America. Anchor Press/Doubleday 1985 270p o.p.; New Am. Lib. paperback available $9.95   **370.19**

1. Literacy   2. Education—Social aspects
ISBN 0-452-26203-8 (pa)   LC 84-20487

The author's "statistics show that one-third of Americans are semiliterate at best, and he finds inadequacies in existing literacy programs. Advocating societal empowerment of the victims of illiteracy, the development of relevant subject matter, and the use of neighborhood facilities, he names elements of successful literacy programs." Booklist

"Passionate and disturbing, 'Illiterate America' is both a consciousness raiser and a primer for action focused on America's 'invisible minority.'" Libr J

Maeroff, Gene I.
The school-smart parent. Times Bks. 1989
434p $19.95   **370.19**
1. Home and school 2. Education—United States
ISBN 0-8129-1631-X   LC 88-29506
Also available in paperback from Holt & Co.

This book contains "suggestions for preparing a young
child for pre-school programs, evaluating nursery and
elementary schools and child care facilities, assessing a
child's progress, understanding responsibilities of teachers,
presenting concepts in many subject fields, and building
character. . . . The tone is encouraging, the advice
detailed and sound. An invaluable guide for parents,
teachers, students of education, and informed citizens."
Libr J

Unger, Harlow G., 1931-
What did you learn in school today? a
parent's guide for evaluating your child's
school. Facts on File 1991 168p il $19.95
370.19
1. Education—United States 2. Public schools
ISBN 0-8160-2510-X   LC 90-21724
"Part 1 discusses the issues, pointing out that the lack
of national standards and the fact that schools are often
more politically than professionally administered make
parental concern necessary. Part 2 provides report cards
or checklists, with which parents can evaluate school
districts, individual schools, teachers and administrators.
Part 3 tells what children should be learning at specific
grade levels." Libr J

370.25 Education—Directories

The **Handbook** of private schools; an annual
descriptive   survey   of   independent
education. Sargent Pubs. il maps $75
370.25
1. Private schools—Directories 2. Education—United
States—Directories
ISSN 0072-9884
First published 1915 with title: Handbook of the best
private schools of the United States and Canada
"Lists and describes nearly 2,000 private elementary
and secondary schools in the United States. Gives information on type, tuition, staff, enrollment, facilities, etc.
Contains a directory of summer academic programs and
camps; classified directories of firms and agencies; and
an alphabetical index of schools." Sheehy. Guide to Ref
Books. 10th edition

Patterson's American education. Educational
Directories $75   **370.25**
1. Education—United States—Directories
Annual. First published 1904. Title varies
"Comprehensive list of schools at all levels, private
and public; educational associations; and school systems."
N Y Public Libr Book of How & Where to Look It
Up

Private independent schools. Bunting &
Lyon $95   **370.25**
1. Private schools—Directories 2. Education—United
States—Directories
ISSN 0079-5399
Annual. First published 1943 with title: Independent
schools, a directory. Title varies

"Gives fairly lengthy descriptions of more than 1,000
private schools and brief listings of others. Includes a
list of educational associations." Sheehy. Guide to Ref
Books. 10th edition

370.5 Education—Serial publications

Education index. Wilson, H.W. service basis
370.5
1. Education—Periodicals—Indexes   2. Education—
Bibliography
ISSN 0013-1385
Also available on CD-ROM
Published monthly, except in July and August, with
quarterly cumulations and permanent bound annual
cumulations
A cumulative index to approximately 400 English-
language periodicals, yearbooks, and monographs. The
main body consists of subject and author entries arranged
in one alphabet. In addition there is an author listing
of citations to book reviews
"A cornerstone for information and research in the
field of education." Am Ref Books Annu, 1982

370.7 Education, research, related topics

Kramer, Rita
Ed school follies; the miseducation of
America's teachers. Free Press 1991 228p
$22.95   **370.7**
1. Teachers—Training
ISBN 0-02-917642-5   LC 91-9774
This is a study of teacher training in the United
States. "During the 1988-89 school year, [the author]
visited 14 schools of education in New York, Tennessee,
Michigan, Southern California, Washington, and Texas,
observing classes and interviewing students and profes-
sors. In this account, she concludes that most students
are idealistic and eager, but are being misguided." Libr
J

The author "saw and heard enough to provide this
remarkable ethnography, marked by even-handedness,
lucid writing, and—given the cant she endured—an admirable degree of patience." Commentary

371 School organization and management; special education

Fiske, Edward B.
Smart schools, smart kids; why do some
schools work? Simon & Schuster 1991 303p
$21.95; pa $11   **371**
1. Public schools 2. Education—United States
ISBN 0-671-69063-9; 0-671-79212-1 (pa)
LC 91-19530
The author "presents an optimistic overview of some
alternatives to what he calls the outmoded 'factory
model' of public school education that predominates in
this country. He looks at schools that have decentralized
management, adopted shared decision making, rearranged
their schedules, and developed new standards of accountability." Booklist
Includes bibliographic references

Martz, Larry

Making schools better; what parents, teachers, and communities can do to breathe new life into America's classrooms; introduction by Robert Coles. Times Bks. 1992 270p pa $12   **371**

1. Public schools 2. Education—United States
ISBN 0-8129-1939-4   LC 91-51018

"Here are 12 concrete, school-tested improvement programs to enhance the quality of American educational systems. They range from preschools to homework hotlines to peer support for dropouts and drug addicts. Martz does not philosophize on the woes of today's schools but delivers positive examples of how parents, teachers, students, and principals have transformed sorry situations into promising ones." Booklist

Includes bibliographic references

Wood, George H.

Schools that work; America's most innovative public education programs. Dutton 1992 xxiii, 290p $22   **371**

1. Public schools 2. Education—United States
ISBN 0-525-93421-9   LC 91-29607
Also available in paperback from New Am. Lib.

The author "presents examples of what he considers excellence in education for others to model within their bailiwick. Time is spent explicating programs in Raban Gap, Georgia (Foxfire), Central Park East Secondary School (CPESS) in Harlem, Hubbard Woods Elementary (Winnetka, Illinois), the Fratney School in Milwaukee, and schools in Athens County, Ohio. He states that these schools struggle against the misguided mandates of those who know little of how schools really operate." Libr J

Includes bibliographic references

371.1   Teaching and teaching personnel

Barzun, Jacques, 1907-

Begin here; the forgotten conditions of teaching and learning; editor, Morris Philipson. University of Chicago Press 1991 222p $24.95; pa $11.95   **371.1**

1. Teaching 2. Learning, Psychology of
ISBN 0-226-03846-7; 0-226-03847-5 (pa)
     LC 90-25877

"Some of the topics Barzun addresses include the inadequate ways in which reading is taught; the demeaning methods of teacher training; the counterfeit 'social studies' programs which are the offshoot of combined geography and history curriculums; the benefits of reading the classics; and how television effects learning." Libr J

Includes bibliographic references

Johnson, LouAnne

My posse don't do homework. St. Martin's Press 1992 226p $19.95   **371.1**

1. Teaching
ISBN 0-312-07638-X   LC 92-3899

"In funny but also poignant vignettes of her classroom experiences, Johnson, who taught non-English-speaking teenagers in an inner city school, writes with concern about the educational bureaucracy she encountered." Booklist

Kobrin, David, 1941-

In there with the kids; teaching in today's classrooms. Houghton Mifflin 1992 256p $19.95   **371.1**

1. Teaching
ISBN 0-395-50083-4   LC 91-26600

"The actions and attitudes of a fourth and a tenth grade teacher and their students are presented here in narrative form. Sample lesson plans, timelines, and teaching through lectures, group work, interviews, homework, and discussions are included." Libr J

"Kobrin's analysis of each approach and his perceptions on the teaching/learning relationship make this a useful resource for prospective teachers as well as others concerned with what should go on in the classroom." Publ Wkly

Kohl, Herbert R.

Growing minds; on becoming a teacher; foreword by Joseph Featherstone. Harper & Row 1984 163p (Harper & Row ser. on the professions) $13.95; pa $10   **371.1**

1. Teaching
ISBN 0-06-015257-5; 0-06-132089-7 (pa)
     LC 82-48671

"In a memoir that highlights peak experiences in his 21 years as an educator, Kohl . . . affirms that he finds teaching children 'more romantic' than any other career choice. . . . In his innovative and informal approaches to the classroom, Kohl . . . is validly critical of our national public schools but, in general, espouses a practical optimism that should inspire new teachers as well as sustain veteran educators and parents." Publ Wkly

On teaching; with a new introduction by the author. Schocken Bks. 1986 184p il pa $6.36   **371.1**

1. Teaching
ISBN 0-8052-0801-1   LC 85-30408
First published 1976

This book "is about the specifics of working with children and developing curriculum material. It is also about educational politics, the social structure of the school, and the ways in which the feelings we have as adults affect the work we do . . . in regular public schools and alternative schools, with children from kindergarten through senior high school." Preface

Includes bibliography

371.3   Methods of instruction and study

Britton, Lesley

Montessori play & learn; a parents' guide to purposeful play from two to six; with an introduction by Joy Starrey Turner. Crown 1992 144p il pa $18   **371.3**

1. Montessori method of education 2. Parenting
ISBN 0-517-59182-0   LC 92-5446

This describes educational activities for two to six year olds according to the Montessori method which parents can introduce at home

Hainstock, Elizabeth G.
Teaching Montessori in the home. Random House 1968 117p il o.p.; New Am. Lib. paperback available $8   371.3
1. Montessori method of education
ISBN 0-452-26268-2 (pa)

This volume covers the pre-school years. Companion volume Teaching Montessori in the home: the school years (1971) available in paperback for $9 (ISBN 0-452-26403-0)

After an introduction to the Montessori method, this book provides specific exercises in practical life skills, sensorial experiences, reading and writing, and arithmetic. It concludes with instructions for making Montessori equipment at home

Includes bibliography

Holt, John Caldwell, 1923-1985
Teach your own; a hopeful path for education; [by] John Holt. Delacorte Press; Lawrence, S. 1981 369p hardcover o.p. paperback available $8.95   371.3
1. Education—Experimental methods 2. Home instruction
ISBN 0-385-29006-3 (pa)   LC 81-1244
"A Merloyd Lawrence book"

The author "not only advocates but provides concrete guidance for home schooling. Disdaining compulsory education systems, he demonstrates how children can be kept away from conventional institutions of learning and offers direction in handling their out-of-school education." Booklist

Lillard, Paula Polk
Montessori; a modern approach. Schocken Bks. 1972 174p il hardcover o.p. paperback available $8.95   371.3
1. Montessori method of education
ISBN 0-8052-0920-4 (pa)

This book contains "historical background of the Italian teacher's life and work." Chicago Public Libr
The author "discusses Montessori in a logical and organized way. . . . Of interest to many will be an appendix with an appraisal of . . . testing of Montessori children in comparison with children from a non-Montessori background." America

Includes bibliography

Montessori, Maria, 1870-1952
The Montessori method; introduction by J. McV. Hunt. Schocken Bks. 1964 xxxix, 376p il hardcover o.p. paperback available $14   371.3
1. Montessori method of education
ISBN 0-8052-0922-0 (pa)

Originally published in Italy; first published 1912 in the United States

This is an introduction to the author's teaching methods. The Montessori system emphasizes the development of individuality in the child and the careful training of the senses. Education is controlled by interpersonal relations between the children rather than between teacher and child

371.3025 Audio and visual materials—Directories

AV market place; the complete business directory of: audio, audiovisual, computer systems, film, video, programming, with industry yellow pages. Bowker il pa $132   371.3025
1. Audiovisual materials—Directories
ISSN 1044-0445

Annual. First published 1969 with title: Audiovisual market place

This volume identifies more than "6,300 companies that create, supply, or distribute an extraordinary range of audiovisual equipment and services. An index of . . . products and services is cross-referenced to companies in the main body. The products, services, and company index identifies all firms geographically. . . . Companies are also indexed by name." Nichols. Guide to Ref Books for Sch Media Cent. 4th edition

371.9 Special education

Armstrong, Thomas
In their own way; discovering and encouraging your child's personal learning style. Tarcher, J.P. 1987 211p $16.95; pa $8.95   371.9
1. Learning disabilities 2. Exceptional children—Education
ISBN 0-87477-439-X; 0-87477-446-2 (pa) LC 87-6445

"Believing that schools have failed to develop children's special abilities, [Armstrong] suggests different ways that parents can help children to learn any subject according to their own style and to develop self-esteem. He also discusses testing and alternative methods of evaluating learning. Parents, teachers, and mental health professionals will find much of interest here." Libr J

Includes bibliography

Bloom, Jill
Help me to help my child; a sourcebook for parents of learning disabled children; with a foreword by David K. Urion. Little, Brown 1990 324p $18.95; pa $9.95   371.9
1. Learning disabilities
ISBN 0-316-09981-3; 0-316-09982-1 (pa)
LC 89-12854

"Writing as a parent of an LD child, Bloom tries to define LD, describes testing, and outlines educational goals. She understands the difficulties that can arise at home when a child is judged learning disabled and offers concrete advice on coping." Libr J

Includes bibliographic references

Conroy, Pat
The water is wide; illustrated with photographs by William and Paul Keyserling. Houghton Mifflin 1972 306p il o.p.; Bantam Bks. paperback available $4.95   371.9
1. Socially handicapped children 2. Blacks—Education
3. Public schools—South Carolina
ISBN 0-553-26893-7 (pa)

Conroy, Pat—*Continued*

"A young white teacher goes to an island off the coast of South Carolina to teach a group of functionally illiterate black children. Yamacraw Island is backward and primitive, a world for the most part left untouched by the 20th Century. . . . By ignoring the textbooks and concentrating on meaningful situations and dialogue . . . he begins to make headway. He also, unfortunately arouses the ire of the powers that be and, after fierce struggle, is fired." Libr J

The **Directory** for exceptional children. Sargent Pubs. il $50   **371.9**

1. Exceptional children—Education—Directories
ISSN 0070-5012

Biennial. First published 1954

"Contains questionnaire data on over 2600 public and private facilities and organizations. Fourteen lengthy sections, arranged by state, list resources for learning disabled, emotionally disturbed, autistic, neurologically impaired, mentally retarded, blind, deaf, hard of hearing, and speech-handicapped persons. Entries include a brief nonevaluative descriptive paragraph." Ref Sources for Small & Medium-sized Libr. 5th edition

Encyclopedia of special education; a reference for the education of the handicapped and other exceptional children and adults; editors, Cecil R. Reynolds, Lester Mann. Wiley 1987 3v il $325   **371.9**

1. Special education—Dictionaries 2. Handicapped
ISBN 0-471-82858-0   LC 86-33975

"Some 380 specialists contributed the more than 2000 succinct, signed, alphabetically arranged entries on leaders in the field of special education, educational and psychological tests, techniques of intervention, handicapping conditions, major court cases and laws, and the services needed to support special education. Brief bibliographies accompany each entry." Ref Sources for Small & Medium-sized Libr. 5th edition

Hayden, Torey L.

Just another kid. Putnam 1988 318p o.p.; Avon Bks. paperback available $4.95 **371.9**

1. Mentally ill children 2. Emotionally disturbed children
ISBN 0-380-70564-8 (pa)   LC 87-7229

The author presents an account of her work with a class of six emotionally disturbed children, and her relationship with the troubled mother of one of her students

"Torey Hayden inspires us by displaying her humane qualities as nurturer to children who test her compassion." N Y Times Book Rev

Kozol, Jonathan

Savage inequalities; children in America's schools. Crown 1991 262p $20   **371.9**

1. Public schools 2. Socially handicapped children 3. Segregation in education
ISBN 0-517-58221-X   LC 91-17574

Also available in paperback from HarperCollins Pubs.

In 1988, Kozol "visited schools in over 30 neighborhoods, including East St. Louis, Harlem, the Bronx, Chicago, Jersey City, and San Antonio. In this account, he concludes that real integration has seriously declined and education for minorities and the poor has moved backwards by at least several decades." Libr J

"Jonathan Kozol has written an impassioned book, laced with anger and indignation, about how our public education system scorns so many of our children. 'Savage Inequalities' is also an important book, and warrants widespread attention." N Y Times Book Rev

Lyman, Donald E.

Making the words stand still; a master teacher tells how to overcome specific learning disability, dyslexia, and old-fashioned word blindness; foreword by Robert S. Sloat. Houghton Mifflin 1986 272p hardcover o.p. paperback available $10.70   **371.9**

1. Learning disabilities 2. Reading—Remedial teaching 3. Dyslexia
ISBN 0-395-48681-5 (pa)   LC 85-14550

Using "anecdotes from his teaching experiences with learning disabled children and his own personal experiences in overcoming a learning disability, the author sets forth a conceptual framework for the causes of learning disabilities. . . . Techniques for assisting children in overcoming learning disabilities are presented." Readings

"So inspirational are the many success stories Lyman relates, and so clear, precise, and workable are his techniques, that this book should be required reading for all parents and teachers of learning-disabled children." Booklist

Porter, Rosalie Pedalino

Forked tongue; the politics of bilingual education. Basic Bks. 1990 285p $22.95; pa $11.95   **371.9**

1. Bilingual education
ISBN 0-465-02487-4; 0-465-02488-2 (pa)
     LC 89-77422

This book offers a history and critique of bilingual education in American schools over the past twenty years

"This book refutes the notion that children's abilities to learn are somehow enhanced by being taught first in their native languages to develop self-esteem and pride in their native culture." Natl Rev

Includes bibliographic references

Rose, Mike

Lives on the boundary; the struggles and achievements of America's underprepared. Free Press 1989 255p $29.95   **371.9**

1. Socially handicapped 2. Teaching 3. Literacy
ISBN 0-02-926821-4   LC 88-21469

Available in paperback from Penguin Bks.

The author addresses "society's prejudices about the academic abilities of the underprivileged. . . . In a series of vividly written vignettes, [Mr. Rose] describes how he has taught inner-city public school pupils, Vietnam veterans, adult literacy students and poorly prepared college students who were admitted under special circumstances to boost minority enrollment." N Y Times Book Rev

Includes bibliography

Smith, Sally Liberman
Succeeding against the odds; how the learning-disabled can realize their promise; [by] Sally L. Smith. Tarcher, J.P. 1992 304p $18.95; pa $12.95   **371.9**
1. Special education 2. Learning disabilities
ISBN 0-87477-674-0; 0-87477-731-3 (pa)
                                    LC 91-34819

In this work the author "stresses that 'learning disabilities are not a single condition but a group of related and often overlapping conditions that lead to low achievement by people who have the potential to do much better.' Specific ways for doing better are outlined here, in a book that is filled with practical suggestions and profiles of success stories, from Tom Cruise to American Express executive Malcolm Goodridge." Booklist

371.95   Gifted students

Saunders, Jacquelyn, 1950-
Bringing out the best; a resource guide for parents of young gifted children; [by] Jacquelyn Saunders with Pamela Espeland. rev & updated ed. Free Spirit 1991 234p il pa $12.95   **371.95**
1. Gifted children—Education 2. Parent and child
ISBN 0-915793-30-X   LC 90-24625
First published 1986

The authors "discuss such subjects as how to tell if a child is gifted, the emotional problems that result from being 'a child of promise,' ways to stimulate a child and the advantages and disadvantages of early schooling. . . . They also offer valuable advice on how to avoid parent burnout. . . . The book concludes with a directory of organizations for parents of gifted children and a list of books on the subject." Publ Wkly [review of 1986 edition]

Vail, Priscilla L.
Smart kids with school problems; things to know and ways to help. Dutton 1987 256p hardcover o.p. paperback available $10
                                        371.95
1. Gifted children—Education 2. Learning disabilities
ISBN 0-452-26242-9 (pa)   LC 87-502
Addresses learning problems of gifted children from pre-school through college age. Topics covered include visual learning, motor functioning, auditory learning, and psychological problems
Includes bibliography

372   Elementary education

Dewey, John, 1859-1952
The school and society, and The child and the curriculum; introduction by Philip W. Jackson. University of Chicago Press 1990 xli, 209p $15.95; pa $7.95   **372**
1. Elementary education
ISBN 0-226-14395-3; 0-226-14396-1 (pa)
                                    LC 90-43528
A combined edition of two essays first published separately in 1899 and 1902 respectively

Both of these works stress the functional relationship between classroom learning activities and real life experiences and analyze the social and psychological nature of the learning process. They present and defend the underlying tenets of Dewey's philosophy of education

Holt, John Caldwell, 1923-1985
How children fail. rev ed. Delacorte Press; Lawrence, S. 1982 298p hardcover o.p. paperback available $9.95   **372**
1. Elementary education
ISBN 0-440-53837-8 (pa)   LC 81-19566
"A Merloyd Lawrence book"
First published 1964 by Pitman

Based on the author's "experiences in teaching elementary-school students. 'Most children in school fail', he wrote. 'They fail because they are afraid, bored, and confused'. . . . He offers more specific reasons for the problems, and more ways to solve them. . . . An intelligent, compassionate look at the classroom experience." Booklist

Learning all the time; [by] John Holt. Addison-Wesley 1989 169p $15.95; pa $8.95
                                            372
1. Elementary education 2. Learning, Psychology of
ISBN 0-201-12095-X; 0-201-12095-X (pa)
                                    LC 89-35038
"A Merloyd Lawrence book"
"The book includes extensive sections on language, arts, and math, with additional information on science and music. Included are specific ideas on what parents can do to aid in the learning process of their children, and it also gives information on the nature of learning." Sci Teach

372.1   Generalities of elementary schools

Kidder, Tracy
Among schoolchildren. Houghton Mifflin 1989 340p $19.95   **372.1**
1. Teaching 2. Elementary education
ISBN 0-395-47591-0   LC 89-34378
Also available Thorndike Press large print edition and in paperback from Avon Bks.
"A Richard Todd book"
This book tells "the story of a young teacher's daily life and work in the Kelly School, a part of the Holyoke, Massachusetts school system. From September to June, Chris Zajac . . . struggles with the . . . task of teaching inner-city children, many from impoverished and broken homes." Libr J
This "is more than a book about needy children and a valiant teacher; it is full of the author's genuine love, delight and celebration of the human condition." N Y Times Book Rev
Includes bibliography

Paley, Vivian Gussin, 1929-
You can't say you can't play. Harvard Univ. Press 1992 134p il $15.95   **372.1**
1. Elementary education 2. Play
ISBN 0-674-96589-2   LC 91-47700

Paley, Vivian Gussin, 1929-—Continued

The author "explores how to keep students from being ignored by their classmates. She describes what happened when she asked students ranging from kindergarten to fifth grade to debate the proposition 'You Can't Say You Can't Play.' Woven throughout Paley's lessons is a parable about loneliness and rejection, which enables readers to share a child's view of the world. What the kids have to say is enchanting and surprisingly wise." Publ Wkly

372.2 Levels of elementary education

Encyclopedia of early childhood education; edited by Leslie R. Williams, Doris Pronin Fromberg. Garland 1992 518p il (Garland reference lib. of social science) $95   **372.2**

1. Elementary education 2. Child development
ISBN 0-8240-4626-9   LC 92-4579

This work "focuses on the education and care of children from birth to age eight, preparation of the adults who work with them, and important policy issues. Some 240 contributors . . . have written articles on the history of early childhood education, the evolution of curriculum materials, and the pioneers in early childcare." Libr J

For a fuller review see: Booklist, Sept. 1, 1992

Marzollo, Jean

The new kindergarten; full-day, child-centered, academic; a book for teachers, administrators, practice teachers, teacher aides, and parents; illustrated by Irene Trivas. Harper & Row 1987 226p il $16.95; pa $7.95   **372.2**

1. Kindergarten
ISBN 0-06-015786-0; 0-06-091512-9 (pa)
     LC 87-45071

In her proposal for an all-day kindergarten, the author suggests organizational techniques and appropriate subjects and themes. A sample program for an entire school year is included

372.4 Reading

Bettelheim, Bruno

On learning to read; the child's fascination with meaning; [by] Bruno Bettelheim & Karen Zelan. Knopf 1982 306p hardcover o.p. paperback available $9.95   **372.4**

1. Reading
ISBN 0-394-71194-7 (pa)   LC 81-47492

This book's "thesis says that children in America have trouble learning to read because the books they are taught to read from are so dull and vacuous, so mindless and simple that the children's innate desire to read is stifled." Best Sellers

"Whether conceptually right or wrong, the authors have something of practical importance to say to anybody interested in early literacy." N Y Rev Books

Flesch, Rudolf Franz, 1911-1986

Why Johnny can't read—and what you can do about it. Harper & Row 1955 222p hardcover o.p. paperback available $10   **372.4**

1. Reading 2. Phonetics—Study and teaching
ISBN 0-06-091340-1 (pa)

The author advocates the alphabetic-phonetic system of teaching children to read. He includes step-by-step directions and phonetic drills for use by parents

Why Johnny still can't read; a new look at the scandal of our schools; [by] Rudolf Flesch; foreword by Mary L. Burkhardt. Harper & Row 1981 xxii, 191p hardcover o.p. paperback available $9   **372.4**

1. Reading 2. Phonetics—Study and teaching
ISBN 0-06-091031-3 (pa)   LC 80-8686

"An unabashed proponent of the phonics system for reading instructions. . . . Flesch, in this updated evaluation of the state of the art of teaching reading, focuses on 50 years of 'cover-up, window dressing and gimmickry,' practices that doom children and label them 'dyslexic,' 'disadvantaged' or 'learning disabled.'" Publ Wkly

Includes bibliographic references

372.6 Language arts. Storytelling

Baker, Augusta, 1911-

Storytelling: art and technique; by Augusta Baker and Ellin Greene. 2nd ed. Bowker 1987 182p il $31   **372.6**

1. Storytelling
ISBN 0-8352-2336-1   LC 87-26539

First published 1977

"The first part of the work gives a history of storytelling in U.S. libraries . . . followed by a chapter on the purpose and values of storytelling. Several chapters are devoted to the practice of storytelling, with attention given to selection of the stories, preparation for story hour and the actual presentation." Am Libr

Includes bibliography

Sawyer, Ruth, 1880-1970

The way of the storyteller. Viking 1962 360p il o.p.; Penguin Bks. paperback available $11   **372.6**

1. Storytelling
ISBN 0-14-004436-1 (pa)

First published 1942

Chapters on the art and philosophy of storytelling, based mainly on the author's own experience. The second section of the book has a collection of stories

373.1 Generalities of secondary schools

Freedman, Samuel G.
Small victories: the real world of a teacher, her students, and their high school. Harper & Row 1990 431p $22.95; pa $12
373.1
1. Siegel, Jessica 2. Seward Park High School 3. High schools
ISBN 0-06-016254-6; 0-06-092087-4 (pa)
LC 89-45654

This is an account of the author's year as an observer at Seward Park High School on the Lower East Side of Manhattan. He focuses on the classroom of Jessica Siegel, an English teacher

Includes bibliographic references

GED: high school equivalency test examination; by Seymour Barasch [et al.] Prentice Hall General Ref. $12   **373.1**
1. High school equivalency examination

First published 1962 with title: High school equivalency diploma test (GED). (13th edition 1993) Frequently revised. Title varies

At head of title: Arco

Includes a diagnostic test; review sections in writing skills, social studies, science, reading skills, and math; and two complete sample tests with explanatory answers

The New GED; coordinating editor, Patricia Mulcrone; contributing authors, Patrick Mulcrone [et al.] Contemporary Bks. 1987 xxi, 791p il pa $11.95   **373.1**
1. High school equivalency examination
ISBN 0-8092-5032-2
LC 87-462
Revised edition of Contemporary's new GED, published 1985

"A new General Educational Development test [became] effective in 1988 . . . and with it this book becomes the standard source for anyone hoping to pass the exam and secure a high school equivalency certificate. . . . Every subject area, from biology to decimals, is covered with equal thoroughly. Pretests and practice tests (with answers) are supplied." Booklist

Rockowitz, Murray
How to prepare for the GED high school equivalency examination; [by] Murray Rockowitz, Samuel C. Brownstein, Max Peters. Barron's Educ. Ser. pa $11.95
373.1
1. High school equivalency examination

First published 1968. (8th edition 1990) Frequently revised. Title varies

General advice on how to study and specific suggestions on reviewing for and taking the tests are followed by sample questions in the five areas covered—English, mathematics, social studies, science, and literature

Sizer, Theodore R.
Horace's compromise; the dilemma of the American high school. Houghton Mifflin 1992 257p pa $9.95   **373.1**
1. High schools 2. Education—United States
ISBN 0-395-61158-X
LC 92-145238
A reissue with a new introduction of the title first published 1984

"The first report from a study of American high schools, co-sponsored by the National Association of Secondary School Principals and the Commission on Educational Issues of the National Association of Independent Schools." Title page

"The dilemma of Horace, the capable teacher who wants to teach his students how to think, is that in order to hold his job he must compromise ideals and accept mediocre learning because the school provides conditions that are not conducive to optimum learning. Sizer proposes drastic surgery to eliminate these conditions." Choice

Includes bibliographic references

Horace's school; redesigning the American high school. Houghton Mifflin 1992 238p $19.95; pa $9.95   **373.1**
1. High schools 2. Education—United States
ISBN 0-395-57230-4; 0-395-65973-6 (pa)   LC 91-869
The author continues the discussion of American education he began in Horace's compromise (entered above). "The fictional character Horace Smith, a dedicated English teacher in the also fictional (but typical) American high school, is now a chair of a Committee on Redesign of his school." Libr J
"This book can serve as a practical handbook for anyone—teacher, student, parent, or concerned citizen—who is interested in pursuing change at the local high school." Christ Sci Monit

Includes bibliographic references

373.2 Types and levels of secondary education

Peterson's guide to independent secondary schools. Peterson's Guides il pa $22.95
373.2
1. Private schools—Directories
ISSN 0894-9409
Annual. First published 1980. Title varies

This guide describes more than 1,300 private secondary schools in the U.S. and abroad. Included are day and boarding schools, military schools, religious schools, and schools for students with special needs

374 Adult education

Anderson, Walter, 1944-
Read with me. Houghton Mifflin 1990 179p $14.95   **374**
1. Literacy 2. Adult education
ISBN 0-395-52393-1
LC 90-33915
"A Marc Jaffe book"
The author discusses adult literacy programs, and includes interviews with adults who have benefited from them; also included are comments from literacy tutors
This book "will be of interest to tutors, adult new readers, and those who wish to know more about the impact of the literacy movement on our society." Libr J

Includes bibliographic references

The **Macmillan** guide to correspondence study; compiled and edited by Modoc Press, Inc. Macmillan $90   **374**

1. Correspondence schools and courses

First published 1983. (5th edition 1993) Periodically revised

"Indicates subject areas available from accredited schools, courses offered, admission requirements and procedures, tuition and fees. Includes formal degree programs, professional noncredit courses, home-study programs, vocational programs, and computer-based programs. Comprehensive subject index to courses." Sheehy. Guide to Ref Books. 10th edition

376 Education of women

Solomon, Barbara Miller, 1919-1992
In the company of educated women; a history of women and higher education in America. Yale Univ. Press 1985 298p il hardcover o.p. paperback available $14.95   **376**

1. Women—Education 2. Higher education
ISBN 0-300-03639-6 (pa)   LC 84-19681

"The work examines popular attitudes towards women's intellectual capabilities, women's struggles to gain access to educational institutions, and the relationship of education to women's later lives and to feminism, from the Colonial era to the present." Choice

"This study raises many of the important issues regarding women's education and provides a valuable foundation on which to explore those, and other issues further." J Am Hist

Includes bibliography

378 Higher education

Aisenberg, Nadya
Women of academe; outsiders in the sacred grove; [by] Nadya Aisenberg and Mona Harrington. University of Mass. Press 1988 207p hardcover o.p. paperback available $13.95   **378**

1. Women teachers 2. Sex discrimination 3. Colleges and universities—Faculty
ISBN 0-87023-607-5 (pa)   LC 87-30067

Based on interviews with more than sixty women, this work examines the role of women in the academic community and their struggle for acceptance and recognition

The authors' "conclusions offer thoughts on what women should do; the possible actions provide no real solutions for individuals but collectively motivate and stimulate self-esteem. A definitive, thought-provoking study." Libr J

Includes bibliography

Boswick, Storm
Guide to the universities of Europe. Facts on File 1991 296p $35   **378**

1. Colleges and universities—Europe
ISBN 0-8160-2359-X   LC 90-19169

This guide "covers more than 275 schools in 26 European countries. While most of the volume is devoted to Western Europe, a small section covers Czechoslovakia, Hungary, Poland, the Soviet Union, and Yugoslavia. It is arranged alphabetically by country and by school within each country." Libr J

For a fuller review see: Booklist, Dec. 15, 1991

Bromwich, David, 1951-
Politics by other means; higher education and group thinking. Yale Univ. Press 1992 257p $30   **378**

1. Higher education 2. United States—Intellectual life
ISBN 0-300-05702-4   LC 92-7914

A "definitive analysis of the threat to liberal education . . . by those who advance antiquarian-reactionary and academic radical ideas of tradition. . . . In the process of attacking the right-wing culture outside the university and left-wing culture inside it, [Bromwich] redefines such key concepts as culture, community, and professionalism. Various campus incidents at Brown, Yale, and Clark, are examined." Choice

Includes bibliographic references

Hayden, Thomas C.
Handbook for college admissions; a family guide. 3rd ed. Peterson's Guides 1989 210p pa $11.95   **378**

1. College choice 2. Colleges and universities—Entrance requirements
ISBN 0-87866-799-7   LC 89-8544

First published 1981 by Atheneum Pubs.

This handbook for students and their families includes information on the selection process, financial aid, and the college experience at large and small schools

Paige, Michele Anna
After the SATs; an insider's guide to freshman year; illustrated by Tom Kerr. Barron's Educ. Ser. 1991 199p il pa $9.95   **378**

1. Study skills 2. College students
ISBN 0-8120-4477-0   LC 91-13511

"Tips on career choices, grades, coursework, instructors, note-taking, writing papers, studying, tests, and alternative study opportunities as well as advice regarding living arrangements, social activities, health, and finances are presented clearly and logically." SLJ

Pelikan, Jaroslav Jan, 1923-
The idea of the university; a reexamination. Yale Univ. Press 1992 238p $30   **378**

1. Newman, John Henry, Cardinal, 1801-1890. Idea of a university 2. Higher education 3. Colleges and universities
ISBN 0-300-05725-3   LC 92-2928

The author "conducts an 'ungoing dialogue with one book,' John Henry Cardinal Newman's *The Idea of a University*. Written more than 150 years ago by the towering 19th century thinker whose efforts to establish a Catholic university in Dublin were cruelly frustrated, Newman's book offers illuminating parallels to, and contrasts, current university crises, and Pelikan draws attention to these in the present work." Publ Wkly

Pelikan, Jaroslav Jan, 1923—— *Continued*
"Written in a style whose clarity is the next best thing to elegance, and expounded with the grace that flows from a cultivated as well as a learned mind." N Y Times Book Rev

Includes bibliographic references

378.1 Generalities of higher education

Brownstein, Samuel C., 1909-
How to prepare for SAT I; [by] Samuel C. Brownstein, Mitchel Weiner [and] Sharon Weiner Green. Barron's Educ. Ser. pa $12.95
378.1
1. Scholastic aptitude test 2. Colleges and universities—Entrance requirements

First published 1954. (18th edition 1994) Title varies

This guide to the new SAT includes a review of skills, test-taking strategies, and sample tests with answers

How to prepare for the ACT, American College Testing Assessment Program; [by] George Ehrenhaft [et al.] Barron's Educ. Ser. il pa $11.95
378.1
1. ACT assessment 2. Colleges and universities—Entrance requirements

Also available in a concise edition

First published 1972 with title: Barron's how to prepare for the American College Testing Program (ACT). (9th edition 1991) Frequently revised. Editors vary

A guide to achieving higher scores on the ACT which includes subject reviews and practice exams with answers

Includes bibliography

Preparation for the CLEP: College Level Examination Program; the 5 general examinations; [by] Leo Lieberman [et al.] Prentice Hall General Ref. pa $12 **378.1**
1. College Level Examination Program

First published 1982 with title: CLEP: College-Level Examination Program. (4th edition 1993) Frequently revised

At head of title: Arco

A study guide for the testing program that allows the nontraditional student to transform what he knows into traditional college credit. It includes sample examinations in English composition, humanities, mathematics, natural sciences, and social sciences and history

378.3 Student finances

College Entrance Examination Board
The college cost book. College Entrance Examination Bd. pa $14.95
378.3
1. College costs 2. Student loan funds

Annual. First published 1980

"Covers 3,000 colleges and universities. Provides information on what each college really costs, including personal expenses, travel and books; how to get financial aid; and how to interpret financial aid packages. Includes tables in the back to help you work out applications for financial aid." N Y Public Libr Book of How & Where to Look It Up

Dennis, Marguerite J., 1946-
Complete college financing guide. Barron's Educ. Ser. 1992 251p pa $13.95
378.3
1. Student loan funds 2. Scholarships, fellowships, etc.
ISBN 0-8120-4950-0
LC 91-42484

First published 1989 with title: Dollars for scholars

This guide explains how to apply for financial assistance from a variety of sources. Attention is given to veterans, minority students, women, handicapped students, and others in special situations

Includes bibliographic references

Edelstein, Scott
Putting your kids through college; [by] Scott Edelstein and the editors of Consumer Reports Books. Consumers Union of U.S. 1989 199p pa $12
378.3
1. College costs 2. Student loan funds 3. Scholarships, fellowships, etc.
ISBN 0-89043-233-3
LC 88-25744

"This volume offers useful background information on college selection, admissions procedures, and just a brief note on graduate school. . . . Some extra notes are directed at parents of foreign students and those with disabilities. A list of state financial aid agencies is appended." Booklist

Includes bibliography

Keeslar, Oreon
Financial aids for higher education. Brown, W.C. pa $35
378.3
1. Scholarships, fellowships, etc. 2. Student loan funds

Biennial. First published 1963 with title: A national catalog of scholarships and other financial aids for students entering college. Subtitle varies

"Alphabetically arranged guide to more than 3000 financial assistance programs for undergraduates. Entries provide sponsor, description, restrictions, value, eligibility, basis of award, application procedures and deadlines, and source of further information. . . . A unique program finder leads students to appropriate programs." Ref Sources for Small & Medium-sized Libr. 5th edition

Krefetz, Gerald
How to pay for your children's college education. College Entrance Examination Bd. 1988 158p pa $12.95
378.3
1. College costs 2. Student loan funds
ISBN 0-87447-248-2
LC 87-72156

New edition in preparation

The author "details various strategies that may make the costly college education of the future a reality. . . . Krefetz outlines all the financial options available (loans, trusts, lines of credit, IRAs, etc.) and shows how they are best suited to different economic circumstances. An excellent selection for public libraries everywhere." Booklist

Paying less for college. Peterson's Guides pa $23.95
378.3
1. College costs 2. Student loan funds 3. Scholarships, fellowships, etc.
ISSN 1062-3205

Annual. First published 1983 with title: The College money handbook. Title varies

Paying less for college—*Continued*
A guide to costs and financial aid at more than 1,700 four-year colleges in the United States

Schlachter, Gail A.
Directory of financial aids for women; [by] Gail Ann Schlachter. Reference Service Press $45   **378.3**
1. Scholarships, fellowships, etc. 2. Women—Education

Biennial. First published 1978

Describes "scholarships, fellowships, loans, grants, awards, and internships designed primarily or exclusively for women. . . . Lists state sources of educational benefits and offers an annotated bibliography of directories that list general financial aid programs. Program title, sponsoring organization, geographic, subject, and filing date indexes." Ref Sources for Small & Medium-sized Libr. 5th edition

Financial aid for the disabled and their families; [by] Gail Ann Schlachter, R. David Weber. Reference Service Press $37.50
    378.3
1. Scholarships, fellowships, etc. 2. Physically handicapped

Biennial. First published 1988

"Provides information on a wide range of funding needs in such areas as education, career development, research, and travel. Includes multiple indexes; cross-referenced." N Y Public Libr Book of How & Where to Look It Up

378.73 Institutions of higher education—United States

American universities and colleges. De Gruyter $149.95   **378.73**
1. Colleges and universities—United States—Directories 2. Education—United States—Directories
ISSN 0066-0922

First published 1928. (14th edition 1992) Frequently revised

Sponsored by the American Council on Education

"A directory of institutions organized by state forms the bulk of this compendium. Entries present characteristics, accreditation, structure, history, degree requirements, and additional information in somewhat greater detail than most directories. Particularly valuable for providing descriptions of individual colleges and schools within some institutions." Ref Sources for Small & Medium-sized Libr. 5th edition

Barron's guide to law schools; introduction by Gary A. Munneke. Barron's Educ. Ser. pa $14.95   **378.73**
1. Colleges and universities—United States—Directories

First published 1967. 1st-8th editions published under the authorship of Elliott M. Epstein, Jerome Shostak, and Lawrence M. Troy. (10th edition 1992) Frequently revised

Information includes profiles of American Bar Association approved law schools, guidelines for preparing for the LSAT, and prospects for employment

Barron's profiles of American colleges. Barron's Educ. Ser. pa $18.95   **378.73**
1. Colleges and universities—United States—Directories 2. Education—United States—Directories

First published 1964

"Published annually since the 1991 and 1992 editions, this popular volume features comprehensive profiles of 1500 accredited four-year schools, an index by major, lists of colleges by costs, and selective rankings." Libr J

Barron's top 50; an inside look at America's best colleges; Tom Fischgrund, editor. 2nd ed. Barron's Educ. Ser. 1993 682p pa $13.95   **378.73**
1. Colleges and universities—United States—Directories 2. College choice
ISBN 0-8120-1447-2   LC 92-39776

First published 1991

This list is based on such criteria as acceptance rate, SAT scores, and academic resources. Comments from recent graduates are included in the description of each college

Cass, James, 1915-1992
Comparative guide to American colleges; for students, parents, and counselors; by James Cass and Max Birnbaum. HarperCollins Pubs. pa $19.95   **378.73**
1. Colleges and universities—United States—Directories 2. Education—United States—Directories

First published 1964. (15th edition 1991) Periodically revised

"Provides analytical and comparative data on individual colleges, with an emphasis on the scholastic achievements of the student body, academic opportunities offered, and the quality of faculty. State, selectivity, and religious indexes. Comparative listing of majors." Ref Sources for Small & Medium-sized Libr. 5th edition

Choose a Christian college; a guide to academically challenging colleges committed to a Christ-centered campus life. 3rd ed. Peterson's Guides 1992 131p il pa $12.95   **378.73**
1. Christian education 2. Colleges and universities—United States—Directories
ISBN 1-56079-217-5   LC 92-22622

First published 1988 with title: Consider a Christian college

"Published in association with the Christian College Coalition." Title page

"This work presents a rationale for selecting a Christian college that cannot be found in other college guides. It goes on to describe in depth the 78 member institutions of the Christian College Coalition." Libr J

The College blue book. Macmillan 5v maps set $200   **378.73**
1. Colleges and universities—United States—Directories 2. Education—United States—Directories
ISSN 0069-5572

Also available on CD-ROM

Biennial. First published 1923

The College blue book—*Continued*

This guide "covers more schools than any other single source. It lists trade schools, specialized institutions, as well as two- and four-year colleges in the United States and Canada." Libr J

College Entrance Examination Board

The college handbook. College Entrance Examination Bd. pa $20 **378.73**

1. Colleges and universities—United States—Directories 2. Education—United States—Directories

First published 1941 by Ginn with title: Annual handbook

"*The College Handbook* is an authoritative annual that supplies information on about 3200 accredited U.S. colleges, both two- and four-year. It covers subjects from admissions to special facilities and offers expert guidelines on choosing a school." Libr J

Index of majors and graduate degrees. College Entrance Examination Bd. pa $15.95 **378.73**

1. Colleges and universities—United States—Directories 2. Colleges and universities—Curricula

Annual. First published 1977 with title: The college handbook index of majors. Variant title: Index of majors

Lists major fields of study and the colleges, state by state, that currently offer them. Also includes separate sections for major programs leading to associate degrees and to bachelor's degrees and graduate degrees, and lists of colleges that have religious affiliations, special academic programs, and special admissions procedures

Doughty, Harold R.

Guide to American graduate schools. Penguin Bks. pa $20 **378.73**

1. Colleges and universities—United States—Directories 2. Professional education—Directories

First published 1967 by Viking. (6th edition 1990) Periodically revised

This guide "describes graduate schools and course work, naming more than 1,100 institutions throughout the U.S., and citing admission standards, tuition and housing costs, financial aid, degree requirements, and fields of study for each entry. The index lists participating institutions under general headings of the fields of study." Booklist

Fiske, Edward B.

The Fiske guide to colleges. Times Bks. pa $16 **378.73**

1. Colleges and universities—United States—Directories 2. College choice

Annual. First published 1982 with title: The New York Times selective guide to colleges

This guide to some 300 of the best colleges and universities nationwide includes information on admissions, costs, financial aid, housing, social life, and academic strengths and weaknesses

The **Insider's** guide to the colleges; compiled and edited by the staff of The Yale Daily News. St. Martin's Press $26.95; pa $15.95 **378.73**

1. Colleges and universities—United States—Directories 2. College choice

Annual. First published 1978

This guide describes admission policies, costs, and academic programs at over 300 selected colleges in all 50 states and Canada. It also features candid student opinions on campus life

Lovejoy's college guide; edited by Charles T. Straughn II and Barbarasue Lovejoy Straughn. Prentice-Hall $40; pa $21 **378.73**

1. Colleges and universities—United States—Directories 2. Education—United States—Directories
ISSN 0076-132X

"A Monarch book"

First published 1940 by Simon & Schuster with title: So you're going to college, compiled by Clarence E. Lovejoy. (22nd edition 1993) Frequently revised

"Lovejoy's provides profiles of more than 2,500 four-year and two-year colleges and universities, along with admissions requirements, application procedures, tuition figures, selectivity rankings, and information on many other topics." N Y Public Libr Book of How & Where to Look It Up

Meltzer, Tom

The student access guide to the best colleges; by Tom Meltzer, Zach Knower and John Katzman. Villard Bks. 1992 566p pa $16 **378.73**

1. Colleges and universities—United States—Directories 2. College choice
ISBN 0-679-73866-5   LC 92-19452

At head of title: The Princeton Review

Information for this guide was gathered from admissions offices, financial aid offices, independent counselors, and more than 30,000 college students. Information for each institution includes: competition level, entrance requirements and financial information. Students rank their colleges in categories including: faculty, work load, class size, location, social life, and sports

Peterson's colleges with programs for students with learning disabilities; Charles T. Mangrum and Stephen S. Strichart, editors; with a foreword by Rhona C. Hartman. 3rd ed. Peterson's Guides 1992 660p pa $24.95 **378.73**

1. Learning disabilities 2. Colleges and universities—United States—Directories
ISBN 1-560-79080-6   LC 92-20684

First published 1985 with title: Peterson's guide to colleges with programs for learning-disabled students

Contains profiles of more than 1,000 two-and four-year colleges with services to learning-disabled students. Includes information on selecting a college and on how to maximize chances for academic success

Peterson's competitive colleges. Peterson's Guides pa $14.95 **378.73**

1. Colleges and universities—United States—Directories
ISSN 0887-0152

Annual. First published 1981

This guide "devotes one page to each of 330 of the 'most challenging' four-year schools in the country. Advice on applying and financial planning, as well as numerous helpful lists and a geographical index, is included." Libr J

Peterson's guide to certificate programs at
American colleges and universities; editors,
George J. Lopos [et al.] Peterson's Guides
1988 343p pa $35.95   **378.73**

1. University extension 2. Continuing education
ISBN 0-87866-741-5   LC 88-43018

"This 'Guide' was developed by Peterson's in conjunction with the National University Continuing Education
Association. . . . Over 1,400 programs, representing 260
schools, are presented in alphabetical order by state, then
by institution, and finally by program classification. . .
. Each entry includes information about program content,
format, evaluation criteria, enrollment requirements, cost,
student services, and contact person." Booklist

Peterson's guide to four-year colleges.
Peterson's Guides il pa $18.95   **378.73**

1. Colleges and universities—United States—Directories 2. Education—United States—Directories
ISSN 0894-9336

Also available on CD-ROM

Annual. First published 1966 as part of Peterson's
annual guide to undergraduate study

This guide provides information on almost 2,000 colleges and universities and includes information on admissions, financial aid, courses, and extracurricular activities

Peterson's guide to two-year colleges.
Peterson's Guides il pa $16.95   **378.73**

1. Colleges and universities—United States—Directories 2. Education—United States—Directories
ISSN 0894-9328

Also available on CD-ROM

Annual. First published 1966 as part of Peterson's
annual guide to undergradute study

This guide profiles more than 1,400 accredited two-
year colleges which grant associate degrees

Smith, Page
Killing the spirit: higher education in
America. Viking 1989 315p o.p.; Penguin
Bks. paperback available $11   **378.73**

1. Higher education
ISBN 0-14-012183-8 (pa)   LC 89-40333

This history of higher education in the United States
presents an analysis of tendencies within academia that
the author considers detrimental

"Smith meticulously yet engagingly details the modern
university's free fall from the ideal of seeking and teaching truth. . . . [But] the cures [the book] offers . . .
are, if not impractical, nearly impossible to get from here
to there. . . . This in no way detracts from the work
as an excellent history of higher education in America."
Christ Sci Monit

379 Government regulation, control, support of education

DelFattore, Joan, 1946-
What Johnny shouldn't read; textbook
censorship in America. Yale Univ. Press
1992 209p $25   **379**

1. Censorship
ISBN 0-300-05709-1   LC 92-3585

DelFattore "discusses the process of textbook censorship, the litigation of specific cases, the role of publishers, and the issues that have an impact on censorship.
. . . She lists state policies on textbook selection and
explores issues of gender, race, and ethnicity, as well as
science and religion." Libr J

The author "thoughtfully presents six specific cases
and their immediate and long-term effects in order to
open the eyes and, hopefully, to raise the voices of those
who treasure intellectual freedom." Booklist

Includes bibliographic references

381 Internal commerce (Domestic trade)

Eiler, Andrew
The consumer protection manual. Facts on
File 1984 658p $40   **381**

1. Consumer protection
ISBN 0-87196-310-8   LC 82-1464

"For anyone who has purchased inferior merchandise
and wondered what recourse the consumer has under the
law, this book provides guidance through the maze of
state and federal regulations and describes what
consumers must do to protect themselves. One of the
most helpful features of the *Manual* is its variety of
sample letters for initiating complaints." Ref Sources for
Small & Medium-sized Libr. 5th edition

Mann, Charles C.
The aspirin wars; money, medicine, and
100 years of rampant competition; by
Charles C. Mann and Mark L. Plummer.
Knopf 1991 420p il $25   **381**

1. Farbenfabriken vorm. Friedrich Bayer & Co.
2. Aspirin 3. Drug industry
ISBN 0-394-57894-5   LC 90-28735

Also available in paperback from Harvard Business
School Press

The authors discuss "the history of the marketing of
aspirin as a drug from its introduction in 1899 to the
present. . . . Some of the events they describe include
the activities of Farbenfabriken Bayer in the United
States in the early 1900s." Libr J

"A very thoroughly researched and truly fascinating
history of a little pill whose story may have only just
begun." N Y Times Book Rev

Includes bibliographic references

Portnoy, J. Elias
Let the seller beware! the complete
consumer guide to getting your money's
worth. Collier Bks. 1991 c1990 242p pa
$9.95   **381**

1. Consumer protection 2. Consumer education
ISBN 0-02-036047-9   LC 90-46831

The author presents guidelines to enable consumers
to combat fraud and deception in the marketplace

383 Postal communication

National five digit zip code and post office directory. U.S. Postal Service maps pa $15
383

1. Zip code
ISSN 0731-9185

Annual. Continuation of National zip code and post office directory

"Besides ZIP codes and post offices, this directory includes information on the organization of the Postal Service, addressing, parcel weights and sizes, delivery statistics, and other matters." Recomm Ref Books in Paperback. 2d edition

384.1 Telegraph. Facsimile transmission

National FAX directory. Gale Res. $85
384.1

1. Facsimile transmission—Directories
ISSN 1045-9499

Annual. First published 1989

Provides fax numbers for U.S. companies, organizations, government agencies, and libraries. Each entry includes name, fax and voice phone numbers, and mailing address

384.55 Television

Auletta, Ken
Three blind mice; how the TV networks lost their way. Random House 1991 642p $25; pa $14
384.55

1. Television broadcasting
ISBN 0-394-56358-1; 0-679-74135-6 (pa)
LC 90-52925

This look at the television broadcast industry focuses on the 1980s when all three of the major networks were taken over by new owners

"In his zest for detail, Auletta trudges dutifully through events that are now just so much TV-industry ephemera. Still, if he is occasionally too fascinated by the trees, Auletta never loses sight of the forest. On a shelf overflowing with behind-the-scenes tomes and tell-all memoirs, his is the network book to beat." Time

Includes bibliographic references

385.09 Railroad transportation— Historical and geographic treatment

Hubbard, Freeman H.
Encyclopedia of North American railroading; 150 years of railroading in the United States and Canada; [by] Freeman Hubbard. McGraw-Hill 1981 377p il $72.40
385.09

1. Railroads—History
ISBN 0-07-030828-4
LC 81-1975

This work includes "biographies, anecdotes, achievements, disasters, and histories of individual railroad companies, locomotive and car builders, rail labor unions, 'railfan' clubs, etc." Booklist

"This is a very useful, reliable source for brief histories and expositions of American railroad topics." Wilson Libr Bull

The **Railroaders**; by the editors of Time-Life Books; with text by Keith Wheeler. Time-Life Bks. 1973 240p il maps (Old West) $19.93
385.09

1. Railroads—History 2. West (U.S.)—History

This book, illustrated with photographs, maps, drawings and newspaper clippings of the period, shows the advent of the railroad into the Old West and its effect on the wilderness and settlers of the late nineteenth century

Includes bibliography

386 Inland waterway and ferry transportation

The **Rivermen**; by the editors of Time-Life Books; with text by Paul O'Neil. Time-Life Bks. 1975 240p il maps (Old West) $19.93
386

1. Inland navigation 2. Steamboats—History 3. West (U.S.)—History

Text and numerous illustrations depict America's waterways and the men and river boats that plied the waters in search of fur, gold and riches

Includes bibliography

387.2 Ships

Hoehling, A. A. (Adolph A.)
Ships that changed history. Madison Bks. 1992 182p il $19.95
387.2

1. Navigation 2. Ships 3. Naval history
ISBN 0-8191-8072-6
LC 92-10990

The author describes "the clippers, the *Great Eastern*, the USS *Monitor*, the RMS *Lusitania*, the ships of Dunkirk, and the USS *Arizona*." Libr J

"Hoehling's text is highly readable, although the quote-ridden chapter on the *Arizona* is disappointing." Publ Wkly

Includes bibliographic references

388.1 Roads and highways

Hokanson, Drake, 1951-
The Lincoln Highway; main street across America; text and photographs by Drake Hokanson. University of Iowa Press 1988 159p il hardcover o.p. paperback available $19.95
388.1

1. Roads
ISBN 0-87745-261-X (pa)
LC 87-30167

Hokanson presents a photo essay on "the earliest transcontinental American highway. . . . Half the book follows the highway, as it was constructed, east to west; half covers later developments, political, technological [and] social." Christ Sci Monit

Hokanson, Drake, 1951-—*Continued*
"A masterly photographer and writer creates a classic of Americana." Booklist

Includes bibliography

388.3   Vehicular transportation

The **Expressmen**; by the editors of Time-Life Books; with text by David Nevin. Time-Life Bks. 1974 240p il maps (Old West) $19.93   **388.3**
1. Postal service—West (U.S.) 2. Express service 3. Transportation—History

This book describes the stagecoach services by which mail, freight, and passengers reached the western settlements. The origins of the Pony Express, Wells Fargo and Company, the so-called "Jackass Mail" (San Antonio and San Diego Mail), and the Oxbow Route are discussed as are the Oregon and Santa Fe trails

Includes bibliography

391   Costume and personal appearance

Barton, Lucy, 1891-1979
Historic costume for the stage; illustrated by David Sarvis. Baker, W.H. 1961 609p il $27.95   **391**
1. Costume—History
ISBN 0-87440-002-3
First published 1935

Covers all periods from the Egyptian (4000 BC) to the 20th century. Each chapter is preceded by a historic overview of the period. Descriptions of garments, the way they were constructed, and how they were worn accompany the illustrations

Includes bibliographies

Boucher, François, b. 1885
20,000 years of fashion; the history of costume and personal adornment; by François Boucher, with a new chapter by Yvonne Deslandres. expanded ed. Abrams 1987 459p il $49.50   **391**
1. Costume—History
ISBN 0-8109-1693-2   LC 86-72852

First published 1967; published in the United Kingdom with title: A history of costume in the West

"Begins divided into historical-regional sections but quickly moves to the history of European costume. Discusses materials, ornaments, accessories, and functions." N Y Public Libr Book of How & Where to Look It Up

Brooke, Iris, 1908-
A history of English costume; written and illustrated by Iris Brooke. [4th ed]. Theatre Arts Bks. 1972 196p il hardcover o.p. paperback available $10.95   **391**
1. Costume—History
ISBN 0-87830-569-6 (pa)
First published 1937 in the United Kingdom

A history of English costume from the Norman Conquest to the present day with detailed sketches of the various styles of dress

Calasibetta, Charlotte Mankey
Fairchild's dictionary of fashion. 2nd ed. Fairchild Publs. 1988 749p il $50   **391**
1. Fashion design—Dictionaries 2. Costume—Dictionaries
ISBN 0-87005-635-2   LC 88-80198
First published 1975

"This work provides 15,000 definitions along with about 500 well-executed line drawings and another 500 biographical sketches of designers." Ref Sources for Small & Medium-sized Libr. 5th edition

Cassin-Scott, Jack
The illustrated encyclopaedia of costume and fashion, 1550-1920. Blandford Press; [distributed by] Sterling 1986 160p il $24.95   **391**
1. Costume—History
ISBN 0-7137-1811-0

"Some 150 colorplates of men, women, and children dressed in period fashions are the highlight of this costume primer. From the stiff silhouette of the mid-sixteenth-century Spanish court dress to the 1920s flapper outfit, each sample includes a brief description of the costume and an illustration. . . . A handy, easy-to-use guide for novice costume designers and artists." Booklist

Davis, Fred
Fashion, culture, and identity. University of Chicago Press 1992 226p il $24.95   **391**
1. Fashion 2. Sex role
ISBN 0-226-13808-9   LC 91-44012

The author examines "fashion's social and psychological significance in modern culture. What makes clothes fashion; how fashions evolve; how fashion choices express social status, gender identity, sexuality, and conformity; and how fashion is (or is not) accepted are [discussed]." Libr J

"Davis has wise things to say about fashion and status, fashion as an element in the economy, and more." Christ Century

Includes bibliographic references

De Marly, Diana
Dress in North America. v1: The New World, 1492-1800. Holmes & Meier 1990 221p il $59.95   **391**
1. Costume—History 2. United States—Social life and customs—1600-1775, Colonial period
ISBN 0-8419-1199-1   LC 90-4905

"Volume 1 of this projected three-volume series is a historical narrative of the development of clothing styles and industries in Colonial America. Beautifully reproduced art works, mostly portrait paintings, are accompanied by excellent fashion commentary." Libr J

Includes bibliography

Ewing, Elizabeth
History of twentieth century fashion; revised and updated by Alice Mackrell. [3rd ed]. Barnes & Noble Bks. 1992 298p il $59.95   **391**

    1. Costume—History 2. Fashion—History
    ISBN 0-389-20993-7   LC 92-10774
    First published 1974 in the United Kingdom; 1975 in the United States by Scribner
    Arranged chronologically from the Edwardian period to the early 1990s, this illustrated history of fashion looks at how social, economic, and technical changes in this century have affected fashion trends. The discussion includes the impact of two world wars, new fibers and manufacturing techniques, and the influence of radical young designers
    Includes bibliographic references

Hunnisett, Jean
Period costume for stage & screen; patterns for women's dress, 1500-1800; illustrations by Janette Haslam. Players Press 1991 176p il $39.95   **391**

    1. Costume—History 2. Dressmaking
    ISBN 0-88734-610-3   LC 90-50385
    Also available volume covering years 1800-1909 $39.95 (ISBN 0-88734-609-X)
    First published 1986 in the United Kingdom
    Contains patterns, illustrations, and instructions for more than twenty garments
    Includes bibliography

Laver, James, 1899-1975
Costume and fashion; a concise history; concluding chapter by Christina Probert. new ed. Thames & Hudson 1982 288p il (World of art lib) pa $14.95   **391**

    1. Costume—History 2. Fashion—History
    ISBN 0-500-20190-0   LC 82-12493
    Also available in paperback from Oxford Univ. Press
    First published 1969 with title: A concise history of costume
    "Offers a historical survey of fashion and social change from earliest times through the 1970s. Illustrations are placed close to pertinent text and their sources are identified." Sheehy. Guide to Ref Books. 10th edition

Lister, Margot
Costume; an illustrated survey from ancient times to the twentieth century. Plays 1968 346p il $24.95   **391**

    1. Costume—History
    ISBN 0-8238-0096-2
    "A comprehensive reference work on costume from the old Egyptian kingdom to 1914, effectively illustrated with line drawings. Attention to details such as hair style, footwear, jewelry, colors and materials, suggestions for constructing the garments, and inclusion of the dress of all classes of society give it practical value." Booklist

Men and women; dressing the part; edited by Claudia Brush Kidwell and Valerie Steele. Smithsonian Institution Press 1989 188p il hardcover o.p. paperback available $24.95   **391**

    1. Fashion 2. Sex role
    ISBN 0-87474-559-4 (pa)   LC 88-18259
    This book "analyzes what changes in fashion say about gender, class, and morality. . . . Changing hair styles and body types are also examined. . . . The book also covers work clothes, sports clothes, military uniforms, blue jeans, and lingerie. A concise and lively book that works on all levels, for casual reader or scholar." Libr J
    Includes bibliography

Milbank, Caroline Rennolds
New York fashion; the evolution of American style. Abrams 1989 303p il $49.50   **391**

    1. Costume 2. Clothing trade 3. Fashion
    ISBN 0-8109-1388-7   LC 89-60
    A "visual documentary of American fashion. . . . Throughout, Milbank intertwines a virtual who's who of the women's clothing industry . . . with the story of the rise of American department stores and ready-to-wear clothing. Beginning with the 1940s, entries are arranged alphabetically by individual designers and include brief biographical information along with their notable signature or trademark design concepts and features. A welcome addition to any type of library collection." Libr J
    Includes bibliography

Nunn, Joan
Fashion in costume, 1200-1980. Schocken Bks. 1984 256p il o.p.; New Amsterdam Bks. paperback available $16.95   **391**

    1. Costume—History
    ISBN 0-941533-79-4 (pa)   LC 83-27089
    The author "surveys European and American dress from the late Middle Ages to the present. Each chapter begins with a brief discussion of historical, social, economic, and artistic events, then moves on to men's, women's, and children's dress, accessories and jewelry, fabrics, and color." Libr J
    Includes bibliography

O'Hara, Georgina
The encyclopaedia of fashion; introduction by Carrie Donovan. Abrams 1986 272p il $29.95   **391**

    1. Fashion—Dictionaries 2. Costume—Dictionaries
    ISBN 0-8109-0882-4   LC 86-3542
    "Beginning in the 1840s and continuing up to the mid-1980s, O'Hara traces the important developments in costume and textile design with emphasis on the individuals who have achieved distinction in this field. It is an impressive list that includes major designers, illustrators, photographers, and fashion trendsetters as well as those individuals whose influence was short lived. The entries in this encyclopaedia are well illustrated and the cross-reference system is very helpful." Choice

Peacock, John, 1943-
The chronicle of Western fashion; from ancient times to the present day. Abrams 1991 224p il $29.95   **391**

1. Costume—History 2. Fashion—History
ISBN 0-8109-3953-3   LC 90-1053

A survey of "Western costume from ancient Egypt to 1980. Presented chronologically, the 8 to 10 illustrations per page are lavishly colored and use color schemes appropriate to each period. All illustrations are labeled with country of origin and wearer's societal status. Every century is followed up by concise captions corresponding to the illustrations." Booklist

Includes bibliographic references

Schnurnberger, Lynn Edelman
Let there be clothes; 40,000 years of fashion; [by] Lynn Schnurnberger. Workman 1991 412p il pa $19.95   **391**

1. Costume—History 2. Fashion—History
ISBN 0-89480-833-8   LC 91-315

"From cave dwellers to twentieth-century revivals, every facet of . . . [Western fashion] is touched on, conveying how what we wear serves as messenger of distinct cultural values. Aside from numerous engrossing facts, Schnurnberger's absorbing presentation features colorful, electric visuals." Booklist

Wilcox, R. Turner, 1888-1970
The dictionary of costume. Scribner 1969 406p il $60   **391**

1. Costume—Dictionaries
ISBN 0-684-15150-2   LC 68-12503

"This fully illustrated dictionary of historic costume covers all facets on a worldwide basis. The entries are primarily succinct descriptions of items of clothing." Ref Sources for Small & Medium-sized Libr. 5th edition

Five centuries of American costume. Scribner 1963 207p il $40   **391**

1. Costume—History
ISBN 0-684-15161-8

"Arranged chronologically, emphasis is on the dress of American men, women, and children from the Vikings, Eskimos, and early settlers to 1960. Clear line drawings illustrate the text." Ref Sources for Small & Medium-sized Libr. 5th edition

Includes bibliography

Folk and festival costume of the world. Scribner 1965 unp il $55   **391**

1. Costume
ISBN 0-684-15379-3   LC 65-23986

"Traditional costumes from 150 countries, described and illustrated in black and white." N Y Public Libr. Ref Books for Child Collect. 2d edition

Includes bibliography

Yarwood, Doreen
The encyclopedia of world costume. Scribner 1979 c1978 471p il o.p.; Outlet reprint available $16.99   **391**

1. Costume—Dictionaries
ISBN 0-517-61943-1

"With over 2000 drawings and eight pages of color illustrations, this is a comprehensive guide to costume from ancient times to the present day. Related subjects are covered in one large entry. There are 650 articles on such topics as: hairstyles, face, fabrics, baby clothes, eyeglasses, cosmetics, political influences, and costumes of various countries." Ref Sources for Small & Medium-sized Libr. 5th edition

Fashion in the Western world, 1500-1990. Drama Bk. Pubs. 1992 176p il $29.95   **391**

1. Fashion—History 2. Costume—History
ISBN 0-89676-118-5   LC 92-239581

Illustrated with "line drawings and photographs, the book traces the succession of styles of women's, men's, and children's dress and accessories against their contemporary social and cultural background as well as the technological developments in fabrics and the manufacture and care of garments." Publisher's note

Includes bibliographic references

392 Customs of life cycle and domestic life

Brill, Mordecai L.
Write your own wedding; [by] Mordecai L. Brill, Marlene Halpin, William H. Genné. rev & updated ed. New Century Pubs. 1985 122p pa $7.95   **392**

1. Weddings 2. Marriage customs and rites
ISBN 0-8329-0398-1   LC 85-7156

First published 1979

The authors present liturgies, original prayers, and vows appropriate for couples wishing to design their own marriage ceremonies

Includes bibliography

Clark, Leta W.
Affordable weddings; how to have the wedding of your dreams on the budget of your choice; illustrations by Robert Curet. Simon & Schuster 1988 223p il pa $10.95   **392**

1. Weddings 2. Marriage customs and rites
ISBN 0-671-64056-9   LC 87-28612

"A Fireside book"

"This book describes all the basics: ceremony, protocol, location, invitations, flowers, sound and lighting, catering, cake, and photography. Of great advantage are the book's worksheets for both Christian and Jewish ceremonies, which help to organize volunteers, resources, and budget." Libr J

Diamant, Anita
The new Jewish wedding. Summit Bks. 1985 268p il hardcover o.p. paperback available $10   **392**

1. Weddings 2. Marriage customs and rites 3. Judaism—Customs and practices
ISBN 0-671-62882-8 (pa)   LC 84-24102

Covers traditional Jewish weddings as well as modern alternatives, and ceremonies which combine the two

Wedding readings; centuries of writing and rituals on love and marriage; selected and with an introduction by Eleanor Munro. Viking 1989 xxiv, 262p il $20 **392**

1. Weddings 2. Marriage customs and rites 3. Love poetry
ISBN 0-670-81088-6 LC 88-40334

"Munro has selected prose, poetry, ethnic love songs, and prayers that are appropriate readings for Catholic, Jewish, and Protestant wedding ceremonies. North American Indian love songs, Chinese prayers, Japanese poems, Persian love poems, and Hindu wedding prayers are included, as well as the more standard Greek classical writings and Biblical passages." Libr J

393 Death customs

Tierney, Patrick
The highest altar; the story of human sacrifice. Viking 1989 480p il maps o.p.; Penguin Bks. paperback available $11.95
393

1. Sacrifice 2. Indians of South America—Rites and ceremonies
ISBN 0-14-013974-5 (pa) LC 87-40666

The author reports that human sacrifice is still practiced today in Chile, Bolivia and Peru. He cites various recent examples, and gives an account of the ethnohistorical background of ritual killings in the Inca empire

"Even if in the end we are left with the doubt that all or most of Mr. Tierney's examples in the Andes illustrate human sacrifice rather than certain ritual aspects of common murder, he gives us abundant and valuable ethnographic material." N Y Times Book Rev

Includes bibliographic references

394.2 Customs—Special occasions

The **American** book of days; compiled and edited by Jane M. Hatch. 3rd ed. Wilson, H.W. 1978 xxvi, 1214p $85 **394.2**

1. Holidays 2. Fasts and feasts 3. Festivals—United States
ISBN 0-8242-0593-6 LC 78-16239

First edition by George W. Douglas, published 1937

"Reports the American ways, both solemn and fanciful, of marking anniversaries and commemorating achievements. Arranged by day, January to December, with full, descriptive articles. Emphasis is on religious and civil holidays and on days honoring events in the founding and growth of the United States." Ref Sources for Small & Medium-sized Libr. 5th edition

Chase's annual events. Contemporary Bks. $42.95 **394.2**

1. Calendars 2. Holidays 3. Almanacs
ISSN 0740-5286

Annual. First published 1958 with title: Chase's calendar of annual events, under the editorship of William D. and Helen M. Chase

Current editor: Mary M. Eley

"Day-by-day listing of national and state holidays, religious observances, special events, festivals and fairs, and historical anniversaries and birthdays. Covers U.S. events primarily, but some international occasions and anniversaries are included." N Y Public Libr Book of How & Where to Look It Up

Dunkling, Leslie, 1935-
A dictionary of days. Facts on File 1988 156p il $22.95; pa $10.95 **394.2**

1. Holidays 2. Festivals
ISBN 0-8160-1916-9; 0-8160-2138-4 (pa) LC 88-3703

This "book is divided into two parts: the dictionary of over 800 entries; then a calendar of named days. It is intended to fill the need for a reader's guide to named days, with entries drawn from 27 categories: political, folkloric, ethnic, literary, etc., with a substantial number from religious feasts and holy days." Libr J

The **Folklore** of American holidays; Hennig Cohen and Tristram Potter Coffin, editors. 2nd ed. Gale Res. 1991 xxxi, 509p $85
394.2

1. Holidays 2. Festivals—United States 3. Folklore—United States
ISBN 0-8103-7602-4 LC 91-14994

"A compilation of more than 500 beliefs, legends, superstitions, proverbs, riddles, poems, songs, dances, games, plays, pageants, fairs, foods, and processions associated with over 120 American calendar customs and festivals." Title page

Arranged in chronological order by holiday date, this work provides information on both religious and secular holidays

The **Folklore** of world holidays; Margaret Read MacDonald, editor. Gale Res. 1992 xxix, 739p $80 **394.2**

1. Holidays 2. Festivals 3. Folklore
ISBN 0-8103-7577-X LC 91-38032

"This compilation explains the folklore surrounding 340 holidays in over 150 countries, excluding the United States. The contents section lists holidays in chronological order, and countries are arranged below each holiday." Libr J

For a fuller review see: Booklist, April 15, 1992

Gregory, Ruth W. (Ruth Wilhelme), 1910-
Anniversaries and holidays. 4th ed. American Lib. Assn. 1983 262p $30 **394.2**

1. Holidays 2. Calendars 3. Birthdays
ISBN 0-8389-0389-4 LC 83-3784

First edition by Mary Emogene Hazeltine published 1928

"A comprehensive record of important dates in calendar-year order: first, calendar of fixed dates with the reason for celebration; second, calendar of movable days, subdivided by various calendars (Jewish, Christian, etc.), with explanations of the differences." Ref Sources for Small & Medium-sized Libr. 5th edition

Holidays and anniversaries of the world; Jennifer Mossman, editor. 2nd ed. Gale Res. 1990 xxix, 1080p $85 **394.2**

1. Holidays 2. Fasts and feasts 3. Chronology, Historical
ISBN 0-8103-4870-5 LC 90-127165

First published 1985

"A comprehensive catalogue containing detailed information of every month and day of the year, with extensive coverage of holidays, anniversaries, fasts and feasts, holy days, days of the saints, the blesseds, and other days of heortological significance, birthdays of the famous, important dates in history, and special events and their sponsors." Title page

Stewart, Martha

Martha Stewart's Christmas; photography, Christopher Baker; design, Virginia Edwards. Potter 1989 144p il $21.95 **394.2**

1. Christmas
ISBN 0-517-57416-0 LC 89-8672

"The author, with the assistance of a whole crew of cooks, decorators, and craftspeople, has transformed her rural Connecticut estate into a glittering symbol of the holiday, all of which is portrayed in seductive color photographs and described in a series of not-too-complicated recipes and craft instructions." Booklist

395 Etiquette (Manners)

Baldrige, Letitia

Letitia Baldrige's complete guide to the new manners for the 90's; illustrations by Denise Cavalieri Fike. Rawson Assocs. 1990 xxi, 646p il $25.95 **395**

1. Etiquette
ISBN 0-89256-320-6 LC 89-43052

Among the topics covered are "adult children returning home; extended families; aged parents living with adult children; . . . live-in relationships and second and third marriages; support of a family with an AIDS victim; and dealing with telephone answering machines." Libr J

"Detailed and accessible, her advice is an extension of the Golden Rule." Publ Wkly

Letitia Baldrige's new complete guide to executive manners. Rawson Assocs. 1993 xxx, 590p il $35 **395**

1. Business etiquette
ISBN 0-89256-362-1 LC 93-14166

First published 1985 with title: Letitia Baldrige's complete guide to executive manners

The author provides advice on such current issues in the workplace as sexual harassment; using nonsexist, ethnically correct forms of address and language; romantic involvement among co-workers; dealing with HIV-positive employees and clients; working with the physically-challenged; and international business manners

"Baldrige's suggestions will serve well those in the corporate world; no business person should be without her well-mannered guidance." Publ Wkly [review of 1985 edition]

Bride's book of etiquette; [by] the editors of Bride's magazine. Perigee Bks. il pa $15.95 **395**

1. Etiquette 2. Weddings 3. Marriage customs and rites

First published 1948. (1993 edition has title: Bride's all new book of etiquette) Periodically revised. Publisher and title vary

A guide to planning a wedding ceremony and reception, from announcements to honeymoon plans

Includes bibliographic references

Bride's new ways to wed; a guide to personalizing your wedding; the editors of Bride's magazine with Antonia van der Meer. Putnam 1990 144p pa $6.95 **395**

1. Etiquette 2. Weddings 3. Marriage customs and rites
ISBN 0-399-51575-5 LC 89-39073

"A Perigee book"

This book "offers various alternatives to the traditional wedding—for couples who are older, for those who live distances from family, for those entering second marriages. Guidelines, check lists, and charts are provided for a travel wedding, theme weddings, long weekend weddings, and the 'ultimate wedding.' Highlighted are numerous ethnic customs surrounding various celebrations." Libr J

Ford, Charlotte

Etiquette; Charlotte Ford's guide to modern manners. Potter 1988 524p o.p.; Outlet paperback available $7.99 **395**

1. Etiquette
ISBN 0-517-05600-3 (pa) LC 87-32893

First published 1980 by Simon & Schuster with title: Charlotte Ford's book of modern manners

"Ford's common-sense approach to relationships—which blends tradition with imagination . . . [include] information about and for single mothers, teenagers, contemporary rules of dating, and a businesswoman's guide to office etiquette and entertaining." Libr J

Lalli, Cele Goldsmith, 1933-

Modern bride wedding celebrations; the complete wedding planner for today's bride; [by] Cele Goldsmith Lalli and Stephanie H. Dahl. Wiley 1992 217p il pa $14.95 **395**

1. Etiquette 2. Weddings 3. Marriage customs and rites
ISBN 0-471-56882-1 LC 91-45504

"The A-Z of wedding planning, this thorough guide even has a section on special situations such as marrying a foreign national. Most issues are discussed from both traditional and contemporary perspectives." Libr J

Martin, Judith, 1938-

Miss Manners' guide for the turn-of-the-millennium; illustrated by Gloria Kamen. Pharos Bks. 1989 742p il $24.95 **395**

1. Etiquette
ISBN 0-88687-551-X LC 89-33717

Also available in paperback from Simon & Schuster

"In ten topical chapters with a variety of subdivisions, Miss Manners explains in her witty, patient manner how to handle nearly every conceivable social situation. An excellent index makes each situation easily accessible." Wilson Libr Bull

Miss Manners' guide to excruciatingly correct behavior; illustrated by Gloria Kamen. Atheneum Pubs. 1982 745p il o.p.; Warner Bks. paperback available $15.95

395

1. Etiquette
ISBN 0-446-38632-4 (pa) LC 81-69135

"A humorously presented, but determinedly correct, guide to modern social behavior. Incorporates questions and answers from the United Feature Syndicate column by 'Miss Manners.'" Sheehy. Guide to Ref Books. 10th edition

Martin, Judith, 1938-—*Continued*
Miss Manners' guide to rearing perfect children; illustrated by Gloria Kamen. Atheneum Pubs. 1984 405p il o.p.; Penguin Bks. paperback available $9.95 **395**

1. Etiquette
ISBN 0-14-008308-1 (pa)   LC 84-45041

"Subjects treated range from pregnancy through children's schooling to their marriage. Dress, dating, parties, eating all are equally well covered with a characteristic tongue-in-cheek humor and a genteel charm that are at once tasteful, honest, and funny." Libr J

Moore, Cindy
Planning a wedding with divorced parents; [by] Cindy Moore and Tricia Windom, with Martha Giddens Nesbit. Crown 1992 198p il pa $13   **395**

1. Weddings 2. Children of divorced parents
ISBN 0-517-58451-4   LC 91-39795

The authors discuss how to deal with the special problems that arise when children of divorced parents plan a wedding

Post, Elizabeth L.
Emily Post's complete book of wedding etiquette. rev ed. HarperCollins Pubs. 1991 243p il $21   **395**

1. Etiquette 2. Weddings 3. Marriage customs and rites
ISBN 0-06-270006-5   LC 90-55548
First published 1982

This guide covers all stages of planning a wedding. Topics include announcing the engagement, choosing the attendants, invitations, prewedding events, the ceremony, the reception, gifts, and second marriages. Special situations such as elopements, home weddings, and civil ceremonies are discussed

Emily Post's etiquette. HarperCollins Pubs. il $27.50; thumb indexed $29.95   **395**

1. Etiquette

First published 1922 under the authorship of Emily Post. (15th edition 1992) Periodically revised and updated. Title varies. Revised by Elizabeth Post beginning with 11th edition (1965)

"The classic reference for which fork to use has been expanded to include such modern situations as dating, living together, second marriages, and co-ed business traveling." N Y Public Libr Book of How & Where to Look It Up

Rogers, Jennifer, 1940-
Tried and trousseau; the bride guide. Simon & Schuster 1992 237p il pa $9.95   **395**

1. Weddings
ISBN 0-671-73935-2   LC 91-29589
"A Fireside book"

The author "covers the bridal front, touching on history, engagements, showers, clothing, ceremonies, catering, and honeymoons, among other topics." Booklist

Includes bibliographic references

Stewart, Marjabelle Young
Can my bridesmaids wear black?—and 325 other most-asked etiquette questions. St. Martin's Press 1989 174p pa $8.95   **395**

1. Etiquette
ISBN 0-312-03300-1   LC 89-30430

"In a question-and-answer format, Stewart provides guidance regarding wedding planning, business affairs, gift giving and receiving, and the protocols of various joyful and solemn occasions." Booklist

Van Buren, Abigail, 1918-
Dear Abby on planning your wedding. Andrews & McMeel 1989 c1988 170p pa $8.95   **395**

1. Weddings 2. Marriage customs and rites 3. Etiquette
ISBN 0-8362-7943-3   LC 88-31224

"Besides regaling readers with some of the zaniest nuptial happenings imaginable, Van Buren offers counsel on wedding attire, guests, stationery, even nudist ceremonies. Parts of the book are designed as a personal planner—with sections designed for notes or lists—in which case libraries will want to encourage single-use photocopying." Booklist

Vanderbilt, Amy
The Amy Vanderbilt complete book of etiquette; a guide to contemporary living; revised and expanded by Letitia Baldrige; drawings by Mona Marks. Doubleday 1978 xxix, 879p $18.95; thumb indexed $27.50   **395**

1. Etiquette
ISBN 0-385-13375-8; 0-385-14238-2 (thumb indexed)
        LC 77-16896

First published 1952 with title: Amy Vanderbilt's complete book of etiquette

New edition in preparation

"Emphasizes 'good manners' in contemporary American society, offering options in many social situations rather than merely hard and fast rules (although attention is still given to formal etiquette). Includes a section 'manners in business.'" Sheehy. Guide to Ref Books. 10th edition

Warner, Diane, 1937-
How to have a big wedding on a small budget; cut your wedding costs in half—or more! rev & updated 2nd ed. Writer's Digest Bks. 1992 137p il $12.95   **395**

1. Weddings
ISBN 0-89879-521-4   LC 92-13810
First published 1990

The author "shows how to cut costs on clothing, music, flowers, food, and photography without being tacky. Includes sample budgets ranging from $1200 to $5500." Libr J

398 Folklore

Barber, Paul, 1941-
Vampires, burial, and death; folklore and reality. Yale Univ. Press 1988 236p $30; pa $9.95 **398**
1. Vampires
ISBN 0-300-04126-8; 0-300-04859-9 (pa)   LC 88-143
"Both scholarly and gruesome, this examines folklore and legends about vampires in the light of modern medical knowledge of post-mortem changes." Booklist
Includes bibliography

Bettelheim, Bruno
The uses of enchantment; the meaning and importance of fairy tales. Knopf 1976 328p $27 **398**
1. Fairy tales—History and criticism 2. Child psychology
ISBN 0-394-49771-6
Also available in paperback from Vintage Bks.
"Premising that unlike other childhood literature, fairy tales function as a necessary aid to emotional growth, a noted child psychologist analyzes some of the old favorites in terms of such concepts as sibling rivalry, the onset of puberty, the threat of adult prerogatives, and reveals how folktales help children accomplish the psychological tasks of development common to the human race." Booklist
"An indispensable handbook for those concerned with child development and children's literature, and fascinating reading for anyone interested in human psychology." Libr J

A **Dictionary** of superstitions; edited by Iona Opie and Moira Tatem. Oxford Univ. Press 1989 494p $35; pa $13.95 **398**
1. Superstition—Dictionaries
ISBN 0-19-211597-9; 0-19-282916-5 (pa)
LC 89-32327
"Predominantly British Isles superstitions arranged alphabetically by central idea. Includes example of superstition and year of oral or written occurrences of its use. Analytical index and cross-references." Ref Sources for Small & Medium-sized Libr. 5th edition

Dorson, Richard Mercer, 1916-1981
American folklore; by Richard M. Dorson. University of Chicago Press 1959 328p (Chicago history of American civilization) hardcover o.p. paperback available $12.95 **398**
1. Folklore—United States
ISBN 0-226-15859-4 (pa)
This survey ranges from colonial times to the present. Aspects covered include the rise of native folk humor, regional cultures, immigrant and black folklore, and folk heroes. Appended are a chronological table and a table of motifs and tale types

Hathaway, Nancy
The unicorn. Viking 1980 191p il o.p.; Avenel Bks. reprint available $12.98 **398**
1. Unicorns
ISBN 0-517-44902-1
LC 80-5364

"A Studio book"
The author "enumerates the many stories, drawn from historical tradition, about the unicorn. . . . [She] deals with the magical creature from ancient times through the medieval age and the Renaissance to the present not only in the European tradition but also in China, Japan, and the Near East." Choice
Includes bibliography

Huygen, Wil
Gnomes; text by Wil Huygen; illustrated by Rien Poortvliet. Abrams 1977 unp il maps music $29.95 **398**
1. Fairies
ISBN 0-8109-0965-0
LC 77-82805
Also available in paperback from Bantam Bks.
Original Dutch edition, 1976
"Dutch writer Huygen and popular Dutch illustrator Poortvliet team up to tell-and-show everything that's known (and much they surmise) about those most private and lovable of all little people, the Gnomes." Publ Wkly

Mascetti, Manuela Dunn
Vampire; the complete guide to the world of the undead. Viking Studio Bks. 1992 224p il $20 **398**
1. Vampires
ISBN 0-670-84664-3
LC 92-53515
First published 1991 in the United Kingdom with title: Chronicles of the vampire
This is an illustrated compendium of vampire lore, describing the vampires of literature, movies, and legends

Mythical and fabulous creatures; a source book and research guide; edited by Malcolm South. Greenwood Press 1987 xlix, 393p il $49.95 **398**
1. Mythical animals 2. Monsters 3. Fairies
ISBN 0-313-24338-7
LC 86-14964
"Pt. I describes 20 fabulous creatures in separate chapters: Birds and beasts, Human-animal composites, Creatures of darkness, and Giants and fairies. Their appearances in literature, history, and art are cited and their functions noted. . . . Pt. II, A miscellany and taxonomy, briefly discusses creatures not previously mentioned or given only passing attention earlier, and classifies some 145 creatures in five categories." Sheehy
Guide to Ref Books. 10th edition. suppl

Tuleja, Tad, 1944-
Curious customs; the stories behind 296 popular American rituals. Harmony Bks. 1987 210p hardcover o.p. paperback available $9.95 **398**
1. Manners and customs 2. Folklore—United States 3. United States—Social life and customs
ISBN 0-517-56654-0 (pa)
LC 87-4098
"A Stonesong Press book"
The origins of "nearly 300 customs and traditions . . . are detailed in this readable compendium. The text is loosely divided into thematic headings, including 'The Mating Game,' 'Foodways,' 'Holidays,' and 'Superstitions.' [An] informative, eminently browsable item." Booklist
Includes bibliography

398.03 Folklore—Encyclopedias and dictionaries

Briggs, Katharine Mary

An encyclopedia of fairies; hobgoblins, brownies, bogies, and other supernatural creatures; [by] Katherine Briggs. Pantheon Bks. 1977 c1976 481p il hardcover o.p. paperback available $19   **398.03**

1. Fairies—Dictionaries
ISBN 0-394-73467-X (pa)

First published 1976 in the United Kingdom with title: A dictionary of fairies

"All kinds of fairies in their broadest definition are included, as well as terms with significance in the folklore of fairies. The entries are authoritative, with generous quotes from sources." Ref Sources for Small & Medium-sized Libr. 5th edition

Funk & Wagnalls standard dictionary of folklore, mythology, and legend; Maria Leach, editor; Jerome Fried, associate editor. Harper & Row 1984 1236p il hardcover o.p. paperback available $34.95   **398.03**

1. Folklore—Dictionaries   2. Legends—Dictionaries
3. Mythology—Dictionaries
ISBN 0-06-250511-4 (pa)   LC 72-78268

This is a reissue, with minor corrections, of a title first published 1949-1950 in two volumes

"Embraces various aspects of folklore. With many anthropologists and sociologists among the contributors, the ethnic rather than the literary side is emphasized." Ref Sources for Small & Medium-sized Libr. 5th edition

Radford, Edwin, 1891-1973

Encyclopaedia of superstitions; by E. and M. A. Radford; with a foreword by Sir John Hammerton. Philosophical Lib. 1949 269p o.p.; Greenwood Press reprint available $55   **398.03**

1. Superstition—Dictionaries 2. Folklore—Dictionaries
ISBN 0-8371-2115-9

First published 1948 in the United Kingdom

This volume "contains over two thousand superstitions of Britain ranging over the past six hundred years, with many references to present day beliefs." Wilson Libr Bull

398.2 Folk literature

Afro-American folktales; stories from black traditions in the New World; selected and edited by Roger D. Abrahams. Pantheon Bks. 1985 xxii, 327p il hardcover o.p. paperback available $16   **398.2**

1. Blacks—Folklore 2. Folklore—Caribbean region
ISBN 0-394-72885-8 (pa)   LC 84-16601

"These 107 tales show how the content and style of African storytelling traditions were transformed in the New World." Publ Wkly

"From creation myths to coded tales in which plantation masters are outwitted, the stories range across the heritage of an African past. . . . The ones from urban America crackle with raw emotion." N Y Times Book Rev

Includes bibliography

American Indian myths and legends; selected and edited by Richard Erdoes and Alfonso Ortiz. Pantheon Bks. 1984 527p il hardcover o.p. paperback available $17   **398.2**

1. Indians of North America—Legends 2. Indians of North America—Religion
ISBN 0-394-74018-1 (pa)   LC 84-42669

"This volume comprises 160 tales of native folklore and myth ranging from one geographical end of our continent to the other. The book is organized according to type of myth. . . . Erdoes and Ortiz seek to keep Indian myth intact and pure through their retellings, using, as often as possible, primary sources." Booklist

Includes bibliography

Arab folktales; translated and edited by Inea Bushnaq. Pantheon Bks. 1986 xxviii, 386p hardcover o.p. paperback available $15   **398.2**

1. Arabs—Folklore
ISBN 0-394-75179-5 (pa)   LC 85-9569

"Ranging throughout the Arab world from Africa to the Middle East, this collection contains animal stories, tales of mischief and trickery, ghost and magic stories, and religious and moral instructions." Booklist

"The importance of [this] book is not only in the pleasure and delight it gives but in the way it participates in the retrieval of a cultural heritage by making that culture available to today's English-language reader." N Y Times Book Rev

Includes bibliography

Ashe, Geoffrey

Mythology of the British Isles. Trafalgar Sq. 1990 304p il hardcover o.p. paperback available $19.95   **398.2**

1. Mythology, British 2. Legends—Great Britain
ISBN 0-413-66540-2 (pa)   LC 89-52192

The author "presents a group of Welsh, Irish, Scottish, and English folklore that, taken together, creates a collective British mythology. . . . Each chapter is divided in two sections. The first part is a narrative of the myth; the second, an explanation of the reality behind it. . . . The volume is valuable to both layperson and scholar." Libr J

Includes bibliographic references

Brunvand, Jan Harold

The choking Doberman and other "new" urban legends. Norton 1984 240p il hardcover o.p. paperback available $8.95   **398.2**

1. Folklore—United States 2. Legends—United States
ISBN 0-393-30321-7 (pa)   LC 83-22031

"These fictitious narratives . . . circulate widely as true incidents. Brunvand details more than 40 . . . anecdotes, ranging from grisly reports of alleged mutilations to comical tales of sexual mishaps." Libr J

"Brunvand is especially adept at tracing apparently fresh stories to ancient roots." Time

Includes bibliography

Brunvand, Jan Harold—*Continued*

The vanishing hitchhiker; American urban legends and their meaning. Norton 1981 208p hardcover o.p. paperback available $8.95   **398.2**

1. Folklore—United States 2. Legends—United States
ISBN 0-393-95169-3 (pa)   LC 81-4744

A collection of modern urban folktales with an ironic or supernatural twist. The author reports on how such tales are disseminated and discusses their inherent messages for contemporary society

Includes bibliographic references

Edmonds, Margot

Voices of the winds: native American legends; [by] Margot Edmonds, Ella E. Clark. Facts on File 1989 368p il $27.95; pa $14.95   **398.2**

1. Indians of North America—Legends
ISBN 0-8160-2067-1; 0-8160-2749-8 (pa)
     LC 89-35431

"Traditional stories from 60 Native cultures of North America are prefaced by brief headnotes. Sources include government documents, periodicals, histories, and field research." Libr J

"The best feature of this . . . work is that it collects less frequently anthologized tales from lesser-known religious traditions." Booklist

Includes bibliography

Favorite folktales from around the world; edited by Jane Yolen. Pantheon Bks. 1986 498p hardcover o.p. paperback available $16   **398.2**

1. Folklore 2. Fairy tales
ISBN 0-394-75188-4 (pa)   LC 86-42644

"Selections include tales from the American Indians, the brothers Grimm, Italo Calvino's Italian folk-tales, as well as stories from Iceland, Afghanistan, Scotland, and many other countries. Yolen provides each section with a relevant introduction, often including historical and literary factors, thus alerting readers as to what to look for." SLJ

Folktales told around the world; edited by Richard M. Dorson. University of Chicago Press 1976 c1975 xxvi, 622p il hardcover o.p. paperback available $23.95   **398.2**

1. Folklore
ISBN 0-226-15874-8 (pa)

In this collection, "the selection is truly international; and if some great folktale traditions are neglected (Armenian, for instance), many riches are offered which the reader is otherwise unlikely to encounter (the Asian and African material, especially). The librarian should note that these are 'real' folktales, oral prose narratives created by adults for adults." Libr J

Includes bibliographic references

Grimm, Jacob, 1785-1863

The complete fairy tales of the Brothers Grimm; translated and with an introduction by Jack Zipes; illustrations by John B. Gruelle. Bantam Bks. 1987 xxxiv, 733p il $25; pa $5.50   **398.2**

1. Fairy tales
ISBN 0-553-05184-9; 0-553-21238-9 (pa)
     LC 86-47728

"Zipes has produced a faithful idiomatic version of the stories in the Grimms' definitive 1857 edition. To the two hundred ten tales then included, he has added thirty-two narratives which were eliminated from that edition. . . . The biographical essay on the Grimm Brothers stresses their historical, social, and cultural context and considers the folkloristic and psychological points of view of various modern critics." Horn Book

Homespun: tales from America's favorite storytellers; edited by Jimmy Neil Smith. Crown 1988 xxi, 390p $19.95   **398.2**

1. Folklore—United States 2. Storytelling
ISBN 0-517-56936-1   LC 87-32989

"Thirty-four stories from 21 of America's most recognized storytellers are prefaced by black-and-white photographs of the tellers and brief biographical sketches. . . . The final 50 pages include a comprehensive bibliography of books on storytelling and of stories; annotations of American storytellers, their works and recordings; and lists of storytelling organizations and festivals. This is a real find for those interested in performing arts, folklore, or good stories." SLJ

Index to fairy tales; including folklore, legends, and myths in collections. Scarecrow Press 1985-1989 3v   **398.2**

1. Folklore—Indexes   2. Fairy tales—Indexes
3. Legends—Indexes 4. Mythology—Indexes

Volumes covering 1949-1972 and 1973-1977 first published by Faxon 1973 and 1979 respectively

A continuation of Index to fairy tales, myths and legends and its two supplements, compiled by Mary Huse Eastman, published 1926-1952 by Faxon and now o.p.

Third supplement covering 1949-1972 compiled by Norma Olin Ireland $45 (ISBN 0-8108-2011-0); fourth supplement covering 1973-1977 compiled by Norma Olin Ireland $29.50 (ISBN 0-8108-1855-8); fifth supplement covering 1978-1986 compiled by Norma Olin Ireland and Joseph W. Sprug $49.50 (ISBN 0-8108-2194-X)

"Although this is an essential reference book for the children's department, it is also a valuable source for the location of much folklore and fairy-tale material and should be available in adult book collections as well." Ref Sources for Small & Medium-sized Libr. 5th edition

Lester, Julius

Black folktales; illustrated by Tom Feelings. Baron, R.W. 1969 159p il o.p.; Grove Press paperback available $7.95   **398.2**

1. Blacks—Folklore 2. Folklore—Africa
ISBN 0-8021-3242-1 (pa)

"Lester gives 12 African and Afro-American folk tales such twentieth-century touches as the Lord's reading of the 'TV Guide' and the mention of Rap Brown and Aretha Franklin but his sprightly versions retain the spirit and shape of the original story. . . . These stories of creation, love, folk heroes, and everyday people have

Lester, Julius—*Continued*
a direct simplicity and laconic humor that is both effective and appealing." Booklist

Malory, Sir Thomas, 15th cent.
Le morte d'Arthur   398.2
1. Arthur, King
Hardcover and paperback editions available from various publishers
Originally published 1485
"The work is a skillful selection and blending of materials taken from the mass of Arthurian legends. The central story consists of two main elements: the reign of King Arthur ending in catastrophe and the dissolution of the Round Table; and the quest of the Holy Grail." Oxford Companion to Engl Lit

Tales of King Arthur; edited and abridged, with an introduction by Michael Senior. Schocken Bks. 1981 c1980 351p il hardcover o.p. paperback available $19   398.2
1. Arthur, King
ISBN 0-8052-0891-7 (pa)   LC 81-40412
This is an "illustrated abridgment of Malory's Arthurian legends from the William Caxton edition of 'Morte d'Arthur' and from manuscripts that differ interestingly from that classic edition. Emphasizing pleasurable reading, Senior has eliminated some extraneous, rambling passages and modernized some spelling for the sake of clarity. . . . The illustrations chosen from medieval manuscripts (all sources are cited in a single list) add to this exciting version of a literary classic." Booklist

Talk that talk: an anthology of African-American storytelling; edited by Linda Goss & Marian E. Barnes. Simon & Schuster 1989 521p hardcover o.p. paperback available $12.95   398.2
1. Blacks—Folklore
ISBN 0-671-67168-5 (pa)   LC 89-10582
The selections included range "from slave stories and the animal legends of Brer Rabbit and Brer Fox to the comedy monologues of Dick Gregory and rap routines. . . . Interspersed throughout are brief sections of commentary and analysis." Booklist
Includes bibliographic references

A **Treasury** of American folklore; stories, ballads, and traditions of the people; edited by B.A. Botkin; with a foreword by Carl Sandburg. American Legacy Press 1989 xxvii, 932p il pa $14.99   398.2
1. Folklore—United States
ISBN 0-517-67978-7   LC 88-29634
A reissue of the title first published 1944 by Crown
This anthology contains ballads of railroad men and miners, black songs and stories, tall tales, and true accounts of frontier characters and sea captains. Classic American jokes and expressions are also included
Includes bibliographic references

A **Treasury** of Jewish folklore; stories, traditions, legends, humor, wisdom, and folk songs of the Jewish people; edited by Nathan Ausubel. Crown 1989 c1948 xxiv, 741p $17.95   398.2
1. Jews—Folklore
ISBN 0-517-50293-3   LC 89-597
A reissue of the title first published 1948
A compilation of the stories, traditions, legends, wit, wisdom and folk songs of the Jewish people in English. It spans some 2000 years, going back to the days of Hillel, and continuing to modern times

398.8 Rhymes and rhyming games

The **Oxford** dictionary of nursery rhymes; edited by Iona and Peter Opie. Oxford Univ. Press 1951 xxvii, 467p il $47.50
398.8
1. Nursery rhymes—Dictionaries
ISBN 0-19-869111-4
"A scholarly collection of nursery rhymes with notes and explanations concerning history, literary associations, social uses, and possible portrayal of real people. Both standard and earliest recorded versions (where available) are included. Indexes for 'notable figures' and first lines." Ref Sources for Small & Medium-sized Libr. 5th edition

The **Oxford** nursery rhyme book; assembled by Iona and Peter Opie; with additional illustrations by Joan Hassall. Oxford Univ. Press 1955 223p il $29.95   398.8
1. Nursery rhymes
ISBN 0-19-869112-2
"Gathered here are 800 rhymes and ditties. They are the infant jingles, riddles, catches, tongue-trippers, baby games, toe names, maxims, alphabets, counting rhymes, prayers, and lullabies, with which generation after generation of mothers and nurses have attempted to please the youngest." Preface

398.9 Proverbs

The **Concise** Oxford dictionary of proverbs; [compiled by] John Simpson with the assistance of Jennifer Speake. 2nd ed. Oxford Univ. Press 1992 316p $23
398.9
1. Proverbs
ISBN 0-19-866177-0   LC 91-39366
First published 1982
This volume "contains over 1000 proverbs commonly used in 20th-century Britain. . . . Arranged alphabetically by the first significant word, each one includes illustrative quotations, beginning with the earliest known use." SLJ
For a fuller review see: Booklist, Jan. 1, 1993

A **Dictionary** of American proverbs; Wolfgang Mieder, editor in chief; Stewart A. Kingsbury and Kelsie B. Harder, editors. Oxford Univ. Press 1992 710p $49.95   **398.9**

1. Proverbs
ISBN 0-19-505399-0   LC 91-15508

"This scholarly work includes 15,000 proverbs with variants currently used in the United States and parts of Canada. Entries are arranged alphabetically under key words and are often followed by variants and cross references. . . . This collection differs from most such compilations because the proverbs were collected by field workers rather than from written sources. The work sets new standards for understanding the oral tradition in America and is an essential purchase for ready-reference collections." Libr J

The **Oxford** dictionary of English proverbs; with an introduction by Joanna Wilson. 3rd ed, revised by F. P. Wilson. Oxford Univ. Press 1970 930p $55   **398.9**

1. Proverbs
ISBN 0-19-869118-1

First published 1935. The first two editions were compiled by William George Smith

Proverbs are "alphabetized under significant words (usually the first). . . . Liberal cross references are included from all other significant words, usually with enough of the phrase so that it is readily identifiable. . . . Dated references are given for each proverb to the earliest uses and sources found, with variant usages at succeeding times, shown by examples from literature." Sheehy. Guide to Ref Books. 10th edition

400 LANGUAGE

Crystal, David, 1941-
The Cambridge encyclopedia of language. Cambridge Univ. Press 1987 472p il maps $49.50; pa $24.95   **400**

1. Language and languages—Dictionaries
ISBN 0-521-26438-3; 0-521-42443-7 (pa)
    LC 86-32637

This "encyclopedia covers all major (and some minor) aspects of language, from its structure and acquisition to artificial languages, spelling reform, and word games." Kister's Best Dict for Adults & Young People

Pei, Mario, 1901-
The story of language. rev ed. Lippincott 1965 491p o.p.; New Am. Lib. paperback available $12.95   **400**

1. Language and languages
ISBN 0-452-00870-0 (pa)

First published 1949

"Mr. Pei deals with the family relationship of languages, with dialects, place names, personal names, slang, cant, jargon, with the sounds and structures of languages. He describes all the modern spoken tongues and discusses problems of language learning." N Y Times Book Rev

The **World's** major languages; edited by Bernard Comrie. Oxford Univ. Press 1987 1025p hardcover o.p. paperback available $29.95   **400**

1. Language and languages
ISBN 0-19-506511-5 (pa)   LC 86-12795

"Ranging from English, French, Spanish, and Russian to Swahili, this comprehensive reference work provides [a] . . . detailed guide to the world's forty major languages. With a general introduction on languages and language families, and authoritative entries written by acknowledged specialists, this is an indispensable resource for anyone seeking a fuller appreciation of the origins of and nature of language." Univ Press Books for Public Libr

401 Language—Philosophy and theory

Chomsky, Noam
Language and mind. enl ed. Harcourt Brace & Co. 1972 194p hardcover o.p. paperback available $16   **401**

1. Language and languages—Psychology 2. Thought and thinking
ISBN 0-15-549257-8 (pa)

First published 1968

Six essays in which the author explores "linguistic theories and philosophy. A leading researcher in language, Chomsky writes for other students and reasonably well-informed laymen." Booklist

Includes bibliographic references

Farb, Peter
Word play; what happens when people talk. Knopf 1974 c1973 350p hardcover o.p. paperback available $12   **401**

1. Communication 2. Language and languages—Psychology
ISBN 0-679-73408-2 (pa)

"The latest knowledge of tongues—an interdiscipline involving psychology, sociology and even a touch of metaphysics—is summed up here for the layman. . . . When the theorizing becomes heavy, Farb knows how to entertain himself and his readers with a rich miscellany of random facts and provocative (if not always documented) opinions that spill beyond his outline." Time

Includes bibliography

410 Linguistics

Crystal, David, 1941-
An encyclopedic dictionary of language and languages. Blackwell 1992 428p il $29.95   **410**

1. Language and languages—Dictionaries
ISBN 0-631-17652-7   LC 92-34195

This work "defines hundreds of terms connected with language, from A to Zoosemiotics. Many entries are the names of languages, language groups, or countries. Others cover such topics as writing systems, punctuation, traditional grammar, and poetics, while still others are terms from phonetics, language typology, transformational

Crystal, David, 1941—— *Continued*

grammar, case grammar, neurolinguistics, and related fields." Libr J

For a fuller review see: Booklist, April 1, 1993

International encyclopedia of linguistics; William Bright, editor-in-chief. Oxford Univ. Press 1992 4v maps set $425

410

1. Language and languages—Dictionaries
ISBN 0-19-505196-3   LC 91-7349

"Comprising approximately seven hundred alphabetically ordered entries, the *International Encyclopedia of Linguistics* provides detailed and up-to-date information on all branches of linguistics. The *IEL* encompasses the full range of the contemporary field of linguistics, including historical, comparative, formal, mathematical, functional, and philosophical linguistics." Univ Press Books for Public and Second Sch Libr

Pei, Mario, 1901-

The world's chief languages; formerly, Languages for war and peace. [5th rev ed]. Vanni 1960 c1946 xxiv, 663p il maps $38

410

1. Philology, Comparative
ISBN 0-913298-07-7

First published 1944 with title: Languages for war and peace

This work describes the seven major languages of the world (French, German, Spanish, Portuguese, Italian, Russian, and Japanese), giving the geographic distribution and identifying characteristics of each. It also includes for each of these languages an outline of pronunciation and grammar as well as a limited vocabulary

411 Writing systems

Logan, Robert K., 1939-

The alphabet effect; the impact of the phonetic alphabet on the development of Western civilization. Morrow 1986 272p o.p.; St. Martin's Press paperback available $9.95

411

1. Alphabet 2. Writing 3. Civilization
ISBN 0-312-00993-3 (pa)   LC 86-5349

In this study, the author aims to show "that communication technologies affect man's thought processes. He [seeks to] trace the products of Western civilization (the codification of law, monotheism, logic, individualism, science, and nationalism) to the phonetic alphabet's abstract and organizational properties." Sci Books Films

An "excellent overview of linguistic, educational, and communications theory." Booklist

412 Etymology

Hayakawa, S. I.

Language in thought and action; [by] S.I. Hayakawa and Alan R. Hayakawa. 5th ed. Harcourt Brace Jovanovich 1990 287p il $21.50; pa $8.95

412

1. Semantics 2. Thought and thinking 3. English language
ISBN 0-15-550120-8; 0-15-648240-1 (pa)

LC 89-84371

First published 1939 with title: Language in action

The author analyzes the nature of language, discusses the processes of thinking and writing, and gives advice on thinking and writing clearly

Includes bibliography

413 Dictionaries

Rheingold, Howard

They have a word for it; a light-hearted lexicon of untranslatable words & phrases. Tarcher, J.P. 1988 224p il pa $8.95   **413**

1. Polyglot dictionaries 2. English language—Foreign words and phrases—Dictionaries
ISBN 0-87477-464-0   LC 87-17999

This "word book proffers terms from other languages for incorporation into English. . . . In topical chapters of words about human relationships, sex, beauty, politics, and other large domains of thought, Rheingold thoroughly and entertainingly describes both the narrow and broader meanings of foreign idioms that usually condense sentences, even paragraphs, of English into a few syllables." Booklist

Includes bibliography

419 Verbal language not spoken and written

Bornstein, Harry

The signed English school book; [by] Harry Bornstein and Karen L. Saulnier; illustrated by Ralph R. Miller, Sr. Gallaudet Univ. Press 1987 165p il pa $13.95   **419**

1. Sign language 2. Deaf—Education
ISBN 0-930323-30-0   LC 87-15042

"A Kendall Green publication"

This topically arranged sign language guide provides school-related vocabulary for parents and teachers of deaf children and adolescents

Includes bibliography

Butterworth, Rod R.

Signing made easy; a complete program for learning sign language. Includes sentence drills and exercises for increased comprehension and signing skill; [by] Rod R. Butterworth and Mickey Flodin. Putnam 1989 224p il pa $11.95   **419**

1. Sign language
ISBN 0-399-51490-2   LC 88-23878

"A Perigee book"

Butterworth, Rod R.—*Continued*

This volume "is organized into general subject areas such as Family and Friends, Work, Food, and Travel. Each chapter builds progressively on the vocabulary and grammar of the previous lesson." Publisher's note

Costello, Elaine

Signing; how to speak with your hands; illustrated by Lois A. Lehman. Bantam Bks. 1983 248p il pa $16.50   **419**

1. Sign language

ISBN 0-553-34612-1   LC 82-45947

An illustrated introduction to American Sign Language (ASL) and its different uses by both the hearing and the deaf

Fant, Louie J.

Say it with hands; [by] Louie J. Fant, Jr. illustrated by Elizabeth G. Miller. National Assn. of the Deaf 1964 153p il pa $8.50   **419**

1. Sign language

ISBN 0-913072-02-8

Beginning sign language book containing illustrations of signs plus practice exercises. Signs are arranged in chapters according to one basic hand shape

Includes bibliography

Lane, Leonard G.

Gallaudet survival guide to signing; illustrations by Jan Skrobisz. new rev ed. Gallaudet Univ. Press 1990 203p il pa $4.95   **419**

1. Sign language

ISBN 0-930323-67-X   LC 89-25686

First published 1987

Line drawings illustrate approximately five hundred signs representing words and concepts as expressed in American Sign Language. Separate charts of the basic handshapes, the American Manual Alphabet, and signed numbers are also included

Riekehof, Lottie L.

The joy of signing; the illustrated guide for mastering sign language and the manual alphabet. 2nd ed. Gospel Pub. House 1987 352p il $16.95   **419**

1. Sign language

ISBN 0-88243-520-5   LC 86-80173

First published 1963 with title: Talk to the deaf

This manual presents over 1300 signs used for communicating with deaf adults, and provides basic vocabulary needed for entering interpreter training programs. Signs are arranged in 25 categories with an alphabetical index. For each sign there is a line drawing, description of how to make the sign, origin (concept) and notes on usage

Includes bibliography

Sternberg, Martin L. A.

American sign language: a comprehensive dictionary; illustrated by Herbert Rogoff. Harper & Row 1981 xlv, 1132p il $65   **419**

1. Sign language

ISBN 0-06-014097-6   LC 75-25066

Also available in an abridged paperback edition

This guide "contains some 5000 alphabetically arranged entries, each providing a pronunciation guide, grammatical notes, and a description and illustration of the appropriate sign and its formation. Extensive bibliography with a subject index, and seven foreign language indexes." Ref Sources for Small & Medium-sized Libr. 5th edition

Includes bibliography

420   English and Old English

Bryson, Bill

The mother tongue: English & how it got that way. Morrow 1990 270p $18.95   **420**

1. English language—History

ISBN 0-688-07895-8   LC 89-77521

Also available in paperback from Avon Bks.

Topics discussed include "etymology, pronunciation, spelling, dialects, grammar, the origins of proper names, [and] wordplay." N Y Times Book Rev

Includes bibliographic references

Burchfield, R. W. (Robert W.)

The English language; [by] Robert Burchfield. Oxford Univ. Press 1985 194p il hardcover o.p. paperback available $8.95   **420**

1. English language

ISBN 0-19-289161-8 (pa)   LC 84-9677

The author examines English language "history in three chapters; glances at literary language and laments modern translations of religious works in a fourth; highlights particular aspects of English and surveys dictionaries and grammars in four more brief chapters; and concludes with a chapter on world Englishes and international English." Choice

Includes bibliography

Unlocking the English language; [by] Robert Burchfield; with an introduction by Harold Bloom. Hill & Wang 1991 202p $18.95; pa $12   **420**

1. English language

ISBN 0-8090-9490-8; 0-374-52339-8 (pa)

LC 90-43282

First published 1989 in the United Kingdom

"The author illustrates how language has changed in this century and how modern political and ideological pressures can make defining words a hazardous occupation. A defender of the historical approach to language, Burchfield attacks modern linguistic theories that block out past meanings of words and past patterns for putting words together." Booklist

Includes bibliographic references

Claiborne, Robert
Our marvelous native tongue; the life and times of the English language. Times Bks. 1983 339p hardcover o.p. paperback available $12 **420**

1. English language—History
ISBN 0-8129-1635-2 (pa)   LC 82-40363

This is a "history of the English language from the prehistoric Indo-Europeans to present-day U.S.A." Libr J

The author "deluges the reader with history, anthropology, linguistics and a dozen other disciplines as he traces our language's past. . . . Although most of the text moves swiftly, there are boggy patches. . . . Still, even these patches contain fascinating tidbits." NY Times Book Rev

Includes bibliography

McCrum, Robert
The story of English; [by] Robert McCrum, William Cran, Robert MacNeil. new & rev ed. Penguin Bks. 1993 c1992 394p il maps pa $17.50 **420**

1. English language—History
ISBN 0-14-015405-1   LC 92-20181

First published 1986 by Viking; present edition first published 1992 in the United Kingdom

A "companion to the PBS television series of the same name. . . . The text covers the history of our language from its roots in Latin through its transplanting to other shores and its infusions from other cultures and languages. . . . Good for browsing, this book is a must for word and history buffs." SLJ [review of 1986 edition]

Includes bibliographic references

The **Oxford** companion to the English language; edited by Tom McArthur; managing editor, Feri McArthur. Oxford Univ. Press 1992 xxvii, 1184p il $49.95 **420**

1. English language—Dictionaries
ISBN 0-19-214183-X

"This Oxford companion—part dictionary, part usage guide, part linguistic encyclopedia—offers the broadest range of reference information to be found in any single source. Included are entries on grammar, prosody, language acquisition, and sexist language, on every nation where English is widely spoken, and on writers and lexicographers whose works have significantly affected the development of the language—about 5,000 entries all told." Am Libr

For a fuller review see: Booklist, Oct. 15, 1992

421 Written and spoken codes of standard English

NBC handbook of pronunciation; introduction by Edwin Newman. 4th ed, revised and updated by Eugene Ehrlich and Raymond Hand, Jr. Harper & Row 1984 539p hardcover o.p. paperback available $13 **421**

1. English language—Pronunciation
ISBN 0-06-273056-8 (pa)   LC 84-47592

First published 1943 by Crowell

"Entries include words or proper names frequently used by broadcasters, common words often mispronounced, and 'difficult' names from history and the arts." Libr J

421.03 Written and spoken codes of standard English—Dictionaries

Acronyms, initialisms, & abbreviations dictionary; a guide to acronyms, initialisms, abbreviations, contractions, alphabetic symbols, and similar condensed appellations. Gale Res. 3v set $235 **421.03**

1. Acronyms—Dictionaries 2. Abbreviations—Dictionaries
ISSN 0270-4404

Also available: Reverse acronyms, initialisms, & abbreviations dictionary

First published 1960 in one volume with title: Acronyms dictionary. (18th edition 1994) Frequently revised

Covers "Aerospace, associations, banking, biochemistry, business, data processing, domestic and international affairs, economics, education, electronics, genetics, government, information technology [etc.]." Title page

Kept current by New acronyms, initialisms, and abbreviations

De Sola, Ralph, 1908-
Abbreviations dictionary. CRC Press $69.95 **421.03**

1. Abbreviations—Dictionaries 2. Acronyms—Dictionaries 3. Signs and symbols

First published 1958 by Duell, Sloan and Pearce. (8th edition 1992) Frequently revised

"Covers most standard abbreviations, including euphemisms, slang, some technical and professional shorthand, historical/mythological references, geographical data, eponyms, airlines/airports of the world." N Y Public Libr Book of How & Where To Look It Up

422 Etymology of standard English

Black, Donald Chain
Spoonerisms, sycophants, and sops. Harper & Row 1988 134p $15.95 **422**

1. English language—Etymology
ISBN 0-06-015886-7   LC 87-45832

Also available in paperback from Dell

This book takes "the form of a multiple-choice exam. [The author] proffers groups of words and asks (most often) how one differs from the others (variations include how they're all alike or where they came from in the first place). . . . Along with the etymological nitty-gritty, an awesome amount of cultural trivia is imparted." Booklist

Carver, Craig M., 1947-

A history of English in its own words.
HarperCollins Pubs. 1991 275p il $22.95; pa
$9   **422**

1. English language—Etymology
ISBN 0-06-270013-8; 0-06-272033-3 (pa)
                                            LC 90-56004

This is an "account of some 750 of the more interesting (and in some cases controversial) etymologies
of English words, arranged in chronological groups from
Anglo-Saxon times to the 20th century." Libr J

Howard, Philip, 1933-

Weasel words. Oxford Univ. Press 1979
175p $21.95   **422**

1. English language—Etymology 2. English language—
Usage 3. Vocabulary
ISBN 0-19-520107-8   LC 78-15583

"This collection of 44 brief essays, one for each word,
published originally in The London Times, discusses the
uses and abuses of words and incidentally includes bits
of etymology and history of the English language."
Choice

Pei, Mario, 1901-

The families of words. Harper & Row
1962 288p o.p.; AMS Press reprint available
$27.50   **422**

1. English language—Etymology
ISBN 0-404-07929-6

The author discusses how various families of words
have evolved, with changes in form and meaning, from
individual Indo-European roots through such separate
branches as Sanskrit, Greek, Latin and Anglo-Saxon into
English. He also shows how English has taken over
words from French, German, Italian, and other modern
languages

Includes bibliography

Thomas, Lewis, 1913-1993

Et cetera, et cetera; notes of a
word-watcher. Little, Brown 1990 197p
$17.95   **422**

1. English language—Etymology
ISBN 0-316-84099-8   LC 90-38741

Also available in paperback from Penguin Bks.

"In each of these mini-essays, Mr. Thomas takes a
word or handful of words and discusses their genealogy.
. . . The book is brief, and some of the essays are
shapelier than others, but anybody who loves words and
wordplay will be entertained by the history behind everyday words and by some of the author's provocative
speculations about language." N Y Times Book Rev

Includes bibliographic references

422.03 Etymology of standard English—Dictionaries

The **Barnhart** dictionary of etymology;
Robert K. Barnhart, editor; Sol Steinmetz,
managing editor. Wilson, H.W. 1988 xxvii,
1284p $59   **422.03**

1. English language—Etymology—Dictionaries
ISBN 0-8242-0745-9   LC 87-27994

This dictionary "focuses on words used in contemporary American English and words of American origin
and incorporates current American scholarship. Entries
give spelling variations, pronunciation for difficult words,
part of speech, definition, and information on word
origins. Written for a wide audience, this is a very
attractive, readable work suited for most library users."
Ref Sources for Small & Medium-sized Libr. 5th edition

The **Concise** Oxford dictionary of English
etymology; edited by T. F. Hoad. Oxford
Univ. Press 1986 $29.95   **422.03**

1. English language—Etymology—Dictionaries
ISBN 0-19-861182-X   LC 85-31970

Based on The Oxford dictionary of English etymology,
entered below

"Provides concise statements on the origins of words
and their development once they became part of the
English language." N Y Public Libr Book of How &
Where to Look It Up

Guinagh, Kevin, 1897-

Dictionary of foreign phrases and
abbreviations; translated and compiled by
Kevin Guinagh. 3rd ed. Wilson, H.W. 1983
261p $40   **422.03**

1. English language—Foreign words and phrases—Dictionaries 2. Quotations 3. Abbreviations—Dictionaries
ISBN 0-8242-0675-4   LC 82-8486

First published 1965

This dictionary "contains more than 5000 foreign
phrases, proverbs, and abbreviations frequently used in
written and spoken English. Provides translations and
pronunciations, and for some entries brief explanatory
notes; includes a list of phrases by languages." Ref
Sources for Small & Medium-sized Libr. 5th edition

Hendrickson, Robert, 1933-

The Facts on File encyclopedia of word
and phrase origins. Facts on File 1987 581p
$50   **422.03**

1. English   language—Etymology—Dictionaries
2. English language—Terms and phrases
ISBN 0-8160-1012-9   LC 86-2067

Also available in a paperback edition from Holt &
Co. with title: The Henry Holt encyclopedia of word and
phrase origins

"A popular etymological dictionary covering some
7500 words and phrases. Written in a less formal style,
this entertaining work will appeal to the general reader
curious about the origins of certain words or expressions
used in everyday speech." Ref Sources for Small &
Medium-sized Libr. 5th edition

Mawson, C. O. Sylvester (Christopher Orlando Sylvester), 1870-1938
The Harper dictionary of foreign terms; based on the original edition by C.O. Sylvester Mawson. 3rd ed, revised & edited by Eugene Ehrlich. Harper & Row 1987 423p $20; pa $10.95 **422.03**
1. English language—Foreign words and phrases—Dictionaries
ISBN 0-06-181576-4; 0-06-091686-9 (pa)
LC 86-46061

First published 1934 with title: Dictionary of foreign terms found in English and American writings of yesterday and today

"Covers some 15,000 foreign words, phrases and quotations from more than fifty languages, including Swahili, American Indian, ancient Greek, and modern Russian. Entries include foreign terms, plural and feminine forms as needed, and definitions. Authoritative, up-to-date, broad coverage." Ref Sources for Small & Medium-sized Libr. 5th edition

Morris, William, 1913-
Morris dictionary of word and phrase origins; [by] William and Mary Morris; foreword by Isaac Asimov. 2nd ed. Harper & Row 1988 669p $28 **422.03**
1. English language—Etymology—Dictionaries
2. English language—Terms and phrases
ISBN 0-06-015862-X
LC 87-45651

Original three volume edition published 1962-1971; one volume edition first published 1977

"Traces the origins of several thousand words and phrases in the English language, including slang terms and clichés not usually found in more formal works. Entries are listed alphabetically by the first word in the phrase, with an index at the end." Ref Sources for Small & Medium-sized Libr. 5th edition

The Oxford dictionary of English etymology; edited by C. T. Onions; with the assistance of G. W. S. Friedrichsen and R. W. Burchfield. Oxford Univ. Press 1966 1024p $60 **422.03**
1. English language—Etymology—Dictionaries
ISBN 0-19-861112-9

"Authoritative work tracing the history of common English words back to their Indo-European roots." Ref Sources for Small & Medium-sized Libr. 5th edition

Tuleja, Tad, 1944-
Foreignisms; a dictionary of foreign expressions commonly (and not so commonly) used in English. Macmillan 1988 205p hardcover o.p. paperback available $8.95 **422.03**
1. English language—Foreign words and phrases—Dictionaries
ISBN 0-02-038020-8 (pa)
LC 88-21563

Provides "spellings, pronunciations, and the meanings of confusing Latin, French, Italian, and other foreign terms. Beyond a genial 'A-Z' listing of definitions, Tuleja offers special sections on popular expressions, subdivided by nationality or purpose. . . . Handy for reference or casual enlightenment." Booklist

Webster's word histories. Merriam-Webster 1989 526p $19.95 **422.03**
1. English language—Etymology—Dictionaries
ISBN 0-87779-048-5
LC 89-12427

This volume presents entries that discuss the origins of some 1500 English words

The "articles (described as 'stories') are well researched and entertaining. . . . This work is great fun to browse, but its reference value is limited by the criterion that to be included a word must be 'interesting.'" Choice

423 English language— Dictionaries

The American heritage dictionary of the English language. 3rd ed. Houghton Mifflin 1992 xliv, 2140p il $39.95 **423**
1. English language—Dictionaries
ISBN 0-395-44895-6
LC 92-851

First published 1969

This dictionary "provides approximately 200,000 main entries. . . . Abbreviations, acronyms, people, and places are all in the A-Z main text. . . . Population figures from the 1980 census . . . are given for U.S. places. Meanings of a word are ordered so that the one most often sought, not the oldest one, is first. Etymologies appear for more than 30,500 entries." Booklist

Ammer, Christine
Have a nice day—no problem! a dictionary of clichés. Dutton 1992 454p $25 **423**
1. English language—Terms and phrases 2. English language—Usage
ISBN 0-525-93394-8
LC 91-21883

"This book examines some 3000 familiar expressions. First, a plain meaning is given for a term, like 'singularly rare' for *scarce as hen's teeth*. Next follow informed remarks on history (*sink or swim* began as *float or sink*), though, as the author notes, the derivation of many clichés is unclear. Whether a cliché is still popular or fading is also noted." Libr J

For a fuller review see: Booklist, April 15, 1992

Bernstein, Theodore Menline, 1904-
Bernstein's reverse dictionary; revised and expanded by David Grambs. 2nd ed. Times Bks. 1988 351p $19.95 **423**
1. English language—Synonyms and antonyms
2. English language—Dictionaries
ISBN 0-8129-1593-3
LC 87-40596

"For people who know there is a word for something, but can't think of it, *Bernstein's* lists meanings alphabetically and supplies the words. Index of target words." Ref Sources for Small & Medium-sized Libr. 5th edition

Bragonier, Reginald
What's what: a visual glossary of the physical world; [by] Reginald Bragonier, Jr., and David Fisher. rev ed. Hammond 1990 581p il $34.95 **423**
1. Picture dictionaries
ISBN 0-8437-3322-5
LC 89-51862

Bragonier, Reginald—*Continued*
First published 1981

"This unique visual glossary provides access to words through pictures of hundreds of common objects and the parts of which they are composed. Arranged in broad categories (e.g. living things, transportation, arts and crafts) with a detailed index, so that users can find both pictures of things for which they have names and names of things for which they have pictures. An excellent source." Ref Sources for Small & Medium-sized Libr. 5th edition

The **Doubleday** Roget's thesaurus in dictionary form; Sidney I. Landau, editor in chief; Ronald J. Bogus, managing editor. rev ed. Doubleday 1987 804p $11.95; thumb-indexed $13.95 **423**
1. English language—Synonyms and antonyms 2. Americanisms
ISBN 0-385-23996-3; 0-385-23997-1 (thumb-indexed)
LC 86-24184

First published 1977

"Despite the words 'Roget' and 'thesaurus' in the title, which may imply a classified arrangement, the entry words in this volume are listed in alphabetical order. Some 250,000 synonyms and antonyms, including slang, are provided, but with little guidance in word selection. This work's arrangement will appeal to those who find *Roget's International Thesaurus* awkward to use." Nichols. Guide to Ref Books for Sch Media Cent. 4th edition

Espy, Willard R.
Words to rhyme with; for poets and song writers. Facts on File 1986 656p $55 **423**
1. English language—Rhyme
ISBN 0-8160-1237-7
LC 85-31216

Also available in paperback from Holt & Co.

This dictionary includes 80,000 rhyming words, divided by sound into single, double, and triple rhyme lists. A glossary defining the more obscure words, and one hundred of Espy's verses are included, plus an introduction which discusses topics such as meter, rhyme scheme and various poetical forms

Glazier, Stephen
Random House word menu. Random House 1992 xxx, 977p $22 **423**
1. English language—Synonyms and antonyms 2. English language—Terms and phrases
ISBN 0-679-40030-3
LC 92-13539

This work "classifies approximately 65,000 words into seven general categories (Nature, Science and Technology, Domestic Life, Arts and Leisure, etc.), which in turn are divided into numerous subcategories and sub-subcategories. . . . A detailed table of contents provides access to the classification scheme and an A-Z index lists all words included in the book." Libr J

For a fuller review see: Booklist, Jan. 1, 1993

Hayakawa, S. I.
Choose the right word; a modern guide to synonyms. Perennial Lib. 1987 726p hardcover o.p. paperback available $14.95
423
1. English language—Synonyms and antonyms
ISBN 0-06-091393-2 (pa)
LC 86-46071

Reprint of the edition first published 1968 by Funk & Wagnalls with title: Funk & Wagnalls Modern guide to synonyms and related words

"Over 1,000 key words are presented, and under these are grouped 6,000 synonyms and related words. The meaning and nuances of the synonyms are described in short essays that provide concise definitions and illustrative sentences." Wilson Libr Bull

Holder, R. W.
The Faber dictionary of euphemisms. Faber & Faber 1989 408p hardcover o.p. paperback available $11.95 **423**
1. Euphemism—Dictionaries
ISBN 0-571-15125-6 (pa)

"Holder, who developed this work from his earlier 'Dictionary of American and British Euphemisms,' includes at least 5,000 terms with definitions and sometimes a quotation from a printed source. . . . Words that are obsolete or of only American or only British usage are so noted. Holder's unique contribution is an index in which the entries are classified under 65 headings." Booklist

Includes bibliography

Illustrated reverse dictionary; find the words on the tip of your tongue. Reader's Digest Assn. 1990 608p il $25 **423**
1. English language—Synonyms and antonyms 2. English language—Dictionaries
ISBN 0-89577-352-X
LC 90-39606

At head of title: Reader's Digest
Based on Reader's Digest reverse dictionary
"Editor: John Ellison Kahn; Americanized and expanded by Walter D. Glanze"

"Part dictionary, part thesaurus, and part book of lists, this work is a compilation of helpful information on over 70,000 English-language words and phrases. Organized in an attractive and readable format, it leads the reader from entry to entry until the desired term is found." Am Libr

For a fuller review see: Booklist, April 15, 1991

Kipfer, Barbara Ann
Roget's 21st century thesaurus in dictionary form; the essential reference for home, school, or office. Dell 1992 978p $18
423
1. English language—Synonyms and antonyms
ISBN 0-440-50386-8
LC 91-37916

"Produced by The Philip Lief Group, Inc."

This thesaurus "follows the now-popular dictionary format for its 17,000 main entries (*abandon-zoom*) and provides other innovations as well. The part of speech, very brief definition, synonyms (over 450,000), and references to an 837-term Concept Index are indicated for each entry. . . . The lexicographer-author's selections reflect contemporary usage, gender sensitivity, and recently evolved words." Libr J

For a fuller review see: Booklist, Oct. 15, 1992

Kister, Kenneth F., 1935-
Kister's best dictionaries for adults & young people; a comparative guide. Oryx Press 1992 xxi, 438p $39.50 **423**
1. English language—Dictionaries—Reviews
ISBN 0-89774-191-9
LC 91-40679

Kister, Kenneth F., 1935—— *Continued*

A revision of Dictionary buying guide (1977)

"The first section contains essays concerning the history, evaluation, content, purchasing, and future of dictionaries by type (e.g., college, unabridged, pocket). It features 132 titles under the Adult listings and 168 under Children and Young Students. The book concludes with appendixes listing language associations, additional dictionary evaluative sources, a bibliography of books and journal articles, language publications, and publishers and distributors." Libr J

For a fuller review see: Booklist, June 1, 1992

Lees, Gene

The modern rhyming dictionary; how to write lyrics; including a practical guide to lyric writing for songwriters and poets. Cherry Lane Bks. 1981 360p $19.95; pa $14.95   **423**

1. English language—Rhyme
ISBN 0-89524-129-3; 0-89524-317-2 (pa)   LC 81-4832

"Lees' dictionary is arranged in three sections—masculine (one-syllable), feminine (two-syllable), and three-syllable rhymes—with each section subdivided by vowels and then into subgroups by the consonant beginning the final syllable of the word." Ref Sources for Small & Medium-sized Libr. 5th edition

Merriam-Webster's collegiate dictionary. 10th ed. Merriam-Webster 1993 1559p   **423**

1. English language—Dictionaries (indexed)
LC 93-20206

Prices vary according to binding

First published 1898. Previous edition had title: Webster's ninth new collegiate dictionary

"Includes 160,000 entries (211,000 definitions), 35,000 verbal illustrations and illustrative quotations, 35,000 etymologies, 4,400 usage paragraphs and notes, and 700 black-and-white drawings. . . . Abbreviations, foreign words and phrases, biographical and geographic names, signs, symbols, and a handbook of style conclude the volume." Booklist

The New Merriam-Webster dictionary for large print users. Hall, G.K. & Co. 1989 xxvii, 1106p $40.95   **423**

1. English language—Dictionaries
ISBN 0-8161-4754-X   LC 89-15437

First published 1977 with title: The Merriam-Webster dictionary for large print users

This dictionary "contains some 60,000 entries. . . . In addition to the usual explanatory notes and the main vocabulary body, the dictionary includes several useful sections such as an extensive list of foreign words and phrases, a list of nations of the world and their population figures, and population tables of United States and Canadian cities and townships. The enlarged type of the dictionary conforms to the standards of the National Association for the Visually Handicapped." Am Ref Books Annu, 1991

The New shorter Oxford English dictionary; edited by Lesley Brown. Oxford Univ. Press 1993 2v $125   **423**

1. English language—Dictionaries
ISBN 0-19-861271-0

First published 1933 with title: The Shorter Oxford English dictionary on historical principles

"Large in scope, the reference contains 500,000 definitions and 87,400 illustrative quotations. . . . Unique among abridged dictionaries is the consistent historical/literary approach the *New Shorter* takes in displaying the changing meanings of words. The *New Shorter* offers the huge scope and scholarship of its parent, the *OED*, [entered below] without the difficulties of a 20-volume set or the nuisance of a magnifying glass and at an affordable price." Libr J

For a fuller review see: Booklist, Jan. 15, 1994

Oxford American dictionary; [compiled by] Eugene Ehrlich [et al.] Oxford Univ. Press 1980 816p $18.95   **423**

1. English language—Dictionaries 2. Americanisms
ISBN 0-19-502795-7   LC 80-16510

Also available in paperback from Avon Bks.

This work, "which contains in the neighborhood of 70,000 entries, offers brief but very clear definitions, numerous illustrative examples, and about 600 frankly prescriptive usage notes." Kister's Best Dict for Adults & Young People

The Oxford dictionary of new words; a popular guide to words in the news; compiled by Sara Tulloch. Oxford Univ. Press 1991 322p $22   **423**

1. English language—Dictionaries 2. Words, New—Dictionaries
ISBN 0-19-869170-X   LC 91-18814

In this "dictionary, about 2000 contemporary words and phrases are given international Phonetic Alphabet pronunciation, one or more definitions, accounts of origin and usage, and readable, useful summaries of their background. All the information provided is first-rate. Examples of usage are quoted, with citations, and a set of 11 'subject icons' highlight graphically the fields of interest (business, drugs, music, etc.) in which the terms operate." Libr J

For a fuller review see: Booklist, Feb. 15, 1992

The Oxford English dictionary. 2nd ed, prepared by J.A. Simpson and E.S.C. Weiner. Oxford Univ. Press 1989 20v set $2750   **423**

1. English language—Dictionaries
ISBN 0-19-861186-2   LC 88-5330

Also available CD-ROM version; three volume compact edition reproduced micrographically from first edition and supplements available for $395

First published 1888 with title: New English dictionary on historical principles

"This is an etymological or word-source dictionary. In addition to definitions, this work gives the history of 290,500 words, both current and archaic, in the English language. Slang entries are very limited. Word histories include early forms, variant forms and roots, and first or exemplary usages in English from ancient to modern times. Short explanatory notes are provided for more common words." N Y Public Libr Book of How & Where to Look It Up

The Random House thesaurus; edited by Jess Stein and Stuart Berg Flexner. college ed. Random House 1984 812p thumb-indexed $14.95   **423**

1. English language—Synonyms and antonyms
ISBN 0-394-52949-9   LC 84-4914

Also available in paperback from D. McKay

"Based upon the Reader's Digest family word finder, c1975." Verso of title page

The Random House thesaurus—*Continued*

An alphabetical listing of over 11,000 main-entry word lists which group together more than 200,000 synonyms and antonyms by meaning. Also included are sample sentences for every main entry (and for each meaning)

Random House unabridged dictionary; Stuart Berg Flexner, editor in chief; Leonore Crary Hauck, managing editor. 2nd ed newly rev & updated. Random House 1993 xlii, 2478p il maps $100   **423**

1. English language—Dictionaries
ISBN 0-679-42917-4   LC 93-84591

Also available on CD-ROM

First published 1966 with title: Random House dictionary of the English language

Entries reflect current usage of words, and include date of first use, pronunciation, syntax, usage, and etymology. Brief biographical entries are included. Supplementary sections include signs and symbols used in various fields; a directory of colleges and universities; concise bilingual dictionaries for French, German, Italian, and Spanish; a manual of style; and a full-color atlas
For a review see: Booklist, Feb. 1, 1994

Random House Webster's college dictionary. Random House 1992 xxxi, 1568p il $17.50; thumb indexed $20   **423**

1. English language—Dictionaries
ISBN 0-679-41420-7; 0-679-41410-X (thumb indexed)
                                      LC 92-1030

First published 1991 as a successor to The Random House College dictionary

Based on the Random House dictionary of the English language, second unabridged edition, entered above
"This *Dictionary* contains 180,000 entries in an A-Z format that includes abbreviations, commonly used foreign words and phrases, biographical names, and geographic names, along with approximately 800 small but detailed black-and-white illustrations." Booklist

Roget's II: the new thesaurus; by the editors of the American heritage dictionary. expanded ed. Houghton Mifflin 1988 1135p $12.95   **423**

1. English language—Synonyms and antonyms
ISBN 0-395-48317-4   LC 88-8842

Also available on CD-ROM with The American Heritage dictionary

This is a revised edition of a thesaurus first published in 1980. The work uses a dictionary format, with words and numbered definitions on the left column of a page, and corresponding numbered synonyms, near-synonyms, antonyms and near-antonyms on the right column

Roget's international thesaurus. 5th ed, edited by Robert L. Chapman. HarperCollins Pubs. 1992 1139p $17.95; thumb indexed $18.95   **423**

1. English language—Synonyms and antonyms
ISBN 0-06-270046-4; 0-06-270014-6 (thumb indexed)
                                      LC 92-7615

First copyright edition published 1911 with title: The standard thesaurus of English words and phrases classified and arranged so as to facilitate the expression of ideas and assist in literary composition
"Roget's 150-year-old plan of organizing words within eight broad classes has been revised by Chapman to create a simpler, more natural, and contemporary arrangement of 15 new classes." Libr J

Similes dictionary; Elyse Sommer, editorial director, Mike Sommer, editor. Gale Res. 1988 xlviii, 950p $72   **423**

1. English language—Terms and phrases 2. English language—Synonyms and antonyms
ISBN 0-8103-4361-4   LC 87-36109

"A collection of more than 16,000 comparison phrases from ancient times to the present, compiled from books, folklore, magazines, newspapers, plays, politics, stage, screen, and television and arranged under more than 500 thematic categories." Title page

"Authors are given for each simile, but not sources. . . . While *Similes Dictionary* overlaps with quotation books and phrase books that include similes, this overlap is not sufficient to detract from its usefulness as a reference tool." Booklist

Includes bibliography

Third Barnhart dictionary of new English; [edited by] Robert K. Barnhart, Sol Steinmetz with Clarence L. Barnhart. Wilson, H.W. 1990 xxi, 565p $49   **423**

1. Words, New—Dictionaries 2. English language—Dictionaries
ISBN 0-8242-0796-3   LC 90-33483

Revised edition of: The Second Barnhart dictionary of new English, published 1980

This work "treats 12,000 new words, abbreviations, and acronyms 'which have come into the common or working vocabulary of the English-speaking world' during the past 30 years. . . . Definitions are as simple and brief as possible, since the *Dictionary* relies on documented quotations. Each entry records the year during which the term became current. . . . Some entries include explanatory notes regarding usage, word formation, or relevant cultural or historical facts. Pronunciation is given only for difficult or familiar words. . . . Highly recommended." Booklist

Webster's collegiate thesaurus. Merriam-Webster 1988 26, 868p $15.95
                                      423

1. English language—Synonyms and antonyms
ISBN 0-87779-069-8   LC 88-13218

A concise paperback edition based on this work is available with title: The Merriam-Webster concise school and office thesaurus $7.95 (ISBN 0-87779-601-7)

First published 1976. Present edition also known as Merriam-Webster's collegiate thesaurus

Arranged alphabetically, entries in this thesaurus list synonyms, related words, idioms, contrasted words, and antonyms

Webster's new dictionary of synonyms; a dictionary of discriminated synonyms with antonyms and analogous and contrasted words. Merriam-Webster thumb-indexed $19.95   **423**

1. English language—Synonyms and antonyms

First published 1942 with title: Webster's dictionary of synonyms. (1984 edition). Periodically revised

"Lists synonyms with notes on connotational distinctions; some antonyms also given. Includes context sentences, as well as contrasted and analogous words. Features long introductory article on distinctions. Cross-referenced. This is not just a basic word list, but more a reference concerning distinctions between related words

Webster's new dictionary of synonyms —
Continued
and word groups." N Y Public Libr Book of How &
Where to Look It Up

Webster's New World dictionary of
American English; Victoria Neufeldt,
editor in chief; David B. Guralnik, editor
in chief emeritus. 3rd college ed.
Prentice-Hall 1994 xxvi, 1574p il $17.95;
thumb-indexed $20   **423**
1. English language—Dictionaries 2. Americanisms
ISBN 0-671-88289-9; 0-671-88243-0 (thumb-indexed)
                                    LC 93-2961
First published 1953 by Collins with title: Webster's
New World dictionary of the American language

"This update of the third edition . . . continues the
New World tradition of currency with a special emphasis
on American colloquialisms and slang as well as words,
senses, forms of words, and idioms that are American
in origin. . . . With its emphasis on Americanisms, this
dictionary continues to make a unique contribution to
any dictionary collection." Booklist

Webster's third new international dictionary
of the English language; unabridged.
Merriam-Webster il   **423**
1. English language—Dictionaries
Prices vary according to binding
First published 1828 with title: An American dictionary of the English language, by Noah Webster. Also
appeared with titles: Webster's unabridged dictionary,
Webster's international dictionary of the English language,
and Webster's new international dictionary of the English
language. This edition first published 1961. Frequently
reprinted with additions and changes to keep it up to
date
"Clear, accurate definitions are given in historical
order. Outstanding for its numerous illustrative quotations, impeccable authority, and etymologies, *Webster's
third* is regarded as the most reliable, comprehensive
general unabridged dictionary." Ref Sources for Small &
Medium-sized Libr. 5th edition

Young, Sue
The new comprehensive American
rhyming dictionary. Morrow 1991 622p
$24.95   **423**
1. English language—Rhyme 2. Americanisms
ISBN 0-688-10360-X   LC 90-19165
Also available in paperback from Avon Bks.

This book contains over 65,000 words and phrases
categorized by sound, rather than spelling. It includes
many colloquialisms and slang expressions

425 English language—Grammar

Booher, Dianna Daniels
Good grief, good grammar; [by] Dianna
Booher. Facts on File 1988 238p $19.95
                                    425
1. English language—Grammar 2. English language—
Business English
ISBN 0-8160-1344-6   LC 87-27525
"Topics discussed include parts of speech, agreement
of tenses, prepositional phrases, capitalization, punctua-
tion, and basic sentence structure. . . . Booher even

offers a refresher course on diagramming sentences. A
handy guide for writers wanting to improve their correspondence." Booklist

427 English language variations

Clark, Gregory R., 1948-
Words of the Vietnam War. McFarland
& Co. 1990 604p $45   **427**
1. English language—Slang 2. Military art and
science—Dictionaries 3. Vietnam War, 1961-1975—
Dictionaries
ISBN 0-89950-465-5   LC 89-43639
"The slang, jargon, abbreviations, acronyms, nomencla-
ture, nicknames, pseudonyms, slogans, specs, euphemisms,
double-talk, chants, and names and places of the era of
United States involvement in Vietnam." Title page

"Approximately 10,000 entries, with over 4300 definitions, are divided into two sections, a long alphabetical
list followed by a short numerical list. Although
specialized, this dictionary may be of particular interest
because of its focus on such a momentous period in
recent history. It should also serve as a useful resource
for locating and defining words which have not yet
found their way into traditional dictionaries." Ref Sources
for Small & Medium-sized Libr. 5th edition

A **Dictionary** of American idioms; based on
the earlier edition; [edited] by M. T.
Boatner, J. E. Gates, and Adam Makkai.
2nd ed, revised and thoroughly updated
by Adam Makkai. Barron's Educ. Ser.
1987 398p pa $11.95   **427**
1. English language—Terms and phrases
2. Americanisms
ISBN 0-8120-3899-1   LC 84-9247
First published 1966 by the American School for the
Deaf with title: A Dictionary of idioms for the deaf

This work "lists over 5000 idioms used in contemporary American speech. Gives definitions, an illustrative
sentence, and in some cases usage notes and etymology.
Of particular interest to ESL students." Ref Sources for
Small & Medium-sized Libr. 5th edition

Dictionary of American regional English;
Frederic G. Cassidy, chief editor. Belknap
Press 1985-1991 2v maps   **427**
1. English language—Dictionaries 2. Americanisms
The first two volumes of a projected five volume
work
Contents: v1 Introduction and A-C $66 (ISBN 0-674-
20511-1); v2 D-H $70 (ISBN 0-674-20512-X)
This dictionary "offers detailed information on
nonstandard, regional, or folk American speech. . . .
Entries do not merely define, but include part of speech,
pronunciation, variant forms, etymology, geographic
range, usage, cross-references, editorial notes, and dated
quotations defining the word. Where appropriate, a
computer-generated map . . . illustrates the regional
distribution of a word. When it is completed . . . this
work will definitely take its place beside the OED as
a classic." Am Libr

Dillard, J. L. (Joey Lee), 1924-
Black English; its history and usage in the United States. Random House 1972 861p il hardcover o.p. paperback available $11
427

1. Blacks—Language 2. Americanisms
ISBN 0-394-71872-0 (pa)

The author contends "that black English is a legitimate descended scion of the English pidgins spoken in West Africa and the Caribbean, and he convincingly details this relationship. He also shows that the grammar of black English, while differing from that of Standard English is regular and functional." Libr J

Hendrickson, Robert, 1933-
American talk; the words and ways of American dialects. Viking 1986 230p o.p.; Penguin Bks. paperback available $7.95
427

1. English language—Dialects 2. Americanisms
ISBN 0-14-009421-0 (pa)   LC 86-40119
"Hendrickson combines informal anecdotes and scholarly research on some 20 native dialects, from Black English to Brooklynese. In addition to pronunciation charts and glossaries, Hendrickson provides samplers of distinctive words and expressions that each dialect has contributed to the language. . . . A wonderful, colorful look at the diversity of American speech." Booklist

Herman, Lewis
American dialects; a manual for actors, directors, and writers; by Lewis Herman and Marguerite Shalett Herman. Theatre Arts Bks. 1959 $22.50
427

1. English language—Dialects 2. Americanisms
ISBN 0-87830-003-1

First published 1947 with title: Manual of American dialects, for radio, stage, screen, and television
"An invaluable guide to reproducing the sounds, rhythms, lilts, and stresses of representative dialects of every major section of the continental United States." Libr J

Lewin, Esther
The thesaurus of slang; 150,000 uncensored contemporary slang terms, common idioms, and colloquialisms arranged for quick and easy reference; [by] Esther Lewin and Albert E. Lewin. Facts on File 1988 435p $50
427

1. English language—Slang 2. English language—Synonyms and antonyms
ISBN 0-8160-1742-5   LC 88-6985
"Organized under 15,000 standard English synonyms, this thesaurus leads the user to alternatives that range widely in their proximity to standard English and appropriate usage context. . . . The working writer, whether student, copy writer, or other professional, will find this book useful when writing informally. It will also appeal to word buffs and other browsers." Libr J

Includes bibliography

Lutz, William, 1940-
Doublespeak; from "revenue enhancement" to "terminal living" how government, business, advertisers, and others use language to deceive you. Harper & Row 1989 290p $17.95; pa $8.95
427

1. English language—Jargon
ISBN 0-06-016134-5; 0-06-091993-0 (pa)
LC 89-45051
The author "identifies four varieties of deliberate linguistic distortion: euphemism, jargon, gobbledygook and inflated language. He has found many instances of each in the officialese of government and politics, science and medicine, economics, business and other great citadels of language abuse. . . . Taken as a whole, the book is an irrefutable indictment of those who subvert language to distort the truth." N Y Times Book Rev

Mencken, H. L. (Henry Louis), 1880-1956
The American language; an inquiry into the development of English in the United States. 4th ed, corrected and rewritten. Knopf 1936 769, xxix p $40
427

1. English language 2. Names 3. Americanisms
ISBN 0-394-40075-5
Supplements 1-2 ea $50 (ISBN 0-394-40076-3; 0-394-40077-1)
Also available in an abridged edition for $35, pa $22.95 (ISBN 0-394-40081-X; 0-394-73315-0)
Analyzed in Essay and general literature index
First published 1919
An historical treatment of the development of American English covering such subjects as pronunciation and spelling, slang, proper names, and common speech
Includes bibliographic references

New Dictionary of American slang; edited by Robert L. Chapman. Harper & Row 1986 485p $32.50
427

1. English language—Slang 2. Americanisms
ISBN 0-06-181157-2   LC 86-45086
Also available for $12 in an abridged paperback edition with title: American slang (ISBN 0-06-096160-0)
First published 1960 by Crowell with title: Dictionary of American slang
This dictionary "defines over 15,000 terms, many with examples of usage, derivations, and periods of usage. Based in part on Wentworth and Flexner's 1960 'Dictionary of American Slang,' the new work has been completely revised, reformatted, and updated to reflect the thousands of expressions that have entered the language over the past two decades from the counterculture, drug scene, blacks, college campuses, and other subcultures." Am Libr

The Oxford dictionary of modern slang; [by] John Ayto, John Simpson. Oxford Univ. Press 1992 299p $25
427

1. English language—Slang
ISBN 0-19-866181-9   LC 93-108616
This dictionary defines "more than 5,000 slang terms currently or recently in use in the English-speaking world. . . . Entries give the date of earliest written use and include indicators that tell where or among what group a slang term originated or is used. Surprisingly, ODMS is divided evenly between US and UK-Commonwealth slang." Choice
For a fuller review see: Booklist, April 15, 1993

Partridge, Eric, 1894-1979

A concise dictionary of slang and unconventional English; edited by Paul Beale; from: A dictionary of slang and unconventional English, by Eric Partridge. Macmillan 1990 xxvi, 534p $35   **427**

1. English language—Slang
ISBN 0-02-605350-0   LC 90-38042

Based on the eighth edition of A dictionary of slang and unconventional English, entered below

First published 1989 in the United Kingdom

"This concise version omits words, phrases, and senses that are known to have originated prior to this century; approximately 1,500 new expressions coined in the 1980s have been added. . . . The emphasis seems to be on British and Commonwealth words. . . . Entries include (to varying degrees) part-of-speech designations, register, definitions, date information, and sources in which early recording of the word can be found." Booklist

Includes bibliographic references

A dictionary of slang and unconventional English; colloquialisms and catch-phrases, solecisms and catachreses, nicknames, vulgarisms and such Americanisms as have been naturalized. Macmillan $85   **427**

1. English language—Slang 2. Americanisms

First published 1937. (8th edition 1984). Periodically revised

Entries are "in one alphabet; front matter includes a helpful note, 'Arrangement Within Entries.' Entries trace, in a way that recalls the 'Oxford English Dictionary,' the development of terms and usages." Booklist
"Partridge remains essential for all reference collections, an irresistable distraction to browsers." Am Ref Books Annu, 1986

Spears, Richard A.

NTC's American idioms dictionary; associate editor, Linda Schinke-Llano. National Textbook 1987 463p $16.95; pa $12.95   **427**

1. English language—Idioms 2. Americanisms
ISBN 0-8442-5452-5; 0-8442-5450-9 (pa)
    LC 86-63996

"Some 8,000 contemporary expressions are included. . . . Access by keyword is provided through a 100-page phrase-finder index." Booklist

428   Standard English usage

Bernstein, Theodore Menline, 1904-

The careful writer; a modern guide to English usage; [by] Theodore M. Bernstein. Atheneum Pubs. 1965 487p hardcover o.p. paperback available $16.95   **428**

1. English language—Usage 2. English language—Idioms
ISBN 0-689-70555-7 (pa)

Alphabetical entries on the writer's problems of English usages: questions of meaning, grammar, punctuation, precision, logical structure, and color

Follett, Wilson

Modern American usage; a guide; edited and completed by Jacques Barzun, in collaboration with Carlos Baker [et al.] Hill & Wang 1966 436p hardcover o.p. paperback available $14.95   **428**

1. English language—Usage 2. English language—Idioms 3. English language—Grammar
ISBN 0-8090-0139-X (pa)

"Provides introductory essays on grammar and usage, followed by a lexicon of troublesome words, phrases, and constructions. Two appendixes cover 'Shall (should), will (would),' and 'Punctuation.'" Ref Sources for Small & Medium-sized Libr. 5th edition

Fowler, H. W.

A dictionary of modern English usage. 2nd ed, revised by Sir Ernest Gowers. Oxford Univ. Press 1965 xx, 725p $21.95; thumb-indexed $24.95; pa $10.95   **428**

1. English language—Etymology 2. English language—Idioms 3. English language—Usage
ISBN 0-19-500153-2; 0-19-500154-0 (thumb-indexed); 0-19-281389-7 (pa)

First published 1926

"Alphabetically arranged; definitions of terms—sometimes with disputed spellings and spelling of plurals, pronunciation, etc.—are interspersed with brief essays on the use and misuse of words and expressions, parts of speech, etc. Reflects the author's personal opinions, and comments are often astringent and witty." Sheehy. Guide to Ref Books. 10th edition

Lewis, Norman, 1912-

How to read better and faster. 4th ed. Crowell 1978 xxiii, 239p hardcover o.p. paperback available $25   **428**

1. Reading
ISBN 0-690-01528-3 (pa)   LC 78-19141

First published 1944

"How an average reader may improve his reading ability, speed, [vocabulary] and comprehension is presented in a series of lessons." Chicago Public Libr

Includes bibliographies

Maggio, Rosalie

The dictionary of bias-free usage; a guide to nondiscriminatory language. Oryx Press 1991 293p pa $25   **428**

1. English language—Usage 2. English language—Terms and phrases 3. Sexism
ISBN 0-89774-653-8   LC 91-13819

"A glossary of words and phrases designed to assist writers in finding alternatives to sexist language. Suggested substitutes are given in italics and listed in order of usefulness. Appendix A, which the author suggests be read first, contains useful guidelines, rationale, and many examples. Appendix B contains eight short essays. Four-page bibliography." Sheehy. Guide to Ref Books. 10th edition. suppl

Morris, William, 1913-
Harper dictionary of contemporary usage; [by] William and Mary Morris; with the assistance of a panel of 165 distinguished consultants on usage. 2nd ed. Harper & Row 1985 xxx, 641p $22.50; pa $13   **428**

1. English language—Usage 2. English language—Dictionaries
ISBN 0-06-181606-X; 0-06-272021-X (pa)

LC 83-48797

First published 1975

"The work contains entries explaining the correct usage of words, phrases, or parts of speech, and 'usage panel questions,' in which literary figures such as John Ciardi, Isaac Asimov, and Harrison Salisbury offer their wit and opinions on debatable points of usage." Libr J

Newman, Edwin
A civil tongue. Macmillan 1976 207p $9.95   **428**

1. English language—Errors
ISBN 0-672-52267-5

First published by Bobbs-Merrill

This is an analysis of flaws in English usage illustrated by examples

Strictly speaking; will America be the death of English? Macmillan 1974 205p $9.95   **428**

1. English language—Errors
ISBN 0-672-51990-9

First published by Bobbs-Merrill

The author derides the misuse of the English language which he interprets as a reflection of society's sad situation. He quotes many cliches, malapropisms, solecisms, redundances and other errors made by such people as journalists, broadcasters, government officials, advertisers, social scientists, and sportsmen

Safire, William
Coming to terms. Doubleday 1991 402p $25   **428**

1. English language—Usage 2. English language—Idioms
ISBN 0-385-41300-9

LC 90-23376

Also available in paperback from Holt & Co.

"Compiled from Safire's 1988-89 *New York Times Magazine* columns 'On Language,' this book contains about 160 essays along with many letters commenting on them." Libr J

Fumblerules: a lighthearted guide to grammar and good usage. Doubleday 1990 153p o.p.; Dell paperback available $5.99   **428**

1. English language—Grammar 2. English language—Usage
ISBN 0-440-21010-0 (pa)

LC 89-48617

"A *fumblerule* is 'a mistake that calls attention to the rule.' For example: 'No sentence fragments.' Each chapter is headlined by a separate example that is followed by a brief explanatory passage illuminating the grammatical rules that have been so cavalierly broken." Booklist

Language maven strikes again. Doubleday 1990 447p $22.95   **428**

1. English language—Usage 2. English language—Idioms
ISBN 0-385-41299-1

LC 89-38624

Also available in paperback from Holt & Co.

In this collection of the author's columns Safire expounds upon word usage, grammar and sentence construction

What's the good word? Times Bks. 1982 325p o.p.; Avon Bks. paperback available $5.95   **428**

1. English language—Usage 2. English language—Idioms
ISBN 0-380-64550-5 (pa)

LC 81-52568

A collection of the author's New York Times columns. Entries include word history, slang, regional pronunciation, usage, and common misuses

You could look it up; more On language from William Safire. Times Bks. 1988 357p il $22.50   **428**

1. English language—Usage 2. English language—Idioms
ISBN 0-8129-1234-8

LC 87-40595

Also available in paperback from Holt & Co.

This "volume of selections from Safire's *New York Times* weekly 'On Language' column talks about word usage, grammar, pronunciation, and punctuation in a witty, colloquial style that both comments on and demonstrates the way we speak now." Booklist

Success with words; a guide to the American language; [by] Reader's Digest; prepared in association with Peter Davies. Reader's Digest Assn. 1983 692p il maps $24.95   **428**

1. English language—Usage
ISBN 0-89577-168-3

LC 82-62542

This guide to American English offers advice on usage and provides examples and recommendations. Also included are articles on style, punctuation, the history of the language and the sources of English words

Webster's dictionary of English usage. Merriam-Webster 1989 978p $18.95   **428**

1. English language—Usage
ISBN 0-87779-032-9

LC 88-37248

"A 500-entry dictionary of English usage supported by 20,000 illustrative quotations from Shakespeare to *Playboy*. In a clear, readable nonprescriptive manner the dictionary looks at English usage from both historical and contemporary perspectives. The emphasis is on how language is currently used. . . . There is an informative essay on the history of English usage, a pronunciation key, and a bibliography." Am Libr

433 German language—Dictionaries

Cassell's German-English, English-German dictionary; completely revised by Harold T. Betteridge. Macmillan 2v in 1 $23.95; thumb-indexed $24.95   **433**

1. German language—Dictionaries (thumb-indexed)

Cassell's German-English, English-German dictionary—*Continued*
Also available in a concise edition for $13.95 (ISBN 0-02-522650-9)

First compiled 1888 by Elizabeth Weir and published by Heath. Periodically revised. Previous American editions published by Funk & Wagnalls with title: The New Cassell's German dictionary

This dictionary incorporates "many new words and usages. Gives phonetic transcriptions of head words. One of the most useful bilingual dictionaries." Sheehy. Guide to Ref Books. 10th edition

Collins concise **German-English, English-German** dictionary. Simon & Schuster 1987 508, 528p $16.95 **433**
1. German language—Dictionaries
ISBN 0-671-63815-7   LC 87-4388
Spine title: Webster's New World German dictionary

Covers current usage in over 100,000 references, with phrases and examples to show how words are used in various contexts. Includes pronunciation guides, and German and English irregular verb tables

The **Oxford-Harrap** standard German-English dictionary; edited by Trevor Jones. Oxford Univ. Press 1977-1978 3v ea $84 **433**
1. German language—Dictionaries

Volumes one to three of a projected five volume set
First published 1963-1974 in England with title: Harrap's standard German and English dictionary

Contents: v1 A-E (ISBN 0-19-864129-X); v2 F-K (ISBN 0-19-864130-3); v3 L-R (ISBN 0-19-864131-1)

437 German language variations

Harkavy, Alexander, 1863-1939
Yiddish-English-Hebrew dictionary; with a new introduction by Dovid Katz. Yivo Inst. for Jewish Res.; Schocken Bks. 1987 xlv, 583p $34.50 **437**
1. Yiddish language—Dictionaries   2. Hebrew language—Dictionaries
ISBN 0-8052-4027-6   LC 86-31414
First published 1925 by the author. This is a reprint of the expanded second edition, published 1928 by the Hebrew Publishing Company

This trilingual dictionary describes the Yiddish language as it was actually used by American Yiddish speakers in the nineteenth and early twentieth centuries

Rosten, Leo Calvin, 1908-
Hooray for Yiddish! a book about English. Simon & Schuster 1982 363p hardcover o.p. paperback available $10 **437**
1. Yiddish language   2. English language—Foreign words and phrases
ISBN 0-671-43026-2 (pa)   LC 82-646
"A cheerful lexicon of Yiddish words which have become part of the English language, plus English words and phrases which have been transformed into Yinglish; the whole garnished with stories, jokes, parables, reverent quotations from the Talmud and a glittering gallery of writers, rabbis, sages, wits, with impulse side trips into the faith, folklore, genius and history of the Jews—from their servitude in Babylon to their magnitude in Beverly Hills." Title page

The joys of Yiddish; by Leo Rosten. McGraw-Hill 1968 xxxviii, 533p o.p.; Simon & Schuster paperback available $5.95 **437**
1. Yiddish language   2. English language—Foreign words and phrases
ISBN 0-671-72813-X (pa)
"A relaxed lexicon of Yiddish, Hebrew and Yinglish words often encountered in English, plus dozens that ought to be, with serendipitous excursions into Jewish humor, habits, holidays, history, religion, ceremonies, folklore, and cuisine; the whole generously garnished with stories, anecdotes, epigrams, Talmudic quotations, folk sayings and jokes—from the days of the Bible to those of the beatnik." Title page

Includes bibliographic references

The joys of Yinglish; [by] Leo Rosten. McGraw-Hill 1989 xxiii, 584p o.p.; New Am. Lib. paperback available $5.99 **437**
1. Yiddish language   2. English language—Foreign words and phrases
ISBN 0-451-17378-3 (pa)   LC 89-8094
"Samples of Yiddish words and phrases that have found their way into mainstream American life (along with those that, according to Rosten, ought to be assimilated). Within each entry are spelling variations, clues on derivation, definitions, pronunciation, and, perhaps best of all, a joke (or several) to clarify meaning and usage." Booklist

438 Standard German usage

Berlitz, Charles, 1914-
German step by step. Wynwood Press 1990 313p pa $11.99 **438**
1. German language—Conversations and phrases
ISBN 0-922066-43-4
A reissue of the title first published 1979 by Everest House

This beginners' guide to the German language contains conversational phrases. Grammatical points of importance are presented within each dialogue. Each sentence used in the conversation is given in three ways: in German, in syllables that facilitate pronunciation and in English. Also included is a short English-German dictionary

439.3 Dutch, Flemish, Afrikaans languages

Cassell's New English-Dutch, Dutch-English dictionary; compiled by J.A. Jockin-La Bastide and G. van Kooten. Macmillan $55 **439.3**
1. Dutch language—Dictionaries   LC 81-11766
First published 1951 in England with title: Cassell's English-Dutch, Dutch-English dictionary. Previous editions were edited by F. P. H. Prick van Wely

"A practical, up-to-date work for the student, business person, or general reader." Sheehy. Guide to Ref Books. 10th edition

439.7   Swedish language

McKay's modern English-Swedish and Swedish-English dictionary. McKay, D. 1954 2v in 1 $12.95   **439.7**

1. Swedish language—Dictionaries
ISBN 0-679-10079-2

Contents: English-Swedish, by Ruben Nöjd; Swedish-English, by Astrid Tornberg and Margareta Angström

The emphasis is on practical modern terminology. Obsolete and uncommon terms are ommitted

439.8   Danish and Norwegian languages

McKay's modern Norwegian-English, English-Norwegian dictionary (Gyldendal's); by H. Scavenius and B. Berulfsen. [5th ed]. McKay, D. 1953? $15.95   **439.8**

1. Norwegian language—Dictionaries
ISBN 0-679-10076-8

First published 1941 under title: Gyldendal's English-Norwegian & Norwegian-English dictionary

A standard work. The Norwegian spelling used is that authorized by law in 1938

443   French language— Dictionaries

Cassell's French dictionary: French-English, English-French; completely revised by Denis Girard with the assistance of Gaston Dulong, Oliver Van Oss, and Charles Guinness. Macmillan 1977 762, 655p $22.95; thumb-indexed $24.95   **443**

1. French language—Dictionaries
ISBN 0-02-522610-X; 0-02-522620-7 (thumb-indexed)
     LC 77-7669

Also available in a concise edition for $12.95 (ISBN 0-02-522670-3)

First published 1920 with title: Cassell's French-English, English-French dictionary. Previous American editions published by Funk & Wagnalls with title: The New Cassell's French dictionary

"New words including colloquialisms, slang, American English and French-Canadian terms [are included]. . . . There are also sections on French verbs and French and English abbreviations. Reliable, standard dictionary. A first choice." N Y Public Libr. Ref Books for Child Collect. 2d edition

The **Concise** Oxford French dictionary; French-English edited by H. Ferrar; English-French edited by J. A. Hutchinson and J.-D. Biard. 2nd ed. Oxford Univ. Press 1980 2v in 1 $32.50; pa $13.95   **443**

1. French language—Dictionaries
ISBN 0-19-864126-5; 0-19-864157-5 (pa)
     LC 80-40695
Previous edition compiled by A. Chevalley published 1940

"The French-English section, the larger portion, provides full definitions and phonetic pronunciations; the English-French section (which uses British spellings) gives only French equivalents. Labels indicate how meaning changes with use and identify vulgar and popular expressions." Nichols. Guide to Ref Books for Sch Media Cent. 4th edition

Harrap's concise French-English dictionary; edited by Patricia Forbes and Muriel Holland Smith. rev, by Helen Knox and Richard Northcott. Harrap; [distributed by] Prentice Hall Press 1989 415, 535p $16.95; pa $12.95   **443**

1. French language—Dictionaries
ISBN 0-13-383035-7; 0-13-383050-0 (pa)
     LC 91-175352

First published 1949 in the United Kingdom
Spine title: Harrap's concise French dictionary
Aims to provide "an up-to-date practical work . . . giving translations of modern English and French vocabulary. Includes scientific and technical terms." Sheehy. Guide to Ref Books. 10th edition. suppl

448   Standard French usage

Berlitz, Charles, 1914-
French step by step. Wynwood Press 1990 302p pa $11.99   **448**

1. French language—Conversations and phrases
ISBN 0-922066-33-7   LC 89-25106

A reissue of the title first published 1979 by Everest House

Aimed at the person with little or no knowledge of the language, this book contains a number of situational conversations with vocabulary. Within each dialogue grammatical points of importance are presented. Sentences used in the conversations are given in three ways: in French, in syllables that facilitate pronunciation and in English. A short English-French dictionary is included

453   Italian language— Dictionaries

Cassell's Italian dictionary; Italian-English, English-Italian; compiled by Piero Rebora with the assistance of Francis M. Guercio and Arthur L. Hayward. Macmillan $19.95; thumb-indexed $23.95   **453**

1. Italian language—Dictionaries

First published 1958 in the United Kingdom with title: Cassell's Italian-English, English-Italian dictionary. Periodically revised. Previous United States editions published by Funk & Wagnalls

"A general dictionary of the Italian language as currently written and spoken." Ref Sources for Small & Medium-sized Libr. 5th edition

458 Standard Italian usage

Berlitz, Charles, 1914-
Italian step by step. Wynwood Press 1990
360p pa $11.99   **458**
1. Italian language—Conversations and phrases
ISBN 0-922066-42-6   LC 90-12128
A reissue of the title first published 1979 by Everest
House
A beginners' guide to Italian with situational conversations containing vocabulary. Grammatical points are presented within each dialogue. A short English-Italian dictionary is appended

463 Spanish language— Dictionaries

The **American** Heritage Larousse Spanish
dictionary;   Spanish/English;
English/Spanish. Houghton Mifflin 1986
xxx, 532, 572p $21.95   **463**
1. Spanish language—Dictionaries
ISBN 0-395-32429-7   LC 86-7202
Also available in a concise edition for $14.45 (ISBN
0-395-43412-2)
Based on The American Heritage Dictionary and the
Pequeño Larousse, this work includes 120,000 words and
phrases representing American English and Latin American Spanish usage

Cassell's Spanish-English, English-Spanish
dictionary. Completely rev and reset ed,
completely rev by Anthony Gooch, Angel
García de Paredes. Macmillan 1978 xxv,
1109p $19.95; thumb-indexed $22.95 **463**
1. Spanish language—Dictionaries
ISBN 0-02-522900-1; 0-02-522910-9 (thumb-indexed)
LC 77-18453
Also available in a concise edition for $13 (ISBN
0-02-522660-6)
First published 1959 in the United Kingdom. First
American edition published 1960 by Funk & Wagnall's
with title: Cassell's Spanish dictionary
This dictionary emphasizes the Spanish of Latin America, and includes both classical and literary Spanish as
well as the language of the modern Spanish-speaking
world

Cuyás, Arturo, 1845-1925
Appleton's new Cuyás English-Spanish and
Spanish-English dictionary; rev and enl by
Lewis E. Brett (part 1) and Helen S. Eaton
(part 2) with the assistance of Walter
Beveraggi-Allende. Revision editor, 5th ed,
Catherine B. Avery. 5th ed rev.
Prentice-Hall 1972 2v in 1 $26.95;
thumb-indexed $28.95   **463**
1. Spanish language—Dictionaries
ISBN 0-13-611749-X; 0-13-611756-2 (thumb indexed)
First published 1903 with title: Appleton's New
English-Spanish and Spanish-English dictionary
"Containing about 130,000 entries, this dictionary
concentrates on meaning equivalents. Pronunciation for
English words. Legible typography. Excludes archaic and

vulgar terms, emphasizing scientific and sociological
changes, technological terms with the current usage illustrated in the examples in context." Ref Sources for
Small & Medium-sized Libr. 5th edition

Smith, Colin
Collins Spanish English, English Spanish
dictionary; by Colin Smith in collaboration
with Diarmuid Bradley [et al.] 3rd ed
unabridged. HarperCollins Pubs. 1993 xxxvii,
775, 908p $27.50   **463**
1. Spanish language—Dictionaries
ISBN 0-06-275504-8   LC 91-36013
First published 1971 in the United Kingdom
"The main body of the book contains up-to-date word
lists that cover main areas of modern life, including
regional usages and slang items. Many illustrative expressions show how particular words are used in context,
and style labels indicate whether a word is literary or
vulgar, formal or informal, and dated or euphemistic.
The value of the dictionary is greatly enhanced by the
'Language in Use' section that concludes the volume. .
. . On the whole, this is a masterpiece of a dictionary
that will be cherished by users on all levels of
proficiency." Am Ref Books Annu, 1993

The **University** of Chicago Spanish
dictionary; compiled by Carlos Castillo &
Otto F. Bond, with the assistance of
Barbara M. García. 4th ed, revised and
enlarged by D. Lincoln Canfield.
University of Chicago Press 1987 475p
$19.95; pa $7.95   **463**
1. Spanish language—Dictionaries
ISBN 0-226-10400-1; 0-226-10402-8 (pa)
LC 86-24886
First published 1948
"A new concise Spanish-English and English-Spanish
dictionary of words and phrases basic to the written and
spoken languages of today, plus a list of 500 Spanish
idioms and sayings with variants and English equivalents." Title page
"The dictionary covers pronunciation, grammar, a
short history of the Spanish language, a Spanish-English
list of five hundred common idioms and proverbs with
dialectal variants, etc. The English-Spanish section
provides similar information on the English language."
Am Ref Books Annu, 1988

468 Standard Spanish usage

Berlitz, Charles, 1914-
Spanish step by step. Wynwood Press
1990 336p pa $11.99   **468**
1. Spanish language—Conversations and phrases
ISBN 0-922066-28-0   LC 89-25104
A reissue of the title first published 1979 by Everest
House
This beginner's guide to Spanish contains situational
conversations which present vocabulary and grammar. A
short English-Spanish dictionary is provided

469.3   Portuguese language—Dictionaries

Taylor, James L.
A Portuguese-English dictionary; revised with corrections and additions by the author and Priscilla Clark Martin. Stanford Univ. Press 1970 c1958 xx, 655p $39.50   **469.3**

1. Portuguese language—Dictionaries
ISBN 0-8047-0480-5

First published 1958

"Contains some 60,000 entries, including Brazilian Portuguese. Planned 'to provide an everyday working tool for as large a number of persons as possible.' Gives not only English equivalents, but often one or more synonyms and, in some cases, examples of usage. Includes many technical and scientific terms, particularly the names of Brazilian fauna and flora." Sheehy. Guide to Ref Books. 10th edition

473   Latin language—Dictionaries

Cassell's Latin dictionary; Latin-English, English-Latin; by D. P. Simpson. Macmillan 1977 c1959 883p thumb-indexed $24.95   **473**

1. Latin language—Dictionaries
ISBN 0-02-522580-4

Also available in a concise edition for $12.95 (ISBN 0-02-522630-4)

First published 1854. This edition first published 1959. Previous United States editions published by Funk & Wagnalls with title: Cassell's New Latin dictionary

"Cassell's incorporates current English idiom and Latin spelling into the traditional presentation of classical Latin. The 30,000 entries include generic terms, geographical and proper nouns. Etymological notes and illustrative quotations are provided within entries." Wynar. Guide to Ref Books for Sch Media Cent. 3d edition

Oxford Latin dictionary; edited by P. G. W. Glare. Oxford Univ. Press 1982 xxiii, 2126p $225   **473**

1. Latin language—Dictionaries
ISBN 0-19-864224-5   LC 82-8162

"Authorized in 1931 and begun two years later, [this dictionary] appeared in eight fascicles published between 1968 and 1982. These have been combined in a single volume." Wilson Libr Bull

This dictionary looks at the meaning and development of more than 40,000 classical Latin words and phrases

483   Classical Greek language—Dictionaries

Liddell, Henry George, 1811-1898
A Greek-English lexicon; compiled by Henry George Liddell and Robert Scott; revised and augmented throughout by Sir Henry Stuart Jones, with the assistance of Roderick McKenzie and with the co-operation of many scholars. With a supplement, 1968. Oxford Univ. Press 1968 2042, 153p $125   **483**

1. Greek language—Dictionaries
ISBN 0-19-864214-8

First edition 1843; this is a reprint of the 9th edition (1925-1940) with a new supplement edited by E. A. Barber and others. The supplement is also available separately for $49.95 (ISBN 0-19-864210-5)

Issued in ten parts. Frequently reprinted. Preliminary leaves include: List of authors and works; Epigraphical publications; Papyrological publications; Periodicals; General list of abbreviations. Addenda and corrigenda

"The standard Greek and English lexicon, covering the language to about 600 A.D., omitting Patristic and Byzantine Greek." Ref Sources for Small & Medium-sized Libr. 5th edition

489   Other Hellenic languages. Modern Greek language

The **Oxford** dictionary of modern Greek; Greek-English and English-Greek; compiled by J. T. Pring. Oxford Univ. Press 1982 370p $35; pa $13.95   **489**

1. Greek language, Modern—Dictionaries
ISBN 0-19-864137-0; 0-19-864148-6 (pa)

"Concise, accurate, inexpensive dictionary. Includes about 20,000 words in modern conversational and written language." Ref Sources for Small & Medium-sized Libr. 5th edition

491.7   East Slavic languages. Russian

The **Oxford** English-Russian dictionary; edited by P. S. Falla. Oxford Univ. Press 1984 1052p $85; flexible binding $29.95; pa $25   **491.7**

1. Russian language—Dictionaries
ISBN 0-19-864117-6; 0-19-864168-0 (flexible binding); 0-19-864192-3 (pa)   LC 83-17344

Companion volume to: The Oxford Russian-English dictionary, by Marcus Wheeler, entered below

This dictionary includes over 90,000 "English words, phrases, and items. The editor has paid special attention to correct translation of colloquial and idiomatic language. His explanatory glosses enable the user to select the appropriate Russian equivalents of English words. He has also included the more important or familiar Americanisms." Am Ref Books Annu, 1985

Wheeler, Marcus

The Oxford Russian-English dictionary; general editor: B. O. Unbegaun with the assistance of D. P. Costello and W. F. Ryan. 2nd ed. Oxford Univ. Press 1984 930p $85; flexible binding $27.50; pa $25
491.7

1. Russian language—Dictionaries
ISBN 0-19-864154-0; 0-19-864167-2 (flexible binding); 0-19-864193-1 (pa)   LC 83-13447
First published 1972

This volume "contains 70,000 entries, including colloquial vocabulary, idioms, and some technical language." Nichols. Guide to Ref Books for Sch Media Cent. 4th edition

491.8 Slavic languages

The **Kosciuszko** Foundation dictionary: English-Polish, Polish-English. Mouton de Gruyter 1959-1961 2v o.p.; Kosciuszko Foundation reprint available ea $27.50
491.8

1. Polish language—Dictionaries
ISBN 0-917004-00-0; 0-917004-16-7

Contents: v1 English-Polish, by K. Bulas and F.J. Whitfield; v2 Polish-English, by K. Bulas, L. L. Thomas and F. J. Whitfield

"The second volume emphasizes 'twentieth century standard Polish'; the first volume includes some English dialect and slang. Examples of usage are given. A substantial bilingual dictionary." Sheehy. Guide to Ref Books. 10th edition

492 Afro-Asiatic languages. Semitic languages

The **Oxford** English-Arabic dictionary of current usage; edited by N. S. Doniach. Oxford Univ. Press 1972 1392p $85
492

1. Arabic language—Dictionaries
ISBN 0-19-864312-8

"Intended both for the English-speaking students of Arabic and the Arabic-speaking students of English. Includes formal literary English, colloquial and slang usage, with the closest Arabic equivalent at the same level of usage." Sheehy. Guide to Ref Books. 10th edition

Wortabet, John, 1827-1908

English-Arabic and Arabic-English dictionary; [by] John Wortabet and Harvey Porter; with a supplement of modern words and new meanings by John L. Mish. Ungar 1954 2v in 1 $60   **492**

1. Arabic language—Dictionaries
ISBN 0-8044-0875-0

Also available in paperback from Hippocrene Bks.

"The reprint of a basic dictionary, with a supplement containing modern words and expressions." Sheehy. Guide to Ref Books. 10th edition

492.4 Hebrew language

Baltsan, Hayim

Webster's New World Hebrew dictionary; Hebrew/English, English/Hebrew. Prentice-Hall 1992 xxx, 827p $35   **492.4**

1. Hebrew language—Dictionaries
ISBN 0-13-944547-1   LC 91-32079

"The work includes two main sequences with a total of 60,000 entries: a Hebrew-English section in which headwords or proper names are Romanized, and an English-Hebrew section in which definitions are given in Roman characters. . . . Besides the guide to the dictionary, there is a 13-page introduction to Hebrew that contains basic information about the alphabet and the structure of the language." Am Ref Books Annu, 1993

493 Non-Semitic Afro-Asiatic languages

Roth, Ann Macy, 1954-

Hieroglyphs without mystery; an introduction to ancient Egyptian writing; translated and adapted for English-speaking readers by Ann Macy Roth. University of Tex. Press 1992 xii, 121p il $35; pa $14.95
493

1. Egyptian language 2. Hieroglyphics
ISBN 0-292-73060-8; 0-292-79804-0 (pa)
                                        LC 91-47600

"Written for ordinary people with no special language skills, the book quickly demonstrates that hieroglyphic writing can be read, once a few simple principles are understood." Univ Press Books for Public and Second Sch Libr

Includes bibliographic references

495.1 Chinese language

The **Basic** English-Chinese, Chinese-English dictionary, using simplified characters; with an appendix containing the original complex characters: transliterated in accordance with the new, official Chinese phonetic alphabet; joint compilers, Teruko Hayashi, Miyuko Hayashi, Yoko Nagano; editor in chief, direction of Peter Bergman. Humanities Press 1980 135p o.p.; New Am. Lib. paperback available $5.95   **495.1**

1. Chinese language—Dictionaries
ISBN 0-451-16826-7 (pa)   LC 79-28325

"A dictionary of 1000 words, arranged in four sections: English to Chinese, Chinese to English, pinyin transliteration, and an appendix of classical or original complex characters. Each word is assigned a number that is then used to identify it in either language throughout the dictionary. Each entry consists of an English or a Chinese definition (English arranged alphabetically, Chinese by number of strokes), and pinyin transliteration." Ref Sources for Small & Medium-sized Libr. 5th edition

Chan, Shau Wing
A concise English-Chinese dictionary; with romanized standard pronunciation; by Shau Wing Chan (Shou-jung Ch'en). 2d ed. Stanford Univ. Press 1955 416p pa $12.95
495.1

1. Chinese language—Dictionaries
ISBN 0-8047-0384-1
First published 1946

Translates from English into Chinese only. Gives written Chinese and tonal equivalents, including neutral tones

Chang, Raymond
Speaking of Chinese; [by] Raymond Chang, Margaret Scrogin Chang. Norton 1978 197p il hardcover o.p. paperback available $8.95
495.1

1. Chinese language
ISBN 0-393-30061-7 (pa)   LC 78-5553

The authors examine written and spoken Chinese from mythical times to the mid-20th century while focusing on political and literary history as well. Sections on calligraphy, proverbs and cooking are included

Includes bibliography

A **New** English-Chinese dictionary; compiled by the Editing Group of A New English-Chinese dictionary. rev & enl ed. University of Wash. Press 1988 1769p $19.95
495.1

1. Chinese language—Dictionaries
ISBN 0-295-96609-2
First published 1975

"The dictionary defines a total of more than 80,000 English words, including derivations and compound words. Entries include pronunciation, part of speech, derivation, usage, knowledge, definition (in Chinese simplified characters), compounds and phrases including the word, and illustrative sentences." Best Ref Books, 1986-1990

495.6 Japanese language

Basic Japanese-English dictionary; [by] the Japan Foundation. Oxford Univ. Press 1989 c1986 958p il pa $17.95
495.6

1. Japanese language—Dictionaries
ISBN 0-19-864162-1   LC 88-30642

"Considered the best of its type, this dictionary is designed for nonnative students of the language. Some 3,000 of the most common words and phrases are arranged on the basis of pronunciation with sentences in Japanese script (*hiragana, katakana, kanji*, and *romanization*) in the left column and English equivalents on the right." Nichols. Guide to Ref Books for Sch Media Cent. 4th edition

The **Kodansha** English-Japanese dictionary. [2d ed]. Kodansha Int./USA 1987 1557p flexible bdg $29.95; pa $28
495.6

1. Japanese language—Dictionaries
ISBN 0-87011-420-4 (flexible bdg); 0-87011-672-X (pa)
First published 1969

A compact dictionary which contains 90,000 entries. Both written and spoken styles are given, and poetic expressions and slang are included

The **Oxford-Duden** pictorial English-Japanese dictionary. Oxford Univ. Press 1983 864p il hardcover o.p. paperback available $19.95
495.6

1. Japanese language—Dictionaries 2. Picture dictionaries
ISBN 0-19-864327-6 (pa)   LC 83-163303

"This topically arranged picture dictionary will be of value chiefly to Japanese speakers engaged in the conversion of English into Japanese (though, with some limitations, thanks to its English and Japanese indexes, it can serve as a regular bilingual dictionary as well). . . . Needless to say, the entries are largely nouns (or nominal phrases). Within the narrow domain of its usability, a fine piece of lexicography." Libr J

495.9 Annam-Muong, Mon-Khmer, Thai (Tai) languages

Lê, Bá-Khanh
Vietnamese-English and English-Vietnamese dictionary. Ungar 1975 2v in 1 o.p. **495.9**

1. Vietnamese language—Dictionaries

Available only in paperback from Hippocrene Bks.

First published 1955 with title: Standard Vietnamese-English dictionary

Contents: v1 Vietnamese-English dictionary, by Lê-Bá-Khanh and Lê-Bá-Kông; v2 English-Vietnamese dictionary, with a supplement of new words: English-Vietnamese, by Lê-Bá-Kông

These two volumes in one, which have separate title pages, give Vietnamese and English equivalents and pronunciation of English words. A list of English synonyms and antonyms is included at the end of the first volume and a supplement of new words is included at the end of the second volume

496 African languages

A **Standard** Swahili-English dictionary; (founded on Madan's Swahili-English dictionary); by the Interterritorial language committee for the East African dependencies under the direction of the late Frederick Johnson. Oxford Univ. Press 1939 $59
496

1. Swahili language—Dictionaries
ISBN 0-19-864403-5

"Origin of word is given in Arabic, Persian, Hindustani, etc. characters. Good layout. Many idioms." Walford. Guide to Ref Mater. 4th edition

497 North American native languages

Boas, Franz, 1858-1942
Introduction to Handbook of American Indian languages [and] Indian linguistic families of America north of Mexico; edited by Preston Holder. University of Neb. Press 1966 221p pa $9.95 **497**
1. Indians of North America—Languages
ISBN 0-8032-5017-7

"A Bison book"

Title on spine: American Indian languages
Handbook of American Indian languages, by Franz Boas; Indian linguistic families of America, north of Mexico, by J. W. Powell

"This volume contains two fundamental contributions to the study of American Indian languages. Although both bear on the problem of the exact nature of North American native language, they are of quite different intent: Franz Boas . . . is concerned with basic linguistic characteristics, while J. W. Powell . . . treats the classification of languages in terms of lexical elements." Preface

Includes bibliographic references

499 Nonaustronesian languages of Oceania, Austronesian languages, miscellaneous languages

Pukui, Mary Kawena, 1895-
Hawaiian dictionary; Hawaiian-English, English-Hawaiian; [by] Mary Kawena Pukui, Samuel H. Elbert. rev & enl ed. University of Hawaii Press 1986 xxvi, 572p $29.95 **499**
1. Hawaiian language—Dictionaries
ISBN 0-8248-0703-0 LC 85-24583
Originally published in two separate parts in 1957 and 1964. First combined edition published 1971

"The Hawaiian-English part comprises about 26,000 entries and is the most comprehensive and up-to-date dictionary for the language. . . . The English-Hawaiian part supplies Hawaiian equivalents for about 12,500 English terms." Sheehy. Guide to Ref Books. 10th edition [review of 1971 edition]

Includes bibliography

500 NATURAL SCIENCES AND MATHEMATICS

The **Almanac** of science and technology; what's new and what's known; prepared by World Information Systems; edited by Richard Golob and Eric Brus. Harcourt Brace & Co. 1990 530p $59.95; pa $29.95 **500**
1. Science 2. Technology
ISBN 0-15-105050-3; 0-15-600050-4 (pa)
LC 89-34650
This book provides a "cross section of key theories, discoveries, and events in astronomy, biology, brain and behavior research, computer and earth sciences, medicine, and physics. Each article is organized in such a way that a generalist can get an idea of the state of the art without a prior knowledge of the field." Libr J

Asimov, Isaac, 1920-1992
Asimov's new guide to science. Basic Bks. 1984 940p il $34.95 **500**
1. Science
ISBN 0-465-00473-3 LC 83-46093
First published 1960 with title: Asimov's Guide to science

"Through chapters on the universe, the solar system, earth, the atmosphere, the elements, particles, waves, machines, and the reactor, the author shows his encyclopedic knowledge of astronomy, geology, physics, and chemistry." Sci Books Films

Includes bibliography

Bronowski, Jacob, 1908-1974
Science and human values; revised edition with a new dialogue, The abacus and the rose. Harper & Row 1965 119p il hardcover o.p. paperback available $9 **500**
1. Science
ISBN 0-06-097281-5 (pa)
Also available in hardcover from P. Smith
First published 1958 by Messner
Contains the following three essays, which were first given as lectures at the Massachusetts Institute of Technology in 1953: The creative mind; The habit of truth; The sense of human dignity. The abacus and the rose was originally broadcast by the BBC Third Programme in 1962
The dialogue "discusses the theme that 'science is as integral a part of the culture of our age as the arts are.'" Sci Am

Bunch, Bryan H.
The Henry Holt handbook of current science and technology; a sourcebook of facts and analysis covering the most important events in science and technology; by Bryan Bunch. Holt & Co. 1992 689p $50 **500**
1. Science 2. Technology
ISBN 0-8050-1829-8 LC 92-6119
"A Henry Holt reference book"
This work contains "articles covering astronomy and space, chemistry, earth science, the environment, life science (excluding medicine), mathematics, physics, and technology." Am Libr
For a fuller review see: Booklist, Dec. 15, 1992
Includes bibliographic references

Dyson, Freeman J., 1923-
From Eros to Gaia; [by] Freeman Dyson. Pantheon Bks. 1992 371p $24.50 **500**
1. Science 2. Physics 3. Astronomy
ISBN 0-679-41307-3 LC 91-50889
"A Cornelia & Michael Bessie book"
"Three dozen essays, including an amazing boyhood composition, explore the whys and hows of scientific pursuits. Dyson examines the 'ecology of science' and how the drive for status all too often overwhelms practicality in the design and economy of important

Dyson, Freeman J., 1923-—*Continued*
projects." Booklist

Includes bibliographic references

Eiseley, Loren C., 1907-1977
The unexpected universe. Harcourt Brace & World 1969 239p hardcover o.p. paperback available $8.95 **500**

1. Natural history 2. Science
ISBN 0-15-692850-7 (pa)

This volume contains personal interpretative meditations on mankind's relationship to nature

Includes bibliography

Flatow, Ira
Rainbows, curve balls and other wonders of the natural world explained; illustrations by Howard Coale. Morrow 1988 240p il $15.95 **500**

1. Science
ISBN 0-688-06705-0 LC 88-2654

Also available in paperback from HarperCollins Pubs.

The author "has chosen everyday situations and looked at the science in them. . . . There are chapters on being at the seaside, in the kitchen, at a concert, in the bathroom, and so on. . . . The material is eclectic, ranging through geophysics, chemistry, toxicology, cosmology, aerodynamics, [and] meteorology." New Sci

Gardner, Martin, 1914-
On the wild side. Prometheus Bks. 1992 257p il $24.95 **500**

1. Science
ISBN 0-87975-713-2 LC 91-43151

"This is a collection of 32 reviews and essays that Gardner has written over the past four or five years. All deal with one aspect or another of pseudoscience. . . . Gardner is a witty and good-humored antidote to the occult, psychic, New Age trash we are inundated with." Sci Books Films

Includes bibliographic references

Hall, Stephen S.
Mapping the next millennium; the discovery of new geographies. Random House 1992 477p il $29.50; pa $16 **500**

1. Science 2. Map drawing
ISBN 0-394-57635-7; 0-679-74175-5 (pa)
LC 91-52667

The author "argues that virtually all modern scientific research can be seen as a process for making maps. Just as the voyages of Columbus and Magellan resulted in new maps of the world, the work of modern scientists produces maps of the brain, of chaotic systems, of the far reaches of the solar system, of the universe itself. Mr. Hall looks at 18 scientific fields and ties them loosely together with this map-making theme." N Y Times Book Rev

Includes bibliographic references

Hazen, Robert M., 1948-
Science matters: achieving scientific literacy; [by] Robert M. Hazen and James Trefil. Doubleday 1991 294p il $19.95; pa $12 **500**

1. Science
ISBN 0-385-24796-6; 0-385-26108-X (pa) LC 90-3786

"This book attempts to acquaint the educated (or miseducated) layperson with the major concepts of modern science. . . . Although many concepts are, perforce, oversimplified, offering the reader only a superficial understanding of some of them, this book is a step in the right direction." Libr J

Includes bibliography

Mysteries of life and the universe; new essays from America's finest writers on science; edited by William H. Shore. Harcourt Brace Jovanovich 1992 317p il $24.95 **500**

1. Science
ISBN 0-15-163972-8 LC 92-15677

"Thirty contributors, including Diane Ackerman (on the Grand Canyon and geologic time), Martin Gardner (on artificial life) and James Trefil (on Neanderthal man) give this amiable collection of personal reflections a pleasantly challenging range. While surely not all of our 'finest' science writers are represented, readers will find essays that spark and satisfy their sense of wonder in this assortment." Publ Wkly

The New York Times book of science literacy; by the editors and reporters of Science times; edited by Richard Flaste. Times Bks. 1991 385p il $24.95 **500**

1. Science
ISBN 0-8129-1880-0 LC 90-50244

Also available in paperback from HarperCollins Pubs.

These "science-related articles which appeared in the *New York Times* 'Science Times' column, cover such topics as coincidences, cocaine, pain control, obsessive-compulsive behavior, night skies, and the solar system. An informative, entertaining choice for larger science collections." Booklist

Perutz, Max F.
Is science necessary? essays on science and scientists. Dutton 1989 285p il o.p.; Oxford Univ. Press paperback available $9.95 **500**

1. Science 2. Scientists
ISBN 0-19-286118-2 (pa) LC 88-20425

This collection of writings about science and scientists consists of "four essays, nine book reviews, one personal reminiscence and a brief newspaper item." N Y Times Book Rev

This is "a readable volume that offers some useful insights into how science is done and what its role in society can and should be." Christ Sci Monit

Includes bibliography

Rensberger, Boyce
How the world works; a guide to science's greatest discoveries. Morrow 1986 378p il hardcover o.p. paperback available $10
500
1. Science
ISBN 0-688-07293-3 (pa)   LC 85-25836
This book lists and summarizes twenty-four "major areas of scientific discovery that Rensberger feels shaped our modern perception of the natural world. . . . Included are an essay on 'What Is Science,' and more than 300 brief articles on scientific concepts and biographies of [scientists]." Sci Books Films
"For an enjoyable and informative look at major science ideas in short essays this is an excellent choice." Choice

Sagan, Carl, 1934-
Broca's brain; reflections on the romance of science. Random House 1979 347p $14.95
500
1. Science 2. Philosophy
ISBN 0-394-50169-1   LC 78-21810
Also available in paperback from Ballantine Bks.
"Sagan considers a variety of themes within the context of contemporary scientific developments, including the quest for extraterrestrial life, popular science, and religious questions, as well as numerous concerns more immediate to his own specialty, astronomy." Libr J
The author "is a lucid, logical writer with a gift for explaining science to the layman and infecting the reader with his own boundless enthusiasm and curiosity." Natl Rev
Includes bibliographic references

Schwartz, Joseph, 1938-
The creative moment; how science made itself alien to modern culture. HarperCollins Pubs. 1992 252p $25
500
1. Science and civilization 2. Technology and civilization 3. Creative ability
ISBN 0-06-016788-2   LC 91-59933
The author "explores the contradiction between science and technology's tremendous impact on our world and most people's ignorance of scientific and technological theories and processes. He assigns much of the blame to science, criticizing both the form of today's science . . . and the ends to which it is applied." Libr J
"Schwartz is a graceful writer and a thoughtful scientist; even unconcerned readers will find themselves brought round the back way to the idea that science is an inherently human activity whose roots in wonder must be reclaimed." Publ Wkly
Includes bibliographic references

Science at the frontier; by Addison Greenwood [et al.] for the National Academy of Sciences. National Acad. Press 1992 277p il $24.95
500
1. Science
ISSN 1065-3082
This first volume of a projected Academy of Sciences series based on national symposia "explores the movement to expand scientific theory and measurement; the relationship between science and government in the search for effective pollution control; the increasing usefulness of computer modeling in science; the search for the secrets of gene transcription; how geologists are probing deep inside the earth as astrophysicists reach to the limits of the observable universe; current developments in magnetic resonance imaging; and more." Publisher's note

Trefil, James S., 1938-
1001 things everyone should know about science; [by] James Trefil. Doubleday 1992 305p il $20
500
1. Science
ISBN 0-385-24795-8   LC 91-2425
Also available in paperback from Simon & Schuster with title: Sharks have no bones: 1001 things you should know about science
"This book is a collection of 1,001 scientific facts and explanations. The lengths of the entries range from about 50 to 500 words, and their significance from the most powerful foundations of modern scientific thinking to whimsical impressions of everyday life. The intelligently selected and clearly presented entries are collected in seven major topics: classical biology, evolution, molecular biology, classical physical science, modern physical science, earth science, and astronomy." Sci Books Films

500.2 Physical sciences

Magill's survey of science, physical science series; edited by Frank N. Magill; consulting editor, Thomas A. Tombrello. Salem Press 1992 6v il set $475   **500.2**
1. Science
ISBN 0-89356-618-7   LC 91-32962
This set includes "380 signed articles, averaging seven pages in length, by 163 academic contributors aimed at the nonspecialist needing an overview of a theory or phenomena. Fields of coverage include physics, mathematics, physical chemistry, computation science, and astronomy/astrophysics." Libr J
Includes bibliographic references

501 Science—Philosophy and theory

Bronowski, Jacob, 1908-1974
The ascent of man. Little, Brown 1974 c1973 448p il hardcover o.p. paperback available $29.95
501
1. Science—Philosophy 2. Science—History 3. Man
ISBN 0-316-10933-9 (pa)
First published 1973 in the United Kingdom, based on the BBC television series
The author "explores the great monuments of human ideas and inventions from the origin of Man to our own day, from primitive tool to relativity." Choice
"This book is a lavishly illustrated paraphrase of the telefilm, resplendent with color photographs that can only be described as a multiple of gorgeous. The text, written with serious contemplation and an amazing perspicacity, reveals the late Dr. Bronowski as a profound and deeply humanistic man concerned with all the activities of man, from the ritual of his society to his curious preoccupation with nature." Sci Books

Medawar, P. B. (Peter Brian), 1915-1987
The limits of science. Harper & Row
1984 108p il o.p.; Oxford Univ. Press
paperback available $9.95   **501**
1. Science—Philosophy
ISBN 0-19-505212-9 (pa)   LC 83-48841
"A Cornelia & Michael Bessie book"
This "book consists of three essays: one on the nature
of science, one titled 'Can Scientific Discovery Be
Premeditated,' and one titled 'The Limits of Science.'"
Choice
This is a "brief, elegantly rational and profoundly
insightful book. . . . Medawar has the rare ability to
speak lucidly to his readers, on an almost personal level,
about technical points that would bog down lesser
authors." Libr J

The threat and the glory; reflections on
science and scientists; [by] Peter Medawar;
edited by David Pyke; forward by Lewis
Thomas. HarperCollins Pubs. 1990 291p
o.p.; Oxford Univ. Press paperback available
$9.95   **501**
1. Science—Philosophy 2. Scientists
ISBN 0-19-286128-X (pa)   LC 89-46107
"A Cornelia & Michael Bessie book"
First published 1959 in the United Kingdom
This is a collection of twenty-three essays, speeches
and book reviews on "genetics, evolution, philosophy,
creativity, scientific fraud, how to survive a stroke, and
attitudes toward death." Publisher's note
"The core [of this book] is a set of six provocative
BBC lectures on 'The Future of Man.' . . . Good reading
about tough subjects for informed lay readers." Libr J
Includes bibliographic references

Prigogine, Ilya
Order out of chaos; man's new dialogue
with nature; by Ilya Prigogine and Isabelle
Stengers; foreword by Alvin Toffler. New
Science Lib. 1984 xxxi, 349p o.p.; Bantam
Bks. paperback available $12.50   **501**
1. Science—Philosophy 2. System theory
ISBN 0-553-34363-7 (pa)   LC 84-8415
Original French edition, 1979
This book is a treatise on the "interactions of scientific problems. . . . Prigogine analyzes the universe as
a set of open fluctuating systems and less frequently
occuring closed systems. Order can appear spontaneously
from chaos, through a process of self-organization. New-
tonian physics, thermodynamics, time, and entropy are
[discussed]." Libr J

Waldrop, M. Mitchell
Complexity: the emerging science at the
edge of order and chaos. Simon & Schuster
1992 380p $23   **501**
1. Science—Philosophy
ISBN 0-671-76789-5   LC 92-28357
"Written not as a rigorous analysis but rather as a
series of intertwining stories, the book chronicles the
trailblazing efforts of a dozen iconoclasts in various disciplines (computer science, physics, economics, biology,
neurology) who came together to establish a daring new
research organization, the Santa Fe Institute. Devoted to
exploring how self-organizing systems develop, this unlikely intellectual community has dissolved traditional

disciplinary boundaries while formulating fruitful new
conceptions of ecology, artificial intelligence, brain function, and fundamental physics. Readers may glimpse a
radical new paradigm aborning." Booklist
Includes bibliography

503 Science—Encyclopedias and dictionaries

Academic Press dictionary of science and
technology; edited by Christopher Morris.
Academic Press 1992 xxxii, 2432p il $115
     503
1. Science—Dictionaries 2. Technology—Dictionaries
ISBN 0-12-200400-0   LC 90-29032
"With over 133,000 entries, this title provides current,
concise definitions of the specialized vocabulary used in
124 designated fields from acoustical engineering to
zoology. . . . This authoritative, attractive dictionary will
be useful to anyone seeking to understand the language
of science and technology." Am Libr
For a fuller review see: Booklist, Jan. 15, 1993

Brennan, Richard P.
Dictionary of scientific literacy. Wiley
1991 334p il (Wiley science editions) $22.95
     503
1. Science—Dictionaries 2. Technology—Dictionaries
ISBN 0-471-53214-2   LC 91-4307
"The terms that are defined are those related to contemporary scientific and technical concepts about which
an intelligent lay audience is likely to be curious. Further, each definition is expressed in nontechnical
language, and most relate the concept to something from
common, everyday experience." Libr J
For a fuller review see: Booklist, Feb. 1, 1992

McGraw-Hill concise encyclopedia of science
& technology; Sybil P. Parker, editor in
chief. 2nd ed. McGraw-Hill 1989 lxxvi,
2222p il $114.50   **503**
1. Science—Dictionaries 2. Technology—Dictionaries
ISBN 0-07-045512-0   LC 88-33275
Also available on CD-ROM as part of McGraw-Hill
science and technical reference set
First published 1984
New edition in preparation
A condensed version of the McGraw-Hill encyclopedia
of science & technology, entered below
"This excellent one-volume science encyclopedia has
been created by extracting 'the essential text from each
article in the parent work while retaining the same
proportionality between subjects.'" Malinowsky. Best Sci
& Technol Ref Books for Young People

McGraw-Hill dictionary of scientific and
technical terms; Sybil P. Parker, editor in
chief. McGraw-Hill il $110.50   **503**
1. Science—Dictionaries 2. Technology—Dictionaries
Also available on CD-ROM as part of McGraw-Hill
science and technical reference set
First published 1974. (4th edition 1989) Periodically
revised
This work "specializes in providing definitions of
scientific and technical terms for the general public as
well as the professional community. . . . The terms

McGraw-Hill dictionary of scientific and technical terms—*Continued*
appear in alphabetical order in boldface type. Each term is followed by a field identifier, a definition, and a pronunciation. . . . The definitions are written clearly and concisely." Topical Ref Books

McGraw-Hill encyclopedia of science & technology; an international reference work in twenty volumes including an index. McGraw-Hill 20v set $1900 **503**
1. Science—Dictionaries 2. Technology—Dictionaries
Also available on CD-ROM
First published 1960 in fifteen volumes. (7th edition 1992) Periodically revised
This work provides "ready-reference information in all areas of modern science and technology. . . . The entries are broad survey articles written for the nonspecialist by an authority in the field." Topical Ref Books
Supplemented by: McGraw-Hill yearbook of science & technology

Van Nostrand's scientific encyclopedia. Van Nostrand Reinhold 2v $195 **503**
1. Science—Dictionaries 2. Technology—Dictionaries
First published 1938. (7th edition, 1989) Frequently revised
"Animal life; biosciences; chemistry; earth and atmospheric sciences; energy source and power technology; mathematics and information sciences; materials and engineering sciences, medicine, anatomy, and physiology; physics; plant science; space and planetary sciences." Subtitle
"This work is an invaluable source of concise, ready-reference information." Topical Ref Books

505 Science—Serial publications

General science index. Wilson, H.W. service basis **505**
1. Science—Periodicals—Indexes
ISSN 0162-1963
Also available on CD-ROM
First published July 1978. Monthly, except June and December, with quarterly and bound annual cumulations
"This index has proven its usefulness through its selective, quality indexing. . . . Its accessible subject headings, extremely broad coverage, and identification of articles on current topics in widely owned periodicals are helpful for high school and college students and public library patrons alike." Ref Sources for Small & Medium-sized Libr. 5th edition

508 Natural history

Attenborough, David, 1926-
The first Eden; the Mediterranean world and man. Little, Brown 1987 240p il maps $24.95 **508**
1. Natural history—Mediterranean region
2. Civilization, Mediterranean
ISBN 0-316-05750-9 LC 87-22801
The author "popularizes the natural and human history of the Mediterranean Sea and its surrounding environs. Arranged in four parts, the text traces the formation and evolution of the sea, humanity's relationship with the flora and fauna of the region, the environmental impact of centuries of war and migration, and the devastating ecological consequences of our disruption and disregard of the natural rhythms and patterns of the area." Booklist
Includes bibliography

Caras, Roger A.
Roger Caras' treasury of classic nature tales; [by] Roger Caras. Dutton 1992 509p $25 **508**
1. Natural history
ISBN 0-525-93422-7 LC 92-52887
"Truman Talley books"
In this volume Caras "offers a diverting mix of prose about flora and fauna, from Edward Abbey to Ann Zwinger. Stephen Jay Gould discourses on the Irish elk, Thomas Bledsoe on the Alaskan brown bear, G. Murray Levick on penguins, Sally Carrighar on whales and Caras himself on hummingbird migration. We also find pieces by John Muir, Mark Twain, Mary Austin, Rachel Carson, Ernest Thompson Seton, Loren Eisley and Joseph Wood Krutsch. The collection covers a wide range of subjects richly and vividly; it is well-termed a 'treasury.'" Publ Wkly

Cousteau, Jacques Yves
Jacques Cousteau's Amazon journey; by Jacques-Yves Cousteau and Mose Richards. Abrams 1984 235p il $45 **508**
1. Natural history—South America 2. Amazon River
ISBN 0-8109-1813-7 LC 83-15374
"This book covers the entire Amazon basin from the mountains of Peru to the delta on the Atlantic. Cousteau traverses it using boats, airplanes, helicopters, and even a hydrofoil, in addition to various land modes of transportation." Libr J
Richards' "narrative combines with Cousteau's personal journal for an exciting story of travel and adventure. . . . With stunning photographs, this is fine fare for any armchair traveler." Publ Wkly
Includes bibliography

Darwin, Charles, 1809-1882
The voyage of the Beagle **508**
1. Beagle Expedition (1831-1836) 2. Natural history
3. South America—Description
Available in hardcover and paperback from various publishers
First published 1839 with title: Journal of researches into the geology and natural history of the various countries visited by H.M.S. Beagle
This journal records the author's five year voyage around the world as naturalist aboard H.M.S. Beagle. The trip was influential in the formulation of Darwin's theories of evolution. During the journey he collected data on wildlife, geological formations, weather, and local customs

Durrell, Gerald Malcolm, 1925-
The amateur naturalist; [by] Gerald Durrell with Lee Durrell. Knopf 1983 320p il o.p.; McKay, D. paperback available $25 **508**
1. Nature study
ISBN 0-679-72837-6 (pa) LC 83-47940

Durrell, Gerald Malcolm, 1925——*Continued*
This guide describes field observation and experiments in a variety of natural habitats, beginning with the backyard and moving on to meadows, woodlands, marshlands, the seashore, and other environments
Includes bibliography

Gould, Stephen Jay, 1941-
Bully for brontosaurus; reflections in natural history. Norton 1991 540p il $22.95; pa $10.95   **508**
1. Natural history 2. Evolution
ISBN 0-393-02961-1; 0-393-30857-X (pa) LC 91-6916
"Most of the essays in this volume, some with added postscripts and notes, were selected from [the author's] column in *Natural History* magazine (1985-1990). . . . These pithy essays focus on evolution and the workings of science." Libr J

The flamingo's smile; reflections in natural history. Norton 1985 476p il hardcover o.p. paperback available $10.95   **508**
1. Natural history
ISBN 0-393-30375-6 (pa)   LC 85-4916
In this collection "the theme is history, both natural and human. . . . The essays are marked by Gould's usual careful scholarship and erudition and clear and nontechnical language." Sci Books Films
Includes bibliography

Leopold, Aldo, 1886-1948
A Sand County almanac; and sketches here and there; illustrated by Charles W. Schwartz; introduction by Robert Finch. Oxford Univ. Press 1987 c1949 xxviii, 228p il $25; pa $8.95   **508**
1. Natural history—United States 2. Nature conservation
ISBN 0-19-505305-2; 0-19-505928-X (pa)
     LC 87-22015
Also available Companion to Sand County almanac (1987)
A reissue of the title first published 1949
The essays in the first section of the book record natural changes observed by the author on his Wisconsin farm during the course of a year. In the other two sections are personal experiences ranging over a wide expanse of country and forty years in time
This "collection of poetic vignettes about run-down farmland and wilderness trips, seasoned with erudite historical reflections . . . has added a significant ethical concept to the prophecies of Thoreau, John Muir and other voices in the wilderness." N Y Times Book Rev

Lincoln, Roger J.
The Cambridge illustrated dictionary of natural history; [by] R. J. Lincoln and G. A. Boxshall; illustrations by Roberta Smith. Cambridge Univ. Press 1987 413p il $34.95; pa $17.95   **508**
1. Natural history—Dictionaries
ISBN 0-521-30551-9; 0-521-39941-6 (pa) LC 87-8018
This "is principally a dictionary of taxonomic groups down to the level of family, with common names cross-referenced to Latin ones, and frequent illustrations. Technical terms are few, and paleontology is given less atten-

tion than current classes of plants, animals, and microorganisms." Recomm Ref Books in Paperback. 2d edition

Matthiessen, Peter
Shadows of Africa; [by] Peter Matthiessen; Mary Frank. Abrams 1992 120p il $34.95
     508
1. Natural history—Africa 2. Wildlife conservation
ISBN 0-8109-3828-6   LC 92-5246
"Essays about Africa, some of them drawn from Matthiessen's previous books, are combined with Frank's 71 evocative portrayals of wildlife. Matthiessen's work, written between 1961 and 1986, covers trips from South Sudan to Zaire; his eye is keen, his knowledge deep, his prose sparkling." Publ Wkly
Includes bibliographic references

Moorehead, Alan, 1910-1983
Darwin and the Beagle. Harper & Row 1969 280p il maps o.p.; Penguin Bks. paperback available $14.95   **508**
1. Darwin, Charles, 1809-1882 2. Beagle Expedition (1831-1836) 3. Natural history—South America
ISBN 0-14-003327-0 (pa)
In this account of the Beagle Expedition, the author describes the countries and areas visited by Darwin, as well as the animals, plants and minerals which Darwin studied. Finally, he discusses Darwin's conclusions about his scientific observation

Nelson, Richard K.
The island within; [by] Richard Nelson. North Point Press 1989 284p $18.95   **508**
1. Natural history—Alaska
ISBN 0-86547-404-4   LC 89-16196
Also available in paperback from Vintage Bks.
In this tale of the author's "trips to an uninhabited island in the Haida Strait, we see him adopting the attitudes and seasonal rituals of the native people. This is a totally enthralling adventure, whether the author is observing animals in land or at sea." Booklist
Includes bibliography

The **Norton** book of nature writing; edited by Robert Finch and John Elder. Norton 1990 921p $29.95   **508**
1. Natural history
ISBN 0-393-02799-6   LC 89-35531
"Nature writers such as Darwin, Emerson, Thoreau, Melville, Audubon, and Muir have captured the essence of wilderness and beast. This anthology draws upon the works of these and 83 other authors, spanning two centuries of English and American literature to provide a concise introduction to this literary form." Libr J
Includes bibliography

The **Oxford** dictionary of natural history; edited by Michael Allaby; foreword by David Attenborough. Oxford Univ. Press 1985 688p $49.95   **508**
1. Natural history—Dictionaries
ISBN 0-19-217720-6   LC 85-13758
This dictionary contains "definitions for the earth and atmospheric sciences, botany, geology, and zoology. Entries are arranged by scientific term with cross-references

The Oxford dictionary of natural history—
Continued

from common names. Public and academic collections will find Allaby's work particularly useful for students, amateur naturalists, and scholars working outside their discipline." Am Libr

Quammen, David, 1948-
The flight of the iguana; a sidelong view of science and nature. Delacorte Press 1988 302p il $17.95; pa $9.50   **508**

1. Natural history
ISBN 0-385-29592-8; 0-385-26327-9 (pa)
          LC 87-30578

This is a collection of twenty-nine natural history essays first published in Outside magazine
"The author instills a sense of fascination and concern for the natural world, both familiar and exotic, and he does so without being preachy or pedantic. . . . The writing flows well, and the concepts discussed are easily understood." Sci Books Films

Includes bibliography

Sparks, John
Realms of the Russian bear; a natural history of Russia and the Central Asian Republics. Little, Brown 1992 288p il map $29.95   **508**

1. Natural history—Russia 2. Natural history—Central Asia
ISBN 0-316-80494-0   LC 92-24368

This companion to the PBS television series is an illustrated introduction to the animals, plants, and ecosystems of Russia and Central Asia including the Volga Delta, the Ural mountains, the Steppes, the Arctic, Siberia and the Russian Far East

Includes bibliography

The Way nature works. Macmillan 1992 359p il maps $35   **508**

1. Natural history 2. Science
ISBN 0-02-508110-1   LC 92-12283

"By presenting information in a series of two-page spreads made up of short essays and diagrams with lengthy captions, the editors of this nature encyclopedia intend to give nonspecialists a basic overview of earth systems, animal behavior, and plant ecology." Libr J
For a fuller review see: Booklist, Feb. 15, 1993

509   Science—Historical and geographic treatment

Asimov, Isaac, 1920-1992
Asimov's chronology of science and discovery. Harper & Row 1989 707p il $29.95   **509**

1. Science—History 2. Inventions—History
ISBN 0-06-015612-0   LC 89-45024

"Along with accurate accessible information on landmark scientific events, the author has placed these achievements in the context of concurrent social, political, and cultural events. . . . Also included is a quick reference timetable of over 4,000 years of discovery and an excellent index." Am Libr

Ferris, Timothy
Coming of age in the Milky Way. Morrow 1988 495p il $19.95   **509**

1. Science—History 2. Universe
ISBN 0-688-05889-2   LC 88-5153

Also available in paperback from Doubleday
Developments in astronomy, physics and geology are featured in this overview of scientific endeavor

Includes bibliography

Gornick, Vivian
Women in science; portraits from a world in transition. Simon & Schuster 1983 172p hardcover o.p. paperback available $8.95   **509**

1. Women scientists
ISBN 0-671-69592-4 (pa)   LC 83-4742

Paperback edition has subtitle: 100 journeys into the territory
This "is a 'group portrait' of women as scientists and their vicissitudes in this male-dominated field. Gornick, who spent a year talking with more than 100 women . . . relates their accounts of the difficulties that beset them." Publ Wkly

Includes bibliography

Great events from history II, Science and technology; edited by Frank N. Magill. Salem Press 1991 5v set $375   **509**

1. Science—History 2. Technology—History
ISBN 0-89356-637-3   LC 91-23313

Contents: v1, 1888-1910; v2, 1910-1931; v3, 1931-1952; v4, 1952-1969; v5, 1969-1991

These volumes cover the major events in the history of science and technology from 1888 through 1991 in 458 chronologically arranged articles
"The articles in the set are well written and most are accessible to the general reader. Although many of the discoveries can be found in other sources, the set provides a clear description of each event and places it in its proper historical context." Booklist

Harré, Rom, 1927-
Great scientific experiments; twenty experiments that changed our view of the world. Oxford Univ. Press 1983 c1981 216p il $27.95; pa $9.95   **509**

1. Science—Experiments 2. Science—History 3. Scientists
ISBN 0-19-520436-0; 0-19-286036-4 (pa)
          LC 82-19035

First published 1981 in the United Kingdom by Phaidon
"Aristotle's study of the embryology of the chick, Pasteur's preparation of artificial vaccines, Jacob and Wollman's discoveries about genetics—these are among the twenty case histories that [are presented in this book]." Publisher's note

Includes bibliography

Hellemans, Alexander, 1946-

The timetables of science; a chronology of the most important people and events in the history of science; [by] Alexander Hellemans and Bryan Bunch. Simon & Schuster 1988 656p o.p. paperback available $19.95   **509**

1. Science—History
ISBN 0-671-73328-1 (pa)   LC 88-23920

"Contains over 10,000 entries organized chronologically and by discipline, interspersed with more than 100 short essays on science and technology and nine overviews of the main periods of scientific history. Indexed by subject and name." N Y Public Libr Book of How & Where to Look It Up

Lindberg, David C.

The beginnings of Western science; the European scientific tradition in philosophical, religious, and institutional context, 600 B.C. to A.D. 1450. University of Chicago Press 1992 455p il maps $57; pa $19.95   **509**

1. Science—History
ISBN 0-226-48230-8; 0-226-48231-6 (pa)
LC 91-37741

Lindberg "chronicles the development of scientific ideas, practices, and institutions from pre-Socratic Greek philosophy to late-medieval scholasticism. . . . [Coverage includes] developments in mathematics, astronomy, mechanics, optics, alchemy, natural history, and medicine." Publisher's note

"Written with commendable thoroughness and erudition." Choice

Includes bibliographic references

Science: a history of discovery in the twentieth century; [edited by] Trevor I. Williams. Oxford Univ. Press 1990 256p il $40   **509**

1. Science—History 2. Technology—History
ISBN 0-19-520843-9   LC 90-39705
"An Equinox book"

This survey of science and technology in the twentieth century relates advances in aeronautics, transportation, physics, medicine, and agriculture, and includes brief biographies of prominent scientists

Includes bibliographic references

510 Mathematics

Barrow, John D., 1952-

Pi in the sky; counting, thinking, and being. Clarendon Press 1992 317p il $25
510

1. Mathematics
ISBN 0-19-853956-8   LC 92-20217
Also available in paperback from Back Bay Bks.

"This broad history of—and reflection upon—the role of mathematics in the human enterprise of figuring reality spans recorded civilization." Publ Wkly

"Rich in philosophical insights and literary allusions, this remarkable study will stimulate and challenge serious readers." Booklist

Includes bibliographic references

Boyer, Carl B. (Carl Benjamin), 1906-

A history of mathematics; revised by Uta C. Merzbach. 2nd ed. Wiley 1989 762p il $59.95; pa $24.95   **510**

1. Mathematics
ISBN 0-471-09763-2; 0-471-54397-7 (pa)   LC 89-5325
First published 1969

"This good general history of mathematics is understandable to the student as well as authoritative for the mathematician." Malinowsky. Best Sci & Technol Ref Books for Young People

Includes bibliographies

Burington, Richard Stevens

Handbook of mathematical tables and formulas. 5th ed. McGraw-Hill 1973 500p $41.03   **510**

1. Mathematics—Tables
ISBN 0-07-009015-7
First published 1933 by Handbook Pubs.

This handbook "is designed for use by students and workers in mathematics, engineering, physics, chemistry, and other fields. The first part includes a summary of the more important formulas and theorems. . . . Part 2 consists of tables." Wynar. Guide to Ref Books for Sch Media Cent. 3d edition

CRC standard mathematical tables and formulae. CRC Press $39.95   **510**

1. Mathematics—Tables
First published 1929 with title: Math tables from the Handbook of Chemistry and Physics. (29th edition, 1991) Periodically revised

"This standard mathematical handbook contains both textual and tabular material. The contents include constants and conversion factors; algebra; combinatorial analysis; geometry; trigonometry; logarithmic, exponential, and hyberbolic functions; analytical geometry; calculus; differential equations; special functions; numerical methods; probability and statistics; and financial tables." Malinowsky. Best Sci & Technol Ref Books for Young People

Dunham, William, 1947-

Journey through genius; the great theorems of mathematics. Wiley 1990 300p il (Wiley science editions) $22.95   **510**

1. Mathematics 2. Mathematicians
ISBN 0-471-50030-5   LC 89-27366
Also available in paperback from Penguin Bks.

This book explains twelve important mathematical theorems as proved by nine mathematicians: Hippocrates, Euclid, Archimedes, Heron, Cardano, Newton, Johann Bernoulli, Euler, and Cantor. Historical background and brief biographies are included

"The book is remarkably easy to read. Careful step-by-step proofs are given for these important theorems. The mathematical background needed for the proofs is, with two exceptions, high school algebra and geometry. The book is appropriately illustrated." Sci Books Films

Includes bibliographic references

McLeish, John
Number. Fawcett Columbine 1992 266p
il $19.50   **510**
1. Mathematics
ISBN 0-449-90693-0   LC 91-58331
This "focuses on the cultural history of number systems. . . . The author goes on to explain clearly a
variety of numerical procedures, from reckoning Mayan
calendars to calculating logarithms." N Y Times Book
Rev

Includes bibliographic references

Paulos, John Allen
Beyond numeracy; ruminations of a
numbers man. Knopf 1991 285p il $21.50;
pa $12   **510**
1. Mathematics
ISBN 0-394-58640-9; 0-679-73807-X (pa)
                                      LC 90-44999
These seventy short essays "range from summaries of
whole disciplines (calculus, trigonometry, topology) to
biographical and historical asides (Gödel, Pythagoras,
non-Euclidean geometry) to bits of mathematical or
quasi-mathematical folklore (infinite sets, Platonic solids,
QED)." Introduction
"This well-written and easy-to-follow book gently
guides readers through many interesting mathematical
topics." SLJ

Includes bibliography

Innumeracy; mathematical illiteracy and its
consequences. Hill & Wang 1989 135p
$16.95   **510**
1. Mathematics
ISBN 0-8090-7447-8   LC 88-17001
Also available in paperback from Random House
The author contends that "innumeracy, an inability
to deal comfortably with the fundamental notions of
number and chance, plagues far too many otherwise
knowledgeable citizens." Introduction
Paulos presents "his concepts entirely in words. Such
hitherto abstruse topics as conditional probability, or
permutations and combinations, are treated in a brief,
entertaining, and comprehensible way without use of a
single equation." Christ Sci Monit

Peterson, Ivars
Islands of truth; a mathematical mystery
cruise. Freeman, W.H. 1990 325p il maps
$19.95; pa $12.95   **510**
1. Mathematics
ISBN 0-7167-2113-9; 0-7167-2148-1 (pa)
                                      LC 89-49501
This explores modern mathematics in the form of an
imaginary journey and covers such topics as minimal
surfaces, topological knots, tilings, fractal geometry, number theory, optimization algorithms, chaos theory, and
mathematical truth

Includes bibliographies

The mathematical tourist; snapshots of
modern mathematics. Freeman, W.H. 1988
240p il $17.95; pa $12.95   **510**
1. Mathematics
ISBN 0-7167-1953-3; 0-7167-2064-7 (pa)
                                      LC 87-33078

"Explanations of terms on the cutting edge in
mathematical research are accompanied here by practical
applications or arresting thoughts. . . . Peterson's writing
and use of terms to describe these complex topics is
clear, and the text is accompanied by numerous examples, diagrams, and color plates." Sci Books Films

Includes bibliography

Sperling, Abraham Paul, 1912-
Mathematics made simple; [by] Abraham
Sperling and Monroe Stuart; edited and
prepared for publication by the Stonesong
Press, Inc. 5th ed, rev. by Christine M.
Peckaitis. Doubleday 1991 272p il pa $12
                                             510
1. Mathematics
ISBN 0-385-26584-0   LC 89-49249
"A Made simple book"
First published 1943 by Kenmore Pub. Co.
"This book serves as a review of arithmetic, and an
introduction to algebra, geometry, and trigonometry.
Combinations and permutations are covered . . . in the
Probability chapter. The exercises and answers in this
book provide readers with opportunities to test their
mastery of each step in these common branches of math-
ematics." Introduction

Tobias, Sheila
Overcoming math anxiety. Norton 1978
278p il $16.95   **510**
1. Mathematics
ISBN 0-393-06439-5   LC 78-17583
"The author concentrates on some common
misconceptions about fractions, decimals, and other
aspects of everyday math; difficulties with spatial
visualization; word problems; and basic algebraic and
statistical concepts. Tobias writes from the non-
mathematician's point of view, and her 'you-can-do-it-too'
approach is supportive and convincing." SLJ

Includes bibliographic references

The **World** of mathematics; a small library
of the literature of mathematics from
A'h-mosé the scribe to Albert Einstein;
presented with commentaries and notes by
James R. Newman. Microsoft Press 1988
4v il set $99.95; pa set $50   **510**
1. Mathematics
ISBN 1-55615-149-7; 1-55615-148-9 (pa)
                                      LC 88-20040
"A Tempus book"
A reissue of the title first published 1956 by Simon
& Schuster
"The anthology covers the history of mathematics,
pure mathematics, a variety of applications and many
articles of incidental mathematical interest." N Y Times
Book Rev

Includes bibliographies

510.3 Mathematics— Encyclopedias and dictionaries

Mathematics dictionary; [by Robert C.] James [and Glenn] James; contributors, Armen A. Alchian [et al.] 5th ed. Van Nostrand Reinhold 1992 548p il $42.95; pa $29.95   **510.3**

1. Mathematics—Dictionaries
ISBN 0-442-00741-8; 0-442-01241-1 (pa)   LC 92-6757
First published 1942 by Digest Press

"Gives definitions of terms and phrases in the various fields of pure and applied mathematics. Includes tables, formulas, mathematical symbols, and vocabularies giving English equivalents of mathematical terms in French, German, Russian, and Spanish." Sheehy. Guide to Ref Books. 10th edition

510.7 Mathematics—Education and related topics

Kaye, Peggy, 1948-
Games for math; playful ways to help your child learn math from kindergarten to third grade; written by Peggy Kaye; with illustrations by the author. Pantheon Bks. 1987 236p il hardcover o.p. paperback available $13   **510.7**

1. Mathematics—Study and teaching 2. Mathematical recreations
ISBN 0-394-75510-3 (pa)   LC 87-45221

This book includes over 60 games for children from kindergarten to third grade intended to improve their math skills

Ruedy, Elisabeth
Where do I put the decimal point? how to conquer math anxiety and increase your facility with numbers; [by] Elisabeth Ruedy and Sue Nirenberg. Holt & Co. 1990 227p il $19.95   **510.7**

1. Mathematics—Study and teaching
ISBN 0-8050-1145-5   LC 89-48728
Also available in paperback from Avon Bks.

This book uses various strategies and quizzes to help the reader conquer math anxiety. Such topics as computing per cents, converting currencies and balancing checkbooks are included

Includes bibliography

512 Algebra and number theory

Reid, Constance
From zero to infinity; what makes numbers interesting. 4th ed. Mathematical Assn. of Am. 1992 186p pa $19   **512**

1. Number theory
ISBN 0-88385-505-4
First published 1955 by Crowell

"This book covers selected topics in number theory. Partly expository, it nonetheless challenges the reader's mind in clever and nonthreatening ways." Sci Books Films

513 Arithmetic

Kogelman, Stanley
The only math book you'll ever need; [by] Stanley Kogelman and Barbara R. Heller. Facts on File 1986 268p il $19.95   **513**

1. Arithmetic 2. Mathematics
ISBN 0-87196-846-0   LC 86-2157
Also available in paperback from Dell

Step-by-step operations are reviewed by presenting problems encountered on a daily basis, such as tipping in restaurants, buying paint, or converting dollars into foreign currency

514 Topology

McGuire, Michael
An eye for fractals; a graphic & photographic essay. Addison-Wesley 1991 165p il $29.95   **514**

1. Fractals
ISBN 0-201-55440-2   LC 90-47632

In text and photographs the author examines the characteristics of fractals and demonstrates how the beauty of nature can be expressed mathematically

"McGuire has produced a book to delight the eye and the mind. An accomplished photographer in the style of Ansel Adams—as attested by the more than 90 black-and-white nature studies in this book—McGuire is, by profession, a scientist. The text is a clear presentation of the fundamental concepts of fractals." Choice

Includes bibliography

520 Astronomy and allied sciences

Asimov, Isaac, 1920-1992
Isaac Asimov's guide to earth & space. Random House 1991 285p il $19.50   **520**

1. Astronomy 2. Earth
ISBN 0-679-40437-6   LC 91-11097
Also available in paperback from Fawcett Bks.

Written as if "Asimov were chatting with an interesting but unsophisticated companion, this guide covers a wide range: ancient history; new discoveries; specific properties of the sun, moon, stars and Earth; as well as general information about the universe." Voice Youth Advocates

Calvin, William H., 1939-
How the Shaman stole the moon; in search of ancient prophet-scientists: from Stonehenge to the Grand Canyon; with illustrations by Malcolm Wells and photographs by the author. Bantam Bks. 1991 223p il maps $21.50; pa $13   **520**
1. Astronomy—History 2. Eclipses, Lunar 3. Eclipses, Solar
ISBN 0-553-07740-6; 0-553-37082-0 (pa)
LC 91-13528
This "book is a foray into archeoastronomy, the study of prehistoric humankind's preoccupation with sun, moon and stars. 'How the Shaman Stole the Moon' sets forth the methods by which ancient sky watchers might have learned to predict eclipses (with occasional success) and how shamans and priests, armed with such knowledge, might have enhanced their status among prescientific people eager for miracles." N Y Times Book Rev
Includes bibliographic references

Goldsmith, Donald
The astronomers. St. Martin's Press 1991 332p il $24.95; pa $14.95   **520**
1. Astronomy 2. Astronomers
ISBN 0-312-05380-0; 0-312-09245-8 (pa)
LC 90-49205
"This book explores some of the major areas of contemporary astronomy. Although there are numerous, brief biographical sketches of individual scientists, the emphasis is chiefly and properly on their works. . . . Color photographs make this book visually spectacular." Libr J
Includes bibliographic references

Harrison, Edward Robert
Darkness at night; a riddle of the universe; [by] Edward Harrison. Harvard Univ. Press 1987 293p il $29.95; pa $12.95   **520**
1. Astronomy—History 2. Universe 3. Astrophysics
ISBN 0-674-19270-2; 0-674-19271-0 (pa)
LC 86-32701
Following a history of cosmology the author attempts to answer Olber's paradox: how can the sky be dark if there are an infinite number of stars?
The author "has done an excellent job. Much of the book centers around the people involved in trying to understand the puzzle, and because of this it is quite easy to read. Contributions of such scientists as Edmond Halley, W. Herschel, W. de Sitter, S. L. Jaki, and H. Bondi are discussed. Four appendixes, a long section of 'notes,' and an extensive bibliography are included." Choice

Moore, Patrick
The amateur astronomer. Norton il $35   **520**
1. Astronomy
First published 1957. (11th edition, 1990) Periodically revised
This guide for beginning and advanced astronomers describes types of telescopes and how to use them, planets, comets, stars, meteors, eclipses, and galaxies which can be seen through them

The **New** astronomy; by the editors of Time-Life Books. Time-Life Bks. 1992 144p il (Voyage through the universe) $19.93   **520**
1. Astronomy
LC 91-46214
This work describes the latest instruments used by astronomers including radio and infrared waves, visible and ultraviolet light, x-rays, and electro-magnetic radiation
Includes bibliography

Ronan, Colin A.
The natural history of the universe; from the big bang to the end of time. Macmillan 1991 212p il maps $39.95   **520**
1. Astronomy 2. Universe
ISBN 0-02-604511-7
LC 91-17063
"A Marshall edition"
This "volume discusses the origin of the universe and basic theories such as quantum mechanics and relativity; the solar system and what's known about pulsars and quasars, and galaxies and stars; and current theories about the future of the cosmos." Booklist
"Imaginatively organized and lavishly illustrated, this book spans such an enormous breadth of topics that it is really a miniature encyclopedia of astrophysics. Above all, Ronan has mastered the enormously difficult art of writing in down-to-earth language about the most esoteric features of our universe." Sci Books Films

Sagan, Carl, 1934-
Cosmos. Random House 1980 365p il $34.95; pa $30   **520**
1. Astronomy 2. Universe
ISBN 0-394-50294-9; 0-394-71596-9 (pa) LC 80-5286
Also available in paperback from Ballantine Bks.
Based on the author's television series of the same name, this volume covers "the 10- to 20-billion-year history of the universe, from the big bang and subsequent evolution of molecular material through the evolution of human culture." Libr J
Includes bibliography

The **Skywatcher's** handbook; night and day, what to look for in the heavens above; consultant editor Colin A. Ronan. Crown 1985 224p il hardcover o.p. paperback available $13.95   **520**
1. Astronomy
ISBN 0-517-57326-1 (pa)
LC 85-3810
Written primarily as a guide for sky observers, this helpful manual discusses cloud formation, stars, planets, precipitation, and mirages, as well as providing advice for amateur sky photographers and telescope users

520.3 Astronomy—Encyclopedias and dictionaries

Moore, Dianne F.
The HarperCollins dictionary of astronomy and space science. HarperCollins Pubs. 1992 338p il $25; pa $13   **520.3**

1. Astronomy—Dictionaries 2. Space sciences—Dictionaries
ISBN 0-06-271542-9; 0-06-461023-3 (pa)
   LC 91-55394

Spine title: Astronomy & space science

"This book covers astronomy and space science literally, from Abenezra (a lunar crater on the near side of the moon) to Zurich number (a measure of relative sunspot activity). As a dictionary, it is surprisingly readable and, for its compactness, remarkably complete. It gives concise, accessible explanations and descriptions of more than 2,300 terms, proper names, and abbreviations used in space science, including NASA terminology." Sci Books Films

521 Celestial mechanics

Zee, A. (Anthony)
An old man's toy; gravity at work and play in Einstein's universe. Macmillan 1989 xxxii, 272p il hardcover o.p. paperback available $9.95   **521**

1. Gravitation 2. Universe
ISBN 0-02-040915-X (pa)
   LC 88-19013

"This book tells of the role of gravity in the formation and evolution of the universe, and also in the beginnings and growth of physics. There are many intriguing biographical sketches of some of the more colorful figures in the history of physics. . . . This is popular science writing at its best." Sci Books Films

Includes bibliography

522 Techniques, equipment, materials of astronomy

Dickinson, Terence
The backyard astronomer's guide; all astronomical photographs by amateur astronomers; [by] Terence Dickson & Alan Dyer. Camden House (Camden East) 1991 295p il $39.95   **522**

1. Astronomy
ISBN 0-921820-11-9

"The authors survey astronomy from the hobbyist's viewpoint, acknowledging some of the most active amateurs and their accomplishments and encouraging readers to contribute to knowledge of the heavens. The book's three parts, respectively on optical equipment, observing techniques, and astrophotography, are full of specifics on their subjects. Equipment reviews are detailed; techniques covered include naked-eye, binocular, and telescope observation; and photography is suggested for a range of camera equipment and film capabilities." Booklist

523 Specific celestial bodies and phenomena

The **Cambridge** atlas of astronomy; edited by Jean Audouze and Guy Israël. 2nd ed. Cambridge Univ. Press 1988 431p il $100   **523**

1. Astronomy
ISBN 0-521-36360-8   LC 84-73453
First published 1985

This resource contains major sections on: the sun, the solar system, the stars and galaxy, the extra-galactic domain, and the scientific perspective (e.g. cosmology, astronomy). Over 700 photographs accompany texts contributed by forty-four astronomers

Chartrand, Mark R.
The Audubon Society field guide to the night sky; astronomical charts by Wil Tirion. Knopf 1991 714p il maps $17.50   **523**

1. Astronomy
ISBN 0-679-40852-5   LC 91-52708

"A Chanticleer Press edition. The Audubon Society field guide series"

"This is a comprehensive guide to the night sky useful for students and amateur astronomers." Voice Youth Advocates

Includes bibliography

Cosmic mysteries; by the editors of Time-Life Books. [rev ed]. Time-Life Bks. 1992 144p il (Voyage through the universe) $19.93   **523**

1. Stars 2. Universe   LC 91-45193
First published 1990

This describes such mysteries of astronomy as black holes and worm holes, and the formation and demise of stars and galaxies, and nebulae

Includes bibliography

Kals, W. S.
Stars and planets; the Sierra Club guide to sky watching and direction finding. Sierra Club Bks. 1990 244p il maps pa $15 **523**

1. Astronomy 2. Stars 3. Planets
ISBN 0-87156-671-0   LC 90-33711

This guide shows how to locate bright stars, planets, and constellations with the naked eye. Among the features are constellation maps, a calendar for phases of the moon and positions of the visible planets to the year 2000, how to get compass directions from the sun and stars, and a pronouncing gazeteer

Moore, Patrick
Stargazing; astronomy without a telescope. Barron's Educ. Ser. 1985 176p il maps $21.95   **523**

1. Astronomy
ISBN 0-8120-5644-2   LC 85-6091

Moore, Patrick—*Continued*

"This guide for finding celestial objects with the naked eye provides copious star charts and maps as aids to the identification of constellations, important stars, and other objects. There are separate sets of maps for viewers in the southern and northern hemispheres, and in equatorial regions." Libr J

"Information is presented in prose that is clear, concise, nontechnical, and readily comprehensible." Booklist

Schaaf, Fred

Seeing the sky; 100 projects, activities, and explorations in astronomy; with illustrations by Doug Myers. Wiley 1990 212p il (Wiley science editions) $24.95; pa $12.95 **523**

1. Astronomy
ISBN 0-471-52093-4; 0-471-51067-X (pa)
LC 89-70673

This introduction to the science of astronomical observation of celestial bodies and sky phenomena details more than 100 projects and experiments

Includes bibliographic references

523.1 The universe; space, galaxies, quasars

Cohen, Nathan

Gravity's lens; views of the new cosmology. Wiley 1988 237p il $19.95; pa $14.95 **523.1**

1. Universe 2. Radio astronomy
ISBN 0-471-63282-1; 0-471-51054-8 (pa)
LC 88-14353

This brief introduction to cosmology includes such topics as gravity lenses, black holes, quasars, supernovas, the Doppler effect, galaxy clusters, and superstring theory

The author "does a good job of simplifying potentially difficult subjects, using commonplace examples to make points clear to the general reader." Booklist

Includes bibliography

Darling, David J.

Deep time; [by] David Darling. Delacorte Press 1989 192p $17.95 **523.1**

1. Universe 2. Particles (Nuclear physics)
ISBN 0-440-50195-4 LC 88-26710

The author attempts to present modern theories about cosmology by tracing the life of an atomic particle. "Spawned in the Big Bang, the proton wanders the cosmos, encounters black holes and quasars, visits the Earth, hitches a ride with the Voyager spacecraft, and ultimately witnesses the collapse of the universe." Libr J

"Partly conjectural and speculative, this book is well grounded in the latest scientific theories of the universe, which are explained with accommodating clarity." Booklist

Includes bibliographic references

Fritzsch, Harald, 1943-

The creation of matter; the universe from beginning to end; translated by Jean Steinberg. Basic Bks. 1984 307p $19.95; pa $9.95 **523.1**

1. Universe
ISBN 0-465-01446-1; 0-465-01447-X (pa)
LC 84-12334

The author relates quantum theory and cosmology in this history of the universe from the big bang to the end of the universe

The "presentation is clear and authoritative." Choice

Frontiers of time; by the editors of Time-Life Books. Time-Life Bks. 1991 144p il (Voyage through the universe) $19.93 **523.1**

1. Universe 2. Time LC 90-11029

Numerous illustrations complement a text that examines various scientific theories of time and their cosmological implications

Includes bibliography

Galaxies; by the editors of Time-Life Books. Time-Life Bks. 1988 144p il (Voyage through the universe) $19.93 **523.1**

1. Galaxies LC 88-2281

An examination of the Milky Way and its neighboring galaxies. After a brief history of galactic astronomy, the book focuses on the breakthroughs brought about by the development of the radio telescope. Various theories of galaxy formation are also discussed

Includes bibliography

Greenstein, George, 1940-

Frozen star. Freundlich Bks. 1983 274p il $16.95 **523.1**

1. Universe
ISBN 0-88191-011-2 LC 83-25459

This overview of astronomy and cosmology includes a look at the history of research on black holes and pulsars

Hawking, S. W. (Stephen W.)

A brief history of time; from the big bang to black holes; [by] Stephen W. Hawking; introduction by Carl Sagan; illustrations by Ron Miller. Bantam Bks. 1988 198p il $22.50; pa $13.95 **523.1**

1. Universe
ISBN 0-553-05340-X; 0-533-34614-8 (pa)
LC 87-33333

Also available G.K. Hall large print edition

This book is an "attempt to simplify and outline some of the most complex and compelling ideas in modern science. The first five chapters are an introduction for the general reader. . . . Where Hawking really hits his stride is in the last six chapters. This is where he describes his own discoveries and work on black holes, the origin and fate of the universe, the arrow of time, and the unification of physical theories. Here the reader really gets an insight into Hawking's mind, and the ideas he puts forth are fascinating." Sci Books Films

Henbest, Nigel
Universe; a computer-generated voyage
through time and space; photography, Philip
Chudy. Macmillan 1992 c1991 80p il $25
523.1

1. Universe 2. Computer graphics
ISBN 0-02-550921-7   LC 91-29171

First published 1991 in the United Kingdom

Using computer graphics and special-effects photography this large format book explores the birth of the
universe, the formation of the Earth, the collision of
heavenly bodies, the Milky Way, black holes, and the
eventual destruction of the universe

Jastrow, Robert, 1925-
God and the astronomers. 2nd ed. Norton
1992 149p il $18.95   523.1

1. Universe 2. Astronomy 3. Religion and science
ISBN 0-393-85005-6   LC 92-32186

First published 1978

The author examines the theological implications of
the big bang theory of creation. Recent scientific findings
about stars and relativity theory are incorporated

Includes bibliographic references

Lerner, Eric J.
The big bang never happened. Times Bks.
1991 466p il $21.95   523.1

1. Universe
ISBN 0-8129-1853-3   LC 89-40789

Also available in paperback from Vintage Bks.

The author argues against the big bang theory of the
origin of the universe and proposes an alternative cosmology: "an eternal, self-sustaining 'plasma' universe
where electromagnetic fields within conducting gases
provide other . . . explanations for observed
phenomena." Libr J

"Lay readers will need familiarity with the basics of
quantum theory or a science dictionary to fully appreciate this grand tour of three centuries of cosmology.
. . . Lerner holds open the door to one of science's
inner rooms for a popular audience." Publ Wkly

Includes bibliographic references

Lightman, Alan P., 1948-
Ancient light; our changing view of the
universe; [by] Alan Lightman. Harvard
Univ. Press 1991 170p il $18.95; pa $10.95
523.1

1. Universe 2. Astronomers
ISBN 0-674-03362-0; 0-674-03363-9 (pa)
LC 91-12459

"Adapted from Origins: the lives and worlds of
modern cosmologists, by Alan Lightman and Roberta
Brawer, published by Harvard University Press, 1990"

The author discusses the development of modern cosmology, the big bang model, and recent challenges to
that model

"Lightman's book is a short and simple introduction
to modern cosmology, with a strong emphasis upon
observation and its interaction with theory. . . . Its
merits are that it is accurate and does not go further
than current observations warrant." Nat Hist

Includes bibliographic references

Overbye, Dennis, 1944-
Lonely hearts of the cosmos; the scientific
quest for the secret of the universe.
HarperCollins Pubs. 1991 438p $25; pa $13
523.1

1. Universe
ISBN 0-06-015964-2; 0-06-092271-0 (pa)
LC 89-45700

The author "focuses on the people who contributed
to contemporary theories of the universe. Through interviews and personal anecdotes, Overbye presents an
insider's view of the lives, works, and personalities of
such legendary figures as [Stephen] Hawking; John
Wheeler, the 'father of the black hole'; and Alan Guth,
architect of the 'inflationary universe' concept." Libr J

Parker, Barry R.
Creation; the story of the origin and
evolution of the universe; [by] Barry Parker;
drawings by Lori Scoffield. Plenum Press
1988 297p il $22.95   523.1

1. Universe
ISBN 0-306-42952-7   LC 88-17893

The author recounts the history of a number of
discoveries in cosmology. "The scope of Parker's topics
ranges from the large-scale structure of the universe and
the details of its creation to the synthesis of the elements
and their evolution into living matter." Choice

Includes bibliography

Silk, Joseph, 1942-
The big bang. rev & updated ed.
Freeman, W.H. 1988 485p il $24.95; pa
$14.95   523.1

1. Universe
ISBN 0-7167-1997-5; 0-7167-1812-X (pa)
LC 88-16497

First published 1980

The author covers the history of the universe, from
the big bang to current speculation on quasars, black
holes, matter and antimatter, superstrings and cosmic
symmetry

Includes bibliography

Stephen Hawking's A brief history of time:
a reader's companion; edited by Stephen
Hawking; prepared by Gene Stone.
Bantam Bks. 1992 194p il $25   523.1

1. Hawking, S. W. (Stephen W.) 2. Universe
ISBN 0-553-07772-4   LC 92-6526

Companion volume to A brief history of time, entered
above, under Hawking, S. W.

This book "features first person commentary divided
among Hawking's companions. . . . The remarks of his
family, mates from Oxford, tutors from Cambridge, and
fellow physicists add up to a humanized picture of the
intuitive genius and his cosmological achievements."
Booklist

Swimme, Brian
The universe story; from the primordial flaring forth to the ecozoic era—a celebration of the unfolding of the cosmos; [by] Brian Swimme and Thomas Berry. HarperSanFrancisco 1992 305p il $22

523.1

1. Universe 2. Civilization—History
ISBN 0-06-250826-1   LC 91-58907

The authors fashion a cosmology that incorporates an ecological view of the universe with a metaphorical interpretation of recent scientific research

Includes bibliographic references

Trefil, James S., 1938-
The dark side of the universe; a scientist explores the mysteries of the cosmos; by James Trefil; illustrations by Judith Peatross. Scribner 1988 197p il o.p.; Doubleday paperback available $9.95   **523.1**

1. Universe 2. Astronomy
ISBN 0-385-28212-4 (pa)   LC 88-1061

The subject of this book "is modern cosmology and elementary particles, and their interconnection." Choice
The author shows "that he can describe the history and philosophy of science humorously, anecdotally and yet profoundly. He can also make a persuasive case for the pure esthetics of physics and astronomy." N Y Times Book Rev

The moment of creation; big bang physics from before the first millisecond to the present universe; illustrations by Gloria Walters. Scribner 1983 234p il o.p.; Collier Bks. paperback available $10.95   **523.1**

1. Universe 2. Nuclear physics
ISBN 0-02-096770-5 (pa)   LC 83-9011

Trefil begins with an overview of the big bang theory and some of its "problems: lack of antimatter, galaxy formation, isotropy, and flatness. From here he . . . [takes] the reader into elementary particles and unified field theory. This is followed by a more detailed discussion of the Big Bang and the early universe." Choice

523.4   Planets

Cattermole, Peter John
Mars; the story of the red planet; [by] Peter Cattermole; with a foreword by Patrick Moore. Chapman & Hall 1992 224p il $35

523.4

1. Mars (Planet)
ISBN 0-412-44140-3   LC 93-112933

This "summarizes what the author and his NASA colleagues have done with the huge data set compiled by the *Mariner 9* and *Viking 1* and *2* missions of the 1970s. The most current theories and speculations are here. . . . In a strong subordinate role to the text are 80 astounding views of plains, ice caps, dune fields, craters, and enough Earth-like weather phenomena to pique the wonder of nontechnical observers." Booklist

Includes bibliography

The **Far** planets; by the editors of Time-Life Books. Time-Life Bks. 1989 144p il (Voyage through the universe) $19.93

523.4

1. Planets 2. Project Voyager   LC 88-15994

Making use of color photographs, this book portrays the planets furthest from the sun including Jupiter, Saturn, Uranus, Neptune and Pluto, and gives a brief history of their study and exploration

Includes bibliography

Littmann, Mark, 1939-
Planets beyond; discovering the outer solar system. Wiley 1988 286p il (Wiley science editions) $22.95; pa $16.95   **523.4**

1. Uranus (Planet) 2. Neptune (Planet) 3. Pluto (Planet)
ISBN 0-471-61128-X; 0-471-51053-X (pa)
LC 88-20498

This book "describes the search for and discovery and exploration of the cold and distant worlds beyond Saturn—Uranus, Neptune, and Pluto. . . . The text is clear and more elaborate than other books on this subject. The historical perspective is enlightening and entertaining." Sci Books Films

Includes bibliographic references

The **Near** planets; by the editors of Time-Life Books. Time-Life Bks. 1992 144p il (Voyage through the universe) $19.93   **523.4**

1. Mars (Planet) 2. Mercury (Planet) 3. Venus (Planet)   LC 92-8443

An illustrated survey of current knowledge about Mars, Mercury and Venus

Includes bibliography

Wilford, John Noble
Mars beckons; the mysteries, the challenges, the expectations of our next great adventure in space. Knopf 1990 244p il $24.95; pa $12   **523.4**

1. Mars (Planet)
ISBN 0-394-58359-0; 0-679-73531-3 (pa)
LC 89-43365

The author has produced a "general introduction to the planet Mars. He examines our fascination with Mars as the other planet in the solar system likely to harbor life, speculation that began with the ancients and took hold in the 19th century. . . . He details the findings of the unmanned probes that in recent years characterized Mars as it really is—a cold, dry world." Libr J

Includes bibliographic references

523.6   Comets

Comets, asteroids, and meteorites; by the editors of Time-Life Books. [rev ed]. Time-Life Bks. 1992 144p il (Voyage through the universe) $19.93   **523.6**

1. Comets 2. Asteroids 3. Meteors   LC 91-39078
First published 1990

Comets, asteroids, and meteorites — *Continued*

Text and numerous illustrations explore current astronomical knowledge of comets, meteors and asteroids. A chapter on Halley's Comet is included and famous scientists and astronomers are profiled

Includes bibliographic references

Sagan, Carl, 1934-

Comet; [by] Carl Sagan and Ann Druyan. Random House 1985 398p il $27.50　**523.6**

1. Comets 2. Halley's comet
ISBN 0-394-54908-2　　　　LC 85-8308

Also available in paperback from Outlet

"The authors explore the myth and science of comets in a lavishly illustrated, slightly oversize volume that is both fascinating and authoritative." Booklist

Includes bibliography

Yeomans, Donald K.

Comets; a chronological history of observation, science, myth, and folklore. Wiley 1991 485p il (Wiley science editions) $35　　　　**523.6**

1. Comets
ISBN 0-471-61011-9　　　　LC 90-12657

This is a "history of comet research from the ancient Greeks and Chinese to the observational results obtained during Halley's Comet's latest visit in 1986. [Yeomans'] story makes fascinating reading for all comers until the narrative reaches the present century, wherein the scientific details become formidable for those lacking a good background in the physical sciences. However, lay readers can surely understand at least the general import of recent discoveries." Libr J

Includes bibliographic references

523.7　Sun

Gribbin, John R.

Blinded by the light; the secret life of the sun; [by] John Gribbin. Harmony Bks. 1991 240p il $20　　　　**523.7**

1. Sun 2. Astrophysics
ISBN 0-517-57827-1　　　　LC 91-9941

Drawing on the findings of current solar research, the author discusses the structure and inner workings of the sun

"It is the science of neutrino astronomy to which Gribbin rightly gives major emphasis. The discovery of the neutrino distinguishes present opportunities from those of history." New Sci

Includes bibliography

Hufbauer, Karl

Exploring the sun; solar science since Galileo. Johns Hopkins Univ. Press 1991 370p il maps (New ser. in NASA history) $39.95; pa $19.95　　　　**523.7**

1. Sun 2. Astronomy
ISBN 0-8018-4098-8; 0-8018-4599-8 (pa)
LC 90-44033

This "volume traces the history of our understanding of the sun from the time of Galileo to the present." Choice

"The book is well illustrated . . . and contains an extensive bibliography of other accounts of the history of solar research, as well as citations of the original research. Hufbauer presents an easily readable, non-mathematical account of the progress of solar science over a 400-year period." Sci Books Films

The Sun; by the editors of Time-Life Books. Time-Life Bks. 1990 144p il (Voyage through the universe) $19.93　　　　**523.7**

1. Sun
LC 89-4468

This covers the history of astronomical research about the sun, the sun's composition, neutrinos, effects of the sun on the earth, solar telescopes, sunspots and flares, solar energy, and solar wind

Includes bibliography

Wentzel, Donat G., 1934-

The restless sun. Smithsonian Institution Press 1989 279p il $29.95　　　　**523.7**

1. Sun 2. Astrophysics
ISBN 0-87474-982-4　　　　LC 88-18491

This book presents, "without recourse to mathematics, phenomena scientists spend their lives unraveling. Luminosity, solar chemistry, nuclear fusion, solar winds, and the Van Allen belts are a few of the complex subjects well described by illustrations and text. Later chapters consider the sun's effects upon the weather and climate of Earth." Booklist

Includes bibliography

523.8　Stars

Beyer, Steven L. (Steven Larsen)

The star guide; a unique system for identifying the brightest stars in the night sky. Little, Brown 1986 c1985 404p il maps hardcover o.p. paperback available $12.95
523.8

1. Stars 2. Astronomy
ISBN 0-316-09268-1 (pa)　　　　LC 85-13039

A guide to "105 of the brightest stars visible in the continental U.S. . . . For each star, the author notes the time of its greatest visibility, its history, lore, description, and the meaning of its name." Booklist

Includes bibliography

Gribbin, John R.

Unveiling the edge of time; black holes, white holes, worm holes; [by] John Gribbin. Harmony Bks. 1992 248p il $20　　　　**523.8**

1. Black holes (Astronomy) 2. Astrophysics
ISBN 0-517-58591-X　　　　LC 92-10485

"The idea of black holes is the unifying theme of this volume. Gribbin follows a historical account in the first few chapters, starting with Newton and continuing on to Einstein's general relativity theory. The solution of Einstein's equations leads to the concept of black holes. Gribbin then shows how the ideas of stellar interiors and evolution gradually led first to the idea of white dwarfs and then to black holes as end points of stellar evolution." Choice

Halpern, Paul

Cosmic wormholes; the search for interstellar shortcuts. Dutton 1992 236p $21

523.8

1. Black holes (Astronomy) 2. Astrophysics 3. Space flight
ISBN 0-525-93477-4   LC 92-52868

The author "outlines concepts and ideas for the twenty-first (if not the twenty-second) century that may allow space travelers to enter a 'wormhole' in the very fabric of space-time in one corner of the universe and exit in another. . . . These concepts are only speculative, and the practical engineering for them may be impossible, but, challenging commonsense notions of what space and time really are, they're sure intriguing on paper." Booklist

Includes bibliographic references

Levitt, I. M. (Israel Monroe), 1908-

Star maps for beginners; by I. M. Levitt & Roy K. Marshall. Newly rev and updated, 50th anniversary ed. Simon & Schuster 1992 64p il pa $10   **523.8**

1. Stars—Atlases 2. Planets
ISBN 0-671-79187-7   LC 93-121137

"A Fireside book"

First published 1942 by the authors. First Simon & Schuster edition 1964

The authors present an overview of the solar system, information on the history and development of constellations, and twelve maps—one for each month—showing star positions

Marschall, Laurence A.

The supernova story. Plenum Press 1988 296p il $22.95   **523.8**

1. Supernovas
ISBN 0-306-42955-1   LC 88-17978

The author describes the history of supernova research and observation and explains the life cycles of stars, pulsars, neutron stars, planetary nebulae, and related phenomena

"This book is beautifully illustrated, accurate, well organized, and complete." Sci Books Films

Includes bibliography

Moore, Patrick

Astronomers' stars. Norton 1989 c1987 164p il $17.95   **523.8**

1. Stars
ISBN 0-393-02663-9   LC 88-22376

First published 1987 in the United Kingdom

"Insights into the observations of ancient astronomers and the theories of modern ones as well as concise, not too technical explanations of such phenomena as black holes, pulsars, quasars, and supernovae are neatly incorporated into discussion of 16 particular bodies. . . . An excellent book, technical enough for the knowledgeable amateur yet accessible to the novice." Booklist

Includes bibliography

Motz, Lloyd, 1910-

The constellations; enthusiast's guide to the night sky; [by] Lloyd Motz and Carol Nathanson. Doubleday 1988 411p il $24.95

523.8

1. Stars
ISBN 0-385-17600-7   LC 86-13568

This book provides an "introduction to the nature of many types of astronomical phenomena—variable stars, stages of star life, galaxies, planetary nebulae, and much more. The history of discoveries involving objects in different constellations is told in a detailed and interesting manner." Sci Teach

Includes bibliography

Stars; by the editors of Time-Life Books. [rev ed]. Time-Life Bks. 1992 144p il (Voyage through the universe) $19.93

523.8

1. Stars   LC 92-3146

First published 1988

This illustrated overview discusses starlight, the birth and death of stars, red giants, supernovas, neutron stars and black holes

Includes bibliography

525 Earth (Astronomical geography)

Hartmann, William K.

The history of earth; an illustrated chronicle of an evolving planet; written by William K. Hartmann; paintings by Ron Miller and William K. Hartmann. Workman 1991 260p il maps $35; pa $19.95   **525**

1. Geology 2. Universe 3. Earth—Age
ISBN 1-56305-122-2; 0-89480-756-0 (pa)
LC 91-50387

"The history of the Earth from its birth to its postulated end, with more emphasis given to Earth's early evolution and the early history of life than is typically the case in books for the general public." Libr J

528 Nautical almanacs

The **Astronomical** almanac; issued by the Nautical Almanac Office, United States Naval Observatory. . . . U.S. Govt. Ptg. Office $23   **528**

1. Nautical almanacs

Annual

Formed by the union in 1981 of The American ephemeris and nautical almanac and The Astronomical ephemeris published by Her Majesty's Nautical Almanac Office

"With basic information contributed by the ephemeris offices of a number of countries, this collection of tables is the authoritative source for annual astronomical data from the movement of heavenly bodies to the calculation of calendars." Ref Sources for Small & Medium-sized Libr. 5th edition

529 Chronology

Aveni, Anthony F.

Empires of time: calendars, clocks, and cultures. Basic Bks. 1989 371p il $24.95; pa $12.95   **529**

1. Time 2. Calendars
ISBN 0-465-01950-1; 0-465-01951-X (pa)

LC 89-42529

This "book about cultural aspects of time begins with a discussion of biological and astronomical cycles and then goes on to describe how ancient people of the west have considered time, including clocks and calendars." Sci Books Films

Includes bibliography

Coveney, Peter

The arrow of time; a voyage through science to solve time's greatest mystery; [by] Peter Coveney and Roger Highfield; foreword by Ilya Prigogine. Fawcett Columbine 1991 c1990 378p il $22.50; pa $12.50   **529**

1. Time
ISBN 0-449-90630-2; 0-449-90723-6 (pa)

LC 90-85770

First published 1990 in the United Kingdom

The authors "demonstrate how the everyday perception that time moves in one direction is consistent with advanced scientific theory. At the center of their theory is an intriguing interpretation of the second law of thermodynamics, which describes the forces of entropy. The authors show that this concept has broad relevance in such fields as cosmology, evolution, and the emerging science of chaos." Libr J

Includes bibliographic references

Parker, Barry R.

Cosmic time travel; a scientific odyssey; [by] Barry Parker; drawings by Lori Scoffield. Plenum Press 1991 308p il $24.50   **529**

1. Time 2. Relativity (Physics)
ISBN 0-306-43966-2   LC 91-18098

The author discusses whether time travel is scientifically possible. He examines "the history of the development of general relativity, the concept of curved space-time and the early evolution of the universe. The remainder of the book [seeks to] explain the problems that arise when we attempt to turn theoretical holes in space-time into time machines." N Y Times Book Rev

"Parker shows clearly how scientific research proceeds on a fascinating subject. The many illustrations (diagrams and portraits of scientists) are good, and there is also a good 11-column index." Sci Books Films

Includes bibliographic references

530 Physics

Davies, P. C. W., 1946-

The matter myth; dramatic discoveries that challenge our understanding of physical reality; [by] Paul Davies and John Gribbin. Simon & Schuster 1992 320p il hardcover o.p. paperback available $12   **530**

1. Reality 2. Physics
ISBN 0-671-72841-5 (pa)   LC 91-39522

"The authors choose for discussion many important and currently popular topics, including chaos, solitons, the topology of space, quantum field theory, antimatter, magnetic monopoles, special and general relativity, the big bang, inflationary cosmology, the omega point, dark matter, cosmic strings and superstrings, wormholes, and the many-universe model." Sci Books Films

Includes bibliographic references

Einstein, Albert, 1879-1955

The evolution of physics; the growth of ideas from early concepts to relativity and quanta; by Albert Einstein and Leopold Infeld. Simon & Schuster 1938 320p il hardcover o.p. paperback available $12

     530

1. Physics—History 2. Relativity (Physics) 3. Quantum theory
ISBN 0-671-20156-5 (pa)

"A simple exposition for the layman of the growth of ideas in physical science from the earliest concepts to the theories of modern times." Publ Wkly

Motz, Lloyd, 1910-

The story of physics; [by] Lloyd Motz and Jefferson Hane Weaver. Plenum Press 1989 412p il $24.50   **530**

1. Physics
ISBN 0-306-43076-2   LC 88-33655

Also available in paperback from Avon Bks.

This book attempts "to tell the whole story of physics from the Greeks to modern developments. . . . The authors have succeeded admirably, and they have done so in an interesting way—each scientific advance is presented in a thumbnail biographical sketch of the person most responsible for that advance." Sci Books Films

Pais, Abraham, 1918-

Inward bound; of matter and forces in the physical world. Oxford Univ. Press 1986 666p $39.95; pa $17.95   **530**

1. Physics—History
ISBN 0-19-851971-0; 0-19-851997-4 (pa)

LC 85-21587

This is a history of particle physics from Roentgen's discovery of x-rays in 1895 to the present

This work is "illuminated by Pais's felicitous style, his extraordinary scholarship, and the wealth of detail he has incorporated in the text. The references alone make Inward Bound an invaluable historical document." Science

Includes bibliographies

The **Physical** world; edited by Martin Sherwood and Christine Sutton. Oxford Univ. Press 1988 183p il $40; pa $22.50
530

1. Physics 2. Chemistry, Physical and theoretical
ISBN 0-19-520632-0; 0-19-520849-8 (pa)
LC 87-26333

"An Equinox book"

This "volume accessibly discusses the roles of physics and chemistry in our everyday lives. Sound, light, electricity, magnetism, and atomic structure are covered, as are data on how various products—e.g., petroleum, fertilizers, cosmetics, explosives and insecticides—are manufactured. . . . The emphasis here is on the impact of complex scientific principles on casual human existence." Booklist

Includes bibliography

Teller, Edward, 1908-
Conversations on the dark secrets of physics; [by] Edward Teller, Wendy Teller, and Wilson Talley. Plenum Press 1991 247p il $23.95
530

1. Physics
ISBN 0-306-43772-4
LC 91-8626

The authors discuss the work of major physicists starting with Pythagoras and the ancient Greeks and including Einstein, Galileo, Johann Kepler, Isaac Newton, Niels Bohr, and Louis de Broglie, and explain such topics as quantum theory, superconductivity, and lasers

"Each chapter starts at a low level of understanding, but often ends up at a dramatically high one. Questions at the end of each chapter have answers that are both expansive and illuminating." New Sci

Includes bibliographic references

Trefil, James S., 1938-
A scientist at the seashore; [by] James Trefil; illustrations by Gloria Walters. Scribner 1984 208p il o.p.; Collier Bks. paperback available $9.95
530

1. Physics 2. Beaches
ISBN 0-02-025920-4 (pa)
LC 84-14112

The author discusses "the natural laws and forces that control the tides, waves, surf, and other physical aspects of the seashore. He also shows how other phenomena, such as the moon's rate of rotation, are related to such processes." Libr J

"Following Mr. Trefil's leads offers as much suspense as a good mystery story, yet 'A Scientist at the Seashore' is a book to learn from. No matter how far afield he takes us, he ties everything back to something familiar; his direct, unpretentious style makes the book painless and enjoyable reading." N Y Times Book Rev

530.1 Physics—Theories and mathematical physics

Calder, Nigel, 1931-
Einstein's universe. Viking 1979 154p il o.p.; Penguin Bks. paperback available $10
530.1

1. Relativity (Physics) 2. Astrophysics 3. Universe
ISBN 0-14-005499-5 (pa)
LC 78-26087

"Calder undertakes to explain the theory of relativity to the layman without using mathematics. . . . Einstein's theory of general relativity . . . is presented first; the historically earlier special relativity theory . . . is introduced late in the book. Calder goes on to discuss developments in science that have borne out Einstein's deductions." Libr J

"The author writes with competence and simplicity. It is a proper tribute to the man who revolutionized our ideas of space, time, and motion." Choice

Chaisson, Eric
Relatively speaking; relativity, black holes, and the fate of the universe; illustrated by Lola Judith Chaisson. Norton 1988 254p il hardcover o.p. paperback available $10.95
530.1

1. Relativity (Physics) 2. Universe 3. Black holes (Astronomy)
ISBN 0-393-30675-5 (pa)
LC 87-11134

"To introduce the subject, Chaisson devotes several chapters to background information on astronomy, subatomic particles, and the major principles that govern them. Concepts such as the Doppler effect, Hubbard's theory, red and blue shifts, and Einstein's famous $E=MC^2$ are then fully explained. A short biography of Einstein will help readers understand the environment in which the great physicists are working." Booklist

Davies, P. C. W., 1946-
The cosmic blueprint; new discoveries in nature's creative ability to order the universe; [by] Paul Davies. Simon & Schuster 1988 223p il hardcover o.p. paperback available $9.95
530.1

1. Force and energy 2. Matter 3. Universe
ISBN 0-671-67561-3 (pa)
LC 87-26442

"This book explicates contemporary thought and experimentation suggesting that the universe is able to organize itself. . . . Writers and scientists discussed include Ilya Prigogine, Karl Popper, Erich Jantsch, John von Neumann, James Crutchfield, Jacques Monod, Roger Penrose, Roger Sperry, and Stephen Hawking." Sci Books Films

Includes bibliography

Einstein, Albert, 1879-1955
The meaning of relativity; including the Relativistic theory of the non-symmetric field. 5th ed. Princeton Univ. Press 1956 166p $35
530.1

1. Relativity (Physics)
ISBN 0-691-08007-0

First published 1922. Translated by Edwin Plimpton Adams, Ernst G. Straus and Bruria Kaufman

The Stafford Little lectures of Princeton University, May 1921

"Though few can understand it, most readers in physics and librarians in charge of science collections know this book as one of the landmarks of modern knowledge. . . . The book is not intended for general reading. Instead it is addressed to . . . [those whose training enables] them to understand the mathematical expressions of relativity." N Y Public Libr. New Tech Books

Gribbin, John R.
In search of Schrödinger's cat; quantum physics and reality. Bantam Bks. 1984 302p il $12   **530.1**

1. Quantum theory 2. Reality
ISBN 0-553-34253-3 (pa)   LC 84-2975

This history of quantum mechanics discusses the work of Huygens, Einstein, Schrödinger, Bohr, Planck and Everett

"This book is quite interesting. It contains many vignettes from the history of science and many insights into the researchers and the work that has led to our current understanding of the quantum theory. Excellent analogies and graphic illustrations are used to present difficult ideas." Sci Books Films

Includes bibliography

530.8   Testing and measurement

Blocksma, Mary
Reading the numbers; a survival guide to the measurements, numbers, and sizes encountered in everyday life. Viking 1989 224p il hardcover o.p.; Penguin Bks. paperback available $11.95   **530.8**

1. Measurement
ISBN 0-14-010654-5 (pa)   LC 88-40336

"This practical work focuses on numerical concepts such as roman numerals, radio frequency, time, prime rate, calendars, money, lumber, nails, and age. Arranged alphabetically by subject, the explanations are clear, concise, and nontechnical." Nichols. Guide to Ref Books for Sch Media Cent. 4th edition

Includes bibliography

535   Light and related radiations

Bova, Ben, 1932-
The beauty of light. Wiley 1988 350p il (Wiley science editions) $24.95   **535**

1. Light
ISBN 0-471-62580-9   LC 88-12228

This book "explores the relevance of light to the human race. The topics are diverse: art, blue-green algae, creation, DNA, . . . lasers, moonlight, Newton, optics, painting, and the list goes on." Sci Teach

"In a clear, conversational style, Bova makes accessible for the general reader a wealth of scientific facts, techniques, and theories." Choice

Includes bibliography

Sobel, Michael I.
Light. University of Chicago Press 1987 263p il hardcover o.p. paperback available $14.95   **535**

1. Light
ISBN 0-226-76151-5 (pa)   LC 86-25024

The author looks "at light and how it is studied and used in all areas of science and technology. He traces the development of physical theories of light through the centuries and shows how general laws of physics can explain a wide variety of light phenomena." Univ Press Books for Public Libr

"The author's technical genius and communications skills are combined with excellent lucid sketches, concise meaty captions, and fascinating photographs to make this a 'must read' book by everyone." Sci Books Films

539.7   Atomic and nuclear physics

Asimov, Isaac, 1920-1992
Atom; journey across the subatomic cosmos; illustrated by D.F. Bach. Dutton 1991 319p il $21.95; pa $12   **539.7**

1. Atoms 2. Nuclear physics
ISBN 0-525-24990-7; 0-452-26834-6 (pa)
     LC 90-21343

"A Truman Talley book"

The author "presents the history of atomic and subatomic research from the speculation of ancient Greek philosophers to the cosmological theorizing of the late 20th century. Somewhat less than half the book is devoted to the story of how the existence of atoms was confirmed and their structure was determined. The remainder of the work deals with the internal structure of the nucleus and with the many particles . . . disclosed by modern physicists." Libr J

Boorse, Henry A. (Henry Abraham), 1904-
The atomic scientists; a biographical history; [by] Henry A. Boorse, Lloyd Motz, and Jefferson Hane Weaver. Wiley 1989 472p il (Wiley science editions) $27.95
     539.7

1. Nuclear physics 2. Atomic theory
ISBN 0-471-50455-6   LC 88-35181

The authors present biographical sketches of scientists who have been involved in atomic physics from the 1st century B.C. to the present

"The authors have not merely replanted bones from the graveyards of forgotten biographies but have read widely and then interpreted what they have learned." Sci Books Films

Includes bibliographic references

Close, F. E.
Too hot to handle; the race for cold fusion. Princeton Univ. Press 1991 376p il $24.95   **539.7**

1. Fleischmann, Martin 2. Pons, Stanley 3. Nuclear physics
ISBN 0-691-08591-9   LC 91-11378

The author recounts the story of B. Stanley Pons and Martin Fleischmann who claimed in 1989 to have discovered a process of producing energy by nuclear cold fusion, and who were subsequently discredited

"'Too Hot to Handle' is a valuable cautionary tale of what can happen when greed displaces good science." N Y Times Book Rev

Includes bibliographic references

Feynman, Richard Phillips

QED; the strange theory of light and matter; [by] Richard Feynman. Princeton Univ. Press 1985 158p (Alix G. Mautner memorial lectures) $18.50; pa $9.95   **539.7**

1. Electrons 2. Light 3. Quantum theory
ISBN 0-691-08388-6; 0-691-02417-0 (pa)

LC 85-42685

The author attempts to describe the interaction between light and electrons

"Feynman describes with accuracy, insight, self-deprecating humor, and clarity the centerpiece of modern elementary particle theory—quantum electrodynamics. . . . 'QED' will challenge the mind." Christ Sci Monit

Mallove, Eugene F.

Fire from ice; searching for the truth behind the cold fusion furor. Wiley 1991 334p il (Wiley science editions) $22.95
539.7

1. Fleischmann, Martin 2. Pons, Stanley 3. Nuclear physics
ISBN 0-471-53139-1   LC 91-8036

The author describes the controversy surrounding Martin Fleischmann and B. Stanley Pons, who announced in 1989 that they had achieved cold nuclear fusion, and decrys what he views as a backlash of the press and researchers against the concept of cold fusion

Includes bibliographic references

Peat, F. David, 1938-

Cold fusion; the making of a scientific controversy. Contemporary Bks. 1989 188p il hardcover o.p. paperback available $8.95
539.7

1. Nuclear physics
ISBN 0-8092-4085-8 (pa)   LC 89-25160

"Peat begins with the controversial March 1989 announcements that cold fusion had been accomplished at the University of Utah and room temperature fusion at Brigham Young University. He masterfully presents previous research in fusing atoms, quantum tunnelling, and how muons (electron-type subatomic particles) can act as fusion catalysts, then returns to the two announced fusion processes. . . . Peat turns next to confirming and dissenting opinions about the Utah experiments, objectively reviewing them." Booklist

540   Chemistry and allied sciences

CRC handbook of chemistry and physics; a ready-reference book of chemical and physical data. CRC Press $99.50   **540**

1. Chemistry—Tables 2. Physics—Tables
First published 1913. (74th edition 1993) Periodically revised

A "reference book containing much-used information on mathematics, chemistry, and physics, including tables, physical constants of chemical elements and compounds, definitions, formulae, etc." AAAS Sci Book List for Young Adults

Includes bibliographic references

Hudson, John, 1943-

The history of chemistry. Chapman & Hall 1992 285p il $59.95; pa $24.95   **540**

1. Chemistry—History
ISBN 0-412-03641-X; 0-412-03651-7 (pa) LC 92-8311

This is a "general introduction to the entire history of chemistry. . . . The illustrations of persons and apparatuses are sharp and crisp. Numerous brief biographies in the text, set off by boxes, help the reader understand how the lives of various chemists affected their scientific work." Sci Books Films

Includes bibliographic references

Lange's handbook of chemistry. McGraw-Hill $79.50   **540**

1. Chemistry—Tables
First published 1934. (14th edition 1992) Periodically revised

"A standard reference source for both the student and the professional chemist. Sections for mathematics, general information and conversion tables, atomic and molecular structure, inorganic chemistry, analytical chemistry, electrochemistry, organic chemistry, spectroscopy, thermodynamic properties, physical properties, and miscellaneous." Sheehy. Guide to Ref Books. 10th edition

Salzberg, Hugh W.

From caveman to chemist; circumstances and achievements. American Chemical Soc. 1991 294p il maps $24.95; pa $14.95   **540**

1. Chemistry—History
ISBN 0-8412-1786-6; 0-8412-1787-4 (pa)

LC 90-44612

"A world history of chemistry from ancient times to the dawn of the 20th century. Like astronomy, chemistry developed from a discipline shrouded in myth and magic into a legitimate science, and Salzberg, a retired chemist, describes this evolution in a sweeping historical sketch. Further, the author shows that advancements in the understanding of chemistry invariably led to improvements in medicine and technology." Libr J

Includes bibliographic references

540.3   Chemistry—Encyclopedias and dictionaries

Hawley's condensed chemical dictionary. Van Nostrand Reinhold $69.95   **540.3**

1. Chemistry—Dictionaries
First published 1919. (12th edition 1993) Periodically revised

Editors vary

"Describes industrial and scientific chemicals, terms, processes, reactions, and related terminology and phenomena. Charts chemical structures; gives uses and trademarked products that employ these chemicals. Some emphasis is on environment and energy sources. Includes appendices." N Y Public Libr Book of How & Where to Look It Up

Van Nostrand Reinhold encyclopedia of chemistry; Douglas M. Considine, editor-in-chief; Glenn D. Considine, managing editor. 4th ed. Van Nostrand Reinhold 1984 1082p il $94.95   **540.3**

1. Chemistry—Dictionaries
ISBN 0-685-19115-X   LC 83-23336

First published 1957 with title: The Encyclopedia of chemistry

"The roughly 1,300 entries range from brief definitions to articles, some of them signed, which may include tabular data and references. Includes topics from fields related to chemistry, such as materials science, energy sources and conversion, biochemistry and biotechnology, wastes and pollution. Cross references; index." Sheehy. Guide to Ref Books. 10th edition

546   Inorganic chemistry

Heiserman, David L., 1940-
Exploring chemical elements and their compounds. TAB Bks. 1992 376p il $26.95; pa $17.95   **546**

1. Chemical elements
ISBN 0-8306-3018-X; 0-8306-3015-5 (pa)
        LC 91-17687

"The book provides the following information for each of the first 94 elements: a chart of basic data; a structural diagram; and a discussion of the historical background, chemical properties, laboratory and commercial productions, and the compounds and isotopes. Elements 95 through 107 are discussed individually but more briefly. Elements 108 and up are lumped together in a short discussion." SLJ

548   Crystallography

Holden, Alan
Crystals and crystal growing; [by] Alan Holden and Phylis Morrison; introduction by Philip Morrison. MIT Press 1982 318p il pa $10.95   **548**

1. Crystallography
ISBN 0-262-58050-0   LC 81-23639

First published 1960 by Anchor Bks.

This book "sets for itself three major goals: 1. Describing the atomistic character of crystallinity; 2. Describing some techniques for preparing large single crystals; and 3. Describing some experiments that display the unexpected properties which flow from crystallinity." Preface

"An excellent introduction to crystallography (and, incidentally, to much basic physics) written in plain language. . . . The text is supplemented by descriptions of simple (and cheap!) experiments and suggestions for additional reading." Libr J

549   Mineralogy

Chesterman, Charles W.
The Audubon Society field guide to North American rocks and minerals; scientific consultant, Kurt E. Lowe. Knopf 1979 c1978 850p il $17.95   **549**

1. Mineralogy 2. Rocks
ISBN 0-394-50269-8   LC 78-54893

"Pocket guide providing color photos and descriptions of some 232 mineral species and forty types of rocks. Includes guide to mineral environments, glossary, bibliography, and indexes by name and locality." Ref Sources for Small & Medium-sized Libr. 5th edition

Manual of mineralogy (after James D. Dana). Wiley il $51.95   **549**

1. Mineralogy

First published 1848 under the authorship of James D. Dana. (21st edition 1993) Periodically revised

Current edition by Cornelis Klein and Cornelius S. Hurlbut

This is a standard introductory reference book for the use of students and collectors. It covers physical, chemical, determinative, and descriptive mineralogy, discusses mineral occurrence, association, and use, and includes both a subject and mineral index

Pellant, Chris
Rocks and minerals; Helen Pellant, editorial consultant; photography by Harry Taylor. Dorling Kindersley 1992 256p il (Eyewitness handbks) $29.95; pa $17.95
       549

1. Mineralogy 2. Rocks
ISBN 1-56458-033-4; 1-56458-061-X (pa)
        LC 91-58222

This field guide to identification of rocks and minerals includes techniques for collection and classification and facts about physical and chemical composition and formation

"Visually attractive, with many color photographs [this provides] detail and information that would benefit either new or experienced naturalists." SLJ

Pough, Frederick H.
A field guide to rocks and minerals; illustrated with photographs and drawings. 4th ed. Houghton Mifflin 1976 317p il $21.45; pa $14.45   **549**

1. Mineralogy 2. Rocks
ISBN 0-395-24047-6; 0-395-24049-2 (pa)

"The Peterson field guide series"

First published 1953

This handbook "has photos of 270 specimens. Pough uses traditional identification methods (in contrast to Audubon's visual method) and includes chapters on crystallography, mineralogy, and home laboratory techniques." Wynar. Guide to Ref Books for Sch Media Cent. 3d edition

Includes bibliography

Simon and Schuster's guide to rocks and minerals; edited by Martin Prinz, George Harlow, and Joseph Peters. Simon & Schuster 1978 607p il hardcover o.p. paperback available $14 **549**

1. Mineralogy 2. Rocks
ISBN 0-671-24417-5 (pa) LC 78-8610

Original Italian edition, 1977

"Half of this book consists of color plates; the other half is an authoritative text which describes the elements of mineralogy and petrology. Crystal system or family, physical and chemical properties, occurrence, uses, and rarity are included for each species." Libr J

Sofianides, Anna S.
Gems & crystals from the American Museum of Natural History; [by] Anna S. Sofianides and George E. Harlow; photographs by Erica and Harold Van Pelt. Simon & Schuster 1990 208p il $40 **549**

1. Mineralogy 2. Precious stones
ISBN 0-671-68704-2 LC 89-11574

Color photographs "picture familiar gems, which are briefly described in terms of their particular properties and the legends associated with them." Booklist

Includes bibliography

550 Earth sciences

Brown, Bruce
The miracle planet; [by] Bruce Brown and Lane Morgan. Gallery Bks. (NY) 1990 257p il o.p.; Knapp Press reprint available $29.95 **550**

1. Earth
ISBN 0-318-42503-3 LC 89-23825

"The intricate process that spawned planet Earth and the intricate network that Earth sustains are among the topics treated in a beautifully illustrated companion to a PBS TV series." Booklist

Includes bibliographic references

Magill's survey of science, earth science series; edited by Frank N. Magill; consulting editor, James A. Woodhead. Salem Press 1990 5v il set $425 **550**

1. Earth sciences
ISBN 0-89356-606-3 LC 89-10923

"The 377 earth science essays, written by contributors from universities, companies, professional societies, and governmental agencies, cover the subdisciplines of geology, oceanography, meteorology, astronomy, geophysics, geochemistry, paleontology, hydrology, seismology, and soil science. The methodologies and environmental issues of earth sciences are also included." Am Ref Books Annu, 1991

Includes bibliographic references

Weiner, Jonathan
Planet Earth. Bantam Bks. 1986 370p il $27.95 **550**

1. Earth sciences
ISBN 0-553-05096-6 LC 85-47795

Published as a companion volume to a public television series this book discusses "plate tectonics, oceanography, climatic change, the composition of the other planets, the workings of the sun, the origin of natural resources, and the origin and future of life on Earth. . . . [It] can serve as a useful introduction to the earth sciences for the layperson." Libr J

Includes bibliography

550.3 Earth sciences— Encyclopedias and dictionaries

The **Concise** Oxford dictionary of earth sciences; edited by Ailsa Allaby and Michael Allaby. Oxford Univ. Press 1990 xxi, 410p hardcover o.p. paperback available $9.95 **550.3**

1. Earth sciences—Dictionaries
ISBN 0-19-286125-5 (pa) LC 89-16387

"Some 6,000 alphabetically organized headwords from all disciplines in the earth sciences are defined and explained. Brief, two- to three-sentence definitions include biographical entries for important figures and cross-references to terms defined elsewhere in the dictionary. Prepared by 33 contributors and advisors, with about a third of the terms drawn from *The Oxford Dictionary of natural history* [entered in class 508]. Useful bibliography of sources." Sheehy. Guide to Ref Books. 10th edition. suppl

551 Geology

Lambert, David, 1932-
Field guide to geology; [by] David Lambert and the Diagram Group. Facts on File 1988 256p il $24.95; pa $14.95 **551**

1. Geology
ISBN 0-8160-1697-6; 0-8160-2032-9 (pa) LC 88-3751

This "introductory field guide to geology for students and the general public is well-illustrated, depicting all aspects of geology." Malinowsky. Best Sci & Technol Ref Books for Young People

Includes bibliography

551.1 Gross structure and properties of the earth

Ballard, Robert D.
Exploring our living planet. National Geographic Soc. 1983 366p il maps $19.95 **551.1**

1. Earth sciences 2. Plate tectonics
ISBN 0-87044-459-X LC 83-2336

"After a discussion of the theory and geological background of plate tectonics, Ballard takes the reader to a number of sites of current plate movement—Iceland, Hawaii, and Italy among them." Choice

"Computer-drawn block diagrams in several chapters provide brilliant vehicles for visual presentation of complex information." Sci Books Films

Includes bibliography

551.2 Volcanoes, earthquakes, thermal waters and gases

Bullard, Fred M. (Fred Mason), 1901-
Volcanoes of the Earth. 2nd rev ed.
University of Tex. Press 1984 629p il $40
551.2

1. Volcanoes
ISBN 0-292-78706-5   LC 83-21738
"The Dan Danciger publication series"
First published 1962 with title: Volcanoes in history, in theory, in eruption

Using nontechnical language, the author describes the history and mythology of volcanoes and their effect on the environment, as well as volcanic cycles, birth of new volcanoes and the relationship of volcanoes to plate tectonics

Includes bibliography

Carson, Rob, 1950-
Mount St. Helens: the eruption and recovery of a volcano; with selected photographs by Geff Hinds, Cheryl Haselhorst and Gary Braasch. Sasquatch Bks. 1990 160p il hardcover o.p. paperback available $19.95   **551.2**

1. Mount Saint Helens (Wash.)
ISBN 0-912365-32-3 (pa)   LC 90-31009
The author "describes the eruption of Mount St. Helens in 1980, and goes on to report what has happened in the devastated area since then. . . . Mr. Carson has a lively story to tell and does it well. The photographs . . . provide beauty as well as information." Atlantic

Cone, Joseph
Fire under the sea; the discovery of the most extroardinary environment on earth—volcanic hot springs on the ocean floor.
Morrow 1991 285p il $25; pa $12   **551.2**

1. Ocean bottom
ISBN 0-688-09834-7; 0-688-11905-0 (pa)
          LC 90-15574
The author examines the undersea hot springs on the Galapagos Rift and their biological and geological significance

Includes bibliographic references

Erickson, Jon, 1948-
Volcanoes and earthquakes. TAB Bks.
1988 308p il $22.95; pa $15.95   **551.2**

1. Volcanoes 2. Earthquakes
ISBN 0-8306-1942-9; 0-8306-2842-8 (pa)
          LC 87-18030
"The major tectonic areas of the world are reviewed, and specific examples of recent volcanic and earthquake activity are analyzed. Predictions regarding these natural disasters are discussed, and the effects of bomb testing and ozone depletion are suggested as possible problem-causing factors for the future. An excellent general text for anyone with a basic understanding of geology." Booklist

Van Rose, Susanna
Volcanoes; [by Susanna van Rose and Ian Mercer] 2nd ed. Harvard Univ. Press 1991
59p il maps pa $9.95   **551.2**

1. Volcanoes
ISBN 0-674-94307-4   LC 90-24036
First published 1974 in the United Kingdom
Cover title
This defines volcanoes, explains why and how they erupt, consequences of eruption and includes information about several famous volcanoes

Walker, Bryce S.
Earthquake; by Bryce Walker and the editors of Time-Life Books. Time-Life Bks.
1982 176p il (Planet earth) $18.60   **551.2**

1. Earthquakes   LC 81-16662
The history of earthquakes is studied, as well as the scientific advances made in predicting and preparing for future earthquakes

Includes bibliography

551.4 Geomorphology and hydrosphere

Jackson, Donald Dale, 1935-
Underground worlds; by Donald Dale Jackson and the editors of Time-Life Books.
Time-Life Bks. 1982 176p il (Planet earth) $18.60   **551.4**

1. Caves   LC 82-782
Describes cave formations, various caves around the world and the science of speleology. Illustrated with color photographs and drawings

Includes bibliography

551.46 Hydrosphere. Oceanography

Carson, Rachel, 1907-1964
The sea around us; [by] Rachel L. Carson; introduction by Ann H. Zwinger; afterword by Jeffrey S. Levinton. Oxford Univ. Press 1989 xxvii, 250p $24.95; pa $8.95   **551.46**

1. Ocean
ISBN 0-19-506186-1; 0-19-506997-8 (pa)
          LC 89-16333
First published 1951; revised edition published 1961; this is a reissue of the 1979 edition which added the introduction and afterword

Beginning with a description of how the earth acquired its oceans, the book covers such topics as how life began in the primeval sea, the hidden lands, the life discovered in the abyss by highly delicate sounding apparatus, currents and tides, the formation of volcanic islands, and mineral resources

Includes bibliography

The **Facts** on File dictionary of marine science; [edited by] Barbara Charton. Facts on File 1988 325p il $24.95; pa $12.95

551.46

1. Oceanography—Dictionaries
ISBN 0-8160-1031-5; 0-8160-2369-7 (pa)

LC 82-15715

This work "includes nearly 2,000 entries covering a wide range of marine phenomena, including water chemistry, marine ecosystems, physical features of the oceans, currents and their effects, and fauna and flora of the ocean." Topical Ref Books

Groves, Donald G.
The oceans: a book of questions and answers; [by] Don Groves. Wiley 1989 203p il maps (Wiley nature editions) pa $14.95

551.46

1. Oceanography
ISBN 0-471-60712-6

LC 88-32625

An introduction to oceanography presented in a question-and-answer format

Includes bibliography

The **Random** House atlas of the oceans; introduction by Jacques Cousteau. Random House 1991 200p il maps $39.50

551.46

1. Ocean 2. Marine biology
ISBN 0-679-40830-4

LC 91-675019

Published in the United Kingdom with title: Oceans
"Published in association with the World Conservation Union (IUCN)"
This volume is "organized in six sections: origins of the oceans, living resources, environment for life; harvesting the seas; the atlas itself; and the challenge of conservation. . . . The atlas is divided by ocean with information on fishing areas, industrial centers, oil and gas fields, threatened species, coastal development, coastal eco-systems, regional agreements, peoples, problems and pollution provided for each ocean." Libr J
For a fuller review see: Booklist, May 1, 1992

The **Times** atlas and encyclopedia of the sea; edited by Alastair Couper. 2nd ed. Harper & Row 1989 272p il maps $65

551.46

1. Ocean—Atlases
ISBN 0-06-016287-2

LC 89-675164

First published 1983 in the United Kingdom with title: The Times atlas of the oceans

Illustrated with photos, maps, tables, and charts, the 105 articles discuss the geography, natural resources, commercial use and environmental status of the world's oceans

551.48 Hydrology

Pringle, Laurence P.
Rivers and lakes; by Laurence Pringle and the editors of Time-Life Books. Time-Life Bks. 1985 176p il (Planet earth) $18.60

551.48

1. Rivers 2. Lakes 3. Freshwater biology

LC 84-24463

Covers the natural history of rivers and lakes of the United States and the ecology of plant and animal life therein

Includes bibliography

551.5 Meteorology

Lockhart, Gary
The weather companion; an album of meteorological history, science, legend, and folklore. Wiley 1988 230p il maps (Wiley science editions) pa $12.95

551.5

1. Meteorology 2. Weather
ISBN 0-471-62079-3

LC 88-6884

This "is a compendium of weather lore, facts, history, and science and covers everything from ancient myths to current research." Sci Teach

Includes bibliography

551.6 Climatology and weather

Ludlum, David M., 1910-
The Audubon Society field guide to North American weather. Knopf 1991 656p il maps $18

551.6

1. Weather forecasting
ISBN 0-679-40851-7

LC 91-52707

"A Chanticleer Press edition"
"The opening essays provide in-depth information on topics such as clouds, snowstorms, floods, etc. About half of the book is comprised of labelled, high-quality photographs. The third section gives description, environment, season, range, and significance of each type of weather. Clear diagrams, simple definitions, and a readable text make this an excellent selection." SLJ

Includes glossary

Pearce, E. A.
The Times Books world weather guide; [by] E.A. Pearce and Gordon Smith. updated ed. Times Bks. 1990 480p maps pa $17.95

551.6

1. Meteorology 2. Weather
ISBN 0-8129-1881-9

LC 90-50319

First published 1984
"Seasonal weather conditions for almost 500 cities worldwide make up the content of this volume. . . . The introductory material contains explanations of weather conditions, charts of heat and humidity, the windchill index, and a glossary of terms. The main body of the work, arranged by continent and then by nation and city, includes a survey of the country's climate, followed by charts for cities." Nichols. Guide to Ref Books for Sch Media Cent. 4th edition

Weather almanac. Gale Res. il maps $120

551.6

1. United States—Climate—Statistics 2. Weather—Statistics

First published 1974. (6th edition 1991) Periodically revised

Current editor: Frank E. Bair
"Definitions and articles on major weather events and meteorological issues. Includes layperson's guide to 'weather fundamentals' and a glossary. Provides meteoro-

Weather almanac—*Continued*
logical and climatological information and statistics for
major U.S. and world cities." N Y Public Libr Book
of How & Where to Look It Up

Weather of U.S. cities. Gale Res. $200
551.6

1. United States—Climate—Statistics 2. Weather—
Statistics

First published 1981 as a two volume set. (4th edition
1992) Periodically revised

Current editor: Frank E. Bair

"A guide to the weather histories of 270 key cities
and weather observation stations in the United States
and its island territories, providing narrative summaries
and records of weather normals, means and extremes for
each observation point." Title page

Williams, Jack, 1936-
The weather book. Vintage Bks. 1992
212p il maps pa $18   **551.6**

1. Weather 2. United States—Climate
ISBN 0-679-73669-7   LC 91-50697

At head of title: USA today

This illustrated book contains information about U.S.
weather and climate, including storms, precipitation, and
forecasting. Profiles of atmospheric scientists and an
explanation of the greenhouse effect are included

Includes bibliography

551.7 Historical geology

Gould, Stephen Jay, 1941-
Time's arrow, time's cycle; myth and
metaphor in the discovery of geological
time. Harvard Univ. Press 1987 222p il
(Jerusalem-Harvard lectures) $18.95   **551.7**

1. Burnet, Thomas, 1635?-1715 2. Hutton, James,
1726-1797 3. Lyell, Sir Charles, 1797-1875 4. Geology
5. Time
ISBN 0-674-89198-8   LC 86-29485

In this historical account of the discovery of geological
time, the author reexamines three British classics of
geology; Thomas Burnet's Sacred theory of the earth
(1690), James Hutton's Theory of the earth (1795) and
Sir Charles Lyell's Principles of geology (1833) in the
light of the two conceptions of time (sequential and cyclical) evoked by the book's metaphorical title

Includes bibliography

553.8 Gems

Arem, Joel E., 1943-
Color encyclopedia of gemstones. 2nd ed.
Van Nostrand Reinhold 1987 248p il $59.95
553.8

1. Precious stones
ISBN 0-442-20833-2   LC 86-26759
First published 1977

"This well-written encyclopedia covers over 200 gemstones, giving chemical formula, crystal structure, colors,
luster, hardness, density, cleavage, optics, spectral data,
luminescence, and size. The color photography is outstanding, capturing the cut and brilliance of each gem."
Malinowsky. Best Sci & Technol Ref Books for Young
People

Includes bibliography

Webster, Robert
Gems; their sources, descriptions and
identification. 4th ed, revised by B. W.
Anderson. Butterworths 1983 xxii, 1006p il
$95   **553.8**

1. Precious stones
ISBN 0-408-01148-3   LC 83-182288

First published 1962

This guide to gemstones also includes "descriptions of
the newer synthetic stones (cubic zirconia, for example)
and of the methods used to change the colors of gemstones. Intended primarily for the professional gemologist,
this . . . edition will appeal to all serious collectors and
to many mineralogists." Am Ref Books Annu, 1985

Includes bibliography

557 Earth sciences—North America

McPhee, John A.
Basin and range; [by] John McPhee.
Farrar, Straus & Giroux 1981 215p $19.95;
pa $8.95   **557**

1. Deffeyes, Kenneth S. 2. Geology—West (U.S.)
ISBN 0-374-10914-1; 0-374-51690-1 (pa)

LC 80-28679

"An essay on the earth's history. It concentrates on
telling the story of the series of parallel mountain ranges
and valleys that can be found from Utah to California—
formed by the stretching apart of the earth's crust—that
is known as the Basin and Range. McPhee tells of his
travels across the arid region . . . in the company of
Princeton geologist Kenneth Deffeyes." Libr J

In suspect terrain; [by] John McPhee.
Farrar, Straus & Giroux 1983 209p $19.95;
pa $11   **557**

1. Harris, Anita 2. Geology—Northeastern States
ISBN 0-374-17650-7; 0-374-51794-0 (pa)

LC 82-21031

"McPhee tells of his travels with U.S. Geological Survey geologist Anita Harris into Brooklyn and along Interstate 80 through New Jersey, Pennsylvania, Ohio, and
into Indiana. McPhee describes the origins of the bedrock
and glacial features they encounter and recounts the
geologic history of the Appalachians. He also tells of
Harris' accomplishments and of her objections to some
current theories of the origin of the easternmost portion
of North America." Libr J

Rising from the plains; [by] John McPhee.
Farrar, Straus & Giroux 1986 213p il
$19.95; pa $8.95   **557**

1. Love, David 2. Geology—Rocky Mountain region
ISBN 0-374-25082-0; 0-374-52065-8 (pa)

LC 86-14891

The author offers an "account of the life of David
Love—a native of Wyoming and its preeminent geological authority. . . . McPhee's explanations of both the
wonders of land formations and Love's lifelong devotion
to a solitary, self-absorbing science make for fascinating
reading." Booklist

Redfern, Ron
The making of a continent; text and photographs by Ron Redfern; color illustrations by Gary Hincks; designed by Betty Binns. Times Bks. 1983 242p il hardcover o.p. paperback available $19.95

557

1. Geology—North America
ISBN 0-8129-1617-4 (pa)　　　LC 83-45041

This book is an "attempt to outline the geologic history of North America by looking at a number of pertinent aspects of earth history and a number of selected areas of the continent. . . . The text is quite well done and will appeal to most readers even though there are places where even the informed lay reader may get bogged down." Libr J

Includes bibliographic references

560 Paleontology. Paleozoology

Arduini, Paolo
Simon & Schuster's guide to fossils; [by] Paolo Arduini and Giorgio Teruzzi. Simon & Schuster 1986 317p il $22.95; pa $12.95

560

1. Fossils
ISBN 0-671-63219-1; 0-671-63132-2 (pa)
　　　　　　　　　　　　　LC 86-22043

Original Italian edition, 1986

"This is an excellent field guide to identifying collecting fossils. Each fossil is described and locations of where they can be found are indicated. Notes are given on the preservation of fossil sites so that areas are not destroyed." Malinowsky. Best Sci & Technol Ref Books for Young People

Cvancara, Alan M.
Sleuthing fossils; the art of investigating past life. Wiley 1990 203p il (Wiley science editions) $24.95; pa $12.95　　　**560**

1. Fossils
ISBN 0-471-51046-7; 0-471-62077-7 (pa)
　　　　　　　　　　　　　LC 89-36282

This book "has been designed for those seeking to know more about paleontology and what its practitioners, the paleontologists, actually do. . . . The book is organized into 10 well-written chapters that are crammed full of information, personal experiences, and descriptions of the work of several well-known paleontologists. . . . Beginners will appreciate the printing of technical terms in boldface type throughout the book and the phonetic spellings of unfamiliar terms. Well-chosen lists of recommended readings appear at the end of each chapter and also in the appendix." Sci Books Films

Eldredge, Niles
Fossils; the evolution and extinction of species; photography by Murray Alcosser; introduction by Stephen Jay Gould. Abrams 1991 xx, 220p il $60　　　**560**

1. Fossils 2. Evolution
ISBN 0-8109-3305-5　　　LC 91-302

The author "examines what the fossilized remains of earth's ancient flora and fauna reveal about mass extinction and the origin of species." Publisher's note

"Full-page photographs adorn about half the pages of this beautiful book. . . . These essays are not intended as detailed academic treatments; rather, they provide a touch of the history of discovery, and the excitement of delving into the unknown—doing paleontology. The anatomical descriptions are easy to understand. This is a 'coffee table book' of the highest quality." Sci Books Films

Includes bibliography

Life pulse; episodes from the story of the fossil record; with illustrations by Lisa C. Heilman Lomauro and photographs by Sidney S. Horenstein. Facts on File 1987 246p il $21.95　　　**560**

1. Fossils 2. Geology, Stratigraphic 3. Life (Biology)
ISBN 0-8160-1151-6　　　LC 86-4558

Eldredge discusses "events in life history, including the origin of life, the Pharenozoic radiation, and the Cambrian, Paleozoic, and Cretaceous extinctions. . . . He argues that evolutionary history is episodic, rather than slow and continuous." Libr J

"Few of the facts presented are unknown to most paleontologists, but the nonscientist will perhaps find a new perspective on evolution that avoids invoking long periods of time for significant changes to appear." Sci Books Films

The miner's canary; unravelling the mysteries of extinction. Prentice Hall Press 1991 246p il $20　　　**560**

1. Extinct animals 2. Fossils
ISBN 0-13-583659-X　　　LC 91-9140

The author "reviews the evidence for extinction and its causes, primarily using fossil evidence and focusing on climatic change and loss of habitat." Libr J

The book "rings with integrity. The author seems almost apologetic about offering views of his own that stray somewhat from his self-imposed syllabus, and he takes care to present opposing views." N Y Times Book Rev

Includes bibliographic references

Erickson, Jon, 1948-
An introduction to fossils and minerals; seeking clues to the earth's past. Facts on File 1992 184p il maps $24.95　　　**560**

1. Fossils 2. Mineralogy 3. Geology
ISBN 0-8160-2587-8　　　LC 91-34390

"The volume begins by detailing the earth's early history, then explains how fossils are used as clues to the earth's past, how they tell us about evolution and the rise and extinction of species, and how they are laid down in the earth's rocks. . . . The book also discusses the formation of crystals and minerals, how they grow, and how to identify and classify them. The volume concludes with information on . . . where and how to collect fossils and minerals." Publisher's note

The book is "quite comprehensive. . . . Outstanding, clear diagrams and various charts and maps clarify the material." SLJ

Includes bibliography

Fenton, Carroll Lane, 1900-

The fossil book; a record of prehistoric life; [by] Carroll Lane Fenton and Mildred Adams Fenton. rev and expanded, by Patricia Vickers Rich, Thomas Hewitt Rich, and Mildred Adams Fenton. Doubleday 1989 740p il $65   **560**

1. Fossils
ISBN 0-385-19327-0   LC 86-16245
First published 1958

This book "ranges with admirable thoroughness and clarity over all 3.5 billion years of living things and the remains they left. It describes what fossils are, how they formed, found and studied." N Y Times Book Rev

Includes bibliographic references

Fortey, Richard A.

Fossils; the key to the past; [by] Richard Fortey. new ed. Harvard Univ. Press 1991 187p il $29.95   **560**

1. Fossils
ISBN 0-674-31135-3   LC 90-24760
First published 1982 by Van Nostrand Reinhold

In this volume, fossils "from earliest Precambrian forms onward are discussed, emphasizing evolutionary trends and extinctions, and relationships with habitat environments and geologic processes, such as volcanism and meteorite impacts, are evaluated. . . . Aspects of preservation, discovery, collection, and identification are discussed." Choice

Gould, Stephen Jay, 1941-

Wonderful life: the Burgess Shale and the nature of history. Norton 1989 347p il $19.95; pa $10.95   **560**

1. Fossils 2. Evolution
ISBN 0-393-02705-8; 0-393-30700-X (pa)
                                      LC 88-37469

"The Burgess Shale is a rock formation containing the fossilized remains of a large number of marine creatures that no longer exist, and also the remains of some that do. The nonsurvivors appear to have been as well equipped to flourish as their contemporaries. Why did they not? . . . [This is an] account of the studies, the misinterpretations, and the revisions of opinion arising from the Burgess Shale material." Atlantic

"With his usual grace and wit Gould guides readers through the technical terminology and explains the significance of these fossils that exploded past assumptions about the history of life." Libr J

Includes bibliography

Lambert, David, 1932-

The field guide to prehistoric life; [by] David Lambert and the Diagram Group. Facts on File 1985 256p il maps $24.95
                                      560

1. Fossils
ISBN 0-8160-1125-7   LC 84-21237

"Presents to the amateur fossil hunter a complete, systematic means of identifying and understanding fossil life. More than 500 illustrations, maps, and charts." NY Public Libr Book of How & Where to Look It Up

Includes bibliography

Parker, Steve

The practical paleontologist; Raymond L. Bernor, editor. Simon & Schuster 1991 159p il maps hardcover o.p. paperback available $14.95   **560**

1. Fossils
ISBN 0-671-69307-7 (pa)   LC 90-45178
"A Fireside book"

This volume includes a "history of paleontology, a discussion of the nature of fossils and their use in geology, an examination of evolution as illustrated by fossil lineages, and . . . information about the practical problems of finding, collecting, preparing, and preserving fossils." Sci Books Films

Raup, David M.

Extinction; bad genes or bad luck? Norton 1991 210p hardcover o.p. paperback available $9.95   **560**

1. Mass extinction of species
ISBN 0-393-30927-4 (pa)   LC 90-27192

In this study of extinction, the author challenges the view that internal factors are critical in explaining the death of a species. Surveying past extinctions, Raup seeks to locate their cause in external factors, specifically the impact of meteorites

"Neither his readers nor his scientific colleagues are likely to endorse everything he says, but his book is an eminently entertaining and informative read." N Y Times Book Rev

Includes bibliographies

Thompson, Ida

The Audubon Society field guide to North American fossils; with photographs by Townsend P. Dickinson; visual key by Carol Nehring. Knopf 1982 846p il maps flexible bdg $18   **560**

1. Fossils
ISBN 0-394-52412-8   LC 81-84772
"A Chanticleer Press edition. The Audubon Society field guide series"

"This softbound field guide to fossils is divided into a section of color photographs followed by a section of detailed descriptions. It covers 420 fossils of marine and freshwater invertebrates, insects, plants, and vertebrates that are likely to be found by the amateur." Malinowsky. Best Sci & Technol Ref Books for Young People

Ward, Peter Douglas, 1949-

On Methuselah's trail; living fossils and the great extinctions. Freeman, W.H. 1992 212p il $18.95; pa $12.95   **560**

1. Fossils 2. Evolution 3. Life (Biology)
ISBN 0-7167-2203-8; 0-7167-2488-X (pa)
                                      LC 91-17071

"Living fossils are species that have survived nearly unchanged since prehistoric times. For scientists they are a window to the past. Ward, an expert on the nautilus, tells us a fascinating story of scientific discovery through a combination of personal narratives and examples of how the study of living creatures helps to interpret the fossil record." Libr J

This is an "excellent account of the practice of modern paleontology that includes the all-important role of fieldwork." Sci Books Films

567 Fossil cold-blooded vertebrates

The **Macmillan** illustrated encyclopedia of dinosaurs and prehistoric animals; a visual who's who of prehistoric life; [by] Dougal Dixon [et al.]; foreword by Malcolm C. McKenna. Macmillan 1988 312p il $39.95; pa $25 **567**

1. Prehistoric animals 2. Dinosaurs 3. Fossils
ISBN 0-02-580191-0; 0-02-042981-9 (pa) LC 88-1800

This "encyclopedia details over 600 species of dinosaurs and other prehistoric animals. Each chapter covers a specific type, such as birds, reptiles, or mammal-like reptiles. The illustrations are excellent and add much to the text." Malinowsky. Best Sci & Technol Ref Books for Young People

567.9 Fossil reptiles. Dinosaurs

Bakker, Robert T.
The dinosaur heresies; new theories unlocking the mystery of the dinosaurs and their extinction. Morrow 1986 481p il $24.95 **567.9**

1. Dinosaurs
ISBN 0-688-04287-2 LC 86-12643
Also available in paperback from Zebra Bks.

"Bakker analyzes the controversies surrounding dinosaur extinction and advances original theories of his own, while painting a picture of very active, adaptable animals. Easily understandable, well illustrated and without scientific jargon." N Y Public Libr Book of How & Where to Look It Up

Dinosaurs past and present; edited by Sylvia J. Czerkas and Everett C. Olson; introduction by John M. Harris. University of Wash. Press 1987 2v il hardcover o.p. paperbacks available ea $29.95 **567.9**

1. Dinosaurs
ISBN 0-295-96707-2 (v1); 0-295-96708-0 (v2) LC 87-60944
Published in association with the Natural History Museum of Los Angeles County

Essays by subject specialists are illustrated with artistic restorations of dinosaurs and their environment

Includes bibliography

Dixon, Dougal, 1947-
The new dinosaurs; an alternative evolution; foreword by Desmond Morris. Salem House 1988 120p il o.p.; Fawcett Bks. paperback available $14.95 **567.9**

1. Dinosaurs
ISBN 0-449-90442-3 (pa) LC 88-1994
The author has written this book "under the guise of 'what if.' What if the dinosaurs had not disappeared? What if they had then continued to evolve? What if they were still around us today? What would they look like? . . . All of these questions are answered in this well-written and well-constructed book." Voice Youth Advocates

Horner, John R.
Digging dinosaurs; [by] John R. Horner and James Gorman; illustrated by Donna Braginetz and Kris Ellingsen. Workman 1988 210p il maps $17.95 **567.9**

1. Dinosaurs 2. Fossils
ISBN 0-89480-220-8 LC 88-40226
Also available in paperback from HarperCollins Pubs.

"Paleontologist Horner reviews his landmark findings from a six-year dig in Montana, which provided the basis for his revolutionary theories that dinosaurs were communal-living, warm-blooded creatures." Booklist

Lambert, David, 1932-
A field guide to dinosaurs; [by] the Diagram Group. Avon Bks. 1983 256p il pa $9.95 **567.9**

1. Dinosaurs
ISBN 0-380-83519-3 LC 83-2820
This dinosaur book "is done in field guide style, with succinct text descriptions emphasizing differences between similar species and a wealth of illustrations, together with locations found and special features of each group. While other books emphasize reconstructions, this one pays attention to skeletal remains." Libr J

Includes bibliography

Lessem, Don
Kings of creation; how a new breed of scientists is revolutionizing our understanding of dinosaurs; illustrated by John Sibbick. Simon & Schuster 1992 367p il maps $25 **567.9**

1. Dinosaurs
ISBN 0-671-73491-1 LC 91-47904
The author "introduces taphonomy, the study of circumstances of dinosaur death and preservation, and cladistics, a classification system that helps define relationships among dinosaurs. We meet scientists Robert Bakker, Peter Dodson, John Ostrum, Phil Currie, Paul Soreno, Jack Horner and others who have upended the traditional world of dinosaur studies with theories of warm-bloodedness, nurture and migration." Publ Wkly

"The writing is nontechnical, but quite clear, and colorful in places, but never florid." Sci Books Films

Includes bibliographic references

McGowan, Chris, 1942-
Dinosaurs, spitfires, and sea dragons; [by] Christopher McGowan. Harvard Univ. Press 1991 365p il $29.95; pa $14.95 **567.9**

1. Reptiles, Fossil 2. Evolution
ISBN 0-674-20769-6; 0-674-20770-X (pa) LC 90-41552

First published 1983 with title: The successful dragons: a natural history of extinct reptiles

"The author deals comprehensively with dinosaurs, flying reptiles—including birds—and marine reptiles. His style is authoritative, clear, and concise. The book is a delight to read." Sci Books Films

Includes bibliography

Norman, David
Dinosaur! Prentice-Hall 1991 192p il $25
                                  567.9

1. Dinosaurs 2. Fossils
ISBN 0-13-218140-1   LC 91-15332
"Conveys the geological time scale, evolution, and
natural history of dinosaurs, as well as the paleon-
tological discoveries that have enabled their story to be
reconstructed." N Y Public Libr Book of How & Where
to Look It Up
Includes bibliography

Paul, Gregory S.
Predatory dinosaurs of the world; a
complete illustrated guide; written and
drawn by Gregory S. Paul. Simon &
Schuster 1988 464p il hardcover o.p.
paperback available $14   **567.9**

1. Dinosaurs
ISBN 0-671-68733-6 (pa)   LC 88-23052
"A New York Academy of Sciences book"
"In the first part of the book Paul describes how the
predatory dinosaurs (meat-eating dinosaurs, as opposed
to herbivorous dinosaurs) evolved, what they looked like
and how they lived. He dispels some commonly held
notions: dinosaurs were not cold-blooded, slow or stupid;
they were, in fact, the ancestors of birds. The second
part of the book is an illustrated catalogue of all important predatory dinosaurs known to date, a new
reorganization of predatory dinosaur taxonomy and
systematics." Publ Wkly
Includes bibliography

The **Ultimate** dinosaur; past-present-future;
Byron Preiss and Robert Silverberg,
editors; Peter Dodson, science editor;
Howard Zimmerman and William R.
Alschuler, associate editors; Martin H.
Greenberg, consulting editor. Bantam Bks.
1992 336p il $35   **567.9**
1. Dinosaurs
ISBN 0-553-07676-0   LC 91-33829
"A Byron Preiss book"
This combines "essays by distinguished scientists (e.g.,
David Gillette and Philip Currie), stories by noted
science fiction writers (e.g., Ray Bradbury and Poul Anderson), and artworks by first-rate illustrators in a single
book on dinosaurs. And, despite the disparate nature of
these genres, it all fits together pretty well. . . . Chapters,
each including fictional and nonfictional contributions,
span the time from the dawn of the age of dinosaurs
to its end. The book also includes some helpful charts
and diagrams." Libr J
Includes bibliographic references

Wilford, John Noble
The riddle of the dinosaur; drawings by
Douglas Henderson. Knopf 1985 304p il
$24.95; pa $13   **567.9**
1. Dinosaurs
ISBN 0-394-52763-1; 0-394-74392-X (pa)
                                  LC 85-40015
The author "traces some of the scientific debates
about dinosaurs: which creatures were their ancestors,
their rivals, their descendants? Were they hot- or cold-
blooded, fast or slow, smart or dumb, sociable or
solitary?" N Y Times Book Rev

"Wilford tells the tales and elucidates the theoretical
controversies in superlative popular style." Booklist
Includes bibliography

573.2   Evolution and genetics of humankind

Calvin, William H., 1939-
The ascent of mind; Ice Age climates and
the evolution of intelligence. Bantam Bks.
1991 302p il $19.95   **573.2**
1. Man—Origin 2. Brain 3. Consciousness
ISBN 0-553-07084-3   LC 90-45037
The author discusses "the question of why humanity
increased its mental faculties fourfold during the Ice Age
spans of 2.5-million years, while other species perished
or changed very little. . . . [He] postulates that cold
climates can increase mental activity as humans force
themselves to adapt or perish." Quill Quire
These "essays are lovely and evocative, and should
be of particular interest to those concerned with current
climatic and ecological trends." Libr J
Includes bibliography

Diamond, Jared M.
The third chimpanzee; the evolution and
future of the human animal; [by] Jared
Diamond. HarperCollins Pubs. 1992 407p il
maps $25; pa $12   **573.2**
1. Man—Origin 2. Evolution
ISBN 0-06-018307-1; 0-06-098403-1 (pa)
                                  LC 91-50455
First published 1991 in the United Kingdom with
title: The rise and fall of the third chimpanzee
The author "argues that the human being is just a
third species of chimpanzee but nevertheless a unique
animal essentially due to its capacity for innovation,
which caused a great leap forward in hominoid evolution. After stressing the significance of spoken language,
along with art and technology, Diamond focuses on the
self-destructive propensities of our species." Libr J
Includes bibliography

Johanson, Donald C.
Lucy: the beginnings of humankind; [by]
Donald C. Johanson and Maitland A. Edey.
Simon & Schuster 1981 409p il hardcover
o.p. paperback available $14   **573.2**
1. Man—Origin 2. Mammals, Fossil
ISBN 0-671-72499-1 (pa)   LC 80-21759
In November 1974 at a place called Hadar in Ethiopia
Donald Johanson "discovered the partial skeleton of an
extremely primitive female, erect-walking primate or
hominid. . . . The skeleton received the name 'Lucy.'
Much later, Lucy received the scientific name,
Australopithecus afarensis, and it was determined she was
some 3.5 million years old. . . . This book is Johanson's
own story of the events leading up to and subsequent
to Lucy's discovery." Best Sellers
Includes bibliography

Johanson, Donald C.—*Continued*

Lucy's child: the discovery of a human ancestor; [by] Donald Johanson and James Shreeve. Morrow 1989 318p il maps $22.95

573.2

1. Man—Origin 2. Mammals, Fossil
ISBN 0-688-06492-2   LC 89-9461
Also available in paperback from Avon Bks.

This is an account of archaeological excavations in Tanzania in 1986. The authors also discuss current research and debates in paleoanthropology

"Although the descriptions of digging fossils are rich in detail and dialogue, . . . it becomes clear that the book's real value lies elsewhere, in the lengthy digressions. There Mr. Johanson provides a lively review of the latest thinking about human origins." N Y Times Book Rev

Includes bibliography

Leakey, Richard E., 1944-

Origins; what new discoveries reveal about the emergence of our species and its possible future; [by] Richard E. Leakey and Roger Lewin. Dutton 1977 264p il o.p.; Penguin Bks. paperback available $9.95

573.2

1. Man—Origin 2. Evolution
ISBN 0-14-015336-5 (pa)   LC 77-77941
In this examination of human origins the authors discuss early predecessors of modern man and study species survival and development as part of the process of biological evolution

Includes bibliographic references

Origins reconsidered; in search of what makes us human; [by] Richard Leakey and Roger Lewin. Doubleday 1992 375p il $25

573.2

1. Man—Origin 2. Evolution
ISBN 0-385-41264-9   LC 92-6661
"Leakey and Lewin discuss how conceptions of human anatomical and behavioral development have been radically altered within the last 12 years by new discoveries and research in other fields. They review the developments and assert Leakey's own hypotheses based on these discoveries. . . . This is an engrossing book written for the layperson, fully explaining anthropological terms and theories when necessary. It's a solid introduction to current theory concerning human development." SLJ

Lee, Thomas F.

The Human Genome Project; cracking the genetic code of life. Plenum Press 1991 323p il $24.50

573.2

1. Human Genome Project 2. Genetic mapping
ISBN 0-306-43965-4   LC 91-21358
The author "gives some history, explains what genes and DNA are and what they do, describes maps and markers, and then turns to an examination of the Human Genome Project: its plans, people, potential products, funding, and ethics." Booklist

Includes bibliography

Lewin, Roger

In the age of mankind; a Smithsonian book of human evolution. Smithsonian Bks. 1988 255p il $37.50; pa $19.95   **573.2**

1. Man—Origin 2. Evolution
ISBN 0-89599-022-9; 0-89599-025-3 (pa)
          LC 88-42686
This book provides an "introduction to selected aspects of human evolution. Lewin . . . presents some pertinent evidence (including data derived from paleontology, archeology, ethnography, biochemistry, genetics, and ecology) and various interpretations based on that evidence." Sci Books Films

Shapiro, Robert, 1935-

The human blueprint; the race to unlock the secrets of our genetic script. St. Martin's Press 1991 xx, 412p il $24.95   **573.2**

1. Human Genome Project 2. Genetic mapping
ISBN 0-312-05873-X   LC 90-29153
Also available in paperback from Bantam Bks.

This is an account of the Human Genome Project, an attempt to map and interpret the entire human genetic code

Includes bibliography

Willis, Delta

The Hominid Gang; behind the scenes in the search for human origins; introduction by Stephen Jay Gould. Viking 1989 352p il maps o.p.; Penguin Bks. paperback available $12   **573.2**

1. Man—Origin 2. Mammals, Fossil
ISBN 0-14-01473-2 (pa)   LC 88-40281
The author discusses current research into human origins and interviews paleontologists such as Richard Leakey, Stephen Jay Gould, Donald Johanson and Alan Walker

"By describing her subject in terms of the individuals currently involved in research, [the author] manages to infuse life into the abraded bones and stones of the archeological record." N Y Times Book Rev

Includes bibliographic references

573.3   Prehistoric humankind

Spencer, Frank

Piltdown; a scientific forgery. Oxford Univ. Press 1990 xxvi, 272p il $24.95

573.3

1. Piltdown forgery
ISBN 0-19-858522-5   LC 90-7688
The Piltdown Man is "a specimen consisting of a partial skull and lower jaw which were once purported to belong to a prehistoric human ancestor. Its discovery was announced in 1912, but it was not until the 1950s that Piltdown Man was proved to be a fraud. . . . [The author discusses] the context of the Piltdown discovery, describes subsequent controversies over the interpretation of these remains, and discusses possible [forgers]." Libr J

"An impressive piece of historical research." Archaeology

574   Biology

Attenborough, David, 1926-
The living planet; a portrait of the Earth.
Little, Brown 1984 320p il hardcover o.p.
paperback available $17.95   **574**

1. Biology 2. Life (Biology)
ISBN 0-316-05749-5 (pa)   LC 84-14323

Companion volume Life on Earth, entered in class
575

This book "is a study of habitats—the polar regions,
jungle and desert, grass plain, the shore-line, islands, the
oceans and the sky. Each is discussed separately." Grow
Point

"It's an armchair naturalist's delight, fact rich and full
of splendid colorplates that provide extra impetus for
browsers." Booklist

Gould, Stephen Jay, 1941-
An urchin in the storm; essays about
books and ideas. Norton 1987 255p il
$18.95; pa $7.95   **574**

1. Biology
ISBN 0-393-02492-X; 0-393-30537-6 (pa)
    LC 87-21718

Analyzed in Essay and general literature index

This collection of Gould's book reviews is arranged
in broad subject areas: evolutionary theory, biological
determinism, time and geology

Lovelock, James
The ages of Gaia; a biography of our
living earth. Norton 1988 xx, 252p il $16.95
    574

1. Biology—Philosophy   2. Gaia   hypothesis
3. Biosphere 4. Life (Biology)
ISBN 0-393-02583-7   LC 87-36567

Also available in paperback from Bantam Bks.

"A volume of the Commonwealth Fund Book Program, under the editorship of Lewis Thomas"

"Gaia is the Greek goddess of the earth. For James
Lovelock she is the embodiment of a hypothesis: the
earth is not merely the abode of life but is a single
living organism. He proposes that all living species are
components of that organism, as cells are components
of the human body." N Y Times Book Rev

Includes bibliographic references

Healing Gaia; practical medicine for the
planet. Harmony Bks. 1991 192p il maps
$25   **574**

1. Biology—Philosophy 2. Gaia hypothesis 3. Ecology
4. Environmental protection
ISBN 0-517-57848-4   LC 91-72678

"A Gaia original"

In this work the author "takes the view of a
'planetary physician' to diagnose and propose cures for
many of the planet's environmental ills, such as global
warming and ozone depletion." Sci Books Films

This features "lavish illustrations. Both students of
ecology and those with only the most modest scientific
credentials will find the ingenious displays, charts and
diagrams of enormous heuristic value." Times Lit Suppl

Includes bibliographic references

Magill's survey of science, life science series;
edited by Frank N. Magill; consulting
editor, Laura L. Mays Hoopes. Salem
Press 1991 6v set $475   **574**

1. Life sciences
ISBN 0-89356-612-8   LC 90-19102

This reference work contains "articles by 188 academic
contributors. Each article . . . [discusses] recent developments, provides a glossary of principal terms, describes
methods of study, includes an essay that places the topic
within the context of scientific knowledge, and contains
cross references to related subjects. Entries are arranged
alphabetically. . . . Areas of coverage include animal and
plant anatomy and physiology, cell biology, ecology, evolution, genetics, and the origin of life." Libr J

Includes bibliographic references

Margulis, Lynn, 1938-
Five kingdoms; an illustrated guide to the
phyla of life on earth; [by] Lynn Margulis,
Karlene V. Schwartz. 2nd ed. Freeman,
W.H. 1988 376p il $37.95; pa $26.95 **574**

1. Biology
ISBN 0-7167-1885-5; 0-7167-1912-6 (pa)   LC 87-210

First published 1982

"After a general discussion of life based on cells, each
kingdom is described and includes a phylogeny showing
the possible evolutionary relationships that occur among
the phyla of that kingdom. It is arranged from the simplest to the most complex. A list of the better known
genera of the phylum being discussed is given and followed by an illustration and fully labeled anatomic
drawing of a representative species. The most typical
habitat on earth is indicated for each phylum. This is
a good introductory guide." Malinowsky. Best Sci &
Technol Ref Books for Young People

Includes bibliography

Thomas, Lewis, 1913-1993
The lives of a cell; notes of a biology
watcher. Viking 1974 153p o.p.; Penguin
Bks. paperback available $9   **574**

1. Biology—Philosophy
ISBN 0-14-004743-3 (pa)

Also available in paperback from Bantam Bks.

In this collection of twenty-nine short essays "the
author does not confine his scientist's eye to a
microscope. He takes a much wider view of the world,
looking at insect behavior and the possibility of intelligent life in outer space or bird songs and the evolution
of language. He also offers a modest proposal for saving
ourselves from nuclear self-destruction." Time

Includes bibliography

574.03   Biology—Encyclopedias and dictionaries

Hale, W. G.
The HarperCollins dictionary of biology;
[by] W.G. Hale and J.P. Margham.
HarperCollins Pubs. 1991 569p il hardcover
o.p. paperback available $13   **574.03**

1. Biology—Dictionaries
ISBN 0-06-461015-2 (pa)   LC 90-55500

Hale, W. G.—*Continued*

First published 1988 in the United Kingdom with title: Collins dictionary of biology

This dictionary "offers 2,000 well-written entries accompanied by plentiful line drawings, diagrams, and tables. Thumbnail biographies of biology notables are included." Recomm Ref Books in Paperback. 2d edition

Henderson's Dictionary of biological terms, [edited by] Eleanor Lawrence. Wiley $57.95   **574.03**

1. Biology—Dictionaries

Also available in Spanish from French & Spanish Bk. Corp.

"A Wiley-Interscience publication"

First published 1920 with title: Dictionary of scientific terms. (10th edition 1989) Periodically revised. Variant title: Dictionary of biological terms

Current editor: Eleanor Lawrence

This biological dictionary "contains over 22,000 entries, including expanded definitions and many new terms. Acronyms and biochemical terms are included; British spelling. Appendixes contain structural formulae of important biochemical compounds and outline classifications of the various kingdoms and phyla." Sheehy. Guide to Ref Books. 10th edition. suppl

574.1 Physiology

Campbell, Jeremy, 1931-

Winston Churchill's afternoon nap; a wide-awake inquiry into the human nature of time. Simon & Schuster 1986 432p $18.95   **574.1**

1. Biological rhythms 2. Time
ISBN 0-671-47547-9   LC 86-13743

In this "exploration of the nature of human time, Campbell . . . [attempts to explain the] ways in which our minds and bodies keep track of time—and how our sense of time is linked to our sense of self." Publisher's note

"An intelligent, carefully researched and instructive book. I know of no work of scientific exposition that packs between two covers so much information on chronobiology." N Y Times Book Rev

Includes bibliography

574.5 Ecology

Amos, William Hopkins

Atlantic & Gulf coasts; by William H. Amos and Stephen H. Amos. Knopf 1985 670p il maps (Audubon Society nature guides) pa $19   **574.5**

1. Atlantic Coast (North America) 2. Gulf Coast (U.S.) 3. Seashore ecology
ISBN 0-394-73109-3   LC 84-48676

"A Chanticleer Press edition"

"Along with companion volumes in the series by Brown, McConnaughey, MacMahon, Niering, Sutton, and Whitney [entered below], these similarly formatted guides contain detailed information on the habitat's features and characteristics, followed by vibrant colorplates of the indigenous flora and fauna as well as descriptive comments for each." Booklist

Includes bibliography

The **Atlas** of endangered species; edited by John Burton. Macmillan 1991 256p il maps $90   **574.5**

1. Endangered species 2. Wildlife conservation 3. Environmental protection
ISBN 0-02-897081-0   LC 91-12611

This "atlas proposes to educate and familiarize readers with the land, sea, air, and water species in all parts of the world threatened by extinction due to commercial hunting, pollution, and habitat destruction. . . . Insert maps, spotlight boxes, and captioned photographs illuminate each section." SLJ

For a fuller review see: Booklist, Feb. 1, 1992

Includes bibliographic references

Bodanis, David

The secret garden; dawn to dusk in the astonishing hidden world of the garden. Simon & Schuster 1992 187p il $25   **574.5**

1. Garden ecology
ISBN 0-671-66353-4   LC 92-23901

The author "takes us on a one-day trip, often at microscopic level, through the garden soil and among the plants and animals found there." Libr J

Brown, Lauren

Grasslands. Knopf 1985 606p il (Audubon Society nature guides) pa $19   **574.5**

1. Grassland ecology
ISBN 0-394-73121-2   LC 84-48675

"A Chanticleer Press edition"

Following the format of Atlantic & Gulf coasts by William Hopkins Amos, entered above, this covers the ecology of grasslands of the United States

Includes bibliography

Caufield, Catherine

In the rainforest. Knopf 1985 c1984 304p $24.95   **574.5**

1. Rain forests 2. Man—Influence on nature
ISBN 0-394-52701-1   LC 84-47644

Also available in paperback from University of Chicago Press

This "volume on the rain forests of the world includes discussion of human . . . impact and of the ecological roles that rain forests serve for humankind." Choice

"This forthright account makes a valuable contribution to our understanding and awareness of ecological repercussions." Booklist

Includes bibliography

Cowell, Adrian

The decade of destruction; the crusade to save the Amazon rain forest. Holt & Co. 1990 215p il maps $19.95   **574.5**

1. Rain forests 2. Man—Influence on nature 3. Amazon River valley
ISBN 0-8050-1494-2   LC 90-55473

Also available in paperback from Anchor Bks.

"Cowell has seen firsthand the encroachment of the government of Brazil and private developers on this great rain forest, and his keen descriptive abilities and straight-

Cowell, Adrian—*Continued*
forward approach afford his readers a good view as
well." Booklist

DiSilvestro, Roger L.
The endangered kingdom: the struggle to
save America's wildlife. Wiley 1989 241p il
(Wiley science editions) $19.95; pa $10.95
                                          574.5
1. Wildlife conservation 2. Endangered species
ISBN 0-471-60600-6; 0-471-52822-6 (pa)
                                   LC 88-38884

The author "considers the fate of American wildlife
from the advent of the European settlers to the present.
. . . Occasional optimism appears in his lucid analysis
of the numerous political and social forces that affect
the destiny of American wildlife. . . . Overall, however,
DeSilvestro's outlook is bleak." Publ Wkly

Includes bibliography

Hecht, Susanna B.
The fate of the forest; developers,
destroyers, and defenders of the Amazon;
[by] Susanna Hecht and Alexander
Cockburn. Verso Eds. [distributed by]
Routledge, Chapman & Hall 1989 266p il
$24.95   574.5
1. Rain forests 2. Man—Influence on nature
3. Amazon River valley
ISBN 0-86091-261-2   LC 89-39145

Also available in hardcover from Borgo Press and in
paperback from HarperCollins Pubs.

"The environmental and social issues at stake in the
battle over Brazilian forests are defined and analyzed in
this study. . . . The vanishing Amazon rain forest is
seen as an ecological disaster area. The authors describe
the forest's history and how it is now being destroyed
. . . by human exploitation. Both sides of the ecology
question are addressed, but the emphasis is on those
trying to save the forests from death." Booklist

Includes bibliography

Kricher, John C.
A field guide to eastern forests: North
America; text and photographs by John C.
Kricher; illustrated by Gordon Morrison.
Houghton Mifflin 1988 368p il $22.95; pa
$15.45   574.5
1. Forest ecology
ISBN 0-395-35346-7; 0-395-47953-3 (pa)
                                   LC 87-35247

"The Peterson field guide series"

"Sponsored by the National Audubon Society, the National Wildlife Federation, and the Roger Tory Peterson
Institute"

This "field guide introduces the forests of the eastern
half of the United States, treating each of twenty-seven
forest types as a complex ecological system. . . . Sixty
plates of Kricher's photographs and Morrison's drawings,
many in color, depict major plant and animal species."
Wilson Libr Bull

MacMahon, James
Deserts; by James A. MacMahon. Knopf
1985 638p il (Audubon Society nature
guides) pa $19   574.5
1. Desert ecology
ISBN 0-394-73139-5   LC 84-48674

"A Chanticleer Press edition"

Following the format of Atlantic & Gulf coasts by
William Hopkins Amos, entered above, this covers the
desert ecology of North America, from Oregon to Mexico

Includes bibliography

McConnaughey, Bayard Harlow, 1916-
Pacific   Coast;   by   Bayard   H.
McConnaughey and Evelyn McConnaughey.
Knopf 1985 633p il (Audubon Society
nature guides) pa $19   574.5
1. Pacific Coast (North America) 2. Seashore ecology
ISBN 0-394-73130-1   LC 84-48673

"A Chanticleer Press edition"

Following the format of Atlantic & Gulf coasts by
William Hopkins Amos, entered above, this covers the
ecology of the Pacific shore from Alaska to Southern
California

Includes bibliography

Nichol, John, 1939-
The mighty rain forest; [by] John Nichol
in association with Worldforest 90. David
& Charles; [distributed by] Sterling 1990
200p il $29.95   574.5
1. Rain forest ecology 2. Man—Influence on nature
ISBN 0-7153-9461-4

"The author looks at rain forests around the world,
describing the animals, plants and people who inhabit
them and showing how humans are destroying vital
natural resources at an alarming rate. He explains how,
why and by whom the rain forests are being exter-
minated, and presents ideas on what can be done to
save them." Publ Wkly

"While other recent books provide in-depth studies of
the issues, this visual, accessible approach focuses eloquently on the forest itself." Booklist

Includes bibliography

Niering, William A.
Wetlands. Knopf 1985 638p il maps
(Audubon Society nature guides) pa $19
                                          574.5
1. Marsh ecology 2. River ecology 3. Lake ecology
ISBN 0-394-73147-6   LC 84-48672

"A Chanticleer Press edition"

Following the format of Atlantic & Gulf coasts by
William Hopkins Amos, entered above, this covers the
flora, fauna and other natural wonders of North
America's rivers, lakes, swamps and marshes

Includes bibliography

The **Official** World Wildlife Fund guide to endangered species of North America. Beacham Pub. 1990-1992 3v il v1-2 set $195; v3 $85   **574.5**

1. Nature conservation 2. Endangered species 3. Rare animals 4. Rare plants
ISBN 0-933833-17-2 (v1-2); 0-933833-29-6 (v3)

Contents: v1 Plants, mammals; v2 Birds, reptiles, amphibians, fishes, mussels, crustaceans, snails, insects & arachnids; v3 Species listed August 1989 to December 1991

"An examination of plant and animal species that have been officially declared 'endangered' or 'threatened' by the United States Congress. . . . Each article includes a locator map showing primary habitats, a short bibliography, and contact organizations for more information." SLJ

Sutton, Ann Livesay, 1923-
Eastern forests; by Ann and Myron Sutton. Knopf 1985 638p il maps (Audubon Society nature guides) pa $19   **574.5**

1. Forest ecology
ISBN 0-394-73126-3   LC 84-48671

"A Chanticleer Press edition"

Following the format of Atlantic & Gulf coasts by William Hopkins Amos, entered above, this covers ecology of North American forests from Hudson Bay to Florida

Includes bibliography

Whitney, Stephen, 1942-
Western forests. Knopf 1985 671p il (Audubon Society nature guides) pa $19
574.5

1. Forest ecology
ISBN 0-394-73127-1   LC 84-48670

"A Chanticleer Press edition"

Following the format of Atlantic & Gulf coasts by William Hopkins Amos, entered above, this covers the ecology of North American woodlands from Alaska to California and the Rockies

Includes bibliography

Wilson, Edward O., 1929-
The diversity of life. Harvard Univ. Press 1992 424p il maps (Questions of science) $29.95   **574.5**

1. Ecology 2. Nature conservation
ISBN 0-674-21298-3   LC 92-9018

"Wilson focuses on the abundance of life forms within tropical rain forests, especially pointing out that both vanishing species and their threatened natural habitats (hot spots) must be saved if we are to maintain the earth's rich and needed genetic reservoir. Identifying five natural events that have disrupted evolution and global diversity (climatic changes, meteorite strikes), Wilson maintains that the present sixth great extinction is being caused by human neglect and ignorance. This important book is highly recommended." Libr J

Includes bibliographic references

574.87 Cytology (Cell biology)

Hall, Stephen S.
Invisible frontiers; the race to synthesize a human gene. Atlantic Monthly Press 1987 334p o.p.; Microsoft Press paperback available $8.95   **574.87**

1. Genetic engineering 2. Recombinant DNA 3. Biotechnology
ISBN 1-55615-172-1 (pa)   LC 87-934

"A Morgan Entrekin book"

An "account of the race, run from the spring of 1976 to the fall of 1978, to achieve not only the synthesis of the human insulin gene but also the genetically engineered production of human insulin itself." N Y Times Book Rev

"Demonstrated is the nature of scientific investigations—not only the excitement, disappointments, and hopes of those involved—but also the fact that the value of experiments lies not in the conclusions reached but in the refinement of the various steps along the way." Sci Books Films

Watson, James D., 1928-
The double helix; a personal account of the discovery of the structure of DNA. Atheneum Pubs. 1968 226p il hardcover o.p. paperback available $11.95   **574.87**

1. DNA 2. Biochemistry—Research
ISBN 0-689-70602-2 (pa)

Also available in paperback from New Am. Lib. and Norton

This book is a "personal, day-by-day account of how Watson, [Francis] Crick and their collaborators in the years between 1951 and 1963 hit upon the famous 'double helix' model of the 'DNA' (deoxyribonucleic acid) molecule, the fundamental genetical material." America

574.9 Geographic treatment of organisms

Berrill, Michael
A Sierra Club naturalist's guide to the North Atlantic coast: Cape Cod to Newfoundland; by Michael and Deborah Berrill; illustrated by Rob Tuckerman. Sierra Club Bks. 1981 464p il $24.95; pa $16
574.9

1. Natural history—New England 2. Natural history—Atlantic Coast (Canada)
ISBN 0-87156-242-1; 0-87156-243-X (pa)
LC 80-23086

"The geology of the region is discussed as well as climate and oceanography. The largest portion of the book is organized according to the major marine habitats of the region. . . . Each of these habitats is discussed in terms of the structure of the environment, the plants and animals found there, and the advantages and disadvantages the habitat offers to the organisms living there. This is a very thorough treatment." Libr J

Includes bibliography

Douglas, Marjory Stoneman

The Everglades; river of grass; illustrated by Robert Fink. rev ed. Pineapple Press (Sarasota) 1988 448p il maps $17.95

574.9

1. Everglades (Fla.)
ISBN 0-910923-38-8   LC 87-18478

Also available in paperback from Mockingbird Bks.

First published 1947 by Rinehart

The author traces the history of the region from its discovery to the present-day battles to control development and preserve its unique ecology

Includes bibliography

Larson, Peggy Pickering, 1931-

A Sierra Club naturalist's guide to the deserts of the Southwest; by Peggy Larson, with Lane Larson; foreword by Ed Abbey; drawings by Lynn Larson. Sierra Club Bks. 1977 286p il $12   **574.9**

1. Natural history—Southwestern States 2. Deserts
ISBN 0-87156-186-7 (pa)   LC 76-24835

The ecology of the deserts and their unusual flora and fauna are discussed and identified in this field guide to the Southwest

Includes bibliography

Perry, Bill, 1918-

A Sierra Club naturalist's guide to the Middle Atlantic Coast; Cape Cod to Cape Hatteras; illustrations by Casey French Alexander. Sierra Club Bks. 1985 470p il maps $25; pa $14   **574.9**

1. Natural history—Atlantic States 2. Seashore
ISBN 0-87156-810-1; 0-87156-816-0 (pa)
                                       LC 83-18691

The author "describes the forces that shape the coast—geology, climate, currents, and waves—and the life forms that inhabit its major biotic communities: barrier beaches, estuaries, salt marshes, and seagrass beds. Hundreds of plants and animals are described in detail . . . with emphasis on their ecological relationships and how to observe them in the field." Publisher's note

Includes bibliography

Whitney, Stephen, 1942-

A Sierra Club naturalist's guide to the Sierra Nevada. Sierra Club Bks. 1979 526p il $24.95; pa $16   **574.9**

1. Natural history—Sierra Nevada Mountains
ISBN 0-87156-215-4; 0-87156-216-2 (pa)   LC 79-766

Geography, landforms, weather, and ecology of this mountain range is discussed, including eight National Forests located along the Sierra Nevada range

This guide "is essential for those wanting to learn more about this magnificent natural resource: hikers, campers, and armchair travellers will find a wealth of information in this compact volume." Libr J

Includes bibliography

Zwinger, Ann

The mysterious lands; an award-winning naturalist explores the four great deserts of the Southwest; [by] Ann Haymond Zwinger; illustrated by the author. Dutton 1989 388p il hardcover o.p. paperback available $12.95

574.9

1. Desert ecology 2. Natural history—Southwestern States
ISBN 0-452-26513-4 (pa)   LC 88-23319

"Truman Talley books"

This describes the plants, animals, and ecology of American Southwestern deserts including the Chihauhuan, Sonoran, Mohave, and Great Basin

"From how desert snails retain moisture to the movements of sand dunes, [the author] captures the spirit of the land. . . . Excellent nature writing for a general audience." Libr J

Includes bibliography

574.92 Aquatic biology. Marine biology

Carson, Rachel, 1907-1964

The edge of the sea; with illustrations by Bob Hines. Houghton Mifflin 1955 276p il hardcover o.p. paperback available $10.70

574.92

1. Marine biology 2. Seashore
ISBN 0-395-28519-4 (pa)

"The seashores of the world may be divided into three basic types: the rugged shores of rock, the sand beaches, and the coral reefs and all their associated features. Each has its typical community of plants and animals. The Atlantic coast of the United States [provides] clear examples of each of these types. I have chosen it as the setting for my pictures of shore life." Preface

Under the sea wind; [by] Rachel L. Carson; illustrations by Bob Hines. 50th anniversary ed. Dutton 1991 304p il $19.95; pa $11   **574.92**

1. Marine biology
ISBN 0-525-24971-0; 0-452-26918-0 (pa)
                                       LC 90-47451

"A Truman Talley book"

A newly illustrated edition of the title first published 1941 by Simon & Schuster

A series of narratives describe the birds and sea creatures that inhabit the Eastern coasts of North America

"Miss Carson's unemotional handling of her subject matter is anything but dull. There is drama in every sentence. She rouses our interest in this ocean world and we want to watch it." N Y Her Trib Books

Cousteau, Jacques Yves

The ocean world; [by] Jacques Cousteau. Abrams 1979 446p il $29.98   **574.92**

1. Marine biology 2. Ocean
ISBN 0-8109-8068-1 (pa)   LC 77-20197

"An Abradale book"

This text is based on the author's twenty-volume series, first published 1972-1974. A compendium of marine fact and lore, it covers a number of aspects of the undersea world: evolution, reproduction, food-getting,

Cousteau, Jacques Yves—*Continued*
motion in the sea, communication, attack and defense mechanisms, legends and tales, life in the polar regions, and the future of the oceans

Includes bibliography

Gosner, Kenneth L., 1925-
A field guide to the Atlantic seashore; invertebrates and seaweeds of the Atlantic Coast from the Bay of Fundy to Cape Hatteras; text and illustrations by Kenneth L. Gosner. Houghton Mifflin 1979 c1978 329p il (Peterson field guide ser) $20.45; pa $13.45   **574.92**
1. Marine biology 2. Seashore
ISBN 0-395-24379-3; 0-395-31828-9 (pa)
LC 78-14784

"Intended as a field guide for amateurs, it covers 907 species of invertebrate animals and 140 species of seaweeds, with explanations of how and where to find them as well as comparisons with similar species." Libr J

Includes bibliography

Stafford-Deitsch, Jeremy
Reef; a safari through the coral world; photographs and text by Jeremy Stafford-Deitsch. Sierra Club Bks. 1991 200p il $30; pa $20   **574.92**
1. Coral reefs and islands 2. Marine ecology
ISBN 0-87156-649-4; 0-87156-541-2 (pa)
LC 90-25432

This volume offers underwater photographs and a commentary on the natural history of coral reefs

Includes bibliography

574.999 Astrobiology

Drake, Frank Donald, 1930-
Is anyone out there? the scientific search for extraterrestrial intelligence; by Frank D. Drake and Dava Sobel. Delacorte Press 1992 272p il $22   **574.999**
1. Life on other planets
ISBN 0-385-30532-X   LC 92-3884

The author "has spent over half his life looking for scientific evidence to support his hypothesis that alien civilizations exist and are probably trying to say 'hello' to their neighbors. Drake began his search in 1959 with Project Ozma, using a radio telescope he set up in the hills of West Virginia. NASA [was scheduled to] join the hunt in the fall of 1992 with its SETI Microwave Observing Project, marking the first coordinated effort to search for interstellar signals. Drake's memoirs provide a fascinating account of a scientist not afraid to probe the fringes of 'respectable' science or to enlist the support of colleagues like Carl Sagan, Freeman Dyson, and Philip Morrison." Libr J

Includes bibliography

First contact: the search for extraterrestrial intelligence; edited by Ben Bova and Byron Preiss; science editor: William R. Alschuler; associate editor: Howard Zimmerman. New Am. Lib. 1990 337p il hardcover o.p. paperback available $12.95
574.999
1. Life on other planets
ISBN 0-452-26645-9 (pa)   LC 89-77089
"A Byron Preiss book"

This book includes contributions by major scientists involved in the search for extraterrestrial intelligence (SETI) and philosophical essays by such speculative thinkers as Arthur C. Clarke, Isaac Asimov and Gregory Benford

Includes bibliography

McDonough, Thomas R.
The search for extraterrestrial intelligence; listening for life in the cosmos. Wiley 1987 244p il $19.95; pa $14.95   **574.999**
1. Life on other planets
ISBN 0-471-84684-8; 0-471-84683-X (pa)
LC 86-15905

The author traces "the evolution of mankind's search for evidence of extraterrestrial intelligence (SETI). Beginning with ancient speculations, he examines both the scientific discoveries concerning the origin and evolution of life on earth and the advances in astronomy that fixed man's place in the cosmos." Libr J

Includes bibliography

575 Evolution and genetics

Attenborough, David, 1926-
Life on Earth: a natural history. Little, Brown 1979 319p il $40; pa $24.95   **575**
1. Evolution 2. Zoology 3. Life (Biology)
ISBN 0-316-05745-2; 0-316-05747-9 (pa)
LC 79-90108

The author presents a "survey of the evolution of life on earth, with a decided emphasis on vertebrates, culminating in Homo sapiens. Based on a 13-part BBC television series, the book is . . . illustrated both pictorially and anecdotally." Choice

Dawkins, Richard, 1941-
The blind watchmaker. Norton 1986 332p il hardcover o.p. paperback available $10.95
575
1. Evolution 2. Natural selection
ISBN 0-393-30448-5 (pa)   LC 85-4960

"This book seeks 'to persuade the reader, not just that the Darwinian world view *happens* to be true, but that it is the only known theory that *could*, in principle, solve the mystery of our existence.'" Sci Teach

"Mr. Dawkins succeeds admirably in showing how natural selection allows biologists to dispense with such notions as purpose and design, and he does so in a manner readily intelligible to the modern reader." N Y Times Book Rev

Dawkins, Richard, 1941-—*Continued*
The selfish gene. new ed. Oxford Univ.
Press 1989 352p il $27.95; pa $10.95 **575**
1. Genetics 2. Evolution
ISBN 0-19-217773-7; 0-19-286092-5 (pa)
               LC 89-16077
First published 1976
The author examines evolution and contends that
genes that benefit individual members of a species will
be passed on to future generations, rather than those
which may benefit the entire group
Includes bibliography

Edey, Maitland Armstrong, 1910-1992
Blueprints; solving the mystery of
evolution; [by] Maitland A. Edey, Donald
C. Johanson. Little, Brown 1989 418p
$19.95   **575**
1. Evolution
ISBN 0-316-21076-5   LC 88-31737
Also available in paperback from Penguin Bks.
This book is a "recounting of evolutionary theory
from its roots in the 18th century, through Darwin's and
Wallace's revolutionary interpretation of natural selection
as evolution's moving force, to the 20th-century un-
raveling of the genetic code." Libr J
"It would be hard to imagine a more readable,
comprehensive survey of the story of evolution." Publ
Wkly
Includes bibliography

Eiseley, Loren C., 1907-1977
The immense journey; [by] Loren Eisley.
Random House 1957 210p $16.95; pa $8
                           575
1. Evolution 2. Man—Origin
ISBN 0-394-43014-X; 0-394-70157-7 (pa)
"Essays on biology and paleontology by an anthropologist speculating on the origin of man and the
theory of evolution." Publ Wkly
Dr Eiseley's "style is beautiful, compelling in impact
and poetic in its imagery. His subject is one of the epics
of natural science—the 'immense journey' of life as
known on this planet." Christ Sci Monit

Gould, Stephen Jay, 1941-
Eight little piggies; reflections in natural
history. Norton 1993 479p il $22.95 **575**
1. Natural history 2. Evolution
ISBN 0-393-03416-X   LC 92-18737
In this collection of essays originally published in
Natural History magazine "Gould critically explores a
cascade of ideas that shed new light on ecology, human
nature, vertebrate anatomy, neo-Darwinism, and mass
extinctions; he even includes personal musings." Libr J
Includes bibliography

Hen's teeth and horse's toes. Norton 1983
413p il hardcover o.p. paperback available
$6.95   **575**
1. Evolution
ISBN 0-393-30200-8 (pa)   LC 82-22259
The theme of this collection is "biological evolution.
[The author] has grouped the 30 essays into seven
categories: Sensible Oddities, Personalities, Adaptation

and Development, Teilhard and Piltdown, Science and
Politics, Extinction and a Zebra Trilogy." America
Includes bibliography

The panda's thumb; more reflections in
natural history; Stephen Jay Gould. Norton
1980 343p il hardcover o.p. paperback
available $9.95   **575**
1. Evolution 2. Natural selection
ISBN 0-393-30819-7 (pa)   LC 80-15952
In these essays "a variety of creatures, including
humans, dinosaurs, pandas, turtles, and microscopic organisms, are considered in light of their reflection of
Darwin's theory. One intriguing theme which runs
throughout the selections is how imperfectly designed
anatomy or haphazardly applied anatomical evolution
best supports Darwinism." Booklist
Includes bibliography

Lewin, Roger
Thread of life; the Smithsonian looks at
evolution. Smithsonian Bks. 1982 256p il
maps hardcover o.p. paperback available
$19.95   **575**
1. Evolution
ISBN 0-89599-029-6 (pa)   LC 82-16834
"Lewin begins with an overview of the geological history and the background of modern evolutionary theory.
He then explores the origin of life and life in the sea."
Sci Books Films
"A profusion of handsome—sometimes startling—color
photos, augmented by charts, diagrams, drawings, and
paintings, enriches this cohesive popularization of evolution." Booklist

Margulis, Lynn, 1938-
Microcosmos; four billion years of
evolution from our microbial ancestors; [by]
Lynn Margulis and Dorion Sagan; foreword
by Dr. Lewis Thomas. Summit Bks. 1986
301p il hardcover o.p. paperback available
$10   **575**
1. Evolution 2. Microorganisms
ISBN 0-671-74798-3 (pa)   LC 86-4432
"Beginning with the chemistry of 'minimal life,' Margulis details the contributions of the microbial world to
the evolution of life on our planet. . . . Concluding
chapters discuss man's place in our present ecosystem,
our continued dependence on microorganisms, and our
debt to our humble microbial origins for the way our
physiology functions. No other book for the lay reader
or interested professional interprets this material as
thoroughly or accurately." Libr J
Includes bibliography

575.01   Evolution and genetics— Theories

Darwin, Charles, 1809-1882
The Darwin reader; edited by Mark
Ridley. Norton 1987 271p il $19.95; pa
$8.95   **575.01**
1. Evolution 2. Natural selection
ISBN 0-393-02476-8; 0-393-95673-3 (pa) LC 87-5480

Darwin, Charles, 1809-1882—*Continued*
First published 1986 in the United Kingdom with title: The essential Darwin

Annotated with introductions and notes, this selection of key passages from Darwin's works are illustrated with pictures from the original editions

Includes bibliography

The essential Darwin; Robert Jastrow, general editor; selections and commentary by Kenneth A. Korey. Little, Brown 1984 327p il (Masters of modern science ser) $19.95; pa $12.95 **575.01**
1. Evolution 2. Natural selection
ISBN 0-316-45826-0; 0-316-45827-9 (pa)
LC 84-15502

"This book presents excerpts from Darwin's most important writings: 'The Voyage of the Beagle,' 'The Origin of Species,' 'The Descent of Man,' and his autobiography. Included in the text are critical evaluations that put Darwin into modern perspective in light of the most recent scientific findings. A fine, well-rounded introduction to Darwin's scientific contributions." Booklist

Includes bibliography

The origin of species **575.01**
1. Evolution 2. Natural selection 3. Man—Origin 4. Heredity

Available in hardcover and paperback from various publishers

First published 1859. Variant title: The origin of species by means of natural selection

The classic exposition of the "theory of evolution by natural selection. Darwin argues that every species develops or evolves from a previous one and that all life is a continuing pattern. His objects of study were the variations from generation to generation in domestic plants and animals. . . . While subsequent investigation has superseded some of Darwin's arguments, *Origin of Species* remains one of the most influential books ever published." Reader's Ency. 3d edition

Eiseley, Loren C., 1907-1977
Darwin's century; evolution and the men who discovered it; by Loren Eiseley. Doubleday 1958 378p il o.p.; Anchor Bks. paperback available $9.95 **575.01**
1. Darwin, Charles, 1809-1882 2. Evolution
ISBN 0-385-08141-3; 0-385-08141-3 (pa)

Analyzed in Essay and general literature index

"The story of Darwin's theory of evolution and the scientific thought and discoveries that foreshadowed and paced this theory. Lyell's theories, the doctrine of uniformitarianism, Lamarckian theory, and the philosophical significance of Darwin's theory are especially stressed." Publ Wkly

Includes bibliography

Gould, Stephen Jay, 1941-
Ever since Darwin; reflections in natural history. Norton 1977 285p il $19.95; pa $9.95 **575.01**
1. Darwin, Charles, 1809-1882 2. Evolution 3. Natural selection
ISBN 0-393-06425-5; 0-393-30818-9 (pa)
LC 77-22504

"In a series of essays written originally for Natural History magazine Gould explores the impact of Darwin's evolutionary theory on the study of man and other organisms." Libr J

Gould "not only explains scientific theory but comments on science itself, with clarity and wit, simultaneously entertaining and teaching." N Y Times Book Rev

Includes bibliography

576 Microbiology

Scott, Andrew, 1955-
Pirates of the cell; the story of viruses from molecule to microbe. Blackwell 1987 247p il $34.95; pa $12.95 **576**
1. Viruses
ISBN 0-631-14046-8; 0-631-15637-2 (pa) LC 85-7347

Scott explains "exactly what viruses are, how they react biologically, and why they are so difficult to control, in addition to the current research on treatment and cure. While the author does discuss some individual viruses—herpes, cancer, AIDS, and polio—the majority of his book is devoted to . . . the viral molecular structure. Useful diagrams and illustrations supplement the text. An excellent primer for anyone interested in understanding the enigma of viruses." Booklist

Includes bibliography

577 General nature of life

Asimov, Isaac, 1920-1992
Beginnings; the story of origins—of mankind, life, the earth, the universe. Walker & Co. 1987 284p il o.p.; Berkley Bks. paperback available $4.95 **577**
1. Life—Origin 2. Man—Origin
ISBN 0-425-11586-0 (pa) LC 87-15325

The author "traces the ancestry of humankind, starting with historical times and moving backward to find the origins of ancient man, hominids, mammals, chordates." Libr J

Jastrow, Robert, 1925-
Until the sun dies. Norton 1977 172p il $12.95 **577**
1. Life—Origin 2. Universe 3. Astronomy
ISBN 0-393-06415-8 LC 77-5613

Companion volumes The enchanted loom, entered in class 153, and Red giants and white dwarfs (1990)

"The author's story starts with the riddle of creation some 20 billion years ago, then moves swiftly forward through the creation of the galaxies and the formation of our planet. Jastrow continues from molecular evolution through the first cell, to the age of dinosaurs and mammals, and finally to the emergence of the human race." Sci Books Films

Sagan, Carl, 1934-
Shadows of forgotten ancestors; a search for who we are; [by] Carl Sagan, Ann Druyan. Random House 1992 505p $22.50 **577**
1. Life—Origin 2. Evolution
ISBN 0-394-53481-6 LC 92-50155

Sagan, Carl, 1934-—*Continued*
The authors' "goal is to explain how luck and natural selection combined to produce human beings after three and a half billion years of life on earth. Human behavior . . . [they argue] results more from similarities with our animal ancestors than from any unique qualities we may possess." Libr J

Includes bibliographic references

581 Botany

Gray, Asa, 1810-1888
Gray's Manual of botany. 8th (centennial) ed, largely rewritten and expanded by Merritt Lyndon Fernald; with assistance of specialists in some groups. American Bk. Co. 1950 lxiv, 1632p il o.p.; Dioscorides Press reprint available $59.95   **581**
1. Plants
ISBN 0-931146-09-7
First published 1848 by J. Munroe and Company with title: A manual of the botany of the northern United States
"A handbook of the flowering plants and ferns of the Central and Northeastern United States and adjacent Canada." Subtitle
"This standard work contains many basic botanical data as well as descriptions of some 8000 species of plants. This material includes a synopsis of the orders and families of vascular plants, a summary of the families, a glossary, and indexes to the Latin, English, French-Canadian, and colloquial." Murphey. How & Where to Look It Up

581.6 Economic botany

Angier, Bradford
Field guide to edible wild plants; jacket and book illustrated by Arthur J. Anderson. Stackpole Bks. 1974 256p il hardcover o.p. paperback available $14.95   **581.6**
1. Edible plants
ISBN 0-8117-2018-7 (pa)
Also available in hardcover from P. Smith
"Plants are arranged alphabetically by one of their common names. Each entry includes genus, family affiliation, other common names, a lengthy plant description (including many interesting facts about the plant), notes on distribution, and a statement concerning edibility and preparation of the plant parts." Libr J

Field guide to medicinal wild plants; illustrated by Arthur J. Anderson. Stackpole Bks. 1978 320p il hardcover o.p. paperback available $16.95   **581.6**
1. Botany, Medical 2. Materia medica
ISBN 0-8117-2076-4 (pa)   LC 78-19112
The author provides the family, common and Latin names, history, characteristics, habitat, and medical uses of 108 wild medicinal plants. Included are the plants used for medicinal purposes by the American Indians. Full-color illustrations accompany the text

Elias, Thomas S.
Edible wild plants; a North American field guide; [by] Thomas S. Elias & Peter A. Dykeman. Sterling 1990 286p il pa $14.95   **581.6**
1. Edible plants 2. Cookery
ISBN 0-8069-7488-5   LC 90-39506
Also available in hardcover from Borgo Press
"An Outdoor life book"
This is a guide to identifying, gathering, and preparing over 200 wild elible plants found in the United States and Canada, illustrated with 400 photographs, most in color

Gibbons, Euell
Stalking the wild asparagus; with illustrations by Margaret F. Schroeder; including a remembrance of the author by John McPhee. 25th anniversary ed. Hood, A.C. 1987 c1962 303p il $19.95; pa $12.95   **581.6**
1. Edible plants 2. Cookery
ISBN 0-911469-04-4; 0-911469-03-6 (pa)
    LC 87-16933
A reprint of the title first published 1962 by McKay
In this series of brief anecdotal essays the naturalist discourses on the identification and preparation of roots, flowers and plants, old Indian legends, and wilderness survival

Hobhouse, Henry
Seeds of change; five plants that transformed mankind. Harper & Row 1986 c1985 252p il maps hardcover o.p. paperback available $12   **581.6**
1. Botany, Economic 2. Civilization
ISBN 0-06-091440-8 (pa)   LC 86-45114
First published 1985 in the United Kingdom
"This book, devoted to quinine, sugar, tea, cotton, and the potato . . . shows how certain plants influenced the course of human affairs, often negatively." Libr J
"Filled with juicy historical snippets, crammed with cultural, herbal and pharmacological lore, this original book by a British journalist deserves to become a classic." Publ Wkly

Includes bibliography

Peterson, Lee
A field guide to edible wild plants of Eastern and Central North America; line drawings by Lee Peterson and Roger Tory Peterson; photographs by Lee Peterson. Houghton Mifflin 1978 c1977 330p il (Peterson field guide ser) $19.45; pa $15.45   **581.6**
1. Edible plants
ISBN 0-395-20445-3; 0-395-31870-X (pa)
    LC 77-27323
The author "describes 373 of the more important and better-known edible species, as well as 37 species of poisonous plants that might be confused with edible species. The usage symbols and open-line illustrations of each species are simple to understand, useful and informative. The 78 color photographs are excellent." Sci

Peterson, Lee—*Continued*
Books Films

Includes bibliography

Turner, Nancy J.
Common poisonous plants and mushrooms of North America; [by] Nancy J. Turner and Adam F. Szczawinski. Timber Press 1991 311p il $55 **581.6**

1. Poisonous plants 2. Mushrooms
ISBN 0-88192-179-3   LC 90-37574

This "presents over 150 of the most common and dangerous poisonous plants, describing not only those of wild areas of temperate North America but also garden and crop plants, house plants, and plant products. Information about each plant includes a description, occurrence, toxicity, symptoms, and treatment for poisoning." Am Libr

For a fuller review see: Booklist, May 15, 1991

Includes bibliography

582.1 Herbaceous and woody plants

Petrides, George A.
A field guide to trees and shrubs; illus. by George A. Petrides, Roger Tory Peterson. 2nd. Houghton Mifflin 1972 xxxii, 428p il hardcover o.p. paperback available $14.45 **582.1**

1. Trees—North America 2. Shrubs 3. Climbing plants
ISBN 0-395-17579-8 (pa)   LC 76-157132

"The Peterson field guide series"

First published 1958

"Field marks of all trees, shrubs, and woody vines that grow wild in the northeastern and north-central United States and in southeastern and south-central Canada." Title page

"Descriptions and clear drawings compare similar species. Includes silhouettes showing typical branching of many of the trees." AAAS. Sci Book List. 3d edition

Symonds, George W. D.
The shrub identification book; photographs by A. W. Merwin. Barrows 1963 379p il hardcover o.p. paperback available $20 **582.1**

1. Shrubs
ISBN 0-688-05040-9 (pa)

"The visual method for the practical identification of shrubs, including woody vines and ground covers." Subtitle

"Part I gives pictorial keys for thorns, leaves, flowers, fruit, twigs and bark of broad-leaved upright shrubs. Part II contains 200 master pages arranged under four categories, with data on habitat, blooming period, etc., accompanying the photographs." Wilson Libr Bull

Includes bibliography

582.13 Herbaceous flowering plants

Johnson, Lady Bird, 1912-
Wildflowers across America; [by] Lady Bird Johnson and Carlton B. Lees; photographs selected by Les Line. Abbeville Press 1988 309p il $39.95 **582.13**

1. Wild flowers
ISBN 0-89659-770-9   LC 88-1275

"The former first lady . . . shares recollections of wildflowers she has loved, especially in the Southwest; the founding of the National Wildflower Research Center; and her work with highway beautification. Lees writes of native plants, their distribution, introductions now at home in America, and wildflowers in the new trend toward natural landscaping. This handsome book abounds with color photographs." Libr J

Includes bibliography

Niering, William A.
The Audubon Society field guide to North American wildflowers: eastern region; [by] William A. Niering and Nancy C. Olmstead; visual key by Susan Rayfield and Carol Nehring. Knopf 1979 863p il $18 **582.13**

1. Wild flowers
ISBN 0-394-50432-1   LC 78-20383

"A Chanticleer Press edition"

"Covers the area east of the Rockies and east of the Big Bend area of Texas to the Atlantic. Color photographs together with family and species descriptions make this a most useful field guide." Sci News

Peterson, Roger Tory, 1908-
A field guide to wildflowers of northeastern and north-central North America; a visual approach arranged by color, form, and detail; by Roger Tory Peterson and Margaret McKenny. Houghton Mifflin 1968 xxviii, 420p il map $21.95; pa $15.95 **582.13**

1. Wild flowers
ISBN 0-395-08086-X; 0-395-18325-1 (pa)

Also available in abridged form in paperback with title: Peterson first guide to wildflowers of northeastern and north-central North America

"The Peterson field guide series"

A "guide to the most frequently encountered flowering plants of Northeastern and North-central North America. There are 1344 illustrations, many in color, of nearly 1300 species." Sci Books

Spellenberg, Richard
The Audubon Society field guide to North American wildflowers: western region; visual key by Susan Rayfield and Carol Nehring. Knopf 1979 862p il $18 **582.13**

1. Wild flowers
ISBN 0-394-50431-3   LC 78-20384

"A Chanticleer Press edition"

Spellenberg, Richard—*Continued*
This is an illustrated guide to wildflowers found from Alaska through California. Subjects are arranged by color and shape to facilitate identification. More than 600 species are covered in detail with notes on 400 others

582.16   Trees

Brockman, C. Frank (Christian Frank), 1902-
Trees of North America; a field guide to the major native and introduced species north of Mexico; illustrated by Rebecca Merrilees; under the editorship of Herbert S. Zim. Golden Press Bks. 1968 280p il hardcover o.p. paperback available $11.95
582.16

1. Trees—North America
ISBN 0-307-13658-2 (pa)   LC 68-23523
"A Golden field guide"

This book identifies 594 species of trees "native to North America north of Mexico, plus some important foreign species that have become naturalized, and some that are grown commercially or as ornamentals. Each of the 730 species is illustrated and described briefly. Technical terms are held to a minimum and the brief descriptions emphasize only the most obvious field characteristics that may not be apparent in the illustrations." Appraisal

Collingwood, G. H. (George Harris), 1890-1958
Knowing your trees; by G. H. Collingwood and Warren D. Brush, revised and edited by Devereux Butcher. American Forestry Assn. il maps $9.50   582.16

1. Trees—United States

First published 1937. Revised with each printing

"Discusses in detail the characteristics of 188 species of trees that grow in the United States and explains the importance of trees. Photos show winter and summer forms of trees, with detail of leaves, flowers, fruit, and bark. A map for each species shows its distribution; a map of the 10 hardiness zones is on the inside front cover." Wynar. Guide to Ref Books for Sch Media Cent. 3d edition

Little, Elbert Luther, 1907-
The Audubon Society field guide to North American trees; [by] Elbert L. Little; photographs by Sonja Bullaty and Angelo Lomeo [et. al.]; visual key by Susan Rayfield and Olivia Buehl. Knopf 1980 2v il v1 $15.95; v2 $14.95   582.16

1. Trees—North America   LC 79-3474
"A Chanticleer Press edition. The Audubon Society field guide series"

Contents: [v1] Eastern region (ISBN 0-394-50760-6); [v2] Western region (0-394-50761-4)

These "guides are unusual in that they contain many color photographs of parts of a living tree. The identification keys are easy to use, being based on an arrangement by leaf shapes, flowers, fruit, and fall leaves, and giving drawings of winter silhouettes. The eastern guide covers 364 species, the western guide describes 314

species; they divide the country at central Texas and the Rockies." Libr J

Simon and Schuster's guide to trees; English translation by Hugh Young. Simon & Schuster 1978 c1977 various paging il hardcover o.p. paperback available $14
582.16

1. Trees
ISBN 0-671-24125-7 (pa)   LC 77-17896
"A Fireside book"

Original Italian edition by P. Lanzara and M. Pizzetti

This is "a field guide to 300 species of trees from around the world. A 50-page introduction ranges over the history of the trees, their ecosystems and names, wood, and its uses, leaves, flowers, seeds, and ecological concerns. The descriptions cover habitat, physical characteristics, propagation, and conditions of growth. Each is accompanied by a drawing showing the tree's shape and a handsome color photograph." Wilson Libr Bull

587   Pteridophytes (Vascular seedless plants)

Cobb, Boughton
A field guide to the ferns and their related families of northeastern and central North America; with a section of species also found in the British Isles and western Europe; illustrated by Laura Louise Foster. Houghton Mifflin 1956 281p il $19.45; pa $14.45   587

1. Ferns
ISBN 0-395-07560-2; 0-395-19431-8 (pa)
"The Peterson field guide series"

All the species are illustrated with drawings of the full plant as well as detailed sketches of spore cases, leaf patterns and other points of identification. Included also are descriptions of the morphology and life cycle of a fern, a cross reference key to closely related species in Europe and a bibliography

Lellinger, David B.
A field manual of the ferns & fern-allies of the United States & Canada; with photographs by A. Murray Evans. Smithsonian Institution Press 1985 389p il $55; pa $29.95   587

1. Ferns
ISBN 0-87474-602-7; 0-87474-603-5 (pa)
LC 84-22216

This guide includes information "on 406 native and naturalized species, subspecies, and important varieties with mention of hybrids and minor varieties. Included are names and classification; frequency and range; habitats and ecology; structure and life cycle; and horticultural notes. . . . This book should be included in all libraries." Choice

Includes bibliography

589.2 Fungi

Lincoff, Gary
The Audubon Society field guide to North American mushrooms; [by] Gary H. Lincoff; visual key by Carol Nehring. Knopf 1981 926p il flexible bdg $17.50   **589.2**
1. Mushrooms
ISBN 0-394-51992-2   LC 81-80827
"A Chanticleer Press edition. The Audubon Society field guide series"
This guide to 703 species of common mushrooms provides 762 color photographs and descriptions as keys to identifying these plants
"The author is an expert on mushroom toxins and instills responsible cautions. The photos are uncommonly beautiful." SLJ

McKnight, Kent H.
A field guide to mushrooms, North America; [by] Kent H. McKnight and Vera B. McKnight; illustrations by Vera B. McKnight. Houghton Mifflin 1987 429p il $19.95; pa $15.45   **589.2**
1. Mushrooms
ISBN 0-395-42101-2; 0-395-42102-0 (pa)
LC 86-27799
"The Peterson field guide series"
"Sponsored by the National Audubon Society and the National Wildlife Federation"
More than 500 species of mushrooms are described and depicted. Edibility of each species is noted

Phillips, Roger, 1932-
Mushrooms of North America; by Roger Phillips, assisted by Geoffrey Kibby & Nicky Foy; with editing help from Alick Henrici [et al.] Little, Brown 1991 319p il $39.95; pa $24.95   **589.2**
1. Mushrooms
ISBN 0-316-70612-4; 0-316-70613-2   LC 89-37050
"This book is a collection of more than 1,000 color photographs of mushrooms and other fungi of North America. The accompanying text includes information on where and when to find each mushroom and how to make a positive identification. . . . There is an introduction that offers data on poisonous species, poisoning symptoms, edible species, and how to dry mushrooms." Booklist
Includes bibliographic references

Smith, Alexander Hanchett, 1904-1988
The mushroom hunter's field guide; [by] Alexander H. Smith and Nancy Smith Weber. all color & enlarged. University of Mich. Press 1980 316p il $18.95   **589.2**
1. Mushrooms
ISBN 0-472-85610-3   LC 80-10514
First published 1958
This is a "field guide for both novices and experts alike. The introductory chapter explains basic terminology and what to look for when identifying fungi. More than 280 mushrooms are described, including identifying marks, edibility, habitat, native range, and type of spore.

A color photograph . . . of each mushroom is most valuable for accurate information." Booklist
Includes bibliography

590.74 Zoological museums, collections, exhibits

Luoma, Jon R.
A crowded ark. Houghton Mifflin 1987 209p $17.95   **590.74**
1. Zoos
ISBN 0-395-40879-2   LC 87-17784
Following a chapter on the history of zoos the author discusses genetic inbreeding, "managing cooperative breeding programs, the potential for frozen gamete banks, the problems of returning zoo animals to the wild, the need for habitat conservation, and the problems of balancing the political, social, and ethical pressures zoos face." Choice
Includes bibliography

591 Zoology

Ackerman, Diane
The moon by whale light; and other adventures among bats, penguins, crocodilians, and whales. Random House 1991 xxii, 249p il $19.50; pa $11   **591**
1. Animals
ISBN 0-394-58574-7; 0-679-74226-3 (pa)
LC 91-52665
The author describes her experiences working with field biologists who study the behavior of bats, crocodiles, whales, and penguins
"A unique blend of poetic essays and scientific descriptions of usually unlovely animals. Ackerman writes with the precision of a scientist and the soul of a romantic." SLJ

Muir, John, 1838-1914
Muir among the animals; the wildlife writings of John Muir; Lisa Mighetto, editor. Sierra Club Bks. 1986 xxviii, 196p il hardcover o.p. paperback available $10   **591**
1. Animals
ISBN 0-87156-607-9 (pa)   LC 86-3914
These "essays convey renowned nineteenth-century naturalist Muir's respect for all types of animals and his gradual evolution into an advocate for animal rights. . . As astute and relevant now as when first composed, Muir's essays make a vital contribution to the natural history of wildlife." Booklist
Includes bibliography

591.5 Ecology of animals

Adams, Douglas, 1952-
Last chance to see; [by] Douglas Adams and Mark Carwardine. Harmony Bks. 1991 220p il $20   **591.5**
1. Endangered species
ISBN 0-517-58215-5   LC 90-42756

Adams, Douglas, 1952-—Continued

Also available in paperback from Ballantine Bks.

This volume recounts the authors' worldwide expeditions in search of endangered species in their native habitats. The komodo dragon, northern white rhinoceros, mountain gorilla, kakapo, baiji dolphin, and rodrigues fruit bat are described

Attenborough, David, 1926-

The trials of life; a natural history of animal behavior. Little, Brown 1990 320p il $29.95   **591.5**

1. Animals—Behavior
ISBN 0-316-05751-7   LC 90-53592

In text and photographs, this volume examines aspects of animal behavior. "Each of 12 chapters concentrates on one phase in the life cycle of any organism: birth, youth, foraging (and, separately, the special foraging that is termed hunting, as well as the avoidance thereof), locating and announcing location, social interactions (again, separately, aggression and competition), interspecific interactions, courtship, and mating." Choice

Benyus, Janine M.

Beastly behaviors; a zoo lover's companion: what makes whales whistle, cranes dance, pandas turn somersaults, and crocodiles roar: a watcher's guide to how animals act and why; illustrations by Juan Carlos Barberis. Addison-Wesley 1992 366p il $29.95   **591.5**

1. Animals—Behavior 2. Zoos
ISBN 0-201-57008-4   LC 92-5381

"Designed as a companion for zoo visits, Benyus' guide details the physical characteristics and basic behaviors (social, feeding, parenting, and sexual) of more than 20 captive animals, such as elephants, whales, flamingos, and crocodiles, including a critique checklist that encourages readers to evaluate their zoo, and outlines ways to improve it." Booklist

"This is one of the best books published on animal behavior for the general reader. . . . [It] is highly recommended for its ability to convey concise yet readable information for the reader." Libr J

Includes bibliography

Griffin, Donald Redfield, 1915-

Animal minds. University of Chicago Press 1992 310p $24.95   **591.5**

1. Animals—Behavior
ISBN 0-226-30863-4   LC 92-6538

The author posits that "animals are cognizant of objects and events and experience conscious thoughts. In an involving, important, scholarly report that should force a reconsideration of animal studies, Griffin reviews animals' remarkable adaptability to novel challenges and their apparent ability to communicate thoughts to others." Publ Wkly

Includes bibliographic references

Lorenz, Konrad

King Solomon's ring; new light on animal ways; illustrated by the author and with a foreword by Julian Huxley. Crowell 1952 202p il o.p.; HarperPerennial paperback available $11   **591.5**

1. Animals—Behavior
ISBN 0-06-131976-7 (pa)

Also available in hardcover from P. Smith

A famous naturalist recounts his experiences with and observations on the behavior of animals and birds, among them fish, water-shrews, greylag geese, dogs, and jackdaws

Morris, Desmond

Animalwatching. Crown 1990 256p il $35   **591.5**

1. Animals—Behavior
ISBN 0-517-57859-X   LC 90-34433

"In this heavily illustrated volume, Morris covers everything from microscopic creatures to mammalian giants, but he concentrates on the higher forms. His writing style is fresh and conversational in tone, and it is apparent that he is at once charmed and intrigued by the creatures he has so intensely observed." SLJ

Includes bibliography

Morton, Eugene S.

Animal talk; science and the voices of nature; [by] Eugene S. Morton, Jake Page. Random House 1992 xxvii, 273p $19.50   **591.5**

1. Animal communication 2. Evolution
ISBN 0-394-58337-X   LC 90-52894

The authors "seek to show ways in which animal communication differs radically from human language. Examples are drawn from a wide range of species—bats, bees, whales, chimpanzees, prairie dogs, moths and vervet monkeys, as well as the song-birds in which Mr. Morton himself specializes. However, the authors intend not to produce 'a Baedeker to an animal Babel' but to explain exactly what animals do when they communicate." NY Times Book Rev

Includes bibliographic references

Murie, Olaus Johan, 1889-1963

A field guide to animal tracks; text and illustrations by Olaus J. Murie. 2nd ed. Houghton Mifflin 1975 c1974 xxi, 375p il $19.45; pa $14.45   **591.5**

1. Tracking and trailing 2. Animals—Behavior
ISBN 0-395-19978-6; 0-395-18323-5 (pa)

"The Peterson field guide series"

First published 1954

"Murie's handbook is recognized as the classic work on the subject. . . . The illustrated guide describes the tracks, droppings, and marks left on bones and leaves by an army of wild animals—bats, bears, rabbits, reptiles, moles, weasels, and others. A fascinating collection of miscellaneous information about the habits of these creatures is part of the descriptive text." Wynar. Ref Books in Paperback. 2d edition

591.92 Marine zoology

The **Encyclopedia** of aquatic life; edited by Keith Banister and Andrew Campbell. Facts on File 1985 349, xxxiii p il $45
591.92

1. Marine animals 2. Freshwater animals
ISBN 0-8160-1257-1   LC 85-10245
"An Equinox book"

"The articles are arranged in three main sections: fishes, aquatic invertebrates, and sea mammals. Each section begins with an overview of the animals to be discussed, then individual taxonomic groups are covered." Topical Ref Books

592 Invertebrates

Barnes, Robert D.
Invertebrate zoology. Saunders College Pub. il $40   **592**

1. Invertebrates   LC 86-10023
First published 1963. (5th edition 1987) Periodically revised

A comprehensive text which discusses all aspects of the biology of the invertebrates
Includes bibliographies

Meinkoth, Norman August, 1913-
The Audubon Society field guide to North American seashore creatures; [by] Norman A. Meinkoth. Knopf 1981 799p il maps flexible bdg $18   **592**

1. Invertebrates 2. Marine biology
ISBN 0-394-51993-0   LC 81-80828
"A Chanticleer Press edition. The Audubon Society field guide series"

This "unique field guide covers some 850 marine invertebrate animals living in or around the shallow waters of the temperate seacoasts of the United States and Canada. Excellent color photographs are grouped at the beginning of the book, followed by text that gives, for each animal, a short description, common and scientific names, habitat, range, and comments." Malinowsky. Best Sci & Technol Ref Books for Young People

594 Mollusks and mollusk-like animals

Morris, Percy A.
A field guide to Pacific coast shells; including shells of Hawaii and the Gulf of California. 2d ed rev and enl. Houghton Mifflin 1974 c1966 xxxiii, 279p il $19.45; pa $15.45   **594**

1. Shells 2. Mollusks
ISBN 0-395-08029-0; 0-395-18322-7 (pa)
"The Peterson field guide series"

First published 1952 with title: A field guide to shells of the Pacific coast and Hawaii

The book is divided into three parts. The first part covers the marine shells occurring from Alaska to southern California; the second includes the Gulf of California; and the third part deals with the shells of Hawaii

Includes bibliography

Rehder, Harald Alfred, 1907-
The Audubon Society field guide to North American seashells; [by] Harald A. Rehder; with photographs by James H. Carmichael, Jr.; visual key by Carol Nehring and Mary Beth Brewer. Knopf 1981 894p il flexible bdg $17.95   **594**

1. Shells 2. Mollusks
ISBN 0-394-51913-2   LC 80-84239
"A Chanticleer Press edition. The Audubon Society field guide series"

"The more than 700 color plates are arranged according to shape and color rather than family or genus, making identification very simple for even the rankest amateur. . . . The text gives the common name, scientific name, description, habitat, range, and comments for each species. This is the most comprehensive field guide to North American seashells." Libr J

Wye, Kenneth R.
The encyclopedia of shells. Facts on File 1991 288p il $45   **594**

1. Shells
ISBN 0-8160-2702-1   LC 91-12191
"Over 1000 types of shells are illustrated in color photographs. . . . Distribution, habitat depth, and relative availability to collectors are explained in descriptions. Coverage is worldwide with extensive representation from the Far East, including many shells rarely seen by casual shell collectors." Libr J

For a fuller review see: Booklist, Jan. 15, 1992

595.7 Insects

Arnett, Ross H., Jr.
Simon and Schuster's guide to insects; by Ross H. Arnett, Jr., and Richard L. Jacques, Jr. Simon & Schuster 1981 511p il hardcover o.p. paperback available $14
595.7

1. Insects
ISBN 0-671-25014-0 (pa)   LC 80-29485
"A Fireside book"

This field guide identifies 350 insect species found in North America. Entries include information about the habits and biology of each species, as well as the scientific and common names of the species and its impact on the environment. Also included is a history of the study of insects, and instructions for collecting insects

Berenbaum, M. (May)
Ninety-nine gnats, nits, and nibblers; [by] May R. Berenbaum; with illustrations by John Parker Sherrod. University of Ill. Press 1989 xxi, 254p il hardcover o.p. paperback available $10.95   **595.7**

1. Insects
ISBN 0-252-06027-X (pa)   LC 88-15420

Berenbaum, M. (May)—*Continued*

This book consists "of 99 vignettes devoted mostly to insects but also including . . . spiders, ticks, and mites. Berenbaum focuses on those insects most frequently encountered by humans in their houses, gardens, fields, and yards, as well as those found on their bodies and the bodies of pets and livestock." Choice

Includes bibliographies

Borror, Donald Joyce, 1907-1988

A field guide to the insects of America north of Mexico; by Donald J. Borror and Richard E. White; color and shaded drawings by Richard E. White; line drawings by the authors. Houghton Mifflin 1970 404p il hardcover o.p. paperback available $14.45
595.7

1. Insects
ISBN 0-395-18523-8 (pa)

Also available in abridged form in paperback with title: Peterson first guide to insects of North America, by Christopher W. Leahy

"The Peterson field guide series"

This book aids in the "identification of the more common of the 88,000 species that have been identified in North America. . . . The last part of the book consists of insect orders with descriptions of the order and the families in them." Sci Books

The **Encyclopedia** of insects; edited by Christopher O'Toole. Facts on File 1986 141p il $24.95
595.7

1. Insects
ISBN 0-8160-1358-6   LC 85-29226

"An Equinox book"

"The emphasis is placed on recent advances in our understanding of the ecology, behavior, morphology, and evolution of each group. Excellent color photographs and illustrations accompany the text. All species are identified by family and scientific name as well as common name." Choice

Includes bibliography

Hölldobler, Bert, 1936-

The ants; [by] Bert Hölldobler and Edward O. Wilson. Belknap Press 1990 732p il $65
595.7

1. Ants
ISBN 0-674-04075-9   LC 89-30653

This volume includes coverage of ant "evolution, taxonomy, life history, chemical ecology, kin recognition, community organization, [and] symbiosis. . . . Army ants, fungus growers, harvesting ants and weaver ants . . . are each given a chapter of their own. . . . The book's last chapter tells the reader how to collect, culture and observe live ants." Sci Am

"Science is rarely good literature. 'The Ants' is an exalting exception." N Y Times Book Rev

Includes bibliography

Milne, Lorus Johnson, 1912-

The Audubon Society field guide to North American insects and spiders; [by] Lorus and Margery Milne; visual key by Susan Rayfield. Knopf 1980 989p il flexible bdg $17.50
595.7

1. Insects 2. Spiders
ISBN 0-394-50763-0   LC 80-7620

"A Chanticleer Press edition. The Audubon Society field guide series"

The authors "have based their field guide on 702 excellent color photographs (75 of which are of spiders and other arachnids). In addition to some general information, the text (two thirds of the book) is made up of brief comments on each kind of arthropod pictured." Choice

Pyle, Robert Michael

The Audubon Society field guide to North American butterflies; visual key by Carol Nehring and Jane Opper. Knopf 1981 916p il $17.95
595.7

1. Butterflies
ISBN 0-394-51914-0   LC 80-84240

"A Chanticleer Press edition. The Audubon Society field guide series"

This guide "introduces more than 600 species of North American butterfly, including those native to the Hawaiian Islands. A section of brilliant color plates (more than 1,000 of them) featuring butterflies in their natural habitats, follows a general introduction and notes on text organization and use." Booklist

The Audubon Society handbook for butterfly watchers; illustrations by Sarah Anne Hughes. Scribner 1984 274p il hardcover o.p.; Houghton Mifflin paperback available $11.70
595.7

1. Butterflies
ISBN 0-395-61629-8 (pa)   LC 83-27106

This book provides "information on a variety of topics: watching versus catching, finding butterflies, equipment, photography, behavior, butterfly gardening, rearing, conservation, and much more." Libr J

Includes bibliography

Scott, James A., 1946-

The butterflies of North America; a natural history and field guide. Stanford Univ. Press 1986 583p il maps $65; pa $24.95
595.7

1. Butterflies
ISBN 0-8047-1205-0; 0-8047-2013-4 (pa)

LC 82-60737

This is an "encyclopedic work covering all 679 species of butterfly from Canada to northern Mexico, plus Bermuda and Hawaii. Part I is a substantial discussion of butterfly ecology and biology, and Part II covers the identification of eggs, larvae, pupae, and adults. Part III comprises 350 pages of species descriptions in phylogenetic sequence, complete with range maps and keyed to 64 gorgeous color plates of butterflies." Am Libr

Stokes, Donald W.

The butterfly book; an easy guide to butterfly gardening, identification, and behavior; [by] Donald and Lillian Stokes and Ernest Williams. Little, Brown 1991 95p il maps pa $10.95   595.7

1. Butterflies
ISBN 0-316-81780-5   LC 91-15323

This book discusses plants which will attract butterflies, explains butterfly life cycles and behavior, and provides information for identification of over 140 species

A guide to observing insect lives; illustrations by Deborah Prince. Little, Brown 1983 371p il $17.95; pa $12.95
595.7

1. Insects
ISBN 0-316-81724-4; 0-316-81727-9 (pa)
LC 82-23927

"The book is organized by season, beginning with spring, and for each season the reader is introduced to some 14 different insects that can be found and observed during that time. Each section begins with a brief description of where to look for insects, and a handy insect location guide is provided. Insects are illustrated in their habitats, and their relationships to other insects are described." Sci Books Films

Includes bibliography

Wilson, Edward O., 1929-

Insect societies. Belknap Press 1971 548p il hardcover o.p. paperback available $22.50
595.7

1. Insects
ISBN 0-674-45495-2 (pa)

In addition to "descriptions of specific groups of organisms, Wilson attempts to bring much diverse information, including fundamental concepts of evolution and ecology, into a conceptual format he terms unified sociobiology. He devotes several chapters to detailed descriptions of various activities necessary to maintenance of the societies, including a chapter on genetic theories relating to social behavior." Libr J

Includes bibliography

597 Cold-blooded vertebrates. Fishes

The **Audubon** Society field guide to North American fishes, whales, and dolphins; [by] Herbert T. Boschung, Jr. [et al.]; visual key by Carol Nehring and Jordan Verner. Knopf 1983 848p il flexible bdg $15.95   597

1. Fishes—North America 2. Whales 3. Dolphins
ISBN 0-394-53405-0   LC 83-47962

"A Chanticleer Press edition. The Audubon Society field guide series"

This guide has "a first section containing excellent photographs of 529 marine and freshwater fishes and 45 cetacean species found in or near North America north of Mexico, and a second section giving brief descriptions of each species. . . . The well-organized and well-written text includes descriptions of physical features, habitat,

range (generally with a small map), and related or similar species." Choice

Cousteau, Jean-Michel

Cousteau's great white shark; [by] Jean-Michel Cousteau and Mose Richards. Abrams 1992 173p il $39.95   597

1. Sharks
ISBN 0-8109-3181-8   LC 92-7983

This book reports on an expedition, lead by the author, to study the great white shark off the coast of Australia. Illustrated with color photographs by underwater specialists

Ellis, Richard, 1938-

Great white shark; [by] Richard Ellis and John E. McCosker; with photographs by Al Giddings and others, and paintings by Richard Ellis. HarperCollins Pubs. 1991 270p il maps $50   597

1. Sharks
ISBN 0-06-016451-4   LC 89-46528

"In collaboration with Stanford University Press"

The authors discuss the great white shark's "unique biology (it's warm blooded), size, distribution, and evolution. They also describe the sport of shark fishing and the efforts . . . [to save] the white from threats of extinction. Handsomely illustrated with Ellis's paintings and many simply awesome photographs, . . . the text has enough scientific fact for armchair icthyologists but not enough to confuse the casual reader." Libr J

Includes bibliographic references

Eschmeyer, William N.

A field guide to Pacific coast fishes of North America; from the Gulf of Alaska to Baja California; [by] William N. Eschmeyer, Earl S. Herald; illustrations by Howard Hammann; Katherine P. Smith, associate illustrator. Houghton Mifflin 1983 336p il map $19.45; pa $15.45   597

1. Fishes—North America
ISBN 0-395-26873-7; 0-395-33188-9 (pa)
LC 82-11989

"The Peterson field guide series"

"Sponsored by the National Audubon Society and National Wildlife Federation"

"A comprehensive, well-illustrated, nearly jargon-free field guide that describes the more than 500 marine fish species likely to be found in depths, less than 650 feet, from the Gulf of Alaska to Baja California." Sci Books Films

Includes bibliography

Page, Lawrence M.
A field guide to freshwater fishes: North America north of Mexico; [by] Lawrence M. Page, Brooks M. Burr; illustrations by Eugene C. Beckham III, John Parker Sherrod, Craig W. Ronto. Houghton Mifflin 1991 432p il maps $24.45; pa $16.45 **597**

1. Fishes—North America
ISBN 0-395-35307-6; 0-395-53933-1 (pa)
LC 90-42049

"The Peterson field guide series"

"Sponsored by the National Audubon Society, the National Wildlife Federation, and the Roger Tory Peterson Institute"

This guide "covers all 790 species known in North America north of Mexico. Over 700 illustrations, most in color, show identifying marks. Also includes 377 distribution maps and additional line drawings of key details." Publisher's note

Includes bibliography

Robins, C. Richard
A field guide to Atlantic coast fishes of North America; [by] C. Richard Robins, G. Carleton Ray; illustrations by John Douglass and Rudolf Freund. Houghton Mifflin 1986 354p il $21.45; pa $15.45 **597**

1. Fishes—North America
ISBN 0-395-31852-1; 0-395-39198-9 (pa)
LC 85-18144

"The Peterson field guide series"

"Sponsored by the National Audubon Society and the National Wildlife Federation"

This guide describes and illustrates 1,100 species that inhabit the waters between the Canadian Arctic and the Gulf of Mexico

Includes bibliography

Sharks; consulting editor, John D. Stevens; illustrations by Tony Pyrzakowski. Facts on File 1987 240p il $35 **597**

1. Sharks
ISBN 0-8160-1800-6
LC 87-601

"A Kevin Weldon production"

This volume is "divided into three parts: the biology of sharks, shark attacks, and miscellanea; legends, use of shark parts by humans, shark cages, repelling sharks." Choice

Includes bibliography

Springer, Victor Gruschka, 1928-
Sharks in question; the Smithsonian answer book; [by] Victor G. Springer and Joy P. Gold. Smithsonian Institution Press 1989 187p il hardcover o.p. paperback available $15.95 **597**

1. Sharks
ISBN 0-87474-877-1 (pa)
LC 88-18185

"At first, the book deals with the general life history of these fish and presents detailed answers to the most commonly asked questions. The remainder of the book discusses the biology of some spectacular shark species and presents a balanced picture of the question of shark attack on humans. Several appendices with information on shark classification, taxonomy, and sizes of selected

sharks are also included." Sci Books Films

Includes bibliography

Stafford-Deitsch, Jeremy
Shark; a photographer's story; foreword by Samuel H. Gruber. Sierra Club Bks. 1987 200p il hardcover o.p. paperback available $24 **597**

1. Sharks
ISBN 0-87156-733-4 (pa)
LC 87-4798

"An Eddison-Sadd edition"

The author, a marine photographer, reports on "his expeditions to the Bahamas, the Red Sea reefs, the open Pacific, and South Australia. His introduction tells how he got hooked on sharks, the first chapter gives an overview of the fish's biology, and he does not forget to bring up fine points of shark behavior, ecology, etc., in the succeeding text. But the totally engrossing photos are what make the book another must for most library collections." Booklist

Includes bibliography

Steel, Rodney
Sharks of the world. Facts on File 1985 192p il $24.95 **597**

1. Sharks
ISBN 0-8160-1086-2
LC 85-6849

This volume contains "information on shark classification, anatomy, evolution, reproduction, and behavior. Written for the nonspecialist, this book is easily readable, save for a few sections where technical terminology is not defined in either the text or the brief glossary. Shark attack descriptions are a bit overwritten." Libr J

Includes bibliography

Thomson, Keith Stewart
Living fossil; the story of the coelacanth. Norton 1991 252p il maps $19.95; pa $9.95 **597**

1. Coelacanth
ISBN 0-393-02956-5; 0-393-30868-5 (pa)
LC 90-43053

This study of the coelacanth discusses "the 1938 discovery of a fish thought to be extinct for 70 million years and the subsequent collection and examination of this [species]." Libr J

"Brisk and engrossing, this is a winning mix of science and adventure." Booklist

597.6 Amphibians

Behler, John L.
The Audubon Society field guide to North American reptiles and amphibians; [by] John L. Behler, F. Wayne King. Knopf 1979 743p il flexible bdg $18 **597.6**

1. Reptiles 2. Amphibians
ISBN 0-394-50824-6
LC 79-2217

"A Chanticleer Press edition. The Audubon Society field guide series"

"Photographs of the reptiles and amphibians are arranged in six main groups: salamanders, frogs and toads, crocodilians, turtles, lizards, and snakes, then subarranged by color. The marine turtles of coastal waters

Behler, John L.—*Continued*
are also included. The text describes each of the species and gives common and scientific names, description, voice, breeding, habitat, subspecies, range, and descriptive comments." Malinowsky. Best Sci & Technol Ref Books for Young People

Conant, Roger, 1909-
A field guide to reptiles and amphibians, eastern and central North America; [by] Roger Conant and Joseph T. Collins; illustrated by Isabelle Hunt Conant and Tom R. Johnson. 3rd ed. Houghton Mifflin 1991 450p il maps $24.45; pa $16.45
597.6
1. Reptiles 2. Amphibians
ISBN 0-395-37022-1; 0-395-58389-6 (pa)
LC 90-21053
"The Peterson field guide series"
First published 1958 with title: A field guide to reptiles and amphibians of the United States and Canada east of the 100th meridian
"Sponsored by the National Audubon Society, the National Wildlife Federation, and the Roger Tory Peterson Institute"
This guide describes 595 species and subspecies. Full-color illustrations and drawings highlight key details and over 300 distribution maps show ranges
Includes bibliographic references

The **Encyclopedia** of reptiles and amphibians; edited by Tim R. Halliday and Kraig Adler. Facts on File 1986 143p il maps $27.95
597.6
1. Reptiles 2. Amphibians
ISBN 0-8160-1359-4
LC 85-29249
"An Equinox book"
"This encyclopedia includes entries for representative species of all the families in Reptilia and Amphibia. The descriptions are very accurate and concise, with excellent illustrations. Range maps are included." Malinowsky. Best Sci & Technol Ref Books for Young People
Includes bibliography

Stebbins, Robert C. (Robert Cyril), 1915-
A field guide to western reptiles and amphibians; text and illustrations by Robert C. Stebbins. 2nd ed rev. Houghton Mifflin 1985 336p il maps $21.45; pa $16.45
597.6
1. Reptiles 2. Amphibians
ISBN 0-395-38254-8; 0-395-38253-X (pa)
LC 84-25125
"The Peterson field guide series"
First published 1966
"Sponsored by the National Audubon Society and National Wildlife Federation"
"Field marks of all species in western North America, including Baja California." Title page
This field guide features over 240 species, most accompanied by illustration and distribution map. Coverage includes Baja California and information on reptile reproduction
Includes bibliography

Tyning, Thomas F.
A guide to amphibians and reptiles; edited by Donald W. Stokes and Lillian Q. Stokes; illustrations by Andrew Finch Magee; range maps by Thomas F. Tynning and Timothy J. Flanagan. Little, Brown 1990 400p il $19.95; pa $10.95
597.6
1. Amphibians 2. Reptiles
ISBN 0-316-81719-8; 0-316-81713-9 (pa)
LC 89-28444
This guide covers common frogs, salamanders, alligators, snakes, turtles, and lizards
Includes bibliographic references

597.9 Reptiles

Ernst, Carl H.
Venomous reptiles of North America. Smithsonian Institution Press 1992 236p il maps $35
597.9
1. Snakes
ISBN 1-56098-114-8
LC 91-3535
"In articles ranging from four to 20 pages, each of the 20 snakes and one lizard is given a detailed portrait including fossil record, karotype, distribution, habitat, behavior, reproduction, food, venom and bite, predators, defense, and population. There is also a range map for each reptile. Illustrating the text are 55 color plates and 61 black-and-white photographs and drawings." Am Libr
For a fuller review see: Booklist, Oct. 1, 1992
Includes bibliography

Klauber, Laurence Monroe, 1883-1968
Rattlesnakes; their habits, life histories, and influence on mankind; abridged by Karen Harvey McClung. University of Calif. Press 1982 xxii, 350p il maps $35; pa $14.95
597.9
1. Rattlesnakes
ISBN 0-520-04038-4; 0-520-04039-2 (pa)
LC 80-16660
Abridgment of two volume edition first published 1956
Published for the Zoological Society of San Diego
This includes "history, myth and folklore in addition to the natural history of the snake. . . . [The author] discusses the temperature limitations of snakes, . . . denning, prey, the bite and its effects on humans." Publ Wkly
Includes bibliography

Mattison, Christopher
Snakes of the world; [by] Chris Mattison. Facts on File 1986 190p il $24.95 **597.9**
1. Snakes
ISBN 0-8160-1082-X
LC 84-24733
Snake morphology, reproduction, diet, self-defense, ecology and behavior are discussed
"Mattison provides an enjoyable introduction to snake biology and snake diversity for the interested general reader. . . . Many of the numerous color photographs are spectacular." Choice
Includes bibliography

Mehrtens, John M.

Living snakes of the world in color.
Sterling 1987 480p il $55   **597.9**

1. Snakes

ISBN 0-8069-6460-X   LC 87-9932

This book presents more than 500 "color photographs
of captive snakes, each with a one-page description of
the reptile's geographic range, ecological niche, and captive care requirements. Special precautions are noted for
venomous species." Libr J

"This is an interesting introduction to the living
snakes of the world. . . . The information is not only
accurate but well presented." Sci Books Films

598 Birds

Alcorn, Gordon Dee

Birds and their young; courtship, nesting,
hatching, fledging, the reproductive cycle;
illustrations by Michelle LaGory. Stackpole
Bks. 1991 183p il $19.95   **598**

1. Birds

ISBN 0-8117-1016-5   LC 90-39204

The author describes the reproductive cycles of birds
including courtship and mating, nest building and egg
laying, embryo development and the hatching and growth
of the young

Includes bibliographic references

The **Audubon** Society master guide to
birding; John Farrand, Jr., editor. Knopf
1983 3v il set $49.35   **598**

1. Birds—North America

ISBN 0-394-54121-9   LC 83-47945

Also available individual volumes ea $16.95

"A Chanticleer Press edition" •

Contents: v1 Loons to sandpipers; v2 Gulls to dippers;
v3 Warblers to sparrows

"These three volumes fill a need in the world of
birdwatching. . . . The 61 authors . . . are outstanding
in this field, and they show their expertise with concise
descriptions. This reviewer particularly liked the excellent
photographs of birds, with small insects with red arrows
to call reader attention to pertinent and distinctive identification points. Some birds are depicted by paintings—
also well done." Choice

Book of North American birds. Reader's
Digest Assn. 1990 576p il maps $32.95
     598

1. Birds—North America

ISBN 0-89577-351-1   LC 89-70261

This book "consists of over 450 page-length species
accounts which feature a . . . color painting, a half-page
anecdotal narrative essay, a range map, a drawing, plus
small sections detailing the bird's identification, habitat,
and food. Smaller accounts (three per page) for 117 scar-
cer birds follow the full-page ones. Appended is a 40-
page section with thumbnail sketches of the best birding
areas in the United States and Canada." Libr J

Includes bibliography

Bull, John L.

The Audubon Society field guide to North
American birds: Eastern region; [by] John
Bull and John Farrand; visual key developed
by Susan Rayfield. Knopf 1977 775p il
flexible bdg $18   **598**

1. Birds—North America

ISBN 0-394-41405-5   LC 76-47926

Companion volume The Audubon Society field guide
to North American birds: Western region, by Miklos D.
F. Udvardy, entered below

"A Chanticleer Press edition. The Audubon Society
field guide series"

The first half of this book consists of color
photographs of various birds. The second half is devoted
to profiles of species including descriptions of voice,
habitat, range and nesting information

Burton, Robert, 1941-

Bird behavior; consulting editor Bruce
Campbell. Knopf 1985 224p il $18.95 **598**

1. Birds—Behavior

ISBN 0-394-53957-5   LC 84-48677

"The book is divided into ten chapters . . . as follows:
the living bird, flight, senses and intelligence, finding
food, diet and way of life, communication, social life,
courtship and mating, rearing the young, and migration."
Choice

"This excellent book features almost 600 original color
photographs with detailed captions which illustrate very
well the salient features of the text. The layout is inviting. The text is crammed with interesting facts and
is a pleasure to read." Libr J

National Audubon Society North
American birdfeeder handbook; foreword,
Stephen W. Kress. Dorling Kindersley 1992
224p il maps $22.95   **598**

1. Birds—North America

ISBN 1-56458-027-X   LC 91-58218

This book offers information about "how to identify,
attract, and feed birds: how to build bird houses, nest-
boxes, and feeders or where to buy them; and why these
backyard visitors behave the way they do. Included are
80 profiles, illustrated with more than 500 . . . color
photographs, of the most commonly observed birds in
North America, with details of their nesting habits, songs,
and feeding preferences." Publisher's note

Includes bibliography

The **Cambridge** encyclopedia of ornithology;
edited by Michael Brooke and Tim
Birkhead. Cambridge Univ. Press 1991
362p il maps (Cambridge reference bk)
$49.50   **598**

1. Birds

ISBN 0-521-36205-9   LC 91-214229

"Following an introduction to ornithology and
coverage of basic evolutionary principles, there are sections on anatomy and physiology, movement (including
flying, walking, and swimming), modern and fossil birds,
daily activities of birds, distribution, migration, population, breeding, behavior, and people and birds." Sci
Books Films

For a fuller review see: Booklist, March 1, 1992

Clark, William S., 1937-
A field guide to hawks, North America; illustrations by Brian K. Wheeler. Houghton Mifflin 1987 198p il maps $19.45; pa $13.95
598

1. Hawks
ISBN 0-395-36001-3; 0-395-44112-9 (pa)   LC 87-4528
"The Peterson field guide series"
"Sponsored by the National Audubon Society and the National Wildlife Federation"
This field guide describes 39 birds. "Each account includes a description, similar species, flight patterns, status and distribution, behavior, unusual plumage, and more. The birds, arranged in phylogenetic sequence, are illustrated by color plates and black-and-white photographs." Nichols. Guide to Ref Books for Sch Media Cent. 4th edition
Includes bibliography

Darlington, David
In condor country. Houghton Mifflin 1987 242p o.p.; Holt & Co. paperback available $13.95
598

1. McMillan, Eben 2. McMillan, Ian I. 3. Condors 4. Birds—Protection
ISBN 0-8050-1750-X (pa)   LC 87-2595
"Condor country is located in eastern San Luis Obispo County, California, an arid region between the interior Coast Range and the San Joaquin Valley. It is home to the six California condor known to be living in the wild and to Eben McMillan and his brother Ian, ranchers, naturalists, and environmentalists who have become uniquely involved with the fate of their avian neighbors. David Darlington invites us to share in the McMillans' daily routines as modern-day ranchers and in their avocation as 'radical amateurs' of the movement to save the condor." Publisher's note
Includes bibliography

Ehrlich, Paul R.
The birder's handbook; a field guide to the natural history of North American birds: including all species that regularly breed north of Mexico; [by] Paul R. Ehrlich, David S. Dobkin, Daryl Wheye. Simon & Schuster 1988 xxx, 785p il hardcover o.p. paperback available $17
598

1. Birds—North America
ISBN 0-671-65989-8 (pa)   LC 87-32404
This volume contains "basic information on each of the 646 species of birds in North America, enriched by 250 short essays on all aspects of avian behavior and biology. This book is a companion volume to any illustrated field guide." Am Libr
Includes bibliography

Encyclopedia of birds; edited by Christopher M. Perrins and Alex. L.A. Middleton. Facts on File 1985 xxxi, 445p il maps $45
598

1. Birds
ISBN 0-8160-1150-8   LC 84-26024
"An Equinox book"
This work "presents an overview of the world's living bird groups. . . . Illustrations are great in number. The full-color drawings are nicely presented, as are the range maps and drawings showing general size compared to humans." Topical Ref Books
Includes bibliography

Field guide to the birds of North America. 2nd ed. National Geographic Soc. 1987 464p il maps pa $16.95
598

1. Birds—North America
ISBN 0-87044-692-4   LC 86-33249
First published 1983
An identification guide to more than 800 species of North American birds. Arranged in family groups, the information for each species includes a full-color illustration, a range map, common and scientific names, measurement, and a description of plumage, distinctive songs and calls, behavior, abundance, and habitat

Gooders, John
Ducks of North America and the northern hemisphere; [by] John Gooders, Trevor Boyer. Facts on File 1986 176p il $27.95
598

1. Ducks
ISBN 0-8160-1422-1   LC 86-6333
The authors cover 52 species of ducks found in the northern hemisphere, with information on physical characteristics, social behavior, breeding habits, geographical distribution and migrating habits
"Good as the text is, Boyer's marvelous illustrations are definitely the book's most salient aspect." Booklist
Includes bibliography

Gorman, James, 1949-
The total penguin; photographs by Frans Lanting. Prentice-Hall 1990 191p il $29.95
598

1. Penguins
ISBN 0-13-925041-7   LC 89-48364
This book considers "penguin natural history, mating and breeding, the bird's remarkable aquatic adaptation, and its interactions with humans, respectively. The 90 color photos that illustrate are of high quality." Booklist

Handbook of North American birds; edited by Ralph S. Palmer. v4-5: Diurnal raptors. Yale Univ. Press 1988 2v il maps ea $45
598

1. Birds of prey
ISBN 0-300-04059-8 (v1); 0-300-04060-1 (v2)
"An exceptional, very thorough standard ornithological work. Intended to be comprehensible by general readers, hence unfamiliar terminology and concepts are kept to a minimum. For each species, gives detailed textual description of both sexes, as well as of any known subspecies, including field identification marks, voice, habitat, distribution, banding status, reproduction, survival, general habits and food. Vol. 4 has its own index, v. 5 an index for both volumes and a list of literature cited in both volumes. Illustrations consist of a few simple ink drawings and distribution maps." Sheehy. Guide to Ref Books. 10th edition. suppl

Harrison, George H.

The backyard bird watcher; technical and graphic assistance by Kit Harrison. Simon & Schuster 1979 284p il hardcover o.p. paperback available $10.95   **598**

1. Bird watching
ISBN 0-671-66374-7 (pa)   LC 78-25956

This guide "gives basic data on planting, feeding, birdhouses, and water; advice on coping with common problems; and a few pointers on bird photography. . . . Harrison writes clearly, enthusiastically, and, above all, sensibly." Libr J

Includes bibliography

Harrison, Kit

America's favorite backyard birds; [by] Kit and George Harrison. Simon & Schuster 1983 288p il hardcover o.p. paperback available $10.95   **598**

1. Birds—United States
ISBN 0-671-67341-6 (pa)   LC 83-11341

This book presents "life histories and behavior of ten of the most popular American birds. One chapter each is devoted to the robin, black-capped chicadee, mockingbird, cardinal, mourning dove, American goldfinch, downy woodpecker, house wren, blue jay, and whitebreasted nut-hatch, describing their habits, and how to attract them." Libr J

Includes bibliography

Hayman, Peter

Shorebirds; an identification guide to the waders of the world; [by] Peter Hayman, John Marchant and Tony Prater. Houghton Mifflin 1986 412p il $49; pa $24.45   **598**

1. Birds
ISBN 0-395-37903-2; 0-395-60237-8 (pa)   LC 85-8230

Companion volume to Seabirds, by Peter Harrison (1983)

"Sponsored by the American Birding Association"

"This is an excellent field guide to the shore birds or waders of the world. The color photographs are outstanding, and the descriptions cover all aspects of the birds: plumage, voice, habits, movements, and measurements." Malinowsky. Best Sci & Technol Ref Books for Young People

Includes bibliography

Heinrich, Bernd, 1940-

One man's owl; with drawings and photographs by the author. Princeton Univ. Press 1987 224p il $29.50   **598**

1. Owls
ISBN 0-691-08470-X   LC 87-3758

The author describes his raising of an orphaned horned owl and his struggle to develop the bird's survival and hunting instincts

The author "writes clearly and engagingly throughout, even when tackling detailed scientific explanations of owl behavior." Wilson Libr Bull

Includes bibliography

Hosking, Eric John, 1909-1991

Eric Hosking's birds of prey of the world; [by] Eric and David Hosking with Jim Flegg. Greene 1988 176p il hardcover o.p. paperback available $14.95   **598**

1. Birds of prey
ISBN 0-8289-642-4 (pa)   LC 87-23608

"This excellent book contains good photographs, both black-and-white and color, and a readable, up-to-date text. Most of the pictures of hawks, eagles, falcons, and vultures, taken by professional wildlife photographers, show the birds in their natural habitats. The text explains the classification of birds, their unusual behaviors, and their ecology. Conservation and the sport of falconry are also covered." Nichols. Guide to Ref Books for Sch Media Cent. 4th edition

The **Illustrated** encyclopedia of birds of the world; the definitive reference to birds of the world; consultant-in-chief, Christopher M. Perrins. Prentice Hall Press 1991 420p il maps $50   **598**

1. Birds
ISBN 0-13-083635-4   LC 90-34400

Published in association with the International Council for Bird Preservation

This illustrated survey has "three sections: a short summary of basic bird biology, an illustrated catalog of about 1200 species representing all living orders and families, and a checklist of all 9300-plus currently recognized species. Both the catalog and the checklist use standard taxonomic arrangement. The entries in the catalog, the heart of the book, include name, range, habitat, size and a concise but clear and not overly technical account of the birds' biology." Libr J

For a fuller review see: Booklist, June 15, 1992

Johnsgard, Paul A.

Hawks, eagles & falcons of North America; biology and natural history. Smithsonian Institution Press 1990 403p il maps $45   **598**

1. Birds of prey
ISBN 0-87474-682-5   LC 89-48558

"The book has two main sections: the biology of these birds of prey (migration, conservation, etc.); and . . . species accounts. The accounts, occupying several to a dozen pages for each species, contain descriptions of plumage, habitats, ecology, and behavior." Choice

"A limited reference series of field-guide-type drawings have been included, although the book is not intended to substitute for a good field guide." Booklist

Includes bibliography

Kress, Stephen W.

The Audubon Society guide to attracting birds; illustrations by Anne Senechal Faust; foreword by Roger Tory Peterson. Scribner 1985 xx, 377p il $24.95   **598**

1. Bird watching
ISBN 0-684-18362-5   LC 85-10813

"Sponsored by the Laboratory of Ornithology, at Cornell University"

The author provides "sections on land-scaping, selecting plants, pools and ponds, nesting structures, and references. The chapters on plants are especially good, with fine illustrations and a section on each major area

Kress, Stephen W.—*Continued*
of the United States. Appendixes detail agencies and organizations, state nurseries, and sources for plants and supplies." Libr J

Includes bibliography

Madge, Steve
Waterfowl; an identification guide to the ducks, geese, and swans of the world; [by] Steve Madge and Hilary Burn. Houghton Mifflin 1988 298p il maps hardcover o.p. paperback available $24.45 **598**

1. Water birds
ISBN 0-395-46726-8 (pa)   LC 87-26186

This is a field guide to the 155 species of aquatic birds. For each species, the author "describes field identification, voice, description of males, females, juveniles and other morphs, bare parts (bill, legs, etc.), measurements, geographical variation and races, habits, habitat, distribution, population, and references. . . . An excellent guide that should be made widely available." Choice

Includes bibliography

Peterson, Roger Tory, 1908-
A field guide to the birds; a completely new guide to all the birds of eastern and central North America; text and illustrations by Roger Tory Peterson; maps by Virginia Marie Peterson. 4th ed, completely rev and enl. Houghton Mifflin 1980 384p il maps $21.45; pa $15.45 **598**

1. Birds—North America
ISBN 0-395-26621-1; 0-395-26619-X (pa)
                                    LC 80-14304

Also available in abridged form in paperback with title: Peterson first guide to birds of North America

"The Peterson field guide series"

First published 1934

"Sponsored by the National Audubon Society and National Wildlife Federation"

This guide to birds found east of the Rocky Mountains contains colored illustrations painted by the author, with description of each species on the facing page. Views of young birds and seasonal variations in plumage are included. Birds are arranged in eight major groups of body shape

A field guide to the birds of Britain and Europe; [by] Roger Tory Peterson, Guy Mountfort, P.A.D. Hollom. 5th ed, in collaboration with D.I.M. Wallace. Houghton Mifflin 1993 261p il $24.95; pa $19.95 **598**

1. Birds—Great Britain 2. Birds—Europe
ISBN 0-395-66931-6; 0-395-66922-7 (pa)
                                    LC 93-22426

"The Peterson field guide series"

First published 1954

"Sponsored by the National Audubon Society, the National Wildlife Federation, and the Roger Tory Peterson Institute"

Covers the British Isles, Iceland, continental Europe and the islands of the Mediterranean. Includes identification, voice and habitat, and names in the foreign language pertinent to location

A field guide to western birds; text and illustrations by Roger Tory Peterson; maps by Virginia Marie Peterson. 3rd ed, completely rev and enl. Houghton Mifflin 1989 432p il maps $22.45; pa $16.45 **598**

1. Birds—West (U.S.)
ISBN 0-395-51749-4; 0-395-51424-X (pa)
                                    LC 89-31517

"The Peterson field guide series"

First published 1941

"A completely new guide to field marks of all species found in North America west of the 100th meridian and north of Mexico." Title page

"Sponsored by the National Audubon Society, the National Wildlife Federation, and the Roger Tory Peterson Institute"

This guide illustrates over 1,000 birds (700 species) on 165 color plates. In addition, over 400 distribution maps are included

Penguins. Houghton Mifflin 1979 238p il $49 **598**

1. Penguins
ISBN 0-395-27092-8   LC 79-10101

With a combination of photographs, sketches and text, naturalist Roger Tory Peterson gives an account of penguins. "Their evolution, behavior, habitat, habits, predators, food, and interactions with seals and humans are discussed. There are also brief accounts of each of the 17 penguin species plus a chapter on their Arctic counterpart, the alcids." Libr J

Includes bibliography

Robbins, Chandler S.
Birds of North America; a guide to field identification; by Chandler S. Robbins, Bertel Bruun, and Herbert S. Zim; illustrated by Arthur Singer. expanded rev ed. Golden Press Bks. 1983 360p il maps $14.95; pa $11.95 **598**

1. Birds—North America
ISBN 0-307-37002-X; 0-307-33656-5 (pa)
                                    LC 83-60422

"A Golden field guide"

First published 1966

Full-color illustrations and range maps facilitate the identification of North American land and water birds

Stap, Don
A parrot without a name; the search for the last unknown birds on earth. Knopf 1990 239p il $19.95 **598**

1. Birds—Peru 2. Bird watching
ISBN 0-394-55596-1   LC 89-43291

Also available in paperback from University of Texas Press

"The author follows the adventures of ornithologists John O'Neill and Ted Parker in the rain forests and jungles of Peru as they observe and collect exotic specimens of birds while trying to stay out of the way of insects, poisonous snakes, and jaguars." Booklist

Stokes, Donald W.

The bird feeder book; an easy guide to attracting, identifying, and understanding your feeder birds; [by] Donald and Lillian Stokes; illustrations of feeders by Gordon Morrison; range maps by Leslie Cowperthwaite. Little, Brown 1987 90p il maps pa $10.95   **598**

1. Bird watching
ISBN 0-316-81733-3   LC 87-3016

"This guide for beginners features 72 dramatic color photographs of the most common backyard birds. The text offers chapters on attracting and identifying birds (which types of feeders to use, etc.), dealing with squirrels and other yard pests, and planting shrubbery layouts that offer food and nest sites. A nicely illustrated, logically organized handbook." Booklist

Includes bibliography

Terres, John K.

The Audubon Society encyclopedia of North American birds; with a foreword by Dean Amadon. Knopf 1980 1280p il $75
     598

1. Birds—North America
ISBN 0-394-46651-9   LC 80-7617

"Provides detailed, authoritative, descriptive accounts of all 847 species of birds recorded in the United States and Canada, grouped by family. Also includes 625 articles on important aspects of avian biology (e.g., courtship, flight, migration, songs and singing, etc.), brief definitions of hundreds of terms, biographical sketches of prominent American ornithologists, and histories of national ornithological societies of the United States. High quality color photographs and black-and-white artists' illustrations accompany entries." Ref Sources for Small & Medium-sized Libr. 5th edition

Udvardy, Miklos D. F., 1919-

The Audubon Society field guide to North American birds: Western region; [by] M. D. F. Udvardy; visual key developed by Susan Rayfield. Knopf 1977 855p il $18   **598**

1. Birds—West (U.S.) 2. Birds—North America
ISBN 0-394-41410-1   LC 76-47938

Companion volume The Audubon Society Field guide to North American birds: Eastern region, by John Bull and John Farrand, Jr., entered above

"A Chanticleer Press edition. The Audubon Society field guide series"

"The area covered embraces Alaska, parts of the Yukon, most of British Columbia and Alberta, and part of all of the thirteen western states of the United States. Altogether, 508 species are described and illustrated." Introduction

599   Mammals

Burt, William Henry, 1903-1987

A field guide to the mammals; text and maps by William Henry Burt; illustrated by Richard Philip Grossenheider. 3d ed. Houghton Mifflin 1976 xxv, 289p il maps $21.45; pa $14.45   **599**

1. Mammals
ISBN 0-395-24082-4; 0-395-24084-0 (pa)
"The Peterson field guide series"
First published 1952
"Sponsored by the National Audubon Society and National Wildlife Federation"
"Field marks of all North American species found north of Mexico." Title page

"This field guide covers 380 species of mammals, including whales, dolphins, and porpoises. Each one is described in detail and most are depicted in color photographs and additional black-and-white sketches. Range maps are included. The description includes information on distinguishing marks, habitat, litter size, appearance of young, specimen tracks, and representations of nests." Malinowsky. Best Sci & Technol Ref Books for Young People

The **Encyclopedia** of mammals; edited by David Macdonald. Facts on File 1984 895, xlviiip il $65   **599**

1. Mammals
ISBN 0-87196-871-1   LC 84-1631

"The 700 entries in this beautifully written encyclopedia cover all of the major species, giving basic evolutionary facts, appearance, social patterns, and environmental concerns. The unique charts show the relative size of each animal compared to man. Other information includes the average body size, gestation period, longevity, and distribution." Malinowsky. Best Sci & Technol Ref Books for Young People

Grzimek's encyclopedia of mammals. McGraw-Hill 1990 5v il $500   **599**

1. Mammals
ISBN 0-07-909508-9 ((set))   LC 89-12542
Original German edition, 1988

"Just over 100 authorities from a handful of countries contributed the 300 or so articles that are arranged in 50 main sections. There are specific articles that include coverage of whales, seals, rodents, carnivores, deer, camels, and other mammal groups, and other articles designed to explain more general aspects of mammal biology and behavior (evolution, ecology, ethology, conservation, and life in captivity)." Topical Ref Books

Walker, Ernest P. (Ernest Pillsbury), 1891-1969

Walker's mammals of the world. 5th ed, by Ronald M. Nowak. Johns Hopkins Univ. Press 1991 2v il set $89.95   **599**

1. Mammals
ISBN 0-8018-3970-X   LC 91-27011
First published 1964

This reference work "covers 4,000 species. . . . Each account includes a physical description, life history, and précis of biological, behavioral, and ecological traits, as well as discussions of economic importance, population status, and efforts to conserve or restore declining species." Sci Books Films

Whitaker, John O., Jr.
The Audubon Society field guide to North American mammals; [by] John O. Whitaker, Jr.; Robert Elman, text consultant; visual key by Carol Nehring. Knopf 1980 745p il maps flexible bdg $18   **599**

1. Mammals
ISBN 0-394-50762-2   LC 79-3525

"A Chanticleer Press edition. The Audubon Society field guide series"

"This field guide, describing the mammals of North America found north of Mexico, is notable for the use of attractive color photographs to illustrate most species. . . . There is considerable information on the habits of individual species in the text of this compact but substantial volume. . . . It also includes animal distribution maps, lists of diagnostic characters, and notes on habitat." Libr J

599.5   Cetaceans and sirenians

Ellis, Richard, 1938-
The book of whales; written and illustrated by Richard Ellis. Knopf 1980 202p il hardcover o.p. paperback available $24.95   **599.5**

1. Whales
ISBN 0-394-73371-1 (pa)   LC 80-7640

"Introductory discussion centers on the whale's evolutionary development and general anatomic and behavioral characteristics. Various species are then profiled." Booklist
"Well written, this is a beautifully illustrated and comprehensively documented account." Choice

Includes bibliography

Dolphins and porpoises. Knopf 1982 270p il hardcover o.p. paperback available $24.95   **599.5**

1. Dolphins 2. Porpoises
ISBN 0-679-72286-6 (pa)   LC 82-47823

"Forty-three species are illustrated and discussed in some detail. After an introductory chapter on classification, behavior, maintenance in captivity, reproduction, intelligence, mythology, etc., there follow individual sections on each porpoise or dolphin. Wash, stipple, or outline drawings of each species are included." Choice

Includes bibliography

Evans, Peter G. H.
The natural history of whales & dolphins. Facts on File 1987 343p il maps $24.95   **599.5**

1. Whales 2. Dolphins
ISBN 0-8160-1732-8   LC 86-24037

The author discusses "the evolution of cetaceans (from the days when they possessed reduced hindlimbs and lived in shallow marshes, to when they graduated to the great oceans); their classification, distribution and feeding habits; their complex and advanced social organization and behavior." Publisher's note

Includes bibliography

Hoyt, Erich, 1950-
The whale watcher's handbook; illustrations by Pieter Folkens. Doubleday 1984 208p il maps $12.95   **599.5**

1. Whales 2. Marine mammals
ISBN 0-385-19036-0 (pa)   LC 83-45167

"A Madison Press book"

"Illustrated with black-and-white drawings, photographs, and maps on almost every page, this book is a field guide to seventy-seven whales, dolphins, and porpoises. Twenty-three introductory pages provide [an introduction to these mammals]. . . . The last part of the book is devoted to a . . . listing of places all over the world where you can go to watch whales in the wild." CM
"This book contains key information needed by serious whale watchers." Sci Books Films

Includes bibliography

Whales, dolphins, and porpoises; consulting editors, Richard Harrison, M.M. Bryden; illustrations by Tony Pyrzakowski. Facts on File 1988 240p il $35   **599.5**

1. Whales 2. Dolphins 3. Porpoises
ISBN 0-8160-1977-0   LC 88-11700

This work "covers the distribution, ecology, evolution, and kinds of whales along with their anatomy, adaptations to aquatic environments, reproduction and development, behavior, intelligence, relations with humans in captivity and in the wild, whales in art and in literature, and the International Whaling Commission. The writing is clear and enjoyable. . . . The illustrations are finely executed." Sci Books Films

Includes bibliography

Winn, Lois King, 1944-
Wings in the sea; the humpback whale; [by] Lois King Winn & Howard E. Winn. University Press of New England 1985 151p il hardcover o.p. paperback available $10.95   **599.5**

1. Whales
ISBN 0-87451-336-7 (pa)   LC 84-40598

This book discusses the life of the humpback whale
This "will serve as a good reference for both amateurs and professionals. More than 70 selected photographs and drawings and 212 literature references supplement the text. The writing style is non-demanding and accurate." Sci Books Films

Includes bibliography

599.6   Paenungulata

Chadwick, Douglas H.
The fate of the elephant. Sierra Club Bks. 1992 492p $25   **599.6**

1. Elephants 2. Wildlife conservation
ISBN 0-87156-635-4   LC 92-4520

The author "examines the major threats to the survival of the world's largest land mammal in a book filled with facts and anecdotes. Natural history buffs as well as readers concerned about the environment will enjoy this glimpse of the elephant's evolution and impact

Chadwick, Douglas H.—*Continued*
on global ecology." Booklist

Includes bibliography

Elephants; the deciding decade; edited by Ronald Orenstein; introduction by Richard Leakey; photography by Brian Beck. Contributors: Jeheskel Shoshani [et al.] Sierra Club Bks. 1991 160p il $35
     599.6

1. Elephants 2. Wildlife conservation
ISBN 0-87156-565-X   LC 91-15254

"Nontechnical and educational chapters by five experts and Richard Leakey's introduction provide excellent information on the ivory trade and ban as well as a fascinating discussion of elephant life history and ecology. Many little-known facts are covered. . . . Because the authors include their personal thoughts and perspective, their far-reaching text is compelling and moving. The photographs are splendid, technically and emotionally." Libr J

Includes bibliography

Moss, Cynthia
Elephant memories; thirteen years in the life of an elephant family. Morrow 1988 336p il maps o.p.; Fawcett Bks. paperback available $10.95   **599.6**

1. Elephants 2. Amboseli National Park (Kenya)
ISBN 0-449-90362-1 (pa)   LC 87-25082

Also available in paperback from Ivy Bks.

"For more than 13 years Cynthia Moss followed the histories of 25 or so elephants living in four related families near the center of Amboseli National Park in Kenya. 'Elephant Memories' is about the park and the researchers who live and work there, but mostly it is the story of Ms. Moss's exotic six-ton neighbors." N Y Times Book Rev

Includes bibliography

599.74 Carnivores

Adamson, Joy, 1910-1980
Born free; a lioness of two worlds. Pantheon Bks. 1987 220p il $11.95; pa $12.95   **599.74**

1. Lions 2. Kenya—Description
ISBN 0-679-56141-2; 0-394-74635-X (pa)
     LC 86-42972

A reissue of the title first published 1960

The "story of a lioness who bridged the gulf between two worlds, that of the jungle and of man. The author and her husband, a Kenya game warden, reared a cub to kill and fend for herself when she was returned to the jungle. At the same time they were able to preserve the bond of confidence and affection established with her as a pet." Cincinnati Public Libr

Catton, Chris
Pandas. Facts on File 1990 152p il $22.95
    599.74

1. Giant panda
ISBN 0-8160-2331-X   LC 89-23401

Relates how pandas were discovered, their habitat and behavior, and recent efforts to restore the panda's population in the wild

"The lengthy and comprehensive study Catton has given to the subject matter is obvious. Arranged into six chapters, the report is a valuable contribution to scientific literature." Sci Books Films

Includes bibliographies

Domico, Terry
Bears of the world; photographs by Terry Domico and Mark Newman. Facts on File 1988 189p il $29.95   **599.74**

1. Bears
ISBN 0-8160-1536-8   LC 88-3881

Following an introduction to ursine development the author examines the American black, brown, polar, Asian black and panda bear species

Includes bibliography

Fox, Michael W., 1937-
The soul of the wolf. Little, Brown 1980 131p il o.p.; Lyons & Burford paperback available $14.95   **599.74**

1. Wolves
ISBN 1-55821-150-0 (pa)   LC 80-13954

Fox "discusses the behavioral traits shared by man and wolf, from eye contact and touch as primary channels of communication to a similar use of body language. . . . [He] also traces the ways in which modern man has deviated from his own primitive ancestors and compares this with the example of the wolf." Publisher's note

Includes bibliographic references

Great cats; consulting editors, John Seidensticker and Susan Lumpkin; illustrations, Frank Knight. Rodale Press 1991 240p il maps (Majestic creatures of the wild) $40   **599.74**

1. Cats, Wild
ISBN 0-87857-965-6   LC 90-29179

"Thirty-eight contributing editors from around the world have written informative chapters about cat species, about the image of cats perpetuated in the art and culture of various civilizations, about cats' survival in zoos and in the wild, and about the outlook for preserving threatened species." Libr J

Hyde, Dayton O., 1925-
Don Coyote; the good times and the bad times of a much maligned American original. Arbor House 1986 245p il $16.95
    599.74

1. Coyotes
ISBN 0-87795-783-5   LC 85-30729

Also available in paperback from Ballantine Bks.

The author describes how he befriended coyotes on his Oregon ranch. He also aims to show how coyotes may be considered useful to humans

"Readers will enjoy Hyde's graceful writing, good humor, and cogent arguments for working with, not against, nature." Libr J

Kitchener, Andrew
The natural history of the wild cats. Comstock 1991 xxi, 280p il maps (Natural history of mammals ser) $27.50   **599.74**
1. Cats, Wild
ISBN 0-8014-2596-4   LC 90-45833

The author provides a "synthesis of what we know about cats, his account always strengthened by the comparative point of view. There are eight vivid chapters packed with graphs, maps and feline parameters. He includes a cat Who's Who in fine color photographs; it shows us most of the small cat species, plus three big cats that, unlike lions and tigers and leopards, are not in the public eye." Sci Am

Includes bibliography

Lawrence, R. D., 1921-
In praise of wolves. Holt & Co. 1986 245p il o.p.; Ballantine Bks. paperback available $4.95   **599.74**
1. Wolves 2. Mammals
ISBN 0-345-34916-4 (pa)   LC 85-21887

The author "uses his encounters with a captive group of wolves in Michigan's Upper Peninsula to develop his theories about the similarities between wolf and human societies; the importance of hormones in aggression, stress and recognition; and the role of predators in a habitat." N Y Times Book Rev
"Even though the book is principally about wolf behavior, Lawrence includes some good natural history of other animals as well. . . . This work is well written, very interesting, and highly recommended." Sci Books Films

Includes bibliography

Lopez, Barry Holstun, 1945-
Of wolves and men. Scribner 1978 309p il hardcover o.p. paperback available $17   **599.74**
1. Wolves
ISBN 0-684-16322-5 (pa)   LC 78-6070

"In succeeding chapters we see the wolf as an expert if cruel killer and as part of a highly organized, loving family and social group. Some myths about the animal are disproved, others are confirmed." Publ Wkly
"This is a history of ideas, written without prejudice, a successful contribution to the difficult study of the relationship between man and the world around him." Booklist

McCall, Karen, 1950-
Cougar; ghost of the Rockies; [by] Karen McCall and Jim Dutcher; foreword by Wallace Stegner; introduction by Maurice Hornocker. Sierra Club Bks. 1992 146p il $30   **599.74**
1. Pumas
ISBN 0-87156-564-1   LC 92-3691

This "book on the largest extant wild native American cat is the accompaniment to Dutcher's film on the same subject. As much an account of wildlife moviemaking as of the animal, it unfolds the parallel stories of one female cougar and her offspring and of the filming of the same cats." Booklist

Includes bibliography

McNamee, Thomas, 1947-
The grizzly bear; with drawings by Gordon Allen. Knopf 1984 308p il $24.95   **599.74**
1. Grizzly bear
ISBN 0-394-52998-7   LC 84-47640

Also available in paperback from Penguin Bks.
A "study of the day-to-day existence and behavior of a Yellowstone Park grizzly bear and her two cubs." Am Libr
This is "a well-balanced and provocative book which blends a wealth of scientific fact with a fine literary style." Libr J

Includes bibliography

Mech, L. David
The Arctic wolf; living with the pack; foreword by Roger Caras. Voyageur Press 1988 128p il $29.95; pa $19.95   **599.74**
1. Wolves
ISBN 0-89658-099-7; 0-89658-211-6 (pa)
                                      LC 89-131699

The author presents "general background information about wolf natural history. . . . Most of the text is an account of the behavior of a single pack of wolves living in the high arctic region north of Hudson Bay." Choice

The way of the wolf; foreword by Robert Bateman; photography by Tom Brakefield [et. al] Voyageur Press 1991 120p il maps $29.95   **599.74**
1. Wolves
ISBN 0-89658-163-2   LC 91-14415

This covers wolf behavior, biology, reproduction, communication and feeding habits and pleads for wolf conservation. Illustrated with color photographs

Includes bibliographic references

Mowat, Farley
Never cry wolf. Little, Brown 1963 247p $18.95   **599.74**
1. Wolves
ISBN 0-316-58639-0

Also available in paperback from Bantam Bks.
"An Atlantic Monthly Press book"
"A biologist for the Canadian government describes his experiences in the Arctic watching and tracking the activities of a wolf family." Publ Wkly

The **Secret** world of pandas; Byron Preiss & Gao Xueyu, editors; introduction by Jane Goodall. Abrams 1990 80p il pa $24.95   **599.74**
1. Giant panda
ISBN 0-8109-2457-9   LC 90-31121

"New China pictures book"
This work offers "glimpses of the 1000 pandas currently estimated to populate the earth—a few kept in zoos, but most roaming Chinese forests. . . . Pictures are the closest many of us will get, and these photos, with accompanying essays on panda history, habitat and habits, generally serve the cause well." Publ Wkly

Stirling, Ian
Polar bears; photographs by Dan Guravich. University of Mich. Press 1988 220p il maps hardcover o.p. paperback available $22.95   **599.74**

1. Polar bear
ISBN 0-472-08108-X (pa)   LC 88-14244

"The author discusses current knowledge regarding polar bear populations, seasonal migration, hibernation, reproduction and denning, the seal-hunting methods of polar bears, and their relation to humans." Sci Teach

Includes bibliography

599.8 Primates

Strum, Shirley
Almost human; a journey into the world of baboons; [by] Shirley C. Strum; drawings by Deborah Ross. Random House 1987 294p il maps $22.50   **599.8**

1. Baboons
ISBN 0-394-54724-1   LC 86-29712

Also available in paperback from Norton

This is an account of the author's "research on the Pumphouse Gang, a troop of olive baboons living on the Kenyan savannah. It is also a fascinating report of the implications and reception of her findings indicating that baboon society, thought to resemble closely that of our hominid ancestors, is far less dependent on male aggression and dominance hierarchy than had previously been supposed." Booklist

Includes bibliography

599.88 Apes

Fossey, Dian
Gorillas in the mist. Houghton Mifflin 1983 326p il hardcover o.p. paperback available $10.95   **599.88**

1. Gorillas
ISBN 0-685-06802-1 (pa)   LC 82-23332

This book "recounts some of the events of the thirteen years that I have spent with the mountain gorillas in their natural habitat and includes data from the fifteen years of continuing field study." Preface

Includes bibliography

Ghiglieri, Michael Patrick, 1946-
East of the Mountains of the Moon; chimpanzee society in the African rain forest; [by] Michael P. Ghiglieri. Free Press 1988 315p il maps $32.95   **599.88**

1. Chimpanzees
ISBN 0-02-911580-9   LC 87-21203

This is an account of the author's study of chimpanzees in the Kibale Forest of Uganda

"Ghiglieri's patient observations not only engender some original scientific conclusions, but also provide a rare insight into the social and political fabric of Idi Amin's Uganda. An exciting, incisive, and multileveled study." Booklist

Includes bibliography

Goodall, Jane
The chimpanzees of Gombe; patterns of behavior. Belknap Press 1986 673p il $39.95   **599.88**

1. Chimpanzees
ISBN 0-674-11649-6   LC 85-20030

This book is based on the author's and her students' observation of chimpanzees in the Gombe National Park in Tanzania. It is an attempt to provide synthesis of twenty-five years of research on these primates

This "densely written book covers almost every aspect of [chimpanzee] behavior observed in the wild. . . . Goodall's book will be a major source for decades and must be considered an essential holding for any life science collection." Choice

Includes bibliography

In the shadow of man; photographs by Hugo van Lawick. rev ed. Houghton Mifflin 1988 297p il map $9.70   **599.88**

1. Chimpanzees
ISBN 0-395-33145-5 (pa)   LC 87-36965

First published 1971

The author describes the chimpanzee group she studied during ten years of field observation in the Gombe Stream Chimpanzee Reserve in Tanzania

Includes bibliography

Through a window; my thirty years with the chimpanzees of Gombe. Houghton Mifflin 1990 268p il map $21.45; pa $9.70   **599.88**

1. Chimpanzees
ISBN 0-395-50081-8; 0-395-59925-3 (pa)
                                    LC 90-36974

Updates the author's In the shadow of man, entered above

This book "tells two stories: first of how the chimps of Gombe in Tanzania have grown, changed and died, and second, how Goodall and her dedicated group of Tanzanian observers have survived the rigours of the past thirty years." Times Lit Suppl

600 TECHNOLOGY (APPLIED SCIENCES)

Brennan, Richard P.
Levitating trains and kamikaze genes; technological literacy for the 1990's. Wiley 1989 262p il (Wiley science editions) $18.95   **600**

1. Technology
ISBN 0-471-62295-8   LC 89-37349

Also available in paperback from HarperCollins

"The author distills basic information about the current state of research on space, biology, computers, the environment, energy, superconductivity, medicine, transportation and weaponry down to 262 pages of usually easy-to-read text. . . . Mr. Brennan answers a lot of the questions you felt too foolish to ask." N Y Times Book Rev

Includes bibliographic references

How in the world? Reader's Digest Assn.
1990 448p il $32 **600**
1. Technology 2. Science 3. Curiosities and wonders
ISBN 0-89577-353-8 LC 90-30663
An illustrated look at the science behind natural and mechanical processes

Macaulay, David, 1946-
The way things work. Houghton Mifflin
1988 384p il $29.95 **600**
1. Technology 2. Machinery 3. Inventions
ISBN 0-395-42857-2 LC 88-11270
In a "combination of illustration and text, Macaulay introduces the science behind mechanization as he explains the functioning of familiar devices, ranging in variety from camshafts to computers." Booklist

604.2 Technical drawing

Technical drawing; [by] Frederick E.
Giesecke [et. al] Macmillan $67; pa $28 **604.2**
1. Mechanical drawing
First published 1936. (9th edition 1991). Periodically revised
This text presents fundamental principles of technical drawing, including dimensioning and drawing techniques for specific areas of modern technology

604.7 Hazardous materials technology

Lewis, Richard J.
Hazardous chemicals desk reference. 3rd ed. Van Nostrand Reinhold 1993 1742p $99.95 **604.7**
1. Hazardous substances—Dictionaries
ISBN 0-442-01408-2 LC 92-46784
First published 1987
Based on N. Irving Sax's Dangerous properties of industrial materials
A guide to hazardous chemicals encountered in industrial situations

608 Inventions and patents

Pressman, David, 1937-
Patent it yourself; edited by Stephen Elias; illustrations by Linda Allison. 3rd ed. Nolo Press (Berkeley) 1991 various paging il $34.95 **608**
1. Patents 2. Inventions
ISBN 0-87337-167-4 LC 91-34546
First published 1979 by McGraw-Hill
This guide for the amateur inventor covers patent searching, filing and infringement
Includes bibliography

609 Technology—Historical and geographic treatment

Diebold, John, 1926-
The innovators; the discoveries, inventions, and breakthroughs of our time. Dutton 1990 303p il o.p.; New Am. Lib. paperback available $9.95 **609**
1. Inventions 2. Technology
ISBN 0-452-26575-4 (pa) LC 89-34510
"A Truman Talley book"
This book examines such innovations as transistors, lasers, fiber optics, VCRs, superconductivity, gene mapping and electronic banking
This book "contains many useful insights into corporate strategies that nurture scientific creativity—skills that will play a key role in shaping the future of the American economy." N Y Times Book Rev
Includes bibliography

Flatow, Ira
They all laughed; from lightbulbs to lasers, the fascinating stories behind the great inventions that have changed our lives. HarperCollins Pubs. 1992 238p il $20; pa $10 **609**
1. Inventions
ISBN 0-06-016445-X; 0-06-092415-2 (pa)
LC 91-58336
"From teflon to lasers, from xerography to velcro, the author humorously describes the often serendipitous events leading to the particular breakthrough. The treatment is enthusiastic and lighthearted and not organized in any thematic or chronological fashion. It's a quick read and informative." Libr J
Includes bibliographic references

Macdonald, Anne L., 1920-
Feminine ingenuity; women and invention in America; [by] Anne Macdonald. Ballantine Bks. 1992 xxiv, 514p il $22 **609**
1. Women inventors 2. Inventions
ISBN 0-345-35811-2 LC 91-55502
This is a "study of American women's contribution to science, engineering, and technology as represented in the issuance of U.S. patents. From the first patent issued to a woman in 1809, Macdonald traces the uphill struggle women have faced in their efforts to obtain equal rights—in the area of patent awards as well as in the broader educational, economic, and social arenas." Libr J
Includes bibliographic references

Mumford, Lewis, 1895-1990
Technics and civilization. Harcourt Brace & Co. 1934 495p il hardcover o.p. paperback available $18.95 **609**
1. Technology—History 2. Technology and civilization
ISBN 0-15-688254-X (pa)
The first volume of a study of modern man which includes The culture of cities (entered in class 307.7), The condition of man (entered in class 909) and The conduct of life (entered in class 128)

Mumford, Lewis, 1895-1990—*Continued*
"A history of machine civilization, going back to the 10th century for its beginnings. The author divides his history into three periods: the eotechnic, or era of wind, water and wood; the paleotechnic, coal and iron; and the neotechnic, electrical energy." Wis Libr Bull

Includes bibliography

Patton, Phil
Made in U.S.A; the secret histories of the things that made America. Grove Weidenfeld 1992 403p il $19.95 **609**
1. Technology 2. Industrial arts
ISBN 0-8021-1276-5 LC 91-19961
Also available in paperback from Penguin Bks.

"In 17 separate essays (each of which includes a brief but informative bibliography), Patton recounts the history of a wide array of typical American objects, ranging from Bowie knives and Winchester rifles to laptop computers and designer jeans. Patton has a vigorous style and a knack for capturing the personalities of people involved in many of the innovations he writes about, and he skillfully places each invention in the social-cultural context of its origins and in its eventual impact." Libr J

Petroski, Henry
The evolution of useful things. Knopf 1992 288p il $24 **609**
1. Inventions 2. Patents
ISBN 0-679-41226-3 LC 91-39524
The author "provides an intricate look, in lay reader's terms, at the technology and basic rationale behind a number of items we often take for granted. The list is comprehensive: kitchen utensils, zippers, tools, paper clips, fast-food packaging, and more. The text is far from a recital of mere facts. Petroski's anecdotes and stories about individual designers and inventors are told with warm regard. He also provides illuminating thoughts on the theoretical, historical, and cultural frameworks that influenced these creations." Libr J

Includes bibliography

Williams, Trevor Illtyd
The history of invention. Facts on File 1987 352p il $40 **609**
1. Technology—History 2. Inventions—History
ISBN 0-8160-1788-3 LC 87-8880
The author "presents a history of technology in five sections: ancient civilizations, the rise of Islam to 1500, Renaissance to the birth of industrialism, early twentieth century to World War II, and postwar civilization to the frontiers of science." Appraisal
"Well written and well illustrated, this book also contains an excellent biographical dictionary of inventors through the ages." Sci Books Films

Includes bibliography

610 Medical sciences. Medicine

Achterberg, Jeanne, 1942-
Woman as healer. Shambhala Publs. 1990 241p il hardcover o.p. paperback available $13 **610**
1. Women in medicine
ISBN 0-8773-616-2 (pa) LC 89-43314

The author "traces the connection of women with the healing arts from prehistoric shamanism to present-day holistic medicine. . . . From Hygeia, Greek goddess of health, to Florence Nightingale and beyond, Achterberg reveals the continuity of experience among women healers." Booklist

Includes bibliography

Borysenko, Joan
Minding the body, mending the mind; [by] Joan Borysenko with Larry Rothstein. Addison-Wesley 1987 241p il $14.38 **610**
1. Mind and body 2. Holistic medicine
ISBN 0-201-10707-4 LC 86-32235
Also available in paperback from Bantam Bks.

The author describes a "ten-week program for learning to 'mind the body' through a medical synthesis of neurology, immunology, and psychology." Libr J
"This volume challenges individuals to take control of their minds and bodies and thus more effectively handle stress-related illnesses and the pressures of daily life. Contains helpful chapter summaries." Booklist

Includes bibliography

Cousins, Norman
Anatomy of an illness as perceived by the patient; reflections on healing and regeneration; introduction by René Dubos. Norton 1979 173p $16.95 **610**
1. Holistic medicine 2. Medicine 3. Mind and body
ISBN 0-393-01252-2 LC 79-10597
Also available in paperback from Bantam Bks.

The author examines how the will to live, modern medicine, and laughter therapy helped him conquer a debilitating disease

Includes bibliography

Head first; the biology of hope. Dutton 1989 368p o.p.; Penguin Bks. paperback available $9.95 **610**
1. Medicine 2. Mind and body
ISBN 0-14-013965-6 (pa) LC 89-7789
Also available Thorndike Press large print edition

"Anecdotal research combines with scientific data in this effort to show that a positive attitude can aid the healing process." Publ Wkly

Includes bibliography

Medicine. Time-Life Bks. 1991 144p il (How things work) $19.93 **610**
1. Medicine LC 90-26963
Text and numerous illustrations introduce the reader to medical research, diagnostic devices, lab tests, immunization, surgery and transplants

The New holistic health handbook; living well in a new age; edited by Shepherd Bliss [et al.] Greene 1985 429p il o.p.; Penguin Bks. paperback available $14.95 **610**
1. Holistic medicine 2. Health
ISBN 0-8289-0561-4 (pa) LC 85-70528
First published 1978 by the Berkeley Holistic Health Center with title: The holistic health handbook

The New holistic health handbook — *Continued*

This is a "compilation of essays on alternative and complementary therapies and systems of healing. The individual contributors have addressed some 120 diverse topics such as homeopathy, yoga, dreams, native American healing, holistic approaches to surgery, and how to choose a holistic practitioner. . . . A comprehensive reference book." Booklist

Includes bibliography

Siegel, Bernie S.

Love, medicine & miracles; lessons learned about self-healing from a surgeon's experience with exceptional patients. Harper & Row 1986 243p il $19.95; pa $12 **610**

1. Holistic medicine 2. Mind and body
ISBN 0-06-015496-9; 0-06-091983-3 (pa)

LC 85-45664

Also available G.K. Hall large print edition

The author "believes that the power of healing stems from the human mind and will, that his scalpel only buys time against cancer, and that self-love and determination are more important than choice of therapy." Libr J

Includes bibliography

Peace, love & healing; bodymind communication and the path to self-healing: an exploration. Harper & Row 1989 290p hardcover o.p. paperback available $12

610

1. Holistic medicine 2. Mind and body
ISBN 0-06-091705-9 (pa)

LC 88-45906

Also available Walker & Co. large print edition

The author explains ways to "give ourselves healing messages through techniques of meditation, visualization, relaxation and peace of mind." Publisher's note

"Highly recommended reading for just about everyone who wants to live and die in a meaningful way." Libr J

Includes bibliographic references

Thomas, Lewis, 1913-1993

The fragile species. Scribner 1992 193p $20; pa $10 **610**

1. Medicine 2. Biology
ISBN 0-684-19420-1; 0-02-054555-X (pa)

LC 91-34315

"A Robert Stewart book"

A "collection of essays, ruminations, and observations on topics ranging from becoming a doctor to the process of aging to the threat of nuclear annihilation. . . . The two essays on AIDS in particular are blueprints of reasoned thought and fine examples of an eloquent writer and sensitive observer at work." Libr J

The **Visual** encyclopedia of natural healing; a step-by-step pictorial guide to solving 100 everyday health problems; by the editors of Prevention Magazine Health Books; edited by Alice Feinstein. Rodale Press 1991 423p il $26.95 **610**

1. Medicine, Popular 2. Health
ISBN 0-87857-928-1

LC 90-45937

"This self-care encyclopedia presents natural healing techniques in a step-by-step format for a variety of common complaints and ailments, from allergies to wrinkles. Its more than 700 illustrations—of massage and acupressure techniques, the Heimlich maneuver, therapeutic exercises, breast self-examination, et al.—are its chief attraction." Libr J

610.3 Medical sciences— Encyclopedias and dictionaries

The **American** Medical Association encyclopedia of medicine; medical editor, Charles B. Clayman. Random House 1989 1184p il $44.45 **610.3**

1. Medicine—Dictionaries
ISBN 0-394-56528-2

LC 88-29693

This "dictionary describes diseases, conditions, symptoms, medications, tests, procedures, and surgical operations for the layperson. Its authority, broad coverage, and excellent diagnostic charts distinguish it from similar works." Libr J

Black's medical dictionary. Barnes & Noble Bks. $77.50 **610.3**

1. Medicine—Dictionaries

First published 1906. (37th edition 1992) Frequently revised

Current editor: C. W. H. Havard

"The entries in this dictionary are encyclopedic in nature, often stretching to several paragraphs, in language understandable to the educated layperson. Illustrated with line drawings and graphs, the work includes extensive articles on parts of the body and diseases." Ref Sources for Small & Medium-sized Libr. 5th edition

Current medical diagnosis and treatment. Appleton & Lange pa $39.95 **610.3**

1. Medicine—Handbooks, manuals, etc.
ISSN 0092-8682

Annual. First published 1974 as a successor to Current diagnosis & treatment

Editors vary

"Provides concise information on the diagnosis and treatment of diseases and disorders for medical practitioners. Uses common medical terminology, but is generally understandable to the layperson." N Y Public Libr Book of How & Where to Look It Up

Dorland's illustrated medical dictionary. Saunders il $39.95 **610.3**

1. Medicine—Dictionaries

First published 1900. (27th edition 1988) Frequently revised

This standard reference includes terms used in medicine, surgery, dentistry, pharmacy, chemistry, nursing, veterinary science, biology, and medical biology. Pronunciation, derivation, and definitions are given

"This is considered one of the most comprehensive medical dictionaries in print." N Y Public Libr Book of How & Where to Look It Up

Merck manual of diagnosis and therapy. Merck & Co. $26 **610.3**

1. Medicine—Handbooks, manuals, etc.

First published 1899. (16th edition 1992) Periodically revised

Merck manual of diagnosis and therapy—
Continued

"A one-volume reference that attempts to cover all but the most obscure diseases. Sections are organized by type of disease or medical specialty." N Y Public Libr Book of How & Where to Look It Up

Merriam-Webster's medical desk dictionary. Merriam-Webster 1993 26a, 790p $24.95
610.3

1. Medicine—Dictionaries
ISBN 0-87779-125-2   LC 93-7965

First published 1986 with title: Webster's medical desk dictionary

This medical dictionary features "part-of-speech labels, pronunciation respelling for all entries. British spellings where needed . . . prefixes, suffixes, and combining forms, an essay on the history of medical English, and over 1,000 biographies of men and women whose names have become part of the medical vocabulary." Publisher's note

Mosby's medical, nursing, and allied health dictionary. 3rd ed, managing editor, Walter D. Glanze; revision editor, Kenneth N. Anderson; consulting editor and writer, Lois E. Anderson. Mosby 1990 xx, 44, 1608p il $25.95
610.3

1. Medicine—Dictionaries 2. Nursing—Dictionaries
ISBN 0-8016-3227-7   LC 90-183154

Also available in abridged form with title: Mosby's pocket dictionary of medicine, nursing & allied health

First published 1983 with title: Mosby's medical & nursing dictionary

"Complete and geared towards nurses and other health professionals. Has exhaustive appendices, including a 44-page color atlas of human anatomy." N Y Public Libr Book of How & Where to Look It Up

The **Oxford** companion to medicine; edited by John Walton, Paul B. Beeson, Ronald Bodley Scott; associate editors and principal contributors, S.G. Owen, Philip Rhodes. Oxford Univ. Press 1986 2v il $150
610.3

1. Medicine—Dictionaries
ISBN 0-19-261191-7   LC 85-29846

Covers "topics such as diagnosis, experimental method, health insurance in the United States, law and medicine in the United Kingdom, medical microbiology, physiology, rehabilitation, and veterinary medicine." Wilson Libr Bull

Includes bibliographies

Stedman's abbrev: abbreviations, acronyms & symbols. Williams & Wilkins 1992 664p (Stedman's word bks) $24   **610.3**

1. Medicine—Dictionaries   2. Abbreviations—Dictionaries 3. Acronyms—Dictionaries
ISBN 0-683-07926-3   LC 91-30701

Spine title: Stedman's abbreviations, acronyms, & symbols

This "directory is a companion work to *Stedman's Medical Dictionary* [entered below] enhancing Stedman's coverage with more than 20,000 clinically relevant and alphabetically arranged abbreviations, acronyms, and symbols used in the medical profession. . . . This specialized dictionary is highly recommended for medical libraries

as well as special and public libraries that have *Stedman's Medical Dictionary*." Am Ref Books Annu, 1993

Stedman's medical dictionary. Williams & Wilkins $49.95   **610.3**

1. Medicine—Dictionaries

Also available from Macmillan

First published 1911. (25th edition 1990) Periodically revised

Provides definitions, pronunciation and derivations for terms used in general medicine, veterinary medicine, biochemistry and other related fields

610.69   Medical personnel

Directory of medical specialists. Marquis Who's Who 3v $295   **610.69**

1. Physicians—Directories
Biennial. First published 1939

"For each physician includes: name, certification(s), type of practice, birth date and place, education, career history, teaching positions, military record, professional memberships, office address and phone number. Includes an outline of certification requirements for each specialty and a statement of its purpose and function." Sheehy. Guide to Ref Books. 10th edition

Directory of physicians in the United States. American Medical Assn. 4v $545 **610.69**

1. Physicians—Directories

Also available CD-ROM version

First published 1906 with title: American medical directory. (33rd edition 1993) Periodically revised

At head of title: American Medical Association

This directory lists names, addresses, and zip codes; includes information on medical school of graduation; year first licensed in state; primary and secondary practice specialties; type of practice; American Board of Medical Specialties Certification; and Physician's Recognition Award status

M.D. doctors talk about themselves; [compiled by] John Pekkanen. Delacorte Press 1988 294p $18.95   **610.69**

1. Physicians
ISBN 0-440-50028-1   LC 88-15351

Also available in paperback from Dell

The compiler "offers the results of interviews with some 70 doctors, eliciting their views on medical education; the financial, psychological, and emotional costs of practice; patients; malpractice; dying and death; drugs; ethics; and greed." Booklist

Laymen "will not find another book that exposes the worries of the average doctor with such honesty and feeling." N Y Times Book Rev

Wischnitzer, Saul
Barron's guide to medical & dental schools. Barron's Educ. Ser. il maps pa $14.95   **610.69**

1. Medicine—Vocational guidance 2. Dentistry—Vocational guidance 3. Osteopathy—Vocational guidance

First published 1982. (6th edition 1993) Periodically revised

Wischnitzer, Saul—*Continued*

This guide profiles "AMA-accredited American and Canadian schools, ADA-accredited dental schools, as well as osteopathic schools, accredited by the American Osteopathic Association. Advice is also given on applying to schools, with specific recommended courses and procedures for maximizing chances of acceptance." Publisher's note

610.7 Medical sciences—Education, nursing, related topics

Ludmerer, Kenneth M.

Learning to heal; the development of American medical education. Basic Bks. 1985 346p $21.95; pa $12.95   **610.7**

1. Medicine—Study and teaching
ISBN 0-465-03880-8; 0-465-03381-6 (pa)

LC 85-47554

This is a history and assessment of American medical education from the 19th century to the present
"A thoroughly researched, well-documented, and readable study that may long serve as a definitive work." Booklist

Includes bibliography

610.73 Nursing and services of medical technicians and assistants

Donahue, M. Patricia

Nursing, the finest art; an illustrated history; illustrations edited and compiled by Patricia A. Russac. Mosby 1985 508p il $42.95   **610.73**

1. Nursing
ISBN 0-8016-1424-4

LC 84-29450

Also available from Abrams

This volume seeks to "trace 'the art' of nursing from primitive peoples to the current 'age of specialization.'" N Y Times Book Rev
"This is an exquisite book both visually and textually. . . . This book is not just a chronicle of heroines and events. It is a subtle weave of the history of medicine and women within the tapestry of civilization." Libr J

Includes bibliography

Kraegel, Janet M.

Just a nurse; from the clinic to hospital ward, battleground to cancer unit: the hearts and minds of nurses today; [by] Janet Kraegel and Mary Kachoyeanos. Dutton 1989 304p o.p.; Dell paperback available $4.95   **610.73**

1. Nurses
ISBN 0-440-20763-0 (pa)

LC 88-30921

This book "features interviews with more than 50 nurses from a variety of medical environments—burn units, cancer wards, delivery rooms, AIDS wards, and HMO offices. In short takes, the nurses frankly discuss their experiences, current issues, and the risks and problems of everyday work." Booklist

610.9 Medical sciences—Historical and geographic treatment

Cassedy, James H.

Medicine in America: a short history. Johns Hopkins Univ. Press 1991 187p (American moment) $36; pa $11.95   **610.9**

1. Medicine—United States—History
ISBN 0-8018-4207-7; 0-8018-4208-5 (pa) LC 91-7058

This history of American medicine traces medical and health-related matters from colonial times to the present
This book "is scholarly, well written, very useful, and fills a void." Choice

Includes bibliographic references

Fisher, Jeffrey A., 1943-

Rx 2000; breakthroughs in health, medicine, and longevity by the year 2000 and beyond. Simon & Schuster 1992 271p $22   **610.9**

1. Medical forecasting 2. Medical technology
ISBN 0-671-73844-5

LC 92-9668

The author "explores the medical trends of the future. In the acknowlegements, Fisher expresses appreciation to 70 biomedical experts he interviewed, and the 22-page bibliography further establishes the author's research. . . He predicts a medicine in which the body will be seem as a 'finely tuned electrochemical engine' and the emphasis will be on preventive care and 'enhancement therapy' from conception to euthanasia." Libr J

Nuland, Sherwin B.

Doctors; the biography of medicine. Knopf 1988 xxi, 519p il hardcover o.p. paperback available $12.95   **610.9**

1. Physicians 2. Medicine—History
ISBN 0-679-72215-7 (pa)

LC 88-9337

This is a "history of medicine told through the biographies of prominent contributors to the healing arts. . . . Among the figures profiled in this collection of knowledgeable and entertaining essays are Hippocrates, Galen, William Harvey, Rudolf Virchow, and William Stewart Halsted. A welcome addition to any medical collection." Booklist

Includes bibliography

Weisse, Allen B.

Medical odysseys; the different and sometimes unexpected pathways to twentieth-century medical discoveries. Rutgers Univ. Press 1991 250p $36; pa $13.95   **610.9**

1. Medicine—History 2. Medicine—Research
ISBN 0-8135-1616-1; 0-8135-1617-X (pa) LC 90-8387

The author "recounts the sometimes serendipitous discoveries that concluded in some milestones of modern medicine: open heart surgery, the artificial kidney, chemotherapy, and others. Although some of these stories 'have been told before,' in Weisse's judgment they have been told incompletely, and he has exploited primary sources to bring 'an important added dimension to the telling.' Well written." Libr J

Includes bibliographic references

611   Human anatomy, cytology, histology

Netter, Frank H., 1906-1991
Atlas of human anatomy; Sharon Colacino, consulting editor. CIBA-GEIGY Corp. 1989 36p, 514p of plates $120; pa $49.95   **611**

1. Human anatomy
ISBN 0-914168-18-5; 0-914168-19-3 (pa)
     LC 89-60477

"The illustrations in [this] Atlas are arranged in seven sections: the head and neck, the back and spinal cord, the thorax, the abdomen, the pelvis and perineum, the upper limb, and the lower limb." Booklist
This is a "book of outstanding artistic and scientific merit that is destined to become a classic both in the field of human anatomy and in artistic portrayal of the human body." Libr J

612   Human physiology

ABC's of the human body; a family answer book. Reader's Digest Assn. 1987 336p il $28   **612**

1. Human anatomy 2. Physiology
ISBN 0-89577-220-5   LC 85-14470

At head of title: Reader's Digest
"The text clearly explains the systems and functions of the human body, answers common questions, probes the mysteries of sickness and health, and gives brief but accurate explanations of human body processes and phenomena. The easy-to-read question-and-answer format enhances accessibility. In addition, the book features wonderful illustrations and photos, ranging from pictures of ancient works of art to computer-enhanced images. Highly recommended for all collections." Booklist

The **Incredible** machine. National Geographic Soc. 1986 384p il $26.95
     612

1. Physiology 2. Human anatomy
ISBN 0-87044-619-3   LC 85-29731

"Photographs of cells, chromosomes, bones, viruses, and organs are coupled with instructive, lucid essays detailing the operation of the world's most incredible machine—the human body. The authors integrate recent scientific findings—on osteoporosis and artificial heart implantation, for example—in their engrossing coverage of reproduction, nutrition, the brain, the effects of aging, and the nervous, circulatory, and immune systems." Booklist

Includes bibliography

Mysteries of the human body; by the editors of Time-Life Books. Time-Life Bks. 1990 143p il (Lib. of curious and unusual facts) $17.27   **612**

1. Physiology 2. Human anatomy   LC 90-30146

An illustrated look at the systems and functions of the human body. Various aspects of sickness and health are explored

Podell, Richard N.
Doctor, why am I so tired? Pharos Bks. 1988 c1987 255p $17.95   **612**

1. Fatigue
ISBN 0-88687-321-5   LC 87-60161

Also available in paperback from Fawcett Bks.
A discussion of the possible causes of fatigue and a look at treatment options
Includes bibliography

Rose, Kenneth Jon
The body in time. Wiley 1988 237p il hardcover o.p. paperback available $10.95
     612

1. Physiology 2. Biological rhythms
ISBN 0-471-51200-1 (pa)   LC 87-21666

A "presentation of human body processes—reflexes, injuries, growth, abuse, rhythms, aging, and interaction with the environment—that uses time as a frame of reference." Sci Teach
"Throughout, the information is accurate, well organized, and clearly presented, and high-quality illustrations complement the text." Sci Books Films

612.1   Blood and circulation

Vogel, Steven, 1940-
Vital circuits; on pumps, pipes, and the workings of circulatory systems; illustrated by Rosemary Anne Calvert. Oxford Univ. Press 1992 315p il $24.95; pa $12.95
     612.1

1. Cardiovascular system 2. Heart
ISBN 0-19-507155-7; 0-19-508269-9 (pa)
     LC 91-23954

An overview of the physiology of the heart and circulatory system
The author "writes clearly and informatively and with just the right touch of humor. . . . even the illustrations he chooses are not just pertinent (and legibly labeled): they increase the understanding gathered from the text." Booklist
Includes bibliography

612.6   Reproduction, development, maturation

Nilsson, Lennart, 1922-
A child is born. completely new ed, text by Lars Hamberger. Delacorte Press 1990 213p il $27.50   **612.6**

1. Pregnancy 2. Embryology 3. Childbirth
ISBN 0-385-30237-1   LC 90-33633

"A Merloyd Lawrence book"
Original Swedish edition, 1965; first United States edition, 1966
An illustrated look at male and female reproductive anatomy and physiology, the processes of ovulation and fertilization, fetal development, and labor and delivery

Wolpert, L. (Lewis)
The triumph of the embryo; [by] Lewis Wolpert; with illustrations drawn by Debra Skinner. Oxford Univ. Press 1991 211p il $22.95   **612.6**
1. Embryology
ISBN 0-19-854243-7   LC 91-7583
Drawing on current embryological research, the author traces the development of the embryo from fertilized egg to whole human being
"Wolpert makes this difficult subject interesting and easy for a layperson to understand." Libr J

612.7 Motor functions and skin (integument), hair, nails

Alexander, R. McNeill
The human machine; illustrated by Mark Iley & Sally Alexander. Columbia Univ. Press 1992 176p il $34.95   **612.7**
1. Physiology 2. Human anatomy
ISBN 0-231-08066-2   LC 92-10517
This is a study "of body motion and . . . aspects of human movement from everyday activities such as writing to sporting techniques such as weightlifting. . . . [Alexander outlines] the mechanical principles involved, detailing such activities as swimming and cycling. [He] also discusses mechanical faults and accidents—medical problems that might disturb the working of the body—including sprains, bone, fractures, arthritis and heart attacks." Publisher's note
Includes bibliographic references

612.8 Nervous functions. Sensory functions

Ackerman, Sandra
Discovering the brain; [by] Sandra Ackerman for the Institute of Medicine, National Academy of Sciences. National Acad. Press 1992 180p il $22.95   **612.8**
1. Brain 2. Nervous system
ISBN 0-309-04529-0   LC 92-1231
Based on presentations at a July 1990 symposium organized by the Institute of Medicine, held in Washington, D.C.
The author details "what we know about the brain and what researchers may be able to accomplish in the next 10 years." Univ Press Books for Public and Second Sch Libr
Includes bibliographic references

Alkon, Daniel L.
Memory's voice; deciphering the brain-mind. HarperCollins Pubs. 1992 285p il $22.50   **612.8**
1. Memory 2. Brain
ISBN 0-06-018300-4   LC 92-52573
"The hunt for a memory storage 'site' in the brain is the subject of this engrossing scientific memoir. Alkon . . . describes, often in elegant prose, his search to explain human memory and learning in biological terms. . . . This fascinating blend of neurobiology and psy-

chology is appropriate for popular science collections." Libr J

Bourke, Dale Hanson
The sleep management plan; foreword by Wallace B. Mendelson. Harper & Row 1990 148p il $14.95; pa $5.50   **612.8**
1. Sleep
ISBN 0-06-250110-0; 0-06-104214-5 (pa)
    LC 89-45554
The author "describes how she relearned her own sleep habits. She argues convincingly for altering sleep patterns and sleep times to fit the individual. . . . This is a good addition to general collections." Libr J
Includes bibliographic references

Dotto, Lydia
Losing sleep; how your sleeping habits affect your life. Morrow 1990 342p $21.95; pa $10   **612.8**
1. Sleep 2. Fatigue 3. Insomnia
ISBN 0-688-09131-8; 0-688-11275-7 (pa)
    LC 90-36466
"The major focus of this book is on the impact of sleep deprivation, sleep disturbances and sleep disorders on alertness and performance on the job." Preface
Includes bibliographic references

Gonzalez-Crussi, F.
The five senses. Harcourt Brace Jovanovich 1989 162p il $17.95   **612.8**
1. Senses and sensation
ISBN 0-15-131398-9   LC 88-28966
Also available in paperback from Random House
This is a collection of essays which explain our senses using a combination of history, science, theology, philosophy, and personal experiences
Includes bibliography

Hauri, Peter
No more sleepless nights; [by] Peter Hauri, Shirley Linde. Wiley 1990 262p $19.95; pa $10.95   **612.8**
1. Insomnia
ISBN 0-471-50770-9; 0-471-54796-4 (pa)
    LC 89-22606
The authors "provide guidelines for finding the underlying causes of insomnia by using checklists, questionnaires, and sleep logs. They also discuss the latest sleep-promoting habits and relaxation techniques and offer suggestions for diet and exercise regimens to promote sleep." Booklist
Includes bibliographic references

Restak, Richard M., 1942-
The brain. Bantam Bks. 1984 371p il $27.95; pa $17.50   **612.8**
1. Brain
ISBN 0-553-05119-9; 0-553-35307-1 (pa)
    LC 84-45177
Also available in paperback from Warner Bks.

Restak, Richard M., 1942——*Continued*
"In chapters on topics such as vision and movement, rhythms and drives, stress and emotion, Restak provides the reader with historical perspective but concentrates on . . . findings and research into the brain/mind. Illustrations effectively support the discussions and technical descriptions are clear." Libr J

Includes bibliography

The brain has a mind of its own; insights from a practicing neurologist; [by] Richard Restak. Harmony Bks. 1991 210p $18; pa $12 **612.8**
1. Brain
ISBN 0-517-57483-7; 0-517-88080-6 (pa)
LC 91-12503

"How much of human behavior is the result of free will? What is the relationship between mind and brain, between conscious thought and the unconscious? What is the effect on the brain of seeing incessant violence in the news media? These are samples of the . . . issues addressed by this collection of over 40 essays on new brain research and its social implications." Quill Quire
The author "delves into every corner of the brain, finding fascinating humanity in it everywhere." Sci Books Films

Includes bibliography

Yager, Jan
The encyclopedia of sleep and sleep disorders; [by] Jan Yager and Michael J. Thorpy. Facts on File 1990 xli, 298p $45 **612.8**
1. Sleep—Dictionaries
ISBN 0-8160-1870-7
LC 89-71520

This work "describes technical, common, and slang sleep terminology in readable entries ranging from one sentence to several pages in length." Booklist

Includes bibliographic references

613 Promotion of health

The **Black** women's health book; speaking for ourselves; edited by Evelyn C. White. Seal Press 1990 301p pa $14.95 **613**
1. Black women—Health and hygiene
ISBN 0-931188-86-5
LC 90-30876

"Here, 41 literary compositions by Alice Walker, Faye Wattleton, Byllye Avery, Angela Davis, Lucille Clifton, and other well-known African American women give a . . . view of the kinds of health problems common among many black women. While some contributors diagnose symptoms and causes of poor health—abuse, addiction, ignorance, incurable disease, life-styles, and neglect—others share advice and information, offer spiritual and human support, and reveal . . . facts about health issues." Booklist

Includes bibliographic references

Brody, Jane E.
Jane Brody's The New York Times guide to personal health; illustrations by Karen Karlsson. Times Bks. 1982 xxvii, 723p il $19.95 **613**
1. Health 2. Medicine, Popular
ISBN 0-8129-1014-1
LC 82-50050

Also available in paperback from Avon Bks.

"A collection of Brody's 'Personal Health' columns, it is divided into 12 parts covering a spectrum of health topics, including nutrition, exercise, sexuality and reproduction, mental health, dental care, abused substances (drugs, alcohol, etc.), environmental health effects, safety, and common illnesses." Publ Wkly

The **Columbia** University College of Physicians and Surgeons complete home medical guide; medical editors: Donald F. Tapley [et al.] rev ed. Crown 1989 930p il $39.95 **613**
1. Medicine, Popular
ISBN 0-517-57216-8
LC 89-9831

First published 1985 with title: Complete home medical guide

"The text in each chapter of this guide describes a disease or presents an overview of a body system. The narrative includes few statements about specific treatments and avoids attempts at diagnosis. The result is a lucid compilation of current, general information about each topic selected. . . . A good first choice when directing the layperson to writings on medical conditions." Ref Sources for Small & Medium-sized Libr. 5th edition

The **Columbia** University School of Public Health 40+ guide to good health; [by] Robert J. Weiss, Genell J. Subak-Sharpe, and the editors of Consumer Reports Books. Consumer Repts. Bks. 1993 452p il $27.95 **613**
1. Health 2. Middle age 3. Aging
ISBN 0-89043-541-3
LC 92-43953

First published 1988 by Times Bks. with title: The Columbia University School of Public Health complete guide to health and well-being after 50

Among the topics discussed in this guide to both the physiological and psychological aspects of middle age are: menopause, alcohol and drug abuse, osteoporosis, stress, exercise, the immune system, and cosmetic surgery. Text is accompanied by charts, tables, illustrations and self-tests

Cooper, Robert K.
Health & fitness excellence; the scientific action plan; foreword by Tom Ferguson; preface by Harold H. Bloomfield. Houghton Mifflin 1989 523p il hardcover o.p. paperback available $12.70 **613**
1. Health 2. Physical fitness
ISBN 0-395-54453-X (pa)
LC 88-25790

The fitness plan which the author presents here "consists of aerobic exercise, a vegetarian or semi-vegetarian diet, a program of stress reduction, improved sensory perception, and positive mental imagery. The author stresses the importance of a healthy environment—indoor and outdoor—and suggests ways in which contaminants can be reduced or eliminated. . . . An excellent contribution to the literature." Booklist

Includes bibliography

The **Good** health fact book; a complete question-and-answer guide to getting healthy and staying healthy. Reader's Digest Assn. 1992 480p il map $26.50
613

1. Health
ISBN 0-89577-416-X   LC 91-44169

Topics covered "include diet and exercise, choosing and consulting health care professionals, mental health, sex and family life, managing chronic health problems, the healthy workplace, and making healthy choices during the middle and later years." Booklist

Gordon, Michael, 1941-
Old enough to feel better; a medical guide for seniors. rev & updated ed. Johns Hopkins Univ. Press 1989 392p $42.50; pa $14.95
613

1. Elderly—Health and hygiene 2. Elderly—Diseases
ISBN 0-8018-3806-1; 0-8018-3807-X (pa) LC 89-1682

First published 1981 by Chilton Book Company

The author "explains what happens to our bodies as we age, why it happens, and what we can do about it." Univ Press Books for Public Libr

Indoor air pollution; a health perspective; edited by Jonathan M. Samet and John D. Spengler. Johns Hopkins Univ. Press 1991 407p il (Johns Hopkins ser. in environmental toxicology) $65; pa $24.95
613

1. Air pollution 2. Environmental health
ISBN 0-8018-4124-0; 0-8018-4125-9 (pa)
LC 90-49482

This volume describes the sources and health effects of indoor air pollution from tobacco smoke, nitrogen dioxide, carbon monoxide, wood smoke, formaldehyde, radon, and other pollutants

Includes bibliographic references

Mayo Clinic family health book; David E. Larson, editor-in-chief. Morrow 1990 1378p il $40
613

1. Health 2. Medicine, Popular
ISBN 0-688-07819-2   LC 90-6065

"The editors have arranged the material in five broad divisions: lifecycles, the world around us, keeping fit, human disease and disorders, and modern medical care." Libr J

The **New** Good Housekeeping family health and medical guide. rev ed. Hearst Bks. 1989 788p il $24.95
613

1. Medicine, Popular 2. Health
ISBN 0-688-06164-8   LC 88-11257

First published 1980 with title: Good Housekeepng family health & medical guide

This guide is divided into four sections, the first of which serves to define terms, diseases, and medical procedures. Sections two, three and four cover family health issues and preventative medicine, as well as special health concerns related to aging and the elderly

Includes bibliography

The **New** our bodies, ourselves; a book by and for women. Updated and expanded for the 1990s. Simon & Schuster 1992 751p il pa $20
613

1. Women—Health and hygiene 2. Women—Psychology
ISBN 0-671-79176-1   LC 92-1627

"A Touchstone book"

First published 1971 with title: Our bodies, ourselves

"This encyclopedia of women's health is organized by broad subject areas: relationships and sexuality, fertility, childbearing, aging. Each chapter has comprehensive information about the subject, quotations from women who have experience with the condition, notes and references and referrals for further information. . . . It is an outstanding resource written by and for women with accessible information for all collections." Libr J

Includes bibliographic references

Paige, Judith
Choice years; health, happiness, and beauty through menopause and beyond; [by] Judith Paige and Pamela Gordon. Villard Bks. 1991 xxiii, 293p il $22
613

1. Menopause 2. Women—Health and hygiene 3. Women—Psychology
ISBN 0-394-58397-3   LC 91-50065

Also available in paperback from Fawcett Bks.

This book "debunks myths, explains clearly physical changes and coping, offers advice on a healthy life-style, and, above all, gives women positive reinforcement for embracing the changes of age and rethinking their concepts of self, beauty, and sexuality." Booklist

Includes bibliographic references

Prevention's giant book of health facts; the ultimate reference for personal health; by the editors of Prevention magazine health books; introduction by Mark Bricklin; edited by John Feltman. Rodale Press 1990 599p il maps $29.95
613

1. Health 2. Medicine, Popular
ISBN 0-87857-909-5   LC 90-45939

This is a "reference book on topics ranging from aging, AIDS, back problems, and caffeine to headaches, mental illness, pet health, and weight loss." Libr J

Vickery, Donald M.
Take care of yourself; the complete guide to medical self-care; [by] Donald M. Vickery, James F. Fries. 5th ed. Addison-Wesley 1993 xxvii, 511p il pa $17.26
613

1. Medicine, Popular 2. Health self-care
ISBN 0-201-63292-6   LC 92-48678

First published 1976

This guide "covers some 99 common medical problems from oral poisoning to genital herpes. Charts help the reader decide whether to treat at home or see a physician." Sci Books Films

Includes bibliographic references

Weil, Andrew
Natural health, natural medicine; a comprehensive manual to wellness and self-care. Houghton Mifflin 1990 356p $19.45; pa $10.70   **613**
1. Health 2. Nutrition 3. Health self-care
ISBN 0-395-49340-4; 0-395-58122-2 (pa)
     LC 89-26926
The author "is one of a minority of physicians recommending alternative medicine, coupled with elements of standard thinking and practice. . . . Here he provides basic information on weight, fitness, vitamins, stress and cancer risk, and gives advice on the use of herbal home remedies as antidotes for common ailments." Publ Wkly
Includes bibliographic references

Weisse, Allen B.
The man's guide to good health; [by] Allen B. Weisse and the editors of Consumer Reports Books. Consumer Repts. Bks. 1991 272p il $25.95   **613**
1. Men—Health and hygiene
ISBN 0-89043-303-8   LC 91-18886
This book "provides basic information for men on the common health problems and diseases that particularly affect them from puberty through old age." Publisher's note
"The guide is straightforward and factual. . . . a good resource." Booklist

The **Wellness** encyclopedia; the comprehensive family resource for safeguarding health and preventing illness; from the editors of the University of California, Berkeley wellness letter. Houghton Mifflin 1991 541p il $29.45; pa $17.45   **613**
1. Health 2. Preventive medicine
ISBN 0-395-53363-5; 0-395-61330-2 (pa)   LC 90-5228
This volume includes "chapters on evaluating health risks, on the importance of diet and exercise in preserving health, on digestive disorders, dental care and weight control. A critical summary of food groups, nutrients, food supplements, vitamins and minerals [is also provided]." Publ Wkly

The **Woman's** guide to good health; [by] Mary Jane Gray [et al.] and the editors of Consumer Reports Books. Consumer Repts. Bks. 1991 468p il $25.95   **613**
1. Women—Health and hygiene
ISBN 0-89043-382-8   LC 91-27256
This book "contains information on how to keep healthy and fit and describes common problems and diseases that women may face at every stage of life, from puberty through old age." Publisher's note

Women's health; medical editor, Charles B. Clayman. Reader's Digest Assn. 1992 144p il (American Medical Association home medical lib) $16.98   **613**
1. Women—Health and hygiene 2. Women—Diseases
ISBN 0-89577-398-8   LC 91-15417
At head of title: The American Medical Association
This book addresses health concerns of women of all ages. The first chapter is an overview of the female life cycle. The next chapter concerns staying healthy and

covers diet, exercise, dealing with stress, and health hazards. The third chapter deals with sex and contraception. The final chapter discusses specific health problems and medical treatments

Your good health; how to stay well, and what to do when you're not; edited by William I. Bennett, Stephen E. Goldfinger, G. Timothy Johnson. Harvard Univ. Press 1987 510p il $24.95; pa $12.95   **613**
1. Health 2. Preventive medicine
ISBN 0-674-96631-7; 0-674-96632-5 (pa)
     LC 87-19671
This is a "guide to health maintenance that stresses prevention and the adoption of habits likely to increase life expectancy and quality." Publ Wkly
"The information offered is essentially sound, extremely helpful to both the doctor and the patient, worth having, and, best of all, offered in a brief, easy-to-understand manner." Sci Books Films

613.2   Dietetics

Bennion, Lynn J.
Straight talk about weight control; taking the pounds off and keeping them off; [by] Lynn J. Bennion, Edwin L. Bierman, James M. Ferguson and [edited by] the editors of Consumer Reports Books. Consumers Union of U.S. 1991 351p il hardcover o.p. paperback available $15.95   **613.2**
1. Obesity 2. Reducing
ISBN 0-89043-246-5 (pa)   LC 90-37950
This surveys and evaluates various weight reduction methods including low-calorie diet plans, franchised weight-reduction centers, surgery and pills, and provides basic information about overweight and nutrition
Includes bibliographic references

Bricklin, Mark
Prevention magazine's complete nutrition reference handbook; over 1,000 foods and meals analyzed and rated for health effect; by Mark Bricklin and the editors of Prevention magazine. Rodale Press 1992 596p $29.95   **613.2**
1. Nutrition 2. Food—Composition
ISBN 0-87596-117-7   LC 91-46322
"The book has three sections: an introduction, an analysis of 1,000 foods, and nutrition tables. . . . The reference tables list the top-ranked food sources for vitamins, minerals, and fiber; healthy substitutes for high-fat foods; the nutrients in cereals; and fast-food comparisons." Booklist

Brody, Jane E.
Jane Brody's good food book; living the high-carbohydrate way; illustrations by Ray Skibinski. Norton 1985 xxviii, 700p il $25   **613.2**
1. High-carbohydrate diet 2. Cookery
ISBN 0-393-02210-2   LC 85-2966
Also available in paperback from Bantam Bks.

Brody, Jane E.—*Continued*

The author "emphasizes a diet in starchy foods (potatoes, rice, pasta, etc.) low in fats and added sugars, and moderate in protein. . . . Over 300 different recipes are included." Libr J

"All health-conscious Americans should read this book, especially those who are on low fat, low-salt diets." Best Sellers

Carper, Jean

Jean Carper's total nutrition guide. Bantam Bks. 1987 424p pa $12.95 **613.2**

1. Nutrition 2. Food—Composition
ISBN 0-553-34350-5   LC 86-47628

This volume offers information "on cholesterol, calcium, and various nutrients. Carper accessibly discusses how nutrients affect health (positively or negatively) and lists what foods hold the most of each nutrient with the least amount of calories. Carper also cogently looks at the health aspects of sugar, dietary fiber, low-calorie diets, vegetarianism, and the nutritional needs required at different stages of life. An exemplary guide for public libraries." Booklist

The **Columbia** encyclopedia of nutrition; [by] the Institute of Human Nutrition, Columbia University College of Physicians and Surgeons; compiled and edited by Myron Winick [et al.] Putnam 1988 349p hardcover o.p. paperback available $12.95 **613.2**

1. Nutrition—Dictionaries
ISBN 0-399-51573-9 (pa)   LC 87-10782

"Clear, readable prose gives an accessible guide to vitamins, additives, dieting, hypertension, and other nutritionally related disorders. Includes section on nutrition for nursing and pregnant women." N Y Public Libr Book of How & Where to Look It Up

Conners, C. Keith

Feeding the brain; how foods affect children. Plenum Press 1989 277p $23.95 **613.2**

1. Children—Nutrition 2. Hyperactive children
ISBN 0-306-43306-0   LC 89-16071

"Can certain foods really improve brain function? Do food additives cause hyperactivity? Is sugar bad for kids? How safe is Nutrasweet, and can it cause brain damage? These are some of the questions Conners addresses. . . . Conners tends to be academic in approach and style, yet is quite readable for interested parents and educators." Booklist

Includes bibliographic references

The **Duke** University Medical Center book of diet and fitness; developed by the Duke Diet and Fitness Center, Michael Hamilton [et al.] Fawcett Columbine 1991 417p il $19.95; pa $12 **613.2**

1. Reducing 2. Exercise
ISBN 0-449-90256-0; 0-449-90785-6 (pa)
                                      LC 88-47813

"This book makes available to the general public the three-part program of behavioral, nutritional, and fitness modification used at Duke University's diet and fitness center. . . . The scheme requires participants to first complete a detailed self-assessment revealing motivations, attitudes, and emotions associated with eating. They then may design individual diet and fitness programs. Specifics, including menus and recipes, are provided for diet planning while well-illustrated exercises make up the fitness component." Booklist

Eat for life; the Food and Nutrition Board's guide to reducing your risk of chronic disease; Catherine E. Woteki and Paul R. Thomas, editors; Committee on Diet and Health, Food and Nutrition Board, Institute of Medicine, National Academy of Sciences. National Acad. Press 1992 179p il $18.95 **613.2**

1. Nutrition 2. Preventive medicine
ISBN 0-309-04049-3   LC 91-37837

"The heart of the book is the first chapter: the nine-point dietary plan to reduce your risk of diet-related chronic diseases (e.g., heart disease, cancer, osteoporosis, and obesity). . . . 'Eat For Life' gives practical recommendations on which foods should comprise the backbone of a healthful eating pattern and, in a how-to section, provides tips on shopping, cooking, and eating out." Publisher's note

Includes bibliographic references

Eisman, Eugene

Your child and cholesterol; by Eugene Eisman and Diane Batshaw Eisman. Fell 1990 189p $9.95 **613.2**

1. Children—Nutrition 2. Low-cholesterol diet
ISBN 0-8119-0034-7   LC 88-83600

This book suggests a program for lowering the amount of fat and cholesterol in the family's diet in order to have a healthier lifestyle. Includes some recipes and a short table of fat and cholesterol content of common foods

Gershoff, Stanley N.

The Tufts University guide to total nutrition; Stanley Gershoff, with Catherine Whitney, and the Editorial Advisory Board of the Tufts University diet & nutrition letter; foreword by Jean Mayer. Harper & Row 1990 xxi, 312p $22.50; pa $14 **613.2**

1. Nutrition 2. Food 3. Diet
ISBN 0-06-015918-9; 0-06-272007-4 (pa)
                                      LC 89-46124

The authors "evaluate current nutritional knowledge and research, thereby providing the basics for creating a personal plan for eating right as they discuss the fundamentals of proper nutrition and the controversies over cholesterol, recommended daily allowances, calcium, caffeine, the connections between food and disease, etc. They advise on wise food purchasing, how to read food labels, and how to choose wisely in restaurants; and they address the nutritional requirements of various age groups as well as foods beneficial to persons suffering from health problems such as heart disorders and allergies." Booklist

Goor, Ron, 1940-

The choose to lose diet; a food lover's guide to permanent weight loss; [by] Ron Goor, Nancy Goor, and Katherine Boyd. Houghton Mifflin 1990 332p $17.45; pa $10.70   **613.2**

1. Low-cholesterol diet   2. Food—Composition
3. Reducing
ISBN 0-395-49336-6; 0-395-60571-7 (pa)

           LC 89-24467

The authors present a plan for weight loss using a low-fat high carbohydrate diet, list the fat content of a variety of foods, and provide sample menus and recipes

Includes bibliographic references

Margen, Sheldon

The wellness encyclopedia of food and nutrition; how to buy, store, and prepare every fresh food; by Sheldon Margen and the editors of the University of California at Berkeley wellness letter. Rebus; [distributed by] Random House 1992 512p il $29.95   **613.2**

1. Food 2. Nutrition
ISBN 0-929661-03-6   LC 92-13017

"The key word in this book is fresh. There are chapters on the preparation, availability, storage, and preparation of more than 500 vegetables, fruits, grains, fish, meat, and legumes. The excellent color photographs will help in purchasing the foodstuffs. Boxes and sidebars give nutritional information and health hints." Booklist

The **Mount** Sinai School of Medicine complete book of nutrition; Victor Herbert and Genell J. Subak-Sharpe, editors; Delia A. Hammock, associate editor. St. Martin's Press 1990 xx, 796p il $35

           613.2

1. Nutrition 2. Food—Composition
ISBN 0-312-05129-8   LC 90-8624

This encyclopedic volume of nutrition basics, includes a discussion of the effects of nutrition on diseases such as diabetes and kidney disease, information about food allergies, weight problems, vegetarianism, sports and nutrition, and a table listing nutrient values of common foods

Includes bibliographic references

Pauling, Linus C., 1901-

How to live longer and feel better; [by] Linus Pauling. Freeman, W.H. 1986 322p o.p.; Avon Bks. paperback available $5.50

           613.2

1. Nutrition 2. Vitamins
ISBN 0-380-70289-4 (pa)   LC 85-25321

The author argues that large doses of Vitamin C can improve longevity and the quality of life

Includes bibliography

Pritikin, Nathan

Diet for runners. Simon & Schuster 1985 256p il hardcover o.p. paperback available $8.95   **613.2**

1. Low-cholesterol diet 2. Athletes—Nutrition
ISBN 0-671-55623-1 (pa)   LC 85-2285

This book "provides dietary guidelines for runners and others who exercise. The author covers the pros and cons of different food groups, takes a look at proteins, fats, carbohydrates, vitamins and minerals, and stresses the importance of drinking enough water." Publ Wkly

The Pritikin permanent weight-loss manual; by Nathan Pritikin; illustrated by Joann T. Rounds. Grosset & Dunlap 1981 401p il o.p.; Bantam Bks. paperback available $5.50   **613.2**

1. Reducing
ISBN 0-553-26320-X (pa)   LC 80-84945

The author "outlines a dietary lifestyle . . . that he claims will permanently cure obesity and reduce the chances that one will develop heart disease and other ailments." Publ Wkly

The Pritikin promise; 28 days to a longer, healthier life. Simon & Schuster 1983 432p il o.p. paperback available $5.99   **613.2**

1. Diet 2. Nutrition 3. Physical fitness 4. Cookery
ISBN 0-671-73267-6 (pa)   LC 83-17546

The author believes "that the high fat/high protein diet consumed by most Americans causes heart disease and that a change in eating habits can prevent onset of heart problems. . . . [He] presents a 28-day program to follow on a 'trial basis' before making a lifetime commitment." Libr J

Robbins, John

May all be fed; diet for a new world; including recipes by Jia Patton and friends. Morrow 1992 415p il $23   **613.2**

1. Vegetarianism 2. Diet 3. Cookery
ISBN 0-688-11625-6   LC 92-12596

Also available in paperback from Avon Bks.

"Citing the disproportionate amount of grain raised for livestock feed, the author suggests vegetarian diets to help the world's hungry. Numerous scientific studies quoted point to overconsumption of protein and high rates of osteoporosis, cancer, and heart disease. . . . Accompanied by nearly 200 highly varied recipes, a dictionary of ingredients, and a resource list of pertinent organizations." Booklist

Includes bibliographic references

Stuart, Richard B.

Weight, sex, and marriage; a delicate balance; [by] Richard B. Stuart and Barbara Jacobson. Norton 1987 189p o.p.; Simon & Schuster paperback available $8   **613.2**

1. Obesity 2. Reducing
ISBN 0-671-67008-5 (pa)   LC 86-33148

"After sensitively analyzing the relationship between weight, sex, and marriage, the authors explain why it is so difficult to lose weight and sustain that loss without first confronting the psychological conditions that prompted overeating. Finally, they provide suggestions on devel-

Stuart, Richard B.—*Continued*

oping and following a personalized program." Booklist

Includes bibliography

Tracy, Lisa

The gradual vegetarian. Evans & Co. 1985 297p o.p.; Dell paperback available $12

613.2

1. Vegetarianism
ISBN 0-440-53124-1 (pa)   LC 84-28629

The author "provides a sensible guide to the adoption of sound eating habits. Rather than urging readers to a radical overnight change in diet, she recommends they accomplish this in three gradual stages." Publ Wkly

Includes bibliography

Tver, David F.

The nutrition and health encyclopedia; [by] David F. Tver and Percy Russell. 2nd ed. Van Nostrand Reinhold 1989 639p il $46.95

613.2

1. Nutrition 2. Health—Dictionaries
ISBN 0-442-23397-3   LC 88-33957

First published 1981

Terms in nutrition and health are arranged in dictionary format; appendixes include tables and lists, charts, cross-references

Vartabedian, Roy E., 1956-

Nutripoints; the breakthrough point system for optimal nutrition; [by] Roy E. Vartabedian, Kathy Matthews. Harper & Row 1990 450p $19.95   **613.2**

1. Nutrition 2. Food—Composition
ISBN 0-06-016275-9   LC 89-45796

"This numerical rating system is based on the food's good factors (vitamins, minerals, fiber content, and protein) weighed against the bad factors (including calories, fat, sodium, sugar, and cholesterol). The Nutripoint system as introduced here calls for individuals to make daily choices from six food groups while trying to achieve a total numerical rating of 100 points." Booklist

Includes bibliography

613.7 Physical fitness

Berland, Theodore, 1929-

Fitness for life; exercises for people over 50. American Assn. of Retired Persons; Scott, Foresman 1986 171p il pa $12.95

613.7

1. Exercise 2. Physical fitness 3. Aging
ISBN 0-673-24812-7   LC 85-18267

"An AARP book"

In this book "the elements of a successful exercise program are explained, and the building blocks to tailor an individualized program are provided. Relaxation and diet, as important complements to exercise, are addressed." Foreword

Includes bibliography

Cooper, Kenneth H.

The aerobics program for total well-being; exercise, diet, emotional balance. Evans & Co. 1982 320p il hardcover o.p.; Bantam Bks. paperback available $11.95   **613.7**

1. Aerobics 2. Physical fitness
ISBN 0-553-34422-6 (pa)   LC 82-16361

This guide includes recommendations on nutrition, exercise, and emotional health

The "program is presented in brisk, no-nonsense prose, supplemented by easily deciphered charts. Appendixes include geographical listings of sports-medicine clinics and an extended reference guide." Booklist

The new aerobics for women; [by] Kenneth H. Cooper and Mildred Cooper. rev ed. Bantam Bks. 1988 324p il pa $14.50

613.7

1. Aerobics 2. Physical fitness
ISBN 0-553-34513-3   LC 88-966

First published 1972 by M. Evans & Company with title: Aerobics for women, and with authors' names in reverse order

This book on aerobics, written exclusively for women, is based on their lifestyle and physical makeup

DeLyser, Femmy

Jane Fonda's new pregnancy workout and total birth program; photographs by Lynn Houston; additional photographs by Femmy DeLyser. Simon & Schuster 1989 336p il hardcover o.p. paperback available $12.95

613.7

1. Exercise 2. Pregnancy 3. Childbirth
ISBN 0-671-73307-9 (pa)   LC 89-36959

First published 1982 with title: Jane Fonda's workout book for pregnancy, birth and recovery

This book offers "exercises and information on all stages of pregnancy, birth and infant care. The author conveys familiar basic knowledge on fitness and nutrition, urging the elimination of toxins from one's life and the birthing procedure. Good advice is given on choosing medical care for the mother-to-be and on where to give birth." Publ Wkly

The **Gym** workout; body sculpting. Time-Life Bks. 1988 144p il (Fitness, health & nutrition) $17.27   **613.7**

1. Weight lifting 2. Exercise   LC 88-2209

This introduction to bodybuilding provides a step-by-step approach to the use of variable resistance machines and freeweights. Other topics covered include home gym equipment and proper diet and exercise

Joyner, Stephen Christopher, 1967-

The joy of walking; more than just exercise. Betterway Publs. 1992 160p il pa $9.95   **613.7**

1. Walking
ISBN 1-55870-232-6   LC 91-43800

This introductory guide discusses walking fundamentals, the importance of diet and value of walking in a comprehensive exercise plan

Includes bibliographic references

Lansbury, Angela

Angela Lansbury's positive moves; my personal plan for fitness and well-being; with Mimi Avins. Delacorte Press 1990 164p il $18.95   **613.7**

1. Physical fitness 2. Health 3. Personal grooming 4. Diet

ISBN 0-385-30223-1   LC 90-3291

Also available Thorndike Press large print edition and in paperback from Dell

"Lansbury emphasizes seeking a realistic level of comfort and activity to enhance physical and psychological fitness. . . . The book is divided into sections, including Diet, Recipes, Exercises, and Advice, with many personal anecdotes." Libr J

Levine, Suzanne M.

Walk it off! 20 minutes a day to health and fitness. New Am. Lib. 1990 257p pa $9   **613.7**

1. Physical fitness 2. Walking

ISBN 0-452-26535-5   LC 90-41033

"A Plume book"

The author discusses ways of incorporating walking in an overall fitness program

Lyons, Pat

Great shape; the first exercise guide for large women; [by] Pat Lyons and Debby Burgard. Arbor House; Morrow 1988 196p il o.p.; Bull paperback available $14.95   **613.7**

1. Physical fitness 2. Exercise 3. Women—Health and hygiene 4. Obesity

ISBN 0-923521-01-1 (pa)   LC 87-25455

This "book proves that fit and fat are not mutually exclusive, and explores the myriad activities large women can enjoy. . . . The book emphasizes creating a positive exercise experience, which will help to generate self-esteem and eliminate the self-defeating diet cycle." Libr J

Includes bibliography

Monro, Robin

Yoga for common ailments; based on a system developed by the Vivekananda Yoga Therapy and Research Foundation; [by] Robin Monro, R. Nagarathna, H.R. Nagendra; Nancy Ford-Kohne, consulting editor. Simon & Schuster 1990 95p il pa $10.95   **613.7**

1. Yoga

ISBN 0-671-70528-8   LC 90-33732

"A Fireside book. A Gaia original"

"Yoga has been gaining popularity as a holistic alternative to traditional Western therapeutics. Addressed to beginning students, this book takes the middle ground by encouraging better health through yoga but also advocating regular care by a health professional." Booklist

Includes bibliographic references

Prevention's practical encyclopedia of walking for health; from age-reversal to weight loss, the most complete guide ever written; by Mark Bricklin, editor; and Maggie Spilner, walking editor, Prevention magazine. Rodale Press 1992 274p il hardcover o.p. paperback available $12.95   **613.7**

1. Walking

ISBN 0-87596-165-7 (pa)   LC 91-47878

This "volume considers walking from every angle—health benefits, getting started, proper form and technique, safety factors, getting motivated, staying psyched, and best places and times." Publisher's note

"Besides discussing the new concept of terrain therapy, Bricklin and Spilner provide, as an added bonus to this information-packed volume, a one-year walking program that's so detailed and encouraging, it's like having a personal walking coach." Libr J

Prudden, Suzy

Starting right; Suzy Prudden's fitness program for children 5-11; [by] Suzy Prudden and Joan Meijer-Hirschland; photographs by Nancy De Pra. Doubleday 1988 167p il pa $10.95   **613.7**

1. Physical fitness 2. Exercise 3. Children—Health and hygiene

ISBN 0-385-23635-2   LC 87-586

"This book defines fitness as preparedness for the demands that life puts on the body. . . . The special needs of skilled, obese, and slow children are addressed. The carefully explained and well-illustrated exercises are grouped by body part emphasis and skill category." Libr J

Suzy Prudden's exercise program for young children; foreword by Burton L. White; photographs by Douglas Hopkins. Workman 1983 191p il pa $6.95   **613.7**

1. Exercise 2. Children—Health and hygiene

ISBN 0-89480-371-9   LC 82-40506

"The exercises are in no way a rigorous training program. They are suggestions for the parent or other adult to spend pleasurable time with a child and give the child an opportunity to develop control and learn about his or her body." Libr J

Suzy Prudden's Pregnancy & back-to-shape exercise program; by Suzy Prudden and Jeffrey Sussman; introductory comments by Alan Davidson and Howard R. Rappaport; photographs by Maje Waldo. Workman 1980 223p il hardcover o.p. paperback available $9.95   **613.7**

1. Exercise 2. Pregnancy

ISBN 0-89480-129-5 (pa)   LC 80-51614

The authors have developed an exercise program specifically for pregnant women. Illustrated with photographs showing the sequence of each routine, the book is divided into three parts: exercises to be done during the months of pregnancy, exercises to reshape the body after childbirth, and exercises for the newborn to be done with either parent

Schwarzenegger, Arnold

Arnold's bodybuilding for men; by Arnold Schwarzenegger, with Bill Dobbins. Simon & Schuster 1981 240p il hardcover o.p. paperback available $16   **613.7**

1. Bodybuilding
ISBN 0-671-53163-8 (pa)   LC 80-28764

An illustrated program of weight training supplemented by a variety of isometric and stretching exercises

Arnold's bodyshaping for women; by Arnold Schwarzenegger, with Douglas Kent Hall. Simon & Schuster 1979 100p il hardcover o.p. paperback available $12.95   **613.7**

1. Weight lifting 2. Exercise 3. Women—Health and hygiene
ISBN 0-671-42479-3 (pa)   LC 79-17911

"Recommending resistance training as the best way to reshape the figure while producing physical fitness, [the author] offers a series of exercises geared to a three-or four-month span of graduated strenuousness. . . . Instructions are clear and detailed, and the oversized format makes the photos especially helpful." Publ Wkly

Shangold, Mona M.

The complete sports medicine book for women; [by] Mona Shangold, Gabe Mirkin; photographs by Dick Bell. rev ed. Simon & Schuster 1992 240p il pa $13   **613.7**

1. Exercise 2. Women—Health and hygiene 3. Sports medicine
ISBN 0-671-74427-5   LC 92-36

"A Fireside book"

First published 1985

This health guide for women athletes covers such topics as weight training; exercise techniques; treating injuries; choosing the right sport; "recent medical research on birth control, beta blockers, and steroids; what and when to eat; keeping fit during pregnancy; the effects of exercise on menstruation and menopause." Publisher's note

Yanker, Gary

Walking medicine; the lifetime guide to preventive and rehabilitative exercise walking programs; by Gary Yanker and Kathy Burton, and 50 medical experts. McGraw-Hill 1990 xxix, 480p il hardcover o.p. paperback available $14.95   **613.7**

1. Walking
ISBN 0-07-072265-X (pa)   LC 90-5443

"This book is divided into seven sections: walking at different times of your life, walking to strengthen muscles and bones, increasing stamina and speed, losing weight, controlling stress, shoes and feet, and a directory of 'walking doctors.'" Libr J

613.9 Birth control and sex hygiene

Comfort, Alex, 1920-

The new joy of sex; illustrated by John Raynes; photography by Clare Park. Crown 1991 251p il $30   **613.9**

1. Sexual behavior
ISBN 0-517-58583-9   LC 91-15542

Also available in paperback from Pocket Bks.

First published 1972 with title: The joy of sex

Describes with illustrations a variety of sexual behaviors, addresses causes and risks of sexually transmitted diseases, and emphasizes the importance of love

Kroll, Ken

Enabling romance; a guide to love, sex, and relationships for the disabled (and the people who care about them); [by] Ken Kroll & Erica Levy Klein; illustrations by Mark Langeneckert. Harmony Bks. 1992 209p il $22.50   **613.9**

1. Sex education 2. Physically handicapped 3. Human relations
ISBN 0-517-57532-9   LC 91-20560

"A unique, important book that acknowledges the sexuality of the disabled and frankly deals with the practical and social aspects of sex life for those with a variety of disabilities, e.g., spinal cord injuries, cerebral palsy, blindness, and deafness. It discusses contraception, sex for couples, masturbation, and dealing with home care attendants in intimate situations." Libr J

Includes bibliography

Pearsall, Paul

Super marital sex; loving for life. Doubleday 1987 xx, 388p $18.95   **613.9**

1. Sex education
ISBN 0-385-24018-X   LC 87-6705

Also available in paperback from Ivy Bks.

Pearsall offers "advice for improving or enhancing the sexual aspect of a marital or committed relationship. . . . There is also a series of questions to help the reader determine if his or her marriage needs therapy. A deft mixture of psychology, self-help, and sexual instruction." Booklist

Includes bibliography

Pietropinto, Anthony

Not tonight, dear: how to reawaken your sexual desire; [by] Anthony Pietropinto and Jacqueline Simenauer. Doubleday 1990 321p $18.95   **613.9**

1. Sexual behavior
ISBN 0-385-23775-8   LC 89-25807

The authors "describe causes and types of desire loss and provide self-evaluation questionnaires and quizzes to help readers assess their personality type and sexual attitudes. Personal vignettes illustrate therapeutic approaches used by 22 leading sex therapists that can be categorized as either behavioral, cognitive, or experiential." Libr J

Stoppard, Miriam
The magic of sex. Dorling Kindersley
1992 256p il $29.95   **613.9**
1. Sex education
ISBN 1-564-58045-8   LC 91-29292
First published 1991 in the United Kingdom
This look at sexual relationships approaches "each
aspect—anatomy, attraction, foreplay, and making love—
from both male and female points of view. There are
also sections on sex during pregnancy and illness, changes
in sexual response with age, improving one's sex life,
sexual problems, STDs, safe sex, reproduction, and
contraception." Libr J

Winikoff, Beverly
The contraceptive handbook; a guide to
safe and effective choices; [by] Beverly
Winikoff, Suzanne Wymelenberg, and the
editors of Consumer Reports Books.
Consumer Repts. Bks. 1992 248p il $18.95
     613.9
1. Birth control
ISBN 0-89043-430-1   LC 92-98
The authors "present basic facts about anatomy and
physiology and the latest information about barrier
methods, pills, intrauterine devices, male and female
sterilization, and natural methods of contraception. They
discuss the advantages, disadvantages, costs, and methods
of obtaining each type of contraceptive. . . . Thorough,
objective coverage makes *The Contraceptive Handbook*
an excellent choice for all collections." Libr J
Includes bibliography

614   Forensic medicine, incidence & prevention of disease

Joyce, Christopher, 1950-
Witnesses from the grave; the stories
bones tell; [by] Christopher Joyce and Eric
Stover. Little, Brown 1991 333p il $19.95
     614
1. Snow, Clyde 2. Forensic anthropology 3. Skeleton
ISBN 0-316-47399-5   LC 90-44068
Also available in paperback from Ballantine Bks.
An introduction to the history and methods of
forensic anthropology. Clyde Snow, one of the disciplines
foremost practitioners, is profiled and his most famous
cases examined
"Those interested in archeology, anthropology, the history of science and criminal investigation will find this
study . . . vastly interesting and awe-inspiring." Publ
Wkly

615   Pharmacology and therapeutics

AARP pharmacy service prescription drug
handbook. 2nd ed. HarperCollins Pubs.
1992 1137p il $35; pa $18   **615**
1. Drugs
ISBN 0-06-271553-4; 0-06-277037-3 (pa)
     LC 91-58281
First published 1988 by Scott, Foresman

This "is intended for the consumer over 50. It contains nearly 1,000 separate entries organized by specific
medical disorder. . . . It describes the cause of the
malady, diagnosis, treatment, and outlook, followed by
a list of the drugs that are used in treatment. . . . The
drug descriptions are written for the layperson, giving
generic and brand names, dosage forms and strengths,
and detailed information on what to do before using the
drug, special restrictions while taking it, possible side
effects, storage instructions, stopping or interrupting
therapy, and special considerations for those over 65.
Concluding the book are a color guide to the various
medications and indexes of drugs and medical conditions." Booklist

Beinfield, Harriet
Between heaven and earth; a guide to
Chinese medicine; [by] Harriet Beinfield and
Efrem Korngold. Ballantine Bks. 1991 432p
il $19.50; pa $12   **615**
1. Medicine, Chinese 2. Herbs—Therapeutic use
3. Acupuncture
ISBN 0-345-35943-7; 0-345-37974-8 (pa)
     LC 90-93214
An overview of the history and current state of
medicine in China. The therapeutic use of herbs,
acupuncture, and the role of psychology in healing are
discussed
Includes bibliographic references

Carper, Jean
The food pharmacy; dramatic new
evidence that food is your best medicine.
Bantam Bks. 1988 367p $18.95; pa $12.50
     615
1. Herbs—Therapeutic use 2. Food—Therapeutic use
ISBN 0-553-05280-2; 0-553-34524-9 (pa)
     LC 87-47899
The author presents "information on the pharmacological effects of food apart from its common nutritional benefits. The first part of the book documents the
scientific investigations for 12 foods (e.g., onions, chili
peppers, and cranberries), providing evidence on how
they fight disease. Then Carper offers a modern pharmacopoeia for 55 common foods." Booklist
Includes bibliography

Castleman, Michael
The healing herbs; the ultimate guide to
the curative power of nature's medicines;
medical reviewer, Sheldon Saul Hendler.
Rodale Press 1991 436p il $27.95   **615**
1. Herbs—Therapeutic use
ISBN 0-87857-934-6   LC 91-6400
"After chapters discussing the history of herbal
therapy, the controversies waged over the safety of herbal
remedies, and strategies for herb storage and preparation,
Castleman offers encyclopedic entries on 100 of the most
common healing herbs." Publ Wkly
Includes bibliographic references

Complete drug reference. Consumer Repts.
Bks. il $39.95   **615**
1. Drugs
Annual. First published 1980 with title: United States
Pharmacopeia drug information for the consumer

Complete drug reference—*Continued*

"Published simultaneously by USPC, Inc., under the title USP DI, Volume II (Advice for the patient)." Verso of title page

"Including more than 5,500 drugs, this work presents drug information to the patient in clear and easy-to-read language. The drugs are listed by their generic names. The drug monographs make up the greatest portion of the source. Information provided for each drug includes brand names, general description, risks to be considered before taking the medicine (e.g., allergies, pregnancy, breast-feeding), proper use, precautions to be taken while using the medicine, and side effects." Am Ref Books Annu, 1993

Drugs available abroad; a guide to therapeutic drugs available and approved outside the U.S.; international data compiled by Derwent Publications, Ltd.; edited by Jerry L. Schlesser. Gale Res. $89.95   **615**

1. Drugs
ISSN 1051-7723

"A Medic book"

Biennial. First published 1990

This volume "lists over 1,000 medically important drugs approved in Canada, Mexico, Western Europe, Central America, the Caribbean, Australia, South Africa, or Scandinavia. . . . Complied from foreign pharmacopoeias and drug compendiums, entries contain generic names, brand names, drug action, dosage, warnings and side-effects, and the names of comparable U.S.-approved drugs. Unproved 'miracle drugs' are not listed. Included also are addresses of foreign manufacturers and regulatory authorities and brief directions on how to obtain these drugs." Am Libr

Goldman, Martin E., 1953-
The handbook of heart drugs; a consumer's guide to safe and effective use. Holt & Co. 1992 xxii, 297p $29.95; pa $12.95   **615**

1. Drugs 2. Heart—Diseases
ISBN 0-8050-1720-8; 0-8050-1721-6 (pa)
                                                  LC 91-39966

"Part one deals with issues affecting the use of cardiovascular drugs: how they work; how their action can be modified by diet, exercise, life-style, and other medications; choosing a cardiologist; the value of diagnostic tests; and how to keep a cardiovascular diary. Part two contains profiles of more than 90 heart drugs." Booklist

Graedon, Joe
50 +; the Graedons' People's pharmacy for older adults; [by] Joe Graedon and Teresa Graedon. Bantam Bks. 1988 459p il $24.95; pa $14.95   **615**

1. Drugs 2. Elderly—Medical care
ISBN 0-553-05245-4; 0-553-34485-4 (pa) LC 88-3304

"A general reference book for persons older than 50. In addition to providing tips on when and how to take certain medications, this book also contains a wealth of data on the drugs most frequently prescribed." Booklist

Includes bibliographies

Graedons' best medicine; from herbal remedies to high-tech Rx breakthroughs; [by] Joe Graedon and Teresa Graedon. Bantam Bks. 1991 444p il $29.95; $14.95   **615**

1. Drugs 2. Herbs—Therapeutic use
ISBN 0-553-07232-3; 0-553-35274-1 (pa)
                                                  LC 90-85030

The authors provide "ratings and recommendations for more than 100 medicines, from herbs to the newest prescription drugs, for complaints including digestive, heart, skin, and metabolic problems as well as pain, mental disturbances, allergies, and problems of the reproductive system. Besides rating medications, the Graedons discuss alternative therapies (e.g., exercise and nutrition), experimental drug trials, and the FDA regulations regarding access to unapproved medicines for life-threatening disease. They use plenty of charts, tables, and lists to relay further information. In all, a comprehensive guide." Booklist

Includes bibliographic references

Griffith, H. Winter (Henry Winter), 1926-
Complete guide to prescription & non-prescription drugs. Body Press/Perigee il pa $15.95   **615**

1. Drugs 2. Nonprescription drugs

Annual. First published 1983

"This guide contains information on more than 5,000 brand-name and more than 700 generic drugs. The charts are arranged alphabetically by generic name or drug class—*Analgesics, Ephedrine*. Each chart contains brief information about brand names, uses, dosages, adverse reactions or side effects, overdose symptoms and treatment, and precautions with other drugs or foods." Booklist

Handbook of nonprescription drugs. American Pharmaceutical Assn. pa $109
                                                         615

1. Nonprescription drugs

First published 1969. (10th edition 1993) Periodically revised

"Chapters are organized by the type of preparation (cold and allergy, contact lens) and describe the conditions they are designed to treat, relevant symptoms, physiology, treatments, ingredients, effectiveness, and safety guidelines. Addressed to the pharmacist, but very useful to the layperson." N Y Public Libr Book of How & Where to Look It Up

Hausman, Patricia
The right dose; how to take vitamins & minerals safely. Rodale Press 1987 528p il $24.95   **615**

1. Nutrition 2. Vitamins
ISBN 0-87857-678-9   LC 86-31367

Also available in paperback from Ballantine Bks.

"The book includes information about the specific role of each vitamin or mineral in the diet, possible interactions with drugs, and stories about supplement misuse. Brand name comparisons for supplements are provided as well as a list of the best natural food sources for each. Recipes are included." Libr J

Includes bibliography

Long, James W.

The essential guide to prescription drugs.
HarperCollins Pubs. $35; pa $16   **615**

1. Drugs

Annual. First published 1977

This reference work gives "drug profiles, including
major prescription drugs, arranged by generic name. Each
profile provides brand names, dosage, actions, and
precautions for use. Supplementary tables present drug
interactions with food, diseases, light, and other drugs.
Access is available through the index by brand or generic
name. Considered the standard of directories compiled
for the layperson." Ref Sources for Small & Medium-
sized Libr. 5th edition

The **Merck** index; an encyclopedia of
chemicals, drugs and biologicals. Merck &
Co. il $35   **615**

1. Materia medica 2. Drugs

First published 1889. (11th edition 1989) Periodically
revised

"Technical descriptions of the preparation, properties,
uses, commercial names, and toxicity of drugs and
medicines." N Y Public Libr Book of How & Where
to Look It Up

Physician's desk reference. Medical
Economics Bks. $57.95   **615**

1. Materia medica
ISSN 0093-4461

Annual. First published 1947. Title varies

"Latest available information intended for physicians
on over 2,000 products. Covers dosage, contraindications,
precautions, side effects, and undesirable interactions. The
information is furnished by the manufacturers of the
various products. Product identification in color." N Y
Public Libr Book of How & Where to Look It Up

Physicians desk reference for nonprescription
drugs. Medical Economics Bks. $37.95
    615

1. Nonprescription drugs
ISSN 1044-1395

Annual. First published 1980

"A companion to the *Physician's Desk Reference* [en-
tered above]. Provides essential information on nonprescription drugs. Indexed by manufacturer, product name,
product category, and active ingredients." N Y Public
Libr Book of How & Where to Look It Up

The **United** States Pharmacopeia. The
National formulary. U.S. Pharmacopeial
Convention $350   **615**

1. Materia medica
ISSN 0-195-7996

Supersedes The pharmacopoeia of the United States
of America and The national formulary. First published
with this title 1980. Revised at five-year intervals (USP
XXII, NF XVII published 1990)

"This is an official compendium of drug information
of the USPC which is responsible for setting drug standards and specifications." Sheehy. Guide to Ref Books.
10th edition

Yudofsky, Stuart C.

What you need to know about psychiatric
drugs; [by] Stuart Yudofsky, Robert E.
Hales, Tom Ferguson. Grove Weidenfeld
1991 xxii, 646p il $21.95   **615**

1. Psychotropic drugs
ISBN 0-8021-1281-1   LC 90-41453

Also available in paperback from Ballantine Bks.

This guide to psychiatric drugs includes "side effects,
interaction, chances of addiction. Discussed are an-
tidepressants, tranquilizers, sleeping pills, and sedatives,
as well as drugs for panic disorders, attention-deficit
hyperactivity disorder, and Alzheimer's disease. More
than a hundred of the most commonly used drugs are
listed, along with benefits, risks, and guidelines for use.
Balanced and reliable, this up-to-date information is
needed in libraries of any size in the reference and circulating collections." Am Libr

Zimmerman, David R.

Zimmerman's complete guide to
nonprescription drugs. 2nd ed. Gale Res.
1992 lix, 1125p $42.95; pa $19.95   **615**

1. Nonprescription drugs
ISBN 0-8103-8874-X; 0-8103-9421-9 (pa)

                   LC 92-32693

First published 1983 by Harper & Row with title: The
essential guide to nonprescription drugs

"Zimmerman rates the safety and efficacy of the active
ingredients in nonprescription medications, relying on
data from the FDA's Over-The-Counter Drug Review.
Each chapter covers a general area such as 'eye-care aids'
or 'toothache relievers' and contains background information on the ailments, descriptions of the active
ingredients used to treat them, and charts rating the
brand-name products." Libr J

For a fuller review see: Booklist, Feb. 15, 1993

615.8   Specific therapies and kinds of therapies

Bauer, Cathryn

Acupressure for everybody; gentle, effective
relief for more than 100 common ailments;
illustrated by Jackie Aher. Holt & Co. 1991
144p il pa $11.95   **615.8**

1. Acupressure
ISBN 0-8050-1579-5   LC 90-25135

"An Owl book"

The author "proposes the Eastern technique of healing
touch as first aid for relieving the minor symptoms of
a panoply of complaints." Booklist

Includes bibliographic references

Massage; total relaxation. Time-Life Bks.
1987 144p il (Fitness, health & nutrition)
$17.27   **615.8**

1. Massage   LC 87-10175

Describes how different types of massage can add to
one's mental and physical health. Includes basic techniques, shiatsu, reflexology, sports massage, and a chapter
on fiber and high-fiber recipes

Randi, James
The faith healers; foreword by Carl Sagan. Prometheus Bks. 1987 314p il hardcover o.p. paperback available $17.95 **615.8**

1. Spiritual healing
ISBN 0-87975-535-0 (pa)   LC 87-17241

An account of how the author and his team of researchers gathered evidence of fraud and greed on the part of many faith-healers. Among those investigated were such leading televangelists as Peter Popoff, W.V. Grant, Pat Robertson, and Oral Roberts

615.9 Toxicology

Dadd, Debra Lynn
The nontoxic home & office; protecting yourself and your family from everyday toxics and health hazards. Tarcher, J.P. 1992 212p pa $10.95 **615.9**

1. Poisons and poisoning 2. Product safety 3. Housing—Environmental aspects
ISBN 0-87477-676-7   LC 91-37870

First published 1986 with title: The nontoxic home

The author provides "information on household and work items that are potential health dangers. . . . Dadd also outlines the possible perils in food and tap water and how to best protect ourselves from them. For each product Dadd offers a safe, often less expensive alternative." Publ Wkly

Includes bibliographic references

Lampe, Kenneth F.
AMA handbook of poisonous and injurious plants; [by] Kenneth F. Lampe, Mary Ann McCann. American Medical Assn. 1985 432p il pa $28 **615.9**

1. Poisonous plants—Toxicology
ISBN 0-89970-183-3   LC 84-28532

"This handbook is intended for health care professionals confronted with cases of plant poisoning, but it may also serve as a help in identifying poisonous plants. Short treatments of plant poisoning in general and botanical names are followed by a long section in which plants are listed by their scientific names. . . . There are 437 colored illustrations of the plants and an index of common and scientific names." Recomm Ref Books in Paperback. 2d edition

Includes bibliographies

Lappé, Marc
Chemical deception; the toxic threat to health and the environment. Sierra Club Bks. 1991 360p il $27; pa $15 **615.9**

1. Environmental health 2. Hazardous substances 3. Public health
ISBN 0-87156-603-6; 0-87156-511-0 (pa) LC 90-9043

In this book the author "examines the public health crisis brought on by the proliferation of chemicals in the workplace, in agriculture and in medicine. . . . Lappé discusses the toxicity of heavy metals, solvents, radiation; environmental pollution caused by CFCs and carbon dioxide." Publ Wkly

"Well written and well documented, it is highly recommended for both public and academic libraries." Libr J

Includes bibliographic references

Toxics A to Z; a guide to everyday pollution hazards; [by] John Harte [et al.] University of Calif. Press 1991 479p il $75; pa $29.95 **615.9**

1. Hazardous substances 2. Environmental health 3. Consumer education
ISBN 0-520-07223-5; 0-520-07224-3 (pa)
    LC 90-25860

This "reference covers the full range of ordinary toxic substances. Part 1, 'All about Toxics,' discusses general issues concerning the hazards of toxics, and part 2, 'A Guide to Commonly Encountered Toxics,' contains information on over 100 individual toxics arranged alphabetically from *Acetic Acid* through *Zinc*." Booklist

Includes bibliography

Winter, Ruth, 1930-
A consumer's dictionary of household, yard, and office chemicals. Crown 1992 329p pa $12 **615.9**

1. Poisons and poisoning 2. Household equipment and supplies
ISBN 0-517-58722-X   LC 91-33189

An introduction to the chemical ingredients found in cleaners, pesticides, cosmetics, etc.

"In addition to the dictionary listings, which are cross-indexed by subject and by synonym, Winter's book includes an informative and well-documented introduction, a directory that lists associations, poison control centers, Environmental Protection Agency (EPA) regional offices, and a . . . bibliography." Libr J

616 Diseases

Bishop, Jerry E., 1931-
Genome; the story of the most astonishing scientific adventure of our time—the attempt to map all the genes in the human body; [by] Jerry E. Bishop & Michael Waldholz. Simon & Schuster 1990 352p hardcover o.p. paperback available $10.95 **616**

1. Genetic mapping
ISBN 0-671-74032-6 (pa)   LC 90-9940

This book discusses "the government-funded program to map every gene in human DNA and the medical, ethical, and scientific questions that effort raises." Libr J

Donoghue, Paul J.
Sick and tired of feeling sick and tired; living with invisible chronic illness; [by] Paul J. Donoghue, Mary E. Siegel. Norton 1992 284p $22.95 **616**

1. Diseases
ISBN 0-393-03408-9   LC 92-6400

"In Part One, the authors define ICI [invisible chronic illness] and include brief descriptions of 13 diseases that fit their criteria. They discuss in clinical, detached language the impact of ICI on the patient, family, friends and employers. In Part Two, Donoghue and Siegel speak directly to the patient, offering coping mechanisms to enhance quality of life through positive thinking, effective communication, and pain management techniques." Libr J

Includes bibliography

Feiden, Karyn

Hope and help for chronic fatigue syndrome; the official guide of the CFS/CFIDS network. Prentice Hall Press 1990 xxiii, 216p $17.95   **616**

1. Chronic fatigue syndrome
ISBN 0-13-809708-9   LC 89-8729

Also available in paperback from Simon & Schuster

This "is a comprehensive reference work on CFS, covering the range from economics (applying for Supplemental Security Income) to pharmacology to library services. Information is current and well-balanced; this book will be of practical value to patients and their families and friends." Libr J

Includes bibliography

Fettner, Ann Giudici

Viruses: agents of change. McGraw-Hill 1990 287p $19.95   **616**

1. Diseases 2. Viruses
ISBN 0-07-020664-3   LC 90-5628

Also available in paperback from Morrow

"Combining fact and speculation, Fettner tells what viruses are, describes various types (flu, herpes, hepatitis, and HIV among them), and explains how they work. . . . Throughout, she smoothly weaves many personal interviews and her broad knowledge of the scientific literature into the text." Booklist

Includes bibliography

Radetsky, Peter

The invisible invaders; the story of the emerging age of viruses. Little, Brown 1991 415p il $22.95   **616**

1. Viruses
ISBN 0-316-73216-8   LC 90-6612

This book presents "the history, nature and operation of viruses responsible for AIDS, cancer and other lethal diseases." Publ Wkly

"Radetsky succeeds in his aim to inform and intrigue general readers while remaining 'absolutely accurate in terms of the workings of these invisible invaders and the people who spend their lives dealing with them.' This fascinating and important book is highly recommended." Libr J

Includes bibliography

Rosenfeld, Isadore

The best treatment. Simon & Schuster 1991 332p $22   **616**

1. Therapeutics
ISBN 0-671-69339-5   LC 91-30759

Also available G. K. Hall large print edition and in paperback from Bantam Bks.

The author "outlines what he considers the best treatments and remedies for a variety of conditions, ranging from chlamydia infections and asthma to psoriasis and migraines. . . . The style is breezy and accessible, especially well suited to those who need immediate advice." Publ Wkly

Second opinion; your comprehensive guide to treatment alternatives. 2nd ed. Bantam Bks. 1988 435p pa $10.95   **616**

1. Medicine, Popular 2. Diagnosis 3. Therapeutics
ISBN 0-553-34478-1   LC 87-47787

First published 1981 by Lincoln Press/Simon & Schuster

The author describes common medical problems, then symptoms, and the range of treatment available for each condition

Roueché, Berton, 1911-

The medical detectives. New Am. Lib. 1991 c1988 421p pa $10.95   **616**

1. Medicine
ISBN 0-452-26588-6   LC 90-14267

"A Truman Talley book"

A collection of medical investigative articles culled from The New Yorker between 1947-1988. Some of the articles were previously published in the 1980 Times Books edition

Sternbach, Richard A.

Mastering pain; a twelve step program for coping with chronic pain. Putnam 1987 239p o.p.; Ballantine Bks. paperback available $4.95   **616**

1. Pain
ISBN 0-345-35428-1 (pa)   LC 86-25553

"Topics include taking pain medication on a strict schedule, improving general physical shape, and learning to relax. Sternbach also examines new research inroads into the theories of pain and psychological techniques for pain control." Booklist

Stoff, Jesse A.

Chronic fatigue syndrome; the hidden epidemic; [by] Jesse A. Stoff, Charles R. Pellegrino. Random House 1988 304p il $18.95   **616**

1. Chronic fatigue syndrome 2. Holistic medicine
ISBN 0-394-56956-3   LC 88-42663

Also available in paperback from HarperCollins Pubs.

The author "discusses the disease, its symptoms, the virus that causes it, and presents a new treatment using traditional and experimental therapies. Entries from the diary of a patient helped by this program is an integral part of the text. Visualization techniques are used to focus the immune system on destroying the viruses, and recipes are provided for the program's recommended diet." Libr J

Includes bibliography

Wingerson, Lois

Mapping our genes; the Genome Project and the future of medicine. Dutton 1990 338p il o.p.; New Am. Lib. paperback available $9.95   **616**

1. Genetic mapping 2. Diseases
ISBN 0-452-26673-4 (pa)   LC 89-48560

The author "combines human interest and scientific information in her report on efforts to ferret out genetic bases for disease. She uses Friedreich's ataxia, cystic

Wingerson, Lois—*Continued*

fibrosis, sickle-cell anemia, Tourette's syndrome, manic-depressive illness, and insulin-dependent diabetes as major examples of successful gene-mapping. She also touches upon various cancers and everyday life in the laboratory." Booklist

Includes bibliography

616.02 Domestic medicine and medical emergencies

The **American** Medical Association family medical guide; edited by Jeffrey R. M. Kunz and Asher J. Finkel. rev ed. Random House 1987 832p il (American Medical Association home health lib) $35
616.02

1. Medicine, Popular 2. Health self-care
ISBN 0-394-55582-1   LC 86-17659
First published 1982

"Layperson's text featuring articles on diseases and disorders, diagnostic charts, and an index of drugs and medications. Extensively illustrated; uses charts when possible. Emphasizes prevention." N Y Public Libr Book of How & Where to Look It Up

The **American** Medical Association guide to your family's symptoms; medical editors: Charles B. Clayman, Raymond H. Curry. Random House 1993 c1992 319p il pa $15
616.02

1. Medicine, Popular
ISBN 0-679-74128-3   LC 91-51014
First published 1988 with title: American Medical Association home medical adviser

This is a self-help guide to symptoms, diseases and medical emergencies

The **American** Medical Association handbook of first aid & emergency care; developed by the American Medical Association; medical editors: Stanley M. Zydlo, Jr., James A. Hill; illustrations by Larry Frederick. rev ed. Random House 1990 332p il (American Medical Association home reference lib) pa $10
616.02

1. First aid
ISBN 0-679-72959-3   LC 89-43545
First published 1980

"A general introduction to procedures is followed by an alphabetical section that has entries on diseases and injuries, giving background information, symptoms, a list of what to do, immediate action to take, and continual care." Nichols. Guide to Ref Books for Sch Media Cent. 4th edition

Auerbach, Paul S.

Medicine for the outdoors; a guide to emergency medical procedures and first aid; with illustrations by Christine Gralapp and Alexandrine Bartlett. rev & updated ed. Little, Brown 1991 412p il $27.95; pa $14.95
616.02

1. First aid 2. Outdoor life—Accidents
ISBN 0-316-05932-3; 0-316-05931-5 (pa)
LC 90-13339
First published 1986

This is an "emergency medical guide for the serious wilderness traveler. Sections deal with major medical problems, disorders related to specific environments, and commonly used drugs and sources of information." Sci Books Films

Includes bibliographic references

The **Doctors** book of home remedies; thousands of tips and techniques anyone can use to heal everyday health problems; by the editors of Prevention Magazine Health Books; edited by Debora Tkac. Rodale Press 1990 676p $27.95
616.02

1. Medicine, Popular
ISBN 0-87857-873-0   LC 89-38656
Also available in paperback from Bantam Bks.

"This source book includes more than 2000 self-help remedies for everyday health problems, alphabetically arranged in an easy-to-read format. Each entry provides a description, tips, techniques, and causes for medical concern." Libr J

The **Doctors** book of home remedies II; over 1,200 new doctor-tested tips and techniques anyone can use to heal hundreds of everyday health problems; by Sid Kirchheimer and the editors of Prevention magazine health books. Rodale Press 1993 613p $27.95
616.02

1. Medicine, Popular
ISBN 0-87596-158-4   LC 93-7754
This volume "adds some 100 new complaints and more than 1,000 new remedies." Booklist

Gill, Paul G., Jr.

Simon & Schuster's pocket guide to wilderness medicine. Simon & Schuster 1991 204p il pa $9.95
616.02

1. First aid 2. Mountaineering
ISBN 0-671-70615-2   LC 90-27523
"A Fireside book"

This layman's guide to first aid for the outdoors "provides advice on treating such ailments as snake and insect bites, sprains and fractures, and heatstroke and hyperthermia." Libr J

616.07   Pathology

Gonzalez-Crussi, F.

Notes of an anatomist. Harcourt Brace Jovanovich 1985 134p $12.95; pa $4.95

616.07

1. Pathology
ISBN 0-15-167285-7; 0-15-667430-0 (pa)   LC 85-776

The author "takes medical subjects as his jumping-off points in these meditative philosophical essays. Such topics as embalming, child abuse, and male genital anatomy are explored as cultural phenomena, drawing on elements of folklore, mythology, and literature." Booklist

Includes bibliographic references

Pagana, Kathleen Deska, 1952-

Mosby's diagnostic and laboratory test reference; [by] Kathleen Deska Pagana, Timothy James Pagana. Mosby-Year Bk. 1992 843p $23.95   **616.07**

1. Diagnosis 2. Nursing
ISBN 0-8016-3756-2   LC 91-27324

This reference to 564 laboratory and diagnostic tests lists explanations of tests and related physiology, test procedures and patient care, contraindications and potential complications, normal and abnormal findings, and possible interfering factors

Includes bibliography

Rosenfeld, Isadore

Symptoms. Simon & Schuster 1989 366p o.p.; Bantam Bks. paperback available $13.95   **616.07**

1. Medicine, Popular

LC 89-4049

"The text is organized by symptoms and each chapter contains a boxed chart, 'Points to Remember,' which succinctly reiterates the various symptoms associated with a partcular condition and what to do about them. This is a readable, useful volume." Booklist

616.1   Diseases of the cardiovascular system

Cooper, Kenneth H.

Controlling cholesterol; Dr. Kenneth H. Cooper's preventive medicine program. Bantam Bks. 1988 357p il $17.95; pa $5.99

616.1

1. Low-cholesterol diet 2. Heart—Diseases—Prevention
ISBN 0-553-05254-3; 0-553-27775-8 (pa)

LC 87-19530

The author discusses "diet, exercise regimens, recipes, and food-content tables and provides brief treatment of lipoproteins, triglycerides, fiber, monounsaturates, smoking, cancer, and alcohol." Libr J

Includes bibliography

Overcoming hypertension; Dr. Kenneth H. Cooper's preventive medicine program. Bantam Bks. 1990 399p $19.95; pa $5.99

616.1

1. Hypertension
ISBN 0-553-05743-X; 0-553-28937-3 (pa)

LC 89-18242

Also available Bantam Doubleday Dell Pub. Group large print edition

Offering a non-pharmacological approach to the prevention and treatment of hypertension, this book presents relaxation techniques, exercise and diet programs, and information about risk factors, medications, and how to monitor one's own blood pressure levels

Includes bibliographic references

Cousins, Norman

The healing heart; antidotes to panic and helplessness. Norton 1983 302p $13.95

616.1

1. Heart—Diseases
ISBN 0-393-01816-4   LC 83-11449

Also available in paperback from Avon Bks.

The author recounts how self-determination and regimentation helped him recover from congestive heart failure

Includes bibliography

Diethrich, Edward B., 1935-

Women and heart disease; what you can do to stop the number-one killer of American women; [by] Edward B. Diethrich and Carol Cohan. Times Bks. 1992 304p $22   **616.1**

1. Heart—Diseases—Prevention 2. Women—Health and hygiene
ISBN 0-8129-1974-2   LC 92-53670

The authors cover "such basic topics as normal heart anatomy and function, signs of heart disease, risk factors, diagnoses, and treatments. They also do an excellent job of explaining why women are at high risk for heart disease and how they can protect themselves." Libr J

Horovitz, Emmanuel

Cholesterol control made easy; how to lower your cholesterol for a healthier heart; foreword by David H. Blankenhorn. Health Trend Pub. 1990 213p il $19.95   **616.1**

1. Low-cholesterol diet 2. Heart—Diseases—Prevention
ISBN 0-9619329-4-5   LC 90-80651

In this exploration of the link between cholesterol and heart disease the author focuses on diet, exercise and weight loss

"Charts and sidebars scattered through the text provide excellent quick-reference information, and helpful appended tables list the sodium, cholesterol, fat, and fiber contents of several hundred familiar foods. An accessible overview that makes good sense." Booklist

Kowalski, Robert E.

8 steps to a healthy heart; the complete guide to heart disease prevention and recovery from heart attack and bypass surgery; forewords by Jack Sternlieb and other leading physicians. Warner Bks. 1992 430p il $21.95   **616.1**

1. Heart—Diseases
ISBN 0-446-51664-3   LC 91-50082

"Targeting readers diagnosed with heart disease, Kowalski . . . presents a comprehensive program covering those lifestyle and emotional changes needed for recovery and future optimum health. He is strongest in addressing the often-overlooked emotional aspects of heart disease, and he covers sexual issues in a sensitive manner." Libr J

The 8-week cholesterol cure; how to lower your blood cholesterol by up to 40 percent without drugs or deprivation; foreword by Albert A. Kattus. rev ed. Harper & Row 1989 xxii, 362p $19.95; pa $9.95   **616.1**

1. Low-cholesterol diet 2. Heart—Diseases—Prevention
ISBN 0-06-016183-3; 0-06-091471-8 (pa)
                                LC 89-45254

First published 1987

The author presents a program for lowering blood cholesterol using diet modifications, oat bran, niacin, and exercise and demonstrates how lower cholesterol reduces the risk of heart disease

Includes bibliography

Kwiterovich, Peter

Beyond cholesterol; the Johns Hopkins complete guide for avoiding heart disease; by Peter O. Kwiterovich. Johns Hopkins Univ. Press 1990 395p il $21.95   **616.1**

1. Low-cholesterol diet 2. Heart—Diseases—Prevention
ISBN 0-8018-3828-2   LC 89-2548

"A complete, information-packed reference guide to everything from the causes of heart disease to its prevention." Univ Press Books for Public Libr

Legato, Marianne J., 1935-

The female heart; the truth about women and coronary artery disease; by Marianne J. Legato and Carol Colman. Simon & Schuster 1991 252p $21   **616.1**

1. Heart—Diseases 2. Women—Diseases
ISBN 0-671-76110-2   LC 90-24478

Also available in paperback from Avon Bks.

"Stress, heredity, and poor living habits can have the same deleterious effect on the female heart as on the male. The author points out the ways in which diagnosis, treatment, and prognosis of cardiovascular disease differ in females. However, the sound principles of regular medical checkups, proper eating, and exercise habits apply equally to men and women. Recommended as authoritative." Libr J

Includes bibliography

Levin, Rhoda F.

Heartmates; a survival guide for the cardiac spouse; foreword by David V. Keith. Prentice Hall Press 1987 249p il o.p.; Pocket Bks. paperback available $5.50   **616.1**

1. Heart—Diseases 2. Domestic relations
ISBN 0-671-72904-7 (pa)   LC 87-11392

A guidebook for spouses and families of those who have survived heart attacks

Includes bibliography

The **Living** heart diet; [by] Michael E. DeBakey [et al.] Simon & Schuster 1984 xxiv, 397p il hardcover o.p. paperback available $13   **616.1**

1. Heart—Diseases—Diet therapy 2. Cookery
ISBN 0-671-61998-5 (pa)   LC 84-10693

"Beginning with a concise description of the heart and how diet can affect its ability to function [the authors] provide menus and recipes for several different heart care diets. The 500 recipes can be used for the author's basic living heart diet, low-calorie and very low fat, low-sodium, and hyperlipidemia diets, as well as for diabetic diets. Each recipe is accompanied by a breakdown of its nutrients." Libr J

Moore, Thomas J., 1944-

Heart failure; a critical inquiry into the revolution in heart care. Random House 1989 308p $19.95   **616.1**

1. Heart—Diseases—Prevention 2. Heart—Surgery
ISBN 0-394-56958-X   LC 88-43222

The author argues that "because there are no accurate nationwide statistics on . . . survival after any form of coronary therapy (open heart surgery, balloon therapy, etc.), it is impossible to compare the beneficial effects of particular treatments. He also says the popular belief that high cholesterol in the blood is related to coronary disease has no firm scientific basis." Libr J

Includes bibliography

Pantano, James A., 1944-

Living with angina; a practical guide to dealing with coronary artery disease and your doctor. Harper & Row 1990 214p il hardcover o.p. paperback available $8.95
                                616.1

1. Heart—Diseases
ISBN 0-06-092055-6 (pa)   LC 89-45701

The author "defines and explains angina and its origin and manifestation, then briefly covers the risk factors leading to coronary artery disease." Libr J

Roth, Eli

Good cholesterol, bad cholesterol; [by] Eli M. Roth, Sandy L. Streicher. Prima Pub. & Communications 1988 179p $15.95; pa $8.95   **616.1**

1. Low-cholesterol diet 2. Heart—Diseases—Prevention
ISBN 0-914629-85-9; 1-55958-025-9 (pa)
                                LC 88-31625

Roth, Eli—*Continued*

This "is a guide to how to reduce the risk of arteriosclerosis by changing the amounts and kinds of lipids in the diet. . . . The writing is clear and can be easily understood by someone without a background in nutrition." Sci Books Films

Includes bibliography

Samuels, Mike

Hypertension; how to work with your doctor and take charge of your health; [by] Mike Samuels and Nancy Samuels. Summit Bks. 1991 151p pa $5   **616.1**

1. Hypertension
ISBN 0-671-68216-4   LC 91-27778

The authors argue that a controlled program of stress control, exercise and diet can successfully combat hypertension

Includes bibliographic references

Selzer, Arthur

Understanding heart disease. University of Calif. Press 1992 211p il $27   **616.1**

1. Heart—Diseases
ISBN 0-520-06560-3   LC 92-4854

"Beginning with a description of the normal heart's structure and function, Selzer turns to the diagnosis of heart disease, including the use of such diagnostic tools as echocardiography, coronary arteriography, magnetic resonance imaging, CAT scan, and other current tests. He surveys treatments such as diet, exercise, use of drugs, and a variety of interventions, among them heart surgery." Publisher's note

The **Yale** University School of Medicine heart book; editors, Barry L. Zaret, Marvin Moser, Lawrence S. Cohen. Morrow 1992 432p il $30   **616.1**

1. Heart—Diseases
ISBN 0-688-09719-7   LC 91-28057

"This reference covers the heart and its function, discusses ways to lower one's risk of heart disease, and explains how diagnoses are made. It also includes an Encyclopedia of Common Heart Disorders that lists major cardiovascular disorders and treatments, and special sections on women, different ethnic and racial groups, and age groupings." Libr J

"One of the most comprehensive looks yet taken at cardiovascular health." Publ Wkly

Includes bibliographic references

616.2 Diseases of the respiratory system

Boggs, Peter B.

Sneezing your head off? how to live with your allergic nose. Simon & Schuster 1992 270p il pa $10   **616.2**

1. Hay fever 2. Allergy
ISBN 0-671-76115-3   LC 91-21733

"A Fireside book"

The author "provides insight into how noses work, what it means to be allergic, and conditions that masquerade as allergic rhinitis. He provides a questionnaire to help determine what kind of nose problem is present, following it with advice on how to remove dust, molds, and pollens from the home. In the rest of the book, he proffers advice on how to take care of your nose." Booklist

Includes bibliographic references

Haas, Francois

The chronic bronchitis and emphysema handbook; [by] Francois Haas, Sheila Sperber Haas; with illustrations by Kenneth Axen. Wiley 1990 272p il (Wiley science editions) pa $12.95   **616.2**

1. Bronchitis 2. Emphysema
ISBN 0-471-62263-X   LC 89-70661

Among the areas covered in this guide to two common respiratory ailments are: selecting the right medication, finding a physician, managing stress, physical therapy, job retraining, and sex

Harrington, Geri

The asthma self-care book; how to take control of your asthma. HarperCollins Pubs. 1991 272p il $19.95; pa $10   **616.2**

1. Asthma 2. Health self-care
ISBN 0-06-016584-7; 0-06-092270-2 (pa)

LC 90-55538

The author discusses "the illness, what prompts attacks, and the pros and cons of medications. She also offers practical advice to help asthmatics reduce stress, get proper exercise, and manage their diets. Harrington is thorough, firm, and sensible." Booklist

Weinstein, Allan

Asthma; the complete guide to self-management of asthma and allergies for patients and their families. McGraw-Hill 1987 350p il o.p.; Fawcett Bks. paperback available $5.99   **616.2**

1. Asthma
ISBN 0-449-21562-8 (pa)   LC 86-10574

"This compendium discusses causes, treatments, and special problems relating to asthma. . . . This clearly written account urges patients to become participants in their own care and offers solid suggestions on how to do so." Booklist

Young, Stuart, 1938-

The asthma handbook; a complete guide for patients and their families; [by] Stuart H. Young, with Susan A. Shulman and Martin D. Shulman. Bantam Bks. 1989 384p pa $9.95   **616.2**

1. Asthma
ISBN 0-553-34712-8   LC 89-6589

Among the subjects covered are: the rights and responsibilities of the asthma patient, medications, special diets, and the treatment of asthma during pregnancy

616.3 Diseases of the digestive system

Carper, Steve
No milk today; how to live with lactose intolerance; foreword by Tarun Kothari, Ravendra N. Sharma, Krisnan D. Thanik. Simon & Schuster 1986 286p $15.95
616.3

1. Lactose intolerance
ISBN 0-671-62020-7   LC 86-2008
"A Fireside book"

The author "explains what lactose intolerance is and how one can learn to live with it by changing dietary practices, and he also devotes several chapters to interpreting food labels and discussing available lactose-free products. Helpful tips on eating out, traveling, and caring for lactose-intolerant children are also included. An excellent and well-researched sourcebook." Booklist

Includes bibliographies

The **Crohn's** disease and ulcerative colitis fact book; [by the] National Foundation for Ileitis & Colitis; edited by Peter A. Banks, Daniel H. Present, and Penny Steiner. Scribner 1983 194p il $18.95
616.3

1. Colon (Anatomy)—Diseases
ISBN 0-684-17967-9   LC 83-11602

This book "traces the causes, symptoms and diagnosis of the diseases, discusses the various treatment options from medication to surgery, and concludes with advice on coping with the illnesses." Libr J

Includes bibliography

Harris, Ann, 1956-
Cystic fibrosis; the facts; [by] Ann Harris and Maurice Super. new ed. Oxford Univ. Press 1991 118p il $22.95
616.3

1. Cystic fibrosis
ISBN 0-19-262024-X   LC 90-14272
First published 1987

This discussion of cystic fibrosis includes an introduction to the physiology of breathing and digestion along with chapters on symptoms and management. The genetics of the disease are explored and psychological issues are addressed

616.4 Diabetes

Biermann, June
The diabetic's total health book; [by] June Biermann, Barbara Toohey; foreword by Fred Whitehouse. 3rd rev ed. Tarcher, J.P. 1992 302p il pa $10.95
616.4

1. Diabetes
ISBN 0-87477-689-9   LC 92-7076
First published 1980

This guide for diabetics covers diet, exercise, stress reduction techniques, lifestyle and emotional well-being, recipes, and tips on obtaining good medical care

Includes bibliography

Edelwich, Jerry
Diabetes; caring for your emotions as well as your health; [by] Jerry Edelwich, Archie Brodsky; foreword by Ronald A. Arky. Addison-Wesley 1987 276p $17.95; pa $12.95
616.4

1. Diabetes
ISBN 0-201-10609-4; 0-201-10608-6 (pa)
     LC 86-10868

"A Merloyd Lawrence book"

The authors "look at the psychosocial aspects of the disease, discussing how the diabetic patient can adjust to life with the minimum of stress. Drawing upon case histories, the authors examine various aspects of living that are affected by the disease, particularly family relations. Sexual problems and possible pregnancy complications are also covered." Booklist

Includes bibliography

Guthrie, Diana W.
The diabetes sourcebook; today's methods and ways to give yourself the best care; [by] Diana W. Guthrie and Richard A. Guthrie; foreword by June Biermann and Barbara Toohey. Lowell House 1990 242p il $21.95; pa $12.95
616.4

1. Diabetes
ISBN 0-929923-30-8; 0-929923-79-0 (pa)   LC 90-2239

The authors "provide the basics about diabetes—types and causes, methods of control, complications. . . . Their book's strengths are its extensive appendixes, illustrations that include lists of exercise/calorie expenditures, a glossary, bibliography, a guide to diabetes camps for children, tables illustrating foot care and various forms of insulin. Particularly useful is the consumer's guide to insulin injection devices." Libr J

Learning to live well with diabetes; editorial committee: Marion J. Franz [et al.]; editor: Cheryl Weiler. rev and updated. DCI Pub. 1991 511p il pa $24.95
616.4

1. Diabetes
ISBN 0-937721-79-4   LC 91-15874
First published 1985

At head of title: International Diabetes Center

This guide discusses diabetes in relation to nutrition, exercise, monitoring, insulin, emotional adjustment, avoiding complications, pregnancy, sports and travel

Includes bibliography

616.5 Diseases of the skin, hair, nails

MacKie, Rona M.
Healthy skin; the facts. Oxford Univ. Press 1992 148p il $24; pa $12
616.5

1. Skin—Care and hygiene
ISBN 0-19-262246-3; 0-19-262244-7 (pa)
     LC 91-39238

This book "explains how the skin is structured and how it works, before giving information on healthy skin and the prevention of skin disease." Univ Press Books for Public and Second Sch Libr

Siegel, Mary-Ellen
Safe in the sun; foreword by Albert M. Lefkowits. Walker & Co. 1990 258p $21.95; pa $13.95   **616.5**

1. Skin—Care and hygiene
ISBN 0-8027-1100-6; 0-8027-7338-9 (pa)

LC 90-11947

The author describes "the sun's inimical effects from the common to the relatively rare—sunburn and sunstroke, premature aging, cataracts and cancers. Varying risks for people of different skin shades, as well as for those suffering from conditions (or taking certain medications) that may increase sun sensitivity, are also discussed, as are the perils of tanning salons and devices." Publ Wkly

Includes bibliographic references

Walzer, Richard A., 1930-
Treating acne; [by] Richard A. Walzer and the editors of Consumer Reports Books. Consumer Repts. Bks. 1992 100p il $16.95   **616.5**

1. Acne
ISBN 0-89043-449-2   LC 91-40262

This overview of acne discusses its causes, various self-help treatments, seeing a dermatologist, choosing the right cosmetics, and methods available for repairing scars

616.6 Diseases of the urogenital system. Diseases of the urinary system

Berger, Gary S.
The couple's guide to fertility; how new medical advances can help you have a baby; [by] Gary S. Berger, Marc Goldstein, Mark Fuerst. Doubleday 1989 442p $22.95; pa $14.95   **616.6**

1. Fertility, Human 2. Infertility
ISBN 0-385-24546-7; 0-385-26390-2 (pa)   LC 89-7863

"This book emphasizes the need for careful testing and identification of the causes of infertility before treatment is considered. Basic reproductive techniques, fertility tests, and treatments are clearly described and evaluated. The authors' description of drug side-effects and success probabilities of surgery is particularly useful." Libr J

Burgio, Kathryn
Staying dry: a practical guide to bladder control; [by] Kathryn L. Burgio, K. Lynette Pearce, Angelo J. Lucco. Johns Hopkins Univ. Press 1989 169p il $30; pa $12.95   **616.6**

1. Bladder—Diseases
ISBN 0-8018-3912-2; 0-8018-3909-2 (pa)

LC 89-45480

"Based on a highly successful program developed at the National Institute on Aging in association with the Johns Hopkins University School of Medicine, this book combines expert medical advice with a simple but comprehensive step-by-step action plan that can solve an incontinence problem." Univ Press Books for Public Libr

Chalker, Rebecca
Overcoming bladder disorders; compassionate, authoritative medical and self-help solutions for incontinence, cystitis, interstitial cystitis, prostate problems, and bladder cancer; by Rebecca Chalker and Kristene E. Whitmore. Harper & Row 1990 337p $19.95; pa $11   **616.6**

1. Bladder—Diseases
ISBN 0-06-016277-5; 0-06-092083-1 (pa)

LC 89-45789

This book provides information on diagnosis, treatment and prevention of bladder disorders
"Although other books on cystitis and prostate problems are available, this is the only comprehensive title on this sensitive subject. A thorough, accessible guide." Libr J

Includes bibliographic references

Corson, Stephen L.
Conquering infertility; a guide for couples; illustrations by Ray Tschoepe. rev ed. Prentice Hall Press 1990 258p il $19.95; pa $9.95   **616.6**

1. Fertility, Human 2. Infertility
ISBN 0-13-168188-5; 0-13-171562-3 (pa)

LC 89-15991

First published 1983 by Appleton-Century-Crofts
The author discusses every aspect of infertility including psychological and emotional problems and techniques available to overcome the condition

Phillips, Robert H., 1948-
Coping with kidney failure; a guide to living with kidney failure for you and your family. Avery Pub. Group 1987 309p pa $9.95   **616.6**

1. Kidneys—Diseases
ISBN 0-89529-370-6   LC 87-17477

"The functions of the kidneys and the options for dialysis or transplantation are described. The emotional impact and lifestyle changes necessitated by renal failure are covered extensively. Diet, medication, pain, and financial impact are also discussed." Libr J

Rous, Stephen N. (Stephen Norman), 1931-
The prostate book; sound advice on symptoms and treatment; illustrations by Betty Goodwin. updated ed. Norton 1992 285p il $22.95   **616.6**

1. Prostate—Diseases
ISBN 0-393-03387-2   LC 91-38775

First published 1988
The author explains "the function of the healthy prostate and discusses the causes, symptoms, and treatment of the most common prostate problems—including inflammation, benign prostatic disease, and cancer of the prostate." Publisher's note

616.7 Diseases of the musculoskeletal system

Aladjem, Henrietta, 1917-
Understanding lupus. Scribner 1985 xxxi, 255p il hardcover o.p. paperback available $11.95   **616.7**

1. Lupus erythematosus, Systemic
ISBN 0-684-18349-8 (pa)   LC 85-1963

First published 1982 with title: Lupus, hope through understanding

The author explains what is known about Systemic lupus erythematosus, what treatments are available, and what research is being done to find a cure. Also includes information on dental care, physician-patient relations, pregnancy, clinical developments, and therapies

Includes bibliography

Appleton, Nancy
Healthy bones; what you should know about osteoporosis. Avery Pub. Group 1990 139p il pa $8.95   **616.7**

1. Osteoporosis
ISBN 0-89529-462-1   LC 90-20404

The author discusses body chemistry and outlines a diet to prevent osteoporosis

Includes bibliographic references

Brewerton, Derrick
All about arthritis; past, present, future. Harvard Univ. Press 1992 317p il $29.95
                                                616.7

1. Arthritis
ISBN 0-674-01615-7   LC 92-11557

The author tells the "story of arthritis research, from the days before germs were recognized as causes of disease and when the reasons for inflammation were obscure, to the present. . . . As he leads us through the historic search for cures, Brewerton introduces relevant basic information on diagnosis, the role of germs and bacteria, body defenses, the nervous system, hormones, DNA, RNA, proteins, crystals, and cells." Publisher's note

Includes bibliographic references

Cooper, Kenneth H.
Preventing osteoporosis; Dr. Kenneth H. Cooper's preventive medicine program. Bantam Bks. 1989 278p il $18.95   **616.7**

1. Osteoporosis
ISBN 0-553-05335-3   LC 88-47826

The author "coaches people on fighting the bone degeneration caused by osteoporosis, prescribing tactics such as exercise, proper nutrition, dietary supplements, and hormone treatments, all geared to a variety of age groups, abilities, and interests." Booklist

Includes bibliography

Eades, Mary Dan
If it runs in your family—arthritis; reducing your risk; foreword by Kent Johnson; developed by the Philip Lief Group, Inc. Bantam Bks. 1992 176p il pa $9   **616.7**

1. Arthritis
ISBN 0-553-35478-7   LC 91-18159

A discussion of risk factors associated with arthritis. Diagnostic tests, treatment, and research are explored

Includes bibliographic references

Fries, James F.
Arthritis; a comprehensive guide to understanding your arthritis. 3rd ed. Addison-Wesley 1990 265p il $10.53 **616.7**

1. Arthritis
ISBN 0-201-52402-3   LC 90-659

First published 1979

This volume discusses the symptoms, causes, treatment and management of over 100 types of arthritis

Includes bibliographic references

Gach, Michael Reed
Arthritis relief at your fingertips; the complete self-care guide to easing aches and pains without drugs. Warner Bks. 1989 231p il hardcover o.p. paperback available $14.95
                                                616.7

1. Arthritis 2. Acupressure
ISBN 0-446-39156-5 (pa)   LC 88-40098

The author "confines himself to acupressure—the application of finger pressure to specific points on the body—as well as techniques of self-massage and stretching exercises to ease the pain of arthritis." Publ Wkly

Includes bibliography

Heaney, Robert P.
Calcium and common sense; [by] Robert P. Heaney and Janet Barger-Lux. Doubleday 1988 266p il pa $16.95   **616.7**

1. Osteoporosis
ISBN 0-385-24219-0   LC 87-19848

"Heaney explodes some of the myths of the current calcium fad and presents solid information on calcium supplements, estrogen therapy, exercise, bone scans, and osteoporosis treatment." Booklist

Includes bibliography

Kantrowitz, Fred G.
Taking control of arthritis. HarperCollins Pubs. 1990 244p o.p. paperback available $10   **616.7**

1. Arthritis
ISBN 0-06-092113-7 (pa)   LC 89-46539

Also available Thorndike Press large print edition

The author explains the disease and offers "information on the symptoms, diagnosis, laboratory tests, medications, and such other forms of treatment as physical and occupational therapy." Libr J

Phillips, Robert H., 1948-
Coping with lupus; a guide to living with lupus for you and your family. Avery Pub. Group 1991 276p il pa $9.95   **616.7**

1. Lupus erythematosus, Systemic
ISBN 0-89529-475-3   LC 90-1270

First published 1984

The author explains the background and diagnosis of lupus and suggests strategies for living with the disease and its emotional and practical problems

Includes bibliographic references

Coping with rheumatoid arthritis. Avery Pub. Group 1988 258p pa $9.95   **616.7**

1. Arthritis
ISBN 0-89529-371-4   LC 88-3450

The author "describes the nature of RA, its diagnosis, and treatment. Phillips also explores the psychological side of this . . . condition, presenting sections on depression, fear, anxiety, anger, guilt, and how to cope with these manifestations." Booklist

Includes bibliography

Pisetsky, David S.
The Duke University Medical Center book of arthritis; [by] David Pisetsky with Susan Flamholtz Trien. Fawcett Columbine 1992 407p il $22   **616.7**

1. Arthritis
ISBN 0-449-90254-4   LC 91-42623

A review of the causes, symptoms, diagnosis and treatment of various arthritic conditions. An outline of the Duke University Basic Arthritis Program is included

Sobel, Dava
Arthritis: what works; [by] Dava Sobel and Arthur C. Klein. St. Martin's Press 1989 471p $22.95; pa $13.95   **616.7**

1. Arthritis
ISBN 0-312-03289-7; 0-312-05379-7 (pa)
LC 89-30422

"An Arthritis Survey publication"

The authors "interviewed over 1000 arthritis sufferers in this survey of remedies ranging from prescription drugs and over-the-counter cures to strategies advised by general physicians and rheumatologists, orthopedists and alternative healers (also included are recipes and meal plans.)" Publ Wkly

"Easy to understand, the book is a good choice for all public libraries." Booklist

Includes bibliography

616.8   Diseases of the nervous system and mental disorders

Atwood, Glenna Wotton, 1931-
Living well with Parkinson's; [by] Glenna Wotton Atwood with Lila Green Hunnewell. Wiley 1991 198p pa $10.95   **616.8**

1. Parkinsonism
ISBN 0-471-52539-1   LC 90-42200

Atwood, a Parkinson's patient offers "her personal experiences, advice, and observations. . . . There's also valuable information regarding medications, nutrition, and exercise." Libr J

Heller, Joseph
No laughing matter; [by] Joseph Heller & Speed Vogel. Putnam 1986 335p o.p.; Avon Bks. paperback available $4.95   **616.8**

1. Guillain-Barré syndrome
ISBN 0-380-70267-3 (pa)   LC 85-19421

"In alternating chapters, Heller and Vogel recount Heller's bout with Guillain-Barre syndrome, a paralyzing affliction that struck him in 1981." Publ Wkly

Josephs, Arthur
The invaluable guide to life after stroke; an owner's manual. Amadeus Press 1992 152p pa $14.95   **616.8**

1. Brain—Diseases
ISBN 0-9631493-9-3   LC 91-77440

"After discussing the causes of stroke [the author] turns to what to expect in the hospital and when returning home. Using stories from other stroke victims, he also provides insights for dealing with the emotions and activities of daily life as well as compelling evidence of the importance of continual therapy and support groups." Booklist

"Of the many books dealing with this topic, this one possibly is the best yet; it is so practical and hopeful for the victim as well as the caregiver." Libr J

Klawans, Harold L.
Life, death, and in between; tales of clinical neurology. Paragon House 1992 270p $21.95   **616.8**

1. Nervous system—Diseases 2. Medical ethics
ISBN 1-55778-526-0   LC 92-4663

Based upon his experiences as a practicing clinical neurologist the author "recounts such philosophical and ethical dilemmas as: treating an obviously dying patient, risking serum hepatitus from blood transfusions for pregnant women, dealing with overprotective family members, misdiagnosed ailments, the environment in which death occurs (in hospitals instead of at home), removing life support systems for comatose patients, and more. Klawans is . . . the masterful and compassionate storyteller, and his book is interesting, thought provoking, and entertaining." Libr J

Newton's madness; further tales of clinical neurology. Harper & Row 1990 218p $17.95; pa $8.95   **616.8**

1. Nervous system—Diseases
ISBN 0-06-016256-2; 0-06-092050-5 (pa)
LC 89-45678

The author recounts twenty-two case histories of neurological disorders, some of them historical, some from the author's practice as a clinical neurologist

Toscanini's fumble; and other tales of clinical neurology. Contemporary Bks. 1988 229p o.p.; Bantam Bks. paperback available $8.95   **616.8**

1. Nervous system—Diseases
ISBN 0-553-34662-8 (pa)   LC 87-36585

Klawans, Harold L.—*Continued*
"Case histories from neurologist Klawans' own practice provide an intriguing springboard to accessible explanations of the structure and functioning of the human brain and nervous system and descriptions of some of the illnesses that can affect them." Booklist

Lance, James W. (James Waldo), 1926-
Migraine and other headaches. rev & updated ed. Scribner 1986 228p il pa $14 **616.8**

1. Headache
ISBN 0-684-18654-3 LC 86-3733
First published 1975 with title: Headache

The author discusses the "etiology and treatment of all types of headaches, concentrating not only on migraines but also vascular, cluster, and tension headaches." Booklist
Includes bibliography

Living well with epilepsy; [edited by] Robert J. Gumnit. Demos Publs. 1990 166p $19.95; pa $12.95 **616.8**

1. Epilepsy
ISBN 0-939957-24-8; 0-939957-21-3 (pa)
LC 89-85237

This explains the diagnosis and management of epilepsy with an emphasis on active participation of patient and family working with health care professionals to allow an epileptic to live as well as possible

McGoon, Dwight C.
The Parkinson's handbook. Norton 1990 174p il $18.95 **616.8**

1. Parkinsonism
ISBN 0-393-02880-1 LC 90-7677

The author "explains the basics of this mysterious disease, describes his own innovative program to combat its symptoms, and tells Parkinsonians how to maintain that strength of spirit which can be their best defense." Publisher's note
Includes bibliography

Richard, Adrienne
Epilepsy; a new approach; [by] Adrienne Richard and Joel Reiter; foreword by Robert Efron. Prentice-Hall 1990 272p il pa $17.45 **616.8**

1. Epilepsy
ISBN 0-13-551847-4 LC 89-25577

"Richard, who has controlled her seizures without drugs for 15 years, and Reiter, a neurologist, suggest medical and self-help techniques that can help ease or control suffering, including biofeedback, psychotherapy, nutrition, relaxation, exercise, stress reduction, and journal keeping." Libr J
Includes bibliographic references

Rosner, Louis J., 1929-
Multiple sclerosis; [by] Louis J. Rosner and Shelley Ross. Prentice Hall Press 1987 246p $19.95 **616.8**

1. Multiple sclerosis
ISBN 0-13-604695-9 LC 87-13426

Also available in paperback from Simon & Schuster
The authors "answer the usual questions regarding MS—causes, symptoms, diagnosis, course of the disease, and possibilities for cure. But they also devote a large part of the text to discussing . . . the emotions of the person with MS and of family members, friends, and caregivers." Libr J

Sacks, Oliver W.
The man who mistook his wife for a hat and other clinical tales; [by] Oliver Sacks. Summit Bks. 1985 233p il o.p.; Perennial Lib. paperback available $12 **616.8**

1. Nervous system—Diseases
ISBN 0-06-097079-0 (pa) LC 85-17220
Also available in hardcover from P. Smith

"Sacks introduces the reader to real people who suffer from a variety of neurological syndromes which includes symptoms such as amnesia, uncontrolled movements, and musical hallucinations. Sacks recounts their stories in a riveting, compassionate, and thoughtful manner." Libr J
Includes bibliography

Migraine; [by] Oliver Sacks. rev and expanded [ed]. University of Calif. Press 1992 xxiii, 338p il $30; pa $13 **616.8**

1. Migraine
ISBN 0-520-08101-3; 0-520-08223-0 (pa) LC 92-407
First published 1970

The author describes many types of migraine and the situations that may provoke them. Comments on treatment are included, as well as discussions of the disease's physiological and psychological aspects. A color section presents paintings by migraine patients, illustrating the visual hallucinations which often precede an attack
Includes bibliography

Shirk, Evelyn Urban
After the stroke; coping with America's third leading cause of death; [by] Evelyn Shirk. Prometheus Bks. 1991 114p (Golden age bks) $19.95; pa $14.95 **616.8**

1. Brain—Diseases
ISBN 0-87975-693-4; 0-87975-694-2 (pa) LC 91-3902

"Evelyn Shirk, wife of stroke patient Jay, describes the couple's 17-year losing battle against the malady. Her account will especially interest patients, family members, and friends in similar predicaments." Booklist

Shuman, Robert
Understanding multiple sclerosis; a guidebook for families; [by] Robert Shuman and Janice Schwartz; foreword by Robert J. Slater. Scribner 1988 219p $19.95 **616.8**

1. Multiple sclerosis
ISBN 0-684-18989-5 LC 88-11488

The authors "discuss how the disease affects self-image, family life, intimate relationships, and career. Real solutions are proffered . . . and sources explain where the reader can find help on these matters. A reassuring guide for MS patients and their families." Booklist
Includes bibliography

Smith, Jane S.

Patenting the sun: polio and the Salk vaccine. Morrow 1990 413p $22.95   **616.8**

1. Salk, Jonas, 1914- 2. Poliomyelitis
ISBN 0-688-09494-5   LC 89-13802

Also available in paperback from Doubleday

The author examines medical, social, cultural, psychological, and political aspects of poliomyelitis and discusses the search for a vaccine

"This exciting, dramatic narrative tells a comprehensive story of the conquest of polio and sheds fresh light on the politics of medicine." Publ Wkly

Includes bibliographic references

Solomon, Seymour

The headache book; [by] Seymour Solomon and Steven Fraccaro. Consumers Union of U.S. 1991 191p pa $14.95

     616.8

1. Headache
ISBN 0-89043-351-8   LC 90-49894

A guide to the symptoms, causes, and treatment of headaches. Prescriptions and non-drug therapies, common headache triggers, children's headaches, and when to see a doctor are among the topics discussed

Includes bibliographic references

616.85 Neuroses, disorders of personality and intellect, speech and language disorders

Abraham, Suzanne

Eating disorders; the facts; [by] Suzanne Abraham and Derek Llewellyn-Jones. 3rd ed. Oxford Univ. Press 1992 201p il $18.95

     616.85

1. Eating disorders
ISBN 0-19-262199-8   LC 91-47619

First published 1984

This work focuses on diagnosis and treatment of anorexia nervosa, bulimia and obesity

Includes bibliographic references

Boskind-White, Marlene

Bulimarexia; the binge/purge cycle; [by] Marlene Boskind-White, William C. White, Jr. 2nd ed. Norton 1987 284p $19.95; pa $10.95   **616.85**

1. Bulimia
ISBN 0-393-02368-0; 0-393-30117-6 (pa)

     LC 86-23733

First published 1983

The authors discuss "findings about the psychological consequences of binge-ing, the relationship of dieting to eating disorders, and the need for nutritional counseling. In addition to group therapy, treatment of individuals, families, and couples is covered. The negative aspects of pharmacological ('magic bullet') cures are discussed." Publisher's note

Includes bibliography

Braiker, Harriet B., 1948-

Getting up when you're feeling down; a woman's guide to overcoming and preventing depression. Putnam 1988 304p o.p.; Pocket Bks. paperback available $5.99

     616.85

1. Depression, Mental 2. Women—Psychology
ISBN 0-671-68327-6 (pa)   LC 88-11484

The author "offers a drugless 'Triple A' program to help head off, shorten or alleviate emotional mood swings often due to fatigue, stress and hormonal variations." Publ Wkly

Bruch, Hilde, 1904-1984

The golden cage; the enigma of anorexia nervosa. Harvard Univ. Press 1978 150p $17.50   **616.85**

1. Anorexia nervosa
ISBN 0-674-35650-0   LC 77-10674

Also available in paperback from Random House

The author "demonstrates that the causes of the disorder rest in psychological factors: the pervasive message that slim is beautiful, the pressure on youngsters to excel, resulting in a distorted self-image. Using 70 case histories of patients with 'the hunger disease,' Bruch reveals the complex nature of its onset and methods of treatment." Publ Wkly

Brumberg, Joan Jacobs

Fasting girls; the emergence of anorexia nervosa as a modern disease. Harvard Univ. Press 1988 366p il $27.50   **616.85**

1. Anorexia nervosa
ISBN 0-674-29501-3   LC 87-25092

Also available in paperback from New Am. Lib.

In this historical view of anorexia nervosa, "Brumberg considers three models for understanding [the disease]— the biological, the psychological, and the cultural." Atlantic

"Brumberg's book is written with verve and grace, and it makes an important contribution to the literature on the history of medical treatment and on the nature of women and of the society in which they live." Science

Includes bibliography

Byrne, Katherine

A parent's guide to anorexia and bulimia; understanding and helping self-starvers and binge/purgers; with an afterword by Bernard Mackler. Schocken Bks. 1987 xx, 167p o.p.; Holt & Co. paperback available $9.95

     616.85

1. Anorexia nervosa 2. Bulimia
ISBN 0-8050-1037-8 (pa)   LC 87-4878

"The author, the mother of an anorexic, has written a practical guide for parents of children with eating disorders. While she does go into the signs and symptoms to watch for, Byrne concentrates on how to live with someone who has anorexia or bulimia. . . . An excellent guide." Booklist

Includes bibliography

Controlling eating disorders with facts, advice, and resources; Raymond Lemberg, consulting editor. Oryx Press 1992 xxi, 218p pa $29.50 **616.85**

1. Eating disorders
ISBN 0-89774-691-0   LC 91-42850

A discussion of "eating disorders, their causes, descriptions, health and psychological effects, and treatments. Lembert also includes a directory of facilities and programs state by state, an extensive bibliography . . . and a list of organizations devoted to this problem. Not only an excellent volume for research, the book has a positive tone that will encourage those personally affected by eating disorders." SLJ

DePaulo, J. Raymond
How to cope with depression; a complete guide for you and your family; [by] J. Raymond DePaulo, Jr. and Keith Russell Ablow. McGraw-Hill 1989 xx, 216p $19.95 **616.85**

1. Depression, Mental
ISBN 0-07-016409-6   LC 89-2317

The authors examine the possible causes, treatments, and professional 'perspectives' of depression

Includes bibliography

Dix, Carol
The new mother syndrome; coping with postpartum stress and depression. Doubleday 1985 264p $17.95 **616.85**

1. Postpartum depression 2. Stress (Psychology) 3. Women—Psychology
ISBN 0-385-27986-8   LC 85-1638

Also available in paperback from Pocket Bks.

"Dix cogently argues that this condition is an unavoidable hormonal and biochemical reaction to childbirth and should be treated accordingly. The often obscure symptoms of postpartum depression are carefully enumerated, and a valuable list of support groups are appended. An intelligible and heartening evaluation of a misunderstood malady." Booklist

Includes bibliography

Doctor, Ronald M.
The encyclopedia of phobias, fears, and anxieties; [by] Ronald M. Doctor and Ada P. Kahn. Facts on File 1989 487p $45 **616.85**

1. Phobias—Dictionaries 2. Fear—Dictionaries
ISBN 0-8160-1798-0   LC 88-31057

"Arranged alphabetically, the *Encyclopedia* offers psychological, pharmacological, diagnostic, and historical information in entries varying in length from a few lines to a few pages and concludes with a brief index and an extensive bibliography. Authoritative yet easier to use than existing resources, this guide's clear presentation makes it useful to both the layperson and the professional." Am Libr

Dowling, Colette
You mean I don't have to feel this way? new help for depression, anxiety, and addiction; with a foreword by Harrison G. Pope, Jr., and James I. Hudson. Scribner 1991 293p $19.95 **616.85**

1. Depression, Mental 2. Stress (Psychology) 3. Compulsive behavior
ISBN 0-684-19257-8   LC 91-20162

Also available in paperback from Bantam Bks.

The author "here challenges the popular belief that depression, panic disorder, addictions and a host of other psychiatric problems result from events in childhood or moral weakness. . . . She presents the latest research in brain chemistry and argues that a lack of serotonin—a natural 'feel-good' chemical—is responsible for an array of mental and mood disorders." Publ Wkly

Includes bibliography

Engel, Beverly
Partners in recovery; how mates, lovers, & other prosurvivors can learn to support & cope with adult survivors of childhood sexual abuse. Lowell House 1991 160p $19.95 **616.85**

1. Child molesting 2. Human relations
ISBN 0-929923-61-8   LC 91-20688

Also available in paperback from Fawcett Bks.

"Engel explains terms and explodes myths as she delineates seven phases of recovery and explains what the prosurvivor should expect in each." Booklist

Includes bibliography

Fieve, Ronald R.
Moodswing; Dr. Fieve on depression. rev & expanded ed. Morrow 1989 276p $22.95 **616.85**

1. Depression, Mental
ISBN 0-688-08879-1   LC 88-34525

Also available in paperback from Bantam Bks.

First published 1975

The author writes about the successes in treating some depression with lithium. Using case histories from his practice, Dr. Fieve explains the main causes of depression and other mood disorders. He also includes a chapter on teenage and adult suicide

Includes bibliography

Fraser, Malcolm, 1903-1994
Self-therapy for the stutterer. Speech Foundation of Am. pa $3 **616.85**

1. Speech disorders

First published 1978. (8th edition 1992) Periodically revised

This manual for overcoming the problem includes such techniques as relaxation, rules for speaking and breath control

Gold, Mark S.

The good news about depression; cures and treatments in the new age of psychiatry; [by] Mark S. Gold, with Lois B. Morris. Villard Bks. 1987 328p $18.95   **616.85**

1. Depression, Mental
ISBN 0-394-54039-5   LC 85-40720

A discussion of the diagnosis, treatment and prevention of depression. Brain anatomy is also examined

Includes bibliography

Goodwin, Donald W.

Anxiety. Oxford Univ. Press 1986 234p $25   **616.85**

1. Stress (Psychology)
ISBN 0-19-503665-4   LC 85-7179

This book "offers a prescriptive evaluation of recent research on anxiety disorders, including the major phobias." Libr J

"Professor Goodwin has a talent for explaining things clearly and memorably." Times Lit Suppl

Includes bibliography

Herman, Judith Lewis

Trauma and recovery. Basic Bks. 1992 276p $27   **616.85**

1. Stress (Psychology) 2. Victims of crime
ISBN 0-465-08765-5   LC 91-45346

This volume "addresses parallels between private and public traumas. Part 1 covers a . . . [series] of traumatic events, including the experiences of rape survivors, combat veterans, battered women, physically abused children, and concentration camp victims. . . . [Part 2] identifies three stages of recovery—safety, remembrance and mourning, and reconnection—which form the framework for the discourse in the second part of the book." Choice

"This book will surely become a landmark work on the social impact of psychological trauma and on its treatment." Women's Rev Books

Includes bibliographic references

Heston, Leonard L.

Mending minds; a guide to the new psychiatry of depression, anxiety, and other mental disorders. Freeman, W.H. 1992 233p $24.95; pa $13.95   **616.85**

1. Psychiatry 2. Mental illness
ISBN 0-7167-2158-9; 0-7167-2167-8 (pa)

LC 91-25061

The author discusses psychiatric illnesses and their treatment. "The diseases covered include those of mood (depression and manic depression), thought (schizophrenia and Alzheimer's disease), anxiety (obsessive-compulsive disorder and panic), drug abuse (alcohol and narcotics), and behavior (antisocial and AIDS-related activities)." Sci Books Films

Includes bibliographic references

Keyes, Daniel, 1927-

The minds of Billy Milligan. Random House 1981 374p il o.p.; Bantam Bks. paperback available $4.50   **616.85**

1. Milligan, Billy 2. Multiple personality
ISBN 0-553-26381-1 (pa)   LC 81-40229

"Billy Milligan was arrested in Ohio in 1977 on three counts of rape, but in a precedent-setting legal decision, he was found not guilty by reason of his 24 multiple personalities. Out of this bizarre case, Keyes . . . has constructed a spellbinding psychological thriller." Publ Wkly

Levenkron, Steven, 1941-

Obsessive-compulsive disorders; treating & understanding crippling habits. Warner Bks. 1991 192p $17.95; pa $10.99   **616.85**

1. Obsessive-compulsive neurosis
ISBN 0-446-51435-7; 0-446-39348-7 (pa)

LC 90-50280

The author emphasizes the role of environmental factors in the development of obsessive-compulsive disorders in children and uses case histories from his psychotherapy practice to explain therapeutic techniques

Includes bibliographic references

Levinson, Harold N.

Phobia free; a medical breakthrough linking 90% of all phobias and panic attacks to a hidden physical problem; [by] Harold N. Levinson with Steven Carter. Evans & Co. 1986 298p hardcover o.p. paperback available $8.95   **616.85**

1. Phobias 2. Stress (Psychology)
ISBN 0-87131-539-4 (pa)   LC 86-6303

"Rejecting the traditional view that phobias are a mental disorder, Levinson . . . offers strong evidence that most phobias have a physiological basis and can be treated simply and safely. Inner ear dysfunction-based phobias, according to Levinson, can be triggered by such disorders as sinus infections, mononucleosis or concussion." Publ Wkly

Includes bibliography

Matsakis, Aphrodite

Vietnam wives; women and children surviving life with veterans suffering post traumatic stress disorder. Woodbine House 1988 xxiv, 423p $16.95   **616.85**

1. Stress (Psychology) 2. Veterans 3. Vietnam War, 1961-1975
ISBN 0-933149-22-0   LC 87-51346

The author "describes post-traumatic stress disorder (PTSD) and ways it manifests itself in psychic numbness and social isolation and, more specifically, in depression, alcoholism, drug addiction and family violence. . . . The book also offers an array of coping techniques for the afflicted wives, along with suggestions on how to find professional help." Publ Wkly

Includes bibliography

Mondimore, Francis Mark, 1953-

Depression; the mood disease. rev ed. Johns Hopkins Univ. Press 1993 237p il $22.95   **616.85**

1. Depression, Mental
ISBN 0-8018-4592-0   LC 92-40513

First published 1990

Mondimore, Francis Mark, 1953- — *Continued*

The author discusses symptoms, diagnosis, and treatment of depression and mood disorders and offers advice to families

Includes bibliographic references

Papolos, Demitri F.

Overcoming depression; [by] Demitri F. Papolos and Janice Papolos. Harper & Row 1987 319p il $25; pa $13 **616.85**

1. Depression, Mental
ISBN 0-06-015756-9; 0-06-096594-0 (pa)
LC 86-46094

"In this exploration of the nature and course of depression [the authors] . . . describe an ideal approach, contrasting it with the actual treatment most patients receive. . . . A wealth of information—model treatments, resources for coping with the social implications of affective disorders, etc.—is made accessible to the layperson in a concise, clear format." Publ Wkly

Includes bibliography

Peele, Stanton

The truth about addiction and recovery; the life-process program for outgrowing destructive habits; [by] Stanton Peele, Archie Brodsky, with Mary Arnold. Simon & Schuster 1991 430p $22.95; pa $12 **616.85**

1. Compulsive behavior
ISBN 0-671-66901-X; 0-671-75530-7 (pa)
LC 90-27678

"In contrast to popular thinking, Peele and Brodsky view addiction as a problem rather than a disease. In lieu of 12-step treatment programs, they advocate 'the life process program,' which focuses on developing personal skills to moderate behavior as opposed to merely accepting addiction as an incurable disease. . . . Essential for all dependency and recovery collections." Libr J

Includes bibliographic references

Rapoport, Judith L., 1933-

The boy who couldn't stop washing; the experience & treatment of obsessive-compulsive disorder. Dutton 1989 260p $18.95 **616.85**

1. Obsessive-compulsive neurosis
ISBN 0-525-24708-4
LC 88-15014

Also available in paperback from New Am. Lib.

The author presents accounts of patients who suffer from obsessive-compulsive disorder and discusses possible causes and methods of treatment with an emphasis on the use of the drug clomipramine

This "book, with its new information and lively writing, and informed by the author's obvious compassion for her patients, makes an important contribution to understanding an intriguing and irrational illness." NY Times Book Rev

Includes bibliography

Schreiber, Flora Rheta

Sybil. Regnery Bks. 1973 350p o.p.; Warner Bks. paperback available $5.95 **616.85**

1. Multiple personality
ISBN 0-446-35940-8 (pa)

This is the "true story of Sybil I. Dorsett, a battered child possessed by 16 different personalities. . . . The author skillfully evokes Sybil's patient work during 11 years of pschoanalysis and her eventual success in integrating these selves into a unified personality." Libr J

Schwartz, Martin F., 1936-

Stutter no more. Simon & Schuster 1991 144p $18.95; pa $9 **616.85**

1. Speech disorders
ISBN 0-671-72612-9; 0-671-75504-8 (pa)   LC 91-286

The author has developed a treatment for stuttering called the "passive airflow technique" that addresses the underlying physiological cause—a locking of the vocal cords. He also describes the basic types of stuttering, lists the stresses that cause it and names famous people who were stutterers

Styron, William, 1925-

Darkness visible; a memoir of madness. Random House 1990 84p $15.95; pa $8 **616.85**

1. Depression, Mental
ISBN 0-394-58888-6; 0-679-73639-5 (pa)
LC 90-53141

Also available in large print for $17.50 (ISBN 0-679-40402-3)

This is an account of the author's experience of suicidal depression and his recovery

"The book's virtues—considerable—are twofold. First, it is a pitiless and chastened record of a nearly fatal human trial far commoner than assumed—and then a literary discourse on the ways and means of our cultural discontents." Publ Wkly

Thigpen, Corbett H.

The three faces of Eve; by Corbett H. Thigpen and Hervey M. Cleckley. McGraw-Hill 1957 38p il o.p. **616.85**

1. Multiple personality

Reprint available from Cleckley-Thigpen Psychiatric Associates

A case study of a woman suffering manifestations of multiple personality. The psychiatrist authors call their patient Eve White, Eve Black and Jane to differentiate between her three distinct personalities

Wilson, R. Reid

Don't panic; taking control of anxiety attacks. Harper & Row 1986 288p hardcover o.p. paperback available $12 **616.85**

1. Stress (Psychology) 2. Phobias
ISBN 0-06-091438-6 (pa)   LC 85-45670

The author "offers a self-help guide to those who suffer from phobias, depression, and other types of compulsive behavior. . . . Simply and clearly presented." Booklist

Includes bibliography

616.86 Substance abuse (Drug abuse)

Beattie, Melody
Beyond codependency; and getting better all the time. Harper & Row 1989 252p pa $9.95   **616.86**

1. Psychology, Applied 2. Substance abuse
ISBN 0-06-255418-2   LC 88-45986

Also available Walker & Co. large print edition

"A Harper/Hazelden book"

The author "focuses here on the process of recovering from the self-defeating behaviors adopted as survival tactics by adult children of families rendered dysfunctional by parental alcoholism or similar traumas. Beattie's strength is short, sharply delineated portraits of ordinary people learning to recognize and avoid unhealthy practices." Publ Wkly

Includes bibliographic references

Codependents' guide to the twelve steps. Prentice Hall Press 1990 273p pa $9.95   **616.86**

1. Substance abuse
ISBN 0-13-140054-1   LC 90-52819

"A Prentice Hall/Parkside book"

"Beattie offers an interpretation of the 12 steps based on her own experience as a recovering addict, codependent, and practicing therapist. This includes an excellent annotated bibliography of recovery titles." Libr J

The **Encyclopedia** of drug abuse; [edited by] Robert O'Brien [et al.] 2nd ed. Facts on File 1992 xxvii, 500p il $45   **616.86**

1. Drug abuse—Dictionaries
ISBN 0-8160-1956-8   LC 89-71531

First published 1984

Over 500 entries provide facts about the medical, legal, social, and biological aspects of drug abuse
For a review see: Booklist, Feb. 15, 1992

Farquhar, John W., 1927-
The last puff; ex-smokers share the secrets of their success; [by] John W. Farquhar, Gene A. Spiller. Norton 1990 252p $18.95; pa $9.95   **616.86**

1. Tobacco habit
ISBN 0-393-02789-9; 0-393-30803-0 (pa)
     LC 89-16182

"Thirty interviews—including Patrick Reynolds, the grandson of R. J. Reynolds, and actress Celeste Holm—describe how smokers get started, the tricks they use to break the habit, and how they feel after successfully kicking the evil weed. Farquhar and Spiller discuss addiction and what happens in the body once nicotine is removed from the system." Booklist

Mann, Peggy
Marijuana alert. McGraw-Hill 1985 526p il o.p. paperback available $10.95   **616.86**

1. Marijuana
ISBN 0-07-039906-9 (pa)   LC 84-4398

The author writes "about the use, abuse, and harmful effects of marijuana. Crowded with facts and figures, the book explores marijuana use in all segments of society; what has been done historically to combat its use; and what is being done now to prevent its use in the armed forces, schools, the workplace, and society as a whole." Libr J

Includes bibliography

Mueller, L. Ann, 1942-
Recovering; how to get and stay sober; [by] L. Ann Mueller and Katherine Ketcham. Bantam Bks. 1987 303p il pa $9.95   **616.86**

1. Alcoholism
ISBN 0-553-34303-3   LC 86-32088

The authors "emphasize the genetic etiology of alcoholism and explain how alcoholics and their families can get help. . . . They describe the various stages of treatment and recovery and outline a nutrition program for the postdetoxification period. An excellent guide to a pervasive problem." Booklist

Includes bibliography

Viscusi, W. Kip
Smoking; making the risky decision. Oxford Univ. Press 1992 170p il $24.95   **616.86**

1. Smoking 2. Tobacco habit
ISBN 0-19-507486-6   LC 91-47138

"Using new empirical data based on several national and regional surveys, Viscusi addresses several issues, including: the sources of information that people have about the risks of smoking, the accuracy of their perceptions of risks associated with smoking, and the consistency of smoking decisions with other risky behavior." Univ Press Books for Public and Second Sch Libr

Includes bibliographic references

Weiss, Roger D., 1951-
Cocaine; [by] Roger D. Weiss and Steven M. Mirin. American Psychiatric Press Corp. 1987 178p $19.50   **616.86**

1. Cocaine 2. Substance abuse
ISBN 0-88048-216-8   LC 86-17245

This is a discussion of cocaine, its history, and the effects of cocaine use

Includes bibliography

616.89 Mental disorders

Ablow, Keith R.

To wrestle with demons; a psychiatrist struggles to understand his patients and himself; by Keith Russell Ablow; foreword by Robert Coles; illustrations by Richard Downs. American Psychiatric Press 1992 158p il $17.95 **616.89**

1. Psychiatry
ISBN 0-88048-546-9 LC 92-10468

"In these 25 three to four-page essays, all but one of which first appeared in the *Washington Post*, Ablow writes of his training; of such mental illnesses as depression, mania, and schizophrenia; and of such treatments as Prozac and ECT." Booklist

Berger, Diane, 1942-

We heard the angels of madness; one family's struggle with manic depression; [by] Diane and Lisa Berger; foreword by Alexander Vuckovic. Morrow 1991 308p $19.95; pa $10 **616.89**

1. Depression, Mental
ISBN 0-688-09178-4; 0-688-11615-9 (pa)
LC 90-48215

"The 'angels of madness' are the voices that Mark Berger, a manic depressive, heard during his manic episodes. They also represent the emotional upheaval his family experienced when they learned of his illness. Mark's mother, Diane, and her sister, Lisa, alternate their personal story with care-giving advice and specifics about the disease." Libr J

Includes bibliographic references

The **Columbia** University College of Physicians and Surgeons complete home guide to mental health; health editors, Frederic I. Kass, John M. Oldham, Herbert Pardes; editorial director, Lois B. Morris; managing editor, Ellen Watson. Holt & Co. 1992 476p il $35 **616.89**

1. Mental illness 2. Psychiatry
ISBN 0-8050-0724-5 LC 92-1534

"A G.S. Sharpe Communications, Inc. Publication"

"Four broad sections cover mental illness assessment and treatment, common problems and disorders among adults, common problems and disorders among children and adolescents, and special issues and problems. The chapters within these divisions are written by experts and contain an impressive amount of accessible information. Subjects include, but are not limited to, the therapeutic use of drugs, eating and sleep disorders, aging, suicide, AIDS, and ethical issues." Libr J

Duke, Patty

A brilliant madness; living with manic-depressive illness; [by] Patty Duke and Gloria Hochman. Bantam Bks. 1992 285p $22.50 **616.89**

1. Manic-depressive psychoses
ISBN 0-553-07256-0 LC 92-5878

This work "alternates between the actress's first-person description of her experiences as a manic-depressive and Ms. Hochman's informative narrative about this sickness.

. . . Ms. Duke is a comforting guide through the terror of mental illness, and Ms. Hochman lightens a weighty topic with interesting, animated writing." N Y Times Book Rev

Includes bibliographic references

Masson, J. Moussaieff (Jeffrey Moussaieff), 1941-

Final analysis; the making and unmaking of a psychoanalyst; [by] Jeffrey Moussaieff Masson. Addison-Wesley 1990 212p $18.22 **616.89**

1. Psychoanalysis
ISBN 0-201-52368-X LC 90-38639

Also available in paperback from HarperCollins Pubs.

In this work the author condemns "the whole practice of psychoanalysis—and, by extension, psychotherapy . . . by holding up his own training analysis as an example of all that's wrong with the field, even going so far as to call orthodox Freudian psychoanalysis a 'cult.'" Booklist

This is "is a terrific story; full of passion, insight, wit and revelation." N Y Times Book Rev

May, Rollo

The cry for myth. Norton 1990 320p $22.95 **616.89**

1. Mythology 2. Psychotherapy
ISBN 0-393-02768-6 LC 90-30451

Also available in paperback from Delacorte Press

May "directs our attention to the psychology of our culture by providing a distinctly American portrait of the place—and displacements—of myth in our society. As is customary for this author, the text weaves case studies and considerable literary exegesis into his cogent analyses." Libr J

Menninger, Karl A. (Karl Augustus), 1893-1990

Man against himself. Harcourt Brace & Co. 1938 485p hardcover o.p. paperback available $10.95 **616.89**

1. Psychology, Pathological 2. Suicide 3. Psychoanalysis
ISBN 0-15-656514-5 (pa)

A study of suicide and the self-destructive instinct underlying certain mental diseases and physical states

Minuchin, Salvador

Family healing; tales of hope and renewal from family therapy; [by] Salvador Minuchin, Michael P. Nichols. Free Press 1992 287p $22.95 **616.89**

1. Psychotherapy 2. Domestic relations
ISBN 0-02-921295-2 LC 92-23854

Family therapist Minuchin "presents nine case studies of families he has worked with. These histories represent four topics: couples, parents and children, remarriage, and aging. As the details of family therapy unfold, the reader is given a rare look at the amazingly adaptive and intricate mechanisms of relationships." Libr J

Porter, Roy, 1946-
A social history of madness; the world through the eyes of the insane. Weidenfeld & Nicolson 1988 c1987 261p $18.95
616.89

1. Mental illness
ISBN 1-55584-185-6   LC 87-33979
First published 1987 in the United Kingdom
This work explores "the writings of insane persons, mostly over the past two or three hundred years, in Europe and the United States as well as in Britain. Its guiding principle is that these outpourings are in their way coherent utterances, just as capable of historical interpretation as the writings of the sane." Times Lit Suppl
"Porter's nonpolemical but measured critical stance and credible reassessments make for enjoyable reading." Libr J
Includes bibliography

Rogers, Carl R. (Carl Ransom), 1902-1987
On becoming a person; a therapist's view of psychotherapy. Houghton Mifflin 1961 420p hardcover o.p. paperback available $8.70
616.89

1. Psychotherapy
ISBN 0-395-08409-1 (pa)
This collection begins with "two talks in which Dr. Rogers gives some biographical data and outlines his progress toward his concept of client-centered therapy; succeeding chapters express his views on helping others toward personal growth, the therapeutic process, his philosophy of the fully functioning person, the place of research in psychotherapy, its implications for living and the new discipline of behavioral sciences." Booklist
Includes bibliography

Seager, Stephen B.
Psychward; a year behind locked doors. Putnam 1991 249p o.p.; Berkley Pub. Group paperback available $4.99
616.89

1. Psychiatry
ISBN 0-425-13297-8 (pa)   LC 90-49911
This is an account of the author's year of internship in a Los Angeles psychiatric hospital
"Seager provides a number of sympathetic profiles of both patients and personnel, infusing the often horrific narrative with compassion, respect, and humanity. A sensitive and riveting firsthand account of the overburdened and understaffed mental-healthcare system." Booklist

Torrey, E. Fuller (Edwin Fuller)
Surviving schizophrenia; a family manual. rev ed. Harper & Row 1988 460p hardcover o.p. paperback available $13
616.89

1. Schizophrenia
ISBN 0-06-096249-6 (pa)   LC 87-45673
First published 1983
A "description of the nature, causes, symptoms, and treatment of schizophrenia." Publisher's note
Includes bibliography

Walsh, Maryellen
Schizophrenia; straight talk for family and friends. Morrow 1985 264p $17.95; pa $9.75
616.89

1. Schizophrenia
ISBN 0-688-04178-7; 0-688-12580-8 (pa)
                    LC 84-20558
"Walsh, the relative of a schizophrenic, explains symptoms, diagnosis, causes, and treatment, while focusing on how family members can deal with the problem and keep a productive family environment going. This quite personal account . . . is reliable without being overly clinical" Booklist
Includes bibliography

Weinberg, George H.
Nearer to the heart's desire; tales of psychotherapy; [by] George Weinberg. Grove Press 1992 237p $22.50
616.89

1. Psychotherapy
ISBN 0-8021-1471-7   LC 91-39386
A psychotherapist "presents eight cases, fictionalized from his own practice, in which he describes both the patients' conditions and his own reasoning and feelings. . . . These well-written, understanding stories of the lives of mentally or emotionally tortured human beings should appeal to many diverse readers." Booklist

Williams, Donna
Nobody nowhere; the extraordinary autobiography of an autistic. Times Bks. 1992 219p il $20.50
616.89

1. Autism
ISBN 0-8129-2042-2   LC 92-53669
In this autobiography, the author discusses her autism and chronicles her life from early childhood through to her mid-twenties
The author's "insights will help 'translate' autistic behaviors for researchers, parents, and therapists working to help autistic people make the painful transition to 'the world.'" Choice

Yalom, Irvin D., 1931-
Love's executioner and other tales of psychotherapy. Basic Bks. 1989 270p $19.95
616.89

1. Psychotherapy
ISBN 0-465-04280-5   LC 89-42522
Also available in paperback from HarperCollins Pubs.
The author presents case studies of some of the clients with whom he has worked as a psychiatrist
This "book moves at the pace of a suspense thriller, with each chapter providing a fascinating look at the patient-therapist relationship." Libr J

616.9 Other diseases

Benzaia, Diana

Protect yourself from Lyme disease; the New York Medical College guide to prevention, detection, and treatment; foreword by John J. Connolly; afterword by Durland Fish. Dell 1989 118p pa $4.99

616.9

1. Lyme disease
ISBN 0-440-20437-2   LC 89-170494

A look at the cause, diagnosis and treatment of lyme disease

"This pocket paperback is the first for the layperson on this important disease and is highly recommended; it is clear, informative, and reasonable." Libr J

616.97 Diseases of the immune system

AIDS and the law; a guide for the public; edited by Harlon L. Dalton, Scott Burris and the Yale AIDS Law Project. Yale Univ. Press 1987 382p $35; pa $12

616.97

1. AIDS (Disease)
ISBN 0-300-04077-6; 0-300-04078-4 (pa)
    LC 87-50492

"This collection of articles addresses legal issues surrounding AIDS. . . . Each section is extensively documented. This is a unique contribution to the literature." Libr J

Includes bibliography

AIDS in the world; [by] The Global AIDS Policy Coalition, Jonathan Mann, general editor; Daniel J.M. Tarantola, scientific editor; Thomas W. Netter, managing editor. Harvard Univ. Press 1992 1037p il $45; pa $22.95   **616.97**

1. AIDS (Disease)
ISBN 0-674-01265-8; 0-674-01266-6 (pa)   LC 92-1545

"The first book ever written on worldwide AIDS . . . in which mountains of data were organized into fantastic illustrations and tables. . . . The authors succeed in bringing international concepts to readers on strategy, research, training, prevention, and care." Choice

Includes bibliographic references

The **AIDS** information sourcebook; edited by H. Robert Malinowsky and Gerald J. Perry. Oryx Press pa $39.95   **616.97**

1. AIDS (Disease)

First published 1988. (3rd edition 1991) Frequently revised

This reference work "lists treatment and counseling centers, information sources, and drugs for AIDS, with a bibliography and other information." Recomm Ref Books in Paperback. 2d edition

Altman, Dennis

AIDS in the mind of America. Anchor Press/Doubleday 1986 228p hardcover o.p. paperback available $8.95   **616.97**

1. AIDS (Disease)
ISBN 0-385-19524-9 (pa)   LC 85-15055

The author "discussess the AIDS epidemic as it affects both the gay community and the views of heterosexuals on sex, disease, medicine and death." Publ Wkly

Includes bibliography

Callaway, C. Wayne

Surviving with AIDS; a revolutionary program of nutritional co-therapy; by C. Wayne Callaway with Catherine Whitney; food plans designed by Kristine Mehring. Little, Brown 1991 192p il pa $14.95

616.97

1. AIDS (Disease) 2. Diet in disease
ISBN 0-316-12467-2   LC 90-13679

"The authors discuss the dietary problems of AIDS patients and suggest practical ways to overcome them. They also provide a nutritional inventory, guidelines for eating to reduce various symptoms, and information on easy food preparation and dining out, in addition to specialized food plans, daily menus, recipes, and information on liquid formulas and tube feeding." Libr J

Includes bibliographic references

Cohen, Donna

The loss of self; a family resource for the care of Alzheimer's disease and related disorders; [by] Donna Cohen, Carl Eisdorfer. Norton 1986 381p $19.95   **616.97**

1. Alzheimer's disease
ISBN 0-393-02263-3   LC 85-15515

Also available in paperback from New Am. Lib.

This book examines the "criteria for recognizing serious memory problems, obtaining a thorough diagnosis, working effectively with a patient, dealing with financial and legal problems, and institutionalizing a patient." Choice

Includes bibliography

Gallo, Robert C.

Virus hunting; AIDS, cancer, and the human retrovirus: a story of scientific discovery. Basic Bks. 1991 352p $22.95; pa $13   **616.97**

1. AIDS (Disease) 2. Medicine—Research
ISBN 0-465-09806-1; 0-465-09815-0 (pa)
    LC 90-55600

"A New Republic book"

The author describes his biomedical research of the cancer-causing retrovirus, how it led to the discovery of the AIDS virus, and the political and ethical controversies surrounding AIDS research

Gershwin, M. Eric, 1946-

Conquering your child's allergies; [by] M. Eric Gershwin, Edwin L. Klingelhofer. Addison-Wesley 1989 xxii, 250p il $18.22; pa $9.57   **616.97**

1. Allergy
ISBN 0-201-12967-1; 0-201-52340-X (pa)

LC 88-29248

This is a "comprehensive guide to allergic symptoms, the variety of allergic 'triggers' (foods, colds, effluents, insect bites, etc.), the common allergic diseases, and how to get effective, long-term care." Booklist

Grmek, Mirko D.

History of AIDS; emergence and origin of a modern pandemic; translated by Russell C. Maulitz and Jacalyn Duffin. Princeton Univ. Press 1990 279p $29.95   **616.97**

1. AIDS (Disease)
ISBN 0-691-08552-8   LC 90-32514

Original French edition, 1989

In this "medical and social history of the disease, Dr. Grmek . . . speculates about the prehistory of AIDS, before its seemingly sudden appearance from nowhere in 1981. He argues that while today's runaway epidemic is a new phenomenon, the viruses that cause AIDS have infected people for many decades, if not for centuries." N Y Times Book Rev

Includes bibliography

Joseph, Stephen C.

Dragon within the gates; the once and future AIDS epidemic. Carroll & Graf Pubs. 1992 272p $20.95   **616.97**

1. AIDS (Disease)
ISBN 0-88184-905-7

"Convinced that 'society, acting through public health, has a right and a duty to protect itself, even at the price of depriving an individual of liberty,' Joseph argues persuasively for quarantine, contact tracing, mandatory reporting, voluntary testing, and needle exchange and condom distribution programs." Libr J

Includes bibliography

Langone, John, 1929-

AIDS: the facts. rev & updated. Little, Brown 1991 266p pa $10.95   **616.97**

1. AIDS (Disease)
ISBN 0-316-51414-4   LC 90-25072

First published 1988

This book describes the symptoms of AIDS, the AIDS virus and its origins, methods of transmission, and the latest medical research, and examines the limitations and advantages of testing methods now being used to detect the virus

Includes bibliographic references

Masters, William H.

CRISIS; heterosexual behavior in the age of AIDS; [by] William H. Masters, Virginia E. Johnson, Robert C. Kolodny. Grove Press 1988 243p $15.95   **616.97**

1. AIDS (Disease)
ISBN 0-8021-1049-5   LC 87-37175

The authors offer "an unequivocal warning to America's heterosexuals that AIDS may soon hit them as hard or harder than it has gays. . . . This is the most cogent and cautious AIDS polemic to date and a major contribution to public policy discussions of the epidemic." Booklist

Includes bibliography

Mobilizing against AIDS; [by] Institute of Medicine, National Academy of Science; Eve K. Nichols, [writer] rev & enl ed. Harvard Univ. Press 1989 387p il $27.50; pa $12.95   **616.97**

1. AIDS (Disease)
ISBN 0-674-57763-9; 0-674-57762-0 (pa)

LC 88-30100

First published 1986

This book discusses "the epidemic, the spectrum of the disease, the effects of HIV on the body, and the best ways to prevent its transmission. . . . Also included are sections on the discovery of the virus, the effectiveness of drugs (limited) and the possibilities of a vaccine (some time in the future), the psychological and social effects of AIDS on an individual and the family, and the impact of AIDS on the health care system." Sci Books Films

Includes bibliography

Orenstein, Neil S.

Food allergies; how to tell if you have them; what to do about them if you do; [by] Neil S. Orenstein and Sarah L. Bingham. Putnam 1987 161p pa $9.95   **616.97**

1. Food allergy
ISBN 0-399-51383-3   LC 87-10926

"A Perigee book"

"Anxiety, digestive disorders, behavioral problems in children, headaches, and fatigue—all can be common symptoms of food allergies. Orenstein and Bingham endorse the Simplification Diet Program as a remedy, which eliminates the most common allergy-producing foods from the diet, then 'challenges' the body by reintroducing the individual foods in two-day intervals." Booklist

Includes bibliography

616.99   Tumors and cancers

Altman, Roberta

The cancer dictionary; [by] Roberta Altman, Michael Sarg. Facts on File 1992 334p il $40   **616.99**

1. Cancer—Dictionaries
ISBN 0-8160-2608-4   LC 91-46941

"Intended for the nonspecialist, the *Cancer Dictionary* contains virtually every term the cancer patient is likely to encounter in the course of investigation, diagnosis, and treatment. Ranging from a few sentences to several

Altman, Roberta—*Continued*
paragraphs in length, the 2,500 entries define for the layperson types of cancer, symptoms, tests, therapies, and surgical procedures." Am Libr

Includes bibliographic references

The **American** Cancer Society cancer book; prevention, detection, diagnosis, treatment, rehabilitation, cure; editor, Arthur I. Holleb; associate editors, Genell J. Subak-Sharpe, William H. White, Philip Kasofsky; illustrator, Robin Lazarus. Doubleday 1986 xxii, 650p il $24.95
616.99

1. Cancer
ISBN 0-385-17847-6   LC 85-25318

This reference work is intended to "educate the public about cancer by providing information regarding early detection and prevention. Each chapter is written by a specialist who describes a particular aspect of cancer. The first half of the book discusses cancer's psychological impact on patients as well as what cancer therapy entails. In part 2, the contributors consider specific cancers and their diagnosis, treatment, and prevention based on current research." Booklist

Cancer sourcebook; edited by Frank E. Bair. Omnigraphics 1990 932p il $75 **616.99**
1. Cancer
ISBN 1-55888-888-8   LC 90-166195

"Basic information on cancer types, symptoms, diagnostic methods, and treatments, including statistics on cancer occurrences worldwide and the risks associated with known carcinogens and activities." Title page

"This reference tool has been specifically created for the nontechnical reader searching for current information about the diagnosis of, and therapies for, various forms of this disease. This volume is a compilation of 37 bulletins, papers, and booklets published between January 1986 and July 1989 by the branches of the National Institutes of Health, particularly the National Cancer Institute." Am Ref Books Annu, 1991

Includes bibliographic references

The **Complete** book of cancer prevention; foods, lifestyles & medical care to keep you healthy; by the editors of Prevention magazine health books. Rodale Press 1988 562p $27.95; pa $16.95 **616.99**
1. Cancer
ISBN 0-87857-740-8; 0-87857-874-9 (pa)
                            LC 87-26594

This guide "first reviews current medical thinking regarding 19 different 'lifestyle cancers' and then examines various risk factors and their connection with particular carcinomas. Further material offers advice on planning an anticancer program, including a discussion of modern treatment methods, nontraditional alternatives among them." Booklist

Dollinger, Malin
Everyone's guide to cancer therapy; [by] Malin Dollinger, Ernest H. Rosenbaum, and Greg Cable. Andrews & McMeel 1991 xxiii, 624p il $29.95; pa $19.95 **616.99**
1. Cancer
ISBN 0-8362-2418-3; 0-8362-2417-5 (pa) LC 91-8397
"A Somerville House book"

This guide "allows its readers to grasp the complexities of diagnosis, of deciding on appropriate therapy, and of the procedures and outcomes of surgery, radiation therapy, and chemotherapy. . . . The lengthy section on treatment for more than 40 specific cancers is contributed to by a host of experts. Each entry in it covers the risk factors, screening test, symptoms, diagnosis, and treatment processes for that particular cancer and concludes with a short list of questions to ask a physician about the disease." Booklist

"This authoritative but readable reference stands out in the literature as a uniquely comprehensive, thorough source of up-to-date information." Libr J

Includes bibliographic references

Hirshaut, Yashar
Breast cancer; the complete guide; [by] Yashar Hirshaut and Peter I. Pressman. Bantam Bks. 1992 322p il $24.50 **616.99**
1. Breast—Diseases 2. Cancer
ISBN 0-553-08960-9   LC 92-7576

This guide "gives comprehensive, up-to-date, and highly detailed information on everything from the first suspicion, through diagnosis and treatments, to follow-up care and recurrence." Libr J

Kaye, Ronnie
Spinning straw into gold; your emotional recovery from breast cancer. Simon & Schuster 1991 218p pa $9.95 **616.99**
1. Breast—Diseases 2. Cancer
ISBN 0-671-70164-9   LC 90-10238
"A Fireside book"

The author discusses problems "that arise during the treatment and recovery process, which she outlines in sections dealing with diagnosis and various treatments, emotional and body issues, and finally, how a woman relates to the world around her during recovery." Booklist

Includes bibliographic references

Laszlo, John, 1931-
Understanding cancer. Harper & Row 1987 305p il hardcover o.p. paperback available $8.95 **616.99**
1. Cancer
ISBN 0-06-091491-2 (pa)   LC 86-46079

The author describes the many types of cancer, explains various treatment options and points out risk factors related to life-style, smoking, diet, etc.

"This comprehensive discussion of the physical and psychological aspects of cancer should prove useful to patients and their families." Booklist

Includes bibliography

Lerner, Max, 1902-1992
Wrestling with the angel; a memoir of my triumph over illness. Norton 1990 210p $18.95 **616.99**
1. Cancer
ISBN 0-393-02846-1   LC 89-26503
Also available in paperback from Simon & Schuster

"Drawing on his diaries, noted journalist, teacher and writer Lerner here narrates and meditates on how, starting at age 78, he survived two bouts of cancer and a

Lerner, Max, 1902-1992—*Continued*

heart attack—all within five years. Though giving most of the credit for this feat to his fortunate access to sophisticated medical therapy, Lerner also made a mighty effort to retain his 'selfhood' and control his options." Publ Wkly

"A keen, analytic observer, this feisty octogenarian offers many unique perspectives in discussing illness, the healing process, aging, and death. A remarkable zest for living emerges in this book." Libr J

Includes bibliography

LeShan, Lawrence L., 1920-

Cancer as a turning point; a handbook for people with cancer, their families, and health professionals; [by] Lawrence LeShan. Dutton 1989 207p o.p.; New Am. Lib. paperback available $10   **616.99**

1. Cancer 2. Holistic medicine
ISBN 0-452-26419-7 (pa)   LC 88-30978

The author counsels "readers on how to realize their self-healing abilities by employing methods dramatized here in case histories. The book details strategies to promote psychological change and teaches techniques (active visualization, classical meditation) that encourage cancer victims to fight the disease." Publ Wkly

Includes bibliography

Murcia, Andy

Man to man; when the woman you love has breast cancer; [by] Andy Murcia and Bob Stewart. St. Martin's Press 1989 220p il hardcover o.p. paperback available $10.95
616.99

1. Breast—Diseases 2. Cancer
ISBN 0-312-04347-3 (pa)   LC 88-30563

The authors, both married to women who have had breast cancer, describe coping with the disease from the husband's point of view

"In this frank volume, the authors offer support to other men and, perhaps more importantly, tell them how they can support their wives." Booklist

Includes bibliography

Nessim, Susan

Cancervive; the challenge of life after cancer; [by] Susan Nessim and Judith Ellis. Houghton Mifflin 1991 xxii, 264p hardcover o.p. paperback available $8.70   **616.99**

1. Cancer
ISBN 0-395-62432-0 (pa)   LC 91-7710

Also available Wheeler Pub. large print edition

Based on the experiences of members of Cancervive, a nationwide support group for survivors of cancer. This offers advice on dealing with problems faced by cancer survivors including ostracism, infertility, fear of recurrence, obtaining medical insurance, job discrimination, and emotional problems

Includes bibliographic references

Reich, Paul Richard

The facts about chemotherapy; a guide for cancer patients and their families; [by] Paul R. Reich with Janice E. Metcalf. Consumer Repts. Bks. 1991 212p $19.95   **616.99**

1. Cancer 2. Chemotherapy
ISBN 0-89043-206-6   LC 90-20256

The author addresses "concerns that emerge when chemotherapy is prescribed: how cancer drugs are developed; what the drugs can and can't accomplish; how to choose and evaluate physicians, treatment centers, and treatment plans; how to interpret survival and cure rates; what should be considered before participating in research programs; and what is involved in refusing or discontinuing treatment." Publisher's note

Includes bibliography

Rosenberg, Steven A.

The transformed cell; unlocking the mysteries of cancer; [by] Steven A. Rosenberg and John M. Barry. Putnam 1992 353p il $24.95   **616.99**

1. Cancer 2. Medicine—Research
ISBN 0-399-13749-1   LC 92-11864

Also available in paperback from Avon Bks.

Rosenberg "details the years of clinical and laboratory research that led to his developing the controversial cancer therapy using interleukin-2 (IL-2), a protein produced by the human immune system and synthesized in the lab." Publ Wkly

"A story that will fascinate adults who have been exposed directly or indirectly to one of the many forms of cancer and motivate active-minded students who have not yet chosen a career but want to do something to make their—and others'—lives worthwhile." Booklist

Royak-Schaler, Renee, 1946-

Challenging the breast cancer legacy; a program of emotional support and medical care for women at risk; [by] Renee Royak-Schaler and Beryl Lieff Benderly. HarperCollins Pubs. 1992 257p $20; pa $10
616.99

1. Breast—Diseases 2. Cancer
ISBN 0-06-016625-8; 0-06-092373-3 (pa)
LC 91-50449

"What makes this book unique is its intended audience: women *at risk* for breast cancer, not those *with* it. Based on studies at the Georgetown University Comprehensive Breast Center, this guide makes a valuable and timely contribution to high-risk women by offering a systematic program of medical and emotional self-care that focuses on, among other things, early detection, diet, exercise, and methods for reducing risk of the disease." Libr J

Includes bibliographic references

Williams, Chris

Lung cancer; the facts. 2nd ed. Oxford Univ. Press 1992 148p il map $21.95
616.99

1. Lungs—Diseases 2. Cancer
ISBN 0-19-262251-X   LC 91-46202

"Oxford medical publications"

First published 1984

Williams, Chris—*Continued*

This volume provides "answers to questions commonly asked by patients with lung cancer, including queries about the causes, diagnosis, and progression of the disease. It also describes curative and symptomatic treatments available for the different types of lung cancer." Univ Press Books for Public and Second Sch Libr

Includes bibliographic references

617 Miscellaneous branches of medicine. Surgery

Bean, Constance A.

The better back book; simple exercises for the prevention and care of back pain. Morrow 1989 232p il hardcover o.p. paperback available $7.95   **617**

1. Backache

ISBN 0-688-10003-1 (pa)   LC 88-12925

Following an explanation of the causes of back pain the author details an exercise program for strengthening back muscles

Includes bibliography

Levine, Suzanne M.

My feet are killing me! Dr. Levine's complete footcare program. McGraw-Hill 1987 213p il $15.95   **617**

1. Podiatry

ISBN 0-07-037458-9   LC 86-19985

Also available in paperback from Fawcett Bks.

"A podiatrist, Levine cogently discusses how to prevent life-style from ruining one's feet. . . . Corns, calluses, bunions, and blisters are just some of the conditions that the author discusses and, when appropriate, she provides suggestions for home remedies. In addition, Levine reviews over-the-counter products." Booklist

Pritt, Donald S.

The complete foot book; [by] Donald S. Pritt, Morton Walker. Avery Pub. Group 1992 162p il pa $12.95   **617**

1. Podiatry

ISBN 0-89529-434-6   LC 91-33326

"A Dr. Morton Walker health book"

"After a brief, illustrated introduction to basic foot physiology and care and to footwear selection, the [authors] devote separate chapters to such common complaints as bunions, hammertoes, athlete's foot, toenail problems, corns, calluses, and warts. A lucid description of each is accompanied by discussion of causes and of self-help and physician-assisted treatments. . . . A well-rounded effort that avoids technical medical jargon and confusing terminology." Booklist

Root, Leon

No more aching back; Dr. Root's new, fifteen-minute-a-day program for a healthy back; illustrations by Elisa Root. Villard Bks. 1990 xxii, 215p il $17.95   **617**

1. Backache 2. Exercise

ISBN 0-394-58794-4   LC 90-12090

Also available in paperback from New Am. Lib.

The author explains "how back pain is evaluated (diagnostic tests and treatments), how the back works, the kinds and causes of back pain. . . . He counsels on how to minimize the risk of back injury in everyday life. His 15-minute-a-day program, with clear line drawings that demonstrate techniques, spells out a series of exercises designed to strengthen the back." Booklist

Schommer, Nancy

Stopping scoliosis. Doubleday 1987 183p il $16.95   **617**

1. Scoliosis 2. Spine—Surgery

ISBN 0-385-23386-8   LC 87-546

Also available in paperback from Avery Pub. Group

This guide to diagnosis and treatment of scoliosis discusses surgical and nonsurgical treatments and current research and stresses the importance of early detection

Includes bibliography

Scott, Judith, 1937-

Good-bye to bad backs; stretching and strengthening exercises for alignment and freedom from lower back pain; foreword by Richard M. Bachrach; photographs by John Vidol; line drawings by David Chevtaikin. 2nd ed. Princeton 1993 269p il $16.95   **617**

1. Backache 2. Exercise

ISBN 0-87127-186-9   LC 92-34672

"A Dance Horizons book"

First published 1988 by Scribner

An illustrated program of exercises designed to stretch lower back muscles to help alleviate pain. Includes advice on better posture, relaxation and stress reduction

Includes bibliographic references

White, Augustus A.

Your aching back; a doctor's guide to relief. Simon & Schuster 1990 332p il hardcover o.p. paperback available $9.95   **617**

1. Backache

ISBN 0-671-71000-1 (pa)   LC 90-9879

"A Fireside book"

A revised edition of the title first published 1983 by Bantam Bks.

An orthopedic surgeon offers advice on preventing and relieving back pain

The author's "focus is on incapacitating pain, usually caused by a verifiable disc disorder. Sufferers with less severe or purely muscular backaches are not often considered, but they may find White's many general recommendations, including furniture specifications, exercises and low-risk sexual positions, quite helpful." Publ Wkly

Includes bibliographic references

617.1 Wounds and injuries

Duff, John F.

Youth sports injuries; a medical handbook for parents and coaches. Collier Bks. 1992 366p il pa $12 **617.1**

1. Sports medicine
ISBN 0-02-013691-9 LC 91-37789

The author "includes first-aid information for 13 of the most common injuries as well as an exhaustive 'Head to Toe' ailment inventory that briefly describes injury symptoms and causes along with what can be done to prevent recurrence." Booklist

Includes bibliography

Restoring the body; treating aches and injuries. Time-Life Bks. 1987 144p il (Fitness, health & nutrition) $17.27
617.1

1. Sports medicine 2. Exercise LC 87-33523

Discusses causes of injury, methods of prevention, exercises designed to strengthen different muscle groups, and suggestions for equipment, first-aid, and tips for fluid replacement during exercise and eating properly

Sheehan, George

Dr. George Sheehan's Medical advice for runners; by George A. Sheehan. World Publs. 1978 303p il $11.95 **617.1**

1. Physical fitness 2. Running 3. Sports medicine
ISBN 0-89037-134-2 LC 78-55788

"In this question-and-answer format, there is a wealth of sensible advice directed both to novice runners and marathon men and women preventing injuries, recognizing symptoms, and seeking professional care. Moreover, much of this information applies to other sports as well." Booklist

617.6 Dentistry

Friedman, Jay W.

Complete guide to dental health; how to avoid being overcharged and overtreated; [by] Jay W. Friedman and the editors of Consumer Reports Books. Consumer Repts. Bks. 1991 307p il $22.95 **617.6**

1. Dentistry 2. Consumer education
ISBN 0-89043-436-0 LC 90-27157

The author provides information and treatment guidelines for the following: lifetime dental health; dental caries; common diseases of the gum and soft tissues of the mouth; chronic destructive periodontal disease; cosmetic dentistry and orthodontics; replacement of missing teeth; endodontics; oral surgery; drugs and anesthetics; how to choose a good dentist; financing dental care

Includes bibliographic references

Taintor, Jerry F.

The oral report; the consumer's common-sense guide to better dental care; by Jerry F. Taintor with Mary Jane Taintor. Facts on File 1988 194p il $18.95 **617.6**

1. Dentistry 2. Consumer education
ISBN 0-8160-1392-6 LC 87-15446

The author explains "dental terminology, then outlines a program of self-care designed to prevent common problems. In addition, the text describes more specialized services including endontics, orthodontics, and prosthodontics. Financing dental services and the average fees charged for particular services are also discussed." Booklist

617.7 Ophthalmology

Anshel, Jeffrey

Healthy eyes, better vision; everyday eye care for the whole family. Body Press (Los Angeles) 1990 276p il pa $12.95 **617.7**

1. Eye
ISBN 0-89586-868-7 LC 90-531

This guide to eye care includes advice on eye protection, nutrition, how to identify eye problems, when to see an eye doctor, and choosing glasses and contact lenses

Includes bibliographic references

Eden, John

The physician's guide to cataracts, glaucoma, and other eye problems; [by] John Eden and the editors of Consumer Reports Books. Consumer Repts. Bks. 1992 312p il $18.95 **617.7**

1. Eye—Diseases 2. Cataract 3. Glaucoma
ISBN 0-89043-425-5 LC 92-7413

"In addition to presenting a comprehensive discussion of diagnosis and treatment for both cataracts and glaucoma, Eden provides basic information about other eye disorders and eye care. . . . Solid, up-to-date, comprehensive information about eye problems and their treatment." Booklist

Seiderman, Arthur

20/20 is not enough; the new world of vision; [by] Arthur S. Seiderman and Steven E. Marcus, in collaboration with David Hapgood. Knopf 1989 196p il $18.95
617.7

1. Vision disorders 2. Vision
ISBN 0-394-57103-7 LC 89-45269

Also available in paperback from Fawcett Bks.

The authors "discuss the promise of vision therapy, the nonsurgical treatment of vision disorders such as nearsightedness, vision-based learning disabilities, and strabismus. Remarkable case histories illustrate that vision—as opposed to sight—is a learned activity; hence, people of all ages can be trained to have better vision skills for reading, driving, video display terminal use, sports, and general health through exercises, biofeedback, and other methods." Libr J

Includes bibliography

617.8 Otology and audiology

Turkington, Carol
The encyclopedia of deafness and hearing disorders; [by] Carol Turkington and Allen E. Sussman. Facts on File 1992 278p il $45
617.8

1. Deafness—Dictionaries 2. Ear—Diseases
ISBN 0-8160-2267-4　　　LC 91-16451

"A comprehensive overview of deafness and hearing disorders, this reference work by known experts in their field focuses on medical topics and technical terms that pertain to the deaf community as a separate culture. Over 500 entries are organized in an A-Z format." Libr J

For a fuller review see: Booklist, April 1, 1992

617.9 Transplantation of tissue and organs

Dowie, Mark
We have a donor; the bold new world of organ transplants. St. Martin's Press 1988 242p $16.95
617.9

1. Transplantation of organs, tissues, etc.
ISBN 0-312-02316-2　　　LC 88-17650

This book examines the ethical and scientific aspects of organ transplantation

"The often gory details are not for the fainthearted; nevertheless, Dowie has written a fascinating and informative survey of a topic that remains, provocatively, in the public eye." Booklist

Gutkind, Lee
Many sleepless nights; the world of organ transplantation. Norton 1988 367p o.p.; University of Pittsburgh Press paperback available $12.95
617.9

1. Transplantation of organs, tissues, etc.
ISBN 0-8229-5905-4 (pa)　　　LC 87-24597

The author discusses "organ transplantation surgery, its successes and failures, and . . . the patients, donors, surgeons, [and] transplant coordinators." Libr J

This "is a fascinating look at the emotional and physical complexities of a harrowing process." Booklist

Organ transplants; a patient's guide; [by] the Massachusetts General Hospital Organ Transplant Team and H.F. Pizer. Harvard Univ. Press 1991 243p $24.95
617.9

1. Transplantation of organs, tissues, etc.
ISBN 0-674-64235-X　　　LC 91-7083

"The book describes transplants of the heart, lung, kidney, pancreas, liver, and bone marrow. . . . Heavy going at times, but recommended." Libr J

618 Gynecology and obstetrics

Dally, Ann G.
Women under the knife; a history of surgery; [by] Ann Dally. Routledge 1991 xxv, 289p il $27.50
618

1. Surgery　　2. Women—Health and hygiene
3. Medical care
ISBN 0-415-90554-0　　　LC 91-38860

In this history of obstetric and gynecological surgery, the author argues "that procedures now seen as brutal and unnecessary were not inherently anti-feminist, but symptomatic of an unbalanced social contract." Libr J

The author "condemns abuses but seeks to uncover a kernel of hope in the therapeutic efficacy of medicine." Times Lit Suppl

Includes bibliographic references

618.1 Gynecology

Cutler, Winnifred Berg
Hysterectomy: before & after; a comprehensive guide to preventing, preparing for, and maximizing health after hysterectomy. Harper & Row 1988 449p il hardcover o.p. paperback available $13
618.1

1. Hysterectomy
ISBN 0-06-091629-X (pa)　　　LC 87-46132

The author "offers comprehensive and clear coverage of uterine diseases that require surgical intervention (e.g., cancer and endometriosis) surgical options, hormonal replacement therapy, sexuality, and post-surgery depression." Booklist

Includes bibliography

Menopause; a guide for women and the men who love them; [by] Winnifred B. Cutler, Celso-Ramón García. rev ed. Norton 1992 431p $25
618.1

1. Menopause
ISBN 0-393-02922-0　　　LC 91-30149

First published 1983

This book "reflects the most recent findings about the role of hormone replacement therapy in the lives of menopausal women. The authors . . . explain the physiological changes that occur during this time and offer detailed information about the benefits and risks of hormone replacement therapy. They emphasize the prevention of osteoporosis and heart disease." Libr J

Includes bibliography

Gillespie, Clark
Hormones, hot flashes and mood swings; living through the ups and downs of menopause. Harper & Row 1989 205p hardcover o.p. paperback available $11
618.1

1. Menopause
ISBN 0-06-096355-7 (pa)　　　LC 88-45934

The author "discusses the physical and emotional effects of menopause. . . . He details what women can expect as they approach menopause and gives advice on proper diet and exercise to help maintain maximum health." Libr J

Goldfarb, Herbert A.
The no-hysterectomy option; your body, your choice; [by] Herbert A. Goldbarb with Judith Greif. Wiley 1990 xx, 265p il $29.95; pa $12.95   **618.1**
1. Hysterectomy
ISBN 0-471-53232-0; 0-471-51615-5 (pa)
LC 90-12692
The author "describes all treatment options and alternatives including hysteroscopy, laser myomectomy, and laser surgery. Also excellent is his coverage of endometriosis, fibroid tumors, cervical cancer, and other medical problems that often lead up to this surgery." Libr J

Includes bibliographic references

Greer, Germaine, 1939-
The change; women, aging, and the menopause. Knopf 1992 422p $23.50
618.1
1. Menopause   2. Women—Psychology   3. Self-realization 4. Aging
ISBN 0-394-58269-1   LC 92-52949
This is a discussion of menopause in Western society. Greer looks at medical, psychological and social aspects of the cessation of menstruation and the aging process. She views the climacteric as an important turning-point in a woman's life
"In a wise, witty and inspiring book, Greer rebukes doctors, psychiatrists—and women themselves—who blame the aging female for her menopausal distress. . . . Greer dispels all manner of myths and misconceptions about menopause." Publ Wkly

Includes bibliographic references

Gross, Amy
Women talk about breast surgery; from diagnosis to recovery; [by] Amy Gross and Dee Ito. Potter 1990 333p $22.95   **618.1**
1. Breast—Surgery
ISBN 0-517-56353-3   LC 89-22793
Also available in paperback from HarperCollins Pubs.
"The book begins with brief descriptions of available treatments, ranging from lumpectomy to total mastectomy, including radiation, chemotherapy, and reconstructive surgery, and a glossary of terms is provided. The bulk of the book consists of interviews, reproduced in a loose question-and-answer format, with women who have had these procedures and with physicians specializing in various forms of treatment." Libr J

Lauersen, Niels
The endometriosis answer book; new hope, new help; [by] Niels H. Lauersen and Constance deSwaan. Rawson Assocs. 1988 255p il o.p.; Ballantine Bks. paperback available $10   **618.1**
1. Endometriosis
ISBN 0-449-90361-3 (pa)   LC 86-43246
The author describes what endometriosis is, the importance of early and accurate diagnosis, and various forms of treatment. Included also is a special diet believed to alleviate some of the distress of the disease

Includes bibliographies

It's your body; a woman's guide to gynecology; [by] Niels Lauersen and Steven Whitney, with Eileen Stukane. completely rev & updated ed. Body Press/Perigee 1993 565p il pa $18.95   **618.1**
1. Women—Health and hygiene
ISBN 0-399-51830-4   LC 93-13395
First published 1977 by Grosset; published 1987 by Putnam with title: A woman's body
This guide to women's health covers such topics as choosing a gynecologist, the reproductive cycle, sexually transmitted diseases, contraception, abortion, infertility, uterine and ovarian abnormalities, sex, and sexual dysfunctions

Love, Susan M.
Dr. Susan Love's breast book; [by] Susan M. Love with Karen Lindsey; illustrations by Marcia Williams. Addison-Wesley 1990 xxiii, 455p il $18.22; pa $13.41   **618.1**
1. Breast—Diseases
ISBN 0-201-09665-X; 0-201-57097-1 (pa)
LC 90-32071
"A Merloyd Lawrence book"
Dr. Love "answers the standard questions related to development, self-examination, breast-feeding, and plastic surgery for augmentation or reduction. She discusses in depth common problems, presenting detailed description, with drawings, of breast biopsy. She devotes the rest of the book to comprehensive information about breast cancer—its risk, prevention, detection, diagnosis, and treatment, and finally, living with it." Booklist

Includes bibliographic references

Malesky, Gale
Take this book to the gynecologist with you; a consumer's guide to women's health; [by] Gale Malesky and Charles B. Inlander. Addison-Wesley 1991 235p pa $9.57 **618.1**
1. Women—Diseases 2. Consumer education
ISBN 0-201-52379-5   LC 90-23365
"A People's Medical Society book"
Presented in question and answer format "Malesky's advice runs from choosing a physician through examining the setting for gynecological services, what to expect during a typical office visit, and a variety of conditions and procedures, from breast cancer to pap smears." Booklist

Includes bibliography

Milan, Albert R.
Breast self-examination; illustrated by the author. Workman 1980 125p il hardcover o.p. paperback available $3.50   **618.1**
1. Breast—Examination
ISBN 0-89480-124-4 (pa)
"A Liberty Publishing Company book"
"A manual devoted exclusively to breast self-examination (BSE) that makes highly effective use of graphics and photos to explain the anatomy of both the normal and the diseased breast and also the cancer detection techniques of palpation and visual observation." Booklist

Perry, Susan
Natural menopause; the complete guide to a woman's most misunderstood passage; [by] Susan Perry and Katherine O'Hanlan. Addison-Wesley 1992 208p $19.18 **618.1**
1. Menopause
ISBN 0-201-58142-6 LC 91-45172
This book about menopause "covers the basic medical and physiological information from a holistic point of view. . . . This is a good book for public libraries that need additional material about menopause." Libr J
Includes bibliographic references

Sheehy, Gail
The silent passage; menopause. Random House 1992 161p $15.50 **618.1**
1. Menopause
ISBN 0-679-41388-X LC 91-51064
Also available Wheeler Pub. large print edition and in paperback from Pocket Bks.
"Interviewing over 100 women in various stages of menopause and 75 experts, [Sheehy] examines the medical, psychological, and social aspects of this 'silent passage.' A biological change that spans five to seven years, this 'second adulthood,' according to Sheehy, has three stages: peri-menopause, menopause, and coalescence." Libr J
"Sheehy includes discussion of herbal remedies, exercise and dietary defenses against osteoporosis. While remaining somewhat inconclusive, her review of this stage of life for women in anti-aging America is detailed and sympathetic." Publ Wkly

Utian, Wulf H., 1939-
Managing your menopause; [by] Wulf H. Utian and Ruth S. Jacobowitz. Prentice Hall Press 1990 225p o.p.; Simon & Schuster paperback available $10 **618.1**
1. Menopause
ISBN 0-671-76426-8 (pa) LC 89-26441
"With the help of medical writer Jacobowitz, Utian, director of the Cleveland Menopause Clinic, offers clear explanations of what happens to the body during menopause and why. The authors discuss finding the right doctor and the pros and cons of hormone replacement therapy, and they offer advice concerning diet, lifestyle, and exercise, as well as sexuality and aging." Libr J
Includes bibliography

618.2 Obstetrics

Complete guide to pregnancy; [by] The Columbia University College of Physicians and Surgeons; medical editors, Donald F. Tapley, W. Duane Todd; editorial director, Genell J. Subak-Sharpe; associate editor, Diane M. Goetz. Crown 1988 358p il $24.95 **618.2**
1. Pregnancy 2. Childbirth
ISBN 0-517-57030-0 LC 88-7079
"A compilation of chapters, written by physicians, devoted to the myriad aspects of pregnancy and childbirth. . . . A pleasant surprise is the information on infertility and genetics. The role of the father is promi-

nently featured, and controversial issues are given balanced treatment." Libr J

Eastman's expectant motherhood; revised by Keith P. Russell. Little, Brown $9.95 **618.2**
1. Pregnancy
First published 1940 under the authorship of Nicholson J. Eastman. (8th edition 1989) Periodically revised
This handbook gives essential information on pregnancy and its hygiene for expectant mothers. Also discussed are diet and weight control, common discomforts and their treatments, danger signals, 'painless childbirth' and convalescence from childbirth

Gillespie, Clark
Your pregnancy month by month. 4th ed. HarperCollins Pubs. 1992 290p il $22; pa $11 **618.2**
1. Pregnancy
ISBN 0-06-055271-9; 0-06-096533-9 (pa)
LC 91-58473
First published 1977
This guide to pregnancy covers genetics, obstetrics, fetology and anesthesiology, and answers questions on such aspects as weight gain, sexual relations during pregnancy, options for labor and delivery, teenage and over age 35 pregnancies

Kitzinger, Sheila, 1929-
Your baby, your way; making pregnancy decisions and birth plans. Pantheon Bks. 1987 352p il hardcover o.p. paperback available $15 **618.2**
1. Pregnancy 2. Childbirth
ISBN 0-394-75249-X (pa) LC 86-42983
This guide demonstrates "how mothers and their labor coaches can create a detailed, personal birthing plan from pregnancy through bonding. Basic advice on nutrition, medical care, midwifery, emotional and physical changes wrought by pregnancy, and on the birth process itself is carefully delivered, but actual choices are left up to the mother." Booklist
Includes bibliography

Martin, Margaret, 1954-
The illustrated book of pregnancy and childbirth. Facts on File 1991 126p il $19.95 **618.2**
1. Childbirth 2. Pregnancy
ISBN 0-8160-2570-3 LC 91-9050
Beginning with an explanation of the reproductive cycle, the author goes on to discuss the following: pregnancy and childbirth, conception, the growth of the fetus, diet and exercise, the effects of drugs and alcohol, changes in a woman's body [and] the stages of labor." Publisher's note

McCartney, Marion

The midwife's pregnancy and childbirth book; having your baby your way; [by] Marion McCartney [and] Antonia van der Meer. Holt & Co. 1990 239p il $19.95

        618.2

1. Pregnancy 2. Childbirth
ISBN 0-8050-1049-1   LC 89-39853

Also available in paperback from HarperCollins Pubs.

"A certified nurse midwife (CNM—a registered nurse with additional, intensive childbirth training) and a medical writer advise on choosing a CNM as primary practitioner during pregnancy and birth. They compare what to expect from either CNM- or physician-attended birth in various settings; sketch the differences in midwives' and physicians' philosophical backgrounds; consider economic, social, and personal motivations for selecting a midwife; and discuss prenatal care, nutrition, basic health issues during pregnancy, labor, delivery, and postpartum concerns." Booklist

Morales, Karla

Take this book to the obstetrician with you; a consumer's guide to pregnancy and childbirth; [by] Karla Morales and Charles B. Inlander. Addison-Wesley 1991 224p pa $9.95

        618.2

1. Pregnancy 2. Childbirth 3. Consumer education
ISBN 0-201-52380-9   LC 90-27768

"A People's Medical Society book"

This guide offers advice on prepregnancy planning and genetic testing, infertility, choosing a birth practitioner and birth setting, as well as how to make decisions and ask questions about obstetric care and birth

This is "thorough and readable, effective in offering the reader a model, a method of inquiry so that she can choose, instead of being intimidated by forms, routines, technology, and personnel." Libr J

Noble, Elizabeth, 1945-

Having twins; a parent's guide to pregnancy, birth, and early childhood; [by] Elizabeth Noble with Leo Sorger; foreword by Louis Keith; illustrated with line drawings by Maya M. Jacob. 2nd ed. Houghton Mifflin 1991 430p il $24.45; pa $12.70

        618.2

1. Twins 2. Pregnancy 3. Childbirth 4. Infants—Care
ISBN 0-395-51088-0; 0-395-49338-2 (pa)

     LC 90-38969

First published 1980

This guide to multiple pregnancy covers pregnancy, birth, how to care for twins and the care of special needs babies

This is an "indispensible tool on the history and physiology of twinning. . . . Both physical and emotional needs are equally considered by Noble, as her realistic treatment of possible complications is balanced by her sensitive, and at time personal, insights." Libr J

Includes bibliography

Planning for pregnancy, birth, and beyond; [by] the American College of Obstetricians and Gynecologists. Dutton 1992 c1990 260p il $20

        618.2

1. Pregnancy 2. Childbirth 3. Infants—Care
ISBN 0-525-93473-1   LC 91-42702

First published 1990 by the American College of Obstetricians and Gynecologists with title: ACOG guide to planning for pregnancy, birth, and beyond

This guide contains information about preconception, prenatal, and postpartum care. All aspects of pregnancy and birth are covered, including special needs or complications

Sears, William

300 questions new parents ask; about pregnancy, childbirth, and infant & child care; [by] William Sears, Martha Sears. New Am. Lib. 1991 294p il pa $9

        618.2

1. Pregnancy 2. Childbirth 3. Infants—Care 4. Child care
ISBN 0-452-26599-1   LC 90-20042

"A Plume book"

In question and answer format, this covers pregnancy and childbirth, care and development of infants and young children

Verny, Thomas R.

Nurturing the unborn child; a nine-month program for soothing, stimulating, and communicating with your baby; by Thomas Verny and Pamela Weintraub. Delacorte Press 1991 xxxv, 219p il $18; pa $11

        618.2

1. Pregnancy 2. Parent and child
ISBN 0-385-30092-1; 0-385-30673-3 (pa)

     LC 90-47950

This work "introduces the Womb Harmonics System, techniques for nurturing an unborn child toward a life of confidence and ease. Presented in simple, step-by-step format, the program features exercises for relaxing parents and for nurturing the unborn child through pregnancy, delivery, and postdelivery." Booklist

Includes bibliographic references

618.3   Diseases and complications of pregnancy

Abrams, Richard S. (Richard Stephen), 1946-

Will it hurt the baby! the safe use of medications during pregnancy and breastfeeding. Addison-Wesley 1990 347p pa $12.95

        618.3

1. Pregnancy 2. Breast feeding 3. Drugs
ISBN 0-201-51809-0   LC 89-29434

The author "discusses common medical disorders seen during pregnancy and the impact that their usual treatment may have on the pregnant woman. He provides specific information about particular drugs—generic and brand names, side effects, dosage, safety during pregnancy, and possible alternatives." Libr J

Includes bibliographic references

Huggins, Kathleen
The nursing mother's companion; foreword by Ruth A. Lawrence; photographs by Harriette Hartigan. rev ed. Harvard Common Press 1990 220p il $16.95; pa $11.95 **618.3**
1. Breast feeding
ISBN 1-55832-025-3; 1-55832-026-1 (pa)
LC 90-38863
First published 1986
This "book covers common questions of new mothers—such as how to prevent soreness, how to ensure an ample milk supply, and how to manage nursing while working—as well as not-so-common medical problems. This . . . includes an up-to-date review of breast pumps currently available. Also [included is an] appendix on drugs and their safety during breastfeeding." Publisher's note

Scher, Jonathan
Preventing miscarriage; the good news; [by] Jonathan Scher, Carol Dix. Harper & Row 1990 240p il hardcover o.p. paperback available $10 **618.3**
1. Miscarriage
ISBN 0-06-092056-4 (pa)
LC 89-45063
"In a loose question-and-answer format, Scher readably provides clinical information on the known causes of miscarriage. Between discussions of hormonal imbalances, physical anomalies, and immunological incompatibilities come poignant stories from women who have suffered numerous miscarriages and subsequent, anxiety-filled pregnancies that finally resulted in birth." Booklist

618.4 Childbirth. Labor

Davis, Elizabeth, 1950-
Heart & hands; a midwife's guide to pregnancy & birth; photographs by Suzanne Arms Wimberley; illustrated by Linda Harrison. 2nd ed. Celestial Arts 1987 229p il $22.95; pa $19.95 **618.4**
1. Childbirth
ISBN 0-89087-495-6; 0-89087-494-8 (pa)
LC 87-13256
First published 1981 by John Muir Publications with title: A guide to midwifery
Describes what a midwife does, how she does it, and presents options to prospective parents on modes of delivery and the choice of a midwife
Includes bibliography

Kitzinger, Sheila, 1929-
Homebirth; the essential guide to giving birth outside of the hospital; photography by Marcia May. Dorling Kindersley 1991 208p il $18.95 **618.4**
1. Childbirth
ISBN 1-87943-101-7
LC 91-60141
The author "examines alternatives to hospital births, conceding that this is not the right choice for everyone. She outlines important considerations in choosing a birth setting, then details the process of preparing for birth at home or in a birth center." Libr J
Includes bibliographic references

Leboyer, Frédérick
Birth without violence. Knopf 1975 114p il $18.95 **618.4**
1. Childbirth
ISBN 0-394-49581-0
Also available in paperback from Fawcett Bks.
Original French edition, 1974
A French obstetrician describes his techniques of childbirth
"The work's stylistic qualities, in addition to the beautiful photographs, jar the reader into thinking about childbirth in a unique and revolutionary way." Choice

Mitford, Jessica, 1917-
The American way of birth. Dutton 1992 322p $23 **618.4**
1. Childbirth 2. United States—Social conditions
ISBN 0-525-93523-1
LC 92-52875
"A William Abrahams book"
"Mitford's probe into American obstetrics as well as the hospitals, clinics, and welfare agencies that supervise the prenatal care and births of American babies results in an indictment against the medical practices surrounding that which should not make us sick—giving birth." Libr J
"Nobody could ask for a more astute guide to modern mores in the delivery room." Newsweek

Savage, Beverly
Preparation for birth; the complete guide to the Lamaze method; [by] Beverly Savage and Diana Simkin; photographs by Mary Motley Kalergis; illustrations by Dana Burns and Laura Hartman. Ballantine Bks. 1987 461p il pa $12 **618.4**
1. Natural childbirth
ISBN 0-345-31230-9
LC 85-90884
"Among the topics covered are Lamaze breathing techniques, the physical process of labor, choosing a doctor or midwife, exercise and relaxation, medication, the role of the partner, postpartum, and the second baby. 'Preparation for Birth' is an essential guide and should be in all public libraries." Libr J
Includes bibliography

618.8 Obstetrical surgery

Flamm, Bruce L.
Birth after Cesarean. Prentice Hall Press 1990 xxv, 197p o.p.; Simon & Schuster paperback available $11 **618.8**
1. Cesarean section 2. Natural childbirth
ISBN 0-671-79218-0 (pa)
LC 89-22900
The author describes and defends the "newly popular concept of vaginal birth after Cesarean (VBAC). He discusses the subject in depth, using a question-and-answer format which, along with a very complete table of contents, makes this book an easily accessible text for library patrons." Libr J
Includes bibliographic references

618.92 Pediatrics

Bain, Lisa J.

A parent's guide to attention deficit disorders; foreword by C. Everett Koop. Dell 1991 216p pa $10   **618.92**

1. Hyperactive children
ISBN 0-385-30031-X   LC 91-24652

"A Delta book"

"The controversy over the definition of ADHD (attention deficit-hyperactivity disorder) is clearly described along with historic views of, and changes in, medical and public opinion. Bain describes the management methods for helping children with ADHD cope with school and family interactions. The pluses and minuses of Ritalin and other medications are considered. In addition, the author stresses the necessity of behavior management therapy." Booklist

Includes bibliographic references

Bearison, David J.

They never want to tell you; children talk about cancer. Harvard Univ. Press 1991 194p $19.95   **618.92**

1. Cancer 2. Children—Diseases
ISBN 0-674-88370-5   LC 90-49945

Eight children who have cancer discuss their experiences and feelings

"This remarkable book . . . will help child cancer patients as well as parents, friends, and professionals to open up their hearts and minds during this most difficult time. Very highly recommended." Libr J

Includes bibliographic references

Bombeck, Erma

I want to grow hair, I want to grow up, I want to go to Boise; children surviving cancer. Harper & Row 1989 174p il $16.95; pa $5.50   **618.92**

1. Cancer 2. Children—Diseases
ISBN 0-06-016170-1; 0-06-109905-8 (pa)
          LC 89-45026

A "collection of poignant yet often funny anecdotes about and conversations with children who have cancer." Booklist

Brace, Edward R.

Childhood symptoms; every parent's guide to childhood illnesses; [by] Edward R. Brace, John P. Pacanowski. rev ed, by Ed Weiner. HarperCollins Pubs. 1992 338p il $30; pa $15   **618.92**

1. Children—Diseases
ISBN 0-06-271532-1; 0-06-273078-9 (pa)
          LC 91-55391

"A Stonesong Press book"

First published 1985

"Easy-to-follow references guide the parent or caregiver through an analysis of the potential problem and alert the reader as to when medical help is needed. Specific symptoms are cross-referenced to conditions in which the symptom plays a part." N Y Public Libr Book of How & Where to Look It Up

Bracken, Jeanne Munn

Children with cancer; a comprehensive reference guide for parents. Oxford Univ. Press 1986 407p il $35; pa $10.95 **618.92**

1. Cancer 2. Children—Diseases
ISBN 0-19-503482-1; 0-19-505659-0 (pa)   LC 86-867

Describes "the types of childhood cancer—how they affect the child, what treatments are available, how to cope with the changes this diagnosis will bring to the entire family, and where to go for help, both emotional and medical." Publisher's note

This "is comprehensive, well written, accurate, and compassionate." Sci Books Films

Includes bibliography

Children with cerebral palsy; a parents' guide; edited by Elaine Geralis; foreword by Tom Ritter. Woodbine House 1991 434p il pa $14.95   **618.92**

1. Cerebral palsy 2. Children—Diseases
ISBN 0-933149-15-8   LC 88-40660

"Designed as an introduction to cerebral palsy, this collection of informative articles written by leading professionals covers several subjects parents of CP children need to know about during the first five years of life. Particularly helpful are lengthy sections on medical treatment and daily care, which offer in-depth discussion without being confusing." Booklist

Includes bibliography

Doft, Norma

When your child needs help; [by] Norma Doft with Barbara Aria. Harmony Bks. 1991 224p $18   **618.92**

1. Child psychiatry 2. Parenting
ISBN 0-517-58046-2   LC 91-15576

In this work the authors "explain how to 'distinguish between appropriate upsets and those problems' that will benefit from counseling or psychotherapy. . . . They explain how to locate a professional who will work well with both child and parents, and they also delineate the specialized focus of various professionals from psychiatrists to social workers." Booklist

Feingold, Ben F.

Why your child is hyperactive. Random House 1975 211p hardcover o.p. paperback available $10   **618.92**

1. Hyperactive children 2. Food additives 3. Diet in disease
ISBN 0-394-73426-2 (pa)   LC 74-9078

"The author's hypothesis [is] that diet is the major cause of hyperactivity. More specifically, he insists that artificial colorings and flavors along with environmental pollutants are the villainous agents. . . . The addendum [contains] sample menus and suggested recipes." Libr J

Ferber, Richard

Solve your child's sleep problems. Simon & Schuster 1985 251p hardcover o.p. paperback available $10   **618.92**

1. Sleep 2. Children—Health and hygiene
ISBN 0-671-62099-1 (pa)   LC 84-22132

Ferber, Richard—*Continued*
The author "discusses in some detail children's sleep cycles, stages of sleep, and biological rhythms and gives advice for preventing sleep problems in children." Sci Books Films
"A practical, informative, and sensitive guide. Appended are addresses for two helpful organizations and a list of useful children's books." Booklist

Garber, Stephen W., 1946-
If your child is hyperactive, inattentive, impulsive, distractible; —helping the ADD (attention deficit disorder) hyperactive child; [by] Stephen W. Garber, Marianne Daniels Garber, Robyn Freedman Spizman. Villard Bks. 1990 235p $20 **618.92**
1. Hyperactive children
ISBN 0-394-57205-X LC 90-35992
"Garber lists the symptoms and discusses current thinking on causes and treatments. Most important, he supplies concrete suggestions for calmness training, controlling distraction, building attention spans, and encouraging rule following." Booklist
Includes bibliography

Ingersoll, Barbara D., 1945-
Your hyperactive child; a parent's guide to coping with attention deficit disorder; foreword by Judith L. Rapoport and Alan J. Zametkin. Doubleday 1988 219p $16.95; pa $9.95 **618.92**
1. Hyperactive children
ISBN 0-385-24069-4; 0-385-24070-8 (pa)
LC 87-36535
This overview of hyperactivity in young children examines many of the difficulties parents face and suggests strategies for managing the behavior problems associated with this condition
Includes bibliography

Jason, Janine
Parenting your premature child; [by] Janine Jason, Antonia van der Meer. Holt & Co. 1989 278p il o.p.; Doubleday paperback available $9.95 **618.92**
1. Infants, Premature 2. Infants—Care
ISBN 0-385-29906-0 (pa) LC 88-8367
"The authors discuss why babies are born prematurely, what to expect with such a delivery, and how 'preemies' differ from full-term newborns. Preemies' early development, later progress, and their impact on couples' decisions to have another child are astutely covered." Booklist

Klass, Perri, 1958-
Baby doctor. Random House 1992 330p $21.50 **618.92**
1. Children—Health and hygiene
ISBN 0-679-40957-2 LC 91-51022
Also available in paperback from Ivy Bks.
This is an "account of the author's year of residency at a major pediatric hospital and her description of the process of becoming a pediatrician. Klass also discusses her own experiences as a mother and the difficulty of finding a balance between motherhood and a career." Libr J
"Dr. Klass's candid discussions of her experiences raise important ethical questions in medicine, such as when a premature baby is simply too small to try to save." N Y Times Book Rev

Marion, Robert
The boy who felt no pain. Addison-Wesley 1990 203p $17.26 **618.92**
1. Children—Diseases
ISBN 0-201-55049-0 LC 90-31289
Also available in paperback from Fawcett Bks.
A New York pediatrician provides fourteen accounts of his more memorable patients
"This is a lively, intriguing account of hospital life by a most engaging and compassionate doctor." SLJ

Neill, Catherine A.
The heart of a child; what families need to know about heart disorders in children; [by] Catherine A. Neill, Edward B. Clark, Carleen Clark. Johns Hopkins Univ. Press 1992 331p il $24.95 **618.92**
1. Heart—Diseases 2. Children—Diseases
ISBN 0-8018-4234-4 LC 92-25198
The authors "outline how the heart develops in a child and show what can go wrong during the growing process. They also discuss the risk factors for heart defects and explain how heart problems are recognized. Neill and Clark also cover treatment options. While the severity of heart problems in children is not minimized, the authors emphasize that most conditions are now treatable." Libr J
Includes bibliographic references

The New child health encyclopedia; the complete guide for parents; [by] Boston Children's Hospital; Frederick H. Lovejoy, medical editor; David Estridge, executive editor. Delacorte Press 1987 xxiv, 740p il hardcover o.p. paperback available $19.95 618.92
1. Children—Health and hygiene 2. Children—Diseases
ISBN 0-385-29597-9 (pa) LC 87-6809
"A Merloyd Lawrence book"
First published 1975 with title: Child health encyclopedia
"Specialized, practical advice book for parents. Divided into four sections: 'Keeping Children Healthy,' 'Finding Health Care for Children,' 'Emergencies,' and 'Diseases and Symptoms.' Provides reliable , up-to-date information on every subject by experts associated with one of the nation's leading child-care facilities." N Y Public Libr Book of How & Where to Look It Up

Rapp, Doris J.
Is this your child? discovering and treating unrecognized allergies. Morrow 1991 626p il $23; pa $12 **618.92**
1. Allergy 2. Children—Health and hygiene
ISBN 0-688-08623-3; 0-688-11907-7 (pa)
LC 90-48676

Rapp, Doris J.—*Continued*

"Parents frequently recognize the classic symptoms of allergy in their children. . . . But allergist Rapp contends that reactivity to particular substances is also responsible for a host of more subtle physical and emotional complications, ranging from childhood depression to headaches to aggressive behavior and suicidal tendencies. Using numerous case histories from her own practice, she demonstrates her controversial theories, explaining how allergies to foods and chemicals trigger some of these unusual responses." Booklist

Includes bibliography

Selikowitz, Mark

Down syndrome; the facts. Oxford Univ. Press 1990 205p il $18.95   **618.92**

1. Down's syndrome 2. Children—Diseases
ISBN 0-19-261872-5   LC 89-15961

"Oxford medical publications"

Discusses possible causes of Down's syndrome, development of the child with the disease, medical problems and educational strategies, and includes advice for parents about future pregnancies

Stevens, Maryann

Breathing easy; a parent's guide to dealing with your child's asthma. Prentice Hall Press 1991 221p il pa $9.95   **618.92**

1. Asthma 2. Children—Diseases
ISBN 0-13-083692-3   LC 90-25564

The author "addresses asthma from a parent's view, with an eye toward prevention. This practical approach answers basic questions about triggers, environment, medications, and living with asthma day by day. Ideas on ways to make hospitalization less traumatic are reassuring to both parent and child." Libr J

Includes bibliography

Taylor, John F., 1944-

Helping your hyperactive child. Prima Pub. & Communications 1990 483p $19.95   **618.92**

1. Hyperactive children
ISBN 1-55958-013-5   LC 89-39849

This guide for parents discusses effective ways of dealing with hyperactive children including the pros and cons of medication, nutrition and other methods

Includes bibliographic references

Terr, Lenore, 1936-

Too scared to cry: psychic trauma in childhood. Harper & Row 1990 372p $23   **618.92**

1. Child psychology 2. Stress (Psychology)
ISBN 0-06-016335-6   LC 89-46121

Also available in paperback from Basic Bks.

Focusing on the 1976 kidnapping of 26 children in Chowchilla California the author examines the lifelong effects of childhood trauma

"Written in an anecdotal format, the book is penetrating and illuminating." Publ Wkly

Includes bibliographic references

618.97   Geriatrics

Alzheimer's disease; a handbook for caregivers; [by] Ronald C. Hamdy [et al.] Mosby 1990 282p $31.95   **618.97**

1. Alzheimer's disease
ISBN 0-8016-2026-0   LC 90-5682

This describes the symptoms and stages of Alzheimer's disease, the options for treatment, and addresses practical problems

Includes bibliographic references

Caring for the Alzheimer patient; a practical guide; edited by Raye Lynne Dippel and J. Thomas Hutton. 2nd ed. Prometheus Bks. 1991 192p il $21.95; pa $14.95   **618.97**

1. Alzheimer's disease
ISBN 0-87975-662-4; 0-87975-663-2 (pa)
     LC 90-25139

"A Golden age book"

First published 1988

Seventeen essays "address a wide variety of topics of concern to Alzheimer caregivers, families, and professionals. . . . The book emphasizes: managing the medical and physical problems of the Alzheimer patient; managing the patient's environmental and behavioral problems and supporting the psychological well-being of the caregiver; bringing together patient care and community resources; and dealing with ethical and legal considerations." Publisher's note

Includes bibliographic references

Griffith, H. Winter (Henry Winter), 1926-

Complete guide to symptoms, illness & surgery for people over 50; surgical illustrations by Mark Pederson. Body Press/Perigee 1992 xxvii, 868p il $29.95; pa $17.95   **618.97**

1. Elderly—Diseases 2. Elderly—Health and hygiene
ISBN 0-685-56436-3; 0-399-51749-9 (pa)
     LC 91-44129

"This guide provides information about diseases, preventive medicine, and health maintenance for older people. . . . It is a fine ready-reference tool and an excellent aid for encouraging people to participate in their own health care." Booklist

Includes bibliography

The **Johns** Hopkins medical handbook; the 100 major medical disorders of people over the age of 50; plus a directory to the leading teaching hospitals, research organizations, treatment centers, and support groups; medical editors: Simeon Margolis, Hamilton Moses; prepared by the editors of The Johns Hopkins medical letter health after 50. Rebus 1992 638p il $39.95   **618.97**

1. Elderly—Diseases 2. Elderly—Health and hygiene 3. Medical care—Directories
ISBN 0-929661-04-4   LC 92-15420

This handbook covers such disorders as "cancer, hearing loss, depression, insomnia. The text . . . is authoritative, clearly written, and illustrated with drawings and diagrams." Libr J

Mace, Nancy L.
The 36-hour day; a family guide to caring for persons with Alzheimer's disease, related dementing illnesses, and memory loss in later life; [by] Nancy L. Mace, Peter V. Rabins. rev ed. Johns Hopkins Univ. Press 1991 xxi, 329p $35; pa $11.95   **618.97**

1. Alzheimer's disease
ISBN 0-8018-4033-3; 0-8018-4034-1 (pa)

LC 90-49523

Also available in paperback from Warner Bks.

First published 1981

A guide designed for families of Alzheimer's sufferers. Current research on the brain, behavior and personality is included

Includes bibliography

Oliver, Rose
Coping with Alzheimer's; a caregiver's emotional survival guide; [by] Rose Oliver, Frances A. Bock. Dodd, Mead 1987 230p o.p.; Wilshire paperback available $10
      618.97

1. Alzheimer's disease
ISBN 0-87980-424-6 (pa)   LC 87-20213

"The authors describe and illustrate how Rational Emotive Therapy (RET), a system of psychotherapy, can help caregivers deal with the situation; specific strategies for handling feelings of depression, shame, anger, guilt, and loneliness are presented." Libr J

Includes bibliography

Roberts, D. Jeanne
Taking care of caregivers; for families and others who care for people with Alzheimer's disease and other forms of dementia. Bull 1991 181p il pa $14.95   **618.97**

1. Alzheimer's disease
ISBN 0-923521-09-7   LC 90-26102

This guide offers exercises and solutions for people who care for those suffering from Alzheimer's disease and other forms of dementia in dealing with stress, guilt, exhaustion, grief, and other problems affecting caregivers physical and mental health

Includes bibliography

Understanding Alzheimer's disease; what it is, how to cope with it, future directions; [by] Alzheimer's Disease and Related Disorders Association; edited by Miriam K. Aronson; foreword by Robert N. Butler. Scribner 1988 380p $15.95
      618.97

1. Alzheimer's disease
ISBN 0-684-18475-3   LC 87-5037

"Diagnosis, treatment, possible etiology, and the emotional impact of Alzheimer's on family members are just some of the topics discussed. Each contributing author concentrates on offering practical advice on coping with the Alzheimer's patient. Particularly useful is the section on the legal and financial aspects of the disease." Booklist

Includes bibliography

620.1   Engineering mechanics and material science

Brady, George S. (George Stuart)
Materials handbook; an encyclopedia for managers, technical professionals, purchasing and production managers, technicians, supervisors, and foremen; [by] George S. Brady, Henry R. Clauser. McGraw-Hill $79.50   **620.1**

1. Materials—Dictionaries 2. Building materials—Dictionaries 3. Commercial products—Dictionaries

First published 1929. (13th edition 1991) Periodically revised. Subtitle varies

"A long established encyclopedic work of technical and trade information, frequently including trade names, for over 15,000 materials of commercial importance, ranging from brick to walrus hide. The bulk of the work is alphabetically arranged descriptive essays that vary in length but consistently detail source, physical properties, and uses of the substance under discussion." Ref Sources for Small & Medium-sized Libr. 5th edition

621   Applied physics

Marks' standard handbook for mechanical engineers. McGraw-Hill il $109.50   **621**

1. Mechanical engineering—Handbooks, manuals, etc.

Also available from American Soc. of Mechanical Engs.

First published 1916 under the editorship of Lionel S. Marks with title: Mechanical engineers' handbook. (9th edition 1987) Periodically revised. Editors vary

This volume presents concisely the basic scientific and technical data of mechanical engineering, covering theory, basic mechanism, standard practice, often-needed mathematical formulae and technical data

Includes bibliographies

Nelson, Carl A.
Millwrights and mechanics guide. 4th ed. Macmillan 1989 1032p il $31   **621**

1. Mechanical engineering—Handbooks, manuals, etc.
2. Building—Handbooks, manuals, etc.
ISBN 0-02-588591-X   LC 89-8323

"An Audel book"

First published 1940 under the authorship of Edwin P. Anderson with title: Audels millwrights & mechanics guide for plant maintenance, builders, riggers, erectors, operators, construction men and engineers

Descriptions and illustrations guide in construction and operation of industrial plants, subsequent maintenance, and machinery and equipment installation

621.3   Superconductivity

American electricians' handbook. McGraw-Hill il $69.50   **621.3**

1. Electric engineering—Handbooks, manuals, etc.

First published 1913. (12th edition 1992) Periodically revised

American electricians' handbook—*Continued*

This handbook for electricians includes "detailed information to lead to the intelligent design, selection, installation, and maintenance of electrical equipment." Am Ref Books Annu, 1993

McGraw-Hill's National Electrical Code handbook. McGraw-Hill $54.50   **621.3**

1. Electric engineering—Handbooks, manuals, etc.

First published 1932 with title: National Electrical Code handbook. (21st edition 1993) Frequently revised to reflect changes in the code. Title varies

This handbook presents analysis and commentary on the National Electrical Code, as it pertains to wiring of appliances, buildings, emergency systems, and other types of electrical construction

Middleton, Robert Gordon, 1908-

Practical electricity; by Robert G. Middleton. 4th ed, rev. by L. Donald Meyers and Joseph A. Tedesco. Macmillan 1988 498p il $22.50   **621.3**

1. Electric engineering
ISBN 0-02-584561-6   LC 87-35550

First published 1969 by Audel

At head of title: Audel

Magnetism, conductors, circuits, wiring, lighting, switching and generation are among the topics discussed

National Electrical Code handbook. National Fire Protection Assn. $65   **621.3**

1. Electric engineering—Handbooks, manuals, etc.

First published 1978. (6th edition 1993) Periodically revised

This "is a nationally accepted guide to the safe installation of electrical conductors and equipment, and is, in fact, the basis for all electrical codes used in the United States." Ref Sources for Small & Medium-sized Libr. 5th edition

Palmquist, Roland E.

Questions and answers for electricians examinations. Macmillan il pa $20   **621.3**

1. Electric engineering—Examinations

"An Audel book"

First published 1945 under the authorship of Edwin P. Anderson with title: Audels questions and answers for electricians examinations. (11th edition 1993 revised by Paul Rosenberg) Periodically revised

Includes information on the National Electrical Code, questions & answers for license tests, Ohm's law with applied examples, hook-ups for motors, lighting & instruments

Standard handbook for electrical engineers. McGraw-Hill $104.50   **621.3**

1. Electric engineering—Handbooks, manuals, etc.

First published 1908. (12th edition 1986) Periodically revised

Contains data on all branches of electrical engineering including material in the field of nuclear physics, plastics and resins, transistors and television

621.319   Transmission of electric power

Armpriester, Kate, 1947-

Do your own wiring. Sterling 1991 123p il pa $12.95   **621.319**

1. Electric wiring
ISBN 0-8069-8472-4   LC 91-18970

Also available from Borgo Press

"A Popular Science book"

First published 1987 by Popular Science Bks.

A basic guide to wiring circuitry, safety, tools, materials and basic skills. Common repairs and improvements are discussed

Basic wiring; by the editors of Time-Life Books. rev ed. Time-Life Bks. 1989 127p il (Home repair and improvement) $15.93   **621.319**

1. Electric wiring   LC 89-4381

First published 1976

This manual provides safety rules for household electrical repairs as well as household improvement projects such as instructions for adding outlets, changing switches, running wires to the exterior of the house for post lanterns, and rewiring lamps

Clifford, Martin, 1910-

Electrical wiring and repair; a guide to improving and maintaining residential electrical systems. Prentice-Hall 1991 258p il $28   **621.319**

1. Electric wiring
ISBN 0-13-247867-6   LC 90-33840

This guide to indoor and outdoor electrical wiring describes correct tools, explains how to make electrical joints and connections, and provides step-by-step instructions for lighting projects

Kittle, James L., 1913-

Home electrical repair and maintenance. McGraw-Hill 1985 219p il pa $9.95   **621.319**

1. Electric wiring
ISBN 0-07-034899-5   LC 84-23347

An "introduction to electricity and housewiring geared to the needs of the average do-it-yourselfer. Topics covered include tools, standard household electrical devices, wiring techniques, minor electrical repairs, and safety measures." Libr J

621.38   Electronics and communications engineering

Grob, Bernard

Basic electronics. McGraw-Hill $40.68   **621.38**

1. Electricity 2. Electronics

First published 1959. (7th edition 1992) Periodically revised

Grob, Bernard—*Continued*
An introductory text on the fundamentals of electricity and electronics for technicians in radio, television, and industrial electronics

Includes bibliography

621.381   Electronics

Electronics engineers' handbook; Donald G. Fink, editor, Donald Christiansen, editor. 3rd ed. McGraw-Hill 1989 various paging il $105.50   **621.381**
1. Electronics—Handbooks, manuals, etc.
ISBN 0-07-020982-0   LC 88-13187
First published 1975
Covers essential principles, data, and design information on the components, circuits, equipment, and systems of electronics engineering. Emphasizes practical use of basic principles. Includes computer-aided design and electronic data processing

Includes bibliographies

Encyclopedia of electronics; Stan Gibilsco, editor-in-chief. TAB Bks. 1985 xxxviii, 983p il $58   **621.381**
1. Electronics—Dictionaries
ISBN 0-8306-2000-1   LC 84-16437
Contains "clear, concise, and jargon-free explanations of . . . electrical, electronics, and communication technology terms. . . . A table of standard schematic symbols precedes over 3,000 alphabetically arranged entries. Copious diagrams and cross-references are provided throughout, and there is a thorough index to articles, illustrations, and tables." Am Libr

Sinclair, Ian Robertson
The   HarperCollins   dictionary   of electronics;   [by]   Ian   R.   Sinclair. HarperCollins Pubs. 1991 363p il $25; pa $12.95   **621.381**
1. Electronics—Dictionaries
ISBN 0-06-271528-3; 0-06-461022-5 (pa)
                                      LC 90-56001
This dictionary includes over 2000 entries with in-depth explanations and examples in the various fields of electronics including microprocessor technology and telecommunications and features over 100 diagrams and charts

Turner, Rufus P.
The illustrated dictionary of electronics; [by] Rufus P. Turner, Stan Gibilsco. 5th ed. TAB Professional & Ref. Bks. 1991 723p il $39.95; pa $26.45   **621.381**
1. Electronics—Dictionaries
ISBN 0-8306-7345-8; 0-8306-3345-6 (pa)
                                      LC 90-22674
First published 1980
This work "deals with electronics in the broadest sense, covering standard terminology as well as jargon and related trade terms. There are 27,000 entries in all. Definitions are concise, cross-referenced, and illustrated with line drawings." Nichols. Guide to Ref Books for Sch Media Cent. 4th edition

621.382   Communications engineering

Weems, David B.
Designing, building, and testing your own speaker system—with projects. [3rd ed]. TAB Bks. 1990 214p il $24.95; pa $16.95
                                      621.382
1. Intercommunication systems
ISBN 0-8306-8374-7; 0-8306-3374-X (pa)
                                      LC 90-30651
First published 1981
This manual offers instructions on building low cost high quality loudspeaker systems using Radio Shack components and the latest audio technology

621.384   Radio and radar

Carr, Joseph J.
Old time radios! restoration and repair. TAB Bks. 1991 256p il $25.95; pa $16.95
                                      621.384
1. Radio—Repairing
ISBN 0-8306-7342-3; 0-8306-3342-1 (pa)
                                      LC 90-44411
This guide includes the history, theory and practical operation of old-time radio sets and detailed instructions and schematics for repairing and rebuilding them

Lewis, Thomas S. W.
Empire of the air; the men who made radio; [by] Tom Lewis. Burlingame Bks. 1991 421p il $25; pa $13   **621.384**
1. De Forest, Lee 2. Armstrong, Edwin Howard, 1890-1954 3. Sarnoff, David, 1891-1971 4. Radio—History
ISBN 0-06-018215-6; 0-06-098119-9 (pa)
                                      LC 90-56385
This history of the development of radio focuses on the careers and contributions of Lee de Forest, Edwin H. Armstrong, and RCA head David Sarnoff
"Lewis' ability to combine telling detail with broad strokes enlivens every facet of this story of man and machine. Published in conjunction with a PBS documentary." Booklist

Includes bibliographic references

621.3841   Amateur (Ham) radio

The **ARRL** handbook for the radio amateur. American Radio Relay League il $25
                                      621.3841
1. Radio—Handbooks, manuals, etc. 2. Amateur radio stations—Handbooks, manuals, etc.
Annual. Began publication 1926. (69th edition 1992) Editions 1 through 61 published with title: The Radio amateur's handbook
"The handbook offers most of the instruction and information needed to begin and enjoy ham-radio activity. . . . This is both authoritative and comprehensive." Wynar. Guide to Ref Books for Sch Media Cent. 3d edition

Bennett, Hank

The complete shortwave listener's handbook; [by] Hank Bennett, Harry L. Helms, and David T. Hardy; foreword by Eugene R. Reich. 3rd ed. TAB Bks. 1986 294p il hardcover o.p. paperback available $17.95   **621.3841**

1. Shortwave radio
ISBN 0-8306-2655-7 (pa)   LC 86-5858

First published 1974

"An excellent introductory guide to shortwave listening. . . . [This] explains the basics of radio waves, terminology, frequencies, monitoring, DXing, and so forth." Recomm Ref Books in Paperback. 2d edition

Kaufman, Milton

Radio operator's license Q & A manual. Sams pa $24.95   **621.3841**

1. Radio—Examinations

First published 1949. (11th edition 1987) Frequently revised. Publisher varies

Designed as a study aid and reference volume, this book covers the information necessary for the successful completion of the FCC examination for commercial radio operators

621.385 Telephone

Oppedahl, Carl

The phone book; how to get the telephone equipment and service you want—and pay less; [by] Carl Oppedahl and the editors of Consumer Reports Books. rev & updated ed. Consumers Union of U.S. 1991 368p il pa $15.95   **621.385**

1. Telephone—Equipment and supplies 2. Consumer education
ISBN 0-89043-364-X   LC 90-19394

First published 1987 with title: The telephone book

This is a consumers guide to telephone equipment and service including long distance and local service, installation and repair, choosing equipment, cellular phones, answering machines and fax machines

621.388 Television

Capelo, Gregory R.

VCR troubleshooting & repair guide; [by] Gregory R. Capelo, Robert C. Brenner. 2nd ed. Sams 1991 286p il pa $24.95 **621.388**

1. Videotape recorders and recording—Maintenance and repair
ISBN 0-672-22749-5   LC 91-60545

First published 1987 with authors names in reverse order

This is a guide to caring for VCRs including preventative maintenance, diagnosing problems and making repairs

Includes bibliographic references

Clifford, Martin, 1910-

The camcorder; use, care, and repair. Prentice-Hall 1989 xx, 279p il $43
621.388

1. Camcorders
ISBN 0-13-113689-5   LC 88-19072

The author supplies "background on the types of camcorders available as well as various features, accessories, tapes, and techniques. [He] provides training and numerous tips on quality 'picture making' and good audio recording, including use of a story line and background music, even for taping family holiday scenes." Booklist

Davidson, Homer L.

Troubleshooting and repairing camcorders. TAB Bks. 1990 533p il $35.95; pa $22.95
621.388

1. Camcorders—Maintenance and repair
ISBN 0-8306-8337-2; 0-8306-3337-5 (pa)
LC 89-29141

This guide to repairing home video cameras includes circuit diagrams, a list of abbreviations used by manufacturers and the addresses of camcorder producers

McComb, Gordon

Troubleshooting and repairing VCR's. 2nd ed. TAB Bks. 1991 413p il $29.95; pa $19.95   **621.388**

1. Videotape recorders and recording—Maintenance and repair
ISBN 0-8306-7777-1; 0-8306-3777-X (pa) LC 91-6782

First published 1988

Basic maintenance and repairs for various models of VCRs

Includes bibliography

Prentiss, Stan

HDTV: high-definition television. 2nd ed. TAB Bks. c1994 322p $29.95; pa $16.95
621.388

1. High definition television
ISBN 0-8306-4296-X; 0-8306-4295-1 (pa)
LC 92-43819

First published 1990

This introduction to high definition television discusses the advantages and disadvantages of various transmission and receiving systems, methods used to produce them, and FCC involvement in choosing a standard for the U.S. market

Wilkins, Richard C.

Home VCR repair illustrated; [by] Richard C. Wilkins, Cheryl A. Hubbard. TAB Bks. 1991 383p il $29.95; pa $19.95   **621.388**

1. Videotape recorders and recording—Maintenance and repair
ISBN 0-8306-7711-9; 0-8306-3711-7 (pa)
LC 91-12590

The authors "reveal the secrets of repairing VCRs with household items and without expensive test equipment. Together, they virtually boast that a two-hour professional repair, e.g., a roller-guide alignment, takes only 15 minutes when you follow their methodology. Their

Wilkins, Richard C.—*Continued*
matter-of-fact, nontechnical presentation makes for easy reading and for easily finding the solutions to particular problems. . . . The illustrations—photos of the parts and procedures under discussion—further enhance this troubleshooting manual." Booklist

621.389 Sound recording, security, related systems

Pohlmann, Ken C.
The compact disc handbook. 2nd ed. A-R Eds. 1992 349p il (Computer music and digital audio ser) $49.95; pa $34.95

621.389

1. Compact discs 2. Compact disc players
ISBN 0-89579-301-6; 0-89579-300-8 (pa)

LC 92-13287

First published 1989 with title: The compact disc
This work offers detailed coverage of all aspects of compact disc technology
Includes bibliographic references

621.39 Computers

Held, Gilbert, 1943-
The PC upgrader's manual; how to build and extend your system. rev ed. Wiley 1991 356p il $24.95

621.39

1. Computers 2. Microcomputers
ISBN 0-471-52452-2

LC 90-12585

First published 1988
This is a guide to personalizing any PC by adding circuit boards, peripherals and other hardware and to fine-tuning software and troubleshooting PC problems

Kidder, Tracy
The soul of a new machine. Little, Brown 1981 293p $19.95

621.39

1. Computers
ISBN 0-316-49170-5

LC 81-6044

Also available in paperback from Avon Bks.
"An Atlantic Monthly Press book"
This book details the work lives of the people who developed a new super-mini computer at the Data General Corporation in the short span of a year and a half from mid-1978 to early 1980
The author "has endowed the tale with such pace, texture and poetic implication that he has elevated it to a high level of narrative art." N Y Times Book Rev

Margolis, Art
Troubleshooting and repairing personal computers. 2nd ed. Windcrest Bks. 1991 679p il $34.95; pa $23.95

621.39

1. Microcomputers—Maintenance and repair
ISBN 0-8306-2187-3; 0-8306-2186-5 (pa)

LC 91-14381

First published 1983; published 1987 with title: Troubleshooting and repairing the new personal computers

This illustrated guide covers the most common microcomputer problems, input and output testing techniques, and diagnosis and repairing techniques

621.43 Internal-combustion engines and propulsion

Wulforst, Harry
The rocketmakers. Orion Bks. (NY) 1990 296p il $18.95

621.43

1. Rocketry
ISBN 0-517-56586-2

LC 90-32532

This is a history of rocket making from the 1920s to the present
Includes bibliographic references

621.46 Electric and related propulsion

Anderson, Edwin P., 1895-
Electric motors; by Edwin P. Anderson and Rex Miller. 5th ed. Macmillan 1991 684p il $35

621.46

1. Electric motors
ISBN 0-02-501920-1

LC 90-40621

"An Audel book"
First published 1947 with title: Audels electric motor guide
Gives practical guidance in the selection, installation, operation, and maintenance of electric motors, with descriptions, illustrations, and some troubleshooting guidance for maintenance and installation personnel

621.6 Fans, blowers, pumps

Stewart, Harry L.
Pumps. 5th ed, rev. by Rex Miller. Macmillan 1991 529p il $35

621.6

1. Pumping machinery 2. Hydraulic machinery
ISBN 0-02-614725-4

LC 90-40618

"An Audel book"
First published 1965 under the authorship of F. D. Graham with title: Audels pumps, hydraulics, air compressors

This guide for operators, engineers, maintenance workers, inspectors, superintendents, and mechanics covers the fundamentals and operating principles of pumps, pump controls, and hydraulics

621.9 Tools and fabricating equipment

Davidson, Homer L.
Troubleshooting and repairing power tools. TAB Bks. 1990 243p il $26.95; pa $17.95

621.9

1. Power tools
ISBN 0-8306-7347-4; 0-8306-3347-2 (pa)

LC 90-37846

Davidson, Homer L.—*Continued*
This repair guide offers step-by-step illustrated procedures for troubleshooting and fixing 35 portable and stationary power tools

Sloane, Eric
A museum of early American tools. Holt & Co. 1990 c1964 108p il $16.95   **621.9**
1. Tools—History
ISBN 0-8050-1292-3   LC 89-27958
Also available in paperback from Ballantine Bks.
A reissue of the title first published 1964 by Funk & Wagnalls
"Tools used in America in the 17th, 18th and early 19th centuries are illustrated with drawings by the author, the originals being in his own collection." Libr J

Watson, Aldren Auld, 1917-
Hand tools; their ways and workings. Norton 1982 416p il $24.95   **621.9**
1. Tools
ISBN 0-393-01654-4   LC 82-8191
"A practical guide for the home craftsperson, with line drawings and detailed descriptions of how to use each tool in the best manner. Also includes a section on sharpening tools, and an appendix on purchasing them, along with plans for a workbench and other pieces of shop equipment." Ref Sources for Small & Medium-sized Libr. 5th edition

623.4   Ordnance

Gun digest. DBI Bks. pa $19.95   **623.4**
1. Firearms 2. Shooting
Annual. First published 1944. Editors vary
This reference work covers information relating to shotguns, rifles, cartridges, sights and scopes, availability of arms and accessories, technical articles on hunting, gun control, foreign arms, etc.

Rhodes, Richard
The making of the atomic bomb. Simon & Schuster 1986 886p il hardcover o.p. paperback available $14.95   **623.4**
1. Atomic bomb
ISBN 0-671-65719-4 (pa)   LC 86-15445
This book chronicles the development of the bomb "from the birth of modern physics in the late 19th century to the first tests of hydrogen bombs, by the United States in 1954 and the Soviet Union in 1955." Science
"The book provides portraits of the many players from Szilard and Einstein to Oppenheimer. . . . The book is heavily documented and includes a 13-page bibliography. This is a definitive work, well written, with a gripping story. It is not an easy book to read, but is well worth the effort." Libr J

Shooter's bible. Stoeger il pa $19.95 **623.4**
1. Firearms—Catalogs
Annual. First published 1925 by Follett
Contains specifications and manufacturers' current prices for a variety of firearms and accessories. Also includes articles on related subjects, gun finder index, and caliber finder index

623.8   Nautical engineering and seamanship

Jane's fighting ships. Jane's Information Group $245   **623.8**
1. Warships 2. Navies
Annual. First published 1898. Title and publisher vary
"Arranged by country with subdivisions according to type of ship. Gives numbers and names of ships within each class; builders; dates of laying down, launching, and completion; and a photograph of a ship within the class. Specifications for each class are also given." Sheehy. Guide to Ref Books. 10th edition

623.88   Seamanship

Day, Cyrus Lawrence, 1900-1968
The art of knotting & splicing; edited by Ray O. Beard, Jr. and M. Lee Hoffman, Jr. 4th ed. Naval Inst. Press 1986 235p il $24.95   **623.88**
1. Knots and splices
ISBN 0-87021-062-9   LC 86-16299
First published 1947 by Dodd, Mead
A series of photographs in sequence demonstrates splicing and the tying of knots in actual use today, giving their origins, backgrounds, comparative strengths and uses
Includes bibliography

623.89   Navigation of nautical craft

Dutton's navigation & piloting. Naval Inst. Press il $44.95   **623.89**
1. Navigation
First published 1926 under the authorship of Benjamin Dutton with title: Navigation and nautical astronomy. (14th edition 1985 by Elbert S. Maloney)
This guide for the coastal and seagoing mariner focuses on piloting, celestial navigation, radio navigation and dead reckoning

624   Civil engineering

The **Backyard** builder; over 150 build-it-yourself projects for your garden, home, and yard; edited by John Warde; illustrated by Frank Rohrbach. Rodale Press 1985 xxiii, 631p il $21.95   **624**
1. Building—Handbooks, manuals, etc.
ISBN 0-87857-531-6   LC 84-24846
An "assemblage of functional outdoor building projects, ranging in scale from bird feeders to storage sheds. . . . An introductory chapter does a brief but creditable job of reviewing materials and methods appropriate for outdoor building. A basic knowledge of hand and power tools and construction techniques is assumed." Libr J

Hawkes, Nigel
Structures; the way things are built.
Macmillan 1990 240p il maps $39.95 **624**
1. Civil engineering 2. Buildings
ISBN 0-02-549105-9   LC 90-35928
"A Marshall edition"

The author "has chosen more than 40 monumental structures for discussion, from Egyptian obelisks to the Vatican, the Great Wall of China, and a nuclear power station. . . . Each is described in detail and shown in color photographs and schematics." Booklist

Includes bibliographic references

Standard handbook for civil engineers; Frederick S. Merritt, editor. 3rd ed. McGraw-Hill 1983 various paging il $124.50 **624**
1. Civil engineering—Handbooks, manuals, etc.
ISBN 0-07-041515-3   LC 82-14902
First published 1968

Seeks to "provide in a single volume a compendium of the best of current civil engineering practices. . . . Emphasis is on fundamental principles and their practical applications, with special attention to simplified procedures."—*Pref.* Signed contributions by specialists include tabular data, line drawings, references." Sheehy. Guide to Ref Books. 10th edition

629.13   Aeronautics

Boyne, Walter J., 1929-
The Smithsonian book of flight. Smithsonian Bks. 1987 288p il $35 **629.13**
1. Aeronautics—History
ISBN 0-89599-020-2   LC 87-9699
Also available from Orion Bks. (NY)

Historical photographs and color paintings illustrate this history of aviation. From contemporaries of the Wright Brothers to modern test pilots, aeronautical engineers' comments about various feats and inventions augment the text

Bryan, C. D. B. (Courtlandt Dixon Barnes)
The National Air and Space Museum; art directed and designed by David Larkin; photographs by Michael Freeman, Robert Golden and Dennis Rolfe. 2nd ed, photographs by Jonathan Wallen. Abrams 1988 498p il $75; pa $39.98 **629.13**
1. National Air and Space Museum (U.S.)
ISBN 0-8109-1380-1; 0-8109-8126-2 (pa) LC 88-3383
First published 1979

An illustrated look at the National Air and Space Museum's exhibits and galleries

"Bryan's text presents descriptions, poetry, history, and anecdotes, with the photographs providing breathtaking scenes of early aircraft, warplanes, and spaceships." Booklist

Includes bibliography

Lindbergh, Charles, 1902-1974
The Spirit of St. Louis. Scribner 1975 c1953 513p $50 **629.13**
1. Aeronautics—Flights 2. Spirit of St. Louis (Airplane)
ISBN 0-684-14421-2
Also available from Buccaneer Bks.
"Hudson River editions"
First published 1953

This is an account of the first solo transatlantic flight from New York to Paris, as well as a detailed description of the preparation for the flight which in turn mirrors aviation of the 1920's

Moolman, Valerie
Women aloft; by Valerie Moolman and the editors of Time-Life Books. Time-Life Bks. 1981 176p il (Epic of flight) $18.60 **629.13**
1. Women air pilots 2. Aeronautics—History
          LC 80-29475

An illustrated chronicle of women in aeronautics from the early 19th century to World War II. Includes women of many nationalities and their fight against sex discrimination

Includes bibliography

Prendergast, Curtis
The first aviators; by Curtis Prendergast and the editors of Time-Life Books. Time-Life Bks. 1981 176p il (Epic of flight) $18.60 **629.13**
1. Aeronautics—History   LC 79-25919

Text and a variety of illustrations trace the burgeoning age of aviation from the "reinvention" of the airplane in France some years after the Wright Brothers' first flight through the beginning of World War I

Includes bibliography

629.132   Principles of aerial flight

Flight. Time-Life Bks. 1990 144p il (How things work) $19.93 **629.132**
1. Flight   LC 90-37365

Text and numerous illustrations explain the principles and methods of flight. Diagrams and cutaway drawings illustrate the similarities in design that allow insects, birds, and aircraft to become airborne

629.133   Aircraft types

Jane's all the world's aircraft. Jane's Information Group il $225 **629.133**
1. Aeronautics
ISSN 0075-3017
Also available on CD-ROM
Annual. First published 1909

This reference offers illustrations, descriptions and specifications of all the aircraft of various countries of the world

629.222   Passenger automobiles

Fariello, Sal

The people's car book; the one essential handbook for people who don't trust mechanics, car salesmen, or car manufacturers. St. Martin's Press 1993 c1992 250p il $15.95   **629.222**

1. Automobiles 2. Consumer education

ISBN 0-312-08278-9   LC 92-26608

A Thomas Dunne book

This is a "guide on what consumers should watch for when they shop. Written for lay readers, the text gives guidance on buying and leasing, preventive maintenance, and repair." Libr J

Gillis, Jack

The car book; the definitive buyer's guide to car safety, fuel economy, maintenance, and much more; with Karen Fierst and Jay Einhorn; foreword by Clarence Ditlow. HarperPerennial il pa $11   **629.222**

1. Automobiles 2. Consumer education

Annual. First published 1981 by Tilden Press

In this consumer guide to automobiles U.S. and foreign models are appraised in terms of safety, fuel economy, maintenance costs, and insurance rates. Special sections cover such topics as buying tires and used cars

Hirsch, Jay

Great American dream machines; classic cars of the 50s and 60s. Macmillan 1985 240p il o.p.; Random House paperback available $23   **629.222**

1. Automobiles

ISBN 0-679-72160-6 (pa)   LC 85-10454

A photographic survey of 65 popular American automobiles from the late 1940s to the early 1970s. The text accompanying the photos includes a list of each model's technical specifications and accessories

Nader, Ralph

The lemon book: auto rights; [by] Ralph Nader and Clarence Ditlow. Moyer Bell 1989 368p hardcover o.p. paperback available $12.95   **629.222**

1. Automobiles 2. Consumer education

ISBN 1-55921-020-6 (pa)   LC 89-37111

"The authors proffer advice on car buying, education on the laws pertaining to it, and a plea for greater consumer involvement in auto industry reforms. Authentic letters from disgruntled buyers abound throughout, as do the names, phone numbers . . . and addresses of sources of help." Booklist

629.227   Cycles

Sloane, Eugene A.

The complete book of bicycling. all new 4th ed. Simon & Schuster 1988 542p il hardcover o.p. paperback available $15.95   **629.227**

1. Bicycles and bicycling

ISBN 0-671-65802-6 (pa)   LC 88-404

"A Fireside book"

First published 1970 by Trident Press. Variant titles: The new complete book of bicycling; The all new complete book of bicycling

Covers choosing a bicycle, repair and tools, preventive maintenance, safety tips for commuters, new technologies, bike touring, all-terrain and mountain bikes, and facts on health

Includes bibliography

629.25   Engines

Crouse, William Harry, 1907-

Automotive electronics and electrical equipment. McGraw-Hill il $29.95   **629.25**

First published 1942. (10th edition 1986) Periodically revised

The author explains the theory of operation, maintenance procedures, checks and adjustments, of the electrical units used on passenger cars, trucks, and buses. The purpose of the book is to enable the owner to test, adjust, or repair all types of motor vehicle electrical units

Automotive engines; [by] William H. Crouse, Donald L. Anglin. McGraw-Hill il $27.95   **629.25**

1. Automobiles—Engines

First published 1955. (7th edition 1986) Periodically revised

Includes material on engine design and servicing techniques, including high-performance engines, pistons, bearings, combustion-chamber design, valves, pollution-control devices, and diagnostic equipment

Automotive fuel, lubricating, and cooling systems; [by] William H. Crouse, Donald L. Anglin. McGraw-Hill il $29.95   **629.25**

1. Automobiles—Engines 2. Automobiles—Fuel systems 3. Automobiles—Lubrication

First published 1955. (6th edition 1981) Periodically revised

Covers engine and fuel-system design and servicing techniques, ventilation, pollution-control devises, and electronic fuel systems

629.28   Motor land vehicles and cycles—Tests, driving, maintenance, repairs

American Automobile Association

Sportsmanlike driving. McGraw-Hill il maps $22.16; pa $14.48   **629.28**

1. Automobile drivers—Education 2. Traffic regulations

American Automobile Association — *Continued*

First published 1947. (9th edition 1987) Periodically revised

This textbook on driver education includes information on technical, mechanical, and safety matters, as well as data on selecting and insuring a car, and travel planning

Basic car care. Time-Life Bks. 1988 144p il (Fix it yourself) $18.60   **629.28**

1. Automobiles—Maintenance and repair
LC 87-28732

An illustrated guide to locating and repairing automotive problems. Engine systems, transmissions, brakes, and cooling systems are discussed

Berto, Frank J.

Bicycling magazine's complete guide to upgrading your bike. Rodale Press 1988 308p il pa $14.95   **629.28**

1. Bicycles and bicycling—Maintenance and repair
ISBN 0-87857-751-3   LC 87-28886

The author "covers most brands and models of all components and the frame. He freely admits his biases, and includes comparisons of index vs. friction shifting, toe clip/strap vs. Look release-type pedals, brakes, saddles, handlebars . . . hubs, rims, and tires. The tables are full of good detail and are complete." Libr J

Bicycling magazine's complete guide to bicycle maintenance and repair; by the editors of Bicycling. rev & updated ed. Rodale Press 1990 310p il $24.95; pa $16.95   **629.28**

1. Bicycles and bicycling—Maintenance and repair
ISBN 0-87857-895-1; 0-87857-896-X (pa) LC 90-8057
First published 1986

This "guide is an excellent, comprehensive manual that covers all repairs from flat tires to complex overhauls. The clear text is supplemented by well-labeled drawings and photographs." Nichols. Guide to Ref Books for Sch Media Cent. 4th edition

Chilton's auto repair manual. Chilton il $26.95   **629.28**

1. Automobiles—Maintenance and repair
ISSN 0069-3634

Annual. First published 1953 with title: Chilton's automobile repair manual

"Covers all mass-produced American cars of the past six or seven years plus the current year. Illustrated; includes charts to help diagnose problems. Useful for both novices and experts." N Y Public Libr Book of How & Where to Look It Up

Chilton's import car repair manual. Chilton il $26.95   **629.28**

1. Automobiles, Foreign—Maintenance and repair
ISSN 0271-3608

Annual. First published 1971-1972 in two volumes with title: Chilton's foreign car repair manual. Title varies

This manual covers maintenance, specifications and repair of European and Japanese cars and pick-up trucks. Many photographs and diagrams are included

Chilton's motorcycle & ATV repair manual. Chilton il $28.95   **629.28**

1. Motorcycles—Maintenance and repair 2. All terrain vehicles—Maintenance and repair

First published 1974 with title: Chilton's motorcycle repair manual. (1945-85 edition 1986) Periodically revised

This is a guide to the tune-up, maintenance and repair of component systems for the more popular motorcycles and for ATVs (all terrain vehicles) sold in the United States

Crouse, William Harry, 1907-

Automotive mechanics; [by] William H. Crouse and Donald L. Anglin. Glencoe il $44.95   **629.28**

1. Automobiles—Maintenance and repair

First published 1946 by McGraw-Hill. (10th edition 1992) Periodically revised

This book tells how an automobile is constructed, how it operates, how to maintain it, and how to repair it

Motor's auto repair manual. Morrow il $23.50   **629.28**

1. Automobiles—Maintenance and repair

Annual. First published 1937

This book gives specific instructions on the removal, replacement, fitting and adjustment of all mechanical parts on all cars currently in operation. Each chapter begins with an index of service operations

Plas, Rob van der, 1938-

The bicycle repair book; the new complete manual of bicycle care; illustrated by the author. 2nd fully updated ed. Bicycle Bks. 1993 192p il pa $9.95   **629.28**

1. Bicycles and bicycling—Maintenance and repair
ISBN 0-933201-55-9   LC 92-83822
First published 1985

Among the topics covered are: selecting tools; preventative maintenance; adjusting brakes, gears, and bearings; wheel building and spoke replacement, and troubleshooting

Sloane, Eugene A.

Sloane's new bicycle maintenance manual. Simon & Schuster 1991 301p il $14.95   **629.28**

1. Bicycles and bicycling—Maintenance and repair
ISBN 0-671-61947-0   LC 91-14699

"A Fireside book"

First published 1981 with title: Eugene A. Sloane's bicycle maintenance manual

This "volume illustrates the proper maintenance and repair of a bicycle's main mechanical systems, from changing a tire to complete overhaul of major elements. Up-to-date information on the latest technological improvements is included, as are suggestions for such specialized machines as tandem bicycles." Booklist

629.4 Astronautics

Collins, Michael, 1930-
Liftoff; the story of America's adventure in space; illustrated by James Dean. Grove Press 1988 288p il hardcover o.p. paperback available $12.95   **629.4**

1. Astronautics—United States
ISBN 0-8021-3188-3 (pa)   LC 88-1706

This "history of the United States space program concentrates on . . . the actual space flights that made up the Mercury, Gemini, Apollo, Skylab, Apollo-Soyuz and space shuttle programs." N Y Times Book Rev

Gibson, Roy
Space. Oxford Univ. Press 1992 153p il (Science, technology, and society ser) $36
629.4

1. Astronautics 2. Outer space—Exploration
ISBN 0-19-858343-5   LC 91-43590

"Written for nonspecialists, the book surveys the history of space flight and considers manned missions, space science, and the uses of different spacecraft." Univ Press Books for Public and Second Sch Libr

In space. Time-Life Bks. 1991 144p il maps (How things work) $19.93   **629.4**

1. Astronautics   LC 90-21496

This book explores what humans have seen in space, from ancient times to the present, and the equipment and machines now used to explore the universe including satellites, spacecraft, and space stations of the future

Magill's survey of science, space exploration series; edited by Frank N. Magill. Salem Press 1989 5v set $425   **629.4**

1. Astronautics 2. Outer space—Exploration
ISBN 0-89356-600-4   LC 88-38267

"This five-volume encyclopedia covers not only space exploration through early 1989 but also some fundamental astronomy. Articles averaging a half-dozen pages each cover individual space craft and space missions." Sci Books Films

Includes bibliographies

629.45 Manned space flight

Lewis, Richard S., 1916-
Challenger: the final voyage. Columbia Univ. Press 1988 249p il $29.95   **629.45**

1. Challenger (Spacecraft)
ISBN 0-231-06490-X   LC 87-17929

The author "examines the accident, the salvage effort that discovered the cause, the Rogers Commission's inquiry, and its recomendations for fixing the shuttle hardware and NASA itself." Libr J

Wolfe, Tom
The right stuff. new ed. Farrar, Straus & Giroux 1983 436p $30   **629.45**

1. Astronauts 2. Astronautics—United States
ISBN 0-374-25033-2   LC 84-162805

Also available in paperback from Bantam Bks.

A reissue of the title first published 1979

This is a "history of the early years of the space program. Starting with an account of the lives of military pilots [the book progresses] through the selection of the first seven astronauts, their training, and the Mercury flights." Libr J

629.47 Astronautical engineering

Stine, G. Harry (George Harry), 1928-
Handbook of model rocketry. Wiley 367p il pa $17.95   **629.47**

1. Rockets (Aeronautics)—Models

First published 1965 by Follett. (6th edition 1994) Periodically revised. Publisher varies

"NAR official handbook"

"Stine, an authority on model rocketry, describes all aspects of the subject from basics to international competition." Ref Sources for Small & Medium-sized Libr. 4th edition

629.8 Automatic control engineering

Caudill, Maureen
In our own image; building an artificial man. Oxford Univ. Press 1992 242p il $23
629.8

1. Robotics 2. Artificial intelligence
ISBN 0-19-507338-X   LC 91-42524

An overview of the technology utilized in android research

Includes bibliographic references

McComb, Gordon
The robot builder's bonanza; 99 inexpensive robotics projects. TAB Bks. 1987 326p il hardcover o.p. paperback available $16.95   **629.8**

1. Robotics
ISBN 0-8306-2800-2 (pa)   LC 87-5040

Following an introduction to the general principles of robotics, tools, supplies and parts, the author presents do-it-youself projects with practical applications

Includes bibliography

Robotics; by the editors of Time-Life Books. [rev ed]. Time-Life Bks. 1991 128p il (Understanding computers) $21.27   **629.8**

1. Robotics   LC 91-16459

First published 1987

An illustrated look at the history of robotics, the various uses and types of robots, and the social and economic ramifications of artificial intelligence

Includes bibliography

631.5 Cultivation and harvesting of crops

Jones, J. L. (John Lemuel), 1907-
Home hydroponics—and how to do it! by Lem Jones with Paul and Cay Beardsley. rev & updated ed. Crown 1990 c1977 142p il pa $12 **631.5**

1. Hydroponics
ISBN 0-517-53760-5 LC 90-1823

First published 1975 by Beardsley; this is a reissue of the 1977 edition published by Ward Ritchie Press

This guide covers equipment, caring for plants and dealing with plant diseases, where to buy supplies and how to grow fruits and vegetables using hydroponic methods

Includes bibliographic references

632 Plant injuries, diseases, pests

Hart, Rhonda Massingham, 1959-
Bugs, slugs & other thugs; controlling garden pests organically. Storey Communications 1991 214p il $21.95; pa $9.95 **632**

1. Agricultural pests 2. Organiculture
ISBN 0-88266-665-7; 0-88266-664-9 (pa)
LC 90-50607

"A Down-to-earth book"

This book, about combating pests without pesticides is "entirely garden-oriented and covers a wide variety of pests, including nematodes, spider mites, aphids, beetles, bugs, moth larvae, turtles, birds, and a long list of mammals, such as armadillos, bears, and the neighbor's kids." Libr J

Includes bibliographic references

634.9 Forestry

MacLean, Norman, 1902-1990
Young men & fire. University of Chicago Press 1992 301p il $19.95; pa $10.95 **634.9**

1. United States. Forest Service 2. Forest fires 3. Fire fighters
ISBN 0-226-50061-6; 0-226-50062-4 (pa)
LC 92-11890

Also available G.K. Hall large print edition

This book "focuses on the death of 13 firefighters . . . who perished in the 1949 Mann Gulch fire along the Missouri River not far from Helena, Mont." Christ Sci Monit

This is a "magnificent drama of writing, a tragedy that pays tribute to the dead and offers rescue to the living. . . . Maclean's search for the truth, which becomes an exploration of his own mortality, is more compelling even than his journey into the heart of the fire. His description of the conflagration terrifies, but it is his battle with words, his effort to turn the story of the 13 men into tragedy, that makes the book a classic." N Y Times Book Rev

635 Garden crops (Horticulture)

Ball, Jeff
Rodale's garden problem solver; vegetables, fruits, and herbs; illustrations by Pamela and Walter Carroll and Robin Brickman; photographs by Liz Ball. Rodale Press 1988 550p il map $23.95 **635**

1. Gardening
ISBN 0-87857-762-9 LC 88-1714

This "guide provides advice on more than 700 specific problems and thousands of other general gardening questions dealing with insect and other animal pests, weeds, propagation, diseases, storage, and nutrient and environmental deficiencies. Ball tells how to identify and control insects (from aphids to wireworms) and diseases that destroy vegetables, fruits and berries, and herbs." Booklist

Includes bibliography

Forsell, Mary
Heirloom herbs; using old-fashioned herbs in gardens, recipes, and decorations; photographs by Tony Cericola; foreword by Rosemary Verey. Villard Bks. 1990 160p il $29.95 **635**

1. Herbs
ISBN 0-394-58336-1 LC 90-50195

"A Running Heads book"

In addition to offering tips on growing and harvesting herbs, the author explores their use in cooking and handicrafts

Halpin, Anne Moyer
Foolproof planting; how to successfully start and propagate more than 250 vegetables, flowers, trees, and shrubs; by Anne Moyer Halpin and the editors of Rodale Press. Rodale Press 1990 319p il $22.95; pa $14.95 **635**

1. Plant propagation 2. Gardening
ISBN 0-87857-876-5; 0-87857-994-X (pa)
LC 89-10991

"A Roundtable Press book"

"Part 1 explains the basic techniques for sprouting plants from seeds and transplanting them; propagation from hard- and softwood cuttings; layering; grafting; and division—of bulbs as well as perennials and shrubs. A planting guide can be found in Part 2, not exhaustive in plants covered (these number 240), but fundamentally sound in guidance given for garden spacing and placement, where and when to plant, and sundry troubleshooting tips." Publ Wkly

Joyce, David
The complete guide to pruning and training plants; [by] David Joyce; technical consultant, Christopher Brickell; foreword by Elvin McDonald. Simon & Schuster 1992 224p il $30 **635**

1. Pruning 2. Plants
ISBN 0-671-73842-9 LC 91-30134

This book offers "information on pruning for plant control. coupled with advice on renovating a vast range of ornamental and fruit-bearing vines, shrubs and trees,

Joyce, David—*Continued*
including camellia, heather, apricot, passion fruit and box. Superb photographs accompany the clear directions." N Y Times Book Rev

Includes bibliographic references

Lawn & garden. Time-Life Bks. 1988 144p il (Fix it yourself) $18.60   **635**
1. Gardening 2. Lawns   LC 88-2373

Discusses problems with indoor and outdoor gardens, soils, flowers, grasses, shrubs, trees, pests and diseases. Also includes sections on tools, safety, and emergencies

The **Organic** gardener's handbook of natural insect and disease control; a complete problem-solving guide to keeping your garden & yard healthy without chemicals; edited by Barbara W. Ellis and Fern Marshall Bradley; contributing writers, Helen Atthowe [et al.] Rodale Press 1992 534p il $26.95   **635**
1. Insect pests 2. Organiculture 3. Plant diseases
ISBN 0-87596-124-X   LC 92-3372

"This book, with 394 color photographs, focuses on how to overcome the problems of insects and diseases in the chemical-free garden. Part one, a plant-by-plant guide to problem solving and prevention, contains a plant encyclopedia with symptoms and solutions for major problems of popular plants, including fruits, vegetables, annuals, bulbs, perennials, trees, and shrubs. Part two contains information on managing pest insects and attracting beneficials." Booklist

Includes bibliographic references

Reader's Digest guide to creative gardening. Reader's Digest Assn. 1986 c1984 384p il $32   **635**
1. Gardening
ISBN 0-278-35223-8   LC 89-113721

First published 1984 in the United Kingdom

Numerous color illustrations accompany a text that describes a wide variety of flowers, and provides instructions on planting, tending, soils, etc.

Rodale's all-new encyclopedia of organic gardening; the indispensable resource for every gardener; edited by Fern Marshall Bradley and Barbara W. Ellis. Rodale Press 1992 690p il $29.95   **635**
1. Organiculture
ISBN 0-87857-999-0   LC 91-32088

First published 1959 with title: Rodale's encyclopedia of organic gardening

"Entries are cross referenced and include further reading lists, related organizations, and key words. Common and botanical names are listed, and while food plants are entered under their common names, ornamentals and herbs are entered under their botanical names. This is an important, complete, well-arranged, and attractive reference tool." Libr J

Rodale's chemical-free yard & garden; the ultimate authority on successful organic gardening; [by] Anna Carr [et al.] Rodale Press 1991 456p il $26.95   **635**
1. Organiculture
ISBN 0-87857-951-6   LC 90-24327

A compendium of "information about biological controls, insect barriers, and the importance of healthy soil. Dealing primarily with pest and disease management, this book addresses vegetables, flowers, fruit, trees and shrubs, and lawns." Libr J

Includes bibliographic references

Rodale's illustrated encyclopedia of herbs; Claire Kowalchik & William H. Hylton, editors; writers: Anna Carr [et al.] Rodale Press 1987 545p il $24.95   **635**
1. Herbs 2. Botany, Medical
ISBN 0-87857-699-1   LC 87-16019

Provides "the history, uses, and cultivation of over 100 herbs, plus information on making teas, lotions, scents, and dyes. Other sections include herbs as houseplants, the history and botany of herbs, and a particularly valuable chapter on the dangers of herbs. The book is attractive and well illustrated." Libr J

Includes bibliography

Smith, Miranda, 1944-
Rodale's garden insect, disease & weed identification guide; [by] Miranda Smith and Anna Carr; illustrations by Robin Brickman. Rodale Press 1988 328p il $21.95   **635**
1. Plant diseases 2. Agricultural pests
ISBN 0-87857-758-0   LC 88-4969

Color photographs and line drawings enable the reader to identify 200 garden insects, diseases, and weeds. Beneficial insects, predators, parasites and pollinators are discussed

Includes bibliography

635.03 Garden crops (Horticulture)—Encyclopedias and dictionaries

Hortus third; a concise dictionary of plants cultivated in the United States and Canada; initially compiled by Liberty Hyde Bailey and Ethel Zoe Bailey; revised and expanded by the staff of the Liberty Hyde Bailey Hortorium. Macmillan 1976 1290p il $150   **635.03**
1. Gardening—Dictionaries   2. Botany—Dictionaries
3. Agriculture—Dictionaries
ISBN 0-02-505470-8

First published 1930 with title: Hortus

"More than 34,000 A-to-Z listings cover all plants cultivated in North America, from a botanical point of view. Almost 200 general entries treat such subjects as bulbs, evergreens, and propagation. Illustrated, and has glossary of terms." N Y Public Libr Book of How & Where to Look It Up

The **New** Royal Horticultural Society dictionary of gardening; editor in chief, Anthony Huxley; editor, Mark Griffiths; managing editor, Margot Levy. Stockton Press 1992 4v il set $795   **635.03**
1. Gardening—Dictionaries
ISBN 1-56159-001-0   LC 92-3261

First published 1951 by Clarendon Press with title: Dictionary of gardening

The New Royal Horticultural Society dictionary of gardening—*Continued*

"The combined effort of 250 of the world's leading horticultural and botanical talents has produced descriptions of 50,000 plants and articles on every conceivable aspect of gardening from soil maintenance to urban greening. . . . With its 4000 line drawings, numerous illustrations, a full index of popular names, and a complete glossary of sources, not to mention an extensive bibliography, this outstanding compilation seems likely to be the standard reference for the next several decades." Libr J

For a fuller review see: Booklist, Sept. 1, 1992

The Wise garden encyclopedia. [rev ed]. Harper & Row 1990 1043p il $45

635.03

1. Gardening—Dictionaries
ISBN 0-06-016114-0   LC 89-46559

First published 1936 by W. H. Wise & Co. with title: The garden encyclopedia; published 1970 by Grosset & Dunlap

"A-to-Z reference for specialists and backyard gardeners alike. . . . Covers flowers, trees, shrubs, lawns, herbs, soil, fertilizers, pesticides, garden design, and many other topics." N Y Public Libr Book of How & Where to Look It Up

Wyman, Donald, 1903-
Wyman's gardening encyclopedia. new expanded 2nd ed. Macmillan 1986 xxvi, 1221p il $55   635.03

1. Gardening—Dictionaries 2. Plants, Cultivated—Dictionaries
ISBN 0-02-632070-3   LC 86-12509

First published 1961

Contains information on major horticultural practices, including use of pesticides and herbicides, and on ornamental and agricultural plant species. Includes scientific names according to Hortus third, entered above, with cross-references for common names

635.9 Flowers and ornamental plants

Annuals. Time-Life Bks. 1988 144p il maps (Time-Life gardener's guide) $18.60 **635.9**

1. Annuals (Plants)   LC 88-2308

Among the topics discussed in this illustrated introduction to annuals are: hybrids, fertilizing, indoor sowing, and flower drying

Includes bibliography

Ball, Jeff
Rodale's flower garden problem solver; annuals, perennials, bulbs, and roses; by Jeff and Liz Ball; illustrations by Pamela and Walter Carroll and Robin Brickman. Rodale Press 1990 422p $23.95   **635.9**

1. Flowers 2. Flower gardening 3. Organiculture
ISBN 0-87857-868-4   LC 89-10992

"Plant-by-plant descriptions provide information on their care and most common afflictions. Recommendations for treatment emphasize natural controls and discourage use of harmful chemicals. Advice on planting

and propagation is also given. The latter part of the book is arranged by pest and disease." Libr J

Rodale's landscape problem solver; a plant-by-plant guide; by Jeff and Liz Ball; illustrations by Pamela and Walter Carroll and Robin Brickman; photographs by Liz Ball and the Rodale Press photography staff. Rodale Press 1989 439p il $24.95   **635.9**

1. Landscape gardening 2. Plant diseases 3. Agricultural pests
ISBN 0-87857-802-1   LC 89-30190

"For distraught gardeners, the Balls list many typical problems and also provide the answers. The authors assure the reader that insects, diseases, and animal pests won't strike all at once; but in any case, they describe the ways in which to strike back, emphasizing preventative measures." Booklist

Includes bibliography

Bonsai; culture and care of miniature trees; by the editors of Sunset Books and Sunset Magazine. 2nd ed. Lane 1976 80p il pa $8.99   **635.9**

1. Bonsai
ISBN 0-376-03044-5

"A Sunset book"

First published 1965

A step-by-step illustrated introduction to the cultivation and care of miniature trees. The aesthetic aspects of bonsai are discussed

Crockett, James Underwood
Crockett's flower garden; by James Underwood Crockett; with the assistance of Marjorie Waters; photography by Russell Morash. Little, Brown 1981 311p il $29.95; pa $19.95   **635.9**

1. Flower gardening
ISBN 0-316-16132-2; 0-316-16133-0 (pa) LC 80-9018

"Each of the monthly chapters contains a series of entries in alphabetical order, covering individual plants that need attention during the month. . . . There is an essay-length feature at the end of each monthly chapter." Introduction

Crockett's indoor garden; by James Underwood Crockett, with the assistance of Marjorie Waters; photography by Russell Morash. Little, Brown 1978 325p il hardcover o.p. paperback available $19.95

635.9

1. House plants 2. Greenhouses
ISBN 0-316-16126-8 (pa)   LC 78-8939

Crockett offers a month-by-month guide to the cultivation of about "one-hundred-thirty plants. These are indicated as easy, difficult, and 'greenhouse only.' Every plant discussed appears in a color photograph and/or a . . . line drawing." Libr J

Includes bibliography

Hériteau, Jacqueline
The National Arboretum book of outstanding garden plants; the authoritative guide to selecting and growing the most beautiful, durable, and care-free garden plants in North America; by Jacqueline Hériteau with H. Marc Cathey and the staff and consultants of the U.S. National Arboretum; introduction by H. Marc Cathey. Simon & Schuster 1990 xxvi, 292p il $39.95
635.9

1. Ornamental plants 2. Landscape gardening
ISBN 0-671-66957-5   LC 89-19704
"A Stonesong Press book"

This is a "reference guide listing 1,700 flowers, herbs, shrubs, trees, ground covers, vines, ornamental grasses, and aquatics—plants that Heriteau and Cathey call 'carefree.' The description of each plant gives information on growth rate and light, soil, and moisture requirements, as well as a rundown of its appearance. The book is an essential guide for serious gardeners." Booklist

Herwig, Rob, 1935-
The Good Housekeeping encyclopedia of house plants. rev 2nd US ed. Hearst Bks. 1990 204p il $22.95   **635.9**
1. House plants
ISBN 0-688-09433-3

Original Dutch edition, 1984; first United States edition, 1985

Spine title: The new Good Housekeeping encyclopedia of house plants

The 350 entries contain information on 1,500 varieties of house plants; popular names, description, geographic origin, and information on care, watering, feeding and growth are provided. Symbols indicate growth requirements

Includes bibliography

House plants; contributing editor, John Brookes. Reader's Digest Assn. 1990 240p il (RD home handbooks) pa $16   **635.9**
1. House plants
ISBN 0-89577-349-X   LC 89-70332

This guide to indoor plants is illustrated in color and provides basic information about each plant and techniques and tips about repotting and progapation of house plants

How to grow African violets; by the editors of Sunset Books and Sunset Magazine. 5th ed. Lane 1977 79p il $7.95   **635.9**
1. African violets
ISBN 0-376-03058-5
"A Sunset book"
First published 1959

Contains suggestions for growing and propagation, entering horticultural shows, and tips on purchasing. Also discusses species related to African violets

How to grow bulbs; by the editors of Sunset Books and Sunset magazine. 4th ed. Lane 1985 96p il pa $8.99   **635.9**
1. Bulbs
ISBN 0-376-03086-0   LC 85-50846

First published 1962 with title: How to grow and use bulbs

At head of title: Sunset

Describes bulbs, corms, rhizomes, tuberous roots and tubers. Includes information about growth needs, containers, diseases and pests, landscape uses, indoor plants, flower arrangement, and miniature plants. An alphabetically arranged list of common bulb flowers concludes the volume

Perennials. Time-Life Bks. 1988 158p il (Time-Life gardener's guide) $18.60 **635.9**
1. Perennials   LC 87-26700

This illustrated introduction to perennials discusses soil preparation, propagation, and care

Includes bibliography

Pizzetti, Mariella
Simon & Schuster's guide to cacti and succulents; U.S. editor, Stanley Schuler; photographs by Giuseppe Mazza; translated by Cynthia Munro. Simon & Schuster 1985 384p il hardcover o.p. paperback available $13.95   **635.9**
1. Cactus 2. Succulent plants
ISBN 0-671-60231-4 (pa)   LC 85-11736

An illustrated "handbook to more than 300 members of the cactus and succulent families, with color photographs matched to brief descriptions and graphic symbols for each plant's place of origin, temperature requirments, and subgenus or subtribe." Booklist

Includes bibliography

Sedenko, Jerry
The butterfly garden; creating beautiful gardens to attract butterflies; foreword by Beth Callaway. Villard Bks. 1991 144p il $24.50   **635.9**
1. Gardening 2. Butterflies
ISBN 0-394-58982-3   LC 91-50067
"A Running Heads book"

This illustrated guide offers advice on the creation of gardens designed to attract and support native butterflies
"This well-organized and beautifully illustrated book will serve as an excellent guide for launching an attractive, pleasurable project." Sci Books Films

Includes bibliography

Smith, Shane
The greenhouse gardener's companion; growing food and flowers in your greenhouse or sunspace. Fulcrum 1992 531p il pa $19.95   **635.9**
1. Greenhouses 2. Gardening
ISBN 1-55591-106-4   LC 92-53031

The author "begins with an overview of the greenhouse environment, which he follows with a long chapter on interior design. Then he focuses on such details as plant layout, selecting plants, propagation, pollination, fertilizers, and pests and diseases. The longest section of the book is an encyclopedia of fruits, vegetables, ornamental plants, and herbs." Booklist

Includes bibliographic references

Taylor's guide to annuals. Houghton Mifflin 1986 479p il (Taylor's guides to gardening) pa $18.95 **635.9**
1. Annuals (Plants) 2. Flower gardening
ISBN 0-395-40447-9 LC 85-30496
"A Chanticleer Press edition"

Taylor's guide to bulbs. Houghton Mifflin 1986 463p il (Taylor's guides to gardening) pa $16.95 **635.9**
1. Bulbs 2. Flower gardening
ISBN 0-395-40449-5 LC 85-30508
"A Chanticleer Press edition"

Taylor's guide to ground covers, vines & grasses. Houghton Mifflin 1987 495p il (Taylor's guides to gardening) pa $16.45 **635.9**
1. Ornamental plants 2. Climbing plants 3. Grasses
ISBN 0-395-43094-1 LC 86-20022
"A Chanticleer Press edition"

Taylor's guide to houseplants. Houghton Mifflin 1987 463p il (Taylor's guides to gardening) pa $16.95 **635.9**
1. House plants
ISBN 0-395-43091-7 LC 86-20023
"A Chanticleer Press edition"

Taylor's guide to perennials. Houghton Mifflin 1986 479p il (Taylor's guides to gardening) pa $18.95 **635.9**
1. Perennials 2. Flower gardening
ISBN 0-395-40448-7 LC 85-30495
"A Chanticleer Press edition"

Taylor's guide to roses. Houghton Mifflin 1986 495p il (Taylor's guides to gardening) pa $16.95 **635.9**
1. Roses 2. Flower gardening
ISBN 0-395-40450-9 LC 85-30492
"A Chanticleer Press edition"

Taylor's guide to shrubs. Houghton Mifflin 1987 479p il (Taylor's guides to gardening) pa $18.95 **635.9**
1. Shrubs
ISBN 0-395-43093-3 LC 86-20024
"A Chanticleer Press edition"

Taylor's guide to vegetables & herbs. Houghton Mifflin 1987 479p il (Taylor's guides to gardening) pa $16.95 **635.9**
1. Vegetable gardening 2. Herb gardening
ISBN 0-395-43092-5 LC 86-20018
"A Chanticleer Press edition"

These volumes are "drawn from 'Taylor's Encyclopedia of gardening'. . . . Each volume begins with general horticultural information and points of basic botany. Following this is a section of color photographs of individual species arranged as an identification guide. Particular information on each species is supplied in a third section, which is also keyed to the color illustrations. This comprehensive and authoritative set features a lucid text and easy-to-follow instructions." Booklist

Williams, T. Jeff
Greenhouses; created and designed by the editorial staff of Ortho Books; manuscript editor, Susan Lang; consulting editors, Doc and Katy Abraham; writers, T. Jeff Williams, Larry Hodgson; photographers, Saxon Holt, Michael Landis; illustrators, Ron Hildebrand, Pamela Manley. Ortho Bks. 1991 112p il pa $8.95 **635.9**
1. Greenhouses
ISBN 0-89721-229-0 LC 90-84633
First published 1978 with title: How to build & use greenhouses

This book offers information about buying and building greenhouses. Plans for nine units, including two solar models are included

Wilson, Jim
Landscaping with container plants. Houghton Mifflin 1990 212p il $34 **635.9**
1. Gardening
ISBN 0-395-49864-3 LC 89-39866
"Topics discussed include selecting and making containers; using container plants in landscapes and limited spaces; making artificial soils; and caring for the special needs of plants grown in confined spaces." Libr J
"A thorough, utterly practical guide to container gardening, from asparagus to zinnias. . . . With its beautiful photographs, Wilson's essential practicality, and colorful humor, this book is both a joy to read and a pleasure to use." Christ Sci Monit

Yang, Linda
The city gardener's handbook; from balcony to backyard; line drawings by Stephen K-M. Tim; garden plans rendered by Sharon Bradley Papp; book design by Martin Moskof. Random House 1990 316p il $26.95 **635.9**
1. Gardening
ISBN 0-394-58371-X LC 89-24382
The author discusses problems faced by city gardeners, such as "pollution, excessive wind and/or shade, and the need to limit growth and weight of plants. . . . [She recommends] trees, shrubs, and flowers for use in the city." Libr J
This book "compactly combines the virtues of extensive knowledge, organization, clear-eyed design and—last but not least—a sympathetic, briskly dedicated authorial tone." Publ Wkly

Includes bibliography

636 Animal husbandry

Faivre, Milton I.
How to raise rabbits for fun and profit. Nelson-Hall 1973 212p il $27.95 **636**
1. Rabbits
ISBN 0-911012-47-8

"All aspects of rabbit raising—selecting stock and equipment, mating, housing, feeding, showing, marketing, and even cooking rabbits—are clearly and concisely discussed." Libr J

636.088 Animals for specific purposes

Brann, Donald R.
How to build pet housing. rev ed. Easi-Bild Directions Simplified 1978 178p il pa $7.95   **636.088**
1. Pets
ISBN 0-87733-751-9   LC 78-103130
First published 1975 by Directions Simplified

An illustrated step-by-step guide to building pet cages and shelters. Includes projects for kennels, hutches, doghouses, bird cages and cat entries

636.089 Veterinary sciences. Veterinary medicine

Black's veterinary dictionary. Barnes & Noble Bks. il $77.50   **636.089**
1. Veterinary medicine—Dictionaries
First published 1928 by Macmillan under the editorship of W. C. Miller with title: Black's veterinary cyclopedia. (17th edition 1992) Title and publisher vary

"Gives comprehensive coverage of terms in veterinary medicine and animal husbandry, as well as the anatomy and physiology of domesticated animals. Some inclusion of public health matters and techniques of interest to farmers." Sheehy. Guide to Ref Books. 10th edition

Merck veterinary manual; a handbook of diagnosis and therapy for the veterinarian. Merck & Co. $24   **636.089**
1. Veterinary medicine—Handbooks, manuals, etc.
Also available on CD-ROM
First published 1955. (7th edition 1991) Periodically revised

"Technical manual for use by veterinarians in the diagnosis and treatment of animal diseases. Authoritative, up-to-date information presented in a brief, convenient format; includes recommended prescriptions." Ref Sources for Small & Medium-sized Libr. 5th edition

Pinney, Chris C.
The illustrated veterinary guide for dogs, cats, birds & exotic pets. TAB Bks. 1992 xxiv, 711p il $29.95   **636.089**
1. Veterinary medicine
ISBN 0-8306-1986-0   LC 91-28718
This guide offers information about choosing, caring for and training all kinds of pets, disease identification and treatment, first aid, and breeding

636.1 Horses and related animals

Clemens, Virginia Phelps, 1941-
A horse in your backyard; a first-time owner's primer of horse keeping. Prentice Hall Press 1991 212p il $19.95   **636.1**
1. Horses
ISBN 0-13-395088-3   LC 90-46769

This book offers advice for first-time horse owners about selecting a horse, grooming, equipment, medical care, trail riding, costs, and showing
This is a "well-organized, easy-to-read, and sensible guide." Libr J
Includes bibliography

The **Complete** horse book; edited by Elwyn Hartley Edwards & Candida Geddes. Trafalgar Sq. 1988 c1987 344p il $29.95; pa $19.95   **636.1**
1. Horses
ISBN 0-943955-00-9; 0-943955-41-6 (pa)
     LC 87-50763
First published 1982 by Larousse with title: The Complete book of the horse; this edition first published 1987 in the United Kingdom

"Separate articles by specialists provide comprehensive coverage of such topics as the physiological and cultural history of the horse, the development of specific breeds around the world, and the horse's anatomy and health. Practical information is also included on keeping and housing horses, breeding, training and riding, and participating in competitions." Booklist

Hartley Edwards, Elwyn
The ultimate horse book; introduced by Sharon Ralls Lemon; photography by Bob Langrish. Dorling Kindersley 1991 240p il $29.95   **636.1**
1. Horses
ISBN 1-87943-103-3   LC 91-60138
The author "delves into the origins of the equine species, the 6,000-year relationship between horse and human, and equine anatomy and behavior. More than 80 breeds of horse and pony are described in elegantly designed two-page spreads highlighting each breed's history and distinctive physical traits and temperaments. Owning and caring for a horse are covered in equally well illustrated discussions of equipment, health, and stable management." Booklist

Morris, Desmond
Horsewatching. Crown 1989 c1988 150p il $13   **636.1**
1. Horses
ISBN 0-517-57267-2   LC 88-34019
First published 1988 in the United Kingdom
"Morris answers many questions about the anatomy, history, traditions, physiology, and interrelationships of horses. The inquiries on how a horse sleeps, eats, sees, hears, and mates give way to more complex questions that are just as succinctly answered in a page or two. . . . An intriguing browsing item and reference that will have wide appeal." Booklist

636.2 Ruminants. Bovines. Cattle

Rifkin, Jeremy
Beyond beef; the rise and fall of the cattle culture. Dutton 1992 353p $21   **636.2**
1. Beef cattle 2. Eating customs
ISBN 0-525-93420-0   LC 91-32285
Also available in paperback from New Am. Lib.

Rifkin, Jeremy—*Continued*

This is an account of cattle raising and beef consumption and their effect on the world economy and the ecosystem

"Backed by persuasive evidence, Rifkin states that cattle are a major cause of pollution, deforestation, desertification and, through the methane they produce, global warming. Charting the human-bovine relationship from the Lascaux caves to the junk-food hamburger, he suggestively argues that beef-eating has helped support male dominance, gender and class hierarchies, and myths of meat as a sign of strength and virility." Publ Wkly

Includes bibliographic references

636.6 Birds other than poultry

Alderton, David

You & your pet bird; photography by Cyril Laubscher. Knopf 1992 224p il pa $15
636.6

1. Cage birds
ISBN 0-679-74061-9   LC 91-58565

"A Dorling Kindersley book"

"This well-illustrated book pictures more than 80 popular varieties of budgies, finches, canaries, parrots, cockatoos, and softbills (such as the toucan and mynah) and reviews their virtues, drawbacks, and requirements." Libr J

Harper, Don

The practical encyclopedia of pet birds for home & garden. Harmony Bks. 1987 c1986 208p il $17.95
636.6

1. Cage birds
ISBN 0-517-56546-3   LC 86-31874

"A Salamander book"

First published 1986 in the United Kingdom with title: Pet birds for home and garden

Color photographs illustrate this guide to over 200 species of birds including finches, parrots, pigeons, quail and doves. Tables are provided showing distribution, size, diet, sexing, and compatibility

Includes bibliography

Lantermann, Werner, 1956-

The new parrot handbook; everything about purchase, acclimation, care, diet, disease, and behavior of parrots, with a special chapter on raising parrots; 50 color photographs by outstanding animal photographers, 30 drawings by Fritz W. Köhler, and 35 maps indicating distribution; translated from the German by Rita and Robert Kimber; American advisory editor, Matthew M. Vriends. Barron's Educ. Ser. 1986 144p il maps pa $7.95
636.6

1. Parrots
ISBN 0-8120-3729-4   LC 86-17289

This book "is divided into two parts, the first about selecting, housing, and caring for a bird; the other devoted to breeding and behavior and including a large section of descriptions of individual species." Booklist

Includes bibliography

636.7 Dogs

American Kennel Club

The complete dog book. Howell Bk. House il $27.50
636.7

1. Dogs

First published 1935. (18th edition 1992) Frequently revised

"The official guide to 124 AKC registered breeds and their history, appearance, selection, training, care and feeding, and first aid. Some color plates." N Y Public Libr. Ref Books for Child Collect. 2d edition

American Kennel Club dog care and training. Howell Bk. House 1991 214p il pa $11.50
636.7

1. Dogs
ISBN 0-87605-405-X   LC 91-8404

This book "describes the dog's basic needs and the owner's responsibilities. The message is clear: people who cannot fulfill these obligations should not buy a dog. Topics discussed include: 'think' before buying, care, showing, training, breeding, and illness." Libr J

Includes bibliography

Carlson, Delbert G.

Dog owner's home veterinary handbook; [by] Delbert G. Carlson and James M. Giffin. rev. and expanded. Howell Bk. House 1992 xxiii, 423p il $25
636.7

1. Dogs—Diseases
ISBN 0-87605-537-4   LC 91-43575

First published 1980

"The authors discuss all of the major organ systems with descriptions of normal functions and infectious and parasitic diseases. Writing in easy-to-understand terms, they identify emergency situations and explain first-aid care. . . . It contains information on Lyme disease and other recently recognized problems." Libr J

Curtis, Patricia, 1923-

The urban dog; how to understand, enjoy, and care for a dog in the city. Bantam Bks. 1986 243p il pa $8.95
636.7

1. Dogs
ISBN 0-553-34270-3   LC 85-48238

"Detailing requirements to consider before bringing a dog into the city home, Curtis discusses such matters as time, money, space and exercise. Her advice on choosing a dog is straightforward, with tips on health, temperament and grooming." Publ Wkly

Includes bibliography

Dibra, Bashkim

Dog training by Bash; tried and true techniques of the dog trainer to the stars; [by] Bashkim Dibra with Elizabeth Randolph. Dutton 1991 312p il $20 **636.7**

1. Dogs—Training
ISBN 0-525-24954-0   LC 90-46462

Also available in paperback from New Am. Lib.

Dibra, Bashkim—*Continued*

The author explains the steps he uses to train and resolve problem behavior in dogs. His technique emphasizes patience, persistence and praise. Contains a section on housebreaking

Evans, Job Michael

The Evans guide for housetraining your dog; with photographs by Charles P. Hornek. Howell Bk. House 1987 127p il $16

636.7

1. Dogs—Training   LC 86-21143

"Evans deals with all the aspects of housetraining, including scheduling, crate training, discipline, and such problems as submissive urination and leg lifting. One of the first books a new puppy owner should read, it belongs in all public libraries." Libr J

Includes bibliography

Fogle, Bruce

Know your dog; an owner's guide to dog behavior; photography by David Ward; additional photography by Jane Burton. Dorling Kindersley 1992 128p il $22.95

636.7

1. Dogs
ISBN 1-56458-080-6   LC 92-4497

Also available Know your cat (1991) for $19.95 (ISBN 1-879431-04-1)

The author "offers a sort of canine psychology here. His premise is that in order to give the best care possible to your dog, and to have the best possible relationship with it, you need to know what various gestures, expressions, and postures mean." Booklist

Fox, Michael W., 1937-

Superdog; raising the perfect canine companion. Howell Bk. House 1990 210p il $17.95

636.7

1. Dogs—Training
ISBN 0-87605-741-5   LC 90-4259

The author "discusses dogs' capabilities, explains various canine postures and sounds, and shows how to 'decode' canine behavior." Libr J

"Spare in its coverage of rudimentary care (there is no information on house-breaking, little on nutrition), the book will gratify dedicated dog owners with its unwavering respect for animals and their powers." Publ Wkly

Hearne, Vicki, 1946-

Bandit; dossier of a dangerous dog. HarperCollins Pubs. 1991 303p $22; pa $11

636.7

1. Dogs—Training 2. Dangerous animals
ISBN 0-06-019005-1; 0-06-099504-1 (pa)

LC 90-56346

This is an account of the author's legal battle to save an impounded dog from being put to death. "In Stamford, Connecticut in 1987, Bandit was condemned to death for being a dangerous dog, an alleged 'pit bull' who had bitten twice, once in defense of his friend and property and once in self-defense. Despite stiff opposition by local animal control officials who wanted Bandit

'disposed of,' Hearne . . . was able to obtain the dog and train him." Libr J

This is "not only a dog story but also a deeply eccentric lesson in justice, linguistics, racism and teleology." N Y Times Book Rev

Herriot, James

James Herriot's dog stories. St. Martin's Press 1986 xxxiii, 426p il $19.95   636.7

1. Veterinary medicine 2. Dogs
ISBN 0-312-43968-7   LC 86-6637

Also available G.K. Hall large print edition

Herriot "has gathered 50 recollections of canines, some of them sentimental, a few tragic and at least one—the story of a terrier male who abruptly becomes attractive to other males—as odd as anything in the Decameron. Herriot recalls that in his student days domestic animals were customarily listed in descending order of importance: horse, ox, sheep, pig, dog. In the latest work, he has brought his favorites to the front and given them a new leash on life." Time

Lowell, Michele

Your purebred puppy; a buyer's guide. Holt & Co. 1990 275p il hardcover o.p. paperback available $10.95   636.7

1. Dogs
ISBN 0-8050-1892-1 (pa)   LC 90-4349

A "guide to purebred puppy selection, this covers all breeds currently granted full or partial recognition by the AKC, plus those recognized by the rival United Kennel Club and a number of up-and-coming rare breeds—175 in all. The right questions to ask, sources to steer away from, breed characteristics, and care requirements are all included here." Libr J

McGinnis, Terri

The well dog book; the classic, comprehensive handbook of dog care; illustrated by Pat Stewart. rev ed. Random House 1991 287p il $22.50   636.7

1. Dogs 2. Dogs—Diseases
ISBN 0-394-58768-5   LC 91-52680

First published 1974

This illustrated manual introduces canine anatomy and offers training, grooming and nutrition guidelines. Diagnostic and preventive information is included

Morris, Desmond

Dogwatching. Crown 1987 c1986 130p il hardcover o.p. paperback available $8

636.7

1. Dogs
ISBN 0-517-88055-5 (pa)   LC 86-23930

Also available Transaction Pubs. large print edition

First published 1986 in the United Kingdom

In this volume "an introductory essay is followed by a question-and-answer section (items one to four pages in length). The questions include ones about mating, hunting behavior, and physical characteristics." Libr J

Morris "is conversational, even amusing at times, but fully informative." Booklist

Ross, John

Dog talk; training your dog through a canine point of view; [by] John Ross and Barbara McKinney. St. Martin's Press 1992 276p il $22.95   **636.7**

1. Dogs—Training
ISBN 0-312-07726-2   LC 92-129

The authors present "easy-to-follow, workable dog-training techniques and guidelines in this readable manual. The techniques are based on common sense, consistency, and an understanding of dog behavior. All facets of dog training are covered, including a simple rundown of reasons for potential failure. . . . Concise, useful advice." Booklist

Siegal, Mordecai

Good dog, bad dog; dog training made easy; [by] Mordecai Siegal & Matthew Margolis; photographs by Mordecai Siegal. new & rev ed. Holt & Co. 1991 350p il $19.95   **636.7**

1. Dogs—Training
ISBN 0-8050-1094-7   LC 90-49749

First published 1973 by Holt, Rinehart & Winston

This work "outlines kind but firm training techniques that are tailored to five different canine temperaments. It also includes training tips for 100 different breeds." Libr J

When good dogs do bad things; [by] Mordecai Siegal, Matthew Margolis. Little, Brown 1986 182p il $18.95   **636.7**

1. Dogs—Training
ISBN 0-316-79008-7   LC 86-7411

The authors "direct owners in resolving most canine deportment flaws. The bulk of the book deals with some 20 specific vexations, including biting . . . jumping, barking, digging, wetting, car chasing and chewing. For each vice, the authors give detailed solutions and preventive measures, and discuss the root causes (human as well as canine)." Publ Wkly

Taylor, David, 1934-

The ultimate dog book; consulting editor, Connie Vanacore; commissioned photography by Dave King, Jane Burton. Simon & Schuster 1990 240p il $29.95   **636.7**

1. Dogs
ISBN 0-671-70988-7   LC 90-32242

"A Dorling Kindersley book"

"Each representative breed . . . is reproduced in a large, vibrantly colored photograph, while smaller illustrations embellish the information on the canine's history, temperament, and physical characteristics. The concluding chapters address dog care, maintenance, and breeding. Highly recommended for browsing and reference." Booklist

Tortora, Daniel F.

The right dog for you; choosing a breed that matches your personality, family, and life-style. Simon & Schuster 1980 381p il hardcover o.p. paperback available $10.95   **636.7**

1. Dogs
ISBN 0-671-47247-X (pa)   LC 80-10845

This book "shows how to match human and canine by temperament and personality traits. Tortora . . . rates characteristics of the 123 AKC-approved breeds according to activity and learning levels, sociability and emotional stability. . . . On the human side, there are questions for readers to answer, to measure their traits and habits with a view to selecting a compatible pet." Publ Wkly

Wilcox, Bonnie

Atlas of dog breeds of the world; [by] Bonnie Wilcox and Chris Walkowicz. T.F.H. Publs. 1989 912p il $129.95   **636.7**

1. Dogs
ISBN 0-86622-930-2

"This is an impressive compilation of the history and development of some 400 breeds of dog, whether recognized by the American Kennel Club or not. Lengthy descriptions note each breed's personality, size, coat type, and origin in a breezy, informal style. Reference librarians will appreciate the inclusion of many obscure breeds, and the excellent, large-color photographs of both puppies and adult dogs." Am Libr

Woodhouse, Barbara

No bad dogs; the Woodhouse way. Summit Bks. 1982 127p il hardcover o.p. paperback available $10   **636.7**

1. Dogs—Training
ISBN 0-671-54185-4 (pa)   LC 81-21530

First published 1978 in the United Kingdom

"A veteran English trainer who runs a school for both dogs and owners, reminisces about her clients and describes her methods for specific behavior problems." Publ Wkly

636.8   Cats

Caras, Roger A.

A cat is watching; a look at the way cats see us. Simon & Schuster 1989 238p il hardcover o.p. paperback available $8.95   **636.8**

1. Cats
ISBN 0-671-72443-6 (pa)   LC 89-19648

Also available G.K. Hall large print edition

"To explain how cats perceive and interact with humans and other animals, Caras explores feline physical and psychological makeup." Libr J

As "thorough and sensitive a tour of the cat's world as a human being can contrive. . . . Serious data and illuminating anecdotes are blended well." N Y Times Book Rev

The **Cornell** book of cats; a comprehensive medical reference for every cat and kitten; by the faculty, staff, and associates, Cornell Feline Health Center, College of Veterinary Medicine, Cornell University; edited by Mordecai Siegal. Villard Bks. 1989 xxvi, 435p il $27   **636.8**
1. Cats—Diseases
ISBN 0-394-56787-0   LC 89-40195

This is a "volume on feline health that includes information on medicine, nutrition and behavior. . . . The heart of the book is devoted to describing the disorders of the various inner systems of the cat, including respiratory, circulatory, nervous and immune. There are complete chapters on a whole range of related subjects—from pediatrics to geriatrics, from nutrition to first aid. An extensive medical glossary is also included." Publisher's note

Edney, A. T. B.
ASPCA complete cat care manual; [by] Andrew Edney; foreword by Roger Caras. Dorling Kindersley 1992 192p il $24.95   **636.8**
1. Cats
ISBN 1-56458-064-4   LC 92-52783

"Cat care is made easy through step-by-step photographs that illustrate grooming, handling, detecting illness, first aid, and other concerns. Difficult-to-explain procedures, such as how to administer medication or transport an injured cat, are clearly understandable." Libr J

Includes bibliographic references

Gebhardt, Richard H.
The complete cat book. Howell Bk. House 1991 224p il $24.95   **636.8**
1. Cats
ISBN 0-87605-841-1   LC 91-13279

This book "begins with brief chapters on the history of the cat and its domestication, and on the anatomical design and function of cats, including muscle structure and diagrams of skeletons. These are followed by an alphabetical set of entries on the breeds. . . . While this book is of primary interest to the breeder/competitor, it will also be a very useful reference tool for identification purposes." SLJ

Includes bibliographic references

McGinnis, Terri
The well cat book; the classic comprehensive handbook of cat care; illustrated by Pat Stewart. 2nd ed. Random House 1993 325p il $23   **636.8**
1. Cats 2. Cats—Diseases
ISBN 0-394-58769-3   LC 92-56834
First published 1975

The author provides "professional advice on nutrition, diagnosing illnesses, treating injuries, and preventing health problems. . . . [She also includes] information on new illnesses such as feline infectious peritonitis and feline immunodeficiency virus, and she clearly explains their symptoms. Among her work's other useful features is the chapter on emergency first aid. . . . Highly recommended for all pet care collections." Libr J

Morris, Desmond
Cat watching. Crown 1987 c1986 136p $13; pa $8   **636.8**
1. Cats
ISBN 0-517-56518-8; 0-517-88053-9 (pa)
LC 86-23938
Also available Transaction Pubs. large print edition
First published 1986 in the United Kingdom
Spine title: Catwatching

In question-and-answer format, the author examines mating, hunting behavior and physical characteristics of cats

Catlore. Crown 1988 180p il $12.95; pa $8   **636.8**
1. Cats
ISBN 0-517-56903-5; 0-517-88057-1 (pa)
LC 87-27268

The author discusses breeds, diets, exercise, games, genetics, communication and medical care

Taylor, David, 1934-
The ultimate cat book; Daphne Negus, consulting editor; commissioned photography by Dave King, Jane Burton. Simon & Schuster 1989 192p il $29.95   **636.8**
1. Cats
ISBN 0-671-68649-6   LC 89-6097
"A Dorling Kindersley book"

"The guide covers not only the origins and specifics of each breed but provides technical information on health, behavior, and reproduction, and advice on showing and traveling. The 750 excellent color photographs and beautiful layout make this a standout." Libr J

638   Insect culture

Hubbell, Sue
A book of bees—and how to keep them; drawings by Sam Potthoff. Random House 1988 193p il $17.95   **638**
1. Bees
ISBN 0-394-55894-4   LC 88-42655
Also available in paperback from Ballantine Bks.

"Following the seasons of the beekeeper's year [the author] imparts practical hints along with literary, mythological, entomological, and anecdotal commentary." Booklist

639.3   Fish culture

The **Aquarium** encyclopedia; [edited by] by Günther Sterba; English editor: Dick Mills; translated by Susan Simpson. MIT Press 1983 605p il $45   **639.3**
1. Aquariums—Dictionaries 2. Fishes—Dictionaries
ISBN 0-262-19207-1   LC 82-247
Original German edition, 1978

"This is a comprehensive reference work, covering all aspects of aquarium-keeping. Informative, readable descriptions are given for the various orders and families of fish, invertebrates, and plants likely to be kept in aquaria. General articles on such topics as filtering sys-

The Aquarium encyclopedia—*Continued*
tems, water chemistry, and fish diseases are also included. . . . The book is handsomely produced with more than 1000 clear illustrations, many of them color photographs." Libr J

Includes bibliography

Axelrod, Herbert R.
Encyclopedia of tropical fishes; with special emphasis on the techniques of breeding; by Herbert R. Axelrod and William Vorderwinkler. T.F.H. Publs. il $17.95   **639.3**

1. Tropical fish 2. Aquariums—Dictionaries
First published 1957. (29th edition 1988) Frequently revised

"A fully illustrated encyclopedia on tropical fish breeding, it contains information on all aspects of the subject—it discusses aquarium water, plants, food, rocks, snails, breeding patterns, and a short section on commercial fish breeding." Wynar. Guide to Ref Books for Sch Media Cent. 2d edition

Handbook of tropical aquarium fishes; [by] Herbert R. Axelrod, Leonard P. Schultz. rev ed. T.F.H. Publs. 1983 718p il $9.95   **639.3**

1. Tropical fish 2. Aquariums
ISBN 0-87666-491-5   LC 83-162328
First published 1969

This book "is basically an illustrated catalog of over 400 tropical fishes, with introductory material about aquariums, plants, ichthyology, and diseases." Wynar. Guide to Ref Books for Sch Media Cent. 3d edition

Includes bibliography

Blasiola, George C.
The new saltwater aquarium handbook; with color photographs by Aaron Norman and drawings by Michele Earle-Bridges; consulting editor, Matthew M. Vriends. Barron's Educ. Ser. 1991 134p il pa $7.95   **639.3**

1. Marine aquariums
ISBN 0-8120-4482-7   LC 91-4358

"Everything about setting up a marine aquarium, aquarium conditioning and maintenance, selecting fish and invertebrates, nutrition, and disease control." Title page

Includes bibliographic references

Levine, Joseph S., 1951-
The complete fishkeeper; everything aquarium fishes need to stay happy, healthy, and alive; principal photographs by Aaron Norman. Morrow 1991 239p il $30 **639.3**

1. Fishes 2. Aquariums
ISBN 0-688-10146-1   LC 91-7415

"Levine gives enthusiastic yet practical advice on every aspect of successful aquarium fish maintenance. Selected freshwater and marine species are photographed and discussed, and in 'Ten Tanks That Work,' tank designs and compatible occupants for ten-, 20- and 55-

gallon tanks are recommended." Libr J

Includes bibliographic references

Mattison, Christopher
A-Z of snake keeping; [by] Chris Mattison; with photographs by the author. Sterling 1991 c1990 143p il maps $24.95; pa $7.95   **639.3**

1. Snakes
ISBN 0-8069-8246-2; 0-8069-8247-0 (pa)
     LC 90-10178
First published 1990 in the United Kingdom

"The alphabetical format mixes detailed descriptions of various snakes from boas to water snakes with topics such as feeding, handling, and sex determination. Cage configurations and heating and hygiene methods are covered, and species most successfully kept in captivity are recommended." Booklist

Includes bibliographic references

The care of reptiles and amphibians in captivity. 3rd rev ed. Blandford Press; [distributed by] Sterling 1992 317p il pa $17.95   **639.3**

1. Reptiles 2. Amphibians
ISBN 0-7137-2338-6   LC 93-114518
First published 1982

"Mattison authoritatively addresses care, health, and breeding of captive reptiles and amphibians. More than half of his book is devoted to descriptions and care requirements of various species of salamanders, newts, frogs, toads, lizards, turtles, tortoises, and snakes. Black-and-white photos are supplemented by a 16-page color insert." Libr J

Includes bibliography

McInerny, Derek, 1909-
All about tropical fish; [by] Derek McInerny, Geoffrey Gerard. 4th ed completely rev, rev. by Chris Andrews. Facts on File 1989 480p il $29.95   **639.3**

1. Tropical fish 2. Aquariums
ISBN 0-8160-2168-6   LC 88-84026
First published 1958 by Macmillan

"The first 10 chapters cover setting up aquariums, selecting plants, and dealing with problems. Giving clear directions, Andrews describes how to build an aquarium or select one from a pet store and how to stock it with fish. . . . Chapters 11 through 23 cover types of fish and recommend easy-to-raise and -breed species. The final two chapters include fish that favor brackish water and marine species. . . . The text is easy to understand, and the directions are especially clear and precise. There are 300 illustrations, 146 of them in color." Booklist

Includes bibliography

Obst, Fritz Jurgen, 1939-
The completely illustrated atlas of reptiles and amphibians for the terrarium; [by] Fritz Jürgen Obst, Klaus Richter, Udo Jacob; translated by U. E. Friese; editor, English-language edition, Jerry G. Walls. T.F.H. Publs. 1988 830p il $129.95 **639.3**

1. Reptiles 2. Amphibians 3. Terrariums
ISBN 0-86622-958-2   LC 92-110201

Obst, Fritz Jurgen, 1939- —*Continued*
This is a "compilation of descriptions, photographs, and instructions for the care of many varieties of reptiles, amphibians, arachnids, and crustaceans that can be kept in captivity. Also included are food animals such as mice, crickets and banana slugs, terrarium plants, and parasites." Libr J
"A remarkable achievement. . . . This work covers thousands of species. . . . The encyclopedia is illustrated with 2,000 beautiful color photographs, and the individual entries are clearly written." Booklist

Includes bibliographic references

639.9   Conservation of biological resources

DeBlieu, Jan
Meant to be wild; the struggle to save endangered species through captive breeding. Fulcrum 1991 302p il $24.95   **639.9**
1. Wildlife conservation   2. Endangered species 3. Breeding
ISBN 1-55591-074-2   LC 91-71365

This study of wildlife conservation in North America examines "efforts that have been made to save certain endangered species through a program of captive breeding and reintroduction. . . . The species discussed in detail are the red wolf, peregrine falcon, whooping crane, Arabian oryx, golden lion tamarin, Puerto Rican parrot, California condor, black-footed ferret, and Florida panther." Sci Books Films

Includes bibliographic references

Merilees, Bill
Attracting backyard wildlife; a guide for nature-lovers. Voyageur Press 1989 159p il pa $10.95   **639.9**
1. Wildlife 2. Gardening
ISBN 0-89658-130-6   LC 89-5516

"For the most part, the backyard wildlife referred to here is birds. . . . Merilees offers detailed instructions on constructing bird houses and feeders. There are also chapters on caring for sick and injured animals, gardens that will attract butterflies and bugs, and gardens that will draw small mammals, reptiles, and amphibians—including mice, squirrels, chipmunks, raccoons, skunks, and bats. With 25 black-and-white photographs and 50 line drawings, this special book will be useful to bird watchers and other nature lovers." Booklist

Includes bibliography

Owens, Delia
The eye of the elephant; an epic adventure in the African wilderness; [by] Delia and Mark Owens. Houghton Mifflin 1992 305p il $22.45   **639.9**
1. Wildlife conservation 2. Elephants
ISBN 0-395-42381-3   LC 92-17691

This is an account of the authors efforts to save elephants in the Luangwa Valley of Zambia from poachers by involving and educating the local people

Includes bibliographic references

640   Home economics and family living

Back to basics; how to learn and enjoy traditional American skills. Reader's Digest Assn. 1981 456p il $25.50   **640**
1. Home economics
ISBN 0-89577-086-5

At head of title: Reader's Digest

This book covers many aspects of self-sufficiency and pioneer crafts. Among the topics discussed are: building adobe homes; making hammocks; drying, threshing and winnowing grain; and playing cat's cradle
"There is much information here, and the range of topics covered is impressive." Booklist

Heloise
All-new hints from Heloise; a household guide for the '90s. Putnam 1989 416p il pa $9.95   **640**
1. Home economics
ISBN 0-399-51510-0   LC 88-33651
Also available Hints from Heloise (1980) from Avon Bks. $8.95 (ISBN 0-380-53066-X)

"A Perigee book"

The author "offers a mother lode of salient tips on cleaning, child-care, pet care, traveling and much more. . . . She is at her most ingenious and credible in the kitchen and on household maintenance." Publ Wkly

Hunter, Linda Mason
The healthy home; an attic-to-basement guide to toxin-free living; [illustrations by Tom Weinman and Scott Ross] Rodale Press 1988 313p il $21.95   **640**
1. Poisons and poisoning 2. Hazardous substances 3. Environmental health
ISBN 0-87857-813-7   LC 88-36490
Also available in paperback from Pocket Bks.

"Covering everything from asbestos in the toaster oven to chlordane insecticide in crawl spaces, the author gathers more valuable information together in this volume than the average reader could easily access elsewhere." Libr J

Includes bibliography

Pinkham, Mary Ellen
Mary Ellen's best of helpful hints. Warner Bks. 1979-1981 2v il v1 pa $5.95; v2 pa $6.95   **640**
1. Home economics
ISBN 0-446-38121-7 (v1); 0-446-97893-0 (v2)

Original volume first published 1976

This collection of household hints includes sections on the kitchen, bathroom, laundry, carpets, sewing, painting, floors, windows, jewelry, shoes, pets, and cars

Reader's Digest practical problem solver; substitutes, shortcuts, and ingenious solutions for making life easier. Reader's Digest Assn. 1991 448p il $26.50   **640**
1. Home economics
ISBN 0-89577-346-5   LC 89-27729

Reader's Digest practical problem solver— *Continued*

"The first three parts—Recycling and Renewing, Common Things with Uncommon Uses, and Formulas and Recipes—are clearly home economics miscellanea giving tips on home repairs and decorating. Parts four and five—A-Z Problem Solver's Dictionary and Charts and Checklists—are mixed bags of advice." Libr J

Rodale's book of practical formulas; easy-to-make, easy-to-use recipes for hundreds of everyday activities and tasks; Paula Dreifus Bakule, editor; contributing writers, Michael Castleman [et al.] Rodale Press 1991 456p il $23.95 **640**

1. Home economics 2. Household equipment and supplies
ISBN 0-87857-979-6   LC 91-17089

This volume provides "information on using ordinary, and some exotic, supplies to help you with everyday household tasks and activities. Written in a cookbook format, it offers do-it-yourselfers hints to save money and/or trips to the store. Each chapter has a brief introduction followed by formulas or recipes to take care of gardens, pots, houses, cars, etc. An appendix lists supply sources." Libr J

641.03 Food and drink— Encyclopedias and dictionaries

Better Homes and Gardens complete guide to food and cooking. Meredith Corp. 1991 480p il $29.95 **641.03**

1. Cookery—Dictionaries 2. Food—Dictionaries
ISBN 0-696-01911-6   LC 90-64090

"Arranged in dictionary format, entries describe foods and cooking techniques and are accompanied by recipes, tips from the kitchen charts, and many color photographs." Booklist

Herbst, Sharon Tyler
Food lover's companion; comprehensive definitions of over 3000 food, wine and culinary terms. Barron's Educ. Ser. 1990 582p il pa $10.95 **641.03**

1. Cookery—Dictionaries
ISBN 0-8120-4156-9   LC 89-140

"This book defines foods, dishes, kitchen equipment, cooking techniques, foreign-food terms, menu terms, and even brand names. Pronunciation is given for foreign words and etymologies are given for some words." Ref Sources for Small & Medium-sized Libr. 5th edition

Mariani, John F.
The dictionary of American food and drink; [by] John Mariani. completely rev and updated. Hearst Bks. 1993 xxxv, 379p pa $19.95 **641.03**

1. Cookery—Dictionaries   2. Food—Dictionaries
3. Beverages—Dictionaries
ISBN 0-688-10139-9   LC 92-44649

First published 1983

"More than 2,000 definitions and descriptions of American classics from Caesar salad to coleslaw, from eggs Benedict to egg foo yung, from hot dogs to heros, from Manhattans to mint juleps." Title page

"Mariani does an excellent job of documenting the terminology of cooking in the U.S." Booklist

Montagné, Prosper, 1865-1948
Larousse gastronomique; the new American edition of the world's greatest culinary encyclopedia; edited by Jenifer Harvey Lang. Crown 1989 1193p il $60 **641.03**

1. Cookery—Dictionaries   2. Food—Dictionaries
3. Cookery, French
ISBN 0-517-57032-7   LC 88-1178

Original French edition, 1938; first United States edition, 1961

This reference work has been "adapted for use in American kitchens. Alphabetically arranged, with many cross-references, the volume includes over 8500 recipes and information on all cooking terms, foods, wines, preservation, serving, organizing, and anything else related to the kitchen. Recipe index and more than 1000 illustrations, most in full color." Ref Sources for Small & Medium-sized Libr. 5th edition

Stobart, Tom
The cook's encyclopedia; ingredients and processes; edited by Millie Owen; illustrations by Ruth Bornschlegel [et al.] Harper & Row 1981 547p il $22.95 **641.03**

1. Cookery—Dictionaries
ISBN 0-06-014127-1   LC 81-47785

First published 1980 in the United Kingdom

"A comprehensive reference source. Ingredients for cooking and cooking techniques are included together with their French, German, Italian, and Spanish equivalents; scientific names are given for most entries. Recipes help to illustrate the use of many of the ingredients." Booklist

641.09 Food and drink— Historical and geographic treatment

Root, Waverley Lewis, 1903-1982
Eating in America: a history; [by] Waverley Root & Richard de Rochemont. Morrow 1976 512p o.p.; Ecco Press paperback available $9.95 **641.09**

1. Food—History 2. Diet 3. Cookery 4. Food industry
ISBN 0-912946-88-1 (pa)

"Surveys the role food has played for more than four centuries in shaping American history. The authors treat, in interesting detail, the influences (political, economic, social, ethnic, climate, etc.) which molded American eating habits." Libr J

Includes bibliography

Visser, Margaret, 1940-
Much depends on dinner; the extraordinary history and mythology, allure and obsessions, perils and taboos, of an ordinary meal. Grove Press 1987 c1986 351p il o.p.; Collier Bks. paperback available $13   **641.09**

1. Food—History 2. Dinners and dining
ISBN 0-02-008851-5 (pa)   LC 87-257

First published 1986 in Canada

The author "describes the preparation of an ordinary dinner of corn, salt, chicken, rice, lettuce, olive oil, lemon juice, and ice cream. In the process, she ponders the history, meaning, physical properties, flavors, hazards, production, social consequences, legendary significance, and appeal of each item." Booklist

Includes bibliography

641.1   Applied nutrition

Bowes, Anna De Planter
Bowes and Church's food values of portions commonly used. Lippincott $29.95   **641.1**

1. Nutrition 2. Food—Composition

First published 1937 with title: Food values of portions commonly served. (16th edition 1994 revised by Jean A. Thompson Pennington) Periodically revised

"Nutrient values derived from computer data banks, tables in journal articles, nutrition textbooks, and information from the food industry are presented by food categories (beverages, candy, cereals, desserts, fast foods, etc.). Brand names are used to help in food identification. Lists calories, carbohydrates, fat, fiber, minerals, vitamins, and amino acid content in an average serving of more than 3500 different foods." Ref Sources for Small & Medium-sized Libr. 5th edition

Includes bibliographic references

Brody, Jane E.
Jane Brody's nutrition book; a lifetime guide to good eating for better health and weight control; by the personal health columnist of The New York Times. Norton 1981 xx, 552p il $22.95   **641.1**

1. Nutrition 2. Diet
ISBN 0-393-01429-0   LC 80-25117

Also available in paperback from Bantam Bks.

This nutrition guide for the layperson covers the basics in addition to popular concerns such as cholesterol, fiber, sugar and additives. Some recipes are included

Kraus, Barbara
Calories and carbohydrates. New Am. Lib. pa $11   **641.1**

1. Food—Composition

First published 1971 by Grosset & Dunlap. (10th edition 1993) Title varies

"More than 8,000 brand-name and basic foods are listed alphabetically in tables with the calorie and carbohydrate count given by measure or quantity. Individual guides for calories or carbohydrates are also published for use in kitchens, supermarkets, or restaurants." Booklist

Nutrition almanac; [pub. in assn. with] Nutrition Search, Inc., John D. Kirschmann, director. 3rd ed. McGraw-Hill 1990 340p pa $17   **641.1**

1. Nutrition 2. Health 3. Food—Composition
ISBN 0-07-034912-6   LC 89-33019

First published 1975

This offers "conveniently selected and arranged information on the effects of various nutrients in the body, problems caused by deficiencies, disorders for which particular vitamins and minerals are helpful, herbal medicine, possible health effects of drinking polluted water, and suggestions on the preparation of healthful food. A table of food composition gives a nutrient analysis for over 600 foods, and a nutrient allowance chart breaks down nutrient requirements by body size, metabolism, and caloric needs." Recomm Ref Books in Paperback. 2nd edition

Includes bibliography

641.2   Beverages (Drinks)

Adams, Leon David, 1905-
The wines of America; [by] Leon D. Adams with Bridgett Novak. 4th ed. McGraw-Hill 1990 528p il $24.95; pa $14.95   **641.2**

1. Wine and wine making
ISBN 0-07-000333-5; 0-07-000332-7 (pa)
     LC 90-31863

First published 1973 by Houghton Mifflin

The author "presents a lively history of U.S. winemaking and escorts readers on an inviting tour of U.S., Canadian, and Mexican wineries. The chapters are arranged regionally, with some larger wine-producing states, such as California and Michigan, receiving their own sections." Booklist

Includes bibliography

Clarke, Oz
The essential wine book. rev and updated. Simon & Schuster 1988 300p il maps pa $17   **641.2**

1. Wine and wine making
ISBN 0-671-67049-2   LC 88-38270

"A Fireside book"

First published 1985 by Viking

This guide describes country-by-country the wines, wine regions, and vineyards of the world with numerous photographs and maps

Cox, Jeff, 1940-
From vines to wines; the complete, step-by-step guide to growing your own grapes and making your own wine; with illustrations by the author. Harper & Row 1985 xxviii, 253p il o.p.; Storey Communications paperback available $10.95   **641.2**

1. Wine and wine making
ISBN 0-88266-528-6 (pa)   LC 84-48590

This is a guide to making wine at home from grape cultivation to storage and aging

Cox, Jeff, 1940-—_Continued_
"Cox uses nontechnical language to describe the things that could go wrong—and right—in the vineyard. An authoritative and readable handbook." Booklist

Johnson, Hugh, 1939-
Hugh Johnson's modern encyclopedia of wine. 3rd ed rev & updated. Simon & Schuster 1991 576p il maps $35   **641.2**
1. Wine and wine making
ISBN 0-671-73638-8   LC 90-20732
First published 1983
"Accepted as the most comprehensive, usable,and well-written book on wine, . . . this work tells you who makes it, where, how good it is, how much it costs, and whether it's worth the price." N Y Public Libr Book of How & Where to Look It Up

Vintage: the story of wine. Simon & Schuster 1989 480p il $39.95; pa $25
641.2
1. Wine and wine making
ISBN 0-671-68702-6; 0-671-79182-6 (pa)
LC 89-33928
The author traces wine's "development, focusing on its importance in human culture from the ancient Egyptians to the recent emergence of the Australian wine industry. In the process, he highlights technical advancements (the wine bottle, corks, and refrigeration equipment), persons of historical importance (Dom Pérignon, Baron Rothschild), and much more. Written in a conversational tone, packed with photographs, illustrations, and interesting sidelights, this book is eminently approachable." Booklist
Includes bibliographic references

Lichine, Alexis, 1913-1989
Alexis Lichine's new encyclopedia of wines & spirits; in collaboration with William Fifield and with the assistance of Jonathan Bartlett [et al.] 5th ed rev. Knopf 1987 771p il maps $45   **641.2**
1. Wine and wine making
ISBN 0-394-56262-3   LC 87-2590
First published 1967 with title: Encyclopedia of wines and spirits
Introductory chapters describe wine history, science and etiquette. Information on wine varieties and regions is provided. Maps show locations of notable vineyards
Includes bibliography

641.3 Food

Chilies to chocolate; food the Americas gave the world; edited by Nelson Foster & Linda S. Cordell. University of Ariz. Press 1992 191p $24.95; pa $13.95   **641.3**
1. Edible plants
ISBN 0-8165-1301-5; 0-8165-1324-4 (pa) LC 92-5243
Essays explore the biological and cultural history of crops cultivated by indigenous peoples of the Americas and trace their dispersion into the fields and kitchens of the Old World
Includes bibliography

The **Encyclopedia** of herbs, spices, & flavorings; contributing editor, Elisabeth Lambert Ortiz. Dorling Kindersley 1992 288p il $34.95   **641.3**
1. Herbs—Dictionaries   2. Spices—Dictionaries
3. Cookery
ISBN 1-56458-065-2   LC 92-6537
"Profusely illustrated with more than 750 full-color photographs, this is a comprehensive sourcebook on 200-plus herbs and spices. . . . This stunning book will be a welcome addition to both the public library reference shelf and its circulating collection." Libr J
Includes bibliography

Mulherin, Jennifer
The Macmillan treasury of spices and natural flavorings; a complete guide to the identification and uses of common and exotic spices and natural flavorings. Macmillan 1988 144p il $17.95   **641.3**
1. Spices 2. Herbs 3. Flavoring essences
ISBN 0-02-587850-6   LC 88-16986
This look at the roles spices and flavorings play in medicine, cosmetics and food preparation contains over 100 recipes
Includes bibliography

Rinzler, Carol Ann
The complete book of herbs, spices, and condiments; from garden to kitchen to medicine chest. Facts on File 1990 199p il $19.95   **641.3**
1. Herbs 2. Spices 3. Condiments
ISBN 0-8160-2008-6   LC 89-23465
"In dictionary format, Rinzler describes a variety of plants and condiments from saccharin to saffron. A unique feature is the inclusion of the nutritional profile of each herb, spice, or condiment." Booklist
Includes bibliographic references

Stobart, Tom
Herbs, spices, and flavorings. Overlook Press 1982 320p il $22.50; pa $9.95
641.3
1. Herbs 2. Spices 3. Flavoring essences
ISBN 0-87951-148-6; 0-87951-228-8 (pa)
LC 81-18886
First published 1970 in the United Kingdom with title: The International Wine and Food Society's guide to herbs, spices, and flavorings; first United States edition published 1973 by McGraw-Hill
"Entries ranging from one to three pages in length inform the reader of the origins and history of natural, synthetic, and harmful cooking flavorings. In addition, the text outlines native, medicinal, and scientific uses for each plant and notes popular and botanical names in several languages. Color plates and black-and-white drawings help identification. An index and an appendix listing plants by family are useful aids." Ref Sources for Small & Medium-sized Libr. 5th edition

641.4   Food preservation and storage

Greene, Janet C.
Putting food by; [by] Janet Greene, Ruth Hertzberg, Beatrice Vaughan. 4th ed newly rev. Greene 1988 420p il $22.95; pa $9.95
641.4

1. Food—Preservation
ISBN 0-8289-0644-0; 0-8289-0645-9 (pa)
LC 87-34262
Also available in paperback from New Am. Lib.
"A Janet Greene book"
First published 1973, with Hertzberg as first author
This is a guide to food preservation methods including freezing, curing, pickling, drying, making jams and jellies, and canning
"A valuable library resource." Booklist
Includes bibliography

641.5   Cooking

Adams, Marcia
Christmas in the heartland; recipes, decorations, and traditions for joyous celebrations; photographs by Jon Jensen; food and prop styling by Fred Derby. Potter 1992 164p il $25
641.5

1. Cookery 2. Christmas decorations 3. Christmas
ISBN 0-517-58572-3   LC 91-44300
The author "has produced a warmly photographed record of several families' traditions, from the Moravian customs of Bethlehem, Pa., to those of a family of gardening enthusiasts near Manchester, Ind. Included are decorating ideas as well as recipes, all with carefully wrought instructions and illustrations." Publ Wkly

The **Africa** News cookbook; African cooking for Western kitchens; [by the] Africa News Service, Inc.; edited by Tami Hultman; designed and illustrated by Patricia Ford. Viking 1986 xxix, 175p il maps o.p.; Penguin Bks. paperback available $17
641.5

1. Cookery, African
ISBN 0-14-046751-3 (pa)   LC 85-40820
This cookbook contains recipes from more than thirty African countries both north and south of the Sahara
"Here, almost everything the cook will need is readily available in local supermarkets or specialty shops. . . . Spices and other special ingredients are well covered in an introductory chapter, and instructions are easy to follow." Booklist
Includes bibliography

Algar, Ayla Esen
Classical Turkish cooking; traditional Turkish food for the American kitchen; [by] Ayla Algar. HarperCollins Pubs. 1991 306p $30
641.5

1. Cookery, Turkish
ISBN 0-06-016317-8   LC 91-55096

"A cuisine that melds the fragrances and flavors of the Far East, Central Asia, Iran, Anatolia, and the Mediterranean is enriched by Algar as she goes well beyond the standard recipes (160 of them) to explain Turkey's historical, cultural, and culinary traditions—and, along the way, to include a glimpse of her personal family heritage." Booklist
Includes bibliographic references

The **American** Diabetes Association, The American Dietetic Association family cookbook; illustrated by Lauren Rosen. rev ed. Prentice Hall Press 1987-1991 4v il ea $23
641.5

1. Diabetes—Diet therapy—Recipes 2. Cookery for the sick
ISBN 0-13-003915-2 (v1); 0-13-003955-1 (v2); 0-13-004145-9 (v3); 0-13-024092-3 (v4) LC 87-42674
Volume one first published 1980; volume two 1984
Volume four has title: The American tradition
This cookbook provides nutritional information and recipes for meal planning for diabetics and their families. Also explains microwave adaptations and new appliances
Includes bibliography

American Heart Association cookbook. Times Bks. $24.50
641.5

1. Cookery 2. Low-cholesterol diet
First published 1973. (5th edition 1991) Periodically revised
This cookbook includes over 600 recipes from appetizers, spreads and snacks to desserts and breakfast dishes. Appendix gives tips for dining out and menus for holidays and special occasions
"No more comprehensive guide to the healthy eating suited to the 1990s is available." Booklist

American Heart Association low-salt cookbook; a complete guide to reducing sodium and fat in the diet; Rodman D. Starke and Mary Winston, editors; illustrations by Regina Scudellari. Times Bks. 1990 349p il $19.95
641.5

1. Cookery 2. Salt free diet
ISBN 0-8129-1852-5   LC 90-10823
This low-salt cookbook is aimed at those seeking to change their eating and cooking habits to avoid cardiovascular disease. In addition to the recipes, the book includes nutritional information and two diet plans

Anderson, Jean, 1929-
The food of Portugal; color photography by the author. Morrow 1986 304p il map $24.95
641.5

1. Cookery, Portuguese
ISBN 0-688-04363-1   LC 86-2510
The author "first covers Portugal's geography and touches on distinctive regional cooking styles. The following glossary delineates Portuguese food, drink, and dining terminology. . . . Part 2, . . . is a guide to the country's best food." Booklist
Includes bibliography

Anderson, Jean, 1929—_Continued_

The new Doubleday cookbook; [by] Jean Anderson and Elaine Hanna. Doubleday 1985 965p il $35   **641.5**

1. Cookery
ISBN 0-385-19577-X   LC 85-16844

First published 1975 with title: The Doubleday cookbook

This book contains 4,700 recipes. Special sections provide information on microwave cooking, food additives and cooking terms

Bailey, Lee

Lee Bailey's Southern food & plantation houses; favorite Natchez recipes; by Lee Bailey and the Pilgrimage Garden Club; photographs by Tom Eckerle; design by Hans Teensma. Potter 1990 176p il $30   **641.5**

1. Cookery—Southern States   2. Mississippi—Social life and customs
ISBN 0-517-57280-X   LC 89-16366

"This gathering of two centuries of the best cooking of Natchez, Mississippi, accompanied by photos of 109 antebellum plantations, includes both traditional and unexpected recipes. . . . Dishes are often rich, but all are beautifully displayed and photographed—as are the furnishings and grounds of many stately homes." Booklist

Barnard, Melanie

Parties; menus for easy good times; [by] Melanie Barnard and Brooke Dojny; photographs by Randy O'Rourke. HarperCollins Pubs. 1992 278p il $27.50   **641.5**

1. Cookery   2. Entertaining
ISBN 0-06-016596-0   LC 92-52582

The authors present "their favorite recipes for entertaining, arranged by seasonal celebrations. They include planning-ahead notes for each menu, and ideas for short-cut substitutions." Libr J

"Though most of the more than 150 recipes might seem old hat to avid culinarians, the combinations in 20 seasonal menus are creative." Booklist

Barr, Nancy Verde

We called it macaroni; an American heritage of southern Italian cooking; illustrations by Kathe Helander. Knopf 1990 344p il (Knopf cooks American) $22.50   **641.5**

1. Cookery, Italian
ISBN 0-394-55798-0   LC 90-53114

This is a collection of 250 recipes favored by immigrants from Calabria, Apulia, Campania, and Sicily

"Barr has produced a memory-laden collection that's a delight for the mind as well as for the palate. What distinguishes this from many of the Italian classics on kitchen shelves are the 30-something sidebars, filled with educational tidbits and remembrances from friends and relatives." Booklist

Beard, James, 1903-1985

James Beard's American cookery; with illustrations by Earl Thollander. Little, Brown 1972 877p il hardcover o.p. paperback available $15.95   **641.5**

1. Cookery
ISBN 0-316-08566-9 (pa)

"Comprehensive in scope the cookbook gives eighteenth-and nineteenth-century recipes as well as modern directions for preparation of a full range of U.S. cookery. . . . The format is attractive and the historical data add to the value of an authoritative guide." Booklist

Includes bibliography

The new James Beard; drawings by Karl Stuecklen. Knopf 1981 625p il hardcover o.p. paperback available $18.95   **641.5**

1. Cookery
ISBN 0-394-72470-4 (pa)   LC 80-29305

In this cookbook the author places "emphasis on fresh foods and lighter foods, and the use of less meat and more vegetables and grains, the more experimental use of seasonings." Libr J

Berkowitz, George

The Legal Sea Foods cookbook; [by] George Berkowitz and Jane Doerfer; illustrations by Bruce Hutchinson. Doubleday 1988 182p il $21.95; pa $14   **641.5**

1. Cookery—Fish   2. Cookery—Seafood
ISBN 0-385-19830-2; 0-385-23183-0 (pa)   LC 87-8922

This is a guide to selecting and preparing fish and other seafood from Boston's Legal Sea Foods restaurants

"The simple and easy-to-follow recipes depend on fresh seafood, of course, in addition to commonly available ingredients and straightforward cooking methods. The chatty advice on seafood buying makes spotting good, fresh fish seem easy." Booklist

Better Homes and Gardens new cook book. Meredith Corp. $24.95; pa $12.95   **641.5**

1. Cookery

Also available in ringbound edition

First published 1930 with title: My Better Homes and Gardens cookbook. (10th edition 1989) Periodically revised

This cookbook includes "recipe choices reflecting concern for lighter meals, more ethnicity, the use of less red meat, and saving time in the kitchen. . . . The _Better Homes_ staff presents clearly written and attractively illustrated recipes ranging from appetizers and snacks to breads and meats, salads, fish and shellfish, sauces and relishes, and soups and stews. Many microwave recipes are included." Booklist

Bracken, Peg, 1920-

The compleat I hate to cook book; drawings by Hilary Knight. Harcourt Brace Jovanovich 1986 278p il $15.95   **641.5**

1. Cookery
ISBN 0-15-120480-2   LC 86-9990

Also available in paperback from Bantam Bks.

A compilation of over 450 easy recipes from the author's I hate to cook book (1960) and two subsequent collections

Brody, Jane E.

Jane Brody's good food gourmet; recipes and menus for delicious and healthful entertaining; illustrations by Ray Skibinski. Norton 1990 xxii, 602p il $25   **641.5**

1. Cookery
ISBN 0-393-02878-X   LC 90-6701

Also available in paperback from Bantam Bks.

A collection of over 500 recipes for entertaining which are low in fat, cholesterol, and salt

Brody, Lora, 1945-

The kitchen survival guide; a hand-holding kitchen primer with 130 recipes to get you started. Morrow 1992 308p $20   **641.5**

1. Cookery
ISBN 0-688-10587-4   LC 91-40663

"Written in a casual style, this primer is an excellent introduction for the person who has never set foot in a kitchen. In addition to 130 recipes for the basics (fried eggs and mashed potatoes), Brody discusses setting up a kitchen and how to shop for food." Booklist

Includes bibliographic references

Bugialli, Giuliano

Giuliano Bugialli's Foods of Italy; photographs by John Dominis. Stewart, Tabori & Chang 1984 304p il $50   **641.5**

1. Cookery, Italian 2. Italy—Social life and customs
ISBN 0-941434-52-4   LC 84-2543

The author "takes the reader on a culinary tour of his country, displaying some of Italy's most famous products, passing on bits of anecdotal history, and preserving a finely honed sense of Italian tradition." Booklist

"The cream of the crop. It combines excellent recipes with sumptuous picture-postcard photographs." N Y Times Book Rev

Burros, Marian Fox

20-minute menus; [by] Marian Burros. Simon & Schuster 1989 254p il pa $19.95   **641.5**

1. Cookery 2. Menus
ISBN 0-671-62390-7   LC 88-38823

This volume consists of 100 menus requiring no more than 20 minutes to prepare. The recipes are low in salt, calories and cholesterol

Casas, Penelope

Tapas, the little dishes of Spain; photographs by Tom Hopkins. Knopf 1985 219p il $24.95; pa $18   **641.5**

1. Cookery, Spanish 2. Cookery—Appetizers
ISBN 0-394-54086-7; 0-394-74235-4 (pa)
LC 85-40160

This book of recipes for Spanish appetizers is divided "by method of preparation: tapas in sauce; marinades, pâtés, salads, and other cold tapas; tapas with bread or pastry; and tapas that are fried, broiled, baked, or otherwise require some last-minute preparation." Libr J

Child, Julia

The French Chef cookbook; drawings and photographs by Paul Child. Knopf 1968 xxxiii, 424p il $19.95   **641.5**

1. Cookery, French
ISBN 0-394-40135-2

Also available in paperback from Bantam Bks.

"This book grew out of the educational television series 'The French Chef.' . . . It ranges from sauces, stews, and meats to appetizers, vegetables, desserts, cakes and pastries, and from the very simple to the fairly complicated. The book represents 119 programs." Introduction

From Julia Child's kitchen; photographs and drawings by Paul Child; additional technical photographs by Albie Walton. Knopf 1975 687, xxvip il $39.95; pa $21.95   **641.5**

1. Cookery, French
ISBN 0-394-48071-6; 0-394-71027-4 (pa)

The author "has taken many of the recipes she demonstrated in her 72 'French Chef' TV shows; grouped them by subject [soups, appetizers, egg dishes, fish, poultry, meat, vegetables, salads, bread] added variations and additional recipes; and introduced each section and most recipes with commentaries." Libr J

Includes bibliography

Julia Child & company; by Julia Child in collaboration with E. S. Yntema; photographs by James Scherer. Knopf 1978 243p il o.p.; Ballantine Bks. paperback available $4.95   **641.5**

1. Cookery 2. Menus
ISBN 0-345-31449-2 (pa)   LC 78-54922

This book was written to accompany the TV series of the same name, which was "based on 13 complete menus to be cooked for company." Libr J

"Breezy, humorous, and lucid." Christ Sci Monit

Mastering the art of French cooking; by Julia Child, Louisette Bertholle, Simone Beck. updated ed. Knopf 1983 2v il set $82.50; pa $41.90   **641.5**

1. Cookery, French
ISBN 0-394-40178-6; 0-394-72114-4 (pa)
LC 83-48113

Also available separately in hardcover and paperback

Volume 1 first published 1961 with Beck's name first; volume 2 by Julia Child and Simone Beck

Volume one includes, in addition to usual categories, a chapter dealing with entrees and luncheon dishes, including quiches, pâtés, and crepes, and other cold buffet items. Volume 2 emphasizes French bread and pastries, with chapters also devoted to soups, meats, chickens, vegetables, and desserts. Appendices discuss stuffings and kitchen equipment

The way to cook; photographs by Brian Leatart and Jim Scherer; food designer, Rosemary Manell. Knopf 1989 511p il $50; pa $30   **641.5**

1. Cookery
ISBN 0-394-53264-3; 0-679-74765-6 (pa)
LC 88-45838

Child, Julia—*Continued*
"With her sensible-as-always approach to food, Child has produced a comprehensive cooking bible, filled with stunning photographs and practical illustrations, that will aid the novice [and] inspire the gourmet. . . . A masterwork from a master chef." Libr J

Claiborne, Craig
Cooking with Craig Claiborne and Pierre Franey; [by] Craig Claiborne and Pierre Franey. Times Bks. 1983 500p o.p.; Fawcett Bks. paperback available $9.95 **641.5**
1. Cookery
ISBN 0-449-90130-0 (pa)   LC 83-45038
The authors "present more than 600 recipes for all courses of a menu, representing many cuisines, fancies, and degrees of elegance and ease of preparation. While there are some extravaganzas, usually the notions of professional chefs . . . these two generally have no peers in taste, judgment and a true sense of the joy of cooking." Libr J

Craig Claiborne's Southern cooking. Times Bks. 1987 364p $19.95 **641.5**
1. Cookery—Southern States
ISBN 0-8129-1599-2   LC 86-14509
Claiborne "offers a selection of Southern fare that runs the gamut from his mother's triple-tiered gelatin mold, circa 1930, to Paul Prudhomme's contemporary Cajun popcorn. . . . From the traditional to the original, these lucid, flavorful recipes will be welcomed by Claiborne's substantial following and by fans of regional American cooking." Publ Wkly

Craig Claiborne's The new New York Times cookbook; [by] Craig Claiborne with Pierre Franey. Times Bks. 1979 751p il $29.95 **641.5**
1. Cookery
ISBN 0-8129-0835-X   LC 79-51428
An illustrated collection of over 1,000 recipes culled from the New York Times that reflect international influences on traditional American cooking. Anecdotes on taste and dining customs are included

The New York Times cook book. rev ed. Harper & Row 1990 799p $27.50 **641.5**
1. Cookery
ISBN 0-06-016010-1   LC 89-45640
First published 1961
A basic collection of recipes covering both traditional American food preparation and more recent culinary trends. Cooking procedures are outlined in a step-by-step approach

The New York Times international cook book; drawings by James J. Spanfeller. Harper & Row 1971 xxvii, 599p il $25
641.5
1. Cookery
ISBN 0-06-010788-X
Full color illustrations accompany the nearly 1000 recipes from 45 countries around the world

Colwin, Laurie
Home cooking; illustrated by Anna Shapiro. Knopf 1988 193p il $17.95 **641.5**
1. Cookery
ISBN 0-394-55969-X   LC 88-45267
Also available in paperback from HarperCollins Pubs.
This "is as much memoir as cookbook and as much about eating as cooking. The recipes are for the kinds of things your mother used to make: baked beans with Boston brown bread, pot roast, potato pancakes—savory, filling and labor-intensive. . . . Even without the recipes, 'Home Cooking' makes a comfy read." N Y Times Book Rev

More home cooking; a writer returns to the kitchen. HarperCollins Pubs. 1993 224p $22 **641.5**
1. Cookery
ISBN 0-06-016849-8   LC 93-29184
This is the second collection of Colwin's "food writings, a number of which have never been printed before, though the majority appeared in Gourmet magazine. Her fans will cherish this final volume, and rightly so, for the cozy, unpretentious good sense that characterizes all her food writing is here in abundance." N Y Times Book Rev

Cone-Esaki, Marcia
Mastering microwave cookery; [by] Marcia Cone and Thelma Snyder; illustrated by Glenn Wolff; photographs by Michael Geiger. Simon & Schuster 1986 639p il $24.95 **641.5**
1. Microwave cookery
ISBN 0-671-54162-5   LC 86-10068
"Four-score pages of directions, tips, and techniques discuss how microwaves work, offer basic ideas on reheating, and present an array of data on cooking times, recipe conversions, utensils, and special equipment." Booklist

Cooking A to Z; the complete culinary reference tool; Jane Horn: editor/writer; Janet Fletcher: contributing writer; Gary Hespenheide: interior designer. Cole 1992 640p il $39.95; pa $24.95 **641.5**
ISBN 1-56426-003-8; 1-56426-002-X (pa)
LC 87-072103
First published 1988 by Ortho Bks.
"This book is both a reference source and a cookbook. The 600 recipes are interspersed among 500 encyclopedic entries for equipment, ingredients, techniques, and other cooking terms. Color photographs and hints in the margins make this a marvelous introductory text for a beginning cook." Booklist

Cooley, Denton A., 1920-
Eat smart for a healthy heart cookbook; by Denton A. Cooley and Carolyn E. Moore. Barron's Educ. Ser. 1987 386p il $21.95; pa $12.95 **641.5**
1. Cookery   2. Heart—Diseases—Diet therapy
3. Heart—Diseases—Prevention
ISBN 0-8120-5745-7; 0-8120-4878-4 (pa)
LC 86-26510

Cooley, Denton A., 1920-—*Continued*

Opening with a "description of various types of heart diseases and the probable dietary causes, the text continues with a discussion of altering diet for a healthy heart and arteries, and then presents some 400 easy-to-prepare recipes, complete with nutritional information." Booklist

Cost, Bruce, 1945-

Bruce Cost's Asian ingredients; buying and cooking the staple foods of China, Japan, and Southeast Asia; foreword by Alice Waters. Morrow 1988 333p il $22.95

641.5

1. Cookery, Oriental 2. Food
ISBN 0-688-05877-9   LC 88-8943

The author provides a guide to selecting and preparing Asian foods available to American consumers

Includes bibliography

Crocker, Betty

Betty Crocker's cookbook. Prentice-Hall il pa $14   641.5

1. Cookery

First published with this title 1969 by Golden Press. (7th edition 1991) Periodically revised

"This book gives easily readable and understandable recipes. Also has a glossary of cooking terms in back, as well as nutritional guidelines and 'special helps.'" N Y Public Libr Book of How & Where to Look It Up

Betty Crocker's microwave cookbook. Prentice Hall Press 1990 367p il loose-leaf bdg $19.95   641.5

1. Microwave cookery
ISBN 0-13-073859-X   LC 89-23140

First published 1981 by Random House

"For beginners, there is a good explanation of how microwave ovens work and how to adapt to their idiosyncrasies. The more than 500 recipes are arranged conventionally—from appetizers and drinks to poultry, fish, meats, vegetables, and desserts." Booklist

Betty Crocker's new international cookbook. Prentice Hall Press 1989 376p il $18.95   641.5

1. Cookery
ISBN 0-13-074378-X   LC 88-32378

First published 1980 with title: Betty Crocker's international cookbook

This includes "450 easy-to-follow recipes culled from over 50 countries. . . . At heart a book intended for the uninitiated cook, the volume includes a glossary of foreign ingredients and terms, informative sidebar explanations, and a regional and general index." Publ Wkly

Betty Crocker's smartcook; the essential everyday cookbook. Prentice-Hall 1988 311p il $16.95   641.5

1. Cookery
ISBN 0-13-074311-9   LC 88-9910

Most of the recipes in this collection "take less than 45 minutes to prepare. . . . The text features salads, soups, eggs and cheese, grains and pasta, desserts, and

sandwiches, including make-ahead calzone or pizza variations. A nice resource for busy people." Booklist

Cunningham, Marion

The breakfast book. Knopf 1987 320p il $19.95   641.5

1. Cookery
ISBN 0-394-55529-5   LC 87-45124

This cookbook offers "plenty of recipes for sweet breads and rolls, inventive dishes such as fresh trout fried in an oatmeal crust, and an array of selections featuring the usual breakfast favorites. . . . These recipes will appeal to a broad range of cooks, both beginners and experts." Booklist

The supper book; illustrated by Donnie Cameron. Knopf 1992 253p il $21.50

641.5

1. Cookery
ISBN 0-679-40144-X   LC 91-41506

An illustrated collection of undemanding recipes for the everyday evening meal or informal company occasion

Curnonsky, 1872-1956

Larousse traditional French cooking. Doubleday 1989 703p il $45   641.5

1. Cookery, French
ISBN 0-385-26532-8   LC 89-1164

Original French edition, 1953

This illustrated cookbook offers over 1,200 recipes for classic French dishes. A command of basic cooking terms and skills is assumed

Deighton, Len, 1929-

ABC of French food; foreword by Egon Ronay; introduction by Jacques Pépin. Bantam Bks. 1990 c1989 256p il map $19.95   641.5

1. Cookery, French
ISBN 0-553-05759-6   LC 89-18157

First published 1989 in the United Kingdom

Novelist Deighton provides alphabetized notes on French food, chefs, restaurants, wines, regions, ingredients, and culinary writing

Del Conte, Anna

A casa; seasonal Italian home cooking. HarperCollins Pubs. 1992 357p $27.50

641.5

1. Cookery, Italian
ISBN 0-06-016524-3   LC 92-52583

The author "outlines, by season and occasion, a number of Italian menus, distinguished by the relaxed attitude and fresh and flavorful dishes of characteristically Italian cooking. . . . The author skillfully interweaves much of the best of Italy's regions into the book, ending up with a happy balance of interesting—and unusual—recipes, cooking techniques and personal recollections." Publ Wkly

De'Medici, Lorenza
The heritage of Italian cooking. Random House 1990 256p il $39.50   **641.5**
1. Cookery, Italian
ISBN 0-394-58876-2   LC 90-8346
A survey of Italian cookery based on early cookbooks, old documents and folk traditions. Art reproductions and color photographs accompany the text
Includes bibliography

Dent, Huntley
The feast of Santa Fe; cooking of the American Southwest; illustrations by Susan Gaber. Simon & Schuster 1985 397p il $22.95   **641.5**
1. Cookery 2. Santa Fe (N.M.)—Social life and customs
ISBN 0-671-47686-6   LC 84-20217
This work presents over 150 recipes and explores associated traditions of the American Southwest
"The cuisine of the southwestern United States is portrayed in all its richness in [this book]. . . . Mr. Dent has written a clear and comprehensive primer on the traditions and foods of Santa Fe, the region's gastronomic capital." N Y Times Book Rev

Dupree, Nathalie
New Southern cooking. Knopf 1986 345p il $25   **641.5**
1. Cookery—Southern States
ISBN 0-394-55818-9   LC 86-18564
This companion volume to the author's Public Television series presents traditional Southern dishes. "The recipes, short and snappy, shouldn't test the technique of even the beginning cook." Booklist
Includes bibliography

Elbert, Virginie
Down-island Caribbean cookery; [by] Virginie F. and George A. Elbert. Simon & Schuster 1991 364p map $24.95   **641.5**
1. Cookery, Caribbean
ISBN 0-671-67203-7   LC 90-48091
This collection of over 300 recipes includes "information on African, Indian, and European influences . . . [and] a full explanation of equipment, as well as a glossary of ingredients and ideas for substitutions. The recipes, one per page, are always identified by island." Booklist

The **Family** Circle cookbook; new tastes for new times; by the editors of Family Circle and David Ricketts; photographs by Steven Mark Needham. Simon & Schuster 1992 648p il loose-leaf bdg $23   **641.5**
1. Cookery
ISBN 0-671-73572-1   LC 92-1146
This "book is packed with charts and tables, cooking tips, sidebars and boxes on a wide range of topics, color photographs of cooking techniques and the finished dishes, and more than 700 recipes. . . . Nutrition information is given for each, and lowfat and low-cholesterol dishes are highlighted, as are quick recipes." Libr J

Farmer, Fannie Merritt, 1857-1915
The Fannie Farmer cookbook. Knopf il $24.95   **641.5**
1. Cookery
First published 1896. (13th edition 1990) Periodically revised
Recent editions by Marion Cunningham
"In more than 1,800 recipes for American dishes, this book pays attention to healthful eating, emphasizing cereals and grains, and has an expanded fish section. Has helpful hints throughout, along with guides to what to look for in ingredients." N Y Public Libr Book of How & Where to Look It Up

Fussell, Betty Harper
Food in good season; a month-by-month harvest of country recipes for cooks everywhere; illustrated by Glenna Putt. Knopf 1988 291p il $18.95   **641.5**
1. Cookery
ISBN 0-394-57117-7   LC 88-45352
The author "takes a look at what's in season during each month of the year across the country and at ways the reader could cook up this harvest. . . . From homey historical favorites to a flirtation with the new American cuisine, Fussell has a finger in every pot and a sure hand on the skillet." Booklist

Gavin, Paola
Italian vegetarian cooking. Evans & Co. 1990 285p $18.95   **641.5**
1. Vegetarian cookery 2. Cookery, Italian
ISBN 0-87131-575-0   LC 89-29699
"Regional vegetarian specialties from all over Italy. Most of these are simple, traditional recipes, dishes from *la cucina casalingua*." Libr J
"Easy-to-follow directions and an introduction explaining the cuisines of the various regions (Veneto, Liguria, Umbria, etc.) make this an enlightening as well as delicious read." Booklist

Gelber, Willa
A feast for the heart; entertaining with elegant and easy low-cholesterol menus; [by] Willa Gelber, with Greg Case; Helen Rothstein Kimmel, nutrition consultant; foreword by Eliot A. Brinton. Little, Brown 1992 246p $21.95   **641.5**
1. Cookery 2. Low-cholesterol diet
ISBN 0-316-30744-0   LC 92-3225
The author "offers seasonal theme menus for special occasions from a fall Spanish Supper to a summer Beat-the-Heat Brunch. Although she relies on a few low-calorie substitutions . . . few of her low-fat recipes seem like diet food. Imaginative, inspired by a variety of cuisines, and simple to prepare, they should be greatly appealing to health-conscious hosts." Libr J

Goldstein, Joyce
Back to square one; old-world food in a new-world kitchen. Morrow 1992 420p il maps $23   **641.5**
1. Cookery
ISBN 0-688-10122-4   LC 92-8366

Goldstein, Joyce—*Continued*
The recipes included are Goldstein's "interpretations
of her favorite dishes from a wide range of cultures,
from Indonesia to the Russian republics to Latin America. . . . The recipes are intriguing, if at times somewhat
daunting for home cooks; excellent headnotes provide the
provenance of each dish as well as suggestions for variations. Highly recommended." Libr J

The Mediterranean kitchen; drawings by
Rachel Goldstein; wine recommendations by
Evan Goldstein. Morrow 1989 410p il $25
641.5

1. Cookery, Mediterranean
ISBN 0-688-07283-6   LC 89-34476

The author "creates superb, earthy foods free from
pretension and fuss. . . . Her eagerness for authentic
cuisine from this ancient region is tempered by a keen,
modern eye for what Americans want to cook and eat
today." Christ Sci Monit

The **Good** Housekeeping illustrated
cookbook. rev & expanded ed. Hearst Bks.
1989 528p il $27   **641.5**

1. Cookery
ISBN 0-688-08074-X   LC 88-2851
First published 1980

This cookbook features over 1,400 recipes. Illustrations
demonstrate such techniques as measuring, dicing, julien-
ning, grating, beating, and folding. Microwave cooking
is also covered

Guide to cooking schools. Shaw Assocs. pa
$16.95   **641.5**

1. Cookery—Study and teaching
ISSN 1040-2616
Annual. First published 1988

"More than 400 cooking school and vacation programs
in the U.S. and selected foreign countries are listed in
this comprehensive guide. Schools are ranked by tuition
and percentage of applicants accepted. The 1994 edition
contains a chapter on wine courses." Booklist

Harris, Jessica B.
Sky juice and flying fish; traditional
Caribbean cooking. Simon & Schuster 1991
242p pa $12.95   **641.5**

1. Cookery, Caribbean
ISBN 0-671-68165-6   LC 90-48012
"A Fireside book"

The author describes "the traditional dishes of the
Caribbean islands. Her lively text is well written and
informative, and she provides historical background and
an excellent glossary as well as an assortment of recipes
both simple and sophisticated." Libr J

Hazan, Marcella
Essentials of classic Italian cooking;
illustrated by Karin Kretschmann. Knopf
1992 688p il $29.50   **641.5**

1. Cookery, Italian
ISBN 0-394-58404-X   LC 92-52954
Revised and updated edition of the author's The classic Italian cookbook (1973) and More classic Italian
cooking (1978)

A guide to the products, techniques and dishes of
classic Italian cooking. Regional specialities are dealt with
at length
This "could readily assume the mantle of *the* definitive resource for Italian cuisine." Booklist

Marcella's Italian kitchen. Knopf 1986
349p il $27   **641.5**

1. Cookery, Italian
ISBN 0-394-50892-0   LC 86-45268

Following an introduction on ingredients, utensils, and
menus, this book of some 250 Italian recipes presents
individual chapters on appetizers, soups, pasta, fish,
meat, vegetables, salads, and desserts

Hewitt, Jean
Cooking for two today; [by] Jean Hewitt
and Marjorie Page Blanchard. Little, Brown
1985 xxiii, 221p hardcover o.p. paperback
available $9.95   **641.5**

1. Cookery
ISBN 0-316-35991-2 (pa)   LC 85-7839

"The authors cover equipment, ingredients, tips for
freezing and storing, and lots of general advice. In addition, the recipes are coded in categories that include
doubling, versatile, quick, leftovers, seasonal, make-ahead,
and elegant. . . . Advanced beginner to intermediate
level." Booklist

The New York Times new natural foods
cookbook. Times Bks. 1982 438p il o.p.;
Avon Bks. paperback available $10   **641.5**

1. Cookery—Natural foods
ISBN 0-380-62687-X (pa)   LC 81-52570

First published 1972 with title: The New York Times
natural foods cookbook

"The recipes provide capable guidelines for constructing wholesome and appetizing meals that utilize vegetables, whole grains and legumes. Highlights include a chapter on fish. . . . These recipes call for reduced amounts
of natural sweeteners, fresh fruits and whole-grain flours."
Publ Wkly

Includes bilbiography

The **International** kosher cookbook; by the
92nd Street Y Kosher Cooking School;
edited by Batia Plotch and Patricia Cobe.
Fawcett Columbine 1992 xlv, 418p il $22
641.5

1. Cookery, Jewish
ISBN 0-449-90366-4   LC 91-73146

"Both traditional Jewish specialties and kosher dishes
developed from cuisines without an established Jewish
tradition are included; there are also sections on the
kosher kitchen and kosher wine, along with special
celebration and holiday menus." Libr J

Jaffrey, Madhur
A taste of India; food photography by
Christine Hanscomb; specially commissioned
location photography by Henry Wilson.
Atheneum Pubs. 1986 c1985 255p il
hardcover o.p. paperback available $26
641.5

1. Cookery, Indic
ISBN 0-689-70726-6 (pa)   LC 85-72598

Jaffrey, Madhur—*Continued*
First published 1985 in the United Kingdom

This "covers India's 16 main culinary regions, with an introductory essay on the history, food customs, and cuisine of each and a selection of regional recipes, some from hotel kitchens, most from private households. The essays are informative, the recipes varied (though there are only about 100 of them all told), glamorous, and not difficult to make once the array of spices is at hand." Libr J

Jones, Jeanne
Cook it light classics. Macmillan 1993 244p $20   **641.5**
1. Cookery
ISBN 0-02-559771-X   LC 92-19255

The author presents low-cal, low-fat and low-cholesterol versions of classic recipes

Jones, Judith
The L.L. Bean book of new New England cookery; [by] Judith and Evan Jones; illustrations by Lauren Jarrett. Random House 1987 669p il $30   **641.5**
1. Cookery
ISBN 0-394-54456-0   LC 87-314

This "collection includes both contemporary and traditional recipes from the six states of New England, . . . often prefaced by notes on regional food history, chefs, and restaurants." Libr J

Kafka, Barbara
Microwave gourmet. Morrow 1987 575p il $25   **641.5**
1. Microwave cookery
ISBN 0-688-06843-X   LC 87-12764

Also available in paperback from Avon Bks.

The author "focuses here on producing interesting, pleasing dishes rather than on teaching readers how to operate their new microwave ovens. . . . Recipes range from family dishes, such as chunky beef chili and pork chops with sauerkraut, to company fare." Publ Wkly

Party food; small & savory; photography by Tom Eckerle. Morrow 1992 xxvii, 323p il $25   **641.5**
1. Cookery 2. Entertaining
ISBN 0-688-11184-X   LC 91-45725

This book includes "more than 300 recipes—of foods meant for entertaining. . . . In raising a party giver's comfort level with feeding 4 to 40, Kafka also manages to expand even a well-practiced cook's horizons, through a variety of sidebars and a homey, personalized narrative." Booklist

Katz, Pat, 1934-
The craft of the country cook; from A-Z, over 1,000 recipes & food ideas. Hartley & Marks 1988 730p il $29.95; pa $19.95
641.5
1. Cookery
ISBN 0-88179-014-1; 0-88179-015-X (pa) LC 88-2671

"In an encyclopedic arrangement, Katz begins with *apples* and ends with *yogurt. Cold storage, gelatin,* and *salt curing* are among the 177 topics described. Recipes and techniques for preparation and preservation are given for each entry." Booklist

Kennedy, Diana
The art of Mexican cooking; traditional Mexican cooking for aficionados; photographs by Michael Calderwood; illustrations by Susana Martinez-Ostos. Bantam Bks. 1989 526p il $24.95   **641.5**
1. Cookery, Mexican
ISBN 0-553-05706-5   LC 89-17649

The author presents recipes for "regional specialties, supplying background material and careful preparation notes for each; there are whole chapters devoted to corn and 'the pig,' as well as invaluable descriptions of chiles and unfamiliar ingredients." Libr J

"Ms. Kennedy is one of the best recipe writers in the business—crisp, unambiguous, always informative." N Y Times Book Rev

Includes bibliographic references

Kowalski, Robert E.
The 8-week cholesterol cure cookbook; more than 200 delicious recipes featuring the foods proven to lower cholesterol. Harper & Row 1989 341p hardcover o.p. paperback available $9.95   **641.5**
1. Low-cholesterol diet 2. Cookery
ISBN 0-06-091689-3 (pa)   LC 88-45896

Companion volume to The 8-week cholesterol cure, entered in class 616.1

This book contains "recipes that cover every kind of dish, literally from soup to nuts, including vegetarian, fish and meat entrées and a considerable variety of tempting desserts. Introductory chapters summarize the 'Cure' diet and explain the more unusual foodstuffs." Publ Wkly

Law, Ruth, b. 1887
The Southeast Asia cookbook. Fine, D.I. 1990 452p il $24.95   **641.5**
1. Cookery, Oriental
ISBN 1-55611-214-9   LC 89-46045

A collection of recipes from Thailand, Singapore, Malaysia, Indonesia, the Philippines, and Vietnam. The author also discusses utensils indispensable to Southeast Asian cuisine

Lemlin, Jeanne
Vegetarian pleasures; a menu cookbook. Knopf 1986 301p hardcover o.p. paperback available $19   **641.5**
1. Vegetarian cookery 2. Menus
ISBN 0-394-74302-4 (pa)   LC 85-45702

The sections of this cookbook are: quick menus; informal menus; elegant menus; summer menus; breakfast and brunch menus; and the basics

"This book is appealing for the range of international flavors and techniques it embraces, making potentially mundane dishes into something special." N Y Times Book Rev

Levy, Faye

Faye Levy's international Jewish cookbook. Warner Bks. 1991 xx, 364p il $29.95   **641.5**

1. Cookery, Jewish
ISBN 0-446-51568-X   LC 91-50083

A "guide to contemporary international Jewish cuisine. Levy includes more than 250 recipes inspired by the cooking of Jewish communities in a variety of cultures, from Moroccan Sea Bass to an Italian-style Braised Cod to Israeli Grilled Chicken. She provides recipes and menus for the holidays (there are six menus for Passover alone) as well as for everyday dishes of all sorts." Libr J

Lindsay, Anne

The American Cancer Society cookbook; [by] Anne Lindsay in consultation with Diane J. Fink. Hearst Bks. 1988 269p il $19.95   **641.5**

1. Cookery 2. Cancer—Diet therapy
ISBN 0-688-07484-7   LC 87-28203

Also available in paperback from Simon & Schuster

Following American Cancer Society dietary guidelines, this includes 200 recipes for low-fat high-fiber dishes

"Lindsay's sensitive palate for herbs and spices enlivens foods' native flavors, and, while she does not entirely eliminate meat from the diet, she cuts consumption to recommended levels." Booklist

Includes bibliography

Lo, Kenneth H. C.

New Chinese vegetarian cooking; [by] Kenneth Lo. Pantheon Bks. 1987 c1986 211p pa $11   **641.5**

1. Vegetarian cookery 2. Cookery, Chinese
ISBN 0-394-75005-5   LC 86-16979

First published 1986 in the United Kingdom

Based on the author's Chinese vegetarian cooking (1974)

The author "has invented dishes that present vegetables in an Oriental equivalent of 'cuisine naturelle.' The recipes are, nonetheless, quintessentially Chinese." Publ Wkly

"This book is destined to be considered definitive, due to Lo's uncompromising good taste and strict attention to the details of fine Chinese cooking." Booklist

Madison, Deborah

The Greens cook book; extraordinary vegetarian cuisine from the celebrated restaurant; by Deborah Madison with Edward Espe Brown. Bantam Bks. 1987 xx, 396p $26.95   **641.5**

1. Vegetarian cookery
ISBN 0-553-05195-4   LC 86-47884

"There are hundreds of delicious recipes for hearty or elegant soups, pastas, salads, casseroles and tarts in which meat products are not missed." N Y Times Book Rev

Includes bibliography

Martínez, Zarela

Food from my heart; cuisines of Mexico remembered and reimagined; foreword by Budd Schulberg. Macmillan 1992 354p $25   **641.5**

1. Cookery, Mexican 2. Mexico—Social life and customs
ISBN 0-02-580471-5   LC 92-25392

"Part memoir/part cultural history/part cookbook, and as heartfelt as its title indicates, [the author's] book is full of delicious recipes, both classic regional specialties and her own creations. . . . The story of how a young Mexican woman from a traditional family becomes a famous New York restauranteur is in fact quite absorbing, and along the way Martinez imparts a lot of information about the foods and cuisine of her country." Libr J

Includes bibliographic references

McGee, Harold

On food and cooking; the science and lore of the kitchen. Scribner 1984 684p il $45   **641.5**

1. Cookery 2. Food
ISBN 0-684-18132-0   LC 82-42667

Also available in paperback from Collier Bks.

This work of the science and history of food blends chemistry, physics, biology, anthropology and cookery. Controversial substances such as nitrate, saccharin and additives are examined

Includes bibliography

Molokhovets, Elena

Classic Russian cooking; Elena Molokhovets' A gift to young housewives; translated, introduced, and annotated by Joyce Toomre. Indiana Univ. Press 1992 680p il (Indiana-Michigan ser. in Russian and East European studies) $39.95   **641.5**

1. Cookery, Russian
ISBN 0-253-36026-9   LC 91-46254

"Molokhovet's book was first published in 1861 but revised by the author up through 1917, thus spanning an important era in Russian history. Her compendium was a sort of a *Fannie Farmer* or *Mrs. Beeton's* that became essential for young Russian housewives. . . . Toomre, a well-known culinary historian, has done an impressive job of presenting Molokhovet's work, providing a lengthy introduction to set the stage and annotations to put the recipes in context. A glimpse into another world that should interest cultural and culinary historians alike." Libr J

Includes bibliographic references

The New Good Housekeeping cookbook; edited by Mildred Ying; with the assistance of Susan Deborah Goldsmith and Ellen H. Connelly. Hearst Bks. 1986 825p il $23   **641.5**

1. Cookery 2. Menus
ISBN 0-688-03897-2   LC 86-81549

Variant title: The Good Housekeeping cookbook

This volume "goes a step beyond the fundamentals by adding a chapter on microwave cooking. Every 'Good Housekeeping' recipe tells not only how many servings it yields, but also how many calories are in each serving.

The New Good Housekeeping cookbook— *Continued*

Each chapter begins with an explanation of basic techniques for cooking the foods it focuses on . . . and progresses to more sophisticated treatments of that fundamental fare." Wilson Libr Bull

Nidetch, Jean

Weight Watchers quick start program cookbook; including the full exchange plan. New Am. Lib. 1984 455p il $18.50 **641.5**

1. Cookery 2. Reducing
ISBN 0-453-01010-5   LC 84-10107
"NAL books"

"Recipes and sample menus designed to start dieters off with a nutritionally sound plan for a quick weight loss, followed by a more gradual loss until a weight goal is achieved." Libr J

Weight Watchers quick success program cookbook; photography by Gus Francisco. New Am. Lib. 1988 440p il $18.95; pa $10.95   **641.5**

1. Cookery 2. Reducing
ISBN 0-453-01016-4; 0-452-26428-6 (pa)
                    LC 88-21045

The 300 recipes in this volume "are both international and down-home in character, with some focusing on quick preparation, others on the budget. . . . Includes menu plans, exchange charts, and cooking tips galore, and each recipe comes with a nutritional breakdown per serving." Booklist

Patout, Alex

Patout's Cajun home cooking. Random House 1986 207p il $19.95   **641.5**

1. Cookery—Louisiana
ISBN 0-394-54725-X   LC 86-10239

The author offers "the best of Cajun tradition combined with some of the new Louisiana cooking styles. . . . The text comes complete with suggested menus and mail-order sources for Cajun and Louisiana ingredients." Booklist

Pépin, Jacques

Jacques Pepin's The art of cooking. Knopf 1987-1988 2v il hardcover o.p. paperbacks available ea $25   **641.5**

1. Cookery
ISBN 0-679-74270-0 (v1); 0-679-74271-9 (v2) (pa)
                    LC 87-4253

Volume 1 covers stocks, soups, eggs, fish, poultry, game, and meat. Volume 2 concentrates on charcuterie and salads, breads, pastries, and desserts. Color photographs accompany the text

Prudhomme, Paul

Chef Paul Prudhomme's Louisiana kitchen; photography by Tom Jimison. Morrow 1984 351p il $23   **641.5**

1. Cookery—Louisiana
ISBN 0-688-02847-0   LC 83-63236

"These 200-plus recipes comprise authentic Cajun, Creole, and southern Louisiana cuisine. That means gumbos (seven kinds here), spicy chicken and seafood dishes, sauces and gravies, pecan-based desserts, and Prudhomme's own specialty—rabbit—along with many other dishes." Booklist

The Prudhomme family cookbook; old-time Louisiana recipes; by the eleven Prudhomme brothers and sisters and chef Paul Prudhomme. Morrow 1987 446p $19.95
                    641.5

1. Cookery—Louisiana
ISBN 0-688-07549-5   LC 87-18345

The Prudhomme brothers and sisters share the recipes of their Cajun upbringing on a farm in southern Louisiana. Biographical information about each family member is included, along with a list of Louisiana fairs and festivals

"This richly fragrant fare, based on lusty ingredients and strong Cajun seasonings, is not for dieters or the faint-palated." Time

Rios, Alicia

The heritage of Spanish cooking; text, Alicia Rios; recipes, Lourdes March. Random House 1992 256p il $45   **641.5**

1. Cookery, Spanish
ISBN 0-679-41628-5   LC 92-53633

Illustrated with reproductions of classic Spanish art and full-color photographs this book contains 150 recipes collected from ancient culinary texts, historic menus and oral traditions

Includes bibliography

Rodale's basic natural foods cookbook; editor, Charles Gerras; collaborating editors and text authors, Camille Cusumano and Carol Munson; editorial assistant, Camille Bucci. Rodale Press 1984 899p $24.95   **641.5**

1. Cookery—Natural foods
ISBN 0-87857-469-7   LC 83-19167

Also available in paperback from Simon & Schuster

"This giant volume, which includes 1500 recipes, aims also to serve as a basic cooking reference. It contains quantities of information . . . on cooking fundamentals. . . . Though appendixes list the calorie and sodium content of some common foods, and recipes . . . use no white flour, white sugar, white rice, salt, or alcohol, this is in no sense a diet book." Libr J

Roden, Claudia

The good food of Italy—region by region. rev ed. Knopf 1990 301p il $30   **641.5**

1. Cookery, Italian
ISBN 0-394-58250-0   LC 89-43353

First published 1989 in the United Kingdom with title: The food of Italy

"Roden's book is divided by subtlety of cuisine in different regions of Italy, including the islands of Sicily and Sardinia. From the top of the boot down, she introduces each section with an essay explaining the type of food considered to be that region's specialty and its culinary history. . . . She concludes each essay with that region's specialty wine. Recipes, listed by type of food (the course in the meal), are appended, as are short

Roden, Claudia—*Continued*
chapters on essential ingredients and choosing a wine."
Booklist

Rojas-Lombardi, Felipe, d. 1991
The art of South American cooking.
HarperCollins Pubs. 1991 xx, 504p $30
    641.5
1. Cookery, Latin American
ISBN 0-06-016425-5   LC 90-56395
The author "includes hundreds of recipes from his
homeland Peru and the other South American countries:
not just ceviche, but 12 different types, unusual tamales
filled with duck or quinoa, empanadas both sweet and
savory, and many more intriguing dishes from Chilean
Clam Chowder to Tomatoes Posing as Strawberries. The
recipes are well written, the text informative and
readable." Libr J

Romagnoli, Margaret
The new Romagnolis' table; by Margaret
and G. Franco Romagnoli; photographs by
G. Franco Romagnoli. Atlantic Monthly
Press 1988 297p il pa $15.95   **641.5**
1. Cookery, Italian
ISBN 0-87113-214-1   LC 87-22871
First published 1975 with title: The Romagnoli's table
In addition to traditional Italian family recipes for
pastas, soups and seafood, this book reflects the influence
of nouvelle and regional cuisines

Rombauer, Irma von Starkloff, 1877-1962
Joy of cooking; [by] Irma S. Rombauer,
Marion Rombauer Becker; illustrated by
Ginnie Hofmann and Ikki Matsumoto.
Macmillan il $21.95   **641.5**
1. Cookery
Also available in paperback from New Am Lib.
First published 1931. (1985 edition) Periodically
revised
"All-purpose cookbook for informal and formal use
with American and foreign recipes. Includes menu plan-
ning suggestions, nutrition, basic information on foods,
basic cooking terminology, and methods of preparation."
N Y Public Libr Book of How & Where to Look It
Up

Rosso, Julee
The new basics cookbook; by Julee Rosso
& Sheila Lukins; illustrated by Sheila
Lukins. Workman 1989 849p il $29.95; pa
$19.95   **641.5**
1. Cookery
ISBN 0-89480-392-1; 0-89480-341-7 (pa)
     LC 88-51581
Also available The Silver palate cookbook in hardcover, paperback and large print
"The authors of *The Silver Palate Cookbook* have
compiled the recipes that made them famous, along with
updates, additions, shopping tips, and suggestions for entertaining. A collection of tried and true recipes covering
soup to nuts. Easy and interesting to read, as well as
being a helpful source of information." N Y Public Libr
Book of How & Where to Look It Up

Sass, Lorna J.
Cooking under pressure. Morrow 1989
268p $18.95   **641.5**
1. Cookery
ISBN 0-688-08814-7   LC 89-31707
This book contains recipes to be prepared in pressure
cookers. Most of the dishes can be completed in 15
minutes

Shapiro, Laura
Perfection salad; women and cooking at
the turn of the century. Farrar, Straus &
Giroux 1986 280p il $16.95   **641.5**
1. Cookery 2. Home economics
ISBN 0-374-23075-7   LC 85-25402
This work is a "history of the American domestic
science movement at the turn of this century. . . .
[Shapiro seeks to show that this was] an era when
science was in ascendency, and the leaders of the
domestic science movement hoped to change the eating
habits of the nation and to do away with the irrational
methods of traditional housekeeping." Libr J
The author "has essentially written a feminist and
sometimes excessively earnest social and intellectual history." Newsweek
Includes bibliography

Simply light cooking; over 250 recipes from
the kitchens of Weight Watchers;
photography by Matthew Klein. New Am.
Lib. 1992 302p il $23   **641.5**
1. Cookery 2. Reducing
ISBN 0-453-01025-3   LC 91-24489
"Singles and families of four alike can call on this
book for quick, nutritious meals. The meticulous recipes
provide nutritional information along with preparation
time and menu suggestions. Recipes are coded to indicate
their cholesterol and/or sodium levels; they derive less
than 30 of their calories from fat." Publ Wkly

Smith, Jeff
The Frugal Gourmet cooks American;
illustrations by Chris Cart. Morrow 1987
477p il $22   **641.5**
1. Cookery
ISBN 0-688-06347-0   LC 87-28163
Also available in paperback from Avon Bks.
A collection of regional American recipes ranging from
Florida crab cakes and peanut soup to Chicago ribs and
green chili stew

The Frugal Gourmet cooks with wine;
illustrations by Gary Jacobsen; with articles
on tasting and selecting wine by Corbet
Clark. Morrow 1986 447p il $22   **641.5**
1. Cookery 2. Wine and wine making
ISBN 0-688-05852-3   LC 86-12679
Also available in paperback from Avon Bks.
"Despite the title, many recipes use no wine, but all,
Smith says, can be enjoyed with wine. Each main course
dish includes a suggested wine accompaniment. . . . Most
recipes are easy and at least fairly frugal." Libr J

Smith, Jeff—*Continued*

The Frugal Gourmet on our immigrant ancestors; recipes you should have gotten from your grandmother; Craig Wollam, culinary assistant; Chris Cart, illustrator; Terrin Haley, D.C. Smith, research assistants. Morrow 1990 539p il maps $19.95 **641.5**

1. Cookery
ISBN 0-688-07590-8 LC 90-48368
Also available in paperback from Avon Bks.

"Smith shares with readers recipes of immigrants who are often overlooked—Basques, Ethiopians, Jamaicans, Latvians, Scottish, Saudi Arabians, and many more. Each chapter begins with an illustration of the people, a map, and a few pages of introduction, including history and food customs. . . . A cookbook bibliography, immigrant history bibliography, source list for unusual ingredients, and an index complete the package." SLJ

The Frugal Gourmet whole family cookbook; recipes and reflections for contemporary living; Craig Wollam, culinary consultant; Chris Cart, illustrator; D.C. Smith, research assistant. Morrow 1992 393p il $22 **641.5**

1. Cookery
ISBN 0-688-06934-7 LC 92-8582
In addition to the recipes, the author includes discussions on the changing American family, cooking for one, cooking with kids, microwave cooking and soda fountains
Includes bibliography

Stern, Jane

Square meals; a cookbook; by Jane and Michael Stern. Knopf 1984 337p il $17.95; pa $8.95 **641.5**

1. Cookery
ISBN 0-394-53112-4; 0-394-74162-5 (pa)
LC 84-47527

A "study of food as popular culture with sections on ladies' lunch; lunch counter and soda fountain food; Sunday dinner; nursery food; homefront food during World War II; and the Cuisine of Suburbia." Libr J

"Conveyed with the [authors'] enduring wit and affection, these 325-plus recipes . . . constitute both a practical cookbook and a revealing study of twentieth-century American social history." Booklist

Vegetarian cooking; contributing editor, Sarah Brown. Reader's Digest Assn. 1992 224p il pa $16 **641.5**

1. Vegetarian cookery
ISBN 0-89577-409-7 LC 91-28308
"RD home handbooks"
First published 1984 in the United Kingdom with title: Vegetarian cookery

"With complete nutritional information and colorful photographs picturing techniques as well as individual dishes and ingredients, this is a fine resource for vegetarians concerned about variety as well as nutritional value." Booklist

Ward, Mary, 1940-

Count out cholesterol cookbook; American Medical Association campaign against cholesterol; [edited by] Art Ulene; recipes by Mary Ward, with additional recipes from Eat well, eat right, the Italian way by Edward Giobbi and Richard Wolff. Knopf 1989 242p il $17.95 **641.5**

1. Cookery 2. Low-cholesterol diet
ISBN 0-394-58194-6 LC 89-15575
"A Feeling fine book"
These 250 recipes are designed to reduce the amount of saturated fat and cholesterol in the diet and to increase the intake of soluble fiber

Weight Watchers 365-day menu cookbook. New Am. Lib. 1981 343p il hardcover o.p. paperback available $9.95 **641.5**

1. Cookery 2. Reducing 3. Menus
ISBN 0-452-25958-4 (pa) LC 81-11183
Each of the more than 500 recipes in this book "lists per serving amounts of calories, protein, fat, sodium, and carbohydrates. Menus, which include considerable variety, provide approximately 1200 calories a day for women, 1600 for men, 1700 for youths." Libr J

Weight Watchers favorite recipes; over 280 winning dishes from Weight Watchers members and staff; photography by Guy Powers. New Am. Lib. 1986 338p il $17.95; pa $11 **641.5**

1. Cookery 2. Reducing
ISBN 0-453-01012-1; 0-452-26465-0 (pa)
LC 86-16174

Displayed in "one-per-page format, the simple, economical dishes . . . feature per-serving counts of calories, protein, fat, carbohydrates, calcium, sodium and cholesterol, and Weight Watchers' exchange information." Publ Wkly

Weight Watchers healthy life-style cookbook; over 250 recipes based on the Personal Choice Program; set design and photography by Gus Francisco. NAL Bks. 1991 358p il $19.95; pa $12 **641.5**

1. Cookery 2. Reducing
ISBN 0-453-01023-7; 0-452-26755-2 (pa)
LC 90-13817

Also available G.K. Hall large print edition

This cookbook features recipes "using a wide variety of foods. . . . Nutritional information includes analysis of calories, protein, fat, carbohydrates, calcium, sodium, cholesterol and dietary fiber." Booklist

Weight Watchers meals in minutes cookbook; photography by Gus Francisco. NAL Bks. 1990 c1989 406p il $19.95; pa $11 **641.5**

1. Cookery 2. Reducing 3. Microwave cookery
ISBN 0-453-01020-2; 0-452-26570-3 (pa)
LC 89-12718

"This cookbook offers a wide variety of . . . recipes low in fat, sodium, and sugar, yet which take 30 minutes or less to prepare. . . . In addition, the book includes quite a few menu planners and an introductory section on speedy food preparation and microwave shortcuts. All recipes include nutrition data, as well as exchange units for those on the Weight Watchers diet plan." Booklist

Weight Watchers new international cookbook; photography by Aaron Rezny. New Am. Lib. 1985 384p il hardcover o.p. paperback available $10.95   **641.5**

1. Cookery 2. Reducing
ISBN 0-452-25951-7 (pa)   LC 85-13443

"Recipes from around the world, adapted to fit the Weight Watchers food plan. Arranged by country, selections feature nutritional and calorie information plus data on the Weight Watchers exchange system." Booklist

Woods, Sylvia
Sylvia's Soul Food; recipes from Harlem's world famous restaurant; [by] Sylvia Woods and Christopher Styler. Hearst Bks. 1992 144p $17   **641.5**

1. Cookery
ISBN 0-688-10012-0   LC 92-16524

This is a collection of over 100 recipes from Sylvia's Soul Food Restaurant in Harlem, New York. "From the familiar hotcakes and grits to smothered steaks and fried chicken, the recipes' directions are easy and require little in the way of exotic ingredients." Booklist

641.6   Cooking specific materials

Aidells, Bruce
Hot links & country flavors; sausages in American regional cooking; [by] Bruce Aidells & Denis Kelly; illustrations by John King. Knopf 1990 380p il maps (Knopf cooks American) $19.95   **641.6**

1. Cookery—Sausages
ISBN 0-394-57430-3   LC 89-19781

"Filled with food lore and written in a lively, personalized sytle . . . [this] sausage-lover's compendium draws on a wide variety of culinary traditions." Booklist

Butel, Jane
Hotter than hell; hot & spicy dishes from around the world. HP Bks. 1987 199p il hardcover o.p. paperback available $9.95   **641.6**

1. Cookery 2. Spices
ISBN 0-89586-542-4 (pa)   LC 87-17795

"Not content with chilis' heat alone, Butel includes ginger, horseradish, mustard, and pepper in her battery of fire starters. At their best, these recipes expand the horizons of Tex-Mex cooking. At the other end of the spectrum, they merely load chili peppers' pungency into otherwise unassuming fare." Booklist

Cameron, Angus
The L.L. Bean game and fish cookbook; by Angus Cameron and Judith Jones; illustrations by Bill Elliott. Random House 1983 475p il $24.95   **641.6**

1. Cookery—Game 2. Cookery—Fish
ISBN 0-394-51191-3   LC 82-15089

This book "explains how to dress, hang, smoke, age and clean fish and game. It . . . covers field dressing of deer, moose, elk and bear. There are also directions

for smoking, grilling, barbecuing, poaching, marinating and larding." N Y Times Book Rev

"With handsome wildlife and botanical drawings by Bill Elliott, the book was written by two experts and is complete and comprehensive." Christ Sci Monit

Choate, Judith, 1940-
The bean cookbook; a celebration of the delicious legume from Hoppin' John to simple cassoulet; principal photography by Peter Johansky; food styling by Dyne Benner. Simon & Schuster 1992 128p il (American kitchen classics) $20   **641.6**

1. Cookery—Beans
ISBN 0-671-73549-7   LC 91-27401

"A Kenan book"

The author "suggests how best to soak dried beans, store beans and freeze cooked beans; she has logically grouped her recipes into sections on appetizers, soups, main courses and accompaniments." Publ Wkly

Greene, Bert, 1923-1988
Greene on greens; illustrations by Norman Green. Workman 1984 432p il $19.95; pa $15.95   **641.6**

1. Cookery—Vegetables
ISBN 0-89480-758-7; 0-89480-659-9 (pa)

    LC 83-40538

The author "provides background information, selection advice, cooking techniques, and recipes for vegetables ranging from artichokes to zucchini." Booklist

Hagman, Bette
The gluten-free gourmet: living well without wheat. Holt & Co. 1990 235p $22.50; pa $12.95   **641.6**

1. Cookery—Grains
ISBN 0-8050-1210-9; 0-8050-1835-2 (pa)

    LC 89-20116

The author "provides more than 200 recipes based on gluten-free flours (primarily rice, potato, tapioca and soy), including breads, cakes, cookies, pies and casseroles." Publ Wkly

The recipes "are easy to prepare. Mail-order sources for gluten-free flours will be especially helpful. The updated and accurate information in this makes it a useful purchase for large cookbook collections." Booklist

Includes bibliographic references

Levy, Faye
Faye Levy's international chicken cookbook. Warner Bks. 1992 422p il $29.95   **641.6**

1. Cookery—Poultry
ISBN 0-446-51569-8   LC 92-54097

"This is in fact a chicken and turkey cookbook (including a separate chapter on game birds), with more than 300 recipes for poultry prepared every way imaginable." Libr J

Marshall, Lydie

A passion for potatoes. HarperCollins Pubs. 1992 xxiii, 248p il $28; pa $14

641.6

1. Cookery—Potatoes
ISBN 0-06-055323-5; 0-06-096910-5 (pa)

LC 91-50516

This book contains "recipes for all courses of a meal, including dessert, along with separate chapters on favorite potato preparations, from mashing through frying. . . . Headnotes include potato and other culinary lore, and the recipes are clear and well written. A charming and knowledgeable work." Libr J

Midgely, John

The goodness of beans, peas and lentils; illustrated by Ian Sidaway. Random House 1992 65p il $12

641.6

1. Cookery—Beans
ISBN 0-679-41624-2

LC 92-13768

This describes various types of beans, their nutritional and health benefits and their history, and includes thirty recipes from many parts of the world, illustrated with watercolor paintings

The goodness of garlic; illustrated by Ian Sidaway. Random House 1992 65p il $12

641.6

1. Cookery 2. Garlic
ISBN 0-679-41626-9

LC 92-14507

This describes types of garlic and related edible alliums such as chives, their health benefits, etymology and history, and includes thirty recipes from around the world, illustrated with watercolor paintings

The goodness of olive oil; illustrated by Ian Sidaway. Random House 1992 65p il $12

641.6

1. Cookery 2. Olive oil
ISBN 0-679-41627-7

LC 92-13767

This describes the health benefits of olive oil, the history of its use and cultivation, how it is extracted, how to choose and cook with olive oil, and includes over 20 recipes, illustrated with watercolor paintings

The goodness of potatoes and other root vegetables; illustrated by Ian Sidaway. Random House 1992 65p il $12   **641.6**

1. Cookery—Vegetables 2. Potatoes
ISBN 0-679-41625-0

LC 92-13766

This describes types of potatoes and other root vegetables, their nutritional and health benefits and their history, and includes recipes, illustrated with watercolor paintings

Morash, Marian

The victory garden cookbook. Knopf 1982 374p il $35; pa $29.95   **641.6**

1. Cookery—Vegetables 2. Vegetable gardening
ISBN 0-394-50897-1; 0-394-70780-X (pa)

LC 81-48132

"Basic gardening methods and preparation and storage techniques are reviewed, as are special characteristics of a particular vegetable. Numerous recipes are included for each vegetable and range from unadorned braising, baking, grilling, and broiling methods to special dishes." Booklist

Shurtleff, William, 1941-

The book of tofu; protein source of the future—now! [by] William Shurtleff & Akiko Aoyagi; illustrated by Akiko Aoyagi. rev & updated ed. Ten Speed Press 1983 v1 335p il hardcover o.p. paperback available $15.95

641.6

1. Cookery—Tofu
ISBN 0-89815-095-7 (pa)

LC 83-70113

Also available in paperback from Ballantine Bks.

"A Soyfoods Center book"

First publsihed 1975

This book contains over 500 recipes from East and West, with step-by-step instructions for making tofu at home, or in a commercial tofu shop. It also features an analysis of tofu's nutritional value

Includes bibliography

Zisman, Honey

The burger book; [by] Honey and Larry Zisman. [rev ed]. St. Martin's Press 1993 112p pa $10.95   **641.6**

1. Cookery—Meat
ISBN 0-312-09256-3

LC 93-18425

First published 1987

"More than 100 delicious and ingenious ways to enjoy the juicy pleasures of hamburgers, plus 41 perfect side-dish recipes for potatoes, relishes, salads, and shakes." Title page

641.7   Specific cooking processes and techniques

Schlesinger, Chris

The thrill of the grill; techniques, recipes & down-home barbecue; [by] Chris Schlesinger & John Willoughby, line drawings by Laura Hartman Maestro; photography by Vincent Lee. Morrow 1990 395p il $25   **641.7**

1. Barbecue cookery
ISBN 0-688-08832-5

LC 89-77522

The authors present a collection of recipes as well as advice about grilling and barbecuing food

Schlesinger "favors what he calls 'equatorial cuisine,' and Caribbean, Mexican, and Southeast Asian influences are evident in his recipes. His grilled dishes are full-flavored and often hot and spicy." Libr J

641.8   Cooking specific kinds of composite dishes

Beard, James, 1903-1985

Beard on bread; drawings by Karl Stuecklen. Knopf 1973 230p il $20   **641.8**

1. Bread
ISBN 0-394-47345-0

Also available in paperback from Ballantine Bks.

Beard, James, 1903-1985—*Continued*
"An inclusive guide to the preparation of a variety of breads with recipes for coffee cakes, rolls, flat breads, fried cakes. . . . The recipes included are those Beard considers the best from around the world which can be made in a U.S. kitchen." Booklist

Beard on pasta. Knopf 1983 236p il $19.95   641.8

1. Cookery—Pasta products
ISBN 0-394-52291-5   LC 82-48727

"A chapter on making pasta, including some non-Italian varieties and gnocchi, is followed by recipes . . . for pasta fresh or dried, used by itself or in combination with other foods." Libr J

Beranbaum, Rose Levy
The cake bible; edited by Maria D. Guarnaschelli; photographs by Vincent Lee; foreword by Maida Heatter. Morrow 1988 555p il $27.95   641.8

1. Cake
ISBN 0-688-04402-6   LC 88-1369

A collection of recipes for classic cakes, buttercreams, icings, fillings and toppings. Ingredients are listed in tabular form with weights given in both ounces and grams. Assembly and storage instructions are included

Includes bibliography

Better Homes and Gardens cookies for Christmas. Meredith Corp. 1985 96p il pa $8.95   641.8

1. Cookies
ISBN 0-696-01290-1   LC 85-60579

A "selection of Christmas cookies, particularly those that can be used as decorations. The recipes are easy to follow, and lovely photographs and clear diagrams aid preparation. The entries include shaped, cutout, bar, drop, and sliced cookies as well as macaroons, meringues, and tartlets." Booklist

Better Homes and Gardens salads. Meredith Corp. 1992 240p il $19.95   641.8

1. Salads
ISBN 0-696-01973-6   LC 91-62189

This book contains more than 230 recipes for main-dish and side-dish salads as well as dressings and vinaigrettes. Includes a section on cleaning, drying and storing salad greens. Illustrated with full-color photographs

Bugialli, Giuliano
Bugialli on pasta; illustrations by Glenn Wolff; photographs by John Dominus. Simon & Schuster 1988 363p il $27.50   641.8

1. Cookery—Pasta products 2. Cookery, Italian
ISBN 0-671-62024-X   LC 88-27460

"From all of Italy's regions, the author has gathered recipes that combine pasta with beans, fish, meat, vegetables, and assorted other ingredients." Booklist

Burnett, George
The breadman's healthy bread book; use your bread machine to make more than 100 delicious, wholesome breads. Morrow 1992 286p $15   641.8

1. Bread
ISBN 0-688-12025-3   LC 92-25402

The author includes over 100 recipes for breads using automatic bread machines

"To his credit, former baker Burnett does understand diet and the benefits of high-fiber eating; he also includes a chart to transcribe his . . . recipes for the workings of other machines. Many of his edibles will be familiar: bagels, English muffins, and tea breads." Booklist

Includes bibliographic references

Clayton, Bernard
Bernard Clayton's new complete book of breads; working drawings by Donnie Cameron. Simon & Schuster 1987 748p il $27.50   641.8

1. Bread
ISBN 0-671-60222-5   LC 87-12758

First published 1973 with title: The complete book of breads

This volume contains recipes for whole wheat and rye breads, buns, biscuits, croissants and a wide selection of ethnic variations. Includes instructions for food processors and high-power mixers

Crocker, Betty
Betty Crocker's cake decorating. Prentice-Hall 1990 c1984 160p il $15   641.8

1. Cake decorating
ISBN 0-671-86501-3   LC 89-16298

A reissue of the title first published 1984 by Random House

This includes over 100 decorated cake recipes for holidays, weddings, birthdays, and other occasions

Betty Crocker's ultimate cookie book. Prentice-Hall 1992 200p il $18   641.8

1. Cookies
ISBN 0-13-084492-6   LC 90-30659

"Whether your preference is oatmeal, fruit, peanut butter, or chocolate, there's something for everyone in this cookie compendium, which features instructions straightforward enough to attract even reluctant bakers." Booklist

Cunningham, Marion
The Fannie Farmer baking book; illustrated by Lauren Jarrett. Knopf 1984 624p il $25   641.8

1. Baking
ISBN 0-394-53332-1   LC 84-47862

"Separate chapters cover pies and tarts, cookies, cakes, yeast breads, quick breads, and crackers in encyclopedic detail with brisk but reassuring professionalism. Many of the 800 recipes are standard favorites." Libr J

Eckhardt, Linda West

Bread in half the time; use your microwave and food processor to make real yeast bread in 90 minutes; [by] Linda West Eckhardt and Diana Collingwood Butts; illustrations by Dolores R. Santoliquido. Crown 1991 344p il $25   **641.8**

1. Bread 2. Microwave cookery
ISBN 0-517-58154-X   LC 91-6285

"The authors have developed dozens of recipes that use the food processor for kneading and the microwave for speeding up the rising process so they can turn out yeast breads in less than the normal time. . . . Recipes for breads, pizzas, bagels, etc., are imaginative and mouth watering. Equally appealing are the ideas and recipes for accompaniments and variations." Libr J

Gubser, Mary

Quick breads, soups & stews; 196 delectable quick breads and classic soups to pair with them for an almost limitless number of superb meals; illustrated by Pat Biggs; edited by Carol Haralson. Council Oak Bks. 1991 287p il pa $16.95   **641.8**

1. Bread 2. Soups 3. Stews
ISBN 0-933031-33-5   LC 90-81820

"Chapter introductions and sidebars provide reliable guidelines on baking and cooking techniques, culinary background, and many suggestions for variations." Libr J

Heatter, Maida

Maida Heatter's best dessert book ever; drawings by Toni Evins. Random House 1990 432p il $24.95   **641.8**

1. Desserts
ISBN 0-394-57832-5   LC 90-8096

The author's recipes for cakes, pies, cookies, and ice creams are prefaced with advice on ingredients, equipment, and techniques

Maida Heatter's book of great chocolate desserts; drawings by Toni Evins. Knopf 1980 428p il $24.50   **641.8**

1. Desserts 2. Cookery—Chocolate
ISBN 0-394-50391-0   LC 79-28282

The author "begins with an introduction to the chocolate tree . . . then covers everything from simple brownies and eleven kinds of chocolate-chip cookies to the original Viennese Sachertorte and a frozen white-chocolate mousse." Newsweek

Maida Heatter's book of great desserts; drawings by Toni Evins. Random House 1991 428p il $24.50   **641.8**

1. Desserts
ISBN 0-679-40509-7   LC 91-52870

A reissue of the title first published 1974 by Knopf

This book includes recipes for both light and rich desserts including nut tortes, "American cakes, desserts with fruits, cookies, and Bavarian creams." Libr J

"The desserts are magnificent, and varied, elegant in style, conventional in taste, and as professional as anything that can be made in a home kitchen." N Y Times Book Rev

Herbst, Sharon Tyler

The joy of cookies. Barron's Educ. Ser. 1987 220p il $15.95   **641.8**

1. Cookies
ISBN 0-8120-5839-9   LC 87-17551

The author maps "out the many avenues of cookie-making: bar, rolled, drop, hand-formed, pressed, refrigerator, chocolate, chocolate-chip and holiday cookies." Publ Wkly

Moore, Marilyn M.

The wooden spoon book of home-style soups, stews, chowders, chilis, and gumbos; favorite recipes from the wooden spoon kitchen. Atlantic Monthly Press 1992 224p $20   **641.8**

1. Soups 2. Stews
ISBN 0-87113-480-2   LC 92-4961

Moore presents "a primer on the making of soup in the home kitchen. She covers such basics as thickenings, stocking a pantry, and equipment for cooking and serving." Booklist

"Soup cooks will find their old-fashioned favorites here, but there are also lighter versions of some old standards as well as unusual variations." Libr J

Includes bibliographic references

Peters, Colette

Colette's cakes; the art of cake decorating. Little, Brown 1991 163p il $24.95   **641.8**

1. Cake decorating
ISBN 0-316-70205-6   LC 90-24676

"This is not intended as a cookbook, although recipes for a white as well as a chocolate cake precede instructions for basic cake decorating. The bulk of the guide contains step-by-step directions for assembling four fabulous cake designs that range from an impressive seashell cake to multitiered wedding cakes." Booklist

Includes bibliographic references

Robertson, Laurel

The Laurel's kitchen bread book; a guide to whole-grain breadmaking; by Laurel Robertson, with Carol Flinders and Bronwen Godfrey. Random House 1984 447p il hardcover o.p. paperback available $18

641.8

1. Bread
ISBN 0-394-72434-8 (pa)   LC 83-43208

A "guide to breadmaking with whole-grain flours. With thorough, easy-to-understand directions, the authors include recipes for rye and whole-wheat breads, rolls, salt-free breads, quick breads, rice breads, and a variety of croutons, stuffings, and crumbs." Booklist

Includes bibliography

Stewart, Martha

Martha Stewart's hors d'oeuvres; the creation and presentation of fabulous finger foods; photographs by Peter Bosch; designed by Vincent Winter; recipes and styling with Sara Foster. Potter 1984 165p il $21.95; pa $16   **641.8**

1. Cookery—Appetizers
ISBN 0-517-55455-0; 0-517-58950-8 (pa)

LC 84-11591

The book "offers menus, recipes, and serving layouts for hors d'oeuvres for all occasions. . . . The photographs are almost awe inspiring, and the master recipes for tartlets, filo, puff pastry, pancakes, crepes, and other bases are excellent. More than 150 recipes and variations. Intermediate to advanced level." Booklist

Wheeler, Steven

The book of cheesecakes. HP Bks. 1988 120p il $9.95   **641.8**

1. Cake
ISBN 0-89586-668-4   LC 87-21252

"The recipes range from tried-and-true classics such as Lindy's famous New York cheesecake to a contemporary variation using exotic passion fruit. . . . Home cooks may be surprised at the diverse evolution of a basically simple food idea." Booklist

642 Meals and table service

Gourmet's holidays and celebrations; from the editors of Gourmet. Condé Nast Publs.; Random House 1992 215p il $24.50   **642**

1. Cookery 2. Entertaining
ISBN 0-679-41767-2   LC 92-50206

This offers recipes and menus for "Thanksgiving, Christmas, Valentine's Day, Passover, Easter, the Fourth of July, and more—plus birthdays, weddings, graduations, and other special occasions. All of the recipes have been developed with an eye toward reducing calories and cholesterol." Publisher's note

Kalish, Susan Schoenfeld

The art of napkin folding; completing the elegant table; by Susan Kalish; text by Nancy Kalish; photography by Tony Cenicola. Running Press 1988 110p il hardcover o.p. paperback available $12.95   **642**

1. Table setting and decoration
ISBN 0-89471-398-1 (pa)   LC 87-42982

"A Running Press/Friedman Group book"

"Kalish shows precisely how to achieve . . . special effects by napkin folding. . . . [She] also shows how kids can embellish paper napkins to make them more colorful or to emphasize a design. Line diagrams delineate folding techniques, and color photographs display the end product." Booklist

Lawrence, Elizabeth

The complete caterer; a practical guide to the craft and business of catering. rev ed. Doubleday 1992 xxii, 346p pa $15   **642**

1. Caterers and catering
ISBN 0-385-23480-5   LC 91-44538

First published 1988

This is an introduction to the business of catering including such issues as taxes, insurance, marketing, kitchen organization, and hiring help

643 Housing and household equipment

Adler, Bill, 1956-

The home remodeler's combat manual; [by] Bill Adler, Jr. HarperPerennial 1991 247p $21.95; pa $9.95   **643**

1. Houses—Remodeling
ISBN 0-06-055279-4; 0-06-096541-X (pa)

LC 90-55487

"Adler's definition of renovation is any change in your house that involves outsiders working in your house. He explains how to work with contractors and begins by expecting the worst. The many useful suggestions for dealing with tradespeople will help keep the homeowner in charge of the project." Libr J

Altman, Roberta

The complete book of home environmental hazards. Facts on File 1990 290p il pa $12.95   **643**

1. Housing—Environmental aspects
ISBN 0-8160-2095-7   LC 89-39982

This is a guide to protecting homes from environmental hazards such as radon, asbestos, lead, formaldehyde, and nuclear waste

Beckstrom, Robert J.

How to build an addition; created and designed by the editorial staff of Ortho Books; writer, Robert J. Beckstrom; illustrator, Ron Hildebrand. Ortho Bks. 1988 96p il pa $8.95   **643**

1. Houses—Remodeling
ISBN 0-89721-103-0   LC 87-72813

"This book proceeds from basic room additions that require framing, roofing, and finish work to more complex additions like kitchens and baths that require plumbing and extra planning. The diagrams are clear and wil help moderate level do-it-yourselfers add on from the foundation up." Libr J

Boyle, Carol, 1934-

From ramshackle to resale; fixing up old houses for profit. TAB Bks. 1990 291p il $24.95; pa $15.95   **643**

1. Houses—Remodeling 2. Real estate investment
ISBN 0-8306-1362-5; 0-8306-3162-3 (pa)

LC 89-35339

"This book is oriented to the investor who wants to add value to houses for resale. Included are a lot of 'extra equity ideas' like using stock moldings to create

Boyle, Carol, 1934——*Continued*
a colonial look, making a Tudor-style ceiling, and recasting plaster ornaments. The emphasis is on quick, practical projects that add value to a house." Libr J

Branson, Gary D.
The complete guide to remodeling your basement; how to create new living space the professional way. Betterway Publs. 1990 170p il pa $14.95   643
1. Basements 2. Houses—Remodeling
ISBN 1-55870-162-1   LC 90-39100

"Branson provides detailed instructions on how to fix up a basement for offices or family rooms. Planning, job sequencing, tool use, and framing walls are all well covered. Tips on doing installations in a concrete floor and using louvered doors are particularly suited to basement needs." Libr J

Chamberlin, Susan
Fences, gates & walls; how to design and build; by S. Chamberlin and J. Pollock. HP Bks. 1983 160p il pa $12.95   643
1. Fences 2. Gates 3. Walls
ISBN 0-89586-189-5   LC 82-84557

Numerous color photographs and line drawings accompany step-by-step instructions for building wood, shingle, picket and solid board fences; concrete, stone, and brick walls; and gates. Appendixes cover building materials and terminology

Decker, Phillip J.
Renovating brick houses; for yourself or for investment; [by] Phillip J. Decker & T. Newell Decker. Storey Communications 1990 247p il $27.95; pa $16.95   643
1. Houses—Maintenance and repair
ISBN 0-88266-593-6; 0-88266-592-8 (pa)
LC 89-46019

"A Garden Way Publishing book"

"Since they focus on one type of house, the authors' recommendations are very specific. They cover cost estimating, planning, demolition, and design as they relate to brick houses, particularly from the Victorian period." Libr J

Designing & remodeling bathrooms; created and designed by the editorial staff of Ortho Books; project editor: Jill Fox; writer: Robert Beckstrom; photographer: Kenneth Rice; illustrator: Rik Olson. Ortho Bks. 1990 111p il pa $8.95   643
1. Bathrooms
ISBN 0-89721-215-0   LC 89-85930

This guide includes full color photographs and plans for bathroom layouts and installation of fixtures
In this book "readers will find a lot of ideas as well as commonsense advice." Libr J

Designing & remodeling kitchens; created and designed by the editorial staff of Ortho Books; project editor: Jill Fox; writer: Robert J. Beckstrom; photographer: Kenneth Rice; illustrator: Rik Olson. Ortho Bks. 1991 111p il pa $8.95   643
1. Kitchens
ISBN 0-89721-216-9   LC 89-85931

This guide includes full color photographs and plans for kitchen layouts and installation of fixtures

Doors and windows; by the editors of Time-Life Books. Time-Life Bks. 1978 128p il (Home repair and improvement) $15.93   643
1. Doors 2. Windows   LC 78-1384

This manual contains instructions for repairing problem windows as well as for installing a variety of types of doors and windows

Duncan, S. Blackwell
Whole house remodeling guide. TAB Bks. 1990 452p il $28.95; pa $19.95   643
1. Houses—Remodeling
ISBN 0-8306-9281-9; 0-8306-3281-6 (pa)
LC 89-39624

"This book focuses on interior work, not additions. Remodeling projects are broken down into five elements—floors, walls, windows, doors, and ceilings. The instructions are clear and explain steps homeowners can take—e.g., noise reduction, structural repairs, cosmetic, and finish work—to improve each element." Libr J

Fine Homebuilding on baths and kitchens. Taunton Press 1990 127p $14.95   643
1. Kitchens 2. Bathrooms
ISBN 0-942391-58-6   LC 89-40581

"Composed of articles from the last ten years of *Fine Homebuilding* magazine, this book gives practical advice that is well supplemented with photographs. The volume will be useful even for libraries that subscribe to the magazine because all related projects are in one place." Libr J

Geiger, Richard H.
Protect your home; a common-sense guide to home security. Storey Communications 1987 150p il hardcover o.p. paperback available $8.95   643
1. Houses—Security measures 2. Burglar alarms
ISBN 0-88266-501-4 (pa)   LC 87-45010

"A Garden Way publishing book"

A basic guide to the selection, installation and maintenance of home alarm systems

Greenfield, Ellen J.

House dangerous; indoor pollution in your home and office—and what you can do about it! foreword by Ralph Nader; introduction by Arthur B. Sacks. rev & updated ed. Interlink Bks. 1991 262p il $24.95; pa $9.95 **643**

1. Housing—Environmental aspects
ISBN 0-940793-68-7; 0-940793-64-4 (pa) LC 90-5018
First published 1987

This discusses causes and solutions for air pollution in the home and office

Includes bibliography

Hamilton, Katie

Don't move--improve! 52 home-enhancement projects that can be completed in one weekend or less; [by] Katie and Gene Hamilton. Holt & Co. 1991 176p il pa $14.95 **643**

1. Houses—Remodeling 2. Interior design
ISBN 0-8050-1378-4 LC 91-29154
"An Owl book"

This do-it-yourself guide contains a "varied assortment of weekend projects: refinishing a piece of furniture, building a garden bench, installing an energy-saving thermostat, lining a closet with cedar, reupholstering a chair, and so on. For each weekend job the Hamiltons provide a brief description of the work involved along with a list of materials and tools." Libr J

Home improvement costs for exterior projects. Means 1991 207p il pa $29.95 **643**

1. Houses—Remodeling 2. Houses—Maintenance and repair 3. Landscape architecture
ISBN 0-87629-222-8 LC 92-120441

This title, part of a two-volume revision of Home Improvement Cost Guide (1989), concentrates exclusively on exterior projects like patio doors or a wheelchair ramp. Each "project includes a list of materials and prices, estimated work-hours, and advice on the difficulty for the do-it-yourselfer." Booklist

Home improvement costs for interior projects. Means 1991 182p il pa $29.95 **643**

1. Houses—Remodeling 2. Houses—Maintenance and repair
ISBN 0-87629-223-6 LC 92-120463

This companion volume to the title entered above concentrates on interior projects like sink replacement or vinyl sheet flooring

Home repair handbook; by the editors of Sunset books and Sunset magazine. Lane 1985 192p il pa $12.95 **643**

1. Houses—Maintenance and repair
ISBN 0-376-01256-0 LC 84-82291
At head of title: Sunset

"Quick emergency fix-ups and major interior and exterior repairs are explained with concise directions and over 600 how-to illustrations." Publisher's note

How things work in your home (and what to do when they don't); by the editors of Time-Life Books. 2nd ed. Holt & Co. 1985 368p il hardcover o.p. paperback available $16.95 **643**

1. Houses—Maintenance and repair 2. Plumbing—Repairing 3. Household equipment and supplies—Repairing
ISBN 0-8050-0126-3 (pa) LC 84-28988
First published 1975 by Time-Life Books

This volume discusses the home toolkit, plumbing, electrical wiring, small and large appliances, heating systems, air conditioners and outdoor repairs

Includes bibliography

Irwin, Robert, 1941-

The home renovation kit. Dearborn Financial Pub. 1992 181p pa $19.95 **643**

1. Houses—Remodeling 2. Real estate investment
ISBN 0-7931-0293-6 LC 91-877

"Irwin thoroughly discusses the financial side of renovation. A rating system to determine the feasibility of a project is described. Part of the book includes problems renovators might discover, with solutions and the time and difficulty of the solutions. Both investors and homeowners will find this book helpful." Libr J

Jackson, Albert, 1943-

The complete home restoration manual; an authoritative, do-it-yourself guide to restoring and maintaining the older house; [by] Albert Jackson & David Day; introduction by Gordon Bock. Simon & Schuster 1992 256p il $40 **643**

1. Houses—Remodeling 2. Historic buildings—Maintenance and repair
ISBN 0-671-73798-8 LC 92-7122

This guide emphasizes that "restoration will take years, not months. . . . Do-it-yourselfers will have no difficulties in following its precepts and instructions. However, this is not truly a how-to manual: most of the restorative chores—tuck-pointing, replacing glass, and so on—demand either a high level of experience or professional knowledge. Nonetheless, it will be a great help to those for whom it is intended." Booklist

Includes bibliographic references

Jones, Jack Payne, 1928-

Remodeling kitchens & baths; a contractor's guide; [by] Jack P. Jones. Craftsman 1989 379p il pa $26.25 **643**

1. Kitchens 2. Bathrooms
ISBN 0-934041-44-X LC 89-15901

"Although written for contractors and including information on advertising and business planning, the descriptions of how to perform work like installing countertops, cabinets, tub surrounds, and ceilings is efficient, clear, and easy to follow." Libr J

Kitchen remodeling. DeCosse 1989 128p il (Black & Decker home improvement lib) $14.95; pa $12.95 **643**

1. Kitchens
ISBN 0-86573-706-1; 0-86573-707-X (pa)
LC 89-11833

Kitchen remodeling—*Continued*

"The entire kitchen project from planning to completion is traced in this book, but its real value lies in its excellent color photographs that guide the reader through installation of cabinets, countertops, appliances, and other kitchen components." Libr J

Kitchens and bathrooms; by the editors of Time-Life Books. rev ed. Time-Life Bks. 1989 128p il (Home repair and improvement) $15.93   **643**

1. Kitchens 2. Bathrooms   LC 88-36841

First published 1977

"Clear diagrams and text describe the most common tasks involved in remodeling these rooms. Information on installing tile, countertops, and running new plumbing is included." Libr J

Lieberman, Dan

Renovating your home for maximum profit; [by] Dan Lieberman, Paul Hoffman. Prima Pub. & Communications 1989 390p il $21.95; pa $14.95   **643**

1. Houses—Remodeling

ISBN 0-914629-93-X; 0-685-47856-4 (pa) LC 89-3934

"Lieberman emphasizes creating monetary value in your home by renovating efficiently. The authors describe where to find bargains for resale and how to approach the project and deal with subcontractors. While not a guide for do-it-yourselfers, the book does include some tricks of the trade like how to create the illusion of space and hominess." Libr J

Litchfield, Michael W.

Renovation; a complete guide; Rosemarie Hausherr, photographer; Terry Murphy, technical editor. 2nd ed. Prentice-Hall 1991 xx, 566p il $36   **643**

1. Houses—Remodeling

ISBN 0-13-159336-6   LC 90-35411

First published 1982 by Wiley

This guide discusses how to assess buildings, both prior to purchase and before renovation, and how to determine what tools and materials to use. Plumbing, electrical work, masonry and carpentry projects are detailed

"If you can afford only one remodeling book, choose this well-illustrated, clearly written, and most comprehensive guide." Libr J

Includes bibliographic references

Madorma, James, 1943-

The home buyer's inspection guide. Betterway Publs. 1990 175p il pa $11.95   **643**

1. Houses—Inspection 2. Houses—Buying and selling

ISBN 1-55870-146-X   LC 89-18323

"Presented here is detailed information to aid potential home buyers in evaluating a house's various systems (electrical, plumbing, heating, etc.) so that they can make more informed decisions. . . . With copious schematic illustrations and a very thorough inspection checklist, Madorma's book is eminently useful." Booklist

Includes bibliography

Major appliances. Time-Life Bks. 1987 144p il (Fix it yourself) $18.60   **643**

1. Household appliances, Electric—Maintenance and repair   LC 86-30136

Discusses basic repair for the handyman in fixing and maintaining major household appliances

Makower, Joel, 1952-

How to buy a house. Perigee Bks. 1990 114, 64p pa $8.95   **643**

1. Houses—Buying and selling

ISBN 0-399-51565-8   LC 89-33668

"A Tilden Press book"

Bound back-to-back with: How to sell a house

The author "gives us one book with two titles, two covers, and two parts. . . . Makower's two topics, home buying and home selling, have already been abundantly covered by others, but he effectively combines them into one convenient package, aiming to reach the established home-owner who is changing residence. Furthermore, *both* parts of the book will be of value to buyers *and* sellers because each needs to know the other's strategy." Booklist

Meyers, L. Donald, 1929-

The complete outdoor building book; patios, decks, fences, landscaping, etc. Prentice-Hall 1992 339p il maps $40   **643**

1. Houses—Remodeling

ISBN 0-13-155276-7   LC 91-12243

This handbook provides instructions for building outdoor home improvements such as decks, patios, walks and driveways, fences and walls. Information on landscape gardening is also included

Miller, Peter G.

Buy your first home now; a practical guide to better deals, cheaper mortgages, and bigger tax breaks for the first-time home buyer. Harper & Row 1990 221p pa $10   **643**

1. Houses—Buying and selling

ISBN 0-06-016233-3   LC 89-45689

The author "explains the benefits of home ownership and the numerous financing options. . . . Also covered is the home-buying process itself, from finding the right community to settlement and possession. Numerous financial examples bring Miller's analysis to life." Libr J

Nash, George, 1949-

Renovating old houses. Taunton Press 1992 343p il $37.95   **643**

1. Houses—Maintenance and repair

ISBN 0-942391-65-9   LC 91-26151

"A Fine homebuilding book"

This do-it-yourself renovation guide covers all house systems from electrical to plumbing and heating. Includes information on preserving exterior details

Includes bibliographic references

New complete do-it-yourself manual. Reader's Digest Assn. 1991 528p il $30
643

1. Houses—Maintenance and repair
ISBN 0-89577-378-3   LC 90-46830
First published 1973 with title: Reader's Digest complete do-it-yourself manual

At head of title: Reader's Digest

"For homeowner and apartment dweller alike, [this] provides details, photographs, and diagrams for projects within the capability of the do-it-yourselfer. It also offers guidance as to when a contractor or specialist is needed." N Y Public Libr Book of How & Where to Look It Up

The **Old** house; by the editors of Time-Life Books. rev ed. Time-Life Bks. 1989 128p il (Home repair and improvement) $15.93
643

1. Houses—Maintenance and repair   LC 89-4277
First published 1979

This is a guide to repair and restoration of old houses. Projects range from the routine to complicated plumbing and electrical system revamping

The **Older** house. Time-Life Bks. 1991 144p il (Fix it yourself) $18.60   **643**
1. Houses—Maintenance and repair   LC 90-21497
This is a guide to repair and maintenance of older houses including exterior walls and trim, foundations, windows, doors, plumbing and heating systems

Owen, David, 1955-
The walls around us; the thinking person's guide to how a house works; illustrations by Polly Roberts Swain. Villard Bks. 1991 308p il hardcover o.p. paperback available $12   **643**
1. Houses—Maintenance and repair 2. Houses—Remodeling
ISBN 0-679-74144-5 (pa)   LC 91-50064
The author discusses "the general fundamentals of house construction and the materials involved . . . [as well as] repairing, remodeling, and maintaining older houses with particular attention to walls, the roof, electricity, kitchens, bathrooms, and plumbing." Libr J
Includes bibliographic references

Pearson, David, 1940-
The natural house book; creating a healthy, harmonious, and ecologically-sound home environment; foreword by Malcolm Wells; U.S. consultants, Richard Freudenberger, Debra Lynn Dadd. Simon & Schuster 1989 287p il hardcover o.p. paperback available $20   **643**
1. Housing—Environmental aspects
ISBN 0-671-66635-5 (pa)   LC 89-10070
"A Gaia original. A Fireside book"
This book examines the design and construction of environmentally healthy homes. The author identifies potentially hazardous products found in the home and offers alternatives
Includes bibliography

Philbin, Tom, 1934-
How to hire a home improvement contractor without getting chiseled. St. Martin's Press 1991 363p il $13.95   **643**
1. Houses—Maintenance and repair 2. Houses—Remodeling
ISBN 0-312-04576-X   LC 90-49538
"In the first part of his how-to, Philbin proffers an eight-point strategy for successfully contracting for home improvements at fair prices. . . . Part two is a virtual directory of common improvement and maintenance jobs, classified by housing element (e.g., flooring, insulation, doors, etc.)." Booklist

Popular mechanics home answer book; edited by Steven Willson; foreword by Joe Oldham. Hearst Bks. 1991 224p il $23
643

1. Houses—Maintenance and repair
ISBN 0-688-10854-7   LC 91-6938
This "is a hands-on manual covering about 50 or so home repair projects. . . . The average homeowner will appreciate the degree of detail in the written procedures as well as the labeling of each job according to level of difficulty, time requirement, and cost of materials." Libr J

Rains, Darrell L.
Major home appliances; a common sense repair manual. TAB Bks. 1987 160p il hardcover o.p. paperback available $15.95
643

1. Household appliances, Electric—Maintenance and repair
ISBN 0-8306-2747-2 (pa)   LC 86-23157
This volume provides "diagnostic and repair procedures for any malady likely to befall a refrigerator, washer, dryer, or dishwasher. It also offers solid advice on preventive maintenance, parts suppliers, safety factors, even things like extended service warranties." Libr J

Rand, Ellen
The complete book of kitchen design; [by] Ellen Rand, Florence Perchuk, and the editors of Consumer Reports Books. Consumer Repts. Bks. 1991 216p il (Homeowner's lib) pa $16.95   **643**
1. Kitchens 2. Consumer education
ISBN 0-89043-474-3   LC 91-8551
"The first part of the book covers kitchen planning: appliance placement, work flow, designing for children and the handicapped, and using a design professional. A variety of floor plans that solve kitchen problems are shown. The second part of the book discusses how to choose the best products, including judging the quality of items like cabinets and flooring." Libr J

Reader's Digest fix-it-yourself manual. Reader's Digest Assn. 1977 480p il $26
643

1. Repairing
ISBN 0-89577-040-7   LC 77-73634
"Information how to repair, clean, and maintain anything in and around your home. Has major sections on furniture repair and upholstering; covers small and large appliances. Illustrated with clear, step-by-step dia-

Reader's Digest fix-it-yourself manual —
Continued
grams and photographs." N Y Public Libr Book of How
& Where to Look It Up

Schnaser, Gene
The home repair emergency handbook.
Taylor Pub. Co. 1992 174p il pa $14.95
643
1. Houses—Maintenance and repair
ISBN 0-87833-797-0　　　　　　LC 92-14253
This "manual leads the user through most common
household and apartment repair problems. For each of
the 118 emergencies covered, it presents background information, how-to advice, and helpful hints that often
include tips on making do until a professional arrives."
Booklist

Small appliances; [by] Time-Life Books.
Time-Life Bks. 1988 128p il (Fix it
yourself) $18.60　　　　　　**643**
1. Household appliances, Electric—Maintenance and
repair　　　　　　LC 88-19922
Discusses the repair of microwave ovens, toasters,
irons, hair dryers, fans, heaters, shavers, mixers, vacuum
cleaners, sewing machines, and other small appliances.
Also includes sections on tools, safety, and emergencies

Sunset bathroom remodeling handbook; by
the editors of Sunset Books and Sunset
Magazine. Sunset Pub. Corp. il pa $8.95
643
1. Bathrooms
First published 1963. (5th edition 1983) Periodically
revised. Title varies
Covers design of bathrooms, decorating and
remodeling ideas, fixtures, plumbing and electrical work,
walls, floors, and cabinets

Sunset kitchens; planning & remodeling; by
the editors of Sunset Books and Sunset
Magazine. Lane il pa $9.99　　　**643**
1. Kitchens
Periodically revised. Title varies
Explains planning and designing the work area, usage
of space, fixtures, appliances, wiring and ventilation.
Includes sample floor plans

Thomas, Steve, 1942-
This Old House kitchens; a guide to
design and renovation; [by] Steve Thomas
and Philip Langdon. Little, Brown 1992
273p il $40; pa $24.95　　　　**643**
1. Kitchens
ISBN 0-316-84106-4; 0-316-84107-2 (pa)
　　　　　　LC 91-20413
"Arguing that there is no single best way to design
a kitchen, the host of the popular PBS program leads
the reader through the process of selecting countertops,
ventilation, heating, lighting, flooring, and equipment."
Libr J

Thomsett, Michael C.
How to buy a house, condo, or co-op;
[by] Michael C. Thomsett and the editors
of Consumer Reports Books. updated ed.
Consumers Union of U.S. 1990 240p $14.95
643
1. Houses—Buying and selling 2. Apartment houses—
Buying and selling
ISBN 0-89043-365-8　　　　　　LC 89-77733
First published 1987
This volume covers dealing with competition,
"reading" the market, formulating and negotiating an offer, mortgage shopping, and closing

Time-Life Books complete home
improvement and renovation manual; by
the editors of the Time-Life Home repair
and improvement series. Prentice Hall
Press 1991 479p il $24.95　　　**643**
1. Houses—Remodeling
ISBN 0-13-921883-1　　　　　　LC 91-6898
"A compilation of the most useful material in Time-
Life's best-selling earlier 36-volume series. Major sections
cover interior improvements; kitchens and bathrooms;
doors and windows; heating, cooling, and electrical systems; exterior improvements; and major additions. Extensively illustrated with clear how-to illustrations and diagrams." N Y Public Libr Book of How & Where to
Look It Up

Time-Life Books complete home repair
manual; by the editors of Time-Life
Books. Prentice Hall Press 1987 479p il
$24.95　　　　　　**643**
1. Houses—Maintenance and repair　　LC 87-16252
"Provides basic information on home-repair tasks such
as fixing water-damaged wallboard, replacing doors and
windows, preparing and painting surfaces, replacing
lighting fixtures, unclogging drains, unfreezing winter
pipes, and repairing roofs, shingles, masonry, and walk-
ways. The step-by-step instructions will assist both
novices and more experienced do-it-yourselfers, and
discussions of necessary tools are complete." Booklist

Vila, Bob
Bob Vila's guide to buying your dream
house; by Bob Vila with Carl Oglesby;
research by Nena Groskind. Little, Brown
1990 283p il pa $11.95　　　　**643**
1. Houses—Buying and selling
ISBN 0-316-90291-8　　　　　　LC 89-8348
In addition to coverage of the physical qualities of
potential "dream houses" Vila explicates the "arcane processes related to purchase and finance. These include
working with a broker; shopping for a mortgage; making
the offer (and negotiating the best price); and surviving
the curious ritual of the closing." Libr J

This Old House guide to building and
remodeling materials. Warner Bks. 1986
486p il pa $16.95　　　　　**643**
1. Houses—Remodeling 2. Building materials
ISBN 0-446-38246-9　　　　　　LC 86-22391
This guide to organizing and outfitting a home workshop concentrates on tools and materials. Includes sections on masonry, roofing, plumbing, electrical systems,
flooring, walls and ceilings

Wacker, David Alan, 1957-
The complete guide to home security; how to protect your family and home from harm. Betterway Publs. 1990 189p il pa $14.95   **643**
1. Houses—Security measures 2. Burglary protection
ISBN 1-55870-163-X   LC 90-39097
While focusing on "measures for securing doors and windows, installing alarm systems, and stashing valuables, [the author] also deals with fire safety, auto and boat theft, sexual assault, child molestation, and consumer fraud. He covers them all in a concise, well-researched manner." Libr J
Includes bibliography

Walls and ceilings; by the editors of Time-Life Books. Time-Life Bks. 1980 136p il (Home repair and improvement) $15.93   **643**
1. Walls 2. Ceilings   LC 80-13045
An illustrated guide on home remodeling which places the emphasis on wall and ceiling replacement, relocation, construction, maintenance and repair

Williams, Gene B.
Chilton's guide to large appliance repair and maintenance. Chilton 1986 255p il pa $14.95   **643**
1. Household appliances, Electric—Maintenance and repair
ISBN 0-8019-7687-1   LC 86-47608
This guide to the repair of home appliances includes basic information on electric motors, heating elements and thermostats

Windows & doors. Time-Life Bks. 1987 127p il (Fix it yourself) $18.60   **643**
1. Windows 2. Doors   LC 87-17981
Detailed explanations of materials, tools, and techniques to be used with how-to diagrams for householders

646.2   Sewing and related operations

Eaton, Jan
The encyclopedia of sewing techniques. Barron's Educ. Ser. 1987 c1986 176p il $19.95   **646.2**
1. Sewing
ISBN 0-8120-5815-1   LC 86-26514
"A Quarto book"
First published 1986 in the United Kingdom
This guide provides information on sewing machines and fabrics as well as sewing techniques and directions for creating clothing and home items

Vogue sewing for the home. Harper & Row 1986 192p il hardcover o.p. paperback available $14.95   **646.2**
1. Sewing 2. Interior design
ISBN 0-06-091409-2 (pa)   LC 85-45033
"Contributions by Butterick Fashion Marketing Co." Title page

This book provides "instructions for dozens of home decorating projects, including curtains, bed coverings, pillows, and tablecloths. Although not designed for the novice, the directions are clear and illustrated with distinct diagrams so that only basic sewing skills are required for most of the projects." Libr J

646.4   Clothing and accessories construction

The **Vogue/Butterick** step-by-step guide to sewing techniques; by the editors of Vogue and Butterick patterns. Prentice Hall Press 1989 415p il $24.95   **646.4**
1. Dressmaking 2. Sewing
ISBN 0-13-944125-5   LC 89-60522
"More than 500 of the 2000 dressmaking procedures regularly used in Vogue and Butterick patterns are demonstrated in this visual encyclopedia of sewing. The table of contents contains 47 broad sewing areas, including instruction for appliqué, bindings, buttonholes, collars, facings, linings, pleats, pockets, shoulderpads, and zippers." Libr J

Vogue fitting; the book of fitting techniques, adjustments, and alterations. Harper & Row 1984 192p il hardcover o.p. paperback available $14.95   **646.4**
1. Dressmaking 2. Tailoring
ISBN 0-06-091410-6 (pa)   LC 84-47561
Based on the Vogue sewing book of fittings, adjustments, and alterations
This volume gives instructions for altering women's patterns to achieve the correct fit for each individual. After a discussion of styles and fabrics the book explains measurements and adjustments

Vogue sewing. Harper & Row 1982 511p il $37.50   **646.4**
1. Dressmaking 2. Sewing
ISBN 0-06-015001-7   LC 81-48031
First published 1970 with title: The Vogue Sewing book; this is a revised edition of The New Vogue Sewing book, published 1980 by Butterick
This book provides step-by-step guidance on fabrics, colors, silhouettes, patterns and accessories for both the novice and the experienced seamstress

646.7   Management of personal and family living. Grooming

Bent, Bob
How to cut your own or anybody else's hair; illustrated by Jack Bozzi. rev and updated ed. Simon & Schuster 1983 128p il spiral bdg $12.95   **646.7**
1. Hair and hairdressing
ISBN 0-671-46776-X   LC 82-19543
"A Fireside book"
First published 1975
This is a guide to hair-cutting techniques and includes advice on hair care and blow-drying

Bozic, Patricia
Cutting hair at home; step-by-step haircutting for everyone; [by] Patricia Bozic and Lee Pola; illustrations by Jack Eckstein. New Am. Lib. 1986 125p il pa $9.95
646.7

1. Hair and hairdressing
ISBN 0-452-25830-8   LC 86-8348
"A Plume book"

The author "provides easy-to-follow guidelines for home haircutting. Her simple guide begins with an overview of haircutting tools and techniques before providing specific step-by-step instructions for various styles for women, men, teens, and children. Also included are helpful guidelines for using hair coloring, conditioning, and permanent-wave products." Booklist

Brumberg, Elaine
Take care of your skin. Harper & Row 1989 271p $18.95; pa $11   **646.7**

1. Skin—Care and hygiene
ISBN 0-06-015793-3; 0-06-091684-2 (pa)
                              LC 88-45888

The author's "guide to skin care goes beyond the usual regimens, showing readers how to resist manipulative sales techniques and the hyperbole that runs rampant in the skin-care industry. Brumberg's tone is that of a wise big sister." Publ Wkly

Chase, Deborah
The new medically based no-nonsense beauty book; illustrations by Margaret Garrison. Holt & Co. 1989 404p il o.p.; Avon Bks. paperback available $8.95 **646.7**

1. Personal grooming 2. Women—Health and hygiene 3. Cosmetics
ISBN 0-380-71203-2 (pa)   LC 88-32870

First published 1974 by Knopf with title: The medically based no-nonsense beauty book

This guide offers "advice on the care of skin, face, nails, and hair. In accessible fashion, Chase discusses and identifies numerous health problems in these areas, introduces specific products, and warns against unsubstantiated claims that cosmetic companies make." Booklist

Includes bibliography

Goodman, Thomas
Smart face; a dermatologist's guide to saving your money and saving your skin; [by] Thomas Goodman and Stephanie Young. Prentice-Hall 1988 207p il pa $9.95
646.7

1. Skin—Care and hygiene 2. Face—Care and hygiene
ISBN 0-13-814377-3   LC 88-6004

The author "introduces skin-care fundamentals, offering information on skin cleansing and moisturizing as well as guidelines for handling wrinkles, acne, and other skin problems." Booklist
This book is "a comprehensive consumer reference guide to cosmetics and facial skin care with medical sections that are refreshingly clear and jargon-free." Publ Wkly

Ludwig, Susan
Petite style; the ultimate fashion guide for women 5'4 and under; [by] Susan Ludwig with Janice Steinberg; illustrations by Barbara Rhodes. New Am. Lib. 1988 183p il $16.95   **646.7**

1. Clothing and dress
ISBN 0-453-00586-1   LC 87-28106

An illustrated guide to coordinating fashions and accessories for the shorter woman

Novick, Nelson Lee
Super skin; a leading dermatologist's guide to the latest breakthroughs in skin care. Potter 1988 308p il $20; pa $13   **646.7**

1. Skin—Care and hygiene
ISBN 0-517-57035-1; 0-517-58533-2 (pa)
                              LC 88-12678

The author "begins with the skin basics (moisturizing, cleansing, and make-up selection) and discusses myriad skin problems, ranging from acne and skin rashes to skin growths and sexually transmitted diseases." Booklist

Powlis, La Verne
Beauty from the inside out; a guide for black women. Doubleday 1988 210p il $19.95   **646.7**

1. Personal grooming 2. Black women—Health and hygiene
ISBN 0-385-23631-X   LC 87-9110

This beauty guide emphasizes nutrition, exercise and self-esteem. Instructions for make-up and hair styling as well as skin and hair care are included

Includes bibliography

Walzer, Richard A., 1930-
Healthy skin: a guide to lifelong skin care; [by] Richard A. Walzer and the editors of Consumer Reports Books. Consumers Union of U.S. 1990 c1989 242p il pa $13.95
646.7

1. Skin—Care and hygiene
ISBN 0-89043-266-X   LC 89-33258

First published 1981 by Appleton-Century-Crofts with title: Skintelligence

This guide to skin care provides information about acne, nail and hair care, allergies, insect bites, sexually transmitted diseases, and skin cancers. Also featured are Consumer Reports ratings of various brands of skin and hair care products

647.9 Multiple dwellings for transients, eating and drinking places

Hotch, Ripley
How to start and run your own bed & breakfast inn; [by] Ripley Hotch & Carl A. Glassman. Stackpole Bks. 1992 182p pa $14.95   **647.9**
1. Hotels, motels, etc.
ISBN 0-8117-2441-7   LC 92-20979
"This work covers the gamut of concerns for the potential innkeeper (acquiring the inn, handling finances, planning for legal and insurance needs, promoting the business, and taking care of guests. . . . This is a good basic practical guide for public library collections." Libr J

The **International** youth hostel handbook; the official guide to budget accommodation. HarperCollins Pubs. 1991 2v pa ea $10.95   **647.9**
1. Youth hostels—Directories
Annual
Prepared by staff of the International Youth Hostel Federation
Contents: v1 Europe and the Mediterranean; v2 Africa, America, Asia, and Australasia
This "directory, in English, French, German, and Spanish, focuses on budget accommodation mainly for young members of the International Youth Hostel Federation." Nichols. Guide to Ref Books for Sch Media Cent. 4th edition
This "is an invaluable annual that no public library should be without." Booklist

Rundback, Betty Revits
Bed & breakfast USA; a guide to tourist homes and guest houses; [by] Betty Revits Rundback and Nancy Kramer. Dutton il pa $14   **647.9**
1. Hotels, motels, etc.
Annual. First published by Tourist House Association of America with title: Guide to guest houses and tourist homes USA; first published with present title 1982
A state-by-state listing of bed and breakfast accommodations in all 50 states, Puerto Rico, and Canada. Entries include contact information, rates, private or shared bath, children or pets permitted, and special features

648 Housekeeping

Adler, Bill, 1956-
Outwitting critters; a surefire manual for confronting devious animals and winning; [by] Bill Adler, Jr.; illustrations by John L. Heinly. HarperCollins Pubs. 1992 256p il $22; pa $10   **648**
1. Pests—Control 2. Wildlife
ISBN 0-06-055292-1; 0-06-096584-3 (pa)
     LC 91-58477

The author "covers dealing with a broad range of potential pests, from the neighbors' pets through such common wild pests as moles, mice, and insects to big intruders like alligators, moose, and sea lions." Booklist
Includes bibliographic references

Aslett, Don, 1935-
Don Aslett's stainbuster's bible; the complete guide to spot removal; illustrated by Craig LaGory. New Am. Lib. 1990 310p il pa $10   **648**
1. Cleaning
ISBN 0-452-26385-9   LC 89-77091
"A Plume book"
The author "discusses how to avoid stains, using common household items (peanut butter, toothpaste, club soda) to remove some stains, and what supplies to have on hand. The book also gives detailed instructions on what to do about dozens of different stains." Libr J
"Humorously enhanced with cartoons, this is an invaluable reference for correcting daily mishaps." Booklist

How to clean practically anything; [by] the editors of Consumer Reports Books with Monte Florman and Marjorie Florman. 3rd edition/updated. Consumer Repts. Bks. 1993 226p pa $11.95   **648**
1. Cleaning 2. House cleaning
ISBN 0-89043-753-X   LC 92-5451
First published 1986
This volume offers advice on buying and using cleaning products and appliances and includes a stain removal chart for fabrics

Janik, Carolyn
Positive moves; the complete guide to moving you and your family across town or across the nation. Weidenfeld & Nicolson 1988 210p hardcover o.p. paperback available $8.95   **648**
1. Moving, Household
ISBN 1-55584-103-1 (pa)   LC 88-4107
The author offers advice on coping with the practical and emotional aspects of moving

Lifton, Bernice
Bug busters. Avery Pub. Group 1990 254p il pa $9.95   **648**
1. Pests—Control
ISBN 0-89529-451-6   LC 90-19678
This book "tells how to get rid of pests that infest home, body, and garden without using chemicals that may kill or sicken the hosts along with the vermin. . . . Always clearly written and illustrated with drawings of pests, their traces, and various apparatus for trapping, *Bugbusters* is a must in household information collections." Booklist
Includes bibliographic references

649 Child rearing

Ames, Louise Bates
Questions parents ask; straight answers from Louise Bates Ames. Potter 1988 306p o.p.; Doubleday paperback available $9.95
649
1. Child rearing 2. Parent and child 3. Child psychology
ISBN 0-385-29902-8 (pa)   LC 87-29078
"Among the topics discussed are adoption, nutrition, gender, siblings, hyperactivity, and personality. The question-and-answer approach is accessible to those who shy away from full-length guides and offers a ready-reference source as well." Booklist
Includes bibliography

Your eight-year-old; lively and outgoing; by Louise Bates Ames and Carol Chase Haber; illustrated with photographs by Betty David. Delacorte Press 1989 147p il $15.95
649
1. Child rearing
ISBN 0-440-50116-4   LC 88-31150
Also available in paperback from Dell
A discussion of the basic personality and typical physical and mental development of the eight-year-old
Includes bibliography

Your five-year-old; sunny and serene; by Louise Bates Ames and Frances L. Ilg, Gesell Institute of Child Development; illustrated with photographs by Betty David. Delacorte Press 1979 123p il o.p.; Dell paperback available $8.95   **649**
1. Child rearing
ISBN 0-385-29145-0 (pa)   LC 78-11622
Beginning with a description of the general characteristics of the five-year-old, the authors go on to discuss how the child relates to parents and others
Includes bibliography

Your four-year-old; wild and wonderful; by Louise Bates Ames and Frances L. Ilg, Gesell Institute of Child Development. Delacorte Press 1976 152p il o.p.; Dell paperback available $8.95   **649**
1. Child rearing
ISBN 0-385-29143-4 (pa)
Following the same format as the titles listed above, this volume discusses the development of the four year old
Includes bibliography

Your one-year-old; the fun-loving, fussy 12-to-24-month-old; by Louise Bates Ames, Frances L. Ilg, and Carol Chase Haber (Gesell Institute of Child Development); illustrated with photographs by Betty David. Delacorte Press 1982 178p il o.p.; Dell paperback available $8.95   **649**
1. Child rearing
ISBN 0-385-29206-6 (pa)   LC 81-17275

This volume on the development of the one year old follows the same format as the titles entered above
Includes bibliography

Your six-year-old; defiant but loving; by Louise Bates Ames and Frances L. Ilg, Gesell Institute of Child Development. Delacorte Press 1976 132p il o.p.; Dell paperback available $8.95   **649**
1. Child rearing
ISBN 0-385-29146-9 (pa)
This book, focusing on the six year old child, follows the same format as the titles entered above
Includes bibliography

Your three-year-old; friend or enemy; by Louise Bates Ames, and Frances L. Ilg, Gesell Institute of Child Development. Delacorte Press 1976 168p il o.p.; Dell paperback available $8.95   **649**
1. Child rearing
ISBN 0-385-29142-6 (pa)
This book focusing on the three year old child follows the same format as the titles entered above
Includes bibliography

Your two-year-old; terrible or tender; by Louise Bates Ames, and Frances L. Ilg, Gesell Institute of Child Development. Delacorte Press 1976 149p il o.p.; Dell paperback available $8.95   **649**
1. Child rearing
ISBN 0-385-29141-8 (pa)
Following the same format as the titles entered above this book explains the development of the two year old
Includes bibliography

Auckett, Amelia D.
Baby massage; parent-child bonding through touching; introduction by Eva Reich. Newmarket Press 1982 128p il hardcover o.p. paperback available $9.95
649
1. Infants—Care 2. Massage 3. Parent and child
ISBN 1-55704-022-2 (pa)   LC 82-2172
"The author, a nurse, worked with a masseur to develop techniques for infant massage. . . . Special instructions are included for handicapped, premature, abused, and adopted babies, as well as for such important events as birthing, weaning, and teething." Libr J
Includes bibliography

Benton, Barbara
The babysitter's handbook. Morrow 1981 215p il $15.50; pa $7.95   **649**
1. Babysitters 2. Child care
ISBN 0-688-00641-8; 0-688-00687-6 (pa) LC 81-3996
"The handbook provides directions for emergencies, what to do about meals, bathing children, bedtime, and gives information about the psychology of children at different stages." Wynar. Guide to Ref Books for Sch Media Cent. 3d edition

Bettelheim, Bruno
A good enough parent; a book on child-rearing. Knopf 1987 377p $18.95; pa $13   **649**
1. Child rearing 2. Parenting
ISBN 0-394-47148-2; 0-394-75776-9 (pa)
LC 86-46152
The author "discusses such topics as anxiety, school performance, discipline, fantasy, and adolescent rebellion, with an extended section on play and competition." Libr J
The author's "background and his detailed exploration of psychological issues in child development . . . lend his book a unique perspective among the plethora of available child care/parenting guides." Booklist

Better Homes & Gardens new baby book. Meredith Corp. il $14.95; pa $9.95 **649**
1. Infants—Care 2. Child care 3. Prenatal care
Also available in paperback from Bantam Bks.
First published 1943 with title: Better Homes & Gardens baby book. Periodically revised
This illustrated book provides information on the care of the baby and child from the prenatal period to the sixth year
Includes bibliography

Brazelton, T. Berry, 1918-
Families; crisis and caring. Addison-Wesley 1989 251p il $17.26   **649**
1. Parenting
ISBN 0-201-09264-6   LC 88-36612
"A Merloyd Lawrence book"
"The author introduces five families and portrays them dealing with such issues as parental rivalry, step-parenting, adoption, critical illness, sibling rivalry, and single parenting. . . . Brazelton's suggestions on communication, time management, and family life are genuinely helpful." Booklist
Includes bibliography

Infants and mothers; differences in development; foreword by Jerome S. Bruner. rev ed. Delacorte Press; Lawrence, S. 1983 xxix, 302p il $19.95; pa $16   **649**
1. Child development 2. Parent and child
ISBN 0-385-29231-7; 0-385-29209-0 (pa)   LC 83-5143
"A Merloyd Lawrence book"
First published 1969
"A description of the physical and psychological growth of an 'average,' a quiet, and an active baby through the first 12 months." Booklist
Includes bibliography

Toddlers and parents; a declaration of independence. rev ed. Delacorte Press; Lawrence, S. 1989 xxi, 249p il $24.95; pa $16   **649**
1. Child development 2. Child rearing
ISBN 0-385-29787-4; 0-385-29790-4 (pa)
LC 89-31336
"A Merloyd Lawrence book"
First published 1974
The author presents case studies in child development from ages one to three in diverse family settings
Includes bibliography

Touchpoints; your child's emotional and behavioral development. Addison-Wesley 1992 xxiv, 479p il $22.95   **649**
1. Child development 2. Child rearing
ISBN 0-201-09380-4   LC 92-23004
"A Merloyd Lawrence book"
The author "defines 'touchpoints' as the periods of development and regression which every child experiences while growing up. He describes the first six years of life and the touchpoints of that period. . . . Worried new parents will be put at ease after reading this book. Brazelton is knowledgeable, warm, and kind, and his book is a pleasure to read." Libr J
Includes bibliography

What every baby knows. Addison-Wesley 1987 274p il $14.38   **649**
1. Child rearing
ISBN 0-201-09262-X   LC 87-14475
Also available in paperback from Ballantine Bks.
"A Merloyd Lawrence book"
The author "recounts his counseling sessions with five couples and their small children, families that differ widely in economic and social backgrounds. . . . Brazelton's questions to the parents and their replies suggest ways for the reader to handle like issues." Publ Wkly
Includes bibliography

Working & caring. Addison-Wesley 1985 xxiii, 197p $16.95; pa $9.57   **649**
1. Parenting 2. Children of working parents
ISBN 0-201-10623-X; 0-201-10629-9 (pa)
LC 85-11189
"A Merloyd Lawrence book"
A guide to help working mothers better balance their careers with child rearing. Among the topics discussed are daycare, caring for a sick child and taking a leave from work
Includes bibliography

Burck, Frances Wells
Babysense; a practical and supportive guide to baby care; written by Frances Wells Burck; with the help of more than 500 parents; illustrations by Diana Thewlis. 2nd ed. St. Martin's Press 1991 313p il hardcover o.p. paperback available $15.95   **649**
1. Infants—Care
ISBN 0-312-05056-9 (pa)   LC 90-19119
First published 1979
The author "uses a question-and-answer format to offer basic advice on feeding, crying, sleeping, and other infant activities, as well as outside childcare. Her book is visually stimulating, with ample illustrations and easy-to-digest sidebars." Libr J

Caplan, Theresa

The early childhood years; the 2- to 6-year-old; [by] The Princeton Center for Infancy and Early Childhood, Theresa and Frank Caplan, authors. Perigee Bks. 1983 334p il hardcover o.p. paperback available $12.95   **649**

1. Child rearing
ISBN 0-399-50862-7 (pa)   LC 83-9587

Also available in paperback from Bantam Bks.

"A GD/Perigee book"

"Includes a minicourse in early childhood development with growth charts and over 120 photographs and a chapter with 14 special parenting topics." Title page

"The Caplans manage to expound with characteristic authority on toilet learning, hyperactivity, day care, temper tantrums, motor development, the effects of divorce, etc." Booklist

Includes bibliography

Caring for your baby and young child; birth to age 5; [by] Steven P. Shelov [et al.] Bantam Bks. 1991 676p il $29.95   **649**

1. Infants—Care 2. Child rearing
ISBN 0-553-07186-6   LC 90-47015

Also available: Caring for your adolescent: ages 12 to 21 (1991); Caring for your school age child: ages 6 to 11 (1993)

At head of title: Seal of the American Academy of Pediatrics

This handbook provides "detailed information on specific health problems in young children. Chapters organized by chronological age cover growth and developmental milestones, basic care, health watch, and safety checks for each age group. An important work." Libr J

Developing your child's potential; by the editors of Time-Life Books. Time-Life Bks. 1987 144p il (Successful parenting) $17.27   **649**

1. Preschool education 2. Child development
LC 86-23130

Advice from child-care authorities on how parents may provide an intellectually stimulating environment for their child from infancy to age six. Illustrations, charts, and checklists supplement the text

Includes bibliography

Driscoll, Jeanne

Taking care of your new baby; a guide to infant care; [by] Jeanne Watson Driscoll & Marsha Walker. Avery Pub. Group 1989 162p il pa $6.95   **649**

1. Infants—Care
ISBN 0-89529-397-8   LC 89-6536

"This sourcebook by two registered nurses reviews basic care for the infant, e.g., feeding, elimination, crying, and bathing, as well as examining postpartum adjustment in both the mother and father." Libr J

Includes bibliography

Eisenberg, Arlene

What to expect the first year; [by] Arlene Eisenberg, Heidi E. Murkoff, Sandee E. Hathaway. Workman 1989 xxiv, 671p il pa $12.95   **649**

1. Infants—Care 2. Child rearing
ISBN 0-89480-577-0   LC 87-40647

The authors of this "guide respond to myriad questions that face parents of newborns. From the age-old debate on the virtues of breast-vs.-bottle feeding to more contemporary ones on father's role and circumcision. . . . A ready-reference section describes recipes, home remedies, common illnesses, and more." Libr J

Experts advise parents; a guide to raising loving, responsible children; [by] Louise Bates Ames [et al.]; edited by Eileen Shiff; illustrated with photographs by Betty David and Suzanne Arms. Delacorte Press 1987 xxi, 370p il $19.95; pa $14.95   **649**

1. Parenting
ISBN 0-385-29522-7; 0-385-29526-X (pa)
LC 86-24024

"A collection of 12 essays on various aspects of parenting, written by highly respected experts that include Louise Bates Ames, Benjamin Spock, and Fitzhugh Dodson." Libr J

"Each section includes a brief bibliography, and the editor has appended a large resource directory, which recommends books for special needs as well as supplying a developmental checklist and hints on selecting a day-care or preschool center." Booklist

Faber, Adele

Siblings without rivalry; how to help your children live together so you can live too; [by] Adele Faber and Elaine Mazlish; illustrations by Kimberly Ann Coe. Norton 1987 219p il $14.95   **649**

1. Brothers and sisters 2. Child rearing
ISBN 0-393-02441-5   LC 86-23919

Also available in paperback from Avon Bks.

This book "outlines ways to defuse such explosive situations as comparing, assigning roles, or taking sides and suggests remedies to avoid conflict. Cartoon-like illustrations and 'quick reminders' help reinforce new behavior." Libr J

Includes bibliography

Finston, Peggy

Parenting plus; raising children with special health needs. Dutton 1990 xxiv, 295p o.p.; Penguin Bks. paperback available $9   **649**

1. Handicapped children 2. Parenting
ISBN 0-14-016837-0 (pa)   LC 89-28527

This "handbook shows parents how to help their disabled children develop self-esteem, reduce bitterness at their condition, increase autonomy, and otherwise make the most of their life circumstances." Libr J

Includes bibliography

Franck, Irene M.

The parent's desk reference; [by] Irene Franck and David Brownstone. Prentice-Hall 1992 615p il $29.95; pa $18   **649**

1. Child rearing 2. Parenting
ISBN 0-13-650003-X; 0-13-650003-X (pa)

LC 92-2707

"This 'desk reference' provides a convenient way for parents to obtain both basic data about a topic and a quick referral to more detailed information and sources of further help. Complete with sidebars and checklists, entries on such subjects as pregnancy and childbirth, infant care, and child development the book also features a directory of agencies that may provide help and a sampling of recent publications." Libr J

Gordon, Sol, 1923-

Raising a child conservatively in a sexually permissive world; [by] Sol Gordon, Judith Gordon. rev and updated ed. Simon & Schuster 1989 241p pa $9.95   **649**

1. Sex education 2. Parent and child
ISBN 0-671-68182-6   LC 89-1545

"A Fireside book"

First published 1983

This "guide offers reassuring advice for parents on communicating with their children on sexual, social and moral matters. At the heart of this approach is the firm belief that informed children will grow into responsible, self-possessed adults, and that it is the parents' responsibility to be the primary sex educators of their children." Publisher's note

Includes bibliography

Gordon, Thomas, 1918-

P.E.T. in action; [by] Thomas Gordon with Judith Gordon Sands. Wyden Bks. 1976 367p o.p.; Bantam Bks. paperback available $4.95   **649**

1. Parenting
ISBN 0-553-24556-2 (pa)

Also available in paperback from New Am. Lib.

Based on questionnaires and interviews with parents who have attended P.E.T. training sessions and have used the method, this book "aims to explore the ways Parent Effectiveness Training has changed the families who have used it." Libr J

Includes bibliography

Parent effectiveness training; the tested new way to raise responsible children. Wyden Bks. [distributed by] Mckay, D. 1970 338p il $12.95   **649**

1. Parenting
ISBN 0-88326-039-5

Also available in paperback from New Am. Lib.

Parent effectiveness training is an alternative parenting approach that "involves active listening, a frank statement of feeling without placing blame, and a true identification of the problem (is it the parent's or the child's?)." Libr J

Guterson, David

Family matters; why homeschooling makes sense. Harcourt Brace Jovanovich 1992 245p $22.95   **649**

1. Home instruction 2. Education—United States
ISBN 0-15-193097-X   LC 92-7877

The author "articulates many of the problems of the American education system and, to a degree, makes a strong case for the role of homeschooling in contributing to the solution. . . . This book is a useful contribution to education literature." Libr J

Includes bibliographic references

Johnson & Johnson from baby to toddler; edited by John J. Fisher; photographs by Bill Parsons; developed by Johnson & Johnson in arrangement with The Child Growth & Development Corporation. Putnam 1988 368p il pa $9.95   **649**

1. Infants 2. Child development
ISBN 0-399-51393-0   LC 87-38207

"A Perigee book"

This volume discusses "how to care for your baby and his or her physical, social, emotional and language development, and also addresses such . . . issues as sleep problems, infant swim classes, adoption and bonding, [and] handling common fears and discipline dilemmas." Publisher's note

Kelly, Marguerite

The mother's almanac; [by] Marguerite Kelly and Elia Parsons; revised by Marguerite Kelly; illustrated by Rebecca Hirsh. rev [ed]. Doubleday 1992 402p il pa $16   **649**

1. Child rearing
ISBN 0-385-46877-6   LC 91-28592

First published 1975

This book provides practical advice for coping with young children. Topics range from discipline and hygiene to cooking, crafts and activities

Includes bibliographic references

The mother's almanac II; illustrated by Katy Kelly. Doubleday 1989 408p il hardcover o.p. paperback available $14.95   **649**

1. Child rearing
ISBN 0-385-13155-0 (pa)   LC 88-25650

On cover: Your child from six to twelve

"In a series of essays written in a charming, witty style that is nonetheless quite informative, Kelly looks at the changes of the middle years through the lenses of developmental cycles, family life, and the outside world." Libr J

Includes bibliography

Kitzinger, Sheila, 1929-

Breastfeeding your baby; photography by Nancy Durrell McKenna; breastfeeding adviser, Chloe Fisher. Knopf 1989 160p il pa $18   **649**

1. Breast feeding
ISBN 0-679-72433-8   LC 88-27225

Kitzinger, Sheila, 1929-—*Continued*

This guide to breastfeeding offers "advice about positioning the baby, interpreting the baby's sucking rhythms, maternal nutrition and breast care. The most valuable parts of the book, however, are not on honing 'technical skills' but those that treat aspects of the intimate communication between mother and baby—during breastfeeding and beyond." Publ Wkly

Includes bibliography

Levant, Ronald F.

Between father and child; how to become the kind of father you want to be; [by] Ronald Levant and John Kelly. Viking 1989 236p hardcover o.p.; Penguin Bks. paperback available $8.95 **649**

1. Fathers 2. Parenting
ISBN 0-14-015261-X (pa)   LC 88-40414

"Drawing upon the counseling and research of Boston University's Fatherhood Project, the authors promote the skills necessary for avoiding father-child conflicts; fostering children's satisfactory moral growth, academic achievement, and sex-role identification; and coping with divorce, stepfathering, and working-parent problems." Booklist

Includes bibliography

Levine, Katherine Gordy

When good kids do bad things; a survival guide for parents. Norton 1991 267p $19.95 **649**

1. Parenting 2. Adolescent psychology
ISBN 0-393-03019-9   LC 91-8580

Also available in paperback from Pocket Bks.

"Caring is the basis of the step-by-step strategy offered in this book for dealing with troubled teenagers. Parents of adolescents who have serious problems, such as substance abuse or violent behavior, will appreciate this guide because it confronts issues beyond messy rooms and pierced ears. The author . . . outlines problems and solutions with warmth, honesty, and guts." Booklist

Includes bibliography

Marks, Jane

We have a problem; a parent's sourcebook. American Psychiatric Press 1992 449p $21.95 **649**

1. Child psychology
ISBN 0-88048-504-3   LC 92-7391

"This book is a collection of stories from Marks's 'We Have a Problem' column in *Parent's Magazine*. It contains physical, psychological, emotional, and discipline problems affecting children of all ages. . . . Parents will appreciate the useful solutions to common problems." Libr J

Melina, Lois Ruskai

Raising adopted children; a manual for adoptive parents. Harper & Row 1986 274p hardcover o.p. paperback available $12 **649**

1. Adopted children 2. Parenting
ISBN 0-06-096039-6 (pa)   LC 85-45648

"A Solstice Press book"

A discussion of "many critical issues faced by parents and their adopted children from infancy through adolescence. Illness, identity problems, adjustments of siblings and relatives, breastfeeding, medical histories, cultural orientation, and birth-parent searches are among the concerns addressed in detail." Booklist

Includes bibliography

Miller, Jo Ann

The parents' guide to daycare; [by] Jo Ann Miller and Susan Weissman. Bantam Bks. 1986 246p pa $8.95 **649**

1. Child care centers
ISBN 0-553-34295-9   LC 86-47581

The author discusses the evaluation and selection of daycare centers. The roles of parent, child and caregiver are examined

Includes bibliographies

Neifert, Marianne R.

Dr. Mom's parenting guide; commensense guidance for the life of your child; [by] Marianne Egeland Neifert. Dutton 1991 274p $19.95 **649**

1. Parenting
ISBN 0-525-93373-5   LC 91-10035

The author "calls on years of practice as a pediatrician and a mother of five to zero in on what can worry parents the most. She dismisses the modern myth of the superparent and assures us that perfection isn't the goal—nurturing solid family values and self-esteem is. Chapters cover the usual hot topics, from discipline to divorce; but rather than claiming to be the definitive word, Neifert encourages further reading and thought through chapter bibliographies." Booklist

Novotny, Pamela Patrick

The joy of twins; having, raising, and loving babies who arrive in groups. Crown 1988 294p il $19.95 **649**

1. Twins 2. Child rearing
ISBN 0-517-56819-5   LC 87-27281

A "guide detailing the care of infant twins and methods for parent survival. . . . The discussion of breast feeding is excellent without being overzealous; in a similar fashion, the author deals with concern such as naps, diapers, and household help." Booklist

Includes bibliography

Olds, Sally Wendkos

The working parents' survival guide. updated & rev ed. Prima Pub. & Communications 1989 404p pa $10.95 **649**

1. Parenting 2. Children of working parents
ISBN 0-914629-82-4   LC 88-38558

First published 1983 by Bantam Bks.

"Learning to balance work, home, marriage, children, and self is the goal of this exploration of the issues that affect working mothers and fathers." Libr J

Includes bibliography

Rosemond, John K., 1947-

Parent power! a common-sense approach to parenting in the '90s and beyond. Andrews & McMeel 1990 xxii, 332p $9.95
649

1. Parenting
ISBN 0-8362-2808-1   LC 90-28239

First published 1981 by East Woods Press with subtitle: a common-sense approach to raising your child in the eighties

The author offers advice on childrearing, emphasizing the need for parents to be authoritative, reviews developmental stages from birth to age 19, and recommends techniques for dealing with problems

Sammons, William A. H.

The self-calmed baby; a liberating new approach to parenting your infant; with a foreword by T. Berry Brazelton. Little, Brown 1989 254p $17.95   **649**

1. Infants—Care
ISBN 0-316-76973-8   LC 88-8322

Also available in paperback from St. Martin's Press

The author "has developed a theory of infant self-calming, a technique in which the baby settles herself down without assistance from anyone. Sammons offers sound advice for new parents coping with feeding and quieting an infant, encouraging them to observe and communicate with the new baby." Libr J

Samuels, Mike

The well baby book; revised and expanded for the 1990s; [by] Mike Samuels and Nancy Samuels; illustrated by Wendy Frost. Summit Bks. 1991 446p il hardcover o.p. paperback available $16.95   **649**

1. Pregnancy 2. Childbirth 3. Infants—Care
ISBN 0-671-73412-1 (pa)   LC 90-26702

First published 1979

This covers prenatal care as well as infant care including feeding, bathing, diapering, immunizations and childhood diseases, daycare and nannies

Includes bibliographic references

Schaffer, Judith

How to raise an adopted child; a guide to help your child flourish from infancy through adolescence; [by] Judith Schaffer and Christina Lindstrom. Crown 1989 310p o.p.; New Am. Lib. paperback available $8.95
649

1. Adopted children 2. Parenting
ISBN 0-452-26560-6 (pa)   LC 89-1243

At head of title: The Center for Adoptive Families

"The well-being of adopted children and the peace of mind of adopting parents are both promoted in this thorough guide. Organizing material by age—from birth to late teens—the authors cogently note the similarities and differences in raising adopted children versus birth children, thus providing a solid reference point for parents." Booklist

Spock, Benjamin, 1903-

Dr. Spock on parenting; sensible advice from America's most trusted child care expert. Simon & Schuster 1988 318p hardcover o.p. paperback available $5.99
649

1. Parenting
ISBN 0-671-68386-1 (pa)   LC 88-15792

"The author presents a personal critique on parenting, often bordering on the autobiographical. . . . He discusses in depth and with great conviction contemporary and traditional parent concerns, such as divorce, discipline, sex education, and the father's role." Libr J

Dr. Spock's baby and child care; [by] Benjamin Spock and Michael B. Rothenberg. Dutton $25   **649**

1. Infants—Care 2. Children—Health and hygiene

Also available in paperback from Pocket Bks.

First published 1946 by Duell with title: The common sense book of baby and child care. (6th edition 1992) Periodically revised

This handbook for parents gives advice on everyday problems that arise in the physical and psychological care of babies and children. Material is topically arranged according to age. Sections on divorce, single and stepparents are included

Turecki, Stanley

The difficult child; by Stanley Turecki with Leslie Tonner. rev ed. Bantam Bks. 1989 258p pa $9.95   **649**

1. Child rearing 2. Hyperactive children 3. Child psychology
ISBN 0-553-34446-3   LC 87-47568

First published 1985

"The authors explore how temperamental factors such as activity level, distractibility, persistence, sensory threshold, and mood influence how a child behaves and in turn how others react. Using case studies, they describe techniques for identifying behavioral traits and managing them within the context of family life." Libr J

Includes bibliography

The **Womanly** art of breastfeeding. 5th rev ed. New Am. Lib. 1991 xxxii, 446p il $11
649

1. Breast feeding
ISBN 0-452-26623-8   LC 91-15005

"A Plume book"

"Thirty-fifth anniversary edition, revised and updated"
"Published in association with La Leche League International"

This guide explains the benefits of breastfeeding and offers advice on avoiding problems, breastfeeding and working mothers, family life, and weaning

Includes bibliographic references

You can say no to your teenager; and other strategies for effective parenting in the 1990s; by Jeanette Shalov [et al.] Addison-Wesley 1991 224p $16.30; pa $8.61   **649**

1. Teenagers 2. Parenting 3. Adolescent psychology
ISBN 0-201-57002-5; 0-201-60826-X (pa)
LC 90-41388

You can say no to your teenager — *Continued*

"More than a guide to discipline, this book examines how parents can clarify their values and thoughtfully guide adolescent children to develop their own identity and beliefs." Libr J

649.8 Home care of sick and infirm

Hastings, Diana

The complete guide to home nursing; U.S. consulting editor: Helen Maule. Barron's Educ. Ser. 1986 224p il $16.95   **649.8**

1. Home nursing
ISBN 0-8120-5754-6

"Basic nursing observation techniques and procedures, such as lifting the patient, taking vitals, changing bedclothes, and giving bed baths, are explained in the first few chapters. Other chapters cover first aid, nutrition, and special needs of children or the elderly. . . . An appendix of health and welfare organizations gives further resources." Libr J

Sankar, Andrea

Dying at home; a family guide for caregiving. Johns Hopkins Univ. Press 1991 xxi, 257p il $22.95   **649.8**

1. Terminally ill 2. Home nursing
ISBN 0-8018-4230-1   LC 91-7060

The author "interviewed 13 caregivers. . . . Chapters are organized around significant issues discussed by the caregivers: the decision to take the patient home to die, use of professional help in the home, caregiving and social support, and death. All of the caregivers evidently felt that they were not 'special' because of their efforts. They were beneficiaries, too." Publ Wkly

Includes bibliography

650 Management and auxiliary services

Business periodicals index. Wilson, H.W. service basis   **650**

1. Business—Periodicals—Indexes   2. Industry—Periodicals—Indexes   3. Economics—Periodicals—Indexes
ISSN 0007-6961

Also available on CD-ROM

Started publication in 1958 as a result of the division of the Industrial arts index to form the Business periodicals index and the Applied Science & technology index

Monthly (except August) with quarterly cumulations and a bound annual volume

A subject guide to periodicals in accounting, advertising, banking, communications, economics, finance and investments, insurance, management, marketing, taxation, and related fields

This work "remains one of the best indexes of business periodicals." Am Ref Books Annu, 1993

Ewing, David W.

Inside the Harvard Business School; strategies and lessons of America's leading school of business. Times Bks. 1990 292p $19.95   **650**

1. Harvard University. Graduate School of Business Administration
ISBN 0-8129-1827-4   LC 89-40188

The author "provides an insider's assessment of the methods and philosophy of the school that is practically synonymous with business and management. . . . The author successfully provides a revealing look at why and how Harvard continues to turn out graduates who turn into leaders." Booklist

Includes bibliography

Louis Rukeyser's business almanac; Louis Rukeyser, editor-in-chief; John Cooney, managing editor; George Winslow, chief researcher. new rev ed. Simon & Schuster 1991 587p il map $25   **650**

1. Business 2. United States—Industries 3. United States—Economic conditions—1974-
ISBN 0-671-70728-0   LC 91-30290

First published 1988

This is a "compendium of business statistics, facts, industry profiles, rankings, analysis, and commentary. This almanac is a browser's treasure and a trivia buff's delight. . . . Rukeyser provides a useful source for identifying trends and historical data and for finding elusive miscellany." Booklist

650.1 Personal success in business

Bernstein, Albert J.

Neanderthals at work; how people and politics can drive you crazy—and what you can do about them; [by] Albert J. Bernstein, Sydney Craft Rozen. Wiley 1992 287p $19.95   **650.1**

1. Job satisfaction
ISBN 0-471-52727-0   LC 91-25866

Also available in paperback from Ballantine Bks.

The authors "identify the three categories of workers found in all companies, defined in terms of how rigidly they approach their jobs. The categories are rebel, believer, and competitor. The thrust of the book is to help understand each type's ways and needs, and then to adopt a personal code of behavior for dealing with each type to ensure one's own personal sanity and professional accomplishment. Case studies both highlight and enliven points made." Booklist

Hamlin, Sonya

How to talk so people listen; the real key to job success. Harper & Row 1988 265p $17.95; pa $10   **650.1**

1. Communication 2. Success
ISBN 0-06-015669-4; 0-06-091573-0 (pa)
LC 87-45624

In this guide to improving speaking skills the author discusses body language, audiences, meetings, small talk, and formal addresses

Kiam, Victor K., II
Live to win; achieving success in life and business. Harper & Row 1989 258p $18.95; pa $4.95   **650.1**

1. Entrepreneurs 2. Business 3. Success
ISBN 0-06-016261-9; 0-06-109907-4 (pa)

LC 89-45677

First published 1988 in the United Kingdom with title: Keep going for it!

The author discusses his experiences as an entrepreneur and presents advice on succeeding in business and in one's personal life

Mackay, Harvey
Swim with the sharks without being eaten alive; outsell, outmanage, outmotivate, & outnegotiate your competition; foreword by Kenneth Blanchard. Morrow 1988 273p $17.95   **650.1**

1. Success 2. Management
ISBN 0-688-07473-1

LC 87-24757

Also available in paperback from Ivy Bks.

This guide to achieving success in the business world focuses on salesmanship, negotiation, and management

Mayer, Jeffrey
If you haven't got the time to do it right, when will you find the time to do it over? Simon & Schuster 1990 159p il $17.95; pa $9   **650.1**

1. Time management
ISBN 0-671-69490-1; 0-671-73364-8 (pa)

LC 90-30065

The author explains organization of "work space and streamline responsibilities of the business day. . . . He discusses how to handle meetings, telephone calls, delegation of work, paperwork, and professional reading. His concise, easy-to-read, easy-to-use, humorously illustrated unclutter-your-desk manual is recommended for business collections." Libr J

McCormack, John, 1944-
Self-made in America; plain talk for plain people about the meaning of success; [by] John McCormack with David R. Legge. Addison-Wesley 1990 226p $19.18; pa $9.95   **650.1**

1. Success
ISBN 0-201-55099-7; 0-201-60823-5 (pa)

LC 90-43883

The author "examines the components of success and how individuals can go about achieving it." Libr J

McCormack, Mark H.
What they don't teach you at Harvard Business School. Bantam Bks. 1984 256p $16.95; pa $12   **650.1**

1. Success 2. Management
ISBN 0-553-05101-6; 0-553-34583-4 (pa)

LC 84-45172

"A John Boswell Associates book"

McCormack's firm, the International Management Group, merchandises professional sports figures and markets the international television rights to sporting events. In this book, McCormack offers advice on business management

Ringer, Robert J.
Million dollar habits. Wynwood Press 1990 237p il o.p.; Fawcett Bks. paperback available $5.95   **650.1**

1. Success 2. Businessmen
ISBN 0-449-21878-3 (pa)

LC 89-29399

"Asserting that achievement in business is more a matter of approach than a result of education, intelligence, or even luck, Ringer pinpoints a variety of common behaviors and attitudes that adversely affect business success and explains how they can be altered for the better." Booklist

Saltzman, Amy, 1958-
Downshifting; reinventing success on a slower track. HarperCollins Pubs. 1991 238p $19.95; pa $10   **650.1**

1. Career changes
ISBN 0-06-016579-0; 0-06-092158-7 (pa)

LC 90-55552

"The author singles out 20 men and women—journalists, doctors, lawyers, academics, salespeople—who have changed both goals and pace to achieve a better-balanced life." Publ Wkly

Includes bibliographic references

650.14   Success in obtaining jobs and promotions

Brennan, Lawrence D. (Lawrence David), 1915-
Resumes for better jobs; [by] Lawrence D. Brennan, Stanley Strand, Edward C. Gruber. 5th ed. Prentice Hall Press 1991 219p il pa $9   **650.14**

1. Résumés (Employment) 2. Applications for positions
ISBN 0-13-773615-0

LC 93-119496

First published 1973 by Simon & Schuster

At head of title: Arco

This volume offers suggestions for writing resumes and cover letters and contains examples. The appendix includes the employment outlook for the year 2000

Includes bibliography

Corwen, Leonard
Your resume; key to a better job. Prentice-Hall $11   **650.14**

1. Résumés (Employment) 2. Applications for positions

First published 1976. (5th edition 1993) Periodically revised

"Designed mainly for higher-level executives and professionals, this bestselling guide . . . features more than 35 sample résumés and 20 model cover letters, worksheets for assessing personal strengths, a resource list for tapping the hidden job market, and a directory of

Corwen, Leonard—*Continued*
information sources by occupation." N Y Public Libr Book of How & Where to Look It Up

Frank, William S.
200 letters for job hunters. Ten Speed Press 1990 345p $17.95   **650.14**
1. Job hunting 2. Applications for positions
ISBN 0-89815-363-8   LC 89-20652
The author offers over 200 sample letters for job hunters. Tips on formats and wording are included

The **Guide** to basic resume writing; [by] Job and Career Information Services Committee of the Adult Lifelong Learning Section, Public Library Association [and] American Library Association. VGM Career Horizons 1991 88p pa $7.95
    650.14
1. Résumés (Employment)
ISBN 0-8442-8123-9   LC 90-50722
At head of title: PLA: Public Library Association, a division of the American Library Association
This volume includes general guidelines for writing resumes, sample resumes and cover letters, a bibliography, a skill groupings list, and a list of action words to use in resume writing

Half, Robert
How to get a better job in this crazy world. Crown 1989 239p $17.95   **650.14**
1. Job hunting
ISBN 0-517-57346-6   LC 89-23894
Also available in paperback from New Am. Lib.
The author discusses how to assess the job market, approach an interview, and insure employment security. Discrimination in the workplace is also examined

Hansen, Katharine
Dynamic cover letters; how to sell yourself to an employer by writing a letter that will get your resume read, get you an interview and get you a job! by Katharine Hansen with Randall S. Hansen. Ten Speed Press 1990 98p il pa $7.95   **650.14**
1. Applications for positions 2. Résumés (Employment)
ISBN 0-89815-356-5   LC 89-77576
A guide to preparing cover letters that will successfully present your credentials to personnel managers

Hyatt, Carole
Shifting gears; how to master career change and find the work that's right for you. Simon & Schuster 1990 271p 18.95; pa $10   **650.14**
1. Career changes
ISBN 0-671-67311-4; 0-671-75676-1 (pa)
    LC 90-38063
The author offers practical advise on how to deal with the emotional and psychological stress that often accompanies a career change

Jackson, Tom
The perfect resume. Doubleday 1990 209p il $12; pa $12.50   **650.14**
1. Résumés (Employment) 2. Applications for positions
ISBN 0-385-26745-2; 0-385-18112-4 (pa)
    LC 90-180347
"Goes beyond the rules of résumé-writing and helps the reader discover potential career objectives, understand the theory and process behind résumé-writing, and target specific employers. . . . The reader is constantly involved through questionnaires and exercises. Sample résumés included." N Y Public Libr Book of How & Where to Look It Up

Koltnow, Emily
Congratulations! you've been fired; sound advice for women who've been terminated, pink-slipped, downsized, or otherwise unemployed; [by] Emily Koltnow and Lynne S. Dumas. Fawcett Columbine 1990 260p pa $8.95   **650.14**
1. Women—Employment 2. Job hunting
ISBN 0-449-90443-1   LC 89-92593
The authors present job-hunting strategies for women who have been fired. The psychological and emotional aspects of job loss are addressed
Includes bibliographic references

Mackay, Harvey
Sharkproof; get the job you want, keep the job you love—in today's frenzied job market; [by] Harvey B. Mackay. HarperBusiness 1993 339p $22   **650.14**
1. Job hunting
ISBN 0-88730-619-5   LC 92-53494
This guide to obtaining and keeping jobs discusses networking, researching potential firms, job interviews and resumes

Résumés that get jobs. Prentice Hall Press pa $7   **650.14**
1. Résumés (Employment) 2. Applications for positions
First published 1963 under the editorship of Edward C. Gruber. (6th edition 1992) Periodically revised
Current editions by Jean Reed
This guide for job-seekers covers job-hunting, interview conduct and focuses on resume writing skills with sample resumes included for a wide variety of positions in various fields

Tarrant, John J., 1924-
Stalking the headhunter; the smart job-hunter's guide to executive recruiters; [by] John Tarrant. Bantam Bks. 1986 270p $17.95   **650.14**
1. Executives—Recruiting 2. Job hunting
ISBN 0-553-05181-4   LC 86-47579
"A Stonesong Press book"
The author "offers a set of strategies for becoming visible to leading recruiters, building a favorable image, handling phone and face-to-face interviews, and negotiating for money, position, protection, and power.

Tarrant, John J., 1924-—*Continued*
He also evaluates the search industry's internal workings." Booklist

Witt, Melanie Astaire, 1953-
Job strategies for people with disabilities; enable yourself for today's job market. Peterson's Guides 1992 292p pa $14.95
650.14

1. Vocational guidance 2. Job hunting 3. Handicapped—Employment
ISBN 1-56079-143-8   LC 92-13864

The author "offers practical, realistic, and sage advice for the 43 million Americans with disabilities who face the open job market. Witt . . . discusses job-search strategies and the self-assessment of realistic career and job skills that can enable and encourage disabled job seekers to put forth their best selves without discrimination." Libr J

Includes bibliographic references

Yate, Martin John
Knock 'em dead; the ultimate job seeker's handbook; [by] Martin Yate. Adams, B. $20, pa $7.95   **650.14**

1. Job hunting
First published 1985. (1993 edition) Periodically revised

This guide to job seeking offers advice on getting and preparing for an interview with over 200 responses to interview questions, and suggestions for negotiating a job offer

651.3   Office management

Doris, Lillian
Complete secretary's handbook; [by] Lillian Doris and Besse May Miller. Prentice-Hall il $39.95, pa $19.95   **651.3**

1. Secretaries—Handbooks, manuals, etc. 2. Office practice—Handbooks, manuals, etc.
First published 1951 and periodically revised. (7th edition 1993) Revised by Mary Ann De Vries beginning with 4th edition

"Contains chapters on filing and follow-up techniques, typing skills, using computers and other automated equipment, and other general secretarial duties. Two sections deal with writing skills and another provides quick references to information needed on a daily basis. Includes glossary of business terms and index." N Y Public Libr Book of How & Where to Look It Up

Merriam-Webster's secretarial handbook. 3rd ed. Merriam-Webster 1993 590p $15.95
651.3

1. Secretaries—Handbooks, manuals, etc. 2. Office practice—Handbooks, manuals, etc.
ISBN 0-87779-236-4   LC 93-10632

First published 1976 with title: Webster's secretarial handbook

Covers various aspects of the business office, including using computers, word processors and other machines; grammar and word usage; and business etiquette
For a review see: Booklist, Feb. 1, 1994

Webster's New World secretarial handbook; prepared under the editorial supervision of In Plain English, Inc. 4th ed. Webster's New World 1989 691p il $15.95; pa $9.95
651.3

1. Secretaries—Handbooks, manuals, etc. 2. Office practice—Handbooks, manuals, etc.
ISBN 0-13-949256-9; 0-13-949249-6 (pa)   LC 89-5698
First published 1968. Title varies

"Guide to many diverse aspects of the profession. Includes information on several professional fields for specialized secretaries, easy-to-understand essay on general legal principles, travel information, and a strong chapter on English usage, including a spelling and syllabification list of 33,000 words. Includes handy general reference section." N Y Public Libr Book of How & Where to Look It Up

651.7   Business communication. Creation and transmission of records

Seglin, Jeffrey L., 1956-
The AMA handbook of business letters. American Mgt. Assn. 1989 352p $65
651.7

1. Business letters
ISBN 0-8144-5835-1   LC 88-48034

"A light review of grammar and usage basics leads off, followed by an extensive section of 270 model letters covering familiar topics in business correspondence, including price queries, proposals, sales pitches, and thank-you notes." Booklist

Includes bibliography

Taintor, Sarah Augusta
The secretary's handbook; [by] Sarah Augusta Taintor and Kate M. Monro. Macmillan $19.95   **651.7**

1. Secretaries—Handbooks, manuals, etc. 2. Office practice—Handbooks, manuals, etc.
First published 1929. (10th edition 1988 revised by Margaret D. Shertzer) Periodically revised

Concentrates on the importance of correct usage of business correspondence. Examples of letters and other standard business forms are included

652.3   Typewriting

Century 21 keyboarding, formatting, and document processing; complete course. South-Western il $43.43   **652.3**

1. Typewriting 2. Word processing
Replaces Century 21 typewriting
5th edition 1992 by Jerry W. Robinson et al.

This complete two-year course aims to build skills for basic typing, personal/business typing, office skills, formatting for electric or electronic machines, and processing of documents (format, contents, grammar, corrections, evaluation of final copy). Technique and speed are emphasized through drills and timed exercises

Levine, Nathan
Typing for everyone. Prentice-Hall pa $13
652.3

1. Typewriting
First published 1971. (9th edition 1994) Periodically revised

Introduces the mechanics of the typewriter, then progresses to skills, reviews, practices, and goals in typing letters, manuscripts, carbon copies, business forms, etc. Includes speed drills, alignment and justification, proofreading, general rules, forms of address, and complimentary close

653 Shorthand

Gregg, John Robert, 1867-1948
Gregg shorthand; series 90; [by] John Robert Gregg, Louis A. Leslie, Charles E. Zoubek; shorthand written by Charles Rader. McGraw-Hill 1985 c1978 320p il $21.95
653

1. Shorthand
ISBN 0-07-024490-1   LC 86-134370
First published 1949 with title: Gregg shorthand manual simplified

This is a simplified version of the shorthand system originally presented by John Robert Gregg. It includes practice suggestions, and reading and writing exercises

Gregg shorthand dictionary; [by] John Robert Gregg [et al.] McGraw-Hill   **653**
1. Shorthand
First published 1963. Periodically revised

Available in various editions and bindings

A compilation of shorthand outlines of words, names and frequently used phrases
"An excellent reference for stenographic students." Wynar. Guide to Ref Books for Sch Media Cent. 2d edition [review of 1963 edition]

657 Accounting

Accountants' handbook. Wiley il $135   **657**
1. Accounting
Supplementary volume available
First published 1923 by Ronald Press. (7th edition 1991) Periodically revised

Current editors: D. R. Carmichael, Steven B. Lilien, Martin Mellman

Presents principles, rules, and procedures of accepted accounting practice
"For many years the authoritative handbook in the field." Sheehy. Guide to Ref Books. 10th edition

Century 21 accounting: advanced course. South-Western il $44.93   **657**
1. Accounting 2. Bookkeeping
First published with title: 20th century bookkeeping and accounting: advanced course. (5th edition 1993) Periodically revised

Current edition by Kenton E. Ross et al.

The second volume in a two-volume textbook teaching accounting principles, procedures and applications. The advanced course is preceded by the first course entered below

Century 21 accounting: first-year course. South-Western il $44.93   **657**
1. Accounting 2. Bookkeeping
First published with title: 20th century bookkeeping and accounting: first year course. (5th edition 1993) Periodically revised

Current edition by Robert M. Swanson, Kenton E. Ross and Robert D. Hanson

The first volume in a two-volume textbook teaching accounting principles, procedures and applications

Siegel, Joel G.
Accounting handbook; [by] Joel G. Siegel, Jae K. Shim. Barron's Educ. Ser. 1990 836p il $29.95   **657**
1. Accounting
ISBN 0-8120-6176-4   LC 89-18394
"Arranged in 12 sections by subject (e.g., financial accounting, government and nonprofit accounting) including a dictionary. Indexed, but lack bibliographies." Sheehy. Guide to Ref Books. 10th edition. suppl

658 General management

Cohen, William A., 1937-
The art of the leader. Prentice-Hall 1990 215p $19.95; pa $9.95   **658**
1. Leadership
ISBN 0-13-046657-3; 0-13-048471-7 (pa)
     LC 89-16359
The author "contends that, with proper training, almost anyone can become a leader. Defining the difference between management and leadership, he recommends 'influence strategies' and how and when to use these. . . . He also discusses staff relations, motivation and fostering teamwork within an organization, basing his advice on sports and military principles." Publ Wkly

Includes bibliographic references

Drucker, Peter Ferdinand, 1909-
The frontiers of management; where tomorrow's decisions are being shaped today; [by] Peter F. Drucker. Dutton 1986 368p o.p.; HarperCollins Pubs. paperback available $10   **658**
1. Management
ISBN 0-06-097111-8 (pa)   LC 86-8004
"A Truman Talley book"
A collection of essays on management and organizational theory. Innovation and flexibility are emphasized

Managing for the future; the 1990s and beyond; [by] Peter F. Drucker. Dutton 1992 370p $25   **658**
1. Management
ISBN 0-525-93414-6   LC 91-31454
"A Truman Talley book"
"Drucker's goal is to explain to busy executives the rapidly changing world in which they are working. Each chapter is 'designed from the beginning to simulate action—identify new opportunities; to point out areas where changes—in process and product, policies, markets, and structure—might be needed.' An interesting view of

Drucker, Peter Ferdinand, 1909- — *Continued*
the future by one of the most widely read business writers." Libr J

Managing the non-profit organization; practices and principles; [by] Peter F. Drucker. HarperCollins Pubs. 1990 235p $22.95; pa $12   **658**
1. Industrial management 2. Corporations
ISBN 0-06-016507-3; 0-06-092263-X (pa)
                                                  LC 89-46525
The author discusses "his ideas on tasks, responsibilities, and practices necessary to manage non-profit organizations." Libr J

The practice of management. Harper & Row 1954 404p hardcover o.p. paperback available $14   **658**
1. Industrial management
ISBN 0-06-091316-9 (pa)
A look at the functions, techniques and responsibilities of management in business and industry. IBM, GM and Sears are used as illustrative examples of successfully managed firms
Includes bibliography

Kanter, Rosabeth Moss
When giants learn to dance: mastering the challenge of strategy, management, and careers in the 1900s. Simon & Schuster 1989 415p $21.95; pa $12   **658**
1. Management
ISBN 0-671-61733-8; 0-671-69625-4 (pa) LC 89-4131
An analysis of the organizational and structural changes that the author contends must be made by American corporations to remain competitive
Includes bibliography

Peters, Thomas J.
Thriving on chaos; handbook for a management revolution. Knopf 1987 561p $25   **658**
1. Management
ISBN 0-394-56784-6   LC 87-45575
Also available in paperback from HarperCollins Pubs.
The author believes that business success is achieved by "enlightened leadership through innovation and flexibility in management style and organizational structure. Essential." Libr J
Includes bibliography

Roberts, Wess
Leadership secrets of Attila the Hun. Warner Bks. 1989 c1987 110p hardcover o.p. paperback available $8.95   **658**
1. Attila, King of the Huns, d. 453 2. Leadership
ISBN 0-446-77806-0 (pa)   LC 88-27739
First published privately in 1987
A slightly tongue-in-cheek presentation of management principles based upon the leadership qualities of Attila the Hun

658.1 Business organization and finance

Blechman, Bruce J.
Guerrilla financing; alternative techniques to finance any small business; by Bruce Jan Blechman and Jay Conrad Levinson. Houghton Mifflin 1991 343p $19.45; pa $10.70   **658.1**
1. Small business
ISBN 0-395-52263-3; 0-395-52264-1 (pa)
                                                  LC 90-24203
"The authors describe the various categories—both traditional and nontraditional—of financial capital, explain how to identify sources within each category, show how to put together a financial proposal, and advise how best to negotiate a deal." Booklist

Burstiner, Irving
The small business handbook; a comprehensive guide to starting and running your own business. rev ed. Prentice Hall Press 1989 356p il pa $17.95   **658.1**
1. Small business
ISBN 0-13-814344-7   LC 88-4585
First published 1979
A guide to starting, building and maintaining a successful business. Location selection, staffing, customer relations, marketing and retailing are among the topics discussed

Edwards, Paul, 1940-
The best home businesses for the 90's; the inside information you need to know to select a home-based business that's right for you; [by] Paul and Sarah Edwards. Tarcher, J.P. 1991 267p hardcover o.p. paperback available $10.95   **658.1**
1. Home business
ISBN 0-87477-633-3 (pa)   LC 91-25210
The authors "researched 70 new businesses that can be started from home. In describing each business, they also discuss: potential earnings; knowledge, skills, and financing needed; the competition; how to price one's service or product; how to attract business; and franchise availability." Libr J
Includes bibliographic references

Hawken, Paul
Growing a business. Simon & Schuster 1987 251p pa $9.95   **658.1**
1. Small business
ISBN 0-671-67164-2   LC 87-16431
The author provides advice on the rewards and risks involved in being an entrepreneur. He advocates attention to detail, fair play, and well thought out programs. Such topics as budgeting, cash flow, credit sources and ratio analysis are also covered

Holtz, Herman
The complete work-at-home companion. Prima Pub. & Communications 1990 354p il pa $15.95 **658.1**

1. Home business
ISBN 1-55958-010-0   LC 89-10849

The author discusses "managing the home work environment and covers finances, marketing, computers, legal concerns, and insurance. Interesting insights into the psychological aspects of home employment are included." Libr J

Includes bibliographic references

How to run a small business; [by] J.K. Lasser Tax Institute. McGraw-Hill $27.95 **658.1**

1. Small business

First edition by J. K. Lasser published 1950. (7th edition 1993) Periodically revised

"Practical advice for small businesses and for people considering opening them. Details everything from choosing a location to financing to tax management, bookkeeping, accounting, personal management, and computer technology. Concisely written and well-organized." N Y Public Libr Book of How & Where to Look It Up

Jessup, Claudia
The woman's guide to starting a business; [by] Claudia Jessup and Genie Chipps. 3rd ed. Holt & Co. 1991 414p pa $14.95 **658.1**

1. Small business 2. Businesswomen
ISBN 0-8050-1140-4   LC 90-4726

"An Owl book"

First published 1976 by Holt, Rinehart & Winston

"The authors explain how to calculate costs, pick a location, set up a corporation, and organize a bookkeeping system. They offer advice on finding a lawyer and choosing an accountant, talking to bankers, hiring and managing help [and] getting effective advertising." Publisher's note

Includes bibliographic references

Mancuso, Joseph
Mancuso's small business resource guide; [by] Joseph R. Mancuso. Prentice Hall Press 1988 557p hardcover o.p. paperback available $19.95 **658.1**

1. Small business
ISBN 0-13-551888-1 (pa)   LC 87-27015

"Portions of this work were originally published by Prentice-Hall, Inc., in the 'The Small Business Survival Guide,' 1980"

The author "lists and describes associations, books, journals, governmental agencies, and private sources offering assistance to those in small business. Chapters arranged alphabetically treat such subjects as advertising, bankruptcy, databases, franchises, mailorder marketing, patents, publicity, real estate, speakers, small business investment companies, and venture capital." Choice

McQuown, Judith H.
Inc. yourself; how to profit by setting up your own corporation. Macmillan $25 **658.1**

1. Corporations 2. Small business

First published 1979. (7th edition 1992) Periodically revised

Covers the legalities of self-incorporation, taxes, employees, accounting, and includes sample forms for incorporation, profit-sharing, retirement plans, and by-laws

Parson, Mary Jean
Managing the one-person business. Dodd, Mead 1988 274p o.p.; Putnam paperback available $10.95 **658.1**

1. Self-employed 2. Small business
ISBN 0-399-51613-1 (pa)   LC 87-20069

This introduction to single-proprietor businesses covers long-term planning, legal issues, financing, marketing and time management

Includes bibliography

Stevens, Mark, 1947-
The Macmillan small business handbook. Macmillan 1988 408p il $35 **658.1**

1. Small business
ISBN 0-02-614490-5   LC 88-13329

This book covers "financing the business, selecting computer hardware and software, marketing the business, and managing employees. . . . Among the most comprehensive of the small business guides, this source is recommended for business reference collections." Libr J

658.3   Personnel management

Half, Robert
Robert Half on hiring. Crown 1985 241p o.p.; New Am. Lib. paperback available $9.95 **658.3**

1. Recruiting of employees
ISBN 0-452-25811-1 (pa)   LC 84-16957

The author "describes key steps and delineates strategies for the elements of hiring, including preparing the job description, determining hiring criteria, advertising the job, interviewing the candidate, obtaining references, and selecting the new employee. Legal ramifications of hiring (and firing) also are treated." Libr J

658.4   Executive management

Davis, George, 1939-
Black life in corporate America; swimming in the mainstream; [by] George Davis and Glegg Watson. Anchor Press/Doubleday 1982 204p hardcover o.p. paperback available $9.95 **658.4**

1. Corporations 2. Black business people 3. Discrimination in employment
ISBN 0-385-14702-3 (pa)   LC 81-22760

Davis, George, 1939-—*Continued*

An examination of African Americans involved in corporate management

"This is an honest but painful book to read, a well-documented glimpse into the managerial world." Choice

Includes bibliography

Drucker, Peter Ferdinand, 1909-

Innovation and entrepreneurship; practice and principles. Harper & Row 1985 277p hardcover o.p. paperback available $12

658.4

1. Entrepreneurs 2. Small business
ISBN 0-06-091360-6 (pa)   LC 84-48593

"Drucker analyzes innovation and entrepreneurship as a practice and discipline. . . . He details the practices and strategies essential to successful entrepreneurial management in both business and public-service enterprises." Publ Wkly

Includes bibliography

Managing for results; economic tasks and risk-taking decisions. Harper & Row 1964 240p hardcover o.p. paperback available $12

658.4

1. Industrial management 2. Decision making
ISBN 0-88730-614-4 (pa)

The author "explains how decisionmakers combine business psychology, economics, management, and intuition to produce greater profits. . . . He deplores complacency and 'stand-patism' while he extols the virtues of enlightened innovation." Libr J

Includes bibliography

Lefferts, Robert

The basic handbook of grants management. Basic Bks. 1983 292p il $21.95

658.4

1. Management 2. Fund raising 3. Grants-in-aid
ISBN 0-465-00600-0   LC 82-72400

"The major focus of the book is on how to manage projects in the broad fields of human services, health, mental health, the arts and humanities, and the social and behavioral sciences." Preface

Includes bibliography

Ouchi, William G.

Theory Z; how American business can meet the Japanese challenge. Addison-Wesley 1981 283p o.p.; Avon Bks. paperback available $10

658.4

1. Industrial management   2. Japan—Industries
3. United States—Industries
ISBN 0-380-71944-4 (pa)   LC 81-8

The author "describes the art of Japanese management and shows how it can be adapted to American companies. He takes readers behind the scenes at several U.S. corporations making the Theory Z change." Publisher's note

Includes bibliography

Peters, Thomas J.

Liberation management; necessary disorganization for the nanosecond nineties; [by] Tom Peters. Knopf 1992 xxxiv, 834p il $27   **658.4**

1. Management
ISBN 0-394-55999-1   LC 90-53071

In this book of management advice and economic analysis Peters argues "that companies have to be flexible enough to readjust to the quick changes of a 'fashion'-driven marketplace." Libr J

"Part pep talk, part grab-bag of business strategies, this energizing, idea-rich handbook will shake up traditional managers and rank-and-file workers alike." Publ Wkly

A passion for excellence; the leadership difference; [by] Tom Peters, Nancy Austin. Random House 1985 xxv, 437p $30 **658.4**

1. Industrial management
ISBN 0-394-54484-6   LC 84-45767

Also available in paperback from Warner Bks.

This examination of quality leaders and leadership techniques focuses on such business success-stories as IBM, Mary Kay Cosmetics and Perdue Chickens

Includes bibliography

658.5   Management of production

Lynn, Gary S.

From concept to market. Wiley 1989 248p il $55; pa $17.95   **658.5**

1. Inventions 2. Entrepreneurs
ISBN 0-471-50126-3; 0-471-50125-5 (pa)

     LC 88-27851

"This is a practical guide designed to answer the questions of entrepreneurs wishing to implement an idea for a new product or concept. . . . Especially helpful are the sample copies of relevant forms, the lists of organizations to contact, and a bibliography." Libr J

658.8   Management of distribution (Marketing)

Davidow, William H.

Total customer service; the ultimate weapon; [by] William H. Davidow and Bro Uttal. Harper & Row 1989 xxii, 227p $19.95; pa $11   **658.8**

1. Customer relations
ISBN 0-06-016180-9; 0-06-092009-2 (pa)

     LC 89-45033

The authors "argue that while most companies in the United States give lip service to customer service, few really invest the money or effort to do it well. . . . The Japanese, meanwhile, have won in many markets because of the level of service they offer to both retail and industrial customers. As global competition increases, as products and features proliferate and as customers get bewildered by look-alikes, survival will depend on the buyer's perceptions of a company's service. . . . [This is] an important book on corporate strategy that still manages to be lively and entertaining." N Y Times Book Rev

Gerhards, Paul
How to sell what you make; the business of marketing crafts. Stackpole Bks. 1990 154p pa $10.95 **658.8**
1. Selling 2. Handicraft
ISBN 0-8117-2244-9   LC 89-36371
The author discusses how to market crafts "at crafts fairs, galleries, and trade shows. Over half the book is devoted to the ins and outs of trade shows; as these shows are a very lucrative and often ignored vehicle for marketing and selling crafts, this book is an invaluable source for all artisans. The last section covers the basic paperwork aspects of a small business as well, and four appendixes cover trade show promoters; a calendar of trade shows; publications; and organizations." Libr J
Includes bibliographic references

Hakuta, Ken
How to create your own fad and make a million dollars; [by] Ken Hakuta a.k.a. Dr. Fad, with Catherine Williams and Margarert B. Carlson. Morrow 1988 226p $12.95
658.8
1. Entrepreneurs   2. Marketing   3. Commercial products
ISBN 0-688-07601-7   LC 88-2732
Also available in paperback from Avon Bks.
The author "offers advice on marketing a fad, emphasizing a fast, lean, tight-budget operation, and discusses finances, rights and protection, exposure, production, pricing, and distribution." Libr J

Hoge, Cecil C., Sr.
Mail order moonlighting. rev ed. Ten Speed Press 1988 359p il pa $9.95 **658.8**
1. Mail-order business
ISBN 0-89815-222-4   LC 87-17953
First edition privately printed 1976; first Ten Speed Press edition published 1977
Among the topics covered in this introduction to the mail order business are: merchandising, advertising, partnerships, finances, and customer relations

Larson, Erik
The naked consumer; how our private lives become public commodities. Holt & Co. 1992 275p $23 **658.8**
1. Market surveys 2. Consumption (Economics) 3. Right of privacy
ISBN 0-8050-1755-0   LC 92-14344
This is a study of how market researchers compile and use information about consumers. The author "asserts that privacy is being silently and rapidly eroded as increasingly sophisticated techniques are used to combine the information that results from marketers' efforts to track everything we watch, buy and use." N Y Times Book Rev
Includes bibliographic references

Levinson, Jay Conrad
Guerrilla marketing weapons; 100 affordable marketing methods for maximizing profits from your small business. Penguin Bks. 1990 258p pa $10 **658.8**
1. Marketing 2. Small business 3. Advertising
ISBN 0-452-26519-3   LC 90-7329
"A Plume book"
The author "defines a weapon 'as a method of communication or contact with customers and prospects designed to render service, improve quality, clarify benefits, enhance credibility, or make the customer or prospect feel good.' Weapons studied include pricing, brand-name awareness, follow-up, speed, neatness, and credibility." Libr J

Simon, Julian L.
How to start and operate a mail-order business; [by] Julian L. Simon with contributions by Paul Bringe [et al.] 5th ed. McGraw-Hill 1993 538p il $39.95 **658.8**
1. Mail-order business
ISBN 0-07-057565-7   LC 93-17657
First published 1965
An introduction to starting and operating a mail-order business. Topics discussed include: products, strategies of mail-order selling, advertising, filling orders and keeping records, and general management
Includes bibliography

659.1 Advertising

Goodrum, Charles A.
Advertising in America; the first 200 years; [by] Charles Goodrum and Helen Dalrymple. Abrams 1990 288p il $60
659.1
1. Advertising
ISBN 0-8109-1187-6   LC 90-130
This "book is an encyclopedia of the print advertising image, with a skeletal timeline delineating influences, styles and techniques, later fleshed out with analyses of why the advertising industry has flourished." Publ Wkly
Includes bibliography

Ogilvy, David, 1911-
Ogilvy on advertising. Crown 1983 224p il o.p.; Random House paperback available $19 **659.1**
1. Advertising
ISBN 0-394-72903-X (pa)   LC 83-1877
The author provides "commentary on the advertising business—how to choose an agency, how to run one, working in advertising, advertising in the various media, profiles of six legendary admen, how to write advertising that sells, and much more. Ogilvy's outspoken and often witty views are heavily illustrated with ads and commercials from around the world." Libr J
Includes bibliography

Standard directory of advertisers. National Register il $525 **659.1**
1. Advertising—Directories
ISSN 0081-4229

Standard directory of advertisers — *Continued*

Annual. First published 1916. Title varies

"A key listing of some 25,000 companies that advertise nationally. Provides addresses, officers (including sales personnel), and kinds of media used. Also notes products (and trademarks)." Ref Sources for Small & Medium-sized Libr. 5th edition

Standard directory of advertising agencies; the agency red book. National Register 3v $525 per year   **659.1**

1. Advertising—Directories
ISSN 0085-6614

Three annual issues (February, June and October). Price includes nine monthly updating supplements
First published 1917

An alphabetically arranged listing of American and foreign advertising agencies. Entries list branches, personnel by title, accounts, affiliation with national media associations, and membership in agency associations. A geographical index is included

659.13   Signs and signboards

Morgan, Hal
Symbols of America. Viking 1986 238p il $40   **659.13**

1. Trademarks
ISBN 0-670-80667-6   LC 85-40560

Also available in paperback from Penguin Bks.

"A Steam Press book"

An illustrated history of American trademarks since the mid-19th century

Includes bibliography

660   Chemical engineering

The **Chemical** formulary. Chemical Pub. Co. v1-29 ea $42; v30 & 31 ea $60   **660**

1. Chemistry, Technical

Cumulative index available for volumes 1-25 for $85
First published 1933. New volumes issued periodically

"These volumes may be useful both to the layman and the chemist requiring information on chemical compounding and treatment in areas foreign to him. Formulas have been provided and reviewed by chemists and engineers engaged in many industries. Each volume presents a collection of new, up-to-date formulas not appearing in previous volumes. Grouping is under broad headings such as: Adhesives, Cosmetics and drugs, Foods and beverages, Paints and lacquers, Soaps and cleaners. Includes lists of chemicals and suppliers." Sheehy. Guide to Ref Books. 10th edition

664   Food technology

Winter, Ruth, 1930-
A consumer's dictionary of food additives. new 3rd rev ed. Crown 1989 352p pa $12   **664**

1. Food additives—Dictionaries
ISBN 0-517-57262-1   LC 89-7899
First published 1972

"Defines food additives in simple, everyday language. The entries are arranged alphabetically by additive, providing information about its origin, its chemical composition, its appearance and taste, what it is used for, what it does, whether it is toxic or beneficial, and its GRAS status." Topical Ref Books

668   Technology of other organic products

Groom, N. St. J. (Nigel St. J.)
The perfume handbook. Chapman & Hall 1992 323p il $29.95   **668**

1. Perfumes
ISBN 0-412-46320-2   LC 92-15183

This "reference provides brief biographical sketches of some of the world's great noses, flacon designers, and other celebrities associated with the perfume business. It also offers profiles of the major companies and houses that produce and sell the world's most sought-after fragrances. About 200 commercial perfumes are reviewed for their key ingredients." Libr J

Winter, Ruth, 1930-
A consumer's dictionary of cosmetic ingredients. new 3rd rev ed. Crown 1989 330p pa $12   **668**

1. Cosmetics—Dictionaries
ISBN 0-517-57263-X   LC 89-7864
First published 1974

This volume describes ingredients used in cosmetics including preservatives, coloring agents, flavorings, fragrances, and processing agents, and their possible toxic or allergic effects

Includes bibliography

671.5   Joining and cutting of metals

Geary, Don
The welder's bible. 2nd ed. TAB Bks. 1993 313p il $29.95; pa $19.60   **671.5**

1. Welding
ISBN 0-8306-3826-1; 0-8306-3825-3 (pa)   LC 92-1677
First published 1980

"A do-it-yourselfer's guide to oxyacetylene welding—with 10 projects. . . . [The author describes] how to identify and use various metals, select tools and gases, put together a welding toolkit, work with fluxes and solder, employ special brazing techniques—even how to assemble a fully functional home workshop." Publisher's note

Giachino, Joseph William
Welding skills; [by] Joseph W. Giachino [and] William Weeks. American Tech. Pubs. il $25.96   **671.5**

1. Welding

First published 1960. (1985 edition) Periodically revised

This volume covers welding theory, techniques, standards, and practices. Also discussed are weld-testing techniques and robotic welding. Exercises are included

Modern welding; complete coverage of the welding field in one easy-to-use volume! by Andrew D. Althouse [et al.] Goodheart-Willcox 1992 736p il $34

671.5

1. Welding 2. Metals
ISBN 0-87006-966-7   LC 91-40908
First published 1965

This is a manual for learning various welding techniques and includes metal identification and technology

674 Lumber processing, wood products, cork

Constantine, Albert
Know your woods. rev ed, by Harry J. Hobbs. Scribner 1975 360p il maps hardcover o.p. paperback available $14

674

1. Trees 2. Wood
ISBN 0-684-18778-7 (pa)
First published 1959 by Home Craftsman

"A ready-reference work devoted primarily to the identification of trees, woods, and veneers for the craftsman and the layman. . . . [Also included are] data on logging, sawmill, and manufacturing methods and operations. Constantine is steeped in his subject and slips in the odd and unusual tidbit as part of his discussion." Booklist

Includes bibliography

Edlin, Herbert L. (Herbert Leeson), 1913-1976
What wood is that? A manual of wood identification. Viking 1969 160p il $26.95

674

1. Wood
ISBN 0-670-75907-4
"A Studio book"

The book discusses timber cutting and sawing, wood identification, including keys for naming timbers, and descriptions of each of the forty trees listed as examples

"The text is of British origin, and does consider some woods little used in our country; it also omits others very much used here. The language is universal, however, and both text and illustrations constitute a notable addition to the woodworker's library." Libr J

The **Encyclopedia** of wood; a tree-by-tree guide to the world's most versatile resource; foreword by John Makepeace; general editor, Aidan Walker. Facts on File 1989 192p il maps $29.95   **674**

1. Wood
ISBN 0-8160-2159-7   LC 89-33439

This book describes the properties, appearance, geographic distribution, and uses of seventy-five types of wood, and discusses trees, forest types, and logging procedures

For a review see: Booklist, Jan. 15, 1990

Petroski, Henry
The pencil; a history of design and circumstance. Knopf 1990 434p il $25; pa $15   **674**

1. Pencils
ISBN 0-394-57422-2; 0-679-73415-5 (pa)
     LC 89-45362

The author discusses the manufacture, design, history, and sociological significance of the pencil

"An incredibly rich and complex history of this entirely unremarkable instrument of communication." SLJ

Includes bibliography

676 Pulp and paper technology

Dawson, Sophie
The art and craft of papermaking. Running Press 1992 144p il $24.95   **676**

1. Papermaking
ISBN 1-56138-158-6   LC 92-50186

This guide "features step-by-step instructions, from selecting the pulp fiber to sculpting and molding the final product. It emphasizes making paper to be used as an artistic medium, rather than for printing. There are good instructions for constructing papermaking equipment such as molds and deckles." Libr J

Includes bibliographic references

677 Textiles

Fairchild's dictionary of textiles. Fairchild Publs. il $40   **677**

1. Textile industry—Dictionaries 2. Fabrics—Dictionaries
First published 1959. (6th edition 1979) Periodically revised
Editor: 1959 Stephen S. Marks; 1967- Isabel B. Wingate

"Reference source for all branches of the industry. Includes entries on fibers, yarns, fabric construction, finishing and sale, inventors and developers, and government standards and regulations. Includes appendix of organizations involved with the textile industry." N Y Public Libr Book of How & Where to Look It Up

683 Hardware and household appliances

Davidson, Homer L.
Microwave oven repair. 2nd ed. TAB Bks. 1991 370p il $29.95; pa $19.60   **683**

1. Microwave ovens—Maintenance and repair
ISBN 0-8306-6457-2; 0-8306-3457-6 (pa)
     LC 90-24054

First published 1984 with title: Practical microwave oven repair

This describes microwave operation, safety, troubleshooting, and tools and equipment used in their repair

Philbin, Tom, 1934-

The complete illustrated guide to everything sold in hardware stores; by Tom Philbin and Steve Ettlinger; illustrations by Robert Strimban; conceived and edited by Stephen R. Ettlinger Editorial Projects. Macmillan 1988 432p il $25.95   **683**

1. Tools
ISBN 0-02-536310-7   LC 88-13615

"Provides complete details on all tools, fasteners, materials, and other home-repair items on the market today, including those for specialized work, where the correct specific tools or materials can make the difference between a successful job and a failure." N Y Public Libr Book of How & Where to Look It Up

Roper, C. A. (Carl A.)

The complete book of locks and locksmithing; [by] C. A. Roper, Bill Phillips. 3rd ed. TAB Bks. 1991 437p il $26.95; pa $19.95   **683**

1. Locks and keys 2. Locksmithing
ISBN 0-8306-7522-1; 0-8306-3522-X (pa)
     LC 90-43543

First published 1976

This guide reveals professional locksmithing techniques in an illustrated, step-by-step format. A list of manufacturers, suppliers of tools, and equipment is appended

683.4   Small firearms

Fadala, Sam, 1939-

The rifleman's bible. Doubleday 1987 190p il pa $12   **683.4**

1. Rifles
ISBN 0-385-23747-2   LC 87-431

In this guide to sporting rifles, special attention is paid to the "selection of the right rifle and ammunition, maintenance, safety, accessories, and creating professional handloads. Also discussed are techniques for improving individual marksmanship, hunting skills, and target shooting." Booklist

684   Furnishings and home workshops

Basic woodworking illustrated; by the editors of Sunset Books and Sunset Magazine. Lane 1986 160p il pa $14.99   **684**

1. Woodwork 2. Furniture
ISBN 0-376-01628-0   LC 85-50847

At head of title: Sunset

"Basic methods of cutting and joining . . . design and assembly procedures for cabinetry, door-hanging, and plain and fancy furniture components are among the subjects covered." Publ Wkly

Blandford, Percy W.

The woodturner's bible. 3rd ed. TAB Bks. 1990 264p il $26.95; pa $16.95   **684**

1. Turning 2. Woodwork
ISBN 0-8306-8404-2; 0-8306-3404-5 (pa)
     LC 89-77066

First published 1979

This guide to woodworking with a lathe includes projects plus plans for building a homemade lathe

DeCristoforo, R. J.

The complete book of portable power tool techniques. Sterling 1987 c1986 258p il pa $17.95   **684**

1. Power tools 2. Woodwork
ISBN 0-8069-6502-9   LC 87-13342

"A Popular Science book"

First published 1986 by Popular Science Books

The author "emphasizes the techniques of safely using portable power tools. . . . He covers in well-illustrated detail the most popular power tools—circular, saber, and reciprocating saws; drills; routers; etc. Appendixes cover wood materials, abrasives, hardware, and shop math." Libr J

The complete book of stationary power tool techniques. Sterling 1988 c1985 388p il pa $19.95   **684**

1. Power tools
ISBN 0-8069-6666-1   LC 87-29625

"A Popular Science book"

This volume covers basic to advanced power tool operations, including the uses, characteristics, and differences among various makers and models. Includes plans for workbenches, tool stands, and storage cabinets

The table saw book. TAB Bks. 1988 342p il $23.95; pa $16.95   **684**

1. Woodwork 2. Saws
ISBN 0-8306-7789-5; 0-8306-2789-8 (pa)
     LC 87-29046

"The author begins with advice on table-saw selection and setup and then proceeds to discussions of the basic types of cuts. All of this information is linked to specific kinds of woodworking operations as the book presents a good deal of technical data in a simple format." Booklist

The **Home** workshop; by the editors of Time-Life Books. rev ed. Time-Life Bks. 1990 128p il (Home repair and improvement) $15.93   **684**

1. Workshops   LC 89-20552

First published 1980

An illustrated discussion of how to set up, best utilize and maintain a home workshop

Jackson, Albert, 1943-

The complete manual of woodworking; [by] Albert Jackson, David Day and Simon Jennings. Knopf 1989 320p il maps $40   **684**

1. Woodwork
ISBN 0-394-56488-X   LC 89-45263

Jackson, Albert, 1943—*Continued*
"This guide covers hand and power tools, joinery, wood selection, carving, finishing, and design. Excellent photos and illustrations make it a physically beautiful book." Libr J

Underhill, Roy
The woodwright's shop; a practical guide to traditional woodcraft. University of N.C. Press 1981 202p il hardcover o.p. paperback available $14.95 **684**
1. Woodwork
ISBN 0-8078-4082-3 (pa) LC 81-2960
"A potpourri of instructions, history, and personal anecdotes, this book, except for a chapter on blacksmithing, is about using the tradiional hand tools that our pioneer ancestors used to fell a tree, split the log into lumber, and produce rakes, hay forks, dough bowls, baskets, and cane-bottom chairs—axes, adzes, froes, shaves, and such homemade helpers as shaving horses and mauls." Libr J
Includes bibliography

Working with metal; by the editors of Time-Life Books. rev ed. Time-Life Bks. 1990 136p il (Home repair and improvement) $15.93 **684**
1. Metalwork
First published 1981
An illustrated presentation of basic metalworking terms, tools and practices. Plumbing, electrical and smithery applications are discussed

684.1 Furniture

Blandford, Percy W.
Country furniture; 114 traditional projects. TAB Bks. 1988 250p il $24.95; pa $15.95 **684.1**
1. Furniture
ISBN 0-8306-1444-3; 0-8306-2944-0 (pa) LC 88-8564
Black-and-white drawings accompany instructions for a range of decorative and functional woodworking projects

Bookshelves & cabinets; by the editors of Sunset Books and Sunset Magazine. 2nd ed. Lane 1987 96p il pa $8.99 **684.1**
1. Cabinet work
ISBN 0-376-01086-X LC 86-82776
First published 1974 with title: How to make bookshelves and cabinets
At head of title: Sunset
This book explains basic procedures, discusses tools and how to select materials and gives step-by-step instructions for various projects such as display modules, serving carts, box cubes, shelving and a variety of cabinets

Brumbaugh, James E.
Upholstering. 3rd ed. Macmillan 1991 various paging il $30 **684.1**
1. Upholstery
ISBN 0-02-517862-8 LC 91-14175

"An Audel book"
First published 1972 by Audel
Presents the fundamentals of furniture styles, tools and equipment, stripping, frame repairs, finishing and refinishing woods, cushions, and fabrics. Covers the uses of foam padding, tie down springs, and putting on the final cover

Wood furniture; finishing, refinishing, repairing. 3rd ed, revised and edited by John Leeke. Macmillan 1992 various paging il $30 **684.1**
1. Furniture finishing 2. Furniture—Repairing 3. Wood finishing
ISBN 0-02-517871-7 LC 91-13108
"An Audel book"
First published 1974 by Audel
This book provides information on how to repair furniture and refinish wood surfaces. Included are sections on various wood grains, stains, and woodworking tools as well as on structural repairs, inlays, and decorative touches
Includes bibliographic references

Built-ins; by the editors of Time-Life Books. Time-Life Bks. 1979 136p il (Home repair and improvement) $15.93 **684.1**
1. Built-in furniture 2. Cabinet work LC 79-18674
This manual gives step-by-step illustrated instructions for building cabinets, room dividers, wall-to-wall bookcases, benches and tables, sleeping lofts, sofas, and beds. A special section is devoted to repairing and remodeling cabinets

Cabinetry; the woodworkers guide to building professional-looking cabinets and shelves; edited by Robert A. Yoder. Rodale Press 1992 440p il $26.95 **684.1**
1. Cabinet work 2. Woodwork
ISBN 0-87857-981-8 LC 91-23894
"Eighteen American woodworkers have designed, built and furnished careful instructions for a variety of objects and furniture to occupy every room in the house, from a modest 'recipe box' to a more elaborate and challenging kneehole desk and cherrywood buffet. . . . Well-put-together step-by-step instructions, amplified visually by excellent cutaway sketches and 'exploded' views, provide a sequential work order that is most useful." Publ Wkly

Furniture; by the editors of Time-Life Books. Time-Life Bks. 1987 128p il (Fix it yourself) $18.60 **684.1**
1. Furniture—Repairing LC 87-25666
This volume shows how to repair or refinish chairs, cabinets, beds, and upholstered furniture. A section on the proper use of basic carpentry tools is included

Grotz, George
The furniture doctor. rev & expanded ed. Doubleday 1989 c1983 366p il $14 **684.1**
1. Furniture—Repairing 2. Furniture finishing
ISBN 0-385-26670-7 LC 89-31315
First published 1962; this is a reissue of the 1983 edition
The author presents practical information on the care, repair and finishing of furniture, using commonly available materials

Hylton, Bill
Outdoor furniture; 30 great projects for the deck, lawn, and garden; [by] Bill Hylton with Fred Matlack & Phil Gehret; illustrations by Frank Rohrbach; photographs by Mitch Mandel. Rodale Press 1992 312p il $26.95   **684.1**
1. Furniture 2. Woodwork
ISBN 0-87596-105-3   LC 91-32271
"This is a guide to the building of outdoor furniture, from 'quick and easy' weekend project to more involved 'classic' designs. The introductions to each project are clear and include a materials list, a cutting list and diagram, step-by-step instructions, and useful tips." Libr J

686.2   Printing

Bove, Tony, 1955-
The art of desktop publishing; using personal computers to publish it yourself; [by] Tony Bove, Cheryl Rhodes, and Wes Thomas; with contributors, Michael Gardner [et al.] 2nd ed. Bantam Bks. 1987 xxiv, 296p il $22.95; pa $19.95   **686.2**
1. Desktop publishing
ISBN 0-553-34565-6; 0-553-34441-2 (pa)
    LC 87-147106
First published 1986
This book explains step-by-step how to create newsletters, brochures, ads, business reports, and other documents, using either a Macintosh, an IBM PC, or IBM PC compatible system and the appropriate software. Among the topics covered are design, layout, computer art, type fonts, and laser printers
Includes bibliography

690   Buildings

Brumbaugh, James E.
Complete roofing handbook; installation, maintenance, repair. 2nd ed, revised by John Leeke. Macmillan 1992 526p il $30
    690
1. Roofs—Maintenance
ISBN 0-02-517851-2   LC 91-43502
"An Audel book"
First published 1986
This home-repair manual addresses such problems as insulation, ventilation, and dormer and skylight requirements. Materials and their uses are discussed. Drawings, diagrams and photographs accompany the text

Floors and stairways; by the editors of Time-Life Books. Time-Life Bks. 1978 128p il (Home repair and improvement) $15.93   **690**
1. Floors 2. Staircases   LC 78-89982
This manual contains instructions for giving life to old floors as well as for installing a range of new floors. Instructions are provided for checking safety features on existing stairways and for constructing new stairways. The final section deals with the installation and maintenance of carpeting

Kidder, Tracy
House. Houghton Mifflin 1985 341p il $17.95   **690**
1. House construction
ISBN 0-395-36317-9   LC 85-7630
Also available in paperback from Avon Bks.
"A Richard Todd book"
"The saga of a couple who supervised the building of their house in Massachusetts, this report interweaves the personal lives of those involved in the project with New England history, the sociology of building, popular lore and practical tips for would-be homebuilders." Publ Wkly
Includes bibliography

Landis, Michael
Patios & decks; how to plan, build & enjoy; by Michael Landis & Ray Moholt. HP Bks. 1983 160p il pa $12.95   **690**
1. Patios
ISBN 0-89586-162-3   LC 82-84041
"Coverage ranges from analysis of the site and planning the design to . . . step-by-step instructions for the actual construction." Booklist

Levy, Matthys
Why buildings fall down; how structures fail; [by] Matthys Levy and Mario Salvadori; illustrations by Kevin Woest. Norton 1992 334p il $24.95   **690**
1. Building failures 2. Structural failures
ISBN 0-393-03356-2   LC 91-34954
"Two structural engineers examine puzzling structural failures and collapses and the destruction of ancient and modern buildings, bridges, dams, and other constructions. Plenty of illustrations accent the lively text." Booklist

Means illustrated construction dictionary; edited by Kornelis Smit & Howard M. Chandler; illustrations by Carl W. Linde. new unabridged ed. Means 1991 691p il $99.95; pa $49.95   **690**
1. Building—Dictionaries
ISBN 0-87629-218-X; 0-87629-219-8 (pa)
    LC 92-129775
First published 1985
Over 14,000 definitions of words, terms, and concepts related to the construction industry. Tables of weights, measures, conversions, size determinations, and symbols are included

Vila, Bob
Bob Vila's This old house; by Bob Vila with Anne Henry [et al.]; photographs by Bill Schwob; illustrations by Anne Henry. Dutton 1981 284p il hardcover o.p. paperback available $19.95   **690**
1. Houses—Remodeling
ISBN 0-525-47670-9 (pa)   LC 81-65115
This book looks at the conversion into condominiums of an 1886 summer cottage complex designed by H. H. Richardson

Vila, Bob—*Continued*

"Included with the excellent photos of work-in-progress are pictures of historic buildings around the country that have been restored and adapted to present-day use, which increase the book's value as a guide and source of ideas on rehabbing and remodeling." Libr J

Includes bibliography

This old house; restoring, rehabilitating, and renovating an older house; [by] Bob Vila with Jane Davison. Little, Brown 1980 270p il hardcover o.p. paperback available $24.95 **690**

1. Houses—Remodeling
ISBN 0-316-17702-4 (pa)   LC 80-36745

"This is the book from the PBS show that spawned much of the interest in home remodeling. . . . [It] covers an actual project from start to finish and describes all of the work that needs to be done for a major renovation." Libr J

Includes bibliography

692   Auxiliary construction practices

American Institute of Architects
Architectural graphic standards. Wiley il $170; pa $67.50   **692**

1. Architecture—Details
"A Wiley-Interscience publication"
First published 1932 under the authorship of Charles G. Ramsey and Harold P. Sleeper. (8th edition 1988) Periodically revised
A guide to structural elements and details, types and dimensions of modern building materials, hardware and furniture

693.8   Construction for specific purposes

Weatherproofing; by the editors of Time-Life Books. Time-Life Bks. 1977 c1976 128p il (Home repair and improvement) $15.93 **693.8**

1. Insulation (Heat) 2. Houses—Maintenance and repair
First published 1976. Second printing revised 1977
This volume discusses how to protect houses against invasion by unwanted air and water, heat and cold, and animals and insects

694   Wood construction. Carpentry

Ball, John E.
Carpenters and builders library. Audel 4v il set $89.95   **694**

1. Carpentry 2. Building
Also available individual volumes ea $21.95
First published 1923 under the authorship of Frank D. Graham with title: Audels carpenters and builders guide. (6th edition 1991) Periodically revised

v1 Tools, steel square, joinery; v2 Builders math, plans specifications; v3 Layouts, foundations, framing; v4 Millwork, power tools, painting

A practical illustrated trade assistant on modern construction for carpenters, joiners, builders, mechanics and all wood workers

Bollinger, Don
Hardwood floors; laying, sanding and finishing. Taunton Press 1990 137p il $19.95 **694**

1. Floors
ISBN 0-942391-62-4   LC 90-11065

The author "addresses the three types of flooring: strip, plank, and parquet—covering such topics as estimating costs; selecting wood types and grades; preparing the underlayment; planning the layout; sanding; and applying various finishes." Libr J

Includes bibliographic references

Burch, Monte, 1943-
Complete guide to building log homes; drawings by Richard J. Meyer and Lloyd P. Birmingham. Sterling 1990 406p il pa $18.95   **694**

1. Log cabins and houses
ISBN 0-8069-7486-9   LC 90-39505

This offers instruction in building log cabins including purchasing the land, making floor plans, shaping the logs, and construction techniques

696   Utilities

Almond, Joseph P.
The plumbers handbook. Macmillan il pa $12.95   **696**

1. Plumbing
"An Audel book"
First published 1971 by Harper Print Co. (8th edition 1991 revised by Rex Miller) Periodically revised
This guide includes information about plumbing and pipefitting for everyone from apprentices to experts

Armpriester, Kate, 1947-
Do your own plumbing; [by] K.E. Armpriester. Sterling 1991 128p il pa $12.95 **696**

1. Plumbing
ISBN 0-8069-8478-3   LC 91-19728
Also available from Borgo Press
First published 1987 by Popular Science Books
This volume "starts with a description of the basic system—water-supply pipes, drain-waste system, and venting. Tools and materials and basic plumbing skills are explained. The author also devotes separate chapters to planning and installing new plumbing in bathrooms, kitchens, utility rooms and basements, and outdoors." Booklist

McConnell, Charles

The home plumbing handbook; by Charles N. McConnell. 4th ed. Macmillan 1992 206p il pa $17 **696**

1. Plumbing
ISBN 0-02-079651-X   LC 92-7382

"An Audel book"

First published 1976 by Audel

"Aided by the book's many illustrations and manufacturers instructions, the home plumber is guided through the most basic plumbing procedures. All techniques and products conform to the latest changes in codes and regulations." Publisher's note

697 Heating, ventilating, air-conditioning engineering

Brumbaugh, James E.

Heating, ventilating, and air conditioning library. 2nd rev ed. Macmillan 1986 3v set $53.95 **697**

1. Heating 2. Ventilation 3. Air conditioning
LC 86-8735

Also available individual volumes ea $26

First published 1976

At head of title: Audel

v1 Heating fundamentals, furnaces, boilers, boiler conversions; v2 Oil, gas, and coal burners, controls, ducts, piping, valves; v3 Radiant heating, water heaters, ventilation, air conditioning, heat pumps, air cleaners

Home heating & cooling. Time-Life Bks. 1988 144p il (Fix it yourself) $18.60 **697**

1. Heating 2. Air conditioning   LC 88-14121

Discusses the repair of burners, furnaces, heaters, heat pumps, and air conditioners. Also includes sections on tools, safety, and emergencies

Kittle, James L., 1913-

Home heating and air conditioning systems; line drawings by Gary McKinney. TAB Bks. 1990 230p il $27.95; pa $15.95 **697**

1. Houses—Heating and ventilation 2. Air conditioning
ISBN 0-8306-9257-6; 0-8306-3257-3 (pa)
LC 89-29159

A guide to the examination and repair of gas- and oil-fired furnaces, boilers, air-conditioning systems, and heat pumps. A troubleshooting chart is appended

698 Detail finishing

Moss, Roger W., 1940-

Victorian exterior decoration; how to paint your nineteenth-century American house historically; [by] Roger W. Moss and Gail Caskey Winkler. Holt & Co. 1987 117p il $29.95; pa $16.95 **698**

1. Architecture, Victorian 2. House painting
ISBN 0-8050-0376-2; 0-8050-2313-5 (pa)
LC 86-15014

"Researching painting schemes from the period, the authors show how to select authentic paints and colors from today's manufacturers with comparative charts and with numerous suggestions on what style of house requires a particular treatment. The application of these paints is also well covered." Booklist

Paint and wallpaper; by the editors of Time-Life Books. Time-Life Bks. 1980 128p il (Home repair and improvement) $15.93 **698**

1. House painting 2. Paper hanging   LC 80-114560

First published 1976

This volume discusses the methods and techniques for interior and exterior painting and the tools required. The section on wallpapering covers tool kits, removal of old paper, repair of damaged paper and specialized techniques for corners, ceilings and stairwells

Pomada, Elizabeth

How to create your own painted lady; a comprehensive guide to beautifying your Victorian home; [by] Elizabeth Pomada and Michael Larsen; line drawings by Richard Spokowski; color renderings by Carole Glosenger Design. Dutton 1989 167p il hardcover o.p. paperback available $19.95 **698**

1. House painting 2. Architecture, Victorian
ISBN 0-525-48474-4 (pa)   LC 89-50697

"This book includes information on paint selection, techniques for special effects (faux marbling, for example), equipment, interior and exterior painting, and more. Color photos and drawing illustrate the painting techniques and color plans for exteriors, and designers are given the opportunity to demonstrate and explain their own particular ideas and color and design preferences." Libr J

Includes bibliographic references

The painted ladies revisited; San Francisco's resplendent Victorians inside and out; [by] Elizabeth Pomada, Michael Larsen; photographs by Douglas Keister. Dutton 1989 160p il $29.95; pa $19.95 **698**

1. House painting 2. Architecture, Victorian
ISBN 0-525-24812-9; 0-525-48508-2 (pa)

LC 89-50696

"San Francisco is the point of reference for a further exploration of the colorist movement and its relationship to domestic, and especially Victorian, architecture. Fabulous interior and exterior shots give the reader a glimpse of the city's mix of modern, traditional, and Victorian and how they harmonize. Richly illustrated in full color, and enhanced by clear annotations, *Painted Ladies Revisited* is a natural for architectural and design collections." Libr J

Includes bibliographic references

700 THE ARTS

Nederveen Pieterse, Jan
White on black; images of Africa and blacks in Western popular culture. Yale Univ. Press 1992 259p il $35   **700**
1. Africa in art 2. Blacks in art 3. Popular culture
ISBN 0-300-05020-8   LC 91-41603
A "visual history of the development of European and American stereotypes of black people over the last two hundred years." Univ Press Books for Public and Second Sch Libr

Includes bibliographic references

Oxford illustrated encyclopedia of the arts; volume editor, John Julius Norwich. Oxford Univ. Press 1990 499p il $49.95   **700**

1. Arts—Dictionaries
ISBN 0-19-869137-8   LC 89-71125
"This arts encyclopedia is one of a series of eight volumes to be published by Oxford that in its entirety will comprise a 'complete encyclopedia of human knowledge and achievement.'. . . This volume encompasses the visual arts, music, theater, film, dance, photography, and literature." Libr J
For a fuller review see: Booklist, April 1, 1991

Schwartz, Lillian, 1927-
The computer artist's handbook; concepts, techniques, and applications; [by] Lillian F. Schwartz with Laurens R. Schwartz. Norton 1992 xxiii, 318p il $55   **700**
1. Computer art
ISBN 0-393-02795-3   LC 89-34830
The author "covers specific utilizations such as drawing, including proportion and perspective, color, animation, sound and music, video and film, and art analysis. Each section is well illustrated and aimed at users of standard personal computers as well as high-end graphic systems. Dynamic, challenging, and creative, this is one computer book that pays as much attention to the creator as to the machine." Booklist

Includes bibliography

701 Philosophy and theory

Arnheim, Rudolf
Art and visual perception; a psychology of the creative eye. new version, expanded and rev ed. University of Calif. Press 1974 508p il $37.50; pa $14.95   **701**
1. Art—Psychology 2. Perception
ISBN 0-520-02327-7; 0-520-02613-6 (pa)
First published 1954
"The concepts of gestalt psychology form the basis for Arnheim's analysis of the visual perception of art. . . . There is [an] . . . attempt to define major variables in visual art in terms of a limited number of basic principles of perception and judgment." Choice
"A unique and highly readable contribution to aesthetics, beautifully produced." J Aesthet Art Crit

Barzun, Jacques, 1907-
The use and abuse of art. Princeton Univ. Press 1974 150p hardcover o.p. paperback available $9.95   **701**
1. Arts
ISBN 0-691-01804-9 (pa)
"Bollingen series"
"The A. W. Mellon lectures in the fine arts, 1973. The National Gallery of Art, Washington, D.C."
This volume presents the "author's less-than-sanguine view of the state of modern art—chiefly the visual arts, but literature and music as well." Publ Wkly

Canaday, John Edwin, 1907-1985
What is art? an introduction to painting, sculpture, and architecture; [by] John Canaday. Knopf 1980 386p il o.p.; McGraw-Hill reprint available $44.50   **701**
1. Art 2. Art appreciation
ISBN 0-07-554329-X   LC 79-23256
"A John L. Hochmann book"
"Updated and expanded from 'The Metropolitan Seminars in Art,' Canaday's series of 12 monographs on the appreciation of painting that was published by the Metropolitan Museum of Art in 1958, this book discusses . . . historical, stylistic, and technical categories of art." Christ Sci Monit
"Of the 450 photos, 150 are well-reproduced color. Of special interest are descriptions of such techniques as egg tempera, fresco painting, etc. " Libr J

702.5 Art—Directories

American art directory. Bowker il $186   **702.5**
1. Art—Directories 2. Art, American—Directories 3. Art, Canadian—Directories
ISSN 0065-6968
Companion volume to Who's who in American art, entered in class 709.2
Biennial. First published 1899 with title: American art annual
"Describes activities of some 2500 U.S. and Canadian museums and art organizations, and 1700 art schools, arranged alphabetically by state, province, and city. Museum listings include names of key officials and data on special collections, exhibitions, activities, and publications. Corporations with art holdings on public view are included in the museum section. Name of head, registration data, majors, degrees granted, and courses are shown for the art schools. Other sections list art magazines, newspapers with art critics, and other sources of information." Ref Sources for Small & Medium-sized Libr. 5th edition

Artist's market. Writer's Digest Bks. il $22.95   **702.5**
1. Art—Marketing—Directories
ISSN 0161-0546
Annual. First published 1974
"Listings of places where art can be sold and exhibited include brokers, studios, agencies, magazines, galleries, and art fairs. Each listing covers who to contact and where, how much they pay, and additional information such as shipping requirements, preparing a portfolio, etc." Ref Sources for Small & Medium-sized Libr. 5th edition

703 Art—Encyclopedias and dictionaries

Encyclopedia of world art. McGraw-Hill; [distributed by] Heraty & Assocs. 1959-1968 15v + 2 supplementary volumes il maps apply to Heraty & Assocs. for price and availability   **703**

1. Art—Dictionaries

Volume 16 supplement, published 1983 has title: World art in our time; volume 17 published 1987

"Survey containing signed articles with extensive bibliographies. This definitive English-language encyclopedia of art embraces architecture, sculpture, painting, and the minor arts. There are numerous cross-references and many illustrations. Volume 15 of the set is a detailed index. Volumes 16 and 17 are updating supplements and can be used independently." Ref Sources for Small & Medium-sized Libr. 5th edition

The **Oxford** companion to art; edited by Harold Osborne. Oxford Univ. Press 1970 1277p il $49.95   **703**

1. Art—Dictionaries 2. Artists—Dictionaries
ISBN 0-19-866107-X

"Articles of varying lengths on the visual arts, designed for the nonspecialist. Handicrafts and the practical arts are not included. Most articles have a coded reference to the bibliography, which numbers about 3000 items. Numerous cross-references." Ref Books for Small & Medium-sized Libr. 5th edition

The **Oxford** dictionary of art; edited by Ian Chilvers and Harold Osborne; consultant editor, Dennis Farr. Oxford Univ. Press 1988 548p $49.95   **703**

1. Art—Dictionaries 2. Artists—Dictionaries
ISBN 0-19-866133-9   LC 88-5138

"Based on earlier Oxford Companions and revised from previous editions, this single-volume reference contains 3000 entries that discuss Western and Western-inspired art from antiquity on. . . . An easy format, accurate facts, and good cross-referencing make this a useful lexicon for the layperson." Libr J

704 Art—Special topics

Hoover, Deborah A.

Supporting yourself as an artist; a practical guide. 2nd ed. Oxford Univ. Press 1989 255p $35; pa $9.95   **704**

1. Art—Marketing 2. Arts—Finance
ISBN 0-19-505971-9; 0-19-505972-7 (pa)
     LC 88-38566

First published 1985

This guide provides information on private, corporate, and federal sources of funding for the arts. Topics covered include proposal writing, budgeting, sponsorship applications, and legal matters

704.9 Iconography

Ferguson, George

Signs & symbols in Christian art; with illustrations from paintings of the Renaissance. Oxford Univ. Press 1959 123p il hardcover o.p. paperback available $9.95   **704.9**

1. Christian art and symbolism
ISBN 0-19-501432-4 (pa)

First published 1954

The most generally and commonly recognized signs and symbols found in Renaissance religious art have been selected and illustrated

Includes bibliography

Honour, Hugh

The image of the black in Western art. [v]4: From the American Revolution to World War I. Menil Foundation 1989 1v in 2pts il ea $50   **704.9**

1. Blacks in art

Contents: pt1 Slaves and liberators (ISBN 0-939594-17-X); pt2 Black models and white myths (ISBN 0-939594-18-8)

This is a study of depictions of black people in American and European art from the eighteenth century to the early twentieth. "This volume is presented in two books. The first book focuses on images of slavery and its abolition, while the second considers blacks in other, typically exotic or orientalist, context." Libr J

This "is a thoroughly sensitive and scholarly work. It is an accessible document of careful research on a deserving topic." Christ Sci Monit

Lippard, Lucy R.

A different war: Vietnam in art. Real Comet Press 1990 131p il pa $18.95   **704.9**

1. Vietnam War, 1961-1975—Art and the war
ISBN 0-941104-43-5   LC 89-70103

Published in conjunction with a traveling exhibition organized by the Whatcom Museum of History and Art

"A collection of art from the Vietnam War created by the citizens at home and soldiers after and during the conflict. The book serves as both a catalogue for the traveling exhibition and a survey of the art of the war." SLJ

"There is little of conventional beauty but much that is moving and provocative in the pictures, and the text enters intelligently into the emotions the artworks stir." Booklist

Includes bibliographic references

McElroy, Guy C., d. 1990

Facing history; the black image in American art, 1710-1940; with an essay by Henry Louis Gates, Jr., and contributions by Janet Levine, Francis Martin, Jr., and Claudia Vess; edited by Christopher C. French. Bedford Arts Pubs. 1990 xlix, 140p il $50; pa $24.95   **704.9**

1. Blacks in art 2. Art, American
ISBN 0-938491-39-3; 0-938491-38-5 (pa)
LC 89-18007

Catalogue of an exhibition held at Corcoran Gallery of Art, January 13-March 25, 1990, and Brooklyn Museum, April 20-June 25, 1990

This work combines "essays on social history with stunning reproductions of visual images. . . . [It] examines the changes in the way blacks have been depicted—from slave and comic grotesque to worker, hero, and symbol of urban life—in works by American artists of all races." Booklist

Includes bibliographic references

705 Art—Serial publications

Art index. Wilson, H.W. service basis **705**

1. Art—Periodicals—Indexes 2. Art—Bibliography
ISSN 0004-3222

Also available on CD-ROM

First published 1930

Quarterly with bound annual cumulations

An author and subject index to more than 200 periodicals. Subjects covered include advertising art, architecture, art history, crafts, graphic arts, and interior design. Current book reviews are indexed in a separate section

"The easiest to use of the major indexes to visual arts and a basic tool for arts research." Walford. Guide to Ref Mater. 3d edition

707 Art—Education and related topics

Silberstein-Storfer, Muriel, 1923-

Doing art together; the remarkable Parent-Child Workshop of the Metropolitan Museum of Art; [by] Muriel Silberstein-Storfer with Mablen Jones; workshop photographs by Seth Joel. Simon & Schuster 1982 287p il hardcover o.p. paperback available $19.95   **707**

1. Art—Study and teaching
ISBN 0-671-43428-4 (pa)
LC 81-9418

"The author details recommended studio set-ups and materials for graduated series of projects in poster paint, paper collage, and clay, with directions in each case for presenting the projects to students of every level from age three to adult beginner." Libr J

Includes bibliography

708 Art—Galleries, museums private collections

The **American** wing at the Metropolitan Museum of Art; [by] Marshall B. Davidson and Elizabeth Stillinger. Metropolitan Mus. of Art 1985 352p il $49.50   **708**

1. Metropolitan Museum of Art (New York, N.Y.). American Wing 2. Art, American
ISBN 0-87099-309-7
LC 85-7250

A tour of the holdings of the "Metropolitan Museum's collection of American decorative arts, architecture, sculpture, and painting. . . . The objects range from a series of period rooms and architectural fragments to furniture and minor decorative arts. The fine arts of painting, drawing, and sculpture are also covered, but in less detail. . . . The museum's native treasures . . . are splendidly showcased in this photogenic presentation." Booklist

Arnold, Bruce, 1936-

The art atlas of Britain & Ireland. Viking 1991 489p il maps $50   **708**

1. Art—Museums 2. Art, British 3. Art, Irish
ISBN 0-670-81925-5

Published in association with the National Trust

This "guide describes some 550 British and Irish fine art collections open to the public, including 81 National Trust properties. . . . Three background chapters are followed by eight chapters on specific collections in geographical arrangement." Choice

"One truly sumptuous feature of this work is that all reproductions are in good quality color. An excellent purchase for public libraries." Libr J

Eisler, Colin T.

Paintings in the Hermitage; by Colin Eisler; introduction by B. B. Piotrovsky and V. A. Souslov. Stewart, Tabori & Chang 1990 653p il $95   **708**

1. Hermitage (Saint Petersburg, Russia)
ISBN 1-55670-159-4
LC 90-34419

This work "includes well over 600 color plates. . . . After a brief chapter on the growth of the collections, seven lengthy and heavily illustrated essays follow. Their subjects are the golden ages, the Bible and the saints, landscape and seascape, domestic interiors, portrait painting, genre painting and still life." N Y Times Book Rev

Includes bibliographic references

Garrett, Robert, 1949-

New York's great art museums; tours of the permanent collections. Chelsea Green 1988 235p il $15.95   **708**

1. Art—Museums 2. Museums—New York (N.Y.)
ISBN 0-930031-13-X
LC 87-35043

A "guide to seven of New York's great museum collections. . . . Garrett has outlined self-guided tours . . . to important galleries in the Metropolitan Museum of Art, the Cloisters, the Museum of Modern Art, the Frick, the Brooklyn Museum, the Guggenheim, and the Whitney. . . . Discussions of selected works in each gallery contain art historical, biographical, and anecdotal information written in an informal, personal style. Gar-

Garrett, Robert, 1949-—*Continued*
rett's scholarship is sound. . . . His enthusiasm makes
this book an excellent companion on a first visit to any
of these museums." SLJ

Includes bibliography

Gowing, Sir Lawrence, 1918-1991
Paintings in the Louvre; introduction by
Michel Laclotte. Stewart, Tabori & Chang
1987 687p il $95   **708**
1. Musée du Louvre 2. Painting, European
ISBN 1-55670-007-5   LC 87-10221

The author "has chosen over 800 paintings from the
Louvre Museum to illustrate that great collection of European art spanning 500 years from 1350 to 1850. . .
. A brief history of the Louvre begins the volume, and
Gowing's . . . remarks on each major painter or school
serve as a kind of personal commentary on the history
of European painting." Libr J

Hibbard, Howard, 1928-1984
The Metropolitan Museum of Art. Harper
& Row 1980 592p il o.p.; Outlet reprint
available $29.99   **708**
1. Metropolitan Museum of Art (New York, N.Y.)
2. Art—History
ISBN 0-517-61201-1   LC 80-7588

"Less a history of the museum than a survey of its
wide-ranging riches [this book] reviews the museum's
holdings in chapters arranged by period of art history.
. . . The superb illustrations (605 color, 442 black and
white) are the splendor of the volume." Booklist

Includes bibliography

Masterpiece paintings from the Museum of
Fine Arts, Boston; selected by Theodore
E. Stebbins, Jr. and Peter C. Sutton; with
commentaries by the curatorial staff of the
Department of Paintings. Abrams 1986
148p il $39.95   **708**
1. Museum of Fine Arts (Boston, Mass.)
ISBN 0-8109-1424-7   LC 86-14200

"A Times Mirror book"

This volume presents reproductions of 125 paintings
in Boston's Museum of Fine Arts. Accompanied by
interpretative commentary, the paintings are arranged in
three sections, American, European, and international,
and date from 1310 to 1975

The **Museum** of Modern Art, New York;
the history and the collection; introduction
by Sam Hunter. Abrams 1984 599p il $75
         708
1. Museum of Modern Art (New York, N.Y.)
ISBN 0-8109-1308-9   LC 83-15769

Published in association with the Museum of Modern
Art

"Following a history of MOMA'a origin and development, the curators of each division highlight the holdings
and discuss the establishment and growth of their individual departments, tracing the broader artistic currents
that have helped to create the museum's total survey
of art in our own time." Booklist

National Museum of Women in the Arts.
Abrams 1987 253p il $45; pa $24.95
         708
1. National Museum of Women in the Arts (U.S.)
2. Women artists
ISBN 0-8109-1373-9; 0-940979-00-4 (pa)
       LC 86-28672

"A Times Mirror book"

This is an illustrated catalog of the National Museum
of Women in the Arts. Reproductions in color and black
and white feature works by women artists from the
Renaissance to the present

Rosenblum, Robert
Paintings in the Musée d'Orsay; foreword
by Françoise Cachin. Stewart, Tabori &
Chang 1989 686p il $95   **708**
1. Musée d'Orsay (Paris, France) 2. Painting, French
3. Painting, Modern—1800-1899 (19th century)
ISBN 1-55670-099-7   LC 89-11338

The author describes the paintings at the Paris
museum of nineteenth-century French art. Some eight
hundred color illustrations are included

"Rosenblum's knowledgeable commentaries place the
works and their creators in their social and artistic
milieu, helping us to see why certain works were praised
or criticized when first exhibited and pointing out common themes or trends." Libr J

Walker, John, 1906-
National Gallery of Art, Washington;
foreword by J. Carter Brown. rev ed.
Abrams 1984 696p il $75   **708**
1. National Gallery of Art (U.S.)
ISBN 0-8109-1370-4   LC 83-27545

First published 1964

This volume provides information on the development
of the collection and its benefactors, and includes
reproductions from the holdings

709   Art—Historical and geographic treatment

Clark, Kenneth, 1903-1983
Civilisation; a personal view. Harper &
Row 1970 c1969 359p il hardcover o.p.
paperback available $22.50   **709**
1. Art—History 2. Civilization, Occidental
ISBN 0-06-090787-8 (pa)

First published 1969 in the United Kingdom

"The text traces the emergence of human values
during crucial periods of man's history from the seventh
century. . . . Clark's interpretations of representative
paintings, sculpture, architectural masterpieces, and such
small pieces as reliquaries and manuscripts afford an
urbane review of archetypes of the past." Booklist

Gombrich, E. H. (Ernst Hans), 1909-
The story of art. Prentice-Hall il pa
$44.50   **709**
1. Art—History

First published 1950 by Phaidon Press. (15th edition
1990) Periodically revised

Gombrich, E. H. (Ernst Hans), 1909- —
Continued

The author examines artistic achievements in their historical context and considers how prevailing social, political, and economic factors may have influenced the succession and popularity of certain artistic styles

Includes bibliography

Janson, H. W. (Horst Woldemar), 1913-1982
History of art. 4th ed, revised and expanded by Anthony F. Janson. Abrams 1991 856p il maps $55   **709**
1. Art—History
ISBN 0-13-388463-5   LC 90-744
Also available from Prentice-Hall   .
First published 1962

A history of art from pre-historic cave paintings to video art. While the focus is primarily on Western art, brief discussions of Oriental, Near Eastern, Islamic, African and Latin American arts are included

Includes bibliographic references

Lippard, Lucy R.
Overlay; contemporary art and the art of prehistory. Pantheon Bks. 1983 266p il hardcover o.p. paperback available $25

709
1. Art, Modern—1900-1999 (20th century) 2. Art, Prehistoric 3. Symbolism
ISBN 0-394-71145-9 (pa)   LC 82-22331

This book "is a juxtaposition of the rock and earth forms of prehistoric Europe and North America and the work of contemporary Western artists who are motivated by a need to create art which is integrated into the fabric of contemporary society at a . . . fundamental and primal level." Choice

This "is an idiosyncratic piece of scholarship, speculative and rich in suggestion. Overlay speaks to those curious about interpreting contemporary art, as well as anyone interested in prehistoric thought, feminism, or the human relationship to nature." Libr J

Includes bibliography

709.01 Arts of nonliterate peoples, and earliest times to 499

Megaw, Ruth
Celtic art; from its beginnings to the book of Kells; [by] Ruth and Vincent Megaw. Thames & Hudson 1989 288p il maps $45; pa $24.95   **709.01**
1. Art, Celtic
ISBN 0-500-05050-3; 0-500-27585-8 (pa)
LC 88-50245

Full color photographs accompany a text that surveys artwork of Celtic origin

Walters, Anna Lee, 1946-
The spirit of native America; beauty and mysticism in American Indian art. Chronicle Bks. 1989 120p il $30; pa $16.95   **709.01**
1. Indians of North America—Art
ISBN 0-87701-651-8; 0-87701-515-5 (pa)
LC 88-31283

"Photographs of more than 250 items, part of the David T. Vernon collection of native American artifacts on display at the Grand Teton National Park. These artifacts from a variety of Indian tribes include whistles, rattles, headdresses, religious articles, baskets, clothing, and tools. Walters, in a well-written text, points out that to the people who created these objects, art and beauty were inseparable from everyday living. A moving and informative work." Booklist

Includes bibliography

709.03   Art—1500-

Canaday, John Edwin, 1907-1985
Mainstreams of modern art; [by] John Canaday. 2nd ed. Harcourt Brace Jovanovich 1981 484p il pa $44   **709.03**
1. Art, Modern 2. Art—History
ISBN 0-03-057638-5   LC 80-25696

First published 1959 by Simon & Schuster; present edition 1981 by Holt, Rinehart & Winston

This is a "history of painting and sculpture in the nineteenth century with their immediate genesis in the late eighteenth and immediate continuations in the first decades of the twentieth." Preface

Harris, Ann Sutherland
Women artists: 1550-1950; [by] Ann Sutherland Harris, Linda Nochlin. Los Angeles County Mus. of Art; Knopf 1976 368p il hardcover o.p. paperback available $24.95   **709.03**
1. Women artists 2. Art, Modern
ISBN 0-394-73326-6 (pa)

Covers "158 paintings by 83 women from 12 countries done over the past 400 years. . . . In collaboration with 15 other scholars, Harris and Nochlin provide biographical sketches of each of the artists represented in the exhibit and comment on their works. Augmented with many full-color plates and black-and-white illustrations." Booklist

Includes bibliography

Rosenblum, Robert
19th century art; painting by Robert Rosenblum, sculpture by H.W. Janson. Abrams 1984 527p il $55   **709.03**
1. Art, Modern—1800-1899 (19th century)
ISBN 0-8109-1362-3   LC 83-3882
Also available from Prentice-Hall

This "survey of 19th-century Western art views the period as a heterogeneous one, marked by reciprocal influences of art, technology, politics, economics, and literature. Coauthored by two distinguished scholars, it is a comprehensive international history that upholds recent interpretations of the period and takes a non-Francocentric approach towards major and minor artists. . . . Over 500 reproductions . . . reinforce the text." Libr J

Includes bibliographic references

709.04   Art—1900-1999

Arnason, H. Harvard
History of modern art: painting, sculpture, architecture. 3rd ed, rev and updated by Daniel Wheeler. Abrams 1986 744p il $55
709.04
1. Art, Modern
ISBN 0-8109-1097-7   LC 86-3411
Also available from Prentice-Hall
First published 1969
Chronologically arranged, with biographical sketches of individual artists
"Arnason attempts to keep abreast of every major development, school, and idiosyncratic individual who may figure in the history of art in our time. The past history of the modern movement from the late nineteenth century on is also adroitly presented. A wealth of illustrations . . . convey the visions of these artists." Booklist
Includes bibliography

Arwas, Victor
Art deco. rev ed. Abrams 1992 316p $75
709.04
1. Art deco
ISBN 0-8109-1926-5   LC 93-102875
First published 1980
The author "traces Art Deco's flowering in furniture, metal, silver, jewelry, enamel, lacquer, figurines, bronzes, sculpture, painting, posters, graphics, book illustrations, bookbinding, glass and ceramics. The extraordinary objects shown in 437 plates (340 in color) are among the finest Art Deco creations ever made." Publ Wkly

Black art ancestral legacy; the African impulse in African-American art. Abrams 1989 305p il $45
709.04
1. Black art
ISBN 0-8109-3104-4   LC 89-23743
"This catalog from the Dallas Museum of Art . . . encompasses the full spectrum of black American visual art from folk to street to fine art. With an impressive selection of illustrated objects and well-written essays and catalog entries, this book will long be the definitive word on the subject and belongs in public and academic libraries." Libr J
Includes bibliographic references

Duncan, Alastair, 1942-
American art deco. Abrams 1986 288p il $60
709.04
1. Art deco
ISBN 0-8109-1850-1   LC 86-3561
This overview of the Art deco period in the United States includes sections on furniture, architecture, painting, and decorative arts
"This book covers much ground, albeit in a generalized manner. Duncan's main contribution has been to bring together many different categories of artistic production, from architecture and painting to various decorative arts, e.g. silver, metalware, ceramics, textiles." Libr J
Includes bibliographic references

Encyclopedia of art deco; edited by Alastair Duncan. Dutton 1988 192p il $29.95
709.04
1. Art deco
ISBN 0-525-24613-4   LC 89-206285
In individual chapters, contributors to this volume discuss Art Deco architecture; sculpture; furniture and interior decoration; lighting; paintings, graphics and bookbinding; glass; ceramics; metalwork; jewelry and accessories; and textiles. Biographical entries on the artists and designers of the Art Deco style appear along the lower portion of the pages throughout the book
"An exhilarating overview of cross-pollination in the decorative arts." N Y Times Book Rev

Gordon, Donald Edward, 1931-1984
Expressionism; art and idea. Yale Univ. Press 1987 263p il hardcover o.p. paperback available $29.95
709.04
1. Expressionism (Art) 2. Art, Modern—1900-1999 (20th century)
ISBN 0-300-05026-7 (pa)   LC 86-9188
The author "delves into the movement's intellectual milieu, subject matter, style, and art criticism as well as the social and cultural traditions of its time to show how Expressionist art embodies the vanguard aesthetic of modern art. Gordon's book is . . . illustrated with 201 black-and-white illustrations and 25 colorplates." Publisher's note
Includes bibliography

Heide, Robert, 1939-
Popular art deco; depression era style and design; [by] Robert Heide and John Gilman. Abbeville Press 1991 228p il $35   **709.04**
1. Art deco
ISBN 1-55859-030-7   LC 90-48164
"The authors track deco's origins, its burst on the American scene, and its influence on the design of everything from ashtrays to radios, graphics to furniture, and, moving into the grand scale, skyscrapers to trains. Lively commentary accompanies excellent illustrations." Booklist
Includes bibliographic references

Hughes, Robert
The shock of the new. rev ed. Knopf 1991 444p il pa $24.95
709.04
1. Art, Modern
ISBN 0-679-72876-7   LC 89-43355
First published 1980 in the United Kingdom
Originally based on a BBC television series, this survey of vanguard art covers the last one hundred years and concludes with a chapter on the 1980s
Includes bibliography

Livingstone, Marco
Pop art: a continuing history. Abrams 1990 271p il $49.50
709.04
1. Pop art
ISBN 0-8109-3707-7   LC 90-99

Livingstone, Marco—*Continued*
With 300 color plates this volume chronicles the work of 130 artists of the Pop Art movement, including Jasper Johns, Robert Rauschenberg, Andy Warhol, and Roy Lichtenstein
"Recommended as the best single historical survey on Pop Art." Libr J
Includes bibliography

Lucie-Smith, Edward, 1933-
Art in the seventies. Cornell Univ. Press 1980 128p il $39.95; pa $17.95   **709.04**
1. Art, Modern—1900-1999 (20th century)
ISBN 0-8014-1328-1; 0-8014-9194-0 (pa) LC 80-7463
"A Phaidon book"
This volume contains "essays, international in scope, on topics ranging from pattern painting to high tech. . . . [Some essays deal with] feminist, political, earth, and fetish art." Libr J
Includes bibliography

Making their mark; women artists move into the mainstream, 1970-85; Randy Rosen, Catherine C. Brawer [compilers] Abbeville Press 1988 300p il $59.95; pa $29.95   **709.04**
1. Women artists 2. Art, Modern—1900-1999 (20th century)
ISBN 0-89659-958-2; 1-55859-161-3 (pa)
LC 88-22261
Catalog of an exhibition held at the Cincinnati Art Museum and other museums
This "volume celebrates and documents the art made by 87 contemporary American women artists. . . . While the heart of the book is the almost 200 illustrations, 70 in color, the essays, written by critics and art historians . . . place the work in a social and historical context." Booklist
Includes bibliography

Modern art: impressionism to post-modernism; edited by David Britt. Little, Brown 1989 416p il $35   **709.04**
1. Art, Modern
ISBN 0-8212-1764-X   LC 89-12103
"A Bulfinch Press book"
"An introduction to the innovations of modern art. Prepared by a team of art historians, this book addresses the lay reader looking for comprehensive treatment of all the major developments." Libr J
Includes bibliography

The **Oxford** companion to twentieth-century art; edited by Harold Osborne. Oxford Univ. Press 1981 656p il $49.95; pa $22.50   **709.04**
1. Art, Modern—1900-1999 (20th century)—Dictionaries 2. Artists
ISBN 0-19-866119-3; 0-19-282076-1 (pa)
LC 82-126560
This book "sketches the careers of hundreds of artists who have done their most significant work between 1900 and 1975. International in scope, it includes articles on movements and on the state of art during the twentieth century in various countries and regions." Wilson Libr Bull

Russell, John, 1919-
The meanings of modern art. rev ed. Museum of Modern Art; HarperCollins Pubs. 1992 473p il $50; pa $30   **709.04**
1. Art, Modern
ISBN 0-06-438496-9; 0-06-430165-6 (pa)
First published in 12 parts, 1974-1975
This survey of modern art discusses the major movements and major artists from the 1860s through the 1980s. Many color plates appear throughout
Includes bibliography

Watson, Peter, 1943-
From Manet to Manhattan; the rise of the modern art market. Random House 1992 xxviii, 558p il $35   **709.04**
1. Art—Collectors and collecting
ISBN 0-679-40472-4   LC 92-5138
An "overview of the development of the art market from the 1880s to the present. It begins with a behind-the-scenes description of the sale of Vincent Van Gogh's *Portrait of Dr. Gachet* at Christie's in 1990 for $82.5 million, and ends with an appendix that lists the record prices set for works of art from 1715 to *Dr. Gachet*. In between is . . . [an] account of the world of auction houses, art collectors, and art dealers." Choice
"Watson's entertaining and expert synthesis and analysis of heretofore widely scattered information greatly enhance our understanding of the mercurial business of art." Booklist
Includes bibliographic references

Yenawine, Philip
How to look at modern art. Abrams 1991 160p il $19.95   **709.04**
1. Art, Modern—1900-1999 (20th century) 2. Art appreciation
ISBN 0-8109-2485-4   LC 91-10152
The author "provides accessible guidelines for deriving meaning from an artwork without knowing any biographical or philosophical data about its creator. Focusing primarily 'on paintings and other two-dimensional art,' the author breaks the act of observation down into five categories: 'physical properties, subject, illusionary and formal properties, and viewer perspectives,' giving examples relevant to each category. . . . This volume offers art neophytes an engaging entry to the fundamental methods of perceiving." Publ Wkly
Includes bibliographic references

709.1   Art—Treatment by areas, regions, places in general

Ettinghausen, Richard
The art and architecture of Islam: 650-1250; [by] Richard Ettinghausen and Oleg Grabar. Penguin Bks. 1987 448p il maps (Pelican history of art) o.p.; Yale Univ. Press paperback available $25 **709.1**
1. Art, Islamic
ISBN 0-300-05330-4 (pa)   LC 86-62813
Presents the decorative arts and architecture created during the spread of Islam through the Middle East
Includes bibliography

709.2   Biographies of artists

Collective biographies

Beckett, Wendy
Contemporary women artists. Universe
Bks. 1988 127p il $24.95   **709.2**
1. Women artists 2. Art, Modern—1900-1999 (20th
century)
ISBN 0-87663-691-1   LC 88-4413
"Brief, perceptive observations introduce the work of
a selection of contemporary women artists, whose styles
run the gamut from realistic to constructivist." Booklist
Includes bibliographies

Cummings, Paul, 1933-
Dictionary of contemporary American
artists. St. Martin's Press il $75   **709.2**
1. Artists, American—Dictionaries
First published 1966. (6th edition in preparation)
Periodically revised
"Information on over 900 artists is provided, giving
education, teaching positions, awards, dealers, exhibitions,
collections, addresses, and sources for further information." Ref Sources for Small & Medium-sized Libr. 5th
edition

Fielding, Mantle, 1865-1941
Mantle Fielding's dictionary of American
painters, sculptors & engravers; edited by
Glen B. Opitz. 2nd newly rev enl &
updated ed. Apollo Bk. 1986 1081p $95
     709.2
1. Artists, American—Dictionaries
ISBN 0-938290-04-5   LC 83-179817
First published privately 1926 in a limited edition
Presents concise biographies of over twelve thousand
American artists of all periods, primarily late 19th and
early 20th century artists. Each biographical entry gives
essential facts of the artist's life and work including date
and place of birth, exhibitions, commissions, awards,
memberships and studies

Garb, Tamar
Women impressionists. Rizzoli Int. Publs.
1986 78p il pa $19.95   **709.2**
1. Women artists 2. Impressionism (Art)
ISBN 0-8478-0757-6   LC 86-42733
The author "examines the lives and work of late 19th
century artists Marie Bracquemond, Mary Cassatt, Eva
Gonzalès and Berthe Morisot. She places the artists into
the context of their times, highlighting their family and
social histories, their educational backgrounds, their circles of friends and colleagues and the limitations imposed
on each by being female. Illustrated by 32 excellent color
plates and several black-and-white reproductions." Publ
Wkly
Includes bibliography

Havlice, Patricia Pate
Index to artistic biography. Scarecrow
Press 1973 2v set $87.50   **709.2**
1. Artists—Indexes
ISBN 0-8108-0540-5
Supplementary volume (published 1981) available for
$67.50 (ISBN 0-8108-1446-3)
The first two volumes list some 70,000 artists'
biographies found in sixty-four reference works. The
supplement covers seventy titles and lists around 47,000
names

Munro, Eleanor C., 1928-
Originals: American women artists; [by]
Eleanor Munro. Simon & Schuster 1979
528p il hardcover o.p. paperback available
$19   **709.2**
1. Women artists 2. Artists, American
ISBN 0-671-42812-8 (pa)   LC 78-31814
An outgrowth of the television series "The originals/
Women in Art" produced by WNET/Thirteen
"In studies of 34 artists, from Cassatt and O'Keeffe
to women working in the Seventies, Munro uses the
artists' lives to illuminate their work, drawing on secondary sources for the earlier generation and interviews for
the later. . . . Munro's thesis is that women, because
they are excluded from the male bonding of bistros and
studios, have tended to be originals." Libr J
Includes bibliography

Petteys, Chris, 1927-
Dictionary of women artists; an
international dictionary of women artists
born before 1900; [by] Chris Petteys, with
the assistance of Hazel Gustow, Ferris Olin,
Verna Ritchie. Hall, G.K. & Co. 1985 851p
il $75   **709.2**
1. Women artists—Dictionaries
ISBN 0-8161-8456-9   LC 84-22511
Includes "over 21,000 . . . painters, sculptors, print-
makers, and illustrators. . . . Entries provide full name,
married name, pseudonym (with cross-references); date
and place of birth; media; location of activity; related
artist (family); education; exhibitions; and references. .
. . A valuable tool for a wide range of uses, from quick
references to scholarly investigation." Libr J

Rosenak, Chuck
Museum of American Folk Art
encyclopedia of twentieth-century American
folk art and artists; [by] Chuck and Jan
Rosenak; contributors, Robert Bishop,
Barbara Cate, Lee Kogan. Abbeville Press
1990 416p il $75   **709.2**
1. Artists, American 2. Folk art, American
ISBN 1-55859-041-2   LC 90-43923
This volume presents "over 250 contemporary folk
artists and their art (paintings and sculpture). After basic
biographical data, the entries describe the artist's cultural
background, subjects and sources, materials and techniques, and formal recognition. Color illustrations provide
a representative example of each person's art." Am Libr
This "is an authoritative and handsome reference
work." Booklist

Who's who in American art. Bowker $176
709.2

1. Artists, American—Dictionaries

Companion volume to American art directory, entered in class 702.5

Biennial. First published 1936 by American Federation of Arts as part of American art annual

"Profiles representatives of all segments of the art world including artists, administrators, and librarians. Entries give vital statistics, professional education and training, commissions and exhibitions, and membership in art societies. Includes geographic and professional classification indexes and cumulative necrology." N Y Public Libr Book of How & Where to Look It Up

Who's who in art. Art Trade Press; [distributed by] Gale Res. $105   **709.2**

1. Artists, British—Dictionaries

Biennial. First published 1927. Subtitle varies

"Includes artists, designers, craftsmen, critics, writers, teachers, collectors, and curators, with appendixes of monograms and signatures, and obituary. British names predominate." Sheehy. Guide to Ref Books. 10th edition

World artists, 1950-1980; an H.W. Wilson biographical dictionary; [edited] by Claude Marks. Wilson, H.W. 1984 912p il $80
709.2

1. Artists—Dictionaries
ISBN 0-8242-0707-6   LC 84-13152

"The 312 painters, sculptors, and graphic artists in this biographical dictionary were selected from the outstanding artistic figures in the US, Europe, and Latin America. . . . The biographical information includes family, working background, and aesthetic beliefs. There are many quotations from the artist and from critics. Also included is a list of significant collections and a bibliography." Choice

World artists, 1980-1990; an H.W. Wilson biographical dictionary; edited by Claude Marks. Wilson, H.W. 1991 413p il $52
709.2

1. Artists—Dictionaries
ISBN 0-8242-0827-7   LC 91-13183

This volume contains brief biographies of 118 artists from around the world who have been influential in the 1980's

Individual biographies

Adams, Ansel, 1902-1984

Adams, Ansel. Ansel Adams, an autobiography; [by] Ansel Adams with Mary Street Alinder. Little, Brown 1985 400p il $60; pa $39.95   **709.2**
ISBN 0-8212-1596-5; 0-8212-1787-9 (pa) LC 85-8135

"A New York Graphic Society book"

The American photographer's "autobiography moves from family reminiscences to his experiences with Edward Weston, Paul Strand, Dorothea Lange, the Newhalls, Georgia O'Keefe, Steiglitz, and Steichen, giving Adams's perspective on developments in the visual arts." Libr J

"Consisting of an almost perfect mix of interacting text and images, including some unexpected candid snapshops of Adams himself, this work is an outstanding

document of 20th-century American photography." Choice

Includes bibliography

Arbus, Diane, 1923-1971

Bosworth, Patricia. Diane Arbus; a biography. Knopf 1984 366p il o.p.; Avon Bks. paperback available $10.95   **709.2**
ISBN 0-380-69927-3 (pa)   LC 84-737

"A Park Avenue princess, [Diane Arbus] grew up to make freaks and misfits the subject of her art. Successfully teamed with her husband in fashion photography, she broke away to the rebellious new ground of 60's photo-journalism. Then, well en route to the status of legend for her haunting camera confrontations, she committed suicide at the age of 48." N Y Times Book Rev

The author "conveys both the beauty and charm that enchanted and enthralled Arbus' friends and the unsettling depression that distanced Arbus from many other people. Unfortunately, there are no Arbus photographs among the volume's illustrations; Bosworth's is an unauthorized biography, but an indispensable and authoritative one." Booklist

Beaton, Sir Cecil, 1904-1980

Vickers, Hugo. Cecil Beaton; a biography. Little, Brown 1986 c1985 xxix, 656p il o.p.; Fine, D.I. paperback available $12.95
709.2

ISBN 1-55611-021-9 (pa)   LC 86-3035

Known primarily for his photography, "Beaton also achieved fame as an Oscar-winning costume and set designer, illustrator, portraitist, writer, and court photographer. Vickers looks closely at Beaton's several great loves, including his years with Greta Garbo, as well as his failure to become a playwright, his greatest dream." Libr J

"Beaton comes alive as Vickers sifts through the wealth of documentation and re-creates a fascinating life." Best Sellers

Includes bibliographic references

Benton, Thomas Hart, 1889-1975

Adams, Henry. Thomas Hart Benton; an American original. Knopf 1989 357p il $60
709.2

ISBN 0-394-57153-3   LC 88-30347

"Noted muralist, regionalist painter, art theorist, instructor of Jackson Pollock, and controversial figure in the world of art and politics, Benton (1889-1975) has received relatively little attention from art historians. In overall format and tone, this . . . biography is aimed at a popular audience. Yet it also contains academic discussions of both abstract and realist art, and nearly half the 340 illustrations are handsome color plates." Libr J

Berenson, Bernard, 1865-1959

Samuels, Ernest. Bernard Berenson; the making of a connoisseur. Belknap Press 1979 477p il hardcover o.p. paperback available $14.95   **709.2**
ISBN 0-674-06777-0 (pa)   LC 78-26748

"Samuels focuses on the first four decades of the long life of the world-famous art critic and writer, from his poor Lithuanian childhood to the years of his elegant

Berenson, Bernard, 1865-1959—*Continued*
Villa I Tatti near Florence and friendship with notables: Santayana, William James, Bertrand Russell, Gertrude Stein, and patroness Mrs. Jack Gardner. Archival materials, letters, and diaries of Mary Smith Costelloe, Berenson's wife, enrich the book and present vivid portraits of both subject and wife." Libr J

Bourke-White, Margaret, 1904-1971
Goldberg, Vicki. Margaret Bourke-White; a biography. Harper & Row 1986 426p il o.p.; Addison-Wesley paperback available $14.38   **709.2**
ISBN 0-201-09819-9 (pa)   LC 85-45199
"In recounting Bourke-White's achievements in a man's field as the first woman photojournalist accredited to the U.S. armed forces and her frontline coverage in WW II, as well as her photos of the liberation of Buchenwald, the partition of India, the Korean War, etc., this . . . biography portrays a brave, dramatic and oddly vulnerable woman." Publ Wkly

Brancusi, Constantin, 1876-1957
Shanes, Eric. Constantin Brancusi. Abbeville Press 1989 128p il (Modern masters ser) $29.95; pa $19.95   **709.2**
ISBN 0-89659-924-8; 0-89659-929-9 (pa) LC 88-7359
The author treats Brancusi's "works thematically, dividing them into categories, following their chronological development and illustrating his analysis with his own photographs of the sculptures." Publ Wkly
Includes bibliography

Cassatt, Mary, 1844-1926
Hale, Nancy. Mary Cassatt; foreword by Eleanor Munro. Doubleday 1975 xxxiii, 333p il o.p.; Addison-Wesley paperback available $14.38   **709.2**
ISBN 0-201-13305-9 (pa)
"The influences shaping Cassatt's life and painting career are examined: membership within a close family, the productive atmosphere the American-born colleague of the French Impressionists found in Paris and Europe, a complex relationship with Edgar Degas, interests in Japanese and ancient Egyptian Art, and—of significance in view of the period and field in which she worked—her femaleness." Booklist
The author "has produced a splendid book; it is beautifully illustrated and contains an extensive bibliography." Best Sellers

Cellini, Benvenuto, 1500-1571
Pope-Hennessy, Sir John. Cellini; principal photography by David Finn; additional photography by Takashi Okamura and others. Abbeville Press 1985 324p il $95   **709.2**
ISBN 0-89659-453-X   LC 85-6111
In this "biographical and critical study . . . the author correlates the sculptor's account of his own life with contemporary evidence to produce a . . . portrait of Cellini and his age." Booklist
"Not only is [this book] a continual excitement to read, but it offers an esthetic adventure of the first order." N Y Times Book Rev

Cézanne, Paul, 1839-1906
Rewald, John. Cézanne; a biography. Abrams 1986 288p il $75; pa $34.98   **709.2**
ISBN 0-8109-0775-5; 0-8109-8100-9 (pa) LC 86-1017
This biography of the French painter is a revised and expanded version of the author's 1936 Sorbonne doctoral dissertation. An English translation was published in 1948 by Simon & Schuster under the title: Paul Cézanne: a biography
"The artist's character is revealed in his own words and in those of his friends . . . making Cézanne accessible in a way simple narrative cannot. Adding greatly to our understanding of Cézanne's development as a painter are the 270 illustrations." Libr J
Includes bibliography

Chagall, Marc, 1887-1985
Kagan, Andrew. Marc Chagall. Abbeville Press 1989 128p il (Modern masters ser) $29.95; pa $19.95   **709.2**
ISBN 0-89659-932-9; 0-89659-935-3 (pa) LC 89-6693
This illustrated biography of the Russian Jewish artist explores his paintings, graphics, mosaics, tapestries, and stained glass works. A biochronology and a selected exhibitions list are appended
Includes bibliography

Dalí, Salvador, 1904-1989
Secrest, Meryle. Salvador Dalí. Dutton 1986 307p il hardcover o.p. paperback available $9.95   **709.2**
ISBN 0-525-48334-9 (pa)   LC 86-8859
This biography of the Spanish artist "draws on interviews with the artist's friends and relatives as well as archival research." Publ Wkly
The author's "lucid account of the artist's neurotic and chaotic life is both riveting and depressing. Dalí seems to have been mad from birth and was a tremendously moody, phobic, and willful child. Secrest does a thorough, jargon-free job of identifying his fears and obsessions as expressed in his paintings and of chronicling his involvement and break with the surrealists." Booklist
Includes bibliography

De Kooning, Willem, 1904-
Waldman, Diane. Willem de Kooning. Abrams 1988 156p il (Lib. of American art) $39.95   **709.2**
ISBN 0-8109-1134-5   LC 87-1385
Published in association with the National Museum of American Art, Smithsonian Institution
The author "traces the artist's life and career from his humble origins in Rotterdam to his triumphant rise as one of the major figures in American art of the 20th century. . . . [This volume offers a] critical essay and a selection of the artist's most important work, much of it reproduced in full color." Publisher's note
Includes bibliography

Dufy, Raoul, 1877-1953

Perez-Tibi, Dora. Dufy. Abrams 1989 335p il $75 **709.2**

ISBN 0-8109-1147-7   LC 89-17517

With its "reproductions of paintings and murals, abstract compositions for fabric design, furniture, ceramics, and especially set designs, the book fulfills the most extravagant wishes of Dufy admirers while offering a splendid introduction for the uninitiated." Choice

Includes bibliographic references

Dürer, Albrecht, 1471-1528

Hutchison, Jane Campbell. Albrecht Dürer; a biography. Princeton Univ. Press 1990 247p il maps $35; pa $12.95 **709.2**

ISBN 0-691-03978-X; 0-691-00297-5 (pa)
LC 89-28971

This "biography illuminates the life of one of the world's true artistic geniuses. . . . The text follows the talented young artist from his childhood and apprenticeship as both a goldsmith and painter in Nuremberg to being a well-traveled journeyman, printmaker, publisher, author, and painter. It closes with a description of the artistic and social impact Dürer had on the Northern Renaissance and future artists." Libr J

"This is a book that presupposes the reader's familiarity with Dürer's art. Most libraries will want to find a place for the book in their collection on Dürer." Choice

Includes bibliographic references

Eakins, Thomas, 1844-1916

Goodrich, Lloyd. Thomas Eakins. Harvard Univ. Press 1982 2v il (Ailsa Mellon Bruce studies in American art) set $90 **709.2**

ISBN 0-674-88490-6   LC 82-12170

Published for the National Gallery of Art

A revised and updated version of Thomas Eakins, his life and work, published 1933 by the Whitney Museum of American Art

The author has combined a chronological survey with thematic treatments of topics such as portraiture and sculpture

"The reader leaves these volumes with the feeling of a personal acquaintance with both Eakins and his art. Goodrich's access to primary sources, especially interviews with family members, friends, and former students of Eakins, plays an important part in this feeling of immediacy. . . . He has created a balanced and in-depth study, providing scholars with a rich mine of ideas for future research." Libr J

Escher, M. C. (Maurits Cornelis), 1898-1972

M. C. Escher; his life and complete graphic work; with a fully illustrated catalogue; by F.H. Bool [et al.]; with essays by Bruno Ernst, M.C. Escher; edited by J.L. Locher. Abrams 1982 349p il $65; pa $29.98 **709.2**

1. Graphic arts
ISBN 0-8109-0858-1; 0-8109-8113-0 (pa)
LC 81-69954

Original Dutch edition, 1981

This book about the Dutch graphic artist "begins with a lengthy biographical essay that draws on the journal of Escher's father, Escher's own letters and diaries, and accounts of Escher's eldest son. A lavish series of photographs and reproductions of drawings and prints accompanies the text and supplements the complete catalog of Escher's graphic works that follows. An essay by Bruno Ernst mathematically analyzes the main subjects of Escher's work, while the artist's own essay, 'The Regular Division of the Plane,' is also reprinted." Booklist

Includes bibliography

Frankenthaler, Helen, 1928-

Elderfield, John. Frankenthaler. Abrams 1987 448p il $150 **709.2**

ISBN 0-8109-0916-2   LC 87-1118

This is a study of the life and work of American abstract artist Helen Frankenthaler

The author "writes with confidence and authority, drawing upon extensive interviews with the artist. With its 262 color and 138 black-and-white illustrations, detailed chronologies, and lengthy bibliography, this superb critical account is highly recommended." Libr J

Gauguin, Paul, 1848-1903

Thomson, Belinda. Gauguin. Thames & Hudson 1987 215p il (World of art) pa $11.95 **709.2**

ISBN 0-500-20220-6   LC 87-50203

This "covers the artist's private life and professional development in great detail and captures the dramatic appeal inherent in both these areas. Some of the controversies of Gauguin's life are also clarified with the help of newly researched material and judicious critical rethinking." Booklist

Includes bibliography

Giacometti, Alberto, 1901-1966

Fletcher, Valerie J. Alberto Giacometti, 1901-1966; [by] Valerie J. Fletcher; with essays by Silvio Berthoud and Reinhold Hohl. Smithsonian Institution Press 1988 250p il $50 **709.2**

ISBN 0-87474-424-5   LC 88-42545

Published on the occasion of the exhibition Alberto Giacometti, 1901-1966, organized by the Hirshhorn Museum and Sculpture Garden, this catalog describes 105 works by the artist in the fields of sculpture, painting, and drawing

"Personal memories by Silvio Berthoud, a nephew, describe the sculptor's irony, humor, and deep interest in people and the world around him. Commentary by Fletcher is clear and concise and is beautifully organized by style, period, and medium." Choice

Includes bibliography

Gogh, Theo van, 1857-1891

Hulsker, Jan. Vincent and Theo van Gogh. See entry under Gogh, Vincent van, 1853-1890   **709.2**

Gogh, Vincent van, 1853-1890

Hulsker, Jan. Vincent and Theo van Gogh; a dual biography; James M. Miller, editor. Fuller Tech. Publs. 1990 470p il $39   **709.2**

1. Gogh, Theo van, 1857-1891
ISBN 0-940537-05-2   LC 89-28907
Original Dutch edition, 1985

The author has "woven together dramatic events in the lives of the van Gogh brothers to produce an in-depth study revealing the role art played in their destinies as well as their personalities, relationships, and desires. . . . Divided into four major stages, the text focuses on their early lives, first interest in art, productive art careers, and tragic endings." Libr J

Includes bibliography

Sweetman, David. Van Gogh: his life & his art. Crown 1990 391p il $30   **709.2**
ISBN 0-517-57793-3   LC 90-32622
Also available in paperback from Simon & Schuster

"Based primarily on the correspondence of Vincent, his brother Theo, and his friends, but also incorporating recent scholarly findings and social history, the book places the artist solidly within the context of his family and his time." Libr J

Includes bibliographic references

Haring, Keith, 1958-1990

Gruen, John. Keith Haring; the authorized biography. Prentice Hall Press 1991 259p il $35   **709.2**
ISBN 0-13-516113-4   LC 90-40600
Also available in paperback from Simon & Schuster

Gruen tells the "story of Haring, from his phenomenal rise on the international art scene as graffiti artist extraordinaire . . . to his tragic death from AIDS at the age of 31. The book focuses on Haring's creative talent—including sculpture, painting, murals, and graphic art projects—and on his compulsive work habits. . . . His life and work are seen through personal and candid interviews with the artist, members of his family, friends, and celebrities." Libr J

Includes bibliographic references

Homer, Winslow, 1836-1910

Cikovsky, Nicolai. Winslow Homer; [by] Nicolai Cikovsky, Jr. Abrams 1990 156p il (Lib. of American art) $39.95   **709.2**
ISBN 0-8109-1193-0   LC 89-17839
Published in association with the National Museum of American Art, Smithsonian Institution

The author attempts "to discern how the meaning and form of Homer's art were shaped by the cultural, social, and political life of the time." Choice

Includes bibliographic references

Kahlo, Frida, 1907-1954

Herrera, Hayden. Frida: a biography of Frida Kahlo. Harper & Row 1983 507p il hardcover o.p. paperback available $20   **709.2**
ISBN 0-06-091127-1 (pa)   LC 80-8688

This biography of the Mexican painter and wife of Diego Rivera "is a mesmerizing story of radical art, romantic politics, bizarre loves and physical suffering. . . . Herrera resolves Kahlo the public figure and Kahlo the artist in a perceptive portrait of a woman who rose above a circumscribed content with a grand style." Time

Zamora, Martha. Frida Kahlo; the brush of anguish; abridged and translated by Marilyn Sode Smith. Chronicle Bks. 1990 143p il $29.95   **709.2**
ISBN 0-87701-746-8   LC 90-33874

This biography of the Mexican painter is an abridgment and translation of a title originally published in Mexico in 1987

Most "important here is the collection of 75 color plates of the artist's original works. Of interest to the initiated because they comprise largely seldom-seen works in various Mexican collections, these plates represent the best collection now available of Kahlo's work." Libr J

Includes bibliographic references

Leonardo, da Vinci, 1452-1519

Bramly, Serge. Leonardo; discovering the life of Leonardo da Vinci; translated by Siân Reynolds. HarperCollins Pubs. 1991 493p il $35   **709.2**
ISBN 0-06-016065-9   LC 90-56356
"An Edward Burlingame book"
Original French edition, 1988

In this account Bramly "sheds light on the more personal aspects of Leonardo. . . . As he follows da Vinci's often frustrating career and ever-widening sphere of inquiries, inventions, and discoveries, he also patches together overlooked clues about his private life, causing us to marvel anew at Leonardo's fertile and versatile mind while acquiring a sharper image of Leonardo the man. A richly detailed, expansive, and thoroughly enjoyable portrait." Booklist

Includes bibliography

Magritte, René, 1898-1967

Sylvester, David. Magritte; the silence of the world. Abrams 1992 352p il $75   **709.2**
ISBN 0-8109-3626-7   LC 91-41676

"Sylvester provides an in-depth portrait of Rene Magritte, a master of the surreal. . . . [This book] details Magritte's early world in Belgium; his longlife marriage; the artistic influences, especially de Chirico; his dealers and colleagues; and the impact of World War II in a well-written narrative. . . . There are 470 reproductions here, with over 340 in beautiful color." Libr J

Includes bibliographic references

Matisse, Henri

Flam, Jack D. Matisse, the man and his art, 1869-1918. Cornell Univ. Press 1986 523p il $79.50 **709.2**

ISBN 0-8014-1840-2 LC 86-4502

The author "presents a thorough and scholarly examination of the artist's life and stylistic development. Each painting is given a complete analysis, revealing Matisse's encounters with the prevailing styles and theories of art to arrive at work distinctly his own." Libr J

Includes bibliography

Gilot, Françoise. Matisse and Picasso; a friendship in art. Doubleday 1990 339p il hardcover o.p. paperback available $16 **709.2**

1. Picasso, Pablo, 1881-1973
ISBN 0-385-42241-5 (pa) LC 90-34869

In Gilot's "memoir, Matisse, whom she greatly admired as kindred soul and fellow painter, seems to be the force holding together her roller-coaster relationship with Picasso. . . . Partly a valentine to a bygone Paris, her narrative also fills in the early years of Matisse and Picasso, with telling glimpses of Colette, Giacometti, Cocteau, Braque, Gertrude Stein, Juan Gris and many others. The book is charmingly illustrated with paintings, graphics and photographs." Publ Wkly

Modigliani, Amedeo, 1884-1920

Rose, June. Modigliani, the pure bohemian. St. Martin's Press 1991 249p il $22.95 **709.2**

ISBN 0-312-06416-0 LC 91-21769

"Rose's 'romantic' biography of Italian modernist Amedeo Modigliani avoids detailed art criticism while engaging the reader in a fully lucid and documented account of his life from a bourgeois childhood in Livorno, Italy to his early death in poverty and despair. In between was a Montparnasse bohemian existence with such contemporaries as Brancusi, Picasso, and Matisse." Libr J

Includes bibliographic references

Morisot, Berthe, 1841-1895

Higonnet, Anne. Berthe Morisot. Harper & Row 1990 240p il hardcover o.p. paperback available $12.95 **709.2**

ISBN 0-06-098101-6 (pa) LC 89-45669

"An Edward Burlingame book"

In this biography of the Impressionist artist the author "argues that Morisot developed a strategy to portray 'a feminine visual culture' in an 'extremely daring unfeminine career while making minimal personal sacrifices'. . . . Overall this is a well argued and convincing study." Libr J

Includes bibliography

Nevelson, Louise, 1900-1988

Lisle, Laurie. Louise Nevelson; a passionate life. Summit Bks. 1990 352p il hardcover o.p. paperback available $12.95 **709.2**

ISBN 0-671-73187-4 (pa) LC 89-29639

"This biographical study aims to unite the two sides of American sculptor Nevelson's personality: the antic and confident grande dame familiar to her public, and the more reclusive artist who privately nurtured her doubts and conflicts over her roles as a creator, mother, and woman." Booklist

This is a "levelheaded biography. It is neither hagiographic nor snide. It is not sensational, even though the life recorded here had its tabloid moments." N Y Times Book Rev

Includes bibliographic references

O'Keeffe, Georgia, 1887-1986

Eisler, Benita. O'Keeffe and Stieglitz; an American romance. Doubleday 1991 546p il $29.50 **709.2**

1. Stieglitz, Alfred, 1864-1946
ISBN 0-385-26122-5 LC 90-46287

Also available in paperback from Penguin Bks.

"A dual biography of painter Georgia O'Keeffe and photographer Alfred Stieglitz, offering a close-up of their relationship, in and out of love, over three decades. Both personal and professional associations occupy Eisler's text." Booklist

Includes bibliographic references

Lisle, Laurie. Portrait of an artist: a biography of Georgia O'Keeffe. University of N.M. Press 1986 408p il o.p.; Washington Sq. Press paperback available $5.95 **709.2**

ISBN 0-671-60040-0 (pa) LC 86-16061

A revised and updated edition of the title first published 1980 by Seaview Books

The author "describes Georgia O'Keeffe's journey from her birth on a midwestern farm, through her controversial career as an art teacher and discovery by Alfred Steiglitz, to her eventual place at the pinnacle of American art in the twentieth century." Univ Press Books for Public Libr

Includes bibliography

Robinson, Roxana. Georgia O'Keeffe: a life. Harper & Row 1989 639p il hardcover o.p. paperback available $14 **709.2**

ISBN 0-06-092000-9 (pa) LC 89-45061

"An Edward Burlingame book"

"This biography, the first to draw on sources unavailable during O'Keeffe's lifetime—and the first to be granted her family's cooperation—offers a persuasive feminist analysis of the life and work of an iconic figure in American art. . . . [The author's] detailed, sensitive critique of O'Keeffe's work . . . alternates with an absorbing, intimate narrative of O'Keeffe's personal life." Publ Wkly

Includes bibliography

Picasso, Pablo, 1881-1973

Gilot, Françoise. Matisse and Picasso. See entry under Matisse, Henri **709.2**

Palau i Fabre, Josep. Picasso; translation by Kenneth Lyons. Rizzoli Int. Publs. 1985 21, 103p il $24.95 **709.2**

ISBN 0-8478-0652-9 LC 85-42962

Original Spanish edition, 1981

The author summarizes Picasso's life, providing illustrations from his work

"Palau i Fabre's quirky, independent reappraisal of Picasso is refreshing. . . . The one- or two-line commentaries on each plate are right on the mark." Publ Wkly

Picasso, Pablo, 1881-1973—*Continued*

Penrose, Sir Roland. Picasso: his life and work. 3rd ed. University of Calif. Press 1981 517p il hardcover o.p. paperback available $13.95   **709.2**

ISBN 0-520-04207-7 (pa)   LC 80-54015

First published 1958 by Harper

The author "has produced a painstaking, comprehensive biography . . . and, what is more, a popular biography, assuming neither knowledge of nor sympathy with twentieth-century art on the part of the reader." Times Lit Suppl [review of 1958 edition]

Includes bibliography

Richardson, John. A life of Picasso; with the collaboration of Marilyn McCully. v1: 1881-1906. Random House 1991 548p il $44.50   **709.2**

ISBN 0-394-53192-2   LC 89-42915

First volume of a projected four volume biography

"Accompanied by 675 black-and-white photographs, Richardson's carefully researched narrative patiently and insightfully traces the outlines of Picasso's first 26 years, from his precarious birth to the brink of success." Booklist

Includes bibliographic references

Stassinopoulos, Arianna. Picasso: creator and destroyer; [by] Arianna Stassinopoulos Huffington. Simon & Schuster 1988 558p il o.p.; Avon Bks. paperback available $4.95   **709.2**

ISBN 0-380-70755-1 (pa)   LC 88-11368

"The Pablo Picasso of [this] highly readable biography . . . is a not-so-sacred monster, more the destroyer than the creator of the subtitle. [The author] does, of course, provide a dutiful account of the highlights in Picasso's artistic development. . . . But little of the creative life is explored in the depth due one of the great masters of modern art. . . . This is a lively and tendentious book." N Y Times Book Rev

Includes bibliography

Pollock, Jackson, 1912-1956

Landau, Ellen G. Jackson Pollock. Abrams 1989 283p il $75   **709.2**

ISBN 0-8109-3702-6   LC 89-241

"The book situates Pollock and his achievement squarely in the social and political context of the time. Movie stars (James Dean, Marlon Brando), Beat writers (Jack Kerouac), and jazz musicians (Charlie 'Bird' Parker) are invoked, inter alia, to provide cultural analogues for 'action painting' and abstract expressionism. In addition, no corner of the artist's life is left unexamined. . . . This is an exciting book on an exciting subject. Its greatest strength lies in Landau's brilliant verbal evocations of the frenzied process of Pollock's magisterial creation." Choice

Includes bibliography

Naifeh, Steven W. Jackson Pollock: an American saga; by Steven Naifeh and Gregory White Smith. Crown 1989 934p il $29.95   **709.2**

ISBN 0-517-56084-4   LC 88-32387

Also available in paperback from HarperPerennial

The authors "take an irreverent slant on Pollock. They are clearly out to show that he was worse than the 'rebel without a cause' the media portrayed. They delve into the fury and frustration behind Pollock's outbursts and

hint that something more sinister was at work. . . . [Their] book is unquestionably readable, and it's fascinating in a voyeuristic sort of way." Christ Sci Monit

Poussin, Nicolas, 1594?-1665

Mérot, Alain. Nicolas Poussin. Abbeville Press 1990 336p il $95   **709.2**

ISBN 1-55859-120-6   LC 90-39623

"Poussin, the great classicist of the baroque period and the father of French painting, receives a fitting tribute in Mérot's monograph. The author covers the painter's career in detail, charting influences and following Poussin's development period by period. Although the author sometimes tends to analyze Poussin studies in much too scholarly a fashion for casual readers, the book nevertheless clearly defines and examines the artist's works and reputation with excellence and intelligence." Booklist

Includes bibliographic references

Rauschenberg, Robert, 1925-

Kotz, Mary Lynn. Rauschenberg, art and life. Abrams 1990 320p il $65   **709.2**

ISBN 0-8109-3752-2   LC 90-217

The author "traces the life and career of American artist Robert Rauschenberg through a narrative that investigates the various stages, developments, and experiments of his artistic life." Booklist

"Kotz has managed to compile a personalized and up-to-date biography of one of the towering geniuses of the 20th century, presenting a richly impressive portrait of the artist with several hundred illustrations, 92 of which are in color." Choice

Includes bibliographic references

Ray, Man, 1890-1976

Baldwin, Neil. Man Ray, American artist. Potter 1988 499p il o.p.; Da Capo Press paperback available $16.95   **709.2**

ISBN 0-306-80423-9 (pa)   LC 87-29181

The biography of "an influential, inventive, determined, and somewhat neglected artist. . . . Baldwin's delineation of the artist's life is fresh and affectionate. He leads his readers through the heady swirl of art and politics during the first half of the century, placing his subject in the creative society of Paris in the 1920s and offering a new perspective on that much scrutinized era. . . . On the personal side, Man Ray's close friendship with Marcel Duchamp and his active love life add spice to the story. An essential volume of art history." Booklist

Includes bibliography

Remington, Frederic, 1861-1909

Samuels, Peggy. Frederic Remington; a biography; by Peggy and Harold Samuels. Doubleday 1982 537p il o.p.; University of Tex. Press paperback available $12.95   **709.2**

ISBN 0-292-72451-9 (pa)   LC 79-6181

This is a biography of the "American artist famous for his dramatic paintings and sculpture of western scenes. As the Samuels . . . reconstruct their subject's life in vast detail, they take the stand that Remington developed from commercial illustrator to quality artist, that he became an outstanding practitioner of American impressionism, and that his early death halted his

Remington, Frederic, 1861-1909—*Continued*
considerable talent at a point of burgeoning power."
Booklist

Includes bibliography

Shapiro, Michael Edward. Frederic
Remington; the masterworks; [by Michael
Edward Shapiro, Peter H. Hassrick; with
essays by David G. McCullough, Doreen
Bolger Burke, John Seelye] Abrams 1988
271p il $35; pa $19.98   **709.2**

ISBN 0-8109-1595-2; 0-89178-032-7 (pa)

LC 87-23167

Published in association with the St. Louis Art
Museum and the Buffalo Bill Historical Center

An exhibition catalog with "essays on Remington's
contributions as magazine illustrator, easel painter, and
sculptor as well as his roles as short story writer, and
novelist. . . . A noteworthy contribution for all academic
and public libraries." Choice

Includes bibliography

Rossetti, Dante Gabriel, 1828-1882
Faxon, Alicia Craig. Dante Gabriel
Rossetti. Abbeville Press 1989 256p il $85
709.2

ISBN 0-89659-928-0   LC 88-37101

This biography of the English poet and painter is
illustrated by 265 illustrations of his work, 140 in color
The author "has concentrated on the intellectual
themes underlying Rossetti's paintings, his brilliant color
technique, his use of symbols, and the development of
his style from medieval angularity to Titianesque rotun-
dity. This is all very fine and useful for appreciating
the excellent plates." Atlantic

Includes bibliography

**Russell, Charles M. (Charles Marion), 1864-
1926**
Hassrick, Peter H. Charles M. Russell.
Abrams 1989 155p il (Lib. of American art)
$39.95   **709.2**

ISBN 0-8109-1571-5   LC 88-7391

A biographical and critical "study of the quintessential
cowboy artist. . . . Hassrick describes Russell's career
ably and verifies his reputation as a most appealing
working-man artist via 52 resplendent colorplates and
nearly as many black-and-white figures." Booklist

Includes bibliography

Seurat, Georges Pierre, 1859-1891
Rewald, John. Seurat; a biography.
Abrams 1990 248p il $75; pa $34.98
709.2

ISBN 0-8109-3814-6; 0-8109-8124-6 (pa)

LC 90-30519

First English translation by Lionel Abel published
1943 by Wittenborn & Co. with title: Georges Seurat

"This new translation of Rewald's French text . . .
includes an updated bibliography and a new series of
illustrations to accompany the author's classic commentary on the French artist. All of Seurat's major works
are reproduced in color, and many studies and sketches
for these masterpieces are also presented in an exceptional sequence of illustrations." Booklist

Stieglitz, Alfred, 1864-1946
Eisler, Benita. O'Keeffe and Stieglitz. See
entry under O'Keeffe, Georgia, 1887-1986
709.2

Stuart, Gilbert, 1755-1828
McLanathan, Richard B. K. Gilbert Stuart;
[by] Richard McLanathan. Abrams 1986
159p il (Lib. of American art) $39.95
709.2

ISBN 0-8109-1501-4   LC 86-1144

Published in association with the National Museum
of American Art, Smithsonian Institution

This is an "interpretation of Stuart's art, his life, and
his sitters and their times. It is a large, beautifully
produced book, with 51 portraits reproduced in excellent
color, 50 in black and white, plus contemporary views
of places important in Stuart's life." Choice

Includes bibliography

Velázquez, Diego, 1599-1660
Brown, Jonathan. Velazquez, painter and
courtier. Yale Univ. Press 1986 322p il $65;
pa $35   **709.2**

ISBN 0-300-03466-0; 0-300-03894-1 (pa)

LC 85-14234

"The life of the great Spanish painter Diego de Velázquez was extraordinary, and Jonathan Brown has made
it enthralling. The painter's astonishing ability to paint
directly from life manifested itself when he was still a
youth, and he quickly became not only the court painter
to King Philip IV but the master of the King's collections. . . . Read in context, the pictures, often interpreted
by critics and artists but never so well as by Mr. Brown,
mean far more than ever before." N Y Times Book Rev

Includes bibliography

Warhol, Andy, 1928?-1987
Bockris, Victor. The life and death of
Andy Warhol. Bantam Bks. 1989 392p il
$21.95; pa $14.95   **709.2**

ISBN 0-553-05708-1; 0-553-34929-5 (pa) LC 89-6856

The author provides an "interpretation of the Warhol
enigma based on interviews with family, friends and associates. Pittsburgh-born Andek Warhola is revealed as
very much a creature of his mother's suffocatingly
provincial upbringing; her naïve old-world exterior hid
a cunning and manipulative personality that shaped her
son's character, according to the author." Publ Wkly

Includes bibliography

Bourdon, David. Warhol. Abrams 1989
432p il $49.50; pa $29.95   **709.2**

ISBN 0-8109-1761-0; 0-8109-8110-6 (pa) LC 89-436

"Woven into Bourdon's very readable text are keen
observations and insights about the work and the artist.
Friendship has not blurred the critic's view of fact or
numbed his willingness to assess the relative merits of
the work. He is unfailingly careful to present opposing
viewpoints about controversial issues, yet his own perceptions are clearly articulated as an informative guide to
the complexities of Warhol's complex career." Choice

Includes bibliography

Warhol, Andy, 1928?-1987—*Continued*

Colacello, Bob. Holy terror: Andy Warhol close-up. Harper & Row 1990 514p il hardcover o.p. paperback available $12.95　　**709.2**

ISBN 0-06-092084-X (pa)　　　　LC 89-46226

"The former editor of Andy Warhol's *Interview* magazine, Colacello has an insider's story to tell. . . . His tone captures perfectly the self-obsessed philosophy that drove Warhol, his hangers-on, and the subculture of sex, drugs, parties, discos, and the New York art scene of the 1970s and early 1980s." Libr J

Ultra Violet. Famous for 15 minutes: my years with Andy Warhol. Harcourt Brace Jovanovich 1988 274p il $18.95　　**709.2**

ISBN 0-15-130201-4　　　　LC 88-24328

Also available in paperback from Avon Bks.

In this memoir the author "focuses on the infamous Factory at its peak with its regulars—Edie Sedgwick, Rod le Rod, and Viva—as well as its celebrity visitors Bob Dylan, Truman Capote, and John Lennon, among others. Fascinating reading, shocking, graphic, and entertaining." Libr J

Warhol, Andy. The Andy Warhol diaries; edited by Pat Hackett. Warner Bks. 1989 807p il $29.95; pa $19.95　　**709.2**

ISBN 0-446-51426-8; 0-446-39138-7 (pa)

LC 88-40565

The entries included in this edition of the American artist's diaries were originally "phoned in each morning (from 1976 to his death in 1987) to his associate Pat Hackett." Newsweek

"Despite their virtuoso triviality, their naïve snobbery and their incredible length, the diaries of Andy Warhol are not without a certain charm. . . . Ms. Hackett's editing, one feels, is affectionate and scrupulous, yet correctly unprotective." N Y Times Book Rev

Wyeth, Andrew, 1917-

Logsdon, Gene. Wyeth people; a portrait of Andrew Wyeth as seen by his friends and neighbors. Taylor Pub. Co. 1988 142p il $13.95　　**709.2**

ISBN 0-87833-634-6　　　　LC 88-12179

This "study of the American realist painter may attract attention as a not-too-indiscreet look at Wyeth's private life and a fond defense of his art. Logsdon has visited Wyeth territory in Maine and Pennsylvania and engaged some of the artist's friends and neighbors in conversations about the man and his life." Booklist

709.32　Ancient Egyptian art

Smith, William Stevenson, 1907-1969

The art and architecture of ancient Egypt; [by] W. Stevenson Smith. rev with additions, by William Kelly Simpson. Penguin Bks. 1981 501p il (Pelican history of art) o.p.; Yale Univ. Press paperback available $26.50　　**709.32**

1. Art, Egyptian 2. Egypt—Antiquities
ISBN 0-300-05328-2 (pa)　　　　LC 79-24561

First published 1958

Chronicles the changes in the architecture and arts throughout the civilization of ancient Egypt

Includes bibliography

709.38　Ancient Greek art

Boardman, John, 1927-

Greek art. rev ed. Praeger Pubs. 1973 252p il (World of art) o.p.; Thames & Hudson paperback available $12.95　　**709.38**

1. Art, Greek
ISBN 0-500-20194-3 (pa)

First published 1964

Partial contents: The beginnings and geometric Greece; Greece and the arts of the East and Egypt; Archaic Greek art; Classical sculpture and architecture; Hellenistic art; Selected bibliography

709.39　Art of other parts of ancient world

Frankfort, Henri, 1897-1954

The art and architecture of the ancient Orient. [4th rev impression]. Penguin Bks. 1970 456p il map (Pelican history of art) o.p.; Yale Univ. Press paperback available $25　　**709.39**

1. Art, Ancient 2. Middle East—Antiquities
ISBN 0-300-05331-2 (pa)

First published 1954 in the United Kingdom, 1955 in the United States

"This volume traces the development of ancient Near Eastern art from 3500 to 539 B.C. The first section covers Sumerian times to the late Assyrian and Neo-Babylonian periods; the second section discusses the art and architecture of Asia Minor and the Hittites, of the Levant in the second millennium B.C., of the Aramaeans and Phoenicians in Syria, and of Ancient Persia." Publisher's note

Includes bibliography

709.44　French art

Blunt, Anthony, 1907-1983

Art and architecture in France, 1500 to 1700. 4th ed. Penguin Bks. 1980 c1981 476p il (Pelican history of art) o.p.; Yale Univ. Press available $50, pa $25　　**709.44**

1. Art, French
ISBN 0-300-05313-4; 0-300-05314-2 (pa)

LC 81-189237

First published 1953

Blunt examines two centuries of French architecture, painting and sculpture, while analyzing artists such as Bellange, Callot, François Mansart and Poussin

Includes bibliography

709.45　Italian art

Andres, Glenn M.

The art of Florence; by Glenn Andres, John Hunisak, A. Richard Turner; principal photography by Takashi Okamura. Abbeville Press 1988 2v set $385　　**709.45**

1. Art, Italian 2. Art, Renaissance
ISBN 0-89659-402-5　　　　LC 83-6394

Andres, Glenn M.—*Continued*
This set "presents the art of Renaissance Florence in two beautiful, oversized volumes. Along with this visual feast comes a substantial and well-written chronological account of Florentine architecture, sculpture, and painting from 1200 to 1600. Basic historical and political background is incorporated into the text, making it informative and accessible to students and others with no prior knowledge of Italian Renaissance art or history." Libr J

Includes bibliography

Labella, Vincenzo
A season of giants: Michelangelo, Leonardo, Raphael, 1492-1508; special photography by John McWilliams. Little, Brown 1990 240p il $45   **709.45**
1. Art, Italian 2. Art, Renaissance
ISBN 0-316-85646-0   LC 90-6252

"Published in conjunction with a . . . cable television series, this lavishly illustrated study of the three leading Italian Renaissance artists examines each individual's creative development and impact on his contemporaries. A well-detailed account that will interest browsers as well as history and art students." Booklist

Wittkower, Rudolf, 1901-1971
Art and architecture in Italy, 1600 to 1750. 3rd rev ed. Penguin Bks. 1980 664p il (Pelican history of art) o.p.; Yale Univ. Press available $60, pa $27.50   **709.45**
1. Art, Italian 2. Art, Baroque
ISBN 0-300-05306-1; 0-300-05308-8 (pa)
                                      LC 80-151645
First published 1958

The author examines works produced during the Early, High, and Late Baroque periods of Italian art, covering such artists as Caravaggio, Bernini, Borromini and Cortona

Includes bibliography

709.47   Russian art

Hamilton, George Heard
The art and architecture of Russia. 3rd ed. Penguin Bks. 1983 482p il (Pelican history of art) o.p.; Yale Univ. Press available $50, pa $25   **709.47**
1. Art, Russian
ISBN 0-300-05326-6; 0-300-05327-4 (pa)
                                      LC 81-10583
First published 1954

Hamilton traces the development of Russian art from the height of the Byzantine Empire, through its flowering under Peter the Great, to contemporary work and the influence of Western European culture

Includes bibliography

709.5   Asian art

Lee, Sherman E.
A history of Far Eastern art. 4th ed. Abrams 1982 548p il maps $55   **709.5**
1. Art, Asian
ISBN 0-8109-1080-2   LC 81-3603
First published 1964
New edition in preparation

"The author's text covers in chronological order the art traditions of China, Japan, and India from 5000 B.C. to A.D. 1850 and also links these major national developments to neighboring cultures. Numerous black-and-white photographs, drawings, maps, and color plates serve as the excellent illustrations." Booklist

Includes bibliography

709.51   Chinese art

Cohen, Joan Lebold
The new Chinese painting, 1949-1986. Abrams 1987 167p il hardcover o.p. paperback available $19.95   **709.51**
1. Painting, Chinese
ISBN 0-8109-2355-6 (pa)   LC 86-22298

"This comprehensive study of modern Chinese painting covers postrevolutionary artists, particularly those active in the period following Mao's death in 1976. Cohen starts by providing useful background material on traditional Chinese ink-and-rice-paper painting, the beginnings of Western influences in 1912, and the development of Communists and social realist esthetics." Publ Wkly

Includes bibliography

Sickman, Laurence, 1906-1988
The art and architecture of China; [by] Laurence Sickman, Alexander Soper. 3rd ed. Penguin Bks. 1968 xxix, 350p il maps (Pelican history of art) o.p.; Yale Univ. Press paperback available $26.50   **709.51**
1. Art, Chinese
ISBN 0-300-05334-7 (pa)
First published 1956

The authors trace the development of painting, sculpture, and architecture from the Shang dynasty to the early twentieth century

Includes bibliography

709.52   Japanese art

Paine, Robert Treat, 1773-1811
The art and architecture of Japan; [by] Robert Treat Paine, Alexander Soper. rev ed. Penguin Bks. 1975 495p il (Pelican history of art) o.p.; Yale Univ. Press available $55, pa $26.50   **709.52**
1. Art, Japanese
ISBN 0-300-05332-0; 0-300-05333-9 (pa)
First published 1955

"Beginning in pre-Buddhist times . . . Paine and Soper explore the divergence between Japanese and Chinese standards in art and show how various cultural forces

Paine, Robert Treat, 1773-1811—*Continued*
encouraged a sensitivity to form and a simplicity of
statement that are fundamental to Japanese art."
Publisher's note

Includes bibliography

709.6   African art

Courtney-Clarke, Margaret, 1949-
African canvas; the art of West African
women; photographs and text by Margaret
Courtney-Clarke; foreword by Maya Angelou.
Rizzoli Int. Publs. 1990 204p il $60
                         709.6
1. Art, African 2. Black art 3. Women artists
ISBN 0-8478-1166-2   LC 89-24037
A photographic survey of West African women's art,
including fabric design, body painting, pottery and murals
These "photographs are vivid, radiant, poised, elegant.
. . . Suffusing both pictures and text is [the author's]
respect, at once powerful and tender, for her subjects
and their dignity, discipline and talent." N Y Times
Book Rev

Includes bibliographic references

Drewal, Henry John
Yoruba; nine centuries of African art and
thought; [by] Henry John Drewal and John
Pemberton, 3rd with Rowland Abiodun;
edited by Allen Wardwell. Abrams 1990
256p il maps $65   **709.6**
1. Art, African 2. Yoruba (African people)
ISBN 0-8109-1794-7   LC 89-22182
Also available in paperback from the Center for
African Art
"Tracing Yoruba civilization from the twelfth through
the twentieth centuries, the authors examine the Yoruba
impetus for artistic creation, the history of their various
kingdoms and empires as illustrated in their artwork, and
the survival of traditional arts in modern Yoruba
society." Booklist
This work "combines immaculate visual documentation of Yoruba art with the highest standards of scholarship." Times Lit Suppl

Includes bibliography

Gillon, Werner
A short history of African art. Facts on
File 1984 405p il $29.95   **709.6**
1. Art, African
ISBN 0-8160-0139-1   LC 84-14075
Also available in paperback from Penguin Bks.
This book "offers an extensive look at the continent's
culture from historical, geographical, and artistic viewpoints. After an opening discussion of Africa's earliest
art, Gillon approaches the subject by region and culture;
painting, sculpture, and architecture are predominant, but
body art, textiles, pottery, and jewelry are also covered."
Booklist

Includes bibliography

Vogel, Susan Mullin
Africa explores; 20th century African art;
[by] Susan Vogel; assisted by Ima Ebong;
contributions by Walter E.A. van Beek [et
al.] Prestel-Verlag; [distributed by] Neues
1991 294p il $70; pa $39.95   **709.6**
1. Art, African
ISBN 3-7913-1143-3; 0-945802-09-9 (pa)
                         LC 90-26683
"Vogel surveys and interprets the diverse creations of
African artists by sorting them into five strains, including
traditional art. . . . Each of these broad and dynamic
categories is defined by a generous sampling of art works
and essays that explore the motivations and styles of
individual artists. A unique and vigorous look at some
of the world's most varied and expressive modern art."
Booklist

Includes bibliographic references

709.72   Mexican art

Mexico: splendors of thirty centuries;
introduction by Octavio Paz. Metropolitan
Mus. of Art 1990 712p il maps $59.95;
pa $39.95   **709.72**
1. Art, Mexican 2. Indians—Art
ISBN 0-87099-595-2; 0-87099-596-0 (pa)
                         LC 90-38083
Issued in conjunction with an exhibition held at the
Metropolitan Museum of Art, the San Antonio Museum
of Art, and the Los Angeles County Museum of Art
"This book explores painting and sculpture, furniture,
textiles, and ceramics, from 1000 B.C. to the mid-20th
century." Libr J

Includes bibliographic references

709.73   American art

Beardsley, John
Hispanic art in the United States; thirty
contemporary painters & sculptors; [by] John
Beardsley, Jane Livingston; with an essay by
Octavio Paz. Abbeville Press 1987 260p il
$55   **709.73**
1. Art, Hispanic American
ISBN 0-89659-688-5   LC 86-28819
Issued in conjunction with an exhibition held at the
Museum of Fine Arts, Houston, May-Sept. 1987, and
other museums
In this introduction to Hispanic art, the authors illustrate "its wide stylistic diversity, discuss its origins,
and identify the influences that have shaped it. Paz, in
his essay, delves into the concept of identity and its
effect on Hispanic art and artists in this country. Brief
biographical sketches of 30 Hispanic painters and sculptors round out this much-needed view of Hispanic art."
Libr J

Includes bibliographies

Coe, Ralph T., 1929-
Lost and found traditions; native American art, 1965-1985; edited by Irene Gordon; photographs by Bobby Hansson. University of Wash. Press; American Federation of Arts 1986 288p il maps hardcover o.p. paperback available $24.95
709.73

1. Indians of North America—Art
ISBN 0-295-96699-8 (pa)   LC 86-70082

This is an exhibition catalog of a collection, assembled by Coe, of contemporary traditional American Indian arts, including pottery, textiles, basketry, jewelry and carvings
"The contemporary vitality of traditional Native American art is unequivocally documented with text and examples in this book. . . . The thoroughness of coverage and visual richness earn this volume the highest recommendation." Libr J

Harlem Renaissance: art of black America; introduction by Mary Schmidt Campbell; essays by David Driskell, David Levering Lewis, and Deborah Willis Ryan. Studio Mus. in Harlem; Abrams 1987 200p il $39.95
709.73

1. Black artists 2. Art, American
ISBN 0-8109-1099-3   LC 86-17229

This book "features four black artists: the sculptor Meta Warrick Fuller and the painters Aaron Douglas, Palmer Hayden and William H. Johnson. Also included are photographs . . . by James Van Der Zee." N Y Times Book Rev
"An eye-catching and eye-opening introduction to the black intelligensia who created the Harlem Renaissance of 1919-1930. . . . Black-and-white figures and color plates are plentiful and of fine quality." Choice
Includes bibliography

Kloss, William
Treasures from the National Museum of American Art. Smithsonian Institution Press 1985 254p il $42; pa $24.95   **709.73**

1. National Museum of American Art (U.S.) 2. Art, American
ISBN 0-87474-594-2; 0-87474-595-0 (pa)
          LC 85-61846

This catalog for a traveling exhibition presents reproductions of and commentary on eighty-one works of art produced from the mid 1700's to the 1970's
Includes bibliographies

Sandler, Irving, 1925-
American art of the 1960s. Harper & Row 1988 412p il hardcover o.p. paperback available $25.95   **709.73**

1. Art, American 2. Art, Modern—1900-1999 (20th century)
ISBN 0-06-430179-6 (pa)   LC 87-45662

This history of American art in the 1960s discusses the work of such artists as Frank Stella, Alex Katz, Andy Warhol, Eva Hesse, and Agnes Martin
"Mr. Sandler never puts himself forward and pushes no favorites. He saw everything, remembers everything and has done a lot of homework. . . . A good book, by a good man." N Y Times Book Rev
Includes bibliography

Scully, Vincent Joseph, 1920-
New World visions of household gods and sacred places; American art and the Metropolitan Museum of Art, 1650-1914; [by] Vincent Scully. Little, Brown 1988 183p il $35   **709.73**

1. Metropolitan Museum of Art (New York, N.Y.)
2. Art, American
ISBN 0-8212-1647-3   LC 87-37860

"A New York Graphic Society book"
"Aided by 200 color and black-and-white plates [the author] tours the Metropolitan Museum of Art's American wing, but veers off to discuss pre-Columbian temples, pueblos, town planning . . . Ashcan School painters, skyscrapers, a Robert Venturi house." Publ Wkly
This "overview is a lively, fascinating necessity for American public libraries." Booklist
Includes bibliography

Tomkins, Calvin, 1925-
Post- to neo-: the art world of the 1980's. Holt & Co. 1988 242p $19.95   **709.73**

1. Art, American 2. Art, Modern—1900-1999 (20th century)
ISBN 0-8050-0663-X   LC 88-4481

Also available in paperback from Penguin Bks.
"In these essays, mostly from 'The New Yorker,' Tomkins looks at the creators and consumers, taste makers and money makers of the contemporary art world." Libr J
"This is a valuable collection, offering many linked and historically grounded perspectives on an extremely pluralistic decade of art making and selling." Booklist

712   Landscape architecture

Better Homes and Gardens step by step landscaping; planning, planting, building. Meredith Corp. 1991 336p il $29.95
712

1. Landscape gardening 2. Landscape architecture
ISBN 0-696-01873-X   LC 90-63292

Offering "solutions for designing typical residential lots, this practical guide for the do-it-yourself landscaper also provides illustrated instructions for building garden structures and features such as garden pools. Major chapters focus on slope solutions, privacy and security, front yards, controlling views, patios and decks, service areas, and maintaining the landscape." Libr J

Brown, Emily L., 1900-
Landscaping with perennials; [by] Emily Brown; illustrated by Leslie J. Haning and Rachel Gage. Timber Press 1986 304p il $39.95   **712**

1. Perennials 2. Landscape gardening
ISBN 0-88192-063-0   LC 87-161554

This book offers information about 2,000 perennials and guidelines for their use in various settings. Sample layouts are included
"This unusual volume combines practicality, common sense, imagination, and good taste." Libr J
Includes bibliography

Cox, Jeff, 1940-
Landscaping with nature; using nature's design to plan your yard. Rodale Press 1991 344p il $26.95   712

1. Landscape gardening
ISBN 0-87857-911-7   LC 90-45938

The authors explain how to create long-lasting plantings of the most environmentally sound trees, shrubs, grasses and groundcovers

Includes bibliographic references

Frey, Susan Rademacher, 1954-
Outdoor living spaces; how to create a landscape you can use & enjoy: featuring hundreds of professional, practical design ideas; [by] Susan Rademacher Frey & Barbara W. Ellis. Rodale Press 1992 342p il $29.95   712

1. Landscape gardening
ISBN 0-87596-132-0   LC 92-17336

This book "presents case histories of ten gardens to demonstrate the process of landscape evaluation, planning and implementation of a design. The gardens range in size from a city courtyard to typical suburban lots and spacious rural properties." Libr J

Includes bibliographic references

Gallup, Barbara
The complete book of topiary; by Barbara Gallup, Deborah Reich; introduction by Rosemary Verey; illustrations by Kimble Pendleton Mead. Workman 1988 318p il pa $12.95   712

1. Ornamental plants 2. Landscape gardening
ISBN 0-89480-318-2   LC 86-40539

The authors "provide chapters on traditional designs for hedges, trees, and espalier displays, and also cover container topiary, ivy training, knot gardens, and frame making. . . . Their advice includes recommended plants, design hints, tools and supplies, and maintenance. The format is clear and readable, and the illustrations appealing. Novices and specialists will be delighted by this highly recommended book." Libr J

Griswold, Mac K.
The golden age of American gardens; proud owners, private estates, 1890-1940; [by] Mac Griswold, Eleanor Weller with research assistance by Helen E. Rollins. Abrams 1991 408p il $75   712

1. Gardens
ISBN 0-8109-3358-6   LC 91-8283

Published in association with the Garden Club of America

A "history of owners, designers, and the ultimate country retreats resulting from their collaborations. . . . Weller's compilation of rare, hand-colored lantern slides and hundreds of black-and-white historical photographs of the era are particularly noteworthy." Booklist

Includes bibliographic references

Landscaping for privacy; by the editors of Sunset books and Sunset magazine. Lane 1985 96p il pa $8.99   712

1. Landscape gardening 2. Landscape architecture
ISBN 0-376-03475-0   LC 84-82289

At head of title: Sunset

"Color photos and other illustrations show effects created by landscaping or redoing existing garden plots with the aim of cutting down on noise and other intrusions on family activities. . . . There are special sections on settings for swimming pools, hot tubs, roof gardens and other projects for urban and surburban dwellings." Publ Wkly

Landscaping illustrated; by the editors of Sunset books and Sunset magazine. Lane 1984 176p il pa $12.95   712

1. Landscape architecture 2. Landscape gardening
ISBN 0-376-03459-9   LC 83-82500

At head of title: Sunset

This book gives step-by-step instructions for planning, designing, and installing a home landscape. There are suggestions for fences, decks, outdoor structures, pools, plants, etc.

Leighton, Phebe
The new American landscape gardener; a guide to beautiful backyards & sensational surroundings; [by] Phebe Leighton and Calvin Simonds. Rodale Press 1987 344p il $21.95   712

1. Landscape gardening 2. Landscape architecture
ISBN 0-87857-672-X   LC 86-27986

This guide to home landscaping covers designing, planting, and maintaining backyard landscapes

Includes bibliography

Lerner, Joel M.
Joel M. Lerner's 101 home landscaping ideas; for every shape & size lot! HP Bks. 1988 136p il pa $9.95   712

1. Landscape architecture
ISBN 0-89586-721-4   LC 87-21258

This book "features scores of landscapes of various shapes and sizes, with much consideration given to pollution, shade, wind, traffic noises, slopes and terraces, unpleasant views, etc., as well as recreational needs. The text also includes an alphabetized list of hundreds of plants delineated by their hardiness zones." Booklist

Macunovich, Janet, 1955-
Easy garden design; 12 simple steps to creating successful gardens and landscapes. Storey Communications 1992 162p il $24.95; pa $14.95   712

1. Landscape gardening
ISBN 0-88266-792-0; 0-88266-791-2 (pa)

LC 91-58926

"A Garden Way Publishing book"

Presenting a "12-step 'recipe' for garden design, Macunovich invites readers to analyze the reasons for the garden, the budget, and the site. Illustrated with numerous scale drawings and sample plans, her book

Macunovich, Janet, 1955-—*Continued*
abounds with practical tips." Libr J

Includes bibliography

Shading our cities; a resource guide for urban and community forests; edited by Gary Moll and Sara Ebenreck; introduction by R. Neil Sampson; foreword by F. Dale Robertson. Island Press (Covelo) 1989 333p il $34.95; pa $19.95 **712**

1. Urban forestry
ISBN 0-933280-96-3; 0-933280-95-5 (pa)

LC 89-15453

Sponsored by the American Forestry Association

This book "addresses the environmental and esthetic roles of trees in the nation's urban areas. Essays by various experts extol both the beauty of the landscaped city and describe trees as economic resources that can reduce pollution and help conserve energy. Pilot projects in selected cities are outlined, while general advice on tree preservation and community organizing is also included." Booklist

Includes bibliographic references

Smith, Mary Riley
The front garden; new approaches to landscape design. Houghton Mifflin 1991 192p il $27.45; pa $18.45 **712**

1. Landscape gardening 2. Landscape architecture
ISBN 0-395-55237-0; 0-395-55236-2 (pa)

LC 90-46192

"A Running Heads book"

"Smith describes a variety of alternatives to the standard front-yard design of foundation shrubbery and lawn. Some of her designs harken back to the dooryard gardens, courtyards, and other period styles found in the United States prior to the mid-19th century, when the park-like style became popular. Other alternatives include edible landscaping, ornamental grasses or meadow gardens, or more formal designs." Libr J

Includes bibliographic references

720 Architecture

Branson, Gary D.
The complete guide to barrier-free housing; convenient living for the elderly and physically handicapped; Hilary W. Swinson, contributing editor. Betterway Publs. 1991 176p il pa $14.95 **720**

1. Elderly—Housing 2. Architecture and the handicapped
ISBN 1-55870-188-5

LC 90-21761

"Barrier-free housing design allows a person with any sort of limited mobility, curtailed dexterity, or a sight/hearing problem to live alone successfully without feeling institutionalized. Branson . . . describes permanent as well as 'adaptable' features which may be adjusted as needs change." Libr J

Kennedy, Roger G.
Greek revival America; photographs by John M. Hall [et al.] Stewart, Tabori & Chang 1989 455p il $85 **720**

1. Architecture, American 2. United States—Social life and customs
ISBN 1-55670-094-6

LC 89-4449

"A National Trust for Historic Preservation book"

The author argues "that the Greek Revival arose not from the desire to emulate ancient Greece but from the psychological and sexual anxieties of individuals. . . . [This study ranges] from Jeffersons's role in shaping the early republic to the stylistic contributions of A.J. Davis and Benjamin Latrobe." Libr J

Includes bibliography

Scully, Vincent Joseph, 1920-
Architecture; the natural and the manmade. St. Martin's Press 1991 388p il maps $40 **720**

1. Architecture
ISBN 0-312-06292-3

LC 91-21550

The essays in this volume discuss the relationship of architecture to nature in buildings, monumental structures, and designed landscapes. Among the topics discussed are "the Greek temple; sacred mountains in Mesopotamia, Egypt, and the Aegean; the Gothic cathedral, Italian towns; Palladio; and the French classic garden." Libr J

"Scully is a consistently thought-provoking and eye-opening guide to the temples, tombs, gardens, and dwelling places humans have made. . . . This handsomely illustrated volume provides a matchless opportunity to survey architectural history from a truly global perspective." Christ Sci Monit

Wright, Frank Lloyd, 1867-1959
Frank Lloyd Wright collected writings; edited by Bruce Brooks Pfeiffer; introduction by Kenneth Frampton. Rizzoli Int. Publs. 1992 2v il **720**

LC 91-40987

Contents: v1 1894-1931 $60, pa $40 (ISBN 0-8478-1699-0; 0-8478-1700-8); v2 1930-1932 $60, pa $40 (ISBN 0-8478-1548-X; 0-8478-1549-8)

These first two volumes of a projected set of six, are comprised of published and unpublished articles, lectures, reminiscences, and essays. Volume 2 includes a reprint of books 1-3 of Wright's autobiography

"Essential for both lay readers and professionals interested in art, art history, and architecture; recommended for both public and academic libraries." Libr J [review of v1]

720.3 Architecture— Encyclopedias and dictionaries

Encyclopedia of architecture; design, engineering & construction; Joseph A. Wilkes, editor-in-chief, Robert T. Packard, associate editor. Wiley 1988-1990 5v il set $950 **720.3**

1. Architecture—Dictionaries
ISBN 0-471-63351-8

LC 87-25222

"A Wiley-Interscience publication"

Encyclopedia of architecture—*Continued*
"This work not only addresses the history of Western architecture over the last 200 years, but it also explores modern concerns such as day-care centers and handicapped-access building codes. The work covers 500 different topics, and each article was written and edited by experts in the field. Accessible to both the art historian and the weekend do-it-yourselfer. Contains 3,000 photographs." N Y Public Libr Book of How & Where to Look It Up

Includes bibliographies

Fleming, John, 1919-
The Penguin dictionary of architecture; [by] John Fleming, Hugh Honour, Nikolaus Pevsner; drawings by David Etherton. 4th ed. Penguin Bks. 1991 497p il $11.95
        720.3

1. Architecture—Dictionaries
ISBN 0-14-051241-1   LC 92-106791

First published 1966

Includes entries on individual architects, architectural terms, building materials, ornamentation, styles and movements, and types of building

720.9   Architecture—Historical and geographic treatment

Fletcher, Banister, 1833-1899
Sir Banister Fletcher's A history of architecture. 19th ed, edited by John Musgrove; consultant editors, John Tarn, Peter Wilis; assistant editor Jane Ferron. Butterworths 1987 xxxii, 1621p il maps $85
        720.9

1. Architecture—History
ISBN 0-408-01587-X   LC 86-31761

Eighteenth edition published 1975 by Scribner available from Macmillan

First published 1896 with title: A history of architecture on the comparative method

"Overarching view of architectural history, newly rewritten and expanded to include worldwide coverage. Extensively illustrated, with glossary, index, and bibliographies appended to each chapter. Includes general introductions and background for each chapter." N Y Public Libr Book of How & Where to Look It Up

Trachtenberg, Marvin
Architecture, from prehistory to post-modernism; the western tradition; [by] Marvin Trachtenberg, Isabelle Hyman. Abrams 1986 606p il $55   **720.9**
1. Architecture—History
ISBN 0-8109-1077-2   LC 85-7369

Also available from Prentice-Hall

This work "emphasizes three aspects of building: as engineering technology, as functional shelter, and as visual art. . . . An opening portfolio of 74 colorplates surveys the entire spectrum of building history, while the numerous text illustrations are reproduced in excellent black and white." Booklist

Includes bibliography

720.973   Architecture—United States

Rifkind, Carole
A field guide to American architecture. New Am. Lib. 1980 322p il hardcover o.p. paperback available $16.95   **720.973**
1. Architecture, American
ISBN 0-452-26269-0 (pa)   LC 79-29651

This volume "covers three centuries of building, generally in chronological order, with chapters on the various stylistic periods. . . . [It includes] ecclesiastical, civic and commercial and utilitarian as well as residential buildings." Libr J

This "is a big book that liberally mixes accurate, concise, cultural history with a survey of American architectural styles, building types, and elements of construction." Choice

Includes bibliography

Whiffen, Marcus
American architecture since 1780; a guide to the styles. rev ed. MIT Press 1992 326p il hardcover o.p. paperback available $12.95
        720.973

1. Architecture, American
ISBN 0-262-73097-9 (pa)   LC 91-32315

First published 1969

This guide contains descriptions, illustrations, and histories of more than forty architectural styles, arranged chronologically from the Adam style to Post-modern styles

724   Architecture from 1400

Bayer, Patricia
Art deco architecture; design, decoration, and detail from the twenties and thirties. Abrams 1992 224p il $49.50   **724**
1. Art deco 2. Architecture, Modern—1900-1999 (20th century)
ISBN 0-8109-1923-0   LC 92-7342

"A profusely illustrated survey of one of the most flamboyant and popular styles of 20th-century architecture. . . . Bayer's effort is distinctive for its truly international coverage and for her inclusion of a chapter devoted to contemporary revivals of Art Deco architecture. The bibliography and fine selection of illustrations are the most valuable part of this effort." Choice

Gropius, Walter, 1883-1969
The new architecture and the Bauhaus; translated from the German by P. Morton Shand; with an introduction by Frank Pick. MIT Press 1965 112p il pa $7.95   **724**
1. Bauhaus 2. Architecture, Modern—1900-1999 (20th century)
ISBN 0-262-57006-8

"The MIT paperback series"

Original German edition, 1925; this is a reissue of the translation first published 1935 in the United Kingdom

Gropius, Walter, 1883-1969—*Continued*
The founder of the Dessau Bauhaus describes the work of that institution, and his own architectural theories

Scully, Vincent Joseph, 1920-
Modern architecture; the architecture of democracy; by Vincent Scully, Jr. rev ed. Braziller 1974 158p il (Great ages of world architecture) hardcover o.p. paperback available $14.95   **724**

ISBN 0-8076-0334-1; 0-8076-0334-1 (pa)

First published 1961

This book attempts to define the historical demensions of modern architecture and to evaluate its meaning in terms of modern life. The author traces the major developments which have taken place in modern architecture from the late nineteenth to the middle of the twentieth century

Includes bibliography

726 Buildings for religious purposes

Adams, Henry, 1838-1918
Mont-Saint-Michel and Chartres; with an introduction by Ralph Adams Cram. Princeton Univ. Press 1981 401p il hardcover o.p. paperback available $13.95
726

1. Mont-Saint-Michel (France). Abbey 2. Notre-Dame (Cathedral: Chartres, France) 3. Middle Ages
ISBN 0-691-00335-1 (pa)   LC 81-47279
Also available in paperback from Penguin Bks.
Privately printed 1904. This is a reprint of the title first published 1913 by Houghton Mifflin

"This classic study of medieval civilization is written as the commentary of Henry Adams to an imaginary niece as they tour the Abbey Church at Mont-Saint-Michel and the Chartres Cathedral." Benet's Reader's Ency of Am Lit

Norman, Edward R.
The house of God; church architecture, style and history. Thames & Hudson 1990 312p il $60   **726**
1. Church architecture
ISBN 0-500-25108-8   LC 90-70073
A study of church architecture from the early days of Christianity to the twentieth century
The author "treats a weighty subject with a light, anecdotal touch. . . . A fine addition to general and specialized collections." Libr J

728 Residential and related buildings

Grow, Lawrence
The seventh old house catalogue. Sterling 1991 224p il pa $14.95   **728**
1. Architecture—Conservation and restoration
ISBN 0-8069-7436-2   LC 90-28644

"A Sterling/Main Street book"

First Old house catalogue published 1976 by Universe Bks.

"For people restoring and furnishing old houses in period styles, Grow offers alphabetically listed products and services, including antiques, architectual elements, and specialists in design and repair. An appendix provides supplier's addresses." Recomm Ref Books in Paperback. 2d edition

Howard, Hugh
How old is this house? a skeleton key to dating, identifying, and understanding three centuries of the American house; by Hugh Howard for Home Renovation Associates. Farrar, Straus & Giroux 1989 224p il $18.95; pa $10.95   **728**
1. Architecture, Domestic
ISBN 0-374-17324-9; 0-374-52179-4 (pa) LC 88-7865
"This is a brief guide on how to read the evidence of the past in older American houses. Focus is on three areas of investigation for the homeowner and renovator: identifying building materials and construction techniques, ascertaining architectural styles, and searching for deeds and other documentation. Although useful as an identification key and primer on gathering historical information, this work is most interesting as a narrative on the house as artifact." Libr J

Includes bibliography

Lind, Carla
The Wright style. Simon & Schuster 1992 224p il $50   **728**
1. Wright, Frank Lloyd, 1867-1959 2. Architecture, Domestic
ISBN 0-671-74959-5   LC 91-44553
"An Archetype Press book"
This book "takes us inside dozens of Frank Lloyd Wright's 'organic' houses, including his home and studio in Oak Park, Illinois, and the two Taliesins. . . . Carla Lind's text traces the development and components of Wright's unique, revolutionary aesthetic while 250 color photographs allow readers to appreciate the harmony of Wright's light-filled, graciously rectilinear rooms." Booklist

Includes bibliographic references

McAlester, Virginia, 1943-
A field guide to American houses; by Virginia and Lee McAlester; with drawings by Lauren Jarrett, and model house drawings by John Rodriquez-Arnaiz. Knopf 1984 525p il $35; pa $21.95   **728**
1. Architecture, Domestic 2. Architecture, American
ISBN 0-394-51032-1; 0-394-73969-8 (pa)
LC 82-48740
A guide to the "numerous architectural styles of American single-family houses. Houses featured range from 17th-century Georgians to Neoeclectics of the late 1970s, with more than 1200 drawings and photographs and brief histories and notable architects of each style." Libr J

Includes bibliography

Nabokov, Peter

Native American architecture; [by] Peter Nabokov, Robert Easton. Oxford Univ. Press 1989 431p il $65; pa $27.50   **728**

1. Indians of North America—Architecture

ISBN 0-19-503781-2; 0-19-506665-0 (pa)   LC 88-9944

This volume examines "the buildings and settlements created by American Indians from prehistoric times to the present." N Y Times Book Rev

"A rich, wide-ranging depiction of American Indian culture, belief, and history. . . . [The] scholarly, well-written text is complemented by a remarkable selection of photographs, drawings, and paintings." Nat Hist

Includes bibliography

Rybczynski, Witold

Home; a short history of an idea. Viking 1986 256p il $16.95   **728**

1. Architecture, Domestic

ISBN 0-670-81147-5   LC 85-40803

Also available in paperback from Penguin Bks.

The author examines "domestic life, from medieval halls to modern kitchens. The study is divided into 10 chapters, each dealing with a particular issue, such as domesticity, efficiency, and austerity, and each citing times and places [Rybczynski feels] best illustrate the advances and changes made in the home." Quill Quire

Includes bibliography

The most beautiful house in the world. Viking 1989 211p il o.p.; Penguin Bks. paperback available $10   **728**

1. Architecture, Domestic

ISBN 0-14-010566-2 (pa)   LC 88-40400

This author describes designing and building his own home. Incorporated into this account are his philosophical reflections on architecture

Rybczynski's "voice—conversational, engaging, learned, very personal—unifies the book, integrating his roles of architect, builder, dweller, teacher and linking the personal story to fascinating little discourses that range through time and the world." N Y Times Book Rev

Includes bibliography

Sinclair, Peg B.

Victorious Victorians; a guide to the major architectural styles; text by Peg B. Sinclair, photographs by Taylor B. Lewis. Holt & Co. 1985 80p il pa $17.95   **728**

1. Architecture, Domestic 2. Architecture, Victorian

ISBN 0-8050-1137-4   LC 85-7612

"An Owl book"

"The text briefly describes various styles (Gothic, stick, Queen Anne, shingle) and identifies their important details. Excellent color photographs, chiefly exterior shots with a few interior settings, then reveal the authentic color schemes of recently restored and renovated structures. A natural item for architecture buffs, decorative arts enthusiasts, and old house owners." Booklist

Includes bibliography

Stewart, Martha

Martha Stewart's new old house; restoration, renovation, decoration, landscaping; photographs by Mathieu Roberts; illustrations by Rodica Prato. Potter 1992 288p il $45   **728**

1. Architecture—Conservation and restoration 2. Interior design

ISBN 0-517-57701-1   LC 92-15900

This work follows the step-by-step renovation, restoration, decoration and landscaping of a 19th-century Federal farmhouse in Connecticut

"Lots of atmospheric photography show workers at their labors." Publ Wkly

728.8   Large and elaborate private dwellings

O'Brien, Jacqueline

Great Irish houses and castles; [by] Jacqueline O'Brien and Desmond Guinness. Abrams 1992 264p il $65   **728.8**

1. Historic buildings—Ireland 2. Architecture, Domestic

ISBN 0-8109-3365-9   LC 91-38155

"Arranged chronologically by period from the pre-Norman through Victorian eras, seven chapters highlight over 60 homes, castles, and ruins. . . . A final chapter focuses on the fine and decorative arts that flourished in 18th-century Ireland. A list of architects and crafts-people with brief biographical citations relating their work and accomplishments in Ireland concludes the volume. . . . This delightful tribute to the outstanding Irish traditions should be enjoyed by all types of libraries." Libr J

Includes bibliography

729   Design and decoration of structures and accessories

Jensen, Robert, 1938-1990

Ornamentalism; the new decorativeness in architecture & design; by Robert Jensen & Patricia Conway; foreword by Paul Goldberger; design by Hermann Strohbach. Potter 1982 297p il $40   **729**

1. Decoration and ornament

ISBN 0-517-54383-4   LC 82-7508

Numerous color and black-and-white photographs examine ornamentalism's influence on interior design, crafts and fine arts

731.4   Sculpture—Techniques and procedures

Bütz, Richard

How to carve wood; a book of projects and techniques. Taunton Press 1984 215p il pa $13.95   **731.4**

1. Wood carving

ISBN 0-918804-20-5   LC 83-50680

Also available in hardcover from P. Smith

"A Fine woodworking book"

Bütz, Richard—*Continued*

The author introduces "the most common types of carving, whittling, chip carving, relief carving, lettering, and architectural carving. The information on tools and their care is very helpful. This is the best book available on the subject." Libr J

Includes bibliography

732 Sculpture to ca. 500 and African sculpture

Segy, Ladislas, 1904-1988

African sculpture speaks. 4th ed enl. Da Capo Press 1975 346p il pa $17.95 **732**

1. Sculpture, African
ISBN 0-306-80018-7

"A Da Capo paperback"

First published 1952 by Wyn

This is a study of the artistic accomplishments of tribal Africa, with emphasis on the art of nineteenth-century West Africa

Includes bibliographies

735 Sculpture from 1400

Janson, H. W. (Horst Woldemar), 1913-1982

19th-century sculpture. Abrams 1985 288p il $55 **735**

1. Sculpture, Modern—1800-1899 (19th century)
ISBN 0-8109-1369-0 LC 84-12508

An illustrated survey of how political, scientific and industrial developments effected major trends in sculpture during the 1800's

Includes bibliography

736 Carving and carvings. Paper cutting and folding

Jackson, Paul

The encyclopedia of origami & papercraft. Running Press 1991 192p il $24.95 **736**

1. Origami 2. Papermaking
ISBN 1-561-38063-6 LC 91-52902

"From a single folded form to sophisticated sculptures using papier-mâché, paper pulp, and casting, this compendium provides technical know-how and a good overview of three-dimensional paper art. . . . Step-by-step color photos indicate all phases of papermaking processes and equipment." Booklist

Sakata, Hideaki

Origami. Kodansha Int./USA 1984 66p il pa $9 **736**

1. Origami
ISBN 0-87040-580-2

Cover-title

This "volume features 30-some foldable variations on eight different traditional themes—crane, pinwheel, 'kabuto,' 'yakko,' balloon, organ, and fish. From those foundations come such decorative objects as boxes, lilies, medallions, etc. The translated text leaves a bit to be desired, but since that is secondary to the step-by-step illustrations, it can be easily overlooked." Booklist

737.4 Coins

Breen, Walter H.

Walter Breen's complete encyclopedia of U.S. and colonial coins; [by] Walter Breen. Doubleday 1988 754p il $100 **737.4**

1. Coins
ISBN 0-385-14207-2 LC 79-6855

This "encyclopedia identifies any major variety of American coin, interprets the historical circumstances surrounding its issue, describes its physical and metallic characteristics, and estimates its level of rarity. Readers seeking background information on federal coinage will find this reference invaluable." Choice

Coin world comprehensive catalog & encyclopedia of United States coins; including pre-federal coinage, pioneer gold, and patterns; edited by David T. Alexander. World Almanac 1990 456p il $35; pa $19.95 **737.4**

1. Coins
ISBN 0-88687-484-X; 0-88687-483-1 (pa)

LC 89-77554

This guide to coins minted in the United States includes an essay on coin collecting and full-size photographs of over 800 coins, with their market values

For a review see: Booklist, Aug. 1990

Cribb, Joe

The coin atlas; the world of coinage from its origins to the present day; [by] Joe Cribb, Barrie Cook, Ian Carradice; cartography by John Flower, with an introduction by the American Numismatic Association. Facts on File 1990 337p il maps $40 **737.4**

1. Coins
ISBN 0-8160-2097-3 LC 89-1353

This book "traces the almost 3000-year history and evolution of coinage in 200 modern nations. Selected coins from each country are described, along with significant political or commercial events which influenced the creation of the nation's currency." Libr J

For a fuller review see: Booklist, Aug. 1990

Fell's international coin book. Fell il $14.95; pa $9.95 **737.4**

1. Coins

First published 1953. (8th edition 1983) Periodically revised

Current edition by Charles J. Andrews

A "companion to 'Fell's United States coin book' [entered below] . . . this brief history of foreign coins is followed by tables showing how to identify and information on how to collect. The coins and paper issues with current values are arranged alphabetically by country. A compact first purchase for the hobby shelf where budgets are small." Booklist

Fell's United States coin book. Fell il $14.95; pa $9.95 **737.4**

1. Coins

First published 1949. (11th edition 1989) Periodically revised

Current edition by Roderick P. Hughes

Fell's United States coin book—*Continued*

This guide contains complete tables showing today's value of every coin minted in the United States. Along with illustrations are information on the history of coins, speculation and investment, how to start a collection, how to sell coins and recognize worthless coins

A **Guide** book of United States coins; fully illustrated catalog and retail valuation list—1616 to date; by R. S. Yeoman; edited by Kenneth Bressett. Western il pa $9.95   **737.4**

1. Coins
ISSN 0072-8829

Annual. First published 1946 by Whitman

At head of title: The official red book of United States coins

A "reference on U.S. coins designed for use in identifying and grading coins. All issues from 1616 to the present are covered. The guide provides historical data, statistics, values, and detailed photographs for each coin. Additional sections deal with specialties such as Civil War and Hard Times tokens, misstruck coins, and uncirculated and proof sets." Nichols. Guide to Ref Books for Sch Media Cent. 4th edition

Handbook of United States coins, with premium list; by R. S. Yeoman; edited by Kenneth Bressett. Western il pa $5.95   **737.4**

1. Coins
ISSN 0072-9949

Annual. First published 1941 by Whitman

At head of title: Official blue book of United States coins

This companion volume to A Guide book of United States coins, entered above, lists average dealer buying price and information on rare coins, new issues and collector trends

Krause, Chester L.

Standard catalog of world coins; by Chester L. Krause and Clifford Mishler. Krause Publs. il pa $47.95   **737.4**

1. Coins

First published 1972. (21st edition 1994) Frequently revised

This volume covers regular and commemorative issue world coinage from 1801 to the present. Coverage of United States coinage is from 1793 to the present. Listing over 120,000 coins, valuations are presented in up to four collectible grades. Other information includes denomination, date, metallic composition, commemorate description, mintage figure and total weight

Yeoman, R. S.

Current coins of the world; revised and edited by Arthur L. Friedberg and Ira S. Friedberg. Coin & Currency Inst. il pa $9.95   **737.4**

1. Coins

First published 1966 by Whitman. (8th edition 1987) Frequently revised

World coinage from 1964 to the present is listed alphabetically by country. Metallic content, Yeoman number, value in two conditions, and date of issue are provided for each coin. Illustrated

738   Ceramic arts

Chaffers, William, 1811-1892

Collectors' handbook of marks & monograms on pottery & porcelain; edited by Frederick Litchfield, assisted by R. L. Hobson and Justus Brinkman. [new ed]. Borden 1947 367p il $10   **738**

1. Pottery—Marks 2. Porcelain—Marks
ISBN 0-87505-066-2

An abridgement of the author's Marks and monograms on European and Oriental pottery and porcelain, 14th edition, published 1932 in the United Kingdom, edited by Frederick Litchfield

Standard work for the identification of porcelain

Godden, Geoffrey A.

Encyclopaedia of British pottery and porcelain marks. Crown 1964 765p il maps o.p.   **738**

1. Pottery, British 2. Pottery—Marks 3. Porcelain—Marks

Available in hardcover from Trafalgar Sq.

"Includes, in alphabetical arrangement, more than 4,000 British china marks ranging in date from 1050 to the present." Sheehy. Guide to Ref Books. 10th edition

Kovel, Ralph M.

Dictionary of marks—pottery and porcelain; by Ralph M. and Terry H. Kovel. Crown 1953 $14.95   **738**

1. Pottery—Marks 2. Porcelain—Marks
ISBN 0-517-00141-1

"A manual which employs a system of the authors' devising to facilitate the user's identification of potters' marks. . . . Maker, place, type of ware, method of producing the mark, color of mark, and approximate date are supplied for each mark. Includes English, European, and American marks from the seventeenth century to the present." Booklist

Kovels' American art pottery; the collector's guide to makers, marks, and factory histories; [by] Ralph and Terry Kovel. Crown 1993 326p il $60   **738**

1. Pottery, American—Collectors and collecting
ISBN 0-517-58012-8   LC 92-20638

Replaces The Kovels' collector's guide to American art pottery, published 1974

Arranged alphabetically by name of factory, this guide covers the history, marks, artists, and product lines of more than 200 art pottery firms

Includes bibliography

Kovels' new dictionary of marks; [by] Ralph and Terry Kovel. Crown 1986 290p il $17.95   **738**

1. Pottery—Marks 2. Porcelain—Marks
ISBN 0-517-55914-5   LC 85-15146

This is regarded as a sequel and complementary volume to . . . [the Dictionary of marks entered above] since only 10 percent of the marks in the present effort were covered in the first one. In scope, the emphasis of the new guide is on nineteenth- and twentieth-century pottery." Am Ref Books Annu, 1987

Levin, Elaine

The history of American ceramics, 1607 to the present; from pipkins and bean pots to contemporary forms. Abrams 1988 351p il $65 **738**

1. Pottery, American
ISBN 0-8109-1172-8 LC 88-3332

"Levin covers the history, traditions, and innovations in American ceramics. . . . Many excellent color and black-and-white illustrations supplement Levin's text, which examines both handmade, single examples and mass-produced items." Booklist

Includes bibliography

738.1 Ceramic arts—Techniques, equipment, materials

Hamer, Frank

The potter's dictionary of materials and techniques; [by] Frank and Janet Hamer. 3rd ed. University of Pa. Press 1991 384p $49.95 **738.1**

1. Pottery—Dictionaries 2. Ceramics—Dictionaries
ISBN 0-8122-3112-0 LC 91-6803

First published 1975 by Watson-Guptill

"A work for the potter, the teacher, and the student. Articles are in dictionary arrangement according to key words and phrases, with cross references to related terms. Generously illustrated with line drawings and photographs. Appendix of tables; brief bibliography." Sheehy. Guide to Ref Books. 10th edition

Kenny, John B., d. 1988

The complete book of pottery making; drawings by Carla Kenny. 2nd ed. Chilton 1976 310p il (Chilton's creative crafts ser) hardcover o.p. paperback available $20.95 **738.1**

1. Pottery
ISBN 0-8019-5933-0 (pa)

First published 1949 by Greenberg

The whole process of pottery making is covered in a series of step-by-step photographs which explain the wheel, modeling, mold work, glaze, coil-building a teapot, etc.

Includes bibliography

Nelson, Glenn C.

Ceramics; a potter's handbook. 5th ed. Holt & Co. 1984 350p il $35; pa $26 **738.1**

1. Pottery
ISBN 0-03-064163-2; 0-03-063227-7 (pa)
LC 83-12633

First published 1960

This manual for beginner to advanced potters presents forming and decorating techniques, body and glaze recipes, and sources for raw materials and equipment

Includes bibliography

Rhodes, Daniel, 1911-1989

Clay and glazes for the potter. rev ed. Chilton 1973 330p il $31.95 **738.1**

1. Pottery 2. Clay 3. Glazes
ISBN 0-8019-5633-1

First published 1957 by Greenberg

The author first considers the composition, physical nature, drying and firing processes, various kinds, mixtures, and preparation of clay. He then focuses on the nature and early types of glazes, their reactions with oxides, glaze materials, technical calculations and formulas, compositions, textures, compounds and mixes, flaws, underglazes and overglazes, reduction firing, and special effects

Includes bibliography

739.2 Work in precious metals

Wyler, Seymour B., d. 1990

The book of old silver: English, American, foreign; with all available hallmarks including Sheffield plate marks. Profusely illustrated. Crown 1937 447p il $25 **739.2**

1. Silverwork 2. Plate 3. Hallmarks
ISBN 0-517-00089-X

Cover title: Old silver

"A short history of old English silver and a description of the varieties of silverware are followed by brief chapters on silversmithing in England, Scotland, the Continental countries, and America. The second half of the book is an unusually comprehensive collection of reproductions of hallmarks, arranged by country and indexed. Illustrated with photographs of old silver." Booklist

739.27 Jewelry

Field, Leslie

The queen's jewels; the personal collection of Elizabeth II. Abrams 1987 192p il $35 **739.27**

1. Elizabeth II, Queen of Great Britain, 1926- 2. Jewelry
ISBN 0-8109-1525-1 LC 86-32187

"Organized alphabetically by gemstones, this historical and visual documentary elegantly displays the world's most famous jewelry collection intertwined with accounts of romance, intrigue, and politics. It offers an inside look at the tastes of each monarch, from Queen Mary's Delhi Durbar emeralds to Elizabeth II's diamond engagement ring designed by Prince Philip." Libr J

Jewelry, 7,000 years; an international history and illustrated survey from the collections of the British Museum; edited by Hugh Tait. Abrams 1987 c1986 255p il $39.95; pa $19.95 **739.27**

1. Jewelry—History
ISBN 0-8109-1157-4; 0-8109-8103-3 (pa)
LC 86-14091

First published 1986 in the United Kingdom with title: Seven thousand years of jewellery

This survey includes "necklaces, Korean earrings, Colombian nose rings, Renaissance pendants, and art deco dress clips. The book, with 400 beautiful photographs, is divided by region and period, placing each piece in a specific time frame and setting. . . .

Jewelry, 7,000 years—*Continued*
For both jewelry lovers and serious students of the decorative arts." Booklist

The **Master** jewelers; edited by A. Kenneth Snowman. Abrams 1990 262p il $49.50
739.27

1. Jewelry
ISBN 0-8109-3606-2   LC 90-32716

The contributors to this volume examine the life and works of 15 master jewelers of the 19th and 20th centuries, among them Cartier, Van Cleef and Arpels, Faberge and Bulgari

"A beautiful publication whose design, layout, and consistent quality of photography maintain the quality of the work described in the text." Choice

Includes bibliographic references

741   Drawing and drawings

Edwards, Betty
Drawing on the artist within; a guide to innovation, invention, imagination and creativity. Simon & Schuster 1986 240p il hardcover o.p. paperback available $12.95
741

1. Drawing 2. Creative ability
ISBN 0-671-63514-X (pa)   LC 85-27688

This book is based on "the concept of dual brain functions, i.e., the idea that the left side of the brain 'specializes in verbal, logical, analytic thinking' and the right in 'visual, spatial, perceptual information'. . . . Edwards pursues the . . . role that seeing plays in creative thought through a series of exercises designed to teach basic drawing and perceptual skills by developing the brain's neglected right side capabilities." Booklist

Includes bibliography

741.2   Drawing—Techniques, equipment, materials

Guptill, Arthur L., 1891-1956
Rendering in pen and ink; edited by Susan E. Meyer. new ed. Watson-Guptill 1976 255p il $29.95   **741.2**

1. Pen drawing 2. Architectural drawing
ISBN 0-8230-4530-7

First published 1928 by Pencil Points Press with title: Drawing with pen and ink

The author combines instruction with many examples by other artists to illustrate his points. He guides the reader step by step, from elementary instruction on the kind of pens, paper and ink to use; through pen handling, value study and sketching to more complex subjects such as life drawings, architectural rendering, trees, interiors and their accessories and reproduction

Hutton-Jamieson, Iain
Colored pencil drawing techniques. North Light Pubs. 1986 176p il $24.95   **741.2**

1. Pencil drawing
ISBN 0-89134-147-1

In this introduction the author discusses materials, color, composition, pencil strokes, matting and framing. Exercises are included

Nicolaides, Kimon
The natural way to draw; a working plan for art study. Houghton Mifflin 1941 221p il hardcover o.p. paperback available $9.70
741.2

1. Drawing
ISBN 0-395-53007-5 (pa)

"After the author's death, the manuscript was prepared for publication . . . by Mamie Harmon." Publisher's note

Among the topics discussed by the author are contour and gesture; drapery; the use of black and white crayon; studies of structure; study from reproductions; and the use of color

741.5   Cartoons, caricatures, comics

Adamson, Joe
Bugs Bunny; fifty years and only one grey hare; prefaces by Friz Freleng and Chuck Jones. Holt & Co. 1990 192p il $35; pa $19.95   **741.5**

1. Warner Bros. Cartoons 2. Bugs Bunny (Fictitious character)
ISBN 0-8050-1190-0; 0-8050-1855-7 (pa)   LC 90-4074

"A Donald Hutter book"

This book is "illustrated with color cels, paintings, and sketches documenting Bugs's career . . . Adamson begins with an anecdotal history of the Rabbit and his creators. He considers the artists who drew Bugs, the writers who worked their magic to create his adventures, and many others who contributed to the Bugs persona." Libr J

Includes filmography and bibliographic references

The **Art** of Mickey Mouse; edited by Craig Yoe and Janet Morra-Yoe; introduction by John Updike. Hyperion Press (Westport) 1991 unp il $35   **741.5**

1. Mickey Mouse (Cartoon character)
ISBN 1-56282-994-7   LC 91-23545

"Paintings, watercolors, collages, drawings, photographs, sculpture, tapestry—the media used vary as much as the representations of Mickey. Artists include Andy Warhol, Charles Schultz, Maurice Sendak, R. Crumb, Peter Max, and William Steig. A drawing of Mickey by longtime fan Michael Jackson is also featured." Libr J

Daniels, Les, 1943-
Marvel; five fabulous decades of the world's greatest comics; introduction by Stan Lee. Abrams 1991 287p il $49.95   **741.5**

1. Marvel comics (New York, N.Y.) 2. Comic books, strips, etc.
ISBN 0-8109-3821-9   LC 91-8783

"Daniels' behind-the-scenes look at the development of Marvel, his profiles of the line's foremost heroes and villains, and biographies of leading writers and artists will entice Boomers who grew up with Marvel's 1960s titles as well as young fans of today's line dominated by those superpowered mutants, the X-Men. But the book's strongest appeal lies in the generous samplings of artwork spread throughout." Booklist

The **Encyclopedia** of American comics; edited by Ron Goulart. Facts on File 1990 408p il $39.95; pa $19.95 **741.5**
1. Comic books, strips, etc.
ISBN 0-8160-1852-9; 0-8160-2582-7 (pa) LC 90-2974

This "guide focuses on comic heroes and villains; the creators, artists, and writers of comic strips and comic books; and the publishers and syndicates of the comics industry. The more than 1,000 entries are arranged in dictionary form." SLJ
For a fuller review see: Booklist, Dec. 15, 1991

Gerberg, Mort
Cartooning; the art and the business. Morrow 1989 272p il pa $14.95 **741.5**
1. Cartoons and caricatures
ISBN 1-55710-017-9 LC 88-27544
First published 1983 by Arbor House with title: The Arbor House book of cartooning

This "guide thoroughly explains the creative techniques of drawing cartoons and explores the use of these illustrations in comic books, editorials, television, greeting cards, and children's books. Gerberg also covers the marketing of the cartoonist's work. . . . Illustrated with the work of such major cartoonists as Charles Addams, Gahan Wilson, and Mort Walker." Booklist

Includes bibliography

Goulart, Ron, 1933-
The great comic book artists. St. Martin's Press 1986-1989 2v il pa ea $12.95 **741.5**
1. Comic books, strips, etc.
ISBN 0-312-34557-7; 0-312-01768-5 LC 86-3711
Alphabetically arranged essays on the lives, careers, styles and works of leading comic book talents; each essay is illustrated with a full page sample of the artist's work

"Although this is a subjective listing of the greatest comic book artists, it could not come from a more informed source than comic book historian Goulart." Libr J

Grant, John, 1949-
Encyclopedia of Walt Disney's animated characters; foreword by David R. Smith. new updated ed, foreword to the revised edition by Roy E. Disney. Hyperion 1993 384p il $40 **741.5**
1. Walt Disney Company 2. Cartoons and caricatures
ISBN 1-56282-904-1 LC 92-25230
First published 1987 by Harper & Row

Divided into two sections, one covering shorts and the other feature-length animated films, this work profiles every Disney character, up to and including the casts of Beauty and the Beast and Aladdin

Includes bibliography

Hanna, William, 1910-
The art of Hanna-Barbera; [by] William Hanna & Joseph Barbera with Ted Sennett. Viking Studio Bks. 1989 270p il $50 **741.5**
1. Animated films
ISBN 0-670-82978-1 LC 88-40627

This volume tells the story of William Hanna and Joe Barbera "complete with hundreds of full-color pictures drawn from the scores of television and feature cartoons that were produced by these industry giants." Booklist

Includes bibliography

Hirschfeld, Al, 1903-
Hirschfeld: art and recollections from eight decades. Scribner 1991 xxix, 306p il $50 **741.5**
1. Cartoons and caricatures
ISBN 0-684-19365-5 LC 91-17349

This is a collection of the artist's cartoon drawings of entertainers, including Katharine Hepburn, Jack Benny, Charles Chaplin, Bette Davis, Judy Garland, the Beatles, Barbara Streisand, and Ethel Merman

"The pleasures of [this book] are multiple. Mr. Hirschfeld as a writer on his art is as astute and to the bone as he is as a draftsman. His brief foreword gives us a clear statement of his goals and an illuminating discussion of drawing as the art of pure line in black and white. . . . There is also brief autobiographical material. Just enough to let us feel closer to the artist without knowing his secrets." N Y Times Book Rev

The **New** comics anthology; edited by Bob Callahan. Collier Bks. 1991 287p il pa $19.95 **741.5**
1. Comic books, strips, etc.
ISBN 0-02-009361-6 LC 91-10444

This "sampling of the new comics for adults touches upon all its modes: outrageous humor, pointed satire, grim and gritty melodrama, humanist realism, and artistic experimentation." Booklist

The **New** Yorker album of drawings, 1925-1975. Viking 1975 unp il o.p.; Penguin Bks. paperback available $16.95 **741.5**
1. Cartoons and caricatures
ISBN 0-14-004968-1 (pa)

This collection of 500 cartoons features the work of such artists as James Thurber, John Held, Jr., Saul Steinberg, Ronald Searle, and Peter Arno

The **New** Yorker book of dog cartoons. Knopf 1992 102p il $18 **741.5**
1. Cartoons and caricatures
ISBN 0-679-41680-3 LC 92-70913
A selection of 101 dog cartoons which have appeared in the New Yorker over the past sixty-five years. An index to contributing artists is included

The **New** Yorker cartoon album, 1975-1985. Viking 1985 unp il o.p.; Penguin Bks. paperback available $15.95 **741.5**
1. Cartoons and caricatures
ISBN 0-14-008111-9 (pa) LC 85-40547
This volume contains "nearly 400 cartoons presented in the 'New Yorker's' pages over the past decade. . . . Among the magazine's brilliant stable of cartoonists whose work is represented here are Charles Addams, George Booth, and Edward Koren." Booklist

O'Sullivan, Judith
The great American comic strip; one hundred years of cartoon art. Little, Brown 1990 200p il hardcover o.p. paperback available $24.95   **741.5**

1. Comic books, strips, etc.
ISBN 0-8212-1754-2 (pa)   LC 90-5752

"A Bulfinch Press book"

"A critical evaluation of some of America's top cartoonists, examining their styles, their themes, and, of course, some of the strips themselves." Booklist

Reidelbach, Maria
Completely Mad; a history of the comic book and magazine. Little, Brown 1991 208p il $50; pa $24.95   **741.5**

1. Mad (Periodical) 2. Comic books, strips, etc.
3. American wit and humor
ISBN 0-316-73890-5; 0-316-73891-3 (pa)
LC 90-26439

"Reidelbach examines the different things *Mad* has done, and been accused of doing, and the tremendous influence it has had on the field of satire and the American consciousness. The book is profusely illustrated, well researched, and has numerous sidebars profiling the many *Mad* contributors over the years." Libr J

Includes bibliographic references

Schulz, Charles M.
You don't look 35, Charlie Brown! Holt & Co. 1985 unp il o.p. paperback available $9.95   **741.5**

1. Comic books, strips, etc.
ISBN 0-03-005624-1 (pa)   LC 85-81217

"To celebrate the 35th anniversary of the comic strip 'Peanuts' Charles Shulz composed this collection of cartoons. The book is divided into sections for each of the recurring characters in the popular strip along with commentaries on the inspiration behind certain episodes. . . Also included are glimpses into the man . . . and his philosophy on humor, heroes and life in general." Voice Youth Advocates

The **Smithsonian** collection of newspaper comics; edited by Bill Blackbeard and Martin Williams; foreword by John Canaday. Smithsonian Institution Press 1978 336p il hardcover o.p. paperback available $14.95   **741.5**

1. Comic books, strips, etc.
ISBN 0-87474-167-X (pa)   LC 77-608090

An assemblage of color and black-and-white selections of comic strips dating from 1896. Buster Brown, Krazy Kat and Blondie are among those featured

"The cartoons in the panoramic collection offer a fascinating commentary on changing mores, styles, and attitudes." Booklist

Includes bibliography

Solomon, Charles
Enchanted drawings; the history of animation. Knopf 1989 322p $75   **741.5**

1. Animated films
ISBN 0-394-54684-9   LC 89-34657

"Starting with primitive early attempts at creating the illusion of motion, this book covers the lore, personalities, techniques, and output of the Hollywood studios and the independents, plus recent efforts such as *Who Framed Roger Rabbit*. Computer and experimental animation are briefly addressed." Libr J

The book is "packed with anecdotes, quotes, budgets and lists as well as lots of odd bits of information. . . . Best of all, the book is beautifully printed (in Japan) and there are more than 400 drawings, cels, filmstrips and photographs." N Y Times Book Rev

Includes bibliography

Thomas, Bob, 1922-
Disney's art of animation; from Mickey Mouse to Beauty and the Beast. Hyperion 1991 208p il $39.95; pa $19.95   **741.5**

1. Walt Disney Company 2. Animated films
ISBN 1-56282-997-1; 1-56282-899-1 (pa)
LC 91-22562

"A Welcome book"

Using the history of the Disney studios as a model, the author touches "on all aspects of making animated films, including conceptualization, scripting, storyboarding, artwork, character development, production, direction, acting, music, layout, animation, and special effects. . . . Highly recommended for general collections." Libr J

Trudeau, G. B. (Garry B.), 1948-
Doonesbury's greatest hits. Holt & Co. 1978 250p il hardcover o.p. paperback available $12.95   **741.5**

1. Comic books, strips, etc.
ISBN 0-8050-0883-7 (pa)   LC 78-53780

A collection of Trudeau's syndicated comic strip depicting American social and political mores of the mid 1970's

Vaz, Mark Cotta
Tales of the Dark Knight: Batman's first fifty years, 1939-1989. Ballantine Bks. 1989 210p il $17.95   **741.5**

1. Batman (Comic strip) 2. Comic books, strips, etc.
ISBN 0-345-36013-3   LC 88-92872

A detailed history of the Batman comic strip from its pulp fiction beginnings through Frank Miller's Dark Knight reinterpretation

Includes bibliographic references

741.6 Graphic design, illustration and commercial art

DeNoon, Christopher
Posters of the WPA; introduction [by] Francis V. O'Connor. Wheatley Press 1987 175p il $40   **741.6**

1. United States. Work Projects Administration
2. Posters
ISBN 0-295-96543-6   LC 87-50519

Published in association with University of Washington Press

"A remembrance of the WPA [by] Anthony Velonis; A design perspective [by] Jim Heimann; A remembrance of the Federal Art Project [by] Richard Floethe." Title page

DeNoon, Christopher—*Continued*

Color reproductions of 280 posters from the Federal Art Project of the Work Projects Administration advertising civic activities, concerts, lectures, health care, plays, and other WPA projects. Several short essays about the WPA and the poster units of the FAP are included to provide background information

Includes bibliography

Heller, Steven

Graphic style; from Victorian to post-modern; by Steven Heller and Seymour Chwast. Abrams 1988 239p il $49.50

741.6

1. Graphic arts 2. Commercial art
ISBN 0-8109-1033-0   LC 88-3287

"A gallery of 640 examples of commercial, propagandistic, and journalistic art is presented in a 150-year chronology of styles. . . . Notes on every other display page treat the histories of the particular styles. More than 200 illustrations are in color." Booklist

"While Heller and Chwast provide us with the who, where, when, and how of style development, they also deal with the peripheral and reactionary trends, making the evolution of graphic styles more understandable. . . . [This] will become a respected reference source for the professional designer, artist, craftsperson, and a fascinating book for the casual reader." Choice

Includes bibliography

Holmes, Nigel, 1942-

Designing pictorial symbols; by Nigel Holmes with Rose DeNeve. Watson-Guptill 1985 143p il hardcover o.p. paperback available $19.95

741.6

1. Signs and symbols 2. Graphic arts
ISBN 0-8230-1330-8 (pa)   LC 85-3143

The author "demonstrates the use of pictorial symbols (pictographs) in modern media. Distinguishing between trademarks and pictographs, he covers the historical evolution of using pictures as symbols and then examines the use of such symbols in front-page news and in sports. . . . Intended for students and practicing professionals as well as a general audience, the book has much to offer all three types of readers." Booklist

Includes bibliography

Illustrators of children's books. Horn Bk. 1947-1978 4v il v1, 3 o.p.; v2 $30.95; v4 $35.95

741.6

1. Illustration of books 2. Illustrators 3. Children's literature—History and criticism

Contents: v1 1744-1945, compiled by Bertha E. Mahony, Louise Payson Latimer and Beulah Folmsbee; v2 1946-1956, compiled by Ruth Hill Viguers, Marcia Dalphin and Bertha Mahony Miller (ISBN 0-87675-016-1); v3 1957-1966, compiled by Lee Kingman, Joanne Foster and Ruth Giles Lontoff; v4 1967-1976, compiled by Lee Kingman, Grace Allen Hogarth and Harriet Quimby (ISBN 0-87675-018-8)

"This standard series contains biographies and bibliographies of outstanding illustrators of children's books. Each book also includes essays on the history and evolution of the art of illustrating children's books. The 1967-1976 volume contains a cumulative index for the series." Nichols. Guide to Ref Books for Sch Media Cent. 4th edition

Lanes, Selma G.

The art of Maurice Sendak. Abrams 1980 278p il $34.95

741.6

1. Sendak, Maurice
ISBN 0-8109-8063-0   LC 80-10796

The author "tells the story of Sendak's career as an illustrator of his own and others' books. . . . Ninety-four full-color illustrations and 165 black and white ones (including many sketches and preliminary drawings) sample the career from 1950 to 1981. The reader will learn a great deal about the planning and execution of children's books along the way." Best Sellers

Meyer, Susan E.

A treasury of the great children's book illustrators. Abrams 1983 272p il hardcover o.p. paperback available $24.95

741.6

1. Illustration of books
ISBN 0-8109-8081-9 (pa)   LC 83-2500

The author presents essays on and reproductions of the work of thirteen illustrators of children's books. These artists include Edward Lear, John Tenniel, Walter Crane, Randolph Caldecott, Kate Greenaway, Beatrix Potter, Ernest H. Shepard, Arthur Rackham, Edmund Dulac, Kay Nielsen, Howard Pyle, N. C. Wyeth, and W. W. Denslow

"The more than 250 illustrations, nearly 100 in color, are painstakingly reproduced. . . . This stunning volume has research and reference value." Booklist

Includes bibliography

The Modern poster. Museum of Modern Art 1988 263p il $50; pa $24.95

741.6

1. Posters
ISBN 0-87070-570-9; 0-87070-571-7 (pa)

    LC 88-60744

Published in conjunction with an exhibition held June 6-September 6, 1988

"The posters, superbly reproduced here, run in a loose chronology from 1879 to 1986, with the most powerful images from the 1930's and World War II. Preceding the plates is an excellent text by Wrede, director of MOMA's Department of Architecture and Design." Libr J

Schwarcz, Joseph H.

The picture book comes of age; looking at childhood through the art of illustration; by Joseph H. Schwarcz and Chava Schwarcz, with a foreword by Betsy Hearne. American Lib. Assn. 1991 217p il $50

741.6

1. Illustration of books 2. Children's literature—History and criticism
ISBN 0-8389-0543-9   LC 90-37809

The author explores "the words and images of Ezra Jack Keats' *Whistle for Willie*, [delves] into such topics as stress, love, the threat of war, and social injustice; and [concludes] with an analysis of Maurice Sendak's trilogy. All are made meaningful through specific comments about particular books and numerous accompanying illustrations." Booklist

Includes bibliographic references

743   Drawing and drawings by subject

Sheaks, Barclay

Drawing figures and faces. Davis Publs. (Worcester); [distributed by] Sterling 1987 183p il $21.95   **743**

1. Figure drawing
ISBN 0-87192-185-5   LC 86-72606

The author teaches "specific drawing techniques for creating pictures of figures and faces. There are 70 exercises, varying in difficulty from experimenting with the textures and strokes of charcoal to drawing abstract 'figurescapes'. In between the formal lessons are black-and-white illustrations and excellent practical tips." Booklist

745   Decorative arts

Fleming, John, 1919-

The Penguin dictionary of decorative arts; [by] John Fleming and Hugh Honour. new ed. Viking 1989 935p il $40   **745**

1. Decorative arts—Dictionaries
ISBN 0-670-82047-4   LC 89-40298

First published 1977 in the United Kingdom with present title; first United States edition published 1977 by Harper & Row with title: Dictionary of decorative arts

"Entries on furniture and furnishings in the Western tradition. Definitions of terms, some biographies of well-known craftspeople and designers, articles on materials and processes, and short histories of factories are included, with 1000 black-and-white illustrations." Ref Sources for Small & Medium-sized Libr. 5th edition

Hartigan, Lynda Roscoe

Made with passion; the Hemphill Folk Art Collection in the National Museum of American Art; [by] Lynda Roscoe Hartigan, with contributions by Andrew L. Connors, Elizabeth Tisdel Holmstead, and Tonia L. Horton. Smithsonian Institution Press 1990 240p il $50   **745**

1. National Museum of American Art (U.S.) 2. Folk art, American
ISBN 0-87474-293-5   LC 90-9622

Published for the National Museum of American Art in conjunction with an exhibition of the Hemphill Folk Art Collection

"This beautifully produced work includes, in addition to the substantial introductory material, detailed entries with physical descriptions and provenance of 196 pieces from the collection. . . . Highly recommended for both art scholars and general readers." Libr J

Includes bibliographic references

Miller, R. Craig

Modern design in the Metropolitan Museum of Art, 1890-1990; photographs by Mark Darley. Abrams 1990 312p il $60   **745**

1. Metropolitan Museum of Art (New York, N.Y.)
2. Design
ISBN 0-8109-3612-7   LC 90-6293

"A selection of objects from the twentieth-century design collection of the Metropolitan Museum of Art, this volume covers examples of applied and decorative arts drawn from the museum's various departments. Miller's historical introductions to each section chart developments from art nouveau to postmodernism." Booklist

745.1   Antiques

Jenkins, Emyl

Emyl Jenkins' appraisal book; identifying, understanding, and valuing your treasures. Crown 1989 326p il $24.95   **745.1**

1. Antiques 2. Collectors and collecting
ISBN 0-517-57086-6   LC 88-22836

The author gives an "account of what inflation has done to the appraised value of antiques and other collectibles, providing information on insurance, estates, gifts, taxes, divorce, theft, and fire. He also includes a guide to making personal inventories and appraisals, as well as stating where to find additional information on appraising. Required reading for all home- and property-owners." Libr J

Kovel, Ralph M.

Kovels' antiques and collectibles price list; [by] Ralph M. Kovel and Terry H. Kovel. Crown il pa $13   **745.1**

1. Antiques 2. Collectors and collecting

First published 1968 with title: The complete antiques price list. Revised annually to reflect current prices. Title varies

Current American market prices for 50,000 antiquities and collectibles. Included are photographs, factory marks and logos, catalogs, reports of sales, auctions, and tips on buying, collecting, restoring, and preserving

Kovels' know your antiques; [by] Ralph & Terry Kovel. rev & updated ed. Crown 1990 349p il pa $14.95   **745.1**

1. Antiques
ISBN 0-05-175786-9   LC 90-2509

First published 1967

"How to recognize and evaluate any antique, large or small, like an expert. Covers pottery, porcelain, silver, pewter, country and formal furniture, pressed and cut glass, prints, bottles, ironware, tinware, letters, sheet music, autographs, books, magazines, and more. Provides advice about caring for antiques and recognizing frauds. Has bibliographies for each specialty." N Y Public Libr Book of How & Where to Look It Up

Kovels' know your collectibles; [by] Ralph and Terry Kovel. Crown 1982 c1981 404p il hardcover o.p. paperback available $15   **745.1**

1. Antiques 2. Collectors and collecting
ISBN 0-517-58840-4 (pa)   LC 81-5515

Kovel, Ralph M.—*Continued*
"Advises on what collectible objects are likely to increase in value and how to preserve, protect, and sell them. Covers ceramics, pottery, furniture, glass, toys, print advertisements, and many other items. Has bibliographies for each major specialty." N Y Public Libr Book of How & Where to Look It Up

Miller, Judith, 1951-
Miller's international antiques price guide; compiled and edited by Judith and Martin Miller. American ed. Viking Studio Bks. il $30 **745.1**
1. Antiques
Annual. First published 1979 with title: Miller's antiques price guide
This guide includes photographs, prices and brief descriptions of museum-quality antiques sold at auction or by dealers during the past year

745.2 Industrial art and design

Murphy, John M., 1944-
How to design trademarks & logos; [by] John Murphy & Michael Rowe. North Light Bks. 1991 c1988 144p il pa $19.95 **745.2**
1. Trademarks 2. Commercial art
ISBN 0-89134-400-4
First published 1988 in the United Kingdom
This guide includes chapters on types of trademarks and logos, aesthetics, developing the design concept, executing the design, developing new brand names, and the legal aspects involved
Includes bibliography

Pulos, Arthur J.
The American design adventure, 1940-1975. MIT Press 1988 446p il hardcover o.p. paperback available $25 **745.2**
1. Industrial design
ISBN 0-262-66068-7 (pa)   LC 87-26266
This study of American design covers "design process, . . . foreign influences, social forces, the affect of World War II, aesthetic factors, design education, the emergence of professional organizations, [and] the affect of the marketplace." Libr J
"The book design is handsome and the volume is beautifully illustrated with 363 excellent photographs and drawings." Choice
Includes bibliography

745.5 Handicrafts

Index to handicrafts, model making, and workshop projects. Faxon (Useful reference ser) **745.5**
1. Handicraft—Indexes 2. Industrial arts education—Indexes
Basic volume (1936) $14 (ISBN 0-87305-057-6); Supplement (1943) $14 (ISBN 0-87305-070-3); Second supplement (1950) $14 (ISBN 0-87305-079-7); Third supplement 1950-1961 (1965) o.p.; Fourth supplement

1962-1967 (1969) $16 (ISBN 0-87305-096-7); Fifth supplement 1968-1973 (1975) $20 (ISBN 0-87305-102-5)
Basic volume and first two supplements compiled by Eleanor Cook Lovell and Ruth Mason Hall; Third supplement compiled by Harriet P. Turner and Amy Winslow; Fourth supplement compiled by E. Winifred Alt; Fifth supplement compiled by Pearl Turner
"An index to books and periodical articles for use in school and home craftwork." Sheehy. Guide to Ref Books. 10th edition

745.592 Toys, models, miniatures, related objects

Schoonmaker, David
Whirligigs & weathervanes; a celebration of wind gadgets with dozens of creative projects to make; [by] David Schoonmaker & Bruce Woods. Sterling 1991 128p il $19.95; pa $12.95 **745.592**
1. Toys 2. Handicraft
ISBN 0-8069-8364-7; 0-8069-8365-5 (pa)
                                       LC 91-12145
An introduction to windtoys and weather vanes. Sections cover history, tools, materials, and construction techniques

745.6 Calligraphy, illumination, heraldic design

Child, Heather
Calligraphy today; twentieth century tradition & practice. [3rd ed]. Taplinger 1988 128p il $22.95 **745.6**
1. Calligraphy
ISBN 0-8008-1206-9
Original edition first published 1963 in the United Kingdom; first United States edition published 1964 by Watson-Guptill
"This largely pictorial survey embraces the development and practice of Western calligraphy. . . . Illustrations include examples of historical scripts and the work of some 100 calligraphers." Publisher's note
Includes bibliography

David, Stuart
Calligraphy A to Z; a new technique for learning the basic hands, step-by-step exercises. Stravon Educ. Press 1985 208p il $17 **745.6**
1. Calligraphy
ISBN 0-87396-088-2   LC 84-16380
The author's "method for teaching calligraphy attempts to simplify the process of learning to write by breaking down the two basic hands—Roman and Italic—into a system of internal structures and basic strokes. . . . Numerous examples, generally of good quality, and a set of exercises accompany each lesson." Libr J

Gourdie, Tom
Calligraphic styles. Taplinger 1979 106p il pa $9.95   **745.6**
1. Calligraphy
ISBN 0-8008-1181-X   LC 79-52316
"A Pentalic book"
This book "shows more than a dozen useful alphabets, discussed letter by letter, and includes samples of works by contemporary masters using the scripts taught." Libr J

745.7 Decorative coloring

Le Grice, Lyn
The stenciled house; an inspirational and practical guide to transforming your home; photography by Michael Murray and David Murray. Simon & Schuster 1988 175p il $24.95   **745.7**
1. Stencil work
ISBN 0-671-66670-3   LC 88-15769
"The book covers just about every situation a stenciler might encounter, from stencil planning for awkward spaces to the treatment of details and decorative objects. . . . Includes photographs and drawings with clear instructions." Publ Wkly

Spencer, Stuart, 1944-
Marbling: how to techniques. Harmony Bks. 1989 127p il pa $14.95   **745.7**
ISBN 0-517-57120-X   LC 88-16576
First published 1988 in the United Kingdom with title: The art of marbling
This manual discusses the uses of faux marble finishes in interior decoration and the tools and techniques required for producing them. A history of the craft and a discussion of the geology of real stone are also included

745.92 Floral arts

Black, Penny
The book of pressed flowers; photography by Geoff Dann. Simon & Schuster 1988 120p il $19.95   **745.92**
1. Flower drying
ISBN 0-671-66071-3   LC 87-26381
"With plants gathered from the seashore or meadow or balcony garden, novice 'pressers' will learn here not only which flora produce what colors and textures, but also how to achieve different moods and effects. The step-by-step color photographs guide hesitant fingers, as do the professional, contemporary tips. . . . Beautiful color photos throughout." Booklist

Hillier, Malcolm
The book of fresh flowers; a complete guide to selecting and arranging. Simon & Schuster 1988 256p il $29.95   **745.92**
1. Flower arrangement
ISBN 0-671-66667-3   LC 88-3173

"The author focuses first on the tools of his trade and how to use them, then offers . . . advice on composition, texture and style. . . . Giving step-by-step instructions for some arrangements pictured, Hillier also recommends seasonal and holiday arrangements." Publ Wkly
"The stunning illustrations offer hundreds of ideas. . . . A fine choice for the public library." Booklist

Penzner, Diana
Everlasting design; ideas and techniques for dried flowers; [by] Diana Penzner with Mary Forsell; principal photography by Tony Cenicola; illustrations by Roman Szolkowski. Houghton Mifflin 1988 144p il pa $10.70   **745.92**
1. Flower arrangement 2. Flower drying
ISBN 0-395-46728-4   LC 88-9459
A guide to making dried flower arrangements and other projects such as pressed-flower notes and pictures
Includes bibliography

746.1 Yarn preparation and weaving

Blumenthal, Betsy, 1943-
Hands on dyeing; [by] Betsy Blumenthal & Kathryn Kreider; illustrations by Ann Sabin. Interweave Press 1988 111p il pa $8.95   **746.1**
1. Dyes and dyeing
ISBN 0-934026-36-X   LC 88-12260
The authors provide techniques and tips on a variety of hand-dyeing projects. Equipment, yarns, dyes, pots, and finishing are covered
Includes bibliography

Brown, Rachel
The weaving, spinning, and dyeing book; illustrated by Rachel Brown and Cheryl McGowen. 2nd ed, rev and expanded. Knopf 1983 430p il pa $35   **746.1**
1. Weaving 2. Spinning 3. Dyes and dyeing
ISBN 0-394-71595-0   LC 83-176576
First published 1978
Following a chapter of general information about weaving the author discusses Navajo weaving, Hopi sash weaving, counterbalanced looms, inkle looms, card weaving, spinning and natural dyeing. Directions are provided for 50 projects. Over 400 line drawings and color illustrations accompany the text

Hecht, Ann
The art of the loom; weaving, spinning, and dyeing across the world. Rizzoli Int. Publs. 1990 208p il $35   **746.1**
1. Weaving 2. Spinning 3. Dyes and dyeing
ISBN 0-8478-1147-6   LC 89-61382
"Hecht focuses on eight areas of the world where outstanding examples of age-old methods of these three interrelated crafts are still practiced today. Visually exceptional . . . as well as informatively superb, her book takes the reader to the American Southwest, the Middle

Hecht, Ann—*Continued*
East, West Africa, Indonesia, Japan, Nepal, Guatemala, and Peru." Booklist

Includes bibliography

746.4 Needle- and handwork

Reader's Digest complete guide to needlework. Reader's Digest Assn. 1979 504p il $27.50 **746.4**

1. Needlework
ISBN 0-89577-059-8   LC 78-71704

Editor: Virginia Colton

A guide to ten different needle crafts, "containing the ABCs, stitches, and techniques anyone would need to start—and finish—a particular crafts project. All aspects of the major forms of needlecraft are covered, from appliqué to rugmaking." Booklist

746.43 Knitting, crocheting, tatting

Coss, Melinda
The Disney book of knitting; by Melinda Coss and Debby Robinson. St. Martin's Press 1987 96p il $19.95; pa $13.95 **746.43**

1. Knitting
ISBN 0-312-01355-8; 0-312-02904-7 (pa)
                                      LC 87-42890

A collection of sweater and accessory projects all featuring well-known Disney characters. An introduction provides basic information on gauge, fairisle, and finishing

Erickson, Mary Anne
Knitting by design; a step-by-step guide to designing and knitting your own clothes; [by] Mary Anne Erickson and Eve Cohen. Bantam Bks. 1986 176p il pa $14.95 **746.43**

1. Knitting
ISBN 0-553-34271-1   LC 86-47582

The authors discuss the basics of knitting: needles, stitches, yarn, and gauge. Instructions for designing a sweater or dress are included

Fassett, Kaffe
Glorious knits; photography by Steve Lovi. Potter 1985 160p il $32.50; pa $20 **746.43**

1. Knitting
ISBN 0-517-55843-2; 0-517-59199-5 (pa) LC 85-6377

This book presents designs and step-by-step instructions for 30 knitting projects, including sweaters, vests and coats. Full color photographs accompany the text

Gibson-Roberts, Priscilla A.
Knitting in the old way; photography by John Van Sant Roberts. Interweave Press 1986 187p il pa $18 **746.43**

1. Knitting
ISBN 0-934026-20-3   LC 85-81330

This book provides an introduction to "traditional knitting, from the color-stranded sweaters of Norway to Icelandic yoke sweaters to the heavy Cowichan sweaters of Western Canada. Included is a chapter on hand spinning yarns for traditional sweater styles." Libr J

Includes bibliography

Hand-knitting techniques from Threads magazine. Taunton Press 1991 125p il pa $17.95 **746.43**

1. Knitting
ISBN 1-56158-012-0   LC 91-13243

"A Threads book"

This compilation of articles spans a variety of subjects, from knitting sweaters from leftover yarns to designing garments from sewing patterns. Schematics for sweaters are included

Hiatt, June
The principles of knitting. Simon & Schuster 1988 571p il $29.95 **746.43**

1. Knitting
ISBN 0-671-55233-3   LC 87-37665

"This is a comprehensive handbook for the knitter who wants to know the 'whys' as well as the 'hows' of hand-knitted fabric construction. Included are chapters on stitch formation, fabric construction, pattern design, project planning, and decorative work (e.g., multi-color knitting, inlay, and needlework embellishment). Superior organization, layout, indexing, and the numerous illustrations add to the value of this work as a basic knitting reference." Libr J

Matthews, Anne
Vogue dictionary of crochet stitches. David & Charles; [distributed by] Sterling 1988 c1987 192p il $24.95; pa $16.95 **746.43**

1. Crocheting
ISBN 0-7153-9086-4; 0-7153-9357-X (pa)
                                      LC 88-114533

First published 1987 in the United Kingdom

This volume "examines 335 crochet stitches in detail, including for each a well-photographed color swatch and pertinent directions. . . . Instructions are provided for a dozen pieces of apparel." Booklist

Newton, Deborah
Designing knitwear. Taunton Press 1992 263p il $39.95 **746.43**

1. Knitting
ISBN 0-942391-06-3   LC 91-36451

"A Threads book"

In this book for experienced knitters the author "lets out all the stops, revealing working methods, knitwear design tips, and techniques that have taken her years to perfect." Libr J

Includes bibliographic references

Righetti, Maggie

Crocheting in plain English. St. Martin's Press 1988 244p il pa $14.95   **746.43**

1. Crocheting
ISBN 0-312-01412-0   LC 87-27512

This guide covers threads and yarns, tools, pattern interpretation, basic stitches, fabric pattern stitches, project assembly, and care of finished articles. Final chapters include instructions for six projects

Knitting in plain English. St. Martin's Press 1986 241p il pa $12.95   **746.43**

1. Knitting
ISBN 0-312-45853-3   LC 86-1800

This compendium is divided into four sections: preliminaries to knitting; the work itself; finishing; and patterns. Black-and-white photos accompany the text

Vogue knitting; the ultimate knitting book; by the editors of Vogue knitting magazine. Pantheon Bks. 1989 280p il $34.95   **746.43**

1. Knitting
ISBN 0-394-57186-X   LC 89-42555

"Following an introductory chapter on the history of knitting, the editors offer tips on how to understand knitting instructions and advice on the whole range of basic and advanced techniques. A stitch dictionary containing instructions and a photo for over 120 stitches is a real bonus. The book also contains patterns for what are referred to as 'classic sweaters.'" Booklist

746.44 Embroidery

Fassett, Kaffe

Glorious needlepoint; photography by Steve Lovi. Potter 1987 160p il hardcover o.p. paperback available $20   **746.44**

1. Needlepoint
ISBN 0-517-59198-7 (pa)   LC 87-2356

The author presents contemporary designs for crafting household items using color and texture in innovative ways

746.46 Patchwork and quilting

Bonesteel, Georgia

Lap quilting with Georgia Bonesteel. Oxmoor House 1982 122p il $24.95; pa $14.95   **746.46**

1. Quilting
ISBN 0-8487-0524-6; 0-8487-1048-7 (pa)
    LC 81-83054

The author describes her method of quilts made in small sections, to quilt "on the go", and gives designs, full size templates, and quilting designs

More lap quilting with Georgia Bonesteel. Oxmoor House 1985 131p il $19.95   **746.46**

1. Quilting
ISBN 0-8487-0634-X   LC 84-60287

"The emphasis here is on more creativity with less labor. The 60-plus designs are enhanced by excellent color photographs, full-size pattern pieces, and a chatty narrative that never loses its charm." Booklist

Goldberg, Rhoda Ochser

The new quilting & patchwork dictionary. Crown 1988 280p il pa $12.95   **746.46**

1. Quilting
ISBN 0-517-56965-5   LC 88-3836

"Quilting techniques, tools and accessories, frames, fabrics, templates, borders, fillers, patchwork and applique patterns, enlarging and reducing, finishing, and more." Title page

"The quilting language is understandable, the writing concise, and the illustrations clear. All in all, a very nice book." Voice Youth Advocates

Linsley, Leslie

The weekend quilt. St. Martin's Press 1986 159p il $19.95   **746.46**

1. Quilting
ISBN 0-312-86016-1   LC 86-1959

Also available More weekend quilts $24.95 (ISBN 0-312-08849-3)

This book features "19 pieced-quilt projects. . . . Carefully chosen for their simplicity, they lend themselves to the strip-piecing method which is the key to their quick assembly. Good color photographs show the finished product. . . . An excellent choice for public libraries." Libr J

McClun, Diana, 1934-

Quilts! Quilts!! Quilts!!! the complete guide to quiltmaking; [by] Diana McClun and Laura Nownes. Quilt Digest Press 1988 159p il pa $19.95   **746.46**

1. Quilting
ISBN 0-913327-16-6   LC 88-18563

"Thirty classic and two new patterns are offered, along with yardage requirements for five standard sizes, templates and specific directions for every stage of construction. McClun and Nownes advise on everything from choosing patterns and color schemes to timesaving techniques. Rich color photographs or diagrams accompany each instruction." Publ Wkly

McMorris, Penny

Crazy quilts. Dutton 1984 127p il hardcover o.p. paperback available $23   **746.46**

1. Quilts
ISBN 0-525-24226-0 (pa)   LC 83-73452

After a historical introduction, examples of crazy quilts are presented in full-color photographs. Biographical information on six nineteenth-century quilt makers is included in a separate section

Includes bibliography

Seward, Linda
Christmas patchwork projects. Sterling 1986 144p il hardcover o.p. paperback available $10.95 **746.46**
1. Quilting 2. Christmas decorations
ISBN 0-8069-6364-6 (pa)   LC 86-5738
The author "presents Christmas projects that are appropriate for beginning and advanced quilters. The text first discusses patchwork techniques, including information on how to select and cut fabrics and quilt the designs. The following chapters detail more than 30 designs for 12-inch-square blocks. While some designs are traditional, others are both innovative and eye-catching." Booklist

Walker, Michele
The complete book of quiltmaking. Knopf 1986 192p il hardcover o.p. paperback available $24.95 **746.46**
1. Quilting
ISBN 0-394-74372-5 (pa)   LC 85-23158
"Color photos display the varied attractions of quilts in both traditional and contemporary designs, adapted and created by the author and her colleagues. Detailed illustrations also accompany Walker's clear instructions on every step of her project. Tips on caring for the handmade quilt are included." Publ Wkly

Includes bibliography

747 Interior decoration

Conran, Terence
Terence Conran's home furnishings; consulting editor: Judy Brittain. Little, Brown 1986 223p il $29.95 **747**
1. Interior design 2. Furniture
ISBN 0-316-15325-7   LC 86-81670
"A how-to-guide to home furnishings complete with sewing directions for individual projects. There are chapters on wall coverings, beds, window treatments, tables and chairs, and cushions. The book is lavishly illustrated with handsome color photographs, line drawings, and charts. . . . Lovely to look at, practical to use." Booklist

Gilliatt, Mary
The complete book of home design. rev ed. Little, Brown 1989 384p il $34 **747**
1. Interior design
ISBN 0-316-31406-4   LC 88-83396
First published 1984
"Emphasis is on use of space; choice of fabrics, prints, furniture, and accessories and their arrangement; and technical considerations, such as lighting. The beautifully designed format makes effective use of many high-quality color photographs and line drawings." Libr J

Designing rooms for children. Little, Brown 1985 c1984 128p il hardcover o.p. paperback available $18.95 **747**
1. Interior design
ISBN 0-316-31419-6 (pa)   LC 84-52849
First published 1984 in the United Kingdom with title: Making the most of children's rooms

The author specifies ideas "complete with color and safety suggestions, with advice and floor plans indicating the flexibility and fore-thought that will make the rooms practical as babies grow into toddlers, school-aged kids, then teenagers. . . . Gilliatt provides inspiration and practical considerations for many appealing designs." Publ Wkly

The Mary Gilliatt book of color. Little, Brown 1985 128p il $24.95 **747**
1. Color 2. Interior design
ISBN 0-316-31379-3   LC 85-50699
This volume is aimed at "people with an interest in, and an eye for, interior design who want to make better use of color in their homes. . . . Each chapter deals with a specific color, exploring the way it can be used to the best effect. . . . The Data File at the back of the book provides ideas and practical advice on how to use color on walls, at windows and on floors." Publisher's note

Mary Gilliatt's new guide to decorating. Little, Brown 1988 256p il $40 **747**
1. Interior design
ISBN 0-316-31385-8   LC 88-80531
This book covers steps of the decorating process "from the first stages of planning and organization through the choosing of fabrics and furnishings. Mary Gilliatt gives advice on finding the right help; outlines successful budgeting; discusses style, inspiration of the past, and various movements; explains the application of color, light, and texture; and finally instructs in the proper techniques for the task at hand." Publisher's note

Setting up home. Little, Brown 1986 128p il hardcover o.p. paperback available $16.95 **747**
1. Interior design
ISBN 0-316-31383-1 (pa)   LC 85-82406
First published 1985 in the United Kingdom
The author "focuses upon decorating a first home, whether an apartment or a house. The ideas presented are useful for anyone looking for fairly inexpensive schemes to highlight, decorate, or renovate their living quarters. . . . The colors are lively and varied in all of the delightful, explanatory photographs. An easy-to-use resource." Booklist

Hatje, Gerd
Rooms by design; houses, apartments, studios, lofts; [by] Gerd Hatje and Herbert Weisskamp. Abrams 1989 208p il $39.95 **747**
1. Interior design
ISBN 0-8109-1598-7   LC 88-34857
"Hatje and Weisskamp explore a variety of options for contemporary living. . . . The work of prominent architects (Gae Aulenti, Robert Venturi), designers (Andrée Putnam), and artists (Keith Haring) is featured." Booklist
"Virtually all interiors—from traditional to contemporary to avant-garde—avoid trendy, fussy, hypercoordinated decorator looks in favor of comfort and livability, offering imaginative yet realizable schemes for readers." Publ Wkly

Laura Ashley complete guide to home decorating; foreword by Nick Ashley; [contributors] Deborah Evans [et al.]; edited by Charyn Jones. Harmony Bks. 1990 c1989 224p il $40; pa $22   **747**

1. Interior design
ISBN 0-517-57338-5; 0-517-59077-8 (pa) LC 89-2229
First published 1989 in the United Kingdom

This guide to home decorating includes instructions for do-it-yourself wallpapering, sewing curtains, framing pictures, making lampshades, bedspreads and accessories, upholstering, offers advice on choosing patterns, textures, lighting, and is illustrated with color photographs and drawings

Varney, Carleton
Room-by-room decorating. Fawcett Columbine 1985 c1984 157p il pa $9.95   **747**

1. Interior design
ISBN 0-449-90114-9   LC 85-113495

The author "first presents a questionnaire to help determine individual style preferences. He then provides general decorating guidelines covering furniture arrangement, balance, color, and accessories. . . . Room-by-room breakdowns include sample ideas for creating traditional, modern, country, or oriental decors." Booklist

"This should be a practical addition to interior design collections, especially in public libraries." Libr J

747.2 Interior decoration—Historical and geographic treatment

Gilliatt, Mary
English country style; photography by Christine Hanscomb. Little, Brown 1987 223p il $29.95   **747.2**

1. Decoration and ornament, English 2. Interior design
ISBN 0-316-31382-3   LC 86-81089
First published 1986 in the United Kingdom

The author discusses "decorating a home (or just a room or two) in the style of an English country house. The noted British decorator not only instructs on how to achieve the desired effect . . . but also offers a lively history of English country style. . . . A lovely, inspiring, practical book." Booklist

Includes bibliography

Grow, Lawrence
American Victorian; a style and source book; [by] Lawrence Grow and Dina Von Zweck. Harper & Row 1984 223p il $35; pa $15.95   **747.2**

1. Decoration and ornament, American 2. Interior design
ISBN 0-06-015209-5; 0-06-091283-9 (pa)
LC 83-48789

The authors "have produced an introductory survey of late 19th-century architecture, decorative treatments, and domestic artifacts, using hundreds of illustrations, many in color or from period prints and photographs."

Libr J
Includes bibliography

Slesin, Suzanne
English style; by Suzanne Slesin & Stafford Cliff; photographs by Ken Kirkwood; foreword by Terence Conran; design by Stafford Cliff; research associate, Lesley Astaire. Potter 1984 288p il $40   **747.2**

1. Decoration and ornament, English 2. Interior design
ISBN 0-517-55276-0   LC 84-2090

"A survey of English style from a variety of periods and living spaces. A brief text supports the 600 excellent color photographs, divided into sections on classic English homes, city houses, flats, lofts, country houses, and collections." Libr J

Japanese style; [by] Suzanne Slesin, Stafford Cliff & Daniel Rosensztroch; photographs by Gilles de Chabaneix. Potter 1987 287p il $45   **747.2**

1. Decoration and ornament, Japanese 2. Interior design
ISBN 0-517-56080-1   LC 87-2269

Photographs and a brief text illustrate traditional and modern extremes in Japanese homes, ranging from centuries-old country houses to contemporary apartments

749.2 Furniture—Historical and geographic treatment

Nutting, Wallace, 1861-1941
Furniture treasury (mostly of American origin). Macmillan 1948-1949 c1928-1933 3v in 2 il v1 $75; v2 $35   **749.2**

1. Furniture, American—History 2. Household equipment and supplies 3. Clocks and watches
ISBN 0-02-590980-0 (v1); 0-02-591040-X (v2)

"All periods of American furniture with some foreign examples in America, also American hardware and household utensils. Five thousand illustrations with descriptions on the same page." Title page

Volume 3 has subtitle: Being a record of designers, details of designs and structure, with lists of clock makers in America, and a glossary of furniture terms. Drawings by Ernest John Donnelly

Sotheby's concise encyclopedia of furniture; general editor, Christopher Payne. Harper & Row 1989 208p il $49.95   **749.2**

1. Furniture—History
ISBN 0-06-016141-8   LC 89-45066

"An illustrated history of furniture from the Renaissance to the present, written by international experts. Details major styles, trends, and innovations. Illustrated dictionary explains furniture styles and construction." NY Public Libr Book of How & Where to Look It Up

750 Painting and paintings

Wright, Christopher, 1945-
The world's master paintings; from the early Renaissance to the present day: a comprehensive listing of works by 1,300 painters and a complete guide to their locations worldwide; compiled by Christopher Wright. Routledge 1992 2v il set $399   **750**

1. Painting—Catalogs
ISBN 0-415-02240-1   LC 91-31694

"Designed to serve as a guide to specific and accurate information about the works of the great painters and the thousands of places that house them." Libr J
For a fuller review see: Booklist, Oct. 15, 1992

751.2 Painting—Materials

Mayer, Ralph, 1895-1979
The artist's handbook of materials and techniques. 5th ed, revised and updated by Steven Sheehan. Viking 1991 761p il $30
751.2

1. Artists' materials 2. Pigments 3. Painting—Technique
ISBN 0-670-83701-6   LC 90-50357
First published 1940

Partial contents: Pigments; Oil painting; Acrylics; Tempera painting; Watercolor and gouache; Pastel; Solvents and thinners; Conservation of pictures

The painter's craft; an introduction to artists' methods and materials. 4th ed, revised and updated by Steven Sheehan. Penguin Bks. 1991 236p il pa $16.95
751.2

1. Painting—Technique 2. Artists' materials
ISBN 0-14-046895-1   LC 90-7768
First published 1948 by Van Nostrand

This book provides a guide to the selection and use of painting materials. Chapter topics include: color; pigments; grounds; oil painting; tempera painting; aqueous paints; pastel; mural painting; synthetic mediums; studio and equipment

Includes bibliography

751.4 Painting—Techniques and procedures

Roukes, Nicholas
Acrylics bold and new. Watson-Guptill 1986 144p il hardcover o.p. paperback available $18.95   **751.4**

1. Painting—Technique
ISBN 0-8230-0059-1 (pa)   LC 85-26541
This book describes the special characteristics of acrylics, then presents 64 experiments showing possible compositions and techniques, including mixed media

751.42 Watercolor painting

Couch, Tony
Watercolor: you can do it! North Light Bks. 1987 175p il $29.95   **751.42**

1. Watercolor painting—Technique
ISBN 0-89134-188-9   LC 86-23597
This beginner's guide to watercolor painting covers materials, composition, and technique. Step-by-step demonstrations show how to proceed from preliminary sketch to finished painting
Includes bibliography

Powers, Alex
Painting people in watercolor; a design approach. Watson-Guptill 1989 144p il $27.50   **751.42**

1. Figure painting 2. Watercolor painting—Technique
ISBN 0-8230-3816-5   LC 88-31426
"Best suited to the amateur watercolorist already accomplished in landscapes and seascapes. Powers' manual on painting the human figure meets the two basic requirements in an art instruction handbook: clarity of directions and an abiding tone of encouragement. . . . The text is augmented by Powers' own phenomenally attractive watercolors." Booklist

Includes bibliography

751.7 Paintings—Specific forms

Chalfant, Henry
Spraycan art; [by] Henry Chalfant and James Prigoff. Thames & Hudson 1987 96p il pa $14.95   **751.7**

1. Street art 2. Graffiti
ISBN 0-500-27469-X   LC 87-50389
"This book showcases handball-court walls, buildings, billboards—and even California's famed 'Hollywood' sign—transformed by the spraycan. Underscoring the intensity and freshness that young 'writers' bring to their work are quotations. . . . [The authors] offer a visual overview of a subject that goes to the heart of today's innercity youth culture." Publ Wkly

Robinson, David
SoHo walls; beyond graffiti. Thames & Hudson 1990 96p il pa $18.95   **751.7**

1. Street art
ISBN 0-550-27602-1   LC 90-70193
This is a collection of photographs of wall art from the area south of Houston Street in New York City
"Robinson's excellent introduction helps to unravel some of the pictorial enigmas shown in this book. By capturing this sampling of contemporary visual urban life, he has preserved wall art that vanishes quickly. Highly recommended for academic, museum, and public library collections." Libr J

Seligman, Patricia, 1950-
Painting murals; images, ideas, and techniques. North Light Bks. 1988 c1987 168p il $26.95   **751.7**

1. Mural painting and decoration
ISBN 0-89134-265-6   LC 88-9963

Seligman, Patricia, 1950-—_Continued_
"A Macdonald Orbis book"

First published 1987 in the United Kingdom

A "do-it-yourself course in mural painting. . . . Seligman covers all the procedures and processes involved, providing clear and thorough instructions. Materials, equipment, techniques, designs, and procedures are all examined as the author shows how to create trompe l'oeil effects ranging from small designs to huge wall-sized murals." Booklist

Includes bibliography

752   Color in painting

Birren, Faber, 1900-1988
Creative color. Schiffer 1987 128p il pa $14.95   **752**

1. Color 2. Painting
ISBN 0-88740-096-5   LC 87-60000

First published 1961 by Reinhold

This introduction to color application discusses the basic concepts of color, how the human eye perceives color, and how color can be changed by qualities of illumination

Includes bibliography

Principles of color; a review of past traditions and modern theories of color harmony. Schiffer 1987 96p il pa $10.95
                                  752

1. Color
ISBN 0-88740-103-1

First published 1969 by Van Nostrand Reinhold

The author presents traditional principles of color harmony, discusses color circles, and gives suggestions for further manipulation based on psychological and natural paths

758   Other subjects in painting

Freeman, Judi
The Fauve landscape; with contributions by Roger Benjamin [et al.] Abbeville Press; Los Angeles County Mus. of Art 1990 350p il maps $65   **758**

1. Fauvism 2. Landscape painting
ISBN 1-55859-025-0   LC 90-664

This is the catalog of an exhibition organized by the Los Angeles County Museum of Art that was devoted to the landscape paintings of Matisse, Derain, Braque and their circle. It contains six essays and a documentary chronology, biographical sketches, and an exhibition checklist

Includes bibliographic references

759.05   Painting—1800-1899

Clark, Kenneth, 1903-1983
The romantic rebellion; romantic versus classic art. Harper & Row 1974 c1973 366p hardcover o.p. paperback available $22.95
                              759.05

1. Art, Modern—1800-1899 (19th century)
ISBN 0-06-430167-2 (pa)

Analyzed in Essay and general literature index

First published 1973 in the United Kingdom

"The works of 13 artists are surveyed, and the period covered runs from the second half of the 18th century to the middle of the 19th century. Except for Goya, Piranesi, Fuseli, Constable, and Turner, all of the artists are French: David to Degas. . . . The essays are eminently readable—as valuable for the specialist as for the general reader." Choice

Rewald, John, 1912-
The history of impressionism. 4th rev ed. Museum of Modern Art 1973 672p il $55; pa $29.95   **759.05**

1. Impressionism (Art)
ISBN 0-87070-360-9; 0-87070-369-2 (pa)

Also available from Abrams

First published 1946

Containing some 600 plates, this chronicle of the impressionist movement discusses the painters that came to be known as impressionists, their struggle for recognition, their meetings, aims, methods and exhibitions and their disbandment after their eighth group show in 1886

Includes bibliography

Post-impressionism: from Van Gogh to Gauguin. 3d ed rev. Museum of Modern Art 1978 590p il $60   **759.05**

1. Postimpressionism (Art) 2. Painters, French
ISBN 0-87070-532-6

First published 1956, and analyzed in Essay and general literature index

A history of post-impressionism from the early days of 1886, when Van Gogh arrived in Paris, to 1893, when Gauguin returned from his first trip to Tahiti

Includes bibliography

759.13   American painting

Discovered lands, invented pasts; transforming visions of the American West; [by] Jules David Prown [et al.] Yale Univ. Press 1992 217p il $35   **759.13**

1. West (U.S.) in art 2. Indians of North America—Pictorial works 3. Art, American
ISBN 0-300-05722-9   LC 92-53537

This "reinterpretation of western American art of the past three centuries reevaluates works by such artists as Bierstadt, Moran, and O'Keeffe from the perspectives of history, art history, and American studies." Univ Press Books for Public and Second Sch Libr

Includes bibliographic references

Finch, Christopher, 1939-
Norman Rockwell's America. Abrams 1975 313p il hardcover o.p. paperback available $24.95   **759.13**

1. Rockwell, Norman, 1894-1978 2. United States—Civilization
ISBN 0-8109-8071-1 (pa)

Artist-illustrator Rockwell's vision of the American dream is examined in such sections as Growing Up in America, Young Love, Home and Family, Democracy, and Americans at Work

Fine, Ruth, 1941-

John Marin; [by] Ruth E. Fine. Abbeville Press; National Gallery of Art 1990 312p il $75
759.13

1. Marin, John, 1870-1953
ISBN 1-558-59015-3
LC 89-17520

Published on the occasion of an exhibition at the National Gallery of Art, Jan. 28-April 15, 1990

"Combining the biographical and the critical . . . the footnoted text is a readable and authentic survey that will serve the novice and scholar alike." Libr J

Includes bibliographic references

George Caleb Bingham; [by] Michael Edward Shapiro [et al.] St. Louis Art Mus.; Abrams 1990 192p il $39.95; pa $24.95
759.13

1. Bingham, George Caleb, 1811-1879
ISBN 0-8109-3102-8; 0-8109-2528-1 (pa)
LC 89-35750

"Five art historians here explore aspects of Bingham's complex personality and varied (and uneven) output. . . . [This] handsome catalog, with glorious color plates, will satisfy a lay as well as scholarly audience." Libr J

Includes bibliographic references

Gerdts, William H.

Art across America; two centuries of regional painting, 1710-1920. Abbeville Press 1990 3v il set $495
759.13

1. Painting, American 2. Painters, American
ISBN 1-558-59033-1
LC 90-598

Contents: v1 New England, New York, Mid-Atlantic; v2 The South, Near Midwest; v3 The Far Midwest, Rocky Mountain West, Southwest, Pacific

This "survey covers American painting outside the main art centers of New York City, Philadelphia, and Boston. . . . The work gives a state-by-state overview of artistic development plus annotations on individual artists. . . . Half of the 1,000 well-chosen illustrations are in color. Nothing of this magnitude or comprehensiveness has previously been attempted. Highly recommended." Choice

Includes bibliographic references

Homer, Winslow, 1836-1910

Winslow Homer in the 1890s; Prout's Neck observed; essays by Philip C. Beam [et al.] Hudson Hills Press 1990 154p il $35
759.13

ISBN 1-55595-042-6
LC 90-80948

Published in association with the Memorial Art Gallery of the University of Rochester

This catalog of an exhibition documents Homer's life and work following his relocation from New York City to the Maine coast. Color plates, family photographs, excerpts from letters and essays are included

Includes bibliographic references

Hopper, Edward, 1882-1967

Edward Hopper: the art and the artist; [by] Gail Levin. Norton 1982 299p il $50; pa $35
759.13

ISBN 0-393-01374-X; 0-393-00082-6 (pa)
LC 79-27958

Published in association with the Whitney Museum of American Art

This "introduction to the paintings and drawings of the American realist stems from a [1981] exhibition at New York City's Whitney Museum. Curator Levin traces Hopper's development as an artist and illustrates the painter's characteristic themes in a lengthy introductory essay. Following this text is a large section of plates, in color and black and white." Booklist

Includes bibliography

Kingsley, April

The turning point; the abstract expressionists and the transformation of American art. Simon & Schuster 1992 414p il $30
759.13

1. Art, Abstract 2. Painting, American
ISBN 0-671-63857-2
LC 92-15359

This "group portrait of American Abstract Expressionists shows how the anguish of their personal lives fed into their art. Kingsley . . . focuses on 1950, the pivotal 'year of greatest interaction' among Jackson Pollock, Willem de Kooning, Mark Rothko and their associates, and the only year when they all lived and worked together in New York City." Publ Wkly

Includes bibliographic references

O'Keeffe, Georgia, 1887-1986

Georgia O'Keeffe. Viking 1976 unp il $75
759.13

ISBN 0-670-33710-2

Also available in paperback from Penguin Bks.

"O'Keeffe traces her artistic evolution in remembrances of her long career. Reproductions of O'Keeffe's work dominate the brief reflections; these oversize color illustrations faithfully represent the artist's style and subjects." Booklist

Georgia O'Keeffe in the West; edited by Doris Bry and Nicholas Callaway. Knopf 1989 98p il $100
759.13

ISBN 0-394-57971-2
LC 89-45287

"In chronological order, the O'Keeffe paintings that were inspired by the landscape of New Mexico are reproduced in this oversize volume." Libr J

759.4 French painting

Courthion, Pierre

Edouard Manet. Abrams 1984 128p il $22.95
759.4

1. Manet, Édouard, 1832-1883
ISBN 0-8109-1318-6

Concise edition of the author's Manet, originally published 1959

The author discusses Manet's technique and choice of subjects, his rejection by the establishment, and the influences of other artists, writers, and society on his work

Courthion, Pierre—*Continued*
Georges Seurat. Abrams 1988 129p il
$22.95   **759.4**

1. Seurat, Georges Pierre, 1859-1891
ISBN 0-8109-1519-7

Concise edition of the author's Georges Seurat,
originally published 1968

This volume features a biographical essay, followed
by an annotated portfolio of 40 full-page color plates.
A selected bibliography is also included

Leymarie, Jean
Gauguin; watercolors, pastels, drawings.
Skira 1989 98p il $25   **759.4**

1. Gauguin, Paul, 1848-1903
ISBN 0-8478-1050-X   LC 88-43447

Original French edition published 1961 in Switzerland

This volume "analyzes the works on paper of the
postimpressionist Gauguin. . . . 50 illustrations [are]
reproduced here, 48 of which are in color—watercolors;
gouaches; drawings executed in pen-and-ink, pencil, chalk
or charcoal; woodcuts; monotypes." Publ Wkly

Matisse: a retrospective; edited by Jack
Flam. Levin Assocs. 1988 392p il o.p.;
Outlet reprint available $34.99   **759.4**

1. Matisse, Henri
ISBN 0-517-03292-9   LC 89-112022

This book discusses the life and career of Matisse.
Color and black-and-white illustrations cover the entire
range of his artistic output

Renoir: a retrospective; edited by Nicholas
Wadley. Levin Assocs. 1987 386p il o.p.;
Outlet reprint available $34.99   **759.4**

1. Renoir, Auguste, 1841-1919
ISBN 0-517-68613-9   LC 88-117274

Illustrated with color reproductions this "anthology of
excerpts from writings on Renoir documents the life and
career of this popular Impressionist artist. More important, however, the book helps to reveal the changing
critical attitudes toward Renoir's work and its relationship to the art of his time and that which came after."
Libr J

Includes bibliographic references

Seitz, William Chapin
Claude Monet. Abrams 1982 126p il
$22.95   **759.4**

1. Monet, Claude, 1840-1926
ISBN 0-8109-1341-0   LC 82-8883

Concise edition of the author's Monet, originally
published 1960

A study of the life and artistic development of one
of the most influential impressionists. 101 illustrations
including 40 full color plates illustrate the text

Thomson, Richard, 1953-
Camille Pissarro; impressionism, landscape
and rural labour. New Amsterdam Bks. 1990
127p il $26.50   **759.4**

1. Pissarro, Camille, 1830-1903 2. Impressionism (Art)
ISBN 0-941533-90-5

Based on a 1990 traveling exhibition organized by the
British South Bank Centre, this book offers a survey of
Pissarro's work in all media

Tucker, Paul Hayes, 1950-
Monet at Argenteuil. Yale Univ. Press
1982 211p il $45; pa $20   **759.4**

1. Monet, Claude, 1840-1926 2. Argenteuil (France) in
art
ISBN 0-300-02577-7; 0-300-03206-4 (pa)
                                  LC 81-12994

This book "covers the period 1871-78, when Monet
lived at Argenteuil and there painted 170 landscapes,
some of his best output. Not the usual art historical
work, this book delves exhaustively into the manner in
which the artist through his art documented the
urbanization and industrialization of the pretty little
French village." Libr J

Includes bibliography

Monet in the '90s; the series paintings.
Yale Univ. Press 1989 307p il $50; pa $30
                                          759.4

1. Monet, Claude, 1840-1926
ISBN 0-300-04659-6; 0-300-04913-7 (pa)
                                  LC 89-63207

Also available in paperback from the Museum of Fine
Arts (Boston)

Published in conjunction with an exhibition organized
by the Museum of Fine Arts, Boston

This work "brings together 90 of Monet's exquisite
paintings . . . created during the 1890s. . . . Tucker
provides a fresh interpretation of these paintings and
Monet's intentions in executing them." Libr J

759.5   Italian painting

Baetjer, Katharine
Canaletto; [by] Katharine Baetjer and J.
G. Links; essays by J. G. Links [et al.]
Metropolitan Mus. of Art 1989 387p il $45;
pa $35   **759.5**

1. Canaletto, 1697-1768
ISBN 0-87099-559-6; 0-87099-561-8 (pa)
                                  LC 89-36404

Also available from Abrams

Catalog of an exhibition held at the Metropolitan
Museum of Art, New York, Oct. 30, 1989-Jan. 31, 1990

A survey of the life and works of the eighteenth-
century Venetian landscape painter

"The five short essays by noted authorities succeed
in capturing many of the essentials of the artist, which
are easily digested by the nonspecialist. The extensive
catalog following the essays contains splendid color
reproductions." Libr J

Includes bibliographic references

Hartt, Frederick, 1914-1991
Michelangelo. Abrams 1984 128p il $22.95
                                          759.5

1. Michelangelo Buonarroti, 1475-1564
ISBN 0-8109-1335-6

Concise edition of the author's Michelangelo, originally
published 1964

At head of title: Michelangelo Buonarroti

Hartt, Frederick, 1914-1991—*Continued*
The forty colorplates in this book include broad views and close details of Michelangelo's frescoes in the Sistine Chapel and of his other paintings

Leonardo, da Vinci, 1452-1519
The notebooks of Leonardo da Vinci
759.5

Available in hardcover and paperback editions from various publishers
Variant title: The literary works of Leonardo da Vinci
Contains drawings, reflections and speculations of the Renaissance genius

Titian: prince of painters; by Francesco Valcanover [et al.]; catalog edited by Susanna Biadene. Prestel-Verlag; [distributed by] Neues 1990 432p il $85
759.5

ISBN 3-7913-1102-6
This is the catalog of an exhibition of the Venetian painter's work held in Venice in the summer of 1990 and subsequently in Washington, D.C.
"The catalog includes a dozen short essays by major Titian scholars covering various aspects of the master's life and milieu, and full, if brief, entries for the more than 75 paintings, drawings, and prints in the Venice show. . . . The overall high quality of its production—from the succulent illustrations to the excellent bibliography—makes this book a most desirable acquisition for all libraries." Choice

759.9492 Dutch painting

Fuchs, Rudolf Herman, 1942-
Dutch painting; [by] R. H. Fuchs. Thames & Hudson 1978 216p il (World of art) $19.95; pa $11.95
759.9492
1. Painting, Dutch
ISBN 0-500-18168-3; 0-500-20167-6 (pa)
LC 78-325580
In this "handbook of Dutch painting of the past 500 years, the author has reasonably weighted his text to the golden age of the 17th Century. Avoiding the too-frequent tendency of surveys of this sort to overwhelm with lists of artists and works, Fuchs instead insightfully focuses on individual paintings and their place within well-formulated conceptual and topical categories." Libr J

Includes bibliography

Gogh, Vincent van, 1853-1890
Vincent van Gogh. Rizzoli Int. Publs. 1990 2v il set $90
759.9492
1. Gogh, Vincent van, 1853-1890
ISBN 0-8478-1288-X
LC 90-60941
Contents: v1 Drawings; v2 Paintings
These volumes "are the catalogs of the exhibitions marking the Netherlands' centennial commemoration of Van Gogh's death, on July 29, 1890." Smithsonian
"Essays by distinguished Dutch art scholars portray a humane genius captivated by peasant life. . . . The analyses of the works, drawing materials, and techniques are fascinating. Yet ultimately, it is the hundreds of exquisite color reproductions that the reader will savor."

Libr J
Includes bibliographic references

Wheelock, Arthur K.
Jan Vermeer; text by Arthur K. Wheelock, Jr. Abrams 1981 168p il (Lib. of great painters) $49.50
759.9492
1. Vermeer, Johannes, 1632-1675
ISBN 0-8109-1730-0
LC 81-1754
This volume includes thirty-five known paintings by the seventeenth century Dutch painter, plus twelve color plates of details from his paintings. Each plate is accompanied by its own commentary. The author also provides a biographical introduction
"A good balance between the scholarly study and the popular application." Libr J
Includes bibliography

759.972 Mexican painting

Herrera, Hayden
Frida Kahlo; the paintings. HarperCollins Pubs. 1991 255p il $40; pa $25 **759.972**
1. Kahlo, Frida, 1907-1954
ISBN 0-06-016699-1; 0-06-092319-9 (pa)
LC 90-56348
This is a critical study of the Mexican artist's life and work
The author's "expressive and fluid prose is able to keep pace with Kahlo's riveting canvases and adds to the experience of viewing them. More than 200 paintings and sketches are reproduced, 80 in color, while numerous photographs illustrate Kahlo's painful, passionate, and creative life. A superb tribute to Kahlo." Booklist
Includes bibliographic references

769 Prints

Mathews, Nancy Mowll
Mary Cassatt: the color prints; by Nancy Mowll Mathews and Barbara Stern Shapiro. Abrams 1989 207p $39.95; pa $24.95 **769**
1. Cassatt, Mary, 1844-1926
ISBN 0-8109-1049-7; 0-8109-2524-9 (pa) LC 88-8107
This catalog "comments on 23 of Cassatt's color prints produced in various states between 1889 and 1897. The prints are examined in terms of theme and working methodology." Choice
"Boasting the completeness of a catalogue raisonné, this sumptuous work surely will remain the leading resource for decades to come." Libr J
Includes bibliography

Slocum, Frank
Topps baseball cards; the complete picture collection, a 40-year history, 1951-1990; foreword by Johnny Bench; introduction and card history by Sy Berger; text by Frank Slocum & Red Foley. Warner Bks. 1990 unp il $99.95
769
1. Baseball cards
ISBN 0-446-51579-5
LC 90-50277
This work includes a facsimile of every baseball card issued by Topps Chewing Gum, Inc. since 1951

769.56 Postage stamps

Scott specialized catalogue of United States stamps. Scott Pub. Co. il $39.95; pa $26 **769.56**

1. Postage stamps—Catalogs

Annual. First published 1923. Title and publisher's name vary

This volume "lists a wide variety of different groups of U.S. stamps such as air post envelopes, first day covers, postal cards, revenue stamps, savings stamps, and telegraph stamps. Listings are in the form used in Scott's 'Standard Catalogue' [entered below]. The 'Information for Collector' section is much more extensive and detailed." Wynar. Guide to Ref Books for Sch Media Cent. 3d edition

Scott standard postage stamp catalogue. Scott Pub. Co. 4v il pa ea $32 **769.56**

1. Postage stamps—Catalogs

Annual. First published 1868. Title, publisher's name and number of volumes vary

"Gives minute details, such as date of issue, design, denomination, color, perforation, and watermark, on all the stamps of the world. Most of the stamps are given a valuation." Ref Sources for Small & Medium-sized Libr. 5th edition

770.1 Photography—Philosophy and theory

Sontag, Susan, 1933-
On photography. Farrar, Straus & Giroux 1977 207p o.p.; Doubleday paperback available $9.95 **770.1**

1. Artistic photography
ISBN 0-385-26706-1 (pa) LC 77-11916

"Six essays originally published in the 'New York Review of Books' examine serious ethical, practical, and aesthetic issues in photography. . . . Within the erudite, critical pieces, Sontag considers famous photographers Walker Evans, Diane Arbus, and Paul Strand and their vocal and visual contributions to the growing field." Booklist

770.2 Photography—Miscellany

Hedgecoe, John
The book of photography; how to see and take better pictures. rev and updated. Knopf 1984 256p il pa $24.95 **770.2**

1. Photography—Handbooks, manuals, etc.
ISBN 0-394-72466-6 LC 83-49189
First published 1976

Among the aspects of photography discussed in this illustrated guide are: camera hardware, visual values, picture composition, portrait techniques, special effects, developing, processing and selecting equipment

The photographer's handbook. 3rd ed rev. Knopf 1992 352p il pa $19 **770.2**

1. Photography—Handbooks, manuals, etc.
ISBN 0-679-74204-2 LC 92-52957
First published 1977

This "work is encyclopedic in nature. Brief sections discuss photographic topics from camera and lens selection, film processing and darkroom technique, how to shoot a variety of subjects in both black and white and color, lighting techniques, through framing and display of prints. . . . High school and public libraries will want to add this to their reference collections." Voice Youth Advocates

Schaub, George
Using your camera. AMPHOTO 1990 144p il hardcover o.p. paperback available $18.95 **770.2**

1. Photography—Handbooks, manuals, etc.
ISBN 0-8174-6351-8 (pa) LC 89-5352

This "volume acquaints us with the modern single-lens-reflex (SLR) camera, how to understand and control various metering systems and focus techniques for sharpness over a particular area, the selection of accessories, films, lenses, contrast control . . . all presented with clarity, authority, and sensitivity." Booklist

770.25 Photography—Directories

Photographer's market. Writer's Digest Bks. il $22.95 **770.25**

1. Photography—Marketing—Directories
ISSN 0147-247X

Annual. First published 1978

"Includes directories of many types of business firms (e.g., advertising agencies, galleries, book and periodical publishers, record companies) with their photographic requirements and name of contact person. Data on contests, foundations and grants, workshops, plus feature articles on the profession and the business of freelancing." Sheehy. Guide to Ref Books. 10th edition

771 Photography—Techniques, equipment, materials

Adams, Ansel, 1902-1984
The negative; [by] Ansel Adams with the collaboration of Robert Baker. New York Graphic Soc. 1981 272p il (New Ansel Adams photography ser) $35 **771**

1. Photography—Processing
ISBN 0-8212-1131-5 LC 81-16808

Companion volume to The print, entered below, and The camera, entered in class 771.3

In this explication of his scientific-aesthetic approach to landscape photography Adams considers: natural and artificial light, film, exposure, filters and darkroom procedures

The print; [by] Ansel Adams with the collaboration of Robert Baker. New York Graphic Soc. 1983 210p il (New Ansel Adams photography ser) $35 **771**

1. Photography—Processing
ISBN 0-8212-1526-4 LC 83-950

Illustrations from Adams' work accompany this step-by-step introduction to photographic printing techniques and materials. Plans for designing a darkroom are included

Hedgecoe, John
John Hedgecoe's darkroom techniques. Simon & Schuster 1985 191p il hardcover o.p. paperback available $9.95 **771**
1. Photography—Processing
ISBN 0-671-66442-5 (pa) LC 84-5457
Step-by-step instructions for developing and printing color and black-and-white photos. Toning, montage, and posterization are discussed

Langford, Michael John, 1933-
The darkroom handbook; photography consultant: Tim Stephens. Knopf 1981 352p il hardcover o.p. paperback available $25 **771**
1. Photography—Processing
ISBN 0-394-72468-2 (pa) LC 80-2703
The author "gives simple explanations and descriptions of the technical processes used in developing color and black-and-white film. Special methods for printing and manipulating the basic negative are also covered. . . . Well illustrated with diagrams, drawings, charts, and a large number of photographic examples." Booklist

Schaefer, John P., 1934-
Basic techniques of photography. Little, Brown 1992 389p il $50; pa $29.95 **771**
1. Adams, Ansel, 1902-1984 2. Photography
ISBN 0-8212-1801-8; 0-8212-1882-4 (pa)
LC 90-27208
At head of title: An Ansel Adams guide
"Based on Ansel Adams' approach to photography as creative expression, this book provides everything a beginner needs to know about camera and darkroom equipment and how to take, develop, and print pictures. Camera systems, accessories, film, and darkroom setups are clearly explained and illustrated with photos and drawings." Booklist

Schaub, George
The Amphoto book of film; a complete guide to current photographic films; George Schaub. 1994 ed. AMPHOTO 1993 176p pa $16.95 **771**
1. Photography—Film
ISBN 0-8174-3484-4 LC 93-3420
First published 1991
Divided by type of film (e.g. color, black-and-white, instant, etc.), this guide lists films based on film speed within each category. Includes other information such as grain structure, degree of enlargement possible, and contrast

771.3 Cameras and accessories

Adams, Ansel, 1902-1984
The camera; Ansel Adams, with the collaboration of Robert Baker. New York Graphic Soc. 1980 203p il (New Ansel Adams photography ser) $35 **771.3**
1. Cameras
ISBN 0-8212-1092-0 LC 80-11402

Companion volumes The negative, and The print, both entered in class 771
"Small, medium, and large format cameras are covered, as are their major accessories. The writing is clear, with a good number of equally clear diagrams and photographs to explain complex points. As expected, the discussion is thorough and sprinkled with just enough recollected experiences to give it the personal touch of this master photographer and teacher." Choice

Meehan, Joseph
The complete book of photographic lenses. AMPHOTO 1991 144p il pa $22.50 **771.3**
1. Photography—Equipment and supplies
ISBN 0-8174-3697-9 LC 91-16236
"Following an overview of lens optics, Meehan explains the uses of normal, long or telephoto, and wide-angle lenses. Standard 35mm format as well as larger formats are included. Good explanations of depth-of-field, focus, and perspective control are given." Libr J
Includes bibliographic references

778.9 Photography of specific subjects

Moeller, Susan D.
Shooting war; photography and the American experience of combat. Basic Bks. 1989 474p il $25.95 **778.9**
1. Photojournalism 2. Documentary photography
ISBN 0-465-07777-3 LC 88-47898
A study of American combat photographers and their work from the Civil War through the Vietnam Conflict
Includes bibliography

779 Photographs

Adams, Ansel, 1902-1984
The American wilderness; edited by Andrea G. Stillman; introduction by William A. Turnage. Little, Brown 1990 146p il $125 **779**
1. Artistic photography 2. Nature photography
ISBN 0-8212-1799-2 LC 90-5402
"A Bulfinch Press book"
This book "takes pertinent quotations from Adams's writings on wilderness conservation and interleaves them with . . . subject groupings of photographs: Yosemite, ocean beaches, Yellowstone, Hawaii, trees, plants, and flowers." Libr J
"Of all the stunning books that have been made from Ansel Adams's photographs, this is the most stunning. Although it does not present him at his most various, it presents him at his very best." Nat Hist

Yosemite and the range of light; introduction by Paul Brooks. New York Graphic Soc. 1979 28p [55 plates] il $150; pa $39.95 **779**
1. Artistic photography 2. Yosemite National Park (Calif.)—Pictorial works
ISBN 0-8212-0750-4; 0-8212-1523-X (pa)
LC 78-72074

Adams, Ansel, 1902-1984—*Continued*

A collection of photographs taken by Adams in California's Sierra Nevada mountain range from the 1920's through the 1970's

"This is a fine showcase for Adams's special brand of romanticism and scientific approach to photography. . . . Paul Brooks, a prominent conservationist, was just the right person to write the text. He has done so with charm and has added another dimension to our appreciation of what nature has wrought and Adams's responses to the beauty of it all." Choice

Arbus, Diane, 1923-1971

Diane Arbus: magazine work; with texts by Diane Arbus; essay by Thomas W. Southall; edited by Doon Arbus and Marvin Israel. Aperture 1984 175p il hardcover o.p. paperback available $29.95   **779**

1. Photography—Portraits 2. Artistic photography
ISBN 0-89381-233-1 (pa)   LC 84-70444

A representative selection of Arbus' photographs "commissioned by magazines during 1960-71. The 151 photographs are mostly portraits of celebrities in several fields." Libr J

This collection "adds significantly to our understanding not only of Arbus's artistic achievement but also of the era in which she worked." N Y Times Book Rev

The Art of photography, 1839-1989; catalogue edited by Mike Weaver; photographs selected by Daniel Wolf with Mike Weaver and Norman Rosenthal. Yale Univ. Press 1989 472p il $65; pa $40   **779**

1. Artistic photography
ISBN 0-300-04457-7; 0-300-04456-9 (pa)

LC 88-28032

This survey of photography was prepared to accompany an exhibition held at the Museum of Fine Arts, Houston, the Australian National Gallery, Canberra, and the Royal Academy of Arts, London, in 1989

"Fifteen chapters organized by genre or stylistic school highlight the finest work of 96 well-known early and modern practitioners and include a fine mix of familiar and unfamiliar works. The images are complemented by a carefully chosen selection of classic 19th- and 20th-century essays on photography. . . . Though there are some curious omissions—no Ansel Adams, and few women photographers—the book is still highly recommended." Libr J

Includes bibliography

The Best of Life. Time-Life Bks. 1973 302p il o.p.; Avon Bks. paperback available $14.95   **779**

1. Photojournalism
ISBN 0-380-00187-X (pa)

A "selection of the magazine's photo-coverage of lensmen who achieved fame in its pages and by lesser-known photographers who had their inspired moments. Here are Eisenstaedt, Bourke-White, Capa, Elisofon, Parks, Mydans, Duncan, Gene Smith and the whole 'Life' gang. Their often historic photos leap at the eye." Publ Wkly

Capa, Cornell, 1918-

Cornell Capa; photographs; edited by Cornell Capa and Richard Whelan. Little, Brown 1992 216p il $60   **779**

1. Photojournalism
ISBN 0-8212-1777-1   LC 92-6533

"A Bulfinch Press book"

"This volume collects 150 of [Capa's] best photographs, taken on assignment for *Life* and other magazines between 1946 and 1974. . . . Capa's accompanying memoirs are at times wry and lighthearted, often erudite and always compassionate." Publ Wkly

Includes bibliographic references

Capa, Robert, 1913-1954

Robert Capa; photographs; edited by Cornell Capa and Richard Whelan. Knopf 1985 242p il o.p.; Pantheon Bks. paperback available $7.95   **779**

1. Photojournalism
ISBN 0-679-72336-6 (pa)   LC 85-40213

"Approximately 260 black-and-white images have been selected by Robert Capa's brother and his biographer as his 'strongest and most memorable' photographs from a career of 30-some years." Libr J

"The photographs are at the highest level of photojournalism: instantaneous records of a newsworthy moment in time, with considerable impact and without guile." Choice

Cartier-Bresson, Henri, 1908-

Henri Cartier Bresson: photographer. Bulfinch Press 1992 343p il $125   **779**

1. Artistic photography
ISBN 0-8212-1986-3   LC 92-53275

An expanded version of the title first published 1979 by the New York Graphic Society, this retrospective volume includes photographs taken by Cartier-Bresson between 1929 and the 1980's

Includes bibliography

Friedlander, Lee, 1934-

Lee Friedlander portraits; foreword by R. B. Kitaj. Little, Brown 1985 71p il $60   **779**

1. Photography—Portraits
ISBN 0-8212-1602-3   LC 85-13791

"A New York Graphic Society book"

"These portraits, taken between 1957 and 1984, include photographs of family, friends, and strangers, as well as such diverse personalities as Blaze Starr and Walker Percy. The painter R. J. Kitaj has written a particularly interesting and thoughtful foreword." Libr J

Karsh, Yousuf, 1908-

Karsh: American legends; photographs and commentary. Bulfinch Press 1992 156p il (Springs of achievement ser. on the art of photography) $50   **779**

1. Photography—Portraits
ISBN 0-8212-1906-5   LC 92-8508

Karsh, Yousuf, 1908——*Continued*
"This book serves two purposes: It offers notable examples of portrait photography as art, and its photographic portraits of 73 celebrities from the arts, the media, and public life make it a visual who's who. Recommended for most libraries." Libr J

Leibovitz, Annie
Photographs, Annie Leibovitz, 1970-1990. HarperCollins Pubs. 1991 232p $85   779
1. Photography—Portraits 2. Artistic photography
ISBN 0-06-016608-8   LC 90-56384
"Leibovitz did many of these 242 photo-portraits (one-third of them in color) for *Rolling Stone* and *Vanity Fair,* yet others included here are previously unpublished. Posed shots and fanzine fare alternate with more penetrating character studies." Publ Wkly

Life: the '60s; edited by Doris C. O'Neil; introduction by Tom Brokaw; commentary by John Neary. Little, Brown 1989 236p il $35   779
1. United States—History—1961-1974—Pictorial works
2. Photojournalism
ISBN 0-8212-1752-6   LC 89-7964
"A Bulfinch Press book"
A selection "of photographs from the archives of 'Life.' . . . Particularly in its condensation of events, this selection of 250 captioned photographs is rather haunting. The images are divided into several categories—Civil Rights, The Kennedy Years, Music, Protest, Fads and Fashions, Space, 1968, and Vietnam— with each category introduced by an essay. . . . A good summary of the decade." Libr J

Livingston, Jane
Odyssey; the art of photography at National Geographic; by Jane Livingston with Frances Fralin and Declan Haun. Thomasson-Grant 1988 363p il hardcover o.p. paperback available $34.98   779
1. National Geographic Society (U.S.) 2. Photography
ISBN 0-934738-45-9 (pa)   LC 88-50159
Catalog of an exhibition held at the Corcoran Gallery of Art
A compilation of nearly 300 photographs from the collection of National Geographic including many that were never published in the magazine
"A must for every photography collection." Booklist

Mapplethorpe, Robert
Certain people; a book of portraits. Twelvetrees Press 1985 unp il $55   779
1. Photography—Portraits 2. Artistic photography
ISBN 0-942642-14-7   LC 85-243883
A selection of the late photographers portraits. Included is an introduction by Susan Sontag
"Mapplethorpe's portraits vividly serve as examples of a formal aesthetic and superb technique. . . . This straightforward presentation displays without the distraction of controversial subjects his icy yet compelling style." Booklist

Some women; introduction by Joan Didion. Little, Brown 1989 114p il $50; pa $24.95   779
1. Artistic photography 2. Women in art 3. Photography—Portraits
ISBN 0-8212-1716-X; 0-8212-1937-5 (pa)
LC 89-31326
This volume comprises some one hundred of Mapplethorpe's black-and-white pictures of women
"Mapplethorpe has taken the vestiges of the glamour shot and united it to a classical study of form. The introduction by Joan Didion is an excellent look into the Mapplethorpe aesthetic. Aside from Mapplethorpe's notoriety, Some Women . . . is a strong compilation from one of the most important photographers of the last decade. It is an essential purchase for all photography collections." Libr J

Museum of Modern Art (New York, N.Y.)
The family of man; the 30th anniversary edition of the classic book of photography; created by Edward Steichen for the Museum of Modern Art, New York; prologue by Carl Sandburg. Museum of Modern Art; [distributed by] Simon & Schuster 1983 192p il hardcover o.p. paperback available $16.95   779
1. Photography—Exhibitions   LC 85-3032
ISBN 0-671-55411-5
First published 1955
Reproductions of the photographs in the exhibition held at the Museum from January 26 to May 8, 1955. Depicts men, women and children playing, working, dreaming, fighting

Photographs that changed the world; the camera as witness, the photograph as evidence; [compiled by] Lorraine Monk. Doubleday 1989 51p il $29.95   779
1. Artistic photography
ISBN 0-385-26195-0   LC 88-33595
This is a collection of some 50 mostly black-and-white photographs that have had a significant impact on society

Ray, Man, 1890-1976
Man Ray: photographs; introduction by Jean-Hubert Martin; with three texts by Man Ray. Thames & Hudson 1982 255p il hardcover o.p. paperback available $24.95
779
1. Artistic photography
ISBN 0-500-27473-8 (pa)   LC 81-53058
This volume is derived from the 1981 retrospective exhibition at the Pompidou Centre in Paris
"Besides the 347 photographs, the book contains three texts by the artist giving a fair sample of the iconoclastic flavor of his thinking. Four critical essays by well-known art critics round out the volume." Booklist

780 Music

Brendel, Alfred
Music sounded out; essays, lectures, interviews, afterthoughts. Farrar, Straus & Giroux 1991 258p il $25; pa $14   **780**
1. Music
ISBN 0-374-21651-7; 0-374-52331-2 (pa)
LC 90-48279

Brendel's essays on concepts, compositions, and composers "have been taken from lectures, expanded from record jacket notes, or were begun as recital program notes. . . . The work is an excellent reference source and more: it is a written legacy from one of the great pianist/thinkers of the last half of the 20th century." Choice

Includes bibliographic references

Gould, Glenn, 1932-1982
The Glenn Gould reader; edited and with an introduction by Tim Page. Knopf 1984 475p music $30   **780**
1. Music
ISBN 0-394-54067-0
LC 84-47819
Also available in paperback from Random House

This is a collection of "Gould's published writings—essays, reviews, profiles, satires, liner notes and anomalies—as well as interviews with Gould . . . and snippets from Gould's . . . output for radio and television." Nation

This book "shows that with [Gould's] passing we not only lost a fine musician and controversial presence but an essayist of wit and daring, energy and elegance." Books Can

Rachlin, Harvey, 1951-
The songwriter's and musician's guide to making great demos. Writer's Digest Bks. 1988 122p il pa $12.95   **780**
1. Popular music—Writing and publishing 2. Sound—Recording and reproducing
ISBN 0-89879-305-X
LC 88-5533

This book "covers preparing lead sheets; lining up vocalists and instrumentalists; booking a recording studio; choosing the various track, tape, and mixing alternatives; and using reverberation and echo effects, home recording equipment, and electronic instruments. Concluding material discusses copyrighting songs, marketing of the demo, and record keeping." Booklist

Riordan, James
Making it in the new music business. rev & updated ed. Writer's Digest Bks. 1991 378p $22.95   **780**
1. Music industry
ISBN 0-89879-458-7
LC 91-21510
First published 1988

"Covering everything from record promotion techniques to handling necessary financial matters, setting goals, and even finding investors, Riordan's compendium of advice to music business novices is suggested for collections where such in-depth materials are in demand." Booklist [review of 1988 edition]

Includes bibliographic references

Shemel, Sidney, 1913-1992
This business of music; by Sidney Shemel and M. William Krasilovsky. Billboard Bks. il $27.50   **780**
1. Music industry 2. Music—Economic aspects 3. Copyright—Music 4. Popular music—Writing and publishing

First published 1964. (6th edition 1990) Periodically revised

"A compendium of useful information on contracts, copyrights, record production, music videos, agents and managers, performing-rights organizations, and other business practices specific to music." Sheehy. Guide to Ref Books. 10th edition. suppl

Includes bibliographic references

780.2 Music—Miscellany

Cook, Richard, 1957-
The Penguin guide to jazz on CD, LP and cassette; [by] Richard Cook and Brian Morton. Penguin Bks. 1992 1287p pa $22.50   **780.2**
1. Jazz music—Discography 2. Sound recordings
ISBN 0-14-015364-0

A "critical guide to currently available recorded jazz from its beginning in 1917 to the present. The book covers more than 1,300 jazz musicians and groups and is organized alphabetically by name. . . . The entry for each recording is preceded by a rating from one to five stars (five is the very best) and includes information about label and catalog number, formats in which available, performers and instrumental credits, and date of the recordings." Booklist

Greenfield, Edward
The Penguin guide to bargain compact discs and cassettes; [by] Edward Greenfield, Robert Layton and Ivan March; edited by Ivan March. Penguin Bks. 1992 689p pa $17.50   **780.2**
1. Compact discs 2. Music—Discography
ISBN 0-14-046919-2

A guide to CDs costing under $12 in the United States and under £10 in the United Kingdom. Entries provide information on cost, quality, recording technology used (i.e. digital or digital remastering) and a brief critical description

March, Ivan
The Penguin guide to compact discs and cassettes; [by] Ivan March, Edward Greenfield, Robert Layton; edited by Ivan March. new ed. Penguin Bks. 1992 1348p pa $23.50   **780.2**
1. Compact discs 2. Music—Discography
ISBN 0-14-046918-4

A distillation of The Penguin guide to compact discs, published 1990; and The Penguin guide to compact discs and cassettes yearbook 1991/2, published 1991, both by Edward Greenfield, Albert Layton, and Ivan March

This guide is arranged by composer, then by type of composition. Entries include evaluations of both performance and recording quality

The **New** Rolling Stone record guide; revised, updated and more complete than ever, this indispensable book reviews and rates over 12,000 rock, pop, soul, country, blues, folk and gospel albums; edited by Dave Marsh and John Swenson. Rolling Stone Press 1983 xxiv, 648p pa $17.95
780.2

1. Popular music—Discography 2. Sound recordings
ISBN 0-394-72107-1   LC 82-40116
"A Random House/Rolling Stone Press book"
First published 1980 with title: The Rolling Stone record guide

"This work is aimed at the consumer and puts albums in a historical context with a critical evaluation. Rock, soul, country, pop, blues, jazz, and gospel are covered, with emphasis on rock. Entries include the catalog number, record company, and arrangement by artist. The reviews are readable and concise; a rating system indicates the relative importance of each album." Ref Sources for Small & Medium-sized Libr. 5th edition

780.3   Music—Encyclopedias and dictionaries

Kennedy, Michael, 1926-
The Oxford dictionary of music. Oxford Univ. Press 1985 810p $49.95   **780.3**

1. Music—Dictionaries 2. Musicians—Dictionaries
ISBN 0-19-311333-3   LC 84-22803
A revised and enlarged edition of The Concise Oxford dictionary of music, third edition published 1980

"There are some 10,000 entries in the new ODM. The book's easy-to-use alphabetically arranged entries include all types of topics related to music: composers, performing artists, orchestras, titles and descriptions of individual works, musical forms and terms, institutions, and writers of music. . . . The ODM will be indispensable to all types of libraries." Booklist

The **New** Grove dictionary of music and musicians; edited by Stanley Sadie. Macmillan 1980 20v il music $2300
780.3

1. Music—Dictionaries 2. Musicians—Dictionaries
ISBN 0-333-23111-2   LC 79-26207
Supersedes Grove's dictionary of music and musicians, first published 1878-1889

"Traditionally the standard multivolume music reference in English. Compared to 'Old Grove,' *New Grove* has twice the amount of information, reflecting the tremendous growth in the field of musicology. Expanded sections include ethnomusicology, popular music, biographies, early music, and bibliographies. The final volume contains multiple appendices and indexes. Very scholarly but accessible to the general readers." N Y Public Libr Book of How & Where to Look It Up

The **New** Harvard dictionary of music; edited by Don Michael Randel. Belknap Press 1986 942p il $37.50   **780.3**

1. Music—Dictionaries
ISBN 0-674-61525-5   LC 86-4780
First published 1944 with title: Harvard dictionary of music, by Willi Apel

"Quick reference entries contrast with longer encyclopedia-length articles on all topics of music including history, popular music, mixed media, and instruments. Also covers non-Western music." N Y Public Libr Book of How & Where to Look It Up

The **New** Oxford companion to music; general editor: Denis Arnold. Oxford Univ. Press 1983 2v il music set $135
780.3

1. Music—Dictionaries 2. Musicians—Dictionaries
ISBN 0-19-311316-3   LC 83-233314
Based on The Oxford companion to music, by Percy A. Scholes, entered below

"Written for the general reader, this standard dictionary covers all areas of musical interest. There are articles about composers and articles on music, covering forms, terms, instruments, acoustical principles, and notation. Some are encyclopedic and others quite short. Numerous cross-references link topics of varying length and depth." Ref Sources for Small & Medium-sized Libr. 5th edition

The **Norton/Grove** concise encyclopedia of music; edited by Stanley Sadie; assistant editor: Alison Latham. Norton 1988 850p il $40
780.3

1. Music—Dictionaries
ISBN 0-393-02620-5   LC 89-200184
Published in the United Kingdom with title: The Grove concise dictionary of music

Based on The New Grove dictionary of music and musicians, entered above, this work offers "some 10,000 short entries for composers, performers, instruments, musical terms, genres, musical works, music publishing, instrument makers, acoustics, and non-Western music. . . . In breadth, balance, and authority, this is a valuable resource." Best Ref Books, 1986-1990

Roche, Jerome
A dictionary of early music; from the troubadours to Monteverdi; by Jerome & Elizabeth Roche. Oxford Univ. Press 1981 208p il $27.95   **780.3**

1. Music—Dictionaries 2. Composers—Dictionaries
ISBN 0-19-520255-4   LC 81-82688
Approximately 1,000 entries dealing with medieval, Renaissance and early baroque music. In addition to entries devoted to composers are terms, types of music, instruments and cross-references. Printed editions of music are cited

"The explanations are necessarily brief, as are the biographical sketches . . . but they're clear, and carefully done. Recommended especially for collections with limited resources for music." Libr J

Scholes, Percy Alfred, 1877-1958
The Oxford companion to music; edited by John Owen Ward. 10th ed rev and reset. Oxford Univ. Press 1970 1189p il music $49.95
780.3

1. Music—Dictionaries 2. Musicians—Dictionaries
ISBN 0-19-311306-6
First published 1938

Alphabetically arranged by subject, this volume contains biographies of composers and articles on every aspect of music, with thousands of cross-references to

Scholes, Percy Alfred, 1877-1958 — *Continued*
related entries and subjects, and detailed accounts of opera plots

Slonimsky, Nicolas, 1894-
Lectionary of music. McGraw-Hill 1989
521p il o.p.; Anchor Bks. paperback
available $14.95   **780.3**
  1. Music—Dictionaries
  ISBN 0-385-41421-8 (pa)   LC 89-2515
"Set out from A to Z, the entries range from music terms, styles, and major concepts to opera synopses and musical trivia; fully a third are names of compositions. The musical poly-math Slonimsky, who has also given us a lexicon of musical invective, treats all entries with an inimitable authority mixed with wit and telling anecdote. . . . Recommended." Libr J

780.79   Music—Competitions, festivals, awards, financial support

The **Music** lover's guide to Europe; a compendium of festivals, concerts, and opera; Roberta Gottesman, editor; Catherine Sentman, associate editor. Wiley 1992 434p il pa $14.95   **780.79**
  1. Music festivals—Directories
  ISBN 0-471-53310-6   LC 91-14409
A "guide to both the major and lesser-known musical events in each of eighteen European countries. It describes 600 events in 300 locations—including Eastern Europe. It tells you when and where the music plays, the type of musical presentation, recent performers, box office and ticket information (including phone and fax numbers), and . . . descriptions of each host city." Publisher's note

Rabin, Carol Price
Music festivals in America; classical, opera, jazz, pops, country, old-time fiddlers, folk, bluegrass, Cajun; illustrated by Celia Elke. 4th ed. Berkshire Traveller Press 1990 271p il maps pa $10.95   **780.79**
  1. Music festivals—Directories
  ISBN 0-930145-01-1   LC 90-901
First published 1979 with title: A guide to music festivals in America

A guide to music festivals in North America arranged by category of music and by state. Information is given on locations, dates, names, addresses and telephone numbers for tickets

780.89   Music of racial, ethnic, national groups

Baraka, Imamu Amiri, 1934-
Black music; [by] LeRoi Jones. Greenwood Press 1980 221p il $42.50   **780.89**
  1. Black music—History and criticism 2. Jazz music
  ISBN 0-313-22518-4   LC 80-15439
A reissue of the title first published 1967 by Morrow

"Thelonius Monk, John Coltrane, and Sonny Murray are a few of the several personalities whose background, distinctive musical efforts, and accomplishments and disappointments are featured in this assemblage of profiles, critical reviews, essays, and other short pieces dating from 1959 to 1967." Booklist
Includes discography

Blues people; Negro music in white America; by LeRoi Jones. Greenwood Press 1980 c1963 244p $49.50   **780.89**
  1. Black music—History and criticism 2. Blues music 3. Jazz music
  ISBN 0-313-22519-2   LC 80-15648
A reissue of the title first published 1963 by Morrow

Contents: The Negro as non-American; The Negro as property; African slaves; American slaves: their music; Afro-Christian music and religion; Slave and post-slave; Primitive blues and primitive jazz; Classic blues: The city; Enter the middle class; Swing—from verb to noun; The blues continuum; The modern scene
Includes bibliographic references

Shaw, Arnold
Black popular music in America; from the spirituals, minstrels, and ragtime to soul, disco, and hip-hop. Schirmer Bks. 1986 386p il $24.95   **780.89**
  1. Black music—History and criticism 2. Popular music
  ISBN 0-02-872310-4   LC 85-24191
"Shaw examines five key black styles—minstrelsy, spirituals, ragtime, jazz, and blues—analyzing the origins and developments of each, profiling important artists and songs, and exploring the 'white synthesis'. . . . Overall this is a worthy, much needed, well-documented history." Libr J
Includes bibliography

Southern, Eileen
The music of black Americans; a history. 2nd ed. Norton 1983 xx, 602p il music hardcover o.p. paperback available $18.95   **780.89**
  1. Black music—History and criticism
  ISBN 0-393-95279-7 (pa)   LC 82-25960
First published 1971

A survey of black music from its West African roots to 20th century jazz and symphonic works

780.9   Music—Historical and geographical treatment

Abraham, Gerald, 1904-1988
The concise Oxford history of music. Oxford Univ. Press 1979 968p il maps $75; pa $22.95   **780.9**
  1. Music—History and criticism
  ISBN 0-19-311319-8; 0-19-284010-X (pa)
                               LC 79-40550
This volume traces the "history of Western music from Sumerian writing-tables dating c. 3000 B. C. through the music of Stravinski. Included . . . [are four sections on] non-Western music: music of Islam, India, Eastern Asia, and Black Africa and America." Choice

Abraham, Gerald, 1904-1988—*Continued*

"The writing style is scholarly but interesting, and Abraham clearly states his critical opinions. . . . Bibliographic essays by music authorities are included, and a detailed index provides access to the wealth of information in the volume." Wilson Libr Bull

Bukofzer, Manfred F., 1910-1955

Music in the Baroque era, from Monteverdi to Bach. Norton 1947 489p il $23.95   **780.9**

1. Music—History and criticism
ISBN 0-393-09745-5

"A general introduction on 'Renaissance versus Baroque Music' prepares us for six chapters that deal with the early, the middle, and the late baroque in Italy, Germany, and the Northern countries, France, England, Spain, and even colonial America. A special chapter is devoted to Bach and another to Handel." Music Libr Assoc Notes

Includes bibliography

Copland, Aaron, 1900-1990

Copland on music. Doubleday 1960 280p o.p.; Norton paperback available $8.95   **780.9**

1. Music—History and criticism
ISBN 0-393-00198-9 (pa)

Analyzed in Essay and general literature index

"A collection of writings about music by the composer, selected over a quite lengthy period of time. Various in quality, generally moderate and intelligent, they are aimed at the 'appreciation' audience rather than at musicians." Publ Wkly

Einstein, Alfred, 1880-1952

Music in the romantic era. Norton 1947 371p il $24.95   **780.9**

1. Music—History and criticism 2. Romanticism
ISBN 0-393-09733-1

Scholarly study of the development of musical thought from the time of Schubert to the death of Wagner. In his foreword the author says: "My aim has been to show how the Romantic movement was manifested in music and how music affected the Romantic movement"

Grout, Donald Jay, 1902-1987

A history of Western music; [by] Donald Jay Grout & Claude V. Palisca. 4th ed. Norton 1988 910p il music $45.95   **780.9**

1. Music—History and criticism
ISBN 0-393-95627-X   LC 88-5204

Also available in a shorter edition $41.95 (ISBN 0-393-95629-6)

First published 1960

The authors survey the course of Western music from the ancient world to modern atonalism and dodecaphony. They cover vocal and instrumental forms, notation, performance, music-printing, the development of instruments, and biographical information on composers

Includes bibliographies

Machlis, Joseph, 1906-

Introduction to contemporary music. 2nd ed. Norton 1979 xxv, 694p il music $28.95   **780.9**

1. Music—History and criticism 2. Music—Analysis, appreciation
ISBN 0-393-09026-4   LC 78-10327

First published 1961

This volume is divided into three sections. Part One describes tonality, form, harmony, rhythm, and orchestration in twentieth-century music. European developments in music are stressed in Part Two, with particular emphasis on the achievements of Stravinsky, Bartok, and Hindemith. Part Three provides a chronological view of American music

Includes bibliography

New Oxford history of music. Oxford Univ. Press 1954-1990 10v il music v1, 3-8, 10 ea $95; v2, 9 ea $99   **780.9**

1. Music—History and criticism

Supersedes The Oxford history of music, first published 1901-1905

A projected 11-volume work

Contents: v1 Ancient and Oriental music, edited by Egon Wellesz (ISBN 0-19-316301-2); v2 2nd ed. The Early Middle Ages to 1300, edited by Richard Crocker and David Hiley (ISBN 0-19-316329-2); v3 Ars nova and the Renaissance, 1300-1540, edited by Dom Anselm Hughes and Gerald Abraham (ISBN 0-19-316303-9); v4 The Age of humanism, 1540-1630, edited by Gerald Abraham (ISBN 0-19-316304-7); v5 Opera and church music, 1630-1750, edited by Nigel Fortune and Anthony Lewis (ISBN 0-19-316305-5); v6 Concert music, 1630-1750, edited by Gerald Abraham (ISBN 0-19-316306-3); v7 The age of enlightenment, 1745-1790, edited by Egon Wellesz and Frederick Sternfeld (ISBN 0-19-316307-1); v8 The age of Beethoven, 1790-1830, edited by Gerald Abraham (ISBN 0-19-316308-X); v9 Romanticism, 1830-1890, edited by Gerald Abraham (ISBN 0-19-316309-8); v10 The modern age, 1890-1960, edited by Martin Cooper (ISBN 0-19-316310-1)

"It would be difficult to find a scholarly multi-volume history of music of comparable statute. . . . [This work is marked by] comprehensiveness, consistency, evenness, and sheer readability." Choice

The **Norton** anthology of western music; edited by Claude V. Palisca. 2nd ed. Norton 1988 2v music pa ea $25.95   **780.9**

1. Music—History and criticism

Contents: v1 Medieval, Renaissance, baroque (ISBN 0-393-95642-3); v2 Classic, romantic, modern (ISBN 0-393-95644-X)

This work is designed to accompany A history of Western music, entered above under Grout, Donald Jay

Rosen, Charles, 1927-

The classical style: Haydn, Mozart, Beethoven. Viking 1971 467p music o.p.; Norton paperback available $14.95   **780.9**

1. Haydn, Joseph, 1732-1809 2. Mozart, Wolfgang Amadeus, 1756-1791 3. Beethoven, Ludwig van, 1770-1827 4. Music—History and criticism
ISBN 0-393-00653-0 (pa)

"Focusing on three giants of the classical period, [the author] follows the development of genres with which each is closely associated." Chicago Public Libr

Rosen, Charles, 1927-—*Continued*
"Rosen's command of his material seems absolute; his insights into the nature of the musical language of the classical masters are penetrating and mature; his prose style is uncommonly rich, yet graceful." Choice

Slonimsky, Nicolas, 1894-
Music since 1900. Schirmer Bks. $100
780.9
1. Music—History and criticism
First published 1937. (5th edition 1994) Periodically revised
"A chronology of musical events (with commentary on the events listed) makes up the bulk of the volume." Sheehy. Guide to Ref Books. 10th edition

780.92   Biographies of musicians
Collective biographies

Ammer, Christine
Unsung; a history of women in American music. Greenwood Press 1980 317p (Contributions in women's studies) $42.95; pa $7.95
780.92
1. Women musicians   2. Women composers 3. Musicians, American
ISBN 0-313-22007-7; 0-313-22909-0 (pa)
LC 79-52324
A socio-cultural assessment of the contributions women have made to American music as musicians, composers and teachers
Includes bibliography

Baker's biographical dictionary of musicians. Schirmer Bks. $125
780.92
1. Music—Bio-bibliography 2. Musicians—Dictionaries
First published 1900 under the authorship of Theodore Baker. (8th edition 1992) Periodically revised
Current editor: Nicolas Slonimsky
"Brief articles about composers, performers, critics, conductors, and teachers arranged alphabetically under surname with pronunciation." Ref Sources for Small & Medium-sized Libr. 5th edition

Composers since 1900; a biographical and critical guide; compiled and edited by David Ewen. Wilson, H.W. 1969 639p il $62
780.92
1. Composers—Dictionaries   2. Music—Bio-bibliography
ISBN 0-8242-0400-X
First supplement published 1981 available for $42 (ISBN 0-8242-0664-9)
Replaces: Composers of today, American composers today, and European composers today, originally published 1934, 1949 and 1954, respectively
This work contains biographical sketches of 220 principal composers of the twentieth century. Included among traditionalists, innovators, eclectics, and romanticists are the avant-garde. The first supplement includes 47 additional composers and updated information on 172 composers from the base volume

The **Concise** Baker's biographical dictionary of musicians; [edited by] Nicholas Slonimsky. Schirmer Bks. $50   780.92
1. Music—Bio-bibliography 2. Musicians—Dictionaries
An abridged version of Baker's biographical dictionary of musicians entered above (8th edition 1993) Periodically revised

Contemporary composers; editors, Brian Morton, Pamela Collins; with a preface by Brian Ferneyhough. St. James Press 1992 1019p $125
780.92
1. Composers—Dictionaries   2. Music—Bio-bibliography
ISBN 1-55862-085-0   LC 93-104306
A "biographical survey of approximately 500 serious living composers. . . . Worldwide in scope, the profiles . . . consist of three main sections: a short biographical sketch; a list of works with dates of completion and first performance; and a brief assessment of each composer's work within the context of his or her day. . . . An important reference work." Libr J

Cross, Milton
The Milton Cross new encyclopedia of the great composers and their music; [by] Milton Cross and David Ewen. rev and expanded. Doubleday 1969 2v $35
780.92
1. Composers—Dictionaries   2. Music—Bio-bibliography
ISBN 0-385-03635-3
First published 1953
"Directed to the comparatively uninformed layperson, this covers biographies of musicians, with sections on the orchestra, the history of music, and a dictionary of musical terms." Ref Sources for Small & Medium-sized Libr. 5th edition

Ewen, David, 1907-1985
American songwriters; an H. W. Wilson biographical dictionary. Wilson, H.W. 1987 489p il $59
780.92
1. Composers, American—Dictionaries 2. Lyricists—Dictionaries
ISBN 0-8242-0744-0   LC 86-24654
Replaces Popular American composers and Popular American composers: First supplement, published 1962 and 1972 respectively
Arranged alphabetically, this reference volume includes 146 biographical entries on American lyricists and composers. Ragtime, minstrel, Tin Pan Alley, Broadway, rock, jazz, blues, folk, country and western, and soul are among the styles represented. Biographees range from Eubie Blake, George Gershwin and George M. Cohan to Chuck Berry, Carole King and Bob Dylan

Feather, Leonard
From Satchmo to Miles; new foreword by the author. Da Capo Press 1984 c1972 258p il (Roots of jazz) $29.50; pa $9.95   780.92
1. Jazz musicians 2. Black musicians
ISBN 0-306-76230-7; 0-306-80302-X (pa)
LC 83-15223
First published 1972 by Stein & Day

Feather, Leonard—*Continued*
A collection of profiles of jazz musicians including Count Basie, Lester Young, Oscar Peterson, Ray Charles, Don Ellis, Duke Ellington, Billie Holiday, Ella Fitzgerald, Louis Armstrong, Dizzy Gillespie, Norman Granz, Miles Davis and Charlie Parker

Flanagan, Bill
Written in my soul; rock's great songwriters talk about creating their music. Contemporary Bks. 1986 432p il hardcover o.p. paperback available $11.95   **780.92**
1. Rock musicians 2. Rock music
ISBN 0-8092-4650-3 (pa)   LC 86-16629
Paperback edition contains added interview with Bruce Springsteen

The author includes only performers "from the 'rock tradition anteceded by Woody Guthrie and Leadbelly.' These narrow parameters are necessary because so many talented songwriters are not interviewed. The 27 who are include Bob Dylan, Kris Kristofferson, Mick Jagger, Joni Mitchell, David Byrne, and Joan Armatrading." SLJ

Friedwald, Will, 1961-
Jazz singing; America's great voices from Bessie Smith to bebop and beyond. Scribner 1990 477p il o.p.; Collier Bks. paperback available $15   **780.92**
1. Jazz music 2. Singers
ISBN 0-02-080131-9 (pa)   LC 89-28172
"Starting with blues singers who laid the foundations for jazz-oriented popular singing, the author follows the development of this vocal style from Bing Crosby and Louis Armstrong through a host of performers to the present day." Publ Wkly
"This is an absolutely essential book for anybody who cares in the slightest about adult popular music." Booklist

Includes discography

Gaar, Gillian G., 1959-
She's a rebel; the history of women in rock & roll. Seal Press 1992 467p il pa $16.95   **780.92**
1. Women musicians 2. Rock music
ISBN 1-87806-708-7   LC 92-16977
"Within a basically chronological context, Gaar combines her astute reassessment of rock and roll trends with scholarly details on a myriad of women rockers (not just performers and composers, but managers, producers, etc.) and punctuates all with the words of the women themselves. What emerges is a rich and lively tapestry documenting the full range of women's involvement in rock and roll." Choice

Geiringer, Karl, 1899-1989
The Bach family; seven generations of creative genius; by Karl Geiringer in collaboration with Irene Geiringer. Da Capo Press 1981 c1954 516p il map music (Da Capo Press music reprint ser) $55   **780.92**
1. Bach family 2. Bach, Johann Sebastian, 1685-1750
ISBN 0-306-79596-5

A reprint of the title first published 1954 by Oxford, with minor emendations by the author

A composite biography of seven generations of the family of Johann Sebastian Bach from the sixteenth-century Thuringia miller Veit to Wilhelm Friedrich Ernst (1759-1845) J. S. Bach's grandson

Includes bibliographies

Gitler, Ira
Jazz masters of the forties; new introduction and discography by the author. Da Capo Press 1983 c1966 290p il (Roots of jazz) hardcover o.p. paperback available $12.95   **780.92**
1. Musicians, American 2. Jazz music
ISBN 0-306-80224-4 (pa)   LC 82-2396
A reprint of the title first published 1966 by Macmillan

The author describes the emergence in the 1940's of bebop and its exponents Charlie 'Yardbird' Parker and Dizzy Gillespie. To their story the author adds those of the jazz musicians of the period: Bud Powell, Lennie Tristano, Dexter Gordon, Lee Konitz, J. J. Johnson, Oscar Pettiford, Kenny Clark, Max Roach, and composer-arranger Tadd Dameron

Includes discographies and bibliography

Great composers, 1300-1900; a biographical and critical guide; compiled and edited by David Ewen. Wilson, H.W. 1966 429p il $55   **780.92**
1. Composers—Dictionaries   2. Music—Bio-bibliography
ISBN 0-8242-0018-7

Companion volume to Composers since 1900, entered above

"Lists of principal works by and works about each composer accompany the biographies. Portraits and appendixes containing chronological and geographical lists add to the value of the work." Ref Sources for Small & Medium-sized Libr. 5th edition

Green, Stanley, 1923-1990
The world of musical comedy; the story of the American musical stage as told through the careers of its foremost composers and lyricists. 4th ed rev and enl. Da Capo Press 1984 c1980 480p il pa $22.50   **780.92**
1. Composers, American 2. Librettists 3. Musicals
ISBN 0-306-80207-4   LC 83-26340
First published 1960 by Ziff-Davis; this is a reprint of the 1980 edition published by A. S. Barnes supplemented with author corrections

"From Victor Herbert to Marvin Hamlisch, Green gives us a classic history of the genre. . . . Thirty-one chapters tell the tale of some 70 individuals or teams that have had a lasting effect on the musical theater. . . . The appendix gives the vitals on every major production of the past 85 years." Booklist

Harris, Sheldon
Blues who's who; a biographical dictionary of blues singers. Da Capo Press 1981 c1979 775p il pa $32.50 **780.92**
1. Blues music 2. Singers
ISBN 0-306-80155-8   LC 81-7873
A reprint of the title first published 1979 by Arlington House
"Covers career histories of 571 blues singers from the turn of the century to contemporary figures. Information is included on dates, places, instruments played, biographical notes, career credits, songs written, awards, and references to sources of further information. There are often photographs with the article and a selected bibliography of blues music. Several useful indexes." Ref Sources for Small & Medium-sized Libr. 5th edition

Harrison, Daphne Duval, 1932-
Black pearls; blues queens of the 1920s. Rutgers Univ. Press 1988 295p il $19.95; $12.95 **780.92**
1. Blues music 2. Black singers
ISBN 0-8135-1279-4; 0-8135-1280-8 (pa)
                                      LC 87-14084
"This book tells the cultural and social impact of the blues during the 1920s when the genre was dominated by women, both on stage and on record. Harrison . . . writes with authority, focusing particularly on Sippie Wallace, Edith Wilson, Victoria Spivey, and Alberta Hunter as she analyzes the music and the collective black experience out of which it grew. A significant book." Libr J
Includes bibliography

Jacobs, Arthur
The Penguin dictionary of musical performers. Viking 1990 250p $21.95
                                      780.92
1. Musicians—Dictionaries
ISBN 0-670-80755-9   LC 91-213281
Also available in paperback from Penguin Bks.
"A biographical guide to significant interpreters of classical music, singers, solo instrumentalists, conductors, orchestras, and string quartets ranging from the seventeenth century to the present day." Title page
"Identifying over 2500 famous performers of classical music from the 1500s to the present, this up-to-date information will be helpful for ready reference and to supplement other titles." Ref Sources for Small & Medium-sized Libr. 5th edition

Musicians since 1900; performers in concert and opera; compiled and edited by David Ewen. Wilson, H.W. 1978 974p il $75
                                      780.92
1. Musicians—Dictionaries 2. Music—Bio-bibliography
3. Opera—Bio-bibliography
ISBN 0-8242-0565-0   LC 78-12727
"Replaces 'Living musicians' and its supplement (1940-57). Gives 'detailed biographical, critical and personal information about 432 of the most distinguished performing musicians in concert and opera since 1900.'—Introd.'
. . . A few bibliographical references are given at the end of each biography; a classified list of musicians concludes the volume." Sheehy. Guide to Ref Books. 10th edition

Richards, Tad
The new country music encyclopedia; [by] Tad Richards & Melvin B. Shestack. Simon & Schuster 1993 270p il pa $14 **780.92**
1. Country musicians 2. Country music—Dictionaries
ISBN 0-671-78258-4   LC 93-17689
"A Fireside book"
Replaces The country music encyclopedia, by Melvin Shestack, published 1974 by Crowell
This volume provides biographies of more than 200 country music singers and songwriters of the past and present. The entries are arranged alphabetically by artist or group, from Alabama to Dwight Yoakam
Includes discography

Schonberg, Harold C.
The great pianists. rev and updated. Simon & Schuster 1987 525p il hardcover o.p. paperback available $14.95 **780.92**
1. Pianists
ISBN 0-671-63837-8 (pa)   LC 87-341
"A Fireside book"
First published 1963
Beginning with the Bach family, the author describes the personal lives and careers of outstanding pianists from the eighteenth century to the present
The lives of the great composers. rev ed. Norton 1981 653p il $27.50 **780.92**
1. Composers
ISBN 0-393-01302-2   LC 80-15058
First published 1970
This book traces the lives of important musical figures from Bach to Schoenberg. The composers are presented in the context of their own times and lesser artists are introduced as they relate to the subject being discussed. A final chapter deals with the aspects and trends of "serious" music after 1945
Includes bibliography

Southern, Eileen
Biographical dictionary of Afro-American and African musicians. Greenwood Press 1982 478p (Greenwood encyclopedia of black music) $75 **780.92**
1. Black musicians—Dictionaries
ISBN 0-313-21339-9   LC 81-2586
"Biographical information on more than 1500 people active in the musical world—composers, performers, educators, etc. . . . Besides a general name index, appendixes list persons by date of birth and musical occupation. Coverage is for people born from 1640 to 1945 and includes all types of musical activity—popular, classical, folk, etc." Ref Sources for Small & Medium-sized Libr. 5th edition

Who's who in American music: classical; edited by Jaques Cattell Press. 2nd ed. Bowker 1985 783p $124.95 **780.92**
1. Musicians—Dictionaries
ISBN 0-8352-2074-5
First published 1983
"Provides biographical information on 9308 professional musicians currently active in 'the creation, performance, preservation, or promotion of serious music in America.' It identifies each person's specialty and lists as appropriate the person's birthdate, place of birth, edu-

Who's who in American music: classical—
Continued
cation, debut performances, works, recorded performances, professional and teaching experience, honors, major publications, address, and other pertinent information. Geographic and professional classifications indexes." Ref Sources for Small & Medium-sized Libr. 5th edition

Individual biographies

Adler, Richard
Adler, Richard. You gotta have heart; an autobiography; [by] Richard Adler with Lee Davis. Fine, D.I. 1989 342p $21.95
780.92
ISBN 1-55611-201-7   LC 89-46032

"For composer-lyricist Adler, success came early, with *The Pajama Game* and *Damn Yankees*. But after the death of his partner, Jerry Ross, finding it impossible to write musicals with a collaborator, he turned from Broadway to a diversified career as a writer of jingles, organizer of White House galas and composer of concert music. Adler has been involved with the most glamorous names in show business, and they, as well as his numerous wives and lovers, all appear in this autobiography." Publ Wkly

Armstrong, Louis, 1900-1971
Collier, James Lincoln. Louis Armstrong, an American genius. Oxford Univ. Press 1983 383p il $30; pa $12.95   **780.92**
ISBN 0-19-503377-9; 0-19-503727-8 (pa)
                                       LC 83-11378
The author tells the story of Armstrong's life and evaluates his musical contributions

"Collier's scholarship is impeccable, his note-by-note musical analysis razor sharp, and his conclusions about Armstrong's place in American music expertly defended. In all respects, a biography worthy of its subject." Booklist

Giddins, Gary. Satchmo. Doubleday 1988 239p il $24.95   **780.92**
ISBN 0-385-24428-2   LC 87-34001
"A Dolphin book"

The author provides an "overview of Armstrong's career, a survey of his major recordings and some interesting observations about Armstrong's contributions to world culture. Especially welcome are the plentiful excerpts from Armstrong's diaries and letters. . . . [This] is a valuable, jubilant look at a great man and artist." N Y Times Book Rev

Includes bibliography

Bach, Johann Sebastian, 1685-1750
Geiringer, Karl. Johann Sebastian Bach; the culmination of an era; by Karl Geiringer in collaboration with Irene Geiringer. Oxford Univ. Press 1966 382p il music $37
780.92
ISBN 0-19-500554-6

The biographical "first third of the book . . . combines historical authority with . . . praise of Bach's craft, honesty, devoutness, and transcendent genius. The remaining two-thirds [is] a critical and analytical discussion of several hundred compositions." Natl Rev

Includes bibliography

Bailey, Pearl, 1918-1990
Bailey, Pearl. Between you and me; a heartfelt memoir on learning, loving and living. Doubleday 1989 270p il $17.95
780.92
ISBN 0-385-27972-8   LC 89-32342
In this memoir the singer and performer reflects on her experiences as an undergraduate at Georgetown University where she received her degree at age 67. She also discusses the breakdown of family life and her years as delegate to the U.S. Mission to the United Nations

Barenboim, Daniel
Barenboim, Daniel. Daniel Barenboim; a life in music; edited by Michael Lewin. Scribner 1992 198p il $23   **780.92**
ISBN 0-684-19326-4   LC 92-7459
"A Robert Stewart book"

Barenboim "traces his career from his wunderkind years in Argentina through his marriage to late cellist Jacqueline du Pre to his recent tenures with the Paris Opera and the Berlin and Israel philharmonics." Libr J

"Barenboim's little book about music is light, seldom controversial, seldom profound or surprising, but certainly not without interest." Booklist

Basie, Count, 1904-1984
Basie, Count. Good morning blues: the autobiography of Count Basie; as told to Albert Murray. Random House 1985 399p il o.p.; Fine, D.I. paperback available $10.95
780.92
ISBN 0-917657-89-6 (pa)   LC 85-2439

"Basie pays tribute to his colleagues and managers (and to John Hammond for 'discovering' him), but does not hesitate to discuss their weaknesses and shortcomings; his language is direct and earthy. Although some of the book reads more like a catalogue or itinerary than an autobiography, it will have strong appeal for jazz buffs and fans of the late bandleader." Publ Wkly

Dance, Stanley. The world of Count Basie. Da Capo Press 1985 c1980 xxi, 399p il pa $13.95   **780.92**
1. Jazz musicians
ISBN 0-306-80245-7   LC 85-12901
A reprint of the title first published 1980 by Scribner

This book "consists of numerous tape-recorded and edited interviews with musicians and vocalists associated with Basie, and each gets to tell his own story. Many overlap and there are interesting confirmations and disputes over details. The language has been polished (and no doubt in some cases cleaned up), but Dance does not noticeably impose his own views on others. There are good photographs." Choice

Includes bibliography and discography

Beethoven, Ludwig van, 1770-1827
Solomon, Maynard. Beethoven. Schirmer Bks. 1977 400p il map music $20.95; pa $12.95   **780.92**
ISBN 0-02-872460-7; 0-02-872240-X (pa) LC 77-5242
"Solomon's four-part biography divides Beethoven's life by geographical, personal, and creative eras, deftly merging the composer's private life with his artistic

Beethoven, Ludwig van, 1770-1827 — *Continued*
accomplishments." Booklist

Includes bibliography

Berlin, Irving, 1888-1989
Bergreen, Laurence. As thousands cheer: the life of Irving Berlin. Viking 1990 658p o.p.; Penguin Bks. paperback available $15.95   **780.92**

ISBN 0-14-010398-8 (pa)   LC 89-40677

The author "brings us the life of a man who, in addition to being an untrained tunesmith of genius . . . was reclusive, insecure and toward the end of his life, paranoid." Publ Wkly

"A substantial contribution to our knowledge, not just of Irving Berlin but of American vernacular music." NY Times Book Rev

Includes bibliography

Berlioz, Hector, 1803-1869
Holoman, D. Kern. Berlioz. Harvard Univ. Press 1989 687p il $35   **780.92**

ISBN 0-674-06778-9   LC 88-35788

This is a biography of the nineteenth-century composer, conductor, and music critic

"There may be aspects of Berlioz's life which Holoman has not fathomed, but be paints as full a picture as has yet been attempted." New Statesman

Includes bibliography

Bernstein, Leonard, 1918-1990
Chapin, Schuyler. Leonard Bernstein; notes from a friend. Walker & Co. 1992 178p $17.95   **780.92**

ISBN 0-8027-1216-9   LC 92-15738

"This informal portrait . . . intimately describes many of the conductor and composer's major projects. . . . The book opens with an excruciating account of the conductor's final illness, then offers glowing vignettes of the 'colorful, explosive, wildly talented, sometimes impossible' human being, as well as detailed accounts of recording sessions and television appearances." N Y Times Book Rev

Peyser, Joan. Bernstein; a biography. Beech Tree Bks. 1987 481p il o.p.; Ballantine Bks. paperback available $5.95   **780.92**

ISBN 0-345-35296-3 (pa)   LC 86-30225

This biography of Leonard Bernstein discusses his personal life and his career as composer and conductor

This study is "thorough, perceptive, and altogether readable. It will appeal to a wide range of readers, and thus belongs in almost any collection." Libr J

Brahms, Johannes, 1833-1897
Geiringer, Karl. Brahms, his life and work; [by] Karl Geiringer in collaboration with Irene Geiringer. 3rd, enl ed, with a new appendix, Brahms as a reader and collector. Da Capo Press 1982 397p il (Da Capo Press music reprint ser) $45; pa $13.95   **780.92**

ISBN 0-306-76093-2; 0-306-80223-6 (pa)
                LC 81-12549

A reprint of the edition published 1947 by Allen & Unwin

This interpretation is based upon over a thousand letters written by Brahms or addressed to him, and upon original manuscripts and printed copies of his compositions with his own corrections and alterations

Includes bibliography

MacDonald, Malcolm. Brahms. Schirmer Bks. 1990 490p il music $29.95   **780.92**

ISBN 0-02-871393-1   LC 90-8545

The author "relates all known facts about the composer, his relationship with friends and acquaintances, and his music. Biography and creative output are interwoven throughout the book, as the author rather laboriously discusses each composition in chronological order. It is assumed that the reader has a fair knowledge of Brahm's works and can read music, for MacDonald includes 68 musical examples that are important to the discussion. MacDonald's verbose style may put off the casual reader, but for a real Brahms lover, the book is a treat." Libr J

Includes bibliographic references

Brown, James
Brown, James. James Brown, the godfather of soul; [by] James Brown, with Bruce Tucker. Macmillan 1986 336p il o.p.; Thunder's Mouth Press paperback available $13.95   **780.92**

ISBN 0-938410-97-0 (pa)   LC 86-12715

"Brown's musical career spans four decades and his style defines the genre called soul. He has chronicled his life, from his birth in 1933 through a troubled youth, prison, and the ups and downs of a spiraling career." Libr J

This "is a solid, informative autobiography, and fans will welcome its vast discography." N Y Times Book Rev

Cage, John
Revill, David. The roaring silence: John Cage, a life. Arcade Pub. 1992 375p il $27.95; pa $12.95   **780.92**

ISBN 1-55970-166-8; 1-55970-220-6 (pa) LC 92-5917

This is a biography of the twentieth-century American composer

"The biography is thoroughly researched and generally sprightly in tone, and risks the occasional reproof to Cage. . . . But Revill's thrust is inevitably to take Cage on his own terms." London Rev Books

Includes bibliographic references

Callas, Maria, 1923-1977

Scott, Michael. Maria Meneghini Callas. Northeastern Univ. Press 1992 372p il $30
780.92

ISBN 1-55553-146-6   LC 92-17103

The author "traces the career of the controversial diva from her teenage appearances as a budding prima donna through the triumphs of the early 1950s to later years when Callas's voice was increasingly frail." Publ Wkly

"We come away from this critical biography with a sound understanding of Callas' complicated personal life and her total commitment to her instrument and career." Booklist

Includes bibliographic references

Carreras, José, 1946-

Carreras, José. Singing from the soul; an autobiography. Y.C.P. Publs. 1991 280p il (Lib. of courage) $27.95   **780.92**

ISBN 1-878756-89-3   LC 90-71130

"The Spanish tenor begins his life story with an account of his diagnosis, treatment, and recovery from leukemia in 1987 and 1988. His return to the concert and operatic stages in the following year provides a triumphant and emotional climax midway through the book. . . . The second half of the book then sketches in Carreras' previous life and career." Booklist

Includes discography

Caruso, Enrico, 1873-1921

Greenfeld, Howard. Caruso. Putnam 1983 275p il o.p.; Da Capo Press paperback available $9.95   **780.92**

ISBN 0-306-80215-5 (pa)   LC 82-13301

This biography "shows how the oldest surviving son of 20 children from a lower-class Neapolitan family developed his voice, musicianship and acting ability into outstanding instruments that won him international acclaim. In addition to recounting Caruso's appearances at opera houses around the world, Greenfeld depicts him as a sensitive colleague and a prankster who nevertheless always suffered from stage fright." Publ Wkly

Includes bibliography

Scott, Michael. The great Caruso. Knopf 1988 322p il $24.95   **780.92**

ISBN 0-394-53681-9   LC 87-46107

Also available in paperback from Northeastern Univ. Press

In this biography "the greatness of the singer is established in terms not only of vocal splendor, but also of an incredibly high level of consistency in performance, and in a giving of self through music for people." Choice

Includes discography and bibliography

Cole, Nat King, 1919?-1965

Gourse, Leslie. Unforgettable: the life and mystique of Nat King Cole. St. Martin's Press 1991 309p il $22.95; pa $12.95
780.92

ISBN 0-312-05982-5; 0-312-07877-3 (pa)
LC 90-27409

This biography looks at "Cole's Chicago childhood, musical roots, early successes, marriages, growing fame, near-disastrous run-in with the IRS, and early death from lung cancer." Booklist

Includes discography and bibliography

Collins, Judy, 1939-

Collins, Judy. Trust your heart; an autobiography. Houghton Mifflin 1987 275p il o.p.; Fawcett Bks. paperback available $4.95   **780.92**

ISBN 0-449-21662-4 (pa)   LC 87-17180

"Folksinger Collins tells her life story from the vantage point of a . . . journal, kept throughout 1985, which launches her on remembrances of the past. The chronology is consistent, and the story is an intriguing one. . . . In addition to reliving her glory days in the sixties, Collins discusses the lesser-known facets of her life since that time." Booklist

Copland, Aaron, 1900-1990

Copland, Aaron. Copland, since 1943; by Aaron Copland and Vivian Perlis. St. Martin's Press 1989 463p il $29.95; pa $14.95   **780.92**

ISBN 0-312-03313-3; 0-312-05066-6 (pa)

LC 89-34847

First volume of autobiography covering the years 1900 through 1942, published 1984 available pa $12.95 (0-312-01149-0)

"This second volume of the well-known Copland-Perlis collaboration is essentially an autobiography interspersed with historical narrative and reminiscences by Copland's associates. Perlis, ever the diligent historian, provides copious documents and footnotes. . . . Scholars and lay readers alike will find this an indispensable source of Copland lore." Libr J

Includes bibliography

Davis, Miles

Davis, Miles. Miles, the autobiography; [by] Miles Davis with Quincy Troupe. Simon & Schuster 1989 431p il hardcover o.p. paperback available $12.95   **780.92**

ISBN 0-671-72582-3 (pa)   LC 89-19652

"The legendary jazz musician Miles Davis . . . takes us on a historical journey that begins with his growing up in the mid-1920s in East St. Louis, then moves on to New York City in the 1940s, where he was a student at the Julliard School of Music, and to his encounters with other jazz greats like Charlie Parker, Dizzy Gillespie, Billie Holiday, Herbie Hancock, and George Duke." Libr J

This book "is profusely detailed, exceedingly candid and eminently readable—by any criterion a major addition to the literature of jazz." N Y Times Book Rev

Dylan, Bob, 1941-

Shelton, Robert. No direction home: the life and music of Bob Dylan. Morrow 1986 573p il o.p.; Ballantine Bks. paperback available $5.95   **780.92**

ISBN 0-345-34721-8 (pa)   LC 85-26781

This is a "biography recounting Dylan's life, analyzing his music, and attempting to place Dylan against the background of his times." Choice

Dylan, Bob, 1941-—*Continued*
"Descriptions of Dylan's family background, his adolescence in Hibbing, Minnesota, and brief university career are without peer. In many respects, [this] supersedes all previous books on Dylan." New Statesman

Includes discography and bibliography

Spitz, Bob. Dylan; a biography. McGraw-Hill 1989 639p il $19.95   **780.92**
ISBN 0-07-060330-8   LC 88-12912

Also available in paperback from Norton

"Lamenting the impenetrable mythology that surrounds singer/songwriter Bob Dylan . . . Spitz accomplishes his demystification through a sometimes fanciful reconstruction of Dylan's life, replete with sordid examples of his reputedly capricious personality. Although the relevance of such treatment is questionable and his often lurid prose will be objectionable to some, Spitz gives a fascinating portrayal of one of the most influential and complex figures in popular music." Choice

Ellington, Duke, 1899-1974
Collier, James Lincoln. Duke Ellington. Oxford Univ. Press 1987 340p il $30
     780.92
ISBN 0-19-503770-7   LC 86-33309

This book, "which includes minibiographies of Ellington's sidemen and detailed musical discussions of individual recordings, is a . . . reflective look at Ellington's career and recordings. The greater part is devoted to Ellington's salad days as a bandleader from the 1920s to the 1940s." Libr J

Includes discography

Dance, Stanley. The world of Duke Ellington. Scribner 1970 311p il o.p.; Da Capo Press paperback available $10.95
     780.92
ISBN 0-306-80136-1 (pa)

The author portrays the jazz maestro, traces his musical career and discusses his music. Also included are interviews with musicians such as Johnny Hodges, Barney Bigard, Ben Webster and Sonny Greer who tell about Duke, their own careers and other musicians

Includes discography

Ellington, Duke. Music is my mistress; by Edward Kennedy Ellington. Doubleday 1973 522p il o.p.; Da Capo Press paperback available $13.95   **780.92**
ISBN 0-306-80033-0 (pa)

"After a prologue there are eight acts unfolding in chronological order—all dealing with Duke Ellington's life. . . . The book is complete with abundant pictures of family, friends, and influential people the composer-bandleader-pianist has met and played with." Best Sellers

Includes bibliography and discography

Foster, Stephen Collins, 1826-1864
Howard, John Tasker. Stephen Foster, America's troubadour. [rev ed]. Crowell 1953 433p il o.p.; Arden Lib. reprint available $50   **780.92**
ISBN 0-8495-2436-9

First published 1934

This volume is a comprehensive and factual biography based on family letters and documents, many of them incorporated in the text

"Mr. Howard has told his story well, recreating the America of Foster with fine skill, revealing the personality of the composer, and discussing his musical ability with knowledge and critical judgment." North Am Rev

Gershwin, George, 1898-1937
Jablonski, Edward. Gershwin. Doubleday 1987 436p il $21.95   **780.92**
ISBN 0-385-19431-5   LC 87-5270

An account of the American composer's life and musical career

"One could complain that the Gershwin encountered in these pages is the debonair newsreel figure whose vexations were mild and few. . . . But the end result of the author's refusal to search Gershwin's closets for skeletons is a healthy emphasis on his music, about which Mr. Jablonsky writes with a contagious enthusiasm." N Y Times Book Rev

Includes bibliographic references

Goodman, Benny, 1909-1986
Collier, James Lincoln. Benny Goodman and the Swing Era. Oxford Univ. Press 1989 404p il $30; pa $10.95   **780.92**
ISBN 0-19-505278-1; 0-19-506776-2 (pa)
      LC 89-16030

Collier "recreates a colorful popular music world of the 1920s and 1930s, as he chronicles the rise and success of Goodman and his band against the social milieu and popular music of the time. The author captures the musician's elusive personality as well as analyzes dozens of Goodman's significant recordings." Univ Press Books for Public Libr

Includes bibliography

Gould, Glenn, 1932-1982
Friedrich, Otto. Glenn Gould; a life and variations. Random House 1989 441p il $24.95; pa $14.95   **780.92**
ISBN 0-394-56299-2; 0-679-73207-1 (pa)
      LC 88-29676

This book "chronicles Gould's development and career . . . and contains tables of all Gould's concert programs, recordings, and broadcasts." Choice

The author "manages to synthesize a vast amount of information into one seamless and compelling life story." N Y Times Book Rev

Includes bibliography

Graham, Bill
Graham, Bill. Bill Graham presents: my life inside rock and out; [by] Bill Graham and Robert Greenfield. Doubleday 1992 568p il $24   **780.92**
ISBN 0-385-24077-5   LC 91-8108

This autobiography by the rock concert promoter consists of "oral interviews with Graham, his family, friends, musicians, [and] agents, . . . with connecting passages by Greenfield." Libr J

Guthrie, Woody, 1912-1967

Guthrie, Woody. Pastures of plenty; a self-portrait; edited by Dave Marsh and Harold Leventhal. HarperCollins Pubs. 1990 xxvi, 259p il $29.95; pa $15 **780.92**

ISBN 0-06-016342-9; 0-06-098419-8 (pa)

LC 89-46547

"Chronicling the dustbowl migrations of the 1930s, the labor struggles of the 1940s, and the Red-scare politics of the 1950s, [Guthrie's] letters, essays, songs, random jottings, and drawings reveal a man struggling to understand why the working men and women who contribute the most are respected the least." Libr J

Klein, Joe. Woody Guthrie; a life. Knopf 1980 475p il o.p.; Ballantine Bks. paperback available $5.95 **780.92**

ISBN 0-345-33519-8 (pa)

LC 80-7634

"The author incorporates into his text a great deal of information sifted from Guthrie's voluminous unpublished writings. . . . He also uses information from historical sources, published works, and hundreds of interviews to place Guthrie in a social and historical perspective. The result of all this research is . . . a very interesting and personal biography." Libr J

Hamlisch, Marvin, 1944-

Hamlisch, Marvin. The way I was; [by] Marvin Hamlisch with Gerald Gardner. Scribner 1992 234p il $22 **780.92**

ISBN 0-684-19327-2

LC 92-20094

"A Robert Stewart book"

"At 48, composer Hamlisch delivers Broadway and Hollywood vignettes from a mid-life perspective." Libr J

"For a dyed-in-the-wool New Yorker, Hamlisch has a narrative style that's long on homespun humor and not without a little pathos. . . . Because of some astounding successes, the composer of *Chorus Line* and *The Way We Were* may well command readers' attention with this chatty and fast-paced account." Booklist

Handel, George Frideric, 1685-1759

Hogwood, Christopher. Handel; chronological table by Anthony Hicks. Thames & Hudson 1985 c1984 312p il maps music hardcover o.p. paperback available $14.95 **780.92**

ISBN 0-500-27498-3 (pa)

LC 85-203040

First published 1984 in the United Kingdom

The author "addresses his book to the serious layman. The composer's comings and goings are documented as accurately as possible, and Mr. Hogwood has added terse critical commentary about the music in sophisticated language but without musical examples." N Y Times Book Rev

Includes bibliography

Haydn, Joseph, 1732-1809

Geiringer, Karl. Haydn: a creative life in music; by Karl Geiringer in collaboration with Irene Geiringer. 3rd rev & enl ed. University of Calif. Press 1982 403p il $37.50; pa $11.95 **780.92**

ISBN 0-520-04316-2; 0-520-04317-0 (pa) LC 82-2821

First published 1946

The author is "one of the few scholars who have devoted themselves almost exclusively to the study of this great master. He has not only collected all the new data that have cast light on Haydn research . . . he has also contributed many valuable observations and ideas." Saturday Rev

Includes bibliography

Landon, H. C. Robbins (Howard Chandler Robbins). Haydn: his life and music; [by] H. C. Robbins Landon and David Wyn Jones. Indiana Univ. Press 1988 383p $45 **780.92**

ISBN 0-253-37265-8

LC 88-2685

This is "the best single-volume biography . . . available on Haydn. More than just a condensation of Landon's five-volume Haydn: Chronicle and Works, this book takes into account the vast amount of Haydn research of the past decade. By alternating chapters on the composer's life and his music, the authors have made this biography more accessible to those who are interested only in Haydn's life and not in technical analyses of his compositions." Choice

Includes bibliography

Hendrix, Jimi

Murray, Charles Shaar. Crosstown traffic: Jimmy Hendrix and the post-war rock'n'roll revolution. St. Martin's Press 1990 c1989 247p il $18.95; pa $9.95 **780.92**

ISBN 0-312-04288-4; 0-312-06324-5 (pa)

LC 89-77681

First published 1989 in the United Kingdom

"The book is a broad-based study of African-American music—blues, jazz, rhythm and blues, and soul—and how the music influenced, and was influenced by, Hendrix." Libr J

"This informed, textured account will be irresistible to devotees of Hendrix and psychedelic rock as well as fans of blues, funk, jazz and rock 'n' roll." Booklist

Includes discography and bibliography

Shapiro, Harry. Jimi Hendrix, electric gypsy; [by] Harry Shapiro and Caesar Glebbeek. St. Martin's Press 1991 723p il $29.95; pa $16.95 **780.92**

ISBN 0-312-05861-6; 0-312-08500-1 (pa)

LC 90-27487

"At once both the definitive biography and reference work on guitar genius Hendrix and his band. . . . This Hendrix cornucopia offers all the bells and whistles of a 100 page discography, with over 200 photographs, mementos and pieces of correspondence, a detailed chronology, and a unique appendix delineating Hendrix's guitars, equipment, and playing techniques, all of which contains sumptuous notes." Libr J

Hodes, Art

Hodes, Art. Hot man; the life of Art Hodes; [by] Art Hodes and Chadwick Hansen; discography by Howard Rye. University of Ill. Press 1992 160p il (Music in American life) $22.50 **780.92**

ISBN 0-252-01753-6

LC 90-19876

Jazz pianist Art Hodes offers "inside views of gangster club owners, the great New York jazz clubs, the vicious critical 'jazz wars' of the 1940s, and his experiences with jazz greats such as Louis Armstrong and Bix Beider-

Hodes, Art—*Continued*
becke." Univ Press Books for Public and Second Sch Libr

Includes discography

Holiday, Billie, 1915-1959
O'Meally, Robert G. Lady Day: the many faces of Billie Holiday; produced by Toby Byron/Multiprises. Arcade Pub. 1991 207p il hardcover o.p. paperback available $16.95 **780.92**

ISBN 1-55970-200-1 (pa)   LC 91-16218

"Narcotics, jail, sexual abuse, and prejudice are often our first associations concerning the life of the great jazz singer, but this biography recalls only Holiday as artist. O'Meally . . . puts her tragedy and talent into perspective, and what emerges is a critique of a singer. The book's first section is outstanding in this regard, employing stories, quotes, and interviews in describing Holiday's technique." Libr J

Includes bibliographic references

Holly, Buddy, 1936-1959
Goldrosen, John. Remembering Buddy; the definitive biography; [by] John Goldrosen and John Beecher. Penguin Bks. 1987 c1986 204p il pa $14.95 **780.92**

ISBN 0-14-010363-5   LC 87-40004

First published 1979 with title: The Buddy Holly story

"The authors trace the career of Buddy Holly, the West Texas rock 'n' roller, in great detail. . . . Appropriately, they take pains to separate fact from legend." Publ Wkly

Includes bibliography and discography

Horowitz, Vladimir, 1904-1989
Schonberg, Harold C. Horowitz; his life and music. Simon & Schuster 1992 427p il $27.50 **780.92**

ISBN 0-671-72568-8   LC 92-24000

"Filled with . . . anecdotes, this intimate biography reveals the positive and negative points of Horowitz's personal life, character and playing style. The book, based in part on interviews with Horowitz taped in 1987, also includes a discography." Publ Wkly

Ives, Charles Edward, 1874-1954
Feder, Stuart. Charles Ives, "my father's song"; a psychoanalytic biography. Yale Univ. Press 1992 396p il $35 **780.92**

ISBN 0-300-05481-5   LC 91-42317

"What happened to [composer] Charles Ives, in relation to his father George, is what happened to America as the United States evolved from rurality into industrialism. There could be no fitter candidate for what is sometimes called psycho-biography; and no author could be better qualified to write it than Stuart Feder, a practicing psychoanalyst, who also holds a degree in music from Harvard." Times Lit Suppl

Includes bibliographic references

Jackson, Mahalia, 1911-1972
Schwerin, Jules. Got to tell it: Mahalia Jackson, queen of gospel. Oxford Univ. Press 1992 204p il $19.95 **780.92**

ISBN 0-19-507144-1   LC 91-43947

A biography of "New Orleans-born contralto Mahalia Jackson (1911-1972), whose career introduced and defined gospel music to white Americans. Set against a backdrop of the growing racial tensions of the 1950s and their explosion in the '60s, the book demonstrates Jackson's remarkable ability to cross boundaries of color on the sheer power of her voice." Publ Wkly

"More of a reminiscence than a true biography, this book offers an intriguing glimpse into the life of an important figure in African American history." Libr J

Includes bibliographic references

Jackson, Michael, 1958-
Taraborrelli, J. Randy. Michael Jackson; the magic and the madness. Birch Lane Press 1991 625p il $21.95 **780.92**

ISBN 1-55972-064-6   LC 91-2792

This biography of the eccentric rock superstar focuses on how his family, in particular his father, has effected his life, music and his adult life

Includes bibliographic references

John, Elton
Norman, Philip. Elton John. Harmony Bks. 1991 520p il $22.50 **780.92**

ISBN 0-517-58762-9   LC 91-41636

A "study of the British singer-songwriter. This well-researched work traces John's career from shy pianist to flamboyant entertainer to subdued middle-aged musician. Norman downplays the more sensational aspects of John's life . . . and provides a balanced and entertaining view of the definitive pop star of the 1970s. This is a worthwhile addition to collections featuring popular music." Libr J

Includes discography

Jolson, Al, d. 1950
Goldman, Herbert G. Jolson; the legend comes to life. Oxford Univ. Press 1988 411p il $30; pa $10.95 **780.92**

ISBN 0-19-505505-5; 0-19-506329-5 (pa) LC 88-4222

"Comprehensively researched and written in a straightforward anecdotal style that is neither endearing nor debunking, Goldman details Jolson's complex life and career, from early beginnings as a street performer through his multifaceted career." Libr J

Joplin, Janis, 1943-1970
Joplin, Laura. Love, Janis. Villard Bks. 1992 342p il $22.50 **780.92**

ISBN 0-679-41605-6   LC 92-53652

"Laura Joplin's deeply personal and touchingly revealing biography of her late, legendary older sister Janis emphasizes their fascinating family history and the emotional and spiritual forces that pushed Janis first to art, then to music. . . . Laura's wise and insightful analysis of Janis, enriched by the inclusion of Janis's ingenuous letters home, is a laudable feat of scholarship and sisterly love." Am Libr

Kern, Jerome, 1885-1945
Bordman, Gerald Martin. Jerome Kern; his life and music; [by] Gerald Bordman. Oxford Univ. Press 1980 438p il $29.95; pa $12.95   **780.92**
ISBN 0-19-502649-7; 0-19-506574-3 (pa)
LC 79-13826
This look at the theatrical composer's career, accomplishments and impact contains interviews with Fred Astaire and Evelyn Laye. Lists of songs of every show and its performers are included

Leadbelly, 1885-1949
Wolfe, Charles K. The life and legend of Leadbelly; by Charles Wolfe and Kip Lornell. HarperCollins Pubs. 1992 333p il $25   **780.92**
ISBN 0-06-016862-5   LC 92-52606
"Drawing on a variety of primary and secondary sources, including numerous interviews, Wolfe and Lornell attempt to separate fact from fiction. . . . Photographs, informative notes, and a full discography are valuable additions." Choice
Includes bibliographic references

Lee, Peggy
Lee, Peggy. Miss Peggy Lee; an autobiography. Fine, D.I. 1989 280p il $18.95   **780.92**
ISBN 1-55611-112-6   LC 88-45420
Also available in paperback from Berkley Bks.
The American singer's "reminiscences are revealing of her difficult North Dakota childhood at the hands of an abusive stepmother, and her innocence in the tough world of show business as she started to shine as a major singer/songwriter. . . . This is a delightful autobiography in her own words, and public libraries should certainly add it to their collections." Libr J

Lennon, John, 1940-1980
Goldman, Albert Harry. The lives of John Lennon; [by] Albert Goldman. Morrow 1988 719p il o.p.; Bantam Bks. paperback available $5.95   **780.92**
ISBN 0-553-28057-0 (pa)   LC 88-8986
"Roughly half of Goldman's immense book deals with Lennon's post-Beatle period, the ten maddest and least productive years of his adult life. The skewed perspective undoubtedly highlights Lennon at his absolute worst. . . . At the same time, Goldman's emphasis dovetails nicely with the revised version of his own life that Lennon peddled during his last years." Time
Robertson, John. The art & music of John Lennon. Carol Pub. Group 1991 218p $17.95   **780.92**
ISBN 1-55972-076-X   LC 90-28953
"A Birch Lane Press book"
This volume "consists of a chronological retracing of Lennon's career, highlighting the impact of his personal situation on the music being developed at that time." Choice
"Vital for Beatles fans and popular music collections, and interesting even to non-Lennon-adoring rockers." Libr J

Includes discography

Liszt, Franz, 1811-1886
Walker, Alan. Franz Liszt. Knopf 1983-1989 2v il ea $39.95   **780.92**
ISBN 0-394-52540-X (v1); 0-394-52541-8 (v2)
LC 82-47821
Contents: v1 The virtuoso years, 1811-1847; v2 The Weimar years, 1848-1861
The first two of a projected three-volume biography of Liszt's life and career. Coverage begins with Liszt's childhood in Hungary and ends in 1861, by which time he was conductor-in-residence for the Weimar court orchestra

Makeba, Miriam, 1932-
Makeba, Miriam. Makeba; my story; by Miriam Makeba with James Hall. New Am. Lib. 1988 c1987 249p il hardcover o.p. paperback available $11   **780.92**
ISBN 0-452-26234-8 (pa)   LC 87-18496
The South African singer's "narrative begins with her childhood and coming-of-age under apartheid. . . . She goes on to describe her international success after arriving in the U.S." Booklist
Makeba's autobiography "brings her strong voice alive in her own words, ringing with simple eloquence." Wilson Libr Bull

Marley, Bob
Davis, Stephen. Bob Marley. rev ed. Schenkman Bks. 1990 286p il $22.95; pa $15.95   **780.92**
ISBN 0-87047-045-0; 0-87047-044-2 (pa) LC 90-8241
First published 1983 in the United Kingdom; first United States edition published 1985 by Doubleday
This portrayal of the reggae star includes interviews, a look at his home life, stage performances and recording sessions with the Wailers, and a chapter about son Ziggy and reggae music after Marley's death in 1981
Includes bibliographic references

McCartney, Paul
Giuliano, Geoffrey. Blackbird: the life and times of Paul McCartney; introduction by Denny Laine. Dutton 1991 384p il $22.95
780.92
ISBN 0-525-93374-3   LC 91-19774
Also available in paperback from New Am. Lib.
"Giuliano relies on extensive interviews with McCartney associates, and the resultant portrait of the most famous pop legend of our time is filled with contradictions. . . . Giuliano is refreshingly frank in assessing McCartney's creative output, particularly in the Wings and post-Wings era, though at other times his subjectivity intrudes. Overall, the book is a quick, entertaining read, and there is quite a bit of new material." Libr J

Includes bibliographic references

Milsap, Ronnie, 1944-

Milsap, Ronnie. Almost like a song; [by] Ronnie Milsap with Tom Carter. McGraw-Hill 1990 259p il $19.95   **780.92**

1. Blind
ISBN 0-07-042374-1   LC 90-5530

An autobiography of the country music singer and songwriter

"A man of obvious natural intellect as well as innate musical ability, Milsap has written a book full of humor, sadness, inspiration, and irony that sheds light not only on his own life but on the diverse worlds of the music industry and the visually impaired." Libr J

Includes discography

Mingus, Charles, 1922-1979

Coleman, Janet. Mingus/Mingus; two memoirs; [by] Janet Coleman and Al Young. Creative Arts 1989 164p il $14.95   **780.92**

ISBN 0-88739-067-6   LC 88-38524

Also available in paperback from Limelight Eds.

The authors were students at the University of Michigan when they first met jazz musician Charles Mingus in the late 1950s. Their book is "the story of the man and the musician and also a story of their own awakening in pre-Kennedy America." N Y Times Book Rev

Coleman and Young "were exposed to sides of Mingus not often shown to the public. They have written about him with much love and tenderness, providing extensive and personal insights into one of the least-understood major figures of modern jazz." Choice

Morrison, Jim, 1943-1971

Hopkins, Jerry. No one here gets out alive; by Jerry Hopkins and Daniel Sugerman. Warner Bks. 1980 387p il hardcover o.p. paperback available $5.95   **780.92**

1. Doors (Musical group)
ISBN 0-446-34268-8 (pa)   LC 79-26611

This biography of rock musician Jim Morrison gives "an idea of how profoundly Morrison, as lyricist and lend singer of the Doors, affected the youth of America in the late 1960s. . . . The book includes a list of the Doors' records, books, and films." Booklist

Jones, Dylan. Jim Morrison, dark star. Viking 1991 191p il $35   **780.92**

ISBN 0-670-83454-8   LC 90-12885

Also available in paperback from Penguin Bks.

In this biography of the controversial rock singer and songwriter "the journalist Dylan Jones charts the star's rise and fall and offers some fresh insights into his motivations and early influences." N Y Times Book Rev

Includes bibliographic references

Riordan, James. Break on through: the life and death of Jim Morrison; [by] James Riordan and Jerry Prochnicky. Morrow 1991 544p il $20; pa $10   **780.92**

ISBN 0-688-08829-5; 0-688-11915-8 (pa)
LC 90-26580

This look at the life and work of Jim Morrison is "well documented and avoids unfounded speculation and unnecessary tales of debauchery common to many other rock 'n' roll biographies. . . . An excellent biography of a true rock icon." Choice

Includes bibliography and discography

Mozart, Wolfgang Amadeus, 1756-1791

Davenport, Marcia. Mozart. [Bicentenary ed]. Scribner 1956 402p il o.p.; Dorset Press reprint available $19.95   **780.92**

ISBN 0-88029-124-9

Also available in paperback from Avon Bks.

"Hudson River editions"

Reprint of the title first published 1932

"This biographer writes of Mozart with an enthusiasm that will be shared by many readers. She has a thorough familiarity with his work, and sympathy and admiration for the man of genius whose difficult life ended at thirty-five. Imaginary conversations lend liveliness to the narrative and the frank treatment of incidents and traits often glossed over is honest and never sensational." Booklist

Includes bibliography

Einstein, Alfred. Mozart; his character, his work; translated by Arthur Mendel and Nathan Broder. Oxford Univ. Press 1945 492p il music $39.95; pa $13.95   **780.92**

ISBN 0-19-500538-4; 0-19-500732-8 (pa)

The author's "examination of the events of Mozart's life in relation to his character, and even more, his analysis of the sources, models, and methods of the musician's creative processes are penetrating and illuminating." Christ Sci Monit

Landon, H. C. Robbins (Howard Chandler Robbins). 1791: Mozart's last year. Schirmer Bks. 1989 240p il $19.95; pa $13.95

780.92

ISBN 0-02-872592-1; 0-02-871315-X (pa) LC 88-3169

This is an account of the year the composer wrote La Clemenza di Tito, The Magic Flute and the Requiem. The author "attempts to demystify Mozart's death by focusing on the last year of his life." N Y Times Book Rev

The author "has produced an amiable little mine of miscellaneous information . . . some of which is old, some quite new, and some entirely original. All of it will be of interest to Mozart buffs." N Y Rev Books

Includes bibliography

Landon, H. C. Robbins (Howard Chandler Robbins). Mozart; the golden years, 1781-1791. Schirmer Bks. 1989 271p il $29.95   **780.92**

ISBN 0-02-872025-3   LC 89-5848

This is a study of the composer, his family, and his music during the last ten years of his life

"As always, Professor Landon is particularly adroit at setting the musical and social scene, and there are valuable sections covering concert life, the organisation of the opera, the pianos of Mozart's day, music publishers, and the Viennese tradition of wind-band music which had such a strong influence on the sonority of Mozart's scores." London Rev Books

Includes bibliography

The Mozart compendium; a guide to Mozart's life and music; edited by H.C. Robbins Landon. Schirmer Bks. 1990 452p $34.95   **780.92**

ISBN 0-02-871321-4   LC 90-9071

This book contains "a chart of Mozart's life and work, side by side with related world events, and . . . a list of compositions by genre, from operas to symphonies, string quartets and songs. Each section is accompanied by musical analysis. Essays on the composer's personal life and work habits [complete the volume.]" N Y Times Book Rev

Includes bibliographic references

Near, Holly

Near, Holly. Fire in the rain—singer in the storm; an autobiography; [by] Holly Near with Derk Richardson. Morrow 1990 290p il $19.95; pa $10   **780.92**

ISBN 0-688-08733-7; 0-688-10964-0 (pa)   LC 90-5784

Near's autobiography "proceeds from her rural northern California beginnings through her Hollywood days and on to her subsequent long career as activist-entertainer on behalf of the radical causes of her time." Booklist

This "is a telling testament to the conservatism of pop culture. It shows how a talented performer can be marginalized because of her sexuality and politics." NY Times Book Rev

Includes discography

O'Day, Anita, 1919-

O'Day, Anita. High times, hard times; [by] Anita O'Day, with George Eells; with a discography compiled by Robert A. Sixsmith and Alan Eichler. Putnam 1981 349p il o.p.; Limelight Eds. paperback available $12.95   **780.92**

ISBN 0-87910-118-0 (pa)   LC 81-1507

This autobiography of the jazz singer recalls her days with the big bands of Krupa and Kenton as well as her battle with heroin addiction

Orbison, Roy, 1936-1988

Amburn, Ellis. Dark star: the Roy Orbison story. Carol Pub. Group 1990 283p il $18.95   **780.92**

ISBN 0-8184-0518-X   LC 90-1740

"A Lyle Stuart book"

"As seen in Amburn's biography, Orbison's life reflects a full range of rock 'n' roll emotions: he rose to stardom in the 1960s, tragically lost his wife and two children, sunk into obscurity, re-emerged to great acclaim, was voted into the Rock 'n' Roll Hall of Fame, then worked himself to death on the crest of a huge comeback. This evenly paced, unbiased, well-researched account of the singer's life is based on recollections of family, friends, and colleagues and material gleaned from print and electronic media." Libr J

Includes discography and bibliography

Parker, Charlie, 1920-1955

Giddins, Gary. Celebrating Bird: the triumph of Charlie Parker. Beech Tree Bks. 1987 128p il hardcover o.p. paperback available $13.20   **780.92**

ISBN 0-688-05951-1 (pa)   LC 86-61275

In addition to his essay the author has "included a series of black-and-white photographs that capture Parker with poetic grace. Addicted to heroin in his teens, Parker led a tragic life. . . . He died in 1955, at 34. This book does not pretend to be a definitive biography; however, it is as penetrating a character study of Bird as any yet written and this is no small accomplishment." N Y Times Book Rev

Includes discography and bibliography

Piaf, Édith, 1915-1963

Crosland, Margaret. Piaf. Putnam 1985 240p il o.p.; Fromm Int. paperback available $8.95   **780.92**

ISBN 0-88064-069-3 (pa)   LC 85-43346

This "first non-French biography of the legendary singer, succeeds in discarding the myths and half-truths promulgated by other biographers and by Piaf herself. . . . Crosland uses both interviews and Piaf's recorded legacy in analyzing the life and work; the result is a fascinating, well-balanced and factual biography that captures the essence of Piaf's tormented life. Appendixes include a complete discography." Libr J

Previn, André, 1929-

Previn, André. No minor chords; my days in Hollywood. Doubleday 1991 148p il $22.50   **780.92**

ISBN 0-385-41341-6   LC 91-19733

A "memoir of Mr. Previn's early life as a movie music maker, with anecdotes of many first-rate colleagues, producers, directors and stars." N Y Times Book Rev

"Consistently clear and lively writing as well as several pages of interesting photos make Previn's . . . literary opus a completely satisfying experience." Publ Wkly

Rich, Buddy, 1917-1987

Tormé, Mel. Traps, the drum wonder: the life of Buddy Rich. Oxford Univ. Press 1991 233p il $21.95; pa $10.95   **780.92**

ISBN 0-19-507038-0; 0-19-507915-9 (pa)   LC 90-22594

"Singer Tormé here celebrates his friend, the late Rich, who was one of the most famous and explosive jazz drummers." Libr J

"Mr. Tormé's account of Rich's struggle with the brain tumor that killed him at the age of 69 is clear-eyed, understated and powerful. Rich was brave, and prickly, to the end. His biographer has managed to present a sympathetic portrait of a difficult person. One comes away from this very touching book with a palpable sense of Buddy Rich's complexity, and with admiration for Mel Tormé's accomplishment." N Y Times Book Rev

Richards, Keith

Bockris, Victor. Keith Richards; the biography. Poseidon Press 1992 409p il $24; pa $12   **780.92**

ISBN 0-671-70061-8; 0-671-87590-6 (pa)   LC 92-17957

This biographical account of Rolling Stones' guitarist Keith Richards includes interviews with Richards, other band members, business associates, friends, and others

"Although this sympathetic portrait doesn't tell fans much they don't already know . . . it is a diverting addition to the rock-bio genre." Publ Wkly

Includes bibliographic references

Scarlatti, Domenico, 1685-1757

Kirkpatrick, Ralph. Domenico Scarlatti. Princeton Univ. Press 1983 c1953 491p il $75; pa $19.95   **780.92**

ISBN 0-691-09101-3; 0-691-02708-0 (pa)   LC 83-11007

Scarlatti, Domenico, 1685-1757—*Continued*
First published 1953

An examination of the life and works of the influential Baroque composer. Discussions of harpsichords, ornamentation and performance are included

Includes bibliography

Schumann, Clara, 1819-1896
Reich, Nancy B. Clara Schumann, the artist and the woman. Cornell Univ. Press 1985 346p il $38.95; pa $14.95   **780.92**

ISBN 0-8014-1748-1; 0-8014-9388-9 (pa)

LC 84-45798

The author "concentrates on the facts of Clara Schumann's life and plays down the romance. She provides a comprehensive bibliography and notes, short chapters . . . on Clara's contribution to music as composer, concert artist, editor and teacher, with a full catalogue and brief discussions of all compositions." Times Lit Suppl

Seeger, Pete
Dunaway, David King. How can I keep from singing: Pete Seeger. McGraw-Hill 1981 386p il o.p.; Da Capo Press paperback available $13.95   **780.92**

ISBN 0-306-80399-2 (pa)   LC 80-29374

"The focus of Seeger's life has been on using music as a force for social change. . . . But he is perhaps best known as the major banjo-playing folksinger who pioneered the folk music revival that flowered in the 1960s. This excellent book provides a well-written and extensively researched account, not only of Seeger's life, but also of the social and political movements of the times in which he lived. An extensive bibliography and discography add to the book's usefulness." Libr J

Sills, Beverly
Sills, Beverly. Beverly; an autobiography; [by] Beverly Sills and Lawrence Linderman. Bantam Bks. 1987 356p il hardcover o.p. paperback available $4.95   **780.92**

ISBN 0-553-26647-0 (pa)   LC 86-47567

"This is a warm and highly ingratiating autobiography of a 'kid-next-door' who grew up to be a superstar of international opera and later manager of New York's second opera house. . . . She relates personal struggles: . . . coping with anti-Semitism and raising a family with two beautiful but severely handicapped children. Her success story makes for fascinating reading that is both rewarding and inspiring." Libr J

Simon, Paul
Humphries, Patrick. Paul Simon, still crazy after all these years. Doubleday 1989 c1988 164p il $17.95   **780.92**

ISBN 0-385-24908-X   LC 88-30030

First published 1988 in the United Kingdom with title: The boy in the bubble

The author has produced a "complete biography of one of popular music's most innovative songwriter/performers. Tempering a fan's reverential treatment with the realism of a professional writer, he examines Simon's legacy as part of the legendary folk duo of Simon and Garfunkel in the 1960s and as a solo artist since the 1970s. . . . Although Humphries's style and leftist politics can be a bit overbearing, he effectively captures his subject as a performer and a human being." Libr J

Includes discography

Springsteen, Bruce
Marsh, Dave. Glory days: Bruce Springsteen in the 1980s. Pantheon Bks. 1987 478p il o.p.; Dell paperback available $5.99   **780.92**

ISBN 0-440-20551-4 (pa)   LC 86-42620

A look at the meteoric rise to stardom of rock musician Bruce Springsteen

"Marsh's book is full of inside gossip. But it is also the first serious book to detail—and analyze—the process of contemporary rock-star-making." Newsweek

Includes bibliography

Tormé, Mel, 1925-
Tormé, Mel. It wasn't all velvet; an autobiography. Viking 1988 384p il o.p.; Zebra Bks. paperback available $4.95   **780.92**

ISBN 0-8217-2862-8 (pa)   LC 88-14249

An autobiographical account of the famous jazz singer, lyricist, and arranger

"Tormé brings a polished prose style and a fine, self-deprecating sense of humor to the task of recounting his wide-ranging career as an entertainer. . . . An engaging life story and a wonderfully vivid look at the music business." Booklist

Toscanini, Arturo, 1867-1957
Horowitz, Joseph. Understanding Toscanini; how he became an American culture-god and helped create a new audience for old music. Knopf 1987 492p il o.p.; University of Minn. Press paperback available $15.95   **780.92**

ISBN 0-8166-1678-7 (pa)   LC 86-45373

The author discusses the conductor's personality and music. He also presents his opinions on Toscanini's promotion by entrepreneurs, acceptance by Americans, and influence upon other conductors

This "is the most detailed examination yet of the man, his work and his audience. . . . The book, however, is only incidentally biographical. In digesting countless reviews, Horowitz has provided a valuable look at the state of American music criticism during the first half of the century." Time

Includes bibliography

Sachs, Harvey. Toscanini. Lippincott 1978 380p il $17.95; pa $10.95   **780.92**

ISBN 0-397-01320-5; 0-06-091473-4 (pa)

LC 78-17245

Also available in paperback from Da Capo Press

This "biography depicts the late maestro as a complex man and an incomparable musician. . . . Sachs discusses Toscanini's musicianship perceptively, but readers will perhaps find more compelling his portrait of the maestro as a person." Publ Wkly

Includes bibliography

Turner, Tina

Turner, Tina. I, Tina; [by] Tina Turner, with Kurt Loder. Morrow 1986 236p il o.p.; Avon Bks. paperback available $5.50
780.92

ISBN 0-380-70097-2 (pa)   LC 86-16455

"Born Anna Mae Bullock in 1939 in Nut Bush, Tennessee, Tina Turner is now—after a fantastic comeback—one of the hottest acts in rock music. . . . The path that Tina . . . followed to pull herself out of sleepy Nut Bush and eventually to gain international stardom is traced here." Booklist

"Kurt Loder has edited I, Tina nicely, letting [Turner's] narrative take center stage, punctuating it with the voices of friends, colleagues, and family." Nation

Verdi, Giuseppe, 1813-1901

Osborne, Charles. Verdi; a life in the theatre. Knopf 1987 360p il o.p.; Fromm Int. paperback available $11.95   **780.92**

ISBN 0-88064-106-1 (pa)   LC 87-45205

A "portrait of the composer, emphasizing the germination, writing, and production of his 28 operas." Libr J

"The account is strictly chronological, relying on letters, reviews, other documents, and recently published research as the bases for a fluent narrative. . . . A usable book for nonspecialists, containing a vivid portrait of Verdi the man." Choice

Includes bibliography

Vishnevskaya, Galina, 1926-

Vishnevskaya, Galina. Galina; a Russian story; translated from the Russian by Guy Daniels. Harcourt Brace Jovanovich 1984 519p il hardcover o.p. paperback available $10.95   **780.92**

ISBN 0-15-634320-7 (pa)   LC 84-10943

Vishnevskaya's autobiography "is a tale of social horror and political intrigue—a poignant, daring, frightening, sometimes even humorous success saga. . . . Vishnevskaya, who retired from opera in 1982, was one of the leading sopranos of her time, and she does offer rare insights into the care and feeding of a Muscovite Aida. But the primary value of her book . . . lies in its candid, often devastating depiction of cultural life in postwar Russia." N Y Times Book Rev

Includes discography

Waller, Fats, 1904-1943

Shipton, Alyn. Fats Waller: his life & times. Universe Bks. 1989 134p il (Jazz life & times) hardcover o.p. paperback available $10.95   **780.92**

ISBN 0-87663-747-0 (pa)   LC 87-35754

The author draws upon "interviews with friends of the legendary performer to present a picture of the man and the musician whose appeal went beyond the jazz world." Publisher's note

Includes bibliography

Whiteman, Paul, 1890-1967

DeLong, Thomas A. Pops: Paul Whiteman, king of jazz. New Century Pubs. 1983 360p il $17.95   **780.92**

ISBN 0-8329-0264-0   LC 83-19291

A "biography of the conductor who played an important role in the acceptance of jazz as an indigenous art form." Publ Wkly

"Offering the right combination of folklore, inside stories and nostalgia, DeLong delivers a first-rate story." West Coast Rev Books

Includes bibliography

Zappa, Frank

Zappa, Frank. The real Frank Zappa book; [by] Frank Zappa, with Peter Occhiogrosso. Poseidon Press 1989 352p il $19.95; pa $10.95   **780.92**

ISBN 0-671-63870-X; 0-671-70572-5 (pa) LC 89-3470

"The outspoken Zappa, one of the most inventive and controversial artists of the past 20 years, is frank, often disgusting, and always entertaining in describing his life. . . . Zappa also relates his opinions about the music performing and recording industries, but then rattles on about a myriad of things: church, drugs, yuppies, politics." Libr J

780.973   Music—United States

Chase, Gilbert, 1906-1992

America's music, from the pilgrims to the present; with a foreword by Richard Crawford and a discographical essay by William Brooks. rev 3rd ed. University of Ill. Press 1987 xxiv, 712p il music (Music in American life) $34.95; pa $24.95
780.973

1. Music, American—History and criticism
ISBN 0-252-00454-X; 0-252-06275-2 (pa)
LC 86-30795

First published 1955 by McGraw-Hill

A critical history of American music, including material on individuals, composers, and groups who have contributed to our musical heritage

Hitchcock, H. Wiley (Hugh Wiley), 1923-

Music in the United States; a historical introduction. 3rd ed. Prentice-Hall 1988 365p (Prentice-Hall history of music ser) pa $31   **780.973**

1. Music, American—History and criticism
ISBN 0-13-608407-9   LC 87-14496

First published 1969

This survey of American music contains information on colonial, sacred, early American secular, nineteenth century vernacular and cultivated, and various types of twentieth century music, including jazz, electronic, pop and rock. The work of composers and performers is also considered

Includes bibliographies

The New Grove dictionary of American music; edited by H. Wiley Hitchcock and Stanley Sadie; editorial coordinator Susan Feder. Grove's Dictionaries of Music 1986 4v il set $695   **780.973**

1. Music, American—Dictionaries
ISBN 0-943818-36-2   LC 86-404

"Includes names and terms germane to the musical tradition of the U.S. Expands articles from *The new Grove* [entered in class 780.3] where appropriate, but adds many more on art music, varieties of popular music, the political and patriotic repertories, specifically American genres, music of the present day, etc. Standard music topics are treated in the American context. Signed articles, many with bibliographies, lists of works, and discographies." Sheehy. Guide to Ref Books. 10th edition. suppl

781   Music—General principles and musical forms

Wilson, Frank R.
Tone deaf and all thumbs? an invitation to music-making for late bloomers and non-prodigies. Viking 1986 210p o.p.; Vintage Bks. paperback available $8.95   **781**

1. Musical ability
ISBN 0-394-75354-2 (pa)   LC 85-40553

"Convinced that everyone has an inborn ability to make music . . . Wilson, who came late to piano playing, here presents a picture of the brain and muscular system to help non-musicians to understand that the human body is a 'natural learner.' . . . Wilson also tries to clarify such mysteries as tone deafness, perfect pitch, sight reading, memorization and 'pumping ivory.'" Publ Wkly

"Much of the material covered . . . is thought-provoking and valuable to both the novice and the accomplished musician." N Y Times Book Rev

Includes bibliographic references

781.1   Music—Aesthetics, appreciation, taste

Copland, Aaron, 1900-1990
Music and imagination. Harvard Univ. Press 1952 116p hardcover o.p. paperback available $6.95   **781.1**

1. Music—Analysis, appreciation
ISBN 0-674-58915-7 (pa)

Analyzed in Essay and general literature index

Charles Eliot Norton lectures, 1951-1952

The author "considers many of the problems of the contemporary composer . . . the qualities of the sensitive listener, the meaning of music, 'the sonorous image,' the creative mind and the interpretive mind, the pull of tradition and the attraction of innovation upon European composers of our day, the twelve-tone procedure, and distinctive contributions of American composers." Libr J

Machlis, Joseph, 1906-
The enjoyment of music; an introduction to perceptive listening. Norton il $41.95   **781.1**

1. Music—Analysis, appreciation

Also available in a shorter edition $34.95 (ISBN 0-393-96070-6)

First published 1955. (6th edition 1990) Periodically revised

This guide to music appreciation brings together biographical, historical, and analytical material, from the music of the Middle Ages to contemporary music

Includes bibliography

Sadie, Stanley
Stanley Sadie's brief guide to music; edited by Stanley Sadie, with Alison Latham. 3rd ed. Prentice-Hall 1993 448p il pa $37.33   **781.1**

1. Music—Analysis, appreciation
ISBN 0-13-086851-5

First published 1987 as an abridgment of Stanley Sadie's music guide

"The book begins with a section on the 'elements' of music, treating pitch, rhythm, harmony, key, etc. . . . The main part of the book, sections III to VIII, discusses the music of six different eras in Western culture, from the Middle Ages to the present day, in chronological order." Preface

Includes bibliographic references

781.2   Elements of music

Piston, Walter, 1894-1976
Counterpoint. Norton 1947 235p music $22.95   **781.2**

1. Counterpoint
ISBN 0-393-09728-5

This work covers the principles and techniques of counterpoint as represented in the works of 18th and 19th century composers

Harmony. 5th ed, revised and expanded by Mark DeVoto. Norton 1987 575p $39.95   **781.2**

1. Harmony
ISBN 0-393-95480-3   LC 86-23901
First published 1941

A presentation of the harmonic structures utilized by composers of the 18th and 19th centuries. Includes examples and exercises

781.4   Techniques of music

Shanet, Howard
Learn to read music. Simon & Schuster 1956 172p il music hardcover o.p. paperback available $10   **781.4**

1. Music—Study and teaching 2. Music—Theory
ISBN 0-671-21027-0 (pa)

The author describes a self-teaching system for learning to read musical notation in a short amount of time

781.6 Traditions of music. Classical music

Swafford, Jan
The Vintage guide to classical music. Vintage Bks. 1992 xxi, 597p il pa $17
781.6

1. Music—Analysis, appreciation 2. Music—History and criticism
ISBN 0-679-72805-8   LC 91-50217

This guide contains "chronologically arranged essays on nearly 100 composers, from Guillaume de Machaut (ca. 1300-1377) to Aaron Copland (1900-1990), that combine biography with detailed analyses of the major works while assessing their role in the social, cultural, and political climate of their times." Publisher's note

Includes bibliography

781.62 Folk music

Greene, Victor R.
A passion for polka; old-time ethnic music in America; [by] Victor Greene. University of Calif. Press 1992 355p il $28   **781.62**

1. Folk music—United States
ISBN 0-520-07584-6   LC 92-954

A "study of the complex interactions among immigrant musicians, urban Americans, and people in the popular music industry from the 1800s." Univ Press Books for Public and Second Sch Libr

Includes bibliographic references

Sandberg, Larry
The folk music sourcebook; [by] Larry Sandberg and Dick Weissman. new updated ed. Da Capo Press 1989 272p il pa $16.95
781.62

1. Folk music
ISBN 0-306-80360-7   LC 89-23389

First published 1976 by Knopf

A "definitive guide to folk music, both popular and scholarly, this traces the orgins, instruments, artists, recordings, books, periodicals, organizations, retail outlets, film archives, and terms in the field." Ref Sources for Small & Medium-sized Libr. 5th edition

781.63 Popular music

Collins, John, 1944-
West African pop roots. Temple Univ. Press 1992 349p il $49.95; pa $19.95
781.63

1. Music, African 2. Popular music
ISBN 0-87722-793-4; 0-87722-916-3 (pa)
LC 91-35089

In "this account of popular music in West Africa [Collins] explores the roots of various styles and genres and the 'feedback' of black music adapted to the New World and returning to Africa to reinfluence its origins." Univ Press Books for Public and Second Sch Libr

Stewart, Gary
Breakout; profiles in African rhythm. University of Chicago Press 1992 157p il maps $24.95; pa $12.95   **781.63**

1. Popular music 2. Music, African
ISBN 0-226-77405-8; 0-226-77406-6 (pa)
LC 91-30279

"Stewart introduces readers to the Afro-beat, soukous, highlife, and palm wine music genres. Stewart's flowing narrative helps blend historical facts with personal experiences to show how and why African music has carved its niche in a world dominated by Western culture." Libr J

Includes bibliographic references and discography

781.64 Western popular music

Berlin, Edward A.
Ragtime; a musical and cultural history. University of Calif. Press 1980 248p il music hardcover o.p. paperback available $11   **781.64**

1. Ragtime music
ISBN 0-520-052196-6 (pa)   LC 78-51759

Berlin traces the evolution of ragtime from popular song and piano rags to its eventual blend with jazz

"While the section on the origins and early history of ragtime will be most attractive to the casual reader, the heart of the book is its analysis of piano ragtime, an analysis filed with musical examples but accessible to a reader minimally trained in music." New Repub

Includes bibliography

Berry, Jason
Up from the cradle of jazz; New Orleans music since World War II; [by] Jason Berry, Jonathan Foose, and Tad Jones. University of Ga. Press 1986 285p il o.p.; Da Capo Press paperback available $16.95   **781.64**

1. Blues music 2. Rock music 3. Jazz music
ISBN 0-306-80493-X (pa)   LC 85-29015

The authors tell the story of New Orleans' music scene "through a series of portraits of major musicians, starting with a chapter on some of the great New Orleans musical families." Booklist

This "carefully documented text, in spite of occasionally strained musical descriptions, is well organized and interesting. An extensive bibliography and discography, and many photographs, enhance the work's value." Choice

Bronson, Fred
The Billboard book of number one hits. rev and enl 3rd ed. Billboard Publs. 1992 xxiv, 822p il pa $21.95   **781.64**

1. Popular music—Discography
ISBN 0-8230-8298-9   LC 92-20318

First published 1985

This book covers hit songs from July 1955 to March 1992, with a brief history of each song and its performer. Included are artist and song title indexes

Gammond, Peter

The Oxford companion to popular music. Oxford Univ. Press 1991 739p $39.95

781.64

1. Popular music—Dictionaries
ISBN 0-19-311323-6   LC 90-14209

"Aims to cover 'all music that would not normally be found in a reference book on "classical" or "serious" music . . . and the essential elements and personalities concerned with popular song of all periods.'—*Introd.* Dictionary arrangement of entries covers roughly 1850-1985, with emphasis on the English-speaking world. Many entries are lengthy, and some have bibliographies." Sheehy. Guide to Ref Books. 10th edition. suppl

The **Guinness** encyclopedia of popular music; edited by Colin Larkin. New England Pub. Assocs. 1992 4v set $295

781.64

1. Popular music—Dictionaries
ISBN 1-88226-700-1   LC 92-33209

This work "provides comprehensive coverage of all forms of twentieth-century music, including pop, rock, heavy metal, country, R&B, rap, reggae, jazz, blues, ragtime, big band, Latin, folk, and gospel. The one hundred contributors have created over 10,000 detailed, well-researched entries." Am Libr

For a fuller review see: Booklist, Feb. 15, 1993

Hamm, Charles

Yesterdays: popular song in America. Norton 1979 xxii, 533p il $24.95 paperback available $14.95   **781.64**

1. Popular music 2. Songs, American
ISBN 0-393-01257-3; 0-393-30062-5 (pa)
                                      LC 79-12953

"The book covers the 'continuous, unbroken, and coherent history' of popular song in America, from its beginnings in Anglo and Irish-American songs, thorugh the heyday of Tim Pan Alley, the advent of Rock and Roll, and the folk music revival in the 1960s." Best Sellers

Includes bibliography

Lees, Gene

Singers and the song; the popular song, its music and lyrics, and the singers who performed them. Oxford Univ. Press 1987 257p $24.95; pa $9.95   **781.64**

1. Popular music 2. Singers
ISBN 0-19-504293-X; 0-19-506087-3 (pa)
                                      LC 86-33233

Analyzed in Essay and general literature index

This is a collection of "essays that have appeared in Jazzletter, a newsletter edited and published by lyricist Lees. The essays concern singers (Frank Sinatra, Jo Stafford, Dick Haymes, et al.), composers, and lyricists of the World War II-Postwar era of popular music." Libr J

Sanjek, Russell

American popular music business in the 20th century; [by] Russell Sanjek, David Sanjek. Oxford Univ. Press 1991 xxii, 334p $27.95   **781.64**

1. Popular music 2. Music, American 3. Music industry
ISBN 0-19-505828-3   LC 90-47745

"This is a reworked and updated edition of Volume 3 of the acclaimed three-volume set by the late Russell Sanjek, *American Popular Music and Its Business* [1988]. While the earlier volume covered the years 1900-84, the new volume, revised by his son David, completes the decade and looks toward the 1990s." Libr J

Includes bibliographic references

Stambler, Irwin

Encyclopedia of folk, country & western music. 2nd ed. St. Martin's Press 1983 902p il hardcover o.p. paperback available $17.95   **781.64**

1. Folk music—Dictionaries 2. Country music—Dictionaries
ISBN 0-312-24819-9 (pa)   LC 82-5702

First published 1969

This book "provides detailed information on individual artists and groups, major variety shows, definitions of terms, instruments, and other areas. Information on awards, a selective discography, and a bibliography are included." Ref Sources for Small & Medium-sized Libr. 5th edition

Whitburn, Joel

The Billboard book of top 40 albums. rev & enl ed. Billboard Bks. 1991 347p il pa $19.95   **781.64**

1. Popular music—Discography
ISBN 0-8230-7534-6   LC 90-22777

First published 1987

This guide lists every album to reach the Top 40 charts since 1955. Each listing includes date, position on the chart, number of weeks in the Top 40, record label, and miscellaneous facts about the artist or group

The Billboard book of top 40 hits; [compiled by] Joel Whitburn. 5th ed, rev and enlarged. Billboard Bks. 1992 674p il pa $19.95   **781.64**

1. Popular music—Discography
ISBN 0-8230-8280-6   LC 91-45488

First published 1983

A guide to all single recordings that have made Billboard's Top 40 lists from 1955 to mid-1991. Entries are alphabetical by artist and give such information as date the record made the charts, number of weeks on the charts, highest position, etc. Biographical data and trivia on most of the artists are also included

781.642   Country music

The **Harmony** illustrated encyclopedia of country music. rev ed. Harmony Bks. 1987 208p il hardcover o.p. paperback available $13.95   **781.642**

1. Country music—Dictionaries
ISBN 0-517-56503-X (pa)   LC 86-18423
New edition in preparation

First published 1977 with title: The Illustrated encyclopedia of country music

Authors: Fred Dellar, Alan Cackett, Roy Thompson, Douglas B. Green

Color photographs of performers and album covers complement discographies and brief biographies of over 450 country music personalities

Roland, Tom
The Billboard book of number one country hits. Billboard Bks. 1991 584p il pa $19.95   **781.642**

1. Country music—Discography
ISBN 0-8230-7553-2   LC 90-15588

Entries list song title, artist, writer, producer, date song became number one, and number of weeks spent in that position on Billboard's country charts. There are indexes by artist and song title

Rosenberg, Neil V.
Bluegrass; a history. University of Ill. Press 1985 447p il (Music in American life) $29.95   **781.642**

1. Bluegrass music
ISBN 0-252-00265-2   LC 84-15747

"'Bluegrass' chronicles the colorful story of the birth and enormous growth of one of America's most popular musical forms. . . . Rosenberg, himself a bluegrass musician, shows how [Bill Monroe, Lester Flatt and Earl Scruggs] and many other performers have shaped the course of this unique music." Publisher's note
"Fans as well as scholars will find much to like in this well-researched, well-indexed work." Libr J

Includes bibliographic references

781.643   Blues music

Scott, Frank, 1942-
The Down Home guide to the blues; by Frank Scott and the staff of Down Home Music. A Cappella Bks. 1990 250p il pa $14.95   **781.643**

1. Blues music—Discography 2. Gospel music—Discography
ISBN 1-55652-130-8   LC 90-37638

A discographical guide to more than 3,000 blues and gospel LPs, CDs, and cassettes with information on the featured artists, and the quality and availability of the recordings

781.65   Jazz music

Collier, James Lincoln, 1928-
The making of jazz; a comprehensive history. Houghton Mifflin 1978 543p il o.p.; Dell paperback available $17.95   **781.65**

1. Jazz music
ISBN 0-385-28668-6 (pa)   LC 77-25030

"Heavily opinionated essays cover the full range of jazz history, from rhythmic African roots, through swing, ragtime, and improv artists, to styles. . . . As a general overview, this is fine, though some details might be in conflict with other sources." Booklist

Includes discography and bibliography

Crowther, Bruce
The big band years; [by] Bruce Crowther, Mike Pinfold; picture editor, Franklin S. Driggs. Facts on File 1988 208p il $24.95   **781.65**

1. Bands (Music) 2. Jazz musicians
ISBN 0-8160-2013-2   LC 88-81981

This heavily illustrated history of big band music includes profiles of Paul Whiteman, Duke Ellington, Benny Goodman, Glenn Miller, Count Basie, Lionel Hampton, and Stan Kenton

Includes discography

Davis, Francis
Outcats: jazz composers, instrumentalists, and singers. Oxford Univ. Press 1990 261p $22.95; pa $9.95   **781.65**

1. Jazz music 2. Jazz musicians
ISBN 0-19-505587-X; 0-19-507470-X (pa)

LC 89-23031

The author "casts a wide net, covering renowned musicians like Cecil Taylor, Sun Ra and Wynton Marsalis; lesser-knowns like the Parisian expatriate Steve Lacy; and jazzwomen like Jane Ira Bloom and Michele Roseworman. . . . Flements of reportage and portraiture give his better critical assessments a sense of intimacy." N Y Times Book Rev

Feather, Leonard
The encyclopedia of jazz in the seventies; by Leonard Feather and Ira Gitler; introduction by Quincy Jones. Horizon Press 1976 393p il o.p.; Da Capo Press paperback available $16.95   **781.65**

1. Jazz music—Dictionaries
ISBN 0-306-80290-2 (pa)

"Articles on jazz, lists of recordings, and brief biographies on all the important figures in the field and many minor ones. Included are a calendar of musicians' birthdays, birthplaces of musicians by state and town, and lists of jazz organizations, schools, booking agencies, and jazz recording companies." Ref Sources for Small & Medium-sized Libr. 5th edition

Feather, Leonard—*Continued*
The encyclopedia of jazz in the sixties; foreword by John Lewis. Horizon Press 1966 312p il o.p.; Da Capo Press paperback available $14.95 **781.65**

1. Jazz music—Dictionaries
ISBN 0-306-80263-5 (pa)

This survey contains 1100 biographies of jazz musicians; a short review of the jazz scene from 1960 to 1966, and an article on folk blues. In addition it includes a list of recordings of the early sixties and one of jazz record companies

The new edition of The encyclopedia of jazz; appreciations by Duke Ellington, Benny Goodman and John Hammond. completely rev, enl and brought up to date. Horizon Press 1960 527p il music o.p.; Da Capo Press paperback available $19.95 **781.65**

1. Jazz music—Dictionaries
ISBN 0-306-80214-7 (pa)

First published 1955 with title: The encyclopedia of jazz

The major part of this reference book is a biographical dictionary of over 2,000 jazz musicians. Also included are a brief history of jazz, an annotated discography, a bibliography and other short articles

The passion for jazz. Horizon Press 1980 208p il o.p.; Da Capo Press paperback available $10.95 **781.65**

1. Jazz music
ISBN 0-306-80402-6 (pa)   LC 80-15133

First published 1980 in the United Kingdom

This is a collection of forty-four articles dealing with people, places, and musical events from the world of jazz

"A generally entertaining and sometimes instructive collection . . . by one of the most durable jazz journalists." Choice

Giddins, Gary
Riding on a blue note; jazz and American pop. Oxford Univ. Press 1981 313p $24.95; pa $10.95 **781.65**

1. Jazz music
ISBN 0-19-502835-X; 0-19-503213-6 (pa)
                                LC 80-21238

A collection of thirty articles which first appeared in the Village Voice

The author "has a keen sense of aesthetics, historical perspective on the art of jazz, and enthusiasm for the subject, and he expresses his ideas with clarity." Choice

Includes bibliography

McRae, Barry
The jazz handbook. Hall, G.K. & Co. 1989 272p il (Performing arts) $25; pa $15.95 **781.65**

1. Jazz music
ISBN 0-8161-9096-8; 0-8161-1828-0 (pa)
                                LC 89-77757

First published 1987 in the United Kingdom

This reference work lists 200 jazz artists with biographical information and critical discographies

For a review see: Booklist, Sept. 1, 1990

The New Grove dictionary of jazz; edited by Barry Kernfeld; editorial consultant Stanley Sadie. Grove's Dictionaries of Music 1988 2v set $350 **781.65**

1. Jazz music—Dictionaries
ISBN 0-935859-39-X   LC 87-25452

"A comprehensive dictionary covering all periods and styles of jazz from many countries. Although it draws on other Grove dictionaries, 90% of the material is newly written. Articles cover individuals, groups and bands, topics and terms, instruments, record companies and labels, and institutions; they are signed, and include bibliographies and selected discographies." Sheehy. Guide to Ref Books. 10th edition. suppl

Schuller, Gunther
The history of jazz. Oxford Univ. Press 1968-1989 2v **781.65**

1. Jazz music

Contents: v1 Early jazz: its roots and musical development $30, pa $11.95 (ISBN 0-19-500097-8; 0-19-504043-0); v2 The swing era: the development of jazz, 1930-1945 $35, pa $17.95 (ISBN 0-19-504312-X; 0-19-507140-9)

Shaw, Arnold
The jazz age; popular music in the 1920's. Oxford Univ. Press 1987 350p $27.95; pa $9.95 **781.65**

1. Popular music 2. Jazz music
ISBN 0-19-503891-6; 0-19-506082-2 (pa)
                                LC 86-33234

The author examines "the fusion of jazz, blues, Harlem piano styles, and Broadway shows that became the legacy of American popular music for subsequent decades." Libr J

Includes discography and bibliography

Simon, George Thomas
The big bands; with a foreword by Frank Sinatra. 4th ed. Schirmer Bks. 1981 614p il hardcover o.p. paperback available $23 **781.65**

1. Bands (Music) 2. Jazz musicians
ISBN 0-02-872430-5 (pa)   LC 81-51633

First published 1967 by Macmillan

The author focuses on America's big bands during their greatest years—from 1935 to 1946. Of the hundreds of bands mentioned, many are profiled at length. The roles of leaders, arrangers, musicians, vocalists, managers, music publishers, the press, and the public are discussed

Includes discography

Tirro, Frank
Jazz: a history. 2nd ed. Norton 1993 xxi, 470, 210p il music $34.95 **781.65**

1. Jazz music
ISBN 0-393-96187-7   LC 92-32682

First published 1977

This book explores jazz history from its beginnings to the present day. Sections on jazz forms, eras, and jazz greats include musical examples and biographical information. Appendices include an annotated listening guide, transcriptions, a chronological table, an annotated bibliography and a selected discography

Williams, Martin T.

The jazz tradition; [by] Martin Williams. 2nd rev ed. Oxford Univ. Press 1993 301p $39.95; pa $12.95 **781.65**

1. Jazz music
ISBN 0-19-507815-2; 0-19-507816-0 (pa)

LC 92-29007

First published 1970

A survey of jazz from its beginnings through the present day as seen through its leading figures

Includes discography

781.66 Rock music

Curry, Jack, 1952-

Woodstock; the summer of our lives. Weidenfeld & Nicolson 1989 xx, 337p il $19.95 **781.66**

1. Woodstock Festival, 1969 2. Rock music
ISBN 1-55584-040-X   LC 88-33757

"Setting out 'to recapture the vibrancy of the Woodstock Festival by repopulating it in microcosm,' author Curry . . . pulls together the stories of a handful of participants at the counterculture's 1969 tour de force. Although the first hundred pages or so are overly preoccupied with giving background information on those interviewed, the pace really picks up when actual memories are shared and, in the last pages, we get a glimpse of where these people are now." Libr J

Escott, Colin

Good rockin' tonight; Sun Records and the birth of rock & roll; [by] Colin Escott with Martin Hawkins. St. Martin's Press 1991 276p il $19.95 **781.66**

1. Sun Records (Firm) 2. Rock music
ISBN 0-312-05439-4   LC 90-48351

The authors offer an "evaluation of the seminal Sun Records and its founder and creative genius Sam Phillips. The developments of Sun and the nascent rock 'n' roll phenomenon in the early 1950s are inextricably entwined through Phillips's recordings of Howlin' Wolf, Elvis Presley, Johnny Cash, Carl Perkins, Roy Orbison, and Jerry Lee Lewis, all of whom began their careers at Sun." Libr J

The **Harmony** illustrated encyclopedia of rock; consultant, Mike Clifford; authors, Peter Frame [et al.] Harmony Bks. il pa $19 **781.66**

1. Rock music—Dictionaries

Originally published 1976 in the United Kingdom with title: The Illustrated new musical express encyclopedia of rock; first United States edition published 1977 with title: The Illustrated encyclopedia of rock. (7th edition 1992) Periodically revised

"Over 700 colorfully illustrated entries profile established British and American artists, giving background information, career highlights, and discographies of outstanding recordings. Illustrations are of individuals, groups, and album covers." Nichols. Guide to Ref Books for Sch Media Cent. 4th edition

Lewisohn, Mark

The complete Beatles chronicles. Harmony Bks. 1992 365p il $40 **781.66**

1. Beatles
ISBN 0-517-58100-0   LC 92-19561

"Laid out in calendar book style, this comprehensive book includes photos, memos, letters, contracts, programs, and newspaper articles. It lists performance places and dates, recording sessions, TV and radio broadcasts. Includes a discography, chart positions (1962-1970), where they played, engagements not played, composer index, and name index. . . . [This] is an outstanding source for Beatles facts." BAYA Book Rev

Nite, Norm N.

Rock on; the illustrated encyclopedia of rock n' roll; special introduction by Dick Clark. Updated ed. Harper & Row 1982-1985 3v il v1 $34.95, v2 $29.95, v3 $25 **781.66**

1. Rock music—Dictionaries   LC 83-48371

Volumes 1-2 first published 1978-1982 by Crowell

Contents: v1 The solid gold years (ISBN 0-06-181642-6); v2 The years of change, 1964-1978 (ISBN 0-06-181643-4); v3 The video revolution, 1979-1984, by Norm N. Nite with Charles Crespo (ISBN 0-06-181644-2)

"This is the most comprehensive of the rock and roll encyclopedias. Brief biographies of rock artists and profiles of groups are arranged alphabetically by artist's last name or the name of the group. Each entry includes a chronological list of hits, and information on the record labels on which these songs were released." Ref Sources for Small & Medium-sized Libr. 5th edition

Rock on almanac; the first four decades of rock 'n' roll: a chronology. 2nd ed. HarperPerennial 1992 581p il $40; pa $20 **781.66**

1. Rock music
ISBN 0-06-271555-0; 0-06-273157-2 (pa)

LC 92-52544

First published 1989

For each year, this book lists the major rock movies, musicals and concerts, the debuts of artists and songs, and the developments in sound and recording. Hits are included for every month and year of rock's history

Pawlowski, Gareth L.

How they became the Beatles; a definitive history of the early years, 1960-1964. Dutton 1989 208p il o.p.; New Am. Lib. paperback available $12.95 **781.66**

1. Beatles 2. Rock musicians
ISBN 0-452-26506-1 (pa)   LC 89-32060

"Numerous vintage black-and-white photographs and reproductions of ticket stubs, programs, album covers, and other memorabilia attractively complement a well-researched chronicle of the early Beatles (1960-1964)." Booklist

Riley, Tim
Tell me why; a Beatles commentary.
Knopf 1988 423p $19.95; pa $9.95   **781.66**
1. Beatles
ISBN 0-394-55061-7; 0-679-72198-3 (pa)
LC 87-40492

"Riley takes the reader through the entire collection of Beatles songs, drawing fresh meanings and imparting new insights to that powerful body of music. Students and fans alike will be helped by the perceptive and accurate annotations in the selected bibliography. An 18-page index makes it an attractive source-book. Highly recommended for general audiences." Choice

The **Rolling** Stone encyclopedia of rock & roll; edited by Jon Pareles, consulting editor, and Patricia Romanowski. Rolling Stone Press; Summit Bks. 1983 615p il hardcover o.p. paperback available $16
781.66
1. Rock music—Dictionaries
ISBN 0-671-44071-3 (pa)   LC 83-4791

This volume presents biographical information, definitions of rock styles and terms, and select discographies
This encyclopedia provides "coverage of too-little-known black and ethnic artists whose important contributions to the development of rock have often been overlooked. It also thoroughly treats new music from punk to funk." Libr J

The **Rolling** Stone illustrated history of rock & roll; the definitive history of the most important artists and their music; edited by Anthony DeCurtis and James Henke with Holly George-Warren; original editor: Jim Miller. [new ed]. Random House 1992 710p il pa $22.50   **781.66**
1. Rock music
ISBN 0-679-73728-6   LC 92-6339
First published 1976

This history of four decades of rock music includes essays and photographs covering individual artists, groups, trends and styles

The **Rolling** Stone interviews: the 1980s; by the editors of Rolling Stone; introduction by Kurt Loder; edited by Sid Holt. St. Martin's Press; Rolling Stone Press 1989 352p il $24.95   **781.66**
1. Rock musicians 2. Entertainers
ISBN 0-312-02973-X   LC 89-30096
A collection of 34 interviews from *Rolling Stone* magazine with rock-music stars, actors, and other performers

Ward, Ed, 1948-
Rock of ages; the Rolling Stone history of rock & roll; by Ed Ward, Geoffrey Stokes, Ken Tucker; with an introduction by Jann S. Wenner. Rolling Stone Press; Summit Bks. 1986 649p il hardcover o.p. paperback available $14.95   **781.66**
1. Rock music
ISBN 0-671-63068-7 (pa)   LC 86-14553

This rock music history consists of three parts: The fifties and before, by E. Ward; The sixties, by G. Stokes; The seventies and beyond, by K. Tucker
"A solid history of the course of rock and roll music." Choice

782 Vocal music

Hines, Jerome, 1921-
Great singers on great singing. Doubleday 1982 356p il o.p.; Limelight Eds. paperback available $13.95   **782**
1. Singing
ISBN 0-87910-025-7 (pa)   LC 81-43280
"Hines interviews 42 prominent opera singers to determine what techniques they employ. He limits his questions to three general areas: 'support,' 'the open throat,' and 'placement.'" Choice

Thomson, Virgil, 1896-1989
Music with words; a composer's view. Yale Univ. Press 1989 178p music $21
782
1. Vocal music 2. Composition (Music) 3. Opera
ISBN 0-300-04505-0   LC 89-30709
The author "offers his thoughts on the art of composing music for words. . . . He is firm in his conviction that the music must be composed first and the words set to the music, not vice versa, and insists also that the text must be arranged in 'word groups' to clarify its meaning." Booklist
"Addressed to composers, of interest to performers, this master class with one of America's most treasured composers is one anyone who loves opera in English could enjoy." Libr J
Includes bibliography

782.27 Hymns

American hymns old and new; [compiled by] Albert Christ-Janer, Charles W. Hughes, Charles Sprague Smith. Columbia Univ. Press 1980 838p music $65   **782.27**
1. Hymns
ISBN 0-231-03458-X
Also published as a two-volume set, with v2 consisting of notes on the hymns and biographies, compiled by Charles W. Hughes (o.p.)
This is an interdenominational compilation of 625 hymns sung in America since 1615

782.28 Carols

The **New** Oxford book of carols; edited by Hugh Keyte and Andrew Parrott; associate editor, Clifford Bartlett. Oxford Univ. Press 1992 xxxiv, 702p music $125
782.28
1. Carols
ISBN 0-19-353323-5   LC 92-756468
First published 1928 with title: The Oxford book of carols

The New Oxford book of carols — *Continued*

This book contains over 300 settings of sacred and secular carols spanning the Catholic and Protestant traditions. The selections are drawn from: folk carols, medieval Latin songs, English medieval carols, Lutheran hymnody, and English "gallery" and American "primitive" carols

A **Treasury** of Christmas songs and carols; edited and annotated by Henry W. Simon. 2nd ed. with guitar chords, illustrated by Rafaello Busoni; piano arrangements by the editor and Rudolph Fellner. Houghton Mifflin 1973 243p il music hardcover o.p. paperback available $15.95   **782.28**

1. Carols 2. Songs
ISBN 0-395-17785-5 (pa)

First published 1955

This book contains over one hundred Christmas songs and carols selected for small informal groups, with sections devoted to Christmas hymns, solo songs, children's carols, rounds and canons

782.42 Songs

The **Books** of American Negro spirituals; edited by James Weldon Johnson and J. Rosamond Johnson. Da Capo Press 1977 pa $14.95   **782.42**

1. Spirituals (Songs)
ISBN 0-306-80074-8

A reprint of the volumes first published separately in 1925 and 1926 by Viking and reissued in the present format 1940. Each volume has special title page

Includes "The book of American Negro spirituals" (1925) and "The second book of Negro spirituals" (1926). Contains words and music of 120 spirituals

Musical arrangements by J. Rosamond Johnson, additional numbers by Lawrence Brown

Braheny, John, 1938-

The craft and business of song writing. Writer's Digest Bks. 1988 322p $19.95   **782.42**

1. Popular music—Writing and publishing
ISBN 0-89879-284-3   LC 87-31744

This guide explains how to write songs, develop a marketing plan, and submit material; work with a music publisher, or self-publish; use songwriting contests to further careers; balance the 'give and take' of contract negotiations to get the best possible deal

Includes bibliography

Ewen, David, 1907-1985

American popular songs; from the Revolutionary War to the present. Random House 1966 507p $19.95   **782.42**

1. Popular music 2. Songs, American
ISBN 0-394-41705-4

Edited by David Ewen

"Approximately 3600 songs are covered, with such imformation provided as date of composition, composer, lyricist, and films or Broadway musicals in which they have been featured." Ref Sources for Small & Medium-sized Libr. 5th edition

Find that tune; an index to rock, folk-rock, disco & soul in collections; edited by William Gargan and Sue Sharma. Neal-Schuman 1984-1988 2v set $85   **782.42**

1. Rock music—Indexes 2. Disco music—Indexes 3. Blues music—Indexes
ISBN 1-55570-020-9

Concentrating on rock, folk-rock, disco, and soul music from the 1950s into the 1980s, these volumes index more than 8,000 songs in over 400 collections of sheet music. Each volume has five parts: collections, song titles, first lines of songs, composer/lyricist, and performer

Furia, Philip, 1943-

The poets of Tin Pan Alley; a history of America's great lyricists. Oxford Univ. Press 1990 322p $24.95; pa $10.95   **782.42**

1. Lyricists 2. Popular music 3. Songs, American
ISBN 0-19-506408-9; 0-19-507473-4 (pa)

     LC 90-35937

This work examines "lyrics from stage and movie musicals and the work of ten lyricists: Irving Berlin, Lorenz Hart, Ira Gershwin, Cole Porter, Oscar Hammerstein, Howard Dietz, Yip Harburg, Dorothy Fields, Leo Robin, and Johnny Mercer. . . . Although primarily a record of one aspect of show business, the book is a good history of American popular culture." Choice

Includes bibliographic references

Havlice, Patricia Pate

Popular song index. Scarecrow Press 1975 933p $59.50 + First, Second, and Third supplements   **782.42**

1. Songs—Indexes 2. Popular music—Indexes
ISBN 0-8108-0820-X

First supplement (1978) $37.50 (ISBN 0-8108-1099-9); Second supplement (1984) $37.50 (ISBN 0-8108-1642-3); Third supplement (1989) $59.50 (ISBN 0-8108-2202-4)

"Indexes 301 song collections published between 1940 and 1972 in the original volume and adds 253 collections in the supplements, mainly from the 1970-87 period, but with some published earlier. 'Popular' includes folk songs, hymns, children's songs, etc. The index is by title, first line of verse, and first line of chorus, all coded to the numbered anthologies." Ref Sources for Small & Medium-sized Libr. 5th edition

Lax, Roger

The great song thesaurus; [by] Roger Lax, Frederick Smith. 2nd ed updated & expanded. Oxford Univ. Press 1989 774p $85   **782.42**

1. Popular music
ISBN 0-19-505408-3   LC 88-31267

First published 1984

A "thesaurus—almanac—index—encyclopedia smorgasbord of popular American and English song information. . . . Among its ten sections, most notable are the year-to-year inventory from 1558 to 1986 of significant songs, the listing of songs delineated by performance medium (theater, film, radio, and television); the thesaurus of

Lax, Roger—*Continued*
songs by subject, key word, and category; and, especially,
the 258-page alphabetically arranged song-title catalog."
Libr J

Lomax, Alan, 1915-
The folk songs of North America in the
English language. Doubleday 1960 xxx, 623p
il hardcover o.p. paperback available $19.95
782.42

1. Folk songs—United States
ISBN 0-385-03772-4 (pa)

"Dolphin books"

"Melodies and guitar chords transcribed by Peggy
Seeger; with one hundred piano arrangements by Matyas
Seiber and Don Banks. Illustrated by Michael Leonard;
editorial assistant: Shirley Collins." Title page

Includes words, music, and origins of over 300 American folk songs including ballads, work songs and
spirituals as well as a book list, guitar guide and a
discography

National anthems of the world; edited by
W.L. Reed and M.J. Bristow. Blandford
Press; [distributed by] Sterling music $90
782.42

1. National songs

First published 1943 in the United Kingdom with
title: National anthems of the United Nations and
France. (8th edition 1993) Periodically revised

This volume contains national anthems of 178 nations,
including melody and accompaniment. Words are presented in the native language with transliteration provided
where necessary. English translations follow. Brief historical notes on the adoption of each anthem are included
and the book concludes with a list of national holidays

The **Oxford** book of sea songs; chosen and
edited by Roy Palmer. Oxford Univ. Press
1986 xxx, 343p il music hardcover o.p.
paperback available $8.95   **782.42**

1. Sea songs
ISBN 0-19-282155-5 (pa)   LC 85-753420

This is a collection of 159 sea songs, "the majority
of them with their music. Editor Palmer provides excellent historical and aesthetic introduction and a little note
for each song detailing the incident that inspired it, the
provenance of its tune, its authorship, or other salient
details about it." Booklist

Includes bibliography

Peterson, Carolyn Sue, 1938-
Index to children's songs; a title, first line,
and subject index; compiled by Carolyn Sue
Peterson and Ann D. Fenton. Wilson, H.W.
1979 318p $36   **782.42**

1. Children's songs—Indexes
ISBN 0-8242-0638-X   LC 79-14265

"A numbered indexed list of 298 children's song books
published between 1909 and 1977, identifying more than
5000 songs (both American and foreign) and variations,
arranged alphabetically by author. There are also a title
and first line index and a subject index using more than
1000 subject headings. The titles are likely to be held
in schools and public libraries." Ref Sources for Small
& Medium-sized Libr. 5th edition

Porter, Cole, 1891-1964
The complete lyrics of Cole Porter; edited
by Robert Kimball; with a foreword by
John Updike. Knopf 1983 xxv, 354p il o.p.;
Da Capo Press paperback available $19.95
782.42

1. Songs, American
ISBN 0-306-80483-2 (pa)   LC 83-48101

The author "has gathered 800 of Porter's lyrics, 400
of which have not been published before. Each section
begins with a full-page photo of Porter or one of the
many celebrated performers of his work. The shows and
films for which he wrote are arranged chronologically,
and each lyric comes with publishing information and
the name of the performer who introduced the song."
Libr J

Sandburg, Carl, 1878-1967
The American songbag; [compiled by] Carl
Sandburg. Harcourt Brace & Co. 1927 xxiii,
495p il music hardcover o.p. paperback
available $16.95   **782.42**

1. Folk songs—United States 2. Ballads, American
ISBN 0-15-605650-X (pa)

The song history of America is traced through this
"collection of 280 songs. . . . The music includes not
merely airs and melodies, but complete harmonizations
or piano accompaniments." Introduction

"Each song is introduced by Mr. Sandburg, who in
a few words gives the story of his discovery or of its
origin. Those notes make fascinating reading, and they
can be enjoyed by those who cannot read notes." Springfield Repub

Songwriter's market. Writer's Digest Bks.
$19.95   **782.42**

1. Popular music—Writing and publishing
ISSN 0161-5971

Annual. First published 1978

The main section of this guide consists of listings of
music publishers, record companies, producers, managers,
booking agents, and firms interested in original music.
Also included are articles which present an overview of
the songwriting field, and listings of resources such as
organizations, workshops, and contests

Wilder, Alec, 1907-1980
American popular song; the great
innovators, 1900-1950; edited and with an
introduction by James T. Maher; a new
foreword by Gene Lees. Oxford Univ. Press
1990 xxxix, 536p music $29.95; pa $14.95
782.42

1. Popular music 2. Music, American—History and
criticism
ISBN 0-19-501445-6; 0-19-501925-3 (pa)
     LC 91-118294

A reissue with a new foreword of the title first
published 1972

This study of American popular songwriting covers
"the emergence of . . . ragtime with Eubie Blake and
Ben Harney in the 1980s, the break from Viennese
'schmaltz,' the emergent sophistication of Gershwin, Porter and the 1920s gang and their successors." Publ Wkly

784 Instruments and instrumental ensembles and their music

Del Mar, Norman, 1919-1994
The Anchor companion to the orchestra. Anchor Press/Doubleday 1987 266p $19.95; pa $10.95 **784**

1. Orchestra—Dictionaries
ISBN 0-385-24081-3; 0-385-24082-1 (pa) LC 87-1359

This is "an encyclopedic dictionary of orchestral terms for the common music lover. Instruments, performance practices, and music preparation terms (e.g. editing, score layout, platform arrangement, etc.) are all amply defined and discussed." Booklist

Piston, Walter, 1894-1976
Orchestration. Norton 1955 477p il music pa $29.95 **784**

1. Instrumentation and orchestration 2. Musical instruments
ISBN 0-393-09740-4

This text on writing for the orchestra begins with a discussion of individual instruments and their playing techniques. The last two sections cover analysis and specific problems of orchestration

784.19 Musical instruments

The New Grove dictionary of musical instruments; edited by Stanley Sadie. Grove's Dictionaries of Music 1984 3v il music set $495 **784.19**

1. Musical instruments—Dictionaries
ISBN 0-943818-05-2 LC 84-9062

This work "includes the history of the field, profiles of over 1000 instrument makers and inventors, bibliographies, and comprehensive coverage of ancient and modern, Western and non-Western musical instruments. Although derived in part from the *New Grove dictionary of music and musicians* [entered in class 780.3], this is a new work that updates, revises, and expands, particularly in the area of non-Western instruments. Over 1600 black-and-white photographs and drawings enhance the articles." Ref Sources for Small & Medium-sized Libr. 5th edition

Waring, Dennis, 1944-
Making wood folk instruments. Sterling 1990 c1979 160p il pa $12.95 **784.19**

1. Musical instruments
ISBN 0-8069-7482-6 LC 90-37056

Originally published 1979 in Canada with title: Folk instruments; first United States edition published 1981 with title: Making folk instruments in wood

This book provides step-by-step instructions for making some fifty musical instruments. Historical background, advice on materials, and playing instructions are included

784.2 Symphony orchestra

Kramer, Jonathan D.
Listen to the music; a self-guided tour through the orchestral repertoire. Schirmer Bks. 1988 xxv, 816p $35; pa $20 **784.2**

1. Orchestral music 2. Composers
ISBN 0-02-871841-0; 0-02-871842-9 (pa) LC 88-9248

"A series of program notes originally written for the concerts of the Cincinnati Symphony Orchestra introduces listeners to 290 musical works. . . . Kramer efficiently covers pertinent aspects of each composer's career, tells his audience what to listen for in each composition, and briefly covers the style and content of each piece. . . . A handy, intelligent guide that manages to hit a large number of high spots in orchestral history." Booklist

Includes bibliography

785 Chamber music

Griffiths, Paul, 1947-
The string quartet; with 82 music examples. Thames & Hudson 1983 240p music hardcover o.p. paperback available $10.95 **785**

1. String quartets
ISBN 0-500-27383-9 (pa) LC 83-70402

This "book follows the quartet from its origins in the middle of the eighteenth century up to the present day." Publisher's note

Griffiths "gives us a very solid survey of the important composers and works in the quartet literature, yet weaves in enough comment about external influences on the genre that the reader gains an excellent sense of its rich and varied historical role in music and society." Choice

786.2 Piano

Schmeckel, Carl D.
The piano owner's guide; how to buy and care for a piano. rev ed. Macmillan 1974 127p il pa $7.95 **786.2**

1. Piano
ISBN 0-684-13872-7

First published 1971

The author offers guidelines on whether to buy a new or used instrument, a grand or an upright. Consideration is given to brand, warranty and tone. He also provides information on player pianos, electronic pianos and organs. For care after the purchase has been made, he advises on tuning, moving, repairs and cleaning. An illustrated discussion of piano structure explains the working of both grand and upright pianos

786.4   Harpsichord

Kottick, Edward L.
The harpsichord owner's guide; a manual for buyers and owners; drawings by Richard Masters; photographs by T. Jorgensen. University of N.C. Press 1987 180p il $32.50; pa $16.95   **786.4**

1. Harpsichord
ISBN 0-8078-1745-7; 0-8078-4388-1 (pa)   LC 87-4981

"Edward Kottick, an experienced harpsicord builder, offers the first practical guide to buying, repairing, and maintaining a harpsicord." Univ Press Books for Public Libr

787.7   Plectral instruments

Ritchie, Jean, 1922-
The dulcimer book. Oak Publs. [distributed by] Music Sales Corp. 1974 45p il pa $9.95   **787.7**

1. Dulcimer
ISBN 0-8256-0016-2

First published 1963 in the United Kingdom

"Being a book about the three-stringed Appalachian dulcimer, including some ways of tuning and playing, some recollections in its local history in Perry and Knott counties, Kentucky; some observations on the probable origins of the instrument in the old countries of Europe; with plentiful photographic illustrations and drawings; and with words and music from some sixteen songs from the Ritchie family of Kentucky." Title page

787.8   Plectral lute family

Seeger, Pete
How to play the 5-string banjo; a manual for beginners. 3rd ed. Oak Publs. [distributed by] Music Sales Corp. 1962 72p il pa $9.95   **787.8**

1. Banjo
ISBN 0-8256-0024-3

First published 1948 by People's Songs

A basic manual for banjo players, with melody line, lyrics, and banjo accompaniment and solos notated in standard form of tablature. Appendix includes material on where to buy a banjo, books on the banjo, books of songs to sing and phonograph records

787.87   Guitar

Bacon, Tony
The ultimate guitar book; [by] Tony Bacon & Paul Day. Knopf 1991 192p il $40   **787.87**

1. Guitar
ISBN 0-394-58955-6   LC 91-52714

This is a "chronological history of the guitar, beginning with an example from 1552 and continuing through current times. Covering acoustic, electrical, and bass guitars, including all the big-name manufacturers such as Fender, Gibson, Martin, and Stratocaster, this informative and beautifully illustrated work will have wide appeal." SLJ

Denyer, Ralph
The guitar handbook. [rev ed]. Knopf 1992 256p il pa $25   **787.87**

1. Guitar
ISBN 0-679-74275-1   LC 92-53164

"A Dorling Kindersley book"

First published 1982

Contains a learning program covering the range of guitar techniques from simple chords to improvised lead solos, profiles of famous and influential guitarists, an illustrated chord dictionary, chapters on guitar customizing and recording techniques, and sections on a variety of acoustic and electric guitars, amplification, special effects and stage sound systems

788   Wind instruments and their music

Wollitz, Kenneth
The recorder book. Knopf 1982 c1981 xxv, 259p il hardcover o.p. paperback available $14   **788**

1. Recorder (Musical instrument)
ISBN 0-394-74999-5 (pa)   LC 81-47518

This "book about playing the recorder offers material for players at every level from novice to master. . . . The text gracefully compresses both detailed and comprehensive knowledge of the instrument—its history, repertory, characteristics, care, and techniques of practicing and performing. . . . Very nearly the ideal one-volume book on the recorder." Booklist

Includes bibliography

791.3   Circuses

Culhane, John
The American circus: an illustrated history. Holt & Co. 1990 xxii, 504p il hardcover o.p. paperback available $19.95   **791.3**

1. Circus
ISBN 0-8050-1647-3 (pa)   LC 89-2182

This book covers the circus from its antecedents in the European equestrian shows first staged in the United States in 1785 to the lavish spectacles of the present

The author "has written an engaging and well-researched history of the American circus. It is sure to be a valuable reference source as well as entertaining reading." Libr J

Includes bibliography

McVicar, Wes
Clown act omnibus; everything you need to know about clowning plus over 200 clown stunts. 2nd ed. Meriwether 1987 184p il pa $10.95   **791.3**

1. Clowns
ISBN 0-916260-41-0   LC 87-42958

First published 1960

This volume covers "the basics of being a clown; clown equipment; walk-ons and walk-arounds; clown acts with special equipment [and includes] over 200 skit ideas, classified." Publisher's note

Includes bibliography

791.4 Motion pictures, radio, television

Bogle, Donald
Blacks in American films and television; an encyclopedia. Garland 1988 510p il (Garland reference lib. of the humanities) o.p.; Simon & Schuster paperback available $24.95   **791.4**
1. Black actors 2. Blacks in motion pictures 3. Blacks in television
ISBN 0-671-67538-9 (pa)   LC 87-29241
"This reference work, filled with facts and strong opinions, provides highly critical evaluations of over 260 films (Hollywood and independent) and over 100 television series, specials, and programs featuring Black performers. A profile section traces the careers of some 100 Black actors and a few directors. Excellent illustrations, a bibliography, and a substantial index support the text." Nichols. Guide to Ref Books for Sch Media Cent. 4th edition

791.43 Motion pictures

The **Actor's** book of movie monologues; edited by Marisa Smith and Amy Schewel. Penguin Bks. 1986 xxx, 240p pa $6.95
                                        791.43
1. Motion pictures 2. Monologues
ISBN 0-14-009475-X   LC 86-8093
"Although designed as a sourcebook for aspiring thespians who need material for auditions, this collection of famous movie monologues makes great browsing for all film buffs. . . . Featuring memorable speeches from more than 80 films, the text is arranged chronologically." Booklist

Caine, Michael, 1933-
Acting in film; an actor's take on movie making; edited by Maria Aitken. Applause Theatre Bk. Pubs. 1990 152p il $14.95; pa $8.95   **791.43**
1. Acting 2. Motion pictures
ISBN 0-936839-86-4; 1-55783-124-6 (pa)
                                        LC 89-39932
"'Acting in Film,' the edited transcript of a BBC program, is largely a book on what stage-trained actors need to unlearn. . . . However, 'Acting in Film' is not a stage-versus-film debate. It is an insider's look at the difference between the two, of as much interest to members of the audience as to actors." N Y Times Book Rev
Includes bibliographic references

Champlin, Charles, 1926-
George Lucas: the creative impulse; Lucasfilm's first twenty years. Abrams 1992 207p il $39.95   **791.43**
1. Lucas, George 2. Lucasfilm Ltd.
ISBN 0-8109-3564-3   LC 92-4547
This book presents a "chronology of over 30 feature and TV movies that Lucas either directed or produced. . . . Fellow directors and good friends Steven Spielberg and Francis Coppola pay tribute to Lucas in brief forewords and the book is capped off with a filmogra-

phy. . . . The many color production stills give the book tremendous browse appeal." Libr J

Cook, David A.
A history of narrative film. 2nd ed. Norton 1990 xxvi, 981p il $40.95   **791.43**
1. Motion pictures—History and criticism
ISBN 0-393-95553-2   LC 88-33274
First published 1981
This historical account provides discussion and analysis of major films, directors, national cinemas, business trends, and technological developments
Includes bibliographic references

Culhane, Shamus
Animation from script to screen. St. Martin's Press 1988 336p il $17.95; pa $12.95   **791.43**
1. Animated films 2. Animation (Cinematography)
ISBN 0-312-02162-3; 0-312-05052-6 (pa)
                                        LC 88-11504
"A Thomas Dunne book"
"This is basically a text for the tyro animator. Culhane, for many years with Walt Disney, discusses the role of each member of an animation team and the uses of computers, storyboarding, and music." Libr J
Includes bibliography

Ebert, Roger
Roger Ebert's movie home companion. Andrews & McMeel pa $14.95   **791.43**
1. Motion pictures 2. Videotapes
Annual. First published 1985
This volume contains full-length reviews of films available on video-cassette. Information provided for each film includes running time, MPAA rating, cast, and year of release. Ebert's essays on recent trends and interviews with interesting film personalities round out the guide

Everson, William K., 1929-
American silent film. Oxford Univ. Press 1978 387p il (History of the American film) $29.95; pa $9.95   **791.43**
1. Motion pictures—History and criticism
ISBN 0-19-502348-X; 0-19-503208-X (pa)
                                        LC 77-25188
The author traces the history of American film from the era of nickelodeons to the introduction of sound movies
"A book that lives up to its ballyhoo as the best modern survey of the silent period, complete with a more-than-ample selection of haunting stills." New Repub
Includes bibliographic references

Fricke, John
The Wizard of Oz: the official 50th anniversary pictorial history; [by] John Fricke, Jay Scarfone, William Stillman; introduction by Jack Haley, Jr. Warner Bks. 1989 245p il $29.95; pa $16.95   **791.43**
1. Wizard of Oz (Motion picture)
ISBN 0-446-51446-2; 0-446-39186-7 (pa) LC 89-5495

Fricke, John—*Continued*

"Fricke and two other Oz fanatics have gathered hundreds of delightful photos—publicity stills, rare archival test shots, samples of advertising pieces, reproductions of vital correspondence, etc.—and wedded them to an informative and enthusiastic text that tells the story of the classic film's creation." Booklist

Gabler, Neal

An empire of their own; how the Jews invented Hollywood. Crown 1988 502p il o.p.; Doubleday paperback available $12.95   **791.43**

1. Motion picture industry 2. Jews—United States 3. Hollywood (Calif.)
ISBN 0-385-26557-3 (pa)   LC 87-27563

The author contends "that the immigrant Jews who started the American film industry had an outsider's yearning to become part of American society; that their films reflected an idealized version of America; and that these films, in turn, became so influential as to have defined American values." Commentary

Includes bibliography

Gallagher, Tag

John Ford; the man and his films. University of Calif. Press 1986 572p il $42.50; pa $17.95   **791.43**

1. Ford, John, 1895-1973 2. Motion pictures
ISBN 0-520-05097-5; 0-520-06334-1 (pa)
    LC 83-18047

"Gallagher's reassessment of John Ford's life and career revels in the complexity of the film director's personality while reconsidering his cinematic achievement. . . . Ford's philosophical and intellectual character is also sketched in this honest yet sympathetic account." Booklist

Includes bibliography

Hamilton, Ian, 1938-

Writers in Hollywood, 1915-1951. Harper & Row 1990 336p $25   **791.43**

1. Motion picture industry 2. Authors, American
ISBN 0-06-016231-7   LC 89-45665

Also available in paperback from Carroll & Graf Pubs.

"An Edward Burlingame book"

This history of screenwriting begins with a discussion of the film The Birth of a Nation and concludes with an account of the blacklist of Hollywood writers in the late 1940s and early 1950s

"This book is based almost entirely on secondary sources but it is valuable to have a survey of this field from a literary critic, particularly from a critic with no axe to grind about great writers demeaning themselves in a lesser medium." New Statesman

Harmetz, Aljean

The making of the Wizard of Oz; movie magic and studio power in the prime of MGM and the miracle of production #1060. Dell 1989 c1977 xx, 331p il $15   **791.43**

1. Wizard of Oz (Motion picture)
ISBN 0-385-29746-7   LC 89-212113

A reissue of the title first published 1977 by Knopf

The book concerns the creation of the musical comedy film based on L. Frank Baum's novel

"Harmetz has done meticulous research into many original sources and interviewed remaining cast members and technicians; she helps to set the record straight on a number of items regarding the production." Libr J

Includes bibliographic references

Round up the usual suspects; the making of Casablanca: Bogart, Bergman, and World War II. Hyperion 1992 402p il $24.95; pa $12.95   **791.43**

1. Casablanca (Motion picture)
ISBN 1-56282-941-6; 1-56282-761-8 (pa)
    LC 92-24020

Harmetz sets this behind-the-scenes look at the making of Casablanca in the context of its wartime production

"Gracefully written and thoroughly researched, 'Round Up the Usual Suspects' deploys telling details and illuminating anecdotes to range far beyond the usual 'Making of . . .' formula." N Y Times Book Rev

Includes bibliographic references

Haskell, Molly

From reverence to rape; the treatment of women in the movies; Molly Haskell. 2nd ed. University of Chicago Press 1987 425p il hardcover o.p. paperback available $15.95   **791.43**

1. Women in motion pictures 2. Motion pictures—History and criticism
ISBN 0-226-31885-0 (pa)   LC 87-14354

First published 1974

Chronologically arranged by decade, this book presents a historical study of the depiction of women in film, from the silent era to the mid-1980's

Hepburn, Katharine, 1907-

The making of The African Queen; or, How I went to Africa with Bogart, Bacall and Huston and almost lost my mind. Knopf 1987 129p il $15.95   **791.43**

1. African Queen (Motion picture)
ISBN 0-394-56272-0   LC 87-45128

Also available G.K. Hall large print edition, and in paperback from New Am. Lib.

"Katharine Hepburn relives the filming of the classic movie, 'The African Queen', in her own inimitable style. . . . The outstanding black-and-white photographs of the actors and crew struggling with the jungle and with the whims of director Huston form a perfect counterpart to Hepburn's humorous and insightful recollections." Booklist

Howard, Jean

Jean Howard's Hollywood; a photo memoir; photographs by Jean Howard; text by Jim Watters. Abrams 1989 248p il $39.95   **791.43**

1. Motion picture industry—Pictorial works
ISBN 0-8109-1190-6   LC 89-264

"Miss Howard has recorded the rarefied behind-the-gates lives of some of the most famous personalities in the history of the motion picture business. No outsider was she, hired for the occasion to 'snap' the swells. Miss

Howard, Jean—*Continued*

Howard is very much one of the swells herself; her pictures are shot from the intimate perspective of the insider, either as a guest at the party or, frequently, as the hostess." N Y Times Book Rev

Hutchison, David, 1944-

Film magic; the art and science of special effects. Prentice-Hall 1987 xxi, 168p il pa $12.95   **791.43**

1. Motion picture photography
ISBN 0-13-314774-6   LC 86-43100

"Citing examples from actual films or easily comprehended hypothetical cases, Hutchison devotes a chapter each to explaining how miniature models (e.g., the L.A. destroyed in *Earthquake* [1974]), model animation (e.g., *King Kong*), matte paintings, traveling mattes, and computer-enabled effects are produced and employed. A generous annotated special effects filmography and an expansive glossary conclude." Booklist

International motion picture almanac. Quigley $85   **791.43**

1. Motion pictures
ISSN 1043-8122

Annual. First published 1929 with title: Motion picture almanac. Variant title: Motion picture and television almanac

This work "is useful for quickly finding out when a motion picture was released. There are lists of producers, exhibitors, motion-picture companies, and other essential data." Ref Sources for Small & Medium-sized Libr. 5th edition

Jones, G. William

Black cinema treasures; lost and found; foreword by Ossie Davis. University of N. Tex. Press 1991 242p il $29.95; pa $16.95   **791.43**

1. Motion pictures 2. Blacks in the motion picture industry
ISBN 0-929398-26-2; 0-929398-36-X (pa)
     LC 91-10882

This book "documents black independent filmmaking from the 1920s to the 1950s, spotlighting sixteen films salvaged from a warehouse in Tyler, Texas, by the author. . . . There are also brief biographies of pioneers such as Oscar Micheaux and Spencer Williams. . . . For anyone with an interest in the social history of the movie industry, this book helps bring to light a much-neglected body of work." San Francisco Rev Books

Includes filmography

Kael, Pauline

Movie love; complete reviews, 1988-1991. Dutton 1991 348p o.p.; New Am. Lib. paperback available $14.95   **791.43**

1. Motion pictures—Reviews
ISBN 0-452-26635-1 (pa)   LC 91-9532

"A William Abrahams book"

"In what may be Kael's best collection, her writing is less hyperbolic, her judgments more considered—yet her enthusiasm seems undimmed." Libr J

Kapsis, Robert E.

Hitchcock; the making of a reputation. University of Chicago Press 1992 313p il $45; pa $16.95   **791.43**

1. Hitchcock, Alfred, 1899-1980 2. Motion pictures
ISBN 0-226-42487-1; 0-226-42489-8 (pa) LC 92-7028

The author examines the evolution of Hitchcock's artistic reputation in the light of the critical reception of his films

Includes bibliographic references

Kendall, Elizabeth, 1947-

The runaway bride; Hollywood romantic comedy of the 1930's. Knopf 1990 285p il $24.95   **791.43**

1. Motion pictures 2. Women in motion pictures
ISBN 0-394-51187-5   LC 90-53164

Also available in paperback from Anchor Bks.

"Focusing on Frank Capra, George Stevens, Gregory La Cava, Leo McCarey and Preston Sturges, Ms. Kendall perceives the evolution of Depression comedy through these directors' relationships—both personal and artistic—with the actresses Barbara Stanwyck, Claudette Colbert, Katharine Hepburn, Ginger Rogers, Jean Arthur, Carole Lombard and Irene Dunne." N Y Times Book Rev

Lebo, Harlan

Citizen Kane; the fiftieth anniversary album; foreword by Robert Wise. Doubleday 1990 xxi, 243p il $29.95   **791.43**

1. Citizen Kane (Motion picture)
ISBN 0-385-41473-0   LC 90-32471

In addition to the script of Citizen Kane, "this volume, illustrated by over 100 never-before-published photographs . . . chronicles the intricacies of this masterpiece's creation. Also included is a detailed account of RKO Studio's imbroglio with William Randolph Hearst, upon whom the character of Charles Foster Kane was based." Libr J

Leff, Leonard J.

The dame in the kimono: Hollywood, censorship, and the production code from the 1920s to the 1960s; [by] Leonard J. Leff and Jerold L. Simmons. Weidenfeld & Nicolson 1990 384p $22.50   **791.43**

1. Breen, Joseph Ignatius, 1890-1965 2. Motion pictures—Censorship 3. Motion picture industry
ISBN 1-555-84224-0   LC 89-14730

"The Production Code Administration (nicknamed the 'Hays Office' for its founder, Will Hays) was empowered for nearly 40 years with the responsibility of censoring Hollywood movies while they were in production. This fascinating history of the office is chock full of blow-by-blow, or cut-by-cut replays of how the censors hacked away at such famous films as *Gone with the Wind, The Outlaw,* and *A Streetcar Named Desire.*" Am Libr

Lenburg, Jeff
The encyclopedia of animated cartoons; foreword by Gary Owens. Facts on File 1991 466p il $40; pa $19.95   **791.43**
1. Animated films
ISBN 0-8160-2252-6; 0-8160-2775-7 (pa)
                   LC 90-21182
First published 1981 by Arlington House with title: The encyclopedia of animated cartoon series

This "history of the American animated cartoon starts in 1906, with the newspaper cartoonist James Stuart Blackton's animated one-reel short, *Humorous Phases of Funny Faces,* crunches along to 1947 and the first black-and-white cartoons shown on television ('Movies for Small Fry') and finishes in 1988, with Disney's comedy/mystery, *Who framed Roger Rabbit.*" Times Lit Suppl

Levy, Emanuel, 1947-
And the winner is—; the history and politics of the Oscar Awards. new expanded ed. Continuum 1990 xx, 390p il pa $15.95
                         791.43
1. Academy awards (Motion pictures)
ISBN 0-8264-0450-2   LC 90-133167
"A Frederick Ungar book"
First published 1987 by Ungar

"This book analyzes the unique place occupied by the Oscar in American culture by describing its distinctive history, characteristics, and multiple functions for the film industry, film artists, moviegoers, and television viewers." Introduction

Includes bibliography

Maltin, Leonard
Leonard Maltin's movie and video guide. New Am. Lib. pa $18   **791.43**
1. Motion pictures 2. Videotapes
Annual. First published 1969 with title: TV movies. Title varies

Contains summaries of films and made-for-television movies playing on both commercial and pay-TV. Films currently available on video cassette are identified

Mamet, David
On directing film. Viking 1991 107p $18.95   **791.43**
1. Motion pictures—Production and direction
ISBN 0-670-83033-X   LC 90-50428
Also available in paperback from Penguin Bks.

"Noted playwright, screenwriter, and director Mamet offers his views on film directing taken, some in transcript form, from lectures and classes at Columbia. . . . Refreshingly untheoretical, particularly regarding acting technique, this is fitfully interesting stuff." Libr J

Mast, Gerald, 1940-1988
A short history of the movies. 5th ed, revised by Bruce F. Kawin. Macmillan 1992 669p il $35; pa $33   **791.43**
1. Motion pictures—History and criticism
ISBN 0-02-580510-X; 0-02-377070-8 (pa)
                   LC 90-28627
First published 1971 by Pegasus Press

The author traces the history of motion pictures from their birth to the present day. Among the topics discussed are the coming of sound, the studio system and the cinemas of the Soviet Union, France and Germany. D. W. Griffith, Mack Sennet and Charlie Chaplin are among the personalities covered

Includes bibliography

Monaco, James
How to read a film; the art, technology, language, history, and theory of film and media. rev ed, with diagrams by David Lindroth. Oxford Univ. Press 1981 533p il $39.95; pa $16.95   **791.43**
1. Motion pictures
ISBN 0-19-502802-3; 0-19-502806-6 (pa)
                   LC 80-16848
First published 1977

This introduction to film study is both a history of film technology and an overview of film theory. Other media—radio, television, and recording—are also considered

Includes bibliography

Morris, L. Robert
Lawrence of Arabia; the official 30th anniversary pictorial history; [by] L. Robert Morris and Lawrence Raskin; foreword by Martin Scorsese. Doubleday 1992 237p il $40; pa $19.50   **791.43**
1. Lawrence of Arabia (Motion picture)
ISBN 0-385-42478-7; 0-385-42479-5 (pa)
                   LC 92-27800
This volume examines the making of the motion picture Lawrence of Arabia in 1962 and its subsequent history, including its restoration and 1989 release

"Morris and Raskin had access to the archives of Columbia Pictures and director Lean, ensuring a generous selection of frame enlargements, stills, design sketches, and other visuals. . . . A useful addition to film collections." Booklist

Includes bibliographic references

The Motion picture guide; [edited by] Jay Robert Nash, Stanley Ralph Ross. CineBooks 1985-1987 12v o.p.   **791.43**
1. Motion pictures—History and criticism
Only annual supplements, covering the films of the year beginning with 1985, are available. Apply to Bowker for prices and availability

This reference work evaluates American feature films released between 1910 and 1984. Volumes 1-9 cover sound movies from 1927 through 1984. Volume 10 is devoted to silent movies from 1910-1936. The next two volumes are indexes

Osborne, Robert A.
60 years of the Oscar; the official history of the Academy Awards; [by] Robert Osborne. Abbeville Press 1989 319p il $49.95   **791.43**
1. Academy awards (Motion pictures)
ISBN 0-89659-952-3   LC 88-30487
New edition in preparation

Osborne, Robert A.—*Continued*

An "account of the awards, which summarizes each event and details nominees and award winners. . . . Coverage begins at the beginning and goes through 1987." Choice

"Movie lovers will find this 'encyclopedic retrospective' to be the ultimate Oscar trivia book. . . . Familiar black-and-white and color photographs, often stills from the movies, don't add much excitement, though pictures of the early award ceremonies are fun." Booklist

Pogel, Nancy

Woody Allen. Twayne Pubs. 1987 247p il (Twayne's filmmaker's series) $22.95; pa $12.95   **791.43**

1. Allen, Woody
ISBN 0-8057-9297-X; 0-8057-9309-7 (pa)
      LC 86-29521

"Covering the 20 years that span Allen's writing and acting debut in 'What's New, Pussycat?' (1965) through his 1985 film 'The Purple Rose of Cairo', Pogel provides an in-depth critical analysis of the distinctive moviemaker's career." Booklist

Includes bibliography

Rebello, Stephen

Alfred Hitchcock and the making of Psycho. Dembner Bks. 1990 224p il $24.95
      791.43

1. Hitchcock, Alfred, 1899-1980 2. Psycho (Motion picture)
ISBN 0-942637-14-3   LC 89-30988

Also available in paperback from HarperPerennial

In this "examination of director Alfred Hitchcock's memorable film *Psycho*, Rebello looks at all aspects of the film's creation, from the acquisition of the original novel to the reaction of the actors during screenings of the rough cuts. For Hitchcock fans as well as film students." Booklist

Includes bibliographic references

Rosenblum, Ralph

When the shooting stops, the cutting begins; a film editor's story; [by] Ralph Rosenblum and Robert Karen. Da Capo Press 1986 c1979 310p il pa $11.95
      791.43

1. Motion pictures—Production and direction
ISBN 0-306-80272-4   LC 86-11495

A reprint of the title first published 1979 by Viking

Rosenblum "mixes personal memoir with a brief history of his profession. . . . His associations with such directors as Sidney Lumet, Mel Brooks, and Woody Allen (he edited every Allen film through Annie Hall) make for absorbing reading and provide the informed lay reader with a new appreciation of the editor's art." Libr J

Scheuer, Steven H.

Movies on TV and videocassette; conceived and edited by Steven H. Scheuer. Bantam Bks. pa $7.50   **791.43**

1. Motion pictures 2. Videotapes

Annual. First published 1958 with title: TV movie almanac & ratings. Title varies

This guide lists movies shown on TV as well as those available on videocassette. Each entry includes a short annotation, partial cast list, running time, etc.

Schneider, Steve

That's all folks! the art of Warner Bros. animation; foreword by Ray Bradbury. Holt & Co. 1988 252p il hardcover o.p. paperback available $19.95   **791.43**

1. Warner Bros. Cartoons 2. Animated films
ISBN 0-8050-1485-3 (pa)   LC 88-81823

"A Donald Hutter book"

The first section of this book "chronicles Warner's growth and development over four decades, while the second part, 'The Stars,' contains short treatments of the major characters and their unique personalities." Libr J

This book is "more than a chronicle of the studio's creative eras under the direction of animators like Friz Freleng, Tex Avery, Bob Clampett and Chuck Jones; it is also something of a treatise on animation. And best of all, this volume is a compendium of classic Warner artwork." N Y Times Book Rev

Screen world; by John Willis. Applause Theatre Bk. Pubs.   **791.43**

1. Motion pictures

Apply to publisher for available volumes and prices

Annual. First published 1949 by Greenberg with title: Daniel Blum's screen world. Publisher varies

"Long-standing series that provides cast and other production information for films released in the United States. Heavily illustrated, it also contains a section of brief biographies of famous screen personalities." Ref Sources for Small & Medium-sized Libr. 5th edition

Sennett, Ted

Great Hollywood westerns. Abrams 1990 272p il $60; pa $29.98   **791.43**

1. Western films
ISBN 0-8109-3352-7; 0-8109-8120-3 (pa)
      LC 90-30520

In this heavily illustrated volume the author "takes a straightforward approach to the subject, systematically surveying the western's various components—the westward march, the loner, the group, the Indians, the women." Publ Wkly

Includes bibliographic references

Shipman, David

The story of cinema; a complete narrative history, from the beginnings to the present; preface by Ingmar Bergman. St. Martin's Press 1984 1280p il hardcover o.p. paperback available $19.95   **791.43**

1. Motion pictures—History and criticism
ISBN 0-312-76280-1 (pa)   LC 84-13254

First published in the United Kingdom as a two volume work, copyrighted 1980 and 1982

This is "an extensive survey of the history of film around the world. Through plot descriptions and critical analyses of 5,000 films—all viewed by him personally—Shipman narrates the course cinema has taken from its Parisian origins to the contemporary work of Coppola, Landis, Scorsese, Lucas, Spielberg, et al." Booklist

Includes bibliography

Taub, Eric
Gaffers, grips, and best boys. St. Martin's
Press 1987 200p pa $10.95   **791.43**
1. Motion pictures—Production and direction
ISBN 0-312-01150-4   LC 87-16364
The author "attempts to convey 'an overall understanding of the entire filmmaking procedure'—from initial
idea to final marketing. Interviews with Hollywood artists
and craftspeople guide the reader through key phases of
the process. . . . Detailed and of interest both to film
students and cinema buffs." Publ Wkly

Thomas, Tony, 1927-
A wonderful life: the films and career of
James Stewart. Citadel Press 1988 255p il
pa $15.95   **791.43**
1. Stewart, James
ISBN 0-8065-1081-1   LC 87-37493
Black-and-white photographs of Stewart's professional
and private life illustrate this look at his 77 films

Van Gelder, Peter, 1953-
That's Hollywood; a behind-the-scenes
look at 60 of the greatest films ever made.
Harper & Row 1990 288p il $22.50; pa
$10.95   **791.43**
1. Motion pictures
ISBN 0-06-055198-4; 0-06-096512-6 (pa)
    LC 89-46491
This "is a collection of general facts, fascinating tid-
bits, and humorous speculation about 60 excellent or
very popular films, ranging from *Frankenstein* (1931) to
Batman (1989). Van Gelder writes with wit throughout.
. . . The book's British origin probably explains Van
Gelder's inclusion of [certain] films. . . . No matter,
American audiences will love this highly browsable item."
Booklist

Wiley, Mason
Inside Oscar; the unofficial history of the
Academy Awards; by Mason Wiley &
Damien Bona; edited by Gail MacColl.
Ballantine Bks. il pa $20   **791.43**
1. Academy awards (Motion pictures) LC 93-105549
First published 1986. (4th edition 1993) Frequently
revised
A chronologically arranged history of the Academy
Awards. Details include excerpts from celebrities, and an
overview of each film's critical reception by the media.
An appendix lists nomination winners, losers, and other
miscellaneous facts

Williams, Alan Larson
Republic of images; a history of French
filmmaking; [by] Alan Williams. Harvard
Univ. Press 1992 458p il $49.95; pa $19.95
    791.43
1. Motion pictures—France
ISBN 0-674-76267-3; 0-674-76268-1 (pa)
    LC 91-25877
"Williams traces the evolution of French filmmaking
since 1895, offering a unique synthesis of history, biography, aesthetics, and theory." Univ Press Books for Public
and Second Sch Libr

"This volume is substantially researched and provides
a wealth of information not previously assembled in a
single study." Libr J
Includes bibliographic references

791.4303 Motion pictures—
Encyclopedias and dictionaries

Green, Stanley, 1923-1990
Encyclopaedia of the musical film. Oxford
Univ. Press 1981 344p $35; pa $15.95
    791.4303
1. Motion pictures—Dictionaries
ISBN 0-19-502958-5; 0-19-505421-0 (pa)   LC 81-735
"In addition to articles on American and British
musical films, there are entries for individual songs and
for performers, composers, lyricists, film directors, and
other persons involved with the genre." Choice
"'The Encyclopaedia' may not be truly encyclopedic;
it concentrates on the musical screen's 'most prominent
individuals, productions, and songs,' which may be
enough for most of us. And its amusing, informative
bits make the book fun to browse through." N Y Times
Book Rev

Halliwell, Leslie, 1929-1989
Halliwell's film guide. HarperCollins Pubs.
$50   **791.4303**
1. Motion pictures—Dictionaries
First published 1977 in the United Kingdom; 1979
in the United States by Scribner. (8th edition 1992) Frequently revised
Covers "English-language feature films, with such information as running time, date of release, country of
origin, production company, color process, major credits,
short plot synopsis, and a critical excerpt. It contains
a rating system to indicate the author's opinion on the
films, an index of alternative titles, and a list of English-
language titles of foreign films." Ref Sources for Small
& Medium-sized Libr. 5th edition

Halliwell's filmgoer's and video viewer's
companion. HarperCollins Pubs. $60; pa $25
    791.4303
1. Motion pictures—Dictionaries
ISBN 0-06-271570-4; 0-06-273239-0 (pa)
First published 1965 in the United Kingdom; 1966
in the United States by Hill & Wang with title: The
filmgoer's companion. (10th edition 1993) Frequently
revised. Publishers vary
"Provides brief entries in dictionary format on directors, cinematographers, composers, actors, films, cinematic
themes, and related subjects. There are some longer entries on major trends in films and film making and some
coverage of film terms and technique. Emphasis on
British and American film scene, with some information
on others." Ref Sources for Small & Medium-sized Libr.
5th edition

Slide, Anthony
The American film industry; a historical
dictionary; research associates, Val
Almendarez [et al.] Greenwood Press 1986
431p $55   **791.4303**
1. Motion pictures—Dictionaries
ISBN 0-313-24693-9   LC 85-27260

Slide, Anthony—*Continued*

Also available in paperback from Limelight Eds.

"A diversity of topics and terms are defined. Film techniques are described. Through a network of extensive cross-references the user can follow the development of significant American film events, companies, organizations, and genres. Good for beginning research and company addresses, yet scholars will find the list of locations of archival materials particularly worthwhile." Ref Sources for Small & Medium-sized Libr. 5th edition

791.44 Radio

Ely, Melvin Patrick

The adventures of Amos 'n' Andy; a social history of an American phenomenon. Free Press 1991 322p il $24.95; pa $12.95
791.44

1. Amos 'n' Andy (Radio program) 2. Amos 'n' Andy (Television program) 3. Blacks in television
ISBN 0-02-909502-6; 0-02-909503-4 (pa)   LC 91-7837

A "historian examines one of America's greatest cultural enigmas—the amazing popularity, among blacks as well as whites, of 'Amos 'n' Andy' on radio for more than 30 years." N Y Times Book Rev

Includes bibliographic references

791.45 Television

Brooks, Tim

The complete directory to prime time network TV shows, 1946-present; [by] Tim Brooks and Earle Marsh. Ballantine Bks. $19
791.45

1. Television programs   LC 91-90655

First published 1979. (5th edition 1992) Periodically revised

"Coverage of all nighttime series on commercial networks is provided, with information on the type of show, broadcast history, cast, spin-offs, and plot or format. Index to actors and actresses." Ref Sources for Small & Medium-sized Libr. 5th edition

Buckley, William F. (William Frank), 1925-

On the firing line; the public life of our public figures; by William F. Buckley, Jr. Random House 1989 xxxix, 533p il $22.50
791.45

1. Firing line (Television program)
ISBN 0-394-57568-7   LC 88-43210

A collection of edited transcripts from Buckley's interview program Firing Line, covering the period 1966 to 1989

"If [the book] has a flaw, it is that it's less about the people who have been Mr. Buckley's subjects than it is about Mr. Buckley himself. This is not unexpected, not meant to disparage the author, whose ideas and expression are often invigorating, if infuriating." N Y Times Book Rev

Gunther, Marc, 1951-

Monday night mayhem; the inside story of ABC's Monday night football; [by] Marc Gunther & Bill Carter. Beech Tree Bks. 1988 384p il $18.95; pa $9.95   **791.45**

1. Monday night football (Television program)
2. Football
ISBN 0-688-07553-3; 0-688-09205-5 (pa)
LC 88-18651

This "account of the program and the people who introduced sports to prime-time television takes the reader from Monday Night's creation on through to the 1988 Super Bowl." Publisher's note

"Monday Night Football was never just sports television, it was prime-time television, and the trappings of the success and stardom, the economics, and the internecine politics and backstabbing make for a fascinating tale. Gunther and Carter have reported the story very thoroughly, and they tell it extremely well." Christ Sci Monit

Hill, Doug, 1950-

Saturday night; a backstage history of Saturday night live; by Doug Hill & Jeff Weingrad. Beech Tree Bks. 1986 510p il o.p.; Random House paperback available $8.95   **791.45**

1. Saturday night live (Television program)
ISBN 0-394-75053-5 (pa)   LC 85-19991

This book is a history of the first ten years of the late-night television show

"In this absorbing account, based on 250 interviews, the authors successfully recreate the chaotic backstage scene." Publ Wkly

International television & video almanac. Quigley $85   **791.45**

1. Television broadcasting 2. Videotapes

Annual. First published 1956 with title: International television almanac

This compendium includes such information as statistics, awards, who's who, network programs, TV producers and distributors, video companies and services, and the world market in television and video

Kessler, Judy, 1947-

Inside Today; the battle for the morning. Villard Bks. 1992 272p $19.50   **791.45**

1. Today show (Television program)
ISBN 0-679-40764-2   LC 92-53657

An "account of the agonies and ecstacies of NBC's morning show from 1978 to the present, written by the program's talent coordinator from 1980 to 1984." Publ Wkly

"Anyone interested in a career in TV news—particularly as a talent booker—should read this book to know the frantic, hilarious, sometimes unethical lengths used to scoop competitors. With its throwaway celebrity gossip, this book will have quick appeal for most readers." Libr J

O'Neil, Thomas
The Emmys; star wars, showdowns, and the supreme test of TV's best. Penguin Bks. 1992 507p il pa $16   **791.45**
1. Emmy awards
ISBN 0-14-016656-4   LC 91-46977
"A Wexford Press book"
This is a year-by-year guide to the Emmy Awards for the years 1948 through 1990-1991. The author's coverage includes the daytime, news, sports, international and special Emmy awards

Paisner, Daniel
Horizontal hold; the making and breaking of a network television pilot. Carol Pub. Group 1992 206p $18.95   **791.45**
1. Television programs 2. Television broadcasting
ISBN 1-55972-148-0   LC 92-24143
"A Birch Lane Press book"
"Paisner traces the progress of . . . a 1990 pilot for a sitcom about White House speech writers called 'E.O.B.' He was present at all stages of the production, from the pitch to the network . . . to the final taping. . . . This behind-the-scenes view provides fascinating insights into what it takes to get a show off the ground." Booklist

Palmer, Edward L.
Television & America's children; a crisis of neglect. Oxford Univ. Press 1988 xxv, 194p $21.95; pa $8.95   **791.45**
1. Children's Television Workshop 2. Television and children
ISBN 0-19-505540-3; 0-19-506321-X (pa) LC 88-4223
The author, one of the founders of the Children's Television Workshop, "reveals why American commercial TV doesn't provide quality programming for young viewers. Contending that a high-quality children's service is within our reach, he outlines the nature and cost of such a service and discusses ways to fund it." Univ Press Books for Public Libr
Includes bibliography

Winn, Marie
The plug-in drug. rev ed. Viking 1985 288p il o.p.; Penguin Bks. paperback available $7.95   **791.45**
1. Television and children
ISBN 0-14-007698-0 (pa)   LC 84-40470
First published 1977
The author "uses professional and parental research to substantiate her position that the major problem with TV for children is not program content, but the stupor-like fixation induced by continued exposure. Watching television, she argues, becomes a 'one-way transaction' requiring little, if any cognitive or physical response. . . . An essential study." Booklist
Includes bibliography

Unplugging the plug-in drug; drawings by Karla Kuskin. Viking 1987 206p il o.p.; Penguin Bks. paperback available $7.95   **791.45**
1. Television and children
ISBN 0-14-008895-4 (pa)   LC 87-8230

The author "has outlined how to go about planning a family, school, or community TV turn-off to help children and others understand the role TV plays in their lives." Libr J
Includes bibliography

791.6   Pageantry

Neil, Randy
The all-new official cheerleader's handbook; [by] Randy L. Neil and Elaine Hart with the staff of the International Cheerleading Foundation, Inc. rev ed. Simon & Schuster 1986 300p il pa $14.95   **791.6**
1. Cheers and cheerleading
ISBN 0-671-61210-7   LC 86-6621
"A Fireside book"
First published 1979 with title: The Official cheerleader's handbook
This volume covers basic cheerleading movements and routines as well as more complex stunts, formations, cheers, and chants. A listing of cheerleading camps is appended

791.8   Animal performances

Hemingway, Ernest, 1899-1961
The dangerous summer; introduction by James A. Michener. Scribner 1985 228p il hardcover o.p. paperback available $11.95   **791.8**
1. Bullfights 2. Spain—Description
ISBN 0-684-18720-5 (pa)   LC 84-27578
Originally written as a series of articles for Life magazine
A look at the "personal and professional rivalry of the two greatest bullfighters since the death of Manolete in 1947: Luis Miguel Dominguín and Antonio Ordóñez. The Dangerous Summer provides an insider's view based on extensive experience, mingles memory and desire, and is essential reading for anyone interested in the subject or the author." Natl Rev

Death in the afternoon. Scribner 1932 517p il $55; pa $19   **791.8**
1. Bullfights
ISBN 0-684-15750-0; 0-684-71796-4 (pa)
"A loosely organized book on bullfighting in Spain. . . . Hemingway depicts the bullfight as an emblematic tragedy, a test of courage, with a bloody and not entirely predictable end. Throughout, he digresses to philosophize on life and death in exchanges with a character he calls the Old Lady." Benet's Reader's Ency of Am Lit

792   Stage presentations

Adler, Stella, 1901-1992
The technique of acting; foreword by Marlon Brando. Bantam Bks. 1988 132p il hardcover o.p. paperback available $11   **792**
1. Acting
ISBN 0-553-34932-5 (pa)   LC 88-47514

Adler, Stella, 1901-1992—*Continued*

"This text capsulizes the exercises and conceptual thinking that have won many converts to Adler's teaching, including focus on physical and vocal techniques, the development of imagination and character, the perfection of stage business, and the interpretation of the playwright's text. . . . A desirable theater how-to for both budding and shopworn actors." Booklist

The **Back** Stage handbook for performing artists; the how-to and who-to contact reference for actors, singers, and dancers; compiled and edited by Sherry Eaker. rev & enl ed. Back Stage Bks. 1991 309p il $16.95   792

1. Acting 2. Performing arts
ISBN 0-8230-7569-9   LC 91-29379

First published 1989

This guide for aspiring actors, singers, and dancers covers such topics as auditioning, writing a good résumé, unions, and how to find temporary work between gigs

Corson, Richard

Stage makeup. Prentice-Hall il $47   792

1. Makeup, Theatrical

First published 1942 by Appleton. (8th edition 1990) Periodically revised

The author discusses the art and technique of theatrical makeup, covering such topics as facial anatomy, various methods for applying greasepaint and other makeup, and the use of beards, wigs, and prosthetic pieces

Gillette, A. S. (Arnold S.), 1904-

Stage scenery: its construction and rigging; [by] A. S. Gillette, J. Michael Gillette. 3rd ed. Harper & Row 1981 448p il $45.50
                    792

1. Theaters—Stage setting and scenery
ISBN 0-06-042332-3   LC 81-568

First published 1959

This is "an introduction to the technical aspects of stage settings and properties, from design and construction through rigging and set changing. . . . The book also includes advice on backstage organization and management as well as the working relationship among designer, director, and stage crew. Amply illustrated with black-and-white photographs, drawings, and diagrams." Booklist

Includes bibliography

Hoggett, Chris

Stage crafts. St. Martin's Press 1977 c1975 282p il $17.50   792

1. Theaters—Stage setting and scenery
ISBN 0-312-75495-7

First published 1975 in the United Kingdom

"Ready-reference guide to various methods and techniques of putting together a limited-budget theater production from A (stage construction) to Z (character makeup)." Booklist

Legat, Michael, 1923-

Putting on a play. St. Martin's Press 1984 208p $12.95   792

1. Amateur theater
ISBN 0-312-07846-3   LC 84-13242

"This book was written with the small, fledgling drama group in mind and covers all aspects of amateur play production, from choosing and casting a play to directing, rehearsals, acting, sets, properties, lighting, costumes, makeup, and publicity. . . . The information provided is sound and practical. A useful addition to theater collections in public, high school, and college libraries." Libr J

Includes bibliography

Moore, Sonia

The Stanislavski system; the professional training of an actor; digested from the teachings of Konstantin S. Stanislavski. 2nd rev ed. Penguin Bks. 1984 96p pa $10
                    792

1. Stanislavsky, Konstantin, 1863-1938 2. Acting
ISBN 0-14-046660-6   LC 84-2855

First published 1960 with title: The Stanislavski method

This is a concise, simplified guide to the teachings of the great master of the Moscow Art Theater

Shurtleff, Michael

Audition; everything an actor needs to know to get the part. Walker & Co. 1978 187p hardcover o.p. paperback available $9.95   792

1. Acting
ISBN 0-8027-7240-4 (pa)   LC 77-90134

The author, a casting director, offers advice on how to approach an audition

Shurtleff discusses the "audition in terms that make it readily understood. . . . He simply lays down some guidelines, twelve in all, to help the talented young person increase the odds of being discovered." Best Sellers

Stanislavsky, Konstantin, 1863-1938

An actor prepares; translated by Elizabeth Reynolds Hapgood; introduction by John Gielgud. Anniversary ed. Theatre Arts Bks. 1948 xx, 295p $39.95; pa $14.95   792

1. Acting
ISBN 0-87830-001-5; 0-87830-983-7 (pa)

First published 1936

"Working examples of good and bad acting described in the form of semi-fiction. The names of the actors are fictitious; the acting principles are based on the experience of the author in the Moscow art theatre." Booklist

Theatre world. Applause Theatre Bk. Pubs. il   792

1. Theater—United States

Apply to publisher for available volumes and prices

Annual. Started publication with the 1944/45 season. Publisher varies

Editor: 1944/45-1962/63, Daniel Blum; 1964/65-date John Willis

Theatre world—*Continued*
This publication "provides a record of performances, casts, and other production information for New York theater and regional theater around the country. There are many photographs and a listing of actors and actresses with brief biographical information." Ref Sources for Small & Medium-sized Libr. 5th edition

792.03 Theater—Encyclopedias and dictionaries

Bordman, Gerald Martin
The Oxford companion to American theatre; [by] Gerald Bordman. 2nd ed. Oxford Univ. Press 1992 735p $49.95
                         792.03
1. Theater—United States—Dictionaries 2. American drama—Dictionaries
ISBN 0-19-507246-4   LC 91-16720
First published 1984
This reference work includes entries on playwrights, plays, actors, directors, producers, songwriters, famous playhouses, dramatic movements, and biographical sketches of prominent theatre personalities and groups

The **Cambridge** guide to world theatre; edited by Martin Banham; editorial advisory board, James Brandon [et al.] Cambridge Univ. Press 1988 1104p il $69.95
                         792.03
1. Theater—Dictionaries
ISBN 0-521-26595-9   LC 88-25804
"Covers dramatists, surveys of national developments, techniques. Emphasizes topics not adequately covered elsewhere: underrepresented areas (e.g., outside Europe and the U.S.), popular theater, popular entertainment. Articles are signed; longer articles have bibliographies." Sheehy. Guide to Ref Books. 10th edition. suppl

The **Oxford** companion to the theatre; edited by Phyllis Hartnoll. 4th ed. Oxford Univ. Press 1983 934p il $55   **792.03**
1. Theater—Dictionaries
ISBN 0-19-211546-4
First published 1951
"Offers definitions or explanations of theater terms, biographical sketches of theater personalities (including many living performers, playwrights, etc.), articles on specific theater companies and theater buildings, and historical sketches of theater in individual countries and cities. International in scope, with some emphasis on British and American theater." Sheehy. Guide to Ref Books. 10th edition

792.3 Pantomime

Mimes on miming; writing on the art of mime; edited with historical notes by Bari Rolfe. Panjandrum Bks. 1979 232p il $15.95; pa $8.95   **792.3**
1. Mime 2. Pantomimes
ISBN 0-915572-32-X; 0-915572-31-1 (pa)
                          LC 79-21659
"The mime tradition is traced chronologically from ancient Greece and Rome up to the present time and geographically from Europe to America and Asia. Mime's

roles in ballet, film, and experimental theater are also discussed. Most of the contributors are mimes themselves—Marcel Marceau, Buster Keaton . . . while an epilogue presents antimime positions by Max Beerbohm, Woody Allen, and others." Booklist
Includes bibliography

792.5 Opera

Alpert, Hollis, 1916-
The life and times of Porgy and Bess; the story of an American classic. Knopf 1990 354p il $35   **792.5**
1. Gershwin, George, 1898-1937. Porgy and Bess
ISBN 0-394-58339-6   LC 89-43367
This book is an account of the origins of the opera and its first and subsequent productions
"Alpert's nice balancing of diverting trivia and dramatic episode makes . . . his entertaining and comprehensive chronicle a special pleasure." Smithsonian
Includes bibliography

Cross, Milton
The new Milton Cross' complete stories of the great operas. rev and enl ed, edited by Karl Kohrs. Doubleday 1955 688p $17.95
                         792.5
1. Operas—Stories, plots, etc.
ISBN 0-385-04324-4
First published 1947 with title: Milton Cross' complete stories of the great operas
This reference work describes over seventy famous operas, giving a plot synopsis and important arias. Also includes a short history of the development of the opera as a musical form and ballet as a traditional part of opera production
Includes bibliographies

The new Milton Cross' more stories of the great operas; by Milton Cross and Karl Kohrs. Revised and expanded by Karl Kohrs. Doubleday 1980 802p $19.95 **792.5**
1. Operas—Stories, plots, etc.
ISBN 0-385-14776-7
First published 1971 with title: Milton Cross' more stories of the great operas
This book adds descriptions of 69 more operas to those covered in the earlier volume entered above
Includes bibliography

Freeman, John W.
The Metropolitan Opera stories of the great operas. Metropolitan Opera Guild; Norton 1984 xxxii, 547p il $24.95   **792.5**
1. Operas—Stories, plots, etc.
ISBN 0-393-01888-1   LC 84-8030
This volume "contains the plots of 150 of the world's most popular operas . . . [plus] biographies of each of the 72 composers represented, and historical background material pertinent to each work." Publisher's note

Grout, Donald Jay, 1902-1987

A short history of opera; [by] Donald Jay Grout with Hermine Weigel Williams. 3rd ed. Columbia Univ. Press 1988 913p il $49

792.5

1. Opera—History and criticism
ISBN 0-231-06192-7 LC 87-9374
First published 1947

"Starting with the lyric theater of the Greeks, medieval dramatic music, and other forerunners, 'A Short History of Opera' then reveals the genre's beginnings in the seventeenth century and follows its progress to the present day. . . . The book is not limited to standard performance repertoire of operas, but includes works considered to be important for the genre's development." Publisher's note

Includes bibliography

Harewood, George Henry Hubert Lascelles, 7th Earl of, 1923-

Kobbé's illustrated opera book; twenty six of the world's favorite operas; by the Earl of Harewood. Putnam 1989 160p il $34.95

792.5

1. Operas—Stories, plots, etc.
ISBN 0-399-13475-1 LC 89-8441

"For each opera, Harewood gives a brief history of its composition and production and critical reception, an act-by-act plot summary, several paragraphs of criticism on storytelling and musical aesthetics." Booklist

Kobbé, Gustav, 1857-1918

The definitive Kobbé's opera book; edited, revised, and updated by the Earl of Harewood. Putnam 1987 1404p $39.95

792.5

1. Operas—Stories, plots, etc.
ISBN 0-399-13180-9 LC 86-18705
First published 1919 with title: The complete opera book

"Reference guide to the world's great operas with plot synopses, performance data, some critical commentary on each opera, and some biographical details about the composers." N Y Public Libr Book of How & Where to Look It Up

Littlejohn, David, 1937-

The ultimate art; essays around and about opera. University of Calif. Press 1992 303p il $25

792.5

1. Opera
ISBN 0-520-07608-7 LC 91-39025
Analyzed in Essay and general literature index

In this collection of essays the author "reaches beyond the pages of the individual opera to deal with its traditions, conventions, and contexts. . . . Aimed primarily at the serious opera-lover, these essays are not scholarly in the usual sense of the term, yet many of the perceptions they contain may well be worth the scholar's attention." Choice

Includes bibliographic references

The New Grove dictionary of opera; edited by Stanley Sadie. Grove's Dictionaries of Music 1992 4v il set $850

792.5

1. Opera—Dictionaries
ISBN 0-935859-92-6 LC 92-36276

This set, "developed from The New Grove Dictionary of Music and Musicians [entered in class 780.3], covers all aspects of the modern Western opera tradition, including composers, performers, directors, companies, stagecraft, theaters, cities, terms, and individual works." Libr J

For a fuller review see: Booklist, April 1, 1993

Osborne, Charles, 1927-

The complete operas of Mozart; a critical guide. Atheneum Pubs. 1978 349p il music o.p.; Da Capo Press paperback available $13.95

792.5

1. Mozart, Wolfgang Amadeus, 1756-1791 2. Operas—Stories, plots, etc.
ISBN 0-306-80190-6 (pa) LC 78-55623

In this introduction to Mozart's operas, "each opera is treated as a separate chapter. . . . Each chapter begins with a separate page containing the dramatis personae and their voice range . . . the date, place, and cast for the first performance . . . the name of the librettist, and the Köchel number." Choice

Includes bibliography

The complete operas of Puccini; a critical guide. Atheneum Pubs. 1982 279p il music o.p.; Da Capo Press paperback available $10.95

792.5

1. Puccini, Giacomo, 1858-1924 2. Operas—Stories, plots, etc.
ISBN 0-306-80200-7 (pa) LC 81-69141

The author "provides general background information on all 13 Puccini operas. . . . Unencumbered by technical language, this enjoyably written book is accessible to all admirers of one of the most popular opera composers of all time." Choice

Includes bibliography

The complete operas of Richard Wagner. Trafalgar Sq. 1991 c1990 288p il $24.95

792.5

1. Wagner, Richard, 1813-1883 2. Operas—Stories, plots, etc.
ISBN 0-943955-33-5 LC 90-70513
Also available in paperback from Da Capo Press
First published 1990 in the United Kingdom

In this book, "biography—often in Wagner's own words—combined with criticism by Wagner's contemporaries, literary background, Wagner's librettos, plot summaries, descriptions of musical elements illustrated with musical examples, and Osborne's own insights form a clear picture of Wagner, his world, and the operas." Libr J

792.6   Musical plays

Bordman, Gerald Martin

American musical comedy; from Adonis to Dreamgirls. Oxford Univ. Press 1982 244p il $24.95   **792.6**

1. Musicals
ISBN 0-19-503104-0   LC 81-22444

"Bordman traces the development of musical comedy from its roots in early ballad operas and burlesques to its present state. . . . Bordman's arguments are convincing and his prose is delightful to read." Libr J

American musical revue; from The passing show to Sugar babies. Oxford Univ. Press 1985 184p il $29.95   **792.6**

1. Musicals
ISBN 0-19-503630-1   LC 85-4816

Using a chronological approach "Bordman traces the revue with critical acumen. . . . He sees the enormous success of such retrospective shows as Sugar Babies and Ain't Misbehavin' as a signal of new life for this revue. An appendix of major Broadway revues is included. In all, a fine conclusion to an important addition to American theater criticism, and one that will be enjoyable to both scholar and theater aficionado alike." Libr J

American musical theatre; a chronicle; [by] Gerald Bordman. 2nd ed. Oxford Univ. Press 1992 821p $49.95   **792.6**

1. Musicals
ISBN 0-19-507242-1   LC 91-15671
First published 1978

This "chronology traces the musical from its origins through the 1989-90 season, providing a delightful mix of history, criticism and theatrical lore." Libr J

American operetta: from H.M.S. Pinafore to Sweeney Todd. Oxford Univ. Press 1981 206p il $29.95   **792.6**

1. Operetta
ISBN 0-19-502869-4   LC 80-20646

The author marks the beginning of this history of the operetta in the United States "with the arrival in 1878 of the English Pinafore. . . . [He explains] the confusing term 'operetta' and charts its progression from Offenbach and Gilbert and Sullivan to Rodgers and Hammerstein and the contemporary musical play." Libr J

Gänzl, Kurt

Gänzl's book of the musical theatre; [by] Kurt Gänzl and Andrew Lamb. Schirmer Bks. 1989 1353p il $85   **792.6**

1. Musicals
ISBN 0-02-871941-7   LC 88-18588

"Detailed plot synopses follow features of first productions and a list of characters. Entries are arranged by country and then chronologically. An essay on the history of musical theater in each geographic area opens every section. A time period spans 1728 to 1987. . . . A selective discography and indexes of titles, authors, composers, lyricists, and of song titles increase its reference value." Ref Sources for Small & Medium-sized Libr. 5th edition

Green, Stanley, 1923-1990

Broadway musicals, show by show. Leonard, H. il pa $16.95   **792.6**

1. Musicals

First published 1985. (4th edition revised by Kay Green, 1994). Periodically revised

Chronologically arranged guide to music productions of the American musical theatre includes statistics, critical reception, cast lists etc.

Lewine, Richard

Songs of the theater; [by] Richard Lewine and Alfred Simon. Wilson, H.W. 1984 897p $78   **792.6**

1. Musicals—Bibliography 2. Popular music—Indexes
ISBN 0-8242-0706-8   LC 84-13068

An updated and largely expanded version of Songs of the American theater, published 1973 by Dodd, Mead

"More than 12,000 songs are listed from musical stage productions, with selected titles from film and television productions. For stage productions, coverage is complete for the years 1925-71 and selected for 1900 to 1924. For each song, the composer, lyricist, show title, and year are listed. A second section lists productions with cast and credits and information on vocal scores and cast albums. Besides a chronological list of productions, there is an index by composer and lyricist." Ref Sources for Small & Medium-sized Libr. 5th edition

Mast, Gerald, 1940-1988

Can't help singin'; the American musical on stage and screen. Overlook Press 1987 389p il $24.95; pa $14.95   **792.6**

1. Musicals 2. Motion pictures
ISBN 0-87951-283-0; 0-87951-362-4 (pa) LC 87-7986

This "book has a chronological arrangement and focuses on those people, composers, lyricists, dancers, and singers, who have gained public attention through their contributions to the American musical." Wilson Libr Bull

"Despite the corny title and chapter headings, this competent, serious, well-illustrated study is attractive and entertaining." Publ Wkly

Includes bibliography

Mordden, Ethan, 1947-

Broadway babies; the people who made the American musical. Oxford Univ. Press 1983 244p $24.95; pa $9.95   **792.6**

1. Musicals
ISBN 0-19-503345-0; 0-19-505425-3 (pa) LC 83-8132

The author's "theme is that the development of musical theater from 1900 to the present reflects the influence of dominant personalities. Sometimes performers have led the way, sometimes composers or directors. Shows through Sondheim's 'Merrily We Roll Along' (1981) are considered. The analysis is not surpassingly novel, but the author is well informed and gives us a different perspective on his subject. . . . The selective discography is of value for its evaluations." Libr J

Rodgers & Hammerstein. Abrams 1992 224p il $45   **792.6**

1. Rodgers, Richard, 1902-1979 2. Hammerstein, Oscar, 1895-1960 3. Musicals
ISBN 0-8109-1567-7   LC 91-46586

Mordden, Ethan, 1947-—*Continued*

The author "devotes one chapter each to the Rodgers and Hammerstein musicals—nine for the stage (Oklahoma! through The Sound of Music), one for film (State Fair), and one for television (Cinderella). He describes the genesis of the show, changes occurring during production, and subsequent history (e.g., film versions, revivals)." Choice

"Lovers of the American musical theater will find a treat in . . . [this] lavishly illustrated sort of glorified scrapbook. . . . Mordden's text provides a diverting, informal, and informative backstage tour." Christ Sci Monit

Includes bibliographic references

Suskin, Steven

Show tunes, 1905-1991; the songs, shows, and careers of Broadway's major composers. rev & expanded ed. Limelight Eds. 1992 xxviii, 769p pa $27.50　　　**792.6**

1. Musicals 2. Composers, American
ISBN 0-87910-146-6　　　LC 91-23643

Replaces Show tunes, 1905-1985, published 1986 by Dodd, Mead

A guide to the works of thirty important composers of Broadway musicals. The entries are arranged chronologically by composer, from Jerome Kern to Stephen Schwartz, and provide production notes, published songs, and additional songs for each musical

Includes bibliographic references

Zadan, Craig

Sondheim & Co. 2nd ed. Harper & Row 1986 408p il $27.95; pa $17.95　　　**792.6**

1. Sondheim, Stephen 2. Musicals
ISBN 0-06-015649-X; 0-06-091400-9 (pa)
　　　LC 86-45165

"This is an updated and revised version of the author's 1974 study of Broadway composer Stephen Sondheim, including the four shows he has produced since A Little Night Music." Libr J

"An essential volume for any collection on the current American musical theater." Choice

792.7　Variety shows

American vaudeville as seen by its contemporaries; edited and with commentary by Charles W. Stein. Knopf 1984 392p il o.p.; Da Capo Press paperback available $11.95　　　**792.7**

1. Vaudeville
ISBN 0-306-80256-2 (pa)　　　LC 84-47526

This book is an "overview of the genre as seen, and recorded, by some of its most illustrious practitioners, including the Four Marx Brothers, George M. Cohan, Buster Keaton, Al Jolson, Mae West, George Burns, Jimmy Durante, Milton Berle, Fanny Brice, Eddie Foy, W. C. Fields, Ed Wynn, Will Rogers, James Cagney, and a host of other Big Time . . . favorites." West Coast Rev Books

Includes bibliographic references

792.8　Ballet and modern dance

Anderson, Jack, 1935-

Choreography observed. University of Iowa Press 1987 294p il $35　　　**792.8**

1. Dancing
ISBN 0-87745-172-9　　　LC 87-6021

Analyzed in Essay and general literature index

This collection of criticism "includes select writings from newspapers and dance magazines . . . which span the years 1965-1985. Anderson comments on choreographers, performances, trends, and problems and pleasures in observing dance. His remarks are often inquisitive and thought-provoking." Libr J

Baryshnikov, Mikhail, 1948-

Baryshnikov at work; Mikhail Baryshnikov discusses his roles; photographs by Martha Swope; text edited and introduced by Charles Engell France. Knopf 1976 252p il hardcover o.p. paperback available $22.95　　　**792.8**

1. Ballet
ISBN 0-394-73587-0 (pa)　　　LC 76-13685

Text and numerous photographs portray Baryshnikov in rehearsal, on stage and in the studio. The dancer also discusses the key roles performed in the United States

Denby, Edwin, 1903-1983

Dance writings; edited by Robert Cornfield and William MacKay. Knopf 1986 608p $40　　　**792.8**

1. Dancing
ISBN 0-394-54416-1　　　LC 85-45935

A chronologically and topically arranged collection of the American dance critic's essays and reviews. Subjects covered are Markova, Balanchine, Nijinsky, Martha Graham, Sonja Henie, Pearl Primus, the Rockettes, and others

"Dance Writings is dance criticism at its very best. . . . [Denby's] criticism is a rare blend: constructively critical and never petty or cruel, and instructive to dancers, viewers, and choreographers." Libr J

Jonas, Gerald, 1935-

Dancing; the pleasure, power, and art of movement; preface by Rhoda Grauer; [pub.] in association with Thirteen/WNET. Abrams 1992 256p il $45　　　**792.8**

1. Dancing
ISBN 0-8109-3212-1　　　LC 92-8038

This "is the companion volume to an eight-part public television series. . . . The eight chapters [seek to present a] cross-cultural look at the meanings and messages embodied in dance around the world. . . . This is an excellent book for anyone who enjoys dance and wants to view it from a cultural perspective." Choice

Includes bibliographic references

Long, Richard A., 1927-
The black tradition in American modern dance; photographs selected and annotated by Joe Nash. Rizzoli Int. Publs. 1989 192p il $29.95   **792.8**

1. Dancing—History 2. Black dancers
ISBN 0-8478-1092-5   LC 89-31739

A look at Afro-American dance influences and traditions. Pearl Primus, Katherine Dunham and Alvin Ailey are among those profiled

Includes bibliographic references

Robertson, Allen
The dance handbook; [by] Allen Robertson, Donald Hutera. Hall, G.K. & Co. 1990 c1988 278p il (Performing arts handbooks) $25; pa $16.95   **792.8**

1. Dancing 2. Ballet
ISBN 0-8161-9095-X; 0-8161-1829-9 (pa)
     LC 89-77759

First published 1988 in the United Kingdom

"The volume consists of 200 main entries—choreographers, dancers, ballets—grouped into eight broad chronological sections. The entries include factual data, a critical evaluation of the subject, lineage or links to related subjects, and a bibliography of books, films and videos." Libr J

For a fuller review see: Booklist, Nov. 1, 1990

Thorpe, Edward
Black dance. Overlook Press 1990 192p il $27.50   **792.8**

1. Black dancers
ISBN 0-87951-379-9   LC 89-8785

This "is a historical chronicle that gives more attention to dance origins in Africa and the Caribbean and that tends to concentrate on specific artists and companies. Historically important figures such as Josephine Baker and Bill ('Bojangles') Robinson and such current artists as Arthur Mitchell and Bill T. Jones are featured in this account." Booklist

Includes bibliography

792.803 Ballet and modern dance—Encyclopedias and dictionaries

Koegler, Horst
The concise Oxford dictionary of ballet. 2nd ed. Oxford Univ. Press 1982 459p il hardcover o.p. paperback available $17.95   **792.803**

1. Ballet—Dictionaries
ISBN 0-19-311330-9 (pa)   LC 82-237993

Original German edition, 1972. First published in the United States 1977 as an English adaptation

Over 5,000 entries discuss ballet history, theaters, dancers, choreographers, composers, schools and companies, and terms

792.9 Stage productions

Gielgud, Sir John, 1904-
Acting Shakespeare; [by] John Gielgud with John Miller. Scribner 1992 c1991 192p il $20   **792.9**

1. Shakespeare, William, 1564-1616—Dramatic production 2. Acting
ISBN 0-684-19511-9   LC 92-8314

"A Robert Stewart book"

First published 1991 in the United Kingdom

In this book the author presents reminiscences and observations concerning his 70-year-career as an actor and director of Shakespeare

"This book will be a delight for those who have followed Gielgud's career, or simply love Shakespeare and tales of the stage. In addition, it will be a welcomed addition to any collection where research may be done of 20th-century Shakespearean performances." Libr J

793 Indoor games and amusements

Maguire, Jack
Hopscotch, hangman, hot-potato, and ha, ha, ha; a rulebook of children's games; foreword by Bob "Captain Kangaroo" Keeshan; produced by the Philip Lief Group, Inc. Prentice Hall Press 1990 304p il pa $13.95   **793**

1. Games
ISBN 0-13-631102-4   LC 89-27200

This book includes "instructions for more than 240 party, sidewalk, ball, water, travel, card, action, and sedentary games. For each entry, Maguire cites the object of the play and lists the number of players, setting, and equipment. . . . This is a straightforward rule book of infinite value to parents, caregivers, teachers, and anyone who likes to play these old favorites." Booklist

Weinstein, Matt
Playfair; everybody's guide to noncompetitive play; by Matt Weinstein & Joel Goodman. Impact Pubs. 1980 249p il pa $10.95   **793**

1. Games
ISBN 0-915166-50-X   LC 80-12591

This "is a compendium of more than 60 games suitable for playing in organizational, educational, family, and party situations. . . . They offer techniques to promote self-disclosure and intimacy or to activate energy in adult groups of sizes varying from ten to the hundreds." Libr J

793.2 Parties and entertainments

Church, Beverly
The joys of entertaining; [by] Beverly Reese Church and Bethany Ewald Bultman. Abbeville Press 1987 336p il $40   **793.2**

1. Entertaining
ISBN 0-89659-752-0   LC 87-1146

Church, Beverly—*Continued*

This guide "merges style, elegance, and reality in covering the basics common to all types of home entertaining. Appendixes treat cocktails, flowers, stain removal, napkin folds, and gifts." Libr J

Includes bibliography

Cooke, Courtney

The best baby shower book; a complete guide for party planners. Meadowbrook 1986 129p il pa $6 **793.2**

1. Showers (Parties) 2. Infants
ISBN 0-671-62276-5 LC 86-12440

This "guide makes suggestions on planning, refreshments, 'keeping the party rolling' without relying too heavily on games, and gifts in various price ranges. It even offers ideas for making your own invitations." Libr J

Dlugosch, Sharon

Bridal showers; 50 great ideas for a perfect shower; [by] Sharon E. Dlugosch and Florence E. Nelson. Perigee Bks. 1987 156p pa $7.95 **793.2**

1. Showers (Parties) 2. Marriage customs and rites
ISBN 0-399-51344-2 LC 86-30387

First published 1984 in a limited edition

This volume features over 50 showerwise themes, including ideas for a wine-and-cheese-tasting shower, a tie-a-quilt shower, and a formal pool shower. The authors provide a checklist, a planning sheet, tips on etiquette, and suggestions for invitations, decorations, activites and gifts

Warner, Penny

Happy birthday parties! written and illustrated by Penny Warner. St. Martin's Press 1985 139p il pa $9.95 **793.2**

1. Children's parties 2. Birthdays
ISBN 0-312-36180-7 LC 85-11824

This volume presents ideas for invitations, party favors, decorations, games, refreshments, etc.

793.73 Puzzles and puzzle games

Pulliam, Tom

The New York Times crossword puzzle dictionary; by Tom Pulliam and Clare Grundman. 2nd ed. Times Bks. 1984 618p $21 **793.73**

1. Crossword puzzles—Dictionaries
ISBN 0-8129-1131-8 LC 84-40108

"A Hudson Group book"

First published 1977

Contains "some 40,000 main entries providing over 500,000 answer words. Essentially a dictionary of undiscriminated synonyms, it is one of the more useful works of its kind." Ref Sources for Small & Medium-sized Libr. 5th edition

The **Random** House cross-word puzzle dictionary. Random House 1989 1093p $19.95 **793.73**

1. Crossword puzzles—Dictionaries
ISBN 0-394-53513-8 LC 88-32554

Each entry lists a variety of terms that may be substituted for the entry term. The arrangement within each term listing is alphabetical and by number of letters

"A useful and entertaining companion for both crossword puzzle and trivia buffs." Ref Sources for Small & Medium-sized Libr. 5th edition

793.8 Magic and related activities

Blackstone, Harry, 1885-1965

The Blackstone book of magic & illusion; [by] Harry Blackstone, Jr., with Charles and Regina Reynolds; foreword by Ray Bradbury; magic effects illustrated by Eric Mason. Newmarket Press 1985 230p il $22.95 **793.8**

1. Magic
ISBN 0-937858-45-5 LC 84-29486

The author "provides a history of magic and the art of illusion, with biographies of some of the pros and an in-depth description of the Great Blackstone's career." Publ Wkly

Includes bibliography

Finnigan, Dave

The complete juggler; illustrated by Bruce Edwards; with special contributions by Todd Strong; technical consultant, Allan Jacobs. 2nd ed. Jugglebug 1991 574p il $19.95; pa $14.95 **793.8**

1. Jugglers and juggling
ISBN 0-9615521-1-5; 0-9615521-0-7 (pa)

LC 91-61138

First published 1987 by Vintage Books

A step-by-step approach to various juggling routines. Includes information about equipment, performing, and business aspects

Randi, James

Conjuring. St. Martin's Press 1992 xx, 314p il $29.95 **793.8**

1. Magic
ISBN 0-312-08634-2 LC 92-21042

"Being a definitive account of the venerable arts of sorcery, prestidigitation, wizardry, deception & chicanery and of the mountebanks & scoundrels who have perpetuated these subterfuges on a bewildered public." Title page

"Randi writes clearly and with a light wit as he guides the reader through this subcultural profession without revealing a single secret. Brightly illustrated, this book will be a valuable item for any library collection." Booklist

Includes bibliography

Summers, Kit

Juggling with finesse; edited by Robert Schwarz; artwork by Tuko Fujisaki. Finesse Press 1987 251p il pa $14.95   **793.8**

1. Jugglers and juggling
ISBN 0-938981-00-5   LC 86-091875

This guide to juggling features "a complete rundown of basic principles, specific tips on handling rings, clubs, balls, and other items in various configurations and numbers, and stylistic suggestions for putting on a first-class act. . . . Photos of top performers in action are supplemented by line drawings that illustrate how the juggling maneuvers are successfully completed." Booklist

Waters, T. A.

The encyclopedia of magic and magicians. Facts on File 1988 372p il $35; pa $19.95   **793.8**

1. Magic—Dictionaries
ISBN 0-8160-1349-7; 0-8160-1981-9 (pa)
     LC 87-13464

This reference work covers a "range of subjects, including biographies, terminology, technical details, and suggested sources for further reading. This book doesn't claim to be totally comprehensive, but the things included are impressive. Very extensive cross-referencing makes it a hard book to put down." Voice Youth Advocates

794   Indoor games of skill

The **World** of games; their origin and history, how to play them, and how to make them; [by] Jack Botermans [et al.] Facts on File 1989 240p il $29.95   **794**

1. Games
ISBN 0-8160-2184-8   LC 89-31359

"More than 150 board games, dice games, card games, domino games, and activity games are featured in this [book]." Libr J

"The value of this book is in its historical and cross-cultural information (e.g., native American games) and its handsome illustrations." Booklist

Includes bibliography

794.1   Chess

Capablanca, José Raúl, 1888-1942

Chess fundamentals. Harcourt Brace & Co. 1921 246p il o.p.; McKay, D. paperback available $8.95   **794.1**

1. Chess
ISBN 0-679-14004-2 (pa)

Explains the general principles of chess through eighteen illustrative games, so that, when grounded in these, the novice may understand the whole elementary science of the game

Divinsky, N. J., 1925-

The chess encyclopedia; [by] Nathan Divinsky. Facts on File 1991 247p il $35
    794.1

1. Chess—Dictionaries
ISBN 0-8160-2641-6   LC 90-47571

First published 1990 in the United Kingdom

This work "explains all technical terms, details the lives of all major figures and grand masters, and discusses all major tournaments. It also includes over 100 of the greatest games ever played." Booklist

Fischer, Bobby, 1943-

Bobby Fischer teaches chess; by Bobby Fischer, Stuart Margulies, Donn Mosenfelder. Basic Systems, Inc. 1966 334p il o.p.; Bantam Bks. paperback available $6.99
    794.1

1. Chess
ISBN 0-553-26315-3 (pa)

In this book the authors give specific advice and hints aimed at both the beginning and advanced player. Each step-by-step lesson is fully illustrated

Gelo, James H., 1948-

Chess world championships; all the games, 1834-1984. McFarland & Co. 1988 706p il $45   **794.1**

1. Chess
ISBN 0-89950-305-5   LC 88-42519

This book "contains every move of every game played in world championship competition, including all 'official' such titles since 1986 and all decisive matches by the world's leading players for the 50 years prior. A diagram of the critical or most interesting moment accompanies every game." Publisher's note

Includes bibliography

Hooper, David, 1915-

The Oxford companion to chess; [by] David Hooper and Kenneth Whyld. 2nd ed. Oxford Univ. Press 1992 483p il $45
    794.1

1. Chess
ISBN 0-19-866164-9   LC 92-9619
First published 1984

This survey provides historical and technical information, including biographies of celebrated players, descriptions of openings and strategies, explanations of terms, and descriptions of ancient and modern variants of chess

United States Chess Federation

U.S. Chess Federation's official rules of chess; compiled and sanctioned by the U.S. Chess Federation; edited by Bill Goichberg, Carol Jarecki, Ira Lee Riddle. 4th ed. McKay, D. 1994 xxix, 370p il pa $12
    794.1

1. Chess
ISBN 0-8129-2217-4   LC 92-40961

"This book, effective 1/1/94, supersedes the Official Rules of Chess First Edition 1974, Second Edition 1978, edited by Martin E. Morrison, and Third Edition 1987, edited by Tim Redman." Title page

In addition to the USCF rules, tournament regulations, equipment standards, code of ethics, and rating system, this handbook also includes tips to winning chess, how to read and write chess notation, and a listing of world and national champions

794.6 Bowling

Anthony, Earl, 1938-
Winning bowling; [by] Earl Anthony and Dawson Taylor. Contemporary Bks. 1977 194p il pa $10.95 **794.6**
1. Bowling
ISBN 0-8092-7791-3 LC 77-75718

The author "has thought through every aspect of the game and offers readers a complete course, in directions so clear they can be visualized even without the accompanying illustrations. Of most obvious benefit to beginners, the manual also contains nuggets for the experienced bowler. . . . The book's excellence lies in providing the learner with a mental picture of precisely what he or she is attempting." Booklist

794.7 Indoor ball games

Byrne, Robert, 1930-
Byrne's standard book of pool and billiards. Harcourt Brace Jovanovich 1978 332p il hardcover o.p. paperback available $15.95 **794.7**
1. Pool (Game) 2. Billiards
ISBN 0-15-614972-9 (pa) LC 78-53913

"Byrne provides basic information about the rules and tactics of the games, and the selection and care of the equipment. The shot diagrams are clear and precise. A good choice for public libraries." Libr J

Includes bibliography

Mosconi, Willie, 1913-1993
Winning pocket billiards. Crown 1965 139p il pa $7.95 **794.7**
1. Pool (Game)
ISBN 0-517-50454-5

This book on pocket billiards has more than 100 step-by-step photographs and diagrams to show how shots should be made. With official rules and a section on trick shots

795 Games of chance

Ainslie, Tom
Ainslie's complete Hoyle; illustrated by Jill Schwartz. Simon & Schuster 1975 526p il hardcover o.p. paperback available $12.95 **795**
1. Games 2. Card games
ISBN 0-671-24779-4 (pa)

Over half of this book is devoted to card games including bridge, rummy, poker, solitaire and related games, as well as children's games. Part two covers board and table games such as backgammon, monopoly, chess, checkers, craps and other dice games, dominoes, mah jong, games of logic, word games (e.g. scrabble, crosswords) and simulation games. Two briefer sections cover gambling-casino games and games suitable for club cars and taverns

Scarne, John, 1903-1985
Scarne's new complete guide to gambling. fully rev expanded updated ed. Simon & Schuster 1973 xxii, 871p il hardcover o.p. paperback available $17.95 **795**
1. Gambling
ISBN 0-671-63063-6 (pa)

First published 1961 with title: Scarne's complete guide to gambling

The author covers horse racing, dice games, betting on sports, off-track betting, greyhound dog racing, Jai-alai, state lotteries, etc. Rules are given and explanations provided on odds, house percentages and playing strategy

This is "virtually a textbook on gambling." Publ Wkly

Sifakis, Carl
Encyclopedia of gambling. Facts on File 1990 340p il $40; pa $19.95 **795**
1. Gambling
ISBN 0-8160-1638-0; 0-8160-2426-X (pa) LC 89-33107

This volume presents some 1,000 alphabetically arranged entries which discuss "wagering games . . . and cheating techniques or cases. . . . Articles average about one-half page in length." Booklist

This work "is comprehensive, accurate, and well-organized. Furthermore, it is well-written in the kind of breezy, informal style best suited to the subject matter." Libr J

Includes bibliography

795.4 Card games

Blackstone, Harry, 1885-1965
Blackstone's modern card tricks. New rev ed. Garden City Bks. 1958 164p il o.p.; Wilshire paperback available $5 **795.4**
1. Card tricks
ISBN 0-87980-282-0 (pa)

First published 1932 by Sully

Emphasizing method and presentation, the author offers instructions for over 100 card tricks of varing difficulty. Directions for card location, discovery, sleight-of-hand, spelling and special tricks are included

Gibson, Walter Brown, 1897-1985
Hoyle's modern encyclopedia of card games; rules of all the basic games and popular variations; [by] Walter B. Gibson. Dolphin Bks. 1974 398p il pa $9.95 **795.4**
1. Card games
ISBN 0-385-07680-0

"A Dolphin handbook"

This guide to the rules and techniques of various card games includes special sections on pinochle, poker and solitaire

Goren, Charles Henry, 1901-1991

Goren's new bridge complete; [by] Chas H. Goren. rev ed. Doubleday 1985 705p il $24.95   **795.4**

1. Bridge (Game)
ISBN 0-385-23324-8   LC 85-10344

First published 1951 with title: Contract bridge complete

Explanations of basic bridge for beginners as well as data on tournament-winning techniques for advanced players

Parlett, David Sidney

The Oxford guide to card games. Oxford Univ. Press 1990 361p il $35; pa $13.95   **795.4**

1. Card games
ISBN 0-19-214165-1; 0-19-282905-X (pa)
     LC 89-77641

A "history of card playing in the Western world, with focus on the distinctions in card play between nations, on the deck of cards itself, and on notable persons in the development of the games. The games, separated into 17 classifications, include such old favorites as euchre, canasta, poker, pinochle, and gin." Booklist

Includes bibliographic references

Patterson, Jerry L.

Blackjack: a winner's handbook. completely rev & updated ed. Perigee Bks. 1990 253p pa $8.95   **795.4**

1. Blackjack (Game)
ISBN 0-399-51598-4   LC 90-7290

First published 1978 by Echelon Enterprises

Following an historical overview and analysis of once popular blackjack systems and methods, the author presents rules and strategies for today's player

Includes bibliographic references

Scarne, John, 1903-1985

Scarne's encyclopedia of card games. Harper & Row 1983 475p il pa $15   **795.4**

1. Card games
ISBN 0-06-091052-6   LC 83-47571

The material in this book has been excerpted, with alterations and additions, from Scarne's encyclopedia of games (1973)

Rules are provided for bridge, pinochle, cribbage, faro and solitaire among many others. In addition the author discusses the histories and variations of the games, odds and probabilities, and how to detect cheating

796   Athletic and outdoor sports and games

American women in sport, 1887-1987; a 100-year chronology; compiled by Ruth M. Sparhawk [et al.] Scarecrow Press 1989 149p il $20   **796**

1. Women athletes 2. Sports
ISBN 0-8108-2205-9   LC 89-6150

The main section of this "chronology is a year-by-year listing of accomplishments made by women in amateur and professional sports. This chronology can be accessed by a subject index to over 70 sports or by an extensive name index." Voice Youth Advocates

Ashe, Arthur

A hard road to glory; a history of the African-American athlete; [by] Arthur R. Ashe, Jr., with the assistance of Kip Branch, Ocania Chalk, and Francis Harris. new ed. Amistad Press 1993 3v il v1 $29.95, v2-3 ea $39.95   **796**

1. Black athletes 2. Sports   LC 93-7395

First published 1988 by Warner Bks.

Contents: v1: 1619-1918 (ISBN 1-56743-006-6); v2: 1919-1945 (ISBN 1-56743-007-4); v3: Since 1946 (ISBN 1-56743-008-2)

"A history of the black athlete in America from 1619 to the present. Each volume contains a sport-by-sport narrative history for the years covered and an extensive reference section documenting the successes of the athletes." N Y Times Book Rev [review of 1988 edition]

"An impressive, important, definitive history of the triumph of a dedicated stratum of African-American society." Libr J [review of 1988 edition]

Includes bibliographic references

Best sports stories. Sporting News il pa $10.95   **796**

1. Sports
ISSN 0067-6292

Annual. First published for the year 1944 by Dutton

This is an anthology of the best sports stories and photographs from newspapers and magazines across the country

Biesel, David B., 1931-

Can you name that team? a guide to professional baseball, football, soccer, hockey, and basketball teams and leagues. Scarecrow Press 1991 232p $37.50   **796**

1. Sports
ISBN 0-8108-2458-2   LC 91-26356

This guide "contains information on professional sports clubs no longer in existence as well as current teams (up to 1991). The contents are divided into three areas, including 950 team names, 38 professional leagues, plus indexes and bibliography." Libr J

For a fuller review see: Booklist, Jan. 15, 1992

Cosell, Howard, 1920-

What's wrong with sports; [by] Howard Cosell with Shelby Whitfield. Simon & Schuster 1991 349p hardcover o.p. paperback available $5.99   **796**

1. Sportsmanship 2. Sports
ISBN 0-671-76919-7 (pa)   LC 91-2178

Cosell's assessment of contemporary sports focuses on boxing, racism, unionism, gambling and drug abuse

The **Guinness** book of sports records. Facts on File il $20.95; pa $13.95   **796**

1. Sports
ISSN 1054-4178

The Guinness book of sports records — Continued

Annual. First published 1972 with title: Guinness sports record book. Variant title: Guinness book of sports records, winners & champions

Taken in part from the Guinness book of world records, entered in class 032.02

This compilation presents records set in over seventy sports, from archery to yachting. Entries are arranged alphabetically by sport and include a brief history of the sport

Guttmann, Allen

Women's sports; a history. Columbia Univ. Press 1991 339p il $29.95; pa $13.95
796

1. Sports 2. Women athletes
ISBN 0-231-06956-1; 0-231-06957-X (pa)
LC 90-28692

The author explores "the social and cultural contexts of women's athletics in ancient civilizations, the Middle Ages, and the Renaissance. This lays the groundwork for a subsequent discussion of the subject's current state, in which he . . . exposes controversial issues which threaten the development of women's sports." Libr J

Includes bibliographic references

Levine, Peter

Ellis Island to Ebbet's Field; sport and the American-Jewish experience. Oxford Univ. Press 1992 328p il (Sports history and society) $25
796

1. Jews—United States 2. Sports
ISBN 0-19-505128-9
LC 91-42016

The author "explores the importance of sport in transforming Jewish immigrants into American Jews. Drawing on interviews with celebrities as well as lesser-known neighborhood stars, Levine vividly recounts the stories of Red Auerbach, Hank Greenberg, Moe Berg, and many others who became Jewish heroes and symbols of the difficult struggle for American success." Univ Press Books for Public and Second Sch Libr

Includes bibliographic references

Micheli, Lyle J., 1940-

Sportswise: an essential guide for young athletes, parents, and coaches; [by] Lyle J. Micheli with Mark D. Jenkins. Houghton Mifflin 1990 300p $19.95; pa $9.95 **796**

1. Sports
ISBN 0-395-51608-0; 0-395-56408-5 (pa)
LC 90-34257

The author discusses sports injuries, psychological aspects of youth sports, and nutrition. Includes chapters that treat the specific concerns of females, handicapped youngsters, and the chronically ill

Nelson, Mariah Burton

Are we winning yet? how women are changing sports and sports are changing women. Random House 1991 238p $19.50
796

1. Women athletes 2. Sports 3. Sex discrimination
ISBN 0-394-57576-8
LC 90-42698

"Using interviews with well-known individuals to personalize her subject, a former Stanford University basketball player discusses a variety of issues facing women athletes—among them, stereotypes, gender roles, and sports ethics. An important and timely discussion." Booklist

Includes bibliographic references

Rules of the game; the complete illustrated encyclopedia of all the sports of the world. [rev ed]. St. Martin's Press 1990 320p il $24.95
796

1. Sports
ISBN 0-312-04574-3
LC 90-37196

First published 1974

This volume covers 150 sports "grouped under 13 headings such as water, court, team, wheels, and air. Each article contains a detailed discussion of major objectives, playing area and equipment, rules, timing and scoring, and participants and officials." Booklist

Sports fan's connection; an all-sports-in-one directory to professional, collegiate, and olympic organizations, events, and information sources; Bradley J. Morgan, editor; Peg Bessette, associate editor. Gale Res. 1992 584p $59.95
796

1. Sports—Directories
ISBN 0-8103-7954-6

"This is a comprehensive guide to information about athletic teams, organizations, events, and media sources of the United States and Canada. There are three sections (professional, college, and Olympic sports) with over 4000 entries subdivided alphabetically. Full descriptive data and contact information for each listing is provided. The 50 sports covered range from archery, biathlon, and canoeing to the luge, rodeo, tae-kwon-do, and yachting. The 'big' four, baseball, basketball, football, and hockey, are also featured." Libr J

For a fuller review see: Booklist, April 15, 1992

796.1 Miscellaneous games

Eden, Maxwell

Kiteworks: explorations in kite building & flying. Sterling 1989 287p il $24.95; pa $16.95
796.1

1. Kites
ISBN 0-8069-6712-9; 0-8069-6713-7 (pa)
LC 89-11372

Color illustrations accompany specific instructions for making a variety of kites. Includes practical advice on materials, repairs, safety, and clubs and events

Includes bibliography

796.323 Basketball

Fox, Robert A.

Basketball: the complete handbook of individual skills. Prentice-Hall 1987 268p il $33
796.323

1. Basketball
ISBN 0-13-066796-X
LC 87-14560

This manual covers the basic basketball skills from footwork to rebounding, with drills and photographs presented for each skill

George, Nelson

Elevating the game; black men and basketball. HarperCollins Pubs. 1992 xxi, 261p il $20   **796.323**

1. Basketball 2. Black athletes
ISBN 0-06-016723-8   LC 91-50465

A history of black involvement with basketball from before World War I

"Understanding the way in which black cultural expressions often knit together, Mr. George even likens basketball to jazz and the nervous, insistent rhythms of rap. It all makes for a rich, welcome addition to sports literature." N Y Times Book Rev

Includes bibliographic references

The **Official** NBA basketball encyclopedia; foreword by Julius Erving; introduction by David J. Stern; edited by Zander Hollander and Alex Sachare. Villard Bks. 1989 766p il $29.95   **796.323**

1. Basketball
ISBN 0-394-58039-7   LC 89-40201

"Covers history, Hall of Fame, all-time records, all-star games, and official NBA rules. Includes complete statistical profile of every player who has ever appeared in the NBA. Illustrated with photographs; indexed." N Y Public Libr Book of How & Where to Look It Up

Ryan, Bob

The Boston Celtics; the history, legends, and images of America's most celebrated team; photographs by Dick Raphael. Addison-Wesley 1989 224p il $23.99; pa $16.30   **796.323**

1. Boston Celtics (Basketball team)
ISBN 0-201-15326-2; 0-201-57001-7 (pa)
    LC 89-36058

"Ryan provides a detailed on- and off-court history of the storied franchise, complete with exciting game accounts, profiles of great players, inside stories, and humorous anecdotes." Booklist

Shaughnessy, Dan

Ever green: the Boston Celtics; a history in the words of their players, coaches, fans, and foes, from 1946 to the present. St. Martin's Press 1990 259p il $18.95; pa $9.95   **796.323**

1. Boston Celtics (Basketball team)
ISBN 0-312-05083-6; 0-312-06348-2 (pa)
    LC 90-37115

The author incorporates recollections of Celtic players and coaches in this history of one of basketball's most successful franchises

Includes bibliography

Smith, Sam, 1948-

The Jordan rules. Simon & Schuster 1992 333p il $22; pa $5.99   **796.323**

1. Jordan, Michael 2. Chicago Bulls (Basketball team)
ISBN 0-671-74491-7; 0-671-79666-6 (pa)
    LC 91-32973

"Smith's account of the Chicago Bulls' 1990-91 championship season is actually a rather honest, in-depth, in-the-locker-room-and-behind-the-scenes portrayal of what is perhaps a typical basketball team—typical, that is, with one exception: the uncanny miracle-worker, Michael Jordan. . . . In these pages, Jordan comes across as arrogant, selfish, pouting, whining, extremely competitive, but also, Smith allows, 'like Shakespeare, . . . the best even though everyone said so.'" Booklist

796.332   American football

Bissinger, H. G.

Friday night lights; a town, a team, and a dream. Addison-Wesley 1990 357p il $19.95   **796.332**

1. Permian High School (Odessa, Tex.) 2. Football
ISBN 0-201-19677-8   LC 90-35694

Also available G.K. Hall large print edition and in paperback from HarperPerennial

In 1988, the author, a "Philadelphia Inquirer editor, left his job to spend a year with a high school sports team. The sport he picked was football, the location, the . . . West Texas oil town of Odessa. . . . Here 20,000 fans turn out regularly to watch their Permian Panthers win." Libr J

"It is a tricky balancing act, but Mr. Bissinger carries it off: 'Friday Night Lights' offers a biting indictment of the sports craziness that grips not only Odessa but most of American society, while at the same time providing a moving evocation of its powerful allure." NY Times Book Rev

Football register. Sporting News il pa $12.95   **796.332**

1. Football—Statistics
Annual. First published 1966
At head of title: The Sporting News

"Here is an alphabetical listing of all active National Football League players. Information for each player includes current and past team affiliations, yearly statistics, and appropriate biographical summaries." Wynar. Ref Books in Paperback. 2d edition

Harrington, Denis J., 1932-

The Pro Football Hall of Fame; players, coaches, team owners, and league officials, 1969-1991. McFarland & Co. 1991 354p il $32.50   **796.332**

1. Pro Football Hall of Fame 2. Football
ISBN 0-89950-550-3   LC 91-52636

The author "first offers a brief history of professional football and the NFL. Then, position by position, he profiles the Hall's members. He provides basic career statistics and information such as rushing yardage and years selected to the Pro Bowl as well as a text that incorporates career highlights with anecdotes." Booklist

"This book is a fine reference work for those wishing biographical and historical information on the people who have had a lasting impact on professional football." Voice Youth Advocates

Klecko, Joe, 1953-
Nose to nose; survival in the trenches of the NFL; [by] Joe Klecko, Joe Fields and Greg Logan. Morrow 1989 287p il $18.95
796.332

1. New York Jets (Football team) 2. National Football League 3. Football
ISBN 0-688-05281-9   LC 89-35071

"Klecko, a defensive lineman who was an integral part of the New York Jets 'Sack Exchange' in the early 1980s, and Joe Fields, the Jets all-pro center, tell their stories in this dual 'autobiography,' written in the third person with sportswriter Greg Logan." Libr J

Telander, Rick
The hundred yard lie; the corruption of college football and what we can do to stop it. Simon & Schuster 1989 223p hardcover o.p. paperback available $8.95   **796.332**

1. Football 2. Sports
ISBN 0-671-72788-5 (pa)   LC 89-38114

The author discusses the corruption and abuses that he argues pervade the majority of college and university football programs

Wilkinson, Bud, 1916-1994
Sports illustrated football: winning defense; illustrations by Robert Handville. rev ed. Sports Illustrated 1987 175p il pa $9.95
796.332

1. Football
ISBN 0-452-26036-1   LC 87-23488

"Sports illustrated winner's circle books"

First published 1973 by Lippincott

The author analyzes basic team and individual defensive strategies and techniques, using diagrams, drawings and photographs

Sports illustrated football: winning offense; illustrations by Robert Handville. rev ed. Sports Illustrated 1987 205p il pa $9.95
796.332

1. Football
ISBN 0-452-26035-3   LC 87-23487

"Sports illustrated winner's circle books"

First published 1972 by Lippincott

The author analyzes basic team and individual offensive strategies and techniques, using diagrams, drawings and photographs

796.334 Soccer

Robson, Bryan, 1957-
Bryan Robson's soccer skills; edited by Tom Tyrrell; specially commissioned photographs by Peter Robinson. Sterling 1987 125p il pa $12.95   **796.334**

1. Soccer
ISBN 0-8069-6654-8

In addition to covering team strategy, the author includes advice on such basic skills as dribbling, tackling and passing. Line drawings and photographs accompany the text

796.342 Tennis

Braden, Vic
Vic Braden's quick fixes; expert cures for common tennis problems; by Vic Braden and Bill Bruns. Little, Brown 1988 135p il $17.95; pa $9.95   **796.342**

1. Tennis
ISBN 0-316-10514-7; 0-316-10515-5 (pa)
LC 87-26099

"A Sports illustrated book"

This book "offers a 'first-aid' approach to veteran players plagued by common tennis ailments. Entire chapters are devoted to specific strokes and problems associated with each, followed by causes and cures designed to provide immediate improvement." Libr J

Burwash, Peter
Total tennis: a complete guide for today's player; [by] Peter Burwash and John Tullius; photographs by Ted Washington. Macmillan 1989 240p il $22.95; pa $12.95   **796.342**

1. Tennis
ISBN 0-02-620401-0; 0-02-079261-1 (pa) LC 89-2837

The authors' primary focus is on stroke instruction. In addition, they offer material on strategy, opponent awareness, and mental toughness

Feinstein, John
Hard courts. Villard Bks. 1991 xx, 457p $22.50   **796.342**

1. Tennis
ISBN 0-394-58333-7   LC 91-50060

This is an account of the year Feinstein spent "on the pro tennis circuit, interviewing dozens of players, coaches, linesmen, ballboys, trainers, and assorted hangers-on." Booklist

796.352 Golf

Blanchard, Kenneth H.
Playing the great game of golf; making every minute count; [by] Ken Blanchard; foreword by Bob Toski; afterword by Chuck Hogan. Morrow 1992 169p il $20 **796.352**

1. Golf
ISBN 0-688-12125-X   LC 92-15319

The author "relates the importance of goal-setting to playing golf. . . . He describes, with lively anecdotes, two desirable golfing goals: performance and satisfaction. . . . For those interested in golf, this delightful book is replete with ideas and wisdom." Libr J

Includes bibliographic references

Golf magazine's encyclopedia of golf; the complete reference; [by] the editors of Golf magazine. 2nd ed. HarperCollins Pubs. 1993 517p il $40   **796.352**

1. Golf—Dictionaries
ISBN 0-06-270019-7   LC 92-16293

First published 1970

Golf magazine's encyclopedia of golf—*Continued*

This volume contains "seven sections: the history of golf, major championships and tournaments, biographies, golf equipment, principles of golf, rules of golf, golf architecture, and a glossary of terms. . . . Black-and-white photographs and tables are used generously throughout the encyclopedia." Booklist

Nicklaus, Jack

Golf my way; by Jack Nicklaus with Ken Bowden; illustrated by Jim McQueen. Simon & Schuster 1974 264p il o.p. paperback available $12   **796.352**

1. Golf
ISBN 0-671-22278-3 (pa)

"This is the only book written by golf's number one player that covers in depth his entire technique of the game as he plays it, from top to bottom. The intellectual and scholarly dedication that Nicklaus brings to his game is explained fully." Choice

Palmer, Arnold, 1929-

Play great golf; mastering the fundamentals of your game. Doubleday 1987 181p il $24.95   **796.352**

1. Golf
ISBN 0-385-24301-4   LC 87-9245

"The book attempts to take the complexity out of the golf swing, reducing it to five fundamentals—grip, address, takeaway, still head, and acceleration. Palmer's advice on how to achieve each is straightforward, free of the kind of pseudo-technical language . . . that is often the bane of golf books." Booklist

Player, Gary

Golf begins at 50; playing the lifetime game better than ever; by Gary Player with Desmond Tolhurst. Simon & Schuster 1988 254p il hardcover o.p. paperback available $14   **796.352**

1. Golf
ISBN 0-671-68319-5 (pa)   LC 88-3148

The author emphasizes an improved short game along with stance and grip adjustments for the senior player. Proper diet and exercise are discussed

Snead, Sam

Golf begins at forty; by Sam Snead with Dick Aultman; with illustrations by James McQueen. Dial Press 1978 175p il o.p.; Doubleday paperback available $14.95
    796.352

1. Golf
ISBN 0-385-27642-7 (pa)   LC 78-5601

Starting with the attitude of the older, experienced golfer, this book proceeds to practical suggestions for lengthening shots and improving the short game, particularly putting

Whitworth, Kathy, 1939-

Golf for women; [by] Kathy Whitworth with Rhonda Glenn. St. Martin's Press 1990 176p il $19.95; pa $12.95   **796.352**

1. Golf
ISBN 0-312-04013-X; 0-312-06984-7 (pa)
    LC 89-78002

This introductory guide covers grip, stance, body alignment, putting fundamentals, trouble shots, and strategy
"A splendidly written, detailed, well-illustrated book." Libr J

Wiren, Gary

The PGA manual of golf; the professional's way to play better golf. Macmillan 1991 451p il $39.95   **796.352**

1. Golf
ISBN 0-02-599291-0   LC 91-13642

"Everything novices and experienced golfers need to know to improve their game is covered within [these] 17 chapters. The history and evolution of the game, laws and fundamentals, proper equipment, psychology of playing, and rules and etiquette are detailed in an easy-to-read format. Many illustrations, photographs, and action sequence photos containing instruction on the fundamentals of grip, basic and specialty strokes, practice drills, and physical training are included." Libr J

Includes bibliographic references

796.357 Baseball

Angell, Roger

Late innings; a baseball companion. Simon & Schuster 1982 429p hardcover o.p. paperback available $12   **796.357**

1. Baseball
ISBN 0-671-75912-4 (pa)   LC 82-764

Also available in paperback from Ballantine Bks.

In these sixteen essays, covering the period from 1977 to 1981, the author "bemoans the changes [in baseball] wrought by TV and million-dollar contracts, scolds the owners for constantly upping the ante, visits Bob Gibson in Omaha and a semipro team in Vermont [and] shows what happens when female reporters finally get into the locker room." Newsweek

Once more around the park. Ballantine Bks. 1991 251p $18.95; pa $10   **796.357**

1. Baseball
ISBN 0-345-36737-5; 0-345-37960-8 (pa)
    LC 90-93223

A collection of 21 pieces, some from Angell's earlier books and others previously uncollected. "Outstanding among the choices . . . are visits with Hall of Famer Bob Gibson and then-91-year-old Smoky Joe Wood." Libr J

Season ticket; a baseball companion. Houghton Mifflin 1988 406p o.p.; Ballantine Bks. paperback available $5.95   **796.357**

1. Baseball
ISBN 0-345-35814-7 (pa)   LC 87-29399

A collection of the author's baseball reports on aspects of the 1983-1987 major league seasons. Includes profiles of Don Mattingly, Dwight Gooden, Dan Quisenberry and Roy Eisenhardt

The **Baseball** encyclopedia; the complete and official record of major league baseball. Macmillan $55 **796.357**

1. Baseball—Statistics

First published 1969. (9th ed. 1993). Periodically revised. Editors vary

"Covers everything about Major League baseball, including awards and special achievements, all-time leaders, teams, players, home/road performance, championships, and major changes in playing and scoring rules, back to 1876." N Y Public Libr Book of How & Where to Look It Up

Bouton, Jim

Ball four; edited by Leonard Shecter. Twentieth-anniversary ed. Collier Bks. 1990 472p il $22.95; pa $13.95 **796.357**

1. Baseball

ISBN 0-02-513980-0; 0-02-030665-2 (pa)

LC 89-49151

First published 1970 by World

The author offers a behind-the-scenes look at major league baseball, its players and management

Brinkman, Joe

The umpire's handbook; [by] Joe Brinkman and Charlie Euchner. rev ed. Greene 1987 162p il pa $9.95 **796.357**

1. Baseball

ISBN 0-8289-0628-9

LC 86-25771

First published 1985

Chapters cover the following: The perils (and rewards) of umpiring; What it takes to be an umpire; The umpire's routine; Making the calls; The plate umpire; The field umpire; The umpire's jurisdiction; Tough plays; The rulebook made easy; Test your knowledge of umpiring; Umpiring softball games

Chadwick, Bruce

When the game was black and white; the illustrated history of the Negro leagues. Abbeville Press 1992 191p il $24.95 **796.357**

1. Baseball 2. Black athletes

ISBN 1-55859-372-1

A "survey of segregated baseball. Topics covered include barnstorming, Latin American ball, and games against white major leaguers. In addition to extremely rare photographs of ball players, including some from Satchel Paige's own scrapbook, there are examples of rare Negro Leagues memorabilia. . . . Highly recommended." Choice

Creamer, Robert W.

Baseball in '41; a celebration of the best baseball season ever—in the year America went to war. Viking 1991 330p il $21.95; pa $12 **796.357**

1. Baseball

ISBN 0-670-83374-6; 0-14-016943-1 (pa)

LC 90-50747

This book "brings back the year Joe DiMaggio hit safely in 56 straight games, Ted Williams hit .406 and the Brooklyn Dodgers won their first pennant in 21 years." N Y Times Book Rev

"For all popular and serious sports collections." Libr J

Includes bibliographic references

Cult baseball players; the greats, the flakes, the weird, and the wonderful; edited by Danny Peary. Simon & Schuster 1990 383p il pa $12.95 **796.357**

1. Baseball

ISBN 0-671-67172-3

LC 89-27907

"A Fireside book"

This is a collection of sixty essays in which the authors write of favorite ball players

"The collection includes essays by Pete Hamill on the heady style of Eddie Stanky, Elmore Leonard on the dedication of George Kell, John Lithgow on the 'gentle giant' Ted Kluzewski, and Stephen Jay Gould on Journeyman Dusty Rhodes's moment in the sun. The articles are interesting not so much for the insight they offer into the ball players, but for the personal attachments the contributors formed for their heroes. . . . An engaging work." Libr J

Geist, Bill

Little League confidential; one coach's completely unauthorized tale of survival. Macmillan 1992 217p $17 **796.357**

1. Little League Baseball, Inc. 2. Baseball

ISBN 0-02-542921-3

LC 91-37562

The author "relates his decade of service as a little-league baseball coach. He admittedly distills his experiences—and those of others—into a season-long 'docudrama' journal. He tells of pompous coaches lecturing their miniplayers on the subtleties of the infield fly rule; he addresses the question of positioning a player with a personal-injury lawyer for a dad. The book is a wonderful effort filled with empathy for kids, impatience for pushy parents, and a good sense of humor." Booklist

Golenbock, Peter, 1946-

The forever boys; the bittersweet world of major league baseball as seen through the eyes of the men who played one more time. Carol Pub. Group 1991 391p il $19.95 **796.357**

1. St. Petersburg Pelicans (Baseball team) 2. Baseball

ISBN 1-55972-034-4

LC 90-25828

"A Birch Lane Press book"

Golenbock describes "the first season (1989-90) of baseball's new Senior League. Traveling with the St. Petersburg Pelicans, he interviewed the players and relates stories about their personal lives, their troubles once they left the majors, and . . . anecdotes from their professional careers. . . . Although one-sided, many stories are heartbreaking and all are interesting. An unusual glimpse at heroes from the not-so-distant past." Libr J

Halberstam, David, 1934-

Summer of '49. Morrow 1989 304p il
$21.95   **796.357**

1. New York Yankees (Baseball team) 2. Boston Red
Sox (Baseball team)
ISBN 0-688-06678-X   LC 89-2886

Also available in paperback from Avon Bks.

"This book is ostensibly about the pennant race between the Yankees and Red Sox [in 1949] and the 'rivalry' between Joe DiMaggio and Ted Williams. . . . It
is a study of all the elements and personalities that
influenced baseball that year and beyond. Halberstam
brings them together in such an enjoyable, interesting,
and informative manner that a reader needn't be a
baseball fan to appreciate the book." Libr J

Honig, Donald

Baseball: the illustrated history of
America's game. Crown 1990 340p il $45
       796.357

1. Baseball
ISBN 0-517-57295-8   LC 89-1223

The author chronicles baseball from its beginnings in
1839 up to the year 1988. For baseball's modern era,
which began in 1901, he provides a year-by-year narrative of the highlights of each season. Included are more
than 1,100 photographs

The New York Yankees; an illustrated
history. rev ed. Crown 1987 344p il $22.50
       796.357

1. New York Yankees (Baseball team)
ISBN 0-517-56542-0   LC 87-8965

First published 1981

This book depicts the ups and downs of the American
League representative from New York from 1903, when
they were known as the Highlanders, to recent times.
The author focuses on the winning tradition of the
franchise that has won more pennants and World Series
titles than any other team

Includes bibliography

James, Bill, 1949-

The baseball book. Villard Bks. 341p il
pa $14.95   **796.357**

1. Baseball
Annual. First published 1990

Provides information about current ballplayers, presented in question-and-answer format; gives statistical
analysis of previous season of individual players; and
presents brief essays on the sport

The Bill James historical baseball abstract.
Villard Bks. 1985 721p il $29.95   **796.357**

1. Baseball—Statistics
ISBN 0-394-53713-0   LC 84-40603

Also available in a revised paperback edition $15.95
(ISBN 0-394-75805-6)

"The book is divided into three parts. The first surveys various aspects of the game, decade by decade,
from the 1870's through the 1970's. The second is
devoted to the relative merits of the game's best players.
. . . The third part contains extensive data on many
of the game's most famous players, past and present."
N Y Times Book Rev

Joy in Mudville; the big book of baseball

humor; edited by Dick Schaap and Mort
Gerberg. Doubleday 1992 xx, 424p il $25
       796.357

1. Baseball
ISBN 0-385-42151-6   LC 91-42417

"Including articles, book excerpts, and comic strips,
this humorous baseball anthology ranges from the
familiar 'Casey at the Bat' and Abbott and Costello's
hilarious 'Who's on First' routine to selections penned
by Garrison Keillor, George Plimpton, and W. P. Kinsella. Suggested for both personal and reference use." Booklist

Kahn, Roger

The boys of summer. Harper & Row 1972
xxii, 442p il hardcover o.p. paperback
available $10   **796.357**

1. Brooklyn Dodgers (Baseball team) 2. Baseball
ISBN 0-06-091416-5 (pa)

Also available in hardcover from Holtzman Press and
Buccaneer Bks.

The author describes attending Brooklyn Dodger games
as a boy, covering Dodger games as a reporter for the
Herald Tribune, and traveling throughout the country to
speak with former Dodgers after the team left New York

Lamb, David

Stolen season; a journey through America
and baseball's minor leagues. Random
House 1991 283p il $20   **796.357**

1. Baseball
ISBN 0-394-57608-X   LC 90-45719

Also available in paperback from Warner Bks.

"The title comes from the leave of absence the author
took from the Los Angeles Times . . . to travel around
the country watching life in the minors. . . . There
ensued a five-month-long, 16,000-mile journey around
America." Natl Rev

"This book should be read by anyone who has yet
to savor the sounds and delights of a minor-league
baseball game." N Y Times Book Rev

Luciano, Ron

The umpire strikes back; by Ron Luciano
& David Fisher. Bantam Bks. 1982 258p
il hardcover o.p. paperback available $3.95
       796.357

1. Baseball
ISBN 0-553-24846-4 (pa)   LC 81-15059

The author, a "major league umpire, tells about his
participation in the national pastime as an umpire. . .
. The anecdotes reveal the relationships of umpires to
players, managers and fans in an array of incidents that
will amuse, surprise and introduce the reader to the real
world of baseball." Best Sellers

Madden, Bill

Damned Yankees: a no-holds-barred account of life with "Boss" Steinbrenner; [by] Bill Madden and Moss Klein; with cartoons by Ed Murawinski. Warner Bks. 1990 292p il hardcover o.p. paperback available $5.95   **796.357**

1. Steinbrenner, George M. (George Michael), 1930-
2. New York Yankees (Baseball team)
ISBN 0-446-36089-9 (pa)   LC 89-29991

"The authors chiefly discuss the period 1977 to 1989, when principal team owner George Steinbrenner converted a stable, conservative, successful franchise into a club characterized by 'chaos, confusion, and craziness' to the point that some top players refuse to sign with the team. . . . The era they survey has seen 18 managers, 11 presidents, 10 PR agents and innumerable here-today, gone-tomorrow players. Such volatility makes for a rollicking though dismaying tale, related here with gusto." Publ Wkly

McCarthy, John P., 1947-

A parent's guide to coaching baseball; [by] John P. McCarthy, Jr. Betterway Publs. 1989 127p il pa $7.95   **796.357**

1. Baseball
ISBN 1-55870-124-9   LC 89-36140

"McCarthy explains all the basics of fielding, hitting, pitching, running, etc., and provides a good overview of the rules of the game, with attention to the modifications of Little League play. But perhaps best of all, he offers sound tips on how parents can become involved without being intrusive. . . . A first-rate addition to public libraries." Booklist

McCrory, G. Jacobs

Softball rules in pictures; revised and illustrated by Michael Brown. Putnam 1992 77p il pa $7.95   **796.357**

1. Softball
ISBN 0-399-51728-6   LC 91-32175

"A Perigee book"
First published 1959

Following a brief discussion of softball equipment and playing field specifications, sections cover pitching, batting, base running, plays, substitutions, and game officials. The book concludes with the text of the Amateur Softball Association of America's Official Playing Rules, revised 1990

Miller, Marvin

A whole different ball game; the sport and business of baseball. Carol Pub. Group 1991 430p il $21.95   **796.357**

1. Baseball 2. Labor unions—United States
ISBN 1-55972-067-0   LC 91-18474

Also available in paperback from Simon & Schuster
"A Birch Lane Press book"

The former executive director of baseball's Players' Association discusses the creation of unionism in baseball, analyzes baseball economics, and details his legal struggles with team owners and management

"The author is not modest in paying tribute to himself, but he is also generous in his comments about the ball players who made sacrifices for their union. A top sports book." Publ Wkly

Neft, David S.

The sports encyclopedia: baseball; [by] David S. Neft, Richard M. Cohen. St. Martin's Press pa $19.99   **796.357**

1. Baseball—Statistics

First published 1974 by Grosset & Dunlap. (1992 edition) Periodically revised

Covers baseball from 1876 to the present and contains team statistics, alphabetical registers of batters and pitchers, and summaries of each season

The World Series; complete play-by-play of every game, 1903-1989; compiled by the authors of The Sports encyclopedia— baseball, David S. Neft & Richard M. Cohen. St. Martin's Press 1990 443p hardcover o.p. paperback available $16.95   **796.357**

1. World series (Baseball)
ISBN 0-685-28832-3 (pa)   LC 89-27092

This book includes box scores and composite statistics for each player in every series and in the regular season. It also provides background stories behind the great moments year by year

Official baseball register. Sporting News pa $11.95   **796.357**

1. Baseball—Statistics

Annual. First published 1940 with title: Baseball register

At head of title: The Sporting News

This book gives information, mostly in tabular form, about active players, managers, coaches and recently retired players in major league baseball. Included are place and date of birth; nicknames; whether right or left-handed; height and weight; hobbies; colleges attended; records and awards; yearly statistics for batting, fielding and pitching in the major and minor leagues and major league career totals; and team records of managers. Includes statistics for play in World Series and All-Star games

Okrent, Daniel

Baseball anecdotes; [by] Daniel Okrent and Steve Wulf. Oxford Univ. Press 1989 356p $21.95   **796.357**

1. Baseball
ISBN 0-19-504396-0   LC 88-37245

Also available in paperback from HarperCollins Pubs.

The authors "essentially have written a history of the game in stories—comic, tragic, controversial—starting with baseball's disputed origins and ending with the 1986 World Series." N Y Times Book Rev

Oleksak, Michael M., 1957-

Béisbol: Latin Americans and the grand old game; [by] Michael M. Oleksak and Mary Adams Oleksak. Masters Press 1991 303p il $22.95   **796.357**

1. Baseball
ISBN 0-940279-35-5   LC 91-10697

"Contains a brief description of the history of Caribbean ball, but the book centers on the fates of Latin players in the United States, with many statistics and stories. It is an enthusiastic, somewhat naïvely written guide for United States fans of Latin players." N Y

Oleksak, Michael M., 1957-—*Continued*
Times Book Rev

Includes bibliographic references

Seidel, Michael
Streak; Joe DiMaggio and the summer of '41. McGraw-Hill 1988 xxi, 260p il o.p.; Penguin Bks. paperback available $8.95
796.357

1. DiMaggio, Joe 2. Baseball
ISBN 0-14-012104-8 (pa)　　　LC 87-33884

Joe DiMaggio's 56-game hitting streak while playing for the New York Yankees is chronicled in this book. Box scores of the games are included in an appendix

The author "faithfully re-creates what life in America was like during that summer before the United States entered World War II. He has interviewed many of the men who played with and against DiMaggio that year and tells just how DiMaggio managed to keep hitting and hitting." N Y Times Book Rev

Seymour, Harold, 1910-1992
Baseball: the people's game. Oxford Univ. Press 1990 672p il $24.95; pa $12.95
796.357

1. Baseball
ISBN 0-19-503890-8; 0-19-506907-2 (pa)　LC 89-3406

Third volume in the author's projected four-volume work. Earlier titles: Baseball: the early years (1960); and Baseball: the golden age (1971)

The author provides a "history of baseball as it was played from sandlot ball to the semipro and professional level in the so-called Negro Leagues; he includes American Legion, Y.M.C.A. and church-sponsored leagues, as well as softball and women's baseball. In short, Mr. Seymour covers the gamut of American baseball outside self-proclaimed Organized Baseball, from the origins of the game to just before World War II." N Y Times Book Rev

"More than a poignant look at fields of dreams, this is a cultural history of America viewed through its national pastime." Libr J

Includes bibliography

Tygiel, Jules
Baseball's great experiment; Jackie Robinson and his legacy. Oxford Univ. Press 1983 392p il $24.95; pa $10
796.357

1. Robinson, Jackie, 1919-1972 2. Baseball 3. United States—Race relations
ISBN 0-19-503300-0; 0-19-507826-8 (pa)　LC 83-4042

This history provides an account of the desegregation of Major League baseball initiated by Jackie Robinson, Branch Rickey, and others

"Tygiel's intelligence, insight, and . . . candor command one's attention; not a facet of civil rights issues passes without his incisive commentary. His book is a definitive statement." Libr J

Includes bibliographic references

Will, George F.
Men at work: the craft of baseball. Macmillan 1990 353p il $19.95　　**796.357**

1. Baseball
ISBN 0-02-628470-7　　　　LC 89-13265

Also available G.K. Hall large print edition and in paperback from HarperCollins Pubs.

This book's four chapters cover these "aspects of baseball: The Manager (Tony LaRussa of Oakland), The Pitcher (Orel Hershiser of Los Angeles), The Batter (Tony Gwynn of San Diego), and The Defense [Cal Ripken, Jr., of Baltimore]." Natl Rev

"The author's own devotion to detail in defining the components of the game is sure to instill in readers a greater appreciation of what is required to master the sport at the major league level, thereby providing a deeper understanding of the foundation of the game. Altogether, this is hardcore baseball presented in fluent style." Libr J

796.4　Weight lifting, track and field, gymnastics

Scott, Dave
Dave Scott's triathlon training; by Dave Scott with Liz Barrett. Simon & Schuster 1986 253p il pa $12.95　　　　**796.4**

1. Triathlon
ISBN 0-671-60473-2　　　　LC 86-9996

"A Fireside book"

This book opens with a "survey of physiology. . . . Following are chapters dealing with swimming, cycling, and running (the three parts of the triathlon) that emphasize technique and training methods. Also, guides to weight training, competition, and nutrition are included. An essential book for triathletes." Booklist

796.42　Track and field

Sheehan, George
George Sheehan on running to win; how to achieve the physical, mental, and spiritual victories of running. Rodale Press 1992 230p il $19.95　　　　**796.42**

1. Running
ISBN 0-87596-145-2　　　　LC 92-19748

The author "offers training tips, diet guidelines, and injury prevention pointers in clear, concise terms that will enhance any runner's enjoyment of the sport." Booklist

796.48　Olympic games

Guttmann, Allen
The Olympics, a history of the modern games. University of Ill. Press 1992 191p il (Illinois history of sport) $24.95　**796.48**

1. Olympic games
ISBN 0-252-01701-3　　　　LC 91-32631

This history traces the modern Olympics from the first games in Athens in 1896 through the 1988 contests

"Although the text emphasizes the political and socioeconomic climate of the Olympics, it also contains memorable accounts of athletic competition. This book, intended for the serious nonspecialist reader, will be a

Guttmann, Allen—*Continued*
valuable addition to both general and specialized collections." Libr J

Includes bibliographic references

Wallechinsky, David, 1948-
The complete book of the Olympics. Little, Brown il $29.95, pa $14.95 **796.48**

1. Olympic games

First published 1984 by Viking. (1992 edition) Periodically revised

This compendium lists final results of all Olympic contests held since 1896. Summaries of selected events are included

796.5 Outdoor life

Bonington, Chris
Mountaineer; thirty years of climbing on the world's great peaks. Sierra Club Bks. 1990 192p il $29.95 **796.5**

1. Mountaineering
ISBN 0-87156-618-4   LC 89-38267

The author has a "record of ascents from Chile to China, Alps to Himalayas and in his native Britain. . . . Here he recaps his adventures, augmenting the text with his spectacular photographs that provide a visual record of his major ascents." Publ Wkly

Fletcher, Colin, 1922-
The complete walker III; the joys and techniques of hiking and backpacking; illustrations by Vanna Prince. 3rd ed rev enl and updated. Knopf 1984 668p il $22.95; pa $18 **796.5**

1. Backpacking
ISBN 0-394-51962-0; 0-394-72264-7 (pa)
                                      LC 83-48870

First published 1969 with title: The complete walker

Covers techniques, equipment, physical conditioning, first aid and other related matters

"Most equipment and technique guides are informative but not very readable; this one is both. . . . Entertaining reading even if you're not planning an outing or expedition." Libr J

Hart, John, 1948-
Walking softly in the wilderness; the Sierra Club guide to backpacking. completely rev and updated. Sierra Club Bks. 1984 500p il pa $12 **796.5**

1. Backpacking
ISBN 0-87156-813-6   LC 83-19592
First published 1977

This guide to backpacking incorporates the environmental concerns of the Sierra Club

Riviere, Bill
The L.L. Bean guide to the outdoors; [by] Bill Riviere, with the staff of L.L. Bean; research by Bruce Willard; illustrated by J. Nicoletti. Random House 1981 xx, 299p il $15.50 **796.5**

1. Outdoor recreation—Equipment and supplies
ISBN 0-394-51928-0   LC 80-6009

"Straightforward information on appropriate, durable types of equipment for cooking, hiking, sleeping (tents and bags), canoeing, backpacking, and chopping wood is supplemented with advice on how to execute these tasks properly." Booklist

796.54 Camping

Guide to summer camps and summer schools. Sargent Pubs. il $26, pa $21 **796.54**

1. Camps—Directories 2. Summer schools—Directories
ISSN 0072-8705

Biennial. First published 1936. Title varies

"Listing of summer camping, travel, pioneering, recreational, and educational programs in the United States and abroad. Entries provide name, location, winter address, age and sex of participants, fees, length of camping period, and a description of important features." Ref Sources for Small & Medium-sized Libr. 5th edition

Kennedy, Richard C.
Choosing the right camp; the complete guide to the best summer camp for your child; [by] Richard C. Kennedy and Michael Kimball. 1993-94 ed. Random House 1992 194p pa $15 **796.54**

1. Camps—Directories
ISBN 0-8129-1926-2   LC 92-4573

"Fifty camps for (boys, girls, or both) are described, with details on staff, age levels, session dates, location, activities, meals, and programs. The focus is on general camps with a steady history, not those specializing in a particular sport or interest." Booklist

Rand McNally RV park & campground directory. Rand McNally il maps pa $13.95 **796.54**

1. Campgrounds—Directories 2. Trailer parks—Directories

Annual. First published 1971 with title: Rand McNally campground and trailer park guide. Combines two previous titles: Rand McNally guidebook to campgrounds, and Rand McNally travel trailer guide

This directory of campgrounds and trailer parks in the United States, Canada, and Mexico includes information on facilities, regulations, size, fees and activities. Full-color maps of each state show campground locations

796.6   Cycling and related activities

Chauner, David
The Tour de France complete book of cycling; [by] David Chauner and Michael Halstead. Villard Bks. 1990 235p il pa $15.95   **796.6**

1. Bicycles and bicycling
ISBN 0-679-72936-4   LC 89-48482

"A John Boswell Associates book"

This book includes a history of bicycles, and information about choosing a bicycle, bicycle hardware and equipment, conditioning, first aid, racing, touring and family cycling, and The Tour de France

LeMond, Greg, 1961?-
Greg LeMond's complete book of bicycling; [by] Greg LeMond and Kent Gordis. Putnam 1987 352p il hardcover o.p. paperback available $10.95   **796.6**

1. Bicycles and bicycling
ISBN 0-399-51594-1 (pa)   LC 87-2273

"At every opportunity, LeMond and coauthor Gordis direct tips to both the competitive cyclist and the weekender who just wants exercise and recreation. . . . In addition to sensible advice on equipment, the text includes valuable suggestions on cycling technique, training, fitness, and nutrition. This is *the* book for libraries needing one quality title on bicycling." Booklist

796.8   Combat sports

Crompton, Paul H. (Paul Howcroft)
The complete martial arts; [by] Paul Crompton. McGraw-Hill 1989 208p il $34.95   **796.8**

1. Martial arts
ISBN 0-07-014450-8   LC 89-8121

This work covers judo, karate, kick boxing, and jujitsu, along with the lesser-known *escrima, savate,* and *pentjak silat*

Ochiai, Hidy
Hidy Ochiai's complete book of self-defense. Contemporary Bks. 1991 340p il $16.95   **796.8**

1. Self-defense 2. Karate
ISBN 0-8092-4055-6   LC 90-19279

"The book is loaded with photos that are accompanied by an easy-to-understand text to help guide the reader from the essential basics to the most advanced self-defense moves. It contains an interesting and practical section on self-defense techniques, as well as an absorbing chapter explaining Ochiai's philosophy of the martial arts." Libr J

Tegnér, Bruce, 1928-1985
Bruce Tegner's complete book of jujitsu. Thor 1977 190p il hardcover o.p. paperback available $10.95   **796.8**

1. Jiu-jitsu
ISBN 0-87407-027-9 (pa)   LC 77-5023

Contents: Introduction; Holds & locks; Hand & foot blows; Trips & throws; Katas; Kneeling & sword katas; Bibliography

From the many martial arts and self-defense systems which have been practiced in Japan under the name jiujitsu the author has selected those routines which he feels are most appropriate for developing and maintaining physical fitness, flexibility and agility, and are most useful for self-expression and self-improvement

Bruce Tegner's complete book of self-defense. completely new ed. Thor 1975 223p il hardcover o.p. paperback available $10.95   **796.8**

1. Self-defense
ISBN 0-87407-030-9 (pa)

First published 1963 by Stein & Day

This book describes various means of self-defense. Safety in practice sessions is stressed. Instructions are given in text and photographs for assertive stances, hand blows, restraints and flexible combinations

Karate: beginner to black belt. Thor 1982 220p il hardcover o.p. paperback available $10.95   **796.8**

1. Karate
ISBN 0-87407-040-6 (pa)   LC 81-18199

This book contains step-by-step instructions on karate techniques ranging from basic to advanced. Emphasis is on safety, health and fitness

796.93   Skiing

Jonas, Bob
Ski magazine's total skiing; [by] Bob Jonas and Seth Masia; illustrations by Ralph Harris. Putnam 1987 189p il hardcover o.p. paperback available $8.95   **796.93**

1. Skis and skiing
ISBN 0-399-51495-3 (pa)   LC 87-10762

This volume covers "ski resorts, selecting and buying equipment, training techniques, and snow conditions . . . [and] provides . . . instruction on alpine skiing and the American Teaching Method for the wedge, the wedge turn, the christie, and the parallel turn. Also covered are cross-country techniques." Publisher's note

796.962   Ice hockey

Diamond, Dan
Hockey hall of fame; the official history of the game and its greatest stars; [by] Dan Diamond, Joseph Romain. Doubleday 1988 160p il $14.95   **796.962**

1. National Hockey League 2. Ice hockey
ISBN 0-385-24830-X   LC 88-18760

This illustrated history of the National Hockey League chronicles biographical and statistical information of over 250 Hall of Fame members

797.1 Boating

Johnson, Peter
The Sail magazine book of sailing. Knopf 1989 352p il maps $40   **797.1**
1. Sailing 2. Boat racing
ISBN 0-394-57457-5   LC 89-2531
"A Dorling Kindersley book"
The author "devotes the bulk of his book to sailing races. He discusses all of the major international contests, including the America's Cup, Olympic events, and both off-shore and in-shore competitions. Racing rules and rating systems are explained. . . . Boardsailing and sand-, land-, and iceboating are also covered." Booklist
"This compares quite favorably with other picture books on the history of yachting and is particularly valuable as a reference source for its statistical information and diagrams of race courses and sailing areas." Libr J

Stapleton, Sid
Stapleton's powerboat bible; how to buy, equip, and organize a boat for coastal and bluewater cruising; with a foreword by Carleton Mitchell; illustrations by Jeff Landis. Hearst Marine Bks. 1989 447p il $22.95   **797.1**
1. Motorboats
ISBN 0-688-08448-6   LC 89-34407
An illustrated guide to the selection, purchase and accessorizing of motorboats. A section on safety and health at sea is included

797.2 Swimming and diving

Counsilman, Doc
The complete book of swimming; [by] James E. Counsilman. Atheneum Pubs. 1977 178p il hardcover o.p. paperback available $10   **797.2**
1. Swimming
ISBN 0-689-70583-2 (pa)   LC 72-82682
After a brief explanation of the elements of swimming, the author discusses the various strokes, training routines, and competitive swimming
"Not as comprehensive or novice-oriented as the title implies, but Counsilman's descriptions of training methods and suggestions for workout routines . . . should make this useful to serious, competitively directed swimmers." Booklist

Katz, Jane
Swimming for total fitness; a progressive aerobic program; by Jane Katz with Nancy P. Bruning; illustrations by Phillip Jones. updated ed. Doubleday 1992 400p il pa $17.50   **797.2**
1. Swimming 2. Physical fitness
ISBN 0-385-46821-0   LC 92-31877
First published 1981
This introduction to swimming covers basic strokes, kicks, turns, starts, and dives. Progressive training regimens for beginning to advanced swimmers are then presented, followed by a chapter on equipment. A question and answer section concludes the book

McCallum, Paul, 1958-
The scuba diving handbook; a complete guide to salt and fresh water diving. Betterway Publs. 1991 192p il $19.95   **797.2**
1. Scuba diving
ISBN 1-55870-180-X   LC 90-21714
This "guide to scuba diving covers all aspects of the sport, from equipment selection and underwater first aid to the proper methods of catching, cooking, and photographing marine life." Booklist
Includes bibliographic references

797.5 Air sports

Wirth, Dick
Ballooning; the complete guide to riding the winds; [by] Dick Wirth, Jerry Young; introduction by Per Lindstrand. rev & updated ed. Random House 1991 168p il pa $22.50   **797.5**
1. Airships
ISBN 0-679-73116-4   LC 90-9105
First published 1980
Partial contents: Two hundred years of flight; The high-tech generation; Sportsmen in the clouds; Solo stats; The great Atlantic challenge; High Alpine flying; Big game ballooning; The art and the science; Take-off; Using wind and weather; Touch-down; High rise research
Includes bibliographic references

798.2 Horsemanship

Gordon-Watson, Mary
The handbook of riding; foreword by William Steinkraus. Knopf 1982 288p il $22.50   **798.2**
1. Horsemanship 2. Horses—Training
ISBN 0-394-52110-2   LC 82-47795
"Instruction on the essentials of horsemanship for every level from beginner to advanced is included in this manual. The classical seat is concentrated on, but Western and side-saddle riding are discussed in separate chapters. Training and keeping a horse, stable and equipment care, competitive and pleasure riding are also set forth." Voice Youth Advocates
"Although the book has a definite British slant, the writing is not only informative but entertaining." Libr J

Practical horseman's book of riding, training, and showing hunters and jumpers; edited by M.A. Stoneridge. Doubleday 1989 c1987 441p il $32.50   **798.2**
1. Horsemanship 2. Horses—Training
ISBN 0-385-19691-1   LC 88-21706
The author "brings together more than 50 well-illustrated essays by famous equestrians, catering to a wide range of interests among hunter/jumper devotees. All of the articles originally appeared in the magazine 'Practical Horseman'. . . . Each essay is prefaced with a brief biography of its author. A convenient, well-rounded anthology. Recommended." Libr J

798.401   Horse race betting

Ainslie, Tom
Ainslie's complete guide to thoroughbred racing. 3rd ed. Simon & Schuster 1986 349p il hardcover o.p. paperback available $11.95
      798.401

1. Horse racing 2. Gambling
ISBN 0-671-65655-4 (pa)   LC 86-3879
First published 1968

A guide to the fundamentals of handicapping races including such topics as breeding, judging condition of the horses, calculating speed, track ratings and other tips for successful betting

The **Best** of thoroughbred handicapping; advice on handicapping from the experts; [edited by] James Quinn. Morrow 1987 341p $22.95   **798.401**

1. Horse racing 2. Gambling
ISBN 0-688-07012-4   LC 87-11128

"Quinn pulls together and distills into 48 essays the systems of the country's most noted handicappers, including Tom Ainslie, Andrew Beyer, William Quirin, and himself. Each essay explains that author's system and provides examples of how it works. Some of the systems are too complex to reduce, and the essays difficult to follow. But for the most part the essays whet the horseplayer's appetite to read the original books, listed in an annotated bibliography." Libr J

799.1   Fishing

Hersey, John, 1914-1993
Blues; with drawings by James Baker. Knopf 1987 205p il $16.95; pa $9   **799.1**
1. Fishing
ISBN 0-394-55960-6; 0-394-75702-5 (pa)
      LC 86-46008

"This book about fishing for bluefish off the coast of Cape Cod features a wide array of information about that one group of fish, but not in straightforward fashion. It is written in the form of fictional conversations between the 'fisherman' and 'the stranger,' who discuss everything from the blues' mating habits to recipes for preparing them. They also cover sea lore, fishing, and ecology, with frequent references to literature and poetry." Libr J
"People who love and care about nature and their place in it, be they fishermen or not, should thoroughly enjoy 'Blues.'" Wilson Libr Bull

Lee, David, 1942-
Fly fishing; a beginner's guide; with illustrations by Daniel D. Feaser; photographs by Katherine G. Lee; foreword by John Randolph. Prentice-Hall 1982 190p il hardcover o.p. paperback available $9.95
      799.1

1. Fishing 2. Fly casting
ISBN 0-13-322529-1 (pa)   LC 81-12110
"A Spectrum book"

"The author has wide experience in the sport, and covers every aspect of it, from equipment to landing the fish itself. The writing style is as enthusiastic as it is informative. The guide is not just for beginners, but for anyone short of an expert." Katz. How to: 1400 Best Books

Includes bibliographies

Lyons, Nick
Confessions of a fly fishing addict. Simon & Schuster 1989 220p hardcover o.p. paperback available $10   **799.1**

1. Fishing 2. Fly casting
ISBN 0-671-67653-9 (pa)   LC 88-36237
"A Fireside book"

"This book of 49 essays (all previously published in the author's 'Seasonable Fisherman' column in *Fly Fishing* magazine) is a handy collection for those fans who feel that Lyons is the best fishing essayist writing today. . . . He has the welcome tendency to not take himself too seriously . . . yet a fluent love of nature and his chosen sport enlighten every page. Recommended for all libraries with fly fishing interests." Libr J

Mojetta, Angelo
Simon & Schuster's guide to saltwater fish and fishing. Simon & Schuster 1992 255p il pa $14   **799.1**

1. Fishing 2. Fishes 3. Marine ecology
ISBN 0-671-77947-8   LC 91-45324
"A Fireside book"

This reference guide to more than 150 species of marine fish provides "the essentials for identifying and catching saltwater fish. An overview of angling methods covers equipment, bait, and various fishing techniques. Each entry—complete with a color photograph—provides facts on each specie's habitat, seasonal activity, behavior, distribution, food, and gastronomic value." Publisher's note

Walton, Izaak, 1593-1683
The compleat angler, 1653-1676; edited, with an introduction and commentary by Jonquil Bevan. Oxford Univ. Press 1983 435p il $115   **799.1**

1. Fishing
ISBN 0-19-812313-2   LC 82-6302
Also available in hardcover and paperback from other publishers

First published 1653

"A treatise on angling with dialogue, which celebrates the countryside and the joys of fishing. It is 'the' classic of piscatory literature." Penguin Companion to Engl Lit

Includes bibliographic references

800 LITERATURE AND RHETORIC

801 Literature—Philosophy and theory

Dickstein, Morris
Double agent; the critic and society. Oxford Univ. Press 1992 220p $23   **801**
1. Criticism 2. Literature—History and criticism
ISBN 0-19-507399-1   LC 91-43271
"Dickstein deplores the way in which serious criticism, ever since its locus of production moved to the university, has been caught in the throes of post-structuralism and cut off from the wider reading public. . . . As a balance to the theoretical weight of most academic criticism, Dickstein proposes a fresh look at the critics who, outside of the academic sphere for the most part, practiced what he calls public criticism. He begins with Matthew Arnold and discusses critics as varied as H. L. Mencken, Lionel Trilling, Northrop Frye, Edmund Wilson, Alfred Kazin, and Constance Rourke." SLJ

Gardner, John, 1933-1982
On moral fiction. Basic Bks. 1978 214p hardcover o.p. paperback available $14
                                        801
1. Literature—Philosophy
ISBN 0-465-05226-6 (pa)   LC 77-20409
Gardner "submits that contemporary U.S. art, primarily that of fiction, is generally not of high quality because it is not moral, in that it strives to devalue rather than improve life. Furthermore, Gardner charges that critics have lost track of true, moral art and have failed to denounce that which is false or immoral." Booklist

Kermode, Frank, 1919-
An appetite for poetry. Harvard Univ. Press 1989 242p $22.50   **801**
1. Poetry—History and criticism 2. Literature—History and criticism 3. Criticism
ISBN 0-674-04093-7   LC 89-31725
Analyzed in Essay and general literature index
This collection contains critical and textual readings of Milton, T. S. Eliot, Wallace Stevens, William Empson and the Bible
"Kermode is not simply a critic but also an artist. . . . In An Appetite for Poetry we encounter writing of balance and decorum, and reading of unflinching audacity." Commonweal
Includes bibliography

Sartre, Jean Paul, 1905-1980
"What is literature?" and other essays. Harvard Univ. Press 1988 361p $39.50; pa $14.95   **801**
1. Literature—Philosophy 2. Authorship
ISBN 0-674-95083-6; 0-674-95084-4 (pa)
                                        LC 87-37931
Analyzed in Essay and general literature index
The title essay was first published in English 1949

Contents: What is literature?; Introducing Les temps modernes; The nationalization of literature; Black Orpheus

803 Literature—Encyclopedias and dictionaries

Abrams, M. H. (Meyer Howard), 1912-
A glossary of literary terms. Harcourt Brace & Co. pa $19.50   **803**
1. Literature—Dictionaries
First published 1957. (6th edition, 1993) Periodically revised
In a series of essays, the author discusses literary terms and definitions ranging from the traditional to the avant-garde. Subsidiary terms are included under major or generic terms

Allusions—cultural, literary, biblical, and historical; a thematic dictionary; Laurence Urdang and Frederick G. Ruffner, Jr., editors; David M. Glixon, associate editor. 2nd ed. Gale Res. 1986 634p $89   **803**
1. Allusions
ISBN 0-8103-1828-8   LC 86-9981
First published 1982
"A thematic dictionary with more than 8700 entries arranged under 712 categories. Contains references to the Bible, literature, history, mythology, and diverse elements of culture such as media, music, and the arts." Ref Sources for Small & Medium-sized Libr. 5th edition

Benét's reader's encyclopedia. 3rd ed. Harper & Row 1987 1091p $45   **803**
1. Literature—Dictionaries
ISBN 0-06-181088-6   LC 87-45022
First published 1948 under the editorship of William Rose Benét
This encyclopedia contains over 9,000 entries and covers world literature from early times to the present. Includes entries on authors, literary movements, characteristics, etc.
"Compiled by many hands, the 3rd ed. emphasizes 20th-century and non-Western literatures, with the result that some of the more obscure classical and European authors, characters, works, and motifs have been excluded." Sheehy. Guide to Ref Books. 10th edition. suppl

Brewer's dictionary of 20th-century phrase and fable. Houghton Mifflin 1992 c1991 662p $30   **803**
1. English language—Terms and phrases 2. English language—Slang 3. Words, New—Dictionaries
ISBN 0-395-61649-2   LC 91-29299
First published 1991 in the United Kingdom
This dictionary features over 8000 new words and phrases coined since 1900. Included are slogans, slang, idioms, catch phrases, acronyms and allusions
For a review see: Booklist, May 15, 1992

Brewer's dictionary of phrase and fable. Harper & Row $35; pa $20   **803**
1. Literature—Dictionaries 2. Allusions
First published 1870. (14th edition 1989) Periodically revised
Current edition edited by Ivor H. Evans

Brewer's dictionary of phrase and fable—
Continued
"Over 15,000 brief entries give the meanings and origins of a broad range of terms, expressions, and names of real, fictitious and mythical characters from world history, science, the arts and literature." N Y Public Libr. Ref Books for Child Collect. 2d edition

Columbia dictionary of modern European literature; Jean-Albert Bédé and William B. Edgerton, general editors. 2d ed fully rev and enl. Columbia Univ. Press 1980 895p $163   **803**
1. Literature—Dictionaries   2. Authors, European—Dictionaries
ISBN 0-231-03717-1   LC 80-17082
First published 1947
"Contains signed articles by some 500 contributors on over 1,800 authors who write (or wrote) in European languages other than English from the late 19th century to the present. General articles on individual literatures are also included." Choice

The **Concise** Oxford dictionary of literary terms; [compiled by] Chris Baldick. Oxford Univ. Press 1990 246p $21.95; pa $8.95   **803**
1. Literature—Dictionaries 2. English language—Terms and phrases
ISBN 0-19-811733-7; 0-19-282893-2 (pa)
    LC 89-71330
Baldick "has collected approximately 1,000 terms relating to literary criticism that he considers to be 'most likely to cause the student or general reader some doubt or bafflement.' . . . The alphabetically arranged entries vary in length from a single phrase to more than a page." Booklist

Cuddon, J. A. (John Anthony), 1928-
A dictionary of literary terms and literary theory. 3rd ed. Blackwell 1991 1051p $44.95   **803**
1. Literature—Dictionaries
ISBN 0-631-17214-9   LC 90-49943
First published 1977 by Doubleday with title: A dictionary of literary terms
In this dictionary each term is defined or described and its origin is usually given. Over a dozen languages are represented

Cyclopedia of literary characters. Salem Press 1963 2v set $75   **803**
1. Literature—Dictionaries 2. Characters and characteristics in literature
ISBN 0-89356-140-1
"Also appears under the title of: Masterplots Cyclopedia of literary characters." Verso of title page
A volume of identification and description, alphabetically arranged by title of work, "of more than sixteen thousand [major and minor] characters from some thirteen hundred novels, dramas, and epics drawn from world literature. . . . Pronunciation is given for names likely to be mispronounced and for unfamiliar foreign names." Preface
Supplemented by Cyclopedia of literary characters II 4v set $300 (ISBN 0-89356-517-2). CD ROM version also available

Encyclopedia of world literature in the 20th century; based on the first edition edited by Wolfgang Bernard Fleischmann; Leonard S. Klein, general editor. rev ed. Ungar; [distributed by] Gale Res. 1981-1993 5v il set $600   **803**
1. Literature—Dictionaries   2. Literature—Bio-bibliography
ISBN 0-8103-9619-X   LC 81-3357
First four volumes originally published 1967-1975
Volume 5 supplement and index, edited by Steven R. Serafin, published by Continuum. Available separately for $150 (ISBN 0-8264-0571-1)
"This multivolume encyclopedia provides extensive up-to-date coverage on international developments in twentieth-century literature. While emphasis is given to writers of Europe and North America, this work also represents one of the most valuable sources of information on national literatures, including Third World countries." Ref Sources for Small & Medium-sized Libr. 5th edition

808   Rhetoric

Achtert, Walter S.
The MLA style manual; by Walter S. Achtert and Joseph Gibaldi. Modern Lang. Assn. of Am. 1985 271p $21   **808**
1. Authorship—Handbooks, manuals, etc.
ISBN 0-87352-136-6   LC 85-4972
This handbook is aimed at users "intent on publishing in the humanities. In addition to advice on publisher selection, query letters, contracts, and the copyright law, the 'Manual' covers questions of style." Booklist

Barzun, Jacques, 1907-
The modern researcher; by Jacques Barzun [and] Henry F. Graff. 5th ed. Harcourt Brace Jovanovich 1992 409p $24.95; pa $13.95   **808**
1. Report writing 2. Research
ISBN 0-395-64494-1; 0-15-562512-8 (pa)
    LC 91-74063
First published 1957
This manual shows "how to gather information, judge its value, verify its accuracy, and sort it for communication in written or oral form." Publisher's note

On writing, editing, and publishing; essays, explicative and hortatory; with a foreword by Morris Philipson. 2nd ed expanded. University of Chicago Press 1986 148p (Chicago guides to writing, editing, and publishing) $20; pa $7.95   **808**
1. Authorship 2. Authors and publishers
ISBN 0-226-03857-2; 0-226-03858-0 (pa)
    LC 85-16562
First published 1971
In this collection of essays, Barzun describes his ideas about writing technique, and also enumerates some of the difficulties encountered in editing and publishing

Bly, Robert W., 1957-
Technical writing; structure, standards, and style; [by] Robert W. Bly and Gary Blake. McGraw-Hill 1982 114p $11.95; pa $6.95
808

1. Technical writing
ISBN 0-07-006174-2; 0-07-006173-4 (pa)
LC 82-15223

"This book is intended as an everyday style and usage guide, filled with rules and examples relevant to common technical writing situations. Among topics covered are expressing numbers, units, equations, and symbols properly, avoiding words and phrases often misused, and shepherding a document through the entire inhouse publishing process." Libr J

Includes bibliography

Bradbury, Ray, 1920-
Zen in the art of writing: essays on writing & creativity. Joshua Odell Eds. 1990 154p il $18.95; pa $8.95   **808**
1. Authorship 2. Creative ability
ISBN 1-877741-02-7; 1-877741-01-9 (pa)
LC 89-25381

"The title piece aims to help the aspiring writer navigate between the self-consciously literary and the calculatingly commercial. Other essays deal with discovering one's imaginative self; feeding one's muse; the germination of Bradbury's novel *Dandelion Wine* in his Illinois boyhood; a trip to Ireland; science fiction as a search for new modes of survival; and the author's stage adaptation of his classic novel *Fahrenheit 451*. Eight poems on creativity round out the volume." Publ Wkly

Brown, Rita Mae
Starting from scratch; a different kind of writer's manual. Bantam Bks. 1988 254p $18.95; pa $9.95   **808**
1. Authorship
ISBN 0-553-05246-2; 0-553-34630-X (pa)
LC 87-19535

"Brown discusses the importance of good dialogue and effective verbs, and she advocates avoiding the passive voice and developing a sound plot. But, speaking from the heart, she also addresses the more personal aspects of becoming a writer—the need to maintain good sleeping habits, to avoid drugs and alcohol, and even to eat balanced meals, among other topics not usually found in this kind of book." Booklist

Includes bibliography

The **Chicago** manual of style. University of Chicago Press il $40   **808**
1. Authorship—Handbooks, manuals, etc. 2. Publishers and publishing—Handbooks, manuals, etc. 3. English language—Usage

First published 1906 with title: A manual of style. (14th edition 1993) Frequently reprinted with minor revisions

"This style manual has become recognized as a reliable standard for writers and editors preparing manuscripts for publication. Major sections cover bookmaking, style, and production and printing." N Y Public Libr Book of How & Where to Look It Up

Coles, Robert
The call of stories; teaching and the moral imagination. Houghton Mifflin 1989 xx, 212p hardcover o.p. paperback available $8.95   **808**
1. Literature—Study and teaching 2. Moral education 3. Books and reading
ISBN 0-395-52815-1 (pa)
LC 88-26659
"A Peter Davison book"

"Using the 'documentary study on psychiatric anthropology' approach of his previous works, Coles presents conversations with college, law, and medical school students that focus on the moral impact of their reading. For Coles, the study of literature is not a purely intellectual exercise but an encounter with exempla that bear on everyday moral dilemmas." Libr J

Collier, Oscar, 1924-
How to write and sell your first nonfiction book; [by] Oscar Collier with Frances Spatz Leighton. St. Martin's Press 1990 279p $17.95   **808**
1. Authorship 2. Authors and publishers
ISBN 0-312-03846-1
LC 89-24190
A guide to assessing the market for and successfully publishing nonfiction. The author offers advice on matters ranging from initial research to post-publication author interviews

Includes bibliography

Cool, Lisa Collier, 1952-
How to sell every magazine article you write. Writer's Digest Bks. 1986 214p hardcover o.p. paperback available $11.95
808
1. Authorship
ISBN 0-89879-355-6 (pa)
LC 86-15864
In this guide to the magazine market, the author discusses the leading magazines, their readership, their pay scales, and their willingness to accept free-lance work
An "excellent resource for writers serious about selling their stories to magazines." Libr J

Includes bibliography

Edel, Leon, 1907-
Writing lives; principia biographica. Norton 1985 270p hardcover o.p. paperback available $6.95   **808**
1. Biography (as a literary form)
ISBN 0-393-30382-9 (pa)
LC 84-5959
Edel "has brought together his various writings on the biographer's art, many previously published and here revised, in an attempt both to define the 'new biography' and suggest criteria by which biography may be evaluated." Libr J

Includes bibliography

First person singular; writers on their craft; compiled by Joyce Carol Oates. Ontario Review Press 1983 280p $15.95; pa $9.95
808
1. Authors, American 2. Authorship
ISBN 0-86538-037-6; 0-86538-045-7 (pa)
LC 83-21927

First person singular—*Continued*

"Twenty-nine well-known novelists and poets, primarily American but also a Canadian or two, discuss their craft in this . . . collection of essays and interviews." Publ Wkly

"If there's any generalization one can make about a group of contributors as diverse as John Updike and Ned Rorem, William Stafford and Bernard Malamud, it's that great writers talk about their work with ease and less great writers talk about their work with . . . less ease." Atlantic

Gibaldi, Joseph, 1942-

MLA handbook for writers of research papers; [by] Joseph Gibaldi, Walter S. Achtert. 3rd ed. Modern Lang. Assn. of Am. 1988 248p pa $9.95   **808**

1. Report writing

ISBN 0-87352-379-2   LC 88-5195

First published 1977 with title: MLA handbook for writers of research papers, theses, and dissertations

"The manual is divided into six chapters: research and writing, the mechanics of writing, the format of the research paper, preparing the list of works cited, documenting sources, and abbreviations and reference works." Nichols. Guide to Ref Books for Sch Media Cent. 4th edition

Giblin, James, 1933-

Writing books for young people; by James Cross Giblin. Writer 1990 132p pa $12

808

1. Authorship 2. Children's literature—Technique

ISBN 0-87116-158-3   LC 89-36417

The author discusses various "aspects of juvenile book writing—picture books, nonfiction books, and novels, including mysteries, science fiction, fantasies, and historical fiction—offering examples from his own and other writers' work to support and illustrate the techniques and methods he recommends." Publisher's note

Harbrace college handbook; [by] John C. Hodges [et al.] Harcourt Brace Jovanovich $21.95   **808**

1. English language—Composition and exercises
2. English language—Grammar   LC 89-85368

First published 1941 with title: Harbrace handbook of English. (12th edition 1993) Frequently revised

A guide to the fundamentals of grammar, composition, and usage

How to be successfully published in magazines; [edited by] Linda Konner. St. Martin's Press 1990 186p $19.95; pa $10.95   **808**

1. Authorship—Handbooks, manuals, etc. 2. Journalism

ISBN 0-312-04406-2; 0-312-04463-1 (pa)

LC 89-78005

"Konner asked 28 magazine editors to comment on what pleases them most in terms of ideas, format, queries, and follow-ups. Advice from successful writers and the basics on writing queries and preparing manuscripts are also supplied." Booklist

Jacobi, Peter

The magazine article; how to think it, plan it, write it; [by] Peter P. Jacobi. Writer's Digest Bks. 1991 247p $17.95

808

1. Authorship—Handbooks, manuals, etc. 2. Journalism

ISBN 0-89879-450-1   LC 90-21253

"Jacobi focuses on article writing as a creative process as opposed to a way of making money. . . . Articles are excerpted from varied publications to exemplify how such techniques as information gathering, structuring, exposition, and description have led to successful results." Libr J

Kilpatrick, James J., 1920-

The writer's art. Andrews, McMeel & Parker 1984 254p hardcover o.p. paperback available $9.95   **808**

1. English language—Usage

ISBN 0-8362-7925-5 (pa)   LC 84-2892

Political columnist Kilpatrick offers a primer on how to write properly and forcefully. Examples of solecism, misspelling and gobbledegook are numerous

"An honest, forthright and at times charming look into American usage." N Y Times Book Rev

McMahan, Elizabeth

The writer's handbook; [by] Elizabeth McMahan, Susan Day. 2nd ed. McGraw-Hill 1988 400p pa $18.95   **808**

1. English language—Grammar 2. Rhetoric

ISBN 0-07-045432-9   LC 87-24160

First published 1980

This guide for acquiring the skills to develop writing proficiency covers grammar, punctuation, style, usage and spelling. A chapter is devoted to business writing

Meredith, Scott

Writing to sell. 3rd rev ed. Harper & Row 1987 xxii, 227p $22.50   **808**

1. Authorship 2. Fiction—Technique

ISBN 0-06-015637-6   LC 86-45128

First published 1950

A guide to the techniques of writing and marketing fiction, nonfiction, and magazine articles

Strunk, William, 1869-1946

The elements of style; by William Strunk, Jr.; with revisions, an introduction, and a chapter on writing by E. B. White. 3d ed. Macmillan 1979 85p $9.95; pa $5.95   **808**

1. Rhetoric

ISBN 0-02-418190-0; 0-02-418200-1 (pa)

LC 78-18444

First appeared 1918, privately printed; first trade edition published 1920 by Harcourt Brace & Co.

"This small volume, revised by award-winning children's writer and essayist White, is a valuable addition to any library. It is prescriptive, conservative, and humorous; in sum, it is the best book available on how to write English prose. Rules of good usage are stated, followed by incorrect and correct examples." Nichols. Guide to Ref Books for Sch Media Cent. 4th edition

Thomas, Frank P., 1916-

How to write the story of your life. Writer's Digest Bks. 1984 230p hardcover o.p. paperback available $11.95 **808**

1. Biography (as a literary form)
ISBN 0-89879-359-9 (pa)   LC 84-19527

The author "notes that writing one's own memoirs is more beneficial personally than getting someone else to do the job. Thomas alternates writing guidance with examples of student work, introduced by salient comments." Libr J

Includes bibliography

Turabian, Kate L., 1893-1987

A manual for writers of term papers, theses, and dissertations. University of Chicago Press (Chicago guides to writing, editing, and publishing) $22; pa $8.95 **808**

1. Report writing 2. Dissertations, Academic
ISBN 0-226-81624-9; 0-226-81625-7 (pa)

First published 1937 with title: A manual for writers of dissertations. (5th edition 1987) Periodically revised

Designed to serve as a guide to suitable style in the presentation of formal papers—term papers, reports, articles, theses, dissertations—both in scientific and in nonscientific fields

Student's guide for writing college papers. 3rd ed. University of Chicago Press 1977 c1976 256p $16; pa $7.95 **808**

1. Report writing 2. Dissertations, Academic
ISBN 0-226-81622-2; 0-226-81623-0 (pa)   LC 76-435

First published 1963

This guide covers selecting a topic, collecting material, planning and writing the paper, and preparing footnotes and bibliographies

United States. Government Printing Office

Style manual. U.S. Govt. Ptg. Office $15, pa $11 **808**

1. Authorship—Handbooks, manuals, etc. 2. Publishers and publishing—Handbooks, manuals, etc. 3. Printing—Style manuals

First published 1908 with title: Manual of style. Frequently revised

"A useful and extensive manual giving the practices of the Government Printing Office on copy preparation, with rules for capitalization, punctuation, abbreviations, etc., and information on foreign languages, including alphabets, with pronunciation, special rules, lists of numbers, etc." Sheehy. Guide to Ref Books. 10th edition

Women writers at work; the Paris review interviews; edited by George Plimpton; introduction by Margaret Atwood. Viking 1989 387p il o.p.; Penguin Bks. paperback available $9.95 **808**

1. Literature—History and criticism 2. Women authors
ISBN 0-14-011790-3 (pa)   LC 88-40332

This volume collects fifteen interviews in which women writers discuss their work, their lives, and the nature of writing in general. Among the interviewees are: Eudora Welty, Marianne Moore, and Edna O'Brien

Writers at work; the Paris Review interviews; edited by George Plimpton. Viking $22 **808**

1. Literature—History and criticism
ISSN 0510-9671

Also available in paperback from Penguin Bks.

First series published 1958 (Ninth series published 1992)

Each volume contains extended interviews with prominent literary figures; biographical notes are included

The **Writer's** handbook. Writer $29.95 **808**

1. Authorship—Handbooks, manuals, etc. 2. Publishers and publishing
ISSN 0084-2710

Annual. First published 1936. Current editor Sylvia K. Burack

"Articles on writing and manuscript preparation make up much of each annual. The main part of the book is a market guide, mainly to the periodical field but including radio, television, and book publishing as well. For each publisher the entry provides name, address, editor, editorial requirements, type of material sought, payment rate, and other useful information. . . . This work is far more than a directory of publishers. Its articles on how to write for specific markets make it a first choice of publications of its kind." Nichols. Guide to Ref Books for Sch Media Cent. 4th edition

The **Writer's** market. Writer's Digest Bks. $26.95 **808**

1. Authorship—Handbooks, manuals, etc. 2. Publishers and publishing
ISSN 0084-2729

Annual. First published 1926

"This guide to markets for prospective writers covers over 4,000 outlets from book and magazine publishers to script producers and greeting card companies. Each entry offers name and address, type of material sought, editorial needs, submission requirements, payment rates, and other useful data." Nichols. Guide to Ref Books for Sch Media Cent. 4th edition

Zinsser, William Knowlton

On writing well; an informal guide to writing nonfiction. 4th ed rev updated & expanded. HarperCollins Pubs. 1990 288p $19.95; pa $9.95 **808**

1. Rhetoric 2. Authorship
ISBN 0-06-055272-7; 0-06-096831-1 (pa)
LC 90-49530

First published 1976

Among the topics discussed are: style, usage, clutter, imprecision and organization

Includes bibliographic references

Writing to learn. Harper & Row 1988 256p hardcover o.p. paperback available $9 **808**

1. Rhetoric—Study and teaching
ISBN 0-06-091576-5 (pa)   LC 87-45825

"Eschewing theory and philosophical breast-beating, Zinsser uses his own experience to reinforce the fact that clear, eloquent writing can be taught for every subject across the curriculum. A practical manual for teachers and a powerful reminder for everyone that good writing makes possible good thinking." Am Libr

Includes bibliography

808.06   Writing children's literature

Aiken, Joan, 1924-
The way to write for children. St. Martin's Press 1983 93p hardcover o.p. paperback available $6.95   **808.06**
1. Authorship 2. Children's literature—Technique
ISBN 0-312-85840-X (pa)   LC 82-10692
First published 1982 in the United Kingdom
This book is directed to authors who seek to write for children. Aiken's suggestions are intended to aid them "in directing their writing toward specific audiences, beginning with the organization of initial ideas and progressing to the choice of voice, plot, and characters." Publisher's note
"In this crisp, informative and often witty survey of 'the market' Aiken is also giving the customers—teachers, librarians, parents, every one concerned with children's literature of quality—a good general idea of what is available already and of what authors are trying to do." Times Lit Suppl

Gates, Frieda
How to write, illustrate, and design children's books. Lloyd-Simone 1986 155p il $23.50   **808.06**
1. Authorship 2. Children's literature—Technique
ISBN 0-938249-25-8   LC 86-81279
The author starts "with a short history of children's books; chapters on markets and creativity resources follow before the author gets to the heart of her subject—advice on writing, illustration techniques, preparation of a dummy, submissions, contracts, copy styling, and printing. The text is explicit and thorough and is nicely complemented by numerous, well-produced graphics in full color and in black and white." Booklist
Includes bibliography

Worlds of childhood: the art and craft of writing for children; [by] Jean Fritz [et al.]; edited by William Zinsser. Houghton Mifflin 1990 213p (Writer's craft) $19.95; pa $8.95   **808.06**
1. Authorship 2. Children's literature—Technique
ISBN 0-395-51428-2; 0-395-51425-8 (pa)
    LC 89-26815
Analyzed in Essay and general literature index
"In transcriptions of talks given at the New York Public Library, six notable children's authors (Jean Fritz, Maurice Sendak, Jill Krementz, Jack Prelutsky, Rosemary Wells, and Katherine Paterson) examine their sources of inspiration and share their insights about the writing process." Booklist
Includes bibliography

808.1   Rhetoric of poetry

Aristotle, 384-322 B.C.
Poetics   **808.1**
1. Poetics 2. Aesthetics
Hardcover and paperback editions available from various publishers
In this basic work of literary criticism, Aristotle discusses the fundamental principles of poetry and its various forms, emphasizing tragedy and the epic

Deutsch, Babette, 1895-1982
Poetry handbook: a dictionary of terms. 4th ed. Funk & Wagnalls 1974 203p o.p.; HarperCollins Pubs. paperback available $10
    808.1
1. Poetics—Dictionaries
ISBN 0-06-463548-1 (pa)
First published 1957
"The craft of verse described in dictionary form. Terms and techniques are defined and illustrated." N Y Public Libr. Ref Books for Child Collect. 2d edition

Eliot, T. S. (Thomas Stearns), 1888-1965
On poetry and poets. Hippocrene Bks. 1975 c1957 308p $21.50   **808.1**
1. Poetry
ISBN 0-374-92530-5
Also available in paperback from Faber & Faber
Analyzed in Essay and general literature index
Reprint of title first published 1957 by Farrar, Straus
This collection of Eliot's essays includes assessments of Johnson, Goethe and Kipling as well as his views on criticism in general

Higginson, William J., 1938-
The haiku handbook; how to write, share, and teach haiku; [by] William J. Higginson with Penny Harter. McGraw-Hill 1985 331p o.p.; Kodansha Int./USA paperback available $10   **808.1**
1. Haiku
ISBN 4-770-01430-9 (pa)   LC 84-17174
The author "surveys the original and related forms (renga, haibun, senryu), inventors and developers (Basho, Buson, Issa, Shiki), and the numerous variations that later authors, especially in other languages, have wrought on haiku's simple principles. He discusses the many uses—artistic, personal, psychological—that the mode can serve, encouraging the reader all along the way to use the form, to experiment, and thus to express thoughts and feelings. . . . An extensive reference section gives word lists, a glossary, and good bibliographies." Booklist

Packard, William
The poet's dictionary; a handbook of prosody and poetic devices. Harper & Row 1989 212p $22.50   **808.1**
1. Poetics—Dictionaries 2. Versification
ISBN 0-06-016130-2   LC 88-45899
This "dictionary gives succinct definitions enhanced by some historical and other explanatory notes, always followed by examples from familiar sources. . . . Reliability and authenticity are hallmarks of this dictionary." Choice
Includes bibliographic references

The **Princeton** handbook of poetic terms; Alex Preminger, editor; Frank J. Warnke and O.B. Hardison, Jr., associate editors; with a select reading list by T.V.F. Brogan. Princeton Univ. Press 1986 309p $44.50; pa $12.95   **808.1**
1. Poetics—Dictionaries
ISBN 0-691-06659-0; 0-691-01425-6 (pa)
    LC 85-43380

The Princeton handbook of poetic terms—
Continued

"Derived from the classic 'Princeton Encyclopedia of Poetry and Poetics' [1975 edition], this compact handbook will provide students of literature with a great deal of information about prosody and poetic terms. The new 'Princeton Handbook of Poetic Terms' includes definitions and articles of varying length, arranged alphabetically by topic, two columns to a page. In order to keep the volume affordable, the decision was made to omit from the original the entries that dealt with national poetries and their history, periods and schools, and most aspects of literary criticism." Booklist

Sidney, Sir Philip, 1554-1586
An apology for poetry **808.1**

Hardcover and paperback editions available from various publishers

Originally "written 1580-1583 in answer to an attack on poetry by the Puritan Stephen Gosson in 'The school of abuse' (1579). Sidney's essay defines as poetry all imaginative writing. In addition to defending its worth and replying to Puritan accusations against it, Sidney gives his own critical appraisal of the poetry, and drama of the time." Reader's Ency. 3d edition

808.2   Rhetoric of drama

Hauge, Michael
Writing screenplays that sell. McGraw-Hill 1988 xxii, 314p o.p.; HarperPerennial paperback available $12 **808.2**

1. Motion picture plays—Technique
ISBN 0-06-272500-9 (pa)   LC 88-2688

This book provides a "discussion of the craft—characters, story development, etc.—and industry; lays out the all-important details of format; then tells how to market the finished product. Hauge's volume is a detailed manual offering a step-by-step methodology, a scriptual analysis of a hit film, 'The Karate Kid,' and handy chapter summaries." Libr J

808.3   Rhetoric of fiction

Conrad, Barnaby, 1922-
The complete guide to writing fiction; [by] Barnaby Conrad and the staff of the Santa Barbara Writers' Conference. Writer's Digest Bks. 1990 309p $18.95 **808.3**

1. Fiction—Technique
ISBN 0-89879-395-5   LC 90-12287

"Keynote editorials, gleaned from speeches given at the annual Santa Barbara Writers' Conference, are written by a range of authors, including Danielle Steel, Ray Bradbury, Eudora Welty, and Alice Adams. This nicely organized tutorial on crafting the major elements of a novel features further significant suggestions on revising a manuscript, selling short stories, hiring an agent, marketing the manuscript, and handling rejection." Booklist

Gardner, John, 1933-1982
The art of fiction; notes on craft for young writers. Knopf 1984 224p $17.95; pa $9 **808.3**

1. Fiction—Technique
ISBN 0-394-50469-0; 0-679-73403-1 (pa)
            LC 83-47850

"This essay distills the late Gardner's ripest thoughts about what fiction is and how to go about learning to write it. The initial section deals with 'literary-aesthetic theory,' the second with 'the fictional process.' . . . The book concludes with two sets of exercises, one for class use and one for individual use. Recommended for any young writer or writing class, and for all readers who care about the craft of fiction." Booklist

On becoming a novelist; foreword by Raymond Carver. Harper & Row 1983 xxv, 150p hardcover o.p. paperback available $10 **808.3**

1. Authorship 2. Fiction—Technique
ISBN 0-06-091126-3 (pa)   LC 82-48662

The author "explores the dynamic chemistry at the heart of the writer's creative process. Gardner's book is a superbly written, thoroughly original, eminently useful volume." Choice

How to write tales of horror, fantasy & science fiction; edited by J.N. Williamson. Writer's Digest Bks. 1987 242p hardcover o.p. paperback available $12.95 **808.3**

1. Science fiction—Technique 2. Fantastic fiction—Technique 3. Horror—Fiction—Technique
ISBN 0-89879-483-8 (pa)   LC 87-6068

"From the pens of master storytellers such as Robert Bloch, Ray Bradbury, and Marion Zimmer Bradley comes valuable advice to the writer starting out in the field of speculative fiction. The emphasis here is on the creative process rather than the business of writing. . . . This book is both indispensable for the novice writer and informative (and fun) for the fan of the various genres discussed." Booklist

Includes bibliography

Irwin, Hadley
Writing young adult novels; [by] Hadley Irwin and Jeannette Eyerly. Writer's Digest Bks. 1988 197p $14.95 **808.3**

1. Authorship 2. Fiction—Technique 3. Young adults' literature—Technique
ISBN 0-89879-313-0   LC 87-29790

The authors "encourage and coach would-be YA writers with thoughtful advice on the youth market, handling sensitive issues, avoiding stereotypes, and submitting to publishers. They cover plot, pace, transitions, grammar, and other nuts and bolts aptly, and avoid too many imperatives, allowing novice writers room for trial and error." Libr J

Keating, H. R. F. (Henry Reymond Fitzwalter), 1926-
Writing crime fiction. St. Martin's Press 1987 88p $13.95; pa $8.95 **808.3**

1. Mystery and detective stories—Technique
ISBN 0-312-01115-6; 0-312-05542-0 (pa)
            LC 87-16346

First published 1986 in the United Kingdom

Keating, H. R. F. (Henry Reymond Fitzwalter), 1926——*Continued*

The author "surveys the history and craft of crime writing. He traces the genre from Poe and cites those examples most worthy of close reading. Sections are devoted to such specialities as detective, police procedural, crime farce, and romantic suspense stories. There are many books on writing crime fiction . . . that may explain mechanics and technique more fully, but this conveys well the thinking behind an effective entertainment. For mystery readers, too." Libr J

Knight, Damon Francis, 1922-

Creating short fiction. Writer's Digest Bks. 1981 215p il hardcover o.p. paperback available $11.95   **808.3**

1. Fiction—Technique 2. Short story
ISBN 0-89879-166-9 (pa)   LC 80-26268

The author "deals with subjects ranging from the psychological bases of writing to technical matters of plot and characterization to short story trouble-shooting. . . . The book includes an annotated Knight story and other interesting features." Libr J

Includes bibliography

Nabokov, Vladimir Vladimirovich, 1899-1977

Lectures on literature; [by] Vladimir Nabokov; edited by Fredson Bowers; introduction by John Updike. Harcourt Brace Jovanovich 1980 xxviii, 385p il $19.95; pa $12.95   **808.3**

1. Fiction—History and criticism
ISBN 0-15-149597-1; 0-15-649589-9 (pa) LC 79-3690

Analyzed in Essay and general literature index

Companion volume Lectures on Russian literature, entered in class 891.7

"A Bruccoli-Clark book"

In the early 1950s, before Nabokov became a famous writer, he taught literature at Wellesley and Cornell. The editor, with the help of Nabokov's wife and son, has collected seven lectures on "Mansfield Park," "Bleak House," "Madame Bovary," "The Strange Case of Dr. Jekyll and Mr. Hyde," "The Walk by Swann's Place," "The Metamorphosis" and "Ulysses." There are two additional lectures on other topics related to literature. The volume includes a sample examination for the course and pages of original manuscripts with maps and diagrams which the author used to illustrate his lectures

The **Western** writer's handbook; edited by James L. Collins. Johnson Bks. 1987 154p $12.95; pa $7.95   **808.3**

1. Western stories—Technique
ISBN 1-55566-023-1; 1-55566-013-4 (pa)
      LC 87-81394

Contributors "offer instruction on how to write Western literature, focusing on the importance of authentic settings, the historical accuracy of the western ambience, treatment of language, and more. Marketing one's book or article, writing for specific audiences (e.g., television, young adult), and utilizing the various methods of research are also discussed cogently. A solid guidebook for budding practitioners." Booklist

Writing mysteries; a handbook; by the Mystery Writers of America; edited by Sue Grafton. Writer's Digest Bks. 1992 208p $18.95   **808.3**

1. Mystery and detective stories—Technique
ISBN 0-89879-502-8   LC 91-34403

"Popular mystery novelist Sue Grafton has pulled together words of wisdom from other celebrated whodunit authors. The excellent suggestions include those on collaborating, establishing a writing schedule, constructing dialogue, doing research, setting the scene, pacing, and selling the finished product through an agent or directly to a publisher. Among the contributors are Bill Granger, Tony Hillerman, Sara Paretsky, Phyllis Whitney, and other members of the Mystery Writers of America." Booklist

Includes bibliographic references

808.5   Rhetoric of speech

Applewhite, Ashton

And I quote; the definitive collection of quotes, sayings, and jokes for the contemporary speechmaker; [by] Ashton Applewhite, William R. Evans III, Andrew Frothingham. St. Martin's Press 1992 xliii, 499p $24.95   **808.5**

1. Public speaking 2. American wit and humor
ISBN 0-312-06897-2   LC 91-36742

"A Thomas Dunne book"

"This collection of over 10,000 quotes is geared to those who seek something witty and appropriate for public presentations. Following some introductory guidance on presenting effective speeches, there is an outline of the book's overall structure and an alphabetical list/index of subject categories. Most quotations are 'one-liners' that may be clever, amusing, profound, or insightful." Libr J

For a fuller review see: Booklist, March 15, 1992

Cook, Jeff Scott

The elements of speechwriting and public speaking. Macmillan 1990 242p il $17.95; pa $6   **808.5**

1. Public speaking
ISBN 0-02-527791-X; 0-02-042782-4 (pa)
      LC 89-31923

The author offers "advice on topic selection, speech construction, and delivery techniques. His suggestions are practical and can be used by a wide audience, ranging from students taking Speech 101 to business executives wanting to improve their presentation skills. Throughout the book are examples from a variety of sources that illustrate specific points explained in the text." Libr J

Includes bibliographic references

Cooper, Morton, 1931-

Winning with your voice. Fell 1990 166p il pa $12.95   **808.5**

1. Voice
ISBN 0-8119-0659-0 (pa)   LC 90-3089

The author "deals seriously with voice production. All kinds of speaking problems are addressed, including stuttering, throat clearing, and hoarseness, and exercises are suggested to eliminate them. The author stresses proper voice placement and gives detailed instruction on how

Cooper, Morton, 1931——*Continued*
to achieve it. Recommended for those who use their voices a lot or whose work requires a great deal of public speaking." Libr J

Includes bibliographic references

Detz, Joan
How to write and give a speech; a practical guide for executives, PR people, managers, fund-raisers, politicians, educators, and anyone who has to make every word count. 2nd ed rev & updated. St. Martin's Press 1992 204p $21.95; pa $8.95 **808.5**
1. Public speaking
ISBN 0-312-08504-4; 0-312-08218-5 (pa)
LC 92-25478
First published 1984
Among the various aspects of public speaking discussed are: tips on topic focus, audience assessment, humor, delivery techniques and media coverage

Hoff, Ron
I can see you naked; a new revised edition, of the national bestseller on making fearless presentations. new rev ed. Andrews & McMeel 1992 326p il $16.95; pa $9.95 **808.5**
1. Public speaking
ISBN 0-8362-8000-8; 0-8362-8008-3 (pa)
LC 92-26641
First published 1988
This "reassuring book is easy for beginners to read and understand. Hoff stresses putting oneself in the listener's shoes, including how to appeal to the audience's concerns, how to make eye contact, and how to let down your guard and really communicate. Sure to be useful." Libr J

Includes bibliographic references

Monkhouse, Bob
Just say a few words; the complete speaker's handbook; illustrations by Ian Dicks. Evans & Co. 1991 189p il $18.95 **808.5**
1. Public speaking
ISBN 0-87131-661-7
LC 91-2346
While the author "gives the usual hints to speakers—rehearse, practice breathing techniques, concentrate—his main thrust seems to be to give advice on making a speech amusing as well as interesting and informative." Libr J

Prochnow, Herbert Victor, 1931-
Speaker's & toastmaster's handbook. Prima Pub. & Communications 1990 357p $19.95; pa 14.95 **808.5**
1. Public speaking 2. Anecdotes 3. Quotations
ISBN 1-55958-038-0; 1-55958-146-8 (pa)
LC 89-48545
"Sections include humorous stories (by topic), definitions, quips, arresting but little-known facts, and proverbs. The book can be of great help in creating a

speech that seizes and holds the attention of its audience." Libr J

Simmons, S. H. (Sylvia H.)
How to be the life of the podium; openers, closers & everything in between to keep them listening. AMACOM 1991 318p $23.95 **808.5**
1. Public speaking 2. Wit and humor
ISBN 0-8144-5069-5
LC 91-23684
The author "tells the neophyte how to capture the audience's attention, how to use quotes and one-liners, and how to exit gracefully while still retaining the audience's interest. The quotes and one-liners deal with general topics and are adaptable to many occasions and groups. Attention here is on crafting a speech rather than delivery." Libr J

Vassallo, Wanda
Speaking with confidence; a guide for public speakers. Betterway Publs. 1990 176p il pa $7.95 **808.5**
1. Public speaking
ISBN 1-55870-147-8
LC 89-29921
The author's "emphasis is on *preparation*, and herein lies her strength. She discusses relaxation techniques and exercises in breath control and voice production. Her audiovisual checklist is a valuable addition. She also considers the many different types of speeches, including impromptu remarks, persuasive speeches, dedications, and introductions; notes how they differ, and delineates the best way to approach each one." Libr J

Includes bibliographic references

808.8 Literature—Collections

Daughters of Africa; an international anthology of words and writings by women of African descent: from the ancient Egyptian to the present; edited and with an introduction by Margaret Busby. Pantheon Bks. 1992 li, 1089p $35 **808.8**
1. Literature—Collections 2. Black authors 3. Women authors
ISBN 0-679-41634-X
LC 92-54116
Arranged chronologically, this anthology includes writings drawn from a variety of genres by women of African descent. Biographical headnotes, annotations and bibliographies are included

The **Norton** book of modern war; edited by Paul Fussell. Norton 1991 830p $24.95 **808.8**
1. Literature—Collections 2. War in literature
ISBN 0-393-02909-3
LC 90-36495
This anthology of 20th century prose and poetry about war covers World War I, the Spanish Civil War, World War II, the Korean War and Vietnam. Authors represented include Heinrich Böll, Marguerite Duras, Ernest Hemingway, Ron Kovic, Norman Mailer, Wilfred Owen and Siegfried Sassoon

The **Paris** review anthology; edited by George Plimpton. Norton 1990 686p il $25   **808.8**

1. Literature—Collections
ISBN 0-393-02769-4   LC 89-35274

"This anthology has historical as well as literary significance since it reminds readers how a new era in writing began. The *Paris Review* was founded in 1953 as a counterblast to what has been called the Age of Criticism; thus, almost all the 187 pieces in this collection are fiction and poetry, with essays about authors replaced by interviews with them." Libr J

The **Penguin** book of First World War prose; edited and with an introduction by Jon Glover & Jon Silkin. Viking 1990 c1989 619p o.p.; Penguin Bks. paperback available $11.95   **808.8**

1. World War, 1914-1918—Literature and the war
ISBN 0-14-005802-8 (pa)   LC 89-51463

First published 1989 in the United Kingdom

"The editors have chosen the prose of nearly 100 individuals who, in their correspondence or published work, attempted to deal with the issues raised by their involvement in the war. The material included is from works of fiction, both best sellers and little-known works, as well as autobiographical sources and letters. Still, the collection should not be viewed merely as war stories. The authors selected are representative of the nations involved in the war and include Sassoon, Remarque, Colette, and Willa Cather, to name just a few. Each selection is introduced by a brief biography of the author." Libr J

The **Portable** medieval reader; edited, and with an introduction by James Bruce Ross and Mary Martin McLaughlin. Viking 1949 690p o.p.; Penguin Bks. paperback available $9.95   **808.8**

1. Literature, Medieval—Collections
ISBN 0-14-015046-3 (pa)

Anthology of "the writings of men and women between the years 1050 and 1500. The aim of the editors is to give, by means of selections from contemporary reports, a picture of the whole structure of the Middle Ages. The less known chronicles have been used whenever possible. The language throughout is modern." Commonweal

Includes bibliography

The **Portable** Renaissance reader; edited, and with an introduction by James Bruce Ross and Mary Martin McLaughlin. Viking 1953 756p o.p.; Penguin Bks. paperback available $9.95   **808.8**

1. Literature—Collections 2. Renaissance
ISBN 0-14-015061-7 (pa)

The editors have covered both the Italian and the North European Renaissance, from about 1400 to 1600. Material is collected under five general headings: An age of gold; The city of man; The study of man; The book of nature; The kingdom of God

Includes bibliographies

Pound, Ezra, 1885-1972
Translations; with an introduction by Hugh Kenner. Greenwood Press 1978 448p $55   **808.8**

1. Literature—Collections
ISBN 0-313-21169-8   LC 78-13153

First published 1954 by New Directions with title: The translations of Ezra Pound; this is a reprint of the enlarged edition published 1963

This collection includes translations from Anglo-Saxon, Chinese, Egyptian, French, Hindi, Italian, Latin and Provencal originals. Fifteen Nō plays are included, with Fenollosa's commentary. The poet has chosen for translation writers whose work marked, in his opinion, a significant turning point in the development of world literature, or, key poems which exemplify what is most vital in a given period or genre

The **Sophisticated** cat; a gathering of stories, poems, and miscellaneous writings about cats; chosen by Joyce Carol Oates and Daniel Halpern. Dutton 1992 391p $23   **808.8**

1. Literature—Collections 2. Cats
ISBN 0-525-93522-3   LC 92-52884

"A William Abrahams book"

"The anthology contains about 100 stories and poems by a diverse group of authors. It begins with classic European writers such as Colette, Anton Chekhov, and Emile Zola. This is followed by 19th-century poets including Emily Dickinson, John Keats, and Alfred, Lord Tennyson. Next, a sampling of 20th-century poets such as T.S. Eliot and W.B. Yeats is offered. Charles Baudelaire and Rainer Maria Rilke honor cats in translated poetry. Joyce Carol Oates, Ted Hughes, Ursula K. Le Guin, and other contemporary writers contribute their insights on cats." Libr J

808.81   Poetry—Collections

An **Anthology** of world poetry; edited by Mark Van Doren; in English translations by Chaucer, Swinburne, Dowson, Symons, Rossetti, Waley, Herrick, Pope, Francis Thompson, E. A. Robinson and others. rev and enl ed. Harcourt Brace & Co. 1936 lxii, 1467p $49.95   **808.81**

1. Poetry—Collections
ISBN 0-15-107665-0

First published 1928 by A. C. Boni

This is a selection from the best English translations of poetry of sixteen ancient and modern languages. Arranged in chronological sequence from the thirty-fifth century B.C. to the twentieth century A.D.

The author "has handled a difficult task with an admirable blend of comprehensiveness and selective taste." Springfield Repub

A **Book** of love poetry; edited and with an introduction by Jon Stallworthy. Oxford Univ. Press 1974 c1973 393p $24.95; pa $11.95   **808.81**

1. Love poetry
ISBN 0-19-519774-9; 0-19-504232-8 (pa)

First published 1973 in the United Kingdom with title: The Penguin book of love poetry

A Book of love poetry—*Continued*

A collection of poems written during the past 2000 years arranged thematically from young love to the "long look back" of the aged

Includes indexes of poets, translators, titles and first lines

The Columbia Granger's index to poetry; indexing anthologies published through June 30, 1993; edited by Edith P. Hazen. 10th ed, completely rev. Columbia Univ. Press 1994 2150p $199 **808.81**

1. Poetry—Indexes 2. English poetry—Indexes

ISBN 0-231-08408-0   LC 93-38761

8th and 9th editions also available as part of Columbia Granger's world of poetry on CD-ROM, which also includes The Columbia Granger's guide to poetry anthologies, by William Katz and Linda Sternberg Katz

First edition, edited by Edith Granger, published 1904 by A. C. McClurg with title: Index to poetry and recitations. Fifth through eighth editions have title Granger's index to poetry

This work is organized into title and first line index, author index, subject index and a list of anthologies with their symbols. Coverage includes poetry translated into English

Confucius to Cummings; an anthology of poetry; edited by Ezra Pound & Marcella Spann. New Directions 1964 xxii, 353p $14.95; pa $12.95 **808.81**

1. Poetry—Collections

ISBN 0-8112-0352-2; 0-8112-0155-4 (pa)

This anthology of poetry of various ages and cultures is a statement by example of the 'Pound critical canon.' Nearly a hundred poets are represented, a number of them in Pound's own translations, with emphasis on the Greek and Latin, Chinese, Troubadour, Renaissance, and Elizabethan. Pound has also supplied commentary on certain of the poems and poets

Index to children's poetry; a title, subject, author, and first line index to poetry in collections for children and youth; compiled by John E. and Sara W. Brewton. Wilson, H.W. 1942-1965 3v **808.81**

1. Poetry—Indexes

Basic volume published 1942 $63 (ISBN 0-8242-0021-7); first supplement published 1954 $40 (ISBN 0-8242-0022-5); second supplement published 1965 $40 (ISBN 0-8242-0023-3)

The main volume indexes 15,000 poems by 2,500 authors in 130 collections. The two supplements analyze another 15,000 poems by 2700 authors in 151 collections

"This tool is an invaluable reference source." Peterson. Ref Books for Child

Index to poetry for children and young people; a title, subject, author, and first line index to poetry in collections for children and young people. Wilson, H.W. 1972-1994 5v **808.81**

1. Poetry—Indexes

A continuation of: Index to children's poetry, entered above. The volume published 1972 covering 1964-1969 compiled by John E. and Sara W. Brewton and G. Meredith Blackburn III $43 (ISBN 0-8242-0435-2); 1970-

1975 published 1978 compiled by John E. Brewton, G. Meredith Blackburn III and Lorraine A. Blackburn $43 (ISBN 0-8242-0621-5); 1976-1981 published 1984 compiled by John E. Brewton, G. Meredith Blackburn III and Lorraine A. Blackburn $43 (ISBN 0-8242-0681-9); 1982-1987 published 1989 compiled by G. Meredith Blackburn III and Lorraine A. Blackburn $48 (ISBN 0-8242-0773-4); 1988-1992 published 1994 compiled by G. Meredith Blackburn III $62 (ISBN 0-8242-0861-7)

Each volume analyzes approximately 10,000 poems by some 2,000 authors in more than 110 collections. Over 2,000 subject headings are used in each volume

The Oxford book of war poetry; chosen and edited by John Stallworthy. Oxford Univ. Press 1984 xxxi, 358p $29.95 **808.81**

1. War poetry 2. Poetry—Collections

ISBN 0-19-214125-2   LC 83-19303

"This comprehensive anthology focuses on poetic treatment of warfare ranging from the battlefields of ancient history to the conflicts in Vietnam, Northern Ireland, and El Salvador." Univ Press Books for Second Sch Libr

This collection "reminds one of the large numbers and great variety of war poems from many centuries that are very good poems. Mr. Stallworthy's selections include most of the best, at least the best in English." N Y Times Book Rev

Includes bibliography

The Penguin book of women poets; edited by Carol Cosman, Joan Keefe, Kathleen Weaver; consulting editors, Joanna Banker, Doris Earnshaw, Deirdre Lashgari. Viking 1979 c1978 399p o.p.; Penguin Bks. paperback available $9.95 **808.81**

1. Poetry—Collections 2. Women poets

ISBN 0-14-058533-8 (pa)   LC 78-26699

First published 1978 in the United Kingdom

This collection "spans 3500 years and 40 literary traditions, from ancient Egypt to modern America. The editors are to be praised for their careful, extensive research." Libr J

Poetry index annual; prepared by the Editorial Board, Roth Publishing, Inc. Poetry Index Press $54.99 **808.81**

1. Poetry—Indexes

Annual. First published 1982 by Granger Book Company

"Each annual volume aims to index, by author, title, and subject, all anthologies of poetry published during the year preceding the date of issue (i.e., 1982 vol. indexes anthologies published 1981). Issues are not cumulative." Sheehy. Guide to Ref Books. 10th edition

808.82 Drama—Collections

The Best American short plays; edited by Howard Stein and Glenn Young. Applause Theatre Bk. Pubs. $29.95, pa $14.95 **808.82**

1. Drama—Collections 2. One act plays

ISSN 1062-7561

This series of annual collections was begun in 1937 under the editorship of Margaret Mayorga with title: Best one-act plays, and published by Dodd, Mead through 1955 (starting in 1953 title changed to The best short plays). Beacon Press published the volumes from 1956

The Best American short plays—*Continued*
through 1961 when publication was suspended. Resumed 1968 under the editorship of Stanley Richards. From 1981 through 1989 edited by Ramon Delgado. Changed to current title and editors with 1990/1991 volume. Volumes prior to 1988 o.p. Apply to publisher for availability and price of retrospective annuals

In addition to the plays each annual contains brief biographical and bibliographical data about dramatists represented

The Best plays of [date]: The Otis Guernsey/Burns Mantle theater yearbook; edited by Otis L. Guernsey, Jr. and Jeffrey Sweet; illustrated with photographs and with drawings by Hirschfeld. Limelight Eds. $39.95   **808.82**

1. Drama—Collections 2. Theater—United States
ISSN 1071-6971

Annual. First published 1920. Variant titles: The Burns Mantle theater yearbook; The Applause/best plays theater yearbook

Some back volumes published by Dodd, Mead available from Applause Theatre Bk. Pubs.; reprints of older annuals available from Ayer; for full information on availability and price contact publishers

The yearbook gives listings of casts and technical personnel for on- and off-Broadway productions, a summary of the season, synopses and lengthy extracts of dialogue from the best plays, and facts and figures on the New York and regional theater

Drury's guide to best plays. 4th ed, [by] James M. Salem. Scarecrow Press 1987 480p $39.50   **808.82**

1. Drama—Indexes
ISBN 0-8108-1980-5   LC 87-380

First published 1953 by F. K. W. Drury

This work includes 1500 entries arranged by playwright. A brief synopsis of each play and royalty information is provided. Coverage ranges from ancient Greece to the 1984-1985 theatrical season

Nine plays of the modern theater; with an introduction by Harold Clurman. Grove Press 1981 896p pa $16.95   **808.82**

1. Drama—Collections
ISBN 0-8021-5032-2   LC 79-52121

This anthology includes plays by Brecht, Beckett, Dürrenmatt, Genet, Pinter, Ionesco, Mrozek, Stoppard, and Mamet

Ottemiller's index to plays in collections; an author and title index to plays appearing in collections published between 1900 and 1985. 7th ed, revised & enlarged by Billie M. Connor and Helene G. Mochedlover. Scarecrow Press 1988 564p $42.50   **808.82**

1. Drama—Indexes
ISBN 0-8108-2081-1   LC 87-34160

First edition compiled by John H. Ottemiller, published 1943 by H.W. Wilson

This index analyzes 1,350 collections and "covers plays by 2,555 authors. The arrangement is by playwright, with lists of plays and collections in which each is designated by symbols. A list of collections analyzed and key to symbols and a title index complete the volume." Nichols. Guide to Ref Books for Sch Media Cent. 4th edition

Our dramatic heritage; edited by Philip G. Hill. v4-6. Fairleigh Dickinson Univ. Press 1989-1992 3v v4 $65, v5-6 ea $55   **808.82**

1. Drama—Collections   LC 81-65294

Also available volumes 1-3 covering classical, Renaissance, golden age and eighteenth century drama

Contents: v4 Romanticism and realism (0-8386-3267-X); v5 Reactions to realism (0-8386-3411-7); v6 Expressing the inexpressible (0-8386-3421-4)

Among the dramatists represented are: Goethe, Ibsen, Strindberg, Brecht, Feydeau and Pirandello

Play index. Wilson, H.W. 1953-1988 7v   **808.82**

1. Drama—Indexes
ISSN 0554-3037

First published 1953 covering the years 1949-1952, and edited by Dorothy Herbert West and Dorothy Margaret Peake $20. Additional volumes: 1953-1960 $25 edited by Estelle A. Fidell and Dorothy Margaret Peake; 1961-1967 $28 edited by Estelle A. Fidell; 1968-1972 $33 edited by Estelle A. Fidell; 1973-1977 $41 edited by Estelle A. Fidell; 1978-1982 $48 edited by Juliette Yaakov; 1983-1987 $58 edited by Juliette Yaakov and John Greenfieldt; 1988-1992 $80 edited by Juliette Yaakov and John Greenfieldt

Play index indexes plays in collections and single plays; one-act and full-length plays; radio, television, and Broadway plays; plays for amateur production; plays for children, young adults, and adults. It is divided into four parts. Part I is an author, title, and subject index; the author or main entry includes the title of the play, brief synopsis of the plot, number of acts and scenes, size of cast, number of sets, and bibliographic information. Part II is a list of collections indexed, and Part III, a cast analysis, lists plays by the type of cast and number of players required. Part IV is a directory of publishers and distributors

"This index is an excellent source for locating published plays." Nichols. Guide to Ref Books for Sch Media Cent. 4th edition

Thirty famous one-act plays; edited by Bennett Cerf and Van H. Cartmell; with an introduction by Richard Watts, Jr. Modern Lib. 1949 c1943 xxii, 617p $16   **808.82**

ISBN 0-394-60473-3   LC 49-9032

"Modern Library giant"

A reprint of a book first published 1943 by Garden City Publishing Company

This anthology contains plays by Anatole France, Strindberg, Schnitzler, O'Neill, Kaufman, Coward, Saroyan and Irwin Shaw. Biographical sketches of each playwright are included

808.83   Fiction—Collections

Short story index. Wilson, H.W. $90 per year   **808.83**

1. Short stories—Indexes
ISSN 0360-9774   LC 75-649762

Also available Short story index: collections indexed 1900-1978 $40 (ISBN 0-8242-0643-6)

Basic volume edited by Dorothy E. Cook and Isabel S. Monro published 1953 $50 (ISBN 0-8242-0384-4); Supplementary volumes: 1950-1954 edited by Dorothy E.

Short story index—*Continued*

Cook and Estelle A. Fidell $40 (ISBN 0-8242-0385-2); 1955-1958 edited by Estelle A. Fidell and Esther V. Flory $40 (ISBN 0-8242-0386-0); 1959-1963 edited by Estelle A. Fidell $40 (ISBN 0-8242-0387-9); 1964-1968 edited by Estelle A. Fidell $45 (ISBN 0-8242-0399-2); 1969-1973 edited by Estelle A. Fidell $60 (ISBN 0-8242-0497-2); 1974-1978 edited by Gary L. Bogart $90; 1979-1983 edited by Juliette Yaakov $100; 1984-1988 edited by Juliette Yaakov $130. Beginning 1974 issued annually with five-year cumulations

This index offers a single-alphabet listing of stories by author, title and subject. The List of collections indexed provides full bibliographic information. Includes a Directory of periodicals and a Directory of publishers and distributors

"An invaluable access to short stories in collections." Ref Sources for Small & Medium-sized Libr. 5th edition

808.85 Speeches—Collections

Lend me your ears; great speeches in history; selected and introduced by William Safire. Norton 1992 957p $35
808.85

1. Speeches, addresses, etc.
ISBN 0-393-03368-6   LC 92-2699

Included in this "volume are 201 great speeches spanning the centuries from the likes of Cicero and Jesus to Ronald Reagan and Boris Yeltsin. Librarians will quickly locate the most famous, including speeches by Lincoln, both Roosevelts, Kennedy, King, and Malcolm X, as well as numerous significant but lesser-known examples of oratorial eloquence. Safire, . . . has grouped his selections chronologically into 13 thematic categories." Libr J

Sutton, Roberta Briggs

Speech index; an index to 259 collections of world famous orations and speeches for various occasions. 4th ed rev & enl. Scarecrow Press 1966 947p $59.50   **808.85**

ISBN 0-8108-0138-8

Supplement, 1966-1980, by Charity Mitchell, published 1982 $45 (ISBN 0-8108-1518-4)

First published 1935 by the H.W. Wilson Company

"Speeches are indexed by orator, type of speech, and by subject, with a selected list of titles given in the appendix. Particularly useful for amateur speakers in locating examples to use in preparing a speech and models they can adapt to their needs." Ref Sources for Small & Medium-sized Libr. 5th edition

The **World's** great speeches; edited by Lewis Copeland and Lawrence W. Lamm. 3rd enl ed. Dover Publs. 1973 pa $11.95
808.85

1. Speeches, addresses, etc.
ISBN 0-486-20468-5

First published 1942 by Garden City Pub. Co.

Contains 255 speeches by 216 speakers arranged under the following headings: Great speeches of earlier times; Great speeches of recent times; Great speeches of our own day; Informal speeches

Includes a Topical index, Index by nations and Index of speakers

808.87 Satire and humor— Collections

Asimov, Isaac, 1920-1992

Isaac Asimov's treasury of humor; a lifetime collection of favorite jokes, anecdotes, and limericks with copious notes on how to tell them and why. Houghton Mifflin 1971 431p pa $10.95   **808.87**

1. Wit and humor 2. Jokes
ISBN 0-395-28412-0

"640 selections are classified under 11 categories: anticlimax, shaggy dog, paradox, putdown, word play, tables turned, Jewish, ethnic, religion, marriage, and bawdy. . . . The subject index includes multiple references to adultery, army life, bigotry, death, Englishmen, farmers, psychiatrists, rabbis, stereotypes, and wives, but most of all to 'Me'—with a 'see' reference under Asimov, Isaac (see Me)." Wilson Libr Bull

808.88 Collections of miscellaneous writings

Bartlett, John, 1820-1905

Familiar quotations. Little, Brown $40
808.88

1. Quotations

First published 1855. Periodically revised. Editors vary

"Comprehensive collection of quotations arranged . . . in chronological order with author and keyword indexes." N Y Public Libr. Ref Books for Child Collect. 2d edition

The **Beacon** book of quotations by women; compiled by Rosalie Maggio. Beacon Press 1992 390p $40   **808.88**

1. Quotations 2. Women—Quotations
ISBN 0-8070-6764-4   LC 92-4697

This volume "contains quotations selected for 'their memorability, their original use of language, their brevity, their ability to shatter conventional patterns of speech or thought, and their potential usefulness to readers needing quotations for speaking and writing.' Arranged alphabetically by topic, this collection includes approximately 8000 quotations under more than 750 topics. The author, source, and date follow each quotation. This work includes cross references to relevant topics, a name index, and a subject index." Libr J

For a fuller review see: Booklist, Oct. 15, 1992

Boller, Paul F.

They never said it; a book of fake quotes, misquotes, and misleading attributions; [by] Paul F. Boller, Jr., and John George. Oxford Univ. Press 1989 xxv, 159p $19.95; pa $6.95   **808.88**

1. Quotations 2. Errors 3. Literary forgeries
ISBN 0-19-505541-1; 0-19-506469-0 (pa)

LC 88-22115

A look at misquotes and misleading attributions. In an alphabetical list of attributees' names or titles the authors expose the truth behind more than 200 phony quotations

Carruth, Gorton
The Harper book of American quotations;
[by] Gorton Carruth and Eugene Ehrlich.
Harper & Row 1988 821p o.p.   **808.88**
1. Quotations   LC 88-45018
Available from Outlet Book Company with title:
American Quotations

"A Hudson Group book"

This book contains "quotations about: American
places, including separate categories for regions, states,
and cities; American events, including the Revolution,
the Civil War, the world wars, and the space age; American wisdom, including ideas and beliefs—reverent and
irreverent—on liberty, religion, politics, sports, and government; American men and women—the famous and
the infamous; American art, literature, and amusements."
Publisher's note

The **Columbia** Granger's dictionary of poetry
quotations; edited by Edith P. Hazen.
Columbia Univ. Press 1992 1132p $99
     808.88
1. Quotations
ISBN 0-231-07546-4   LC 91-42240
This work contains the "most memorable lines written
by the greatest poets of English. Quotations are organized
alphabetically by poet, and coded so one can find full
text in hundreds of current anthologies. With keyword
and subject indexing." Univ Press Books for Public and
Second Sch Libr

The **Concise** Oxford dictionary of quotations.
2nd ed. Oxford Univ. Press 1982 c1981
464p pa $9.95   **808.88**
1. Quotations
ISBN 0-19-281324-2
First published 1964
Collected here are 5800 quotations by 1100 authors
from around the world ranging in time from the 8th
century BC to the 1970's. Arrangement is alphabetical
by the names of authors with sections such as
Anonymous, Ballads, The Bible, the Mass in Latin, etc.
included in the alphabetical order. Foreign quotations are
given in the original language followed by the English
translation. Indexed by key words

The **Dictionary** of war quotations; compiled
and edited by Justin Wintle. Free Press
1989 506p $35   **808.88**
1. War—Quotations
ISBN 0-02-935411-0   LC 89-16818
The editor has "assembled over 4000 quotations offering a history of attitudes as well as behavior. Ranging
from paragraphs to aphorisms, they present war's enduring mix of fascination and horror. The *Dictionary* is
organized in three sections. Part I deals with the general
nature of war. Part II comments on wars and battles
from the Stone Age to the Falklands, with no significant
omissions. Part III features personalities." Libr J
Includes bibliographic references

The **Macmillan** book of proverbs, maxims,
and famous phrases; selected and arranged
by Burton Stevenson. Macmillan 1987
2957p $75   **808.88**
1. Proverbs 2. Quotations
ISBN 0-02-614500-6   LC 86-16275
First published 1948 with title: The Home book of
proverbs, maxims and familiar phrases. This is a reprint
of the 1965 edition

"Provides sources for more than 73,000 English
proverbs and traces their development and variations.
Arranged by subject or key word." N Y Public Libr
Book of How & Where to Look It Up

The **Macmillan** dictionary of quotations.
Macmillan 1989 790p $35   **808.88**
1. Quotations
ISBN 0-02-511931-1   LC 89-12237
This "dictionary includes about 20,000 quotations
grouped in more than 1100 categories. Approximately
100 categories are biographical. . . . Keyword and
biographical indexes are included." Libr J
For a fuller review see: Booklist, Jan. 15, 1990

Magill, Frank Northen, 1907-
Magill's quotations in context; by Frank
N. Magill; associate editor, Tench Francis
Tilghman: [1st-2nd ser] Salem Press
1965-1969 4v each 2v set $75   **808.88**
1. Quotations
ISBN 0-89356-132-0; 0-89356-136-3
"Two thousand quotations in the *First Series* and
1,500 in the *Second Series* come from the classics, fiction, poetry, drama, and nonfiction. Entries, arranged alphabetically by key word, give source, author, date of
first appearance, and type of work, followed by explanations and comments. The value of the work is not in
its number of quotations, which are far fewer than in
most one-volume works, but in the unique information
the volumes provide." Nichols. Guide to Ref Books for
Sch Media Cent. 4th edition

A **New** dictionary of quotations on historical
principles from ancient and modern
sources; selected and edited by H. L.
Mencken. Knopf 1942 1347p $74.50
     808.88
1. Quotations
ISBN 0-394-40079-8
Quotations in prose and poetry arranged under subjects. The quotations are dated and names of authors
and titles of books quoted are given in full

The **New** international dictionary of
quotations; selected by Margaret Miner
and Hugh Rawson. 2nd ed. Dutton 1993
480p $25   **808.88**
1. Quotations
ISBN 0-525-93599-1   LC 92-43136
First published 1986 with Rawson's name appearing
first
This volume "includes almost 4,000 quotations from
ancient times to the present. Most of the selections are
familiar—from the Bible, Shakespeare, other famous
writers, statesmen, and celebrities, as well as the wise
and prolific anonymous. Quotations are arranged by subject. . . . Recommended as a supplementary purchase
for libraries." Booklist

The **New** Quotable woman; compiled and
edited by Elaine Partnow. completely rev
and updated. Facts on File 1992 xxii,
714p $40   **808.88**
1. Quotations 2. Women—Quotations
ISBN 0-8160-2134-1   LC 91-25960

The New Quotable woman—*Continued*
A revised combined edition of: The quotable woman, from Eve to 1799 (1986) and The quotable woman, 1800-1981 (1983)

"More than 2,500 women are represented by over 15,000 quotations." Libr J

For a fuller review see Booklist, Oct. 15, 1992

The New York Public Library book of twentieth-century American quotations; edited by Stephen Donadio [et al.] Warner Bks. 1992 622p $24.95   **808.88**
1. Quotations
ISBN 0-446-51639-2   LC 91-50395

"A Stonesong Press book"

"This compendium's broad subject areas, supported by a detailed index, allow readers to find quotations that delineate a wide array of aspects of American life—from the comic to the serious, the mundane to the important. A must." SLJ

For a fuller review see: Booklist, Jan. 15, 1993

The Oxford book of aphorisms; chosen by John Gross. Oxford Univ. Press 1983 383p $29.95; pa $10.95   **808.88**
1. Quotations
ISBN 0-19-214111-2; 0-19-282015-X (pa)
                                LC 82-14263

"Aphorisms, maxims, quotations, and pensées from ancient times to the present comprise this volume. Entries, arranged under subjects such as good and evil, provide the originator, source, and date for the sayings (if known)." Nichols. Guide to Ref Books for Sch Media Cent. 4th edition

The Oxford book of death; chosen and edited by D.J. Enright. Oxford Univ. Press 1987 351p $30; pa $10.95   **808.88**
1. Death—Quotations
ISBN 0-19-214129-5; 0-19-282013-3 (pa)
                                LC 82-14341

This is a collection of quotations. Enright divides his "subject into 14 parts, beginning with 'Definitons' and ending with 'Epitaphs, Requiems and Last Words.' He introduces each section . . . [and] then presents his selections." Newsweek

"Much work has gone into this compilation, and the individual introductions to the component sections are, as we would expect, elegant, modest and very wise." Times Lit Suppl

Includes bibliography

The Oxford dictionary of modern quotations; edited by Tony Augarde. Oxford Univ. Press 1991 371p $29.95
                                808.88
1. Quotations
ISBN 0-19-866141-X   LC 90-26588

This "collection of 5,000 quotations is arranged alphabetically by personal name. . . . To qualify as 'modern,' persons quoted had to have lived past 1900." Booklist

The Oxford dictionary of quotations; edited by Angela Partington. 4th ed. Oxford Univ. Press 1992 1061p $35   **808.88**
1. Quotations
ISBN 0-19-866185-1   LC 92-244553
First published 1941

A collection of over 20,000 quotations from more than 3,000 poets, novelists, essayists and historians. Entries are alphabetical with attributions and explanatory notes

For a review see: Booklist, Dec. 1, 1992

The Penguin dictionary of modern humorous quotations; compiled by Fred Metcalf. Viking 1986 319p o.p.; Penguin Bks. paperback available $12   **808.88**
1. Quotations 2. Wit and humor
ISBN 0-14-007568-2 (pa)

This is an anthology of humorous remarks arranged by subject

"Here are drolleries and epigrams from the famous and anonymous collected for writers, speechifiers, browsers, office wits, and whoever needs an original joke. Fred Metcalf admits in his foreword that much of the humor is cynical, malicious, scurrilous, and racy. It is, but not all of it." Christ Sci Monit

Quotations in black; compiled and edited by Anita King. Greenwood Press 1981 344p $45   **808.88**
1. Blacks—Quotations 2. Proverbs
ISBN 0-313-22128-6   LC 80-1794

"Arranged chronologically by the birth date of the speaker, [this book] provides an international selection of more than 1100 quotations from over 200 quotable blacks, plus a brief biographical sketch of each. An additional section includes proverbs. Access to all quotations is provided by both author and subject/key word indexes. A unique work, which should stand beside standard collections of quotations." Ref Sources for Small & Medium-sized Libr. 5th edition

Simpson, James Beasley
Simpson's contemporary quotations; compiled by James B. Simpson; foreword by Daniel J. Boorstin. rev ed. Houghton Mifflin 1988 495p $21.95   **808.88**
1. Quotations
ISBN 0-395-43085-2   LC 87-37867

First published 1957 by Crowell with title: Best quotes

This volume "contains about ten thousand quotes from nearly four thousand namecunds. The book is arranged under twenty-four subheads, grouped together under three major headings: the world, humankind, and communications and the arts. Subheadings include topics such as law, business, love, religion, sports, theater, art, and science." Am Ref Books Annu, 1989

Toasts; over 1,500 of the best toasts, sentiments, blessings, and graces; [compiled by] Paul Dickson; illustrated by Rollin McGrail. Crown 1991 256p il $18
                                808.88
1. Toasts 2. Wit and humor
ISBN 0-517-58412-3   LC 91-6967

Originally published in different form 1981 by Delacorte Press

"Covering traditional occasions such as anniversaries and weddings as well as a variety of other 'toastable' events, this book organizes 1,500 toasts under 75 alphabetically arranged subject headings. Included are ethnic, military, birthday, and holiday toasts. There are also toasts related to sports, aging, food, parents, and even cheese and champagne! The toasts have been gathered from a variety of toast books, many of which date from

Toasts—*Continued*

the late nineteenth and early twentieth centuries. An interesting history of toasting is included." Booklist

Includes bibliographic references

Warner, Carolyn

The last word; a treasury of women's quotes; foreword by Erma Bombeck. Prentice-Hall 1992 363p $29.95; pa $14.95

808.88

1. Women—Quotations

ISBN 0-13-524372-6; 0-13-517715-4 (pa)

LC 92-13954

This volume is "intended as a practical reference source for women public speakers, providing over 16,000 quotations arranged alphabetically by author within 40 alphabetically arranged topical chapters. Each chapter begins with tips, emphasizing the speaker's obligation and role in conveying the topical messages to an audience. Warner provides a biographical index with brief identifying data." Libr J

809   Literary history and criticism

Black literature criticism; excerpts from criticism of the most significant works of black authors over the past 200 years; edited by James P. Draper. Gale Res. 1992 3v il set $250   **809**

1. Literature—History and criticism 2. Black authors 3. Blacks in literature

ISBN 0-8103-7929-5   LC 91-33761

Contents: v1 Achebe-Ellison; v2 Emechta-Malcolm X; v3 Marshall-Young

This work covers "significant black writers throughout the world, including Chinua Achebe, Toni Morrison, and Wole Soyinka. Selections were made on the basis of scope, quantity of critical information available, recommendations from notable authorities, retrospective evaluations, seminal articles on authors' works, current commentaries offering recent viewpoints, and interviews and authors' statements regarding their works." Libr J

For a fuller review see: Booklist, Dec. 15, 1991

Bradbury, Malcolm, 1932-

The modern world; ten great writers. Viking 1989 c1988 294p o.p.; Penguin Bks. paperback available $8.95   **809**

1. Literature—History and criticism

ISBN 0-14-011484-X (pa)   LC 88-40304

Analyzed in Essay and general literature index

First published 1988 in the United Kingdom

"This book treats Dostoevsky, Ibsen, Conrad, Mann, Joyce, Proust, Eliot, Pirandello, Woolf, and Kafka, discussing 'their achievement, their interconnections, their influence, and their perception of the modern world.' A brief essay on each author deals with biography and oeuvre, focusing on one major work. In the process, Bradbury highlights various qualities or themes of modernism such as exile, the city, naturalism, symbolism, tragicomedy, fragmentation, etc." Libr J

Contemporary literary criticism. Gale Res.   **809**

1. Literature—History and criticism

ISSN 0091-3421   LC 76-38938

Irregular. Started publication in 1973

Volumes 1 to 75, 1973-1993, available at $115 each

"Excerpts from criticism of the works of today's novelists, poets, playwrights, short story writers, scriptwriters, and other creative writers." Title page

"This multivolume, onging series offers significant passages from contemporary criticism on authors who are now living or who have died since December 31, 1959. . . . Brief author sketches are followed by critical excerpts, presented in chronological order." Ref Sources for Small & Medium-sized Libr. 5th edition

Frye, Northrop

The great code; the Bible and literature. Harcourt Brace Jovanovich 1982 xxiii, 261p il hardcover o.p. paperback available $9.95

809

1. Bible—Criticism, interpretation, etc. 2. Bible as literature

ISBN 0-15-636480-8 (pa)   LC 81-47303

The author "examines the Bible from the standpoint of literary criticism, insisting that this matrix and repository of myth and metaphor for Western civilization stands outside literature and exerts its overpowering influence in part because of its autonomous position." Libr J

This "is an absorbing and intellectually audacious inquiry into 'how or why a poet might read the Bible.'" New Yorker

Includes bibliographic references

Words with power; being a second study of the Bible and literature. Harcourt Brace Jovanovich 1990 342p $24.95; pa $10.95

809

1. Bible as literature

ISBN 0-15-198462-X; 0-15-698365-6 (pa)

LC 90-39460

"The Bible is saturated with myth and metaphor, writes Frye. In this sequel to *The Great Code: The Bible and Literature* [entered above], the eminent critic places biblical imagery and narrative structure within the framework of Western literature." Publ Wkly

Includes bibliographic references

Gilbert, Sandra M.

The madwoman in the attic; the woman writer and the nineteenth-century literary imagination; [by] Sandra M. Gilbert and Susan Gubar. Yale Univ. Press 1979 xiv, 719p il hardcover o.p. paperback available $19.95   **809**

1. Women authors 2. American literature—History and criticism 3. English literature—History and criticism 4. Women in literature

ISBN 0-300-02596-3 (pa)   LC 78-20792

Analyzed in Essay and general literature index

This study of nineteenth-century women writers attempts to "demonstrate that 'women from Jane Austen and Mary Shelley to Emily Brontë and Emily Dickinson produced literary works that are in some sense palimpsestic, works whose surface designs conceal or obscure deeper, less accessible (and less socially acceptable) levels

Gilbert, Sandra M.—*Continued*
of meaning.'" N Y Times Book Rev

Includes bibliographic references

Highet, Gilbert, 1906-1978

The classical tradition; Greek and Roman influences on Western literature. Oxford Univ. Press 1949 xxxviii, 764p hardcover o.p. paperback available $16.95 **809**

1. Literature—History and criticism 2. Literature, Comparative 3. Classical literature—History and criticism

ISBN 0-19-500206-7 (pa)

Analyzed in Essay and general literature index

"The twenty-four chapters fall into four main sections. The first takes in the Dark and Middle Ages—Anglo-Saxon poetry and prose, French epic and romance, Dante, Petrarch, Boccaccio, Chaucer. The second section comprises eight chapters on the Renaissance—drama, epic, pastoral and romance, lyric, the literature of translation, Rabelais, Montaigne. . . . [The] third section [is] 'The Baroque Age.' . . . After baroque, we come to our fourth and last section, the romantic, or . . . the revolutionary period 'and afterwards.'" Spectator

Includes bibliography

James, Henry, 1843-1916

Literary criticism. Library of Am. 1984 2v ea $32.50 **809**

1. Literature—History and criticism

ISBN 0-940450-22-4 (v1); 0-940450-23-2 (v2)

LC 84-11241

Edited by Leon Edel and Mark Wilson

Contents: v1 Essays on literature, American writers, English writers; v2 French writers, other European writers. The prefaces to the New York edition

"Grouped by nationality, alphabetically by author, and chronologically, the essays provide a kind of critical book within a book on such writers as Balzac, George Eliot, and Hawthorne. These groupings enable the reader to see how James approached a writer and to follow the development of his thinking about particular writers over the years." Publisher's note

Includes bibliographies

Lehman, David, 1948-

Signs of the times; deconstruction and the fall of Paul de Man. Poseidon Press 1991 318p $21.95; pa $13 **809**

1. De Man, Paul 2. Literature—Philosophy

ISBN 0-671-68239-3; 0-671-77594-4 (pa)

LC 90-25825

The author discusses the literary movement known as deconstruction and the revelations in 1978 "that the late Paul de Man, one of its chief exponents, had collaborated with the Nazis, writing anti-Semitic articles during the German occupation of Belgium." Libr J

Includes bibliographic references

Magill's survey of world literature; edited by Frank N. Magill. Marshall Cavendish 1992 6v il set $389.95 **809**

1. Literature—History and criticism 2. Literature—Bio-bibliography

ISBN 1-85435-482-5

LC 92-11198

Companion set Magill's survey of American literature, entered in class 810.9

"The 215 alphabetical author entries date from antiquity to the late 20th century and include the gamut of genres. The major emphasis is on European writers, especially the British, with representation of English-language writers from non-European countries; Latin American authors and a smattering of authors from classical Eastern culture are also represented. . . . Each entry begins with a statement of the author's major achievement, followed by a biographical treatment and a critical summary of major works." Libr J

For a fuller review see: Booklist, Dec. 15, 1992

Includes bibliographic references

Masterpieces of world literature; edited by Frank N. Magill. Harper & Row 1989 957p $40 **809**

1. Literature—History and criticism

ISBN 0-06-016144-2

LC 89-45052

"While this volume gives plot information, character descriptions, and critical evaluation of 204 works (novels, plays, stories, and poems), plus analysis of 66 others (mostly essays), the information is straight from the *Critical Surveys* series, the *Masterplots* series, and the *Cyclopedia of Literary Characters* [the latter two entered in classes 808 and 803 respectively]. . . . The unsigned articles are clearly written, objective, accurate, and informative. Arrangement is alphabetical by the best-known English title. . . . Two indexes provide access to authors and original titles." Booklist

Modern black writers; compiled and edited by Michael Popkin. Ungar 1978 xx, 519p (Lib. of literary criticism) $65 **809**

1. American literature—Black authors—History and criticism 2. West Indian literature—History and criticism 3. African literature—History and criticism

ISBN 0-8044-3258-9

LC 76-15656

"Popkin offers a useful summary and a brief but provocative discussion of the contemporary critical debate about the black aesthetic in his introduction. His primary aim, however, is to compile extensive excerpts of criticism dealing with major black poets, dramatists, and novelists from Africa, the Caribbean, and the U.S. . . . The organization is excellent." Choice

Includes bibliographic references

Pound, Ezra, 1885-1972

Literary essays; edited with an introduction by T. S. Eliot. New Directions 1954 464p hardcover o.p. paperback available $12.95 **809**

1. Literature—History and criticism

ISBN 0-8112-0157-0 (pa)

Also available in hardcover from Greenwood Press

First published 1954 and analyzed in Essay and general literature index

T.S. Eliot "believes that Pound has stated a great deal about the art of writing, particularly poetry, that is permanently valid and useful. His chief concerns are the arts as good medicine, techniques, and accuracy of language. He believes that good writing instructs, moves, and delights." Cincinnati Public Libr

Pritchett, V. S. (Victor Sawdon), 1900-

The myth makers; literary essays; [by] Victor Sawdon Pritchett. Random House 1979 190p $11.95   **809**

1. Literature—History and criticism
ISBN 0-394-50472-0   LC 78-21801

Analyzed in Essay and general literature index

This "is a collection of essays on Tolstoy, Dostoyevsky, Flaubert, Stendhal, Genet, Strindberg, Borges, and a dozen other writers. The pieces . . . were done over the years for such magazines as The New Statesman, The New York Review of Books, and The New Yorker." Christ Sci Monit

Includes bibliography

Trilling, Lionel, 1905-1975

Beyond culture; essays on literature and learning. Harcourt Brace Jovanovich 1978 204p (Works of Lionel Trilling. Uniform ed) $10.95   **809**

1. Literature—History and criticism
ISBN 0-15-111987-2   LC 77-17365

First published 1965 and analyzed in Essay and general literature index

Contents: On the teaching of modern literature; Emma and the legend of Jane Austen; The fate of pleasure; Freud: within and beyond culture; Isaac Babel; The Leavis-Snow controversy; Hawthorne in our time; The two environments: reflections on the study of English

The liberal imagination; essays on literature and society. Harcourt Brace Jovanovich 1979 c1978 284p (Works of Lionel Trilling. Uniform ed) $10   **809**

1. Literature—History and criticism
ISBN 0-15-151197-7   LC 78-65749

First published 1950 by Viking Press, and analyzed in Essay and general literature index

Contents: Reality in America; Sherwood Anderson; Freud and literature; The Princess Casamassima; The function of the little magazine; Huckleberry Finn; Kipling; The immortality ode; Art and neurosis; The sense of the past; Tacitus now; Manners, morals, and the novel; The Kinsey Report; F. Scott Fitzgerald; Art and fortune; The meaning of a literary idea

Includes bibliography

Twentieth-century literary criticism. Gale Res. ea volume $109   **809**

1. Literature—History and criticism
ISSN 0276-8178   LC 76-46132

Irregularly published series which began publication in 1978

"Excerpts from criticism of the works of novelists, poets, playwrights, short story writers, and other creative writers who lived between 1900 and 1960, from the first published critical appraisals to current evaluations." Title page

Writers for children; critical studies of major authors since the seventeenth century; Jane M. Bingham, editor. Scribner 1988 661p $95   **809**

1. Children's literature—History and criticism 2. Children's literature—Bio-bibliography
ISBN 0-684-18165-7   LC 87-16011

Analyzed in Essay and general literature index

This volume contains signed essays on eighty-four European and North American writers whose works have become children's classics. Among the authors discussed are Louisa May Alcott, Ludwig Bemelmans, Arna Bontemps, Alexandre Dumas, Wanda Gág, Erich Kästner, George Macdonald, L. M. Montgomery, E. Nesbit, Charles Perrault, Carol Ryrie Brink and Laura Ingalls Wilder

"Each essay knits pertinent details of a writer's life with a critical assessment of his works. . . . A reference tool for teachers, librarians, and college students, especially useful for a research overview." Choice

Includes bibliography

809.1   Poetry—History and criticism

Gioia, Dana

Can poetry matter? essays on poetry and culture. Graywolf Press 1992 257p $25; pa $12   **809.1**

1. Poetry—History and criticism 2. Criticism
ISBN 1-55597-176-8; 1-55597-177-6 (pa)
     LC 92-10550

Analyzed in Essay and general literature index

In addition to addressing the business of being a poet and the New Formalism the author offers readings of Robinson Jeffers, Weldon Kees, Robert Bly and others

"Gioia is an engaged, thoroughgoing, enthusiastic reader, one who infuses his audience with his passion for poetry." Booklist

Lewis, C. S. (Clive Staples), 1898-1963

Allegory of love; a study in medieval tradition. Oxford Univ. Press 1936 378p hardcover o.p. paperback available $15.95   **809.1**

1. Love poetry—History and criticism 2. Literature, Medieval 3. English poetry—History and criticism
ISBN 0-19-281220-3 (pa)

"The theme of Mr. Lewis's book is the slow emergence of the passion of romantic love, and the slow evolution of the literary expression of that passion through the Middle Ages. The process, as he presents it, culminates in Spenser." Times Lit Suppl

The **New** Princeton encyclopedia of poetry and poetics; Alex Preminger and T.V.F. Brogan, co-editors; Frank Warnke, O.B. Hardison, Jr., and Earl Miner, associate editors. Princeton Univ. Press 1993 xlvi, 1383p $125; pa $29.95   **809.1**

1. Poetry—History and criticism 2. Poetry—Dictionaries 3. Poetics—Dictionaries
ISBN 0-691-03271-8; 0-691-02123-6 (pa)
     LC 92-41887

First published 1965 with title: Encyclopedia of poetry and poetics

This work deals with the history, forms, genres, movements and critical approaches to oral and written verse. It examines issues in such areas as: hermenuetics, feminist poetics, Chicano poetry, deconstruction, poststructuralism and cultural criticism. Non-Western and emergent poetries are featured and 106 national poetries are covered

For a review see: Booklist, Dec. 15, 1993

Paz, Octavio, 1914-
The other voice; essays on modern poetry; translated from the Spanish by Helen Lane. Harcourt Brace Jovanovich 1991 160p $16.95 **809.1**
1. Poetry—History and criticism
ISBN 0-15-170449-X   LC 91-4764
Original Spanish edition, 1990
This volume "consists of seven essays on poetry, the modern age, history, and society's sense of time . . . written over a period of 15 years." Christ Sci Monit
What makes Paz an "extraordinary man of letters is his comfort with subjects as dissimilar as the market economy and José Martí, the Hispanic psyche and the architecture of pyramids." Nation

809.2 Drama—History and criticism

Bentley, Eric, 1916-
The life of the drama. Applause Theatre Bk. Pubs. 1991 371p pa $12.95   **809.2**
1. Drama—History and criticism
ISBN 1-55783-110-6   LC 91-28774
Analyzed in Essay and general literature index
First published 1964 by Atheneum
The author discusses plot, character, dialogue, and action in various theatrical genres. Among the dramatists discussed are Aeschylus, Beckett, Brecht, Chekhov, Corneille, Goethe, Ibsen, Ben Jonson, Molière, Pirandello, Racine, Shakespeare, Shaw, and Sophocles
Includes bibliographic references

Brustein, Robert, 1927-
The theatre of revolt; an approach to the modern drama; with a new preface by the author. Dee, I.R. 1991 435p pa $13.95
809.2
1. Drama—History and criticism
ISBN 0-929587-53-7   LC 90-23644
Analyzed in Essay and general literature index
First published 1964 by Little, Brown
The author argues that revolt characterizes 20th century theater in general. He explicates the work of Ibsen, Brecht, Strindberg, Chekhov, Shaw, Pirandello, O'Neill, Artaud and Genet
Includes bibliographic references

Esslin, Martin
The theatre of the absurd. 3rd ed rev & enl. Penguin Bks. 1983 c1980 480p $10.95
809.2
1. Drama—History and criticism
ISBN 0-14-020929-8 (pa)   LC 81-169374
First published 1961 by Anchor Books; this edition first published 1980 in the United Kingdom
A study on the type of drama associated with the names of Samuel Beckett, Eugène Ionesco, Arthur Adamov, Jean Genet, and a number of other avant-garde writers
Includes bibliography

Kerr, Walter, 1913-
Tragedy and comedy; new introduction by William Alfred. Da Capo Press 1985 355p pa $9.95   **809.2**
1. Tragedy 2. Comedy
ISBN 0-306-80249-X   LC 85-11692
First published 1967 by Simon & Schuster
Among the playwrights discussed in this history of the two primary forms of drama are: Aristophanes, Shakespeare, Molière, Chekhov, Beckett, Osborne and Albee
Includes bibliography

Masterplots II, drama series; edited by Frank N. Magill. Salem Press 1990 4v set $365   **809.2**
1. Drama—Stories, plots, etc. 2. Drama—History and criticism
ISBN 0-89356-491-5   LC 89-10989
This "set includes 327 works by 148 playwrights. . . . The selection of plays spans the spectrum from seminal works from the early years of the century to recent Broadway hits and is representative of the wide range of styles, themes, and dramatic techniques that characterize twentieth-century drama. About 70 of the plays treated in the set have been translated into English from other languages." Booklist

McGraw-Hill encyclopedia of world drama; an international reference work in 5 volumes; Stanley Hochman, editor in chief. [2nd ed]. McGraw-Hill 1983 c1984 5v il set $415   **809.2**
1. Drama—Dictionaries 2. Drama—Bio-bibliography
ISBN 0-07-079169-4   LC 83-9919
First published 1972
"A majority of the entries emphasize playwrights and their contributions, with the remaining entries devoted to surveys of the world's dramatic literature, major dramatic genres, important theater groups and companies, and other subjects. The encyclopedia, international in scope and comprehensive in its level of treatment, will meet the needs of critics and theater buffs, as well as historians, educators, and performing artists. More than twenty-five hundred illustrations add dimension and depth to this multi-volume set." RQ

809.3 Fiction—History and criticism

Aldiss, Brian Wilson, 1925-
The trillion year spree; by Brian W. Aldiss with the assistance of David Wingrove. Atheneum Pubs. 1986 511p o.p.; Avon Bks. paperback available $9.95 **809.3**
1. Science fiction—History and criticism
ISBN 0-380-70461-7 (pa)   LC 86-47682
First published 1973 in the United Kingdom with title: Billion year spree
"Aldiss considers Mary Shelley's Frankenstein as the first modern science fiction story and contends that all current science fiction has inherited its literary form from that novel and its Gothic offshoots. Besides Shelley, he examines the writings of Poe, Wells, Edgar Rice Burroughs and John W. Campbell, Jr. Other chapters explore the Victorian era, the major authors of the 1930s through the 1970s, and sf films. [This book] is essential for all libraries." Libr J
Includes bibliography

Asimov, Isaac, 1920-1992

Asimov's galaxy; reflections on science fiction. Doubleday 1989 318p $17.95 **809.3**

1. Science fiction—History and criticism
ISBN 0-385-24120-8   LC 88-15909

This volume contains more than 50 essays originally published as editorials in Isaac Asimov's Science fiction magazine

"Using science fiction as a touchstone, the essays cover a variety of topics, but of particular interest, perhaps, to the Asimov fan, are more than a dozen autobiographical pieces. . . . Other areas covered include 'Women and Science Fiction,' 'Plagiarism,' 'Pseudonyms,' 'Magic,' 'Magazine Covers' and the slush pile." Publ Wkly

Critical survey of mystery and detective fiction; edited by Frank N. Magill. Salem Press 1988 4v set $300   **809.3**

1. Mystery and detective stories—History and criticism 2. Mystery and detective stories—Biobibliography
ISBN 0-89356-486-9   LC 88-28566

These "volumes cover 270 mystery/detective authors, the majority British and American. Signed articles run 2,500 words with major figures receiving longer entries. . . . Entries include: biographical information, pseudonyms, types of plots, series, series characters, critical analysis of the work, bibliographies, and discussion of the author's contribution to the genre." Am Libr

Includes bibliography

Dillard, Annie

Living by fiction. Harper & Row 1982 192p hardcover o.p. paperback available $10
809.3

1. Fiction—History and criticism
ISBN 0-06-091544-7 (pa)   LC 81-47882

"Dillard examines what she calls 'contemporary modernist' fiction as practiced by writers like Borges, Nabokov, Calvino, Barthelme, and Pynchon. She soundly defines terms, compares modernist and traditional styles, and makes fresh observations about fiction's publishers, audience, and critics." Libr J

Includes bibliographic references

The **Encyclopedia** of science fiction; edited by John Clute and Peter Nicholls; contributing editor, Brian Stableford; technical editor, John Grant. [2nd ed]. St. Martin's Press 1993 xxxvi, 1370p il $75
809.3

1. Science fiction—Dictionaries
ISBN 0-312-09618-6   LC 92-47048
First published 1979

"The 4,360 entries cover major and minor authors who have contributed to the evolution of the genre, themes, terminology . . . films, television programs . . . magazines, comics, 64 illustrators, book publishers, and original anthologies from 27 countries. Of particular value for reference and collection development librarians are lengthy entries on small presses and limited editions, bibliographies, notable collections of science fiction (both public and private), the clear distinction of real names and pseudonyms, and entries on individual publications such as *Amazing Stories*." Choice

Kundera, Milan

The art of the novel; translated from the French by Linda Asher. Grove Press 1988 165p $17.95
809.3

1. Fiction—History and criticism 2. Fiction—Technique
ISBN 0-8021-0011-2   LC 87-15564
Also available in paperback from HarperCollins
Original French edition, 1986

"Kundera begins and ends with sections on the European novel. In between he sheds light on many topics, including Hermann Broch and Franz Kafka, polyphonic structure, stupidity, kitsch, and the laughter of God." Choice

McCarthy, Mary, 1912-1989

Ideas and the novel. Harcourt Brace Jovanovich 1980 121p (Northcliffe lectures, 1980) $7.95   **809.3**

1. Fiction—History and criticism
ISBN 0-15-143682-7   LC 80-82344

The author mounts an "attack on the post-modern novel and calls for a return to the philosophical novel, or the 'novel of ideas.' . . . To remind us of what we have lost, she offers a . . . reinterpretation of such 19th-century favorites as Stendhal, Balzac, Hugo, Dostoevsky, and Tolstoy." Saturday Rev

McCormick, Donald, 1911-

Spyfiction: a connoisseur's guide; [by] Donald McCormick & Katy Fletcher. Facts on File 1990 346p $23.95   **809.3**

1. Spies in literature 2. Fiction—Bio-bibliography
ISBN 0-8160-2098-1   LC 89-29524

This alphabetical listing provides biographical, bibliographical and critical information for over 200 authors of spy fiction

The **New** encyclopedia of science fiction; edited by James Gunn. Viking 1988 524p il $24.95   **809.3**

1. Science fiction—Dictionaries
ISBN 0-670-81041-X   LC 87-40637

"More than 500 entries provide bibliographic information on and critical evaluations of writers, artists, and editors. Also included are summary evaluations of more than 250 films—classics, crowd-pleasers, and a few representative stinkers. The heart of the book, however, lies in the nearly 100 essays exploring the science, the business, the history, and the themes, conventions, and forms of science fiction." Choice

Science fiction writers; critical studies of the major authors from the early nineteenth century to the present day; E.F. Bleiler, editor. Scribner 1982 623p $89   **809.3**

1. Science fiction—History and criticism 2. Science fiction—Bio-bibliography
ISBN 0-684-16740-9   LC 81-51032

This book contains "essays on seventy-two American and British and three European authors of the nineteenth and twentieth centuries. Articles . . . have been written by science fiction authorities. . . . With its inclusion of pioneering nineteenth-century authors, [it] gives a desirable fullness to science fiction reference literature." Wilson Libr Bull

Short story criticism; excerpts from criticism of the works of short fiction writers. Gale Res. $85   **809.3**

1. Short stories—History and criticism
ISSN 0895-9439

Biannual. First published 1988

This "series presents significant critical excerpts on the most important short story writers of all eras and nationalities. Each entry gives a biographical and critical overview, a list of principal works, excerpts of criticism, and a selected bibliography." Ref Sources for Small & Medium-sized Libr. 5th edition

Supernatural fiction writers; fantasy and horror; E. F. Bleiler, editor. Scribner 1985 2v set $160   **809.3**

1. Fantastic fiction—History and criticism 2. Fantastic fiction—Bio-bibliography
ISBN 0-684-17808-7   LC 84-27588

"Essays on writers of fantasy and horror from 125 A.D. to the present include an introduction and overview, a selected bibliography, and a list of critical studies. Commentaries containing biographical and critical information, are generally five to ten pages in length." Ref Sources for Small & Medium-sized Libr. 5th edition

Includes bibliography

Symons, Julian, 1912-
Bloody murder; from the detective story to the crime novel. 3rd rev ed. Mysterious Press 1993 c1992 349p $21.95   **809.3**

1. Mystery and detective stories—History and criticism
ISBN 0-89296-496-0   LC 92-54127

First published 1972 in the United Kingdom. Present edition first published 1992 in the United Kingdom

A critical survey of crime fiction, including detective stories, psychological crime stories, thrillers, and espionage, covering authors from Poe to the 1990's

Twentieth-century science-fiction writers; editor, Curtis C. Smith. 2nd ed. St. James Press 1986 933p $95   **809.3**

1. Science fiction—History and criticism 2. Science fiction—Bio-bibliography
ISBN 0-912289-27-9

First published 1981

"Covers primarily English-language writers of science fiction from H. G. Wells to the present. Author entries consist of biographical data, a bibliography of works (both science fiction and non-science fiction), and a signed critical essay." Ref Sources for Small & Medium-sized Libr. 5th edition

810.3 American literature—
Encyclopedias and dictionaries

Benét's reader's encyclopedia of American literature; edited by George Perkins, Barbara Perkins, and Phillip Leininger. HarperCollins Pubs. 1991 1176p $45
                    810.3

1. American literature—Dictionaries
ISBN 0-06-270027-8   LC 91-55001

"Portions of this book appeared in a somewhat modified form in The reader's encyclopedia of American literature, published by T.Y. Crowell in 1962, and in Benét's reader's encyclopedia, third edition, published by Harper & Row in 1987." Verso of title page

This work "covers the literary movements, genres of fiction and nonfiction, and social, political, and religious influences on literature throughout North and South America." Libr J

Includes bibliographic references

The **Cambridge** handbook of American literature; edited by Jack Salzman. Cambridge Univ. Press 1986 286p $24.95
                    810.3

1. American literature—Dictionaries 2. American literature—Bio-bibliography
ISBN 0-521-30703-1   LC 86-2587

This handbook's "750 entries, two thirds of them about authors, briefly describe the contents and contribution of key works, assess the careers of writers, and explain the tenets and characteristics of literary movements." Wilson Libr Bull

Hart, James David, 1911-1990
The concise Oxford companion to American literature. Oxford Univ. Press 1986 497p $30; pa $14.95   **810.3**

1. American literature—Dictionaries 2. American literature—Bio-bibliography
ISBN 0-19-503982-3; 0-19-504771-0 (pa) LC 86-8510

This abridgement is based on The Oxford Companion to American literature, 5th edition, entered below. It contains 2,000 entries, including biographies, plot summaries, and descriptions of literary movements

The **Oxford** companion to American literature. 5th ed. Oxford Univ. Press 1983 896p $49.95   **810.3**

1. American literature—Dictionaries 2. American literature—Bio-bibliography
ISBN 0-19-503074-5   LC 81-22469

First published 1941

"In dictionary arrangement, it includes short biographies of American authors, with lists of their major works and information regarding their style and subject matter; summaries and descriptions of the important American novels, stories, essays, poems and plays; definitions and historical outlines of literary societies, magazines, anthologies, co-operative publications, literary awards, book collectors, printers, etc." Sheehy. Guide to Ref Books. 10th edition

The **Oxford** companion to Canadian literature; general editor, William Toye. Oxford Univ. Press 1983 843p $60
                    810.3

1. Canadian literature—Dictionaries 2. Canadian literature—Bio-bibliography 3. French Canadian literature—Dictionaries 4. French Canadian literature—Bio-bibliography
ISBN 0-19-540283-9

"Entries for writers and genres predominate, the former including novelists, poets, dramatists, biographers, philosophers, and some authors of children's books; the latter extending to criticism, essays, translations, humor and satire, mystery and crime fiction, science fiction, and travel literature as well as the many expected categories (including extensive surveys of novels in English, novels in French, and regional literature). French-Canadian

The Oxford companion to Canadian literature—*Continued*
literature and writers are treated at length." Sheehy. Guide to Ref Books. 10th edition

810.8   American literature— Collections

Afro-American women writers, 1746-1933; an anthology and critical guide; [edited by] Ann Allen Shockley. Hall, G.K. & Co. 1988 xxviii, 465p o.p.; New Am. Lib. paperback available $14.95   **810.8**
1. American literature—Black authors—Collections
2. American literature—Women authors—Collections
ISBN 0-452-00981-2 (pa)   LC 87-35936
"An anthology of poetry, short stories, essays, and excerpts from novels, memoirs, and journals, by exemplary black women writers spanning the many decades from colonial slavery to the Harlem Renaissance of the 1920s and 1930s. . . . Entries in the anthology are prefaced by biographical sketches of the writers. . . . A sensitive gathering of powerful works, for students of black literature or any serious reader." Booklist
Includes bibliography

Black southern voices; an anthology of fiction, poetry, drama, nonfiction, and critical essays; edited by John Oliver Killens and Jerry W. Ward, Jr. New Am. Lib. 1992 608p pa $15   **810.8**
1. American literature—Black authors—Collections
2. American literature—Southern States—Collections
ISBN 0-452-01096-9   LC 92-3700
This anthology "gathers plays, poems, essays, and fiction by a total of 56 writers, as well as classic spiritual and blues lyrics, to represent the black Southern literary tradition. . . . Each excerpt or piece is preceded by a brief biographical sketch of the author and an overview of his or her oeuvre." Booklist

Double stitch; black women write about mothers and daughters; edited by Patricia Bell-Scott [et al.] Beacon Press 1991 271p $19.95   **810.8**
1. American literature—Black authors—Collections
2. American literature—Women authors—Collections
3. Mothers and daughters 4. Black women
ISBN 0-8070-0910-5   LC 91-10284
"Black mother-daughter relationships are explored through the varying perspectives, traditions, and experiences expressed in this anthology of 47 personal and scholarly essays, stories, and poems written by black women. Among the contributors are well-known writers and scholars such as Alice Walker, Audre Lourde, Gloria T. Hull, Bell Hooks, Sonia Sanchez, and Patricia Hill Collins." Libr J
Includes bibliographic references

Memory of kin; stories about family by black writers; edited, with an introduction and commentary, by Mary Helen Washington. Doubleday 1991 416p $24.95; pa $12.95   **810.8**
1. American literature—Black authors—Collections
ISBN 0-385-24782-6; 0-385-24783-4 (pa)
     LC 90-42487

"Organized under 10 familial categories—from wives and husbands to mothers and sons to the extended family—this potpourri of stories, excerpts from novels, and poems explores the many ways the generations connect." Publ Wkly
Includes bibliographic references

The Meridian anthology of early American women writers; from Anne Bradstreet to Louisa May Alcott, 1650-1865; edited by Katharine M. Rogers. New Am. Lib. 1991 516p pa $14.95   **810.8**
1. American literature—Women authors—Collections
ISBN 0-452-01075-6   LC 91-6769
"A Meridian book"
This "collection offers fiction, poetry, autobiography, letters, and essays by a fascinating variety of women, some well known—Abigail Adams, Sojourner Truth, Sarah Moore Grimké—and some who will be known only to a small number of today's readers—Caroline Stansbury Kirkland, Catharine Maria Sedgwick, Fanny Fern." Libr J

A Modern Southern reader; major stories, drama, poetry, essays, interviews, and reminiscences from the twentieth-century South; edited by Ben Forkner and Patrick Samway. Peachtree Pubs. 1986 736p hardcover o.p. paperback available $23.95   **810.8**
1. American literature—Southern States—Collections
ISBN 0-934601-08-9 (pa)   LC 86-21218
Authors represented range from William Faulkner, Eudora Welty, and John Crowe Ransom to such newer voices as Barry Hannah, Dave Smith, and Harry Crews. Biographical notes appended

The Norton anthology of American literature; [edited by] Nina Baym [et al.] 3rd ed. Norton 1989 2v ea pa $31.95   **810.8**
1. American literature—Collections
ISBN 0-393-95736-5 (v1); 0-393-95738-1 (v2)
     LC 88-38038
First published 1979
An anthology of American prose, poetry and drama dating from 1620 to the 20th century. Includes essays and introductions to authors and works

Personal dispatches: writers confront AIDS; edited by John Preston. St. Martin's Press 1989 xxii, 183p hardcover o.p. paperback available $8.95   **810.8**
1. AIDS (Disease) 2. American literature—Collections
3. Gay men
ISBN 0-312-05141-7 (pa)   LC 89-35320
This "anthology reprinting works of gay writers—Andrew Holleran, Edmund White, Robert Gluck and many lesser known authors—reflects the personal and political impact on the gay community and movement of the epidemic. The pieces vary from the lyrical to the polemical, from angry to mystical." Publ Wkly

The Portable beat reader; edited by Ann Charters. Viking 1992 xxxvi, 642p $25   **810.8**
1. American literature—Collections 2. Bohemianism
ISBN 0-670-83885-3   LC 91-16155

The Portable beat reader—*Continued*

Also available in paperback from Penguin Bks.

"Viking portable library"

"The collection proceeds chronologically and from east to west, in effect tracking Kerouac's cross-country journey and linking the East Coast Beats with San Francisco poets such as Kenneth Rexroth, Lawrence Ferlinghetti, Gary Snyder, and Michael McClure. The works of 'second wave' Beat writers Amiri Baraka (LeRoi Jones), Diana DiPrima, Frank O'Hara, Bob Dylan, even Norman Mailer, to name a few, are included, with the connections to the original group discussed." Booklist

"Cutting through bohemian posturing and excess, Charters here reprints much of the most vital, readable and relevant material produced by the Beat generation." Publ Wkly

Includes bibliographic references

The Pushcart prize . . . : best of the small presses; an annual small press reader. Pushcart Press   **810.8**

1. American literature—Collections

Volumes I-XVIII available in hardcover from Pushcart Press and in paperback from Avon Bks. and Penguin Bks. Prices vary

Annual. First published 1976

Edited by Bill Henderson

Each volume "consists of short stories, poems and essays; includes the work of established and beginning writers, and has a faintly subversive character. Its audience would seem to be primarily the young, yet among its contributors are many of the best writers in America. . . . Like all interesting literary journals, 'The Pushcart Prize' is eclectic and uneven. . . . The number and diversity of journals represented and the sheer length of it are impressive." Books of the Times

Reading rooms; edited by Susan Allen Toth and John Coughlan; foreword by Daniel J. Boorstin. Doubleday 1990 486p il o.p.; Pocket Bks. paperback available $12

810.8

1. American literature—Collections 2. Public libraries 3. Books and reading

ISBN 0-671-74764-9 (pa)   LC 90-13927

An "anthology of essays, stories, poems, memoirs and excerpts from novels, each in celebration of a great institution all too often taken for granted: the public library. In works by Eudora Welty, Edith Wharton, E. B. White, Isaac Asimov, Alfred Kazin, Philip Roth and dozens of other notable American writers, we read of libraries large and small, their librarians and the readers, young and old, who use them." Publ Wkly

Includes bibliographic references

The Twentieth century treasury of sports; edited by Al Silverman and Brian Silverman. Viking 1992 xli, 717p $30

810.8

1. Sports

ISBN 0-670-84662-7   LC 92-53516

This anthology of "fiction and nonfiction from the world of sports offers such diversity as the thrills of surfing in 'The Waves of Waikiki' by Jack London, to Senator Bill Bradley's thought-provoking notes of a retired athlete, 'After the Applause.' Among the essays examining the 'intimate relationship between sports and life' are literary works by James Baldwin, William Faulkner, F. Scott Fitzgerald, Stephen King, Ring Lardner, Norman Mailer, George Orwell, and Red Smith." Libr J

810.9   American literature— History and criticism

American women writers; a critical reference guide from colonial times to the present; editor, Lina Mainiero; associate editor, Langdon Lynne Faust. Ungar 1979-1982 4v set $300, ea $75   **810.9**

1. American literature—History and criticism 2. Women authors 3. American literature—Bio-bibliography

ISBN 0-8044-3150-7

"This set contains biocritical essays on over 1,000 American women authors of literary, popular, and juvenile fiction and nonfiction, from colonial times to the present. Entries consist of brief biographical data; an essay on the author's significance and overall contribution, major works, themes, and style; and a list of works by and about her." Nichols. Guide to Ref Books for Sch Media Cent. 4th edition

Black women writers (1950-1980); a critical evaluation; edited by Mari Evans. Anchor Bks. 1984 xxviii, 543p $22.95; pa $13.95

810.9

1. American literature—Black authors 2. American literature—Women authors 3. American literature—History and criticism

ISBN 0-385-17124-2; 0-385-17125-0 (pa)

LC 81-43914

Critical essays on Maya Angelou, Alice Childress, Toni Morisson, Lucille Clifton, and 11 other post World War II Afro-American women writers

"This important work, a tribute to the corpus of literature produced by black women, is an indispensable resource for any serious student, scholar or teacher desiring to probe the depths of the Afro-American literary tradition." Freedomways

Includes bibliographic references

Chicano literature; a reference guide; edited by Julio A. Martínez and Francisco A. Lomelí. Greenwood Press 1984 492p $55

810.9

1. American literature—Mexican American authors—Bio-bibliography

ISBN 0-313-23691-7   LC 83-22583

"Signed critical essays on the life and works of Chicano authors and on other topics relevant to the history and development of Chicano literature, including articles on the novel, poetry, theater, children's literature, and Chicano philosophy." Ref Sources for Small & Medium-sized Libr. 5th edition

Includes bibliography

Columbia literary history of the United States; Emory Elliott, general editor; associate editors, Martha Banta [et al.]; advisory editors, Houston A. Baker [et al.] Columbia Univ. Press 1988 xxviii, 1263p $67.50   **810.9**

1. American literature—History and criticism

ISBN 0-231-05812-8   LC 87-14672

This anthology "expands the traditional subjects of literary history by incorporating current theoretical ideas and newly discovered writers. Includes treatment of recently explored subjects, such as the role of women and minorities in U.S. literature. No separate bibliography

Columbia literary history of the United States—*Continued*
other than what is found in the text." N Y Public Libr Book of How & Where to Look it Up

Conn, Peter J.
Literature in America: an illustrated history; [by] Peter Conn. Cambridge Univ. Press 1989 xx, 587p il $32.95   **810.9**
1. American literature—History and criticism
ISBN 0-521-30373-7   LC 88-30505
"A chronological survey that ranges from 'The Colonial Experience' to the present, [this book seeks to] supply historical contexts for the various periods of American literature, biographical sketches of many . . . authors, and meditations on artistic reactions to religious and political ideas." N Y Times Book Rev
Includes bibliography

Dardis, Tom
The thirsty muse; alcohol and the American writer. Ticknor & Fields 1989 292p il o.p.; Houghton Mifflin paperback available $8.95   **810.9**
1. American literature—History and criticism 2. Authors, American 3. Alcoholism
ISBN 0-395-57422-6 (pa)   LC 88-29394
"Drawing on current addiction research and more than 100 meetings of Alcoholics Anonymous, Dardis examines the careers of Faulkner, Fitzgerald, Hemingway, and O'Neill, presenting harrowing portraits in self-destruction. . . . In spare, lucid prose, the author analyzes the addictive personality and explains the roles of genetics and environment." Booklist
Includes bibliography

Donoghue, Denis
Reading America. Knopf 1987 320p $22.95   **810.9**
1. American literature—History and criticism
ISBN 0-394-55939-8   LC 87-45125
Also available in paperback from University of Calif. Press
Analyzed in Essay and general literature index
The author presents a selection of his essays and commentaries on American literature from Emerson and Whitman through Auden and Ashbery
"The perfect book for those who want insight into American literature without pedantry." Libr J

Harvard guide to contemporary American writing; Daniel Hoffman, editor; with essays by Leo Braudy [et al.] Belknap Press 1979 618p hardcover o.p. paperback available $16.50   **810.9**
1. American literature—History and criticism
ISBN 0-674-37537-8 (pa)   LC 79-10930
Analyzed in Essay and general literature index
This is a critical survey of what the authors consider "the most significant writing in the United States from the end of World War II to the end of the 1970s. In original essays, ten . . . critics describe and assess the work of American novelists, playwrights, and poets, and analyze the intellectual and critical environment in which they worked." Publisher's note

Jackson, Blyden, 1910-
The history of Afro-American literature; v1 The long beginning, 1746-1895. Louisiana State Univ. Press 1989 450p $29.95   **810.9**
1. American literature—Black authors—History and criticism 2. Blacks—Intellectual life
ISBN 0-8071-1511-8   LC 88-26603
"This first volume of a proposed four-volume history of Afro-American writing is divided into two parts: 'The Age of Apprenticeship' and 'The Age of Abolitionists.' The first part discusses . . . early poetry, sermons, histories, and folklore. This early literature displays the efforts of a people to cope with a new land, culture, and language. Subsequently, the book presents the reactions of a people enslaved." Libr J
Includes bibliography

Kazin, Alfred, 1915-
An American procession; the major writers from 1830-1930. Knopf 1984 408p $18.95
     810.9
1. American literature—History and criticism
ISBN 0-394-50378-3   LC 83-26843
Analyzed in Essay and general literature index
This book "starts with Ralph Waldo Emerson in the 1830's and ends a century later with Eliot, Ezra Pound, John Dos Passos, William Faulkner, Ernest Hemingway, and F. Scott Fitzgerald. . . . Between Emerson and the moderns the critical authors . . . are Thoreau, Hawthorne, Poe, Whitman, Melville, Emily Dickinson, Mark Twain, Henry James, Stephen Crane, Theodore Dreiser, and Henry Adams." N Y Times Book Rev
"Over all, 'An American Procession' is a refresher in the best sense: without any fundamental revision of our understanding of our classics, it vivaciously refreshes our awareness of them, and our gratitude for them." New Yorker

A writer's America; landscape in literature. Knopf 1988 240p il $24.95   **810.9**
1. American literature—History and criticism 2. Nature in literature
ISBN 0-394-57142-8   LC 88-1299
The author "reminds us that nature is not only the subject of a genre but a fundamental concern of the American classics, from Poe and Melville to Faulkner and Hemingway. He enhances his argument, and the book's attractiveness, with a lively selection of art and photographs. . . . Mr. Kazin is wonderfully evocative in describing the wilderness dawn of the American literary imagination." N Y Times Book Rev
Includes bibliography

A **Literary** history of the American West; sponsored by the Western Literature Association. Texas Christian Univ. Press 1987 xliii, 1353p il $79.50   **810.9**
1. American literature—West (U.S.)—History and criticism 2. West (U.S.) in literature
ISBN 0-87565-021-X   LC 85-50538
"Dozens of writers—mostly academics—contribute chapters on well-known writers such as Wright Morris and on lesser lights such as Thomas Hornsby Ferril and Frederick Manfred, as well as on neatly categorized groups and issues (e.g. Afro-American western writers and trends in western poetry). The result is an impressive compendium: hefty, scholarly, encyclopedic, and indispensable for serious students of western literature." Booklist
Includes bibliography

Magill's survey of American literature; edited by Frank N. Magill. Marshall Cavendish 1991 6v il set $370   **810.9**
1. American literature—History and criticism 2. American literature—Bio-bibliography
ISBN 1-85435-437-X   LC 91-28113

This set presents coverage of 190 American writers from the seventeenth century to the present

"No one can accuse Magill of elitism, for he combines alphabetically into this manageably sized set both the time-tested and the currently trendy authors of American literature. Nor can he be accused of ignoring women, for 46 of the 190 entries are women. . . . Current black, Hispanic, and Native American writers are well represented." Libr J

Masterpieces of African-American literature; edited by Frank N. Magill. HarperCollins Pubs. 1992 593p $40   **810.9**
1. American literature—Black authors—Dictionaries 2. Blacks in literature
ISBN 0-06-270066-9   LC 92-52542

This work "includes articles on 149 titles in African American literature from various genres. Some 91 authors are represented, 37 of whom are women. Entries, which are generally well written and informative, include sections on the principal characters, plot, analysis, and the critical context. Descriptions of the standard works, including a number of young adult titles, are presented. . . . This is an essential purchase that provides material not always easily available elsewhere." Libr J

For a fuller review see: Booklist, Jan. 15, 1993

Matthiessen, F. O. (Francis Otto), 1902-1950
American renaissance; art and expression in the age of Emerson and Whitman. Oxford Univ. Press 1941 xxiv, 678p il hardcover o.p. paperback available $18.95   **810.9**
1. American literature—History and criticism
ISBN 0-19-500759-X (pa)

Analyzed in Essay and general literature index

A critical study of works by Emerson, Thoreau, Melville, Hawthorne and Whitman and their impact on American intellectual history

Morrison, Toni, 1931-
Playing in the dark; whiteness and the literary imagination. Harvard Univ. Press 1992 91p $14.95   **810.9**
1. American literature—History and criticism 2. Blacks in literature 3. Race in literature
ISBN 0-674-67377-8   LC 91-39671

Also available in paperback from Vintage Bks.

Analyzed in Essay and general literature index

"Citing 'willful critical blindness' to the intrinsic role the 'Africanist presence' played in defining white 'Americanness,' Morrison analyzes the psychological, symbolic, and societal implications of race in the work of Edgar Allan Poe, Henry James, Herman Melville, Willa Cather, Mark Twain, William Faulkner, and Ernest Hemingway. Her frank and eye-opening assessments of 'the impact of racism on those who perpetuate it' broadens and invigorates our understanding of white American literature and the conflicted attitudes it expresses. A savvy and original inquiry." Booklist

Includes bibliographic references

The **Oxford** book of American literary anecdotes; edited by Donald Hall. Oxford Univ. Press 1981 xxiv, 360p hardcover o.p. paperback available $8.95   **810.9**
1. Authors, American—Anecdotes
ISBN 0-19-503388-4 (pa)   LC 80-27436

"Harvested from biographies, letters, interviews and reviews, these anecdotes were selected to reveal what American authors were like as people. Included: almost 150 writers from Anne Bradstreet and Jefferson to James Jones and Sylvia Plath." SLJ

Reading black, reading feminist; a critical anthology; edited by Henry Louis Gates, Jr. Penguin Bks. 1990 534p pa $14.95   **810.9**
1. American literature—Black authors—History and criticism 2. Women authors 3. Blacks in literature 4. Feminism
ISBN 0-452-01045-4   LC 90-35286

Analyzed in Essay and general literature index

"A Meridian book"

"In 26 critical essays, the volume looks at poems, novels, short stories, plays and autobiographies by black women writers ranging from 18th-century slave narratives to contemporary works of writers poised for the '90s." Publ Wkly

Ruas, Charles
Conversations with American writers. Knopf 1985 324p il o.p.; McGraw-Hill paperback available $7.95   **810.9**
1. American literature—History and criticism 2. Authorship
ISBN 0-07-054206-6 (pa)   LC 84-47848

"Most of these 14 interviews took place between 1975 and 1979, when Ruas was at WBAI radio in New York. Three generations of writers are represented: those who began to publish in the 1940s (Welty, Vidal, Capote, Mailer), in the 1950s and 1960s (Sontag, Burroughs, Heller, Doctorow), and in the 1970s (Robert Stone, Toni Morrison, Paul Theroux). Tennessee Williams, Marguerite Young, and Scott Spencer also appear." Libr J

Ruas "has selected and edited wisely. He thumps for no school of thought or critical trend. Indeed, literary culture as a major moral or aesthetic influence has slipped to the sidelines. What remains is not agreed-upon styles but individual voices." Time

Russell, Sandi
Render me my song; African American women writers from slavery to the present. St. Martin's Press 1991 227p $18.95; pa $9.95   **810.9**
1. American literature—Black authors—History and criticism 2. Women authors 3. Blacks in literature
ISBN 0-312-05288-X; 0-312-07074-8 (pa)
LC 90-49209

"From Lucy Terry's earliest recorded rhyme in 1746, to Ntozake Shange's novels of the 1980s, Russell surveys the development of black women's literary traditions in America." Booklist

Sawyer-Lauçanno, Christopher, 1951-
The continual pilgrimage; American writers in Paris, 1944-1960. Grove Press 1992 345p il $22.50   **810.9**
1. American literature—History and criticism 2. Authors, American 3. Paris (France)—Intellectual life
ISBN 0-8021-1371-0   LC 91-41295
This is an "account of American writers who lived in Paris during the decade and a half following World War II—transplanted literary luminaries that include Richard Wright, James Baldwin, William Styron, Lawrence Ferlinghetti, James Jones, Irwin Shaw, Chester Himes, John Ashbery, and the Beat writers." Libr J
"Detailing the material and social conditions that these writers found in Paris, Sawyer-Lauçanno discusses how the city empowered them in ways that American cities could not have." Publ Wkly

Includes bibliographic references

Warren, Robert Penn, 1905-1989
New and selected essays. Random House 1989 423p $24.95   **810.9**
1. American literature—History and criticism
ISBN 0-394-57516-4   LC 88-26470
Analyzed in Essay and general literature index
This book contains essays on Nathaniel Hawthorne, Mark Twain, Joseph Conrad, Ernest Hemingway, William Faulkner, Herman Melville, John Greenleaf Whittier, Robert Frost, and John Crowe Ransom
"Armed with the methods of the New Criticism and the metaphors of a poet, Robert Penn Warren plunges deep into our literary heritage to rescue the hidden meaning of some of our most famous literary works." N Y Times Book Rev

Wiget, Andrew
Native American literature. Twayne Pubs. 1985 147p il (Twayne's United States authors ser) $20.95   **810.9**
1. American literature—American Indian authors—History and criticism
ISBN 0-8057-7408-4   LC 84-19809
The author "includes Arctic, Canadian, Mesoamerican, and American Indian literatures in this critical survey of 50,000 years of indigenous literature. The chapters on oral narrative, oratory, and oral poetry are the strongest, illuminating how creation, emergence, and trickster tales, and lyric and ritual poetry restore harmony through the integration of content and performance." Libr J

Includes bibliography

Wilson, Edmund, 1895-1972
Patriotic gore; studies in the literature of the American Civil War. Oxford Univ. Press 1962 xxxii, 816p o.p.; University Press of New England paperback available $16.95   **810.9**
1. American literature—History and criticism 2. United States—History—1861-1865, Civil War
ISBN 0-930350-61-8 (pa)
Analyzed in Essay and general literature index
"A collection of sixteen essays on writing related to the war including the memoirs of Union generals Grant and Sherman and Confederates Mosby and Lee, diaries, political writing, and fiction by writers such as Ambrose

Bierce and John De Forest." Benet's Reader's Ency of Am Lit

811   American poetry

Ackerman, Diane
Jaguar of sweet laughter; new & selected poems. Random House 1991 254p $18   **811**
ISBN 0-394-57645-4   LC 90-48243
"Ackerman's lyrical voice and her feeling for detail and nuance are omnipresent in this work, assembled from prior books with ten new poems." Libr J

Aiken, Conrad, 1889-1973
Collected poems. 2nd ed. Oxford Univ. Press 1970 1049p $35   **811**
ISBN 0-19-501258-5
First published 1953
This volume contains all of the poet's published verse written since 1953 and the verse he has chosen to preserve from more than five decades of previously published work. The arrangement is chronological
The "work of one of the masters of our time, a poet who can charm, surprise, enlighten, or terrify, varying but never losing a harpsichordist's elegance of touch." Atlantic

Ammons, A. R., 1926-
The really short poems of A. R. Ammons. Norton 1991 160p $17.95; pa $8.95   **811**
ISBN 0-393-02870-4; 0-393-30850-2 (pa)
      LC 89-71357
"The more than 100 poems in this collection span the career of one of the deans of contemporary poetry. . . . Throughout, Ammons makes you laugh and forces you to think hard about the way humans relate to natural phenomena and to themselves." Booklist

Angelou, Maya
And still I rise. Random House 1978 54p $11.95   **811**
ISBN 0-394-50252-3   LC 78-57118
Angelou's "volume of poetry enlarges on themes from her autobiographical writings and earlier poetry." Libr J
"There are certain love poems here that are, in a true sense, as intimate as any by her sister poets of any race; yet they are uniquely Angelou, totally innocent of any exploitation or shock value." Publ Wkly

I shall not be moved. Random House 1990 48p $14.95   **811**
ISBN 0-394-58618-2   LC 89-43550
Also available in paperback from Bantam Bks.
"Angelou's themes include loss of love and youth, human oneness in diversity, the strength of blacks in the face of racism and adversity." Publ Wkly
"Angelou speaks eloquently of black life, unfolding a significant history in poems that are highly controlled and yet powerful." Libr J

Angelou, Maya—Continued

Just give me a cool drink of water 'fore I diiie; the poetry of Maya Angelou. Random House 1971 48p $15   **811**

ISBN 0-394-47142-3

The first part of this poetry collection "contains poetry of love, and therefore of anguish, sharing, fear, affection and loneliness. Part Two features poetry of racial confrontation—of protest, anger and irony." SLJ

Now Sheba sings the song; with art by Tom Feelings. Dutton; Dial Bks. 1987 54p il $18.95; pa $9.95   **811**

ISBN 0-525-24501-4; 0-525-48374-8 (pa)

LC 86-19876

"Feeling's 84 sepia and black-and-white illustrations of black women were drawn in Africa, the U.S., South America and the Caribbean. They inspired Angelou to write this poem celebrating black women's strength, dignity, exuberance and sexuality. Pictures and verse complement each other." Publ Wkly

Oh pray my wings are gonna fit me well. Random House 1975 67p $14.95   **811**

ISBN 0-394-49951-4

This collection contains "good heritage ballads and excellent lyrics such as 'Child Dead in Old Seas,' and the colorful, pleasant 'This Winter Day,' which reminds one of genre paintings." Libr J

Anne Sexton; telling the tale; edited by Steven E. Colburn. University of Mich. Press 1988 481p (Under discussion) $37.50; pa $14.95   **811**

1. Sexton, Anne
ISBN 0-472-09379-7; 0-472-06379-0 (pa)

LC 88-14373

"This book starts with a chronology and biographical essays which recount Anne Sexton's life. . . . The body of the book consists of literary criticism of Sexton's work. . . . Colburn adequately outlines the debate, presenting facts and disparate opinions." West Coast Rev Books

Includes bibliography

Ansen, Alan

Contact highs; selected poems, 1957-1987; introduction by Steven Moore with an afterword by Rachel Hadas. Dalkey Archive Press 1989 xxxiv, 213p $19.95; pa $11.95   **811**

ISBN 0-916583-44-9; 0-916583-45-7 (pa)   LC 89-7768

"Though relatively unknown, Ansen has been a real actor in literary history for the past 30 years. . . . [This collection's] styles range from the drug-induced 'Heroin' through a sestina dedicated to Ashbery to Audenesque formalism that rhymes. Whatever the styles, the cadences are powerfully relentless and informed by an intellectual complexity rare today. As witty as O'Hara, Ansen also plunges into the depths of the human condition. This may be one of the more significant poetry publications of the decade." Libr J

Ashbery, John

April galleons; poems. Viking 1987 97p o.p.; Penguin Bks. paperback available $7.95   **811**

ISBN 0-14-058603-2 (pa)   LC 87-40059

"Elisabeth Sifton books"

The author's "seamless style allows a rich assemblage of voices to move nimbly between high comedy and low, among fable, memory, and meditation. Youthful experience is contrasted with a life in late middle age . . . and while change remains a major theme, life rather than art becomes central." Libr J

Flow chart. Knopf 1991 216p $20   **811**

ISBN 0-679-40201-2   LC 90-52903

This "torrent of invention—a book-length meditation-cum-narrative whose true subject may be the process of its own unfolding—comes as close to an epic poem as our postmodern, nonlinear, deconstructed sensibilities will allow." Libr J

Hotel Lautréamont. Knopf 1992 157p $23   **811**

ISBN 0-679-41512-2   LC 92-52952

"Blandishments, chitchat, jokes, parodies, personae and all kinds of slang circulate freely through Ashbery's . . . collection. As always, his work will frustrate readers who must know just what it's about. Curious and spectacular details no sooner come up than they vanish; distractions and even boredom have their places; and Ashbery's central preoccupations—passing time, the ambiguities of identity—are as ordinary as they are enduring." Publ Wkly

Selected poems. Viking 1985 349p o.p.; Penguin Bks. paperback available $12.95   **811**

ISBN 0-14-058553-2 (pa)   LC 85-40549

"Elisabeth Sifton books"

"Ashbery's work is seductive precisely because it alludes to shared traditions and assumptions about poetry. His poems attract us with their gestures of 'meaningful' discourse, the meditative pace of their syntax and the memories and expectations of meaningfulness that it evokes, the careful use of qualifiers, and the precisions and surprises of his diction." Benet's Reader's Ency of Am Lit

Atwood, Margaret, 1939-

Selected poems. Simon & Schuster 1978 c1976 240p hardcover o.p. paperback available $9.95   **811**

ISBN 0-395-40422-3 (pa)   LC 77-18042

First published 1976 in Canada

"This collection of the best from all of Atwood's published works, dating back to 1966, points out Atwood's progression as a thinker and poet and makes plain her central concern during the years; the transformations that involves us all." Booklist

Selected poems II; poems, selected & new, 1976-1986. Houghton Mifflin 1987 147p hardcover o.p. paperback available $9.95   **811**

ISBN 0-395-45406-9 (pa)   LC 87-3861

"Tighter, more compactly selected than her previous 'Selected poems' [entered above] this volume contains material from Atwood's last three collections, as well as

Atwood, Margaret, 1939----*Continued*
a section incorporating previously uncollected 'New Poems (1985-1986).'" Choice

Baldwin, James, 1924-1987
Jimmy's blues; selected poems. St. Martin's Press 1985 75p $11.95; pa $9.95
811

ISBN 0-312-44247-5; 0-312-05104-2 (pa)

LC 85-25185

The first published collection of poetry from the author of If Beale Street could talk, Another country and The fire next time

Benét, Stephen Vincent, 1898-1943
John Brown's body
811
1. Brown, John, 1800-1859—Poetry 2. United States—History—1861-1865, Civil War—Poetry
Hardcover and paperback editions available from various publishers
Awarded the Pulitzer Prize, 1929
First published 1928 by Doubleday, Doran
"A narrative of the Civil War, it opens with a prelude on the introduction of slavery, which is followed by a description of John Brown and his raid on Harpers Ferry. The poem, which considers both sides of the conflict with sympathy, includes sketches of famous participants, battles, the hardships of those on the home front, etc." Reader's Ency. 3d edition

Berrigan, Daniel
Block Island; afterword by Mary McAnally. Unicorn Press 1985 102p $20; pa $9.95
811
ISBN 0-87775-175-7; 0-87775-176-5 (pa)
This sequence of poems by the Jesuit poet/activist uses Block Island, Rhode Island as its central metaphor

Prison poems; foreword by Philip Berrigan. Unicorn Press 1973 124p hardcover o.p. paperback available $8.95
811
ISBN 0-87775-149-8 (pa)
These poems were "written while Berrigan was imprisoned at Danbury Federal Penitentiary. . . . To his customary range of allusions Berrigan has added penitentiary life as well as references to his activities in opposition to the war." Choice

Berry, Wendell, 1934-
Collected poems, 1957-1982. North Point Press 1985 268p $19.95; pa $9.95
811
ISBN 0-86547-189-4; 0-86547-197-5 (pa)
LC 84-62305
"'What must a man do to be at home in the world?' This is the overriding concern in Wendell Berry's poems, gathered here from eight books from the past 25 years. Though rooted in the rugged rural landscape of Kentucky, the poems ultimately grow from the landscape of the human heart. The interplay of the natural world and the human spirit is the informing principle." Libr J

"As a nature poet Berry has a grass-roots, homespun quality that reminds one of Frost. He moves easily from witty lyrics and graceful elegies to moving love poems, philosophical odes and confessionals." Publ Wkly

Sabbaths. North Point Press 1987 96p $12.95; pa $6.95
811
ISBN 0-86547-289-0; 0-86547-290-4 (pa)
LC 87-60877
"These poems reflect a utopian vision—reminiscent of the religion of the Native American people—that relates human life to the cycles of the Earth. Organized by years rather than by specific titles, Berry's lyrical hymns follow the seasons of birth and death, growth and decay, over a seven-year period, from 1979 to 1986." Publ Wkly

Berryman, John, 1914-1972
Collected poems, 1937-1971; edited and introduced by Charles Thornbury. Farrar, Straus & Giroux 1989 347p hardcover o.p. paperback available $14.95
811
ISBN 0-374-52281-2 (pa)
LC 89-30944
"Brings together in chronological order for the first time the seven collections of short poems Berryman himself arranged and published. 'Homage to Mistress Bradstreet' is included, though 'The Dream Songs,' as a self-contained work, is excluded." N Y Times Book Rev
"A poet at the center of the mid-century's intellectual and emotional life, Berryman records the outcome of human experience as the opposite of what we either hope for or expect in shifts of language from dialect to sophisticated rhetoric that underscore the agony of the poetry." Libr J

The dream songs. Farrar, Straus & Giroux 1969 xx, 427p hardcover o.p. paperback available $14.95
811
ISBN 0-374-51670-7 (pa)
This book contains the author's 385 'dream songs' that originally appeared in various magazines, the Pulitzer Prize winning 77 dream songs (1964) and His toy, his dream, his rest (1968). The poet also provides a brief note about Henry, the poems' central character
"Berryman makes brilliant use of his speaker's indiscriminately retentive perception—the patter of jukeboxes, of cocktail parties, of the gutter and the cathedral—to drop us dizzily into an original world where life is lived naked and unashamed." Va Q Rev

Henry's fate & other poems, 1967-1972. Farrar, Straus & Giroux 1977 93p $7.95
811
ISBN 0-374-16950-0
LC 76-52950
This "posthumous volume of Berryman's verse reproduces previously unpublished Dream Songs as well as several fascinating fragments and unfinished poems. Berryman captures his 'failing life, his whisky curse' in language that is taut and agonized. . . . Berryman articulates his themes—alcoholism, adultery, love of his daughter, and the woes of teaching—by engaging in dialogue with his famous alter egos, Henry and Mr. Bones." Libr J

Bidart, Frank, 1939-
In the western night; collected poems, 1965-90. Farrar, Straus & Giroux 1990 243p $19.95; pa $13.95 **811**

ISBN 0-374-17660-4; 0-374-52271-5 (pa)

LC 89-25993

The poet "confronts head-on the insoluble problems of being: the thirst for meaning, the fathomless abyss of death, the polarities of good and evil. . . . Bidart also draws on wrenching autobiographical incident, Christian tradition, Western philosophy. . . . A poet who believes the poem embodies 'the mind in action,' he synthesizes the flexibility of Pound's *Cantos*, Robert Lowell's sense of argument with the past, and Hart Crane's collage-like structuring into a distinctive, sharp-edged voice raised to an intense pitch." Publ Wkly

Bishop, Elizabeth, 1911-1979
The complete poems, 1927-1979. Farrar, Straus & Giroux 1983 287p hardcover o.p. paperback available $8.95 **811**

ISBN 0-374-51817-3 (pa)

LC 82-21119

Supersedes the author's Complete poems, published 1969

This volume contains poems from four collections: North & South (1946); A cold spring (1955, winner of Pulitzer prize); Questions of travel (1965); and Geography III (1977). Also included are translations, uncollected poems, and sections entitled "Poems written in youth" and "Occasional poems"

Bishop's "reputation is founded on perhaps 25 poems. . . . Altogether that looks like a modest achievement until one considers that most of the larger poetic reputations of the past century have been founded on similar evidence. The difference is that Bishop's masterpieces stand in a higher ratio to her work as a whole." N Y Times Book Rev

Blackburn, Paul, 1926-1971
The collected poems of Paul Blackburn; edited, with an introduction, by Edith Jarolim. Persea Bks. 1985 xxxv, 667p il $37.50 **811**

ISBN 0-89255-086-4

LC 85-9309

"Blackburn wrote over 1200 poems, and Jarolim has rescued 523 of them, working mainly with out-of-print editions. She includes poems from 1945 to 1971, a period when Blackburn became associated with the Black Mountain poets and gained fame as a translator of Spanish and Provencal poetry." Libr J

"Much of Blackburn's poetry is an engaging mix of sharp, allusive adventuring, humor and wordplay, annotated fragments of musical speech, and a moderate but distinctive use of metaphor. Edith Jarolim's introduction provides a concise view of Blackburn's art and life." Choice

Bly, Robert
Loving a woman in two worlds. Dial Press 1985 78p o.p.; Perennial Lib. paperback available $10 **811**

ISBN 0-06-097083-9 (pa)

LC 84-12704

"Bly's intense love poems record the complexity of a lover's relationship with its mood-swings of joy and grief, sharing and independence. Though the verses are not romantic in a conventional sense, the emotional bonds they plumb go deep." Publ Wkly

Selected poems. Harper & Row 1986 213p hardcover o.p. paperback available $9.95 **811**

ISBN 0-06-096048-5 (pa)

LC 84-47556

"The book is arranged in nine sections, each introduced by a short essay. Two longer essays, 'Whitman's Line as a Public Form' and 'The Prose Poem as an Evolving Form,' conclude the book. Although he begins with early poems previously uncollected and ends with excerpts from his most recent volume, Mr. Bly avoids strict chronology. Rather, each section is designed to illustrate a step in the evolution of his poetics." N Y Times Book Rev

Bogan, Louise, 1897-1970
The blue estuaries: poems, 1923-1968. Farrar, Straus & Giroux 1968 136p o.p.; Ecco Press paperback available $8.50 **811**

ISBN 0-88001-192-0 (pa)

LC 76-46175

"Influenced by the English metaphysical poets, Bogan's poetry is subtle, restrained, and intellectual." Benet's Reader's Ency of Am Lit

Booth, Philip, 1925-
Selves; new poems; by Philip Booth. Viking 1990 75p $17.95 **811**

ISBN 0-670-83055-0

LC 89-40317

Also available in paperback from Penguin Bks.

This collection "features contemplative poems born of the observant patience of North country life. The best are based on concrete observation. . . . Booth's strength is that he speaks of significant issues like the ultimate privacy of suffering, the painful hidden destruction of relationships, the coming of aging and death." Libr J

Brooks, Gwendolyn
Selected poems. Harper & Row 1963 127p hardcover o.p. paperback available $8.95 **811**

ISBN 0-06-090989-7 (pa)

LC 63-16503

"The subject of this poetry is the lives of African American residents of Northern urban ghettos, particularly women, and Brooks has been praised for her depiction of that experience in forms ranging from terza rima to blues meter." Benet's Reader's Ency of Am Lit

Bryant, William Cullen, 1794-1878
The poetical works of William Cullen Bryant; with chronologies of Bryant's life and poems and a bibliography of his writings by Henry C. Sturges, and a memoir of his life by Richard Henry Stoddard. Roslyn ed. Appleton & Co. 1903 cxxx, 418p il o.p.; AMS Press reprint available $42.50 **811**

ISBN 0-404-01143-8

Bryant's "poems on Indians, Africans, Greeks and 'William Tell' are typical of his humanitarian liberalism. His language is that of the transitional period between 18th century diction and early-19th-century romanticism. His best poems philosophize about a carefully delineated natural object or scene . . . and exemplify American literature's movement from New England puritanism to

Bryant, William Cullen, 1794-1878 — *Continued*
mild Republican, romantic transcendentalism." Penguin Companion to Am Lit

Budbill, David
Judevine; the complete poems, 1970-1990. Chelsea Green 1991 310p $24.95; pa $14.95
811
ISBN 0-930031-47-4; 0-930031-48-2 (pa)
LC 91-23481
"Poems of dignity and passion spin a tale of rural folk in a poor Vermont town." Booklist

Bukowski, Charles
The roominghouse madrigals; early selected poems, 1946-1966. Black Sparrow Press 1988 256p $20; pa $12.50 **811**
ISBN 0-87685-733-0; 0-87685-732-2 (pa)
LC 88-10426
The poems are "gathered from the prolific poet's early, out-of-print, and now scarce pamphlets. . . . The language is a bit less ostentatious than in later work, permitting a gentle and often self-mocking humor to emerge." Libr J

Bynner, Witter, 1881-1968
Selected poems; edited and with a critical introduction by Richard Wilbur; biographical introduction by James Kraft. Farrar, Straus & Giroux 1978 cxxviii, 254p (Works of Witter Bynner v1) $30 **811**
ISBN 0-374-25863-5
LC 77-21365
This volume "contains verse from 15 of [Bynner's] 18 published volumes, along with a dozen poems previously uncollected." Libr J
This "volume shows Bynner at his best. He was a skilled and polished versifier with a genuine lyrical gift. His close knowledge of Chinese poetry, which he also translated, is reflected in some poems, in a sparseness of language and imagery." Choice

Carruth, Hayden, 1921-
Collected shorter poems, 1946-1991. Copper Canyon Press 1992 417p $23; pa $12 **811**
ISBN 1-55659-048-2; 1-55659-049-0 (pa) LC 92-3389
"This omnibus volume, more than twice the size of *Selected Poetry* offers a sampling from nearly all of Carruth's prior collections, plus a selection of 32 previously ungathered pieces written over the last five years. Even the new poems are surprisingly eclectic, including rhymed sonnet, Beat litany, Objectivist lyric, and dramatic monolog. Such variety notwithstanding, Carruth's personal blend of wit, *Weltanschauung*, and conscience is indelibly his own, one of the lasting literary signatures of our time." Libr J

Tell me again how the white heron rises and flies across the nacreous river toward the distant islands. New Directions 1989 83p pa $8.95 **811**
ISBN 0-8112-1104-5
LC 89-31603

"Rich, long-lined ruminations on poetry, jazz, nature, metaphysics, and love—concluding with an elegy, 'Mother,' of Whitmanian proportions—constitute the finest single collection by one of America's senior poets." Booklist

Carver, Raymond
A new path to the waterfall; poems; introduction by Tess Gallagher. Atlantic Monthly Press 1989 xxxi, 126p hardcover o.p. paperback available $10.95 **811**
ISBN 0-87113-374-1 (pa)
LC 88-34989
"In her moving introduction, Carver's widow, writer Tess Gallagher, notes how often a particular poem calls to mind a corresponding story, and the reverse is also true. Indeed, to know Carver by his prose is to know him only partially. Master at illuminating those often mundane moments that starkly dramatize entire lives, Carver was also master at creating mood, and many of those poems have a striking lyrical intensity, especially when Carver unflinchingly faces death while celebrating life. A coda to a remarkable literary career." Libr J

Ultramarine. Random House 1986 140p hardcover o.p. paperback available $8.95
811
ISBN 0-394-75535-9 (pa)
LC 86-10221
The collection exhibits "an acute eye for significant detail and an unerring ear for authentic speech, precision and economy of means, dramatic drive, and an uncanny knack for melding humor and pathos. To read Carver's poems is to enter, instantly, into a real but specially heightened world, inhabited by real people." Booklist

Ciardi, John, 1916-1986
Poems of love and marriage. University of Ark. Press 1988 35p $12.95; pa $7.95
811
ISBN 1-55728-055-X; 1-55728-054-1 (pa)
LC 88-17229
These lyrics have been collected from both Ciardi's published and unpublished work and focus on the nature of youthful romance and marriage

Selected poems. University of Ark. Press 1984 222p $21; pa $8.95 **811**
ISBN 0-938626-29-9; 0-938626-30-2 (pa)
LC 83-24254
The author "leaves virtually no aspect of modern life untouched, bringing to each subject his particular vision. . . . Whether short lyrics or long, anecdotal verse, Ciardi's poems flow beautifully, without straining for effect." Publ Wkly

Clampitt, Amy
Archaic figure; poems. Knopf 1987 113p $15.95; pa $12.95 **811**
ISBN 0-394-55919-3; 0-394-75090-X (pa)
LC 86-46004
"We admire Clampitt most of all for the degree to which her poetry imitates, in idealized form, the refined but tortuous convolutions of human consciousness of the highest order. She treats her craft as the great synthesizing art. There is no aspect of myth, history, civilization, nature or everyday human existence excluded from her probative meditations." Publ Wkly

Clampitt, Amy—*Continued*
The kingfisher; poems. Knopf 1983 149p
$15.95; pa $14.95   **811**

ISBN 0-394-52840-9; 0-394-71251-X (pa)
LC 82-47963

The images in this collection of Clampitt's poetry are drawn from a "variety of origins—nature (from Iowa to Greece), religion (from Athena to Christ), science (from geology to entomology), art (from manuscript illumination to Beethoven), and literature (from Homer to Hopkins)." N Y Rev Books

Westward; poems. Knopf 1990 107p
$18.95; pa $9.95   **811**

ISBN 0-394-58455-4; 0-679-72867-8 (pa)
LC 89-43359

The author reveals her "sense of landscape, as well as an exceptional gift for recording the subtleties of nature. Here she visits both sides of the Atlantic in Jamesian fashion. Her American journey ranges from a graveyard celebration of Emily Dickinson at Amherst, Mass., to the California coast, where 'the land ends.' Her most ambitious poem, 'The Prairie,' juxtaposes the barren Russian steppes of Chekhov alongside the harsh, isolated Dakota plains where the speaker's great-grandfather settled amid a 'hinterland of grass,' and finds an uneasy moral." Publ Wkly
"No living poet writes with fiercer energy, or is able to transform the diversity of life into such a variegated unity." New Leader

What the light was like. Knopf 1985 110p
$14.95; pa $12.95   **811**

ISBN 0-394-54318-1; 0-394-72937-4 (pa)
LC 84-48652

Clampitt's "nature poems are her centerpieces, be they quick and compressed like 'A Baroque Sunburst' or conversational and expansive like the title poem. She is less convincing with social commentary and the urban scene. Here the verbal fireworks at times get too tricky. It isn't cleverness for its own sake we want, but—as happens when we read her best poems—to be whirled by the language to an unexpected truth." Libr J

Corso, Gregory
Mindfield; with foreword by William S. Burroughs & Allan Ginsberg; and drawings by the author. Thunder's Mouth Press 1989 268p il $24.95; pa $12.95   **811**

ISBN 0-938410-85-7; 0-938410-86-5 (pa)   LC 89-5152

"This volume includes substantial selections from each of [the author's] six volumes of published poetry and 23 previously unpublished poems. Corso has written a number of the most memorable American poems since WW II. His poetry combines a lyrical directness of speech with a unique blend of surrealism and aphoristic statement." Choice

Cowley, Malcolm, 1898-1989
Blue Juniata: a life; collected and new poems. Penguin Bks. 1985 163p pa $8.95
                                               811

ISBN 0-14-058556-7   LC 85-13845
"Elisabeth Sifton books"
"Cowley has gathered the work of six decades, which traces the life and thought of one of the most veritable and venerable men of letters of our time. . . . Cowley's pointed details and insights . . . reveal the excitement

of living through perilous decades, and in the final section's six poems from old age, graceful and alert as always, he looks back with nostalgia and marks the lengthening shadows case by a life filled with activity, well-chosen works, and uncommon reflection." Booklist

Crane, Stephen, 1871-1900
The complete poems of Stephen Crane; edited and with an introduction by Joseph Katz. Cornell Univ. Press 1972 xxxvii, 154p pa $9.95   **811**

ISBN 0-8014-9130-4

This collection of 134 poems, arranged in chronological order, includes poems from the two collections printed during Crane's lifetime: The black riders and other lines (1895) and War is kind (1899), as well as poems which he contributed to periodicals and those surviving in verifiable holographs or typescripts
"Crane's experimental free verse heralded and somewhat influenced the imagist movement of Ezra Pound and Amy Lowell." Herzberg. Reader's Ency of Am Lit

Includes bibliographic references

Creeley, Robert, 1926-
The collected poems of Robert Creeley, 1945-1975. University of Calif. Press 1982 671p $42.50; pa $12.95   **811**

ISBN 0-520-04243-3; 0-520-04244-1 (pa)
LC 81-19668

Thirty years of Creeley's works have been collected from nine previous books, small press publications, and little magazines
"After nearly four decades of writing, [Creeley's] work has become a major influence on contemporary poetics and new generations of writers. Reading through Creeley's poems, you find yourself enticed by his oblique but exacting perceptions." Christ Sci Monit

Selected poems. University of Calif. Press 1991 xxii, 366p $25   **811**

ISBN 0-520-06935-8   LC 91-7152
"A Centennial book"
"This new sampling both refines and builds upon its predecessors, *Selected Poems* and *Collected Poems* [entered above]. From the nearly antagonistic minimalism of 'A Piece' ('One and/one, two,/three') through the philosophical expansiveness of 'Desultory Days' and beyond, it becomes apparent that Creeley's work has not so much opened up over the years as fluctuated in its attentions to self and world." Libr J

Cummings, E. E. (Edward Estlin), 1894-1962
Complete poems, 1904-1962; containing all the published poetry; edited by George J. Firmage. rev corr & expanded ed. Liveright 1991 xxxii, 1102p $50   **811**

ISBN 0-87140-145-2   LC 91-29158
Expanded version of Complete poems, 1913-1962 (1972)
"This volume has been prepared directly from the poet's original manuscripts, preserving the original typography and format. It includes all the previously published works, from *Tulips* (1922) to *Etcetera* (1983), as well as 36 uncollected poems that originally appeared in little magazines or anthologies." Libr J

Cummings, E. E. (Edward Estlin), 1894-1962—*Continued*

W [ViVa] edited, with an afterword, by George James Firmage. Liveright 1979 lxxp (Cummings typescript editions) $9.95; pa $3.95   **811**

ISBN 0-87140-636-5; 0-87140-125-8 (pa) LC 79-4212

First published 1931

This edition is based on "galley and page proofs when needed; and it incorporates all of Cummings's final alterations and corrections (the original edition contained numerous typographical errors). 'ViVa' includes some of Cummings's most experimental work and several of his best-known poems. It is a mixed bag of topics and techniques, with a good measure of satire on city life and characters mixed with poems on love and the lover." Choice

Dickey, James

The central motion; poems, 1968-1979. Wesleyan Univ. Press 1983 148p $30; pa $14.95   **811**

ISBN 0-8195-5091-4; 0-8195-6088-X (pa)

LC 83-21734

This volume collects the author's The eye beaters (1970), The zodiac (1977) and The strength of fields (1980)

"The more James Dickey changes, the more *c'est la même chose*. This is partly because what he does as a poet is to dramatize himself in the act of taking chances, very much including chances with language and form. . . . This man's best poems will be read and admired for a long time to come." N Y Times Book Rev

The eagle's mile. Wesleyan Univ. Press 1990 66p hardcover o.p. paperback available $10.95   **811**

ISBN 0-8195-1187-0 (pa) LC 89-49257

"Although departing from the narrative-based style of his past work, Dickey . . . is still deeply committed to the presentation of reality in incongruous terms. His use of language itself is innovative; words are hitched together to create new, slightly unnatural juxtapositions." Publ Wkly

Poems, 1957-1967. Wesleyan Univ. Press 1978 c1967 299p $30; pa $15.95   **811**

ISBN 0-8195-3073-5; 0-8195-6055-3 (pa)

First published 1967

Most of the poems from "Drowning with Others," "Helmets," the winner of the National Book Award for 1965, "Buckdancer's Choice" and "Into the Stone" are here "augmented by enough new poems for another whole volume. The new poems are stronger and darker in mood than the earlier ones, but some of the same themes—animals in the wild, snakes and snakebite, the father-and-son tie, the perceptive senses of the blind reappear in different form." Publ Wkly

The whole motion; collected poems, 1949-1992. Wesleyan Univ. Press 1992 477p (Wesleyan poetry) $29.95   **811**

ISBN 0-8195-2202-3 LC 91-50811

"A definitive retrospective of an American poet known for his experimental and probing approach. . . . This robust collection embraces more than 200 poems from over a dozen books, including his first, *Into the Stone*, to *Buckdancer's Choice*, winner of the 1966 National

Book Award, his latest monograph, *The Eagle's Mile* (Wesleyan Univ., 1990), as well as a set of previously uncollected or unpublished works." Booklist

Dickinson, Emily, 1830-1886

The complete poems of Emily Dickinson; edited by Thomas H. Johnson. Little, Brown 1960 770p $25; pa $14.95   **811**

ISBN 0-316-18414-4; 0-316-18413-6 (pa)

A chronological arrangement of all known Dickinson poems and fragments

Final harvest; Emily Dickinson's poems; selection and introduction by Thomas H. Johnson. Little, Brown 1961 331p $19.95; pa $11.95   **811**

ISBN 0-316-18416-0; 0-316-18415-2 (pa) LC 62-8061

A selection of 575 poems from The complete poems of Emily Dickinson, entered above. The editor's aim has been to allow the reader to realize the full scope and diversity of the poet's work

Dove, Rita

Grace notes; poems. Norton 1989 73p $16.95; pa $9.95   **811**

ISBN 0-393-02719-8; 0-393-30696-8 (pa)

LC 89-30762

"Dove takes simple memories (drilling with flash cards as a child) or events (her daughter's curiosity about anatomy) and turns them into polished refigurings that are freighted with meaning. . . . Pared yet luminous, these poems should be read by anyone who loves poetry." Libr J

Thomas and Beulah; poems. Carnegie-Mellon Univ. Press 1986 79p $14.95; pa $6.95   **811**

ISBN 0-88748-020-9; 0-88748-021-7 (pa)

LC 85-71965

"Dove has written a sequence of lyrics that traces the lives of a turn-of-the-century Southern black couple, Thomas and Beulah, who emigrate to Akron, Ohio and live there until their deaths in the 1960s." Libr J

"Dove is principally a poet of dramatic force—a quality found relatively rarely in lyric, a genre by its nature reflective, circling, and static. . . . The poems comprise a true sequence: that is, most are richer for, and in fact only intelligible in, the context of the rest." N Y Times Book Rev

Dunbar, Paul Laurence, 1872-1906

The collected poetry of Paul Laurence Dunbar; edited and with an introduction by Joanne M. Braxton. University Press of Va. 1993 xxxvi, 396p $40; pa $14.95   **811**

ISBN 0-8139-1454-X; 0-8139-1438-8 (pa)

LC 92-37190

This volume contains the entire text of The complete poems of Paul Laurence Dunbar published 1913 by Dodd, Mead, and an additional sixty poems, sixteen of which were found in manuscript form

"The poet's predecessors in the use of African-American dialect were white writers, such as Irwin Russell, Stephen Collins Foster, Joel Chandler Harris, and Thomas Nelson Page, but they were unable to portray African-American life with Dunbar's personal insights." Benet's Reader's Ency of Am Lit

Duncan, Robert Edward, 1919-1988
Ground work; before the war; [by] Robert Duncan. New Directions 1984 175p hardcover o.p. paperback available $10.95
811

ISBN 0-8112-0896-6 (pa)   LC 84-4889

Duncan's "work is difficult right on the surface. His sheer reach and range of associations and patterning are so complex that the reader is forced to scan the page as one scans a horizon and register some sense of a visual whole before proceeding to the parts. . . . 'Ground Work: Before the War' is . . . a series of sequences or books within books." N Y Times Book Rev

Ground work II; in the dark; [by] Robert Duncan. New Directions 1987 90p $19.95; pa $9.95
811

ISBN 0-8112-1041-3; 0-8112-1042-1 (pa)

LC 87-11033

"This, [Duncan's] last volume, at least in part a reflection on that upcoming death, may yet turn out to be his most important. . . . In In the Dark, Robert Duncan dares to address an absolute, where no life stirs, where sleep, waking, and dream all are foreign, where a kind of purity reigns—'And purity begins to flame when we see the word fire in it,' as Duncan wrote in his letter. Duncan's poetry makes its way straight into that flame in the dark." Am Book Rev

Eliot, T. S. (Thomas Stearns), 1888-1965
Collected poems, 1909-1962. Harcourt Brace & World 1963 221p $16.95 **811**
ISBN 0-15-118978-1

This volume contains the complete text of 'Collected poems, 1909-1935,' the 'Four quartets,' and several other poems accompanied by brief prefatory notes

Four quartets. Harcourt Brace & Co. 1943 39p hardcover o.p. paperback available $4.95
811

ISBN 0-15-633225-6 (pa)

This volume is "an elaborate, allusive meditation on time and eternity, consisting of four poems named for four different places. . . . The whole work is as elaborately constructed as a piece of music, with its recurrent imagery, series of symbols (the separate poems are concerned, respectively, with air, earth, water, and fire), and literary, historical, and Christian references. Each poem ends with some words about the poet's craft and the problems of creating a work of art." Reader's Ency. 3d edition

Erdrich, Louise
Baptism of desire; poems. Harper & Row 1989 78p hardcover o.p. paperback available $9.95
811

ISBN 0-06-092044-0 (pa)   LC 89-45650

"Evocative and explicit, this collection of poems from novelist Erdrich explores the often mingled spiritualities of her dual Catholic and Native American heritage. .

. . The last poems are domestic and reflective, written, according to the author, in the small hours of the night when pregnancy made her insomniac. Vividly physiological, these celebrate the possibilities of new life against the backdrop of myth and history evoked in the preceding selections." Publ Wkly

Ferlinghetti, Lawrence
A Coney Island of the mind; poems. New Directions 1958 93p hardcover o.p. paperback available $5.95 **811**
ISBN 0-8112-0041-8 (pa)

This collection of new and old poems by the owner of the City Lights bookshop, which served as headquarters for the San Francisco literary movement, "is a grab bag of undergraduate musings about love and art, much hackneyed satire of American life and some real and wry perceptions of it." N Y Times Book Rev

Endless life; selected poems. New Directions 1981 215p hardcover o.p. paperback available $9.95 **811**
ISBN 0-8112-0797-8 (pa)   LC 80-29127

Ferlinghetti's "poetry is not usually lyrical and his images, though pungent, are tightly controlled; his lines are short, sometimes staccato, and scattered at seeming random down the page; and emotion is understated or, more often, the victim of irony. Yet, for sheer, soaring energy, he's hard to beat. Like a run-away train or a child reciting the alphabet all in one breath, the words and lines of his poems flow from one to the next with sure inevitability and grace." Best Sellers

Over all the obscene boundaries; European poems & transitions. New Directions 1984 122p hardcover o.p. paperback available $7.95 **811**
ISBN 0-8112-0920-2 (pa)   LC 84-6919

This is a collection of poems that were inspired by the author's trip to France. Five of the poems are written in French

"While [Ferlinghetti's] sense of observation is still sharp, these poems (written mostly during the last seven years) are quieter, less surreal than other recent work. . . . [The] poems written in French, and the French scattered in poems and titles, are effective. This book is Ferlinghetti at his best." Libr J

When I look at pictures. Peregrine Smith Bks. 1990 47p il $12.95 **811**
ISBN 0-87905-212-0   LC 90-34070

A collection of poems inspired by the paintings of Monet, Picasso, Pissarro, and others

Fowler, Virginia C., 1948-
Nikki Giovanni. Twayne Pubs. 1992 192p (Twayne's United States authors ser) $21.95
811

1. Giovanni, Nikki
ISBN 0-8057-3983-1   LC 92-16731

This introduction to the black poet assesses her work in political, sociological and biographical terms. An interview with Giovanni is included

"The full bibliography contains helpful annotations. This clear introduction provides a base for further study of Giovanni's work." Libr J

Francis, Robert, 1901-1987
Late fire, late snow; new and uncollected poems. University of Mass. Press 1992 72p il $20; pa $8.95 **811**

ISBN 0-87023-813-2; 0-87023-814-0 (pa)   LC 92-7991

"While age is a recurring theme, *Late Fire, Late Snow* is arranged so that the later poems converse with the earlier ones in a . . . mixture of subject and tone, mingling the pastoral with the political, the contemplative with the Chaplinesque." Publisher's note

Frost, Robert, 1874-1963
The poetry of Robert Frost; edited by Edward Connery Lathem. Holt & Co. 1969 607p hardcover o.p. paperback available $12.95 **811**

ISBN 0-8050-0501-3 (pa)

"A one-volume edition of Frost's eleven volumes of poetry and two short blank-verse plays. The collection ranges in time from A Boy's Will (1913) to In the Clearing (1962). . . . [There is] an appendix of bibliographical and textual notes for each of the poems." Nation

The road not taken; illustrated by John O'Hara Cosgrave II. Holt & Co. 1951 xxxvii, 282p il $16.95; pa $10.95 **811**

ISBN 0-8050-0529-3; 0-8050-0528-5 (pa)

"An introduction to Robert Frost; a selection of Robert Frost's poems; with a biographical preface and running commentary by Louis Untermeyer." Title page

Gallagher, Tess
Moon crossing bridge; poetry. Graywolf Press 1992 99p $17 **811**

ISBN 1-55597-156-3   LC 91-32695

"The sequence of poems that together constitute a narrative is the late-twentieth-century equivalent of the epic poem. In this, one of her finest works, Gallagher mourns the loss of her husband (the late short-story writer Raymond Carver), and hers becomes, in the process, a universal voice of grief." Booklist

Gerstler, Amy
Bitter angel; poems. North Point Press 1990 79p $12.95 **811**

ISBN 0-86547-408-7   LC 89-16083

Gerstler's "characters inhabit the fringes of society: they are saints, . . . homeless men, a sleepwalker and a hypnotist, and the 'bitter angel' of the title poem, who unceremoniously appears in a 'tinny, nickel-and-dime light.' Innocents all, these would-be seers bear the burden of a hypersensitivity to the world around them and, because of it, share a kind of grace. . . . Gerstler balances classical allusion with bold experimentation in voice, form and content, creating a tension that gives her work an urgent, honest edge." Publ Wkly

Gibran, Kahlil, 1883-1931
The Prophet. Knopf 1923 107p il $13; pa $11 **811**

ISBN 0-394-40428-9; 0-394-55049-8 (pa)

Also available G.K. Hall large print edition

A collection of poems by the mystical writer/artist, who was born in Lebanon and died in the United States, in which the prophet Almustafa deals with fundamental aspects of human life such as love, friendship, good and evil, self-knowledge, passion and reason, joy and sorrow, freedom, work, marriage and children, prayer and death

Gildner, Gary
Blue like the heavens; new & selected poems. University of Pittsburgh Press 1984 142p hardcover o.p. paperback available $12.95 **811**

ISBN 0-8229-5358-7 (pa)   LC 83-19746

"Generous samples from four previous books (1969-78) and a score of new poems show off this very likable author to good advantage. Never obscure or self-consciously 'poetical,' and very often amusing, Gildner's lines are sure to provide multiple shocks (and laughs) of recognition, as he retraces choice patches all over the American scene." Booklist

Ginsberg, Allen, 1926-
Collected poems, 1947-1980. Harper & Row 1984 xxi, 837p il hardcover o.p. paperback available $15.95 **811**

ISBN 0-06-091494-7 (pa)   LC 84-47573

"A complete collection of the poetry of the most celebrated Beat, gathered from the many small-press volumes and magazines in which they have appeared, with sometimes extraordinary notes by the poet." N Y Times Book Rev

Howl, and other poems. City Lights Bks. 1956 44p pa $4.95 **811**

ISBN 0-87286-017-5

"The Pocket poet series"

"Leading poet of the so-called 'beat generation,' Ginsberg writes a loosely structured, prophetic-sounding line. Howl, is a lament for what society did to his generation, turning some to suicide, drug addiction, homosexuality." Herzberg. Reader's Ency of Am Lit

White shroud; poems, 1980-1985. Harper & Row 1986 89p hardcover o.p. paperback available $11 **811**

ISBN 0-06-091429-7 (pa)   LC 86-45104

"Ginsberg's unique synthesis of Buddhism with urban Jewish roots, of Whitman, Blake, and Williams with the contemporary bardic methods of rock 'n roll, continues to inform his work with an immediacy absent in much of current poetry. Musical notation is provided for poems conceived as songs." Choice

Giovanni, Nikki
Those who ride the night winds. Morrow 1983 62p $9.95; pa $6.95 **811**

ISBN 0-688-01906-4; 0-688-02653-2 (pa)

LC 82-20811

The poet "attempts to evolve a new format for most of these poems, using a prose line with ellipses between phrases. . . . Her subjects are general and mass-market political: Billie Jean King, the death of John Lennon, Martin Luther King." Libr J

Giovanni, Nikki—*Continued*

The women and the men. Morrow 1975 unp il hardcover o.p. paperback available $6.95 **811**

ISBN 0-688-07947-4 (pa)

"The poems are divided into three sections. . . . 'The Women' is a startling group of poems. Primarily portraits, they are clear and honest expressions and statements of black womanhood. . . . The poems in 'The Men' are more personal in nature. They are simple, joyful, tense poems of the poet's emotional response to love. . . . The final group of poems, 'And Other Places,' contains several short, crystal-clear images of life in Africa." Best Sellers

Glück, Louise, 1943-

Ararat. Ecco Press 1990 68p $17.95; pa $9.95 **811**

ISBN 0-88001-247-1; 0-88001-248-X (pa)

LC 89-35647

"The world of Louise Glück's 'Ararat' is one of threat, competition, envy and grief. 'Ararat,' Ms. Glück's fifth book of poetry, works almost as a single poem. The 32 poems tell the story of a wounding, and even though they speak of contemporary Long Island, they echo Greek tragedy. 'Ararat' has a relentlessness more common in fiction than poetry. Coupled with precision and clarity, it makes some of the poems difficult to read. . . . No American poet writes better than Louise Glück; perhaps none can lead us so deeply into our own natures." NY Times Book Rev

The triumph of Achilles. Ecco Press 1985 60p $13.50; pa $7.50 **811**

ISBN 0-88001-081-9; 0-88001-082-7 (pa)

LC 85-10249

This collection shows Glück "experimenting with new types of poems, from Orientalist attempts to capture the moment to songs, narratives and long mixed sequences. Language is looser, embracing the casual as well as the concise, and Glück's sense of the line has broadened too." Nation

The wild iris. Ecco Press 1992 63p $19.95 **811**

ISBN 0-88001-281-1 LC 91-36419

"More than half of the poems address an 'unreachable father,' or are spoken in a voice meant to be his. . . . This ambitious and original work consists of a series of 'matins,' 'vespers,' poems about flowers, and others about the seasons or times of day, carrying forward a dialogue between the human and divine. This is poetry of great beauty, where lamentation, doubt and praise show us a god who can blast or console, but who too often leaves us alone." Publ Wkly

Goldbarth, Albert

Heaven and earth; a cosmology: poems. University of Ga. Press 1991 118p $20; pa $9.95 **811**

ISBN 0-8203-1299-1; 0-8203-1300-9 (pa)

LC 90-45961

"The reader must work hard to interpret the poet's complicated but extraordinary vision. To make his points, Goldbarth links stories from his own experience with interpretive allusions to art and religion, and his imagery often is loaded with esoteric scientific terms. Ultimately, however, the poet's perceptions of life ring so real and true that the reader is more than likely to forgive any verbal and narrative convolution." Publ Wkly

H. D. (Hilda Doolittle), 1886-1961

Collected poems, 1912-1944; edited by Louis L. Martz. New Directions 1983 xxxvi, 629p $35; pa $17.95 **811**

ISBN 0-8112-0876-1; 0-8112-0971-7 (pa) LC 83-6380

This volume includes "H.D.'s poetry, published and unpublished, through her *Trilogy* completed in 1944, excepting her verse dramas and poems in prose works. Also excluded is the late verse in *By Avon River* and *Helen in Egypt*." Libr J

The editor's textual notes "offer valuable and illuminating scholarly commentary and present the most important of the textual variants. An informative and sensitively written introduction discusses aspects of the interpenetration of H.D.'s biography with her poetic sensibility. This volume is an impressive scholarly work." Choice

Selected poems; edited by Louis L. Martz. New Directions 1988 xxvi, 198p $18.95; pa $9.95 **811**

ISBN 0-8112-1065-0; 0-8112-1066-9 (pa) LC 88-1460

"This collection offers new readers the chance to follow the development of H. D.'s voice from its early contained imagism to the late oracular expansiveness; the selections especially emphasize the later, less-available poems, stinting early ones that can be found in most anthologies." Booklist

Hall, Donald, 1928-

Old and new poems. Ticknor & Fields 1990 244p $24.95; pa $12.95 **811**

ISBN 0-89919-926-7; 0-89919-954-2 (pa)

LC 90-31087

This collection "gathers a generous selection of the work from 1947 to the present. Mr. Hall, as this collection makes clear, has improved with the years. . . . In the triumphant work of his maturity, in a burly line not strictly metrical but full-blown in its sonority, Mr. Hall celebrates with grieving joy the transmutation of matter into energy and the consumption of life by death, death seen as the unrefusable essence of life itself. . . . This is poetry that marches in a stately order; classical in its dignity and perfectly readable, it argues the mystical union of dark and light, death and life." N Y Times Book Rev

The one day; a poem in three parts. Ticknor & Fields 1988 67p $16.95; pa $8.95 **811**

ISBN 0-89919-817-1; 0-89919-816-3 (pa)

LC 88-10130

"In this three-part poem, composed of male and female narrative, as well as classic texts—prophecy, pastoral, history and eclogue—the concept of middle age is explored with fresh insight and expressed in brilliant turns of phrase. Though at times esoteric because of its form and the intricacy and spontaneity of Hall's thought processes, the poem maintains a remarkable clarity and elegance of language as vivid, concrete details are interspersed with a stream of consciousness." Publ Wkly

Halliday, Mark, 1949-
Tasker Street. University of Mass. Press
1992 76p $20; pa $9.95   **811**

ISBN 0-87023-776-4; 0-87023-777-2 (pa)

LC 91-41031

"Often autobiographical in nature, but still moving
beyond the personal, the poems work well as a whole.
One can easily appreciate their moments of truth." Libr
J

Harrison, Jim, 1937-
Selected & new poems, 1961-1981;
drawings by Russell Chatham. Delacorte
Press 1982 212p il o.p.; Doubleday
paperback available $8.95   **811**

ISBN 0-385-28945-6 (pa)   LC 82-7435

"A Seymour Lawrence book"

"The persona in these poems lives at the extremes
of experience: 'Asleep again between peach rows, drunk
at mid-morning and something/ conclusive is needed, a
tooth pulled, a fistfight, a girl.' The poems are filled with
sex, drink, love, fishing, hunting, blood." Libr J

Hayden, Robert Earl, 1913-1980
Collected poems; edited by Frederick
Glaysher. Liveright 1985 205p hardcover
o.p. paperback available $8.95   **811**

ISBN 0-87140-138-X (pa)   LC 84-28880

"Hayden's poetry is a blend of unrivaled craftsmanship
with a sharp, unrestrained vision. His subjects encompass
the whole of human experience, from the extremely personal but never obscure ('Approximations') to the historical but never pedantic ('Belsen, Day of Liberation'). His
technique is similarly varied. Hayden is as adept with
haiku, imitations of Eskimo song-poems, or sonnets as
he is with free verse. A particularly important addition
to libraries with black literature collections." Booklist

Hecht, Anthony, 1923-
The transparent man: poems. Knopf 1990
75p $18.95; pa $10   **811**

ISBN 0-394-58506-2; 0-679-73358-2 (pa)

LC 89-43399

This is a "strange, gorgeously moody, occasionally imperfect (even Mr. Hecht can be left-handed) collection
lit by Vermeer or La Tour. It returns to the concerns
that have troubled this troubled poet—death in Venice,
the woe that is in marriage, elegies at the heart of happiness and the Holocaust. The subjects are not unusual—
who isn't afraid of a poet with unusual subjects?—but
the conviction and darkening conscience contribute to the
pressure that blooms into style." N Y Times Book Rev

Hughes, Langston, 1902-1967
Selected poems of Langston Hughes;
drawings by E. McKnight Kauffer. Knopf
1959 297p il $22.50; pa $9.95   **811**

ISBN 0-394-40438-6; 0-679-72818-X (pa)

This collection represents Langston Hughes' own decisions as to which of his poems he wanted to preserve
and reprint

Hugo, Richard F.
Making certain it goes on; the collected
poems of Richard Hugo. Norton 1983 xxi,
456p $25; pa $10.95   **811**

ISBN 0-393-01784-2; 0-393-30139-7 (pa)   LC 83-8016

"Though he would never be a serene poet, his collected poems show Hugo turning toward a calm peace that
would mark his best work in 'White Center' (1980) and
'The Right Madness On Skye' (1981), and in the 22 new
poems in this volume. . . . Among the new poems
included [here] Hugo was still driving, looking, and
naming. If we had not noticed before that his great gift
was the elegy, we see it now." N Y Times Book Rev

Ignatow, David, 1914-
New and collected poems, 1970-1985.
Wesleyan Univ. Press 1986 332p (Wesleyan
poetry) hardcover o.p. paperback available
$16.95   **811**

ISBN 0-8195-6174-6 (pa)   LC 85-15311

"In this collection we see [Ignatow's] extensive and
excellent use of the prose poem, as well as many of
his finest poems of reconciliation with his father. If
poems are to be prized for their emotional intensity and
directness, then Ignatow's poems of old age and of his
relationship with his son must indeed be held in very
high estimation. . . . What will persist about [his] poetry
is a peculiar quality of voice which is intimate, self-
mocking, and gently speculative." Va Q Rev

Shadowing the ground. Wesleyan Univ.
Press 1991 68p (Wesleyan poetry) $22.50; pa
$10.95   **811**

ISBN 0-8195-2195-7; 0-8195-1197-8 (pa)

LC 90-20872

"Here are sixty-five short, spare, untitled poems, their
uniformity of appearance (two-thirds of them ten lines
or fewer) belying the plural perspectives that David
Ignatow brings to his considerations of age and death's
imminence. . . . Shadowing the Ground celebrates contrary responses to unplanned obsolescence." World Lit
Today

**James Dickey; edited and with an
introduction by Harold Bloom. Chelsea
House 1987 168p (Modern critical views)
$24.95   811**

1. Dickey, James

ISBN 1-55546-272-3   LC 86-34321

Among the contributors to this critical overview of
Dickey's work are Joyce Carol Oates, Robert Penn Warren and Linda Wagner

Includes bibliography

Jarrell, Randall, 1914-1965
The complete poems. Farrar, Straus &
Giroux 1969 507p $45; pa $14.95   **811**

ISBN 0-374-12716-6; 0-374-51305-8 (pa)

Collected here are the entire contents of three
published volumes Selected poems (1955), The woman
at the Washington Zoo (1960), and The Lost World
(1965) plus poems published from 1934 to 1964 but
never collected and some never before published

Jarrell, Randall, 1914-1965—*Continued*
Selected poems; edited by William H. Pritchard. Farrar, Straus & Giroux 1990 115p $17.95; pa $10.95 **811**

ISBN 0-374-25867-8; 0-374-52290-1 (pa)

LC 89-61250

"A Michael di Capua book"

"The chronological selection of fifty poems that Pritchard has made from Jarrell's oeuvre is a stringent one, since the Complete Poems [entered above] contains about 300 poems. Certainly this selection contains the strongest poems." New Repub

Jeffers, Robinson, 1887-1962
The collected poetry of Robinson Jeffers; edited by Tim Hunt. Stanford Univ. Press 1988-1991 3v ea $60 **811**

LC 87-18083

Contents: v1 1920-1928 (ISBN 0-8047-1414-2); v2 1928-1938 (ISBN 0-8047-1723-0); v3 1938-1962 (ISBN 0-8047-1847-4)

The first three volumes of a projected four volume set

"Jeffers' strengths and weaknesses as a poet are inextricable, but he wrote nothing trivial. His narratives owe much to the example of Edward Arlington Robinson, but they surpass the model and have not been equaled since. Their plots and characterizations are repetitive and even obsessive, but the narrative pulse of the ten and five stressed lines is both supple and controlled, while the interspersed authorial commentary varies the cadence and lends shrewed perspective. No reevaluation can ignore them. The shorter poems share the same rhythm of lyric thrust checked by terse observation and dicta." Benet's Reader's Ency of Am Lit

Dear Judas, and other poems; afterword by Robert J. Brophy. Liveright 1977 179p hardcover o.p. paperback available $7.95 **811**

ISBN 0-87140-113-4 (pa)

LC 76-56144

"Dear Judas," the title poem, published separately 1929, is a long dramatic piece which represents the betrayal of Christ by Judas as an act of love. A companion narrative poem, "The loving shepherdess," follows. Six short poems complete the volume

The double axe, & other poems, including eleven suppressed poems; with a foreword by William Everson, and an afterword by Bill Hotchkiss. Liveright 1977 xxii, 197p $12.95; pa $7.95 **811**

ISBN 0-87140-625-X; 0-87140-114-2 (pa)

LC 76-55796

First published 1948 by Random House

This collection includes the long narrative title poem followed by 27 short pieces including eleven poems previously suppressed because of their bitter criticism of American involvement in World War II

Rock and hawk; a selection of shorter poems; edited by Robert Hass. Random House 1987 xliii, 290p $19.95 **811**

ISBN 0-394-55769-7

LC 87-9612

A "selection focusing on Jeffers's shorter poems but including a few of the longer poems. As critics have tended to focus on Jeffers's narrative poems, this collection offers a fresh opportunity to reevaluate the shorter poems while reminding us that Jeffers's work must be read in opposition to such modernists as Pound and Eliot. But the most valuable feature of this work is Robert Hass's extensive and probing introduction, which summarizes Jeffers's personal life and explores various pivotal points in his writing career." Libr J

Kenner, Hugh
The Pound era. University of Calif. Press 1971 606p il $40; pa $16.95 **811**

1. Pound, Ezra, 1885-1972
ISBN 0-520-01860-5; 0-520-02427-3 (pa)

"A detailed account of Pound's career from the viewpoint of ideas, movements, and personalities of his age. A main theme of the book is that to Pound and his era, ages and cultures share in a basic continuity. . . . Vorticism, imagism, social credit, China—all receive detailed new treatment as the author probes their impact on Pound's work." Libr J

"As a reader of Pound, Kenner is superb. He moves with ease and authority through the most tangled passages of allusion, ideogram and fragments of Greek and Latin. As an advocate pleading for the 'Cantos' to be recognized as a successful and crucial imaginative achievement, he is perhaps less convincing." N Y Times Book Rev

Includes bibliographic references

Kerouac, Jack, 1922-1969
Pomes all sizes; introduction by Allen Ginsberg. City Lights Bks. 1992 175p pa $8.95 **811**

ISBN 0-87286-269-0

LC 92-1204

"This book, which Kerouac prepared for publication before his death in 1969, collects poems written between 1954 and 1965. Most are playful—comments about friends, variations on the sounds of words. Yet a few extremely sensitive longer pieces appear, including 'Caritas,' in which the poet runs after a barefoot beggar boy to give him money for shoes and then begins to doubt the boy's veracity. Other intriguing poems reflect the poet's religious concerns of the moment, running the gamut of Eastern and Western religions." Libr J

Scattered poems. City Lights Bks. 1971 76p pa $4.95 **811**

ISBN 0-87286-064-7

"The Pocket poets series"

This collection "contains poems that either have previously appeared in periodicals or have not appeared in print at all. The poems are delightfully representative of Kerouac: that free and easy style of writing from the music of the imagination, without a score to follow. Those familiar with the San Francisco school of poetry will readily see Kerouac's affinity in style and content with such writers as Rexroth, Everson, Snyder, Ferlinghetti, Ginsberg, et al. . . . Kerouac sings in the American language to an American tune." Libr J

Kinnell, Galway, 1927-
The past. Houghton Mifflin 1985 57p $13.95; pa $9.95 **811**

ISBN 0-395-39385-X; 0-395-39386-8 (pa)

LC 85-14211

Kinnell's book of poems "ends with elegies for his friends and fellow poets Richard Hugo and James Wright. He looks back to childhood, his first love, his growing children and the breakup of a marriage." N Y Times Book Rev

Kinnell, Galway, 1927-—*Continued*

"This is a book that pleases, even surprises, by gathering weight in the reading, that seems to take on layers and layers of meaning gradually, almost without acknowledging that movement. The early poems are derived from what seem to be simple, even simplistic memories . . . while the poems that conclude the book bring us to less concrete, more evocative meditations on the relationship of those memories to the journey toward death." Commonweal

Selected poems. Houghton Mifflin 1982 148p hardcover o.p. paperback available $11.95   **811**

ISBN 0-395-32046-1 (pa)   LC 81-20254

"This selection comprises 50 lyrics and longer meditations, all from previous collections, though several are newly revised." Libr J

This volume "bears witness to this poet's extraordinary range, depth and command of technique." Publ Wkly

When one has lived a long time alone. Knopf 1990 69p $18.95; pa $11   **811**

ISBN 0-394-58856-8; 0-679-73281-0 (pa)

      LC 90-53163

"The author now in his seventh decade, confronts his own mortality. . . . There are many of Kinnell's trademark long poems, including the title poem, where phrases pile on top of one another to evoke a vivid world. But there are several short gems as well." Libr J

Kizer, Carolyn

The nearness of you; poems. Copper Canyon Press 1986 97p $15; pa $10   **811**

ISBN 0-914742-96-5; 0-914742-97-3 (pa)

      LC 86-71838

A collection of poems about men and their relations with women

"This volume sums up and stands as testament to Kizer's gifts as an artist and as an extraordinary human being." Booklist

Yin; new poems. BOA Eds. 1984 85p $18; pa $9   **811**

ISBN 0-918526-44-2; 0-918526-45-0 (pa)

"Two loving and lovely poems celebrate [Kizer's] joy in her adult daughter, as does the long prose memoir of her early life with her greatly accomplished and ambitious mother, toward whom her emotions are more mixed. . . . With her intelligence and poetic gifts, Kizer cannot help but see, and speak, sharply. Acute but acid, her vision and voice are both witty and wise—and may provoke the more middle-of-the-road reader with their pungency. Still, whether tender or biting, Kizer's poems will demand the kind of attention that other informed hearts can understand." Booklist

Koch, Kenneth, 1925-

Selected poems, 1950-1982. Random House 1985 239p hardcover o.p. paperback available $9.95   **811**

ISBN 0-394-73771-1 (pa)   LC 84-17851

"'Selected Poems' represents work from five collections. Koch's attention to the surfaces of a poem—wordplay, sight, and tone, and particularly to the juxtaposition

of images—often creates comic as well as beautiful effects. This volume reveals an evolution in Koch's work from the high-spirited lyric (in which a conceit is often reworked into hilarious shapes and sizes) to a more restrained irony with deepening philosophical intent. Koch is not a frivolous poet, but one who attempts to expand the serious possibilities of humor." Libr J

Kumin, Maxine, 1925-

The long approach; poems. Viking 1985 80p $14.95   **811**

ISBN 0-670-80429-0   LC 85-7204

This volume of poems is divided into three sections. The first section, entitled "In the Family", deals with ties of kinship. "Out There", the second section, focuses on such places as Israel and Egypt. The final section, "On the Farm", concerns rural life

"Kumin is best known, probably, for her poems on rural life, and this volume adds to her canon several appealing pieces about the New Hampshire farm she lives on. Sometimes, it is true, she lapses into a forced jauntiness in her celebrations of nature. . . . But one appreciates her quieter precisions." Poetry

Nurture; poems. Viking 1989 63p o.p.; Penguin Bks. paperback available $8.95   **811**

ISBN 0-14-058619-9 (pa)   LC 89-31129

"These poems are exhaustive in their sorrow: they are predominantly short, brutal elegies for the natural world. . . . The overall effect is one of anguished enumeration—as if the poet stood on the deck of a sinking Noah's ark, counting again each animal we are losing. This emotional census fails occasionally as poetry and becomes a kind of versified prose. . . . But if we read these poems as exhortations in the plain style, if we read them to learn, they amaze." N Y Times Book Rev

Langland, Joseph

Selected poems. University of Mass. Press 1991 118p $20   **811**

ISBN 0-87023-747-0   LC 90-24604

These sixty-five poems spanning a forty year career "speak in a strong, natural voice that has mastered the craft and moves confidently within it. In them, one hears speech and music together in a wide-ranging world of ideas." Univ Press Books for Public and Second Sch Libr

Laughlin, James, 1914-

Selected poems, 1935-1985. City Lights Bks. 1986 248p $25.95; pa $9.95   **811**

ISBN 0-87286-179-1; 0-87286-180-5 (pa)

      LC 85-27992

The founder and publisher of New Directions Books presents a collection of his poems

"Laughlin's verses are either centered on his personal feelings—his need for love, his frustrations at life's diurnal trivia—or on intellectual games with another writer's work. . . . [In] the largest and opening section of this volume, Mr. Laughlin's linguistic philosophy rests on unadorned simple speech. . . . Other sections of [the] book include poems he has written entirely in French, 'Long-line Poems' and poems written by his alter ego, Hiram Handspring. Some of these last poems demonstrate Laughlin's capability for wit." N Y Times Book Rev

Levertov, Denise, 1923-

Breathing the water. New Directions 1987 86p hardcover o.p. paperback available $8.95
811

ISBN 0-8112-1027-8 (pa)   LC 86-23658

"Levertov's poetry has moved progressively into the realm of spirituality, always combined with the imperative of social activism. . . . These poems are both apocalyptic and hopeful regarding the fate of humankind." Publ Wkly

Collected earlier poems, 1940-1960. New Directions 1979 133p hardcover o.p. paperback available $7.95
811

ISBN 0-8112-0718-8 (pa)   LC 78-26199

This collection gathers "together three previously unpublished poems, selections from . . . *The Double Image* (1946) and all the poems from the three following collections, *Here and Now* (1957), *Overland to the Islands* (1958), *With Eyes at the Back of Our Heads* (1960). . . . Poems appear in chronological order with dates and places of composition added." Libr J

A door in the hive. New Directions 1989 113p $16.95; pa $8.95
811

ISBN 0-8112-1118-5; 0-8112-1119-3 (pa) LC 89-8304

Levertov "displays a newly impressive range in her 19th collection. The rough-hewn jewel of the book is the long poem 'El Salvador: Requiem and Invocation,' stylized with lines as stark, staccato and dramatically moving as the brutalizing subject. In a world-weary mood, the poet addresses issues of human self-destruction and our rapacious consumption of the earth." Publ Wkly

Evening train. New Directions 1992 120p $17.95; pa $8.95
811

ISBN 0-8112-1219-X; 0-8112-1220-3 (pa)
LC 92-20385

This collection "provides one more clue to how this impressive and remarkably prolific poet thinks about the world. The poems touch on a range of subjects that are clearly of great importance to the writer. As in her essays, the two themes revisited most often in these poems are the beauty of nature and the human quest for spiritual fulfillment. In addition, there are poems about love, aging, the environment, AIDS, and war." Libr J

Poems, 1960-1967. New Directions 1983 247p hardcover o.p. paperback available $8.95
811

ISBN 0-8112-0859-1 (pa)   LC 83-2263

A combined edition of three of the poet's collections The Jacob's ladder, O taste and see, and The sorrow dance, published 1961, 1964, and 1967, respectively

The poet's "concern for quotidian realities and eternal verities gives these poems substance meant to last, expressed in a style that is clear, concise, intense. . . . Lyrical but spare, the lines speak of many things—marriage, rivers, the world that is 'not enough' with us—and the faint sounds of biblical and other literary allusions show a sensibility that has assimilated the great tradition with the urgencies of today. A solid achievement." Booklist

Poems, 1968-1972. New Directions 1987 259p $19.95; pa $10.95
811

ISBN 0-8112-1004-9; 0-8112-1005-7 (pa) LC 86-5389

A combined edition of three of the poet's collections Relearning the alphabet, To stay alive, and Footprints, published 1970, 1971, and 1972, respectively

"Here are love poems, elegies, and poems of natural observations as moving as any in modern American literature, written with the immense craft that distinguishes Levertov's work. A necessity for American poetry collections." Booklist

Levine, Philip, 1928-

New selected poems. Knopf 1991 292p $24; pa $15
811

ISBN 0-679-40165-2; 0-679-74056-2 (pa)
LC 90-53422

This selection contains poems Levine chose for his earlier Selected poems (1984), plus 15 new works

"This is a monumental work that somehow remains wonderfully accessible, largely because Levine has chosen pieces carefully, favoring shorter works and poems that address his staple themes of family (like 'Uncle' and 'My Son and I') and childhood ('Coming Home'). Many of the poems are powerfully imagistic." Libr J

What work is; poems. Knopf 1991 77p $19
811

ISBN 0-679-40166-0   LC 90-53421

"This collection amounts to a hymn of praise for all the workers of America. These proletarian heroes, with names like Lonnie, Loo, Sweet Pea, and Packy, work the furnaces, forges, slag heaps, assembly lines, and loading docks at places with unglamorous names like Brass Craft or Feinberg and Breslin's First-Rate Plumbing and Plating. . . . But Levine's characters are also significant for their inner lives, not merely their jobs." Libr J

Lindsay, Vachel, 1879-1931

The poetry of Vachel Lindsay; complete & with Lindsay's drawings; newly edited by Dennis Camp. Spoon River Poetry Press 1984 2v il ea $24.95
811

ISBN 0-933180-45-4   LC 84-197091

"A two-volume definitive edition of Lindsay's poetry superseding 'Collected Poems' which was incomplete and marred by textual errors and omissions. . . . Lindsay is remarkable in that he wrote about anything that attracted his attention, including silent movie stars and the Russian Revolution; the list is long. That he wrote too much, was unselective, and apparently was not self-critical enough is apparent. But Lindsay's faithfulness to his feelings and devotion to his art merit attention and respect. An important addition to collections of early 20th century American poetry." Choice

Logan, John, 1923-1987

Only the dreamer can change the dream; selected poems. Ecco Press 1981 209p (American poetry ser) $14.95; pa $7.95
811

ISBN 0-912946-77-6; 0-912946-78-4 (pa)
LC 80-23184

Logan's "best poems deal with personal relationships, or else try to connect the conscious and the unconscious—the life with others and the inner life—in a searching, analytic way that has become unfashionable in the reaction against the vogue of 'confessional' poetry. . . . Such connections between the grandiose and the immediate are always risky, but they are a real and important human experience; and at his best . . . Logan traces them out delicately, musically and with utter conviction." N Y Times Book Rev

Longfellow, Henry Wadsworth, 1807-1882

The poetical works of Longfellow; with a new introduction by George Monteiro. Houghton Mifflin 1975 xxvii, 689p $39

811

ISBN 0-395-18487-8

"Cambridge editions"

First published 1893 with title: The complete poetical works of Henry Wadsworth Longfellow

This collection contains "The song of Hiawatha" and "The courtship of Miles Standish" plus a few juvenile poems and unacknowledged or uncollected translations. Notes, and index of first lines, and a complete chronological list of Longfellow's poems are also included

Lowell, James Russell, 1819-1891

The poetical works of James Russell Lowell, rev and with a new introduction by Marjorie R. Kaufman. Houghton Mifflin 1978 xxxiv, 494p $15

811

ISBN 0-395-25726-3   LC 77-17274

"Cambridge editions"

First published 1896 with title: The complete poetical works of James Russell Lowell

Following a chronology of Lowell's life and a critical introduction, this volume presents uncollected poems as well as the following separately published works: The vision of Sir Launfal (1848); A fable for critics (1848); The Biglow papers (first series 1848, second series 1865); Under the willows, and other poems (1869); The cathedral (1870); Three memorial poems (1877); Heartsease and rue (1888); Last poems (1895). A chronological list of Lowell's poems and indexes of titles and first lines are included

Lowell, Robert, 1917-1977

Day by day. Farrar, Straus & Giroux 1977 137p $12.95; pa $5.95

811

ISBN 0-374-13525-8; 0-374-51471-2 (pa)   LC 77-6799

These poems deal with "domestic routines and alarms, intrusive memories, new marital discord, children, weather, newspapers." Time

"Lowell has achieved true mastery after a lifetime of writing— he knows fewer answers than he did in his hotly certain youth, but he's learned the subtlest music in which to put the questions." Newsweek

Selected poems. rev ed. Farrar, Straus & Giroux 1977 255p hardcover o.p. paperback available $14

811

ISBN 0-374-51400-3 (pa)   LC 78-104855

First published 1976

A selection of over 200 poems tracing the development of one of the premier confessional poets of his generation

Loy, Mina

The last lunar Baedeker; edited and introduced by Roger L. Conover; with a note by Jonathan Williams. Jargon Soc. 1982 lxxix, 334p il $25

811

ISBN 0-912330-46-5   LC 81-86061

"An advanced member of the true avant-garde early in the century, Loy was universally recognized by literary modernists such as Pound, Eliot, and Williams. . . . In an obvious labor of love, this book's editor Roger L. Conover, has searched out her scattered writings—poems, satires, songs, polemics, profiles, 'ready mades,' and many post-1930 unpublished pieces—sketched out her fascinating life in a charming introduction, and compiled the whole, with several photographs and notes, in a befittingly handsome volume." Booklist

MacLeish, Archibald, 1892-1982

Collected poems, 1917-1982; with a prefatory note to the newly collected poems by Richard B. McAdoo. Houghton Mifflin 1985 524p hardcover o.p. paperback available $14.95

811

ISBN 0-395-39569-0 (pa)   LC 85-14392

Collects all the known poetry of the author/public servant. As an expatriate in Paris his early work was heavily influenced by Pound and Eliot. After returning to the States his verse concerned itself more with America's political, social, and cultural heritage

Matthews, William, 1942-

Selected poems and translations, 1969-1991. Houghton Mifflin 1992 200p $19.95

811

ISBN 0-395-63121-1   LC 91-45716

"This collection brings together more than 100 poems, chosen from eight previously published volumes, and 40 translations from the French, Latin and Bulgarian." Publ Wkly

"Matthews has been widely praised for the solid grounding of his poems, and rightly so. His clear-cut metaphors illuminate the everyday world with the magic of semantic revelation and the grace of otherminded-ness." Booklist

Merrill, James Ingram

The changing light at Sandover; including the whole of The book of Ephraim, Mirabell's books of number, Scripts for the pageant and a new coda, The higher keys. Atheneum Pubs. 1983 560p $25

811

ISBN 0-689-11282-3   LC 82-72995

This is a "collection, under a new general title, of all three 'divine comedies' unabridged, plus a new, 37-page coda." N Y Times Book Rev

The trilogy "is, surely, an astonishing performance, not a masterpiece, but as near to one, I think, as anything else that American poetry has produced in the last two or three decades, and the capstone—for now, anyway—of an extraordinary career." N Y Rev Books

The inner room; poems; by James Merrill. Knopf 1988 95p $16.95; pa $8.95

811

ISBN 0-394-47248-3; 0-679-72049-9 (pa)

LC 88-45265

This volume consists of "poems, prose poems, and a one-act play in verse." Libr J

Merrill "presents in his eleventh collection the lyric voice sounding its greatest depth. Always witty, sometimes coy, Merrill writes a poem elevated but precise—in most cases." Booklist

Merrill, James Ingram—*Continued*

Selected poems, 1946-1985; [by] James Merrill. Knopf 1992 339p $25 **811**

ISBN 0-679-41082-1   LC 91-58622

"By relying on exaggeratedly artificial forms, mixing different stanzaic patterns with blank verse and even prose, cultivating a composite tone, and referring to the writing process within his work, Merrill has continued to resist and interrupt any illusions of unmediated speech. Whatever his ostensible subject, the poet is always placed at the scene of writing, choosing his words, revising, and commenting on what he is doing." Benet's Reader's Ency of Am Lit

Merwin, W. S. (William Stanley), 1927-

Selected poems. Atheneum Pubs. 1988 276p $22.95; pa $14.95 **811**

ISBN 0-689-11970-4; 0-689-70736-3 (pa)

LC 87-31771

"Between 1952 and 1988, Merwin published 11 collections containing a total of 630 poems. For his Selected Poems he has chosen about 100. . . . The poet says his choices were subjective. Nothing was revised. The poet's selection enables a reader to follow the development of his style and to contemplate the range of his concerns: myth, time and memory, the murder of animals, nuclear and ecological disaster, family. His rank as a major 20th-century poet seems secure." Choice

Millay, Edna St. Vincent, 1892-1950

Collected lyrics. Harper & Row 1943 383p hardcover o.p. paperback available $9.95

811

ISBN 0-06-090863-7 (pa)

Companion volume to: Collected sonnets, entered below

This collection includes poems from the following volumes: Renascence; Second April; A few figs from thistles; Harp-weaver, and other poems; Buck in the snow; Wine from these grapes; Huntsman, what quarry

"Rereading this collection of excellent lyrics is a nostalgic experience. It reminds one how simple we all were in the '20s, even in rebellion." Book Week

Collected poems; edited by Norma Millay. Harper & Row 1956 xxi, 738p hardcover o.p. paperback available $16.95 **811**

ISBN 0-06-090889-0 (pa)

The poems in this collection "are divided into two separate sections of lyrics and sonnets, arranged chronologically and printed in groups under the titles of the original volumes, ranging from 'Renascence' of 1917 to 'Mine the harvest,' published in 1954, four years after the poet's death." Booklist

Collected sonnets of Edna St. Vincent Millay. rev & expanded ed. Perennial Lib. 1988 xxiv, 187p hardcover o.p. paperback available $9 **811**

ISBN 0-06-091091-7 (pa)   LC 83-48369

First published 1941

This collection includes three poems not published before in book form and sonnets from the following volumes: Renascence; A few figs from thistles; Second April; Harp-weaver; Buck in the snow; Fatal interview; Wine from these grapes; Huntsman, what quarry; Make bright the arrows

Edna St. Vincent Millay: selected poems. the centenary edition, edited and with an introduction by Colin Falck. HarperCollins Pubs. 1991 xxx, 162p $17.95 **811**

ISBN 0-06-016733-5   LC 91-55102

"Mr. Falck's lucid and tightly written introduction is nearly worth the price of admission to this handsome selection. . . . [His] ear for Millay's remarkable musical flexibility, her sometimes shockingly contemporary innovations, her ironies and sustained passions, allows a poetic appreciation in the best sense. But the poems are their own best evidence." N Y Times Book Rev

Moore, Marianne, 1887-1972

The complete poems of Marianne Moore. Macmillan; Viking 1981 305p o.p.; Penguin Bks. paperback available $8.95 **811**

ISBN 0-14-058601-6 (pa)   LC 80-13586

This "definitive edition of 'The Complete Poems' was prepared by Clive Driver and presents all of Moore's final emendations and cuts, punctuation, hyphens, line arrangements, and revised notes (all critical components of her poetry). It also includes five poems Moore wrote between the publication of the 1967 edition and the time of her death." Libr J

Morgan, Robert, 1944-

At the edge of the orchard country. Wesleyan Univ. Press 1987 68p (Wesleyan poetry) $22.50; pa $10.95 **811**

ISBN 0-8195-5158-9; 0-8195-6164-9 (pa)

LC 85-29506

"There are two types of poems here: short meditations and longer narratives focusing on character. . . . Morgan's genius for imagery is such that ordinary things become new without any contrivance. And no poet writing today has a better ear. The poems' muscular music is in accord with the physical world they embrace." Poetry

Nash, Ogden, 1902-1971

Bed riddance; a posy for the indisposed; illustrated by Milton Glaser. Little, Brown 1970 127p il hardcover o.p. paperback available $6.95 **811**

ISBN 0-316-59853-4 (pa)

A collection of verses on the subject of illness, some of which were previously published in the 'New Yorker.' Included are poems about insomnia, the common cold, doctors and healthy well-wishers

"These little poems make fine company for those convalescing. . . . The poems have wit, rhyme, meaning, verve, and dash. Which is what you always get from Ogden Nash." Libr J

A penny saved is impossible; with drawings by Ken Maryanski. Little, Brown 1981 120p il hardcover o.p. paperback available $7.95 **811**

ISBN 0-316-59806-2 (pa)   LC 81-13742

"This posthumous collection includes verses written throughout Nash's more than 40-year career. Many familiar subjects reappear: money and the lack of it, the difficulty of getting up in the morning, and the despicable failure of the rich to pick up a check. There is also a more-than-liberal sampling of Nash at his cur-

Nash, Ogden, 1902-1971—*Continued*
mudgeonly best, grousing about the cruelties of inexorable fate." Booklist

Verses from 1929 on. Little, Brown 1959 522p $24.95   **811**

ISBN 0-316-59828-3

Includes more than 400 poems selected and revised by the author from these six volumes of his published verse: I'm a stranger here myself (1938); Good intentions (1942); Many long years ago (1945); Versus (1949); Private dining room (1953); You can't get there from here (1957)

Nemerov, Howard
Inside the onion. University of Chicago Press 1984 63p $9.95; pa $6.95   **811**

ISBN 0-226-57244-7; 0-226-57245-5 (pa) LC 83-9312

"Nemerov's gift is for making the casual and the commonplace arresting, and he deliberately avoids dramatic or heroic subjects so that the effect of a volume of his poems is cumulative rather than immediate." World Lit Today

Trying conclusions; new and selected poems, 1961-1991. University of Chicago Press 1991 161p $18.95   **811**

ISBN 0-226-57263-3   LC 91-3217

This is a selection of work from Nemerov's "seven previous volumes, plus a last section of 23 new poems." Christ Sci Monit

"By and large a formalist in style, [Nemerov] nevertheless interpolated a truly American diction and easygoing wit reminiscent of Mark Twain and Will Rogers. Something of a fatalist . . . Nemerov stood undeceived but not smug, wondering at our 'many destinies.'" Libr J

War stories; poems about long ago and now. University of Chicago Press 1987 60p $10.95; pa $7.95   **811**

ISBN 0-226-57242-0; 0-226-57243-9 (pa) LC 87-5097

"By far the most affecting and effective poems here are in the central section, 'The War in the Air.' Recalling Nemerov's World War II service as a fighter pilot, these have weight, pungency, and bite that the occasional verses of the other two parts, 'The War in the Streets' and 'The War in the Heavens,' lack. Throughout the collection Nemerov's adroit, conservative technique makes nearly every line sharply readable." Booklist

Niedecker, Lorine, 1903-1970
From this condensery; the complete writing of Lorine Niedecker; edited by Robert J. Bertholf. Jargon Soc. 1985 336p $30   **811**

ISBN 0-912330-57-0   LC 85-80301

"Painstakingly assembled (the poems in order of their publication), this handsome edition persuasively offers the oeuvre of a poet in process. . . . [Bertholf] has spared no effort to check all [Niedecker's] previously published work, revisions, and manuscripts in several archives to establish a reasonably definitive text. His extensive notes offer publication data, textual variants, and pertinent quotations from Niedecker's letters. This edition belongs in all . . . collections that aim to include the best of postmodernist American poetry." Choice

Oates, Joyce Carol, 1938-
The fabulous beasts; poems; illustrations by A. G. Smith, Jr. Louisiana State Univ. Press 1975 86p il $13.95; pa $6.95   **811**

ISBN 0-8071-0153-2; 0-8071-0285-7 (pa)

"Frailty of human communication is the theme of these melancholy, meditative poems and prose narratives. The main concern here is failed relationship, the lost friend, the telephone line gone suddenly dead. But the four sections of free verse move from frustration to an appreciation for the tenuousness and preciousness of all human contact." Booklist

The time traveler. Dutton 1989 131p $18.95; pa $9.95   **811**

ISBN 0-525-24802-1; 0-525-48505-8 (pa) LC 89-7748

"A William Abrahams book"

"Oates has listened to the voices of contemporary culture and to her own traveler/poet's voice to shape this diverse, appealing collection of 70 poems. Giving particular emphasis to the role of women, she considers nature, art, history, relationships, and travel. This work will engage a variety of poetry readers and fans of the author's other works." Libr J

Women whose lives are food, men whose lives are money; poems; by Joyce Carol Oates; illustrated by Elizabeth Hansell. Louisiana State Univ. Press 1978 80p il $13.95   **811**

ISBN 0-8071-0391-8   LC 77-17220

"While familiar Oates themes are present here—bewilderment in love, anxiety towards the outer world—they are gifted with expression in imagery which, if offhand and random at times, is oftener telling and deft. . . . A fine collection." Choice

O'Hara, Frank, 1926-1966
The selected poems of Frank O'Hara; edited by Donald Allen. Knopf 1974 c1973 233p hardcover o.p. paperback available $14   **811**

ISBN 0-394-71973-5 (pa)

The poems chosen for this collection, arranged chronologically, give voice to "a New York City artist of continuing critical importance. Polishing a variety of poetic styles to reflect his distinctive personality O'Hara pays tribute to artists, poets, and to friends of the urban milieu in which he moved. . . . A brief prefatory essay describes O'Hara's approach to poetry: appended are a chronology of his life and works from 1926 to 1966 and indexes of titles and first lines." Booklist

Oliver, Mary, 1935-
New and selected poems. Beacon Press 1992 255p $20   **811**

ISBN 0-8070-6818-7   LC 92-7767

This collection "joins together poems written over 30 years. One of the astonishing aspects of Oliver's work is the consistency of tone over this long period. What changes is an increased focus on nature and an increased precision with language that has made her one of the very best poets." N Y Times Book Rev

Olson, Charles, 1910-1970

The collected poems of Charles Olson; excluding the Maximus poems; edited by George F. Butterick. University of Calif. Press 1987 xxxvi, 675p $60   **811**

ISBN 0-520-05764-3   LC 86-14652

"Perhaps the most important American postmodernist poet, Olson was little published during his life. This work, . . . should solidify his reputation. Olson burst into poetry in his maturity, sure of his instincts. Though his debt to Pound is evident, he went further in exploring both American language and experience. What amazes us now is not just the profundity and erudition of his themes but the variety of ways he expresses his humanity. Ceaselessly experimental, his poems do not lose their intelligence or intelligibility." Libr J

The Maximus poems; edited by George F. Butterick. University of Calif. Press 1985 652p $49.95; pa $29.95   **811**

ISBN 0-520-04015-5; 0-520-05595-0 (pa)
            LC 79-65759

This edition contains the entire sequence of poems set in Gloucester, Massachusetts, whose protagonist is the mythical figure, Maximus

"It is impossible to describe in this small space the immensity of Charles Olson's achievement—as poet, theoretician and explorer of the 'human universe.' Just as Ezra Pound's writing energized Western poetry in the first half of this century, Olson in the 1950s redefined its direction and inspired the next generation of writers. . . . 'The Maximus Poems' are a complex far-ranging attempt to grasp the history of human thought." Christ Sci Monit

Oppen, George, 1908-1984

The collected poems of George Oppen. New Directions 1975 263p il hardcover o.p. paperback available $9.95   **811**

ISBN 0-8112-0615-7 (pa)

"Encompassing a lifetime of work, these poems reveal a poetic sensibility full of questioning, examining, building, tearing down, rebuilding; Oppen writes 'I have not and never did have any motive of poetry/But to achieve clarity.' He approaches the poetic task intuitively. From one section to the next in this complete collection of previously published volumes these poems grow in depth, concept, and form while retaining Oppen's personality." Booklist

Patchen, Kenneth, 1911-1972

The collected poems of Kenneth Patchen. New Directions 1968 504p hardcover o.p. paperback available $15.95   **811**

ISBN 0-8112-0140-6 (pa)

This collection contains work published between 1936 and 1957

"A remarkable volume, although it is difficult to describe. One could say that it contains the animal honesty of Whitman, and the desperate exaltation of Hart Crane, and the simple delight in sense perception of D. H. Lawrence." N Y Times Book Rev

Piercy, Marge

Available light. Knopf 1988 129p hardcover o.p. paperback available $9.95   **811**

ISBN 0-394-75691-6 (pa)   LC 87-40490

In this collection Piercy's "feminist rhetoric has been replaced by the presence of a woman patiently turning 50, looking back at her life. The same political commitment Piercy exhibits especially well in her fiction is here expressed more concisely, transformed by imagery into understanding. Various temporary causes are merged into an exquisite, life-long struggle: displaying an intellect not previously visible, Piercy permits readers to share the soul searching, forgiveness, and final reclamation of her Jewish heritage that stems from her parents' deaths." Libr J

Circles on the water; selected poems of Marge Piercy. Knopf 1982 299p hardcover o.p. paperback available $16   **811**

ISBN 0-394-70779-6 (pa)   LC 81-17210

In this selection "activist and feminist, Piercy has recorded the thoughtful but equally sensory experience of a woman with the difficult intent to both work and love." Libr J

My mother's body. Knopf 1985 143p hardcover o.p. paperback available $11   **811**

ISBN 0-394-72945-5 (pa)   LC 84-48661

In this "collection Piercy's verse emerges with a new density, precision, and musicality. Justice, daily events, nature are still thematic concerns, but here she concentrates on the personal—her marriage and the death of her mother. Writing feelingly about her mother's self-denial and unfulfilled life, Piercy reveals the source of her own feminism." Libr J

Stone, paper, knife. Knopf 1983 144p $12.95; pa $9.95   **811**

ISBN 0-394-52802-6; 0-394-71219-6 (pa)
            LC 82-48050

"The poems in the first section rehash the breakup of her own and, by implication, the failure of all marriages. Like the poems of rage in the second section, these poems are general rather than specific, and artifice is substituted for emotion. . . . All the themes—love, rage, and nature—combine in the long poems which make up the final section. And if these poems are also rhetorical at times, they have both craft and vision behind them." Libr J

Plath, Sylvia

Ariel. Harper & Row 1966 85p hardcover o.p. paperback available $8   **811**

ISBN 0-06-090890-4 (pa)

First published 1955 in the United Kingdom

A collection of forty of Plath's poems written between 1960 and her death in 1963

"The vehemence and intimacy of the verse is such as to constitute a very powerful rhetoric and sincerity." Reporter

The collected poems; edited by Ted Hughes. Harper & Row 1981 351p hardcover o.p. paperback available $12.95   **811**

ISBN 0-06-090900-5 (pa)

Plath, Sylvia—*Continued*

The collection contains "all the poems Plath wrote, published and unpublished, from 1956 to 1963, as well as a sample of her early work." Publ Wkly

"Although her best poems deal with suffering and death, others are exhilarating and affectionate, and her tone is frequently witty as well as disturbing." Concise Oxford Companion to Engl Lit

Crossing the water; transitional poems. Harper & Row 1971 56p hardcover o.p. paperback available $7.95   **811**

ISBN 0-06-090789-4 (pa)

This posthumous collection of poems written in 1960 and 1961 evidences "Plath's preoccupation with death [which] is conveyed in obsessive use of the word black to connote despair and in other metaphors. . . . Desperate funnels of words, structured in strength and discipline, allude to nature, people, time and painful experiences of living." Booklist

Poe, Edgar Allan, 1809-1849

Poems; edited by Thomas Olive Mabbott. Harvard Univ. Press 1969 xxx, 627p il (Collected works of Edgar Allan Poe, v1) $41   **811**

ISBN 0-674-13935-6

"Belknap Press book"

Volume 1 of a three volume collection of Poe's works. "The editor has included complete versions of all the variants, and he has also included a considerable number of poems that have been attributed to Poe, with . . . editorial comment. He has also included . . . biographical and critical material that might throw light on the poems." Va Q Rev

Includes bibliography

Pound, Ezra, 1885-1972

The cantos of Ezra Pound. New Directions 1970 802p $31.95   **811**

ISBN 0-8112-0350-6

"The first sections of the 'Cantos' were published in magazine form as early as 1917. Pound's conception of his epic changed several times during different phases of his life. Originally intended as a didactic treatise for 'philistine' Americans, it combined elements from classical myth, ancient Oriental poetry, Provençal ballads, and modern economic theory, to create a vast disjointed panorama of the growth of civilization. A monumental work of poetic enterprise." Reader's Ency. 3d edition

Collected early poems of Ezra Pound; edited by Michael John King; with an introduction by Louis L. Martz. New Directions 1982 xxii, 330p hardcover o.p. paperback available $11.95   **811**

ISBN 0-8112-0843-5 (pa)   LC 82-8156

The editor "collects all of Pound's early books from 'A Lume Spento' through 'Ripostes,' including the 99 poems Pound excluded from his 1926 collected poems, 'Personae,' as well as 25 poems previously available only in periodicals, and 38 manuscript poems never published before including the complete 'San Trovaso Notebook.'" Libr J

Selected poems. new ed. New Directions 1957 184p pa $6.95   **811**

ISBN 0-8112-0162-7

First published 1949

This "provides a good sampling of the Pound who wrote 'A Virginal,' the latter-day Renaissance poet, as well as the reincarnate Li Po and the other 'personae' that Ezra wore during the years he spent absorbing the styles (and not the political thinking) of other centuries." Saturday Rev

Ransom, John Crowe, 1888-1974

Selected poems. 3rd ed rev & enl. Knopf 1991 159p $22   **811**

ISBN 0-679-40257-8   LC 90-52904

First published 1945

"These poems boast an unmistakable idiom, that of a 'displaced scholar,' as Robert Penn Warren describes Ransom's typical persona. An ironical voice, whose timbre hints of the poet's training in classics and of his education at Oxford, it is nonetheless capable of relating with tenderness and pity such incidents as the death of children and their pets." Benet's Reader's Ency of Am Lit

Ray, David, 1932-

Sam's book. Wesleyan Univ. Press 1987 81p (Wesleyan poetry) $22.50; pa $10.95   **811**

ISBN 0-8195-5170-8; 0-8195-6180-0 (pa)   LC 86-9195

"Of all the losses, perhaps the most difficult to bear is the death of a child. In 'Sam's Book,' David Ray bears what he can, mourning and lovingly remembering his son, who was killed in a car accident at the age of 19. What is remarkable about this book is the direct manner in which Mr. Ray faces both his son's life and death. The poems are strong and heart-rending because there is no attempt to find a transcendental meaning in this tragedy, nor does his mourning aim at exorcising his torment." N Y Times Book Rev

Reed, Ishmael, 1938-

New and collected poems. Atheneum Pubs. 1988 233p $22.95; pa $9.95   **811**

ISBN 0-689-12003-6; 0-689-12004-4 (pa)

     LC 88-19024

"Expressed through various forms—from short, epigramlike bits to longer, proselike chunks—Reed's most recurring themes are related to social issues, not simply those black causes one would expect, but also the plight of Eskimos, native Americans, even boxers and other athletes. It is his strong sense of the individual's place in history that focuses his sensibility on the underdog." Booklist

Rexroth, Kenneth, 1905-1982

The collected longer poems. New Directions 1968 307p hardcover o.p. paperback available $5.95   **811**

ISBN 0-8112-0177-5 (pa)   LC 68-25549

"Rexroth's pieces proceed with casual narrative, with lumps of prose 'philosophy' barely leavened with syllabics, with lovely lyricism with engaging romanticism, and overwhelming (at times) pretentiousness." Choice

Rexroth, Kenneth, 1905-1982—*Continued*

The collected shorter poems. New Directions 1967 c1966 348p hardcover o.p. paperback available $8.95   **811**

ISBN 0-8112-0178-3 (pa)   LC 66-17818

"Rexroth is probably one of the most learned autodidacts we have. His love poems are unquestionably great. They celebrate woman's body, mutual happiness, the sacramental character of love, and give a naturalist's lyricism which surpasses Keats. Other poems treat the supernatural, the macabre, the evil, and the great events of man's life with a sure, sharp, cerebral skill that is personal and unique. Rexroth is not a stylist and is seldom delicate, but his delicacy will become an ornament in the history of American letters." Choice

Selected poems; edited with an introduction by Bradford Morrow. New Directions 1984 152p hardcover o.p. paperback available $8.95   **811**

ISBN 0-8112-0917-2 (pa)   LC 84-9972

"This selection retrieves the immensely talented teenager of the early '20s and all the other steps toward the authoritative aged poet of the '70s. We see from Morrow's choices the shape of a career, at once distinctive from, but also exemplary of, the grand sweep of American modernism, which Rexroth very obviously helped—along with Pound and Eliot, Williams and Stevens—to create. Morrow's useful notes illuminate the more arcane allusions." Choice

Rich, Adrienne

An atlas of the difficult world; poems, 1988-1991. Norton 1991 60p $17.95; pa $7.95   **811**

ISBN 0-393-03069-5; 0-393-03069-5 (pa)
LC 91-12900

"In passionate, flowing cadences, our most visible poetic proponent of feminism finds ways to balance the conflicting demands of poetry and ideology." N Y Times Book Rev

The fact of a doorframe; poems selected and new, 1950-1984. Norton 1984 341p $18.95; pa $10.95   **811**

ISBN 0-393-01905-5; 0-393-30204-0 (pa)   LC 84-6107

This collection "is a selection from nine previous books, with an additional number of uncollected and more recent poems." Foreword

"Rich's great virtue is her long struggle for authenticity. . . . She will be remembered in literary history as one of the first American women to claim a public voice in lyric." New Repub

Time's power; poems, 1985-1988. Norton 1989 58p hardcover o.p. paperback available $7.95   **811**

ISBN 0-393-30575-9 (pa)

"Rich's poetry is always concerned with the struggle to make meaningful connections with other human beings. Here, Rich looks back on an unhealed mother-daughter conflict, a broken friendship, and other past wounds and events from an age when 'We're serious now/about death we talk to her daily as to a neighbor.'" Libr J

"As ever, Ms. Rich seems wonderfully able to isolate her personal struggles within a wider framework of social concerns, giving her poems resonance and moral force." N Y Times Book Rev

Robinson, Edwin Arlington, 1869-1935

Selected poems of Edwin Arlington Robinson; edited by Morton Dauwen Zabel; with an introduction by James Dickey. Macmillan 1965 xxviii, 257p pa $12.95   **811**

ISBN 0-02-070530-1

"The introduction is a reevaluation of the Robinson opus emphasizing the cerebral nature of his poetry, the deliberateness of his approach, and his indirectness in achieving effect. . . . Appended are the editor's note and a bibliography." Booklist

Roethke, Theodore, 1908-1963

The collected poems of Theodore Roethke. Doubleday 1966 279p hardcover o.p. paperback available $10.95   **811**

ISBN 0-385-08601-6 (pa)

Roethke's "refreshingly original rhythms are keenly articulated and often hypnotic. Although his work is uneven and he sometimes gives way to self-indulgence or to surprising naiveté, many of his best poems recreate disconcertingly intense psychic or mystical experience. He also had a flair for the seductively lyrical and the brashly irreverent. He ranks as one of the best poets of the first postmodern generation." Benet's Reader's Ency of Am Lit

Sandburg, Carl, 1878-1967

The complete poems of Carl Sandburg. rev and expanded ed. Harcourt Brace Jovanovich 1970 xxxi, 797p $27.95   **811**

ISBN 0-15-120773-9

First published 1950

Introduction by Archibald MacLeish

A collection of seven of the author's books: Chicago poems, 1916; Cornhuskers, 1918; Smoke and steel, 1920; Slabs of the sunburnt West, 1922; Good morning, America, 1925; The people, yes, 1936; Honey and salt, 1963

"Known for his free verse, written under the influence of Walt Whitman and celebrating industrial and agricultural America, American geography and landscape, figures in American history, and the American common people, [Sandburg] frequently makes use of contemporary American slang and colloquialisms." Herzberg. Reader's Ency of Am Lit

The people, yes. Harcourt Brace & Co. 1936 286p pa $9.95   **811**

ISBN 0-15-671665-8

"The longest and most sustained piece of work [the author] has yet done in verse. It is a book that will irritate some; and some will find it meaningless. . . . It is as honest as it is questioning and it speaks its deep convictions in a tongue we know." N Y Her Trib Books

Sarton, May, 1912-

Selected poems of May Sarton; edited and with an introduction by Serena Sue Hilsinger and Lois Brynes. Norton 1978 206p hardcover o.p. paperback available $10.95   **811**

ISBN 0-393-04512-9 (pa)   LC 78-14850

Sarton, May, 1912——*Continued*
"What May Sarton does is to follow the round of
a woman's life. Her verse is traditional, warm, ripe with
the wisdom of her years as a poet, novelist,
autobiographer. She draws on the artifacts of the past
for images to live by in the here and now." Christ Sci
Monit

The silence now; new and uncollected
earlier poems. Norton 1988 79p $14.95

811

ISBN 0-393-02651-5   LC 88-12429

In this volume "Sarton confronts the process of aging
and its accompanying losses and gains." Libr J

"The more recent work is exquisitely tender, full of
reverence for the most fleeting of beauties. Death is
present: a huge old tree falls, a favorite cat passes, but
everything is loved the more passionately for its
transience." Booklist

Schnackenberg, Gjertrud
A gilded lapse of time. Farrar, Straus &
Giroux 1992 143p $16   **811**
ISBN 0-374-16226-3   LC 92-13462

"As she tours the ghostly Mausoleum of Galla Placidia
and Dante's tomb at Ravenna, Schnackenberg finds in
Italian Renaissance art the multifarious inspiration for
this . . . collection of poems." Publ Wkly

"Ms. Schnackenberg's poems offer emotional power
without coercive force: her lines unfold from terror to
beauty to terror. . . . The biblical imagery, classical
allusions and philosophy from which the poems are composed might be airless bookishness in another poet, but
Ms. Schnackenberg can spin straw into gold." N Y
Times Book Rev

**Service, Robert W. (Robert William), 1874-
1958**
Best tales of the Yukon. Running Press
1983 159p il $15.90; pa $7.95   **811**
ISBN 0-89471-202-0; 0-89471-201-2 (pa) LC 83-3128

Verses chronicling the Klondike gold rush and immor-
talizing the colorful characters of the Yukon Territory,
chosen from the author's earlier collections The spell of
the Yukon and Ballads of a Cheechako

Sexton, Anne
The complete poems; with a foreword by
Maxine Kumin. Houghton Mifflin 1981
xxiv, 622p $29.95; pa $14.95   **811**
ISBN 0-395-29475-4; 0-395-32935-3 (pa) LC 81-2482

"This collection contains all the poems in the eight
volumes published in Sexton's lifetime, the two published
after her death, and seven poems never before in print."
Libr J

"Even before her death in 1974, Sexton's work was
the subject of critical controversy, often dismissed as
mere confessionalism. But, as Maxine Kumin observes
in an insightful introductory essay, Sexton 'delineated the
problematic position of women—the neurotic reality of
the time' and in so doing 'earned her place in the
canon.'" Choice

Love poems; foreword by Diane Wood
Middlebrook. Houghton Mifflin 1989 c1969
68p hardcover o.p. paperback available $9.95

811

ISBN 0-395-51760-5 (pa)   LC 89-34994

A reissue with a new introduction of the title first
published 1969

Sexton's love poems "are lyrical, frank, and self-
revealing. She is explicit about love's diversions and
perversions. 'The Ballad of the Lonely Masturbator' is
a powerful poem. But it compels the same way that
much of the imagery in the poems compels—with the
fascination born of curiosity and shock. . . . Miss Sexton
is an excellent craftsman. Her poems read true to the
ear." Libr J

Selected poems of Anne Sexton; edited
with an introduction by Diane Wood
Middlebrook and Diana Hume George.
Houghton Mifflin 1988 xxvi, 266p $21.95;
pa $11.95   **811**
ISBN 0-395-44595-7; 0-395-47782-4 (pa)
LC 87-34253

"The poems selected by the editors build a case for
Sexton as a major 20th-century writer who fearlessly
deals with subjects that hitherto were taboo—insanity,
sex, the essential loneliness of the human condition, and
the difficulty in achieving real communication between
men and women, mothers and their children, children
and their parents, the individual and a dehumanizing
society. . . . Highly recommended for academic and
public libraries." Choice

Transformations; with drawings by Barbara
Swan. Houghton Mifflin 1971 lllp il
hardcover o.p. paperback available $9.95

811

ISBN 0-395-12722-X (pa)   LC 71-156489

In these transformations of 17 tales from the Brothers
Grimm, the poet "maintains both the characters and
plots of Grimm; but she has primed them with an
evocative metaphoric fibre, a rich but simple imagery,
and the ironic, often grotesque cast of her own poetic
vision." Best Sellers

Shange, Ntozake
A daughter's geography. St. Martin's Press
1983 77p il hardcover o.p. paperback
available $8.95   **811**
ISBN 0-312-06327-X (pa)   LC 83-9625

The author "has written a series of hardhitting poems
that show her daughter both the internal and external
(Nicaragua, Haiti, Atlanta) geography that are her
heritage. Many of the poems are fueled by Shange's
anger. . . . She writes of various kinds of men—macho,
the flasher, obscene phone caller—with the same anger.
But when she writes in the section titled 'From Okra
to Greens/A Different Kinda Love Story' she calls up
images of her childhood and of black history to throw
light on the present and some of the anger disappears."
Choice

Shapiro, Harvey, 1924-
National Cold Storage Company; new and selected poems. Wesleyan Univ. Press 1988 93p $22.50; pa $10.95   811
    ISBN 0-8195-2152-3; 0-8195-1153-6 (pa)
                                      LC 87-20472
This collection "is a monument to death, disappointment and loss, and it is this Jewish ironist's contemplation of death that gives these poems the ethos of classical Stoicism: virtue based on knowledge, leading to a self-knowledge that, in Mr. Shapiro's work, widens into an engaging and authentic self-mockery." N Y Times Book Rev

Shapiro, Karl Jay, 1913-
New & selected poems, 1940-1986; [by] Karl Shapiro. University of Chicago Press 1987 103p pa $9.95   811
    ISBN 0-226-75033-7   LC 87-10790
This volume includes poems published since the appearance of Collected poems, 1940-1978, o.p. They are accompanied by the poet's own selections from each period of his career
Shapiro "finds cause for personal celebration in the most quotidian occurrences; yet he is equally adept at probing more public subjects. . . . It would have been helpful if the poems had been dated and/or had included an indication of which book they were selected from; but despite that shortcoming, readers will find these 'Selected Poems' a treasure." Libr J

Simic, Charles, 1938-
The book of gods and devils; poems. Harcourt Brace Jovanovich 1990 70p $17.95; pa $8.95   811
    ISBN 0-15-113455-3; 0-15-613546-9 (pa) LC 90-4297
"While Simic's terse, enigmatic poems have always expresssed metaphysical concerns, this volume's title might suggest he is moving in an overtly religious, even visionary, direction. This expectation is only partially fulfilled by the poems. They largely represent a further exploration of styles and themes he has employed the past few years. The dualism implied by the title is played out in the way the poems balance existential dread with the possibility of hope." Libr J

Hotel insomnia; poems. Harcourt Brace Jovanovich 1992 66p $18.95; pa $10.95
                                               811
    ISBN 0-15-142188-9; 0-15-642182-8 (pa)
                                      LC 91-44897
This "volume has the surrealistic clarity sometimes achieved by the sleepless. In the small hours, a drastic simplification takes place by which the infinite particulars of the world seem to point to a mere handful of meanings." Publ Wkly
"There are few poets writing today whose sense of wonder is so palpable." Libr J

Selected poems, 1963-1983. rev & expanded ed. Braziller 1990 229p pa $10.95
                                               811
    ISBN 0-8076-1240-5   LC 89-25129
    First published 1985
"The selections display Simic's ability to take an ordinary object and, through the magic of his poetry, rife with intimations of ritual and chanting, turn it into

a mysterious, complex representation of the dark forces that control our lives." Publ Wkly

Simpson, Louis Aston Marantz, 1923-
Collected poems. Paragon House 1988 385p hardcover o.p. paperback available $12.95   811
    ISBN 1-55778-411-6 (pa)   LC 88-9879
"This collection includes only the poems Simpson wanted to include. By his account, Simpson 'can hardly enjoy a poem that is all idea'—a confession that immediately separates his work from that of many contemporaries." Libr J

People live here; selected poems, 1949-1983; [by] Louis Simpson. BOA Eds. 1983 216p $25; pa $12   811
    ISBN 0-918526-42-6; 0-918526-43-4 (pa)
"The book includes more than 100 poems from previous volumes, some unpublished poems, a chronology of publication dates, and a short autobiography." Libr J
"While capable of lyric rapture, the poet typically holds himself at some distance from his subjects and is by turns satirical, bemused, sorrowing, disdainful, sympathetic, wry." Nation

Smith, William Jay, 1918-
Collected poems, 1939-1989. Scribner 1990 254p $24.95   811
    ISBN 0-684-19167-9   LC 90-40760
"Smith has had a lifelong love affair with the lyric. Unabashedly musical, he grounds the reader in a memorable detail: a willow in winter is 'a frozen harp,' a tulip 'a slender goblet wreathed in flame.' Smith's formal, witty style lends itself to the all-but-forgotten arts of light and occasional verse. But the themes of love and mortality are ever-present and reach fruition in the moving later poems." Libr J

Snodgrass, W. D. (William De Witt), 1926-
Selected poems, 1957-1987. Soho Press 1987 270p $19.95   811
    ISBN 0-939149-04-4   LC 87-9463
"These selected poems reveal an important American poet's impressive array of dramatic powers. Selections from 'Heart's Needle' (his Pulitzer Prize-winning volume), small press poems, and excerpts from the intriguing 'Fuehrer Bunker'—dramatic monologues from the top members of Hitler's Third Reich—are included." Libr J

Snyder, Gary
Axe handles; poems. North Point Press 1983 114p hardcover o.p. paperback available $8.95   811
    ISBN 0-86547-119-3 (pa)   LC 83-61398
"The poet in his 50s recalls his past, also the racial past, the 'long ago.' Some poems are anecdotal; others are notations with various parts of speech omitted, such as articles, connectives, even verbs. This poet likes tools and uses words as tools." Choice

Snyder, Gary—*Continued*

Left out in the rain; new poems, 1947-1985; Gary Snyder. North Point Press 1986 209p hardcover o.p. paperback available $9.95 **811**

ISBN 0-86547-268-8 (pa) LC 86-60994

"The poems in this book do not speak with the voice we have come to regard as Snyderian. Perhaps that is the reason they were not included in any of the eight volumes of poems Snyder published between 1959 and 1985; they would have unbalanced the volumes' unity. Or perhaps some were exercises or experiments: a villanelle, a sestina, formal poems in rhyme, several in the style of Yeats, humorous poems, lyrics. Now we see a more prolific and versatile poet than we previously saw." Choice

No nature; new and selected poems. Pantheon Bks. 1992 390p $25 **811**

ISBN 0-679-41385-5 LC 92-54110

This is a "selection of the best of Snyder's career, spanning from *Riprap* (1959), published at the time of his involvement with the Beatniks and the San Francisco Renaissance, to a previously unpublished group of sixteen poems entitled 'No Nature.'" Libr J

"There is an understated majesty about the ease with which Mr. Snyder puts the present into perspective." NY Times Book Rev

Soto, Gary

Who will know us? new poems. Chronicle Bks. 1990 69p pa $8.95 **811**

ISBN 0-87701-673-9 LC 89-22047

"Childhood, religion, family life, travel—whatever Soto's surface subject, he manages to discover in ordinary situations the soul's struggle with the world and with itself. His straightforward style, relaxed manner, and quiet but assured voice mark him as a poet of great appeal to general readers." Booklist

Stevens, Wallace, 1879-1955

The collected poems of Wallace Stevens. Knopf 1954 534p $34.50 **811**

ISBN 0-394-40330-4

Stevens's "poems range from descriptive and dramatic lyrics to meditative and discursive discourse, but all show a deep engagement in experience and in art. His musical verse, rich in tropic imagery but precise and intense in statement, is marked by concern with means of knowledge, with the contrast between reality and appearance, and the emphasis upon imagination as giving an aesthetic insight and order to life." Oxford Companion to Am Lit. 5th edition

Strand, Mark, 1934-

The continuous life; poems. Knopf 1990 63p $20 **811**

ISBN 0-394-58817-7 LC 90-52947

"The poems are singularly idiosyncratic and searching. Strand, the urbane stoic, returns an elemental poet, his home overlooking a valley. . . . The poems are classical in their postures, converging before us with Aristotelian clarity, even serenity, in spite of the mournful landscapes they often evoke." Poetry

Tate, James, 1943-

Selected poems. Wesleyan Univ. Press; University Press of New England 1991 239p $27.50; pa $14.95 **811**

ISBN 0-8195-2190-6; 0-8195-1192-7 (pa)

LC 90-50918

Tate has "created a voice and a kind of poem that no one else could have written. His comedy works not only to entertain, which it does marvelously—he has the rare ability to be very, very funny on the page—but partly to cover and partly to reveal underlying disorientation and angst." N Y Times Book Rev

Taylor, Henry, 1942-

The flying change; poems; by Henry Taylor. Louisiana State Univ. Press 1985 55p $13.95; pa $6.95 **811**

ISBN 0-8071-1263-1; 0-8071-1264-X (pa)

LC 85-11295

Set in a rural world, these poems comment on tragic events: "a blacksmith severing his finger, a horse cutting its throat on barbed wire. But beauty lies here, too, in the form of a dragonfly." Libr J

"Mr. Taylor's sense of nostalgia for his home territory is a traditional American feeling and one of the strengths of this solidly written, hauntingly conceived volume." NY Times Book Rev

Thoreau, Henry David, 1817-1862

The winged life; the poetic voice of Henry David Thoreau; edited and with commentaries by Robert Bly; wood engravings by Michael McCurdy. Sierra Club Bks. 1986 151p il $18.95 **811**

ISBN 0-87156-762-8 LC 86-60603

"Bly selects the most powerful and revealing of Thoreau's verse, as well as passages from his journals, essays, and travel books. . . . He groups these selections around key themes in Thoreau's work, such as the secret life hidden within every person, the decision not to live one's life 'meanly,' the value of an unhurried gestation period in everyone's young adulthood, the joyful and involving observation of the nonhuman world, and Thoreau's celebration of his own wildness and the wildness he loved in nature." Publisher's note

Includes bibliography

Toomer, Jean, 1894-1967

The collected poems of Jean Toomer; edited by Robert B. Jones and Margery Toomer Latimer; with an introduction and textual notes by Robert B. Jones. University of N.C. Press 1988 xxxv, 111p $17.95; pa $8.95 **811**

ISBN 0-8078-1773-2; 0-8078-4209-5 (pa)

LC 87-19203

"This is the only collected edition of poems by Jean Toomer, the enigmatic Afro-American writer, Gurdjieffian guru, and Quaker convert who is perhaps best known for his 1923 lyrical narrative, Cane. The fifty-five poems here—most of them previously unpublished—chart a fascinating evolution of artistic consciousness." Univ Press Books for Public Libr

Updike, John

The carpentered hen, and other tame creatures. Knopf 1982 84p $16.95   **811**

ISBN 0-394-52394-6   LC 81-48133

A reissue of the title first published 1958 by Harper & Row

This volume "is notable for its skill, variety, and comic sense. The patent absurdities of modern advertising, journalism, and customs strike sparks from the poet's sharp but never cruel wit." Booklist

Facing nature; poems. Knopf 1985 110p $13.95   **811**

ISBN 0-394-54385-8   LC 84-48666

Updike "demonstrates again his superior talent for 'light' verse in several witty, well-crafted lines on 'The Rockettes,' self-service gas stations, food, and foibles of everyday life." Booklist

Midpoint, and other poems. Knopf 1969 98p $16.95   **811**

ISBN 0-394-40383-5

These poems deal with love and death, animals and angels, places and persons, dream artifacts and the naked ape. First is a long semi-autobiographical poem followed by light verse and incidental lyrics

Telephone poles, and other poems. Knopf 1963 83p $19.95   **811**

ISBN 0-394-40457-2

"If Updike's manner is usually playful, who will object? . . . Yet the book seems, in its arrangement, roughly divided inside itself, with some of the most trivial tidbits placed first and nearly all the deep poems pushed back into the second section." N Y Times Book Rev

Wagoner, David

Through the forest; new and selected poems, 1977-1987. Atlantic Monthly Press 1987 223p hardcover o.p. paperback available $7.95   **811**

ISBN 0-87113-153-6 (pa)   LC 87-927

"Wagoner's poetic world teems with salmon, hawks, field mice, frogs, and rattlesnakes in their richly described ambiences of desert arroyo, swamp marsh, seacoast, and orchard—ample evidence that Wagoner is one of our finest nature poets. But one reads (and re-reads) these lovely poems for the pleasures of their craftsmanship." Libr J

Walcott, Derek

The Arkansas testament. Farrar, Straus & Giroux 1987 117p $14.95; pa $8.95   **811**

ISBN 0-374-10582-0; 0-374-52099-2 (pa)   LC 87-323

"Despite its title, this is another evocation of Walcott's St. Lucia, a Caribbean paradise of whelk-gatherers, sea grapes, and sugar cane where the poet reads 'silvery nouns' and deciphers 'scriptures of sand.'" Libr J

"With his mastery of lyric, epic, dramatic and narrative genres, Walcott reminds me of Tintoretto: he is garish and bold, uneven and unequaled in catching observed particulars in the density of stop-time. No modernist mistrust of eloquence unseats Mr. Walcott's confidence and willingness to employ tradition." N Y Times Book Rev

Collected poems, 1948-1984. Farrar, Straus & Giroux 1986 515p $30; pa $15.95   **811**

ISBN 0-374-12626-7; 0-374-52025-9 (pa)

LC 85-20688

"It is difficult to think of a poet in our century who—without ever betraying his native sources—has so organically assimilated the evolution of English literature from the Renaissance to the present, who has absorbed the Classical and Judeo-Christian past, and who has mined the history of Western painting as Walcott has. Throughout his entire body of work he has managed to hold in balance his passionate moral concerns with the ideal of art." Poetry

Includes bibliography

Omeros. Farrar, Straus & Giroux 1990 325p $30; pa $12   **811**

ISBN 0-374-22591-5; 0-374-52350-9 (pa)

LC 90-33592

This epic poem "follows the wanderings of a present-day Odysseus and the inconsolable sufferings of those who are displaced and traveling with trepidation toward their homes. Written in seven circling books and . . . tercets, the poem illuminates the classical past and its motifs through an extraordinary cast of contemporary characters from the island of Santa Lucia." Publ Wkly

"No poet rivals Mr. Walcott in humor, emotional depth, lavish inventiveness in language or in the ability to express the thoughts of his characters and compel the reader to follow the swift mutations of ideas and images in their minds. This wonderful story moves in a spiral, replicating human thought." N Y Times Book Rev

Walker, Alice, 1944-

Her blue body everything we know; earthling poems, 1965-1990, complete. Harcourt Brace Jovanovich 1991 463p $24.95   **811**

ISBN 0-15-140040-7   LC 90-5160

In this volume of Walker's "complete earlier work, joined to new, previously uncollected poems, we see a quarter century of impressive artistic development." Booklist

Horses make a landscape look more beautiful; poems. Harcourt Brace Jovanovich 1984 79p $10.95; pa $6.95   **811**

ISBN 0-15-142169-2; 0-15-642173-9 (pa)   LC 84-6556

In this collection, the author "harks back to her mixed ancestry—Cherokee, white, black—in both the dedication and throughout the work, with references to specific relatives and their exploits." Publ Wkly

Warren, Robert Penn, 1905-1989

Being here: poetry, 1977-1980. Random House 1980 108p $10.95; pa $4.95   **811**

ISBN 0-394-51304-5; 0-394-73935-3 (pa)

LC 80-11520

This volume "marks an interesting return by this most gifted of major American poetic voices to more traditional forms—forms rather resembling those with which Warren began decades ago—embodying, still, the discoveries about the need for telling concrete imagery the poet has made in the lengthy interim." Choice

Warren, Robert Penn, 1905-1989 — *Continued*

Brother to dragons; a tale in verse and voices; Robert Penn Warren. a new version. Random House 1979 141p $12.95   **811**

ISBN 0-394-50551-4   LC 79-10782

First published 1953

This revision of Warren's poem relates the events leading to and resulting from the murder of a young slave by Thomas Jefferson's nephews, Lilburn and Isham Lewis

"Though the tale . . . bears the heavy kind of metaphysical burden typical of Warren's works, it is redeemed by the vividness of its voices." Choice

Includes bibliographic references

Chief Joseph of the Nez Perce; who called themselves the Nimipu "the real people"; a poem. Random House 1983 64p $9.95; pa $7.95   **811**

1. Joseph, Nez Percé Chief, 1840-1904—Poetry
ISBN 0-394-53019-5; 0-394-71356-7 (pa)

LC 82-20431

A narrative poem based on the life of Chief Joseph of the Nez Perce Indians

"Variations of metre and rhythm prevent monotony; prose extracts, mainly from contemporary documents, are effectively intercut. The narrative is limpid, and moves adroitly between the viewpoints of Joseph and the poet, with occasional forays into the minds of the Federal officers." Times Lit Suppl

New and selected poems, 1923-1985. Random House 1985 322p $19.95; pa $15.95   **811**

ISBN 0-394-54380-7; 0-394-73848-9 (pa)

LC 84-45755

"The newly collected poems, 1980-84, are grouped under the apt rubric 'Altitudes and Extensions,' for the poet here takes the long and high view of his personal history, beliefs, and perennial themes. . . . The rest of the volume presents strong poems from 11 previous books, in reverse chronological order. Forward to back, these display a consistency of vision and rhythmic poise that help explain how, after such prolific labors, the poet can still be going strong." Booklist

Now and then; poems, 1976-1978. Random House 1978 75p $11.95; pa $5.95   **811**

ISBN 0-394-50164-0; 0-394-73515-3 (pa)

LC 78-57102

"Divided in two sections, the book celebrates the demands of memory. The first poems are dramatic narratives instigated in part by the poet's visit to his hometown. [The second section offers] speculative poems which enlarge a moment into a lyrical consideration of truth, guilt, or memory." Libr J

"The quality of achievement is consistent almost throughout these poems. Like Hardy, Yeats and Stevens, Warren is at his strongest past 70." New Repub

Or else—poem/poems, 1968-1974. Random House 1974 102p $10.95   **811**

ISBN 0-394-49448-2

"Numerous short poems link to form a unitary expression of incidents and observations dealing directly or abstractly with immortality. Brought forth out of Warren's past, the images are rendered in prose-like style

and frequently indicate the poet's concern with the physical details of death." Booklist

Selected poems, 1923-1975. Random House 1976 325p $17.95   **811**

ISBN 0-394-40531-5

Warren "emerges in this retrospective selection as one of the major American poets. . . . A poet with the courage to imagine apocalypse in more than one of its infinite variations, he speaks of strength and weakness alike." Christ Sci Monit

Wheatley, Phillis, 1753-1784

The poems of Phillis Wheatley; edited with an introduction by Julian D. Mason, Jr. rev & enl ed. University of N.C. Press 1989 235p $27.50; pa $12.95   **811**

ISBN 0-8078-1835-6; 0-8078-4245-1 (pa)

LC 88-23280

First published 1966

This volume contains all of the poems and letters known to have been written by Wheatley, America's first significant black woman writer

Whitman, Walt, 1819-1892

Leaves of grass   **811**

Hardcover and paperback editions available from various publishers

First published 1855

"The book, radical in form and content, takes its title from the themes of fertility, universality, and cyclical life. . . . As he revised and added to the original edition, Whitman arranged the poems in a significant autobiographical order." Reader's Ency

Whittier, John Greenleaf, 1807-1892

The poetical works of Whittier; with a new introduction by Hyatt H. Waggoner. Houghton Mifflin 1975 xxxii, 538p $29.95   **811**

ISBN 0-395-21599-4

"Cambridge editions"

First published 1857 by Ticknor and Fields; first Cambridge edition 1895

The output of "the much-loved American Quaker poet, champion of peace, the abolition of slavery and the rights of man." Pratt Alcove

"Whether his work is poetry or rhymed propaganda, it is literature, for it expresses a man and events in words that are today alive with emotion." Macy's Spirit of Am Lit

Wilbur, Richard, 1921-

New and collected poems. Harcourt Brace Jovanovich 1988 393p $27.95; pa $10.95   **811**

ISBN 0-15-165206-6; 0-15-665491-1 (pa)

LC 87-18175

This "volume includes the complete texts of [the author's] six previous volumes, 23 new poems, three new translations and the text of the cantata 'On Freedom's Ground' (done in collaboration with the composer William Schuman)." N Y Times Book Rev

Wilbur, Richard, 1921-—*Continued*

"Wilbur has done what is most difficult and rare: He has used the full palette of the poetic art to deal with modern experience." Christ Sci Monit

Williams, William Carlos, 1883-1963

The collected poems of William Carlos Williams. New Directions 1986-1988 2v

811

ISBN 9-99-999999-9   LC 86-5448

Contents: v 1, 1909-1939; ed. by A. Walton Litz and Christopher MacGowan $35, pa $19.95 (ISBN 0-8112-0999-7; 0-8112-1187-8); v2, 1939-1962; ed. by Christopher MacGowan $37, pa $19.95 (0-8112-1063-4; 0-8112-1188-6)

"Williams's original approach to poetry, his insistence on the importance of the ordinary, and his successful attempts at making his verse as 'tactile' as the spoken word had a far-reaching effect on American poetry." Reader's Ency

Paterson. rev ed, prepared by Christopher MacGowan. New Directions 1992 311p $38

811

ISBN 0-8112-1225-4   LC 92-22956

First published 1963

"Set in Paterson, N.J., the poem is a statement on contemporary civilization. Williams uses one dominant metaphor throughout: the city is the human mind beside the river of time; the language of contemporary events (the waterfall) gives the only kind of meaning possible in the flux of time. The poem is composed of lyrics, narrative episodes, prose interludes, bits of letters, etc., to comprise an ecstatic statement on human life." Herzberg. Reader's Ency of Am Lit

Winters, Yvor, 1900-1968

The collected poems of Yvor Winters; with an introduction by Donald Davie. Swallow Press 1980 c1978 230p $16.95

811

ISBN 0-8040-0799-3   LC 78-51596

First published 1978 in the United Kingdom

This "collection includes The Early Poems of Yvor Winters 1920-28, Collected Poems, a selection of previously uncollected poems and translations and the short story 'The Brink of Darkness.'" Libr J

"Abstraction, morality, and—let us call it gray diction—keep a close companionship in Winters's poetry, but the love of earth is never far behind. His triumphs are often morality tales in which the wrestling of impulse with reason becomes all-absorbing and the moral quietly slips out the back door, leaving Winters disarmed and his readers delighted." Times Lit Suppl

Wolfe, Thomas, 1900-1938

A stone, a leaf, a door; poems; selected and arranged in verse by John S. Barnes; with a foreword by Louis Untermeyer. Scribner 1945 166p $20; pa $9.95   811

ISBN 0-684-15754-3; 0-684-19313-2 (pa)

An experiment in which some of Thomas Wolfe's prose-poetry has been reprinted in the form of verse. "Here again is great variety, ranging from long, swinging dithyrambs that might have come from Blake's 'Prophetic Books' or Whitman's 'Leaves of Grass' to the crisper phrasing we associate with H. D. or Amy Lowell." NY Times Book Rev

Wright, Charles, 1935-

The world of the ten thousand things; poems, 1980-1990. Farrar, Straus & Giroux 1991 232p hardcover o.p. paperback available $13   811

ISBN 0-374-52326-6 (pa)

"These poems can be read as a single poetic sequence like John Berryman's 'Dream Songs.' They chart a spiritual quest, an investigation of relations between the visible world and the invisible." N Y Times Book Rev

Wright, James Arlington, 1927-1980

Above the river; the complete poems; [by] James Wright; with an introduction by Donald Hall. Farrar, Straus & Giroux; University Press of New England 1990 xxxvii, 387p $27.95; pa $16   811

ISBN 0-374-12749-2; 0-374-52282-0 (pa)

LC 89-16538

"A Wesleyan University Press edition"

"The narrowed range of Wright's characteristic subjects and format, the very delicacy of his instincts, confine him. But his best poems, with their grace and intelligence, not only stand as a rebuke to most of the glib work of his time, but remain among the finest examples of the midcentury American lyric." N Y Times Book Rev

Collected poems; [by] James Wright. Wesleyan Univ. Press 1971 215p $30; pa $16.95   811

ISBN 0-8195-4031-5; 0-8195-6022-7 (pa)

"This collection includes a selection of poems from his first book, 'The Green Wall,' and all of his poems from 'Saint Judas,' 'The Branch Will Not Break' and 'Shall We Gather at the River,' plus 30 translations— . . . from the Spanish of Jiméne Guillén, Salinas, Neruda and Valléjo and the German of Goethe and Georg Trakl—and 33 new poems of his own." Publ Wkly

Zukofsky, Louis, 1904-1978

"A". University of Calif. Press 1978 826p $27.50; pa $10.95   811

ISBN 0-520-03223-3; 0-520-04095-3 (pa)   LC 76-7773

"The poem, whose title comes from the sounding of a musical 'A' in Bach's Passion according to St. Matthew at the beginning of the poem in 1928, has been called 'the most hermetic poem in English.' It recounts the events of history, personal and public, up to 1968." Choice

"Zukofsky's art, in this work, is without equal. No poet of our time can so sound the resources of language, so actuate words to become all that they might be thought otherwise to engender." N Y Times Book Rev

811.008   American poetry— Collections

African-American poetry of the nineteenth century; an anthology; edited by Joan R. Sherman. University of Ill. Press 1992 506p $39.95; pa $15.95   **811.008**
1. American poetry—Black authors—Collections
ISBN 0-252-01917-2; 0-252-06246-9 (pa)
                    LC 91-41709
Companion to Sherman's Invisible poets (1989)
An anthology of work by "African American poets from the 19th century. The introduction surveys the historical and cultural values of African American poetry. The poems themselves have historical as well as lyric value; unfamiliar as well as familiar poets are included. Though the poems are formal, the rhymes are generally unforced. . . . This anthology also includes an extensive bibliography to help researchers find other resources." Libr J

The **Best** American poetry. Scribner $25
                             811.008
1. American poetry—Collections
ISSN 1040-5763
Also available in paperback from Collier Bks.
Series editor: David Lehman
An annual collection of American verse culled from large-circulation magazines and smaller literary reviews

The **Bread** Loaf anthology of contemporary American poetry; edited by Robert Pack, Sydney Lea, Jay Parini; published for the Bread Loaf Writers' Conference, Middlebury College. University Press of New England 1985 347p hardcover o.p. paperback available $14.95   **811.008**
1. American poetry—Collections
ISBN 0-87451-350-2 (pa)   LC 85-40489
"To reflect the various styles and concerns of the foremost voices in contemporary American poetry—from the traditional (Nims) to the less orthodox (Ashbery), from the personal to the public—the editors have selected 231 poems from 72 poets, all of whom have at least two collections to their credit." Booklist

Early ripening; American women's poetry now; edited and introduced by Marge Piercy. Pandora Press 1987 280p pa $14.95   **811.008**
1. American poetry—Women authors—Collections
ISBN 0-86358-141-2   LC 87-6047
A "collection of 64 poets unafraid of writing as women. There are poets known to most readers, such as May Sarton and Denise Levertov; there are poets known to most poetry lovers, such as Sharon Olds and Marilyn Hacker; and there are poets of emerging reputations, including Wendy Rose and Ellen Bass." Booklist

Harper's anthology of 20th century Native American poetry; edited by Duane Niatum. Harper & Row 1988 xxxii, 396p $24.95; pa $18   **811.008**
1. American poetry—American Indian authors—Collections
ISBN 0-06-250665-X; 0-06-250666-8 (pa)
                    LC 86-45023

This collection "contains the work of 36 native American poets, with hearty selections from each. Among the 36 are poets near the mainstream (Scott Momaday, James Welch, Louise Erdrich); those in academe (Gerald Vizenor, Linda Hogan, Jim Barnes; those writing in the tribal oral tradition (Barney Bush, Peter Blue Cloud, Wendy Rose); and those working in a modernist voice (Gladys Cardiff, Paula Gunn Allen). This book belongs in every collection that claims to represent the multiple voices of American literature today." Booklist
Includes bibliography

The **Harvard** book of contemporary American poetry; edited by Helen Vendler. Belknap Press 1985 440p $24.95 **811.008**
1. American poetry—Collections
ISBN 0-674-37340-5   LC 85-5473
Following an introduction which places recent American poetry in its aesthetic and social contexts, the editor presents a representative selection of the work of thirty-five poets. Among those included are: James Merrill, Elizabeth Bishop, Gary Snyder, Jorie Graham, and Amy Clampitt. Brief biographies of the poets are appended

Men of our time; an anthology of male poetry in contemporary America; edited by Fred Moramarco and Al Zolynas. University of Ga. Press 1992 xxxvii, 408p $45; pa $19.95   **811.008**
1. American poetry—Collections
ISBN 0-8203-1404-8; 0-8203-1430-7 (pa)
                    LC 91-31462
"Featuring 257 poems from more than 170 poets, this collection affirms both the diversity and commonality of male experience in the U.S. today. Unapologetically grounded in a distinctly male ethos or imagination, the poems also embrace and celebrate the multicultural tenor of American life through their mix of ethnic and racial perspectives." Univ Press Books for Public and Second Sch Libr

A **New** geography of poets; compiled and edited by Edward Field, Gerald Locklin, Charles Stetler. University of Ark. Press 1992 xxix, 324p il $28; pa $14.95
                             811.008
1. American poetry—Collections
ISBN 1-55728-240-4; 1-55728-241-2 (pa)
                    LC 91-46003
The Geography of poets was first published 1979 in paperback by Bantam Bks.
An anthology of contemporary American poetry representative of various regional voices
In this collection "we find the colloquial, rangy, sometimes racy language of the West; the plainspeech of the Midwest; the direct frankness of the Northwest. This is an exciting, accessible collection." Booklist

The **New** Oxford book of American verse; chosen and edited by Richard Ellmann. Oxford Univ. Press 1976 liv, 1076p $39.95   **811.008**
1. American poetry—Collections
ISBN 0-19-502058-8
Replaces The Oxford book of American verse, edited by F. O. Matthiessen (1950)
"This volume begins with Anne Bradstreet, who died in 1672, and ends with Imamu Amiri Baraka (LeRoy Jones), born in 1934. . . . A few ballads and folk songs, and one hymn, are . . . included. Most of the poets

The New Oxford book of American verse
—*Continued*
are represented with some amplitude so as to give a sense of their range and variety." Introduction

The New Oxford book of Canadian verse in English; chosen and with an introduction by Margaret Atwood. Oxford Univ. Press 1982 xl, 477p $34.75

811.008

1. Canadian poetry—Collections
ISBN 0-19-540396-7   LC 83-208695
Replaces The Oxford Book of Canadian verse, in English and French, edited by A. J. M. Smith (1960)
The editor has made a "selection of 120 poets, ranging from the 16th century to contemporary times. Her choices are, for the most part, perspicacious and sensitive. Most poems are well known, fairly short but representative, and stylistically accessible." Libr J

Out of this world; an anthology of the St. Mark's poetry project, 1966-1991; edited and with an introduction by Anne Waldman; foreword by Allen Ginsburg. Crown 1991 xxx, 690p pa $22   811.008

1. American poetry—Collections
ISBN 0-517-56681-8   LC 90-28382
"The Poetry Project at St. Mark's has been the *de facto* headquarters of the East Coast avant-garde for 25 years. Largely composed of work from the project's magazine *The World*, this anthology 'celebrates the "outrider" tradition,' including selections from progenitors like Creeley, Corso, and Guest through unclassifiables such as Alice Notley and John Yau, to today's best-known language poets." Libr J
"Although Waldman errs on the side of inclusivity, the writing she culls from the latest generation is nearly all galvanizing and diverse." Publ Wkly

The Oxford book of American light verse; chosen and edited by William Harmon. Oxford Univ. Press 1979 l, 540p $29.95

811.008

1. American poetry—Collections 2. Humorous poetry
ISBN 0-19-502509-1   LC 78-12356
Companion volume to The New Oxford book of English light verse, entered in class 821.008
"Light verse may be humorous, or ribald or witty, or satirical, or some combination of those qualities and others. Ogden Nash wrote it, of course, but so, on occasion, did such poets as Nemerov, Corso, and Whitman. . . . [Included are] such well-known poems as 'Yankee Doodle,' 'A visit from St. Nicholas,' 'Paul Revere's Ride,' 'Ten Little Indians'; lyrics by such figures as Stephen Foster, Cole Porter, and Stephen Sondheim; and a wide assortment of satires, puns, and yarns. It is light and it is fun." Libr J

The Poetry of black America; anthology of the 20th century; [edited by] Arnold Adoff; introduction by Gwendolyn Brooks. Harper & Row 1973 $25; pa $24.89

811.008

1. American poetry—Black authors—Collections
ISBN 0-06-020089-8; 0-06-020090-1 (pa)
A collection of over 600 poems by 145 authors. James Weldon Johnson, Paul Laurence Dunbar, Langston Hughes, Gwendolyn Brooks, Sonia Sanchez, Don Lee and Nikki Giovanni are among the poets represented. Biographical sketches are provided

Six American poets; an anthology; edited by Joel Connaroe. Random House 1991 xxxiv, 281p il $27.50; pa $12   811.008

1. American poetry—Collections
ISBN 0-679-40689-1; 0-679-74525-4 (pa)

LC 91-15375
This anthology contains 247 representative poems by Walt Whitman, Emily Dickinson, Wallace Stevens, William Carlos Williams, Robert Frost and Langston Hughes

Songs from this Earth on turtle's back; contemporary American Indian poetry; edited by Joseph Bruchac. Greenfield Review Press 1983 294p il pa $10.95

811.008

1. American poetry—American Indian authors—Collections
ISBN 0-912678-58-5   LC 82-82420
"A biographical statement accompanies each sampling from 50 poets representing more than 35 different Native American nations." Libr J
"The collection provides a balance to the volumes of compiled chants and translated (or mistranslated) songs already in most libraries. . . . [The authors] display a variety of styles and themes and draw from urban, rural, and reservation backgrounds, yet they share a reverence for the earth and the natural world and a keen understanding of the power of language to create and shape that world." Choice

The Voice that is great within us; American poetry of the twentieth century. Bantam Bks. 1970 722p pa $6.95   811.008

1. American poetry—Collections
ISBN 0-553-26263-7
"A Bantam classic"
Compiled by Hayden Carruth
Works by more than 130 American poets of the modern period are represented in this anthology. Biographical sketches and bibliographies are included

811.009 American poetry— History and criticism

Bly, Robert
American poetry; wildness and domesticity. Harper & Row 1990 341p $22.95; pa $9.95   **811.009**
1. American poetry—History and criticism
ISBN 0-06-016265-1; 0-06-092082-3 (pa)

LC 89-45628
Analyzed in Essay and general literature index
"This collection of Bly's critical writings spans four decades and offers a panorama of American poetry as seen through the eyes of one of this country's preeminent poets. . . . Garnished with copious quotation from the poetry, Bly's criticism is idiosyncratic, intense, opinionated, harsh, exuberant, penetrating, political, oracular, and, of course, poetic." Libr J

Voices & visions; the poet in America; edited by Helen Vendler. Random House 1987 xxx, 528p il $29.95   811.009
1. American poetry—History and criticism
ISBN 0-394-53520-0   LC 86-40154
Analyzed in Essay and general literature index

Voices & visions—*Continued*

In this companion volume to the PBS television series, "each of the 13 poets (Whitman, Dickinson, Frost, Stevens, Williams, Pound, Moore, Eliot, Crane, Hughes, Bishop, Lowell, and Plath) is covered in an essay written by a leading critic (Richard Poirier on Frost, Hugh Kenner on Pound, Vendler herself on Stevens, etc.). Like the series, the text scants biography in favor of close reading, focusing on poems rather than poets. As such, however, it provides solid critical overviews of these 13 important poets." Booklist

Williams, William Carlos, 1883-1963

Something to say; William Carlos Williams on younger poets; edited with an introduction by James E. B. Breslin. New Directions 1985 280p $23.95   **811.009**

1. American poetry—History and criticism
ISBN 0-8112-0955-5   LC 85-8890

"Feeling unappreciated himself until late middle-age, Williams made great efforts to further the careers of younger poets (i.e., born after 1900), encouraging, offering criticism, writing letters of introduction and recommendation, prefaces, reviews. . . . In collecting all of the poet's known printed encomia, editor Breslin shows Williams to be consistent (not to say repetitive), sometimes extravagant in his claims, and often far off the critical mark. Still, this historically significant volume has a place in active literature collections." Booklist

Includes bibliography

812   American drama

Albee, Edward, 1928-

The lady from Dubuque; a play. Atheneum Pubs. 1980 161p o.p.; Dramatists Play Service paperback available $4.75 **812**

ISBN 0-8222-0628-5 (pa)   LC 78-3192

Characters: 4 men, 4 women. 2 acts. First produced at the Morosco Theater, New York City, January 31, 1980

A drama "in which a dying woman receives the motherly compassion she needs from a lady who may or may not be her mother." McGraw-Hill Ency of World Drama

The plays. Macmillan 1991 3v ea $75   **812**

ISBN 0-02-501761-6 (v1); 0-02-501762-4 (v2); 0-02-501763-2 (v3)

"Hudson River editions. An Atheneum book"

Contents: v1 Who's afraid of Virginia Woolf?; Tiny Alice; A delicate balance; Box; Quotations from Chairman Mao Tse-tung; v2 All over; Seascape; Counting the ways; Listening; The lady from Dubuque; v3 Everything in the garden; Malcolm; The ballad of the sad cafe

Who's afraid of Virginia Woolf? a play. Atheneum Pubs. 1962 242p hardcover o.p. paperback available $9   **812**

ISBN 0-689-70565-4 (pa)

Characters: 2 men, 2 women. 3 acts. First produced at the Billy Rose Theatre, New York City, October 13, 1962

Set on a college campus, this play exhibits a night of warfare between a professor and his wife, daughter of the college president, as witnessed by a young couple newly arrived on campus

Allen, Woody

The floating light bulb. Random House 1982 104p $10.50   **812**

ISBN 0-394-52415-2   LC 81-15815

Characters: 4 men, 2 women. 2 acts. First presented at the Vivian Beaumont Theater, New York City, April 27, 1981

In this comedy "a mother's nagging expectations have 'crippled' one of two children (who spends his time performing magic in his bedroom) and driven the husband to desire distance. But when Jerry Wexler, a theatrical agent and brother of a neighbor, enters their lives the mother becomes more loving, self-aware, and perceptive." Libr J

Arthur Miller; edited and with an introduction by Harold Bloom. Chelsea House 1987 164p (Modern critical views) $24.95   **812**

1. Miller, Arthur, 1915-
ISBN 0-87754-711-4   LC 86-29962

A collection of critical essays focusing on Death of a salesman, The crucible and A view from the bridge

Includes bibliography

Arthur Miller: a collection of critical essays; edited by Robert W. Corrigan. Prentice-Hall 1969 176p $12.95   **812**

1. Miller, Arthur, 1915-
ISBN 0-13-582973-9

"A Spectrum book. Twentieth century views"

Ten essays explore Miller's dominant themes and his personal and theatrical development

Includes bibliographic references

Baldwin, James, 1924-1987

Blues for Mister Charlie; a play. Dial Press 1964 121p o.p.; Dell paperback available $4.95   **812**

ISBN 0-440-30637-X (pa)

Characters: 10 men, 2 women, extras. 3 acts. First produced at the ANTA Theatre, New York City, April 23, 1964

The "play is based on a trial that took place in Mississippi in 1955. Following the murder of a black youth, the white culprit is acquitted by the court." McGraw-Hill Ency of World Drama

Baraka, Imamu Amiri, 1934-

Dutchman, and The slave; two plays; [by] LeRoi Jones. Morrow 1964 88p hardcover o.p. paperback available $8.95   **812**

ISBN 0-688-21084-8 (pa)

In Dutchman Baraka "explores the revolutionary potential of the educated black middle-class intellectual, represented by the protagonist, Clay, a would-be poet. When Clay is exposed as dangerous—that is, as a latent killer—by white society, seductively imaged as a beautiful white woman named Lula, he is summarily executed by that society. *The Slave* (1964), a fable set in a future of war between the races, continues the theme of black revolutionary militancy." Benet's Reader's Ency of Am Lit

Carpenter, Frederic Ives, 1903-1991
Eugene O'Neill; by Frederic I. Carpenter. rev ed. Twayne Pubs. 1979 192p (Twayne's United States authors ser) $20.95   **812**

1. O'Neill, Eugene, 1888-1953
ISBN 0-8057-7267-7   LC 78-11672
First published 1964

Following a discussion of the relationship between O'Neill's life and his plays, the author describes and criticizes the major plays individually, and concludes with an overview of O'Neill's critical standing

Includes bibliography

DeLillo, Don
The day room; a play. Knopf 1987 101p $15.95   **812**

ISBN 0-394-56918-0   LC 87-46039
Also available in paperback from Dramatists Play Service and Penguin Bks.

Characters: 10 men, 5 women. 2 acts. First produced by The American Repertory Theatre, Cambridge, Massachusetts, April, 1986
Black comedy. Two hospital patients encounter succession of escapees from psychiatric ward

DeRose, David J.
Sam Shepard. Twayne Pubs. 1992 171p il (Twayne's United States authors ser) $21.95   **812**

1. Shepard, Sam, 1943-
ISBN 0-8057-3964-5   LC 92-13511
The author "analyzes Shepard's plays in light of his theatrical as well as thematic intentions. . . . Supported by evidence gleaned from stage directions, visual imagery, and physical staging, DeRose's readings of Shepard's plays are balanced and perceptive. A good general introduction to Shepard and his work." Libr J

Includes bibliographic references

Edward Albee; edited and with an introduction by Harold Bloom. Chelsea House 1987 181p (Modern critical views) $24.95   **812**

1. Albee, Edward, 1928-
ISBN 0-87754-707-6   LC 86-29943
Ronald Hayman, Gerald Weales, and Anthony Hopkins are among the authors who assess Albee's contributions to the theater

Includes bibliography

Elder, Lonne, 1931-
Ceremonies in dark old men; [by] Lonne Elder III. Farrar, Straus & Giroux 1969 179p pa $7.95   **812**

ISBN 0-374-50792-9
Characters: 5 men, 2 women. First produced at the St. Mark's Playhouse, New York City, February 4, 1969
Tragedy about old black vaudevillean and his family trying to escape from despair of Harlem ghetto life

Eliot, T. S. (Thomas Stearns), 1888-1965
The cocktail party; a comedy. Harcourt Brace & Co. 1950 190p pa $6.95   **812**

ISBN 0-15-618289-0
Awarded the New York Drama Critics Circle Award for 1950

Characters: 5 men, 4 women. 3 acts. First produced at the Edinburgh Festival, August 22-27, 1949
"On one level, the play is a contemporary drawing-room comedy dealing with the marriage of Edward and Lavinia and Edward's affair with Celia; on another, it is a profound religious work dealing with redemption. The verse is written in the rhythms of conversation, with passages of incantation and repetition." Reader's Ency. 3d edition

The confidential clerk; a play. Harcourt Brace & Co. 1954 159p hardcover o.p. paperback available $6.95   **812**

ISBN 0-15-622015-6 (pa)
Characters: 4 men, 3 women. 3 acts. First produced at the Edinburgh Festival, 1953
A satirical play in verse concerning Colby Simpson, a new confidential clerk to Sir Claude Mulhammer of London

Murder in the cathedral. Harcourt Brace & Co. 1935 87p hardcover o.p. paperback available $4.95   **812**

1. Thomas, à Becket, Saint, Archbishop of Canterbury, 1118?-1170—Drama 2. Great Britain—History—1154-1399, Plantagenets—Drama
ISBN 0-15-663277-2 (pa)
Characters: 2 men, women's chorus and extras. 2 parts, 14 scenes. First produced at the Canterbury Festival, England, June, 1935
This verse drama of the conflict between church and state in 12th century England (under Henry II) culminates in the murder of Thomas à Becket in Canterbury Cathedral

Falk, Signi Lenea
Tennessee Williams; by Signi Falk. 2nd ed. Twayne Pubs. 1978 194p (Twayne's United States authors ser) lib bdg $19.95   **812**

1. Williams, Tennessee, 1911-1983
ISBN 0-8057-7202-2   LC 77-16575
First published 1962

This study examines Williams' theatrical work with particular emphasis on his characters and his position among other Southern writers

Includes bibliography

Fierstein, Harvey
Safe sex. Atheneum Pubs. 1987 112p il hardcover o.p. paperback available $8.95   **812**

ISBN 0-689-70802-5 (pa)   LC 87-11507
Contents: Manny and Jake; Safe sex; On tidy endings
Three one-act plays examining the psychological effects of AIDS

Fierstein, Harvey—Continued

Torch song trilogy; three plays; with a note from the author. Villard Bks. 1983 c1979 175p il $12.95   **812**

ISBN 0-394-53428-X   LC 83-48075

Awarded the Tony award for best play, 1983

First published 1981 by Gay Presses of New York

Characters: 4 men, 3 women. First produced on Broadway at the Little Theatre, June 10, 1982

Contents: International stud; Fugue in a nursery; Widows and children first!

"Three semi-autobiographical one-act plays. It was the first major gay theater piece to attract and hold non-gay audiences with a comic and honest view of gay life." Libr J

Foote, Horton

Selected one-act plays of Horton Foote; edited by Gerald C. Wood. Southern Methodist Univ. Press 1989 507p $29.95; pa $14.95   **812**

1. One act plays
ISBN 0-87074-274-4; 0-87074-275-2 (pa)

LC 88-42635

"Foote is here represented by a generous selection of one-act plays, eight from the 1950s, and nine from the 1980s. . . . Like his screenplays and stage plays, these pieces are often set in the mythic town of Harrison, Texas, and develop themes that we have come to expect from him. These meticulously observed studies of family tension, the need for belonging to a place and a people, the pressures of personal and cultural change, the inner life of people threatened with the erosion of love and identity, are fine examples of the playwright's art." Libr J

Fuller, Charles

A soldier's play; a play. Hill & Wang 1982 c1981 100p hardcover o.p. paperback available $7.95   **812**

ISBN 0-374-52148-4 (pa)   LC 82-15395

Awarded the Pulitzer Prize, 1982

"A Mermaid dramabook"

Characters: 12 men. 2 acts. First produced at Theater Four, New York City, November 20, 1981

Racial tensions erupt as murder investigation is being conducted in Southern army camp during World War II

Gibson, William, 1914-

The miracle worker; a play for television. Knopf 1957 131p $16.95   **812**

1. Keller, Helen, 1880-1968—Drama   2. Sullivan, Anne, 1866-1936—Drama
ISBN 0-394-40630-3

Dramatic portrayal of relationship between Helen Keller and her teacher Anne Sullivan

"The present text is meant for reading, and differs from the telecast version in that I have restored some passages that read better than they play and others omitted in performance for simple lack of time." Author's note

Goodrich, Frances, 1891-1984

The diary of Anne Frank; dramatized by Frances Goodrich and Albert Hackett; based upon the book, Anne Frank: diary of a young girl; with a foreword by Brooks Atkinson. Random House 1956 174p il $15   **812**

1. Netherlands—History—1940-1945, German occupation—Drama   2. World War, 1939-1945—Jews—Drama   3. Jews—Netherlands—Drama
ISBN 0-394-40564-1

Awarded the Pulitzer Prize and the New York Drama Critics Circle Award for 1956

Characters: 5 men, 5 women. 2 acts. First produced at the Cort Theatre, New York City, October 5, 1955

Dramatization of Anne Frank: diary of a young girl, entered in class 92. Portrays ultimately unsuccessful attempt of Jewish family to remain hidden during the German occupation of Holland

Guare, John

Six degrees of separation; a play. Random House 1990 120p $19.95; pa $10   **812**

ISBN 0-679-40161-X; 0-679-73481-3 (pa)

LC 90-53449

Characters: 13 men, 4 women. First produced at the Mitzi Newhouse Theater, New York City, June 1990

Satirical look at contemporary urban America. Upscale, liberal New York City couple is manipulated by young black man

Gurney, A. R. (Albert Ramsdell), 1930-

Love letters and two other plays: The golden age and What I did last summer; with an introduction by the playwright. Penguin Bks. 1990 209p pa $8.95   **812**

ISBN 0-452-26501-0   LC 90-34177

"A Plume book"

Love letters dramatizes the 30-year epistolary "exchange between an upper-class man and an upper-upper-class woman. . . . The Golden Age is an updated, romantic-comic variation upon Henry James' Aspern Papers in which a young academic locates an old woman who may possess a missing chapter of The Great Gatsby and schemes to get it from her. What I did Last Summer is about 14-year-old Charlie's bohemian season with Anna, the Pig Woman, who fosters his creativity as she once did his mother's." Booklist

Hansberry, Lorraine, 1930-1965

Les blancs: the collected last plays of Lorraine Hansberry; edited with critical backgrounds, by Robert Nemiroff; introduction by Julius Lester. Random House 1972 370p o.p.; New Am. Lib. paperback available $8.95   **812**

ISBN 0-452-25414-0 (pa)

Nemiroff has collected and edited Lorraine Hansberry's last works, giving for each the critical background necessary to place its importance in the canon of her work. "Les blancs," which opened on Broadway in 1970, is an exploration of the making of a black revolutionary. "What use are flowers?," which deals with the perpetuation of the human race, is an example of Miss Hansberry's affirmation of life. "The drinking gourd," is a television drama commissioned—but never produced—by

Hansberry, Lorraine, 1930-1965—_Continued_
NBC. It is a picture of slavery which Miss Hansberry described as 'a serious treatment of family relationships by a slave-owning family and their slaves'

A raisin in the sun; a drama in three acts. Random House 1959 142p il o.p.; New Am. Lib. paperback available $10   **812**

ISBN 0-452-26485-5 (pa)

Awarded the New York Drama Critics Circle Award for the 1958-1959 season

Characters: 8 men, 3 women. 6 scenes in 3 acts. First produced at the Ethel Barrymore Theatre, New York City, March 11, 1959

"A black family seeking passage out of the Chicago ghetto is the focus of _Raisin_, and the growing realization of real values of its leading character, Walter Lee, is the substance of its action." Reader's Ency. 3d edition

Henley, Beth
Crimes of the heart; a play. Viking; Penguin Bks. 1982 125p o.p.; Penguin Bks. paperback available $6.95   **812**

ISBN 0-14-048212-1 (pa)   LC 81-24026

Awarded the Pulitzer Prize and the Drama Critics Circle Award, 1981

Characters: 2 men, 4 women. 3 acts. 1 interior. First produced at Actors Theatre of Louisville in February 1979

Set in Hazelhurst, Mississippi five years after Hurricane Camille, this comedy-drama explores the lives of three young sisters as they gather to await news of the family patriarch, their grandfather, who is near death in the local hospital

Hughes, Langston, 1902-1967
Five plays; edited with an introduction by Webster Smalley. Indiana Univ. Press 1963 258p $20; pa $8.95   **812**

ISBN 0-253-32230-8; 0-253-20121-7 (pa)

Contents: Mulatto; Soul gone home; Little Ham; Simply heavenly; Tambourines to glory

Mule bone; a comedy of Negro life; [by] Langston Hughes and Zora Neale Hurston; edited with introductions by George Houston Bass and Henry Louis Gates, Jr., and the complete story of the Mule bone controversy. HarperPerennial 1991 282p $19.95; pa $9.95   **812**

ISBN 0-06-055301-4; 0-06-096885-0 (pa)
LC 90-55835

Characters: 9 men, 4 women, extras. 2 acts 3 scenes. First produced at the Ethel Barrymore Theater, New York City, February 14, 1991

Comedy set in black community of small southern town. Feud between best friends divides entire population between Baptists and Methodists

"Included are the Hurston story that is the basis of the play, the collaborators' correspondence, and biographical and autobiographical accounts of the play's troubled genesis." Booklist

Inge, William, 1913-1973
4 plays. Grove Press 1979 c1958 304p $9.95   **812**

ISBN 0-8021-3209-X   LC 78-73032

The author was awarded the Pulitzer Prize, 1953, for Picnic

"A Black cat book"

First published 1958 by Random House

Contents: Come back, Little Sheba; Picnic; Bus stop; The dark at the top of the stairs

Jones, Tom, 1928-
The fantasticks; by Tom Jones and Harvey Schmidt; with special 30th anniversary foreword and illustrations by the authors. 30th anniversary ed. Applause Theatre Bk. Pubs. 1990 162p il $19.95; pa $7.95   **812**

ISBN 1-55783-074-6; 1-55783-141-6 (pa)
LC 90-33931

Characters: 9 men 2 women. 2 acts. First presented at the Sullivan Street Playhouse, New York City, May 3, 1960

Musical comedy based on Edmund Rostand's Les romanesques. A tale of young love featuring a boy, a girl, their fathers, and a wall

This anniversary edition includes recollections by Tom Jones and a scrapbook

Kopit, Arthur L.
Wings; a play; by Arthur Kopit. Hill & Wang 1978 78p hardcover o.p. paperback available $7.95   **812**

ISBN 0-8090-1239-1 (pa)   LC 78-10428

"A Mermaid dramabook"

Characters: 5 men, 5 women. 4 scenes. First produced at The Yale Repertory Theater, New Haven, Connecticut, March 3, 1978

Elderly woman suffers stroke and struggles to recover sense of self, world, language and past as hospital surroundings and people gradually penetrate her consciousness

Laurents, Arthur, 1918-
West Side story; a musical (based on a conception of Jerome Robbins). Random House 1958 143p il $13.95   **812**

ISBN 0-394-40788-1

"Book by Arthur Laurents; music by Leonard Bernstein; lyrics by Stephen Sondheim; entire production directed and choreographed by Jerome Robbins." Title page

Characters: 25 men, 14 women. First produced at the Winter Garden Theatre, New York City, September 26, 1957

The feud between two rival New York gangs tragically ends the romantic dreams of two young lovers

Lerner, Alan Jay, 1918-1986

Camelot; a new musical; book and lyrics by Alan Jay Lerner; music by Frederick Loewe. Random House 1961 115p il $13.95
812

1. Arthur, King—Drama
ISBN 0-394-40521-8

Characters: 14 men, 5 women, extras. 19 scenes in 2 acts. First produced at the Majestic Theatre, New York City, December 3, 1960
"Based on The once and future king, by T. H. White." Title page
A musical recreation of the Arthurian legend from the marriage of Arthur and Guenevere to the wars following Lancelot and Guenevere's defections

My fair lady; a musical play in two acts. Coward-McCann 1956 186p o.p.; New Am. Lib. paperback available $2.95 **812**

ISBN 0-451-13890-2 (pa)

Awarded the New York Drama Critics Circle Award for 1956

"Based on 'Pygmalion' by Bernard Shaw; adaptation and lyrics by Alan Jay Lerner; music by Frederick Loewe." Title page
Characters: 28 men, 14 women. First produced at the Mark Hellinger Theatre, New York City, March 15, 1956
A British professor of phonetics transforms a Covent Garden flower girl into a semblance of a duchess

Levin, Ira

Deathtrap; a thriller in two acts. Random House 1979 112p $9.95 **812**

ISBN 0-394-50727-4   LC 78-57128

Characters: 3 men, 2 women. 2 acts. First produced at the Music Box Theater, New York City, February 26, 1978
Play about an aging author of mystery plays who seeks to effect the perfect crime but is thwarted by a new neighbor

MacLeish, Archibald, 1892-1982

Six plays. Houghton Mifflin 1980 216p $10 **812**

ISBN 0-395-28419-8   LC 80-92

Contents: Nobodaddy; Panic; The fall of the city; Air raid; The Trojan horse; This music crept by me upon the waters
"This collection of six plays, written between 1926 and 1953, provides useful insights into MacLeish's growth as a poetic dramatist. Each play is furnished with a new preface by the author." Choice

Mamet, David

American buffalo; a play. Grove Press 1977 c1976 106p $6.95 **812**

ISBN 0-8021-4099-8   LC 77-78079

Awarded the New York Drama Critics Circle Award for best play, 1977, and the Obie Award, 1976
"An Evergreen book"
Characters: 3 men. 2 acts. First produced at St. Clement's Theater, New York City, February 1976
This is a play about three men, small time crooks, who spend the day in a junk shop plotting the theft of a coin collection. The drama focuses on their relationships with one another. Despite mutual distrust, brutality and verbal abuse, the three men's lives remain inextricably bound

Glengarry Glen Ross; a play. Grove Press 1984 108p pa $7.95 **812**

ISBN 0-8021-3091-7   LC 83-49380

Awarded the Pulitzer Prize, 1984
Characters: 7 men. 2 acts, 4 scenes. First produced at The Cottlesoe Theatre, London, England, September 21, 1983
Comedy about sharp dealings of small-time, cutthroat real estate salesmen

McCullers, Carson, 1917-1967

The member of the wedding; a play. New Directions 1951 118p pa $6.95 **812**

ISBN 0-8112-0093-0

Awarded the New York Drama Critics Circle Award for 1950
Characters: 6 men, 7 women. 3 acts with 3 scenes in the last act. First produced at the Empire Theatre, New York City, January 3, 1950
Based on the author's book of the same title, this is "a study of the loneliness of an over-imaginative young Georgian girl." Saturday Rev

Miller, Arthur, 1915-

After the fall; a play. Viking 1964 114p o.p.; Penguin Bks. paperback available $6 **812**

ISBN 0-14-048162-1 (pa)

Reprinted as a revised final stage version
Characters: 15 men, 10 women. First produced at the ANTA-Washington Square Theatre, New York City, January 23, 1964
This autobiographical drama "caused considerable controversy, partly because of the characterization of Maggie, supposedly modeled on Miller's second wife, the actress Marilyn Monroe." Reader's Ency

The crucible; a play in four acts. Viking 1953 145p o.p.; Penguin Bks. paperback available $6.95 **812**

1. Witchcraft—Drama 2. Salem (Mass.)—Drama
ISBN 0-14-048138-9 (pa)

Characters: 11 men, 10 women. First produced at the Martin Beck Theatre in New York City, January 22, 1953
A play based on the Salem witchcraft trials of 1692. It deals particularly with the hounding to death of the nonconformist John Proctor

Death of a salesman; certain private conversations in two acts and a requiem. Viking 1949 139p o.p.; Penguin Bks. paperback available $7 **812**

ISBN 0-14-048134-6 (pa)

Winner of the New York Drama Critics Circle Award and the Pulitzer Prize, 1949
Characters: 8 men, 5 women. First produced at the Morosco Theatre, New York City, February 10, 1949
"The tragedy of a typical American—a salesman who at the age of sixty-three is faced with what he cannot face: defeat and disillusionment. It is a bitter and moving experience of groping for values and for material success." Wis Libr Bull

Miller, Arthur, 1915-—*Continued*
The price; a play. Viking 1968 116p o.p.;
Penguin Bks. paperback available $6   **812**

ISBN 0-14-048194-X (pa)

Characters: 3 men, 1 woman. 2 acts. First produced
at the Morosco Theatre, New York City, February 7,
1968

A "play about two estranged brothers who meet after
[many] years to dispose of their parents' furniture. One
sacrificed a science career and became a policeman to
support their father during the depression while the other
studied to become a surgeon. Questions of self-sacrifice,
self-interest, responsibility, and illusions are explored but
left for the reader to resolve." Wis Libr Bull

The ride down Mt. Morgan. Penguin Bks.
1992 142p pa $7   **812**

ISBN 0-14-048236-9   LC 91-46569

Characters: 4 men, 3 women. 2 acts. First produced
at Wyndam's Theater, London, England, October 31,
1991

Tragicomedy set in upstate New York hospital.
Bigamous life of wealthy middle-aged Jewish insurance
entrepreneur unravels after auto accident

A view from the bridge; a play in two
acts. Viking 1960 86p o.p.; Penguin Bks.
paperback available $6   **812**

ISBN 0-14-048135-4 (pa)

Characters: 12 men, 3 women. First produced at the
Coronet Theatre, New York City, 1955

An Italian warped by jealous love for his wife's niece
brings disaster upon himself and two illegal Italian immigrants

Moss, Leonard, 1931-
Arthur Miller. rev ed. Twayne Pubs. 1980
182p il (Twayne's United States authors ser)
lib bdg $19.95   **812**

1. Miller, Arthur, 1915-
ISBN 0-8057-7311-8   LC 79-25071

First published 1967

The author provides critical readings of Miller's plays
up to The creation of the world and other business
(1973). A 1970 interview with Miller is included

Includes bibliography

Norman, Marsha
'night, mother; a play. Hill & Wang 1983
89p hardcover o.p. paperback available $8.95
    812

ISBN 0-374-52138-7 (pa)   LC 83-10834

Awarded the Pulitzer prize, 1983

"A Mermaid dramabook"

Characters: 2 women. 2 acts. First produced by the
American Repertory Theater, Cambridge, Massachusetts,
December 1982

Drama explores the final hour in the life of a young
woman who has lost interest in living and has decided
to commit suicide

O'Neill, Eugene, 1888-1953
The iceman cometh; a play. Vintage Bks.
1946 260p pa $8   **812**

ISBN 0-394-70018-X

Characters: 16 men, 3 women. First produced at the
Martin Beck Theatre, New York City, October 9, 1946

Thoughts and actions of a group of derelicts, habitués
of a cheap New York saloon. The time is 1912

Long day's journey into night. Yale Univ.
Press 1956 c1955 176p $18.50   **812**

ISBN 0-300-00807-4

Awarded the Pulitzer Prize, 1957

Characters: 3 men, 2 women. 4 acts, 5 scenes. First
produced in Stockholm, Sweden, February, 1956

"Among the papers Eugene O'Neill left when he died
in 1953 was the manuscript of an autobiography. Not
an autobiography in the usual sense, however. For 'Long
Day's Journey Into Night' is in the form of a play—a
true O'Neill tragedy, set in 1912 in the summer home
of a theatrical family that is isolated from the community by a kind of ingrown misery and a sense of
doom." N Y Times Book Rev

A moon for the misbegotten; a play in
four acts. Random House 1952 177p o.p.;
Vintage Bks. paperback available $7   **812**

ISBN 0-394-71236-6 (pa)

Characters: 4 men, 1 woman. First produced at the
Bijou Theatre, New York City, 1957

A tragedy "about the belated romance of two 'misbegotten' people, a drunken ne'er-do-well and a huge
woman who is almost a freak." Publ Wkly

More stately mansions; edited by Martha
Gilman Bower. unexpurgated ed. Oxford
Univ. Press 1988 313p $32.50   **812**

ISBN 0-19-505364-8   LC 88-1467

Also available in shortened version from Yale University Press pa $9.95 (ISBN 0-300-00177-0)

"Merciless drama of greed and power continuing the
history of Simon Hartford, his wife Sara, and his mother
Deborah. The three protagonists are locked in a life-and-
death struggle for dominance, each at the mercy of
drives and appetites seemingly beyond his control."
McGraw-Hill Ency of World Drama

Nine plays; by Eugene O'Neill, selected by
the author. Modern Lib. 1993 829p $20
    812

ISBN 0-679-60028-0   LC 92-27149

First published 1932 by Liveright; first Modern Library edition 1941

Contents: The Emperor Jones; The hairy ape; All
God's chillun got wings; Desire under the elms; Marco
Millions; The Great god Brown; Lazarus laughed; Strange
interlude; Mourning becomes Electra

The plays of Eugene O'Neill. Modern Lib.
1982 3v ea $10.95   **812**

ISBN 0-394-60805-4 (v1); 0-394-60806-2 (v2);
0-394-60807-0 (v3)

First published 1941

Contents: v1 Anna Christie; Beyond the horizon, The
Emperor Jones; The hairy ape; The great god Brown;
The straw; Dynamo; Days without end; v2 Morning
becomes Electra; Ah, wilderness; All God's chillun got
wings; Marco millions; Welded; Diff'rent; First man;
Gold; v3 Strange interlude; Desire under the elms;
Lazarus laughed; The Fountain; The moon of the Carib-
bees; Bound east for Cardiff; The long voyage home;
In the zone; Ile; Where the cross is made; The rope;
The dreamy kid; Before breakfast

Rabe, David

Hurlyburly; a play. [rev ed]. Grove Press 1991 210p hardcover o.p. paperback available $9.95   **812**

ISBN 0-8021-3251-0 (pa)   LC 85-770

"An Evergreen book"

First published 1985

Characters: 4 men, 3 women. 3 acts, 6 scenes. First produced at the Goodman Theatre, Chicago, April 2, 1984

Dramatic comedy chronicles post-Vietnam War American lives among jaded jet set in Los Angeles

Shange, Ntožake

For colored girls who have considered suicide/when the rainbow is enuf; a choreopoem. Macmillan 1977 64p hardcover o.p. paperback available $5.95   **812**

1. Black women—Drama

ISBN 0-02-024891-1 (pa)   LC 77-3034

Choreopoem performed by seven women exploring the joys and sorrows of being a black woman

Three pieces. St. Martin's Press 1981 142p il $12.95   **812**

ISBN 0-312-80280-3   LC 80-28437

Contents: Spell #7; A photograph; Boogie woogie landscapes

Three short theatrical pieces depicting the Afro-American experience

Shepard, Sam, 1943-

Fool for love and The sad lament of Pecos Bill on the eve of killing his wife; words by Sam Shepard; music by Sam Shepard & Catherine Stone. City Lights Bks. 1983 112p hardcover o.p. paperback available $8.95   **812**

ISBN 0-87286-150-3 (pa)   LC 83-18858

In Fool for love the myths of the Old West are evidenced in a violent confrontation between half-brother and half-sister who happen to be lovers. The sad lament of Pecos Bill on the eve of killing his wife is a musical look at the distaff side of the popular Western legend

A lie of the mind; a play in three acts; [and] The war in heaven: angel's monologue, by Joseph Chaikin and Sam Shepard. New Am. Lib. 1987 155p hardcover o.p. paperback available $6.95   **812**

ISBN 0-452-25869-3 (pa)   LC 86-21884

Cast of characters for A lie of the mind: 4 men, 4 women. 3 acts, 14 scenes. First produced at the Promenade Theater, New York City, December 5, 1985

In A lie of the mind violence underlies the destinies of two families, linked by marriage, but kept apart by jealousy and distrust. The war in heaven is a poetic monologue by an angel

Simon, Neil

Barefoot in the park; a new comedy. Random House 1964 143p il $11.95   **812**

ISBN 0-394-40515-3

Characters: 4 men, 2 women. 3 acts. First produced at the Biltmore Theatre, New York City, October 23, 1963

Comedy about young married couple residing in rundown Manhattan brownstone

Biloxi blues. Random House 1986 101p $11.95   **812**

ISBN 0-394-55139-7   LC 85-24173

Characters: 6 men, 2 women. 2 acts, 17 scenes. First produced at the Ahmanson Theatre, Los Angeles, December 8, 1984

Second play in Simon's semi-autobiographical trilogy. Comedy/drama set in basic training camp in Biloxi, Mississippi in the year 1943. Young recruit encounters army life, discipline and shades of anti-semitism

Brighton Beach memoirs. Random House 1984 130p $14.95   **812**

ISBN 0-394-53739-4   LC 83-21216

Also available in paperback from New Am. Lib.

Awarded the New York Drama Critics Circle Award, 1983

Characters: 3 men, 4 women. 2 acts. First produced at the Ahmanson Theatre, Los Angeles, March 27, 1983

First play in author's semi-autobiographical trilogy about growing up in Depression era Brooklyn

Broadway bound. Random House 1987 118p $13.95   **812**

ISBN 0-394-56395-6   LC 87-42653

Also available in paperback from New Am. Lib.

Characters: 4 men, 2 women. 2 acts. First produced at the Broadhurst Theatre, New York City, December 4, 1986

Third play in the author's semi-autobiographical trilogy deals with brothers pursuing radio-comedy career amidst family upheavals

California suite; a new comedy. Random House 1977 112p $9.95   **812**

ISBN 0-394-41284-2   LC 76-53453

First presented at the Eugene O'Neill Theatre, New York City, June 10, 1976

"Four playlets about different couples occupying the same suite at the Beverly Hills Hotel. The parts work well as a whole: the first and third attempting serious comment on love and marriage, the second and fourth as zany physical comedy." Libr J

Chapter two; a new comedy. Random House 1979 132p $11.95   **812**

ISBN 0-394-50293-0   LC 78-57093

Characters: 2 men, 2 women. 2 acts. First produced at the Imperial Theatre, New York City, December 4, 1977

A romance about a recently widowed novelist and a just-divorced actress who meet unwillingly through mutual friends

The collected plays of Neil Simon; with an introduction by Neil Simon. v2-3. Random House 1979-1991 2v v2 $29.95, v3 $34.50   **812**

ISBN 0-394-50770-3 (v2); 0-679-40889-4 (v3)

Volume 2 also available in paperback from New Am. Lib.

Volume 1 entered below with title The comedy of Neil Simon

Simon, Neil—*Continued*

Contents v2: Little me; The gingerbread lady; The prisoner of Second Avenue; The Sunshine Boys; The good doctor; God's favorite; California suite; Chaper two; v3: Sweet Charity; They're playing our song; I ought to be in pictures; Fools; The odd couple (female version); Brighton Beach memoirs; Biloxi blues; Broadway bound

The comedy of Neil Simon; with an introduction by Neil Simon. Random House 1971 657p $25 **812**

ISBN 0-394-47364-7

Contents: Come blow your horn; Barefoot in the park; The odd couple; The star-spangled girl; Promises, promises; Plaza suite: Visitor from Mamaroneck; Plaza suite: Visitor from Hollywood; Plaza suite: Visitor from Forest Hills; Last of the red hot lovers

Fools; a comic fable. Random House 1982 90p $10.50 **812**

ISBN 0-394-52390-3   LC 81-21051

Characters: 7 men, 3 women. 2 acts. First presented at the Eugene O'Neill Theatre, New York City, April 6, 1981

A romantic fable set in 19th century Ukrainian village. Young schoolteacher vows to lift curse off townspeople

I ought to be in pictures; a new comedy. Random House 1981 96p $9.95 **812**

ISBN 0-394-51774-1   LC 80-6048

Characters: 1 man, 2 women. 2 acts. First presented January 17, 1980 at the Mark Taper Forum, Los Angeles

Comedy set in Hollywood. Father-daughter relationship develops between unsuccessful scriptwriter afraid of commitments and his visiting adolescent daughter abandoned at the age of three who longs for parental love

Lost in Yonkers. Random House 1991 120p $17 **812**

ISBN 0-679-40890-8   LC 91-53112

Also available in paperback from New Am. Lib.

Awarded the Pulitzer Prize, 1991

Characters: 4 men, 3 women. 2 acts. First presented at the Stevens Center for the Performing Arts, Winston-Salem, December 31, 1990

This play, "set in 1940s New York, is a sad-funny portrait of a dysfunctional family, headed by a woman who provided for her children but never showed them love." Booklist

The odd couple. Random House 1966 116p il $10.95 **812**

ISBN 0-394-40649-4

Characters: 6 men, 2 women. 4 scenes in 3 acts. First produced at the Plymouth Theatre, New York City, March 10, 1965

Comedy "in which two divorced men share an apartment and learn something about themselves and how they look to their former wives." Booklist

Plaza suite; directed on Broadway by Mike Nichols. Random House 1969 115p il $9.95 **812**

ISBN 0-394-40667-2   LC 69-16467

Characters: 3 men, 2 women. First produced at the Plymouth Theatre, New York City, February 14, 1968

"Three one-act plays, each with the same hotel setting, in which the author [examines] marriage, the generation gap, and human vanity." Booklist

Rumors; a farce. Random House 1990 134p $16.95 **812**

ISBN 0-394-58799-5   LC 90-52998

Characters: 5 men, 5 women. 2 acts. First produced at the Old Globe Theatre, San Diego, September 22, 1988

Farce about wedding anniversary party for deputy mayor of New York that goes awry because of series of domestic crises

The Sunshine Boys; a new comedy. Random House 1973 109p il $9.95 **812**

ISBN 0-394-48808-3   LC 73-5049

Characters: 5 men, 2 women. First produced at the Broadhurst Theater, New York City, December 20, 1972

A comedy about an attempt to reunite a vaudeville team, who though they dislike each other, played together for 43 years. The crisis is reached when the team reluctantly agrees to rehearse their old act for a history of comedy to be shown on television

They're playing our song; a new musical comedy; music by Marvin Hamlisch; lyrics by Carol [sic] Bayer Sager. Random House 1980 113p $9.95 **812**

ISBN 0-394-51069-0   LC 79-5565

Characters: 4 men, 4 women. First produced at the Imperial Theatre, New York City, February 11, 1979

Musical comedy about stormy relationship between aspiring lyricist and successful pop composer

Sondheim, Stephen

Sunday in the park with George; music and lyrics by Stephen Sondheim; book by James Lapine; introduction by Andre Bishop. Applause Theatre Bk. Pubs. 1991 218p (Applause musical lib) $19.95; pa $9.95 **812**

1. Seurat, Georges Pierre, 1859-1891—Drama

ISBN 1-557-83067-3; 1-557-83068-1 (pa)   LC 90-981

Awarded the Pulitzer Prize and the New York Drama Critics Circle Award, 1985

Large mixed cast. 2 acts. First presented at the Booth Theatre, New York City, May 2, 1984

Musical inspired by Georges Seurat's painting

"Instead of mimicking reality through a conventional, naturalistic story, the authors of 'Sunday' deploy music and language in nonlinear patterns that, like Seurat's tiny brushstrokes, become meaningful only when refracted through a contemplative observer's mind." N Y Times Mag

Vonnegut, Kurt, 1922-

Happy Birthday, Wanda June; a play; by Kurt Vonnegut, Jr. Delacorte Press 1971 199p il hardcover o.p. paperback available $11.95 **812**

1. Homer—Parodies, travesties, etc.

ISBN 0-385-28386-5 (pa)

"A Seymour Lawrence book"

Characters: 5 men, 3 women, 1 boy, 1 girl. 3 acts, 12 scenes. First produced at the Theatre de Lys, New York City, October 7, 1970

A satirical retelling of the story of Ulysses' homecoming. After eight years absence, Harold Ryan, a legendary hunter, returns home to his wife Penelope who is engaged to marry someone else

Wagner, Jane
The search for signs of intelligent life in the universe. Harper & Row 1986 223p il hardcover o.p. paperback available $10.95
                                                                    812
ISBN 0-06-092071-8 (pa)   LC 86-45435
Characters: 1 woman. 2 acts. First produced at the Plymouth Theater, New York City, September 26, 1985
One woman show. A dozen diverse comic characters reflect eccentricities of American life

Wasserman, Dale, 1917-
Man of La Mancha; a musical play; lyrics by Joe Darion; music by Mitch Leigh. Random House 1966 82p il $9.95; pa $6.95
                                                                    812
ISBN 0-394-40621-4; 0-394-40619-2 (pa)
Winner of the New York Drama Critics Circle award "Best Musical 1966"
Characters: 14 men, 5 women, extras. First produced at the ANTA Washington Square Theatre, New York City, November 22, 1965
This musical play-adaptation of Don Quixote is built around Cervantes' defense, when imprisoned and held for inquisition. He arranges a mock trial performance to present his case

Wasserstein, Wendy
The Heidi chronicles, and other plays. Harcourt Brace Jovanovich 1990 252p $17.95
                                                                    812
ISBN 0-15-139985-9
Also available in paperback from Vintage Bks.
Contents: Uncommon women and others; Isn't it romantic; The Heidi chronicles
This collection traces "three decades of changing styles, mores, life objectives, and intellectual challenges. Wasserstein examines her characters and their times with great good humor, complexity, depth of feeling, and a firm refusal to accept trite and easy images." Libr J

Wilder, Thornton, 1897-1975
Our town; a play in three acts. Coward-McCann 1938 128p o.p.; HarperCollins Pubs. paperback available $4.95
                                                                    812
ISBN 0-06-080779-2 (pa)
Awarded the Pulitzer Prize, 1938
Characters: Large mixed cast. First produced at McCarter's Theatre, Princeton, N.J., January 22, 1938
Drama of life in a small New Hampshire village, called Grover's Corners. The people of the village go about their daily affairs, through a few years in the early 1900s. Although when produced little or no scenery is used, the play has a stage manager who links together the separate parts of the action with running commentary, somewhat in the manner of the Greek chorus

Three plays: Our town, The skin of our teeth, The matchmaker; with a preface. Harper & Row 1957 401p hardcover o.p. paperback available $13
                                                                    812
ISBN 0-06-091293-6 (pa)

Wilder was awarded the Pulitzer Prize, 1938 for Our town, and 1943 for The skin of our teeth
A collection of three titles first copyrighted 1938, 1942, and 1955 respectively. An earlier version of: The matchmaker, was first copyrighted 1939 with title: The merchant of Yonkers
In Our town (entered separately above) the dead of a New Hampshire village of the early 1900s, appreciate life more than the living. The skin of our teeth is an allegorical fantasy about man's struggle to survive. The matchmaker is a romantic farce set in the 1880's

Williams, Tennessee, 1911-1983
27 wagons full of cotton, and other one-act plays. 3rd ed. New Directions 1966 238p pa $9.95
                                                                    812
1. One act plays
ISBN 0-8112-0225-9
First published 1946
Thirteen one-act plays portraying various aspects of life in the South

Cat on a hot tin roof. New Directions 1975 173p pa $8.95
                                                                    812
ISBN 0-8112-0567-3
Awarded the 1955 Pulitzer Prize and the New York Drama Critics Circle Award
First published 1955; the 1975 edition is based on the American Shakespeare Theatre (Stratford, Connecticut) revival which contains a completely rewritten third act
Characters: 6 men, 5 women, 2 boys, 2 girls. 3 acts. First produced by the Playwright's Company at the Morosco Theatre, New York City, March 24, 1955
A dying Mississippi Delta plantation owner's sons and their wives struggle for the inheritance of his rich estate

The glass menagerie; a play. New Directions 1949 c1945 124p pa $4.95 **812**
ISBN 0-8112-0220-8
Awarded the New York Drama Critics Circle Award, 1945
"The New classics"
A reprint of the edition first published 1945 by Random House, with the addition of a brief essay entitled The catastrophe of success
Characters: 2 men, 2 women. 2 parts. First produced at the Civic Theatre, Chicago, December 26, 1944
"A poignant and painful family drama set in St. Louis, in which a frigid and frustrated mother's dreams of her glamorous past as a Southern belle conflict with the grimness of her reduced circumstances, as she persuades her rebellious son Tom to provide a 'gentleman caller' for her crippled daughter, Laura." Oxford Companion to Engl Lit. 5th edition

A streetcar named Desire. New Directions 1980 c1947 179p $5.95
                                                                    812
ISBN 0-8112-0765-X
Awarded the Pulitzer Prize, 1948
First published 1947
Characters: 6 women, 7 men. 11 scenes. First produced at the Barrymore Theatre, New York City, December 3, 1947
"A study of sexual frustration, violence, and aberration, set in New Orleans, in which Blanche Dubois' fantasies of refinement and grandeur are brutally destroyed by her brother-in-law, Stanley Kowalski, whose animal

Williams, Tennessee, 1911-1983—*Continued*
nature fascinates and repels her." Oxford Companion to
Engl Lit. 5th edition

The theatre of Tennessee Williams. New
Directions 1971-1992 8v   **812**

v1 pa $19.95 (ISBN 0-8112-1135-5); v2 pa $19.95
(ISBN 0-8112-1136-3); v3 $35, pa $19.95 (ISBN 0-8112-
0419-7; 0-8112-1137-1); v4 $35 (ISBN 0-8112-0422-7); v5
$35 (ISBN 0-8112-0593-2); v6 $35 (ISBN 0-8112-0794-3);
v7 $35 (ISBN 0-8112-0795-1); v8 $35 (ISBN 0-8112-1201-
7)

Contents: v1 Battle of angels; The glass menagerie;
A streetcar named Desire; v2 The eccentricities of a
nightingale; Summer and smoke; The rose tatoo; Camino
Real; v3 Cat on a hot tin roof; Orpheus descending;
Suddenly last summer; v4 Sweet bird of youth; Period
of adjustment; The night of the iguana; v5 The milk
train doesn't stop here anymore; Kingdom of earth (The
seven descents of Myrtle); Small craft warnings; The two-
character play; v6 27 wagons full of cotton; The purification; The Lady of Larkspur Lotion; The last of my solid
gold watches; Portrait of a madonna; Auto-da-fé; Lord
Byron's love letter; The strangest kind of romance; The
long good-bye; Hello from Bertha; This property is condemned; Talk to me like the rain and let me listen;
Something unspoken; The unsatisfactory supper; Steps
must be gentle; The demolition downtown; v7 In the
bar of a Tokyo Hotel; I rise in flame, cried the Phoenix;
The mutilated; I can't imagine tomorrow; Confessional;
The frosted glass coffin; The Gnädiges Fraulein; A perfect
analysis given by a parrot; Lifeboat drill; Now the cats
with jewelled claws; This is the peaceable kingdom; v8
Vieux Carré; A lovely Sunday for Creve Coeur; Clothes
for a summer hotel; The Red Devil battery sign

Wilson, August
Fences; a play; introduction by Lloyd
Richards. New Am. Lib. 1986 101p pa
$6.95   **812**
ISBN 0-452-25842-1   LC 86-5264
Awarded the Pulitzer Prize, 1987
"A Plume book"
Characters: 5 men, 1 woman, 1 girl. 2 acts, 9 scenes.
First produced at the Yale Repertory Theater, New
Haven, Connecticut, April 30, 1985
Family drama about black experience in America.
1960's spirit of liberation alienates hard working father
from wife and son

Ma Rainey's black bottom; a play in two
acts. New Am. Lib. 1985 111p pa $7.95
                                                 812
ISBN 0-452-26113-9   LC 84-27156
"A Plume book"
Characters: 8 men, 2 women. 2 acts. First produced
at the Yale Repertory Theater, New Haven, Connecticut,
April 6, 1984
Recording session by black blues great Ma Rainey for
white-owned studio, is setting for exploration of racial
relations and conflicts

The piano lesson. New Am. Lib. 1990
108p $16.95; pa $6.95   **812**
ISBN 0-525-24926-5; 0-452-26534-7 (pa)
                                      LC 90-38734
Awarded the Pulitzer Prize and the New York Drama
Critics Circle Award, 1990

Characters: 5 men, 3 women. 2 acts, 7 scenes. First
presented at the Yale Repertory Theatre, New Haven,
November 26, 1987
Drama set in 1936 Pittsburgh chronicles black experience in America. Family conflict arises over heirloom
piano

Wilson, Lanford, 1937-
5th of July; a play. Hill & Wang 1979
c1978 128p il hardcover o.p. paperback
available $10   **812**
ISBN 0-374-52170-0 (pa)   LC 78-26477
"A Mermaid dramabook"
Characters: 4 men, 4 women. 2 acts. First produced
by the Circle Repertory Company, New York City, April
27, 1978
This drama explores "the tenacious links between college friends—a Vietnam veteran, an aspiring country
singer, lovers, ex-lovers—drawn back to an anxious
reunion that recalls old wounds and traumas." Booklist

Angels fall; a play. Farrar, Straus &
Giroux 1983 102p hardcover o.p. paperback
available $9.95   **812**
ISBN 0-374-52231-6 (pa)   LC 83-97
"A Mermaid dramabook"
Characters: 4 men, 2 women. 2 acts. 1 interior. First
presented by the New World Festival, Inc. Miami,
Florida, June 19, 1982
Road closing because of nuclear power plant accident
strands group of people in remote New Mexico mission

Burn this; a play. Hill & Wang 1988 c1987
99p o.p.; Farrar, Straus & Giroux paperback
available $9.95   **812**
ISBN 0-374-52158-1 (pa)   LC 87-21073
"A Mermaid dramabook"
Characters : 3 men, 1 woman. 2 acts. First produced
at the Mark Taper Forum, Los Angeles, California,
January 22, 1987
Romantic comedy. Dancer falls in love with married
brother of recently deceased dancing partner

The Hot l Baltimore; a play. Hill & Wang
1973 145p hardcover o.p. paperback
available $9.95   **812**
ISBN 0-374-52165-4 (pa)
"A Mermaid dramabook"
Characters: 5 men, 7 women. 3 acts. First produced
at the Circle Theatre, New York City, February 4, 1973
The lobby of a derelict hotel marked for demolition
is the setting for a motley group of residents to reveal
the sad sagas of their lives

Talley's folly; a play. Hill & Wang 1980
c1979 60p hardcover o.p. paperback
available $7.95   **812**
ISBN 0-374-52157-3 (pa)   LC 79-23587
Awarded the Pulitzer Prize and the New York Drama
Critics Award, 1980
"A Mermaid dramabook"
Characters: 1 man, 1 woman. 1 act. First produced
by the Circle Repertory Company, New York City, May
1, 1979
This "drama portrays an unlikely but touching
romance between a Jewish accountant from St. Louis and
a spinsterish nurse's aide who is trying to escape from

Wilson, Lanford, 1937-—*Continued*
the protective custody of her family and the rural way of life." Booklist

Wouk, Herman, 1915-
The Caine mutiny court-martial; a play. Based on his novel "The Caine mutiny". Doubleday 1954 128p $14.95   **812**
ISBN 0-385-04054-7
Characters: 13 men. 2 acts. First produced at the Granada Theatre, Santa Barbara, California, October 12, 1953
"Lieutenant Maryk stands trial for having taken over command of the mine sweeper from the autocratic Captain Queeg. The testimony of witnesses telescopes the events that led up to the mutiny in this stage play which achieves a dramatic intensity denied to the looser form of the novel." Booklist

Zindel, Paul
The effect of gamma rays on man-in-the-moon marigolds; a drama in two acts; drawings by Dong Kingman. Harper & Row 1971 108p il $18   **812**
ISBN 0-06-026829-8
Awarded the Pulitzer Prize, 1971, and the 1969-70 New York Drama Critics Circle Award
Characters: 5 women. First produced at the Mercer-O'Casey Theatre, New York City, April 7, 1970
"The play, in the naturalistic tradition, deals with a widow and her two daughters, the imagination of one of whom has been captured by the atom and the possibilities it offers of producing mutations." McGraw-Hill Ency of World Drama

812.008   American drama— Collections

Best American plays: 3rd series—1945-1951; edited with an introduction by John Gassner. Crown 1952 xxviii, 707p $35
     812.008
1. American drama—Collections
ISBN 0-517-50950-4
First volume of series Twenty best plays of the modern American theatre, second volume Best plays of the modern American theatre and series 5 and 8 o.p.
This collection "includes Arthur Miller's 'Death of a Salesman,' Tennessee Williams' 'A Streetcar Named Desire,' William Inge's 'Come Back, Little Sheba' and 14 others." Publ Wkly

Best American plays: 4th series—1951-1957; edited with an introduction by John Gassner. Crown 1958 xxii, 648p $35
     812.008
1. American drama—Collections
ISBN 0-517-50436-7
"Contains the complete reading texts of 17 plays which were . . . successful stage productions. An introductory essay by the editor assesses trends and achievements in the American theater during the period covered. Each play is prefaced by a brief introduction." Booklist

Best American plays: 6th series—1963-1967; edited by John Gassner and Clive Barnes. Crown 1971 594p $35   **812.008**
1. American drama—Collections
ISBN 0-517-50951-2
An anthology of seventeen plays, produced on and off Broadway. Among the plays included are Tiny Alice, Hogan's goat, The Fantasticks, and Fiddler on the roof

Best American plays: 7th series—1967-1973; edited with an introduction by Clive Barnes. Crown 1975 585p $35   **812.008**
1. American drama—Collections
ISBN 0-517-51387-0
Includes nineteen American plays which have been produced on Broadway and off-Broadway. Among them are Jules Feiffer's 'Little Murders,' Lonne Elder's 'Ceremonies in Dark Old Men,' and Arthur Miller's 'The Price'

Best American plays: 9th series—1983-1992; edited by Clive Barnes; introduction by Clive Barnes; biographical introductions by Lori Weinless. Crown 1993 526p $40
     812.008
1. American drama—Collections
ISBN 0-517-57452-7
This collection includes Tina Howe's Painting Churches, Lanford Wilson's Burn this, Alfred Uhry's Driving Miss Daisy, and 13 other plays

Best American screenplays; complete screenplays; edited by Sam Thomas; foreword by Frank Capra. Crown 1986-1990 2v   **812.008**
1. Motion picture plays
First series $27.50 (ISBN 0-517-55542-5); Second series $35 (ISBN 0-517-57463-2)
Collects final versions of screenplays produced over a 50-year period, 1930-1980. Brief biographies of the screenwriter precede each screenplay

Black female playwrights; an anthology of plays before 1950; [edited by] Kathy A. Perkins. Indiana Univ. Press 1989 288p il (Blacks in the diaspora) $35   **812.008**
1. American drama—Black authors—Collections
2. American drama—Women authors—Collections
ISBN 0-253-34358-5   LC 88-46040
Contents: G.D. Johnson: Plumes, A Sunday morning in the south, Blue blood, Blue-eyed black boy; M.P. Burrill: Aftermath, They that sit in darkness; Z.N. Hurston: The first one, Color struck; E. Spence: Undertow, Fool's errand, Her; M. Miller: Stragglers in the dust, Riding the goat, Christophe's daughters, Harriet Tubman; M. Bonner: The purple flower, Exit: an illusion; S. Graham: It's morning, I gotta home
Includes bibliography

Black theater, U.S.A. forty-five plays by black Americans, 1847-1974; James V. Hatch, editor; Ted Shine, consultant. Free Press 1974 886p $39.95   **812.008**
1. American drama—Black authors—Collections
ISBN 0-02-914160-5
Among the playwrights represented are: Jean Toomer, Langston Hughes, Willis Richardson, Richard Wright, Stanley Richards, James Baldwin, Lorraine Hansberry,

Black theater, U.S.A.—*Continued*
Alice Childress, Adrienne Kennedy, Imamu Amiri Baraka (LeRoi Jones), and Ed Bullins
Includes bibliography

Out front; contemporary gay and lesbian plays; edited and with an introduction by Don Shewey. Grove Press 1988 xxvii, 564p hardcover o.p. paperback available $14.95   **812.008**
1. American drama—Collections
ISBN 0-8021-3025-9 (pa)   LC 88-1257

Contents: Street theater, by D. Wilson; Bent, by M. Sherman; Execution of justice, by E. Mann; The well of horniness, by H. Hughes; A weekend near Madison, by K. Tolan; Remedial English, by E. Smith; Forget him, by H. Fierstein; The Lisbon Traviata, by T. McNally; The fairy garden, by H. Kondoleon; Jerker, by R. Chesley; As is, by W. M. Hoffman

Includes bibliography

Plays by American women, 1900-1930; edited and with an introduction by Judith E. Barlow. Applause Theatre Bk. Pubs. 1985 xxxiii, 261p $24.95; pa $10.95   **812.008**
1. American drama—Women authors—Collections
ISBN 0-87910-226-8; 0-87910-225-X (pa)
LC 84-24606

Revised edition of Plays by American women: the early years, published 1981 by Avon Books

Contents: A man's world, by R. Crothers; Trifles, by S. Glaspell; Miss Lulu Bett, by Z. Gale; Plumes, by G. D. Johnson; Machinal, by S. Treadwell

Includes bibliography

813.009 American fiction—History and criticism

The **American** short story, 1900-1945/1945-1980; a critical history. Twayne Pubs. 1983-1984 2v (Twayne's critical history of the short story)
813.009
1. Short stories—History and criticism 2. American fiction—History and criticism

Contents: Volume 1900-1945, edited by Philip Stevick $22.95, pa $12.95 (ISBN 0-8057-9353-4; 0-8057-9356-9); 1945-1980 volume edited by Gordon Weaver $22.95, pa $12.95 (ISBN 0-8057-9350-X; 0-8057-9355-0)

The influence of social, cultural and historical events is examined and the experimental and innovative stories of the post-war period are analyzed

This "is an excellent guide for student and scholar alike. . . . A notable aspect of the work is the adequate coverage given to the contributions of black and women writers." Choice [review of volume covering 1945-1980]

Includes bibliography

Asals, Frederick
Flannery O'Connor; the imagination of extremity. University of Ga. Press 1982 268p il hardcover o.p. paperback available $13   **813.009**
1. O'Connor, Flannery
ISBN 0-8203-0839-0 (pa)   LC 81-10513
"Asals's critique articulates O'Connor's concern with conflict between faith and reason. . . . [The author considers] O'Connor's duality of images—sight and blindness, sun and moon, trees and sky." Libr J
Includes bibliography

Baker, Carlos, 1909-1987
Hemingway: the writer as artist. [4th ed]. Princeton Univ. Press 1972 xx, 438p hardcover o.p. paperback available $17.95
813.009
1. Hemingway, Ernest, 1899-1961
ISBN 0-691-01305-5 (pa)
First published 1952
Following a discussion of Hemingway's expatriation and his aesthetic principles, Baker analyzes both the fiction and nonfiction focusing on their texture, structure and symbolism. An annotated checklist of Hemingway's poetry, prose, and journalism is included

Bakish, David
Richard Wright. Ungar 1973 114p (Modern literature monographs) o.p.
813.009
1. Wright, Richard, 1908-1960
"The study weighs the impact of Wright's political concepts and personal experiences as dominant factors in the formulation of his writing style and through synopses of both familiar and less-known works shows Wright's critical importance as a black author." Booklist

Brooks, Cleanth, 1906-
William Faulkner: first encounters. Yale Univ. Press 1983 230p hardcover o.p. paperback available $13   **813.009**
1. Faulkner, William, 1897-1962
ISBN 0-300-03399-0 (pa)   LC 83-3634
The author "introduces [what he considers to be] Faulkner's most important novels and stories, focusing on theme, character, and plot as well as on Faulkner's world—the fictional Yoknapatawpha County." Publisher's note
"A simple, lucid, and lively introduction to the major works of William Faulkner." Choice
Includes bibliography

William Faulkner: the Yoknapatawpha country. Yale Univ. Press 1963 499p o.p.; Louisiana State Univ. Press paperback available $16.95   **813.009**
1. Faulkner, William, 1897-1962
ISBN 0-8071-1601-7 (pa)
"Introductory chapters contrast Faulkner with various other regional writers, comment on the social structure in his novels, and discuss his poetic treatment of nature. 'Sanctuary,' 'Light in August,' 'The sound and the fury,' 'Absalom, Absalom!' and other works are analyzed in remaining chapters. Genealogies and a character index

Brooks, Cleanth, 1906-—*Continued*
are included." Booklist

Includes bibliographic references

William Faulkner: toward Yoknapatawpha and beyond. Yale Univ. Press 1978 445p o.p.; Louisiana State Univ. Press paperback available $16.95   **813.009**

1. Faulkner, William, 1897-1962
ISBN 0-8071-1602-5 (pa)   LC 77-10898

In this volume Brooks examines Faulkner's five non-Yoknapatawpha novels: Soldiers' pay, Mosquitoes, Pylon, The wild palms and A fable, as well as his poetry and early prose

Includes bibliographic references

Cannon, P. H.
H.P. Lovecraft; by Peter Cannon. Twayne Pubs. 1989 153p il (Twayne's United States authors ser) $20.95   **813.009**

1. Lovecraft, H. P. (Howard Phillips), 1890-1937
ISBN 0-8057-7539-0   LC 88-34753

"While enthusiastically sympathetic, Cannon avoids claiming too much for Lovecraft, concluding that he will remain the idol of horror fans, largely ignored by the critical establishment. Chronology, notes, selected bibliography appended." Booklist

A **Casebook** on Ken Kesey's One flew over the cuckoo's nest; edited by George J. Searles. University of N.M. Press 1992 209p il $27.50   **813.009**

1. Kesey, Ken. One flew over the cuckoo's nest
ISBN 0-8263-1323-X   LC 91-30704

A resource "comprising fifteen of the most provocative responses to the novel as well as a complete annotated bibliography." Univ Press Books for Public and Second Sch Libr

Critical essays on F. Scott Fitzgerald's Tender is the night; [edited by] Milton R. Stern. Hall, G.K. & Co. 1986 280p (Critical essays on American literature) $40   **813.009**

1. Fitzgerald, F. Scott (Francis Scott), 1896-1940. Tender is the night
ISBN 0-8161-8444-5   LC 85-17601

"Fitzgerald was far from satisfied with the version of 'Tender is the night' published in 1934, and he kept reworking it until he died, ultimately producing a 'final' version with radically altered chronology that was published in 1951 and promptly forgotten. . . . The essays and reviews gathered here are arranged by decade, giving a thorough overview of the novel's original reception and subsequent re-evaluations." Booklist

Includes bibliographies

Critical essays on Philip Roth; [edited by] Sanford Pinsker. Hall, G.K. & Co. 1982 278p (Critical essays on American literature) $35   **813.009**

1. Roth, Philip
ISBN 0-8161-8423-2   LC 81-13300

This is a collection of essays, reviews and articles by scholars and critics on the work of Philip Roth, including a bibliographical essay by the editor

Critical essays on Steinbeck's The grapes of wrath; [edited by] John Ditsky. Hall, G.K. & Co. 1989 168p il (Critical essays on American literature) $40   **813.009**

1. Steinbeck, John, 1902-1968. Grapes of wrath
ISBN 0-8161-8887-4   LC 88-24736

This volume presents selections from 50 years of critical response to Steinbeck's classic novel

Includes bibliographic references

Critical essays on Stephen Crane's The Red badge of courage; [edited by] Donald Pizer. Hall, G.K. & Co. 1990 269p (Critical essays on American literature) $40   **813.009**

1. Crane, Stephen, 1871-1900. Red badge of courage
ISBN 0-8161-8898-X   LC 90-30087

This collection of essays on Crane's classic Civil War novel contains both early reviews and modern scholarship. Among the contributors are William Dean Howells, Harold Frederic, James Nagel and Jean Cazemajou

Includes bibliographic references

Daly, Jay
Presenting S. E. Hinton. updated ed. Twayne Pubs. 1989 148p (Twayne's young adult authors ser) $19.95   **813.009**

1. Hinton, S. E.
ISBN 0-8057-8211-7   LC 89-32347

Also available in paperback from Dell

First published 1987

An introductory look at the life and work of the author of The outsiders, Tex, and Rumble fish

Includes bibliography

Dangerous men & adventurous women; romance writers on the appeal of the romance; edited by Jayne Ann Krentz. University of Pa. Press 1992 186p $24.95; pa $12.95   **813.009**

1. Love stories—History and criticism
ISBN 0-8122-3192-9; 0-8122-1411-0 (pa)
      LC 92-22665

In these essays, best-selling romance "authors dispute some of the notions that plague their profession, including the time-worn theory that the romance genre contains only a single, monolithic story, which is cranked out over and over again. The authors discuss positive, life-affirming values inherent in all romances: the celebration of female power, courage, intelligence, and gentleness; the inversion of the power structure of a patriarchal society; and the integration of male and female. Several of the essays also discuss the issue of reader identification with the characters, a relationship that is far more complex than most critics realize." Publisher's note

Includes bibliographic references

Doyle, Paul A., 1925-
Pearl S. Buck. rev ed. Twayne Pubs. 1980 179p (Twayne's United States authors ser) $19.95   **813.009**

1. Buck, Pearl S. (Pearl Sydenstricker), 1892-1973
ISBN 0-8057-7325-8   LC 80-24376

First published 1965

Doyle, Paul A., 1925——*Continued*
This study examines Buck's thematic interests, plots, arguments, characterization, and style
Includes bibliography

Dutton, Robert R.
Saul Bellow. rev ed. Twayne Pubs. 1982 212p (Twayne's United States authors ser) $20.95   **813.009**
1. Bellow, Saul
ISBN 0-8057-7353-3   LC 81-6977
First published 1971
This study of Bellow attempts to show the symbolism and romantic irony present in his novels
Includes bibliography

Eble, Kenneth Eugene
F. Scott Fitzgerald; by Kenneth Eble. rev ed. Twayne Pubs. 1977 187p (Twayne's United States authors ser) $19.95   **813.009**
1. Fitzgerald, F. Scott (Francis Scott), 1896-1940
ISBN 0-8057-7183-2   LC 77-429
Also available in paperback from Macmillan
First published 1963
This assessment of Fitzgerald's oeuvre places particular emphasis on his achievement in the short story format
Includes bibliography

Ernest Hemingway: six decades of criticism; edited by Linda W. Wagner. Michigan State Univ. Press 1987 341p pa $22   **813.009**
1. Hemingway, Ernest, 1899-1961
ISBN 0-87013-250-4   LC 87-61766
Analyzed in Essay and general literature index
Replaces Ernest Hemingway: five decades of criticism, published 1974
This collection includes critical essays by Scott Donaldson, Paul Rosenfeld, Malcolm Cowley, John Wain, Nelson Algren, and E.L. Doctorow

Ernest Hemingway's The sun also rises; edited and with an introduction by Harold Bloom. Chelsea House 1987 184p (Modern critical interpretations) $29.95   **813.009**
1. Hemingway, Ernest, 1899-1961. The sun also rises
ISBN 1-55546-053-4   LC 87-6342
Eleven essays that represent the critical reception of Hemingway's novel of the "lost generation" and their disillusionment
Includes bibliography

Felgar, Robert, 1944-
Richard Wright; by Robert Felgar. Twayne Pubs. 1980 189p il (Twayne's United States authors ser) $19.95   **813.009**
1. Wright, Richard, 1908-1960
ISBN 0-8057-7320-7   LC 80-16309
"Drawing upon existing biographical information and critical opinion, Felgar attempts a reinterpretation of Wright's 'themes, ideas, and techniques'. . . . [This] is a useful introduction to Wright and his works, particularly for general readers." Choice
Includes bibliography

French, Warren G., 1922-
J.D. Salinger, revisited; by Warren French. Twayne Pubs. 1988 147p (Twayne's United States authors ser) $19.95   **813.009**
1. Salinger, J. D. (Jerome David), 1919-
ISBN 0-8057-7522-6   LC 88-4851
Also available in paperback from Macmillan
First published 1976
"Summarizing contemporary critical thought while advancing his own reading of Salinger's work, French raises a number of fascinating points." Booklist
Includes bibliographies

Jack Kerouac; [by] Warren French. Twayne Pubs. 1986 xx, 147p (Twayne's United States authors ser) $19.95   **813.009**
1. Kerouac, Jack, 1922-1969
ISBN 0-8057-7467-X   LC 86-4817
The author "believes that Kerouac is worth taking seriously, not so much for the oft-misread beat bible 'On the Road' as for the various works constituting the 'Duluoz Legend' (in particular, 'Big Sur'), all of which build on the legend Kerouac tried to create for himself and all of which reveal, in one way or another, his agonizing internal conflicts. A thoughtful, intelligent effort to revise the critical thinking on Kerouac." Booklist
Includes bibliography

John Steinbeck; [by] Warren French. 2nd ed rev. Twayne Pubs. 1975 189p (Twayne's United States authors ser) $19.95   **813.009**
1. Steinbeck, John, 1902-1968
ISBN 0-8057-0693-3
Also available in paperback from Macmillan
First published 1961
The author contrasts theories of nineteenth century naturalism with theories of literary consciousness to arrive at a viable concept of Naturalism, which he uses to review Steinbeck's fiction
Includes bibliography

Friedman, Alan Warren
William Faulkner. Ungar 1985 c1984 220p $19.95   **813.009**
1. Faulkner, William, 1897-1962
ISBN 0-8044-2218-4   LC 82-40274
"With this comprehensive collection of essays, Friedman attempts to document the unity of Faulkner's work. . . . Those familiar with Faulkner's work will find much of interest here, while new readers will profit from an engaging overview of both the author and his work." Booklist
Includes bibliography

Grebstein, Sheldon Norman
John O'Hara. Twayne Pubs. 1966 175p (Twayne's United States authors ser) hardcover o.p. paperback available $10.95   **813.009**
1. O'Hara, John, 1905-1970
ISBN 0-8084-0187-4 (pa)

Grebstein, Sheldon Norman—*Continued*

The author "provides a reasoned if not stylistically distinctive critical interpretation and assessment of O'Hara's novels and short stories after first discussing salient features of O'Hara's childhood bearing on his writing and his reception, or lack thereof, by the scholarly critics over the past three decades." Booklist

Includes bibliography

Greiner, Donald J.

John Updike's novels. Ohio Univ. Press 1984 223p $23.95; pa $12.95   **813.009**

1. Updike, John
ISBN 0-8214-0780-5; 0-8214-0792-9 (pa)   LC 84-7213

This "is a perceptive and thorough discussion of the major fiction of one of America's most important authors since WW II. . . . The heart of Greiner's book is his lenghty and penetrating examination of the Rabbit trilogy." Choice

Includes bibliography

Gunn, James E., 1923-

Isaac Asimov: the foundations of science fiction; [by] James Gunn. Oxford Univ. Press 1982 236p (Science fiction writers) $24.95; pa $7.95   **813.009**

ISBN 0-19-503059-1; 0-19-503060-5 (pa)
             LC 81-19006

"A Galaxy book"

The author "focuses on Asimov's robots and on the Foundation trilogy, emphasizing throughout Asimov's limited use of background, style, and characterization, and his constantly recurring theme of the rational solution of a problem. The Lucky Starr juveniles get comparatively cursory treatment, but otherwise this is a very fine book indeed—well informed, clearly written, and judicious." Booklist

Includes bibliography

Hardy, John Edward

Katherine Anne Porter. Ungar 1973 160p (Modern literature monographs) $18.95
             813.009

1. Porter, Katherine Anne, 1890-1980
ISBN 0-8044-2351-2

The author considers the meaning of Katherine Anne Porter's art through a review of what has been written about her life, followed by an analysis of the stories themselves

Includes bibliography

Hendrick, Willene, 1928-

Katherine Anne Porter; by Willene Hendrick and George Hendrick. rev ed. Twayne Pubs. 1988 160p (Twayne's United States authors ser) $19.95   **813.009**

1. Porter, Katherine Anne, 1890-1980
ISBN 0-8057-7513-7   LC 87-21246

First published 1965 under the authorship of George Hendrick

A critical analysis of Porter's essays and fiction. Ship of fools, her only novel, is reviewed at length

Includes bibliography

Hershinow, Sheldon J., 1942-

Bernard Malamud. Ungar 1980 165p (Modern literature monographs) $18.95
             813.009

1. Malamud, Bernard, 1914-1986
ISBN 0-8044-2377-6   LC 79-48077

In this account of the American author's fiction, Hershinow attempts to demonstrate "the ways in which, as a writer, [Malamud] is a 'moral activist.'" Choice

Includes bibliography

Hillway, Tyrus

Herman Melville. rev ed. Twayne Pubs. 1979 177p (Twayne's United States authors ser) $19.95   **813.009**

1. Melville, Herman, 1819-1891
ISBN 0-8057-7256-1   LC 78-11937

First published 1963

An introductory look at the plots, characters, and dominant themes of Melville's works, beginning with Typee (1846)

Includes bibliography

Hughes, R. S., 1948-

John Steinbeck; a study of the short fiction. Twayne Pubs. 1988 218p il (Twayne's studies in short fiction) $21.95
             813.009

1. Steinbeck, John, 1902-1968
ISBN 0-8057-8302-4   LC 88-19967

"Underscored with the sentiment that Steinbeck's stories are equal if not superior to his more famous novels, Hughes' examination falls into three parts. Part 1 is a critical analysis, story by story. . . . Part 2 is a collection of statements by Steinbeck himself about the writing of short stories. Part 3 brings together a handful of critical essays about Steinbeck." Booklist

Includes bibliography

J.D. Salinger; edited and with an introduction by Harold Bloom. Chelsea House 1987 147p (Modern critical views) $24.95   **813.009**

1. Salinger, J. D. (Jerome David), 1919-
ISBN 0-87754-716-5   LC 86-29941

This collection of nine essays provides a view of Salinger's critical reception. Among the contributors are Alfred Kazin, David Galloway and Gerald Rosen

Includes bibliography

John Steinbeck; edited and with an introduction by Harold Bloom. Chelsea House 1987 172p (Modern critical views) $24.95   **813.009**

1. Steinbeck, John, 1902-1968
ISBN 0-87754-635-5   LC 86-29958

A selection of criticism, arranged in chronological order of publication, devoted to the fiction of John Steinbeck

Includes bibliography

John Updike; edited and with an introduction by Harold Bloom. Chelsea House 1987 172p (Modern critical views) $24.95 **813.009**

1. Updike, John
ISBN 0-87754-717-3 LC 86-29971

Critical interpretations of Updike's fiction from the Rabbit and Bech novels to The coup. Contributors include Joyce Carol Oates, Tony Tanner and Cynthia Ozick

Includes bibliography

Joyce Carol Oates; edited and with an introduction by Harold Bloom. Chelsea House 1987 164p (Modern critical views) $24.95 **813.009**

1. Oates, Joyce Carol, 1938-
ISBN 0-87754-712-2 LC 86-29968

A collection of critical essays on the works of a prolific novelist/short story writer. Oates' rhetorical style is considered

Includes bibliography

L'Amour, Louis, 1908-1988
The Sackett companion; a personal guide to the Sackett novels. Bantam Bks. 1988 341p il maps $19.95; pa $10 **813.009**
ISBN 0-553-05305-1; 0-553-37102-9 (pa)
LC 88-47530

"Each individual profile of the 17 Sackett novels contains a map, a cover painting, brief plot synopsis, and an annotated list of characters. Sackett enthusiasts will also welcome the inclusion of a detailed Sackett genealogy and family tree." Booklist

Levant, Howard
The novels of John Steinbeck; a critical study; with an introduction by Warren French. University of Mo. Press 1974 304p hardcover o.p. paperback available $12 **813.009**

1. Steinbeck, John, 1902-1968
ISBN 0-8262-0424-4 (pa)

This is "a good critical study of all of Steinbeck's longer fiction." Choice

Includes bibliography

Levin, Harry, 1912-
The power of blackness; Hawthorne, Poe, Melville. Knopf 1958 263p o.p.; Ohio Univ. Press paperback available $9.95 **813.009**

1. Hawthorne, Nathaniel, 1804-1864 2. Poe, Edgar Allan, 1809-1849 3. Melville, Herman, 1819-1891
ISBN 0-8214-0581-0 (pa)

"A study of common themes and images and their adaptation by these three writers. Drawn from lectures given at the University of California, Berkeley in 1957." Publ Wkly

The book "manages to isolate and to underscore the essential quality of each writer." Nation

Includes bibliography

Long, Robert Emmet, 1934-
Henry James, the early novels. Twayne Pubs. 1983 195p il (Twayne's United States authors ser) $22.95 **813.009**

1. James, Henry, 1843-1916
ISBN 0-8057-7379-7 LC 82-18721

Companion volume Henry James, the later novels, by William R. Macnaughton, entered below

Critical analyses of: Roderick Hudson; The American; The Europeans; Daisy Miller; Washington Square; The portrait of a lady; and, The Bostonians

Includes bibliography

Lundquist, James
J. D. Salinger. Ungar 1979 194p (Modern literature monographs) $26.95 **813.009**

1. Salinger, J. D. (Jerome David), 1919-
ISBN 0-8044-2560-4 LC 78-4301

"Besides gathering together what little biographical material is available, this makes a competent attempt to place Salinger's achievement within a firm personal and historical context and has the added value of that achievement." Booklist

Includes bibliography

Mackey, Douglas A., 1947-
Philip K. Dick. Twayne Pubs. 1988 157p (Twayne's United States authors ser) $21.95 **813.009**

1. Dick, Philip K.
ISBN 0-8057-7515-3 LC 87-25041

This critical introduction to the prolific and controversial science fiction author also examines some of Dick's posthumously published early, mainstream work

Includes bibliography

Macnaughton, William R., 1939-
Henry James, the later novels. Twayne Pubs. 1987 154p (Twayne's United States authors ser) $22.95 **813.009**

1. James, Henry, 1843-1916
ISBN 0-8057-7505-6 LC 87-15030

Companion volume Henry James, the early novels, by Robert Emmet Long, entered above

This "critical survey examines the novels James wrote during the last half of his career: *The Princess Casamassima* (1886), *The Tragic Muse* (1890), *The Awkward Age* (1899), *The Wings of the Dove* (1902), *The Ambassadors* (1903), and *The Golden Bowl* (1904). Discussions are rigorous but never lose themselves in arcane concepts and expressions." Booklist

Includes bibliography

Marling, William, 1951-
Raymond Chandler. Twayne Pubs. 1986 169p (Twayne's United States authors ser) $20.95 **813.009**

1. Chandler, Raymond, 1888-1959
ISBN 0-8057-7472-6 LC 86-7678

The author provides a "survey of Chandler's biography, his art—its imaginative evolution, scope, thematic direction, and stylistic proclivities—and the literary

Marling, William, 1951-—*Continued*
assessment of his work." Choice

Includes bibliography

Martin, Terence
Nathaniel Hawthorne. rev ed. Twayne
Pubs. 1983 221p (Twayne's United States
authors ser) $20.95   **813.009**

1. Hawthorne, Nathaniel, 1804-1864
ISBN 0-8057-7384-3   LC 82-23419

First published 1965

A critical introduction to the nature and extent of
Hawthorne's achievement in fiction, giving insight into
his romances and tales

Includes bibliography

McDowell, Margaret B.
Carson McCullers. Twayne Pubs. 1980
158p il (Twayne's United States authors ser)
$19.95   **813.009**

1. McCullers, Carson, 1917-1967
ISBN 0-8057-7297-9   LC 79-13361

This "study begins with a solid introductory chapter
of biographical material and a discussion of McCuller's
theory of fiction and then proceeds to allot one chapter
each to her five novels." Choice

Includes bibliography

McElderry, Bruce Robert
Thomas Wolfe; by B. R. McElderry, Jr.
Twayne Pubs. 1964 207p (Twayne's United
States authors ser) $20.95   **813.009**

1. Wolfe, Thomas, 1900-1938
ISBN 0-8057-0833-2

Also available in paperback from College & Univ.
Press

This "reviews the highlights of Thomas Wolfe's career,
then compares recorded fact with Wolfe's fictional or
dramatic versions to show the depth and breadth of his
literary artistry." Booklist

Includes bibliography

McSweeney, Kerry, 1941-
Moby-Dick; Ishmael's mighty book.
Twayne Pubs. 1986 131p (Twayne's
masterwork studies) $20.95; pa $9.95
                    813.009

1. Melville, Herman, 1819-1891. Moby-Dick
ISBN 0-8057-7954-X; 0-8057-8002-5 (pa) LC 86-4839

This study "focuses on the major themes and concepts
of Melville's most widely studied novel. Also covered
are such matters as the novel's historical context and
its critical reception. Introduced by a chronology of Melville's life, the monograph concludes with lists of primary
and, more important for the student, secondary sources."
Booklist

Merrill, Robert, 1944-
Joseph Heller. Twayne Pubs. 1987 153p
(Twayne's United States authors ser) $19.95
                    813.009

1. Heller, Joseph
ISBN 0-8057-7492-0   LC 86-19580

"Merrill is uncommonly well versed in the critical
debates surrounding the work of Joseph Heller, and he
treats the author's critics sensitively and generously—and
then just as sensitively and generously goes on to
disagree with them." Booklist

Includes bibliography

Michener, James A. (James Albert), 1907-
My lost Mexico; with photographs by the
author. State House Press 1992 165p il
$24.95   **813.009**

1. Mexico—Description
ISBN 0-938349-93-7   LC 92-26953

The author "reconstructs the birth of his recently
published novel *Mexico*, which he had originally abandoned in 1961. . . . Discussing the 'colossal' writer's
blocks he has faced over the years, Michener offers advice to aspiring writers as he describes his many trips
to Mexico, divulges his sources of inspiration and relives
the writing of *Mexico* with the aid of reproduced journal
pages, workbook entries and photographs." Publ Wkly

Mogen, David, 1945-
Ray Bradbury. Twayne Pubs. 1986 186p
(Twayne's United States authors ser) $19.95
                    813.009

1. Bradbury, Ray, 1920-
ISBN 0-8057-7464-5   LC 86-11972

"Mogen begins with an overview of Bradbury's personal and literary history. His major works are discussed
and compared. The book, thus, is valuable both as a
source for biographical material and as a collection of
literary criticism of Bradbury's works." SLJ

Includes bibliography

Paulson, Suzanne Morrow
Flannery O'Connor; a study of the short
fiction. Twayne Pubs. 1988 238p (Twayne's
studies in short fiction) $20.95   **813.009**

1. O'Connor, Flannery
ISBN 0-8057-8301-6   LC 88-14681

This study is "divided into three sections: analysis by
thematic subject (such as death, male/female conflicts,
and good/evil conflicts); short excerpts from O'Connor's
letters, lectures, and interviews; and selections of critical
articles and book excerpts about her writing." Booklist

Includes bibliography

Ralph Ellison: a collection of critical essays;
edited by John Hersey. Prentice-Hall 1974
180p $12.95   **813.009**

1. Ellison, Ralph. Invisible man
ISBN 0-13-274357-4

"A Spectrum book. Twentieth century views"

This collection brings together selections by critics and
authors such as Robert Penn Warren, Saul Bellow, Irving
Howe, and Tony Tanner. The essays focus primarily on
Invisible man, Ellison's symbolic, epic narrative of a

Ralph Ellison: a collection of critical essays—*Continued*
black man's maturation in white America
Includes bibliography

Reed, Kenneth T.
Truman Capote. Twayne Pubs. 1981 145p (Twayne's United States authors ser) $19.95 **813.009**

1. Capote, Truman, 1924-1984
ISBN 0-8057-7321-5   LC 80-26056

This "overview of Capote's place in American letters . . . begins with a condensed interpretive biographical section, followed by somewhat more expansive literary criticism of Capote's short fiction, novels, and reportage. Capote's style, themes, characterizations, and influences receive summary interpretation." Booklist
Includes bibliography

Richard Wright's Native son; edited and with an introduction by Harold Bloom. Chelsea House 1988 174p (Modern critical interpretations) $24.95 **813.009**

1. Wright, Richard, 1908-1960. Native son
ISBN 1-55546-055-0   LC 87-30402

A collection of critical essays on Wright's classic portrayal of the black experience, arranged chronologically in the order of their original publication
Includes bibliography

Richman, Sidney
Bernard Malamud. Twayne Pubs. 1967 c1966 160p (Twayne's United States authors ser) $19.95 **813.009**

1. Malamud, Bernard, 1914-1986
ISBN 0-8057-0472-8

Malamud's tragic vision, realism and use of symbolism are emphasized in this discussion of his novels and short stories. A chronology and bibliography are included

Rovit, Earl H.
Ernest Hemingway; [by] Earl Rovit, Gerry Brenner. rev ed. Twayne Pubs. 1986 214p (Twayne's United States authors ser) $20.95 **813.009**

1. Hemingway, Ernest, 1899-1961
ISBN 0-8057-7455-6   LC 85-28916
First published 1963

Hemingway's work is presented through an analysis of his style, his characteristic employment of narrational structures, recurrent themes, and the Hemingway "code" as elements in his total achievement
Includes bibliography

Schatt, Stanley, 1943-
Kurt Vonnegut, Jr. Twayne Pubs. 1976 174p (Twayne's United States authors ser) $19.95 **813.009**

1. Vonnegut, Kurt, 1922-
ISBN 0-8057-7176-X

The author "surveys Vonnegut's philosophy and style, taking into consideration the full spectrum of his work. . . . Schatt examines each work systematically and in depth, calling upon biographical information when needed." Libr J
Includes bibliography

The **Short** stories of Ernest Hemingway; critical essays; edited with an overview and checklist, by Jackson J. Benson. Duke Univ. Press 1975 375p hardcover o.p. paperback available $16.95 **813.009**

1. Hemingway, Ernest, 1899-1961
ISBN 0-8223-0386-8 (pa)
Analyzed in Essay and general literature index

"Benson has put together . . . 30 of the best interpretive and critical writings about the short stories of [Hemingway]. . . . To this collection he has added an introduction and an important essay of his own. . . . Finally, there is a splendid comprehensive bibliography." Choice

Sinclair Lewis; edited and with an introduction by Harold Bloom. Chelsea House 1987 144p (Modern critical views) $24.95 **813.009**

1. Lewis, Sinclair, 1885-1951
ISBN 0-87754-628-2   LC 86-29912

A collection of ten critical essays on the novels of Sinclair Lewis which examine their ironic, satiric and moral dimensions
Includes bibliography

Skaggs, Peggy
Kate Chopin. Twayne Pubs. 1985 130p (Twayne's United States authors ser) $19.95 **813.009**

1. Chopin, Kate, 1851-1904
ISBN 0-8057-7439-4   LC 84-27977

The author "provides careful analyses of Chopin's two volumes of published short stories ('Bayou Folks' and 'A Night in Arcadie'), the stories of her unpublished volume, 'A Vocation and a Voice,' her uncollected short stories, poems, and essays, as well as her two novels, 'At Fault' and 'The Awakening.' A thorough critical study of interest to both general readers and scholars." Booklist
Includes bibliography

Spaeth, Janet
Laura Ingalls Wilder. Twayne Pubs. 1987 110p (Twayne's United States authors ser) $18.95 **813.009**

1. Wilder, Laura Ingalls, 1867-1957
ISBN 0-8057-7501-3   LC 87-15

The author discusses the life and work of Laura Ingalls Wilder, relating the history of pioneer life to the fictional events and characters in her "Little House" books
Includes bibliographies

The **Stephen** King companion; edited by George Beahm. Andrews & McMeel 1989 363p il pa $10.95 **813.009**

1. King, Stephen, 1947-
ISBN 0-8362-7978-6   LC 89-17811

The Stephen King companion—*Continued*
This volume "includes original and reprinted pieces relating to King, many from uncommon sources, including a lengthy 1983 Playboy magazine interview which holds up well. . . . Appendixes list books in print by or about King, films, TV, and audio cassettes based on King tales, and detailed notes on collecting King." Libr J

The Tales of Poe; edited and with an introduction by Harold Bloom. Chelsea House 1987 167p (Modern critical interpretations) $29.95   **813.009**
1. Poe, Edgar Allan, 1809-1849
ISBN 1-55546-011-9   LC 86-34307
A collection of essays analyzing the themes and styles of Poe's tales of horror
Includes bibliography

Thomas Wolfe; edited and with an introduction by Harold Bloom. Chelsea House 1987 174p $24.95   **813.009**
1. Wolfe, Thomas, 1900-1938
ISBN 0-87754-638-X   LC 86-29952
A collection of critical essays that examine the structure, themes and metaphors employed by Wolfe in his fiction. Morris Beja, Leo Gurko and David Herbert Donald are among the contributors
Includes bibliography

Twentieth century interpretations of A farewell to arms; a collection of critical essays; edited by Jay Gellens. Prentice-Hall 1970 121p $9.95   **813.009**
ISBN 0-13-303180-2
"A Spectrum book"
"Hemingway's style, symbolism, and treatment of war are recurring subjects in the articles that date from 1940 to 1966; the authors represented include Carlos Baker, Wyndham Lewis, Malcolm Cowley, and a number of lesser-known university professors or instructors." Booklist
Includes bibliography

Twentieth century interpretations of All the king's men; a collection of critical essays; edited by Robert H. Chambers. Prentice-Hall 1977 161p $9.95; pa $3.45   **813.009**
1. Warren, Robert Penn, 1905-1989. All the king's men
ISBN 0-13-022434-0; 0-13-022426-X (pa)
    LC 77-23876
"A Spectrum book"
"The 11 essays and Chambers's introduction consider most of the important problems in 'All the king's men' and furnish a history of the novel's critical reception as well." Choice
Includes bibliography

Twentieth century interpretations of The great Gatsby; a collection of critical essays. Prentice-Hall 1968 119p $22.50   **813.009**
1. Fitzgerald, F. Scott (Francis Scott), 1896-1940. The great Gatsby
ISBN 0-13-363820-0
"A Spectrum book"
Edited by Ernest Lockridge

This volume, which ranges across forty years of criticism of this American classic, includes contributions by Marius Bewley, Thomas A. Hanzo, Edith Wharton, Lionel Trilling, and Fitzgerald himself
Includes bibliography

Twentieth century interpretations of The scarlet letter; a collection of critical essays; edited by John C. Gerber. Prentice-Hall 1968 120p $15.95   **813.009**
ISBN 0-13-791582-9
"A Spectrum book"
The articles in this volume provide a framework for the analysis of the background, form, technique, and meaning of the novel
Includes bibliography

Wagner-Martin, Linda
The modern American novel, 1914-1945; a critical history. Twayne Pubs. 1989 163p (Twayne's critical history of the novel) $22.95; pa $9.95   **813.009**
1. American fiction—History and criticism
ISBN 0-8057-7851-9; 0-8057-7853-5 (pa)
    LC 89-15515
The author "considers a wide array of authors, including famous ones (Willa Cather, Gertrude Stein, Ernest Hemingway, Frank Norris, William Faulkner, and James Agee) and lesser-knowns (Nella Larsen, Meridel Le Sueur, Martha Gellhorn, and Harry Brown)." Booklist
Includes bibliography

Waldeland, Lynne
John Cheever. Twayne Pubs. 1979 160p (Twayne's United States authors ser) $19.95   **813.009**
1. Cheever, John, 1912-1982
ISBN 0-8057-7251-0   LC 78-26596
"Emphasizing particularly the beauty of Cheever's refined and lyrical style, Waldeland focuses on Cheever basically as a structuralist and largely ignores the finer analysis of image and symbol, yet giving attention at appropriate times to such factors as characterization, themes, and influences." Choice
Includes bibliography

Walters, Dorothy
Flannery O'Connor. Twayne Pubs. 1973 172p (Twayne's United States authors ser) $19.95   **813.009**
1. O'Connor, Flannery
ISBN 0-8057-0556-2
This analysis of O'Connor's short stories and novels focuses on her use of description, dialect, irreverent humor, and religious symbolism
Includes bibliography

Wiggins, Genevieve
L.M. Montgomery. Twayne Pubs. 1992 191p (Twayne's world authors ser) $21.95   **813.009**
1. Montgomery, L. M. (Lucy Maud), 1874-1942
ISBN 0-8057-3980-7   LC 92-6201

Wiggins, Genevieve—*Continued*
Examines the literary career of the author of "Anne of Green Gables" and the influence of her personal life on her writings

Includes bibliography

Wilson, James D. (James Darrell), 1946-
A reader's guide to the short stories of Mark Twain. Hall, G.K. & Co. 1987 297p (Reference publication in literature) $40
813.009
1. Twain, Mark, 1835-1910
ISBN 0-8161-8721-5   LC 86-29578

This book "serves as a critical introduction to 65 works —virtually all Twain's short fiction. . . . Each story is treated in a chapter that uses the following format: publication history; relevant historical and biographical information; theme, style, and method in context; critical synopsis; and bibliography. An excellent reference." Libr J

Winchell, Donna Haisty
Alice Walker. Twayne Pubs. 1992 152p (Twayne's United States authors ser) $20.95
813.009
1. Walker, Alice, 1944-
ISBN 0-8057-7642-7   LC 91-45309

This work assesses Walker's entire body of work including her poetry and her recent novel The temple of my familiar. The author combines biographical information with critical analysis to provide an overview of Walker's accomplishments

Includes bibliography

Winter, Douglas E.
Stephen King; the art of darkness. New Am. Lib. 1984 252p il hardcover o.p. paperback available $5.99   **813.009**
1. King, Stephen, 1947-
ISBN 0-451-16774-0 (pa)   LC 84-1167

An analysis of King's early novels emphasizing their symbolism, social commentary and moral issues. An appendix includes synopses of the short fiction

Includes bibliography

814 American essays

Baldwin, James, 1924-1987
The price of the ticket; collected nonfiction, 1948-1985. St. Martin's/Marek 1985 xx, 690p $29.95   **814**
ISBN 0-312-64306-3   LC 85-11733

"Classic Baldwin pieces are here—'Nobody Knows My Name,' 'Notes of a Native Son,' 'The Fire Next Time'— as well as little-known reviews, all of which demonstrate the stunning articulateness and passion that have prompted critics and the reading public alike to consider his voice, in both fiction and nonfiction, as one of extreme intelligibility in depicting black experiences and attitudes." Booklist

Berry, Wendell, 1934-
Home economics; fourteen essays. North Point Press 1987 192p $20; pa $9.95   **814**
ISBN 0-86547-274-2; 0-86547-275-0 (pa)
LC 86-62838

The author writes about what he views as "the passing of community and farm life, the inherent value of hand labor and well-made objects, the uses of wild lands, the decadence of the university, and especially the sacred economic order of nature, to which human economies must necessarily be subordinate." Libr J

What are people for? essays. North Point Press 1990 210p hardcover o.p. paperback available $10.95   **814**
ISBN 0-86547-437-0 (pa)   LC 89-29848

These essays describe contemporary ecological problems and present the author's view of how people should relate to the earth
"Ever thought provoking and always gracefully and powerfully expressive, Berry, in these essays, proves himself to be arguably the most essential social and cultural critic of our day." Booklist

The **Best** American essays. Ticknor & Fields $22.95; pa $10.95   **814**
ISSN 0888-3742
Annual. First published 1986
Editors vary

Editors select essays from general interest magazines that touch on topics political, scientific, historical, religious, and sociological, in addition to the personal and literary

Bloom, Allan David
Giants and dwarfs; essays, 1960-1990. Simon & Schuster 1990 395p hardcover o.p. paperback available $11   **814**
1. Books and reading 2. United States—Intellectual life 3. Colleges and universities
ISBN 0-671-74726-6 (pa)   LC 90-42050

Analyzed in Essay and general literature index

These essays fall into three groups: memoirs of certain teachers (in particular Bloom's mentor Leo Strauss), interpretive studies of various books, and a discussion of American university education as it is now practiced

Includes bibliographic references

The **Bread** Loaf anthology of contemporary American essays; edited by Robert Pack and Jay Parini. University Press of New England 1989 379p $30; pa $14.95   **814**
ISBN 0-87451-476-2; 0-87451-475-4 (pa)
LC 88-40352

Published for the Bread Loaf Writer's Conference, Middlebury College

This collection "presents 32 essays from diverse authors on varied subjects. Some are by noted scholars and critics, such as Harold Bloom and William Gass, others by familiar authors, such as Joyce Carol Oates and Gore Vidal. The subjects range from Sinclair Lewis and Freud to the Indianapolis 500 and the biology of sex. One might expect a collection like this to be uneven, but the quality of writing is high throughout, and the subjects are not only interesting but educational." Libr J

Includes bibliography

Brodsky, Joseph, 1940-
Less than one; selected essays. Farrar, Straus & Giroux 1986 501p $30; pa $12.95
       814

ISBN 0-374-18503-4; 0-374-52055-0 (pa)
       LC 85-15900

Analyzed in Essay and general literature index

The essays in this volume "begin and end with autobiographical pieces; in between there are alternate homages to favorite poets, both Russian and non-Russian, as well as substantial discussions of such topics as geography and history, political force and ethical choice, and literary tradition." N Y Times Book Rev

Burroughs, William S., 1914-
The adding machine; selected essays. Seaver Bks. [distributed by] Holt & Co. 1986 205p $16.95
       814
ISBN 0-8050-0000-3
       LC 86-3765

Also available in paperback from Arcade Pub.

First published 1985 in the United Kingdom

"This collection of 43 brief essays, written over three decades . . . [includes] lectures on fellow novelists (Hemingway, Fitzgerald, Kerouac, Beckett), on [Burroughs's] own experiments (cut-up, dream transcription, 'routines'), on advice to young writers and old reviewers, and on the . . . vicissitudes of his career." Choice

Davenport, Guy, 1927-
The geography of the imagination; forty essays. North Point Press 1981 384p o.p.; Pantheon Bks. paperback available $15
       814

ISBN 0-679-73859-2 (pa)
       LC 91-53116

In addition to essays on modern and classical literature the author also discusses archaeology, biology, lexicography, music and photography. Among his subjects are: Poe, Agassiz, Pound, Ives, Zukofsky, Meatyard, Tchelitchew and Joyce

Includes bibliographic references

Didion, Joan
After Henry. Simon & Schuster 1992 319p $22
       814

ISBN 0-671-72731-1
       LC 91-46458

Also available in paperback from Random House

This is a collection of reportorial essays reprinted from The New Yorker, The New York Review of Books and New West. They are arranged in three sections: "Washington," "California," and "New York." Topics include the Reagan presidency, the 1988 political campaign, and the 1989 Central Park jogger rape case

"Readers should welcome the chance to savor the vintage sotto voce style that more than 20 years ago distinguished this careful writer from New Journalism's noisier competition." Time

The white album. Simon & Schuster 1979 222p o.p.; Farrar, Straus & Giroux paperback available $10
       814

ISBN 0-374-52221-9 (pa)
       LC 79-10242

This is a collection of essays about California in the 1960s and 1970s

"All of the essays . . . manifest not only [Miss Didion's] intelligence but an instinct for details that continue to emit pulsations in the reader's memory and a style that is spare, subtly musical in its phrasing and exact." N Y Times Book Rev

Eliot, T. S. (Thomas Stearns), 1888-1965
Selected essays. new ed. Harcourt Brace & Co. 1950 460p $19.95
       814
ISBN 0-15-180387-0

Analyzed in Essay and general literature index

First published 1932

"From the literary point of view, Eliot's most valuable essays have been those in which he calls attention to the merits and techniques of the minor Elizabethan dramatists and the 17th-century metaphysical poets, as well as a small group of essays in which he discusses his methods of composition and literary analysis. . . . In his historical, philosophical, and religious essays, he argued brilliantly for the conservative tradition and for the restoration of the unified religio-aesthetic society which he believed to have existed in Europe before the advent of the rationalistic delusions." Benet's Reader's Ency of Am Lit

Ellison, Ralph
Shadow and act. Random House 1964 xxii, 317p hardcover o.p. paperback available $11
       814
ISBN 0-394-71716-3 (pa)

Analyzed in Essay and general literature index

This collection of essays is "concerned with three general themes: with literature and folklore, with Negro musical expression—especially jazz and blues—and with the complex relationship between Negro American subculture and North American culture as a whole." Introduction

Epstein, Joseph, 1937-
A line out for a walk; familiar essays. Norton 1991 331p hardcover o.p. paperback available $10.95
       814
ISBN 0-393-30854-5 (pa)
       LC 90-44698

This is a collection of essays on a variety of subjects

"This acknowledged master of the familiar essay will captivate readers who want to escape life momentarily and guide readers who, like Flaubert, want to live more profoundly." Booklist

Fiedler, Leslie A.
Fiedler on the roof; essays on literature and Jewish identity; by Leslie Fiedler. Godine 1990 184p $19.95; pa $11.95 **814**
1. Jews in literature
ISBN 0-87923-859-3; 0-87923-949-2 (pa)
       LC 90-55282

Analyzed in Essay and general literature index

This volume is a collection of the literary critic's "essays and book reviews since 1970 on more or less Jewish topics. These include: anti-Semitism, the Holocaust, the Book of Job, Isaac Bashevis Singer, Bernard Malamud, . . . and Jewish consciousness in (J.) Joyce's Ulysses." Commentary

"Disturbing, provocative, and brilliant." Libr J

Giovanni, Nikki
Sacred cows—and other edibles. Morrow 1988 167p $12.95; pa $7.75 **814**

ISBN 0-688-04333-X; 0-688-08909-7 (pa)

LC 87-22045

In these essays, the author "expresses (and impresses with) her strong attitudes about poverty, stupidity, prejudice, ineffectual black leadership, insects, credit cards and other inducements to consumerism, female exploitation, TV commercials, ex-smokers, required seat-belting, men who walk a picket line against abortion, dumb sports announcers. She feels more positively about her teenage son, soap, being happy with what she has, *Little House on the Prairie* and the virtues of baseball." Publ Wkly

Gordon, Mary, 1949-
Good boys and dead girls; and other essays. Viking 1991 253p $19.95 **814**

ISBN 0-670-82567-0

LC 90-50467

Also available in paperback from Penguin Bks.

Analyzed in Essay and general literature index

In 28 "essays and reviews (all but the title piece previously published), novelist Gordon describes her pregnancy, visits Marilyn Monroe's grave and gives a feminist reading of American literature from Faulkner to Updike." Publ Wkly

Hoagland, Edward
Balancing acts; essays. Simon & Schuster 1992 351p $23; pa $11 **814**

ISBN 0-671-74681-2; 0-671-87235-4 (pa)

LC 92-17355

This is an "assortment of essays with a broad range of themes. The most common threads here are travel, nature, and literature." Libr J

"Hoagland is an intellectual, but he's also an extraordinary reporter. Whether in Yemen or Wyoming, in Belize or the Okefenokee Swamp, or especially in Alaska, he finds beauty and truth—among his fellow travelers and those he encounters as well as in the landscape." Christ Sci Monit

Howe, Irving
Selected writings, 1950-1990. Harcourt Brace Jovanovich 1990 490p $34.95; pa $14.95 **814**

ISBN 0-15-180390-0; 0-15-680636-3 (pa)

The author "has assembled a 'representative selection,' of his essays, providing 'a reasonably fair picture of an intellectual career spanning four decades.'" N Y Times Book Rev

"Howe on James Baldwin, T. E. Lawrence, Sholom Aleichem, Holocaust writings, and modernist literature— there is plenty to reflect upon in this distinguished collection from one of our most consistently perceptive critics." Booklist

Kosinski, Jerzy N., 1933-1991
Passing by; selected essays, 1962-1991; [by] Jerzy Kosinski. Random House 1992 256p $22.50 **814**

ISBN 0-679-41389-8

LC 91-51065

"A collection of essays, never published in book form, from the author whose 1991 suicide shocked the literary world." Libr J

Kumin, Maxine, 1925-
In deep; country essays. Viking 1987 180p o.p.; Beacon Press paperback available $9.95 **814**

1. Country life—New Hampshire

ISBN 0-8070-6323-1 (pa)

LC 86-40299

These essays are arranged by season. "In 'Bringing Up Boomerang,' Kumin comments on how her life on the farm has fed her poetic vision. . . . Other essays range from instructions on how to hunt and prepare wild mushrooms, to a discourse on the similarities between a poet and a mule, to a homage to Thoreau. In the final essay, 'A Sense of Place,' she addresses the role of the poet in today's society." Publisher's note

Levertov, Denise, 1923-
New & selected essays. New Directions 1992 266p $21.95; pa $11.95 **814**

ISBN 0-8112-1217-3; 0-8112-1218-1 (pa)

LC 92-17887

"This collection of 25 essays, dating from 1965 to 1991, explores several major areas of critical interest to Levertov. . . . Although somewhat uneven and not always convincing, these essays present an opportunity to examine the interests, inspirations, and ideology of one of our most respected poets." Libr J

Mencken, H. L. (Henry Louis), 1880-1956
The impossible H.L. Mencken; a selection of his best newspaper stories; edited by Marion Elizabeth Rodgers; with a foreword by Gore Vidal. Doubleday 1991 lx, 707p $27.50; pa $15 **814**

ISBN 0-385-26207-8; 0-385-26208-6 (pa) LC 91-284

This book collects 170 of Mencken's newspaper articles on a variety of subjects that appeared, from 1908 to 1948

Pound, Ezra, 1885-1972
Selected prose, 1909-1965; edited with an introduction by William Cookson. New Directions 1973 475p hardcover o.p. paperback available $12.95 **814**

ISBN 0-8112-0574-6 (pa)

Among the topics included in this collection of 66 essays are religion, Confucianism, Mencius, American historical figures, civilization, economics, poetry, and Pound's contemporaries. The essay, Patria mia, is included

Price, Reynolds, 1933-
A common room; essays, 1954-1987. Atheneum Pubs. 1987 405p $24.95; pa $11.95 **814**

ISBN 0-689-11948-8; 0-689-70817-3 (pa)

LC 87-27064

Analyzed in Essay and general literature index

Price, Reynolds, 1933-—*Continued*
The novelist, poet and literary critic presents a collection of his essays

"By turns thoughtful, ornery, eloquent, long-winded and wise, Mr. Price reflects on the work of artists as celebrated as Henry James and Eudora Welty and as little known as the American Indian author James Welch." N Y Times Book Rev

Reed, Ishmael, 1938-
Writin' is fightin'; thirty-seven years of boxing on paper. Atheneum Pubs. 1988 226p hardcover o.p. paperback available $9.95   **814**
  ISBN 0-689-70734-7 (pa)   LC 88-10555

This is a collection of the author's "essays—including book reviews and editorials—which were previously published in various periodicals. . . . His attacks on narrow-mindedness—political, racial, or literary—are never without foundation and always provocative. A consistently stimulating collection." Booklist

Rich, Adrienne
Blood, bread, and poetry; selected prose, 1979-1985. Norton 1986 238p $15.95; pa $8.95   **814**
  1. Feminism
  ISBN 0-393-02376-1; 0-393-30397-7 (pa) LC 86-5452
  Analyzed in Essay and general literature index

This work "includes radical feminist philosophy, literary criticism, and personal history—all approached from her white, Jewish, lesbian, middle-class American 'location.'" Booklist

Snyder, Gary
The practice of the wild; essays. North Point Press 1990 190p hardcover o.p. paperback available $10.95   **814**
  ISBN 0-86547-454-0 (pa)   LC 90-7590

"Poet Snyder's tough, beautiful essays combine native American lore, Confucian/Zen philosophy, and a loving respect for the wilderness." Booklist

Sontag, Susan, 1933-
Styles of radical will. Farrar, Straus & Giroux 1969 274p o.p.; Doubleday paperback available $9.95   **814**
  ISBN 0-385-26709-6 (pa)
  Analyzed in Essay and general literature index

"The book contains essays, some previously published, arranged in groups. The first group of three is aesthetic and philosophical; three deal with film; and the last set is . . . a reply to a Partisan Review questionnaire about America and an . . . essay on a trip to North Vietnam." Libr J

Under the sign of Saturn. Farrar, Straus & Giroux 1980 203p $10.95   **814**
  ISBN 0-374-28076-2   LC 80-19199
  Also available in paperback from Doubleday
  Analyzed in Essay and general literature index

This collection "of essays has meditations on Anton Artaud, Elias Canetti, Leni Riefenstahl, Walter Benjamin and Hans-Jürgen Syberberg's film about Hitler, along with brief eulogies for Paul Goodman and Roland Barthes." N Y Times Book Rev

Trilling, Lionel, 1905-1975
The last decade; essays and reviews, 1965-1975; edited by Diana Trilling. Harcourt Brace Jovanovich 1979 241p (Works of Lionel Trilling. Uniform ed) $9.95; pa $7.95   **814**
  ISBN 0-15-148421-X; 0-15-648892-2 (pa) LC 79-1849
  Analyzed in Essay and general literature index

This volume brings together "some of the thoughts on literature, politics, and culture that engaged America's foremost literary critic and educator in the last years of his life. The book begins and ends with autobiographical pieces: the first is a personal memoir of the Thirties; the final piece consists of fragmentary notes which Trilling used for an autobiographical lecture." Libr J
  Includes bibliographic references

Twain, Mark, 1835-1910
The complete essays of Mark Twain; now collected for the first time; edited and with an introduction by Charles Neider; drawings by Mark Twain. Doubleday 1963 xxv, 705p il $15.95   **814**
  ISBN 0-385-06590-6

Some of the 68 essays are: The Sandwich Islands; English as she is taught; Mental telegraphy; The German Chicago; Queen Victoria's jubilee; What is man; Taxes and morals; The bee; Concerning tobacco; Adam's soliloquy; Down the Rhone; Dueling; Letters to Satan; Some national stupidities; The war prayer; Letter from the recording angel

Vidal, Gore, 1925-
At home; essays, 1982-1988. Random House 1988 303p $18.95; pa $9.95   **814**
  ISBN 0-394-57020-0; 0-679-72528-8 (pa)
                                  LC 88-42670

"The essays in this collection cover a wide range of topics, from the early days of aviation through the battle of Armageddon to life in a Roman street. Numerous literary figures are discussed, including Tennessee Williams, Henry James, Italo Calvino, and Dawn Powell, while in the political arena Richard Nixon, the Reagans, and Oliver North come under scrutiny." Libr J

Matters of fact and of fiction; essays 1973-1976. Random House 1977 285p $14.95   **814**
  1. Literature—History and criticism
  ISBN 0-394-41128-5   LC 76-53459
  Analyzed in Essay and general literature index

The first part of this volume "is concerned with aspects of contemporary fiction. . . . The second half examines other matters, with pieces on West Point and on the escapades of E. Howard Hunt and Robert Moses . . . and a personal recollection of Tennessee Williams." Libr J

Vidal, Gore, 1925-—*Continued*
The second American revolution, and other essays (1976-1982). Random House 1982 278p $15   **814**
ISBN 0-394-52265-6   LC 81-48281
Analyzed in Essay and general literature index
This is a "collection of 19 essays on literary figures (F. Scott Fitzgerald, Edmund Wilson, Doris Lessing), . . . presidents (Theodore Roosevelt, Lincoln), and politics (Vidal advocates calling a new constitutional convention), with side excursions into homosexuality, twice-born Christians, and the movies." Libr J

Walker, Margaret, 1915-
How I wrote Jubilee, and other essays on life and literature; edited by Maryemma Graham. Feminist Press 1989 xxi, 157p $35; pa $9.95   **814**
ISBN 1-55861-003-0; 1-55861-004-9 (pa)
LC 89-17017
"The essays . . . compellingly recount the personal history of a woman for whom individual expression is an essential form of the struggle against racism, sexism, and classism. . . . Walker's radical humanist perspective ought to reinvigorate current critical discussions of race, gender, class, and literature." Libr J
Includes bibliographic references

Wasserstein, Wendy
Bachelor girls. Knopf 1990 209p $18.95; pa $9   **814**
ISBN 0-394-56199-6; 0-679-73062-1 (pa)
LC 89-45363
This collection of "essays range from how Jessica Lange is annoyingly perfect; a list of the ten worst boyfriends of all time; and the truly heartbreaking 'Jean Harlow's Wedding Night,' in which Wasserstein both explains and drops her comic facade." Libr J

Weinberger, Eliot
Outside stories, 1987-1991. New Directions 1992 177p pa $10.95   **814**
ISBN 0-8112-1221-1   LC 92-9869
"These 15 essays mix myth and modernism—with Borgesian humor and irony—to throw light on both. . . . Their subjects range wide: Atlantis as a projection of dreaming sea-cucumbers; An outraged chronicle of the Rushdie affair. . . . Discussions of the state of poetry as a business, and of the Tiananmen Square demonstrations." Libr J

White, E. B. (Elwyn Brooks), 1899-1985
Essays of E. B. White. Harper & Row 1977 277p hardcover o.p. paperback available $12   **814**
ISBN 0-06-090662-6 (pa)   LC 77-7717
Analyzed in Essay and general literature index
Most of the essays first appeared in The New Yorker. "They range from a 1934 piece on the St. Nicholas Magazine 'League' and the distinguished writers who were members of it as children, to a 1975 report from Allen Cove, Maine, where White had retreated from the bedlam of the city." Publ Wkly

Writings from the New Yorker. Harper & Row 1990 244p $20; pa $11   **814**
ISBN 0-06-016517-0; 0-06-092123-4 (pa)
LC 89-46564
"Wide-ranging in subject matter, these essays tackle such diverse subjects as Krushchev, Senator McCarthy, revolving doors, and Sunday drivers in New York, all with a sense of humor." Libr J

Williams, William Carlos, 1883-1963
In the American grain. Boni & Liveright 1925 235p o.p.; New Directions paperback available $9.95   **814**
ISBN 0-8112-0230-5 (pa)
Williams portrays "the developing American conscience in sketches of such major figures as Columbus, Cotton Mather, Washington, Franklin, and Poe, and such minor ones as Champlain, Thomas Morton, Père Sebastian Rasles, and Jacataqua. He sought the grain of American character especially in homely, rather than heroic, incidents of national history." Benet's Reader's Ency of Am Lit

815.008   American speeches— Collections

Representative American speeches. Wilson, H.W. (Reference shelf) pa $15   **815.008**
1. Speeches, addresses, etc., American
Annual. First published 1937-1938
Editor: 1980/1981-date Owen Peterson
A compilation containing a selection of speeches of the year made by eminent men and women on major trends and events. Each speech is prefaced by a note about the speaker and the occasion. The appendix in each volume contains biographical notes

817   American satire and humor

Allen, Woody
Side effects. Random House 1980 149p $8.95; pa $4.95   **817**
ISBN 0-394-51104-2; 0-345-34335-2 (pa)   LC 79-5549
"The sixteen sketches—which [are concerned with themes] of love and death, angst and despair, bagels and lox—appeared originally in magazines." Commonweal

Without feathers. Random House 1975 210p o.p.; Ballantine Bks. paperback available $5.99   **817**
ISBN 0-345-33697-6 (pa)
A collection of sixteen satirical sketches, most of which previously appeared in The New Yorker and other periodicals, and two one-act plays: God, and Death. The sketches include "take-offs on other writers (Kafka, Bellow, Strindberg), and several 'intellectual' dissertations on such topics as the Irish genius, the origins of slang, the lesser ballets, psychic phenomena, etc." Libr J

Barry, Dave
Dave Barry does Japan. Random House 1992 210p il $18   **817**
ISBN 0-679-40485-6   LC 92-53634

Barry, Dave—*Continued*

This collection of humor is based on the author's three week trip to Japan

"There are a few sensitive moments in his comical tour, but Barry does not stray long from his typical, sarcastic self, so fans should be delighted." Booklist

Dave Barry slept here; a sort of history of the United States. Random House 1989 178p il $15.95   817

ISBN 0-394-56541-X   LC 88-43205

Also available in paperback from Fawcett Bks.

The author's "idea of making humor out of many familiar events and notable figures in American history is appealingly audacious. . . . Ideal reading for gloomy afternoons and other times that require pleasant diversion." Libr J

Dave Barry talks back; cartoons by Jeff MacNelly. Crown 1991 285p il $18; pa $9
                                                817

ISBN 0-517-58546-4; 0-517-58868-4 (pa)
                                    LC 91-11139

A collection of the humorists's newspaper columns. Topics range from politics to popular culture

Dave Barry turns 40. Crown 1990 179p $16.95   817

ISBN 0-517-57755-0   LC 90-1621

Also available in paperback from Fawcett Bks.

Humorist Dave Barry writes about the onset of middle age and it's effects, both physical and mental

Dave Barry's greatest hits. Crown 1988 287p o.p.; Fawcett Bks. paperback available $10   817

ISBN 0-449-90406-7 (pa)   LC 88-3822

Humor and commentary by the Pulitzer Prize winning columnist

Dave Barry's only travel guide you'll ever need. Fawcett Columbine 1991 171p il maps hardcover o.p. paperback available $10
                                                817

1. Travel
ISBN 0-449-90759-7 (pa)   LC 91-70649

"The popular humor columnist's take on traveling again showcases his scattergun style, which is really best indulged in smaller doses than a whole book's worth. . . . Folks like Barry's farrago of non sequiturs, deliberate stupidity, heavy-handed ironies, flippancy, and lampshade-hat silliness." Booklist

Blount, Roy

Now, where were we? Villard Bks. 1989 252p $17.95   817

ISBN 0-394-57419-2   LC 88-27668

Also available in paperback from Ballantine Bks.

In this collection of essays from various periodicals, the author "tackles the social fabric of America—and himself—from the point of view of a Southerner." Libr J

"These pieces are brilliantly loopy, reassuringly subversive." N Y Times Book Rev

Bombeck, Erma

Family; the ties that bind—and gag! McGraw-Hill 1987 199p o.p.; Fawcett Bks. paperback available $5.95   817

ISBN 0-449-21529-6 (pa)   LC 87-3277

"A gathering of her grown children back under her roof leads Bombeck to wonder how she ever survived bringing these three rapscallions to adulthood; along the way she also recollects various incidents in that tortuous enterprise. The result is rapid-fire commentary featuring such brilliantly sarcastic humor that the reader will convulse with laughter at the turn of nearly every page." Booklist

When you look like your passport photo, it's time to go home. HarperCollins Pubs. 1991 256p $19.95; pa $5.99   817

ISBN 0-06-018311-X; 0-06-109981-3 (pa)
                                    LC 91-55097

Also available HarperCollins large print edition

The humorist "deflates the bloated claims of travel as pure pleasure. . . . With her husband, Bombeck finds risky adventures from primitive New Guinea to supposedly civilized countries. The couple endures carping companions on a tour bus in Rome. . . . Other trials involve the vagaries of renting cars, tipping and, always, finding a working toilet, as problematic in Houston's vaunted Space Center as in the backward places of the world." Publ Wkly

Buchwald, Art

I think I don't remember; illustrated by Steve Mendelson. Putnam 1987 350p il hardcover o.p. paperback available $7.95
                                                817

ISBN 0-399-51482-1 (pa)   LC 87-13920

Also available Thorndike Press large print edition

This volume contains over 100 topical columns by syndicated writer and lecturer Buchwald

"Liberal doses of fun, well suited for light reading and humor collections." Libr J

Whose rose garden is it anyway? illustrated by Steve Mendelson. Putnam 1989 352p il $18.95; pa $9.95   817

ISBN 0-399-13480-8; 0-399-51651-4 (pa)
                                    LC 89-10614

Also available G.K. Hall large print edition

A "collection of reprinted syndicated columns. George Bush's politicking is Buchwald's main target here (although there are a few shots aimed at Reagan, Dukakis, Oliver North, Ed Meese, and others. . . . Nothing startling, just sheer Buchwaldian wit." Booklist

Grizzard, Lewis

Chili dawgs always bark at night. Villard Bks. 1989 220p o.p.; Ballantine Bks. paperback available $5.95   817

ISBN 0-345-36708-1 (pa)   LC 89-40291

Also available G.K. Hall large print edition

Grizzard "presents a collection of his columns. . . . His topics include religion, dining out, journalism, golf, dogs, people named Bubba, teenagers, the sad state of sports in his adopted city. . . . The book is innocuous and amiable and calculated not to offend anyone." Publ Wkly

Grizzard, Lewis—*Continued*

Don't bend over in the garden, Granny, you know them taters got eyes. Villard Bks. 1988 245p $15.95   **817**

ISBN 0-394-57181-9   LC 88-40171

Also available in paperback from Ballantine Bks.

Syndicated columnist Grizzard takes a satirical look at sex, censorship, televangelists and mortality

I haven't understood anything since 1962, and other nekkid truths. Villard Bks. 1992 288p $18   **817**

ISBN 0-679-40685-9   LC 92-53653

Also available Wheeler Pub. large print edition

This is a collection of humor by the syndicated columnist

"Grizzard's tales of growing up in the South are vivid, his analysis of press stereotyping of 'the poor Bubba/redneck/good ol' boy' is on the mark, and even his meaner, more self-pitying diatribes have their share of witty observations." Booklist

When my love returns from the ladies room, will I be too old to care? Villard Bks. 1987 236p $14.95   **817**

ISBN 0-394-56418-9   LC 87-40183

The pieces included in this collection cover such topics as "southerners taking courses to learn not to speak like southerners, the humorlessness of women in the liberation movement, the inability to get a cheeseburger without mushrooms in an eatery for yuppies and the menaces to life and limb at the ordinary salad bar." Publ Wkly

You can't put no boogie-woogie on the king of rock and roll. Villard Bks. 1991 266p $17.50   **817**

ISBN 0-679-40601-8   LC 91-15315

Also available G.K. Hall large print edition and in paperback from Ballantine Bks.

In this work the author "offers a collection of his short, pithy essays—110 in all—covering a wide variety of contemporary topics. Grizzard provides a hilarious denigration of soccer, humorous barbs about 2 Live Crew, Madonna, and MTV, ironic commentary on adultery and the 'new masculinity,' and funny profiles of modern-day personalities, including Ted Turner and Jane Fonda, Jim Bakker, and Donald Trump." Booklist

Ivins, Molly

Molly Ivins can't say that, can she? Random House 1991 284p $22.50; pa $11   **817**

ISBN 0-679-40445-7; 0-679-74183-6 (pa)

LC 91-52662

This is a "collection of previously published pieces from The Progressive, Ms., The Nation and other magazines. . . . Country music, Nancy Reagan's wardrobe, national political conventions, the Iran-contra affair, the Dallas Cowboys cheerleaders, football as the established religion in Texas, the differences between Southerners and other Americans and also the differences between Texans and other Southerners—on all these matters and many others, she has wise and often hilarious things to say." N Y Times Book Rev

Keillor, Garrison

We are still married; stories & letters. Viking 1989 330p o.p.; Penguin Bks. paperback available $8.95   **817**

ISBN 0-14-01356-6 (pa)   LC 88-40283

Also available G.K. Hall large print edition

The "poems, opinions, stories, letters and whatnots in this collection ponder the meaning and nuance of yard sales, sneezes, Woodlawn Cemetery, the last surviving cigarette smokers . . . and traveling with teen-age children." N Y Times Book Rev

King, Florence

Reflections in a jaundiced eye. St. Martin's Press 1989 198p hardcover o.p. paperback available $8.95   **817**

ISBN 0-312-03978-6 (pa)   LC 88-29810

"The author's acerbic humor runs wild in critiques of John Updike and Mary Gordon, and . . . King certainly has plenty to say about WASPs, children, editing, Mrs. Roosevelt . . . and America's rampant disease—'Nice Guyism.' King is way beyond irreverent and definitely a tonic for too many 'Have a nice day's.'" Booklist

McManus, Patrick F.

The good samaritan strikes again. Holt & Co. 1992 211p $17.95; pa $7.95   **817**

ISBN 0-8050-2042-X; 0-8050-2922-2 (pa)

LC 92-10633

Also available G.K. Hall large print edition

"Whether detailing his first kiss, an elusive 'big' fish, or his conversations with a garden snake, McManus will heartily entertain readers with his latest collection of humorous tales." Booklist

Real ponies don't go oink! Holt & Co. 1991 198p $16.95; pa $6.95   **817**

ISBN 0-8050-1651-1; 0-8050-2107-8 (pa)

LC 90-29893

Also available G.K. Hall large print edition

A collection of the humorist's monthly columns from Outdoor Life

O'Rourke, P. J.

Parliament of whores; a lone humorist attempts to explain the entire U.S. government. Atlantic Monthly Press 1991 xx, 233p o.p.; Random House paperback available $12   **817**

ISBN 0-679-73789-8 (pa)   LC 91-8416

"A Morgan Entrekin book"

"In a manner that is more likely to grab a reader by the lapels and throttle him into hysterics than your average high school civics textbook, O'Rourke deftly skewers our three branches of government." Libr J

Peter, Laurence J.

The Peter Principle; by Laurence J. Peter & Raymond Hull. Morrow 1969 179p il hardcover o.p. paperback available $9.45
817

1. Management—Anecdotes
ISBN 0-688-27544-3 (pa)

Also available in paperback from Bantam Bks.

"In a delightful spoof of administrative inefficiency in both public and private enterprise, the authors expound their theory known as the Peter Principle—'in a hierarchy every employee tends to rise to his level of incompetence.' From this they develop their science of hierarchiology." Cincinnati Public Libr

Rooney, Andrew A.

Not that you asked. Random House 1989 270p $15.95
817

ISBN 0-394-57837-6   LC 88-43362

Also available G.K. Hall large print edition and in paperback from Penguin Bks.

In this collection the author "offers tidbits on Sam Donaldson, ladies underwear, fake garage sales, unsung heroes, and realism in real estate, among other topics." Booklist

Sweet and sour. Putnam 1992 254p $18.95
817

ISBN 0-399-13774-2   LC 92-17753

Also available Thorndike Press large print edition

A collection of the author's syndicated newspaper columns covering such topics as: weekend chores, postal abbreviations, help-wanted ads and congressmen. Also includes tributes to Frank Sinatra and William Paley

Thurber, James, 1894-1961

The beast in me, and other animals; a new collection of pieces and drawings about human beings and less alarming creatures. Harcourt Brace & Co. 1948 340p il hardcover o.p. paperback available $5.95
817

ISBN 0-15-610850-X (pa)

Also available from Amereon

"A mixture of Thurber cartoons, drawings, stories and articles. Soap operas, Dewey, animals, prehistoric and otherwise are among the variety of subjects turned into nonsense for the entertainment of the reader. A good assortment." Ont Libr Rev

Fables for our time, and famous poems; illustrated by James Thurber. Harper & Row 1940 124p il hardcover o.p. paperback available $11
817

ISBN 0-06-090999-4 (pa)

Also available from Borgo Press

"The fables and poems are old; the morals and pictures are madly modern. Pure Thurber." Cincinnati Public Libr

The Thurber carnival; written and illustrated by James Thurber. Harper & Row 1945 369p il hardcover o.p. paperback available $12
817

ISBN 0-06-090445-3 (pa)

A Thurber omnibus containing stories mainly from: My world and welcome to it; Let your mind alone; The middle-aged man on the flying trapeze; My life and hard times; Fables for our time and famous poems illustrated; The owl in the attic; The seal in the bedroom; Men, women and dogs; The war between men and women

Trillin, Calvin

Enough's enough (and other rules of life). Ticknor & Fields 1990 251p $19.95 **817**

ISBN 0-89919-958-5   LC 90-36205

Also available in paperback from Houghton Mifflin

A collection of the satirist's columns from 1987 to 1990. "The targets of his wit and scorn include Donald Trump, the 'humble roots' of Senator Bob Dole, word processor spell-checks, teenage talk, telephone solicitors who call you by your first name, George Bush's trying to be taken for a regular guy and Ronald Reagan's selective deafness." Publ Wkly

If you can't say something nice. Ticknor & Fields 1987 257p o.p.; Penguin Bks. paperback available $7.95
817

ISBN 0-14-011483-1 (pa)   LC 87-11259

The sixty-five essays in this collection first appeared either in the Nation or in humorist Trillin's syndicated column

"Trillin moves effortlessly from politics to relatives to polite society, readily bestowing his critical humor upon all." Booklist

Travels with Alice. Ticknor & Fields 1989 195p o.p.; Avon Bks. paperback available $9
817

ISBN 0-380-71209-1 (pa)   LC 89-32735

"In this gathering of 15 recollections of holidays . . . Trillin offers himself as essayist rather than descriptive writer, interpreter rather than guide. With him most of the time were his wife Alice and two daughters, and their experiences—renting a house in the south of France, shopping at the Central Market in Florence, and hanging around the small French town of Uzés—provide the themes of a readable, unexacting book of pleasant rambles and a multiplicity of small happenings and human stories." Libr J

Wyse, Lois

Funny, you don't look like a grandmother; illustrated by Lilla Rogers. Crown 1989 111p il $14
817

ISBN 0-517-57157-9   LC 88-20387

Also available Thorndike Press large print edition and in paperback from Avon Bks.

A collection of anecdotes which describe what it is like to be a contemporary grandmother

817.008 American satire and humor—Collections

The **Best** of modern humor; edited by Mordecai Richler. Knopf 1983 542p il $29.50   **817.008**

1. American wit and humor 2. English wit and humor
ISBN 0-394-51531-5   LC 83-48102

This is a collection of humor from sixty-five American and British writers

"The witless complain that humor is impossible to write in an age when headlines are more absurd than the products of imagination. Richler's contemporary entries offer hilarious refutation." Time

The **Big** book of new American humor; the best of the past 25 years; edited by William Novak [and] Moshe Waldoks with Donald Altschiller. Perennial Lib. 1990 339p il pa $17   **817.008**

1. American wit and humor
ISBN 0-06-096551-7   LC 90-55004

This is a collection of humorous essays, short stories, screenplays, parodies, cartoons and limericks

Fireside treasury of new humor; edited by Al Sarrantonio. Simon & Schuster 1989 328p $22.95   **817.008**

1. American wit and humor 2. English wit and humor
ISBN 0-671-68380-2   LC 89-1599

"A Fireside book"

This book "draws together many of today's best-selling humorists, as well as a few lesser-known yet talented writers. Among those represented here are Art Buchwald, Doug Kenney, Martin Mull, Jonathan Winters, Bob and Ray, Dave Barry, Garrison Keillor, Stephanie Brush, Tom Bodett, Fran Lebowitz, and Cynthia Heimel." Libr J

Laughing matters; a celebration of American humor; selected and edited by Gene Shalit. Doubleday 1987 xxix, 622p il o.p.; Ballantine Bks. paperback available $14.95   **817.008**

1. American wit and humor
ISBN 0-345-36251-9 (pa)   LC 86-24351

"An anthology of some of the funniest writing and drawing in America. . . . [It includes] such contributors as Benchley, Parker, Nash, Keillor, Perelman, Marquis, and Twain among the scribblers; Thurber, Schulz, Feiffer, Gorey, Trudeau, Hollander, Kliban, and Gary Larson among the doodlers; and Burns and Allen, Abbott and Costello, Bob and Ray, the Marxes, Will Rogers, and Fred Allen and Jack Benny among the 'performance artists.'" Booklist

818 American miscellany

Amory, Cleveland
The cat and the curmudgeon; illustrations by Lisa Adams. Little, Brown 1990 295p il $17.95   **818**

ISBN 0-316-03739-7   LC 90-6419

Also available G.K. Hall large print edition

"The latest installment in the continuing saga of how a mature curmudgeon copes with the tribulations of, as the author would say, being owned by a cat who, truth be told, is a curmudgeon himself: administering pills, trips to and visits from the vet, walks in the park and romance (human curmudgeon to woman, not cat to cat), to name a few." N Y Times Book Rev

The cat who came for Christmas; illustrations by Edith Allard. Little, Brown 1987 240p il $15.95   **818**

ISBN 0-316-03737-0   LC 87-3258

Also available G.K. Hall large print edition and in paperback from Penguin Bks.

This is the "story of a white cat rescued by Amory one Christmas Eve. Struggling to understand his feline friend, he becomes devoted to a degree that not everyone will understand. An animal rights activist, Amory shares his feelings about veterinarians, airlines, hotels, human and animal natures, and the complexities of modern life." Libr J

Anderson, Sherwood, 1876-1941
The portable Sherwood Anderson; edited and with an introduction by Horace Gregory. rev ed. Viking 1972 497p o.p.; Penguin Bks. paperback available $9.95   **818**

ISBN 0-14-015076-5 (pa)

First published 1949

Includes Winesburg, Ohio, with linked passages from "Poor white," and other stories, biographical portraits, newspaper writings, and letters

Baker, Nicholson
U and I; a true story. Random House 1991 179p $17.50; pa $9   **818**

1. Updike, John 2. Authorship
ISBN 0-394-58994-7; 0-679-73575-5 (pa)
     LC 90-43565

"In this extended essay on the anxiety of influence, Baker . . . explores his intellectual and emotional debt to John Updike." Libr J

Baker, Russell, 1925-
There's a country in my cellar. Morrow 1990 432p $20.95   **818**

ISBN 0-688-09598-4   LC 90-36699

Also available in paperback from Avon Bks.

"Baker has selected . . . 137 of 3800 or so of his 'Observer' columns, written for the Times between 1963 and 1989." Libr J

Baraka, Imamu Amiri, 1934-
The LeRoi Jones/Amiri Baraka reader; by Amiri Baraka; edited by William J. Harris in collaboration with Amiri Baraka. Thunder's Mouth Press 1991 498p hardcover o.p. paperback available $14.95   **818**

ISBN 1-56025-007-0 (pa)   LC 90-25689

A collection of Baraka's poems; plays, and other writings. "The selections included are arranged chronologically in four distinct periods: The Beat Period

Baraka, Imamu Amiri, 1934——_Continued_
(1957-62), The Transitional Period (1963-65), The Black
Nationalist Period (1965-74), and The Third World
Marxist Period (1974-present)." Libr J

Includes bibliography

Barthelme, Donald
The teachings of Don B. the satires,
parodies, fables, illustrated stories, and plays
of Donald Barthelme; edited by Kim
Herzinger; with an introduction by Thomas
Pynchon. Turtle Bay Bks. 1992 xxii, 352p
il $24.50   **818**
ISBN 0-679-40982-3   LC 92-53663

"The first installment of Barthelme's complete oeuvre
(two additional volumes will follow) contains a compilation of short pieces and plays. Together they form a
witty melange, entertaining and at the same time a
substantial literary entrée to be savored." Booklist

The **Best** of the West; an anthology of
classic writing from the American West;
edited by Tony Hillerman. HarperCollins
Pubs. 1991 528p $27.50; pa $15   **818**
1. West (U.S.) in literature
ISBN 0-06-016664-9; 0-06-093352-0 (pa)
LC 90-55930

This anthology's "nonfiction sources run from 500
B.C. to the late nineteenth century; fictional selections
by Harte, Crane, Scarborough, Davis, Stegner, and Norris
are included. . . . Hillerman's subject groupings (e.g.,
explorers, settlers, Navajos, Hispanics, cowboys, miners,
women, travel, and the military) make sense, and his
juxtapositions encourage a thoughtful response." Booklist

Bierce, Ambrose, 1842-1914?
The collected writings; with an
introduction by Clifton Fadiman. Citadel
Press 1946 810p pa $11.95   **818**
ISBN 0-8065-0180-4

Also available in hardcover from Amereon

Collected works of the American journalist, aphorist,
poet, and short story writer. Fadiman's introduction
locates Bierce's place and influence in the American
literary tradition

Bishop, Elizabeth, 1911-1979
The collected prose; edited, with an
introduction, by Robert Giroux. Farrar,
Straus & Giroux 1984 xxii, 278p $17.50; pa
$12.95   **818**
ISBN 0-374-12628-3; 0-374-51855-6 (pa)
LC 83-16418

A collection of Bishop's autobiographical sketches and
short stories

"Whether she is discussing the sensuous joys and dark
fears of childhood or diamond mining and the preparation of food in Brazil, Elizabeth Bishop provides warm,
unforced revelations on an array of topics. . . . A book
to relish as well as to read." Choice

Includes bibliographic references

Blais, Madeleine, 1947-
The heart is an instrument; portraits in
journalism; foreword by Geneva Overholser.
University of Mass. Press 1992 341p il
$27.95   **818**
ISBN 0-87023-772-1   LC 91-48358

"Readers are drawn into the lives of a fascinating
assortment of people in the 15 feature articles reprinted
in this book. The vivid portrait of Christine Falling, the
baby killer, with her fractured language and world-views
stands next to a sketch of 68-year-old Tennessee Williams as he nears the end of a life devoted to literature.
Blais writes beautifully, telling stories that illustrate the
drama and importance of each life. The reader will care
about these people." Libr J

Bodett, Tom
Small comforts; more comments and
comic pieces. Addison-Wesley 1987 165p
$12.45; pa $8.61   **818**
ISBN 0-201-13417-9; 0-201-13689-9 (pa)
LC 87-12804

"This is a collection of homespun musings on what
[the author] calls his life of 'bone-chilling normalcy.'"
Booklist

"Bodett is genuinely touching when he describes hs
infant son and the joys of being a father, a boy waiting
for his first school bus ride and the beauties of Alaska."
Publ Wkly

Bowden, Mary Weatherspoon
Washington Irving. Twayne Pubs. 1981
201p (Twayne's United States authors ser)
$19.95   **818**
1. Irving, Washington, 1783-1859
ISBN 0-8057-7314-2   LC 80-21364

This study incorporates biographical information with
a critical discussion of Irving's essays, histories and
biographies

Includes bibliography

Brown, J. D. (James Dale), 1948-
Henry Miller. Ungar 1986 147p (Literature
and life, American writers) $19.95   **818**
1. Miller, Henry, 1891-1980
ISBN 0-8044-2077-7   LC 86-6961

The author "displays a deep sensitivity for the
appreciation of his subject . . . while acknowledging his
shortcomings as a writer." Choice

Includes bibliography

Bukowski, Charles
Septuagenarian stew: stories & poems.
Black Sparrow Press 1990 375p il $25; pa
$14   **818**
ISBN 0-87685-795-0; 0-87685-794-2 (pa) LC 90-316

The author's prose subjects "are nearly always the
same: drinking and womanizing; hanging out in bars, at
the racetrack, in low-rent neighborhoods and low-down
apartments; once in a while being recognized as the great
writer fallen on hard times. . . . His loosely constructed
poems range from narratives forced into staggered lines
to spare meditations leavened by a knowing wit." N Y
Times Book Rev

Capote, Truman, 1924-1984
A Capote reader. Random House 1987
722p $35   **818**

ISBN 0-394-55647-X   LC 86-10128

This volume presents the majority of Capote's work, both fiction and nonfiction

This book "includes just about everything that merits preservation and forcefully reminds us of the impact his early short stories and novellas had on the post-war American literary scene." Quill Quire

The dogs bark; public people and private places. Random House 1973 419p o.p.; New Am. Lib. paperback available $11.95   **818**

ISBN 0-452-25909-6 (pa)

This collection of essays, profiles, travel pieces and observations includes The muses are heard, and Local color, originally published 1956 and 1950 respectively

This book "bulges with sharp, subtle observations of people, fascinating reminiscences and travel jottings, wonderful sketches, anecdotes and yarns, and, among other things, the most frightening horror story you've ever heard." N Y Times Book Rev

Music for chameleons; new writing. Random House 1980 262p $11.95   **818**

ISBN 0-394-50826-2   LC 79-5532

Also available in paperback from New Am. Lib.

"There are three sections: one of short stories, or something like; one consisting of the 'In cold blood'-like 'short novel, Handcarved coffins;' and one called 'Conversational portraits,' which is precisely that." Choice

Castronovo, David
Thornton Wilder. Ungar 1986 174p (Literature and life, American writers) $19.95   **818**

1. Wilder, Thornton, 1897-1975
ISBN 0-8044-2119-6   LC 86-19255

In this study a "chronology is followed by a brief biography, then a discussion of the major works and themes, and, finally, a selected bibliography. The formula is useful as an introduction to Wilder and a quick survey of his life and work." Choice

Cather, Willa, 1873-1947
Stories, poems, and other writings. Literary Classics of the U.S. 1992 1039p (Lib. of America) $35   **818**

ISBN 0-940450-71-2   LC 91-62294

This volume contains the novels Alexander's bridge (1912) and My mortal enemy (1926); the poetry collection April twilights, and other poems (1923); the essay collection Not under forty (1936); and the following short story collections: Youth and the bright Medusa (1920); Obscure destinies (1932); The old beauty, and others (1948); and uncollected stories from 1892-1929

Cosby, Bill, 1937-
Time flies; introduction by Alvin F. Poussaint. Doubleday 1987 176p $15.95   **818**

ISBN 0-385-24040-6   LC 87-13083

Also available in paperback from Bantam Bks.
"A Dolphin book"

"At age 50, the author considers the inevitabilities of the aging process, addressing his own mini-crises—gray hairs, trifocals, etc.—with wise witticisms." Publ Wkly

Cowley, Malcolm, 1898-1989
The portable Malcolm Cowley; edited, with an introduction and notes, by Donald W. Faulkner. Viking 1990 xxxiv, 604p o.p.; Penguin Bks. paperback available $9.95   **818**

ISBN 0-14-015101-X (pa)   LC 89-40319

This is a collection of essays, verse, letters, and auto-biographical pieces

"Poet, critic, Boswell of the Lost Generation of which he himself was a member, savior of Faulkner's dwindling reputation, editor of Kerouac's On the Road, discoverer of John Cheever, Cowley knew everybody and wrote about them with sharp insight." Libr J

Includes bibliographic references

Crane, Hart, 1899-1932
Complete poems and selected letters and prose; edited with an introduction and notes by Brom Weber. Liveright 1966 302p $19.95   **818**

ISBN 0-87140-959-3

The book includes poems discovered since the earlier edition of Crane's collected poems; annotations and variant readings; and Waldo Frank's introduction to the 1958 edition of Crane's poetry

Crane, Stephen, 1871-1900
Prose and poetry. Library of Am. 1984 1379p $27.50   **818**

ISBN 0-940450-17-8   LC 83-19908

Edited by J. C. Levenson

"Maggie: a girl of the streets; The red badge of courage; Stories, sketches, and journalism; Poetry." Title page

"This collection also includes both Crane's collections of epigrammatic free verses—'The Black Riders' and 'War is kind'—and selections from his uncollected poems." Publisher's note

Includes bibliographic references

Critical essays on Henry David Thoreau's Walden; [edited by] Joel Myerson. Hall, G.K. & Co. 1988 254p (Critical essays on American literature) $40   **818**

ISBN 0-8161-8885-8   LC 88-1818

Scholars discuss Thoreau's classic from both philosophical and literary perspectives

Includes bibliographies

Critical essays on James Baldwin; [edited by] Fred L. Standley, Nancy V. Burt. Hall, G.K. & Co. 1988 312p (Critical essays on American literature) $40   **818**

1. Baldwin, James, 1924-1987
ISBN 0-8161-8879-3   LC 88-1802

A collection of critical essays examining Baldwin's novels, stories, and prose

Includes bibliographies

Critical essays on Langston Hughes; [edited by] Edward J. Mullen. Hall, G.K. & Co. 1986 207p (Critical essays on American literature) $40   **818**

1. Hughes, Langston, 1902-1967
ISBN 0-8161-8697-9   LC 85-16376

This is a "collection of reviews and essays on the writer's work. Taken together, these pieces make a good starting point for anyone who wants to see Hughes' accomplishment whole." Booklist

Includes bibliographies

Day, Clarence, 1874-1935
Life with father   **818**

Various editions available

First published 1935 by Knopf

Humourous essays on the life of a New York family, during the Brownstone front era. Although most of the members of the Day family come into the picture, it is the author's dominating and very forceful father who occupies center stage

Dickey, James
Night hurdling; poems, essays, conversations, commencements, and afterwords. Bruccoli Clark 1983 356p $25   **818**

ISBN 0-89723-038-8   LC 83-7096

"This collection presents Dickey speaking in a variety of modes, including nine interviews. . . . Dickey returns to the key events of his life: growing up in Georgia, flying combat missions in the South Pacific in World War II, writing 'Deliverance.'" Libr J

Dillard, Annie
Teaching a stone to talk; expeditions and encounters. Harper & Row 1982 177p hardcover o.p. paperback available $10   **818**

1. Natural history
ISBN 0-06-091541-2 (pa)   LC 82-47520

"In the fourteen pensées that make up this book [the author] bears witness, reflects on her observations of the order and disorder, the splendor and horror of the natural world." New Yorker

Du Bois, W. E. B. (William Edward Burghardt), 1868-1963
Writings. Library of Am. 1986 1334p $27.50   **818**

ISBN 0-940450-33-X   LC 86-10565

Edited by Nathan Huggins

Contents: The suppression of the African slave-trade; The souls of black folk; Dusk of dawn; Essays; Articles from The cirisis

Includes bibliography

Eiseley, Loren C., 1907-1977
The night country; [by] Loren Eiseley; illustrated by Leonard Everett Fisher. Scribner 1971 240p il hardcover o.p. paperback available $10.95   **818**

ISBN 0-684-18908-9 (pa)

Also available in hardcover from P. Smith

These poetically expressed reflections "evoke a sense of wonder and appreciation of nature and man's place in the universe. The striking black-and-white illustrations preceding each chapter contribute to the mood and tone." Booklist

Includes bibliography

The star thrower; introduction by W. H. Auden. Times Bks. 1978 319p o.p.; Harcourt Brace & Co. paperback available $7.95   **818**

ISBN 0-15-684909-7 (pa)   LC 77-87827

A collection of the late scientist's essays and poems. "The materials are arranged in three categories, 'Nature and Autobiography,' 'Early Poems,' and 'Science and Humanism'." Christ Sci Monit

"To read this collection is to see the things he points out to us refracted, transmuted, and clarified through the prism of his poetic imagination and literate style." Libr J

Eliot, T. S. (Thomas Stearns), 1888-1965
The complete poems and plays, 1909-1950. Harcourt Brace & Co. 1952 392p $24.95   **818**

ISBN 0-15-121185-X

This book is made up of six individual titles formerly published separately: Collected poems (1909-1935); Four quartets; Old Possum's book of practical cats; Murder in the cathedral; Family reunion; Cocktail party

Ellison, Ralph
Going to the territory. Random House 1986 338p $19.95; pa $12   **818**

ISBN 0-394-54050-6; 0-394-75062-4 (pa)
    LC 85-28117

Analyzed in Essay and general literature index

"This collection of essays, addresses, and reviews deals with topics in literature, music, and race relations. . . . Ellison tries to view American culture as a cloth of one piece. His analysis of the growth of the culture, and of the dynamic interaction of the diverse elements within it, is perceptive and convincing." Libr J

Emerson, Ralph Waldo, 1803-1882
Essays & lectures. Library of Am. 1983 1321p $30   **818**

ISBN 0-940450-15-1   LC 83-5447

Edited by Joel Porte

Contents: Nature; Addresses and lectures; Essays, first and second series; Representative men; English traits; The conduct of life; Uncollected prose

Includes bibliography

Emerson, Ralph Waldo, 1803-1882 — Continued

The portable Emerson. [rev ed], edited by Carl Bode in collaboration with Malcolm Cowley. Penguin Bks. 1981 xxxix, 670p pa $12.50   **818**

ISBN 0-14-015094-3   LC 81-4047

"The Viking portable library"

First published 1946 by Viking and analyzed in Essay and general literature index

The editors have provided the following selections: essays, including History, Self-reliance, The over-soul, Circles and The poet; The complete texts of Nature and English traits; biographical essays on Plato, Napoleon, Henry David Thoreau, Thomas Carlyle, and others as well as twenty-two poems

Includes bibliography

Fitzgerald, F. Scott (Francis Scott), 1896-1940

The crack-up, with other uncollected pieces, note-books and unpublished letters; together with letters to Fitzgerald from Gertrude Stein [et al.] and essays and poems by Paul Rosenfeld [et al.]; edited by Edmund Wilson. New Directions 1945 347p hardcover o.p. paperback available $9.95   **818**

ISBN 0-8112-0051-5 (pa)

The book is made up of autobiographical papers, some pieces written for the magazines from 1931 to 1937; Fitzgerald's notebooks in which he jotted down thoughts for future writings; selected letters to his friends; letters to him; and some essays and poems about him

Fitzgerald, Zelda, 1900-1948

The collected writings; edited by Matthew J. Bruccoli; introduction by Mary Gordon. Scribner 1991 xxvii, 480p $24.95   **818**

ISBN 0-684-19297-7   LC 90-21762

Also available in paperback from Macmillan

This volume brings together a novel entitled Save me the waltz, a play entitled 'Scandalabra,' eleven stories, twelve magazine articles, and a selection of the author's letters to F. Scott Fitzgerald

"While much of her prose is overblown with almost surrealistic descriptions, making for sometimes difficult reading, there is an original mind and wit at work here." Libr J

Includes bibliographic references

Franklin, Benjamin, 1706-1790

Writings. Library of Am. 1987 1605p $30
                                              818

ISBN 0-940450-29-1   LC 87-3303

Edited by J. A. Leo Lemay

This volume contains the text of Franklin's Autobiography "as well as 57 new attributions. Also included are all prefaces and maxims from the full run of Poor Richard's Almanack, plus a . . . selection of other writings, both personal and public. The material is arranged by the eras of Franklin's [life]." Libr J

Includes bibliography

Fulghum, Robert

All I really need to know I learned in kindergarten; uncommon thoughts on common things. Villard Bks. 1988 196p $18.45   **818**

ISBN 0-394-57102-9   LC 88-40144

Also available G.K. Hall large print edition and in paperback from Ivy Bks.

What the author "learned in kindergarten was share everything, play fair, don't hit people, put things back, clean up your own mess, don't take things that aren't yours, say you're sorry, take a nap every afternoon, and so on. . . . The basis of this fairly serious book . . . is that you're best served by periodic self-examination." Christ Sci Monit

It was on fire when I lay down on it. Villard Bks. 1989 218p $18.95; pa $5.95
                                              818

ISBN 0-394-58056-7; 0-804-10582-0 (pa)
                                      LC 89-40193

Also available large print edition

This is a "collection of humorous and poignant anecdotes, observations, and reminiscences." Booklist

"Quoting a man rescued from a burning bed, the title is a clue to the merriment in some of the essays collected here, inviting readers to laugh as they empathize with those who put themselves in absurd situations. . . . The selections beguile and educate, whatever the subject." Publ Wkly

Galvin, James

The meadow. Holt & Co. 1992 230p $19.95; pa $10.95   **818**

1. Natural history—United States 2. Ranch life
ISBN 0-8050-1684-8; 0-8050-2703-3 (pa)
                                      LC 91-34277

The author "blends fiction and fact into a haunting story that explores the high meadow on Sheep Creek in Wyoming, just across the border from Colorado. In an often haunting voice, Mr. Galvin describes the processes by which man and place are shaped and defined by each other." N Y Times Book Rev

Goodman, Ellen

At large. Summit Bks. 1981 245p $12.95
                                              818

ISBN 0-671-43306-7   LC 81-8816

This book is a collection of 104 of the author's newspaper columns from 1979-1981

"In nondoctrinaire observations on an astonishingly wide range of issues—feminism, children, politics, and social ethics among them—the author uses good humor, honest emotions, and home truths as catalysts to initiate her thoughtful commentaries on the world and life today." Booklist

Making sense. Atlantic Monthly Press 1989 xxi, 396p o.p.; Penguin Bks. paperback available $9.95   **818**

ISBN 0-14-013897-8 (pa)   LC 89-34054

In this collection of her newspaper columns Goodman's "perceptions, recorded over the past five years, are drawn together into topical chapters that reflect her primary concerns: people, politics, ethics, and family life." Booklist

Goodman, Ellen—*Continued*

"Reliably witty and original, Goodman proves to have both punch and staying power in these short essays." Publ Wkly

Hawthorne, Nathaniel, 1804-1864

The portable Hawthorne; edited by Malcolm Cowley. rev. and expanded ed. Viking 1969 698p o.p.; Penguin Bks. paperback available $12   **818**

ISBN 0-14-015038-2 (pa)

"The Viking portable library"

First published 1948

This anthology contains the complete text of The scarlet letter with Hawthorne's introduction "The custom house." Thirteen of Hawthorne's stories are also included as are passages from his American notebook plus sections from his European journals and letters and excerpts from his novel The house of the seven gables

Includes bibliography

Headings, Philip Ray, 1922-

T.S. Eliot; by Philip R. Headings. rev ed. Twayne Pubs. 1982 xxii, 235p il (Twayne's United States authors ser) $20.95   **818**

1. Eliot, T. S. (Thomas Stearns), 1888-1965
ISBN 0-8057-7357-6   LC 81-23525

First published 1964

Among Eliot's works examined in this book are: The waste land, The love song of J. Alfred Prufrock, Murder in the Cathedral, and On poetry and poets. The author also discusses developments in Eliot criticism

Includes bibliography

Hecht, Ben, 1894-1964

A thousand and one afternoons in Chicago; design and illustrations by Herman Rosse. University of Chicago Press 1992 288p il pa $15.95   **818**

1. Chicago (Ill.)
ISBN 0-226-32279-3   LC 91-40882

First published 1922 by Covici-McGee

A collection of 64 vignettes about life in 1921 Chicago

Hemingway, Ernest, 1899-1961

The Fifth Column, and four stories of the Spanish Civil War. Scribner 1969 151p $40; pa $9.95   **818**

1. Spain—History—1936-1939, Civil War—Drama
2. Spain—History—1936-1939, Civil War—Fiction
ISBN 0-684-15815-9; 0-684-12723-7 (pa)

"The Scribner library of contemporary classics"

First published 1962

The Fifth Column, Hemingway's only full-length play, was first published in 1938. Set in Madrid under siege during The Spanish Civil War, it deals with an American's involvement in counter-espionage activities against the Fascists. The stories included are: The denunciation; The butterfly and the tank; Night before battle; Under the ridge

Henry David Thoreau; edited and with an introduction by Harold Bloom. Chelsea House 1987 276p (Modern critical views) $29.95   **818**

1. Thoreau, Henry David, 1817-1862
ISBN 0-87754-697-5   LC 86-31020

Stanley Cavell, Loren Eiseley and Walter Ben Michaels are among the contributors who discuss Thoreau's language, narrative technique and philosophy

Includes bibliography

Henry David Thoreau's Walden; edited and with an introduction by Harold Bloom. Chelsea House 1987 150p (Modern critical interpretations) $29.95   **818**

ISBN 1-55546-012-7   LC 87-9306

A collection of eight critical essays on Thoreau's Walden arranged in chronological order of publication

Includes bibliography

Hoagland, Edward

The tugman's passage. Random House 1982 208p $12.50   **818**

ISBN 0-394-52268-0   LC 81-15803

"This collection of 14 essays and 26 short pieces written anonymously for the editorial page of the 'New York Times' covers such diverse subjects as Johnny Appleseed; rambling in Cairo and East Africa; tugboat men in New York's harbor." Publ Wkly

Hughes, Langston, 1902-1967

Good morning, revolution; uncollected social protest writings; edited and with an introduction by Faith Berry; foreword by Saunders Redding. Hill, L. 1973 145p o.p.; Carol Pub. Group paperback available $9.95   **818**

ISBN 0-8065-1308-X (pa)

Poems, essays and a short story address how to combat racism and economic inequality

James, Henry, 1843-1916

The portable Henry James; edited and with an introduction by Morton Dauwen Zabel. rev ed, revised by Lyell H. P. Powers. Viking 1968 696p o.p.; Penguin Bks. paperback available $12   **818**

ISBN 0-14-015055-2 (pa)

"The Viking portable library"

First published 1951 and analyzed in Essay and general literature index

Included are three complete novelettes (The pupil, The beast in the jungle, and The beach of desolation) as well as a number of short stories. There is also a selection of essays, critical writings, letters, and passages from James' autobiographical writings

Includes bibliography

Jefferson, Thomas, 1743-1826
The life and selected writings of Thomas Jefferson; edited and with an introduction by Adrienne Koch and William Peden. Modern Lib. 1993 xlii, 691p $19; pa $12
818

ISBN 0-679-60062-0; 0-679-74894-6 (pa)

First published 1944

Contents: Autobiography, including the Declaration of Independence; The anas; Travel journals; Essay on Anglo-Saxon; Biographical sketches; Notes on Virginia; Public papers; Letters

Writings. Library of Am. 1984 1600p $35
818

ISBN 0-940450-16-X   LC 83-19917

Edited by Merrill D. Peterson

"Autobiography—A summary view of the rights of British America—Notes on the State of Virginia—Public papers—Addresses, messages, and replies—Miscellany—Letters." Title page

This is "the largest and most skillfully edited single-volume Jefferson ever published." N Y Times Book Rev

Includes bibliographic references

Kesey, Ken
The further inquiry; photographs by Ron Bevirt. Viking 1990 215p il $24.95   **818**

1. Cassady, Neal

ISBN 0-670-83174-3   LC 89-40685

"Kesey gained notoriety in 1964 when he and his Merry Pranksters converted a school bus into a psychedelic caravan with Neal Cassady at the wheel—a cross-country safari chronicled in Tom Wolfe's *Electric Kool-Aid Acid Test* [entered in class 92]. This look back at that LSD-laced adventure, written as a dramatic script, conjures a courtroom trial in which Cassady's Spirit and assorted riders on the '64 journey are held accountable for their mad melee." Publ Wkly

King, Stephen, 1947-
Stephen King's danse macabre. Everest House 1981 400p il o.p.; Berkley Pub. Group paperback available $5.99   **818**

1. Horror—Fiction—History and criticism

ISBN 0-425-10433-8 (pa)   LC 79-28056

King includes "childhood reminiscences, anecdotes about fellow writers, plot synopses of favorite films, novels, stories and television programs, a selected reading list, even a quiz—that deals with the genre in which he has so far chosen to work." N Y Times Book Rev

Knapp, Bettina Liebowitz, 1926-
Anaïs Nin; [by] Bettina L. Knapp. Ungar 1979 c1978 168p (Modern literature monographs) $19.95   **818**

1. Nin, Anaïs, 1903-1977

ISBN 0-8044-2481-0   LC 78-57692

Nin's "wide-ranging 'oeuvre,' consisting of diaries, an 'unprofessional study' of D. H. Lawrence, novels and stories (including erotica), is investigated in detail." Libr J

"An excellent critical introduction to Anaïs Nin. . . . The biographical and critical assessments are balanced and perceptive." Choice

Includes bibliography

Kramer, Victor A.
Thomas Merton, monk and artist. Cistercian Publs. 1987 226p (Cistercian studies ser) pa $11.95   **818**

1. Merton, Thomas, 1915-1968

ISBN 0-87907-602-X   LC 87-6418

Revised edition of Thomas Merton, published 1984 by Twayne

An overview of Merton's major published writings. Kramer provides a chronology, a brief biography, an assessment of Merton's dual vocation as writer and monk, and a work-by-work assessment of themes

Includes bibliography

Le Guin, Ursula K., 1929-
Buffalo gals and other animal presences. Capra Press 1987 196p il $15.95   **818**

ISBN 0-88496-270-9   LC 87-11692

Also available in paperback from New Am. Lib.

This is a "collection of stories and poems spanning fifteen years. . . . [The title story] . . . is a Coyote tale . . . about a little girl who survives a plane crash and is nurtured by the (other) animals, whom she sees sometimes as animals and sometimes as people." Am Book Rev

"Among the best pieces is the title story; like many of the others, it works its effect through a reversal of the usual (human) point of view." Libr J

Dancing at the edge of the world; thoughts on words, women, places. Grove Press 1988 306p o.p.; HarperCollins Pubs. paperback available $11   **818**

ISBN 0-06-097289-0 (pa)   LC 88-11266

"Chronologically arranged, these 33 talks and essays and 17 reviews of books and films, dating from 1976 through 1987, record Le Guin's responses to ethical and political climates, the transforming effect of certain literary ideas and the changes of a supple, disciplined mind." Publ Wkly

Levertov, Denise, 1923-
The poet in the world. New Directions 1973 275p hardcover o.p. paperback available $8.95   **818**

ISBN 0-8112-0493-6 (pa)

"Drawing on formal essays, notebook jottings, work sheets, rally speeches, and symposium talks, Levertov offers a . . . sample of her prose writings." Libr J

Includes bibliographic references

Lowell, Robert, 1917-1977
Collected prose; edited and introduced by Robert Giroux. Farrar, Straus & Giroux 1987 377p $25   **818**

1. Poetry—History and criticism

ISBN 0-374-12625-9   LC 86-29098

Analyzed in Essay and general literature index

Lowell, Robert, 1917-1977—*Continued*

This "collection of Robert Lowell's prose ranges in time from an essay on the Iliad written in 1935 at St. Mark's to the unfinished study, 'New England and Further,' on which he was working when he died in 1977." Publisher's note

"Lowell's attention to tradition, social issues and the subtleties of craft gives his Collected Prose energy and lasting value." Nation

Includes bibliography

MacDonald, Betty, d. 1958

The egg and I   **818**

1. Farm life

Hardcover and paperback editions available from various publishers

First published 1946 by Lippincott

These are the reminiscences of the author's life with her husband on a chicken farm in the state of Washington

This is "sprightly, diverting, and excellent entertainment. The whole book crackles with innocent deviltry of acorns hitting the roof-tops." Saturday Rev

Malcolm, Janet

The purloined clinic; selected writings. Knopf 1992 382p $22.50   **818**

ISBN 0-679-41232-8   LC 92-4498

Analyzed in Essay and general literature index

This collection of essays, book reviews and profiles touches on a wide range of subjects: psychoanalysis, literature, art and family therapy. Discussions of works by Freud, Kundera, Havel and Eakins are included

Mamet, David

Some freaks. Viking 1989 180p o.p.; Penguin Bks. paperback available $7.95

                                     818

ISBN 0-14-012434-9 (pa)   LC 88-40650

These "brief sketches include pieces on guns, London, Superman, polls, and a hardware store in Cabot, Vt. While intelligent, sometimes provocative, and sometimes amusing, the pieces have no thread to tie them together. Perhaps they do not need one. It may be telling of Mamet, or of American culture generally, that much more is written in these pages about filmmaking than about theater." Libr J

McCarthy, Mary, 1912-1989

Occasional prose. Harcourt Brace Jovanovich 1985 341p $17.95   **818**

ISBN 0-15-167810-3   LC 85-765

McCarthy's "book comprises uncollected reviews and criticism, obituary pieces, . . . political reporting, several prefaces and afterwords to other people's books, a retelling of 'La Traviata' . . . and one biographical sketch, all culled from the last 15 years or so of her distinguished writing career." N Y Times Book Rev

Mencken, H. L. (Henry Louis), 1880-1956

The American scene; a reader; selected and edited and with an introduction and commentary, by Huntington Cairns. Knopf 1965 xxvii, 542p $20; pa $12.95   **818**

1. United States—Civilization

ISBN 0-394-43594-X; 0-394-75214-7 (pa)

A selection of Mencken's essays arranged under the headings: The critic of American life; American letters; Politics; American journalism; American English; Religion and morals; Persons; Memories; Letters; Miscellany

A choice of days; essays from Happy days, Newspaper days, and Heathen days; selected and with an introduction by Edward L. Galligan. Knopf 1980 xxiii, 337p hardcover o.p. paperback available $7.95

                                     818

ISBN 0-394-74760-7 (pa)   LC 80-7645

"Selections from Mencken's three volumes of delightful autobiographical essays—'Happy Days, 1880-1892,' 'Newspaper Days, 1899-1906,' and 'Heathen Days, 1890-1936.' Droll tales of childhood adventures in Baltimore are followed by equally humorous stories of his career as a budding journalist and grand, opinion-filled accounts of life during Prohibition." Booklist

Merwin, W. S. (William Stanley), 1927-

The lost upland. Knopf 1992 307p $22

                                     818

1. Dordogne (France)

ISBN 0-679-40526-7   LC 91-22199

Also available in paperback from Holt & Co.

In this triptych of narratives Merwin "pays tribute to the people of the uplands of Southwestern France. The book's three sections deal primarily with local characters, including a declining nobleman, a shepherd, and a wine merchant." Libr J

"Mr. Merwin is adept at treating human behavior as part of nature and at fashioning a sense of place from people's conduct. These people view the unwelcome present through the prism of the past, thus the title of the book and the sweet longing it leaves behind." NY Times Book Rev

Miller, Arthur, 1915-

The portable Arthur Miller; edited and with an introduction, by Harold Clurman. Viking 1971 xxv, 566p o.p.; Penguin Bks. paperback available $12.95   **818**

ISBN 0-14-015071-4 (pa)

"The Viking portable library"

This collection contains four complete plays: Death of a salesman, The crucible, Incident at Vichy, The price; the original story: The misfits, and excerpts from the cinema novel based on it; two short stories: Fame, and Fitter's night; excerpts from a non-fiction book: In Russia; a poem: Lines from California; biographical notes and an introductory essay by the editor

Includes bibliography

Miller, Henry, 1891-1980
Henry Miller on writing; selected by Thomas H. Moore from the published and unpublished works of Henry Miller. New Directions 1964 216p pa $9.95 **818**
ISBN 0-8112-0112-0

The author discusses the art and practice of writing with insights on how he set his goals, how he discovered the excitement of using words, how the books he read influenced him, and how he learned to draw on his own experiences

Miller, R. Baxter
The art and imagination of Langston Hughes. University Press of Ky. 1989 149p $18 **818**
1. Hughes, Langston, 1902-1967
ISBN 0-8131-1662-7   LC 89-5645

The author "offers a biocritical reading of Hughes' writings. This literary analysis delves into the conditions of Hughes' own experiences to explore the characteristic themes of the writer's art and to examine how his imagination was fired by black folk culture and his memories of the women in his life." Booklist

Includes bibliography

Mitchell, Joseph, 1908-
Up in the old hotel and other stories. Pantheon Bks. 1992 718p $27.50; pa $14 **818**
ISBN 0-679-41263-8; 0-679-74631-5 (pa)
LC 91-50835

A compendium of Mitchell's stories, profiles and articles written for the New Yorker between 1938 and 1965
"It doesn't take an Aristotle to explain how a book full of people and places and customs that no longer exist could make a reader as happy as 'Up in the Old Hotel' does. Mr. Mitchell always mediates the sadness such subjects bring—the loss of time, the life slipping by, the way the old manners fail to hang on—and he lets the reader feel only the pleasure that comes from his own very personal discoveries." N Y Times Book Rev

Momaday, N. Scott
In the presence of the sun; stories and poems, 1961-1991. St. Martin's Press 1992 xx, 143p il $17.95 **818**
ISBN 0-312-08222-3   LC 92-25225

"Illustrated with 50 of the author's own drawings and paintings, the poems and stories collected here are all somehow engaged with Momaday's Native American heritage and the Plains culture of the past." Publ Wkly
These works convey the "deep sense of place of the Native American oral tradition. . . . Like the Plains Shields he celebrates, these poems and stories are 'meditations that make a round of life.'" Libr J

Moore, Marianne, 1887-1972
The complete prose of Marianne Moore; edited and with an introduction by Patricia C. Willis. Viking 1986 723p $24.95 **818**
ISBN 0-670-80451-7   LC 85-41064
"An Elisabeth Sifton book"

"Except for letters, interviews, quotations, and material she herself did not see to press, this book includes all of [the American poet's] published prose." Libr J
The author's "achievement in prose, as in poetry, is marked by an idiosyncrasy that is no barrier to profundity, by a personal predilection that carries the authority of measured judgment." New Repub

Morrell, David, 1943-
Fireflies. Dutton 1988 218p o.p. **818**
1. Morrell, Matthew 2. Cancer   LC 88-3588
Available Thorndike Press large print edition

Combining reality with fictionalized sequences, the author relates events leading to the tragic death of his 15-year-old son Matthew

Mowat, Farley
The dog who wouldn't be; illustrated by Paul Galdone. Little, Brown 1957 238p il $18.95 **818**
1. Dogs
ISBN 0-316-58636-6

Also available in hardcover from Amereon and paperback from Bantam Bks.

The author reminisces about his boyhood in Saskatchewan and his relationship with his dog Mutt

Nemerov, Howard
A Howard Nemerov reader. University of Mo. Press 1991 534p il $24.95 **818**
ISBN 0-8262-0776-6   LC 90-20174

This volume comprises a selection of Nemerov's poetry, short stories, and critical writing, and one complete novel, Federigo, or, The Power of Love
"This fine, labyrinthine collection will delight readers who are familiar only with Howard Nemerov's poetry. Here we have his fiction, which allows him a much wider emotional and imaginative range than do his poems, and his essays, which reveal Mr. Nemerov as brilliantly incisive, if occasionally curmudgeonly." N Y Times Book Rev

Newman, Edwin
I must say; on English, the news and other matters. Warner Bks. 1988 296p hardcover o.p. paperback available $9.95 **818**
1. United States—Civilization
ISBN 0-446-39099-2 (pa)   LC 88-21625

In this collection of over 150 of his newspaper columns, Newman reflects on good English, the media, sports, travel, world affairs, national character, and music, among other things
"A trenchant, humorous, and thought-provoking work for public libraries." Libr J

Parker, Dorothy, 1893-1967
The portable Dorothy Parker; with a new introduction by Brendan Gill. rev and enl ed. Viking 1973 xxvii, 610p o.p.; Penguin Bks. paperback available $12 **818**
ISBN 0-14-015074-9 (pa)
"The Viking portable library"

Parker, Dorothy, 1893-1967—*Continued*
First published 1944 with title: Dorothy Parker

This collection contains: thirty-two short stories; poems; drama reviews; book reviews, including the entire text of Constant reader; and miscellaneous articles

"It is hard to imagine a library that would not want this book." Choice

Percy, Walker, 1916-1990
Lost in the cosmos; the last self-help book. Farrar, Straus & Giroux 1983 262p $14.95; pa $13   **818**
ISBN 0-374-19165-4; 0-374-52346-0 (pa)   LC 83-1590

"The book consists of a mock self-help quiz. Percy poses 20 questions with didactic overtones. . . . Lost in the Cosmos contains essays, science fiction, one-liners, charts, a script for 'The Last Donahue Show,' and letters to 'Dear Abby.'" Christ Today

"The whole is brought off with that sly humor and intellectual verve that have made the author's novels exceptional." Natl Rev

Signposts in a strange land; edited with an introduction by Patrick Samway. Farrar, Straus & Giroux 1991 428p $25; pa $15   **818**
ISBN 0-374-26391-4; 0-374-52345-2 (pa)
                                          LC 91-12360

This collection includes "speeches, interviews, and essays (some published for the first time) investigate various aspects of Percy's lifelong interests: the South; science, language, and literature; and morality and religion." Booklist

Plimpton, George
The best of Plimpton. Atlantic Monthly Press 1990 368p il hardcover o.p. paperback available $12.95   **818**
ISBN 0-87113-503-5 (pa)   LC 90-42037

"A Morgan Entrekin book"

This "volume collects Plimpton pieces from the last 35 years. Included are the articles that served as the basis for his well-known books—e.g., *Paper Lion, The Bogey Man*—and a wealth of other sport and nonsport accounts. Plimpton watches a World Series game with poet Marianne Moore; probes the enigma that was football legend Vince Lombardi; profiles actor Warren Beatty, novelist William Styron, and . . . provides portraits of places he's known and loved (Newport Beach, Elaine's Restaurant in New York, Norfolk, Nebraska)." Booklist

Poe, Edgar Allan, 1809-1849
The complete poems and stories; with selections from his critical writings; with introduction and explanatory notes by Arthur Hobson Quinn; text established, with bibliographical notes, by Edward H. O'Neill; illustrated by E. McKnight Kauffer. Knopf 1946 2v il o.p.; Vintage Bks. paperback available $13   **818**
ISBN 0-394-71678-7 (pa)

Contents: v1 Introduction; Poems; Tales. v2 Tales (continued) Narrative of Arthur Gordon Pym of Nantucket; Criticism, Marginalia; Bibliographical and textual notes

Essays and reviews. Library of Am. 1984 1544p $35   **818**
ISBN 0-940450-19-4   LC 83-19923
Edited by G. R. Thompson

This volume is divided into six main divisions: Theory of poetry, Reviews of British and Continental authors; Reviews of American authors and American criticism; Magazines and criticism; The literary and social scene; and Articles and marginalia
Includes bibliographic references

Poetry and tales. Library of Am. 1984 1408p $35   **818**
ISBN 0-940450-18-6   LC 83-19931
Edited by Patrick F. Quinn

This volume contains 70 stories and Poe's poetic work in its entirety
Includes bibliographic references

Requiem; new collected works by Robert A. Heinlein and tributes to the grand master; edited by Yoji Kondo. TOR Bks. 1992 341p $21.95; pa $12.95   **818**
1. Heinlein, Robert A. (Robert Anson), 1907-1988
ISBN 0-312-85168-5; 0-312-85523-0 (pa)
                                          LC 91-38909

A collection of fiction, speeches, poems, memorials, and stories about and by Robert Heinlein

Rogers, Will, 1879-1935
Will Rogers' world; America's foremost political humorist comments on the twenties and thirties--and eighties and nineties; [edited by] Bryan B. Sterling and Frances N. Sterling. Evans & Co. 1989 242p il $17.95   **818**
1. American wit and humor
ISBN 0-87131-564-5   LC 89-1129

This book is "primarily a collection of quotations and miscellaneous sayings by the famed newspaper columnist, actor, and rope-twirling cowboy. The selections are grouped under the headings America, Congress, elections, government, presidents, politics, business, and philosophy. The compilers supply a running commentary." Libr J

Sarton, May, 1912-
Sarton selected; an anthology of the journals, novels, and poems of May Sarton; edited, with an introduction and notes, by Bradford Dudley Daziel. Norton 1991 390p $22.95   **818**
ISBN 0-393-02968-9   LC 90-46669

This anthology represents the work of May Sarton from her childhood in Belgium to her recovery from a stroke in her mid-seventies

Sheed, Wilfrid
Essays in disguise. Knopf 1989 xxii, 264p $19.95   **818**
ISBN 0-394-55875-8   LC 89-45293
Analyzed in Essay and general literature index

Sheed, Wilfrid—*Continued*
"Whether writing on Sinatra or Updike, Hemingway or the Catholic Church, the Mafia or Salinger, Sheed's always-exciting prose style and his uncanny way of extracting the most from his subjects never fail to leave his readers satisfied." Libr J

Silko, Leslie
Storyteller; [by] Leslie Marmon Silko. Seaver Bks. 1981 278p il $17.95; pa $14.95
818

ISBN 0-394-51589-7; 0-86579-004-3 (pa)
LC 80-20251

This "consists of short stories, anecdotes, folktales, poems, historical and autobiographical notes, and photographs." N Y Times Book Rev
"Memory and invention are the stuff of Silko's story-telling. Although many of her stories traverse familiar territory—the dislocation of a disinherited people—her perceptions are acute, and her style reflects the breadth, the texture, the mortality of her subjects." Saturday Rev

Sontag, Susan, 1933-
Against interpretation, and other essays. Farrar, Straus & Giroux 1966 304p o.p.; Hippocrene Bks. reprint available $20.50
818

ISBN 0-87052-352-X (pa)

Also available in paperback from Doubleday

Analyzed in Essay and general literature index

These essays, written between 1961 and 1965 "range over the contemporary arts, literature, drama, the movies, with side discussion of the milieu of painting and the graphic arts." Libr J

Stein, Gertrude, 1874-1946
Selected writings; edited with an introduction and notes by Carl Van Vechten and with an essay on Gertrude Stein by F. W. Dupee. Modern Lib. 1962 706p hardcover o.p. paperback available $18
818

ISBN 0-679-72464-8 (pa)

Also available in hardcover from P. Smith

In addition to the autobiography of Alice B. Toklas and the libretto Four saints in three acts, this volume contains representative selections of Stein's poetry, prose, drama, and criticism

The Yale Gertrude Stein; selections; with an introduction by Richard Kostelanetz. Yale Univ. Press 1980 xxxi, 464p hardcover o.p. paperback available $18 **818**
ISBN 0-300-02609-9 (pa)
LC 80-5398

This book contains selections from the eight Yale University Press volumes of 'The unpublished writings of Gertrude Stein' initially published between 1951 and 1958. The editor has included poetry, prose, compressed novels, stories, plays, and essays
The book offers a "sturdy sampling of Stein's work, the charming and the opaque, from the period roughly 1910-40. The selection is both canny . . . and representative." Choice

Steinbeck, John, 1902-1968
Working days; the journals of The grapes of wrath, 1938-1941; edited by Robert DeMott. Viking 1989 lvii, 180p il o.p.; Penguin Bks. paperback available $8.95
818

1. Steinbeck, John, 1902-1968. The grapes of wrath
ISBN 0-14-014457-9 (pa)
LC 88-40276

This is the diary the American novelist kept while he was writing The grapes of wrath. The volume "covers the period of actual composition, from May to October, 1938, followed by a few post-production entries from the period October 1939 to January 1941." San Francisco Rev Books
This book "will provide a field day for Steinbeck aficionados, but for its insights into the creative mind it is also a valuable book for writers, aspiring or arrived." N Y Times Book Rev

Stevens, Wallace, 1879-1955
Opus posthumous; poems, plays, prose. rev enl & corr ed, edited by Milton J. Bates. Knopf 1989 334p $30; pa $14.95
818

ISBN 0-394-57792-2; 0-679-72534-2 (pa)
LC 88-46045

Companion volume to The collected poems of Wallace Stevens, entered in class 811

First published 1957 under the editorship of Samuel French Morse

This is a collection of the author's poetry, drama, aphorisms, and essays
This volume provides a "marvelous chance to discover again the unity in diversity of Stevens's mind. . . . The accumulation of verse and prose makes it a paradoxically good introduction to Stevens's work, even though it was first published after his death." Times Lit Suppl

Theroux, Paul
Sunrise with seamonsters; travels & discoveries, 1964-1984. Houghton Mifflin 1985 365p hardcover o.p. paperback available $8.70 **818**
ISBN 0-394-41501-2 (pa)
LC 85-2343

There are ~~~~ articles in this book, printed in chronological order from 1964 to 1984. . . . Theroux's essays fall into two main categories: on writers he admires—Henry James, Henry Miller, S. J. Perelman, V. S. Pritchett—and on travel (by train whenever possible) in Europe, Africa, Asia, and the New York subway." Natl Rev

Thompson, Hunter S.
The great shark hunt; strange tales from a strange time. Summit Bks. 1979 602p o.p.; Ballantine Bks. paperback available $12
818

ISBN 0-345-37482-7 (pa)
LC 79-831

Also available in paperback from Warner Bks.

"A Rolling Stone Press book"

"A retrospective in journalistic theater, this gathers together excerpts from Thompson's 'Fear and Loathing in Las Vegas' and 'Fear and Loathing on the Campaign Trail,' plus his reportage from such diverse journals as 'Rolling Stone,' 'Playboy,' 'The New York Times,' etc.,

Thompson, Hunter S.—*Continued*
going back to 1962." Publ Wkly

Includes bibliography

Thoreau, Henry David, 1817-1862
The portable Thoreau; edited and with an
introduction by Carl Bode. rev ed. Viking
1964 698p o.p.; Penguin Bks. paperback
available $11   **818**

ISBN 0-14-015031-5 (pa)

"The Viking portable library"

First published 1947 and analyzed in Essay and
general literature index

This volume contains the complete text of Walden
and a large portion of A week on the Concord and
Merrimack Rivers as well as selections from The Maine
Woods, Cape Cod and Excursions. Some of Thoreau's
poems, essays and a portion of his Journal are also
included

Includes bibliography

Walden   **818**

Hardcover and paperback editions available from
various publishers

First published 1854

"Philosophy of life and observations of nature drawn
from the author's solitary sojourn of two years in a
cabin on Walden Pond near Concord, Massachusetts."
Pratt Alcove

Walden and other writings of Henry
David Thoreau; edited by Brooks Atkinson.
Modern Lib. 1992 769p $18.50   **818**

ISBN 0-679-60004-3   LC 92-50225

First Modern Library edition, 1950

In addition to Walden, entered separately above, this
collection of Thoreau's prose includes: A week on the
Concord and Merrimack Rivers; Cape Cod; The Allegash
and East Branch; Walking; Civil disobedience; Slavery
in Massachusetts; A plea for Captain John Brown; Life
without principle

A week on the Concord and Merrimack
rivers; Walden, or, Life in the woods; The
Maine woods; Cape Cod. Library of Am.
1985 1114p il $30   **818**

ISBN 0-940450-27-5   LC 85-5175

Edited by Robert F. Sayre

The first volume of a projected two volume set of
Thoreau's work

"Politically the most conscious of the Transcenden-
talists, an acute observer of natural and social facts,
Thoreau was an outstanding prose stylist." Reader's Ency

Includes bibliography

Thurber, James, 1894-1961
Collecting himself; James Thurber on
writing and writers, humor and himself;
Michael J. Rosen, editor. Harper & Row
1989 xx, 263p il hardcover o.p. paperback
available $8.95   **818**

ISBN 0-06-092017-3 (pa)   LC 89-45062

"A collection of Thurber's writings and drawings not
previously anthologized. . . . A number of the pieces
are excerpts from Thurber's many interviews and com-

mentaries, spanning some 30 years. In these he shares
with the reader his coping with progressive blindness,
his method of drawing, his writing tactics, and his personal relationships. His critical views on theatre, other
writers, and the state of humor itself are also divulged."
Libr J

Trillin, Calvin
American stories. Ticknor & Fields 1991
294p $19.45   **818**

ISBN 0-395-59367-0   LC 91-15939

"Twelve nonfiction narratives on a diverse range of
subjects. . . . Included are pieces as varied as a murder-
for-love in Kansas to the on-and off-screen antics of
eccentric magicians Penn & Teller. Most originally appeared in Trillin's column in *The New Yorker*. . . .
Trillin skillfully draws us into the weird world of drive-
in movie critic Joe Bob Briggs as well as that of a young
American student falling mortally ill in China. We learn
to care about those being reported on, and we also enjoy
the tale being told." Libr J

Twain, Mark, 1835-1910
The innocents abroad; or, The new
Pilgrim's progress, being some account of
the steamship Quaker City's pleasure
excursion to Europe and the Holy Land
                                                 818

1. Voyages and travels   2. Europe—Description
3. Middle East—Description

Available in paperback from various publishers

First published 1869

"Humorous account of a voyage through the Mediterranean and travel in the bordering countries." Carnegie
Libr. of Pittsburgh

Letters from the earth; edited by Bernard
DeVoto; with a preface by Henry Nash
Smith. Harper & Row 1962 303p $15.50;
pa $5.95   **818**

ISBN 0-06-014435-1; 0-06-080331-2 (pa)

Also available in hardcover from Buccaneer Bks.

"A series of controversial, anti-religious essays written
in the late period of the author's life." Chicago Public
Libr

Includes bibliography

Life on the Mississippi   **818**

1. Mississippi River valley

Hardcover and paperback editions available from
various publishers

First published 1874

Mark Twains's famous account of life on the Mississippi in the old steamboat days and his own experiences
as a pilot

"Its historical sketches, its frequent passages of vivid
description, and its humorous episodes combine to make
[this] a masterpiece of the literature of the Middle West."
Eng and Pope's What to Read

Twain, Mark, 1835-1910—*Continued*

The outrageous Mark Twain; some lesser-known but extraordinary works; with "Reflections on religion" now in book form for the first time; selected and edited, with an introduction, by Charles Neider. Doubleday 1987 348p $16.95   **818**

ISBN 0-385-23522-4   LC 86-32912

"The essays, letters, and one story gathered here aren't outrageous; they are outraged. . . . In the single piece receiving its first book publication here, 'Reflections on Religion,' he attacks the depictions of God in both testaments as incommensurate with the qualities of mercy and justice commonly attributed to the deity. . . . Only extensive Twain collections really need this anthology, but it will also be serviceable in libraries where the various essays aren't available in other volumes." Booklist

A pen warmed-up in hell: Mark Twain in protest; edited by Frederick Anderson. Harper & Row 1972 183p hardcover o.p. paperback available $8.95   **818**

ISBN 0-06-090678-2 (pa)

Also available in hardcover from Borgo Press

A selection of two dozen examples of Twain's social criticism. Among the topics represented: war, politics, patriotism, racism, hypocrisy, capitalism, and overpopulation

The portable Mark Twain; edited by Bernard De Voto. Viking 1946 786p o.p.; Penguin Bks. paperback available $9.95   **818**

ISBN 0-14-015020-X (pa)

Analyzed in Essay and general literature index

"The Viking portable library"

Contains the following complete works: Notorious jumping frog of Calavaras County; Private history of a campaign that failed; Adventures of Huckleberry Finn; Fenimore Cooper's literary offenses; Mysterious stranger. Also comprehensive selections from: A tramp abroad; Old times on the Mississippi; Connecticut Yankee in King Arthur's court; Pudd'n-head Wilson; Following the equator; Mark Twain in eruption; Mark Twain's autobiography. Twenty-eight of Twain's letters are also included

Roughing it   **818**

1. Hawaii—Description 2. West (U.S.)—Description

Hardcover and paperback editions available from various publishers

First published 1872

A humorous account of a trip across the plains to California and then to Hawaii in the early 1860's

The wit and wisdom of Mark Twain; edited by Alex Ayres. Harper & Row 1987 265p $19.95   **818**

ISBN 0-06-015783-6   LC 87-45020

Also available in paperback from New Am. Lib.

The editor "provides systematic access to plenty of Twain's bon mots by arranging them in a dictionary of topics from *Adam* to *youth*. . . . Where background is needed, Ayres supplies it succinctly and, as an afterword, proffers 'What Mark Twain might say today' on such ponderables as communism, extraterrestrial intelligence, the national debt, terrorism, and the unborn. Much to Ayres' credit, many of these approximations sound markedly Twainian." Booklist

Includes bibliography

Updike, John

Assorted prose. Knopf 1965 326p $24.95   **818**

ISBN 0-394-41473-X

A collection of parodies, profiles, autobiographical sketches and literary criticism

Hugging the shore; essays and criticism. Knopf 1983 xx, 919p $19.95; pa $14.95   **818**

ISBN 0-394-53179-5; 0-394-72497-6 (pa)   LC 83-47957

In addition to miscellaneous essays, this volume contains pieces on "classic nineteenth-century figures (Flaubert, Hawthorne), and twentieth-century authors." NY Rev Books

"These reviews are models of craft—and something more. Updike summarizes expertly and quotes tellingly, and takes care to seek out the true thematic and moral center of whatever book he's analyzing." Christ Sci Monit

Odd jobs; essays and criticism. Knopf 1991 xxii, 919p $35   **818**

ISBN 0-679-40414-7   LC 91-52738

Analyzed in Essay and general literature index

This collection includes "short notices, a travel piece, and occasional pieces on assigned topics like fiction, women, national monuments, popular music, New York architecture, being on TV, and speeches. But mostly there are essays and reviews, a few on science or technical topics, but generally literary." Libr J

Includes bibliographic references

Picked-up pieces. Knopf 1975 519, xxiiip il o.p.; Fawcett Bks. paperback available $4.50   **818**

ISBN 0-449-21203-3 (pa)

This collection, comprised mostly of book reviews, also includes an assortment of essays, profiles, introductions and speeches on a variety of topics

Vidal, Gore, 1925-

Views from a window; conversations with Gore Vidal; selected, arranged, and introduced by Robert J. Stanton; edited by Robert J. Stanton and Gore Vidal. Stuart, L. 1980 319p $14.95   **818**

ISBN 0-8184-0302-0   LC 80-16808

Vidal comments on his life and work, his contemporaries, sex, politics and popular culture

Vonnegut, Kurt, 1922-

Fates worse than death; an autobiographical collage of the 1980s. Putnam 1991 237p il o.p.; Berkley Pub. Group paperback available $8.95   **818**

ISBN 0-425-13406-7 (pa)   LC 91-10691

Vonnegut, Kurt, 1922-- *Continued*

In this book the author "applies an apocalyptic eye to everything from global starvation to censorship. In this collection of speeches, essays and memoirs, linked together by reflective passages, Mr. Vonnegut is perhaps more intimate with the reader than ever. He reveals a tortured family life and tells stories of alcoholism and insanity and of deep grief and, sometimes, reconciliation." N Y Times Book Rev

Palm Sunday; an autobiographical collage. Delacorte Press 1981 330p il hardcover o.p. paperback available $5.99 **818**

ISBN 0-440-36906-1 (pa)   LC 80-27322

This is a collection of the author's letters, reviews, speeches, memoirs, a "self-interview," a short story, a play and a sermon he delivered on Palm Sunday

Walker, Alice, 1944-

In search of our mothers' gardens; womanist prose. Harcourt Brace Jovanovich 1983 397p 16.95; pa $10.95 **818**

ISBN 0-15-144525-7; 0-15-644544-1 (pa)   LC 83-8584

"Novelist and poet Walker brings together assorted essays and reviews that refocus attention on her own life and literary work. By 'womanist,' Walker means an extended concept of black feminism, and this dual minority consciousness informs the basic ideas and themes behind all of her writing." Booklist

Includes bibliographic references

Living by the word; selected writings, 1973-1987. Harcourt Brace Jovanovich 1988 196p $15.95; pa $8.95 **818**

ISBN 0-15-152900-0; 0-15-652865-7 (pa)

LC 87-29615

The author "presents a collection of miscellaneous essays, speeches, and journal entries that encapsulates the concerns of her writings and her life. Minorities, whether racial or sexual, figure prominently in these pieces as Walker discusses her own identity as a black American woman." Booklist

Warren, Robert Penn, 1905-1989

A Robert Penn Warren reader. Random House 1987 477p $22.50 **818**

ISBN 0-394-55896-0   LC 86-17850

This collection includes the complete texts of Segregation: the inner conflict of the South and The legacy of the Civil War, published separately in 1956 and 1961 respectively; as well as poetry, short stories, novel excerpts, literary criticism and essays

Welty, Eudora, 1909-

The eye of the story; selected essays and reviews. Random House 1978 355p hardcover o.p. paperback available $7.95 **818**

ISBN 0-394-72732-0 (pa)   LC 78-103296

A "collection of non-fiction pieces written over the course of almost four decades. There are essays on individual writers—Jane Austen, Henry Green, Katherine Anne Porter, Willa Cather; essays on the arts of reading and writing; there [are] . . . book reviews; and finally, a number of 'personal and occasional pieces.'" New Repub

White, E. B. (Elwyn Brooks), 1899-1985

One man's meat. new and enl ed. Harper & Row 1944 350p hardcover o.p. paperback available $13 **818**

ISBN 0-06-091081-X (pa)

Analyzed in Essay and general literature index

First published 1942

Fifty-five essays, on a variety of themes, in which the author's memories of his life in New York blend with the everyday life on his salt water farm in Maine. Many of the articles have appeared in Harpers, or the New Yorker

White, Theodore H., 1915-1986

Theodore H. White at large; the best of his magazine writing, 1939-1986; edited and with an introduction by Edward T. Thompson. Pantheon Bks. 1992 xxi, 681p $35 **818**

ISBN 0-679-41635-8   LC 92-54108

"A Cornelia & Michael Bessie book"

This collection of White's magazine reportage begins in 1939 and ends with his death in 1986. World War II China, postwar Europe, the Middle East, Africa and the American political and social scenes are discussed. Profiles of Malraux, J. F. Kennedy, and Chiang Kai-Shek are among those included

Whitman, Walt, 1819-1892

Complete poetry and collected prose. Library of Am. 1982 1380p $30 **818**

ISBN 0-940450-02-X   LC 81-20768

Edited by Justin Kaplan

Contents: Leaves of grass (1855); Leaves of grass (1891-92); Complete prose works (1892); Supplementary prose

Walt Whitman; selected and with notes by Mark Van Doren. Revised by Malcolm Cowley; with a chronology and bibliographical checklist by Gay Wilson Allen. Viking 1974 xxxvii, 648p o.p.; Penguin Bks. paperback available $12 **818**

ISBN 0-14-015078-1 (pa)

"The Viking portable library"

First published 1945

Anthology of the works of Whitman in both poetry and prose, including selections from Leaves of grass, the complete text of Specimen days (1882) and Democratic vistas (1871)

Will, George F.

The morning after; American successes and excesses, 1981-1986. Free Press 1986 430p $24.95; pa $12.95 **818**

ISBN 0-02-934430-1; 0-02-055450-8 (pa)

LC 86-12071

This collection of the author's columns discusses subjects ranging from Gary Hart to modern art to the Baltimore Orioles

Will, George F.—*Continued*
Suddenly; the American idea abroad and at home, 1986-1990. Free Press 1990 429p $19.95; pa $12.95 **818**

ISBN 0-02-934435-2; 0-02-934436-0 (pa)   LC 90-3851

This collection of newspaper columns covers both foreign and domestic issues of the 1980's. Among the topics discussed are: abortion, the Bork nomination, the 1988 presidential election and the collapse of communism

Wilson, Edmund, 1895-1972
The fifties; from notebooks and diaries of the period; edited with an introduction by Leon Edel. Farrar, Straus & Giroux 1986 xxxii, 663p il $25; pa $12.95 **818**

ISBN 0-374-15486-4; 0-374-52066-6 (pa)   LC 86-9997

This installment of the American writer's journals records his travels, family matters, research on literary and historical subjects, and meetings with other writers
Includes bibliographies

The forties; from notebooks and diaries of the period; edited with an introduction by Leon Edel. Farrar, Straus & Giroux 1983 xxviii, 369p il hardcover o.p. paperback available $9.25 **818**

ISBN 0-374-51835-1 (pa)   LC 82-21028

This book records Wilson's assignments for the New Yorker during the decade. Included are notes taken for his travel books as well as more personal reflections

The sixties; the last journal, 1960-1972; edited with an introduction by Lewis Dabney. Farrar, Straus & Giroux 1993 li, 968p il $30 **818**

ISBN 0-374-26554-2   LC 92-16642

In the final volume of the American writer's journals, Wilson discusses travel, his friends, his health and the literary scene during the 1960s
This "journal is at once curiously detached from the 1960s (JFK's assassination gets a single bitter paragraph) and a barometer of that decade's convulsions and of the unraveling of the social fabric. Riddled with passages of great beauty and self-revelation, this hectic daybook is the most wide-ranging of Wilson's journals." Publ Wkly

Upstate; records and recollections of northern New York. Farrar, Straus & Giroux 1971 386p il o.p.; Syracuse Univ. Press paperback available $15.95 **818**

1. Wilson family 2. New York (State)
ISBN 0-8156-2499-9 (pa)

This book opens with historical anecdotes and family reminiscences about persons connected with the development of the area surrounding literary critic Edmund Wilson's ancestral home in the upper New York State community of Talcottville. It continues with selections from his diary-notebook from 1950 to 1970

Wolfe, Tom
Mauve gloves & madmen, clutter & vine, and other stories, sketches and essays; illustrated by the author. Farrar, Straus & Giroux 1976 243p il $18.95; pa $9.95 **818**

ISBN 0-374-20424-1; 0-374-52092-5 (pa)

This collection of short stories, sketches, and essays explores the politics and culture of the 1970s

The purple decades; a reader; selected by Tom Wolfe. Farrar, Straus & Giroux 1982 396p il $17.50 **818**

ISBN 0-374-23927-4   LC 82-11879

"Wolfe comes off as a social anthropologist in this omnibus that he clearly intends as a rounded, tuned-in portrait of our age. His terrain is the subcultures of a fragmented society, their bizarre lifestyles and status rituals, whether among test pilots, hippies, chic artists and their patrons, or the narcissists of the 'me decade,' the '70's." Publ Wkly

820.3 English literature— Encyclopedias and dictionaries

The **Cambridge** guide to English literature; [compiled by] Michael Stapleton; consultant editor: Nicholas Barker. Cambridge Univ. Press 1983 992p il $37.50 **820.3**

1. English literature—Dictionaries 2. English literature—Bio-bibliography 3. American literature—Dictionaries 4. American literature—Bio-bibliography
ISBN 0-521-25647-X   LC 83-1967

"A handbook or 'companion' rather than a 'guide' in the usual bibliographic sense. Includes entries for authors, titles, literary characters, literary terms and movements (although names and titles predominate). Covers English writing of the United States, Australia, Canada, New Zealand, Ireland, and South Africa as well as Great Britain. . . . Articles often include editorial comment as well as factual information. Includes selected living authors." Sheehy. Guide to Ref Books. 10th Edition

The **Cambridge** guide to literature in English; [edited by] Ian Ousby; foreword by Doris Lessing. new ed. Cambridge Univ. Press 1993 1054p il $49.95 **820.3**

1. English literature—Dictionaries 2. English literature—Bio-bibliography 3. American literature—Dictionaries 4. American literature—Bio-bibliography
ISBN 0-521-44086-6   LC 93-7941

This volume covers the English-language literature of India, Africa, the Caribbean, Ireland, Canada, Australia, New Zealand, the United States, and the United Kingdom. It includes entries for authors, titles, movements, genres, poetic forms, critical concepts and literary terms
For a review see: Booklist, April 1, 1994

The **Concise** Oxford companion to English literature; edited by Margaret Drabble and Jenny Stringer. Oxford Univ. Press 1987 631p $24.95 **820.3**

1. English literature—Dictionaries 2. English literature—Bio-bibliography 3. American literature—Dictionaries 4. American literature—Bio-bibliography
ISBN 0-19-866140-1   LC 87-1595

This is an abridgement of the fifth edition of The Oxford companion to English literature, entered below
"More than 5,000 entries illuminate the plots of novels and plays; songs and poems; the lives and works of authors, poets, playwrights, essayists, philosophers, and historians; fictional characters; literary movements; legends; theatres; periodicals." Publisher's note

Dictionary of fictional characters. Completely rev ed, [by] Martin Seymour-Smith. Writer 1992 c1991 598p pa $17.95   **820.3**

1. English literature—Dictionaries 2. American literature—Dictionaries 3. Characters and characteristics in literature—Dictionaries

ISBN 0-87116-166-4   LC 92-5025

First published 1963 under the authorship of William Freeman

This work identifies characters from English and American novels, short stories, poems, plays, and operas. The main section arranges entries alphabetically by name of character giving for each the entrant's relationship to main characters in the work, the title of the work, publication date, and author

The **Oxford** companion to English literature. 5th ed, edited by Margaret Drabble. Oxford Univ. Press 1985 1155p $49.95   **820.3**

1. English literature—Dictionaries 2. English literature—Bio-bibliography 3. American literature—Dictionaries 4. American literature—Bio-bibliography

ISBN 0-19-866130-4   LC 84-27308

First published 1932 under the editorship of Sir Paul Harvey

This reference work "contains over 9,000 entries: some 2,000 plot summaries and outlines of novels, plays, poems, and so forth; over 3,000 concise biographies (for authors born before 1940); entries for literary characters; surveys of literary and artistic movements; and lists of prizes, periodicals, newspapers, and other publications." Nichols. Guide to Ref Books for Sch Media Cent. 4th edition

Wilde, W. H. (William Henry), 1923-

The Oxford companion to Australian literature; [by] William H. Wilde, Joy Hooton, Barry Andrews. Oxford Univ. Press 1985 760p $59; pa $29.95   **820.3**

1. Australian literature—Dictionaries 2. Australian literature—Bio-bibliography

ISBN 0-19-554233-9; 0-19-553273-2 (pa)

    LC 86-146201

This volume contains "entries for authors, literary works, journals, movements, and a few literary characters. Bibliographical information is limited mainly to lists of author's works (with publication dates), and occasional references to biographies of the writers." Sheehy. Guide to Ref Books. 10th edition. suppl

820.8 English literature—Collections

British women writers; an anthology from the fourteenth century to the present; edited by Dale Spender and Janet Todd. Bedrick Bks. 1989 925p $39.95; pa $19.95   **820.8**

1. English literature—Women authors—Collections

ISBN 0-87226-326-6; 0-87226-216-2 (pa) LC 89-6572

This chronologically arranged collection "brings together established literary figures and less familiar writers from the Middle Ages to the present day. . . . The anthology includes poems, plays, short stories, extracts from novels, diaries, letters, autobiography and journalism." Publisher's note

Includes bibliography

The **Norton** anthology of English literature; M. H. Abrams, general editor [et al.] Norton 2v ea $39.95, pa $35.95   **820.8**

1. English literature—Collections

First published 1962. (16th edition 1993) Periodically revised

Contains representative writings of authors which convey the tone and trends of specific literary movements and periods. Both volumes contain explanatory footnotes, selected bibliographies, notes on literary forms and usage, an author-title index, and marginalia glossaries

The **Norton** anthology of literature by women; the tradition in English; [edited by] Sandra M. Gilbert, Susan Gubar. Norton 1985 xxxiv, 2457p $47.50; pa $34.95   **820.8**

1. American literature—Women authors—Collections 2. English literature—Women authors—Collections

ISBN 0-393-01940-3; 0-393-95391-2 (pa)

    LC 84-27276

"From Queen Elizabeth to Alice Walker, the editors have compiled representative selections of prose and poetry reflecting the ongoing attempts of women writers to express the concerns of their sex both in human relationships and in coming to terms with a male-dominated society." Booklist

"Intelligent period introductions focus on historical background and the quality of women's lives and educations. The volume also has biographical headnotes, footnotes, and glosses at the bottom of the page, and bibliographies that suggest texts and sources for study." Libr J

The **Oxford** anthology of Australian literature; edited by Leonie Kramer and Adrian Mitchell. Oxford Univ. Press 1985 589p il $39.95; pa $29.95   **820.8**

1. Australian literature—Collections

ISBN 0-19-554477-3; 0-19-554476-5 (pa)

    LC 85-228185

"This volume surveys Australian poetry and prose from the end of the 18th century to the present. It is intended to represent its range and to document its continuity. It contains samples from early writers such as Henry Lawson and Henry Handel Richardson (Ethel F. Robertson) to modern writers . . . such as Shirley Hazzard and David Malouf. The anthology is divided into four sections, each preceded by a short commentary. The works are presented chronologically within the sections and include biographical data about the writer." Libr J

The **Oxford** anthology of English literature; general editors: Frank Kermode and John Hollander. Oxford Univ. Press 1973 6v in 2 il maps hardcover o.p. paperback available ea $29.95   **820.8**

1. English literature—Collections

ISBN 0-19-501657-2 (v1); 0-19-501658-0 (v2)

Each of the six parts collected here were published separately and are available in paperback at prices indicated below

Contents: v1 The Middle Ages through the eighteenth century: Medieval English literature, edited by J. B. Trapp $19.95 (ISBN 0-19-501624-6); The literature of Renaissance England, edited by John Hollander and Frank Kermode $19.95 (ISBN 0-19-501637-8); The

The Oxford anthology of English literature
—*Continued*
Restoration and the eighteenth century, edited by Martin Price $19.95 (ISBN 0-19-501614-9); v2 1800 to the present: Romantic poetry and prose, edited by Harold Bloom and Lionel Trilling $19.95 (ISBN 0-19-501615-7); Victorian prose and poetry, edited by Lionel Trilling and Harold Bloom $18.95 (ISBN 0-19-501616-5); Modern British literature, edited by Frank Kermode and John Hollander $19.95 (ISBN 0-19-501652-1)

The Oxford anthology of English literature: major authors edition; general editors: Frank Kermode and John Hollander. Oxford Univ. Press 1975 2v il maps pa v1 $13.95, v2 $18.95 **820.8**
1. English literature—Collections
Contents: v1 From Beowulf to Johnson (ISBN 0-19-501900-8); v2 From Blake to Auden (ISBN 0-19-501901-6)
"This edition of the Oxford Anthology of English literature [entered above] is not merely an abridgement. . . . Thirty authors from the 'Beowulf'-poet to W. H. Auden have been selected from the larger version, but significant additions have been made so that the student may have access to a broader range of material by several of these figures." Preface to the Major authors edition
Includes bibliography

The Oxford book of late medieval verse and prose; edited by Douglas Gray; with a note on grammar and spelling in the fifteenth century by Norman Davis. Oxford Univ. Press 1989 xxi, 586p $45; pa $13.95 **820.8**
1. Literature, Medieval—Collections 2. English literature—Collections
ISBN 0-19-812452-X; 0-19-282245-4 (pa)
LC 88-23263
An anthology of English prose and poetry from the beginning of the 15th century to 1525
Includes bibliographic references

820.9 English literature—History and criticism

Donoghue, Denis
England, their England; commentaries on English language and literature. Knopf 1988 365p $24.95 **820.9**
1. English literature—History and criticism
ISBN 0-394-56473-1
LC 87-40482
Also available in paperback from University of Calif. Press
Analyzed in Essay and general literature index
Authors analyzed in this collection include Shakespeare, Swift, Wilde, Wyndham Lewis and T. S. Eliot

We Irish; essays on Irish literature and society. Knopf 1986 275p o.p.; University of Calif. Press paperback available $12 **820.9**
1. Irish literature—History and criticism
ISBN 0-520-06425-9 (pa)
LC 86-45266
Analyzed in Essay and general literature index

"Donoghue here combines three . . . essays with 25 scholarly pieces and review articles. . . . Following sections of four essays each on Yeats and Joyce, there is one on social and political occurrences, and a last one offering a dozen lively assessments of Irish writers." Choice

Ellmann, Richard, 1918-1987
Four Dubliners; Wilde, Yeats, Joyce, and Beckett. Braziller 1987 c1986 122p il $12.95; pa $6.95 **820.9**
1. Yeats, W. B. (William Butler), 1865-1939 2. Wilde, Oscar, 1854-1900 3. Joyce, James, 1882-1941 4. Beckett, Samuel, 1906-1989
ISBN 0-8076-1185-9; 0-8076-1208-1 (pa)
LC 87-13245
In four critical essays, first delivered as lectures at the Library of Congress, the author examines aspects of the lives and work of four twentieth-century writers
"Ellmann's poised vision of these four: Beckett denying, Joyce affirming, Yeats ranging from pole to pole, Wilde yoking contraries, is a stellar example of the 'double vision' in which literary criticism and biography are partners rather than rivals." Christ Sci Monit

The Feminist companion to literature in English; women writers from the Middle Ages to the present; [edited by] Virginia Blain, Patricia Clements, Isobel Grundy. Yale Univ. Press 1990 1231p $49.95 **820.9**
1. English literature—Women authors—Bio-bibliography 2. American literature—Women authors—Bio-bibliography
ISBN 0-300-04854-8
LC 90-70515
"Over 2,700 biographical entries, most of about 500 words, seek to set each writer in the context of her time and to intimate her relevance to us today." Am Libr
For a fuller review see: Booklist, Jan. 1, 1991

Heilbrun, Carolyn G., 1926-
Hamlet's mother and other women. Columbia Univ. Press 1990 266p (Gender and culture) $34.50 **820.9**
1. English literature—Women authors—History and criticism 2. American literature—Women authors—History and criticism 3. Feminism 4. Women in literature
ISBN 0-231-07176-0
LC 89-49208
Also available in paperback from Ballantine Bks.
Analyzed in Essay and general literature index
"In this collection of essays and speeches advocating the application of feminist criticism to the canon of English literature, Heilbrun . . . also offers an acute view of the politics of academia. . . . Calling upon such related fields as psychology and semiotics, she focuses on the lives and writings of Virginia Woolf and James Joyce, E.M. Forster, Vera Brittain, May Sarton and others." Publ Wkly
Includes bibliographic references

Kenner, Hugh
A colder eye; the modern Irish writers. Knopf 1983 301p o.p.; Johns Hopkins Univ. Press paperback available $12.95 **820.9**
1. English literature—History and criticism
ISBN 0-8018-3838-X (pa)
LC 82-48723

Kenner, Hugh—*Continued*
This critical history of Irish literary modernism focuses on the works of Joyce, Beckett, Synge and Yeats

A sinking island; the modern English writers. Knopf 1988 290p $22.95 **820.9**
1. English literature—History and criticism
ISBN 0-394-54254-1   LC 87-45131
Also available in paperback from Johns Hopkins Univ. Press
This survey of major 20th-century British writers includes studies of Conrad, Woolf, Eliot and Lawrence
"As we've come to expect from this master critic, [this] is a perceptive, profoundly learned, and highly readable book about literature that is itself a work of stellar literary quality." Quill Quire

Modern British literature; compiled and edited by Ruth Z. Temple, Martin Tucker. Ungar 1966-1985 5v (Lib. of literary criticism) v1-3 set $225, v4-5 ea $75
820.9
1. English literature—History and criticism
ISBN v1-3 0-8044-3275-9; v4 0-8044-3279-1; v5 0-8044-3140-X
Contents: v1 A-G; v2 H-P; v3 R-Z; v4 Supplement, compiled and edited by Martin Tucker and Rita Stein; v5 Second supplement, compiled and edited by Denis Lane and Rita Stein
"For each of the authors included, excerpts from criticism have been chosen to describe his qualities, define his status, indicate, if he is well known, something of his life and personality." Introduction
The supplementary volume brings criticism up to date on approximately one-third of the authors entered in the 3 main volumes. The second supplementary volume brings criticism up to date covering the years 1975 onward. Each of the 5 volumes includes bibliographies and an index to critics

The **New** Moulton's library of literary criticism; general editor, Harold Bloom. Chelsea House 1985-1990 11v (Chelsea House lib. of literary criticism) set $770
820.9
1. Criticism   2. English literature—History   and criticism 3. American literature—History and criticism
ISBN 0-87754-778-5
Individual volumes also available separately at $70 each
Replaces The Library of literary criticism of English and American authors (also known as Moulton's library of literary criticism) and The Library of literary criticism of English and American authors through the beginning of the twentieth century
"Both abridges and updates earlier Moulton's collections providing excerpts from criticism written before the 20th century concerning 532 authors and anonymous works written from the 8th century up to 1904. Entries, which include biographies as well as critical information, are arranged chronologically by death date within each volume. Figures covered include nonliterary authors, such as Thomas Jefferson and Charles Darwin." Sheehy. Guide to Ref Books. 10th edition. suppl

The **Oxford** history of Australian literature; edited by Leonie Kramer; with contributions by Adrian Mitchell [et al.] Oxford Univ. Press 1981 509p $59
820.9
1. Australian literature—History and criticism
ISBN 0-19-550590-5   LC 81-162174
"The major sections of this history—those on fiction, drama, and poetry—are written by Adrian Mitchell, Terry Sturm, and Vivian Smith, respectively. . . . Lists of general secondary material plus separate bibliographies for 78 writers . . . occupy 60 pages. The index includes authors, titles of longer works, and some thematic headings." Choice

The **Oxford** illustrated history of English literature; edited by Pat Rogers. Oxford Univ. Press 1987 528p il maps $45; pa $18.95 **820.9**
1. English literature—History and criticism
ISBN 0-19-812816-9; 0-19-282728-6 (pa) LC 86-8507
"Covers the whole range of English literature from Anglo-Saxon times to the present day. Contributors are eminent scholars and writers in their respective periods. It is generously illustrated in color and black-and-white, with pictures chosen to illuminate and supplement the text, and includes suggestions for further reading, maps, and a table of important dates." Univ Press Books for Public Libr

Powell, Anthony, 1905-
Miscellaneous verdicts; writings on writers, 1946-1989. University of Chicago Press 1992 501p $34.95 **820.9**
1. English literature—History and criticism 2. American literature—History and criticism
ISBN 0-226-67710-9   LC 92-7756
"These mostly short pieces by the author of the sequence of novels called *A Dance to the Music of Time* are addicting: knowledgeable yet easygoing and graceful, always focusing on interesting or useful information, and wittily understated." Libr J
Includes bibliographic references

Woolf, Virginia, 1882-1941
The second common reader. Harcourt Brace & Co. 1932 295p hardcover o.p. paperback available $7.95 **820.9**
1. English literature—History and criticism
ISBN 0-15-619808-8 (pa)
Analyzed in Essay and general literature index
Published in the United Kingdom with title: The common reader. Second series
Twenty-two essays on a variety of books and their authors—from William Hazlitt to Thomas Hardy, from John Donne to Robinson Crusoe

Women and writing; edited and with an introduction by Michèle Barrett. Harcourt Brace & Co. 1980 c1979 198p pa $8.95
820.9
1. English literature—Women authors—History and criticism
ISBN 0-15-693658-5   LC 79-3371
Also available in hardcover from P. Smith
First published 1979 in the United Kingdom

Woolf, Virginia, 1882-1941—*Continued*
"The selection of essays, reviews, and extracts from longer works presented here manifests the effortless, light intelligence that has awed and enthralled readers since the early decades of this century. The introduction by Michèle Barrett is interesting." Booklist

Yeats, W. B. (William Butler), 1865-1939
Letters to the new island; edited by George Bornstein and Hugh Witemeyer. Macmillan 1990 c1989 xxi, 200p il (Collected works of W. B. Yeats, v7) $29.95 **820.9**

1. Irish literature—History and criticism
ISBN 0-02-513722-0   LC 88-27366
First published 1989 in the United Kingdom

This book contains twenty-one "prose pieces Yeats published between 1888 and 1892 in two American newspapers—the Boston Pilot and the Providence Sunday Journal. The pieces are reviews and brief essays on Irish literature and folklore." Libr J

821 English poetry

Auden, W. H. (Wystan Hugh), 1907-1973
Collected poems; edited by Edward Mendelson. Vintage Bks. 1991 xxvii, 926p pa $22.50 **821**
ISBN 0-679-73197-0   LC 91-158031
Originally published in hardcover in different form by Random House in 1976

A compilation of all the poems Auden wished to preserve, in his final revisions. Previous collected editions and later shorter poems are included. There is also an absurdist play written 1928: Paid on both sides

Thank you, fog; last poems. Random House 1974 61p $8.95 **821**
ISBN 0-394-49496-2
Arranged by the poet himself mostly from pieces completed from 1972, when Auden returned to England, to September 1973 when he died in Austria, this collection also includes two lyrics written in 1963-1964 from his libretto for Don Quixote and an antimasque coauthored with Chester Kallman: The Entertainment of the senses

Blake, William, 1757-1827
The complete writings of William Blake; with variant readings; edited by Geoffrey Keynes. [new ed]. Oxford Univ. Press 1966 944p (Oxford standard authors) $39.95; pa $17.95 **821**
ISBN 0-19-254157-9; 0-19-281050-2 (pa)
First published 1957
Blake's "poetry deals in the subtlest kind of symbolism with a skill that cannot be matched. His philosophy is a series of intuitive flights into the realm of the Absolute, soaring with tranquil and imperious assurance; to our minds they are presented as a group of strange, complicated symbols, which to Blake are the clearest, most familiar realities." Legouis and Cazamian's Hist of Eng Lit

The essential Blake; selected and with an introduction by Stanley Kunitz. Ecco Press 1987 92p (Essential poets, v4) hardcover o.p. paperback available $6 **821**
ISBN 0-88001-139-4 (pa)   LC 86-24087
The editor has selected the poems he feels provide the best introduction to Blake's craft

Songs of innocence and of experience; shewing the two contrary states of the human soul 1789-1794; [by] W. Blake. Oxford Univ. Press 1977 155p il hardcover o.p. paperback available $11.95 **821**
ISBN 0-19-281089-8 (pa)   LC 78-300013
Songs of innocence was first published 1789; Songs of experience 1794

"Two series of poems. . . . The first group exults in the omnipresence of divine love and sympathy, even in face of sorrow; the second group, gloomy in tone, opposes the first and deals with the power of evil. Innocence and experience are two opposing states of the human soul; the poems of one group are set against the poems of the other. . . . Often the same subject is treated in each group, as in 'The Chimney Sweeper' and 'A Little Boy Lost.'" Reader's Ency. 3d edition

Brontë, Emily, 1818-1848
The complete poems of Emily Jane Brontë; edited from the manuscripts by C. W. Hatfield. Columbia Univ. Press 1941 xxi, 262p $39.50 **821**
ISBN 0-231-01222-5
A re-editing of the complete poems of Emily Brontë, based on all the known manuscripts. About half of the 193 poems are those belonging to the so-called Gondal cycle

Browning, Elizabeth Barrett, 1806-1861
The poetical works of Elizabeth Barrett Browning; with a new introduction by Ruth M. Adams. Houghton Mifflin 1974 xxii, 548p $39 **821**
ISBN 0-395-18012-0
"Cambridge editions"
First published 1900 with title: The complete poetical works of Elizabeth Barrett Browning

This collection "does not carry a full biographical sketch of Elizabeth Barrett Browning. . . . Rather the Introduction identifies that part of the poetry which has proved of lasting value or interest, considers two major achievements, 'Sonnets from the Portuguese' and 'Aurora Leigh,' and estimates the place that Elizabeth Barrett Browning may be expected to claim in a reader's attention and in poetic evaluation." Editor's note

Sonnets from the Portuguese **821**
Hardcover and paperback editions available from various publishers

A series of sonnets which "were written during a period of seven years and are considered by some scholars to have been inspired by her love for her husband [poet Robert Browning]." New Century Handb of Engl Lit

Browning, Robert, 1812-1889

The poetical works of Robert Browning; with a new introduction by G. Robert Stange. Houghton Mifflin 1974 1032p $40
821

ISBN 0-395-18485-1
"Cambridge editions"
Based on the 1895 Cambridge edition, The complete poetic and dramatic works of Robert Browning, this book also contains a chronology of Browning's life, notes, index of first lines, and an essay on Shelley

Robert Browning's poetry; authoritative texts, criticism; selected and edited by James F. Loucks. Norton 1980 c1979 604p hardcover o.p. paperback available $14.95
821

ISBN 0-393-09092-2 (pa)   LC 79-10295
"A Norton critical edition"
"Editor Loucks has chosen wisely from Browning's prodigious output (filling 12 volumes in the 'complete' edition), with selections covering the early 'experimental phase' as well as the interesting, though less studied, years of 'later achievement,' but with a greater part of his emphasis upon the poet's middle and major period (1855-69)." Booklist

Includes bibliography

Burns, Robert, 1759-1796

The poetical works of Burns; edited by Raymond Bentman. Houghton Mifflin 1974 xxxii, 414p $39
821

ISBN 0-395-18486-X
"Cambridge editions"
First published 1897 with title: Complete poetical works of Robert Burns
"The greatest of Scottish lyrical poets and song writers. He wrote mainly in dialect. His poems show warm passions and sympathies, and an intense love for man and nature." Pratt Alcove

Byron, George Gordon Byron, 6th Baron, 1788-1824

Don Juan   **821**

Hardcover and paperback editions available from various publishers
"'Don Juan,' begun in 1819, was still unfinished when Byron died. This sixteen-thousand-line poem in sixteen cantos was continually added to by the poet, and as such it can be read as a contemporaneous account of the author's moods and feelings. Byron used 'Don Juan' as a platform to express many of his sardonic opinions of people and events. The protagonist is, of course, Byron himself, only thinly disguised as the famous Spanish rake." Reader's Ency. 3d edition

The poetical works of Byron; revised and with a new introduction by Robert F. Gleckner. Houghton Mifflin 1975 xxvi, 1051p $39
821

ISBN 0-395-20431-3
"Cambridge editions"
First published 1905 with title: The complete poetical works of Lord Byron

The poems are arranged in groups: "Childe Harold's Pilgrimage"; Shorter poems; Satires; Tales, chiefly Oriental; Italian poems; Dramas; "Don Juan" which are in general chronological order. Within each of these groups, the poems are arranged by date of composition, or if this is unknown, by date of publication

Campbell, Roy, 1901-1957

The selected poems of Roy Campbell; chosen by Peter Alexander. Oxford Univ. Press 1982 131p $24.95   **821**

ISBN 0-19-211946-X   LC 81-22338
South African Campbell's "best poetry has a lyrical intensity unique among English-language poets of the 20th c. Neither his sensibility nor his models were British. His early enthusiasm for Elizabethan and Jacobean verse does inform his poetry, but the major influences on his work are French. . . . The combination of these elements gives his best poems a distinctive, ringing certainty of tone, a vividness of imagery, and an insistent energy." Ency of World Lit in the 20th Century

Chaucer, Geoffrey, d. 1400

The Canterbury tales   **821**

Hardcover and paperback editions available from various publishers
"A collection of twenty-four stories, all but two of which are in verse, written by Geoffrey Chaucer mainly between 1386 and his death in 1400. The stories are supposed to be related by members of a company of thirty-one pilgrims (including the poet himself) who are on their way to the shrine of St. Thomas at Canterbury. The prologue which tells of their assembly at the Tabard Inn in Southwark and their arrangement that each shall tell two stories on the way to Canterbury and two on the return journey, is a remarkable picture of English social life in the fourteenth century, inasmuch as every class is represented from the gentlefolks to the peasantry." Keller. Reader's Dig of Books

The complete poetry and prose of Geoffrey Chaucer; edited by John H. Fisher. 2nd ed. Harcourt Brace & Co. 1989 1040p il $54.75   **821**

ISBN 0-03-028612-3   LC 88-29400
First published 1977
Contents: Canterbury tales; Troylus and Criseyde; Book of the Duchess; Parliament of fowls; House of fame; Legend of good women; Short poems; Romaunt of the rose; Boece; Treatise on the astrolabe, and Equatorie of the planets

Includes bibliography

The portable Chaucer; selected, translated and edited by Theodore Morrison. rev ed. Viking 1975 611p o.p.; Penguin Bks. paperback available $8.95   **821**

ISBN 0-14-015081-1 (pa)
"The Viking portable library"
First published 1949
Contains Troilus and Cressida, The Canterbury tales, selections from The book of the duchess and The bird's parliament, and some short verse

Includes bibliography

Coleridge, Samuel Taylor, 1772-1834

The poems of Samuel Taylor Coleridge; including poems and versions of poems herein published for the first time; edited with textual and bibliographical notes by Ernest Hartley Coleridge. Oxford Univ. Press 1957 c1912 xxiii, 614p (Oxford standard authors) $35; pa $18.95 **821**

ISBN 0-19-254120-X; 0-19-281051-0 (pa)

First published 1912

"Of all that is purest and most ethereal in the romantic spirit, [Coleridge's] poetry is the most finished, the supreme embodiment." Camb Hist of Engl Lit

Coward, Noel

The lyrics of Noël Coward. Overlook Press 1973 c1965 418p $25; pa $12.95 **821**

ISBN 0-87951-197-4; 0-87951-187-7 (pa)

This is a reprint of a title first published 1965 in the United Kingdom

Arranged by the decades in which they were written, this book includes the lyrics to songs by Noël Coward spanning from the 1920's to the 1960's

Critical essays on Robert Browning; edited by Mary Ellis Gibson. Hall, G.K. & Co. 1992 275p il (Critical essays on British literature) $40 **821**

1. Browning, Robert, 1812-1889

ISBN 0-8161-8861-0 LC 91-47110

Scholars assess the life and work of the influential English poet

Includes bibliographic references

Critical essays on W.B. Yeats; [edited by] Richard J. Finneran. Hall, G.K. & Co. 1986 258p (Critical essays on modern British literature) $40 **821**

1. Yeats, W. B. (William Butler), 1865-1939

ISBN 0-8161-8758-4 LC 85-30207

"The volume is composed of essays by 14 leading Yeats scholars. . . . The text is supplemented by an annotated bibliography of earlier collections and a review of book-length studies on Yeats in general or his poetry, but (unfortunately) not his plays." Booklist

Donne, John, 1572-1631

The poems of John Donne; edited by Herbert J. C. Grierson. Oxford Univ. Press 1933 460p hardcover o.p. paperback available $16.95 **821**

ISBN 0-19-281113-4 (pa)

In verse John Donne "wrote satires, epistles, elegies, and miscellaneous poems, distinguished by wit, profundity of thought and erudition, passion and subtlety, coupled with a certain roughness of form. . . . He was the greatest of the writers of 'metaphysical' poetry, in which passion is interwoven with reasoning." Oxford Companion to Engl Lit

Ewart, Gavin

The Gavin Ewart show; selected poems, 1939-1985. Bits Press 1986 140p $14.95; pa $8.95 **821**

ISBN 0-933248-05-9; 0-933248-06-7 (pa)

LC 87-108748

A selection from The collected Ewart (1980), The new Ewart (1982), and The young pobble's guide to his toes (1985)

"A clever, lively, often extremely funny writer . . . his work is a display case of inventiveness and adaptation." N Y Times Book Rev

Gardner, John, 1933-1982

The poetry of Chaucer. Southern Ill. Univ. Press 1977 xxxv, 408p hardcover o.p. paperback available $19.95 **821**

1. Chaucer, Geoffrey, d. 1400

ISBN 0-8093-0871-1 (pa) LC 76-22713

Gardner "surveys Chaucer's verse from the early Book of the Duchess, moving chronologically through the 'minor poems' and Troilus, and ending with five chapters on the Canterbury Tales." Libr J

Includes bibliographic references

Gunn, Thom

Selected poems, 1950-1975. Farrar, Straus & Giroux 1979 131p $12.95 **821**

ISBN 0-374-25865-1 LC 79-9158

"Gunn's selections from six of his books give a solid representation of each stage of his development—from cerebral, taut, formal early pieces in 'Fighting terms' (1958) to relaxed, prosy-sounding, but carefully controlled freer forms in 'Jack Straw's castle' (1977)." Choice

Hardy, Thomas, 1840-1928

The complete poems of Thomas Hardy; edited by James Gibson. Macmillan 1978 c1976 xxxvi, 1002p il hardcover o.p. paperback available $23 **821**

ISBN 0-02-069600-0 (pa) LC 77-15579

First published 1976 in the United Kingdom

"With inclusion of 29 previously uncollected poems, such as 'Domicilium,' six of 'The dynasts' extracts (which Hardy treated as poetic entities in his 1916 Selected poems), and deathbed epigraphs for G. K. Chesterton and George Moore, Gibson has produced a volume that should serve as the standard edition for many years. This edition offers minor corrections (such as identations, stanza breaks, word revisions) of the 1930 'Collected poems,' which it now supersedes. Title and first-line indexes help readers find particular poems quickly." Choice

Heaney, Seamus

The haw lantern. Farrar, Straus & Giroux 1987 51p $12.95; pa $7.95 **821**

ISBN 0-374-16837-7; 0-374-52109-3 (pa)

LC 87-17705

"Mr. Heaney is a poet of excision; he knows just what to leave out in order to let the reader in. . . . 'Clearances,' along with his earlier 'Glanmore Sonnets,' rescues an outworn form from cliché and stands among the best sonnet sequences written in English in this century. Some half a dozen poems here signal a new direc-

Heaney, Seamus—*Continued*

tion. These are 'allegories,' in which Mr. Heaney grapples with abstraction in a way he has not previously attempted." N Y Times Book Rev

Seeing things. Farrar, Straus & Giroux 1991 107p $18.95; pa $8 **821**

ISBN 0-374-25776-0; 0-374-52389-4 (pa)

LC 91-21669

This volume is "divided into two sections. Part One is mostly elegiac. The poet listens to Philip Larkin's shade quoting Dante, summons up his 'undrowned' father walking into the yard ('His step unguided, his ghosthood immanent'), and lovingly recalls a host of dead friends. . . . 'Squarings,' [forms] the second half and principal glory of the volume. This highly symmetrical, solidly rigged poem consists of 48 12-line poems arranged in four sections of equal length, each proposing a dominant metaphorical and meditative terrain." N Y Times Book Rev

Selected poems, 1966-1987. Farrar, Straus & Giroux 1990 273p $30; pa $15 **821**

ISBN 0-374-25868-6; 0-374-52280-4 (pa)

This collection "offers an ample selection of some of the best work by one of our finest contemporary poets. The collection emphasizes his recent efforts, although it does not include any new poems. Readers will savor the author's rich Irish-English vocabulary, the sinuous power of his line, and his distinctive music." Libr J

Station Island. Farrar, Straus & Giroux 1985 123p $20; pa $12 **821**

ISBN 0-374-26978-5; 0-374-51935-8 (pa)

LC 84-21067

This collection is "divided into three parts: an opening section of lyric poems; . . . a central sequence inspired by Dante; and a concluding section in which the mythological Irish king Sweeney appears to observe contemporary Ireland, its literary life in particular." New Repub

"As always reading Heaney, the poems offer deep poetic satisfactions. The music is immediately recognizable as his own in its density and resonance. His metrics are varied and complicated, his ear flawless and bold. This is a book of immense conscience and mastery." Wilson Libr Bull

Hopkins, Gerard Manley, 1844-1889

The poems of Gerard Manley Hopkins. 4th ed. Oxford Univ. Press 1967 lxvi, 362p $39.95; pa $16.95 **821**

ISBN 0-19-500164-8; 0-19-281094-4 (pa)

First published 1918 in the United Kingdom; 1948 in the United States

"Based on the first edition of 1918 and enlarged to incorporate all known poems and fragments; edited with additional notes, a foreword on the revised text, and a new biographical and critical introduction by W. H. Gardner and N. H. Mackenzie." Title page

This book brings together all the poems, including the early verses first published in the poet's "Journals and Papers" (1959), the remainder of his Latin verse together with translations into English of all the Latin poems which are entirely original compositions

Housman, A. E. (Alfred Edward), 1859-1936

The collected poems of A. E. Housman. Holt & Co. 1965 254p pa $10.95 **821**

ISBN 0-8050-0547-1

Also available in hardcover from Amereon

This anthology "constitutes the authorized canon of A. E. Housman's verse as established in 1939." Note on the text

Hughes, Ted, 1930-

Crow: from the life and songs of the crow. Harper & Row 1971 84p hardcover o.p. paperback available $12 **821**

ISBN 0-06-090905-6 (pa)

Crow "is one of those rare books of poetry that have the public impact of a major novel. . . . In the figure of Crow, the 40-year-old English poet creates a shocking synthesis of the life-force and the death-force." Newsweek

New selected poems. Harper & Row 1982 242p hardcover o.p. paperback available $15 **821**

ISBN 0-06-090925-0 (pa)

LC 80-8207

"Nearly half of this book is a reprint of Hughes' 'Selected Poems, 1957-1967' [o.p.]; the rest is drawn from his brilliant fourth collection , 'Crow' [entered above], and from five other books published in the past decade—more than 150 pieces all together, but no new, previously unpublished poems." Libr J

Wolfwatching. Farrar, Straus & Giroux 1990 c1989 66p $18.95; pa $9 **821**

ISBN 0-374-29199-3; 0-374-52325-8 (pa)

First published 1989 in the United Kingdom

This collection by England's Poet Laureate contains animal poems, dream sequences and poems about his family and his Yorkshire past

John Dryden; edited and with an introduction by Harold Bloom. Chelsea House 1987 234p (Modern critical views) $29.95 **821**

1. Dryden, John, 1631-1700

ISBN 1-55546-277-4

LC 86-34306

A collection of twelve critical essays on the work of Dryden, arranged in chronological order of original publication

Includes bibliography

Jonson, Ben, 1573?-1637

The complete poems; edited by George Parfitt. Yale Univ. Press 1982 634p (English poets, 12) o.p.; Penguin Bks. paperback available $10.95 **821**

ISBN 0-14-042277-3 (pa)

LC 81-15948

Jonson's "poetry, notable for its balance, its control, its unadorned simplicity that is not without lyricism, prefigured the later lyrics of the 17th-century Cavalier poets, the 'sons of Ben.'" Reader's Ency. 3d edition

Keats, John, 1795-1821
Poetical works; edited by H. W. Garrod. Oxford Univ. Press 1956 xxviii, 477p (Oxford standard authors) hardcover o.p. paperback available $16.95 **821**

ISBN 0-19-281067-7 (pa)

"Probably the most talented of the English romantic poets, Keats wrote a surprisingly large body of poetry before his early death. Practically all the finished poems of the 1818-19 group are the work of a mature poet, and a few of them, such as the magnificent 'To Autumn,' are among the finest examples of English lyric poetry." Reader's Ency. 3d edition

Kipling, Rudyard, 1865-1936
Complete verse; definitive edition. Doubleday 1989 c1940 850p $24.95; pa $15 **821**

ISBN 0-385-26088-1; 0-385-26089-X (pa) LC 88-7364

Replaces Rudyard Kipling's verse: definitive edition, published 1940

This edition includes all of Kipling's published poetry and, in addition, more than 20 poems which have not previously appeared in the inclusive edition of his verse

Langland, William, 1330?-1400?
Piers Plowman **821**

Hardcover and paperback editions available from various publishers

This Middle English poem is "written in 'Alliterative Verse' like Old English poetry and uses a deliberately rustic and archaic dialect. It is an allegorical moral and social satire, written as a 'vision' of the common medieval type." Reader's Ency. 3d edition

Larkin, Philip
Collected poems; edited with an introduction by Anthony Thwaite. Farrar, Straus & Giroux 1989 330p $30; pa $14.95 **821**

ISBN 0-374-12623-2; 0-374-12623-2 (pa) LC 88-83528

"'Larkin's poetry is a bit too easily resigned to grimness don't you think?' Elizabeth Bishop once wrote to Robert Lowell. It is true that his range is narrow, but within its confines is a beguiling variety of tones and forms. He never repeats himself to make the same point, and his poems are more readily memorized than those of almost any other postwar poet. . . . And when most of the flashier, more blustery contemporary literature has passed away, his poetry—ghostly, heartbreaking, exhilarating—will continue to haunt." N Y Times Book Rev

Lewis, C. S. (Clive Staples), 1898-1963
Narrative poems; edited by Walter Hooper. Harcourt Brace Jovanovich 1972 c1969 hardcover o.p. paperback available $4.95 **821**

ISBN 0-15-665327-3 (pa)

First published 1969 in the United Kingdom

"The four long narrative poems which comprise this collection reveal the romantic longing that Lewis says in the preface haunted him from the age of six. *Dymer*, nearly 100 pages in length, recounts the story of a monster who murders his father and becomes a god. The subjects of the other poems reflect Lewis' attachment to Arthurian legend, to Utopias, and to the techniques of Anglo-Saxon verse." Libr J

Longley, Michael, 1939-
Gorse fires. Wake Forest Univ. Press 1991 51p $11.95; pa $6.95 **821**

ISBN 0-916390-49-7; 0-916390-48-9 (pa)

LC 91-72021

This poetic sequence "addresses Irish issues through sustained allusions to epic poems. Interspersed among the poems are seven translations from the second half of the 'Odyssey,' including the recognition scenes involving Odysseus, his wife, Penelope, his father, Laertes, his nurse and his dog. The political position of 'Gorse Fires' . . . shows in the rearrangement of Homers episodes." N Y Times Book Rev

Mahon, Derek, 1941-
Selected poems. Viking 1991 194p $20 **821**

ISBN 0-670-83575-7 LC 91-118111

"Published in association with Oxford University Press"

"Derek Mahon is a key Northern Irish poet trying to 'achieve a synthesis/ Of the archaic and the entirely new.' The stately, measured quality of his verse often belies its discordant subject, the essential dislocation and cultural estrangement at the heart of his enterprise. . . . There is a highly traveled quality to these poems as the poet moves between places, continually turning away from and then back toward his divided country." N Y Times Book Rev

Milton, John, 1608-1674
Complete poetical works; edited by Douglas Bush. Houghton Mifflin 1965 xxxiii, 570p $43.95; pa $8.95 **821**

ISBN 0-395-05574-1; 0-395-07493-2 (pa)

"Cambridge editions"

"Every form that Milton attempted—the masque, the elegy, the sonnet, the long epic, the short epic, the verse drama—seemingly achieved its potentiality at his hands. And distinguishable as Milton's various periods might be from each other, each is unmistakably 'Miltonic,' an epithet suggesting a standard of poetic power and intellect never since challenged." Coll & Adult Read List

Paradise lost **821**

Hardcover and paperback editions available from various publishers

Written ca. 1667

"The only completed sucessful epic in English, a treatment of the Fall ostensibly so as to 'justify the ways of God to men' but in fact so as to illuminate the paradoxes and contraditions of man's condition and the currents of hope, despair and chastened resolve that stirred in Milton's own breast." Penguin Companion to Engl Lit

Muldoon, Paul

Madoc; a mystery. Farrar, Straus & Giroux 1991 261p $19.95; pa $12 **821**

ISBN 0-374-19557-9; 0-374-52344-4 (pa)

LC 90-27876

This poetic "tale of what might have happened if Coleridge had really established his utopia in America, by one of Ireland's best poets, is filled with characteristic Muldoonish pranks that will amuse and puzzle readers." N Y Times Book Rev

Pearl (Middle English poem)

Pearl **821**

Hardcover and paperback editions available from various publishers

One of the greatest works of Middle English poetry, this 14th century poetic romance by the anonymous Pearl Poet tells how the poet loses a beautiful white pearl which symbolizes both the loss of his two-year-old daughter and of theological purity or grace. He dreams of encountering his loved one as a pearl-bedecked maiden who has become one of the mystical brides of Christ and awakens with renewed spiritual strength after being granted a glimpse of her new abode, the New Jerusalem (Heaven)

Pope, Alexander, 1688-1744

The poetical works of Alexander Pope **821**

Various editions available. Variant title: The poems of Alexander Pope

"Pope's metrical skill was apparent very early in his 'Pastorals' (1709), which he said he wrote when he was sixteen. Known for its skillful use of the heroic, or closed, couplet, his poetry is characterized by technical finish, invective, and wit; it is satiric, epigrammatic, and didactic." Reader's Ency. 3d edition

Rossetti, Christina Georgina, 1830-1894

The complete poems of Christina Rossetti; edited, with textual notes and introductions, by R. W. Crump. a variorum ed. Louisiana State Univ. Press 1979-1986 2v il v1 $37.50; v2 $40 **821**

ISBN 0-8071-0358-6 (v1); 0-8071-1246-1 (v2)

LC 78-5571

First two volumes of a projected three volume set

"Three kinds of material will be included: poems published in various collections of hers; uncollected, individually published verse; and work that has remained in manuscript form. For the first time, the poetry will appear in critical texts, with a full list of variants, including punctuation, from all authoritative sources." Choice

Rossetti is "known for her ballads and her mystic religious lyrics, marked by symbolism, vividness of detail, and intensity of feeling." Reader's Ency. 3d edition

Rossetti, Dante Gabriel, 1828-1882

The essential Rossetti; selected and with an introduction by John Hollander. Ecco Press 1990 c1989 159p (Essential poets) pa $6 **821**

ISBN 0-88001-196-3

LC 88-27314

"This selection contains all of Rossetti's major poetry, including ecphrastic sonnets . . . ballads, *The House of Life* complete, the whole of *A Trip to Paris and Belgium* (never before reprinted), and a wealth of others." Introduction

Shakespeare, William, 1564-1616

Sonnets **821**

Hardcover and paperback editions available from various publishers

"A series of 154 sonnets by Shakespeare. Probably composed between 1593 and 1601, they are written in the form of three quatrains and a couplet that has come to be known as Shakespearean. Influenced by, and often reacting against, the popular sonnet cycles of the time, notably Sir Philip Sidney's 'Astrophel and Stella', Shakespeare's sonnets are among the finest examples of their kind." Reader's Ency. 3d edition

Shelley, Percy Bysshe, 1792-1822

The poetical works of Percy Bysshe Shelley; edited by Newell F. Ford. Houghton Mifflin 1975 704p $24.95 **821**

ISBN 0-395-18461-4

"Cambridge editions"

"A poetry of sheer beauty with urgent messages to all mankind." Good Read

Shelley's poetry and prose; authoritative texts, criticism; selected and edited by Donald H. Reiman and Sharon B. Powers. Norton 1977 700p pa $15.95 **821**

ISBN 0-393-09164-3

LC 76-26929

"A Norton critical edition"

"This edition includes all of Shelley's greatest poetry and other poems frequently taught or discussed . . . as well as three of his most important prose works." Preface

Includes bibliography

Smith, Stevie, 1902-1971

Collected poems; edited with a preface by James MacGibbon. New Directions 1983 591p il pa $16.95 **821**

ISBN 0-8112-0882-6

LC 83-43008

First published 1975 in the United Kingdom

Smith "wrote three novels, but has been more widely recognized for her witty, caustic, and enigmatic verse, much of it illustrated by her own comic drawings." Concise Oxford Companion to Engl Lit

Soyinka, Wole

Mandela's earth and other poems. Random House 1988 70p $13.95 **821**

ISBN 0-394-57021-9

LC 88-42656

"Soyinka's verse is dense and difficult, unabashedly political while at the same time retaining the inspiration of Yoruba mythology. For these reasons, he has been accused of obscurity. Yet Mandela's Earth is accessible to those willing to accept a challenge." Choice

Spender, Stephen, 1909-

Collected poems, 1928-1985. Random House 1986 204p $19.95 **821**

ISBN 0-394-54601-6   LC 85-2323

Also available in paperback from Oxford Univ. Press

Updated edition of Collected poems, 1929-1953, published in 1955

In this volume the author has "eliminated poems he considers too wordy and added several early poems—versions of Rilke, Lorca and Altolaguirre. Also included are remembrances of Louis MacNeice, Igor Stravinsky and W. H. Auden, which were written recently. The poems are arranged thematically under such headings as 'War Poems,' 'Diary Poems' and 'Home.'" Publ Wkly

Spenser, Edmund, 1552?-1599

The faerie queene   **821**

Hardcover and paperback editions available from various publishers

"The greatest work of Spenser, of which the first three books were entrusted to the printer in Nov. 1589, and the second three were published in 1596." Oxford Companion to Engl Lit

"An epic to compare with the great epics of the classical world and of Renaissance Italy, *The Faerie Queene* is simultaneously a nationalistic paean to the greatness of Elizabeth and her England, an imaginative romance, and a moral allegory of the soul of man on his quest for salvation." Reader's Ency. 3d edition

The poetical works of Edmund Spenser; edited with critical notes by J. C. Smith and E. De Selincourt; with an introduction by E. De Selincourt, and a glossary. Oxford Univ. Press 1924 various paging il (Standard authors ser) $29.95; pa $18.95   **821**

ISBN 0-19-254144-7; 0-19-281070-7 (pa)

"One of the greatest English poets, and the first major English writer to arise after Chaucer. . . . [His work reflects] the Renaissance conception of poetry as the highest instrument of moral teaching. Deliberately archaic in style, he looked to Chaucer as the pure 'well of English undefiled', but he was no mere imitator of his master, and gave to English poetry both an enriched, romantic language, lines marked by their running sweetness of diction, and stanzas—called Spenserian." Reader's Ency. 3d edition

Tennyson, Alfred Tennyson, Baron, 1809-1892

The poetical works of Tennyson; edited by G. Robert Strange. Houghton Mifflin 1974 xx, 706p $39   **821**

ISBN 0-395-18014-7

"Cambridge editions"

First published 1898 with title: The poetic and dramatic works of Alfred, Lord Tennyson

"Tennyson has made the widest appeal of any English poet of the nineteenth century. His verse is graceful, romantic, elegant, of great pictorial beauty, and imbued with deep religious feeling. Tennyson's poetry perfectly mirrored the spirit of his era in England." Pratt Alcove

Thomas, Dylan, 1914-1953

The collected poems of Dylan Thomas. New Directions 1953 203p hardcover o.p. paperback available $8.95   **821**

ISBN 0-8112-0205-4 (pa)

"The prologue in verse, written for this collected edition of my poems, is intended as an address to my readers, the strangers. This book contains most of the poems I have written, and all, up to the present year, that I wish to preserve. Some of them I have revised a little." Preface

The poems of Dylan Thomas; edited with an introduction and notes by Daniel Jones. New Directions 1971 291p $16.95   **821**

ISBN 0-8112-0398-0

"To the 90 poems Thomas published in Collected Poems, 1934-1952 Jones has added 102 and placed the total, as far as he could determine, in the chronological order of their composition. Some of the poems were still in manuscript form when Thomas died; others had been published in periodicals and anthologies. In an appendix, Jones offers Thomas' early poems—including one written when the poet was 12." Libr J

Includes bibliographic references

Tomlinson, Charles, 1927-

Collected poems. Oxford Univ. Press 1985 xviii, 351p $29.95   **821**

ISBN 0-19-211974-5   LC 85-3016

The present work "reprints all the volumes from The Necklace of 1955 to The Flood of 1981, along with a single poem from [Tomlinson's] 1951 pamphlet, Relations and Contraries." Times Lit Suppl

"Even if his poems are rather cold in their fluency, Tomlinson is never less than true to their imperatives. 'Look. Listen', they command. He does, and we do." Encounter

Wordsworth, William, 1770-1850

The poetical works of William Wordsworth; edited, revised and with a new introduction by Paul D. Sheats. Houghton Mifflin 1982 xlviii, 939p il $39   **821**

ISBN 0-395-18496-7   LC 81-20175

"Cambridge editions"

First published 1904 with title: The complete poetical works of William Wordsworth

"One of England's greatest poets, who revealed the extraordinary beauty and significance of simple people and things." Good Read

William Wordsworth; edited by Stephen Gill. Oxford Univ. Press 1984 xxxii, 752p (Oxford authors) $29.95; pa $18.95   **821**

ISBN 0-19-254175-7; 0-19-281333-1 (pa)
     LC 83-17278

This volume offers a collection of the major poems (including the 1805 Prelude) and a selection of critical prose

"The introduction is of real value and the annotation copious and excellect." Times Lit Suppl

Includes bibliography

Yeats, W. B. (William Butler), 1865-1939
The poems; edited by Richard J.
Finneran. rev ed. Macmillan 1989 xxviii,
751p (Collected works of W. B. Yeats, v1)
$35   **821**

ISBN 0-02-632701-5   LC 88-13700

First published 1983

This edition of the Nobel Laureate's verse contains
texts of all the poems Yeats is known to have written.
The editor has restored Yeat's rhetorical punctuation and
provides textual notes

821.008 English poetry— Collections

The **Best** loved poems of the American
people; selected by Hazel Felleman.
Doubleday 1936 xxxv, 670p $16.95
     821.008

1. English poetry—Collections 2. American poetry—
Collections
ISBN 0-385-00019-7

First published by Garden City Publishing Company

Poems are grouped under the following headings: Love
and friendship; Inspiration; Poems that tell a story; Faith
and reverence; Home and mother; Childhood and youth;
Partriotism and war; Humor and whimsey; Memory and
grief; Nature; Animals; Various themes

Ciardi, John, 1916-1986
How does a poem mean? [by] John
Ciardi, Miller Williams. 2nd ed. Houghton
Mifflin 1975 xxiii, 408p o.p. paperback
available $19.95   **821.008**

1. English poetry—Collections 2. American poetry—
Collections 3. Poetry—History and criticism
ISBN 0-395-18605-6 (pa)

First published 1960

This volume discusses the value and nature of poetry,
its kinds, structure and techniques through detailed
analysis of individual poems from the medieval age
down to the present

Five hundred years of English poetry;
Chaucer to Arnold; edited by Barbara
Lloyd-Evans. Bedrick Bks. 1989 1200p
$39.95; pa $19.95   **821.008**

1. English poetry—Collections
ISBN 0-87226-325-8; 0-87226-215-4 (pa)
     LC 89-42891

An anthology of representative works by major English
poets from Chaucer to the Victorians

"One of the most comprehensive anthologies of major
English poets' works, both epic and short lyrics, available
in one volume. The index to first lines, glossary,
abbreviations, notes on the text, information on versification, verse forms, and types of poetry add to its usefulness as a reference source." SLJ

The **New** Oxford book of Christian verse;
chosen and edited by Donald Davie.
Oxford Univ. Press 1981 xxix, 319p $30;
pa $11.95   **821.008**

1. Religious poetry
ISBN 0-19-213426-4; 0-19-282157-1 (pa)
     LC 80-49703

Replaces The Oxford book of Christian verse, edited
by Lord David Cecil (1940)

The editor "in his introduction sets forth his . . .
guidelines: 'poetry that appeals, either explicitly or by
plain implication . . . to some one or more of the
distinctive doctrines of the Christian church: to the
Incarnation preeminently, to Redemption, Judgement, the
Holy Trinity, the Fall' and yet a poetry which in no
way 'fails to measure up strictly in artistry to the best
of the secular verse written through the same centuries.'"
N Y Times Book Rev

The **New** Oxford book of eighteenth century
verse; chosen and edited by Roger
Lonsdale. Oxford Univ. Press 1984 xlii,
870p $34.95; pa $15.95   **821.008**

1. English poetry—Collections
ISBN 0-19-214122-8; 0-19-282054-0 (pa)
     LC 83-17477

Replaces The Oxford Book of eighteenth century verse,
edited by David Nicol Smith (1926)

This anthology "will be welcome to anyone interested
in the poetry of the period. The casual reader will find
a goodly selection of the familiar . . . [and] a number
of unfamiliar works, since about 25 percent of the inclu-
sions are of such obscure writers as John Hawthorn, J.
Wilde, and that most prolific of authors, Anonymous.
. . . Indexed by first line and author, with brief
biographical and historical notes." Libr J

The **New** Oxford book of English light
verse; chosen by Kingsley Amis. Oxford
Univ. Press 1978 xxxiv, 347p $29.95
     821.008

1. English poetry—Collections 2. Humorous poetry
ISBN 0-19-211862-5

Companion volume to The Oxford Book of American
light verse, entered in class 811.008

Replaces The Oxford Book of light verse, edited by
W. H. Auden (1938)

This anthology of humorous poetry contains work by
mostly British authors. Americans represented include:
Bret Harte, Robert Frost, Peter De Vries and Phyllis
McGinley

The **New** Oxford book of English verse,
1250-1950; chosen and edited by Helen
Gardner. Oxford Univ. Press 1972 974p
$39.95   **821.008**

1. English poetry—Collections
ISBN 0-19-812136-9

Replaces The Oxford Book of English verse, 1250-
1900, edited by Sir Arthur Quiller-Couch (1900)

This anthology covers seven centuries of verse and
brings the terminal date down to 1950. It "covers the
entire spectrum of English poetic genius. As well as
private and personal poems, there are poems dealing
with public events, historic occasions, religious, moral,
and political convictions, satire, and . . . light verse."
Publisher's note

The **New** Oxford book of Irish verse; edited with translations by Thomas Kinsella. Oxford Univ. Press 1986 xxx, 423p $30; pa $13.95 **821.008**

1. Irish poetry—Collections
ISBN 0-19-211868-4; 0-19-282643-3 (pa)

LC 85-21479

Replaces The Oxford Book of Irish verse, XVIIth century-XXth century, chosen by Donagh MacDonagh and Lennox Robinson (1958)

"This selection is divided into three parts. Book I opens with the earliest pre-Christian poetry in Old Irish and ends in the fourteenth century with the first Irish poetry in the English language. Book II covers the fourteenth to the eighteenth centuries and Book III the nineteenth and twentieth centuries." Publisher's note

The **New** Oxford book of Victorian verse; edited by Christopher Ricks. Oxford Univ. Press 1987 xxxiv, 654p $30; pa $14.95 **821.008**

1. English poetry—Collections
ISBN 0-19-214154-6; 0-19-282778-2 (pa)

LC 86-23701

Replaces The Oxford Book of Victorian verse, edited by Sir Arthur Quiller-Couch (1912)

An anthology of 19th century English poetry. Among the poets prominently featured are: Clough, Morris, Arnold, the Decadents, Emily Brontë, Clare, Barnes, and Christina Rossetti

"While general collections should all add Ricks, those retaining [the Quiller-Couch edition] should dust him off and keep him available in order to represent fully Victorian verse and changing attitudes toward it." Libr J

The **Norton** anthology of modern poetry; edited by Richard Ellmann and Robert O'Clair. 2nd ed. Norton 1988 xlix, 1865p pa $38.95 **821.008**

1. English poetry—Collections 2. American poetry—Collections
ISBN 0-393-95636-9

LC 87-28310

First published 1973

An anthology of English and American verse from Whitman to the present day

The **Norton** book of light verse; edited by Russell Baker; with the assistance of Kathleen Leland Baker. Norton 1986 447p $25 **821.008**

1. English poetry—Collections 2. American poetry—Collections 3. Humorous poetry
ISBN 0-393-02366-4

LC 86-18172

Arranged by subject, this anthology presents some four hundred British and American light verse selections. The poems date from the sixteenth-century to the present

The **Oxford** book of ballads; selected and edited by James Kinsley. Oxford Univ. Press 1969 711p hardcover o.p. paperback available $13.95 **821.008**

1. Ballads, English 2. Ballads, Scottish
ISBN 0-19-281330-7 (pa)

Replaces The Oxford Book of ballads, compiled by Sir Arthur Quiller-Couch (1910)

This volume "contains for the most part, ballads from the Child canon. Texts of the 150 ballads are, however, based on single rather than composite versions and aim less for poetic quality than for closeness to oral tradition.

Grouping is by relation in theme or mood without a formal subject arrangement and the compiler has included musical airs for more than 80 of the ballads. Sources for both poetry and music are indicated in the notes; title index." Booklist

The **Oxford** book of children's verse; chosen and edited with notes, by Iona and Peter Opie. Oxford Univ. Press 1973 xxxi, 407p il $29.95 **821.008**

1. Children's poetry—Collections 2. English poetry—Collections 3. American poetry—Collections
ISBN 0-19-812140-7

Arranged chronologically, these 332 selections from British and American children's poetry include works by such poets as Chaucer, Charles and Mary Lamb, Kipling, Farjeon, Milne, Eliot and Nash. Poets still living are not included

This "volume serves as a solid base for a logical presentation of the historical development of children's verse." Choice

The **Oxford** book of narrative verse; chosen and edited by Iona and Peter Opie. Oxford Univ. Press 1983 407p $29.95; pa $11.95 **821.008**

1. English poetry—Collections 2. American poetry—Collections
ISBN 0-19-214131-7; 0-19-282243-8 (pa)

LC 82-22494

This collection of poetry "includes fairy-tales, and folk-stories, broadsides and ballads, adventure and romance, passion and parody." Economist

This is an "anthology predictably freighted with English poets (34 of the 46 selections) but none the worse for that. 'This book,' says the Opies, 'pretends to be nothing more than a story book.' It is nothing less, and leaves you wondering where this admirable kind of verse has gone." Libr J

The **Oxford** book of satirical verse; chosen by Geoffrey Grigson. Oxford Univ. Press 1980 454p hardcover o.p. paperback available $12.95 **821.008**

1. English poetry—Collections 2. American poetry—Collections 3. Satire, English—Collections 4. Satire, American—Collections
ISBN 0-19-281425-7 (pa)

LC 79-41738

This collection includes 232 satirical poems and excerpts from poems from the sixteenth century to the present

"This is a book which will be read and reread, and no-one who loves literature will tire of it. It is impervious to the tides of satiric theory, and proof against new fashions in poetics, for it enshrines strong feelings and imperishable expression." Times Lit Suppl

The **Oxford** book of Scottish verse; chosen by John MacQueen and Tom Scott. Oxford Univ. Press 1967 c1966 xxix, 633p $35 **821.008**

ISBN 0-19-812131-8

First published 1966 in the United Kingdom

This volume includes the work of poets from the thirteenth century up to those contemporary poets born before 1930

"The great merit of this anthology is that it is based on a consensus that has grown up during the past generation's rediscovery of Scottish poetry. . . . More than a quarter of the whole is given to poets born since about 1880." Times Lit Suppl

The **Oxford** book of seventeenth century verse; chosen by H. J. C. Grierson and G. Bullough. Oxford Univ. Press 1934 974p $49.95 **821.008**

1. English poetry—Collections
ISBN 0-19-812125-3

The compilers include "more than 600 poems from more than 100 poets; the text carefully prepared, the spelling modified from the originals in a manner which, though a little hard to justify in theory, in practice gives no offence. The selection from the major poets is a full one, and all the minor poets who deserve a place are here." Times Lit Suppl

The **Oxford** book of short poems; chosen and edited by P.J. Kavanagh and James Michie. Oxford Univ. Press 1985 xl, 307p $30; pa $12.95 **821.008**

1. English poetry—Collections 2. American poetry—Collections
ISBN 0-19-214135-X; 0-19-282073-7 (pa)
LC 84-27294

This anthology of poems contains 658 selections of fewer than fourteen lines

This volume "presents a compact and valuable canon of the best short poems in English. Many good poems have been excluded, but the core of the tradition is there for readers to admire and poets to imitate, if they can." Christ Sci Monit

The **Oxford** book of twentieth-century English verse; chosen by Philip Larkin. Oxford Univ. Press 1973 1,641p $35 **821.008**

1. English poetry—Collections
ISBN 0-19-812137-7

This anthology of more than 600 poems by more than 200 twentieth-century British writers includes works by John Masefield, T. S. Eliot, W. B. Yeats, W. H. Auden, Dylan Thomas and Alan Sillitoe

"A strong vein of neo-Georgianism runs throughout the book, resulting in a clear partiality for work that is explicitly, even documentarily, English in locale, for poems that are narrative or anecdotal, for neat, well-populated fables and for moralistic ruminations." New Statesman

Poems that live forever; compiled by Hazel Felleman. Doubleday 1965 xxiv, 454p $17.95 **821.008**

1. English poetry—Collections 2. American poetry—Collections
ISBN 0-385-00358-7

An anthology of favorite poetry largely by English and American authors

"Arrangement is by subject under such headings as stories and ballads, love, friendship, home and family, patriotism and war, humor, death, faith and inspiration, others." Publ Wkly

The **Top** 500 poems; edited by William Harmon. Columbia Univ. Press 1992 xxx, 1132p $29.95 **821.008**

1. English poetry—Collections 2. American poetry—Collections
ISBN 0-231-08028-X
LC 91-42239

"Harmon devises an interesting method (collecting the 500 most anthologized shorter English and American poems as indexed in the *Columbia Granger's Index to Poetry*, 8th and 9th eds.) to bring together poetry of the last 750 years that he calls the 'greatest successes'. . . . Each of the 500 poems, arranged in chronological order, has a biographical headnote and editorial comments by the editor." Libr J

821.009 English poetry—History and criticism

Brooks, Cleanth, 1906-
The well wrought urn; studies in the structure of poetry. Reynal 1947 o.p.; Harcourt Brace Jovanovich paperback available $9.95 **821.009**

1. English poetry—History and criticism
ISBN 0-15-695705-1 (pa)

Analyzed in Essay and general literature index

"Essays in criticism for critics, in which a theory of poetic structure is explored by analyses of great poems from Donne and Shakespeare to William Butler Yeats. Author dwells on the devices of paradox, irony and metaphor and finally examines the approach to poetry made by other modern critics." Libr J

Pritchard, William H.
Lives of the modern poets. Oxford Univ. Press 1980 316p $27.50; pa $8.95 **821.009**

1. American poetry—History and criticism 2. English poetry—History and criticism
ISBN 0-19-502690-X; 0-19-502989-5 (pa)
LC 79-17615

Analyzed in Essay and general literature index

"This collection of nine critical essays provides introductions and evaluations for the poets Pritchard sees as the most interesting of those writing in English in the early 20th Century: Thomas Hardy, W. B. Yeats, E. A. Robinson, Robert Frost, Ezra Pound, T. S. Eliot, Wallace Stevens, Hart Crane, and William Carlos Williams." Libr J

822 English drama

Behan, Brendan, 1923-1964
The complete plays; introduced by Alan Simpson; with a bibliography by E. H. Mikhail. Grove Weidenfeld 1991 384p pa $12.95 **822**

ISBN 0-8021-3070-4
LC 78-53931

"An Evergreen book"

First published 1978

Contents: The quare fellow; The hostage; Richard's cork leg; Moving out; A garden party; The big house

Besier, Rudolf, 1878-1942
The Barretts of Wimpole Street; a comedy in five acts. Little, Brown 1930 165p $14.95 **822**

1. Browning, Elizabeth Barrett, 1806-1861—Drama 2. Browning, Robert, 1812-1889—Drama
ISBN 0-316-09223-1

Characters: 13 men, 4 women. First produced in England at the Malvern Festival, August 20, 1930

Besier, Rudolf, 1878-1942—*Continued*

"The long-famous courtship and elopement of Elizabeth Barrett and Robert Browning furnish the theme for this drama. . . . The author has followed the known facts faithfully and yet has succeeded in creating a play which is of commanding interest in itself." Carnegie Libr. of Pittsburgh

Bolt, Robert

A man for all seasons; a play in two acts. Random House 1962 xxv, 163p il $10.95; pa $3.50   **822**

1. More, Sir Thomas, Saint, 1478-1535—Drama
2. Great Britain—History—1485-1603, Tudors—Drama
ISBN 0-394-40623-0; 0-394-70321-9 (pa)

Characters: 11 men, 2 women. First produced in the United States at the ANTA Theatre, New York City, November 22, 1961

A play set in sixteenth century England about Sir Thomas More, a devout Catholic, and his conflict with Henry VIII

Burgess, Anthony, 1917-1993

Cyrano de Bergerac; by Edmond Rostand; translated and adapted for the modern stage by Anthony Burgess. Knopf 1971 174p $16.95; pa $9.95   **822**

1. Cyrano de Bergerac, 1619-1655—Drama
ISBN 0-394-47239-X; 0-679-73413-9 (pa)

This version was commissioned for production at the Tyrone Guthrie Theater in Minneapolis. It is adapted and translated from the French play originally produced in 1897. Cyrano, the hero, a Gascon poet and swordsman notorious for his long nose, is in love with Roxana

Christie, Agatha, 1890-1976

The mousetrap and other plays; introduction by Ira Levin. HarperPaperbacks 1993 c1978 742p pa $5.99   **822**

ISBN 0-06-100374-3

First published 1978 by Dodd, Mead

Includes the following plays: Ten little Indians; Appointment with death; The hollow; The mousetrap; Witness for the prosecution; Towards zero; Verdict; Go back for murder

Churchill, Caryl

Serious money. Methuen 1987 112p (Royal Court writers ser) pa $9.95   **822**

ISBN 0-413-16660-0   LC 87-206668

Characters: 14 men, 6 women. Music. 2 acts. First produced at Wyndham's Theatre, London, July 6, 1987

A satire set in the contemporary London financial world. A cartel's efforts to obtain a company go awry when a murder occurs

Congreve, William, 1670-1729

The comedies of William Congreve; edited by Anthony G. Henderson. Cambridge Univ. Press 1982 407p (Plays by Renaissance and Restoration dramatists) $64.95; pa $19.95   **822**

ISBN 0-521-24747-0; 0-521-28932-7 (pa) LC 82-1182

Contents: The old bachelor; The double dealer; Love for love; The way of the world

"*The Old Bachelor* (1693), which was produced under Dryden's auspices, was widely acclaimed. It was followed by three other comedies: *The Double Dealer* (1693), 'Love for Love', and his masterpiece, 'The Way of the World'. In these plays, Congreve revealed a genius for urbane, scintillating wit that rivaled Molière's." Reader's Ency. 3d edition

Coward, Noel

Three plays; introduction by Edward Albee. Grove Press 1979 254p pa $9.95   **822**

ISBN 0-8021-5108-6   LC 79-52122

A reprint of the title first published 1965 by Dell

Contents: Blithe spirit; Hay fever; Private lives

Dryden, John, 1631-1700

All for love; edited by David M. Vieth. University of Neb. Press 1972 xxxiv, 146p (Regents Restoration drama ser) hardcover o.p. paperback available $5.95   **822**

1. Cleopatra, Queen of Egypt, d. 30 B.C.—Drama
ISBN 0-8032-5379-6 (pa)

Also available in paperback from Norton

An English Restoration tragedy which is an adaptation of Shakespeare's "Antony and Cleopatra" done in blank verse

Fry, Christopher

The lady's not for burning, A phoenix too frequent, and an essay "An experience of critics". Oxford Univ. Press 1977 124p pa $6.95   **822**

ISBN 0-19-519916-2

"A Galaxy book"

The lady's not for burning, first produced 1948 in London, is a romantic comedy in verse about witchcraft in 14th century England. A phoenix too frequent, first produced 1946 in London, is set in Ephesus where a widow, determined to die in her husband's tomb, is diverted from her death-wish

Fugard, Athol

Boesman and Lena and other plays. Oxford Univ. Press 1978 xxv, 299p (Oxford paperbacks) pa $9.95   **822**

ISBN 0-19-281242-4   LC 77-30721

Contents: The blood knot; People are living there; Hello and goodbye; Boesman and Lena

Fugard, Athol—*Continued*
"Master Harold"—and the boys. Knopf
1982 60p o.p.; Penguin Bks. paperback
available $6   **822**

1. South Africa—Race relations—Drama
ISBN 0-14-048187-7 (pa)   LC 82-48027

Characters: 3 men. 1 act. First produced at the Yale
Repertory theatre, New Haven, Connecticut, 1982
Drama with racial overtones set in Port Elizabeth tea
room focuses on precocious white South African
teenager's relationship with two black men who work for
his family, both old enough to be his father

Gay, John, 1685-1732
The beggar's opera; edited by Edgar V.
Roberts; music edited by Edward Smith.
University of Neb. Press 1969 xxix, 238p
music (Regents Restoration drama ser) o.p.;
Penguin Bks. paperback available $6.95
                                                    822

ISBN 0-14-043220-5 (pa)
First published 1728
A ballad opera, this is a rogues' comedy satirizing
corrupt politics in 18th century England

Goldsmith, Oliver, 1728-1774
She stoops to conquer   **822**

Available in paperback from various publishers
18th century social comedy about love affairs of two
cousins
"The author's masterpiece. A delightful example of the
best type of English society comedy." Pratt Alcove

Harold Pinter; edited and with an
introduction by Harold Bloom. Chelsea
House 1987 183p (Modern critical views)
$24.95   **822**

1. Pinter, Harold, 1930-
ISBN 0-87754-706-8   LC 86-29964
Among the Pinter works analyzed in this collection
of critical essays are: The homecoming; The birthday
party; Silence; Landscape; and Betrayal
Includes bibliography

Hinchliffe, Arnold P., 1930-
Harold Pinter. rev ed. Twayne Pubs. 1981
177p (Twayne's English authors ser) $20.95
                                                    822

1. Pinter, Harold, 1930-
ISBN 0-8057-6784-3   LC 80-24903
First published 1967
An assessment of the dramatist's work for stage, radio,
and screen. Attention is also given to Pinter's role as
actor, producer, and director
Includes bibliography

Marlowe, Christopher, 1564-1593
Doctor Faustus   **822**

Available in hardcover and paperback editions from
various publishers

"A drama in blank verse and prose . . . published
apparently in 1604, though entered in the Stationer's
Register in 1601, and probably produced in 1588. It is
perhaps the first dramatization of the medieval legend
of a man who sold his soul to the Devil, and who
became identified with a Dr. Faustus, a necromancer of
the 16th cent." Oxford Companion to Engl Lit

O'Casey, Sean, 1880-1964
Seven plays by Sean O'Casey; selected,
with an introduction and notes by Ronald
Ayling. St. Martin's Press 1985 xl, 545p il
$32.50   **822**

ISBN 0-312-71323-1   LC 85-2167
Contents: The shadow of a gunman; Juno and the
paycock; The plough and the stars; The silver tassie; Red
roses for me; Cock-a-doodle dandy; The Bishop's bonfire
Includes bibliography

Osborne, John, 1929-
Look back in anger. Criterion Bks. 1957
96p o.p.; Penguin Bks. paperback available
$6   **822**

ISBN 0-14-048175-3 (pa)
Characters: 3 men, 2 women. First produced at the
Royal Court Theatre, London, May 8, 1956
This play "introduced a new strain of realism to
British theatre and set the tone for the generation of
anti-Establishment writers who became known as the
Angry Young Men. Osborne described his own parents
as 'impoverished middle class,' but his play deals with
the frustrations, crude language, and squalid conditions
of working-class life." Reader's Ency. 3d edition

Pinter, Harold, 1930-
Betrayal. Grove Press 1979 c1978 138p pa
$8.95   **822**

ISBN 0-8021-3080-1   LC 78-65251
First published 1978 in the United Kingdom
Characters: 3 men, 1 woman. 9 scenes. First produced
at the National Theatre, London, November 15, 1978
The development of an adulterous love affair, between
a woman and her husband's best friend, is portrayed
from 1977 backwards in time to its inception in 1968

Complete works; with an introduction,
Writing for the theatre. Grove Weidenfeld
1990 4v pa each $10.95   **822**

ISBN   0-8021-5096-9   (v1);   0-8021-3237-5   (v2);
0-8021-5049-7 (v3); 0-8021-5050-0 (v4) LC 90-13933
"An Evergreen book"
First Grove Press edition published 1977-1981
Plays included are: v1 The birthday party; The room;
The dumb waiter; A slight ache; A night out; v2 The
caretaker; The dwarfs; The collection; The lover; Night
school; Trouble in the works; The black and white [revue
sketch]; Request stop; Last to go; Special offer; v3 The
homecoming; Tea party; The basement; Landscape;
Silence; Night; That's your trouble; That's all; Applicant;
Interview; Dialogue for three; v4 Old times; No man's
land; Betrayal; Monologue; Family voices

Five screenplays. Grove Press 1973 367p
pa $18.95   **822**

1. Motion picture plays
ISBN 0-8021-5119-1

Pinter, Harold, 1930——_Continued_
Contents: The servant; The pumpkin eater; The Quiller memorandum; Accident; The go-between

The homecoming. Grove Press 1966 c1965 82p pa $6.95   **822**

ISBN 0-8021-5105-1

First published 1965 in the United Kingdom

Characters: 5 men, 1 woman. First American production at the Music Box, New York City, January 5, 1967
Professor living in America visits family in London where he introduces his wife to menacing all-male household

Mountain language. Grove Press 1989 c1988 47p $16.95; pa $6.95   **822**

ISBN 0-8021-1157-2; 0-8021-3168-9 (pa)

LC 88-35782

First published 1988 in the United Kingdom

Characters: 6 men, 2 women. 4 scenes. First produced at the National Theatre, London, October 20, 1988
Four brief scenes illustrating the inherent brutality of state-enforced oppression

Old times. Grove Press 1972 c1971 75p pa $7.95   **822**

ISBN 0-8021-5029-2

First published 1971 in the United Kingdom

Characters: 1 man, 2 women. 2 acts. First produced June 1, 1971 at the Aldwych Theatre, London. First American production, November 1971 at the Billy Rose Theatre, New York City
"The basic situation—man, wife, and friend meeting in a lonely seaside farmhouse and talking over old times in London when their relationships were quite different—is a framework upon which Pinter has hung a psychological analysis of the hopes, memories, dreams, and failures of at least two people (the reality of the friend is questionable)." Libr J

Shaffer, Peter
Equus. Atheneum Pubs. 1974 211p o.p.; Penguin Bks. paperback available $6   **822**

ISBN 0-14-048185-0 (pa)

Characters: 5 men, 4 women. 1 act, 35 scenes. First produced by the National Theater, London, July 26, 1973
Drama about "a jolting confrontation between a psychiatrist and a 17-year-old boy who has blinded six horses from the stable where he is employed. As the probe into the boy's attitudes and behavior deepens, this criminal act is revealed to have been a result of his notions of a sexual/religious spirit in horses." Booklist

Lettice & lovage; a comedy. Harper & Row 1990 100p $16.95; pa $12   **822**

ISBN 0-06-039098-0; 0-06-096342-5 (pa)

LC 88-45724

"A Cornelia & Michael Bessie book"

First published 1988 in the United Kingdom

Characters: 2 men, 3 women, extras. 3 acts. 3 settings. First produced at the Theatre Royal, Bath, October 6, 1987

This play is "about the initially chilly, ultimately warm relationship between two middle-aged women rather bogged down in life. Lettice is the daughter of a female theatrical entrepreneur from whom she imbibed a love of history and histrionics. Lotte, daughter of an art-book publisher, is a former student of architecture with a historical turn of mind herself. . . . Both women's

parts, written for star turns, are full of comic invention based upon credible, though eccentric, characterization." Booklist

Peter Shaffer's Amadeus. Harper & Row 1981 97p music hardcover o.p. paperback available $9   **822**

1. Mozart, Wolfgang Amadeus, 1756-1791—Drama
2. Salieri, Antonio, 1750-1825—Drama

ISBN 0-06-090783-5 (pa)   LC 79-3415

Also available in paperback from New Am. Lib.

A revised version of the title first published 1980 in the United Kingdom

Characters: 9 men, 1 woman, extras. 2 acts. First produced at the National Theater of Great Britain, November 1979
Explores relationship between Austrian court composer Antonio Salieri and the divinely gifted young Wolfgang Amadeus Mozart

Sheridan, Richard Brinsley Butler, 1751-1816
Sheridan's plays; edited with an introduction by Cecil Price. Oxford Univ. Press 1975 xxxi, 442p $29.95; pa $14.95
822

ISBN 0-19-254169-2; 0-19-281158-4 (pa)

"Oxford standard authors"

This collection includes: The rivals, St. Patrick's Day, The Duenna, The school for scandal, The critic, A trip to Scarborough, Pizarro, and The camp

Stoppard, Tom
The real thing. Faber & Faber 1983 c1982 84p hardcover o.p. paperback available $8.95
822

ISBN 0-685-26862-4 (pa)

First published 1982 in the United Kingdom

Characters: 4 men, 3 women. 2 acts. First produced at the Strand Theatre, London, November 16, 1982
Relationship between playwright's life and work are reflected in his rocky marriage to an actress

Rosencrantz and Guildenstern are dead. Grove Press 1967 126p hardcover o.p. paperback available $7.95   **822**

1. Shakespeare, William, 1564-1616—Parodies, travesties, etc.

ISBN 0-8021-3275-8 (pa)

Characters: 13 men, 2 women, extras. First produced in this form April 11, 1967 in London
This play "took the theatre world on both sides of the Atlantic by storm. The originality of the idea which put Hamlet's two insignificant friends centerstage was matched by the brilliance of the dialogue between these bewildered nonentities." Reader's Ency. 3d edition

Travesties. Grove Press 1975 99p pa $5.95
822

ISBN 0-8021-5089-6

Characters: 5 men, 2 women. Prologue, 2 acts. First produced at the Aldwych Theatre, London, June 10, 1974
Satire on politics, literature and art. James Joyce, Lenin and Dadaist Tristan Tzara come together in memories of obscure English diplomat in Zurich. Song and dance routines

Synge, J. M. (John Millington), 1871-1909
The complete plays. Vintage Bks. 1960
268p pa $10   **822**

ISBN 0-394-70178-X

Also available in paperback from Heinemann Educ.
Bks.

Contents: In the shadow of the glen; Riders to the
sea; The tinker's wedding; The well of the saints; The
playboy of the Western world; Deirdre of the sorrows

Thomas, Dylan, 1914-1953
Under milk wood; a play for voices. New
Directions 1954 107p music pa $5.95   **822**

ISBN 0-8112-0209-7

"A radio play for voices. Written in poetic, inventive
prose, this play is full of humor, a joyful sense of the
goodness of life and love, and a strong Welsh flavor.
It is an impression of a spring day in the lives of the
people of Llareggub, a Welsh village situated under Milk
Wood. It has no plot, but a wealth of characters who
dream aloud, converse with one another, and speak in
choruses of alternating voices." Reader's Ency. 3d edition

Wilde, Oscar, 1854-1900
The importance of being Earnest   **822**

Hardcover and paperback editions available from
various publishers

Written in 1895

Drawing room comedy exposing quirks and foibles of
Victorian society with plot revolving around amorous
pursuits of two men who face social obstacles when they
woo young ladies of quality

This play "is noted for its witty lines, its clever situations, and its satire on the British nobility and clergy."
Reader's Ency. 3d edition

822.008 English drama—Collections

Everyman, and medieval miracle plays;
edited with an introduction by A. C.
Cawley. Dent o.p.; Tuttle paperback
available $5.95   **822.008**

1. Mysteries and miracle plays
ISBN 0-460-87032-7 (pa)

"Everyman's library"

This edition first published 1909 with title: Everyman,
with other interludes including eight miracle plays

In addition to Everyman, this collection includes plays
from the Towneley, Coventry, York and Chester cycles

Restoration plays; with an introduction by
Brice Harris. Modern Lib. 1953 xx, 674p
o.p.; McGraw-Hill paperback available
$7.43   **822.008**

1. English drama—Collections
ISBN 0-07-553658-7 (pa)

Contents: The rehearsal, by G. Villiers; The country
wife, by W. Wycherley; The man of mode, by G.
Etherege; All for love, by J. Dryden; Venice preserved,
by T. Otway; The relapse, by J. Vanbrugh; The way
of the world, by W. Congreve; The beaux' stratagem,
by G. Farquhar

822.3 William Shakespeare

Bartlett, John, 1820-1905
A complete concordance or verbal index
to words, phrases, and passages in the
dramatic works of Shakespeare; with a
supplementary concordance to the poems. St.
Martin's Press 1953 1910p $118.75   **822.3**

ISBN 0-312-15645-6

First published 1894 by Macmillan with title: a new
and complete concordance or verbal index to words,
phrases & passages in the dramatic works of Shakespeare

"Based upon the text of the Globe edition; gives full
context for each word listed, with exact reference to act,
scene, and line as numbered in the Globe edition 1891."
Sheehy. Guide to Ref Books. 10th edition

Boyce, Charles
Shakespeare A to Z; the essential reference
to his plays, his poems, his life and times,
and more; David White, editorial consultant;
foreword by Terry Hands. Facts on File
1990 742p il $45   **822.3**

1. Shakespeare, William, 1564-1616
ISBN 0-8160-1805-7   LC 90-31239

Also available in paperback from Dell

"A Roundtable Press book"

This book has "synopses of all of Shakespeare's plays
by act and scene; sketches of all of his characters, as
well as the historic personages on whom some of them
were based; biographies of his contemporaries in the
Elizabethan theater; portraits of many of the actors who
achieved fame in his plays; and mentions of many
modern theatrical works that have been influenced by
him." SLJ

Includes bibliographic references

Champion, Larry S.
The essential Shakespeare; an annotated
bibliography of major modern studies. 2nd
ed. Hall, G.K. & Co. 1993 568p $65
     822.3

1. Shakespeare, William, 1564-1616—Bibliography
2. Shakespeare, William, 1564-1616—Criticism,
interpretation, etc.
ISBN 0-8161-7332-X   LC 92-39078

First published 1986

An annotated checklist of significant Shakespearean
scholarship in English since 1900. Entries are arranged
under general studies or under individual works

Chute, Marchette Gaylord, 1909-
Shakespeare of London; [by] Marchette
Chute. Dutton 1949 397p o.p.; Penguin Bks.
paperback available $10.95   **822.3**

1. Shakespeare, William, 1564-1616—Biography
ISBN 0-14-015313-6 (pa)

"Retelling of Shakespeare's life, reconstructed from
documentary evidence and a sound knowledge of
Shakespeare's England. . . . The author's Shakespeare is
a young man of talent, who made good at a congenial
occupation at a time when the political and cultural
atmosphere was conducive to the development of literary

Chute, Marchette Gaylord, 1909- — Con-tinued
and dramatic talent." Booklist

Includes bibliography

Stories from Shakespeare; [by] Marchette Chute. World Pub. Services 1956 351p il o.p.; New Am. Lib. paperback available $6
822.3

1. Shakespeare, William, 1564-1616—Adaptations
ISBN 0-452-01061-6 (pa)

A retelling of the plays, comedies, tragedies, and histories included in Shakespeare's First folio. "Its purpose is to give the reader a preliminary idea of each of the thirty-six plays by telling the stories and explaining in a general way the intentions and points of view of the characters." Introduction

A **Companion** to Shakespeare studies; edited by Harley Granville-Barker and G. B. Harrison. Cambridge Univ. Press 1934 408p il $75
822.3

1. Shakespeare, William, 1564-1616—Criticism, interpretation, etc.
ISBN 0-521-05132-0

Analyzed in Essay and general literature index

A collection of essays by noted academics exploring various aspects of Shakespearean scholarship

Includes bibliography

DeLoach, Charles, 1927-
The quotable Shakespeare; a topical dictionary; compiled by Charles DeLoach. McFarland & Co. 1988 xxiii, 544p $39.95
822.3

1. Shakespeare, William, 1564-1616—Dictionaries
2. Shakespeare, William, 1564-1616—Quotations
ISBN 0-89950-303-9   LC 87-35362

"Some 6,500 quotations are given under about 1,000 topical headings in alphabetical sequence. Reference is given to the exact line of the source in *The Riverside Shakespeare*. Title, character, and topical indexes." Sheehy. Guide to Ref Books. 10th edition. suppl

Fraser, Russell A.
Shakespeare, the later years. Columbia Univ. Press 1992 380p il $32   **822.3**

1. Shakespeare, William, 1564-1616—Biography
ISBN 0-231-06766-6   LC 91-31956

Also available: Young Shakespeare $32 (ISBN 0-231-06764-X)

"Carefully interweaving the story of Shakespeare's works and that of his times, Fraser suggests many new (and some startling) interrelationships. He also limns a glorious poet who is a shrewed businessman and has a cold eye when this is wanted. Not all readers will agree with Fraser's conclusions, but virtually all will find them worthy of reflection. Should become part of every 'standard' Shakespeare collection." Choice

Includes bibliographic references

Frye, Northrop
Northrop Frye on Shakespeare; edited by Robert Sandler. Yale Univ. Press 1986 186p $27; pa $10
822.3

1. Shakespeare, William, 1564-1616—Criticism, interpretation, etc.
ISBN 0-300-03711-2; 0-300-04208-6 (pa)
LC 86-50485

Shakespeare scholar Frye provides in-depth analyses of ten plays

"Frye's work is completely accessible, its style crisp and engaging. Most of all, it is full of basic 'good sense' about our most abused literary figure." Libr J

Greer, Germaine, 1939-
Shakespeare. Oxford Univ. Press 1986 136p (Past masters) $18.95; pa $6.95
822.3

1. Shakespeare, William, 1564-1616—Criticism, interpretation, etc.
ISBN 0-19-287539-6; 0-19-287538-8 (pa)
LC 85-18746

This "study is arranged topically with chapters on teleology, ethics, poetics, politics, and sociology in the Bard's oeuvre. Although she focuses on his plays—more than 30 of them are covered, some far more thoroughly than others—Greer also includes brief commentary on the poetry." Booklist

Includes bibliography

Hughes, Ted, 1930-
Shakespeare and the goddess of complete being. Farrar, Straus & Giroux 1992 524p $35
822.3

1. Shakespeare, William, 1564-1616—Criticism, interpretation, etc.
ISBN 0-374-26204-7   LC 92-73077

"Hughes begins by analyzing *Venus and Adonis* and the *Rape of Lucrece*, suggesting that the two myths that inform these poems—of the hero who rejects the goddess and is killed in return, and of the god who destroys the goddess—form a fundamental mythic and symbolic pattern that underlies Shakespeare's later plays, beginning with *As You Like It* and incorporating all the great tragedies and romances. . . . Every page is lit up with some insight that makes one think about the plays in a new light." Libr J

Lamb, Charles, 1775-1834
Tales from Shakespeare; by Charles and Mary Lamb
822.3

1. Shakespeare, William, 1564-1616—Adaptations

Hardcover and paperback editions available from various publishers

First published 1807

A now classic collection of twenty plays by Shakespeare adapted as prose stories—the comedies by Mary Lamb, the tragedies by Charles Lamb

Levi, Peter, 1931-

The life and times of William Shakespeare. Holt & Co. 1989 xxiii, 392p il maps $29.95; pa $14.95   **822.3**

ISBN 0-8050-1199-4; 0-8050-1552-3 (pa)

                   LC 89-30501

First published 1988 in the United Kingdom

The author "offers information about Shakespeare's background and parentage, the Stratford and London that he knew, events that shaped his experience, and the actors, managers and writers with whom he associated. But most of the facts relate to the times." Publ Wkly

Includes bibliography

Levin, Harry, 1912-

The question of Hamlet. Oxford Univ. Press 1959 178p $16.95; pa $5.95   **822.3**

1. Shakespeare, William, 1564-1616. Hamlet

ISBN 0-19-500621-6; 0-19-500808-1 (pa)

The author examines the various threads of thought, action, style, characterization, and symbolism which pull the play together

Onions, Charles Talbut, 1873-1965

A Shakespeare glossary; [by] C. T. Onions. 3rd ed, enlarged and revised throughout by Robert D. Eagleson. Oxford Univ. Press 1986 326p hardcover o.p. paperback available $14.95   **822.3**

1. Shakespeare, William, 1564-1616—Dictionaries

ISBN 0-19-812521-6 (pa)   LC 84-7912

First published 1911

"Gives definitions of words or senses of words now obsolete, as well as explanations for unfamiliar allusions and for proper names. Illustrative citations from Shakespeare are included for each definition." Ref Sources for Small & Medium-sized Libr. 5th edition

Includes bibliography

Schoenbaum, Samuel, 1927-

Shakespeare's lives; [by] S. Schoenbaum. new ed. Oxford Univ. Press 1991 612p il $35   **822.3**

1. Shakespeare, William, 1564-1616—Biography

ISBN 0-19-818618-5   LC 91-154

First published 1970

The author provides a history of the research into and discoveries related to Shakespeare's life. Various biographers are discussed

Includes bibliographic references

Shakespeare, William, 1564-1616

The complete works of William Shakespeare   **822.3**

Hardcover and paperback editions available from various publishers

For a comparison of most of the editions of Shakespeare see: The Reader's Advisor

A dictionary of quotations from Shakespeare; a topical guide to over 3,000 great passages from the plays, sonnets, and narrative poems; selected by Margaret Miner and Hugh Rawson. Dutton 1992 368p $25   **822.3**

1. Shakespeare, William, 1564-1616—Quotations 2. Quotations

ISBN 0-525-93451-0   LC 92-1354

The focus of this "dictionary, the authors say, is on 'quotations that are likely to be of practical use for writers and speakers today . . . [and] relevant to modern times and present-day problems.' Consequently, among the 400 categories are such headings as democracy, media, public relations, and Star Wars. Nearly half the quotations are annotated, with useful information about meaning and context." Libr J

An Oxford anthology of Shakespeare; selected and introduced by Stanley Wells. Oxford Univ. Press 1987 xx, 396p $24.95; pa $8.95   **822.3**

ISBN 0-19-812935-1; 0-19-282240-3 (pa)   LC 87-5788

"Shakespearean scholar Wells has gleaned from Shakespeare's 43 plays and 14 of his sonnets a collection of poems and passages whose strengths lie in their artistic, rhetorical, and literary value rather than their dramatic qualities. Organized under 13 headings, the passages could supplement a study of Shakespeare or could be used for private readings. . . . An excellent source because truly readable pieces have been chosen." Libr J

The **Shakespeare** handbook; [edited by] Levi Fox. Hall, G.K. & Co. 1987 264p il $35   **822.3**

1. Shakespeare, William, 1564-1616—Criticism, interpretation, etc.

ISBN 0-8161-8905-6   LC 87-16990

This work "offers overview discussions of Elizabethan and Jacobean theater, staging traditions of succeeding centuries, film adaptations of the plays, the society of Shakespeare's day, and the Bard's life. . . . Sidebar articles throughout provide the bricks of fact and detail needed to complement the mortar of generalization and analysis in the text." Wilson Libr Bull

Includes bibliography

Spevack, Marvin

The Harvard Concordance to Shakespeare. Harvard Univ. Press 1973 1600p $80   **822.3**

1. Shakespeare, William, 1564-1616—Concordances

ISBN 0-674-37475-4

A one-volume edition based on volumes IV, V, and VI of A Complete and Systematic Concordance to the Works of Shakespeare, by Marvin Spevack, published in 1968-1970. Based on the modern-spelling Riverside text of Shakespeare, edited by G. Blackmore Evans, it provides entries for every one of the more than 29,000 different words used by the Bard. Since contexts are provided, it can serve as a quotations dictionary to the plays and poems

Twentieth century interpretations of Julius Caesar; a collection of critical essays; edited by Leonard F. Dean. Prentice-Hall 1968 120p $8.95 **822.3**

1. Shakespeare, William, 1564-1616. Julius Caesar
ISBN 0-13-512285-6

"A Spectrum book"

A compilation of scholarly essays analyzing the subject and form of Shakespeare's historical drama

Includes bibliography

Wagenknecht, Edward, 1900-
The personality of Shakespeare. University of Okla. Press 1972 190p hardcover o.p. paperback available $10.95 **822.3**

1. Shakespeare, William, 1564-1616—Biography
2. Shakespeare, William, 1564-1616—Criticism, interpretation, etc.
ISBN 0-8061-1591-1 (pa)

"What can the poems and plays tell us about the temperament of our most impersonal of authors? That is the question Wagenknecht asks. . . . All who love Shakespeare will enjoy this rare glimpse of the middle ground between embellished reviews of the dull facts of his life and disembodied criticism of his plays." Libr J

William Shakespeare; his world, his work, his influence; John F. Andrews, editor. Scribner 1985 3v il set $250 **822.3**

1. Shakespeare, William, 1564-1616—Criticism, interpretation, etc. 2. Great Britain—Intellectual life
ISBN 0-684-17851-6 LC 85-8305

Contents: v1 His world; v2 His work; v3 His influence

"Each volume constitutes a series of signed essays (with selective bibliographies) which together explore 'virtually every aspect of the phenomenon we refer to as Shakespeare.' . . . Contributors (American and British, with two exceptions) are mainly academics but include names from the theater such as John Gielgud, Jonathan Miller and John Simon. Illustrations are fully described in v.3, which includes a general index to the set." Sheehy. Guide to Ref Books. 10th edition. suppl

Includes bibliographies

823.009 English fiction—History and criticism

Baker, James R.
Critical essays on William Golding. Hall, G.K. & Co. 1988 197p (Critical essays on British literature) $40 **823.009**

1. Golding, William, 1911-1993
ISBN 0-8161-8764-9 LC 87-33312

The author examines the moral and philosophical aspects in the work of the British Nobel Laureate

Includes bibliographic references

Benstock, Bernard
James Joyce. Ungar 1985 202p (Literature and life ser) $19.95 **823.009**

1. Joyce, James, 1882-1941
ISBN 0-8044-2047-5 LC 84-28048

An assessment of the Joycean canon. The major works, Ulysses and Finnegans wake, are discussed at length as are the poetry and the author's only play Exiles

Includes bibliography

Berg, Maggie
Jane Eyre; portrait of a life. Twayne Pubs. 1987 134p (Twayne's masterwork studies) lib bdg $20.95; pa $7.95 **823.009**

1. Brontë, Charlotte, 1816-1855. Jane Eyre
ISBN 0-8057-7955-8 (lib bdg); 0-8057-8010-6 (pa)
LC 87-14877

The author considers Brontë's novel as a self-portrait of a female artist, focusing on Jane Eyre as protagonist and narrator

Includes bibliography

Blom, Margaret Howard
Charlotte Brontë. Twayne Pubs. 1977 176p (Twayne's English authors ser) $19.95 **823.009**

1. Brontë, Charlotte, 1816-1855
ISBN 0-8057-6673-1 LC 76-42225

The author "follows the series format—chronology, biography, criticism, notes, annotated bibliography. There are no radical interpretations or flights of fancy. Especially noteworthy is the chapter on Charlotte's early unpublished writings. Blom succeeds admirably in following the contorted paths of this early writing and making sense of it." Libr J

Coale, Samuel
Anthony Burgess. Ungar 1981 223p (Modern literature ser) $10.95 **823.009**

1. Burgess, Anthony, 1917-1993
ISBN 0-8044-2124-2 LC 81-40459

This survey of the English author's fiction examines his novels "in terms of theme, structure, and form, and explores Burgess's experimentation with orchestral forms, ancient myths, linguistic tropes, and structures." Publisher's note

Includes bibliography

Crabbe, Katharyn W., 1945-
J.R.R. Tolkien. rev and expanded ed. Ungar 1988 233p (Literature and life, British writers) $19.95; pa $9.95 **823.009**

1. Tolkien, J. R. R. (John Ronald Reuel), 1892-1973
ISBN 0-8044-2106-4; 0-8044-6106-6 (pa) LC 87-5931

First published 1981

Brief biographical information is followed by analysis of The lord of the rings trilogy and such posthumously published works as The book of lost tales, The lays of Beleriand, and The shaping of Middle-Earth

Includes bibliography

Critical essays on Anthony Burgess; [edited by] Geoffrey Aggeler. Hall, G.K. & Co. 1986 231p (Critical essays on modern British literature) $40 **823.009**

1. Burgess, Anthony, 1917-1993
ISBN 0-8161-8757-6 LC 85-27319

Critical essays on Anthony Burgess—*Continued*

"Though dealing only with Burgess' novels, the contributors assembled here present most of the conceivable modes of criticism that Burgess' work may inspire. . . . Particularly enlightening are the essays that focus on Burgess' variations of Joycean themes and on his attempts to structure novels like sonatas. A revealing 'Paris Review' interview with the novelist is also included." Booklist

Includes bibliographies

Critical essays on Doris Lessing; [edited by] Claire Sprague and Virginia Tiger. Hall, G.K. & Co. 1986 237p $40   **823.009**

1. Lessing, Doris May, 1919-
ISBN 0-8161-8756-8   LC 85-27097

This collection of essays is "organized by broad topic headings under which works from all phases of Lessing's career are discussed together. . . . The long introduction is noteworthy especially for its insights on the 'Jane Somers' hoax as an expression of Lessing's need to break out of the impasse of the Canopus series." Booklist

Includes bibliography

Critical essays on E. M. Forster; [compiled and edited by] Alan Wilde. Hall, G.K. & Co. 1985 181p $40   **823.009**

1. Forster, E. M. (Edward Morgan), 1879-1970
ISBN 0-8161-8754-1   LC 85-2763

A collection of essays "which attempt to isolate not only the meaning and significance of Forster's work, but also his personal stance morally, intellectually, artistically, and politically, as well as sexually." Booklist

Includes bibliographies

Critical essays on Nadine Gordimer; [edited by] Rowland Smith. Hall, G.K. & Co. 1990 226p (Critical essays on world literature) $40   **823.009**

1. Gordimer, Nadine, 1923-
ISBN 0-8161-8847-5   LC 90-31945

Critics examine the novels and short stories of the South African Nobel laureate

Includes bibliographic references

Critical essays on Virginia Woolf; [edited by] Morris Beja. Hall, G.K. & Co. 1985 253p (Critical essay on modern British literature) $40   **823.009**

1. Woolf, Virginia, 1882-1941
ISBN 0-8161-8753-3   LC 85-914

Beja has "gathered 22 items on Woolf (8 brief book reviews, 1922-41; 13 reprints of essays or passages from books, 1937-81; 2 original essays, 1984) by as many hands, representing mostly well-known US academics." Choice

Includes bibliographic references

Critical survey of long fiction, English language series; edited by Frank N. Magill. rev ed. Salem Press 1991 8v $475
     823.009

1. English fiction—History and criticism 2. American fiction—History and criticism 3. English fiction—Bio-bibliography 4. American fiction—Bio-bibliography
ISBN 0-89356-825-2   LC 91-19694

First published 1983

"This Magill study of English-language long fiction provides bio-bibliographical information and a critical evaluation for over 300 authors, together with twenty essays on the history and development of the novel and the novella." Ref Sources for Small & Medium-sized Libr. 5th edition

Includes bibliographic references

D.H. Lawrence's Sons and lovers; edited and with an introduction by Harold Bloom. Chelsea House 1988 170p (Modern critical interpretations) $24.95   **823.009**

1. Lawrence, D. H. (David Herbert), 1885-1930. Sons and lovers
ISBN 1-55546-024-0   LC 87-17831

Contributors offer critical assessments of Lawrence's classic evocation of working-class life

Includes bibliography

D.H. Lawrence's The rainbow; edited and with an introduction by Harold Bloom. Chelsea House 1988 152p il (Modern critical interpretations) $24.95   **823.009**

1. Lawrence, D. H. (David Herbert), 1885-1930. The rainbow
ISBN 1-55546-023-2   LC 87-27463

Alan Friedman, Colin Clarke and Daniel J. Schneider are among the contributors offering critical perspectives on Lawrence's generational novel about love and marriage

Includes bibliography

Davies, Stevie

Emily Bronte. Indiana Univ. Press 1988 180p (Key women writers) $25   **823.009**

1. Brontë, Emily, 1818-1848
ISBN 0-253-30105-X   LC 88-10916

A "feminist perspective on the novels and other writings of Emily Brontë. . . . The highest appeal of this book will be for literary theorists and students of women's studies." Booklist

Includes bibliography

De Vitis, A. A.

Graham Greene. rev ed. Twayne Pubs. 1986 218p (Twayne's English authors ser) $21.95   **823.009**

1. Greene, Graham, 1904-1991
ISBN 0-8057-6911-0   LC 85-17612

First published 1964

The author focuses primarily on Greene's fiction from the early The man within and Brighton Rock to the more recent Monsignor Quixote and The tenth man. Also discussed are pertinent biographical facts that may effect an understanding of the work, and Greene's journalistic contributions, including his film reviews

Includes bibliography

Dick, Bernard F.

William Golding. rev ed. Twayne Pubs. 1987 168p (Twayne's English authors ser) $20.95   **823.009**

1. Golding, William, 1911-1993
ISBN 0-8057-6925-0   LC 86-14857

Dick, Bernard F.—*Continued*
First published 1967

This critical study covers such works as Lord of the flies, The spire, Darkness visible, and Rites of passage

"Complete with chronology, selected bibliography, index, and notes, [this] work provides the perspective necessary to put Golding in his proper place in literary history." Choice

Dircks, Richard J.
Henry Fielding. Twayne Pubs. 1983 143p il (Twayne's English authors ser) $17.95
823.009

1. Fielding, Henry, 1707-1754
ISBN 0-8057-6768-1   LC 83-10723

Critical analysis of: Tom Jones, Amelia, The voyage to Lisbon, John Andrews, Shamela and Jonathan Wild

Includes bibliography

Draper, Michael, 1953-
H.G. Wells. St. Martin's Press 1988 133p (Modern novelists) $24.95   **823.009**

1. Wells, H. G. (Herbert George), 1866-1946
ISBN 0-312-02090-2   LC 88-4675

A critical assessment of the British novelist focusing on the political and social aspects of his work

Includes bibliography

Ermarth, Elizabeth, 1939-
George Eliot; [by] Elizabeth Deeds Ermarth. Twayne Pubs. 1985 163p (Twayne's English authors ser) $19.95
823.009

1. Eliot, George, 1819-1880
ISBN 0-8057-6910-2   LC 85-8603

"In the biographical sketch that opens the book, and in the following chapter devoted to Eliot's translations and essays, Ermarth tallies the influences that contributed to the novelist's intellectual development. . . . Ermarth is consistently successful in locating the central issues of each of the novels and in relating them in turn to Eliot's own system of moral and philosophical belief." Booklist

Includes bibliography

Ford, Paul F.
Companion to Narnia; illustrated by Lorinda Bryan Cauley. Harper & Row 1980 xxxii, 313p il hardcover o.p. paperback available $6.95   **823.009**

1. Lewis, C. S. (Clive Staples), 1898-1963. Chronicles of Narnia
ISBN 0-06-250341-3 (pa)   LC 80-7734

Also available in paperback from Macmillan

C. S. Lewis wrote seven books of fantasy that are collectively called The Chronicles of Narnia. This book "is an encyclopedia of Narnian names and terms and related matters, with . . . footnoted articles, page references to American and British hardcover editions, cross-references, and a running footline for quick location of materials in the alphabet." Choice

Fullbrook, Kate
Katherine Mansfield. Indiana Univ. Press 1986 146p (Key women writers) hardcover o.p. paperback available $7.95   **823.009**

1. Mansfield, Katherine, 1888-1923
ISBN 0-253-20401-1 (pa)   LC 86-45392

This critical study examines the aesthetic and techniques employed by the New Zealand-born short story writer

Includes bibliography

Gidez, Richard B.
P.D. James. Twayne Pubs. 1986 153p (Twayne's English authors ser) $19.95
823.009

1. James, P. D.
ISBN 0-8057-6924-2   LC 86-3073

The author "writes knowledgeably of the classic tradition in detective fiction, ably tracing James's debts to Christie and Allingham and her respectful parody of Dorothy L. Sayers's 'Gaudy Night' (1935) in her own Cambridge novel, 'An Unsuitable Job for a Woman' (1972)." Choice

Includes bibliography

Gillon, Adam, 1921-
Joseph Conrad. Twayne Pubs. 1982 210p (Twayne's English authors ser) $19.95
823.009

1. Conrad, Joseph, 1857-1924
ISBN 0-8057-6820-3   LC 81-13301

This work "ranges over every essential aspect of the writer's life and work. . . . The scope is admirable: the literary heritage (such as Shakespeare's influence on Conrad, for example), the major themes of the fiction, the references to the abiding critical evaluations of others, and the aim to isolate key motifs of both life and work." Choice

Includes bibliography

Hardwick, Michael, 1924-
The complete guide to Sherlock Holmes. St. Martin's Press 1987 c1986 255p il $16.95; pa $10.95   **823.009**

1. Doyle, Sir Arthur Conan, 1859-1930—Characters
2. Holmes, Sherlock (Fictitious character)
ISBN 0-312-00580-6; 0-312-07248-1 (pa)   LC 87-81

First published 1986 in the United Kingdom

The author "begins with the opening chapters of 'A Study in Scarlet' (1888) . . . and then progresses through all the Holmes pieces in chronological order. . . . The textual synopses are effectively cemented together with a running commentary on Arthur Conan Doyle's life. Included are illustrations from the stories as originally published in the 'Strand Magazine' and a who's who of characters." Booklist

Horror: the 100 best books; edited by Stephen Jones and Kim Newman. Carroll & Graf Pubs. 1988 254p $15.95; pa $8.95
823.009

1. Horror—Fiction—History and criticism 2. Books and reading—Best books
ISBN 0-88184-417-9; 0-88184-594-9 (pa) LC 88-7351

Horror: the 100 best books—*Continued*
"Each of 100 writers and editors of horror fiction plugs his or her own favorite book in the genre. Chronologically, the resulting '100 Best' span from 1592 and Marlowe's play, 'Doctor Faustus,' to a novel and a short-story collection both published in 1987. Genre classics such as 'Frankenstein,' 'Dracula,' and 'Dr. Jekyll and Mr. Hyde' are expectably honored, as are contemporary titles by King, Barker, Strieber, Straub, et al., and works by many of Edwardian England's and mid-twentieth-century America's horror specialists." Booklist

Jaffe, Jacqueline A.
Arthur Conan Doyle. Twayne Pubs. 1987 148p (Twayne's English authors ser) lib bdg $19.95   **823.009**
1. Doyle, Sir Arthur Conan, 1859-1930
ISBN 0-8057-6954-4   LC 87-8421
"Jaffe organizes Doyle's diverse canon by genre and discusses it in the context of the late 19th century romantic revival. Devoting two chapters to the Holmes novels and stories, she shows Doyle fusing romantic assumptions with rationalist certainties, to create a uniquely popular hero: the knight-errant as master detective. Jaffe promotes renewed attention for Doyle's historical novels and scientific romances." Publisher's note
Includes bibliography

James Joyce's Ulysses; edited and with an introduction by Harold Bloom. Chelsea House 1987 168p (Modern critical interpretations) $29.95   **823.009**
1. Joyce, James, 1882-1941. Ulysses
ISBN 1-55546-021-6   LC 87-5830
Critical essays assessing Joyce's modernist masterpiece
Includes bibliography

John le Carré; edited and with an introduction by Harold Bloom. Chelsea House 1987 180p (Modern critical views) $24.95   **823.009**
1. Le Carré, John, 1931-
ISBN 0-87754-703-3   LC 86-31026
A selection of critical essays, arranged in chronological order of publication, devoted to the fiction of John le Carré
Includes bibliography

Keating, H. R. F. (Henry Reymond Fitzwalter), 1926-
Crime and mystery: the 100 best books. Carroll & Graf Pubs. 1987 219p $15.95; pa $8.95   **823.009**
1. Mystery and detective stories—Bibliography
2. Books and reading—Best books
ISBN 0-88184-345-8; 0-88184-441-1 (pa)
                                   LC 87-17377
A "collection of essays reflecting one writer's ideas about what constitutes the best in crime and mystery fiction. The two-page essays extend from Poe's *Tales of Mystery and Imagination* through P.D. James's *A Taste for Death*, forming a sort of history of the genre. Each essay contains a synopsis of the plot or theme, a critical assessment, and a list of first and recent editions. Keating, a prolific mystery writer, seems an ideal choice to compile such a work, and his wit and intelligence make these essays as much fun as they are informative." Libr J

Lane, Calvin Warren, 1923-
Evelyn Waugh. Twayne Pubs. 1981 189p (Twayne's English authors ser) $19.95
                                   823.009
1. Waugh, Evelyn, 1903-1966
ISBN 0-8057-6793-2   LC 80-22498
This is a study of the English author's life and works. "The six chapters discuss in turn Waugh and his world, the early satiric novels through Put Out More Flags, 'The Catholic Novels' (Brideshead Revisited), Helena, . . . The Loved One and The Ordeal of Gilbert Pinfold, the war trilogy, Waugh as critic and [Waugh's achievement]." World Lit Today
Includes bibliography

Lee, Hermione
The novels of Virginia Woolf. Holmes & Meier 1977 237p $19.50   **823.009**
1. Woolf, Virginia, 1882-1941
ISBN 0-8419-0314-X   LC 77-4981
This is literary criticism of Virginia Woolf's nine novels
"The criticism is straightforward, closely reasoned, solid, requires knowledge of the fiction involved." Publ Wkly
Includes bibliography

Levin, Harry, 1912-
James Joyce; a critical introduction. rev and augmented ed. New Directions 1960 256p pa $9.95   **823.009**
1. Joyce, James, 1882-1941
ISBN 0-8112-0089-2 (pa)
First published 1941
"A book on Joyce that is not a bare physiognomic map, but a rich, allusive and civilized guide through Joyce's technology, a first-rate study in literary history, an essay full of marginal richness as both literary and social criticism." New Repub
Includes bibliography

Long, Robert Emmet, 1934-
Barbara Pym. Ungar 1986 256p (Literature and life. British writers) $19.95   **823.009**
1. Pym, Barbara
ISBN 0-8044-2545-0   LC 86-7053
In this study of Pym's life and work, the author "analyzes each novel but emphasizes Pym's characteristic use of satire and comedy. . . . This study is recommended for most libraries with an active interest in contemporary fiction." Libr J
Includes bibliography

Mellor, Anne Kostelanetz
Mary Shelley, her life, her fiction, her monsters. Methuen 1988 xx, 275p il $35; pa $14.95   **823.009**
ISBN 0-415-02591-5; 0-415-90147-2 (pa)
                                   LC 87-31249
The author "blends biography and informed criticism here to give a feminist reevaluation of Mary Shelley and her fiction, especially *Frankenstein*. . . . Mellor's book is clearly written and forcefully argued." Choice
Includes bibliography

O'Faoláin, Seán, 1900-1991

The vanishing hero; studies in novelists of the twenties. Books for Libs. 1971 c1957 204p (Essay index reprint ser) $16

823.009

1. English fiction—History and criticism 2. American fiction—History and criticism 3. Heroes and heroines in literature
ISBN 0-8369-2065-1

Reprint of the title first published 1957 by Little, Brown and analyzed in Essay and general literature index

"The Irish novelist-critic-playwright dissects eight modern literary greats, aiming to discover the essence of each individual through his or her written words alone. Huxley, Waugh, Faulkner, Hemingway, Greene, Bowen, Joyce, Woolf are [included]." Publ Wkly

Oleksiw, Susan

A reader's guide to the classic British mystery. Hall, G.K. & Co. 1988 585p $35

823.009

1. Mystery and detective stories—History and criticism
ISBN 0-8161-8787-8   LC 88-1735

"Oleksiw lists annotations of over 1440 novels by 121 authors, arranging them first alphabetically by writer. They are also listed chronologically by the story's time frame, with novels featuring series characters entered first. The 50- to 75-word annotations sketch the plot; numerous specialized indexes are helpful in finding one's way around the unconventional arrangement." Libr J

Page, Norman

A Conrad companion. St. Martin's Press 1986 185p $25   **823.009**

1. Conrad, Joseph, 1857-1924
ISBN 0-312-16261-8   LC 85-11998

The author provides "information on the genesis, composition, publication and reception of Conrad's books together with an indication of some of the main lines of interpretation, criticism and evaluation. There are also a filmography and a select bibliography." Publisher's note

A Dickens companion. Schocken Bks. 1984 369p il hardcover o.p. paperback available $11.95   **823.009**

1. Dickens, Charles, 1812-1870
ISBN 0-8052-0846-1 (pa)   LC 83-16306

"This volume contains a detailed chronology of Dickens's life and works, biographical sketches of the Dickens circle, sections on Dickens's illustrators and topography, and a select bibliography, which contains sections on film adaptations and early dramatizations. . . . Finally, there is an overview of modern criticism and a list of characters with a brief description of each." Choice

Pipes, Daniel, 1949-

The Rushdie affair; the novel, the Ayatollah, and the West. Carol Pub. Group 1990 269p $18.95   **823.009**

1. Rushdie, Salman. Satanic verses 2. Khomeini, Ruhollah
ISBN 1-55972-025-5   LC 89-43091

"A Birch Lane Press book"

"Besides recounting the events that took place between the publication of *The Satanic Verses* and the Ayatollah's edict, . . . this work examines the text of Rushdie's novel to see why the book was considered blasphemous by the Ayatollah. Pipes suggests that with his knowledge of Islam Rushdie must have known that his book would be considered blasphemous. The text and legality of the edict are also considered." Libr J

Includes bibliographic references

Reilly, Patrick

George Orwell: the age's adversary. St. Martin's Press 1986 316p $29.95   **823.009**

1. Orwell, George, 1903-1950
ISBN 0-312-32449-9   LC 85-18425

A critique of Orwell as novelist with particular emphasis on Animal farm and Nineteen eighty-four

"Reilly is perceptive and thorough, and the book offers far more critical light than heated fervor." Choice

Richetti, John J.

Daniel Defoe. Twayne Pubs. 1987 154p (Twayne's English authors ser) $19.95

823.009

1. Defoe, Daniel, 1661?-1731
ISBN 0-8057-6955-2   LC 87-8550

The author surveys "Defoe's life and writings, including the major nonfiction as well as the novels. Employing a lucid and witty style, Richetti deftly sketches the historical and literary context for the beginning student." Choice

Includes bibliography

Rosenthal, Michael, 1937-

Virginia Woolf. Columbia Univ. Press 1979 270p hardcover o.p. paperback available $16   **823.009**

1. Woolf, Virginia, 1882-1941
ISBN 0-231-04849-1 (pa)   LC 79-12161

"Chapters on Woolf's life, Bloomsbury, and the nature of her fiction are followed by discussions of each of the novels plus the biographies and social and literary criticism." Libr J

Includes bibliography

The **Rushdie** file; edited by Lisa Appignanesi and Sara Maitland. Syracuse Univ. Press 1990 266p hardcover o.p. paperback available $13.95   **823.009**

1. Rushdie, Salman. Satanic verses
ISBN 0-8156-0248-0 (pa)   LC 89-48413

"A chronicle of the events that began with the publication of *The Satanic Verses* and led to the disappearance of Salman Rushdie from public life. The book includes reviews, interviews with the author, the decree by Khomeini, and responses and comments as they were made all over the world. . . . These thought-provoking essays and interviews provide moral and philosophical observations that concern Muslims, Christians, and anyone interested in issues of intellectual freedom." SLJ

Sanders, Dennis, 1949-

The Agatha Christie companion; the complete guide to Agatha Christie's life and work; [by] Dennis Sanders & Len Lovallo. Delacorte Press 1984 xxvii, 523p o.p.; Berkley Pub. Group paperback available $12.95   **823.009**

1. Christie, Agatha, 1890-1976
ISBN 0-425-11845-2 (pa)   LC 83-5167

Part 1 is "divided into mystery novels and collections, and miscellaneous books (gothics, etc.). . . . Part 2 is the best available guide to Christie's plays, films, and television adaptations, and includes the story behind each production, plus cast lists. Eighteen alphabetical lists make up the final part, summarizing each detective's titles, plus Christie's total collected 'oeuvre.' Last is a token secondary bibliography." Libr J

Sharrock, Roger

Saints, sinners, and comedians; the novels of Graham Greene. University of Notre Dame Press 1984 298p $10.95   **823.009**

1. Greene, Graham, 1904-1991
ISBN 0-268-01713-1   LC 84-40359

The author "discusses all of Graham Greene's novels individually, up to and including 'Monsignor Quixote,' His book will prove invaluable, especially with its concise plot descriptions, to students, and entertaining and stimulating to everyone who enjoys reading contemporary fiction." Univ Press Books for Public Libr

Includes bibliography

Skal, David J.

Hollywood gothic; the tangled web of Dracula from novel to stage to screen. Norton 1990 242p il $39.95; pa $15.95   **823.009**

1. Stoker, Bram, 1847-1912. Dracula   2. Horror films—History and criticism
ISBN 0-393-02904-2; 0-393-30805-7 (pa) LC 90-7283

The author traces the vampire Dracula from Bram Stoker's 1897 novel through three stage adaptations and various film versions, including the 1931 film featuring Bela Lugosi

"Though neither a book for browsers nor a complete history of film versions, Skal's chronicle of early endeavors to bring Stoker's *Dracula* to the screen will fascinate serious fans and intrigue film students." Booklist

Includes bibliographic references

Trilling, Lionel, 1905-1975

E. M. Forster. 2nd rev ed. New Directions 1964 pa $5.95   **823.009**

1. Forster, E. M. (Edward Morgan), 1879-1970
ISBN 0-8112-0210-0

Also available from Harcourt Brace & Co.

First published 1943

Contents: Introduction: Forster and the liberal imagination; Swaston and Cambridge; The short stories; Where angels fear to tread; The longest journey; A room with a view; Howards end; A passage to India; Mind and will: Forster's literary criticism; Bibliography

824   English essays

Bacon, Francis, 1561-1626

The essays; or, Counsels, civil and moral   **824**

Hardcover and paperback editions available from various publishers

"A collection of brief essays by Francis Bacon, published in three editions during his lifetime: a first edition of ten essays (1597); a second of thirty-eight (1612); and a third of fifty-eight (1625). Generally, they deal with questions of personal or public conduct and philosophical or religious matters. They are written in a witty, pithy, widely metphorical, and highly original style." Reader's Ency. 3d edition

Carlyle, Thomas, 1795-1881

On heroes, hero-worship and the heroic in history. Oxford Univ. Press 1928 245p $12.95   **824**

1. Heroes and heroines
ISBN 0-19-250062-7

Also available in paperback from University of Neb. Press

"The World's classics"

First published 1841

By means of sketches of Mahomet, Dante, Shakespeare, Luther, Samuel Johnson, Cromwell, Napoleon and others, Carlyle aims to prove the importance of the great man in history and to show that the essential heroic qualities have been the same in all great men

Past and present; edited with an introduction and notes by Richard D. Altick. New York Univ. Press 1977 294p hardcover o.p. paperback available $15   **824**

ISBN 0-8147-0562-6 (pa)

First published 1843

In this work Carlyle's "attack on the contemporary failure of democracy, as he saw it, was presented poetically as an account of the ordered life at the medieval abbey of St Edmund's, Bury. Labour and duty are the true ends of life (the 'gospel of work'), and the many voluntarily submit to the leadership of the superior few, such as Abbott Sampson." Penguin Companion to Engl Lit

Sartor resartus; edited with an introduction and notes by Kerry McSweeney and Peter Sabor. Oxford Univ. Press 1987 xlii, 273p (The World's classics) pa $7.95   **824**

ISBN 0-19-281757-4   LC 87-5753

First published 1833-1834, Sartor resartus contains the germ of Carlyle's philosophy. It purports to be an interpretation of the work of an erudite German professor but is really the story of Carlyle's own fierce spiritual conflict between doubt and faith. It presents a philosophy of clothes, or the outward forms of things

Includes bibliographic references

Coleridge, Samuel Taylor, 1772-1834

Biographia literaria.   **824**

Coleridge, Samuel Taylor, 1772-1834—*Continued*

Hardcover and paperback editions available from various publishers

First published 1817

This book "contains essays on literary criticism and develops the author's distinction between fancy and imagination. The book also contains a discussion of the distinction between reason and understanding, an explanation of Coleridge's concept of a willing suspension of disbelief, a trenchant critical analysis of Wordsworth's poetry, and detailed discussions of portions of the philosophies of Kant, Schelling, and Fichte." Reader's Ency. 3d edition

Connolly, Cyril, 1903-1974

The selected essays of Cyril Connolly; edited and with an introduction by Peter Quennell. Persea Bks. 1984 307p $17.95
                                                           824

ISBN 0-89255-072-4   LC 83-22147

Analyzed in Essay and general literature index

"A Stanley Moss book"

This collection of writing by the British editor and book reviewer has three sections: "Travel," "Life and Literature," and "Satires and Parodies"

De Quincey, Thomas, 1785-1859

The confessions of an English opium-eater
                                                           824

1. Drug addiction

Hardcover and paperback editions available from various publishers

First published 1822

This famous account of the English author's ecstasies and sufferings until his drug habit was brought under control "attracted attention, not simply by its personal disclosures, but by the extraordinary power of its dream-painting." Ency Britannica

Forster, E. M. (Edward Morgan), 1879-1970

Two cheers for democracy. Harcourt Brace & Co. 1951 363p hardcover o.p. paperback available $9.95   **824**

ISBN 0-15-692025-5 (pa)

Analyzed in Essay and general literature index

A collection of essays, articles, reviews and broadcasts focusing on literature, society and politics

Greene, Graham, 1904-1991

Collected essays. Viking 1969 463p o.p.; Penguin Bks. paperback available $7.95
                                                           824

ISBN 0-14-003159-6 (pa)

Analyzed in Essay and general literature index

A collection of critical essays on literature, politics, religion and social issues

Orwell, George, 1903-1950

Dickens, Dali & others; studies in popular culture. Reynal & Hitchcock 1946 243p o.p.; Harcourt Brace & Co. paperback available $8.95   **824**

ISBN 0-15-626053-0 (pa)

Analyzed in Essay and general literature index

Contents: Charles Dickens; Boys' weeklies; Wells, Hitler and the world state; The art of Donald McGill; Rudyard Kipling; W. B. Yeats; Benefit of clergy: some notes on Salvador Dali; King Koestler; Raffles and Miss Blandish: In defence of P. G. Wodehouse

Shooting an elephant, and other essays. Harcourt Brace & Co. 1950 200p $12.95
                                                           824

ISBN 0-15-182043-0

Analyzed in Essay and general literature index

A collection of "autobiographical reminiscence, literary criticism and incidental journalism." Time

The **Oxford** book of essays; chosen and edited by John Gross. Oxford Univ. Press 1991 xxiii, 680p $30; pa $16.95   **824**
ISBN 0-19-214185-6; 0-19-282970-X (pa)
                                                    LC 90-34948

"The collection begins in the 17th century with Sir Francis Bacon moralizing on truth and ends with a scathing review of a Judith Krantz best seller by Clive James. In between there is something for just about everyone, e.g., Boswell on war, Thoreau on moonlight, Banham on potato chips. Literary, theological, sociological, political, and humorous essays are included." Libr J

Includes bibliographic references

Woolf, Virginia, 1882-1941

Essays of Virginia Woolf; edited by Andrew McNeillie. Harcourt Brace Jovanovich 1987-1989 3v v1 $19.95, v2-3 ea $22.95   **824**

Contents: v1 1904-1912 (ISBN 0-15-129055-5); v2 1912-1918 (ISBN 0-15-129056-3); v3 1919-1924 (ISBN 0-15-129057-1)

The first three volumes of a projected six-volume collection of Woolf's critical reviews, art and drama notices, travel pieces and extended ruminations on subjects ranging from character in fiction to the social status of women

827 English satire and humor

The **Oxford** book of humorous prose; William Caxton to P.G. Wodehouse: a conducted tour; [chosen and edited] by Frank Muir. Oxford Univ. Press 1990 xxxiv, 1162p $39.95; pa $17.95   **827**
1. English wit and humor 2. American wit and humor
ISBN 0-19-214106-6; 0-19-282959-9 (pa) LC 89-9242

"A sprinkling of American contributors join British humorists in this selection of pieces ranging from the gently witty to the irreverent, the bawdy, and the sexy." Booklist

The Oxford book of humorous prose —
Continued

"Selections are generally very short, with bridges, often fairly humorous of themselves, by Muir. The humor ranges from the broad to the subtle and, in fact, in any other way that humor might range; there's something in here for everyone." Libr J

Swift, Jonathan, 1667-1745

A tale of a tub; to which is added The battle of the books, and the Mechanical operation of the spirit. Together with The history of Martin, Wotton's Observations upon the Tale of a tub, Curll's Complete key, etc. The whole edited with an introduction and notes historical and explanatory, by A. C. Guthkelch and D. Nichol Smith. 2nd ed. Oxford Univ. Press 1958 lxxvii, 374p il $59　　**827**

ISBN 0-19-811404-4

First published in this edition 1920

A tale of a tub, The battle of the books, and A discourse concerning the mechanical operation of the spirit, were first published together in 1704. The first is an allegorical satire ridiculing the corruptions of religion and learning by extremists and pedants. The second is a mock heroic satire on squabbles concerning the relative merits of ancient and modern authors presented as an account of the battle between ancient and modern books in St. James Library. The third ridicules the manner of worship and preaching of religious enthusiasts of the period

Includes bibliographic references

828　English miscellany

Blake, William, 1757-1827

The complete poetry and prose of William Blake; edited by David V. Erdman; commentary by Harold Bloom. newly rev ed. University of Calif. Press 1982 xxvi, 990p $47.50　　**828**

ISBN 0-520-04473-8　　　　LC 81-40323

First published 1965 with title: Poetry and prose of William Blake

This collection contains the complete poetry and prose of Blake, including his letters, as well as critical commentary

The portable Blake; selected and arranged with an introduction by Alfred Kazin. Viking 1946 713p il o.p.; Penguin Bks. paperback available $11　　**828**

ISBN 0-14-015026-9 (pa)

"The Viking portable library"

In addition to the complete text of Songs of innocence and experience, this work includes "a generous selection of verse, prose, letters, and essays. Blake is shown as an artist and poet against all institutions but ever seeking unity (though his was the mystic's quest) while hunting for realism and naturalism." Cincinnati Public Libr

Includes bibliography

Bowen, Elizabeth, 1899-1973

The mulberry tree; writings of Elizabeth Bowen; selected and introduced by Hermione Lee. Harcourt Brace Jovanovich 1987 c1986 325p il $19.95　　**828**

ISBN 0-15-163240-5　　　　LC 86-29446

First published 1986 in the United Kingdom

This is a collection of nonfiction pieces written by the Anglo-Irish novelist between 1934 and 1972. The editor "has arranged her material under six headings: Essays, Prefaces, Reviews, Letters, Broadcasts and Autobiography." Times Lit Suppl

Includes bibliography

Chatwin, Bruce

What am I doing here? Viking 1989 367p o.p.; Penguin Bks. paperback available $9.95
　　828

ISBN 0-14-011577-3 (pa)　　　　LC 89-40165

Also available Transaction Pubs. large print edition

"Most of these 35 sketches are of people encountered worldwide, some famous (Malraux, Indira Gandhi), all distinguished for some unique statement or action—from an aesthetic of violence to political murder to postage stamp painting. Chatwin's prose is a kind of democratic Mandarin, at once enameled, crisp, and colloquial." Libr J

Coleridge, Samuel Taylor, 1772-1834

The portable Coleridge; edited and with an introduction by I. A. Richards. Viking 1950 630p o.p.; Penguin Bks. paperback available $11　　**828**

ISBN 0-14-015048-X (pa)

"The Viking portable library"

Includes: The rime of the ancient mariner (1875); Christabel; Kubla Khan; and most of the shorter poems; ample representation of the "Biographia literaria," generous selections from the other literary criticism, political essays, notebooks, and letters; also a lengthy biographical introduction

Includes bibliography

Selected poetry and prose; edited with an introduction, by Donald A. Stauffer. Modern Lib. 1951 xxviii, 608p o.p.; McGraw-Hill paperback available $8.36　　**828**

ISBN 0-07-553638-2 (pa)

"A representative selection of the works of Coleridge. . . . All the poems included are complete. Among the prose selections many of the letters and occasional chapters from his critical writings are complete, but the majority are cut and vary in length from a paragraph to several pages." Booklist

Includes bibliography

Conrad, Joseph, 1857-1924

The portable Conrad; edited and with an introduction and notes by Morton Dauwen Zabel. rev ed, [edited] by Frederick R. Karl. Viking 1969 762p o.p.; Penguin Bks. paperback available $9.95　　**828**

ISBN 0-14-015033-1 (pa)

Conrad, Joseph, 1857-1924—*Continued*
"The Viking portable library"
First published 1947

Contains two novels: The Nigger of the Narcissus and Typhoon; three long stories; six shorter stories; and a selection from Conrad's prefaces, letters and autobiographical writings

Includes bibliography

Golding, William, 1911-1993
A moving target. Farrar, Straus & Giroux 1982 202p hardcover o.p. paperback available $7.95 **828**

ISBN 0-374-51850-5 (pa)   LC 82-5026

This collection of sixteen occasional pieces contains travel essays on Egypt, Delphi, England, Holland, and Greece as well as a series of writings on literary creation and creativity

"Golding's erudition, wit, and brilliant powers of observation are apparent in each of the selections." Choice

Gordimer, Nadine, 1923-
The essential gesture; writing, politics and places; edited and with an introduction by Stephen Clingman. Knopf 1988 356p o.p.; Penguin Bks. paperback available $11 **828**

1. South Africa—Politics and government 2. South Africa—Race relations
ISBN 0-14-012212-5 (pa)   LC 88-21612

This is a collection of essays, articles and speeches by the South African novelist

"Politics and literature are mixed into a brilliant amalgam as Gordimer reflects on both the changes apartheid has made in South Africa and on the growing opposition to her country's racial policies." Booklist

Includes bibliography

Greene, Graham, 1904-1991
The portable Graham Greene; edited by Philip Stratford. Viking 1973 xxiii, 610p o.p.; Penguin Bks. paperback available $9.95 **828**

ISBN 0-14-015075-7 (pa)
"The Viking portable library"

This collection contains ten selections from autobiographical writings; twelve short stories; two complete novels: The heart of the matter and The third man; nine critical literary essays; and statements about political and social issues

Reflections; selected and introduced by Judith Adamson. Reinhardt Bks. 1990 324p $19.95 **828**

ISBN 1-871061-19-9   LC 90-81666
Also available in paperback from Penguin Bks.

"This volume includes Greene's thoughts on such diverse subjects as the political climates in Cuba, Haiti, and Chile; the French war in Indochina; used bookstores; and praise for Indian writer R.K. Narayan." Libr J

Yours etc.: letters to the press; selected and introduced by Christopher Hawtree. Reinhardt Bks. 1989 xx, 268p o.p.; Penguin Bks. paperback available $9.95 **828**

ISBN 0-14-012372-5 (pa)   LC 89-62859

The letters selected "range in subject matter from Colette and G.B. Shaw to Ronald Reagan; Capri, Cuba, Ghana, Vietnam; contraception, obscenity, torture, tyranny, the right to die." Publ Wkly

"Mr. Greene writes a splendid prose, and his ideas are often persuasive and always thought-provoking." NY Times Book Rev

Holmes, Richard, 1945-
Footsteps; adventures of a Romantic biographer. Viking 1985 288p il maps o.p.; Penguin Bks. paperback available $8.95 **828**

1. Authors, English
ISBN 0-14-013936-2 (pa)   LC 83-47897
"Elisabeth Sifton books"

This "is an unusual mixture of persons adventure and retelling of the stories of Robert Lewis Stevenson, William Wordsworth, Mary Wollstonecraft, and the French writer, Gerard de Nerval, as well as that of Shelley. Organized into four parts, each tells of that year's adventures as the European experiences of these five writers lived among the great and notable moments of history." Best Sellers

Includes bibliography

Hunting, Robert
Jonathan Swift. rev ed. Twayne Pubs. 1989 152p (Twayne's English authors ser) $20.95 **828**

1. Swift, Jonathan, 1667-1745
ISBN 0-8057-6982-X   LC 89-2126
First published 1967

This is a critical introduction to the work and life of the English satirist and poet

Includes bibliography

Huxley, Aldous, 1894-1963
Brave new world, and Brave new world revisited; with a foreword by the author; introduction by Martin Green. Harper & Row 1965 c1960 2v in 1 pa $13 **828**

ISBN 0-06-090101-2

Partially analyzed in Essay and general literature index
"HarperColophon books"

First published 1960; a combined edition of the two titles published 1932 and 1958 respectively

Brave new world revisited is entered separately in class 303.3. Brave new world is a satirical novel "set in the year 632 AF (After Ford), it is a grim picture of the world which Huxley thinks our scientific and social developments have already begun to create." Reader's Ency. 3d edition

Joyce, James, 1882-1941
The portable James Joyce; with an introduction & notes by Harry Levin. Viking 1947 760p o.p.; Penguin Bks. paperback available $12.50   **828**

ISBN 0-14-015030-7 (pa)
"The Viking portable library"
Spine title: James Joyce
Includes the following four complete works: Portrait of the artist as a young man; Collected poems; Exiles (play); Dubliners (short stories); also excerpts from Ulysses and Finnegans wake
Includes bibliography

Lawrence, D. H. (David Herbert), 1885-1930
The portable D. H. Lawrence; edited and with an introduction by Diana Trilling. Viking 1947 692p o.p.; Penguin Bks. paperback available $12   **828**

ISBN 0-14-015028-5 (pa)
Partially analyzed in Essay and general literature index
"The Viking portable library"
This volume contains eight short stories or novelettes: The Prussian officer; Tickets, please; The blind man; Two blue birds; The lovely lady; The rockinghorse winner; The princess; The fox; excerpts from The rainbow, and Women in love; a dozen poems; travel sketches; letters; and a number of essays and critical writings

Lessing, Doris May, 1919-
The Doris Lessing reader. Knopf 1988 635p $24.95   **828**

ISBN 0-394-57307-2   LC 88-12689
"Excerpts from the writer's novels, plus 14 short stories and selections from nonfiction and autobiographical essays, supply a wide-ranging sampling of Lessing's art." Booklist

Prisons we choose to live inside; [by] Doris Lessing. Harper & Row 1987 78p hardcover o.p. paperback available $9   **828**

ISBN 0-06-039077-8 (pa)   LC 87-45064
"A Cornelia & Michael Bessie book"
"Originally prepared as a series of five lectures for the Canadian Broadcasting Corporation, this little book of social-philosophical essays by one of the great novelists of our time is decidedly Tolstoyan in nature." Publ Wkly

Lewis, C. S. (Clive Staples), 1898-1963
The essential C. S. Lewis; edited and with an introduction by Lyle W. Dorsett. Macmillan 1988 536p $27.50; pa $12.95
                                          828

ISBN 0-02-532230-3; 0-02-019550-8 (pa)
                                          LC 88-11882
This work "includes a brief autobiographical sketch, a smattering of letters, and selections from each of the literary categories the versatile Lewis adopted: children's fiction, adult fiction, religion and morality, poetry, philosophy, and literary history and criticism. Arrangement is by genre, and each chapter is preceded by a brief introduction. The entire texts of two novels, *The Lion, the Witch and the Wardrobe* and *Perelandra*, are

included." Booklist
Includes bibliography

Milton, John, 1608-1674
The portable Milton; edited and with an introduction by Douglas Bush. Viking 1949 693p o.p.; Penguin Bks. paperback available $12.50   **828**

ISBN 0-14-015044-7 (pa)
"The Viking portable library"
A selection of the early poems and sonnets; "Areopagitica" complete; lengthy selections from the other chief prose works; and the three major poems, "Paradise lost," "Paradise regained," and "Samson Agonistes," complete
Includes bibliography

Orwell, George, 1903-1950
The Orwell reader; fiction, essays, and reportage; with an introduction by Richard H. Rovere. Harcourt, Brace & Co. 1956 456p hardcover o.p. paperback available $10.95   **828**

ISBN 0-15-670176-6 (pa)
Analyzed in Essay and general literature index
"Twenty-five or so selections from the works of George Orwell, including among other things, generous chunks of all five of his novels, sections of 'Homage to Catalonia,' 'The Road to Wigan Pier,' and 'The Lion and the Unicorn,' and, in their entirety, his essays on Kipling, Tolstoy, and Swift, as well as the autobiographical pieces 'Why I Write' and 'Such, Such Were the Joys.'" New Yorker

Orwell, the lost writings; edited with an introduction by W. J. West. Arbor House 1985 304p o.p.; Avon Bks. paperback available $5.95   **828**

ISBN 0-380-70118-9 (pa)   LC 85-9194
First published in the United Kingdom with title: Orwell, the war broadcasts
"This volume accounts for a significant gap in Orwell's publication, the war years of 1941-43 during which he served as a producer of BBC Indian service programs. Several of his scripts for those shows and a complement of letters make up most of . . . the book." Booklist
Includes bibliographic references

The **Oxford** book of literary anecdotes; edited by James Sutherland. Oxford Univ. Press 1975 382p $29.95; pa $8.95   **828**

1. English literature—Anecdotes 2. Authors, English—Anecdotes
ISBN 0-19-812139-3; 0-19-281936-4 (pa)
"Clarendon Press"
This is a collection of some four hundred anecdotes by and about British literary figures from the seventh-century poet Caedmon down to P. G. Wodehouse and Dylan Thomas
The editor "quotes original sources—memoirs, letters, diaries, early biographies—and his book is more than a succession of quips and repartees. His criteria are elastic enough to include material we might not ordinarily think of as anecdotes." Newsweek
Includes bibliographic references

Pinter, Harold, 1930-
Poems and prose, 1949-1977. Grove Press 1978 101p hardcover o.p. paperback available $5.95 **828**

ISBN 0-8021-5190-6 (pa)   LC 78-56046

"A bitter, gritty realism supports Pinter's poetry. . . . The prose pieces—cryptic, cutting, shaped like absurdist dialogue—are less successful, perhaps because, unlike the poems, they are fragments of plays rather than alternates to them." Booklist

Rushdie, Salman
Imaginary homelands; essays and criticism, 1981-1991. Granta Bks. 1991 432p $24.95 **828**

ISBN 0-670-83952-3   LC 90-50914

Also available in paperback from Penguin Bks.

Analyzed in Essay and general literature index

"The 75 articles collected here, many of them book reviews, range widely over literary, political, and religious themes." Libr J

Swift, Jonathan, 1667-1745
The portable Swift; edited with an introduction by Carl Van Doren. Viking 1948 601p il o.p.; Penguin Bks. paperback available $8.95 **828**

ISBN 0-14-015037-4 (pa)

"The Viking portable library"

A selection of Swift's essays, poems, letters, journals, and the complete text of Gulliver's travels

Includes bibliography

Thomas, Dylan, 1914-1953
A child's Christmas in Wales   **828**

1. Christmas—Wales

Hardcover and paperback editions available from various publishers

First published 1954

A portrait of Christmas Day in a small Welsh town and of the author's childhood there

For any season of the year "the language is enchanting and the poetry shines with an unearthly radiance." NY Times Book Rev

Wilde, Oscar, 1854-1900
The artist as critic; critical writings of Oscar Wilde; edited by Richard Ellman. Random House 1969 xxviii, 446p o.p.; University of Chicago Press paperback available $17.95 **828**

1. Literature—History and criticism
ISBN 0-226-89764-8 (pa)

A collection of the author's shorter pieces written between 1877 and 1895. It includes many unsigned reviews for the Pall Mall Gazette and the revised final version of The Portrait of Mr. W. H., the four essays of Intentions, reviews, letters to editors, and some of Wilde's trial testimony

The portable Oscar Wilde; selected and edited by Richard Aldington and Stanley Weintraub. rev ed. Viking 1981 741p o.p.; Penguin Bks. paperback available $10.95 **828**

ISBN 0-14-015093-5 (pa)   LC 80-39827

"The Viking portable library"

First published 1946

This volume contains The critic as artist, The picture of Dorian Gray, Salomé, The importance of being Earnest, De profundis, and selected poems, reviews, letters and excerpts from other works

Woolf, Virginia, 1882-1941
Flush; a biography. Harcourt Brace & Co. 1933 185p il hardcover o.p. paperback available $7.95 **828**

1. Browning, Elizabeth Barrett, 1806-1861
ISBN 0-15-631952-7 (pa)

Also available Transaction Pubs. large print edition

A fanciful look at Elizabeth Browning through the eyes of her cocker spaniel Flush

"With wit, audacity and penetration Virginia Woolf gives us, as it were, the pre-primitive mind. The result is a poetic biography which awakens in the reader an acute delight in all the physical senses, a renewed knowledge of the way in which concepts may first take shape in a consciousness interpreting entirely through instincts and sensations." N Y Times Book Rev

The Virginia Woolf reader; edited by Mitchell A. Leaska. Harcourt Brace Jovanovich 1984 371p hardcover o.p. paperback available $12.95 **828**

ISBN 0-15-693590-2 (pa)   LC 84-4478

"A Harvest book"

Excerpts from Woolf's "novels form less than 20 percent of a reader whose selections of short stories, essays, letters, and diary entries are excellent. This collection will be useful to those already familiar with Woolf's novels and seeking an introductory selection of her other writings." Libr J

Yeats, W. B. (William Butler), 1865-1939
Mythologies. Macmillan 1959 368p il o.p.; Collier Bks. paperback available $12.95 **828**

ISBN 0-02-055620-9 (pa)

This volume includes: The Celtic twilight (1893); The secret rose (1897); The tables of the law, and The adoration of the Magi (1897); Per amica silentia lunae (1918)

"The early prose remains fresh and lively, and in the meditations that follow, Yeats expresses, with inimitable ease, his mature convictions concerning the life and art of the time." New Yorker

829   Old English (Anglo-Saxon)

An **Anthology** of Old English poetry; translated into alliterative verse by Charles W. Kennedy. Oxford Univ. Press 1960 pa $9.95 **829**

1. Anglo-Saxon poetry
ISBN 0-19-500928-2

An Anthology of Old English poetry —
Continued

"The translator has chosen his selections to illustrate the variety, vigor, and lyricism of this prolog to later English literature. The poems were originally written during the seventh to the tenth centuries." Booklist

Beowulf

Beowulf   **829**

Hardcover and paperback editions available from various publishers

This epic of a dragon-slaying hero "is the earliest extant written composition of such length in English, and indeed in all Teutonic literature. Its content was based on Norse legends merged with historical events of the early sixth century in Denmark; this oral tradition was carried to England by Danish invaders of the mid-sixth century, fused with the Christianity they absorbed there, and finally written down by a single but unknown poet c700." Reader's Ency. 3d edition

Beowulf; edited and with an introduction by Harold Bloom. Chelsea House 1987 144p (Modern critical interpretations) $24.95
     829

1. Beowulf
ISBN 0-87754-904-4   LC 87-8093

A collection of critical essays on the Old English epic poem

Includes bibliography

830.3   German literature— Encyclopedias and dictionaries

Garland, Henry B. (Henry Burnand)
The Oxford companion to German literature; by Henry and Mary Garland. 2nd ed. Oxford Univ. Press 1986 1020p $55
     830.3

1. German literature—Dictionaries 2. German literature—Bio-bibliography
ISBN 0-19-866139-8   LC 85-25962

First published 1976

Entries include biographies, synopses of important works, literary terms and movements, historical events and figures, and material relevant to the social and intellectual background of German literature from the earliest records to the present

831   German poetry

Celan, Paul
Last poems; translated by Katharine Washburn and Margret Guillemin. North Point Press 1986 211p hardcover o.p. paperback available $9.95   **831**

ISBN 0-86547-224-6 (pa)   LC 85-72978

A bilingual selection of the German poet's work

"Celan's verse derives from and reflects his experiences as a Jew in Europe during World War II and, afterwards, as a Jew writing in German." Libr J

Poems of Paul Celan; translated, with an introduction, by Michael Hamburger. rev ed. Persea Bks. 1989 350p $24.95; pa $14.95
     831

ISBN 0-89255-140-2; 0-89255-134-8 (pa)
     LC 88-22567

First published 1980 with title: Paul Celan: poems

"This bilingual German-English selection culled from [the poet's] nine collections reveals that his is a poetry of darkness: anguish over what life offers and denies; the ever-present shadow of death that shades each breath. . . . Yet it also expresses an undefined, perhaps undefinable, joy." Booklist

Rilke, Rainer Maria, 1875-1926
The book of images; a bilingual edition; translated by Edward Snow. North Point Press 1991 258p $25   **831**

ISBN 0-86547-468-0   LC 91-11638

In this collection of poems Rilke analyzes the nature of subjectivity and perception

Duino elegies   **831**

Available in paperback from various publishers

First English translation published 1939

"These elegies, the last great work of the poet, were named for the castle of Duino on the Adriatic, where they were first conceived." New Statesman

New poems (1907); translated by Edward Snow. North Point Press 1984 197p hardcover o.p. paperback available $10
     831

ISBN 0-86547-415-X (pa)   LC 84-60683

In this "translation, Edward Snow renders into believable English the complete text of Rilke's work of early maturity. . . . Maintaining fidelity to Rilke's idiosyncratic and problematic German, Snow does not reproduce his formal structures but does capture the rhythms, tone shifts, and overall feel of the poems to an admirable degree. Bilingual edition." Booklist

New poems (1908); the other part; translated by Edward Snow. North Point Press 1990 221p hardcover o.p. paperback available $10   **831**

ISBN 0-86547-416-8 (pa)   LC 86-62835

This is a bilingual edition of the author's poetry

"These are poems of great beauty and power, brilliantly translated in a fluid, convincing idiom." Publ Wkly

Sonnets to Orpheus   **831**
     LC 87-6146

Available in paperback from various publishers

First English translation 1936 in the United Kingdom; 1942 in the United States by Norton

"Deeply rooted in the symbolist tradition, the 'Sonnets' collapse the barriers that exist between the inner and the outer world and celebrate the inherently musical quality of language. In his masterful translation of the 'Sonnets', Young captures the fluidity of the original with sensitivity and precision." Libr J

Rilke, Rainer Maria, 1875-1926—*Continued*
The unknown Rilke: expanded edition; selected poems; translated with an introduction by Franz Wright. Oberlin College Press 1990 176p (Field translation ser) pa $12.95   **831**

ISBN 0-932440-56-8   LC 90-52880

This collection contains selections from Rilke's New poems and from The life of Mary, as well as a number of other poems and fragments

832 German drama

Butler, Michael, 1935-
The plays of Max Frisch. St. Martin's Press 1985 182p $25   **832**

1. Frisch, Max, 1911-1991
ISBN 0-312-61680-5   LC 84-17906

This "study first places Max Frisch in his social and political context, then looks at each play in turn. . . . Throughout the book references are made to Frisch's diaries, speeches and narrative fiction where these illuminate his concept and practice of theatre." Publisher's note

Includes bibliography

Dürrenmatt, Friedrich
The visit; a tragi-comedy; translated from the German by Patrick Bowles. Grove Press 1962 109p pa $6.95   **832**

ISBN 0-8021-3066-6

"An Evergreen original"

Characters: 28 men, 6 women, extras. 3 acts. First produced in the United States at the Lunt-Fontaine Theatre, New York City, May 5, 1958

This play "concerns millionaire Claire Zachanassian's return to her small home town where, in her youth, she was seduced and abandoned by III. She seeks revenge and, to get it, she bribes the entire population: every man, woman and child will be rich for the rest of their lives if they agree to put III to death. After a feeble moral struggle and a travesty of a trial, the people of Güllen condemn and execute the erstwhile lover. In so doing they condemn themselves and Dürrenmatt condemns society as a whole." Cambridge Guide to World Theatre

Goethe, Johann Wolfgang von, 1749-1832
Faust   **832**

Available in hardcover and paperback from various publishers

In this epic drama "Mephistopheles makes a bargain with the aged Faust. If Faust is granted one moment of complete contentment, he loses his soul. Faust regains his youth and with Mephistopheles he travels about enjoying every form of earthly pleasure." Haydn. Thesaurus of Book Dig

Weiss, Peter, 1916-1982
The persecution and assassination of Jean-Paul Marat as performed by the inmates of the Asylum of Charenton under the direction of the Marquis de Sade; English version by Geoffrey Skelton; verse adaptation by Adrian Mitchell; introduction by Peter Brook. Atheneum Pubs. 1965 117p hardcover o.p. paperback available $6.95   **832**

1. Marat, Jean Paul, 1743-1793—Drama 2. Sade, marquis de, 1740-1814—Drama
ISBN 0-689-70568-9 (pa)

Original German edition, 1964

Characters: 20 men, 7 women. 2 acts, 33 divisions. First produced in the United States at the Martin Beck Theatre, New York City, December 27, 1965

The play takes place at the madhouse of Charenton, where the Marquis de Sade wrote plays and staged them with his fellow-inmates before audiences from Paris. It deals with the conflict in ideas between the proponents of revolution, represented by Marat, and the advocates of resignation, represented by de Sade

833.009 German fiction—History and criticism

Field, George Wallis
Hermann Hesse. Twayne Pubs. 1970 198p (Twayne's world authors ser) $19.95   **833.009**

1. Hesse, Hermann, 1877-1962
ISBN 0-8057-2424-9

In addition to coverage of Hesse's life and works the author also assesses the state of Hesse criticism

Includes bibliography

Franz Kafka's The metamorphosis; edited and with an introduction by Harold Bloom. Chelsea House 1988 149p (Modern critical interpretations) $24.95   **833.009**

1. Kafka, Franz, 1883-1924. The metamorphosis
ISBN 1-55546-070-4   LC 87-17827

Martin Greenberg, Stanley Corngold and Evelyn Torton Beck are among the contributors to this collection of critical assessments of Kafka's classic

Includes bibliography

Franz Kafka's The trial; edited and with an introduction by Harold Bloom. Chelsea House 1987 142p (Modern critical interpretations) $24.95   **833.009**

1. Kafka, Franz, 1883-1924. The trial
ISBN 1-55546-071-2   LC 87-9360

A selection of modern critical interpretations of Franz Kafka's novel

Includes bibliography

838   German miscellany

Dürrenmatt, Friedrich
Plays and essays; edited by Volkmar
Sander; foreword by Martin Esslin.
Continuum 1982 xxii, 312p (German lib)
$27.50; pa $12.95   **838**
   ISBN 0-8264-0257-7; 0-8264-0267-4 (pa)
                       LC 81-22184
"The volume contains two of Dürrenmatt's most
popular and important plays ('Romulus the Great,' 1948,
and 'The Visit,' 1956); rules (a set of theses) for his
famous 1962 play, 'The Physicists,' a novella titled 'The
Judge and His Hangman;' an essay on the problem of
modern theater; and a hypothetical lecture intended 'only
as a rough outline of several of [the world's political]
laws.'" Booklist

Grass, Günter, 1927-
On writing and politics, 1967-1983;
translated by Ralph Manheim; introduction
by Salman Rushdie. Harcourt Brace
Jovanovich 1985 157p $13.95; pa $4.95
                                 838
   ISBN 0-15-169969-0; 0-15-668793-3 (pa)   LC 85-786
   Analyzed in Essay and general literature index
   "A Helen and Kurt Wolff book"
"This volume consists of 13 essays originally published
by Grass between 1978 and 1984. [They deal] with the
interrelation of literature and political action." Libr J

Handke, Peter, 1942-
The weight of the world; translated by
Ralph Manheim. Farrar, Straus & Giroux
1984 243p $18.95   **838**
   ISBN 0-374-28745-7   LC 84-4196
   Also available in paperback from Macmillan
   Original German edition published 1977 in Austria
A combined journal and writer's notebook covering
the period from 1975 to 1977 when the Austrian author
was living in Paris with his small daughter

Hollington, Michael
Günter Grass; the writer in a pluralist
society. Boyars, M. 1980 186p (Critical
appraisals ser) $16   **838**
   1. Grass, Günter, 1927-
   ISBN 0-7145-2678-9
"Hollington writes on each of Grass's novels, and has
a chapter each on the poetry and plays. The book is
helpful on Grass's background and political involvements
and his anti-idealist, gradualist-reformist view of society
and individual psychology." Libr J

Rilke, Rainer Maria, 1875-1926
Rilke on love and other difficulties;
translations and considerations of Rainer
Maria Rilke; [edited by] John J. L. Mood.
Norton 1975 117p hardcover o.p. paperback
available $8.95   **838**
   ISBN 0-393-04404-1 (pa)

A collection of Rilke's letters, prose, poetry and
critical essays, which reveals his insight into the human
condition, especially the juxtaposition of male and female

839   Other Germanic literatures

The **Penguin** book of modern Yiddish verse;
edited by Irving Howe, Ruth R. Wisse,
and Khone Shmeruk. Viking 1987 xxii,
719p o.p.; Penguin Bks. paperback
available $14.95   **839**
   1. Yiddish poetry—Collections
   ISBN 0-14-009472-5 (pa)   LC 85-40788
The editors have "produced an anthology of over 200
poems by 39 poets, arranged chronologically and with
extensive biographical and textual notes. The poets range
from Yitskhok Leybush Perets (1852-1915), . . . to the
inventive Abraham Sutzkever. . . . The poems themselves, all beautifully translated by a variety of translators, with themes ranging from old-country folk tales
to American sweatshops, are accompanied by the
originals." Libr J
   Includes bibliography

839.3   Dutch, Flemish, Afrikaans literatures

Frank, Anne, 1929-1945
Anne Frank's Tales from the secret annex;
with translations by Ralph Manheim and
Michel Mok. Doubleday 1984 c1983 136p
$14.95   **839.3**
   ISBN 0-385-18715-7   LC 82-45871
   Original Dutch edition copyrighted 1949. First English
   translation published 1960 in the United Kingdom with
   title: Tales from the house behind
This volume presents all of Anne Frank's existing
stories, sketches and drafts as well as her personal
reminiscences and essays
"The bulk of the collection is on the sober side: tales
of poor or solitary young girls, and earnest pleas for
understanding and charity among people. Less likely to
appeal to the cynical reader, these stories display Anne
Frank's best talent: a narrative, neither pretentious nor
dull, that is without match for both the compelling message and the elusive sentiment." Best Sellers

839.7   Swedish literature

Hammarskjöld, Dag, 1905-1961
Markings; translated from the Swedish by
Leif Sjöberg & W. H. Auden; with a
foreword by W. H. Auden. Knopf 1964
xxiii, 221p pa $25   **839.7**
   1. Spiritual life
   ISBN 0-394-43532-X
   Also available in paperback from Ballantine Bks.
   Original Swedish edition, 1963
The author described this account as a sort of white
book concerning his negotiations with himself and with
God. A record of his inner life, it opens with a poem
he wrote around 1925; most of the entries were made
during the nineteen forties and fifties—and the book ends
with a poem written only a few weeks before his plane
crashed

Strindberg, August, 1849-1912

Six plays; in new translations by Elizabeth Spriggs. Doubleday 1955 304p pa $7.95
839.7

ISBN 0-385-09272-5

"A Doubleday Anchor book"

Contents: The father; Miss Julie; The stronger; Easter; A dream play; The ghost sonata

Strindberg: five plays; translated, with an introduction by Harry G. Carlson. University of Calif. Press 1983 297p $37.50; pa $14
839.7

ISBN 0-520-04697-8; 0-520-04698-6 (pa)
LC 82-15882

Also available in paperback from New Am. Lib.

Contents: The father; Miss Julie; The dance of death; A dream play; The ghost sonata

839.8 Danish and Norwegian literatures

Ibsen, Henrik, 1828-1906

The complete major prose plays; translated and introduced by Rolf Fjelde. Farrar, Straus & Giroux 1978 1143p o.p.; New Am. Lib. paperback available $16.95
839.8

ISBN 0-452-26205-4 (pa)
LC 77-28349

Contents: Pillars of society; A doll house; Ghosts; An enemy of the people; The wild duck; Rosmersholm; The lady from the sea; Hedda Gabler; The master builder; Little Eyolf; John Gabriel Borkman; When we dead awaken

Includes bibliography

Hedda Gabler and A doll's house; translated by Christopher Hampton. Faber & Faber 1989 176p pa $9.95
839.8

ISBN 0-571-14124-2
LC 90-201183

Hedda Gabler is the tragedy of a woman who shoots herself when her role in her lover's death is discovered. A doll's house is the drama of a woman who leaves her family to pursue personal freedom

840.3 French literature— Encyclopedias and dictionaries

The **Concise** Oxford dictionary of French literature; edited by Joyce M. H. Reid. Oxford Univ. Press 1976 $29.95; pa $12.95
840.3

1. French literature—Dictionaries 2. French literature—Bio-bibliography
ISBN 0-19-866118-5; 0-19-281200-9 (pa)

"Clarendon Press"

An abridged, revised and updated version of The Oxford companion to French literature, entered below

The **Oxford** companion to French literature; compiled and edited by Sir Paul Harvey and J. E. Heseltine. Oxford Univ. Press 1959 771p maps $55
840.3

1. French literature—Dictionaries 2. French literature—Bio-bibliography
ISBN 0-19-866104-5

"Covers French literature from medieval times to approximately 1939, in the manner of other Oxford 'companions,' including: (1) articles on authors, critics, historians, religious writers, savants, scientists, etc.; (2) articles on individual works, allusions, places, and institutions; and (3) general survey articles on phases or aspects of French literary life, movements, etc." Sheehy. Guide to Ref Books. 10th edition

841 French poetry

Baudelaire, Charles, 1821-1867

Les fleurs du mal; the complete text of The flowers of evil; in a new translation by Richard Howard; illustrated with nine original monotypes by Michael Mazur. Godine 1982 xxxii, 365p il hardcover o.p. paperback available $16.95
841

ISBN 0-87923-462-8 (pa)
LC 81-13283

Original French edition, 1857

"Howard puts the original's rhymed alexandrines primarily into iambic pentameter blank verse, which allows him to capture the immediate, concrete, visceral quality of Baudelaire's imagery." Choice

The flowers of evil; selected and edited by Marthiel and Jackson Mathews. rev ed. New Directions 1963 c1962 xxxi, 448p pa $16.95
841

ISBN 0-8112-1117-7

A previous selection of poems translated from the 1857 French work by Geoffrey Wagner was published in 1947 by New Directions. This selection contains translations by various translators. Texts are given in both English and the original French

"Faced with the conflict of good and evil, Baudelaire discards the conventional distinctions, and seeks beauty or good in the perverse, the grotesque, and the morbid. His sensibility, painfully alive to all emotions and sensations, lends unity to the various poems." Reader's Ency. 3d edition

Beckett, Samuel, 1906-1989

Collected poems in English and French. Grove Press 1977 147p $10; pa $8.95
841

ISBN 0-8021-1187-4; 0-8021-3096-8 (pa)
LC 77-77855

This work contains poems written by Beckett in English and French along with his translations and bilingual versions of poems by Eluard, Rimbaud, Apollinaire, and Chamfort

Bédier, Joseph, 1864-1938
The romance of Tristan and Iseult; as retold by Joseph Bédier; translated by Hilaire Belloc and completed by Paul Rosenfeld. Pantheon Bks. 1945 253p il o.p.; Random House paperback available $5.56
841

1. Tristan
ISBN 0-394-70271-9 (pa)

Bédier, a French schoolmaster and poet, attempted a scientific reconstruction of the Tristan story. His work was published in 1900, in French. Hilaire Belloc made an English translation, omitting four of the original chapters. The present edition includes the Belloc translation, with a translation of the missing chapters by Paul Rosenfeld

Césaire, Aimé
Aimé Césaire, the collected poetry; translated, with an introduction and notes by Clayton Eshleman and Annette Smith. University of Calif. Press 1983 408p il $39.95; pa $17
841

ISBN 0-520-04347-2; 0-520-05320-6 (pa)
LC 82-17394

Parallel text in English and French

The collected work of the Martinican poet-statesman. "Translators Eshleman and Smith provide a very lengthy introduction to the author, along with notes, presenting the original poems 'en face.'" Booklist

Chanson de Roland
The song of Roland
841

1. Roland (Legendary character)—Poetry

Available in hardcover and paperback from various publishers

"This heroic poem celebrates the mighty feats of Roland, the great French hero in the time of Charlemagne. The medieval legend has replaced and transformed the actual facts of history to a great extent but the epic poem has continued in popularity." Bookman's Manual

Mallarmé, Stéphane, 1842-1898
Poems; translated by Roger Fry, with commentaries by Charles Mauron. Oxford Univ. Press 1937 c1936 307p o.p.; AMS Press reprint available $32
841

ISBN 0-404-16330-0

"Marked by elliptical phrases, Mallarmé's poetry employes condensed figures and unorthodox syntax. Each poem is built about a central symbol, idea, or metaphor and consists of subordinate images that illustrate and help to develop the idea. Often obscure, his work never fails to be evocative and exciting." Reader's Ency. 3d edition

Rimbaud, Arthur, 1854-1891
Illuminations, and other prose poems; translated by Louise Varèse. rev ed. New Directions 1957 xxxv, 182p pa $8.95
841

ISBN 0-8112-0184-8

This translation first published 1946

These prose poems of the French Symbolist are given in both their original texts and in English translations. This edition also contains two other series of prose poems, together with an introduction in which the translator discusses the complicated ins and outs of 'Rimbaudien' scholarship and the special qualities of Rimbaud's writing

A season in hell & The drunken boat; English translation by Louise Varèse. New Directions 1961 xx, 108p pa $5.95 **841**

ISBN 0-8112-0185-6

Title page and text in French and English

Although he stopped writing at the age of nineteen, Arthur Rimbaud (1854-1891) possessed a revolutionary talent and his poetry and prose have increasingly influenced the major writers of our century. To his A season in hell is here added Rimbaud's longest and possibly greatest single poem The drunken boat

Includes bibliography

Tristan
The romance of Tristan and Isolt; translated from the Old French by Norman B. Spector; with a foreword by Eugène Vinaver. Northwestern Univ. Press 1973 91p hardcover o.p. paperback available $10.95
841

"The earliest, but incomplete, extant version of this medieval romance was that written in Anglo-Norman French verse by Thomas of Britain about 1185. . . . The story is laid in Ireland and Cornwall with some versions adding details from Brittany. Sir Tristram is sent to Ireland to bring Isolde to Cornwall to be the bride of King Mark. A love potion causes Tristram and Isolde to fall in love and after many trysts and separations each dies of love of the other." Reader's Adviser

Verlaine, Paul, 1844-1896
Selected poems; translated by C. F. MacIntyre. University of Calif. Press 1948 xx, 228p il pa $11
841

ISBN 0-520-01298-4

Eighty poems, chosen from Verlaine's first six books. French originals and translations are on facing pages. Contains a preface by the translator

The translator "has done Verlaine a gracious courtesy, and American readers a great kindness. The charm, verbal fireworks, sympathy and nostalgia of this major French poet are Englished with color and convictions." Chicago Sunday Trib

Includes bibliography

Villon, François, b. 1431
The poems of François Villon; translated and with an introduction and notes by Galway Kinnell. Houghton Mifflin 1977 xxiii, 246p o.p.; University Press of New England paperback available $14.95 **841**

ISBN 0-87451-236-0 (pa)
LC 77-12999

This translation first published 1965 by New American Library

French text (based on the Longnon-Foulet edition of 1932) and English translation on facing pages. Includes a critical introduction and explanatory notes

Villon, François, b. 1431—*Continued*

"Using standard academic texts of the medieval French poet, Kinnell exceeds a transliteration of the originals. . . . Villon's ribaldry and humorous despair sparkle throughout." Booklist

Includes bibliography

841.008 French poetry— Collections

The **Random** House book of twentieth-century French poetry; with translations by American and British poets; edited by Paul Auster. Random House 1982 xlix, 635p hardcover o.p. paperback available $24   **841.008**

1. French poetry—Collections
ISBN 0-394-71748-1 (pa)   LC 82-280

This bilingual edition collects the verse of forty-eight poets as translated by eighty-four poets. The volume opens with a section of poems by Guillaume Apollinaire and closes with a group of poems by Philippe Denis. The original and translation appear on facing pages

"This excellent anthology undertakes a double task: to provide a comprehensive view of French poetry in the twentieth century and to show, in the range of translators it offers, the influences of that poetry on American and British poets. . . . Paul Auster has done an excellent job of matching poets and translators." Nation

Includes bibliographic references

842 French drama

Beckett, Samuel, 1906-1989

Cascando, and other short dramatic pieces. Grove Press 1969 c1968 88p $8.95   **842**

ISBN 0-394-47496-1

Contents: Words and music; Cascando; Eh Joe; Play; Come and go; Film

"Included are two radio plays, a television play, a screenplay, and an ultra brief minisketch. The longest but least interesting work, 'Play,' concerns three people inside funeral urns waiting for the last remnants of their lives (their guilt) to burn away. . . . The other five plays are uniformly marvelous. Each is profound and beautiful. 'Film,' the screenplay, concerns the pursuit of 'The Object' by 'The Eye' and the 'anguish of perceivedness.'" Libr J

Collected shorter plays. Grove Press 1984 316p il hardcover o.p. paperback available $15.95   **842**

ISBN 0-8021-5055-1 (pa)   LC 83-49371

Contents: Act without words I; Act without words II; All that fall; Breath; . . . but the clouds . . . ; Cascando; Catastrophe; Come and go; Eh Joe; Embers; Footfalls; Ghost trio; Krapp's last tape; Nacht und Träume; Not I; Ohio impromptu; The old tune; A piece of monologue; Play; Quad; Rockaby; Rough for radio I; Rough for radio II; Rough for theatre I; Rough for theatre II; That time; What where; Words and music; Film

"Because they live only in their minds, Beckett's characters are free to invent other characters, whose existence becomes the proof of their own. The freedom to invent is linked to the compulsive need to express; throughout Beckett's work, language is used as the only weapon against chaos, at the same time that he reveals the incapacity of language for any meaningful expression." Reader's Ency. 3d edition

Ends and Odds; eight new dramatic pieces. Grove Press 1977 c1976 128p $10; pa $8.95   **842**

ISBN 0-8021-1190-4; 0-8021-5046-2 (pa)

Contents: Ends: Not I; That time; Footfalls; Ghost trio; Odds: Theatre I; Theatre II; Radio I; Radio II

"Ends and Odds proclaim imaginary worlds as dense as any [Beckett] has made before. A head, a hand, a lonely voice, or even a faint footfall is filled with as much intensity as silence and darkness itself. . . . It is a tiring style . . . but it does not tire the mind." New Repub

Waiting for Godot; tragicomedy in 2 acts. Grove Press 1954 60p il hardcover o.p. paperback available $6.95   **842**

ISBN 0-8021-3034-8 (pa)

Translated from the French by the author

Originally written in French. The play was first produced in Paris during the winter of 1952

"There are strong biblical references throughout, but Beckett's powerful and symbolic portrayal of the human condition as one of ignorance, delusion, paralysis, and intermittent flashes of human sympathy, hope, and wit has been subjected to many varying interpretations. The theatrical vitality and versatility of the play have been demonstrated by performances throughout the world." Oxford Companion to Engl Lit. 5th edition

Camus, Albert, 1913-1960

Caligula & three other plays; translated from the French by Stuart Gilbert; with a preface written specially for this edition and translated by Justin O'Brien. Knopf 1958 302p hardcover o.p. paperback available $7.95   **842**

ISBN 0-394-70207-7 (pa)

"Four of the author's best-known plays, written between 1938 and 1950. 'Caligula,' about the infamous emperor's self-destroying rebellion against fate; 'The Misunderstanding,' about the murder of a man by his ghoulish mother and sister,' 'The Just Assassins,' on the self-questionings of terrorists; and 'State of Siege,' an allegory about the refusal of one individual in a plague-stricken city to compromise with evil." Publ Wkly

Genet, Jean, 1910-1986

The blacks: a clown show; translated from the French by Bernard Frechtman. Grove Press 1960 128p pa $8.95   **842**

ISBN 0-8021-5028-4

"An Evergreen book"

Original French edition, 1958

"Drama in which a group of bizarrely dressed Negroes give a performance for another group of Negroes who wear white masks and represent the major figures of white society's established authority." McGraw-Hill Ency of World Drama

Genet, Jean, 1910-1986—*Continued*

The maids [and] Deathwatch; two plays; with an introduction by Jean-Paul Sartre; translated from the French by Bernard Frechtman. Grove Press 1954 166p hardcover o.p. paperback available $8.95
842

ISBN 0-8021-5056-X (pa)

Deathwatch, a one-act play written 1947 and first produced 1949 "deals with an insignificant criminal who tries to assume the highly desirable and prestigious role of murderer. . . . In 'The Maids (Les bonnes),' produced in 1947, . . . two servant girls have created an elaborate ritual in which they impersonate their mistress and finally murder her symbolically." McGraw-Hill Ency of World Drama

Giraudoux, Jean, 1882-1944

Four plays; adapted, and with an introduction by Maurice Valency. Hill & Wang 1958 xxi, 255p pa $9.95 842

ISBN 0-8090-0712-6

"A Mermaid dramabook"

Contents: The mad-woman of Chaillot; The Apollo of Bellac; The enchanted; Ondine

Ionesco, Eugène

Rhinoceros, and other plays; translated by Derek Prouse. Grove Press 1960 141p pa $8.95
842

ISBN 0-8021-3098-4

Also available in hardcover from P. Smith

"An Evergreen book"

Contents: Rhinoceros; The future is in eggs; The leader

Three satirical comedies. In Rhinoceros, one man resists the pressure to conform as everyone about him accepts their transformation into rhinoceroses and he finds himself socially isolated. In The future is in eggs, a couple must produce eggs destined to become intellectuals. The leader is a satire on the mass adulation of political figures in which the leader turns out to be a headless figure

Molière, 1622-1673

The misanthrope, and other plays; translated and with an introduction by Donald M. Frame. New Am. Lib. 1968 512p pa $4.95
842

ISBN 0-451-52415-2

"A Signet classic"

Contents: The misanthrope; The doctor in spite of himself; The miser; The would-be gentleman; The mischievous machinations of Scapin; The learned women; The imaginary invalid

Tartuffe, and other plays; translated with an introduction by Donald M. Frame. New Am. Lib. 1967 384p pa $3.50 842

ISBN 0-451-52011-4

Contents: The ridiculous précieuses; The school for husbands; The school for wives; The critique of the school for wives; The Versailles impromptu; Tartuffe;

Don Juan

Includes bibliography

Racine, Jean, 1639-1699

Britannicus; Phaedra; Athaliah; translated, with an introduction and notes, by C. H. Sisson. Oxford Univ. Press 1987 215p $34.50; pa $6.95
842

ISBN 0-19-251037-1; 0-19-281758-2 (pa)

LC 86-19977

Three verse plays. Britannicus presents the political intrigue surrounding the emperor Nero. Phaedra retells the Greek legend about a queen who fell in love with her stepson. Athaliah is based on Old Testament account of the idolatrous Queen of Judah

Sartre, Jean Paul, 1905-1980

No exit, and three other plays. Vintage Bks. 1989 275p pa $10
842

ISBN 0-679-72516-4

LC 89-40097

Also available in paperback from Random House

Contents: No exit; The flies; Dirty hands; The respectful prostitute

The first two plays are entered below. . . . The third concerns a young Communist intellectual's attempt to maintain his integrity as party line changes and personal relationships alter perceptions of his murder of a party boss who had fallen out of favor, but whose memory is later rehabilitated. The last play concerns a prostitute's involvement in false charges of rape against a murdered black man and his companion in a town in the American South

No exit (Huis clos); a play in one act, & The flies (Les mouches); a play in three acts. Knopf 1947 c1946 166p $14.95 842

ISBN 0-394-40642-7

First published 1946 in the United Kingdom with title: The flies and In camera

No exit is a modern morality play. Its three chief characters are contemporary human beings condemned to hell because of crimes against humanity. The flies is a retelling in modern idiom of the Orestes-Electra story

Wiesel, Elie, 1928-

The trial of God; (as it was held on February 25, 1649, in Shamgorod); a play in three acts; translated by Marion Wiesel. Random House 1979 161p o.p.; Schocken Bks. paperback available $12
842

1. Jews—Drama

ISBN 0-8052-0809-7 (pa)

LC 78-21366

Characters: 6 men, 2 women

"Three traveling Purim players arrive to celebrate the holiday but instead stage a mock trial of God in seventeenth-century village where a pogrom has destroyed the Jewish population except for an innkeeper and his mad daughter." Booklist

843.009 French fiction—History and criticism

Murdoch, Iris
Sartre; romantic rationalist. Viking 1987 158p o.p.; Penguin Bks. paperback available $6.95   **843.009**
1. Sartre, Jean Paul, 1905-1980
ISBN 0-14-010143-8 (pa)   LC 86-40566
First published 1963 by Yale University Press
The author "offers a critical reading of the writings of French philosopher Jean-Paul Sartre. . . . She examines the influence and importance of Sartre's thinking on the generation of students and intellectuals following World War II. . . . Murdoch then courses through her subject's writings and offers numerous political and philosophical asides in the process of assessing the man and his style." Booklist
Includes bibliography

Vargas Llosa, Mario, 1936-
The perpetual orgy; Flaubert and Madame Bovary; translated from the Spanish by Helen Lane. Farrar, Straus & Giroux 1986 239p $17.95; $8.95   **843.009**
1. Flaubert, Gustave, 1821-1880. Madame Bovary
ISBN 0-374-23077-3; 0-374-52062-3 (pa)
                                            LC 86-19515
This "is a discussion of the genesis, execution, structure and technique of 'Madame Bovary.' It is the best single account of the novel I know." N Y Times Book Rev
Includes bibliographic references

844 French essays

Camus, Albert, 1913-1960
Lyrical and critical essays; edited and with notes by Philip Thody; translated from the French by Ellen Conroy Kennedy. Random House 1968 365p hardcover o.p. paperback available $11   **844**
ISBN 0-394-70852-0 (pa)
Partially analyzed in Essay and general literature index
"In the autobiographical 'lyrical' essays Camus explores the character of Mediterranean man, the nature of absurdity, the inevitability of death, irony, and the vitality of physical life. The 'critical' essays contain reviews of Sartre's first novels and analyses of Melville, Silone, Gide, Faulkner, and others who influenced him. A closing autobiographical section consists of letters, prefaces, and three interviews." Booklist

The myth of Sisyphus, and other essays; translated from the French by Justin O'Brien. Knopf 1955 212p hardcover o.p. paperback available $9   **844**
ISBN 0-679-73373-6 (pa)
Analyzed in Essay and general literature index
Personal reflections on the meaning of life and the philosophical questions surrounding suicide

Resistance, rebellion, and death; translated from the French and with an introduction by Justin O'Brien. Knopf 1961 c1960 271p hardcover o.p. paperback available $9   **844**
ISBN 0-394-71966-2 (pa)
Analyzed in Essay and general literature index
"A selection of forthright essays on contemporary world politics, on capital punishment and the relations of the state and the individual, and on art, chosen from the three volumes of 'Actuelles,' published in France between 1950 and 1958." Publ Wkly

848 French miscellany

Barthes, Roland
A Barthes reader; edited, and with an introduction by Susan Sontag. Hill & Wang 1982 xxxviii, 495p hardcover o.p. paperback available $16.95   **848**
ISBN 0-374-52144-1 (pa)   LC 80-26762
This volume "offers a rich retrospective of Barthes's work. Susan Sontag has ably selected texts, and given most of them in their entirety." New Repub

Cottrell, Robert D.
Simone de Beauvoir. Ungar 1975 168p (Modern literature monographs) $19.95   **848**
1. Beauvoir, Simone de, 1908-1986
ISBN 0-8044-2132-3
Cottrell blends literary criticism with biographical detail in examining Simone de Beauvoir's many works, her novels, travel books, sociological studies and autobiography. Among the aspects stressed are her early feminism, her relationship with Jean-Paul Sartre, and her contacts with America
Includes bibliography

Maurois, André, 1885-1967
Illusions. Columbia Univ. Press 1968 101p $29.50   **848**
ISBN 0-231-03171-8
"The George B. Pegram lectures"
"In readable, nontechnical language, Maurois uses easy-to-understand examples from everyday life and includes his opinions on why people enjoy the arts, whether the artist can survive in a world ruled by science and technology, and whether the new mass media will allow man to do without the arts." Booklist

Rimbaud, Arthur, 1854-1891
Arthur Rimbaud: complete works; translated from the French by Paul Schmidt. Harper & Row 1975 309p hardcover o.p. paperback available $13   **848**
ISBN 0-06-090490-9 (pa)
This is a compilation of Rimbaud's "poetry, prose, and selected letters and documents. Translator Schmidt has divided the works into chronological segments corresponding to periods in Rimbaud's life, prefacing each division with biographical background. Original French versions not provided." Booklist

Rimbaud, Arthur, 1854-1891—*Continued*
Complete works, selected letters; translation, introduction and notes by Wallace Fowlie. University of Chicago Press 1966 370p hardcover o.p. paperback available $12.95   **848**

ISBN 0-226-71973-1 (pa)

In this bilingual edition of Rimbaud's work the original French texts are accompanied by English prose translations. In addition to the complete poetic works there are two prose fragments, a short story in the form of a seminarian's journal, and a selection of letters chosen to illustrate biographical details and Rimbaud's credo as a poet

Robinson, Joy D. Marie
Antoine de Saint-Exupéry. Twayne Pubs. 1984 179p (Twayne's world authors ser) $20.95   **848**

1. Saint-Exupéry, Antoine de, 1900-1944
ISBN 0-8057-6552-2   LC 84-10769

Biographical and critical assessments of the French aviator-author. The classic The little prince is examined in depth

Includes bibliography

Thody, Philip Malcolm Waller, 1928-
Albert Camus; by Philip Thody. St. Martin's Press 1988 125p (Modern novelists) hardcover o.p. paperback available $12.95
                                        848

1. Camus, Albert, 1913-1960
ISBN 0-333-43705-5 (pa)   LC 88-4444

Camus' "novels, plays, short stories, and essays are examined in the context of the absurd, his rejection of authority (divine or political), his search for moderation in life and art, and the past and present events that helped mold his thought." Choice

Includes bibliography

Valéry, Paul, 1871-1945
Selected writings. New Directions 1950 256p hardcover o.p. paperback available $12.95   **848**

ISBN 0-8112-0213-5 (pa)

"Seventeen poems are translated by eighteen translators, including Denis Devlin, Léonie Adams, and C. Day Lewis. . . . The rest of the book is composed of the French love miscellanies, essays, dialogues, and critiques." New Yorker

Voltaire, 1694-1778
The portable Voltaire; edited, and with an introduction by Ben Ray Redmen. Viking 1949 569p o.p.; Penguin Bks. paperback available $12.50   **848**

ISBN 0-14-015041-2 (pa)

"The Viking portable library"

The selections from Voltaire's works include: Candide, part one; Three stories: Zadig, Micromegas, and Story of a good Brahmin; Letters, and selections from the Philosophical Dictionary and other works. The editor's introduction gives a biographical sketch of Voltaire

Weil, Simone, 1909-1943
Formative writings, 1929-1941; edited and translated by Dorothy Tuck McFarland and Wilhelmina Van Ness. University of Mass. Press 1987 289p $30; pa $15.95   **848**

ISBN 0-87023-539-7; 0-87023-632-6 (pa) LC 86-6976

Contents: Science and perception in Descartes; The situation in Germany; Factory journal; War and peace; Philosophy

"In this collection, moral and political judgments . . . confront the reader often. . . . The editor-translators' work and their meticulous annotations help make these observations vivid and provocative." N Y Times Book Rev

Includes bibliographic references

850.9   Italian literature—History and criticism

Wilkins, Ernest Hatch, 1880-1966
A history of Italian literature; revised by Thomas G. Bergin. Harvard Univ. Press 1974 570p $45   **850.9**

1. Italian literature—History and criticism
ISBN 0-674-39701-0

First published 1954 and analyzed in Essay and general literature index

A chonological record "of the development of Italian literature from the 13th century to the present time. Emphasis, however, is on the writers before 1800; three chapters are devoted to Dante, and one chapter each to such writers as Petrarch, Boccaccio, and Manzoni." Libr J

Includes bibliography

851   Italian poetry

Dante Alighieri, 1265-1321
The divine comedy   **851**

Available in hardcover and paperback from various publishers

An epic poem, completed in 1321, in which the poet describes his visionary spiritual journey through Hell, Purgatory and Paradise—guided first by the classical poet Vergil and then by his beloved Beatrice—which results in a purification of his religious faith

The portable Dante; edited, and with an introduction by Paolo Milano. [rev ed]. Viking 1969 xlii, 662p o.p.; Penguin Bks. paperback available $9.95   **851**

ISBN 0-14-015032-3 (pa)   LC 77-7623

"The Viking portable library"

First published 1947

Contents: The Divine comedy, translated by L. Binyon, with notes from C. H. Grandgent; La vita nuova [The new life] complete, translated by D. G. Rossetti; excerpts from the Rhymes and the Latin prose works

"An excellent idea of the power and variety of 'The Divine Comedy' can be gained from Laurence Binyon's lucid and intelligent version in 'terza rima.' . . . The editor contributes an introduction and notes on the most enlightening contemporary Dante criticism." New Yorker

Includes bibliographic references

Dante Alighieri, 1265-1321—*Continued*

Vita nuova; a translation and an essay by Mark Musa. new ed. Indiana Univ. Press 1973 210p hardcover o.p. paperback available $8.95 **851**

ISBN 0-253-20162-4 (pa)

Also available in paperback from Oxford University Press

Originally written ca. 1292; this translation first published 1962

A series of autobiographical poems in which Dante tells the story of his love for Beatrice

Montale, Eugenio, 1896-1981

Selected poems; introduction by Glauco Cambon. New Directions 1966 xxiv, 161p hardcover o.p. paperback available $8.95 **851**

ISBN 0-8112-0119-8 (pa)

The poems in this collection appear in both the original Italian and in English translations by various English and American poets. They are selected from the three published volumes of the author's poetry: Cuttlefish bones, The occasions, and The storm and other things

Petrarca, Francesco, 1304-1374

Sonnets & songs; translated by Anna Maria Armi; introduction by Theodor E. Mommsen. Pantheon Bks. 1946 521p o.p.; AMS Press reprint available $67.50 **851**

ISBN 0-404-14695-3

Three hundred and sixty-six of the sonnets and odes printed in the original on one page with the translation opposite

The book "presents Petrarch as if he were a modern poet as indeed in these poems he is. It is extraordinary how fresh these poems are: it is as if their beautiful Italian melodies were written within the past ten years." Commonweal

Quinones, Ricardo J.

Dante Alighieri. Twayne Pubs. 1979 212p il (Twayne's world authors ser) $22.95 **851**

1. Dante Alighieri, 1265-1321
ISBN 0-8057-6405-4

"Quinones discusses all of Dante's major works ('Vita nuova,' 'De vulgari eloquentia,' 'Convivio,' 'De monarchia,' and 'Divina commedia'), setting them in their cultural context and appropriately elucidating their interconnections." Choice

Includes bibliography

852   Italian drama

Pirandello, Luigi, 1867-1936

Naked masks; five plays; edited by Eric Bentley. Dutton 1952 xxvii, 386p o.p.; New Am. Lib. paperback available $7.95 **852**

ISBN 0-525-48319-5 (pa)

Contents: Liolà; It is so! (If you think so); Henry IV; Six characters in search of an author; Each in his own way

853.009   Italian fiction—History and criticism

Cottrell, Jane E.

Alberto Moravia. Ungar 1974 166p (Modern literature monographs) $18.95 **853.009**

1. Moravia, Alberto, 1907-1990
ISBN 0-8044-2131-5

Also available in paperback from Columbia Univ. Press

A critical study of the works of the Italian novelist Alberto Pincherle, who writes under the pseudonym of Alberto Moravia

The author exhibits "scholarship and delicacy in evaluating a complex and paradoxical writer. A fine introductory overview, for general as well as academic libraries." Libr J

Includes bibliography

854   Italian essays

Eco, Umberto

Travels in hyper reality; essays; translated from the Italian by William Weaver. Harcourt Brace Jovanovich 1986 307p $15.95; pa $8.95 **854**

ISBN 0-15-191079-0; 0-15-691321-6 (pa)

LC 85-24810

Analyzed in Essay and general literature index

"A Helen and Kurt Wolff book"

"This smorgasbord of 26 pieces ultimately focuses on the boundaries of realism as exemplified by the 'hyperreality' of American phenomena like the Madonna Inn, wax museums, San Simeon, theme parks, etc." Libr J

Levi, Primo, 1919-1987

Other people's trades. Summit Bks. 1989 222p hardcover o.p. paperback available $8.95 **854**

ISBN 0-671-70519-9 (pa)

LC 86-23097

The pieces "collected in 'Other People's Trades,' treat many different subjects; among them are love, chess, poetry, fleas, beetles, wood, snakes, language, Rabelais, fear, frogs, computers, his house in Turin, Italy, and his family. . . . Levi is original, various, always lucid; there is a pleasing natural consistency to him." N Y Times Book Rev

858   Italian miscellany

Levi, Primo, 1919-1987

The mirror maker: stories and essays; translated from the Italian by Raymond Rosenthal. Schocken Bks. 1989 176p hardcover o.p. paperback available $9.95 **858**

ISBN 0-8052-0989-1 (pa)

LC 89-42680

"A collection of short stories and brief, occasional essays. . . . A reporter's interviews with various animals, a tale of national banners that may set a superpatriot's teeth on edge, and depictions of life in a concentration camp are among the subjects of the author's fictional

Levi, Primo, 1919-1987—_Continued_
miniatures. The essays and poems cover many of these
same topics in a sprightly but contemplative manner."
Booklist

860.3   Spanish literature—
Encyclopedias and dictionaries

Dictionary of Mexican literature; edited by
Eladio Cortés. Greenwood Press 1992 xliii,
768p $85   **860.3**

1. Mexican literature—Dictionaries
ISBN 0-313-26271-3   LC 91-10529

This volume contains "500 entries covering the most
important writers, literary schools, and cultural movements in Mexican literary history. The 41 contributors
include American, Mexican, and Hispanic scholars with
assistance from some of the authors themselves." Libr
J

For a fuller review see: Booklist, April 1, 1993

The **Oxford** companion to Spanish literature;
edited by Philip Ward. Oxford Univ.
Press 1978 629p $55   **860.3**

1. Spanish literature—Dictionaries 2. Spanish literature—Bio-bibliography
ISBN 0-19-866114-2   LC 78-325227

This book "covers literature written in the languages
of Spain (Castilian, Catalan, Basque, Galician) from
Roman times to 1977. Central and South America are
covered as well as peninsular Spain. The bulk of the
entries—which range from a paragraph to a page—are
for authors and specific works, but there are also some
for movements, groups, styles, and terms related to literature." Wilson Libr Bull
"This is an indispensable sourcebook." Choice

860.8   Spanish literature—
Collections

The **Borzoi** anthology of Latin American
literature; edited by Emir Rodríguez
Monegal, with the assistance of Thomas
Colchie. Knopf 1977 2v pa ea $19.95
            860.8

1. Latin American literature—Collections
Contents: v 1 From the time of Columbus to the
twentieth century (ISBN 0-394-73301-0); v2 The twentieth
century—from Borges and Paz to Guimarães Rosa and
Donoso (ISBN 0-394-73366-5)

"Brilliantly organized, this two-volume overview of
Latin American literature surveys writers in the context
of their time, the culture, politics, influences which
marked their eras." Publ Wkly

860.9   Spanish literature—History
and criticism

**Chandler, Richard E. (Richard Eugene),
1916-**
A new history of Spanish literature; [by]
Richard E. Chandler [and] Kessel Schwartz.
Louisiana State Univ. Press 1961 696p $45;
pa $18.95   **860.9**

1. Spanish literature—History and criticism
ISBN 0-8071-1699-8; 0-8071-1735-8 (pa)

This text "treats each genre in a separate part,
prefaced with a chapter on Spanish history, culture and
literature. . . . Valuable reference features include well-
written biocritical sketches, appendices listing 'first things
in Spanish literature,' literary and historical chronologies,
an excellent bibliography and detailed index, combining
to make this a valuable addition to the reference collection." Wilson Libr Bull

Handbook of Latin American literature;
edited by David William Foster. 2nd ed.
Garland 1992 799p (Garland reference lib.
of the humanities) $95; pa $18.95 **860.9**

1. Latin American literature—History and criticism
ISBN 0-8153-0343-2; 0-8153-1143-5 (pa)
                 LC 92-16452

First published 1987
This collection surveys the literature of Latin America
with chapters covering individual countries of South and
Central America, Latino writing in the United States,
paraliterature, and film
Includes bibliographies

Modern Latin American literature; compiled
and edited by David William Foster,
Virginia Ramos Foster. Ungar 1975 2v
(Lib. of literary criticism) set $120
            860.9

1. Latin American literature—History and criticism
ISBN 0-8044-3139-6

"The purpose of this two-volume work is to make
available a compilation of international critical commentary on 20th century Latin Amerian writers. The set
includes excerpts in English on 137 writers, extracted
from books, periodicals, newspapers, and encyclopedias.
Each volume includes an alphabetical list of all writers
reviewed and a list of authors by country." Wynar.
Guide to Ref Books for Sch Media Cent. 3d edition

861   Spanish poetry

Cid, ca. 1043-1099
The poem of the Cid   **861**

Paperback editions available from various publishers
"The poem is based on the exploits of Rodrigo or
Ruy Díaz de Bivar (c.1043-1099), who was known as
'el Cid.' . . . Similar in form to the 'Chanson de
Roland,' the poem is notable for its simplicity and
directness and for its exact, picturesque detail. Despite
the inclusion of much legendary material, the figure of
the Cid who is depicted as the model Castillian warrior,
is not idealized to an extravagant degree." Reader's Ency.
3d edition

García Lorca, Federico, 1898-1936
The poetical works of Federico García Lorca; edited by Christopher Maurer. Farrar, Straus & Giroux 1988-1991 2v il v1 pa $11; v2 $50   **861**

ISBN 9-99-999999-9   LC 87-33151

The first installments of a projected three volume edition of the poet's work

Poems in English and Spanish

Contents: v1 Poet in New York (ISBN 0-374-52083-6); v2 Collected poems (ISBN 0-374-12624-0)

Includes bibliographic references

Selected poems; edited by Francisco García Lorca and Donald M. Allen. New Directions 1955 180p hardcover o.p. paperback available $8.95   **861**

ISBN 0-8112-0091-4 (pa)

The poet's brother, in his preface "clearly traces the line of development in Lorca's work from the early lyrics and ballads to the later lyric dramas. The English versions of the poems, by eighteen translators, bring out the contrast and color of the originals, which are included, and there is a chronology of the poet's life." New Yorker

Juana Inés de la Cruz, 1651-1695
A Sor Juana anthology; translated by Alan S. Trueblood; with a foreword by Octavio Paz. Harvard Univ. Press 1988 248p $37.50   **861**

ISBN 0-674-82120-3   LC 87-27693

This volume "offers a useful sampling and English rendition of Sor Juana's work. Poetry predominates among the selections. . . . Given the difficulty of Mr. Trueblood's task—attempting to capture in English the voice of a poet who herself mastered many poetic languages—his translations are admirable." N Y Times Book Rev

Includes bibliographic references

Machado, Antonio, 1875-1939
Times alone; selected poems of Antonio Machado; chosen and translated by Robert Bly. Wesleyan Univ. Press 1983 173p hardcover o.p. paperback available $14.95   **861**

ISBN 0-8195-6081-2 (pa)   LC 83-6955

"This bilingual edition of 50 poems, selected from Machado's major collections, shows Bly the translator at his best. . . . Bly's spirited and intuitive 'notes' before each section allow us to enter the spirit of Machado's world." Libr J

Includes bibliography

Mexican poetry; an anthology; compiled by Octavio Paz; translated by Samuel Beckett; preface by C.M. Bovra. Grove Press 1985 213p $29.95; pa $9.95   **861**
1. Mexican poetry—Collections

ISBN 0-394-55019-6; 0-394-62086-0 (pa)

LC 85-17684

First published 1958 by Indiana University Press with title: Anthology of Mexican poetry

Includes selections from 35 poets whose writings span four centuries (from 1521 to 1910). Among the poets represented are Bernardo de Balbuena, Juan Ruiz de Alarcon, and Ramon Lopez Velarde

"Samuel Beckett has achieved translations which are fluid, colorful, and idiomatic." Booklist

Neruda, Pablo, 1904-1973
Five decades; a selection (poems: 1925-1970); edited and translated by Ben Belitt. Grove Press 1974 xxii, 431p hardcover o.p. paperback available $14.50   **861**

ISBN 0-8021-3035-6 (pa)

Bilingual selection of poems from twenty-one books published between 1925 and 1970. Text in Spanish and English

"Belitt's insight into the intricate metaphysical imagery of Neruda's poetry is quite apparent in these translations." Choice

Includes bibliography

Late and posthumous poems, 1968-1974; introduction by Manuel Duran; edited and translated by Ben Belitt. Grove Press 1988 239p hardcover o.p. paperback available $11.95   **861**

ISBN 0-8021-3145-X (pa)   LC 88-11290

"With the exception of the darker surrealism of the 1930s, Nobel Prize-winning poet Neruda's work was consistently life-affirming, even to his last days. Translated by Belitt, no stranger to Neruda, the 'late and posthumous poems' display an exhilarating variety. These poems attest to Neruda's warmth, profundity, and humility." Libr J

Selected odes of Pablo Neruda; translated, with an introduction by Margaret Sayers Peden. University of Calif. Press 1990 375p (Latin American literature and culture) $40; pa $13   **861**

ISBN 0-520-05944-1; 0-520-07172-7 (pa)

LC 90-10707

"With the Spanish text and the English translation on facing pages, the beautiful odes of the great Chilean poet pay tribute to simple things in simple words, from bicycles and birds to his suit." Booklist

Stones of the sky; translated by James Nolan. Copper Canyon Press 1987 75p $15; pa $10   **861**

ISBN 1-556-59006-7; 1-556-59007-5 (pa)

LC 87-71140

"Typifying a mellow and introspective Neruda . . . this slender bilingual volume redirects the Chilean's amorous, telluric, and quotidian predilections toward rocks and gems." Libr J

The yellow heart; translated by William O'Daly. Copper Canyon Press 1990 109p $17; pa $10   **861**

ISBN 1-55659-028-8; 1-55659-029-6 (pa)

LC 89-81834

"This posthumously published bilingual collection by the Chilean-born Nobel laureate, ably translated and introduced by O'Daly, confirms the mature poet as a sur-

Neruda, Pablo, 1904-1973—*Continued*
passing craftsman with a marvelous range of voice and texture." Publ Wkly

Paz, Octavio, 1914-
The collected poems of Octavio Paz, 1957-1987; edited & translated by Eliot Weinberger; with additional translations by Elizabeth Bishop [et al.] New Directions 1987 669p il $37.50; pa $19.95 **861**

ISBN 0-8112-1037-5; 0-8112-1173-8 (pa)
LC 87-23989

"Dense, weighty, and miraculous, this bilingual edition compresses into one volume all the poems published in book form since 1957. Nearly 200 poems, some newly translated, many new to an English-language edition, conclusively demonstrate Paz's power." Libr J

Includes bibliography

Early poems, 1935-1955; translated from the Spanish by Muriel Rukeyser [et al.] Indiana Univ. Press 1973 145p o.p.; New Directions paperback available $7.95 **861**

ISBN 0-8112-0478-2 (pa)

"This bilingual collection was first published in 1963 [with title: Selected poems of Octavio Paz] and included poems chosen from eight separate works." Libr J

"Paz's early poems reveal a poet of formidable talent, of easy and commanding presence." N Y Rev Books

Selected poems; edited by Eliot Weinberger; translated from the Spanish by G. Aroul [et al.] New Directions 1984 147p hardcover o.p. paperback available $8.95 **861**

ISBN 0-8112-0899-0 (pa) LC 84-9856

"The 67 well-chosen selections show Paz in his several phases and guises—in lyrics and prose poems, in long, free-form pieces and short, impressionistic works—a range of styles representing the best modes of East and West as practiced South over the last half-century. Many of the translations are by his peers (Elizabeth Bishop, Mark Strand, W. C. Williams)." Booklist

862 Spanish drama

García Lorca, Federico, 1898-1936
Five plays; comedies and tragicomedies; translated by James Graham-Lujan and Richard L. O'Connell. New Directions 1963 246p music hardcover o.p. paperback available $8.95 **862**

ISBN 0-8112-0090-6 (pa)

Contents: The billy-club puppets; The shoemaker's prodigious wife; The love of Don Perlimplin and Belisa in the garden; Dōna Rosita, the spinster; The butterfly's evil spell

Three tragedies; translated by James Graham-Luján and Richard L. O'Connell; introduced by Francisco García Lorca. Greenwood Press 1977 212p $49.75 **862**

ISBN 0-8371-9578-0 LC 77-3056

Also available in paperback from New Directions

First published 1947 by New Directions

Contents: Blood wedding; Yerma; Bernarda Alba

A dramatic trilogy comprised of three tragedies of Spanish peasant life

864 Spanish essays

Fuentes, Carlos
Myself with others; selected essays. Farrar, Straus & Giroux 1988 214p $19.95; pa $8.95 **864**

ISBN 0-374-21750-5; 0-374-52237-5 (pa) LC 87-7448

Essays by the Mexican writer on subjects ranging from the cinema of Buñuel to the literary output of Cervantes, Borges and Garcia Marquez

Paz, Octavio, 1914-
Convergences; essays on art and literature; translated from the Spanish by Helen Lane. Harcourt Brace Jovanovich 1987 303p $19.95; pa $10.95 **864**

ISBN 0-15-122585-0; 0-15-622586-7 (pa)
LC 86-31836

Analyzed in Essay and general literature index

This is a collection of fifteen essays written by the Mexican poet between 1967 and 1982. The subjects discussed include Latin American poetry, the Japanese haiku, Picasso's art, André Breton and Miró

The labyrinth of solitude; The other Mexico, Return to the labyrinth of solitude, Mexico and the United States, The philanthropic ogre. Grove Press 1985 398p hardcover o.p. paperback available $11.95 **864**

1. Mexico—Civilization 2. National characteristics, Mexican
ISBN 0-8021-5042-X (pa) LC 82-47999

The labyrinth of solitude and The other Mexico were first published 1961 and 1972 respectively

In this collection of essays and one interview, Paz explorers the cultural and historical influences on the social behavior of his countrymen

The monkey grammarian; translated from the Spanish by Helen R. Lane. Seaver Bks. 1981 162p il o.p.; Arcade Pub. paperback available $9.95 **864**

ISBN 1-55970-135-8 (pa) LC 81-1914

Original Spanish edition, 1974

This book is "an extended meditation on the nature of language. Its title refers to Hanuman, the Indian monkey God, uprooted of mountains, conqueror of space and mythic author of systematic language, the divine simian hero of the Sanskrit epic 'Ramayana.'" N Y Times Book Rev

868   Spanish miscellany

Borges, Jorge Luis, 1899-1986
Labyrinths; selected stories & other writings; edited by Donald A. Yates & James E. Irby; preface by André Maurois. New Directions 1962 248p il hardcover o.p. paperback available $9.95   **868**

ISBN 0-8112-0012-4 (pa)

Also available in hardcover from Modern Lib.

A collection of tales, literary and metaphysical essays, and parables

870.8   Latin literature— Collections

The **Portable** Roman reader; edited, and with an introduction by Basil Davenport. Viking 1951 656p o.p.; Penguin Bks. paperback available $10   **870.8**

1. Latin literature—Collections
ISBN 0-14-015056-0 (pa)

"The Viking portable library"

This anthology includes selections from Plautus, Terence, Caesar, Virgil, Seneca, Juvenal as well as complete plays by Plautus and Terence and the anonymous poem Vigil of Venus

870.9   Latin literature—History and criticism

Hadas, Moses, 1900-1966
History of Latin literature. Columbia Univ. Press 1952 474p $60   **870.9**

1. Latin literature—History and criticism
ISBN 0-231-01848-7

Companion volume to History of Greek literature, entered in class 880.9

"The book traces Roman writing from its earliest beginnings down to the Dark Ages, ending with Saint Augustine and the other Christian writers of his time. In this sweep of some seven centuries every writer, and almost every work, is discussed, described, and, in the best sense of the word, appreciated." N Y Times Book Rev

Hamilton, Edith, 1867-1963
The Roman way. Norton 1932 281p hardcover o.p. paperback available $3.95   **870.9**

1. Latin literature—History and criticism 2. Rome—Civilization
ISBN 0-393-00232-2 (pa)

Companion volume to The Greek way, entered in class 880.9

An interpretation of Roman life from the descriptions in the works of great writers from Plautus and Terence to Virgil and Juvenal

872   Latin dramatic poetry and drama

Terence
Terence, the comedies; translations by Palmer Bovie, Constance Carrier, and Douglass Parker; edited by Palmer Bovie. Johns Hopkins Univ. Press 1992 xxi, 398p (Complete Roman drama in translation) $45; pa $14.95   **872**

ISBN 0-8018-4353-7; 0-8018-4354-5 (pa)

LC 91-33984

First published 1974 by Rutgers University Press with title: The complete comedies of Terence

Includes the following plays: The brothers (Adelphoe); The eunuch (Eunouchus); The girl from Andros (Andria); Her husband's mother (Hecyra); Phormio; The self-tormentor (Heautontimorumenos)

873   Latin epic poetry and fiction

Ovid, 43 B.C.-17 or 18
Metamorphoses   **873**

Hardcover and paperback editions available from various publishers

"A series of tales in Latin verse. . . . Dealing with mythological, legendary, and historical figures, they are written in hexameters, in 15 books, beginning with the creation of the world and ending with the deification of Caesar and the reign of Augustus." Reader's Ency. 3d edition

Virgil
The Aeneid of Virgil   **873**

Hardcover and paperback editions available from various publishers

"The Aeneid is in twelve books: the first six in imitation of the Odyssey; the last six, of the Iliad. The Trojan hero is led to Italy, where he is to be the father of a race and of an empire supreme among nations. On his way thither he tarries at Carthage, whose queen, Dido, loves him as with the first love of a virgin. To her he tells the story of Troy. For love of him she slays herself when the gods lead him from her shores. Arrived in Italy he seeks the underworld, under the protection of the Sibyl of Cumæ. He emerges thence to overcome his enemies." Keller. Reader's Dig of Books

874   Latin lyric poetry

Horace
The Odes and Epodes; with an English translation by C. E. Bennett. rev ed. Harvard Univ. Press 1927 430p pa $15.50   **874**

ISBN 0-674-99037-4

"The Loeb classical library"

This edition first published 1918

English prose translations of the Odes and Epodes, opposite the original Latin. There is a short introductory chapter on the life and works of Horace, followed by a chapter on the meters he used. An index of proper names refer to the Latin originals by number and line

Includes bibliography

877 Latin satire and humor

Erasmus, Desiderius, 1466?-1536
The praise of folly   877

Hardcover and paperback editions available from various publishers

A "satirical monologue in Latin. . . . Folly praises herself and proclaims her superiority over Wisdom. The author's argument, of course, is 'that it is folly not to see things as they really are; scholars should not abandon ideals just because they cannot be fully realized but should apply their learning and reason as best they can to daily living.'" Reader's Adviser

Juvenal
Satires   877

Hardcover and paperback editions available from various publishers

"The sixteen 'Satires' of Juvenal, which contain a vivid picture of contemporary Rome under the Empire, have seldom been equalled as biting diatribes. . . . Juvenal's invectives in powerful hexameters, exact and epigrammatic, were aimed at lax and luxurious society, tyranny, criminal excesses, and the immorality of women." Reader's Adviser

878 Latin miscellany

Caesar, Julius, 100-44 B.C.
The Gallic War; with an English translation by H. J. Edwards. Harvard Univ. Press 1958 xxii, 616p il maps $15.50   878
1. Rome—History
ISBN 0-674-99080-3
"The Loeb classical library"
Caesar's account of his campaign (58-50 B.C.) to bring the province of Gaul (France) under his control

Horace
The essential Horace; odes, epodes, satires, and epistles; translated by Burton Raffel; with a foreword and an afterword by W.R. Johnson. North Point Press 1983 xxiv, 274p hardcover o.p. paperback available $13.95
878
ISBN 0-86547-112-6 (pa)   LC 82-73717
"Satirist, scold, scholar, and old silly . . . Horace ranges far more in subject and particularly in style than most previous, primarily staid translations would suggest, and Raffel's new version—representing about 80 percent and certainly the most memorable parts of the canon—presents the poet in a thoroughly modern mode and in all his mercurial moods." Booklist

Horace's Satires and Epistles; translated by Jacob Fuchs; introduction by William S. Anderson. Norton 1977 105p hardcover o.p. paperback available $3.95   878
ISBN 0-393-09093-0 (pa)   LC 77-22300
"The works translated in this volume constitute slightly more than half the total poetic output of Horace. The 'Satires' are the work of the young poet; the 'Epistles' were produced by a middle-aged man who at least says that he feels age creeping up on him and limiting his choices." Introduction

Satires, Epistles and Ars poetica; with an English translation by H. Rushton Fairlough. Harvard Univ. Press 1926 xxx, 508p pa $15.50   878
ISBN 0-674-99214-8
"The Loeb classical library"
Latin and English on opposite pages
Horace's Satires sketch boldly but good-humoredly the social life of his day. The Epistles are simple, friendly correspondence, in which we find the man Horace, without a trace of the moral teacher or censor. His "Art of poetry," a brief and apparently casual letter, has had great influence on modern literature

Martial
Epigrams; with an English translation by Walter C. A. Ker. Harvard Univ. Press 1919-1920 2v ea $15.50   878
1. Epigrams
"The Loeb classical library"
Latin and English on opposite pages
"Martial's twelve books of 'Epigrams' are written for the most part in elegiac couplets modelled on Ovid and Catullus. They show his acute observation of Roman life in the last third of the first century and were often brutally insulting or grossly obscene." Bookman's Manual
Includes bibliography

Suetonius Tranquillus, C., ca. 69-ca. 122
The twelve Caesars; translated by Robert Graves. Penguin Bks. 1957 315p il pa $8.95
878
1. Roman emperors 2. Rome—History
ISBN 0-14-044072-0
"A detailed account of the life and times of the first twelve emperors from Caesar to Domitian." Reader's Ency. 3d edition

Tacitus, Cornelius
The complete works of Tacitus; translated from the Latin by Alfred John Church and William Jackson Brodribb; edited and with an introduction by Moses Hadas. Modern Lib. 1942 xxv, 773p il o.p.; McGraw-Hill paperback available $9.30   878
1. Rome—History
ISBN 0-07-553639-0 (pa)
Contains: The annals; The history; The life of Cnaeus Julius Agricola; Germany and its tribes; A dialogue on oratory

880.3 Classical Greek literature—Encyclopedias and dictionaries

The **Oxford** companion to classical literature; edited by M. C. Howatson. 2nd ed. Oxford Univ. Press 1989 615p il maps $45   **880.3**

1. Classical literature—Dictionaries
ISBN 0-19-866121-5   LC 88-27330
First published 1937 under the editorship of Sir Paul Harvey

This work "covers classical literature from the appearance of the Greeks, around 2200 B.C., to the close of the Athenian philosophy schools in A.D. 529. It includes articles on authors, major works, historical notables, mythological figures, and topics of literary significance. Short summaries of major works, chronologies, charts, and maps are special features." Nichols. Guide to Ref Books for Sch Media Cent. 4th edition

880.8 Classical Greek literature—Collections

The **Portable** Greek reader; edited, and with an introduction by W. H. Auden. Viking 1948 726p hardcover o.p.; Penguin Bks. paperback available $11   **880.8**

1. Greek literature—Collections
ISBN 0-14-015039-0 (pa)
"The Viking portable library"

"Selections from representative Greek writers, from Homer to Galen, aimed at providing the reader with an introduction to all facets of Greek culture, rather than to its literature alone. Mr. Auden's preface deals chiefly with the various Greek concepts of the hero, in comparison with our own, and points up the immense differences between the two civilizations." New Yorker

880.9 Classical Greek literature—History and criticism

Ancient writers; Greece and Rome; T. James Luce, editor in chief. Scribner 1982 2v $165   **880.9**

1. Classical literature—History and criticism
ISBN 0-684-16595-3   LC 82-50612
Analyzed in Essay and general literature index
Contents: v1 Homer to Caesar; v2 Lucretius to Ammianus Marcellinus

"The forty-seven articles found in this important handbook of Greek and Roman literature were written by noted classicists and vary in length from ten to fifty pages. Arranged chronologically, they primarily treat individual authors, although some cover groups of authors. Each article consists of biographical information, a critical analysis of the author's works, and a selective bibliography of primary and secondary sources. An important resource for libraries supporting an interest in classical studies." Ref Sources for Small & Medium-sized Libr. 5th edition

Hadas, Moses, 1900-1966
History of Greek literature. Columbia Univ. Press 1950 327p $42   **880.9**

1. Greek literature—History and criticism
ISBN 0-231-01767-7
Companion volume History of Latin literarture, entered in class 870.9

This study of Greek literature from its beginnings to the fifth century A.D. examines and analyzes both the less familiar works and the universally acknowledged "classics" relating them to the political and social conditions of the times

Hamilton, Edith, 1867-1963
The echo of Greece. Norton 1957 224p hardcover o.p. paperback available $7.95   **880.9**

1. Greek literature—History and criticism
2. Civilization, Greek
ISBN 0-393-00231-4 (pa)
An interpretive essay on the Greek way of life during the fourth century B.C. It deals particularly with the political philosophies of Greek teachers and leaders—Isocrates, Plato, Aristotle, Demosthenes, and Alexander the Great

The Greek way. Norton 1943 347p hardcover o.p. paperback available $4.95   **880.9**

1. Greek literature—History and criticism
2. Civilization, Greek
ISBN 0-393-00230-6 (pa)
Companion volume to The Roman way, entered in class 870.9

First published 1930. Variant title: The great age of Greek literature

An account of writers and literary forms of the Periclean Age including discussions of Pindar, Aristophanes, Aeschylus, tragedy, Greek religion and philosophy

882 Classical Greek dramatic poetry and drama

Aeschylus
The Oresteia   **882**

Hardcover and paperback editions available from various publishers

The only extant Greek dramatic trilogy. It includes Agamemnon, The libation bearers, and The Eumenides

Suppliants; translated by Janet Lembke. Oxford Univ. Press 1975 104p (Greek tragedy in new translations) $19.95   **882**

ISBN 0-19-501933-4
The classical tragedy is based on the legend of the Argive women who invoked the aid of the gods in recovering from the Thebans the bodies of Argive warriors slain in the battle against Thebes

Aristophanes

The complete plays of Aristophanes; edited and with an introduction by Moses Hadas. Bantam Bks. 1962 501p pa $4.95
882

ISBN 0-553-21343-1

"A Bantam classic"

Includes the following plays: Acharnians; Knights; Clouds; Wasps; Peace; Birds; Lysistrata; Thesmophoriazusae; Frogs; Ecclesiazusae; Plutus

The frogs, and other plays; translated with an introduction by David Barrett. Penguin Bks. 1964 223p pa $5.95   **882**

ISBN 0-14-044152-2

"The Penguin classics"

Contents: The wasps; The poet and the woman; The frogs

Euripides, ca. 485-ca. 406 B.C.

Ten plays; translated by Moses Hadas and John McLean; with an introduction by Moses Hadas. Bantam Bks. 1981 c1960 358p pa $4.95   **882**

ISBN 0-553-21363-6

"A Bantam classic"

A reissue of the 1960 Bantam edition; first published 1936 by Dial Press

Contents: Alcestis; Medea; Hippolytus; Andromache; Ion; Trojan women; Electra; Iphigenia among the Taurians; The Bacchants; Iphigenia at Aulis

Sophocles

Antigone; translated by Richard Emil Braun. Oxford Univ. Press 1973 101p (Greek tragedy in new translations) $19.95; pa $6.95   **882**

ISBN 0-19-501741-2; 0-19-506167-5 (pa)

Disaster follows the refusal of King Creon of Thebes to allow the burial of his nephew, whom he had declared a traitor. When the dead man's sister, Antigone, who is engaged to Creon's son, defies the tyrant, she is condemned to death. Warned of the god's displeasure by the prophet Tiresias, Creon relents too late, for Antigone has already hanged herself. Her suicide is followed by those of Creon's son and his wife

The complete plays of Sophocles; translated by Sir Richard Claverhouse Jebb; edited with an introduction by Moses Hadas. Bantam Bks. 1982 c1967 261p pa $3.95   **882**

ISBN 0-553-21354-7

"A Bantam classic"

A reissue of the 1967 Bantam edition

Contents: Ajax; Electra; Oedipus the King; Antigone; Trachinian women; Philoctetes; Oedipus at Colonus

Oedipus the King   **882**

Hardcover and paperback editions available from various publishers

This classical tragedy deals with the fulfillment of a prophecy as it is revealed that Oedipus has unwittingly killed his father, married his mother and brought the plague to Thebes. He blinds himself in horror and becomes an outcast

Three tragedies: Antigone, Oedipus the King, Electra; translated into English verse by H. D. F. Kitto. Oxford Univ. Press 1962 159p pa $8.95   **882**

ISBN 0-19-500374-8

Antigone and Oedipus the King are entered separately above. Electra describes how Agamemnon's daughter and her brother Orestes slay their mother and her paramour to avenge their father's murder

882.008   Classical Greek dramatic poetry and drama—Collections

Greek drama; [edited by] Moses Hadas. Bantam Bks. 1965 337p (Lib. of world drama) pa $4.95   **882.008**

1. Greek drama—Collections
ISBN 0-553-21221-4

"A Bantam classic"

Includes translations of Agamemnon and Eumenides by Aeschylus; Antigone; Oedipus the King and Philoctetes by Sophocles; Medea, Hippolytus and Trojan women by Euripides; Frogs by Aristophanes

883   Classical Greek epic poetry and fiction

Finley, M. I. (Moses I.), 1912-1986

The world of Odysseus. rev ed. Viking 1978 192p map o.p.; Penguin Bks. paperback available $6.95   **883**

1. Civilization, Greek
ISBN 0-14-020570-5 (pa)   LC 77-28903

Also available in hardcover from P. Smith

First published 1954

The author attempts to present the reader with a picture of Greek society based on a close reading of the Illiad and Odyssey

Includes bibliographic references

Homer

The Iliad   **883**

1. Trojan War—Poetry

Hardcover and paperback editions available from various publishers

A "Greek epic poem (8th century B.C.?) attributed to Homer. In 24 books of dactylic hexameter verse, it details the events of the few days near the end of the Trojan War, focusing on the withdrawal of Achilles from the contest and the disastrous effects of this act on the Greek campaign." Reader's Ency. 3d edition

The Odyssey   **883**

Hardcover and paperback editions available from various publishers

Homer—*Continued*

"An epic poem in Greek hexameters. . . . The 'Odyssey' is a sequel to the 'Iliad' and narrates the ten years' adventures of Ulysses during his return journey from Troy to his own kingdom, the island of Ithaca." Keller. Reader's Dig of Books

884 Classical Greek lyric poetry

Greek lyrics. 2nd ed rev and enl. University of Chicago Press 1960 81p map hardcover o.p. paperback available $5.95   **884**

ISBN 0-226-46944-1 (pa)

First published 1955

Edited and translated by Richard Alexander Lattimore

More than a hundred poems and poetic fragments from the great age of Greek lyric poetry, retaining the original meter in highly idiomatic English

Lattimore "holding closely to the original metres, has produced renderings of great power and beauty. . . . He has completely freed the poems from sentimentality, and the thrilling ancient names—Anacreon, Alceus, Simonides, Sappho—acquire fresh brilliance and vitality under his hand." New Yorker

Pindar

The odes of Pindar   **884**

Hardcover and paperback editions available from various publishers

The Odes (Epinicia) celebrated victories in the great national games, and were accompanied by music, which is lost to us. The fragments represent almost every kind of lyric poem

"Since Pindar's Epinicia are generally concerned with mythical subjects, reserving praise of the mortal victor for the end of the ode, his works are a fine source of legend." Reader's Ency. 3d edition

Pindar's Victory songs; translation, introduction, prefaces [by] Frank J. Nisetich. Johns Hopkins Univ. Press 1980 367p il $45; pa $25.95   **884**

ISBN 0-8018-2350-1; 0-8018-2356-0 (pa) LC 79-3739

Contents: Introduction: Historical background, Pindar's Victory songs, The translation; Olympian odes; Pythian odes; Nemean odes; Isthmian odes; Appendixes: The dating of Pindar's odes, Geographical distribution of Pindar's odes, Myths in the odes of Pindar, Variant readings, Athletic contests

Includes bibliography

888 Classical Greek miscellany

Aristotle, 384-322 B.C.

The basic works of Aristotle; edited, and with an introduction by Richard McKeon. Random House 1941 xxxix, 1487p $34.95   **888**

ISBN 0-394-41610-4

Follows the Oxford translation of 1931

Contains entire texts of the following: Physica; De generatione et corruptione; De anima; Parva naturalia; Metaphysica; Ethica Nicomachea; Politica; De poetica

Some chapters have been omitted from the following included works: Organon; De caelo; Historia animalium; De partibus animalium; De generatione animalium;

Rhetorica

Includes bibliography

Introduction to Aristotle; with a new general introduction and new introductions to the particular works, by Richard McKeon. 2nd ed rev and enl. University of Chicago Press 1974 c1973 lii, 759p $15   **888**

ISBN 0-226-56032-5

First published 1947 by Modern Library

Contents: Analytics posteriora (Posterior analytics); Physica (Physics) the second of the eight books; De anima (On the soul): De partibus animalium (On the parts of animals) book I, chapter I; Metaphysica (Metaphysics) the first and twelfth of the fourteen books; Ethica Nicomachea (Nicomachean ethics); Politica (Politics) the first and third of the eight books; Poetica (Poetics); Rhetorica (Rhetoric) book I, chapters 1-4, book II, chapters 18-22

Plato

The dialogues of Plato; Apology, Crito, Phaedo, Symposium, Republic; Jowett translation edited and with introductory notes by J. D. Kaplan. Washington Sq. Press 1950 386p pa $5.99   **888**

ISBN 0-671-52524-7

"The dialog's chosen for this edition are the best-known of Plato's writings and also the most influential. They are valuable both as literature and as the major statements of his philosophy." Introduction

The portable Plato; edited with an introduction by Scott Buchanan. Viking 1948 696p o.p.; Penguin Bks. paperback available $12.50   **888**

ISBN 0-14-015040-4 (pa)

"The Viking portable library"

"Protagoras, Symposium, Phaedo, and the Republic, complete, in the English translation of Benjamin Jowett." Title page

Includes bibliography

The Republic   **888**

1. Utopias 2. Political science

Hardcover and paperback editions available from various publishers

In this section of the celebrated Dialogues in which Socrates is represented as interlocutor, Plato develops his views of the ideal state. "Political thought in Europe has been more or less consciously influenced by the Republic for twenty-three centuries." Dickinson. Best Books Ser

889 Modern Greek literature

Cavafy, Constantine P., 1863-1933

The complete poems of Cavafy; translated by Rae Dalven; with an introduction by W. H. Auden. Expanded ed. Harcourt Brace Jovanovich 1976 xxiv, 311p pa $10.95   **889**

ISBN 0-15-619820-7   LC 76-22804

"A Harvest book"

Cavafy, Constantine P., 1863-1933 — *Continued*

First published 1961

Contains translations of poems, chronologically arranged, which have never before appeared in book form in English or in Greek. Auden's introduction analyzes Cavafy's poetry

Includes bibliography

Kazantzakis, Nikos, 1883-1957

The Odyssey: a modern sequel; translated into English verse, introduction, synopsis, and notes by Kimon Friar; illustrated by Ghika. Simon & Schuster 1958 xxxviii, 824p il hardcover o.p. paperback available $14.95

                                 889

1. Odysseus (Greek mythology)—Poetry
ISBN 0-671-20247-2 (pa)

Original Greek edition, 1983

"A long, lusty poem, filled with adventures and with the philosophical beliefs of the author. . . . Intended as a sequel to [Homer's] Odyssey, it imagines Odysseus' homecoming to Ithaca and, soon, his departure again for good, his abduction of Helen from Sparta . . . his travels over the Mediterranean and, eventually, his conversion to ascetic philosophy and his wanderings over the earth." Publ Wkly

Seferis, George, 1900-1971

Collected poems; translated, edited, and introduced by Edmund Keeley and Philip Sherrard. Expanded ed. Princeton Univ. Press 1981 xxiii, 550p il $68   **889**

ISBN 0-691-06471-7   LC 80-8731
First published 1967

The collected poems of the Greek Nobel laureate. Translations printed opposite the original Greek text

The translations "succeed admirably in bringing over into English the peculiar qualities of the poet's language." Libr J

Includes chronology and bibliography

891   East-Indo European literatures

Mahābhārata. Bhagavadgītā

The Bhagavad Gita   **891**

Hardcover and paperback editions available from various publishers

"An eighteen-part discussion between the god Krishna, an avatar of Vishnu appearing as a charioteer, and Arjuna, a warrior about to enter battle, on the nature and meaning of life. Sometimes called the New Testament of Hinduism, it is an interpolation in the great Hindu epic the Mahābhārata." Reader's Ency

Narayan, R. K., 1906-

The Ramayana; a shortened modern prose version of the Indian epic: (suggested by the Tamil version of Kamban). Viking 1972 171p o.p.; Penguin Bks. paperback available $7   **891**

ISBN 0-14-004428-0 (pa)

A retelling of Prince Rama's courtship of the fourteen-year-old Sita, their exile, Sita's abduction, the search, and the great battle with her abductor Ravana, involving a pantheon of gods, heroes, and evil spirits

Narayan "has not produced a scholarly translation but rather, by using his skills as a novelist, has given us a short and readable modern version." Libr J

Omar Khayyam

Rubáiyát of Omar Khayyám.   **891**

Hardcover and paperback editions available from various publishers

"The Rubáiyát' (Quatrains) of Omar the Tentmaker, of Persia, is composed of a series of stanzas forming 'a medley of love and tavern songs, tinged with Sufi mysticism, and with the melancholy of Eastern fatalism.'" Dickinson. Best Books Ser

891.6   Celtic literatures

The **Oxford** book of Welsh verse in English; chosen by Gwyn Jones. Oxford Univ. Press 1977 xxxvii, 313p $24.95   **891.6**

1. Welsh poetry—Collections
ISBN 0-19-211858-7   LC 77-359670

This anthology covers Welsh poetry from Taliesin (sixth century) to Dylan Thomas. The first third of this volume is devoted to translations of 141 poems, some done especially for this collection. The modern period begins with the works of Henry Vaughan and George Herbert. The selection of twentieth century poets include those who are little known in translation, as well as the famous

891.7   Russian literature

Akhmatova, Anna Andreevna, 1889-1966

The complete poems of Anna Akhmatova; [by] Anna Akhmatova; translated by Judith Hemschemeyer; edited and with an introduction by Roberta Reeder. Zephyr Press (Somerville) 1990 c1989 2v il hardcover o.p. paperback available $24.95

                                   891.7

ISBN 0-939010-27-5 (pa)   LC 88-51831

"Anna Akhmatova—the high priestess of Russian poetry—saw her husband shot, her son imprisoned twice by Stalin, her work banned in the 1930's and late 40's. . . . Sonorous, calm, deliberate in movement, her Russian has no English equivalent, but in this admirably restrained and accurate translation, sense and message strike with all the weight of the original." N Y Times Book Rev

Brodsky, Joseph, 1940-
A part of speech. Farrar, Straus & Giroux
1980 151p $15.95; pa $10   **891.7**
ISBN 0-374-22987-2; 0-374-51633-2 (pa)   LC 80-613
In addition to new work this collection contains Brodsky's choice of translations of his earlier work
Brodsky "is a poet of dramatic yet delicate vision—a man with a sense of the increasingly obscured loftiness of human life. But under no circumstances is his poetry dully ethereal. His dramatic power cuts both ways: he can portray a luminous moment or a time of seemingly purposeless suffering with equal clarity." Christ Sci Monit
Includes bibliographic references

To Urania. Farrar, Straus & Giroux 1988
173p $14.95; pa $9   **891.7**
ISBN 0-374-17253-6; 0-374-52333-9 (pa)
                                  LC 87-24589
This collection contains translations (by the poet and other translators) "of poems from two previous books, Chast'rechi and Uraniia, along with poems written in English. Included are . . . elegies for parents and friends, . . . historical meditations, evocations of European cities, and a dialogue in fourteen cantos between two inmates of a Soviet psychiatric hospital." Poetry

The **Cambridge** history of Russian literature;
edited by Charles A. Moser. rev ed.
Cambridge Univ. Press 1992 709p $89.95;
pa $27.95   **891.7**
1. Russian literature—History and criticism
ISBN 0-521-41554-3; 0-521-42567-0 (pa)
                                  LC 91-38275
This volume presents "a survey of Russian literature from the beginnings to this decade, in sufficient but not overwhelming detail.' Ten chapters by specialists elucidate this history from 988 to approximately 1980, with a lengthy bibliography at the end of the volume." Sheehy. Guide to Ref Books. 10th edition. suppl

Chekhov, Anton Pavlovich, 1860-1904
Best plays; [by] Anton Chekhov; translated and with an introduction by Stark Young.
Modern Lib. 1956 296p hardcover o.p.
paperback available $3.95   **891.7**
ISBN 0-394-50984-3 (pa)
Contents: The sea gull; Uncle Vanya; The three sisters; The cherry orchard

Five major plays; translated and with an introduction by Ronald Hingley. Oxford
Univ. Press 1977 322p pa $4.95   **891.7**
ISBN 0-19-502250-5   LC 77-11172
Translations in this volume are taken from The Oxford Chekhov, entered below
Contents: Ivanov; The seagull; Uncle Vanya; Three sisters; The cherry orchard

The Oxford Chekhov; translated and edited by Ronald Hingley. Oxford Univ.
Press 1964-1968 3v ea $49.95   **891.7**
This edition of Chekhov's works is complete in nine volumes. Volumes 4-9 are collections of short stories
Contents: v1 Short plays (ISBN 0-19-21349-6); v2 Platonov; Ivanov; The seagull (ISBN 0-19-211347-X); v3 Uncle Vanya; Three sisters; The cherry orchard; The wood-demon (ISBN 0-19-211339-9)

The portable Chekhov; edited and with an introduction by Avrahm Yarmolinsky.
Viking 1947 631p o.p.; Penguin Bks.
paperback available $12.50   **891.7**
ISBN 0-14-015035-8 (pa)
"The Viking portable Library"
This collection contains "two plays, 'The Cherry Orchard' and 'The Boor,' 28 short stories and selections from Chekhov's letters." Publ Wkly

Handbook of Russian literature; edited by
Victor Terras. Yale Univ. Press 1985 558p
hardcover o.p. paperback available $24.95
          891.7
1. Russian literature—Dictionaries
ISBN 0-300-04868-8 (pa)   LC 84-11871
"The volume includes entries on authors, genres, literary movements, and period studies, together with reviews of notable journals. The lengthiest entries run to more than 6,000 words, and the shortest have been kept to a single paragraph." Booklist
"A valuable resource for students, scholars, and general readers." Libr J
Includes bibliography

Kirk, Irina
Anton Chekhov. Twayne Pubs. 1981 165p
(Twayne's world authors ser) $20.95   **891.7**
1. Chekhov, Anton Pavlovich, 1860-1904
ISBN 0-8057-6410-0   LC 80-19110
This introduction to Chekhov's life and works examines and analyzes the Russian author's plays and short stories, placing them in the context of world literature
Includes bibliography

Mirskiĭ, Dmitriĭ Petrovich, 1890-1939
A history of Russian literature, from its beginnings to 1900; edited by Francis J.
Whitfield. Vintage Bks. 1958 383p $9
          891.7
1. Russian literature—History and criticism
ISBN 0-394-70720-6
Contains Mirsky's A history of Russian literature from the earliest times to the death of Dostoyevsky (1881) and the first two chapters of his Contemporary Russian literature, 1881-1925
Summarizes the development of Russian literature, analyzing the influences of foreign models and the contribution of native social elements to literary growth and development. Critical interpretations of the works of major and some minor literary figures are included

Nabokov, Vladimir Vladimirovich, 1899-1977
Lectures on Russian literature; edited with an introduction by Fredson Bowers.
Harcourt Brace Jovanovich 1981 324p il
hardcover o.p. paperback available $11.95
          891.7
1. Russian literature—History and criticism
ISBN 0-15-649591-0 (pa)
Analyzed in Essay and general literature index
Companion volume Lectures on literature, entered in class 808.3

Nabokov, Vladimir Vladimirovich, 1899-1977—Continued

This book is "derived from notes Nabokov made for his literature classes at Wellesley and Cornell. Included are chapters on Gogol, Turgenev, Dostoevsky, Tolstoy, Chekhov, and Gorki, as well as several miscellaneous essays on censorship and the art of translation." Libr J

Nikolai Gogol. New Directions 1944 172p hardcover o.p. paperback available $8.95
891.7

1. Gogol', Nikolaĭ Vasil'evich, 1809-1852
ISBN 0-8112-0120-1 (pa)

"The Makers of modern literature"

The noted Russian modernist presents his own idiosyncratic readings of an author who influenced him

Pushkin, Aleksandr Sergeevich, 1799-1837

Boris Godounov; Russian text with translation and notes by Philip L. Barbour. Greenwood Press 1976 196p $38.50 **891.7**

ISBN 0-8371-8522-X

Also available in paperback from Blackwell

A reprint of the 1953 edition published by Columbia Univ. Press

Characters: Large mixed cast. Five acts. First produced at the Maryinsky Theatre, St. Petersburg, Russia, 1870

Set in early 17th-century Russia, this play depicts the reign of Boris Godounov and the political upheaval that took place in the development of the nation

The bronze horseman; selected poems of Alexander Pushkin; translated and introduced by D.M. Thomas. Viking 1982 261p o.p.; Penguin Bks. paperback available $15.95
891.7

ISBN 0-631-14385-8 (pa)   LC 81-70186

This book contains a "selection of poems, narrative verse, and dramas. . . . The book has two sections: the first is devoted to Pushkin's short lyrics and contains some 38 selections; the second includes 10 longer works, among them such diverse items as 'The Bronze Horseman;' the drama, 'Mozart and Salieri;' the mock epic, 'Gavriliad;' and the fairy-tale drama, 'Rusalka.' There are no prose works." Choice

The **Russian** short story; a critical history; Charles A. Moser, editor. Twayne Pubs. 1986 xxiv, 232p (Twayne's critical history of the short story) $22.95 **891.7**

1. Russian fiction—History and criticism
ISBN 0-8057-9360-7   LC 86-14865

"The Russian short story is examined from the publication in the early nineteenth century of Pushkin's 'Tales of Belkin' . . . to 1980, when the Russian story stood poised between stagnation and rejuvenation. Technique, subject matter, and impact are the focuses here as the authors proceed through the development of the Russian short story both in its organic trends and in its sociopolitical contexts." Booklist

Includes bibliography

Slonim, Marc, 1894-1976

Soviet Russian literature; writers and problems, 1917-1977; Marc Slonim. 2d rev ed. Oxford Univ. Press 1977 437p $25; pa $10.95 **891.7**

1. Russian literature—History and criticism
ISBN 0-19-502151-7; 0-19-502152-5 (pa)
     LC 76-426661

Analyzed in Essay and general literature index

First published 1964

A critical assessment of major post-revolutionary novelists and poets. Major emphasis is placed on the Communist socio-political impact on Russian literature

Includes bibliographic references

Solzhenitsyn, Aleksandr, 1918-

Candle in the wind; translated by Keith Armes with Arthur Hudgins; with an introduction by Keith Armes. University of Minn. Press 1973 141p $11.95 **891.7**

ISBN 0-8166-0681-1

Original Russian edition copyright 1960

In this play "the protagonist, Alex Coriel, a 40-year-old mathematician closely resembling Solzhenitsyn himself, returns a changed man after nine years in a prison camp on false charges (the locale is a fictional 'Caledonia,' not Russia)." Publ Wkly

Terras, Victor

A history of Russian literature. Yale Univ. Press 1991 654p $45 **891.7**

1. Russian literature—History and criticism
ISBN 0-300-04971-4   LC 91-13337

This history of Russian literature begins with a chapter on folklore and then presents a chronological account covering Old Russian literature (eleventh to sixteenth centuries); the seventeenth century; the eighteenth century; the Romantic period; the age of the novel, the Silver Age, and the Soviet period

"The book's minor shortcomings are overshadowed by its numerous merits: its accuracy, keenness of observation, subtle comments, vivid quotations, erudition." Times Lit Suppl

Tsvetaeva, Marina Ivanovna, 1892-1941

Selected poems [of] Marina Tsvetayeva; translated by Elaine Feinstein, with literal versions provided by Angela Livingstone [et al.] rev and enl ed. Oxford Univ. Press 1981 108p pa $14.95 **891.7**

ISBN 0-19-211894-3   LC 80-41681

Also available another edition translated by David McDuff from Dufour Eds.

This translation first published 1971

"As a poet Tsvetayeva impresses with her psychic energy, she is on fire with poetry, and nothing is put in perspective, everything is immediate, emotional in the best sense." N Y Times Book Rev

Includes bibliographic references

Turgenev, Ivan Sergeevich, 1818-1883
A month in the country; a comedy in five acts; by Ivan Turgenev; translated and introduced by Isaiah Berlin. Viking 1982 127p o.p.; Penguin Bks. paperback available $4.95 **891.7**

ISBN 0-14-044436-X (pa)   LC 81-52222
Characters: 7 men, 5 women, 1 boy. 5 acts. First produced at the Maly Theatre, Moscow, January 13, 1872
Month spent by young German tutor on 19th century Russian estate sparks rivalry between bored wife and her young ward

Twentieth century interpretations of Crime and punishment; a collection of critical essays; edited by Robert Louis Jackson. Prentice-Hall 1974 122p pa $8.95 **891.7**

1. Dostoyevsky, Fyodor, 1821-1881. Crime and punishment
ISBN 0-13-193086-9
"A Spectrum book"
These critical essays by Russian, European and American critics examine, analyze and assess the novel, its main characters, its social setting, questions of guilt and evil and the integral role played by the epilogue
Includes bibliography

Yarmolinsky, Avraham, 1890-
A treasury of Russian verse. Books for Libs. 1969 c1949 314p (Granger index reprint ser) $21 **891.7**

1. Russian poetry—Collections
ISBN 0-8369-6093-9
Reprint of the title first published 1949 by Macmillan
An anthology of Russian poetry, in translation. Includes an introductory essay by Yarmolinsky and biobraphical notes on the poets included

Yevtushenko, Yevgeny Aleksandrovich, 1933-
Almost at the end; foreword by Harrison E. Salisbury; translated from the Russian by Antonina W. Bouis, Albert C. Todd, and Yevgeny Yevtushenko. Holt & Co. 1987 146p hardcover o.p. paperback available $8.95 **891.7**

ISBN 0-8050-0785-7 (pa)   LC 86-22800
This collection by the contemporary Russian poet includes translations of "Fuku," an autobiographical work in poetry and prose originally published in the literary magazine Novy Mir in 1985, and twenty-two shorter poems
Yevtushenko's "striking metaphors and startling comparisons, with their unexpected flashes of humor, are just as effective in the bold bluntness of English as in Russian." N Y Times Book Rev

The collected poems, 1952-1990; [by] Yevgeny Yevtushenko; edited by Albert C. Todd with the author and James Ragan. Holt & Co. 1990 659p $29.95 **891.7**

ISBN 0-8050-0696-6   LC 90-44794
"A John Macrae book"

"Based on Yevtushenko's own selections from the complete six-volume Russian edition, this collection is fluently translated by many distinguished poets, among them Richard Wilbur, Stanley Kunitz, and D.M. Thomas. Helpful textual annotations explain the many geographical and historical references, making the poems more accessible to the general reader." Libr J

The poetry of Yevgeny Yevtushenko, 1953-1965; translated with an introduction by George Reavey. Bilingual ed. October House 1965 xxxvii, 215p o.p.; Boyars, M. paperback available $8.95 **891.7**

ISBN 0-7145-0482-3 (pa)
"Fifty-three poems of the well-known Russian poet in the original Russian with sensitive English translations. The translator introduces the selection with a discussion of the equivocal position of poetry in Russian society past and present and a biographical critique of Evtushenko in which he emphasizes Evtushenko's struggle for the freedom of poetry. Appended are the original Russian sources." Booklist

891.8 Slavic literatures

Čapek, Karel, 1890-1938
R.U.R. and The insect play; by the Brothers Čapek. Oxford Univ. Press 1961 179p pa $14.50 **891.8**

ISBN 0-19-281010-3
Translated from the Czech by Paul Selver
"R.U.R." is a fantasy in which robots revolt against their human masters. In "The insect play," a dying tramp dreams about insect life

Toward the radical center; a Karel Čapek reader; edited and with an introduction by Peter Kussi; foreword by Arthur Miller; translated by Norma Comrada [et al.] Catbird Press 1990 407p il $23.95; pa $12.95 **891.8**

ISBN 0-945774-06-0; 0-945774-07-9 (pa)
    LC 89-39708
"A Garrigue book"
This volume contains new and revised translations of the Czech author's writings. Included are the complete texts of three plays: R.U.R., the Makropoulos Secret, and The Mother; Act II of From the Life of the Insects; essays and short stories from Apocryphal Stories, Intimate Things, Tales from Two Pockets and other collections, and travel sketches and essays on gardening
"To a piece, the selections are delightful, compassionate, and modernly conscious of the mysteriousness of everyday life." Booklist
Includes bibliography

Miłosz, Czesław
Beginning with my streets; essays and recollections; translated by Madeline G. Levine. Farrar, Straus & Giroux 1992 288p $30 **891.8**

ISBN 0-374-11010-7   LC 91-33925
Analyzed in Essay and general literature index
This collection of essays "opens with a poetic evocation of images and faces from the streets of Vilnius at a time when life seemed to offer the 'possibility of nor-

Miłosz, Czesław—*Continued*
malcy' and proceeds to discuss a variety of themes: time
and the 'dread mystery of ephemerality,' nationalism and
religion, the seven cardinal sins, the influence of Emmanuel Swedenborg on Dostoyevsky, and a number of
Mr. Milosz's friends and some literary figures who
touched his life and work." N Y Times Book Rev

The collected poems, 1931-1987. Ecco
Press 1988 511p hardcover o.p. paperback
available $14.95   **891.8**
   ISBN 0-88001-174-2 (pa)   LC 87-24479
   "Nobel Prize winner Milosz here includes most works
from his four books of poetry available in English, plus
50 pages of new poems and numerous older poems never
before translated, yet excludes poems not translated to
his satisfaction." Libr J
   "Like other major witnesses of this century—Primo
Levi, Zbigniew Herbert—Milosz is a moralist: his work
does not pronounce or make judgments; it simply takes
as its criterion human decency—disinterested, modes, and
not willingly misled." N Y Rev Books

The history of Polish literature. 2nd ed.
University of Calif. Press 1983 583p il
$42.50; pa $14   **891.8**
   1. Polish literature—History and criticism
   ISBN 0-520-04465-7; 0-520-04477-0 (pa)
                      LC 82-20227
   "This edition reproduces the original hardcover edition
published by The Macmillan Company and Collier Macmillan Ltd., London, in 1969. The book was completed
a couple of years earlier, so the material it covered did
not extend beyond the middle 1960s. In order to give
the reader some idea of later developments in contemporary Polish literature, a brief epilogue has been added
to this edition. The bibliography has also been consider-
ably updated." Preface

Provinces; translated by the author and
Robert Hass. Ecco Press 1991 72p $19.95
      891.8
   ISBN 0-88001-317-6   LC 91-3685
   "In new poems of penetrating honesty, this famous
immigrant from Poland, who won the Nobel Prize in
Literature in 1980, presents a lucid, deceptively straight-
forward, unforgettable portrait of the artist as an old
man." N Y Times Book Rev

Seifert, Jaroslav, 1901-1986
The selected poetry of Jaroslav Seifert;
translated from the Czech by Ewald Osers;
edited and with additional translations by
George Gibian. Macmillan 1986 194p $9.95
      891.8
   ISBN 0-02-609150-X   LC 85-23685
   This volume contains English translations of works
from eighteen of the Czech poet's thirty collections of
poetry "plus prose selections from his reminiscences. .
. . [His themes include:] celebration of his native country, a . . . concern for the sufferings of others, and a
. . . delight in the beauty of the physical world and
the love of women." Libr J

892   Afro-Asiatic literatures. Semitic literatures

Amichai, Yehuda
The selected poetry of Yehuda Amichai;
edited and newly translated by Chana Bloch
and Stephen Mitchell. Harper & Row 1986
173p hardcover o.p. paperback available
$12.50   **892**
   ISBN 0-06-096062-0 (pa)   LC 85-45611
   This is a selection of poems written between 1948
and 1985 by the Israeli poet. The poems are selected
from ten collections previously published in Hebrew
   "Mr. Amichai is an essentially autobiographical poet
with the rare ability to characterize the complex fate of
the modern Israeli, the private individual inevitably affected by the public realm of war, politics and religion."
N Y Times Book Rev

Anthology of modern Palestinian literature;
edited and introduced by Salma Khadra
Jayyusi. Columbia Univ. Press 1992
xxxiii, 744p $34.95   **892**
   1. Arabic literature—Collections
   ISBN 0-231-07508-1   LC 92-5189
   "Presented here are translations of poems, stories, and
excerpts from novels, as well as works by Palestinian
poets who write in English. Also included are personal
narratives by Palestinian writers depicting the varied
aspects of Palestinian life from the turn of the century
to the present. . . . Biographical sketches introduce the
authors, and a chronology of modern Palestinian history
provides background for some of the events and places
referred to in the selections. The introduction by the
editor provides a concise but comprehensive political history of Palestinian literature during the twentieth century." Publisher's note
   Includes bibliography

Gilgamesh
Gilgamesh   **892**
   Hardcover and paperback editions available from
various publishers
   Variant title: The epic of Gilgamesh
   "A Babylonian poem. One of the oldest and most
important major epics in literature, it was first
discovered on clay tablets in the library of 'Assur-Bani-
Pal' (668-626 BC). . . . The epic includes stories,
originally separate, of 'Gilgamesh', a legendary king of
Sumerian origin; 'Enkidu', a sort of primeval man; Ut-
napishtim, the Babylonian 'Noah'; and several other
tales." Reader's Ency. 3d edition

895.1   Chinese literature

Anthology of Chinese literature; compiled
and edited by Cyril Birch. Grove
Weidenfeld 1987 2v   **895.1**
   "UNESCO collection of representative works: Chinese
series"
   Reprint of the 1965-1972 edition
   Contents: [v1] From early times to the 14th century;
Donald Keene, associate editor (ISBN 0-8021-5038-1); v2
From the 14th century to the present day (ISBN 0-8021-
5090-X)

Anthology of Chinese literature—*Continued*

This "set is likely to remain for years to come the best introductory sampler to the literature of China, a model of the anthologizer's art." Choice

Includes bibliographies

Anthology of modern Chinese poetry; edited and translated by Michelle Yeh. Yale Univ. Press 1993 245p $33   **895.1**

1. Chinese poetry—Collections
ISBN 0-300-05487-4   LC 92-16322

Published with assistance from Mary Cady Tew Memorial Fund

"Arranged chronologically, this selection of twentieth-century poetry from China and Taiwan offers a few poems by each of 67 poets born between 1891 and 1963. Its scope is enormous, its range impressive. Editor Yeh's translations are accessible and fluid; her introduction and notes are helpful without being overbearingly scholarly." Booklist

Includes bibliographic references

The Columbia book of Chinese poetry; from early times to the thirteenth century; translated and edited by Burton Watson. Columbia Univ. Press 1984 385p il (Translations from the Oriental classics) $44; pa $17   **895.1**

1. Chinese poetry—Collections
ISBN 0-231-05682-6; 0-231-05683-4 (pa)

LC 83-26182

This anthology's "arrangement is historical, beginning with selections from a first millenium BC collection of Chinese verse (the Shih ching), and ending with tz'u lyrics from the Sung period (AD 960-1279). The 12 selections [are] each prefaced with a two- or three-page introduction." Choice

Includes bibliography

Dillard, Annie

Encounters with Chinese writers. Wesleyan Univ. Press 1984 106p pa $12.95   **895.1**

1. Authors, Chinese 2. China—Intellectual life
ISBN 0-8195-6156-8   LC 84-7322

"This is a collection of reminiscences of [Dillard's] conversations with Chinese writers while she was part of a six-member team of American intellectuals who visited China in 1982, and later when a Chinese delegation visited this country." Christ Sci Monit

One hundred poems from the Chinese; [edited and translated] by Kenneth Rexroth. New Directions 1956 159p hardcover o.p. paperback available $7.95   **895.1**

1. Chinese poetry—Collections
ISBN 0-8112-0180-5 (pa)

Also available: One hundred more poems from the Chinese, $12 in hardcover (ISBN 0-8112-0369-7) and $6.95 in paperback (ISBN 0-8112-0179-1)

Companion volume One hundred poems from the Japanese, entered in class 895.6

"Nine poets, who lived centuries ago, speak with the poignancy of understatement of unchanging things; the brevity of life, the richness of friendship, the beauties of nature, the inevitability of old age and death." Booklist

Includes bibliography

Pei-tao, 1949-

The August sleepwalker; [by] Bei Dao; translated and with an introduction by Bonnie S. McDougall. New Directions 1990 c1988 140p $16.95; pa $8.95   **895.1**

ISBN 0-8112-1131-2; 0-8112-1132-0 (pa)

LC 89-13694

First published 1988 in the United Kingdom

"One of China's most famous poets, and now living in exile, Dao (Zhao Zhenkai) has been ably translated in these 91 poems. Many are love poems; others freeze a beautiful or touching landscape; some capture a fleeting image; a few evoke the horror of a political murder. Only a place name or word in three or four poems reveals that they are by a Chinese author, but knowing the backdrop of political repression adds a particular poignancy to this fine work." Libr J

895.6   Japanese literature

Keene, Donald, 1922-

Dawn to the West; Japanese literature of the modern era. Holt & Co. 1984 2v   **895.6**

1. Japanese literature—History and criticism
LC 82-15445

Analyzed in Essay and general literature index

v1 Fiction $60, pa $29.95 (ISBN 0-03-062814-8; 0-8050-0607-9); v2 Poetry, drama, criticism $40, pa $19.95 (ISBN 0-03-062816-4; 0-8050-0608-7)

This work surveys "figures and literary movements since 1868 when Japan was opened to the West. Starting with the 'new' literature begun with the denial of traditional writing . . . Keene gives examples of imitations and influences while [attempting to] account for the emergence of new [literary] forms." Libr J

Keene "imparts knowledge in unparalleled volume and with unwavering precision. [This work] marks the end of our innocence with regard to modern Japanese literature." N Y Times Book Rev

The pleasures of Japanese literature. Columbia Univ. Press 1988 133p il (Companions to Asian studies) $20; pa $12.95   **895.6**

1. Japanese literature—History and criticism
ISBN 0-231-06736-4; 0-231-06737-2 (pa)

LC 88-18069

The author discusses Japanese aesthetics, poetry, fiction and drama, focusing on works of the premodern period

"If your library has no other introduction to the Japanese classics, nor any need for another, this is the one it ought to include." Booklist

Includes bibliography

Modern Japanese literature; an anthology; compiled and edited by Donald Keene. Grove Press 1960 c1956 440p hardcover o.p. paperback available $14.95   **895.6**

1. Japanese literature—Collections
ISBN 0-8021-5095-0 (pa)

"The selections give a representative sampling of the poetry, prose, and drama from the 1870's through the 1940's. Short enlightening notes on the writers or background for the text are added unobtrusively." Booklist

Includes bibliography

One hundred poems from the Japanese; [edited and translated] by Kenneth Rexroth. New Directions 1956 143p $11.95; pa $7.95 **895.6**

1. Japanese poetry—Collections
ISBN 0-8112-0371-9; 0-8112-0181-3 (pa)

Also available: One hundred more poems from the Japanese, $12 in hardcover (ISBN 0-8112-0618-1) and $7.95 in paperback (ISBN 0-8112-0619-X)

Companion volume One hundred poems from the Chinese, entered in class 895.1

A bilingual collection of poems drawn chiefly from the traditional Manyōshu, Kokinshū, and Hyakunin Isshu collections and also containing examples of haiku and other later forms. The translator's introduction provides background information on the history and nature of Japanese poetry

Includes bibliography

The **Penguin** book of Japanese verse; translated with an introduction by Geoffrey Bownas and Anthony Thwaite. Penguin Bks. 1964 lxxvi, 242p pa $9.95 **895.6**

1. Japanese poetry—Collections
ISBN 0-14-058527-3

An anthology of Japanese poetry from the primitive and Nara periods to the 20th century. Includes a lengthy critical and historical introduction, a chronology and an index of poets

Ten thousand leaves

The ten thousand leaves; a translation of the Man'yōshū, Japan's premier anthology of classical poetry; [translated by] Ian Hideo Levy. Princeton Univ. Press 1981 409p il (Princeton library of Asian translations) hardcover o.p. paperback available $15.95 **895.6**

1. Japanese poetry—Collections   LC 80-8561

"The first of a planned four-volume complete translation of the 8th-century collection regarded . . . as Japan's first poetry anthology. . . . The majority of the works are in tanka form (31 syllables), the whole anthology representing the compositions of 260 named and many anonymous poets, and illustrating a . . . variety of style and subject." Libr J

"This book is notable not just for its handling of a difficult poetic style, but also for its remarkable translations of noble prose passages." Times Lit Suppl

Waley, Arthur, 1889-1966

The Nō plays of Japan; with letters by Oswald Sickert. Grove Press 1957 319p pa $9.95 **895.6**

1. Nō plays
ISBN 0-8021-5206-6

Also available in paperback from Tuttle

"An Evergreen book"

First published 1921 in the United Kingdom; first United States edition published 1922 by Knopf

Contains translation of 20 Nō plays and summaries of 16 more. In his introduction Mr. Waley gives a brief history of the Nō drama, its origin, the text of the plays, and the chief playwrights. He also tells about the stage settings, costumes and properties used in the production

of these plays. The greatest representation is given to the works of Seami and Zenchiku Ujinobu

Includes bibliography

896   African literatures

The **Penguin** book of modern African poetry; edited by Gerald Moore and Ulli Beier. 3rd ed. Penguin Bks. 1988 315p pa $9.95 **896**

1. African poetry—Collections
ISBN 0-14-058573-7

First published 1963 in the United Kingdom with title: Modern poetry from Africa

"The poems are organized by country. . . . The poets are organized by age, from oldest to youngest. . . . Their writing has an urgency that derives from the sense, . . . that there is much to be done and all of it important." N Y Times Book Rev

897   North American native literatures

American Indian literature; an anthology; edited and with an introduction by Alan R. Velie. rev ed. University of Okla. Press 1991 373p il $29.95; pa $14.95 **897**

1. Indians of North America—Literature 2. American literature—American Indian authors—Collections
ISBN 0-8061-2331-1; 0-8061-2345-1 (pa)

LC 90-50700

First published 1979

An illustrated anthology of Native American tales, songs, memoirs, oratory, poetry and fiction. The editor provides critical introductions to each section

Includes bibliographic references

Coltelli, Laura, 1941-

Winged words: American Indian writers speak; [reported by] Laura Coltelli. University of Neb. Press 1990 211p il (American Indian lives) $25; pa $9.95 **897**

1. American literature—American Indian authors—History and criticism
ISBN 0-8032-1445-6; 0-8032-6351-1 (pa)

LC 89-39323

A compilation of interviews with Louise Erdrich, N. Scott Momaday, James Welch and eight other native American writers

"Coltelli's questions probe the writers' sources of inspiration, methods of composition, and perceptions of their own and their works' relationship to tribal culture, among other broad areas. But it's the questions Coltelli has tailored to each individual that hit pay dirt and result in some illuminating moments." Booklist

Includes bibliographic references

The **Portable** North American Indian reader; edited and with an introduction by Frederick W. Turner III. Viking 1974 628 o.p.; Penguin Bks. paperback available $12
897

1. Indians of North America—Literature 2. American literature—American Indian authors—Collections
ISBN 0-14-015077-3 (pa)

"The Viking portable library"

This introduction to the traditions and history of the North American Indian includes: myths, tales, poetry, oratory, and autobiography from the Iroquois, Cherokee, Winnebago, Sioux, and many other tribes

Includes bibliography

900 GEOGRAPHY AND HISTORY

901 History—Philosophy and theory

Durant, William James, 1885-1981
The lessons of history; by Will and Ariel Durant. Simon & Schuster 1968 117p $17.95
901

1. History—Philosophy
ISBN 0-671-41333-3

A series of essays about the nature, the conduct and the prospects of man, seeking in the great lives, the great ideas, the great events of the past for the meaning of man's long journey through war, conquest and creation

Includes bibliography

Spengler, Oswald, 1880-1936
The decline of the West. new rev ed. Knopf 1945 2v set $80
901

1. History—Philosophy 2. Civilization—History
ISBN 0-394-42178-7

Also available in an abridged edition from Oxford Univ. Press

First published 1926-1928

Translated from the German by C. F. Atkinson

Contents: v1 Form and actuality; v2 Perspectives of world-history

This work "reflects the pessimistic atmosphere in Germany after World War I. Spengler maintained that history has a natural development, in which every culture is a distinct organic form that grows, matures, and decays." Reader's Ency. 3d edition

902 History—Miscellany. Chronologies

An **Encyclopedia** of world history; ancient, medieval, and modern, chronologically arranged; compiled and edited by William L. Langer. 5th ed rev and enl, with maps and genealogical tables. Houghton Mifflin 1972 xxxix, 1569p il maps $44
902

1. Chronology, Historical 2. History—Outlines, syllabi, etc.
ISBN 0-395-13592-3
First published 1940

This is "a handbook of historical facts. . . . Emphasis is placed on political, military, and diplomatic history, with lesser attention given to literature, art, science, and economics. Historical coverage extends from prehistory to 1970." Topical Ref Books

Grun, Bernard, 1901-1972
The timetables of history; a horizontal linkage of people and events. new 3rd rev ed. Simon & Schuster 1991 724p $35; pa $20
902

1. Chronology, Historical
ISBN 0-671-74919-6; 0-671-74271-X (pa)
LC 92-100939

"A Touchstone book"
First published 1975
Based on Werner Stein's Kulturfahrplan

"These clearly laid-out timetables relate significant events occuring in various fields of endeavor to their historical and political milieu. Daily life as well as science, literature, religion, the arts, and music are charted in a two-page format that facilitates an easy comparison. More recent times are covered in greater detail." Ref Sources for Small & Medium-sized Libr. 5th edition

The **Timetables** of American history; Laurence Urdang, editor; with an introduction by Henry Steele Commager. Simon & Schuster 1982 c1981 470p il hardcover o.p. paperback available $20
902

1. Chronology, Historical
ISBN 0-671-25246-1 (pa)
LC 81-18206
"A Laurence Urdang reference book"
"Information is presented chronologically in tabular form. Each double-page spread has columns for history and politics, the arts, science and technology, and miscellaneous, with separate columns thereunder for events and developments in America and elsewhere. Covers through 1980. Indexed." Sheehy. Guide to Ref Books. 10th edition

Trager, James
The people's chronology; a year-by-year record of human events from prehistory to the present. rev and updated ed. Holt & Co. 1992 1237p il (Henry Holt reference bk) $45
902

1. Chronology, Historical
ISBN 0-8050-1786-0
LC 91-36734
First published 1979

Trager, James—*Continued*

This volume contains over 30,000 entries covering prehistory through 1991. "Entries typically consist of a brief paragraph describing a particular event. Within a year, events are arranged not by date but by subject. Events are classified with graphic symbols beside them, in 30 different categories, including politics, economics, literature, architecture, crime, music, theater, food, and even tobacco." Booklist

Wetterau, Bruce

The New York Public Library book of chronologies. Prentice-Hall 1990 634p $29.95 **902**

1. Chronology, Historical
ISBN 0-13-620451-1   LC 90-46768

"A Stonesong Press book"

This book contains "250 separate chronologies, each covering an area of history or culture, organized under 14 topics. Within each chapter numerous lists trace subjects that relate to the major one." Libr J

For a fuller review see: Booklist, Dec. 15, 1990

World history; a dictionary of important people, places, and events from ancient times to the present. Holt & Co. 1994 1173p (Henry Holt reference bk) $60 **902**

1. Chronology, Historical 2. History—Dictionaries
ISBN 0-8050-2350-X   LC 93-38510

Revised edition of Macmillan concise dictionary of world history, published 1983

Alphabetically arranged entries focusing mainly on political history but also covering the arts, religion, intellectual life, science and technology. Chronologies are provided for some countries, periods and wars

903 History—Encyclopedias and dictionaries

Cook, Chris, 1945-

Dictionary of historical terms. 2nd ed. Bedrick Bks. 1990 c1989 350p $34.95; pa $14.95 **903**

1. History—Dictionaries
ISBN 0-87226-331-2; 0-87226-241-3 (pa)
                                      LC 89-14934

First published 1983

This reference work "covers political, religious, and social terms, but not people, wars, or battles. . . . The alphabetically arranged entries range from a brief sentence to more than 500 words. The origin and translation of foreign terms appear in parentheses immediately following the terms. . . . A wealth of valuable information." Booklist

Kurian, George Thomas

Encyclopedia of the Third World. Facts on File 3v il maps set $225 **903**

1. Developing countries—Dictionaries

First published 1978 as a two volume set. (4th edition 1992) Periodically revised

"Basic facts, location, weather, population, ethnicity, and language are given for nations of the Third World. Political, economic, educational, military, legal, cultural, and social information is supplied. . . . Comprehensive,

well organized, and convenient, set in large type, with an introduction of relevant international organizations, several valuable appendixes, and a good index, this tool will meet the demands placed on libraries for current Third World data." Ref Sources for Small & Medium-sized Libr. 5th edition

904 Collected accounts of events

Great disasters; dramatic true stories of nature's awesome powers. Reader's Digest Assn. 1989 320p il maps $30 **904**

1. Natural disasters
ISBN 0-89577-321-X   LC 88-26504

"Natural calamities—from the death of the dinosaurs and the eruption of Vesuvius to the Chicago Fire, the Armenian earthquake, and the threat of global warming—are discussed in a profusely illustrated account." Booklist

"This is a well-produced volume. . . . The text is crisp, the photos attractive and relevant, the diagrams clear and informative." Libr J

Macdonald, John, 1945-

Great battlefields of the world; introduction by Len Deighton; foreword by Sir John Hackett. Macmillan 1985 c1984 200p il maps hardcover o.p. paperback available $25.95 **904**

1. Battles
ISBN 0-02-044464-8 (pa)   LC 85-332

First published 1984 in the United Kingdom

"The text and unique battlefield illustrations examine 30 significant battles in world history from Cannae, 216 B.C., to Dien Bien Phu, 20 November 1953, but excludes the eastern front of World War II. The text traces each battle in detail, analyzing tactics, weapons, weather and terrain, commanders, political aspects, outcomes, and resulting consequences." Wynar. Guide to Ref Books for Sch Media Cent. 3d edition

907 History—Education and related topics

Schama, Simon

Dead certainties; unwarranted speculations. Knopf 1991 333p $21; pa $12 **907**

1. Historiography
ISBN 0-679-40213-6; 0-679-73613-1 (pa)
                                      LC 90-52902

This exploration of the nature of historical writing consists of two stories. The first one "is concerned with the battlefield death of James Wolfe, British commander in the North American campaign of the Seven Years' War; the second with the murder ninety years later of a Harvard Medical School professor, George Parkman." New Repub

Tuchman, Barbara Wertheim

Practicing history; selected essays; by Barbara W. Tuchman. Knopf 1981 306p $16.50 **907**

1. Historiography 2. History, Modern
ISBN 0-394-52086-6   LC 81-47509

Also available in paperback from Ballantine Bks.

Tuchman, Barbara Wertheim—*Continued*
A collection of essays on the nature, methodology and writing of history

909 World history. Civilization

Boorstin, Daniel J. (Daniel Joseph), 1914-
The creators. Random House 1992 811p il $30 **909**
1. Civilization 2. Arts 3. Creation (Literary, artistic, etc.)
ISBN 0-394-54395-5 LC 91-39948
In this volume "Boorstin undertakes an interpretive history of creativity in Western civilization. Packed with shrewd, entertaining profiles of Dante, Goethe, Benjamin Franklin and dozens of others, this stimulating synthesis sets the achievements of individual geniuses into a coherent narrative of humanity's advance from ignorance." Publ Wkly
Includes bibliographic references

The discoverers. Random House 1983 745p $27; pa $16 **909**
1. Civilization 2. Discoveries (in geography) 3. Science—History
ISBN 0-394-40229-4; 0-394-25633-6 (pa)
LC 83-42766
The author "leads his reader through . . . anecdotal information of the discoveries of timekeeping, map-making, observations of nature, both large and small, and of insights into human social organizations, past and present, in this popularized, general history of 'mankind's need to know.'" Choice

The **Cambridge** history of Islam; edited by P. M. Holt, Ann K. S. Lambton, Bernard Lewis. Cambridge Univ. Press 1978 2v in 4 il maps **909**
1. Islamic countries—History 2. Civilization, Islamic
First published 1970 in two volumes
Contents: v1A The central Islamic lands from pre-Islamic times to the First World War pa $42.95 (ISBN 0-521-29135-6); v1B The central Islamic lands since 1918 pa $42.95 (ISBN 0-521-29136-4); v2A The Indian subcontinent, South East Asia, Africa, and the Muslim West $64.50, pa $42.95 (ISBN0-521-29137-2); v2B Islamic society and civilization $94.95, pa $42.95 (ISBN 0-521-21949-3; 0-521-29138-0) set pa $95 (ISBN 0-521-08755-4)
"This is a comprehensive history of the Islamic countries in the usual Cambridge form of separate essays written by outstanding scholars in the various fields. . . . Though the text might warrant some criticism, the quality of the essays is generally excellent. . . . This major work . . . is essential for *all* but small neighborhood and secondary school collections." Libr J

Eban, Abba, 1915-
Heritage: civilization and the Jews. Summit Bks. 1984 354p il maps $40 **909**
1. Jews—History
ISBN 0-671-44103-5 LC 84-2696
A "history of the Jewish experience throughout the world . . . tracing 5000 years of Jewish influence on world culture and surveying the interaction between Jews and other nations and peoples." Libr J

My people: the story of the Jews. Random House 1968 534p il hardcover o.p. paperback available $14.95 **909**
1. Jews—History 2. Israel—History
ISBN 0-394-72759-2 (pa)
Following a broad outline of Jewish history the author looks at the modern state of Israel, its place in world affairs, and its relations with its neighbors

Encyclopedia of Jewish history; events and eras of the Jewish people. Facts on File 1986 287p il maps $40 **909**
1. Jews—History—Dictionaries
ISBN 0-8160-1220-2 LC 85-23941
"Provides concise information about Jewish history and key figures from the earliest times to the present. Contains 100 chronologically arranged entries of about 800 words each. Numerous colored illustrations, photographs, maps, and diagrams. Includes index to text and illustrations and a dozen appendixes on culture and ethnography." Sheehy. Guide to Ref Books. 10th edition. suppl

Eyewitness to history; edited by John Carey. Harvard Univ. Press 1988 c1987 xxxviii, 706p $29.95 **909**
1. World history—Sources
ISBN 0-674-28750-9 LC 88-1699
Also available in paperback from Avon Bks.
First published 1987 in the United Kingdom with title: The Faber book of reportage
An anthology of eyewitness accounts to historical events and persons from ancient Greece to the fall of Marcos
Includes bibliography

Fargues, Philippe
The atlas of the Arab world; [by] Philippe Fargues & Rafic Boustani. Facts on File 1991 144p il maps $50 **909**
1. Arab countries
ISBN 0-8160-2346-8 LC 89-675447
"A wealth of information presented in colorful maps, graphs, diagrams, and charts. Arranged by broad cultural topics such as ethnic groups and religions, society, cities, oil and industry, facts not readily available in standard resources are presented and compared." SLJ
For a fuller review see: Booklist, Feb. 15, 1992

Grant, Michael, 1914-
From Alexander to Cleopatra; the Hellenistic world. Scribner 1983 c1982 319p il maps o.p.; Collier Bks. paperback available $14.95 **909**
1. Mediterranean region—History 2. Hellenism
ISBN 0-02-032787-0 (pa) LC 82-10802
First published 1982 in the United Kingdom
The author offers a "survey of the Hellenistic world (323-31 BC) of ancient Greece and the Near East. . . . Grant begins with a quick survey of the struggles of the generals after Alexander's death for power and land, then delves into the vibrant cultural achievements and social developments that formed this important period in Western civilization. . . . An outstanding popular history of a fascinating and important era, and Grant presents it lucidly." Choice

A **Historical** atlas of the Jewish people; from the time of the Patriarchs to the present; general editor, Eli Barnavi; English edition editor, Miriam Eliav-Feldon; cartography, Michel Opatowski. Knopf 1992 299p il maps $50
909

1. Jews—History—Maps
ISBN 0-679-40332-9   LC 92-53169

"Covering three millennia of Jewish history and culture through a combination of concise text, accurate and well-drawn maps, and a sumptuous array of photographs, diagrams, and reproductions of paintings, this atlas succeeds in covering all the main themes of the Jewish experience. The material is arranged chronologically and systematically. . . . The result is a reference that will profit both scholars and lay readers." Libr J

A **History** of civilization. Prentice-Hall 2v il ea $37.33
909

1. Civilization—History

Also available in a one-volume edition and a three-volume edition

First published 1955. (8th edition 1992) Periodically revised

Volume one of this study covers prehistory to 1715 and volume two deals with the years 1648 to the present

Includes bibliographic references

A **History** of private life; Philippe Ariès and Georges Duby, general editors. Harvard Univ. Press 1987-1991 5v il ea $39.95; v1-2 pa ea $18.95
909

1. Civilization 2. Manners and customs 3. Family life
LC 86-18286

Translated by Arthur Goldhammer

Contents: v1 From pagan Rome to Byzantium; Paul Veyne, editor (ISBN 0-674-39975-7; 0-674-39974-9); v2 Revelations of the medieval world; Georges Duby, editor (ISBN 0-674-39976-5; 0-674-40001-1); v3 Passions of the Renaissance; Roger Chartier, editor (ISBN 0-674-39977-3); v4 From the fires of revolution to the Great War; Michelle Perrot, editor (ISBN 0-674-39978-1); v5 Riddles of identity in modern times; Antoine Prost and Gérard Vincent, editors (ISBN 0-674-39979-X)

"An extraordinarily rich compendium of information on virtually all aspects of life in all social classes. . . . The lucid style should appeal to the general reader, for whom the book is intended." Libr J [review of v1]

Includes bibliographic references

Hourani, Albert Habib
A history of the Arab peoples; [by] Albert Hourani. Harvard Univ. Press 1991 xx, 551p il $27.50
909

1. Arab countries—History 2. Civilization, Arab
ISBN 0-674-39565-4   LC 90-48708

Also available in paperback from Warner Bks.

This history of the Arab peoples "is divided into five parts, treating the 7th through 10th centuries, the 11th through 15th centuries, the 16th through 18th centuries and what Mr. Hourani calls 'The Age of European Empires (1800-1939)' and 'The Age of Nation-States (since 1939).' . . . This is history in the grand style. It can lead to a better understanding of the Arabs, past and present." N Y Times Book Rev

Includes bibliographic references

The **Illustrated** atlas of Jewish civilization; 4,000 years of Jewish history; consulting editor, Martin Gilbert. Macmillan 1990 224p il maps $40
909

1. Jews—History—Maps
ISBN 0-02-543415-2   LC 90-675150

"A Quarto book"

A visual survey of Jewish history and culture from patriarchal times to the present

This "is a successful blend of beautiful cartography, arresting illustrations, and informative text." Libr J

Johnson, Paul, 1928-
A history of the Jews. Harper & Row 1987 644p $25; pa $14
909

1. Jews—History
ISBN 0-06-015698-8; 0-06-091533-1 (pa)
LC 85-42575

This narrative attempts to cover the "interplay between Jewish history and Western history, and between the philosophical, ethical, religious, social and political notions of Judaic culture and those of Western culture." Publisher's note

This "is an absorbing, provocative, well-written, often moving book, an insightful and impassioned blend of history and myth, story and interpretation." Christ Sci Monit

Includes bibliography

Lamb, David
The Arabs; journeys beyond the mirage. Random House 1987 333p $19.95; pa $13
909

1. Arab countries
ISBN 0-394-54433-1; 0-394-75758-0 (pa)
LC 86-10136

"The book is both a primer on Arab culture and history, ancient and contemporary, and a selective tour of the Arab world Mr. Lamb saw as a reporter." N Y Times Book Rev

Includes bibliography

Mumford, Lewis, 1895-1990
The condition of man. Harcourt Brace & Co. 1944 467p il hardcover o.p. paperback available $9.95
909

1. Civilization—History 2. Man
ISBN 0-15-621550-0 (pa)

The third in the author's series which begins with Technics and civilization (entered in class 609), The culture of cities (entered in class 307.7), and finishes with The conduct of life (entered in class 128)

This book traces the development of personality and community as it explores the rise of modern man

Includes bibliography

The myth of the machine. Harcourt Brace & Co. 1967-1970 2v hardcover o.p. paperbacks available ea $19.95
909

1. Civilization—History 2. Technology and civilization
ISBN 0-15-622341-2 (v1); 0-15-671610-0 (v2)

Contents: v1 Technics and human development; v2 The pentagon of power

Mumford, Lewis, 1895-1990—*Continued*
In this historical survey of the development of man from prehistoric times through the Space Age, the author explores the forces that have shaped technology, taking "life itself to be the primary phenomenon, and creativity, rather than the 'conquest of nature,' as the ultimate criterion of man's biological and cultural success." Author's note

Includes bibliographies

Ortega y Gasset, José, 1883-1955
The revolt of the masses; translated, annotated, and with an introduction by Anthony Kerrigan; edited by Kenneth Moore; with a foreword by Saul Bellow. University of Notre Dame Press 1985 xxxi, 192p $25.95　　　　　　　**909**
1. Civilization 2. Europe—Civilization 3. Proletariat
ISBN 0-268-01609-7　　　　　　LC 81-40457
Original Spanish edition, 1930; first English translation, 1932

A collection of essays by the Spanish intellectual in which he analyzes the dangers of control of government by the masses. He sees Bolshevism and Fascism as particularly threatening to civilization

Potok, Chaim, 1929-
Wanderings; Chaim Potok's history of the Jews. Knopf 1978 431p il maps $40　**909**
1. Jews—History
ISBN 0-394-50110-1　　　　　　LC 78-54915
Also available in paperback from Fawcett Bks.

This informal history of the Jewish people emphasizes the themes of wandering and persecution

Includes bibliography

Toynbee, Arnold, 1852-1883
A study of history; abridgement of volumes I-X; by D. C. Somervell. Oxford Univ. Press 1946-1957 2v ea $25, pa $14.95
　　　　　　　　　　　　　　909
1. Civilization—History 2. History—Philosophy
Contents: v1 Abridgement of volumes I-VI (ISBN 0-19-500198-2, 0-19-505080-0); v2 Abridgement of volumes VII-X (ISBN 0-19-500199-0, 0-19-505081-9)

An abridgment of the first ten volumes of Toynbee's twelve-volume study on the rise and fall of civilizations. The editor has followed the pattern of the original work and has added a final chapter on how this book came to be written and a summary of the ten volumes

Wells, H. G. (Herbert George), 1866-1946
The outline of history; being a plain history of life and mankind; revised and brought up to date by Raymond Postgate and G. P. Wells; with maps and plans by J. F. Horrabin. Doubleday 1971 xxii, 1103p il maps $24.95　　　　　　　　**909**
ISBN 0-385-02420-7
First published 1920 by Macmillan
"Beginning with the postition of the earth in space it covers geologic time and human history down to the present." Wis Libr Bull

909.07　World history— ca. 500-1450/1500

Billings, Malcolm
The cross & the crescent; a history of the Crusades. Sterling 1988 c1987 239p il hardcover o.p. paperback available $14.95
　　　　　　　　　　　　　　909.07
1. Crusades
ISBN 0-8069-7364-1 (pa)　　　　LC 88-12049
First published 1987 in the United Kingdom
An illustrated look at the 700-year-long attempt by Europeans to gain control of the Holy Land
Includes bibliography

Burns, Thomas S.
A history of the Ostrogoths. Indiana Univ. Press 1984 299p il $19.95　　**909.07**
1. Civilization, Medieval 2. Teutonic peoples
ISBN 0-253-32831-4　　　　　　LC 83-49286
This "study of the Ostrogoths . . . explores the interaction between Rome and her eastern Germanic neighbors with the focus on the Ostrogothic experience. Traditional literary sources are looked at with a fresh eye, and new archaeological materials are thoroughly explored." Libr J
Includes bibliography

The **Cambridge** illustrated history of the Middle Ages; edited by Robert Fossier; translated by Janet Sondheimer. Cambridge Univ. Press il　　**909.07**
　　　　　　　　　　　　　　LC 85-21268
The first and third volumes of a projected four volume set
Volume 3 translated by Sarah Hanbury-Tension
Contents: Volume I: 350-950 (1989) $69.95 (ISBN 0-521-26644-0); Volume III: 1250-1520 (1986) $69.95 (ISBN 0-521-26646-7)
"There is a mine of fresh information here on agricultural, commerical, urban, military, and religious life." Libr J

909.08　Modern history, 1450/1500-

Kennedy, Paul M., 1945-
The rise and fall of the great powers; economic change and military conflict from 1500 to 2000; [by] Paul Kennedy. Random House 1988 xxv, 677p maps $24.95; pa $15
　　　　　　　　　　　　　　909.08
1. History, Modern 2. Economic conditions 3. Balance of power
ISBN 0-394-54674-1; 0-679-72019-7 (pa) LC 87-9690
The author "assesses the interaction between economics and strategy of the past five centuries; the correlation between productive and revenue-sharing capacities on the one hand and military strength on the other." Publ Wkly
"Kennedy's great achievement is that he makes us see our current international problems against a background of empires that have gone under because they were unable to sustain the material cost of greatness; and he does so in a universal historical perspective." N Y Rev Books
Includes bibliography

The New Cambridge modern history. Cambridge Univ. Press 1957-1979 14v apply to publisher for price   **909.08**

1. History, Modern

This 14-volume set replaces The Cambridge Modern history, first published 1902-1912 by Macmillan in thirteen volumes

Contents: v1 The Renaissance, 1493-1520; v2 The Reformation, 1520-1559; v3 The Counter-Reformation and the price of revolution, 1559-1610; v4 The decline of Spain and the Thirty-Years' War, 1609-48/59; v5 The ascendency of France, 1648-88; v6 The rise of Great Britain and Russia, 1688-1715/25; v7 The old regime, 1713-63; v8 The American and French revolutions, 1763-93; v9 War and peace in an age of upheaval, 1793-1830; v10 The zenith of European power, 1830-70; v11 Material progress and world-wide problems, 1870-1898; v12 The shifting balance of world forces, 1893-1945 (Originally titled: The era of violence); v13 Companion volume; v14 Atlas

"The most important general modern history, useful for reference purposes because of its high authority." Sheehy. Guide to Ref Books. 10th edition

Tuchman, Barbara Wertheim

The march of folly; from Troy to Vietnam; [by] Barbara W. Tuchman. Knopf 1984 447p il o.p.; Ballantine Bks. paperback available $12   **909.08**

1. History, Modern
ISBN 0-345-30823-9 (pa)   LC 83-22206

The author analyzes examples of governmental bumbling including the Trojan horse, the U.S. involvement in Vietnam, and the British loss of the American colonies

Includes bibliography

909.81 World history—19th century, 1800-1899

Johnson, Paul, 1928-

The birth of the modern; world society, 1815-1830. HarperCollins Pubs. 1991 xx, 1095p $35; pa $16   **909.81**

1. History, Modern—1800-1899 (19th century)
2. Civilization, Modern
ISBN 0-06-016574-X; 0-06-092282-6 (pa)
    LC 90-55541

This study examines "people, ideas, politics, manners and morals, economics, art, science and technology, diplomacy, business and commerce, literature and revolution." Publisher's note

"This marvelously readable, vivid, immensely illuminating 1120-page chronicle of the epoch of Andrew Jackson, Wordsworth, Goya, Faraday, Beethoven and Bolivar is filled with startlingly original, provocative observations." Publ Wkly

Includes bibliographic references

909.82 World history—20th century, 1900-1999

Beschloss, Michael R., 1955-

The crisis years; Kennedy and Khrushchev, 1960-1963. HarperCollins Pubs. 1991 816p il $29.95; pa $15   **909.82**

1. Kennedy, John F. (John Fitzgerald), 1917-1963
2. Khrushchev, Nikita Sergeevich, 1894-1971 3. World politics—1945-1991 4. United States—Foreign relations—Soviet Union 5. Soviet Union—Foreign relations—United States
ISBN 0-06-016454-9; 0-06-098105-9 (pa)
    LC 90-55946

"An Edward Burlingame book"

This book, based on primary sources, is an account of such Cold War episodes as "the Bay of Pigs, the Vienna summit, the Berlin Wall, the Cuban Missile Crisis, John Kennedy's assassination, and Nikita Khrushchev's overthrow." Publisher's note

Includes bibliography

Drucker, Peter Ferdinand, 1909-

The new realities; in government and politics, in economics and business, in society and world view. Harper & Row 1989 276p $19.95; pa $12   **909.82**

1. World politics—1965- 2. Economic conditions
ISBN 0-06-016129-9; 0-06-091699-0 (pa) LC 89-1992

The author examines societal problems from a managerial point of view

"Peter Drucker is never obscure. He shatters the reader with quite specific insights and forecasts, alternately infuriating right and left." Economist

Facts on file; weekly world news digest with cumulative index. Facts on File $630 per year   **909.82**

1. History, Modern—1900-1999 (20th century)—Periodicals
ISSN 0014-6641

Also available on CD-ROM

Annual bound volume: Facts on file yearbook available at $95

Started publication 1940. Looseleaf. Subtitle varies

"A weekly classified digest of news arranged under such headings as: World affairs, National affairs, Foreign affairs, Latin America, Finance, Economy, Arts, Science, Education, Religion, Sports, Obituaries, Miscellaneous, etc. Indexes are published twice monthly and are cumulative throughout the year." Sheehy. Guide to Ref Books. 10th edition

The **Facts** on File encyclopedia of the 20th century; general editor, John Drexel. Facts on File 1991 1046p il maps $79.95   **909.82**

1. History, Modern—1900-1999 (20th century)—Dictionaries
ISBN 0-8160-2461-8   LC 91-21278

This volume "comprises about 10,000 brief, unsigned articles devoted to the most significant people, places, events, and scientific and artistic developments of this century. The entries, which are arranged alphabetically with access enhanced by numerous internal and external cross references and an index, average about ten per page, and sometimes include bibliographic citations." Libr J

Tuchman, Barbara Wertheim
The proud tower; a portrait of the world before the war, 1890-1914; [by] Barbara W. Tuchman. Macmillan 1966 528p il $60
909.82

1. History, Modern—1900-1999 (20th century) 2. History, Modern—1800-1899 (19th century) 3. Europe—Social conditions 4. United States—Social conditions
ISBN 0-02-620300-6

Also available in paperback from Bantam Bks.

The author describes pre-war social conditions in the U.S., France, England and Germany

Includes bibliographic references

910 Geography and travel

National geographic index, 1888-1988. National Geographic Soc. 1989 1215p il maps $26.95
910

1. National geographic (Periodical)—Indexes 2. Geography—Periodicals—Indexes
ISBN 0-87044-764-5
LC 88-33086

This index to National Geographic magazine "indexes some 7,000 articles published in the 1,148 issues of the magazine over the last 100 years. Articles may be located by subject, title, author, or photographer." Booklist

910.2 Geography—Miscellany. Travel guides

Baedeker guides. Prentice Hall Press il maps prices vary
910.2

Available guides cover countries, regions and major cities. Periodically revised
"Baedeker is one of the classic names in the field of travel literature. This new and revised series . . . emphasizes sites and cultural attractions." Am Ref Books Annu, 1983

Birnbaum travel guides. HarperCollins Pubs. maps pa prices vary
910.2

Series first published by Houghton Mifflin as Get 'em and go travel guides, later as Stephen Birnbaum travel guides. Periodically revised
"Expanding series of guides provides detailed travel and sightseeing information and extensive listings of accommodations, restaurants, museums, and other tourist attractions. Updated annually." N Y Public Libr Book of How & Where to Look It Up

Cities of the world. Gale Res. 4v il maps set $280
910.2

1. Cities and towns
ISSN 0889-2741

First published 1982. (4th edition 1993) Periodically revised

"A compilation of current information on cultural, geographical, and political conditions in the countries and cities of six continents, based on the Department of State's 'Post reports.'" Title page of 1993 edition

Contents v1 Africa; v2 The Western Hemisphere (exclusive of the United States); v3 Europe and the Mediterranean Middle East; v4 Asia, the Pacific, and the Asiatic Middle East, cumulative index

Davis, Kenneth C.
Don't know much about geography; everything you need to know about the world but never learned. Morrow 1992 384p il maps $23; pa $11
910.2

1. Geography 2. Questions and answers
ISBN 0-688-10332-4; 0-380-71379-9 (pa)
LC 92-19142

The author's "survey of geography is intricately tied to world history and interspersed with passages from great historians, explorers, and travel writers. Questions open each chapter and are answered at the end following a neat chronology of the information covered. Davis succeeds admirably in his goal of showing that geography is not a 'dusty mystery, but an exciting art as well as a useful science.'" Booklist

Includes bibliographic references

Fielding's travel books. Travel Bks. prices vary
910.2

Frequently revised these guides cover countries and areas which include Australia, Bermuda and the Bahamas, Brazil, Caribbean, Far East, Mexico, New Zealand, and Scandinavia
Emphasis is on how to travel, although there is also information on where to go and what to see. With hints on tipping, eating, customs, dress, and language

Fodor's travel guides. Fodor's Travel Publs. prices vary
910.2

Formerly: Fodor's modern guides, published by McKay

Revised annually, "Fodor's offers more than 300 guides to the world's nations, regions, and cities—from Acapulco to Williamsburg. The books give details on how to get to all these places and where to stay, where to eat, and what to see once you get there." N Y Public Libr Book of How & Where to Look It Up

Michelin guides. Michelin Tire Corp. prices vary
910.2

The Michelin Red guides issued annually deal primarily with accomodations and restaurants, garages and service stations. Text is in French, English, Italian and German. The Michelin Green guides are mainly concerned with sightseeing, places of interest and suggested itineraries and routes

The **Wall** Street journal guides to business travel. Fodor's Travel Publs. 1991 4v maps ea pa $20
910.2

Individual volumes cover business travel in the United States and Canada; Europe; the Pacific Rim; and international cities

Williams, Anita
The 50+ traveler's guidebook; where to go, where to stay, what to do; by Anita Williams and Merrimac Dillon. St. Martin's Press 1991 270p pa $12.95
910.2

1. Travel
ISBN 0-312-05863-2
LC 90-27709

Williams, Anita—*Continued*

Also available Thorndike Press large print edition in hardcover and paperback

Part one covers "travel destinations, accommodations, and activities. . . . Part two is a resource directory and adviser on airlines, car rental, travel clubs and associations, a variety of travel services, nonsmoking accommodations, tourist bureaus, services for handicapped travelers, and specialty travel publications." Booklist

910.3 Geography—Dictionaries, encyclopedias, gazetteers

Cambridge world gazetteer; a geographical dictionary; edited by David Munro. Cambridge Univ. Press 1990 733p il maps $44.95   910.3

1. Gazetteers

ISBN 0-521-39438-4   LC 90-1515

First published 1988 in the United Kingdom with title: Chambers world gazetteer

This work contains some "20,000 alphabetized entries for political entities (countries, states, cities, etc.) and physical features (rivers, mountains, oceans, etc.). Entries include such information as pronunciation (when not obvious), location, population, land area, elevation, and brief economic and cultural descriptions." Booklist

Canby, Courtlandt

The encyclopedia of historic places; advisory editor, Gorton Carruth. Facts on File 1984 2v il set $175   910.3

1. Geographic names—Dictionaries 2. Gazetteers

ISBN 0-87196-126-1   LC 80-25121

"A Hudson Group book"

"Each entry lists the name, alternative native name, variant spellings, ancient or former name, present-day country, geographic location, and historic significance. Numerous cross-references provide multiple entry points. Battle sites, lakes, rivers, mountains, archaeological digs, empires, and forts are included along with cities, towns, countries, and provinces." Am Libr

"Despite overlap with other reference works, 'Historic Places' has a unique emphasis and should become librarians' first choice." Wilson Libr Bull

Exploring your world: the adventure of geography. National Geographic Soc. 1989 608p il maps $31.95   910.3

1. Geography—Dictionaries

ISBN 0-87044-726-2   LC 89-13099

"Arranged in dictionary form, the 334 encyclopedic entries cover a wide array of geographical topics and range in size from a paragraph (i.e., lagoon) to as many as fifteen pages. . . . Virtually every entry is followed by a large number of cross-references. . . . More than one thousand photographs, diagrams, and charts delight the eye and provide a valuable additional learning modality." SLJ

Kurian, George Thomas

The encyclopedia of the First World. Facts on File 1990 2v il maps $145
910.3

1. Geography—Dictionaries

ISBN 0-8160-1233-4   LC 89-11649

Companion set Encyclopedia of the Third World, entered in class 903

"The editor of this reference defines First World countries as 'advanced, developed, industrial, or post industrial,' and non-Communist. These include Western Europe, North America, Australia, New Zealand, and Japan." Libr J

For a fuller review see: Booklist, Sept. 1, 1990

The Statesman's year-book world gazetteer; [edited by] John Paxton. 4th ed. St. Martin's Press 1991 693p $49.95   910.3

1. Gazetteers

ISBN 0-312-05597-8

First published 1975 in the United Kingdom

This volume supplements The Stateman's yearbook, entered in class 310.5. In addition to the gazetteer entries, which give location, recent history, industries and population, it includes a section which defines geographical terms and a series of statistical tables

For a review see: Booklist, Nov. 1, 1991

Webster's new geographical dictionary. Merriam-Webster il maps $24.95   910.3

1. Geography—Dictionaries 2. Gazetteers

First published 1949 with title: Webster's geographical dictionary. (revised edition 1988) Periodically revised

"Concise and easy-to-read gazetteer, listing both ancient and modern place names. Most entries include pronunciation, brief description, population and brief history. Includes numerous charts and lists, some maps and a list of geographical terms from other languages." NY Public Libr. Ref Books for Child Collect. 2d edition

Worldmark encyclopedia of the nations. Worldmark Press 5v il maps set $375
910.3

1. Geography—Dictionaries 2. World history—Dictionaries 3. World politics—Dictionaries

First published 1960. (7th edition 1988) Periodically revised

"Factual and statistical information on the countries of the world, exhibited in uniform format under such rubrics as topography, population, public finance, language, and ethnic composition. Country articles appear in volumes 2 through 5, arranged geographically by continent. Volume 1 is devoted to the United Nations and its affiliated agencies. Illustrations, maps. No indexes." Ref Sources for Small & Medium-sized Libr. 5th edition

910.4 Accounts of travel. Seafaring life. Buried treasure

Ballard, Robert D.

The discovery of the Titanic; by Robert D. Ballard with Rick Archbold; introduction by Walter Lord; illustrations of the Titanic by Ken Marschall. Warner Bks. 1987 230p il hardcover o.p. paperback available $17.95

910.4

1. Titanic (Steamship) 2. Shipwrecks 3. Underwater exploration

ISBN 0-446-38912-9 (pa)   LC 87-8211

This account of the 1985-1986 discovery and exploration of the sunken liner Titanic is written by the leader of the joint French/American expedition

The author does not "offer any new revelations to clear away some of the mysteries surrounding the sinking. But the eerily beautiful photographs and drawings of the ghostlike hull, garlanded with stalactites of rust, juxtaposed with scenes of the Titanic in its regal glory, poignantly conjure up the mystique of this doomed ship better than any words." N Y Times Book Rev

Berton, Pierre, 1920-

The Arctic grail; the quest for the North West Passage and the North Pole, 1818-1909. Viking 1988 672p il maps o.p.; Penguin Bks. paperback available $12.95

910.4

1. Northwest Passage 2. North Pole 3. Explorers

ISBN 0-14-011680-X (pa)   LC 88-40063

This book covers the "period of Arctic exploration from the . . . expedition of William Edward Parry in 1818 to that of Robert Edwin Peary in 1909." Publisher's note

"Mr. Berton's history of Arctic exploration . . . is largely a chronicle of discomfort, lost ships, and dead men. It should be monotonous, but it is not. . . . The book is well written, the enormous mass of material is clearly organized." Atlantic

Includes bibliography

Columbus, Christopher

The voyage of Christopher Columbus; Columbus' own journal of discovery; newly restored and translated [by] John Cummins. St. Martin's Press 1992 241p il maps $19.95

910.4

1. Voyages and travels 2. America—Exploration

ISBN 0-312-07880-3   LC 92-4012

"A Thomas Dunne book"

"The explorer's shipboard journal details his first voyage to the New World and his fateful encounter with the natives. It exists today only in a later manuscript copy by Bartolome de Las Casas, who paraphrased extensively in the third person. By restructuring this version and supplementing it with other sources, Cummins . . . claims to have restored the original in a nonliteral translation that 'remodels' Columbus's cumbersome Spanish. The resulting lively and highly readable narrative will have historians arguing about the authenticity of its voice." Libr J

Includes bibliography

Dana, Richard Henry, 1815-1882

Two years before the mast   **910.4**

1. Seafaring life 2. Voyages and travels

Hardcover and paperback editions available from various publishers

First published anonymously in 1840

The author "shipped out of Boston in 1834 on the *Pilgrim* and sailed around the Horn to California on a hide-trading expedition. The book is based on the journal he kept during the voyage. Horrified by the brutal captain's mistreatment of the sailors, and shocked by their lack of legal redress, Dana wrote with a burning indignation that did much to rouse the public to the mariners' plight." Benet's Reader's Ency of Am Lit. 2d edition

Eaton, John P.

Titanic, triumph and tragedy; [by] John P. Eaton and Charles A. Haas; foreword by John Maxtone-Graham. Norton 1987 319p il $47.50   **910.4**

1. Titanic (Steamship) 2. Shipwrecks

ISBN 0-393-02380-X   LC 86-23560

The authors seek to present in text and illustrations the story of the steamship Titanic from its construction to its sinking on April 14, 1912. Also included are underwater photographs of the sunken ship taken when it was found in 1985

"This is the definitive book on the transatlantic steamship 'Titanic.' The authors . . . have put together what must be the most complete collection of illustrations and photographs of the 'Titanic' ever assembled in a book." Libr J

García Márquez, Gabriel, 1928-

The story of a shipwrecked sailor; who drifted on a life raft for ten days without food or water, was proclaimed a national hero, kissed by beauty queens, made rich through publicity, and then spurned by the government and forgotten for all time; translated from the Spanish by Randolph Hogan. Knopf 1986 106p $13.95   **910.4**

1. Velasco, Luis Alejandro 2. Survival (after airplane accidents, shipwrecks, etc.)

ISBN 0-394-54810-8   LC 85-45673

Also available in paperback from Ballantine Bks.

Original Spanish edition, 1970

"In 1955 Garcia Marquez was working as a reporter in Colombia. One of his stories was a serialized account of a sailor who was swept overboard with seven other crew members of a Colombian destroyer and who was the only one to survive. This book presents Garcia Marquez' version of the sailor's first-person narrative." Booklist

Heyerdahl, Thor

Kon-Tiki: across the Pacific by raft; translated by F.H. Lyon. Rand McNally 1950 304p il o.p.; Simon & Schuster paperback available $5.50   **910.4**

1. Kon-Tiki Expedition (1947) 2. Pacific Ocean 3. Ethnology—Polynesia

ISBN 0-671-72652-8 (pa)

Original Norwegian edition, 1948

Heyerdahl, Thor—*Continued*
The "story of the six men who crossed the Pacific from Peru to the Polynesians on a primitive balsa-log raft such as Peruvian natives of the fifth century used, to prove that it was possible that the legendary race that came to Easter Island and the Polynesians could have come from Peru." Wis Libr Bull

Lord, Walter, 1917-
The night lives on. Morrow 1986 272p il o.p.; Jove Publs. paperback available $4.50   **910.4**
1. Titanic (Steamship) 2. Shipwrecks
ISBN 0-515-09250-9 (pa)   LC 86-5182
Further thoughts about the steamship disaster prompted by the 1985 discovery and filming of the wreckage

A night to remember. Holt & Co. 1955 209p il $30   **910.4**
1. Titanic (Steamship) 2. Shipwrecks
ISBN 0-8050-1733-X
Also available in paperback from Bantam Bks.
A detailed account of "the tragic drama of that terrible night—April 4, 1912—when the 'Titanic,' the unsinkable ship, struck an iceberg and went down in the icy waters of the Atlantic." Libr J

Maxtone-Graham, John
Crossing & cruising; from the golden era of ocean liners to the luxury cruise ships of today. Scribner 1992 311p il $30 **910.4**
1. Ocean travel 2. Ships
ISBN 0-684-19154-7   LC 92-4131
Companion volume to The only way to cross (1972) and Liners to the sun (1985)
The author describes the ocean-going experiences of emigrants of the past and today's tourists, and the ships upon which they have traveled
This "is a book crammed with but not overburdened by a wealth of information on what's attractive and repellent on various ships, a book whose facts and lore are bolstered by myriad anecdotes and interviews with ship designers, owners, captains and crew. . . . Mr. Maxton-Graham blends past and present . . . in a most shipshape fashion." N Y Times Book Rev
Includes bibliography

McPhee, John A.
Looking for a ship. Farrar, Straus & Giroux 1990 241p $18.95; pa $9.95 **910.4**
1. Stella Lykes (Freighter) 2. Seafaring life
ISBN 0-374-19077-1; 0-374-52319-3 (pa) LC 90-3311
Also available Thorndike Press large print edition
In this book McPhee focuses on the "plight of the U.S. merchant marine. Accompanying Second Mate Andy Chase on a 42-day run down the west coast of South America aboard the S.S. *Stella Lykes,* McPhee provides the reader with stories and tales of modern seafaring life and the problems of making a living as a merchant mariner. . . . An engrossing tale of the sea, with excellent detail and humanity." Libr J

Pellegrino, Charles R.
Her name, Titanic; the untold story of the sinking and finding of the unsinkable ship; [by] Charles Pellegrino. McGraw-Hill 1988 269p il o.p.; Avon Bks. paperback available $5.50   **910.4**
1. Titanic (Steamship) 2. Shipwrecks 3. Underwater exploration
ISBN 0-380-70892-2   LC 88-13212
This book presents a "dramatization of the 1912 disaster, enhanced by unpublished diaries, transcripts of wireless transmissions and interviews of survivors. Woven into the account of the sinking is the story of oceanographer Robert Ballard, whose team of men and robots struggled to find the location of the wreck." Publ Wkly
Includes bibliography

Read, Piers Paul, 1941-
Alive; the story of the Andes survivors. Lippincott 1974 352p il maps o.p.; Avon Bks. paperback available $5.99   **910.4**
1. Survival (after airplane accidents, shipwrecks, etc.) 2. Andes
ISBN 0-380-00321-X (pa)
The author describes the extraordinary hardships endured by the survivors of a horrific plane crash in the Andes

Theroux, Paul
To the ends of the earth; the selected travels of Paul Theroux. Random House 1991 xxi, 342p il $23   **910.4**
1. Voyages and travels
ISBN 0-679-40246-2   LC 91-9533
First published in different form 1990 in the United Kingdom with title: Traveling the world
This volume contains the author's own selection of what he considers to be his best travel writing. Pieces have been chosen from: The great railway bazaar; The old Patagonian express; The kingdom by the sea; Sunrise with seamonsters and Riding the iron rooster (all titles entered separately)

Yeager, Jeana
Voyager; [by] Jeana Yeager and Dick Rutan with Phil Patton. Knopf 1987 337p il $19.95   **910.4**
1. Voyager (Airplane) 2. Aeronautics—Flights
ISBN 0-394-55266-0   LC 86-46163
Relates the story behind "the *Voyager's* nine-day epic flight around the world without refueling. . . . The demanding physical requirements of the flight and the setbacks in its preparation represent a pinnacle of endurance by Yeager and Rutan, who spent six years designing, building, and testing the aircraft." Libr J

911   Historical geography

Atlas of American history. 2nd rev ed. Scribner 1985 c1984 306p maps lib bdg $65   **911**
1. United States—Historical geography—Maps
ISBN 0-684-18411-7   LC 84-675413

Atlas of American history—*Continued*
First published 1943 under the editorship of James Truslow Adams

"Development of the United States illustrated by maps. Provides coverage through the Vietnam War. Includes some demographic maps. Indexed." N Y Public Libr Book of How & Where to Look It Up

Beck, Warren A.
Historical atlas of the American West; by Warren A. Beck and Ynez D. Haase. University of Okla. Press 1989 xlii, 78p maps $37.50; pa $18.95   **911**
1. West   (U.S.)—Historical   geography—Maps
2. Atlases, Historical
ISBN 0-8061-2193-9; 0-8061-2456-3 (pa)
LC 88-40540
"Defining the West as that part of the United States lying west of the 100th meridian, Beck and Haase provide a cartographic survey of the history of the region. In addition to maps illustrating such standard themes as natural resources, exploration and travel routes, the growth of the transportation network, and Indian tribal lands, the authors have included detailed maps on such topics as the Spanish-Mexican land grants and the Mt. St. Helens's eruption. . . . This atlas is an essential purchase for most libraries." Libr J

Goetzmann, William H.
The atlas of North American exploration; from the Norse voyages to the race to the pole; [by] William Goetzmann, Glyndwr Williams. Prentice Hall General Ref. 1992 224p il maps $40   **911**
1. America—Exploration 2. Explorers 3. Atlases, Historical
ISBN 0-13-297128-3
LC 92-8573
"This survey atlas, emphasizing exploration from the late 1400s to the late 1800s, is firmly directed toward a general audience. It features excellent color maps and illustrations with two-page 'spreads,' each devoted to the analysis of a particular explorer and each with extracts from the explorer's journals (translated to English if necessary). The atlas takes Columbus and his predecessors as a starting point, and covers all of North America. . . . The writers have endeavored to maintain an objective tone, and in the bibliography give full citations for works mentioned in the text." Libr J

The **Harper** atlas of world history. rev ed. HarperCollins Pubs. 1992 unp il maps $40
911
1. Atlases, Historical
ISBN 0-06-270067-7
LC 92-52538
First United States edition published 1987
Editor: Pierre Vidal-Naquet
"The period of coverage is 70,000,000 B.C. through the spring of AD 1992. The maps are instructive, colorful, but sometimes rather stylized. Each topic includes a chronological list of relevant events at the bottom of the page. . . . Highly recommended." Libr J

Historical atlas of the United States. National Geographic Soc. 1988 289p il maps $59.95   **911**
1. United States—Historical geography—Maps
ISBN 0-87044-747-5
LC 88-675398
Edited by Wilbur E. Garrett

"The intent of the volume is to provide [a] comprehensive atlas of US history from a geographic perspective. . . . The end result is attractive to look at and entertaining to read." Choice

Oliphant, Margaret
The atlas of the ancient world; charting the great civilizations of the past. Simon & Schuster 1992 unp maps $40   **911**
1. Geography, Ancient
ISBN 0-671-75103-4
LC 91-38075
This "book treats nine ancient civilizations, beginning in Mesopotamia, Egypt, and Persia and culminating in the Roman world. Other chapters are devoted to China, India, and the Americas. . . . Each civilization is presented in text, attractive photographs and drawings (many in color), site plans, and maps." Booklist
Includes bibliography

Rand McNally atlas of world history. 1992 ed. Rand McNally 1992 192p maps $45; pa $24.95   **911**
1. Atlases, Historical
ISBN 0-528-83499-1; 0-528-83498-3 (pa)
First published 1981 in the United Kingdom with title Hamlyn historical atlas. Current British edition has title Philip's atlas of world history
"Nearly 100 chronologically arranged maps trace the progress of humanity from various 'isolated societies' at the dawn of history to what approaches a single 'global community' in 1990. The maps, although often detailed in terms of the places and physical features included, are uncluttered, attractive, and easy to interpret. The well-written text accompanying them may be read as an introductory survey to world history." Am Ref Books Annu, 1993

The **Times** atlas of the Second World War; edited by John Keegan. Harper & Row 1989 254p il maps $50   **911**
1. World War, 1939-1945—Maps 2. Atlases, Historical
ISBN 0-06-016178-7
LC 89-45070
This atlas contains "more than 450 oversized full-color maps, 150 photographs and illustrations, a lengthy text, and a detailed chronology. . . . [It] uses the latest techniques in computer mapping to describe virtually every major and minor conflict of the war. . . . There is extensive treatment of social and economic topics, like the wartime economics of Britain, the United States, and Japan, detailed treatment of the Holocaust, and fascinating charts and maps of intelligence-gathering networks and underground forces. An essential source for every library." Libr J

The **Times** atlas of world history; edited by Geoffrey Barraclough. 3rd ed, edited by Norman Stone. Hammond 1989 358p il maps $95   **911**
1. Atlases, Historical
ISBN 0-7230-0304-1
LC 89-675246
First published 1978
"Outstanding historical atlas. Maps are striking and supplemented with informative text and occasional illustrations. Stresses economic and social as well as political history." Ref Sources for Small & Medium-sized Libr. 5th edition

912 Atlases. Maps

Atlas of the Third World; edited by George Kurian. 2nd ed. Facts on File 1992 384p il maps $125   **912**

1. Developing countries
ISBN 0-8160-1930-4   LC 88-675259
First published 1983

Contains 600 maps and more than 2,000 statistical charts describing the economic, political, demographic, and geographic aspects of the world's developing countries

For a review see: Booklist, April 1, 1993

Atlas of the world. 2nd ed. Oxford Univ. Press 1993 various paging il maps $65   **912**

1. Atlases
ISBN 0-19-521025-5   LC 93-676838
First published 1992

At head of title: Oxford

In addition to the main section of multicolored world maps, this atlas has a "World statistics" section with tables of comparisons; an "Introduction to geography" section with essays, maps, graphs and diagrams; and a "City maps" section with detailed maps of sixty-six major cities of the world

Britannica atlas. Encyclopaedia Britannica il maps $109   **912**

1. Atlases

Supersedes the Encyclopaedia Britannica World atlas, first published 1942, and the 1965 edition with title: Encyclopaedia Britannica World atlas international. Published jointly with Rand McNally in 1969. (1993 edition) Periodically revised

An international atlas with text in English, German, Spanish, French and Portuguese

The Economist atlas of the new Europe. Holt & Co. 1992 unp il maps (Henry Holt reference bk) $75   **912**

1. Europe—Maps
ISBN 0-8050-1982-0   LC 92-10565

"In this atlas, readers get a volume composed of nine sections (e.g., history, business, finance), with each section ranging in length from two to four pages and featuring an overview, maps, charts, and tables. The atlas also contains two time charts and a country-analysis section offering statistics by country. The aim of this atlas is to depict the current borders of the European community and to show how the countries relate to one another economically. . . . Appropriate for any reference department that is besieged with questions about how these countries look now." Libr J

Goode's world atlas; editor, Edward B. Espenshade, Jr. Rand McNally il maps $28.95   **912**

1. Atlases

First published 1922 with title: Goode's school atlas. (18th edition revised 1992) Periodically revised

"Contains thematic maps and tables showing distribution of population, minerals, manufacturing, and other subjects. Also included are metropolitan-area maps, physical-political maps of regions, geographic tables, and ocean-floor maps showing earth movement. Pronouncing index included." N Y Public Libr Book of How & Where to Look It Up

Hammond atlas of the world. Hammond 1992 303p il maps $65   **912**

1. Atlases
ISBN 0-8437-1175-2   LC 92-675635

The maps in this new atlas have been computer-generated from digitized geographic data. The core section of maps is supplemented by several other sections, including "Global Relationships," which presents thematic maps and other graphics on such topics as the environment, population, languages, religions, economic resources, and climate

For a fuller review see: Booklist, Jan. 15, 1993

The Map catalog; every kind of map and chart on earth and even some above it; Joel Makower, editor; Cathryn Poff, Laura Bergheim, associate editors. 2nd ed rev & expanded. Random House 1990 364p il $27.50; pa $18   **912**

1. Maps
ISBN 0-394-58326-4; 0-679-72767-1 (pa)
     LC 89-37566

"A Tilden Press book"

First published 1986 in paperback by Vintage Bks.

This work "provides comprehensive information on how to obtain map-related products, software, and other materials. . . . It addresses more than 50 categories of maps, such as historical, weather, military, travel, bicycle, wildlife, and globes. This is the definitive source for obtaining cartographic products." Nichols. Guide to Ref Books for Sch Media Cent. 4th edition

National Geographic atlas of the world. rev 6th ed. National Geographic Soc. 1992 il maps $80; pa $65   **912**

1. Atlases
ISBN 0-87044-835-8; 0-87044-834-X (pa)
     LC 92-27845

First published 1963

This "atlas begins with a series of thematic and world maps, accompanied by text, that cover such topics as food, minerals, climate, energy, and population. The back of the atlas includes a section that provides brief profiles, including flags, of U.S. states, Canadian provinces, and the nations of the world. Other sections focus on geographic comparisons, climate, and population of selected places around the world. . . . It is the middle portion of this atlas that people recognize and associate with the National Geographic Society. These colorful pages are arranged by continent, followed by sections on the oceans and the heavens." Booklist

The New York Times atlas of the world. new family ed. Times Bks. 1992 156p il maps $37.50   **912**

1. Atlases
ISBN 0-8129-2075-9   LC 92-53666

An adaptation of the Times atlas of the world, comprehensive edition, entered below

"An introductory section includes information about states and territories and lists of geographic comparisons. Beautiful, full-color maps, city plans, views of the solar system, and many other features come together to provide a first-rate atlas." SLJ

For a fuller review see: Booklist, April 15, 1993

Rand McNally commercial atlas & marketing guide. Rand McNally $395

912

1. Atlases
ISSN 0361-9723
Annual. First published 1876
"Primarily an atlas of the United States, with large, detailed, clear maps. Includes many statistical tables of population, business and manufacturers, agriculture, and other commercial features, such as indicators of market potential." Ref Sources for Small & Medium-sized Libr. 5th edition

Rand McNally road atlas; United States/Canada/Mexico. Rand McNally maps pa $7.95

912

1. United States—Maps 2. Road maps
Annual. First published 1926
"Road maps of each state in the United States, Canada, and Mexico. Distances shown on the maps. Index of place names and mileage charts included." Ref Sources for Small & Medium-sized Libr. 5th edition

The **Times** atlas of the world. comprehensive ed. Times Bks. il maps $175

912

1. Atlases
First published 1967. (9th edition 1992) Periodically revised
"This is the most comprehensive world atlas currently available. . . . [It] is an essential purchase for any medium to large public or academic library. Small libraries will also want to consider it, in spite of its price, because it is three sources in one: a mini-geographic-reference source (introductory material), a thorough gazetteer (place-name index); and a detailed, comprehensive world atlas." Booklist

914 Geography of and travel in Europe

Fodor's affordable Europe. Fodor's Travel Publs. pa $17

914

1. Europe—Description
Fodor's Affordable series also includes guides to other destinations
Annual. First published 1972 by McKay. Variant titles: Fodor's Europe on a budget; Fodor's budget Europe
This guide book is designed to help the cost-conscious tourist plan a European vacation. It includes information about different kinds of transportation and suggests specific package tours, hotels, restaurants, sights, shops and "offbeat resorts" in over 25 eastern and western European countries

914.1 Geography of and travel in the British Isles

Theroux, Paul
The kingdom by the sea; a journey around Great Britain. Houghton Mifflin 1983 353p o.p.; Pocket Bks. paperback available $6.99

914.1

1. Great Britain—Description
ISBN 0-671-70923-2 (pa)   LC 83-10838

"Theroux depicts a declining and dreary Britain as he circles its coastlines on foot and by local bus and train. He finds dilapidated and near-empty resorts, tired old people, skinheads and other unsavory young people, closed factories, chronic unemployment, boredom, and hopelessness. . . . But it is a valid and perceptive set of impressions by a skillful writer who wants to like the country." Libr J

914.11 Geography of and travel in Scotland

Boswell, James, 1740-1795
The journal of a tour to the Hebrides with Samuel Johnson

914.11

1. Johnson, Samuel, 1696-1772 2. Hebrides (Scotland)—Description 3. Scotland—Description
Available in paperback editions from various publishers
First published 1785
The renowned biographer here recounts the daily events of a tour which he took in 1773 with Johnson

914.2 Geography of and travel in England and Wales

Herriot, James
James Herriot's Yorkshire; photographs by Derry Brabbs. St. Martin's Press 1979 223p il $18.95

914.2

1. Yorkshire (England)—Description
ISBN 0-312-43970-9   LC 79-5339
Also available in paperback from Bantam Bks.
Noted veterinarian Herriot conducts a guided tour of Yorkshire England. Color photographs accompany the anecdotal text

914.36 Geography of and travel in Austria

Jones, J. Sydney
Viennawalks; photographs by J. Sydney Jones. Holt & Co. 1985 289p il pa $12.95

914.36

1. Vienna (Austria)—Description
ISBN 0-8050-1189-7   LC 84-9028
"A New Republic book"
The author presents four walking tours through Vienna designed to illustrate the city's life, history, and culture
Includes bibliography

914.5 Geography of and travel in Italy

Harrison, Barbara Grizzuti
Italian days. Weidenfeld & Nicolson 1989 479p il $22.95

914.5

1. Italy—Description
ISBN 1-55584-311-5   LC 89-30115
Also available in paperback from Houghton Mifflin

Harrison, Barbara Grizzuti—*Continued*

The author "journeyed to Italy in search of a national ethos as well as her own past. She discovered a great deal about both. . . . Her accounts of living in turn in Milan . . . Florence, Rome . . . Naples and Calabria are captivating—rich with artistic and architectural insights, full of flashing, quirky asides and offbeat encounters. The writing is superb: eloquent, witty, colorful and lyrical." Publ Wkly

Includes bibliography

Simon, Kate

Italy; the places in between. rev and expanded ed. Harper & Row 1984 384p maps $16.95; pa $12.95   **914.5**

1. Italy—Description
ISBN 0-06-015310-5; 0-06-091131-X (pa)

LC 83-48940

First published 1970

A guide to travel in Italy outside the major cities and tourist spots

The author is "superb . . . as a travel companion, guide, and stylist who can untangle the mysteries of a foreign culture, read a route map, and happily direct the tourist on the way to a pleasant and fulfilling adventure." Booklist

914.6   Geography of and travel in the Iberian Peninsula

Michener, James A. (James Albert), 1907-

Iberia; Spanish travels and reflections; photographs by Robert Vavra. Random House 1968 818p il maps $29.95   **914.6**

1. Spain—Description
ISBN 0-394-42982-6

Also available in paperback from Fawcett Bks.

The author presents his impressions of Spain based on visits to ten of its cities

914.99   Geography of and travel in the Aegean Islands

Durrell, Lawrence

The Greek Islands. Viking 1978 287p il o.p.; Penguin Bks. paperback available $14.95   **914.99**

1. Aegean Islands (Greece and Turkey)—Description
ISBN 0-14-005661-0 (pa)   LC 77-18120

In this survey of some of the Greek Islands Durrell weaves together "description, history and myth, architectural and archaeological study, and personal reminiscence." Publisher's note

915   Geography of and travel in Asia

Polo, Marco, 1254-1323?

The travels of Marco Polo   **915**

1. Asia—Description 2. Voyages and travels

Hardcover and paperback editions available from various publishers

An autobiographical account of Marco Polo's thirteenth century travels in Asia

Theroux, Paul

The great railway bazaar: by train through Asia. Houghton Mifflin 1975 342p o.p.; Simon & Schuster paperback available $9.95   **915**

1. Asia—Description 2. Railroads—Asia
ISBN 0-671-72648-X (pa)

The author "took a four-month solitary lecture tour of Asia in 1973, traveling by train wherever possible. His route was through Turkey, Iran, India, Southeast Asia, Japan, and back to London via the Soviet Union. He writes of conversations and impressions of the people encountered." Libr J

915.1   Geography of travel in China and adjacent areas

Jenkins, Peter, 1951-

Across China. Morrow 1986 351p il maps o.p.; Fawcett Bks. paperback available $5.95   **915.1**

1. China—Description
ISBN 0-449-21456-7 (pa)   LC 86-21646

Also available G.K. Hall large print edition

"A William Morrow/Sweet Springs Press book"

"In chronological sequence Jenkins writes three different types of narrative. The first, set at his Tennessee home, recounts the origins of his China trip. Another follows the 1984 American expedition to Mt. Everest via the unclimbed north slope in Tibet. A third narrative shifts Jenkins's own travel to the grasslands of Inner Mongolia and the south China coast at Fuzhou." Libr J

"The book provides an intriguing account of the start of the 1984 China/Everest Expedition, and charming vignettes of life in Inner Mongolia." Best Sellers

Includes bibliography

Salzman, Mark

Iron & silk. Random House 1987 c1986 211p $17.95; pa $10   **915.1**

1. China—Description 2. Martial arts
ISBN 0-394-55156-7; 0-394-75511-1 (pa)

LC 86-11846

The author tells of his two years teaching English to medical students in China's Hunan Province following his graduation from Yale University in 1982

This book is "not so much a treatise on modern Chinese mores as a series of telling vignettes. . . . [The author] describes his encounter with Pan Qingfu, the country's foremost master of wushu, the traditional Chinese martial art." Time

Theroux, Paul

Riding the iron rooster; by train through China. Putnam 1988 480p o.p.; Ivy Bks. paperback available $4.95   **915.1**

1. China—Description 2. Railroads—China
ISBN 0-8041-0454-9 (pa)   LC 87-31574

This is an account of the author's year-long rail journey through China

Theroux, Paul—_Continued_

"For Theroux, traveling is both about people—their thoughts, customs, and peculiarities—and a form of autobiography, and here we learn as much about his own quirks and fancies as we do about the intriguing world of contemporary China." Libr J

915.4 Geography of and travel in South Asia. India

Matthiessen, Peter

The snow leopard. Viking 1978 338p o.p.; Penguin Bks. paperback available $11
915.4

1. Himalaya Mountains—Description 2. Natural history—Himalaya Mountains 3. Zen Buddhism
ISBN 0-14-010266-3 (pa)   LC 78-5

Companion volume Nine-headed dragon river, entered in class 294.3

This book "is based on the journal Matthiessen kept during his trek with the field biologist George Schaller to the Crystal Mountain, in upper Nepal, in 1973. The trek took them 250 miles to the Land of Dolpo, on the Tibetan plateau. . . . The purpose: to observe the November rut of the Himalayan blue sheep in order to determine whether this little-known species is related to the extinct common ancestor of the goat and the sheep." Saturday Rev

Includes bibliographic references

915.6 Geography of and travel in the Middle East

Horwitz, Tony, 1958-

Baghdad without a map, and other misadventures in Arabia. Dutton 1991 276p map o.p.; New Am. Lib. paperback available $10
915.6

1. Middle East—Description
ISBN 0-452-26745-5 (pa)   LC 90-46653

This is an account of the author's travels in Egypt, Libya, the Sudan, Lebanon, Iraq, Iran and other countries in the Middle East. Horwitz accompanied his wife to the region "in the late 1980s and returned to Baghdad in August 1990 following the invasion of Kuwait." Libr J

"Horwitz mixes insight and humor in these observations that illustrate on an everyday level both the contradictions and the idiosyncrasies of the Arab world." Booklist

916 Geography of and travel in Africa

Harris, Eddy L.

Native stranger; a black American's journey into the heart of Africa. Simon & Schuster 1992 315p map $22
916

1. Africa—Description
ISBN 0-671-74897-1   LC 91-40579

Also available in paperback from Random House

"A black American writer describes his painful journey across Africa in search of himself." Booklist

"This is no ordinary travel book. Harris's account of his time in a Liberian jail would do Orwell proud. His descriptions of the people he encountered are memorably sanguine. . . . Harris emerged from Africa unencumbered by the dream of a Promised Land." Newsweek

Matthiessen, Peter

African silences. Random House 1991 225p maps $21; pa $10
916

1. Natural history—Africa 2. Africa—Description
ISBN 0-679-40021-4; 0-679-73102-4 (pa)

LC 90-52893

"In this account of three trips to Central and Western Africa, Matthiessen reports on the almost total devastation of wildlife in Senegal, Gambia, and the Ivory Coast and describes an expedition searching for the rare Congo peacock and gorillas in the Virunga Mountains of Zaire." Libr J

Matthiessen "offers his readers a superb vicarious experience. . . . A dazzling, if dismaying report." Publ Wkly

917 Geography of and travel in North America

America's magnificent mountains; prepared by the Special Publications Division, National Geographic Society. National Geographic Soc. 1980 207p il $8.95 **917**

1. North America—Description 2. Mountains
ISBN 0-87044-281-3   LC 78-21447

Text and numerous illustrations portray the beauty and majesty of America's mountains focusing on the Coast Mountains and Sierra Madre mountain system of Mexico

917.3 Geography of and travel in the United States

American guide series il   **917.3**

All state and city guides are available from Somerset Pubs. at various prices. Some titles are also available from other publishers

Compiled by the Federal Writers' Project (later called the Writers' Program) of the Works Progress Administration, these guides were originally published 1937-1949 by various publishers. Since then they have been reprinted, many in revised editions, by several different publishers

"Includes guides to each state, many cities and regions, and some special subjects. The state guidebooks are particularly useful, giving accurate information about points of interest with some historical and background material and sidelights on the unusual." Sheehy. Guide to Ref Books. 10th edition

Cantor, George, 1941-

Historic landmarks of black America; foreword by Robert L. Harris, Jr. Gale Res. 1991 372p il maps $35
917.3

1. Historic sites 2. Blacks—History 3. United States—History, Local 4. United States—Description
ISBN 0-8103-7809-4   LC 91-12543

Cantor, George, 1941——*Continued*

This is a guide "to over 300 sites in the U.S. and Canada for travelers or students seeking information on landmarks in African-American history. . . . Arranged by region, then by state, entries include a summary of the history and significance of the landmark, exact location, and in most cases, hours and admission charge." SLJ

For a fuller review see: Booklist, Sept. 1, 1991

The **Complete** guide to America's national parks. National Park Foundation maps pa $12.95   **917.3**

1. National parks and reserves—United States

First published 1979. (1994-1995 edition) Periodically revised

This park visitors' guide also covers national monuments, military parks, seashores and lakeshores, historic sites, and battlefields. Entries are listed by State, and include contact information, activities and facilities, travel directories, and nearby attractions and points of interest

Discover America! a scenic tour of the fifty states. National Geographic Soc. 1989 336p il $26.95   **917.3**

1. United States—Description
ISBN 0-87044-804-8   LC 89-12438

At head of title: National Geographic Society

An illustrated look at natural and scenic areas throughout the United States

Heat Moon, William Least

Blue highways; a journey into America; photographs by the author. Little, Brown 1983 c1982 421p il $24.95   **917.3**

1. United States—Description
ISBN 0-316-35395-7   LC 82-14942

Also available in paperback from Houghton Mifflin

"An Atlantic Monthly Press book"

An account of the author's journey across the U.S. in a van taking only secondary roads

Jenkins, Peter, 1951-

A walk across America. Morrow 1979 288p il maps $22.95   **917.3**

1. United States—Description
ISBN 0-688-03427-6   LC 78-10320

Also available in paperback from Fawcett Bks.

This book chronicles the author's journey with his dog from New York to the Gulf of Mexico

The walk west; a walk across America 2; by Peter and Barbara Jenkins. Morrow 1981 349p il maps $20.45; pa $12   **917.3**

1. United States—Description
ISBN 0-688-00666-3; 0-688-11271-4 (pa)
       LC 81-11177

The authors describe their 3 year, 2,000 mile walk from New Orleans to Oregon

Kane, Joseph Nathan, 1899-

Nicknames and sobriquets of U.S. cities, states, and counties. 3rd ed, [by] Joseph Nathan Kane & Gerard L. Alexander. Scarecrow Press 1979 429p $35   **917.3**

1. Geographic names—United States 2. Nicknames
ISBN 0-8108-1255-X   LC 79-20193

First published 1965 with title: Nicknames of cities and states of the U.S.

An enlargement of a section of Kane's "1000 facts worth knowing" plus Alexander's "Nicknames of American cities, towns and villages (past and present)"

"Comprehensive listing of nicknames of cities, counties, and states. Indexed geographically by city and state, and alphabetically by nickname." Ref Sources for Small & Medium-sized Libr. 5th edition

Let's go: the budget guide to USA & Canada. St. Martin's Press maps $18.99
       917.3

1. United States—Description 2. Canada—Description

Annual. First published 1981 by Dutton. Successor to: Let's go: the student guide to America, published 1969 by Harvard Student Agencies, and Let's go: the student guide to the United States and Canada, published 1972 by Dutton

This guide, aimed at students, provides practical information on how to travel inexpensively throughout the United States & Canada

Mobil travel guides. Prentice Hall Travel ea pa $14   **917.3**

1. United States—Description

First published by Simon & Schuster

"Seven regional guides to the United States that contain information about points of interest, annual or seasonal events, restaurant and lodging facilities (with ratings), and suggested auto tours. Organized by state and city. Updated annually." Ref Sources for Small & Medium-sized Libr. 5th edition

National Geographic's guide to the national parks of the United States. rev ed. National Geographic Soc. 1992 432p il maps pa $26.50   **917.3**

1. National parks and reserves—United States
ISBN 0-87044-885-4   LC 92-5851

First published 1989

This guide provides information on each of the fifty national parks, including things to do, campgrounds and accommodations, and facilities for the disabled

Parks directory of the United States; Darren L. Smith, editor. Omnigraphics 1992 525p $85   **917.3**

1. Parks—United States 2. Historic sites
ISBN 1-55888-765-2   LC 91-45072

"A guide to 3,700 national and state parks, recreation areas, historic sites, battlefields, monuments, forests, preserves, memorials, seashores, and other designated recreation areas in the United States administered by national and state park agencies." Title page

For a review see: Booklist, Feb. 15, 1993

Stevens, Joseph E. (Joseph Edward), 1956-
America's national battlefield parks; a
guide; maps by Beth Silverman. University
of Okla. Press 1990 337p il maps $29.95;
pa $19.95 **917.3**

1. National parks and reserves—United States 2. Battles 3. United States—Description
ISBN 0-8061-2268-4; 0-8061-2319-2 (pa)

LC 89-40739

"For each site, Stevens offers brief travel advisories
and lengthier historical summaries. He reports on the
location, nearest town, visitor center, handicapped access,
and available tours; he then enthusiastically tells the
story of the battle. . . . Stevens' skill at explaining the
historical significance of each site extends the book's
usefulness beyond a travel guide to a resource that will
also captivate history and military-literature buffs." Booklist

917.41 Geography of and travel in Maine

Thoreau, Henry David, 1817-1862
The Maine woods **917.41**

1. Maine—Description

Hardcover and paperback editions available from
various publishers

First published 1864

This account of the author's rambles around the lakes
and woods of Maine "records three different excursions:
Thoreau's trip to Mount Katahdin (which he called
'Ktaadn'), published in the 'Union Magazine' in 1848;
'Chesuncook,' which appeared in the 'Atlantic Monthly'
in the same year; and 'The Allegash and the East
Branch,' which is a marvel of precise observation." Herz-
berg. Reader's Ency of Am Lit

917.44 Geography of and travel in Massachusetts

Thoreau, Henry David, 1817-1862
Cape Cod **917.44**

1. Cape Cod (Mass.)—Description

Available in hardcover from Princeton Univ. Press
and in paperback from Penguin Bks.

First published 1865

This "account is based on the author's experiences
during the three short visits to Cape Cod (Oct. 1849;
June 1850; July 1855), and includes ten essays on the
history and character of the inhabitants, 'The Highland
Light,' Nantucket, the sea, the beach, and other aspects
of the Cape." Oxford Companion to Am Lit

917.8 Geography of and travel in Western United States

The **Sierra** Club guides to the national parks
of the Rocky Mountains and the Great
Plains; text by Conger Beasley, Jr. [et al.]
Stewart, Tabori & Chang 1984 272p il
maps $18.95 **917.8**

1. National parks and reserves—Great Plains 2. National parks and reserves—Rocky Mountain region
3. Rocky Mountain region—Description
ISBN 0-394-72754-1 LC 84-2539

This guide covers "seven national parks in the Rocky
Mountain and Great Plains regions. Combining practical
information with beautiful color photographs, the book
describes each park and its natural features, gives a short
history of the area and its development, and outlines
recreational opportunities with emphasis on wilderness
trails and hiking paths." Booklist

Wallis, Michael, 1945-
Route 66: the mother road. St. Martin's
Press 1990 243p $29.95; pa $17.95 **917.8**

1. West (U.S.)—Description
ISBN 0-312-04049-0; 0-312-08285-1 (pa)

LC 89-77813

Over 300 illustrations accompany the text as it examines the highway's history, roadside diners, towns,
motels and people

917.9 Geography of and travel in Great Basin and Pacific Coast states

Brower, Kenneth, 1944-
Yosemite; an American treasure; prepared
by the Special Publications Division.
National Geographic Soc. 1990 199p il map
$12.95 **917.9**

1. Yosemite National Park (Calif.)
ISBN 0-87044-794-7 LC 90-5655

Text and photographs "chronicle how rivers of ice
shaped the valley and relate the saga of Yosemite—from
the time it was the secret refuge of the Ahwahneechee
Indians through its first one hundred years as a national
park. . . . Brower details the captivating variety of
Yosemite's plants and animals. He portrays, too, the
people." Publisher's note

Includes bibliographic references

917.91 Geography and travel in Arizona

Fishbein, Seymour L.
Grand Canyon country; its majesty and
its lore. National Geographic Soc. 1991 199p
il map $13.95 **917.91**

1. Grand Canyon (Ariz.)
ISBN 0-87044-828-5 LC 91-6635

Fishbein, Seymour L.—*Continued*
An illustrated look at the land and people of the Grand Canyon region. Environmental issues are also considered

Includes bibliography

Fletcher, Colin, 1922-
The man who walked through time; with photographs taken en route by the author. Knopf 1967 o.p.; Vintage Bks. paperback available $10   **917.91**
1. Grand Canyon (Ariz.)
ISBN 0-679-72306-4 (pa)

An account of the author's journey on foot through the Grand Canyon National Park

918 Geography of and travel in South America. Latin America

Theroux, Paul
The old Patagonian express; by train through the Americas. Houghton Mifflin 1979 404p hardcover o.p. paperback available $9.70   **918**
1. America—Description 2. Railroads—Latin America
ISBN 0-395-52105-X (pa)   LC 79-15353
Also available in paperback from Pocket Bks.

The author describes his journey from Boston to Patagonia by train

918.1 Geography of and travel in Brazil

Kane, Joe
Running the Amazon. Knopf 1989 277p il $19.95; pa $9.95   **918.1**
1. Amazon River—Description
ISBN 0-394-55331-4; 0-679-72902-X (pa)
                            LC 88-81694

An account of the author's adventures as a member of the first expedition to travel the 4200-mile length of the Amazon
"This is an adventure story, but it also is a thoughtful account of an area little known but increasingly important worldwide. Recommended for most libraries." Libr J

918.2 Geography of and travel in Argentina

Chatwin, Bruce
In Patagonia. Summit Bks. 1977 205p map o.p.; Penguin Bks. paperback available $8.95   **918.2**
1. Patagonia (Argentina and Chile)—Description
ISBN 0-14-011291-X (pa)   LC 78-885
First published 1977 in the United Kingdom

This travelogue "captures the exotic characters and scenery Chatwin encountered in the southern tip of South America on a search for an important prehistoric artifact." Booklist

Nowhere is a place; travels in Patagonia; [by] Bruce Chatwin and Paul Theroux; photographs by Jeff Gnass; introduction by Paul Theroux. Sierra Club Bks. 1992 109p il $25   **918.2**
1. Patagonia (Argentina and Chile)—Description
ISBN 0-87156-500-5   LC 91-46287
First published 1985 in the United Kingdom with title: Patagonia revisited; first United States edition published 1986 by Houghton Mifflin

Originally presented as a lecture before the Royal Geographic Society

The authors "delve together into the region's history and legends, tracing its remarkable impact on the imaginations of a multitude of literary figures. . . . To this feast of erudition, adventure, charming presentation and lovely color photographs, Theroux's introduction adds a vivid memorial of Chatwin." Publ Wkly

Includes bibliographic references

919 Geography of and travel in Pacific Ocean Islands

Evans, Julian, 1955-
Transit of Venus; travels in the Pacific. Pantheon Bks. 1992 277p maps $22.50   **919**
1. Oceania—Description
ISBN 0-679-41637-4   LC 92-54117
This travel narrative covers the author's exploration of the islands of the South Pacific
"Evans describes his adventures in this tropical vastness with candidness and clarity. . . . An obvious strength of the book is the brief but excellent history of the islands and the impact of various cultures upon it. This is a good introduction to the area and the people, places, and politics that make it unique." Libr J

Theroux, Paul
The happy isles of Oceania; paddling the Pacific. Putnam 1992 528p maps $24.95   **919**
1. Oceania—Description
ISBN 0-399-13726-2   LC 91-39687
Also available in paperback from Fawcett Bks.

The author "spent 18 months in a one-man collapsible kayak exploring such exotic Pacific islands as New Zealand, Australia, the Soloman and Cook Islands, Fiji, Samoa, Tahiti, Easter Island, and Hawaii. . . . A brilliant storyteller with an eye for the absurd, Theroux takes the reader to little-known places where time seems to have stood still and people lead simple lives totally unrelated to 20th-century America." Libr J

919.4 Geography of and travel in Australia

Chatwin, Bruce
The songlines. Viking 1987 293p o.p.; Penguin Bks. paperback available $9.95   **919.4**
1. Australia—Description 2. Australian aborigines
ISBN 0-14-009429-6 (pa)   LC 86-40512

Chatwin, Bruce—*Continued*
"An Elisabeth Sifton book"

The author's travels in this book were organized around the concept of "'Songlines'—the invisible pathways along which aboriginal Australians travel to perform their central cultural activities." Publ Wkly

"This is an important book and a challenging one. . . . It is full of odd characters, bizarre incidents, moments of poetry—some of them comic—that spring as much from the writer's own generosity of spirit as from the richness of things." Times Lit Suppl

920 BIOGRAPHY

Books of biography are arranged as follows: 1. Biographical collections (920) 2. Biographies of individuals alphabetically by name of biographee (92)

Almanac of American presidents; from 1789 to the present: an original compendium of facts and anecdotes about politics and the presidency in the United States of America; edited by Thomas L. Connelly and Michael D. Senecal. Facts on File 1991 485p il $45   **920**
1. Presidents—United States
ISBN 0-8160-2219-4   LC 91-18895
"A Manly book"

This reference covers "41 presidents including their families; first ladies; children and other relatives; education; elections, including split-ticket campaigns; close races; contested elections, campaign slogans and songs; personal, political and financial scandals; careers—military, congressional, offices, and odd jobs they held; famous last words [and] where they are buried." Publisher's note

Includes bibliographic references

American leaders, 1789-1991; a biographical summary. Congressional Quarterly 1991 534p $35.95   **920**
1. Politicians—United States 2. United States—Biography
ISBN 0-87187-594-2   LC 90-22351
First published 1987 with title: American leaders, 1789-1987

A compilation of biographical information on elected officials (presidents, vice-presidents, state governors, cabinet officers, members of Congress) and Supreme Court justices

For a review see: Booklist, Feb. 1, 1992

Anthony, Carl Sferrazza
First Ladies; the saga of the presidents' wives and their power. Morrow 1990-1991 2v il ea $30, pa $15   **920**
1. Presidents—United States—Spouses   LC 90-5858
Contents: v1 1789-1961 (ISBN 0-688-07704-8; 0-688-11272-2); v2 1961-1990 (ISBN 0-688-10562-9; 0-688-12575-1)

This work combines political analysis, social history, and biography in examining the White House years of the First Ladies

"Exhaustively researched and meticulously presented, these sensitive and insightful portraits contain a wealth of invaluable biographical material." Booklist

Includes bibliography

Auchincloss, Louis
The Vanderbilt era; profiles of a gilded age. Scribner 1989 214p il o.p.; Collier Bks. paperback available $8.95   **920**
1. Vanderbilt family 2. Upper classes 3. New York (N.Y.)—Social life and customs
ISBN 0-02-030310-6 (pa)   LC 89-5973

The author "examines the lives of New York's 'acceptable' families, the privileged wealthy, in the period 1880-1920. . . . Dubbed The Four Hundred, . . . the 'elite' were heirs of railroad tycoon Cornelius Vanderbilt or merchant John Jacob Astor, among others." Publ Wkly

"Mr. Auchincloss has a fine ear for anecdote, and his accounts are burnished with family feeling." N Y Times Book Rev

Bell, Eric Temple, 1883-1960
Men of mathematics; [by] E. T. Bell. Simon & Schuster 1937 xxi, 592p il hardcover o.p. paperback available $14.95
                                  920
1. Mathematicians
ISBN 0-671-62818-6 (pa)
Analyzed in Essay and general literature index

This volume looks at the lives and contributions of 35 pioneers of modern mathematics

Bentley, Phyllis, 1894-1977
The Brontës. Thames & Hudson 1986 c1969 144p il pa $9.95   **920**
1. Brontë family
ISBN 0-500-26016-8   LC 85-51359
First published 1969 with title: The Brontës and their world

"This volume contains much factual material about the famous literary family. . . . Intended as enrichment for those already well versed in Brontë lore and literature, this succinctly written summary tantalizes the uninitiated to delve more deeply into the lives and writings of the Brontës." Publ Wkly

Biography index; a cumulative index to biographical material in books and magazines. Wilson, H.W. annual subscription $120   **920**
1. Biography—Indexes 2. Biography—Bibliography
ISSN 0006-3053
Also available on CD-ROM
First issued September 1946

Published quarterly, November, February, May, and August, with bound annual and permanent two-year cumulations. Permanent volumes $180 each

"'Biography Index' is a dependable and time-tested source that is basic in reference collections. It will serve many needs and holds a positive place in the vast area of biographical research." Am Ref Books Annu, 1982

Boller, Paul F.
Presidential anecdotes; [by] Paul F. Boller, Jr. Oxford Univ. Press 1981 410p $24.95
                                  920
1. Presidents—United States—Anecdotes
ISBN 0-19-502915-1   LC 80-27092
Also available in paperback from Penguin Bks.

Boller, Paul F.—*Continued*

"A collection of the words spoken by the 40 men who have served as Presidents of the U.S. The Presidents, presented in order of their service in office, are 'exposed' in capsule summaries and then anecdotes are arranged in general topic areas for each President." Choice

Includes bibliographic references

Presidential wives; [by] Paul F. Boller, Jr. Oxford Univ. Press 1988 533p $24.95; pa $9.95 **920**

1. Presidents—United States—Spouses
ISBN 0-19-503763-4; 0-19-505976-X (pa)
LC 87-31573

This is a collection of "essays about each of the Presidents' wives; each essay is followed by an assortment of amusing anecdotes. Boller focuses primarily on the relationship between the wife and her presidential husband, with little attention to her outside activities or children. The approach is friendly and uncritical." Libr J

Includes bibliography

Brenner, Marie

House of dreams: the Bingham family of Louisville. Random House 1988 452p il o.p.; Avon Bks. paperback available $4.95 **920**

1. Bingham family
ISBN 0-380-70727-6 (pa)
LC 87-28609

This is the story of "a liberal, socially active family whose fortune was based on a communications empire. . . . Over a relatively short, three-generational time span, this family reached its apogee and . . . the empire and the relationships between family members collapsed." Booklist

This book "can be read in several ways: as a love story between Barry Bingham Sr. and his wife Mary, as a guide to how not to rear children, as a cautionary tale about self-deception." Time

Includes bibliography

Caroli, Betty Boyd

First Ladies. Oxford Univ. Press 1987 xxii, 398p il $30; pa $11.95 **920**

1. Presidents—United States—Spouses
ISBN 0-19-503768-5; 0-19-505654-X (pa)
LC 86-28586

The "First Ladies (some of them daughters or other relatives) have been a highly varied group. . . . Caroli takes a look at each of them and their effect on the job, and also examines the ways the role of First Lady has changed over the years." Libr J

This book "gives the reader intimate glimpses into presidential marriages. A must for historical buffs." Choice

Includes bibliography

Ching, Frank, 1940-

Ancestors; 900 years in the life of a Chinese family. Morrow 1988 528p il $22.95 **920**

1. Chin family
ISBN 0-688-04461-1
LC 87-28289

"Shortly after Frank Ching arrived in the People's Republic of China in June of 1979, . . . he found himself embarked on an odyssey of personal and historical discovery. . . . The result is [this book], a stunning accomplishment in which, by recounting individual lives of members of his own clan, Mr. Ching brings to life the last nine centuries of Chinese history and culture as almost no other work in the English language has done." N Y Times Book Rev

Includes bibliography

Collier, Peter, 1939-

The Fords; an American epic; [by] Peter Collier and David Horowitz. Summit Bks. 1987 496p il hardcover o.p. paperback available $14 **920**

1. Ford family 2. Ford, Henry, 1863-1947
ISBN 0-671-66951-6 (pa)
LC 87-18948

A biography of three generations of the Henry Ford family

The authors "give us, with a novelistic flair for pacing and the effective use of anecdote, an exciting portrait that will not fail to satisfy even the heartiest appetite for the perversities and extravagances of the powerful." Commentary

Includes bibliography

The Kennedys; an American drama; [by] Peter Collier, David Horowitz. Summit Bks. 1984 576p il o.p.; Warner Bks. paperback available $6.99 **920**

1. Kennedy family
ISBN 0-446-35738-3 (pa)
LC 84-2502

The authors "have written a family history, from Patrick Kennedy's arrival in Boston in 1849 to the 1984 death of the troubled David Kennedy. They trace a legacy of amorality and all-consuming competitiveness to Joseph Kennedy. . . . Collier and Horowitz write in a splendid journalistic style." Libr J

Includes bibliography

The Rockefellers; an American dynasty; by Peter Collier and David Horowitz. Holt, Rinehart & Winston 1976 746p il o.p.; New Am. Lib. paperback available $4.95 **920**

1. Rockefeller family
ISBN 0-451-13455-9 (pa)

This "account of the family's story over the past four generations starts with John D. Rockefeller, Sr., who amassed the family's financial power. The authors survey the . . . philanthropies of J.D.R., Jr., the . . . influence of the brothers (J.D.R. III, Laurance, Winthrop, Nelson, and David), and the . . . generation of the 21 cousins." Libr J

Includes bibliographic references

Davis, John H., 1929-

The Guggenheims (1848-1988); an American epic. Shapolsky Pubs. 1988 512p il $19.95; pa $12.95 **920**

1. Guggenheim family
ISBN 0-944007-07-4; 0-56171-072-5 (pa)
LC 88-39902

First published 1978 by Morrow

This book provides a look at the Guggenheim family, from the patriarch Meyer to the present-day generation

Davis, John H., 1929-—*Continued*
The Kennedys; dynasty and disaster, 1848-1983. McGraw-Hill 1984 722p il o.p.; Shapolsky Pubs. paperback available $6.95
920
1. Kennedy family
ISBN 1-56171-060-1 (pa)　　　LC 83-19566
An account of four generations of the Kennedy family
"Mr. Davis has clearly done much research, and at his most convincing he dogs his facts like a courtroom lawyer. Those who simply can't get enough of the Kennedys will find their favorite sordid details between these covers." N Y Times Book Rev
Includes bibliography

Fraser, Antonia, 1932-
The warrior queens. Knopf 1989 c1988 383p il $22.95; pa $12.95　　　**920**
1. Women—Biography 2. Kings, queens, rulers, etc. 3. Women soldiers
ISBN 0-394-54939-2; 0-679-72816-3 (pa)
LC 88-45778
First published 1988 in the United Kingdom with title: Boadicea's chariot
The author "covers 17 women, from Queen Boadicea to Margaret Thatcher, who have ruled, specifically in time of war. Her character vignettes are sharp and incisive, and along the way she offers some intriguing thoughts on how societies through time have reacted to females cast in a role of military leadership. . . . Highly recommended." Libr J
Includes bibliographic references

The wives of Henry VIII. Knopf 1993 c1992 479p il $25　　　**920**
1. Henry VIII, King of England, 1491-1547 2. Great Britain—History—1485-1603, Tudors
ISBN 0-394-58538-0　　　LC 92-52950
First published 1992 in the United Kingdom with title: The six wives of Henry VIII
This work examines the lives of the six women— Catherine of Aragon, Anne Boleyn, Jane Seymour, Anna of Cleves, Katherine Howard, and Catherine Parr—who became Queens of England between 1509 and 1547. The author discusses their marriages to Henry VIII
"Fraser's readable style, empathy for her subjects, and piquant use of historical details and anecdotes make this a satisfying addition to the history shelves." Libr J
Includes bibliography

Fraser, Rebecca
The Brontës; Charlotte Brontë and her family. Crown 1988 543p il $25　　　**920**
1. Brontë family
ISBN 0-517-56438-6　　　LC 88-29918
Also available in paperback from Fawcett Columbine
This "biography sets Charlotte Brontë in her rightful place as the central figure in a remarkable and gifted family. Fraser gives a full account of the parents, home, teachers, publishers, friends, fellow writers and finally the husband of the woman who chose the masculine *nom-de-plume* 'Currer Bell.' The writings of Emily ('Ellis Bell') and Anne ('Action') are described and evaluated, as are the unpublished effusions of their wastrel brother Branwell." Publ Wkly
Includes bibliography

Goodwin, Doris Kearns
The Fitzgeralds and the Kennedys. Simon & Schuster 1987 932p il o.p.; St. Martin's Press paperback available $19.95　　　**920**
1. Fitzgerald family 2. Kennedy family
ISBN 0-312-06354-7 (pa)　　　LC 86-21994
"Beginning with the baptism of John Francis Fitzgerald (Rose's father) in 1863 and ending with a stirring account of JFK's inauguration in 1961, the story sweeps from the immigrant ghetto of Boston's North End to Camelot and takes in just about everything along the way." Publ Wkly
Includes bibliography

Grafton, David
The sisters; Babe Mortimer Paley, Betsey Roosevelt Whitney, Minnie Astor Fosburgh: the lives and times of the fabulous Cushing sisters. Villard Bks. 1992 316p il $22　**920**
1. Paley, Babe Mortimer 2. Whitney, Betsey Cushing Roosevelt, 1908- 3. Fosburgh, Minnie Astor 4. Cushing family
ISBN 0-394-58416-3　　　LC 91-50061
Grafton "chronicles the fascinating lives of three of high-society's biggest trendsetters: Babe Mortimer Paley, Minnie Astor Fosburgh, and Betsey Roosevelt Whitney. . . . Readers will be captivated by the dramatic and tragic events that Grafton discloses about these grand dames of the 1930s, whose influence was felt up through the 1970s." Booklist
Includes bibliography

Grobel, Lawrence
The Hustons. Scribner 1989 xx, 812p il o.p.; Avon Bks. paperback available $12.95
920
1. Huston family 2. Huston, John, 1906-1987
ISBN 0-380-71224-5 (pa)　　　LC 89-10076
This biography of three generations of the Huston family (Walter, John, Angelica, Danny, and Tony) focuses mainly on the late film director John Huston
"The author's biographical method in dealing with these assorted . . . people appears to have been to interview everyone who ever knew any of them and to record, with very little critical appraisal, whatever he was told. The result is a great deal of trivia intermixed with information, which will fascinate enthusiasts of show business." Atlantic
Includes bibliography

Haley, Alex
Roots. Doubleday 1976 587p $25　　　**920**
1. Haley family 2. Kinte family
ISBN 0-385-03787-2
Also available in paperback from Dell
This book details Haley's "search for the genealogical history of his family. He describes his trip to Gambia, the African homeland of his ancestors, and recounts the lives of his forebears." Benet's Reader's Ency of Am Lit

Hernon, Peter, 1947-
Under the influence; the unauthorized story of the Anheuser-Busch dynasty; [by] Peter Hernon and Terry Ganey. Simon & Schuster 1991 461p il $24.95   **920**
1. Busch family 2. Anheuser-Busch, Inc.
ISBN 0-671-69024-8   LC 91-13974
Also available in paperback from Avon Bks.

In this history of Anheuser Busch "what emerges is a colorful portrait of a family whose ambition and political connections over a period of 130 years led to an enduring and commanding success in the brewing industry. Rather than treat this as social history or as a business case study, the authors . . . focus on family personalities and their sometimes dubious business dealings." Libr J

Includes bibliographic references

Herzog, Chaim, 1918-
Heroes of Israel; profiles of Jewish courage. Little, Brown 1989 295p il $22.95   **920**
1. Jews—Biography 2. Heroes and heroines
ISBN 0-316-35901-7   LC 89-7966
"Ranging from biblical to modern times, this biographical survey . . . profiles those who fought for the Jewish people, such as Samson, Deborah, Hannah Szenes, David Ben-Gurion, and the Entebbe rescue team." Booklist
The author "has written a passionate, sensitive, and compelling book. . . . Feats of the modern-day figures are illuminated by extensive background material on major historic events." Libr J

Hibbert, Christopher, 1924-
The House of Medici; its rise and fall. Morrow 1975 c1974 364p il maps hardcover o.p. paperback available $13.50   **920**
1. Medici family 2. Florence (Italy)—History
ISBN 0-688-05339-4 (pa)
First published 1974 in the United Kingdom with title: The rise and fall of the House of Medici

This book is concerned with "heads of the Medici family [who] directed the government of the Florentine state from 1434, with Cosimo's return from exile, until the death of the Grand Duke Giovanni Gastone in 1737." Times Lit Suppl

Includes bibliography

Ione, Carole, 1937-
Pride of family; four generations of American women of color. Summit Bks. 1991 224p il $19.95   **920**
1. Whipper family 2. Wheeler family 3. Lewis family 4. Black women
ISBN 0-671-54453-5   LC 91-11761
Also available in paperback from Avon Bks.

"An African American writer seeks to understand her own life by uncovering the histories of her foremothers in this sensitive, detailed portrait of black women's lives over the last 150 years." Booklist

Includes bibliography

Kane, Joseph Nathan, 1899-
Facts about the presidents; a compilation of biographical and historical information. 6th ed. Wilson, H.W. 1993 433p il $55   **920**
1. Presidents—United States
ISBN 0-8242-0845-5   LC 93-9207
First published 1959

The main part of this work provides an individual chapter on each President, from Washington through Clinton, presenting such information as family, education, election, Vice President, main events and accomplishments of his administration, and First Lady. Part two contains tables and lists presenting comparative data on all the Presidents

Kennedy, John F. (John Fitzgerald), 1917-1963
Profiles in courage; special foreword by Robert F. Kennedy. Commemorative ed. Perennial Lib. 1988 c1964 282p pa $6   **920**
1. Politicians—United States 2. Courage
ISBN 0-06-080698-2
Also available G.K. Hall large print edition
First published 1956 by Harper & Brothers

This series of profiles of Americans who took courageous stands at crucial moments in public life includes John Quincy Adams, Daniel Webster, Thomas Hart Benton, Sam Houston, Edmund G. Ross, Lucius Q. C. Lamar, George Norris, Robert A. Taft and others

Includes bibliography

Kingston, Maxine Hong
China men. Knopf 1980 308p o.p.; Vintage Bks. paperback available $10   **920**
1. Chinese Americans—Biography
ISBN 0-679-72328-5 (pa)   LC 79-3469
This book "paints a rich picture of the writer's male family members, but those portraits of her grandfathers, father, and brothers are interspersed with fascinating bits of historical data. . . . The whole is held together by pieces of folklore that one feels compelled to go back to and reread." Libr J

Lacey, Robert
Ford, the men and the machine. Little, Brown 1986 778p il o.p.; Ballantine Bks. paperback available $5.95   **920**
1. Ford family 2. Ford, Henry, 1863-1947 3. Automobile industry
ISBN 0-345-34312-3 (pa)   LC 86-10642
"The book's first half covers the first Henry Ford, his building of the Model T and his introduction of the moving assembly line in mass production. [The second half covers the exploits of the Ford family.]" Economist
"Thoroughly researched, well-illustrated, this volume is balanced and readable and will have broad appeal." Libr J

Includes bibliography

Lewis, R. W. B. (Richard Warrington Baldwin)

The Jameses; a family narrative. Farrar, Straus & Giroux 1991 695p il $35   **920**

1. James family
ISBN 0-374-17861-5   LC 91-10501

Also available in paperback from Anchor Bks.

The author traces the "James family from William James of Albany, N.Y., who emigrated from Ireland in 1789 and founded the clan's fortune, to the death of novelist Henry in 1916. The main focus is on Henry Sr. and his three most prominent children: leading psychologist and thinker William; great novelist Henry, 'inveterate collector of impressions'; and Alice, political radical and frequent invalid." Publ Wkly

"This very full and fascinating account of one of America's major families will interest students of literature and history as well as the general reader." Libr J

Includes bibliographic references

Montgomery, Sy

Walking with the great apes; Jane Goodall, Dian Fossey, Biruté Galdikas. Houghton Mifflin 1991 280p il $19.95; pa $9.70   **920**

1. Goodall, Jane 2. Fossey, Dian 3. Galdikas, Biruté 4. Women scientists
ISBN 0-395-51597-1; 0-395-61156-3 (pa)
      LC 90-48043

"A Peter Davison book"

The author tells the story of three primatologists, "Birute Galdikas, who studies orangutans in Borneo, Jane Goodall, who observes chimpanzees in Tanzania, and Dian Fossey, who died fighting for the mountain gorillas of Rwanda." N Y Times Book Rev

"This is an exciting book. Montgomery provides an outstanding, popularized synthesis. . . . The author also conveys a fine sense of the diverse personalities of the three." Booklist

Includes bibliographic references

Nagel, Paul C.

The Adams women; Abigail and Louisa Adams, their sisters and daughters. Oxford Univ. Press 1987 310p il $30; pa $10.95   **920**

1. Adams, Abigail, 1744-1818 2. Adams, Louisa Catherine, 1775-1852 3. Adams family
ISBN 0-19-503874-6; 0-19-505920-4 (pa)
      LC 86-31262

The author describes "the lives of the Adams wives and daughters as women in the society where the Adams men were so prominent. Using their letters and journals as his principal source, and quoting from them liberally, he has brought these strong and intelligent women to the center of the stage." Wilson Libr Bull

Includes bibliography

Nash, Jay Robert

Bloodletters and badmen; a narrative encyclopedia of American criminals from the Pilgrims to the present. Evans & Co. 1973 640p il hardcover o.p. paperback available $17.95   **920**

1. Criminals
ISBN 0-87131-200-X (pa)

Among the notorious Americans profiled are John Wilkes Booth, Lee Harvey Oswald, Jesse James and Al Capone

Includes bibliography

O'Toole, Patricia

The Five of Hearts: an intimate portrait of Henry Adams and his friends, 1880-1918. Potter 1990 459p il $25   **920**

1. Adams, Henry, 1838-1918 2. Hay, John Milton, 1838-1905 3. King, Clarence, 1842-1901 4. Hay, Clara 5. Adams, Marian, 1843-1885 6. United States—Intellectual life
ISBN 0-517-56350-9   LC 89-16378

This is the "story of a friendship among five little people, three small men and two small women, in Washington from the 1880's onward. Henry and Clover Adams, John and Clara Hay and the eternal bachelor Clarence King were *soigné*, intellectual and influential. They were also in the thick of political activity. . . . The book gives us a new perception of America during a period of erupting violence." N Y Times Book Rev

Peters, Margot

The house of Barrymore. Knopf 1990 641p il $29.95   **920**

1. Barrymore family
ISBN 0-394-55321-7   LC 89-43451

Also available in paperback from Simon & Schuster

This is a biography of the American actors John, Ethel, and Lionel Barrymore

The author "has made an outstanding contribution to the history of the American theater in her thoroughly readable account of three of its most illustrious artists." Libr J

Includes bibliographic references

Plutarch, ca. 46-ca. 120

Plutarch: the lives of the noble Grecians and Romans; the Dryden translation; edited and revised by Arthur Hugh Clough. Modern Lib. 1992 2v ea $19   **920**

1. Greece—Biography 2. Rome—Biography
ISBN 0-679-60008-6 (v1); 0-679-60009-4 (v2)
      LC 92-50223

First Modern Library edition published 1932

This work is "arranged mainly in pairs in which a Greek and a Roman are contrasted. His subjects, who include Demosthenes and Cicero, were statesmen or generals. In the process of writing about them, he invents dialogue and describes the emotions of the personages involved." Reader's Ency. 3d edition

Reynolds, Patrick

The gilded leaf; triumph, tragedy, and tobacco: three generations of the R.J. Reynolds family and fortune; by Patrick Reynolds, and Tom Shachtman. Little, Brown 1989 353p il $19.95   **920**

1. Reynolds family 2. R. J. Reynolds Tobacco Co. 3. Tobacco industry
ISBN 0-316-74121-3   LC 88-31437

"This multigenerational biography of the wealthy Reynolds tobacco family concentrates on the family squabbles and the excessive, abusive lifestyles of many of the heirs." Booklist

Includes bibliography

Ritter, Lawrence S.
The glory of their times; the story of the early days of baseball told by the men who played it. new enl ed. Morrow 1984 360p il hardcover o.p. paperback available $10
920

1. Baseball—Biography
ISBN 0-688-11273-0 (pa)   LC 84-221549
First published 1966 by Macmillan
A collection of 26 oral histories of baseball's early days by veteran players

Talese, Gay
Unto the sons. Knopf 1992 635p $25
920

1. Talese family 2. Italian Americans
ISBN 0-679-41034-1   LC 91-53178
Also available in paperback from Ivy Bks.
This is a history of the author's family in southern Italy and the United States
"With fine storytelling voice, Talese penned this odyssey with affection, but also with the clear-eyed sense of the dramatic and noble lives of his forebears. The result . . . is a grand epic." Libr J
Includes bibliography

Vanderbilt, Arthur T., 1950-
Fortune's children: the fall of the house of Vanderbilt; [by] Arthur T. Vanderbilt II. Morrow 1989 496p il hardcover o.p. paperback available $12.95
920

1. Vanderbilt family
ISBN 0-688-10386-3 (pa)   LC 89-32421
This account of four generations of the Vanderbilt family chronicles railroad magnate Cornelius Vanderbilt's accumulation of wealth and the ways in which his heirs spent the family fortune
"Vanderbilt dramatizes both the successes and excesses of America's Gilded Age—the enormous new wealth, the lavish lifestyles, and, later, the desperate schemes to maintain social status and fortune (contesting wills, matchmaking with nobility, and, most notably, battling for custody of 'Little Gloria'). . . . An absorbing social history." Libr J
Includes bibliography

Vare, Ethlie Ann
Mothers of invention; from the bra to the bomb: forgotten women & their unforgettable ideas; [by] Ethlie Ann Vare & Greg Ptacek; with a foreword by Julie Newmar. Morrow 1988 256p il hardcover o.p. paperback available $8.95
920

1. Women inventors
ISBN 0-688-08907-0 (pa)   LC 87-23982
This book presents information on women inventors and their inventions from the first century of our era to the present

This is "a fascinating and gratifying book. It's a book not to be read all at once, but to be dipped into, to be shown to your friends and your kids. . . . It gives us a positive view of women's inventiveness, from the frivolous to the noble." N Y Times Book Rev

Warner, Ezra J.
Generals in blue; lives of the Union commanders. Louisiana State Univ. Press 1964 xxiv, 679p il $29.95
920

1. Generals 2. United States—History—1861-1865, Civil War—Biography
ISBN 0-8071-0822-7
This book contains biographical sketches of the 583 men who attained the rank of general during the Civil War years. A photograph of each man is also included
Includes bibliography

Generals in gray; lives of the Confederate commanders. Louisiana State Univ. Press 1959 xxvii, 420p il $24.95
920

1. Generals 2. United States—History—1861-1865, Civil War—Biography 3. Confederate States of America—Biography
ISBN 0-8071-0823-5
"Biographical sketches of the Confederate generals; concise outlines of their military careers, also giving dates of birth and death and places of burial. The product of ten years of research, much of it done in interviews with descendants. Illustrated with 425 portraits." Publ Wkly
Includes bibliography

Weir, Alison
The six wives of Henry VIII. Grove Weidenfeld 1992 643p il $24.95
920

1. Henry VIII, King of England, 1491-1547 2. Great Britain—History—1485-1603, Tudors
ISBN 0-8021-1497-0   LC 91-29522
First published 1991 in the United Kingdom
This is a collective biography of the wives of the Tudor king of England
"Wonderfully detailed, extensively researched. . . . The narrative is free flowing, humorous, informative, and readable." SLJ
Includes bibliographic references

Wilson, A. N. (Andrew Norman), 1950-
Eminent Victorians. Norton 1990 240p il $25
920

1. Great Britain—Intellectual life
ISBN 0-393-02848-8
First published 1989 in the United Kingdom
The author "examines the lives of Prince Albert, William Gladstone, Charlotte Brontë, Josephine Butler, Cardinal Newman, and Julia Margaret Cameron." Booklist
"The six individuals [the author] profiles . . . are treated with sympathy and accuracy. His portraits are balanced (even to an equal division between the sexes in coverage), and equally important, he provides a better understanding of the age through the lives of key Victorians." Libr J

Wiser, William

The great good place; American expatriate women in Paris. Norton 1991 336p il $20.95 **920**

1. Paris (France)—Intellectual life 2. Women—Biography
ISBN 0-393-02999-9   LC 90-22763

The author "examines the lives of five expatriate American women of the early [twentieth] century: Mary Cassatt, Edith Wharton, Caresse Crosby, Zelda Fitzgerald and Josephine Baker. His thesis is that to understand these women it is necessary to understand their relationship to the city they chose to live in." N Y Times Book Rev

This "is an informative and highly readable collection of stories that nonspecialist readers will find literate and interesting." Choice

Includes bibliography

Women of mathematics; a biobibliographic sourcebook; edited by Louise S. Grinstein and Paul J. Campbell. Greenwood Press 1987 xx, 292p $65 **920**

1. Women mathematicians
ISBN 0-313-24849-4   LC 86-25711

"This collection includes biographic sketches and bibliographies of 43 women mathematicians ranging from Hypatia (370-415) to Grace Murray Hopper (1906-). Criteria for inclusion is most often attainment of an advanced math degree. . . . This is a valuable collection, with most of the biographies proving entertaining as well as educational." Libr J

920.003 Biographical reference works

Abrams, Irwin

The Nobel Peace Prize and the laureates; an illustrated biographical history, 1901-1987. Hall, G.K. & Co. 1988 269p $40 **920.003**

1. Nobel prizes 2. Biography—Dictionaries
ISBN 0-8161-8609-X   LC 88-16313

This "volume contains biographies of the 87 famous and not-so famous individuals who have been recipients of the prize from 1901 to 1987, and also discusses each prize period separately, providing an overview of the social, political, and historical decision-making environment that influenced the selection choice." Libr J

American authors, 1600-1900; a biographical dictionary of American literature; edited by Stanley J. Kunitz and Howard Haycraft. Wilson, H.W. 1938 846p il (Authors ser) $72 **920.003**

1. Authors, American—Dictionaries 2. American literature—Bio-bibliography
ISBN 0-8242-0001-2

"Complete in one volume with 1300 biographies and 400 portraits." Title page

"This standard biographical source contains some 1300 popularly written biographies and 400 portraits. Sketches vary in length from 150 to 2500 words and include brief bibliographies of works by and about the author." Ref Sources for Small & Medium-sized Libr. 5th edition

American men & women of science; a biographical directory of today's leaders in physical, biological and related sciences. Bowker 8v set $750 **920.003**

1. Scientists—Dictionaries
ISSN 0192-8570

Also available on CD-ROM

Irregular. First published 1906 with title: American men of science. Some editions were divided into two sections: Physical and biological sciences and Social sciences

"Provides brief biographical sketches of . . . scientists active in all natural science fields in the United States and Canada. Arranged alphabetically, with discipline index." Ref Sources for Small & Medium-sized Libr. 5th edition

American writers; a collection of literary biographies; Leonard Unger, editor in chief. Scribner 1974-1981 4v + supplement I-II (in 4v) set $625 **920.003**

1. Authors, American—Dictionaries 2. American literature—Bio-bibliography 3. American literature—History and criticism
ISBN 0-684-17322-0

Also available: British writers 8v set $625 (ISBN 0-684-18253-X)

Contents: v1 Henry Adams to T. S. Eliot; v2 Ralph Waldo Emerson to Carson McCullers; v3 Archibald MacLeish to George Santayana; v4 Isaac Bashevis Singer to Richard Wright; supplement I pt 1 Jane Addams to Sidney Lanier; supplement I pt 2 Vachel Lindsay to Elinor Wylie; supplement II pt 1 W. H. Auden to O'Henry; supplement II pt 2 Robinson Jeffers to Yvor Winters

"In general, readable essays, the lives, careers, and works of 155 American authors are introduced. A selected bibliography of the author's principal works and critical studies concludes each essay." Ref Sources for Small & Medium-sized Libr. 5th edition

Attwater, Donald, 1892-1977

Penguin dictionary of saints. 2nd rev ed, revised and updated by Catherine Rachel John. Penguin Bks. 1983 352p (Penguin reference bks) pa $11 **920.003**

1. Saints—Dictionaries
ISBN 0-14-051123-7

First published 1965

"A good brief dictionary. Includes a short glossary of terms preceding the alphabetical listing of more than 750 saints. The saint's symbol in art is frequently indicated." Sheehy. Guide to Ref Books. 10th edition

The **Biographical** dictionary of scientists. Bedrick Bks. 1984-1986 6v il ea $28 **920.003**

1. Scientists—Dictionaries

First published 1983-1985 in the United Kingdom

Contents: v1 Astronomers (ISBN 0-911745-80-7); v2 Biologists (ISBN 0-911745-82-3); v3 Chemists (ISBN 0-911745-81-5); v4 Physicists (ISBN 0-911745-79-3); v5 Engineers and inventors (ISBN 0-87226-009-7); v6 Mathematicians (ISBN 0-87226-008-9)

"Each of these volumes follows an identical format: after a brief historical overview of the subject field, there is an alphabetically arranged collection of about 200 very readable biographies of leading scientists in that field throughout history, and including some living individuals.

The Biographical dictionary of scientists—
Continued
Each volume has a glossary of terms peculiar to its
field." Libr J

The **Book** of saints; a dictionary of servants
of God; compiled by the Benedictine
monks of St. Augustine's Abbey,
Ramsgate. 6th ed, entirely rev and re-set.
Morehouse 1989 605p il hardcover o.p.
paperback available $24.95   **920.003**
1. Christian saints—Dictionaries
ISBN 0-8192-1611-9 (pa)   LC 89-33515
First published 1921

"Each entry includes the saint's name, appellation,
feast day, dates, liturgical group, hagiographic rank (saint
or blessed), religious order, and a short description of
the saint's life. . . . One of the best single-volume
reference works on hagiography." Best Ref Books, 1986-
1990

British authors before 1800; a biographical
dictionary; edited by Stanley J. Kunitz
and Howard Haycraft; complete in one
volume with 650 biographies and 220
portraits. Wilson, H.W. 1952 584p il
(Authors ser) $60   **920.003**
1. Authors, English—Dictionaries 2. English literature—Bio-bibliography
ISBN 0-8242-0006-3

Companion volume British authors of the nineteenth
century, entered below

"Short biographical essays on principal and marginal
figures in British literature. Bibliographies appended to
essays." N Y Public Libr Book of How & Where to
Look It Up

British authors of the nineteenth century;
edited by Stanley J. Kunitz; associate
editor: Howard Haycraft; complete in one
volume with 1000 biographies and 350
portraits. Wilson, H.W. 1936 677p il
(Authors ser) $64   **920.003**
1. Authors, English—Dictionaries 2. English literature—Bio-bibliography
ISBN 0-8242-0007-1

"More than a thousand authors of the British Empire
(including Canada, Australia, South Africa, and New
Zealand) are represented by sketches varying in length
from approximately 100 to 2500 words, roughly propor-
tionate to the importance of the subjects." Preface

Butler, Alban, 1711-1773
Butler's Lives of the saints; complete
edition; edited, revised and supplemented by
Herbert Thurston and Donald Attwater.
Christian Classics 1981 4v set $140; pa $95
920.003
1. Christian saints—Dictionaries
ISBN 0-87061-045-7; 0-87061-137-2 (pa)

Also available in a concise edition, edited by Michael
Walsh, in paperback from HarperSanFrancisco

A reprint of the four volume set published 1956 by
Kenedy

New edition of a work first published 1756-1759. The
calendar arrangement is retained, but the number of entries has almost doubled and many of the entries have

been rewritten in whole or part

"The biographies of the saints and beati are arranged
by their feast days with each of the four volumes containing three months. . . . Each volume has a table of
contents arranged by the days of the month with a list
of the feasts for each day." Booklist

Cambridge biographical dictionary; general
editor, Magnus Magnusson; assistant
editor, Rosemary Goring. Cambridge
Univ. Press 1990 1604p $44.95   **920.003**
1. Biography—Dictionaries
ISBN 0-521-39518-6   LC 90-1542

Replaces Chambers biographical dictionary; United
Kingdom edition retains former title

"As a single-volume, worldwide, all-period biographical
dictionary this has no peers." Libr J
For a fuller review see: Booklist, Feb. 15, 1991

Concise dictionary of American biography.
4th ed complete to 1970. Scribner 1990
1536p $150   **920.003**
1. United States—Biography—Dictionaries
ISBN 0-684-19188-1   LC 90-8951
First published 1964

"Edited under the sponsorship of the American Council of Learned Societies." Book jacket

This one-volume abridgement of the Dictionary of
American biography "contains concise versions of all
18,110 biographies contained in the original work and
its supplements. . . . The *CDAB* is a valuable reference
work. For many users, these brief entries will be exactly
what they are seeking." Booklist

Contemporary authors. Gale Res. apply to
publisher for price and availability
920.003
1. Authors—Dictionaries   2. Literature—Bio-
bibliography

Started publication 1967. Frequency varies. Indexes
cumulate at frequent intervals. Editors vary

Revised and updated biographies from this series are:
1st revision, Permanent series, and New revision series

"A bio-bibliographical guide to current writers in fiction, general nonfiction, poetry, journalism, drama, motion pictures, television, and other fields." Title page

"Published to give an up-to-date source of biographical
information on current authors in many fields—
humanities, social sciences, and sciences—and from many
countries. Sketches attempt to give, as pertinent: personal
facts (including names of parents, children, etc.), career,
writings (as complete a bibliography as possible), work
in progress, sidelights, and occasional biographical
sources." Sheehy. Guide to Ref Books. 10th edition

Contemporary black biography; profiles from
the international black community. Gale
Res. il $42   **920.003**
1. Blacks—Biography
ISSN 1058-1316

Started publication 1992. Editors vary

"This new serial is to be published twice a year.
Included in each volume are biographies of innovators
in the black global community who are currently living
and/or who have had a lasting impact on society. Every
field of endeavor imaginable is represented, from science,
politics, and creative arts to sports. More than 70 individuals . . . are profiled in two- to four-page entries
in volume 1. . . . This new title will be useful for its
coverage of current people in the news who are not as
easy to find elsewhere." Booklist

Contemporary dramatists; preface to the third edition, Ruby Cohn; preface to the fifth edition, Michael Billington; editor, K.A. Berney. 5th ed. St. James Press 1993 843p (Contemporary writers of the English language) $135 **920.003**

1. Dramatists, English—Dictionaries 2. Dramatists, American—Dictionaries 3. English drama—Bio-bibliography 4. American drama—Bio-bibliography
ISBN 1-55862-185-7

First published 1972 by St. Martin's Press

"Biographies, published work, and critical essays on living dramatists, with supplements for screen, radio, and television writers, musical librettists, and theater groups." N Y Public Libr Book of How & Where to Look It Up

Contemporary poets; preface to the first edition, C. Day Lewis; preface to the fifth edition, Diane Wakoski; editor, Tracy Chevalier. 5th ed. St. James Press 1991 1179p (Contemporary writers of the English language) $135 **920.003**

1. Poets, English—Dictionaries 2. Poets, American—Dictionaries 3. English poetry—Bio-bibliography 4. American poetry—Bio-bibliography
ISBN 1-558-62035-4 LC 90-63664

First published 1970 with title: Contemporary poets of the English language. Editors vary

"A biographical handbook of contemporary poets, arranged alphabetically. Entries consist of a short biography, full bibliography, comments by some of the poets, and a signed critical essay." Ref Sources for Small & Medium-sized Libr. 5th edition

Current biography: cumulated index, 1940-1990; edited by Jill Kadetsky. Wilson, H.W. 1991 133p $25 **920.003**

1. Biography—Periodicals—Indexes
ISBN 0-8242-0819-6

This index lists the subjects of all the profiles published from 1940 through 1990 in a single alphabet, providing access to almost 20,000 biographies. Updates and obituaries are noted. Cross-references cover name variants, pseudonyms and changes in titles of nobility

Current biography yearbook. Wilson, H.W. il $60 **920.003**

1. Biography—Periodicals
ISSN 0084-9499

Annual. First published 1940 with title: Current biography

Also issued monthly except December at a subscription price of $60 per year (ISSN 0011-3344). Yearbooks 1940-1985 available ea $54; 1986-date ea $60

"Biographies of prominent people written in lively, popular prose. Emphasis is on entertainers, star athletes, politicians, and other celebrities. Series is cumulative, with biographies revised and updated occasionally. Each volume has seven-year index." N Y Public Libr Book of How & Where to Look It Up

Dictionary of American biography; edited by Allen Johnson and Dumas Malone. Scribner 1958-1988 11v + index and supplements 3-8 set $1399 **920.003**

1. United States—Biography—Dictionaries
ISBN 0-684-17323-9

First published 1928-1937 as 20 volume set plus index, with supplementary volumes added in 1944 and 1958. Supplements 3-8 were published 1973-1988. A complete index guide for volumes 1-10 and supplements 1-7 is available in paperback $13.45 (ISBN 0-684-17152-X). Supplement 8 contains an index to supplements 1-8

Published under the auspices of the American Council of Learned Societies

"The scholarly American biographical dictionary designed on the lines of the English 'Dictionary of national biography' . . . with signed articles and bibliographies. . . . More than 13,600 biographies in the basic set. Does not include living persons." Sheehy. Guide to Ref Books. 10th edition

Dictionary of American Negro biography; edited by Rayford W. Logan and Michael R. Winston. Norton 1983 c1982 $65 **920.003**

1. Blacks—Biography—Dictionaries
ISBN 0-393-01513-0 LC 81-9629

"Biographies of black Americans who have had an impact on history, excluding those still living. Bibliographies follow entries. Includes index of entries by profession or field of endeavor." N Y Public Libr Book of How & Where to Look It Up

The **Dictionary** of national biography; edited by Sir Leslie Stephen and Sir Sidney Lee. Oxford Univ. Press 1908-1909 22v set $2250 + 9 supplementary volumes at various prices **920.003**

1. Great Britain—Biography—Dictionaries
ISBN 0-19-865101-5

Second supplement, 1901-1911 Edited by Sir Sidney Lee (ISBN 0-19-865201-1); Third supplement, 1912-1921 Edited by H. W. C. Davis and J. R. H. Weaver (ISBN 0-19-865202-X); Fourth supplement, 1922-1930 Edited by J. R. H. Weaver (ISBN 0-19-865203-8); Fifth supplement, 1931-1940 Edited by L. G. Wickham Legg (ISBN 0-19-865204-6); Sixth supplement, 1941-1950 Edited by L. G. Wickham Legg and E. T. Williams (ISBN 0-19-865205-4); Seventh supplement, 1951-1960 Edited by E. T. Williams and Helen M. Palmer (ISBN 0-19-865206-2); Eighth supplement, 1961-1970 Edited by E. T. Williams and C. S. Nicholls (ISBN 0-19-865207-0); Ninth supplement, 1971-1980 Edited by Lord Blake and C. S. Nicholls (ISBN 0-19-865208-9); Tenth supplement, 1981-1985 Edited by Lord Blake and C. S. Nicholls

"Founded in 1882 by George Smith. From the earliest times to 1900." Title page

The main work and first supplement were originally published in sixty-six volumes, in 1885-1901, and reissued 1908-1909 in twenty-two volumes

"Authoritative and comprehensive British biography. Well-documented and signed biographies of notable inhabitants of the British Isles and colonies. Each article includes a bibliography, and every supplement has a cumulative index to all entries beginning from 1901 in one alphabetical sequence." Ref Sources for Small & Medium-sized Libr. 5th edition

The **Dictionary** of national biography: the concise dictionary. Oxford Univ. Press 1953-1982 2v pt.1 $95; pt.2 $39.95 **920.003**

1. Great Britain—Biography—Dictionaries
Half title: The concise dictionary of national biography
Contents: pt.1 From the beginnings to 1900; Being an epitome of the main work and its supplement (ISBN 0-19-865301-8); pt.2 1901-1970 (ISBN 0-19-865303-4)

The Dictionary of national biography: the concise dictionary—*Continued*

"'The concise dictionary' serves a double purpose, i.e., it is both an index [to the work entered above] and also an independent biographical dictionary (since it gives abstracts, each about one-fourteenth of the length of the original article)." Sheehy. Guide to Ref Books. 10th edition

Dictionary of scientific biography; Charles Coulston Gillispie, editor in chief. Scribner 1981 16v in 8 set $1199   **920.003**

ISBN 0-684-16962-2

Also available Volumes 17-18 designated Supplement II published 1990 set $180 (ISBN 0-684-18294-7)

This is a reprint of the title published 1970-1980 in 16 volumes, now bound in double volumes, retaining original numbering on spine. Volumes 15-16 are Supplement I and Index

Published under the auspices of the American Council of Learned Societies

This "biographical dictionary covers over forty-five hundred people ranging from Einstein, Newton, and Pasteur to Marx, Columbus, and Abailard. Its focus is on the biographee's place in the history of science, rather than on his or her life story. The signed entries run from part of a page to many pages and include excellent bibliographies." RQ

European authors, 1000-1900; a biographical dictionary of European literature; edited by Stanley J. Kunitz and Vineta Colby; complete in one volume with 967 biographies and 309 portraits. Wilson, H.W. 1967 1016p il (Authors ser) $73   **920.003**

1. Authors, European—Dictionaries 2. Literature—Bio-bibliography
ISBN 0-8242-0013-6

Includes continental European writers born after the year 1000 and dead before 1925. Nearly a thousand major and minor contributors to thirty-one different literatures are discussed

"These biographies provide quick, satisfactory introductions to a staggering variety of authors and literatures." Choice

Grant, Michael, 1914-

Greek and Latin authors, 800 B.C.-A.D. 1000; a biographical dictionary. Wilson, H.W. 1980 490p il (Authors ser) $65   **920.003**

1. Authors, Greek—Dictionaries 2. Authors, Latin—Dictionaries 3. Classical literature—Bio-bibliography
ISBN 0-8242-0640-1   LC 79-27446

Covers more than 370 classical authors. Each entry includes "the pronunciation of the author's name, biographical background, an overview of major works with critical commentary on the nature and quality of those works, and, where relevant, a brief discussion of the influence of the author's works on later literature." Ref Sources for Small & Medium-sized Libr. 5th edition

Hawkins, Walter L. (Walter Lee), 1949-

African American biographies; profiles of 558 current men and women. McFarland & Co. 1992 490p il $39.95   **920.003**

1. Blacks—Biography
ISBN 0-89950-664-X   LC 91-50938

This "is a compendium of profiles of 558 of the nation's most notable blacks who are currently living or who died since 1968. . . . These individuals were chosen for their achievements in sports or in their professions, as well as for political and community leadership. . . . Entries are arranged alphabetically, giving personal data, achievements, and organizational affiliations. Most entries are a page in length." Booklist

Index to Marquis Who's Who books. Marquis Who's Who $79.50   **920.003**

1. Biography—Dictionaries—Indexes

Annual. Published 1974-1984 with title: Marquis Who's Who publications index to all books. Title varies

"An index to the names of all persons whose biographical sketches appear in current editions of [all the] Marquis biographical directories, with reference to the work in which the biography appears." Sheehy. Guide to Ref Books. 10th edition

The International who's who. Europa Publs. [distributed by] Gale Res. $260   **920.003**

1. Biography—Dictionaries
ISSN 0074-9613

Annual. First published 1935

"Offers brief biographical data on prominent persons throughout the world." Sheehy. Guide to Ref Books. 10th edition

Kelly, J. N. D. (John Norman Davidson)

The Oxford dictionary of popes. Oxford Univ. Press 1986 347p $29.95; pa $11.95   **920.003**

1. Popes—Dictionaries
ISBN 0-19-213964-9; 0-19-282085-0 (pa)
    LC 85-15599

"An excellent source of information, which is arranged chronologically with an alphabetical index. Contains popes, antipopes, and an appendix on Pope Joan." Ref Sources for Small & Medium-sized Libr. 5th edition

Latin American writers; Carlos A. Solé, editor in chief; Maria Isabel Abreu, associate editor. Scribner 1989 3v set $275   **920.003**

1. Authors, Latin American 2. Latin American literature—History and criticism
ISBN 0-684-18463-X   LC 88-35481

This work "presents an overview of Latin American literature from the colonial period to the present. Articles covering 176 writers of Spanish America and Brazil include a signed biographical and critical essay, followed by a selected bibliography of primary and secondary sources." Ref Sources for Small & Medium-sized Libr. 5th edition

The **McGraw-Hill** encyclopedia of world biography; an international reference work. McGraw-Hill; [distributed by] Heraty & Assocs. 1973 12v il maps set $550

920.003

1. Biography—Dictionaries
ISBN 0-07-079633-5

Set of five supplementary volumes covering 20th century world biography published 1987-1992 by Heraty & Assocs. with title: Encyclopedia of world biography: 20th century, available for $354

"Features 5000 signed articles about persons relevant to social and cultural history. Each article has a brief synopsis and includes portraits and illustrations. Text sections are headlined; brief bibliography follows each article. Volume 12 contains the index and study guides that place the individuals into historical/cultural perspective." Ref Sources for Small & Medium-sized Libr. 5th edition

Nobel Prize winners; an H.W. Wilson biographical dictionary; editor, Tyler Wasson; consultants, Gert H. Brieger [et al.] Wilson, H.W. 1987 xxxiv, 1165p il $90

920.003

1. Nobel prizes 2. Biography—Dictionaries
ISBN 0-8242-0756-4   LC 87-16468

First supplement covering 1987-1991 available for $35 (ISBN 0-8242-0834-X)

This reference book "begins with an alphabetical listing of winners, a listing of prize categories (broken down chronologically by years), an article on Alfred Nobel, and another on the process by which the prizes are awarded. . . . Included are all winners (persons and institutions) from 1901-1986 in entries of 1200-1500 words." SLJ

The **Nobel** Prize winners: literature; edited by Frank N. Magill. Salem Press 1987 3v il set $210

920.003

1. Authors—Dictionaries 2. Nobel prizes
ISBN 0-89356-541-5   LC 88-6469

Also available at $210 per set are volumes covering prizewinners in physics, chemistry, and physiology or medicine, published 1989, 1990, and 1991 respectively

Contents: v1 1901-1926; v2 1927-1961; v3 1962-1987

"Arranged chronologically, the articles average 3,500 words, synopsizing the prizewinners' lives and works. . . . Entries have special sections on the presentation of the award, the Nobel lecture, and the critical reception of the prizewinner." Booklist

Notable American women, 1607-1950; a biographical dictionary; Edward T. James, editor; Janet Wilson James, associate editor; Paul S. Boyer, assistant editor. Harvard Univ. Press 1971 3v hardcover o.p. paperback set available $45 **920.003**

1. Women—United   States—Biography   2. United States—Biography—Dictionaries
ISBN 0-674-62734-2 (pa)

1,359 American "women—art patrons, astronomers, Indian captives, circus performers, entrepreneurs, inventors, philosophers—are treated in well written articles which range from 400 to 7,000 words. . . . Each article is followed by bibliographical references." Choice

Notable American women: the modern period; a biographical dictionary; edited by Barbara Sicherman [et al.] Harvard Univ. Press 1980 xxii, 773p $50; pa $24.95

920.003

1. Women—United   States—Biography   2. United States—Biography—Dictionaries
ISBN 0-674-62732-6; 0-674-62733-4 (pa)

LC 80-18402

This companion volume to the title entered above adds 442 biographies and extends coverage to women who died between 1951 and 1975

Notable black American women; Jessie Carney Smith, editor. Gale Res. 1992 xlvii, 1334p il $75 **920.003**

1. Black women—Dictionaries 2. United States—Biography—Dictionaries
ISBN 0-8103-4749-0   LC 91-35074

A shorter version profiling 100 women is available in paperback from Visible Ink Press with title Epic lives

"This biographical encyclopedia documents the achievements of 500 African-American women who have made significant contributions to American culture from the colonial era to the present. . . . Subjects include women active in all fields of endeavor, from education, science, and the arts, to business, law and politics. . . . Authoritative and entertaining at the same time, these sketches are appropriate for high school and college students as well as the general reader." Am Libr

For a fuller review see: Booklist, April 15, 1992

Peterson, Bernard L.
Contemporary black American playwrights and their plays; a biographical directory and dramatic index; foreword by James V. Hatch. Greenwood Press 1988 xxvi, 625p $75 **920.003**

1. American drama—Black authors—Bio-bibliography 2. American drama—Black authors—Dictionaries
ISBN 0-313-25190-8   LC 87-17814

"Provides information on more than 700 contemporary dramatists, screenwriters, and scriptwriters. Depending upon a availability of data, entries include biographical and bibliographical information, together with annotations of dramatic works." Ref Sources for Small & Medium-sized Libr. 5th edition

Roses, Lorraine Elena, 1943-
Harlem Renaissance and beyond: literary biographies of 100 black women writers, 1900-1945; [by] Lorraine Elena Roses, Ruth Elizabeth Randolph. Hall, G.K. & Co. 1989 413p il $45 **920.003**

1. Black authors—Dictionaries 2. Women authors—Dictionaries 3. American literature—Black authors—Bio-bibliography
ISBN 0-8161-8926-9   LC 89-38731

"Included are the major figures, such as Zora Neale Hurston, as well as many writers who have published only two or three pieces but whose work deserves attention. These short sketches, augmented by bibliographical listings and critical commentary, should provide the impetus for further interest and investigation into long-neglected works. A valuable reference tool." Libr J

Twentieth century authors; a biographical dictionary of modern literature; edited by Stanley J. Kunitz and Howard Haycraft. Wilson, H.W. 1942 1577p il (Authors ser) $92   **920.003**

1. Authors—Dictionaries   2. Literature—Bio-bibliography
ISBN 0-8242-0049-7

First supplement published 1955 available for $82 (ISBN 0-8242-0050-0). Continued by: World authors, 1950-1970, entered below

"Complete in one volume with 1850 biographies and 1700 portraits." Title page

"Covers authors throughout the world whose works have been published in English. The main volume contains 1850 sketches. The supplement includes an additional 700 authors and updates sketches for most of the authors in the main volume." Ref Sources for Small & Medium-sized Libr. 5th edition

Waldman, Carl
Who was who in Native American history; Indians and non-Indians from early contacts through 1900. Facts on File 1989 410p il $45   **920.003**

1. Indians of North America—Biography—Dictionaries
ISBN 0-8160-1797-2   LC 89-35088

"Approximately 1,000 brief biographical sketches are provided for Indians and non-Indians; coverage is split evenly between the two groups. There is no index, but cross-references are used throughout the descriptions. The appendix contains a listing of Native Americans by tribes and a listing of non-Indians by major categories." Booklist

Who was who in world exploration; [by] Carl Waldman and Alan Wexler. Facts on File 1992 712p il maps $65   **920.003**

1. Explorers—Dictionaries
ISBN 0-8160-2172-4   LC 91-21277

This work "includes information on more than 800 explorers from ancient times up to the 20th century. Each entry begins with a chronology of an explorer's accomplishments and concludes with a discussion of his or her place in world exploration. . . . Two excellent appendixes and an extensive bibliography enhance the usefulness of this essential reference work for public/academic libraries." Libr J

Webster's American biographies; Charles Van Doren, editor; Robert McHenry, associate editor. Merriam-Webster 1984 1233p $21.95   **920.003**

1. United States—Biography—Dictionaries
ISBN 0-87779-253-4   LC 83-26706

First published 1974

"Entries range from paragraph to column in length and include persons both living and dead. Subjects chosen by their likelihood to be looked up. Includes geographical index." Ref Sources for Small & Medium-sized Libr. 5th edition

Webster's new biographical dictionary. Merriam-Webster $24.95   **920.003**

1. Biography—Dictionaries

Replaces Webster's biographical dictionary

"Brief biographies of more than 30,000 figures from ancient times to the present. Pronunciation, dates, and chief contribution to civilization are given. Valuable for ready reference." Ref Sources for Small & Medium-sized Libr. 5th edition

Who was who; a companion to Who's who. St. Martin's Press 1920-1992 8v ea $99.95   **920.003**

1. Great Britain—Biography—Dictionaries

A cumulated index to volumes 1-8 is available for $99.95 (ISBN 0-312-06817-4)

Contents: v1 1897-1915 (ISBN 0-312-87570-3); v2 1916-1928 (ISBN 0-312-87605-X); v3 1929-1940 (ISBN 0-312-87640-8); v4 1941-1950 (ISBN 0-312-87675-0); v5 1951-1960 (ISBN 0-312-87710-2); v6 1961-1970 (ISBN 0-312-87745-5); v7 1971-1980 (ISBN 0-312-87746-3); v8 1981-1990 (ISBN 0-312-06818-2)

"For the most part the original sketches as they last appeared in 'Who's who' [entered below] are reprinted with the date of death added, but in a few instances additional information has been incorporated." Sheehy. Guide to Ref Books. 10th edition

Who was who in America; a companion biographical reference work to Who's who in America. Marquis Who's Who 1942-1993 10v + 2 supplementary volumes [index volume and historical volume] set $767.50   **920.003**

1. United States—Biography—Dictionaries

Also available on CD-ROM

Contents: v1 1897-1942; v2 1943-1950; v3 1951-1960; v4 1961-1968; v5 1969-1973; v6 1974-1976; v7 1977-1981; v8 1982-1985; v9 1985-1989; v10 1989-1993

"This set includes . . . listings for persons who were once included in *Who's who in America*, but are no longer (owing to death or other reasons, such as fall from prominence). Can be useful for identifying historical personages." Ref Sources for Small & Medium-sized Libr. 5th edition

Who was who in the Greek world, 776 BC-30 BC; edited by Diana Bowder. Cornell Univ. Press 1982 227p il maps $39.95   **920.003**

1. Greece—Biography—Dictionaries 2. Greece—History
ISBN 0-8014-1538-1   LC 82-71594

Companion volume to Who was who in the Roman world, 753 BC-AD 476 (1980)

"A Phaidon book"

"More than 750 entries, arranged alphabetically, give brief but readable biographical data about notable Greeks (and non-Greeks important in Greek history). . . . Specialized, but a worthwhile addition to the reference shelf." Booklist

Who's who; an annual biographical dictionary. St. Martin's Press $185   **920.003**

1. Great Britain—Biography—Dictionaries
ISSN 0083-937X

"The pioneer work of the who's who type and still one of the most important. Until 1897, it was the handbook of titled and official classes and included lists of names rather than biographical sketches. . . . It is principally British, but a few prominent names of other nationalities are included. Biographies are reliable and fairly detailed; they give main facts, addresses, and in

Who's who—_Continued_
case of authors, lists of works." Sheehy. Guide to Ref Books. 10th edition

Who's who among black Americans. Gale Res. $115   920.003
1. Blacks—Biography—Dictionaries
ISSN 0362-5753

First published 1976 by Educational Communications. Biennial schedule after 5th edition

"Short entries focusing on career achievements and positions. Indexes list entries by place of birth and profession." N Y Public Libr Book of How & Where to Look It Up

Who's who in America. Marquis Who's Who 3v $429.95   920.003
1. United States—Biography—Dictionaries
ISSN 0083-9396

Also available on CD-ROM

Biennial. First published 1899. Kept up to date between editions by a supplement, beginning with 1987-1988 edition

"The standard dictionary of contemporary biography, containing concise biographical data, prepared according to established practices, with addresses and, in the case of authors, lists of works. . . . Each edition is thoroughly revised, new biographies added, and others dropped. For names of persons dropped because of death, see 'Who was who' [entered above]." Sheehy. Guide to Ref Books. 10th edition

Who's who in American politics. Bowker 2v set $225   920.003
1. Politicians—United States—Dictionaries
ISSN 0000-0205

Biennial. First published 1967

"Biographical directory of political leaders in the Congress, the executive branch of the federal government, state legislatures, state executive branches, mayors of cities with populations over 50,000, national and state party chairs, national party committee members, county chairs, and state supreme court justices. Entries are arranged by state, then alphabetically by name. Indexed by name." Ref Sources for Small & Medium-sized Libr. 5th edition

Who's who in finance and industry. Marquis Who's Who $250   920.003
1. Business—Biography—Dictionaries
ISSN 0083-9523

Also available on CD-ROM

Biennial. First published 1936 with title: Who's who in commerce and industry

"Gives international coverage of businessmen. Includes index of firms with references to personnel for whom sketches are included." Sheehy. Guide to Ref Books. 10th edition

Who's who in the world. Marquis Who's Who $319   920.003
1. Biography—Dictionaries
ISSN 0083-9825

Also available on CD-ROM

Biennial. First published for 1971/1972

"About 25,000 biographies in the first edition, representing some 150 countries; the number of entries has increased significantly in later editions. . . . Invites comparison with the 'International who's who' [listed above] and includes many of the same names, though each work includes some that the other does not." Sheehy. Guide to Ref Books. 10th edition

Who's who of American women. Marquis Who's Who $225   920.003
1. Women—United States—Biography   2. United States—Biography—Dictionaries
ISSN 0083-9841

Also available on CD-ROM

Biennial. First published for 1958/1959

"Includes short biographies in the standard Marquis format of . . . American women who are currently prominent in various professions and government." Ref Sources for Small & Medium-sized Libr. 5th edition

World authors, 1950-1970; a companion volume to Twentieth century authors; edited by John Wakeman; editorial consultant: Stanley J. Kunitz. Wilson, H.W. 1975 1594p il (Authors ser) $95   920.003
1. Authors—Dictionaries   2. Literature—Biobibliography
ISBN 0-8242-0419-0

This volume includes 959 "authors who came into prominence between 1950 and 1970. . . . Authors were chosen for literary importance or outstanding popularity." Wilson Libr Bull

World authors, 1970-1975; editor, John Wakeman; editorial consultant, Stanley J. Kunitz. Wilson, H.W. 1980 894p il (Authors ser) $80   920.003
1. Authors—Dictionaries   2. Literature—Biobibliography
ISBN 0-8242-0641-X   LC 79-21874

This volume provides biographical or autobiographical sketches for 348 of the most influential and popular men and women of letters who have come into prominence between 1970 and 1975

World authors, 1975-1980; editor, Vineta Colby. Wilson, H.W. 1985 829 il (Authors ser) $80   920.003
1. Authors—Dictionaries   2. Literature—Biobibliography
ISBN 0-8242-0715-7   LC 85-10045

This work profiles the lives and works of 379 writers

World authors, 1980-1985; editor, Vineta Colby. Wilson, H.W. 1990 938p il (Authors ser) $82   920.003
1. Authors—Dictionaries   2. Literature—Biobibliography
ISBN 0-8242-0797-1   LC 90-49782

This volume covers 320 contemporary writers

World explorers and discoverers; editor, Richard E. Bohlander; consultants, John L. Allen [et al.] Macmillan 1991 531p il maps $85   920.003
1. Explorers—Dictionaries
ISBN 0-02-897445-X   LC 91-23156

"Over 300 explorers and discoverers are featured in this attractive compilation that covers exploration from ancient times to the present and includes such notable moderns as Jacques Cousteau and Edmund Hillary." Am Libr

92 Individual biography

Lives of artists and musicians will be found in this catalog in class 709.2 and 780.92 respectively

Aaron, Hank, 1934-
Aaron, Hank. I had a hammer: the Hank Aaron story; [by] Henry Aaron with Lonnie Wheeler. HarperCollins Pubs. 1991 333p il $21.95; pa $5.50   **92**
 ISBN 0-06-016321-6; 0-06-109956-2 (pa)
                                        LC 90-55521
This biography traces "Aaron's incredible career— which saw him, from 1954 to 1976, break Babe Ruth's all-time home run record, win the Most Valuable Player Award, and appear in many All-Star games, two World Series, and one League Championship Series." Booklist

Abdul-Jabbar, Kareem, 1947-
Abdul-Jabbar, Kareem. Kareem; [by] Kareem Abdul-Jabbar with Mignon McCarthy. Random House 1990 233p il $18.95   **92**
 1. Los Angeles Lakers (Basketball team)
 ISBN 0-394-55927-4   LC 89-28067
Also available in paperback for Warner Bks.
In addition to reviewing his playing days basketball superstar Abdul-Jabbar also examines the role of the black athlete in society
"This pleasant memoir by the man many believe to be basketball's greatest player will be welcomed by his fans." Booklist

Abernathy, Ralph D.
Abernathy, Ralph D. And the walls came tumbling down; an autobiography; [by] Ralph David Abernathy. Harper & Row 1989 638p il hardcover o.p. paperback available $12.95   **92**
 1. Blacks—Civil rights
 ISBN 0-06-091986-8 (pa)   LC 89-45023
"Abernathy's autobiography . . . documents the conditions of growing up as a black person in the South in the 1930s and 1940s; . . . [it is also] an account of the civil rights crusade of the 1960s and 1970s." Booklist
"Readers interested primarily in factual accuracy should look elsewhere, but when Mr. Abernathy sticks to accounts of his own direct involvement, his storytelling is gripping, even moving." N Y Times Book Rev

Acheson, Dean, 1893-1971
Brinkley, Douglas. Dean Acheson; the Cold War years, 1953-71. Yale Univ. Press 1992 429p il $35   **92**
 1. United States—Foreign relations
 ISBN 0-300-04773-8   LC 91-48188
This account of Acheson's life after retiring as Truman's secretary of state considers his role in "NATO-related debates and task forces, the Berlin and Cuban missile crises, Vietnam War decision-making, the Cyprus dispute of 1964, the anti-de Gaulle initiative of the 1960s, and U.S.-African policy." Publisher's note

"What Brinkley has done, by focusing on the phase of Acheson's life when his native conservatism was most outspokenly revealed, is to highlight the reckless perversity of the charges laid against him by his enemies, and so to restore to him the reputation he does deserve, as the grandmaster of the anti-Communist grand alliance." New Repub
Includes bibliographic references

Adams, Ansel. See class 709.2

Adams, Henry, 1838-1918
Adams, Henry. The education of Henry Adams   **92**
Hardcover and paperback editions available from various publishers
First published in a popular edition 1918
"Henry Adams was the son of Charles Francis Adams, U.S. Minister to Britain during the Civil War, and a grandson of John Quincy Adams. His 'education' consists of everything that happened to him or about him from his birth to his death." St Louis Public Libr
"Not a complete autobiography, the book omits any mention of the thirteen years of Adams's marriage and the seven years following his wife's suicide. It does, however, present a vivid picture of the people and places the author knew." Reader's Ency. 3d edition

Adler, Richard. See class 780.92

Alexandra, Empress, consort of Nicholas II, Emperor of Russia, 1872-1918
Massie, Robert K. Nicholas and Alexandra. See entry under Nicholas II, Emperor of Russia, 1868-1918   **92**

Alfred, the Great, King of England, 849-899
Duckett, Eleanor Shipley. Alfred the Great. University of Chicago Press 1956 220p hardcover o.p. paperback available. $8.95
                                          92
 1. Great Britain—History—0-1066
 ISBN 0-226-16779-8 (pa)
"The life of Alfred the Great set against the social and political background of ninth-century England. King Alfred's accomplishments as soldier, ruler, translator, and author show him to be a many-sided man who, despite his prowess on the battlefield, loved the serenity and the solitude of the scholarly life." Booklist

Algren, Nelson, 1909-1981
Drew, Bettina. Nelson Algren; a life on the wild side. Putnam 1989 416p il o.p.; University of Tex. Press paperback available $16.95   **92**
 ISBN 0-292-75543-0 (pa)   LC 89-10299
This "presentation of the life and career of the Chicago writer most widely known for his 1949 novel, *The Man with the Golden Arm*, and his celebrated romance with Simone de Beauvoir, is fluidly narrated, closely detailed, and warmly sympathetic. Without glossing over Algren's severe character flaws . . . Drew portrays Algren as a kind of populist of the demimonde."

Algren, Nelson, 1909-1981—*Continued*
Libr J
Includes bibliography

Ali, Muhammad, 1942-
Hauser, Thomas. Muhammad Ali; his life and times. Simon & Schuster 1991 544p il hardcover o.p. paperback available $14   92
ISBN 0-671-77971-0 (pa)   LC 91-10395
In this biography the author quotes the recollections of more than 200 acquaintances, friends, enemies, associates, relations, opponents, and observers of the American boxer
Includes bibliographic references

Allen, Gracie, 1906?-1964
Burns, George. Gracie, a love story. Putnam 1988 319p il o.p.; New Am. Lib. paperback available $4.95   92
ISBN 0-451-16886-0 (pa)   LC 88-23904
Also available G.K. Hall large print edition
"This is a tribute to Gracie Allen, Burns's wife and partner, and the story of their life together, from vaudeville through early radio and television." Libr J
"Candid, witty, touching, this memoir is more than the usual show-biz bio. As the chronicle of an entertainer's love affair, it is all the more special because the love still continues." Booklist

Alvarez, Everett, 1937-
Alvarez, Everett. Chained eagle; by Everett Alvarez, Jr. and Anthony S. Pitch. Fine, D.I. 1989 308p il $18.95   92
1. Vietnam War, 1961-1975—Personal narratives
2. Prisoners of war, American
ISBN 1-55611-167-3   LC 89-45547
Also available in paperback from Dell
"Shot down during the Gulf of Tonkin incident in 1964, Alvarez survived more than eight years of brutal treatment by the North Vietnamese, then faced the challenge, which he seems to have met effectively, of rebuilding his career and personal life." Booklist
"Told in a controlled and quiet tone, this story grips the reader in a way no sensational telling could." Libr J

Anderson, Laurie, 1947-
Howell, John. Laurie Anderson; with photos by f-Stop Fitzgerald. Thunder's Mouth Press 1992 150p il (American originals) pa $11.95   92
ISBN 1-56025-029-1   LC 92-10434
This book presents an essay on Anderson's career, an interview with the performance artist/visual artist/rock musician/composer, a chronological list of her works in various media, and many photographs

Angelou, Maya
Angelou, Maya. All God's children need traveling shoes. Random House 1986 210p $15.95; pa $9   92
ISBN 0-394-52143-9; 0-679-73404-X (pa)
                    LC 85-19351
In the fifth "of Angelou's series of memoirs, the author describes her attempt with other black expatriates to find a home in Ghana in the 1960s." Booklist

Angelou, Maya. Conversations with Maya Angelou; edited by Jeffrey M. Elliot. University Press of Miss. 1989 246p (Literary conversations ser) $32.50; pa $14.95   92
ISBN 0-87805-361-1; 0-87805-362-X (pa)
                    LC 88-37291
A compilation of interviews with the poet/memoirist

Angelou, Maya. Gather together in my name. Random House 1974 214p $22   92
ISBN 0-394-48692-7
Also available in paperback from Bantam Bks.
Second autobiographical volume "begins when the author, still in her teens, has given birth to a son, and continues through the time when she goes to work as a prostitute." Publisher's note

Angelou, Maya. The heart of a woman. Random House 1981 272p $24.95   92
ISBN 0-394-51273-1   LC 81-40232
Also available in paperback from Bantam Bks.
The "fourth autobiographical installment . . . covers the years 1957 to the early 60s, conjuring some of the issues and the excitement of the Civil Rights Movement." SLJ

Angelou, Maya. I know why the caged bird sings. Random House 1970 c1969 281p $21   92
ISBN 0-394-42986-9
Also available in paperback from Bantam Bks.
The first volume in the author's autobiographical series covers her childhood and adolescence in rural Arkansas, St. Louis, and San Francisco
"Angelou is a skillful writer; her language ranges from beautifully lyrical prose to earthy metaphor, and her descriptions have power and sensitivity." Libr J

Angelou, Maya. Singin' and swingin' and gettin' merry like Christmas. Random House 1976 269p $19.95   92
ISBN 0-394-40545-5
Also available in paperback from Bantam Bks.
"The third installment of Angelou's moving autobiography covers her brief marriage and early struggles to get a foothold in show business. . . . As in her previous books . . . Angelou's writing exudes black pride and upbeat courage in the face of countless setbacks." Booklist

Angleton, James

Mangold, Thomas. Cold warrior: James Jesus Angleton; the CIA's master spy hunter; [by] Tom Mangold. Simon & Schuster 1991 462p il $24.95; pa $13 **92**

1. United States. Central Intelligence Agency

ISBN 0-671-66273-2; 0-671-77880-3 (pa)

LC 91-15084

This is a biography of the Central Intelligence Agency's former chief of counterintelligence. Having served the C.I.A. "for 20 years until his dismissal in 1974, Angleton is best known for his decade-long hunt for K.G.B. moles." N Y Times Book Rev

"Based on exhaustive research, Mangold's fascinating account argues persuasively that Angleton did more to damage U.S. intelligence than all the Soviet spies put together." Libr J

Includes bibliographic references

Anthony, Susan B., 1820-1906

Barry, Kathleen. Susan B. Anthony: a biography of a singular feminist. New York Univ. Press 1988 426p il $35 **92**

ISBN 0-8147-1105-7   LC 88-1228

Also available in paperback from Ballantine Bks.

The author explores "the 'subjectivity' of Anthony and the transformation of her political consciousness. . . . Although the text occasionally suffers from polemics, adulation, and novelistic twists, Barry is to be praised for her prodigious research and for her success in placing Anthony, as a major historical actor, in her own social-historical milieu." Choice

Includes bibliography

Arbus, Diane. See class 709.2

Armstrong, Louis. See class 780.92

Arnaz, Desi, 1917-1986

Harris, Warren G. Lucy & Desi. See entry under Ball, Lucille, 1911-1989 **92**

Bach, Johann Sebastian. See class 780.92

Bailey, Pearl. See class 780.92

Baker, Josephine, 1906-1975

Rose, Phyllis. Jazz Cleopatra: Josephine Baker in her time. Doubleday 1989 321p il $22.50 **92**

ISBN 0-385-24891-1   LC 88-35585

Also available in paperback from Vintage Bks.

The author "traces Baker's life from her impoverished childhood in St. Louis on through to her theatrical successes in a series of Parisian revues. The book also investigates Baker's later activities in various civil rights and humanitarian causes." Booklist

"Not simply the story of a complex and influential woman, this indispensable biography treats in full the two cultures—American and Continental—that formed Baker, and sets a new standard for critical studies of performing artists." Publ Wkly

Includes bibliography

Baker, Russell, 1925-

Baker, Russell. The good times. Morrow 1989 351p il $19.95 **92**

ISBN 0-688-06170-2   LC 89-46

Also available G.K. Hall large print edition and in paperback from New Am. Lib.

"A Thomas Congdon book"

"This is a sequel to Baker's Pulitzer Prize-winning 'Growing up' [entered below]. Here, he recounts the mischances and lucky breaks that have guided his journalism career." Libr J

This "is a superb autobiography, wonderfully told, often hilarious, always intelligent and unsparing." N Y Times Book Rev

Baker, Russell. Growing up. Congdon & Weed 1982 278p il o.p.; New Am. Lib. paperback available $8.95 **92**

ISBN 0-452-25275-X (pa)   LC 82-12534

This book "recounts the first 24 years of [Baker's] life as the son of an independent and deep-rooted Virginian family. . . . Here is a modest book, a modest autobiographical story." Natl Rev

Baldwin, James, 1924-1987

Campbell, James. Talking at the gates: a life of James Baldwin. Viking 1991 306p il $21.95 **92**

ISBN 0-670-82913-7   LC 90-50744

Also available in paperback from Penguin Bks.

This biography "of the writer's life, explores the often vitriolic relationships between Baldwin and Langston Hughes, Richard Wright, Norman Mailer and other writers." N Y Times Book Rev

Includes bibliographic references

Weatherby, William J. James Baldwin: artist on fire; a portrait; by W. J. Weatherby. Fine, D.I. 1989 412p il $19.95 **92**

ISBN 1-55611-126-6   LC 88-45852

Also available in paperback from Dell

"Drawing on many interviews and various published and unpublished sources, Weatherby functions as reporter and interrogator rather than as analytical biographer. The resulting portrait of Baldwin is a decidedly personal document that captures the many facets of the man's personality and the love and convictions that filled his life." Booklist

Ball, Lucille, 1911-1989

Harris, Warren G. Lucy & Desi; the legendary love story of television's most famous couple. Simon & Schuster 1991 351p il o.p. **92**

1. Arnaz, Desi, 1917-1986   LC 91-19840

Available only in a large print edition from Thorndike Press

The author describes the personal and professional lives of the couple who created the popular TV series "I love Lucy"

"What sets this bio apart from run-of-the-mill Hollywood fare is Harris' lively prose. . . . Harris displays style and a sense of humor. Though never blind to his subjects' many foibles, he also shows genuine affection for them as people." Booklist

Baraka, Imamu Amiri, 1934-
Baraka, Imamu Amiri. The autobiography of LeRoi Jones/Amiri Baraka. Freundlich Bks. 1984 329p $16.95 **92**

ISBN 0-88191-000-7   LC 83-20576

An "account of a talented black writer's quest for meaning and identity, from diaper days through 40th birthday (1974)." Libr J

"The impressions, justifications, motivations, and expectations that Jones/Baraka is able to articulate here reveal a brilliance and earnestness about art and blackness beneath his notorious stridency. . . . In addition, the account is leavened by a surprising sense of humor." Booklist

Barenboim, Daniel. See class 780.92

Barkley, Charles
Barkley, Charles. Outrageous! the fine life and flagrant good times of basketball's irresistible force; [by] Charles Barkley and Roy S. Johnson. Simon & Schuster 1992 315p il $20 **92**

ISBN 0-671-73799-6   LC 91-40301

Also available in paperback from Avon Bks.

This is an autobiography of the basketball star

"Basketball fans will relish Barkley's critiques of players, his insider's view of the NBA life-style, and his self-deprecating wit." Booklist

Barnum, P. T. (Phineas Taylor), 1810-1891
Saxon, A. H. P.T. Barnum: the legend and the man. Columbia Univ. Press 1989 437p il $32.95 **92**

ISBN 0-231-05686-9   LC 89-982

"Working primarily from Barnum's letters, business papers, family members' and associates' diaries, and legal documents, Saxon has pieced together a picture of the legendary circus owner. Saxon's detailed coverage of Barnum's life . . . is rich with anecdotes yet scholarly enough to please any researcher. Saxon succeeds admirably in capturing the essence of Barnum." Booklist

Includes bibliography

Basie, Count. See class 780.92

Beach, Sylvia
Fitch, Noel Riley. Sylvia Beach and the lost generation; a history of literary Paris in the twenties and thirties. Norton 1983 447p il $25; pa $14.95 **92**

1. Paris (France)—Intellectual life
ISBN 0-393-01713-3; 0-393-30231-8 (pa)
LC 82-24621

"Sylvia Beach earned her place in modern literary history by publishing Ulysses in 1922. Her bookshop and lending library, Shakespeare and Company, was a center for the literary avant-garde in Paris in the 1920's and 30's. . . . The book focuses on Beach's . . . friend Adrienne Monnier, the career of Joyce, and the daily workings of the bookshop." Libr J

Includes bibliographic references

Beaton, Cecil. See class 709.2

Beauvoir, Simone de, 1908-1986
Bair, Deirdre. Simone de Beauvoir; a biography. Summit Bks. 1990 718p il hardcover o.p. paperback available $14.95 **92**

ISBN 0-671-74180-2 (pa)   LC 89-22029

"Bair's biography of the French author, philosopher, and feminist aims to restore the balance between interest in de Beauvoir's personal life—as the lifelong companion of Jean-Paul Sartre and sometime lover of Nelson Algren—and the question of her achievements as a writer and thinker." Booklist

Includes bibliographic references

Francis, Claude. Simone de Beauvoir; a life, a love story; by Claude Francis and Fernande Gontier; translated from the French by Lisa Nesselson. St. Martin's Press 1987 412p il hardcover o.p. paperback available $12.95 **92**

1. Sartre, Jean Paul, 1905-1980
ISBN 0-312-02324-3 (pa)   LC 86-27908

Original French edition, 1985

"Drawing on interviews with de Beauvoir before her death in 1986 and other sources, the authors have unearthed some family skeletons. . . . The authors also tracked down hundreds of unpublished letters between the celebrated feminist and writer Nelson Algren. . . . At the core of this biography is de Beauvoir's 'revolutionary romance' with Jean-Paul Sartre." Publ Wkly

"This is a lucid, appealingly human account of the life of the French feminist." N Y Times Book Rev

Includes bibliography

Beethoven, Ludwig van. See class 780.92

Begin, Menachem, 1913-1992
Perlmutter, Amos. The life and times of Menachem Begin. Doubleday 1987 444p il $21.95 **92**

1. Israel—Politics and government
ISBN 0-385-18926-5   LC 86-19745

The author seeks to "trace Begin from his early days in Poland to his last days as prime minister of Israel." Libr J

This is "an interesting, breathless study of Menachem Begin that is rich in information that will be new to most American readers. It is intended as a political biography, not a personal one." N Y Times Book Rev

Includes bibliography

Bell, Vanessa, 1879-1961
Dunn, Jane. A very close conspiracy: Vanessa Bell and Virginia Woolf. See entry under Woolf, Virginia, 1882-1941   **92**

Bellow, Saul
Miller, Ruth. Saul Bellow; a biography of the imagination. St. Martin's Press 1991 xxiii, 385p il $24.95   **92**

ISBN 0-312-03927-1   LC 89-28983

This is an "account of just how Bellow's personal life has influenced the literary world of his novels and stories." Booklist

"What distinguishes this book is Miller's point of view. Using her journal entries to record countless informal conversations, she peppers her unique account with personal vignettes of Bellow. . . . Her high regard of her subject is never hidden." Libr J

Includes bibliographic references

Belushi, John, 1949-1982
Woodward, Bob. Wired: the short life and fast times of John Belushi. Simon & Schuster 1984 461p il hardcover o.p. paperback available $5.99   **92**

ISBN 0-671-64077-1 (pa)   LC 84-5334

A biography of the late comedian who rose to fame on television's Saturday Night Live and went on to appear in the films Animal house and The Blues Brothers

"Woodward conducted extensive interviews, read Jacklin's [Belushi's wife] diaries, and put together the facts: an excellent who, what, and where of Belushi. Unfortunately, he left out the why—the soul of the man." Libr J

Includes bibliographic references

Ben-Gurion, David, 1886-1973
Teveth, Shabtai. Ben-Gurion; the burning ground, 1886-1948. Houghton Mifflin 1987 967p il hardcover o.p. paperback available $12.95   **92**

1. Zionism
ISBN 0-395-48358-1 (pa)   LC 86-27485

"Ben-Gurion, Israel's first prime minister, spent 66 years of his life in politics. . . . This biography, which ends with the founding of the state of Israel, covers the political events and Zionist fervor that formed Ben-Gurion's personality and goals." Booklist

"There is many a detailed page, but never a dull one. Politics are interwoven with innumerable personal vignettes." N Y Times Book Rev

Includes bibliography

Benga, Ota, d. 1914?
Bradford, Phillips Verner. Ota Benga; the pygmy in the zoo; [by] Phillips Verner Bradford & Harvey Blume. St. Martin's Press 1992 xxi, 281p il $22.95   **92**

1. Pygmies
ISBN 0-312-08276-2   LC 92-22296

"In 1904, white missionary Samuel Phillips Verner (grandfather of the author) brought eight Congolese pygmies, including Ota Benga, out of Kasailand in Africa in order to exhibit them for the anthropology department at the St. Louis World's Fair. Then in 1906, Ota was placed on display with an orangutan in a primate house cage at the Bronx Zoo. . . . Ten years later, Ota committed suicide in Lynchberg, Virginia. This fascinating book is a tragic glimpse at financial greed, human exploitation, religious arrogance, scientific abuse . . . and, especially unfounded racism." Libr J

Benjamin, Judah Philip, 1811-1884
Evans, Eli N. Judah P. Benjamin, the Jewish Confederate. Free Press 1988 xxi, 469p il $27.95; pa $12.95   **92**

ISBN 0-02-908880-1; 0-02-909911-0 (pa)

LC 87-19256

"Judah Benjamin served in the Confederate cabinet as secretary of state and of war, as well as attorney general; he sat at President Jefferson Davis' right hand. But, as he wished it, little information about him exists in the history books. Evans rectifies the situation and does it well. . . . Evans places particular focus on the nature of that relationship with Jefferson Davis, as well as on Benjamin's sense of himself as a Jew in the nineteenth-century South." Booklist

Includes bibliography

Benny, Jack, 1894-1974
Benny, Jack. Sunday nights at seven; the Jack Benny story; by Jack Benny and his daughter Joan; with a foreword by George Burns. Warner Bks. 1990 302p il $19.95; pa $8.99   **92**

ISBN 0-446-51546-9; 0-446-39321-5 (pa)

LC 90-50286

Also available G.K. Hall large print edition

This book consists of parts of an unpublished autobiography the comedian wrote in the late 1960s, interspersed with reminiscences and commentary by Joan Benny

"Whenever the words are Jack Benny's, which is about half the time . . . [this] is a delightful book. His passages may be a bit short on depth and on details of his personal life, but they are long on warmth and wit." N Y Times Book Rev

Benton, Thomas Hart. See class 709.2

Berenson, Bernard. See class 709.2

Bergman, Ingmar, 1918-
Bergman, Ingmar. The magic lantern; an autobiography; translated from Swedish by Joan Tate. Viking 1988 308p il o.p.; Penguin Bks. paperback available $10.95   **92**

ISBN 0-14-010469-0 (pa)   LC 87-40659
Original Swedish edition, 1987

"As a filmmaker, Bergman stands alone among postwar artists in his relentless dissection of the human soul's dark side. . . . This autobiography although naturally of great interest, proffers a mixed blessing. . . . What Bergman does relate, particularly his tangled relationships with his parents, is not only illuminating but quite moving. No 'tell-all' book this one, but revealing in ways that much longer and allegedly 'franker' books are not." Libr J

Bergman, Ingrid, 1915-1982

Bergman, Ingrid. Ingrid Bergman, my story; by Ingrid Bergman and Alan Burgess. Delacorte Press 1980 504p il hardcover o.p. paperback available $4.95   **92**

   ISBN 0-440-14086-2 (pa)   LC 80-15420

"In essence, this is a very long monologue by Bergman about her emotional life, with factual continuity and interviews with others by Alan Burgess. . . . This 'double' narrative, awkward at first, finally enhances the book's extraordinary authority and immediacy. . . . It is filled with the compelling romance and suspense of some of Bergman's best films." Best Sellers

Berlin, Irving. See class 780.92

Berlioz, Hector. See class 780.92

Bernhardt, Sarah, 1844-1923

Gold, Arthur. The Divine Sarah: a life of Sarah Bernhardt; [by] Arthur Gold, Robert Fizdale. Knopf 1991 351p il $30; pa $17   **92**

   ISBN 0-394-52879-4; 0-679-74185-2 (pa)
                  LC 89-45361

This biography details "Bernhardt's triumphs and tragedies, her political passions (she supported Dreyfus and America's entry into WW I), her countless love affairs and frustrating quest for sexual fulfillment, her paradoxical neglect of the illegitimate son she adored." Publ Wkly

"So well written is this novel-like biography that even those unfamiliar with Bernhardt or her body of work will find the book an irresistibly good read." Booklist

   Includes bibliography

Bernstein, Carl

Bernstein, Carl. Loyalties; a son's memoir. Simon & Schuster 1989 262p hardcover o.p. paperback available $8.95   **92**

   1. Bernstein, Alfred 2. Bernstein, Sylvia
   ISBN 0-671-69598-3 (pa)   LC 88-36655

The author recalls his childhood in a progressive Washington Jewish family during the McCarthy era. Both of his parents invoked the Fifth Amendment when asked about their membership in the Communist Party. Bernstein seeks the truth about his parents' political commitment and its meaning for their lives and his relationship to them

"The book fairly crackles with emotional intensity and unsettling historical questions. With his rich depiction of his parents and pungent evocation of the period, Bernstein has been able to explore his controversial issues with the finesse of a jazz musician." Time

Bernstein, Leonard. See class 780.92

Billy, the Kid

Utley, Robert Marshall. Billy the Kid; a short and violent life; [by] Robert M. Utley. University of Neb. Press 1989 302p il $30; pa $10.95   **92**

   ISBN 0-8032-4553-X; 0-8032-9558-8 (pa)
                  LC 89-30022

Examines the career of the young outlaw whose life and death were an expression of the violence prevalent on the American frontier

"Robert M. Utley does what countless books, movies, television shows, musical compositions, and paintings have failed to do: he successfully strips off the veneer of legendry to expose the reality of Billy the Kid." Univ Press Books for Public Libr

   Includes bibliography

Bird, Larry

Bird, Larry. Drive: the story of my life; by Larry Bird with Bob Ryan; foreword by Magic Johnson. Doubleday 1989 259p il $18.95   **92**

   ISBN 0-385-24921-7   LC 89-37228

Also available in paperback from Bantam Bks.

"Presented as a memoir about 'overcoming obstacles,' the discussions of the events that shaped Bird's life, including his parents' divorce and father's suicide . . . serve as mere asides to innocuous, though entertaining basketball anecdotes." Publ Wkly

Bismarck, Otto, Fürst von, 1815-1898

Crankshaw, Edward. Bismarck. Viking 1981 451p il maps o.p.; Penguin Bks. paperback available $10.95   **92**

   1. Germany—Politics and government—1818-1866
   2. Germany—Politics and government—1866-1918
   ISBN 0-14-006344-7 (pa)   LC 80-29171

"In this scrupulously detailed, eloquently written biography, the 19th-century master of Realpolitik emerges as a peculiarly fascinating kind of scoundrel. . . . This is not only a distinguished biography, but also a somber meditation on how easily people are seduced into worshiping naked power." Saturday Rev

   Includes bibliography

Black, Shirley Temple, 1928-

Black, Shirley Temple. Child star: an autobiography. McGraw-Hill 1988 546p il o.p.; Warner Bks. paperback available $5.95   **92**

   ISBN 0-446-35792-8 (pa)   LC 88-23286

"Shirley Temple, the archetypal child star, tells what it was like to be a national phenomenon at an age when most kids have barely started school. . . . Temple's prose can be weighty . . . but once readers come to grips with the labyrinthine sentences, they will enjoy the look at Shirley's remarkable life, from 'Good Ship Lollypop' days to marriage and her second career as a diplomat." Booklist

Black Elk, 1863-1950

Black Elk. Black Elk speaks; being the life story of a holy man of the Oglala Sioux; as told through John G. Neihardt (Flaming Rainbow); introduction by Vine Deloria, Jr.; illustrated with drawings by Standing Bear and a portfolio of photographs. University of Neb. Press 1979 299p il $25; pa $9.95
92

1. Oglala Indians
ISBN 0-8032-3301-9; 0-8032-8359-8 (pa)
LC 79-12367
A reprint of the title first published 1932 by Morrow

The Indian whose life story this is, was born in 1863. He was a famous warrior and hunter in his youth, and became a practicing medicine man among his people. Of him Neihardt says, "As an indubitable seer, he seemed to represent the consciousness of the Plains Indian more fully than any other I had ever known."

This "is about as near as you can get to seeing life and death, war and religion, through an Indian's eyes." Outlook

Bonner, Elena

Bonner, Elena. Alone together; translated from the Russian by Alexander Cook. Knopf 1986 269p il $17.95; pa $8.95
92
1. Sakharov, Andreï Dmitrievich, 1921-1989
ISBN 0-394-55835-9; 0-394-75538-3 (pa)
LC 86-82152
Also available G.K. Hall large print edition

The wife of the late Soviet civil rights advocate and Nobel Peace Prize laureate Andrei Sakharov tells of her trials at the hands of the KGB, her illnesses, her travels in the West, and her relationship with her husband

Bonner's memoir "is a very human story of love and trust between two people trapped in a hostile environment, of their refusal to succumb, and their determination to remain in charge of their own lives, if not of their immediate circumstance. At the same time we are given a most illuminating picture of Soviet life." Times Lit Suppl

Boone, Daniel, 1734-1820

Faragher, John Mack. Daniel Boone; the life and legend of an American pioneer. Holt & Co. 1992 429p il maps $27.50
92

ISBN 0-8050-1603-1
LC 92-21873
"The popular image of Daniel Boone is that of an unlettered backwoodsman, skilled hunter and Indian fighter. But evidence argues that he was reasonably well educated for his time and place, that he was a landowner, businessman and a respected leader of frontier society. Faragher . . . has sifted through folklore and fact to reconstruct a realistic portrait of Boone and the expanding frontier. . . . Faragher has written an absorbing, definitive biography." Publ Wkly

Includes bibliographic references

Bourke-White, Margaret. See class 709.2

Bradley, Omar Nelson, 1893-1981

Bradley, Omar Nelson. A general's life; an autobiography; by Omar N. Bradley and Clay Blair. Simon & Schuster 1983 752p il o.p.; TAB Bks. reprint available $19.95 92
ISBN 0-8306-3312-X
LC 82-19404
"Written in the first person by collaborator Blair and not completed until after Bradley's death (1981), this 'joint autobiography' is actually better described as a fluent and historically sound 'authorized' biography. . . . Blair's prose is readable . . . and his research impeccable." Libr J

Includes bibliographic references

Brady, James S.

Dickenson, Mollie. Thumbs up: the life and courageous comeback of White House press secretary Jim Brady. Morrow 1987 560p il $19.95
92
ISBN 0-688-06497-3
LC 87-17385
An "authorized biography of James Brady, President Reagan's likable press secretary who was wounded during the 1981 presidential assassination attempt by John Hinckley. At times, the book reads like a testimonial to Brady and his wife, Sarah; but for the most part it offers rounded, personal, sympathetic portraits." Libr J

Includes bibliographic references

Brahms, Johannes. See class 780.92

Braithwaite, E. R.

Braithwaite, E. R. To Sir, with love. Prentice-Hall 1960 c1959 o.p.
92
1. Great Britain—Race relations 2. London (England)—Social conditions 3. Teaching

Available only in paperback from Jove Publs.

First published 1959 in the United Kingdom

A "book about the problems and joys of a black teacher from British Guiana, teaching in a school for difficult teenagers in a white slum in London. Parts of the book deal with effects of the race problem. . . . But the author focuses on his attempts to win the respect of his students and to develop their own self-respect." Black Lit for High Sch Stud

Brancusi, Constantin. See class 709.2

Brandeis, Louis Dembitz, 1856-1941

Baker, Leonard. Brandeis and Frankfurter; a dual biography. Harper & Row 1984 567p il o.p.; New York Univ. Press paperback available $17.50
92
1. Frankfurter, Felix, 1882-1965 2. United States. Supreme Court
ISBN 0-8147-1086-7 (pa)
LC 83-48319
"The author "has drawn together the stories of Justices Brandeis and Frankfurter. He examines their working lives and interests and attempts to use similarities in their careers and their joint friendship as the basis for this book." Choice

Brandeis, Louis Dembitz, 1856-1941—*Continued*
"The book fully captures the personalities and fortunes of the two men as they set their individual and collective marks on society and on the history of their country." Booklist

Includes bibliography

Brando, Marlon, 1924-
Schickel, Richard. Brando; a life in our times. Atheneum Pubs. 1991 218p il $21.95
92
ISBN 0-689-12108-3   LC 91-9735
In this biography the author "provides the outlines of Brando's life, but his primary concern is the reason much of a generation idolized and identified with Brando." Libr J
"A remarkably perceptive, searching, and illuminating look at Brando the man and the performer, as well as his loyal audience." Booklist

Brice, Fanny, 1891-1951
Grossman, Barbara Wallace. Funny woman: the life and times of Fanny Brice. Indiana Univ. Press 1991 287p il $35; pa $12.95
92
ISBN 0-253-32653-2; 0-253-20762-2 (pa)
LC 90-39331
This biography of the American entertainer "offers not only a detailed chronology of Brice's four-decade career in the context of the times but perceptively analyzes her material and methods, providing vivid reconstructions of some of her more successful routines." Choice

Includes bibliographic references

Brickman, Arlyne
Carpenter, Teresa. Mob girl; a woman's life in the underworld. Simon & Schuster 1992 288p il $21
92
ISBN 0-671-68345-4   LC 91-43256
This is the biography of a woman involved with the Mafia in New York who turned informer
The author "has done a superb rendering of Brickman's story. She goes far beyond naming names and retelling events as she digs into Brickman's underlying motivations and vividly recreates Brickman's exhilaration over her triumphs and pain over her defeats in her pursuit of the mob girl lifestyle." Libr J

Includes bibliographic references

Brontë, Charlotte, 1816-1855
Gaskell, Elizabeth Cleghorn. The life of Charlotte Brontë; [by] Elizabeth C. Gaskell; with an introduction by Clement Shorter
92
Available in paperback from Penguin Bks.
First published 1857
"Mrs. Gaskell was herself a popular novelist, who commanded a very wide audience. She brought to bear upon the biography of Charlotte Brontë all those literary gifts which had made the charm of her seven volumes of romance . . . . It is quite certain that Charlotte Brontë would not stand on so splendid a pedestal today

but for the single-minded devotion of her accomplished biographer." Clement K. Shorter

Brooks, Louise, 1906-1985
Brooks, Louise. Lulu in Hollywood; introduction by William Shawn. Knopf 1982 109p il o.p.; Limelight Eds. paperback available $13.95
92
ISBN 0-87910-125-3 (pa)   LC 81-48108
"These seven discontinuous autobiographical essays, which Brooks wrote over many years time, vividly reincarnate the milieu of her stage and screen years and offer counterimages of several great contemporaries: Bogart, W. C. Fields, Lillian Gish, and Garbo. . . . Brooks' well-crafted observations reveal things about the undersides of revue-stage and silent-film industries that are rarely discussed." Booklist

Paris, Barry. Louise Brooks. Knopf 1989 609p il $24.95
92
ISBN 0-394-55923-1   LC 89-45540
Also available in paperback from Anchor Bks.
"Despite a brief career (24 films, only a handful of any merit), Louise Brooks led a life that is the stuff of Hollywood legend. . . . This is the first book-length portrait of Brooks, and Paris takes full advantage of cooperation from numerous sources as well as access to Brooks's papers." Libr J

Includes filmography and bibliographic references

Brown, Claude, 1937-
Brown, Claude. Manchild in the promised land. Macmillan 415p $55
92
ISBN 0-02-517325-1
Also available in paperback from New Am. Lib.
"Hudson River editions"
First published 1965
This is "the autobiography of a young black man raised in Harlem. [It is] a realistic description of life in the ghetto. . . . The core of the book concerns the 'plague' of heroin addiction that swept through Harlem in the 1950s taking the lives of many of Brown's contemporaries." Publ Wkly

Brown, James. See class 780.92

Browning, Elizabeth Barrett, 1806-1861
Forster, Margaret. Elizabeth Barrett Browning; a biography. Doubleday 1989 c1988 400p il $19.95
92
ISBN 0-385-24959-4   LC 88-25063
First published 1988 in the United Kingdom
This "biography offers arresting new information on Elizabeth Barrett Browning, her family and associates. . . . The book covers [her] 15-year marriage and Robert Browning's life with their son after his wife died in 1861. This biography is an invaluable addition to the record of the great Victorian romance." Publ Wkly

Includes bibliographic references

Broyard, Anatole

Broyard, Anatole. Intoxicated by my illness; and other writings on life and death; compiled and edited by Alexandra Broyard; foreword by Oliver Sacks. Potter 1992 135p $18   **92**

1. Cancer—Personal narratives
ISBN 0-517-58216-3   LC 91-43719

"In October 1990 the author, an editor at the *New York Times Book Review*, died of prostate cancer that had been diagnosed 14 months earlier. During that time he wrote the essays and journal entries that are printed, along with the autobiographical story 'What the Cystoscope Said' and earlier pieces on dying from the early 1980's, in this slim, affecting volume." Publ Wkly

Bryan, William Jennings, 1860-1925

Ashby, LeRoy. William Jennings Bryan; champion of democracy. Twayne Pubs. 1987 245p il (Twayne's twentieth-century American biography ser) $26.95; pa $12.95   **92**

1. United States—Politics and government
ISBN 0-8057-7760-1; 0-8057-7776-8 (pa) LC 87-8407

This biography of the politician, lecturer, and lawyer is "thoughtful and well-balanced. . . . For a generation who know Bryan only in terms of the Scopes trial, if at all, this biography is a richly deserved, lively rendering of an important American hero. It is highly readable and enjoyable." SLJ

Includes bibliography

Buber, Martin, 1878-1965

Friedman, Maurice S. Encounter on the narrow ridge: a life of Martin Buber; [by] Maurice Friedman. Paragon House 1991 496p il $31.95; pa $18.95   **92**
ISBN 1-55778-453-1; 1-55778-596-1 (pa)
LC 90-44502

This biography (based on the author's three volume Martin Buber's life and work) "traces Buber's career showing the pivotal events in his life as well as the influences of Judaism, Christianity, general philosophical thought, and linguistics on his writings and lectures. Friedman analyzes succinctly, but with great care, Buber's responses to the important events of the 20th century." Libr J

Includes bibliographic references

Buchanan, James M., 1919-

Buchanan, James M. Better than plowing and other personal essays. University of Chicago Press 1992 184p il $23.95   **92**
ISBN 0-226-07816-7   LC 91-44417

"This collection of 12 broadly autobiographical essays represents a personal history of a well-known and controversial economist (and avid rusticator) Buchanan, the Nobel Prize winner who originated public choice theory." Libr J

Buchanan, Patrick

Buchanan, Patrick. Right from the beginning; by Patrick J. Buchanan. Little, Brown 1988 392p il o.p.; Regnery Gateway paperback available $12.95   **92**
ISBN 0-89526-745-4 (pa)   LC 87-35354

In this memoir, the conservative columnist and television commentator recounts his Washington, D.C. childhood, his college years, and his career to 1966, when he began working for Richard Nixon

"For anyone seeking a concise summary of the tenets of modern American conservatism, Buchanan's clear, sharp-as-a-jab prose is a good place to start." Christ Sci Monit

Buck, Pearl S. (Pearl Sydenstricker), 1892-1973

Stirling, Nora B. Pearl Buck, a woman in conflict; [by] Nora Stirling. New Century Pubs. 1983 357p il $17.95   **92**
ISBN 0-8329-0261-6   LC 83-19455

"As a missionary family child, Buck's immersion in Chinese life to the point of considering herself Chinese explains her ability to identify with her fictional Chinese characters, according to this sympathetic biography. The spectacular success of 'The Good Earth' established Buck not only as a Nobel Prize-winning novelist, but as the West's chief interpreter of the Chinese." Publ Wkly

Includes bibliography

Buckley, William F. (William Frank), 1925-

Judis, John B. William F. Buckley, Jr., patron saint of the conservatives. Simon & Schuster 1988 528p il hardcover o.p. paperback available $10.95   **92**
ISBN 0-671-69593-2 (pa)   LC 87-28797

In this biography Judis covers these periods of Buckley's life: "prep schools, Yale University, the Army, the Central Intelligence Agency, his work in books, his . . . [involvement with] Joe McCarthy, the founding and operation of the National Review, his race for mayor of New York." Nation

"No one can write a truly definitive biography of a man whose career is still far from over. But in telling the story of William F. Buckley, Jr.'s successful life, John B. Judis has come remarkably close." New Repub

Buffalo Bill, 1846-1917

Russell, Don. The lives and legends of Buffalo Bill. University of Okla. Press 1960 514p il hardcover o.p. paperback available $18.95   **92**
ISBN 0-8061-1537-8 (pa)

This is a "dissection of Cody's authentic life and its recounting in dime novels and autobiographies of that period. . . . While strongly biographical, this work is not a perceptive study of Cody's life and personality. But it certainly is a thorough discussion of the growth of his career and record into a melodramatic legend." Libr J

Includes bibliography

Buñuel, Luis, 1900-1983
Buñuel, Luis. My last sigh; translated by Abigail Israel. Knopf 1983 256p il hardcover o.p. paperback available $8.95   **92**

ISBN 0-394-72501-8 (pa)   LC 83-48105

Original French edition, 1982; published in the United Kingdom with title: My last breath

This autobiography of the Spanish surrealist filmmaker "may be quite simply the loveliest testament ever left by a film director. . . . It has the same startling but delectable perversity and deep humor as Buñuel's best films and, like most of them, is a work of old age." N Y Times Book Rev

Burdick, Carol
Burdick, Carol. Woman alone: a farmhouse journal; introduction by Olive Ann Burns. Eriksson 1989 209p $17.95   **92**

ISBN 0-8397-8642-5   LC 89-16787

"Reeling from a divorce after 20 years of marriage, aspiring writer Burdick held a full-time job as she helped care for her dying father. Her only release was in weekend or evening escapes to the family's farm in upper New York State. The house, without plumbing or electricity, and its 70 acres offered Burdick serenity and solitude. . . . Readers will find her journal inspiring." Publ Wkly

Burgess, Anthony, 1917-1993
Burgess, Anthony. Little Wilson and big God. Weidenfeld & Nicolson 1986 460p o.p.; Grove Press paperback available $14.95   **92**

ISBN 0-8021-3240-5 (pa)   LC 86-26721

"The first installment of Anthony Burgess' autobiography is a moving, impressively written exegesis of the first 42 years of his life." Booklist

Burgess, Anthony. You've had your time; the second part of the confessions. Grove Weidenfeld 1991 403p $23.50   **92**

ISBN 0-8021-1405-9   LC 90-22029

First published 1990 in the United Kingdom

"Picking up where he left off in *Little Wilson and Big God* [entered above] . . . Burgess gives us the rest of his life story, starting in 1959. Facing death, after a doctor's diagnosis of a fatal brain tumor, Burgess the erstwhile writer becomes Burgess the machine, cranking out novels and all manner of high and low journalism in order to pay his bills and leave his wife a legacy. But Burgess lives—and stays living—and the writerly career is launched." Booklist

Burke, Chris
Burke, Chris. A special kind of hero; Chris Burke's own story; [by] Chris Burke and Jo Beth McDaniel. Doubleday 1991 248p il $18   **92**

ISBN 0-385-41645-8   LC 91-3536

Also available in paperback from Dell

"Burke, who was born with Down syndrome and is severely handicapped, has gained national recognition as 'Corky' on the television series, *Life Goes On*. Three short chapters are in his own words and the rest of the third-person narrative recounts his parents refusal to institutionalize him and his family's unfaltering efforts to shower love, support, and approval on the happy-go-lucky boy. It is an intensely personal biography that can be read for pleasure and inspiration." SLJ

Burns, George, 1896-
Burns, George. All my best friends; [by] George Burns, written with David Fisher. Putnam 1989 320p il o.p.   **92**

LC 89-10920

Available G.K. Hall large print edition

Burns "describes life in show business from the 1900s onward, recalling how he and his young friends broke into vaudeville and made it to stardom on radio, in films and on TV. The master raconteur invigorates his story with anecdotes about Eddie Cantor, Sophie Tucker, Jolson, Fannie Brice, Jack Benny, the Marx Brothers et al." Publ Wkly

Burns, George. Wisdom of the 90s; [by] George Burns written with Hal Goldman. Putnam 1991 189p il $12.95; pa $5.95   **92**

ISBN 0-399-13695-9; 0-399-51777-4 (pa)

LC 91-18730

This is a collection of reminiscences of the aged actor and comedian

"Anecdotes ranging from his vaudeville debut at age seven through his heyday on stage and screen display the wit and timing that still draw audiences." Publ Wkly

Burroughs, John, 1837-1921
Renehan, Edward. John Burroughs; an American naturalist; [by] Edward J. Renehan, Jr. Chelsea Green 1992 356p il $24.95   **92**

ISBN 0-930031-59-8   LC 92-19579

In this biography of the naturalist, "we learn not only about his life but also about his friendships with such shapers of American life as Emerson, Whitman, Henry Ford, Thomas Edison, Theodore Roosevelt, John Muir, and Jay Gould. Renehan has a good sense for interesting anecdotes. . . . We also learn something about the cultural events and trends of the late 19th-century and early 20th-century America." Choice

Includes bibliography

Burroughs, William S., 1914-
Morgan, Ted. Literary outlaw: the life and times of William S. Burroughs. Holt & Co. 1988 659p il o.p.; Avon Bks. paperback available $12.95   **92**

ISBN 0-380-70882-5 (pa)   LC 88-9290

This book "covers Burroughs' life and works as well as his circle of friends and fellow writers." Booklist

"While not a definitive portrait, Morgan's book is an accurate and serviceable biography of one of America's foremost authors. Essential reading for anyone interested in Burroughs, it belongs in all serious literature collections." Libr J

Burton, Richard, 1925-1984

Bragg, Melvyn. Richard Burton; a life. Little, Brown 1989 c1988 533p il $22.95

92

ISBN 0-316-10595-3   LC 88-31275

Also available in paperback from Warner Bks.

First published 1988 in the United Kingdom with title: Rich

"Bragg had access to Burton's letters and his 350,000-word diaries. The extensive quotations from the diaries enrich the book not only with details about show business and Burton's personal and social life but also with a great deal of material about Burton's emotional and intellectual life. Some of this material is shocking; all of it is honest and revealing." Choice

Burton, Sir Richard Francis, 1821-1890

Rice, Edward. Captain Sir Richard Francis Burton; the secret agent who made the pilgrimage to Mecca, discovered the Kama Sutra, and brought the Arabian nights to the West. Scribner 1990 522p il $35   **92**

ISBN 0-684-19137-7   LC 89-10898

Also available in paperback from HarperPerennial

"Explorer, swordsman, linguist, scholar, writer, lover of women and pursuer of hidden knowledge, Burton was *par excellence* the Victorian version of Renaissance man." Publ Wkly

"Rice is a good storyteller, and he knows more than previous biographers . . . about his subject's absorption in Islam and about the lands he explored." Newsweek

Includes bibliographic references

Cage, John. See class 780.92

Caldwell, Erskine, 1903-1987

Caldwell, Erskine. With all my might; an autobiography. Peachtree Pubs. 1987 332p il $19.95   **92**

ISBN 0-934601-11-9   LC 86-63528

"The controversial author of the novels 'Tobacco Road' (1932) and 'God's Little Acre' (1933) has always borne the reputation for enjoying the seamy underside of poor southern life a little too much. . . . Caldwell sits back now and recounts his life experiences in an honest, intimate, and articulate memoir. . . . One cannot help but admire and listen to his charming voice." Booklist

Caligula, Emperor of Rome, 12-41

Barrett, Anthony A. Caligula; the corruption of power. Yale Univ. Press 1990 xxvi, 334p il maps $30   **92**

1. Rome—History
ISBN 0-300-04653-7   LC 89-51310

Also available in paperback from Simon & Schuster

In this study of the Roman emperor who ruled from A.D. 37-41, the author "challenges the popular notion that dismisses Caligula as just a deranged madman." Booklist

"The defects and achievements of the . . . Emperor are assessed critically and with full exploitation of the nonliterary sources—epigraphical, archaeological, and, especially important, numismatic—that often throw light on or raise doubts about the evidence provided by the

ancient writers. The result is a sober, balanced estimate." Atlantic

Includes bibliographic references

Callas, Maria. See class 780.92

Campbell, Joseph, 1904-1987

Campbell, Joseph. The hero's journey: the world of Joseph Campbell; Joseph Campbell on his life and work; edited and with an introduction by Phil Cousineau; foreword by Stuart L. Brown, executive editor. Harper & Row 1990 xxix, 225p il $24.95   **92**

1. Mythology
ISBN 0-06-250102-X   LC 89-45561

"A spiritual autobiography of sorts, the book ranges widely, from Cro-Magnon art to Arthurian legend to marriage as a 'sacrificial field,' as it follows Campbell from his Catholic boyhood and early interest in American Indians to his years in Paris and Munich, through his travels and teaching at Sarah Lawrence." Publ Wkly

Includes bibliographic references

Larsen, Stephen. A fire in the mind: the life of Joseph Campbell; [by] Stephen and Robin Larsen. Doubleday 1991 xx, 636p il $30; pa $15   **92**

ISBN 0-385-26635-9; 0-385-26636-7 (pa)

LC 91-19737

"A penetrating, moving, and suitably complex portrait of the man who rekindled our interest in myths and what they tell us about life. The authors illuminate Campbell the man as well as the philosopher, tracing his influences and the evolution of his vast knowledge." Booklist

Cantwell, Mary

Cantwell, Mary. American girl; scenes from a small-town childhood. Random House 1992 209p $20   **92**

ISBN 0-394-57502-4   LC 91-51021

Also available Thorndike Press large print edition and in paperback from Penguin Bks.

The author "recounts her days in the small town of Bristol, Rhode Island, a place where she knew everyone and everyone knew her. . . . She remembers teachers, storekeepers, the rich summer people, and the Portugese kids from Back Road." Libr J

"Cantwell limns the Bristol of her youth with prose as quick, translucent, and deft as watercolors. . . . A tender and captivating narrative." Booklist

Capote, Truman, 1924-1984

Clarke, Gerald. Capote; a biography. Simon & Schuster 1988 631p il $18.45

92

ISBN 0-671-22811-0   LC 88-3144

Also available in paperback from Ballantine Bks.

This biography "tackles the writer's whole life and attempts an incisive psychological investigation of what made Capote tick as man and artist." Booklist

"In this work of prodigious research gracefully presented, Mr. Clarke, who had his subject's confidence during the last years, gives Capote what the writer himself, in a last grand, gutsy gesture, declared he wanted: a book

Capote, Truman, 1924-1984—*Continued*
in which nothing, nothing at all, was left out." N Y
Times Book Rev

Includes bibliography

Capra, Frank, 1897-1991
McBride, Joseph. Frank Capra; the
catastrophe of success. Simon & Schuster
1992 768p il $27.50; pa $16   **92**

ISBN 0-671-73494-6; 0-671-79788-3 (pa)   LC 92-1311

In this "biography the Sicilian immigrant filmmaker,
admired for the liberal and proletarian sentiments of his
movies, emerges as a deeply contradictory figure. . . .
McBride presents a man seething with bitterness, rage,
self-doubt and sexual anxiety with his two wives. He
analyzes Capra's reactionary idealization of small-town
America and the misogynist undertones of his films."
Publ Wkly

"This definitive biography belongs in even the smallest
film study collections." Booklist

Caputo, Philip
Caputo, Philip. Means of escape.
HarperCollins Pubs. 1991 405p $25; pa $12
92

ISBN 0-06-018312-8; 0-06-098402-3 (pa)
LC 91-55098

These are the recollections of Caputo's "career as a
correspondent during which he witnessed the horrors of
war in the Middle East and in Vietnam." Booklist

"This is, make no mistake about it, a startlingly
honest and brutal book. . . . The writing is superb."
Libr J

Carles, Emilie, 1900-1979
Carles, Emilie. A life of her own; a
countrywoman in twentieth-century France;
as told to Robert Destanque; translated and
with an introduction and afterword by
Avriel H. Goldberger. Rutgers Univ. Press
1991 271p il $19.95   **92**

ISBN 0-8135-1641-2   LC 90-41861

Also available in paperback from Penguin Bks.

Original French edition, 1977

"This is the memoir of a mountain peasant born at
the turn of the century who was lucky and persevering
enough to finish school, work in Paris, attend the Sorbonne, and become a schoolteacher. Carles married an
intellectually inclined housepainter, and they returned to
her village in the Alps of southeastern France to raise
their family." Libr J

"The memoir brings to life a captivating woman."
Publ Wkly

Carnegie, Andrew, 1835-1919
Wall, Joseph Frazier. Andrew Carnegie.
University of Pittsburgh Press 1989 1137p
il $49.95; pa $19.95   **92**

ISBN 0-8229-3828-6; 0-8229-5904-6 (pa)
LC 88-38160

A reissue of the title first published 1970 by Oxford
University Press

This biography follows Carnegie from his boyhood in
Scotland through his emigration to America, his rise in
the business world, and his early ventures in oil, railroads, telegraphy, and the iron and steel industries

Includes bibliography

Carreras, José. See class 780.92

Carson, Rachel, 1907-1964
Hynes, H. Patricia. The recurring silent
spring. Pergamon Press 1989 227p (Athene
ser) $30; pa $14.95   **92**

ISBN 0-08-037117-5; 0-08-037116-7 (pa)
LC 88-29049

Also available in paperback from Teachers College
Press

"Hynes reexamines the life and work of Rachel Carson, . . . maintaining that Carson wrote in part in refutation of the view, long held by professional men, that
women had 'lesser mental ability and stamina to do
science.' Hynes contends that . . . Carson's Silent Spring
[entered in class 363.7] continues to serve 'as a fundamental text on evolution—neither outdated nor inac-
curate.'" Choice

Includes bibliographic references

Carter, Jimmy, 1924-
Carter, Jimmy. Everything to gain; making
the most of the rest of your life; [by]
Jimmy and Rosalynn Carter. Random House
1987 198p o.p.; Fawcett Bks. paperback
available $4.95   **92**

ISBN 0-449-14538-7 (pa)   LC 86-27885

Also available Thorndike Press large print edition

"The former president and First Lady alternate first-
person reminiscences with sections written jointly to tell
the story of their lives after leaving the White House
in 1980. Frankly acknowledging the trauma of the lost
election, the Carters record their efforts to overcome the
difficulties of making a fresh start while deeply in debt,
adjusting to life in a small house in Plains, Ga., and
other challenges." Publ Wkly

Carter, Jimmy. Keeping faith: memoirs of
a president. Bantam Bks. 1982 622p il maps
hardcover o.p. paperback available $17.50
92

1. United States—Politics and government—1974-1989
ISBN 0-553-34571-0 (pa)   LC 82-90323

These memoirs treat such matters as "improving relations with China; enacting energy legislation; negotiating
the second Strategic Arms Limitation treaty (SALT II);
concluding the Panama Canal treaties; and convincing
Menachem Begin and Anwar Sadat to reach agreement
at Camp David." N Y Rev Books

This is "vintage Jimmy Carter, a mirror, in fact, of
its author: honest, sincere, intelligent, dry, humorless and
impersonal." N Y Times Book Rev

Caruso, Enrico. See class 780.92

Cary, Lorene
Cary, Lorene. Black ice. Knopf 1991 237p
$24; pa $10   **92**
1. St. Paul's School (Concord, N.H.)
ISBN 0-394-57465-6; 0-679-73745-6 (pa)
      LC 90-52988
"In the early 1970's, an Eastern prep school recruiting
minority students opened its doors to Cary, then a 15-
year-old Philadelphia high school girl. These affecting
recollections explore her experiences—interactions with
teachers, an affair with another student, friendships, and
problems with prejudice—as well as her struggle to determine her own black identity." Booklist

Cassady, Carolyn
Cassady, Carolyn. Off the road: my years
with Cassady, Kerouac, and Ginsberg.
Morrow 1990 436p il $22.95   **92**
1. Kerouac, Jack, 1922-1969 2. Ginsberg, Allen, 1926-
3. Cassady, Neal
ISBN 0-688-08891-0   LC 90-5588
Also available in paperback from Penguin Bks.
The author "describes the complex, intense relationships that developed between her husband [Neal Cas-
sady], Kerouac, and Ginsberg, and she analyzes their
effects on her marriage." Libr J
"Cassady re-creates, with fresh surprise, the roller
coaster of pain and pleasure she endured, as well as the
tremendous discipline she acquired that enabled her to
survive and grow, unlike her men, who self-destructed.
A moving and unstinting account of potent personalities
in pivotal times." Booklist

Cassatt, Mary. See class 709.2

Castro, Fidel, 1927-
Szulc, Tad. Fidel; a critical portrait.
Morrow 1986 703p o.p.; Avon Bks.
paperback available $5.95   **92**
1. Cuba—History
ISBN 0-380-69956-7 (pa)   LC 86-16460
The author "devotes the greater part of this book to
Castro's early, formative years and the forging and
triumph of his revolutionary movement. The years of
Castro's rule after the Bay of Pigs invasion receive
briefer treatment. Well written and very readable."
Choice
Includes bibliography

Cather, Willa, 1873-1947
Lee, Hermione. Willa Cather; double lives.
Pantheon Bks. 1989 410p il $29.95; pa $15
     92
ISBN 0-394-53703-3; 0-679-73649-2 (pa)
     LC 89-43233
"This interpretive biography . . . examines the rela-
tionship between Cather's work and her personal life."
Booklist
The author's "discussion of Cather's 12 novels and
numerous stories is so absorbing that it provokes a
rereading of the work, which makes it a valuable critical
study." N Y Times Book Rev
Includes bibliography

O'Brien, Sharon. Willa Cather; the
emerging voice. Oxford Univ. Press 1987
464p il $29.95   **92**
ISBN 0-19-504132-1   LC 86-12710
Also available in paperback from Fawcett Bks.
"The first volume in a two-part biography, O'Brien's
feminist study examines Cather's formative years. She
argues convincingly that not until the Nebraska writer
developed a sense of herself as a woman was she able
to achieve the power demonstrated in her later novels
and stories." Am Libr
Includes bibliographies

Sergeant, Elizabeth Shepley. Willa Cather;
a memoir. Ohio Univ. Press 1992 312p il
pa $16.95   **92**
ISBN 0-8214-1009-1   LC 91-13075
This is a reissue of the title first published 1953 by
Lippincott
The author, an intimate friend of Cather's, has
provided an "illuminating glimpse of a lively, likable,
and immensely gifted young writer whom time and a
thousand tributes turned into a formidable, self-absorbed,
and somewhat baffled woman." New Yorker
Includes bibliographic references

Woodress, James Leslie. Willa Cather; a
literary life; [by] James Woodress. University
of Neb. Press 1987 xx, 583p il hardcover
o.p. paperback available $14.95   **92**
ISBN 0-8032-9708-4 (pa)   LC 86-30894
The author "does a fine job of describing Willa
Cather's colorful public life and of piecing together the
puzzle of her unconventional private life. . . . Mr.
Woodress does not try to superimpose on Cather's life
any theories—feminist, Freudian, Lacanian, or otherwise.
Instead, he recounts in straightforward and lively prose
the life of a remarkable woman." N Y Times Book Rev
Includes bibliography

**Catherine II, the Great, Empress of Russia,
1729-1796**
Troyat, Henri. Catherine the Great;
translated by Joan Pinkham. Dutton 1980
377p il o.p.; Berkley Bks. paperback
available $5.99   **92**
ISBN 0-425-07981-3 (pa)   LC 79-25613
Original French edition, 1977
"Relying heavily on Catherine's own memoirs, plus
her correspondence with her Western idolaters-publicists,
such as Friedrich Grimm, Voltaire and Diderot, Troyat
gives us a portrait the Empress herself might have
decreed for posterity." Publ Wkly
Includes bibliography

Cellini, Benvenuto. See class 709.2

Cézanne, Paul. See class 709.2

Chace, James
Chace, James. What we had: a memoir.
Summit Bks. 1990 187p $17.95   **92**
ISBN 0-671-69478-2   LC 89-78431

Chace, James—*Continued*
The author has written a "memoir about coming-of-age in the 1940s and '50s. He grew up in Fall River, Mass., a once-thriving textile town whose decline seemed to parallel the limbo of his parents' marriage. . . . As he reminisces about Pearl Harbor, Billie Holiday, hearing T.S. Eliot at Harvard, Paris in the early 1950s, Chace evokes the experience of a generation." Publ Wkly

Chagall, Marc. See class 709.2

Chamberlain, Wilt, 1936-
Chamberlain, Wilt. A view from above. Villard Bks. 1991 290p il $19.50   **92**
ISBN 0-679-40455-4   LC 91-16771
Also available in paperback from New Am. Lib.

In this book Chamberlain expresses "his views on various subjects. Former and current sports figures, race relations, celebrities, sex, women, and money are topics upon which he has very candid opinions. Sprinkled liberally throughout the book are 'Wiltisms,' his interesting and often humorous philosophies on life. He devotes a full chapter to sex and love, and tells why he has remained a bachelor after all these years." Libr J

Chambers, Whittaker
Chambers, Whittaker. Witness. Random House 1952 808p o.p.; Regnery Gateway reprint available $21.95, pa $11.95   **92**
1. Communist Party (U.S.) 2. Communism—United States
ISBN 0-89526-571-0; 0-89526-789-6(pa)

Whittaker Chambers' own account of his life, his connection with the Communist Party and his repudiation of it, and his role in the Hiss-Chambers trial

Chanel, Coco, 1883-1971
Madsen, Axel. Chanel; a woman of her own. Holt & Co. 1990 388p il $21.95; pa $12.95   **92**
ISBN 0-8050-0961-2; 0-8050-1639-2 (pa)
                                      LC 89-24692
"Intertwining Chanel's business ventures, wealth, glamour, and influences, the biography is filled with . . . stories of personal triumph, success and tragedy, social intrigue, and sexual escapades with nobility, artists, and politicians. The text, broken down into four parts, focuses on her life from her birth and childhood years to her early business success, her decline following the demoralizing events of World War II, and her amazing comeback at the age of 70 to the haute couture world she helped create." Libr J
Includes bibliography

Chaucer, Geoffrey, d. 1400
Gardner, John. The life & times of Chaucer; ornaments by J. Wolf. Knopf 1977 328p il hardcover o.p. paperback available $9.95   **92**
1. Great Britain—History—1154-1399, Plantagenets
ISBN 0-394-72500-X (pa)   LC 76-1915

This "biography provides a . . . portrait of Chaucer as man and poet. Valet, civil servant, soldier, prisoner of war, lover, cuckold perhaps, diplomat who undertook perilous journeys for his king—Chaucer's life was almost as full and varied as his 'Canterbury Tales.'" Publ Wkly
"This is speculative biography, but based on careful assumptions. Gardner agrees and disagrees with his predecessors in judicious fashion." Christ Sci Monit
Includes bibliographic references

Howard, Donald Roy. Chaucer; his life, his works, his world; [by] Donald R. Howard. Dutton 1987 636p il o.p.; Fawcett Bks. paperback available $12.95   **92**
1. Great Britain—History—1154-1399, Plantagenets
ISBN 0-449-90341-9 (pa)   LC 86-32899
"A William Abrahams book"

This literary biography "employs Chaucer's own writing as a telescope into the era, the man, and his work. . . . Howard's work is immersed in period detail along with frequent references to Chaucer's verse. It is an absorbing study, enlightening and enhancing our perception of the era and the author." Booklist
Includes bibliography

Cheever, John, 1912-1982
Cheever, John. The journals of John Cheever. Knopf 1991 399p $24.50   **92**
ISBN 0-394-57274-2   LC 91-52728
This "volume contains extensive personal journals. . . . The journals served Cheever both as writer's notebook and memoir, clarifying much of his method of working. The inner life of a writer is revealed in these highly introspective memoirs. . . . A candid, beautiful, often startling portrait of a 20th-century American writer." Libr J

Cheever, Susan. Home before dark. Houghton Mifflin 1984 243p il o.p.; Bantam Bks. paperback available $10   **92**
ISBN 0-553-35150-8 (pa)   LC 84-9057
A memoir "of how one man's talents, faults and contradictions (all immense) shaped the life of a family, and the daughter's life in particular. Relying on both her memories and research, and quoting liberally from the brilliant and previously unpublished journals kept by the elder Cheever throughout his life, she provides outlines of a biography." Publ Wkly
"The close observation, rueful domestic detail and puzzled love evident in the book make it one of the best portraits of an American writer." Newsweek

Donaldson, Scott. John Cheever; a biography. Random House 1988 416p il $22.50   **92**
ISBN 0-394-54921-X   LC 86-29682
"Donaldson delves into the writer's deteriorating marriage, his alcoholism, persistent phobias and self-disgust, his affairs with actress Hope Lange and composer Ned Rorem, blending in . . . appraisals of the short stories and novels." Publ Wkly
"One mark of a good literary biography is that it send the reader back to the writer's work with new insights and appreciation. This is certainly the case with Scott Donaldson's fine biography of John Cheever." West Coast Rev Books

Chekhov, Anton Pavlovich, 1860-1904

Pritchett, V. S. (Victor Sawdon). Chekhov; a spirit set free. Random House 1988 235p $17.95; pa $8.95   **92**

ISBN 0-394-54650-4; 0-679-72546-6 (pa)

LC 87-43213

This is a biographical study of the Russian writer and an analysis of his work

"Chekhov's originality and artistry take on new vitality in part because Pritchett's English imagination harmonizes with the Russian's." Choice

Troyat, Henri. Chekhov; translated from the French by Michael Henry Heim. Dutton 1986 364p il o.p.; Fawcett Bks. paperback available $10.95   **92**

ISBN 0-449-90281-1 (pa)   LC 86-8897

Original French edition, 1984

"Troyat documents the harshness of Chekhov's up-bringing and carefully chronicles the engendering and maturation of his simultaneous careers—his true calling as a writer and his day-to-day work as a doctor. . . . The general reader comes away comprehending Chekhov's sensitive nature and appreciating his creative genius." Booklist

Includes bibliography

Cheng, Nien, 1915-

Cheng, Nien. Life and death in Shanghai. Grove Press 1987 c1986 547p $24.95   **92**

1. China—History—1949-1976

ISBN 0-8021-1205-6   LC 86-45254

Also available in paperback from Penguin Bks.

First published 1986 in the United Kingdom

"For six and a half years, from 1966 until 1973, Nien Cheng, an upper-class Chinese widow . . . was held in solitary confinement at Shanghai Detention House No. 1, charged with espionage, but never tried. Her book . . . [is an] account of that experience and its aftermath." Ms

This "is a volume that belongs on the shelf alongside the writings of Primo Levi, Elie Wiesel, Dith Pran, and other chroniclers of ideological fanaticism, its dehumanizing consequences, and its all too rare resisters." Christ Sci Monit

Chesnut, Mary Boykin Miller, 1823-1886

Chesnut, Mary Boykin Miller. The private Mary Chesnut; the unpublished Civil War diaries; [edited by] C. Vann Woodward, Elisabeth Muhlenfeld. Oxford Univ. Press 1984 xxix, 292p $24.95; pa $13.95   **92**

1. United States—History—1861-1865, Civil War

ISBN 0-19-503511-9; 0-19-503513-5 (pa)

LC 84-12219

"The picture that emerges of Chesnut's private world throughout the Civil War years is fascinating; she was married to a Southern senator who helped draft the secession document and friend to such high ranking confederates as President and Mrs. Jefferson Davis. . . . The diary entries are an intriguing historical and personal record." Booklist

Includes bibliographic references

Chesterton, G. K. (Gilbert Keith), 1874-1936

Coren, Michael. Gilbert, the man who was G.K. Chesterton. Paragon House 1990 304p il $22.95   **92**

ISBN 1-55778-256-3   LC 89-16202

Published in a slightly different version in the United Kingdom, 1989

The author examines Chesterton's life by "quoting extensively from letters, journals, and his autobiography. In workmanlike prose he chronicles Chesterton's sometimes naive economic and political ideas, occasional bigotry, efforts to maintain his bloated body, and influential conversion to Catholicism." Libr J

Includes bibliography

Chestnut, J. L., Jr.

Chestnut, J. L., Jr. Black in Selma: the uncommon life of J.L. Chestnut, Jr. [by] J.L. Chestnut, Jr., Julia Cass. Farrar, Straus & Giroux 1990 431p il $22.95   **92**

1. Blacks—Civil rights

ISBN 0-374-11404-8   LC 89-77436

"Born in Selma, Alabama, in 1930, Chestnut became the town's first black attorney. His participation in the civil rights movement of the 1960s was full and consequential. In collaboration with Pulitzer Prize-winning journalist Julia Cass, Chestnut recounts his coming of age in Selma, his endeavors to advance professionally, and his continued efforts to ensure that doors are opened to other blacks." Booklist

Chopin, Kate, 1851-1904

Toth, Emily. Kate Chopin. Morrow 1990 528p il $27.95   **92**

ISBN 0-688-09707-3   LC 90-37894

Also available in paperback from University of Tex. Press

This is a biography of the writer who, born in St. Louis in 1850, "eventually moved to Louisiana when she married. Left a widow with six children in 1882, she turned to writing for her livelihood, and she was successful until the publication of her controversial novel The Awakening in 1899." Libr J

"Reflective of much research and careful consideration, Toth's biography paints a rich portrait of a woman who, at the turn of the century, held firm convictions often at variance with the conventions of her time." Booklist

Includes bibliography

Christie, Agatha, 1890-1976

Gill, Gillian. Agatha Christie; the woman and her mysteries. Free Press 1990 243p il $24.95; pa $10.95   **92**

ISBN 0-02-911702-X; 0-02-911703-8 (pa)

LC 90-38545

Also available G.K. Hall large print edition

This biocritical assessment of the mystery writer examines her novels in relation to actual events in Christie's life. The author places special emphasis on the works Christie wrote under the pseudonym Mary Westmacott

"Gill is convincing in her defense of the quality of Christie's work and equally persuasive in depicting the novelist as a fascinating character in her own right." Booklist

Includes bibliographic references

Christie, Agatha, 1890-1976—*Continued*
Morgan, Janet. Agatha Christie; a biography. Knopf 1985 c1984 393p il $24.95
92

ISBN 0-394-52554-X   LC 84-48678

First published 1984 in the United Kingdom

"As the first authorized biographer, Morgan had access to Christie's papers and personal effects, as well as introductions to 200 friends and associates. She has rendered an intelligent and good-humored account of Christie's life and work." Libr J

Churchill, Lady Clementine, 1885-1977
Hough, Richard Alexander. Winston and Clementine: the triumphs and tragedies of the Churchills. See entry under Churchill, Sir Winston, 1874-1965
92

Churchill, Sir Winston, 1874-1965
Gilbert, Martin. Churchill: a life. Holt & Co. 1991 1066p il maps $35; pa $19.95
92

ISBN 0-8050-0615-X; 0-8050-2396-8 (pa)
LC 91-20288

This is a one-volume distillation of the author's multi-volume biography of Churchill entered below

Though Gilbert "has his own, debatable, view of Churchill as a reformer always ill-at-ease with the Tories, he doesn't argue. He displays. He ushers rather than nags you past his evidence." New Statesman Soc

Gilbert, Martin. Churchill: a photographic portrait. Houghton Mifflin 1988 364p il $24.95
92

ISBN 0-395-48680-7   LC 88-9084

This is a new and slightly expanded edition of a volume of photographs first published 1974

"An interesting and valuable companion [to the author's eight-volume biography of Churchill, entered below]. Most of the more than 400 photographs Mr. Gilbert presents are new to this reader; they show Winston Churchill in every phase and mood of his long life; and they are accompanied by a commentary that is highly informative." N Y Times Book Rev

Gilbert, Martin. Winston Churchill, the wilderness years. Houghton Mifflin 1982 c1981 279p il $16.95
92

1. Great Britain—Politics and government—1900-1999 (20th century)
ISBN 0-395-31869-6   LC 82-9279

First published 1981 in the United Kingdom

"This is a companion piece to the PBS 'Masterpiece Theatre' series to which Gilbert also contributed. Dealing with Churchill's years out of the government, when he was vigorously critical of its policy of inaction and appeasement, the book is a crisp, readable narrative for the general reader." Libr J

Includes bibliography

Gilbert, Martin. Winston S. Churchill; illustrated with photographs and maps. Houghton Mifflin 1986-1988 2v il maps v7 $40; v8 $39
92

1. Great Britain—Politics and government—1900-1999 (20th century)

Volumes one and two by Randolph S. Churchill o.p.; volumes three through six by Martin Gilbert o.p.

Contents: v7 Road to victory, 1941-1945 (ISBN 0-395-37859-1); v8 Never despair, 1945-1965 (ISBN 0-395-41918-2)

"The whole vast work . . . despite the dual authorship, is of a piece—and if it is not as uniquely great in literary quality as it is in physical bulk it is certainly a stupendous achievement." N Y Times Book Rev

Hough, Richard Alexander. Winston and Clementine: the triumphs and tragedies of the Churchills; [by] Richard Hough. Bantam Bks. 1991 c1990 528p il hardcover o.p. paperback available $6.99
92

1. Churchill, Lady Clementine, 1885-1977 2. Great Britain—Politics and government—1900-1999 (20th century)
ISBN 0-553-29365-6 (pa)   LC 90-46638

"In this portrait of Churchill's married and family life, Hough offers views of the man at his most heroic and of his wife at her most sufferingly noble." Booklist

Includes bibliographic references

Manchester, William. The last lion: Winston Spencer Churchill. Little, Brown 1983-1988 2v il maps v1 $29.95, v2 $35
92

1. Great Britain—Politics and government—1900-1999 (20th century)   LC 82-24972

Both volumes also available in paperback from Dell

Contents: v1 Visions of glory, 1874-1932 (ISBN 0-316-54503-1); v2 Alone, 1932-1940 (ISBN 0-316-54512-0)

The first two volumes of a projected three volume biography cover the life of the British statesman from birth to the Nazi blitzkrieg and Churchill's appointment as prime minister

"Manchester is not only master of detail, anecdote, and setpiece, but also of 'the big picture'. . . . Some critics may find his prose rather purple, but his style is entirely appropriate to his subject, and the panoramic sweep of his work." Natl Rev

Includes bibliographies

Soames, Mary. Winston Churchill; his life as a painter: a memoir by his daughter; with a foreword by Derek Hill. Houghton Mifflin 1990 224p il $39
92

ISBN 0-395-56319-4   LC 90-4809

The daughter of the English statesman describes her father's Post-Impressionist style paintings and his activities during the times he produced them

Includes bibliographic references

Cid, ca. 1043-1099
Fletcher, R. A. (Richard A.). The quest for El Cid; [by] Richard Fletcher. Knopf 1990 c1989 217p il maps $24.95
92

1. Spain—History
ISBN 0-394-57447-8   LC 89-43289

Cid, ca. 1043-1099—*Continued*
Also available in paperback from Oxford Univ. Press

First published 1989 in the United Kingdom

This is an attempt to examine the historical realities behind the legend of Rodrigo Diaz de Vivar, a medieval warrior who became the hero of the Spanish national epic poem El Poema de Mio Cid

"Beginning students, sophisticated scholars, and the general reader interested in Spanish medieval history will benefit from this provocative, learned, and elegantly written study." Libr J

Includes bibliographies

Clay, Lucius D. (Lucius DuBignon), 1897-1978
Smith, Jean Edward. Lucius D. Clay; an American life. Holt & Co. 1990 835p il hardcover o.p. paperback available $19.95
            92

ISBN 0-8050-1787-9 (pa)   LC 89-24720

Clay "headed the military procurement effort in WW II, served as U.S. military governor in occupied Germany until his retirement from the Army in '49, and went on to careers in business and banking. He was also active in politics, playing a pivotal role in Eisenhower's '52 presidential campaign. . . . The biography is based in part on interviews Smith . . . conducted with Clay over a six-year period." Publ Wkly

"An unusual biography that uses a question-and-answer format to cut to the quick of the issues and events that moved its subject to become, arguably, one of our nation's great soldiers and statesmen." Booklist

Includes bibliographic references

Clinton, Bill, 1946-
Allen, Charles F. (Charles Flynn). The comeback kid: the life and career of Bill Clinton; by Charles F. Allen and Jonathan Portis. Carol Pub. Group 1992 294p il maps $18.95
            92

ISBN 1-55972-154-5   LC 92-19745

"A Birch Lane Press book"

"The book's texture reflects the authors' professional provenances as educrat and political reporter, respectively, and therefore holds a plenitude of information on the two areas of Arkansan life in which Clinton has made his mark: elections and school reform. . . . The prime value of this work is furnishing patrons with background information about the Clintons' lives before they became national celebrities." Booklist

Includes bibliographic references

Cohn, Roy, 1927-1986
Von Hoffman, Nicholas. Citizen Cohn. Doubleday 1988 483p il $19.95   **92**

ISBN 0-385-23690-5   LC 87-27450

Also available in paperback from Bantam Bks.

This biography of the American lawyer presents coverage of "Cohn's Washington years as counsel to Senator Joe McCarthy . . . [as well as] indictments by Bobby Kennedy's Justice Department, the . . . years as New York power broker, and finally disbarment and death from AIDS." Libr J

This is "a big, colorful book, loaded with anecdotes and reminiscences, but not to be taken as the final word on any of the scores of controversial subjects it treats."

Natl Rev

Includes bibliography

Cole, Nat King. See class 780.92

Coleridge, Samuel Taylor, 1772-1834
Holmes, Richard. Coleridge; early visions. Viking 1990 409p il o.p.; Penguin Bks. paperback available $9.95   **92**

ISBN 0-14-012440-3 (pa)   LC 89-40652

First published 1989 in the United Kingdom

This first of a projected two-volume biography of the English writer "follows Coleridge from childhood to his departure for the Mediterranean, in 1804." Atlantic

"There really have been few literary biographies better than this. . . . The tempo is quick and the direction of the narrative focused." Booklist

Includes bibliography

Colette, 1873-1954
Massie, Allan. Colette. Penguin Bks. 1986 152p il (Lives of modern women) pa $4.95
            92

ISBN 0-14-008160-7   LC 85-52211

The author discusses "the major factors in Colette's life, including the experience of her being forced by her first husband to write for profit, her lesbian relations, her years as a performer in music halls, and how her sensuous reactions to nature were transferred to the written page. This is simply a brilliantly economical assessment of one person's uncommon life and unique literary accomplishment. Selected bibliography." Booklist

Collins, Judy. See class 780.92

Columbus, Christopher
Morison, Samuel Eliot. Admiral of the ocean sea: a life of Christopher Columbus; maps by Erwin Raisz; drawings by Bertram Greene. Little, Brown 1942 xx, 680p il maps $45; pa 24.95   **92**

ISBN 0-316-58354-5; 0-316-58478-9 (pa)

"An Atlantic Monthly Press book"

A condensation of the author's two-volume work with same title also published in 1942 but now o.p.

"An authoritative . . . biography of Columbus which is also decidedly original in its emphasis on the ability of Columbus as seaman and navigator and in the amount of space given to tracing the routes of the voyages and landings." Libr J

Conway, Jill K., 1934-
Conway, Jill K. The road from Coorain; [by] Jill Ker Conway. Knopf 1989 238p il $24; pa $10   **92**

1. Australia
ISBN 0-394-57456-7; 0-679-72436-2 (pa)
            LC 88-25932

Also available G.K. Hall large print edition

This is a memoir by "the historian and former president of Smith College, who grew up on a sheep station in the western grasslands of New South Wales, Australia." N Y Times Book Rev

Conway, Jill K., 1934-—*Continued*
The author's "inspiring story is told with rich, vivid details." Voice Youth Advocates

Cooper, Lady Diana, 1892-1986
Waugh, Evelyn. The letters of Evelyn Waugh and Diana Cooper. See entry under Waugh, Evelyn, 1903-1966 **92**

Copland, Aaron. See class 780.92

Corman, Roger
Corman, Roger. How I made a hundred movies in Hollywood and never lost a dime; [by] Roger Corman with Jim Jerome. Random House 1990 237p il $18.95 **92**
ISBN 0-394-56974-1   LC 89-33766
Also available in paperback from Delacorte Press
"Corman has had two careers in Hollywood. From 1955 to 1971, he produced and directed dozens of low-budget science fiction, horror, and action movies. . . . In his second incarnation, Corman became an executive whose company nurtured young talent [including Jack Nicholson, Martin Scorsese, and Francis Coppola, among others.]" Libr J
"This account of Corman's life and career includes reminiscences by those who have worked with him: performers, directors, assistant producers, writers. The book is a significant contribution to the history of American movies." Publ Wkly

Cousins, Norman
Cousins, Norman. Human options. Norton 1981 224p il $9.95 **92**
ISBN 0-393-01430-4   LC 80-29181
The author presents an "'autobiographical notebook' focusing on what he has learned during 40 years in public and cultural life. . . . Cousins also includes brief portraits of major figures he has known, from Churchill and Casals to Hemingway, Faulkner, and various 'Saturday Review' editors, as well as a selection of his personal photographs." Publ Wkly

Cowley, Malcolm, 1898-1989
Cowley, Malcolm. The dream of the golden mountains; remembering the 1930s. Viking 1980 328p il o.p.; Penguin Bks. paperback available $8.95 **92**
1. United States—Civilization
ISBN 0-14-005919-9 (pa)   LC 79-18485
Also available in hardcover from P. Smith
Sequel to Exile's return (1934)
Cowley's memoir of the Depression era "carries a sense of impressive presence—of both the writer and the years recalled. . . . Though journal notes, reworked essays, and memory are slightly disjunctive at the seams, the whole is nonetheless a quietly brilliant and thoughtful tour de force of recall and interpretation of both literary and social history." Booklist

Crane, Stephen, 1871-1900
Benfey, Christopher E. G. The double life of Stephen Crane; [by] Christopher Benfey. Knopf 1992 294p il $25 **92**
ISBN 0-394-56864-8   LC 91-36726
The author puts forth the "hypothesis that Crane's life was foreshadowed and dictated by his fiction. As a reporter Crane experienced the horrors of war (Spanish-American) only after he wrote *The Red Badge of Courage*; years before a common-law marriage to a former madam, he wrote *Maggie: A Girl of the Streets*. Benfey supports his thesis with a detailed analysis of Crane's life and works including the often overlooked poetry." Publ Wkly
"This is a movingly mystical biography, pulsing with predestination and wonder at the way art forged a code for life." Booklist
Includes bibliographic references

Cromwell, Oliver, 1599-1658
Fraser, Antonia. Cromwell, the Lord Protector. Knopf 1973 xx, 774p il maps o.p.; Fine, D.I. paperback available $14.95 **92**
1. Great Britain—History—1642-1660, Civil War and Commonwealth
ISBN 0-917657-90-X (pa)
Published in the United Kingdom with title: Cromwell: our chief of men
This book presents a portrait of the 17th-century genius, who in roles of legislator, soldier, and ruler dominated Britain during and after the Great Civil War
The author has "presented her findings in a smooth-flowing narrative which is a pleasure to read. . . . To some extent the book lacks historical background and depth. But as a portrait of a man it is a genuine work of art: complete, subtle, understanding and convincing." New Statesman
Includes bibliography

Cronyn, Hume
Cronyn, Hume. A terrible liar; a memoir. Morrow 1991 431p il $23 **92**
ISBN 0-688-10080-5   LC 91-7936
A memoir by the prominent actor, scriptwriter, director and producer
This "is a thoroughly charming, witty, and often funny autobiography not only because it represents a splendid piece of writing, or because of the absence of jarring personal 'revelations,' but mainly because Cronyn emerges as such a decent, intelligent, fair, sensitive, and likable human being. . . . The book easily combines personal stories, comments, and happenings onstage and offstage." Christ Sci Monit

Crow Dog, Mary
Crow Dog, Mary. Lakota woman; by Mary Crow Dog and Richard Erdoes. Grove Weidenfeld 1990 263p il $18.95 **92**
1. Dakota Indians
ISBN 0-8021-1101-7   LC 89-24862
Also available in paperback from HarperPerennial
"Born in 1955 and raised in poverty on the Rosebud Reservation, Mary Crow Dog escaped an oppressive Catholic boarding school but fell into a marginal life of urban shoplifting and barhopping. A 1971 encounter with

Crow Dog, Mary—*Continued*

AIM (the American Indian Movement), participation in the 1972 Trail of Broken Treaties march on Washington, and giving birth to her first child while under fire at the 1973 siege of Wounded Knee radicalized her." Libr J

"The story of Mary Crow Dog's coming of age in the Indian civil rights movement is simply told—and, at times, simply horrifying." N Y Times Book Rev

Cukor, George, 1899-1983

McGilligan, Patrick. George Cukor, a double life; a biography of the gentleman director. St. Martin's Press 1991 404p il $24.95 **92**

ISBN 0-312-05419-X   LC 90-48352

Also available in paperback from HarperPerennial

This is a biography of the director of such films as Dinner at Eight, Little Women, David Copperfield, Sylvia Scarlett, Camille, A Double Life, and The Chapman Report

"Patrick McGilligan's book is that rarity of rarities among Hollywood biographies: a full-bodied study of a man and his métier, equally insightful about the life and the art. . . . The important thing, however, is that Mr. McGilligan does make distinctions and render useful value judgments, based on a detailed knowledge of all the intricacies and intrigues of film making." N Y Times Book Rev

Cunningham, Laura

Cunningham, Laura. Sleeping arrangements. Knopf 1989 195p $18.95 **92**

ISBN 0-394-56112-0   LC 88-27023

Also available in paperback from New Am. Lib.

This memoir of the author's life through high school "is a paean to Cunningham's mother, Rosie, who died when the author was eight, and to the two eccentric uncles who raised her." Booklist

This "is a touching, funny book about growing up in the Bronx in the 1950s. . . . Laura Cunningham has captured the neighborhood, the times, even the ways people think and talk." Christ Sci Monit

Cuomo, Mario

McElvaine, Robert S. Mario Cuomo; a biography. Scribner 1988 449p il $19.95

92

ISBN 0-684-18970-4   LC 88-2041

This "portrait of the New York State governor . . . is based on interviews with Cuomo, his friends and peers." Publ Wkly

"In an attempt to produce an objective account of Cuomo's life, personality, and political career, journalist McElvaine diligently tries to find faults, flaws, and dirty little secrets, but he is remarkably unsuccessful in this pursuit. Only minimal lapses are unearthed, and even these prove less damaging to the subject's character than illustrative of his essential humanity." Booklist

Includes bibliography

Curley, James Michael, 1874-1958

Beatty, Jack. The rascal king: the life and times of James Michael Curley, 1874-1958. Addison-Wesley 1992 571p il $25   **92**

1. Massachusetts—Politics and government
ISBN 0-201-17599-1   LC 92-9718

"A William Patrick book"

This is the biography "of a man who over the course of a half-century in politics was four times mayor of Boston, once governor of Massachussetts, twice a congressional representative, and twice a prisoner in jail. . . . Indicting Curley here, praising him there, Beatty's assessment is fair-minded, his research solid, his asides on today's political parallels enlightening, and his style appropriate to a flamboyant subject." Libr J

Includes bibliographic references

Custer, Elizabeth Bacon

Custer, Elizabeth Bacon. Boots and saddles; or, Life in Dakota with General Custer   **92**

1. Custer, George Armstrong, 1839-1876

Hardcover and paperback editions available from various publishers

First published 1885 by Harper

Written partly to protect her husband's memory against detractors, this memoir by George Armstrong Custer's wife deals primarily with their life in the Dakota Territory in the 1870's, just prior to the fatal Battle of the Little Big Horn

Dalai Lama XIV, 1935-

Dalai Lama XIV. Freedom in exile; the autobiography of the Dalai Lama. HarperCollins Pubs. 1990 288p il maps $22.95; pa $11   **92**

ISBN 0-06-039116-2; 0-06-098701-4 (pa)
          LC 89-46523

"A Cornelia & Michael Bessie book"

"The Dalai Lama's story is, in part, a chapter in the 2,500-year history of Buddhism as well as a testament to the 'mendacity and barbarity' of Communist China. He shares the details of his amazing life, a glimpse at some of the mysteries of Tibetan Buddhism, and his unshakable belief in the basic good of humanity." Booklist

Dali, Salvador. See class 709.2

Darrow, Clarence, 1857-1938

Stone, Irving. Clarence Darrow for the defense; a biography. Doubleday 1949 c1941 570p o.p.; New Am. Lib. paperback available $5.95   **92**

ISBN 0-451-15930-6 (pa)

First published 1941

This life of a famous American defense lawyer shows him as a man who never compromised with his principles, who was willing to give up everything for the cause he believed to be right

"Irving Stone's informal biography begins a little too much like a novel, but it becomes full, rich and fascinating." N Y Her Trib Books

Includes bibliography

Darwin, Charles, 1809-1882

Desmond, Adrian J. Darwin; [by] Adrian Desmond & James Moore. Warner Bks. 1992 c1991 808p il $35 **92**

ISBN 0-446-51589-2   LC 91-50412

First published 1991 in the United Kingdom

The authors portray "Darwin as a freethinking agnostic fearful of being labeled an anarchist, a scientific titan trapped on a literary treadmill, a voyager on the *Beagle* appalled at 'low' races of savages, and a paterfamilias who subordinated women but was completely dependent on his wife." Publ Wkly

"No other biography of Darwin has anywhere near the density of detail this book has. This rich tapestry, supplemented with 91 fine illustrations, is intended to provide the basis for relating Darwin the creative scientist to his social and political milieu." N Y Times Book Rev

Includes bibliography

Davis, Benjamin O., Jr.

Davis, Benjamin O., Jr. Benjamin O. Davis, Jr., American; an autobiography. Smithsonian Institution Press 1991 442p il $19.95 **92**

ISBN 0-87474-742-2   LC 90-9905

"Lt. General Benjamin Davis, the first black to graduate from West Point, describes his experiences and achievements in the military and as a civilian in the face of blatant racial discrimination." Booklist

Davis, Bette, 1908-1989

Moseley, Roy. Bette Davis: an intimate memoir. Fine, D.I. 1990 192p il $18.95 **92**

ISBN 1-55611-218-1   LC 89-46319

This biography of Bette Davis is based on the author's fifteen year friendship with the actress. "A very personal account, it includes Davis's likes and dislikes (from fellow actors to foods) and intimate accounts of events omitted from more objective biographies. . . . A nice addition to the Davis literature." Libr J

Quirk, Lawrence J. Fasten your seat belts: the passionate life of Bette Davis. Morrow 1990 464p il $21.95 **92**

ISBN 0-688-08427-3   LC 89-29771

"Although he takes a warts-and-all approach, Quirk is sympathetic to his subject, without fawning. Along with all the requisite movie lore and bedtime revelries, the account provides plenty of inside Hollywood stories, many of them about the men in the center and on the periphery of Davis' life. . . . This in-depth look at an enduring legend is likely to establish itself as the definitive Davis bio." Booklist

Davis, Jefferson, 1808-1889

Davis, William C. Jefferson Davis; the man and his hour. HarperCollins Pubs. 1991 784p il $35 **92**

1. United States—History—1861-1865, Civil War
ISBN 0-06-016706-8   LC 90-56352

The author "explores how Davis's attitudes and values were developed at West Point and during his Mexican War service and how they were put to the test in his

years as U.S. senator, as secretary of war under Franklin Pierce and as president of the Southern Confederacy." Publ Wkly

What makes this book "so interesting to read is that it is much more than a chronicle of the life of the Confederate President. It is, in addition, a carefully thought out and persuasively argued psychological interpretation of that life." N Y Times Book Rev

Includes bibliography

Davis, Miles. See class 780.92

Davis, Patti

Davis, Patti. The way I see it; an autobiography. Putnam 1992 335p il $22.95 **92**

ISBN 0-399-13748-3   LC 91-46575

The daughter of Ronald and Nancy Reagan recounts her life as daughter and sister, public figure, critic of her father's policies, drug addict, actress and author. Davis also discusses her decision to reverse a surgical procedure she once elected to prevent her from bearing children

Davis, Sammy, Jr.

Davis, Sammy, Jr. Why me? the Sammy Davis, Jr. story; [by] Sammy Davis, Jr., Jane Boyar and Burt Boyer. Farrar, Straus & Giroux 1989 373p il o.p.; Warner Bks. paperback available $5.75 **92**

ISBN 0-446-36025-2 (pa)   LC 88-36327

An account of the entertainer's personal and private life as played out against the black struggle for equality

This "book is 'totally' readable. He reveals things about the Kennedys, about his love affairs, his involvement with civil rights, his strange fascination with the 'forbidden' (including Satanism), and surprisingly, facing bankruptcy." West Coast Rev Books

Dayan, Moshe, 1915-1981

Dayan, Yaël. My father, his daughter. Farrar, Straus & Giroux 1985 289p il $17.95 **92**

ISBN 0-374-21695-9   LC 85-15995

Also available in paperback from Shapolsky Pubs.

This biography of the Israeli general and cabinet minister, "is not limited to purely personal reflections, but also features [the author's] recollections of her father's military and political careers as well as his archaeological interests." Booklist

"Miss Dayan, who is a novelist, blends biography and autobiography in a disarming account of her father's life and their relationship. . . . It is a melancholy and vibrant portrait of a man who may have become a legend to many but whose daughter knew him better." N Y Times Book Rev

De Kooning, Willem. See class 709.2

Defoe, Daniel, 1661?-1731
Backscheider, Paula R. Daniel Defoe; his life. Johns Hopkins Univ. Press 1989 671p il $40; pa $19.95   **92**
ISBN 0-8018-3785-5; 0-8018-4512-2 (pa)
                                    LC 88-26752
"Multifaceted and multitalented—journalist, merchant, novelist, spy—Defoe emerges as complex yet comprehensible. The work also paints a clear picture of Defoe's political, social, and economic milieu." Libr J
Includes bibliography

Dershowitz, Alan M.
Dershowitz, Alan M. Chutzpah. Little, Brown 1991 378p il $22.95   **92**
1. Jews—United States
ISBN 0-316-18137-4   LC 91-6443
Also available in a large print edition pa $15.95 (0-316-18138-2) and in paperback from Simon & Schuster
This is an account of the author's life as an American Jew, from an Orthodox boyhood in Brooklyn as the child of Polish immigrants through Yale Law School, a professorship at Harvard, and involvement in Jewish causes. Dershowitz discusses the Holocaust and its meaning for a post-Holocaust generation of Jews, Zionism and Israel, Soviet Jewry and his role in the Sharansky case, his defense of Jonathan Pollard, and his position on the separation of church and state
The author "has written a bold, powerful book because he has lived a bold, powerful life." N Y Times Book Rev
Includes bibliographic references

Des Barres, Pamela
Des Barres, Pamela. Take another little piece of my heart; a groupie grows up. Morrow 1992 304p il $20   **92**
ISBN 0-688-09149-0   LC 92-19882
In this sequel to I'm with the band (1987), the author "tells us about her trying life as a wife, a mother, and the daughter of aging parents." Booklist
This book "is indisputably juicy, thanks to Des Barres's effervescence and no-holds-barred approach to celebrity gossip." Publ Wkly

Dick, Philip K.
Sutin, Lawrence. Divine invasions: a life of Philip K. Dick. Harmony Bks. 1989 352p il o.p.; Carol Pub. Group paperback available $12.95   **92**
ISBN 0-8065-1228-8 (pa)   LC 89-2014
"Using Dick's novels and stories as an autobiographical key to Dick's life . . . [the author traces] the intellectual and social development of a struggling writer on the rocky road to success." Booklist
"Sutin's street-wise biography does the man full justice and should be a hit with Dick's many readers." Libr J
Includes bibliography

Dickens, Charles, 1812-1870
Ackroyd, Peter. Dickens. HarperCollins Pubs. 1990 1195p il hardcover o.p. paperback available $16   **92**
ISBN 0-06-092265-6 (pa)
This biography of the 19th century English novelist covers his life and work and the world in which he lived
The author "is a master biographer with a seductive prose style, and this massive volume is likely to stand as the Dickens biography for decades to come." Publ Wkly
Includes bibliography

Kaplan, Fred. Dickens; a biography. Morrow 1988 607p il $24.95   **92**
ISBN 0-688-04341-0   LC 88-12859
Also available in paperback from Avon Bks.
"In tracing Dickens's career from 'boy prodigy' to grizzled Victorian giant of letters . . . Kaplan covers his roles as journalist, novelist, social reformer and businessman." Publ Wkly
"Kaplan has synthesized the vast amount of biodata into a coherent account of Dickens's public and private selves. . . . Important to Dickens scholars while accessible to the general public." Libr J

Tomalin, Claire. The invisible woman: the story of Nelly Ternan and Charles Dickens. Knopf 1991 317p il $25; pa $13   **92**
1. Ternan, Ellen Lawless, 1839-1914
ISBN 0-394-57959-3; 0-679-73819-3 (pa)
                                    LC 90-44499
This is an account "of Dickens's secret 12-year relationship with the young actress Ellen Ternan, which lasted from his 45th year until his death in 1870." Christ Sci Monit
"Besides offering a marvelous whirl through the 'disreputable' world of the theater, Tomalin provides a new slant on Dickens as a writer uncomfortably trapped in his own conventional morality." Publ Wkly

Diderot, Denis, 1713-1784
Furbank, Philip Nicholas. Diderot; a critical biography; [by] P. N. Furbank. Knopf 1992 524p il $29.50   **92**
ISBN 0-679-41421-5   LC 92-52960
The author "surveys Diderot's life, offering critical examinations of his major works, including . . . discussions of Letter on the Blind, The Nun, D'Alembert's Dream, and Jacques the Fatalist as well as Rameau and the Encyclopédie." Libr J
"Mr. Furbank's book is directed to the general reader, but the specialist will appreciate the vast quantity of new material on Diderot, along with accounts of the political and cultural events of 18th-century France." N Y Times Book Rev
Includes bibliographic references

Dietrich, Marlene, 1901-1992
Bach, Steven. Marlene Dietrich; life and legend. Morrow 1992 626p il $25   **92**
ISBN 0-688-07119-8   LC 92-23507
In this biography of the actress, Bach "plumbs Dietrich's special blend of erotic power, irony and humor and limns a strong-willed woman whose innumerable sexual affairs satisfied a simple need for companionship. . . . This engrossing biography is especially good on Dietrich's early career, her valiant anti-Nazi efforts and

Dietrich, Marlene, 1901-1992—*Continued*
her phoenixlike rebirth as a troubadour-actress." Publ
Wkly

Includes bibliographic references

Dillard, Annie
Dillard, Annie. An American childhood.
Harper & Row 1987 255p hardcover o.p.
paperback available $11   **92**
   ISBN 0-06-091518-8 (pa)   LC 87-45042

   In this autobiography, Dillard presents as account of
her life from her childhood in Pittsburgh until her entrance into college
   "Dillard's luminous prose painlessly captures the pain
of growing up in this wonderful evocation of childhood.
. . . The events of childhood often loom larger than
life; the magic of Dillard's writing is that she sets down
typical childhood happenings with their original immediacy and force." Publ Wkly

Dillard, Annie. The writing life. Harper
& Row 1989 111p hardcover o.p. paperback
available $10   **92**
   ISBN 0-06-091988-4 (pa)   LC 89-45034

   The author "probes the sorcery that levitates her own
writing, discussing with clear eye and wry wit how,
where and why she writes." Publ Wkly

DiMaggio, Joe
Kahn, Roger. Joe & Marilyn; a memory
of love. Morrow 1986 269p o.p.; Avon Bks.
paperback available $4.95   **92**
   1. Monroe, Marilyn, 1926-1962
   ISBN 0-380-70462-5 (pa)   LC 86-17990

   The author "doesn't repeat exhaustively covered accounts of the lives of DiMaggio and the late Monroe.
The two legendary figures assume humanity in this
recreation of baseball's 'Yankee Clipper' and 'the world's
most famous blond.'" Publ Wkly
   "The numerous anecdotes and pithy quotes, combined
with Kahn's ingratiating, laid-back writing style, make
this account diverting, if at times depressing, reading."
Booklist

Dinesen, Isak, 1885-1962
Dinesen, Isak. Letters from Africa,
1914-1931; edited for the Rungstedlund
Foundation by Frans Lasson; translated by
Anne Born. University of Chicago Press
1981 xli, 474p il hardcover o.p. paperback
available $16.95   **92**
   ISBN 0-226-15311-8 (pa)   LC 80-25856

   Original Danish edition, 1978

   "Isak Dinesen (Baroness Karen Blixen) kept up a
lively correspondence with Danish relatives and friends
throughout her 17 years on a Kenyan coffee farm—the
period that was to form the basis of her *Out of Africa*.
. . . The range and depth of these letters . . . provide
deep insight into the popular Danish writer, as well as
a wealth of precise details concerning her years in
Africa." Booklist

Includes bibliographic references

Thurman, Judith. Isak Dinesen; the life
of a storyteller. St. Martin's Press 1982 495p
il $19.95; pa $10.95   **92**
   ISBN 0-312-43737-4; 0-312-43738-2 (pa) LC 82-5573

   This biography traces Dinesen's life from her childhood in Denmark through her years in Kenya and her
return to Denmark to focus on her literary career
   "With great insight and a novelist's gift for nuance
and narrative sweep, Thurman shows the extraordinary
degree to which Dinesen's life and art meshed. In addition, Thurman's sensitive criticism of Dinesen's work
reveals exceptional artistry in its own right." Booklist

Includes bibliographies

Dix, Dorothea Lynde, 1802-1887
Schlaifer, Charles. Heart's work: Civil War
heroine and champion of the mentally ill,
Dorothea Lynde Dix; [by] Charles Schlaifer
and Lucy Freeman. Paragon House 1991
175p $19.95   **92**
   ISBN 1-55778-419-1   LC 91-10328

   This is the life story of a woman who "won the
respect of men and women alike through her quiet
determination and selfless dedication to help those imprisoned in troubled minds." Publ Wkly
   "An excellent portrait of an amazing and energetic
woman." Booklist

Donoghue, Denis
Donoghue, Denis. Warrenpoint. Knopf
1990 193p il $19.45   **92**
   ISBN 0-394-53966-4   LC 89-77855

   In this intellectual autobiography the Irish literary
critic "has written a seductive book. Perhaps it could
be said that he has spliced together two books, one of
which is more seductive than the other. One of them
narrates. The other contemplates. Warrenpoint is a series
of passages, not unlike journal entries, some of which
deal with his youth in the Northern Irish seaside town
of that name, . . . while the others consist of the annotations of the professor and man of letters. . . . The
conjunction of the young Donoghue with the savant is
among the attractions of the book." London Rev Books

Doolittle, James Harold, 1896-1993
Doolittle, James Harold. I could never be
so lucky again; an autobiography; by
General James H. "Jimmy" Doolittle, with
Carroll V. Glines. Bantam Bks. 1991 574p
il $22.50; pa $5.99   **92**
   ISBN 0-553-07807-0; 0-553-29725-2 (pa) LC 91-3353

   In this "memoir, World War II flying ace Doolittle
. . . recalls his sterling military career and the importance of his family." Booklist
   "The book recalls vividly Doolittle's days as an aviation pioneer—and retells the exciting story of the Tokyo
raid." Publ Wkly

Includes bibliographic references

Dostoyevsky, Fyodor, 1821-1881

Dostoyevsky, Fyodor. Complete letters; edited and translated by David Lowe and Ronald Meyer. Ardis Pubs. 1988-1991 5v il ea $35   **92**

LC 87-17510

Contents: v1 1832-1859 (ISBN 0-88233-897-8); v2 1860-1867 (ISBN 0-88233-926-5); v3 1868-1871 (ISBN 0-88233-542-1); v4 1872-1877 (ISBN 0-88233-543-X); v5 1878-1881 (ISBN 0-88233-544-8)

These letters afford a "marvelous self-portrait of the Russian novelist teetering between farce and tragedy while seeking literary fame." Publ Wkly

Includes bibliographies

Frank, Joseph. Dostoevsky. Princeton Univ. Press 1976-1986 3v il   **92**

Also available in paperback

Contents: [v1] The seeds of revolt, 1821-1849 $58 (ISBN 0-691-06260-9); [v2] The years of ordeal, 1850-1859 $47 (ISBN 0-691-06576-4); [v3] The stir of liberation, 1860-1865 $58 (ISBN 0-691-06652-3)

The first three volumes of a projected five volume biography of Dostoevsky, these volumes trace his life from his boyhood to 1865. His writings are discussed in relation to influences and themes which recur in his greatest works

Includes bibliographic references

Douglas, Kirk, 1916-

Douglas, Kirk. The ragman's son; an autobiography. Simon & Schuster 1988 510p il hardcover o.p. paperback available $5.95
92

ISBN 0-671-73789-9 (pa)   LC 88-11563

Also available G.K. Hall large print edition

"The son of a Jewish immigrant, Douglas fought brutal poverty and prejudice to make his own way through college and into acting. His book is full of wonderful celebrity anecdotes and insider's details on a Hollywood that has now disappeared. More importantly, Douglas shares surprising vulnerability and insight, which belie his hard-jawed image." Libr J

Douglass, Frederick, 1817?-1895

Douglass, Frederick. My bondage and my freedom   **92**

1. Abolitionists

Hardcover and paperback editions available from various publishers

First published 1855 by Orton & Mulligan

In this autobiography Douglass tells of his life as a slave and his early years in the abolitionist movement

Douglass, Frederick. Narrative of the life of Frederick Douglass, an American slave; written by himself   **92**

1. Abolitionists

Hardcover and paperback editions available from various publishers

Originally published 1845 by the Boston Anti-slavery office

"Frederick Douglass became famous as a slave who escaped to the North and spent his life-time in the abolitionist movement. His 'Narrative,' one of three auto-biographical works written by the self-taught slave, is the story of his life up to his escape to freedom." Libr J

Huggins, Nathan Irvin. Slave and citizen: the life of Frederick Douglass; edited by Oscar Handlin. Little, Brown 1980 194p (Lib. of American biography) $21   **92**

1. Abolitionists

ISBN 0-316-38001-6   LC 79-89336

Also available in paperback from Scott, Foresman

"Huggins has written the preeminent biography of the preeminent black man of the 19th Century. . . . This intelligent, insightful, and even angry, book offers an excellent introduction to Douglass, black life, and the snarls of race relations in the last century." Libr J

Includes bibliographic references

McFeely, William S. Frederick Douglass. Norton 1991 465p il map $24.95   **92**

ISBN 0-393-02823-2   LC 89-36517

This "biography of Frederick Douglass supplies a welcome portrait of the slave-turned-abolitionist-orator and a careful reconsideration of his ideas and writings." Booklist

Includes bibliographic references

Doyle, Sir Arthur Conan, 1859-1930

Symons, Julian. Conan Doyle: portrait of an artist. Mysterious Press 1987 c1979 137p il hardcover o.p. paperback available $9.95
92

ISBN 0-89296-926-1 (pa)   LC 87-20432

First published 1979 in the United Kingdom

Symons "writes knowledgeably and empathetically about the prolific Victorian doctor turned author. . . . The book contains perceptive comments on the Holmesian adventures and other literary works that Doyle considered superior to the detecting tales that made him enduringly famous." Publ Wkly

Includes bibliography

Dravecky, Dave

Dravecky, Dave. Comeback; [by] Dave Dravecky with Tim Stafford. Zondervan 1990 252p il $17.99; pa $8.99   **92**

ISBN 0-310-52880-1; 0-310-52881-X (pa)

LC 89-49238

The former baseball pitcher describes his career and his brief return to baseball in 1989 following his 1988 cancer surgery

Dreiser, Theodore, 1871-1945

Lingeman, Richard R. Theodore Dreiser; [by] Richard Lingeman. v2: an American journey, 1908-1945. Putnam 1990 544p il $39.95   **92**

ISBN 0-399-13520-0   LC 86-9380

This volume completes the biography begun with Theodore Dreiser: At the gates of the city, 1871-1907 (1987)

"Able to reconcile contrarieties in Dreiser's personality, Lingeman is particularly good in detailing Dreiser's run-ins with censors and publishers, his uneasy alliance/friendship with Mencken, his use of the Gillette-Brown

Dreiser, Theodore, 1871-1945—*Continued*
murder case in An American Tragedy, his compulsive
affairs with younger women, and his unflagging search
for purpose in an apparently chaotic universe." Libr J

Includes bibliography

Duberman, Martin B.
Duberman, Martin B. Cures; a gay man's
odyssey; [by] Martin Duberman. Dutton
1991 305p o.p.; New Am. Lib. paperback
available $11   **92**

ISBN 0-452-26780-3 (pa)   LC 90-46658

"Duberman, a noted playwright, historian, gay activist,
and author . . . chronicles his slow emergence from the
closet of the late 1960's by slaying the dragons of his
deeply internalized homophobia. He candidly describes
his involvement with 1960's psychoanalysis and his half-
hearted desire to be heterosexual." Libr J

The author "kept a meticulous journal that has allowed him to construct a moving chronicle of his transition from closet case to liberated gay man in an autobiography that is at once historically significant and personally instructive." Nation

Includes bibliographic references

Dubus, Andre, 1936-
Dubus, Andre. Broken vessels; essays.
Godine 1991 155p $19.95; pa $11.95   **92**

ISBN 0-87923-885-2; 0-87923-948-4 (pa) LC 91-6711

Biographical "essays dating from 1977 to 1990, in
which short-story writer Dubus, the victim of a 1986
automobile accident, poignantly confronts a turbulent
period of critical success, medical crisis, and marital
failure. Body and mind battered, Dubus endures both
as a man and as a writer." Booklist

Dufy, Raoul. See class 709.2

Dukakis, Kitty
Dukakis, Kitty. Now you know; [by] Kitty
Dukakis with Jane Scovell. Simon &
Schuster 1990 315p il hardcover o.p.
paperback available $9.95   **92**

1. Dukakis, Michael
ISBN 0-671-74179-9 (pa)   LC 90-39952

The author discusses her recovery from addictions to
alcohol and amphetamines

"Dukakis is candid about her life; her problems with
her mother seem to have had particular impact on her,
especially the discovery that her mother was an adopted
child whose own birth mother was her nanny. What she
is not very open about in the book is her husband
Michael's role in the maelstrom that has been Kitty's
life." Booklist

Duke, Patty
Duke, Patty. Call me Anna: the
autobiography of Patty Duke; [by] Patty
Duke and Kenneth Turan. Bantam Bks.
1987 298p il $17.95; pa $5.99   **92**

ISBN 0-553-05209-8; 0-553-27205-5 (pa)
                                                LC 87-47591

The actress discusses her life and career; her relationship with the theatrical managers who raised her and
changed her name from Anna; her suicide attempts and
eventual treatment for manic-depressive illness; and her
1985 election as president of the Screen Actors Guild

Dunne, John Gregory, 1932-
Dunne, John Gregory. Harp. Simon &
Schuster 1989 235p hardcover o.p.
paperback available $8.95   **92**

ISBN 0-671-72514-9 (pa)   LC 89-32701

"Growing up in Hartford, Conn., the Irish Catholic
author who would one day write *True Confessions* felt
like a social outcast, a 'harp' among WASPs whom he
pejoratively called 'Yanks.' After being drafted into the
army this 'quintessential Princeton prig' shed some of
his snobbery, likewise his shame over his Irish roots.
. . . [A] 'mordant, defiant, raunchy, sarcastic memoir.'"
Publ Wkly

Durante, Jimmy, 1893-1980
Robbins, Jhan. Inka dinka doo: the life
of Jimmy Durante. Paragon House 1991
194p il $19.95   **92**

ISBN 1-55778-418-3   LC 91-15305

The author "relates how Durante's career began in
Coney Island honky-tonks and endured burlesque, vaudeville, radio, and film before progressing to television. He
combines interview quotes with previously published
material padded out with asides of social history." Libr
J

Includes bibliographic references

Duranty, Walter, 1884-1957
Taylor, S. J. Stalin's apologist: Walter
Duranty, the New York Times's man in
Moscow. Oxford Univ. Press 1990 404p il
$24.95   **92**

ISBN 0-19-505700-7   LC 89-16108

This is a biography of Walter Duranty "the flamboyant, controversial newsman who headed The New
York Times's Moscow bureau from 1922 to 1936. . .
. He wielded great influence in shaping American attitudes toward the Soviet Union during its fledgling
years. . . . The principal strength of S. J. Taylor's indif-
ferently written but beautifully researched volume is that
it exposes the very amoral pragmatism of Duranty's
character." N Y Times Book Rev

Includes bibliographic references

Dürer, Albrecht. See class 709.2

Dylan, Bob. See class 780.92

Eakins, Thomas. See class 709.2

Earhart, Amelia, 1898-1937
Lovell, Mary S. The sound of wings: the
life of Amelia Earhart. St. Martin's Press
1989 xxv, 420p il hardcover o.p. paperback
available $12.95   **92**

ISBN 0-312-05160-3 (pa)   LC 89-34935

Earhart, Amelia, 1898-1937—*Continued*
This biography concentrates on Earhart's "personality and character and the relationships with family and friends as they contributed to her accomplishments. . . . The book also contains excerpts from *Last Flight*, Earhart's reworked logbook and notes on the fateful 1937 flight." Libr J
Includes bibliographic references

Rich, Doris L. Amelia Earhart; a biography. Smithsonian Institution Press 1989 321p il $24.95   **92**
ISBN 0-87474-836-4   LC 89-32181
Also available in paperback from Dell
"Rich emphasizes Earhart's flying career and the stories and personalities behind her accomplishments. It is a scholarly account of her life, highlighting her goals, enthusiasm, and competitive pioneer spirit." Libr J
A "fast-paced, richly detailed biography." Publ Wkly
Includes bibliography

Early, Jubal Anderson, 1816-1894
Osborne, Charles C. Jubal; the life and times of General Jubal A. Early, CSA, defender of the lost cause. Algonquin Bks. 1992 560p il maps $29.95   **92**
ISBN 0-945575-35-1   LC 92-11982
This biography of the Confederate general is "a well-written and balanced account of Early's life and career that will appeal to general readers and scholars alike. Osborne explains the source of Early's extraordinary ambition, describes his antebellum political career, including his antisecessionist vote in the 1861 Virginia convention, and traces his development throughout the war into the bitter and unreconstructed rebel he always remained. The bulk of the book consists of Osborne's careful campaign history." Libr J
Includes bibliographic references

Eban, Abba, 1915-
Eban, Abba. Personal witness; Israel through my eyes. Putnam 1992 671p il $29.95   **92**
1. Zionism 2. Israel—Foreign relations
ISBN 0-399-13589-8   LC 91-15808
This memoir by the former Israeli foreign minister and ambassador to the United States and the United Nations describes his involvement in Israel's history from WW II to the 1980's
"With his graceful prose and his eye for detail, Mr. Eban makes the history of Israel, as seen through his career, a true delight to read." N Y Times Book Rev

Einstein, Albert, 1879-1955
Pais, Abraham. 'Subtle is the Lord'—the science and life of Albert Einstein. Oxford Univ. Press 1982 552p il $35; pa $16.95   **92**
ISBN 0-19-853907-X; 0-19-520438-7 (pa) LC 82-2273
The author "organizes his account of Einstein's scientific activities around five topics: Statistical Physics; Relativity, the Special Theory; Relativity, the General Theory; The Later Journey (on unified field theory); and the Quantum Theory. Within each section, the account is basically chronological." Science

This is "a splendid scientific biography of Einstein. . . . As Einstein would surely have desired, physics is given priority, but it is illuminated by precise historical details that make its development come alive for the reader." Choice
Includes bibliographic references

Eiseley, Loren C., 1907-1977
Christianson, Gale E. Fox at the wood's edge: a biography of Loren Eiseley. Holt & Co. 1990 517p il hardcover o.p. paperback available $16.95   **92**
ISBN 0-8050-1858-1 (pa)   LC 89-24714
A biography of archaeologist, professor, and literary naturalist Eiseley who was a poet and writer as well as a cult hero to members of the 1960's counterculture
"A competent, literate, well-documented chronicle of Eiseley's life. Mr. Christanson shows us the haunting of Eiseley, but cannot quite conjure up the ghost himself. If the subject remains elusive, undoubtedly Eiseley meant it to be." N Y Times Book Rev
Includes bibliography

Eisenhower, Dwight D. (Dwight David), 1890-1969
Ambrose, Stephen E. Eisenhower; soldier and president. Simon & Schuster 1990 635p il hardcover o.p. paperback available $16   **92**
ISBN 0-671-74758-4 (pa)   LC 90-9701
Condensed version of a two volume work published 1983-1984
"Tracing Eisenhower's family background, education, military and political careers, and influence as elder statesman, the author chronicles Eisenhower's triumphs and failures and at the same time provides a vivid picture of the off-duty Ike. . . . This is the definitive one-volume biography of Eisenhower." Publ Wkly
Includes bibliographic references

Eisenhower, David. Eisenhower: at war, 1943-1945. Random House 1986 xxvii, 977p il maps $29.95   **92**
ISBN 0-394-41237-0   LC 81-40212
The author "intially envisaged a book about his grandfather's second Presidential term. . . . Eventually he decided that he could not treat the White House years at all without examining the way World War II had prepared Eisenhower for the Presidency. 'Eisenhower: At War' is, in consequence, the first of three projected volumes on the age of Eisenhower." N Y Times Book Rev
"A highly detailed, virtually day-by-day chronicle . . . , the book is meticulously researched, carefully written, imposing in its sheer massiveness." Newsweek
Includes bibliography

Eleanor, Queen, consort of Henry II, King of England, 1122?-1204

Kelly, Amy Ruth. Eleanor of Aquitaine and the four kings; [by] Amy Kelly. Harvard Univ. Press 1950 431p il hardcover o.p. paperback available $12.95   **92**

1. Middle Ages—History 2. Great Britain—History—1154-1399, Plantagenets
ISBN 0-674-24254-8 (pa)

This life story of Eleanor of Aquitaine, wife of two kings and mother of two others, is also a study of the twelfth century in which she lived

Includes bibliography

Eliade, Mircea, 1907-1986

Eliade, Mircea. Autobiography; translated from the Romanian by Mac Linscott Ricketts. Harper & Row 1981-1988 2v il v1 pa $15.95; v2 $19.95   **92**

ISBN 0-226-20407-3 (v1 pa); 0-226-20411-1 (v2)
LC 81-6308

Volume two published by University of Chicago Press. Volume one hardcover o.p.; paperback reprint published 1990 by University of Chicago Press

Contents: v1 Journey east, journey west, 1907-1937; v2 Exile's odyssey, 1937-1960

This is an autobiography by the writer and teacher on mythology and religion. The first volume traces Eliade's life and intellectual development from his birth in Bucharest in 1907 to his sojourn in India to his return to Romania. Volume two begins in 1937 and relates his experiences in Romania during World War II, in Paris after the war, and in the United States after his emigration in 1956

Includes bibliographic references

Eliot, George, 1819-1880

Eliot, George. Selections from George Eliot's letters; edited by Gordon S. Haight. Yale Univ. Press 1985 567p il hardcover o.p. paperback available $19.95   **92**

ISBN 0-300-04050-4 (pa)   LC 84-13222

"This one-volume condensation of the nine-volume edition of 'The George Eliot Letters' (Yale Univ. Pr., 1954-78) generously represents the mind and heart of the great Victorian writer. Haight arranges the letters (11 are published for the first time) into a helpful format spanning 14 significant periods in GE's life. . . . Also, the letters often illuminate, in fascinating detail, the evolution of Eliot's works as well." Libr J

Taylor, Ina. A woman of contradictions: the life of George Eliot. Morrow 1989 255p il $19.95   **92**

ISBN 0-688-09405-8   LC 89-38405

"Considering the early years as crucial to Eliot's later intellectual, social, and creative development, Taylor presents a woman who was 'everything a Victorian female was not supposed to be': sensual, materialistic, assertive, and subtly deceptive. . . . Although this biography seems sketchy at times, it sheds new light on a major novelist." Libr J

Includes bibliography

Eliot, T. S. (Thomas Stearns), 1888-1965

Gordon, Lyndall. Eliot's new life. Farrar, Straus & Giroux 1988 356p il hardcover o.p. paperback available $9.95   **92**

ISBN 0-374-52205-7 (pa)   LC 88-7235

This biography, by the author of Eliot's early years begins with the poet's 1927 conversion to Anglicanism. The author "argues that Eliot's entire work should be interpreted as a spiritual autobiography." N Y Times Book Rev

"Gordon has fashioned an engrossing, highly original biography that uses previously unavailable letters to forge dozens of new links between [Eliot's] personal life and the poems and plays." Publ Wkly

Includes bibliography

Elizabeth I, Queen of England, 1533-1603

Erickson, Carolly. The first Elizabeth. Summit Bks. 1984 c1983 447p il hardcover o.p. paperback available $14   **92**

1. Great Britain—History—1485-1603, Tudors
ISBN 0-671-50393-6 (pa)   LC 82-19274

"Readers will find this Elizabeth to be a spellbinding figure. That Erickson adds to our knowledge of the queen is no mean accomplishment, given the quality of previous biographies. This work ranks with the best and will appeal both to a general audience and to scholars. It is a deft blend of the public and private life of Elizabeth, stemming from Erickson's interpretation of the written records. An exciting book." Libr J

Includes bibliography

Hibbert, Christopher. The virgin queen: Elizabeth I; genius of the Golden Age. Addison-Wesley 1991 287p il maps $24; pa $14.42   **92**

1. Great Britain—History—1485-1603, Tudors
ISBN 0-201-15626-1; 0-201-60817-0 (pa)
LC 90-23275

First published 1990 in the United Kingdom

In this biography of Elizabeth I "Hibbert goes for personality and colour. He has the good gossip writer's nose for human foibles. . . . A wonderfully rich and interesting personality emerges from Mr. Hibbert's pages and he parades [the Queen's] whims, wisely without trying to reconcile them." Hist Today

Includes bibliographic references

Somerset, Anne. Elizabeth I. Knopf 1991 636p il $29.50   **92**

1. Great Britain—History—1485-1603, Tudors
ISBN 0-394-54435-8   LC 91-52731

Also available in paperback from St. Martin's Press

The author "offers some fresh thinking about various factors and actions of Elizabeth, queen and woman, including the influence on her sense of identity played by the execution and infamy of her mother, Anne Boleyn, and, toward the end of her reign, her refusal to name a successor." Booklist

The author "painstakingly reconstructs the world of the late 16th century. The research behind her portrayal of Elizabeth is prodigious, and her attention to particulars is unfailing." N Y Times Book Rev

Includes bibliographic references

Elizabeth I, Queen of England, 1533-1603
—Continued
Strachey, Lytton. Elizabeth and Essex; a
tragic history. Harcourt Brace & Co. 1928
296p il hardcover o.p. paperback available
$6.95   92
1. Essex, Robert Devereux, Earl of, 1566-1601
2. Great Britain—History—1485-1603, Tudors
ISBN 0-15-628310-7 (pa)
The story "begins where the conventional biography
recedes, when the queen at fifty-three falls in love with
a lad of twenty—a favorite whom she forgives again and
again and sends at last to the scaffold." Chicago Public
Libr
Includes bibliography

Ellington, Duke. See class 780.92

Engels, Friedrich, 1820-1895
Carver, Terrell. Friedrich Engels; his life
and thought. St. Martin's Press 1990 274p
il $39.95   92
ISBN 0-312-04501-8   LC 89-77153
This biography emphasizes Engel's early years, his
relationship with his capitalist family, and the ambiguity
of his collaboration with Marx
Includes bibliographic references

Escher, M. C. See class 709.2

Essex, Robert Devereux, Earl of, 1566-1601
Strachey, Lytton. Elizabeth and Essex. See
entry under Elizabeth I, Queen of England,
1533-1603   92

Farrell, Suzanne, 1945-
Farrell, Suzanne. Holding on to the air;
an autobiography; by Suzanne Farrell with
Toni Bentley. Summit Bks. 1990 322p il
o.p.; Penguin Bks. paperback available $13
                                                         92
ISBN 0-14-015722-0 (pa)   LC 90-38824
"An account of the private and professional life of
the American dancer. As Balanchine's muse and center
of his attentions, she collaborated with him in the creation of his most enduring ballets." Libr J
Includes bibliographic references

Fast, Howard, 1914-
Fast, Howard. Being red. Houghton
Mifflin 1990 370p il $22.45   92
ISBN 0-395-55130-7   LC 90-37492
Also available in paperback from Dell
"Fast tells of his lower-class Bronx childhood, World
War II work for Voice of America, disillusioning jour-
nalistic travels in the Third World, and activities in the
Communist Party, to which be remained doggedly loyal
until 1957." Libr J
"There are few autobiographies which touch the heart
and soul with such searing passion as this one. Howard
Fast has put all the energies which have distinguished

his books into this all-encompassing memoir. It definitely
should not be missed." West Coast Rev Books

Father Divine
Watts, Jill. God, Harlem U.S.A.: the
Father Divine story. University of Calif.
Press 1992 249p il $30   92
ISBN 0-520-07455-6   LC 91-21662
"Born George Baker Jr. (1876-1965), Father Divine
was a charismatic African-American religious leader who
in 1919 established the Peace Mission movement. . . .
[The author] argues that Father Divine should be
recognized as a theologian rather than as a cult figure."
Publ Wkly
"Watts is perfectly credible in fathoming the often
contradictory nature of Father Divine's personality and
ideas, and the result is the final word on the man for
some time to come." Booklist
Includes bibliography

Faulkner, William, 1897-1962
Blotner, Joseph Leo. Faulkner; a
biography; [by] Joseph Blotner. Random
House 1984 778p il hardcover o.p.
paperback available $16.95   92
ISBN 0-679-73053-2 (pa)   LC 83-17663
A revised, updated, and condensed one-volume edition
of the two volume work published 1974
"Using recent scholarship and posthumously published
Faulkner writings, Blotner effectively brushes up and
streamlines his detailed and indelible portrait of the
writer; he has also refined his critical analysis of
Faulkner's art in the light of recent reassessments and
reevaluations. Notes, chronology, genealogy." Booklist

Karl, Frederick Robert. William Faulkner,
American writer; a biography; [by] Frederick
R. Karl. Weidenfeld & Nicolson 1989 1131p
il $37.50   92
ISBN 1-55584-088-4   LC 88-13966
Also available in paperback from Fawcett Bks.
What the author "manages to accomplish is a par-
ticularly successful interweaving of the life and works of
the late Mississippian, one in which Faulkner's paradox-
ical self, warts and all, is a strongly felt presence. . .
. This is a tightly written volume in spite of its length;
nothing about it sprawls." Choice
Includes bibliography

Oates, Stephen B. William Faulkner, the
man and the artist; a biography. Harper &
Row 1987 363p il o.p.; Outlet paperback
available $6.99   92
ISBN 0-517-05345-4 (pa)   LC 86-46266
"Copiously researched, this biography is not geared to
the literary scholar; Oates invites any well-read individual
to follow him as he accessibly traces the major events
in William Faulkner's life. Oates reacts to Faulkner's
books not so much in terms of what they did to and
for American literature as what they did to and for
Faulkner as a person." Booklist
Includes bibliography

Ferlinghetti, Lawrence

Silesky, Barry. Ferlinghetti: the artist in his time. Warner Bks. 1990 294p il $24.95; pa $13.99   **92**

ISBN 0-446-51491-8; 0-446-39289-8 (pa)

LC 89-40473

"Now mainly a painter, Lawrence Ferlinghetti has been an influential and noted American poet . . . and promoter of avant-garde literature (as a publisher and through his San Francisco bookstore, City Lights). Silesky here works through his subject's lonely childhood, college and military life, and subsequent diverse travels before moving to the beat scene." Libr J

Includes bibliographic references

Feynman, Richard Phillips

Feynman, Richard Phillips. Surely you're joking, Mr. Feynman! adventures of a curious character; [by] Richard P. Feynman as told to Ralph Leighton; edited by Edward Hutchings. Norton 1985 350p $18.95   **92**

ISBN 0-393-01921-7   LC 84-14703

Also available in paperback from Bantam Bks.

An "unusual scientific autobiography by a most unusual Nobel Prize winner. . . . The anecdotes here range from his involvement in serious scientific projects to reminiscences about his boyhood experiments and college fraternity pranks. A vivid portrait of a lively, brilliant thinker." Booklist

Feynman, Richard Phillips. What do you care what other people think? further adventures of a curious character; [by] Richard P. Feynman, as told to Ralph Leighton. Norton 1988 255p il o.p.; Bantam Bks. paperback available $12.95   **92**

ISBN 0-553-34784-5 (pa)   LC 88-22390

Also available G.K. Hall large print edition

The first part of the memoir "contains stories from Feynman's personal life, the most poignant of which describes the tragic, misdiagnosed, and fatal illness of his first wife, Arlene. . . . The second part is the most gripping; it is an account of Feynman's frustrating encounter with Washington politics and diplomacy as a member of the Rogers Commission appointed to investigate the cause of the shocking explosion of the space shuttle, 'Challenger.'" Sci Books Films

Gleick, James. Genius: the life and science of Richard Feynman. Pantheon Bks. 1992 532p $27.50   **92**

ISBN 0-679-40836-3   LC 92-6577

"Although it would be hard to relate personal stories about Feynman more engagingly than Feynman himself did in *What Do You Care What Other People Think?* [entered above] the late Nobelist could not hope for better than his biographer here delivers—a portrait in which the physicist remains a person and is not reduced to an icon of science." Publ Wkly

Includes bibliography

Fielding, Henry, 1707-1754

Battestin, Martin C. Henry Fielding: a life; [by] Martin C. Battestin with Ruthe R. Battestin. Routledge 1989 738p il $45   **92**

ISBN 0-415-01438-7   LC 89-27717

This is a biography of the eighteenth-century playwright, novelist, and jurist

This biography "supersedes all previous lives of Fielding. . . . As the foremost present-day Fielding scholar, Battestin (University of Virginia) has produced a study that is a must for all academic and public libraries supporting an interest in Tom Jones and Joseph Andrews and the English theater, novel, and social history." Choice

Includes bibliographic references

Fisher, M. F. K. (Mary Frances Kennedy), 1908-1992

Fisher, M. F. K. (Mary Frances Kennedy). As they were. Knopf 1982 261p hardcover o.p. paperback available $12   **92**

ISBN 0-394-71348-6 (pa)   LC 81-48130

"An assortment of genial reminiscences and lasting impressions . . . that Fisher has collected over the years. A childhood in Whittier, California, two of the author's kitchens in Provence, travels and excursions throughout Europe, the harshness of a Long Island winter, and meals throughout the world are the stuff of which Fisher's pungent memories are made and which the writer conveys in the most graceful and gratifying of styles." Booklist

Fisher, M. F. K. (Mary Frances Kennedy). To begin again; stories and memoirs, 1908-1929. Pantheon Bks. 1992 179p $21
92

ISBN 0-679-41576-9   LC 92-54113

This volume "collects memoirs of the noted culinary writer's early years, reaching back to her infancy in Michigan and her childhood in California. . . . These are the work of a first-rate raconteur who learned to write and cook as well as she told stories." Libr J

Fitzgerald, Zelda, 1900-1948

Milford, Nancy. Zelda; a biography. Harper & Row 1970 424p il hardcover o.p. paperback available $15   **92**

1. Fitzgerald, F. Scott (Francis Scott), 1896-1940
ISBN 0-06-091069-0 (pa)

This biography of Zelda Sayre Fitzgerald, the wife of F. Scott Fitzgerald, draws upon many unpublished letters and interviews with friends of the Fitzgeralds, such as Edmund Wilson and Carl Van Vechten. It traces the life of Zelda Sayre through her marriage to Fitzgerald and their relationship, to her breakdown and, finally, her death in a sanatorium fire

Includes bibliographic references

Flanner, Janet, 1892-1978

Wineapple, Brenda. Genêt: a biography of Janet Flanner. Ticknor & Fields 1989 361p il $24.45   **92**

ISBN 0-89919-442-7   LC 89-5215

Also available in paperback from University of Neb. Press

"From 1925 to 1975, under the pseudonym Genêt, Janet Flanner wrote 'Letters from Paris' for The New Yorker. . . . [The author seeks to] document Flanner's reporting of the great events of the century (e.g., Lindbergh's landing, the Nuremberg trials), her profiles (e.g., De Gaulle, Picasso, Hitler), her . . . travels, her brief

Flanner, Janet, 1892-1978—*Continued*
marriage and her lesbian liaisons . . . and her long
friendships with . . . [such people] as Hemingway."
Choice

"Wineapple has written with great care about Janet
Flanner's inner state and her literary accomplishments.
. . . A thorough and reverent biography of an important
woman of letters." Booklist

Includes bibliography

Flaubert, Gustave, 1821-1880
Lottman, Herbert R. Flaubert; a
biography. Little, Brown 1989 396p il $24.95
92

ISBN 0-316-53342-4   LC 88-21919

Also available in paperback from Fromm Int.

"Lottman regards Flaubert as a master of his craft
and as perhaps the first truly modern author. Instead
of depending on opinions on Flaubert's habits and talent,
the biographer has researched his subject in many
original documents. . . . The reassessment made possible
by this method corrects some previous misconceptions
and redefines the impressive acclaim that Flaubert has
already been accorded." Booklist

Includes bibliography

Ford, Betty
Ford, Betty. Betty, a glad awakening; [by]
Betty Ford with Chris Chase. Doubleday
1987 217p il $16.95   **92**

ISBN 0-385-23502-X   LC 86-19646

Mrs. Ford presents a "description of her treatment for
addiction to prescription drugs and alcohol, as well as
an account of her first seven years of recovery. The joy
and enthusiasm with which she discusses her activities
and projects testify to the benefits of sobriety. Many
people contribute to the story: family members, professionals, and friends." Libr J

Ford, Ford Madox, 1873-1939
Judd, Alan. Ford Madox Ford. Harvard
Univ. Press 1991 476p il $27.50   **92**

ISBN 0-674-30815-8   LC 90-47379

A look at the public and private life of the influential
English novelist and editor

Forrest, Nathan Bedford, 1821-1877
Wills, Brian Steel. A battle from the start:
the life of Nathan Bedford Forrest.
HarperCollins Pubs. 1992 457p il maps $30
92

1. United States—History—1861-1865, Civil War
ISBN 0-06-016832-3   LC 91-58380

This is a biography of the Confederate Civil War
general

"The book is readable, Forrest emerges as a complex
though not entirely attractive human being, and the notes
and bibliography will give serious students plenty to sink
their teeth into." Booklist

Forrestal, James V., 1892-1949
Hoopes, Townsend. Driven patriot: the life
and times of James Forrestal; by Townsend
Hoopes and Douglas Brinkley. Knopf 1992
587p il $30   **92**

ISBN 0-394-57761-2   LC 91-23074

This is a biography of the financier and military organizer who, in 1947, became the first United States
Secretary of Defense

This "is an illuminating and at times haunting book
that will surely stand as the definitive account of James
Forrestal's triumphant yet tragic life." N Y Times Book
Rev

Includes bibliography

Forster, E. M. (Edward Morgan), 1879-1970
Furbank, Philip Nicholas. E. M. Forster;
a life; [by] P. N. Furbank. Harcourt Brace
Jovanovich 1978 2v in 1 il hardcover o.p.
paperback available $8.95   **92**

ISBN 0-15-628651-3 (pa)   LC 78-54671

First published 1977-1978 in the United Kingdom in
a two volume edition

The first part of this biography of the British writer,
entitled "The growth of the novelist, 1879-1914,"
describes Forster's childhood, travels to Italy, Greece, and
India, first novels, and early awareness of his homosexuality. The second part, "Polycrates' ring, 1914-1970,"
relates his experiences in Alexandria during World War
I, his second trip to India, his writing of A passage to
India, and his life as an active public figure

This biography "draws on all the available diaries and
correspondence, as well as on innumerable conversations.
Graceful, intimate, evocative, it is that rare thing, a
study of a major writer by a major critic who was also
a close friend." New Statesman

Includes bibliographic references

Fortas, Abe, 1910-1982
Kalman, Laura. Abe Fortas; a biography.
Yale Univ. Press 1990 499p il $29.95   **92**

ISBN 0-300-04669-3   LC 90-31482

An account of Fortas' career "as a government official
during the New Deal, as founder of a powerful Washington law firm that represented both business interests and
societal underdogs, as a long-time confidante and adviser
to Lyndon Johnson, and as a Supreme Court Justice."
Libr J

Includes bibliographic references

Foss, Joe
Foss, Joe. A proud American; the
autobiography of Joe Foss; [by] Joe Foss
with Donna Wild Foss. Pocket Bks. 1992
359p il $22   **92**

ISBN 0-671-75735-0   LC 92-28200

The autobiography of the WWII hero who served as
governor of South Dakota, commissioner of the American Football League and host of the TV series The
Outdoorsman and The American Sportsman

The author "emerges as a man with a broad combative streak, unlikely to win Mr. Nice Guy awards but
as honest about himself as he is about others." Booklist

Includes bibliographic references

Fosse, Bob

Gottfried, Martin. All his jazz; the life & death of Bob Fosse. Bantam Bks. 1990 483p il $24.95　　**92**

ISBN 0-553-07038-X　　LC 90-38650

This is a biography of the choreographer of the musical comedies The Pajama Game, Damn Yankees, Sweet Charity, and Chicago as well as the film musicals Cabaret and All That Jazz

Grubb, Kevin Boyd. Razzle dazzle: the life and work of Bob Fosse. St. Martin's Press 1989 xxviii, 292p il $29.95　　**92**

ISBN 0-312-03414-8　　LC 89-35077

"Fosse drew upon his early days as a dancer in vaudeville and strip joints to create a highly charged, stylistic choreography that reshaped the Broadway musical for three decades. He also directed four films and a TV special. . . . Grubb has produced a fascinating, lively, and balanced biography that is a fitting tribute to Fosse's genius. Required reading for theater and dance buffs." Libr J

Includes bibliographic references

Fossey, Dian

Hayes, Harold. The dark romance of Dian Fossey; [by] Harold T.P. Hayes. Simon & Schuster 1990 351p il hardcover o.p. paperback available $10.95　　**92**

1. Gorillas
ISBN 0-671-74231-0 (pa)　　LC 90-34941

This is a biography of the American ethologist noted for her field work with the mountain gorillas of Africa

This "is a compassionate, fascinating portrait of a driven woman, a portrayal that does not downplay the ugly side of her nature . . . but still shows her as a woman of great courage and dedication." Booklist

Includes bibliographic references

Mowat, Farley. Woman in the mists: the story of Dian Fossey and the mountain gorillas of Africa. Warner Bks. 1987 380p il hardcover o.p. paperback available $10.95　　**92**

1. Gorillas
ISBN 0-446-38720-7 (pa)　　LC 87-40166

The author has "organized Fossey's journals into a biography that quotes her writings so heavily as to be autobiographical. Much of the text parallels material in Fossey's Gorillas in the Mist [entered in class 599.8] but provides additional insights into her personal life, difficulties in maintaining funding, and the continuation of her work up to her death in 1985. This gripping, action-packed story is essential reading for all who understand the sacrifice of self for the preservation of other species." Libr J

Foster, Stephen Collins. See class 780.92

Fox, Charles Elmer

Fox, Charles Elmer. Tales of an American hobo; preface by Albert E. Stone; introduction by Lynne M. Adrian. University of Iowa Press 1989 xxiii, 226p (Singular lives) $19.95; pa $9.95　　**92**

ISBN 0-87745-251-2; 0-87745-252-0 (pa) LC 89-5055

Fox "left a broken home in 1928, when he was not quite 15, and quickly became part of the network of those who traveled wherever the trains and their imaginations could carry them, picking up odd jobs at factories or farms until wanderlust struck again. . . . At times Fox rambles, and some stories fall flat. Taken as a whole, however, the book is a lively picture of an unjustly neglected part of American culture." Publ Wkly

Includes bibliographic references

Frank, Anne, 1929-1945

Frank, Anne. The diary of a young girl; translated from the Dutch by B. M. Mooyaart-Doubleday　　**92**

1. World War, 1939-1945—Jews 2. Netherlands—History—1940-1945, German occupation 3. Jews—Netherlands

Available in various bindings and editions including a large print edition

This is the diary of a "German-Jewish girl who hid from the Nazis with her parents, their friends, and some other fugitives in an Amsterdam warehouse from 1942 to 1944. Her diary, covering the years of hiding, was found by friends and published as Het achterhus (1947); it was later published in English as The Diary of a Young Girl (1952). . . . Written with humor as well as insight, it shows a growing girl with all the preoccupations of adolescence and first love. The diary ends three days before the Franks and their group were discovered by the Nazis." Reader's Ency. 3d edition

Frank, Anne. The diary of Anne Frank: the critical edition. Doubleday 1989 719p il $35　　**92**

1. World War, 1939-1945—Jews 2. Netherlands—History—1940-1945, German occupation 3. Jews—Netherlands
ISBN 0-385-24023-6　　LC 88-9678

"Prepared by the Netherlands State Institute for War Documentation; introductions by Harry Paape, Gerrold van der Stroom and David Barnouw; with a summary of the report by the State Forensic Science Laboratory of the Ministry of Justice compiled by H.J.J. Hardy; edited by David Barnouw and Gerrold van der Stroom; translated by Arnold J. Pomerans and B. M. Mooyaart-Doubleday." Title page

This version of the diary (entered above) also includes several related studies and reports

Includes bibliographic references

Frankenthaler, Helen. See class 709.2

Frankfurter, Felix, 1882-1965

Baker, Leonard. Brandeis and Frankfurter. See entry under Brandeis, Louis Dembitz, 1856-1941　　**92**

Franklin, Benjamin, 1706-1790

Benjamin Franklin: his life as he wrote it; edited by Esmond Wright. Harvard Univ. Press 1990 c1989 297p il $25　　**92**

ISBN 0-674-06654-5　　LC 89-39795

First published 1989 in the United Kingdom

"Wright's new edition of Franklin's Autobiography [entered below] supplements the usual text with other autobiographical writings. . . . The book is divided into eight chapters, and the Autobiography, itself reorganized, is

Franklin, Benjamin, 1706-1790—*Continued*
heavily interspersed with some five dozen letters and
numerous other notes, essays, diary entries, speeches, interviews, and articles. The result both plugs some holes
in the original and extends the life beyond 1758, when
the *Autobiography* ends." Libr J

Bowen, Catherine Drinker. The most
dangerous man in America: scenes from the
life of Benjamin Franklin. Little, Brown
1986 c1974 274p pa $8.95   **92**

ISBN 0-316-10379-9

"An Atlantic Monthly Press book"

A reissue of the title first published 1974

"Bowen utilizes Franklin's autobiographical writings, in
addition to . . . secondary works on him . . . in order
to detail five 'scenes' from his life. They include, for
example, a discussion of Franklin at the Albany Congress
of 1754, and two views of him in London, 1757-1766."
Libr J

"In spare, unflamboyant prose, [this book] evokes the
essences, rather than the surfaces and details, of Franklin's first 68 years." New Repub

Includes bibliography

Franklin, Benjamin. The autobiography of
Benjamin Franklin   **92**

Hardcover and paperback editions available from
various publishers

Written between 1771 and 1788

"Franklin's account of his life, written for his son
William. . . . During the Revolutionary War, the
manuscript was put aside. . . . Franklin later more than
doubled the length . . . but still took the story only
to 1757-1759, ending before the period of his greatest
public service. Still, the book remains the first undisputed classic of American literature and one of the
most interesting autobiographies in English." Benet's
Reader's Ency of Am Lit

Fraser, Sylvia
Fraser, Sylvia. My father's house; a
memoir of incest and of healing. Ticknor
& Fields 1988 c1987 254p o.p.; Perennial
Lib. paperback available $10   **92**

1. Incest
ISBN 0-06-097218-1 (pa)   LC 87-37456

First published 1987 in Canada

"In this stunningly powerful memoir, Fraser, a successful Canadian journalist and novelist, recaptures a childhood that had been repressed for 40 years. She had no
conscious memory of the incestuous sexual abuse to
which she had been subjected. . . . [However] memories
seeped through in dreams and in the sexual violence of
her novels. Here, she tells her story with eloquence,
compassion, and almost unbearable candor." Libr J

Freud, Anna, 1895-1982
Coles, Robert. Anna Freud; the dream of
psychoanalysis. Addison-Wesley 1991 xxv,
220p (Radcliffe biography ser) $19.95   **92**

ISBN 0-201-57707-0   LC 91-30542

"A Merloyd Lawrence book"

As the first child psychoanalyst, Freud "contributed
theoretical rigor to the new discipline, and as a teacher,
she trained a generation of analysts. But it is as a
humanitarian that she was most profoundly gifted.

Founder of care facilities for children during the London
Blitz and lifelong advocate for children, she dedicated
herself to helping innumerable individual youngsters."
Booklist

"Adhering closely to Freud's own words as written and
recorded on tape, Coles highlights—and cogently analyzes—her contributions to psychoanalysis and our understanding of child development in this comprehensive, not
exclusively admiring tribute." Publ Wkly

Includes bibliographic references

Freud, Sigmund, 1856-1939
Freud, Sigmund. The Freud/Jung letters;
the correspondence between Sigmund Freud
and C. G. Jung; edited by William
McGuire; translated by Ralph Manheim and
R. F. C. Hull. Princeton Univ. Press 1974
xlii, 650p o.p.; Harvard Univ. Press
paperback available $16.95   **92**

1. Jung, C. G. (Carl Gustav), 1875-1961
ISBN 0-674-323330-0 (pa)

"Bollingen series"

"The birth, nurturing, and ultimate termination of
friendship pervades the 360 letters written between 1906
and 1914, and the early twentieth-century psychological
concepts exposed are enlivened by case histories and
personal sidelights." Booklist

Includes bibliography

Gay, Peter. Freud; a life for our time.
Norton 1988 xx, 810p il $30   **92**

ISBN 0-393-02517-9   LC 87-20454

Also available in paperback from Anchor Bks.

This biography provides an "updating of our knowledge of the life of the founder of psychoanalysis . . .
and it also delineates the continuing impact of Freud's
thought on modern endeavors in a number of fields."
Sci Books Films

"The book is beautifully written. Gay's approach is
to try to understand Freud and his alliances and environment rather than to worship or challenge him." Choice

Includes bibliography

Jones, Ernest. The life and work of
Sigmund Freud. Basic Bks. 1953-1957 3v il
v1 $30, v2-3 ea $40   **92**

Contents: v1 The formative years and the great
discoveries, 1856-1900 (ISBN 0-465-04016-0); v2 Years
of maturity, 1901-1919 (ISBN 0-465-04017-9); v3 The last
phase, 1919-1939 (ISBN 0-465-04018-7)

A "standard reference not only to Freud and his work
but to the intellectual history of our time." Times Lit
Suppl

Includes bibliographic references

Frost, Robert, 1874-1963
Burnshaw, Stanley. Robert Frost himself.
Braziller 1986 342p il hardcover o.p.
paperback available $12.95   **92**

ISBN 0-8076-1234-0 (pa)   LC 86-20793

This "book has an important purpose: to rescue Frost
from the negative image that has lingered like a dark
storm cloud since Lawrance Thompson's three-volume
biography. [A condensed one-volume edition entered
below]. The final two chapters in particular argue for
the humane and generous Frost, in contrast to the

Frost, Robert, 1874-1963—*Continued*
maniacal monster of Thompson's account." Libr J

Includes bibliography

Thompson, Lawrance Roger. Robert Frost; a biography; by Lawrance Thompson and R.H. Winnick; the authorized life of the poet condensed into a single volume edited by Edward Connery Lathem. Holt & Co. 1982 c1981 543p il $25   **92**

ISBN 0-03-050921-1   LC 80-28337

Condensation of the author's three volume biography originally published 1966-1976

Examines the craft and both the public and private life of the influential American poet

Gage, Nicholas
Gage, Nicholas. A place for us. Houghton Mifflin 1989 419p il o.p.; Simon & Schuster paperback available $10.95   **92**

1. Gatzoyiannis family
ISBN 0-671-72585-8 (pa)   LC 89-35429

"A Marc Jaffe book"

In this sequel to Elenei [entered below under Gatzoyiannis, Eleni] Gage "tells what happened to Eleni's children after they escaped from their Greek mountain village. Gage was nine years old when he and three of his sisters boarded a ship to America in 1949, to meet the father they had never known." Publisher's note

"Gage's story is moving and humorous, a tale of adjustment to an unknown culture." Libr J

Galbraith, John Kenneth, 1908-
Galbraith, John Kenneth. A life in our times; memoirs. Houghton Mifflin 1981 563p $16.45   **92**

1. United States—Politics and government—1900-1999 (20th century)
ISBN 0-395-30509-8   LC 80-27373

The author describes his "experiences in diverse roles, including service in the Roosevelt administration during the depression; wartime price control during WW II; editor of 'Fortune'; ambassador to India; educator and celebrated author of widely read books on economics." Choice

In this book Galbraith "re-establishes the fact that as a raconteur and a literary stylist he stands with the best." N Y Times Book Rev

Gandhi, Mahatma, 1869-1948
Gandhi, Mahatma. Gandhi's autobiography; the story of my experiments with truth; translated from the original in Gujarati by Mahadev Desai   **92**

1. India—Politics and government

Hardcover and paperback editions available from various publishers

First published 1927-1929 in the United Kingdom in two volumes with title: My experiments with truth

Written by Gandhi during a prison term in the early 1920's and originally published as a series of articles in an Indian magazine, this book reveals the basic forces and factors which molded Gandhi's life. It describes his colorful childhood, his varied education, his singular career as a lawyer, his complex religious and intellectual development, his championship of the untouchables of his native land, and his epic fight for Indian independence

Garbo, Greta, 1905-1990
Daum, Raymond W. Walking with Garbo; conversations and recollections; [by] Raymond Daum; edited and annotated by Vance Muse. HarperCollins Pubs. 1991 222p il $25; pa $13   **92**

ISBN 0-06-016492-1; 0-06-092355-5 (pa)

LC 90-55925

This is a pictorial biography of the actress, accompanied by Garbo's words, as recorded by Daum, and a historical text by Muse

García Lorca, Federico, 1898-1936
Gibson, Ian. Federico García Lorca: a life. Pantheon Bks. 1989 xxii, 551p il hardcover o.p. paperback available $15.95   **92**

ISBN 0-679-73157-1 (pa)   LC 88-28871

Loosely based on the two-volume Spanish work published 1985-1987

This is a biography of the Spanish writer who was assassinated during the Spanish Civil War

"Gibson's sense of place is equalled by his sense of person. His re-creation of the teeming artistic talent and the café life of Spain in the 1930s is superb. So effective is Gibson's account of Lorca's vitality and fecundity that along with admiration for the poet's opulent talent, he provokes a fierce outrage at his ultimate fate." Times Lit Suppl

Includes bibliography

Gardner, Alexander, 1821-1882
Katz, D. Mark. Witness to an era: the life and photographs of Alexander Gardner; the Civil War, Lincoln, and the West. Viking Studio Bks. 1991 305p il $50   **92**

ISBN 0-670-82820-3   LC 89-40696

A "tribute to the life and work of pioneer photographer Gardner, whose documentation of the Civil War era—especially famous battles and President Lincoln—and the faces and places of the Old West has left an indelible mark on the history of photojournalism." Booklist

Includes bibliographic references

Gardner, Ava, 1922-1990
Gardner, Ava. Ava; my story. Bantam Bks. 1990 315p il $19.95; pa $5.99   **92**

ISBN 0-553-07134-3; 0-533-29306-0 (pa) LC 90-1102

Also available Thorndike Press large print edition

In this account of her life, the film star "describes her drunken and amatory excesses, her abortions, the battering she took at the hands of George C. Scott, the failures of her three marriages—and the failures of her husbands." N Y Times Book Rev

Gates, Daryl F.

Gates, Daryl F. Chief: my life in the LAPD; [by] Daryl F. Gates with Diane K. Shah. Bantam Bks. 1992 371p il $22.50

92

1. Los Angeles (Calif.). Police Dept.
ISBN 0-553-07301-X   LC 91-40060

This is the autobiography of the Los Angeles Chief of Police

"'Chief' is a lively, readable defense of the Los Angeles style of hard-nosed policing to which Mr. Gates has devoted most of his life." N Y Times Book Rev

Gatzoyiannis, Eleni

Gage, Nicholas. Eleni. Random House 1983 470p $19.95   **92**

1. Greece—History—1900-1999 (20th century)
ISBN 0-394-52093-9   LC 82-42803

Also available in paperback from Ballantine Bks.

"On August 28, 1948, a Greek peasant woman, Eleni Gatzoyiannis, was executed by guerrillas in her village of Lia. Some 30 years later, her son . . . wrote this book . . . weaving together three stories: World War II and the civil war in Greece; Eleni's life and how the catastrophic events in Greece smashed her world; and his own search for vengeance." Libr J

"The separate strands lead to an intensely moving climax, making Eleni one of the rare books in which the power of art re-creates the full historical truth." NY Rev Books

An account of Nicholas Gage's life in America, A place for us, is entered above

Gauguin, Paul. See class 709.2

Gaulle, Charles de, 1890-1970

Lacouture, Jean. De Gaulle. Norton 1990-1992 2v il ea $29.95; pa $15.95   **92**

1. France—Politics and government   LC 90-37997

This is an abridgement of the original French edition

Contents: v1 The rebel, 1890-1944; translated from the French by Patrick O'Brian (ISBN 0-393-02699-X; 0-393-30999-1); v2 The ruler, 1945-1970; translated from the French by Alan Sheridan (ISBN 0-393-03084-9; 0-393-31000-0)

This is a biography of the French general and political figure. The first volume covers De Gaulle's life from his childhood in Lille to the liberation of Paris in 1944. Volume two continues to his death in 1970

Includes bibliographic references

Gehrig, Lou, 1903-1941

Robinson, Ray. Iron horse: Lou Gehrig in his time. Norton 1990 300p il $22.50   **92**

ISBN 0-393-02857-7   LC 89-29272

Also available Thorndike Press large print edition and in paperback from HarperCollins Pubs.

"Playing in the considerable shadow of Babe Ruth, Lou Gehrig's accomplishments as baseball's 'Iron Horse' include a legendary record of 2,130 consecutive games played. . . . Robinson's narrative not only traces Gehrig's life and career but also provides an insightful look at baseball in the 1920s and the Depression years." Libr J

Genghis Khan, 1162-1227

Ratchnevsky, Paul. Genghis Khan: his life and legacy; translated and edited by Thomas Nivison Haining. Blackwell 1992 313p il $34.95

92

ISBN 0-631-16785-4   LC 91-2295

Original German edition, 1983

This is a biography of "the man responsible for unifying the scattered Mongol tribes into an empire-building nation." Libr J

"This is an outstanding piece of historical writing that will enthrall both specialists and those with a more casual interest in the field." Booklist

Includes bibliographic references

Geronimo, Apache Chief, 1829-1909

Debo, Angie. Geronimo; the man, his time, his place. University of Okla. Press 1976 xx, 480p il maps (Civilization of the American Indian ser) hardcover o.p. paperback available $17.95   **92**

1. Apache Indians
ISBN 0-8061-1828-8 (pa)   LC 76-13858

The author "interviewed people who knew Geronimo, who fought with him and lived with him in captivity. She has written a colorful narrative of revenge and raids, of escape, pursuit and surrender. . . . Her portrait of Geronimo the old celebrity is touching, and a tribute to an exceptional leader." Publ Wkly

Includes bibliography

Gershwin, George. See class 780.92

Giacometti, Alberto. See class 709.2

Gifford, Kathie Lee

Gifford, Kathie Lee. I can't believe I said that! an autobiography; [by] Kathie Lee Gifford with Jim Jerome. Pocket Bks. 1992 300p il $22   **92**

ISBN 0-671-74241-8   LC 92-56723

This autobiography looks at the author's childhood, singing career, religious convictions, successful TV career as Regis Philbin's sidekick, and her marriage to sports broadcaster Frank Gifford

Gilbreth, Frank Bunker, 1868-1924

Gilbreth, Frank B. (Frank Bunker). Cheaper by the dozen; [by] Frank B. Gilbreth, Jr. and Ernestine Gilbreth Carey; drawings by Vasiliu. [updated ed]. Crowell 1963 245p il $19.95   **92**

1. Gilbreth family
ISBN 0-690-18632-0

Also available in hardcover from Amereon

First published 1948

This biographical portrait of family life highlights the reminiscences of the twelve Gilbreth children and their adventures with their father, whose time and efficiency studies were applied to domestic life

Gill, Brendan, 1914-

Gill, Brendan. Here at the New Yorker. Random House 1975 406p il o.p.; Carroll & Graf Pubs. paperback available $12.95

92

1. New Yorker (Periodical)
ISBN 0-88184-350-4 (pa)

This book chronicles Brendan Gill's years as a member of the staff. He presents an "insider's view of his colleagues (Gibbs, Hellman, E. B. White), artists (Addams, Arno, Steinberg), and contributors (Benchley, Flanner, O'Hara, Edmund Wilson), their traditions and idiosyncrasies, attitudes toward fame, money, literature, drink, and fellow-toilers." Publ Wkly

Ginsberg, Allen, 1926-

Miles, Barry. Ginsberg: a biography. Simon & Schuster 1989 588p il $24.95

92

ISBN 0-671-50713-3   LC 89-6422
Also available in paperback from HarperPerennial

"Describing his world travels, mantra-chanting, meditation, musical compositions and achievements as a photographer, Miles traces Ginsberg's development into a member of the establishment." Publ Wkly
This "book skillfully evokes the poet's childhood, authoritatively expresses his opinions on sundry matters of later life and work, gives him his due as life force of youthful rebellion and the 60's counterculture. Read it; you'll enjoy yourself." N Y Times Book Rev

Includes bibliography

Schumacher, Michael. Dharma lion: a critical biography of Allen Ginsberg. St. Martin's Press 1992 769p il $35   92
ISBN 0-312-08179-0   LC 92-25224

"Allen Ginsberg, choreographer of the Beat movement, ambassador of the counterculture and great communicator of several hip generations, attracts attention that crosses natural, generational, sexual and literary boundaries. . . . Given access to Ginsberg's private archives and having interviewed more than 100 people in 10 years of research, Schumacher weaves a monumental cultural biography. . . . Beat veterans will be delighted with this book, and newcomers well-informed by it." Publ Wkly

Includes biliographic references

Giovanni, Nikki

Giovanni, Nikki. Gemini: an extended autobiographical statement on my first twenty-five years of being a black poet. Bobbs-Merrill 1972 c1971 149p o.p.; Penguin Bks. paperback available $6.95   92
ISBN 0-14-004264-4 (pa)

These autobiographical essays trace Giovanni's life from her early years in Cincinnati to her years as successful poet and black activist

Gleason, Jackie

Henry, William A. The great one: the life and legend of Jackie Gleason; [by] William A. Henry III. Doubleday 1992 321p il $22.50   92
ISBN 0-385-41533-8   LC 91-40090

Also available G.K. Hall large print edition
This is a biography of the popular TV comedian and movie actor
"This is a thorough, penetrating, uncompromising study. . . . The book presents diverse sentiments from those who knew him well." Publ Wkly

Godden, Jon, 1906-1985

Godden, Jon. Two under the Indian sun; [by] Jon and Rumer Godden. Beech Tree Bks. 1987 c1966 199p il pa $8.95   92
1. Godden, Rumer, 1907- 2. India—Description
ISBN 0-688-07422-7   LC 87-20742

First published 1966 by Knopf

The authors here "evoke their Indian childhood. In 1914, after a year in London, the girls come home to Bengal where their father is a steamship agent. They are six and seven-and-a-half years of age, and their stories cover the next five years." Publ Wkly

Godden, Rumer, 1907-

Godden, Jon. Two under the Indian sun. See entry under Godden, Jon, 1906-1985

92

Godden, Rumer. A house with four rooms. Morrow 1989 319p il $18.95; pa $10.95   92
ISBN 0-688-08629-2; 0-688-10382-0 (pa)
                    LC 89-12147

"In this installment in her autobiography—covering from 1946 to 1978—Godden weaves personal drama, reflection, and revelations into the ongoing narrative about the time in which many of her books were written. . . . The volume opens with Godden's arrival in war-torn Liverpool and concludes with her seventieth birthday." Booklist
"Godden is a born storyteller with an eye for quality of detail. . . . This second volume of [her] memoirs shimmers with charisma and gives an intimate, precious glimpse into her life and work." Libr J

Godden, Rumer. A time to dance, no time to weep. Beech Tree Bks. 1987 243p il $16.95; pa $7   92
ISBN 0-688-07421-9; 0-688-08904-6 (pa)
                    LC 87-22697

"This first volume of autobiography by an English novelist who resided much of her life in India covers the years 1907-46." Booklist

Gogh, Theo van. See class 709.2

Gogh, Vincent van. See class 709.2

Goldwater, Barry M. (Barry Morris), 1909-

Goldwater, Barry M. (Barry Morris). Goldwater; by Barry M. Goldwater with Jack Casserly. Doubleday 1988 414p il $21.95   92
1. United States—Politics and government—1900-1999 (20th century)
ISBN 0-385-23947-5   LC 87-38136

Also available in paperback from St. Martin's Press

Goldwater, Barry M. (Barry Morris), 1909-—*Continued*

"In this memoir, Goldwater focuses primarily on his political career and his role in helping the conservative arm of the Republican Party gain . . . legitimacy and power. In addition to his discussion of the 1964 presidential race . . . he provides chapters on Vietnam, Nixon, Watergate, and Reagan." Libr J

Goldwyn, Samuel, 1882-1974

Berg, A. Scott (Andrew Scott). Goldwyn; a biography. Knopf 1989 579p il $24.95

92

ISBN 0-394-51059-3   LC 88-8395

This is a life of the producer of such films as Stella Dallas, Wuthering Heights, The Best Years of Our Lives, The Little Foxes, and Pride of the Yankees

"Berg dusts off a few skeletons in the Goldwyn closet, telling both what Goldwyn wanted people to believe about his past and giving a more truthful picture of the mogul's life. Both accounts are inventively colorful and compelling. . . . Embedded into this life story is a riveting account of Hollywood history in general and of Goldwyn's MGM studios in its heyday." Booklist

Includes bibliographic references

Goodman, Benny. See class 780.92

Gorbachev, Mikhail

Doder, Dusko. Gorbachev; heretic in the Kremlin; [by] Dusko Doder and Louise Branson. Viking 1990 450p o.p.; Penguin Bks. paperback available $9.95   92

1. Soviet Union—Politics and government
ISBN 0-14-011535-8 (pa)   LC 89-40665

This book "explores the evolution of Gorbachev as a political visionary and describes the resistance Gorbachev's plans . . . received from both ends of the political spectrum." Libr J

Includes bibliographic references

Kaiser, Robert Greeley. Why Gorbachev happened; his triumphs and his failure; [by] Robert G. Kaiser. Simon & Schuster 1991 476p map hardcover o.p. paperback available $14   92

1. Soviet Union—Politics and government
ISBN 0-671-77878-1 (pa)   LC 91-6986

The author "shows how Gorbachev succeeded in creating 'real politics' in the Soviet Union but failed to redeem his achievements in stable living conditions. The impact of the Chernobyl disaster and the roles of rival politicians like Boris Yeltsin are especially well documented." Libr J

Includes bibliographic references

Mikhail S. Gorbachev: an intimate biography; by the editors of Time Magazine; with an introduction by Strobe Talbott; edited by Donald Morrison. New Am. Lib. 1988 264p il $14.95; pa $4.50   92

1. Soviet Union—Politics and government
ISBN 0-451-82179-3; 0-451-15700-1 (pa)
                                   LC 88-50093

"Treatment of Gorbachev's early years relies on hearsay, his reminiscences, and those of fellow student Zdenek Mlynar. . . . The chapter on the 1987 Washington summit is the best. Readers will find none of the promised intimacy, but may enjoy the match of the authors' style with Gorbachev's celebrity." Libr J

Sheehy, Gail. The man who changed the world: the lives of Mikhail S. Gorbachev. HarperCollins Pubs. 1990 401p il hardcover o.p. paperback available $11   92

1. Soviet Union—Politics and government
ISBN 0-06-092120-X (pa)   LC 90-55173

"Gorbachev's humble origins in rural, famine-ridden Stalinist Russia, his rise through the Communist Party machinery, and his revolutionary overhaul of an inept, inflexible sociopolitical and economic system are charted." Booklist

"A riveting book. Sheehy's narrative style is conversational and breezy, but the ease with which this book may be read should not mislead anyone as to its serious and rigorous scholarship." SLJ

Includes bibliographic references

Gordimer, Nadine, 1923-

Gordimer, Nadine. Conversations with Nadine Gordimer; edited by Nancy Topping Bazin and Marilyn Dallman Seymour. University Press of Miss. 1990 xxiv, 321p (Literary conversations ser) $32.50; pa $14.95   92

ISBN 0-87805-444-8; 0-87805-445-6 (pa)
                                   LC 90-12556

This is a collection of interviews in which Gordimer talks "about her life as a white South African, about her fiction, and about writers she admires." Booklist

Includes bibliographic references

Gordon, Lyndall

Gordon, Lyndall. Shared lives. Norton 1992 285p il $24.95   92

1. Jews—South Africa
ISBN 0-393-03164-0   LC 92-8414

Gordon "offers a candid and touching memoir of her friendship with three women, all now dead, who grew up with the author in the middle-class liberal Jewish society of Cape Town, South Africa, during the 1950s." Publ Wkly

Gordon, Ruth, 1896-1985

Gordon, Ruth. My side; the autobiography of Ruth Gordon. Fine, D.I. 1986 502p il pa $9.95   92

ISBN 0-917657-81-0   LC 86-80029

In this memoir, stage and motion picture actress and screenwriter Gordon recalls her career from 1915 to the mid-1970's

Göring, Hermann, 1893-1946

Irving, David John Cawdell. Göring; a biography; [by] David Irving. Morrow 1989 573p il $22.95   92

1. Germany—History—1933-1945
ISBN 0-688-06606-2   LC 88-21776

Göring, Hermann, 1893-1946—*Continued*
Also available in paperback from Avon Bks.

This is a life of the German political and military leader who was head of the Luftwaffe and the organizer of Germany's economic mobilization under Hitler
"The merit of this Göring biography lies in its mass of biographical detail and in numerous (though not complete) source references." N Y Times Book Rev

Gould, Glenn. See class 780.92

Graham, Bill. See class 780.92

Graham, Martha
De Mille, Agnes. Martha: the life and work of Martha Graham. Random House 1991 509p il $30; pa $15   **92**
    ISBN 0-394-55643-7; 0-679-74176-3 (pa)
                                   LC 87-36964

"De Mille traces Graham's uphill path to greatness, chronicling the long, arduous hours of practice, the austere discipline of her teaching methods, her poverty, and uncompromising dedication to her visions." Booklist
"DeMille's strong writing, combined with her personal knowledge of Graham and all the important players in Graham's life . . . provide insights into the 20th century American dance world and Graham's life that only a fellow dancer, choreographer, and woman could." Libr J

Includes bibliography

Graham, Martha. Blood memory. Doubleday 1991 279p il $25   **92**
    ISBN 0-385-26503-4   LC 91-15444
Also available in paperback from Pocket Bks.

In this memoir Graham "recounts her early apprenticeship with the Denishawn School, her stint as 'Art' in the Greenwich Village Follies, and the struggle to form and maintain her own company." Libr J
"Like [Graham's] dances, her book 'Blood Memory' explores life inside out and in many roles and guises." N Y Times Book Rev

Graham, Maury, 1917-
Graham, Maury. Tales of the iron road; my life as king of the hobos; [by] "Steam Train" Maury Graham and Robert J. Hemming. Paragon House 1990 222p il $19.95   **92**
    ISBN 1-55778-129-X   LC 89-8682
"'Steam Train' Graham began hoboing in 1931 and by 1980 had traveled countless miles across the nation. In more recent years, he has become a celebrity of sorts. In this remarkable book he relates a saga of his life and travels." Libr J

Grant, Cary, 1904-1986
Higham, Charles. Cary Grant; the lonely heart; [by] Charles Higham and Roy Moseley. Harcourt Brace Jovanovich 1989 358p il $18.95   **92**
    ISBN 0-15-115787-1   LC 88-34801
Also available in paperback from Avon Bks.

A look at the actor's career and private life based on interviews with some 150 people

Grant, Ulysses S. (Ulysses Simpson), 1822-1885
Anderson, Nancy Scott. The generals: Ulysses S. Grant and Robert E. Lee; [by] Nancy Scott Anderson, Dwight Anderson. Knopf 1988 c1987 523p o.p.; Vintage Bks. paperback available $15   **92**
    1. Lee, Robert E. (Robert Edward), 1807-1870
    2. United States—History—1861-1865, Civil War
    ISBN 0-394-75985-0 (pa)   LC 87-45341

In this dual biography the authors "create a parallel reconstruction and interpretation of the lives and careers of Grant and Lee. In a narrative iridescent in its fluidity, applaudable in its respectable and responsible approach, the authors limn the two famous protagonists' heritages, boyhoods, military educations and initiations, their wives and families, their Civil War operations and successes and failures, and, of course, their characters." Booklist

Includes bibliography

Catton, Bruce. Grant moves south; with maps by Samuel H. Bryant. Little, Brown 1960 564p maps $27.95; pa $15.95   **92**
    1. United States—History—1861-1865, Civil War—Campaigns
    ISBN 0-316-13207-1; 0-316-13244-6 (pa)

"Grant's development as a man and leader is brilliantly shown in this reconstruction of his Mississippi campaign." Booklist

Includes bibliography

Catton, Bruce. Grant takes command; with maps by Samuel H. Bryant. Little, Brown 1969 556p maps $27.95; pa $15.95   **92**
    1. United States—History—1861-1865, Civil War—Campaigns
    ISBN 0-316-13210-1; 0-316-13240-3 (pa)

This sequel to Grant moves south, entered above, "takes up Ulysses S. Grant's career just after his capture of Vicksburg in 1863. . . . It carries the action right up to Richmond and Lee's surrender at Appomattox." Publ Wkly

Includes bibliography

Grant, Ulysses S. (Ulysses Simpson). Memoirs and selected letters; personal memoirs of U.S. Grant, selected letters, 1839-1865. Library of Am. 1990 2v in 1 il maps $35   **92**
    1. United States—History—1861-1865, Civil War
    ISBN 0-940450-58-5   LC 90-60013

This volume includes Grant's personal memoirs, first published in 1885 and 175 letters written between 1839 and 1865

Includes bibliographic references

McFeely, William S. Grant; a biography. Norton 1981 592p il hardcover o.p. paperback available $15.95   **92**
    ISBN 0-393-30046-3 (pa)   LC 80-25279

The author "traces the life of Grant from his youth to his death from throat cancer in 1885, all the while assessing Grant's character and the impact of events on his life." Booklist

Includes bibliography

Grant, Ulysses S. (Ulysses Simpson), 1822-1885—*Continued*

Smith, Gene. Lee and Grant. See entry under Lee, Robert E. (Robert Edward), 1807-1870   **92**

Graves, Robert, 1895-1985

Graves, Richard Perceval. Robert Graves; the years with Laura, 1926-1940. Viking 1990 380p il o.p.; Penguin Bks. paperback available $16   **92**

1. Jackson, Laura, 1901-1991

ISBN 0-14-016948-2 (pa)   LC 90-50114

This work "focuses on the passionate relationship between two leading poets of our time, Robert Graves and Laura Riding. A sequel to *Robert Graves: The Assault Heroic 1895-1926* [1987] it begins with the slightly shell-shocked WW I veteran Graves, a close friend of T. E. Lawrence, setting off for a teaching stint in Egypt accompanied by his wife and Laura, a ménage à trois. The Mallorca years follow, a period that sees the production of much of Graves's best work. . . . Richard Graves writes of his uncle with cool objectivity, letting the emotionally and intellectually surcharged facts speak for themselves." Publ Wkly

Includes bibliographic references

Graves, Robert. Conversations with Robert Graves; edited by Frank L. Kersnowski. University Press of Miss. 1989 183p (Literary conversations ser) $32.50; pa $14.95   **92**

ISBN 0-87805-413-8; 0-87805-414-6 (pa)

LC 89-32216

A compilation of brief interviews with the British poet, novelist and mythographer culled from a wide variety of sources

"The diversity of viewpoints here is admirably opinionated and will complement more traditional biographies of Graves." Booklist

Greeley, Andrew M., 1928-

Greeley, Andrew M. Confessions of a parish priest; an autobiography. Simon & Schuster 1986 507p il $18.95   **92**

ISBN 0-671-61084-8   LC 86-13090

In this memoir, the author, a Roman Catholic priest, social scientist, and novelist, writes about the "difficult daily life of a priest, the ways of Irish Catholics in Chicago, ethnicity in American life and the meaning and relevance of religious sociology." N Y Times Book Rev

"Although judgments are often very harsh, Greeley's is not a vindictive or libelous tract. . . . In sum, Greeley's is a candid look at his church, its leaders, his colleagues, himself in his several roles." Commonweal

Greene, Graham, 1904-1991

Sherry, Norman. The life of Graham Greene. v1: 1904-1939. Viking 1989 xxiii, 783p il o.p.; Penguin Bks. paperback available $15.95   **92**

ISBN 0-14-014450-1 (pa)   LC 88-40559

"This first of a projected two-volume biography concludes with the composition of Greene's masterpiece, 'The Power and the Glory.'" Libr J

"Drawing on Greene's revealing personal diary, the autobiography *A Sort of Life* [1971], and the uncanny parallels between reality and art found in Greene's fiction, Sherry has produced a massive volume covering the author's formative years. . . . A major biocritical opus of a major figure in world literature." Booklist

Greer, Reg, 1904-1983

Greer, Germaine. Daddy we hardly knew you. Knopf 1990 c1989 311p $19.95   **92**

ISBN 0-394-58313-2   LC 89-45867

Also available in paperback from Fawcett Bks.

First published 1989 in the United Kingdom

"Driven to know if the father who returned from World War II a cold and vacant man had loved her once, feminist Greer follows a trail of false leads and outright lies to know the truth about the man who called himself Reg Greer." Libr J

"This is a very sad story, which [Ms. Greer] glosses with her rage and transcends with her vast knowledge of all sorts of things. At the same time it's a significant allegorical tale of a daughter's search for identity." NY Times Book Rev

Gromyko, Andreï Andreevich, 1909-1989

Gromyko, Andreï Andreevich. Memoirs; [by] Andrei Gromyko; foreword by Henry A. Kissinger; translated by Harold Shukman. Doubleday 1989 414p il $27.50   **92**

1. Soviet Union—Foreign relations

ISBN 0-385-41288-6   LC 89-27763

Original Russian edition, 1988

Gromyko "tells of his early years in a small Russian village; his experience in the traumatic Russian Civil War; and his steady rise to the top (Foreign Minister for over half a century) of the Soviet political hierarchy. He also renders portraits of the century's most fascinating personalities, ranging from Richard Nixon to Charlie Chaplin. His personal views of Stalin [are] presented in a separate chapter." Libr J

"Re-created conversations with JFK, Mao, FDR, Truman, Churchill, Nelson Rockefeller, Sadat and dozens of others spice a fast-moving narrative." Publ Wkly

Guinness, Alec

Dear Alec: Guinness at 75; edited by Ronald Harwood. Limelight Eds. 1989 140p il $16.95   **92**

ISBN 0-87910-127-X   LC 89-33976

"A collection of reminiscences and tributes by more than a dozen of Guinness' friends and colleagues on the occasion of his 75th birthday. . . . Contributors . . . include actresses Peggy Ashcroft, Eileen Atkins, Coral Browne and Irene Worth; actors John Gielgud and Cyril Cusak; filmmakers Franco Zeffirelli and George Lucas; and critic J.C. Trewin." Publisher's note

Guinness, Alec. Blessings in disguise. Knopf 1986 c1985 238p il $17.95   **92**

ISBN 0-394-55237-7   LC 85-45705

Also available in paperback from Warner Bks.

First published 1985 in the United Kingdom

The "English actor remembers his life, family, friends, and career, all the way from an unpromising first entrance on the legitimate stage to Star Wars." Booklist

Guinness, Alec—*Continued*

Guinness "has a real talent for writing: he isn't part of the usual gosh-and-gush school, but is a cool, ironic stylist who . . . is also highly entertaining, with unusual portraits of people one had thought had been done to death." New Statesman

Gunther, John, 1929-1947

Gunther, John. Death be not proud; a memoir. Harper & Row 1949 261p il hardcover o.p. paperback available $6 **92**

ISBN 0-06-080973-6 (pa)

A memoir of John Gunther's seventeen-year-old son, who died after a series of operations for a brain tumor. Not only a tribute to a remarkable boy but an account of a brave fight against disease

Guthrie, Woody. See class 780.92

Haig, Alexander Meigs, 1924-

Haig, Alexander Meigs. Inner circles; how America changed the world: a memoir; [by] Alexander M. Haig, Jr., with Charles McCarry. Warner Bks. 1992 610p il maps $24.95 **92**

1. United States—Foreign relations
ISBN 0-446-51571-X   LC 91-50409

A memoir emphasizing the author's participation in policy making during the Nixon, Ford and Reagan administrations

This book "contains some of the most perceptive and candid analyses of Korea, Vietnam and other major episodes in modern American foreign policy yet offered by any of the senior participants." N Y Times Book Rev

Includes bibliographic references

Haines, John Meade, 1924-

Haines, John Meade. The stars, the snow, the fire; twenty-five years in the northern wilderness: a memoir; by John Haines. Graywolf Press 1989 182p $17.95 **92**

1. Alaska—Description
ISBN 1-55597-117-2   LC 88-37719

Also available in paperback from Washington Sq. Press

"A Graywolf memoir"

"Mr. Haines, who was born in Virginia in 1924, homesteaded a wild spot north of Fairbanks, Alaska, in 1947. He has spent much of the intervening time there, at his cabin outside the hamlet of Richardson. These essays, all published previously, mostly in magazines, tell of his life under the harsh and sublime circumstances the land allowed." N Y Times Book Rev

Halston

Gaines, Steven S. Simply Halston; the untold story; [by] Steven Gaines. Putnam 1991 320p il $22.95 **92**

ISBN 0-399-13612-6   LC 91-13850

Also available in paperback from Jove Publs.

This look at the life and career of designer Halston who died of AIDS in 1990 includes interviews with friends and business acquaintances

Hamilton, Alexander, 1757-1804

Flexner, James Thomas. The young Hamilton; a biography. Little, Brown 1978 497p il $19.95 **92**

ISBN 0-316-28594-3   LC 77-13877

"This study thoroughly covers the first 26 years of Hamilton's life, from his squalid boyhood in Nevis through his experiences in the Revolutionary War. Flexner's is primarily a character study, designed to discover the incipient statesman in the insecure immigrant youth, student, and soldier." Libr J

Includes bibliography

Hamilton, Mary, 1866-1936

Hamilton, Mary. Trials of the earth; the autobiography of Mary Hamilton; edited by Helen Dick Davis; with a foreword by Ellen Douglas. University Press of Miss. 1992 xxii, 259p maps $25 **92**

ISBN 0-87805-579-7   LC 92-17772

"This autobiography of a Delta country pioneer woman is a unique addition to the history of the Mississippi lumber industry. Set in the late 19th and early 20th century, it is the account of Mary Hamilton, wife of a mysterious Englishman, Frank Hamilton, who came into the Delta as a lumberman. Hamilton details life in lumber camps where she was usually the only woman cooking for dozens of her husband's workers. . . . A true gem of regional history." Choice

Hamlisch, Marvin. See class 780.92

Hammer, Armand, 1898-1990

Weinberg, Steve. Armand Hammer; the untold story. Little, Brown 1989 501p il o.p.; Crown paperback available $3.99 **92**

ISBN 0-517-06282-8 (pa)   LC 89-12220

"This is an unauthorized biography of the medical doctor who built the Occidental Petroleum Corporation. . . . It attempts to convey a factual account of Hammer's extraordinary business career from mostly secondary sources." Libr J

"Weinberg's impressive book is the most complete portrait available of one of the twentieth century's most fascinating individuals." Booklist

Includes bibliography

Hammer, Signe

Hammer, Signe. By her own hand: memoirs of a suicide's daughter. Soho Press 1991 200p $18.95 **92**

ISBN 0-939149-49-4   LC 91-8564

Also available in paperback from Vintage Bks.

"If a mother takes her own life, how does her daughter identify herself? Signe Hammer was presented with that question. . . . The author's search is sometimes painfully gentle; sometimes it seethes with anger against her father. And when Signe traces that cataclysmic act back through family histories, she is calm, sensitive, and analytical all at once." Booklist

Hammett, Dashiell, 1894-1961

Johnson, Diane. Dashiell Hammett, a life. Random House 1983 xxi, 344p il o.p.; Fawcett Bks. paperback available $8.95   **92**

     ISBN 0-449-90223-4 (pa)   LC 82-40122

This is a biography of the writer whose works include Red harvest, The Dain curse, The Maltese falcon, The glass key, and The thin man

Hammett "began writing late and was finished at 40; for more than a quarter of a century he tried to write another book. It's to Diane Johnson's credit that she devotes two-thirds of her excellent life of Hammett to those burnt-out years. . . . Johnson has done her research well. A novelist, she writes her biography as a fiction writer would—which is to say with appropriate twists and a breezy style." Newsweek

Includes bibliography

Handel, George Frideric. See class 780.92

Hansberry, Lorraine, 1930-1965

Hansberry, Lorraine. To be young, gifted and black; Lorraine Hansberry in her own words; adapted by Robert Nemiroff; with original drawings and art by Miss Hansberry; and an introduction by James Baldwin. Prentice-Hall 1969 xxii, 266p il o.p.; New Am. Lib. paperback available $5.50   **92**

     ISBN 0-451-15952-7 (pa)

Work on this book and on the script for the play of the same title, which was presented at New York's Cherry Lane Theatre in 1969, "proceeded concurrently, each drawing upon the experiences and creative discoveries of the other, but ultimately diverging quite drastically." Postscript

Haring, Keith. See class 709.2

Harris, Jean

Harris, Jean. Marking time; letters from Jean Harris to Shana Alexander. Scribner 1991 189p $19.95   **92**

     1. Alexander, Shana
     ISBN 0-684-19367-1   LC 91-13799

Also available in paperback from Zebra Bks.

"A Robert Stewart book"

This book "consists solely of letters Harris wrote to famed journalist-turned-biographer Shana Alexander from New York's Bedford Hills Correctional Facility from January 1989 through February 1991." Booklist

"Harris describes with eloquence and ironic wit the vindictive cruelty, the petty small-mindedness, the rare joyous moments, and the human tragedies that are found in a woman's prison." Libr J

Harrison, Rex

Harrison, Rex. A damned serious business; my life in comedy. Bantam Bks. 1991 288p il $21.95   **92**

     ISBN 0-553-07341-9   LC 90-20364

This memoir focuses "primarily on Harrison's career on stage and in front of the camera. From middle-class Liverpool beginnings to modest success on the London stage to international acclaim as Henry Higgins in *My*

Fair Lady, Harrison regales readers with his acting philosophies while also offering anecdotes featuring the beknighted of theater and the movies." Booklist

Haskell, Molly

Haskell, Molly. Love and other infectious diseases; a memoir. Morrow 1990 302p $18.95   **92**

     1. Sarris, Andrew
     ISBN 0-688-07006-X   LC 89-28554

Also available in paperback from Carol Pub. Group

The author presents "a chronicle of her psychological journey through her husband's . . . collapse and recovery from an encephalitic virus infection. . . . Just as her husband gets well, [Molly Haskell] gets sick—ultimately needing surgery three times for bowel obstructions. And then, in a freak coincidence, he requires the identical surgery." N Y Times Book Rev

"Blessed with a remarkable gift for clarity and self-reflection, Haskell uses Sarris' illness as a lantern by which she can shine a light on the dark corners of her life." Time

Havel, Václav

Havel, Václav. Letters to Olga; June 1979-September 1982; translated from the Czech with an introduction by Paul Wilson. Knopf 1988 397p o.p.; Holt & Co. paperback available $16.95   **92**

     1. Havel, Olga
     ISBN 0-8050-0973-6 (pa)   LC 87-45434

"During his three-year imprisonment for human rights activities, Czech dissident and . . . playwright Havel was allowed to write nothing but one letter a week to his wife. In these 144 letters that made it through the prison censor, Havel meditates on theatre, religion, and philosophy, his personal world-view; the meaning of his actions; and the issues of human identity and personal responsibility in modern society." Libr J

Hawking, S. W. (Stephen W.)

White, Michael. Stephen Hawking; a life in science; [by] Michael White and John Gribbin. Dutton 1992 304p $23   **92**

     ISBN 0-525-93447-2   LC 92-699

Hawking's "British biographers, both scientists, examine their subject's personal history and ably fill in the spaces between his great leaps of theory. They avoid sentimentalizing the physicist's disabling ALS (Lou Gehrig's disease), which struck him in his early 20s, while acknowledging that the condition has had a dramatic impact on his life and reputation." Publ Wkly

Includes bibliographic references

Hawthorne, Nathaniel, 1804-1864

Miller, Edwin Haviland. Salem is my dwelling place: a life of Nathaniel Hawthorne. University of Iowa Press 1991 596p il $35; pa $16.95   **92**

     ISBN 0-87745-332-2; 0-87745-381-0 (pa)
     LC 91-14543

This is a biography of the 19th century American novelist

Hawthorne, Nathaniel, 1804-1864 — Continued

"Psychologically probing (but free of all jargon), Miller's elegantly written study gives us a fresh, sympathetic picture of an immensely complex, repressed man. . . . A masterful work, wholly satisfying." Libr J

Includes bibliographic references

Hayden, Tom

Hayden, Tom. Reunion; a memoir. Random House 1988 539p il o.p.; Collier Bks. paperback available $12.95   **92**

ISBN 0-02-033105-3 (pa)   LC 87-43224

"In a journey spanning more than 25 years, Hayden has gone from co-founding Students for a Democratic Society, to marriage to actress Jane Fonda, to serving in the California legislature. This political autobiography covers that tumultuous odyssey, concentrating on the 1960s." Libr J

"This book is a valuable addition to the archive of the Sixties, by one of the architects of that decade. It deserves to be read." West Coast Rev Books

Includes bibliographic references

Haydn, Joseph. See class 780.92

Hayes, Helen, 1900-1993

Hayes, Helen. My life in three acts; [by] Helen Hayes with Katherine Hatch. Harcourt Brace Jovanovich 1990 266p il $19.95   **92**

ISBN 0-15-163695-8   LC 89-15614

Also available Thorndike Press large print edition and in paperback from Simon & Schuster

"A Helen and Kurt Wolff book"

"Miss Hayes reflects on her . . . life and career as the first lady of the American theater, beginning with her Broadway debut in 1909, when she was 9 years old." N Y Times Book Rev

"A frank, pleasant, and heartfelt memoir sure to appeal to Hayes' many fans." Booklist

Hayworth, Rita, 1918-1987

Leaming, Barbara. If this was happiness: a biography of Rita Hayworth. Viking 1989 404p il o.p.; Ballantine Bks. paperback available $5.95   **92**

ISBN 0-345-36931-9 (pa)   LC 88-40649

This biography follows "Hayworth's life from reluctant child performer to incest victim, glamour queen and wife to Orson Welles and Prince Aly Kahn." Publ Wkly

Ms. Leaming "has created a convincing historical portrait of Rita Hayworth's world. The meticulous research makes the painful story of Hayworth's personal problems vivid." N Y Times Book Rev

Includes bibliography

Hearn, Lafcadio, 1850-1904

Cott, Jonathan. Wandering ghost: the odyssey of Lafcadio Hearn. Knopf 1991 xxi, 438p il $24.45   **92**

ISBN 0-394-57152-5   LC 90-4412

Also available in paperback from Kodansha Int./USA

This is a biography of the American writer who lived in Japan and published twenty books, many of them concerned with the culture of his adopted country

The author "resurrects a lively and unique personality and collection of nineteenth-century writings in this penetrating biography. . . . Hearn's cross-cultural quest for a meaningful life is a remarkable tale, well told by both the subject himself and his biographer." Booklist

Includes bibliographic references

Hearst, William Randolph, 1863-1951

Swanberg, W. A. Citizen Hearst: a biography of William Randolph Hearst. Scribner 1961 555p il hardcover o.p. paperback available $7.95   **92**

ISBN 0-684-17147-3 (pa)

In this book the author examines every side of his subject: Hearst the millionaire, the newspaper tycoon, the politician, the kingmaker; his influence on the Spanish-American War, his sumptuous life at San Simeon, and his art collecting

Includes bibliography

Heinlein, Robert A. (Robert Anson), 1907-1988

Heinlein, Robert A. (Robert Anson). Grumbles from the grave; edited by Virginia Heinlein. Ballantine Bks. 1990 c1989 281p il hardcover o.p. paperback available $5.95   **92**

ISBN 0-345-36941-6 (pa)   LC 89-6859

"A Del Rey book"

"Through a series of letters, selected by Heinlein and linked by commentary from his wife, we learn the history of sf writing in this country from the 1940s to 1972. Many of the letters are frank about the prudishness of early sf publishing, which censored some of Heinlein's work, and about his own antagonism toward religion." Libr J

"Entertaining for the general reader, invaluable for the serious student of sf or Heinlein." Booklist

Includes bibliography

Hellman, Lillian, 1906-1984

Hellman, Lillian. Pentimento. Little, Brown 1973 297p o.p.; New Am. Lib. paperback available $4.50   **92**

ISBN 0-451-15442-8 (pa)

This continuation of An unfinished woman—a memoir (1969) offers sketches of events and people from the author's past. She reminisces about her childhood in the South, some of her eccentric relatives including Cousin Bethe and Uncle Willy, Julia, her childhood friend who was trapped by the Nazis, Dashiell Hammett, who was her lover, and her experiences in the theater

"Pentimento is valuable as a picture of a woman and writer in the making." New Repub

Rollyson, Carl E. (Carl Edmund). Lillian Hellman; her legend and her legacy; [by] Carl Rollyson. St. Martin's Press 1988 xxii, 613p il hardcover o.p. paperback available $13.95   **92**

ISBN 0-312-03481-4 (pa)   LC 87-28398

Hellman, Lillian, 1906-1984—*Continued*

This biography "discusses Hellman's plays and other published writings, her work for Hollywood, political involvements and numerous sexual liaisons." Publ Wkly

"Rollyson's detailed and balanced biography effectively argues that the playwright, self-centered and harshly authoritarian, orchestrated her life and writing to create the glowing but false image of grande dame and heroine of culture." Libr J

Includes bibliography

Wright, William. **Lillian Hellman; the image, the woman.** Simon & Schuster 1986 507p il o.p.; Ballantine Bks. paperback available $4.95   **92**

ISBN 0-345-34740-4 (pa)   LC 86-17794

"The late playwright led a luridly colorful life, full of love affairs, wrangling, and skulduggery. Her supporting cast included literary and theatrical stars of the highest luminescence. Yet for all that, Wright reveals that Hellman was a liar about herself. . . . How thorough a liar is the question that makes this skillfully written biography fascinating down to the last paragraph." Booklist

Includes bibliographic references

Helmsley, Harry B., 1909-

Moss, Michael. **Palace coup: the inside story of Harry and Leona Helmsley.** Doubleday 1989 346p il $18.95   **92**

1. Helmsley, Leona
ISBN 0-385-24973-X   LC 88-36759

The author "traces how Harry built his empire, how Leona wooed Harry, how she built 'her' hotel empire, and finally, how they both ended up on the front page of the 'New York Post' with headlines blaring tax evasion and conspiracy charges." Booklist

Helmsley, Leona

Moss, Michael. **Palace coup: the inside story of Harry and Leona Helmsley.** See entry under Helmsley, Harry B., 1909- **92**

Hemingway, Ernest, 1899-1961

Baker, Carlos. **Ernest Hemingway; a life story.** Scribner 1976 c1969 697p il $47.50; pa $12.95   **92**

ISBN 0-684-14740-8; 0-02-001690-5 (pa)

"Hudson River editions"

A reprint of the title first published 1969

"Most of the story is drawn directly or indirectly from manuscript sources, including many pages of his unpublished work, approximately 2500 of his letters, and at least an equal number of letters to him from friends, members of his family, and chance associates. These materials have been supplemented with numerous interviews." Foreword

The author has "organized his book in such a way that it can be enjoyed by the general reader and at the same time used by scholars." Saturday Rev

Includes bibliographic references

Burgess, Anthony. **Ernest Hemingway and his world.** Scribner 1978 128p il hardcover o.p. paperback available $10.95   **92**

ISBN 0-684-18504-0 (pa)   LC 77-93899

This "pictorial biography gives us a big hunk of Hemingway, shorn of self-made legend and myth. Burgess delves behind the tough-guy persona of the warrior, hunter, fisherman, drinker." Publ Wkly

The author's "capsule criticism of the most notable fiction and nonfiction are brilliant and incisive. . . . His book is a pleasure to read and is valuable to students of both authors." Choice

Includes bibliography

Griffin, Peter. **Along with youth: Hemingway, the early years.** Oxford Univ. Press 1985 258p il $22.95; pa $8.95   **92**

ISBN 0-19-503680-8; 0-19-505066-5 (pa)

                              LC 85-11422

This "biography, the first of a projected three-volume work, deals with Ernest Hemingway's life from birth to the age of 22 and his first marriage, to Hadley Richardson." Choice

This is a "wonderful and intimate book." N Y Times Book Rev

Includes bibliography

Griffin, Peter. **Less than a treason: Hemingway in Paris.** Oxford Univ. Press 1990 197p il $17.95   **92**

ISBN 0-19-505332-X   LC 89-26606

This continuation of the biography entered above covers the period 1922-1929 which Hemingway and his first wife spent in Paris, Italy, Spain, and Switzerland

Hemingway, Ernest. **A moveable feast.** Scribner 1964 211p il $35; pa $11   **92**

1. Paris (France)—Description
ISBN 0-684-17340-9; 0-684-71804-9 (pa)

A posthumously published collection of sketches, which Hemingway said might be regarded as fiction, about the author's early life in Paris during the 1920's. In addition to picturing the Parisian scene, Hemingway portrays F. Scott Fitzgerald, Gertrude Stein, Ezra Pound, Ford Maddox Ford, and others

Hotchner, A. E. **Hemingway and his world.** Vendome Press 1989 207p il $45   **92**

ISBN 0-86565-082-9   LC 89-16444

This biography includes "photos of Hemingway and others, as well as color photos of book jackets, memorabilia and scenes from such favorite locales as Paris, Italy, Spain and Africa. The text is arranged chronologically, with entries on the novelist's friends, wives and favorite places, as well as cities and historical events identified with him. . . . This handsome, appealing book provides a satisfying overview of the trajectory of the novelist's life." N Y Times Book Rev

Includes bibliography

Kert, Bernice. **The Hemingway women.** Norton 1983 555p il hardcover o.p. paperback available $14.95   **92**

1. Women in literature
ISBN 0-393-30270-9 (pa)   LC 82-18988

Hemingway, Ernest, 1899-1961—*Continued*

The author "examines the lives of Ernest Hemingway's mother, sisters, wives, and other female friends and lovers—the influential nature of their relationships with him and their lives apart from him." Booklist

"Comprehensive and well researched, Kert's book will be of interest to scholars, undergraduate students, and general readers." Choice

Includes bibliography

Lynn, Kenneth Schuyler. Hemingway; by Kenneth S. Lynn. Simon & Schuster 1987 702p il o.p.; Fawcett Bks. paperback available $14.95   92

ISBN 0-449-90308-7 (pa)   LC 87-82

"Taking as his premise Hemingway's glib assertion that the only analyst he relied upon was his 'portable Corona Number 3,' Lynn tracks the exploration of a disordered inner world as Hemingway sought to find some sort of resolution to the agony of his personal conflicts through 'his cunningly wrought fiction.' The man who emerges from Lynn's biography is a vastly more complex and compelling figure than the white-bearded, pontificating 'Papa' of myth." Publ Wkly

Includes bibliography

Mellow, James R. Hemingway: a life without consequences. Houghton Mifflin 1992 704p il $29.50   92

ISBN 0-395-37777-3   LC 92-9549

"In sheer number of pages, Mr. Mellow's version of the life is most heavily weighed toward the years 1921 to 1930, when Hemingway lived in Paris during his first two marriages and published the novels and stories that built his early reputation as one of this country's most important writers. Mr. Mellow seems in a hurry to get through the rest of the story, but he does dutifully summarize Hemingway's childhood, adolescence and the major events of the later years. . . . Mr. Mellow takes careful note of Hemingway's publications in the context of his life and gives sensitive readings, both biographical and critical, to them all." N Y Times Book Rev

Includes bibliographic references

Meyers, Jeffrey. Hemingway; a biography. Harper & Row 1985 644p il hardcover o.p. paperback available $12.95   92

ISBN 0-06-091364-9 (pa)   LC 84-48611

"Taking pains to illuminate the more controversial issues that surround Hemingway as an artist and man, Meyers carefully documents the evolution of the writer's public persona, which also was reflected in his fiction, as he moved from wounded soldier to lost-generation bohemian to beloved but irascible Papa." Booklist

Includes bibliography

Reynolds, Michael S. Hemingway; [by] Michael Reynolds. Blackwell 1989-1992 2v il maps ea $24.95   92

Contents: [v2] The Paris years (ISBN 0-631-15352-7); [v3] The American homecoming (ISBN 0-631-18481-3)

These volumes continue the author's study of Hemingway's life begun with The young Hemingway (entered below). The Paris years covers the period from 1922 to 1925, while The American homecoming discusses Hemingway's experiences and works from 1926 to 1929

Includes bibliographic references

Reynolds, Michael S. The young Hemingway; [by] Michael Reynolds. Blackwell 1987 c1986 291p il hardcover o.p. paperback available $12.95   92

ISBN 0-631-14787-X (pa)   LC 85-22936

First published 1986 in the United Kingdom

This is a "study of Hemingway from his early youth to the time just before his expatriate years." N Y Times Book Rev

"This incisive, well-written biography . . . will prove useful at almost every readership level, from general reader to scholar." Choice

Includes bibliography

Hendrix, Jimi. See class 780.92

Henry, O., 1862-1910

Stuart, David. O. Henry; a biography of William Sydney Porter. Scarborough House 1990 267p il $19.95   92

ISBN 0-8128-3057-1   LC 85-40242

The author "argues that William Sydney Porter's conviction and imprisonment in 1898 for embezzling was decisive in converting a somewhat nomadic jack of all trades into the celebrated short-story writer famed for the surprise ending. The biographer produces persuasive evidence of Porter's innocence, and cites the writer's depression over the incident as the cause of his passive, ineffectual self-defense." N Y Times Book Rev

Includes bibliographic references

Henson, Matthew Alexander, 1866-1955

Henson, Matthew Alexander. A black explorer at the North Pole; by Matthew A. Henson; foreword by Robert E. Peary; introduction by Booker T. Washington; introduction to the Bison book edition by Susan A. Kaplan. University of Neb. Press 1989 xxxvi, 195p il pa $6.95   92

1. Peary, Robert Edwin, 1856-1920 2. Arctic regions
ISBN 0-8032-7245-6   LC 88-27002

Available in hardcover with original title from Ayer

First published 1912 by Stokes with title: A Negro explorer at the North Pole

An account of the author's "trek to the North Pole with Robert E. Peary and four Eskimos in the spring of 1909. . . . [Henson] learned Eskimo language and Arctic survival techniques, then served as teacher to white men like Peary and MacMillan." Book World

Hentoff, Nat

Hentoff, Nat. Boston boy. Knopf 1986 175p o.p.; Faber & Faber paperback available $7.95   92

ISBN 0-571-12951-X (pa)   LC 85-45675

"Hentoff, known variously for his 'Village Voice' column, his novels and books, . . . here looks at his youth and the forces that shaped his views as a staunch libertarian. . . . Told with frankness and gently self-deprecating wit, Hentoff's recollections pleasantly define a very particular place in time." Publ Wkly

Hepburn, Katharine, 1907-

Andersen, Christopher P. Young Kate; [by] Christopher Andersen. Holt & Co. 1988 270p il o.p.; Delacorte Press paperback available $12.95   **92**

ISBN 0-385-29891-9 (pa)   LC 88-8819

Also available Thorndike Press large print edition

"A Donald Hutter book"

This biography of the American actress, based on conversations the author had with her, covers her experiences up to her graduation from Bryn Mawr

"Much has already been written about Hepburn, but what sets Andersen's biography apart is that she is only a featured player in the story of her childhood: Her parents are the stars. . . . [One] of the finest of [its] genre." Libr J

Includes bibliography

Bryson, John. The private world of Katharine Hepburn; written and photographed by John Bryson; foreword by Katharine Hepburn. Little, Brown 1990 175p il $39.95; pa $24.95   **92**

ISBN 0-316-11332-8; 0-316-11333-6 (pa) LC 90-5490

This is a collection of candid photographs of the actress taken over a fifteen year period, accompanied by a brief text

Edwards, Anne. A remarkable woman: a biography of Katharine Hepburn. Morrow 1985 511p il o.p.; Pocket Bks. paperback available $5.99   **92**

ISBN 0-671-72756-7 (pa)   LC 85-11523

"Edwards has the knack of making her subject flesh and blood rather than mere movie icon. She avoids the biographer's trap of reciting her subjects' accomplishments, choosing instead to divine Hepburn's motivations for her choices in life. For those not familiar with Hepburn's unusual childhood, strong personal will, 30-year friendship with Spencer Tracy, and movie and stage career, this could be enlightening reading." Booklist

Includes bibliography

Hepburn, Katharine. Me; stories of my life. Knopf 1991 420p il $24.50   **92**

ISBN 0-679-40051-6   LC 90-50805

Also available Random House large print edition in hardcover and paperback; paperback available from Ballantine Bks.

This book "sounds just like its author—lots of cropped sentences, dashes, Hepburnian phrasing. But it's not a full-dress autobiography; as the subtitle proclaims, this is a collection of stories. . . . Still, fans will not be disappointed. Beginning with her early years . . . and concluding with her relationship with Tracy, Hepburn delivers all kinds of wry moments and, of course, a most interesting cast of characters." Booklist

Herbst, Josephine, 1892-1969

Herbst, Josephine. The starched blue sky of Spain; and other memoirs; introduction by Diane Johnson. HarperCollins Pubs. 1991 xxv, 178p $19.95; pa $10   **92**

ISBN 0-06-016512-X; 0-06-092305-9 (pa)
                                      LC 90-55931

In four "essays written in her sixties about her life between ages six and 51, Herbst easily re-creates the artistic climate of the Twenties and Thirties, as well as the passion for art, conversation, and travel that drew many talented Midwesterners to New York and Europe." Libr J

Herriot, James

Herriot, James. All creatures great and small. 20th anniversary ed. St. Martin's Press 1992 442p $18.95   **92**

1. Veterinary medicine
ISBN 0-312-08498-6   LC 92-18975

Also available G.K. Hall large print edition and in paperback from Bantam Bks.

First published 1972

The first volume of Herriot's autobiographical account of the practice of veterinary medicine in Yorkshire, England in the 1930s

Herriot, James. All things bright and beautiful. St. Martin's Press 1974 378p $17.95   **92**

1. Veterinary medicine
ISBN 0-312-02030-9

Also available in paperback from Bantam Bks.

A continuation of Herriot's reminiscences of pre-World War II Yorkshire

Herriot, James. All things wise and wonderful. St. Martin's Press 1977 432p $17.95   **92**

1. Veterinary medicine
ISBN 0-312-02031-7   LC 77-76640

Also available in paperback from Bantam Bks.

This installment of Herriot's memoirs focuses on his RAF service during the war

Herriot, James. Every living thing. St. Martin's Press 1992 342p $22.95   **92**

1. Veterinary medicine
ISBN 0-312-08188-X   LC 92-18526

Also available G.K. Hall large print edition

This book continues Herriot's "anecdotal recollections of work among the animals and people of his beloved Yorkshire Dales, this time in the 1950s." Booklist

Herriot, James. The Lord God made them all. St. Martin's Press 1981 373p $17.95   **92**

1. Veterinary medicine
ISBN 0-312-49834-9   LC 80-29097

Also available in paperback from Bantam Bks.

This volume deals with post-war changes in veterinary medicine and Herriot's trips to Russia and Turkey

Herzl, Theodor, 1860-1904

Pawel, Ernst. The labyrinth of exile: a life of Theodor Herzl. Farrar, Straus & Giroux 1989 554p $30; pa $15   **92**

1. Zionism
ISBN 0-374-18256-6; 0-374-52351-7 (pa) LC 89-7905

"Herzl, a Hungarian-born Viennese Jew, at age 35 transformed himself from journalist and dandified minor playwright to leader of the secular Zionist movement." Publ Wkly

Herzl, Theodor, 1860-1904—*Continued*

"Pawel has a sharp eye and he writes easily and incisively, penetrating the inner chambers of the man and the movement. There are many interesting new facts and a fresh analysis. Highly recommended to both scholars and those who wish to learn about the early years of Zionism." Libr J

Includes bibliography

Hesburgh, Theodore Martin

Hesburgh, Theodore Martin. God, country, Notre Dame: the autobiography of Theodore M. Hesburgh; [by] Theodore M. Hesburgh with Jerry Reedy. Doubleday 1990 331p il $21.95 **92**

1. University of Notre Dame
ISBN 0-385-26680-4   LC 90-33371

Also available in paperback from Fawcett Bks.

The former president of the University of Notre Dame "describes his Catholic upbringing and then his eminent role in the church, education, and politics, including his work for civil rights, the peace corps, and immigration reform." Booklist

This book "reads like oral history—easily, at times breezily, without a lot of distracting detail, as if the author were just chatting about himself." N Y Times Book Rev

Hillerman, Tony

Hillerman, Tony. Talking mysteries: a conversation with Tony Hillerman; [by] Tony Hillerman and Ernie Bulow; illustrations by Ernest Franklin. University of N.M. Press 1991 135p il $16.95 **92**

1. Mystery and detective stories—History and criticism
ISBN 0-8263-1279-9   LC 91-2467

This book "contains an introduction and interview by Ernie Bulow, a memoir by Hillerman, [and] 'The Witch, Yazzie, and the Nine of Clubs,' . . . [a story in which] Jim Chee of the Navajo Tribal Police investigates a murder made to look like witchcraft. . . . Hillerman discusses his writing habits, pitfalls, ambitions, and influences . . . and his insights into the crime novel." San Francisco Rev Books

Includes bibliographic references

Himmler, Heinrich, 1900-1945

Breitman, Richard. The architect of genocide: Himmler and the final solution. Knopf 1991 335p $22.50 **92**

1. National socialism 2. Germany—Politics and government—1933-1945
ISBN 0-394-56841-9   LC 90-52956

Also available in paperback from University Press of New England

The author "focuses on Himmler's role in the decision making of the final solution, on how Himmler and the SS gained control of Nazi Germany's Jewish policy, and on other related World War II activities." Booklist

"This engrossing, detailed study constitutes a powerful refutation of revisionist scholars who claim that Hitler did not plan the Final Solution in advance but instead improvised it out of either military or political frustration." Publ Wkly

Includes bibliographic references

Hirohito, Emperor of Japan, 1901-1989

Behr, Edward. Hirohito; behind the myth. Villard Bks. 1989 xxvi, 437p il $22.50; pa $14.95 **92**

1. Japan—Politics and government
ISBN 0-394-58072-9; 0-679-73171-7 (pa)   LC 89-5677

The author "presents a well-researched (though in English-language sources only) study that provides a fascinating and probing look at the life of the 20th century's longest-reigning monarch." Libr J

Includes bibliography

Hoyt, Edwin Palmer. Hirohito: the emperor and the man; [by] Edwin P. Hoyt. Praeger Pubs. 1992 214p il $24.95 **92**

1. Japan—Politics and government
ISBN 0-275-94069-1   LC 91-4189

"This biography is based on the premise that Hirohito was not responsible for the military expansions of the 1930s and 1940s but rather was at the mercy of an aggressive military that kept him an imperial 'prisoner.' Hirohito is presented as a man of peace and goodwill who was not in line with his times." Booklist

Includes bibliographic references

Kawahara, Toshiaki. Hirohito and his times; a Japanese perspective; introduction [by] W.G. Beasley. Kodansha Int./USA 1990 216p il $18.95 **92**

1. Japan—Politics and government
ISBN 0-87011-979-6   LC 89-77698

"At once colorless and highly controversial, Hirohito (1901-1989), we're shown, was vaguely 'for peace' in the early days of his 62-year reign and made an attempt to demystify the throne, but he was unable to override court rigidity or control the expansionist tendencies of the militarists, which led to war in China and the attack on Pearl Harbor. Kawahara describes the stormy controversy during the U.S. Occupation over whether the emperor should remain on the throne as a 'living god,' or be tried as a war criminal." Publ Wkly

Hitchcock, Alfred, 1899-1980

Spoto, Donald. The dark side of genius: the life of Alfred Hitchcock. Little, Brown 1983 594p il o.p.; Ballantine Bks. paperback available $5.95 **92**

ISBN 0-345-31462-X (pa)   LC 82-23997

This is a biography of the director of such films as The man who knew too much, The thirty-nine steps, The lady vanishes, Rebecca, Spellbound, Strangers on a train, Rear window, and Psycho

This "is a vivid and perceptive portrait of a man whose character was as strange and shadowed as his films. . . . Hitchcock's final obsession was secretiveness, but he has been well served by a knowledgeable and revealing biography." Time

Includes bibliography

Hitler, Adolf, 1889-1945

Bullock, Alan. Hitler and Stalin; parallel lives. Knopf 1992 c1991 1081p il maps $34.50; pa $20   **92**

1. Stalin, Joseph, 1879-1953 2. Germany—Politics and government—1933-1945 3. Soviet Union—Politics and government

ISBN 0-394-58601-8; 0-679-72994-1 (pa)

LC 91-52711

First published 1991 in the United Kingdom

This biography of Hitler and Stalin "places the lives of the dictators side by side and follows them from beginning to end." Christ Sci Monit

"The twentieth century cannot be understood without close examination of the work of Stalin and Hitler. It is particularly important to note what their regimes and aims had in common and where they differed. Alan Bullock has put us all in his debt by placing their actions side by side, in enormous detail, and in chronological sequence to make the comparison easy." Times Lit Suppl

Includes bibliographic references

Hitler, Adolf. Mein Kampf; translated by Ralph Manheim. Houghton Mifflin 1943 xxi, 694p $21.45; pa $10.70   **92**

1. National socialism 2. Germany—Politics and government—1918-1933

ISBN 0-395-07801-6; 0-395-08362-1 (pa)

"Hitler's steady rise to power was interrupted only by the Beer Hall Putsch (1923), an unsuccessful attempt to overthrow the Weimar Republic. . . . During the nine months of imprisonment that followed he wrote 'Mein Kampf' (1924; tr. 'My struggle,' 1940). This book contained autobiographical and reflective passages, rife with hysterical anti-Semitism and paranoia, as well as the program he intended to implement; for the West it was a warning that went unheeded." Reader's Ency. 3d edition

Toland, John. Adolf Hitler. Anchor Bks. 1992 xx, 1035p il $18   **92**

1. Germany—Politics and government—1933-1945 2. National socialism

ISBN 0-385-42053-6

LC 91-31242

Also available in paperback from Ballantine Bks.

A reissue of the title first published 1976

This biography is based on more than 250 interviews with people acquainted with Hitler and materials from U.S. and British archives

"In the course of detailed and painstaking investigations [Toland] has disposed of a number of myths." NY Times Book Rev

Includes bibliography

Hobson, Laura Keane Zametkin, 1900-1986

Hobson, Laura Keane Zametkin. Laura Z, a life; years of fulfillment; [by] Laura Z. Hobson; introduction by Norman Cousins; afterword by Christopher Z. Hobson. Fine, D.I. 1986 331p il $18.95   **92**

ISBN 0-917657-19-5

LC 87-111759

Continues the author's autobiography, the first volume published 1983 by Arbor House without subtitle. Paperback edition containing both volumes available from D.I. Fine

Hobson's autobiography begins with an account of the screen version of her novel, Gentleman's Agreement and concludes with a discussion of the writing of Consenting Adult

"This is a remarkable self-portrait of an exceptional woman. She focuses on the importance of her need to write. . . . Unsparing of her own faults, she tells a fascinating and inspiring story." Libr J

Hodes, Art. See class 780.92

Hoffman, Abbie

Jezer, Marty. Abbie Hoffman, American rebel. Rutgers Univ. Press 1992 345p il $22.95   **92**

ISBN 0-8135-1850-4

LC 92-7766

In this biography of the social activist, Jezer "traces Hoffman's evolution from Brandeis beatnik to Yippie leader and spokesperson for the Woodstock nation." Libr J

"A solid account of the life of an inventive, destructive *luftmensch*, and a valuable cautionary tale for both the left and the right." N Y Times Book Rev

Includes bibliographic references

Hoffman, Eva

Hoffman, Eva. Lost in translation; a life in a new language. Dutton 1989 280p o.p.; Penguin Bks. paperback available $10   **92**

ISBN 0-14-012773-9 (pa)

LC 88-18962

An autobiographical account of the author's experiences as a teenage emigre from Poland to Canada in the 1950s

The author's "obsession with words has paid off handsomely: her language is crisp and precise when summing up essential experience, and richly evocative when lingering on detail." Nation

Holiday, Billie. See class 780.92

Holly, Buddy. See class 780.92

Homer, Winslow. See class 709.2

Hook, Sidney, 1902-1989

Hook, Sidney. Out of step; an unquiet life in the 20th century. Harper & Row 1987 628p il o.p.; Carroll & Graf Pubs. paperback available $14.95   **92**

ISBN 0-88184-399-7 (pa)

LC 86-45117

This autobiography by the American political philosopher is "filled with people, incidents, ideas, arguments, drama, anecdote, conflict, and contrast. Not technically 'philosophical', it sparkles nonetheless with the fireworks of ideas and theories. Not, in the usual sense, personal, it is nonetheless alive with personality, passion, conviction, and opinions." Christ Sci Monit

Hoover, J. Edgar (John Edgar), 1895-1972

Gentry, Curt. J. Edgar Hoover; the man and the secrets. Norton 1991 846p il $29.95   **92**

1. United States. Federal Bureau of Investigation

ISBN 0-393-02404-0

LC 90-30576

Hoover, J. Edgar (John Edgar), 1895-1972
—*Continued*

Also available in paperback from New Am. Lib.

The author "has based his account of Hoover on more than 300 interviews and on access to previously classified FBI documents. . . . Gentry paints a portrait of Hoover as the 'indispensable man,' with many provocative revelations about his political dealings." Libr J

Includes bibliographic references

Hope, Bob, 1903-

Hope, Bob. Don't shoot, it's only me; Bob Hope's comedy history of the United States; [by] Bob Hope with Melville Shavelson. Putnam 1990 315p il o.p.; Jove Publs. paperback available $5.99   **92**

ISBN 0-515-10565-1 (pa)   LC 90-8119

Also available Thorndike Press large print edition

"Hope, the official comedian of the U.S. armed forces since 1941, tells his own version of American military history. Stories of war, peacetime, and presidents are interspersed with one-liners, gags, and sentimental memories." Booklist

"This book is an odds-on crowd pleaser, funny and touching." Publ Wkly

Horney, Karen, 1885-1952

Quinn, Susan. A mind of her own: the life of Karen Horney. Summit Bks. 1987 479p il o.p.; Addison-Wesley paperback available $12.45   **92**

ISBN 0-201-15573-7 (pa)   LC 87-18432

"An independent mind and spirited character led Karen Horney to become one of the first women to study medicine in repressive pre-World War I Germany, to be the first psychoanalyst to challenge Freud's ideas about women, to lead a walkout from the New York Psychoanalytic Institute, and through her own teachings and writings to alter the course of psychoanalytic history. Quinn's well-researched and lively telling gives suitable attention to unconscious as well as conscious forces in Horney's development." Libr J

Includes bibliography

Horowitz, Vladimir. See class 780.92

Houghton, Norris, 1909-

Houghton, Norris. Entrances and exits; a life in and out of the theatre. Limelight Eds. 1991 377p il $29.95   **92**

ISBN 0-87910-144-X   LC 90-40527

The author "director, designer, producer, educator, and much more is a treasure of American theater, partly because he is a direct link to Stanislavsky and the first generation of the Moscow Art Theater. . . . [This autobiography] helps put his career in perspective and provides real insight into the stages of growth U.S. theater has experienced." Libr J

Hu, John, 18th cent.

Spence, Jonathan D. The question of Hu. Knopf 1988 187p $18.95   **92**

1. Foucquet, Jean-François, 1665-1741
ISBN 0-394-57190-8   LC 88-21564

Also available in paperback from Vintage Bks.

The author examines the story of John Hu, a Chinese convert who accompanied Jean-François Foucquet, a Jesuit missionary, to France in 1722 where his exuberant response to the West led to his confinement in an asylum

This book "addresses the larger question of how we define madness and to what degree the madhouse was an instrument of social control. . . . Mr. Spence's delicate but nevertheless ambitious approach makes him one of the most original and exciting historians writing now." N Y Times Book Rev

Includes bibliography

Hughes, Langston, 1902-1967

Hughes, Langston. I wonder as I wander; an autobiographical journey. Rinehart 1956 405p o.p.; Hippocrene Bks. reprint available $27.50   **92**

ISBN 0-374-94031-2

Continuing the autobiography begun in The big sea (1940), this volume contains an account of Hughes' journeys through Russia, Spain, China, and Japan, as well as some incidents of his poetry readings in this country

Rampersad, Arnold. The life of Langston Hughes. Oxford Univ. Press 1986-1988 2v il ea $32.50   **92**

LC 86-2565

Both volumes also available in paperback

Contents: v1 1902-1941: I, too, sing America (ISBN 0-19-504011-2); v2 1941-1967: I dream a world (ISBN 0-19-504519-X)

"Rampersad is an unsparing but sympathetic analyst of Hughes's life and work; he has written an absorbing critical biography that is also a deft social history of black America in the 20th century." Publ Wkly

Includes bibliographic references

Hunter-Gault, Charlayne

Hunter-Gault, Charlayne. In my place. Farrar, Straus & Giroux 1992 257p il $19
                    92

ISBN 0-374-17563-2   LC 92-16331

In this memoir Hunter-Gault "reflects on her childhood and young adulthood, including her historic role as one of two black students who desegregated the University of Georgia in 1961." Publ Wkly

This work "offers up the example of a single life that journeyed from small-town South Carolina to Manhattan, from the Turner High School newspaper to 'MacNeil/Lehrer,' from one end to another of an extraordinary social spectrum." N Y Times Book Rev

Includes bibliographic references

Hurston, Zora Neale, 1891-1960

Hurston, Zora Neale. Dust tracks on a road; with a new foreword by Maya Angelou. HarperCollins Pubs. 1991 277p hardcover o.p. paperback available $12 **92**

ISBN 0-06-096567-3 (pa)   LC 90-55501

First published 1942 by Lippincott

The author describes her wanderings in and out of schools and jobs as a young girl, finishing her course work at Barnard, and beginning her life's work

Includes bibliography

Zora! Zora Neale Hurston: a woman and her community; compiled and edited by N. Y. Nathiri. Sentinel Communications Co. 1991 134p il $24.95 **92**

ISBN 0-941263-21-5   LC 90-63868

An illustrated look at the life, work and influence of the novelist, folklorist, and anthropologist who was a major figure in the Harlem Renaissance

Hussein, Ṣaddām

Karsh, Efraim. Saddam Hussein; a political biography; [by] Efraim Karsh and Inari Rautsi. Free Press 1991 309p $22.95 **92**

1. Iraq—Politics and government
ISBN 0-02-917063-X   LC 91-10867

An "account of Hussein's rise to power and the political milieu in which he thrived. Relying on Western, Soviet, Arab, and Israeli sources, the authors meticulously trace the violent history of modern Iraq and the coming to power of the Ba'th Party. . . . Recommended for scholars of the modern Middle East as well as informed laypersons." Libr J

Huxley, Aldous, 1894-1963

Dunaway, David King. Huxley in Hollywood. Harper & Row 1989 458p il $24.95 **92**

ISBN 0-06-039095-6   LC 89-45036

Also available in paperback from Anchor Bks.

"A Cornelia & Michael Bessie book"

"Dunaway has based his research not only on the standard sources but also on numerous interviews with Huxley's friends, relatives, and acquaintances. . . . Dunaway attempts to appeal to the general reader as well as to the academic, and at times the book includes digressive and trivial material of little value. Yet, for anyone wishing a complete portrait of Huxley in Hollywood, this study is recommended reading." Choice

Includes bibliographic references

Huxley, Elspeth, 1907-

Huxley, Elspeth. The flame trees of Thika; memories of an African childhood. Morrow 1959 288p il o.p.; Penguin Bks. paperback available $7.95 **92**

1. Kenya—Social life and customs
ISBN 0-14-001715-1 (pa)

This is an account of the author's childhood on a coffee plantation in Kenya. She describes the landscape, the Kikuya peoples, the European settlers and the difficulties her parents faced adjusting to life in the bush

Iacocca, Lee A.

Iacocca, Lee A. Iacocca; an autobiography; [by] Lee Iacocca with William Novak. Bantam Bks. 1984 352p il $21.95; pa $5.99 **92**

1. Automobile industry
ISBN 0-553-05339-6; 0-553-25147-3 (pa)

LC 84-45174

The author provides "a behind-the-scenes account of the corporate boardrooms of Ford and Chrysler. Along the way he provides his 'key to management' and recounts the Mustang success story, his acrimonious split with Henry Ford II, and the saving of Chrysler." Libr J

"Whatever Iacocca's private life, he tells us very little about it. No matter. Because the corporate life he writes about is so much his world, the book stands as autobiography." Publ Wkly

Iacocca, Lee A. Talking straight; [by] Lee Iacocca with Sonny Kleinfield. Bantam Bks. 1988 324p il $21.95; pa $5.50 **92**

1. United States—Economic conditions—1974-
ISBN 0-553-05270-5; 0-553-27805-3 (pa)

LC 88-175522

Also available G.K. Hall large print edition

The author "addresses such public policy problems as corporate takeovers, the trade deficit, the plight of farmers, education, and the declining quality of American products. More personally, he talks about raising his two daughters, coping with his wife's death, his recent divorce, growing old, and what he would do if he were president." Libr J

"Not surprisingly, Mr. Iacocca is at his best when he discusses the business world. . . . Flaws and all, 'Talking Straight' manages to give off a nice shine, probably because of Mr. Iacocca's integrity and his large sense of accountability." N Y Times Book Rev

Ickes, Harold L. (Harold LeClair), 1874-1952

Watkins, T. H. (Tom H.). Righteous pilgrim: the life and times of Harold L. Ickes, 1874-1952. Holt & Co. 1990 1010p il $35; pa $19.95 **92**

1. United States—Politics and government—1933-1945
ISBN 0-8050-0917-5; 0-8050-2112-4 (pa)

LC 89-35746

A biography of the "articulate reform politician, F.D.R.'s Secretary of the Interior, who did so much to define liberalism in his time." N Y Times Book Rev

The author "is especially strong on personality and private life. . . . A fine example of the biographer's art." Booklist

Includes bibliography

Ireland, Jill

Ireland, Jill. Life lines. Warner Bks. 1989 358p hardcover o.p. paperback available $5.99 **92**

ISBN 0-446-35939-4 (pa)   LC 88-30863

"A Dove book"

In this autobiographical sequel to Life wish (1987) the author writes of her life before and after marriage to Charles Bronson, the illness of her elderly father, and the drug addiction problems of her adopted son Jason

Ireland, Jill—*Continued*
"This heartfelt story . . . will not win any literary prizes, but it might get honorable mention for 'most sincere.'" N Y Times Book Rev

Isabella I, Queen of Spain, 1451-1504
Liss, Peggy K. Isabel the Queen; life and times. Oxford Univ. Press 1992 398p il $30
92
1. Spain—History
ISBN 0-19-507356-8   LC 91-46645
In this "chronologically arranged political and social history of the Queen of Renaissance Spain, the author ventures to explain Isabel's actions in the religious and social contexts of the time and to show her as a product of her environment. Liss makes no excuses for the often brutal reign and gives readers vast amounts of information so they can arrive at their own conclusions." Libr J

Includes bibliographic references

Rubin, Nancy. Isabella of Castile; the first Renaissance queen. St. Martin's Press 1991 468p il maps $29.95; pa $14.95   **92**
1. Spain—History
ISBN 0-312-05878-0; 0-312-08511-7 (pa)
LC 90-27079
This is a biography of the wife of Ferdinand of Aragon and sponsor of Columbus' 1492 voyage. The political, social and religious life of 15th century Spain is examined

Includes bibliographic references

Ishi
Kroeber, Theodora. Ishi in two worlds; a biography of the last wild Indian in North America. University of Calif. Press 1976 262p il $32.50; pa $10.95   **92**
1. Yana Indians
ISBN 0-520-03152-0; 0-520-00675-5 (pa)
First published 1961
An account "of the life of the sole survivor of a California Indian tribe. The author, wife of the famed anthropologist, reconstructs the decimation of Ishi's [Yana] people and his reluctant entry in 1911 into the world of his conquerors." Booklist

Ivan IV, the Terrible, Czar of Russia, 1530-1584
Bobrick, Benson. Fearful majesty: the life and reign of Ivan the Terrible. Putnam 1987 398p il o.p.; Paragon House paperback available $12.95   **92**
1. Russia—History
ISBN 1-55778-226-1 (pa)   LC 86-30638
"In probing this Czar's complex character [the author] . . . wisely avoids amateur psychologizing. Instead he finds clues to Ivan's aberrant behavior in biology and politics. . . . It is the chief merit of Mr. Bobrick's biography that it gives us a portrait of Ivan the Terrible as a figure of high tragedy rather than a madman or villain." N Y Times Book Rev

Includes bibliography

Ives, Charles Edward. See class 780.92

Jackson, Bo
Jackson, Bo. Bo knows Bo; the autobiography of a ballplayer; [by] Bo Jackson and Dick Schaap. Doubleday 1990 218p il $18.95   **92**
ISBN 0-385-41620-2   LC 90-41073
Also available in paperback from Jove Publs.
The versatile athlete "tells of his rise from grinding poverty as one of 10 children in a fatherless Alabama family. . . . Athletics were Jackson's salvation: he starred in track and field in high school, then in football at Alabama's Auburn University, where he won the prestigious Heisman trophy. His story is heartwarming." Publ Wkly

Jackson, Mahalia. See class 780.92

Jackson, Michael. See class 780.92

Jackson, Stonewall, 1824-1863
Bowers, John. Stonewall Jackson; portrait of a soldier. Morrow 1989 367p il maps $19.95   **92**
1. United States—History—1861-1865, Civil War—Campaigns
ISBN 0-688-05747-0   LC 88-37918
Also available in paperback from Avon Bks.
In this "biography of a consummate soldier, Bowers takes a novelistic approach that serves him well in relating Jackson's military achievements, as well as providing the reader with penetrating insights into the character of a man who was something of an enigma to friend and foe alike. . . . The author's vivid prose style and unerring sense of the dramatic (especially in describing the flow of battle) make for absorbing reading. An appealing volume for Civil War buffs." Booklist

James, Daniel, 1920-1978
Phelps, J. Alfred. Chappie; America's first black four-star general: the life and times of Daniel James, Jr. Presidio Press 1991 366p il maps $19.95; pa $9.95   **92**
ISBN 0-89141-396-0; 0-89141-464-9 (pa)
LC 90-43537
"'Chappie' James (1920-1978) became one of the legendary Tuskegee Airmen during World War II, took part in the struggle of black officers for racial equality in the Army Air Corps, flew combat missions in Korea and Vietnam, served as Air Force PR chief during the height of the anti-war protests, and concluded a brilliant career as a four-star general." Publ Wkly

Includes bibliography

James, Henry, 1843-1916
Edel, Leon. Henry James. Lippincott 1953-1972 5v il o.p.; Avon Bks. paperback set available $14.75   **92**
ISBN 0-380-39636-X (pa)
Only volume five available in hardcover from Lippincott for $13.95 (ISBN 0-397-00733-7)

James, Henry, 1843-1916—*Continued*

Contents: v1 The untried years, 1843-1870; v2 The conquest of London, 1870-1881; v3 The middle years, 1882-1895; v4 The treacherous years, 1895-1901; v5 The master, 1901-1916

"Edel has delivered James from the stultifying hand of legend and in the process allowed us a clearer focus upon his work than had seemed possible. . . . [This] monument to an artist is itself a great work of art—the single greatest work of biography produced in our century." Book World

Includes bibliographic references

James, Henry. Henry James and Edith Wharton; letters: 1900-1915; edited by Lyall H. Powers. Scribner 1990 412p il $29.95
92

1. Wharton, Edith, 1862-1937
ISBN 0-684-19146-6   LC 89-36809

"This volume contains all 180 items of the correspondence [considered] extant between Henry James and Edith Wharton. Published here for the first time are 131 of the 164 letters of James to Wharton and 5 of the 8 letters from Wharton to James that survived his burning of his papers in 1909 and 1915. Also included are 30 letters of Wharton and Theodora Bosanquet, James's secretary." Choice

"Sadly, very few letters survive from Wharton's side, but she's still a strong presence here as James admires her travels and projects, his awe alternating with delicious irony. Though full of references to her failing marriage and his failing health and hopes, his letters are buoyed up by an unfailingly playful wit. Most of them have not appeared before, and few with such helpful clarifications." Libr J

Includes bibliographic references

Kaplan, Fred. Henry James; the imagination of genius: a biography. Morrow 1992 620p il $25
92

ISBN 0-688-09021-4   LC 92-12246

"Similar in emotional complexity and cunning insights to James's own novels, this nuanced depiction reveals the author as an ambivalent Victorian, a voluntary expatriate who paid the price for his independence in loneliness and alienation." Publ Wkly

Includes bibliographic references

Jarrell, Randall, 1914-1965

Pritchard, William H. Randall Jarrell; a literary life. Farrar, Straus & Giroux 1990 338p il $25; pa $14.95
92

ISBN 0-374-24677-7; 0-374-52277-4 (pa)
LC 91-166233

"A Michael di Capua book"

"Though he was active for three decades, [Jarrell's] name is largely unfamiliar today. Using a lucid and detailed critical style, Pritchard offers a fairly advanced level of analysis of this gifted and undervalued writer, particularly of his poetry. He provides no gossipy retellings of incidents, instead demonstrating influences through the usage of vocabulary, cadence, and structure." Libr J

Includes bibliographic references

Jefferson, Thomas, 1743-1826

Brodie, Fawn McKay. Thomas Jefferson; an intimate history; [by] Fawn M. Brodie. Norton 1974 591p il o.p.; Bantam Bks. paperback available $6.95
92

ISBN 0-553-27335-3 (pa)

"Emphasis on Jefferson's personality, the private thoughts and experiences which influenced his political evolution and in turn shaped the course of history, marks a compelling psychological biography." Booklist

Includes bibliography

Cunningham, Noble E. In pursuit of reason: the life of Thomas Jefferson; [by] Noble E. Cunningham, Jr. Louisiana State Univ. Press 1987 414p il (Southern biography ser) $24.95
92

ISBN 0-8071-1375-1   LC 86-27626

Also available in paperback from Ballantine Bks.

"Cunningham's Jefferson is a man occasionally given to emotional turmoil . . . but mainly he is a personification of the Enlightenment's faith in human reason, progress, and education. It is a traditional interpretation, even conservative—Jefferson's faults and mistakes are down-played or excused—but consistent with the weight of academic evidence. This is now the beginning biography for students and scholars alike." Libr J

Includes bibliography

Dabney, Virginius. The Jefferson scandals; a rebuttal. Madison Bks. 1991 154p il $24.95; pa $12.95
92

1. Hemings, Sally, 1773-1835
ISBN 0-8191-7863-2; 0-8191-7821-7 (pa)
LC 90-45905

A reissue of the title first published 1981 by Dodd, Mead

"The American public has long been fascinated by the allegation that Thomas Jefferson had a 38-year affair with Sally Hemings, a light-skinned slave, who supposedly bore him five children. . . . Dabney offers a concise, forceful broadside asserting that there is no solid historical evidence for this 'fantastic slander,' first made by a disreputable journalist in 1802." Publ Wkly

Includes bibliographic references

Malone, Dumas. Jefferson and his time. Little, Brown 1948-1981 6v il ea $27.50
92

1. United States—Politics and government—1783-1809

Volumes three and six also available in paperback for $12.95

Contents: v1 Jefferson the Virginian (ISBN 0-316-54474-4); v2 Jefferson and the rights of man (ISBN 0-316-54473-6); v3 Jefferson and the ordeal of liberty (ISBN 0-316-54475-2); v4 Jefferson the President, first term, 1801-1805 (ISBN 0-316-54467-1); v5 Jefferson the President, second term, 1805-1809 (ISBN 0-316-54465-5); v6 The sage of Monticello (ISBN 0-316-54463-9)

A comprehensive biography covering Jefferson's personal and public life

"Other students of Jefferson there will be, but none will be able to ignore Malone and his observations; and few, if any, will displace this study best described as definitive." Libr J

Includes bibliographies

Jefferson, Thomas, 1743-1826—*Continued*
McLaughlin, Jack. Jefferson and Monticello; the biography of a builder. Holt & Co. 1988 481p il $29.95; pa $14.95 **92**

ISBN 0-8050-0482-3; 0-8050-1463-2 (pa)

LC 87-23664

In this work the author focuses on the domestic life of the third U.S. President, and his near lifetime involvement with the building of his home, Monticello

"McLaughlin's book is that rare combination: a scholarly but immensely readable work that provides new insights into Jefferson's personality through a detailed examination of his home." Libr J

Includes bibliography

John XXIII, Pope, 1881-1963
Hebblethwaite, Peter. Pope John XXIII; shepherd of the modern world. Doubleday 1985 c1984 550p il hardcover o.p. paperback available $10.95 **92**

ISBN 0-385-23537-2 (pa)

LC 82-45483

First published 1984 in the United Kingdom with title: John XXIII, Pope of the council

A look at John's humble beginnings and his brief, but influential tenure as head of the Roman Catholic Church

Includes bibliography

John, Elton. See class 780.92

John Paul I, Pope, 1912-1978
Cornwell, John. A thief in the night: the mysterious death of Pope John Paul I. Simon & Schuster 1989 366p il $21.95

92

ISBN 0-671-68394-2

LC 89-36326

The author reports on his investigation of the death of Albino Luciani, who died on September 28, 1978, 33 days after his elevation to the papacy. Cornwell concludes that Pope John Paul I "died a natural death of pulmonary embolism; that there never was a murder plot, though some of his staff may have covered up their own negligence; and that Curia officials, although not guilty of murder, may have contributed to the Pope's death by their incompetence." Economist

"With meticulous record-keeping and dogged tracking, Cornwell takes us into the labyrinthine, byzantine society of Vatican City, piecing together a sad and compelling story." Publ Wkly

Johnson, Earvin, 1959-
Johnson, Earvin. Magic's touch; [by] Earvin "Magic" Johnson, Jr., and Roy S. Johnson. Addison-Wesley 1989 xxviii, 236p il $17.26 **92**

ISBN 0-201-51794-9

LC 89-17494

This book traces "Johnson's career from his boyhood roots in Lansing, Michigan, through his ten-year career as leader of the Los Angeles Lakers. Johnson discusses his friendship and rivalry with Larry Bird, his NCAA championship at Michigan State, and his five NBA championships with the Lakers. Interesting are the discussions of basketball's finer points, such as dribbling and passing." Libr J

Johnson, Earvin. My life; [by] Earvin "Magic" Johnson with William Novak. Random House 1992 329p il $22 **92**

ISBN 0-679-41569-6

LC 92-53637

"In this autobiography, Johnson recounts his life, culminating with his now well-known participation as a member of the 'Dream Team' at the Barcelona Olympics." Libr J

"Basketball superstar Johnson's straight talk on AIDS gives his autobiography its thrust and power. . . . Fans will enjoy his replays of key games and seasons, as well as his frank impressions of his former Los Angeles Lakers teammates, coach Pat Riley, the Boston Celtics' Larry Bird and other players." Publ Wkly

Johnson, Lyndon B. (Lyndon Baines), 1908-1973
Califano, Joseph A. The triumph & tragedy of Lyndon Johnson; the White House years; [by] Joseph A. Califano, Jr. Simon & Schuster 1991 398p il $25; pa $13

92

1. United States—Politics and government—1961-1974
ISBN 0-671-66489-1; 0-671-79209-1 (pa)

LC 91-24439

The author, who was Lyndon Johnson's top aide for domestic affairs from 1965 to 1969, presents his observations and recollections of the President

Califano "has written an intimate, balanced and basically sympathetic portrait of the 36th president." Publ Wkly

Includes bibliographic references

Caro, Robert A. The years of Lyndon Johnson. Knopf 1982-1990 2v il v1 $29.95; v2 $24.95 **92**

1. United States—Politics and government—1900-1999 (20th century)

LC 82-47811

Also available in paperback from Vintage Bks.

Contents: v1 The path to power (ISBN 0-394-49973-5); v2 Means of ascent (ISBN 0-394-52835-2)

These are the first two volumes in a projected four-volume biography of President Johnson. The path to power covers the years 1908-1941, and Means of ascent continues from 1941 to Johnson's election to Congress in 1948

Includes bibliographies

Dallek, Robert. Lone star rising: Lyndon Johnson and his times, 1908-1960. Oxford Univ. Press 1991 721p il $30; pa $16.95

92

1. United States—Politics and government—1900-1999 (20th century)
ISBN 0-19-505435-0; 0-19-507904-3 (pa)

LC 90-39830

This first volume of a projected two volume biography chronicles Johnson's formative years, his congressional tenure, and his nomination for vice-president in 1960

"The author combines painstaking historical research with acute sociological insight, producing a fascinating and balanced account of the life and times of one of the most influential legislators of the twentieth century." Booklist

Includes bibliography

Johnson, Samuel, 1709-1784

Bate, Walter Jackson. Samuel Johnson; [by] W. Jackson Bate. Harcourt Brace Jovanovich 1977 xxii, 646p il hardcover o.p. paperback available $10.95   **92**

ISBN 0-15-679259-1 (pa)   LC 77-73044

In this study of Johnson's life, character and work Bate seeks to portray a man who with an erratic, unprepossessing personality, lived on the edge of poverty for fifty years, was beset by trial and tragedy, illness and fears, and yet through his monumental genius, made his life a triumph

"Dr. Johnson's life is a portrait of his century. . . . We can see him in every mood, reacting to most forms of human tribulation, and discover just what it was like to be alive two centuries ago, in every class of society. . . . This biography is written with intense admiration." New Repub

Includes bibliography

Boswell, James. The life of Samuel Johnson   **92**

Hardcover and paperback editions available from various publishers

First published 1791

Variant title: The life of Johnson

"The most famous biography in the English language. It is an intimate and minute delineation of the great lexicographer's life, character and person, enlivened with small-talk, gossip and bits of familiar correspondence. It is also an admirable portrayal of the society of which Johnson was the outstanding figure." Pratt Alcove

Jolson, Al. See class 780.92

Jones, Hettie, 1934-

Jones, Hettie. How I became Hettie Jones. Dutton 1990 239p o.p.; Penguin Bks. paperback available $8.95   **92**

1. Baraka, Imamu Amiri, 1934-
ISBN 0-14-015388-8 (pa)   LC 89-17087

"Hettie Jones, née Cohen, for seven years the wife of writer and black militant LeRoi Jones (later Amiri Baraka), has written a thoughtful, intimate memoir of their life in the burgeoning movement of new jazz, poetry and politics that flourished in lower Manhattan in the late 1950s and early 1960s. In it she re-creates an important moment in our cultural history." Nation

Jones, John Paul, 1747-1792

Morison, Samuel Eliot. John Paul Jones; a sailor's biography; with an introduction by James C. Bradford; charts and diagrams by Erwin Raisz. Naval Inst. Press 1989 xxvi, 537p il (Classics of naval literature) $29.95   **92**

1. United States—History, Naval
ISBN 0-87021-323-7   LC 89-13423

Also available in paperback from Northeastern Univ. Press

A reissue with a new introduction of the title first published 1959 by Little, Brown

This "documented chronicle of the American sea captain's life . . . is particularly concerned with his ability as a seaman and with the naval engagements in which he took part." Booklist

"Morison has destroyed the myth of John Paul Jones but has left us a more human, more understandable character." Best Sellers

Includes bibliographic references

Joplin, Janis. See class 780.92

Joyce, James, 1882-1941

Beja, Morris. James Joyce; a literary life. Ohio State Univ. Press 1992 150p il $30; pa $12.50   **92**

ISBN 0-8142-0598-4; 0-8142-0599-2 (pa)
          LC 92-20068

In this biography Beja traces the correspondence between the events of Joyce's life and his literary oeuvre

"This concise yet thorough biography of James Joyce fills a void in Joycean studies by offering students and general readers a short, readable account of the writer's life." Univ Press Books for Public and Second Sch Libr

Includes bibliographic references

Ellmann, Richard. James Joyce. new and rev ed. Oxford Univ. Press 1982 887p il $50; pa $21.95   **92**

ISBN 0-19-503103-2; 0-19-503381-7 (pa)
          LC 81-22455

First published 1959

This biography describes "Joyce's working methods, views on life and literature, political opinions, familial relationships and problems, and incessant struggle against poverty and threatening blindness." Publ Wkly

This "is a vast undertaking and continuing achievement—massive, masterly, and definitive, rich in anecdote and detail. It is also extremely readable; the easy, often sympathetic style communicates gracefully not only facts but analysis." Choice

Includes bibliographic references

Joyce, Nora Barnacle, 1884-1951

Maddox, Brenda. Nora; the real life of Molly Bloom. Houghton Mifflin 1988 xx, 472p il $24.95   **92**

1. Joyce, James, 1882-1941
ISBN 0-395-36510-4   LC 88-3023

Also available in paperback from Fawcett Bks.

The author "gives us the woman behind the man James Joyce, the woman who, the great novelist said, 'made him a man.' . . . For many readers, Nora's real life will have an interest beyond fiction." Christ Sci Monit

Includes bibliography

Juana Inés de la Cruz, 1651-1695

Paz, Octavio. Sor Juana; or, The traps of faith; translated by Margaret Sayers Peden. Belknap Press 1988 547p il $37.50; pa $15.95   **92**

ISBN 0-674-82105-X; 0-674-82106-8 (pa) LC 88-3002

Original Spanish edition, 1982

This is a study of the life and work of the seventeenth-century Mexican poet

"Paz's book on Sor Juana displays an extraordinary sweep of imagination and intelligence, and it is many things: a biography, a critical study, a re-creation of an era, a meditation on Mexican history, a dialogue of poet

Juana Inés de la Cruz, 1651-1695 — *Continued*

with poet, a reflection on the role of the intellectual in the modern world." N Y Rev Books

Includes bibliography

Jung, C. G. (Carl Gustav), 1875-1961

Freud, Sigmund. The Freud/Jung letters. See entry under Freud, Sigmund, 1856-1939
92

Jung, C. G. (Carl Gustav). Memories, dreams, reflections; recorded and edited by Aniela Jaffé; translated from the German by Richard and Clara Winston. rev ed. Vintage Bks. 1989 c1963 430p pa $12 **92**

ISBN 0-679-72395-1   LC 88-37040

First published 1963 by Pantheon Bks.

"This volume of recollections reveals the intellectual and spiritual development of an eminent Swiss psychologist and psychiatrist while only touching upon the outward events of his long and productive life. . . . An important, firsthand document for readers who wish to understand this seminal writer and thinker." Booklist

Includes bibliography

Kafka, Franz, 1883-1924

Pawel, Ernst. The nightmare of reason: a life of Franz Kafka. Farrar, Straus & Giroux 1984 466p il $25.50; pa $15 **92**

ISBN 0-374-22236-3; 0-374-52335-5 (pa)

LC 83-25376

This "biography recounts Kafka's parentage, schooling, employment, loves, and friendships." Libr J

"The author, with great sensitivity, has amassed every relevant detail of Kafka's life, worked through all the useful—and occasionally useless—biographical and critical material, and produced a work of such thoroughness that it is difficult to imagine any work that might supersede it." Choice

Includes bibliography

Kahlo, Frida. See class 709.2

Karpov, Anatoly, 1951-

Karpov, Anatoly. Karpov on Karpov; a memoir of a chess world champion; translated from the Russian by Todd Bludeau. Atheneum Pubs. 1991 232p il $24.95 **92**

1. Chess

ISBN 0-689-12060-5   LC 91-16031

Karpov, world chess champion between 1975 and 1985, reviews his career and his intense rivalry with Gary Kasparov. Commentary on legendary players and match-ups is included

Kaye, M. M. (Mary Margaret), 1908-

Kaye, M. M. (Mary Margaret). The sun in the morning; my early years in India and England. St. Martin's Press 1990 454p il o.p.
92

LC 90-37514

Available in hardcover from Viking and in paperback from Penguin Bks.

The first volume of the author's autobiography contains "recollections of a carefree childhood in British-governed India (The Raj) and of a more restricted adolescence in school at 'home'—in . . . England." Libr J

Kazin, Alfred, 1915-

Kazin, Alfred. New York Jew. Knopf 1978 307p $18 **92**

ISBN 0-394-49567-5   LC 78-1932

"Continuing the autobiography of his Walker in the City and Starting Out in the Thirties [both entered below, Kazin] picks up in 1938 and carries us into the Seventies. . . . [He includes sketches of a number of] cultural figures . . . and [recalls] . . . the magazines he worked for, the colleges he taught in, the countries he visited, the women he loved." Libr J

Kazin, Alfred. Starting out in the thirties. Little, Brown 1965 166p o.p.; Cornell Univ. Press paperback available $7.95 **92**

ISBN 0-8014-9562-8 (pa)

A "tour of the Depression in New York and the generation of radical writers—John Steinbeck, William Saroyan, Clifford Odets, James T. Farrell, Robert Cantwell—who, like Author Kazin, were starting out in the Thirties." Time

Kazin, Alfred. A walker in the city; drawings by Marvin Bileck. Harcourt Brace & Co. 1951 176p hardcover o.p. paperback available $9.95 **92**

ISBN 0-15-694176-7 (pa)

Also available in hardcover from P. Smith

Reminiscences of a boy's life in New York, branching out in walks and excursions from the center, the kitchen of the home of poor Jewish immigrants in Brownsville

Keith, Nancy

Keith, Nancy. Slim; memories of a rich and imperfect life; [by] Slim Keith with Annette Tapert. Simon & Schuster 1990 319p il $22.95 **92**

ISBN 0-671-63164-0   LC 90-31452

Also available in paperback from Warner Bks.

Social celebrity 'Slim' Keith recalls her marriages to director Howard Hawks, Broadway producer Leland Hayward, and banker Kenneth Keith, and friendships with Clark Gable, Ernest Hemingway, and others

Slim "writes about famous people, decorative people and interesting people. At her best she's vivid and pungent . . . at her worst she's pleasantly superficial." NY Times Book Rev

Keller, Helen, 1880-1968

Keller, Helen. The story of my life. Doubleday 1954 382p il $15.95 **92**

1. Blind 2. Deaf
ISBN 0-385-04453-4

Also available in paperback from various publishers

First published 1903

This biography of the inspirational Keller contains accounts of her home life and her relationship with her devoted teacher Anne Sullivan

Lash, Joseph P. Helen and teacher: the story of Helen Keller and Anne Sullivan Macy. Delacorte Press 1980 811p il (Radcliffe biography ser) hardcover o.p. paperback available $6.95 **92**

1. Sullivan, Anne, 1866-1936 2. Blind 3. Deaf
ISBN 0-440-53509-3 (pa)   LC 79-25599

"A Merloyd Lawrence book"

The author "tells the life stories of both Keller and the educator who devoted her life to her, the woman Helen referred to simply as 'Teacher.'" Ms

"This is a deeply absorbing portrait of two intertwined lives whose meanings can't be understood separately." NY Times Book Rev

Includes bibliography

Kelly, Jim

Kelly, Jim. Armed and dangerous; [by] Jim Kelly with Vic Carucci. Doubleday 1992 249p il $20 **92**

1. Buffalo Bills (Football team)
ISBN 0-385-42451-5   LC 92-13807

All-pro Buffalo Bills quarterback Kelly "writes movingly of growing up with five brothers and a machinist father who worked in a steel mill, and of his feats at the University of Miami, where he quarterbacked the Hurricanes to national prominence. The strength of the book is Kelly's candid portrayal of teammates, games and off-field controversies." N Y Times Book Rev

Kelly, Katie

Kelly, Katie. A year in Saigon; how I gave up my glitzy job in television to have the time of my life teaching Amerasian kids in Vietnam. Simon & Schuster 1992 254p il $22 **92**

ISBN 0-671-75090-9   LC 92-5989

The author "tells of the year she spent trying to help young Amerasians in Vietnam. After Kelly visited in 1988, she decided to return to teach English and facts about the United States to the children abandoned by their American fathers and shunned by the Vietnamese. She held classes in the American Transit Center and then, when that privilege was denied her, in parks, restaurants, bars, and a student's home. She describes her experiences, which ranged from pathetic to humorous and portrays life in contemporary Saigon." Libr J

Kennan, George Frost, 1904-

Kennan, George Frost. Sketches from a life; [by] George F. Kennan. Pantheon Bks. 1989 365p $22.95; pa $12.95 **92**

1. United States—Foreign relations
ISBN 0-394-57504-0; 0-679-72877-5 (pa)
LC 88-43282

"This is a collection of very private reflections spanning some 60 years of foreign service in Nazi Germany, the Baltic states, the Low Countries, the Soviet Union, as well as nonofficial travels covering the entire globe. Kennan has marvelous insight into his ever-changing surroundings—an insight that is always sharp, sometimes melancholy, and punctuated frequently by dry, Midwestern wit." Libr J

Kennedy, Edward Moore, 1932-

Damore, Leo. Senatorial privilege; the Chappaquiddick cover-up. Regnery Gateway 1988 496p il maps $21.95 **92**

1. Kopechne, Mary Jo, 1941-1969
ISBN 0-89526-564-8   LC 88-11535

Also available in paperback from Dell

The author presents his investigation into the 1969 death of Mary Jo Kopechne, who was the passenger in a car driven off a bridge after a party on Chappaquiddick Island, Massachusetts, by Senator Edward M. Kennedy

This is "an exciting and meticulously researched job of investigative reporting. . . . Exciting as the fastest-paced mystery novel, but at the same time utterly responsible, thorough, and convincing." Natl Rev

Kennedy, John F. (John Fitzgerald), 1917-1963

Hamilton, Nigel. JFK, reckless youth. Random House 1992 xxiv, 898p il $30 **92**

ISBN 0-679-41216-6   LC 92-8207

This is an "account of John F. Kennedy from the future president's birth in 1917 in Brookline, Mass., through his school years . . . to his years in Europe before World War II, when his father was United States ambassador to Great Britain. The first of three planned volumes, Hamilton's book ends in 1946 when JFK was elected to congress at the age of 29." Christ Sci Monit

The author "has written a remarkably fresh work that promises to be the fullest, most revealing portrait of Kennedy's personal and political development." Publ Wkly

Includes bibliographic references

Manchester, William. One brief shining moment: remembering Kennedy. Little, Brown 1983 280p il hardcover o.p. paperback available $16.95 **92**

1. United States—Politics and government—1961-1974
ISBN 0-316-54511-2 (pa)   LC 83-17590

Some two hundred "photographs supplement the author's reminiscences and those of 150 members of the Kennedy entourage." Libr J

"The tone is elegiac and at times almost mawkishly reverential . . . but the telling is saved from idolatry by a colloquial, fair reporting of Kennedy's tempers, humors, graces, and failures." Horn Book

Kennedy, John F. (John Fitzgerald), 1917-1963—*Continued*

O'Donnell, Kenneth P. "Johnny, we hardly knew ye": memories of John Fitzgerald Kennedy; by Kenneth P. O'Donnell and David F. Powers, with Joe McCarthy. Little, Brown 1972 434p hardcover o.p. paperback available $13.95 **92**

1. United States—Politics and government—1953-1961
2. United States—Politics and government—1961-1974
ISBN 0-316-63000-4 (pa)

This memoir focuses "on Kennedy's development as a 'total politician,' from his race for Congress in 1946 to his death." Libr J

Kennedy, Robert F., 1925-1968

Kennedy, Robert F. Robert Kennedy, in his own words; the unpublished recollections of the Kennedy years; edited by Edwin O. Guthman and Jeffrey Shulman. Bantam Bks. 1988 493p il $22.50; pa $16 **92**

1. United States—Politics and government—1961-1974
ISBN 0-553-05316-7; 0-553-34661-X (pa)
                                            LC 88-47680
Published in cooperation with Twenty-first Century Books

The text of this volume is based on interviews conducted with Robert F. Kennedy in 1964, 1965, and 1967 by Anthony Lewis, John Bartlow Martin, Arthur M. Schlesinger, Jr., and John Francis Stewart. The interviews were part of the John F. Kennedy Library's oral history project, initiated by Robert Kennedy to record the recollections of members of the Kennedy administration

"Terse, frequently pungent, RFK's transcribed remarks are valuable for the immediacy they impart to events that quickly became history." Libr J

Schlesinger, Arthur M. Robert Kennedy and his times; [by] Arthur M. Schlesinger, Jr. Houghton Mifflin 1978 1066p il o.p.; Ballantine Bks. paperback available $6.95 **92**

1. United States—Politics and government—1900-1999 (20th century)
ISBN 0-345-32547-8 (pa)   LC 78-8469

"A highly sympathetic and readable political biography covering in depth Robert Kennedy's tenure in public life. At times extremely partisan, at times dispassionate, Schlesinger's study effectively captures Kennedy's impact on national politics and the main currents of American politics during the 1950s and 1960s." Choice

Includes bibliographic references

Kern, Jerome. See class 780.92

Kerouac, Jack, 1922-1969

McNally, Dennis. Desolate angel: Jack Kerouac, the Beat generation, and America. Random House 1979 400p il o.p.; Delta Bks. paperback available $12.95 **92**

1. Bohemianism
ISBN 0-385-30095-6 (pa)   LC 78-23786

A biography of the author of On the road, Desolation angels, Dharma bums, and Big Sur, among others. Kerouac's contemporaries among the "Beats," Allen Ginsberg, Neal Cassady, John C. Holmes, and William S.

Burroughs are also discussed as reflections of the changing fabric of society following World War II

Includes bibliography

Nicosia, Gerald. Memory babe: a critical biography of Jack Kerouac. Grove Press 1983 767p il o.p.; Penguin Bks. paperback available $9.95 **92**

1. Bohemianism
ISBN 0-14-058016-6 (pa)   LC 82-24212
"A Fred Jordan book"

"The best thing about [this book] is that it meshes well with Kerouac's own books, paraphrasing them, putting their story in chronological order and fleshing out the autobiographical legend." N Y Times Book Rev

Includes bibliographic references

Kesey, Ken

Wolfe, Tom. The electric kool-aid acid test. Farrar, Straus & Giroux 1968 416p o.p.; Bantam Bks. paperback available $5.95 **92**

1. LSD (Drug)
ISBN 0-553-26491-5 (pa)

A portrait of the novelist Ken Kesey and the West Coast "Merry Pranksters" during a several years pursuit of the LSD experience and development of psychedelia

Khrushchev, Nikita Sergeevich, 1894-1971

Khrushchev, Sergei. Krushchev on Khrushchev; an inside account of the man and his era; by his son, Sergei Khrushchev; edited and translated by William Taubman. Little, Brown 1990 423p il $24.95 **92**

1. Soviet Union—Politics and government
ISBN 0-316-49194-2   LC 90-5618

The son of the former Soviet leader writes of Khrushchev's overthrow and final years

"Sergei Khrushchev does not try to hide his affection for his father, or his anguish at the man's political fate. At the same time, he strains admirably to be objective and balanced." N Y Times Book Rev

King, Larry, 1933-

King, Larry. Tell me more; by Larry King with Peter Occhiogrosso. Putnam 1990 301p o.p.; St. Martin's Press paperback available $4.99 **92**

ISBN 0-312-92690-1 (pa)   LC 90-8458

Companion volume to Tell it to the King (1988)

The author "interviews innumerable celebrities from show business, politics, sports and the media. Here with freelancer Occhiogrosso he presents high and low moments of those occasions. . . . This storehouse of anecdote is well worth readers' attention." Publ Wkly

King, Martin Luther, 1929-1968

Bennett, Lerone. What manner of man: a biography of Martin Luther King, Jr. by Lerone Bennett, Jr.; with an introduction by Benjamin E. Mays. [3rd rev ed]. Johnson 1968 251p il $17.95   **92**

1. Blacks—Civil rights
ISBN 0-87485-027-4

First published 1964

The author recalls Martin Luther King from his childhood, education, accomplishments as a Baptist minister, his leadership in the black Civil Rights movement, his winning the 1964 Nobel Peace Prize to the tragic end of his life in 1968

Colaiaco, James A. Martin Luther King, Jr; apostle of militant nonviolence. St. Martin's Press 1988 238p $29.95; pa $14.95   **92**

1. Blacks—Civil rights
ISBN 0-312-02365-0; 0-312-08843-4 (pa)
                                            LC 88-14900

"Colaiaco's book fills a very important place in the historiography of Martin Luther King Jr. It is a short, thorough work that touches all the main issues and themes, and puts them into the context of the times. . . . More than a fact-by-fact biography, Colaiaco's study reveals the ideological contradictions . . . underlying the events he describes." Choice

Includes bibliography

Garrow, David J. Bearing the cross: Martin Luther King, Jr., and the Southern Christian Leadership Conference. Morrow 1986 800p $22.95   **92**

1. Southern Christian Leadership Conference
2. Blacks—Civil rights
ISBN 0-688-04794-7   LC 86-8594

Also available in paperback from Vintage Bks.

This book is a "study of King's participation in the civil rights revolution. It [seeks to] portray his interaction with the staff members of the major civil rights institutions and . . . [other participants] in that struggle." Christ Century

"Granting its limitations, Bearing the Cross is likely to remain for a long time the most informative life of Martin Luther King, Jr., and the most thorough study of the civil rights movement, or the large part of it in which King and the SCLC was active." N Y Rev Books

Includes bibliography

Oates, Stephen B. Let the trumpet sound: the life of Martin Luther King, Jr. Harper & Row 1982 560p il o.p.; New Am. Lib. paperback available $14.95   **92**

1. Blacks—Civil rights
ISBN 0-452-25627-5 (pa)   LC 81-48046

"Mr. Oates treats King's personality with insight and tact, but his focus, understandably, is on the public man. He is particularly successful in tracing the origins of King's ideas in his early upbringing and preparation for the ministry. . . . [The author] displays a remarkable understanding of King's individual role in the civil rights movement." N Y Times Book Rev

Includes bibliographic references

We shall overcome: Martin Luther King, Jr., and the Black freedom struggle; edited by Peter J. Albert and Ronald Hoffman. Pantheon Bks. 1990 294p il $22.95   **92**

1. Blacks—Civil rights
ISBN 0-394-58399-X   LC 89-71016

Also available in paperback from Da Capo Press

"This is a collection of papers and comments from a symposium sponsored by the U.S. Capitol Historical Society. Contributors range from leading academics like David Garrow to Civil Rights activists like Robert Moses. As a group, the essays have two main focuses: the role of religion in King's life and ideas; and the issue of the relative importance of King's personality as opposed to historical forces in creating the modern Civil Rights movement." Libr J

Includes bibliographic references

King, Stephen, 1947-

King, Stephen. Bare bones; conversations on terror with Stephen King; Tim Underwood and Chuck Miller, editors. McGraw-Hill 1988 211p $16.95   **92**

ISBN 0-07-065759-9   LC 87-31078

Also available in paperback from Warner Bks.

A collection of "interviews conducted from 1979 through 1987 in journals ranging from *Playboy* to *Yankee.*" Booklist

"This book will be of interest to King fans who enjoy knowing more about their favorite author. King is open and honest to many questions that stray beyond what an author needs to share with his audience. His answers are thoughtful and insightful and not without a mixture of humor and a touch of the macabre." West Coast Rev Books

King, Stephen. Feast of fear; conversations with Stephen King; Tim Underwood and Chuck Miller, editors. Carroll & Graf Pubs. 1992 282p $18.95   **92**

ISBN 0-88184-811-5   LC 92-6902

"Sprinkled with personal revelations, these interviews, a feast for fans, furnish a rare glimpse into King's private universe. Underwood and Miller . . . have cleverly stitched together 47 newspaper and magazine interviews, many published in obscure places, which follow the novelist chronologically from his years working in an industrial laundry to his phenomenal success and cozy family life in Bangor, Maine." Publ Wkly

Kirkland, Gelsey

Kirkland, Gelsey. Dancing on my grave; an autobiography; by Gelsey Kirkland with Greg Lawrence. Doubleday 1986 286p il $17.95   **92**

1. American Ballet Theatre
ISBN 0-385-19964-3   LC 86-8857

Also available in paperback from Jove Pubs.

This is an autobiographical account of the dancer's life and career, written in collaboration with her husband. Kirkland discusses her experiences with George Balanchine's New York City Ballet, her partnership with Mikhail Baryshnikov in the American Ballet Theatre, her emotional difficulties, anorexia, unhappy love affairs, and addiction to cocaine

The author "has provided an unnervingly vivid statement about the perils of a profession in which your instrument is yourself." N Y Times Book Rev

Kirkland, Gelsey—*Continued*

Kirkland, Gelsey. The shape of love; [by] Gelsey Kirkland and Greg Lawrence. Doubleday 1990 237p il $19.95   **92**

ISBN 0-385-24918-7   LC 89-28476

Also available in paperback from Berkley Pub. Group

This sequel to the title entered above "tells what has happened to Kirkland and Lawrence since recovery and their marriage. After an absence of two years Kirkland triumphantly returned to the stage to perform with the Royal Ballet in *Romeo and Juliet* and *The Sleeping Beauty*." Libr J

"Although less gossipy than the previous book, this will appeal to aspiring ballerinas and fans." SLJ

Kisor, Henry, 1940-

Kisor, Henry. What's that pig outdoors? A memoir of deafness; foreword by Walker Percy. Hill & Wang 1990 270p $18.95 **92**

1. Deaf

ISBN 0-8090-9689-7   LC 89-26765

Also available G.K. Hall large print edition and in paperback from Penguin Bks.

"Deaf since the age of three, Kisor overcame this disability by learning to lip-read and to speak with the help and support of his family and teacher. With these skills he became a part of the hearing world and . . . a prize-winning journalist and adjunct instructor of journalism at Northwestern University." Libr J

"All the way along, there were setbacks and heart-aches, challenges and triumphs. [Mr. Kisor] has set them down in a clean, deft prose style that is a pleasure to read and that lets the rest of us realize what an easy time we have in moving through our customary encounters from sunup to sundown." N Y Times Book Rev

Kissinger, Henry, 1923-

Isaacson, Walter. Kissinger; a biography. Simon & Schuster 1992 893p il $30   **92**

ISBN 0-671-66323-2   LC 92-16009

This "biography provides plenty of ammunition for the former Secretary of State's supporters *and* detractors. . . . Isaacson . . . sees Kissinger as the foremost American negotiator of this century, but one whose furtive, conspiratorial, at times deceitful personality shaped his conservative realpolitik and diplomatic maneuvering." Publ Wkly

Includes bibliographic references

Kissinger, Henry. White House years. Little, Brown 1979 xxiv, 1521p il $29.95
92

1. United States—Foreign relations

ISBN 0-316-49661-8   LC 79-90006

This book covers the period from 1969, when Kissinger became Richard Nixon's national-security advisor, to the signing of the Vietnam peace agreement in January 1973

"Writing with the combined insights of an accomplished historian and statesman, Kissinger exposes the readers to the foreign policy-making process in the U.S. as well as the form and content of specific policies woven primarily by him under Presidents Nixon and Ford." Choice

Includes bibliographic references

Kissinger, Henry. Years of upheaval. Little, Brown 1982 xxi, 1283p il $29.95
92

1. United States—Foreign relations

ISBN 0-316-28591-9   LC 81-86320

This volume deals with the "unraveling of the Paris agreement, the continuation of triangular diplomacy with Peking and Moscow . . . the overthrow of Salvador Allende, the . . . October 1973 war in the Middle East, the first oil crisis, Kissinger's shuttle diplomacy, the beginning of the anti-détente campaign in the United States, Richard Nixon's . . . Middle East journal—and [Watergate]." N Y Rev Books

"Dr. Kissinger's account of these [years] is a literary and historical masterpiece that makes superb reading." Christ Sci Monit

Includes bibliographic references

Koch, Ed, 1924-

Koch, Ed. Citizen Koch; an autobiography; [by] Edward I. Koch with Daniel Paisner. St. Martin's Press 1992 281p il $22.95 **92**

1. New York (N.Y.)—Politics and government

ISBN 0-312-08161-8   LC 92-18669

"A Thomas Dunne book"

In this autobiography the former mayor of New York City, "who has been a private citizen since 1990 after a political career that began in 1963, talks pridefully about his life after the mayoralty as an attorney, radio and TV host, movie reviewer, lecturer, etc." Publ Wkly

"For all his vaunted candor, the man comes across as a touchy, self-protective, oddly provincial figure. Still, some of the anecdotes are funny, and thanks no doubt to Mr. Paisner, the Koch voice is here." N Y Times Book Rev

Koller, Alice

Koller, Alice. The stations of solitude. Morrow 1990 364p $19.95   **92**

ISBN 0-688-07940-7   LC 89-29899

Also available in paperback from Bantam Bks.

"Koller constructs a contemplation on the place of Truth within daily life around such daily themes as waking, working, relationships, and dealing with money. The result is mostly autobiographical." Libr J

"Ms. Koller's exemplary life provides a wealth of instructive anecdote. . . . This book's uneven tone calls to mind the patter of a brilliant but eccentric performer: it enthralls one minute and gets querulous the next." NY Times Book Rev

Koop, C. Everett

Koop, C. Everett. Koop; the memoirs of America's family doctor. Random House 1991 342p il $22   **92**

ISBN 0-394-57626-8   LC 91-52671

Also available in paperback from HarperCollins Pubs.

"After describing his life before and shortly after becoming Surgeon General, Dr. Koop discusses the major issues he addressed in his new job: smoking, AIDS, the rights of handicapped children and abortion. While not dramatic, Dr. Koop's memoirs are quietly revealing and provocative." N Y Times Book Rev

Kuralt, Charles, 1934-

Kuralt, Charles. A life on the road.
Putnam 1990 253p il o.p.; Ivy Bks.
paperback available $5.99 **92**

ISBN 0-8041-0869-2 (pa)   LC 90-39461

Also available Thorndike Press large print edition

"Kuralt reviews his career in print journalism and as
a reporter for the electronic media. He recalls his most
unusual and memorable programs and interviewees." Publ
Wkly

Kurosawa, Akira, 1910-

Kurosawa, Akira. Something like an
autobiography; translated by Audie E. Bock.
Knopf 1982 205p il hardcover o.p.
paperback available $12 **92**

1. Motion picture industry
ISBN 0-394-71439-3 (pa)   LC 81-48100

These are the memoirs of the Japanese filmmaker,
covering his life up to 1951-52, when his film Rashōmon
won international awards

This "is a fascinating, moving record of one man's
pursuit of excellence in a single art." N Y Times Book
Rev

Kusz, Natalie

Kusz, Natalie. Road song. Farrar, Straus
& Giroux 1990 258p $18.95 **92**

ISBN 0-374-25121-5   LC 90-34777

Also available Thorndike Press large print edition and
in paperback from HarperPerennial

In this memoir the author recalls her "close-knit
family and youth in Alaska—the tragic accident that left
her blind in one eye, her relationship with her strong
mother, her teenage rebellion, and her return to the land
her family loved." Booklist

"Eschewing sentimentality and self-pity, Kusz paints
a moving portrait of herself and her funny and heroic
family in this engrossing, poetically written memoir."
Publ Wkly

La Guardia, Fiorello Henry, 1882-1947

Kessner, Thomas. Fiorello H. La Guardia
and the making of modern New York.
McGraw-Hill 1989 700p il o.p.; Penguin
Bks. paperback available $12.95 **92**

1. New York (N.Y.)—Politics and government
ISBN 0-14-014358-0 (pa)   LC 89-2293

This biography covers "La Guardia's entire life . .
. enhancing the existing record with interviews, archival
work, and a reading of the contemporary press." Libr
J

The author "has produced a panoramic history and
character study [with] sweep and lucidity." N Y Times
Book Rev

Includes bibliographic references

L'Amour, Louis, 1908-1988

L'Amour, Louis. Education of a wandering
man. Bantam Bks. 1989 232p il $16.95
92

ISBN 0-553-05703-0   LC 89-14903

"These unfinished memoirs by the noted Western
author possess a raw enthusiasm for life and for books
that is too rarely encountered today. For most of the
book, L'Amour recounts scattered anecdotes of his
knockabout years as a sailor, prize fighter, silver miner,
and longshoreman who ranged from New Orleans to
Singapore with a book in his hip pocket." Libr J

Includes bibliography

Landry, Tom

Landry, Tom. Tom Landry: an
autobiography; [by] Tom Landry with Gregg
Lewis. Zondervan 1990 302p il o.p.;
HarperPaperbacks $5.50 **92**

1. Dallas Cowboys (Football team)
ISBN 0-06-104057-6 (pa)   LC 90-33913

Also available Walker & Co. large print edition

"Landry briefly recounts his Texas boyhood and his
high school, college, and professional playing days before
settling into a detailed account of the coaching career
that got him into the Hall of Fame. There are some
interesting anecdotes centering around the Cowboy greats
(Roger Staubach, Bob Lilly, and Tony Dorsett, to name
a few), but this is as much organizational history as
autobiography." Booklist

Lansky, Meyer, 1902-1983

Lacey, Robert. Little man: Meyer Lansky
and the gangster life. Little, Brown 1991
547p il maps $24.95; pa $5.99 **92**

1. Mafia
ISBN 0-316-51168-4; 0-316-51163-3 (pa)

LC 91-18324

This is a biography of the reputed racketeer

"Based on new research and interviews with Lansky's
friends and family, [this] book presents an emotionally
cold businessman, a survivor who exacts grudging
admiration but little compassion. . . . [This is a] lively
deconstruction of the gangster life." Time

Includes bibliographic references

Larsen, Wanwadee

Larsen, Wanwadee. Confessions of a mail
order bride; American life through Thai
eyes. New Horizon Press 1989 324p $21.95
92

ISBN 0-88282-051-6   LC 89-43331

"When her existence in Thailand is abruptly shattered
by the murder of her brother, Wanwadee decides to
utilize the services of an Asian mail-order bride agency
in the hopes of pursuing a college education in America.
Fortunately, the man she marries is sympathetic, and her
memoirs record her growing relationship with him and
her attempts to come to terms with her adopted home"
Libr J

"Larsen cogently compares and contrasts her birth culture with her adopted one, on topics such as gender
behavior, individualism and community, racism, and education." Booklist

Lattimore, Owen, 1900-1989

Newman, Robert P. Owen Lattimore and the "loss" of China. University of Calif. Press 1992 669p il $32 **92**

1. China—Foreign relations—United States 2. United States—Foreign relations—China

ISBN 0-520-07388-6 LC 91-21888

"A Philip E. Lilienthal book"

This biography of the American Sinologist focuses on the accusations brought against Lattimore in the 1950s by Joseph R. McCarthy, the Senate Internal Security subcommittee, the Justice Department and the FBI. They alleged that Lattimore was a Soviet agent and played a part in the Communist revolution in China. The case was dismissed in 1955. The volume concludes with an account of Lattimore's subsequent career at Leeds, his retirement, return to the United States, and death

"Newman's forays into a wide range of archives have been so adventuresome that his book stands on its own as a valuable contribution to modern American history. . . . It is hard to imagine that this comprehensive and engrossing study of Lattimore's life, works, and tribulations will ever be superseded." New Repub

Includes bibliographic references

Lawrence, D. H. (David Herbert), 1885-1930

Meyers, Jeffrey. D.H. Lawrence; a biography. Knopf 1990 445p $24.95; pa $14 **92**

ISBN 0-394-57244-0; 0-679-73065-6 (pa)

LC 89-43294

"Meyers tells the story of D.H. Lawrence's life—one of the saddest and at the same time most hopeful chapters in literary history—with the focus right where it belongs: on showcasing the unquenchable passion of a man who spent 44 years wrestling with the question of how to be fully alive." Booklist

Includes bibliographic references

Worthen, John. D.H. Lawrence. v1: the early years, 1885-1912. Cambridge Univ. Press 1991 626p il (Cambridge biography) $49.95; pa $18.95 **92**

ISBN 0-521-25419-1; 0-521-43772-5 (pa)

LC 90-23423

"Worthen's biography of Lawrence's early years is the first volume of Cambridge's new three-volume life of Lawrence, each to be written by a different scholar. Worthen takes the young writer through his elopement with Frieda. . . . This persuasive biography is compulsive good reading from cover to cover. A major event in modern literary studies." Libr J

Includes bibliographic references

Worthen, John. D.H. Lawrence: a literary life. St. Martin's Press 1989 xxvi, 196p (Literary lives) hardcover o.p. paperback available $14.95 **92**

ISBN 0-312-08752-7 (pa) LC 89-34364

"In concentrating on contracts, agreements, and the demands made on DHL's writings by 'practical' considerations, Worthen shows how he reacted with compromise. Yet on other occasions, Lawrence maintained a heroic struggle to contain the integrity of his manuscripts, and in this book he surfaces as a man caught in the web of professional survival. . . . [This is] an impressive summary of DHL's career." Choice

Includes bibliography

Lawrence, T. E. (Thomas Edward), 1888-1935

Wilson, Jeremy. Lawrence of Arabia; the authorized biography of T.E. Lawrence. Atheneum Pubs. 1990 1188p il maps $35 **92**

ISBN 0-689-11934-8 LC 89-49008

Also available in an abridged paperback edition from Collier Bks.

First published 1989 in the United Kingdom

Wilson "depicts all aspects of Lawrence's strengths and accomplishments, including his development as a literary figure and his friendships with writers and political leaders." Libr J

"This vast biography of one of the most enigmatic figures in modern times will endure beside T.E. Lawrence's own book 'The Seven Pillars of Wisdom' as Lawrence's monument, and future books about the great soldier and adventurer will be merely commentaries on it." N Y Times Book Rev

Includes bibliographic references

Leadbelly. See class 780.92

Lee, Peggy. See class 780.92

Lee, Robert E. (Robert Edward), 1807-1870

Anderson, Nancy Scott. The generals: Ulysses S. Grant and Robert E. Lee. See entry under Grant, Ulysses S. (Ulysses Simpson), 1822-1885 **92**

Flood, Charles Bracelen. Lee—the last years. Houghton Mifflin 1981 308p il $24.45; pa $12.70 **92**

ISBN 0-395-31292-2; 0-395-34637-1 (pa) LC 81-4231

This book "tells the story of Robert E. Lee from the surrender of his army in April 1865 until his death in October 1870. . . . Much of the book is devoted to the attitudes and actions of the great Virginian as a spokesman and symbol of national reconciliation and as an innovative yet practical-minded president of Washington College (now Washington and Lee University), in Lexington, Virginia." Hist Rev New Books

Includes bibliography

Freeman, Douglas Southall. Lee; an abridgment in one volume, by Richard Harwell, of the four-volume R. E. Lee; with a new foreword by James M. McPherson. Scribner 1991 xxiii, 601p il maps $35 **92**

1. United States—History—1861-1865, Civil War

ISBN 0-684-19378-7 LC 91-20088

First published 1961

"Students of history will continue to want and to use the original four-volume work [entered below] but most general readers will find this abridgment more convenient and adequate to their interest. All footnotes and all of the appendix have been omitted as well as details of Civil War action that are not necessary to show the main course of Lee's life and action." Booklist

Freeman, Douglas Southall. R. E. Lee; a biography. Scribner 1934-1935 4v v1-2, 4 ea $60; v3 $55 **92**

1. United States—History—1861-1865, Civil War

Lee, Robert E. (Robert Edward), 1807-1870—*Continued*

v1 ISBN 0-684-15482-X; v2 ISBN 0-684-15483-8; v3 ISBN 0-684-15484-6; v4 ISBN 0-684-15485-4

The official biography of Robert E. Lee based on exhaustive research, which won the Pulitzer Prize 1935. Includes a critical bibliography of manuscripts and printed sources

The author's "narrative has vitality and color, a sustained vividness. But it is never falsely dramatic or rhapsodic. His prose is firm and never tedious." N Y Times Book Rev

Nolan, Alan T. Lee considered; General Robert E. Lee and Civil War history. University of N.C. Press 1991 231p il $22.50   **92**

1. United States—History—1861-1865, Civil War
ISBN 0-8078-1956-5   LC 90-48296

In this biography of the Confederate Civil War general, the author contends "that Lee the slaveholder was not antislavery, that the reluctant secessionist endorsed Southern independence, that the general lost the war by his repeated offensive thrusts and provincial vision—and more." Libr J

"Nolan uses sources cleverly to build his case and adroitly pits this new 'truth' against the words of Lee's historically staunchest promoters." Booklist

Includes bibliographic references

Smith, Gene. Lee and Grant; a dual biography. McGraw-Hill 1984 412p il o.p.; New Am. Lib. paperback available $10.95   **92**

1. Grant, Ulysses S. (Ulysses Simpson), 1822-1885
2. United States—History—1861-1865, Civil War
ISBN 0-452-00773-9 (pa)   LC 83-25555

This "dual biography features alternating chapters that depict the ironic contrasts in the lives of two of the nineteenth century's most prominent personalities." Booklist

"The action rapidly shifts between the two protagonists at various points throughout their lives, a literary technique that Smith manages with nimbleness and aplomb. The result is a satisfying look at the early years of both men and a revealing run-through of the war itself." Libr J

Includes bibliography

LeMond, Greg, 1961?-

Abt, Samuel. LeMond: the incredible comeback of an American hero. Random House 1990 206p il $18.95   **92**

1. Bicycle racing
ISBN 0-394-58476-7   LC 89-43428

"A behind-the-scenes look at international bicyclist Greg LeMond, who made an 'incredible comeback' from a nearly fatal hunting accident. Journalist Abt spent time with LeMond during his victorious Tour de France. . . . The inside look at the Tour de France, bicycling teams and agents, other European races, and famous bicyclists such as Bernard Hinault, will appeal to avid bicyclists as well as interested readers." Libr J

L'Engle, Madeleine, 1918-

L'Engle, Madeleine. Two-part invention; the story of a marriage. Farrar, Straus & Giroux 1988 232p $18.95   **92**

1. Franklin, Hugh, d. 1986
ISBN 0-374-28020-7   LC 88-81547

Also available Walker & Co. large print edition and in paperback from HarperCollins Pubs.

This book is the author's "memoir of her nearly forty-five-year marriage to Hugh Franklin, a successful stage and television actor who died of cancer in the fall of 1986. . . . The book follows [the] two lives from the time of their first meeting to their final separation." Commonweal

"Ms. L'Engle does not shrink from describing the difficult trials as well as the joys of her married life. And she deals with the challenge to her religious belief brought on by her husband's painful dying." N Y Times Book Rev

Lenin, Vladimir Il'ich, 1870-1924

Clark, Ronald William. Lenin; [by] Ronald W. Clark. Harper & Row 1988 564p il $27.95; pa $10.95   **92**

ISBN 0-06-015802-6; 0-06-091698-2 (pa)
LC 87-45090

"An Edward Burlingame book"

Published in the United Kingdom with subtitle: The man behind the mask

A "portrait of Lenin the man, as opposed to the politician and revolutionary. Clark . . . depicts Lenin's attraction to the outdoors, his appreciation of music and poetry, his capacity for passion and emotion, his love for both his wife, Nadezhda Krupskaya, and his revolutionary companion Inessa Armand." N Y Times Book Rev

"This brilliant, dispassionate biography . . . separates the man from the myths which cling to him. . . . Though his tone is brisk and businesslike, Clark conveys the human side of a zealot." Publ Wkly

Includes bibliography

Lennon, John. See class 780.92

Leonardo. See class 709.2

Leonowens, Anna Harriette, 1834-1914

Landon, Margaret. Anna and the King of Siam; illustrated by Margaret Ayer. Harper & Row 1944 391p il map $16.95   **92**

1. Mongkut, King of Siam, 1804-1868 2. Thailand—Social life and customs
ISBN 0-381-98135-5

Also available in hardcover from Buccaneer Bks.

Anna Leonowens' experiences at the Siamese court in the 1860's. From her experiences she wrote two books, "The English governess at the Siamese court," and "The romance of the harem." The author has put these two books into one story with additions to make a complete tale

Levi, Primo, 1919-1987

Levi, Primo. The periodic table; translated from the Italian by Raymond Rosenthal. Schocken Bks. 1984 233p hardcover o.p. paperback available $10   **92**

ISBN 0-8052-0811-9 (pa)   LC 84-5453

Original Italian edition, 1975

"This curious memoir, organized in 21 chapters from Argon to Zinc, ransacks the periodic table of the elements for strained metaphors as it traces one adolescent's search for identity. Levi ironically portrays himself as a young aspiring chemist eager to fathom nature's secrets." Publ Wkly

Lewis, C. S. (Clive Staples), 1898-1963

Lewis, C. S. (Clive Staples). Surprised by joy; the shape of my early life. Harcourt Brace & Co. 1955 238p $14.95; pa $6.95   **92**

ISBN 0-15-187011-X; 0-15-687011-8 (pa)

Also available Walker & Co. large print edition

"The book is primarily an account of the author's religious ups and downs . . . [including] his glad retreat into atheism, and . . . the long involved return through nature, spiritualism and philosophy to Theism and finally to Christianity." N Y Her Trib Books

Wilson, A. N. (Andrew Norman). C.S. Lewis; a biography. Norton 1990 334p il $22.50   **92**

ISBN 0-393-02813-5   LC 89-27361

Also available in paperback from Fawcett Columbine

This biography "brings to light the most important episodes and aspects of Lewis' life: for instance, his curious and longstanding relationship with Janie ('Minto') Moore, his troubled friendship with J. R. R. Tolkien, his secret marriage to Joy Gresham, his conversion to Christianity, and his unending and increasingly subtle scrutiny of what it meant to be a Christian." Booklist

"The mixture presented in Wilson's biography of the life of learning, the college life at Magdalen where he taught, of domestic drama and bad temper, religion, and sex, is irresistible." N Y Rev Books

Includes bibliographic references

Lincoln, Abraham, 1809-1865

Handlin, Oscar. Abraham Lincoln and the Union; [by] Oscar and Lilian Handlin. Little, Brown 1980 204p il (Lib. of American biography) o.p.; Scott, Foresman paperback available $13.50   **92**

1. United States—Politics and government—1815-1861
ISBN 0-673-39340-2 (pa)   LC 80-81259

"An Atlantic Monthly Press book"

This is a "character study of Abraham Lincoln which surveys his entire life but places the greatest emphasis on his early formative years. . . . The authors . . . outline his philosophical views in a clear, concise, and highly readable fashion." Choice

Includes bibliography

Oates, Stephen B. Abraham Lincoln, the man behind the myths. Harper & Row 1984 224p $19.95   **92**

1. United States—History—1861-1865, Civil War
ISBN 0-06-015304-0   LC 83-48798

Also available in paperback from New Am. Lib.

This book first suggests some myths about Lincoln and then includes chapters on his political development; "themes in his personal life; his abilities as a war leader, especially as emancipator; and the assassination. Oates also [presents a section on Mary Lincoln]." Libr J

"Oates re-creates the life and world of Abraham Lincoln with the skill of a master painter, using images and colors on a canvas. . . . [The author] succeeds in portraying both the facts and myths of history as essential to our understanding it." Christ Sci Monit

Includes bibliography

Sandburg, Carl. Abraham Lincoln: The prairie years; with 105 illustrations from photographs, and many cartoons, sketches, maps, and letters. Harcourt Brace & Co. 1926 2v il maps set $40   **92**

1. Frontier and pioneer life
ISBN 0-15-100777-2

This biography of Lincoln is an account of the first fifty-one years of his life before he became President. Mr. Sandburg shows Lincoln growing along with the growth of the nation—product and expression of his times and the soil that bore him

Sandburg, Carl. Abraham Lincoln: The prairie years and The war years. illustrated ed. Harcourt Brace Jovanovich 1970 c1954 640p il maps $49.95; pa $19.95   **92**

1. Frontier and pioneer life 2. United States—History—1861-1865, Civil War
ISBN 0-15-100638-5; 0-15-602611-2 (pa)

First published 1954

A condensation of the two volumes of "The prairie years" (entered above) and the four volumes of "The war years" (1939). The author has taken advantage of material made available since the original volumes were published to include in this edition of his lifetime study of Lincoln

Includes bibliographic references

Lincoln, Mary Todd, 1818-1882

Baker, Jean H. Mary Todd Lincoln; a biography. Norton 1987 429p il hardcover o.p. paperback available $9.95   **92**

ISBN 0-393-30586-4 (pa)   LC 86-23757

The author "portrays Mrs. Lincoln as a woman tortured by a series of family bereavements and thwarted from developing her natural talents by a patriarchal society that branded as 'unwomanly' her involvement in her husband's political career. Ms. Baker establishes her first argument with a lengthy investigation of Mary Todd's early family history in Lexington, Ky., and sustains the second by enlarging upon such topics as 19th-century domesticity, childbirth, mourning customs, spiritualism and America's deplorable insanity laws." NY Times Book Rev

Includes bibliography

Lindbergh, Anne Morrow, 1906-
Lindbergh, Anne Morrow. War within and
without; diaries and letters of Anne Morrow
Lindbergh, 1939-1944. Harcourt Brace
Jovanovich 1980 xxxi, 471p il $14.95   **92**
    ISBN 0-15-194661-2   LC 79-21614
    "A Helen and Kurt Wolff book"
    This is the final volume of the author's letters and
diaries; previous volumes: Bring me a unicorn (1972);
Hour of gold, hour of lead (1973); Locked rooms and
open doors (1974) and The flower and the nettle (1976)
    This volume "covers the prewar and war years, during
which she and her celebrated husband took their stand
against the Roosevelt administration and interventionist
lobbies at home and abroad, to serve as spokesmen for
the isolationist position. . . . [The volume also deals
with such experiences as] having babies, engaging nurses
and secretaries, finding suitable rental properties on Long
Island, Martha's Vineyard, and so forth." Christ Sci
Monit
    Includes bibliographic references

Lindbergh, Charles, 1902-1974
Lindbergh, Charles. The wartime journals
of Charles A. Lindbergh. Harcourt Brace
Jovanovich 1970 xx, 1038p il map $19.95
                                    92
    1. World War, 1939-1945
    ISBN 0-15-194625-6
    The journals "cover the pre-World War II period,
when the celebrated flier was in Europe surveying military aviation . . . [and] the war years when . . . he
served as a civilian aeronautical expert in private industry and in the Pacific, also managing to work in 50
combat missions; and the weeks just after the Nazi surrender, which found him again in Europe, attached to
a Naval Mission studying wartime developments in plane
design and missiles." N Y Times Book Rev

Lippmann, Walter, 1889-1974
Steel, Ronald. Walter Lippmann and the
American century. Little, Brown 1980 669p
il o.p.; Vintage Bks. paperback available
$15.95   **92**
    ISBN 0-394-74731-3 (pa)   LC 80-11691
    "An Atlantic Monthly Press book"
    This "biography takes noted journalist Lippmann from
Harvard in 1906 where he studied with James and Santayana to his first journalistic job as assistant to Lincoln
Steffens through an astonishing career as a political
columnist that included a personal relationship with
every President from Wilson to Johnson." Libr J
    This biography "is important both as history and as
the story of a mind that influenced the American journey
from the beginnings of world powers under 'Teddy'
Roosevelt to the discovery in Vietnam of the limit on
that power." Christ Sci Monit
    Includes bibliography

Liszt, Franz. See class 780.92

Liu Binyan, 1925-
Liu Binyan. A higher kind of loyalty; a
memoir by China's foremost journalist;
translated by Zhu Hong. Pantheon Bks.
1990 294p $22.95   **92**
    1. China—Politics and government
    ISBN 0-394-57471-0   LC 89-42654
    "Liu describes the devotion to truth and independence
of mind that motivated him and thousands of other
Chinese to speak out against tyranny. . . . Rich with
detail and inside stories on Chinese politics and
propaganda, Liu's recollections will captivate specialists
as well as the general reader." Christ Sci Monit

London, Jack, 1876-1916
Stone, Irving. Jack London, sailor on
horseback; a biography. Doubleday 1978
c1938 305p $12.95   **92**
    ISBN 0-385-14084-3
    Also available in paperback from New Am. Lib.
    First published 1938 by Houghton with title: Sailor
on horseback; the biography of Jack London
    A life of the novelist, adventurer, revolutionist based
on his correspondence, on his private papers, and on
interviews with many people who played an important
part in his tempestuous career

Long, Earl K.
Kurtz, Michael L. Earl K. Long; the saga
of Uncle Earl and Louisiana politics; [by]
Michael L. Kurtz and Morgan D. Peoples.
Louisiana State Univ. Press 1990 312p il
(Southern biography ser) hardcover o.p.
paperback available $9.95   **92**
    1. Louisiana—Politics and government
    ISBN 0-8071-1765-X (pa)   LC 89-37883
    "Earl was a key figure in his brother 'Kingfish' Huey
Long's rise to power and, after Huey's assassination,
launched a notable career of his own, serving as
lieutenant governor and three times as governor of
Louisiana; he was elected to Congress shortly before his
death in 1960." Publ Wkly
    The book's "primary (and controversial) contributions
to current knowledge about Long are: material on Long's
ties with organized crime taken from FBI files; an
analysis of Long's efforts to protect black voting rights;
and evidence that Long suffered from manic depression.
This is a necessary book for all libraries with collections
on Southern politics." Libr J
    Includes bibliographic references

Long, Huey Pierce, 1893-1935
Hair, William Ivy. The Kingfish and his
realm: the life and times of Huey P. Long.
Louisiana State Univ. Press 1991 406p il
map $24.95   **92**
    1. Louisiana—Politics and government
    ISBN 0-8071-1700-5   LC 91-18546
    This is a biography of the man who was governor
of Louisiana from 1928 to 1932 and senator from 1932
until his assassination in 1935

Long, Huey Pierce, 1893-1935—*Continued*

"Written with passion and mordant wit, the book is literally hard to put down; the Kingfish seems to stimulate good writing. Overall, [this] is one of the more convincing negative biographies of recent years." Rev Am Hist

Includes bibliographic references

Williams, T. Harry (Thomas Harry). Huey Long. Knopf 1969 884, xxiip il $40; pa $20
92

1. Louisiana—Politics and government
ISBN 0-394-42954-0; 0-394-74790-9 (pa)

"Huey Long's enemies considered him to be a dangerous demagogue and radical while his loyal followers looked upon him as the champion of the poor against the power of the big corporations. . . . Professor T. Harry Williams . . . interviewed almost 300 individuals who knew Huey Long. He analyzed the development of Long's personality from his early childhood days in the northern parish of Winn to his career in the United States' Senate." Best Sellers

Includes bibliographic references

Lorenz, Konrad

Lorenz, Konrad. On life and living; Konrad Lorenz in conversation with Kurt Mündl; translated by Richard D. Bosley. St. Martin's Press 1990 166p $17.95; pa $9.95
92

ISBN 0-312-03901-8; 0-312-05937-X (pa)
LC 89-24118

"This book comprises ten years of the recollections and thoughts of Nobel Prize-winning ethologist Lorenz, recorded in conversation with journalist Mündl before Lorenz's death in 1989. It includes reflections on Lorenz's life and on his lifelong relationship with animals; and his views on maladies of the modern world. . . . This work, . . . is especially relevant in a time of reawakening environmental consciousness." Libr J

Louis, Joe, 1914-1981

Barrow, Joe Louis. Joe Louis; 50 years an American hero; [by] Joe Louis Barrow, Jr. & Barbara Munder. McGraw-Hill 1988 270p il o.p.
92

LC 88-9019

Available only in G.K. Hall large print edition

This "biography is the result of Barrow's search for his father. He interviewed dozens of Louis' contemporaries, who fondly recall a warm, witty, and generous individual. . . . This intimate human saga of a son seeking to learn whatever he can concerning a father he barely knew offers a whole new perspective on Joe Louis as a man." Booklist

Includes bibliography

Lowell, Robert, 1917-1977

Hamilton, Ian. Robert Lowell; a biography. Random House 1982 527p il $19.95
92

ISBN 0-394-50965-X
LC 82-40121

"This book subjects to rigorous yet sympathetic scrutiny both the life and the achievement of the man generally considered America's leading poet of the post-Pound-Eliot-Frost generation." Publ Wkly

Luce, Clare Boothe, 1903-1987

Martin, Ralph G. Henry and Clare: an intimate portrait of the Luces. See entry under Luce, Henry Robinson, 1898-1967
92

Luce, Henry Robinson, 1898-1967

Martin, Ralph G. Henry and Clare: an intimate portrait of the Luces. Putnam 1991 463p il $24.95; pa $14.95
92

1. Luce, Clare Boothe, 1903-1987
ISBN 0-399-13652-5; 0-399-51781-2 (pa)
LC 91-10986

The subjects of this biography are Henry Luce, founder of Time mangazine, and Clare Booth Luce, member of Congress and Ambassador

"A Martin book means a well-integrated storyline, written from a somewhat analytical and detached perspective, told in a captivating manner for a gossip-loving general audience." Libr J

Includes bibliographic references

Luther, Martin, 1483-1546

Bainton, Roland Herbert. Here I stand: a life of Martin Luther. Abingdon Press 1950 422p il music hardcover o.p. paperback available $5.95
92

1. Europe—Church history 2. Reformation
ISBN 0-687-16895-3 (pa)

Also available in hardcover from P. Smith

This biography of Martin Luther interprets his work, writings, and lasting contributions. It recreates the spiritual setting of the sixteenth century and shows Luther's place within it

Includes bibliography

Erikson, Erik H. (Erik Homburger). Young man Luther; a study in psychoanalysis and history. Norton 1958 288p hardcover o.p. paperback available $9.95
92

ISBN 0-393-31036-1 (pa)

"This study of Martin Luther as a young man was planned as a chapter in a book on emotional crises in late adolescence and early adulthood. But Luther proved too bulky a man to be merely a chapter." Preface

Includes bibliography

Oberman, Heiko Augustinus. Luther: man between God and the Devil; [by] Heiko A. Oberman; translated by Eileen Walliser-Schwarzbart. Yale Univ. Press 1990 c1989 xx, 380p il $35
92

1. Europe—Church history 2. Reformation
ISBN 0-300-03794-5
LC 89-5747

Original German edition, 1982

The author "posits that to understand Luther the reformer is to first realize he was a medieval man for whom Satan was as real as God and human. By placing Luther back into the context of his own age, Oberman strips away any simplistic, post-Enlightenment notions of Luther as the savior of humanity from the darkest obscurantism of the Catholic Church. . . . A triumph of scholarship that brings Luther to life in all of his furious, outspoken, and violent passion." Booklist

Includes bibliography

MacArthur, Douglas, 1880-1964

Manchester, William. American Caesar: Douglas MacArthur, 1880-1964. Little, Brown 1978 793p il maps $29.95   **92**

ISBN 0-316-54498-1   LC 78-8004

Also available in paperback from Dell

Manchester examines the life of the American general who was United Nations commander-in-chief in Korea

"William Manchester concentrates on MacArthur's character and personality and the reactions of others to him, giving only sketches of his battles." Harpers

Includes bibliography

MacLaine, Shirley

MacLaine, Shirley. Dance while you can. Bantam Bks. 1991 303p il $22.50; pa $5.99   **92**

ISBN 0-553-07607-8; 0-553-29786-4 (pa)

LC 91-13527

Also available G.K. Hall large print edition

MacLaine focuses primarily on her relationships with her aging mother, her daughter Sachi, and her brother Warren Beatty

MacLaine, Shirley. Dancing in the light. Bantam Bks. 1985 421p $17.95; pa $5.99   **92**

ISBN 0-553-05094-X; 0-553-27557-7 (pa)

LC 85-47621

In this memoir MacLaine "pursues spiritual matters further by investigating her soul's previous incarnations on earth. By undergoing 'past-life recall treatments through the process of acupuncture', she was able to visualize her past lives." N Y Times Book Rev

MacLaine, Shirley. Out on a limb. Bantam Bks. 1983 372p $18.95; pa $5.99   **92**

ISBN 0-553-05267-5; 0-553-27370-1 (pa)

LC 82-45955

In this book MacLaine "interweaves her explorations into reincarnation with tales of her affair with an unidentified married British politician." N Y Times Book Rev

MacLaine "touches the reader with her sincerity; we never doubt her faith. The accomplished actress is an able writer." Publ Wkly

Maclean, Donald Duart, 1913-1983

Cecil, Robert. A divided life: a personal portrait of the spy Donald Maclean. Morrow 1989 212p il $18.95; pa $7.95   **92**

1. Espionage, Russian

ISBN 0-688-08119-3; 0-688-09431-7 (pa)

LC 88-38794

First published 1988 in the United Kingdom

This is an account of the British diplomat who worked as a Soviet spy. Cecil discusses "how he believes Maclean was first recruited and how he fled to Moscow, the background of Maclean's nervous breakdown in Cairo, the nature of his marriage to his American wife, Melinda, and the extent to which Maclean had access to American atomic secrets." Publisher's note

This is "a clear and detailed account by a foreign office colleague who knew Maclean. . . . It is a valuable aid to perceiving how and why he went wrong, while giving a balanced assessment of how much harm he did." Economist

Includes bibliography

MacLeish, Archibald, 1892-1982

MacLeish, Archibald. Archibald MacLeish: reflections; edited by Bernard A. Drabeck and Helen E. Ellis; foreword by Richard Wilbur. University of Mass. Press 1986 291p il $30; pa $15.95   **92**

ISBN 0-87023-511-7; 0-87023-623-7 (pa)

LC 85-28912

"In these long interviews, conducted during the last five years of his life, a noted writer talks about his professional life as a poet, playwright, lawyer, editor of 'Fortune,' Librarian of Congress and Harvard professor." Publ Wkly

"In this genial, relaxed book we have a golden view of the candidly retrospective statesman-poet in his old age as he really was, with most pretension and all rhetoric abandoned." N Y Times Book Rev

Includes bibliography

MacNeil, Robert, 1931-

MacNeil, Robert. Wordstruck; a memoir. Viking 1989 230p il o.p.; Penguin Bks. paperback available $9.95   **92**

ISBN 0-14-010401-1 (pa)   LC 88-40293

Also available G.K. Hall large print edition

In this memoir the PBS journalist "tells how, as a child, he began a lifelong fascination with language. . . . Growing up during World War II in Halifax, Nova Scotia, where his naval father was based, MacNeil drank in the seacoast atmosphere but more avidly feasted on books." Publ Wkly

Madden, John

Madden, John. One size doesn't fit all; [by] John Madden with Dave Anderson. Villard Bks. 1988 227p o.p.   **92**

LC 87-40577

Available only in paperback from Jove Publs.

"Mr. Madden guides us on a lighthearted cross-country tour as he muses on 'pets and golf and broadcasting and having kids.' He comes across much as he does on television, as an emphatic, unpretentious, slightly goofy sports enthusiast who also loves to eat. Mr. Madden's homespun charm can be delightful." N Y Times Book Rev

Magritte, René. See class 709.2

Mahler, Alma, 1879-1964

Keegan, Susanne. The bride of the wind: the life and times of Alma Mahler-Werfel. Viking 1992 346p il $25   **92**

ISBN 0-670-80513-0   LC 92-6727

First published 1991 in the United Kingdom

"Mahler-Werfel lived in the center of the Viennese artistic community in the early decades of this century, surrounded by the likes of Arnold Schönberg, Thomas Mann, Oskar Kokoschka, and her husbands Gustav Mahler, Walter Gropius, and Franz Werfel. To present this multifaceted personality and the turbulent society of her time, Keegan draws on a variety of factual sources, successfully weaving together a fascinating story that is well organized and well written." Libr J

Includes bibliographic references

Mahmoody, Betty

Mahmoody, Betty. For the love of a child; [by] Betty Mahmoody with Arnold D. Dunchock. St. Martin's Press 1992 293p $21.95   92

1. Parental kidnapping
ISBN 0-312-08194-4   LC 92-20974

"A Thomas Dunne book"

In this sequel to the title entered below, the author "tells about her life after her escape from Iran. . . . [Ms. Mahmoody also presents] cases of other bereft parents who resorted to extreme measures to be reunited with their children who now live in other countries, including Israel, Pakistan and Jordan." N Y Times Book Rev

Mahmoody, Betty. Not without my daughter; a true story; [by] Betty Mahmoody, with William Hoffer. St. Martin's Press 1987 420p hardcover o.p. paperback available $5.99   92

1. Iran—Social conditions
ISBN 0-312-92588-3 (pa)   LC 87-16421

Also available G.K. Hall large print edition

"A Thomas Dunne book"

"When an American woman married to an Iranian doctor goes with her husband and their young daughter to his native country in 1984, culture shock turns to personal tragedy as the husband reveals a secret plan to remain with his family in Iran." Booklist

"Her frantic efforts to escape from a husband turned deceitful and violent, his hostile, fanatic Shiite family and, to her, a repulsive mode of life in the war-torn capital are here dramatically recounted." Publ Wkly

Mailer, Norman

Rollyson, Carl E. (Carl Edmund). The lives of Norman Mailer; a biography; by Carl Rollyson. Paragon House 1991 xxii, 425p il $26.95   92

ISBN 1-55778-193-1   LC 91-8120

This is a biography of the "novelist, essayist, journalist, movie director . . . amateur pugilist, reputed misogynist six times married, Pulitzer Prize winner." Publ Wkly

"What really sets this book apart is Rollyson's provocative critiques of Mailer's major novels, essays, and reportage and the author's attempt to link Mailer's art with real events in Mailer's life in order to prove his thesis that this larger-than-life and highly controversial, if not downright repugnant, contemporary writer has invented multiform identities for himself precisely to be controversial." Booklist

Includes bibliography

Makeba, Miriam. See class 780.92

Malcolm, Andrew H., 1943-

Malcolm, Andrew H. Someday. Knopf 1991 295p il $22   92

ISBN 0-394-58782-0   LC 90-5048

Also available in paperback from HarperPerennial

In this memoir the author focuses on his life with his mother and ponders the legal and ethical questions about death raised by her terminal illness

Malcolm X, 1925-1965

Carson, Clayborne. Malcolm X: the FBI file; introduction by Spike Lee; edited by David Gallen. Carroll & Graf Pubs. 1991 514p il $23.95; pa $12.95   92

ISBN 0-88184-751-8; 0-88184-758-5 (pa)

LC 91-26697

"This is a collection of declassified documents from the FBI surveillance of the orator and religious (later political) leader that, with historian Carson's studious commentary, focuses less on Malcolm's relation to the FBI and more on that to the larger civil rights movement. These excerpts . . . follow his travels and speeches, media interviews and FBI interviews, oftentimes including transcripts as written or summarized by Gallen and Carson." Booklist

Gallen, David. Malcolm X: as they knew him. Carroll & Graf Pubs. 1992 288p il $21.95; pa $11.95   92

ISBN 0-88184-851-4; 0-88184-850-6 (pa) LC 92-6436

"The first section is a richly woven narrative—oral reminiscences by a variety of people who knew Malcolm intimately or professionally. Familiar (Maya Angelou, the late Alex Haley, Kenneth B. Clark, Mike Wallace) and unfamiliar names blend together in this testimony to Malcolm's prophetic and charismatic nature. . . . The second section of the book consists of seven interviews with Malcolm. . . . Part Three contains six reflective essays on Malcolm's role in African American history." Libr J

Malcolm X. The autobiography of Malcolm X; with the assistance of Alex Haley; introduction by M. S. Handler; epilogue by Alex Haley; afterword by Ossie Davis. Ballantine Bks. 1992 500p $20; pa $12   92

1. Black Muslims
ISBN 0-345-37975-6; 0-345-37671-4 (pa)

LC 92-52659

First published 1965 by Grove Press

Based on tape-recorded conversations with Alex Haley, this account of the life of the Black Muslim leader was completed shortly before his murder

Alex Haley "did his job with sensitivity and with devotion. . . . [The book] will have a permanent place in the literature of the Afro-American struggle." N Y Rev Books

Perry, Bruce. Malcolm; the life of a man who changed black America. Station Hill Press 1991 542p il $24.95; pa $14.95   92

ISBN 0-88268-103-6; 0-88268-121-4 (pa)

LC 90-23350

"Perry traces Malcolm X's footsteps from birth in 1925 to death in 1965, using several hundred interviews to fill in detail and correct the autobiography Alex Haley edited [entered above]. Probing what he labels as the deep-seated and hidden causes that made Malcolm who and what he was, Perry produces a portrait of an emotionally abused and abandoned boy who grew to manipulate his fearful helplessness into emotional and political power." Libr J

Includes bibliographic references

Mandela, Nelson

Benson, Mary. Nelson Mandela; the man and the movement; foreword by Desmond M. Tutu. Norton 1986 268p il hardcover o.p. paperback available $8.95   92

1. African National Congress 2. South Africa—Race relations
ISBN 0-393-30322-5 (pa)   LC 85-31017

"This thorough political biography does a good job of explicating Mandela's philosophy (non-Communist and nonracist) and describing his involvement with the . . . African National Congress." Am Libr

Includes bibliography

Kumalo, Alf. Mandela; echoes of an era; [by Alf Kumalo; text by Es'kia Mphahlele] Penguin Bks. 1990 160p il pa $16.95   92

1. South Africa—Race relations—Pictorial works
ISBN 0-14-014316-5   LC 90-217614

Pictorial presentation of the life and times of the South African anti-apartheid leader

Mandela, Winnie. Part of my soul went with him. See entry under Mandela, Winnie   92

Meer, Fatima. Higher than hope: the authorized biography of Nelson Mandela. Harper & Row 1990 c1988 426p il hardcover o.p. paperback available $10.95   92

1. South Africa—Race relations
ISBN 0-06-092066-1 (pa)   LC 89-45053
First published 1988 in South Africa

"Meer has a unique perspective—as academic, long-time family friend, and fellow activist—and she was allowed to interview Mandela for three days in prison [in 1989]. She describes not only the Mandelas' personal lives, but also the history of anti-apartheid struggle and the role of the ANC and other political groups." Booklist

Mandela, Winnie

Mandela, Winnie. Part of my soul went with him; edited by Anne Benjamin; and adapted by Mary Benson. Norton 1985 163p il $14.95; pa $6.95   92

1. Mandela, Nelson 2. South Africa—Race relations
ISBN 0-393-02215-3; 0-393-30290-3 (pa)
                LC 85-21632

An autobiographical account of Winnie Mandela's life as wife of controversial ANC activist Nelson

Mantle, Mickey, 1931-

Mantle, Mickey. The Mick; [by] Mickey Mantle with Herb Gluck. Doubleday 1985 248p il o.p.   92
                LC 85-2000

Available only in paperback from Jove Publs.

Baseball Hall-of-Famer Mantle recounts his playing days with the New York Yankees and his turbulent private life

Mantle, Mickey. My favorite summer, 1956; by Mickey Mantle & Phil Pepe. Doubleday 1991 246p il $18.95   92

ISBN 0-385-41261-4   LC 90-48551

Also available in paperback from Dell

"Mantle focuses on the 1956 season, when he won the triple crown by leading the American League in batting average, home runs, and runs batted in. It was also the year the Yankees played a . . . World Series against . . . the Brooklyn Dodgers." Quill Quire

Marie Antoinette, Queen, consort of Louis XVI, King of France, 1755-1793

Haslip, Joan. Marie Antoinette. Weidenfeld & Nicolson 1988 c1987 306p il $19.95 92

1. France—History—1589-1789, Bourbons
ISBN 1-55584-183-X   LC 87-34031

First published 1987 in the United Kingdom

"Marie Antoinette was born an Austrian archduchess into a happy family, but her peace of mind was sacrificed to the alliance between Austria and France when she was sent to Versailles to marry the uninspiring dauphin, the future and ill-fated Louis XVI. . . . Haslip, in sumptuous but significant detail, emphasizes both the grandness of the French queen's station and her decline into total unpopularity." Booklist

Includes bibliography

Maris, Roger, 1934-1985

Allen, Maury. Roger Maris; a man for all seasons. Fine, D.I. 1986 272p il $16.95
                92

ISBN 0-917657-94-2   LC 86-81476

"A warmly admiring view of the slugger whose career reached a climax with the Yankees in the 1960s. . . . Though Maris's saga is touched on in other books about the Yankees, this is the definitive Maris story." Libr J

Markham, Beryl, 1902-1986

Lovell, Mary S. Straight on till morning: the biography of Beryl Markham. St. Martin's Press 1987 xxiv, 408p il hardcover o.p. paperback available $10.95   92

ISBN 0-312-01895-9 (pa)   LC 87-16329

This is a life of the British aviatrix. "Raised in Kenya alongside the sons of Nandi hunters, Markham was the first person to fly west across the Atlantic solo." Libr J

Lovell does not "record only the high points of Beryl's life, nor does she eulogize her; rather, she gives the whole picture of a woman. . . . Her biography provides an enthralling study, not simply of a remarkable personality, but of a place, a period, and a culture." Wilson Libr Bull

Includes bibliography

Marley, Bob. See class 780.92

Marshall, Thurgood
Davis, Michael D. Thurgood Marshall; warrior at the bar, rebel on the bench; [by] Michael D. Davis and Hunter R. Clark. Carol Pub. Group 1992 400p il $24.95
92

1. United States. Supreme Court
ISBN 1-55972-133-2   LC 92-26996
"A Birch Lane Press book"
This book "focuses on the professional life of the eloquent, hard-driven man who spearheaded the greatest legal victories for desegregation and civil rights for all people in this century. . . . As a guide to the legal struggles of this American leader, this book is written clearly and with obvious affection and admiration for Marshall." Booklist
Includes bibliographic references

Goldman, Roger L. Thurgood Marshall; justice for all; by Roger Goldman with David Gallen. Carroll & Graf Pubs. 1992 509p $24.95; pa $13.95   **92**
ISBN 0-88184-805-0; 0-88184-965-0 (pa) LC 92-5400
This is a "collection of original material, previously published personal recollections, and a representative sampling of opinions and dissents. . . . Marshall helped to change America, and this fine study of his legal career and jurisprudence is a fitting testament to his unflagging pursuit of social and legal justice. Wisely, this collection is not hagiographic; it offers proper perspective and accurate analysis, not idol worship." Libr J
Includes bibliographic references

Martin, Dean
Tosches, Nick. Dino; living high in the dirty business of dreams. Doubleday 1992 572p il $24   **92**
ISBN 0-385-26216-7   LC 91-22313
"An immigrant barber's son, high-school dropout Dino Crocetti—aka Dean Martin—left a job in an Ohio steel mill to achieve what no one before him had pulled off: simultaneous fame as a star of stage, movies, TV and records. . . . Although this is a deeply unflattering portrait of Martin . . . it will nevertheless be a feast for fans because of its detailed coverage of the star's multiple careers." Publ Wkly

Marx, Groucho, 1891-1977
Marx, Groucho. Love, Groucho: letters from Groucho Marx to his daughter Miriam; edited by Miriam Marx Allen. Faber & Faber 1992 241p il $21.95; pa $14.95 **92**
ISBN 0-571-12915-3; 0-571-19809-0 (pa)
LC 91-44205
"Groucho's daughter has collected his correspondence to her in this volume. . . . Allen's cursory notes do little to explain the contents of the letters, and in any case Groucho's comments on his radio show and Hollywood friends are so entertaining on their own that they hardly require annotation." Libr J

Mary I, Queen of England, 1516-1558
Loades, D. M. Mary Tudor; a life; [by] David Loades. Blackwell 1989 410p il $29.95; pa $17.95   **92**

1. Great Britain—History—1485-1603, Tudors
ISBN 0-631-15453-1; 0-631-18449-X (pa) LC 89-7163
"Mary Tudor has been variously depicted by historians and biographers, but the prevailing tendency has been to see her as a narrowly pious incompetent, richly deserving of the sobriquet 'Bloody Mary.' As this fine life shows, the real Mary was a much more complex personality and has deserved a better fate at the hands of posterity. This full, well-rounded biography provides the best treatment of Mary yet." Libr J
Includes bibliography

Mary, Queen, consort of George V, King of Great Britain, 1867-1953
Edwards, Anne. Matriarch: Queen Mary and the House of Windsor. Morrow 1984 527p il hardcover o.p. paperback available $15.95   **92**

1. House of Windsor
ISBN 0-688-06272-5 (pa)   LC 84-60447
"Queen Mary was royalty personified. Her immense dignity and sense of propriety were a source of great strength to her husband, King George V, and to the British people, but her personal coldness, particularly toward her children, probably shaped history by its effect on her elder son, Edward VIII. . . . This is personal biography, with cursory attention to external events." Libr J
Includes bibliography

Mary, Queen of Scots, 1542-1587
Fraser, Antonia. Mary Queen of Scots. illustrated abridged ed. Delacorte Press 1978 208p il hardcover o.p. paperback available $6.95   **92**

1. Great Britain—History—1485-1603, Tudors
2. Scotland—History—1500-1599 (16th century)
ISBN 0-440-35476-5 (pa)   LC 78-703
A condensation of the title first published 1969
A look at the tragic life of Mary Stuart, the 16th century Catholic ruler of Protestant Scotland, and her incessant struggle with political and religious opponents
Includes bibliography

Mason, Robert, 1942-
Mason, Robert. Chickenhawk: back in the world; life after Vietnam. Viking 1993 388p il $22.50   **92**
ISBN 0-670-84835-2   LC 92-50518
This companion volume to the author's Vietnam memoir (entered in class 959.704) "picks up the story and details the author's inability to readjust to civilian life after months of combat duty as a helicopter pilot." N Y Times Book Rev

Mathabane, Mark

Mathabane, Mark. Kaffir boy; the true story of a black youth's coming of age in apartheid South Africa. Macmillan 1986 354p il o.p.; New Am. Lib. paperback available $9.95   **92**

1. South Africa—Race relations
ISBN 0-452-25943-6 (pa)   LC 86-53

"Born in the township of Alexandra in 1960, the author of this memoir experienced hunger, crime, and [segregation] . . . during his formative years. His mother and grandmother worked hard to enable him to finish school. . . . The narrative ends in 1978, as Mathabane takes up a U.S. tennis scholarship." Libr J

"Mathabane's account has a fierce physical and psychological authenticity. . . . The searing indictment of the apartheid system stems from personal experience and social observation." Booklist

Mathabane, Mark. Kaffir boy in America; an encounter with apartheid. Scribner 1989 303p il $19.95; pa $10   **92**

1. South Africa—Race relations 2. United States—Race relations
ISBN 0-684-19043-5; 0-02-034530-5 (pa) LC 89-4199

In this sequel to the title entered above, Mathabane describes his life in the United States

Mather, Cotton, 1663-1728

Silverman, Kenneth. The life and times of Cotton Mather. Harper & Row 1984 479p il o.p.; Columbia Univ. Press paperback available $20   **92**

1. Massachusetts—History—1600-1775, Colonial period
ISBN 0-231-06125-0 (pa)   LC 83-48385

"Taking Mather and his contemporaries on their terms, Silverman's sympathetic yet critical study succeeds in making Cotton Mather understandable to a readership far removed from the culture of 17th-century New England." Choice

Includes bibliographic references

Mather, Increase, 1639-1723

Hall, Michael G. (Michael Garibaldi). The last American Puritan: the life of Increase Mather, 1639-1723. Wesleyan Univ. Press 1988 438p il maps hardcover o.p. paperback available $19.95   **92**

1. Puritans
ISBN 0-8195-6238-6 (pa)   LC 87-7367

This "biography of an important colonial clergyman is based on a thorough mastery of primary sources. In addition to serving as Harvard's president, Mather was active in politics and religion, and he demonstrated an active interest in science. Since Mather was a prolific author as well, his life can serve to document the intellectual history of his generation." Libr J

Includes bibliography

Matisse, Henri. See class 709.2

Maugham, W. Somerset (William Somerset), 1874-1965

Calder, Robert Lorin. Willie: the life of W. Somerset Maugham; [by] Robert Calder. St. Martin's Press 1989 429p il $22.95; pa $14.95   **92**

ISBN 0-312-03954-9; 0-312-08337-8 (pa)
                                     LC 89-27127

This biography "reconstructs the woof and warp of the English writer's life. . . . Mr. Calder discusses Maugham's homosexuality, his Victorian sense of propriety, his unhappy marriage that ended in divorce, his wanderlust, . . . his verbal and financial generosity, his irrational outbursts and parsimony and his turbulent relations with his daughter, Liza. The portrait, three-dimensional and detailed, suffers not from the writing, but from Maugham's own seemingly impenetrable persona." N Y Times Book Rev

Includes bibliographic references

Maxwell, Robert

Greenslade, Roy. Maxwell; the rise and fall of Robert Maxwell and his empire. Carol Pub. Group 1992 376p il $19.95
                                     92

ISBN 1-55972-123-5   LC 92-23957
"A Birch Lane Press book"

A biography of the controversial press baron by a former employee

Includes bibliographic references

Mays, Willie, 1931-

Mays, Willie. Say hey: the autobiography of Willie Mays; [by] Willie Mays with Lou Sahadi. Simon & Schuster 1988 286p il hardcover o.p. paperback available $4.50
                                     92

ISBN 0-671-67836-1 (pa)   LC 88-6699

The life and career of one of baseball's greats

This "autobiography reveals Mays to be a fine man as well as someone who played baseball for the love of the game." Libr J

McCarthy, Joseph, 1908-1957

Oshinsky, David M. A conspiracy so immense: the world of Joe McCarthy. Free Press 1983 597p il $24.95; pa $16.95   **92**

1. Internal security—United States 2. Communism—United States
ISBN 0-02-923490-5; 0-02-923760-2 (pa)
                                     LC 77-18474

This is a biography of the Senator who achieved prominence in the early 50s with his accusations against U.S. officials he considered Communist or subversive

The author has done "exhaustive research in both primary and secondary sources, including interviews with many of the people who knew McCarthy personally. Although clearly anti-McCarthy, the author makes a genuine attempt to be objective and present both sides of his subject." Choice

Includes bibliography

McCarthy, Mary, 1912-1989

Brightman, Carol. Writing dangerously: Mary McCarthy and her world. Potter 1992 714p il $30   **92**

    ISBN 0-517-56400-9   LC 92-7180

"This book considers McCarthy's career as reviewer, critic, editor, author, investigative journalist, and political commentator. . . . The author's approach has been to analyze the provocative elements in McCarthy's temperament, which led to promiscuity, radical politics, character assassinations, and feuds with other writers." Libr J

"The achievement of [this book] is Ms. Brightman's placement of McCarthy's personal and literary selves in historical, intellectual and social contexts, and her willingness to explore her subject's multiplicity." N Y Times Book Rev

Includes bibliographic references

Gelderman, Carol W. Mary McCarthy; a life; [by] Carol Gelderman. St. Martin's Press 1988 430p il hardcover o.p. paperback available $12.95   **92**

    ISBN 0-312-03482-2 (pa)   LC 87-27953

"A carefully researched, nicely paced and always readable work that avoids sycophancy and modestly allows the subject, as much as possible, to speak for herself." N Y Times Book Rev

Includes bibliography

McCarthy, Mary. How I grew. Harcourt Brace Jovanovich 1987 278p il hardcover o.p. paperback available $8.95   **92**

    ISBN 0-15-642185-2 (pa)   LC 86-29480

Also available Thorndike Press large print edition

In this memoir, the author of Memories of a Catholic girlhood writes about her life and intellectual development from ages thirteen to twenty-one

McCarthy, Mary. Intellectual memoirs; New York 1936-1938; with a foreword by Elizabeth Hardwick. Harcourt Brace Jovanovich 1992 xxii, 114p $15.95   **92**

    ISBN 0-15-144820-5   LC 91-40333

In this companion volume to the title entered above McCarthy recalls her early years in New York before she began writing novels and stories

McCartney, Paul. See class 780.92

McClellan, George Brinton, 1826-1885

Sears, Stephen W. George B. McClellan; the young Napoleon. Ticknor & Fields 1988 482p il hardcover o.p. paperback available $12.70   **92**

    1. United States—History—1861-1865, Civil War
    ISBN 0-89919-914-3 (pa)   LC 88-2138

This biography of the Civil War general "covers both the awkward character traits that led to McClellan's incompetence and the battlefield actions that he regularly bungled. In addition to its merit as Civil War history, the book is of great interest as the portrait of an intelligent man working at what he failed to realize was the wrong profession." Atlantic

Includes bibliography

McCloy, John Jay, 1895-1989

Bird, Kai. The chairman: John J. McCloy; the making of the American establishment. Simon & Schuster 1992 800p il $30   **92**

    ISBN 0-671-45415-3   LC 91-44255

This is a biography of the Wall Street lawyer whose professional activities involved government service along with work in the corporate sector. McCloy's business experience included stints as president of the World Bank and chair of Chase Manhattan Bank

"This fine study of McCloy's accomplishments is also a searching look into the exclusive club of men who make our political decisions." Publ Wkly

Includes bibliography

McCullers, Carson, 1917-1967

Carr, Virginia Spencer. The lonely hunter: a biography of Carson McCullers. Doubleday 1975 600p il o.p.; Carroll & Graf Pubs. paperback available $12.95   **92**

    ISBN 0-88184-123-4 (pa)

"This full-scale biography is heavily documented, and, judging by her hundreds of notes, Carr has done a thorough job of research, having interviewed dozens of people who knew McCullers, steeped herself in McCullers' books and the environments in which she lived, and read and assimilated the written materials—reviews, essays, articles, books, etc.—already published on McCullers." Choice

Includes bibliography

McDaniel, Hattie, 1898-1952

Jackson, Carlton. Hattie: the life of Hattie McDaniel. Madison Bks. 1989 220p il $18.95; pa $12.95   **92**

    ISBN 0-8191-7295-2; 1-56833-004-9 (pa)

               LC 89-30903

"For those of us who knew her only as 'Mammy' in Gone with the Wind, Hattie McDaniel's life story holds lots of surprises. She was also a singer, songwriter, and radio, stage, and TV performer. With an anecdotal style, the author clears up a lot of errors concerning her career." Booklist

Includes bibliography

McFadden, Cyra

McFadden, Cyra. Rain or shine; a family memoir. Knopf 1986 177p il hardcover o.p. paperback available $4.95   **92**

    1. Taillon, Cy 2. Qualley, Pat
    ISBN 0-394-74879-4 (pa)   LC 85-45597

In this biography the author describes her "interaction with her family, particularly her love-hate relationship with her father, Cy Taillon, the dean of American rodeo announcers from the 1940s through the 1970s; and . . . life on the American rodeo circuit during that period." Libr J

"This funny, affecting memoir achieves a series of satisfying reconciliations. . . . McFadden has the rare skill of stripping away pretensions without making the people exposed seem ridiculous." Time

McGraw, John, 1873-1934

Alexander, Charles C. John McGraw. Viking 1988 358p il o.p.; Penguin Bks. paperback available $8.95   **92**

ISBN 0-14-009600-0 (pa)   LC 87-23149

This is a biography of the man who "managed the New York Giants from 1902 through 1932, winning 10 pennants and 3 World Series." Booklist

"With great erudition and meticulous research [the author] brings to life not only a game and its competitors but a whole period of U.S. history." America

Includes bibliography

McLaurin, Tim

McLaurin, Tim. Keeper of the moon. Norton 1991 316p $19.95   **92**

ISBN 0-393-02996-4   LC 91-10719

Also available in paperback from Anchor Bks.

In this memoir, the American novelist reminisces about growing up in the rural South in the 1960s

"It was quite wonderful to encounter Mr. McLaurin's eloquence and an elegance of language that does arise, in his case, from a hardscrabble Southern upbringing. . . . Mr. McLaurin has real talent. He is a moving writer—never cute, nor overly colloquial—and his prose has a lyrical clarity that conveys with unusual dignity the integrity of his own experience." N Y Times Book Rev

McLuhan, Marshall, 1911-1980

Marchand, Philip. Marshall McLuhan; the medium and the messenger. Ticknor & Fields 1989 320p il $19.95; pa $11.95   **92**

ISBN 0-89919-485-0; 0-89919-947-X (pa)

LC 88-39455

This is an "account of McLuhan's life, with the facts and phases of his career presented in chronological order. The author has drawn in other pertinent material into the narrative, including excerpts of McLuhan's writings and talks, the comments of those who knew him, and this original thinker's emotional reactions to life." Libr J

Includes bibliography

McNamara, Robert S., 1916-

Shapley, Deborah. Promise and power: the life and times of Robert McNamara. Little, Brown 1993 734p il $29.95   **92**

ISBN 0-316-78280-7   LC 92-15614

This "biography of McNamara chronicles his youth and education before focusing on his varied career. Shapley taps a profusion of secondary and primary sources, including her own interviews with McNamara, to track the 'whiz kid' from his early days teaching statistical control to Army Air Force officers in World War II through his climb to the presidency of Ford Motor Company, his pivotal role as secretary of defense in shaping America's Vietnam policy, to his impact on development as president of the World Bank." Libr J

"Shapley goes far in unraveling the complexities of this enigmatic man." Publ Wkly

Includes bibliographic references

Mead, Margaret, 1901-1978

Howard, Jane. Margaret Mead, a life. Simon & Schuster 1984 527p il map hardcover o.p.; Fawcett Bks. paperback available $4.95   **92**

ISBN 0-449-20836-2 (pa)   LC 84-5525

This is a biography of the American anthropologist whose first book was Coming of age in Samoa

One of the author's "greatest strengths is her energetic gathering of comments and reminiscences from all kinds of informants and then incorporating them aptly into her narrative." Choice

Includes bibliography

Mead, Margaret. Blackberry winter; my earlier years. Morrow 1972 305p il o.p.

92

Available in hardcover from P. Smith

"About one-third of Mead's autobiography covers the years before she became an anthropologist and another third her field work in Samoa, in New Guinea, among the Omaha Indians, and in Bali. . . . The concluding chapters . . . describe in subjective detail her role as mother and grandmother." Choice

Mehta, Ved, 1934-

Mehta, Ved. The stolen light; continents of exile. Norton 1989 462p hardcover o.p. paperback available $9.95   **92**

1. Blind

ISBN 0-393-30673-9 (pa)   LC 88-15102

Previous titles in the Continents of exile series are: Daddyji (1972); Mamaji (1979); Vedi (1982); The ledge between the streams (1984); and Sound: shadows of the new world (1985)

This "sixth volume in Mehta's . . . memoirs finds the writer beginning his college education in California and continuing his process of assimilation—more often as observer than participant—into American culture." Booklist

"A delightful book that will appeal to a variety of readers." Libr J

Mehta, Ved. Up at Oxford; continents of exile. Norton 1993 432p il $25   **92**

1. Blind

ISBN 0-393-03544-1   LC 92-42491

In the seventh installment of his autobiographical series Mehta "relives his undergraduate years at Oxford's Balliol College. . . . Despite his constant struggle to find his footing on the English class ladder, and the inconveniences and frustrations caused by his blindness, Mehta became an irrepressible Anglophile in the small, intimate, yet worldly Oxford of 1956-1959." Publ Wkly

Mencken, H. L. (Henry Louis), 1880-1956

Mencken, H. L. (Henry Louis). The diary of H.L. Mencken; edited by Charles A. Fecher. Knopf 1989 xxx, 476p il $30; pa $16.95   **92**

ISBN 0-394-56877-X; 0-679-73176-8 (pa) LC 89-2523

"This is about one-third of the diary that Mencken kept from 1930 to 1948. . . . The diary, which was sealed by Mencken's request for 25 years, reveals Mencken's daily thoughts about his activities and friends, as well as his attitudes and biases." Libr J

Mencken, H. L. (Henry Louis), 1880-1956
—Continued

"What can one say about Mencken? He was as brilliant a writer and polemicist as we have ever had, he was a great wit, a deeply loyal friend, a champion of good and great writing, a bully, a racist and a simultaneous champion of both aristocracy and democracy. He contained multitudes, and they are all alive and kicking in these outrageous, brilliantly written and exasperating pages." N Y Times Book Rev

Includes bibliographic references

Mengele, Josef
Posner, Gerald L. Mengele: the complete story; [by] Gerald L. Posner and John Ware. McGraw-Hill 1986 364p il o.p.; Dell paperback available $4.95 **92**

1. World War, 1939-1945—Atrocities
ISBN 0-440-15579-7 (pa)   LC 85-23170

This is an account of the Nazi doctor's escape from the Allies and life as a fugitive in Brazil

Includes bibliography

Merton, Thomas, 1915-1968
Merton, Thomas. The seven storey mountain. Harcourt Brace Jovanovich 1990 473p $15.95; pa $9.95 **92**

ISBN 0-15-181354-X; 0-15-680679-7 (pa)
                                        LC 90-37477

Also available in hardcover from Buccaneer Bks.
"An HBJ modern classic"
First published 1948
"The autobiography of a poet who became a convert to Catholicism and at the age of 26 after a full and traveled worldly career as student and teacher, entered a Trappist monastery." Publ Wkly

Mott, Michael. The seven mountains of Thomas Merton. Houghton Mifflin 1984 xxvi, 690p il maps hardcover o.p. paperback available $15.45 **92**

ISBN 0-395-40451-7 (pa)   LC 84-10944

An authorized biography of the influential monk and writer
"Mott's Merton is neither rose nor dark-colored. In a corpse-littered genre, that is no small accomplishment. Mertoniana will go on and on, but no life will likely emerge as balanced in pathos, as tempered in hero-worship and as genuinely Catholic as this one." America

Includes bibliography

Shannon, William Henry. Silent lamp: the Thomas Merton story; [by] William H. Shannon. Crossroad 1992 304p il $22.95 **92**

ISBN 0-8245-1166-2   LC 91-44042

The author "focuses on significant moments in the famous monk's life. . . . Charting the monk's journeys within a historical context, Shannon also traces Merton's internal conflicts over his role as a contemplative and his sense of mission in the world." Publ Wkly
"This is a wonderful biography . . . told simply but compellingly. . . . An essential book for anyone interested in this fascinating man." Booklist

Includes bibliographic references

Merwin, W. S. (William Stanley), 1927-
Merwin, W. S. (William Stanley). Unframed originals; recollections. Atheneum Pubs. 1982 236p $14.95 **92**

ISBN 0-689-11284-X   LC 81-70063

In this autobiographical volume Merwin recalls his parents, aunts, uncles and cousins in rural Pennsylvania
The author presents "an original, self-questioning voice, poetically rich in each detail yet haunting in the final realization that the past cannot be reconstructed, only glimpsed during privileged moments." World Lit Today

Michener, James A. (James Albert), 1907-
Michener, James A. (James Albert). The world is my home: a memoir. Random House 1992 519p il $25 **92**

ISBN 0-679-40134-2   LC 91-18447

Also available large print paperback edition $19 (0-679-73981-5)
This memoir "explores the personal history and intellectual, political, and philosophical landscape of the prolific . . . writer and storyteller—terms he prefers to *author*. . . . This book is a recommended addition to the Michener collection in any library." Libr J

Mill, John Stuart, 1806-1873
Mill, John Stuart. Autobiography **92**

Various editions available

"A human document of unusual interest. Mill, a noble spirit educated by a narrow-minded pedant, shut off from all normal contact, developed an egotism that makes this book so completely an autobiography that besides his father and [his] wife he seems to exist alone in a world of which he has both center and circumference." Pratt Alcove

Miller, Henry, 1891-1980
Dearborn, Mary V. The happiest man alive: a biography of Henry Miller; by Mary Dearborn. Simon & Schuster 1991 368p il $24.95; pa $13 **92**

ISBN 0-67: 57704-7; 0-671-77982-6 (pa)
                                        LC 90-19898

This biography of the American novelist describes "the events of his life, drawing on his autobiographical fiction, nonfiction, and letters. . . . Dearborn discusses Miller's experiences in terms of his development as a writer. She provides thorough descriptions of how and when various works were written and their publishing history." Libr J

Includes bibliographic references

Ferguson, Robert. Henry Miller; a life. Norton 1991 397p il $24.95; pa $12.95 **92**

ISBN 0-393-02978-6; 0-393-31019-1 (pa)
                                        LC 91-13729

In this "biography Ferguson measures the cheerful amoralist of *Tropic of Cancer* and *The Rosy Crucifixion* against the guilt-ridden, insecure male in revolt against his bourgeois Brooklyn family. . . . The Miller in these pages is neither the macho bully portrayed by feminists nor the adolescent sexual philosopher dismissed by the academic establishment, but a 'unique . . . and necessary

Miller, Henry, 1891-1980—*Continued*
literary figure,' a popular American sage." Publ Wkly
Includes bibliographic references

Miller, Lee, 1907-1977
Penrose, Antony. The lives of Lee Miller.
Holt, Rinehart & Winston 1985 216p il o.p.;
Thames & Hudson paperback available
$19.95   **92**
ISBN 0-500-27509-2 (pa)   LC 85-5878
Written by her son, this work examines the life and
work of the model and photographer
"Part memoir, part photo essay, part search for the
real woman behind an unconventional mother, this
straight-forward narrative, and its 171 accompanying
illustrations, never idealizes its subject, but allows the
telling of her story to reveal a complex, ambiguous personality who shared all of herself with no one." Art Am
Includes bibliography

Millett, Kate
Millett, Kate. The loony-bin trip. Simon
& Schuster 1990 316p hardcover o.p.
paperback available $10.95   **92**
1. Psychotherapy 2. Manic-depressive psychoses
ISBN 0-671-74028-8 (pa)   LC 90-30227
Millett recounts her personal experience of mental illness and treatment. "Diagnosed as a manic depressive,
she endured forced hospitalization by family and friends,
suicide attempts, depression, and her fight for freedom
from the prescribed drug lithium and the stigma of being
'crazy.'" Libr J

Milne, A. A. (Alan Alexander), 1882-1956
Thwaite, Ann. A. A. Milne: the man
behind Winnie-the-Pooh. Random House
1990 xx, 553p il $29.95   **92**
ISBN 0-394-58724-3   LC 90-52999
This biography depicts Milne's "happy childhood,
solidly middle-class background, ardent pacifism, and
complex relations . . . with his wife and son." Libr J
This "long, leisurely narrative is meticulously detailed
and full of allusive anecdotes and reminiscences." Horn
Book
Includes bibliography

Milsap, Ronnie. See class 780.92

Minatoya, Lydia Y. (Lydia Yuriko), 1950-
Minatoya, Lydia Y. (Lydia Yuriko).
Talking to high monks in the snow; an
Asian American odyssey; [by] Lydia Yuri
Minatoya. HarperCollins Pubs. 1992 269p
$20; pa $11   **92**
1. Japanese Americans
ISBN 0-06-016809-9; 0-06-092372-5 (pa)
     LC 91-50450
This is an account "of a Japanese American woman's
youth in upstate New York, caught between her immigrant parents' culture and her own American experience." Publ Wkly
"Minatoya's memoir rings with the pure energy of
stories well told. Her deftly sketched vignettes and
animated anecdotes vibrate with sorrow, revelation, and

delight. Her family's odyssey is the journey from Japan
to America; her own odyssey takes her to Japan, China,
Nepal, and, finally, back home, feeling refreshed and
renewed." Booklist

Mingus, Charles. See class 780.92

Mitchell, Margaret, 1900-1949
Pyron, Darden Asbury. Southern daughter:
the life of Margaret Mitchell. Oxford Univ.
Press 1991 xxii, 533p il $26   **92**
ISBN 0-19-505276-5   LC 90-20833
Also available in paperback from HarperPerennial
This is a "biography of the author of *Gone with the
Wind*. Included is . . . analysis of the 1936 novel and
of David Selznick's 1940 film epic about the Civil War
in Georgia. But the book's major achievement is the
sympathetic yet objective coverage of Mitchell, from her
birth in Atlanta in 1900 to her death in 1949 in a car
accident." Publ Wkly

Modigliani, Amedeo. See class 709.2

**Moltke, Helmuth James, Graf von, 1907-
1945**
Moltke, Helmuth James, Graf von. Letters
to Freya: 1939-1945; edited and translated
from the German by Beate Ruhm von
Oppen. Knopf 1990 441p il $24.95   **92**
1. Moltke, Freya von 2. Germany—Politics and
government—1933-1945
ISBN 0-394-57923-2   LC 89-45268
These letters "constitute a day-by-day account of the
count's official work at military headquarters in Berlin,
mixed with comments on his visits to various European
capitals, expressions of affection toward his family, and
the deepening of his Christian faith. Arrested by the
Gestapo in 1944 for his secret activities, his continuing
letters to his wife were smuggled out by the prison
chaplain. . . . His letters confirm the exalted character
of this authentic hero and provide vivid word pictures
of conditions in wartime Germany." Publ Wkly
Includes bibliographic references

Monette, Paul
Monette, Paul. Becoming a man; half a
life story. Harcourt Brace Jovanovich 1992
278p $19.95   **92**
ISBN 0-15-111519-2   LC 91-39475
Also available in paperback from HarperSanFrancisco
The author recounts "his early life in Andover, Massachusetts, his college years at Yale University, his teaching career at a prep school, and the struggle between
his gay identity and society's homophobic attitudes." Libr
J
"Although the elegiac memory of his lovers and
friends who have been lost to the plague frames his
autobiography, Mr. Monette concentrates on life, not
death. . . . Fiercely committed to bequeathing a map
of his psychic terrain, to spare others the pain of his
solitary journey, his fine memoir is affirmative and ultimately celebratory." N Y Times Book Rev

Monroe, Marilyn, 1926-1962

Kahn, Roger. Joe & Marilyn. See entry under DiMaggio, Joe   **92**

Steinem, Gloria. Marilyn; text by Gloria Steinem; photographs by George Barris. Holt & Co. 1987 c1986 182p il o.p.; New Am. Lib. paperback available $5.99   **92**

    ISBN 0-451-15596-3 (pa)   LC 86-19442

This biography of Marilyn Monroe by feminist and journalist Steinem includes information and photographs from an interview conducted by Barris shortly before the actress's death in 1962

"Steinem for the most part admirably avoids the ideological excess that we have come to associate with the women's movement—Monroe emerges from her book a far more dimensional figure than she would have been if she had been presented as simply the victim of a male-dominated society." N Y Times Book Rev

Strasberg, Susan. Marilyn and me; sisters, rivals, friends. Warner Bks. 1992 282p il $21.95   **92**

    1. Strasberg, Susan
    ISBN 0-446-51592-2   LC 91-50609

"These personal recollections are underlined by the author's passionate quest to stand equal to Marilyn Monroe in her famous father's eyes. Virtually adopted into the Strasberg household at age 29, Monroe soon absorbed the special attention of acting coach Lee Strasberg and his self-abnegating wife Paula. Susan, in her late teens at the outset, was at once fascinated, repelled, and cowed by the power of this unusual relationship which lasted until Monroe's untimely death. Her book, a mixture of autobiography, pop show biz history, and personal catharsis, is touching and disturbing." Libr J

Summers, Anthony. Goddess: the secret lives of Marilyn Monroe. Macmillan 1985 415p il $18.95   **92**

    ISBN 0-02-615460-9   LC 85-8929
    Also available in paperback from New Am. Lib.

This biography focuses on the private life of the actress. It "is a sensible and sensitive—but definitely not sensationalist—piece of investigative journalism that should enthrall readers of all sorts." Quill Quire

    Includes bibliography

Montand, Yves

Montand, Yves. You see, I haven't forgotten; [by] Yves Montand with Hervé Hamon and Patrick Rotman; translated from the French by Jeremy Leggatt. Knopf 1992 465p il $25   **92**

    ISBN 0-679-41012-0   LC 91-58647

This account of Montand's life and career "captures the excitement and surprise of its subject's unusual background: his childhood as the son of political refugees from Fascist Italy, his early years as a manual laborer in Marseilles, his rapid rise to stardom as a singer, then an actor." Publ Wkly

Montgomery of Alamein, Bernard Law Montgomery, Viscount, 1887-1976

Hamilton, Nigel. Master of the battlefield: Monty's war years, 1942-1944. McGraw-Hill 1984 c1983 xxxi, 863p il maps $25.95   **92**

    ISBN 0-07-025806-6   LC 83-11262

First published 1983 in the United Kingdom with title: Monty: master of the battlefield, 1942-1944

This sequel to Monty: the making of a general, 1887-1942 (1981) "continues the saga of one of the greatest generals of all time, from his triumph at El Alamein in 1942 through the Italian Campaign of 1943 to victory in Normandy in 1944." Libr J

    Includes bibliography

Hamilton, Nigel. Monty: final years of the Field-Marshall, 1944-1976; Nigel Hamilton. McGraw-Hill 1986 xxvii, 996p il maps $29.95   **92**

    ISBN 0-07-025807-4   LC 86-10369

"This third and final volume of Hamilton's definitive biography follows Montgomery from the period after the Normandy landings, to the German surrender and through his postwar career, which included proconsulship of British-occupied Germany." Publ Wkly

    Includes bibliography

Moore, Marianne, 1887-1972

Molesworth, Charles. Marianne Moore; a literary life. Atheneum Pubs. 1990 xxii, 472p il o.p.; Northeastern Univ. Press paperback available $16.95   **92**

    ISBN 1-55553-115-6 (pa)   LC 90-709

"Molesworth charts the growth of a major modernist through careful critical readings of her poetry and prose, her work as an editor of the Dial, and an examination of Moore as an active, social New York literary figure whose colleagues and admirers included T.S. Eliot and Ezra Pound." Publ Wkly

    Includes bibliographic references

Morisot, Berthe. See class 709.2

Morris, Jan, 1926-

Morris, Jan. Pleasures of a tangled life. Random House 1989 209p $18.95; pa $12.95   **92**

    ISBN 0-394-57649-7; 0-679-73131-8 (pa)   LC 89-4004

Among the subjects the author reflects upon in this memoir are "Abyssinian cats, dining in restaurants, the public versus the private American character, the real joys of nontouristic travel, the pain of bad reviews and the evanescence of fame." N Y Times Book Rev

"The memories here are in random order, but the style and vivid imagery that have won Morris acclaim as a travel writer and journalist are evident." Libr J

Morrison, Jim. See class 780.92

Moses, Robert, 1888-1981
Caro, Robert A. The power broker: Robert Moses and the fall of New York. Knopf 1974 1246, xxxiv p il $40; pa $24
92

ISBN 0-394-48076-7; 0-394-72024-5 (pa)

This is a biographical critique of the man who in four decades as a public official "built most of the parks, bridges and highways in and around New York City." Newsweek

Includes bibliography

Mountbatten of Burma, Edwina Ashley Mountbatten, Countess, 1901-1960
Morgan, Janet. Edwina Mountbatten; a life of her own. Scribner 1991 489p il $27.50
92

1. Mountbatten of Burma, Louis Mountbatten, Earl, 1900-1979
ISBN 0-684-19346-9   LC 91-546

This is a biography of "the wife of Lord Louis Mountbatten, who was an auxiliary member of the British royal family, the last viceroy of India before its independence and its split into Hindu and Muslim republics, and an admiral of the Royal Navy." Booklist

"A definitive biography of an important, fascinating woman. Using the private diaries and letters of the Mountbatten family as well as letters and interviews with their intimates, Morgan creates a rich, detailed tapestry of Edwina Mountbatten's life, family, and relationships." Choice

Includes bibliographic references

Mozart, Wolfgang Amadeus. See class 780.92

Muir, John, 1838-1914
Fox, Stephen R. (Stephen Russell). John Muir and his legacy; the American conservation movement; [by] Stephen Fox. Little, Brown 1981 436p il $29.95   **92**

1. Nature conservation
ISBN 0-316-29110-2   LC 81-1852

"The first portion of this study examines the career and influences of John Muir, while the balance of the volume delineates the growth of the American conservation movement since his death in 1914. . . . The growth of the Sierra Club, Audubon Society, Isaak Walton League, and the Wilderness Society are also chronicled." Choice

Includes bibliographic references

Muir, John. The story of my boyhood and youth   **92**

Various editions available

First published 1913 by Houghton Mifflin

"The naturalist's childhood in a strict Presbyterian home in Scotland, his boyhood experiences of the privations and out-of-door delights of pioneer life on a Wisconsin farm, and his shifts and contrivances while earning his way through the state university." Cleveland Public Libr

Mura, David
Mura, David. Turning Japanese; memoirs of a sansei. Atlantic Monthly Press 1991 376p $22.95   **92**

1. Japan—Social life and customs
ISBN 0-87113-431-4   LC 90-49529

Also available in paperback from Anchor Bks.

This memoir is a "journey of discovery by a poet and third-generation Japanese-American who explores the sense of difference that haunts him both at home and in Japan." N Y Times Book Rev

Murrow, Edward R.
Persico, Joseph E. Edward R. Murrow; an American original. McGraw-Hill 1988 562p il $24.95   **92**

ISBN 0-07-049480-0   LC 88-9080

Also available in paperback from Dell

A look at the private and professional life of the pioneering radio and television journalist

"In comprehensive detail, with dramatic, well-told anecdotes and insight and perceptiveness, Joseph E. Persico describes a man of extraordinary natural gifts, human failings and stunning accomplishments." N Y Times Book Rev

Includes bibliography

Sperber, Ann M. Murrow, his life and times; [by] A. M. Sperber. Freundlich Bks. 1986 xx, 795p il $25   **92**

ISBN 0-88191-008-2   LC 85-27534

Also available in paperback from Bantam Bks.

This "ambitious exploration of Murrow's life places his story in the foreground of what is, as well, a panorama of the years 1935-65." N Y Times Book Rev

Includes bibliography

Nabokov, Vladimir Vladimirovich, 1899-1977
Boyd, Brian. Vladimir Nabokov. Princeton Univ. Press 1990-1991 2v il   **92**

Contents: [v1] The Russian years $29.95; pa $15.95 (ISBN 0-691-06794-5; pa ISBN 0-691-02470-7) [v2] The American years $35; pa $16.95 (ISBN 0-691-06797-X; pa ISBN 0-691-02471-5)

This biography follows the life of the novelist and poet from his childhood in czarist Russia and European exile to his final years in the United States. The author provides extensive critical analysis of Nabokov's literary output

Includes bibliographic references

Nabokov, Vladimir Vladimirovich. Speak, memory; an autobiography revisited. rev ed. Vintage Bks. 1989 316p il pa $9.95   **92**

ISBN 0-679-72339-0

A revised version of the memoir first published 1951 in the United States with title: Conclusive evidence

These recollections of the author's youthful years give an account of a vanishing world. They offer a picture of the author's family, their flight from Russia, education in England, and émigré life in Paris and Berlin

Nabokov, Vladimir Vladimirovich, 1899-1977—*Continued*

Nabokov, Vladimir Vladimirovich. Vladimir Nabokov: selected letters, 1940-1977; edited by Dmitri Nabokov and Matthew J. Bruccoli. Harcourt Brace Jovanovich 1989 xxvi, 582p il $29.95; pa $14.95 **92**

ISBN 0-15-164190-0; 0-15-693610-0 (pa)

LC 88-26793

"A Bruccoli Clark Layman book"

"These articulate if often astringent letters follow the novelist's life from his arrival in America until his death in Switzerland. Two subjects, literature and lepidoptera (a passionate avocation), predominate. Recipients range from friends and relatives to editors, translators, and interviewers." Libr J

Napoleon I, Emperor of the French, 1769-1821

Mackenzie, Norman Ian. The escape from Elba: the fall and flight of Napoleon, 1814-1815; [by] Norman MacKenzie. Oxford Univ. Press 1982 299p il $30 **92**

ISBN 0-19-215863-5

LC 81-18672

"Relying heavily on the memoirs of both feature and bit players, Norman MacKenzie offers a lively account of how, in April 1814 [Napoleon] . . . was made King of Elba, an island rich in rocks, and within a year was again threatening the assembled powers of Europe." N Y Times Book Rev

Includes bibliography

Navratilova, Martina, 1956-

Navratilova, Martina. Martina; [by] Martina Navratilova with George Vecsey. Knopf 1985 287p il $16.95 **92**

ISBN 0-394-53640-1

LC 84-48894

Also available in paperback from Fawcett Bks.

"The tennis champ opens up about her life in Czechoslovakia, her defection at 18, and her relationships with women who have played important roles in her life." SLJ

Neal, Patricia

Neal, Patricia. As I am; an autobiography; [by] Patricia Neal with Richard Deneut. Simon & Schuster 1988 384p il o.p. **92**

LC 88-1990

Available G.K. Hall large print edition

"Actress Neal's life has been one of great tragedy: her much-publicized stroke, the death of her small daughter, the brain-damaging accident of her son, her broken love affair with Gary Cooper, and the betrayal by her husband, Roald Dahl, after 30 years of marriage. . . . Her autobiography covers her early aspirations and later successes and . . . details her tempestuous marriage. Neal's honesty and strength infuse the book with life." Libr J

Near, Holly. See class 780.92

Nevelson, Louise. See class 709.2

Newman, John Henry, Cardinal, 1801-1890

Newman, John Henry, Cardinal. Apologia pro vita sua; being a history of his religious opinions **92**

1. Catholic Church

Hardcover and paperback editions available from various publishers

First published 1864 in the United Kingdom

"The Apologia, a masterpiece of English autobiographical writing, is a defense of the religious convictions which led Newman to abandon the Church of England for the Church of Rome." Reader's Adviser

Newman, Phyllis

Newman, Phyllis. Just in time; notes from my life. Simon & Schuster 1988 207p il o.p.; Limelight Eds. paperback available $12.95 **92**

ISBN 0-87910-138-5 (pa)

LC 88-11566

"Actress Newman breezes through an account of her life's joys and tribulations, putting a brave face on her bout with cancer and the infidelities of an otherwise compatible husband, Adolph Green. She records her professional triumphs . . . and recalls with obvious relish the celebrities with whom she hobnobbed." Publ Wkly

Nicholas II, Emperor of Russia, 1868-1918

Massie, Robert K. Nicholas and Alexandra. Atheneum Pubs. 1967 584p il $35 **92**

1. Alexandra, Empress, consort of Nicholas II, Emperor of Russia, 1872-1918 2. Russia—History
ISBN 0-689-10177-5

Also available in paperback from Dell

This study provides an intimate account of the Romanov family and the coming of the Russian Revolution. Kerensky, Lenin and Rasputin are among the personalities profiled

This book, "solid with research, reads as lightly as a novel, as authoritatively as a textbook. Dialogue and lively description lend a sense of immediacy, but his notes, discretely relegated to the back of the book, show how carefully he has avoided slipping into fiction." Christ Sci Monit

Includes bibliography

Radzinsky, Edvard. The last tsar: the life and death of Nicholas II; translated from the Russian by Marian Schwartz. Doubleday 1992 462p il $25; pa $14.95 **92**

ISBN 0-385-42371-3; 0-385-46962-4 (pa)

LC 91-46348

In this biography of Tsar Nicholas II the author offers new evidence that Lenin ordered the execution of the Tsar and his family and that two members of the family survived

"A convoluted, utterly absorbing tale by a popular Russian playwright, trained as an archivist, who has pursued the assassination of the Russian royals since the 1970's and struck gushers of information in the glasnost era." N Y Times Book Rev

Includes bibliographic references

Nicolson, Sir Harold George, 1886-1968
Sackville-West, V. (Victoria). Vita and Harold. See entry under Sackville-West, V. (Victoria), 1892-1962   **92**

Nin, Anaïs, 1903-1977
Nin, Anaïs. The diary of Anaïs Nin. Harcourt Brace & Co. 1966-1980 7v il hardcover o.p. paperbacks available   **92**

Published in the United Kingdom with title: The journals of Anaïs Nin

Contents: v1 1931-1934 $10.95 (ISBN 0-15-626025-5); v2 1934-1939 $10.95 (ISBN 0-15-626026-3); v3 1939-1944 $10.95 (ISBN 0-15-626027-1); v4 1944-1947 $9.95 (ISBN 0-15-626028-X); v5 1947-1955 $10.95 (ISBN 0-15-626030-1); v6 1955-1966 $10.95 (ISBN 0-15-626032-8); v7 1966-1974 $10.95 (ISBN 0-15-626035-2)

"A record of avant-garde life in Paris and New York, with portraits of friends like Henry Miller and Lawrence Durrell, the diaries essentially chronicle a woman's coming to terms with her feminine identity." Reader's Ency. 3d edition

Nin, Anaïs. The early diary of Anaïs Nin; with a preface by Joaquin Nin-Culmell. Harcourt Brace Jovanovich 1978-1985 4v il hardcover o.p. paperbacks available   **92**
LC 77-20314

Contents: [v1] has title: Linotte: the early diary of Anaïs Nin, 1914-1920 $7.50 (ISBN 0-15-652386-8); v2 1920-1923 $12.95 (ISBN 0-627248-2); v3 1923-1927 $12.95 (ISBN 0-15-627250-4); v4 1927-1931 $12.95 (ISBN 0-15-627251-2)

These volumes cover Nin's childhood from age eleven to her marriage to banker Hugo Guiler, at age 20. They chronicle her father's desertion, family relationships and her growing love for literature

Nitze, Paul H.
Nitze, Paul H. From Hiroshima to glasnost; at the center of decision: a memoir; [by] Paul H. Nitze with Ann M. Smith and Steven L. Rearden. Grove Weidenfeld 1989 xxii, 504p il $25   **92**

1. United States—Foreign relations
ISBN 1-55584-110-4   LC 89-8985

"Nitze, the man who was at the center of the American arms control negotiations for 40 years, reveals the policies and personalities on both sides and gives a unique look at why the Cold War never turned into WW III. . . . This memoir is also a miniautobiography of this advisor to presidents from Roosevelt to Reagan, with miniature personality portraits of all those presidents as well as of many leading politicians and advisors." Choice

Nixon, Patricia, 1912-1993
Eisenhower, Julie Nixon. Pat Nixon; the untold story. Simon & Schuster 1986 480p il o.p.; Zebra Bks. paperback available $4.50
92

1. Nixon, Richard M. (Richard Milhous), 1913-1994
ISBN 0-8217-2300-6 (pa)   LC 86-20209

The author portrays her mother as "devoted, loyal, thrifty, courageous—a remarkable woman whose 'grit' kept her going from her struggling student days in the Depression through the vicissitudes of political life to the nightmare of Watergate." Publ Wkly

Nixon, Richard M. (Richard Milhous), 1913-1994
Ambrose, Stephen E. Nixon. Simon & Schuster 1987-1991 3v il   **92**

1. United States—Politics and government—1900-1999 (20th century)   LC 86-26126
Contents: v1 The education of a politician, 1913-1962, pa $14 (ISBN 0-671-65722-4); v2 The triumph of a politician, 1962-1972 o.p.; v3 Ruin and recovery, 1973-1990 $27.50, pa $16 (ISBN 0-671-69188-0; 0-671-79208-3)

Ambrose "makes a unique contribution in balancing Nixon's stunning political abilities and glaring personal deficiencies, noting the consequences for the country and its president. His is a captivating work, written with fairness and skill. No library should omit this from its collection." Libr J

Includes bibliographies

Morris, Roger. Richard Milhous Nixon; the rise of an American politician. Holt & Co. 1990 1005p il $29.95; pa $15.95   **92**
ISBN 0-8050-1121-8; 0-8050-1834-4 (pa)   LC 89-7451

This first volume of a projected three-volume biography covers "the future President from distant ancestry through the 1952 election." Time
This is a "massive, powerful biography, absorbing in its research and in its skillful use of anecdote and illustrative detail. . . . Mr. Morris has exhaustively established the human story of Mr. Nixon's early years in all their day-to-day detail, illuminating, for better or worse, defenders or critics, the public man." N Y Times Book Rev

Includes bibliography

Nixon, Richard M. (Richard Milhous). In the arena: a memoir of victory, defeat, and renewal; [by] Richard Nixon. Simon & Schuster 1990 384p il hardcover o.p. paperback available $5.95   **92**

1. United States—Politics and government—1900-1999 (20th century)
ISBN 0-671-72934-9 (pa)   LC 90-30013

"This volume serves as a kind of omnibus collection: Nixon on China, Nixon on glasnost, Nixon on the press, Nixon on philosophy of life, Nixon on campaigning, and so on." Booklist
"The memoir adds nothing new on Watergate. What it does is subtly round out our picture of a man." Christ Sci Monit

Nixon, Richard M. (Richard Milhous), 1913-1994—*Continued*

Wicker, Tom. One of us: Richard Nixon and the American dream. Random House 1991 731p $24.45 **92**

1. United States—Politics and government—1900-1999 (20th century)
ISBN 0-394-55066-8 LC 89-42779

This is an assessment of the former president's life and career and its meaning for United States politics

"Wicker succeeds in humanizing Nixon to a remarkable degree in this notably fair and evenhanded portrait of the public and private man." Publ Wkly

Includes bibliographic references

Nofziger, Lyn

Nofziger, Lyn. Nofziger. Regnery Gateway 1992 370p $21.95 **92**

1. United States—Politics and government—1900-1999 (20th century)
ISBN 0-89526-513-3 LC 92-15908

The author discusses his career in journalism and politics, and his experiences working with Ronald "Reagan as governor in California, then with presidents Nixon and Reagan, and finally as a lobbyist." Libr J

"Nofziger portrays with unflinching honesty the personalities of those attracted to the conservative banner. . . . Irreverent, sometimes cynical, Nofziger never allows his own political passions to kill his sense of humor." Booklist

Nolan, Christopher, 1965-

Nolan, Christopher. Under the eye of the clock; the life story of Christopher Nolan; preface by John Carey. St. Martin's Press 1988 c1987 163p o.p.; Doubleday paperback available $7.95 **92**

ISBN 0-385-29713-0 (pa) LC 87-22161

First published 1987 in the United Kingdom

The author, severely disabled, "tells his life story—to date—as viewed 'under the eye of the clock' of memory: family (constantly encouraging), school days and friendships, a term at Trinity College, literary acclaim, and media attention. Using the third person, Nolan writes with detachment and without self-pity." Libr J

Noonan, Peggy

Noonan, Peggy. What I saw at the revolution: a political life in the Reagan era. Random House 1990 353p $19.95 **92**

1. United States—Politics and government—1981-
ISBN 0-394-56495-2 LC 89-42908

Also available G.K. Hall large print edition and in paperback from Ivy Bks.

This book "is about CBS, where I worked, about the media in general and their dance with politics. It is also about speechwriting, what it's like to be a writer in politics, a woman in politics, and a visitor for five years to its capital. . . . Most of . . . [this book is] about Reagan, . . . and what his presidency meant." Introduction

Noonan "has written the funniest, most richly textured, nervously self-effacing and deftly observed political memoir likely to come out of the 1980s." Time

North, Oliver L., Jr.

Bradlee, Ben. Guts and glory: the rise and fall of Oliver North; by Ben Bradlee, Jr. Fine, D.I. 1988 572p il $21.95 **92**

1. Iran-Contra Affair, 1985-1990
ISBN 1-55611-053-7 LC 87-46034

This account of Oliver North's life and military career focuses on his involvement in the Iran-Contra Affair

Includes bibliography

Nostradamus, 1503-1566

Randi, James. The mask of Nostradamus. Scribner 1990 256p il o.p.; Prometheus Bks. paperback available $16.95 **92**

ISBN 0-87975-830-9 (pa) LC 89-70189

A biographical study of "Michel de Notredame, better known as Nostradamus, the famous 16th-century French physician, astrologer and seer. Commentators claim that Nostradamus's cryptic verses accurately prophesied such events and personalities as Napoleon, Hitler, the French Revolution, the Great Fire of London and the invention of the Montgolfier balloon. Nonsense, argues Randi, and his meticulous readings of key quatrains make a potent case for his contention." Publ Wkly

Includes bibliography

Oakley, Annie, 1860-1926

Kasper, Shirl. Annie Oakley. University of Okla. Press 1992 288p il $22.95 **92**

ISBN 0-8061-2418-0 LC 91-50864

This biography of the legendary sharpshooter "not only paints a picture of a woman with an unusual occupation for her time; it also colors the whole era of Wild West performers from Buffalo Bill to Will Rogers." Booklist

Includes bibliographic references

Oates, Joyce Carol, 1938-

Oates, Joyce Carol. Conversations with Joyce Carol Oates; edited by Lee Milazzo. University Press of Miss. 1989 192p (Literary conversations ser) $32.50; pa $14.95 **92**

ISBN 0-87805-411-1; 0-87805-412-X (pa)
LC 89-16673

A collection of interviews with, and essays about the prolific novelist, poet and short story writer

O'Connor, Flannery

O'Connor, Flannery. The habit of being; letters; edited and with an introduction by Sally Fitzgerald. Farrar, Straus & Giroux 1979 617p $30; pa $16 **92**

ISBN 0-374-16769-9; 0-374-52104-2 (pa)
LC 78-11559

This collection includes letters to friends in the literary establishment: Robert Lowell and Elizabeth Hardwick, Caroline Gordon Tate, Robert and Sally Fitzgerald and others

O'Day, Anita. See class 780.92

O'Keeffe, Georgia. See class 709.2

Olivier, Laurence, 1907-1989
Spoto, Donald. Laurence Olivier; a biography. HarperCollins Pubs. 1992 460p il $23   92

ISBN 0-06-018315-2   LC 90-56398

First published 1991 in the United Kingdom

"A remarkably versatile actor, the extraordinarily rare kind impossible to typecast, Sir Larry possessed a repute that brooked no challenge as the greatest Shakespearean of the century, both as director and as player. . . . Supported by numerous photos, Spoto's biography wonderfully dissolves the barrier between the private and the public Olivier." Booklist

Includes bibliographic references

Olson, Charles, 1910-1970
Clark, Tom. Charles Olson; the allegory of a poet's life. Norton 1991 403p $27.95   92

ISBN 0-393-02958-1   LC 90-43054

"Best known for his innovative poetic theory and the famous 'Maximus' poems, Olson served as a mentor to an entire generation of poets, among them Robert Duncan and Robert Creeley. In this critical biography, Clark provides new insight into the conflicts and struggles of Olson's life and the influence they had on his work." Libr J

Includes bibliographic references

Onassis, Christina
Wright, William. All the pain that money can buy: the life of Christina Onassis. Simon & Schuster 1991 399p il $22.95   92

ISBN 0-671-68459-0   LC 90-20347

Also available G.K. Hall large print edition

In this biography of the Greek heiress the author covers "Christina's difficult childhood, during which she was both ignored and adored; her many unsuccessful attempts at a happy romantic life; the specter of death that hung over her as first her mother, then brother, then father died; and, finally, her own mysterious demise." Booklist

Onassis, Jacqueline Kennedy
Heymann, C. David (Clemens David). A woman named Jackie. Stuart, L. 1989 715p il $21.95   92

ISBN 0-8184-0472-8   LC 89-4463

Also available G.K. Hall large print edition and in paperback from New Am. Lib.

"In his attempt to unravel the personality of Jacqueline Kennedy Onassis, C. David Heymann . . . has painted a portrait of a good-looking woman of one-dimensional talents, intelligence, sensitivity and self-awareness, whose personality was dominated by three men: her father and her two husbands." N Y Times Book Rev

Includes bibliography

O'Neill, Eugene, 1888-1953
O'Neill, Eugene. Conversations with Eugene O'Neill; edited by Mark W. Estrin. University Press of Miss. 1990 xxxv, 242p il (Literary conversations ser) $32.50; pa $14.95   92

ISBN 0-87805-446-4; 0-87805-447-2 (pa)

LC 90-38144

A collection of interviews with, and essays about the famous playwright

Includes bibliographic references

O'Neill, Tip
O'Neill, Tip. Man of the House; the life and political memoirs of Speaker Tip O'Neill; [written] with William Novak. Random House 1987 387p il o.p.; St. Martin's Press paperback available $4.95   92

1. United States—Politics and government—1900-1999 (20th century)

ISBN 0-312-91191-2 (pa)   LC 87-4805

This autobiography of the Democratic Congressional leader provides the reader "with many things: a personal credo, an incisive history of the functioning of the U.S. House of Representatives during the past quarter-century, and a personal view of the political and socioeconomic history of the United States in the past half-century." Wilson Libr Bull

Orbison, Roy. See class 780.92

Orton, Joe
Lahr, John. Prick up your ears: the biography of Joe Orton. Knopf 1978 302p il o.p.; Limelight Eds. paperback available $14.95   92

ISBN 0-87910-057-5 (pa)   LC 78-7130

"The life and works of the British playwright who turned farce into outrageous social criticism are examined. . . . Lahr investigates how Orton's disturbing family relationships and a notorious private life, which centered on anonymous homosexual activities, are reflected on the stage in audacious attacks on bourgeois tastes." Booklist

Includes bibliography

Orwell, George, 1903-1950
Shelden, Michael. Orwell; the authorized biography. HarperCollins Pubs. 1991 497p il $25; pa $15   92

ISBN 0-06-016709-2; 0-06-092161-7 (pa)

LC 90-56396

This biography of the English author focuses on his private life

"George Orwell (born Eric Blair) lives on in this inspired treatment. Not a dry summation of facts and figures, obsessions and works, this book brims with humor and compassion." Booklist

Includes bibliographic references

Owens, Jesse, 1913-1980

Baker, William J. (William Joseph). Jesse Owens; an American life. Free Press 1986 289p il $27.95; pa $12.95 **92**

ISBN 0-02-901780-7; 0-02-901760-2 (pa) LC 86-4671

This biography of the gifted black track athlete intertwines the chronological story of Owens's life with the major political and social events of his time

Includes bibliography

Paine, Thomas, 1737-1809

Ayer, A. J. (Alfred Jules). Thomas Paine. Atheneum Pubs. 1988 195p il $19.95 **92**

ISBN 0-689-11996-8 LC 88-16622

Also available in paperback from University of Chicago Press

"Tracing Paine's life from his birth in England to his emigration to America just before the Revolutionary War, Ayer considers the effect of Paine's pamphlet *Common Sense* upon that war. *Rights of Man* is then discussed in the light of Burke's attacks upon the French Revolution and of the thought of Hobbes, Locke, Hume, and Rousseau. The saga concludes with an account of the acrimony heaped upon Paine for his diatribes against Christian religious beliefs and his espousal of deism in *The Age of Reason.*" Libr J

Includes bibliography

Paley, William S., 1901-1990

Smith, Sally Bedell. In all his glory: the life of William S. Paley; the legendary tycoon and his brilliant circle. Simon & Schuster 1990 782p il hardcover o.p. paperback available $15 **92**

1. CBS Inc.
ISBN 0-671-74917-X (pa) LC 90-42704

This is a biography of "the Chicago cigarmaker's son who built the CBS television empire and reigned as its chairman until 1983." Publ Wkly

"As a book about the rise of CBS, this is an invaluable source for historians of the industry. As a book about a man, it is an engaging, glamorous, glitzy adventure story." New Leader

Includes bibliographic references

Pallone, Dave

Pallone, Dave. Behind the mask; my double life in baseball; [by] Dave Pallone with Alan Steinberg. Viking 1990 331p il o.p.; New Am. Lib. paperback available $5.99 **92**

ISBN 0-451-17029-6 (pa) LC 90-50059

In this memoir the author writes about the effect being gay had upon his career as an umpire

"Pallone talks honestly about his controversial career. . . . The book captures Pallone's torment: he wanted to admit his homosexuality publicly, but feared the consequences because of baseball's ingrained homophobia." Libr J

Parker, Charlie. See class 780.92

Parker, Dorothy, 1893-1967

Meade, Marion. Dorothy Parker; what fresh hell is this? Villard Bks. 1988 c1987 459p il $22.50 **92**

ISBN 0-394-54440-4 LC 87-40189

Also available in paperback from Penguin Bks.

"The author has written a disturbing story of a writer whose life was marked by endless disturbances and self-depreciation, and who left behind no correspondence, manuscripts, or private papers. Under the circumstances, Ms. Meade has brilliantly reconstructed her subject's life. . . . The book is a tribute to a woman who left her mark on the literary history of her times and whose coruscating wit is still remembered." West Coast Rev Books

Includes bibliography

Parker, Idella

Parker, Idella. Idella: Marjorie Rawlings' "perfect maid"; [by] Idella Parker with Mary Keating. University Press of Fla. 1992 135p il map $22.95; pa $12.95 **92**

1. Rawlings, Marjorie Kinnan, 1896-1953
ISBN 0-8130-1143-4; 0-8130-1144-2 (pa) LC 92-8893

This "memoir, written by the black woman who was cook, housekeeper and comfort to the famous author from 1940 to 1950, tells two stories—one of their spirited (and tempestuous) friendship, the other of race relations in rural Florida in the days before integration." Univ Press Books for Public and Second Sch Libr

Parks, Gordon

Parks, Gordon. Voices in the mirror; an autobiography. Doubleday 1990 351p il $22.95; pa $12 **92**

ISBN 0-385-26698-7; 0-385-26699-5 (pa)
LC 90-34871

"A Nan A. Talese book"

An autobiography by the black photographer, film director, painter, composer and author

"Mr. Parks is a superb example of what talent, courage, and determination can accomplish against odds. He started out from Kansas poor, black, homeless, and unschooled—but also unstoppable. He encountered bigotry, which he recalls with anger, and help, which he recalls with appreciation. His autobiography is eloquent and thoughtful." Atlantic

Pasolini, Pier Paolo, 1922-1975

Schwartz, Barth David. Pasolini requiem. Pantheon Bks. 1992 785p il $35 **92**

ISBN 0-394-57744-2 LC 90-53403

This "biography reconstructs the turbulent life and times of Pier Paolo Pasolini, the Italian novelist (*A Violent Life*), poet and filmmaker who continually jousted with society's conventions." Publ Wkly

"Mr. Schwartz's ambitious biography fills out much of the historical background of Pasolini's life. . . . As a judicious account of this volatile artist it will likely become the standard Pasolini biography of our time." N Y Times Book Rev

Includes filmography and bibliographic references

Pasternak, Boris Leonidovich, 1890-1960

Barnes, Christopher J. Boris Pasternak; a literary biography; [by] Christopher Barnes. v1: 1890-1928. Cambridge Univ. Press 1989 507p il $84.95 **92**

ISBN 0-521-25957-6   LC 88-39638

This is the first part of a projected two-volume biography of the Russian poet and prose-writer

Barnes's biography "will certainly become the standard and indispensable guide for students not only of the poet but of his age and literary milieu. . . . His approach is factual, his perception quite unsentimental: but his awareness of the youthful Pasternak's problems and evolution as a writer of verse, a student musician, a highly emotional and volatile being, is extraordinarily delicate and comprehensive." London Rev Books

Includes bibliography

Pasternak, Boris Leonidovich. I remember; sketch for an autobiography. Pantheon Bks. 1959 191p il o.p.; Harvard Univ. Press paperback available $9 **92**

ISBN 0-674-43950-3 (pa)

Also available in hardcover from P. Smith

"Translated with a preface and notes by David Magarshack; with an essay on Translating Shakespeare, translated by Manya Harari." Title page

"The author tells little about his personal life, but lingers instead over descriptions of his literary contemporaries of the pre-World War I era. The brief concluding essay deals primarily with Shakespeare's poetic style and use of rhythm in several plays." Booklist

Paton, Alan

Paton, Alan. Towards the mountain; an autobiography. Scribner 1980 320p il hardcover o.p. paperback available $9.95 **92**

ISBN 0-684-18892-9 (pa)   LC 80-19634

Also available in hardcover from P. Smith

This first volume of the South African writer's autobiography, followed by Journey continued (1988), "covers the period 1903-1948, from Paton's birth to the publication of Cry, the Beloved Country." Libr J

"Novelist Paton writes a brilliant autobiography; his self-assessment is done with deep thought and admirable balance." Booklist

Patton, George S. (George Smith), 1885-1945

Blumenson, Martin. Patton: the man behind the legend, 1885-1945. Morrow 1985 320p il maps $17.95 **92**

1. World War, 1939-1945—Campaigns

ISBN 0-688-06082-X   LC 85-15301

This biography of the World War II general uses quotes from Patton and his family

"At a glance, the book is deceptive. It appears to be a short popular biography written in a pleasing style, but it rests on a solid foundation of research." N Y Times Book Rev

Includes bibliography

Pauling, Linus C., 1901-

Serafini, Anthony. Linus Pauling; a man and his science; foreword by Isaac Asimov. Paragon House 1989 xxii, 310p il hardcover o.p. paperback available $13.95 **92**

ISBN 1-55778-440-X (pa)   LC 88-28348

"The life story of Linus Pauling, the brilliant two-time Nobel Prize winner—first in chemistry and later for peace—profiles a scientist who is often difficult and a little eccentric but always courageous and dedicated. . . . A fascinating biography." Booklist

Includes bibliography

Pei, I. M., 1917-

Wiseman, Carter. I.M. Pei; a profile in American architecture. Abrams 1990 320p il $55 **92**

ISBN 0-8109-3709-3   LC 90-30727

The author "surveys the work and career of the Chinese-born American architect who is best known for the glass pyramid he designed for the Louvre courtyard. . . . An excellent series of architectural photographs along with other illustrations accompanies Wiseman's assessment and appreciation." Booklist

Includes bibliography

Pepper, Claude

Pepper, Claude. Pepper, eyewitness to a century; by Claude Denson Pepper with Hays Gorey. Harcourt Brace Jovanovich 1987 320p il $17.95 **92**

ISBN 0-15-171695-1   LC 87-8662

The autobiography of the Florida Congressman, who was an advocate of rights for the elderly

"Pepper sensitively blends private feelings and events from his personal life into this tale of a lengthy, stimulating career in public office." Booklist

Pepys, Samuel, 1633-1703

Pepys, Samuel. The diary of Samuel Pepys, a new and complete transcription edited by Robert Latham and William Matthews. Contributing editors: William A. Armstrong [et al.] University of Calif. Press 1970-1983 11v il maps v1-9 ea $38; v10-11 ea $40 **92**

1. Great Britain—History—1603-1714, Stuarts
2. Great Britain—Social life and customs

"Written in shorthand between 1660 and 1669 and not deciphered until 1825, when it was published in part, the Diary was never intended for the public eye. It not only presents a vivid picture of an age, but is also a uniquely uninhibited and spontaneous revelation of its author's life and character." Reader's Ency. 3d edition

Percy, Walker, 1916-1990

Tolson, Jay. Pilgrim in the ruins: a life of Walker Percy. Simon & Schuster 1992 544p il $27.50 **92**

ISBN 0-671-65707-0   LC 92-20101

Percy, Walker, 1916-1990—*Continued*
"Percy the novelist was arguably the most legitimate apologist for orthodox Christianity in modern letters. A convert to Catholicism, Percy mourned this century's loss of sense of sin. . . . Tolson's biography is a skillful synthesis of the trivia of Percy's life, the evolution of his thought, and the substance of his novels." Libr J

Includes bibliographic references

Pericles, 499-429 B.C.
Kagan, Donald. Pericles of Athens and the birth of democracy. Free Press 1991 287p il maps $24.95 **92**

1. Athens (Greece)—Politics and government
ISBN 0-02-916825-2 LC 90-43197

Also available in paperback from Simon & Schuster

First published 1990 in the United Kingdom

This is a "chronicle of the years leading up to and into the . . . [Peloponnesian War] between the Athenians and Spartans. Pericles is cast as the tragic hero whose flaw is the very rationality with which he so skillfully guided the Athenians and forged an empire." Libr J

The author "has produced an engaging and informative book which brings to life both Pericles and classical Athens itself." Commentary

Includes bibliographic references

Peter I, the Great, Emperor of Russia, 1672-1725
Massie, Robert K. Peter the Great; his life and world. Knopf 1980 909p il $40 **92**

1. Russia—History
ISBN 0-394-50032-6 LC 80-7635

Also available in paperback from Ballantine Bks.

The author "explains Russia's foreign relations in the late 1600's and early 1700's and the opening of Russia to westernization. This is a sympathetic appraisal of Peter's accomplishments. . . . The lives of the aristocracy are explored . . . and the changes wrought upon them emphasized. This lengthy and informative book reads like a novel full of romance and intrigue." Libr J

Includes bibliography

Philby, Kim, 1912-1988
Knightley, Phillip. The master spy: the story of Kim Philby. Knopf 1989 292p il $19.95; pa $9.95 **92**

ISBN 0-394-57890-2; 0-679-72688-8 (pa)
LC 88-46162

First published 1988 in the United Kingdom with title: Philby

This biography of British spy Harold Adrian "Kim" Philby "travels familiar territory, of course, for we already know a great deal about the Cambridge spies. . . . Still, there are some surprises here, and a good bit of intriguing detail cunningly worked into a highly readable text, so that the familiar landscape takes on new colors." N Y Times Book Rev

Includes bibliographic references

Piaf, Édith. See class 780.92

Picasso, Pablo. See class 709.2

Pickford, Mary, 1893-1979
Eyman, Scott. Mary Pickford; America's sweetheart. Fine, D.I. 1990 342p il $19.95; pa $11.95 **92**

ISBN 1-55611-147-9; 1-55611-243-2 (pa)
LC 89-45346

In addition to tracing Pickford's screen career the author also delves into her checkered personal life and her founding of United Artists with Fairbanks, Chaplin and Griffith

Includes bibliography and filmography

Pirsig, Robert M.
Pirsig, Robert M. Zen and the art of motorcycle maintenance; an inquiry into values. Morrow 1974 412p $23.40; pa $13.50 **92**

ISBN 0-688-00230-7; 0-688-05230-4 (pa)

A collection of the author's philosophical musings inspired by a motorcycle trip with his son

Plath, Sylvia
Alexander, Paul. Rough magic: a biography of Sylvia Plath. Viking 1991 402p il $24.95 **92**

ISBN 0-670-81812-7 LC 91-50155

Also available in paperback from Penguin Bks.

"Choosing to write Plath's life without the consent and probable constraints of the estate, Alexander eschews quoting from Plath's work; his is not a literary study. Yet the results are impressive: a thorough, beautifully fashioned chronicle rich in new materials and significant minutiae, beginning with the convergence of her parents' lives, continuing with Plath's precocious childhood and tumultuous adulthood, and concluding with her posthumous literary career." Publ Wkly

Includes bibliographic references

Hayman, Ronald. The death and life of Sylvia Plath. Carol Pub. Group 1991 235p il $19.95 **92**

ISBN 1-55972-068-9 LC 91-3835

"A Birch Lane Press book"

"In his study of the American poet, Hayman . . . organizes new and familiar material into thematic, not chronological chapters, and poses challenging questions in the hope of stirring further discussion and dislodging recalcitrant information from those who knew Plath." Publ Wkly

Includes bibliography

Plath, Sylvia. The journals of Sylvia Plath; foreword by Ted Hughes; Ted Hughes, consulting editor and Frances McCullough, editor. Dial Press 1982 370p il o.p.; Ballantine Bks. paperback available $5.99 **92**

ISBN 0-345-35168-1 (pa) LC 81-19435

Plath, Sylvia—*Continued*

These edited selections from Plath's journals cover the period from July, 1950 (the summer before she entered college) to December 1959 when she and her husband Ted Hughes left for England

Stevenson, Anne. Bitter fame: a life of Sylvia Plath; with additional material by Lucas Myers, Dido Merwin, and Richard Murphy. Houghton Mifflin 1989 413p il hardcover o.p. paperback available $10.95
92

ISBN 0-395-53846-7 (pa)   LC 89-7530

"A Peter Davison book"

This biography, "aims to correct many of the popular misconceptions about Plath, whose brief life and suicide made her a legendary figure and feminist symbol in contemporary literature." Booklist

"The author's objectivity and her success in assembling . . . sources pay off richly. . . . We are enabled, with Stevenson's guidance, to draw fresh conclusions about the late poet's conflicts between her fierce drive to succeed and keen appetite for self-destruction." Publ Wkly

Includes bibliography

Poe, Edgar Allan, 1809-1849

Meyers, Jeffrey. Edgar Allan Poe; his life and legacy. Scribner 1992 348p il $30 **92**

ISBN 0-684-19370-1   LC 92-17890

In this biography of the American writer, the author draws "parallels with insight and style between Poe's eminently difficult life and his body of decidedly strange work." Booklist

Includes bibliography

Silverman, Kenneth. Edgar A. Poe; mournful and never-ending remembrance. HarperCollins Pubs. 1991 564p il hardcover o.p. paperback available $13 **92**

ISBN 0-06-092331-8 (pa)   LC 90-56397

The author explains "how Poe's early life influenced his work. He details Poe's turbulent career as poet, short story writer, and editor . . . and traces his literary development through bouts of alcoholism and hallucinations and disputes with literary rivals. An excellent addition to the literature that furthers understanding of America's gothic tale-teller." Libr J

Includes bibliographic references

Pogrebin, Letty Cottin

Pogrebin, Letty Cottin. Deborah, Golda, and me; being female and Jewish in America. Crown 1991 396p $22 **92**

1. Jews—United States
ISBN 0-517-57517-5   LC 90-28499

Also available in paperback from Anchor Bks.

"Pogrebin, best known as a founder of *Ms.* magazine, confronts head-on her struggles as a feminist to maintain a sense of Judaism. . . . While Pogrebin adopts a heartfelt confessional tone, especially when discussing family secrets and her reasons for eschewing religion for 20 years, she never gets lost in a morass of feelings; instead, she views both her religion and her political stance clearly." Booklist

Includes bibliography

Pollock, Jackson. See class 709.2

Pope, Alexander, 1688-1744

Mack, Maynard. Alexander Pope; a life. Norton 1985 975p il $25.95; pa $14.95
92

ISBN 0-393-02208-0; 0-393-30529-5 (pa) LC 85-2941

Published in association with Yale Univ. Press

The author blends criticism of Pope's "poetry, from the early pastorals and Homer translations to such masterpieces as 'The Rape of the Lock' and the 'Dunciad,' with copious and intriguing detail regarding the private life. . . . Pope held a mirror to his age, catching its follies and foibles, grandeur and viciousness with unrivaled precision; and Mack brings us both Pope and the age in a biography as entertaining as it is masterly." Publ Wkly

Includes bibliography

Porter, Katherine Anne, 1890-1980

Givner, Joan. Katherine Anne Porter; a life. rev ed. University of Ga. Press 1991 576p il $45; pa $19.95 **92**

ISBN 0-8203-1348-3; 0-8203-1340-8 (pa)
LC 90-23496

"Brown thrasher books"

First published 1982 by Simon & Schuster

A biography of the American writer whose works include: Flowering Judas, Hacienda, Noon wine, Ship of fools, and Pale horse, pale rider

"Givner has plumbed Porter's every year thoroughly in this comprehensive and well-rounded study. . . . With patience and understanding, she presents this woman as the 'aristocrat first lady of American letters, linguist, musician, femme fatale, and raconteur.'" Christ Sci Monit [review of 1982 edition]

Includes bibliographic references

Porter, Katherine Anne. Letters of Katherine Anne Porter; selected and edited and with an introduction by Isabel Bayley. Atlantic Monthly Press 1990 xlii, 642p il hardcover o.p. paperback available $16.95
92

ISBN 0-87113-453-5 (pa)   LC 89-31242

In this collection of her correspondence from 1930 to 1963 Porter comments "on topics ranging from literature, publishing, and current events to concerns about love, illness, and finances." Libr J

"This wide selection of letters provides the best possible antidote to any suspicion that the whole of her life was wretched, a rudderless voyage. Now we have hundreds of pages of firsthand evidence that—whatever her struggles with work, love and a means of subsistence—Porter was rarely less than a solid kind help to a broad range of friends." N Y Times Book Rev

Includes bibliography

Potter, Beatrix, 1866-1943

Lane, Margaret. The tale of Beatrix Potter; a biography. rev ed, with eight colour and thirty black and white plates. Warne 1968 173p il o.p.; Penguin Bks. paperback available $9.95 **92**

ISBN 0-14-007364-7 (pa)

Potter, Beatrix, 1866-1943—*Continued*
First published 1946

Beatrix Potter's life was divided into two distinct periods: her early years as the only daughter in a wealthy English home, and her happy married life when she farmed and raised sheep on her own lands in the Lake District. The author has discovered as much detail as possible about both periods

Potter, Beatrix. Beatrix Potter's letters; selected and introduced by Judy Taylor. Warne 1990 c1989 478p il $29.95   92
ISBN 0-7232-3437-X

First published 1989 in the United Kingdom

"From more than 1400 extant letters, Taylor has chosen 400 that range over the whole course of Potter's life. The famous 'picture letters' are printed in facsimile, other drawings are reproduced on virtually every other page, and a few pages of color plates appear." Libr J

"The editorial notes throughout the text of 'Beatrix Potter's Letters' are admirably brief and helpful; the index is gratifyingly full, though not without holes; and the illustrations, particularly the Potter pencil sketches and studies, have been chosen with marked sensitivity to the texts they punctuate." N Y Times Book Rev

Includes bibliography

Taylor, Judy. Beatrix Potter; artist, storyteller and countrywoman. Warne 1987 c1986 224p il $24.95   92
ISBN 0-7232-3314-4   LC 86-50799

First published 1986 in the United Kingdom

"In this brief but copiously illustrated biography, Judy Taylor adds much fresh information to what was previously known about her sanguine-spirited and intensely private subject's life. . . . Ms Taylor's more sharply drawn accounts of her subject's typically shrewd but evenhanded business dealings . . . seem a truer reflection not just of Potter's temperament but of her esthetic sense as well." N Y Times Book Rev

Includes bibliography

Pound, Ezra, 1885-1972
Carpenter, Humphrey. A serious character: the life of Ezra Pound. Houghton Mifflin 1988 1005p il $39   92
ISBN 0-395-41678-7   LC 87-37836

Also available in paperback from Dell

Along with assessing Pound's achievements as poet and critic the author also examines his pro-Fascist and virulently anti-Semitic political views

Includes bibliography

Laughlin, James. Pound as wuz: essays and lectures on Ezra Pound. Graywolf Press 1987 203p il $17; pa $9.50   92
ISBN 1-55597-097-4; 1-55597-098-2 (pa)
          LC 87-81376

Pound's publisher and friend "offers a personal reminiscence of Ezra Pound together with some idiosyncratic and often rather casual appraisals of his work. . . . Laughlin's views are decidedly sympathetic, and his personal approach to Pound is always evident in the intimate, nonscholarly tone he adopts. . . . A valuable, insightful personal glimpse of one of the great geniuses and great cranks of the twentieth century." Booklist

Includes bibliography

Tytell, John. Ezra Pound; the solitary volcano. Anchor Press 1987 368p il $19.95   92
ISBN 0-385-19694-6   LC 86-25912

"In this incisive interpretative biography, based on interviews with those who knew him and a mass of published and unpublished Poundiana, Tytell examines the circumstances behind the poems and thereby generates new understanding of the man." Publ Wkly

Includes bibliography

Poussin, Nicolas. See class 709.2

Powell, Adam Clayton, 1908-1972
Hamilton, Charles V. Adam Clayton Powell, Jr; the political biography of an American dilemma. Atheneum Pubs. 1991 545p il $24.95   92
ISBN 0-689-12062-1   LC 90-28505

Chronicling "Powell's rise and fall, Hamilton moves from the 1930s, when Powell became a New York City councilman, to his service starting in 1945 as a U.S. Representative, and then to his chairing of the House Education and Labor Committee, his expulsion from the House in 1967, and his defeat at the polls in 1970." Libr J

"Hamilton's admirable study not only provides insight into this complex and contradictory personality but helps illuminate a neglected period in the civil rights struggle." Nation

Includes bibliographic references

Powell, Colin L.
Means, Howard B. Colin Powell; soldier/statesman, statesman/soldier; by Howard Means. Fine, D.I. 1992 369p il $23   92
ISBN 1-55611-335-8   LC 92-53079

This biography of the American general tells of his "upbringing in the South Bronx in the 1930's and 40's, his schooling at City College, his rise through the Army and his role during the Persian Gulf War." N Y Times Book Rev

"Based in part on interviews with Powell, this is a singular, thorough, and balanced work." Libr J

Previn, André. See class 780.92

Price, Eugenia
Price, Eugenia. Inside one author's heart; a deeply personal sharing with my readers. Doubleday 1992 115p il $15   92
ISBN 0-385-42321-7   LC 91-35734

"In this tribute to close personal and professional friends, Price thanks editors, agents, publishers, confidants, and readers for the festivities and fan mail marking her 75th birthday. . . . Her fans will relish these intimate musings rife with spiritual reflections and emotional kudos to her readers." Booklist

Price, Reynolds, 1933-

Price, Reynolds. Clear pictures; first loves, first guides. Atheneum Pubs. 1989 304p il $19.95   92

ISBN 0-689-12075-3   LC 88-34395

Also available in paperback from Ballantine Bks.

North Carolina novelist Price "trains his lenses on family, neighbors, rural surroundings, and a few significant 'snapshot' scenes that provide a kind of narrative continuity to a sensitive, much-loved and loving, child's slow realization of himself. . . . The achievements of the autobiography are multiple, among them a clear-sighted chronicle of the rural South in the Thirties and Forties." Libr J

Price, Reynolds. Conversations with Reynolds Price; edited by Jefferson Humphries. University Press of Miss. 1991 xx, 294p (Literary conversations ser) $32.50; pa $14.95   92

ISBN 0-87805-482-0; 0-87805-483-9 (pa)
                                            LC 90-49284

A collection of interviews with Reynolds Price in which he discusses his writings and views on literature and society

Proust, Marcel, 1871-1922

Painter, George Duncan. Marcel Proust; a biography; [by] George D. Painter. 2nd ed. Random House 1989 2v in 1 il $39.95
                                                          92

ISBN 0-394-57669-1   LC 89-42913

First published 1959 in two volumes in the United Kingdom; 1959-1965 in the United States by Little, Brown with title: Proust

In this biography the author points out the real-life counterparts of characters, events, and places in Proust's Remembrance of things past

Pulitzer, Joseph, 1885-1955

Pfaff, Daniel W. Joseph Pulitzer II and the Post-dispatch; a newspaperman's life. Pennsylvania State Univ. Press 1991 455p il $29.95   92

1. St. Louis post-dispatch (Newspaper)
ISBN 0-271-00748-6   LC 90-49036

The author examines Joseph Pulitzer's tenure as editor of the St. Louis Post-Dispatch and his uneasy relationship with his legendary father

The author "has written an outstanding biography, one that may set students of journalistic history to wondering whether Pulitzer II was not a better newsman than his revered father." Publ Wkly

Includes bibliographic references

Puller, Lewis B., Jr.

Puller, Lewis B., Jr. Fortunate son; the autobiography of Lewis B. Puller, Jr. Grove Weidenfeld 1991 389p $21.95   92

1. Vietnam War, 1961-1975—Personal narratives
ISBN 0-8021-1218-8   LC 91-4463

Also available in paperback from Bantam Bks.

This is a "Vietnam memoir by a veteran who survived a truly horrifying array of wounds (the loss of both legs, one hand, and most of the remaining hand), then went on to survive a bout with alcoholism, earn a law degree, preserve his marriage, and become active in veterans affairs. Puller managed all this in the long shadow of his father, the legendary marine general Chesty Puller." Booklist

Pullman, George Mortimer, 1831-1897

Leyendecker, Liston E. Palace car prince: a biography of George Mortimer Pullman. University Press of Colo. 1992 323p il $29.95   92

1. Pullman Palace Car Company
ISBN 0-87081-223-8   LC 91-37716

"A detailed and personal biography of the creator of the Pullman car and his family and times . . . useful for reference and general reading about the man and the period." Choice

Includes bibliographic references

Pym, Barbara

Holt, Hazel. A lot to ask: a life of Barbara Pym. Dutton 1991 308p il $19.95
                                                          92

ISBN 0-525-24937-0   LC 90-23515

Also available G.K. Hall large print edition and in paperback from New Am. Lib.

First published 1990 in the United Kingdom

This biography of the British novelist includes "details about Barbara Pym's private life as well as her published and unpublished writings." Publ Wkly

Includes bibliographic references

Quayle, Dan

Broder, David S. The man who would be president: Dan Quayle; by David S. Broder, Bob Woodward. Simon & Schuster 1992 207p il $18   92

ISBN 0-671-79183-4   LC 92-8183

"Quayle is presented as a decent politician (and parent), who is able to get along with others and who is adept at promoting himself. . . . This is likely to become the definitive work on the Quayle vice presidency." Libr J

Raban, Jonathan

Raban, Jonathan. For love & money: a writing life, 1969-1989. Harper & Row 1989 c1987 344p $22.50; pa $10   92

ISBN 0-06-016166-3; 0-06-098102-4 (pa)
                                            LC 89-45058

"An Edward Burlingame book"

First published 1987 in the United Kingdom

This "collection of short works is cemented together with an extended memoir in which Raban describes the many genres in which he's worked—scriptwriting, reviews, fiction, travel writing, . . . autobiography. In discussing the peculiar difficulties and pleasures of each, Raban explores all the choices and temptations of a writer's life." Booklist

Rabi, Isidor Isaac

Rigden, John S. Rabi, scientist and citizen. Basic Bks. 1987 302p il $21.95; pa $9.95 **92**

ISBN 0-465-06792-1; 0-465-06793-X (pa)

LC 86-47736

"The Alfred P. Sloan Foundation series"

This is a biography of the American scientist who won the Nobel Prize in physics in 1944. This works aims to "trace Rabi's life and work from his birth in 1898 in Rymanow, a small town in Galicia. . . . Rabi's life makes for fascinating reading, but the power of this book for the general readers lies in its interwoven, readily understandable explanation of many of the ideas of modern physics." Sci Books Films

Includes bibliography

Radner, Gilda, 1946-1989

Radner, Gilda. It's always something. Simon & Schuster 1989 269p il o.p.; Avon Bks. paperback available $5.95 **92**

1. Cancer—Personal narratives

ISBN 0-380-71072-2 (pa)

LC 89-6303

In this account of her struggle with ovarian cancer "the spirited star of 'Saturday Night Live' has laid out all the horrors of surgery and chemotherapy, but there are also lighter moments, like her 1984 marriage to the actor Gene Wilder. . . . 'It's Always Something' is compelling as testimony from the cancer wars by a courageous and much-loved entertainer." N Y Times Book Rev

Saltman, David. Gilda; an intimate portrait. Contemporary Bks. 1992 246p il $19.95; pa $8.95 **92**

ISBN 0-8092-4102-1; 0-8092-3815-2 (pa) LC 92-3831

This is a biography of the popular TV and movie comedienne "who brought such memorable characters as Judy Miller, Rhonda Weiss, Baba Wawa, Candy Slice, Roseanne Roseannadana, and Lisa Loopner to life. . . . Radner is depicted as a fully rounded woman with all of the special qualities needed to possess comic genius." Libr J

Ramanujan Aiyangar, Srinivasa, 1887-1920

Kanigel, Robert. The man who knew infinity: a life of the genius, Ramanujan. Scribner 1991 438p il maps $27.95 **92**

ISBN 0-684-19259-4 LC 90-49788

Also available in paperback from Washington Sq. Press

This biography traces the life of the Indian mathematician. "Working alone in relative obscurity and lacking the usual academic credentials [Ramanujan] could easily have passed unnoticed. However, with the help of a handful of friends and the ultimate support of renowned English mathematician G.H. Hardy, his work was brought to the attention of the world." Libr J

"Kanigel deserves high praise for a work of arduous research and rare insight." Booklist

Includes bibliographic references

Rasputin, Grigorii Efimovich, 1871-1916

Fuhrmann, Joseph T. Rasputin; a life. Praeger Pubs. 1990 276p il $24.95 **92**

ISBN 0-275-93215-X LC 89-3651

"The author distinguishes fact and probability from myth in the life of Grigory Rasputin, a Siberian peasant known as a profligate, religious leader, and faith healer. Fuhrmann documents how Rasputin's ability to aid the hemophiliac heir, Alexis, led to his power to influence Empress Alexandra and through her, Nicholas II, Russia's last tsar." Libr J

Includes bibliography

Rather, Dan

Rather, Dan. I remember; [by] Dan Rather with Peter Wyden. Little, Brown 1991 261p il $19.95 **92**

ISBN 0-316-73440-3 LC 91-21773

"Recollections of living in small-town Texas during the Great Depression and World War II with his extended family, schoolmates and townsfolk fill Rather's book with anecdotes both engaging and warmly nostalgic." Libr J

Ratushinskaya, Irina

Ratushinskaya, Irina. Grey is the color of hope; translated by Alyona Kojevnikov. Knopf 1988 355p il hardcover o.p. paperback available $8.95 **92**

1. Political prisoners

ISBN 0-679-72447-8 (pa) LC 88-45322

"In March 1983, on her 29th birthday, the Soviet poet Irina Ratushinskaya received a seven-year prison sentence for expressing 'anti-Soviet agitation and propaganda' in her verse. This . . . prose text is a memoir of the three and a half years she served in a work camp. . . . One of the many fascinations of Ms. Ratushinskaya's memoir is that it records [Soviet camp life] . . . through the prism of an acutely female sensitivity." N Y Times Book Rev

Rauschenberg, Robert. See class 709.2

Ray, James Earl, 1928-

Ray, James Earl. Who killed Martin Luther King? the true story by the alleged assassin. National Press Bks. 1992 285p il hardcover o.p. paperback available $12.95 **92**

1. King, Martin Luther, 1929-1968—Assassination

ISBN 1-882605-02-0 (pa) LC 91-34847

"Here, Ray, convicted assassin of Martin Luther King, Jr., gives us the story as he sees it. Ray denies that he did the awful deed, claiming that he was in a car driving away from Memphis on April 4, 1968, when he heard the news of King's death on his car radio. . . . The first half of the book, in which Ray details his pathetic life drifting across the country and landing in and out of jail, is the best part, reading often like a Jim Thompson novel." Booklist

Ray, Man. See class 709.2

Reagan, Nancy, 1923-
Kelley, Kitty. Nancy Reagan; the unauthorized biography. Simon & Schuster 1991 603p il hardcover o.p. paperback available $5.99   **92**
ISBN 0-671-64647-8 (pa)   LC 91-6650
Also available G.K. Hall large print edition
This is a biography of the former First Lady which lists her many alleged misdeeds
Includes bibliographic references

Reagan, Nancy. My turn: the memoirs of Nancy Reagan; by Nancy Reagan with William Novak. Random House 1989 384p il $21.95   **92**
1. Reagan, Ronald, 1911-
ISBN 0-394-56368-9   LC 89-42786
Also available Thorndike Press large print edition and in paperback from Dell
"This is a book about people rather than politics, except where political matters touched me directly, as they did during the long months of the Iran-contra affair, and during [the] five election campaigns." Foreword
"The title is well chosen. Mrs. Reagan takes the opportunity to get back at her critics, settle some scores, and, in a few cases, mend fences." Booklist

Reagan, Ronald, 1911-
Cannon, Lou. President Reagan; the role of a lifetime. Simon & Schuster 1991 948p il hardcover o.p. paperback available $16
92
1. United States—Politics and government—1974-1989
ISBN 0-671-75576-5 (pa)   LC 91-6960
This portrait of the fortieth President of the United States focuses on his career in politics, especially his tenure in the White House
The author's "tone is judicious, the hyperbole limited and the coverage comprehensive." N Y Times Book Rev
Includes bibliographic references

Wills, Garry. Reagan's America; innocents at home. Doubleday 1987 472p il $19.95
92
1. United States—Politics and government—1981-
ISBN 0-385-18286-4   LC 86-16493
Also available in a revised paperback edition with a chapter on the legacy of the Reagan era, from Penguin Bks.
"Despite the fast-forward quality of the presidential chapters, Reagan's America is a prodigious feat of research and popular history. The author has synthesized disparate incidents and uncovered revealing data." Time
Includes bibliography

Remington, Frederic. See class 709.2

Reston, James, 1909-
Reston, James. Deadline; a memoir. Random House 1991 525p il $25   **92**
ISBN 0-394-58558-5   LC 91-52679

Also available in paperback
This is an autobiography by the journalist who served as a reporter and columnist for The New York Times from 1940 to 1987
This memoir "offers a healthy portion of insider dope about past events as well as an overly generous assortment of homespun wisdom about America, the Times, the journalism business generally, and [his wife] Sally Fulton Reston." Columbia J Rev

Rexroth, Kenneth, 1905-1982
Hamalian, Linda. A life of Kenneth Rexroth. Norton 1991 444p il $25; pa $12.95   **92**
ISBN 0-393-02944-1; 0-393-30915-0 (pa)
LC 90-38002
A biography of the American poet and translator
"Hamalian depicts the virtues and flaws of this fascinating man, with cool, evenhanded balance. . . . With its multifaceted portrait, rendered with photographic accuracy, this instructive book augments our appreciation of the man and his era." Libr J
Includes bibliography

Rhodes, Cecil John, 1853-1902
Rotberg, Robert I. The founder: Cecil Rhodes and the pursuit of power; [by] Robert I. Rotberg with the collaboration of Miles F. Shore. Oxford Univ. Press 1988 xxii, 800p il maps $39.95; pa $16.95   **92**
ISBN 0-19-504968-3; 0-19-506668-5 (pa) LC 88-5960
"Imperialist, financier, politician, and mining magnate, Rhodes was a larger-than-life figure in southern Africa whose influence is still felt through his scholarships and the DeBeers diamond monopoly." Libr J
"A massive though fluid treatment of a life of infinite controversy. . . . Rotberg establishes with care where Rhodes can be faulted for opportunism and even inhumanity and where he can be credited with greatness. The last word on the man, for some time to come." Booklist
Includes bibliography

Rhodes, Richard
Rhodes, Richard. A hole in the world; an American boyhood. Simon & Schuster 1990 271p il hardcover o.p. paperback available $10   **92**
ISBN 0-671-74725-8 (pa)   LC 90-9949
The author "begins the story of his boyhood with his mother's suicide, which occurred when he was 13 months old. This act touched every aspect of his life from that day forward. After several itinerant years, his father finally landed Rhodes and his brother Stanley in the house of a ghastly woman who was to become Rhodes's stepmother. . . . This book is a testament to the incredible resiliency of the human spirit." Libr J

Rhodes, Richard. Making love; an erotic odyssey. Simon & Schuster 1992 175p $18; pa $10   **92**
ISBN 0-671-78227-4; 0-671-87072-6 (pa)
LC 92-12467
The author presents an account of "his own sexual life. . . . Emphasing the 'verity' of everything in the book, Rhodes offers explicit descriptions that may titillate

Rhodes, Richard—*Continued*

some readers and shock others. This well-written, if sometimes self-indulgent, volume provocatively and perceptively provides one perspective on male heterosexuality." Libr J

Includes bibliographic references

Rhys, Jean

Angier, Carole. Jean Rhys; life and work. Little, Brown 1991 c1990 762p il $35 **92**

ISBN 0-316-04263-3　　　　　LC 91-6819

"Rhys (1890-1979), author of several novels and short stories, drew on her life experience as a colonial exile from the British West Indies who became a chorus girl, bohemian, and writer living by her wits in London and Paris. Angier . . . painstakingly links Rhys's difficult life to events and characters in her fiction." Libr J

Includes bibliographic references

Rice, Anne, 1941-

Ramsland, Katherine M. Prism of the night: a biography of Anne Rice; [by] Katherine Ramsland. Dutton 1991 385p il $22.95 **92**

ISBN 0-525-93370-0　　　　　LC 91-15904

Also available in paperback from New Am. Lib.

"Born in 1941, [Rice] grew up in a New Orleans full of Southern gothic ambience; her father enjoyed taking her through cemeteries. The death of her alcoholic, highly religious mother, and the later loss of her own daughter to leukemia, plunged her into grief, obsessive-compulsive behavior and nearly fragmented her. Through her supernatural tales and erotica written under a number of pseudonyms, she explored her own masochistic impulses." Publ Wkly

"Ramsland is thorough, but she spends more time recounting plot than showing how the themes she uncovers are carried out in Rice's work. Nevertheless, her painstaking biography will be useful for both lay and scholarly readers." Libr J

Rice, Sarah, 1909-

Rice, Sarah. He included me: the autobiography of Sarah Rice; transcribed and edited by Louise Westling. University of Ga. Press 1989 181p il $22.50; pa $11.95 **92**

ISBN 0-8203-1141-3; 0-8203-1337-8 (pa)

　　　　　　　　　　　LC 88-38690

The author "tells of growing up in poverty with seven siblings, of marrying three times and bearing a son, of becoming a certified teacher but working as a maid because jobs for black teachers were few. Intertwined in Mrs. Rice's story are glimpses of what rural Alabama was like in the early part of the century." N Y Times Book Rev

This oral history tells "a compelling, instructive, and otherwise unavailable story. It provides insight into black women struggling with the world of black males as well as with contemporary American society." Choice

Rich, Buddy. See class 780.92

Richards, Keith. See class 780.92

Robeson, Paul, 1898-1976

Duberman, Martin B. Paul Robeson; by Martin Bauml Duberman. Knopf 1988 804p il $24.95 **92**

ISBN 0-394-52780-1　　　　　LC 88-45297

Also available in paperback from Ballantine Bks.

This is a biography of the black singer, actor and political activist

"It is the wonderful achievement of Martin Bauml Duberman to have recaptured the greatness of Paul Robeson and the ambiguity and treacherousness of his time, while guarding his own critical sense, avoiding many partisan and ideological traps." Nation

Includes bibliography

Rodriguez, Richard, 1944-

Rodriguez, Richard. Hunger of memory; the education of Richard Rodriguez; an autobiography. Godine 1982 195p o.p.; Bantam Bks. paperback available $4.95 **92**

ISBN 0-553-27293-4 (pa)　　　　LC 81-81810

An account "of the coming of age of a person of Mexican descent and culture in American society and the inevitable transition in the private life of his family. Rodriguez focuses on his educational experiences, from his parochial elementary school . . . to his university years and subsequent experience as an educator." Libr J

Rogers, Ginger, 1911-

Rogers, Ginger. Ginger: my story. HarperCollins Pubs. 1991 450p il $22; pa $5.99 **92**

ISBN 0-06-018308-X; 0-06-109114-6 (pa)

　　　　　　　　　　　LC 90-56394

Also available G.K. Hall large print edition

In this autobiography the author "chronicles her rise to stardom and describes her various dramatic and musical film roles. She also reviews her five marriages and various romances, while charmingly setting the record straight on her partnership with Fred Astaire. . . . This delightful chronicle of 50 years in entertainment is refined, well-written fun." Libr J

Rogers, Will, 1879-1935

Rogers, Will. The autobiography of Will Rogers; selected and edited by Donald Day; with a foreword by Bill and Jim Rogers **92**

Various reprint editions available

First published 1949 by Houghton Mifflin

"Everyone loved Rogers, the man and the humorist, and this volume will allow a wide public to have access to much of his philosophy and accurate political, theatrical, and purely human comment." Libr J

Rogers, Will, 1879-1935—*Continued*

Rogers, Will. Will Rogers at the Ziegfeld Follies; edited by Arthur Frank Wertheim; foreword by Joseph H. Carter. University of Okla. Press 1992 268p il $24.95   **92**

1. Ziegfeld, Florenz, 1869-1932
ISBN 0-8061-2357-5   LC 92-54137

"Will Rogers and Florenz Ziegfeld are two magic names in show business. A fascinating exchange of telegrams and letters brings to life the rare friendship between them. Included here are Rogers writings that have never been published. As the only book dealing with Rogers on the stage, this fills an important gap in the life story of the famous humorist." Univ Press Books for Public and Second Sch Libr

Includes bibliographic references

Rollin, Ida, 1908-1983

Rollin, Betty. Last wish. Linden Press/Simon & Schuster 1985 236p o.p.; Warner Bks. paperback available $8.95   **92**

1. Cancer—Personal narratives 2. Right to die
ISBN 0-446-37032-0 (pa)   LC 85-12903

"In this book TV journalist Rollin chronicles her mother's two-and-a-half year illness with ovarian cancer, from the diagnosis to her decision to end her unrelenting pain and nausea through suicide." Libr J

"The most remarkable aspect of this book is that it manages not to be depressing. Betty Rollin's loving portrait of her mother's life . . . is as compelling as the account of her death." N Y Times Book Rev

Rooney, Mickey

Rooney, Mickey. Life is too short. Villard Bks. 1991 374p il $22   **92**

ISBN 0-679-40195-4   LC 90-50665

Also available large print edition $24.50 (ISBN 0-679-40287-X); paperback available from Ballantine Bks.

In this autobiography Rooney presents an account of his show business career and his personal life

"Rooney's self-deprecating humor powers this book. He's not a brutal kiss-and-teller, and he's more of a connoisseur of stories and observations than of finely matched facts. . . . This will appeal to fans who have enjoyed his work over the years. Not without flaws, but it works." Libr J

Includes filmography

Roosevelt, Eleanor, 1884-1962

Cook, Blanche Wiesen. Eleanor Roosevelt. v1: 1884-1933. Viking 1992 587p il $27.50   **92**

ISBN 0-670-80486-X   LC 87-40632

Also available in paperback from Penguin Bks.

This installment of Cook's biography "spans the years from Eleanor's birth to her husband Franklin Delano's inauguration." Publisher's note

"A feminist biography that regards its subject not only as a mostly 19th-century woman who invented her own life with very little help, but also as a self-created political figure of considerable significance." N Y Times Book Rev

Includes bibliographic references

Lash, Joseph P. Eleanor; the years alone; foreword by Franklin D. Roosevelt, Jr. Norton 1972 368p il $14.95   **92**

ISBN 0-393-07361-0

The author describes Mrs. Roosevelt's private and public life in the years following President Roosevelt's death, during which she served as a delegate to the UN, and became known as the First Lady of the World

Includes bibliographic references

Lash, Joseph P. Eleanor and Franklin; the story of their relationship; based on Eleanor Roosevelt's private papers; foreword by Arthur M. Schlesinger, Jr.; introduction by Franklin D. Roosevelt, Jr. Norton 1971 765p il o.p.; New Am. Lib. paperback available $5.95   **92**

1. Roosevelt, Franklin D. (Franklin Delano), 1882-1945
ISBN 0-451-14076-1 (pa)

Focusing upon Mrs. Roosevelt's private and public life, the author gives insight into her childhood and reconstructs the relationship between the famous couple

Includes bibliographic references

Roosevelt, Eleanor. Eleanor Roosevelt's My day. Pharos Bks. 1989-1991 3v il v1 $18.95; v2-3 ea $19.95   **92**

ISBN 0-88687-407-6 (v1); 0-88687-457-2 (v2); 0-88687-503-X (v3)   LC 88-28821

Volume one edited by Rochelle Chadakoff; volumes two and three edited by David Emblidge

Contents: v1 Her acclaimed columns, 1936-1945; v2 The post-war years, her acclaimed columns, 1945-1952; v3 First lady of the world, her acclaimed columns, 1953-1962

"This sampling of Eleanor Roosevelt's 'My Day' columns . . . reflect her high moral values and broad interests, from the mundane and personal to the sweeping and reformist." Libr J

Roosevelt, Franklin D. (Franklin Delano), 1882-1945

Davis, Kenneth Sydney. FDR, into the storm, 1937-1940; a history; [by] Kenneth S. Davis. Random House 1993 691p $35   **92**

1. United States—Politics and government—1933-1945
ISBN 0-679-41541-6   LC 92-21640

In this fourth volume of a projected five-volume biography "particular emphasis is laid on Roosevelt's attempt to 'pack' the Supreme Court, his response to the growing threat of fascism in Europe, and the unexpectedly strong challenge by Republican Wendell Wilkie in the 1940 presidential campaign." Publ Wkly

Includes bibliographic references

Davis, Kenneth Sydney. FDR, the New Deal years, 1933-1937; a history; [by] Kenneth S. Davis. Random House 1986 756p $29.95   **92**

1. United States—Politics and government—1933-1945
ISBN 0-394-52753-4   LC 85-31704

This is the third volume of Davis's biography of Franklin D. Roosevelt, preceded by FDR, the beckoning destiny, 1882-1928 (1972) and FDR, the New York years,

Roosevelt, Franklin D. (Franklin Delano), 1882-1945—*Continued*
1928-1933 (1985)

Davis "recounts FDR's rise to the presidency amid the deepening Depression . . . and the extraordinary burst of activity that comprised the New Deal. . . . The author's dramatic recounting of the tumultuous period nicely captures the unusual bond between FDR and the American people, and includes revealing explorations of his relationship with his wife, Eleanor, and hers with Lorena Hickok." Publ Wkly

Includes bibliography

Lash, Joseph P. Eleanor and Franklin. See entry under Roosevelt, Eleanor, 1884-1962

92

Ward, Geoffrey C. Before the trumpet: young Franklin Roosevelt, 1882-1905. Harper & Row 1985 390p il $19.95; pa $9.95 **92**

ISBN 0-06-015451-9; 0-06-091344-4 (pa)

LC 84-48755

This book "covers FDR's family history for two generations prior to his birth, and traces his development to his marriage." Best Sellers

"If the outlines of the broad story are familiar, if some of the family anecdotes have been told before, the texture is nonetheless richer, the detail more finely tuned than in any other portrait of Franklin Roosevelt's early years." N Y Times Book Rev

Includes bibliography

Ward, Geoffrey C. A first class temperament: the emergence of Franklin Roosevelt. Harper & Row 1989 889p il $27.95; pa $14.95 **92**

ISBN 0-06-016066-7; 0-06-092026-2 (pa)

LC 88-45908

This continuation of the biographical study entered above "carries the story from Roosevelt's marriage to Eleanor to his return to public life in 1928, subsequent to his recovery from severe illness." Booklist

"A fascinating, well-balanced, scholarly treatment and a significant contribution to the understanding of FDR." Libr J

Includes bibliography

Roosevelt, Theodore, 1858-1919

Cooper, John Milton. The warrior and the priest: Woodrow Wilson and Theodore Roosevelt. See entry under Wilson, Woodrow, 1856-1924 **92**

McCullough, David G. Mornings on horseback; [by] David McCullough. Simon & Schuster 1981 445p il hardcover o.p. paperback available $14.95 **92**

1. Roosevelt family
ISBN 0-671-44754-8 (pa)

LC 81-1697

This biography follows Theodore Roosevelt from his childhood to his defeat for mayor of New York and marriage to Edith Carow in 1886

"Based on diligent and thorough research, with emphasis on family, physical ailments, and friends, and written with verve and color, this is a stimulating book that will appeal to the general reader." Libr J

Includes bibliography

Morris, Edmund. The rise of Theodore Roosevelt. Coward, McCann & Geoghegan 1979 886p il o.p.; Ballantine Bks. paperback available $16 **92**

ISBN 0-345-33902-9 (pa)

LC 78-23789

A study of the life and times of Theodore Roosevelt tracing events from his birth until the death of President McKinley in 1901

Includes bibliography

Rose, Pete, 1941-

Rose, Pete. Pete Rose: my story; [by] Pete Rose and Roger Kahn. Macmillan 1989 300p il $18.95 **92**

ISBN 0-02-560611-5

LC 89-13166

"There is much more to read about than just the gambling issue in 'Pete Rose: My Story.' There is baseball, including chapters on Mr. Rose's boyhood and minor league years. There is also, of course, a good deal about major league baseball. The baseball stories are presented in bursts, punctuated with prose snapshots of Mr. Rose today." N Y Times Book Rev

Rossetti, Dante Gabriel. See class 709.2

Roth, Herman, 1901-1989

Roth, Philip. Patrimony; a true story. Simon & Schuster 1991 238p il hardcover o.p. paperback available $10 **92**

1. Roth, Philip
ISBN 0-671-75862-4 (pa)

LC 90-35891

This "is an account of how Roth cared for his eighty-six-year-old father during the last stages of the parent's incurable brain tumor." Time

This "ordinary, crucial story is well suited to a comic master, and Mr. Roth brings to the tale his gift for attention, his worldly, vernacular heart and the tremendous inventive force that here he keeps largely in check." N Y Times Book Rev

Roth, Philip

Roth, Philip. The facts; a novelist's autobiography. Farrar, Straus & Giroux 1988 195p $17.95 **92**

ISBN 0-374-15212-8

LC 88-14187

Also available in paperback from Penguin Bks.

Following a prologue about his parents, Roth recounts "five stages of his life: his New Jersey youth; his college days at Bucknell; meeting his wife-to-be while as instructor at the University of Chicago; his early writing days, including [his conflict with] . . . the Jewish community; and his life in the sixties." Libr J

"The Facts is a lively and serious version of a novelist's life, but it seems even more interesting as a new way of formulating the questions about the imagination that Roth has been pursuing with increasing complication in the Zuckerman novels." N Y Rev Books

Rousseau, Jean-Jacques, 1712-1778

Cranston, Maurice. The noble savage: Jean-Jacques Rousseau, 1754-1762. University of Chicago Press 1991 399p il $32.50 **92**

ISBN 0-226-11863-0

LC 90-28111

Rousseau, Jean-Jacques, 1712-1778 — Continued

"The second part of a projected trilogy, this sequel to Volume 1, *Jean-Jacques: The Early Life and Work of Jean-Jacques Rousseau* (1983) covers the most productive, turbulent, and controversial eight years of Rousseau's life. His *Discourse on Inequality, Letter to Voltaire on Providence, Letter to d'Alembert, La Nouvelle Héloise, The Social Contract*, and *Emile* emerge from this period." Choice

"Cranston offers the finest and most richly detailed portrait ever assembled of these vagabond years." New Statesman Soc

Includes bibliographic references

Rousseau, Jean-Jacques. Confessions; edited and introduced by P. N. Furbank. Knopf 1992 2v in 1 $20   **92**

ISBN 0-679-40998-X   LC 91-53194

Also available in paperback from Penguin Bks.

"Everyman's library"

First Everyman's library edition, 1931

"An autobiography by Jean-Jacques Rousseau. The twelve volumes, written between 1766 and 1770, were published posthumously (I-VI, 1781; VII-XII, 1788). In this work, Rousseau 'frankly and sincerely' reveals the details of his erratic and rebellious life. Scholars find, however, that his unconscious motivation was to justify himself in the eyes of his supposedly numerous persecutors." Reader's Ency. 3d edition

Rowan, Carl Thomas, 1925-

Rowan, Carl Thomas. Breaking barriers; a memoir; [by] Carl T. Rowan. Little, Brown 1991 395p il $22.95   **92**

ISBN 0-316-75977-5   LC 90-42827

Also available in paperback from HarperPerennial

Black syndicated columnist Rowan examines his career in journalism and his service in the Kennedy and Johnson administrations

Runyon, Damon, 1880-1946

Breslin, Jimmy. Damon Runyon. Ticknor & Fields 1991 410p $24.95   **92**

ISBN 0-89919-984-4   LC 91-16073

"The life of colorful journalist/short story writer Runyon, whose authentic depiction of New York lowlife became the basis for the musical *Guys and Dolls*." Libr J

"Breslin paints Runyon's life on a mural-sized canvas, cramming in as much detail as the surface can hold. . . . A commanding and dynamic portrait of a legendary writer and his world." Booklist

Rusk, Dean, 1909-

Rusk, Dean. As I saw it; by Dean Rusk as told to Richard Rusk; edited by Daniel S. Papp. Norton 1990 672p il $29.95   **92**

1. United States—Foreign relations
ISBN 0-393-02650-7   LC 89-34461

Also available in paperback from Penguin Bks.

"Dean Rusk, talking into a tape recorder to his son, reminisces about his family background, his education, his military service during World War II, his accomplishments in various State Department posts and, finally,

his eight years as secretary of state under Kennedy and Johnson." Publ Wkly

"Historians and others would do well to welcome this account, both because Richard Rusk has not hesitated to ask his father tough questions and because he was in a better position than Mr. Rusk's previous biographers to press for answers." N Y Times Book Rev

Includes bibliography

Russell, Bertrand, 1872-1970

Clark, Ronald William. The life of Bertrand Russell; [by] Ronald W. Clark. Knopf 1976 c1975 766p il o.p.; Da Capo Press paperback available $17.95   **92**

ISBN 0-306-80397-6 (pa)

First published 1975 in the United Kingdom

The author sets out to "reconstruct Russell's development—philosophically, politically, sexually—at each stage of his life." Libr J

"Clark has done a commendable job of weaving a quantity of detail into a flowing account." Booklist

Includes bibliography

Russell, Bertrand. The autobiography of Bertrand Russell. Allen & Unwin; [distributed by] Routledge, Chapman & Hall 1967-1969 3v v1 pa $16.95; v2-3 ea $34.95   **92**

Contents: v1 1872-1914 (ISBN 0-04-921022-X); v2 1914-1944 (ISBN 0-04-921009-2); v3 1944-1969 (ISBN 0-04-921010-6)

This is a three-volume autobiography of the English philosopher and mathematician

Russell, Bertrand. The selected letters of Bertrand Russell; edited by Nicholas Griffin. v1: The private years, 1884-1914. Houghton Mifflin 1992 xxi, 553p $35   **92**

ISBN 0-395-56269-4   LC 91-47644

In this first selection "Griffin presents more than 200 previously unpublished letters . . . which show various facets of Russell's life between the ages of 12 and 44. The letters illuminate an aspect of Russell that does not come through in his more formal and technical writings, giving him humanity and dimension." Libr J

Includes bibliographic references

Russell, Charles M. See class 709.2

Ruth, Babe, 1895-1948

Creamer, Robert W. Babe; the legend comes to life. Simon & Schuster 1974 443p il o.p. paperback available $12   **92**

ISBN 0-671-76070-X (pa)

This biography of the baseball player covers his personal life and his professional career

Ritter, Lawrence S. The Babe; a life in pictures; Lawrence S. Ritter, text and captions; Mark Rucker, picture editor. Ticknor & Fields 1988 282p il $40; pa $17.95   **92**

ISBN 0-89919-768-X; 0-89919-915-1 (pa) LC 88-8579

"A Baseball Ink book"

Ruth, Babe, 1895-1948—_Continued_
Numerous photographs highlight this look at the career of baseball's first superstar

Includes bibliography

Sacagawea, 1786-1884
Clark, Ella Elizabeth. Sacagawea of the Lewis and Clark expedition; [by] Ella E. Clark and Margot Edmonds. University of Calif. Press 1979 171p il hardcover o.p. paperback available $11.95   **92**
1. Lewis and Clark Expedition (1804-1806)
ISBN 0-520-05060-6 (pa)   LC 78-65466
"Sacagawea, the Shoshone Indian woman who accompanied the Lewis and Clark expedition, has been a regional heroine and a feminist celebrity for most of this century. But, as these writers show, her role as 'the guide' was more fictive than actual. . . . Based on careful interpretation of the explorer's journals, this revisionist study does a good job of redefining her actual contributions." Booklist

Includes bibliography

Sackville-West, V. (Victoria), 1892-1962
Glendinning, Victoria. Vita: the life of V. Sackville-West. Knopf 1983 436p il o.p.; Quill paperback available $12   **92**
ISBN 0-688-04111-6 (pa)   LC 83-47961
"The story of Vita Sackville-West and Harold Nicolson's unorthodox marriage is known from their son Nigel's Portrait of a Marriage [entered below. This] authorized biography [attempts to] fill in the gaps." Libr J
"It is one of Victoria Glendinning's skills as a biographer that she succeeds in commanding the reader's interest in someone whose personality one may find inherently distasteful." Encounter

Includes bibliographic references

Nicolson, Nigel. Portrait of a marriage. Atheneum Pubs. 1973 249p il hardcover o.p. paperback available $12.95   **92**
1. Nicolson, Sir Harold George, 1886-1968
ISBN 0-689-70597-2 (pa)
"Shortly after his mother's death, Nigel Nicolson . . . [found] an autobiography account, written in the early years of her marriage, of her . . . love affair with another woman. . . . [He] decided to publish that manuscript, along with a longer narrative by himself amplifying the story." Newsweek

Sackville-West, V. (Victoria). Vita and Harold; the letters of Vita Sackville-West and Harold Nicolson; edited by Nigel Nicolson. Putnam 1992 452p il $29.95 **92**
1. Nicolson, Sir Harold George, 1886-1968
ISBN 0-399-13666-5   LC 91-4340
"Their son selected from 10,000 existing letters (hitherto available only to researchers) to create this epistolary chronicle of the relationship between Sackville-West and Nicolson from 1910 to 1962. Their beautifully written, tender, and intimate correspondence reveals an extraordinarily talented, witty, articulate, sophisticated, upper-class English literary couple." Libr J

Sakharov, Andreĭ Dmitrievich, 1921-1989
Bonner, Elena. Alone together. See entry under Bonner, Elena   **92**

Sakharov, Andreĭ Dmitrievich. Memoirs; [by] Andrei Sakharov; translated from the Russian by Richard Lourie. Knopf 1990 xxi, 773p il $29.95; pa $16   **92**
ISBN 0-394-53740-8; 0-679-73595-X (pa)
LC 90-53068
The Soviet physicist and political dissident discusses his life and career up until 1986
"Virtually everyone . . . is likely to find the second half of the book unforgettable. It describes, blow by blow, Sakharov and [his wife Elena] Bonner's . . . battle for their personal as well as universal rights." New Leader

Includes bibliographic references

Sakharov, Andreĭ Dmitrievich. Moscow and beyond, 1986-1989; [by] Andrei Sakharov; translated by Antonina Bouis. Knopf 1991 c1990 168p il $19.95; pa $11 **92**
ISBN 0-394-58797-9; 0-679-73987-4 (pa)
LC 90-52865
"The second volume of memoirs by the heroic Soviet physicist and democratic idealist covers his final years, from the end of exile to his last speech to the Congress of People's Deputies." N Y Times Book Rev

Salinger, J. D. (Jerome David), 1919-
Hamilton, Ian. In search of J.D. Salinger. Random House 1988 222p $17.95; pa $8.95   **92**
ISBN 0-394-53468-9; 0-679-72220-3 (pa)
LC 85-25591
Hamilton's intended biography, "scheduled for release in August 1986, was abandoned after Salinger successfully sued to enjoin publication on the grounds of copyright violation." Libr J
"In addition to drawing parallels between Salinger's fiction and his personal life, Hamilton provides a sketchy overview of the author's early schooling, military career, first brief marriage, initial attempts to get published, and sudden, overwhelming success with Catcher in the Rye. In discussing the now-celebrated court case, Hamilton raises important questions about freedom of information versus the right to privacy." Booklist

Includes bibliography

Salisbury, Harrison Evans, 1908-1993
Salisbury, Harrison Evans. A journey for our times; a memoir; [by] Harrison E. Salisbury. Harper & Row 1983 546p il o.p.; Carroll & Graf Pubs. paperback available $10.95   **92**
ISBN 0-88184-037-8 (pa)   LC 81-47904
"A Cornelia & Michael Bessie book"
In this autobiography "Salisbury relives his childhood, his work as a UPI reporter during the Depression, his World War II journalistic adventures in the U.S. and London, and his poignant years in Russia." Booklist

Sandburg, Carl, 1878-1967

Callahan, North. Carl Sandburg; his life and works. Pennsylvania State Univ. Press 1987 258p il $29.75   **92**

ISBN 0-271-00486-X   LC 86-43031

"North Callahan has written a creditable biography of the writer and the man, often using his own extensive recollections of the poet. . . . He has enhanced this work with telling anecdotes that give the man from Galesburg, Ill., a dimension beyond the printed page." N Y Times Book Rev

Includes bibliography

Niven, Penelope. Carl Sandburg; a biography. Scribner 1991 843p il $35   **92**

ISBN 0-684-19251-9   LC 90-20664

"A Robert Stewart book"

The author presents Sandburg, the "son of immigrant Swedes in his roles as hobo, soldier, journalist, orator, socialist, biographer of Abraham Lincoln and poet." Publ Wkly

"Niven has done a notable job in humanizing Sandburg through the portrayal of his family life and in outlining some of his professional torments and struggles." Booklist

Includes bibliography

Sanger, Margaret, 1879-1966

Chesler, Ellen. Woman of valor: Margaret Sanger and the birth control movement in America. Simon & Schuster 1992 639p il $27.50   **92**

1. Birth control

ISBN 0-671-60088-5   LC 92-11496

Also available in paperback from Anchor Bks.

"Margaret Sanger's belief in the right of women to control their lives and bodies drove her to dedicate her life to making sex education and contraception available to all women. Risking imprisonment, she opened the first American birth-control clinic in 1916 and wrote groundbreaking publications about female sexuality and reproductive choices. . . . Chesler not only tracks Sanger's eventful life, but also articulates the moral, medical, and political aspects of the ongoing debate over birth control." Am Libr

Includes bibliographic references

Saroyan, William, 1908-1981

Saroyan, William. Chance meetings. Norton 1978 135p hardcover o.p. paperback available $3.50   **92**

ISBN 0-393-00969-6 (pa)   LC 77-17505

The author describes "the encounters he has had from boyhood and young manhood in Fresno and San Francisco to his years of 'fame' in New York and Paris." Publ Wkly

Saroyan's "special ability to see a wholeness, a unity, in an episode . . . makes him a great storyteller." NY Times Book Rev

Sarton, May, 1912-

Sarton, May. After the stroke; a journal. Norton 1988 280p il hardcover o.p. paperback available $5.95   **92**

ISBN 0-393-30630-5 (pa)   LC 87-18562

Also available G.K. Hall large print edition

"Sarton suffered a stroke at the age of 73. This journal detailing her year-long, arduous recovery is a brutally honest look at the pain and debilitation that come with illness." Booklist

Sarton, May. At seventy; a journal. Norton 1984 334p il hardcover o.p. paperback available $9.95   **92**

ISBN 0-393-31030-2 (pa)   LC 83-19369

The author is "willing to grapple with the hard facts of experience—old age, the death of close friends, her homosexuality—and she writes about them with characteristic honesty and insight. Moreover, she is a keen observer, and her reflections on a great variety of topics give this book its spark." N Y Times Book Rev

Sarton, May. Encore; a journal of the eightieth year. Norton 1993 332p il $21.95   **92**

ISBN 0-393-03529-8   LC 92-40014

"Throughout this minutely detailed journal, poet and novelist Sarton emphasizes one's individual obligation to be as happy as possible yet remain aware of the suffering that cripples the lives of others." Libr J

Sarton, May. Endgame; a journal of the seventy-ninth year. Norton 1992 345p il $21.95   **92**

ISBN 0-393-03346-5   LC 91-30172

"Like all of Sarton's journals, this is a testament to the joys of nature from a courageous and loving woman. It is different from the others . . . in that now, at age 79 and living alone in her house in Maine, she must struggle with frailty and illness that make fierce inroads on her independence." Publ Wkly

Sarton, May. The house by the sea; a journal; photographs by Beverly Hallam. Norton 1977 287p il hardcover o.p. paperback available $5.95   **92**

ISBN 0-393-00069-9 (pa)   LC 77-7490

This installment in the author's journal includes thoughts on international crises, memorials to friends, and the writing life

Sarton, May. Journal of a solitude. Norton 1973 208p il hardcover o.p. paperback available $8.95   **92**

ISBN 0-393-30928-2 (pa)

"This is a year-long account of Sarton's struggle to come to terms with herself and her creative potential. . . . Although Sarton knows she has much to be thankful for, she's dissatisfied with her progress both as human being and as artist. Her fears are subtly enervating." Libr J

Sarton, May. Plant dreaming deep. Norton 1968 189p il hardcover o.p. paperback available $5.95   **92**

ISBN 0-393-30108-7 (pa)

Also available in hardcover from P. Smith

In this memoir the author "tells how she bought a house in a small New Hampshire town, how she remade it, what she experienced as the seasons passed, and what she learned from the house, its surroundings, and the village." Saturday Rev

Sarton, May, 1912-—*Continued*

This is a "small, but tender and often poignant book by a woman of many insights." N Y Times Book Rev

Sarton, May. A world of light; portraits and celebrations. Norton 1976 254p il hardcover o.p. paperback available $4.95
92

ISBN 0-393-30500-7 (pa)

"Poet-novelist Sarton's long, successful artistic career has been blessed by the friendship of many extraordinary people, including her mother and father. Here, in a dozen reminiscences, she brings to life men and women now dead who left indelible marks on her body and spirit." Publ Wkly

Sartre, Jean Paul, 1905-1980

Cohen-Solal, Annie. Sartre: a life; translated by Anna Cancogni; edited by Norman MacAfee. Pantheon Bks. 1987 591p il hardcover o.p. paperback available $12.95
92

ISBN 0-394-75662-2 (pa)   LC 86-42615

Original French edition, 1985

This book "chronicles Sartre's odd, fatherless childhood, his meteoric rise to the front ranks of French intellectual life, his drastic ideological shifts and changes, his consistent failures in practical politics and his equally consistent successes as a lover of women." Newsweek

"An engaging and highly readable biography. The vivid narration moves at a quick pace and is almost journalistic in its attention to detail and to the extensive reporting of facts and events." Choice

Includes bibliography

Gerassi, John. Jean-Paul Sartre; hated conscience of his century. v1: Protestant or protester? University of Chicago Press 1989 213p il $19.95
92

ISBN 0-226-28797-1   LC 88-27945

This first volume of a biography of the French philosopher and writer covers the years from his birth through the end of World War II

"A dazzlingly original work. . . . 'Jean-Paul Sartre'is an intellectual biography that effectively explores the complexities of Sartre's thinking and the successive philosophical and political positions he espoused and publicized." N Y Times Book Rev

Includes bibliography

Hayman, Ronald. Sartre; a life. Simon & Schuster 1987 572p il $19.95
92

ISBN 0-671-45942-2   LC 86-29842

Also available in paperback from Carroll & Graf Pubs.

A "portrait that chronicles Sartre's professional and private lives in detail. The book captures the link between thought and political action that best characterizes Sartre's experiences and also describes his influential relationships, not only with Beauvior but also with a whole range of notable writers and celebrities of his time." Booklist

Includes bibliography

Sartre, Jean Paul. Witness to my life; the letters of Jean-Paul Sartre to Simone de Beauvoir, 1926-1939; edited by Simone de Beauvoir; translated by Lee Fahnestock and Norman McAfee. Scribner 1992 448p $27.50
92

ISBN 0-684-19338-8   LC 92-5068

Original French edition, 1983

This is a translation of letters written by the French philosopher between 1926, when he was a student at the Ecole Normale Superieure in Paris, and the beginning of World War II. In addition to Simone de Beauvoir, the correspondents include Simone Jollivet and Louise Vedrine

"This collection offers an accessible and rounded version of the relationship between de Beauvoir and Sartre. The collection includes several letters to others important to both of them, so that Sartre's relationship with de Beauvoir is illuminated by his discussion of her with others." Libr J

Includes bibliography

Sartre, Jean Paul. The words; translated from the French by Bernard Frechtman. Braziller 1964 255p o.p.; Vintage Bks. paperback available $10
92

ISBN 0-394-74709-7 (pa)

The French existentialist writer "examines the formation of his character during his childhood years, which were passed in a completely adult world between his widowed mother and her parents. The central event of his childhood was the discovery of the world of words, of language." Libr J

Scarlatti, Domenico. See class 780.92

Schreiber, Le Anne

Schreiber, Le Anne. Midstream. Viking 1990 309p il o.p.; Penguin Bks. paperback available $8.95
92

ISBN 0-14-012187-0 (pa)   LC 89-40345

"At forty, journalist Schreiber (Time and the New York Times) decided to . . . leave behind her career. The same season in which she began house hunting in the rural Catskills, her mother was diagnosed as having pancreatic cancer. . . . [The author aims to] balance her own and her family's experiences of her mother's . . . [dying] with a parallel account of her search for spiritual rebirth in the country." Libr J

"If 'Midstream' were no more than another record of a painful progress toward death, there'd be little point in reading it. It is instead a book about how the lingering death of an uncooperative and demanding parent affected a daughter, of the toll it took on her." Newsweek

Schumann, Clara. See class 780.92

Schwarzkopf, H. Norman

Cohen, Roger. In the eye of the storm: the life of General H. Norman Schwarzkopf; [by] Roger Cohen, Claudio Gatti. Farrar, Straus & Giroux 1991 342p il maps $19.95
92

ISBN 0-374-17708-2   LC 91-15581

Schwarzkopf, H. Norman—*Continued*
Also available G.K. Hall large print edition and in paperback from Berkley Pub. Group

This biography of the U.S. general covers his life in the military, his family, and his role in the Persian Gulf War

"On the whole it is a rather serious and highly readable book that provides important insights into the general, especially into his origins, character and psychology." N Y Times Book Rev

Schwarzkopf, H. Norman. It doesn't take a hero: General H. Norman Schwarzkopf; the autobiography; written with Peter Petre. Bantam Bks. 1992 530p il maps $25   **92**
1. Persian Gulf War, 1991
ISBN 0-553-08944-7   LC 92-20762
Also available in large print from Doubleday

"The whole book is a description of General Schwarzkopf's relations with people. It is remarkably emotional. To an unusual degree he sees events as secondary to the personalities he has been affected by. He emphasizes his sensitive side. . . . 'It Doesn't Take a Hero' is not a military record. . . . It covers the gulf war, of course, but General Schwarzkopf devotes so much space to his life before that event that he has produced two books in one." N Y Times Book Rev

Includes bibliographic references

Schweitzer, Albert, 1875-1965
Bentley, James. Albert Schweitzer: the enigma. HarperCollins Pubs. 1992 208p $20   **92**

ISBN 0-06-016364-X   LC 91-50458
This biography of Albert Schweitzer "traces the theological and philosophical development of this 20th-century avatar of morality, placing him in the German tradition. The author provides ample detail about Schweitzer's tormented childhood, the teachers who shaped his character and intellect, his musical brilliance . . . his visits to a psychiatrist. Entering the long-standing controversy about his missionary work in Africa, Bentley offers evidence to refute those who brand Schweitzer a racist." Publ Wkly

Includes bibliographic references

Schweitzer, Albert. Out of my life and thought; an autobiography; newly translated by A. B. Lemke; preface by Rhena Schweitzer Miller and A. B. Lemke. rev ed. Holt & Co. 1990 272p il $24.95; pa $12.95   **92**

ISBN 0-8050-1467-5; 0-8050-1862-X (pa)
    LC 90-37697
First English translation by C. T. Campion published 1933

This is "the autobiography of the world-famous missionary doctor, organist, philosopher, theologian, and Nobel Peace Prize winner, newly translated, researched, and corrected." Booklist

Includes bibliographic references

Scott, Paul, 1920-1978
Spurling, Hilary. Paul Scott; a life of the author of the Raj quartet. Norton 1991 438p il $24.95   **92**
ISBN 0-393-02938-7   LC 91-11762

This biography of the British writer "explores his family background in North London, his war years in India and the Far East, his experiences as a literary agent, and the development of his fiction and the people on whom his most famous characters were based." Publisher's note

The author "has woven a seamless story of a complex, troubled and conflicted man so that even those who haven't read a word of Scott's work can still enjoy her book. It is remarkably rich in its understanding of human psychology and its mastery of the biographers's art." N Y Times Book Rev

Scribner, Charles, 1921-
Scribner, Charles. In the company of writers; a life in publishing; [by] Charles Scribner, Jr.; based on the oral history by Joel R. Gardner. Scribner 1990 193p il $22.50   **92**
1. Charles Scribner's Sons
ISBN 0-684-19250-0   LC 90-33309
"Begun as a series of interviews for the Columbia Oral History Project, this book is an informal account of Scribner's life and career. . . . His wonderful anecdotes about Ernest Hemingway, Max Perkins, and P. D. James are the chief attractions." Booklist

Sedgwick, Edie, 1943-1971
Stein, Jean. Edie; an American biography; edited with George Plimpton. Knopf 1982 455p il o.p.; Delacorte Press paperback available $10.95   **92**
ISBN 0-385-29791-2 (pa)   LC 81-48118
A biographical pastiche of the model and Warhol film star who died from an overdose of barbituates at the age of 28

"This is oral history as it should be. The interviewing is probing and encyclopedic, but the editing is truly extraordinary." Ms

Seeger, Pete. See class 780.92

Seldes, George, 1890-
Seldes, George. Witness to a century; encounters with the noted, the notorious, and the three SOBs. Ballantine Bks. 1987 xxi, 490p il $19.95; pa $12.95   **92**
ISBN 0-345-33181-8; 0-345-35329-3 (pa)
    LC 86-47804
These memoirs are "built . . . around the personalities, major and minor, that [Seldes] encountered from the time that he took his first newspaper job, on the Pittsburgh Leader, on February 9, 1909." Columbia J Rev

"Woodrow Wilson, Bernard Baruch, Eleanor Roosevelt, Cole Porter, Errol Flynn, Sinclair Lewis, and a hundred less-celebrated travelers through Seldes's century pass quickly on and off the stage, leaving indelible impressions through Seldes's deft and very human sketches." Christ Sci Monit

Selzer, Richard

Selzer, Richard. Down from Troy; a doctor comes of age. Morrow 1992 300p $20 **92**

ISBN 0-688-09715-4   LC 91-39541

The author "traces the arc of his life from his 1930s childhood in Troy, N.Y., through his medical training and career as a surgeon in New Haven, Conn., to his retirement in 1985. He returns again and again here to his boyhood home near Albany, where he lived with his artistic mother, a singer who expected him to become a writer, his admired older brother Billy and his father, a general practitioner." Publ Wkly

"This is a terrible beauty of a book, full of love and pain and a palpable rich sadness that will stay with a reader forever. This is Selzer's finest work." Libr J

Selznick, David O., 1902-1965

Thomson, David. Showman: the life of David O. Selznick. Knopf 1992 792p il $35 **92**

1. Motion picture industry
ISBN 0-394-56833-8   LC 91-47886

This is a biography of the producer of such films as Dinner at Eight, King Kong, David Copperfield, Gone With the Wind, Rebecca, Since You Went Away, Duel in the Sun, and Portrait of Jennie

"The story Mr. Thomson tells is rich in film scholarship and richer in human drama, astute and sensitive to the tenous border between personal and professional narratives in show business lives." N Y Times Book Rev

Includes bibliography

Seurat, Georges Pierre. See class 709.2

Sexton, Anne

Middlebrook, Diane Wood. Anne Sexton; a biography. Houghton Mifflin 1991 xxiii, 488p il $24.45 **92**

ISBN 0-395-35362-9   LC 91-13701

Also available in paperback from Vintage Bks.

"A Peter Davison book"

For this biography of the troubled American confessional poet the author "plumbed psychiatric records, including tapes made of therapy sessions; interviewed family members, fellow poets, friends and lovers; and closely read the poems themselves to reconstruct Sexton's life—its interior sequences and external chronology." Publ Wkly

"Ms. Middlebrook has written a wonderful book: just, balanced, insightful, complex in its sympathies and in it's judgment of Sexton both as a person and as a writer." N Y Times Book Rev

Includes bibliographic references

Shaw, Bernard, 1856-1950

Holroyd, Michael. Bernard Shaw. Random House 1988-1993 4v il **92**

LC 88-42660

Also available in paperback (v3-4 in a combined edition)

Contents: v1 1856-1898, The search for love $24.95 (ISBN 0-394-52577-9); v2 1898-1918, The pursuit of power $24.95 (ISBN 0-394-57553-9); v3 1918-1950, The lure of fantasy $30 (ISBN 0-394-57554-7); v4 1950-1991,

The last laugh $34.50 (ISBN 0-679-41987-X)

Includes bibliographic references

Shelley, Mary Wollstonecraft, 1797-1851

Spark, Muriel. Mary Shelley. Dutton 1987 248p il o.p.; New Am. Lib. paperback available $8.95 **92**

ISBN 0-452-00951-0 (pa)   LC 86-31901

"A William Abrahams book"

A revision of the author's Child of light, first published 1951 in the United Kingdom

"Spark covers the facts of Mary's life (her upbringing, elopement with Shelley, friendship with Byron, the struggle to support herself and her son by the pen after Shelley's death); in part two she brings her astute critical intelligence to bear on Mary's novels, principally 'Frankenstein' and the futuristic 'The Last Man,' and Mary's posthumous editing of Shelley's poetry." Publ Wkly

Includes bibliography

Sunstein, Emily W. Mary Shelley; romance and reality. Little, Brown 1989 478p il $24.95 **92**

ISBN 0-316-82246-9   LC 88-12990

Also available in paperback from Johns Hopkins Univ. Press

A "revisionist account of a woman who 'literally embodies the English Romantic movement'. . . . Sunstein provides substantial documentation of the breadth of Shelley's education and the extent of her writing. . . . Most rewarding, perhaps, are Sunstein's astute insights into Shelley's emotional life." Choice

Includes bibliography

Shelley, Percy Bysshe, 1792-1822

Holmes, Richard. Shelley: the pursuit. Dutton 1975 c1974 829p il o.p.; Penguin Bks. paperback available $12.95 **92**

ISBN 0-14-058037-9 (pa)

First published 1974 in the United Kingdom

"Holmes delves deeply into records and studies pertaining to Percy Bysshe Shelley to reassess the English Romantic poet and his works." Booklist

Includes bibliography

Sherman, William T. (William Tecumseh), 1820-1891

Marszalek, John F. Sherman; a soldier's passion for order. Free Press 1993 635p il $29.95 **92**

1. United States—History—1861-1865, Civil War
ISBN 0-02-920135-7   LC 92-24533

This "biography depicts William Tecumseh Sherman (1820-1891) as unable to accept disorder and uncertainty because of an unstable childhood, reinforced by economic failure in post-Jacksonian America. The Civil War offered the general both an ultimate challenge and an ultimate opportunity. . . . This provocative volume stands as an outstanding modern study of one of this country's great public figures." Publ Wkly

Includes bibliography

Shevchenko, Arkady N.

Shevchenko, Arkady N. Breaking with Moscow. Knopf 1985 378p $18.95 **92**

1. Soviet Union—Foreign relations
ISBN 0-394-52055-6 LC 85-5204

Also available in paperback from Ballatine Bks.

"Shevchenko was a top advisor to the Soviet Foreign Ministry and the Politburo and an Under Secretary General of the United Nations who became the highest-ranking Soviet official ever to go over to the West. He tells his story here." Natl Rev

This work "contains an abundance of unique material and intimate details about the functioning of Soviet foreign policy." Commentary

Includes bibliographic references

Shirer, William L. (William Lawrence)

Shirer, William L. (William Lawrence). 20th century journey; a memoir of a life and the times. Little, Brown 1976-1990 3v il **92**

LC 84-21279

v1 available only in paperback from Bantam Bks.; v2-3 available in hardcover and paperback from Bantam Bks.

Contents: v1 The start, 1904-1930; v2 The nightmare years, 1930-1940 ($29.95 ISBN 0-316-78703-5); v3 A native's return, 1945-1988 ($24.95 ISBN 0-316-78713-2)

"The books of journalist Shirer have been received with excitement by a wide audience for many years, and the reasons are clear: with great powers of description and analysis, he is able to reconstruct the pivotal events in international politics and government over the past half century." Booklist

Shoemaker, Bill, 1931-

Shoemaker, Bill. Shoemaker; [by] Bill Shoemaker and Barney Nagler. Doubleday 1988 267p il $17.95 **92**

ISBN 0-385-23945-9 LC 87-28743

"The autobiography of Bill Shoemaker, the greatest race-rider ever to grace the American turf, will be of intense interest to any devotee of thoroughbred racing. . . . The jockey's judgments and opinions about the game carry a unique stamp of authority, and he isn't shy about making pronouncements." Booklist

Sills, Beverly. See class 780.92

Simenon, Georges, 1903-1989

Simenon, Georges. Intimate memoirs; including Marie-Jo's book; translated by Harold J. Salemson. Harcourt Brace Jovanovich 1984 815p $22.95 **92**

ISBN 0-15-144892-2 LC 83-18679

"A Helen and Kurt Wolff book"

"This massive work begins in 1980, two years after Simenon's daughter Marie-Jo committed suicide, and flashes back through time as an apologia to her for his life. . . . In tracing his rise from a poor Belgian clerk to a prolific, wealthy, and internationally acclaimed mystery writer, Simenon vividly details his passion for life." Booklist

Simon, Herbert Alexander, 1916-

Simon, Herbert Alexander. Models of my life; [by] Herbert A. Simon. Basic Bks. 1991 xxix, 415p il $26.95; pa $15 **92**

ISBN 0-465-04640-1; 0-465-04641-X (pa)

LC 90-55595

"The Alfred P. Sloan Foundation series"

"The autobiography of an intellectual, this volume traces the dauntingly diverse career of a pioneer in artificial intelligence. Aside from his work in computer science, Simon has achieved important breakthroughs in economics (Nobel laureate), political theory, and cognitive psychology." Booklist

Includes bibliographic references

Simon, Kate

Simon, Kate. Etchings in an hourglass. Harper & Row 1990 240p hardcover o.p. paperback available $9.95 **92**

ISBN 0-06-092080-7 (pa) LC 89-46117

Sequel to: Bronx primitive (1982); A wider world (1986)

"In the third volume of her memoirs . . . travel writer Simon recalls the joys and sorrows of her adult life." Libr J

"Few people in our time have so keenly remembered, and so frankly recounted in print, the vagaries, defeats, successes and losses of a gallant and independent life." N Y Times Book Rev

Simon, Paul. See class 780.92

Singer, Isaac Bashevis, 1904-1991

Singer, Isaac Bashevis. In my father's court. Farrar, Straus & Giroux 1966 307p hardcover o.p. paperback available $12 **92**

1. Jews—Poland
ISBN 0-374-50592-6 (pa)

"A series of reminiscences of the author's childhood, focused on the Beth Din, the rabbinical court that is a fundamental part of Jewish institutions." Best Sellers

"These penetrating, philosophical little studies of human nature faithfully show the richness of life, the volatile emotions, the depth of religious feeling in old-time Jewish Warsaw." Publ Wkly

Smith, Joseph, 1805-1844

Brodie, Fawn McKay. No man knows my history: the life of Joseph Smith, the Mormon prophet; by Fawn M. Brodie. 2nd ed rev and enl. Knopf 1971 499, xx p il $35 **92**

1. Mormons
ISBN 0-394-46967-4

First published 1945

Taking as her title a phrase from a sermon by Joseph Smith himself, the author has attempted to discover as much of the truth concerning Joseph Smith and the beginnings of Mormonism, as can be found in an intensive research into documents, diaries, unpublished manuscripts, etc.

Includes bibliography

Smith, Red, 1905-1982

Berkow, Ira. Red: a biography of Red Smith. Times Bks. 1986 302p il $17.95
92

ISBN 0-8129-1203-9   LC 85-40829

A biography of the Pulitzer Prize-winning sports columnist whose career spanned 55 years with the Milwaukee Sentinel, the New York Herald Tribune and finally the New York Times

Includes bibliography

Smith, Stevie, 1902-1971

Barbera, Jack. Stevie: a biography of Stevie Smith; [by] Jack Barbera and William McBrien. Oxford Univ. Press 1987 c1985 378p il $35; pa $10.95   **92**

ISBN 0-19-520549-9; 0-19-505657-4 (pa)
          LC 86-23916

First published 1985 in the United Kingdom

"Using a large number of Smith's poems in whole and in lengthy excerpts to illustrate both her expressions as a poet and the artistic uses she made of her personal experiences, this book is a thorough and engrossing record of a notable career." Booklist

Includes bibliography

Snider, Duke, 1926-

Snider, Duke. The Duke of Flatbush; [by] Duke Snider, with Bill Gilbert; introduction by Carl Erskine. Kensington Pub. Corp. 1988 288p il $17.95; pa $3.95   **92**

ISBN 0-8217-2469-X; 0-8217-2698-6 (pa)
          LC 88-50408

"A Zebra book"

"Snider joined the Brooklyn Dodgers in the same year as Jackie Robinson, relocated with the team to Los Angeles, then played with the Mets and the San Francisco Giants in the twilight of his career. With co-author Gilbert, . . . 'The Dook,' as he was dubbed in Flatbush, tells the story of those years excitingly and movingly." Publ Wkly

Soyinka, Wole

Soyinka, Wole. Aké; the years of childhood. Random House 1981 230p $14.95; pa $11   **92**

ISBN 0-394-52807-7; 0-679-72540-7 (pa)
          LC 82-40148

The "African dramatist, poet, novelist, and critic recreates his childhood. . . . In the western Nigerian village of Aké he grew up in an environment both Yoruba and Christian, initiated into traditional African cults but also steeped in Christian teachings by his father Essay, headmaster of a primary school, and his mother, aptly nicknamed Wild Christian." Libr J

"Soyinka's account of the first eleven years of his life is delightful. Soyinka excels at the difficult task of credibly capturing the child's point of view." World Lit Today

Springsteen, Bruce. See class 780.92

Stafford, Jean, 1915-1979

Goodman, Charlotte Margolis. Jean Stafford: the savage heart. University of Tex. Press 1990 394p il $24.95   **92**

ISBN 0-292-74022-0   LC 89-37293

"Goodman's biography of the American fiction writer shows how Stafford took the raw materials of her often unhappy lot in life and made out of these sad experiences a memorable body of work. Sketching these connections between life and art, Goodman traces her subject's impoverished childhood and sorts through a series of unsettling family relationships." Booklist

Includes bibliographic references

Hulbert, Ann. The interior castle: the art and life of Jean Stafford. Knopf 1992 430p il $25   **92**

ISBN 0-394-55704-2   LC 91-22978

Hulbert "traces her subject's childhood in Colorado and California, probing Stafford's uneasy family relationships, particularly with her father, a failed writer, and follows the writer East and into her marriages to Robert Lowell, Oliver Jensen and A. J. Liebling." Publ Wkly

The author "avoids jargon and reductive readings while providing a thorough analysis of Stafford's work and its literary context." Libr J

Includes bibliographic references

Stalin, Joseph, 1879-1953

Bullock, Alan. Hitler and Stalin. See entry under Hitler, Adolf, 1889-1945   **92**

Conquest, Robert. Stalin; breaker of nations. Viking 1991 346p il $25   **92**

1. Soviet Union—Politics and government
ISBN 0-670-84089-0   LC 91-28782

Also available in paperback from Penguin Bks.

The author "portrays the Soviet dictator as an insufferably rude husband, a Georgian who hated his roots and Russified himself, a crude boor who yearned to be a backslapping man to the people." Publ Wkly

"Intended for the general reader, [this work] provides a superb portrait of the man who terrorized his country for 30 years. . . . Briskly written, authoritative yet not pedantic, filled with interesting incidents and anecdotes, [it] makes for fascinating reading." N Y Times Book Rev

Includes bibliographic references

Deutscher, Isaac. Stalin; a political biography. 2nd ed. Oxford Univ. Press 1967 c1966 661p il pa $17.95   **92**

1. Soviet Union—Politics and government
ISBN 0-19-500273-3

First published 1949

This biography is neither an apologia for, nor an indictment of, Stalin, but an attempt to describe and analyze his complex role and personality with as much detachment as is possible. The author shows the forces that shaped Stalin's life and placed him in the dominating position on the Russian scene

Includes bibliography

Stanton, Elizabeth Cady, 1815-1902

Griffith, Elisabeth. In her own right: the life of Elizabeth Cady Stanton. Oxford Univ. Press 1984 xx, 268p il hardcover o.p. paperback available $12.95   92

1. Feminism

ISBN 0-19-503729-4 (pa)   LC 83-25120

A "portrait of the radical feminist leader whose crusade for women's suffrage antedated that of her close friend and rival, Susan B. Anthony, by three years. Stanton's broader aims of total independence for herself and for all women conflicted with those of other reformers who focused on specific goals such as abolition." Publ Wkly

Includes bibliographic references

Steffan, Joseph

Steffan, Joseph. Honor bound; a gay American fights for the right to serve his country. Villard Bks. 1992 245p il $22.50   92

ISBN 0-679-41660-9   LC 92-53654

"Discharged from the U.S. Naval Academy in 1987 for being a homosexual, Steffan filed suit a year later challenging the regulations that ban gays and lesbians from the armed services. In this memoir he narrates his discovery and affirmation of his sexual identity, then criticizes Annapolis for intolerance and inflexibility." Publ Wkly

This "is more than just a book about a young gay man who wants to serve his country in the U.S. Navy. It is an interesting, timely account of life in a military academy." Libr J

Steffens, Lincoln, 1866-1936

Kaplan, Justin. Lincoln Steffens; a biography. Simon & Schuster 1974 380p il hardcover o.p. paperback available $12.95   92

ISBN 0-671-22035-7 (pa)

"Kaplan's approach is a traditional, chronological one, carrying the reader from Steffins' California boyhood through his early years as a journalist-reformer, and then to his dalliance with Bohemia, his flirtation with fascism, and to the connubial bliss he ultimately found with Bolshevism. It is the portrayal of this intellectual and emotional odyssey from reformer to revolutionary that rightfully stands out." Choice

Includes bibliographic references

Steffens, Lincoln. The autobiography of Lincoln Steffens. Harcourt Brace & Co. 1931 2v il   92

v1 o.p.; v2 available in paperback for $10.95 (ISBN 0-15-609396-0)

The life of an American reporter, journalist, student of ethics and politics

"Here is a text-book on journalism; a treasure house for the historian of that wave of social idealism that shook the United States from 1900 to 1917; a casebook for the psychologist of political types. Above all it is the vivid diary of a bold and humane pilgrim." Survey

Stein, Gertrude, 1874-1946

Mellow, James R. Charmed circle: Gertrude Stein & company. Praeger Pubs. 1974 528p il o.p.; Houghton Mifflin paperback available $12.70   92

ISBN 0-395-47982-7 (pa)

An account of the artists, writers and musicians drawn to Gertrude Stein's salon in early 20th century Paris

"Drawn primarily from memoirs and letters, [this study] consolidates rather than extends our understanding of an extraordinary time and its heroic actors." N Y Times Book Rev

Includes bibliography

Stein, Gertrude. The autobiography of Alice B. Toklas. Modern Lib. 1993 342p $14.50; pa $9   92

1. Toklas, Alice B. 2. Paris (France)—Intellectual life

ISBN 0-679-60081-7; 0-679-72463-X (pa)

LC 93-15339

Also available in hardcover from P. Smith

First published 1933 by Harcourt Brace & Co.

"The book is really Stein's autobiography, presented as though written by her secretary, Alice Toklas. The book provoked a rejoinder from various Parisian artists and writers, *Testimony Against Gertrude Stein* (1935). . . . For the average reader, however, Stein's book holds much fascination in its views of Parisian life and personalities, and the whole is offered in a genuinely witty style." Benet's Reader's Ency of Am Lit

Steinbeck, John, 1902-1968

Steinbeck, John. Conversations with John Steinbeck; edited by Thomas Fensch. University Press of Miss. 1988 xxi, 116p (Literary conversations ser) $32.50; pa $14.95   92

ISBN 0-87805-359-X; 0-87805-360-3 (pa)

LC 88-17538

"This collection of Steinbeck's interviews allows him to speak on his own behalf in an illuminating expression of his intentions, goals, and achievements. From the beginning of his career through his last years the interviews reveal a fascinating, controversial, and captivating personality." Univ Press Books for Second Sch Libr

Includes bibliography

Stengel, Casey

Creamer, Robert W. Stengel; his life and times. Simon & Schuster 1984 349p il hardcover o.p. paperback available $9.95   92

ISBN 0-671-70131-2 (pa)   LC 83-17508

"Casey Stengel is remembered as either the shrewd, innovative New York Yankee manager who won 10 pennants and seven World Series from 1949 to 1960 or as the seemingly senile, aged master of malaprop who (mis)managed the legendarily inept New York Mets in the early 1960s. Creamer . . . dissolves the apparently disparate images and melds them into an inclusive vision of an unexpectedly complex man." Booklist

Stevens, Wallace, 1879-1955

Richardson, Joan. Wallace Stevens. Beech Tree Bks. 1986-1988 2v il v1 $21.95; v2 $27.95 **92**

LC 86-5393

Contents: [v1] The early years, 1879-1923 (ISBN 0-688-05401-3); [v2] The later years, 1923-1955 (ISBN 0-688-06860-X)

A look at both the public and private life of the influential American poet, aesthetician, and insurance executive

Includes bibliographies

Stevenson, Adlai E. (Adlai Ewing), 1900-1965

McKeever, Porter. Adlai Stevenson: his life and legacy. Morrow 1989 591p il $25; pa $14.95 **92**

ISBN 0-688-06661-5; 0-688-10387-1 (pa)

LC 89-30055

A biography of "the former Governor of Illinois, Presidential candidate and United Nations Ambassador. . . . The book takes us from his family roots to his childhood and up through the world of public service." West Coast Rev Books

"If Stevenson is remembered more for his words than his deeds, more for his phrases than his ideas or policies, all the more reason to quote him extensively, as Mr. McKeever does. If it was Stevenson's private life that makes compelling reading, all the more reason to show it in its full turmoil, complexity and emotion, as Mr. McKeever does." N Y Times Book Rev

Includes bibliography

Stieglitz, Alfred. See class 709.2

Stone, I. F. (Isidor Feinstein), 1907-1989

Cottrell, Robert C. Izzy: a biography of I. F. Stone. Rutgers Univ. Press 1992 388p il $25.95 **92**

ISBN 0-8135-1847-4   LC 91-45763

This is a biography of the "journalist, muckraker, and indomitable critic of the Establishment. An editorialist at the *New York Post* during the Depression, Stone went on to chronicle the rise of McCarthyism, the fall of segregation, and the emergence of the anti-Vietnam War movement. His newspaper, *I.F. Stone Weekly*, which ran from 1953-1971, exposed many forms of corruption at the highest levels of government." Libr J

Includes bibliographic references

Strasberg, Susan

Strasberg, Susan. Marilyn and me. See entry under Monroe, Marilyn, 1926-1962 **92**

Stuart, Gilbert. See class 709.2

Stuart, Jeb, 1833-1864

Thomas, Emory M. Bold dragoon: the life of J.E.B. Stuart. Harper & Row 1986 354p il maps o.p.; Vintage Bks. paperback available $8.95 **92**

1. United States—History—1861-1865, Civil War
ISBN 0-394-75775-0 (pa)   LC 85-45577

The life and military exploits of the controversial Confederate officer

Thomas "makes scattered and complex cavalry actions admirably clear. More important, he examines with sympathy but without sentimentality the process by which a high-spirited, ambitious and rather insecure young man managed to make himself a demigod." N Y Times Book Rev

Includes bibliography

Sturges, Preston

Jacobs, Diane. Christmas in July: the life and art of Preston Sturges. University of Calif. Press 1992 525p il $30 **92**

ISBN 0-520-07926-4   LC 92-19690

A critical biography of the American filmmaker

"An insightful and highly perceptive biography of comic film master Sturges. Jacobs brings Sturges fully to life in all his creative, egotistical, generous, and contradictory glory." Libr J

Includes bibliography

Sullivan, Anne, 1866-1936

Lash, Joseph P. Helen and teacher: the story of Helen Keller and Anne Sullivan Macy. See entry under Keller, Helen, 1880-1968 **92**

Swift, Jonathan, 1667-1745

Nokes, David. Jonathan Swift, a hypocrite reversed; a critical biography. Oxford Univ. Press 1985 427p il $35 **92**

ISBN 0-19-812834-7   LC 85-5657

A biography of Swift from his early life and his early poetry, through his declining years, portraying his various roles as satirist, politician, churchman and friend

"Throughout, Nokes's comments on Swift's works are fresh and sensible. He uses Swift's obsessively autobiographical verse well." Times Lit Suppl

Includes bibliographic references

Taulbert, Clifton L.

Taulbert, Clifton L. Once upon a time when we were colored. Council Oak Bks. 1989 153p il $16.95; pa $9.95 **92**

ISBN 0-933031-19-X; 0-933031-34-3 (pa)

LC 88-63115

"A businessman included in 'Time' magazine's . . . issue on blacks 'making it in white America,' the author lives with his wife and childen in Tulsa, Okla. It's a long way from tiny Glen Allen, Miss., where Taulbert grew up in the 1950s, a time and place he describes

Taulbert, Clifton L.—*Continued*
with love in this funny, sweet, touching memoir." Publ Wkly

Taylor, Maxwell D., 1901-1987
Taylor, John M. General Maxwell Taylor; the sword and the pen; foreword by Lewis F. Powell, Jr. Doubleday 1989 457p il o.p.; Bantam Bks. paperback available $5.99 **92**
ISBN 0-553-29159-9 (pa)   LC 88-31055
A "biography of General Maxwell D. Taylor, commander of the 101st Airborne Division in World War II, the Eighth Army at the end of the Korean War, and twice chairman of the Joint Chiefs of Staff. . . . The author is Taylor's son, but what he may lack in objectivity does not affect the thoroughness of his research or the excellence of his writing." Booklist

Includes bibliographic references

Taylor, Paul, 1930-
Taylor, Paul. Private domain. Knopf 1987 371p il $22.95   **92**
ISBN 0-394-51683-4   LC 86-45366
Dancer/choreographer "Taylor's insights on fellow artists—Graham, Balanchine, Robert Rauschenberg—are unusually trenchant and fresh. The book is blessedly free of the cleaned-up quality that such memoirs often have. . . . For readers who want to hear about pressures and strains on the professional dancer—the drugs, the drink, the penury—they are all here." Time

Tecumseh, Shawnee Chief, 1768-1813
Eckert, Allan W. A sorrow in our heart: the life of Tecumseh. Bantam Bks. 1992 862p maps $27.50; pa $6.99   **92**
1. Shawnee Indians
ISBN 0-553-08023-7; 0-553-56174-X (pa)
                                LC 91-31858
This is a "narrative biography of Tecumseh, the remarkable Shawnee warrior and statesman who succeeded in organizing a group of disparate tribes into a cohesive confederacy of nations. . . . Eckert places his subject firmly within his proper social and historical context by providing a tremendous amount of meticulously researched and authenticated background information, including illuminating details of tribal life and Shawnee culture." Booklist

Includes bibliographic references

Gilbert, Bil. God gave us this country; Tekamthi and the first American Civil War. Atheneum Pubs. 1989 369p maps o.p.; Anchor Bks. paperback available $12.95
                                        92
1. Indians of North America—Wars
ISBN 0-385-41357-2 (pa)   LC 88-38148
A "narrative that tells the entire story of the Shawnee wars from the middle of the 18th century to its conclusion in 1811. Much of it consists of a history of the Shawnees themselves, a vivid description of their customs and an authoritative biography of Tecumseh, who emerges as a fully rounded character and a distinct part of American history." N Y Times Book Rev

Includes bibliography

Ternan, Ellen Lawless, 1839-1914
Tomalin, Claire. The invisible woman: the story of Nelly Ternan and Charles Dickens. See entry under Dickens, Charles, 1812-1870
                                        92

Tharp, Twyla
Tharp, Twyla. Push comes to shove. Bantam Bks. 1992 376p il $24.50   **92**
ISBN 0-553-07306-0   LC 92-17977
"Linda Grey Bantam Books"
The choreographer and dancer discusses "her artistic development and personal life. . . . The book ends with a chronology of her work from 1965-1992." Libr J
"Tharp is a frank and giving autobiographer as well as an intuitive, fluid writer, balancing the professional with the private, the emotional with the aesthetic, and sharing the painful and demanding process by which the intimate lessons of life are translated into performance." Booklist

Thatcher, Margaret
Young, Hugo. The Iron Lady: a biography of Margaret Thatcher. Farrar, Straus & Giroux 1989 569p il $30; pa $14.95   **92**
1. Great Britain—Politics and government—1952-
ISBN 0-374-22651-2; 0-374-52251-0 (pa)
                                LC 89-11875
This "political biography reveals how Thatcher changed the face of the Conservative Party in a series of 'mighty battles' with the old guard, tamed the trade unions, controlled inflation and unemployment and, by her conduct of the Falkland War and her dealings with Reagan and Gorbachev, emerged as a global leader." Publ Wkly
This "is a model political biography, admirably organized, intellectually serious. . . . It is solid, comprehensive, well written, analytical rather than judgmental." NY Times Book Rev

Includes bibliography

Thomas, Dylan, 1914-1953
Ferris, Paul. Dylan Thomas; by Paul Ferris. Dial Press 1977 399p il o.p.; Paragon House paperback available $12.95   **92**
ISBN 1-55778-215-6 (pa)   LC 76-54936
This biography "disentangles Thomas from the cocoon of legend that he wove about himself. . . . Beneath Thomas's womanizing horseplay and drinking, Ferris claims, was a tormented man who never once in print described an ordinary, successful act of sex. Obsessed with his role as a poet, Thomas became his own worst enemy." Publ Wkly

Includes bibliography

Thomas, Dylan. Selected letters of Dylan Thomas; edited and with commentary by Constantine FitzGibbon. New Directions 1967 c1966 420p $10   **92**
ISBN 0-8112-0399-9
First published 1966 in the United Kingdom
This collection covers the years 1931 to 1953 and includes letters that relate to the poet's methods of composition and general views of poetry. Correspondents include Pamela Hansford Johnson, John Davenport,

Thomas, Dylan, 1914-1953—*Continued*
Henry Treece, T. W. Earp, Oscar Williams and John Brinnin

Thomas, Piri, 1928-
Thomas, Piri. Down these mean streets. Knopf 1967 333p hardcover o.p. paperback available $11   **92**

1. Puerto Ricans—New York (N.Y.)
ISBN 0-679-73238-1 (pa)

The author, the son of Puerto Rican parents—one dark, one white—was born in New York's Spanish Harlem. He records the story of his growth to manhood, in the midst of street fights, gang rumbles, drugs, homosexuality, petty thievery, illegitimate parenthood, and a long prison sentence

"The book's literary qualities are primitive. Yet it has an undeniable power. . . . It claims our attention and emotional response because of the honesty and pain of life led in outlaw, fringe status where the dream is always to escape." N Y Times Book Rev

Thompson, Dorothy
Kurth, Peter. American Cassandra: the life of Dorothy Thompson. Little, Brown 1990 587p il $24.95; pa $12.95   **92**

ISBN 0-316-50723-7; 0-316-50724-5 (pa)
LC 89-14000

This biography "not only details the life of one of America's great political journalists, but also admits us to the marvelous circles in which she traveled: from foreign correspondents in Europe between the wars to the literati who surrounded her husband, Sinclair Lewis. . . . Expelled from Germany by Hitler himself, she began her anti-fascist campaign in her syndicated column." Booklist

Includes bibliographic references

Timerman, Jacobo, 1923-
Timerman, Jacobo. Prisoner without a name, cell without a number; translated from the Spanish by Toby Talbot. Knopf 1981 164p $12.50; pa $10   **92**

ISBN 0-394-51448-3; 0-679-72048-0 (pa) LC 80-2715

The author "an outspoken Zionist and formerly a newspaper publisher in Buenos Aires, relates his 30-month political incarceration—torture and isolation in a clandestine prison, then detention in an official penal institution—which preceded his expulsion from [Argentina] in 1979." Publ Wkly

Tocqueville, Alexis de
Jardin, André. Tocqueville: a biography; translated from the French by Lydia Davis with Robert Hemenway. Farrar, Straus & Giroux 1988 550p $35   **92**

ISBN 0-374-27836-9
LC 88-10255

Original French edition, 1984

The author traces "Tocqueville's life from his noble birth in postrevolutionary France, through his travels around the world in his youth, and on to his roles as a leader and government office holder in the Second Republic." Booklist

"Jardin gives us a concise and balanced account of Tocqueville's public positions and passions. He does this with economy, grace, thoroughness, and reliability." New Repub

Includes bibliography

Tolkien, J. R. R. (John Ronald Reuel), 1892-1973
Carpenter, Humphrey. Tolkien; a biography. Houghton Mifflin 1977 286p il hardcover o.p. paperback available $10.70   **92**

ISBN 0-395-48676-9 (pa)   LC 77-9081

The author "presents a chronological biography of John Ronald Reuel Tolkien from his birth in South Africa, his childhood with brother Hilary after their early orphaning, his education, army life, marriage and death." Publ Wkly

"Much that the reader of Tolkien is grateful to know—his ambitions as poet and work as lexicographer, his range of friendships and the ordinariness of his life style, his innocence and his orthodoxy—comes through unromanticized." Choice

Includes bibliography

Tolstoy, Leo, graf, 1828-1910
Wilson, A. N. (Andrew Norman). Tolstoy. Norton 1988 xxviii, 572p il $25   **92**

ISBN 0-393-02585-3   LC 88-12485

Also available in paperback from Fawcett Bks.

"Investigating how Tolstoy's life and personality shaped his art, Wilson reassesses the presumed autobiographical content in Tolstoy's writings by documenting many of the deceptions and lies perpetuated both in the writer's fiction and in his own journals and correspondence." Booklist

"At times the opinionated biographer comes close to edging his protagonist off the stage altogether, but overall the book is a highly readable introduction to Tolstoy and his world." Libr J

Includes bibliography

Tormé, Mel. See class 780.92

Toscanini, Arturo. See class 780.92

Toth, Susan Allen
Toth, Susan Allen. Ivy days; making my way out East. Little, Brown 1984 199p hardcover o.p. paperback available $6.95   **92**

1. Smith College
ISBN 0-316-85079-9 (pa)   LC 84-2912

This is a memoir of Toth's college experiences at Smith in the late 1950's and early 1960's

"Mrs. Toth's prose is compassionate and poised; she is graceful, humourous, wry, pointed and altogether unembarrassed." N Y Times Book Rev

Toynbee, Arnold Joseph, 1889-1975

McNeill, William Hardy. Arnold J. Toynbee, a life; [by] William H. McNeill. Oxford Univ. Press 1989 346p il $30; pa $10.95   **92**

ISBN 0-19-505863-1; 0-19-506335-X (pa)

LC 88-23188

A "portrait of the British scholar, historian, and author of the monumental 10-volume 'Study of History,' examining Toynbee's work and personal life." Booklist

"Throughout this carefully documented and eminently readable account Mr. McNeil keeps the reader aware of Toynbee's limitations, both personal and professional." N Y Times Book Rev

Includes bibliographic references

Tracy, Spencer, 1900-1967

Davidson, Bill. Spencer Tracy, tragic idol. Dutton 1988 c1987 232p il o.p.; Zebra Bks. paperback available $5.99   **92**

ISBN 0-8217-3738-4 (pa)   LC 87-36428

First published 1987 in the United Kingdom

This biographical account of the actor's life "tells his story from a slightly different angle, viewing his alcoholism and depression as the primary shapers of his life." Booklist

Trollope, Anthony, 1815-1882

Hall, N. John. Trollope; a biography. Clarendon Press 1991 581p il $35; pa $17.95   **92**

ISBN 0-19-812627-1; 0-19-283071-6 (pa) LC 91-8011

This is a biography of the Victorian novelist

The author of this "leisurely and wonderfully informative biography . . . has used [a] wealth of material well. He gives the reader not only a lively portrait of the man but a picture of an age in all its variety." New Leader

Includes bibliographic references

Trotsky, Leon, 1879-1940

Deutscher, Isaac. The prophet outcast: Trotsky, 1929-1940. Oxford Univ. Press 1963 543p il $35; pa $10.95   **92**

1. Soviet Union—History

ISBN 0-19-500147-8; 0-19-281066-9 (pa)

Concluding volume of Deutscher's study of the life of Leon Trotsky. Previous titles The prophet armed: Trotsky, 1879-1921 and The prophet unarmed: Trotsky, 1921-1929 o.p.

This final volume covers Trotsky's years in exile which ended with his assassination in Mexico

Includes bibliography

Truman, Harry S., 1884-1972

McCullough, David G. Truman; [by] David McCullough. Simon & Schuster 1992 1117p il $30; pa $15   **92**

ISBN 0-671-45654-7; 0-671-86920-5 (pa) LC 92-5245

This biography of the 33rd president "not only conveys in rich detail Truman's accomplishments as a politician and statesman, but also reveals the character and personality of this constantly-surprising man—as school-boy, farmer, soldier, merchant, county judge, senator, vice president and chief executive. The book relates how Truman overcame the stigma of business failure and debt . . . and acquired a reputation for honesty, reliability and common sense." Publ Wkly

Includes bibliographic references

Miller, Merle. Plain speaking: an oral biography of Harry S. Truman. Berkley Pub. Group 1974 448p hardcover o.p. paperback available $5.99   **92**

1. United States—Politics and government—1945-1953

ISBN 0-425-09499-5 (pa)

Parts of this book deal with the memories of people who knew the President before 1935, the year he first went to Washington as Senator from Missouri. Other parts deal with his Presidency and the period following it. The work is based on tapes Miller compiled from interviews with Truman and others in 1961-1962 in Independence, Missouri

Truman, Harry S. Where the buck stops: the personal and private writings of Harry S. Truman; edited by Margaret Truman. Warner Bks. 1989 388p hardcover o.p. paperback available $12.95   **92**

1. United States—Politics and government—1945-1953

ISBN 0-446-39175-1 (pa)   LC 89-40366

"President Harry S. Truman's consuming interest in American history, his irreverent attitude toward Presidential predecessors and his painful honesty make 'Where the Buck Stops' fascinating reading. . . . The book [is] a potpourri of anecdote and opinion." N Y Times Book Rev

Turner, Tina. See class 780.92

Twain, Mark, 1835-1910

Kaplan, Justin. Mr. Clemens and Mark Twain; a biography. Simon & Schuster 1966 424p il hardcover o.p. paperback available $15   **92**

ISBN 0-671-74807-6 (pa)

"Although this biography of Mark Twain begins when Twain is 31 . . . the book is a full account of Twain, his life and his work related both to his early years and to the 'Gilded Age' of his mature life." Publ Wkly

Includes bibliography

Sanborn, Margaret. Mark Twain: the bachelor years; a biography. Doubleday 1990 508p $24.95   **92**

ISBN 0-385-23702-2   LC 88-31287

The author discusses the early life of Samuel Clemens: "his boyhood in Hannibal, Mo., his years on the Mississippi riverboats, his travels to the Nevada mining towns and to California, to Hawaii and to Europe and the Holy Land." N Y Times Book Rev

"This study certainly captures with a vivid appeal the amusing experiences that were transformed into literary art by Twain. On a more serious note, however, Sanborn also probes into the darker, tragic events of her subject's life." Booklist

Includes bibliography

Twain, Mark, 1835-1910—*Continued*

Twain, Mark. The autobiography of Mark Twain; as arranged and edited with an introduction and notes, by Charles Neider. Harper & Row 1959 xxvi, 388p il hardcover o.p. paperback available $10   **92**

ISBN 0-06-092025-4 (pa)

The editor "has arranged the selections in coordinated chronological order, ending with the death of Clemens' daughter Jean in December, 1909." Booklist

Tz'u-hsi, Empress dowager of China, 1835-1908

Seagrave, Sterling. Dragon lady; the life and legend of the last empress of China; by Sterling Seagrave with the collaboration of Peggy Seagrave. Knopf 1992 601p il maps $30; pa $16   **92**

1. China—History
ISBN 0-679-40230-6; 0-679-73369-8 (pa)
         LC 91-52712

This is a biography of the Empress Dowager. "As Regent for the young T'ung-chih and Kuang-hsu (her son and nephew), she ruled China almost continuously between 1861 and her death in 1908." Times Lit Suppl

"The last empress of China is conventionally portrayed as an evil, ruthless tyrant, a murderer and a depraved concubine. . . . Now along comes this superb, impeccably researched, absorbing biography-cum-history to explode the myth of the dragon empress." Publ Wkly

Includes bibliography

Updike, John

Updike, John. Self-consciousness; memoirs. Knopf 1989 257p $18.95   **92**

ISBN 0-394-57222-X   LC 88-13022

Also available in paperback from Fawcett Bks.

"In this book's six chapters, Updike reflects upon the salient influences on his life and writing: his psoriasis, asthma, stuttering, bad teeth, and an ineffectual father who was barely able to make ends meet during the Depression. Updike treats these difficulties with grace and charm." Choice

Vanderbilt, Gloria, 1924-

Vanderbilt, Gloria. Once upon a time; a true story. Knopf 1985 301p il o.p.; Fawcett Bks. paperback available $4.50   **92**

ISBN 0-449-12902-0 (pa)   LC 84-48667

"This book offers a view of Vanderbilt from age two to seventeen and includes more than two dozen family photographs. Vanderbilt says that finding one of the photographs inspired her account, which covers the infamous trial for her custody. Though the struggle was between her rather absent mother and her aunt, Gloria saw it only as her battle to stay with her beloved nurse 'Big Elephant.'" Libr J

Velázquez, Diego. See class 709.2

Verdi, Giuseppe. See class 780.92

Victoria, Queen of Great Britain, 1819-1901

St. Aubyn, Giles. Queen Victoria; a portrait. Atheneum Pubs. 1992 669p il $29.95   **92**

1. Great Britain—History—1800-1899 (19th century)
ISBN 0-689-12141-5   LC 91-29123

First published 1991 in the United Kingdom

"St. Aubyn has produced a vivacious and engaging portrait of the queen that is knowledgeable and familiar without being patronizingly over-familiar. He has an excellent grasp of detail and a gift for making almost anything, from a political crisis to a domestic dispute, thoroughly fascinating." Christ Sci Monit

Includes bibliography

Strachey, Lytton. Queen Victoria. Harcourt Brace & Co. 1921 434p il $15.95; pa $10.95   **92**

1. Great Britain—History—1800-1899 (19th century)
ISBN 0-15-175695-3; 0-15-675696-X (pa)

"Harbrace modern classics"

This portrait includes Queen Victoria and her time, characterizations of Lord Melbourne, Palmerston, Gladstone, Disraeli, and the prince consort

Includes bibliography

Thompson, Dorothy. Queen Victoria; the woman, the monarchy, and the people. Pantheon Bks. 1990 167p il $18.45   **92**

1. Great Britain—History—1800-1899 (19th century)
ISBN 0-394-53709-2   LC 90-52563

United Kingdom edition has subtitle: gender and power

The author "approaches Victoria's life from a feminist viewpoint, exploring her changing image in the eyes of a paternalistic British society." SLJ

Includes bibliographic references

Woodham Smith, Cecil Blanche Fitz Gerald. Queen Victoria; from her birth to the death of the Prince Consort; [by] Cecil Woodham-Smith. Knopf 1972 486p il o.p.; Fine, D.I. paperback available $9.95   **92**

1. Great Britain—History—1800-1899 (19th century)
ISBN 0-917657-95-0 (pa)

"This important scholarly biography with excerpts from Victoria's journals and letters is based on meticulous research in the Royal Family Archives at Windsor. British historian and biographer Woodham-Smith, gives a detailed chronology of the life, times, and entourage of Queen Victoria from childhood to widowhood." Booklist

Includes bibliographic references

Vidal, Gore, 1925-

Vidal, Gore. Screening history. Harvard Univ. Press 1992 96p il $14.95   **92**

ISBN 0-674-79586-5   LC 92-2912

"Mr. Vidal's provocative meditation on perceptions of history are based on his Massey Lectures, at Harvard. . . . Written versions of history are, in Mr. Vidal's

Vidal, Gore, 1925-—*Continued*
opinion, no more to be trusted than movie versions, and
a lot less memorable besides being a lot less fun. Mr.
Vidal is a movie-lover and a veteran observer of politicians and their histrionics. He relates history on the
screen to the general concept of events, his personal
experience, and his acerbic view of doings in Washington." Atlantic

Villella, Edward
Villella, Edward. Prodigal son; dancing for
Balanchine in a world of pain and magic;
[by] Edward Villella with Larry Kaplan.
Simon & Schuster 1992 317p il $23; pa $13
92

   ISBN 0-671-72370-7; 0-671-79717-4 (pa)
                             LC 91-39937
   "The title of this autobiography refers to a ballet with
which Villella is closely associated. It also defines the
dancer's perception of his complex relationship with the
choreographer George Balanchine. As a street kid from
Queens, Villella entered the rarefied world of classical
ballet and danced with Balanchine's New York City Ballet for more than 20 years. . . . This is a testimony
to Villella's achievements, an homage to a great
choreographer, and a reconciliation between the dancer
and his artistic father." Libr J

Vishnevskaya, Galina. See class 780.92

Wałęsa, Lech, 1943-
Wałęsa, Lech. The struggle and the
triumph; an autobiography; by Lech Walesa
with the collaboration of Arkadiuz Rybicki;
translated by Franklin Philip in collaboration
with Helen Mahut. Arcade Pub. 1992 330p
il $24.95
92

   1. Solidarity (Labor union) 2. Poland—Politics and
government
   ISBN 1-55970-149-8   LC 91-35875
   In this sequel to A way of hope (1987), Walesa "continues his autobiography from 1983 to his election to
the Polish presidency in 1990. . . . From his power base
in Solidarity, Walesa portrays his maturing role as a
national and international leader and his commitment to
non-violence to achieve political and economic reform."
Libr J

Waller, Fats. See class 780.92

Walton, Sam
Trimble, Vance H. Sam Walton; the
inside story of America's richest man.
Dutton 1990 319p il $19.95   92
   1. Wal-Mart Stores, Inc.
   ISBN 0-525-24922-2   LC 90-38232
   Also available in paperback from New Am. Lib.
   This biography of the man Forbes magazine once
listed as the richest man in America "recounts how Walton's chain of stores grew from a single store in a tiny
northwestern Arkansas town into a giant firm." Booklist

Walton, Sam. Sam Walton, made in
America; my story; by Sam Walton with
John Huey. Doubleday 1992 269p il $22.50
92

   1. Wal-Mart Stores, Inc.
   ISBN 0-385-42615-1   LC 92-18874
   Also available in large print for $26.50 (ISBN 0-385-
42617-8)
   The founder of Wal-Mart Stores, the largest retail
chain in the world, recounts how he made his fortune
   "Readers will enjoy the folksy narrative of the small-
town millionaire who revolutionized retail distribution.
. . . Coauthor Huey does a fine job of incorporating
candid testimonials from family members and associates."
Libr J
   Includes bibliographic references

Warhol, Andy. See class 709.2

Warren, Earl, 1891-1974
Schwartz, Bernard. Super chief: Earl
Warren and his Supreme Court; a judicial
biography. unabridged ed. New York Univ.
Press 1983 853p il hardcover o.p. paperback
available $25   92
   1. United States. Supreme Court
   ISBN 0-8147-7826-7 (pa)   LC 82-18868
   This biography, based on documentary sources, por-
trays Chief Justice Earl Warren's influence on the U.S.
Supreme Court during the years 1953 to 1969
   Includes bibliography

Warren, Robert Penn, 1905-1989
Warren, Robert Penn. Talking with Robert
Penn Warren; edited by Floyd C. Watkins,
John T. Hiers, Mary Louise Weaks.
University of Ga. Press 1990 419p $45; pa
$19.95   92
   ISBN 0-8203-1219-3; 0-8203-1220-7 (pa)
                             LC 89-20570
   This is a collection of interviews in which Warren
discusses such topics as racial segregation, "writing, its
relation to criticism, and the value of ambivalence and
individual virtue in contrast to legislated morality."
Booklist
   Includes bibliographic references

Washington, Booker T., 1856-1915
Harlan, Louis R. Booker T. Washington:
the making of a black leader, 1856-1901.
Oxford Univ. Press 1972 379p il $39.95; pa
$14.95   92
   ISBN 0-19-501596-7; 0-19-501915-6 (pa)
   This book "covers Washington's life from his birth
as a slave in western Virginia up to [the year 1901,
when he dined] with Theodore Roosevelt at the White
House, an event signifying white recognition of Washington as the chief spokesman for black interests in the
period before World War I." Libr J

Washington, Booker T., 1856-1915 — Continued

Harlan, Louis R. Booker T. Washington: the wizard of Tuskegee, 1901-1915. Oxford Univ. Press 1983 548p il $39.95; pa $15.95
92

1. Tuskegee Institute
ISBN 0-19-503202-0; 0-19-504229-8 (pa)
LC 82-14547

This is the second and concluding volume of a life of the black educator and founder of Tuskegee Institute
"Having avoided the pitfalls of white guilt and black rage and the temptation to judge the past by standards of the present, Mr. Harlan deserves honors for his remarkable achievement." N Y Times Book Rev
Includes bibliographic references

Washington, Booker T. Up from slavery; an autobiography **92**

1. Tuskegee Institute
Hardcover and paperback editions available from various publishers
First published 1901
"The classic autobiography of the man who, though born in slavery, educated himself and went on to found Tuskegee Institute." N Y Public Libr

Washington, George, 1732-1799

Ferling, John E. The first of men: a life of George Washington. University of Tenn. Press 1988 598p il maps $44.95; pa $22.50
92

1. United States—History
ISBN 0-87049-562-3; 0-87049-628-X (pa)
LC 87-26037

The author "probes the contradictions and complexities of character that led to Washington's success." Publ Wkly
Ferling "incorporates a wealth of traditional primary material. . . . This is a well-documented, gracefully written and engaging history." Choice
Includes bibliography

Flexner, James Thomas. George Washington. Little, Brown 1965-1972 4v il v1 $27.50; v2-4 ea $29.95
92

1. United States—History
Contents: [v1] The forge of experience (1732-1775) (ISBN 0-316-28597-8); [v2] George Washington in the American Revolution (1775-1783) (ISBN 0-316-28595-1); [v3] George Washington and the new nation (1783-1793) (ISBN 0-316-28600-1); [v4] Anguish and farewell (1793-1799) (ISBN 0-316-28602-8)
Includes bibliographies

Flexner, James Thomas. Washington, the indispensable man. Little, Brown 1974 423p il $24.95
92

ISBN 0-316-28605-2
Also available in paperback from New Am. Lib.
This study is based on the author's four volume biography, entered above
"This more popular account has been rewritten rather than patched together from the larger work." Libr J
Includes bibliography

Freeman, Douglas Southall. Washington; an abridgment in one volume, by Richard Harwell, of the seven-volume George Washington; with a new introduction by Michael Kammen; afterword by Dumas Malone. Collier Bks. 1993 c1992 xxviii, 792p il maps pa $21
92

1. United States—History
ISBN 0-02-043214-3
LC 92-31779

An abridgment of seven volumes first published 1948-1957 by Scribner; abridgment first published 1968 by Scribner
In this compression of Washington's life the emphasis "is necessarily heavily on biography; to emphasize the story of Washington, the background descriptive of his time has been reduced as much as possible." Introduction
Includes bibliographic references

Washington, George. The diaries of George Washington; Donald Jackson, editor; Dorothy Twohig, associate editor. University Press of Va. 1976-1979 6v il maps v2-6 ea $37.50
92

Contents: v1 1748-65 o.p.; v2 1766-70 (ISBN 0-8139-0688-1); v3 1771-75, 1780-81 (ISBN 0-8139-0721-7); v4 1784-June 1786 (ISBN 0-8139-0722-5); v5 July 1786-December 1789 (ISBN 0-8139-0801-9); v6 January 1790-December 1799 (ISBN 0-8139-0807-8)
"Here is the little-known Washington: the adventurer, surveyor, novice soldier, slave-owner, experimental farmer. And here, too—beautifully illustrated—are the routine and rhythm of life in 18th-century Virginia." Choice
Bibliography included for each volume

Waugh, Evelyn, 1903-1966

Carpenter, Humphrey. The Brideshead generation: Evelyn Waugh and his friends. Houghton Mifflin 1990 523p il $27.95; pa $12.70
92

ISBN 0-395-44142-0; 0-395-59769-2 (pa)
LC 89-19770

"A Peter Davison book"
First published 1989 in the United Kingdom
The author addresses the life and work of the English novelist Evelyn Waugh and examines the careers of some of his contemporaries, such as Anthony Powell, John Betjeman, Graham Greene, Cyril Connolly, and Henry Yorke (who wrote as Henry Green)
"Having established in fascinating and often richly repulsive detail the ethos out of which Waugh's early fiction came, The Brideshead Generation then concentrates on his career. What was happening to his contemporaries is never lost sight of." Times Lit Suppl
Includes bibliography

Stannard, Martin. Evelyn Waugh. Norton 1987-1992 c1986-c1992 2v il v1 $24.95; v2 $29.95
92

Volume one first published 1986 in the United Kingdom
Contents: [v1] The early years, 1903-1939 (ISBN 0-393-02450-4); [v2] The later years, 1939-1966 (ISBN 0-393-03412-7)

Waugh, Evelyn, 1903-1966—*Continued*

The first volume of this literary biography of the British writer discusses his education and his travels to several countries. Volume two examines Waugh's military career as an army officer during World War II and concludes with his death. Both volumes relate Waugh's writings to his life and beliefs, and discuss his relations with his wives and children

Includes bibliographies

Waugh, Evelyn. The letters of Evelyn Waugh and Diana Cooper; edited by Artemis Cooper. Ticknor & Fields 1992 344p il $27 **92**

1. Cooper, Lady Diana, 1892-1986
ISBN 0-395-56265-1   LC 91-30271

First published 1991 in the United Kingdom with title: Mr. Wu and Mrs. Stitch

"This correspondence between the renowned British novelist and his close friend, socialite-actress and writer Diana Cooper, began in 1932 and continued until Waugh's death in 1966." Publ Wkly

"The letters have been edited to eliminate libelous and redundant passages, but the importance and the artistry of the correspondence remain intact, the letters quite delightful in their literary as well as historical contexts." Booklist

Includes bibliography

Webb, Beatrice Potter, 1858-1943

Seymour-Jones, Carole. Beatrice Webb; a life. Dee, I.R. 1992 369p il $30 **92**

ISBN 1-56663-001-0   LC 92-16656

"Upper-class social reformer and Fabian socialist, Webb experienced the difficulties and contradictions facing autonomous, independent women who sought to effect social and political change. Seymour-Jones does a nice job in illuminating the psychological price exacted for her rebellion against convention and for her renunciation of personal fulfilment." Choice

Includes bibliography

Weil, Simone, 1909-1943

McLellan, David. Utopian pessimist: the life and thought of Simone Weil. Poseidon Press 1990 316p il maps $22.95 **92**

ISBN 0-671-68521-X   LC 89-48195

This biography of the French philosopher "makes for compelling reading. . . . It is especially valuable for two chapters analysing her major political works, Oppression and Liberty (completed in 1934) and The Need for Roots (1943) within the context of her life." New Statesman

Includes bibliographic references

Welles, Orson, 1915-1985

Brady, Frank. Citizen Welles: a biography of Orson Welles. Scribner 1989 655p il o.p.; Anchor Bks. paperback available $12.95

92

ISBN 0-385-26759-2 (pa)   LC 88-6531

"The focus of the book is largely on Welles's professional life. As an exhaustively detailed catalogue of everything he ever did on the stage, on radio and in film, as well as everything he ever wanted to do, 'Citizen Welles' may well be definitive." N Y Times Book Rev

Includes bibliography

Leaming, Barbara. Orson Welles; a biography. Viking 1985 562p il o.p.; Penguin Bks. paperback available $10.95 **92**

ISBN 0-14-012762-3 (pa)   LC 83-40657

This biography "chronologically catalogs Welles' eventful artistic career, interspering it . . . with a narrative describing Leaming's interviews with the man himself." Booklist

Includes bibliography

Welles, Orson. This is Orson Welles; [by] Orson Welles and Peter Bogdanovich; Jonathan Rosenbaum, editor. HarperCollins Pubs. 1992 xxxv, 533p il $30 **92**

ISBN 0-06-016616-9   LC 92-52601

"This is the transcript of interviews with Welles that filmmaker Bogdanovich conducted over a ten-year period. Throughout, Welles reminisces on his remarkable career. But along with remembrances of the entertainment world, he offers his thoughts on everything from writers and literature to comic strips, bullfighting, and gangsters. . . . Bogdanovich and editor Rosenbaum have done a great service to make this material available after years in storage." Libr J

Welty, Eudora, 1909-

Welty, Eudora. One writer's beginnings. Harvard Univ. Press 1984 104p il (William E. Massey, Sr. lectures in the history of American civilization) $10 **92**

ISBN 0-674-63925-1   LC 83-18638

Also available in paperback from Warner Bks.

A series of lectures in which the author reflects on her Southern heritage and her early artistic influences

West, Jessamyn, d. 1984

West, Jessamyn. Hide and seek; a continuing journey. Harcourt Brace Jovanovich 1973 310p hardcover o.p. paperback available $8.95 **92**

ISBN 0-15-640150-9 (pa)

In this autobiography West "reminisces about her childhood and youth, depicting family life and travels. Along the way she reflects on a variety of subjects, such as education, language, death, love, religion, dreams." Libr J

"An insightful and humorous reflection on continuity and change in the American culture over a period of years." Choice

Wharton, Edith, 1862-1937

James, Henry. Henry James and Edith Wharton. See entry under James, Henry, 1843-1916 **92**

Lewis, R. W. B. (Richard Warrington Baldwin). Edith Wharton; a biography. Harper & Row 1975 592p il o.p.; Fromm Int. paperback available $12.95 **92**

ISBN 0-88064-020-0 (pa)

This is a "scholarly biography of the sometimes enigmatic but always fascinating Edith Wharton. Dr. Lewis is showing us Edith Wharton as a woman and as an author of first rank with the specific intent of asking

Wharton, Edith, 1862-1937—*Continued*
us to understand her in relation to her age and to her contemporary artists. . . . Her development as a writer and as a person is documented thoroughly." Best Sellers

Includes bibliography

Wharton, Edith. The letters of Edith Wharton; edited by R.W.B. Lewis and Nancy Lewis. Scribner 1988 654p il o.p.; Collier Bks. paperback available $14.95 **92**

ISBN 0-02-034400-7 (pa)   LC 87-23526

"Selected from some 4000 letters that span over 60 years, these 400 letters serve to represent Wharton's life and personality." Libr J

"Though the individual letters tend in their social routine to be very much alike, the collection as a whole makes a sumptuous historical record, annotated to perfection, and fills out R. W. B. Lewis's remarkably informative biography [entered above]." New Repub

White, E. B. (Elwyn Brooks), 1899-1985
Elledge, Scott. E.B. White; a biography. Norton 1984 400p il hardcover o.p. paperback available $9.95 **92**

ISBN 0-393-30305-5 (pa)   LC 83-4032

This biography "follows White from his birth in Mount Vernon, N.Y. to his . . . octogenarian retreat in Maine." Libr J

The author is "fair, respectful, thorough, entertaining, skillful and unpedantic. He has performed a splendid exercise in scholarship and literary analysis, and the result is fun." N Y Times Book Rev

Includes bibliography

White, E. B. (Elwyn Brooks). Letters of E. B. White; collected and edited by Dorothy Lobrano Guth. Harper & Row 1976 686p il hardcover o.p. paperback available $20 **92**

ISBN 0-06-091517-X (pa)

Also available in hardcover from Borgo Press

This collection of letters by the essayist, poet, novelist and author of several classic children's books is chronologically arranged. Written between the year 1908 when White was nine, and 1974 when he was retired and living on his farm in Maine they concern his relationships with his wife, Katherine White and his family and friends, which include Harold Ross, James Thurber, Robert Benchley, Alexander Woollcott and others

White, Ryan
White, Ryan. Ryan White: my own story; by Ryan White and Ann Marie Cunningham. Dial Bks. 1991 277p il $16.95 **92**

1. AIDS (Disease)
ISBN 0-8037-0977-3   LC 90-21038

Also available in paperback from New Am. Lib.

Ryan White describes how he got AIDS, engaged in a legal battle to return to school, and became a celebrity and spokesperson for issues concerning the deadly disease

The book contains "surprising snatches of humor and insight that lend dimension to the vulnerable young man whose positive outlook shines through so clearly. Not saccharine, not angry, not bitter, this unusual book, delivered without an ounce of self-pity, seems as honest as it is inspiring." Booklist

White, Theodore H., 1915-1986
White, Theodore H. In search of history; a personal adventure. Harper & Row 1978 561p o.p.; Warner Bks. paperback available $7.95 **92**

ISBN 0-446-34657-8 (pa)   LC 78-2177

In this book White "looks back on the major events he has reported during his journalistic career—China just prior to and during World War II, the Marshall Plan, the 1960 presidential campaign, etc.—and attempts to place them in historical perspective. The work in some sense also constitutes an autobiography." Libr J

Whiteman, Paul. See class 780.92

Whitman, Walt, 1819-1892
Callow, Philip. From noon to starry night: a life of Walt Whitman. Dee, I.R. 1992 394p il $28.50 **92**

ISBN 0-929587-95-2   LC 92-5311

The author "attempts to illuminate Walt Whitman's life . . . by focusing primarily on the poet's experiences before the Civil War. . . . Callow adds a historical sketch of early-19th-century America to show how the nation Whitman celebrated so eloquently in *Leaves of Grass* formed his complex personality." Publ Wkly

"Infused with tenderness and respect, this fine biography deciphers the complexity of Whitman's sexuality and passionate creativity while celebrating his abiding compassion and grandeur of spirit." Booklist

Includes bibliographic references

Wiesenthal, Simon
Wiesenthal, Simon. Justice not vengeance; translated from the German by Ewald Osers. Grove Weidenfeld 1989 372p il $22.50 **92**

1. War crime trials 2. Holocaust, Jewish (1933-1945)
ISBN 0-8021-1278-1   LC 89-23283

The author recounts "his liberation from Mauthausen; his capture of Adolf Eichmann; his dealings with Franz Stangl, the commandant of Treblinka, and other Nazis. He devotes a whole chapter to Raoul Wallenberg, the Swede who saved thousands of Jews and was taken prisoner by the Russians in 1945." Booklist

"In all, this book provides a sense of a formidable presence, of a force larger than life that seems equal to an enormous task it has taken on." N Y Times Book Rev

Wilde, Oscar, 1854-1900
Ellmann, Richard. Oscar Wilde. Knopf 1988 c1987 680p il $24.95; pa $11.95 **92**

ISBN 0-394-55484-1; 0-394-75984-2 (pa)
     LC 87-45354

First published 1987 in the United Kingdom

"Wilde's life epitomizes the classic formula for a tragic history, the man who, by hubris, falls from greatness. In Mr. Ellmann's hands, the story becomes as compelling as fiction while never deviating from the facts. Humour and elegance illuminate the accounts of Wilde's family, his friends and the enemies he earned." Economist

Includes bibliography

Wilder, Laura Ingalls, 1867-1957

Anderson, William T. Laura Ingalls Wilder country; text by William Anderson; color photography by Leslie A. Kelly. HarperPerennial 1990 119p il hardcover o.p. paperback available $20   **92**

1. Literary landmarks—United States
ISBN 0-06-097346-3 (pa)   LC 89-46512

Cover subtitle: The people and places in Laura Ingalls Wilder's life and books

"Contemporary and period photographs of the places in the Laura Ingalls Wilder books have been combined with a narrative about the actual historical settings." Horn Book

Wilder, Laura Ingalls. A Little House sampler; [by] Laura Ingalls Wilder, Rose Wilder Lane; edited by William T. Anderson. University of Neb. Press 1988 243p il $20   **92**

1. Frontier and pioneer life
ISBN 0-8032-1022-1   LC 87-19208

Also available in paperback from Perennial Lib.

Before she wrote Little House in the Big Woods and other novels in the series about her pioneer childhood, Laura Ingalls "Wilder wrote a column for the Missouri Ruralist describing her life on the frontier. These writings, and some by her daughter Rose Wilder Lane, form the basis of this collection. Anderson has arranged these items to give a chronological, biographical account of the two writers, and has supplied . . . introductions to place each item in context." Libr J

Williams, Edward Bennett

Thomas, Evan. The man to see: Edward Bennett Williams; ultimate insider: legendary trial lawyer. Simon & Schuster 1991 587p il $28; pa $15   **92**

ISBN 0-671-68934-7; 0-671-79211-3 (pa)
      LC 91-25131

"Capital trial lawyer Williams provided legal, political, business and personal counsel to government leaders, including U.S. presidents. Superbly capturing his subject's complex, often contradictory personality, Thomas . . . interviewed hundreds of people who knew the controversial attorney." Publ Wkly

Includes bibliographic references

Williams, Ted, 1918-

Seidel, Michael. Ted Williams; a baseball life. Contemporary Bks. 1991 400p il $19.95; pa $10.95   **92**

ISBN 0-8092-4254-0; 0-8092-3931-0 (pa)
      LC 90-23894

This is a biography of the player who spent his entire nineteen year career with the Boston Red Sox

"Seidel manages to keep his account balanced, painting a larger picture of the nature of baseball in the 1940s and 1950s. . . . Seidel's work should stand the test of time as an accurate, evenhanded portrait." Libr J

Includes bibliographic references

Williams, Tennessee, 1911-1983

Spoto, Donald. The kindness of strangers: the life of Tennessee Williams. Little, Brown 1985 409p il $19.95   **92**

ISBN 0-316-80781-8   LC 84-27772

Also available in paperback from Ballantine Bks.

"Based on hundreds of interviews with those who knew him and on other previously unpublished material, [the author] presents a portrait of Tennessee Williams which is both respectful and sensitive." Wilson Libr Bull

Includes bibliography

Williams, Tennessee. Five o'clock angel: letters of Tennessee Williams to Maria St. Just, 1948-1982; with commentary by Maria St. Just; preface by Elia Kazan. Knopf 1990 407p il $24.95   **92**

ISBN 0-394-56427-8   LC 89-43354

Also available in paperback from Penguin Bks.

"Written to the Russian-born English actress who furnished Williams with moral support and practical advice from his first success to the end of his life, . . . these witty, often moving letters reveal a courageous, dedicated playwright increasingly beset by the hazards of fame, self-doubt, [and] addiction to alcohol and drugs. . . . Though they shed little light on the plays, these brilliantly edited letters offer a wonderful picture of Broadway in the late 1940s and 1950s and of the later international theater scene." Libr J

Wilson, Woodrow, 1856-1924

Cooper, John Milton. The warrior and the priest: Woodrow Wilson and Theodore Roosevelt; [by] John Milton Cooper, Jr. Belknap Press 1983 442p il hardcover o.p. paperback available $12.95   **92**

1. Roosevelt, Theodore, 1858-1919 2. United States—Politics and government—1898-1919
ISBN 0-674-94751-7 (pa)   LC 83-6021

This "book is divided into four sections dealing respectively with the origins and early careers of both men, the parallel presidencies of Theodore Roosevelt (US) and Woodrow Wilson (Princeton), the election of 1912, and WW I." Choice

The author's "distinctions are sharp, his insights original, his judgments balanced and his narrative unfailingly graceful." N Y Times Book Rev

Includes bibliographic references

Heckscher, August. Woodrow Wilson. Scribner 1991 743p il $35   **92**

ISBN 0-684-19312-4   LC 91-6767

Also available in paperback from Collier Bks.

This biography of Wilson "tracks his family background, his education, his transition from academician to political leader." Publ Wkly

Heckscher has written a "well-organized and serviceable work, blending political and personal history in a readable, generally sympathetic narrative." Libr J

Includes bibliography

Wilson, Woodrow, 1856-1924—*Continued*
Smith, Gene. When the cheering stopped: the last years of Woodrow Wilson; with an introduction by Allan Nevins. Morrow 1964 307p il hardcover o.p. paperback available $12.95   **92**
1. Wilson, Edith Bolling Galt, 1872-1961 2. United States—Politics and government—1898-1919
ISBN 0-688-06011-0 (pa)

A look at the final years of the Wilson administration, when, with the President in physical decline his wife Edith basically handled his office
Includes bibliography

Windsor, Edward, Duke of, 1894-1972
Ziegler, Philip. King Edward VIII; a biography. Knopf 1991 552p il $24.95   **92**
ISBN 0-394-57730-2   LC 90-53073
Also available in paperback from Ballantine Bks.

This biography discusses "Edward's years as Prince of Wales, his brief reign, his governorship of the Bahamas and the sad exile as Duke of Windsor." Publ Wkly
Includes bibliography

Windsor, Wallis Warfield, Duchess of, 1896-1986
Higham, Charles. The Duchess of Windsor; the secret life. McGraw-Hill 1988 482p il o.p.; Berkley Pub. Group paperback available $5.50   **92**
ISBN 1-55773-227-2 (pa)   LC 87-36662
This is a biography of Wallis Warfield Simpson, Duchess of Windsor, the Baltimore woman for whom England's King Edward VIII gave up his throne in 1936
Includes bibliography

Wittgenstein, Ludwig, 1889-1951
Monk, Ray. Ludwig Wittgenstein; the duty of genius. Free Press 1990 654p il $32.95
92
ISBN 0-02-921670-2   LC 90-37619
Also available in paperback from Penguin Bks.

"Wittgenstein the philosopher and Wittgenstein the man have generated two largely separate industries. In a full-scale biography of him, British philosopher Monk tries to show that this possibly acutest and most influential mind of the century and the obsessional personality were one, driven by spiritual as much as by intellectual concerns." Publ Wkly
"The story is well told; the narrative is vivid, clear, sympathetic and credible." N Y Times Book Rev
Includes bibliography

Wodehouse, P. G. (Pelham Grenville), 1881-1975
Wodehouse, P. G. (Pelham Grenville). Yours, Plum; the letters of P.G. Wodehouse; edited with an introduction by Frances Donaldson. Heineman, J.H. 1990 269p il $22.95   **92**
ISBN 0-87008-130-6

A collection of letters addressed primarily to a small group of close friends and Wodehouse's stepdaughter. They reflect on the author's public and private life including his opinions of fellow writers

Wolfe, Thomas, 1900-1938
Donald, David Herbert. Look homeward: a life of Thomas Wolfe. Little, Brown 1987 579p il o.p.; Fawcett Bks. paperback available $12.95   **92**
ISBN 0-449-90286-2 (pa)   LC 86-10460
This biography is based on Wolfe's manuscripts and the "extensive body of documentation and commentary associated with the life of a writer whose material was his life and family. Donald's story is masterful as an evocation of a character and a period; you don't have to share his convictions about Wolfe's literary achievement to be engaged by it." New Repub
Includes bibliography

Wolff, Tobias, 1945-
Wolff, Tobias. This boy's life: a memoir. Atlantic Monthly Press 1989 288p o.p.; Perennial Lib. paperback available $10   **92**
ISBN 0-06-097277-7 (pa)   LC 88-17600
The novelist and short story writer "offers an engrossing and candid look into his childhood and adolescence in his first book of nonfiction. In unaffected prose he recreates scenes from his life that sparkle with the immediacy of narrative fiction. The result is an intriguingly guileless book, distinct from the usual reflective commentary of autobiography." Libr J

Woolf, Leonard, 1880-1969
Alexander, Peter. Leonard and Virginia Woolf. See entry under Woolf, Virginia, 1882-1941   **92**

Woolf, Virginia, 1882-1941
Alexander, Peter. Leonard and Virginia Woolf; a literary partnership; [by] Peter F. Alexander. St. Martin's Press 1992 265p il $29.95   **92**
1. Woolf, Leonard, 1880-1969
ISBN 0-312-09082-X   LC 92-29034
"In this dual biography, Alexander charts the lives of Bloomsbury's famous couple, emphasizing their influence on each other and taking issue with those who consider Virginia one of the most important novelists of the 20th century." Libr J
Includes bibliographic references

Bell, Quentin. Virginia Woolf: a biography. Harcourt Brace Jovanovich 1972 2v in 1 il hardcover o.p. paperback available $14.95
92
ISBN 0-15-693580-5 (pa)
The author, Mrs. Woolf's nephew, "shows how Virginia Woolf grew from a frail child to a woman with confidence enough to fly in the face of many of the traditions of her time, how the Bloomsbury group was born and how Virginia Woolf fitted into the society of men like Lytton Strachey, Keynes, Roger Fry, E. M.

Woolf, Virginia, 1882-1941—*Continued*
Forster, T. S. Eliot." Publ Wkly
Includes bibliography

Dunn, Jane. A very close conspiracy: Vanessa Bell and Virginia Woolf. Little, Brown 1991 c1990 338p il $29.95 **92**
1. Bell, Vanessa, 1879-1961
ISBN 0-316-19653-3   LC 91-6807
First published 1990 in the United Kingdom
This is a biography of Virginia Woolf and her relationship with her artist sister, Vanessa Bell
"This well-written, well-documented study of the Stephen sisters' relationship is organized thematically rather than chronologically to describe the strong devotion and mutual dependence of Bell and Woolf." Libr J

Includes bibliographic references

Gordon, Lyndall. Virginia Woolf, a writer's life. Norton 1985 c1984 341p il hardcover o.p. paperback available $8.95 **92**
ISBN 0-393-30342-X (pa)   LC 84-25424
First published 1984 in the United Kingdom
"Gordon combines literary criticism with biographical investigation in her life of Virginia Woolf. . . . Using the major novels *To the Lighthouse* and *The Waves*, Gordon explores in detail the autobiographical ramifications of these works as she traces Woolf's childhood, marriage, and literary career." Booklist
Includes bibliography

Woolf, Virginia. A moment's liberty: the shorter diary; abridged and edited by Anne Olivier Bell; introduction by Quentin Bell. Harcourt Brace Jovanovich 1990 516p $22.95; pa $16.95 **92**
ISBN 0-15-161894-1; 0-15-661912-1 (pa)
LC 90-33428
An abridged edition of the five volumes of Woolf's Diary, published 1977-1984
"The diaries here may appeal to a larger audience, not least because each year represented is prefaced by a wonderfully succinct overview. Here are Woolf's superbly drawn portraits of Max Beerbohm, T.S. Eliot, John Maynard Keynes, Katherine Mansfield—and her occasionally acerbic remarks on what they said and did. But the diaries are also a repository for luminous thoughts on birds and weather, the pleasures of walking or listening to music." Publ Wkly

Woolf, Virginia. Moments of being; edited, with an introduction and notes, by Jeanne Schulkind. 2nd ed. Harcourt Brace Jovanovich 1985 230p pa $7.95 **92**
ISBN 0-15-661918-0   LC 85-8521
"A Harvest/HBJ book"
First published 1976
This volume consists of unpublished autobiographical writings, including several "Reminiscences" written at the start of Woolf's career, a piece entitled "A sketch of the past" written shortly before her suicide, and papers read to the Memoir Club
Includes bibliographic references

Woolf, Virginia. A passionate apprentice; the early journals, 1897-1909; edited by Mitchell A. Leaska. Harcourt Brace Jovanovich 1990 444p $24.95; pa $14.95 **92**
ISBN 0-15-171287-5; 0-15-671160-5 (pa)
LC 90-42126
This is a collection "of journals and diaries printed in their entirety, kept by Virginia Woolf (then Virginia Stephen) from age 15-27." Booklist
"The impression to be gained from [this work], the contents of seven notebooks that have been scrupulously edited and most sensitively introduced and linked by Mitchell A. Lesaka, is of resilience and determination, and an unquenchable appetite for life." N Y Times Book Rev

Includes bibliographic references

Wordsworth, William, 1770-1850
Gill, Stephen Charles. William Wordsworth; a life; [by] Stephen Gill. Clarendon Press 1989 525p il $35; pa $13.95 **92**
ISBN 0-19-812828-2; 0-19-282747-2 (pa)
LC 88-15622
"Gill does a superb job of interrelating the life and work of this particularly autobiographical poet. . . . Readable at once as pure biography, intellectual biography, and literary criticism, this book will appeal to anyone with an interest in Wordsworth." Libr J
Includes bibliography

Wright, Frank Lloyd, 1867-1959
Gill, Brendan. Many masks: a life of Frank Lloyd Wright. Putnam 1987 544p il o.p.; Ballantine Bks. paperback available $12.95 **92**
ISBN 0-345-35698-5 (pa)   LC 87-13202
This biography describes the architect's long career and turbulent private life
"Gill evaluates which of Wright's projects failed by the architect's own standards, and which ones succeeded." Publ Wkly
Includes bibliography

Wright, Jim, 1922-
Barry, John M. The ambition and the power. Viking 1989 768p o.p.; Penguin Bks. paperback available $12.95 **92**
1. United States—Politics and government—1981-
ISBN 0-14-010488-7 (pa)   LC 88-40408
"Barry scrutinizes the political career of the . . . ousted Speaker of the House of Representatives, Jim Wright of Texas." Booklist
"Mr. Barry does a credible job of inside reporting and analysis on a variety of subjects. In addition to his detailing of Mr. Wright's business dealings, the author is especially sharp on Mr. Wright's involvement in the . . . savings and loan calamity and on legislative showdowns on the House floor." N Y Times Book Rev

Wright, Orville, 1871-1948

Crouch, Tom D. The Bishop's boys: a life of Wilbur and Orville Wright. See entry under Wright, Wilbur, 1867-1912   **92**

Howard, Fred. Wilbur and Orville: a biography of the Wright brothers. See entry under Wright, Wilbur, 1867-1912   **92**

Wright, Richard, 1908-1960

Gayle, Addison. Richard Wright; ordeal of a native son. Anchor Press/Doubleday 1980 342p o.p.   **92**

Available only in hardcover from P. Smith

This biography of the black author was written with access to "previously classified documents from the files kept on Wright by the US government from the mid-1930s until his death in 1960. . . . [These included] 187 bits and pieces from the FBI along with a handful of sheets from the CIA and other government agencies." New Repub

Includes bibliography

Walker, Margaret. Richard Wright, daemonic genius; a portrait of the man, a critical look at his work. Warner Bks. 1988 428p il o.p.; Amistad Press paperback available $9.95   **92**

ISBN 1-56743-004-X (pa)   LC 87-19902

"An Amistad book"

"Combining biography, literary criticism and memoir, Walker's passionately committed portrait gets closer to the inner Wright than any previous volume. The unjustly neglected author of *Native Son* emerges as an angry and deeply ambivalent man who conceived of himself as 'a white American with a black skin.'" Publ Wkly

Includes bibliography

Wright, Richard. American hunger; afterword by Michel Fabre. Harper & Row 1977 146p hardcover o.p. paperback available $10   **92**

1. Blacks—Social conditions
ISBN 0-06-090991-9 (pa)   LC 76-47248

Black boy, Wright's autobiography of his early years entered below "ended with his decision to leave his Southern home for Chicago, a denouement which seemed to project an optimistic faith in America. 'American Hunger,' originally intended for publication as an integral part of 'Black Boy,' forces us to see Wright's classic autobiography in a totally new light." Publ Wkly

Wright, Richard. Black boy; a record of childhood and youth. Harper & Row 1964 c1945 285p $19.95; pa $6   **92**

1. Blacks—Social conditions
ISBN 0-06-014761-X; 0-06-081250-8 (pa)

A reissue of the title first published 1945 by World Publishing Company

This autobiographical work concludes with Wright "newly arrived in Chicago in 1927 as a fugitive from the white South that never knew him. [It] relates his nomadic life in Tennessee, Arkansas, and Mississippi, abandoned by his father and with his mother working at menial jobs or incapacitated by illness." Benet's Reader's Ency of Am Lit

Wright, Wilbur, 1867-1912

Crouch, Tom D. The Bishop's boys: a life of Wilbur and Orville Wright. Norton 1989 606p il hardcover o.p. paperback available $14.95   **92**

1. Wright, Orville, 1871-1948
ISBN 0-393-30695-X (pa)   LC 88-19585

"This book is both a biography of these great American heroes and a history of early aviation. Crouch discusses the Wrights' early life in Dayton, which was dominated by their father, the controversial Bishop Wright. He provides a detailed account of the development of the airplane. . . . A well-researched book which uses often overlooked original source material." Libr J

Includes bibliography

Howard, Fred. Wilbur and Orville: a biography of the Wright brothers. Knopf 1987 530p il $24.95   **92**

1. Wright, Orville, 1871-1948
ISBN 0-394-54269-X   LC 86-46022

"Written in an engaging style as an adventure story, this book is a fascinating account. It proceeds from the brothers' childhood through their years at Kitty Hawk and Huffman Prairie to the legal battles and final disposition of the 1903 Wright Flyer." Sci Books Films

Includes bibliography

Wyeth, Andrew. See class 709.2

Wynn, Ned

Wynn, Ned. We will always live in Beverly Hills; growing up crazy in Hollywood. Morrow 1990 285p il $19.95   **92**

ISBN 0-688-08509-1   LC 90-37030

Also available in paperback from Penguin Bks.

"The author son of Keenan Wynn, grandson of Ed Wynn, and stepson of Van Johnson, writes an often bitter and cynical account of growing up in Hollywood. A substance abuser at an early age, he describes his aimless, self-indulgent life. The narrative is sometimes confused, but the general effect is one of catharsis. . . . The book may appeal to those who are fascinated by the dark side of fame." Libr J

Yeager, Chuck, 1923-

Yeager, Chuck. Yeager; an autobiography; [by] Chuck Yeager & Leo Janos. Bantam Bks. 1985 342p il $17.95; pa $5.95   **92**

ISBN 0-553-05093-1; 0-553-25674-2 (pa)   LC 85-3959

Yeager "describes his early life in the hills of West Virginia; his years as fighter pilot in World War II, where he was shot down in occupied France and escaped with the help of the French Resistance. . . . He tells his story vividly and pulls no punches in describing the events and the people who made history with him." SLJ

Yeats, W. B. (William Butler), 1865-1939

Archibald, Douglas N. Yeats; [by] Douglas Archibald. Syracuse Univ. Press 1983 280p (Irish studies) hardcover o.p. paperback available $14.95   **92**

ISBN 0-8156-2391-7 (pa)   LC 82-19638

Yeats, W. B. (William Butler), 1865-1939
—Continued

"This book is organized around Yeats's interaction with the Romantic and modernist traditions in literature; his relationships with his family, especially his father, and his friends, especially Maud Gonne and Lady Gregory; the burden of his Anglo-Irish heritage and his celebrations of its major exemplars; his involvement with the occult, spiritism, and magic." Introduction

"Thoroughly informed, sensitive, and readable, this book is perhaps the best introduction we have to the whole of Yeats." Choice

Includes bibliography

Jeffares, A. Norman (Alexander Norman). W. B. Yeats: a new biography. Farrar, Straus & Giroux 1989 374p il $30   92
ISBN 0-374-28588-8   LC 90-187998
First published 1988 in the United Kingdom

The author "opts for an entirely new biography of Yeats rather than a revised version of his 1948 study, *W. B. Yeats: Man and Poet*. With the results of more than 30 years of new critical opinion and research of his own and by other people, Jeffares is able to supply a sensitive investigation of the contradictions that Yeats experienced as he developed into one of the world's great poets." Booklist

Includes bibliography

Yeats, W. B. (William Butler). The autobiography of William Butler Yeats; consisting of Reveries over childhood and youth, The trembling of the veil, and Dramatis personae. Macmillan 1987 c1965 404p $35   92
ISBN 0-02-632710-4   LC 87-14069
"A Macmillan Hudson River edition"
First published 1938

This volume contains "three long personal narratives telling the story of the Irish poet's childhood and early manhood. To these have been added two short extracts from a diary kept in 1909 . . . and a later account of his reception in Sweden when he was awarded the Nobel Prize for literature." N Y Her Trib Books

Yeltsin, Boris
Morrison, John. Boris Yeltsin; from Bolshevik to Democrat. Dutton 1991 303p map $20   92
1. Russia   (Republic)—Politics   and   government
2. Soviet Union—Politics and government
ISBN 0-525-93431-6   LC 91-34999
Also available in paperback from New Am. Lib.

This is a study of the "political struggle to democratize the Communist oligarchy in the Soviet Union . . . and the resistance to and leadership of this struggle within the vast Russian republic. Boris Yeltsin— one-time Communist Party member, now elected president of the Russian republic—demands the focus of this study." Booklist

Includes bibliographic references

Solovyov, Vladimir. Boris Yeltsin; a political biography; [by] Vladimir Solovyov and Elena Klepikova; translated by David Gurevich in collaboration with the authors. Putnam 1992 320p il $24.95   92
1. Russia   (Republic)—Politics   and   government
2. Soviet Union—Politics and government
ISBN 0-399-13715-7   LC 91-45102

The authors "have probed into Yeltsin's background, seeking to better understand this radical Russian who took control from Mikhail Gorbachev. A section comparing the lives of Yeltsin and Gorbachev is quite instructive. . . . The authors grant Yeltsin heroic status for his courage during the August 1991 coup, but they are not certain he can survive his revolution." Libr J

Includes bibliography

Young, Brigham, 1801-1877
Arrington, Leonard J. Brigham Young; American Moses. Knopf 1985 522p il $24.95   92
1. Mormons
ISBN 0-394-51022-4   LC 84-48650
Also available in paperback from University of Ill. Press

The author "starts his narrative with a description of Young's early years and how he and his family came into contact with the new faith. It follows him to Illinois, where sect founder Joseph Smith was assassinated, and across the plains and mountains as he leads the faithful to their promised land." Booklist

Includes bibliography

Young, Whitney Moore, 1921-1971
Weiss, Nancy J. (Nancy Joan). Whitney M. Young, Jr., and the struggle for civil rights. Princeton Univ. Press 1989 286p il $27.95   92
1. Blacks—Civil rights
ISBN 0-691-04757-X   LC 89-4045

This is a biography of the civil rights leader and executive director of the National Urban League

"This book is useful for anyone wishing to gain more understanding of the forces at work in the civil rights movement in the 1940s through the 1960s. Weiss's biography is concise and easy to read. . . . Weiss succeeds in conveying a complete sense of who Young was as a person." Christ Sci Monit

Includes bibliographic references

Zappa, Frank. See class 780.92

929   Genealogy, names, insignia

American & British genealogy & heraldry; a selected list of books; compiled by P. William Filby. 3rd ed. New England Hist. Genealogical Soc. 1983 736p $35   929
1. Genealogy—Bibliography 2. Heraldry—Bibliography
ISBN 0-88082-004-7   LC 83-865
Supplement published 1987 available for $15
First published 1970 by American Library Association

"Provides in classified order a selected list of books that American libraries should have to meet the needs of genealogists. Does not list family histories as such,

American & British genealogy & heraldry
—*Continued*
but rather the basic bibliographies, indexes, manuals, and auxiliary aids needed to pursue genealogical research." Ref Sources for Small & Medium-sized Libr. 5th edition

Baxter, Angus, 1912-
In search of your European roots; a complete guide to tracing your ancestors in every country in Europe. Genealogical 1985 289p pa $14.95 **929**
1. Genealogy
ISBN 0-8063-1114-2 LC 84-73426
This work covers the various types of genealogical records available in 30 European countries. Archival resources from the national to local level are described
Includes bibliography

Bentley, Elizabeth Petty
Directory of family associations. 1993-94 ed. Genealogical 1993 336p pa $29.95 **929**
1. Genealogy—Directories
ISBN 0-8063-1383-8
First published 1991
"An A-Z directory of 5000 family associations in the United States, it provides current addresses, phone numbers, contact persons, and publications. It is a much-needed, current resource for identifying U.S. family associations. . . . It will greatly assist planning for family reunions, contacting lost family members, or searching for missing heirs." Libr J [review of 1991 edition]

The genealogist's address book. 1992-93 ed. Genealogical 1992 539p $29.95 **929**
1. Genealogy—Directories
ISBN 0-8063-1348-X LC 92-71672
First published 1991
A "source for names, addresses, phone numbers, hours, and publications for national and state genealogical institutions and organizations. Included are ethnic and religious organizations that can help with genealogical research, as well as research centers and lineage societies. Special sections address adoption research and the use of computers." Libr J

Doane, Gilbert Harry, 1897-1984
Searching for your ancestors; the how and why of genealogy; [by] Gilbert H. Doane and James B. Bell. 6th ed. University of Minn. Press 1992 334p pa $17.95 **929**
1. Genealogy
ISBN 0-8166-1990-5 LC 91-32606
First published 1937
This guide shows how to "construct a family tree, trace elusive ancestors, discriminate between promising leads and false information, [and] use new computer research methods. . . . Also included is information on how to utilize the Family History Library in Salt Lake City and its Family Centers, the Library of Congress's Local History and Genealogy Room, the National Archives, and regional public library systems." Publisher's note
Includes bibliography

Fletcher, William P.
Recording your family history. Dodd, Mead 1986 313p o.p.; Ten Speed Press paperback available $11.95 **929**
1. Genealogy
ISBN 0-89815-324-7 (pa) LC 86-13598
First published 1983 in mimeograph format with title: Talking your roots
"A guide to preserving oral history with videotape, audiotape, suggested topics and questions, interview techniques." Title page
Includes bibliography

Gilmer, Lois C.
Genealogical research and resources; a guide for library use. American Lib. Assn. 1988 70p pa $17 **929**
1. Genealogy—Bibliography
ISBN 0-8389-0482-3 LC 87-32534
This book presents "coverage of genealogical reference service, genealogical research and its organization, primary sources, and secondary sources, and gives an overview of foreign research, with a selected bibliography for each chapter." Choice

Greenwood, Val D.
The researcher's guide to American genealogy. 2nd ed. Genealogical 1990 609p il $24.95 **929**
1. Genealogy 2. Archives—United States
ISBN 0-8063-1267-X LC 89-81464
First published 1973
"This classic textbook for the more experienced researcher gives detailed answers to questions about primary records, including vital, census, probate, land, court (including adoption), church, military, cemetery, and wills. Completely updated, it remains the outstanding text and reference book in American genealogy and the benchmark against which others must be judged." Libr J
Includes bibliographic references

Neagles, James C.
The Library of Congress; a guide to genealogical and historical research; by James C. Neagles, assisted by Mark C. Neagles. Ancestry 1990 381p il $35.95 **929**
1. Library of Congress 2. Genealogy 3. United States—History, Local
ISBN 0-916489-48-5 LC 89-18594
"This book describes significant materials in the Local History and Genealogy Reading Room as well as other areas of the Library of Congress. It is divided into three sections. Part 1 is an introduction to the Library, its divisions, services, and catalogs. Part 2 discusses categories of records and publications pertinent to genealogy, while part 3, which makes up more than half the book, describes key source materials by region and state." Booklist
Includes bibliographic references

The **Source**; a guidebook of American genealogy; edited by Arlene Eakle and Johni Cerny. Ancestry 1984 786p il $39.95
929

1. Genealogy
ISBN 0-916489-00-0　　　　　LC 84-70206

"A compilation of resources, research techniques, and record sources for American genealogical study. Useful for beginners and professionals." N Y Public Libr Book of How & Where to Look It Up

929.4 Personal names

Handbook of pseudonyms and personal nicknames; compiled by Harold S. Sharp. Scarecrow Press 1972 2v $59.50 + First and Second supplements　　**929.4**

1. Pseudonyms 2. Nicknames
ISBN 0-8108-0460-3

First supplement (1975) $74.50 (ISBN 0-8108-0807-2); Second supplement (1982) $29.50 (ISBN 0-8108-1539-7)

"Standard ever-expanding source for identification of the real persons behind pen names, stage names, pseudonyms, aliases, sobriquets, and nicknames. Each real name entry contains dates, brief identification, and a listing of all known pseudonyms, etc. Entries are listed by real name and by pseudonym." Ref Sources for Small & Medium-sized Libr. 5th edition

Lansky, Bruce
The best baby name book in the whole wide world. rev ed. Meadowbrook 1990 c1984 140p il pa $5　　　　**929.4**

1. Personal names
ISBN 0-915658-17-8

First published 1982; this is a reissue of the revised edition, published 1984

Offers advice to parents on choosing a name. Includes a listing of over 13,000 names

Latham, Edward
A dictionary of names, nicknames, and surnames of persons, places, and things. Omnigraphics 1990 334p $48　　**929.4**

1. Names—Dictionaries 2. Nicknames 3. Personal names—Dictionaries
ISBN 1-55888-901-9　　　　　LC 89-26513

A reissue of the title first published 1904 by Dutton

Compiled as a supplemnt to the "ordinary dictionaries of biography, geography, mythology, etc. [wherein] a person or place is often alluded to by means of a surname or nickname without any clue being given to the reader, who does not happen to be aware of the actual name of the person or place." Preface

Rosenkrantz, Linda
Beyond Jennifer and Jason; an enlightened guide to naming your baby; by Linda Rosenkrantz and Pamela Redmond Satran. St. Martin's Press 1988 300p $18.95; pa $9.95　　　　**929.4**

1. Personal names
ISBN 0-312-01907-6; 0-312-01908-4 (pa) LC 88-1840

This book contains nearly one hundred lists of names, organized into four sections: Style, Image, Sex, and Tradition

Shankle, George Earlie
American nicknames; their origin and significance. 2nd ed. Wilson, H.W. 1955 524p $42　　　　**929.4**

1. Nicknames 2. Personal names—United States 3. Geographic names—United States
ISBN 0-8242-0004-7

First published 1937

"Not limited to nicknames of persons, but includes also those applied to places, institutions, or objects, arranged by real names with cross references from nicknames. Information under the real names includes some explanation of the nicknames and their origin, and gives references to sources of information in footnotes." Sheehy. Guide to Ref Books. 10th edition

Stewart, George Rippey, 1895-
American given names; their origin and history in the context of the English language; [by] George R. Stewart. Oxford Univ. Press 1979 264p $29.95; pa $8.95
929.4

1. Personal names—United States
ISBN 0-19-502465-6; 0-19-504040-6 (pa)
LC 78-17603

This "is a dictionary of more than 800 names, including slave names used on antebellum plantations. Each entry gives derivation, meaning, [and] times of greatest popularity." Libr J

Includes bibliographic references

Twentieth century American nicknames; edited by Laurence Urdang; compiled by Walter C. Kidney and George C. Kohn; with a foreword by Leslie Alan Dunkling. Wilson, H.W. 1979 398p $40　　**929.4**

1. Nicknames 2. Personal names—United States 3. Geographic names—United States
ISBN 0-8242-0642-8　　　　　LC 79-23390

"Nicknames and the real names of persons, places, etc., are listed in a single alphabet. Includes variant nicknames. Editor attempted to avoid duplication of nicknames appearing in Shankle's *American nicknames* [entered above]." Ref Sources for Small & Medium-sized Libr. 5th edition

Withycombe, Elizabeth Gidley
The Oxford dictionary of English Christian names; by E. G. Withycombe. 3d ed. Clarendon Press 1977 xlvii, 310p $15.95; pa $10.95　　　　**929.4**

1. Personal names, English
ISBN 0-19-869124-6; 0-19-281213-0 (pa)
LC 77-373402

First published 1945 in the United Kingdom

"For each name the author gives its derivation, a brief history of usage through the ages including sources for earliest use, and cross-references from variant forms. A brief supplement lists 'Some common words derived from Christian names.'" Booklist

929.9 Flags

Shearer, Benjamin F.
State names, seals, flags, and symbols; a historical guide; [by] Benjamin F. Shearer and Barbara S. Shearer. Greenwood Press 1987 239p il $39.95   **929.9**

1. Geographic names—United States 2. Seals (Numismatics) 3. Flags—United States
ISBN 0-313-24559-2   LC 86-27135

Also available in paperback from New Am. Lib.

"Separate chapters cover state names and nicknames, mottoes, seals, flags, capitols, flowers, trees, birds, and songs. In each chapter, individual states are given ample coverage, with one or more paragraphs devoted to each. . . . The excellent index offers easy access to the contents." SLJ

Includes bibliography

Talocci, Mauro
Guide to the flags of the world; illustrations by Guido Canestrari, Carlo Giordana, Paolo Riccioni; translated from the Italian by Ronald Strom. rev & updated ed, by Whitney Smith. Morrow 1982 271p il hardcover o.p. paperback available $14.95   **929.9**

1. Flags
ISBN 0-688-01141-1 (pa)   LC 81-16890

Original Italian edition, 1977

"Descriptions and histories of national, state, and provincial flags, coats of arms, and international flags. Arranged by continent, then by country." N Y Public Libr Book of How & Where to Look It Up

930 History of ancient world

The **Atlas** of mysterious places; the world's unexplained sacred sites, symbolic landscapes, ancient cities, and lost lands; edited by Jennifer Westwood. Weidenfeld & Nicolson 1987 240p il maps $34.95   **930**

1. Antiquities 2. Historic sites 3. Cities and towns, Ruined, extinct, etc. 4. Civilization, Ancient
ISBN 1-55584-130-9   LC 86-28170

An illustrated look at such ancient sites as Knossos, Stonehenge, the Nazca lines, and the Great Pyramids
"An exemplary study for public and school libraries." Booklist

The **Cambridge** ancient history. Cambridge Univ. Press 1970-1991 il maps apply to publisher for price   **930**

1. History, Ancient

Original 12 volume set published 1923-1939 with 5 volumes of plates. Revised editions of volumes 5, 6, 9-11 in preparation

Contents: v 1, pt 1 Prolegomena and prehistory 3rd ed. 1970; v 1, pt 2 Early history of the Middle East 3rd ed. 1971; v2, pt 1 History of the Middle East and the Aegean Region, ca. 1800-1380 B.C. 3rd ed. 1973; v2, pt 2 History of the Middle East and the Aegean Region, ca. 1380-1000 B.C. 3rd ed. 1975; v3, pt 1

Prehistory of the Balkans; and the Middle East and the Aegean world, tenth to eighth centuries B.C. 2nd ed. 1982; v3, pt 2 The Assyrian and Babylonian Empires and other states of the Near East, from the eighth to the sixth centuries B.C. 2nd ed. 1991; v3, pt 3 Expansion of the Greek world, eighth to sixth centuries B.C. 2nd ed. 1982; v4 Persia, Greece and the Western Mediterranean, ca. 525 to 479 B.C. 2nd ed. 1988; v5 Athens, 478-401 B.C. o.p.; v6 Macedon, 401-301 B.C. o.p.; v7, pt 1 The Hellenistic World 2nd ed. 1984; v7, pt 2 The rise of Rome to 220 B.C. 2nd ed. 1990; v8 Rome and the Mediterranean to 133 B.C. 2nd ed. 1990; v9 The Roman Republic, 133-44 B.C.; v11 The imperial peace, A.D. 70-192; v12 The imperial crises and recovery, A.D. 193-324

Only available volume of plates illustrating v1-2, 2nd ed. 1977; other volumes of plates o.p.

An "excellent reference history, each chapter written by a specialist, with full bibliographies at the end of each volume." Sheehy. Guide to Ref Books. 10th edition

Mysteries of the ancient world; prepared by the Special Publications Division, National Geographic Society. National Geographic Soc. 1979 223p il maps $9.95   **930**

1. Civilization, Ancient 2. Excavations (Archeology)
ISBN 0-87044-254-6   LC 77-93402

Contents: Ice Age hunters: artists in hidden caves; Roots of the city: Jericho and Catal Hüyük; Egypt's pyramids: monuments of the Pharaohs; Ancient India: cities lost in time; Megaliths: Europe's silent stones; Minoans: a joyous people vanishes in myth; Mycenaeans: warrior-merchants of Greece; Etruscans: festive in life, lavish in death; Easter Island: brooding sentinels of stone

Includes bibliography

Splendors of the past; lost cities of the ancient world; prepared by the Special Publications Division, National Geographic Society. National Geographic Soc. 1981 295p il maps $19.95   **930**

1. Cities and towns, Ruined, extinct, etc. 2. Civilization, Ancient
ISBN 0-87044-358-5   LC 80-7827

This volume "focuses on the lost cities of seven ancient civilizations, among them those of Sumeria, Pompeii, Angkor, and the Hittite empire. The popularly written articles convey the meticulous labor involved in the cities' construction, provide a glimpse of ancient ways of life, and suggest the excitement of archaeological discovery." Booklist

Includes bibliography

930.1 Archaeology

Marek, Kurt W., 1915-1972
Gods, graves, and scholars; the story of archaeology; by C. W. Ceram; translated from the German by E. B. Garside and Sophie Wilkins. 2nd rev and substantially enl ed. Knopf 1967 441p il maps $30; pa $10   **930.1**

1. Archeology
ISBN 0-394-42661-4; 0-394-74319-9 (pa)

Original German edition, 1949; first English language edition, 1951

"The story of Champollion and the reading of the Rosetta Stone, the decipherment of the inscriptions on the monument of Darius the Great, Leonard Woolley's

Marek, Kurt W., 1915-1972—*Continued*
famous excavations at Ur, and John Lloyd Stephens'
discovery of the ruins of a great Mayan city are . . .
told in this book." Doors to More Mature Read

Includes bibliography

Robbins, Lawrence H.
Stones, bones, and ancient cities; the
greatest archaeological discoveries of all
time. St. Martin's Press 1990 267p il $18.95
930.1

1. Antiquities 2. Archeology 3. Civilization, Ancient
ISBN 0-312-04431-3   LC 89-77948

The author "has compiled facts, theories, and personal
experience into seven chapters exploring missing links to
human ancestors, cave art, burial practices, the discovery
of lost cities, underwater archaeology, archaeoastronomy
(the study of 'ancient monuments of an astronomical
nature'), and the origin of writing. . . . A fascinating,
highly readable, and informative excursion into the richness of the past and the secrets it still holds." Booklist

Includes bibliography

932 Egypt to 640 A.D.

Aldred, Cyril, 1914-1991
Akhenaten: King of Egypt. Thames &
Hudson 1988 320p il $35; pa $19.95   **932**

1. Akhenaton, King of Egypt, fl. ca. 1388-1358 B.C.
2. Egypt—Antiquities
ISBN 0-500-05048-1; 0-500-27621-8 (pa)
     LC 87-51153

The author "relates the archaeological processes
whereby Akhenaten's existence and his impact on Egyptian life were reconstructed through unearthed physical
evidence." Booklist

Aldred "ranges over archaeology, art-history, morbid
pathology, social and political history and the evolution
of ideas. This is a book to which one will return, and
gain each time one does so." Times Lit Suppl

Includes bibliography

Bucaille, Maurice
Mummies of the pharaohs; modern
medical investigations; translated from the
French by Alastair D. Pannell and the
author. St. Martin's Press 1990 xx, 236p il
$18.95   **932**

1. Mummies 2. Egypt—Antiquities
ISBN 0-312-05131-X   LC 90-37420

Original French edition, 1987

The author "presents a record of modern medical research conducted on Egyptian mummies in Paris to
foster an understanding of the process of mummifica-
tion." Booklist

Bunson, Margaret R.
The encyclopedia of ancient Egypt; [by]
Margaret Bunson. Facts on File 1991 291p
il maps $40   **932**

1. Egypt—Civilization—Dictionaries   2. Egypt—Antiquities—Dictionaries
ISBN 0-8160-2093-0   LC 89-27473

This work "consists of more than 1,500 alphabetically
arranged entries covering Egypt from around 3200 B.C.
to the fall of the New Kingdom in 1070 B.C. There
are several broad entries such as *Egypt, Agriculture, and
Religion*. The bulk of the book, however, consists of
specific entries for kings and queens, gods and goddesses,
cities, important documents, etc." Booklist

Includes bibliographic references

Hobson, Christine
The world of the pharaohs; foreword by
Thomas J. Logan. Thames & Hudson 1987
192p il maps $19.95   **932**

1. Egypt—Antiquities
ISBN 0-500-05046-5   LC 87-50390

Contents: Discovering the past; Egyptian origins;
Pyramids: houses for eternity; The shifting sands; Temples: mansions of the gods; Egypt's legacy

Includes bibliography

Hoffman, Michael A., 1944-
Egypt before the pharaohs; the prehistoric
foundations of Egyptian civilization. rev and
updated. University of Tex. Press 1991 xxi,
409p il pa $17.95   **932**

1. Egypt—Antiquities 2. Prehistoric man
ISBN 0-292-72073-4   LC 90-70161

First published 1979 by Knopf

This volume studies the cultural development of prehistoric Egyptian society

Includes bibliographic references

Lepre, J. P.
The Egyptian pyramids; a comprehensive,
illustrated reference. McFarland & Co. 1990
341p il $49.95   **932**

1. Egypt—Antiquities 2. Pyramids
ISBN 0-89950-461-2   LC 89-43623

This "study of the pyramids built during the reigns
of 42 different pharaohs, incorporates details pertaining
to the history of each of the pharaohs who constructed
a pyramid, concise chronological listings of the pyramids,
relevant textual studies from the ancient Egyptian
sources, and a review of the material remains associated
with the pyramids." Choice

Includes bibliographic references

Reeves, C. N. (Carl Nicholas), 1956-
The complete Tutankhamun; the king, the
tomb, the royal treasure; by Nicholas
Reeves; foreword by the Seventh Earl of
Carnarvon. Thames & Hudson 1990 224p
il maps $24.95   **932**

1. Tutankhamen, King of Egypt 2. Egypt—Antiquities
3. Excavations (Archeology)—Egypt
ISBN 0-500-05058-9   LC 90-70202

This book covers ancient Egyptian history and
describes events that took place during Tutankhamen's
rule. The author then focuses on the discovery of Tut's
tomb and the artifacts found there

"Reeves has produced a beautiful book with significant
new information. The extent, wealth, and quality of the
illustrations alone make it an important and attractive

Reeves, C. N. (Carl Nicholas), 1956- —
Continued
book." Libr J
Includes bibliography

Romer, John, 1941-
Ancient lives; daily life in Egypt of the pharaohs. Holt & Co. 1984 235p il maps hardcover o.p. paperback available $16.95
932
1. Egypt—Antiquities 2. Egypt—Civilization
ISBN 0-8050-1244-3 (pa)   LC 84-12908
Published in the United Kingdom with subtitle: The story of the pharaohs' tombmakers
The author "re-creates in rich, sensory detail the rhythms and textures of ordinary life in an extraordinary time and place. We learn what the villagers' houses were like, what they ate and wore, what they dreamt about. . . . Some readers may be put off by the dense accumulation of archeological detail. But for those who stay with it, this book has rewards." N Y Times Book Rev
Includes bibliography

Tompkins, Peter
Secrets of the Great Pyramid; with an appendix by Livio Catullo Stecchini. Harper & Row 1971 416p il hardcover o.p. paperback available $30   **932**
1. Pyramids
ISBN 0-06-090631-6 (pa)
The subject of this book "is Cheops' pyramid at Giza, which Tompkins believes was built not as a tomb but as a monumental record of Egyptian mathematical and astronomical data." Libr J
Includes bibliography

933 Palestine to 70 A.D.

Dothan, Trude Krakauer
People of the sea; the search for the Philistines; [by] Trude Dothan, Moshe Dothan. Macmillan 1992 276p il maps $25
933
1. Philistines 2. Middle East—Antiquities
ISBN 0-02-532261-3   LC 91-47880
"Through their narratives and descriptions of finds . . . the Dothans reconstruct the life of a people whom the Bible perceived as barbarous, yet whom they have found to be sophisticated city planners with advanced technology who profoundly affected the cultures around them in the Late Bronze and Early Iron Age. Written in a direct, engaging style, this is for lay readers as well as scholars." Libr J
Includes bibliography

935 Mesopotamia and Iranian Plateau to 637 A.D.

Woolley, Sir Leonard, 1880-1960
The Sumerians. Norton 1965 198p il maps hardcover o.p. paperback available $8.95
935
1. Sumerians 2. Civilization, Assyro-Babylonian
ISBN 0-393-00292-6 (pa)
Also available in hardcover from AMS Press
"The Norton library"
First published 1929 in the United Kingdom
A reconstruction of Sumerian civilization based on the excavations at Ur, the King-lists and legends

936.2 England to 410 A.D.

Fowles, John, 1926-
The enigma of Stonehenge; [by] John Fowles & Barry Brukoff. Summit Bks. 1980 126p il hardcover o.p. paperback available $9.95   **936.2**
1. Stonehenge (England) 2. Great Britain—Antiquities
ISBN 0-671-43758-5 (pa)   LC 80-11472
A collaboration between John Fowles, who investigates the meaning and history of the ancient monument, and Barry Brukoff whose numerous contemporary photographs illustrate the text

Ross, Anne
The life and death of a Druid prince; the story of Lindow Man, an archaeological sensation; [by] Anne Ross and Don Robins. Summit Bks. 1989 176p il maps hardcover o.p. paperback available $10.95   **936.2**
1. Lindow Man 2. England—Antiquities
ISBN 0-671-74122-5 (pa)   LC 90-9616
"Lindow Man is the name given to remains found in an English peat bog of a corpse that has been proven to be at least 1,800 years old. . . . Using evidence gathered from stomach contents (Robins' specialty) and the body's physical appearance, as well as known events in Celtic history, the two authors surmise that this person was a Druid prince from Ireland who was sacrificed to help turn the tide in the Roman invasion of England." Booklist
Includes bibliographic references

937 Roman Empire

Carcopino, Jérôme, 1881-1970
Daily life in ancient Rome; the people and the city at the height of the empire; edited with bibliography and notes by Henry T. Rowell; translated from the French by E. O. Lorimer. Yale Univ. Press 1940 342p il hardcover o.p. paperback available $14
937
1. Rome—Social life and customs 2. Rome—Civilization
ISBN 0-300-00031-6 (pa)

Carcopino, Jérôme, 1881-1970—*Continued*

An exploration of the economy, social customs, education and religious practices of Rome during the second century

Durant, William James, 1885-1981

Caesar and Christ; by Will Durant. Simon & Schuster 1944 751p il maps (Story of civilization, pt3) $35   **937**

1. Rome—History 2. Rome—Civilization 3. Church history

ISBN 0-671-11500-6

"A history of Roman civilization and of Christianity from their beginnings to A.D.325." Title page

Includes bibliography

Gibbon, Edward, 1737-1794

The decline and fall of the Roman Empire   **937**

1. Rome—History 2. Byzantine Empire

Hardcover and paperback editions available from various publishers

First published 1776-1788 in the United Kingdom with title: The history of the decline and fall of the Roman Empire

"In this substantial history of the Roman Empire, Gibbon bridges the abyss between the ancient and the modern world. It is the one historical work of the eighteenth century that is still accepted as authoritative. It covers thirteen centuries of history, during which time paganism was breaking down and Christianity was taking its place." Reader's Adviser

Pompeii; the vanished city; by the editors of Time-Life Books. Time-Life Bks. 1992 168p il (Lost civilizations) $19.93   **937**

1. Pompeii (Ancient city)   LC 92-1277

A heavily illustrated look at the social life and customs of Pompeii at the time of Vesuvius' eruption. The excavations at Herculaneum are also discussed

Includes bibliography

938   Greece to 323 A.D.

Civilization of the ancient Mediterranean: Greece and Rome; edited by Michael Grant and Rachel Kitzinger. Scribner 1988 3v il maps set $259   **938**

1. Civilization, Greek 2. Rome—Civilization

ISBN 0-684-17594-0   LC 87-23465

This reference work contains "97 chapters by 88 authorities on everything from farming and cooking to taxes, warfare and divinities in Greece and Rome. . . . The bibliographies following each chapter are . . . comprehensive, the photographs and illustrations are as instructive as they are delightful and the maps are easy to read." N Y Times Book Rev

Durant, William James, 1885-1981

The life of Greece; [by] Will Durant. Simon & Schuster 1939 754p il (Story of civilization, pt2) $35   **938**

1. Greece—History 2. Civilization, Greek

ISBN 0-671-41800-9

"Being a history of Greek civilization from the beginnings, and of civilization in the Near East from the death of Alexander, to the Roman conquest; with an introduction on the prehistoric culture of Crete." Title page

Includes bibliography

Grant, Michael, 1914-

The classical Greeks. Scribner 1989 337p il $27.50   **938**

1. Greece—History

ISBN 0-684-19126-1   LC 89-6131

This book "centers on the lives and times of 37 great figures of classical Greece—artists, politicians, philosophers, soldiers—to create a detailed picture of the era, from the fifth century B.C. to the accession of Alexander the Great in 336 B.C." Booklist

Includes bibliography

The founders of the Western world; a history of Greece and Rome. Scribner 1991 352p maps $27.50   **938**

1. Greece—History 2. Rome—History

ISBN 0-684-19303-5   LC 90-23818

This history covers "the rise of Hellenistic culture and philosophies, its political collapse in the Peloponnesian War, Alexander the Great's immortal but insubstantial conquests, and everything's absorption by and propagation to the future under the auspices of the Pax Romana. . . . A cornerstone acquisition for any and every library." Booklist

Includes bibliography

The rise of the Greeks. Scribner 1988 c1987 391p il maps o.p.; Collier Bks. paperback available $14.95   **938**

1. Greece—History

ISBN 0-02-032781-1 (pa)   LC 87-34741

First published 1987 in the United Kingdom

This work "focuses on the years c.1000-490 B.C., following the collapse of the Mycenaean palace regimes and before the Peloponnesian Wars." Publisher's note

"For an age from which so little literary material survives, it is inevitable that much of the information comes from recent archaeological finds—and this work makes great use of such material. Much more attention than usual is paid to Sicily, Cyrene, Cyprus, and South Russia; this geographical organization is one of the book's great virtues." Choice

Includes bibliography

Levi, Peter, 1931-

Atlas of the Greek world. Facts on File 1981 c1980 239p il maps (Historical atlas ser) $45   **938**

1. Greece—Maps 2. Civilization, Greek 3. Greece—Antiquities

ISBN 0-87196-448-1   LC 81-122477

First published 1980 in the United Kingdom

Levi, Peter, 1931——Continued
"After a part on 'the land in context,' the material is arranged chronologically: the ages of Bronze, of tyranny, of Pericles, and of Alexander. A final part on 'the fate of Hellenism' deals with Greece's influence on later Western civilization." Libr J
"A great deal of information is presented in a generally attractive manner. Recommended for public and undergraduate libraries." Choice

MacKendrick, Paul Lachlan, 1914-
The Greek stones speak; the story of archaeology in Greek lands. 2nd ed. Norton 1981 534p il maps $24.95; pa $13.95 **938**
1. Greece—Antiquities 2. Excavations (Archeology)—Greece
ISBN 0-393-01463-0; 0-393-30111-7 (pa) LC 81-4349
First published 1962
This is a "survey of Greek archaeology from prehistory to the third century A.D. . . . While readable, the guide is for those with background in ancient history and archaeology." Booklist
Includes bibliographic references

The **Oxford** history of the classical world; edited by John Boardman, Jasper Griffin, Oswyn Murray. Oxford Univ. Press 1986 882p il maps $49.95 **938**
1. History, Ancient 2. Civilization, Ancient
ISBN 0-19-872112-9 LC 85-21774
Also available in a two-volume paperback edition ea $21.50 (v1 ISBN 0-19-282165-2; v2 ISBN 0-19-282166-0)
"Thirty-two chapters (with select bibliographies) by different authors, plus an introduction and conclusion, survey antiquity from the time of Homer to the fall of the Roman Empire. Part 1 covers Greece, Part 2, the Hellenistic age and the evolution of the Roman republic, and part 3, Imperial Rome." Libr J
"This is a finely produced book, treating not only the political and social history of the classical world but its cultural history as well—especially well, since the latter constitutes a major emphasis." Choice

Robinson, Cyril Edward, b. 1884
Everyday life in ancient Greece; [by] C. E. Robinson. Oxford Univ. Press 1933 159p il maps o.p.; Greenwood Press reprint available lib bdg $45 **938**
1. Civilization, Greek 2. Greece—Social life and customs
ISBN 0-8371-9078-9 (lib bdg)
Also available in hardcover from AMS Press
The development of Greek society is traced from its origins to the end of the classical age. Special focus is on Athens and its economy, politics, art, religion and education

Thucydides
The history of the Peloponnesian War **938**
1. Greece—History—431-404 B.C., Peloponnesian War
Hardcover and paperback editions available from various publishers
Variant title: The Peloponnesian War

Thucydides' "chosen subject was the Peloponnesian War, which covered 27 years of his own lifetime, 431-404 B.C., and in which he fought as a commander of the Athenian troops in Thrace. His ideal of history is said to have been first accuracy, and then relevancy. . . . He rarely digressed. His history is unfinished, breaking off in the middle of the year 411 B.C." Reader's Adviser

938.003 Classical dictionaries

Grant, Michael, 1914-
A guide to the ancient world; a dictionary of classical place names. Wilson, H.W. 1986 728p maps $68 **938.003**
1. Classical dictionaries 2. Mediterranean region—Gazetteers
ISBN 0-8242-0742-4 LC 86-15785
"This dictionary provides background for about nine hundred places important to an understanding of the cultures of the ancient Greeks, Etruscans, and Romans. . . . The time period covered is from the first millennium B.C. until the fall of the Roman empire in the fifth century A.D. Depending on the subject, a typical entry includes information about history, geography, archaeology, and sometimes art and mythology." Am Ref Books Annu, 1987

The **Oxford** classical dictionary; edited by N. G. L. Hammond and H. H. Scullard. 2nd ed. Oxford Univ. Press 1970 xxii, 1176p $55 **938.003**
1. Classical dictionaries
ISBN 0-19-869117-3
First published 1949 under the editorship of M. Cary and others
"A scholarly dictionary, with signed articles, covering biography, literature, mythology, philosophy, religion, science, geography, etc. Most of the articles are brief, but there are some longer survey articles, e.g. Rome, music, scholarship, etc." Sheehy. Guide to Ref Books. 10th edition

939 Other parts of ancient world to ca. 640

Wood, Michael, 1948-
In search of the Trojan War. Facts on File 1985 272p il maps o.p.; New Am. Lib. paperback available $12.95 **939**
1. Troy (Ancient city) 2. Civilization, Ancient 3. Bronze Age
ISBN 0-452-25960-6 (pa) LC 85-16113
The author "outlines the path the legend took through medieval, Renaissance and modern society. The bulk of this . . . book is devoted to archeological efforts to prove the truth of Homer's epic and confirm that Troy was actually at Hissarlik. Mr. Wood also describes the history and archeology of Mycenae." N Y Times Book Rev
"This is a first-rate book. . . . The book makes a readable and clear approach to some of the knottiest problems of Bronze Age archaeology." Choice
Includes bibliography

940.1 Europe—Early history to 1453

The **Cambridge** medieval history; planned by J. B. Bury. Cambridge Univ. Press 1929-1967 8v in 9 il maps **940.1**

1. Middle Ages—History

Contents: v1 The Christian Roman Empire and the foundation of the Teutonic kingdoms (o.p.); v2 The rise of the Saracens and the foundation of the Western Empire (o.p.); v3 Germany and the Western Empire (o.p.); v4 The Byzantine Empire 2d ed. Pt.1 Byzantium and its neighbors 2nd ed. (o.p.); pt.2 Government, church and civilization 2nd ed. $150 (ISBN 0-521-04536-3); v5 Contest of empire and papacy (o.p.); v6 Victory of the papacy $185 (ISBN 0-521-04538-X); v7 Decline of the empire and papacy (o.p.); v8 Close of the Middle Ages (o.p.)

"An excellent reference history, written by specialists, with full bibliographies at the end of each volume." Sheehy. Guide to Ref Books. 10th edition

Dictionary of the Middle Ages; Joseph R. Strayer, editor in chief. Scribner 1982-1989 12v + index il maps set $990 **940.1**

1. Middle Ages—Dictionaries

ISBN 0-684-19073-7   LC 82-5904

"Authoritative and modern, this interdisciplinary dictionary spans the years from A.D. 500 to 1500, taking cognizance of the Byzantine, Islamic, and Jewish contributions to medieval life as well as the European. . . . The contents are in alphabetical sequence, some articles providing brief definitions or identifications, others offering extensive background and analysis." Ref Sources: a brief guide

Durant, William James, 1885-1981

The age of faith; [by] Will Durant. Simon & Schuster 1950 1196p il (Story of civilization, pt4) $35 **940.1**

1. Civilization, Medieval 2. Middle Ages—History 3. Religion

ISBN 0-671-01200-2

"A history of medieval civilization—Christian, Islamic, and Judaic—from Constantine to Dante: A.D. 325-1300." Title page

Includes bibliography

Gies, Frances

The knight in history. Harper & Row 1984 255p il maps $16.95; pa $12 **940.1**

1. Knights and knighthood 2. Middle Ages—History

ISBN 0-06-015339-3; 0-06-091413-0 (pa)

LC 84-47571

This book describes the rise and fall of the institution of knighthood and the influence of the medieval knight throughout history

Includes bibliography

Life in a medieval village; [by] Frances and Joseph Gies. Harper & Row 1990 257p il maps $22.95; pa $12 **940.1**

1. Civilization, Medieval 2. Middle Ages—History

ISBN 0-06-016215-5; 0-06-092046-7 (pa)

LC 89-33759

"Elton, England, is the focal point of the authors' efforts to portray the everyday life and social structure of the High Middle Ages. After giving a brief summary of Elton's origins and development in the Roman and Anglo-Saxon periods, the book examines just how the residents lived and worked within the feudal structure at the beginning of the fourteenth century." Booklist

"The Gieses provide a highly readable and soundly researched picture." Libr J

Includes bibliography

Gies, Joseph

Life in a medieval city; [by] Joseph and Frances Gies. Crowell 1969 274p il maps o.p.; HarperCollins Pubs. paperback available $12 **940.1**

1. Civilization, Medieval 2. Middle Ages—History

ISBN 0-06-090880-7 (pa)

"A portrait of a medieval city [Troyes], a flourishing settlement of a type not known in Europe before the Middle Ages." Cincinnati Public Libr

The **Middle** Ages; by Morris Bishop. American Heritage 1985 c1968 350p il (American Heritage lib) pa $9.95 **940.1**

1. Middle Ages—History 2. Civilization, Medieval

ISBN 0-8281-0487-5   LC 85-23013

First published 1968 with title: The Horizon book of the Middle Ages

This volume covers the period from the conversion of Constantine in 312 A.D. through the conclusion of the Hundred Years War in 1461

The **Oxford** illustrated history of medieval Europe; edited by George Holmes. Oxford Univ. Press 1988 398p il maps $45; pa $21.95 **940.1**

1. Europe—History—476-1492

ISBN 0-19-820073-0; 0-19-285220-5 (pa)

LC 87-11122

An "account of medieval Europe from the fall of Rome to the eve of the Reformation. This popular history, well-written by professional historians, is for the intelligent general reader. . . . Maps, charts, and illustrations deserve high praise. Highly recommended." Libr J

Includes bibliography

940.2 Europe—1453-

Durant, William James, 1885-1981

The age of Louis XIV; by Will and Ariel Durant. Simon & Schuster 1963 802p il (Story of civilization, pt8) $35 **940.2**

1. Europe—Civilization 2. Europe—History—1492-1789

ISBN 0-671-01215-0

"A history of European civilization in the period of Pascal, Molière, Cromwell, Milton, Peter the Great, Newton and Spinoza: 1648-1715." Title page

Includes bibliography

Durant, William James, 1885-1981 — *Continued*

The age of Napoleon; by Will and Ariel Durant. Simon & Schuster 1975 xxi, 872p il (Story of civilization, pt11) $35 **940.2**

1. Napoleon I, Emperor of the French, 1769-1821 2. Europe—Civilization 3. Europe—History—1789-1900
ISBN 0-671-21988-X

"A history of European civilization from 1789-1815." Subtitle

This look at the social and political history of 1789-1815 Europe focuses on the influence of Napoleon

Includes bibliography

The age of reason begins; by Will and Ariel Durant. Simon & Schuster 1961 732p il (Story of civilization, pt7) $35 **940.2**

1. Europe—Civilization 2. Europe—History—1492-1789
ISBN 0-671-01320-3

"A history of European civilization in the period of Shakespeare, Bacon, Montaigne, Rembrandt, Galileo, and Descartes: 1558-1648." Title page

Includes bibliography

The age of Voltaire; by Will and Ariel Durant. Simon & Schuster 1965 898p il (Story of civilization, pt9) $35 **940.2**

1. Voltaire, 1694-1778 2. Europe—Civilization 3. Europe—History—1492-1789
ISBN 0-671-01325-4

"A history of civilization in Western Europe from 1715 to 1756, with special emphasis on the conflict between religion and philosophy." Title page

Includes bibliography

The Reformation; [by] Will Durant. Simon & Schuster 1957 1025p il (Story of civilization, pt6) $35 **940.2**

1. Europe—Civilization 2. Reformation 3. Europe—History—476-1492 4. Europe—History—1492-1789
ISBN 0-671-61050-3

"A history of European civilization from Wyclif to Calvin: 1300-1564." Title page

Among the personalities discussed are Charles V, Chaucer, Knox, Luther, Mary I, More, Rabelais and Wolsey

Includes bibliography

Rousseau and revolution; by Will and Ariel Durant. Simon & Schuster 1967 xx, 1091p il maps (Story of civilization, pt10) $35 **940.2**

1. Europe—Civilization 2. Europe—History—1492-1789 3. Eighteenth century
ISBN 0-671-63058-X

"A history of civilization in France, England, and Germany from 1756 and in the remainder of Europe from 1715 to 1789." Title page

There is "no popular history that is so encyclopedic in scope, so brightly readable in style." Saturday Rev

Includes bibliography

Hobsbawm, E. J. (Eric J.), 1917-

The age of revolution, 1789-1848. World Pub. Co. 1962 356p il maps (World histories of civilization) o.p.; New Am. Lib. paperback available $5.95 **940.2**

1. Europe—History—1789-1900 2. Industry—History
ISBN 0-451-62720-2 (pa)

"This book traces the transformation of the world between 1789 and 1848 insofar as it was due to what is here called the 'dual revolution'—the French Revolution of 1789 and the contemporaneous (British) Industrial Revolution." Preface

Includes bibliography

Manchester, William

A world lit only by fire; the medieval mind and the Renaissance: portrait of an age. Little, Brown 1992 318p il maps $24.95; pa $11.95 **940.2**

1. Renaissance
ISBN 0-316-54531-7; 0-316-54556-2 (pa)

LC 91-39928

The author covers "the tumultuous span from the Dark Ages to the dawn of the Renaissance. He delineates an age when invisible spirits infested the air, when tolerance was seen as treachery and 'a mafia of profane popes desecrated Christianity.' Besides re-creating the arduous lives of ordinary people, . . . [Manchester] peoples his tapestry with such figures as Leonardo, Machiavelli, Lucrezia Borgia, Erasmus, Luther, Henry VIII and Anne Boleyn." Publ Wkly

Includes bibliographic references

Nicolson, Sir Harold George, 1886-1968

The Congress of Vienna; a study in allied unity: 1812-1822; by Harold Nicolson. Harcourt Brace & Co. 1946 312p il hardcover o.p. paperback available $10.95 **940.2**

1. Congress of Vienna (1814-1815) 2. Europe—Politics and government—1789-1900
ISBN 0-15-622061-X (pa)

The author examines the Conference which convened to settle the problems that arose following Napoleon's defeat

Includes bibliographic references

940.3 World War I, 1914-1918

Churchill, Sir Winston, 1874-1965

The world crisis; an abridgment of the classic 4-volume history of World War I; [by] Winston S. Churchill. Scribner 1992 866p il maps $35 **940.3**

1. World War, 1914-1918 2. World War, 1914-1918—Great Britain
ISBN 0-684-19453-8

LC 92-17003

This is Churchill's comprehensive account of World War I from the British standpoint as seen by him from the position of authority he held

Ferrell, Robert H.

Woodrow Wilson and World War I, 1917-1921. Harper & Row 1985 346p il maps (New American nation ser) $19.95; pa $8.95   **940.3**

1. Wilson, Woodrow, 1856-1924 2. World War, 1914-1918—United States 3. United States—Politics and government
ISBN 0-06-011229-8; 0-06-091216-2 (pa)
         LC 84-48160

A look at how Wilson directed American policy throughout the First World War

This book "is grounded on solid scholarship and though the writing is informal at times it is an engaging style nonetheless. . . . There is a useful bibliography." Best Sellers

Massie, Robert K., 1929-

Dreadnought; Britain, Germany, and the coming of the great war. Random House 1991 xxxi, 1007p il map $35   **940.3**

1. World War, 1914-1918—Causes 2. Germany—History—1866-1918 3. Great Britain—History—1900-1999 (20th century)
ISBN 0-394-52833-6   LC 91-52672

Also available in paperback from Ballantine Bks.

The author discusses the race for naval superiority between Great Britain and Germany leading up to the First World War

"Dreadnought is history in the grand manner, as most readers prefer it: how people shaped, or were shaped by, events that consensus has declared to be landmarks. At his vivid best, Massie does not simply retell the past. He allows one, in a way, to relive it." Time

Includes bibliography

Stokesbury, James L.

A short history of World War I. Morrow 1981 348p maps hardcover o.p. paperback available $11   **940.3**

1. World War, 1914-1918
ISBN 0-688-00129-7 (pa)   LC 80-22206

This chronologically arranged history of World War I presents both the political and military perspectives

Includes bibliography

Toland, John

No man's land; 1918, the last year of the Great War. Doubleday 1980 xx, 651p il maps o.p.; Ballantine Bks. paperback available $5.95   **940.3**

1. World War, 1914-1918
ISBN 0-345-33577-5 (pa)   LC 78-22761

The author "writes primarily of the fighting on the Western Front during the last year of the Great War, with secondary attention given to the struggles among the political and military leaders of the countries involved." Choice

Includes bibliography

Tuchman, Barbara Wertheim

The guns of August; [by] Barbara W. Tuchman. anniversary ed. Macmillan 1988 c1962 511p il maps $19.95   **940.3**

1. World War, 1914-1918
ISBN 0-02-620311-1   LC 88-29330

Also available in paperback from Bantam Bks.

A reissue with a new preface by the author of the title first published 1962

A history of the negotiations that preceded World War I and the course of the war's first month

Includes bibliography

The Zimmermann telegram; [by] Barbara W. Tuchman. [new ed]. Macmillan 1966 244p il o.p.; Ballantine Bks. paperback available $10   **940.3**

1. World War, 1914-1918—Causes
ISBN 0-345-32425-0 (pa)

First published 1958

The author discusses the German plan to induce Mexico to attack the U.S. during World War I

Includes bibliographic references

940.4 World War I, 1914-1918 (Military conduct of the war)

Lawrence, T. E. (Thomas Edward), 1888-1935

Seven pillars of wisdom; a triumph. Doubleday 1935 672p il maps hardcover o.p. paperback available $15   **940.4**

1. World War, 1914-1918—Middle East 2. Arabs 3. Bedouins 4. Wahhabis
ISBN 0-385-41895-7 (pa)

Also available in hardcover from Dorset Press

"Not only a history of the Arab revolt during the [First] World War, but a commentary on the national characteristics, and political policies of Arabs, Turks and British." Cleveland Public Libr

Liddell Hart, Sir Basil Henry, 1895-1970

The real war, 1914-1918; with twenty-five maps; by B. H. Liddell Hart. Little, Brown 1930 508p maps hardcover o.p. paperback available $14.95   **940.4**

1. World War, 1914-1918
ISBN 0-316-52505-7 (pa)

A short history of World War I in which the action of the book ranges wherever Germany and the Allies locked in combat: Poland, Mesopotamia, Gallipoli, Caporetto, Baghdad, the North Sea, and the Mediterranean

Includes bibliography

Simpson, Colin, 1931-

The Lusitania. Little, Brown 1973 c1972 303p il o.p.; Penguin Bks. paperback available $5.95   **940.4**

1. Lusitania (Steamship)
ISBN 0-14-006803-1 (pa)

First published 1972 in the United Kingdom

Simpson, Colin, 1931-—*Continued*
The author argues that the circumstances in which the Lusitania "would be attacked were 'created' by prominent officials both British and American, most cynically so by Churchill who wanted to draw America into the war." Publ Wkly

Includes bibliography

940.53 World War II, 1939-1945

Armor, John
Manzanar; by John Armor and Peter Wright; commentary by John Hersey; photographs by Ansel Adams. Times Bks. 1988 xx, 167p il $27.50 **940.53**
1. Manzanar War Relocation Center 2. Japanese Americans—Evacuation and relocation, 1942-1945
ISBN 0-8129-1727-8 LC 88-40155
Also available in paperback from Vintage Bks.

Armor, Wright, and Hersey describe the "relocation of Japanese Americans in World War II. Specific attention to Manzanar, the first camp, appears in the form of 100 photographs taken by Ansel Adams in 1943." Libr J

Churchill, Sir Winston, 1874-1965
Closing the ring. Houghton Mifflin 1951 749p maps (Second World War, v5) $29.95; pa $11.70 **940.53**
1. World War, 1939-1945 2. World War, 1939-1945—Great Britain
ISBN 0-395-07535-1; 0-395-41059-2 (pa)
"'Closing the Ring' sets forth the year of conflict from June 1943 to June 1944. Aided by the command of the oceans, the mastery of the U-boats, and our ever growing superiority in the air, the Western Allies were able to conquer Sicily and invade Italy, with the result that Mussolini was overthrown and the Italian nation came over to our side." Preface

The gathering storm. Houghton Mifflin 1948 784p maps (Second World War, v1) hardcover o.p. paperback available $11.70 **940.53**
1. World War, 1939-1945 2. World War, 1939-1945—Great Britain
ISBN 0-395-41055-X (pa)
The first volume of Churchill's monumental history of the Second World War describes the days between the false peace and Hitler's near-victory just before Dunkirk

The grand alliance. Houghton Mifflin 1950 903p maps (Second World War, v3) $29.95; pa $11.70 **940.53**
1. World War, 1939-1945 2. World War, 1939-1945—Great Britain
ISBN 0-395-07538-6; 0-395-41057-6 (pa)
This volume begins with the German drive in the East, covers the War in Africa and describes the entrance into the war of Russia and, after Pearl Harbor, the United States

The hinge of fate. Houghton Mifflin 1950 1000p maps (Second World War, v4) $29.95; pa $11.70 **940.53**
1. World War, 1939-1945 2. World War, 1939-1945—Great Britain
ISBN 0-395-07539-4; 0-395-41058-4 (pa)
Describing events leading to the invasion of Sicily, warfare in Africa, the discouragingly slow job of reconquest in Europe, meetings with Roosevelt, and efforts at collaboration with Stalin, this volume covers the period from January 1942 to May 1943

Their finest hour. Houghton Mifflin 1949 751p maps (Second World War, v2) $29.95; pa $11.70 **940.53**
1. World War, 1939-1945 2. World War, 1939-1945—Great Britain
ISBN 0-395-07536-X; 0-395-41056-8 (pa)
This volume starts with the problems confronting Churchill as he assumed the office of Prime Minister in 1940 and continues with accounts of the Battle of Britain, the Battle of France and Dunkirk

Triumph and tragedy. Houghton Mifflin 1953 800p maps (Second World War, v6) $29.95; pa $11.70 **940.53**
1. World War, 1939-1945 2. World War, 1939-1945—Great Britain
ISBN 0-395-07540-8; 0-395-41060-6 (pa)
The concluding volume of Churchill's history of World War II begins with D-Day and covers campaigns leading to the defeat of Germany and Japan

Dawidowicz, Lucy S.
The war against the Jews, 1933-1945. 10th anniversary ed. Free Press 1986 c1975 xxxx, 466p maps o.p.; Bantam Bks. paperback available $14.95 **940.53**
1. Holocaust, Jewish (1933-1945) 2. Jews—Europe
ISBN 0-553-34532-X (pa) LC 86-6516
A reissue with new introduction and supplementary bibliography of the title first published 1975 by Holt, Rinehart & Winston

"One of the best histories of the mass murder of Jews in World War II. Argues for the centrality of anti-Semitism in Hitler's program." Reader's Adviser

Edmonds, Robin
The big three; Churchill, Roosevelt, and Stalin in peace & war. Norton 1991 608p il maps $27.95; pa $14.95 **940.53**
1. Churchill, Sir Winston, 1874-1965 2. Roosevelt, Franklin D. (Franklin Delano), 1882-1945 3. Stalin, Joseph, 1879-1953 4. World War, 1939-1945—Diplomatic history
ISBN 0-393-02889-5; 0-393-30914-2 (pa) LC 90-6854
The author "explores the intricate relationship of the triumvirate responsible for the success of the Allies in World War II—Churchill, Roosevelt, and Stalin. A worthwhile addition to any collection covering the war years and the cold war that followed." Booklist

Includes bibliographic references

Encyclopedia of the Holocaust; Israel Gutman, editor in chief; [published in association with] Yad Vashim, Sifriat Poalim Publishing House. Macmillan 1990 4v il maps set $360   **940.53**

1. Holocaust, Jewish (1933-1945)

ISBN 0-02-896090-4   LC 89-13466

"This set provides a wealth of information about a major event in the history of Western civilization. Entries treat countries, people, reflections in the arts and theology, sites of camps and massacres, and contemporary documentation centers. There are also entries on non-Jewish victims like gypsies and homosexuals." Ref Sources for Small & Medium-sized Libr. 5th edition

Feig, Konnilyn G.

Hitler's death camps; the sanity of madness. Holmes & Meier 1981 xxiv, 547p il $47.95; pa $34.50   **940.53**

1. Holocaust, Jewish (1933-1945) 2. Concentration camps

ISBN 0-8419-0675-0; 0-8419-0676-9 (pa)   LC 81-140

This work "presents the concentration camp network as a key element in a Holocaust interpreted as manifesting Western civilization's general moral crisis. . . . [Feig's] focus on the human, moral element results in the occasional submergence of analysis beneath undifferentiated horror stories." Libr J

Includes bibliography

Feis, Herbert, 1893-1972

Churchill, Roosevelt, Stalin; the war they waged and the peace they sought. 2nd ed. Princeton Univ. Press 1967 c1957 702p maps $89   **940.53**

1. World War, 1939-1945—Diplomatic history

ISBN 0-691-05607-2

First published 1957

"The story of the American-British-Russian coalition during World War II. Examines the ideas and purposes of each member of the alliance, the clashes between them and the attitudes of the three dominating figures." Publ Wkly

Includes bibliographic references

The road to Pearl Harbor; the coming of the war between the United States and Japan. Princeton Univ. Press 1950 356p map hardcover o.p. paperback available $16.95   **940.53**

1. United States—Foreign relations—Japan 2. Japan—Foreign relations—United States 3. World War, 1939-1945—Diplomatic history

ISBN 0-691-01061-7 (pa)

The author looks at the diplomatic origins of the war between the U.S. and Japan

Includes bibliographic references

Gies, Miep, 1909-

Anne Frank remembered; the story of the woman who helped to hide the Frank family; [by] Miep Gies with Alison Leslie Gold. Simon & Schuster 1987 252p il maps hardcover o.p. paperback available $8.95   **940.53**

1. Frank family 2. Netherlands—History—1940-1945, German occupation 3. Holocaust, Jewish (1933-1945)

ISBN 0-671-66234-1 (pa)   LC 86-25991

"A memoir by the courageous Dutch woman who helped hide the Frank family, this book augments the Anne Frank story. Perceptive characterizations, with insight into life in Amsterdam during the Nazi occupation." SLJ

Gilbert, Martin, 1936-

Atlas of the Holocaust. Morrow 1993 282p il maps $20   **940.53**

1. Holocaust, Jewish (1933-1945)

ISBN 0-688-12364-3   LC 92-33895

First published 1982 with title: The Macmillan atlas of the Holocaust

Over 300 black-and-white maps arranged in chronological sequence depict the Nazi assault on European Jews. Acts of resistance, revolts, escapes and rescues are also documented

For a review see: Booklist, Nov. 15, 1993

Includes bibliography

The Holocaust; a history of the Jews of Europe during the Second World War. Holt & Co. 1986 c1985 959p il maps hardcover o.p. paperback available $16.95   **940.53**

1. Holocaust, Jewish (1933-1945)

ISBN 0-8050-0348-7 (pa)   LC 85-5523

"Proceeding chronologically from Hitler's rise to power in 1933 to Germany's surrender and the liberation of the concentration camps, [the author] documents the countless horrors of this 'unprecedented explosion of evil over good,' drawing extensively on records and testimonies of those who survived (as well as some who eventually perished)." Booklist

Includes bibliography

The Second World War; a complete history. Holt & Co. 1989 846p il maps $29.95; pa $17.95   **940.53**

1. World War, 1939-1945

ISBN 0-8050-0534-X; 0-8050-1788-7 (pa)

      LC 89-11129

The author begins this study "with the invasion of Poland. Gilbert's flowing narrative is spiced with anecdotal details culled from diaries, memoirs and official documents. He is especially skillful at interweaving summaries of military strategy with vignettes of civilian suffering—the genocide of the Jews is never far from view." Newsweek

Includes bibliography

Japan at war; by the editors of Time-Life Books. Time-Life Bks. 1980 208p il (World War II) $19.93   **940.53**

1. World War, 1939-1945—Japan 2. Japan—History—1868-1945

      LC 80-24612

Text and numerous illustrations portray the Japanese people prior to and during the Second World War. The effect of the war is described and the military ex-

Japan at war—*Continued*
pansionist policy of Tojo is dealt with

Includes bibliography

Japanese Americans, from relocation to redress; edited by Roger Daniels, Sandra C. Taylor, Harry H.L. Kitano; contributions by Leonard J. Arrington [et al.] rev ed. University of Wash. Press 1991 xxi, 242p il pa $17.95 **940.53**
1. Japanese Americans—Evacuation and relocation, 1942-1945 2. World War, 1939-1945—Reparations
ISBN 0-295-97117-7 LC 91-2892

First published 1986 by University of Utah Press

A collection of essays on Japanese Americans focusing on their wartime relocation and their efforts to seek reparations

Includes bibliographic references

Kalib, Goldie Szachter, 1931-
The last selection; a child's journey through the Holocaust; by Goldie Szachter Kalib, with Sylvan Kalib and Ken Wachsberger. University of Mass. Press 1991 xx, 266p il maps $29.95 **940.53**
1. Jews—Poland 2. Holocaust, Jewish (1933-1945)—Personal narratives
ISBN 0-87023-758-6 LC 91-3869

"Goldie Szachter was the daughter of a well-to-do Jewish family in a small Polish town. After an idyllic early childhood, the German occupation of Poland turned her world upside down, as she was first sheltered from the full force of the Holocaust by Christian families, then sent with her family to a labor camp and, at age 13, to Auschwitz and Bergen-Belsen where most of her family perished. Because the family was able to evade some of the initial brutality of the Nazi's Jewish policies, this account differs from some others." Libr J

Keegan, John, 1934-
The Second World War. Viking 1990 c1989 608p il maps $29.95 **940.53**
1. World War, 1939-1945
ISBN 0-670-82359-7 LC 89-16682

Also available in paperback from Penguin Bks.

First published 1989 in the United Kingdom

This military and stategic history contains sections covering the Eastern and Western fronts and the war in the Pacific

"Keegan accompanies his narrative with a series of set battlepieces, of strategic analyses, and of 'themes of war'. . . . [The book] is beautifully ordered and . . . a pleasure to read." New Statesman Soc

Includes bibliographic references

Levi, Primo, 1919-1987
The drowned and the saved; translated from the Italian by Raymond Rosenthal. Summit Bks. 1988 203p o.p.; Vintage Bks. paperback available $10 **940.53**
1. Holocaust, Jewish (1933-1945)—Personal narratives
2. Auschwitz (Poland: Concentration camp)
ISBN 0-679-72186-X (pa) LC 87-18052

Auschwitz survivor Levi, an Italian Jewish chemist from Turin, wrote this final contemplation of the Holocaust before his suicide in 1987

"If the unending tragedy of the Holocaust can ever be said to make sense, then it does so in these pages." New Yorker

Lifton, Robert Jay, 1926-
The Nazi doctors; medical killing and the psychology of genocide. Basic Bks. 1986 561p $22.95; pa $16 **940.53**
1. Holocaust, Jewish (1933-1945) 2. World War, 1939-1945—Atrocities 3. Concentration camps
ISBN 0-465-04904-4; 0-465-04905-2 (pa)
LC 85-73874

"How could German physicians trained as scientist-healers carry out Nazi orders for mass killings? . . . Lifton, an American Jewish physician, seeks answers through interviews with surviving doctors, family members, and victims and by painstakingly gleaning Holocaust archives." Sci Books Films

Includes bibliography

Lindwer, Willy
The last seven months of Anne Frank; translated from the Dutch by Alison Meersschaert. Pantheon Bks. 1991 204p il o.p.; Anchor Bks. paperback available $12 **940.53**
1. Frank, Anne, 1929-1945 2. Holocaust, Jewish (1933-1945)—Personal narratives 3. Netherlands—History—1940-1945, German occupation
ISBN 0-385-42360-8 (pa) LC 90-53437

"Six Dutch Jewish women who survived the concentration camps in the last months of the war bear witness to the kind of suffering that Anne Frank endured before she died." Booklist

Miller, Judith, 1948-
One, by one, by one: facing the Holocaust. Simon & Schuster 1990 319p hardcover o.p. paperback available $10.95 **940.53**
1. Holocaust, Jewish (1933-1945)
ISBN 0-671-74034-2 (pa) LC 90-30091

This is an account "of memories of the Holocaust in six countries, of the ways that each nation attempts to preserve, to interpret, or to expunge the historical truth. Miller looks at Germany, Austria, France, the Netherlands, the USSR, and the United States." Libr J

"The journalist's trade—interviewing extensively, searching for the telling anecdote, talking to historians, sociologists and psychologists, who often speak more superficially than they write—has shortcomings. Yet Judith Miller has had access that few freelance writers could equal." N Y Times Book Rev

Includes bibliographic references

Miller, Russell
The resistance; by Russell Miller and the editors of Time-Life Books. Time-Life Bks. 1979 208p il maps (World War II) $19.93 **940.53**
1. World War, 1939-1945—Underground movements
LC 79-14316

Miller, Russell—*Continued*

An illustrated account of the various resistance movements which existed in Europe during Nazi occupation

Includes bibliography

Overy, R. J. (Richard James)

The road to war; [by] Richard Overy with Andrew Wheatcroft. Random House 1990 c1989 364p il maps $24.95   **940.53**

1. World War, 1939-1945—Causes

ISBN 0-394-58260-8   LC 89-10435

First published 1989 in the United Kingdom

"Overy presents the 1920s and 1930s as perceived by the major powers at the time without the benefit of hindsight. There are no 'pure knights' here preparing for the 'good war,' only paranoid politicians haunted by the effects of World War I, the Russian Revolution, and the Great Depression." Libr J

"The book is a concise, highly readable account of how WW II came about." Publ Wkly

Includes bibliography

Polmar, Norman

World War II; America at war, 1941-1945; [by] Norman Polmar, Thomas B. Allen. Random House 1991 940p il maps $35   **940.53**

1. World War, 1939-1945—United States

ISBN 0-394-58530-5   LC 91-16212

"Covers the standard political and military personalities, events, battles, and equipment as well as social issues like children, homosexuals, the Holocaust, segregation, and popular culture. . . . This book is organized in two main parts: a 48-page chronology and a 'War Guide A-Z.'" Booklist

"Highly recommended for reference collections." Libr J

Includes bibliographic references

Pyle, Ernie, 1900-1945

Ernie's war; the best of Ernie Pyle's World War II dispatches; edited with a biographical essay by David Nichols; foreword by Studs Terkel. Random House 1986 432p il $19.95   **940.53**

1. World War, 1939-1945

ISBN 0-394-54923-6   LC 85-18390

Also available in paperback from Simon & Schuster

"Organized chronologically and following Pyle's path from Britain during the Blitz to North Africa, Sicily, Italy, France, and the Pacific, the text reveals vivid details about the day-to-day life of the infantry soldier as well as offering a unique view of the basics of warfare." Booklist

Includes bibliography

Silver, Eric

The book of the just; the silent heroes who saved Jews from Hitler. Grove Weidenfeld 1992 175p il $19.95   **940.53**

1. World War, 1939-1945—Jews—Rescue 2. Holocaust, Jewish (1933-1945)

ISBN 0-8021-1347-8   LC 92-10075

This "volume contains short accounts of gentiles—Christians, Moslems, and a Japanese diplomat—who risked their careers and their lives to save Jews from Hitler's death factories." Libr J

Includes bibliographic references

Smith, Gene

The dark summer; an intimate history of the events that led to World War II. Macmillan 1987 314p il hardcover o.p. paperback available $9.95   **940.53**

1. World War, 1939-1945—Causes 2. Europe—Politics and government—1914-1945

ISBN 0-02-037390-2 (pa)   LC 87-7897

This book "details the personalities and events of the summer of 1939 as the world was drawn into a war that no one but Adolf Hitler wanted. England, Germany, and Russia are the focus; memories of prominent and 'ordinary' folk are interwoven to give the feel of the time." Libr J

Includes bibliography

Sulzberger, C. L. (Cyrus Leo), 1912-1993

World War II. American Heritage 1985 372p il maps pa $10.70   **940.53**

1. World War, 1939-1945

ISBN 0-8281-0331-3   LC 85-3978

Also available in hardcover from P. Smith

In this volume "the emphasis is on the people involved—the leaders, the victims, and the fighters. . . . Over a third of the book consists of eyewitness accounts from Edward R. Murrow, William L. Shirer, Antoine de Saint-Exupéry, and many others." Publisher's note

Includes bibliography

Terkel, Studs, 1912-

"The good war"; an oral history of World War Two. Pantheon Bks. 1984 589p o.p.; Ballantine Bks. paperback available $6.95   **940.53**

1. World War, 1939-1945—Personal narratives

ISBN 0-345-32568-0 (pa)   LC 84-42710

In a series of interviews Terkel depicts how WWII affected the lives of average Americans

Toland, John

The last 100 days. Random House 1966 622p il o.p.; Bantam Bks. paperback available $6.95   **940.53**

1. World War, 1939-1945—Europe

ISBN 0-553-28640-4 (pa)

Basing his report on hundreds of interviews with eyewitnesses the author relates the military and diplomatic strategy that defeated Nazism and fascism at the close of World War II

Includes bibliographic references

The rising sun; the decline and fall of the Japanese Empire, 1936-1945. Random House 1970 xxxv, 954p il maps o.p.; Bantam Bks. paperback available $7.95   **940.53**

1. World War, 1939-1945—Japan

ISBN 0-553-26435-4 (pa)

Toland, John—*Continued*

This study begins in 1936 "when rebellious army units . . . occupied much of central Tokyo and assassinated several government leaders. It continues with the invasion of China, the pact with Germany and Italy, the nonaggression pact with the Soviet Union, and the . . . negotiations with the United States that ended in the attack on Pearl Harbor." Saturday Rev

Includes bibliography

Watt, Donald Cameron

How war came; the immediate origins of the Second World War, 1938-1939. Pantheon Bks. 1989 736p il maps $29.45; pa $17.95
940.53

1. World War, 1939-1945—Causes
ISBN 0-394-57916-X; 0-679-73093-1 (pa) LC 89-8802

The author "examines the political and diplomatic atmosphere during the pivotal 11-month prewar period that included the signing of the Munich agreement, German occupation of the Sudetenland, the Nazi-Soviet nonaggression pact, the invasion of Poland and the British declaration of war." Publ Wkly

"This is well-written history of the most serious sort." N Y Times Book Rev

Includes bibliography

Weatherford, Doris

American women and World War II. Facts on File 1990 338p il (History of women in America) $29.95
940.53

1. World War, 1939-1945—Women 2. Women—United States—History
ISBN 0-8160-2038-8 LC 89-71489

"The author provides information on the role of women in World War II, covering such topics as their jobs, their 'new' status, and their image in the eyes of their fellow citizens." Booklist

"This is a fascinating and immensely readable account." Libr J

Includes bibliographic references

The **World** almanac of World War II; the complete and comprehensive documentary of World War II; edited by Peter Young. rev ed. World Almanac 1986 c1981 613p il maps pa $18.95
940.53

1. World War, 1939-1945 2. Chronology, Historical
ISBN 0-88687-712-1 LC 86-196736

"A Bison book"

First published 1981 with title: The World Almanac book of World War II

"Gives chronology, information on weapons and equipment, biographies, and a summation. Has full-color photographs, maps, and clear analysis." N Y Public Libr Book of How & Where to Look It Up

The **World** at arms: the Reader's Digest illustrated history of World War II. Reader's Digest Assn. 1989 480p il maps $29.95
940.53

1. World War, 1939-1945
ISBN 0-89577-333-3

"Detailed information about campaigns and individual battles is side by side with short boxed biographies of the commanders involved. Maps show troop movements

during campaigns and battles and dioramas are included for decisive battles." Voice Youth Advocates

WW II: Time-Life Books history of the Second World War. Prentice Hall Press 1989 496p il maps $39.95
940.53

1. World War, 1939-1945
ISBN 0-13-922022-4 LC 89-15969

Based on the Time-Life World War II series

This volume "features an entirely original (and excellent) text, a contemporary typeface, hundreds of maps and photographs, numerous color illustrations of important tanks and aircraft, and paintings by some of the war's foremost artists." Booklist

Wyman, David S.

The abandonment of the Jews; America and the Holocaust, 1941-1945. Pantheon Bks. 1984 444p hardcover o.p. paperback available $16
940.53

1. Holocaust, Jewish (1933-1945) 2. World War, 1939-1945—United States
ISBN 0-394-74077-7 (pa) LC 84-42711

"Wyman identifies three factors which led the United States to abandon the Jews in Europe (despite full knowledge of what that abandonment would mean): anti-Semitism; a sense of helplessness; and . . . fear of being branded as pro-Jewish." Nation

"A first-rate book for both specialists and generalists." Choice

Includes bibliography

Yahil, Leni

The Holocaust; the fate of European Jewry, 1932-1945; translated from the Hebrew by Ina Friedman and Haya Galai. Oxford Univ. Press 1990 808p il maps (Studies in Jewish history) $39.95; pa $17.95
940.53

1. Holocaust, Jewish (1933-1945) 2. Jews—Europe
ISBN 0-19-504522-X; 0-19-504523-8 (pa)
LC 89-37750

Original Hebrew edition, 1987

This volume "covers all aspects of the subject, such as Jewish resistance and emigration, and the various worldwide efforts, successful and otherwise, at rescue. . . . The most important original contribution to the study of the Holocaust made by Ms. Yahil is that she places it in the political context of that era." N Y Times Book Rev

Includes bibliographic references

940.54 World War II, 1939-1945 (Military conduct of the war)

Ambrose, Stephen E.

Band of brothers; E Company, 506th Regiment, 101st Airborne: from Normandy to Hitler's Eagle's Nest. Simon & Schuster 1992 335p il maps $25; pa $13 **940.54**

1. United States. Army. Parachute Infantry Regiment, 506th. Company E 2. World War, 1939-1945—Europe
ISBN 0-671-76922-7; 0-671-86736-9 (pa)
LC 91-47684

Ambrose, Stephen E.—*Continued*
"Here is the story of the daring E Company, which began the war by parachuting into France on D-Day and ended it by capturing Eagle's Nest, Hitler's outpost in Bavaria." Libr J

"Moving, poignant, and uplifting, this book is highly recommended for medium and large World War II collections." Booklist

Includes bibliographic references

Astor, Gerald, 1926-
A blood-dimmed tide; the Battle of the Bulge by the men who fought it. Fine, D.I. 1992 532p il maps $28   940.54
1. Ardennes, Battle of the, 1944-1945 2. World War, 1939-1945—Personal narratives
ISBN 1-55611-281-5   LC 91-58657

"Interviewing more than 50 veterans from both sides of the Bulge, Astor . . . has written an objective account of the Ardennes campaign that delineates a complex mix of cowardice and courage, stupidity and brilliance, brutality and grace under fire." Libr J

Includes bibliography

Bailey, Ronald H.
The air war in Europe; by Ronald H. Bailey and the editors of Time-Life Books. Time-Life Bks. 1979 208p il maps (World War II) $19.93   940.54
1. World War, 1939-1945—Aerial operations
LC 78-2937

This book explains the strategies employed by the RAF and the U.S. Air Force for their missions into Germany during World War II. Picture essays alternate with descriptions of the planning and execution of bombing raids

Includes bibliography

Casey, William J.
The secret war against Hitler; by William Casey. Regnery Gateway 1988 304p il $19.95   940.54
1. United States. Office of Strategic Services 2. World War, 1939-1945—Secret service
ISBN 0-89526-563-X   LC 88-2013
Also available in paperback from Berkley Bks.

"The author examines the clandestine intelligence maneuvers prior to D-Day, where misinformation was able to disguise the true Allied landing site. Casey also believed that the Allied high command, faced with creditable intelligence reports, missed several military opportunities, hastening both Pearl Harbor and the dropping of atomic bombs on Japan." Booklist

Clarke, Thurston
Pearl Harbor ghosts; a journey to Hawaii, then and now. Morrow 1991 411p il maps $22   940.54
1. Pearl Harbor (Oahu, Hawaii), Attack on, 1941 2. World War, 1939-1945—Campaigns—Pacific Ocean
ISBN 0-688-08301-3   LC 91-382

The author aims to recreate the events of December 7, 1941 with a combination of travelogue, historical analysis, and personal reminiscences. In addition, Clarke

attempts to analyze American attitudes to Japan before, during, and fifty years after the attack

Clausen, Henry C., 1905-
Pearl Harbor; final judgement; [by] Henry C. Clausen and Bruce Lee. Crown 1992 485p il map $25   940.54
1. Pearl Harbor (Oahu, Hawaii), Attack on, 1941
ISBN 0-517-58644-4   LC 92-5216

This "look at the puzzling reasons why U.S. officials were totally unprepared for the 1941 Japanese attack on Pearl Harbor is . . . written by the prosecuting attorney who was appointed in 1944 to investigate the Pearl Harbor debacle."

This "book possesses the assets of fresh perspectives, sound research, a lively style and an exciting, suspenseful plot." N Y Times Book Rev

Includes bibliographic references

Collier, Richard
The war in the desert; by Richard Collier and the editors of Time-Life Books. Time-Life Bks. 1977 208p il maps (World War II) $19.93   940.54
1. World War, 1939-1945—North Africa 2. World War, 1939-1945—Campaigns   LC 77-81945

Text and numerous illustrations portray the North African war zone and the commanders in charge. The British campaign in Egypt and Libya and the joint Anglo-American military actions in Tunisia are dealt with

Includes bibliography

Costello, John
The Pacific War. Rawson, Wade 1981 742p il maps o.p.; Quill paperback available $17.95   940.54
1. World War, 1939-1945—Pacific Ocean
ISBN 0-688-01620-0 (pa)   LC 81-7381

A "history of World War II as it was played out in the Pacific theater. . . . Emphasizing the role played by Allied intelligence sources during the early period of the war, Costello analyzes the actual battles from Pearl Harbor to the atomic bombing of Japan." Booklist

Includes bibliography

Descent into nightmare; by the editors of Time-Life Books. Time-Life Bks. 1992 183p il maps (Third Reich) $22.60
940.54
1. World War, 1939-1945—Campaigns 2. Germany—History—1933-1945   LC 91-28936

An illustrated look at the Third Reich's crushing military defeat. Chapters also focus on Nazi atrocities and the Nuremberg trials

Includes bibliography

Ford, Daniel

Flying Tigers; Claire Chennault and the American Volunteer Group. Smithsonian Institution Press 1991 450p il (Smithsonian history of aviation ser) $24.95 **940.54**

1. Chennault, Claire Lee, 1890-1958 2. China. Air Force. American Volunteer Group 3. World War, 1939-1945—Aerial operations
ISBN 1-56098-011-7 LC 90-26953

This is a study of Claire Chennault and the American Volunteer Group aviators who flew for China early in World War II

"Myths and exaggerations that surround the Flying Tigers create a difficult task for any author seeking truth. Based on careful research that includes documents, diaries, and interviews, Ford's book appears to come close to the actual facts." Choice

Includes bibliographic references

Fortress Europe; by the editors of Time-Life Books. Time-Life Bks. 1992 174p il maps (Third Reich) $22.60 **940.54**

1. World War, 1939-1945—Campaigns—France 2. Germany—History—1933-1945 LC 91-29938

Nazi military efforts to defend the Reich are explored in this heavily illustrated volume. Life in wartorn Berlin is also examined

Includes bibliography

Frank, Richard B.

Guadalcanal. Random House 1990 800p il maps $34.95 **940.54**

1. Guadalcanal Island (Solomon Islands), Battle of, 1942-1943
ISBN 0-394-58875-4 LC 90-8265

Also available in paperback from Penguin Bks.

The author "establishes Guadalcanal's decisive place in the history of World War II. . . . Frank evaluates the adversaries' strengths and weaknesses, stressing in particular the shortcomings of the U.S. Navy and the Japanese Army." Libr J

"Within its scope this is a first-rate book that will be enormously interesting to military historians, WW II buffs, officers in the armed forces, and veterans." Choice

Includes bibliographic references

Fussell, Paul, 1924-

Wartime: understanding and behavior in the Second World War. Oxford Univ. Press 1989 330p il $24.95; pa $10.95 **940.54**

1. World War, 1939-1945—United States 2. World War, 1939-1945—Great Britain 3. World War, 1939-1945—Propaganda
ISBN 0-19-503797-9; 0-19-506577-8 (pa) LC 89-2875

In this book Fussell "seeks to evoke the psychological and emotional culture of Americans and Britons during the Second World War." Newsweek

"Fussell's version of the war doesn't, perhaps, exactly 'balance the scales,' but it is a useful corrective. Nobody who reads it will come away thinking about the war complacently." New Repub

Includes bibliography

Goldstein, Donald M.

The way it was; Pearl Harbor, the original photographs; [by] Donald M. Goldstein, Katherine V. Dillon and J. Michael Wenger. Pergamon-Brassey's 1991 181p il maps $29.95 **940.54**

1. Pearl Harbor (Oahu, Hawaii), Attack on, 1941—Pictorial works
ISBN 0-08-040573-8 LC 90-49572

This is a collection of photographs of the Japanese attack on Pearl Harbor in 1941

"The 430 prints in this . . . collection were gathered from various Japanese and U.S. sources, and most have never been seen by the general public. The majority were taken during the height of the air raid itself, many from Japanese cockpits. . . . The overall effect is to give the reader an uncanny sense of being present at the battle." Libr J

Hastings, Max

Overlord: D-Day and the battle for Normandy. Simon & Schuster 1984 368p il maps hardcover o.p. paperback available $12 **940.54**

1. Operation Overlord 2. Normandy (France), Attack on, 1944
ISBN 0-671-55435-2 (pa) LC 83-20439

Hastings presents an "analysis of the Normandy campaign. He . . . [considers] the limits of the Allied armies' fighting power compared to the Wehrmacht." Libr J

"Hastings' reportage of the battle is not unworthy to stand with that of the best journalists and writers who witnessed it. . . . He has managed to recreate what it was like for almost everyone who was there." N Y Times Book Rev

Includes bibliography

Victory in Europe; D-Day to V-E Day; photographs by George Stevens; introduction by George Stevens, Jr. Little, Brown 1985 192p il maps $25 **940.54**

1. World War, 1939-1945—Campaigns—Pictorial works
ISBN 0-316-81334-6 LC 85-50176

An account of the war in Europe from the Normandy invasions to V-E Day featuring stills from a documentary film by George Stevens

Includes bibliography

Hersey, John, 1914-1993

Hiroshima; a new edition with a final chapter written forty years after the explosion. Knopf 1985 196p il $21; pa $4.50 **940.54**

1. Hiroshima (Japan)—Bombardment, 1945 2. Atomic bomb 3. World War, 1939-1945—Japan
ISBN 0-394-54844-2; 0-679-72103-7 (pa)
LC 85-40346

First published 1946

An account of the aftermath of the first atomic bomb as reflected in the lives of six survivors

Hough, Richard Alexander, 1922-

The Battle of Britain; the greatest air battle of World War II; [by] Richard Hough and Denis Richards. Norton 1989 413p il maps hardcover o.p. paperback available $14.95   **940.54**

1. Britain, Battle of, 1940
ISBN 0-393-30734-4 (pa)   LC 89-12697

"Drawing on interviews and correspondence with more than 300 surviving air and ground crew, Hough and Richards . . . cover the battle in its entirety, from July through the end of October 1940, including chapters on prewar air defense measures, the outbreak of war in 1939, and events leading up to the battle." Booklist

Includes bibliographic references

The longest battle; the war at sea, 1939-45; [by] Richard Hough. Morrow 1987 c1986 371p il maps hardcover o.p. paperback available $9.95   **940.54**

1. World War, 1939-1945—Naval operations
ISBN 0-688-07953-9 (pa)   LC 86-23632

First published 1986 in the United Kingdom

The author "has drawn from a wide range of personal reminiscences, published and unpublished, and although his accounts of campaigns and battles follow a fairly standard pattern, to provide a framework, the details provided by these personal perspectives add depth and colour." Times Lit Suppl

Includes bibliography

Hoyt, Edwin Palmer

The airmen; the story of American fliers in World War II; by Edwin P. Hoyt. McGraw-Hill 1990 418p il $22.50   **940.54**

1. World War, 1939-1945—Aerial operations
ISBN 0-07-030633-8   LC 90-6563

An account of the feelings and contributions of veteran pilots, bombardiers, gunners and navigators

Includes bibliographic references

The GI's war; the story of American soldiers in Europe in World War II; [by] Edwin P. Hoyt. McGraw-Hill 1988 620p il maps o.p.; Da Capo Press paperback available $16.95   **940.54**

1. World War, 1939-1945—Campaigns 2. Soldiers—United States
ISBN 0-306-80448-4 (pa)   LC 87-29868

The author "uses simple, almost stark, stories to establish the matter-of-fact attitude of rank-and-file American soldiers who fought the Germans. A reporter and foxhole-level narrator, he relies heavily on letters, tapes, and interviews from junior officers and enlisted men who served in the U.S. Army's combat arms in the European theater." Libr J

Includes bibliography

Japan's war; the great Pacific conflict, 1853 to 1952; by Edwin P. Hoyt. McGraw-Hill 1986 514p il maps o.p.; Da Capo Press paperback available $14.95   **940.54**

1. World War, 1939-1945—Japan 2. World War, 1939-1945—Pacific Ocean 3. Japan—History—1868-1945
ISBN 0-306-80348-8 (pa)   LC 85-24192

"The 'conflict' in the title refers to the threat Japan's military leaders saw . . . as the West began to dominate East Asia and the Pacific Basin. The conflict took on new dimensions in the early 20th century with the clash between militarists and fledgling democrats, and with the ultimate disaster that followed Japan's attack on the West in World War II." N Y Times Book Rev

Includes bibliography

Keil, Sally Van Wagenen

Those wonderful women in their flying machines; the unknown heroines of World War II. rev and expanded ed. Four Directions Press 1990 418p il $24.95   **940.54**

1. Women's Air Service Pilots (U.S.) 2. World War, 1939-1945—Women 3. World War, 1939-1945—Aerial operations
ISBN 0-9627659-0-2   LC 90-84246

First published 1979 by Rawson, Wade

"Using a narrative approach, Keil views the courageous endeavors of World War II women flyers who served in a division of the U.S. Army Air Force as Women's Airforce Service Pilots (WASPs)." Booklist

Knox, Donald, 1936-

Death march; the survivors of Bataan. Harcourt Brace Jovanovich 1981 xxv, 482p il maps hardcover o.p. paperback available $11.95   **940.54**

1. World War, 1939-1945—Prisoners and prisons 2. World War, 1939-1945—Campaigns—Philippines 3. Prisoners of war, American
ISBN 0-15-625224-4 (pa)   LC 81-47555

The author records "recollections of some 68 survivors of the Japanese capture of Bataan. . . . Some of these soldiers, nurses, pilots, sailors, and others went to prison camp, some escaped to join guerrilla bands, some ended the war working in Japan and Manchuria as slave labor." Libr J

Liddell Hart, Sir Basil Henry, 1895-1970

History of the Second World War. Putnam 1971 c1970 768p maps hardcover o.p. paperback available $17.95   **940.54**

1. World War, 1939-1945
ISBN 0-399-50445-1 (pa)

First published 1970 in the United Kingdom

This "comprehensive military history of World War II . . . examines motivations, actions, and justifications of prewar entanglements, battles, campaigns, and the military and political aftermath of World War II." Booklist

Includes bibliography

Lord, Walter, 1917-
Day of infamy. Holt & Co. 1991 243p il maps $24.95   940.54
1. Pearl Harbor (Oahu, Hawaii), Attack on, 1941
ISBN 0-8050-1898-0
Also available in paperback from Bantam Bks.
A reissue of the title first published 1957
Based on over 500 eyewitness reports, this book provides a minute-by-minute account of the Japanese attack on Pearl Harbor

Lovell, Mary S.
Cast no shadow; the life of the American spy who changed the course of World War II. Pantheon Bks. 1992 398p il $24.50   940.54
1. Pack, Amy Thorpe, 1910-1963 2. World War, 1939-1945—Secret service
ISBN 0-394-57556-3   LC 91-52625
"This is the story of a real-life spy heroine, Pack, a diplomat's wife who was one of Britain's most successful spies during World War II. . . . This carefully crafted, well-written, and readable book should appeal to a variety of readers, from World War II buffs to intrigue aficionados." Libr J
Includes bibliography

Lukacs, John, 1924-
The duel; 10 May-31 July 1940, the eighty-day struggle between Churchill and Hitler. Ticknor & Fields 1991 c1990 258p o.p.; Houghton Mifflin paperback available $10.70   940.54
1. Churchill, Sir Winston, 1874-1965 2. Hitler, Adolf, 1889-1945 3. World War, 1939-1945—Great Britain 4. World War, 1939-1945—Germany
ISBN 0-395-61863-0 (pa)   LC 90-11263
First published 1990 in the United Kingdom
This book attempts to reconstruct events beginning "with the appointment of Churchill as British Prime Minister (May 10th, 1940) and ending with Hitler's order to his generals to prepare for an attack on the Soviet Union for the Spring of 1941 (July 10th, 1940)." Publisher's note
"Lukacs ably narrates the train of events within the interval, but the distinctive feature of his writing is a tight weaving of social and psychological insight into the well-known story." Booklist
Includes bibliographic references

Macdonald, John, 1945-
Great battles of World War II; foreword by Sir John Hackett. Macmillan 1986 192p il maps o.p.; Courage Bks. reprint available $19.98   940.54
1. World War, 1939-1945—Campaigns
ISBN 1-56138-329-5   LC 86-8681
Companion volume: Great battlefields of the world, entered in class 904
This volume covers "30 battles and campaigns of World War II. The centerpiece of each entry is a computer-generated painting showing key or typical moments of the conflict. The accompanying text deals with the strategy, tactics, weaponry, commanders, and any

notable battle features." Booklist
Includes bibliography

Manchester, William
Goodbye, darkness; a memoir of the Pacific War. Little, Brown 1980 401p il o.p.; Dell paperback available $6.99   940.54
1. World War, 1939-1945—Pacific Ocean 2. World War, 1939-1945—Personal narratives
ISBN 0-440-32907-8 (pa)   LC 80-17310
This memoir arises from a 1978 trip the author made "to Pacific battlefields, seeking to exorcise three decades of nightmares dating to wartime days as a Marine Corps sergeant. . . . First tracing his family background, youth, enlistment, training, and embarkation from San Diego, Manchester unravels a memoir featuring historical reconstruction, disjointed flash-forwards, shocking vignettes, [and] redoubtable vocabulary." Choice

Morison, Samuel Eliot, 1887-1976
History of United States naval operations in World War II. Little, Brown 1947-1962 15v il maps ea $40   940.54
1. World War, 1939-1945—Naval operations
Contents: v1 Battle of the Atlantic, September 1939-May 1943 (ISBN 0-316-58301-4); v2 Operations in North African waters, October 1942-June 1943 (ISBN 0-316-58302-2); v3 Rising Sun in the Pacific, 1931-April 1942 (ISBN 0-316-58303-0); v4 Coral Sea, Midway and submarine actions, May 1942-August 1942 (ISBN 0-316-58304-9); v5 Struggle for Guadalcanal, August 1942-February 1943 (ISBN 0-316-58305-7); v6 Breaking the Bismarck's barrier, 22 July 1942-1 May 1944 (ISBN 0-316-58306-5); v7 Aleutians, Gilberts and Marshalls, June 1942-April 1944 (ISBN 0-316-58307-3); v8 New Guinea and the Marianas, March 1944-August 1944 (ISBN 0-316-58308-1); v9 Sicily—Salerno—Anzio, January 1943-June 1944 (ISBN 0-316-58316-2); v10 Atlantic battle won, May 1943-May 1945 (ISBN 0-316-58310-3); v11 Invasion of France and Germany, 1944-1945 (ISBN 0-316-58311-1); v12 Leyte, June 1944-January 1945 (ISBN 0-316-58317-0); v13 The liberation of the Philippines: Luzon, Mindanao, the Visayas, 1944-1945 (ISBN 0-316-58313-8); v14 Victory in the Pacific, 1945 (ISBN 0-316-58314-6); v15 Supplement and general index (ISBN 0-316-58315-4)
Includes bibliographic references

The two-ocean war; a short history of the United States Navy in the Second World War. Little, Brown 1989 c1963 xxvii, 611p il maps $37.50; pa $19.95   940.54
1. World War, 1939-1945—Naval operations
ISBN 0-316-58366-9; 0-316-58352-9 (pa)
                LC 89-12549
A reissue of the title first published 1963
This is a rewritten and condensed version of the title entered above
Includes bibliographic references

Mowat, Farley
And no birds sang. Little, Brown 1980 c1979 219p $14.95   940.54
1. World War, 1939-1945—Personal narratives
ISBN 0-316-58695-1   LC 79-23231
Also available in paperback from Bantam Bks.
"An Atlantic Monthly Press book"

Mowat, Farley—*Continued*

First published 1979 in Canada

Mowat "shares memories of his experiences as a young World War II Canadian soldier, recalling both his early heroic preconceptions of war and the devastating truth he came to understand." Booklist

Patton, George S. (George Smith), 1885-1945

War as I knew it; by George S. Patton, Jr.; annotated by Paul D. Harkins. Houghton Mifflin 1947 425p il maps $19.45

940.54

1. World War, 1939-1945—Campaigns
ISBN 0-395-08074-6

Also available in paperback from Bantam Bks.

Edited by Beatrice Ayer Patton

An account of the General's WWII European campaigns from the fight for Sicily to the conquest of Germany based on a series of "open letters" written to his wife

Prange, Gordon William, 1910-1980

At dawn we slept; the untold story of Pearl Harbor; [by] Gordon W. Prange in collaboration with Donald M. Goldstein and Katherine V. Dillon. Viking 1991 889p il $35

940.54

1. Pearl Harbor (Oahu, Hawaii), Attack on, 1941
ISBN 0-670-84074-2   LC 91-50176

Also available in paperback from Penguin Bks.

First published 1981 by McGraw-Hill

The author "offers a comprehensive account of Japanese preparations for the attack, the origins and extent of American unpreparedness, and the aftermath of the attack on both sides." Booklist

Includes bibliographic references

December 7, 1941; the day the Japanese attacked Pearl Harbor; [by] Gordon W. Prange with Donald M. Goldstein and Katherine V. Dillon. McGraw-Hill 1988 493p il o.p.; Warner Bks. paperback available $14.95

940.54

1. Pearl Harbor (Oahu, Hawaii), Attack on, 1941
ISBN 0-446-38997-8 (pa)   LC 87-3019

This account of the attack on Pearl Harbor is based on eyewitness testimony of participants on both sides

"The final volume of the late Prange's seminal trilogy maintains the luminous quality of his earlier works. Like *At Dawn We Slept* [entered above] and *Pearl Harbor: the verdict of history* [1986] it is thoroughly documented and detailed yet captivatingly readable as well." Libr J

Includes bibliography

Miracle at Midway; [by] Gordon W. Prange, Donald M. Goldstein and Katherine V. Dillon. McGraw-Hill 1982 469p il maps o.p.; Penguin Bks. paperback available $15

940.54

1. Midway, Battle of, 1942
ISBN 0-14-006814-7 (pa)   LC 82-4691

This is an account of the American victory over the Japanese at Midway in June 1942

"The authors present a clear, balanced, technically accurate account with penetrating insights into the nature of military command as well as the battle's lessons for naval warfare." America

Includes bibliography

Ross, Bill D.

Peleliu; tragic triumph: the untold story of the Pacific war's forgotten battle. Random House 1991 381p il maps $21.50   **940.54**

1. World War, 1939-1945—Campaigns—Pacific Ocean
ISBN 0-394-56588-6   LC 89-43420

This account covers "not only the events on the battlefield but the strategic background, unit histories, and relations (good and bad) among the commanders." Booklist

Includes bibliography

Sandler, Stanley, 1937-

Segregated skies; all-black combat squadrons of WW II. Smithsonian Institution Press 1992 217p il (Smithsonian history of aviation ser) $24.95   **940.54**

1. United States. Army Air Forces 2. World War, 1939-1945—Aerial operations 3. World War, 1939-1945—Blacks
ISBN 1-56098-154-7   LC 91-39452

The author "details the World War II experiences of blacks in the three fighter groups that shattered the U.S. Army Air Corps' all-white policy. He begins with the government's 1940 decision to develop 'colored personnel for the aviation service' by training them in isolation outside Tuskegee, Alabama, and concludes with descriptions of combat in North Africa and southern Europe." Libr J

Includes bibliographic references

Spector, Ronald

Eagle against the sun; the American war with Japan; [by] Ronald H. Spector. Free Press 1985 589p il $29.95   **940.54**

1. World War, 1939-1945—Campaigns—Pacific Ocean 2. World War, 1939-1945—United States 3. World War, 1939-1945—Japan
ISBN 0-02-930360-5   LC 84-47888

Also available in paperback from Vintage Bks.

This is a "one-volume history of the American-Japanese conflict during WW II." Choice

While "policy, strategy and military operations are emphasized . . . Mr. Spector makes a real attempt to give readers some idea of what the war was like for the men and women who fought it. It is here that the book is at its best." N Y Times Book Rev

Includes bibliography

Stevenson, William, 1924 or 5-

Intrepid's last case. Villard Bks. 1983 xxvii, 321p o.p.; Ballantine Bks. paperback available $4.95   **940.54**

1. Stephenson, Sir William Samuel, 1896-1989 2. World War, 1939-1945—Secret service
ISBN 0-345-30091-2 (pa)   LC 83-48077

Stevenson, William, 1924 or 5-—*Continued*
In this volume "Stephenson works to clear his chief deputy, Dick Ellis, from postwar allegations of treason." Libr J

Includes bibliographic references

A man called Intrepid; the secret war. Harcourt Brace Jovanovich 1976 xxv, 486p il maps o.p.; Ballantine Bks. paperback available $5.95 **940.54**
1. Stephenson, Sir William Samuel, 1896-1989 2. World War, 1939-1945—Secret service
ISBN 0-345-31023-3 (pa)
An examination of World War II Allied secret intelligence operation coordinated by William Stephenson a.k.a. Intrepid

Toland, John
Infamy; Pearl Harbor and its aftermath. Doubleday 1982 366p il maps hardcover o.p. paperback available $14 **940.54**
1. Pearl Harbor (Oahu, Hawaii), Attack on, 1941
ISBN 0-385-42051-X (pa)   LC 81-43300
This book concentrates "on the investigations into the attack on Pearl Harbor. . . . Toland's thesis is that President Roosevelt and other high officials knew about the planned Japanese attack, but through a combination of political reasons and blunders failed to pass on the information." Libr J
"Mr. Toland has written a thriller. He recounts the attack dramatically and then reviews the investigations in a way that raises doubts and questions." N Y Times Book Rev

Includes bibliography

Travers, Paul J. (Paul Joseph), 1951-
Eyewitness to infamy: an oral history of Pearl Harbor; [by] Paul Joseph Travers. Madison Bks. 1991 270p il $24.95 **940.54**
1. Pearl Harbor (Oahu, Hawaii), Attack on, 1941
ISBN 0-8191-8058-0   LC 91-4259
This volume features "accounts of 43 survivors. The eyewitnesses cover all the services, most of the major ships and installations, and all phases of the attack as well as the clean up that began the day after. Most of the pieces are brief, some are more vivid than others, but they all add up to a fairly substantial contribution to our knowledge of how the attack looked on December 7, 1941." Booklist

Weintraub, Stanley, 1929-
Long day's journey into war; December 7, 1941. Dutton 1991 706p il maps $26.95 **940.54**
1. Pearl Harbor (Oahu, Hawaii), Attack on, 1941 2. World War, 1939-1945
ISBN 0-525-93344-1   LC 91-8352
Also available in paperback from New Am. Lib.
"A Truman Talley book"
This is an hour by hour account of events taking place around the world and at Pearl Harbor during the weekend of the Japanese attack
"To make and place the thousands of minute tiles that make up this great mosaic of war is a remarkable feat; to have done it so artfully is astounding." Natl Rev

Includes bibliographic references

Wheeler, Keith
War under the Pacific; by Keith Wheeler and the editors of Time-Life Books. Time-Life Bks. 1980 208p il (World War II) $19.93 **940.54**
1. World War, 1939-1945—Pacific Ocean 2. World War, 1939-1945—Naval operations—Submarine 3. Submarines   LC 80-13222
Numerous photographs and accompanying text chronicle submarine warfare in the Pacific theater of operations

Includes bibliography

940.55 Europe—1945-

Lewis, Flora
Europe; road to unity. rev ed. Simon & Schuster 1992 590p maps pa $14 **940.55**
1. Europe—Description 2. Europe—Civilization
ISBN 0-671-77828-5   LC 92-234710
"A Touchstone book"
First published 1987 with subtitle: a tapestry of nations
The author surveys the history, geography, politics, economy, culture, and "national character" of western and eastern European nations

Includes bibliographic references

941 British Isles

Britain; by the editors of Time-Life Books. Time-Life Bks. 1986 160p il maps (Lib. of nations) $28.60 **941**
1. Great Britain   LC 86-22995
An illustrated look at the peoples and history of the various regions of Great Britain. Regional, social and religious differences are noted as is Britain's colonial past

Includes bibliography

The **Cambridge** historical encyclopedia of Great Britain and Ireland; editor, Christopher Haigh. Cambridge Univ. Press 1985 392p il maps hardcover o.p. paperback available $21.95 **941**
1. Great Britain—History—Dictionaries
ISBN 0-521-39552-6 (pa)   LC 85-47568
"Broad chronological overview of seven themes ranging from government to culture. The essays on topics such as government and politics, warfare, society, the economy, and international relations are supported by short identification paragraphs in the margins. The time period covered extends from 100 B.C. to 1975. There is a biographical section with about 800 entries." Ref Sources for Small & Medium-sized Libr. 5th edition

The **Cambridge** illustrated dictionary of British heritage; edited by Alan Isaacs and Jennifer Monk. Cambridge Univ. Press 1986 484p il maps $39.95 **941**
1. National characteristics, British 2. Great Britain—Civilization—Dictionaries 3. Great Britain—Social life and customs—Dictionaries
ISBN 0-521-30214-5   LC 86-13708

The Cambridge illustrated dictionary of British heritage—*Continued*

Among the topics covered are British art, buildings, cuisine, customs, education, geography, history, language, law, monarchy, politics, religion and sports

"Most entries offer descriptions comparable to those in standard reference sources. . . . Some of the illustrations provide valuable information not so readily accessible." Choice

Cannon, John, 1929-

The Oxford illustrated history of the British monarchy; [by] John Cannon and Ralph Griffiths. Oxford Univ. Press 1988 727p il $49.95   **941**

1. Great Britain—Kings, queens, rulers, etc. 2. Great Britain—Politics and government
ISBN 0-19-822786-8   LC 88-5172

"A dynastic account of the history, public and private, of the British monarchy. Augmented by many illustrations that show the visual magnificence that is a part of the monarchy." N Y Public Libr Book of How & Where to Look It Up

Includes bibliography

Hibbert, Christopher, 1924-

The English; a social history, 1066-1945. Norton 1987 785p il $39.95   **941**

1. England—Social life and customs 2. National characteristics, British
ISBN 0-393-02371-0   LC 86-8752

This is a chronicle of the daily life of the English people from the Norman Conquest to the present age

"In place of analysis here we find anecdotes. The emphasis is local, the facts are fascinating, the tone is often amusing." N Y Times Book Rev

Includes bibliography

Johnson, Paul, 1928-

Castles of England, Scotland and Wales. Harper & Row 1989 215p il maps $29.95; pa $20   **941**

1. Castles 2. Great Britain—Description
ISBN 0-06-016103-5; 0-06-092351-2 (pa)
                                            LC 89-45046

First published 1978 in the United Kingdom with title: The National Trust book of British castles

"Johnson's survey of castle-building and restoration leads the reader through the architectural, military, and political history of England, Wales, and Scotland. . . . Johnson provides a fascinating tour, via excellent color photographs and sharp diagrams, of these surviving structures and their historical importance." Booklist

The Oxford illustrated history of Britain; edited by Kenneth O. Morgan. Oxford Univ. Press 1984 640p il maps $45; pa $22.95   **941**

1. Great Britain—History
ISBN 0-19-822684-5; 0-19-285174-8 (pa)
                                            LC 83-21990

"2,000 years of British history as told by ten leading historians. Details how the past has shaped British character, patriotism, and ethnocentrism. Includes over 250 illustrations, chronologies, genealogies of monarchs,

and a table of Prime Ministers." N Y Public Libr Book of How & Where To Look It Up

941.082   British Isles—1901-

Churchill, Sir Winston, 1874-1965

Blood, toil, tears, and sweat: the speeches of Winston Churchill; edited and with an introduction by David Cannadine. Houghton Mifflin 1989 355p il hardcover o.p. paperback available $10.95   **941.082**

1. Great Britain—Politics and government—1900-1999 (20th century)
ISBN 0-395-55998-7 (pa)   LC 89-19939

This selection ranges from Churchill's "1901 maiden speech in the House of Commons defending Britain's conduct in the Boer War, to his witty attack on the House of Lords, his impassioned denunciation of Bolshevist tyranny in the wake of the Russian Revolution, his gallant . . . tributes to Franklin Roosevelt and Neville Chamberlain, his stern warning about the postwar 'Iron Curtain,' and his prescient prophecy of European unity." Christ Sci Monit

941.085   British Isles—1945-

Jenkins, Peter, 1934-1992

Mrs. Thatcher's revolution; the ending of the socialist era. Harvard Univ. Press 1988 c1987 xxxvi, 417p il $27.50; pa $12.95
                                          941.085

1. Thatcher, Margaret 2. Great Britain—Politics and government—1952-
ISBN 0-674-58832-0; 0-674-58833-9 (pa) LC 88-7231

First published 1987 in the United Kingdom

"Jenkins takes as his canvass not simply the Iron Lady or her government, but the texture of contemporary British society. This is as full, vibrant, and moving a portrait as we are liable to have." Libr J

Includes bibliography

941.5   Ireland

Newman, Peter R.

A companion to Irish history, 1603-1921. Facts on File 1991 244p maps $27.95
                                           941.5

1. Ireland—History—Dictionaries 2. Ireland—Biography—Dictionaries
ISBN 0-8160-2572-X   LC 91-23677

"Newman takes as his starting point the destruction of the native order after the defeat of Hugh O'Neill and Hugh O'Donnell at Kinsale (1601) and the subsequent confiscation of their lands in the northern province. His ending point is the signing of the Anglo-Irish Treaty in December 1921. . . . Entries are arranged in alphabetical order followed by appendixes listing administrators, a chronology, a bibliography, and six maps." Choice

"Providing objective treatment of a controversial subject, Newman's encyclopedia will help a wide variety of patrons." Libr J

The **Oxford** illustrated history of Ireland; edited by R.F. Foster. Oxford Univ. Press 1989 382p il maps $45; pa $19.95

941.5

1. Ireland—History
ISBN 0-19-822970-4; 0-19-285245-0 (pa)

LC 89-16168

This illustrated history includes "six essays by Irish scholars, five covering chronological periods in Irish history and the sixth a . . . discussion of the interplay between Irish literature and history." Libr J

"A thoughtful and highly informative volume that manages to underscore the ancient and rooted aspects of Irish culture, even while it explores in depth the mobility and shifting of the Irish people into 'fractured and sometimes unexpected patterns.'" Booklist

Includes bibliographic references

942.01 England—Early history to 1066

Goodrich, Norma Lorre
King Arthur. Watts 1986 406p il maps o.p.; Harper & Row paperback available $14

942.01

1. Arthur, King 2. Great Britain—History—0-1066
ISBN 0-06-097182-7 (pa)

LC 85-22558

The author examines historical and literary materials relating to Arthur as both an actual and legendary figure

Includes bibliography

942.05 England—Tudor period, 1485-1603

Martin, Colin, 1939-
The Spanish Armada; [by] Colin Martin & Geoffrey Parker. Norton 1988 296p il hardcover o.p. paperback available $11.95

942.05

1. Spanish Armada, 1588
ISBN 0-393-30926-6 (pa)

LC 89-102323

"A concise history describing the power struggles and political intrigues of Europe that led to the launching of the armada." Publ Wkly

Includes bibliographic references

Mattingly, Garrett, 1900-1962
The Armada. Houghton Mifflin 1988 c1959 443p il maps hardcover o.p. paperback available $11.70

942.05

1. Spanish Armada, 1588
ISBN 0-395-08366-4 (pa)

LC 87-26210

A reissue of the title first published 1959; 1984 edition had title: The defeat of the Spanish Armada

This account of the defeat of the Spanish Armada by the British in 1588 describes in detail the "military measures and actions, the sentiments and passions of the public, political intrigue, and the motives and maneuvering of the royal figures involved, notably Elizabeth." Publ Wkly

Includes bibliographic references

942.06 England—Stuart and Commonwealth periods, 1603-1714

Trevelyan, George Macaulay, 1876-1962
The English Revolution, 1688-1689. Holt & Co. 1939 c1938 281p o.p.; Oxford Univ. Press paperback available $6.95

942.06

1. Great Britain—History—1603-1714, Stuarts
ISBN 0-19-500263-6 (pa)

First published 1938 in the United Kingdom

This study covers not only the revolution itself but also the events of the reign of James II, which led up to it and the political changes which followed

Includes bibliography

942.08 England—Period of Victoria and House of Windsor, 1837-

Taylor, A. J. P. (Alan John Percivale), 1906-1990
English history, 1914-1945. Oxford Univ. Press 1965 xxvii, 708p maps (Oxford history of England) $65; pa $16.95

942.08

1. Great Britain—History—1900-1999 (20th century)
ISBN 0-19-821715-3; 0-19-285268-X (pa)

A study of the political, economic, and social changes in England over a thirty year span

943 Central Europe. Germany

Craig, Gordon Alexander, 1913-
The Germans; [by] Gordon A. Craig. Putnam 1982 350p maps o.p.; New Am. Lib. paperback available $12

943

1. Germany—Civilization 2. Germany—History
ISBN 0-452-01085-3 (pa)

LC 81-8650

This work examining the social history of Germany contains "chapters on religion, money, Germans and Jews, women, professors and students, romantics, literature and society, soldiers, Berlin—and an appendix called 'The Awful German Language.'" Publisher's note

Includes bibliography

Fulbrook, Mary, 1951-
A concise history of Germany. Cambridge Univ. Press 1991 c1990 263p il maps (Cambridge concise histories) $49.95; pa $12.95

943

1. Germany—History
ISBN 0-521-36283-0; 0-521-36836-7 (pa)

LC 90-32506

First published 1990 in the United Kingdom

"Covering German history from the medieval period to the nation's current reunification, the book examines the political, social, and cultural context. . . . Major figures on the German scene such as Martin Luther, Immanuel Kant, and Adolf Hitler are given appropriate attention in Fulbrook's account, but her main emphasis is . . . on broader historical currents." Booklist

Includes bibliography

Gay, Ruth
The Jews of Germany; a historical portrait; with an introduction by Peter Gay. Yale Univ. Press 1992 297p il maps $35
943

1. Jews—Germany
ISBN 0-300-05155-7   LC 91-30235
This is a history of Germany's Jews from the first century to the Holocaust
"Illustrated sumptuously with paintings, photographs and excerpts from letters and historical documents, . . . this affirming history survives the sad end of the centuries-old German Jewish way of life." N Y Times Book Rev

Germany; by the editors of Time-Life Books. Time-Life Bks. 1986 160p il maps (Lib. of nations) $28.60   **943**

1. Germany   LC 86-5766
This illustrated volume discusses the history, economy and society of Germany
Includes bibliography

943.08   Germany since 1866

Craig, Gordon Alexander, 1913-
Germany, 1866-1945; by Gordon A. Craig. Oxford Univ. Press 1978 825p (Oxford history of modern Europe) $39.95; pa $21
943.08

1. Germany—History
ISBN 0-19-822113-4; 0-19-502724-8 (pa)
LC 78-58471
"A Clarendon Press book"
A "predominantly military and political history of modern Germany." Libr J
"An impressive . . . survey of modern German history, this book is an indispensable reference." New Statesman
Includes bibliography

943.086   Germany—Period of Third Reich, 1933-1945

The **Encyclopedia** of the Third Reich; edited by Christian Zentner and Friedemann Bedürftig; English translation edited by Amy Hackett. Macmillan 1991 2v il set $190   **943.086**

1. Germany—History—1933-1945—Dictionaries
ISBN 0-02-897500-6   LC 90-49885
Original German edition, 1985
"Over 3000 entries on specific subjects from Otto Abetz to Zyklon B are accompanied by two dozen longer essays on such general themes as the Final Solution and women in the Third Reich. The text is supplemented by over 1200 . . . illustrations." Libr J
"The depth and breadth of coverage make this an outstanding source of information on this era for school, public, and academic libraries." Am Libr
Includes bibliographic references

Engelmann, Bernt, 1921-
In Hitler's Germany; daily life in the Third Reich; translated from the German by Krishna Winston. Pantheon Bks. 1986 335p o.p.; Schocken Bks. paperback available $16
943.086

1. World War, 1939-1945—Germany 2. National socialism 3. Germany—History—1933-1945
ISBN 0-8052-0864-X (pa)   LC 85-6251
Original German edition published in two volumes, 1982-1983
This book is an attempt by a journalist to combine memoir, oral history and aspects of "social, political, and cultural history of the Third Reich. . . . He has interviewed . . . doctors, waiters, family members, old school friends, a professor of religion, labor union activist, Protestant pastor, resistance workers, and others." Choice

Fleming, Gerald
Hitler and the final solution; with an introduction by Saul Friedlander. University of Calif. Press 1984 xxxvi, 219p il hardcover o.p. paperback available $13   **943.086**

1. Hitler, Adolf, 1889-1945 2. Holocaust, Jewish (1933-1945)
ISBN 0-520-06022-9 (pa)   LC 83-24352
Original German edition, 1982
This work attempts to prove "that the Final Solution was deliberately designed and personally willed and ordered by Hitler. Fleming reveals the elaborate precautions taken not only to disguise the nature of the operation but also to ensure that it could not be connected with Hitler." Publisher's note
Includes bibliography

Koonz, Claudia
Mothers in the fatherland; women, the family, and Nazi politics. St. Martin's Press 1987 xxxv, 556p il $25; pa $16.95
943.086

1. Women—Germany 2. Germany—History—1933-1945 3. National socialism
ISBN 0-312-54933-4; 0-312-02256-5 (pa)
LC 86-13815
The author analyzes "the question of women's participation in the Third Reich. The dominant figure here is Gertrud Scholtz-Klink, chief of the Women's Bureau under Hitler. . . . Koonz concludes that Nazi women, no less than men, 'destroyed ethical vision, debased human traditions, and rendered decent people helpless.'" Publ Wkly
"In the history of women in general, the Nazi chapter is a particularly painful one, but it is written with forthrightness and an authority based upon enormous work in the archives and in the field." N Y Rev Books
Includes bibliography

Posner, Gerald L.
Hitler's children; sons and daughters of leaders of the Third Reich talk about their fathers and themselves. Random House 1991 239p il $20.50   **943.086**

1. National socialism 2. Germany—History—1933-1945
ISBN 0-394-58299-3   LC 90-9128

Posner, Gerald L.—*Continued*

Also available in paperback from Berkley Pub. Group

The author "located a representative group of the children of Third Reich leaders willing to talk about their experiences during those dark German days. Within each interview piece, Posner provides a rundown of the life and Nazi career of the leader in question, the group including Reichsmarschall Hermann Göring, Admiral Karl Donitz, Reichsbank president Hjalman Schacht, governor general of Poland Hans Frank, 'Angel of Death' Josef Mengele, Reichsminister Rudolf Hess, and would-be Hitler assassin Claus von Stauffenberg." Booklist

Includes bibliography

Read, Anthony

Kristallnacht; the Nazi night of terror; [by] Anthony Read and David Fisher. Times Bks. 1989 294p il $19.95   **943.086**

1. Germany—History—1933-1945   2. Holocaust, Jewish (1933-1945) 3. Jews—Germany
ISBN 0-8129-1723-5   LC 89-40184

Also available in paperback from Bedrick Bks.

This is an account of the events of the night of November 9-10, 1938, in Germany and Austria. Almost all of the synagogues were burned down, shops owned by Jews were destroyed, and thousands of Jews were taken to concentration camps. The authors describe how Kristallnacht was organized

"This tightly written, soundly researched, popular narrative by two British historians supplies an excellent overview of the events." Libr J

Includes bibliography

Rempel, Gerhard

Hitler's children; the Hitler youth and the SS. University of N.C. Press 1989 354p il hardcover o.p. paperback available $12.95
943.086

1. Germany—History—1933-1945   2. National socialism
ISBN 0-8078-4299-0 (pa)   LC 88-28036

The author examines the alliance between the Nazi SS and the Hitler Youth

"Rempel's objective work brings into focus one aspect of the sordid history of the Third Reich." Booklist

Includes bibliography

Shirer, William L. (William Lawrence)

The rise and fall of the Third Reich; a history of Nazi Germany; with a new afterword by the author. Simon & Schuster 1990 1249p $35; pa $14.95   **943.086**

1. Germany—History—1933-1945
ISBN 0-671-72869-5; 0-671-72868-7 (pa)
LC 90-221762

"A Touchstone book"

First published 1960

This is a comprehensive, documented history of Germany from the beginning of the Nazi party in 1918 to the World War II defeat of Germany in 1945. Here is a detailed account of the events, and the leading figures of the Nazi era, especially Adolf Hitler

Includes bibliographic references

Speer, Albert, 1905-1981

Inside the Third Reich; memoirs; translated from the German by Richard and Clara Winston; introduction by Eugene Davidson. Macmillan 1970 596p il hardcover o.p. paperback available $16
943.086

1. Hitler, Adolf, 1889-1945 2. Germany—History—1933-1945 3. World War, 1939-1945—Germany
ISBN 0-02-037500-X (pa)

Original German edition, 1969

The author, Hitler's "architect and later his armaments minister, was in the dictator's inner circle for almost 12 years. . . . [After the war] Speer used the enforced leisure of his 20 prison years as a war criminal to plan and write these memoirs." Libr J

Includes bibliographic references

943.087   Germany—1945-

Grass, Günter, 1927-

Two states—one nation? translated from the German by Krishna Winston with A.S. Wensinger. Harcourt Brace Jovanovich 1990 123p $18.95; pa $8.95   **943.087**

1. German reunification question (1949-1990) 2. Germany—Politics and government
ISBN 0-15-192270-5; 0-15-692060-3 (pa)
LC 90-42125

"A Helen and Kurt Wolff book"

A collection of the author's speeches, essays, and newspaper interviews on the subject of German reunification dating from 1961 to the spring of 1990

Schneider, Peter, 1940-

The German comedy; scenes of life after the wall; translated by Philip Boehm and Leigh Hafrey. Farrar, Straus & Giroux 1991 211p $21; pa $11   **943.087**

1. Germany—Social conditions 2. Germany—Description
ISBN 0-374-10201-5; 0-374-52358-4 (pa)
LC 91-20416

The author "presents his analysis of the new Berlin/Germany and what lies ahead. Personal anecdotes abound, and readers will enjoy the author's 'man-on-the spot' style. . . . The big questions, such as a possible revival of German nationalism, militarism, and anti-Semitism, are deftly treated by the author." Libr J

943.1   Northeastern Germany

Borneman, John

After the wall; east meets west in the new Berlin. Basic Bks. 1991 258p il $21.95; pa $12   **943.1**

1. Berlin (Germany)
ISBN 0-465-00083-5; 0-465-00084-3 (pa)
LC 90-55589

The author "interviewed a variety of East Germans to learn what it was like to live in the German Democratic Republic and how the Autumn Revolution of 1989 affected their lives. The picture that emerges is one of warped lives, stunted productive capacities and

Borneman, John—*Continued*
an entire generation 'perverted to passivity.'" Publ Wkly

Includes bibliographic references

Darnton, Robert
Berlin journal, 1989-1990. Norton 1991
352p il $22.95; pa $10.95   **943.1**
1. Germany (East)—Politics and government 2. Berlin (Germany)
ISBN 0-393-02970-0; 0-393-31018-3 (pa)
                 LC 90-19745
"Darnton spent parts of 1989 and 1990 in Germany, witnessing the end of that country's division into East and West as the Berlin Wall fell. . . . [He] focuses more on events and aftereffects in East Germany as experienced by ordinary citizens, rather than trying to write a definitive study. Darnton talks with workers, bureaucrats, and government officials and describes what was happening and what the people understood about these momentous events." Booklist

943.6   Austria and Liechtenstein

Crankshaw, Edward, 1909-1984
The fall of the House of Habsburg. Viking 1963 459p il map o.p.; Penguin Bks. paperback available $11   **943.6**
1. Franz Joseph I, Emperor of Austria, 1830-1916 2. House of Habsburg 3. Austria—History
ISBN 0-14-006459-1 (pa)
"Events between the time of Franz Josef's accession as emperor of the Habsburg monarchy in 1848 and his death in the middle of World War I are reconstructed in this fascinating analysis." Booklist

Includes bibliographic references

943.7   Czechoslovakia

Havel, Václav
Summer meditations; translated from the Czech by Paul Wilson. Knopf 1992 151p $20   **943.7**
1. Czechoslovakia—Politics and government 2. Political ethics
ISBN 0-679-41462-2   LC 91-58931
Also available in paperback from Vintage Bks.
These meditations by the Czech president "were written 18 months into office, from July to August 1991, and revised for the English edition. . . . Havel made these revisions, he says, in light of changes in the Soviet Union and in view of 'the resistance' some of his proposals met in the Czechoslovak parliament." Christ Sci Monit

943.8   Poland

The **Chronicle** of the Łódź ghetto, 1941-1944; edited by Lucjan Dobroszycki; translated by Richard Lourie [et al.] Yale Univ. Press 1984 lxviii, 551p il $50; pa $25   **943.8**
1. Jews—Poland 2. Holocaust, Jewish (1933-1945) 3. Łódź (Poland)—Social conditions
ISBN 0-300-03208-0; 0-300-03924-7 (pa)   LC 84-3614

"This English edition comprises about one fourth of the original surviving German and Polish manuscript. Day-by-day entries of one to ten pages recorded events and living conditions from January 1941 to the ghetto's liquidation in July 1944. The chronicle was composed by a team of writers, employees of the Jewish ghetto administration." Libr J
"The record is made more profoundly melancholic by the restrained archivist style employed by the chroniclers." New Statesman

Davies, Norman
Heart of Europe; a short history of Poland. Clarendon Press 1984 xxi, 511p il o.p. paperback available $11.95   **943.8**
1. Poland—History
ISBN 0-19-285152-7 (pa)   LC 83-22003
The author uses a reverse chronological approach to examine Poland during WW II and its aftermath, the Partitions, and the independent monarchies

Includes bibliographic references

943.9   Hungary

Michener, James A. (James Albert), 1907-
The bridge at Andau. Random House 1957 270p map $19.95   **943.9**
1. Hungary—History—1956, Revolution 2. Refugees, Hungarian
ISBN 0-394-41778-X
Also available in paperback from Fawcett Bks.
"The heroism, horror and tragedy of the 1956 Hungarian revolt is revealed through interviews with many refugees [who crossed the bridge at Andau to freedom]." Cleveland Public Libr

944   France and Monaco

France; by the editors of Time-Life Books. Time-Life Bks. 1985 c1984 160p il maps (Lib. of nations) $28.60   **944**
1. France   LC 85-20531
A portrait in text and color photographs of the land, people, culture and history of France and present day life in that country

Includes bibliography

Tuchman, Barbara Wertheim
A distant mirror; the calamitous 14th century; [by] Barbara W. Tuchman. Knopf 1978 xx, 677p il maps $45   **944**
1. Coucy, Enguerrand de, 1340-1397 2. France—History—1328-1589, House of Valois 3. Fourteenth century 4. Civilization, Medieval
ISBN 0-394-40026-7   LC 78-5985
Also available in paperback from Ballantine Bks.
The author traces the history of the fourteenth century by following the career of a "feudal lord, Enguerrand de Coucy VII, the seigneur of some 150 towns and villages in Picardy. He was born in 1340, and he died in captivity in 1397, having been made a prisoner by the Turks." Time

Includes bibliography

Weber, Eugen Joseph, 1925-
My France; politics, culture, myth; [by] Eugen Weber. Belknap Press 1991 412p $27.50; pa $14.95 **944**

1. France—History 2. France—Civilization
ISBN 0-674-59575-0; 0-674-59576-9 (pa)
LC 90-35780

Analyzed in Essay and general literature index

A collection of essays on French history and civilization "by a resolutely untheoretical Romanian-born historian whose life's work has transformed the study of the French past." N Y Times Book Rev

Includes bibliographic references

944.04   France—Revolutionary period, 1789-1804

Burke, Edmund, 1729?-1797
Reflections on the Revolution in France **944.04**

1. France—History—1789-1799, Revolution
Hardcover and paperback editions available from various publishers
First published 1790

"A treatise by Edmund Burke, written in the form of a letter to a Frenchman. It attacks the leaders and principles of the French Revolution for their violence and excesses, and urges reform, rather than rebellion, as a means of correcting social and political abuses." Reader's Ency. 3d edition

Lefebvre, Georges, 1874-1959
The French Revolution. Columbia Univ. Press 1962-1964 2v v1 hardcover o.p., v2 $54; pa ea $17.50 **944.04**

1. France—History—1789-1799, Revolution
Original French edition, 1930; this translation is based on 1957 reprintings

Contents: v1 From its origins to 1793, translated by Elizabeth Moss Evanson (ISBN 0-231-08598-2); v2 From 1793 to 1799, translated by John Hall Stewart and James Friguglietti (ISBN 0-231-02519-X; 0-231-08599-0)

An account of the political, military, social, economic and intellectual aspects of the French Revolution

Includes bibliographies

Schama, Simon
Citizens: a chronicle of the French Revolution. Knopf 1989 xx, 948p il maps $39.50; pa $16.95 **944.04**

1. France—History—1789-1799, Revolution
ISBN 0-394-55948-7; 0-679-72610-1 (pa)
LC 88-45320

The author "offers a narrative in the form of a nineteenth-century chronicle that delves into the events and meaning of that momentous series of historical events." Booklist

"Baroque eloquence and rococo sparkle make the book long but never long-winded. All in all, it is an intelligent book for intelligent readers that is also a delight to read." N Y Times Book Rev

Includes bibliography

944.05   France—Period of First Empire, 1804-1815

Schom, Alan
One hundred days; Napoleon's road to Waterloo. Atheneum Pubs. 1992 398p il maps $28 **944.05**

1. Napoleon I, Emperor of the French, 1769-1821 2. Waterloo, Battle of, 1815
ISBN 0-689-12097-4
LC 92-4249

Also available in paperback from Oxford Univ. Press

This is an account of "Napoleon's escape from Elba in February 1815 and his return . . . to France. Rallying the nation behind him, he mustered his army and marched off to meet Wellington at Waterloo. . . . This is a first-class reconstruction of Napoleon's final campaign." Publ Wkly

Includes bibliography

944.07   France—Period of Second Republic and Second Empire, 1848-1870

Friedrich, Otto, 1929-
Olympia; Paris in the age of Manet. HarperCollins Pubs. 1992 329p il $28 **944.07**

1. Manet, Édouard, 1832-1883 2. Paris (France)—History 3. Art, French
ISBN 0-06-016318-6
LC 91-50443

Also available in paperback from Simon & Schuster

"Edouard Manet and his masterful, once controversial portrait *Olympia* serve as touchstones for Friedrich's . . . anecdotal sketches of the lives of Napoleon and Eugenie, Flaubert, Zola, Jacques Offenbach, and of course, Manet and his 'network of women.'" Booklist

"Mr. Friedrich does a good job of presenting both the world that inspired 'Olympia' and the society that rejected it, and of providing lots of pertinent facts and colorful anecdotes along the way." N Y Times Book Rev

Includes bibliographic references

944.08   France—1870-

Flanner, Janet, 1892-1978
Paris journal; [by] Janet Flanner (Genêt); edited by William Shawn. Harcourt Brace Jovanovich 1988 c1965-1971 3v v1-2 ea pa $12.95; v3 o.p. **944.08**

1. Paris (France)—History 2. France—Politics and government 3. Paris (France)—Intellectual life
LC 88-2300

"A Harvest/HBJ book"

First two volume edition published 1965-1971 by Atheneum Pubs.

Contents: v1 1944-1955 (ISBN 0-15-670948-1); v2 1956-1964 (ISBN 0-15-670949-X); v3 1965-1970 (o.p.)

In these bulletins, written for the New Yorker, the author comments on the political, social, and artistic aspects of life in France during the period covered

It is the author's "total tapestry, her brilliantly colored and intricately patterned portrait of Paris itself, that will enchant, educate, and inspire the reader." Saturday Rev

944.081   France—Period of Third Republic, 1870-1945

Bald, Wambly
On the Left Bank, 1929-1933; edited by Benjamin Franklin V. Ohio Univ. Press 1987 xxvii, 159p il $21.95   **944.081**
1. Paris (France)—Intellectual life 2. Bohemianism
ISBN 0-8214-0852-6   LC 86-23638

The author, an American reporter, wrote an irreverent gossip column for the Paris edition of the Chicago Tribune from 1929-1933. This book reproduces much of the column, which focused on the social activities of such personalities as Henry Miller, Ford Madox Ford, Gertrude Stein, and Louise Bryant

Includes bibliographies

Bredin, Jean-Denis
The affair; the case of Alfred Dreyfus; translated from the French by Jeffrey Mehlman. Braziller 1986 628p il hardcover o.p. paperback available $12.95   **944.081**
1. Dreyfus, Alfred, 1859-1935 2. Trials (Espionage) 3. Antisemitism 4. France—Politics and government—1815-1914
ISBN 0-8076-1175-1 (pa)   LC 85-22374
Original French edition, 1983

In his examination of the case, the author seeks to "set the affair within the . . . currents of French history and the rising tide of anti-Semitism." Choice
"That Bredin manages to be both passionate and exact is his first outstanding virtue. He is admirably free of the baroque conspiracy theories that sprout so luxuriantly on both sides of this case." N Y Rev Books

Includes bibliography

944.083   France—Period of Fifth Republic, 1958-

Mayle, Peter
Toujours Provence; illustrations by Judith Clancy. Knopf 1991 241p il $20   **944.083**
1. Provence (France)—Social life and customs
ISBN 0-679-40253-5   LC 90-50804
Also available Thorndike Press large print edition

This companion volume to the title entered below continues the author's account of life in the South of France

A year in Provence; illustrations by Judith Clancy. Knopf 1990 c1989 207p il $23; pa $10   **944.083**
1. Provence (France)—Social life and customs
ISBN 0-394-57230-0; 0-679-73114-8 (pa)
              LC 89-38475
First published 1989 in the United Kingdom

The author "emigrated to the South of France, where he has bought and modernized a house close to the village of Ménerbes in the Lubéron. A Year in Provence is his account of a settler's experiences, beginning with his arrival in January and ending with a party for the builders to celebrate the house's completion the following Christmas." Times Lit Suppl

"A Francophile's delight, this is a highly entertaining book which also teaches a lesson in social life and customs." Libr J

945   Italian Peninsula and adjacent islands. Italy

Barzini, Luigi Giorgio, 1908-1984
The Italians; by Luigi Barzini. Atheneum Pubs. 1964 352p maps hardcover o.p. paperback available $13   **945**
1. National characteristics, Italian 2. Italy—Civilization
ISBN 0-689-70540-9 (pa)
Also available in hardcover from P. Smith

"The Italians as they are and as foreigners think they are . . . described by an Italian journalist whose probing examination of national life and character does not oversimplify a society webbed with contradiction and incongruity." Booklist

Durant, William James, 1885-1981
The Renaissance; [by] Will Durant. Simon & Schuster 1953 776p il (Story of civilization, pt5) $35   **945**
1. Renaissance 2. Italy—Civilization 3. Italy—History—0-1559
ISBN 0-671-61600-5
"A history of civilization in Italy from 1304-1576 A.D." Title page

"A mosaic of biographical sketches interspersed with lively passages on manners, morals, dress, food, festivals, plagues, pastimes and artistic preferences among the Italian élite, during some eight generations." N Y Her Trib Books

Includes bibliography

Italy; by the editors of Time-Life Books; with photographs by Romano Cagnoni. Time-Life Bks. 1986 160p il maps (Lib. of nations) $28.60   **945**
1. Italy   LC 86-14456
An illustrated look at the history, geography, and development of Italy's culture, including craftsmanship, the film industry, and family structure

Includes bibliography

Norwich, John Julius, 1929-
A history of Venice. Knopf 1982 xxiv, 673p il maps hardcover o.p. paperback available $16.95   **945**
1. Venice (Italy)—History
ISBN 0-679-72197-5 (pa)   LC 81-48116
First published 1977-1981 in the United Kingdom in two volumes with title: Venice

"An account of the Venetian Republic, from its obscure 5th century origins to its demise in 1797. . . . This is largely a political history, the greater part of which concentrates on Venice's prime between the 13th and 16th centuries." Libr J
This "history is complete, accurate, elegantly written, and easily readable by nonspecialists." N Y Times Book Rev

Includes bibliography

Parks, Tim
Italian neighbors; or, A lapsed Anglo-Saxon in Verona. Grove Weidenfeld 1992 272p $19.95 **945**

1. Italy—Social life and customs
ISBN 0-8021-1531-4   LC 91-44046

"A 10-year resident, with his Italian-born wife, of a village close to Verona, British-born novelist Parks . . . here celebrates the endearing and exasperating traits of his adoptive home and the 'magical duplicity' of its people." Publ Wkly

Parks "splendidly characterizes his Italian neighbors and their hang-ups: almost everybody seems obsessed by health worries, keeping doctors and pharmacists busy with an unending chain of tests. Mr. Parks also has a keen ear for everyday speech." N Y Times Book Rev

946 Iberian Peninsula and adjacent islands. Spain

Fuentes, Carlos
The buried mirror; reflections on Spain and the New World. Houghton Mifflin 1992 399p il $35 **946**

1. Spain—Civilization 2. Latin America—Civilization
ISBN 0-395-47978-9   LC 91-34312

The author "believes that a common cultural heritage can help the countries of Latin America transcend disunity and fragmentation. . . . He . . . explores Spanish America's love-hate relationship with Spain and its search for an identity in its multicultural roots." Publ Wkly

"Every page in this lapidary essay offers profound insight into the Spanish American psyche." Libr J

Includes bibliographic references

Hughes, Robert
Barcelona. Knopf 1992 573p il $27.50; pa $14 **946**

1. Barcelona (Spain)—History
ISBN 0-394-58027-3; 0-679-74383-9 (pa)
     LC 91-53179

The author discusses the history, art, architecture, culture and politics of the Catalan capital from Roman times to the twentieth century

"The great distinction of Hughes' approach is that he can move, commandingly, from a Miró canvas to transvestite hookers in the street without missing a beat—and bring to both the same kind of rigorous attention and full-bodied sensibility." Time

Includes bibliography

Spain; by the editors of Time-Life Books. Time-Life Bks. 1987 160p il maps (Lib. of nations) $28.60 **946**

1. Spain   LC 87-1922

"The book traces Spain's long, and many times bloody, history from the first invasions of the Phoenicians, through Roman rule, three centuries of German occupation, and the Moorish dynasties to the beginning of the modern era with Ferdinand and Isabella. Period photographs capture the drama of the Spanish Civil War, the years of Franco's rule, and today's constitutional monarchy." Publisher's note

Includes bibliography

947 Russia. Eastern Europe

The **Cambridge** encyclopedia of Russia and the Soviet Union; general editors: Archie Brown [et al.]; consultant editors: John Bowlt, H.B.F. Dixon. Cambridge Univ. Press 1982 492p il maps o.p. **947**

1. Russia—Dictionaries   LC 81-9965
New edition due Spring 1994

Contents: Territory and peoples; History; Religion; Art and architecture; Language and literature; Music, theatre, dance and film; The sciences; The Soviet political system; The economy; Soviet society; Military power and policy; The world role

Crankshaw, Edward, 1909-1984
The shadow of the Winter Palace; Russia's drift to revolution, 1825-1917. Viking 1976 429p il o.p.; Penguin Bks. paperback available $10.95 **947**

1. House of Romanov 2. Russia—History
ISBN 0-14-004622-4 (pa)   LC 76-10636
Also available in hardcover from P. Smith

This book traces the political, economic, intellectual and diplomatic history of Russia from the Decembrist uprising to the Revolution

Includes bibliography

Eastern Europe; by the editors of Time-Life Books. Time-Life Bks. 1987 160p il maps (Lib. of nations) $28.60 **947**

1. Eastern Europe   LC 87-10224

An illustrated overview of the history, culture, people, religion, geography, and economy of Czechoslovakia, Hungary, and Poland

Includes bibliography

Massie, Suzanne
Land of the firebird; the beauty of old Russia. Simon & Schuster 1980 493p hardcover o.p. paperback available $20 **947**

1. Russia—Civilization 2. Art, Russian
ISBN 0-671-46059-5 (pa)   LC 80-12860
"A Touchstone book"

The author's intent "is to give 'a sense of the whole, now-vanished culture of old Russia . . . to describe that beauty which the Russians once knew how to create, what they loved, and admired and how they once lived and rejoiced.'" N Y Times Book Rev

Includes bibliography

Paxton, John, 1923-
Encylopedia of Russian history; from the Christianization of Kiev to the break-up of the U.S.S.R. ABC-CLIO 1993 483p maps $45 **947**

1. Russia—Dictionaries 2. Soviet Union—Dictionaries
ISBN 0-87436-690-9   LC 93-29564
First published 1983 with title: Companion to Russian history

Paxton, John, 1923-—*Continued*
This volume includes more than 2,500 entries covering people, events, places and politics. Other features include a separate chronology and a section of maps

Riasanovsky, Nicholas Valentine, 1923-
A history of Russia; [by] Nicholas V. Riasanovsky. 5th ed. Oxford Univ. Press 1993 xx, 711p il maps $37   **947**
1. Russia—History
ISBN 0-19-507462-9   LC 91-43254
First published 1963
This narrative history includes discussions of economics, social organization, religion, and culture
Includes bibliographic references

Russia and the independent states; edited by Daniel C. Diller. Congressional Quarterly 1993 342p il maps $34.95; pa $24.95   **947**
1. Soviet Union—History   2. Russia—History
3. Eastern Europe—History
ISBN 0-87187-862-3; 0-87187-617-5 (pa)
      LC 92-33273
Replaces Congressional Quarterly's Soviet Union
"Part 1 traces Russian and Soviet history (primarily 19th and 20th century) through the August 1991 coup and Mikhail Gorbachev's subsequent resignation. . . . Part 2 covers the new Commonwealth of Independent States: its defenses, economy, and foreign relations. Part 3 profiles the newly independent republics individually." Libr J
For a fuller review see: Booklist, Sept. 15, 1993
Includes bibliography

947.08   Russia since 1855

Pipes, Richard
The Russian Revolution. Knopf 1990 xxiv, 944p il maps $40; pa $18   **947.08**
1. Russia—History
ISBN 0-394-50241-8; 0-679-73660-3 (pa)
      LC 89-35129
The author provides a "history of great turmoil, from the last decade of the nineteenth century, when student ferment reached troublesome proportions, to the Bolshevik takeover in October 1917 and the party's subsequent establishment of its own authoritarian regime." Booklist
This is a "massive, wonderfully vivid, gripping chronicle. . . . No other book so brilliantly clarifies the inner dynamics of the Russian Revolution." Publ Wkly
Includes bibliography

Salisbury, Harrison Evans, 1908-1993
Black night, white snow: Russia's revolutions, 1905-1917; [by] Harrison E. Salisbury. Doubleday 1978 c1977 746p o.p.; Da Capo Press paperback available $16.95
    947.08
1. Russia—History
ISBN 0-306-80154-X (pa)   LC 74-18830
The author explores "the major political, economic, social, and intellectual developments of the period and their influence on the revolutions. But his account is

mainly structured around an analysis on the lives of . . . Nicholas II and Lenin." Christ Sci Monit
Includes bibliography

947.084   Russia (Soviet Union)—1917-1991

Medvedev, Roy Aleksandrovich, 1925-
Let history judge; the origins and consequences of Stalinism; [by] Roy Medvedev. rev and expanded ed, edited and translated by George Shriver. Columbia Univ. Press 1989 xxi, 903p $68.50; pa $19.50   **947.084**
1. Stalin, Joseph, 1879-1953 2. Soviet Union—Politics and government
ISBN 0-231-06350-4; 0-231-06351-2 (pa)   LC 89-758
Original Russian edition copyrighted 1967; first United States edition published 1972 by Knopf
"Never have Stalin's crimes against humanity been more forcefully or more thoroughly documented than in . . . [this book, which] distills firsthand testimonies of the mass arrests, torture, imprisonment and executions that befell millions of innocent Soviet citizens." Publ Wkly
Includes bibliographic references

Moynahan, Brian
Comrades: 1917—Russia in revolution. Little, Brown 1991 374p il maps $24.95
    947.084
1. Soviet Union—History—1917-1921, Revolution
ISBN 0-316-58698-6   LC 91-28727
This is a "narrative of the principal personalities and events surrounding the Russian Revolution of 1917, told from the vantage point of eyewitnesses. . . . Moynahan writes well and skillfully weaves quotations and descriptions from many well-known personal accounts into a coherent whole, characterizing not only the political but the social and cultural life of the times." Libr J
Includes bibliographic references

Reed, John, 1887-1920
Ten days that shook the world   **947.084**
1. Soviet Union—History—1917-1921, Revolution
Hardcover and paperback editions available from various publishers
First published 1919 by International Pubs.
"A reportorial, firsthand, and sympathetic account of the November Revolution in Russia (1917). . . . After prefatory explanation of political groups and other organizations, and of the background of the uprising, the work tells with graphic detail of the fall of the provisional government, the revolution and counterrevolution, the solidifying of power, and the resultant congress." Oxford Companion to Am Lit. 5th edition

947.085   Russia (Soviet Union)—1953-1991

Cohen, Stephen F.

Voices of glasnost; interviews with Gorbachev's reformers; [by] Stephen F. Cohen, Katrina vanden Heuvel. Norton 1989 339p il $19.95; pa $12.95   **947.085**

1. Soviet Union—Politics and government
ISBN 0-393-02625-6; 0-393-30735-2 (pa)

LC 89-32441

In a "series of interviews, this book presents fourteen Soviet public figures, leaders of Mikhail Gorbachev's radical reforms, or perestroika, talking about their personal and political struggles to change the Soviet system." Publisher's note

"Usually a book-length collection of interviews is unpromising fare, but this work is exceptional." Libr J

The **Decline** and fall of the Soviet empire; edited by Bernard Gwertzman and Michael T. Kaufman. Times Bks. 1992 xxii, 522p $15   **947.085**

1. Soviet Union—Politics and government
ISBN 0-8129-2046-5   LC 91-51038

An anthology of articles by New York Times staff members documenting the events that led to the collapse of the Soviet empire. Special emphasis is paid to the reforms set in motion by Gorbachev

Felshman, Neil

Gorbachev, Yeltsin, and the last days of the Soviet empire. St. Martin's Press 1992 276p il $22.95   **947.085**

1. Gorbachev, Mikhail 2. Yeltsin, Boris 3. Soviet Union—Politics and government
ISBN 0-312-08200-2   LC 92-24154

"A Thomas Dunne book"

This account of the collapse of the Soviet Union in 1991 includes a look at the political careers of Mikhail Gorbachev and Boris Yeltsin

This work "has something distinct to say about the developments leading to the collapse of a fearsome power and the directions history may take in its wake." New Leader

Gorbachev, Mikhail

The August coup; the truth and the lessons. HarperCollins Pubs. 1991 127p il $18   **947.085**

1. Gorbachev, Mikhail 2. Soviet Union—Politics and government
ISBN 0-06-016890-0   LC 91-58635

This is an account of the abortive August 1991 coup against Soviet President Gorbachev

"This quickly written account . . . does not merely repeat the news accounts of what happened but offers an inside interpretation of why the coup occurred . . . and why it eventually failed. . . . Gorbachev discusses the Union of Sovereign States he had proposed and the needed economic union." Libr J

Gray, Francine du Plessix

Soviet women: walking the tightrope. Doubleday 1990 c1989 213p $19.95; pa $10   **947.085**

1. Women—Soviet Union 2. Soviet Union—Social conditions
ISBN 0-385-24757-5; 0-385-41733-0 (pa)

LC 89-23589

"The book documents the conditions of medical care, education, and employment as well as considers the worlds of fashion, art, and literature, where women play important roles." Booklist

Includes bibliographic references

Khrushchev, Nikita Sergeevich, 1894-1971

Khrushchev remembers; the glasnost tapes; foreword by Strobe Talbott; translated and edited by Jerrold L. Schecter with Vyacheslav V. Luchkov. Little, Brown 1990 219p il $19.95   **947.085**

1. Soviet Union—Politics and government
ISBN 0-316-47297-2   LC 90-52878

In his retirement Khrushchev "recorded his recollections and reflections. Smuggled abroad, portions of 'Khrushchev Remembers' [1970-1974] appeared in the West; . . . [this] third installment contains those fragments that the deceased leader's family had felt could not be published—until the coming of glasnost." N Y Times Book Rev

Medvedev, Roy Aleksandrovich, 1925-

Khrushchev: the years in power; [by] Roy A. Medvedev, Zhores A. Medvedev; translated by Andrew R. Durkin. Columbia Univ. Press 1976 198p il map $38   **947.085**

1. Khrushchev, Nikita Sergeevich, 1894-1971 2. Soviet Union—Politics and government
ISBN 0-231-03939-5

Also available in paperback from Norton

The authors "outline the issues surrounding Krushchev's rise to power and the failures of his domestic policies, primarily agricultural, that led to his political demise." Choice

Includes bibliographic references

Smith, Hedrick

The new Russians. rev ed. Random House 1991 734p map $29.50   **947.085**

1. Soviet Union—Social life and customs 2. Soviet Union—Social conditions 3. National characteristics, Russian
ISBN 0-679-41294-8

First published 1990

"In this sequel to The Russians [entered below], Smith draws on several visits to the Soviet Union since his days as a New York Times correspondent to survey the changes wrought under Gorbachev and the obstacles to further reform. . . . Smith organizes his chapters around general themes (for example, the new role of Soviet television) and provides three chapters on the non-Russian republic." Libr J [review of 1990 edition]

Smith, Hedrick—*Continued*
The Russians. updated ed. Times Bks.
1983 578p il map $30   **947.085**

1. Soviet Union—Social life and customs 2. Soviet
Union—Social conditions 3. National characteristics,
Russian
ISBN 0-8129-1086-9   LC 83-9289
First published 1976

Smith, who was the New York Times former bureau
chief in Moscow from 1971 to 1974, describes how Russians feel about their government, the West, the housing
situation, schools, marriage, abortion, children, pre-marital
sex, sports, crime, drink, the quality of consumer goods,
books, and food

Includes bibliographic references

948   Scandinavia

Roesdahl, Else
The Vikings; translated by Susan M.
Margeson and Kirsten Williams. Allen Lane;
[distributed by] Viking 1991 322p il maps
$24.95   **948**

1. Vikings
ISBN 0-7139-9048-1
Also available in paperback from Penguin Bks.
Original Danish edition, 1987

A survey of Viking civilization from c.750-c.1050.
"About one-third of the book deals with Viking expan-
sion into Russia, Normandy, the British Isles, Iceland,
Greenland, etc. . . . . Most of the book surveys the
geography, people, society, religion, art, etc., of the
Vikings' Scandinavian homelands." Libr J

Includes bibliography

Scandinavia; by the editors of Time-Life
Books. Time-Life Bks. 1987 160p il maps
(Lib. of nations) $28.60   **948**

1. Scandinavia   LC 86-30132

An introduction to the geography, history, economy,
government, and people of Denmark, Norway, Sweden,
Iceland, and Finland

Includes bibliography

949.2   Netherlands

Schama, Simon
The embarrassment of riches; an
interpretation of Dutch culture in the
Golden Age. Knopf 1987 698p il maps
$39.95   **949.2**

1. Netherlands—Civilization
ISBN 0-394-51075-5   LC 86-45418
Also available in paperback from University of Calif.
Press

The author aims to show "how, in the seventeenth
century, a modest assortment of farming, fishing and
shipping communities, without shared language, religion
or government, transformed themselves into a formidable
world empire—the Dutch Republic." Publisher's note

"Delving into customs, beliefs, popular art and quirks
of behavior, Schama has fashioned a tour de force, a
profound, unconventional and rewarding portrait of a
people." Publ Wkly

Includes bibliography

949.5   Greece

Clogg, Richard, 1939-
A concise history of Greece. Cambridge
Univ. Press 1992 257p il maps $44.95; pa
$12.95   **949.5**

1. Greece—History
ISBN 0-521-37228-3; 0-521-37830-3 (pa)
          LC 91-25872

An "illustrated introduction to the history of modern
Greece, from the first stirrings of the national movement
in the late eighteenth century to the present day." Univ
Press Books for Public and Second Sch Libr

Includes bibliographic references

Norwich, John Julius, 1929-
Byzantium. Knopf 1989-1992 c1988-1991
2v il maps v1 $35; v2 $30   **949.5**

1. Byzantine Empire
First published 1988-1991 in the United Kingdom

The first two volumes of a projected trilogy on the
history of the Byzantine Empire

Contents [v1] The early centuries (ISBN 0-394-53778-
5); [v2] The apogee (ISBN 0-394-53779-3)

"If the third volume is as enjoyable and exhaustive
as the first two, history fans will have the definitive
work on the subject." Libr J

Includes bibliographies

Toynbee, Arnold Joseph, 1889-1975
The Greeks and their heritages; [by]
Arnold Toynbee. Oxford Univ. Press 1981
334p $25   **949.5**

1. Greece—History 2. Civilization, Greek
ISBN 0-19-215256-4   LC 81-198525

"Toynbee's history of Greece focuses upon the legacies
that three major civilizations—Mycenaean, Hellenic, and
Byzantine—passed to their successors and how this
cumulative heritage has affected and been incorporated
into modern Greece." Booklist

Includes bibliography

949.8   Romania

Behr, Edward, 1926-
Kiss the hand you cannot bite: the rise
and fall of the Ceausescus. Villard Bks. 1991
xxiii, 293p il $22.50   **949.8**

1. Ceauşescu, Nicolae 2. Ceauşescu, Elena
3. Romania—History
ISBN 0-679-40128-8   LC 90-22263

"Behr studies the reign of Nicolae Ceausescu in
Romania and the fall of his dictatorship in 1989. Behr
believes that the case of Romania, although it coincided
with the political unrest in Eastern Europe at the same
time, represents a special situation, both for unique
conditions in that nation and for the excessively brutal
system of rulership that was hidden from world scrutiny
for many years." Booklist

Includes bibliographic references

Codrescu, Andrei, 1946-
The hole in the flag; a Romanian exile's story of return and revolution. Morrow 1991 249p $21   **949.8**

1. Romania—History
ISBN 0-688-08805-8   LC 90-26046

Also available in paperback from Avon Bks.

The author "was born in Romania, left as a teenager and returned to observe the shocks and joys of revolution from December 1989 to January 1991." Publ Wkly
"Codrescu has succeeded at a disconcerting task: writing a delightful book about a harrowing subject. . . . Wit and irony color nicely his observations on political society and, by extension, human nature." Libr J

Manea, Norman
On clowns; the dictator and the artist: essays. Grove Weidenfeld 1992 178p $18.95
                                                949.8

1. Romania—History
ISBN 0-8021-1415-6   LC 91-23866

In this collection of essays, the Romanian writer describes life under the Ceausescu regime
"Manea's struggle to retain his humanity and artistic integrity is an emotionally powerful story. Both Manea's personal and professional life were subject to unthinkable oppression that is made all too real by his vivid prose." Libr J

Includes bibliographic references

950 Asia. Orient. Far East

Durant, William James, 1885-1981
Our Oriental heritage; [by] Will Durant. Simon & Schuster 1935 1049p il (Story of civilization, pt1) $35   **950**

ISBN 0-671-54800-X

"Being a history of civilization in Egypt and the Near East to the death of Alexander, and in India, China and Japan from the beginning to our own day; with an introduction on the nature and foundations of civilization." Title page

Includes bibliography

Encyclopedia of Asian history; prepared under the auspices of the Asia Society; Ainslie T. Embree, editor in chief. Scribner 1988 4v il maps set $360 **950**

1. Asia—History—Dictionaries
ISBN 0-684-18619-5   LC 87-9891

"This reference undertakes to 'make available the highest level of contemporary scholarship on Asia to a nonspecialist audience.' Political, socioeconomic, and intellectual movements are treated equally, but with an emphasis on historical significance." N Y Public Libr Book of How & Where to Look It Up

951 China and adjacent areas

The **Cambridge** encyclopedia of China; editor, Brian Hook; consultant editor, Denis Twitchett. 2nd ed. Cambridge Univ. Press 1991 502p il maps $55   **951**

1. China—Dictionaries
ISBN 0-521-35594-X   LC 91-18600

First published 1982
"Topics cover history, law, medicine, religion, literature, and architecture, with less emphasis on social conditions. . . . A useful purchase, especially for smaller libraries." Libr J
For a fuller review see: Booklist, Feb. 15, 1992

The **Cambridge** history of China; general editors, Denis Twitchett and John K. Fairbank. Cambridge Univ. Press 1993 8v
                                                951

1. China—History   LC 76-29852

Ten volumes of a projected fifteen volume set
Contents: v1 The Ch'in and Han Empires, 221 B.C.-A.D. 220 $145 (ISBN 0-521-24327-0); v3 Sui and T'ang China, 589-906, pt.1 $155 (ISBN 0-521-21446-7); v6 Alien regimes and border states, 710-1368 $120 (ISBN 0-521-24331-9); v7 The Ming Dynasty, 1368-1644, pt.1 $135 (ISBN 0-521-24332-7); v10 Late Ch'ing, 1800-1911, pt.1 $145 (ISBN 0-521-21447-5); v11 Late Ch'ing, 1800-1911, pt.2 $145 (ISBN 0-521-22029-7); v12 Republican China, 1912-1949, pt.1 $165 (ISBN 0-521-23541-3); v13 Republican China, 1912-1949, pt.2 $150 (ISBN 0-521-24338-6); v14 The People's Republic, pt.1 $120 (ISBN 0-521-24336-X); v15 The People's Republic, pt.2 $125 (ISBN 0-521-24337-8)

"An important series for scholars, this is also a valuable reference tool for general collections." Libr J
Includes bibliographies

Dalai Lama XIV, 1935-
My Tibet; text by His Holiness the fourteenth Dalai Lama of Tibet; photographs and introduction by Galen Rowell. University of Calif. Press 1990 162p il $40
                                                951

1. Tibet (China)—Description—Pictorial works
ISBN 0-520-07109-3   LC 90-10868

"A Mountain Light Press book"
This is "a volume of photographs taken in recent years by Galen Rowell, with a text drawn from interviews with the Dalai Lama or essays written previously by him." N Y Times Book Rev
"Nowhere has the logic of merging Buddhist philosophy and environmentalism received a clearer and more compelling expression than in My Tibet. . . . It is a model of the kind of chemistry that can develop when both a wonderful photographer and a thoughtful writer care deeply about their subject." Nat Hist

Fairbank, John King, 1907-1991
China; a new history. Belknap Press 1992 519p il maps $27.95   **951**

1. China—History
ISBN 0-674-11670-4   LC 91-44164

This book aims to cover the "span of China's history from the paleolithic cultures of 400,000 B.C. to the Tiananmen massacre of 1989." N Y Times Book Rev

Fairbank, John King, 1907-1991 — Continued

"No American scholar of China was better known to the public and academia alike than Fairbank. This history of China, completed two days before his death in 1991, is a fitting final work." Libr J

Includes bibliography

China: tradition & transformation; [by] John K. Fairbank, Edwin O. Reischauer. rev ed. Houghton Mifflin 1989 551p il pa $34
                                                     951

1. China—History
ISBN 0-395-49692-6   LC 88-83732
First published 1978

Also issued as part of East Asia: tradition & transformation, by John Fairbank, Edwin O. Reischauer, Albert Craig

This study of the history and culture of China focuses on the traditions of the Chinese people and the changes imposed on the country by foreign influences

The great Chinese revolution: 1800-1985. Harper & Row 1986 396p maps hardcover o.p. paperback available $12   **951**

1. China—History
ISBN 0-06-039076-X (pa)   LC 86-665
"A Cornelia & Michael Bessie book"

Contents: Late imperial China: growth and change, 1800-1895; The transformation of the late imperial order, 1895-1911; The era of the first Chinese Republic, 1912-1949; The Chinese People's Republic, 1949-1985

"The book is never pedantic, but gathers together a lifetime of scholarship plus a true gift for presentation of complex issues and a fine eye for telling illustration." Libr J

Includes bibliography

Hsü, Immanuel Chung-yueh, 1923-

The rise of modern China; [Chung-kuo chin tai shih] [by] Immanuel C.Y. Hsü. 4th ed. Oxford Univ. Press 1990 xxxi, 971p il maps $38   **951**

1. China—History
ISBN 0-19-505867-4   LC 89-32568
First published 1970

An examination of China's social, economic, intellectual, and political history, from 1600 to the present

Includes bibliographies

Seagrave, Sterling

The Soong dynasty. Harper & Row 1985 532p il $22.50; pa $15   **951**

1. Sung family 2. China—History—1912-1949
ISBN 0-06-015308-3; 0-06-091318-5 (pa)
                                      LC 83-48802

The author examines the impact that the influential Soong family had on modern China. One of T.V. Soong's daughters married Sun Yat-sen and the other Chiang Kai-shek

Includes bibliography

Spence, Jonathan D.

The search for modern China. Norton 1990 xxv, 876p il maps $32.95; pa $22.95
                                                     951

1. China—History
ISBN 0-393-02708-2; 0-393-30780-8 (pa)   LC 89-9241

"Beginning with the decline of the Ming dynasty and ending with the Tiananmen Square massacre, Spence chronicles the cultural and social transformations of the country, concentrating on the many wars and rebellions." Booklist

Spence's "own sense of China's past is so vivid, his understanding so sure and his writer's skill so powerful that the reader apprehends distant events as if they were contemporary." New Statesman

Includes bibliography

951.04 China—Period of Republic, 1912-1949

Salisbury, Harrison Evans, 1908-1993

The Long March; the untold story; [by] Harrison E. Salisbury. Harper & Row 1985 419p il maps $22.95   **951.04**

1. Mao Zedong, 1893-1976 2. China—History—1912-1949 3. Communism—China
ISBN 0-06-039044-1   LC 84-48618
"A Cornelia & Michael Bessie book"

An account of Mao's Long March based on interviews with many of the participants

Includes bibliography

Snow, Edgar, 1905-1972

Edgar Snow's China; a personal account of the Chinese revolution; compiled from the writings of Edgar Snow by Lois Wheeler Snow. Random House 1981 xx, 284p il $19.95   **951.04**

1. China—History—1912-1949 2. Communism—China
ISBN 0-394-50954-4   LC 80-5267

This scrapbook contains a collection of photographs, many by Snow, interspersed with snippets from his journalistic sketches and books. The photographs and text cover events in China from 1928 to 1949

Includes bibliographies

Wilson, Dick, 1928-

The Long March, 1935; the epic of Chinese communism's survival. Viking 1972 c1971 xx, 331p il map o.p.; Penguin Bks. paperback available $7.95   **951.04**

1. China—History—1912-1949
ISBN 0-14-006113-4 (pa)
First published 1971 in the United Kingdom

This is an account of the year-long, 6,000 miles march of the Chinese Communist Army

"As well as recounting the numerous examples of heroism which occured, Mr. Wilson also treats the political events of the march in the greatest detail." Economist

Includes bibliography

951.05 China—Period of People's Republic, 1949-

Chang, Jung, 1952-
Wild swans; three daughters of China. Simon & Schuster 1991 524p il $25
951.05

1. China—History 2. Women—China
ISBN 0-671-68546-5   LC 91-20696
Also available in paperback from Anchor Bks.

The author "tells the harrowing life stories of her maternal grandmother, her mother, and herself. Their tales span a period of radical change in China that has touched every aspect of life." Booklist

Fang Lizhi
Bringing down the Great Wall; writing on science, culture, and democracy in China; introduction by Orville Schell; editor and principal translator, James H. Williams. Knopf 1991 c1990 xlviii, 336p $19.95
951.05

1. Human rights 2. China—Politics and government
ISBN 0-394-58493-7   LC 90-53064
Also available in paperback from Norton
Analyzed in Essay and general literature index

"A comprehensive selection of the written (and spoken) words of the witty, passionate, tenacious and articulate Chinese scientist and dissident who at present is living in the United States." N Y Times Book Rev

Link, E. Perry (Eugene Perry), 1944-
Evening chats in Beijing; probing China's predicament; [by] Perry Link. Norton 1992 321p $24.95; pa $10.95   **951.05**
1. China—Intellectual life 2. China—Politics and government
ISBN 0-393-03052-0; 0-393-31065-5 (pa)
    LC 91-29724

This book is based on the author's conversations with Chinese writers and scholars. In 1988-89 Link "served as an academic exchange coordinator in Beijing, where he came into contact with a broad cross section of Chinese intellectuals. . . . [He attempts to portray] the mental, emotional and physical universe that Chinese intellectuals inhabit." Libr J

"The discussions are frank and incisive. . . . The Chinese in these 'Evening Chats' are brilliantly and brutally honest, and it is a pleasure to eavesdrop." NY Times Book Rev

Lord, Bette Bao
Legacies: a Chinese mosaic. Knopf 1990 245p $19.95   **951.05**
1. China—Social life and customs 2. China—Politics and government
ISBN 0-394-58325-6   LC 89-43452
Also available G.K. Hall large print edition and in paperback from Fawcett Columbine

The author lived in China from 1985 to 1989. Her book is based on interviews with Chinese people, including an actress, a teacher, a veteran of the Long March, an artist, a journalist, a peasant, an entrepreneur and a Communist Party cadre, who recount their experiences of persecution during the Cultural Revolution. The author also describes her own experiences and her family history

"A vivid and startling mosaic of the political struggles that foreshadowed the Tiananmen Square uprising." Time

Salisbury, Harrison Evans, 1908-1993
The new emperors; China in the era of Mao and Deng; [by] Harrison E. Salisbury. Little, Brown 1992 544p il maps $24.95
951.05

1. Mao Zedong, 1893-1976 2. Deng Xiaoping, 1904- 3. China—History—1949-
ISBN 0-316-80910-1   LC 91-31017
Also available in paperback from Avon Bks.

This is an account of recent Chinese history and a "biography of two men who have ruled China since 1949: Mao Zedong and his lieutenant and successor Deng Xiaoping." Christ Sci Monit

"As a master reporter, the author has a keen eye for the dramatic scene and for personal relationships. His anecdotes are pearls, though they are not strung together with an overarching theory." N Y Times Book Rev

Includes bibliographic references

Terrill, Ross
China in our time; the epic saga of the People's Republic from the Communist victory to Tiananmen Square and beyond. Simon & Schuster 1992 366p il map $25
951.05

1. China—History—1949-
ISBN 0-671-68096-X   LC 92-7699

This is an account of political developments and social conditions in China since 1964. Terrill also writes about his experiences within the country and the changes in his perception of Communist rule

"An informal but fact-filled view of China's revolution and evolution." Booklist

Includes bibliographic references

951.7 Mongolia

Severin, Timothy
In search of Genghis Khan; photography by Paul Harris. Atheneum Pubs. 1992 241p il maps $25   **951.7**
1. Genghis Khan, 1162-1227 2. Mongols 3. Mongolia—Description
ISBN 0-689-12134-2   LC 91-33870
Also available in paperback from Collier Bks.

"Curious about how much of the traditional way of life survived in Mongolia after 70 years of Communist oppression, Severin hooked up with a group of Mongols attempting an ambitious cross-country journey on horseback in the old manner." Booklist

"A fascinating and rewarding blend of history, adventure and contemporary reporting." N Y Times Book Rev

951.9 Korea

Brady, James, 1928-
The coldest war: a memoir of Korea.
Orion Bks. (NY) 1990 248p il $19.95
951.9

1. Korean War, 1950-1953—Personal narratives
ISBN 0-517-57690-2   LC 89-28348
Also available in paperback from Pocket Bks.

"From November 1951 to July 1952, the author was a marine lieutenant who frequently found himself called upon to fight and kill Chinese and North Korean soldiers on the battlefields of Korea. His memoir of that experience is a well-crafted piece told in a voice that skillfully mixes the sardonic insight of an older man looking back on a highly extraordinary episode of his past with the naïveté of the young warrior he once was." Booklist

Hastings, Max
The Korean War. Simon & Schuster 1987 391p il maps hardcover o.p. paperback available $12.95   **951.9**

1. Korean War, 1950-1953
ISBN 0-671-66834-X (pa)   LC 87-16547
The author covers the political and military background of the Korean War, and also discusses how it served as a prelude to the American involvement in the Vietnam War, 15 years later

Includes bibliography

Knox, Donald, 1936-
The Korean War; an oral history.
Harcourt Brace Jovanovich 1985-1988 2v il v1 $24.95, v2 $29.95   **951.9**

1. Korean War, 1950-1953   LC 85-8567
Contents: v1 Pusan to Chosin (ISBN 0-15-147288-2); v2 Uncertain victory, with additional text by Alfred Coppel (ISBN 0-15-147289-0)

The first volume "covers the conflict in 1950; the second part continues through the armistice in 1953. There are excerpts from books and battle diaries, and occasional discussions of events in wider context, but it is the front-line soldiers who tell the story." Libr J

Includes bibliographic references

MacDonald, C. A.
Korea: the war before Vietnam; [by] Callum A. MacDonald. Free Press 1987 c1986 330p il maps $29.95   **951.9**

1. Korean War, 1950-1953
ISBN 0-02-919621-3   LC 86-22943
First published 1986 in the United Kingdom

This is an account of "how the Korean War started, how the U.S. became involved, what the high-level decisions were that determined the course of the fighting, why Truman dismissed MacArthur and why it took two years to negotiate a ceasefire." Publ Wkly

Includes bibliography

Summers, Harry G.
Korean War almanac; [by] Harry G. Summers, Jr. Facts on File 1990 288p il maps $24.95; pa $14.95   **951.9**

1. Korean War, 1950-1953
ISBN 0-8160-1737-9; 0-8160-2463-4 (pa)
LC 89-33560
"This reference book on the war contains an overview of the entire conflict, a chronology of events, and 375 articles on the people, battles, weapons, military units, and key concepts of the war." N Y Public Libr Book of How & Where to Look It Up

Toland, John
In mortal combat: Korea, 1950-1953.
Morrow 1991 624p il maps $25.50; pa $13
951.9

1. Korean War, 1950-1953
ISBN 0-688-10079-1; 0-688-12579-4 (pa) LC 91-9320
In this history of the Korean War the author "covers strategic and tactical maneuvers, correspondents, political struggles, behind-the-lines activities, prisoners of war, and numerous acts of combat and leadership heroism (and failure)." Libr J

"Though the tale of the Korean War has been told many times before, Mr. Toland's rendition is panoramic, gripping and, to a remarkable degree, original in its insights." N Y Times Book Rev

Includes bibliographic references

952 Japan

Beasley, William G., 1919-
The rise of modern Japan. St. Martin's Press 1990 306p maps hardcover o.p. paperback available $14.95   **952**

1. Japan—History
ISBN 0-312-04077-6 (pa)   LC 89-70070
"This is a survey of modern Japanese history from its origins in the Tokugawa period to the present, bringing the story up through the death of Hirohito and the Recruit-Cosmos scandal in Japanese politics in the early part of 1989. While there is nothing astoundingly new in interpretation here, the book . . . is good, solid history." Libr J

Includes bibliography

Benedict, Ruth, 1887-1948
The chrysanthemum and the sword; patterns of Japanese culture. Houghton Mifflin 1946 324p hardcover o.p. paperback available $10.95   **952**

1. Japan—Civilization   2. Japan—Social life and customs 3. National characteristics, Japanese
ISBN 0-395-50075-3 (pa)

In this book an anthropologist writes of the Japanese view of life and of themselves. She sketches in the main outlines of their society and then describes their system of practical ethics, their ideas of good and evil and the disciplines which make them able to live according to their code

Reischauer, Edwin O. (Edwin Oldfather), 1910-1990

Japan: the story of a nation. 4th ed. Knopf 1989 375p il $29.45   **952**

1. Japan—History
ISBN 0-394-58527-5

First published 1970

This history of the Japanese people from their origins to the present examines their civilization, cultural heritage, militarism, and economy

Includes bibliographic references

Japan, tradition & transformation; [by] Edwin O. Reischauer, Albert M. Craig. rev ed. Houghton Mifflin 1989 352p il $34.36   **952**

1. Japan—History
ISBN 0-395-49696-9   LC 88-83734

First published 1978

This text on the history and culture of Japan examines the traditions of the Japanese people and analyzes the changes wrought by foreign influences

The Japanese today; change and continuity. Belknap Press 1988 426p il maps $29.50; pa $12.95   **952**

1. Japan 2. National characteristics, Japanese
ISBN 0-674-47181-4; 0-674-47182-2 (pa)
  LC 87-14904

First published 1977 with title: The Japanese

The author "shows how change within continuity has been the most enduring characteristic of the Japanese experience—throughout the nation's history. He analyzes and explains in detail the government, education, business, and social structure of the country in modern times." Christ Sci Monit

Includes bibliography

Seidensticker, Edward, 1921-

Tokyo rising; the city since the great earthquake. Knopf 1990 362p il maps $24.95   **952**

1. Tokyo (Japan)—History
ISBN 0-394-54360-2   LC 89-33150

Also available in paperback from Harvard Univ. Press

Companion volume to Low city, high city: Tokyo from Edo to the earthquake (1983)

The author describes "Tokyo's growth from the point of its recovery from the earthquake, through the even worse havoc wrought by World War II, to the present day. . . . A deep, richly expressed evocation of a vital city's constantly renewed personality." Booklist

Includes bibliographic references

952.04   Japan—1945-

Field, Norma, 1947-

In the realm of a dying emperor. Pantheon Bks. 1991 273p map $22; pa $12   **952.04**

1. Hirohito, Emperor of Japan, 1901-1989 2. Japan—Civilization 3. Japan—Politics and government
ISBN 0-679-40504-6; 0-679-74189-5 (pa)   LC 91-2292

"Field, the daughter of a Japanese mother and an American father . . . returned to Japan for a year's study just prior to the final illness and death of Emperor Hirohito on January 7, 1989. Using this event as a means to probe the nature of contemporary Japanese society, Field presents an in-depth study of three individuals who stood up against what she sees as 'the death-in-life quality of daily routine' in contemporary Japan. . . . An intelligent and thought-provoking analysis." Libr J

Iyer, Pico

The lady and the monk; four seasons in Kyoto. Knopf 1991 337p $22; pa $12   **952.04**

1. Kyoto (Japan)—Description
ISBN 0-679-40308-6; 0-679-73834-7 (pa)   LC 91-413

"British born and Harvard educated, Iyer arrived in Japan in 1987 with no organized plans, contacts, or living arrangements. This poetic account of his yearlong sojourn offers fascinating insight into Japanese culture and the people he met." Booklist

953   Arabian Peninsula and adjacent areas

Theroux, Peter

Sandstorms: days and nights in Arabia. Norton 1990 281p $18.95; pa $10.95   **953**

1. Arab countries—Description
ISBN 0-393-02841-0; 0-393-30797-2 (pa)
  LC 89-28609

The author "recounts his experiences in the Middle East of the 1980s. The author went to Egypt to teach English and wound up chronicling the disappearance of Lebanon's Shia Iman Moussa Sadr. But *Sandstorms* is the human side of an American in Arabia. . . . Theroux's Arabia is rough but undeniably real, poignant and elemental." Libr J

953.8   Saudi Arabia

Lacey, Robert

The kingdom; Arabia and the House of Saud. Harcourt Brace Jovanovich 1982 630p il maps o.p.; Avon Bks. paperback available $5.95   **953.8**

1. Saudi Arabia—History
ISBN 0-380-61762-5 (pa)   LC 81-83741

This study "of Arabia in this century focuses on the formation of the modern state with Abdul Aziz ibn Saud's restoration of family dominance in 1902, the solidification of tribal rule based on adherence to fundamentalist Islam, and Arabia's emergence as a world power fueled by vast oil resources and the strategic importance of the Middle East in the Cold War." Libr J

Includes bibliography

954 South Asia. India

The **Cambridge** encyclopedia of India, Pakistan, Bangladesh, Sri Lanka, Nepal, Bhutan, and the Maldives; editor, Francis Robinson. Cambridge Univ. Press 1989 520p il maps $55   **954**

1. India—Dictionaries 2. South Asia—Dictionaries
ISBN 0-521-33451-9   LC 88-26737

"A regional encyclopedia focusing on the history and sociology of the area. Seventy contributors provide an in-depth and comprehensive picture of South Asia and the Indian subcontinent. Includes 75 maps, 69 tables, and dynastic charts from 500 B.C. to the present." N Y Public Libr Book of How & Where to Look It Up

Lapierre, Dominique
The City of Joy; translated from the French by Kathryn Spink. Doubleday 1985 464p o.p.; Warner Bks. paperback available $5.99   **954**

1. Calcutta (India)—Social conditions
ISBN 0-446-35556-9 (pa)   LC 85-10128

An account of life in the most squalid of Calcutta's slums, Anand Nagar (The City of Joy). The author focuses on the lives of a rickshaw driver, a Polish Catholic priest, an American doctor and an Assamese nurse

Wolpert, Stanley A., 1927-
A new history of India. 4th ed. Oxford Univ. Press 1993 505p maps $39.95; pa $18.95   **954**

1. India—History
ISBN 0-19-507659-1; 0-19-507660-5 (pa)
                    LC 92-12573
First published 1977

A comprehensive survey of Indian history from its early beginnings to the present. Coverage since 1988 includes discussion of the assassination of Rajiv Ghandi; violence in Kashmir, Punjab, and Assam; and the effects of rural development

Includes bibliographic references

954.04 India—1947-1971

Collins, Larry, 1929-
Freedom at midnight; [by] Larry Collins and Dominique Lapierre. Simon & Schuster 1975 572p il maps o.p.; Avon Bks. paperback available $5.95   **954.04**

1. India—History
ISBN 0-380-00693-6 (pa)

"The authors skillfully reconstruct the years during which India gained independence and delineate the people who played important roles in the dramatic event." Booklist

Includes bibliography

954.05 India—1971-

Bumiller, Elisabeth
May you be the mother of a hundred sons; a journey among the women of India. Random House 1990 306p il $19.95
                    954.05

1. Women—India 2. India—Social life and customs
ISBN 0-394-56391-3   LC 89-27120
Also available in paperback from Fawcett Bks.

"In addition to the usual discussion of arranged marriages, movie stars, and Indira Gandhi, India's late prime minister, Bumiller portrays a wide cross section of Indian society. Her discussion of bride burning, family planning, village health programs, the outlook of village women, and female infanticide will generate much comment and discussion. Essential for libraries with women's studies and Third World collections." Libr J

Includes bibliography

Mehta, Ved, 1934-
A family affair; India under three prime ministers. Oxford Univ. Press 1982 166p $25   **954.05**

1. Gandhi, Indira, 1917-1984 2. India—History
ISBN 0-19-503118-0   LC 81-22508

The author "uses family relationships as the framework for his episodic narrative about the three prime ministers of India from 1977 to the [early 1980s]. He relates how each one from Mrs. Gandhi to Moraji Desai to Charan Singh have allegedly or actually favored their sons or sons-in-law with political or economic concessions and then have ostensibly been forced from office because of this nepotism." Hist Rev New Books

Naipaul, V. S. (Vidiadhar Surajprasad), 1932-
India: a million mutinies now. Viking 1991 521p o.p.; Penguin Bks. paperback available $13   **954.05**

1. India
ISBN 0-14-015680-1 (pa)   LC 90-50424
First published 1990 in the United Kingdom

This book contains Naipaul's impressions of socioeconomic conditions in present day India and reflects the societal changes he witnessed since his 1962 visit which he related in India: a wounded civilization (1977)

954.93 Sri Lanka

McGowan, William
Only man is vile; the tragedy of Sri Lanka. Farrar, Straus & Giroux 1991 397p $25   **954.93**

1. Sri Lanka
ISBN 0-374-22652-0   LC 91-20655

In a "mix of travelogue, history and hard-edged reporting McGowan traces the country's failure to become a stable multiethnic society to the disfiguring heritage of British colonialism and a self-aggrandizing Sinhalese ruling elite that fosters racism, jingoist nationalism and 'war-lust.' McGowan's memorable prose captures the noise, passions and violence of a country that seems bent on destroying itself." Publ Wkly

955 Iran

American hostages in Iran; the conduct of a crisis; [by] Warren Christopher [et al.]; with commentaries by Oscar Schachter, Abraham A. Ribicoff; under the editorial direction of Paul H. Kreisberg. Yale Univ. Press 1985 443p $45 **955**
1. Iran hostage crisis, 1979-1981 2. United States—Foreign relations—Iran 3. Iran—Foreign relations—United States
ISBN 0-300-03233-1   LC 84-19592
"A Council on Foreign Relations book"
"The long and complex negotiations between the U.S. and Iran that led to the release of the American hostages at the U.S. embassy in Teheran is re-created in this collection of essays by some of the people who worked out that delicate agreement. . . . Among the topics treated are international law, foreign policy, economic reprisal, and military rescue missions." Booklist

Follett, Ken, 1949-
On wings of eagles. Morrow 1983 444p il maps o.p.; New Am. Lib. paperback available $5.95 **955**
1. Iran hostage crisis, 1979-1981
ISBN 0-451-16353-2 (pa)   LC 83-9328
The author "recounts the efforts of successful Texas industrialist Ross Perot to rescue from a Teheran jail two senior corporate executives arrested during the anti-American and revolutionary period in Iran in 1979." Libr J

Hiro, Dilip
The longest war; the Iran-Iraq military conflict. Routledge 1991 xxiv, 323p il maps $49.95; pa $16.95 **955**
1. Iran-Iraq War, 1980-1988
ISBN 0-415-90406-4; 0-415-90407-2 (pa)
     LC 90-45641
First published 1989 in the United Kingdom
This is an account of the 1980-1988 war between Iran, under the rule of the Ayatollah Khomeini and Iraq, under the rule of Saddam Hussein
The author "writes clearly and, although the style is somewhat journalistic, the end product is balanced, well researched, and carefully done." Choice
Includes bibliographic references

Saikal, Amin, 1951-
The rise and fall of the Shah. Princeton Univ. Press 1980 279p il maps $42 **955**
1. Mohammed Reza Pahlavi, Shah of Iran, 1919-1980 2. Iran—Politics and government 3. Iran—Foreign relations—United States 4. United States—Foreign relations—Iran
ISBN 0-691-03118-5   LC 80-7462
A look at Mohammed Reza Pahlavi's rule and in particular his effort to transform Iran into an economic and military regional power
Includes bibliography

Wright, Robin
In the name of God: the Khomeini decade. Simon & Schuster 1989 284p il maps hardcover o.p. paperback available $10.95 **955**
1. Iran—Politics and government
ISBN 0-671-72511-4 (pa)   LC 89-21632
This book "chronicles Iran under Khomeini, a . . . decade that began with his arrival in 1979 and ended with his death in 1989." N Y Times Book Rev
"This sympathetic yet balanced study is one of the few that cogently presents the events following Khomeini's seizure of power in Iran." Libr J
Includes bibliography

956 Middle East

The **Cambridge** encyclopedia of the Middle East and North Africa; executive editor, Trevor Mostyn, advisory editor, Albert Hourani. Cambridge Univ. Press 1988 504p il maps $55 **956**
1. Middle East
ISBN 0-521-32190-5   LC 88-10866
"Offers an overview of various subject areas for the region: e.g., history, quick survey by major periods; culture, including religion, literature, arts, music, Islamic science, Islamic law; economics, with statistics as current as 1986. Pt. 5 is a survey of individual countries, Mauritania to Afghanistan to Somalia. The volume ends with 'peoples without a country,' e.g., Kurds, Armenians, Palestinians." Sheehy. Guide to Ref Books. 10th edition. suppl
Includes bibliographies

Dickey, Christopher
Expats: travels in Arabia, from Tripoli to Teheran. Atlantic Monthly Press 1990 228p hardcover o.p. paperback available $9.95
     956
1. Middle East—Description 2. Middle East—Politics and government
ISBN 0-87113-463-2 (pa)   LC 90-151
The author "traversed the Arab Middle East as Newsweek's bureau chief in Cairo in the last half of the Eighties, covering stories such as the American bombing of Libya, the disintegration of Lebanon, and more. Here, he draws on his experiences for a series of vignettes of individuals he met." Libr J
"Moving across the Middle East, Mr. Dickey constructs a richly hued collage of foreigners enmeshed in the Arab world." N Y Times Book Rev

Fisher, Sydney Nettleton, 1906-1987
The Middle East; a history; [by] Sydney Nettleton Fisher, William Ochsenwald. 4th ed. McGraw-Hill 1990 xxv, 776p maps $22.42 **956**
1. Middle East—History
ISBN 0-07-557262-1   LC 89-12155
First published 1959 by Knopf
"Beginning with the rise of Islam, this history covers the Middle Eastern Crescent and adjoining Arab lands to the present time. Emphasizes the role of history in the current debates and conflicts." N Y Public Libr Book of How & Where to Look It Up
Includes bibliographic references

Friedman, Thomas L.
From Beirut to Jerusalem. Farrar, Straus
& Giroux c1990 541p il maps $25   **956**

1. Middle East—Politics and government 2. Jewish-
Arab relations 3. Lebanon—History 4. Israel—Politics
and government
ISBN 0-374-15895-9   LC 92-148666

Also available in paperback from Anchor Bks.

First published 1989

The author presents an account of the political situation in the Middle East as he witnessed it in his years
as a reporter in Lebanon and Jerusalem

"When recounting his frequently harrowing experiences
in that troubled region, Friedman can be absolutely
riveting; similarly, his historical insights, his explanation
of the root causes of the Arab-Israeli conflict, and his
impressions of people and places in the Holy Land never
fail to fascinate." Booklist

Glass, Charles
Tribes with flags; a dangerous passage
through the chaos of the Middle East.
Atlantic Monthly Press 1990 510p hardcover
o.p. paperback available $12.95   **956**

1. Middle East
ISBN 0-87113-457-8 (pa)   LC 89-157

This is an account of the author's travels in the Middle East. In 1987, Glass set out from Iskenderun (Alex-
andretta) "in southern Turkey, to Aqaba in Jordan. . .
. His odyssey ended abruptly when . . . the Hizballah
kidnapped and held him hostage in Beirut for two
months until his escape. The trip is the framework for
this book." Time

"Interestingly, the retelling of Glass's days as hostage
fills only a relatively few pages; instead, this is a literate,
erudite, and leisurely stroll through the Middle East."
Libr J

Herzog, Chaim, 1918-
The Arab-Israeli wars; war and peace in
the Middle East. Random House 1982 392p
il maps hardcover o.p. paperback available
$15   **956**

1. Jewish-Arab relations
ISBN 0-394-71746-5 (pa)   LC 80-5291

This book traces "the Arab-Israeli wars and military
conflicts from the 1948 War of Independence through
the 1973 Yom Kippur War." Libr J

Includes bibliography

The Middle East. Congressional Quarterly il
maps pa $25.95   **956**

1. Middle East—Politics and government
First published 1974. (7th edition 1991) Periodically
revised

Covers topics such as oil, Islam, the Arab-Israeli conflict, the Persian Gulf, and the arms trade in the Middle
East. Also presents profiles of Middle Eastern nations
and twentieth-century leaders and includes documents
such as UN resolutions and peace treaties

Includes bibliography

Ziring, Lawrence, 1928-
The Middle East; a political dictionary.
ABC-CLIO 1992 401p (Clio dictionaries in
political science ser) $56.50; pa $29.95
                                         956

1. Middle East—Politics and government—Dictionaries
ISBN 0-87436-612-7; 0-87436-697-6 (pa)
                                         LC 92-15379

First published 1984 with title: The Middle East political dictionary

"Included in this volume are 271 numbered entires
on events, movements, diplomacy, conflict, culture, and
characteristics relevant to Middle East politics in the
second half of the twentieth century. Entries are grouped
in seven broad categories (e.g., ethnicity and culture, Islam) and then arranged alphabetically within the sections.
Each entry includes a definition of the topic and a
synopsis of its significance in the political schema." Am
Ref Books Annu, 1993

For a fuller review see: Booklist, Sept. 1, 1992

956.04 Middle East—1945-1980

Hammel, Eric M.
Six days in June; how Israel won the
1967 Arab-Israeli War; [by] Eric Hammel.
Scribner 1992 xxiii, 452p maps $30
                                         956.04

1. Israel-Arab War, 1967 2. Israel—History, Military
ISBN 0-684-19390-6   LC 92-4596

This account of the Six Day War analyzes "the war's
four campaigns—in the Sinai against Egypt, in the West
Bank against Jordan, in the Golan Heights against Syria,
and for the capture of Old Jerusalem." N Y Times Book
Rev

"Hammel does an excellent job of detailing how Israel
prepared for the war and describing combat. Moreover,
his highly readable style will be popular with public
library patrons, especially if this is the first book they
read on the subject." Libr J

Includes bibliographic references

956.1 Turkey

Settle, Mary Lee
Turkish reflections; a biography of a place;
introduction by Jan Morris. Prentice Hall
Press 1991 233p $19.95   **956.1**

1. Turkey
ISBN 0-13-917675-6   LC 91-3126

Also available in paperback from Simon & Schuster

"A Destinations book"

In a "journey deep into the heart of Turkey, Settle
. . . revisits a country where past and present are everywhere intertwined. Contradicting the unflattering Western
stereotypes of Turks, she depicts a people she admires
for their capacity for friendship, their essential warmth
and honesty." Publ Wkly

956.7 Iraq

Allen, Thomas B., 1929-
War in the Gulf; [by Thomas B. Allen, F. Clifton Berry, Norman Polmar] Turner Pub. (Atlanta) 1991 240p il maps $29.95; pa $19.95   **956.7**

1. Persian Gulf War, 1991
ISBN 1-878685-00-7; 1-878685-01-5 (pa)
                                            LC 91-65803

At head of title: CNN

The authors "provide background on the war, detail its progress, discuss the international reaction to events, chart the use of the various forms of military hardware, and profile the key leaders involved. The clearly presented text does a good job of stating the facts and venturing opinions, but it's probably the photos—all well printed and very colorful—that will draw an audience." Booklist

David, Peter, 1951-
Triumph in the desert; the challenge, the fighting, the legacy; text by Peter David; foreword by General Colin L. Powell; edited by Ray Cave and Pat Ryan; additional text by C.D.B. Bryan [et al.] Random House 1991 209p il $25   **956.7**

1. Persian Gulf War, 1991
ISBN 0-679-40722-7   LC 91-15404

Photojournalists and armed forces artists illustrate this account of the Gulf War from the invasion of Kuwait by Iraq, through the deployment of Allied forces, to the return of the troops

Desert Storm; the war in the Persian Gulf; by the editors of Time magazine; edited by Otto Friedrich. Little, Brown 1991 232p il $19.45   **956.7**

1. Persian Gulf War, 1991
ISBN 0-316-85100-0   LC 91-52896

"A Time book"

This volume assesses the actual military engagement, and the aftermath of the international coalition's defeat of Saddam Hussein

Dunnigan, James F.
From shield to storm; high-tech weapons, military strategy, and coalition warfare in the Persian Gulf; [by] James F. Dunnigan and Austin Bay. Morrow 1992 512p il maps $20   **956.7**

1. Persian Gulf War, 1991
ISBN 0-688-11034-7   LC 91-24588

This is an "account of the causes of the Persian Gulf war and how it was fought. . . . Dunnigan and Bay discuss the strategy, tactics and operational problems on both sides of the battlefront. . . . The book explores the ratio of friendly-fire casualties, the performance of female GIs in the field, the reaction of journalists to war-zone restrictions, and other issues of concern to the general reader." Publ Wkly

Includes bibliographic references

Friedman, Norman, 1946-
Desert victory; the war for Kuwait. Naval Inst. Press 1991 435p il $24.95; pa $18.95
                                            956.7

1. Persian Gulf War, 1991
ISBN 1-55750-254-4; 1-55750-255-2 (pa)
                                            LC 91-21088

"The narrative deals with the background of the conflict, the buildup of the war, and the blockade of Iraq, and outlines the main naval, air, and ground operations." Choice
"A thoughtful book, almost certainly of permanent value." Booklist

Hilsman, Roger, 1919-
George Bush vs. Saddam Hussein; military success! political failure? Lyford Bks. 1992 273p maps $21.95   **956.7**

1. Persian Gulf War, 1991
ISBN 0-89141-470-3   LC 92-11929

The author, examines Saddam Hussein's rise to power, events in the Gulf region prior to U.S. involvement, negotiation attempts, military compaigns, and political and economic consequences of the war. Concluding sections on Hussein and Bush offer an assessment of each leader's personality and background

Includes bibliographic references

MacArthur, John R.
Second front; censorship and propaganda in the Gulf war. Hill & Wang 1992 260p $19.95   **956.7**

1. Persian Gulf War, 1991 2. Freedom of the press
ISBN 0-8090-8517-8   LC 91-41338

Also available in paperback from University of Calif. Press

The author discusses the Pentagon's program of news censorship during the Gulf War and argues that the response of the American media to this program was less than satisfactory

The author presents a "solidly documented indictment of media performance during the war. He faults both print and broadcasting for ineffective or nonexistent protests against censorship and for poor war reporting." Libr J

Miller, Judith, 1948-
Saddam Hussein and the crisis in the Gulf; [by] Judith Miller and Laurie Mylroie. Times Bks. 1990 268p maps pa $5.95
                                            956.7

1. Hussein, Ṣaddām   2. Persian Gulf War, 1991
3. Iraq—Politics and government
ISBN 0-8129-1921-1   LC 90-48403

This book discusses the career of the Iraqi president, the political history of Iraq, the Iran-Iraq war, Iraq's acquisition of modern weapons, the role of oil, and the background of the Iraqi invasion of Kuwait

Includes bibliographic references

Sciolino, Elaine
The outlaw state; Saddam Hussein's quest for power and the Gulf crisis. Wiley 1991 320p il maps $22.95   **956.7**
1. Hussein, Ṣaddām 2. Persian Gulf War, 1991 3. Iraq—Politics and government
ISBN 0-471-54299-7   LC 91-12940
This is "a critical examination of Saddam Hussein's rise to power, his effect on international politics, and the events surrounding the Gulf War." Booklist
"The blow-by-blow account is taut, in the fashion of news reporting at its best, and is embellished with rich historical background. . . . General readers will find this account authoritative and highly readable." Choice
Includes bibliography

Smith, Jean Edward
George Bush's war. Holt & Co. 1992 325p $24.95   **956.7**
1. Bush, George, 1924- 2. Persian Gulf War, 1991
ISBN 0-8050-1388-1   LC 91-31059
The author, "who questions whether the Gulf war was necessary, places the responsibility for Desert Storm on Bush. . . . He provides a virtual day-by-day chronicle of the decisions of 1990 that led to war." Libr J
"The best thing about the book—which must be reckoned *the* one to read if you want to know what happened and who did it—is Smith's disinclination to moralize." Booklist
Includes bibliographic references

956.94   Palestine. Israel

Bellow, Saul
To Jerusalem and back; a personal account. Viking 1976 182p o.p.; Penguin Bks. paperback available $6.95   **956.94**
1. Israel
ISBN 0-14-007273-X (pa)
Using an extended visit to Israel in late 1975 as his framework, Bellow "addresses the question of what it means to be Jewish in the 20th Century and in particular, what it means to be an Israeli Jew living on the brink of extinction." Libr J

Binur, Yoram
My enemy, my self. Doubleday 1989 215p il $18.95   **956.94**
1. Palestinian Arabs 2. Jewish-Arab relations
ISBN 0-385-23995-5   LC 88-29934
"Binur, an Israeli Jew and a journalist, posed as an Arab for six months to examine closely the relationship between Jews and Arabs in Israel. Binur lived as an Arab in a variety of settings, including a refugee camp in the Gaza Strip, a number of jobs in Tel Aviv, and as a volunteer on a kibbutz. . . . The result: a depressing picture of fear, and mistrust on both sides." Booklist

Collins, Larry, 1929-
O Jerusalem! [by] Larry Collins and Dominique Lapierre. Simon & Schuster 1972 637p il maps hardcover o.p. paperback available $14   **956.94**
1. Jerusalem—History—1948, Siege 2. Israel-Arab War, 1948-1949
ISBN 0-671-66241-4 (pa)
This is an account of the struggle for the city of Jerusalem during the Israel-Arab War of 1948
Includes bibliography

Elon, Amos
Jerusalem, city of mirrors. Little, Brown 1989 286p maps $19.95   **956.94**
1. Jerusalem
ISBN 0-316-23388-9   LC 89-34155
"Throughout his well-paced, gentle narrative, Elon proceeds to explore his premise that Jerusalem is a necropolis wherein the dead hand of the past often has more weight than the living hand of the present. To emphasize this, Elon drifts back and forth between Islamic, Jewish, and Christian viewpoints as well as historic events." Libr J
Includes bibliography

Israel; by the editors of Time-Life Books; with photographs by Hans Wiesenhofer. Time-Life Bks. 1987 160p il maps (Lib. of nations) $28.60   **956.94**
1. Israel   LC 86-23176
Following a brief look at the history of the Jewish people this illustrated guide focuses on the founding of the nation, its relations with frequently hostile neighbors, minority populations, the quest for self-sufficiency and the connection between religion and government. Picture essays include a look at a kibbutz and at various biblical landscapes
Includes bibliography

Laqueur, Walter, 1921-
A history of Zionism; with a new preface by the author. Schocken Bks. 1989 xxii, 639p il $16.95   **956.94**
1. Zionism
ISBN 0-8052-0899-2   LC 88-38221
A reissue with new introduction of the title first published 1972 by Holt, Rinehart & Winston
The author examines the history of Zionism over the past three centuries from its European roots to the establishment of the state of Israel
Includes bibliography

Sachar, Howard Morley, 1928-
A history of Israel; [by] Howard M. Sachar. Knopf 1976-1987 2v il maps   **956.94**
1. Israel—History 2. Zionism
Volume two published by Oxford University Press
Contents: v1 From the rise of Zionism to our time pa $19.95 (ISBN 0-394-73679-6); v2 From the aftermath of the Yom Kippur War $27.95, pa $12.95 (ISBN 0-19-504386-3; 0-19-504623-4)

Sachar, Howard Morley, 1928-—_Continued_
"Sachar is long recognized as one of the most eminent and productive scholars in the field of Middle Eastern and Jewish history. . . . As with all his books, Sachar demonstrates here, too, his enormous erudition and good sense." Choice

Includes bibliography

Schiff, Zeev, 1932-
Intifada; the Palestinian uprising: Israel's third front; [by] Ze'ev Schiff & Ehud Ya'ari; edited and translated by Ina Friedman. Simon & Schuster 1990 352p hardcover o.p. paperback available $10.95 **956.94**
1. Israel—Politics and government 2. Jewish-Arab relations 3. Palestinian Arabs
ISBN 0-671-73291-9 (pa) LC 89-48864

"The authors present a balanced account of the _intifada's_ progress since 1987, and their tight chronological focus highlights events and issues developed during this period while also sketching in needed historical background." Booklist

Shipler, David K.
Arab and Jew; wounded spirits in a promised land. Times Bks. 1986 596p o.p.; Penguin Bks. paperback available $10.95
956.94
1. Jewish-Arab relations 2. Israel—Social conditions 3. Palestinian Arabs
ISBN 0-14-010376-7 (pa) LC 86-5882

An attempt "to examine the attitudes, images, and stereotypes that Arabs and Jews have of one another, the roots of their aversions, and the complex interactions between them in the small territory where they live together under Israeli rule." Foreword

956.95 Jordan

Grossman, David
The yellow wind; translated from the Hebrew by Haim Watzman. Farrar, Straus & Giroux 1988 216p map $17.95 **956.95**
1. Palestinian Arabs 2. West Bank 3. Jewish-Arab relations
ISBN 0-374-29345-7 LC 87-37527

Also available in paperback from Delta Bks.

Original Hebrew edition, 1987

"Grossman was assigned to report for a weekly newspaper on life for both occupied and occupier on the West Bank during the 20th anniversary of its conquest. With an eye and ear for revealing detail, he argues that the Jews are now doing to Palestinians what has been done to them through the ages." Libr J

958.1 Afghanistan

Bonner, Arthur
Among the Afghans. Duke Univ. Press 1987 366p il maps (Central Asia book ser) $29.95 **958.1**
1. Afghanistan—History—Soviet occupation, 1979-1989
ISBN 0-8223-0783-9 LC 87-22260

The author relates his personal experiences covering recent Afghan history for the New York Times

Borovik, Artem, 1960-
The hidden war; a Russian journalist's account of the Soviet war in Afghanistan; [by] Artyrom Borovik. Atlantic Monthly Press 1990 288p il map hardcover o.p. paperback available $10.95 **958.1**
1. Afghanistan—History—Soviet occupation, 1979-1989
ISBN 0-87113-521-3 (pa) LC 90-42028

"A Morgan Entrekin book"

"Borovik covered the Soviet military involvement in Afghanistan from early 1980 through the final phase of withdrawal in February 1989. . . . He offers in this work an introductory essay which speculates on the scenario for the Soviet Union's entry into Afghanistan in late December 1979, followed by two gripping accounts of Russian soldiers under fire." Libr J

959.1 Burma

Aung San Suu Kyi
Freedom from fear, and other writings; foreword by Václav Havel; edited with an introduction by Michael Aris. Viking 1991 338p il pa $12 **959.1**
1. Myanmar—Politics and government
ISBN 0-670-84560-4 LC 91-40692

This is a collection of essays, letters, speeches, and other writings by the Burmese opposition leader, winner of the 1991 Nobel Peace Prize

"Mrs. Aung San Suu Kyi's excellent book offers inspiration to many other peoples in the region as much as it reflects Myanmar's own desire for change." N Y Times Book Rev

959.3 Thailand

Wyatt, David K.
Thailand; a short history. Yale Univ. Press 1984 351p il maps $40; pa $16 **959.3**
1. Thailand—History
ISBN 0-300-03054-1; 0-300-03582-9 (pa)
LC 83-25953

This volume provides a "general history of the country. Beginning with the migrations of the Tai peoples from southern China into the Indo-Chinese peninsula, the author records how they created a political system that produced the modern country we know today. The interlocking relations with Burma, Cambodia, Laos, and Vietnam point out how skillfully forged this hegemony was. About half the book deals with the Chakri dynasty's efforts to modernize the country." Libr J

Includes bibliography

959.6   Cambodia

Chandler, David P.

The tragedy of Cambodian history; politics, war, and revolution since 1945. Yale Univ. Press 1991 396p il maps $37.50; pa $17   **959.6**

1. Cambodia—History
ISBN 0-300-04919-6; 0-300-05752-0 (pa)
LC 91-17074

The author "examines Cambodia's five governments from the end of WW II to the beginning of the Vietnamese protectorate in 1979." Publ Wkly

"Mr. Chandler's spadework in French, American and British archives, the multitude of interviews he conducted with participants and observers of many nationalities, and his readings in the largely French-language Cambodian press going back to colonial days have enabled him to construct as complete a historical narrative as has ever been compiled." N Y Times Book Rev

Includes bibliographic references

Criddle, Joan D.

To destroy you is no loss; the odyssey of a Cambodian family; [by] Joan D. Criddle and Teeda Butt Mam. Atlantic Monthly Press 1987 289p map o.p.; Doubleday paperback available $9.95   **959.6**

1. Cambodia—History—1975- 2. Refugees, Cambodian
ISBN 0-385-26628-6 (pa)   LC 87-1396

"With the Khmer Rouge takeover in 1975, gently bred, 15-year-old Teeda and 15 members of her upper-class family were among millions driven from Phnom Penh into the countryside. . . . Before Teeda's family emigrated to America in 1980, they led a slavelike existence . . . a life of constant terror." Publ Wkly

"Mam's story, told to Criddle (who sponsored the family's emigration to the United States), reveals with simple sensitivity and insight another perspective of the nightmare. . . . A moving, difficult, important book." Libr J

959.704   Vietnam—1949-

America in Vietnam; a documentary history; edited with commentaries by William Appleman Williams [et al.] Anchor Press/Doubleday 1985 345p map $19.95
     959.704

1. Vietnam War, 1961-1975
ISBN 0-385-19752-7   LC 84-9321

Also available in paperback from Norton

In this collection of original essays and documentary sources, historians try to explain the U.S.-Vietnamese War of 1963-75 within the greater context of two centuries of American involvement in Asia

Includes bibliography

The **American** experience in Vietnam; a reader; edited by Grace Sevy. University of Okla. Press 1989 319p hardcover o.p. paperback available $12.95   **959.704**

1. Vietnam War, 1961-1975
ISBN 0-8061-2390-7 (pa)   LC 89-40222

"Thirty essays, speeches, and interviews on the subject of America's involvement in the Vietnam War. The selections . . . include sections on American policy, the nature of the war and the soldiers who fought it, the role of the press, and the antiwar movement. The writers hail from all points on the political spectrum, but mostly from the center and the left; among their number are Norman Podhoretz, Martin Luther King, Jr., Paul Goodman, and John Kerry." Booklist

Includes bibliographic references

Bilton, Michael

Four hours in My Lai; [by] Michael Bilton and Kevin Sim. Viking 1992 430p il maps o.p.; Penguin Bks. paperback available $13.50   **959.704**

1. Mỹ Lai Massacre, Vietnam, 1968
ISBN 0-14-017709-4 (pa)   LC 91-47651

The authors "have reconstructed perhaps the ugliest day in recent American history: March 16, 1968, when 105 soldiers of Charlie Company, 11th Brigade, Americal Division . . . massacred approximately 500 children, women and old men in the Vietnamese hamlet of My Lai. . . . The authors . . . recount circumstances leading up to the massacre, the horrific event itself and the subsequent cover-up and investigation." N Y Times Book Rev

"Any collection organized around the Vietnam War that does not carry this work is not complete." Libr J

Includes bibliographic references

Bloods: an oral history of the Vietnam War by black veterans; [edited by] Wallace Terry. Random House 1984 311p il o.p.; Ballantine Bks. paperback available $5.95
     959.704

1. Vietnam War, 1961-1975—Personal narratives
2. Black soldiers
ISBN 0-345-31197-3 (pa)   LC 83-42775

Black Vietnam War veterans discuss their experiences in battle and stateside

This is "an intimate overview that often makes the reader stop, sit back, and think about this war that tore at America. . . . The accounts are moving, powerful and offer several views." Voice Youth Advocates

Includes bibliography

Butler, David, 1941-

The fall of Saigon; scenes from the sudden end of a long war. Simon & Schuster 1985 510p il o.p.; Dell paperback available $5.95   **959.704**

1. Vietnam War, 1961-1975 2. Ho Chi Minh City (Vietnam)
ISBN 0-440-12431-X (pa)   LC 85-1788

"Glimpses of South Vietnam in retreat, from the North Vietnamese offensive in early March 1975 to the fall of Saigon in late April, are provided by American journalist Butler, who witnessed the proceedings as an NBC reporter." Booklist

Includes bibliography

Caputo, Philip
A rumor of war. Holt, Rinehart & Winston 1977 346p o.p.; Ballantine Bks. paperback available $5.95 **959.704**
1. Vietnam War, 1961-1975—Personal narratives
ISBN 0-345-33122-2 (pa)　　　LC 76-29900
"The combat recollections of a very young Marine officer in Vietnam in 1965-1966. Caputo later became a newspaperman. . . . He remembers himself as a patriotic youngster, eager to prove his manhood, and then . . . he takes us through his step-by-step discovery that war and manhood and their interrelation are more complicated than he had dreamed." New Yorker

Engelmann, Larry
Tears before the rain; an oral history of the last days of South Vietnam. Oxford Univ. Press 1990 375p il $22.95 **959.704**
1. Vietnam War, 1961-1975—Personal narratives
ISBN 0-19-505386-9　　　LC 89-26629
This book presents interviews with Americans and Vietnamese "about their experiences during the last days of the fall of Saigon in 1975." N Y Rev Books
"The book's only weakness is that it slights the American antiwar perspective. Otherwise, this is a very strong collection of interviews." Choice

FitzGerald, Frances, 1940-
Fire in the lake; the Vietnamese and the Americans in Vietnam. Little, Brown 1972 491p maps o.p.; Random House paperback available $14 **959.704**
1. Vietnam War, 1961-1975 2. Vietnam—Politics and government
ISBN 0-679-72394-3 (pa)
"An Atlantic Monthly Press book"
This book looks at the effects American intervention had on the Vietnamese social and intellectual landscape
Includes bibliography

Franklin, H. Bruce (Howard Bruce), 1934-
M.I.A.; or, Mythmaking in America. Hill Bks. 1992 225p $17.95 **959.704**
1. Vietnam War, 1961-1975—Missing in action
ISBN 1-55652-118-9　　　LC 91-34068
"Franklin reviews the astonishing numbers games the Pentagon and POW/MIA activists have played, traces the deliberate manipulation of this issue by a generation of self-serving politicians . . . analyzes the roles of groups like the National League of Families and VIVA and of individuals like Henry Kissinger and H. Ross Perot in developing and sustaining true believers' faith, and reveals the interplay between life and art in POW/MIA books and films, from *The Deerhunter* to *Rambo* and beyond." Booklist
Includes bibliographic references

Glasser, Ronald J.
365 days. Braziller 1971 292p hardcover o.p. paperback available $9.95 **959.704**
1. Vietnam War, 1961-1975—Personal narratives 2. Vietnam War, 1961-1975—Medical care
ISBN 0-8076-0995-1 (pa)

The author, a military doctor who was stationed in Japan, recounts his experiences treating wounded American military personnel during the Vietnam War

Gottlieb, Sherry Gershon
Hell no, we won't go! resisting the draft during the Vietnam War. Viking 1991 xxvi, 274p $21.95 **959.704**
1. Vietnam War, 1961-1975—Draft resisters
ISBN 0-670-83935-3　　　LC 90-50768
"Arranged by type of draft evasion (psychologically unstable, physically unfit, expatriate, etc.) and based on interviews with men who successfully avoided military service during the Vietnam War, this collection of first-person recollections offers an intriguing perspective on antiwar sentiments during the 1960s and 1970s." Booklist

Karnow, Stanley
Vietnam: a history. [rev and updated]. Viking 1991 768p il maps $30 **959.704**
1. Vietnam War, 1961-1975 2. Vietnam—History
ISBN 0-670-84218-4
Also available in paperback from Penguin Bks.
First published 1983
A summation "of over two centuries of conflict in Indochina. Chronicling a tragic history, Karnow presents a balanced and sympathetic view of Vietnamese aspirations and the mishaps that led to American involvement in a 'war nobody won.'" Voice Youth Advocates [review of 1983 edition]

Mason, Patience H. C.
Recovering from the war; a woman's guide to helping your Vietnam vet, your family, and yourself. Viking 1990 444p o.p.; Penguin Bks. paperback available $9.95
959.704
1. Vietnam War, 1961-1975 2. Adjustment (Psychology)
ISBN 0-14-009912-3 (pa)　　　LC 88-40422
This "book is a primer for women (or anyone else, for that matter) who have relationships with Vietnam veterans. Writing at all times from the female perspective, she tackles the problems that arose out of the Vietnam experience and offers counsel on what family members can and cannot do about them." Booklist
"Compelling, well researched, and important." Libr J
Includes bibliography

Mason, Robert, 1942-
Chickenhawk. Viking 1983 339p il map o.p.; Penguin Bks. paperback available $10
959.704
1. Vietnam War, 1961-1975—Personal narratives 2. Vietnam War, 1961-1975—Aerial operations
ISBN 0-14-007218-7 (pa)　　　LC 82-42737
Companion volume Chickenhawk: back in the world, entered in class 92
This book describes Mason's experiences as an Army helicopter pilot in Vietnam
The author's "prose, low-keyed and carefully unemotional, lets the facts of misjudgment, destruction, mutilation, and death make their own cumulative and devastating effect. His report is exciting, and moving, and the ending is a bitter shock." Atlantic

McCloud, Bill, 1948-

What should we tell our children about Vietnam? University of Okla. Press 1989 155p $17.95   **959.704**

1. Vietnam War, 1961-1975
ISBN 0-8061-2229-3   LC 89-40218

Also available in paperback from Berkley Pub. Group

"President Bush, William Westmoreland, Gary Trudeau, and Philip Caputo are among some of the best known of 128 individuals who gave their views when McCloud, a junior high school teacher and veteran, wrote to ask them what young people should understand about the war." Booklist

Includes bibliography

Moore, Harold G.

We were soldiers once—and young; Ia Drang: the battle that changed the war in Vietnam; [by] Harold G. Moore and Joseph L. Galloway. Random House 1992 412p il maps $25   **959.704**

1. Vietnam War, 1961-1975—Personal narratives
ISBN 0-679-41158-5   LC 92-53642

"On Nov. 14, 1965, the 1st Battalion of the 7th Cavalry, commanded by Col. Moore and accompanied by UPI reporter Galloway, helicoptered into Vietnam's remote Ia Drang Valley and found itself surrounded by a numerically superior force of North Vietnamese regulars. Moore and Galloway here offer a detailed account, based on interviews with participants and on their own recollections, of what happened during the four-day battle." Publ Wkly

Includes bibliographic references

Prados, John

Valley of decision: the siege of Khe Sanh; [by] John Prados and Ray W. Stubbe. Houghton Mifflin 1991 551p il $29.95   **959.704**

1. Khe Sanh, Battle of, 1968 2. Vietnam War, 1961-1975
ISBN 0-395-55003-3   LC 91-25531

Also available in paperback from Dell

"A Marc Jaffe book"

This is a study of the battle of Khe Sanh, fought during the Vietnam War

This is a "good blend of documentary research and personal experience drawn from oral interviews." Choice

Includes bibliography

Safer, Morley

Flashbacks: on returning to Vietnam. Random House 1990 206p $18.95 **959.704**

1. Vietnam—Description 2. Vietnam War, 1961-1975—Personal narratives
ISBN 0-394-58374-4   LC 89-24242

Also available in paperback from St. Martin's Press

"In 1965 Morley Safer accompanied a force of U.S. Marines on a search-and-destroy mission to the hamlet of Cam Ne. It was mostly destroy. The footage of troops burning peasant huts was seen by millions on the CBS News. It was an era of 'tragic foolishness,' says Safer in Flashbacks, an artful contrast of past and present that recalls a time when the typewriter, not the portable hair dryer, was the essential tool of the TV journalist." Time

Sheehan, Neil

After the war was over; Hanoi and Saigon. Random House 1992 131p map hardcover o.p. paperback available $9   **959.704**

1. Vietnam—Description
ISBN 0-679-74507-6 (pa)   LC 91-51063

The author, who was a New York Times correspondent during the Vietnam War, reports on current conditions in Vietnam based on his 1989 return visit to that country

"Filled with insightful and informed observations, this brief book offers help toward understanding the past and breaking down the emotional and cultural barriers of the present." Libr J

A bright shining lie: John Paul Vann and America in Vietnam. Random House 1988 861p il $24.95; pa $15   **959.704**

1. Vann, John Paul 2. Vietnam War, 1961-1975
ISBN 0-394-48447-9; 0-679-72414-1 (pa)

     LC 87-43330

The author "tells the story of the war through the focus of John Paul Vann, an army officer who faced down South Vietnamese politicians and American generals to expose the corruption that undermined our efforts and later was President Nixon's civilian adviser in Vietnam until he was killed in a helicopter crash in 1972. It is a dramatic device that lets Mr. Sheehan bring the very palpable feel of the war to us with passionate power." N Y Times Book Rev

Includes bibliography

Summers, Harry G.

Vietnam War almanac; [by] Harry G. Summers, Jr. Facts on File 1985 414p il $27.95; pa $14.95   **959.704**

1. Vietnam War, 1961-1975
ISBN 0-8160-1017-X; 0-8160-1813-8 (pa)

     LC 83-14054

"Provides a clear, accessible, and objective look at the conflict that shaped a generation. Includes an introductory history of the country and a description of the physical and historical conditions that shaped American policy there; a chronology of events, both in Vietnam and in the United States; and 500 articles." N Y Public Libr Book of How & Where to Look It Up

The **Vietnam** War and American culture; edited by John Carlos Rowe and Richard Berg. Columbia Univ. Press 1991 275p il pa $13.95   **959.704**

1. Vietnam War, 1961-1975 2. United States—Civilization
ISBN 0-231-06733-X   LC 90-22418

Analyzed in Essay and general literature index

"Veterans, journalists, poets, and scholars show how American culture represents the Vietnam War in newspapers, popular films, music, plays, and on television." Univ Press Books for Public and Second Sch Libr

Includes bibliographic references

The **Wall**; images and offerings from the Vietnam Veterans Memorial; conceived by Sal Lopes; introduction by Michael Norman. Collins 1987 128p il $19.95

959.704

1. Vietnam Veterans Memorial (Washington, D.C.)
ISBN 0-00-217974-1   LC 87-10375

"A Floyd Yearout production"

"A collection of photographs and commentary on the Vietnam Veterans Memorial, better known as the Wall. . . . The book is extremely powerful in content—almost overwhelming. It is well organized, yet eloquent and even cathartic to a nation coming to terms with regret and restoration." Libr J

959.9 Philippines

Karnow, Stanley
In our image; America's empire in the Philippines. Random House 1989 494p il maps $24.95   **959.9**

1. Philippines—History
ISBN 0-394-54975-9   LC 88-42676

Also available in paperback from Ballantine Bks.

A history of American involvement in the Philippines from 1898 to the present

The author's "treatment of the indecisiveness of President McKinley over the issue of empire and of the egotistical General MacArthur make the work a definite purchase for libraries. . . . Those who love swashbuckling history will enjoy this work." Libr J

Includes bibliographic references

Seagrave, Sterling
The Marcos dynasty. Harper & Row 1988 485p il $22.50   **959.9**

1. Marcos, Ferdinand E., 1917-1989 2. Marcos, Imelda 3. Philippines—Politics and government
ISBN 0-06-015815-8   LC 87-45075

Also available in paperback from Fawcett Bks.

This book, based on interviews and intelligence leaks, traces the rise and fall of the political careers of Ferdinand and Imelda Marcos

Includes bibliography

960 Africa

Davidson, Basil, 1914-
Africa in history; themes and outlines. rev and expanded ed. Collier Bks. 1991 425p $14.95   **960**

1. Africa—History
ISBN 0-02-042791-3   LC 90-23905

First published 1966 with title: Africa: history of a continent

Among the topics discussed are Africa's diverse regional differences, apartheid, the rise of Islam, tribal mores, slavery and colonization

Includes bibliographic references

Harden, Blaine
Africa; dispatches from a fragile continent. Norton 1990 333p il $22.50   **960**

1. Africa—Politics and government 2. Africa—Social conditions
ISBN 0-393-02882-8   LC 89-77789

Also available in paperback from Houghton Mifflin

"After 30 years of independence, Africa relies on foreign aid that is based more on Western computations than on the domestic needs of countries that lack national identities. . . . Focusing on individuals but combining travel, history, politics, economics and generalities of African society, . . . Harden explores the indigenous systems that help hold 'the whole sorry mess' together." Publ Wkly

Includes bibliographic references

Pakenham, Thomas, 1933-
The scramble for Africa, 1876-1912. Random House 1991 xxv, 738p il maps $32   **960**

1. Africa—History
ISBN 0-394-51576-5   LC 91-52681

Also available in paperback from Avon Bks.

This book is an account of the colonization and conquest of Africa by five European nations—Great Britain, France, Belgium, Germany, and Italy

This is a "sweeping narrative, refreshingly old fashioned in its appreciation of the fact that imperialism did have some virtues, which offers as good an introduction to the 'scramble' as has ever been written." Libr J

Includes bibliography

967 Central Africa and offshore islands

Africa south of the Sahara. Europa Publs. [distributed by] Gale Res. maps $295   **967**

1. Sub-Saharan Africa
ISSN 0065-3896

Annual. First published 1971

"In three main parts: (1) Background to the continent; (2) Regional organizations; (3) Country surveys. The third part includes information for each country on physical and social geography, recent history, economy, statistics. The directory section gives names of political parties, members of government, media, banks, trade unions, shipping companies, periodicals, etc. Country surveys include select bibliographies." Sheehy. Guide to Ref Books. 10th edition

967.6 Uganda and Kenya

East Africa; by the editors of Time-Life Books. Time-Life Bks. 1987 160p il maps (Lib. of nations) $28.60   **967.6**

1. East Africa   LC 87-10222

An illustrated overview of the history, geography, culture, agriculture and economy of Kenya, Tanzania, and Uganda

Includes bibliography

967.62 Kenya

Bentsen, Cheryl
Maasai days. Summit Bks. 1989 286p il
o.p.; Anchor Bks. paperback available $11
      967.62
1. Masai (African people) 2. Kenya
ISBN 0-385-41630-X (pa)   LC 89-34257
The author "describes her six-year-long friendship with
a group of Maasai villagers, whose problems in adapting
to or resisting new ways of life (the effects on the
Maasai of alcohol, politics and modern education) she
came to understand and respect." Publ Wkly

Dinesen, Isak, 1885-1962
Isak Dinesen's Africa; images of the wild
continent from the writer's life and words;
with text chosen from the memoirs and
letters of Isak Dinesen; and photographs by
Yam Arthus-Bertrand [et al.]; introduction
by Judith Thurman. Sierra Club Bks. 1985
142p il map $35   **967.62**
1. Kenya
ISBN 0-87156-821-7   LC 85-8366
This volume combines "excerpts from Dinesen's autobiographical writings, stories and letters with color
photographs of Africa's land, people and wildlife." Publ
Wkly

Out of Africa. Modern Lib. 1992 399p
$15.50   **967.62**
1. Kenya
ISBN 0-679-60021-3   LC 92-50213
A reissue of the title first published 1938 by Random
House
A record of the author's life on a Kenya coffee plantation, and of the natives and their primitive festivals, of
big game and of Lulu the gazelle who came to live at
the farm

Out of Africa and Shadows on the grass.
Vintage Bks. 1989 462p pa $12   **967.62**
1. Kenya
ISBN 0-679-72475-3   LC 89-40144
A combined edition of two titles first published 1938
and 1960 respectively
Out of Africa is entered separately above. Shadows
on the grass consists of four short essays which present
the author's recollections of her servants in Africa

968 Southern Africa. Republic of South Africa

Sparks, Allister
The mind of South Africa. Knopf 1990
424p $24.95   **968**
1. South Africa—Race relations
ISBN 0-394-58108-3   LC 89-45890
Also available in paperback from Ballantine Bks.
"An eminent liberal Johannesburg journalist looks at
his country from the earliest times when blacks first
came there through the present seething confrontation
between the 'neo-apartheid' government and the forces
of resistance. Sparks synthesizes individual experience and

global politics, past and present." Booklist
Includes bibliography

Thompson, Leonard Monteath
A history of South Africa; [by] Leonard
Thompson. Yale Univ. Press 1990 xxi, 288p
il maps $29.95; pa $15   **968**
1. South Africa—History
ISBN 0-300-04815-7; 0-300-05171-9 (pa)
     LC 89-22594
"Thompson's history of South Africa begins not with
the European entry into southern Africa but with the
presence of black Africans—farmers and hunters—who
lived in or migrated to the area from adjoining regions
and who are the earliest known inhabitants of the
present-day country. . . . The account of colonization
of Africa by various European countries and the territorial battles that ensued in the eighteenth and nineteenth centuries set the scene for Thompson's intensive
study of more recent historical events, particularly apartheid." Booklist
Includes bibliographic references

968.04 Southern Africa— 1814-1910

Pakenham, Thomas, 1933-
The Boer War. Random House 1979 xxix,
718p il $29.95   **968.04**
1. South African War, 1899-1902
ISBN 0-394-42742-4   LC 79-4779
"Pakenham's history of the Boer War of 1899-1902
. . . is based heavily on oral and original manuscript
sources, most unpublished." Booklist
"The writing is balanced, combining readability with
perception and insight, and the interpretations at once
convincing and departures from conventional wisdom. A
splendid achievement." Libr J
Includes bibliography

968.06 Republic of South Africa, 1961-

Holland, Heidi
The struggle: a history of the African
National Congress. Braziller 1990 252p il
$19.95; pa $10.95   **968.06**
1. African National Congress 2. South Africa—Race
relations 3. South Africa—Politics and government
ISBN 0-8076-1238-3; 0-8076-1255-3 (pa)
     LC 89-70782
Relying on interviews and drawing on written accounts
the author "has produced a concise and informative history of the African National Congress—a history that will
enable readers to better comprehend South Africa's political complexities." N Y Times Book Rev
Includes bibliographic references

Mallaby, Sebastian
After apartheid; the future of South Africa.
Times Bks. 1992 275p maps $22; pa $12
968.06

1. South Africa—Race relations 2. South Africa—Politics and government
ISBN 0-8129-1938-6; 0-8129-2204-2 (pa)
LC 91-50190

The author discusses "the present situation in South Africa, the factors involved in the transition to a black majority government, and the possibilities of success." Libr J

"Mallaby writes with verve and flair, interspersing long personal anecdotes with thumbnail analyses of African and Third World development issues. An up-to-date, serious introduction to vital and informative post-Apartheid questions of political economy in South Africa." Choice

Includes bibliographic references

Paton, Alan
Save the beloved country. Scribner 1989
315p $22.50
968.06

1. South Africa—Race relations 2. South Africa—Politics and government
ISBN 0-684-19127-X
LC 89-6290

First published 1987 in South Africa

"These collected journalistic pieces of the last 25 years are inevitably political. Paton writes of prominent South Africans—Luthuli, Mandela, Tutu, Smuts, Botha, Buthelezi—of Soweto, Sharpeville, and Crossroads, of detentions and bannings, of Afrikaners and apartheid, of hopes and fears; they are a *cri de coeur* for South Africa." Libr J

Wilson, Francis, 1939-
South Africa: the cordoned heart. Norton
1986 186p il maps hardcover o.p. paperback
available $14.95
968.06

1. South Africa—Race relations 2. South Africa—Economic conditions 3. South Africa—Social conditions
ISBN 0-393-30335-7 (pa)
LC 85-31015

Edited by Omar Badsha; introduction and text by Francis Wilson; foreword by Bishop Desmond Tutu

This book of photographic essays by twenty South African photographers is a project of The Second Carnegie Inquiry into Poverty and Development in Southern Africa

This volume "includes extensive and valuable text from the [Carnegie Inquiry] conference's research papers. A compelling portrait of South Africa that belongs in all subject collections." Libr J

968.91 Zimbabwe

Lessing, Doris May, 1919-
African laughter; four visits to Zimbabwe;
[by] Doris Lessing. HarperCollins Pubs. 1992
442p $25; pa $13
968.91

1. Zimbabwe
ISBN 0-06-016854-4; 0-06-092433-0 (pa)
LC 92-52590

"After the wars fought by black nationalists for the liberation of Rhodesia ended in 1980 and the nation of Zimbabwe came into being, Lessing was able to return to the homeland that had officially exiled her 25 years earlier because of her opposition to the white govern-ment. The distinguished novelist . . . details four trips she made to Zimbabwe in 1982, 1988, 1989, and 1992 in a series of haunting vignettes dealing with facets of life there." Publ Wkly

970.004 North American native peoples

Apes, William, b. 1798
On our own ground; the complete writings
of William Apess, a Pequot; edited and with
an introduction by Barry O'Connell.
University of Mass. Press 1992 lxxxi, 344p
$50; pa $17.95
970.004

1. Indians of North America—New England 2. Pequot Indians
ISBN 0-87023-766-7; 0-87023-770-5 (pa)
LC 91-27750

This volume contains the work of William Apess (usually called Apes), a "Pequot Indian born in Massachusetts in 1798. He was . . . a political/religious leader who successfully led a movement for self government among a Native community, the so-called Mashpee Revolt (1833)." Choice

Includes bibliographic references

Boyer, Ruth McDonald, 1918-
Apache mothers and daughters; four
generations of a family; [by] Ruth
McDonald Boyer and Narcissus Duffy
Gayton. University of Okla. Press 1992 xx,
393p il maps $24.95
970.004

1. Apache Indians
ISBN 0-8061-2447-4
LC 92-54149

A family history of four generations of Chiricahua Apache women. "Woven into this account are factual details about the Apaches." Publisher's note

"The voice throughout the narrative is an Apache one, emphasizing the continuation of Chiricahua culture. . . . It's a treat for anyone interested in cultural change and persistence." Libr J

Includes bibliographic references

Brown, Dee Alexander
Bury my heart at Wounded Knee; an
Indian history of the American West. Holt
& Co. 1970 487p il $27.95; pa $14.95
970.004

1. Indians of North America—West (U.S.) 2. West (U.S.)—History 3. Indians of North America—Wars
ISBN 0-8050-1045-9; 0-8050-1730-5 (pa)

This is an account of the experience of the American Indian during the white man's expansion westward

Includes bibliography

Deloria, Vine
Custer died for your sins; an Indian
manifesto; by Vine Deloria, Jr. Macmillan
1969 279p o.p.; University of Okla. Press
paperback available $12.95
970.004

1. Indians of North America
ISBN 0-8061-2129-7 (pa)

Deloria, Vine—*Continued*
The author examines how anthropologists, missionaries, and government agencies have mistreated American Indians

The First Americans; by the editors of Time-Life Books. Time-Life Bks. 1992 183p il maps (American Indians) $19.93
970.004
1. Indians of North America.   LC 92-6548
An illustrated look at Native American social customs, crafts, religion and culture
Includes bibliography

Goetzmann, William H.
The first Americans; photographs from the Library of Congress; text by William H. Goetzmann. Starwood Pub. 1991 144p il (Lib. of Congress classics) $34.95   **970.004**
1. Indians of North America—Pictorial works
ISBN 0-912347-96-1   LC 91-12662
"This volume demonstrates that melodramatic images created by commercial photographers of the late 19th and early 20th centuries perpetuated fallacies about Native Americans. Goetzmann . . . selects photos of 'real Indians' and costumed actors, and explains how professional photographers and artists interpreted Native American culture according to classical and romantic ideals. The work of Edward S. Curtis, who attempted to document the tribal way of life, is well represented here." Publ Wkly
Includes bibliographic references

Handbook of North American Indians; William C. Sturtevant, general editor. Smithsonian Institution Press 1978 il maps prices vary per volume   **970.004**
1. Indians of North America   LC 77-17162
Also available in hardcover from U.S. Government Printing Office, Superintendent of Documents
Volumes available are: v4 History of Indian-white relations; William C. Sturtevant, volume editor $47 (ISBN 0-87474-184-X); v5 Arctic; David Damas, volume editor $29 (ISBN 0-87474-185-8); v6 Subarctic; June Helm, volume editor $25 (ISBN 0-87474-186-6); v7 Northwest coast; Wayne Suttles, volume editor $38 (ISBN 0-87474-187-4); v8 California; Robert F. Heizer, volume editor $25 (ISBN 0-87474-188-2); v9-10 Southwest; Alfonso Ortiz, volume editor v9 $23, v10 $25 (ISBN 0-87474-189-0; 0-87474-190-4); v11 Great Basin; Warren L. D'Azevedo, volume editor $27 (ISBN 0-87474-191-2); v15 Northeast; Bruce G. Trigger, volume editor $27 (ISBN 0-87474-195-5)
"This projected twenty-one volume set . . . gives an encyclopedic summary of current historical-cultural knowledge of North American Indians. Extensively researched, readable essays are accompanied by illustrations, maps, and bibliographies." Ref Sources for Small & Medium-sized Libr. 5th edition

Indian reservations; a state and federal handbook; compiled by Confederation of American Indians. McFarland & Co. 1986 329p $45   **970.004**
1. Indians of North America—Reservations—Directories
ISBN 0-89950-200-8   LC 85-43573

"Indian reservations are arranged here alphabetically within state listings. Information on land status, culture, government, climate, tribal economy, transportation, community facilities, recreation, and vital statistics is included in a typical entry." Booklist

Ishi, the last Yahi; a documentary history; edited by Robert F. Heizer and Theodora Kroeber. University of Calif. Press 1979 242p il maps $29.95; pa $13.95 **970.004**
1. Ishi 2. Yana Indians
ISBN 0-520-03296-9; 0-520-04366-9 (pa)
    LC 76-19966
"Captured in Mill Creek, California, in 1911, Ishi (a name given him by anthropologists; no one knows his real name) was the last of a band of 'prehistoric' Indians known as the Yahi, a subdivision of the Yana tribe, probably the earliest settlers in the California region. Ishi was studied, befriended, and allowed a good deal of freedom to pursue life as it was before his capture. These documents record both the chronology of the way anthropologists work and the way Ishi changed in response to Western culture, until his death from tuberculosis in 1916." Booklist

Josephy, Alvin M., 1915-
The Nez Perce Indians and the opening of the Northwest; by Alvin M. Josephy, Jr. abridged ed. University of Neb. Press 1979 c1971 667p maps $35; pa $16.95   **970.004**
1. Nez Percé Indians 2. Pacific Northwest—History
ISBN 0-8032-2555-5; 0-8032-7551-X (pa)
    LC 79-14847
"A Bison book"
First published 1965; this is a reprint of the abridged edition published 1971 by Yale Univ. Press
This history of the Nez Perce tribe traces its contact with white settlers from Lewis and Clark to Chief Joseph and war in 1877
Includes bibliography

Now that the buffalo's gone; a study of today's American Indians; by Alvin M. Josephy, Jr. Knopf 1982 300p il $25
    970.004
1. Indians of North America 2. Indians of North America—Government policy
ISBN 0-394-46672-1   LC 82-47797
Also available in paperback from University of Okla. Press
This look at American Indians focuses primarily on the Seminoles, the Pequots, the Senecas, and the Taos Pueblo Indians
Includes bibliography

Manzione, Joseph A., 1957-
I am looking to the North for my life: Sitting Bull, 1876-1881. University of Utah Press 1990 172p il (University of Utah publications in the American West) $19.95
    970.004
1. Sitting Bull, Dakota Chief, 1831-1890 2. Dakota Indians
ISBN 0-87480-354-3   LC 90-52747
"After the defeat of Custer at the Battle of the Little Big Horn, many of the participating Sioux fled to Canada with Sitting Bull. This action, which is so often over-

Manzione, Joseph A., 1957-—*Continued*
looked in popular accounts, precipitated an international
incident involving the U.S., Canada, and Britain for a
period of five years. . . . Primary source material is
skillfully employed to fill in the details on this neglected
yet significant chapter in native Americans' heroic attempt to preserve their traditional culture." Booklist

Includes bibliographic references

Matthiessen, Peter
Indian country. Viking 1984 338p o.p.;
Penguin Bks. paperback available $11
970.004
1. Indians of North America—Claims 2. Human ecology
ISBN 0-14-013023-3 (pa)   LC 83-47996
This "is a collection of essays about various
'traditional' Indians who are seeking to preserve their
old ways and beliefs in the face of the destructive
exploitation of their environment by large energy, mining,
and lumber companies, backed by the U.S. government."
Sci Books Films

McReynolds, Edwin C.
The Seminoles. University of Okla. Press
1957 397p il maps (Civilization of the
American Indian ser) hardcover o.p.
paperback available $14.95   970.004
1. Seminole Indians
ISBN 0-8061-1255-7 (pa)
"This is almost strictly a military and political history,
in great detail, spiced with a few incidents which reveal
the courageous character of the Seminoles, and stressing
their relations with the Creeks." Libr J

Includes bibliography

Native American testimony; a chronicle of
Indian-white relations from prophecy to
the present, 1492-1992; edited by Peter
Nabokov; with a foreword by Vine
Deloria, Jr. Viking 1991 474p il maps
$27.50   970.004
1. Indians of North America—Government policy
2. Indians of North America—History—Sources
ISBN 0-670-83704-0   LC 90-23579
Also available in paperback from Penguin Bks.
First published 1978 by Crowell with subtitle: An anthology of Indian and white relations, first encounter to
dispossession
"A collection of primary-source material, grouped by
key issues that arose during 500 years of Indian and
white encounters in North America. Nabokov uses
traditional narratives, old government transcripts, reservation newspapers, and firsthand interviews to highlight this
chronological volume. Photographs appear throughout."
SLJ

Includes bibliographic references

Reedstrom, Ernest Lisle
Apache wars; an illustrated battle history;
[by] E. Lisle Reedstrom. Sterling 1990 256p
il $24.95; pa $16.95   970.004
1. Apache Indians—Wars
ISBN 0-8069-7254-8; 0-8069-7255-6 (pa)
LC 90-38971

An "illustrated study of the battles, leaders, and equipment of the Apache wars, with full credit given to the
most tenacious and skilled of the U.S. Army's Indian
opponents. The pictures, the book's strong point, cover
forts, leaders, animals, clothing, weapons, and uniforms."
Booklist

Includes bibliographic references

Reference encyclopedia of the American
Indian; edited by Barry T. Klein. Todd
Publs. $125   970.004
1. Indians of North America—Dictionaries
First published 1967 by B. Klein. (6th edition 1993).
Periodically revised
"This volume is actually a multipurpose resource:
encyclopedia, directory, bibliography, and biographical
source. . . . The consolidation and incorporation of a
variety of resources on Native Americans here make this
a very useful reference volume." Booklist

Schultz, Duane P.
Over the earth I come; the great Sioux
uprising of 1862; [by] Duane Schultz. St.
Martin's Press 1992 307p il $21.95; pa
$12.95   970.004
1. Dakota Indians—Wars
ISBN 0-312-07051-9; 0-312-09360-8 (pa)
LC 91-36453
"A Thomas Dunne book"
"The largest mass execution in U.S. history took place
in December 1862, when 38 Dakota Indians were hanged
on President Lincoln's order for their participation in
what has come to be called 'The Great Sioux Uprising.'"
Libr J
The author's "capably researched and tautly written
'Over the Earth I Come' reminds us that responsibility
for the abominable events that occurred during the In-
dian wars cut across ethnic boundaries." N Y Times
Book Rev

Includes bibliographic references

The **Smithsonian** book of North American
Indians; before the coming of the
Europeans; by Philip Kopper and the
editors of Smithsonian Books. Smithsonian
Bks. 1986 288p il $39.95   970.004
1. Indians of North America 2. North America—Antiquities
ISBN 0-89599-018-0   LC 86-20239
Also available from Abrams
This "book attempts to reconstruct the picture of
those people's lives, religious customs, hunting tools, artistic achievements, and architecture. Arranged by
geographical location, the text examines the cultures of
the Arctic, North America, and Central America." Booklist

Stewart, Hilary
Totem poles; written and illustrated by
Hilary Stewart. University of Wash. Press
1990 192p il maps $35   970.004
1. Totems and totemism 2. Indians of North America—Northwest coast of North America
ISBN 0-295-97052-9   LC 90-12614
The author has put together a "study of the culture
and history of totem poles and their symbolism and
significance. She relates the legends depicted in the poles,

Stewart, Hilary—*Continued*
distinguishes between various styles, and provides information on how totem poles are carved and raised."
Booklist

Includes bibliographic references

Viola, Herman J.
After Columbus; the Smithsonian chronicle of the North American Indians. Smithsonian Bks.; Orion Bks. (NY) 1990 288p il maps $45; pa $24.95　　　**970.004**
1. Indians of North America
ISBN 0-517-58108-6; 0-89599-031-8 (pa)　LC 90-9990

The author has drawn upon Native American oral history, archaeological records, and the resources of the Smithsonian Institution to present approximately 500 years of North American Indian history. The volume is heavily illustrated with photographs of artifacts, portraits, historical paintings, and maps

Visions of the people; a pictorial history of Plains Indian life; with essays by Evan M. Maurer [et al.]; exhibition organized by Evan M. Maurer and Louise Lincoln; catalogue entries by Evan M. Maurer [et al.] Minneapolis Inst. of Arts; [distributed by] University of Wash. Press 1992 298p il pa $35　　　**970.004**
1. Indians of North America—Great Plains
ISBN 0-295-97229-7　　　LC 92-85422

"Among native peoples of the North American Plains there is a long history of making representational imagery, both sacred and personal. This . . . illustrated book explores that tradition, setting a large variety of objects in their social context and against a background of sweeping historical change." Univ Press Books for Public and Second Sch Libr

Waldman, Carl
Atlas of the North American Indian; maps and illustrations by Molly Braun. Facts on File 1985 276p il maps $29.95; pa $17.95　　　**970.004**
1. Indians of North America
ISBN 0-87196-850-9; 0-8160-2136-8 (pa)　LC 83-9020

"Details the migration of prehistoric tribes to North America from Asia. A unique section on 'Lifeways' provides information on all socioeconomic and religious aspects of Native American cultures, both pre- and post-contact with European Americans. Covers the Indian Wars, the Land Cessions, and contemporary Native American conditions." N Y Public Libr Book of How & Where to Look It Up

Encyclopedia of Native American tribes; illustrations by Molly Braun. Facts on File 1988 293p il $45　　　**970.004**
1. Indians of North America—Dictionaries
ISBN 0-8160-1421-3　　　LC 86-29066

"Discusses more than 150 tribes of North America and gives summaries of the historic record including locations, migrations, languages, war, culture, contact with Europeans, and present conditions." N Y Public Libr Book of How & Where to Look It Up

Weatherford, J. McIver
Native roots; how the Indians enriched America; [by] Jack Weatherford. Crown 1991 310p il $21　　　**970.004**
1. Indians of North America
ISBN 0-517-57485-3　　　LC 91-6520

Also available in paperback from Fawcett Bks.

The author "writes about some 20 different aspects of the material and intellectual culture of Native Americans, in . . . [an attempt] to show how present-day America was built on Indian foundations." Voice Lit Suppl

"A valuable corrective to the sentimentality with which we regard the first U.S. settlers and developers." Booklist

Includes bibliographic references

White, Jon Ewbank Manchip, 1924-
Everyday life of the North American Indian; [by] Jon Manchip White. Holmes & Meier 1979 256p il $24.50　　　**970.004**
1. Indians of North America—Social life and customs
ISBN 0-8419-0488-X

"A concise well-organized review of prehistoric culture (before the white man) precedes general chapters on hunters, warriors, medicine men, artists, and home life before and after the formation of reservations. Within each topic, regional and tribal practices are differentiated." Booklist

Includes bibliography

Wright, Ronald
Stolen continents; the Americas through Indian eyes since 1492. Houghton Mifflin 1992 424p il maps $22.95; pa $12.70　　　**970.004**
1. Indians 2. America—Exploration
ISBN 0-395-56500-6; 0-395-65975-2 (pa)
　　　LC 91-36202
"A Peter Davison book"

The author "views the past 500 years from the native American perspective by drawing on long-neglected post-Columbian documents. Maintaining a five-track narrative, he follows the history of the distinct groups that survived the European invasion: the Aztecs of Mexico, The Maya of Guatemala and Yucatan, the Incas of Peru, and the Cherokees and Iroquois of North America. . . . Compelling, important, and well told." Booklist

Includes bibliography

970.01　North America—Early history to 1599

America in 1492; the world of the Indian peoples before the arrival of Columbus; edited and with an introduction by Alvin Josephy, Jr.; developed by Frederick E. Hoxie. Knopf 1992 477p il maps $35; pa $17　　　**970.01**
1. Indians—History 2. Indians—Antiquities 3. America—Exploration 4. America—Antiquities
ISBN 0-394-56438-3; 0-679-74337-5 (pa)
　　　LC 90-26222

America in 1492—*Continued*

These essays depict "the diverse lives of the approximately 75 million people living in the Americas around the turn of the fifteenth century. Geography guides the first section. . . . Another section focuses on languages, spiritual beliefs and customs, art, and 'systems of knowledge.'" Booklist

Includes bibliographic references

The **Christopher** Columbus encyclopedia; Silvio A. Bedini, editor; editorial board, David Buisseret [et al.] Simon & Schuster 1992 2v il maps set $175   **970.01**

1. Columbus, Christopher 2. America—Exploration—Dictionaries
ISBN 0-13-142662-1   LC 90-29253

The encyclopedia contains articles by some 150 contributors on the explorer and his age

"This encyclopedia's strength lies in the many excellent entries on various scientific and technical issues related to European maritime activities in the 15th and 16th centuries." N Y Times Book Rev

Enterline, James Robert

Viking America; the Norse crossings and their legacy. Enterline, 144 W. 95th St., New York, NY 10025 1972 217p il maps $9.95   **970.01**

1. America—Exploration 2. Vikings
ISBN 0-385-02585-8

First published by Doubleday

"Reconstructing the early Norse 'crossings' [the author] seeks to show that Leif Eriksson's 'Vinland' . . . lay in the Ungava Bay area north of Newfoundland and south of Baffin Island. Further, he is convinced that some Norse settlements endured on this continent for two centuries." Publ Wkly

Includes bibliography

Fagan, Brian M.

The great journey; the peopling of ancient America. Thames & Hudson 1987 288p il maps $19.95; pa $12.95   **970.01**

1. America—Antiquities 2. Indians 3. Prehistoric man 4. Archeology
ISBN 0-500-05045-7; 0-500-27515-7 (pa)
LC 87-50196

"Topics covered include the environment of the Bering Land Bridge . . . and the linguistic, dental, and skeletal evidence for the Asian ancestry of North American Indians. Also included are the history of the debate and necessary background coverage of the evolution of culture in the Old World." Sci Books Films

This book "succeeds in telling a complex story lucidly. This is an admirable introduction to questions that have exercised men ever since the discovery of the Americas." N Y Times Book Rev

Includes bibliography

Lucena Salmoral, Manuel

America 1492; portrait of a continent 500 years ago. Facts on File 1990 240p il maps $50   **970.01**

1. Indians—Social life and customs 2. Indians—Antiquities 3. America—Antiquities
ISBN 0-8160-2483-9   LC 89-77029

Also available Spanish language edition $50 (ISBN 0-8160-2484-7)

The author describes the "Inca, Aztec, and Mayan societies of Latin America, and also of the native cultures of the U.S. Southwest. Catchy, appealing headlines for each topic, a lively style of writing, and thousands of illustrations make this comprehensive work attractive." SLJ

Includes bibliographic references

Phillips, William D.

The worlds of Christopher Columbus; [by] William D. Phillips, Jr. and Carla Rahn Phillips. Cambridge Univ. Press 1992 322p il maps $29.95; pa $13.95   **970.01**

1. Columbus, Christopher 2. America—Exploration
ISBN 0-521-35097-2; 0-521-44652-X (pa)
LC 91-18790

This work discusses the explorer in the "context of 200 years of earlier European maritime efforts aimed at gaining wealth through trade with Asia and expanding Christianity." Libr J

The authors "write clearly, simply and conscientiously. . . . Theirs is an excellent book for the Columbus beginner." N Y Times Book Rev

Includes bibliographic references

Sale, Kirkpatrick

The conquest of paradise; Christopher Columbus and the Columbian legacy. Knopf 1990 453p maps $30   **970.01**

1. Columbus, Christopher 2. America—Exploration
ISBN 0-394-57429-X   LC 90-53069

Also available in paperback from New Am. Lib.

The author "views Columbus as seed-bearer of a European civilization of conquest, violence, ecological plunder and intolerance. Cast as a magnificent voyage of discovery into Columbus's psyche and the character of the New World, this demythologizing biographical adventure profiles an isolated, unattached explorer given to self-deception, full of millennial obsessions about the end of the world." Publ Wkly

Includes bibliographic references

971 Canada

Canada; by the editors of Time-Life Books. Time-Life Bks. 1988 160p il maps (Lib. of nations) $28.60   **971**

1. Canada   LC 87-33641

This book covers the history, geography, people, culture and economy of Canada

Includes bibliography

The **Canadians**; by the editors of Time-Life Books; with text by Ogden Tanner. Time-Life Bks. 1977 240p il (Old West) $19.93   **971**

1. Canada—History—0-1763 (New France) 2. Canada—History—1800-1899 (19th century)   LC 76-26845

Photographs and reproductions accompany a text that explores the history of Canada's westward expansion. Competition for natural resources and the early activities of the North West Mounted Police are covered

Includes bibliography

Malcolm, Andrew H., 1943-
The Canadians. Times Bks. 1985 385p il
o.p.; St. Martin's Press paperback available
$13.95   **971**

1. Canada—Civilization   2. National characteristics,
Canadian
ISBN 0-312-06921-9 (pa)   LC 84-40425
Also available in paperback from Bantam Bks.

Following an overview of Canada's history and
geography the author discusses the nation's people,
economy, and close ties with the United States
Includes bibliography

Morris, Jan, 1926-
O Canada; travels in an unknown country.
HarperCollins Pubs. 1992 c1990 173p $20
         971

1. Canada—Description
ISBN 0-06-018328-4   LC 91-50456
First published 1990 in Canada with title: City to city

In "profiles of 10 Canadian cites and towns, [the
author] demonstrates the rich diversity of the country's
mores, values and social and political systems, which,
she insists, differ widely from those of the U.S. The
French flavor of Quebec and Montreal; Britain's imperial
imprint on St. Andrews and Toronto; and the Indian,
Metis and Inuit customs of northern reaches recall
Canada's origins and colonial beginnings." Publ Wkly

972 Middle America. Mexico

Bazant, Jan
A concise history of Mexico; from Hidalgo
to Cárdenas, 1805-1940. Cambridge Univ.
Press 1977 222p hardcover o.p. paperback
available $17.95   **972**

1. Mexico—History
ISBN 0-521-29173-9 (pa)   LC 76-50086
This history focuses on the struggle of various classes
to own and control land. Foreign relations, military campaigns, art and other cultural achievements are
considered
Includes bibliographic references

Coe, Michael D.
The Maya. 5th ed fully rev & expanded.
Thames & Hudson 1993 224p il $29.95; pa
$14.95   **972**

1. Mayas
ISBN 0-500-02115-5; 0-500-27716-8 (pa)
First published 1966 by Praeger

An illustrated survey of the Maya civilization, focusing
on the achievements of the Classic Period, A.D. 300-900
Includes bibliography

Díaz del Castillo, Bernal, 1496-1584
The discovery and conquest of Mexico,
1517-1521. Farrar, Straus & Giroux 1956
xxxi, 478p il maps o.p.   **972**

1. Mexico—History
Available in hardcover from Buccaneer Bks.

"Edited from the only exact copy of the original ms
(and published in Mexico) by Genaro García. Translated
with an introduction and notes by A. P. Maudslay.
Introduction to the American edition by Irving A.
Leonard." Title page

"The memoirs of an old man, who began to write
of his experiences half a century after they occurred and
completed his account at the age of 84, they are not
free from minor inaccuracies, but they are the most
reliable narrative that exists." Chicago Sunday Trib

Mexico; by the editors of Time-Life Books.
Time-Life Bks. 1985 160p il maps (Lib.
of nations) $28.60   **972**

1. Mexico—History   LC 85-51036
Color and black-and-white photographs illustrate this
introduction to Mexican history, culture, social life, and
politics
Includes bibliography

Meyer, Michael C.
The course of Mexican history; [by]
Michael C. Meyer, William L. Sherman. 4th
ed. Oxford Univ. Press 1991 718, xxxviip
il maps hardcover o.p. paperback available
$22   **972**

1. Mexico—History
ISBN 0-19-506600-6 (pa)   LC 90-7205
First published 1979

A chronologically arranged survey of the political, economic, social, and cultural history of Mexico, ranging
from the pre-Columbian period to the present
Includes bibliographic references

Prescott, William H.
The history of the conquest of Mexico
and History of the conquest of Peru.
Modern Lib. 1936 xxxvi, 1288p il maps $22
         972

1. Mexico—History   2. Peru—History   3. Aztecs
4. Incas
ISBN 0-394-60471-7
"Modern Library giant"
The first title was originally published 1843 in three
volumes

This comprehensive history "involves studies ranging
from the Spain of Charles V to the fabulous empire and
court of the great Montezuma, to the heroic figure of
Hernando Cortes. The ancient, shadowy story of the Aztecs, their society, military organizations, and religion, is
traced in a manner both scholarly and glamorous. . .
. The 'History of the Conquest of Peru' (1847) is a
companion volume about the sequel to that wave of
Spanish exploration." Haydn. Thesaurus of Book Dig

Ridley, Jasper Godwin
Maximilian and Juárez; [by] Jasper Ridley.
Ticknor & Fields 1992 353p il $24.95
         972

1. Maximilian, Emperor of Mexico, 1832-1867
2. Juárez, Benito, 1806-1872 3. Mexico—History
ISBN 0-89919-989-5   LC 92-22732

An "account of the French intervention in Mexico
during the mid-19th century and of the subsequent rule
by Austrian Archduke Maximilian. *Maximilian and*

Ridley, Jasper Godwin—*Continued*

Juárez is intended for a general audience; therefore, it contains abundant background information and brief descriptions of most participants in the struggle. Ridley impressively places Mexican events in the context of world politics to illustrate the futile position in which the Archduke found himself." Choice

Includes bibliographic references

Ruiz, Ramón Eduardo

Triumphs and tragedy; a history of the Mexican people. Norton 1992 512p $29.95; pa $14.95   **972**

1. Mexico—History
ISBN 0-393-03023-7; 0-393-31066-3 (pa)

LC 91-13136

A narrative study of Mexico's "tumultuous origin and development—from its Olmec, Aztec, and Mayan heritage to its present-day incarnation as a dependent, struggling, and economically unstable modern country. This history of Mexico . . . is one long tragedy intermittently punctuated by triumph." Publisher's note

"A valuable introduction for the novice and a rich resource for the student or specialist." Booklist

Includes bibliography

Schele, Linda

A forest of kings: the untold story of the ancient Maya; [by] Linda Schele and David Freidel; color photographs by Justin Kerr. Morrow 1990 542p il maps $29.95; pa $15   **972**

1. Mayas
ISBN 0-688-07456-1; 0-688-11204-8 (pa)   LC 90-5809

"Using deciphered Mayan hieroglyphics, the authors lead readers through the discovery and description of Mayan civilization, from its beginning to the Spanish conquest." Booklist

"What makes this volume more accessible and of greater impact than the average scholarly study are the frequent vignettes of great events, kingly acts, etc., told dramatically, in a fictive but plausible style that allows the ancient Maya at last to speak for themselves." Libr J

Includes bibliographic references

Townsend, Richard

The Aztecs; [by] Richard F. Townsend. Thames & Hudson 1992 224p il (Ancient peoples and places) $29.95; pa $14.95 **972**

1. Aztecs
ISBN 0-500-02113-9; 0-500-27720-6 (pa)

"In addition to analyzing the advancement and eventual dissolution of the extensive Aztec empire, the author also provides a fascinating record of the minutiae of daily life. . . . A compact introduction to the historical and sociological evolution of a prominent Meso-American civilization." Booklist

Includes bibliography

972.08   Mexico since 1867

Lewis, Oscar, 1914-1970

The children of Sánchez; autobiography of a Mexican family. Random House 1961 xxxi, 499p hardcover o.p. paperback available $16   **972.08**

1. Mexico City (Mexico)—Social conditions 2. Poor—Mexico City (Mexico) 3. Family
ISBN 0-394-70280-8 (pa)

"First-person autobiographical narratives by the members of a poor family in Mexico City. One by one, the father and his four grown children told the anthropologist author their stories of fights, sex, struggles for jobs, bitterness, hate, sickness, death, and only a little happiness." Publ Wkly

"Oscar Lewis has made something brilliant and of singular significance, a work of such unique concentration and sympathy." N Y Times Book Rev

Riding, Alan

Distant neighbors; a portrait of the Mexicans. Knopf 1984 385p hardcover o.p. paperback available $10   **972.08**

1. Mexico—Social life and customs 2. National characteristics, Mexican
ISBN 0-679-72441-9 (pa)   LC 84-47811

This is an examination of Mexico's economy, society, and politics, and of the relationship between the United States and Mexico

Includes bibliography

Womack, John

Zapata and the Mexican Revolution. Knopf 1969 c1968 435p il hardcover o.p. paperback available $14   **972.08**

1. Zapata, Emiliano, 1879-1919 2. Mexico—History
ISBN 0-394-70853-9 (pa)

The author reconstructs the "history of the agrarian revolution in southern Mexico from the late Díaz period to about 1920. The work is well written [and] carefully conceived." Choice

972.8   Central America

Ford, Peter

Around the edge; a journey among pirates, guerrillas, former cannibals and turtle fishermen along the Miskito Coast. Viking 1991 349p $22.95   **972.8**

1. Atlantic Coast (Central America)—Description
ISBN 0-670-82827-0   LC 90-50756

The author "tells of his journey down the Caribbean coastline of Central America. He traveled the route from Belize to Panama mainly by boat and foot, staying with the people of the small villages along the way." Libr J

"Risk and hazard punctuate 'Around the Edge,' yet its finest moments are those in which Ford contemplates the complexion of life and politics along the coast and deftly lures readers into the region's human and natural history." Christ Sci Monit

Krauss, Clifford
Inside Central America; its people, politics, and history. Summit Bks. 1991 316p maps hardcover o.p. paperback available $11　　　　　**972.8**

1. Central America—Politics and government 2. Central America—Foreign relations—United States 3. United States—Foreign relations—Central America
ISBN 0-671-76072-6 (pa)　　　　LC 90-25462

This book "presents portraits of Guatemala, El Salvador, Nicaragua, Honduras, Costa Rica and Panama and shows how the history, culture and economics of each shape their politics and their volatile relationship with the U.S." Publisher's note

Includes bibliographic references

Nuccio, Richard
What's wrong, who's right in Central America? [by] Richard A. Nuccio. 2nd ed. Holmes & Meier 1989 170p il maps pa $14.95　　　　　**972.8**

1. Central America—Foreign relations—United States 2. United States—Foreign relations—Central America
ISBN 0-8419-1177-0　　　　LC 89-1796

First published 1986

A look at the U.S. relations with El Salvador, Nicaragua, Costa Rica, Honduras, and Guatemala

Pérez-Brignoli, Héctor
A brief history of Central America; translated by Ricardo B. Sawrey A. and Susana Stettri de Sawrey. University of Calif. Press 1989 223p maps $45; pa $13　　　　　**972.8**

1. Central America—History
ISBN 0-520-06049-0; 0-520-06832-7 (pa)
　　　　　　　　　LC 89-31889

This book presents the economic, political and cultural history of Guatemala, Honduras, El Salvador, Nicaragua and Costa Rica, the five national states of Central America

"For interested laypersons, this is an excellent introduction with an accurate sense of the region, past and present." Libr J

Includes bibliography

972.81　Guatemala

Simon, Jean-Marie
Guatemala; eternal spring, eternal tyranny. Norton 1988 256p il $35; pa $22.50
　　　　　　　　　972.81

1. Guatemala 2. Civil rights
ISBN 0-393-02488-1; 0-393-30506-6 (pa)
　　　　　　　　　LC 88-15101

The author, a photographer, presents in text and photographs a view of contemporary Guatemala. She focuses on political repression, human rights violations and the poverty of the peasantry

972.84　El Salvador

El Salvador; Central America in the new Cold War; edited by Marvin E. Gettleman [et al.] rev and updated. Grove Press 1987 450p il maps hardcover o.p. paperback available $13.95　　　　　**972.84**

1. Communism—El Salvador 2. El Salvador—Politics and government
ISBN 0-8021-5209-0 (pa)　　　　LC 86-33499

First published 1981

"Covering the political spectrum from Jeane Kirkpatrick to Shirley Christian and from Henry Kissinger to Senator Edward Kennedy, the contributors consider various aspects of the turmoil that is afflicting the country. Background information on the revolutionary struggle, particularly in the areas of land reform and liberation theology, helps to fill out the balanced presentation." Booklist

Includes bibliography

972.85　Nicaragua

Davis, Peter, 1937-
Where is Nicaragua? Simon & Schuster 1987 347p hardcover o.p. paperback available $8.95　　　　　**972.85**

1. Nicaragua—Politics and government 2. Nicaragua—Foreign relations—United States 3. United States—Foreign relations—Nicaragua
ISBN 0-671-65720-8 (pa)　　　　LC 86-29814

The author visited Nicaragua in 1983 and 1986. He discusses the country's political situation, life under the Sandinista government, and relations between Nicaragua and the United States
A "cogent, thoroughly integrated portrait of Nicaragua's history, culture, politics, personalities, and . . . ambience." Libr J

Kinzer, Stephen
Blood of brothers; life and war in Nicaragua. Putnam 1991 450p il maps hardcover o.p. paperback available $14
　　　　　　　　　972.85

1. Nicaragua—Politics and government—1974-
ISBN 0-385-42258-X (pa)　　　　LC 90-19763

An account of "the ill-fated attempt by the Sandinistas to govern Nicaragua following their overthrow of the Somoza dictatorship in 1979. . . . While critical of the U.S. role in the creation and support of the Contras, Kinzer allocates much of the blame for the failure of the Sandinistas on their own policies of militarism and economic mismanagement." Booklist

Includes bibliography

972.87　Panama

Buckley, Kevin
Panama; the whole story. Simon & Schuster 1991 304p hardcover o.p. paperback available $11　　　　　**972.87**

1. Panama—Foreign relations—United States 2. United States—Foreign relations—Panama
ISBN 0-671-77876-5 (pa)　　　　LC 91-2727

Buckley, Kevin—*Continued*

The author "describes events leading up to the 'Just Cause' invasion of Panama by U.S. troops. His book covers the complexities of Panamanian political intrigues, the corruption, the political culture, the involvement of the United States with Manuel Noriega, and the interaction between Noriega and the major domestic and international actors from 1986 through January 1990." Libr J

Includes bibliographic references

Dinges, John

Our man in Panama; how general Noriega used the United States—and made millions in drugs and arms. Random House 1990 402p il $21.95   **972.87**

1. Noriega, Manuel Antonio 2. Panama—Foreign relations—United States 3. United States—Foreign relations—Panama
ISBN 0-394-54910-4   LC 89-42769

Also available in paperback from Times Bks.

This is an account of Manuel Noriega's rise to power in Panama and of his relations with the United States from the 1950s up to 1989

The author "focuses on allegations of Noriega drug trafficking. . . . He makes it clear that he has reported only what he can absolutely prove, and he dismisses much of the Bush-Noriega scuttlebutt." Nation

Includes bibliographic references

Donnelly, Thomas

Operation Just Cause; the storming of Panama; by Thomas Donnelly, Margaret Roth, Caleb Baker. Lexington Bks. 1991 453p il $24.95   **972.87**

1. Panama—History—American invasion, 1989
ISBN 0-669-24975-0   LC 91-2732

"Drawing on hundreds of interviews, the authors describe the invasion of 26,000 U.S. troops against the Panama Defense Forces, and the toppling of Manuel Noriega. In addition to crisp accounts of conventional firefights during the brief campaign—December '89-January '90—the book describes a wide variety of military situations, affording readers a close look at how U.S. troops make war in the post-Vietnam era." Publ Wkly

Includes bibliographic references

McCullough, David G., 1933-

The path between the seas; the creation of the Panama Canal, 1870-1914; [by] David McCullough. Simon & Schuster 1977 698p il maps hardcover o.p. paperback available $14.95   **972.87**

1. Panama Canal
ISBN 0-671-24409-4 (pa)   LC 76-57967

This is a "history of the canal project, beginning with de Lesseps' bold and ultimately disastrous investment and ending with the triumph of American enterprise in 1914." Libr J

"Not only is this a well-told story of the building of the Panama Canal but it also supplies welcome background for the . . . debate on the canal's role in inter-American relations." Booklist

Includes bibliography

972.91   Cuba

Castro, Fidel, 1927-

Nothing can stop the course of history; interview by Jeffrey M. Elliot and Marvyn M. Dymally; photographs by Gianfranco Gorgoni. Pathfinder Press 1986 258p il $45; pa $17.95   **972.91**

1. Cuba—Politics and government 2. Latin America—Politics and government 3. World politics
ISBN 0-87348-660-9; 0-87348-661-7 (pa)
                                      LC 86-61524

Original Spanish edition published 1985 in Cuba

This is a transcript of an interview with the Cuban premier conducted by U.S. congressman Mervyn Dymally and his foreign affairs advisor, Jeffrey Elliot. Castro discusses his country, Latin America, and international affairs

Miller, Tom, 1947-

Trading with the enemy; a Yankee travels through Castro's Cuba. Atheneum Pubs. 1992 353p maps $24   **972.91**

1. Cuba—Description
ISBN 0-689-12094-X   LC 92-15415

The author spent several "months living in and traveling through Castro's Cuba. His topic is timely. In an age when other communist governments are toppling faster than Babel's tower, Cuba remains a mystery to the West. Miller does an admirable, if somewhat erratic, job of introducing his readers to the people, culture, idiosyncracies, and wonders of these nearby yet unknown neighbors." Libr J

Includes bibliographic references

Pérez, Louis A., 1943-

Cuba; between reform and revolution; [by] Louis A. Pérez, Jr. Oxford Univ. Press 1988 504p maps $30; pa $14.95   **972.91**

1. Cuba—History
ISBN 0-19-504587-4; 0-19-504586-6 (pa)
                                      LC 87-34892

"A narrative history that emphasizes the antecedents of the Cuban revolution and concludes with an analysis of Fidel Castro's successes and failures." N Y Public Libr Book of How & Where to Look It Up

Includes bibliography

Smith, Wayne S.

Portrait of Cuba. Turner Pub. (Atlanta) 1991 192p il map $39.95   **972.91**

1. Cuba—History
ISBN 1-87868-507-4   LC 91-66125

The author provides an "overview of Cuban history, which moves quickly through the island's colonial period and difficult separation from Spain to the book's particular focus: the context in which Castro gained power, his effect on Cuba over the 30-year run of his dictatorship, and the significance to Cuban welfare of Soviet involvement and continued U.S. hostility. With a bounty of fascinating period photographs from earlier decades of this century and lovely ones of contemporary Cuba . . . this book is distinguished by its cogency and balance." Booklist

Timerman, Jacobo, 1923-
Cuba; a journey; translated by Toby Talbot. Knopf 1990 125p $18.95   **972.91**
1. Cuba—Politics and government
ISBN 0-394-53910-9   LC 90-53120

"The Argentine journalist recounts traveling around Cuba in the summer of 1987, talking to all levels of Cubans from prostitutes to officials. Beneath the tattered exterior of Cuban life, Timerman discovered even shabbier underpinnings." Booklist

972.94   Haiti

Gold, Herbert, 1924-
The best nightmare on Earth; a life in Haiti. Prentice Hall Press 1991 303p il $19.95   **972.94**
1. Haiti
ISBN 0-13-372327-5   LC 90-24895
Also available in paperback from Simon & Schuster

The author "decribes his fascination with Haiti, which began when he first visited the island in the early 1950s. Over the years he cultivated a cadre of friends who provided him entrance into the inner circle of Haitian society. His memoir is a kaleidescope of impressions and experiences." Libr J

972.97   Leeward Islands

Kincaid, Jamaica
A small place. Farrar, Straus & Giroux 1988 81p o.p.; New Am. Lib. paperback available $7   **972.97**
1. Antigua and Barbuda
ISBN 0-452-26235-6 (pa)   LC 88-376
Antiguan Kincaid addresses foreign visitors to her country. In this essay, she discusses the poverty and political corruption of the island, which she views as a legacy of British colonialism and also as a result of an economy controlled by tourism

973   United States

America then & now; great old photographs of America's life and times, and how those same scenes look today; edited by David Cohen; text by Susan Wels. HarperCollins Pubs. 1992 232p il maps $40   **973**
1. United States—Social life and customs—Pictorial works
ISBN 0-06-250176-3   LC 91-76080
This book matches old photographs of the American scene with contemporary images

"The editors have carefully avoided nostalgia or evoking a sense that there were only good old days. . . . Cohen and Wels have no great point to make, but their diversions are informative and evocative." Christ Century

Includes bibliographic references

The **Annals** of America. Encyclopaedia Britannica 1968-1986 24v il maps set $549   **973**
1. United States—History—Sources
ISBN 0-87827-199-6
Each volume has a distinctive title

"Volumes 1 through 21 comprise approximately 2300 selections from speeches, diaries, journals, books, and articles illustrating and documenting the history of America from 1493 to 1986. Companion volumes include a name index and a conspectus." Ref Sources for Small & Medium-sized Libr. 5th edition

Bailey, Thomas Andrew, 1902-1983
The American pageant; a history of the Republic; by Thomas A. Bailey, David M. Kennedy. Heath il $38   **973**
1. United States—History
Also available in a two-volume paperback edition v1 $24, v2 $27

First published 1956. (10th edition 1994) Frequently revised

A general history which uses a chronological approach to events from the discovery of America and colonization through recent events

Includes bibliographic references

Billington, Ray Allen, 1903-
Westward expansion; a history of the American frontier; [by] Ray Allen Billington, Martin Ridge. 5th ed. Macmillan 1982 892p maps $72   **973**
1. United States—Territorial expansion 2. United States—History 3. Mississippi River valley 4. West (U.S.)—History
ISBN 0-02-309860-0   LC 81-8450
First published 1949

The book traces the advance of the frontier across America from colonial beginnings along the Atlantic Coast in the 16th century to the closing of the frontier nearly four hundred years later

Includes bibliography

Boorstin, Daniel J. (Daniel Joseph), 1914-
The Americans: The democratic experience. Random House 1973 717p $39.95; pa $15   **973**
1. United States—Civilization 2. United States—Social conditions 3. United States—Economic conditions
ISBN 0-394-48724-9; 0-394-71011-8 (pa)
Concluding volume of the author's trilogy which began with The Americans: The colonial experience, entered in class 973.2 and continued with The Americans: The national experience, entered below

This volume is concerned with the democratization of the national character over the past hundred years and the growth of technology

Includes bibliographic references

Boorstin, Daniel J. (Daniel Joseph), 1914-
—*Continued*
The Americans: The national experience.
Random House 1965 517p $35; pa $14
973
1. United States—Civilization 2. National charac-
teristics, American 3. United States—Intellectual life
ISBN 0-394-41453-5; 0-394-70358-8 (pa)
This is the second volume of the author's trilogy
A cultural interpretation of American history, this
book traces "the roots of contemporary American life
to the years between the Revolution and the Civil War."
Booklist
Includes bibliographic references

The exploring spirit; America and the
world, then and now; [by] Daniel Boorstin.
Random House 1976 102p $6.95 **973**
1. United States—Civilization 2. Technology and
civilization 3. National characteristics, American
ISBN 0-394-40602-8
"This volume consists of the Reith Lectures for the
BBC (recorded in the fall of 1975) in slightly expanded
form. The lectures probe the meaning of exploration
from the Renaissance to the present." Libr J

Hidden history; selected and edited by
Daniel J. Boorstin and Ruth F. Boorstin.
Harper & Row 1987 xxv, 332p $19.95
973
1. United States—Civilization
ISBN 0-06-039071-9 LC 87-45023
Also available in paperback from Vintage Bks.
"A Cornelia & Michael Bessie book"
"A collection of essays and abridgments from [Boor-
stin's] books that investigates certain overlooked or dis-
regarded corners of history. . . . History engagingly writ-
ten, deeply felt, widely appealing." Booklist

Burns, James MacGregor
The American experiment. Knopf
1982-1989 c1981-1989 3v maps **973**
1. United States—History
Also available in paperback from Vintage Bks.
Contents: v1 The vineyard of liberty $39.95 (ISBN
0-394-50546-8); v2 The workshop of democracy $30
(ISBN 0-394-51275-8); v3 The crosswinds of freedom $35
(ISBN 0-394-51276-6)
This three-volume history of the United States
celebrates the American experience from the American
Revolution and the development of the Constitution to
the election of George Bush
Includes bibliographic references

Commager, Henry Steele, 1902-
The American mind; an interpretation of
American thought and character since the
1880's. Yale Univ. Press 1950 476p
hardcover o.p. paperback available $16
973
1. United States—Civilization 2. National characteristics, American 3. United States—Intellectual life
ISBN 0-300-00046-4 (pa)
Analyzed in Essay and general literature index

Partial contents: John Fiske and the evolutionary philosophy; William James and the impact of pragmatism;
Determinism in literature; Religious thought and practice;
Lester Ward and the science of society; Thorstein Veblen
and the new economics; Innovators in historical
interpretation; Applications of political theory; Evolution
of American law; Architecture and society; Bibliography

The empire of reason; how Europe
imagined and America realized the
Enlightenment. Anchor Press/Doubleday
1977 342p il o.p.; Oxford Univ. Press
paperback available $9.95 **973**
1. United States—Intellectual life 2. Enlightenment
3. United States—History
ISBN 0-19-503062-1 (pa) LC 76-2837
This is a "study of how the New World's
'philosophes'—predominantly rural, practical men of action—successfully extended and carried out the ideas of
Old Europe's philosophers of the Enlightenment." Publ
Wkly
This is "a work of considerable erudition, supported
by a great stack of notes. There are delightful vignettes
of some of the lesser-known worthies of both the European and American Enlightenments." Saturday Rev
Includes bibliographic references

Documents of American history; edited by
Henry Steele Commager and Milton
Cantor. Prentice-Hall 2v il ea $59 **973**
1. United States—History—Sources
First published 1934 by Crofts. (10th edition 1988)
Periodically revised
"Compilation of official and archival documents that
illustrate American history. All constitutional amend-
ments, important Supreme Court decisions, and many
presidential addresses are included. Useful for beginning
documentary research." N Y Public Libr Book of How
& Where to Look It Up

Facts about the states; editors, Joseph
Nathan Kane, Janet Podell, Steven
Anzovin. 2nd ed. Wilson, H.W. 1994
c1993 624p il $60 **973**
1. United States—History, Local 2. State governments
ISBN 0-8242-0849-8 LC 93-30328
First published 1989
Provides geographic, demographic, economic, political,
and cultural facts about the fifty states, Puerto Rico, and
the District of Columbia. Part I presents state entries
in alphabetical order. Part II provides comparative tables
that rank states in categories such as population,
geography, education, and finance

The **Hispanic** experience in North America;
sources for study in the United States;
edited by Lawrence A. Clayton. Ohio
State Univ. Press 1992 189p il $35 **973**
1. Spaniards—United States 2. America—Exploration
ISBN 0-8142-0568-2 LC 91-39274
"Growing out of a conference hosted by the Library
of Congress, this collection of bibliographic essays covers
the historical legacy of Spain in North America from
the first sighting of the continent by Juan Ponce de Leon
in 1512." Univ Press Books for Public and Second Sch
Libr
Includes bibliographic references

Hofstadter, Richard, 1916-1970

The American political tradition, and the men who made it; with a foreword by Christopher Lasch. 25th anniversary ed. Knopf 1973 xxxiii, 378p $24.95; pa $12
973

1. United States—Politics and government
ISBN 0-394-48880-6; 0-679-72315-3 (pa)

First published 1948 and analyzed in Essay and general literature index

This volume contains twelve essays, ten of which analyze the political careers of Lincoln, Jefferson, Jackson, Calhoun, Wendell Phillips, Bryan, Theodore Roosevelt, Wilson, Hoover and Franklin D. Roosevelt

Includes bibliography

Images of America: a panorama of history in photographs. Smithsonian Bks. 1989 255p il $39.95
973

1. United States—History—Pictorial works
ISBN 0-89599-023-7   LC 89-11322

"Nostalgia is the essence of *Images of America*, a compendium of photos owned by the Smithsonian Institution and chosen for their historical rather than artistic value." Booklist

Langdon, William Chauncy, 1871-1947

Everyday things in American life, 1776-1876. Scribner 1941 398p il map $45
973

1. United States—Social life and customs
ISBN 0-684-17416-2

Companion volume: Everyday things in American life, 1607-1776, entered in class 973.2

The emphasis in this book "is on expansion, with chapters on Roads and turnpikes, Covered bridges, River transportation, The passing of canals, The development of steam. Other chapters treat of home life upstairs and down, clothes and their materials, and the improvements in farm machinery, all illustrated with well chosen pictures." Wis Libr Bull

Includes bibliography

Making America; the society & culture of the United States; edited by Luther S. Luedtke. University of N.C. Press 1992 554p il $34.95; pa $16.95
973

1. National characteristics, American 2. United States—Civilization
ISBN 0-8078-2030-X; 0-8078-4370-9 (pa)
LC 91-50786

Analyzed in Essay and general literature index

"Scholars address 'America' from a diversity of disciplines, personal histories, regions, and political points of view. *Making America* is a dynamic account of the American experience, from matters of landscape, immigration, and urbanization; to manners, literature, and the arts; social organization and values; religion, political thought, philosophy, and law." Univ Press Books for Public and Second Sch Libr

Includes bibliographic references

Morison, Samuel Eliot, 1887-1976

A concise history of the American Republic; [by] Samuel Eliot Morison, Henry Steele Commager, William E. Leuchtenburg. 2nd ed. Oxford Univ. Press 1983 765p il maps hardcover o.p. paperback available $29.95
973

1. United States—History
ISBN 0-19-503180-6 (pa)   LC 82-3621

Also available in a two volume paperback edition, each $22: v1 To 1877 (ISBN 0-19-503181-4); v2 Since 1865 (ISBN 0-19-503182-2)

First published 1977

"An abbreviated and revised edition of The growth of the American Republic." Title page

Includes bibliography

The growth of the American Republic; [by] Samuel Eliot Morison, Henry Steele Commager, and William E. Leuchtenburg. 7th ed. Oxford Univ. Press 1980 2v il maps ea $31
973

1. United States—History
ISBN 0-19-502593-8 (v1); 0-19-502594-6 (v2)
LC 79-52432

First published 1930 in a single volume

A history of the United States that deals with military, political, economic, social, literary and spiritual aspects of the nation's development

"A good general history, well-written." Sheehy. Guide to Ref Books. 10th edition

The Oxford history of the American people. Oxford Univ. Press 1965 xxvii, 1150p il maps o.p.
973

1. United States—History 2. United States—Civilization

Available only in a three-volume paperback edition from New Am. Lib.

A political, social, and military history of the United States from prehistoric man to President Kennedy's assassination, including such aspects of American life as sports, science, art, and music. Also includes comments on Canadian history

Schlesinger, Arthur M., 1917-

The cycles of American history; [by] Arthur M. Schlesinger, Jr. Houghton Mifflin 1986 498p hardcover o.p. paperback available $11.70
973

1. United States—History 2. United States—Foreign relations 3. United States—Politics and government
ISBN 0-395-45400-X (pa)   LC 86-7706

"For this volume, Schlesinger has revised and updated papers, reviews, and essays that have appeared in various forms over the past quarter-century. . . . Each of the 14 essays that make up the book offers a fresh, demanding, and lively argument about important issues in American intellectual, political, or diplomatic history." Choice

Includes bibliography

Schlesinger, Arthur M., 1917— *Continued*
The disuniting of America. Norton 1992
160p $10.95; pa $7.95 **973**

1. Multiculturalism 2. Intercultural education 3. United States—History—Historiography 4. United States—Civilization
ISBN 0-393-03380-5; 0-393-30987-8 (pa)
LC 91-38884

"This book examines the contemporary controversy regarding the teaching of history and its ramifications for a multiethnic society. The author argues that the critical traditions of scholarship based on diversity, dissent, and close scrutiny of broad claims must not be abandoned. . . . [He contends] that schools and colleges must not degrade history by allowing its contents to be dictated by pressure groups, whether political, economic, religious, or ethnic." N Y Rev Books

This is "a sane and temperate book." N Y Times Book Rev

Steinbeck, John, 1902-1968
Travels with Charley; in search of America. Viking 1962 246p o.p.; Penguin Bks. paperback available $6 **973**

1. United States—Civilization 2. United States—Description
ISBN 0-14-005320-4 (pa)

The Nobel laureate recounts his impressions and observations of America gathered during a trip through forty states in the company of his French poodle Charley

973.02 United States—History—Miscellany. Chronologies

The **Encyclopedia** of American facts and dates; edited by Gorton Carruth. HarperCollins Pubs. $40 **973.02**

1. United States—History—Chronology

Also available from New Am Lib. in a paperback abridged edition with title: What happened when

First published 1956 by Crowell. (9th edition 1993) Periodically revised

Entries that deal with a variety of topics are chronologically arranged in parallel columns to show concurrent events in American life, from around 1000 A.D. to the present

Shenkman, Richard
Legends, lies, and cherished myths of American history. Morrow 1988 202p $15.95 **973.02**

1. United States—History—Miscellanea
ISBN 0-688-06580-5
LC 88-9293

Also available G.K. Hall large print edition and in paperback from HarperCollins Pubs.

The author "debunks a host of popular myths associated with U.S. history. From the Founding Fathers to the Reagan presidency, heretofore undisputed facts are exposed as fiction. Misquotes, misinterpretations, and downright fabrications are all duly recorded in an amusing and illuminating fashion. An irresistible browsing item." Booklist

Includes bibliography

973.03 United States—History—Encyclopedias and dictionaries

Concise dictionary of American history. Scribner 1983 1140p $95 **973.03**

1. United States—History—Dictionaries
ISBN 0-684-17321-2
LC 82-42731

A one volume abridgement of the eight volume Dictionary of American history, entered below

This volume "contains over 6,200 entries abridged from the parent set and updated plus new articles that bring coverage up to 1982. Arranged in dictionary format, it provides quick access to a wide range of topics." Wynar. Guide to Ref Books for Sch Media Cent. 3d edition

Dictionary of American history. rev ed. Scribner 1976 8v set $625 **973.03**

1. United States—History—Dictionaries
ISBN 0-684-13856-5

First published 1940

"The set contains readable articles that explain the concepts, events, and places of American history. It covers political, economic, social, industrial, and cultural history. It does not include biographical sketches." Ref Sources for Small & Medium-sized Libr. 5th edition

Johnson, Thomas Herbert
The Oxford companion to American history; [by] Thomas H. Johnson in consultation with Harvey Wish. Oxford Univ. Press 1966 906p $49.95 **973.03**

1. United States—History—Dictionaries
ISBN 0-19-500597-X

"Concise introductory articles on a variety of topics and historical personages." N Y Public Libr Book of How & Where to Look It Up

The **Reader's** companion to American history; Eric Foner and John A. Garraty, editors; sponsored by the Society of American Historians. Houghton Mifflin 1991 xxii, 1226p $34 **973.03**

1. United States—History—Dictionaries
ISBN 0-395-51372-3
LC 91-19508

"The nearly 1000 entries, ranging from concise explanations to multipage essays, are all equally well written, crisp, and entertaining. Most entries are signed by the nearly 400 contributors, many of whom are acknowledged experts in their fields. . . . Brief bibliographies and thorough 'See also' references to related articles follow each entry." Libr J

For a fuller review see: Booklist, Jan. 1, 1992

973.06 United States—History—Organizations

Directory of historical organizations in the United States and Canada. American Assn. for State & Local Hist. pa $79.95 **973.06**

1. United States—History—Societies—Directories
2. Canada—History—Societies—Directories
ISSN 1045-456X

Directory of historical organizations in the United States and Canada—*Continued*

Biennial. First published 1956 with title: Directory of historical societies and agencies in the United States and Canada

"Libraries should acquire the latest edition of this publication, which lists historical societies geographically, giving mailing address, number of members, museums, hours and size of library, publication program, etc." Ref Sources for Small & Medium-sized Libr. 5th edition

973.1   United States—Early history to 1607

Morison, Samuel Eliot, 1887-1976

The European discovery of America. Oxford Univ. Press 1971-1974 2v il maps ea $39.95; pa $19.95   **973.1**

1. America—Exploration 2. Voyages and travels

Contents: v1 The northern voyages, A.D.500-1600 (ISBN 0-19-501377-8; 0-19-508271-0); v2 The southern voyages, A.D.1492-1616 (ISBN 0-19-501823-0; 0-19-508272-9)

Includes bibliographic references

The great explorers; the European discovery of America. Oxford Univ. Press 1978 xxv, 752p il maps $39.95; pa $18.95   **973.1**

1. America—Exploration 2. Voyages and travels
ISBN 0-19-502314-5; 0-19-504222-0 (pa)

LC 77-21831

A one-volume abridgement of the author's The European discovery of America, entered above

This book "is an exact reprinting of 11 of the 20 chapters from The northern voyages and 18 of the 31 chapters from The southern voyages. Though it includes accounts of the more popular explorers (Cabot, Columbus, Magellan, Drake, and others), it excludes Morison's descriptions of the Irish and Norse explorations, his analysis of nations' maritime policy, his account of a mariner's life, and his 'Bibliography and notes,' upon which the narrations were based." Choice

973.2   United States—Colonial period, 1607-1775

Bailyn, Bernard

The peopling of British North America; an introduction. Knopf 1986 177p $19.95; pa $8   **973.2**

1. United States—History—1600-1775, Colonial period
ISBN 0-394-55392-6; 0-394-75779-3 (pa)

LC 85-82144

In this introductory volume of a projected multivolume work, the author "gives first airing to his overall argument on settling patterns in history. Though designed to introduce the subsequent volumes, this superbly articulate study is understandable on its own." Booklist

Includes bibliography

Voyagers to the West; a passage in the peopling of America on the eve of the Revolution; [by] Bernard Bailyn, with the assistance of Barbara DeWolfe. Knopf 1986 xxvii, 668p il maps $35; pa $14.95   **973.2**

1. Great Britain—Immigration and emigration 2. United States—History—1600-1775, Colonial period
ISBN 0-394-51569-2; 0-394-75778-5 (pa)

LC 86-45358

"The five sections of this book present a . . . depiction of the pre-Revolutionary emigration from Britain." Publisher's note

"Mr. Bailyn has complied with modern historical demands for the statistical and quantifiable. . . . He has also gone far beyond number, and made us understand this epic of hardship and adaptability as if we had been part of it." New Yorker

Includes bibliographic references

Boorstin, Daniel J. (Daniel Joseph), 1914-

The Americans: The colonial experience. Random House 1958 434p $34.95; pa $12   **973.2**

1. United States—Civilization 2. United States—History—1600-1775, Colonial period 3. National characteristics, American 4. United States—Intellectual life
ISBN 0-394-41506-X; 0-394-70513-0 (pa)

The first volume of the author's trilogy entitled: The Americans; following volumes entered in class 973

"This study of colonial America attempts to show that it was not merely an offshoot of the mother country, but a new civilization. . . . The author centers his highly informative work on colonial education, the special qualities of American speech, and the growth of a distinct culture." Booklist

Includes bibliography

Earle, Alice Morse, 1851-1911

Child life in colonial days   **973.2**

1. United States—Social life and customs—1600-1775, Colonial period 2. Children—United States

Hardcover and paperback editions available from various publishers

Companion volume to Home life in colonial days (1898)

First published 1899 by Macmillan

An account of how children spent their days in school and at home

Hawke, David Freeman

Everyday life in early America. Harper & Row 1988 195p il (Everyday life in America) hardcover o.p. paperback available $11   **973.2**

1. United States—History—1600-1775, Colonial period 2. United States—Social life and customs
ISBN 0-06-091251-0 (pa)   LC 87-17667

The author "provides enlightening and colorful descriptions of early Colonial Americans and debunks many widely held assumptions about 17th century settlers." Publ Wkly

Includes bibliography

Langdon, William Chauncy, 1871-1947

Everyday things in American life, 1607-1776. Scribner 1937 xx, 353p il map $55   **973.2**

1. United States—Social life and customs—1600-1775, Colonial period
ISBN 0-684-17415-4

Companion volume: Everyday things in American life, 1776-1876, entered in class 973

"How the early colonists lived, what they ate, what they worked at, how they travelled, all helped out with a variety of illustrative material." New Yorker

Includes bibliography

Schlesinger, Arthur M., 1888-1965

The birth of the Nation; a portrait of the American people on the eve of independence; with an introduction by Arthur M. Schlesinger, Jr. Knopf 1968 258p o.p.; Houghton Mifflin paperback available $11.70   **973.2**

1. United States—Social life and customs—1600-1775, Colonial period 2. United States—History—1600-1775, Colonial period 3. National characteristics, American
ISBN 0-395-31675-8 (pa)

The author describes the terrain and resources of the new world; the settlers, the ideas they brought with them, and the modifications these ideas underwent in the new land; the role of the family; the agricultural way of life; the first emergence of cities; the stirrings of class consciousness, the evolution of the American mind and the early gropings of the artistic consciousness

Includes bibliography

973.3 United States—Periods of Revolution and Confederation, 1775-1789

Becker, Carl, 1873-1945

The Declaration of Independence; a study in the history of political ideas. Knopf 1942 286p hardcover o.p. paperback available $6.95   **973.3**

1. Jefferson, Thomas, 1743-1826 2. United States. Declaration of Independence 3. United States—Politics and government—1775-1783, Revolution
ISBN 0-394-70060-0 (pa)

Also available in hardcover from P. Smith

A reprint, with a new preface, of a book first published 1922 by Harcourt Brace & Co.

"A study of the Declaration, the philosophy that lay behind it, the history of its several drafts, an estimate of its literary quality." Wis Libr Bull

Includes bibliographic references

Foner, Eric

Tom Paine and Revolutionary America. Oxford Univ. Press 1976 xx, 326p il maps hardcover o.p. paperback available $14.95   **973.3**

1. Paine, Thomas, 1737-1809—1 2. United States—Politics and government—1775-1783, Revolution 3. United States—Economic conditions—1775-1783, Revolution 4. United States—Social conditions
ISBN 0-19-502182-7 (pa)   LC 75-25456

The author examines the roots of Paine's thought within the social, economic and political context of colonial America

Includes bibliographic references

Hibbert, Christopher, 1924-

Redcoats and rebels; the American Revolution through British eyes. Norton 1990 xx, 375p il maps $29.95   **973.3**

1. United States—History—1775-1783, Revolution
ISBN 0-393-02895-X   LC 90-31753

Also available in paperback from Avon Bks.

Beginning with the Stamp Act of 1765 "the author interprets the War for Independence as viewed by the mother country: more a dirty insurrection than the sacred pursuit of liberty." Booklist

"Mr. Hibbert has an eye for the telling anecdote and the graphic quotation, and his bibliography indicates that he has consulted a wealth of manuscript material as well as research published during the last 30 years that illuminates what lay behind the British defeat." N Y Times Book Rev

Morgan, Edmund Sears

The birth of the Republic, 1763-89; [by] Edmund S. Morgan. 3rd ed. University of Chicago Press 1992 206p (Chicago history of American civilization) $29.95; pa $8.95   **973.3**

1. United States—History—1775-1783, Revolution 2. United States—History—1783-1809
ISBN 0-226-53756-0; 0-226-53757-9 (pa) LC 92-8871

First published 1956

A brief study of the American revolutionary period from 1763 to 1789

Includes bibliographic references

Morris, Richard Brandon, 1904-1989

Witnesses at the creation; Hamilton, Madison, Jay, and the Constitution; [by] Richard B. Morris. Holt, Rinehart & Winston 1985 279p il o.p.; New Am. Lib. paperback available $4.50   **973.3**

1. United States—Politics and government—1783-1809
ISBN 0-451-62686-9 (pa)   LC 85-810

"A Lou Reda book"

"The nationalist convictions of Hamilton, Madison, and Jay . . . are examined as the book illustrates how the Constitution was debated, amended, and ratified through the persuasive support of these three men." Booklist

Includes bibliography

Smith, Page

A new age now begins; a people's history of the American Revolution. McGraw-Hill 1976 2v il maps o.p.; Penguin Bks. paperbacks available ea $16.95   **973.3**

1. United States—History—1775-1783, Revolution
ISBN 0-14-012253-2 (v1); 0-14-012254-0 (v2)

The author relates the "disparate elements that together fed the evolution of the U.S. from the earliest English settlements, through colonization, and on to the Revolutionary War." Booklist

"This is a compelling, readable book written by a trained historian whose knowledge of the subject is matched by his enthusiasm." Christ Sci Monit

Includes bibliographic references

Followed by: The shaping of America, entered in class 973.4

Tuchman, Barbara Wertheim

The first salute; [by] Barbara W. Tuchman. Knopf 1988 347p il maps $22.95
973.3

1. United States—History—1775-1783, Revolution
ISBN 0-394-55333-0   LC 88-45216

Also available Thorndike Press large print edition and in paperback from Ballantine Bks.

"'The first salute' accorded to the striped flag of the thirteen States was given by a Dutch colony, St. Eustatius, in November, 1776. The subject of this study is the contribution of the Dutch and the French, to the independence of the United States." West Coast Rev Books

"The book is a tightly woven narrative, ingeniously structured. It is not a blow-by-blow account of the conflict; familiarity with issues and events is assumed. Instead, Tuchman takes a specific incident and through it elucidates the course and outcome of the war." Christ Sci Monit

Includes bibliography

Wood, Gordon Stewart

The radicalism of the American Revolution; [by] Gordon S. Wood. Knopf 1992 447p $27.50; pa $15   **973.3**

1. United States—Politics and government—1775-1783, Revolution 2. United States—History—1775-1783, Revolution 3. United States—Social life and customs
ISBN 0-679-40493-7; 0-679-73688-3 (pa)

LC 91-19719

"Under the broad categories of monarchy, republicanism, and democracy, Wood explains how the US was transformed from a society that took for granted a nonworking elite and a dependent servile underclass to one in which the free-standing individualist, who worked for a living, became the norm. . . . [A] readable book based on hundreds of primary and secondary sources." Choice

Includes bibliographic references

The **World** almanac of the American Revolution; edited by L. Edward Purcell and David F. Burg. World Almanac 1992 386p il pa $18.95   **973.3**

1. United States—History—1775-1783, Revolution
ISBN 0-88687-574-9   LC 91-32057

A chronological examination of the events of the American Revolution and its aftermath, describing political and military actions. A separate section provides biographical information on important figures. Beginning with 1775, a one-page summary begins each year's events. Interspersed in the chronology are essays on special topics

For a review see: Booklist, August 1992

973.4 United States— Constitutional period, 1789-1809

Miller, John Chester, 1907-1991

The Federalist era, 1789-1801. Harper & Row 1960 304p il map (New American nation ser) hardcover o.p. paperback available $10.95   **973.4**

1. Federal Party (U.S.) 2. United States—History—1783-1809
ISBN 0-06-133027-2 (pa)

A chronicle of the administrations of George Washington and John Adams, concentrating on the politics and diplomacy

Includes bibliography

Smith, Page

The shaping of America; a people's history of the young republic. McGraw-Hill 1980 xxiv, 870p il o.p.; Penguin Bks. paperback available $15.95   **973.4**

1. United States—History—1783-1865 2. United States—Politics and government—1783-1865
ISBN 0-14-012259-1 (pa)   LC 79-13592

Sequel to: A new age now begins, entered in class 973.3

"Smith's second installment in his popular traversal of American history . . . covers the period from 1783 to 1826, as the young nation experienced strains, conflicts, development, and expansion." Booklist

"Smith has avoided pedantry and brought history to life in colorfully human terms. His vast narrative moves with cinematic flexibility in a flow of essay-like chapters." Publ Wkly

Includes bibliography

Followed by: The nation comes of age, entered in class 973.5

973.5 United States—1809-1845

Elting, John Robert

Amateurs, to arms!: a military history of the War of 1812; by John R. Elting. Algonquin Bks. 1991 353p il maps (Major battles and campaigns) $24.95   **973.5**

1. United States—History—1812-1815, War of 1812
ISBN 0-945575-08-4   LC 91-8705

"No other conflict in our history found us so unready or ill-prepared as the War of 1812, argues Elting, who here presents the military side of the war and emphasizes the amateurishness of the Americans. . . . This is a lively, well-written account." Publ Wkly

Includes bibliography

Schlesinger, Arthur M., 1917-
The age of Jackson; by Arthur M. Schlesinger, Jr. Little, Brown 1945 577p $22.50; pa $14.95 **973.5**

1. United States—History—1815-1861   2. United States—Politics and government—1815-1861
ISBN 0-316-77344-1; 0-316-77343-3 (pa)

The author shows the relation of Jacksonian democracy to law, industrialism, religion and literature, the beginning of the Free Soil movement and the growing intensity of sectional disputes

Includes bibliography

Smith, Page
The nation comes of age; a people's history of the ante-bellum years. McGraw-Hill 1981 1231p il o.p.; Penguin Bks. paperback available $16.95 **973.5**

1. United States—History—1815-1861
ISBN 0-14-012260-5 (pa)   LC 80-16889

Sequel to: The shaping of America, entered in class 973.4

"The opening chapter covers the election of 1828, the final chapter the election of 1860—Andrew Jackson to Abraham Lincoln. Besides politics, whole sections discuss religion, the family, women, utopian societies, literature, art, reformers." Choice

"A rich, popular history enlivened by well-chosen infusions from contemporary diaries and autobiographies." Saturday Rev

Followed by: Trial by fire, entered in class 973.7

Tocqueville, Alexis de
Democracy in America   **973.5**

1. United States—Social conditions 2. United States—Politics and government 3. Democracy 4. National characteristics, American

Hardcover and paperback editions available from various publishers

First part originally published in France, 1835; the second in 1840

Based partly on the French author's observations of American political and social conditions during a visit in 1831-1832. "It remains the best philosophical discussion of Democracy illustrated by the experience of the United States, up to the time when it was written, which can be found in any language." Pratt Alcove

973.6   United States—1845-1861

The **Mexican** War; by the editors of Time-Life Books, with text by David Nevin. Time-Life Bks. 1978 240p il maps (Old West) $19.93 **973.6**

1. United States—History—1845-1848, War with Mexico   LC 77-95212

This heavily illustrated book examines the causes, campaigns and soldiers of the war with Mexico

Includes bibliography

973.7   United States— Administration of Abraham Lincoln, 1861-1865. Civil War

Bishop, Jim, 1907-1987
The day Lincoln was shot; with illustrations selected and arranged by Stefan Lorant. Harper & Row 1955 304p il hardcover o.p. paperback available $6 **973.7**

1. Lincoln, Abraham, 1809-1865—Assassination
ISBN 0-06-080005-4 (pa)

The complete record of the dramatic events which occurred on the day Lincoln was shot in Ford's Theatre. The chapters start with one for 7 A.M. April 14, 1865 and close with one for 7 A.M. April 15, 1865

Includes bibliography

The **Blue** and the Gray; the story of the Civil War as told by participants; edited by Henry Steele Commager; foreword by Douglas Southall Freeman. rev and abridged. New Am. Lib. 1973 2v pa ea $5.99 **973.7**

1. United States—History—1861-1865, Civil War

Also available in a one-volume hardcover edition from Outlet

"A Mentor book"

An abridged edition of title first published 1950 by Bobbs-Merrill

Contents: v1 The nomination of Lincoln to the eve of Gettysburg (ISBN 0-451-62778-4); v2 The Battle of Gettysburg to Appomattox (ISBN 0-451-62640-0)

The author includes non-miliatry aspects and quotes from civilian accounts as well as military writings. Includes poetry as well as prose

Includes bibliographies

Boatner, Mark Mayo, 1921-
The Civil War dictionary; by Mark Mayo Boatner III; maps and diagrams by Allen C. Northrop and Lowell I. Miller. rev ed. McKay, D. 1988 974p maps $29.45 **973.7**

1. United States—History—1861-1865, Civil War—Dictionaries
ISBN 0-8129-1689-1   LC 87-40599

Also available in paperback from Vintage Bks.

First published 1959

"With more than 4,000 entries . . . this dictionary remains the most comprehensive and consistently accurate reference tool on the American Civil War. In addition to the biographical sketches there are entries relating to campaigns and battles, naval engagements, weapons, issues and incidents, military terms and definitions, politics, literature, and statistics." Choice

Includes bibliography

Brother against brother; Time-Life Books history of the Civil War; by the editors of Time-Life Books. Prentice Hall Press 1990 431p il maps $39.95 **973.7**

1. United States—History—1861-1865, Civil War
ISBN 0-13-921818-1   LC 89-23142

Based on the Time-Life Civil War series

Brother against brother—*Continued*

James McPherson "contributes some typically lucid and on-the-mark introductory comments. Deserving of special mention are the photographs, many of them—particularly those of Grant and Sherman—so rare as to impart a thrill to the reader who encounters them for the first time." Booklist

Catton, Bruce, 1899-1978

Gettysburg; the final fury. Doubleday 1974 114p il maps $17.95; pa $10.95   **973.7**

1. Gettysburg (Pa.), Battle of, 1863
ISBN 0-385-02060-0; 0-385-41145-6 (pa)

An account of the causes, events and consequences of the Civil War battle which turned the tide in favor of the Union forces

"What is truly distinguished about Catton's retelling of the Gettysburg story is his nearly total focus on the significant human and military details and, most important, the lucid serenity of his descriptive writing." Publ Wkly

Never call retreat. Doubleday 1965 555p maps (Centennial history of the Civil War, v3) o.p.   **973.7**

1. United States—History—1861-1865, Civil War
Available in hardcover from Buccaneer Bks.

This concluding volume of Catton's Civil War trilogy deals with the South's decline in strength and unity from December 1862, to Lee's surrender

Includes bibliographic references

Reflections on the Civil War; edited by John Leekley. Doubleday 1981 xxiv, 246p il o.p.; Berkley Bks. paperback available $4.95   **973.7**

1. United States—History—1861-1865, Civil War
ISBN 0-425-10495-8 (pa)   LC 79-6164

"In this work, Bruce [Catton] reflects on a wide range of subjects, including the cause and meaning of the Civil War; the actual experience of army life for the common soldier; and the major campaigns." Foreword

A stillness at Appomattox. Doubleday 1953 438p maps o.p.   **973.7**

1. Appomattox Campaign, 1865 2. United States—History—1861-1865, Civil War—Campaigns
Available in hardcover from P. Smith

Concluding volume of trilogy which began with Mr. Lincoln's army (1951) and Glory road (1952). This final volume of the author's study of the Army of the Potomac covers the period from early 1864 to April, 1865

The author's "approach is judicious, his interpretation unbiased and his coverage comprehensive." N Y Times Book Rev

Includes bibliography

Terrible swift sword. Doubleday 1963 559p maps (Centennial history of the Civil War, v2) $17.95   **973.7**

1. United States—History—1861-1865, Civil War
ISBN 0-385-02614-5

Also available in paperback from Washington Sq. Press

The second book in a trilogy, preceded by: The coming fury (1961) and followed by: Never call retreat, entered above

This volume begins just after the Battle of Bull Run in 1861 and continues until General McClellan was relieved of his command of the Army of the Potomac in 1862

Includes bibliography

This hallowed ground; the story of the Union side of the Civil War. Doubleday 1956 437p maps (Mainstream of America ser) $17.95   **973.7**

1. United States—History—1861-1865, Civil War
ISBN 0-385-04664-2

This history deals with the entire scope of the Civil War—from the months of unrest and hysteria that led to Fort Sumter through the Union victory

Includes bibliography

The **Causes** of the Civil War; edited by Kenneth M. Stampp. 3rd rev ed. Simon & Schuster 1991 255p pa $10   **973.7**

1. United States—History—1861-1865, Civil War—Causes 2. United States—History—1861-1865, Civil War—Sources
ISBN 0-671-75155-7   LC 91-36819

"A Touchstone book"

First published 1959 by Prentice-Hall

This book integrates the conclusions of various postwar historians with the thoughts of contemporary commentators like Jefferson Davis, Horace Greeley, and Lincoln. Political, cultural and economic aspects are emphasized

Includes bibliographic references

Chesnut, Mary Boykin Miller, 1823-1886

Mary Chesnut's Civil War; edited by C. Vann Woodward. Yale Univ. Press 1981 lviii, 886p il $48; pa $19.95   **973.7**

1. United States—History—1861-1865, Civil War 2. Confederate States of America
ISBN 0-300-02459-2; 0-300-02979-9 (pa)

     LC 80-36661

Mary Chesnut's "diary chronicles the early months of the Confederacy in Montgomery, gives a firsthand account of the attack on Fort Sumter, records events in Richmond and Columbia, S.C., during the critical periods of the war, and relates the return to the Chesnut family's plantation in Camden, S.C., after Lee's surrender at Appomattox." Christ Sci Monit

Includes bibliographic references

The **Civil** War almanac; executive editor, John S. Bowman; Ian V. Hogg and Antony Preson, technical consultants. Facts on File 1983 c1982 400p il maps o.p.; Pharos Bks. paperback available $14.95   **973.7**

1. United States—History—1861-1865, Civil War
ISBN 0-88687-401-7 (pa)   LC 82-15514

Also available G.K. Hall large print edition

"A Bison book"

This book is "divided into three main parts: a chronology spanning August 1619 (first slaves purchased by English colonists) to April 1877, which is subdivided by subject headings . . . a weapons and equipment section; and biographical listings: 133 brief sketches of personalities deemed important." Choice

"This is a fine one-volume reference work." Libr J

Davis, Burke, 1913-
The long surrender. Random House 1985
319p il $19.95; pa $12   **973.7**
1. Davis, Jefferson, 1808-1889 2. United States—History—1861-1865, Civil War 3. Confederate States of America
ISBN 0-394-52083-1; 0-679-72409-5 (pa)
LC 83-42767
A "chronicle of the Confederate leadership's flight and capture and the beginnings of the unrepentant Davis's role as 'martyr of the Lost Cause.' Based on papers, diaries and other primary sources, the book captures nicely the high emotions of the war's end." Publ Wkly
Includes bibliographic references

Sherman's march. Random House 1980
335p il maps $21.95; pa $11   **973.7**
1. United States—History—1861-1865, Civil War—Campaigns
ISBN 0-394-50739-8; 0-394-75763-7 (pa) LC 79-5550
The author "reconstructs Sherman's infamous, but vastly consequential march through Georgia and the Carolinas, which sent the Confederacy into its death throes. Basing his narrative on eyewitness accounts, Davis brings the event down to a personal level." Booklist
Includes bibliography

To Appomattox; nine April days, 1865.
Rinehart 1959 433p il maps o.p.; Eastern
Acorn Press paperback available $4.25
973.7
1. United States—History—1861-1865, Civil War 2. Appomattox Campaign, 1865
ISBN 0-915992-17-5 (pa)
"The story of the last nine days of the Civil War from the march on Richmond to the surrender at Appomattox. Quotations from diaries, letters, newspapers and military reports create a sense of immediacy as the reader follows each day's events in the city, in the Confederate camp, and with the Union Army." Publ Wkly
Includes bibliography

Davis, William C., 1946-
Battle at Bull Run; a history of the first major campaign of the Civil War. Doubleday 1977 298p il maps o.p.; Louisiana State Univ. Press paperback available $11.95   **973.7**
1. Bull Run, Battle of, 1861
ISBN 0-8071-0867-7 (pa)   LC 76-42322
In this account of the war's first major engagement Davis' "sketches of the commanders, which will particularly delight Civil War enthusiasts, delve into the officer's backgrounds and unusual characteristics and include critical appraisals of their leadership capabilities. In addition, Davis includes fascinating human interest stories about the troops." Libr J
Includes bibliography

Foote, Shelby
The Civil War; a narrative. Random
House 1958-1974 3v maps set $119.95, pa
$72   **973.7**
1. United States—History—1861-1865, Civil War
ISBN 0-394-49517-9; 0-394-749138
Volumes also available separately

Contents: v1 Fort Sumter to Perryville; v2 Fredericksburg to Meridian; v3 Red River to Appomattox
"In objectivity, in range, in mastery of detail, in beauty of language and feeling for the people involved, this work surpasses anything else on the subject." New Repub
Includes bibliography

Freeman, Douglas Southall, 1886-1953
Lee's lieutenants; a study in command.
Scribner 1942-1944 3v il maps v1-2 $60, v3
$65; pa ea $21   **973.7**
1. United States—History—1861-1865, Civil War—Campaigns 2. United States—History—1861-1865, Civil War—Biography 3. Confederate States of America
Contents: v1 Manassas to Malvern Hill (ISBN 0-684-15486-2; 0-684-8748-5); v2 Cedar Mountain to Chancellorsville (ISBN 0-684-15487-0; 0-684-18749-3); v3 Gettysburg to Appomattox (ISBN 0-684-15488-9; 0-684-18750-7)
A "detailed treatment of the military history of the Civil War as seen through the performance of the Confederate officers. The clarity of Freeman's description of battles lies in his use of only the information known to the Confederate officers at the time of the battle." Enoch Pratt Free Libr
Includes bibliography

Furgurson, Ernest B., 1929-
Chancellorsville, 1863; the souls of the brave. Knopf 1992 405p il maps $25; pa
$14   **973.7**
1. Chancellorsville, Battle of, 1863
ISBN 0-394-58301-9; 0-679-72831-7 (pa)
LC 91-47059
Furgurson presents an account of "the battle's separate phases, the strategic thinking on both sides, the confusion and hesitation in Richmond and Washington, and the events surrounding Stonewall Jackson's death." Choice
"Mr. Furgurson has written what should become the standard account of the battle. He is especially good at discussing both larger tactical issues and the experiences of ordinary soldiers. He is also evenhanded." N Y Times Book Rev
Includes bibliographic references

Glatthaar, Joseph T., 1956-
Forged in battle: the Civil War alliance of black soldiers and white officers. Free Press 1990 370p il $27   **973.7**
1. United States. Army—History 2. United States—History—1861-1865, Civil War 3. Black soldiers
ISBN 0-02-911815-8   LC 89-11620
Also available in paperback from New Am. Lib.
"In 1861 hardly anyone could picture so radical a notion as a black man wearing Union blue and carrying a rifle. . . . By the end of the war 180,000 blacks had served in the United States Colored Troops, commanded by 7,000 white officers. . . . [This book] is more social history than military narrative. 'My object is to explore the inner working of these black commands,' Mr. Glatthaar writes, 'to investigate conduct, attitudes, and experiences among the participants.'" N Y Times Book Rev
Includes bibliography

Jordan, Robert Paul

The Civil War; prepared by the Special Publications Division, National Geographic Society. National Geographic Soc. 1982 c1969 215p il maps $8.95   **973.7**

1. United States—History—1861-1865, Civil War
ISBN 0-87044-077-2   LC 82-18807
First published 1969

This account of the American Civil War offers an historical survey of the decades before the clash and descriptions of numerous battles, leaders and personalities
"A magnificent book. . . . Fascinating drawings, photographs, and paintings supplement the absorbing text." Keating. Build Bridges of Understanding Between Cultures

Includes bibliography

Katcher, Philip R. N.

The Civil War source book; [by] Philip Katcher. Facts on File 1992 318p il maps $35   **973.7**

1. United States—History—1861-1865, Civil War
ISBN 0-8160-2823-0   LC 92-8180

The author "focuses on the experiences, equipment, uniforms, and tactics of army, navy, and state forces of both sides. Short biographies of major figures and an annotated 'sources' section are provided, and illustrations and quotations or excerpts from first-person accounts abound." Libr J

Leckie, Robert

None died in vain; the saga of the American Civil War. HarperCollins Pubs. 1990 682p maps $29.95; pa $15   **973.7**

1. United States—History—1861-1865, Civil War
ISBN 0-06-016280-5; 0-06-092116-1 (pa)
     LC 89-45832

This account of the Civil War examines contributing social, political and economic causes, recounts major and minor battles, and provides biographical information about key people

Includes bibliography

Lee takes command: from Seven Days to Second Bull Run; by the editors of Time-Life Books. Time-Life Bks. 1984 176p il maps (Civil War) $19.93   **973.7**

1. Lee, Robert E. (Robert Edward), 1807-1870
2. Peninsular Campaign, 1862 3. Shenandoah Valley Campaign, 1862   LC 83-24382

This volume describes how the Confederate army under the command of Robert E. Lee thwarted a drive against the capital in Richmond, Virginia, by Union forces under George McClellan in June, 1862. Driving the enemy back in a series of battles called the Seven Days, Lee took the offensive and moved north in maneuvers climaxing in the second major battle at Bull Run in August, 1862. Illustrations include photographs, engravings, paintings and battle maps

Includes bibliography

Lincoln, Abraham, 1809-1865

The portable Abraham Lincoln; edited and with an introduction by Andrew Delbanco. Viking 1992 xxxvii, 341p il $25   **973.7**

1. United States—Politics and government—1815-1861
2. United States—Politics and government—1861-1865
ISBN 0-670-84088-2   LC 91-37488
Also available in paperback from Penguin Bks.
"The Viking portable library"
Material drawn from Speeches and writings, entered below
"This collection shows Lincoln at work in law, politics, and war. All the great Lincoln works are here, with the added bonus of several personal memos that show Lincoln's humor." Libr J

Includes bibliography

Speeches and writings; speeches, letters, and miscellaneous writings. Literary Classics of the U.S. 1989 2v (Lib. of America) set $70   **973.7**

1. United States—Politics and government—1815-1861
2. United States—Politics and government—1861-1865
ISBN 0-940450-68-2

Volumes available separately at $35
Also available in an abridged one-volume paperback edition from Vintage Bks. with title: Selected speeches and writings
[v1] 1832-1858; [v2] 1859-1865

These volumes are based upon The collected works of Abraham Lincoln (1953). Included are all seven of the Lincoln-Douglas debates, political speeches, business and personal letters, poems, and telegrams to generals in the field
"Replete with extremely helpful notes on the texts and an extensive chronology, this edition makes a momentous and thrilling addition to any . . . library." N Y Times Book Rev

Macdonald, John, 1945-

Great battles of the Civil War; foreword by John Keegan. Macmillan 1988 200p il maps $19.95; pa $22.95   **973.7**

1. United States—History—1861-1865, Civil War—Campaigns
ISBN 0-02-577300-3; 0-02-034554-2 (pa) LC 88-1782

The author "has selected 17 crucial Civil War engagements and applied computer mapping to their geography. . . . The cartography is accompanied by an intelligent text, clear graphs of force and loss ratios, and well-chosen illustrations. This unique Civil War atlas is valuable, if not indispensable, for library collections." Libr J

McPherson, James M.

Abraham Lincoln and the second American Revolution. Oxford Univ. Press 1991 173p $17.95; pa $8.95   **973.7**

1. Lincoln, Abraham, 1809-1865 2. United States—History—1861-1865, Civil War
ISBN 0-19-505542-X; 0-19-507606-0 (pa) LC 90-6885

A "volume of short essays that go right to the heart of the meaning of the war and Abraham Lincoln's role in it. How could the two sides have espoused such opposite notions of liberty? . . . And what, finally, did it all achieve? Such questions linger for many students of the war despite all the books. Mr. McPherson . . . goes right at them in crystal clear, well-reasoned,

McPherson, James M.—*Continued*
supremely informed essays." N Y Times Book Rev

Includes bibliographic references

Battle cry of freedom; the Civil War era. Oxford Univ. Press 1988 904p il maps (Oxford history of the United States) $39.95 **973.7**

1. United States—History—1861-1865, Civil War
ISBN 0-19-503863-0 LC 87-11045

Also available in paperback from Ballantine Bks.

This narrative looks at political and economic events from the Mexican War through Appomattox. Military campaigns and personalities are discussed

This volume "is comprehensive yet succinct, scholarly without being pedantic, eloquent but unrhetorical. It is compellingly readable." N Y Times Book Rev

Includes bibliography

Ordeal by fire. 2nd ed. McGraw-Hill 1993 2v il maps v1 $16.95; v2 $18.95 **973.7**

1. United States—History—1861-1865, Civil War 2. United States—History—1865-1898 3. Reconstruction (1865-1876) LC 92-23635

First published 1982 in one volume by Knopf

Contents: v1 The coming of war (ISBN 0-07-045837-5); v2 The Civil War (ISBN 0-07-045838-3)

The author "goes back to 1800 to explain the social, political, and economic developments leading up to the war, proceeds to the intricate maneuvers, civil and military, of the war itself, and continues through the tangle of interests and influences that brought Reconstruction and black progress to . . . [an] end in 1894." Atlantic [review of 1982 edition]

Includes bibliographic references

Nevin, David, 1927-
Sherman's march: Atlanta to the sea; by David Nevin and the editors of Time-Life Books. Time-Life Bks. 1986 175p il maps (Civil War) $19.93 **973.7**

1. Sherman, William T. (William Tecumseh), 1820-1891 2. United States—History—1861-1865, Civil War—Campaigns LC 86-5764

This illustrated volume portrays the destruction of civilian property and resources as Sherman marched across Georgia and through the Carolinas

Includes bibliography

Randall, J. G. (James Garfield), 1881-1953
The Civil War and Reconstruction; [by] J. G. Randall, David Donald. 2nd ed rev, with enlarged bibliography. Heath 1969 866p il maps $21 **973.7**

1. United States—History—1861-1865, Civil War 2. Reconstruction (1865-1876)
ISBN 0-669-06428-9

First published 1937

This documented account of American history includes the period from about 1850 to 1877. The causes and consequences of the Civil War are studied in detail, and comprise about two thirds of the book; about one third is devoted to the Reconstruction period

Royster, Charles
The destructive war; William Tecumseh Sherman, Stonewall Jackson, and the Americans. Knopf 1991 523p il maps $29.50; pa $15 **973.7**

1. Sherman, William T. (William Tecumseh), 1820-1891 2. Jackson, Stonewall, 1824-1863 3. United States—History—1861-1865, Civil War
ISBN 0-394-52485-3; 0-679-73878-9 (pa)
LC 90-26458

The author examines "the impact William Tecumseh Sherman and Thomas 'Stonewall' Jackson had on public thinking about the military conduct of the Civil War." Libr J

"Perhaps the achievement of Mr. Royster's book is not so much its ability to explain, which remains very considerable, but its power to make the reader feel the force of Civil War Americans' idea of violence." N Y Times Book Rev

Includes bibliographic references

Sears, Stephen W.
Landscape turned red; the Battle of Antietam. Ticknor & Fields 1983 431p il maps $18.95; pa $12.70 **973.7**

1. Antietam (Md.), Battle of, 1862
ISBN 0-89919-172-X; 0-395-65668-0 (pa)
LC 82-19519

Also available in paperback from Warner Bks.

This "account of the Battle of Antietam, the bloodiest day of the Civil War, is wide-ranging, detailed, and copiously documented. Stephen Sears . . . describes the tension-filled days preceding September 17, 1862, especially the political climate of Union pessimism and Confederate optimism. . . . The battle itself is then exhaustively recounted." Booklist

Includes bibliography

To the gates of Richmond; the Peninsula Campaign. Ticknor & Fields 1992 468p il maps $24.95 **973.7**

1. Peninsular Campaign, 1862
ISBN 0-89919-790-6 LC 92-6923

"The campaign on the peninsula between the James and York rivers in Virginia in the spring of 1862 was McClellan's major strategic effort and the first major Union offensive in the East. . . . Sears does an outstanding job in making intelligible an extremely complex campaign." Booklist

Includes bibliographic references

Shadows of the storm. Doubleday 1981 464p il (Image of war, 1861-1865, v1) $19 **973.7**

1. United States—History—1861-1865, Civil War—Pictorial works
ISBN 0-385-15466-6 LC 80-1659

"A project of the National Historical Society."

"The first in a series of six picture books called 'The Image of War: 1861-1865' [other volumes o.p.] The emphasis of this volume is placed on the early stages of the war. It contains over 650 photographs and is supported with articles by a number of well-known Civil War authors. . . . This volume alone is a valuable addition for any library." Choice

Smith, Page

Trial by fire; a people's history of the Civil War and Reconstruction. McGraw-Hill 1982 1038p o.p.; Penguin Bks. paperback available $20   **973.7**

1. United States—History—1861-1865, Civil War 2. Reconstruction (1865-1876)

ISBN 0-14-012261-3 (pa)   LC 81-18573

Sequel to: The nation comes of age, entered in class 973.5

In this fifth volume of his history of the United States, the author "gleans his material from diaries, letters and other writings of individuals ranging from Southern gentlewomen to black slaves. . . . This rich cross-section provides insights into virtually every emotion and attitude generated by the Civil War. . . . Smith's eye-opening examination of the Reconstruction era is important history for our time." Publ Wkly

Followed by: The rise of industrial America, entered in class 973.8

Stampp, Kenneth M. (Kenneth Milton)

And the war came; the North and the secession crisis, 1860-1861. Louisiana State Univ. Press 1950 331p il hardcover o.p. paperback available $12.95   **973.7**

1. United States—History—1861-1865, Civil War—Causes 2. United States—Politics and government—1815-1861

ISBN 0-8071-0101-X (pa)

Also available in hardcover from Greenwood Press

"Out of the complex pattern of events leading up to the Civil War, Kenneth Stampp has selected one thread and subjected it to keen examination. In doing so he illuminates the whole pattern. The object of his analysis is the evolution of northern public opinion regarding the mounting crisis which came to a climax in mid-April, 1861." Publisher's note

Includes bibliography

Still, William, 1821-1902

The Underground Railroad   **973.7**

1. Underground railroad 2. United States—History—1861-1865, Civil War

Reprint editions available from Ayer and from Johnson

First published 1872 by Porter & Coates

"A record of facts, authentic narratives, letters, &c., narrating the hardships, hairbreadth escapes and death struggles of the slaves in their efforts for freedom, as related by themselves and others, or witnessed by the author; together with sketches of some of the largest stockholders and most liberal aiders and advisers of the road." Title page

Ward, Geoffrey C.

The Civil War; an illustrated history; [by] Geoffrey C. Ward with Ken Burns and Ric Burns. Knopf 1990 425p il maps $60; pa $30   **973.7**

1. United States—History—1861-1865, Civil War

ISBN 0-394-56285-2; 0-679-74277-8 (pa)

LC 89-43475

This is a companion to a nine-part Public Broadcasting System documentary

The authors aim to "present the war as the central defining event of American history and of the lives of those Americans caught up in it. In four separate, additional essays, professional historians briefly discuss the causes of the war, emancipation, the politics of the war, and its long-term meaning." Libr J

Includes bibliographic references

Wert, Jeffry D.

Mosby's Rangers. Simon & Schuster 1990 384p il hardcover o.p. paperback available $11   **973.7**

1. Confederate States of America. Army. Virginia Cavalry Battalion, 43rd 2. United States—History—1861-1865, Civil War

ISBN 0-671-74745-2 (pa)   LC 90-37917

In this "history of Mosby's Rangers, one of the most successful irregular army units to operate during the Civil War, Wert details the guerrilla group's exploits which provided Jeb Stuart and Robert E. Lee with valuable intelligence on the enemy's movements." Booklist

"Well-researched, objectively written, this is a first-class history." Publ Wkly

Includes bibliographic references

Wheeler, Richard

Witness to Appomattox. Harper & Row 1989 255p il maps $19.95; pa $10.95   **973.7**

1. Appomattox Campaign, 1865

ISBN 0-06-016078-0; 0-06-092068-8 (pa)

LC 88-45532

The author links together the words of participants and eyewitnesses in a narrative of the Appomattox Campaign of 1865

"A distinctly engrossing book, one that is likely to be particularly useful for smaller Civil War collections." Booklist

Includes bibliography

Witness to Gettysburg. Harper & Row 1987 273p il maps $19.95   **973.7**

1. Gettysburg (Pa.), Battle of, 1863

ISBN 0-06-015760-7   LC 86-46108

Also available in paperback from New Am. Lib.

A "detailed, eyewitness version of the Battle of Gettysburg. The preparatory events by both civilians and soldiers, the skirmishes and marches, the agonizing three days of battle—all are authentically reenacted. The realism generated by the quotations that Wheeler cohesively spins into his narrative is enhanced by period maps and illustrations adapted from sketches or photographs made at the time of battle." Booklist

Includes bibliography

Wiley, Bell Irvin, 1906-

The life of Billy Yank; the common soldier of the Union. Bobbs-Merrill 1952 454p il o.p.; Louisiana State Univ. Press paperback available $11.95   **973.7**

1. United States. Army—Military life 2. United States—History—1861-1865, Civil War

ISBN 0-8071-0476-0 (pa)

"'The soldiers' own writings—their letters and diaries—are . . . used as chief source for a picture of the response of the Union men to the call to arms, their training, army life, reactions to Southerners they encoun-

Wiley, Bell Irvin, 1906—_Continued_
tered, opinions of Negroes, and comments on their Reb counterparts." Booklist

Includes bibliography

The life of Johnny Reb; the common soldier of the Confederacy. Bobbs-Merrill 1943 444p o.p.; Louisiana State Univ. Press paperback available $11.95   **973.7**
1. Confederate States of America. Army—Military life
2. United States—History—1861-1865, Civil War
ISBN 0-8071-0475-2 (pa)

"Composite biography of the ordinary soldier of the Confederacy—his behavior in camp and under fire, his food, clothing, weapons, religion, amusements, attitude toward women, and so on. Taken mostly from firsthand accounts in letters, diaries, and records." New Yorker

Includes bibliography

Williams, T. Harry (Thomas Harry), 1909-1979
Lincoln and his generals. Knopf 1952 363p il maps o.p.; McGraw-Hill paperback available $6.95   **973.7**
1. Lincoln, Abraham, 1809-1865—1 2. United States—History—1861-1865, Civil War—Campaigns
3. Generals
ISBN 0-07-553705-2 (pa)

Also available in hardcover from Dorset Press

"Lincoln in a new guise, as a great military strategist and forerunner of modern tactics in warfare. The book discusses the North's unpreparedness at the outbreak of the Civil War and the lack of competent generals until Grant and Sherman proved their abilities." Booklist

Includes bibliography

Wills, Garry, 1934-
Lincoln at Gettysburg; the words that remade America. Simon & Schuster 1992 317p $23; pa $12   **973.7**
1. Lincoln, Abraham, 1809-1865
ISBN 0-671-76956-1; 0-671-86742-3 (pa) LC 92-3546
The author "argues that in the Gettysburg Address Abraham Lincoln, with consummate skill, changed the Constitution from within, making the hope it embodies triumph over its words by insinuating the ringing affirmation of equality from the Declaration of Independence into people's minds as the foundation of the American Government." N Y Times Book Rev
This is a "tour de force that will cause much discussion and argument." Libr J

Includes bibliographic references

973.8 United States—Reconstruction period, 1865-1901

Connell, Evan S., 1924-
Son of the Morning Star. North Point Press 1984 441p il o.p.; HarperCollins Pubs. paperback available $12.95   **973.8**
1. Custer, George Armstrong, 1839-1876 2. Little Big Horn, Battle of the, 1876
ISBN 0-06-097003-0 (pa)   LC 84-60681

The author "explores the whole context of the defeat of General Custer at the Battle of the Little Bighorn." Booklist
This book is "impressive in its massive presentation of information, and in the conclusions it draws about the probable events that led to the fracas on the banks of the Little Bighorn. But its strength lies in the way the author has shaped his material." N Y Times Book Rev

Includes bibliography

Foner, Eric
Reconstruction; America's unfinished revolution, 1863-1877. Harper & Row 1988 xxvii, 690p il maps $29.95; pa $18   **973.8**
1. Reconstruction (1865-1876) 2. United States—History—1865-1898
ISBN 0-06-015851-4; 0-06-091453-X (pa)
LC 87-45615

"Incorporating much eyewitness material, this book emphasizes the centrality of the Black experience. The book also examines the themes of race and class, the remodeling of Southern society, and the national context. A complete, modern, scholarly text." N Y Public Libr Book of How & Where to Look It Up

Includes bibliography

Franklin, John Hope, 1915-
Reconstruction: after the Civil War. University of Chicago Press 1961 258p il (Chicago history of American civilization) hardcover o.p. paperback available $12.95
973.8
1. Reconstruction (1865-1876) 2. United States—History—1865-1898
ISBN 0-226-26076-3 (pa)

This is an "account of American life in a time of great challenge, unfamiliar problems, and uncertain leadership. Discusses the Radicals' effort to secure racial justice in the South, the fact that corruption existed not only in the South, and that some worthwhile measures emerged from 'carpetbag' legislatures." Guide to Read in Am Hist

Includes bibliography

Sandoz, Mari, 1896-1966
The Battle of the Little Bighorn. Lippincott 1966 191p maps (Great battles of history ser) o.p.; University of Neb. Press paperback available $6.95   **973.8**
1. Custer, George Armstrong, 1839-1876 2. Little Big Horn, Battle of the, 1876
ISBN 0-8032-9100-0 (pa)

Also available in hardcover from Amereon

"An account of the United States Army expedition against the Sioux Nation with emphasis on the political motives and ambitions of General Custer." Publ Wkly

Includes bibliography

Schlereth, Thomas J.

Victorian America; transformations in everyday life, 1876-1915. HarperCollins Pubs. 1991 363p (Everyday life in America) $30; pa $11   **973.8**

1. United States—Social life and customs
ISBN 0-06-016218-X; 0-06-092160-9 (pa)
LC 89-46555

The author surveys the objects, events, experiences, products and tastes that comprised what he terms America's Victorian culture (1876-1915) and shows how its values shaped modern life

"What a wonderful book. . . . Schlereth is no wry compiler of trivia. His analysis of social context reveals truly profound, intangible transformations in how and where Americans spent their time during four pivotal decades." Booklist

Includes bibliographic references

Smith, Page

The rise of industrial America; a people's history of the post-Reconstruction era, v6. McGraw-Hill 1984 965p il o.p.; Penguin Bks. paperback available $16.95   **973.8**

1. United States—History—1865-1898
ISBN 0-14-012262-1 (pa)
LC 83-9332

Sequel to: Trial by fire, entered in class 973.7

The sixth volume of the author's history of the United States "focuses on the fierce war between capital and labor that divided the country in the last quarter of the nineteenth century." Publisher's note

Followed by: America enters the world, entered in class 973.91

Stampp, Kenneth M. (Kenneth Milton)

The era of reconstruction, 1865-1877. Knopf 1965 228p o.p.; Random House paperback available $7.96   **973.8**

1. Reconstruction (1865-1876) 2. United States—Politics and government—1865-1898
ISBN 0-394-70388-X (pa)

A politicql history of the brief "radical" rule in the post Civil War South

Includes bibliography

Utley, Robert Marshall, 1929-

Cavalier in buckskin; George Armstrong Custer and the western military frontier; by Robert M. Utley. University of Okla. Press 1988 226p il maps (Oklahoma western biographies) $22.95; pa $10.95   **973.8**

1. Custer, George Armstrong, 1839-1876 2. Indians of North America—Wars 3. West (U.S.)—History
ISBN 0-8061-2150-5; 0-8061-2292-7 (pa) LC 88-5426

The author "gives the facts and some . . . theories behind the Custer mythology and tells how this legendary army officer worked hard to promote himself as a hero to the American people so he could rise through the army ranks." West Coast Rev Books

This "is a fair and full-bodied account that cogently interprets the facts, provides the proper psychological analysis, and offers solid grounding for the development of the considerable myth." Booklist

973.9   United States—1901-

Boorstin, Daniel J. (Daniel Joseph), 1914-

Democracy and its discontents; reflections on everyday America. Random House 1974 136p $5.95   **973.9**

1. United States—Civilization 2. United States—History—1900-1999 (20th century)
ISBN 0-394-49146-7

"Based on a series of lectures given at the University of Michigan, this collection of interpretative essays focuses on the problem of overabundance in . . . American life. Boorstin asserts that most of America's problems 'arise not so much from our failures as from our successes'—especially successes in technology." Libr J

Lemann, Nicholas

The promised land; the great black migration and how it changed America. Knopf 1991 401p $24.95   **973.9**

1. Blacks—Social conditions 2. Migration, Internal
ISBN 0-394-56004-3   LC 90-52951

Also available in paperback from McKay, D.

An "account of the migration of 6.5 million black people from rural South to urban North between 1910-1970." N Y Times Book Rev

The author "describes why the war on poverty did not succeed and why the civil rights movement yielded only partial victories in trying to win improvements. While Lemann's interviews establish the human drama of this process, his assessment of the consequences of this great movement both for African Americans and for the entire country raises substantial questions of justice and equality that cut to the heart of the social situation of the impoverished and oppressed today." Booklist

Includes bibliographic references

Manchester, William

The glory and the dream; a narrative history of America, 1932-1972. Little, Brown 1974 1397p $35   **973.9**

1. United States—History—1900-1999 (20th century) 2. United States—Civilization 3. United States—Social conditions
ISBN 0-316-54496-5

Also available in paperback from Bantam Bks.

This is a history of "the major events, sensational happenings, and news-making personalities from the Great Depression through the second inauguration of Richard Nixon." Libr J

Includes bibliography

Slotkin, Richard, 1942-

Gunfighter nation; the myth of the frontier in twentieth-century America. Atheneum Pubs. 1992 850p $40   **973.9**

1. Frontier and pioneer life—West (U.S.) 2. United States—Popular culture
ISBN 0-689-12163-6   LC 92-4446

Also available in paperback from HarperCollins Pubs.

"This is the final volume of Slotkin's . . . trilogy on the influence of the frontier on the American character (*Regeneration Through Violence*, [1973]; *The Fatal Environment*, [1985]). . . . On the premise that myth is spread by mass media, Slotkin examines numerous

Slotkin, Richard, 1942-—*Continued*
elements of popular culture ranging from James Fenimore Cooper's Hawkeye in *The last of the Mohicans* to John Wayne's *Green Berets* film to demonstrate how the myth affects American perceptions regarding foreign and domestic issues." Libr J

Includes bibliographic references

Stern, Jane
Jane & Michael Stern's encyclopedia of pop culture; an A to Z guide of who's who and what's what, from aerobics and bubble gum to Valley of the Dolls and Moon Unit Zappa. HarperCollins Pubs. 1992 593p il hardcover o.p. paperback available $17.50

973.9

1. United States—Popular culture
ISBN 0-06-096972-5 (pa)   LC 92-52546

A "compendium of more than 200 people, objects and phenomena that have entered the collective consciousness since WW II. . . . For anyone who wants to remember pet rocks, pop rocks and pop-tarts—and many more cultural artifacts—this volume is eminently browse-able." Publ Wkly

Terkel, Studs, 1912-
American dreams: lost and found. Pantheon Bks. 1980 xxv, 470p o.p.; Ballantine Bks. paperback available $6.99

973.9

1. United States—Civilization 2. United States—Social conditions
ISBN 0-345-32993-7 (pa)   LC 80-7703

A collection of statements by individual Americans expressing their personal aspirations and disappointments and feelings about the American dream, gathered by Terkel in his travels around the country

973.91   United States—1901-1953

Allen, Frederick Lewis, 1890-1954
The big change; America transforms itself, 1900-1950. Harper & Row 1952 308p hardcover o.p. paperback available $11

973.91

1. United States—History—1900-1999 (20th century)
2. United States—Social conditions 3. United States—Economic conditions—1900-1999 (20th century)
ISBN 0-06-132082-X (pa)

Also available in hardcover from Greenwood Press

Sketches of "some of the major changes that took place in the United States during the years 1900-1950. Art, literature, manners, morals, sports, business, politics, and the everyday living that took place during this period come under the scrutiny of the author." Guide to Read in Am Hist

Includes bibliographic references

Only yesterday; an informal history of the nineteen-twenties. Harper & Row 1957 370p hardcover o.p. paperback available $6.95

973.91

1. United States—History—1919-1933 2. United States—Social conditions 3. United States—Economic conditions—1919-1933
ISBN 0-06-080004-6 (pa)

"An account of the years from the spring of 1919 to . . . [1931]. It is a kaleidoscopic picture of American politics, society, manners, morals, and economic conditions." Booklist

Includes bibliographic references

Since yesterday; the nineteen-thirties in America, September 3, 1929-September 3, 1939. Harper & Row 1940 362p il hardcover o.p. paperback available $12

973.91

1. United States—History—1919-1933 2. United States—History—1933-1945 3. United States—Social conditions 4. United States—Economic conditions
ISBN 0-06-091322-3 (pa)

A look at the decade from September 3, 1929, when the great bull market reached its peak, to September 3, 1939, when England declared war on Germany. Since the years covered are those of the Great Depression, the chronicle focuses more politics and economics than manners, customs and the arts

Hofstadter, Richard, 1916-1970
The age of reform from Bryan to F.D.R. Knopf 1955 328, xxp $16.95; pa $9

973.91

1. United States—Politics and government—1900-1999 (20th century)
ISBN 0-394-41442-X; 0-394-70095-3 (pa)

This analysis of the reform movements in American politics from 1890-1940 reviews: (1) The agrarian uprising that found its expression in the Populist movement of the 1890's; (2) The Progressive movement from about 1900-1914; (3) The New Deal of the 1930's. Emphasis is placed upon the ideas of the leading political reformers

Includes bibliographic references

Schlesinger, Arthur M., 1917-
The crisis of the old order, 1919-1933. Houghton Mifflin 1988 557p (Age of Roosevelt) pa $11.95

973.91

1. Roosevelt, Franklin D. (Franklin Delano), 1882-1945 2. United States—History—1919-1933
ISBN 0-395-48903-2   LC 88-8210

"The American Heritage library"

A reissue of the title first published 1957

This is the first of three volumes which interpret the political, economic, social, and intellectual life of the United States during the time when Franklin D. Roosevelt was in office. This volume covers the years preceding his first term

Includes bibliographic references

Followed by: The coming of the New Deal, and The politics of upheaval, both entered in class 973.917

Smith, Page

America enters the world; a people's history of the Progressive era and World War I, v7. McGraw-Hill 1985 1089p il maps o.p.; Penguin Bks. paperback available $16.95 **973.91**

1. United States—History—1900-1999 (20th century) 2. United States—Politics and government—1900-1999 (20th century)

ISBN 0-14-012263-X (pa) LC 84-14372

Sequel to: The rise of industrial America, entered in class 973.8

This seventh volume of the author's history of the United States covers the "twenty-year period from 1901 to 1921 [that] was marked by the heightened war between capital and labor and the resultant progressive movement." Publisher's note

Followed by: Redeeming the time, entered below

Redeeming the time; a people's history of the 1920s and the New Deal, v8. McGraw-Hill 1987 1205p il o.p.; Penguin Bks. paperback available $18.95 **973.91**

1. United States—History—1900-1999 (20th century)

ISBN 0-14-012264-8 (pa) LC 86-2922

This is the concluding volume of the author's history of the United States. "Beginning with the Roaring Twenties—the time of Lindbergh and Fitzgerald, Sacco and Vanzetti—Smith sets the stage for the devastating Depression. . . . Here, the dominant figure is, of course, Franklin Delano Roosevelt." Publisher's note

"This gifted historian succeeds brilliantly in revealing historic turns through their more dramatic and colorful moments." Publ Wkly

Terkel, Studs, 1912-

Hard times; an oral history of the Great Depression. Pantheon Bks. 1970 462p hardcover o.p. paperback available $12
973.91

1. United States—Social conditions 2. United States—Economic conditions—1919-1933 3. United States—Economic conditions—1933-1945 4. Depressions, Economic

ISBN 0-394-74691-0 (pa)

"Persons of all ages, occupations, and classes scattered across the U.S. remember what they experienced or were told about the economic crisis of the 1930's. The result is a social document of immense interest." Booklist

973.917 United States—Administration of Franklin D. Roosevelt, 1933-1945

Larrabee, Eric

Commander in chief; Franklin Delano Roosevelt, his lieutenants, and their war. Harper & Row 1987 723p maps $25
973.917

1. Roosevelt, Franklin D. (Franklin Delano), 1882-1945 2. World War, 1939-1945—United States

ISBN 0-06-039050-6 LC 85-42609

Also available in paperback from Simon & Schuster

"A Cornelia and Michael Bessie book"

"Larrabee's story concerns 10 World War II heroes from the U.S., all in positions of high command. Chief of the group is FDR. . . . Larrabee's account focuses on Roosevelt's role in selecting commanders and directing their efforts." Booklist

"The book is well researched and superbly written—and studded with the author's blunt opinions." Publ Wkly

Includes bibliography

Lash, Joseph P., 1909-1987

Dealers and dreamers; a new look at the New Deal. Doubleday 1988 510p il $24.95
973.917

1. Cohen, Benjamin V., 1894-1983 2. Corcoran, Thomas 3. United States—History—1933-1945 4. United States—Economic conditions—1933-1945

ISBN 0-385-18716-5 LC 87-6706

The author "explores how character and personality traits influenced New Deal programs as he places primary focus on two particular leaders of the era, Benjamin V. Cohen and Thomas G. Corcoran. Adept at handling biographical, political, economic, and social angles simultaneously, Lash sees the New Deal as a once-in-a-lifetime combination of the practical and the ideological. Few writer compose history as fluidly and as warmly personalized as he." Booklist

Includes bibliography

Leuchtenburg, William Edward, 1922-

Franklin D. Roosevelt and the New Deal, 1932-1940; [by] William E. Leuchtenburg. Harper & Row 1963 393p il (New American nation ser) hardcover o.p. paperback available $14
973.917

1. Roosevelt, Franklin D. (Franklin Delano), 1882-1945 2. United States—History—1933-1945 3. United States—Economic conditions—1933-1945

ISBN 0-06-133025-6 (pa)

This treatment of Roosevelt's first two terms in office emphasizes the economic crisis and New Deal reforms. The author shows how social forces influenced government action: the San Francisco strike in 1934, the careers of Huey Long and Father Coughlin, the sharecroppers' revolt, and unemployment

This book "is comprehensive, logically organized, and written with clarity and detachment." Am Hist Rev

Includes bibliography

Roosevelt, Franklin D. (Franklin Delano), 1882-1945

FDR's fireside chats; edited by Russell D. Buhite and David W. Levy. University of Okla. Press 1992 xx, 326p $24.95 **973.917**

1. United States—Politics and government—1933-1945 2. United States—Foreign relations

ISBN 0-8061-2370-2 LC 91-50299

Transcriptions of Roosevelt's radio broadcasts concerning economics, social reform and international relations

Includes bibliographic references

Schlesinger, Arthur M., 1917-

The coming of the New Deal. Houghton Mifflin 1988 669p (Age of Roosevelt) pa $11.95　　　**973.917**

1. Roosevelt, Franklin D. (Franklin Delano), 1882-1945 2. United States—History—1933-1945
ISBN 0-395-48905-9　　　LC 88-8209

"The American Heritage library"

A reissue of the title first published 1959

"This second volume of 'The Age of Roosevelt' continues the work begun with 'The Crisis of the Old Order, 1919-1933' [class 973.91]. . . . The dramatic story of how representative democracy began the battle to conquer economic collapse is followed through the first two years of the New Deal." Libr J

Includes bibliographic references

The politics of upheaval. Houghton Mifflin 1988 749p (Age of Roosevelt) pa $11.95　　　**973.917**

1. Roosevelt, Franklin D. (Franklin Delano), 1882-1945 2. United States—History—1933-1945
ISBN 0-395-48904-0　　　LC 88-8207

"The American Heritage library"

A reissue of the title first published 1960

This third volume of The age of Roosevelt "concentrates on the turbulent years of 1935-1936—years when the revived American energies seem to be shooting off in every direction." Publisher's note

Includes bibliographic references

973.92　United States—1953-

Bloom, Allan David

The closing of the American mind. Simon & Schuster 1987 392p hardcover o.p. paperback available $10.95　　　**973.92**

1. Higher education 2. United States—Intellectual life
ISBN 0-671-65715-1 (pa)　　　LC 86-24768

This is the author's assessment of liberal arts education today. "In essence, he argues that over the last 25 years the academy has all but abandoned the intellectual and moral principles that have traditionally informed and given substance to liberal education, becoming prey to the enthusiasms—increasingly politicized—of the moment." N Y Times Book Rev

Cooke, Alistair, 1908-

America observed; from the 1940s to the 1980s; selected and introduced by Ronald A. Wells. Knopf 1988 232p $19.95 **973.92**

1. United States—Social life and customs 2. United States—Politics and government
ISBN 0-394-57342-0　　　LC 88-45441

"Reprinted here are 58 of [Cooke's] brief essays from 1946 to 1985, almost all of them from [the Guardian]. . . . Some deal with presidential politics in Washington, others with . . . life in small towns around the country." Libr J

Gitlin, Todd

The sixties; years of hope, days of rage. Bantam Bks. 1987 513p $19.95; pa $14.95　　　**973.92**

1. United States—History—1961-1974 2. United States—Social conditions 3. Students—Political activity
ISBN 0-553-05233-0; 0-553-34601-6 (pa)
　　　LC 87-47575

"Though ex-SDS leader Gitlin occasionally falls prey to the self-indulgence that snares most sixties' commentators, his analysis of the decade's politics is thought-provoking and clearheaded. Rather than singing the familiar hymn of praise to youthful idealism, Gitlin carefully dissects why the activist spirit developed when it did and what its legacy has been." Am Libr

Includes bibliography

Goodwin, Richard N.

Remembering America; a voice from the sixties. Little, Brown 1988 552p $19.95　　　**973.92**

1. United States—Politics and government—1961-1974
ISBN 0-316-32024-2　　　LC 88-15596

Also available in paperback from HarperCollins Pubs.

The author, a speechwriter for John Kennedy, Robert Kennedy, Eugene McCarthy and Lyndon Johnson, recounts his experiences in politics from the late 1950's through 1968

Habits of the heart; individualism and commitment in American life; [by] Robert N. Bellah [et al.] University of Calif. Press 1985 355p $29.95　　　**973.92**

1. National characteristics, American 2. United States—Social life and customs 3. United States—History—1900-1999 (20th century)
ISBN 0-520-05388-5　　　LC 84-16370

Also available in paperback from HarperCollins Pubs.

This "study is an attempt to see if there have been any significant changes in the way Americans think and behave in regard to their private and public lives since Tocqueville undertook his famous analysis in the 1800s." Libr J

"Blending interviews with historical analysis, this report offers a telling portrait of the isolated American. It should be noted that the vast majority of subjects interviewed were white and middle-class, and roughly half, it appears, live in California." Publ Wkly

Kuralt, Charles, 1934-

On the road with Charles Kuralt. Putnam 1985 316p il o.p.; Fawcett Bks. paperback available $5.95　　　**973.92**

1. United States—Social life and customs 2. United States—Description
ISBN 0-449-13067-3 (pa)　　　LC 85-6330

"As a CBS reporter specializing in 'soft' news, Kuralt has been roaming around the U.S. since 1967 in search of 'just plain folks.' Some 100 of the television interviews that resulted from that search have been transcribed for this collection. Loosely organized by themes emphasizing the individuality, altruism, and humor that characterize small town and rural Americans, the interviews and anecdotes are consistently entertaining." Booklist

Mills, C. Wright (Charles Wright), 1916-1962

The power elite. Oxford Univ. Press 1956
423p $39.95; pa $13.95   **973.92**

1. United States—Civilization 2. United States—Social
conditions 3. Power (Social sciences)
ISBN 0-19-500020-X; 0-19-500680-1 (pa)

An "analysis of the elite of America: celebrities, admirals and generals, politicians, businessmen, and their
relation to the society they lead." Chicago Public Libr

Includes bibliographic references

Moyers, Bill

A world of ideas; conversations with
thoughtful men and women about American
life today and the ideas shaping our future.
Doubleday 1989 513p il $39.95; pa $25
    973.92

1. United States—Civilization 2. United States—Politics and government—1981-
ISBN 0-385-26278-7; 0-385-26346-5 (pa) LC 89-1109

"This book is a compilation of the 41 interviews that
Moyers conducted for his 1988 PBS TV series, [a] mix
of authors, scientists, educators, and philosophers,
including the late Barbara Tuchman on the lessons of
history; Tom Wolfe on political activism on the local
scale; and former New York Public Library Director Vartan Gregorian." Libr J

A world of ideas II; public opinions from
private citizens; Andie Tucher, editor.
Doubleday 1990 284p il $35; pa $22.95
    973.92

1. United States—Civilization 2. United States—Politics and government—1981-
ISBN 0-385-41664-4; 0-385-41665-2 (pa)
    LC 90-38334

"This collection encompasses 29 more interviews,
including conversations with writer Maxine Hong Kingston, theater director Peter Sellars, medical researcher
Jonas Salk, and journalist William L. Shirer." Libr J

Smith, Hedrick

The power game; how Washington works.
Random House 1988 xxii, 793p $24.95
    973.92

1. United States—Politics and government—1974-1989
2. Power (Social sciences)
ISBN 0-394-55447-7   LC 87-42669

Also available in paperback from Ballantine Bks.

The author "relies primarily on anecdotes and case
studies from the Reagan era to illustrate how the use
of power determines the effectiveness of government."
Libr J

Smith "has an insider's awareness of the alliances,
machinations and turf-battles that make the capital work;
he knows what he is talking about." Economist

Includes bibliography

Stevens, Jay

Storming heaven: LSD and the American
dream. Atlantic Monthly Press 1987 396p
o.p.; HarperCollins Pubs. paperback available
$13   **973.92**

1. LSD (Drug) 2. Counter culture 3. United States—
Social conditions
ISBN 0-06-097172-X (pa)   LC 87-1191

The author seeks to trace the use of hallucinogenic
drugs in America from the first synthesis of LSD in
1943 to its role in the counterculture of the 1960's

This is "the most compelling account yet of how these
hallucinogenic, or 'psychedelic,' drugs became an explosive force in postwar American history." Newsweek

Includes bibliography

White, Theodore H., 1915-1986

America in search of itself; the making
of the President, 1956-1980. Harper & Row
1982 465p $15.95   **973.92**

1. United States—Politics and government—1900-1999
(20th century) 2. Presidents—United States—Election
ISBN 0-06-039007-7   LC 81-47679

Also available in paperback from Warner Bks.

"A Cornelia & Michael Bessie book"

The author interprets "the forces that diminished our
'culture of hope' and led to the repudiation of liberality
signaled by the 1980 election." Publ Wkly

"It is difficult to read this book . . . without being
seduced by [White's] rare literary grace, his matchless
knowledge of the political system." Harpers

973.921 United States—Administration of Dwight D. Eisenhower, 1953-1961

Branch, Taylor

Parting the waters: America in the King
years, 1954-63. Simon & Schuster 1988
1064p il hardcover o.p. paperback available
$16   **973.921**

1. King, Martin Luther, 1929-1968 2. United States—
History—1953-1961 3. Blacks—Civil rights
ISBN 0-671-68742-5 (pa)   LC 88-24033

This history of the American civil rights movement
from 1954 to 1963 focuses on the life of Dr. Martin
Luther King

The author "has searched out the hidden reality and
often tragic human drama of the King years. On his
best pages, the past, miraculously, seems to spring back
to life. King himself appears human, all too human. Yet
when the reader is done, his remarkable virtues and
ordinary vices seem of a piece, the component parts of
a coherent, towering personality." Newsweek

Includes bibliography

973.922 United States— Administration of John F. Kennedy, 1961-1963

Bernstein, Irving, 1916-
Promises kept; John F. Kennedy's new frontier. Oxford Univ. Press 1991 342p il $24.95   **973.922**
1. Kennedy, John F. (John Fitzgerald), 1917-1963
2. United States—Politics and government—1961-1974
3. United States—Economic policy 4. United States—Social policy
ISBN 0-19-504641-2   LC 90-33287

"Considering in turn the major policy decisions—civil rights, taxes, unemployment, education, Medicare, and the Peace Corps—Bernstein traces Kennedy's selection of advisers and directors on each issue, uses the vast quantity of written literature to piece together the president's decision-making process, explains the actions he took, and then calculates the probability that the policy would have been successfully implemented." Booklist

Includes bibliographic references

Brugioni, Dino A.
Eyeball to eyeball; the inside story of the Cuban missile crisis; edited by Robert F. McCort. Random House 1991 622p il $35
973.922
1. Cuban Missile Crisis, Oct. 1962
ISBN 0-679-40523-2   LC 91-52820

The author, a former supervisor of aerial reconnaissance photographs for the Central Intelligence Agency, offers an account of the Cuban missile crisis with special emphasis on the role played by the intelligence community
"This is a solid, gripping, detailed chronicle of the crisis." Publ Wkly

Includes bibliographic references

Halberstam, David, 1934-
The best and the brightest. 20th anniversary ed. Random House 1992 xx, 688p $30   **973.922**
1. United States—Politics and government—1961-1974
2. United States—Foreign relations—Vietnam 3. Vietnam—Foreign relations—United States
ISBN 0-679-41062-7   LC 91-51020
Also available in paperback from Fawcett Bks.
First published 1972

"The author describes analytically rather than narratively, how the Kennedy-Johnson intellectual (McNamara, Bundy, Rusk, Ball, Taylor, et al.) men praised as 'the best and the brightest' men of this century, became the architects of the disastrous American policy of Indochina." Libr J

Includes bibliography

Kennedy, Robert F., 1925-1968
Thirteen days; a memoir of the Cuban missile crisis; with introductions by Robert S. McNamara and Harold Macmillan. Norton 1969 224p il hardcover o.p. paperback available $6.95   **973.922**
1. Cuban Missile Crisis, Oct. 1962 2. United States—Politics and government—1961-1974 3. United States—Foreign relations—Soviet Union 4. Soviet Union—Foreign relations—United States
ISBN 0-393-09896-6 (pa)
Also available in paperback from New Am. Lib.
A behind-the-scenes account of the Cuban Missile Crisis of 1962. Includes reproductions of pertinent documents and speeches by both President Kennedy and Nikita Khrushchev

Lane, Mark, 1927-
Plausible denial; was the CIA involved in the assassination of JFK? Thunder's Mouth Press 1991 393p il hardcover o.p. paperback available $13.95   **973.922**
1. Kennedy, John F. (John Fitzgerald), 1917-1963—Assassination 2. United States. Central Intelligence Agency
ISBN 1-56025-048-8 (pa)   LC 91-30931

"This volume describes Lane's . . . probe into CIA involvement in Kennedy's death, with special focus on his 1978 defense of a small newspaper against renowned spy/Watergater E. Howard Hunt's charges of libel." Booklist
"Lane's book is a substantive contribution to the field, which will undoubtedly be controversial." Libr J

Includes bibliographic references

Wofford, Harris, 1926-
Of Kennedys and Kings; making sense of the sixties. University of Pittsburgh Press 1992 516p il $29.95; pa $16.95   **973.922**
1. Kennedy, John F. (John Fitzgerald), 1917-1963
2. Kennedy, Robert F., 1925-1968 3. King, Martin Luther, 1929-1968 4. United States—Politics and government—1961-1974
ISBN 0-8229-3832-4; 0-8229-5808-2 (pa)

LC 92-12624

First published 1980 by Farrar, Straus & Giroux

The title refers to President Kennedy and his brother Robert, and to Martin Luther King, Jr. his father and his wife Coretta. The author, who "worked in the 1960 Kennedy campaign, served as JFK's advisor on civil rights, helped Sargent Shriver set up the Peace Corps, and was involved in the civil rights movement . . . combines memoir and narrative in this . . . treatment, mingling others' opinions with his own." Libr J

973.924 United States— Administration of Richard Nixon, 1969-1974

Bernstein, Carl
All the President's men; by Carl Bernstein [and] Bob Woodward. Simon & Schuster 1974 349p il hardcover o.p. paperback available $9.95   **973.924**

1. Washington post 2. Watergate Affair, 1972-1974
ISBN 0-671-64644-3 (pa)

The two Washington Post reporters whose investigative journalism first revealed the Watergate scandal tell the way it happened from the first suspicions, through the trail of false leads, lies, secrecy, and high-level pressure, to the final moments when they were able to put the pieces of the puzzle together and write the series that won the Post a Pulitzer Prize

Greene, John Robert, 1955-
The limits of power; the Nixon and Ford administrations. Indiana Univ. Press 1992 296p $29.95   **973.924**

1. Nixon, Richard M. (Richard Milhous), 1913-1994
2. Ford, Gerald R., 1913- 3. United States—Politics and government—1961-1974 4. United States—Politics and government—1974-1989
ISBN 0-253-32637-0   LC 91-47014

This "analysis of eight years of Republican leadership (1969-1977) seeks to explain why the 'Myth of the Omnipotent President,' as Greene dubs it, came to an end. . . . Greene recounts the familiar Watergate story, then shows how Richard Nixon left the office of President 'infinitely more limited' than it had been when he was sworn in. He goes on to describe the populace's brief romance with Gerald Ford, which ended abruptly when Ford pardoned Nixon." Publ Wkly

Includes bibliographic references

Kutler, Stanley I.
The wars of Watergate; the last crisis of Richard Nixon. Knopf 1990 733p il $24.95   **973.924**

1. Nixon, Richard M. (Richard Milhous), 1913-1994
2. Watergate Affair, 1972-1974 3. United States—Politics and government—1961-1974
ISBN 0-394-56234-8   LC 89-43351

Also available in paperback from Norton

The author "provides comprehensive documentation detailing the Watergate crisis. Though the facts are familiar, the passage of time and the availability of new material afford a fresh historical perspective." Booklist

Includes bibliography

Nixon, Richard M. (Richard Milhous), 1913-1994
From the President; Richard Nixon's secret files; edited by Bruce Oudes. Harper & Row 1988 lxvi, 661p $22.50; pa $12.95   **973.924**

1. Watergate Affair, 1972-1974 2. United States—Politics and government—1961-1974
ISBN 0-06-015953-7; 0-06-091621-4 (pa)
    LC 88-45050

This volume contains a "sampling of the Nixon 'Special Files,' opened to the public by the National Archives in May 1987. A useful contribution to documenting the Nixon administration, the collection reveals attitudes, goals, and priorities of the President and his staff. Chronologically arranged, the documents range from trivial notes to important position papers written by Nixon, H.R. Haldeman, Patrick Buchanan, Charles Colson (whose contributions outnumber Nixon's), and other staff members." Choice

Woodward, Bob, 1943-
The final days; [by] Bob Woodward, Carl Bernstein. Simon & Schuster 1976 476p il o.p. paperback available $8.95   **973.924**

1. Nixon, Richard M. (Richard Milhous), 1913-1994
2. Watergate Affair, 1972-1974 3. United States—Politics and government—1961-1974
ISBN 0-671-69087-6 (pa)

The title refers to the final days of the Nixon Presidency. The authors have "constructed a two-part narrative, the first half covering the period from April 30, 1973—the day John Dean was fired as White House counsel—until late July 1974, and the second half covering the last two weeks in detail." N Y Times Book Rev

973.926 United States— Administration of Jimmy Carter, 1977-1981

Haas, Garland A., 1919-
Jimmy Carter and the politics of frustration. McFarland & Co. 1992 217p $25.95   **973.926**

1. Carter, Jimmy, 1924- 2. United States—Politics and government—1974-1989
ISBN 0-89950-705-0   LC 91-51000

"Haas's treatment of the Carter presidency examines how and why Carter gained the Democratic nomination and the presidency; his relationship with Congress, the media, and members of his administration; and his defeat by Ronald Reagan." Choice

Includes bibliographic references

973.927 United States— Administration of Ronald Reagan, 1981-1989

Abrams, Elliott
Undue process; a story of how political differences are turned into crimes. Free Press 1993 243p $22.95   **973.927**

1. Iran-Contra Affair, 1985-1990
ISBN 0-02-900167-6   LC 92-24945

"The former Assistant Secretary of State for Inter-American Affairs from mid-summer 1985 through the end of the Reagan Administration was indicted by the [office of] Independent Counsel in the fall of 1990 for his role in the Iran-Contra affair. He recounts here the events between the indictment and his guilty plea on Oct. 7, 1991 on two counts of withholding information from Congress. Abrams' account bristles with indignation not only over the actions of the Independent Counsel

Abrams, Elliott—_Continued_

but also at the Reagan Administration's failure to stand by him." Libr J

Bennett, William John, 1943-

The de-valuing of America; the fight for our culture and our children; [by] William J. Bennett. Summit Bks. 1992 271p $20; pa $12   **973.927**

1. Social values 2. United States—Social conditions 3. United States—Moral conditions

ISBN 0-671-68305-5; 0-671-79719-0 (pa)

LC 91-42629

"This volume chronicles my decade of service in the Reagan and Bush administrations, as chairman of the National Endowment for the Humanities, Secretary of Education, and director of the Office of National Drug Control Policy." Preface

"This book is Bennett's war diary, consisting of dispatches from the front in the struggle between, on the one hand, the combined forces of Washington's 'Beltway' culture, academia, and the media and, on the other hand, mainstream America and its traditional bourgeois values." Commentary

Draper, Theodore, 1912-

A very thin line; the Iran-contra affairs. Hill & Wang 1991 690p il $27.95
                                                 973.927

1. Iran-Contra Affair, 1985-1990

ISBN 0-8090-9613-7   LC 90-21751

Also available in paperback from Simon & Schuster

The author has "reconstructed from the voluminous documentary records the Washington connection that linked the arms sales to Khomeini's Iran with the support of the anti-Sandinista forces in Nicaragua." Libr J

Includes bibliographic references

Johnson, Haynes Bonner, 1931-

Sleepwalking through history; America in the Reagan years; [by] Haynes Johnson. Norton 1991 524p il $24.95   **973.927**

1. Reagan, Ronald, 1911- 2. United States—Politics and government—1974-1989 3. United States—History—1974-1989

ISBN 0-393-02937-9   LC 90-38623

Also available in paperback from Anchor Bks.

This is a study of American politics, history, and culture during the 1980s

The author "concentrates on major events like the Iran-contra affair and the Wall street scene, and briefly touches on other domestic scandals. . . . Not the definitive history of the 1980s, but recommended as an important book by an important author." Libr J

Includes bibliographic references

Speakes, Larry Melvin

Speaking out; the Reagan presidency from inside the White House; [by] Larry Speakes with Robert Pack. Scribner 1988 322p il o.p.; Avon Bks. paperback available $4.95
                                                 973.927

1. Reagan, Ronald, 1911- 2. United States—Politics and government—1974-1989

ISBN 0-380-70726-8 (pa)   LC 88-3247

"Starting with the 1981 assassination attempt on President Reagan that crippled press secretary Jim Brady, whom he succeeded, Speakes . . . recounts his part as White House spokesman in the six years that followed." Publ Wkly

This book "will be looked at over the years by those researchers trying to get a better fix on what went on and what went wrong with the Reagan administration." West Coast Rev Books

Terkel, Studs, 1912-

The great divide; second thoughts on the American dream. Pantheon Bks. 1988 439p $18.95   **973.927**

1. United States—Social conditions

ISBN 0-394-57053-7   LC 88-42543

Also available in paperback from Avon Bks.

"Ordinary people reflect on the issues of the 1980s—Reaganism, greed, farming, race relations, education, and religion. . . . The 'divide' exists when inner beliefs conflict with public policy; when family members harbor differing views on heartfelt issues; when the ideas of the 1960s are compared with those of the 1980s. . . . There are no answers here, just very timely and provocative commentary in Terkel's inimitable style." Libr J

973.928 United States— Administration of George Bush, 1989-1993

Woodward, Bob, 1943-

The commanders. Simon & Schuster 1991 398p il o.p.; Pocket Bks. paperback available $5.99   **973.928**

1. Bush, George, 1924- 2. United States. Dept. of Defense 3. United States—Foreign relations 4. Persian Gulf War, 1991

ISBN 0-671-76960-X (pa)   LC 91-13037

This book discusses "top-level White House [and] Pentagon decisionmaking, first in the attack on Panama, and then in the 5½ months of diplomatic and especially military maneuvering that preceded the war with Iraq." Christ Sci Monit

974.4 Massachusetts

Bradford, William, 1588-1657

Of Plymouth Plantation, 1620-1647; the complete text, with notes and an introduction by Samuel Eliot Morison. Knopf 1952 xliii, 448p maps $24   **974.4**

1. Massachusetts—History—1600-1775, Colonial period 2. Pilgrims (New England colonists)

ISBN 0-394-43895-7

Also available in paperback from Modern Lib.

Bradford, William, 1588-1657—*Continued*
Written between 1630 and 1650; first published 1856
with title: History of Plymouth Plantation

"The opening book sketches the origin of the
Separatist movement, the flight from England to Holland,
the settlement at Leiden, the plans for the settlement
in New England, and the *Mayflower* voyage. The second
book, which includes the major part of the history, is
in the form of annals from 1620 to 1646, and describes
every aspect of the life of the Pilgrims. Besides being
a primary historical source, the work has artistic value
because of its dignified, sonorous style, deriving from the
Geneva Bible." Oxford Companion to Am Lit. 5th edition

974.8   Pennsylvania

Serrin, William
Homestead; the glory and tragedy of an
American steel town. Times Bks. 1992 xxvi,
452p $25   **974.8**
1. Homestead (Pa.) 2. Steel industry
ISBN 0-8129-1886-X   LC 90-50246
Also available in paperback from Vintage Bks.

The author traces the history of Homestead, Pennsylvania, a town that grew up around the Homestead Steel
Works in the 1880s. The mill closed in 1986. Serrin also
discusses the history of the labor movement in the town

This book "sympathetically presents business, labor,
and human history from a strongly pro-labor working-
class perspective. . . . This is not a scholarly work but
a moving biography of a town that the general reader
will find informative." Libr J

Includes bibliographic references

975   Southeastern United States. Southern States

Cash, Wilbur Joseph, 1900-1941
The mind of the South; with a new
introduction by Bertram Wyatt-Brown.
Vintage Bks. 1991 xliv, 444p pa $12   **975**
1. Southern States—Civilization
ISBN 0-679-73647-6   LC 91-50042
First published 1941 by Knopf

A psychological, cultural, and social history of the old
South

975.3   District of Columbia (Washington)

Brinkley, David
Washington goes to war. Knopf 1988 286p
il $18.95   **975.3**
1. World War, 1939-1945—United States 2. Washington (D.C.)—History
ISBN 0-394-51025-9   LC 87-46017
Also available in paperback from Ballantine Bks.

"Brinkley's account of Washington, D.C., in the hal-
cyon days of World War II, when the capitol was the
fulcrum of world power and human folly, is exceptionally
well written and enriched with wry wit and engaging
anecdotes." Libr J

Includes bibliography

975.5   Virginia

Bridenbaugh, Carl, 1903-1992
Jamestown, 1544-1699. Oxford Univ. Press
1980 199p il $40   **975.5**
1. Jamestown (Va.)—History
ISBN 0-19-502650-0   LC 79-13989

This is an account of the earliest permanent English
settlement in the New World. The author relies almost
exclusively on the surviving original sources as he seeks
to revise the accepted ideas about Virginia and correct
many sentimental myths. He also deals with the economic and social life of the community, and assesses the
early attempts at self-government in the town

Includes bibliography

975.8   Georgia

Carter, Jimmy, 1924-
Turning point; a candidate, a state, and
a nation come of age. Times Bks. 1992 xxv,
223p il $22   **975.8**
1. Georgia—Politics and government
ISBN 0-8129-2079-1   LC 92-53671
Also available Thorndike Press large print edition and
in paperback from Random House

The former president gives an account of his first
political campaign, in which he successfully challenged
the old regime for a seat in the Georgia State Senate
in 1962

"The story of how Carter and a few loyal friends saw
this episode through to success is good reading for
anyone who cares about democracy. It's a simply told
tale, but the author acknowledges the complexities of the
experience." Christ Sci Monit

Foxfire [1]-10. Doubleday 1972-1993 10v il
                               975.8
1. Country life—Georgia 2. Appalachian region—
Social life and customs 3. Handicraft

Editors: v1-6 Eliot Wigginton; v7 Paul F. Gillespie;
v8-9 Eliot Wigginton and Margie Bennett; v10 George
P. Reynolds and Susan Walker
First book in series has title: The Foxfire book

Available: v1 $15.95, pa $14 (ISBN 0-385-07350-X;
0-385-07353-4); v2 pa $14 (ISBN 0-385-02267-0); v3 pa
$14 (ISBN 0-385-02272-7); v4 pa $14 (ISBN 0-385-12087-
7); v5 $19.95, pa $14 (ISBN 0-385-14307-9; 0-385-14308-
7); v6 $14.95, pa $14 (ISBN 0-385-15271-X; 0-385-15272-
8); v7 $19.95, pa $14 (ISBN 0-385-15243-4; 0-385-15244-
2); v8 pa $14 (ISBN 0-385-17741-0); v9 $24.95, pa $14
(ISBN 0-385-17743-7; 0-385-17744-5); v10 $30, pa $14
(ISBN 0-385-46910-1; 0-385-42276-8)

"A chronicle of the economic, historic, and cultural
changes of an Appalachian village as perceived through
the inquisitive minds of its younger generation. . . .
Begun . . . as an experiment in getting students more
directly involved in their classwork, the 'Foxfire' volumes
have developed into an enduring example of a practical
and effective educational philosophy." Booklist

**Foxfire: 25 years; edited by Eliot Wigginton
and his students. Anchor Bks. 1991 xxi,
359p il $24.95; pa $14.95   975.8**
1. Country life—Georgia 2. Appalachian region—
Social life and customs 3. Handicraft
ISBN 0-385-41345-9; 0-385-41346-7 (pa)
                                LC 90-22834

Foxfire: 25 years—*Continued*

An "oral history of both the school and the publications [entered above] whose educational philosophy sparked 25 years of experimentation and achievement among the residents of Appalachia." Booklist

976.1 Alabama

Agee, James, 1909-1955

Let us now praise famous men; three tenant families; [by] James Agee, Walker Evans; with an introduction to the new edition by John Hersey. Houghton Mifflin 1988 c1941 liv, 471p il $24.95; pa $12.95 **976.1**

1. Alabama—Social conditions 2. Farm tenancy
ISBN 0-395-48901-6; 0-395-48897-4 (pa)
LC 88-18110

First published 1941

This republication of the classic work based on a 1936 journalistic assignment contains "about twice as many photographs [by Evans] as the original contained. These photographs are all snapshots in black and white and contain a story in themselves; they were not meant to illustrate but, as the original preface says, 'they and the text are coequal, mutually independent, and fully collaborative.' The book is an account of the actual daily lives of three families of tenant farmers." Best Sellers

Maharidge, Dale

And their children after them; the legacy of Let us now praise famous men: James Agee, Walker Evans, and the rise and fall of cotton in the South; [by] Dale Maharidge and Michael Williamson; with a foreword by Carl Mydans. Pantheon Bks. 1989 xxiv, 262p il $24.95; pa $14.95 **976.1**

1. Agee, James, 1909-1955 2. Evans, Walker, 1903-1975 3. Alabama—Social conditions 4. Alabama—Description 5. Farm tenancy
ISBN 0-394-57766-3; 0-679-72878-3 (pa)
LC 88-43136

"Maharidge and Williamson have revisited, photographed, and interviewed the surviving members and descendants of the Gudger, Ricketts, and Woods families shown in [the title entered above]." Libr J

976.4 Texas

The **Texans**; by the editors of Time-Life Books; with text by David Nevin. Time-Life Bks. 1975 240p il maps (Old West) $19.93 **976.4**

1. Texas—History

Text and numerous illustrations portray the history of Texas and the pioneers and colonizers that settled in the territory

Includes bibliography

978 Western United States

The **Chroniclers**; by the editors of Time-Life Books; with text by Keith Wheeler. Time-Life Bks. 1976 240p il (Old West) $19.93 **978**

1. Journalists 2. West (U.S.)—History 3. Frontier and pioneer life—West (U.S.) LC 75-34961

This book describes the Western frontiers of the 19th century as represented by contemporary reporters, artists, and photographers

Includes bibliography

The **Cowboys**; by the editors of Time-Life Books; with text by William H. Forbis. Time-Life Bks. 1973 240p il maps (Old West) $19.93 **978**

1. Cowhands 2. West (U.S.)—History

"The lore of the western frontier is graphically presented in this diverting look at the world of the American cowboy and the heyday of the cattle barons from the early 1860s through the late 1880s." Booklist

Includes bibliography

Frazier, Ian

Great Plains. Farrar, Straus & Giroux 1989 290p il maps $17.95 **978**

1. Great Plains—Description 2. West (U.S.)—Description
ISBN 0-374-21723-8 LC 88-31106

Also available in paperback from Penguin Bks.

The author recounts his experiences and observations traveling in the Western United States

"This is a colorful and engaging blend of travelogue, local color, geography and folklore." Publ Wkly

The **Frontiersmen**; by the editors of Time-Life Books; with text by Paul O'Neil. Time-Life Bks. 1977 240p il maps (Old West) $19.93 **978**

1. Frontier and pioneer life—West (U.S.) 2. West (U.S.)—History LC 76-47101

Portrays the people and times, the drama and danger of the developing frontier in eighteenth- and early nineteenth-century United States

Includes bibliography

The **Gamblers**; by the editors of Time-Life Books. Time-Life Bks. 1978 240p il (Old West) $19.93 **978**

1. Gambling 2. West (U.S.)—History 3. Frontier and pioneer life—West (U.S.) LC 78-12281

This volume "examines the role of gambling on the American frontier: among the Indians, on the rivers, in the mining camps, and in the boom towns. . . . The book is packed with interesting anecdotes, and covers the race track and boxing ring, lotteries and steamboat racing, as well as all of the traditional card and table games. The text is arresting, with well-placed illustrations." Libr J

Includes bibliography

Lewis, Meriwether, 1774-1809

The journals of Lewis and Clark; edited by Bernard De Voto; maps by Erwin Raisz. Houghton Mifflin 1953 lii, 504p maps hardcover o.p. paperback available $10.70
978

1. Lewis and Clark Expedition (1804-1806) 2. West (U.S.)—Exploration 3. Columbia River 4. Missouri River
ISBN 0-395-08380-X (pa)

This condensation is based on "Original journals of the Lewis and Clark Expedition," edited by Reuben Gold Thwaites, published in 1904-1905

"A tightfisted narrative, often illiterate but always engrossing, of forty-odd brave and resourceful men immersed for twenty-eight months in a wilderness where no white man had ever before set foot. A most successful operation." New Yorker

McPhee, John A.

Outcroppings; photographs by Tom Till; edited by Christopher Merrill. Smith, G.M. 1988 130p il $34.95
978

1. West (U.S.)—Description 2. Geology—West (U.S.)
ISBN 0-87905-262-7
LC 88-5422

Excerpts from McPhee's books on the West are accompanied by some 70 color photographs. "The insight into the American West provided by the photos and excerpts does not explain the geology of the west, nor is it intended to do so. Instead, Till and McPhee provide a means to hear and understand men like geologists Ken Deffeyes and David Love, conservationist David Brower, dam builder Floyd Dominy, and the woman to whom the book is dedicated, Ethel Waxham Love, mother of David Love. This book is about the conflict between the urge to protect and the urge to subjugate the western landscape and its resources to economic needs." Choice

The Miners; by the editors of Time-Life Books; with text by Robert Wallace. Time-Life Bks. 1976 240p il (Old West) $19.93
978

1. Gold mines and mining 2. Silver mines and mining 3. Frontier and pioneer life—West (U.S.)

Text and photographs present a description of mining and miners in the West and Alaska during the last half of the nineteenth century

Includes bibliography

Parkman, Francis, 1823-1893

The Oregon Trail
978

1. Oregon Trail 2. West (U.S.)—Description 3. Indians of North America 4. Frontier and pioneer life—West (U.S.)

Available only in paperback from New Am. Lib. and Penguin Bks.

Originally published serially in Knickerbocker Magazine; first published in book form, 1849, with title: The California and Oregon Trail

"An account of a trip made in 1846 by the author and his cousin Quincy Adams Shaw. They traveled together from St. Louis to Fort Laramie; there they separated, Parkman going to live for some weeks with a tribe of Sioux Indians. The Oregon Trail provides valuable descriptions of the prairies at the most fascinating period of their history and a remarkable ethnological study of the Indians." Benet's Reader's Ency of Am Lit

Includes bibliography

The Pioneers; by the editors of Time-Life Books; with text by Huston Horn. Time-Life Bks. 1974 240p il maps (Old West) $19.93
978

1. West (U.S.)—History 2. Overland journeys to the Pacific 3. Frontier and pioneer life—West (U.S.)

This book traces the routes traveled by the pioneers who made the difficult overland journey across America to the West. The political and economic reasons for such migrations are discussed

Includes bibliography

The Ranchers; by the editors of Time-Life Books; with text by Ogden Tanner. Time-Life Bks. 1977 240p il maps (Old West) $19.93
978

1. Ranch life 2. West (U.S.)—History 3. Frontier and pioneer life—West (U.S.)
LC 77-85283

Describes in text and illustrations the development of large ranches in the western plains, the impact of these establishments on the economy of the area, their organization, and some famous ranches and their owners

Includes bibliography

Schlissel, Lillian

Far from home; families of the westward journey; [by] Lillian Schlissel, Byrd Gibbens, Elizabeth Hampsten; foreword by Robert Coles. Schocken Bks. 1989 264p il $19.95; pa $13
978

1. Frontier and pioneer life—West (U.S.) 2. West (U.S.)—Social life and customs
ISBN 0-8052-4052-7; 0-8052-0977-8 (pa)
LC 88-42685

"The authors relate the story of three pioneering families—largely through the words of mothers and daughters preserved in old correspondence and later autobiographical writings." Christ Sci Monit

"An immensely readable book that peers closely into the lives of ordinary American frontier families." Booklist

Includes bibliographic references

The Scouts; by the editors of Time-Life Books; with text by Keith Wheeler. Time-Life Bks. 1978 240p il (Old West) $19.93
978

1. West (U.S.)—History 2. Frontier and pioneer life—West (U.S.)
LC 78-1364

This book "examines the critical role of the scout in the expansion of the Western frontier. It begins with the first generation of white scouts and recounts their services to emigrants, surveyors, and soldiers. It then turns to Indians and describes how whites were able to effectively exploit their talents by capitalizing on animosities among tribes." Libr J

Includes bibliography

The Townsmen; by the editors of Time-Life Books; with text by Keith Wheeler. Time-Life Bks. 1975 240p il (Old West) $19.93
978

1. West (U.S.)—History 2. Frontier and pioneer life—West (U.S.)

The Townsmen—*Continued*
This book describes the growth of towns in the West—the establishment of schools and businesses, the apportionment of building lots, the governing ordinances, and the entertainments of frontier towns such as music-halls, saloon-theaters, and boxing matches. Includes photographic essays of the growth of such towns as Denver, Colorado, Runnymede, Kansas, and Guthrie, Oklahoma
Includes bibliography

The **Trailblazers**; by the editors of Time-Life Books; with text by Bil Gilbert. Time-Life Bks. 1973 236p il maps (Old West) $19.93
978
1. West (U.S.)—Exploration
This is an illustrated account of the men who explored and charted the American West. It describes the Lewis and Clark Expedition; the lives of the fur trappers and mountain men; expeditions to California led by Joseph Reddeford Walker, Zebulon Pike and others; the work of naturalists, artists and photographers who went out West; the explorations by the Army's Corps of Topographical Engineers led by John Fremont and William Emory; and, the post-Civil War surveys led by three civilians—Ferdinand Hayden, Clarence King, and John Wesley Powell—and by George Wheeler, an Army lieutenant
Includes bibliography

Tunis, Edwin, 1897-1973
Frontier living; written and illustrated by Edwin Tunis. Crowell 1976 c1961 165p il maps $25.95
978
1. Frontier and pioneer life—West (U.S.) 2. West (U.S.)—History
ISBN 0-690-01064-8
Companion volume Colonial living (1976) also available
A reprint of the title first published 1961 by World Publishing Company
This volume "portrays the manners and customs of the frontiersman and his family from the beginning of the westward movement through the 19th century in . . . text and more than 200 drawings." Wis Libr Bull

978.1 Kansas

Heat Moon, William Least
PrairyErth; (a deep map). Houghton Mifflin 1991 624p maps $24.95; pa $13.45
978.1
1. Chase County (Kan.)
ISBN 0-395-48602-5; 0-395-63752-X (pa)
LC 91-23250
"A Peter Davison book"
This book is concerned with "Chase County in south central Kansas. Located in the heart of the Flint Hills, the sparsely populated area contains one of the best remaining tracts of tallgrass prairie that once covered much of the Midwest. ('PrairyErth' is an old geologic term for prairie soils). . . . [The author] examines the county's geological, natural, and human history." Libr J
"The author's range of knowledge and his talent for linking fascinating memorabilia with the issue of quality of life are impressive." Sci Books Films

Stratton, Joanna L.
Pioneer women; voices from the Kansas frontier; introduction by Arthur M. Schlesinger, Jr. Simon & Schuster 1981 319p il hardcover o.p. paperback available $12.95
978.1
1. Women—Kansas 2. Frontier and pioneer life—Kansas 3. Kansas—History
ISBN 0-671-44748-3 (pa)
LC 80-15960
"A unique book based on the memoirs of nearly 800 pioneer women who lived in Kansas between 1854 and 1890. . . . The book presents personal and detailed accounts of life inside homes, the schools, and the social organizations of early Kansas." Choice
Includes bibliography

978.9 New Mexico

Nolan, Frederick W., 1931-
The Lincoln County War; a documentary history. University of Okla. Press 1992 607p il maps $49.95
978.9
1. Frontier and pioneer life—New Mexico 2. Lincoln County (N.M.)—History
ISBN 0-8061-2377-X
LC 91-22210
An account of the "brutal scramble for control of a chunk of south central New Mexico Territory in 1878. . . . The traders and beef suppliers Lawrence G. Murphy and Jimmy Dolan maintained an economic and political stranglehold on a county peopled primarily by small farmers, ranchers and reservation Indians. The two were challenged by a lawyer, Alexander McSween, and an English rancher and investor, John Tunstall. . . . Each pair drew to their camp a number of opportunistic and combative drifters." N Y Times Book Rev
"An admirably full and thoughtful treatment of the Lincoln County troubles . . . captures the climate of violence that fed the myth of the Wild West." N Y Rev Books
Includes bibliographic references

979.1 Arizona

Shelton, Richard, 1933-
Going back to Bisbee. University of Ariz. Press 1992 329p $35; pa $15.95
979.1
1. Arizona—Description
ISBN 0-8165-1302-3; 0-8165-1289-2 (pa)
LC 91-41131
This is an "annal of place— a paean to the Sonoran desert south of Tucson, a landscape as prickly as the cacti that grow in it and yet as refreshing as a rainy-season rainstorm. Shelton imbues landscapes, flora and fauna with resonance, imprinting themes of memory, history and human nature in the reader's mind. . . . Shelton knows the lore and the life of Southern Arizona, and his diction, both precise and evocative, reflects his poetic skills." Publ Wkly
Includes bibliographical references

979.4   California

The **Forty-niners**; by the editors of Time-Life Books; with text by William Weber Johnson. Time-Life Bks. 1974 240p il maps (Old West) $19.93   **979.4**

1. California—Gold discoveries 2. California—History 3. Frontier and pioneer life—California

This illustrated account of the gold rush in California in the 1840's and 50's describes the gold discoveries, the migrations of gold seekers from across the country, the work of the prospector, life in the mining communities, the effects of the gold rush on California's development, and the big winners and losers in the quest for wealth

Includes bibliography

Muir, John, 1838-1914

The Yosemite; the original John Muir text; illustrated with photographs by Galen Rowell; each photograph accompanied by an excerpt from the works of John Muir and an annotation by Galen Rowell; introduction by the photographer. Sierra Club Bks. 1989 218p il $40   **979.4**

1. Yosemite National Park (Calif.)
ISBN 0-87156-653-2   LC 88-34919

"A Yolla Bolly Press book"

New "photos complement the Sierra Club's edition of Muir's 1912 classic *The Yosemite*. . . . The combined artistry and shared passion of Muir and of Rowell . . . make this a stunning tribute to one of America's favorite national parks." Libr J

Includes bibliographic references

979.8   Alaska

The **Alaskans**; by the editors of Time-Life Books; with text by Keith Wheeler. Time-Life Bks. 1977 240p il maps (Old West) $19.93   **979.8**

1. Alaska—History   LC 77-79673

A pictorial history of Alaska, from its purchase by the United States in 1867 through 1912, chronicling the exploration of the wilderness, the discovery of gold, and the development of the whaling, fishing, and fur industries

Includes bibliography

Leo, Richard

Edges of the earth; a man, a woman, a child in the Alaskan wilderness. Holt & Co. 1991 303p $19.95   **979.8**

1. Alaska—Social life and customs
ISBN 0-8050-1575-2   LC 91-589

Also available in paperback from Zebra Bks.

This is an account of the author's experiences homesteading in Alaska

"As much as anything, this is a story of how the isolation of the wilderness can destroy some relationships while nurturing others." Booklist

McPhee, John A.

Coming into the country; [by] John McPhee. Farrar, Straus & Giroux 1977 438p maps $22.95; pa $9.95   **979.8**

1. Alaska—Description
ISBN 0-374-12645-3; 0-374-52287-1 (pa)
     LC 77-12249

This book "is actually three lengthy bulletins about Alaska. . . . The first describes a canoe trip that McPhee and four companions took. . . . Second, McPhee tells of a helicopter ride with a committee looking for a site on which to build a new state capital. The last and longest section covers some wintry months spent in Eagle, a tiny settlement on the Yukon River." Time

980   South America. Latin America

The **Cambridge** encyclopedia of Latin America and the Caribbean; general editors, Simon Collier, Thomas E. Skidmore, Harold Blakemore. 2nd ed. Cambridge Univ. Press 1992 479p il maps $55   **980**

1. Latin America—Dictionaries
ISBN 0-521-41322-2   LC 92-14496

First published 1985

"Broad coverage for the general reader of history and economic development, culture and society, and flora and fauna." N Y Public Libr Book of How & Where to Look It Up

The **Cambridge** history of Latin America; edited by Leslie Bethell. Cambridge Univ. Press 1984-1991 7v   **980**

1. Latin America—History

First seven volumes of a projected ten volume set

Contents: v1-2 Colonial Latin America v1 $105, v2 $115 (ISBN 0-521-23223-6; 0-521-24516-8); v3 From independence to c.1870 $115 (ISBN 0-521-23224-4); v4-5 c.1870 to 1930 v4 $105, v5 $120 (ISBN 0-521-23225-2; 0-521-24517-6); v7-8 Latin America since 1930 v7 $110, v8 $94.95 (ISBN 0-521-24518-4; 0-521-26652-1)

"History of the areas south of the United States from just prior to the European invasions to the present. . . . Covers general themes in Latin American history with chronological accounts of the individual countries. Bibliographical essays are appended to each chapter." NY Public Libr Book of How & Where to Look It Up

The **South** American handbook. Prentice-Hall maps $40   **980**

1. Latin America 2. South America

Annual. First published 1924 by Rand McNally

"For each country, brief historical and socioeconomic information is followed by detailed descriptions of individual cities—their museums, libraries, art exhibitions, hotels (with rates), shops, transportation, etc. Though chiefly used for up-to-date travel information, the series has historical value in libraries." Booklist

Williamson, Edwin
The Penguin history of Latin America. Allen Lane 1992 o.p.; Penguin Bks. paperback available $15   **980**
1. Latin America—History
ISBN 0-14-012559-0 (pa)

"The book is organized topically, rather than by country, and the author wisely selected regional examples of his major themes, rather than attempting a detailed analysis of each country. The work ends with an unusual exploration of literature and culture in relation to identity and modernization, followed by a helpful bibliographic essay." Libr J

985 Peru

Bingham, Hiram, 1875-1956
Lost city of the Incas; the story of Machu Picchu and its builders. Duell 1948 263p il o.p.; Greenwood Press reprint available $59.50   **985**
1. Machu Picchu (Peru) 2. Peru—Antiquities 3. Incas
ISBN 0-313-22950-3

"In 1911 Bingham, an American explorer, found the Inca city of Machu Picchu, which had been lost for 300 years. In this volume he tells of its origin, how it came to be lost and how it was finally discovered." Libr J

Includes bibliography

Hemming, John, 1935-
The conquest of the Incas. Harcourt Brace Jovanovich 1970 641p il maps hardcover o.p. paperback available $17.95   **985**
1. Incas 2. Peru—History
ISBN 0-15-622300-7 (pa)

"This [study] focuses on relations of Spaniards and Incas during the Spanish conquest of Peru launched by Pizarro and partners. Spaniards and Incas speak frequently in their own words as preserved in Spanish documents. . . . Inca ways and achievements, the empire's tragic vulnerability because of rivalrous leaders and civil war, and conquest aftermath are made sharply manifest." Booklist

Includes bibliography

Incas: lords of gold and glory; by the editors of Time-Life Books. Time-Life Bks. 1992 168p il (Lost civilizations) $19.93   **985**
1. Incas   LC 92-5149

An illustrated look at the social, political, economic, religious and cultural aspects of Inca civilization. The Spanish conquest is also examined

Includes bibliography

Moseley, Michael Edward
The Incas and their ancestors; the archaeology of Peru; [by] Michael E. Moseley. Thames & Hudson 1992 272p il maps $35   **985**
1. Incas 2. Peru—Antiquities
ISBN 0-500-05063-5   LC 91-65309

This account of Andean prehistory and archaeology takes us from the first settlement of 10,000 years ago to the Spanish conquest

"Clearly presented, with a generous ration of maps and illustrations, [the volume] is thoughtful and welcome." Times Lit Suppl

989.2 Paraguay

Macintyre, Ben, 1963-
Forgotten fatherland; the search for Elisabeth Nietzsche. Farrar, Straus & Giroux 1992 256p il $22   **989.2**
1. Förster-Nietzsche, Elisabeth, 1846-1935 2. Germans—Paraguay
ISBN 0-374-15759-6   LC 92-9699

"In 1886, Nietzsche's sister, Elisabeth, together with her husband Bernhard Foerster and 14 German families, founded a colony in Paraguay that they christened 'Nueva Germania.' Their purpose was to escape a fatherland they believed to be in serious decline and to live in a place where their beliefs—anti-Semitism, vegetarianism, nationalism, Lutheranism—could flourish. Macintyre vividly recounts the sights and sounds of the villages and jungles, the flora and fauna he encountered in his arduous adventure to locate the remains of this colony." Libr J

Includes bibliographic references

990 Other parts of world. Pacific Ocean islands

Michener, James A. (James Albert), 1907-
Return to paradise. Random House 1951 437p $24   **990**
1. Islands of the Pacific
ISBN 0-394-44291-1

Also available in paperback from Fawcett Bks.

Partially analyzed in Essay and general literature index

Essays included are: The atoll; Polynesia; Fuji; Guadalcanal; Espiritu Santo; New Zealand; Australia; New Guinea; Rabaul; What I learned. Short stories included are: Mr. Morgan; Povenaa's daughter; Mynah birds; The story; Good life; Until they sail; The jungle; The fossickers

"Alternate chapters describe each island followed by a short story set against the region described." Ont Libr Rev

994 Australia

Hughes, Robert
The fatal shore. Knopf 1987 688p il maps $24.95; pa $15   **994**
1. Australia—History 2. Penal colonies
ISBN 0-394-50668-5; 0-394-75366-6 (pa)
LC 86-45272

"This epic account chronicles the history of Australia during the 80 years (1788-1868) of England's convict transportation system, when some 160,000 convicts reached 'the fatal shore.' Interweaving his own lucid narrative with untapped original sources—including the diaries and letters of the prisoners themselves—Hughes shows the evolution of the system and of the fledgling nation that emerged from the brutal penal colony." Libr J

Includes bibliographic references

Morris, Jan, 1926-
Sydney. Random House 1992 256p il maps $22   **994**
1. Sydney (Australia)—Description
ISBN 0-394-55098-6   LC 91-41141

Founded in 1788, Sydney, Australia is, "Morris states, 'one of the great cities of the world,' booming from its participation in Pacific Rim trade, blessed with a splendid climate and a spectacularly beautiful harbor. . . . The author capably describes Sydney's social structure and memorably captures its architectural ambience." Publ Wkly

996   Polynesia and Micronesia

Heyerdahl, Thor
Easter Island—a mystery solved. Random House 1989 255p il $24.95   **996**
1. Easter Island—Antiquities
ISBN 0-394-57906-2   LC 88-32204

In this "book, the occasion for his return to Easter Island after 30 years, Heyerdahl tells the history of the island through the eyes of explorers and travelers, from its discovery by the Dutch in 1722, through Heyerdahl's

. . . visit in 1986, during which he and his staff resumed limited excavations, and aided by residents and their recall of ancient myths, resolved the puzzle of how the statues had 'walked' from the quarries to their places on the island." Libr J

Includes bibliography

998   Arctic islands and Antarctica

Lopez, Barry Holstun, 1945-
Arctic dreams; imagination and desire in a northern landscape; [by] Barry Lopez. Scribner 1986 xxix, 464p maps $22.95   **998**
1. Arctic regions 2. Natural history—Arctic regions
ISBN 0-684-18578-4   LC 85-24979
Also available in paperback from Bantam Bks.

Based on his experiences in the region Lopez discusses "Arctic exploration, geography, weather, animal migration, and behavior." Libr J

"What compels the reader to enter this frozen world of the far north is Lopez's beautiful prose style and the breadth and strength of his understanding. He lavishes attention on and achieves precise expression of this world." Choice

Includes bibliography

PART 2

AUTHOR, TITLE, SUBJECT, AND ANALYTICAL INDEX

AUTHOR, TITLE, SUBJECT, AND ANALYTICAL INDEX

This index to the books in the Classified Catalog includes author, title, subject, and analytical entries; added entries for joint authors and for editors of works entered under title; and name and subject cross-references, all arranged in one alphabet. The number in boldface type at the end of each entry refers to the Dewey Decimal Classification where the main entry for the book will be found.

For further directions for use of this index and for examples of analytical entries, see Directions for Use of the Catalog.

The **Audubon** Society field guide to North American butterflies. Pyle, R. M.   **595.7**

The **Audubon** Society field guide to North American fishes, whales, and dolphins   **597**

The **Audubon** Society field guide to North American fossils. Thompson, I.   **560**

The **Audubon** Society field guide to North American insects and spiders. Milne, L. J.   **595.7**

The **Audubon** Society field guide to North American mammals. Whitaker, J. O., Jr.   **599**

The **Audubon** Society field guide to North American mushrooms. Lincoff, G.   **589.2**

The **Audubon** Society field guide to North American reptiles and amphibians. Behler, J. L.   **597.6**

The **Audubon** Society field guide to North American rocks and minerals. Chesterman, C. W.   **549**

The **Audubon** Society field guide to North American seashells. Rehder, H. A.   **594**

The **Audubon** Society field guide to North American seashore creatures. Meinkoth, N. A.   **592**

The **Audubon** Society field guide to North American trees. Little, E. L.   **582.16**

The **Audubon** Society field guide to North American weather. Ludlum, D. M.   **551.6**

The **Audubon** Society field guide to North American wildflowers: eastern region. Niering, W. A.   **582.13**

The **Audubon** Society field guide to North American wildflowers: western region. Spellenberg, R.   **582.13**

The **Audubon** Society field guide to the night sky. Chartrand, M. R.   **523**

The **Audubon** Society guide to attracting birds. Kress, S. W.   **598**

The **Audubon** Society handbook for butterfly watchers. Pyle, R. M.   **595.7**

The **Audubon** Society master guide to birding   **598**

Auerbach, Paul S.
Medicine for the outdoors   **616.02**

Augarde, Tony
(ed) The Oxford dictionary of modern quotations. See The Oxford dictionary of modern quotations   **808.88**

The **August** coup. Gorbachev, M.   **947.085**

The **August** sleepwalker. Pei-tao   **895.1**

Augustine, Saint, Bishop of Hippo
The confessions of St. Augustine   **242**
See/See also pages in the following book(s):
Russell, B. A history of Western philosophy p352-66   **109**

Augustus, Emperor of Rome, 63 B.C.-14 A.D.
See/See also pages in the following book(s):
Suetonius Tranquillus, C. The twelve Caesars   **878**

Auletta, Ken
Greed and glory on Wall Street   **332.6**
Three blind mice   **384.55**

Aultman, Dick
(jt. auth) Snead, S. Golf begins at forty   **796.352**

Aung San Suu Kyi
Freedom from fear, and other writings   **959.1**

Auschwitz (Poland: Concentration camp)
Levi, P. The drowned and the saved   **940.53**

Austen, Jane, 1775-1817
Emma; criticism
In Trilling, L. Beyond culture p28-49   **809**
Mansfield Park; criticism
In Nabokov, V. V. Lectures on literature p9-61   **808.3**
See/See also pages in the following book(s):
Gilbert, S. M. The madwoman in the attic p107-83   **809**
Trilling, L. The last decade p204-14   **814**
Woolf, V. Women and writing p109-20   **820.9**

Auster, Paul, 1947-
(ed) The Random House book of twentieth-century French poetry. See The Random House book of twentieth-century French poetry   **841.008**

Austin, Nancy
(jt. auth) Peters, T. J. A passion for excellence   **658.4**

Australia
Conway, J. K. The road from Coorain   **92**
Description
Chatwin, B. The songlines   **919.4**
History
Hughes, R. The fatal shore   **994**

Australian aborigines
Chatwin, B. The songlines   **919.4**

Australian literature
Bio-bibliography
Wilde, W. H. The Oxford companion to Australian literature   **820.3**
Collections
The Oxford anthology of Australian literature   **820.8**
Dictionaries
Wilde, W. H. The Oxford companion to Australian literature   **820.3**
History and criticism
The Oxford history of Australian literature   **820.9**

Austria
History
Crankshaw, E. The fall of the House of Habsburg   **943.6**
See/See also pages in the following book(s):
Durant, W. J. The age of Napoleon p558-66   **940.2**
Durant, W. J. Rousseau and revolution p341-66   **940.2**

Ausubel, Nathan, 1899-1986
(ed) A Treasury of Jewish folklore. See A Treasury of Jewish folklore   **398.2**

Authoritarianism *See* Totalitarianism

Authors
See also Black authors; Literature—Bio-bibliography; Women authors
Newbery and Caldecott Medal books, 1966-1975   **028.5**
Newbery and Caldecott Medal books, 1976-1985   **028.5**
Newbery Medal books, 1922-1955   **028.5**
Dictionaries
Contemporary authors   **920.003**
The Nobel Prize winners: literature   **920.003**
Twentieth century authors   **920.003**
World authors, 1950-1970   **920.003**
World authors, 1970-1975   **920.003**
World authors, 1975-1980   **920.003**
World authors, 1980-1985   **920.003**
Homes and haunts
See Literary landmarks

Authors, American
Dardis, T. The thirsty muse   **810.9**
First person singular   **808**
Hamilton, I. Writers in Hollywood, 1915-1951   **791.43**
Mitgang, H. Dangerous dossiers   **363.2**
Robins, N. S. Alien ink   **363.2**
Sawyer-Lauçanno, C. The continual pilgrimage   **810.9**
Anecdotes
The Oxford book of American literary anecdotes   **810.9**
Dictionaries
American authors, 1600-1900   **920.003**
American writers   **920.003**

Authors, Chinese
Dillard, A. Encounters with Chinese writers   **895.1**

Authors, English
Holmes, R. Footsteps   **828**
See/See also pages in the following book(s):
Woolf, V. The second common reader p127-55   **820.9**
Anecdotes
The Oxford book of literary anecdotes   **828**
Dictionaries
British authors before 1800   **920.003**
British authors of the nineteenth century   **920.003**

Authors, European
Dictionaries
Columbia dictionary of modern European literature   **803**
European authors, 1000-1900   **920.003**

Authors, Greek
Dictionaries
Grant, M. Greek and Latin authors, 800 B.C.-A.D. 1000   **920.003**

Authors, Indic
See/See also pages in the following book(s):
Rushdie, S. Imaginary homelands p9-25   **828**

Authors, Latin
Dictionaries
Grant, M. Greek and Latin authors, 800 B.C.-A.D. 1000   **920.003**

Gordon-Watson, Mary
The handbook of riding   798.2
Gore, Albert, Jr.
Earth in the balance   304.2
Goren, Charles Henry, 1901-1991
Goren's new bridge complete   795.4
Goren's new bridge complete. Goren, C. H.   795.4
Gorey, Hays
(jt. auth) Pepper, C. Pepper, eyewitness to a century   92
Gorgas, William Crawford, 1854-1920
See/See also pages in the following book(s):
McCullough, D. G. The path between the seas   972.87

Gorge-purge syndrome *See* Bulimia
Gorillas
Fossey, D. Gorillas in the mist   599.88
Hayes, H. The dark romance of Dian Fossey   92
Mowat, F. Woman in the mists: the story of Dian Fossey and the mountain gorillas of Africa   92
Gorillas in the mist. Fossey, D.   599.88
Göring, Hermann, 1893-1946
See/See also pages in the following book(s):
Posner, G. L. Hitler's children p190-201   943.086
Goring, Rosemary
(ed) Cambridge biographical dictionary. See Cambridge biographical dictionary   920.003
Gorky, Maksim, 1868-1936
The lower depths
In Our dramatic heritage v4   808.82
See/See also pages in the following book(s):
Mirskiĭ, D. P. A history of Russian literature, from its beginnings to 1900 p376-86   891.7
Nabokov, V. V. Lectures on Russian literature   891.7
Gorman, James, 1949-
The total penguin   598
(jt. auth) Horner, J. R. Digging dinosaurs   567.9
Gorman, Michael, 1941-
The concise AACR2, 1988 revision   025.3
(ed) Anglo-American cataloguing rules, 2d ed., 1988 revision. See Anglo-American cataloguing rules, 2d ed., 1988 revision   025.3
Gornick, Vivian
Women in science   509
Gorse fires. Longley, M.   821
Gosner, Kenneth L., 1925-
A field guide to the Atlantic seashore   574.92
The **gospel** according to Jesus. Mitchell, S.   226
Gospel music
See also Spirituals (Songs)
Discography
Scott, F. The Down Home guide to the blues   781.643
Gospels (Books of the New Testament) *See* Bible. N.T. Gospels
Goss, Linda
(ed) Talk that talk: an anthology of African-American storytelling. See Talk that talk: an anthology of African-American storytelling   398.2
Got to tell it: Mahalia Jackson, queen of gospel. Schwerin, J.   780.92
Gottesman, Roberta
(ed) The Music lover's guide to Europe. See The Music lover's guide to Europe   780.79
Gottfried, Martin
All his jazz   92
Gottlieb, Annie
(jt. auth) Sher, B. Teamworks!   302.3
Gottlieb, Linda
(jt. auth) Hyatt, C. When smart people fail   158
Gottlieb, Sherry Gershon
Hell no, we won't go!   959.704
Gottschalk, Louis Moreau, 1829-1869
See/See also pages in the following book(s):
Schonberg, H. C. The great pianists p217-29   780.92
Gough, Michael, 1939-
Dioxin, Agent Orange   363.1
Goulart, Ron, 1933-
The great comic book artists   741.5
(ed) The Encyclopedia of American comics. See The Encyclopedia of American comics   741.5
Gould, Glenn, 1932-1982
The Glenn Gould reader   780
About
Friedrich, O. Glenn Gould   780.92

See/See also pages in the following book(s):
Schonberg, H. C. The great pianists p475-81   780.92
Gould, Stephen Jay, 1941-
Bully for brontosaurus   508
Eight little piggies   575
Ever since Darwin   575.01
The flamingo's smile   508
Hen's teeth and horse's toes   575
The mismeasure of man   153.9
The panda's thumb   575
Time's arrow, time's cycle   551.7
An urchin in the storm   574
Wonderful life: the Burgess Shale and the nature of history   560
Gourdie, Tom
Calligraphic styles   745.6
Gourmet's holidays and celebrations   642
Gourmont, Remy de, 1858-1915
See/See also pages in the following book(s):
Pound, E. Literary essays p339-58   809
Pound, E. Selected prose, 1909-1965 p413-23   814
Gourse, Leslie
Unforgettable: the life and mystique of Nat King Cole   780.92

Government *See* Political science
Government, Local *See* Local government
Government, Resistance to
See also Passive resistance; Revolutions
Government and business *See* Industry—Government policy
Government and the press *See* Press—Government policy
Government by the people   320.4
Government debts *See* Public debts
Government housing *See* Public housing
Government information
Law and legislation
Marwick, C. M. Your right to government information   342
Government Printing Office (U.S.) *See* United States. Government Printing Office
Government procurement *See* Government purchasing
Government property surplus *See* Surplus government property
Government purchasing
Traub, J. Too good to be true: the outlandish story of Wedtech   364.1
Government reference books   015.73
Government regulation of industry *See* Industry—Government policy
Government research centers directory. See Government research directory   001.4
Government research directory   001.4
Government spending policy *See* United States—Appropriations and expenditures
Governmental investigations
United States
See/See also pages in the following book(s):
Newman, R. P. Owen Lattimore and the "loss" of China   92
Gowing, Sir Lawrence, 1918-1991
Paintings in the Louvre   708
Goya, Francisco, 1746-1828
See/See also pages in the following book(s):
Clark, K. The romantic rebellion p69-95   759.05
Durant, W. J. Rousseau and revolution p300-09   940.2
Goya y Lucientes, Francisco José de *See* Goya, Francisco, 1746-1828
GPO *See* United States. Government Printing Office
Grabar, Oleg
(jt. auth) Ettinghausen, R. The art and architecture of Islam: 650-1250   709.1
Grace notes. Dove, R.   811
Gradstein, Bonnie
(jt. auth) Friedman, R. Surviving pregnancy loss   155.9
The **gradual** vegetarian. Tracy, L.   613.2
The **graduate.** Willingham, C.
In Best American screenplays   812.008
Graedon, Joe
50 +   615
Graedons' best medicine   615
Graedon, Teresa, 1947-
(jt. auth) Graedon, J. 50 +   615
(jt. auth) Graedon, J. Graedons' best medicine   615
Graedons' best medicine. Graedon, J.   615

Kunitz, Stanley, 1905-
(ed) American authors, 1600-1900. See American authors, 1600-1900 **920.003**
(ed) British authors before 1800. See British authors before 1800 **920.003**
(ed) British authors of the nineteenth century. See British authors of the nineteenth century **920.003**
(ed) European authors, 1000-1900. See European authors, 1000-1900 **920.003**
(ed) Twentieth century authors. See Twentieth century authors **920.003**
Kunz, Jeffrey R. M.
(ed) The American Medical Association family medical guide. See The American Medical Association family medical guide **616.02**
Kuomintang (China)
See/See also pages in the following book(s):
Fairbank, J. K. The United States and China **327.51**
Kuralt, Charles, 1934-
A life on the road **92**
On the road with Charles Kuralt **973.92**
Kurian, George Thomas
The encyclopedia of the First World **910.3**
Encyclopedia of the Third World **903**
(ed) Atlas of the Third World. See Atlas of the Third World **912**
Kurosawa, Akira, 1910-
Something like an autobiography **92**
Kurth, Peter
American Cassandra: the life of Dorothy Thompson **92**
Kurtz, Michael L., 1941-
Earl K. Long **92**
Kurzweil, Raymond
The age of intelligent machines **006.3**
Kushites *See* Cushites
Kushner, Harold S., 1935-
When bad things happen to good people **296.3**
Who needs God **296.7**
Kusz, Natalie
Road song **92**
Kutler, Stanley I.
The wars of Watergate **973.924**
Kutzner, Patricia L.
World hunger **363.8**
Kuvshinoff, Boris W.
(jt. auth) Henle, R. A. Desktop computers **004**
Kuwait
History—1991, Persian Gulf War
See Persian Gulf War, 1991
Kwanze, Kiyotsugu, 1355-1406
Sotoba Komachi
In Waley, A. The Nō plays of Japan **895.6**
Kwiterovich, Peter
Beyond cholesterol **616.1**
Kwitny, Jonathan
Acceptable risks **362.1**
Kyoto (Japan)
Description
Iyer, P. The lady and the monk **952.04**

L

The L.L. Bean book of new New England cookery. Jones, J. **641.5**
The L.L. Bean game and fish cookbook. Cameron, A. **641.6**
The L.L. Bean guide to the outdoors. Riviere, B. **796.5**
La Bastide, J. A. Jockin- *See* Jockin-La Bastide, J. A.
La Guardia, Fiorello Henry, 1882-1947
About
Kessner, T. Fiorello H. La Guardia and the making of modern New York **92**
La Leche League International
The Womanly art of breastfeeding. See The Womanly art of breastfeeding **649**
Labella, Vincenzo
A season of giants: Michelangelo, Leonardo, Raphael, 1492-1508 **709.45**

Labor
See also Agricultural laborers; Migrant labor; Proletariat; Work
United States
Dulles, F. R. Labor in America **331.8**
Encyclopedia of career change and work issues **331.7**
Geoghegan, T. Which side are you on? **331.8**
Terkel, S. Working **331.2**
See/See also pages in the following book(s):
Howe, I. World of our fathers p287-324 **305.8**
Labor, Hours of *See* Hours of labor
Labor and laboring classes *See* Labor
Labor in America. Dulles, F. R. **331.8**
Labor movement *See* Labor
Labor of love, labor of sorrow. Jones, J. **305.4**
Labor Statistics Bureau (U.S.) *See* United States. Bureau of Labor Statistics
Labor unions
United States
Dulles, F. R. Labor in America **331.8**
Foner, P. S. Women and the American labor movement **331.8**
Freeman, R. B. What do unions do? **331.8**
Geoghegan, T. Which side are you on? **331.8**
Miller, M. A whole different ball game **796.357**
Outten, W. N. The rights of employees and union members **344**
See/See also pages in the following book(s):
Galbraith, J. K. The new industrial state **338.973**
Laboratory animal experimentation *See* Animal experimentation
Laborers *See* Labor
Labrunie, Gérard *See* Nerval, Gérard de, 1808-1855
The **labyrinth** of exile: a life of Theodor Herzl. Pawel, E. **92**
The **labyrinth** of solitude. Paz, O.
In Paz, O. The labyrinth of solitude [and other essays] p7-212 **864**
The **labyrinth** of solitude [and other essays]. Paz, O. **864**
Labyrinths. Borges, J. L. **868**
Lacey, Robert
Ford, the men and the machine **920**
The kingdom **953.8**
Little man: Meyer Lansky and the gangster life **92**
Lacouture, Jean
De Gaulle **92**
Lactose intolerance
Carper, S. No milk today **616.3**
Lader, Lawrence
RU 486 **363.4**
Ladies' voices. Stein, G.
In Stein, G. Selected writings p555-56 **818**
The **lady** and the monk. Iyer, P. **952.04**
Lady Day: the many faces of Billie Holiday. O'Meally, R. G. **780.92**
The **lady** from Dubuque. Albee, E. **812**
also in Albee, E. The plays v2 **812**
The **lady** from the sea. Ibsen, H.
In Ibsen, H. The complete major prose plays p587-688 **839.8**
Lady of Larkspur Lotion. Williams, T.
In Williams, T. 27 wagons full of cotton, and other plays p65-72 **812**
In Williams, T. The theatre of Tennessee Williams v6 p81-89 **812**
The **lady's** not for burning. Fry, C.
In Fry, C. The lady's not for burning, A phoenix too frequent, and an essay "An experience of critics" p13-87 **822**
The **lady's** not for burning, A phoenix too frequent, and an essay "An experience of critics". Fry, C. **822**
Lagrange, Joseph Louis, comte de, 1736-1813
See/See also pages in the following book(s):
Bell, E. T. Men of mathematics p153-71 **920**
Lahr, John, 1941-
Prick up your ears: the biography of Joe Orton **92**
Lake ecology
Niering, W. A. Wetlands **574.5**
Lakers (Basketball team) *See* Los Angeles Lakers (Basketball team)
Lakes
Pringle, L. P. Rivers and lakes **551.48**
Lakota woman. Crow Dog, M. **92**

Mamiya, Lawrence H.
(jt. auth) Lincoln, C. E. The black church in the African
American experience   **277.3**
Mammals
   See also groups of mammals; and names of mam-
mals
Burt, W. H. A field guide to the mammals   **599**
The Encyclopedia of mammals   **599**
Grzimek's encyclopedia of mammals   **599**
Lawrence, R. D. In praise of wolves   **599.74**
Walker, E. P. Walker's mammals of the world   **599**
Whitaker, J. O., Jr. The Audubon Society field guide to
North American mammals   **599**
Mammals, Fossil
Johanson, D. C. Lucy: the beginnings of humankind
   573.2
Johanson, D. C. Lucy's child: the discovery of a human
ancestor   **573.2**
Willis, D. The Hominid Gang   **573.2**
Mammals, Marine *See* Marine mammals
Man
Bronowski, J. The ascent of man   **501**
Mumford, L. The condition of man   **909**
Teilhard de Chardin, P. The phenomenon of man
   113

Influence of environment
   See also Environmental health
Influence on nature
Caufield, C. In the rainforest   **574.5**
Commoner, B. Making peace with the planet   **304.2**
The Conservation atlas of tropical forests: Africa
   333.75
Cowell, A. The decade of destruction   **574.5**
Ehrlich, P. R. Healing the planet   **363.7**
The Green lifestyle handbook   **363.7**
Hecht, S. B. The fate of the forest   **574.5**
Mason, R. J. Atlas of United States environmental issues
   363.7
McKibben, B. The end of nature   **363.7**
McPhee, J. A. The control of nature   **304.2**
Nichol, J. The mighty rain forest   **574.5**
Origin
   See also Evolution; Prehistoric man
Asimov, I. Beginnings   **577**
Calvin, W. H. The ascent of mind   **573.2**
Darwin, C. The origin of species   **575.01**
Diamond, J. M. The third chimpanzee   **573.2**
Eiseley, L. C. The immense journey   **575**
Johanson, D. C. Lucy: the beginnings of humankind
   573.2
Johanson, D. C. Lucy's child: the discovery of a human
ancestor   **573.2**
Leakey, R. E. Origins   **573.2**
Leakey, R. E. Origins reconsidered   **573.2**
Lewin, R. In the age of mankind   **573.2**
Willis, D. The Hominid Gang   **573.2**
   See/See also pages in the following book(s):
Jastrow, R. Until the sun dies p130-43   **577**
Man, Prehistoric *See* Prehistoric man
Man (Theology)
   See/See also pages in the following book(s):
Teilhard de Chardin, P. Toward the future p13-39
   194
Man against himself. Menninger, K. A.   **616.89**
Man and aggression   **152.4**
Man and his symbols. Jung, C. G.   **150.19**
A man called Intrepid. Stevenson, W.   **940.54**
A man for all seasons. Bolt, R.   **822**
Man for himself. Fromm, E.   **171**
Man-made minds. Waldrop, M. M.   **006.3**
Man of La Mancha. Wasserman, D.   **812**
The man of mode. Etherege, Sir G.
   In Restoration plays   **822.008**
Man of the House. O'Neill, T.   **92**
Man Ray *See* Ray, Man, 1890-1976
Man Ray: photographs. Ray, M.   **779**
Man to man. Murcia, A.   **616.99**
The man to see: Edward Bennett Williams. Thomas, E.
   92
The man who changed the world: the lives of Mikhail S.
Gorbachev. Sheehy, G.   **92**
The man who climbed the pecan trees. Foote, H.
   In The Best American short plays, 1990   **808.82**
   In Foote, H. Selected one-act plays of Horton Foote
p265-89   **812**

The man who knew infinity: a life of the genius, Ramanu-
jan. Kanigel, R.   **92**
Man who married a dumb wife. France, A.
   In Thirty famous one-act plays p5-24   **808.82**
The man who mistook his wife for a hat and other clinical
tales. Sacks, O. W.   **616.8**
The man who walked through time. Fletcher, C.
   917.91
The man who would be president: Dan Quayle. Broder, D.
S.   **92**
Management
   See also Industrial management
Drucker, P. F. The frontiers of management   **658**
Drucker, P. F. Managing for the future   **658**
Kanter, R. M. When giants learn to dance: mastering the
challenge of strategy, management, and careers in the
1900s   **658**
Lefferts, R. The basic handbook of grants management
   658.4
Mackay, H. Swim with the sharks without being eaten
alive   **650.1**
McCormack, M. H. What they don't teach you at Har-
vard Business School   **650.1**
Peters, T. J. Liberation management   **658.4**
Peters, T. J. Thriving on chaos   **658**
Anecdotes
Peter, L. J. The Peter Principle   **817**
Managing for results. Drucker, P. F.   **658.4**
Managing for the future. Drucker, P. F.   **658**
Managing the non-profit organization. Drucker, P. F.
   658
Managing the one-person business. Parson, M. J.   **658.1**
Managing your menopause. Utian, W. H.   **618.1**
Manchester, William
American Caesar: Douglas MacArthur, 1880-1964   **92**
The glory and the dream   **973.9**
Goodbye, darkness   **940.54**
The last lion: Winston Spencer Churchill   **92**
One brief shining moment: remembering Kennedy
   92
A world lit only by fire   **940.2**
Manchild in the promised land. Brown, C.   **92**
Manchus
   See/See also pages in the following book(s):
Fairbank, J. K. The United States and China   **327.51**
Mancuso, Joseph
Mancuso's small business resource guide   **658.1**
Mancuso's small business resource guide. Mancuso, J.
   658.1
Mandela, Nelson
About
Benson, M. Nelson Mandela   **92**
Kumalo, A. Mandela   **92**
Mandela, W. Part of my soul went with him   **92**
Meer, F. Higher than hope: the authorized biography of
Nelson Mandela   **92**
Mandela, Winnie
Part of my soul went with him   **92**
Mandela's earth and other poems. Soyinka, W.   **821**
Manea, Norman
On clowns   **949.8**
Manes, Christopher, 1957-
Green rage   **363.7**
Manet, Édouard, 1832-1883
About
Courthion, P. Edouard Manet   **759.4**
Friedrich, O. Olympia   **944.07**
Mangold, Thomas
Cold warrior: James Jesus Angleton   **92**
Manhoff, Bill
The owl and the pussycat
   In Best American plays: 6th series—1963-1967 p495-
525   **812.008**
Manhunt. Maas, P.   **364.1**
Manic-depressive psychoses
   See also Depression, Mental
Duke, P. A brilliant madness   **616.89**
Millett, K. The loony-bin trip   **92**
Mankiewicz, Herman J., 1897-1953
Citizen Kane
   In Best American screenplays   **812.008**
Manley, Deborah
(ed) The Guinness book of records 1492. See The Guin-
ness book of records 1492   **031.02**

S

Sobel, Michael I.
Light   535

Soccer
Robson, B. Bryan Robson's soccer skills   796.334

Social action
The Global ecology handbook   363.7
Hollender, J. How to make the world a better place   361.2
Steger, W. Saving the earth   363.7

Social anthropology *See* Ethnology

Social behavior *See* Human behavior

Social change
Aburdene, P. Megatrends for women   305.4
Bettelheim, B. Social change and prejudice, including Dynamics of prejudice   305.8
Hardison, O. B. Disappearing through the skylight   303.4
Meyrowitz, J. No sense of place   302.23
Naisbitt, J. Megatrends   303.4
Naisbitt, J. Megatrends 2000   303.4
Toffler, A. Future shock   303.4
Toffler, A. Powershift   303.4
Toffler, A. The third wave   303.4
See/See also pages in the following book(s):
Fromm, E. To have or to be? p168-202   302

Social change and prejudice, including Dynamics of prejudice. Bettelheim, B.   305.8

Social classes
See also Labor; Middle classes; Upper classes
Veblen, T. The theory of the leisure class   305.5

Social conditions
See also names of groups of people and names of countries, cities, etc. with the subdivision *Social conditions*
Gay, P. The bourgeois experience: Victoria to Freud   306

The **social** contract. Rousseau, J.-J.   320.1

Social customs *See* Manners and customs

Social democracy *See* Socialism

Social equality *See* Equality

Social ethics
See also Bioethics
Bok, S. Secrets   177
Hook, S. Convictions   191
Leinberger, P. The new individualists   306

Social groups
Sher, B. Teamworks!   302.3

A **social** history of madness. Porter, R.   616.89

Social insecurity. Hardy, D.   368.4

Social learning *See* Socialization

Social life and customs *See* Manners and customs

Social medicine
Beasley, J. D. The betrayal of health   362.1

Social problems
See also Discrimination
Harrington, M. The new American poverty   305.5
Hollender, J. How to make the world a better place   361.2

Social problems and the church *See* Church and social problems

Social psychology
See also Alienation (Social psychology); Hysteria (Social psychology); Psychology, Applied
Allport, G. The nature of prejudice   152.4
Bettelheim, B. Surviving, and other essays   155.9

Social sciences

Dictionaries
International encyclopedia of the social sciences   300.3

Periodicals—Indexes
Social sciences & humanities index v19-27   050
Social sciences index   300.5
Social sciences & humanities index. See Social sciences index   300.5
Social sciences & humanities index v19-27   050
Social sciences index   300.5

Social security
Hardy, D. Social insecurity   368.4
Jehle, F. F. The complete & easy guide to Social Security & Medicare   368.4
McCormack, T. P. The AIDS benefits handbook   362.1
Robertson, A. H. Social security   368.4
Social Security handbook   368.4

Social Security Administration *See* United States. Social Security Administration

Social Security handbook   368.4

Social values
Bennett, W. J. The de-valuing of America   973.927
Galbraith, J. K. The culture of contentment   330.973

Social work

Dictionaries
Encyclopedia of social work   361

Socialism
Harrington, M. Socialism: past and future   335
See/See also pages in the following book(s):
Durant, W. J. The lessons of history p56-67   901
Galbraith, J. K. The new industrial state   338.973
Naisbitt, J. Megatrends 2000 p93-117   303.4
Seymour-Jones, C. Beatrice Webb   92
Tuchman, B. W. The proud tower p407-62   909.82

Socialization
Kotre, J. N. Seasons of life   155

Socialized medicine *See* Medicine, State

Socially handicapped
Rose, M. Lives on the boundary   371.9

Socially handicapped children
Conroy, P. The water is wide   371.9
Kozol, J. Savage inequalities   371.9

Societies
See also Associations
Encyclopedia of associations   061.025

Directories
The World of learning   060.25

Society, Primitive *See* Nonliterate folk society

Society of Biblical Literature
Harper's Bible commentary. See Harper's Bible commentary   220.7

Society of Friends
Barbour, H. The Quakers   289.6
Trueblood, E. The people called Quakers   289.6
See/See also pages in the following book(s):
Backman, M. V. Christian churches of America p138-46   277.3
Boorstin, D. J. The Americans: The colonial experience p33-69   973.2
Langdon, W. C. Everyday things in American life, 1607-1776 p48-62   973.2

Society of Jesus *See* Jesuits

Sociology
See also Educational sociology
See/See also pages in the following book(s):
Buber, M. Pointing the way   100

Dictionaries
Encyclopedia of sociology   301

Sociology, Christian
See also Liberation theology
Niebuhr, H. R. Christ and culture   261

Socrates

About
Stone, I. F. The trial of Socrates   183
See/See also pages in the following book(s):
Russell, B. A history of Western philosophy p82-93   109

Sofianides, Anna S.
Gems & crystals from the American Museum of Natural History   549

Soft drink industry
Enrico, R. The other guy blinked   338.7

Softball
McCrory, G. J. Softball rules in pictures   796.357

Softball rules in pictures. McCrory, G. J.   796.357

Software   005
The Software encyclopedia   005
Software Reviews on File   005

Sogyal, Rinpoche
The Tibetan book of living and dying   294.3

SoHo walls. Robinson, D.   751.7

Solal, Annie Cohen- *See* Cohen-Solal, Annie

Solar eclipses *See* Eclipses, Solar

Solar radiation
See also Greenhouse effect

Solar system
See/See also pages in the following book(s):
Asimov, I. Asimov's new guide to science p79-153   500

Soldiers
See also Women soldiers; names of countries with the subdivision *Army—Military life*

Soto, Gary
Who will know us? 811
Soto, Hernando de, ca. 1500-1542
See/See also pages in the following book(s):
Williams, W. C. In the American grain p45-58 814
Sotoba Komachi. Kwanze, K.
In Waley, A. The Nō plays of Japan 895.6
Soul gone home. Hughes, L.
In Hughes, L. Five plays p37-42 812
The **soul** of a new machine. Kidder, T. 621.39
The **soul** of the wolf. Fox, M. W. 599.74
Soul on ice. Cleaver, E. 305.8
The **souls** of black folk. Du Bois, W. E. B. 305.8
also in Du Bois, W. Writings 818
Souls on fire. Wiesel, E. 296.8
Sound
Recording and reproducing
Rachlin, H. The songwriter's and musician's guide to making great demos 780
See/See also pages in the following book(s):
Clifford, M. The camcorder p207-34 621.388
Sound and fury. Alterman, E. 302.23
The **sound** of a miracle. Stehli, A. 155.45
The **sound** of wings: the life of Amelia Earhart. Lovell, M. S. 92
Sound recordings
See also Compact discs
Cook, R. The Penguin guide to jazz on CD, LP and cassette 780.2
The New Rolling Stone record guide 780.2
Bibliography
Words on cassette 011
Sounder. Elder, L.
In Best American screenplays 812.008
Soups
Gubser, M. Quick breads, soups & stews 641.8
Moore, M. M. The wooden spoon book of home-style soups, stews, chowders, chilis, and gumbos 641.8
The **Source** 929
South, Malcolm, 1937-
(ed) Mythical and fabulous creatures. See Mythical and fabulous creatures 398
South (U.S.) *See* Southern States
South Africa
Economic conditions
Wilson, F. South Africa: the cordoned heart 968.06
History
Thompson, L. M. A history of South Africa 968
Politics and government
Gordimer, N. The essential gesture 828
Holland, H. The struggle: a history of the African National Congress 968.06
Mallaby, S. After apartheid 968.06
Paton, A. Save the beloved country 968.06
Race relations
Benson, M. Nelson Mandela 92
Gordimer, N. The essential gesture 828
Holland, H. The struggle: a history of the African National Congress 968.06
Mallaby, S. After apartheid 968.06
Mandela, W. Part of my soul went with him 92
Mathabane, M. Kaffir boy 92
Mathabane, M. Kaffir boy in America 92
Meer, F. Higher than hope: the authorized biography of Nelson Mandela 92
Paton, A. Save the beloved country 968.06
Sparks, A. The mind of South Africa 968
Wilson, F. South Africa: the cordoned heart 968.06
See/See also pages in the following book(s):
Thompson, L. M. A history of South Africa p154-242 968
Race relations—Drama
Fugard, A. "Master Harold"—and the boys 822
Race relations—Pictorial works
Kumalo, A. Mandela 92
Social conditions
Wilson, F. South Africa: the cordoned heart 968.06
South African War, 1899-1902
Pakenham, T. The Boer War 968.04
South America
The South American handbook 980
Description
Darwin, C. The voyage of the Beagle 508
The **South** American handbook 980

South Asia
Dictionaries
The Cambridge encyclopedia of India, Pakistan, Bangladesh, Sri Lanka, Nepal, Bhutan, and the Maldives 954
South Pacific Region *See* Oceania
South Sea Islands *See* Oceania
South Seas *See* Oceania
The **Southeast** Asia cookbook. Law, R. 641.5
Southern, Eileen
Biographical dictionary of Afro-American and African musicians 780.92
The music of black Americans 780.89
Southern Christian Leadership Conference
Garrow, D. J. Bearing the cross: Martin Luther King, Jr., and the Southern Christian Leadership Conference 92
Southern cooking, Craig Claiborne's. Claiborne, C. 641.5
Southern daughter: the life of Margaret Mitchell. Pyron, D. A. 92
Southern food & plantation houses, Lee Bailey's. Bailey, L. 641.5
Southern literature *See* American literature—Southern States
Southern Rhodesia *See* Zimbabwe
Southern States
Civilization
Cash, W. J. The mind of the South 975
See/See also pages in the following book(s):
Mencken, H. L. The American scene p157-68 818
Economic conditions
See/See also pages in the following book(s):
The Causes of the Civil War 973.7
Race relations
Morris, A. D. The origins of the civil rights movement 305.8
Race relations—Pictorial works
Durham, M. Powerful days 323.1
Lyon, D. Memories of the Southern civil rights movement 323.1
Southwest Pacific Region *See* Oceania
Sovereigns *See* Kings, queens, rulers, etc.
Soviet Russian literature. Slonim, M. 891.7
Soviet Union
See also Russia; Russia (Republic)
Dictionaries
Paxton, J. Encyclopedia of Russian history 947
Environmental policy
See Environment—Government policy—Soviet Union
Foreign relations
Gorbachev, M. Perestroika 327.1
Gromyko, A. A. Memoirs 92
Shevchenko, A. N. Breaking with Moscow 92
Foreign relations—United States
Beschloss, M. R. The crisis years 909.82
Kennan, G. F. American diplomacy 327.73
Kennedy, R. F. Thirteen days 973.922
History
Deutscher, I. The prophet outcast: Trotsky, 1929-1940 92
Russia and the independent states 947
History—1917-1921, Revolution
Moynahan, B. Comrades: 1917—Russia in revolution 947.084
Reed, J. Ten days that shook the world 947.084
Politics and government
Bullock, A. Hitler and Stalin 92
Cohen, S. F. Voices of glasnost 947.085
Conquest, R. Stalin 92
The Decline and fall of the Soviet empire 947.085
Deutscher, I. Stalin 92
Doder, D. Gorbachev 92
Felshman, N. Gorbachev, Yeltsin, and the last days of the Soviet empire 947.085
Gorbachev, M. The August coup 947.085
Gorbachev, M. Perestroika 327.1
Kaiser, R. G. Why Gorbachev happened 92
Khrushchev, N. S. Khrushchev remembers 947.085
Khrushchev, S. Krushchev on Khrushchev 92
Medvedev, R. A. Khrushchev: the years in power 947.085
Medvedev, R. A. Let history judge 947.084
Mikhail S. Gorbachev: an intimate biography 92

White, Elwyn Brooks *See* White, E. B. (Elwyn Brooks), 1899-1985

White, Evelyn C., 1954-
(ed) The Black women's health book. See The Black women's health book   613

White, Jon Ewbank Manchip, 1924-
Everyday life of the North American Indian   970.004

White, Margaret Bourke- *See* Bourke-White, Margaret, 1904-1971

White, Marlene Boskind- *See* Boskind-White, Marlene

White, Michael, 1959-
Stephen Hawking   92

White, Phyllis Dorothy James *See* James, P. D.

White, Richard E.
(jt. auth) Borror, D. J. A field guide to the insects of America north of Mexico   595.7

White, Ryan
Ryan White: my own story   92

White, T. H. (Terence Hanbury), 1906-1964
Once and future king; dramatization. See Lerner, A. J. Camelot   812

White, Terence Hanbury *See* White, T. H. (Terence Hanbury), 1906-1964

White, Theodore H., 1915-1986
America in search of itself   973.92
In search of history   92
The making of the president, 1960   324.6
Theodore H. White at large   818

White, Welsh S., 1940-
The death penalty in the nineties   364.6

White, William C., Jr.
(jt. auth) Boskind-White, M. Bulimarexia   616.85

The white album. Didion, J.   814

White bears and other unwanted thoughts. Wegner, D. M.   153.4

White House years. Kissinger, H.   92

White lies. Davies, N.   345

White on black. Nederveen Pieterse, J.   700

White shroud. Ginsberg, A.   811

Whitehead, Alfred North, 1861-1947
Process and reality   113

Whitehead, Mary Beth
A mother's story   306.8

Whiteman, Paul, 1890-1967
About
DeLong, T. A. Pops: Paul Whiteman, king of jazz   780.92

Whitfield, Shelby
(jt. auth) Cosell, H. What's wrong with sports   796

Whitman, Walt, 1819-1892
Complete poetry and collected prose   818
Democratic vistas
In Whitman, W. Walt Whitman   818
Leaves of grass   811
also in Whitman, W. Complete poetry and collected prose   818
Leaves of grass [selections]
In Whitman, W. Walt Whitman   818
Specimen days
In Whitman, W. Walt Whitman   818
Walt Whitman   818
About
Callow, P. From noon to starry night: a life of Walt Whitman   92
See/See also pages in the following book(s):
Kazin, A. An American procession p103-27   810.9
Matthiessen, F. O. American renaissance p517-625   810.9
Voices & visions p3-50   811.009

Whitmore, Kristene E., 1952-
(jt. auth) Chalker, R. Overcoming bladder disorders   616.6

Whitney, Betsey Cushing Roosevelt, 1908-
About
Grafton, D. The sisters   920

Whitney, Catherine
Whose life?   363.4
(jt. auth) Callaway, C. W. Surviving with AIDS   616.97
(jt. auth) Gershoff, S. N. The Tufts University guide to total nutrition   613.2

Whitney, Elinor, 1889-
(ed) Newbery Medal books, 1922-1955. See Newbery Medal books, 1922-1955   028.5

Whitney, Stephen, 1942-
A Sierra Club naturalist's guide to the Sierra Nevada   574.9
Western forests   574.5

Whitney, Steven
(jt. auth) Lauersen, N. It's your body   618.1

Whitney M. Young, Jr., and the struggle for civil rights. Weiss, N. J.   92

Whitney Museum of American Art
See/See also pages in the following book(s):
Garrett, R. New York's great art museums   708

Whittemore, Hank
CNN   070.1

Whittier, John Greenleaf, 1807-1892
The poetical works of Whittier   811
See/See also pages in the following book(s):
Warren, R. P. New and selected essays p235-83   810.9

Whittling *See* Wood carving

Whitworth, Jerry A.
About
Earley, P. Family of spies   327.12

Whitworth, Kathy, 1939-
Golf for women   796.352

Who killed Martin Luther King?. Ray, J. E.   92

Who killed my daughter?. Duncan, L.   364.1

Who needs God. Kushner, H. S.   296.7

Who was who   920.003

Who was who in America   920.003

Who was who in Native American history. Waldman, C.   920.003

Who was who in the Greek world, 776 BC-30 BC   920.003

Who was who in world exploration. Waldman, C.   920.003

Who will know us?. Soto, G.   811

Who will tell the people. Greider, W.   324

Who wrote the Bible?. Friedman, R. E.   222

"Whoever fights monsters—". Ressler, R. K.   364.1

A whole different ball game. Miller, M.   796.357

Whole house remodeling guide. Duncan, S. B.   643

The whole library handbook. Eberhart, G. M.   027

The whole motion. Dickey, J.   811

Wholey, Dennis
(ed) Becoming your own parent. See Becoming your own parent   362.29
(ed) When the worst that can happen already has. See When the worst that can happen already has   128

Wholistic medicine *See* Holistic medicine

Who's afraid of Virginia Woolf?. Albee, E.   812
also in Albee, E. The plays v1   812

Who's calling the shots?. Carlsson-Paige, N.   155.4

Who's who   920.003

Who's who among black Americans   920.003

Who's who in America   920.003

Who's who in American art   709.2

Who's who in American music: classical   780.92

Who's who in American politics   920.003

Who's who in art   709.2

Who's who in finance and industry   920.003

Who's who in the Bible. Calvocoressi, P.   220.9

Who's who in the world   920.003

Who's who of American women   920.003

Whose broad stripes and bright stars?. Germond, J.   324

Whose life?. Whitney, C.   363.4

Whose rose garden is it anyway?. Buchwald, A.   817

Why Americans hate politics. Dionne, E. J., Jr.   320.5

Why black people tend to shout. Wiley, R.   305.8

Why buildings fall down. Levy, M.   690

Why do clocks run clockwise? and other imponderables. Feldman, D.   031.02

Why do dogs have wet noses? and other imponderables of everyday life. Feldman, D.   031.02

Why Gorbachev happened. Kaiser, R. G.   92

Why I am not a Christian, and other essays on religion and related subjects. Russell, B.   211

Why Johnny can't concentrate. Moss, R. A.   153.1

Why Johnny can't read—and what you can do about it. Flesch, R. F.   372.4

Why Johnny can't tell right from wrong. Kilpatrick, W.   370.1

Why Johnny still can't read. Flesch, R. F.   372.4

Why me?. Davis, S., Jr.   92

Why we can't wait. King, M. L.   323.1

Woolf, Virginia, 1882-1941—*About*—*Continued*
Critical essays on Virginia Woolf   823.009
Dunn, J. A very close conspiracy: Vanessa Bell and Virginia Woolf   92
Gordon, L. Virginia Woolf, a writer's life   92
Lee, H. The novels of Virginia Woolf   823.009
Rosenthal, M. Virginia Woolf   823.009
   See/See also pages in the following book(s):
Bradbury, M. The modern world p229-51   809
Heilbrun, C. G. Hamlet's mother and other women p58-97, 134-39   820.9
O'Faoláin, S. The vanishing hero p170-204   823.009
Woolley, Sir Leonard, 1880-1960
The Sumerians   935
Word books *See* Picture dictionaries
Word games
   See also Crossword puzzles
Word histories, Webster's   422.03
Word play. Farb, P.   401
Word processing
Century 21 keyboarding, formatting, and document processing   652.3
Word skills *See* Reading
Words *See* Vocabulary
Words, New
Dictionaries
Brewer's dictionary of 20th-century phrase and fable   803
The Oxford dictionary of new words   423
Third Barnhart dictionary of new English   423
The **words**. Sartre, J. P.   92
Words and music. Beckett, S.
   In Beckett, S. Cascando, and other short dramatic pieces p21-32   842
   In Beckett, S. Collected shorter plays   842
The **words** of Albert Schweitzer. Schweitzer, A.   210
The **words** of Martin Luther King, Jr.. King, M. L.   323.1
Words of the Vietnam War. Clark, G. R.   427
Words on cassette   011
Words on tape. See Words on cassette   011
Words to rhyme with. Espy, W. R.   423
Words with power. Frye, N.   809
Wordstruck. MacNeil, R.   92
Wordsworth, William, 1770-1850
Ode: intimations of immortality from recollections of early childhood; criticism
   In Brooks, C. The well wrought urn   821.009
   In Trilling, L. The liberal imagination p123-51   809
The poetical works of William Wordsworth   821
William Wordsworth   821
About
Gill, S. C. William Wordsworth   92
   See/See also pages in the following book(s):
Holmes, R. Footsteps   828
Work
   See also Labor
Levering, R. A great place to work   331.2
Terkel, S. Working   331.2
The **work** of nations. Reich, R. B.   330.9
Work Projects Administration *See* United States. Work Projects Administration
Work, study, travel abroad. Council on International Educational Exchange   370.19
Working. Terkel, S.   331.2
Working & caring. Brazelton, T. B.   649
Working at home *See* Home business
Working class *See* Labor
Working days. Steinbeck, J.   818
Working hours *See* Hours of labor
Working parents, Children of *See* Children of working parents
The **working** parents' survival guide. Olds, S. W.   649
Working with metal   684
Working women *See* Women—Employment
Works Progress Administration *See* United States. Work Projects Administration
The **workshop** of democracy. Burns, J. M.
   In Burns, J. M. The American experiment v2   973
Workshops
The Home workshop   684
The **World** almanac and book of facts   031.02
The **World** almanac book of World War II. See The World almanac of World War II   940.53

The **World** almanac of the American Revolution   973.3
The **World** almanac of World War II   940.53
World artists, 1950-1980   709.2
World artists, 1980-1990   709.2
The **World** at arms: the Reader's Digest illustrated history of World War II   940.53
World atlas, Goode's   912
World authors, 1950-1970   920.003
World authors, 1970-1975   920.003
World authors, 1975-1980   920.003
World authors, 1980-1985   920.003
The **World** Book encyclopedia   031
The **World** Book year book. See The World Book encyclopedia   031
World Christian encyclopedia   203
World coins. See Krause, C. L. Standard catalog of world coins   737.4
The **world** crisis. Churchill, Sir W.   940.3
World economics *See* Economic conditions
World encyclopedia of 20th century murder. Nash, J. R.   364.03
World encyclopedia of organized crime. Nash, J. R.   364.03
World explorers and discoverers   920.003
World history
Dictionaries
Worldmark encyclopedia of the nations   910.3
Sources
Eyewitness to history   909
World history. Wetterau, B.   902
World hunger. Kutzner, P. L.   363.8
The **world** is burning. Shoumatoff, A.   333.7
The **world** is my home: a memoir. Michener, J. A.   92
A **world** lit only by fire. Manchester, W.   940.2
The **world** of biblical literature. Alter, R.   221.6
The **world** of Count Basie. Dance, S.   780.92
The **world** of Duke Ellington. Dance, S.   780.92
The **World** of games   794
A **world** of ideas. Moyers, B.   973.92
A **world** of ideas II. Moyers, B.   973.92
The **World** of learning   060.25
A **world** of light. Sarton, M.   92
The **World** of mathematics   510
The **world** of musical comedy. Green, S.   780.92
The **world** of myth. Leeming, D. A.   291
The **world** of Odysseus. Finley, M. I.   883
World of our fathers. Howe, I.   305.8
The **world** of the pharaohs. Hobson, C.   932
The **world** of the ten thousand things. Wright, C.   811
World on fire. Mitchell, G. J.   363.7
World politics
Castro, F. Nothing can stop the course of history   972.91
Fulbright, J. W. The price of empire   327.73
Nixon, R. M. 1999   327.73
Yergin, D. The prize   338.2
1945-1991
Beschloss, M. R. The crisis years   909.82
   See/See also pages in the following book(s):
Prados, J. Presidents' secret wars p13-29   327.12
1965-
Drucker, P. F. The new realities   909.82
Gorbachev, M. Perestroika   327.1
Halberstam, D. The next century   303.49
Dictionaries
Worldmark encyclopedia of the nations   910.3
World records
The Guinness book of records 1492   031.02
World religions   291
World Resources Institute
The Information please environmental almanac. See The Information please environmental almanac   363.7
World series (Baseball)
Neft, D. S. The World Series   796.357
The **World** treasury of modern religious thought   200
World War, 1914-1918
Churchill, Sir W. The world crisis   940.3
Liddell Hart, Sir B. H. The real war, 1914-1918   940.4
Stokesbury, J. L. A short history of World War I   940.3
Toland, J. No man's land   940.3
Tuchman, B. W. The guns of August   940.3
Causes
Massie, R. K. Dreadnought   940.3

Z

A Cappella Bks., 106 W. Franklin Ave., Pennington, N.J. 08534 Tel 609-737-6525 Fax 609-737-3787; refer orders to 814 N. Franklin St., Chicago, Ill. 60610 Tel 312-337-0747 Fax 312-337-5985

A-R Eds. Inc., 801 Deming Way, Madison, Wis. 53717 Tel 608-836-9000; 800-736-0070 (orders only)

Abbeville Press Inc., 488 Madison Ave., New York, N.Y. 10022 Tel 212-888-1969; 800-227-7210 Fax 212-644-5085

ABC-CLIO Inc., 50 S. Steele St., Suite 805, Denver, Colo. 80209 Tel 303-333-3003 Fax 303-333-4037; refer orders to P.O. Box 1911, Santa Barbara, Calif. 93116-1911 Tel 800-422-2546 Fax 805-685-9685

Abingdon Press, P.O. Box 801, Nashville, Tenn. 37202-0801 Tel 615-749-6000; 800-251-3320 (orders) Fax 615-749-6512; 749-6577 (orders)

Abrams: Harry N. Abrams Inc., 100 5th Ave., New York, N.Y. 10011 Tel 212-206-7715; 800-345-1359 Fax 212-645-8437; refer orders to Editions Publisol, P.O. Box 339, Gracie Station, New York, N.Y. 10028 Tel 212-289-3981

Academic Press Inc., 525 B St., Suite 1900, San Diego, Calif. 92101-4495 Tel 619-231-6616; 800-321-5068 Fax 619-699-6320; refer orders to 6277 Sea Harbor Dr., Orlando, Fla. 32887 Tel 407-345-2000; 800-321-5068 Fax 800-336-7377

Access Press (NY): Access Press Ltd., 10 E. 53rd St., New York, N.Y. 10022-5299 Tel 212-207-7493; 800-328-3443; refer orders to HarperCollins Pubs.

Adams, B.: Bob Adams Inc., 260 Center St., Holbrook, Mass. 02343 Tel 617-767-8100; 800-872-5627

Addison-Wesley Pub. Co., Jacob Way, Reading, Mass. 01867 Tel 617-944-3700; 800-447-2226 (orders only)

Adler & Adler Pubs., Inc., 4550 Montgomery Ave., Suite 705, Bethesda, Md. 20814 Tel 301-654-4271; refer orders to Woodbine House

Algonquin Bks.: Algonquin Bks. of Chapel Hill, 307 W. Weaver St., Carrboro, N.C. 27510 Tel 919-967-0108 Fax 919-933-0272; refer orders to Workman Pub. Co. Inc., 708 Broadway, New York, N.Y. 10003 Tel 212-254-5900; 800-722-7202 Fax 212-254-8098; 800-521-1832 (orders)

AMACOM, 135 W. 50th St., New York, N.Y. 10020 Tel 212-903-8315 Fax 212-903-8168; refer orders to P.O. Box 319, Saranac Lake, N.Y. 12983 Tel 518-891-5510; 800-262-9699 Fax 518-891-3653

Amadeus Press, 133 S.W. 2nd Ave., Suite 450, Portland, Or. 97204 Tel 503-227-2878; 800-327-5680 (U.S. & Can.) Fax 503-227-3070

Amereon Ltd., P.O. Box 1200, Mattituck, N.Y. 11952-9500 Tel 516-298-5100; Fax 516-298-5631

American Assn. for State & Local Hist., 172 2nd Ave. N., Suite 202, Nashville, Tenn. 37201 Tel 615-255-2971

American Assn. of Mus. (The), 1225 Eye St. N.W., Suite 200, Washington, D.C. 20005 Tel 202-289-9127 Fax 202-289-6578

American Assn. of Retired Persons, 601 E St. N.W., Washington, D.C. 20049 Tel 202-434-2500

American Bible Soc., 1865 Broadway, New York, N.Y. 10023 Tel 212-581-7400 Fax 212-582-7245; refer orders to P.O. Box 5656, Grand Central Station, New York, N.Y. 10163 Tel 800-543-8000

American Bk. Co., 125 Spring St., Lexington, Mass. 02173; refer orders to Heath

American Chemical Soc., 1155 16th St. N.W., Washington, D.C. 20036 Tel 202-872-4600; 800-333-9511 Fax 202-872-4615; refer orders to Distribution Office, Dept. 451, P.O. Box 57136, West End Station, Washington, D.C. 20037 Tel 202-872-4363; 800-227-5558 Fax 202-872-6067

American Council of Life Insurance, 1001 Pennsylvania Ave. N.W., Washington, D.C. 20004-2599 Tel 202-624-2000

American Federation of Arts, 41 E. 65th St., New York, N.Y. 10021 Tel 212-988-7700 Fax 212-861-2487

American Forestry Assn., 1516 P St. N.W., Washington, D.C. 20005 Tel 202-667-3300 Fax 202-667-7751

American Foundation for the Blind Inc., 15 W. 16th St., New York, N.Y. 10011 Tel 212-620-2155; 800-232-5463 Fax 212-620-2105

American Guidance Service Inc., 4201 Woodland Rd., Circle Pines, Minn. 55014-1796 Tel 612-786-4343; 800-328-2560 Fax 612-786-5603

American Heritage Pub. Co. Inc., 60 5th Ave., New York, N.Y. 10011 Tel 212-206-5500; refer orders to Houghton Mifflin

American Legacy Press, 40 Engelhard Ave., Avenel, N.J. 07001 Tel 908-827-2700; 800-223-6804; refer orders to Random House

American Lib. Assn., 50 E. Huron St., Chicago, Ill. 60611 Tel 312-280-2424; 800-545-2433 Fax 312-944-2641 (orders only)

American Medical Assn., 515 N. State St., Chicago, Ill. 60610 Tel 312-464-5000; 800-621-8335 Fax 312-464-5600

American Mgt. Assn., 135 W. 50th St., New York, N.Y. 10020 Tel 212-586-8100; refer orders to P.O. Box 1026, Saranac Lake, N.Y. 12983-9986 Tel 800-262-9699 Fax 518-891-0368

American Pharmaceutical Assn., 2215 Constitution Ave. N.W., Washington, D.C. 20037 Tel 202-628-4410; 800-237-2742 (orders only)

American Psychiatric Press Inc., 1400 K St. N.W., Suite 1101, Washington, D.C. 20005 Tel 202-682-6262; 800-368-5777 Fax 202-789-2648

American Psychiatric Press Corp. See American Psychiatric Press Inc.

American Radio Relay League Inc., 225 Main St., Newington, Conn. 06111 Tel 203-666-1541

American Source Bks., P.O. Box 280353, Lakewood, Colo. 80228 Tel 303-980-0580

American Tech. Pubs. Inc., 1155 W. 175th St., Homewood, Ill. 60430 Tel 708-957-1100; 800-323-3471 Fax 708-957-1137

Amistad Press Inc., Time & Life Bldg., Rockefeller Center, Room 3845, New York, N.Y. 10020 Tel 212-522-6936; refer orders to Penguin USA, P.O. Box 999, Bergenfield, N.J. 07621 Tel 201-387-0600; 800-253-6476 Fax 201-385-6521

AMPHOTO, 1515 Broadway, New York, N.Y. 10036 Tel 212-536-5121; 800-451-1741 Fax 212-536-5359; refer orders to 1695 Oak St., Lakewood, N.J. 08701 Tel 908-363-4511

AMS Press, 56 E. 13th St., New York, N.Y. 10003 Tel 212-777-4700 Fax 212-995-5413

Ancestry Pub. Co. Inc., 400 S. 400W, Bldg. D, Salt Lake City, Utah 84101 Tel 801-531-1790; 800-531-1790; refer orders to P.O. Box 476, Salt Lake City, Utah 84110

Anchor Bks., 1540 Broadway, New York, N.Y. 10036 Tel 212-354-6500; 800-223-6834 Fax 212-492-9698

Anchor Press, 1540 Broadway, New York, N.Y. 10036 Tel 212-354-6500; 800-223-6834 Fax 212-492-9698

Anchor Press/Doubleday, 1540 Broadway, New York, N.Y. 10036 Tel 212-354-6500; 800-223-6834 Fax 212-492-9698

Andrews & McMeel Inc., 4900 Main St., Kansas City, Mo. 64112 Tel 816-932-6700; 800-826-4216 Fax 816-932-6706

Andrews, McMeel & Parker, 4900 Main St., Kansas City, Mo. 64112 Tel 816-932-6700; 800-826-4216

Aperture Foundation Inc., 20 E. 23rd St., New York, N.Y. 10010 Tel 212-505-5555; 800-631-3577 Fax 212-979-7759; refer orders to Farrar, Straus & Giroux

Apollo Bk., 5 Schoolhouse Lane, Poughkeepsie, N.Y. 12603 Tel 914-462-0040; 800-942-8222; 800-431-5003 (outside N.Y.)

Applause Theatre Bk. Pubs., 211 W. 71st St., New York, N.Y. 10023 Tel 212-595-4735; 800-873-6775 Fax 212-721-2856

Appleton & Lange, 25 Van Zant St., East Norwalk, Conn. 06855 Tel 203-838-4400; 800-423-1359 Fax 203-854-9486

Arbor House Pub. Co., 1350 Ave. of the Americas, New York, N.Y. 10019 Tel 212-261-6500; 800-843-9389; refer orders to 39 Plymouth St., Fairfield, N.J. 07007 Tel 201-227-7200

Arcade Pub., 141 5th Ave., New York, N.Y. 10010 Tel 212-475-2633; 800-343-9204 Fax 212-353-8148; refer orders to Little, Brown

Arden Lib., Mill & Main Sts., Darby, Pa. 19023

Ardis Pubs., 2901 Heatherway, Ann Arbor, Mich. 48104 Tel 313-971-2367 Fax 313-973-0039; refer orders to Maxway Data Corp., 225 W. 34th St., Room 1105, New York, N.Y. 10001 Tel 212-947-6100; 800-877-7133

Aronson, J.: Jason Aronson Inc., 230 Livingston St., Northvale, N.J. 07647 Tel 201-767-4093 Fax 201-767-4330; refer orders to 1205 O'Neill Highway, Dunmore, Pa. 18512 Tel 717-342-1449; 800-782-0015 Fax 717-348-9297

Association for Educ. Communications & Technology, 1126 16th St. N.W., Washington, D.C. 20036 Tel 202-466-4780

Atheneum Pubs., 866 3rd Ave., New York, N.Y. 10022 Tel 212-702-2000; 800-257-5755; refer orders to Macmillan

Atlantic Monthly Press See Grove/Atlantic

Audel: Theodore Audel & Co., c.o. Macmillan Pub. Co., 866 3rd Ave., New York, N.Y. 10022 Tel 212-702-2000; refer orders to 100 Front St., Box 500 Riverside, N.J. 08075-7500 Tel 609-461-6500

Avenel Bks., 40 Engelhard Ave., Avenel, N.J. 07001 Tel 908-827-2700; 800-223-6804; refer orders to Random House

Avery Pub. Group Inc., 120 Old Broadway, Garden City Park, N.Y. 11040 Tel 516-741-2155; 800-548-5757 Fax 516-742-1892

Avon Bks., 1350 Ave. of the Americas, New York, N.Y. 10019 Tel 212-261-6800 Fax 212-261-6895; refer orders to Route 2, Swanson Dr., Dresden, Tenn. 38225 Tel 901-364-5742; 800-238-0658 Fax 800-223-0239

Back Stage Bks., 1515 Broadway, New York, N.Y. 10036 Tel 212-764-7300; 800-451-1741 (orders)

Baker Bk. House, P.O. Box 6287, Grand Rapids, Mich. 49516-6287 Tel 616-676-9185; 800-877-2665 Fax 616-676-9573

Baker, W.H.: Walter H. Baker Co., 100 Chauncy St., Boston, Mass. 02111 Tel 617-482-1280

Ballantine Bks., 201 E. 50th St., New York, N.Y. 10022 Tel 212-751-2713; 800-638-6460 Fax 212-572-4912; refer orders to 400 Hahn Rd., Westminster, Md. 21157 Tel 800-726-0600

Bantam Bks. Inc., 1540 Broadway, New York, N.Y. 10036 Tel 212-354-6500; 800-223-6834 Fax 212-492-9698

Barnes & Noble Bks., 4720 Boston Way, Lanham, Md. 20706 Tel 301-306-0400 Fax 301-459-3366

Barricade Bks. Inc., 61 4th Ave., New York, N.Y. 10003 Tel 212-228-8828 Fax 212-673-1039; refer orders to Publishers Group West, P.O. Box 8843, Emeryville, Calif. 94662 Tel 800-788-3123

Barron's Educ. Ser. Inc., 250 Wireless Blvd., Hauppauge, N.Y. 11788 Tel 516-434-3311; 800-257-5729; 800-645-3476 (outside NY) Fax 516-434-3723

Barrows Co. Inc., 116 E. 66th St., New York, N.Y. 10021 Tel 212-772-1199

Basic Bks. Inc. Pubs., 10 E. 53rd St., New York, N.Y. 10022 Tel 212-207-7057; 800-242-7737; 800-331-3761 (individual orders) Fax 212-207-7203; 800-822-4090 (orders); refer orders to HarperCollins Pubs., 1000 Keystone Ind. Park, Scranton, Pa. 18512-4621 Tel 800-331-3761

BBC/Parkwest Publs., 451 Communipaw Ave., Jersey City, N.J. 07304 Tel 201-432-3257 Fax 201-432-3708; 800-727-5937

Beacham Pub., 2100 S St. N.W., Washington, D.C. 20009 Tel 202-234-0877 Fax 202-234-1402

Beacon Press, 25 Beacon St., Boston, Mass. 02108 Tel 617-742-2110 Fax 617-723-3097; refer orders to Farrar, Straus & Giroux

Bedford Arts Pubs., 301 Brannan St., Suite 410, San Francisco, Calif. 94107 Tel 415-882-7870; refer orders to Publisher Resources Inc., 1224 Heil Quaker Blvd., P.O. Box 7001, La Vergne, Tenn. 37086-7001 Tel 615-793-5090; 800-937-5557

Bedrick Bks.: Peter Bedrick Bks. Inc., 2112 Broadway, Room 318, New York, N.Y. 10023 Tel 212-496-0751 Fax 212-496-1158

Beech Tree Bks., 1350 Ave. of the Americas, New York, N.Y. 10019 Tel 212-261-6500; 800-237-0657 Fax 212-779-0965; refer orders to 39 Plymouth St., Fairfield, N.J. 07007 Tel 201-227-7200; 800-843-9389 Fax 201-227-6849

Belknap Press, 79 Garden St., Cambridge, Mass. 02138 Tel 617-495-2480

Benziger Pub. Co., 15319 Chatsworth St., Mission Hills, Calif. 91395

Berkley Bks., 200 Madison Ave., New York, N.Y. 10016 Tel 212-951-8800; 800-631-8571; refer orders to P.O. Box 506, E. Rutherford, N.J. 07073 Tel 201-933-9292; 800-223-0510 Fax 201-933-4927

Berkley Pub. Group (The), 200 Madison Ave., New York, N.Y. 10016 Tel 212-951-8800; 800-631-8571 Fax 212-545-8917; refer orders to P.O. Box 506, E. Rutherford, N.J. 07073 Tel 201-933-9292 Fax 201-933-4927

Berkshire Traveller Press (The), P.O. Box 297, Stockbridge, Mass. 01262 Tel 413-298-3636 Fax 413-298-5323

Betterway Publs. Inc., 1507 Dana Ave., Cincinnati, Ohio 45207 Tel 513-531-2222; 800-289-0963 Fax 513-531-4082

Bicycle Bks. Pub. Inc., P.O. Box 2038, 32 Glen Dr., Mill Valley, Calif. 94941 Tel 415-381-2515 Fax 415-381-6912; refer orders to Bookpeople, 7900 Edgewater Dr., Oakland, Calif. 94621 Tel 510-632-4700; 800-999-4650

Billboard Bks., 1515 Broadway, New York, N.Y. 10036 Tel 212-536-5121; refer orders to 1695 Oak St., Lakewood, N.J. 08701 Tel 908-363-5679; 800-451-1741

Billboard Publs. Inc., 1515 Broadway, New York, N.Y. 10036 Tel 212-536-5121; refer orders to 1695 Oak St., Lakewood, N.J. 08701 Tel 908-363-5679; 800-451-1741

Birch Lane Press, 600 Madison Ave., 11th Floor, New York, N.Y. 10022 Tel 212-486-2200 Fax 212-486-2231; refer orders to 120 Enterprise Ave., Secaucus, N.J. 07094 Tel 201-866-8159

Bits Press, Dept. of English, Case Western Reserve Univ., Cleveland, Ohio 44106

Black Sparrow Press, 24 10th St., Santa Rosa, Calif. 95401 Tel 707-579-4011 Fax 707-579-0567

Blackwell Pubs., 108 Cowley Rd., Oxford OX4 1JF, Eng. Tel (0865) 791 100 Fax (0865) 791 347; refer orders to Marston Bk. Services Ltd., P.O. Box 87, Osney Mead, Oxford OX2 0DT, Eng. Tel (0865) 791 155 Fax (0865) 791 927

Branch offices

U.S.: Blackwell, 238 Main St., Suite 501, Cambridge, Mass. 02142 Tel 617-547-7110 Fax 617-547-0789; refer orders to American Int. Distr. Corp., 64 Depot Rd., Colchester, Vt. 05446 Tel 802-878-0315; 800-488-2665 (outside Vt.) Fax 802-878-1102

BOA Eds. Ltd., 92 Park Ave., Brockport, N.Y. 14420 Tel 716-637-3844

Body Press/Perigee, 200 Madison Ave., New York, N.Y. 10016 Tel 212-951-8400; 800-631-8571

Body Press (Los Angeles): Body Press, 11150 Olympic Blvd., Suite 650, Los Angeles, Calif. 90064

Bonus Bks., 160 E. Illinois St., Chicago, Ill. 60611 Tel 312-467-0580; 800-225-3775 Fax 312-467-9271

Books for Libs., 3 Park Ave., New York, N.Y. 10016

Borden Pub. Co., 1855 W. Main St., Alhambra, Calif. 91801

Borgo Press (The), P.O. Box 2845, San Bernardino, Calif. 92406-2845 Tel 909-884-5813 Fax 909-888-4942

Bowker: R. R. Bowker Co., 121 Chanlon Rd., New Providence, N.J. 07974 Tel 908-464-6800; 800-521-8110 Fax 908-464-3553

Boyars, M.: Marion Boyars Pubs. Ltd., 24 Lacy Rd., London SW15 1NL, Eng. Tel (081) 788 9522 Fax (081) 789 8122; refer orders to Clipper Distr. Services Ltd., Windmill Grove, Portchester, Fareham, Hampshire PO16 9HT, Eng. Tel (0705) 200 080

Branch offices

U.S.: Marion Boyars Pubs. Inc., 237 E. 39th St., No. 1A, New York, N.Y. 10016-2110 Tel 212-697-1599; refer orders to Inland Bk. Co., 140 Commerce St., East Haven, Conn. 06512 Tel 203-467-4257; 800-243-0138

Braziller: George Braziller Inc., 60 Madison Ave., Suite 1001, New York, N.Y. 10010 Tel 212-889-0909 Fax 212-689-5405

Brown, W.C.: William C. Brown Co. Pubs., 2460 Kerper Blvd., P.O. Box 539, Dubuque, Iowa 52004-0539 Tel 319-588-1451; 800-338-5558 Fax 319-589-4668

Bruccoli Clark, 2006 Sumter St., Columbia, S.C. 29201 Tel 803-771-4642; refer orders to Independent Pubs. Group, 1 Pleasant Ave., Port Washington, N.Y. 11050 Tel 516-944-9325

Bulfinch Press, 34 Beacon St., Boston, Mass. 02108 Tel 617-227-0730 Fax 617-227-0790; refer orders to 200 West St., Waltham, Mass. 02154 Tel 800-343-9204 Fax 617-890-0875

Bull Pub. Co., 110 Gilbert Ave., Menlo Park, Calif. 94025 Tel 415-322-2855 Fax 415-327-3300; refer orders to P.O. Box 208, Palo Alto, Calif. 94302 Tel 800-676-2855

Bunting & Lyon Inc., 238 N. Main St., Wallingford, Conn. 06492 Tel 203-269-3333

Burlingame Bks.: Edward Burlingame Bks., 10 E. 53rd St., New York, N.Y. 10022-5299 Tel 212-207-7000

Business One Irwin, 1333 Burr Ridge Parkway, Burr Ridge, Ill. 60521 Tel 708-789-4000; 957-5800 (Alaska & Hawaii); 800-634-3961 (except Alaska & Hawaii)

Butterworths, Halsbury House, 35 Chancery Lane, London WC2A 1EL, Eng. Tel (071) 400 2500 Fax (071) 400 2842

Branch offices

U.S.: Butterworths, 8 Industrial Way, Bldg. C, Salem, N.H. 03071 Tel 603-898-9664 Fax 603-898-9858

Cambridge Univ. Press, Edinburgh Bldg., Shaftesbury Rd., Cambridge CB2 2RU, Eng. Tel (0223) 312 393 Fax (0223) 315 052

Branch offices

U.S.: Cambridge Univ. Press, 40 W. 20th St., New York, N.Y. 10011-4211 Tel 212-924-3900; refer orders to 110 Midland Ave., Port Chester, N.Y. 10573-4930 Tel 914-937-9600; 800-227-0247; 800-872-7423 (orders only)

Camden House (Camden East): Camden House Pub. Ltd., 7 Queen Victoria Rd., Camden East, Ont., Can. K0K 1J0 Tel 613-378-6661 Fax 613-378-6123

Cameron & Co. Inc., 543 Howard St., San Francisco, Calif. 94105 Tel 415-777-5582; 800-779-5582 Fax 415-777-4814; refer orders to Baker & Taylor Bks., Western Div., 380 Edison Way, Reno, Nev. 89564 Tel 702-786-6700; 800-775-1900

Capra Press, P.O. Box 2068, Santa Barbara, Calif. 93120 Tel 805-966-4590 Fax 805-965-8020

Carnegie-Mellon Univ. Press, P.O. Box 21, Schenley Park, Pittsburgh, Pa. 15213 Tel 412-578-2861; refer orders to Cornell Univ. Press Services, 512 E. State St., P.O. Box 250, Ithaca, N.Y. 14850 Tel 607-277-2338; 800-666-2211

Carol Pub. Group, 600 Madison Ave., 11th Floor, New York, N.Y. 10022 Tel 212-486-2200 Fax 212-486-2231; refer orders to 120 Enterprise Ave., Secaucus, N.J. 07094 Tel 201-866-8159

Carroll & Graf Pubs. Inc., 260 5th Ave., New York, N.Y. 10001 Tel 212-889-8772 Fax 212-545-7909; refer orders to Publishers Group West, P.O. Box 8843, Emeryville, Calif. 94662 Tel 800-788-3123

Catbird Press, 16 Windsor Rd., North Haven, Conn. 06473 Tel 203-230-2391 Fax 203-230-8029; refer orders to Independent Pubs. Group, 814 N. Franklin St., Chicago, Ill. 60610 Tel 312-337-0747; 800-888-4741 Fax 312-337-5985

Catholic Univ. of Am. Press (The), 620 Michigan Ave. N.E., Room 303, Washington, D.C. 20064 Tel 202-635-5052 Fax 202-319-5802; refer orders to P.O. Box 4852, Hampden Station, Baltimore, Md. 21211 Tel 410-516-6953 Fax 410-516-6998

Celestial Arts, P.O. Box 7123, Berkeley, Calif. 94707 Tel 510-845-8414; 800-841-2665 Fax 510-524-1052

Chapman & Hall, 29 W. 35th St., New York, N.Y. 10001-2291 Tel 212-244-3336 Fax 212-563-2269

Chelsea Green Pub. Co., Route 113, Box 130, Post Mills, Vt. 05058-0130 Tel 802-333-9073; 800-639-4099 (orders only) Fax 802-333-9092

Chelsea House Pubs., 95 Madison Ave., New York, N.Y. 10016 Tel 212-683-4400; 800-848-2665

Chemical Pub. Co., 80 8th Ave., New York, N.Y. 10011

Cherry Lane Bks., 110 Midland Ave., Port Chester, N.Y. 10573; refer orders to P.O. Box 430, Port Chester, N.Y. 10573 Tel 914-937-8601

Children's Bk. Council Inc., 568 Broadway, Suite 404, New York, N.Y. 10012 Tel 212-966-1990 Fax 212-966-2073

Chilton Bk. Co., 201 King of Prussia Rd., Radnor, Pa. 19089-0230 Tel 215-964-4000; 800-695-1214; refer orders Dunmore Distr. Center, Reeves St. & Monahan Ave., Dunmore, Pa. 18512

Christian Classics Inc., 77 W. Main St., P.O. Box 30, Westminster, Md. 21158 Tel 410-848-3065; 800-888-3065 Fax 410-857-2805

Christian Science Pub. Soc. (The), 1 Norway St., Boston, Mass. 02115 Tel 617-450-2790; 800-288-7090; 800-877-8400 (orders) Fax 617-450-2017

Chronicle Bks., 275 5th St., San Francisco, Calif. 94103 Tel 415-777-7240; 800-445-7577; 800-722-6657 (outside Calif.) Fax 415-777-8887

CIBA-GEIGY Corp., c.o. Medical Educ. Div., 14 Henderson Dr., West Caldwell, N.J. 07006 Tel 201-882-4881; 800-631-1162; refer orders to P.O. Box 18060, Newark, N.J. 07191 Tel 800-631-1181

CineBooks Inc., 990 Grove St., Evanston, Ill. 60201 Tel 312-475-8400; 800-544-5701; refer orders to Independent Pubs. Group, 814 N. Franklin St., Chicago, Ill. 60610 Tel 312-337-0747; 800-888-4741

Cistercian Publs. Inc., Western Mich. Univ. Station, Kalamazoo, Mich. 49008 Tel 616-387-5090

Citadel Press, 600 Madison Ave., 11th Floor, New York, N.Y. 10022 Tel 212-486-2200; refer orders to 120 Enterprise Ave., Secaucus, N.J. 07094 Tel 201-866-8156

City Lights Bks., 261 Columbus Ave., San Francisco, Calif. 94133 Tel 415-362-1901 Fax 415-362-4921; refer orders to The Subterranean Co., P.O. Box 160, 265 S. 5th St., Monroe, Or. 97456 Tel 800-274-7826 Fax 503-847-6018

Clarendon Press See Oxford Univ. Press

Cleckley-Thigpen Psychiatric Associates, P.O. Box 2619, Augusta, Ga. 30904 Tel 706-724-7492

Cleis Press, P.O. Box 8933, Pittsburgh, Pa. 15221 Tel 412-937-1555; refer orders to Bookpeople, 7900 Edgewater Dr., Oakland, Calif. 94621 Tel 510-632-4700; 800-999-4650

Coin & Currency Inst. Inc (The), P.O. Box 1057, Clifton, N.J. 07014 Tel 201-471-1441

Cole Pub. Co. Inc., 4415 Sonoma Highway, Santa Rosa, Calif. 95409 Tel 707-538-0492 Fax 707-538-0497

College Entrance Examination Bd., 45 Columbus Ave., New York, N.Y. 10023 Tel 212-713-8000 Fax 212-713-8184; refer orders to College Bd. Publs., P.O. Box 886, New York, N.Y. 10101-0886 Tel 800-323-7155 (credit card orders)

Collier Bks., 866 3rd Ave., New York, N.Y. 10022 Tel 212-702-2000; 800-257-5755; refer orders to Macmillan

Collins: William Collins Sons & Co. Ltd., c.o. HarperCollins Pubs., 77/85 Fulham Palace Rd., Hammersmith, London W6 8JB, Eng. Tel (081) 741 7070 Fax (081) 307 4440; refer orders to P.O. Box, Glasgow G4 0NB, Scotland Tel (041) 772 3200 Fax (041) 772 3200

Columbia Bks. Inc. Pubs., 1212 New York Ave. N.W., Suite 330, Washington, D.C. 20005 Tel 202-898-0662

Columbia Univ. Press, 562 W. 113th St., New York, N.Y. 10025 Tel 212-316-7100; refer orders to 136 S. Broadway, Irvington-on-Hudson, N.Y. 10533 Tel 914-591-9111; 800-944-8648 Fax 800-944-1844

Commerce Clearing House Inc., 4025 W. Peterson Ave., Chicago, Ill. 60646 Tel 312-583-8500; 800-248-3248 Fax 708-940-0113

Comstock Pub. Assocs., P.O. Box 250, Ithaca, N.Y. 14853 Tel 607-257-7000; 277-2211 (orders only)

Condé Nast Publs. Inc., 350 Madison Ave., New York, N.Y. 10017 Tel 212-880-6649 Fax 212-880-8289

Congdon & Weed, 180 N. Michigan Ave., Chicago, Ill. 60601-7401 Tel 312-782-9181; 800-221-7945; refer orders to Contemporary Bks.

Congressional Quarterly Inc., 1414 22nd St. N.W., Washington, D.C. 20037-1003 Tel 202-822-1475; 800-638-1710 (orders) Fax 202-887-6706

Consumer Repts. Bks., 101 Truman Ave., Yonkers, N.Y. 10703 Tel 914-378-2000; 800-272-0722 (orders) Fax 914-378-2901

Consumers Union of U.S. Inc., 101 Truman Ave., Yonkers, N.Y. 10703 Tel 914-378-2000; 800-272-0722 (orders) Fax 914-378-2901

Contemporary Bks. Inc., 2 Prudential Plaza, Suite 1200, Chicago, Ill. 60601 Tel 312-540-4500; 800-621-1918 Fax 312-540-4687

Continuum, 370 Lexington Ave., New York, N.Y. 10017-6550 Tel 212-532-3650 Fax 212-532-4922; refer orders to Publisher Resources Inc., 1224 Heil Quaker Blvd., P.O. Box 7001, La Vergne, Tenn. 37086 Tel 615-793-5090; 800-937-5557 Fax 615-793-3915

Copper Canyon Press, P.O. Box 271, Port Townsend, Wash. 98368 Tel 206-385-4925 Fax 206-385-4985

Cornell Univ. Press, Sage House, 512 E. State St., P.O. Box 250, Ithaca, N.Y. 14851-0250 Tel 607-277-2338; refer orders to C.U.P. Services, 750 Cascadilla St., Ithaca, N.Y. 14850 Tel 607-277-2211

Council Oak Bks., 1350 E. 15th St., Tulsa, Okla. 74120 Tel 918-587-6454; 800-247-8850 Fax 918-583-4995

Council of State Govts., Iron Works Pike, P.O. Box 11910, Lexington, Ky. 40578-1910 Tel 606-231-1939; 800-800-1910

Courage Bks., 125 S. 22nd St., Philadelphia, Pa. 19103 Tel 215-567-5080; 800-345-5359 (orders only) Fax 800-453-2884

Coward-McCann, 200 Madison Ave., New York, N.Y. 10016 Tel 212-951-8400; 800-631-8571; refer orders to 390 Murray Hill Parkway, East Rutherford, N.J. 07073

Coward, McCann & Geoghegan See Coward-McCann

CQ Press, 1414 22nd St. N.W., Washington, D.C. 20037-1003 Tel 202-822-1475; 800-638-1710 (orders) Fax 202-887-6706

Craftsman Bk. Co., 6058 Corte Del Cedro, P.O. Box 6500, Carlsbad, Calif. 92008 Tel 619-438-7828; 800-829-8123 Fax 619-438-0398

CRC Press Inc., 2000 Corporate Blvd. N.W., Boca Raton, Fla. 33431 Tel 407-994-0555; 800-272-7737 (orders) Fax 407-997-7249; 998-9114 (orders)

Creative Arts Bk. Co., 833 Bancroft Way, Berkeley, Calif. 94710 Tel 510-848-4777 Fax 510-848-4844

Creative Therapeutics, 155 County Rd., P.O. Box R, Cresskill, N.J. 07626-0317 Tel 201-567-7295; 800-544-6162 Fax 201-567-8956

CrimeBooks Inc., 1213 Wilmette Ave., Suite 203, Wilmette, Ill. 60091-2557 Tel 708-251-8350

Crossroad, 370 Lexington Ave., 26th Floor, New York, N.Y. 10017-6550 Tel 212-532-3650 Fax 212-532-4922; refer orders to Publisher Resources Inc., 1224 Heil Quaker Blvd., P.O. Box 7001, La Vergne, Tenn. 37086-7001 Tel 615-793-5090; 800-937-5557 Fax 615-793-3915

Crowell See HarperCollins Pubs.

Crown Pubs. Inc., 201 E. 50th St., New York, N.Y. 10022 Tel 212-751-2600 Fax 212-572-6192; refer orders to Random House

CSA Publs., State Univ. of N.Y., Binghamton, N.Y. 13901 Tel 607-777-2116

Da Capo Press Inc., 233 Spring St., New York, N.Y. 10013 Tel 212-620-8000; 800-221-9369; 800-321-0050 (orders only) Fax 212-463-0742

Dalkey Archive Press (The), 4241 Illinois State Univ., Normal, Ill. 61790-4241 Tel 309-438-7555 Fax 309-438-7422

David, J.: Jonathan David Pubs. Inc., 68-22 Eliot Ave., Middle Village, N.Y. 11379 Tel 718-456-8611 Fax 718-894-2818

Davidson, H.: Harlan Davidson Inc., 3110 N. Arlington Heights Rd., Arlington Heights, Ill. 60004 Tel 708-253-9720 Fax 708-253-9728

DBI Bks. Inc., 4092 Commercial Ave., Northbrook, Ill. 60062 Tel 708-272-6310; 800-767-6310 Fax 708-272-2051

DCI Pub., 13911 Ridgedale Dr., Minnetonka, Minn. 55343 Tel 612-541-0239; 800-848-2793 Fax 612-541-4969; refer orders to P.O. Box 739, Wayzata, Minn. 55391

De Gruyter: Walter de Gruyter & Co., Genthinerstr. 13, 10785 Berlin, Germany Tel (030) 260050 Fax (030) 26005251
  Branch offices
  U.S.: Walter De Gruyter Inc., 200 Saw Mill River Rd., Hawthorne, N.Y. 10532 Tel 914-747-0110 Fax 914-747-1326

Dearborn Financial Pub. Inc., 520 N. Dearborn St., Chicago, Ill. 60610 Tel 312-836-4400 Fax 312-836-1021

DeCosse: Cy DeCosse Inc., 5900 Green Oak Dr., Minnetonka, Minn. 55343 Tel 612-936-4700; 800-328-3895 Fax 612-933-1456

Dee, I.R.: Ivan R. Dee Inc., 1332 N. Halsted St., Chicago, Ill. 60622-2637 Tel 312-787-6262 Fax 312-787-6269; refer orders to 62 Imlay St., Brooklyn, N.Y. 11231-1227 Tel 800-634-0226 (orders only)

Delacorte Press, 1540 Broadway, New York, N.Y. 10036 Tel 212-354-6500; 800-223-6834 Fax 212-492-9698

Dell Pub. Co. Inc., 1540 Broadway, New York, N.Y. 10036 Tel 212-354-6500; 800-223-6834 Fax 212-492-9698

Delta Bks., 1540 Broadway, New York, N.Y. 10036 Tel 212-354-6500; 800-223-6834 Fax 212-492-9698

Dembner Bks., 61 4th Ave., New York, N.Y. 10011 Tel 212-228-8828; 800-365-3453; refer orders to Publishers Group West, P.O. Box 8843, Emeryville, Calif. 94662 Tel 800-788-3123

Demos Publs., 386 Park Ave. S., Suite 201, New York, N.Y. 10016 Tel 212-683-0072 Fax 212-683-0118

Dial Bks., 375 Hudson St., New York, N.Y. 10014 Tel 212-366-2000 Fax 212-366-2666

Dial Press (The), 666 5th Ave., New York, N.Y. 10103 Tel 212-765-6500; 800-223-6834

Dioscorides Press Inc., 133 S.W. 2nd Ave., Suite 450, Portland, Or. 97204 Tel 503-227-2878; 800-327-5680 (U.S. & Can.) Fax 503-227-3070

Dodd, Mead Out of business; list acquired by Putnam Pub. Group and others

Dolphin Bks., 666 5th Ave., New York, N.Y. 10103 Tel 212-765-6500; 800-223-6834

Dorling Kindersley Ltd., 9 Henrietta St., Covent Garden, London WC2E 8PS, Eng. Tel (071) 836 5411 Fax (071) 836 7570; refer orders to Tiptree Bk. Services Ltd., Church Rd., Tiptree, Colchester CO5 0SR, Eng. Tel (0621) 816 362 Fax (0621) 819 011
  Branch offices

U.S.: Dorling Kindersley Inc., 232 Madison Ave., Suite 1206, New York, N.Y. 10016 Tel 212-684-0404 Fax 212-684-0111; refer orders to Houghton Mifflin

Dorset Press, 120 5th Ave., New York, N.Y. 10011 Tel 212-924-8395 Fax 212-675-0413

Doubleday, 1540 Broadway, New York, N.Y. 10036 Tel 212-354-6500; 800-223-6834 Fax 212-492-9698

Dover Publs. Inc., 180 Varick St., New York, N.Y. 10014 Tel 212-255-3755 Fax 212-626-9670; refer orders to 31 E. 2nd St., Mineola, N.Y. 11501 Tel 516-294-7000; 800-223-3130 Fax 516-742-5049

Dow Jones-Irwin, 1818 Ridge Rd., Homewood, Ill. 60430 Tel 708-798-6000; 800-448-3343; 800-634-3966 (orders only) Fax 708-798-6388; 798-1490 (orders only)

Drama Bk. Pubs., 260 5th Ave., New York, N.Y. 10001 Tel 212-725-5377 Fax 212-725-8506

Dramatists Play Service Inc., 440 Park Ave. S., New York, N.Y. 10016 Tel 212-683-8960 Fax 212-213-1539

Duke Univ. Press, P.O. Box 90660, Durham, N.C. 27708-0660 Tel 919-687-3600 Fax 919-684-8644

Dustbooks, P.O. Box 100, Paradise, Calif. 95967 Tel 916-877-6110; 800-477-6110

Dutton: E. P. Dutton, 375 Hudson St., New York, N.Y. 10014-3657 Tel 212-366-2000 Fax 212-366-2020; refer orders to Penguin USA, P.O. Box 999, Dept. 1709, Bergenfield, N.Y. 07621

Easi-Bild Directions Simplified Inc., 529 N. State Rd., Briarcliff Manor, N.Y. 10510

Eastern Acorn Press, 339 Walnut St., Philadelphia, Pa. 19106 Tel 215-597-7129

Eastman Kodak. Professional Photography Div., 343 State St., Bldg. 10, 6th Floor, Rochester, N.Y. 14650-0132 Tel 716-724-1580 Fax 716-724-0774

Ecco Press, 100 W. Broad St., Hopewell, N.J. 08525 Tel 609-466-4748; refer orders to Norton

Educational Directories Inc., P.O. Box 199, Mount Prospect, Ill. 60056-0346

Eerdmans: Wm. B. Eerdmans Pub. Co., 255 Jefferson Ave. S.E., Grand Rapids, Mich. 49503 Tel 800-253-7521 (U.S. & Can. orders only) Fax 616-459-6540

Element Bks. Ltd., The Old School House, The Courtyard, Bell St., Shaftesbury, Dorset SP7 8BP, Eng.

Encyclopaedia Britannica Inc., 310 S. Michigan Ave., Chicago, Ill. 60604 Tel 312-347-7959; 347-7005 (orders only); 800-554-9862 Fax 312-347-7914; 347-7135 (orders only)

Enoch Pratt Free Lib. Publs., 400 Cathedral St., Baltimore, Md. 21201-4484

Eriksson: Paul S. Eriksson Pub., 208 Battell Bldg., Middlebury, Vt. 05753 Tel 802-388-7303 Fax 802-388-2940

Evans & Co.: M. Evans & Co. Inc., 216 E. 49th St., New York, N.Y. 10017 Tel 212-688-2810 Fax 212-486-4544; refer orders to National Bk. Network, 4720 Boston Way, Lanham, Md. 20706 Tel 301-459-8696; 800-462-6420 Fax 301-459-2118

Everest House Pubs., 33 W. 60th St., New York, N.Y. 10023 Tel 212-685-6464

Excellent Bks., 221 S. Reeves Dr., No. 305, Beverly Hills, Calif. 90212 Tel 310-275-6945

Faber & Faber Ltd., 3 Queen Sq., London WC1N 3AU, Eng. Tel (071) 465 0045 Fax (071) 465 0034; refer orders to 16 Burnt Mill, Elizabeth Way, Harlow, Essex CM20 2HX, Eng. Tel (0279) 421 352

Branch offices

U.S.: Faber & Faber Inc., 50 Cross St., Winchester, Mass. 01890 Tel 617-721-1427 Fax 617-721-1427; refer orders to C.U.P. Services, 750 Cascadilla St., Ithaca, N.Y. 14851 Tel 607-666-2211; 800-688-2877

Facts on File Inc., 460 Park Ave. S., New York, N.Y. 10016-7382 Tel 212-683-2244; 800-322-8755 (except Alaska & Hawaii) Fax 212-683-3633; 800-678-3633 (except Alaska & Hawaii)

Fairchild Publs. Inc., 7 W. 34th St., New York, N.Y. 10001 Tel 212-630-3880; 800-247-6622 Fax 212-630-3868

Fairleigh Dickinson Univ. Press, 285 Madison Ave., Madison, N.J. 07940 Tel 201-377-4700 Fax 201-593-8510; refer orders to Associated Univ. Presses, 440 Forsgate Dr., Cranbury, N.J. 08512 Tel 609-655-4770 Fax 609-655-8366

Farrar, Straus & Giroux Inc., 19 Union Sq. W., New York, N.Y. 10003 Tel 212-741-6900; 800-631-8571 Fax 212-633-9385

Fast Forward Pub., P.O. Box 45153, Seattle, Wash. 98145-0153 Tel 206-527-3112

Fawcett Bks., 201 E. 50th St., New York, N.Y. 10022 Tel 212-751-2600; refer orders to Ballantine Bks.

Fawcett Columbine, 201 E. 50th St., New York, N.Y. 10022 Tel 212-751-2600; refer orders to 400 Hahn Rd., Westminster, Md. 21157 Tel 800-733-3000

Faxon: F. W. Faxon Co. Inc., 15 Southwest Park, Westwood, Mass. 02090

Fell: Frederick Fell Pub. Inc., 2131 Hollywood Blvd., Suite 204, Hollywood, Fla. 33020 Tel 305-925-5242; 800-635-6366 (orders only)

Feminist Press: The Feminist Press at the City Univ. of N.Y., 311 E. 94th St., New York, N.Y. 10128 Tel 212-360-5790; refer orders to The Talman Co. Inc., 131 Spring St., Suite 201E-N, New York, N.Y. 10012 Tel 212-431-7175; 800-537-8894 (orders only)

Ferguson, J.G.: J. G. Ferguson Pub. Co., 200 W. Monroe, Suite 250, Chicago, Ill. 60606 Tel 312-580-5480 Fax 312-580-4948

Financial Planning Inst., P.O. Box 135, Boston, Mass. 02258 Tel 617-965-8120 Fax 617-332-7786

Fine, D.I.: Donald I. Fine Inc., 19 W. 21st St., New York, N.Y. 10010 Tel 212-727-3270 Fax 212-727-3277; refer orders to Penguin USA, P.O. Box 120, Bergenfield, N.J. 07621-0120 Tel 201-387-0600; 800-526-0275 Fax 201-385-6521; 800-227-9604

Finesse Press, 2068 Via Las Cumbres, Suite 7, P.O. Box 11244, San Diego, Calif. 92111 Tel 619-569-7728

Fodor's Travel Publs. Inc., 201 E. 50th St., New York, N.Y. 10022 Tel 212-572-8757 Fax 212-572-2248; refer orders to Random House

Forest Press (Albany): Forest Press, 85 Watervliet Ave., Albany, N.Y. 12206 Tel 518-489-8549; refer orders to 6565 Frantz Rd., Dublin, Ohio 43017-3395 Tel 614-764-6000; 800-848-8286; 800-848-5878 (outside Ohio) Fax 614-764-6096

Fortress Press, 426 S. 5th St., P.O. Box 1209, Minneapolis, Minn. 55440-1209 Tel 612-330-3300; 800-752-8153; 800-328-4648 (outside Minn.) Fax 612-330-3455

Foundation Center (The), 79 5th Ave., New York, N.Y. 10003-3076 Tel 212-620-4230; 800-424-9836 Fax 212-807-3677

Four Directions Press, 611 Broadway, Suite 426, New York, N.Y. 10012-2608 Tel 212-529-7272; 800-556-6200

Four Walls Eight Windows Pub. Co., 39 W. 14th St., Room 503, New York, N.Y. 10011-7489 Tel 212-206-8965; 800-444-2524 Fax 212-206-8799; refer orders to P.O. Box 548, Village Station, New York, N.Y. 10014-0548

Fraser-Vance Pub., 38 Academy St., Madison, Conn. 06443 Tel 203-245-0366 Fax 203-245-1830; refer orders to Williamson

Free Press, 866 3rd Ave., New York, N.Y. 10022 Tel 212-702-3130; 800-257-5755 Fax 212-605-9364

Free Spirit Pub. Inc., 400 1st Ave. N., Suite 616, Minneapolis, Minn. 55401 Tel 612-338-2068; 800-735-7323

Freeman, W.H.: W. H. Freeman & Co., 41 Madison Ave., 37th Floor, New York, N.Y. 10010 Tel 212-576-9400 Fax 212-689-2383; refer orders to 4419 W. 1980 S., Salt Lake City, Utah 84104 Tel 801-973-4660; 800-877-5351 Fax 801-977-9712

French & Spanish Bk. Corp., 115 5th Ave., New York, N.Y. 10003

Freundlich Bks., 212 5th Ave., Suite 1305, New York, N.Y. 10010 Tel 212-532-9666

Friends United Press, 101 Quaker Hill Dr., Richmond, Ind. 47374 Tel 317-962-7573; 800-537-8838

Fromm Int. Pub. Corp., 560 Lexington Ave., New York, N.Y. 10022 Tel 212-308-4010 Fax 212-371-5187; refer orders to Kampmann & Co., 226 W. 26th St., New York, N.Y. 10001 Tel 212-727-0190; 800-462-6420

Fulcrum Pub., 350 Indiana St., Suite 350, Golden, Colo. 80401 Tel 303-277-1623; 800-992-2908 Fax 303-279-7111

Fuller Tech. Publs., 2392 Fuller Rd., Ann Arbor, Mich. 48105 Tel 313-662-9953

Funk & Wagnalls Inc., 53 E. 77th St., New York, N.Y. 10021 Tel 212-570-4500; refer orders to HarperCollins Pubs.

Gale Res. Co., 835 Penobscot Bldg., Detroit, Mich. 48226-4094 Tel 313-961-2242 Fax 313-961-6083; refer orders to P.O. Box 33477, Detroit, Mich. 48232-5477 Tel 800-877-4253

Gallaudet Univ. Press, 800 Florida Ave. N.E., Washington, D.C. 20002-3625 Tel 202-651-5488; 800-451-1073 Fax 202-651-5489

Gallery Bks. (NY): Gallery Bks., 112 Madison Ave., New York, N.Y. 10016 Tel 212-532-6600

Garland Pub. Inc., 717 5th Ave., Suite 2500, New York, N.Y. 10022 Tel 212-751-7447 Fax 212-308-9399; refer orders to 1000A Sherman Ave., Hamden, Conn. 06514 Tel 203-281-4487; 800-627-6273 (orders only) Fax 203-230-1186

Genealogical Pub. Co. Inc., 1001 N. Calvert St., Baltimore, Md. 21202 Tel 410-837-8271

Georgia State Univ. Business Press, University Plaza, Atlanta, Ga. 30303-3093 Tel 404-651-4253

Glencoe, 15319 Chatsworth St., Mission Hills, Calif. 91345 Tel 818-898-1391; 800-334-7344; refer orders to 100 Front St., Box 500, Riverside, N.J. 08075-7500 Tel 609-461-6500; 800-323-7445 Fax 609-461-7070; 800-562-1272

Globe Pequot Press (The), P.O. Box 833, 6 Business Park Rd., Old Saybrook, Conn. 06475-4238 Tel 203-395-0440; 800-243-0495 Fax 203-395-0312

Godine: David R. Godine Pub., Horticultural Hall, 300 Massachusetts Ave., Boston, Mass. 02115 Tel 617-536-0761; 800-445-6638 Fax 617-421-0934

Golden Press Bks., 850 3rd Ave., New York, N.Y. 10022 Tel 212-753-8500

Goodheart-Willcox Co. Inc., 123 W. Taft Dr., South Holland, Ill. 60473-2089 Tel 708-333-7200; 800-323-0440 Fax 708-333-9130

Gospel Pub. House, 1445 Boonville Ave., Springfield, Mo. 65802 Tel 417-831-8000; 800-641-4310 Fax 417-862-2781

Graywolf Press, 2402 University Ave., Suite 203, St. Paul, Minn. 55114 Tel 612-641-0077 Fax 612-641-0036; refer orders to Consortium Bk. Sales & Distr., 213 E. 4th St., St. Paul, Minn. 55101 Tel 612-221-9035; 800-283-3572 Fax 612-221-0124

Greene: Stephen Greene Press Inc., 375 Hudson St., New York, N.Y. 10014 Tel 212-366-2000; refer orders to Viking, P.O. Box 120, Bergenfield, N.J. 07621-0120 Tel 201-387-0600; 800-526-0275

Greenfield Review Press (The), 2 Middle Grove Rd., P.O. Box 308, Greenfield Center, N.Y. 12833 Tel 518-584-1728 Fax 518-583-9741

Greenwood Press, 88 Post Road W., P.O. Box 5007, Westport, Conn. 06881 Tel 203-226-3571; 800-225-5800 Fax 203-222-1502

Grey House Pub. Inc., Pocket Knife Sq., Lakeville, Conn. 06039 Tel 203-435-0868 Fax 203-435-0867

Grolier Inc., Sherman Turnpike, Danbury, Conn. 06816 Tel 203-797-3500; 800-356-5590

Grosset & Dunlap Pubs., 200 Madison Ave., New York, N.Y. 10016 Tel 212-951-8400; 800-631-8571 Fax 212-532-3693; refer orders to 390 Murray Hill Parkway, East Rutherford, N.J. 07073

Grove/Atlantic 841 Broadway, New York N.Y. 10003-4793 Tel 212-614-7850; 800-638-6460 Fax 212-614-7886; refer orders to Publishers Group West, P.O. Box 8843, Emeryville, Calif. 94662 Tel 800-788-3123

Grove Weidenfeld See Grove/Atlantic

Grove's Dictionaries of Music Inc., 15 E. 26th St., Suite 1503, New York, N.Y. 10010 Tel 212-481-1332; 800-221-2123

Hall, G.K. & Co.: G. K. Hall & Co., P.O. Box 159, Thorndike, Me. 04921 Tel 800-223-6121; lib. & general ref. bks. available from 866 3rd Ave., New York, N.Y. 10022 Tel 212-702-6789; 800-257-5755

Hammond Inc., 515 Valley St., Maplewood, N.J. 07040-1396 Tel 201-763-6000; 800-526-4953 Fax 201-763-7658

Harcourt Brace & Co., 1250 6th Ave., San Diego, Calif. 92101 Tel 619-231-6616; 800-543-1918 Fax 800-235-0256

Harcourt Brace Jovanovich See Harcourt Brace & Co.

Harmony Bks., 201 E. 50th St., New York, N.Y. 10022 Tel 212-751-2600 Fax 212-572-6192; refer orders to Random House

Harper & Row See HarperCollins Pubs.

HarperBusiness, 10 E. 53rd St., New York, N.Y. 10022-5299 Tel 212-207-7581; 800-242-7737 Fax 212-207-7145

HarperCollins College Pubs., 10 E. 53rd St., New York, N.Y. 10022-5299 Tel 212-207-7021; 800-782-2665; refer orders to 1900 E. Lake, Glenview, Ill. 60025 Tel 708-657-3900

HarperCollins Pubs., 10 E. 53rd St., New York, N.Y. 10022-5299 Tel 212-207-7000; 800-242-7737 Fax 212-207-7145; refer orders to 1000 Keystone Ind. Park, Scranton, Pa. 18512 Tel 717-343-4761; 800-982-4377; 800-242-7737 (outside Pa.) Fax 800-822-4090

HarperPaperbacks, 10 E. 53rd St., New York, N.Y. 10022-5299 Tel 212-207-7000; refer order to 1000 Keystone Ind. Park, Scranton, Pa. 18512 Tel 717-343-4761; 800-982-4377; 800-242-7737 (outside Pa.) Fax 800-822-4090

HarperPerennial, 10 E. 53rd St., New York, N.Y. 10022-5299 Tel 212-207-7000; 800-328-3443 Fax 212-207-7145; refer orders to 1000 Keystone Ind. Park, Scranton, Pa. 18512 Tel 717-343-4761; 800-982-4377; 800-242-7737 (outside Pa.) Fax 800-822-4090

HarperSanFrancisco, 1160 Battery St., San Francisco, Calif. 94111-1213 Tel 415-477-4400; 800-328-5125 Fax 415-477-4444; refer orders to 1000 Keystone Ind. Park, Scranton, Pa. 18512-0588 Tel 717-343-4761; 800-982-4377; 800-242-7737 (outside Pa.) Fax 800-822-4090

Hartley & Marks Inc., P.O. Box 147, Point Roberts, Wash. 98281 Tel 206-945-2017 Fax 604-738-1913

Harvard Common Press (The), 535 Albany St., Boston, Mass. 02118 Tel 617-423-5803 Fax 617-695-9794

Harvard Univ. Press, 79 Garden St., Cambridge, Mass. 02138 Tel 617-495-2600; 495-2480 (orders) Fax 617-495-8924; 800-962-4983

Hastings House Pubs., Inc., 141 Halstead Ave., Mamaroneck, N.Y. 10543 Tel 914-835-4005; refer orders to Publishers Group West, P.O. Box 8843, Emeryville, Calif. 94662 Tel 800-788-3123

Health Trend Pub., P.O. Box 17420, Encino, Calif. 91416-7420 Tel 818-345-1471

Hearst Bks., 1350 Ave. of the Americas, New York, N.Y. 10019 Tel 212-261-6770; 800-843-9389 Fax 212-779-0965

Hearst Marine Bks., 1350 Ave. of the Americas, New York, N.Y. 10019 Tel 212-261-6500; 800-843-9389 Fax 212-779-0965; refer orders to 39 Plymouth St., Fairfield, N.J. 07007 Tel 201-227-7200

Heath: D. C. Heath & Co., 125 Spring St., Lexington, Mass. 02173 Tel 617-862-6650; 800-235-3565 Fax 617-860-1493; refer orders to 2700 N. Richardt Ave., Indianapolis, Ind. 46219 Tel 317-359-5585

Heineman, J.H.: James H. Heineman Inc., 475 Park Ave., New York, N.Y. 10022 Tel 212-688-2028

Hemlock Soc. (The), P.O. Box 11830, Eugene, Or. 97440-4030 Tel 503-342-5748; 800-247-7421

Herald House, P.O. Box HH, Independence, Mo. 64055 Tel 816-252-5010; 800-767-8181

Herald Press, 616 Walnut Ave., Scottdale, Pa. 15683-1999 Tel 412-887-8500; 800-245-7894 Fax 412-887-3111; refer orders to Provident Bookstore, Lancaster Shopping Center, 1625 Lititz Pike, Lancaster, Pa. 17601-6599 Tel 800-759-4447 Fax 717-397-8299

Heraty & Assocs.: Jack Heraty & Assocs. Inc., 330 W. Colfax, Palatine, Ill. 60067 Tel 312-991-0255

Hill & Wang Inc., 19 Union Sq. W., New York, N.Y. 10003 Tel 212-741-6900; 800-638-3030 Fax 212-633-9385

Hill Bks.: Lawrence Hill Bks., 230 Park Pl., Suite 6A, Brooklyn, N.Y. 11238 Tel 718-857-1015; refer orders to Independent Pubs. Group, 814 N. Franklin St., Chicago, Ill. 60610 Tel 312-337-0747; 800-888-4741

Hippocrene Bks. Inc., 171 Madison Ave., New York, N.Y. 10016 Tel 212-454-2366

Holmes & Meier Pubs. Inc., 30 Irving Pl., New York, N.Y. 10003 Tel 212-254-4100 Fax 212-254-4104; refer orders to H & M Distributors, 300 Long Beach Blvd., Stratford, Conn. 06497-7116 Tel 800-437-7840 Fax 203-386-9333

Holt & Co.: Henry Holt & Co., 115 W. 18th St., New York, N.Y. 10011 Tel 212-886-9200 Fax 212-633-0748; refer orders to 4375 W. 1980 S., Salt Lake City, Utah 84104 Tel 801-972-2221; 800-488-5233 Fax 801-977-9712

Hood, A.C.: Alan C. Hood Pub., 28 Birge St., Brattleboro, Vt. 05301 Tel 802-254-2200

Horizon Press, P.O. Box 402, Times Sq. Station, New York, N.Y. 10108 Tel 212-757-4420

Horn Bk. Inc., 14 Beacon St., Boston, Mass. 02108 Tel 617-227-1555; 800-325-1170

Houghton Mifflin Co., 222 Berkeley St., Boston, Mass. 02116 Tel 617-351-5000; refer orders to Wayside Rd., Burlington, Mass. 01803 Tel 617-272-1500; 800-225-3362

Howell Bk. House, 866 3rd Ave., New York, N.Y. 10022 Tel 212-702-3800; 800-257-5755 Fax 212-605-9346; refer orders to Macmillan

HP Bks., 11150 Olympic Blvd., Suite 650, Los Angeles, Calif. 90064 Tel 310-477-6100; 800-421-0892 Fax 213-855-8993

Hudson Hills Press Inc., 230 5th Ave., Suite 1308, New York, N.Y. 10001-7704 Tel 212-889-3090

Human Sciences Press Inc., 233 Spring St., New York, N.Y. 10013-1578 Tel 212-620-8000; 800-221-9369 Fax 212-807-1047

Humanities Press See Humanities Press Int. Inc.

Humanities Press Int. Inc., 165 1st Ave., Atlantic Highlands, N.J. 07716-1289 Tel 908-872-1441 Fax 908-872-0717

Hunter House Inc., P.O. Box 2914, Alameda, Calif. 94501-0914 Tel 510-865-5282; refer orders to Unique Bks., 4230 Grove Ave., Gurnee, Ill. 60031 Tel 708-623-9171

Hyperion, 114 5th Ave., New York, N.Y. 10011 Tel 212-633-4400 Fax 212-633-4833; refer orders to Little, Brown

Hyperion Press (Westport): Hyperion Press Inc., 47 Riverside Ave., Westport, Conn. 06880 Tel 203-226-1091

Image Bks., 1540 Broadway, New York, N.Y. 10036-6500 Tel 212-354-6500; 800-223-6834 Fax 212-492-9700; refer orders to Doubleday Consumer Services, P.O. Box 5071, Des Plaines, Ill. 60017-5071

Impact Pubs. Inc., 874 Via Esteban, San Luis Obispo, Calif. 93401 Tel 805-543-5911 Fax 805-543-4093; refer orders to P.O. Box 1094, San Luis Obispo, Calif. 93406 Tel 800-246-7228

Indiana Univ. Press, 601 N. Morton St., Bloomington, Ind. 47404-3797 Tel 812-855-6804; 800-842-6796 (orders) Fax 812-855-7931

Interlink Bks., 99 7th Ave., Brooklyn, N.Y. 11215 Tel 718-797-4292; 800-238-5465 Fax 718-855-7329

International City Mgt. Assn., 777 N. Capitol St. N.E., Suite 500, Washington, D.C. 20002-4201 Tel 202-962-3620; 800-745-8780 (orders only) Fax 202-962-3500

International Specialized Bk. Services, 5804 N. E. Hassalo St., Portland, Or. 92713-3644 Tel 503-287-3093 Fax 503-284-8859

InterVarsity Press, P.O. Box 1400, 5206 Main St., Downers Grove, Ill. 60515 Tel 708-964-5700; 800-843-9487 (orders) Fax 708-964-1251

Interweave Press, 201 E. 4th St., Loveland, Colo. 80537 Tel 303-669-7672; 800-272-2193; refer orders to Contemporary Bks.

Irvington Pubs. Inc., 740 Broadway, Suite 905, New York, N.Y. 10003 Tel 212-777-4100

Island Press (Covelo): Island Press, Star Route 1, Box 38, Covelo, Calif. 95428 Tel 707-983-6432; refer orders to P.O. Box 7, Covelo, Calif. 95428 Tel 800-828-1302

Ivy Bks., 201 E. 50th St., New York, N.Y. 10022 Tel 212-572-2573; 800-733-3000 (orders)

Jane's Information Group, Sentinel House, 163 Brighton Rd., Coulsdon, Surrey CR5 2NH, Eng. Tel (081) 763 1030
Branch offices
U.S.: Jane's Information Group, 1340 Braddock Pl., Suite 300, Alexandria, Va. 22313-2036 Tel 703-683-3700

Jargon Soc. Inc. (The), 1000 W. 5th St., Winston-Salem, N.C. 27101 Tel 919-724-7619; refer orders to Inland Tel 800-243-0138

Jewish Publ. Soc., 1930 Chestnut St., Philadelphia, Pa. 19103-4599 Tel 215-564-5925; 800-234-3151

Johns Hopkins Univ. Press (The), 701 W. 40th St., Suite 275, Baltimore, Md. 21211 Tel 410-516-6990; 800-537-5487 (orders only) Fax 410-516-6998

Johnson Pub., 820 Michigan Ave., Chicago, Ill. 60605

Johnson Bks., 1880 S. 57th Ct., Boulder, Colo. 80301 Tel 303-443-9766; 800-258-5830 Fax 303-443-1679

Joshua Odell Eds., 629 State St., No. 215, Santa Barbara, Calif. 93101 Tel 805-966-4606; refer orders to Capra Press, P.O. Box 2068, Santa Barbara, Calif. 93120 Tel 805-966-4590

Jossey-Bass Inc. Pubs., 350 Sansome St., San Francisco, Calif. 94104 Tel 415-433-1740 Fax 415-433-0499

Jove Publs. Inc., 200 Madison Ave., New York, N.Y. 10016 Tel 212-951-8800; 800-631-8571 Fax 212-545-8917; refer orders to P.O. Box 506, E. Rutherford, N.J. 07073 Tel 201-933-9292 Fax 201-933-4927

Jugglebug, 7506 J Olympic View Dr., Edmonds, Wash. 98026 Tel 206-774-2127; 800-523-1776 Fax 206-774-5811

Kensington Pub. Corp., 475 Park Ave. S., New York, N.Y. 10016 Tel 212-889-2299 Fax 212-779-8073

Kiplinger Bks., 1729 H St. N.W., Washington, D.C. 20006 Tel 202-887-6680 Fax 202-331-1206

Knapp Press (The), 5900 Wilshire Blvd., Los Angeles, Calif. 90036 Tel 213-937-5486

Knopf: Alfred A. Knopf Inc., 201 E. 50th St., New York, N.Y. 10022 Tel 212-751-2600; 800-726-0600; refer orders to 400 Hahn Rd., Westminster, Md. 21157 Tel 410-848-1900; 800-733-3000 Fax 800-659-2436

Kodansha Int./USA, 114 5th Ave., 18th Floor, New York, N.Y. 10011 Tel 212-727-6460; 800-631-8571 Fax 212-727-9177; refer orders to Farrar, Straus & Giroux

Kosciuszko Foundation, 15 E. 65th St., New York, N.Y. 10021

Krause Publs. Inc., 700 E. State St., Iola, Wis. 54990 Tel 715-445-2214 Fax 715-445-4087

Lane Pub. Co., 80 Willow Rd., Menlo Park, Calif. 94025-3691 Tel 415-321-3600; 800-321-0372; 800-227-7346 (outside Calif.)

Lawrence, S.: Seymour Lawrence Inc., 1 Beacon St., Boston, Mass. 02108 Tel 617-725-5173; 800-225-3362; refer orders to Wayside Rd., Burlington, Mass. 01803 Tel 617-272-1500

Learning Publs. Inc., 5351 Gulf Dr., Holmes Beach, Fla. 33509 Tel 813-778-6651; refer orders to P.O. Box 1338, Holmes Beach, Fla. 33509 Tel 813-778-6818; 800-222-1525

Leonard, H.: Hal Leonard Pub. Corp., 7777 W. Bluemound Rd., P.O. Box 13819, Milwaukee, Wis. 53213 Tel 414-774-3630; 800-642-6692 Fax 414-774-3259

Levin Assocs.: Hugh Lauter Levin Assocs. Inc., 2507 Post Rd., Southport, Conn. 06490 Tel 203-254-7733 Fax 203-254-7586

Lexington Bks., 866 3rd Ave., New York, N.Y. 10022 Tel 212-702-2000; 800-257-5755 Fax 212-605-4872

Libraries Unlimited Inc., P.O. Box 6633, Englewood, Colo. 80155-6633 Tel 303-770-1200; 800-237-6124 Fax 303-220-8843

Library of Am. (The), 14 E. 60th St., New York, N.Y. 10022 Tel 212-308-3360; 800-631-3577 Fax 212-750-8352; refer orders to Viking Penguin, P.O. Box 120, Bergenfield, N.J. 07621-0120 Tel 201-387-0600; 800-526-0275

Library of Congress, Washington, D.C. 20540 Tel 202-707-6095 Fax 202-707-9898; refer orders to U.S. Govt. Ptg. Office, Washington, D.C. 20402 Tel 202-783-3238

Library Professional Publs., 925 Sherman Ave., Hamden, Conn. 06514 Tel 203-248-6307 Fax 203-230-9275

Limelight Eds., 118 E. 30th St., New York, N.Y. 10016 Tel 212-532-5525; 800-426-0489 Fax 212-532-5526; refer orders to Maxway Data Corp., 225 W. 34th St., New York, N.Y. 10001 Tel 212-947-6100 Fax 212-563-5703

Linden Press/Simon & Schuster Inc., Simon & Schuster Bldg., 1230 Ave. of the Americas, New York, N.Y. 10020 Tel 212-698-7000 Fax 212-698-7336

Lippincott See HarperCollins Pubs.

Literary Classics of the U.S., 14 E. 60th St., New York, N.Y. 10022 Tel 212-308-3360; 800-631-3577; refer orders to Viking, P.O. Box 120, Bergenfield, N.J. 07621-0120 Tel 201-387-0600; 800-526-0275

Little, Brown & Co. Inc., 34 Beacon St., Boston, Mass. 02108 Tel 617-227-0730 Fax 617-227-0790; refer orders to 200 West St., Waltham, Mass. 02254 Tel 617-890-0250; 800-343-9204 Fax 617-890-0875

Liveright Pub. Corp., 500 5th Ave., New York, N.Y. 10110 Tel 212-354-5500

Lloyd-Simone Pub. Co., 32 Hillside Ave., Monsey, N.Y. 10952 Tel 914-356-7273; refer orders to Library Res. Assocs., Dunderberg Rd., RD #5 Box 41, Monroe, N.Y. 10950 Tel 914-783-1144

Los Angeles County Mus. of Art, 5905 Wilshire Blvd., Los Angeles, Calif. 90036 Tel 213-857-6044; refer orders to University of Wash. Press

Lothrop, Lee & Shepard Bks., 1350 Ave. of the Americas, New York, N.Y. 10019 Tel 212-261-6500; 800-237-0657 Fax 212-779-0965; refer orders to 39 Plymouth St., Fairfield, N.J. 07007 Tel 201-227-7200; 800-843-9389 Fax 201-227-6849

Louisiana State Univ. Press, Baton Rouge, La. 70893 Tel 504-388-6294; 388-8271 (orders only) Fax 504-388-6461

Lowell House, 2029 Century Park E., Suite 3290, Los Angeles, Calif. 90067 Tel 310-552-7555

Lyford Bks., c.o. Presidio Press, 505 B San Marin Dr., Suite 300, Novato, Calif. 94945-1340 Tel 415-898-1081 Fax 415-898-0383

Lyons & Burford, 31 W. 21st St., New York, N.Y. 10010 Tel 212-620-9580 Fax 212-929-1836

Macmillan Pub. Co., 866 3rd Ave., New York, N.Y. 10022 Tel 212-702-2000; 800-257-5755; refer orders to 100 Front St., Box 500, Riverside, N.J. 08075-7500 Tel 609-461-6500; 800-323-7445 Fax 609-461-7070; 800-562-1272

Macmillan Educ. Co., 866 3rd Ave., New York, N.Y. 10022 Tel 212-702-2000; 800-257-5755

Madison Bks., 4720 Boston Way, Lanham, Md. 20706 Tel 301-459-5308; 800-462-6420 Fax 301-459-2118

Marquis Who's Who Inc., 3002 Glenview Rd., Wilmette, Ill. 60091 Tel 708-441-2264; 800-621-9669

Marshall Cavendish Bks. Ltd., 119 Wardour St., London W1V 3TD, Eng. Tel (071) 734 6710 Fax (071) 439 1423

Branch offices

U.S.: Marshall Cavendish Corp., 2415 Jerusalem Ave., N. Bellmore, N.Y. 11710 Tel 516-826-4200; 800-821-9881

Masters Press, 2647 Waterfront Parkway, East Rd., Indianapolis, Ind. 46214-2041 Tel 317-298-5706; 800-722-2677; refer orders to National Bk. Network, 4720 Boston Way, Lanham, Md. 20706 Tel 301-459-8696; 800-462-6420 Fax 301-459-2118

Mathematical Assn. of Am. (The), 1529 18th St. N.W., Washington, D.C. 20036 Tel 202-387-5200; 800-331-1622 Fax 202-265-2385

McFarland & Co. Inc. Pubs., P.O. Box 611, Jefferson, N.C. 28640 Tel 919-246-4460 Fax 919-246-5018

McGraw-Hill Int. Bk. Co., 1221 Ave. of the Americas, New York, N.Y. 10020 Tel 212-512-2000; 800-722-4726; refer orders to 13311 Monterey Ave., Blue Ridge Summit, Pa. 17294-0850 Tel 717-794-2194; 800-822-8138 Fax 717-794-2080

McKay, D.: David McKay Co. Inc., 201 E. 50th St., New York, N.Y. 10022 Tel 212-751-2600; 800-638-6460 Fax 212-872-8026; refer orders to Random House Inc., 400 Hahn Rd., Westminster, Md. 21157 Tel 800-492-0782

Meadowbrook Inc., 18318 Minnetonka Blvd., Deephaven, Minn. 55391 Tel 612-473-5400; 800-338-2232 Fax 612-475-0736; refer orders to Simon & Schuster

Means: R. S. Means Co. Inc., 100 Construction Plaza, P.O. Box 800, Kingston, Mass. 02364-0800 Tel 617-585-7880; 800-334-3509 (orders)

Medical Economics Bks., 5 Paragon Dr., Montcale, N.J. 07654 Tel 201-358-7200 Fax 201-262-6543

Menil Foundation, c.o. Harvard Univ. Press, 79 Garden St., Cambridge, Mass. 02138 Tel 617-495-2480

Merck & Co. Inc., P.O. Box 2000, Rahway, N.J. 07065 Tel 201-574-5403

Meredith Corp., 1716 Locust St., Des Moines, Iowa 50309 Tel 515-284-3000; 800-678-8091 Fax 515-284-2700

Meriwether Pub. Ltd., 885 Elkton Dr., Colorado Springs, Colo. 80907 Tel 719-594-4422; 800-937-5297 Fax 719-594-9916

Merriam-Webster Inc., 47 Federal St., Springfield, Mass. 01102 Tel 413-734-3134; 800-828-1880 Fax 413-731-5979

Methuen See Chapman & Hall

Metropolitan Mus. of Art, 1000 5th Ave., New York, N.Y. 10028 Tel 212-879-5500 Fax 212-535-4830

Metropolitan Opera Guild, 1865 Broadway, New York, N.Y. 10023 Tel 212-582-3285

Michelin Tire Corp., P.O. Box 3305, Spartanburg, S.C. 29304-3305

Michigan State Univ. Press, 1405 S. Harrison Rd., 25 Manly Miles Bldg., Suite 25, East Lansing, Mich. 48823-5202 Tel 517-355-9543 Fax 800-678-2120

Microsoft Press, 1 Microsoft Way, Redmond, Wash. 98052-6399 Tel 206-882-8080; 800-677-7377; refer orders to Ingram Bk. Co., 1125 Heil Quaker Blvd., La Vergne, Tenn. 37086-7005 Tel 615-793-5000; 800-251-5900 (orders only)

Microtrend Bks., 165 Vallecitos de Oro, San Marcos, Calif. 92069 Tel 619-744-2299; 800-752-9766

Mills & Sanderson Pubs., 41 Worth Rd., Suite 201, Bedford, Mass. 01730 Tel 617-861-0992; 800-441-6224 Fax 617-275-1713

Minneapolis Inst. of Arts, 2400 3rd Ave. S., Minneapolis, Minn. 55404 Tel 612-870-3029

MIT Press (The), 55 Hayward St., Cambridge, Mass. 02142 Tel 617-253-8189; 800-356-0343 Fax 617-258-6779; 625-6660 (orders)

Modern Lang. Assn. of Am. (The), 10 Astor Pl., New York, N.Y. 10003-6981 Tel 212-475-9500 Fax 212-477-9863

Modern Lib. (The), 201 E. 50th St., New York, N.Y. 10022 Tel 212-751-2600; 800-726-0600

Moody Press, 820 N. LaSalle Dr., Chicago, Ill. 60610 Tel 312-329-2108; 800-678-6928 Fax 312-329-2144

Morehouse Pub. Co., 871 Ethan Allen Highway, Suite 204, Ridgefield, Conn. 06877 Tel 203-431-3927; refer orders to P.O. Box 1321, Harrisburg, Pa. 17105 Tel 717-541-8130; 800-877-0012

Morning Glory Press, 6595 San Haroldo Way, Buena Park, Calif. 90620-3748 Tel 714-828-1998 Fax 714-828-2049

Morrow: William Morrow & Co. Inc., 1350 Ave. of the Americas, New York, N.Y. 10019 Tel 212-261-6500; 800-237-0657 Fax 212-779-0965; refer orders to 39 Plymouth St., Fairfield, N.J. 07007 Tel 201-227-7200; 800-843-9389 Fax 201-227-6849

Mosby: C. V. Mosby Co. (The), 11830 Westline Ind. Dr., St. Louis, Mo. 63146 Tel 314-872-8370; 800-426-4545 (individuals); 800-633-6699 (institutions) Fax 314-432-1380

Mosby-Year Bk., 11830 Westline Ind. Dr., St. Louis, Mo. 63146 Tel 314-872-8370; 800-426-4545 (individuals); 800-633-6699 (institutions) Fax 314-432-1380

Mouton de Gruyter, Genthiner Str. 13, D-1000 Berlin 30, Germany Tel (030) 26005235

Branch offices

U.S.: Mouton de Gruyter, 200 Saw Mill River Rd., Hawthorne, N.Y. 10532 Tel 914-747-0110 Fax 914-747-1326

Moyer Bell Ltd., Kymbolde Way, Wakefield, R.I. 02879 Tel 401-789-0074 Fax 401-789-3793

Museum of Modern Art (The), 11 W. 53rd St., New York, N.Y. 10019 Tel 212-708-9443 Fax 212-708-9779

Mysterious Press, 1271 Ave. of the Americas, New York, N.Y. 10021 Tel 212-522-7200 Fax 212-522-7991; refer orders to Little, Brown

NAL Bks., 375 Hudson St., New York, N.Y. 10014 Tel 212-366-2000; refer orders to Penguin USA, P.O. Box 120, Bergenfield, N.J. 07621 Tel 201-387-0600; 800-526-0275

National Acad. Press, P.O. Box 285, 2101 Constitution Ave. N.W., Washington, D.C. 20418 Tel 202-334-3313; 800-624-6242 (orders only) Fax 202-334-2451

National Assn. of Social Workers, 750 1st St. N.E., Washington, D.C. 20002-4241 Tel 202-408-8600; 800-638-8799; refer orders to P.O. Box 431, Annapolis JCT, Md. 20701 Tel 800-227-3590 Fax 301-206-7989

National Assn. of the Deaf, 814 Thayer Ave., Silver Spring, Md. 20910 Tel 301-587-1788

National Fire Protection Assn., 1 Batterymarch Park, P.O. Box 9101, Quincy, Mass. 02269-9101 Tel 617-770-3000; 800-344-3555

National Gallery of Art, Constitution Ave. at 6th St. N.W., Washington, D.C. 20565 Tel 202-737-4215 Fax 202-842-2356; refer orders to 2000 S. Club Dr., Landover, Md. 20785 Tel 301-322-5900 Fax 301-322-1578

National Geographic Soc., 1145 17th St. N.W., Washington, D.C. 20036 Tel 202-857-7000; refer orders to P.O. Box 1640, Washington, D.C. 20013-9861 Tel 301-921-1200; 800-638-4077

National Journal, 1730 M St. N.W., Washington, D.C. 20036 Tel 202-857-1400; 800-424-2921 Fax 202-833-8069

National Park Foundation, P.O. Box 57473, Washington, D.C. 20037; refer orders to Viking

National Press Bks., 7200 Wisconsin Ave., Suite 212, Bethesda, Md. 20814 Tel 301-657-1616; 800-275-8888 Fax 301-657-8475; refer orders to National Bk. Network, 4720 Boston Way, Lanham, Md. 20706 Tel 301-459-8696; 800-462-6420 Fax 301-459-2118

National Register Pub. Co. Inc., 121 Chanlon Rd., New Providence, N.J. 07974 Tel 908-464-6800; 800-526-4902 Fax 908-464-3553

National Textbook Co., 4255 W. Touhy Ave., Lincolnwood, Ill. 60646-1975 Tel 708-679-5500; 800-323-4900

Naval Inst. Press, U.S. Naval Inst., Preble Hall, 118 Maryland Ave., Annapolis, Md. 21402-5035 Tel 410-268-6110 Fax 410-269-7940; refer orders to 2062 Generals Highway, Annapolis, Md. 21401-6780 Tel 410-224-3378; 800-233-8764 Fax 410-224-2406

Neal-Schuman Pubs. Inc., 100 Varick St., New York, N.Y. 10013 Tel 212-925-8650 Fax 212-219-8916

Nelson-Hall Pubs., 111 N. Canal St., Chicago, Ill. 60606 Tel 312-930-9446 Fax 312-930-5903 (orders)

Nelson, T.: Thomas Nelson Pubs., Nelson Pl. at Elm Hill Pike, P.O. Box 14100, Nashville, Tenn. 37214-1000 Tel 615-889-9000; 800-251-4000 Fax 615-391-5225

New Am. Lib. Inc. (The), 375 Hudson St., New York, N.Y. 10014 Tel 212-366-2000; refer orders to Penguin USA, P.O. Box 120, Bergenfield, N.J. 07621 Tel 201-387-0600; 800-526-0275

New Amsterdam Bks., 101 Main St., P.O. Box C, Franklin, N.Y. 13775 Tel 607-829-2800; 800-944-4040 Fax 607-829-2057

New Century Pubs. Inc., RR1, Box 384C, Route 173 W., Hampton, N.J. 08827 Tel 908-735-9701

New Directions Pub. Corp., 80 8th Ave., New York, N.Y. 10011 Tel 212-255-0230 Fax 212-255-0231; refer orders to W. W. Norton & Co. Inc., 500 5th Ave., New York, N.Y. 10110 Tel 212-354-5500; 800-233-4830 (orders) Fax 212-869-0856; 800-458-6515 (orders)

New England Hist. Genealogical Soc., 101 Newbury St., Boston, Mass. 02116 Tel 617-536-5740

New England Pub. Assocs., P.O. Box 5, Chester, Conn. 06412 Tel 203-345-3660

New Horizon Press Pubs. Inc., P.O. Box 669, Far Hills, N.J. 07931 Tel 908-604-6311; 800-533-7978 Fax 908-604-6330

New Press (NY), c.o. McGraw-Hall, 1221 Ave. of the Americas, New York, N.Y. 10020 Tel 212-512-2000; 800-722-4726

New Science Lib., 300 Massachusetts Ave., Boston, Mass. 02115 Tel 617-424-0030 Fax 617-236-1563; refer orders to Random House

New Soc. Pubs., 4527 Springfield Ave., Philadelphia, Pa. 19143 Tel 215-382-6543; 800-333-9093 Fax 215-222-1993

New York Graphic Soc., 34 Beacon St., Boston, Mass. 02106 Tel 617-227-0730; refer orders to Little, Brown

New York Univ. Press, 70 Washington Sq. S., New York, N.Y. 10012 Tel 212-998-2575 Fax 212-995-3833

Newmarket Press, 18 E. 48th St., New York, N.Y. 10017 Tel 212-832-3575; 800-669-3903 Fax 212-832-3629

Nolo Press (Berkeley): Nolo Press, 950 Parker St., Berkeley, Calif. 94710 Tel 510-549-1976; 800-992-6656 (orders only) Fax 800-645-0895

North Light Bks., 1507 Dana Ave., Cincinnati, Ohio 45207 Tel 513-531-2222; 800-289-0963 Fax 513-531-4082

North Light Pubs., 1507 Dana Ave., Cincinnati, Ohio 45207 Tel 513-531-2222; 800-551-0963; Fax 513-531-4082

North Point Press, 1563 Solano Ave., Suite 353, Berkeley, Calif. 94707-2116 Tel 510-704-8046 Fax 510-704-0167; refer orders to Farrar, Straus & Giroux

Northeastern Univ. Press, 360 Huntington Ave., 272HN, Boston, Mass. 02115 Tel 617-437-5480 Fax 617-437-5483; refer orders to C.U.P. Services, P.O. Box 6525, Ithaca, N.Y. 14851 Tel 607-277-2211 Fax 607-277-6292

Northwestern Univ. Press, 625 Colfax St., Evanston, Ill. 60201-2807 Tel 708-491-5313; 800-621-2736 Fax 708-491-8150

Norton: W. W. Norton & Co. Inc., 500 5th Ave., New York, N.Y. 10110 Tel 212-354-5500; 800-233-4830 (orders) Fax 212-869-0856; 800-458-6515 (orders)

Nova Pub. Co., 1103 W. College St., Carbondale, Ill. 62901 Tel 618-457-3521; refer orders to National Bk. Network, 4720 Boston Way, Lanham, Md. 20706 Tel 301-459-8696; 800-462-6420 Fax 301-459-2118

Oak Knoll Bks., 414 Delaware St., New Castle, Del. 19720 Tel 302-328-7232 Fax 302-328-7274

Oberlin College Press, Rice Hall, Oberlin, Ohio 44074 Tel 216-775-8407 Fax 216-775-8124

October House, P.O. Box 454, Stonington, Conn. 06378

Ohio State Univ. Press, 1070 Carmack Rd., Room 180, Pressey Hall, Columbus, Ohio 43210-1002 Tel 614-292-6930 Fax 614-292-2065

Ohio Univ. Press, Scott Quadrangle, Athens, Ohio 45701-2979 Tel 614-593-1155; 800-242-7737 Fax 614-563-4536; refer orders to Chicago Distr. Center, 11030 S. Langley Ave., Chicago, Ill. 60628 Tel 312-568-1550; 800-621-2736 (outside Ill.) Fax 312-660-2235

Omnigraphics Inc., 2400 Penobscot Bldg., Detroit, Mich. 48226 Tel 313-961-1340; 800-234-1340 Fax 313-961-1383

Ontario Review Press, 9 Honey Brook Dr., Princeton, N.J. 08540 Tel 609-737-7497; refer orders to George Braziller Inc., 60 Madison Ave., New York, N.Y. 10010 Tel 212-889-0909

Open Hand Pub. Inc., P.O. Box 22048, Seattle, Wash. 98122 Tel 206-323-3868

Orbis Bks., Fathers & Brothers of Maryknoll, Walsh Bldg., Maryknoll, N.Y. 10545 Tel 914-941-7636; 800-258-5838 Fax 914-945-0670; 941-7005 (orders)

Orion Bks. (NY): Orion Bks., 201 E. 50th St., New York, N.Y. 10022 Tel 212-751-2600 Fax 212-572-6192; refer orders to Random House

Ortho Bks., 6001 Bollinger Canyon Rd., Bldg. T, San Ramon, Calif. 94583 Tel 415-842-5530; refer orders to Ballantine Bks.

Oryx Press (The), 4041 N. Central Ave., No. 700, Phoenix, Ariz. 85012-3397 Tel 602-265-2651; 800-279-6799 Fax 602-265-6250; 800-279-4663

Our Sunday Visitor Inc., 200 Noll Plaza, Huntington, Ind. 46750-9983 Tel 219-356-8400; 800-348-2440 Fax 219-356-8472

Outlet Bk. Co. Inc., 40 Engelhard Ave., Avenel, N.J. 07001 Tel 908-827-2700; 800-223-6804; refer orders to Random House

Overlook Press (The), 149 Wooster St., 4th Floor, New York, N.Y. 10012 Tel 212-477-7162 Fax 212-477-7525; refer orders to Rural Route 1, Box 496, Woodstock, N.Y. 12498

Oxford Univ. Press, Walton St., Oxford OX2 6DP, Eng. Tel (0865) 56767; refer orders to Oxford Univ. Press Distr. Services, Saxon Way West, Corby, Northamptonshire NM1 9ES, Eng. Tel (0536) 741 519

Branch offices

U.S.: Oxford Univ. Press Inc., 200 Madison Ave., New York, N.Y. 10016 Tel 212-679-7300; 800-458-5833; refer orders to 2001 Evans Rd., Cary, N.C. 27513 Tel 800-451-7556 Fax 919-677-1303

Oxmoor House Inc., P.O. Box 2262, Birmingham, Ala. 35201 Tel 205-877-6249; 800-633-4712; refer orders to Sunset Bks., 80 Willow Rd., Menlo Park, Calif. 94025-3691 Tel 415-321-3600; 800-321-0372; 800-227-7346 (outside Calif.)

Pandora Press, 77/85 Fulham Palace Rd., Hammersmith, London W6 8JB, Eng. Tel (081) 741 7070; refer orders to HarperCollins Distr. Services, P.O. Box, Glasgow G4 0NB, Scotland Tel (041) 772 3200

Branch offices

U.S.: Pandora, 1160 Battery St., San Francisco, Calif. 94111-1213 Tel 415-477-4400; 800-328-5125 Fax 415-477-4444

Panjandrum Bks., 11321 Iowa Ave., Suite 1, Los Angeles, Calif. 90025

Pantheon Bks. Inc., 201 E. 50th St., New York, N.Y. 10022 Tel 212-872-8238; 800-638-6460; Fax 212-572-6030; refer orders to Random House Inc., 400 Hahn Rd., Westminster, Md. 21157 Tel 410-848-1900; 800-733-3000 Fax 800-659-2436

Paragon House Pubs., 401 5th Ave., New York, N.Y. 10016 Tel 212-725-3380 Fax 212-725-3617

Pathfinder Press, 410 West St., New York, N.Y. 10014 Tel 212-741-0690 Fax 212-727-0150

Paulist Press, 997 MacArthur Blvd., Mahwah, N.J. 07430 Tel 201-825-7300 Fax 201-825-8345; 825-6921 (orders); 800-836-3161 (orders)

Peachtree Pubs. Ltd., 494 Armour Circle N.E., Atlanta, Ga. 30324-4088 Tel 404-876-8761; 800-241-0113 Fax 404-875-2578; 800-875-8909

Penguin Bks. Ltd., 27 Wright's Lane, London W8 5TZ, Eng. Tel (071) 938 2200; refer orders to Bath Rd., Harmondsworth, Middlesex UB7 0DA, Eng. Tel (081) 759 1984

Branch offices

U.S.: Penguin Bks., 375 Hudson St., New York, N.Y. 10014 Tel 212-366-2000; refer orders to Penguin USA, P.O. Box 120, Bergenfield, N.J. 07621 Tel 201-387-0600; 800-526-0275

Pennsylvania State Univ. Press, 820 N. University Dr., Suite C, Barbara Bldg., University Park, Pa. 16802 Tel 814-865-1327; 800-326-9180 (orders) Fax 814-863-1408

Peregrine Smith Bks., P.O. Box 667, Layton, Utah 84041 Tel 801-544-9800; 800-421-8714

Perennial Lib., 10 E. 53rd St., New York, N.Y. 10022-5299 Tel 212-207-7000; refer orders to HarperCollins Pubs., Keystone Ind. Park, Scranton, Pa. 18512 Tel 800-982-4377; 800-242-7737 (outside Pa.)

Pergamon-Brassey's Int. Defense Pubs., 8000 Westpark Dr., 1st Floor, McLean, Va. 22102 Tel 703-442-0900; refer orders to 100 Front St., Box 500, Riverside, N.J. 08075-7500 Tel 609-461-6500

Pergamon Press, Headington Hill Hall, Oxford OX3 0BW, Eng. Tel (0865) 743 685 Fax (0865) 743 946

Perigee Bks., 200 Madison Ave., New York, N.Y. 10016 Tel 212-951-8400; 800-631-8571; refer orders to 390 Murray Hill Parkway, East Rutherford, N.J. 07073

Persea Bks. Inc., 60 Madison Ave., New York, N.Y. 10010 Tel 212-779-7668

Peterson's Guides Inc., 202 Carnegie Center, Princeton, N.J. 08540 Tel 609-243-9111; 800-338-3282 Fax 609-452-0966

Pharos Bks., 200 Park Ave., New York, N.Y. 10166 Tel 212-692-3824 Fax 212-692-3758; refer orders to St. Martin's Press

Phillips: S. G. Phillips Inc., P.O. Box 83, Chatham, N.Y. 12037 Tel 518-392-3068

Philosophical Lib. Inc., 31 W. 21st St., 11th Floor, New York, N.Y. 10010 Tel 212-727-7870; 800-336-7870 Fax 212-727-7874

Pineapple Press (Sarasota): Pineapple Press Inc., P.O. Drawer 16008, Southside Station, Sarasota, Fla. 34239 Tel 813-952-1085 Fax 813-952-1085

Players Press Inc., P.O. Box 1132, Studio City, Calif. 91614-0132 Tel 818-789-4980 Fax 818-980-9756

Plays Inc., 120 Boylston St., Boston, Mass. 02116 Tel 617-423-3157

Plenum Press, 233 Spring St., New York, N.Y. 10013-1578 Tel 212-620-8047; 800-221-9369 (orders) Fax 212-463-0742; 807-1047 (orders)

Pocket Bks., Simon & Schuster Bldg., 1230 Ave. of the Americas, New York, N.Y. 10020 Tel 212-698-7000; 800-223-2348; refer orders to Simon & Schuster Inc., 200 Old Tappan Rd., Old Tappan, N.J. 07675 Tel 201-767-5937; 800-223-2336

Poetry Index Press, 185 Great Neck Rd., Great Neck, N.Y. 11021 Tel 516-466-3676; 800-327-0295; refer orders to P.O. Box 406, Great Neck, N.Y. 11022

Poseidon Press, Simon & Schuster Bldg., 1230 Ave. of the Americas, New York, N.Y. 10020 Tel 212-698-7000; 800-223-2348; refer orders to Simon & Schuster Inc., 200 Old Tappan Rd., Old Tappan, N.J. 07675 Tel 201-767-5937; 800-223-2336

Potter: Clarkson N. Potter Inc. Pubs., 201 E. 50th St., New York, N.Y. 10022 Tel 212-751-2600 Fax 212-572-6192; refer orders to Random House

Praeger Pubs., 88 Post Rd. W., P.O. Box 5007, Westport, Conn. 06881 Tel 203-226-3571 Fax 203-222-1502

Prentice-Hall Inc., Route 9W, Englewood Cliffs, N.J. 07632 Tel 201-592-2000; 800-223-1360; refer orders to Simon & Schuster Inc., 200 Old Tappan Rd., Old Tappan, N.J. 07675 Tel 201-767-5937; 800-223-2336

Prentice Hall General Ref., 15 Columbus Circle, New York, N.Y. 10023 Tel 212-373-8500; 800-223-2348; refer orders to Paramount Pub., 200 Old Tappan Rd., Old Tappan, N.J. 07675 Tel 201-767-5937; 800-223-2336 Fax 201-767-5852 (orders)

Prentice Hall Press, 15 Columbus Circle, New York, N.Y. 10023 Tel 212-373-8500; 800-223-2348; refer orders to Simon & Schuster Inc., 200 Old Tappan Rd., Old Tappan, N.J. 07675 Tel 201-767-5937; 800-223-2336

Prentice Hall Travel, 15 Columbus Circle, New York, N.Y. 10023 Tel 212-373-8500; 800-223-2348; refer orders to Simon & Schuster Inc., 200 Old Tappan Rd., Old Tappan, N.J. 07675 Tel 201-767-5937; 800-223-2336

Presidio Press, 505 B San Marin Dr., Suite 300, Novato, Calif. 94945-1340 Tel 415-898-1081 Fax 415-898-0383

Price/Stern/Sloan Inc., 11150 Olympic Blvd., Suite 650, Los Angeles, Calif. 90064 Tel 310-477-6100; 800-421-0892 Fax 310-445-3933; refer orders to P.O. Box 64575, Los Angeles, Calif. 90064 Fax 310-445-3934

Prima Pub. & Communications, 1830 Sierra Gardens, Suite 130, Roseville, Calif. 95661 Tel 916-786-0426 Fax 916-624-2385; refer orders to St. Martin's Press

Princeton Bk. Co. Pubs., 12 W. Delaware Ave., P.O. Box 57, Pennington, N.J. 08534 Tel 609-737-8177; 800-326-7149

Princeton Univ. Press, 41 William St., Princeton, N.J. 08540 Tel 609-258-4900 Fax 609-258-6305; refer orders to California-Princeton Fulfillment, Services, 1445 Lower Ferry Rd., Ewing, N.J. 08618 Tel 609-883-1759; 800-777-4726 Fax 609-883-7413; 800-999-1958

PRO-ED, 8700 Shoal Creek Blvd., Austin, Tex. 78758-6897 Tel 512-451-3246 Fax 512-451-8542

Prometheus Bks., 700 E. Amherst St., Buffalo, N.Y. 14215-1674 Tel 716-837-2475 Fax 716-835-6901; refer orders to Warehouse & Fulfillment Center, 59 John Glenn Dr., Amherst, N.Y. 14228-2197 Tel 716-691-0133; 800-421-0351 (orders only) Fax 716-691-0137

Pushcart Press (The), P.O. Box 380, Wainscott, N.Y. 11975 Tel 516-324-9300; refer orders to Norton

Putnam: G. P. Putnam's Sons, 200 Madison Ave., New York, N.Y. 10016 Tel 212-951-8400; 800-631-8571; refer orders to 390 Murray Hill Parkway, East Rutherford, N.J. 07073

Quigley Pub. Co. Inc., 159 W. 53rd St., New York, N.Y. 10019 Tel 212-247-3100

Quill, 1350 Ave. of the Americas, New York, N.Y. 10019 Tel 212-261-6500; 800-843-9389 Fax 212-779-0965; refer orders to 39 Plymouth St., Fairfield, N.J. 07007 Tel 201-227-7200

Quilt Digest Press (The), P.O. Box 1331, Gualala, Calif. 95445 Tel 707-884-4100; refer orders to Publishers Group West, P.O. Box 8843, Emeryville, Calif. 94662 Tel 800-788-3123

Rand McNally, 8255 N. Central Park Ave., Skokie, Ill. 60076 Tel 708-329-8100

Random House Inc., 201 E. 50th St., New York, N.Y. 10022 Tel 212-751-2600; 800-726-0600; refer orders to 400 Hahn Rd., Westminster, Md. 21157 Tel 410-848-1900; 800-733-3000 Fax 800-659-2436

Rawson Assocs., 866 3rd Ave., New York, N.Y. 10022 Tel 212-702-2000; 800-257-5755; refer orders to 100 Front St., Box 500, Riverside, N.J. 08075 Tel 609-461-6500; 800-257-8247

Rawson, Wade Pubs. Inc., 630 3rd Ave., New York, N.Y. 10017; refer orders to Scribner

RB Bks., 1006 N. 2nd St., Harrisburg, Pa. 17102 Tel 717-232-7944; 800-497-1497 Fax 717-238-3280

Reader's Digest Assn. Inc. (The), 260 Madison Ave., New York, N.Y. 10016 Tel 212-850-7007; refer orders to Reader's Digest Rd., Pleasantville, N.Y. 10570 Tel 800-431-1246

Real Comet Press (The), 3131 Western Ave., Suite 410, Seattle, Wash. 98121-1028 Tel 206-283-7827; refer orders to Consortium Bk. Sales & Distr., 287 E. 6th St., Suite 365, St. Paul, Minn. 55101 Tel 612-221-9035; 800-283-3572

Rebus Inc., 632 Broadway, New York, N.Y. 10012 Tel 212-505-2255

Reference Service Press, 10 Twin Dolphin Dr., Suite B-308, Redwood City, Calif. 94065 Tel 415-594-0743

Regency Ref. Lib., 5300 Patterson Ave. S.E., Grand Rapids, Mich. 49530 Tel 616-698-6900; refer orders to HarperCollins Pubs.

Regnery Bks., 1130 17th St. N.W., Suite 600, Washington, D.C. 20036 Tel 202-457-0978 Fax 202-457-0774

Regnery Gateway Inc., 1130 17th St. N.W., Suite 600, Washington, D.C. 20036 Tel 202-457-0978 Fax 202-457-0774; refer orders to National Bk. Network, 4720 Boston Way, Lanham, Md. 20706 Tel 301-459-8696; 800-462-6420 Fax 301-459-2118

Retirement Policy Inst., 2203 Wittstock Dr., Charlotte, N.C. 28210 Tel 704-553-9193

Revell: Fleming H. Revell Co., P.O. Box 6287, Grand Rapids, Mich. 49516 Tel 616-676-9185; 800-877-2665 Fax 616-676-9573; 398-3111 (orders)

Rizzoli Int. Publs. Inc., 300 Park Ave. S., New York, N.Y. 10010 Tel 212-387-3400; 800-433-1238 (orders only); refer orders to St. Martin's Press

Rodale Press Inc., 33 E. Minor St., Emmaus, Pa. 18098 Tel 215-967-5171; 800-322-6333; 800-527-8200 (outside Pa.); refer orders to St. Martin's Press

Rolling Stone Press, 745 5th Ave., New York, N.Y. 10151 Tel 212-758-3800

Routledge, 11 New Fetter Lane, London EC4P 4EE, Eng. Tel (071) 583 9855 Fax (071) 583 0701
Branch offices
U.S.: Routledge, 29 W. 35th St., New York, N.Y. 10001-2291 Tel 212-244-3336 Fax 212-563-2269

Routledge & Kegan Paul See Chapman & Hall

Routledge, Chapman & Hall See Chapman & Hall

Running Press Bk. Pubs., 125 S. 22nd St., Philadelphia, Pa. 19103 Tel 215-567-5080; 800-345-5359 (orders only) Fax 800-453-2884

Rutgers Univ. Press, 109 Church St., New Brunswick, N.J. 08901 Tel 908-932-7764 Fax 908-932-7039; refer orders to R.U.P. Distr. Center, P.O. Box 4869, Hampden Station, Baltimore, Md. 21211 Tel 410-516-6947; 800-446-9323 Fax 410-516-6998

Rutledge Hill Press, 513 3rd Ave. S., Nashville, Tenn. 37210 Tel 615-244-2700; 800-234-4234 Fax 615-244-2978

Salem House Pubs., 462 Boston St., Topsfield, Mass. 01983 Tel 717-343-4761; refer orders to HarperCollins Pubs., Keystone Ind. Park, Scranton, Pa. 18512 Tel 800-982-4377; 800-242-7737 (outside Pa.)

Salem Press Inc., P.O. Box 1097, Englewood Cliffs, N.J. 07632 Tel 201-871-3700; 800-221-1592

Sams, 201 W. 103rd St., Indianapolis, Ind. 46290 Tel 317-573-2500; 800-428-5331 Fax 800-448-3804 (orders)

Sargent Pubs.: Porter Sargent Pubs. Inc., 11 Beacon St., Boston, Mass. 02108 Tel 617-523-1670

Sasquatch Bks., 1931 2nd Ave., Seattle, Wash. 98101 Tel 206-441-5555 Fax 206-441-6213; refer orders to Pacific Pipeline Inc., 19215 66th Ave. S., Kent, Wash. 98032 Tel 206-872-5523; 800-562-4647

Saunders: W. B. Saunders Co., The Curtis Center, Independence Sq. W., Philadelphia, Pa. 19106-3399 Tel 215-238-7800 Fax 215-238-7883; refer orders to 6277 Sea Harbor Dr., Orlando, Fla. 32821 Tel 407-345-2525; 800-782-4479

Saunders College Pub., The Curtis Cts., Independence Sq. W., Philadelphia, Pa. 19106 Tel 215-238-7800; refer orders to 6277 Sea Harbor Dr., Orlando, Fla. 32821 Tel 407-345-2525; 800-782-4479

Saur: K. G. Saur Verlag KG, Ortlerstr. 8, Postfach 701620, 81373 Munich, Germany Tel (089) 76902 Fax (089) 76902
Branch offices
U.S.: K. G. Saur Inc., 121 Chanlon Rd., New Providence, N.J. 07974 Tel 908-464-6800; 800-521-8110 Fax 908-464-3553

Scarborough House, 4720 Boston Way, Lanham, Md. 20706 Tel 301-459-5308

Scarecrow Press Inc., 52 Liberty St., P.O. Box 4167, Metuchen, N.J. 08840 Tel 908-548-8600; 800-537-7107 Fax 908-548-5767

Schenkman Bks. Inc., 118 Main St., P.O. Box 119, Rochester, Vt. 05767 Tel 802-767-3702

Schiffer Pub. Ltd., 77 Lower Valley Rd., Atglen, Pa. 19310 Tel 215-593-1777 Fax 215-593-2002

Schirmer Bks., 866 3rd Ave., New York, N.Y. 10022 Tel 212-702-3445 Fax 212-605-9368; refer orders to Macmillan Pub. Co., 100 Front St., Box 500, Riverside, N.J. 08075-7500 Tel 609-461-6500; 800-323-7445 Fax 609-461-7070; 800-562-1272

Schocken Bks. Inc., 201 E. 50th St., New York, N.Y. 10022 Tel 212-751-2600; 800-726-0600 Fax 212-572-6030; refer orders to Random House Inc., 400 Hahn Rd., Westminster, Md. 21157 Tel 410-848-1900; 800-733-3000 Fax 800-659-2436

Scholarly Press Inc., P.O. Box 160, St. Clair Shores, Mich. 48080

SCM Press Ltd., 26-30 Tottenham Rd., London N1 4BZ, Eng. Tel (071) 249 7262 Fax (071) 249 3776
Agents
U.S.: Trinity Press Int.

Scott, Foresman & Co., 1900 E. Lake Ave., Glenview, Ill. 60025 Tel 708-729-3000

Scott Pub. Co., 911 Vandemark Rd., Sidney, Ohio 45365 Tel 513-498-0802; refer orders to P.O. Box 828, Sidney, Ohio 45365 Tel 800-327-1259; 800-448-3611 (outside Ohio)

Scribner: Charles Scribner's Sons, 866 3rd Ave., New York, N.Y. 10022 Tel 212-702-2000; 800-257-5755; refer orders to Macmillan

Seal Press (The), 3131 Western Ave., Suite 410, Seattle, Wash. 98121-1028 Tel 206-283-7844; refer orders to Consortium Bk. Sales & Distr., 213 E. 4th St., St. Paul, Minn. 55101

Seaver Bks., c.o. Arcade Pub., 141 5th Ave., New York, N.Y. 10010 Tel 212-475-2633

Self-Help Clearinghouse, St. Clares-Riverside Medical Center, Pocono Rd., Denville, N.J. 07834

Sentinel Communications Co., 75 E. Amelia St., MP106, Orlando, Fla. 32801 Tel 407-420-5275; 800-347-6868

Seven Locks Press, 7307 MacArthur Blvd., Suite 213, Bethesda, Md. 20816 Tel 301-320-2130; 800-537-9359 Fax 301-320-9323; refer orders to P.O. Box 27, Cabin John, Md. 20818

Shambhala Publs. Inc., 300 Massachusetts Ave., Boston, Mass. 02115 Tel 617-424-0030 Fax 617-236-1563; refer orders to Random House

Shapolsky Pubs. Inc., 136 W. 22nd St., New York, N.Y. 10011 Tel 212-633-2022; 800-288-8889 Fax 212-633-2123

Shaw Assocs., 625 Biltmore Way, Suite 1406, Coral Gables, Fla. 33134 Tel 305-446-8888

Shoe String Press Inc. (The), 925 Sherman Ave., Hamden, Conn. 06514 Tel 203-248-6307 Fax 203-230-9275

Sierra Club Bks., 100 Bush St., 13th Floor, San Francisco, Calif. 94103 Tel 415-291-1600; refer orders to Random House

Signature Bks. (Salt Lake City): Signature Bks. Inc., 350 South 400 E., Suite G4, Salt Lake City, Utah 84111 Tel 801-531-1483 Fax 801-531-1488

Simon & Schuster Inc. Pubs., Simon & Schuster Bldg., 1230 Ave. of the Americas, New York, N.Y. 10020 Tel 212-698-7000; 800-223-2348; refer orders to Simon & Schuster, 200 Old Tappan Rd., Old Tappan, N.J. 07675 Tel 800-223-2336 (orders)

Skira: Editions d'Art Albert Skira, 89 Route de Chene, CH-1208 Geneva, Switzerland Tel (022) 495533 Fax (020) 495535

Agents

U.S.: Rizzoli Int. Publs.

Slack Inc., 6900 Grove Rd., Thorofare, N.J. 08086 Tel 609-848-1000; 800-257-8290 Fax 609-853-5991

Smith, G.M.: Gibbs M. Smith Inc., P.O. Box 667, Layton, Utah 84041 Tel 801-544-9800; 800-421-8714

Smith, P., 6 Lexington Ave., Magnolia, Mass. 01930 Tel 508-525-3562

Smithsonian Bks., 955 L'Enfant Plaza, Room 2100, Washington, D.C. 20560 Tel 202-287-3388; 800-223-2584; refer orders to Norton

Smithsonian Institution Press, 470 L'Enfant Plaza, Suite 7100, Washington, D.C. 20560 Tel 202-287-3738 Fax 202-287-3184; refer orders to TAB Bks.

Snow Lion Publs., P.O. Box 6483, Ithaca, N.Y. 14851 Tel 607-273-8506; 800-950-0313 (orders) Fax 607-272-8634

Soho Press Inc., 853 Broadway, New York, N.Y. 10003 Tel 212-260-1900; 800-631-8571 Fax 212-260-1902; refer orders to Putnam Pub. Group, 390 Murray Hill Parkway, East Rutherford, N.J. 07073

Sourcebooks Trade, 26 N. Webster St., Naperville, Ill. 60540 Tel 708-961-2161; 800-798-2475 (orders only) Fax 708-961-2168

South-Western Pub. Co., 5101 Madison Rd., Cincinnati, Ohio 45227 Tel 513-271-8811; 800-543-0487 Fax 513-527-6328; refer orders to Cincinnati Customer Service Center, 4770 Duke Dr., Suite 200, Mason, Ohio 45040 Tel 513-398-1122 Fax 513-398-9867

Southern Ill. Univ. Press, P.O. Box 3697, Carbondale, Ill. 62902-3697 Tel 618-453-2281; 453-6619 (orders) Fax 618-453-1221

Southern Methodist Univ. Press, P.O. Box 415, Dallas, Tex. 75275 Tel 214-768-1432 Fax 214-768-1428; refer orders to Texas A&M Univ. Press

Speech Foundation of Am., P.O. Box 11749, Memphis, Tenn. 38111 Tel 800-992-9392

Spoon River Poetry Press, P.O. Box 1443, Peoria, Ill. 61655 Tel 507-537-6463; refer orders to Bookslinger, 502 N. Prior, St. Paul, Minn. 55104 Tel 612-649-0271

Sporting News Pub. Co. (The), 1212 N. Lindbergh Blvd., St. Louis, Mo. 63132 Tel 314-993-7734; refer orders to P.O. Box 44, St. Louis, Mo. 63166

Sports Illustrated, Time & Life Bldg., 1271 Ave. of the Americas, New York, N.Y. 10020 Tel 212-522-1212

Springer Pub. Co. Inc., 536 Broadway, New York, N.Y. 10012 Tel 212-431-4370 Fax 212-941-7842

St. James Press, 835 Penobscot Bldg., Detroit, Mich. 48226-4094 Tel 800-345-0392; refer orders to P.O. Box 33477, Detroit, Mich. 48232-5477

St. Louis Art Mus. (The), Forest Park, St. Louis, Mo. 63110 Tel 314-721-0067

St. Martin's/Marek, 175 5th Ave., New York, N.Y. 10010 Tel 212-674-5151; 800-221-7945

St. Martin's Press Inc., 175 5th Ave., New York, N.Y. 10010 Tel 212-674-5151; 800-221-7945 Fax 212-420-9314

Stackpole Bks. Inc., P.O. Box 1831, Cameron & Kelker Sts., Harrisburg, Pa. 17105 Tel 717-234-5041; 800-732-3669 Fax 717-234-1359

Standard & Poor's Corp., 25 Broadway, New York, N.Y. 10004 Tel 212-208-8702; 208-8786 (orders only)

Stanford Univ. Press, Stanford, Calif. 94305-2235 Tel 415-723-1593 Fax 415-725-3457

Starwood Pub., 5230 MacArthur Blvd. N.W., Washington, D.C. 20016 Tel 202-362-7404 Fax 202-362-6001

State House Press, 8906 Wall St., Suite 702, Austin, Tex. 78754 Tel 800-421-3378

Station Hill Press, Station Hill Rd., Barrytown, N.Y. 12507 Tel 914-758-5840; 800-342-1993 (credit card orders only)

Sterling Pub. Co. Inc., 387 Park Ave. S., New York, N.Y. 10016-8810 Tel 212-532-7160; 800-367-9692

Stewart, Tabori & Chang Inc., 575 Broadway, 6th Floor, New York, N.Y. 10012 Tel 212-941-2929 Fax 212-941-2982

Stockton Press, 257 Park Ave. S., New York, N.Y. 10010 Tel 212-673-4400; 800-221-2123 Fax 212-673-9842

Stoeger Pub. Co., 55 Ruta Ct., S. Hackensack, N.J. 07606 Tel 201-440-2700; 800-631-0722

Stonehill Pub. Co. Inc., New York, N.Y.

Storey Communications Inc., Schoolhouse Rd., Pownal, Vt. 05261-9990 Tel 802-823-5811 Fax 413-662-3429

Stravon Educ. Press, 845 3rd Ave., New York, N.Y. 10022 Tel 212-371-2880

Stuart, L.: Lyle Stuart, Inc., 120 Enterprise Ave., Secaucus, N.J. 07094 Tel 201-866-4199; 800-572-6657

Studio Mus. in Harlem, 144 W. 125th St., New York, N.Y. 10027 Tel 212-864-4500

Summit Bks., 1230 Ave. of the Americas, New York, N.Y. 10020 Tel 212-698-7501; 800-223-2336; refer orders to Prentice Hall Trade, Simon & Schuster Inc., 200 Old Tappan Rd., Old Tappan, N.J. 07675 Tel 201-767-5937; 800-223-2336 (orders only)

Sunset Pub. Corp., 80 Willow Rd., Menlo Park, Calif. 94025-3691 Tel 415-321-3600; 800-321-0372; 800-227-7346 (outside Calif.)

Superintendent of Docs., U.S. Govt. Ptg. Office, Washington, D.C. 20402

Swallow Press, Scott Quadrangle, Athens, Ohio 45701-2979 Tel 614-593-1155; 800-242-7737 Fax 614-593-4536; refer orders to Chicago Distr. Center, 11030 S. Langley Ave., Chicago, Ill. 60628 Tel 312-568-1550; 800-621-2736 (outside Ill.) Fax 312-660-2235

Syracuse Univ. Press, 1600 Jamesville Ave., Syracuse, N.Y. 13244-5160 Tel 315-443-5534; 443-2597 (orders); 800-365-8929 (orders) Fax 315-443-5545

T.F.H. Publs. Inc., 1 TFH Plaza, Union & 3rd Aves., Neptune City, N.J. 07753 Tel 908-988-8400; 800-631-2188

TAB Bks., P.O. Box 40, Blue Ridge Summit, Pa. 17294-0850 Tel 717-794-2191; 800-822-8138 Fax 717-794-2080

TAB Professional & Ref. Bks., 13311 Montery Ave., Blue Ridge Summit, Pa. 17214-9989 Tel 717-794-2191; 800-822-8138

Taplinger Pub. Co. Inc., P.O. Box 1324, New York, N.Y. 10185; refer orders to Parkwest Publs. Inc., 451 Communipaw Ave., Jersey City, N.J. 07304 Tel 201-432-3257 Fax 201-432-3708

Tarcher, J.P.: Jeremy P. Tarcher Inc., 5858 Wilshire Blvd., Suite 200, Los Angeles, Calif. 90036 Tel 213-935-9980; refer orders to Putnam Pub. Group, 390 Murray Hill Parkway, East Rutherford, N.J. 07073

Taunton Press Inc. (The), 63 S. Main St., Box 5506, Newtown, Conn. 06470-5506 Tel 203-426-8171; 800-243-7252 Fax 203-426-3434; refer orders to Norton

Taylor Pub. Co., 1550 W. Mockingbird Lane, Dallas, Tex. 75235 Tel 214-819-8100; 800-677-2800 (orders only) Fax 214-819-8580

Temple Univ. Press, 1601 N. Broad St., Univ. Services Bldg., Room 305, Philadelphia, Pa. 19122 Tel 215-787-8787; 800-447-1656 Fax 215-787-4119

Ten Speed Press, P.O. Box 7123, Berkeley, Calif. 94707 Tel 510-845-8414; 800-841-2665 (orders only) Fax 510-524-1052

Texas Christian Univ. Press, P.O. Box 30783, Fort Worth, Tex. 76129 Tel 817-921-7822; refer orders to Texas A&M Univ. Press, Drawer C, College Station, Tex. 77843-4354 Tel 409-845-1436; 800-826-8911 Fax 409-847-8752

Thames & Hudson Ltd., 30-34 Bloomsbury St., London WC1B 3QP, Eng. Tel (071) 636 5488 Fax (071) 636 1695; refer orders to 44 Clockhouse Rd., Farnborough, Hampshire GU14 7QZ, Eng. Tel (0252) 541 602 Fax (0252) 377 380
Branch offices
U.S.: Thames & Hudson Inc., 500 5th Ave., New York, N.Y. 10110 Tel 212-354-3763 Fax 212-869-0856; refer orders to Norton

Theatre Arts Bks., 29 W. 35th St., New York, N.Y. 10001 Tel 212-244-3336

Thomas More Press, 205 W. Monroe St., Chicago, Ill. 60606 Tel 312-609-8880; 800-835-8965

Thomasson-Grant Pub., 1 Morton Dr., Suite 500, Charlottesville, Va. 22901 Tel 804-977-1780; 800-999-1780 Fax 804-977-1696

Thor Pub. Co., P.O. Box 1782, Ventura, Calif. 93002; refer orders to Crossing Press

Thunder's Mouth Press, 54 Greene St., Suite 4S, New York, N.Y. 10013-2651 Tel 212-226-0277 Fax 212-226-7682

Ticknor & Fields, 215 Park Ave. S., New York, N.Y. 10003 Tel 212-420-5841; 800-225-3362 Fax 212-420-5850; refer orders to Houghton Mifflin

Timber Press Inc., 133 S.W. 2nd Ave., Suite 450, Portland, Or. 97204 Tel 503-227-2878; 800-327-5680 (U.S. & Can.) Fax 503-227-3070

Time-Life Bks. Inc., 777 Duke St., Alexandria, Va. 22314 Tel 703-838-7000; refer school & lib. orders to Silver Burdett Co., 250 James St., CN1918, Morristown, N.J. 07960-1918 Tel 201-285-7700; 800-631-8081

Times Bks., 201 E. 50th St., New York, N.Y. 10022 Tel 212-751-2600; 800-726-0600; refer orders to Random House Inc., 400 Hahn Rd., Westminster, Md. 21157 Tel 410-848-1900; 800-733-3000 Fax 800-659-2436

Todd Publs., 18 N. Greenbush Rd., W. Nyack, N.Y. 10994 Tel 914-358-6213

TOR Bks., 175 5th Ave., New York, N.Y. 10010 Tel 212-388-0100; 800-221-7945 Fax 212-420-9314; refer orders to St. Martin's Press

Trafalgar Sq. Inc., Howe Hill Rd., N. Pomfret, Vt. 05053 Tel 802-457-1911; 800-423-4525 Fax 802-457-1913

Transaction Pubs., Rutgers Univ., New Brunswick, N.J. 08903 Tel 908-932-2280 Fax 908-932-3138

Trinity Press Int., P.O. Box 851, Valley Forge, Pa. 19460 Tel 215-768-2120 Fax 215-768-2056; refer orders to P.O. Box 13008, Hauppauge, N.Y. 11788 Tel 800-421-8874 Fax 516-582-2736

Turner Pub. (Atlanta): Turner Pub. Inc., 1 CNN Center, P.O. Box 105366, Atlanta, Ga. 30348 Tel 404-827-3617 Fax 404-827-3665; refer orders to Andrews & McMeel Inc., 4900 Main St., Kansas City, Mo. 64112 Tel 816-932-6700; 800-826-4216

Turtle Bay Bks., 201 E. 50th St., New York, N.Y. 10022 Tel 212-751-2600; 800-726-0600

Tuttle: Charles E. Tuttle Co. Inc., 77 Central St. at McKinley Sq., Boston, Mass. 02109 Tel 617-338-9390 Fax 617-338-9690; refer orders to P.O. Box 410, Rutland, Vt. 05702-0410 Tel 802-773-8930; 800-526-2778 Fax 802-773-6993

Twayne Pubs., 866 3rd Ave., New York, N.Y. 10022 Tel 212-702-2000; 800-257-5755 Fax 212-605-9350; refer orders to Macmillan Distr. Center, Front & Brown Sts., Riverside, N.J. 08075 Tel 609-461-6500; 800-323-7445 Fax 609-461-7070; 800-562-1272

Twelvetrees Press, 2400 N. Lake Ave., Altadena, Calif. 91001 Tel 818-798-5207

Tyndale House Pubs. Inc., 351 Executive Dr., Carol Stream, Ill. 60188 Tel 708-668-8300; 800-323-9400 Fax 708-668-8905; refer orders to P.O. Box 80, Wheaton, Ill. 60189

U.N. Publs., Palais des Nations, CH-1211 Geneva 10, Switzerland Tel (022) 7400921 Fax (022) 7400931

Branch offices

U.S.: U.N. Publs., 2 United Nations Plaza, Room DC2-853, New York, N.Y. 10017 Tel 212-963-8302; 800-253-9646 Fax 212-963-3489

U.S. Govt. Ptg. Office, USGPO Stop SSMR, Washington, D.C. 20401; refer orders to Superintendent of Docs., Washington, D.C. 20402-9325 Tel 202-783-3238

U.S. Pharmacopeial Convention Inc., 12601 Twinbrook Parkway, Rockville, Md. 20852 Tel 800-227-8772 Fax 301-816-8148

U.S. Postal Service, Philatelic Marketing Div., 475 L'Enfant Plaza S.W., Washington, D.C. 20260

Ungar Pub. Co. (The), 370 Lexington Ave., New York, N.Y. 10017 Tel 212-532-3650; refer orders to Publisher Resources Inc., P.O. Box 7017, LaVergne, Tenn. 37086 Tel 800-937-5557

Unicorn Press Inc., P.O. Box 3307, Greensboro, N.C. 27402 Tel 919-852-0281

Universe Bks., 300 Park Ave. S., 5th Floor, New York, N.Y. 10010 Tel 212-387-3400

University of Ariz. Press (The), 1230 N. Park, Suite 102, Tucson, Ariz. 85719-4140 Tel 602-621-1441; 800-426-3797 Fax 602-621-8899

University of Ark. Press, 201 Ozark St., Fayetteville, Ark. 72701 Tel 501-575-3246; 800-525-1823 Fax 501-575-6044

University of Calif. Press, 2120 Berkeley Way, Berkeley, Calif. 94720 Tel 510-642-4247; 800-822-6657 Fax 510-643-7127; refer orders to California-Princeton Fulfillment Services, 1445 Lower Ferry Rd., Ewing, N.J. 08618 Tel 609-883-1759; 800-822-6657 Fax 800-999-1958

University of Chicago Press, 5801 S. Ellis Ave., 4th Floor, Chicago, Ill. 60637 Tel 312-702-7700 Fax 312-702-9756; refer orders to 11030 S. Langley Ave., Chicago, Ill. 60628 Tel 312-568-1550; 800-621-2736 Fax 312-660-2235

University of Ga. Press (The), 330 Research Dr., Athens, Ga. 30602-4901 Tel 706-369-6130 Fax 706-369-6131

University of Hawaii Press, 2840 Kolowalu St., Honolulu, Hawaii 96822 Tel 808-956-8694; 956-8255 (orders only) Fax 808-988-6052

University of Ill. Press, 54 E. Gregory Dr., Champaign, Ill. 61820 Tel 217-333-0950 Fax 217-244-8082; refer orders to P.O. Box 4856, Hampden Post Office, Baltimore, Md. 21211 Tel 800-545-4703 Fax 410-516-6969

University of Iowa Press, 119 W. Park Rd., 100 Kuhl House, Iowa City, Iowa 52242-1000 Tel 319-335-2000 Fax 319-335-2055; refer orders to Publications Order Dept., 100 Oakdale Campus, No. M105 OH, Iowa City, Iowa 52242-5000 Tel 319-335-4645; 800-235-2665 Fax 319-335-4039

University of Mass. Press, P.O. Box 429, Amherst, Mass. 01004 Tel 413-545-2217; 545-2219 (orders) Fax 413-545-1226

University of Mich. Press, 839 Greene St., P.O. Box 1104, Ann Arbor, Mich. 48106-1104 Tel 313-764-4388; 764-4392 (orders) Fax 313-936-0456; 800-876-1922 (orders)

University of Minn. Press, 2037 University Ave. S.E., Minneapolis, Minn. 55455-3092 Tel 612-624-2516; 624-0005 (orders); 800-388-3863 (orders) Fax 612-626-7313

University of Mo. Press (The), 2910 LeMone Blvd., Columbia, Mo. 65201 Tel 314-882-0180; 800-828-1894 (orders only) Fax 314-884-4498

University of N.C. Press (The), P.O. Box 2288, Chapel Hill, N.C. 27515-2288 Tel 919-966-3561; 800-848-6224 (orders) Fax 919-966-3829; 800-272-6817 (orders)

University of N.M. Press, 1720 Lomas Blvd. N.E., Albuquerque, N.M. 87131-1591 Tel 505-277-2346; 277-4810 (orders) Fax 505-277-9270; 800-622-8667 (orders)

University of N. Tex. Press, P.O. Box 13856, Denton, Tex. 76203-3856 Tel 817-565-2142 Fax 817-565-4590; refer orders to Texas A&M Univ. Press

University of Neb. Press, 901 N. 17th St., Lincoln, Neb. 68588-0520 Tel 402-472-3581 Fax 402-472-6214; refer orders to P.O. Box 880484, Lincoln, Neb. 68588-0484 Tel 800-755-1105 Fax 800-526-2617

University of Notre Dame Press, Notre Dame, Ind. 46556 Tel 219-239-6346 Fax 219-631-8148; refer orders to P.O. Box 635, South Bend, Ind. 46624 Tel 800-677-3232

University of Okla. Press, 1005 Asp Ave., Norman, Okla. 73019-0445 Tel 405-325-5111 Fax 405-325-4000; refer orders to P.O. Box 787, Norman, Okla. 73070-0787 Tel 405-325-2000; 800-627-7377 Fax 405-364-5798

University of Pa. Press, 418 Service Dr., 1300 Blockley Hall, Philadelphia, Pa. 19104-6097 Tel 215-898-6261 Fax 215-898-0404; refer orders to P.O. Box 4836, Hampden Station, Baltimore, Md. 21211 Tel 410-516-6948; 800-445-9880 Fax 410-516-6998

University of Pittsburgh Press, 127 N. Bellefield Ave., Pittsburgh, Pa. 15260 Tel 412-624-4110 Fax 412-624-7380; refer orders to C.U.P. Services, P.O. Box 6525, Ithaca, N.Y. 14851 Tel 800-666-2211 Fax 800-688-2877

University of Tenn. Press (The), 293 Communications Bldg., Knoxville, Tenn. 37996-0325 Tel 615-974-3321 Fax 615-974-3724; refer orders to 11030 S. Langley, Chicago, Ill. 60628 Tel 312-568-1550; 800-621-2736 Fax 312-660-2235

University of Tex. Press, P.O. Box 7819, Austin, Tex. 78713-7819 Tel 512-471-7233; 800-252-3206 Fax 512-320-0668

University of Utah Press, 101 University Services Bldg., Salt Lake City, Utah 84112 Tel 801-581-6771; 800-444-8638 Fax 801-581-3365

University of Wash. Press, P.O. Box 50096, Seattle, Wash. 98145-5096 Tel 206-543-8870; 800-441-4115 Fax 206-543-3932

University Press of Am. Inc., 4720 Boston Way, Lanham, Md. 20706 Tel 301-459-3366; 800-462-6420 Fax 301-459-2118

University Press of Colo., P.O. Box 849, Niwot, Colo. 80544 Tel 303-530-5337 Fax 303-530-5306

University Press of Fla., 15 N.W. 15th St., Gainesville, Fla. 32611-2079 Tel 904-392-1351; 800-226-3822 Fax 904-392-7302

University Press of Ky., 663 S. Limestone St., Lexington, Ky. 40508-4008 Tel 606-257-2951; 257-5200 (orders) Fax 606-257-2984; refer orders to P.O. Box 6525, Ithaca, N.Y. 14851 Tel 607-277-2211; 800-666-2211 Fax 607-277-6292; 800-688-2877

University Press of Miss., 3825 Ridgewood Rd., Jackson, Miss. 39211-6492 Tel 601-982-6205 Fax 601-982-6217

University Press of New England, 23 S. Main St., Hanover, N.H. 03755 Tel 603-643-7100; 643-7110 (orders); 800-421-1561 (orders) Fax 603-643-1540; 643-1560 (orders)

University Press of Va., P.O. Box 3608, University Station, Charlottesville, Va. 22903-0608 Tel 804-924-3468 Fax 804-982-2655

Van Nostrand Reinhold Co. Inc., 115 5th Ave., New York, N.Y. 10003 Tel 212-254-3232; 800-543-2681 Fax 212-254-9499; refer orders to 7625 Empire Dr., Florence, Ky. 41042-0668 Tel 606-525-6600; 800-354-9706 Fax 606-525-7778

Vanni: S. F. Vanni, 30 W. 12th St., New York, N.Y. 10011

Vendome Press, 515 Madison Ave., New York, N.Y. 10022 Tel 212-838-8991; refer orders to Rizzoli Int. Publs.

VGM Career Horizons, 4255 W. Touhy Ave., Lincolnwood, Ill. 60646-1975 Tel 708-679-5500; 800-323-4900 Fax 708-679-2494

Viking: Viking Penguin, 375 Hudson St., New York, N.Y. 10014 Tel 212-366-2000; 800-331-4624 Fax 212-366-2666; refer orders to P.O. Box 999, Bergenfield, N.J. 07621 Tel 201-387-0600; 800-253-6476 Fax 201-385-6521

Viking Studio Bks., 375 Hudson St., New York, N.Y. 10014 Tel 212-366-2000

Villard Bks., 201 E. 50th St., New York, N.Y. 10022 Tel 212-751-2600; 800-726-0600; refer orders to Random House Inc., 400 Hahn Rd., Westminster, Md. 21157 Tel 410-848-1900; 800-733-3000 Fax 800-659-2436

Vintage Bks., 201 E. 50th St., New York, N.Y. 10022 Tel 212-751-2600; 800-726-0600; refer orders to Random House Inc., 400 Hahn Rd., Westminster, Md. 21157 Tel 410-848-1900; 800-733-3000 Fax 800-659-2436

Voyageur Press, 123 N. 2nd St., P.O. Box 338, Stillwater, Minn. 55082 Tel 612-430-2210; 800-888-9653 Fax 612-430-2211

Wake Forest Univ. Press, P.O. Box 7333, Winston-Salem, N.C. 27109 Tel 919-761-5448

Walker & Co., 435 Hudson St., New York, N.Y. 10014 Tel 212-727-8300; 800-289-2553 Fax 212-727-0984 .

Warne: Frederick Warne & Co. Ltd., 27 Wright's Lane, London W8 5TZ, Eng. Tel (071) 416 3000 Fax (071) 416 3199

Branch offices

U.S.: Warne, 375 Hudson St., New York, N.Y. 10014 Tel 212-366-2000; 800-331-4624 Fax 212-366-2666; refer orders to Penguin USA, P.O. Box 999, Bergenfield, N.J. 07621 Tel 201-387-0600; 800-253-6476 Fax 201-385-6521

Warner Bks., Time & Life Bldg., 1271 Ave. of the Americas, New York, N.Y. 10020 Tel 212-522-7200 Fax 212-522-7158; refer orders to Little, Brown

Washington Sq. Press, Simon & Schuster Bldg., 1230 Ave. of the Americas, New York, N.Y. 10020 Tel 212-698-7000; 800-223-2348; refer orders to Prentice Hall Trade, Simon & Schuster Inc., 200 Old Tappan Rd., Old Tappan, N.J. 07675 Tel 201-767-5937; 800-223-2336 (orders only)

Watson-Guptill Publs., 1515 Broadway, New York, N.Y. 10036 Tel 212-536-5121 Fax 212-536-5359; refer orders to 1695 Oak St., Lakewood, N.J. 08701 Tel 908-363-5679; 800-451-1741 (orders) Fax 908-363-0338

Watts: Franklin Watts Inc., 95 Madison Ave., New York, N.Y. 10016 Tel 212-951-2650 Fax 212-689-7803; refer orders to 5450 N. Cumberland Ave., Chicago, Ill. 60656-1484 Tel 800-672-6672 Fax 800-374-4329

Webster's New World, 15 Columbus Circle, New York, N.Y. 10023 Tel 212-373-8500; 800-223-2348; refer orders to Simon & Schuster Inc., 200 Old Tappan Rd., Old Tappan, N.J. 07675 Tel 800-223-2336 (orders only)

Weidenfeld & Nicolson See Grove/Atlantic

Wesleyan Univ. Press, 110 Mt. Vernon St., Middletown, Conn. 06457 Tel 203-344-7918; refer orders to University Press of New England, 23 S. Main St., Hanover, N.H. 03755 Tel 603-643-7100; 643-7110 (orders); 800-421-1561 (orders) Fax 603-643-1540; 643-1560 (orders)

West Pub. Co., 50 W. Kellogg Blvd., St. Paul, Minn. 55164 Tel 612-228-2973; 800-328-2209; refer orders to 615 Opperman Dr., P.O. Box 64833, St. Paul, Minn. 55164-1803

Western Pub. Co. Inc., 1220 Mound Ave., Racine, Wis. 53404 Tel 414-633-2431; refer orders to 5945 Erie St., Racine, Wis. 53402 Tel 800-225-9514

Westminster Press (The), 100 Witherspoon St., Louisville, Ky. 40202-1396; refer orders to 925 Chestnut St., Philadelphia, Pa. 19107 Tel 215-928-2745; 800-462-0405; 800-523-1631 (orders only)

Westview Press Inc., 5500 Central Ave., Boulder, Colo. 80301-2847 Tel 303-444-3541; 800-456-1995 Fax 303-449-3356

Wheatley Press (The), 3518 Cahuenga Blvd. W., Suite 205, Los Angeles, Calif. 90068 Tel 213-850-5311; refer orders to University of Wash. Press

Wheeler Pub. (Hingham), 34 Leavitt St., Hingham, Mass. 02043 Tel 617-740-8071 Fax 617-740-8074

Wiley: John Wiley & Sons Inc., 605 3rd Ave., New York, N.Y. 10158-0012 Tel 212-850-6000 Fax 212-850-6088; refer orders to 1 Wiley Dr., Somerset, N.J. 08873-1272 Tel 908-469-4400; 800-879-4539 Fax 908-302-2300

Williams & Wilkins, 428 E. Preston St., Baltimore, Md. 21202 Tel 410-528-4000; 800-638-0672 Fax 410-528-4422; refer orders to P.O. Box 1496, Baltimore, Md. 21203

Wilshire Bk. Co., 12015 Sherman Rd., N. Hollywood, Calif. 91605-3781 Tel 213-875-1711

Wilson, H.W.: The H. W. Wilson Co., 950 University Ave., Bronx, N.Y. 10452 Tel 718-588-8400; 800-367-6770 Fax 718-590-1617

Windcrest Bks., c.o. TAB Bks. Inc., 13311 Montery Ave., Blue Ridge Summit, Pa. 17214-9989 Tel 717-794-2191; 800-822-8138 Fax 717-794-2080

Woodbine House, 5615 Fishers Lane, Rockville, Md. 20852 Tel 301-468-8800; 800-843-7323

Woodrow Wilson Int. Center for Scholars, 1000 Jefferson Dr. S.W., Smithsonian Institution Bldg., Washington, D.C. 20560 Tel 202-357-2429

Word Bks., 5221 N. O'Connor Blvd., Suite 1000, Irving, Tex. 75039 Tel 214-556-1900; refer orders to P.O. Box 2518, Waco, Tex. 76702

Workman Pub. Co. Inc., 708 Broadway, New York, N.Y. 10003 Tel 212-254-5900; 800-722-7202 Fax 212-254-8098; 800-521-1832 (orders)

World Almanac, 200 Park Ave., New York, N.Y. 10166 Tel 212-692-3824; refer orders to St. Martin's Press

World Bk. Inc., 525 W. Monroe, 20th Floor, Chicago, Ill. 60661 Tel 312-258-3700; 800-621-8202

World Pub. Services, Fredericksburg, Tex. 78624

World Publs., 809 S. Orlando Ave., Suite H, Winter Park, Fla. 32789 Tel 407-628-4802

Worldmark Press, 242 E. 50th St., New York, N.Y. 10022 Tel 212-355-3118

Writer Inc. (The), 120 Boylston St., Boston, Mass. 02116-4615 Tel 617-423-3157

Writer's Digest Bks., 1507 Dana Ave., Cincinnati, Ohio 45207 Tel 513-531-2222; 800-289-0963 Fax 513-531-4082

Wynwood Press, P.O. Box 6287, Grand Rapids, Mich. 49516 Tel 616-676-9185; 800-877-2665 Fax 616-676-9573; 398-3111 (orders)

Y.C.P. Publs. Inc., P.O. Box 931766, Los Angeles, Calif. 90093 Tel 213-857-8683

Yale Univ. Press, 302 Temple St., New Haven, Conn. 06520 Tel 203-432-0940; refer orders to 92A Yale Station, New Haven, Conn. 06520 Fax 203-432-0948

Yankee Bks., 33 E. Minor St., Emmaus, Pa. 18098 Tel 215-967-5171; 800-527-8200

Yivo Inst. for Jewish Res., 1048 5th Ave., New York, N.Y. 10028 Tel 212-535-6700

Zebra Bks., 475 Park Ave. S., New York, N.Y. 10016 Tel 212-889-2299; 800-221-2647 Fax 212-779-8073

Zephyr Press (Somerville): Zephyr Press, 13 Robinson St., Somerville, Mass. 02145 Tel 617-628-9726; refer orders to Bookslinger, 2402 University Ave., Suite 507, St. Paul, Minn. 55114 Tel 612-649-0271; 800-397-261

Zondervan Pub. House, 5300 Patterson Ave. S.E., Grand Rapids, Mich. 49530 Tel 616-698-6900; 800-727-1309 (orders) Fax 616-698-3439; 698-3255 (orders)